The Interlinear Hebrew-Aramaic OLD TESTAMENT

The Interlinear Hebrew-Aramaic OLD TESTAMENT

With Strong's Concordance Numbers
Above Each Word

This is VOLUME III of
The Interlinear Hebrew-Greek-English Bible

Jay P. Green, Sr.
General Editor and Translator

HENDRICKSON
PUBLISHERS

The Interlinear Bible, 4 volumes
© 1976, 1977, 1978, 1979, 1980, 1981, 1984.
2nd Edition © 1985 by Jay P. Green, Sr.

The English translation in the side column, *A Literal Translation of the Bible,* © 1985 by Jay Green, Sr.

The Greek text © 1976 by the Trinitarian Bible Society, London, England. Used by permission.

Hendrickson Publishers edition published by permission.
ISBN 1565639804   4 volume set
ISBN 1565639839   Old Testament (Volumes 1–3)
ISBN 1565639790   New Testament (Volume 4)

Printed in the United States of America

Printed in December 2005

PUBLISHER'S PREFACE
REPRINT EDITION

Since the release of the second edition of *The Interlinear Hebrew-Greek-English Bible,* Bible students around the world have found this work to be a valuable resource for gaining insight into the original languages of Scripture. Because an interlinear Bible is a helpful aid for those who may not have had a formal course of study in the Hebrew and Greek languages, demand for such an accessible tool as this has grown steadily despite its sometimes limited availability.

The addition of *Strong's* numbers to the second edition has enabled those with little or no prior knowledge of Greek or Hebrew to access a wealth of language reference works keyed to *Strong's Exhaustive Concordance*—Greek/Hebrew dictionaries, analytical lexicons, concordances, word studies, and others. Moreover, the inclusion of the *Literal Translation of the Bible* has offered readers at-a-glance insight into the roots of many biblical words. For example biblical names reveal rich meanings (*e.g.* the *Nethinim* are temple-slaves). The names of biblical places convey more (*e.g. Kibroth-Hattaavah* means "The Graves of Lust"). Official positions are explained (captain of the guard is more literally rendered "chief of the executioners").

The volumes that make up this set are an exact reprint of the second edition and are being produced under license from the original editor and copyright holder. Because it is an exact reprint, no editorial changes—additions or corrections—have been made. As such, it will reflect the original editor's work including the inevitable imperfections that accompany such a typographically complex project. Nonetheless, this affordable reprint is offered in the hope that the reissue of this classic reference tool will meet an important need for all who seek a better understanding of Scripture.

PREFACE

After nearly forty centuries of desperate failure, has Satan, aided and cheerfully abetted by deceitful and desperately wicked men (Jer. 17:9), finally succeeded in destroying the written word of God, the Bible, as a single-voiced witness to his great arch-enemy, our God and Savior Jesus Christ? Has the old Devil, like a sleight-of-hand shell-game artist, finally brought us to the point where we are searching desperately for the true word of God? Are we to believe that it cannot now be intact after all this time, having been run through the shredder of unholy hands and heads? Let it not be said! For not only has God warned us that, "*Man shall not live by bread alone, but by every word that proceeds out of the mouth of God,*" (Deut. 8:3; Matt. 4:4), but God has provided us with the very words that we are to live by, and He has most certainly also preserved for us the very words by which we are to live. Else, how could He plainly say, "*And if anyone hears My words and does not believe, I do not judge him . . . the word which I spoke is that which will judge him in the last day,*" (John 12:47,48)?

God has given us His life-giving words in words which all men may receive and believe. From the least intelligent to the most brilliant, men from all backgrounds and in all lands and languages must be able to hear, understand, believe and obey; else the Divine purpose cannot be fulfilled. In order to leave every person without excuse, God the Holy Spirit breathed out through the divinely chosen penmen words in common use among the Hebrew people, and, later, words commonly in use by the Greek-speaking world. However, since few today read Hebrew and Greek, and since the Scriptdures are intended for every nation and tongue, a translation into the common language of each person is needed. This Tyndale wrote in his preface, "which thing moved me to translate the New Testament. Because I had perceived by experience that it was impossible to establish the lay people in any truth except the Scripture were plainly laid before their eyes in their mother tongue, that they might see the process, order and meaning of the text." Tyndale labored to translate so that "every plowboy might understand," and such a great spiritual revolution followed that J. R. Green, the noted English historian, felt compelled to write, "No greater moral change ever passed over a nation than passed over England in the latter part of the reign of Queen Elizabeth. England became the people of a Book, and that Book was the Bible. Itwas read by every class of people. And the effect was amazing. The whole moral tone of the nation was changed."

With these considerations in mind, and also with much fear and trembling before our majestic and awesome God, we have sought to provide in *The Interlinear Hebrew-Greek-English Bible* both the original God-breathed Hebrew, Aramaic and Greek words (as incorporated in the texts received by the vast majority of Bible-believing peoples), and two literal English translations of these words. Our purpose in doing so is that the reader and student of this work might be led to *"receive in meekness the implanted word, which is able to save your souls"* (James 1:21). It now is submitted to you in the hope that the Almighty God who enabled us to conceive and to execute this monumental task will also enable you to grow in grace and in the knowledge of our Lord Jesus Christ by the use of it.

THE INTERLINEAR BIBLE

This work, we believe, contains all the Hebrew and Aramaic words which have been preserved for us by the Masoretes, and which in total has come to be known as the Masoretic Text. This work also contains the Greek words as printed in the Stephens Edition of 1550, which has become known as the Textus Receptus, or, Received Text, for the past four centuries. We have not followed the order of the Hebrew Bible (The Law, The Prophets, The Writings), but the order of the English Bible.

Why did we use these particular texts? It is simply because these are the only texts which can justly be designated as 'received' texts. In worldwide acceptance they tower so far above any other original Hebrew or Greek texts that there is no doubt but what they must be used in a work such as this is, a work that is intended to become a standard work for all the English-speaking peoples in the world. They are the 'Received Texts' because no other text has been able to win the adherence of any group powerful enough to displace either the Masoretic or the Received Text from their place as the standard by which all others are measured.

Since there will be separate prefaces supplied with each volume of this work, we will confine our remarks here to matters concerning the Hebrew and English printed in this volume. The Hebrew text in the Old Testament volumes of this work was first typeset in 1866 by the British and Foreign Bible Society, and it is from the Masoretic text. It was chosen over other beautiful Hebrew texts simply because it provided, for the most part, adequate room for the interlineary addition of the English equivalents under the original words.

The English, both that under the Hebrew words and that in the translation on the side, constitutes the original translation work of Jay P. Green, Sr., improved by scholars on a Board of Review, and from a volunteer Editorial Board. For purposes of fixing responsibility, the English translations are both those of Jay P. Green, Sr., since he was the sole judge of what changes would, or would not, be allowed in either the English equivalents placed under the Hebrew words, or the translation in the column at the side of the page.

THE INTERLINEAR BIBLE: WHAT IT IS; WHAT IT IS NOT.

This being the only complete interlineary Bible in existence, we give our concept of what this work is, and what it is not:

1. This *Interlinear Bible* is a Bible in every sense of the word, having both the original words, and two English translations for English-speaking people. Some may use this Bible in order to read the Bible in the original languages; others may read only the English translation, referring to the original words only in order to further investigate the meaning in lexicons or other reference works. It is our firm belief that all the benefits promised within the Bible itself may fairly be expected from the reading studying of this Bible.

2. It is the most literal English translation every produced, certainly the only one with literal meanings placed under the original words. Still, it is not in a true sense an absolutely literal representation of the Hebrew or Greek words. To begin with, no foreign language could adequately capture all the fullness of expression of either the Hebrew or Greek languages. In the Hebrew particularly, it being a pictorially-based language, it is impossible for the English translator to bring out in English the many shades of thought which are found in the Hebrew Bible (*e.g.* when the translation reads "*meek*", this will hardly convey to you that the word is derived from a root signifying to "afflict"; and when you read "*delight*", you will not realize that the original word pictures out a bending down toward the object being delighted in).

3. It not only gives the English reader insight into the literal meanings of the original languages, but opens to the understanding many idiomatic expressions. However, at this point, it must be admitted that the final product is somewhat of a hybrid production. On the one hand, it is not possible to express all the Hebrew idiom in English. On the other hand, if all idioms were attempted in English, many English readers would not always receive the sense, being unfamiliar with the background of the idiomatic expression. It is for this reason that two English translations are sometimes provided, one under each word of the original, it being more literal and more idiomatic at times; and the other on the side, giving a more standard treatment of translation so that the reader might more easily collect the sense of the entire context. There is another reason for the lack of expression of some of the idiom of the Hebrew language, and that is the limitation in space with which the translator was faced in this format. The cost of resetting the Hebrew to fit a fully literal translation into English would have been so great that the average serious Bible student would have found the final cost to be prohibitive. Also this work being intended for general use among all English-understanding peoples, it was necessary to avoid expressions which could only be comprehended by the more advanced Hebrew scholars. It is hoped that this work as you now see it will be useful to all classes of Bible readers, whatever may be their educational

level, and that it will be the most useful Bible ever produced in the matter of conveying spiritual truths and insights to the reader.

4. This Bible should prove to be a word book of considerable value for the study of Biblical vocabulary, both Hebrew and English.

5. It is intended to be a reader, both for those who are reading the English only, and for those who desire to read the original and at the same time to have help in understanding the meaning of each word. It will provide a much more rapid-reading Hebrew Bible than any that has been in existence until now. It will give the English reader a feel for Hebrew expressions which may not have been experienced before.

6. Although it gives some immediate lexiconal help, it is not intended to serve as a lexicon (dictionary).

7. It is most certainly not a grammar. Students must not use it in learning Hebrew or Greek grammar.

8. It is not intended to be a substitute for the person, in-depth study of the original. Students of the word should continue to make their own studies, using every reference work available to them. Each one should attempt to make his own independent translation. It would be neither seemly nor wise for anyone to take these words and present them as his own translation.

9. This work should be of considerable use to pastors and teachers. To those who have been trained in the original Biblical languages this work will be a refresher. It should help the trained student to remain sharp and fresh in his recognition of the meanings of all the words in any context. To the untrained pastor or teacher, it should be realized that without some knowledge of the literal meanings of the Hebrew, Aramaic and Greek words, one cannot be certain in a single instance that the sermon or lesson based on a text of Scripture is the accurate teaching of that text. This work is intended to give you encouragement and help in attaining such a knowledge of the meanings of the original Hebrew, Aramaic and Greek words.

10. Because all the nearly nineteen hundred Hebrew root words and the seven hundred and fifty or so Greek root words are here, along with English equivalents, this work is ideal for the use of those who must prepare written manuscripts or articles for publication. To find the original word with which you are concerned, one needs only to know the Biblical reference in order to quickly refer to them in this work.

11. *The Interlinear Bible* is the fulfillment of a long-recognized need. Martin Luther is reported as saying that he would not part with his knowledge of Hebrew for untold gold. Yet the vast majority of English-speaking people have been shut out of this precious knowledge, not having the time, or the money, to attend schools that teach Hebrew. One of the most often-voiced desires, especially since the hundreds of thou-

sands of interlineary New Testaments have been distributed in the past century, is the desire for a complete interlineary Bible. And this obviously is because it is the next best thing to a formal opportunity to study the Hebrew and Greek languages in depth. Until now, however, the formidable task of producing such an immeasureably useful Bible had never been completed.

There has been some progress for several centuries. First, for the purpose of creating study tools of the magnitude that the Bible necessitates, there must have been provided a standard translation in English. This came to us in the form of the King James Version of the Bible, the first edition issued in 1611, and the final form of it being established by 1730 a.d. Then it was possible to make a concordance which could be used by one and all, whether learned or unlearned — only the ability to read being necessary for its use. After another century or so, lexicon-dictionaries and grammars found fertile soil, and these added their input to the growing knowledge of the Bible. These at first were for the learned, or those formally trained. Then came the two big concordances, one by James Strong, the other by Robert Young. These gave abundant help to those who had only been trained in the English language. By the use of these one could laboriously make a study of the original individual words of the Bible. In the past century useful Bible dictioaries have helped in word studies, and wordbooks such as W. E. Vine's *Expository Dictionary of New Testament Words*, other studies by Trench and Girdlestone, etc. have advanced Biblical knowledge. Now in this present age there are more Biblical helps than ever before, a time when *The Interlinear Bible* can now be used as a means to shorten the time and effort to make Biblical studies in the lexicons, dictionaries, concordances, etc. Anyone who will learn the Hebrew alphabet and the Greek alphabet (the work of only one or two days) will be blessed with even more help from this *Interlinear Bible*.

12. *The Interlinear Bible* is up-to-date, having used the latest lexicons and study helps in the fixing of meanings, and a trustworthy guide to an accurate understanding of the Biblical words.

SPECIFIC DIFFICULTIES ENCOUNTERED.

It should be kept in mind in the use of this word that there is a wide difference in time and culture and language, not only between Hebrew and Greek, but also between those languages, times and cultures, and those of our day. In rendering the Biblical languages into English we particularly found it difficult to deal with the following:

A. Figures of Speech. The Hebrew speaks of the 'lip' of the river, rather than the 'bank'; sometimes the 'mouth' of Jehovah, rather than the 'word' or 'command' of Jehovah; 'lifting the heads' rather than counting, etc. If the figure of speech were considered intelligible to the English reader, the literal meaning is often given in this work.

B. Parts of Speech. It is not always possible to render the parts of speech in literal form, and at the same time convey the meaning to the English reader.

C. Interpretation. There is always interpretation in rendering one language into another, and it is necessary to consider the entire context before making a translation. There may be differences of opinion as to what the context teaches, but the purpose of this work has been to give the sense of the original language as we interpreted it after lengthy study.

D. Untranslated Words. There are some Hebrew words which are not translated in this work. For instance, אֶת־ an untranslated sign defining the direct object of a verb, and at places, אֲשֶׁר , the relative particle, which is sometimes redundant.

E. Implied Words. There are many instances in which the verb, or other words, are implied within the Hebrew word, either by the sentence structure, the syntax, or the context. In such cases the translator has supplied the word, even though it is not represented by Hebrew characters. In these instances the word supplied has been put in parentheses so that the reader will know that they were supplied by the translator. In the marginal translation these supplied words may be in italic type.

F. Punctuation and Capitalization. It should be realized that in the original Biblical languages, both Hebrew and Greek, all letters were capital letters, as we think of them. Therefore in the use of capitals and small letters, as we do in modern-day English, any capital letter can be counted as supplied. Capital letters have been used in this work for the following: for the beginning of all sentences; for the beginning word in all speeches; for specific events or places, such as, The Passover, The Feast of Tabernacles, The Negeb, The River (either Nile, or Euphrates), etc.; and we have also capitalized all pronouns which we deem to refer to the Deity, whether God the Father, God the Son, or God the Holy Spirit.

It should also be noted that there was no punctuation in the original manuscripts, either in the Hebrew or Greek. In the Hebrew text which we are using for this volume, the Masoretes (*c.* 700 a.d.) have placed certain punctuation marks for the benefit of the Hebrew reader. In this work we have generally followed the Masoretic punctuation, keeping in mind that punctuation is an aid to the reader. For this reason the punctuation may seen strange to the English reader at first, but since the reader is reading the English in Hebrew order (from right to left), and is oftentimes reading very literally, the reader will be aided by the punctuation as it appears under the Hebrew words. In the English translation in the margin we have followed modern English punctuation rules, our authority being *The Chicago Manual of Style.*

In regard to the use of question marks and the indication of interrogation, it should be noted that a question is often indicated in the Hebrew at the beginning of a sentence, sometimes by interrogative words, or at times only by the context.

G. The name of Jehovah, יְהֹוָה. The Old Testament contained this name in some fifty-five hundred places, and in this *Interlinear Bible* we have always rendered it Jehovah, or in its shortened form, Jah. The Jews, of course, considered this name to be incommunicable, never pronouncing it. The root bears the meaning of continuing being, a personal, absolute, self-determining Existence. It is very likely best translated as in Exodus 3:14, where the Lord said to Moses, "*I AM THAT I AM*" — "*Thus you shall say to the sons of Israel, I AM has sent me to you . . . .*" Because of the vagueness of the Hebrew tense (which is the same in both parts of the sentence) other renderings are possible, but in our opinion none better than "*I AM THAT I AM*". The name Jehovah is, of course, an English word which is based on the Masorete's choice of writing. They so revered this holy name that they wrote the vowels of the word signifying Lord (*adonai*) with the consonants of the name which God gave to Himself, JHWH, resulting in יְהוָֹה Jehovah —or as some prefer to render it, Yahweh, the consonants being in the Hebrew properly transliterated YHWH. In the history of the English language, however, the letter *J* has a written counterpart in the German *J*, although the letter *J* in German is pronounced like an English *Y*. The bulk of theological studies having come from German sources, there has been an intermixed usage in English of the *J* and the *Y*. Our English translations of the Bible reflect this, so we have chosen to use *J*, thus Jehovah, rather than Yahweh, because this is established English usage for Biblical names beginning with this Hebrew letter. No one suggests that we ought to change Jacob, Joseph, Jehoshaphat, Joshua, etc. to begin with a *Y*, and neither should we at this late date change Jehovah to Yahweh.

H. Non-literal Translation. Various forms of the Hebrew verb, idioms, and repetitions are sometimes rendered here by their intention, rather than by their exact expression. Examples of such are: (1) The Hebrew superlative (literally קֹדֶשׁ קָדָשִׁים is herein as "*most holy*. In Genesis 10:L9 it is said, "*Nimrod was a mighty hunter before the Lord*", or, *a hunter of God*, indicating that he was the greatest of hunters. (2) The Hebrew infinitive absolute, (literally מוֹת יָמוּת is "*dying, he shall die*", but it is usually translated by such words as surely, or certainly. (3) Hebrew idioms (literally *the mouth of the sword* may be translated herein as *the edge of the sword*. In successive editions the more literal idioms have been inserted. (4) Figures of Speech. (Literally אֵין לוֹ is *non-existence to him*, or, *not to him is*, but herein it is often rendered as, "he does not have," or, "not to him

Also, *seven years and twenty years and one hundred years* will appear herein as "*twenty-seven and one hundred years*", the word years being printed only once in English).

I. Non-concordant Translation. As in all languages, parts of speech may be fluid enough to have many meanings for one word or particle, usually depending on its contextual circumstance. For example, in Hebrew, we have וְ — *and, but, then, or*, and many others. Also דָּבָר for *word, thing, matter*. Although an attempt is made in *The Interlinear Bible* to translate certain Hebrew words with the same English word throughout a book, especially translating those words which have distinct doctrinal meaning, it is not always possible to fulfill the sense of the context by using the same English word. Many times reference to the English translation in the margin will help to explain difficult expressions.

J. Non-agreement of Number. Singular pronouns are often translated by the plural (normally a Hebrew collective) — for example, literally *to him* may appear as *to them*. Numbered objects are often singular in Hebrew. For example, literally it is written *four hundred man* but herein it will be rendered in the plural, *four hundred men*.

K. Space Limitations. Apart from the linguistic considerations, the interlineary format posed many mechancial problems as well. A moment's reflection on the difficult task of putting English meanings under Hebrew words will show that many short words require long English translations, or even more than one English word at places. In order to serve the reader best, a two-line format has been chosen in order to allow in nearly all instances a full expression of the meaning of the Hebrew words. At times the English, especially on the second line, is allowed to extend beyond the space under the Hebrew word, if no confusion results. Nevertheless, in certain places, and particularly in translating certain words, it has been necessary for us to adopt either a different word for translation, or a shortened form of construction. For example, in dealing with the Hebrew verb construct state, the possessive form was used to meet space requirements, such as *the sons of Israel* being rendered as *Israel's sons*. And whereas כְּ is normally *according to*, because of space limitations it is sometimes rendered as *by, as to*, etc. Also normally וַיְהִי would be rendered *and it came to be*, herein it is rendered *and it was*, because of the shortness of the Hebrew word. You will find in causative verb tenses that a shortening is often unavoidable, but happily in English the sense still comes through. Literally it may be, *he shall cause to put to death*, but herein, *he will execute*, especially where judicial execution is intended.

Jay P. Green, Sr., General Editor and Translator

HOW TO USE THE NUMBERING SYSTEM IN THIS WORK

The number over each Hebrew word is designed to be the key to a fuller understanding of that word, and of the context. The student will obtain more information on the word by referring to any or all of the reference works which are also keyed to Strong's numbering system. To find every single place where the word is used in the Bible, look up that number in *The New Englishman's Hebrew Concordance*, at which place will be listed in Biblical order all the places the holy penmen have used that word. This will help fix the meaning by Biblical usage. To discover more information on the root, the origin, the usage in other languages, and particularly the variations in the conjugations of verbs, look up the number in *The New BrownDriver-Briggs Hebrew-Aramaic Lexicon with Index* (or for quicker reference use *A Concise Lexicon to the Biblical Languages*). Also there is a Hebrew lexicon in the back of *Strong's Exhaustive Concordance.*

By this quick means of searching the individual usages of the words in a phrase, a sentence, or a paragraph, a far more accurate knowledge of the spiritual meaning of that passage will develop in the mind of the student. Thus spiritual heights will be climbed; ever higher will the spirit of the searcher rise, and the soul will soar with blessing on top of blessing, nevermore to return to its former state.

The editor wishes to express his deep appreciation to Dr. Allan A. MacRae for his encouragement through the years, and to the staff of Biblical School of Theology for their help in this work, particularly in improving the translation of the New Testament. We also want to express our appreciation for the space provided for the work of the Board of Review by Faith Theological Seminary and Westminster Theological Seminary. We owe particular appreciation to Rev. Maurice Robinson and Rev. Frank Coho, who have spent more time in improving this work than any other. We also owe a deep debt of gratitude to the many others who have contributed to this work, whether in the original edition, or by sending in their suggestions for the present improved edition.

Despite a widespread scepticism that such a work could ever be completed, now by God's grace, it is our pleasure to commend this work to you for your spiritual benefit. May Jehovah be praised!

Jay P. Green, Sr., General Editor

HOW TO READ THE ENGLISH LINES UNDER THE HEBREW, OR GREEK

1. Read the English in Hebrew order, that is from right to left.
2. Read the top line first, the line directly under the Hebrew.
3. Read from right to left on the first line, then on the second line.
4. Proceed to the next Hebrew word, reading the top English line first.

In reading the Greek New Testament section, however:

1. You will read in English order, that is from left to right.
2. Since Greek sentence structure is different, words will not be in order.
3. Refer to the English translation on the side to pick up word order.

PSALM 56

To the chief musician, concerning the silent dove —those far off. Of David, a secret treasure — when the Philistines seized him in Gath.

[1]Favor me, O God, for man snuffs me up; all the day fighting oppresses me. [2]My watchers panted for me all the day; for many are proudly fighting over me. [3]The day I am afraid, I will trust in You. [4]In God I will praise His word; in God I have trusted; I will not fear; what will flesh do to me? [5]All the day they pervert my words; all their thoughts *are* against me for evil. [6]They stir up strife; they hide; they observe my footprints as they wait *for* my soul. [7]Is escape for them by iniquity? In anger the peoples cast down, O God.

[8]You have counted my wandering; O put my tears in Your bottle; *are they* not in Your Book? [9]Then my enemies will turn back in the day I call; this I know, for God *is* for me. [10]In God I will praise the word; in Jehovah I will praise the word. [11]In God I have trusted; I will not fear; what will man do to me? [12]On me, O God, *are* Your vows; I will render to You thank offerings. [13]For You have delivered my soul from death. *Do you* not keep my feet from falling, *so that I* may walk before God in the light of the living?

PSAL. LVI. נו

PSALM 56

270 4387 1732 7350 482 3128 5329
1 לַמְנַצֵּחַ עַל־יוֹנַת אֵלֶם רְחֹקִים לְדָוִד מִכְתָּם בֶּאֱחֹז אֹתוֹ
him in secret a of those silent the concern- chief the To
seizing —treasure David ;off far dove ing musician

3117 3605 582 7602 430 2603 1661 6430
2 פְלִשְׁתִּים בְּגַת׃ חָנֵּנִי אֱלֹהִים כִּי־שְׁאָפַנִי אֱנוֹשׁ כָּל־הַיּוֹם
the all ;man snuffs for O Favor in the
day up me ,God ,me .Gath Philistines

3898 7227 3117 3605 8324 7602 3905 3898
3 לֹחֵם יִלְחָצֵנִי׃ שָׁאֲפוּ שׁוֹרְרַי כָּל־הַיּוֹם כִּי־רַבִּים לֹחֲמִים
are many for the all my Panted oppresses fighting
fighting ;day watchers me for .me

1984 430 982 3372 3117 4791
4 לִי מָרוֹם׃ יוֹם אִירָא אֲנִי אֵלֶיךָ אֶבְטָח׃ בֵּאלֹהִים אֲהַלֵּל
5 will I God In will in I am I The .proudly over
praise .trust You .afraid day me

1320 6213 4100 3372 3808 982 430 1697
דְּבָרוֹ בֵּאלֹהִים בָּטַחְתִּי לֹא אִירָא מַה־יַּעֲשֶׂה בָשָׂר לִי׃
to flesh will what will I not have I in His
?me do ;fear ;trusted God ;word

1481 7451 4284 3605 6087 1697 3117 3605
6 כָּל־הַיּוֹם דְּבָרַי יְעַצֵּבוּ עָלַי כָּל־מַחְשְׁבֹתָם לָרָע׃ יָגוּרוּ
7 stir they for their (are) against they my the All
;strife up .evil thoughts all me ;pervert words day

205 5315 6960 8104 6119 6845
8 יִצְפִּינוּ הֵמָּה עֲקֵבַי יִשְׁמֹרוּ כַּאֲשֶׁר קִוּוּ נַפְשִׁי׃ עַל־אָוֶן
iniquity By (for) they as ,mark my they they
.soul my wait footprints ,hide

5608 5112 430 3381 5971 639 6405
9 פַּלֶּט־לָמוֹ בְּאַף עַמִּים הוֹרֵד אֱלֹהִים׃ נֹדִי סָפַרְתָּה אַתָּה
;You have wan-My O cast the In for escape
counted dering ,God ,down peoples anger ?them is

341 7725 5612 3808 4997 1832 7760
10 שִׂימָה דִמְעָתִי בְנֹאדֶךָ הֲלֹא בְּסִפְרָתֶךָ׃ אָז יָשׁוּבוּ אוֹיְבַי
my will Then ?Book Your in (they are) Your into my O
enemies turn not ;bottle tears put

430 430 3045 2088 7121 3117 268
11 אָחוֹר בְּיוֹם אֶקְרָא זֶה־יָדַעְתִּי כִּי־אֱלֹהִים לִי׃ בֵּאלֹהִים
In for God for I this I the in back
God .me (is) ,know ;call day

3372 3808 430 1697 1984 3068 1697 1984
12 אֲהַלֵּל דָּבָר בַּיהוָה אֲהַלֵּל דָּבָר׃ בֵּאלֹהִים בָּטַחְתִּי לֹא אִירָא
will I not have I In the will I in the will I
.fear ;trusted God .word praise Jehovah ;word praise

8426 7999 5088 430 5921 120 6213
13 מַה־יַּעֲשֶׂה אָדָם לִי׃ עָלַי אֱלֹהִים נְדָרֶיךָ אֲשַׁלֵּם תּוֹדֹת
thank will I Your (are) O On to man do will What
offerings render ;vows ,God ,me ?me

1980 1762 7272 3808 4194 5315 5337
14 לָךְ׃ כִּי הִצַּלְתָּ נַפְשִׁי מִמָּוֶת הֲלֹא רַגְלַי מִדֶּחִי לְהִתְהַלֵּךְ
(I that so) from my (You Do) from my have You For to
walk may ,falling feet (keep) not .death soul delivered .You

2416 216 430 6440
לִפְנֵי אֱלֹהִים בְּאוֹר הַחַיִּים׃
the the in God before
?living of light

PSAL. LVII נז

PSALM 57

1 לַמְנַצֵּחַ אַל־תַּשְׁחֵת לְדָוִד מִכְתָּם בְּבָרְחוֹ מִפְּנֵי־שָׁאוּל

Saul's from he when secret a of do not chief the To
face fled ,treasure ;David ;destroy ,musician

2 בַּמְּעָרָה׃ חָנֵּנִי אֱלֹהִים ׀ חָנֵּנִי כִּי בְךָ חָסָיָה נַפְשִׁי וּבְצֵל־

in ,Yea my takes in for merciful be O merciful Be the in
shadow ;soul refuge You ,me to ,God ,me to .cave

3 כְּנָפֶיךָ אֶחְסֶה עַד־יַעֲבֹר הַוּוֹת׃ אֶקְרָא לֵאלֹהִים עֶלְיוֹן

Most God to will I .calamities passes until take I Your
;High call by ,refuge wings

4 לָאֵל גֹּמֵר עָלָי׃ יִשְׁלַח מִשָּׁמַיִם ׀ וְיוֹשִׁיעֵנִי חֵרֵף שֹׁאֲפִי

who him will He save and from shall He for who to
.me crushes shame ;me Heaven send .me works God

5 סֶלָה יִשְׁלַח אֱלֹהִים חַסְדּוֹ וַאֲמִתּוֹ׃ נַפְשִׁי ׀ בְּתוֹךְ לְבָאִם

;lions (is) My His and His God shall .Selah
among soul .truth mercy send

אֶשְׁכְּבָה לֹהֲטִים בְּנֵי־אָדָם שִׁנֵּיהֶם חֲנִית וְחִצִּים וּלְשׁוֹנָם

their and and (are) their ;men the those lie I
tongue ;arrows spears teeth of sons ,fire on (among)

6 חֶרֶב חַדָּה׃ רוּמָה עַל־הַשָּׁמַיִם אֱלֹהִים עַל כָּל־הָאָרֶץ

the all over ,God O the above Be .sharp a (is)
earth ,heavens exalted sword

7 כְּבוֹדֶךָ׃ רֶשֶׁת ׀ הֵכִינוּ לִפְעָמַי כָּפַף נַפְשִׁי כָּרוּ לְפָנַי שִׁיחָה

;pit a before they my bowed is my for they net A Your
me dig ;soul down ,steps prepared .glory

8 נָפְלוּ בְתוֹכָהּ סֶלָה׃ נָכוֹן לִבִּי אֱלֹהִים נָכוֹן לִבִּי אָשִׁירָה

will I my fixed O My is .Selah .it into have they
sing ;heart is ,God ,heart fixed fallen

9 וַאֲזַמֵּרָה׃ עוּרָה כְבוֹדִי עוּרָה הַנֵּבֶל וְכִנּוֹר אָעִירָה שָּׁחַר׃

the will I and harp Wake my Wake give and
.dawn awaken .lyre ,up !glory ,up .praise

10
11 אוֹדְךָ בָעַמִּים ׀ אֲדֹנָי אֲזַמֶּרְךָ בַּלְאֻמִּים׃ כִּי־גָדֹל עַד־שָׁמַיִם

the to (is) For the among sing will I O among will I
heavens great .nations You to ,Lord ,peoples the You praise

12 חַסְדֶּךָ וְעַד־שְׁחָקִים אֲמִתֶּךָ׃ רוּמָה עַל־שָׁמַיִם אֱלֹהִים עַל

over O the above Be Your the and Your
,God ,heavens exalted .truth clouds to ,mercy

כָּל־הָאָרֶץ כְּבוֹדֶךָ׃

Your the all
.glory earth

PSAL. LVIII נח

PSALM 58

1
2 לַמְנַצֵּחַ אַל־תַּשְׁחֵת לְדָוִד מִכְתָּם׃ הַאֻמְנָם אֵלֶם צֶדֶק

righteous- in ,Indeed secret a of do not chief the To
ness silence .treasure ;David ;destroy ;musician

3 תְּדַבֵּרוּן מֵישָׁרִים תִּשְׁפְּטוּ בְּנֵי אָדָם׃ אַף־בְּלֵב עוֹלֹת

wicked- in ,Yes ?men O You Do uprightly you will
ness heart of sons ,judge ?speak

PSALM 57

To the chief musician. Do not destroy. A secret treasure of David, when he fled from Saul in the cave.

1Be merciful to me, O God, be merciful to me, for my soul trusts in You; yea, in the shadow of Your wings I will make my hiding-place, until the great destruction passes by. 2I will cry to God most High, to God who works for me. 3He shall send from Heaven and save me; He will shame the one who crushes me. Selah. God shall send His mercy and His truth. 4My soul *is* among lions; I lie *among* those who are set on fire, the sons of men, whose teeth *are* spears and arrows, and their tongue is a sharp sword. 5Be praised above the heavens, O God; let Your glory *be* over the whole earth.

6They have prepared a net for my steps; my soul is bowed down; *they have* dug a pit before me; they have fallen into it. Selah. 7My heart is fixed, O God, my heart is fixed; I will sing and give praise. 8Wake up my glory! Wake up, harp and lyre! I will stir the morning-dawn with praise. 9I will praise You among the peoples, O Lord, I will sing to You among the nations. 10For Your mercy *is* great to the heavens, and Your truth to the clouds. 11Be exalted above the heavens, O God; Your glory over the whole earth.

PSALM 58

To the chief musician. Do not destroy. A secret treasure of David.

1Will you indeed speak righteousness in silence? Do you judge uprightly, O sons of men? 2Yes, in heart you work the evil of your hands in the land. 3The wicked are estranged from the womb; *they go* astray from the belly, speaking lies. 4Their poison *is* like the poison of a snake; like the deaf adder, he stops his ear, 5which will not hear the charmer's voice, skillful caster of spells. 6O God, break their teeth in their mouth; break out the big teeth of the young lions, O Jehovah. 7Let them melt away like waters; they flow off to them; he bends his arrows; *let them be* as though *they were* cut off, 8as a snail goes *into* melting, a miscarriage of a woman; they do not see the sun. 9Before your pots can feel the thorns, whether green *or* glowing, He shall sweep it away. 10The righteous shall rejoice when he sees vengeance; he shall wash his feet in the blood of the wicked. 11And man will say, Truly, a fruit *is* to the righteous; truly, there is a God judging in the earth.

7358 7563 2114 6424 3027 2555 776 6466
4 תִּפְעָלוּן בָּאָרֶץ חֲמַס יְדֵיכֶם תְּפַלֵּסוּן׃ זֹרוּ רְשָׁעִים מֵרָחֶם
the from the Are you your the the in ;work You
;womb wicked estranged .weigh hands of violence land

3644 5175 2534 1823 2534 3577 1696 990 8582
5 תָּעוּ מִבֶּטֶן דֹּבְרֵי כָזָב׃ חֲמַת־לָמוֹ כִּדְמוּת חֲמַת־נָחָשׁ כְּמוֹ־
like a the like is to poison lies speakers the from they
;snake of poison them (is) of ,belly stray

3907 6963 8085 3808 834 241 331 2795 6620
6 פֶתֶן־חֵרֵשׁ יַאְטֵם אָזְנוֹ׃ אֲשֶׁר לֹא־יִשְׁמַע לְקוֹל מְלַחֲשִׁים
the the will not which his he ,deaf the
,charmers of voice hear ;ear stops adder

4459 6310 8127 2040 430 2449 2266 2266
7 חוֹבֵר חֲבָרִים מְחֻכָּם׃ אֱלֹהִים הֲרָס־שִׁנֵּימוֹ בְּפִימוֹ מַלְתְּעוֹת
big the their in their break ,God O .skillful spells a
of teeth ;mouth teeth of caster

8557 4325 3644 3988 3068 5422 3715
8 כְּפִירִים נְתֹץ ׀ יְהוָה׃ יִמָּאֲסוּ כְמוֹ־מַיִם יִתְהַלְּכוּ־לָמוֹ
to they ;waters like them Let O break young the
;them off flow away melt .Jehovah ,out lions

5209 1980 8557 7642 4135 2671 1869
9 יִדְרֹךְ חִצָּו כְּמוֹ יִתְמֹלָלוּ׃ כְּמוֹ שַׁבְּלוּל תֶּמֶס יַהֲלֹךְ נֵפֶל
mis- a ,goes (into) snail a as were they as his he
of carriage melting ,off cut though ;arrows bends

329 5518 995 2962 8121 2372 802
10 אֵשֶׁת בַּל־חָזוּ שָׁמֶשׁ׃ בְּטֶרֶם יָבִינוּ סִּירֹתֵיכֶם אָטָד כְּמוֹ־
as the your can Before the they not a
,thorns pots feel .sun see ,woman

6471 5359 2372 6662 8056 8175 2740 2416
11 חַי כְּמוֹ־חָרוֹן יִשְׂעָרֶנּוּ׃ יִשְׂמַח צַדִּיק כִּי־חָזָה נָקָם פְּעָמָיו
his ;vengeance he when The shall sweep shall He glowing as ,green
feet sees righteous rejoice .away it

3426 637 6662 6529 120 559 7563 1818 7364
12 יִרְחַץ בְּדַם הָרָשָׁע׃ וְיֹאמַר אָדָם אַךְ־פְּרִי לַצַּדִּיק אַךְ יֵשׁ־
there truly the to (is) fruit ,Truly ,man will And the the in shall he
is ;righteous say .wicked of blood wash

776 8199 430
אֱלֹהִים שֹׁפְטִים בָּאָרֶץ׃
the in judging God a
.earth

PSAL. LIX נט

PSALM 59

To the chief musician. Do not destroy. A secret treasure of David, when Saul sent, and they watched the house to kill him.

1Deliver me from my enemies, O my God; set me on high from the ones who rise up against me. 2Deliver me from the workers of evil, and save me from bloody men. 3For, lo, they lie in wait for my soul; mighty ones gather against me; not *for* my transgression, and not my sin, O Jehovah. 4Without *my* fault they run and prepare themselves; awaken to help me, and look.

5And You, O Jehovah God of hosts, the God of Israel: Awake to visit all the

8104 7586 7971 4387 1732 7843 408 5329
1 לַמְנַצֵּחַ אַל־תַּשְׁחֵת לְדָוִד מִכְתָּם בִּשְׁלֹחַ שָׁאוּל וַיִּשְׁמְרוּ
they and ,Saul when secret a of do not chief the To
watched sent treasure ;David ;destroy ;musician

6965 430 341 5337 4191 1004
2 אֶת־הַבַּיִת לַהֲמִיתוֹ׃ הַצִּילֵנִי מֵאֹיְבַי ׀ אֱלֹהָי מִמִּתְקוֹמְמַי
rising those from my O my from Deliver kill to the
me against ;God ,enemies me .him house

3462 1818 582 205 5337 7682
3 תְּשַׂגְּבֵנִי׃ הַצִּילֵנִי מִפֹּעֲלֵי אָוֶן וּמֵאַנְשֵׁי דָמִים הוֹשִׁיעֵנִי׃
save ,blood from and ;evil the from Deliver me set
.me of men of workers me .high on

3808 6588 3808 5794 1481 5315 693 2009
4 כִּי הִנֵּה אָרְבוּ לְנַפְשִׁי יָגוּרוּ עָלַי עַזִּים לֹא־פִשְׁעִי וְלֹא־
and my (for) not mighty against they my for lie they ,lo ,For
not ,transgression —men ,me gather ;soul wait in

7200 7125 5782 3559 7323 5771 3068 2403
5 חַטָּאתִי יְהוָה׃ בְּלִי־עָוֺן יְרוּצוּן וְיִכּוֹנָנוּ עוּרָה לִקְרָאתִי וּרְאֵה׃
and meet to awaken and they (my) Without O my (for)
.see me ;prepare run fault .Jehovah ,sin

6485 6974 3478 430 6635 430 3068
6 וְאַתָּה יְהוָה־אֱלֹהִים צְבָאוֹת אֱלֹהֵי יִשְׂרָאֵל הָקִיצָה לִפְקֹד
visit to awake ;Israel the ,hosts God O And
of God (of) Jehovah ,You

nations; be not merciful to any plotting evil. Selah. [6]They return at evening; they howl like a dog, and go around the city. [7]Behold, they bellow with their mouth; swords *are* in their lips; for *they say,* Who hears? [8]But You, O Jehovah, shall laugh at all the nations. [9]O my Strength, to You let me watch; for God *is* my strong tower.

[10]The God of my mercy shall meet me; God shall let me see *my desire* on my enemies. [11]Do not kill them, lest my people forget; scatter them by Your power and bring them down, O Jehovah our shield. [12]*For* the sin of their mouth is the word of their lips, and let them be captured in their pride, and for cursing and lying *which* they tell. [13]Consume *them* in *Your* anger; consume, so that they may not be; and they shall know that God *is* ruling in Jacob, to the ends of the earth. Selah.

[14]Yes, they shall return at evening; let them howl like the dog and go around the city; [15]let them wander up and down for food, and growl if they are not satisfied. [16]But I will sing of Your power; yes, I will sing of Your mercy in the morning. For You have been my strong tower, and my hiding-place in the day of my trouble. [17]To You, O my strength, I will sing; for God *is* my strong tower, the God of my mercy.

PSALM 60

To the chief musician, on the Lily of Testimony. A secret treasure of David, to teach; when he struggled with Aram-naharaim, and with Aram-Zobah, when Joab returned, and struck twelve thousand of Edom in the Valley of Salt.

[1]O God! You cast us off; You broke us; You who were angry; take us back.

6153 7725 5542 205 898 2603 1471 3605
8 כָּל־הַגּוֹיִם אַל־תָּחֹן כָּל־בֹּגְדֵי אָוֶן סֶלָה׃ יָשׁוּבוּ לָעֶרֶב
at They .Selah .evil slyly any Be not the all
;evening return plotting to merciful .nations

2719 6310 5042 2009 5892 5437 3611 1993
9 יֶהֱמוּ כַכָּלֶב וִיסוֹבְבוּ עִיר׃ הִנֵּה ׀ יַבִּיעוּן בְּפִיהֶם חֲרָבוֹת
swords their with they ,Behold the go and the like they
;mouth bellow .city around ,dog howl

7832 3068 8085 4310 8193
10 בְּשִׂפְתוֹתֵיהֶם כִּי־מִי שֹׁמֵעַ׃ וְאַתָּה יְהוָה תִּשְׂחַק־לָמוֹ
at shall O But ?hears Who for their in (are)
;them laugh ,Jehovah ,You (say they) ;lips

4869 430 8104 3212 5797 1471/3605 3932
11 12 תִּלְעַג לְכָל־גּוֹיִם׃ עֻזּוֹ אֵלֶיךָ אֶשְׁמֹרָה כִּי־אֱלֹהִים מִשְׂגַּבִּי׃
my (is) God for me let to My nations all at will You
.tower strong ,watch You ;strength mock

2026 408 8324 7200 430 6923 2617 430
אֱלֹהֵי חַסְדּוֹ יְקַדְּמֵנִי אֱלֹהִים יַרְאֵנִי בְשֹׁרְרָי׃ אַל־תַּהַרְגֵם ׀
slay do Not my on me let will God shall my The
,them .foes look ;me meet mercy of God

136 4043 3381 2428 5128 5971 7911
פֶּן־יִשְׁכְּחוּ עַמִּי הֲנִיעֵמוֹ בְחֵילְךָ וְהוֹרִידֵמוֹ מָגִנֵּנוּ אֲדֹנָי׃
O our bring and Your by scatter my forget lest
.Lord ,shield ,down them strength them ,people

3585 422 1347 3920 8193 1697 6310 2403
13 חַטַּאת־פִּימוֹ דְּבַר־שְׂפָתֵימוֹ וְיִלָּכְדוּ בִגְאוֹנָם וּמֵאָלָה וּמִכַּחַשׁ
for and for and their in them let and their the (is) their sin The
lying (the) ,cursing ;pride taken be ,lips of word mouth of

4910 430 3045 369 3615 2534 3615 5608
14 יְסַפֵּרוּ׃ כַּלֵּה בְחֵמָה כַּלֵּה וְאֵינֵמוֹ וְיֵדְעוּ כִּי־אֱלֹהִים מֹשֵׁל
(is) God that they that they that con- in Consume they
ruling know may ,not be ,sume ;anger (them) .speak

3611 1993 6153 7725 5542 776 657 3290
15 בְּיַעֲקֹב לְאַפְסֵי הָאָרֶץ סֶלָה׃ וְיָשֻׁבוּ לָעֶרֶב יֶהֱמוּ כַכָּלֶב
the like shall they at they And .Selah the the to in
dog howl ;evening return shall .earth of ends ,Jacob

3885 7646 3808/518 398 5128 5892 5437
16 וִיסוֹבְבוּ עִיר׃ הֵמָּה יְנִיעוּן לֶאֱכֹל אִם־לֹא יִשְׂבְּעוּ וַיָּלִינוּ׃
they then are they not if ;eat to wander they the go and
.growl ,satisfied around ;city around

4869 1961 2617 1242 7442 5797 7891
17 וַאֲנִי ׀ אָשִׁיר עֻזֶּךָ וַאֲרַנֵּן לַבֹּקֶר חַסְדֶּךָ כִּי־הָיִיתָ מִשְׂגָּב לִי
to strong a you for Your the in will I Yes Your will But
,me tower been have ;mercy morning of sing ,strength of sing I

4869 430 2167 5797 6862 3117 4498
18 וּמָנוֹס בְּיוֹם צַר־לִי׃ עֻזִּי אֵלֶיךָ אֲזַמֵּרָה כִּי־אֱלֹהִים מִשְׂגַּבִּי
my (is) God for will I You to my O to distress the in a and
.tower strong praise sing ,strength .me of day refuge

2611 430
אֱלֹהֵי חַסְדִּי׃
my the
.mercy of God

PSAL. LX ס

PSALM 60

5327 3925 1732 4387 5715 7799 5921 5329
1 2 לַמְנַצֵּחַ עַל־שׁוּשַׁן עֵדוּת מִכְתָּם לְדָוִד לְלַמֵּד׃ בְּהַצּוֹתוֹ ׀
he when ,teach to of secret a ;Testimony the on chief the To
struggled ;David ;treasure of Lily ;musician

5221 3097 7725 6678 758 5104 763
אֶת אֲרַם נַהֲרַיִם וְאֶת־אֲרַם צוֹבָה וַיָּשָׁב יוֹאָב וַיַּךְ אֶת־
and Joab when ,Zobah Aram and naharaim Aram- with
struck returned with

6555 2146 430 505 6240 8147 4417/1516 123
3 אֱדוֹם בְּגֵיא־מֶלַח שְׁנֵים עָשָׂר אָלֶף׃ אֱלֹהִים זְנַחְתָּנוּ פְרַצְתָּנוּ
You cast You O .thousand twelve Salt the in (of)
;us broke ;off us ,God of Valley Edom

[2]You made the earth tremble; You tore it; heal its breaks, for it is shaking. [3]You have shown Your people hardship; You made us drink the wine of trembling. [4]You have given a banner to those who fear You, to lift it up because of the truth. Selah.

[5]Save *with* Your right hand and answer me, that Your beloved may be delivered. [6]God has spoken in His holiness; I will rejoice; I will divide Shechem, and measure out the valley of Succoth. [7]Gilead *is* Mine, and Manasseh *is* Mine; Ephraim *is* the strength of My head; Judah *is* My lawgiver; [8]Moab *is* My washpot; over Edom I will cast out My shoe; over me, Philistia, shout in triumph. [9]Who will bring me *into* the strong city? Who will lead me into Edom? [10]Have not You, O God, cast us aside? And will You not go forth with our armies, O God? [11]Give us help against *our* foe, for vain is the deliverance of man. [12]Through God we shall do mighty things; for He shall tread on our foes.

PSALM 61

To the chief musician, on stringed instruments. Of David.

[1]Hear my cry, O God, and listen to my prayer. [2]From the end of the earth I call to You when my heart faints; O lead me to the Rock *that* is higher than I. [3]For You have been my shelter, a strong tower before the enemy. [4]I will dwell in Your tabernacle forever; I will trust in the shelter of Your wings. Selah.

[5]For You, O God, have heard my vows; You appointed the inheritance

7667 7495 6480 776 7493 7725 599
4 אָנַפְתָּ תְּשׁוֹבֵב לָנוּ׃ הִרְעַשְׁתָּה אֶרֶץ פְּצַמְתָּהּ רְפָה שְׁבָרֶיהָ
its heal tore You the to made You .us take were You
,breaks ;it ;earth tremble back ;angry

8055 3196 8248 7186 5971 7200 4131
5 כִי־מָטָה׃ הִרְאִיתָ עַמְּךָ קָשָׁה הִשְׁקִיתָנוּ יַיִן תַּרְעֵלָה׃
.trembling the us make You hard- Your have You is it for
of wine drink ;ship people shown .shaking

6440 5542 7189 5127 5251 3373 5414
6
7 נָתַתָּה לִּירֵאֶיךָ נֵּס לְהִתְנוֹסֵס מִפְּנֵי קֹשֶׁט סֶלָה׃ לְמַעַן
That .Selah the because be to a those to have You
.truth of ,displayed banner You fearing given

1696 430 6030 3225 3462 3039 2502
8 יֵחָלְצוּן יְדִידֶיךָ הוֹשִׁיעָה יְמִינְךָ וַעֲנֵנוּ׃ אֱלֹהִים ׀ דִּבֶּר
has God answer and Your save Your be may
spoken .me hand right (with) ,beloved delivered

4053 5523 6010 7927 2505 5937 6944
9 בְּקָדְשׁוֹ אֶעְלֹזָה אֲחַלְּקָה שְׁכֶם וְעֵמֶק סֻכּוֹת אֲמַדֵּד׃ לִי
To measure Succoth the and ,Shechem will I will I His in
Me .out of valley divide ;rejoice ;holiness

2710 3063 7200 4581 669 4519 1568
גִלְעָד ׀ וְלִי מְנַשֶּׁה וְאֶפְרַיִם מָעוֹז רֹאשִׁי יְהוּדָה מְחֹקְקִי׃
My Judah My the Ephraim (is) to and ,Gilead
;lawgiver (is) ;head of strength (is) ;Manasseh Me (is)

6429 5275 7993 123 7366 5518 4124
10 מוֹאָב ׀ סִיר רַחְצִי עַל־אֱדוֹם אַשְׁלִיךְ נַעֲלִי עָלַי פְּלֶשֶׁת
,Philistia on My will I Edom over My pot the Moab
me ;shoe out cast ;washing of (is)

3808 123 5148 4310 4692 5892 2986 4310 7321
11
12 הִתְרוֹעָעִי׃ מִי יֹבִלֵנִי עִיר מָצוֹר מִי נָחַנִי עַד־אֱדוֹם׃ הֲלֹא־
Have ?Edom into will Who ?strong the bring will Who in shout
not me lead city (into) me .triumph

6635 430 3318 3808 2186 430
אַתָּה אֱלֹהִים זְנַחְתָּנוּ וְלֹא־תֵצֵא אֱלֹהִים בְּצִבְאוֹתֵינוּ׃
our with ,God O You will And us cast ,God O You
?armies ,forth go not ?aside

430 120 8668 7723 6862 5833 3053
13
14 הָבָה־לָּנוּ עֶזְרָת מִצָּר וְשָׁוְא תְּשׁוּעַת אָדָם׃ בֵּאלֹהִים
Through .man the vain for against help us to Give
God of deliverance (is) ,foe (our)

6862 947 1931 2428 6213
נַעֲשֶׂה־חָיִל וְהוּא יָבוּס צָרֵינוּ׃
our shall He for mighty shall we
.foes on tread ,things do

PSAL. LXI סא

PSALM 61

3478 7440 430 8085 1732 5058 5329
1
2 לַמְנַצֵּחַ עַל־נְגִינַת לְדָוִד׃ שִׁמְעָה אֱלֹהִים רִנָּתִי הַקְשִׁיבָה
listen and ,cry my ,God O ,Hear .David of stringed on chief the To
to ;instruments ;musician

6697 3820 5848 7121 776 7097 8605
3 תְּפִלָּתִי׃ מִקְצֵה הָאָרֶץ ׀ אֵלֶיךָ אֶקְרָא בַּעֲטֹף לִבִּי בְּצוּר־
the in my when will I to the the From my
rock ;heart faints ,call You earth of end .prayer

6440 5797/4024 4268 1961 5148 7311
4 יָרוּם מִמֶּנִּי תַנְחֵנִי׃ כִּי־הָיִיתָ מַחְסֶה לִי מִגְדַּל־עֹז מִפְּנֵי
before strong a for a You For lead I than is (that)
tower ,me shelter been have ,me higher

3671 5643 2620 5769 168 1481 341
5= אוֹיֵב׃ אָגוּרָה בְאָהָלְךָ עוֹלָמִים אֶחֱסֶה בְסֵתֶר כְּנָפֶיךָ
Your the in me let ;forever Your in me Let the
.wings of shelter hide tent dwell .enemy

3373 3425 5414 5088 8085 430 5542
6 סֶלָה׃ כִּי־אַתָּה אֱלֹהִים שָׁמַעְתָּ לִנְדָרָי נָתַתָּ יְרֻשַּׁת יִרְאֵי
fearers heritage a You my have O ,You For .Selah
of to gave ;vows heard ,God

of those who fear Your
name. 6You will add days
to the days of the king; his
years will be as generations
to generations. 7He shall
sit enthroned forever before
God; appoint mercy and
truth to preserve Him. 8So I
will sing praise to Your
name forever, so that I may
pay my vows day *by* day.

PSALM 62

To the chief musician, to Jeduthun. A Psalm of David.

1Only to God is my soul
silent; from Him *comes* my
salvation. 2He alone *is* my
rock and my salvation, my
strong tower; I shall not be
greatly moved. 3How long
will you break in against a
man? You will shatter him,
all of you, like a bowing
wall, a tottering fence.
4Surely, they plotted to cast
him down from his
excellent dignity; they
delight in lies; they bless
with their mouth, but they
curse in their heart. Selah.
5Only be silent to God, O
my soul, for my hope comes
from Him. 6He alone *is* my
rock and my salvation, my
strong tower; I shall not be
shaken. 7On God *is* my
salvation and my glory; my
strong rock, my refuge *is* in
God. 8Trust in Him at every
time, you people; pour out
your heart before Him; God
is a refuge for us. Selah.
9Surely the sons of men
are vanity, the sons of man
are a lie; they go up in the
scales; they *are higher* than
vanity together. 10Trust not
in oppression, and do not
be vain in robbery; if riches
increase to you, do not set
your heart *on them*. 11God
has spoken once; twice I
have heard this, that power
belongs to God; 12Also
mercy *belongs* to You, O
Lord, for You reward a man
according to his work.

1755 1755 81 41 3254 4428 3117 3117 8034
7 שְׁמֶךָ׃ יָמִים עַל־יְמֵי־מֶלֶךְ תּוֹסִיף שְׁנוֹתָיו כְּמוֹ־דֹר וָדֹר׃
genera- genera- as his will You the the to Days Your
.tion to tion years ;add king of days .name

3651 5341 4487 571 2617 430 6440 5769 3427
8 יֵשֵׁב עוֹלָם לִפְנֵי אֱלֹהִים חֶסֶד וֶאֱמֶת מַן יִנְצְרֻהוּ׃
9 כֵּן
So will they ;appoint and mercy ;God before forever shall He
.him keep truth sit

3117 3117 5088 7999 5703 8034 2167
אֲזַמְּרָה שִׁמְךָ לָעַד לְשַׁלְּמִי נְדָרַי יוֹם ׀ יוֹם׃
(by) day my I that ,forever Your me let
.day vows pay may name praise

PSAL. LXII סב

PSALM 62

1747 430 389 1732 4210 3038 5329
1 לַמְנַצֵּחַ עַל־יְדוּתוּן מִזְמוֹר לְדָוִד׃
2 אַךְ אֶל־אֱלֹהִים דּוּמִיָּה
(in) God to Only of psalm a ;Jeduthun to chief the To
silence .David ;musician

38 08 4869 3444 6697 389 3444 53 15
נַפְשִׁי מִמֶּנּוּ יְשׁוּעָתִי׃ 3 אַךְ־הוּא צוּרִי וִישׁוּעָתִי מִשְׂגַּבִּי לֹא־
not strong my my and my He alone my (comes) from my (is)
;tower ,salvation rock (is) .salvation Him ;soul

3605 7523 376 2050 5704 7227 4131
אֶמּוֹט רַבָּה׃ 4 עַד־אָנָה ׀ תְּהוֹתְתוּ עַל־אִישׁ תְּרָצְּחוּ כֻלְּכֶם
of all will You a against will you when Until .greatly shall I
,you ,him shatter ?man in break shaken be

5080 3289 7613 389 1760 1449 5186 7023
כְּקִיר נָטוּי גָּדֵר הַדְּחוּיָה׃ 5 אַךְ מִשְּׂאֵתוֹ ׀ יָעֲצוּ לְהַדִּיחַ
cast to they his from Surely .tottering fence a ;leaning a like
;down (him) plotted exaltation wall

430 389 55 42 7043 71 30 1288 6310 3577 7521
יִרְצוּ כָזָב בְּפִיו יְבָרֵכוּ וּבְקִרְבָּם יְקַלְלוּ־סֶלָה׃ 6 אַךְ לֵאלֹהִים
God to Only .Selah they in but they their with ;lies they
.curse heart their ,bless mouth in joy

3468 6697 389 8615 53 15 1826
דּוֹמִּי נַפְשִׁי כִּי־מִמֶּנּוּ תִּקְוָתִי׃ 7 אַךְ־הוּא צוּרִי וִישׁוּעָתִי
my and my He alone my (is) from for my be
,salvation rock (is) .hope Him ,soul ,silent

5797/6697 3519 3468 430 5921 4131 38 08 4869
מִשְׂגַּבִּי לֹא אֶמּוֹט׃ 8 עַל־אֱלֹהִים יִשְׁעִי וּכְבוֹדִי צוּר־עֻזִּי
strong my my and my God On shall I not strong my
;rock ;glory salvation (is) .shaken be ;tower

6440 8210 5971 6256 982 430 4268
מַחְסִי בֵּאלֹהִים׃ 9 בִּטְחוּ בוֹ בְכָל־עֵת ׀ עָם שִׁפְכוּ־לְפָנָיו
before pour (you) ,time in in Trust in (is) my
Him out ;pledge every Him .God refuge

120 1121 1892 389 55 42 4268 430 3824
לְבַבְכֶם אֱלֹהִים מַחֲסֶה־לָּנוּ סֶלָה׃ 10 אַךְ ׀ הֶבֶל בְּנֵי־אָדָם
.men the vanity Surely .Selah for a God Your
of sons (are) .us refuge (is) ;heart

3808 3162 1892 59 27 3976 376 1121 3577
כָּזָב בְּנֵי־אִישׁ בְּמֹאזְנַיִם לַעֲלוֹת הֵמָּה מֵהֶבֶל יָחַד׃ 11 אַל־
not .together (lighter) they ;up go to the in ,man the lie a
vanity than (are) scales of sons (are)

7896 408 5107 2428 1891 38 08 1498 62 33 982
תִּבְטְחוּ בְעֹשֶׁק וּבְגָזֵל אַל־תֶּהְבָּלוּ חַיִל ׀ כִּי־יָנוּב אַל־תָּשִׁיתוּ
set do not be if riches become do not in and in Trust
(on them) increased ;vain ;robbery ,oppression

430 5797 8085 2098 430 16 96 259 38 20
לֵב׃ 12 אַחַת ׀ דִּבֶּר אֱלֹהִים שְׁתַּיִם־זוּ שָׁמָעְתִּי כִּי עֹז לֵאלֹהִים׃
;God to power that have I thus twice ;God has Once your
(is) ,heard spoken .heart

4639 376 7999 2617 136
13 וּלְךָ־אֲדֹנָי חָסֶד כִּי־אַתָּה תְשַׁלֵּם לְאִישׁ כְּמַעֲשֵׂהוּ׃
to according man a reward You for (is) O also
.work his ;mercy ,Lord ,you to

PSALM 63

A Psalm of David, when he was in the wilderness of Judah.

[1]O God, You *are* my God; I earnestly seek You; my soul thirsts for You; my flesh longs for You, as in a dry and weary land without water. [2]Therefore I have seen you in the holy place, seeing Your power and Your glory. [3]For Your loving-kindness *is* better than life; my lips give praise to You. [4]So I will bless You while I live; I will lift up my hands in Your name. [5]My soul shall be satisfied, as *with* marrow and fatness; and my mouth shall praise *You* with joyful lips, [6]when I remember You upon my bed, I will think on You in the night-watches. [7]For You have been a help to me, and I will rejoice under the shadow of Your wings. [8]My soul is cleaved after You — Your right hand upholds me. [9]And those who seek to destroy my life shall go into the depths of the earth. [10]They shall pour him out by the sword; they shall be a serving for jackals. [11]But the king shall rejoice in God; everyone who swears by Him shall glory, because the mouth of liars shall be stopped.

PSALM 64

To the chief musician. A Psalm of David.

[1]O God, hear my voice in my complaint; guard my life from the terror of the enemy. [2]Hide me from the secret company of plunderers, from the tumult of evildoers, [3]who sharpen their tongue like a sword; they tread their arrows, a bitter word, [4]so that they may shoot at the innocent from a lurking place; suddenly they shoot at him, and fear not. [5]They make themselves strong *in* an evil

PSAL. LXIII סג

PSALM 63

1 2 410 430 3063 4057 1961 1732 4210
מזמור לדוד בהיותו במדבר יהודה: אלהים | אלי אתה
You my ,God O .Judah the in he when of psalm A
;(are) God of wilderness was ,David

3004 776 1320 3642 5315 6770 7836
אשחרך צמאה לך | נפשי כמה לך בשרי בארץ־ציה
dry a in my for faints my for thirsts earnestly I
land ,flesh You ;soul You ;You seek

3 3519 5797 7200 2372 6944 4325 1097 5889
ועיף בלי־מים: כן בקדש חזיתך לראות עזך וכבודך:
Your and Your seeing have I the in So .water without and
glory power ;You seen place holy weary

4 5 1288 3651 7623 8193 2416 2617 2896
כי־טוב חסדך מחיים שפתי ישבחונך: כן אברכך
will I So .You praise lips my ;life than Your better For
You bless (is) mercy

6 5315 7646 1880 2459 3709 5375 8034 2416
בחיי בשמך אשא כפי: כמו חלב ודשן תשבע נפשי
my be shall and marrow As my will I Your in while
;soul satisfied fatness (with) .palms up lift name ;live I

7 821 3326 5921 2142 6310 1984 7445 8193
ושפתי רננות יהלל־פי: אם־זכרתיך על־יצועי באשמרות
the in my upon remember I When my shall joy (with) and
watches night bed you .mouth praise of lips

8 9 1692 7442 3671 6738 5833 1961 1897
אהגה־בך: כי־היית עזרתה לי ובצל כנפיך ארנן: דבקה
is will I Your in and to help a You For on will I
cleaved .shout wings' shadow me been have .You think

10 1245 7722 3225 8551 310 5315
נפשי אחריך בי תמכה ימינך: והמה לשואה יבקשו
seek destroy to And Your upholds me after My
they .hand right ,You soul

11 4521 2719 3027 5064 776 8482 935 5315
נפשי יבאו בתחתיות הארץ: יגירהו על־ידי־חרב מנת
lot a the hand by shall They the the into shall they my
for ;sword's out him pour .earth of depths come ;life

12 3605 1984 430 8056 4428 1961 7776
שעלים יהיו: והמלך ישמח באלהים יתהלל כל־
everyone shall ;God in shall the But they jackals
glory. rejoice king .be shall

8267 1696 6310 5534 7650
הנשבע בו כי יסכר פי דוברי־שקר:
a (one the) the be shall for by who
.lie speaking of mouth shut Him swears

PSAL. LXIV סד

PSALM 64

1 2 6343 7879 6963 430 8085 1732 4210 5329
למנצח מזמור לדוד: שמע־אלהים קולי בשיחי מפחד
the from my in my ,God O ,Hear of a chief the To
of dread ;complaint voice .David psalm ;musician

3 6466 7285 7489 5475 5640 2416 5341 341
אויב תצר חיי: תסתירני מסוד מרעים מרגשת פעלי
doers the from ;spoilers the from me Hide my guard the
of of tumult of council .life enemy

4 4751 1697 2671 1869 3956 2719 8150 834 205
און: אשר שננו כחרב לשונם דרכו חצם דבר מר:
,bitter a their they their a like sharpen who ;evil
word arrows tread ;tongues sword

5 6 2388 3372/3808 3384 6597 8535 4565 3384
לירות במסתרים תם פתאם ירהו ולא ייראו: יחזקו־
They they and shoot they suddenly the from shoot to
strengthen .fear not ,him at ;perfect ambush

plan; they talk of laying snares secretly; they say, Who shall see them? [6]They search into injustice, *saying*, We have finished a *well*-laid plan. And the inward part of man and *the* heart *are* deep! [7]But God shall shoot an arrow at them; their wounds shall suddenly appear. [8]So they shall be confounded; their tongue falls upon themselves; everyone seeing them shall flee. [9]And all men shall fear and shall declare the work of God; yea, they shall in wisdom consider His work. [10]The righteous shall rejoice in Jehovah, and shall trust in Him; and all the upright in heart shall glory.

PSALM 65

To the chief musician. A Psalm and Song of David.

[1]To You silence *is* praise, O God, in Zion; and to You is a vow paid. [2]To You who hears prayer, all flesh comes. [3]Things of iniquity are mightier than I; our transgressions, You atone for them. [4]Blessed is *the one* You choose and cause to come near You, he shall dwell *in* Your courts; we shall be satisfied with the goodness of Your house, Your holy temple. [5]You will answer us in righteousness *by* awesome things, O God of our salvation; the Confidence of all the ends of the earth and the sea, of those afar off. [6]By Your strength the mountains are set, banded together with might. [7]*You* still the roaring of the sea, the roar of their waves, and the tumult of the peoples. [8]And the inhabitants of the uttermost parts are afraid of Your signs; You make the outgoings of the morning and the evening to rejoice. [9]You visit the earth and water it; You greatly enrich it; the river of God is full of water—You provide their grain, for in this way You have prepared it. [10]You fill its terraces with water. You

7200 4310 559 4170 2934 5608 7451 1697

לָמוֹ ׀ דְּבַר רָע יְסַפְּרוּ לִטְמוֹן מוֹקְשִׁים אָמְרוּ מִי יִרְאֶה־

see shall Who they ;snares slyly of they an (in) them-
,say laying talk ;evil thing selves

3820 376 7130 2665 2665 8552 5766 2664

7 לָמוֹ׃ יַחְפְּשׂוּ־עוֹלֹת תַּמְנוּ חֵפֶשׂ מְחֻפָּשׂ וְקֶרֶב אִישׁ וְלֵב

and man's in- And hidden a hiding have We in- They ?them
heart part ward .(plot) finished ;justice investigate

3782 4347 6597 2671 430 3384 6013

8
9 עָמֹק׃ וַיֹּרֵם אֱלֹהִים חֵץ פִּתְאוֹם הָיוּ מַכּוֹתָם׃ וַיַּכְשִׁילוּהוּ

shall they So their shall ;suddenly an God shoot But (are)
confounded be .wounds appear arrow them at !deep

120 3605 3372 7200 3605 5074 3956 5921

10 עָלֵימוֹ לְשׁוֹנָם יִתְנֹדְדוּ כָּל־רֹאֵה בָם׃ וַיִּירְאוּ כָּל־אָדָם

men all fear And .them seeing every- shall their them on
one flee ;tongue (is)

3068 6662 8056 7919 4639 430 6467 5046

11 וַיַּגִּידוּ פֹּעַל אֱלֹהִים וּמַעֲשֵׂהוּ הִשְׂכִּילוּ׃ יִשְׂמַח צַדִּיק בַּיהוָה

in the Shall wisely they His ,yea ;God the and
Jehovah righteous rejoice .consider work of work declare

3820 3477 3605 1984 2620

וְחָסָה בוֹ וְיִתְהַלְלוּ כָּל־יִשְׁרֵי־לֵב׃

.heart the all shall and in take and
in upright glory ;Him refuge

PSAL. LXV סה

PSALM 65

430 8416 1747 7892 1732 4210 5329

1
2 לַמְנַצֵּחַ מִזְמוֹר לְדָוִד שִׁיר׃ לְךָ דֻמִיָּה תְהִלָּה אֱלֹהִים

God O ,praise silence To .song a of a chief the To
(is) You ;David psalm ;musician

935 1320 3605 5704 8605 8085 5088 7999 6726

3 בְּצִיּוֹן וּלְךָ יְשֻׁלַּם־נֶדֶר׃ שֹׁמֵעַ תְּפִלָּה עָדֶיךָ כָּל־בָּשָׂר יָבֹאוּ׃

.comes flesh all to ;prayer (You) a is and in
You hear .vow paid You to ;Zion

835 3722 6588 1396 5771 1697

4 דִּבְרֵי עֲוֺנֹת גָּבְרוּ מֶנִּי פְּשָׁעֵינוּ אַתָּה תְכַפְּרֵם׃ אַשְׁרֵי ׀

Blessed for atone You our ;I than are iniquity Things
is .them ,transgressions mightier of

6918 1004 2898 7646 2691 7931 7126 977

5 תִּבְחַר וּתְקָרֵב יִשְׁכֹּן חֲצֵרֶיךָ נִשְׂבְּעָה בְּטוּב בֵּיתֶךָ קְדֹשׁ

holy Your the with shall we Your shall he will and You (one)
,house of goodness satisfied be ;courts in dwell ;near bring choose

3605 4009 3468 430 6030 6664 3372 1964

6 הֵיכָלֶךָ׃ נוֹרָאוֹת ׀ בְּצֶדֶק תַּעֲנֵנוּ אֱלֹהֵי יִשְׁעֵנוּ מִבְטָח כָּל־

all con- the our God O will You in awesome (By) Your
of fidence ;salvation of ,us answer righteousness things .temple

1369 247 3581 2022 3559 7350 3220 776 7099

7 קַצְוֵי־אֶרֶץ וְיָם רְחֹקִים׃ מֵכִין הָרִים בְּכֹחוֹ נֶאְזָר בִּגְבוּרָה׃

;might in is Your by the set are ;off far of and the the
girded ,strength mountains seas the ,earth of ends

3372 3816 1995 1530 7588 3220 7588 7623

8 מַשְׁבִּיחַ ׀ שְׁאוֹן יַמִּים שְׁאוֹן גַּלֵּיהֶם וַהֲמוֹן לְאֻמִּים׃ וַיִּירְאוּ

are And the the and their the the the still (You)
afraid .peoples of tumult ,waves of roar ,seas of roaring

6485 7442 6153 1242 4161 226 7099 3427

9 יֹשְׁבֵי קְצָוֺת מֵאוֹתֹתֶיךָ מוֹצָאֵי־בֹקֶר וָעֶרֶב תַּרְנִין׃ פָּקַדְתָּ

visit You make You and the out- the Your of furthest the those
.rejoice to evening morning of goings ;signs limits in living

4325 4390 430 6388 6238 7227 7783 776

10 הָאָרֶץ ׀ וַתְּשֹׁקְקֶהָ רַבַּת תַּעְשְׁרֶנָּה פֶּלֶג אֱלֹהִים מָלֵא מָיִם

—water is God the enrich You greatly and the
of full of river ;it ;it overflow earth

1418 5181 7301 8525 3559 3651 1715 6186

11 תָּכִין דְּגָנָם כִּי־כֵן תְּכִינֶהָ׃ תְּלָמֶיהָ רַוֵּה נַחֵת גְּדוּדֶיהָ

its You fill You Its have You thus for their You
;ridges press ;water with furrows .it prepared grain provide

deepen its furrows; You make it soft with showers; You bless the sprouting of it. 11You crown the year of Your goodness, and Your tracks drop with fruitfulness. 12The pastures of the wilderness drop, and the little hills gird themselves *with* joy. 13The meadows are outfitted with flocks; the valleys are also covered with grain; they shout for joy and sing.

PSALM 66

To the chief musician. A Son. A Psalm.

1Make a joyful noise to God, all the earth; 2Sing out the honor of His name; give glory to His praise. 3Say to God, How fearful *are* Your works! Through the greatness of Your power, Your enemies pretend obedience to You. 4All the earth shall worship You; and they sing to You; they praise Your name. Selah.

5Come and see God's works, who is awesome in His acts toward the sons of men. 6He turns the sea into dry land; they go through the river on foot; there we will rejoice with Him. 7He rules by His power forever; His eyes search out the nations; let not the rebels exalt themselves. Selah.

8Bless our God, O peoples, and make heard the voice of His praise; 9who holds our soul in life, and does not allow our foot to slide. 10For You, O God, have proved us; You have tested us as silver is refined. 11You have brought us into the net; You laid afflictions on our loins. 12You have let men ride at our head; we went through fire and through water; but You brought us out to plenty. 13I will go into Your house with burnt offerings; I will

2896 8141 5850 1288 6780 4127 7241
12 ברביבים תמגגנה צמחה תברך: עטרת שנת טובתך
Your with the You You its it make You with
,goodness year crown .bless sprouting ;soft showers
1389 15 2r4 4057 4999 7491 1880 7491 4570
13 ומעגליך ירעפון דשן: ירעפו נאות מדבר וגיל גבעות
the and wilder- the the drip with drop Your and
hills joy (with) ,ness of pastures ;fatness tracks
1250 5848 6010 6629 3733 38,47 2296
14 תחגרנה: לבשו כרים הצאן ועמקים יעטפו בר
;grain are the also the The fitted are gird
with covered valleys ;flocks meadows with .themselves
7891 7321
יתרועעו אף ישירו:
.sing and shout they
joy for

PSAL. LXVI סו

PSALM 66

2167 776 3605 430 7321 4210 7892 5329
1 2 למנצח שיר מזמור הריעו לאלהים כל הארץ: זמרו
Shout the all ,God to a Make a ;song a chief the To
;earth noise joyful .psalm ;musician
430 559 8416 3519 7760 8034 3519
3 כבוד שמו שימו כבוד תהלתו: אמרו לאלהים מה
How ,God to Say His (to) glory put His the
.praise forth ;name of honor
776 3605 341 3581 5797 7230 4639 3372
4 נורא מעשיך ברב עזך יכחשו לך איביך: כל הארץ
the All Your to pretend Your the in Your fearful
earth .enemies You obedience ,power of might works (are)
7200 3212 5412 8034 1984 2167 7812
5 ישתחוו לך ויזמרו לך יזמרו שמך סלה: לכו וראו
and Come .Selah Your they to they and ;You shall
see .name praise ;you sing worship
3220 2015 120 1121 5949 3372 430 4659
6 מפעלות אלהים נורא עלילה על בני אדם: הפך ים
the He .men the toward His in is who ,God works the
sea turns of sons acts awesome of
4910 8056 8033 7272 5674 5104 3006
7 ליבשה בנהר יעברו ברגל שם נשמחה בו: משל
He in will we there on pass they through dry into
rules .Him rejoice ;foot river the ;land
408 5637 6822 1471 5869 5769 1369
בגבורתו עולם עיניו בגוים תצפינה הסוררים אל
not the search the His ;forever His by
rebels ;out nations eyes power
6963 8085 430 5971 1288 5542 7311
8 ירימו למו סלה: ברכו עמים אלהינו והשמיעו קול
the make and our O Bless .Selah them- let
of voice heard ,God ,peoples .selves exalt
7272 4132 5414/3808 2416 5315 7760 8416
9 תהלתו: השם נפשנו בחיים ולא נתן למוט רגלנו:
our slip to does and ,life in our who ;praise His
.foot allow not soul places
935 3701 6884 6884 430 974
10 11 כי בחנתנו אלהים צרפתנו כצרף כסף: הבאתנו
have You .silver one as have You ;God O have You For
us brought refines us refined ,us proved
7218 882 7392 4975 4157 7760 4486
12 במצודה שמת מועקה במתנינו: הרכבת אנוש לראשנו
our at men have You our on afflictions You the into
;head ride let .loins laid ;net
5930 1004 935 7310 3318 4325 784 935
13 באנו באש ובמים ותוציאנו לרויה: אבוא ביתך בעולות
burnt with Your will I to You but through and through we
offerings house into go .plenty out us brought ;water fire went

pay You my vows,
14 which my lips have opened, and in my trouble my mouth has spoken.
15 I will make go up burnt offerings of fatlings to You, with the incense of rams; I will do *it* with bulls and he-goats. Selah.

16 Come, hear, and let me tell, all you who fear God, what He has done to my soul.
17 I cried to Him with my mouth, and exaltations were under my tongue.
18 If I had regarded iniquity in my heart, Jehovah would not have heard.
19 Surely God has heard; He has attended to the voice of my prayer.
20 Blessed *be* God, who has not turned away my prayer, and His mercy from me!

6862 63,10 1696 8193 6475 834 5088 7999
14 אֲשַׁלֵּם לְךָ נְדָרָי׃ אֲשֶׁר־פָּצוּ שְׂפָתָי וְדִבֶּר־פִּי בַּצַּר־לִי׃
to the in my has and my have which my You will I
.me trouble mouth spoken ,lips opened vows pay

1241 6213 352 7004 5927 4220 5930
15 עֹלוֹת מֵחִים אַעֲלֶה־לָּךְ עִם־קְטֹרֶת אֵילִים אֶעֱשֶׂה בָקָר
bulls will I ;rams the with to make will I fatlings Burnt
(it) do of incense ,You up go of offerings

430 3373 3605 5608 8085 3212 5542 6260
16 עִם־עַתּוּדִים סֶלָה׃ לְכוּ־שִׁמְעוּ וַאֲסַפְּרָה כָּל־יִרְאֵי אֱלֹהִים
,God you all let and ,hear ,Come .Selah .he-goats with
fear who ,tell me

3956 8478 7311 6310 7121 413 5315 6213 834
17 אֲשֶׁר עָשָׂה לְנַפְשִׁי׃ אֵלָיו פִּי־קָרָאתִי וְרוֹמַם תַּחַת לְשׁוֹנִי׃
my under (were) and I (with) to my for has He what
.tongue exaltations ,cried mouth my Him ,soul done

430 8085 403 136 8085 3808 3820 7200 518 205
18
19 אָוֶן אִם־רָאִיתִי בְלִבִּי לֹא יִשְׁמַע אֲדֹנָי׃ אָכֵן שָׁמַע אֱלֹהִים
;God has Surely the have would not my in had I If evil
heard .Lord heard ,heart seen

5493 3808 834 430 1288 8605 6963 7181
20 הִקְשִׁיב בְּקוֹל תְּפִלָּתִי׃ בָּרוּךְ אֱלֹהִים אֲשֶׁר לֹא־הֵסִיר
has not who ,God Blessed my the to has He
away turned (be) .prayer of voice attended

854 2617 8605
תְּפִלָּתִי וְחַסְדּוֹ מֵאִתִּי׃
from His and my
.me mercy ,prayer

PSALM 67

To the chief musician, for stringed instruments. A Psalm. A song.

1 May God be merciful to us and bless us, *and* cause His face to shine *upon* us. Selah.
2 That Your way may be known on earth, Your salvation among all nations.
3 Let the peoples thank You, O God; let all the peoples thank You.
4 O let the peoples be glad and sing for joy; for You shall judge the peoples uprightly and govern the peoples on earth. Selah.
5 Let the peoples give thanks to You, O God; let all the peoples give thanks to You.
6 The earth has given its increase; God, our own God, shall bless us.
7 God shall bless us; and all the ends of the earth shall fear Him.

PSAL. LXVII סז

PSALM 67

215 1288 2603 430 7892 4210 5058 5329
1
2 לַמְנַצֵּחַ בִּנְגִינֹת מִזְמוֹר שִׁיר׃ אֱלֹהִים יְחָנֵּנוּ וִיבָרְכֵנוּ יָאֵר
making bless and be May God A A stringed for chief the To
shine ,us us to merciful .song .psalm .instrument ;musician

3444 1471 3605 1870 776 3045 5542 854 6440
3 פָּנָיו אִתָּנוּ סֶלָה׃ לָדַעַת בָּאָרֶץ דַּרְכֶּךָ בְּכָל־גּוֹיִם יְשׁוּעָתֶךָ׃
Your nations among Your the in may That .Selah with His
.salvation all ,way earth known be .us face

7442 8056 3605 5971 3034 430 5971 3034
4 יוֹדוּךָ עַמִּים ׀ אֱלֹהִים יוֹדוּךָ עַמִּים כֻּלָּם׃ יִשְׂמְחוּ וִירַנְּנוּ
sing and let O of all the thank ;God O the Thank
joy for glad be .them ,peoples You ,peoples You

5148 776 3816 4334 5971 8199 3816
5 לְאֻמִּים כִּי־תִשְׁפֹּט עַמִּים מִישֹׁר וּלְאֻמִּים ׀ בָּאָרֶץ תַּנְחֵם
.guide the on the and ,uprightly the shall You for the
earth peoples peoples judge ;peoples

776 3605 5971 3034 430 5971 3034 5542
6
7 סֶלָה׃ יוֹדוּךָ עַמִּים ׀ אֱלֹהִים יוֹדוּךָ עַמִּים כֻּלָּם׃ אֶרֶץ
The of all the let ;God O the Let .Selah
earth .them ,peoples You thank ,peoples You thank

430 1288 430 430 1288 2981 5414
8 נָתְנָה יְבוּלָהּ יְבָרְכֵנוּ אֱלֹהִים אֱלֹהֵינוּ׃ יְבָרְכֵנוּ אֱלֹהִים
,God shall own our ,God shall its has
us bless .God us bless ;increase given

776 657 3605 3372
וְיִירְאוּ אוֹתוֹ כָּל־אַפְסֵי־אָרֶץ׃
the the all Him shall and
.earth of ends fear

PSALM 68

To the chief musician. A Psalm of David. A song.

1 God rises up *and* His enemies are scattered; and

PSAL. LXVIII . סח

PSALM 68

342 6327 430 6965 7892 4210 1732 5329
1
2 לַמְנַצֵּחַ לְדָוִד מִזְמוֹר שִׁיר׃ יָקוּם אֱלֹהִים יָפוּצוּ אוֹיְבָיו
His are (and) ,God shall A A of chief the To
;enemies scattered arise .song .psalm .David ;musician

those who hate Him flee
from His face. 2 As smoke
is driven away, You drive
them away; as wax melts
before the fire, the wicked
perish in God's presence.
3 But the righteous are glad;
they shout for joy before
God; yea, they exult with
gladness. 4 Sing to God,
sing praise to His name; lift
up for Him who rides in the
deserts; by His name
Jehovah; yea, exult in His
presence. 5 God in His
holy dwelling *is* a father of
the fatherless, and a judge
of the widows. 6 God
causes the lonely to live at
home; He brings out those
who are bound with chains,
while the rebellious dwell
in a dry land.
7 O God, when You
marched before Your
people, when You walked
on through the wilderness.
Selah. 8 The earth shook,
and the heavens dropped
before God, this Sinai
before God, the God of
Israel. 9 O God, You sent
down a shower of plenty, by
which You upheld Your
inheritance when it was
weary: You established it.
10 Your flock lived in it; You,
O God, have prepared for
the poor in Your goodness.
11 Jehovah gave the
word; those who bore it
were a great army. 12 Kings
of armies fled, they ran
away; yea, she who stayed
home has divided the
plunder. 13 When you lie
among the sheepfolds, the
wings of a dove are covered
with silver, and their
feathers with gleaming
gold. 14 When the Almighty
scatters kings in it, it snows
on *Mount* Salmon. 15 The
mountain of Bashan *is*
God's mountain; the Ba-
shan range *is* a mountain of
peaks. 16 Why do you gaze
in envy, O mountain range,
at the mountain God
desired for His dwelling?
Yea, Jehovah will dwell *in it*
forever. 17 The chariots of

1749 4549 5086 6227 5086 6440 8130 5127
3 וְיָנוּסוּ מְשַׂנְאָיו מִפָּנָיו׃ כְּהִנְדֹּף עָשָׁן תִּנְדֹּף כְּהִמֵּס דּוֹנַג
wax as drive You ,smoke is As His from who those and
melts ,away (them) away driven .face Him hate flee

8056 6662 430 6440 7563 6 784 6440
4 מִפְּנֵי־אֵשׁ יֹאבְדוּ רְשָׁעִים מִפְּנֵי אֱלֹהִים׃ וְצַדִּיקִים יִשְׂמְחוּ
be shall the But .God's in the perish the before
;glad righteous presence wicked ,fire

430 7891 8057 7797 430 6440 5970
5 יַעַלְצוּ לִפְנֵי אֱלֹהִים וְיָשִׂישׂוּ בְשִׂמְחָה׃ שִׁירוּ לֵאלֹהִים
.God to Sing with they and ;God before shall they
.gladness exult shall rejoice

6440 5937 8034 3050 6160 7392 5549 2167
זַמְּרוּ שְׁמוֹ סֹלּוּ לָרֹכֵב בָּעֲרָבוֹת בְּיָהּ שְׁמוֹ וְעִלְזוּ לְפָנָיו׃
His in and His by the in Him for up lift His Sing
.presence exult —name Jah ;deserts rides who (song a) ;name to praise

430 6944 4583 430 490 1781 3490 1
6
7 אֲבִי יְתוֹמִים וְדַיַּן אַלְמָנוֹת אֱלֹהִים בִּמְעוֹן קָדְשׁוֹ׃ אֱלֹהִים ׀
God His in (is) the and the father
.holy dwelling God widows' judge ,orphans'

3574 615 3318 1004 3173 3427
מוֹשִׁיב יְחִידִים ׀ בַּיְתָה מוֹצִיא אֲסִירִים בַּכּוֹשָׁרוֹת אַךְ
while with who those He at the makes
chains bound are out brings ;home lonely dwell

5971 6440 3318 430 6707 7931 5637
8 סוֹרְרִים שָׁכְנוּ צְחִיחָה׃ אֱלֹהִים בְּצֵאתְךָ לִפְנֵי עַמֶּךָ
Your before Your in God O a in dwell the
.people outgoing .land dry rebellious

5197 8064 637 7493 776 5542 3453 6805
9 בְּצַעְדְּךָ בִישִׁימוֹן סֶלָה׃ אֶרֶץ רָעָשָׁה ׀ אַף־שָׁמַיִם נָטְפוּ
dropped the ,yea ;trembled the ;Selah the through Your in
(rain) heavens earth ;wilderness stepping

1653 3478 430 430 6440 5514 2088 430 6440
10 מִפְּנֵי אֱלֹהִים זֶה סִינַי מִפְּנֵי אֱלֹהִים אֱלֹהֵי יִשְׂרָאֵל׃ גֶּשֶׁם
A .Israel the ,God before Sinai this ;God before
of shower of God

2416 3559 3811 5159 430 5130 5071
11 נְדָבוֹת תָּנִיף אֱלֹהִים נַחֲלָתְךָ וְנִלְאָה אַתָּה כוֹנַנְתָּהּ׃ חַיָּתְךָ
Your established You it (when) Your ;God O shed You plenty
flock .it ,weary was inheritance ,abroad

561 5414 136 430 6041 2896 3559 3427
12 יָשְׁבוּ־בָהּ תָּכִין בְּטוֹבָתְךָ לֶעָנִי אֱלֹהִים׃ אֲדֹנָי יִתֶּן־אֹמֶר
the gave The .God O the for Your in You ;it in dwelt
;word Lord poor goodness provided

5116 5074 5074 6635 4428 7227 6635 1319
13 הַמְבַשְּׂרוֹת צָבָא רָב׃ מַלְכֵי צְבָאוֹת יִדֹּדוּן יִדֹּדוּן וּנְוַת
she and they ,flee armies Kings .great a army bearers the
staying flee of (were) it of

3128 3671 8240 996 7901 518 7998 2505 1004
14 בֵּית תְּחַלֵּק שָׁלָל׃ אִם־תִּשְׁכְּבוּן בֵּין שְׁפַתָּיִם כַּנְפֵי יוֹנָה
a the the among you If the divided (at)
dove of wings ,sheepfolds down lie .spoil home

7706 6566 2742 3422 84 3701 2645
15 נֶחְפָּה בַכֶּסֶף וְאֶבְרוֹתֶיהָ בִּירַקְרַק חָרוּץ׃ בְּפָרֵשׂ שַׁדַּי
the When .gold with its and with are
Almighty scatters gleaming feathers ,silver covered

2022 1316 2022 430 2022 6756 7949 4428
16 מְלָכִים בָּהּ תַּשְׁלֵג בְּצַלְמוֹן׃ הַר־אֱלֹהִים הַר־בָּשָׁן הַר
a ;Bashan the (is) God's mountain (mount) in it ,it in kings
of mount of mountain .Salmon snows

2530 2022 1386 2022 7520 4100 1316 2022 1386
17 גַּבְנֻנִּים הַר־בָּשָׁן׃ לָמָּה ׀ תְּרַצְּדוּן הָרִים גַּבְנֻנִּים הָהָר חָמַד
desired the (at) of O you do Why .Bashan (is) peaks
mountain ,peaks mount ,envy in gaze of mount the

430 7393 5331 3427 3068 637 7931 430
18 אֱלֹהִים לְשִׁבְתּוֹ אַף־יְהוָה יִשְׁכֹּן לָנֶצַח׃ רֶכֶב אֱלֹהִים
God The .forever dwell will Jehovah ,Yea His for God
of chariots (it in) ?dwelling

God are myriads, thousands
of changes, the Lord among
them; *in* Sinai, in the holy
place. [18]You have gone
up on high; You have led
captivity captive; You have
received gifts among men;
yea, to dwell *among* the
rebellious, O Jehovah God.
[19]Blessed *be* the Lord:
day by day He bears
burdens for us, the God of
our salvation. Selah.
[20]Our God *is* the God of
salvation; and to Jehovah
the Lord *are* the issues of
death. [21]Yea, God will
crush His enemies' head;
the hairy crown of him who
walks on in his guilt.
[22]The Lord said, I will bring
back from Bashan; I will
bring back *My people* from
the depths of the sea; [23]so
that your foot may be
dashed in the blood of your
enemies, the tongue of *your*
dogs in it. [24]They have
seen Your processions, O
God; the goings of my God
my King, in the holy place
[25]The singers went before
then the musicians *came*
among *them were* the
virgins playing the timbrels
[26]O bless God in the
congregations, the Lord,
from the fountain of Israel.
[27]There is little Benjamin
their ruler; the leaders of
Judah *in* their crowd, *and*
the leaders of Zebulun, the
leaders of Naphtali.
[28]Your God has com-
manded your strength; O
God, be strong, *in* this You
have worked out for us.
[29]Because of Your temple
over Jerusalem, kings shall
bring a present to You.
[30]Rebuke the wild beasts of
the reeds, the herd of bulls,
with the calves of the
peoples, trampling down
with pieces of silver. He
scatters the people who
delight in war. [31]Let nobles
be brought out of Egypt;
Ethiopia shall run up her
hands to God. [32]Sing to
God, kingdoms of the earth;
and praises to the Lord.
Selah.
[33]To Him who rides on
the heavens of heavens of
old; lo, He sends out His

4791 5927 6944 5514 136 8136 505 7239
19 רִבֹּתַיִם אַלְפֵי שִׁנְאָן אֲדֹנָי בָם סִינַי בַּקֹּדֶשׁ׃ עָלִיתָ לַמָּרוֹם |
;high on have You the in (in) among the ,changes thousands twenty
up gone .place holy Sinai ;them Lord of ,thousand

7931 5637 637 120 4979 3947 7628 7617
שָׁבִיתָ שֶּׁבִי לָקַחְתָּ מַתָּנוֹת בָּאָדָם וְאַף סוֹרְרִים לִשְׁכֹּן |
dwell to the and among gifts have You cap- have You
,(among) rebellious also ;men received ;tivity captive led

3444 410 6006 3117 3117 136 1288 430 3050
20 יָהּ אֱלֹהִים׃ בָּרוּךְ אֲדֹנָי יוֹם | יוֹם יַעֲמָס־לָנוּ הָאֵל יְשׁוּעָתֵנוּ
our the for bears He by day the Blessed .God O
.salvation of God ,us burdens day ;Lord Jah

4194 136 3068 4190 410 410 5542
21 סֶלָה׃ הָאֵל | לָנוּ אֵל לְמוֹשָׁעוֹת וְלֵיהוִה אֲדֹנָי לַמָּוֶת
for the to and of the to God .Selah
death Lord Jehovah ;salvation God us (is)

8181 6936 341 7218 4272 430 389 8444
22 תּוֹצָאוֹת׃ אַךְ־אֱלֹהִים יִמְחַץ רֹאשׁ אֹיְבָיו קָדְקֹד שֵׂעָר
hairy the His the will God ,Yea the
crown ;enemies of head crush .issues

7725 7725 1316 136 559 816 1980
23 מִתְהַלֵּךְ בַּאֲשָׁמָיו׃ אָמַר אֲדֹנָי מִבָּשָׁן אָשִׁיב אָשִׁיב
will I bring will I from the said his in who him of
back bring ;again ,Bashan Lord .guilt on walks

3611 3956 1818 7272 4272 3220 4688
24 מִמְּצֻלוֹת יָם׃ לְמַעַן | תִּמְחַץ רַגְלְךָ בְּדָם לְשׁוֹן כְּלָבֶיךָ
Your the the in Your (may You) so the the from
dogs of tongue blood foot shatter that ;sea of depths

4428 410 1979 430 1979 7200 341
25 מֵאֹיְבִים מִנֵּהוּ׃ רָאוּ הֲלִיכוֹתֶיךָ אֱלֹהִים הֲלִיכוֹת אֵלִי מַלְכִּי
my my goings the ;God O Your They from (Your)
,King ,God of processions seen have .it enemies

8608 5959 8432 5059 310 7891 6923 6944
26 בַקֹּדֶשׁ׃ קִדְּמוּ שָׁרִים אַחַר נֹגְנִים בְּתוֹךְ עֲלָמוֹת תּוֹפֵפוֹת׃
the playing the among the then The went holy the in
.timbrels virgins (were) them ;musicians (came) ,singers before .place

8033 3478 4726 136 430 1288 4721
27 28 בְּמַקְהֵלוֹת בָּרְכוּ אֱלֹהִים אֲדֹנָי מִמְּקוֹר יִשְׂרָאֵל׃ שָׁם
There .Israel the from the ,God O the in
is of fountain Lord bless .assemblies

8269 2074 8269 7277 3063 8269 7287 6810 1144
בִּנְיָמִן | צָעִיר רֹדֵם שָׂרֵי יְהוּדָה רִגְמָתָם שָׂרֵי זְבֻלוּן שָׂרֵי
princes Zebu- the their (in) Judah the their little Benja-
lun of princes ;crowd of princes ;ruler min

6466 2098 430 5810 5797 430 6680 5320
29 נַפְתָּלִי׃ צִוָּה אֱלֹהֶיךָ עֻזֶּךָ עוּזָּה אֱלֹהִים זוּ פָּעַלְתָּ לָּנוּ׃
for have You this O be your Your com- has.Naphtali's
.us worked ,God ,strong ;strength God manded

2416 1605 7862 2831 2986 3389 1964
30 31 מֵהֵיכָלֶךָ עַל־יְרוּשָׁלָםִ לְךָ יוֹבִילוּ מְלָכִים שָׁי׃ גְּעַר חַיַּת
the Rebuke a kings shall to Jerusalem over of Because
of beast .present bring You temple Your

3701 7518 7511 5971 5695 47 5712 7070
קְנֵה עֲדַת אַבִּירִים | בְּעֶגְלֵי עַמִּים מִתְרַפֵּס בְּרַצֵּי־כָסֶף
;silver with trampling the the with the com- the the
of pieces down peoples of calves ,bulls of pany ,reeds

4714 2830 857 2654 7128 5971 967
32 בִּזַּר עַמִּים קְרָבוֹת יֶחְפָּצוּ׃ יֶאֱתָיוּ חַשְׁמַנִּים מִנִּי מִצְרָיִם
;Egypt out bronze be Let who war the He
of brought .in delight peoples scatters

430 7891 776 4467 430 3027 7323 3568
33 כּוּשׁ תָּרִיץ יָדָיו לֵאלֹהִים׃ מַמְלְכוֹת הָאָרֶץ שִׁירוּ לֵאלֹהִים
;God to sing the Kingdoms .God to her shall Ethiopia
earth of hands up run

6963 5414 2005 6924 8064 8064 7392 5542 136 2167
34 זַמְּרוּ אֲדֹנָי סֶלָה׃ לָרֹכֵב בִּשְׁמֵי שְׁמֵי־קֶדֶם הֵן יִתֵּן בְּקוֹלוֹ
His He ,lo ;old heavens the on Him To .Selah the praises
,voice gives of of heavens rides who .Lord

voice, a mighty voice. 34 Ascribe strength to God over Israel; His majesty and His strength in the skies. 35 O God, *You are* overwhelming out of Your holy places; the God of Israel *is* He who gives strength and powers to the people. Blessed *be* God!

PSALM 69

To the chief musician, Concerning the Lilies of David.

1 Save me, O God, for the waters have come in to *my* soul. 2 I sink in deep mire, and there is no standing; I have come into deep waters where the floods overflow me. 3 I am weary from my crying, my throat is scorched; my eyes fail while I wait for my God. 4 They who hate me without a cause are more than the hairs of my head; they who would destroy me are mighty, my lying enemies; then I restored what I did not take by violence.

5 O God, You know my foolishness; and my guiltiness *is* not hidden from You. 6 O Jehovah of hosts, do not let those who wait on You be ashamed for my sake; let not the ones who seek You be ashamed for my sake, O God of Israel. 7 Because I suffered reproach for Your sake, shame has covered my face. 8 I have become a stranger to my brothers, and a foreigner to my mother's children. 9 For the zeal of Your house has consumed me; and the reproaches of the ones who reproach You have fallen on me. 10 When I humbled my soul with fasting, it also was to my reproach; 11 I also made sackcloth my clothing, and I became a mockery to them. 12 They who sit in the gate spoke of me; and I *was* the song of drunkards. 13 But *as for* me, my prayer *is* to You, O Jehovah, at a time of favor, O God! In the plentitude of

7834 5797 1346 3478/ 59 21 430 5797/5414/5797 6963
35 קוֹל עֹז׃ תְּנוּ עֹז לֵאלֹהִים עַל־יִשְׂרָאֵל גַּאֲוָתוֹ וְעֻזּוֹ בַּשְּׁחָקִים׃
the in His and His ;Israel over God to strength As- .mighty a
.skies strength majesty scribe voice

8592 5797/ 5414 3478 410 4720 430 3372
36 נוֹרָא אֱלֹהִים מִמִּקְדָּשֶׁיךָ אֵל יִשְׂרָאֵל הוּא נֹתֵן עֹז וְתַעֲצֻמוֹת
and strength who He ,Israel the Your of out ;God Awe-
powers gives of God ,places holy (is) some

430 1288 5971
לָעָם בָּרוּךְ אֱלֹהִים׃
!God Blessed the to
(be) .people

PSAL. LXIX סט

PSALM 69

935 430 3462 1732 7999 53 29
1 לַמְנַצֵּחַ עַל־שׁוֹשַׁנִּים לְדָוִד׃
2 הוֹשִׁיעֵנִי אֱלֹהִים כִּי בָאוּ
have for ,God O ,me Save Of the according chief the To
come .David .Lilies to ;musician

935 4613 369 4688 3121 2883 53.15 5704 4325
3 מַיִם עַד־נָפֶשׁ׃ טָבַעְתִּי בִּיוֵן מְצוּלָה וְאֵין מָעֳמָד בָּאתִי
have I ;standing and ,deep in sunk I (my) to the
come no is mire .soul waters

2787 7121 3021 7857 7641 4325 4615
4 בְמַעֲמַקֵּי־מַיִם וְשִׁבֹּלֶת שְׁטָפָתְנִי׃ יָגַעְתִּי בְקָרְאִי נִחַר
is my with am I overflowed His and waters into
burnt ,crying weary .me floods deep

7.21.8 8185 7231 430 31 76 3615 1627
5 גְּרוֹנִי כָּלוּ עֵינַי מְיַחֵל לֵאלֹהָי׃ רַבּוּ מִשַּׂעֲרוֹת רֹאשִׁי
my hairs the More my for while my fail my
head of than .God wait I eyes ;throat

1497 380 8 834 8267 341 6789 6105 2600 8130
שֹׂנְאַי חִנָּם עָצְמוּ מַצְמִיתַי אֹיְבַי שֶׁקֶר אֲשֶׁר לֹא־גָזַלְתִּי
,stole I not what ;lying my my are without my are
enemies ,destroyers mighty ;cause haters

819 200 3045 430 7725 227
6 אָז אָשִׁיב׃ אֱלֹהִים אַתָּה יָדַעְתָּ לְאִוַּלְתִּי וְאַשְׁמוֹתַי מִמְּךָ
from my and my know You God O must I then
You guiltiness ;foolishness :restore

3808 6635 30 68 136 6960 954 3582
7 לֹא־נִכְחָדוּ׃ אַל־יֵבֹשׁוּ בִי ׀ קֹוֶיךָ אֲדֹנָי יְהוִה צְבָאוֹת אַל־
not ;hosts Jehovah O on waiters in let Do not are not
of Lord ,You me ashamed be .hidden

2781 5375 5668/3588 3478 430 1245 3637
8 יִכָּלְמוּ בִי מְבַקְשֶׁיךָ אֱלֹהֵי יִשְׂרָאֵל׃ כִּי־עָלֶיךָ נָשָׂאתִי חֶרְפָּה
;reproach I for Because .Israel God O seekers in be let
bore sake Your of ,You for me ashamed

517 1121 5237 251 1961 2114 6440 3639 3680
9 כִּסְּתָה כְלִמָּה פָנָי׃ מוּזָר הָיִיתִי לְאֶחָי וְנָכְרִי לִבְנֵי אִמִּי׃
my sons to a and my to have I a my shame has
.mother's foreigner ,brothers become stranger .face covered

59 21 5307 27 78 2781 398 1004 7068
10 כִּי־קִנְאַת בֵּיתְךָ אֲכָלָתְנִי וְחֶרְפּוֹת חוֹרְפֶיךָ נָפְלוּ עָלָי׃
on have reproachers the and con- has Your the For
.me fallen You of of reproaches ;me sumed house of zeal

3830 5414 2781 1961 53.15 6680 1058
11 וָאֶבְכֶּה בַצּוֹם נַפְשִׁי וַתְּהִי לַחֲרָפוֹת לִי׃
12 וָאֶתְּנָה לְבוּשִׁי
my also I to reproach it and my with I And
clothing made .me was ,soul fasting ,wept

5058 8179 3427 7878 1491 2 1961 82 42
13 שָׂק וָאֱהִי לָהֶם לְמָשָׁל׃ יָשִׂיחוּ בִי יֹשְׁבֵי שָׁעַר וּנְגִינוֹת
the and the who They on meditated a to I and sack-
of song ;gate in sit me .proverb them became cloth

430 75 22 6256 30 68 8605 7941 8354
14 שׁוֹתֵי שֵׁכָר׃ וַאֲנִי תְפִלָּתִי־לְךָ ׀ יְהוָה עֵת רָצוֹן אֱלֹהִים
!God O ,favor a at O to my (as) But strong drinkers
of time ,Jehovah ,You (is) prayer ,me (for) .drink of

Your mercy answer me, in the truth of Your salvation.
14Deliver me out of the mire, that I may not sink; let me be delivered from those who hate me; and out of the deep waters.
15Let not the floodwaters overflow me, nor let the deep swallow me up; and let not the pit shut its mouth on me.

16Hear me, O Jehovah, for Your mercy *is* good; in the plentitude of Your mercies, turn toward me.
17And do not hide Your face from Your servant; for I am distressed; hear me quickly;
18draw near my soul; redeem it; ransom me because of my enemies.
19You know my reproach and my shame, and my dishonor; my enemies *are* all before You.
20Reproach has broken my heart, and I am faint; and I waited for one to show pity, but *there was* no one; and for comforters, but I found none.
21They also gave me gall in my food; and in my thirst they gave me vinegar to drink.
22Let their table be a trap before them; and to those at ease a snare.
23Let their eyes be darkened, that they may not see; and cause their loins *to* be troubled continually.
24Pour out Your wrath on them; and let the glow of Your anger overtake them.
25Let their home be made desolate; let no one dwell in their tents.
26For whom You have stricken, they have persecuted; and they gossip to the pain of those You pierced.
27Put iniquity to their iniquity; and do not let them enter into Your righteousness.
28Blot them out from the Book of Life; yea, let them not be written with the righteous.

29But I *am* poor and in pain; O God, Your salvation shall set me on high.
30I will praise God's name in a song; and I will magnify Him with thanks.
31And it shall please Jehovah more than bulls, horned *or* hoofed bull.
33The humble

15 ברב־חסדך ענני באמת ישעך׃ הצילני מטיט ואל־
3808 2916 5337 3468 571 6030 2617 7230
that not | of out mire the | Deliver me | Your salvation. | the in of truth | answer me, | Your mercy; | the in of plenty

16 אטבעה אנצלה משנאי וממעמקי־מים׃ אל־תשטפני ׀
7857 3808 4325 4615 8130 5337 2882
overflow me | let not | waters; | of out and deep the | my from haters, | be me let delivered | may I sink;

שבלת מים ואל־תבלעני מצולה ואל־תאטר־עלי באר
875 332 408 4688 1104 3808 4325 7641
the pit | on me | let shut | and not | the deep; | swallow let up me | and not; waters | the of flood

17 פיה׃ ענני יהוה כי־טוב חסדך כרב רחמיך פנה אלי׃
6437 7356 7230 2617 2896 3068 6030 6310
toward me. | turn | Your mercies | the in of plenty | Your mercy; | (is) good | for | O Jehovah, | Answer me, | its mouth.

18 19 ואל־תסתר פניך מעבדך כי־צר־לי מהר ענני׃ קרבה
7126 6030 4118 6887 5650 6440 5640
draw near | answer me; | quickly | to distress me; | for (is) | Your from servant; | Your face | do hide | And not

20 אל־נפשי גאלה למען איבי פדני׃ אתה ידעת חרפתי
2781 3045 6299 341 4616 1350 5315
my reproach, | know | You | ransom me. | my enemies, | because of | redeem it; | my soul; | to

21 ובשתי וכלמתי נגדך כל־צוררי׃ חרפה ׀ שברה לבי
3820 7665 2781 6887 3605 5048 3639 1322
my heart, | has broken | Reproach | my enemies. | all | (are) You before | my and dishonor; | my and shame,

22 ואנושה ואקוה לנוד ואין ולמנחמים ולא מצאתי׃ ויתנו
5414 4672 3808 5162 369 5110 6960 5136
they And (me) gave | found. I | and none | for and comforters, | but none; | for pity, | I and looked | am I and sick;

23 בברותי ראש ולצמאי ישקוני חמץ׃ יהי־שלחנם לפניהם
6440 7979 1961 2558 8248 6772 7219 1267
before them | their table | Let be | vinegar. | gave they drink to me | my in and thirst | gall; | my in food

24 לפח ולשלומים למוקש׃ תחשכנה עיניהם מראות
7200 5869 2821 4170 7965 6341
from seeing; | their eyes, | be Let darkened | snare a. | the to and peace at ones | a for trap;

25 ומתניהם תמיד המעד׃ שפך־עליהם זעמך וחרון אפך
639 2740 2195 5921 8210 4571 8548 4975
Your anger | the and of glow | Your wrath, | upon them | Pour out | make quiver. | continually | their and loins

26 ישיגם׃ תהי־טירתם נשמה באהליהם אל־יהי ישב׃
3427 1961 3808 168 8074 2918 1961 5381
one dwell. | let | no | their in tents | made desolate; | their home | be Let | over- let them take.

27 כי־אתה אשר־הכית רדפו ואל־מכאוב חלליך יספרו׃
5608 2491 4341 7291 5221 834
they gossip; | You those pierced, | the of pain | and to | per- they secuted; | have stricken, | whom | You | For

28 29 תנה־עון על־עונם ואל־יבאו בצדקתך׃ ימחו מספר חיים
2416 5612 4229 6666 935 408 5771 5414
Life; | the from of Book | Blot them | Your in righteousness. | let do enter them | and not | their to iniquity; | iniquity | put

30 ועם צדיקים אל־יכתבו׃ ואני עני וכואב ישועתך אלהים
430 3444 3510 6041 3789 408 6662
God O, | Your salvation, | and pain in; | poor, | But (am) I | be let written. | not | the righteous | and with

31 תשגבני׃ אהללה שם־אלהים בשיר ואגדלנו בתודה׃
8426 1430 7892 430 8034 1984 7682
with thanks. | will I Him magnify | a in song; | God's | name | will I praise | set shall me on high.

32 33 ותיטב ליהוה משור פר מקרן מפריס׃ ראו ענוים ישמחו
8056 6035 7200 6531 7160 6499 7794 3068 3190
are (and) glad; | The humble | have seen | (and) hoofed. | horned | (or) bull, | more than bulls, | to Jehovah | shall it And be good

who seek God, your heart shall live. [33]For Jehovah hears the needy, and He does not despise His prisoners. [34]Let the heavens and the earth praise Him, the seas, and everything that moves in them. [35]For God will save Zion; and He will build the cities of Judah, and they shall live there and possess it. [36]And His servants' seed shall inherit; and they who love His name shall live in it.

PSALM 70

To the chief musician. A Psalm of David, to bring to remembrance.

[1]O God, deliver me! Hurry, O Jehovah, to help me! [2]Let those who seek after my soul be ashamed and turned pale; let them be turned backward and shamed, those who desire my evil. [3]Let them be turned back for a reward of their shame, those who say, Aha, aha! [4]Let all those who seek You rejoice, and be glad in You; and let those who love Your salvation forever say, Let God be magnified. [5]But I *am* poor and needy, come quickly to me, O God; You *are* my help and my deliverer; O Jehovah, do not wait any longer.

PSALM 71

[1]I put my trust in You, O Jehovah, let me not be put to shame forever. [2]In Your righteousness deliver me and rescue me; bow down Your ear to me and save me. [3]Be a rock of strength for me, to which I may always go; You have given a commandment to save me; for You *are* my rock and my fortress. [4]O my God, deliver me out of the hand of the wicked, and out of the palm of the unjust and the ruthless. [5]For You *are*

34 8085 3824 2421 130 1875
34 דֹּרְשֵׁי אֱלֹהִים וִיחִי לְבַבְכֶם׃ כִּי־שֹׁמֵעַ אֶל־אֶבְיוֹנִים
the hears For your let ,God who You
needy .heart live seek

3220 776 8064 1984 959 38 08 615 3068
35 יְהוָה וְאֶת־אֲסִירָיו לֹא בָזָה׃ יְהַלְלוּהוּ שָׁמַיִם וָאָרֶץ יַמִּים
the the and the praise Let does He not His and ,Jehovah
seas ,earth heavens Him .despise prisoners

3063 5892 1129 67.26 3462 430 7430 3605
36 וְכָל־רֹמֵשׂ בָּם׃ כִּי אֱלֹהִים יוֹשִׁיעַ צִיּוֹן וְיִבְנֶה עָרֵי יְהוּדָה
,Judah the He and ;Zion save will God For in moving and
of cities build will .them thing every

8034 157 5157 5650 2233 3423 8033 3427
37 וְיָשְׁבוּ שָׁם וִירֵשׁוּהָ׃ וְזֶרַע עֲבָדָיו יִנְחָלוּהָ וְאֹהֲבֵי שְׁמוֹ
His they and shall His And and there they and
name love who ;it inherit servants' seed .it possess live shall

7931
יִשְׁכְּנוּ־בָהּ׃
.it in shall
dwell

PSAL. LXX ע

PSALM 70

5833 30 68 53 37 430 2142 1732 53 29
1 2 לַמְנַצֵּחַ לְדָוִד לְהַזְכִּיר׃ אֱלֹהִים לְהַצִּילֵנִי יְהוָה לְעֶזְרָתִי
help to O deliver to ,God O to bring to of chief the To
,me Jehovah !me .remembrance ;David ;musician

36 37 268 5472 53.15 1245 2659 9 54 2363
3 חוּשָׁה׃ יֵבֹשׁוּ וְיַחְפְּרוּ מְבַקְשֵׁי נַפְשִׁי יִסֹּגוּ אָחוֹר וְיִכָּלְמוּ
and backward them let my who those con- and be Let !hurry
,shamed turned be ;soul seek founded ashamed

1889 559 1322 6118 7451 26.55
4 חֲפֵצֵי רָעָתִי׃ יָשׁוּבוּ עַל־עֵקֶב בָּשְׁתָּם הָאֹמְרִים הֶאָח ׀
!Aha who those their a for them Let my who those
,say shame of reward back turn .evil desire

8548 559 1245 3605 80 56 7 797
5 הֶאָח׃ יָשִׂישׂוּ וְיִשְׂמְחוּ ׀ בְּךָ כָּל־מְבַקְשֶׁיךָ וְיֹאמְרוּ תָמִיד
,continually let and who those all in be and Let !Aha
say ;You seek You glad ,rejoice

430 34 6041 3444 157 430 1430
6= יִגְדַּל אֱלֹהִים אֹהֲבֵי יְשׁוּעָתֶךָ׃ וַאֲנִי ׀ עָנִי וְאֶבְיוֹן אֱלֹהִים
,God O and poor I But Your lovers ,God be Let
,needy (am) .salvation of magnified

309 38 08 30 68 6403 5828 2363
חוּשָׁה־לִּי עֶזְרִי וּמְפַלְטִי אַתָּה יְהוָה אַל־תְּאַחַר׃
wait do not O You my and my to come
.longer any ;Jehovah ;(are) deliverer help ;me quickly

PSAL. LXXI עא

PSALM 71

5337 6666 57 09 954 408 2620 3068
1 2 בְּךָ־יְהוָה חָסִיתִי אַל־אֵבוֹשָׁה לְעוֹלָם׃ בְּצִדְקָתְךָ תַּצִּילֵנִי
deliver Your in .forever be me let not seek I O In
me righteousness shame to put ,refuge Jehovah You

6697 1961 3462 241 5186 6403
3 וּתְפַלְּטֵנִי הַטֵּה־אֵלַי אָזְנְךָ וְהוֹשִׁיעֵנִי׃ הֱיֵה לִי ׀ לְצוּר
a for Be save and Your to bow and
of rock me .me ear me down ;me rescue

4486 55 53 3462 6680 8548 935 45 83
מָעוֹן לָבוֹא תָּמִיד צִוִּיתָ לְהוֹשִׁיעֵנִי כִּי־סַלְעִי וּמְצוּדָתִי אָתָּה׃
You my and my for save to have You ;always to ,refuge
.(are) fortress rock ;me commanded to come

2556 5767 3709 75 63 3027 6403 430
4 5 אֱלֹהַי פַּלְּטֵנִי מִיַּד רָשָׁע מִכַּף מְעַוֵּל וְחוֹמֵץ׃ כִּי־אַתָּה
You For the and the the from the the from deliver my O
(are) .ruthless unjust of palm ,wicked of hand me ,God

my hope, O Lord Jehovah,
my trust from my youth. [6]I
have rested on You from the
belly; You are He who took
me out of my mother's
womb; my praise *shall*
always *be* of You. [7]I am
like a wonder to many, but
You *are* my strong tower.
[8]My mouth is filled *with*
Your praise, *with* your glory
all the day long.

[9]Do not cast me off now
at the time of my old age.
Do not forsake me when my
strength fails. [10]For my
enemies speak against me;
and those who lurk for my
soul plot together. [11]And
they say, God has forsaken
him; pursue him and take
him, for there is no one to
deliver. [12]O God, do not be
far from me; O my God,
come quickly to help me.
[13]Let them be ashamed; let
those who are enemies of
my soul be consumed; let
them be covered with re-
proach, and let those seeking evil for me *be* dis-
honored; [14]and I will
always hope, and I will add
more on all your praise.
[15]My mouth shall tell of
Your righteousness *and*
Your salvation all the day;
for I do not know the
numbers. [16]I will come in
the strength of the Lord
Jehovah; I will speak of Your
righteousness, of Yours
alone. [17]O God, You have
taught me from my youth;
and until now I have
declared Your wonders.
[18]And now that I am old and
gray-headed, O God, do not
leave me; until I have mani-
fested Your strength to the
generation, Your power to
everyone who is to come.

[19]And, Your righteous-
ness, O God, *is* to the
heights, *You* who have done
great things. O God, who *is*
like You? [20]Who has shown
me great and evil distresses;
You will turn *me*; You make
me live; and You will turn
from the depths of the earth;
You will bring me up.
[21]You will multiply my greatness and surround and
comfort me. [22]I will also
thank You with a harp; O my

990 5564 5921 5271 4009 3068 136 8615
6 תקותי אדני יהוה מבטחי מנעורי׃ עליך נסמכתי מבטן
the from ;womb | have I leaned | on You | my from .youth | my trust | ,Jehovah O Lord | my ,hope

1961 4159 8548 8416 1491 517 4578
7 ממעי אמי אתה גוזי בך תהלתי תמיד׃ כמופת הייתי
am I | a like wonder | (shall) .(be) always | my praise | in who He You ;me took | You (are) | my mother's | of out belly

3117 3605 8416 6310 4390 5797 4268 7227
8 לרבים ואתה מחסי עז׃ ימלא פי תהלתך כל היום
day the long | all | your (with) ,praise | My mouth | is filled | .strong | my refuge | You but (are) | to ,many

408 3581 3615 2209 6256 7993 408 8597
9 תפארתך׃ אל תשליכני לעת זקנה ככלות כחי אל
not | my ,strength | when fails | old ;age | the at of time | cast Do off me | not | Your (with) .glory

3162 3289 5315 8104 341 559 5800
10 תעזבני׃ כי אמרו אויבי לי ושמרי נפשי נועצו יחדו׃
,together | plot | my soul | those and watching | against ;me | my enemies | speak | For | forsake do .me

430 5337 369 8610 7291 5800 430 559
11 12 לאמר אלהים עזבו רדפו ותפשוהו כי אין מציל׃ אלהים
God O | .deliverer | there for no is | take and ;him | pursue (him) | has ;him forsaken | God | ,saying

7853 3615 954 2439 5833 430 7368 408
13 אל תרחק ממני אלהי לעזרתי חישה׃ יבשו יכלו שטני
foes the of | be let consumed | them Let ;blush | come .quickly | help to me | my O God | from ;me | be do far | not

8548 7451 1245 3639 2781 5844 5315
14 נפשי יעטו חרפה וכלמה מבקשי רעתי׃ ואני תמיד
continually | and I | for evil ;me | those seeking | and dishonor | reproach | be Let with covered | my .soul

3605 6666 5608 6310 8416 3605 3254 3176
15 איחל והוספתי על כל תהלתך׃ פי יספר צדקתך כל
all | Your righteousness | shall tell | My mouth | Your .praise | all | in | will I and more add | will hope

1369 935 5615 3045 3808 8668 3117
16 היום תשועתך כי לא ידעתי ספרות׃ אבוא בגברות
strength in | will I come | the .numbers | do I know | not | For | Your .salvation | the ,day

3920 430 905 6666 2142 3068 136
17 אדני יהוה אזכיר צדקתך לבדך׃ אלהים למדתני
have You me taught | ,God O | Yours .alone | Your ,righteousness | will I mention | ;Jehovah's | the Lord

7872 2208 5704 1571 6381 5046 4994 5704 5271
18 מנעורי ועד הנה אגיד נפלאותיך׃ וגם עד זקנה ושיבה
gray- and ,headed | (am I) old | when | And even | Your .wonders | have I declared | now | and until | my from ;youth

935 3605 1755 2220 5046 5704 5800 408 430
אלהים אל תעזבני עד אגיד זרועך לדור לכל יבוא
is who coming | to everyone | gen- the ;ation | Your arm | I reveal | until | leave do ;me | not | ,God O

1419 6213 834 4791 5704 430 6666 1369
19 גבורתך׃ וצדקתך אלהים עד מרום אשר עשית גדלות
great ;things | has done | who | the ,heights | to | (is) ,God O | Your And ,righteousness | Your .power

7451 7227 6864 7200 834 4310 430
20 אלהים מי כמוך׃ אשר הראיתנו צרות רבות ורעות
,evil and | great | distresses | shown has me | Who | like ?You | who (is) | ,God O

7235 5927 7725 776 8415 2421 7725
21 תשוב תחיינו ומתהומות הארץ תשוב תעלני׃ תרב
will You multiply | will You up me bring | will You turn | the earth | from and of depths the | make You ;live me | will You ;(me) turn

571 5035 3627 3034 1571 5162 5437 1420
22 גדלתי ותסב תנחמני׃ גם אני אודך בכלי נבל אמתך
Your truth | harp a with ;instrument | thank will you | I also | (and) .me comfort | sur- and round | my ,greatness

God, I will sing Your truth to You with the lyre, O holy One of Israel. 23My lips shall shout for joy, for I will sing praise to You; also my soul which you have redeemed. 24And my tongue shall muse on Your righteousness all the day; because those seeking my evil are disgraced; they are put to shame.

PSALM 72

Of Solomon.

1Give the king Your judgments, O God; and Your righteousness to the king's son. 2Your people He shall judge in righteousness, and Your poor in justice. 3The mountains will lift up peace to the people; and the little hills through righteousness. 4He shall judge the poor of the people; and He shall save the sons of the needy; and He shall crush the oppressor. 5They shall fear You with the sun; and before the moon in all generations. 6He shall descend like rain on the mown grass; like showers that water the earth. 7In His days the righteous shall flourish, and plenty of peace, till the moon *is* not. 8He shall also rule from sea to sea, and from the River to the ends of the earth. 9Those dwelling in the desert will bow before Him, and His enemies will lick the dust. 10The kings of Tarshish and of the isles shall bring presents; the kings of Sheba and Seba shall offer gifts. 11Yea, all kings shall fall down before Him; all nations shall serve Him. 12For He shall save the needy who cries, and the poor *with* no helper. 13He shall have pity on the poor and needy; and He saves the souls of the needy ones. 14He shall redeem their souls from oppression and violence; and their blood shall be precious in His eyes.

15And He shall live, and the gold of Sheba shall be given to Him; and prayer shall be made for Him continually; He shall bless Him all the day long. 16A fullness

23 אֱלֹהָי אֲזַמְּרָה לְךָ בְכִנּוֹר קְדוֹשׁ יִשְׂרָאֵל׃ תְּרַנֵּנָּה שְׂפָתַי כִּי
24 אֲזַמְּרָה־לָּךְ וְנַפְשִׁי אֲשֶׁר פָּדִיתָ׃ גַּם־לְשׁוֹנִי כָּל־הַיּוֹם תֶּהְגֶּה
צִדְקָתֶךָ כִּי־בֹשׁוּ כִּי־חָפְרוּ מְבַקְשֵׁי רָעָתִי׃

PSAL. LXXII עב

PSALM 72

1 לִשְׁלֹמֹה ׀ אֱלֹהִים מִשְׁפָּטֶיךָ לְמֶלֶךְ תֵּן וְצִדְקָתְךָ לְבֶן־מֶלֶךְ׃
2 יָדִין עַמְּךָ בְצֶדֶק וַעֲנִיֶּיךָ בְמִשְׁפָּט׃ יִשְׂאוּ הָרִים שָׁלוֹם
3
4 לָעָם וּגְבָעוֹת בִּצְדָקָה׃ יִשְׁפֹּט ׀ עֲנִיֵּי־עָם יוֹשִׁיעַ לִבְנֵי אֶבְיוֹן
5 וִידַכֵּא עוֹשֵׁק׃ יִירָאוּךָ עִם־שָׁמֶשׁ וְלִפְנֵי יָרֵחַ דּוֹר דּוֹרִים׃
6 יֵרֵד כְּמָטָר עַל־גֵּז כִּרְבִיבִים זַרְזִיף אָרֶץ׃ יִפְרַח־בְּיָמָיו
7
8 צַדִּיק וְרֹב שָׁלוֹם עַד־בְּלִי יָרֵחַ׃ וְיֵרְדְּ מִיָּם עַד־יָם וּמִנָּהָר
9 עַד־אַפְסֵי־אָרֶץ׃ לְפָנָיו יִכְרְעוּ צִיִּים וְאֹיְבָיו עָפָר יְלַחֵכוּ׃
10 מַלְכֵי תַרְשִׁישׁ וְאִיִּים מִנְחָה יָשִׁיבוּ מַלְכֵי שְׁבָא וּסְבָא
11 אֶשְׁכָּר יַקְרִיבוּ׃ וְיִשְׁתַּחֲווּ־לוֹ כָל־מְלָכִים כָּל־גּוֹיִם
12 יַעַבְדוּהוּ׃ כִּי־יַצִּיל אֶבְיוֹן מְשַׁוֵּעַ וְעָנִי וְאֵין־עֹזֵר לוֹ׃ יָחֹס
13
14 עַל־דַּל וְאֶבְיוֹן וְנַפְשׁוֹת אֶבְיוֹנִים יוֹשִׁיעַ׃ מִתּוֹךְ וּמֵחָמָס
15 יִגְאַל נַפְשָׁם וְיֵיקַר דָּמָם בְּעֵינָיו׃ וִיחִי וְיִתֶּן־לוֹ מִזְּהַב
16 שְׁבָא וְיִתְפַּלֵּל בַּעֲדוֹ תָמִיד כָּל־הַיּוֹם יְבָרֲכֶנְהוּ׃ יְהִי פִסַּת־

of grain shall be in the earth on the top of the mountains; its fruit shall shake like Lebanon, and *they* of the city shall flourish like the grass of the earth.

[17]His name shall be forever; His name shall continue before the sun, and they shall bless themselves by Him; all nations shall call Him blessed.

[18]Blessed *is* Jehovah God, the God of Israel, who alone does wonderful things. [19]And blessed *is* His glorious name forever; and all the earth *is* filled with His glory! Amen and amen!

[20]The prayers of David the son of Jesse have ended.

PSALM 73

A Psalm of Asaph.

[1]Truly God *is* good to Israel, to the pure of heart. [2]And I, my foot had almost stumbled; my steps nearly were made to slip. [3]For I was jealous of the proud; I looked on the peace of the wicked. [4]For there *are* no pangs to their death, and their body fat. [5]They are not in the toil of man; yea, they are not touched with men! [6]So pride enchains them; violence covers them *like* a garment. [7]Their eyes go out from fatness; they have passed the imaginations of the heart. [8]They scoff and speak in malice *of* cruelty; from on high they speak. [9]They set their mouth against the heavens, and their tongue walks through the earth. [10]Because of this His people shall return here; and waters of a full *cup is* drained by them. [11]And they say, How does God know? Also, is there knowledge in the Most High? [12]Behold! These *are* the wicked that *are* always at ease; they increase riches. [13]Surely I have purified my heart in vain, and I have washed my hands in

---

PSALM 72:17 (interlinear)

6692	6529	3844	7493	2022	7.218	776	1250
shall flourish	and its fruit	like Lebanon	shall shake	the mountains;	the on top of	the in earth	grain

51·25 8.121 6440	57L·69	80L34. 1961	776	6212	5892·
shall continue before	;forever	His Shall name be	the earth.	the like of grass	the of city

17 shall the before ;forever His Shall the the like the of
continue sun name be .earth of grass city

18 | 430 | 3068 | 1288 | 833 | 147.1 | 3605 | 1288 | 8034·
,God Jehovah Blessed call shall nations all by bless they and His
(is) .blessed Him ;Him themselves ;name

19 | .3519 | 8034. | 1288 | 905 | 6381 | 62.13. | 3478 | 430
His name blessed And .alone wonderful who ,Israel God the
glorious (is) things does of

20 | 13615 | 543 | 543 | 776· | 3605 | 3519 | 4390 | 57 69·
have and ,Amen the all His is and ;forever
ended !amen .earth glory with filled

3348. 1121 17·32 8605
.Jesse the David The
of son of prayers

PSAL. LXXIII   עג

PSALM 73 (interlinear)

1 | 3820 | 1249· | 430 | 3478 | 2896 | 389 | 623 | 4210
.heart the to ,God Israel to (is) Truly of A
of pure good ·Asaph psalm

2
3 | 7065 | 838 | 8210 | 369· | 7272 | 5186 | 4592
was I For my made were nearly my had almost And
jealous .steps slip to ;foot stumbled ,I

4 | 4194· | 2784 | 369 | 7200 | 7563 | 7965 | 1984
their to pangs there For looked I the the the of
;death no are .on wicked of peace ;proud

5 | 5060 | 38·08 | .120 | 5973 | 582 | 5999 | 1193 | 1277
are they not men and are they man the in their but
touched ;not with :not of trouble ;body fat

6
7 | 2459 | 3318 | 2555 | 7897· | 5848 | 1346 | 6059 | 3651
from out go .them to violence gar- a covers ,pride enchains So
fatness of ment (like) them

8 | 6233 | 7451 | 1696 | 4167 | 3820 | 4906 | 5674· | 5869
(of) in and They the imagina- the have they Their
;cruelty malice speak scoff .heart of tions passed ;eyes

9 | 776 | 1980 | 3956 | 6310 | 8064 | 8371 | 1696 | 4791
through walks their and their the against They they from and
.earth the tongue ;mouth heavens set .speak high on

10
11 | 4680 | 559 | 43·92 | 4325 | 1988 | 5971 | 77·25
How they And by (is) full a and ;here His shall So
,say .them drained (cup) of waters people return

12 | 7961 | 7563 | 428 | 2009 | 5945 | 1844 | 3426 | 410 | 3045
are who the These !Behold the in knowledge Is ?God does
ease at ,wicked (are) ?High Most there know

13 | 5356 | 7364 | 3820 | 2135 | 7385 | 389 | 2428 | 7685 | 57 6 9·
in I and ;heart my have I in Surely (their) they ;always
innocency washed have cleansed vain .riches increase

innocence. 14For all the day I was touched; and my chastening *is* at the mornings. 15If I say, I will speak in this way, behold, I would deceive a generation of Your sons. 16And I thought to know this. It *was* painful in my eyes; 17until I went into the sanctuary of God, *then* I discerned their end. 18Surely You will set them in slippery places; You will make them fall into ruins. 19How they have become desolation in an instant, finished, consumed from terrors. 20Like a dream from dreaming, O Lord; in awaking You will despise their image. 21For my heart *was in* ferment and I was pierced *in* my reins. 22And I *was* brutish and I did not know; I was *like* animals with You. 23Yet I *was* with You continually; You have taken my right hand. 24You shall guide me by Your counsel and afterward shall take me *to* glory. 25Whom *is* to me in Heaven? And I have no desire on earth besides You. 26My flesh and my heart waste away; God *is* the rock of my heart and my portion forever. 27For, lo, those who are far from You shall perish; You have cut off all who go whoring from You. 28*As for* me, the nearness of God *is* good to me; I have made my refuge in the Lord Jehovah, to declare all Your works.

559 518 1242 8433 3117 3605 5060 3709
14 15 כַפָּי׃ וָאֱהִי נָגוּעַ כָּל־הַיּוֹם וְתוֹכַחְתִּי לַבְּקָרִים׃ אִם־אָמַרְתִּי
,say I If the at (is) my and the all touched For my
.mornings chastening ;day was I .palms

3045 2803 898 1121 1755 2009 3644 5608
16 אֲסַפְּרָה כְמוֹ הִנֵּה דוֹר בָּנֶיךָ בָגָדְתִּי׃ וָאֲחַשְּׁבָה לָדַעַת
know to I And would I Your gener- a ,behold this in will I
thought .deceive sons of ation ,way speak

995 410 4720 935 5704 5869 5999 2088
17 זֹאת עָמָל הִיא בְעֵינָי׃ עַד־אָבוֹא אֶל־מִקְדְּשֵׁי־אֵל אָבִינָה
dis- I ;God the into went I until my in it painful ,this
cerned of sanctuary ,eyes (was)

4876 5307 7896 2513 389 319
18 לְאַחֲרִיתָם׃ אַךְ בַּחֲלָקוֹת תָּשִׁית לָמוֹ הִפַּלְתָּם לְמַשּׁוּאוֹת׃
.ruins into will You ;them will You slippery in Surely their
fall them make set places .end

2472 1091 8552 5486 7281 8047 1961 349
19 אֵיךְ הָיוּ לְשַׁמָּה כְרָגַע סָפוּ תַמּוּ מִן־בַּלָּהוֹת׃ כַּחֲלוֹם
a Like !terrors from consumed fin- an in desolation they How
dream ;ished ,instant become have

3820 2556 959 6757 5782 136 2472
20 21 מֵהָקִיץ אֲדֹנָי בָּעִיר ׀ צַלְמָם תִּבְזֶה׃ כִּי יִתְחַמֵּץ לְבָבִי
my (in was) For will You their In O from
,heart ferment .despise image awaking ,Lord ,dreaming

1961 929 3045 3808 1198 8150 3629
22 וְכִלְיוֹתַי אֶשְׁתּוֹנָן׃ וַאֲנִי־בַעַר וְלֹא אֵדָע בְּהֵמוֹת הָיִיתִי
was I (like) did I and brutish And was I (in) and
animals ;know not (was) I .pierced reins my

5148 6098 3225 3027 270 8548
23 24 עִמָּךְ׃ וַאֲנִי תָמִיד עִמָּךְ אָחַזְתָּ בְּיַד־יְמִינִי׃ בַּעֲצָתְךָ תַנְחֵנִי
shall You Your By .right my have You with continually Yet with
;me guide counsel hand taken You (was) I .You

2654 3808 5973 8064 4310 3947 3519 310
25 וְאַחַר כָּבוֹד תִּקָּחֵנִי׃ מִי־לִי בַשָּׁמָיִם וְעִמְּךָ לֹא־חָפַצְתִּי
do I not And in to Whom shall (to) and
desire You besides ?Heaven me (is) .me take glory afterward

430 2506 3820 6697 3820 7607 3615 776
26 בָאָרֶץ׃ כָּלָה שְׁאֵרִי וּלְבָבִי צוּר־לְבָבִי וְחֶלְקִי אֱלֹהִים
God (is) my and my the my and my Waste on
portion heart of rock ;heart flesh away .earth

2181 3605 6789 6 7369 2009 5769
27 לְעוֹלָם׃ כִּי־הִנֵּה רְחֵקֶיךָ יֹאבֵדוּ הִצְמַתָּה כָּל־זוֹנֶה מִמֶּךָּ׃
from go who all have You shall far those ,lo ,For .forever
.You whoring off cut ;perish You from ,behold

4268 3068 136 7896 2896 430 7132 589
28 וַאֲנִי ׀ קִרֲבַת אֱלֹהִים לִי־טוֹב שַׁתִּי ׀ בַּאדֹנָי יֱהוִה מַחְסִי
my Jehovah the in have I (is) to God near- the ,I And
,refuge Lord set ;good me of ness

4390 3605 5608
לְסַפֵּר כָּל־מַלְאֲכוֹתֶיךָ׃
Your all to
.works declare

PSAL. LXXIV עד

PSALM 74

A Lesson, of Asaph.

1O God, have You cast *us* off forever; will Your anger smoke against the sheep of Your pasture? 2Remember Your congregation; You purchased *them* in days before; You redeemed *us as* the rod of Your inheritance, this Mount Zion in which You have dwelt. 3Lift up Your steps to the perpetual

639 6225 5331 2186 430 4100 623 7919
1 מַשְׂכִּיל לְאָסָף לָמָה אֱלֹהִים זָנַחְתָּ לָנֶצַח יֶעְשַׁן אַפְּךָ
Your Will ?forever You have O ,Why .Asaph of ;lesson A
anger smoke off us cast ,God

7626 1350 6924 7069 5712 2142 4830 6629
2 בְּצֹאן מַרְעִיתֶךָ׃ זְכֹר עֲדָתְךָ ׀ קָנִיתָ קֶּדֶם גָּאַלְתָּ שֵׁבֶט
the (as) re- You of You Your Remember Your the against
of rod deemed .old gained assembly ?pasture of sheep

4876 6471 7311 7931 2088/6726 2022 5159
3 נַחֲלָתֶךָ הַר־צִיּוֹן זֶה ׀ שָׁכַנְתָּ בּוֹ׃ הָרִימָה פְעָמֶיךָ לְמַשֻּׁאוֹת
the to Your up Lift in have You ,this Zion Mount Your
.desolations steps .which dwelt ,inheritance

desolations; *the* enemy who has done all evil in the sanctuary. 4Your vexers have roared in the middle of Your congregation; they set up their own signs *for* signs. 5He is known as one bringing axes in on high, against the thick trees. 6And now together they break down its carved work with the axe and hammers. 7They have cast fire in Your sanctuary; they have polluted the place where Your name dwells on the earth. 8They said in their hearts, Let us rage against them together; they have burned up all the meeting-places of God in the land. 9We did not see our signs; there is no longer a prophet; nor *any* among us who knows how long. 10O God, how long shall the enemy defame *You*? Shall the enemy scorn Your name forever? 11Why do You withdraw Your hand, even Your right hand? From out of Your bosom, consume *them*.

12For God *is* my King of old, who works salvation in the midst of the land. 13You broke the sea by Your strength; You burst the heads of sea-monsters in the waters. 14You cracked open the heads of leviathan; You made him food for the people of the wilderness. 15You divided the fountain and the torrent; You dried up mighty rivers. 16The day *is* Yours, the night *is* also Yours; You have established the light and the sun. 17You have fixed all the boundaries of the earth; You have formed the summer and winter. 18Remember this: the enemy has defamed, O Jehovah; and a foolish people have scorned Your name. 19Do not give the soul of Your turtle-dove to the wild beasts; You will not forever forget the life of Your afflicted ones. 20Look to *Your* covenant; for the dark places of the earth are full, the abodes of violence. 21O let not the ill-treated ones turn back ashamed; let the poor and needy praise Your

4150 7130 6884 7580 6944 341 7489 3605 5331
4 נצח כל־הרע אויב בקדש׃ שאגו צרריך בקרב מועדך
Your the in Your have the in (the) done has per-
;sanctuary of middle vexers roared .sanctuary enemy evil all ,petual

6086 5442 4605 935 3045 226 226 7760
5 שמו אותתם אתות׃ יודע כמביא למעלה בסבך־עץ
the against high on one as is He (for) their setting
trees thick in bringing known .signs signs up

1984 3597 3781 3162 6603 6258 7134
6 קרדמות׃ ועת פתוחיה יחד בכשיל וכילפות יהלמון׃
break they and the in ,together carved its And .axes
.down hammers ax work now

559 8034 4908 2490 776 4720 784 7971
7 8 שלחו באש מקדשך לארץ חללו משכן־שמך׃ אמרו
They Your place the have they the on Your fire have They
said .name dwells where polluted earth ;sanctuary into sent

226 776 410 4150 3605 8313 3162 3238 3820
9 בלבם נינם יחד שרפו כל־מועדי־אל בארץ׃ אותתינו
signs Our the in God the all have they ;together us Let their in
.land of meeting-places up burned them oppress ,hearts

5704 5704 3045 5030 5750 369 7200 3808
10 לא־ראינו אין־עוד נביא ולא־אתנו ידע עד־מה׃ עד־
Until .when until (one) with and a longer not we not
knowing us not ;prophet (is) (any) ;see did

4100 5331 8034 341 5006 6862 2778 430
11 מתי אלהים יחרף צר ינאץ אויב שמך לנצח׃ למה
Why ?forever Your the shall the shall ,God O ,when
name enemy scorn ,enemy evil speak

4428 430 3615 2436 7130 3225 3027 7725
12 תשיב ידך וימינך מקרב חוקך כלה׃ ואלהים מלכי
my (is) God For consume Your From Your even Your You do
king !(them) ,bosom of out ?hand right ,hand withdraw

5797 6565 776 7130 3444 6466 6924
13 מקדם פעל ישועות בקרב הארץ׃ אתה פוררת בעזך
with divided You the the in salvation who ,old of
might Your .land of midst works

7218 7533 4325 8577 7218 7665 3220
14 ים שברת ראשי תנינים על־המים׃ אתה רצצת ראשי
the broke You the on sea- the You the
of heads pieces in .waters monsters of heads broke ;sea

5158 4599 1234 6728 5971 3978 5414 3882
15 לויתן תתננו מאכל לעם לציים׃ אתה בקעת מעין ונחל
the and the divided You the of the for food made You levia-
;torrent fountain .wilderness people him ;than

3915 637 3117 386 5104 3001
16 אתה הובשת נהרות איתן׃ לך יום אף־לך לילה אתה
You the to (is) also The to (is) .mighty rivers up dried You
;night You ,day You

7019 776 1367 3605 5324 8121 3974 3559
17 הכינות מאור ושמש׃ אתה הצבת כל־גבולות ארץ קיץ
summer the the a; have You the and the have
;earth of boundaries stationed .sun light fixed

5971 3068 2778 341 2088 2142 3335 2779
18 וחרף אתה יצרתם׃ זכר־זאת אויב חרף ׀ יהוה ועם־
a O has the :thus Remember have You and
people ;Jehovah blasphemed enemy .them formed ,winter

6041 2416 8549 5315 2416 5414 408 8034 5006 5036
19 נבל נאצו שמך׃ אל־תתן לחית נפש תורך חית עניך
Your the Your the the to Do not Your has foolish
afflicted of life ;dove of soul beasts wild give .name despised

776 4285 4390 1285 5027 5331 7911 408
20 אל־תשכח לנצח׃ הבט לברית כי־מלאו מחשכי־ארץ
the dark the full are for the to Look .forever will You not
earth of places of ,covenant forget

8034 1984 34 6041 3637 1790 7725 408 2555 4999
21 נאות חמס׃ אל־ישב דך נכלם עני ואביון יהללו שמך׃
Your praise let the and the ;ashamed the of Let not .violence the
.name needy poor oppressed back turn of abodes

name. 22Arise, O God, contend for Your cause; remember Your reproach from the fool all the day. 23Do not forget the voice of Your enemies; the noise of those rising up against You is going up continually.

22 36 105 50 3 6 2781 2142 7379 7378 430 6965
קוּמָה אֱלֹהִים רִיבָה רִיבֶךָ זְכֹר חֶרְפָּתְךָ מִנִּי־נָבָל כָּל־
all the from Your remember Your contend,God O ,Arise
fool reproach ;cause own (for)

23 8548 5927 6965 7588 6887 6963 7911 408 3117
הַיּוֹם׃ אַל־תִּשְׁכַּח קוֹל צֹרְרֶיךָ שְׁאוֹן קָמֶיךָ עֹלֶה תָמִיד׃
.continually is Your the Your the Do not .day the
up going foes of noise ;enemies of voice forget

PSAL. LXXV עה

PSALM 75

To the chief musician. Do not destroy. A Psalm of Asaph. A Song.

1We have given thanks to You, O God; we have given thanks; for Your name is near; Your wonderful works have been told. 2When I take the appointed time, I shall judge in uprightness. 3The earth and all of its inhabitants are melting away; I set firm its pillars. Selah.

4I said to the boastful, Do not boast; and to the wicked, Do not lift up the horn. 5Do not lift up your horn on high, do *not* speak with a stiff neck. 6For exaltations are not from the east, nor from the west, nor from the desert; 7but God *is* the judge; *He* puts down this *one* and lifts up this *other*. 8For a cup is in the hand of Jehovah; and the wine foams, it is fully mixed; and He pours out from it; surely all the wicked of the earth must drain its dregs *and* all drink. 9But I will witness forever; I will sing praises to the God of Jacob. 10And I will cut off all the horns of the wicked; *but* the horns of the righteous shall be lifted up.

1
2 3034 7892 623 4210 7843 408 5329
לַמְנַצֵּחַ אַל־תַּשְׁחֵת מִזְמוֹר לְאָסָף שִׁיר׃ הוֹדִינוּ לְּךָ ׀
to have We A of psalm A do not chief the To
,You thanks given .song .Asaph .destroy ;musician

3 3947 6387 5608 8034 7138 3034 430
אֱלֹהִים הוֹדִינוּ וְקָרוֹב שְׁמֶךָ סִפְּרוּ נִפְלְאוֹתֶיךָ׃ כִּי אֶקַּח
take I When Your wonderful have Your is for have we ;God O
.works told been ;name near ;thanks given

4 3427 3605 776 4127 8199 4339 4150
מוֹעֵד אֲנִי מֵישָׁרִים אֶשְׁפֹּט׃ נְמֹגִים־אֶרֶץ וְכָל־יֹשְׁבֶיהָ
its all and The melting are shall upright- in I set the
;inhabitants of earth away .judge ness ,time

5 1984 1984 559 5542 5982 8505
אָנֹכִי תִכַּנְתִּי עַמּוּדֶיהָ סֶּלָה׃ אָמַרְתִּי לַהוֹלְלִים אַל־תָּהֹלּוּ
Do not the to say I .Selah its set I
;boast ,boastful .pillars firm

6 7161 4791 7311 7161 7311 408 7563
וְלָרְשָׁעִים אַל־תָּרִימוּ קָרֶן׃ אַל־תָּרִימוּ לַמָּרוֹם קַרְנְכֶם
,horn your high on lift Do not the lift Do not the to and
up .horn up .wicked

7 3808 4628 4161 3808 6277 6677 1696
תְּדַבְּרוּ בְצַוָּאר עָתָק׃ כִּי לֹא מִמּוֹצָא וּמִמַּעֲרָב וְלֹא
and from nor the from not For .stiff a with do (not)
not ,west the ,east neck speak

8 7311 2088 8213 2088 8199 430 7311 4057
מִמִּדְבַּר הָרִים׃ כִּי־אֱלֹהִים שֹׁפֵט זֶה יַשְׁפִּיל וְזֶה יָרִים׃
lifts and puts this the (is) God but (are) the from
.up this down ;judge ;exaltations desert

9 389 2088 5064 4538 4392 2564 3196 3068 3027 3563
כִּי כוֹס בְּיַד־יְהוָה וְיַיִן חָמַר ׀ מָלֵא מֶסֶךְ וַיַּגֵּר מִזֶּה אַךְ־
surely from He and is it fully ,foams the and ;Jehovah (is) cup a For
;it out pours ;mixed wine of hand the in

10 5769 5046 776 7563 3605 8354 4680 8105
שְׁמָרֶיהָ יִמְצוּ יִשְׁתּוּ כֹּל רִשְׁעֵי־אָרֶץ׃ וַאֲנִי אַגִּיד לְעֹלָם
;forever will I But the the all (and) must dregs its
declare .earth of wicked drink drain

11 7311 1438 7563 7161 3605 3290 430 2167
אֲזַמְּרָה לֵאלֹהֵי יַעֲקֹב׃ וְכָל־קַרְנֵי רְשָׁעִים אֲגַדֵּעַ תְּרוֹמַמְנָה
shall (but) will I the the And .Jacob the to will I
up lifted be ;off cut wicked of horns all of God praises sing

6662 7161
קַרְנוֹת צַדִּיק׃
the horns the
.righteous of

PSAL. LXXVI עו

PSALM 76

To the chief musician. For stringed instruments. A Psalm of Asaph. A Song of Praise.

1God *is* known in Judah; His name *is* great in Israel. 2And His abode is in Salem; and His dwelling-place in Zion. 3There He broke the

1
2 430 3063 3045 7892 623 4210 5058 5329
לַמְנַצֵּחַ בִּנְגִינֹת מִזְמוֹר לְאָסָף שִׁיר׃ נוֹדָע בִּיהוּדָה אֱלֹהִים
;God Judah in (is) .song A of psalm A with chief the To
known .Asaph .instruments stringed ;musician

3 6726 4585 5520 8004 1961 8034 1419 3478
בְּיִשְׂרָאֵל גָּדוֹל שְׁמוֹ׃ וַיְהִי בְשָׁלֵם סֻכּוֹ וּמְעוֹנָתוֹ בְצִיּוֹן׃
in His and His Salem in is And His (is) Israel in
.Zion dwelling-place ;abode .name great

fiery arrows of the bow, the shield, and the sword, and the battle. Selah. [4]You *are* glorious, *more* excellent than the mountains of prey. [5]The stout-hearted have been stripped; they slept their sleep; and none of the men of might have found their hands. [6]By Your rebuke, O God of Jacob, both the horse and chariot have sunk into a sleep. [7]You, *even* You, are terrifying; and who can stand before You when You are angry? [8]You have caused judgment to be heard from Heaven; the earth feared and was stilled, [9]when God arose to judgment, to save all the meek of the earth. Selah. [10]For the wraths of man thank You; You encircle Yourself *with* the wraths left over. [11]Vow and pay to Jehovah your God; let all that are around Him bring presents to the Fearful One. [12]He shall cut off the spirit in princes; *He is* feared by the kings of the earth.

215 5542 4421 2719 4043 7198 7565 7665 8033
4 5 שמה שבר רשפי־קשת מגן וחרב ומלחמה סלה: נאור
glorious .Selah the and the and the the fiery the He There
.battle ,sword ,shield ,bow of arrows broke

5123 38 20 47 7997 2964 2042 117
6 אתה אדיר מהררי־טרף: אשתוללו | אבירי לב נמו
they ;heart The been have .prey the than (more) You
slept of stout stripped of mountains excellent ,(are)

430 1606 3027 2428 582 3605 4672 3808 8142
7 שנתם ולא־מצאו כל־אנשי־חיל ידיהם: מגערתך אלהי
God O Your By their might the any have and their
of ,rebuke .hands of men found not ;sleep

5975 4310 3372 5483 7393 7290 3290
8 יעקב נרדם ורכב וסוס: אתה | נורא אתה ומי־יעמד
can and (even) be to are You the and the both sunk ,Jacob
stand who ,You ,feared .horse chariot ,sleep into

3372 776 1779 8085 8064 639 227 6440
9 לפניך מאז אפך: משמים השמעת דין ארץ יראה
feared the ;judgment caused You from You when before
earth heard be to Heaven ?angry (are) You

776 6035 3605 3462 430 4941 6965 8252
10 ושקטה: בקום־למשפט אלהים להושיע כל־ענוי־ארץ
the the all save to God judgment to when was and
.earth of humble arose ,still

5087 2296 2534 7611 3034 120 2534 5542
11 12 סלה: כי־חמת אדם תודך שארית חמת תחגר: נדרו
Vow gird You wraths The thank man the For .Selah
.Yourself on of residue ;You of wraths

4172 7862 2986 5439 3605 430 3068 7999
ושלמו ליהוה אלהיכם כל־סביביו יובילו שי למורא:
the to gifts let are who all Your to and
.One Fearful bring Him around ;God Jehovah repay

776 4428 3372 5057 7307 1219
13 יבצר רוח נגידים נורא למלכי־ארץ:
the the by (is He) ;princes the shall He
.earth of kings feared of spirit off cut

PSAL. LXXVII עז

PSALM 77

PSALM 77

To the chief musician on Jeduthun. A Psalm of Asaph.

[1]My voice *is* to God, and I cry; my voice *is* to God, and He gave ear to me. [2]In the day of my distress I sought the Lord; my hand was open in the night and did not grow numb; my soul refused to be comforted. [3]I remember God and am troubled; I meditate and my spirit faints. Selah. [4]You seized the watches of my eyes; I am troubled, and I cannot speak. [5]I thought upon the days of old, the years of *bygone* ages. [6]I will remember my song in the night; I will speak with my own heart, and my spirit carefully searches. [7]Will the Lord cast off forever; and will He not add to be

430 6963 4210 623 3038 5329
1 2 למנצח על־ידיתון לאסף מזמור: קולי אל־אלהים
,God to My .psalm A Of .Jeduthun ac- chief the To
(is) voice .Asaph to cording musician

136 6864 3117 238 430 6963 6817
3 ואצעקה קולי אל־אלהים והאזין אלי: ביום צרתי אדני
the my the In to He and ,God to my I and
Lord distress of day .me ear gave (is) voice ;cry

5315 5162 3985 6313 3808 5064 3915 3027 1875
דרשתי ידי | לילה נגרה ולא תפוג מאנה הנחם נפשי:
my be to refused did and was the in my ;sought I
.soul comforted ;numb grow not poured night hand

5542 7307 5848 7878 1993 430 2142
4 אזכרה אלהים ואהמיה אשיחה | ותתעטף רוחי סלה:
.Selah my and meditate I am and God I
.spirit faints .troubled remember

3117 2803 1696 3808 6470 5869 8109 270
5 6 אחזת שמרות עיני נפעמתי ולא אדבר: חשבתי ימים
the thought I can I and am I my watches the You
days on .speak not troubled ;eyes of seized

3820 3915 5058 2142 5769 8141 6924
7 מקדם שנות עולמים: אזכרה נגינתי בלילה עם־לבבי
my with the in my will I .ages the the ,old of
heart own ;night song remember of years

3254 3808 136 2186 5769 7307 2664 7878
8 אשיחה ויחפש רוחי: הלעולמים יזנח | אדני ולא־יסיף
will He And the Will forever my and will I
add not ?Lord off cast .spirit searches ,meditate

pleased any more? [8]Is His mercy gone forever? Has *His* word failed for all generations? [9]Has God forgotten to be gracious; has He in anger shut up His tender mercies? Selah.

[10]And I said, This *is* my sickness, the years of the right hand of the Most High; [11]I will remember the works of Jehovah; surely I will remember Your wonders of old. [12]I will also meditate on all Your works and muse of Your doings. [13]O God, your way *is* in holiness; who *is* a God great like God? [14]You *are* the God who does wonders; You have revealed Your strength among the peoples. [15]You have redeemed Your people with Your power, the sons of Jacob and Joseph. Selah.

[16]The waters saw You, O God, the waters saw You; they were afraid; yea, the deeps trembled. [17]The clouds poured out water; the skies uttered a voice; and Your arrows flew out. [18]The voice of Your thunder in the tempest; lightnings lit up the world; the earth trembled and quaked! [19]Your way *is* in the sea; and Your path *is* in the great waters; and Your footsteps are not known. [20]You led Your people like a flcok by the hand of Moses and Aaron.

1755 1755 561 1584 2617 5331 656 5750 7521
9 לִרְצוֹת עוֹד׃ הֶאָפֵס לָנֶצַח חַסְדּוֹ גָּמַר אֹמֶר לְדֹר וָדֹר׃
and genera- to (His) Has His forever Has any be to
?generation tion word failed ?mercy ceased ?more pleased

559 5542 7356 639 7092 410 2603 7911
10
11 הֲשָׁכַח חַנּוֹת אֵל אִם־קָפַץ בְּאַף רַחֲמָיו סֶלָה׃ וָאֹמַר
I And .Selah tender His in He has Or ?God be to Has
said ?mercies anger up shut gracious forgotten

2142 3588 3050 4611 2142 5945 3225 8141 2470
12 חַלּוֹתִי הִיא שְׁנוֹת יְמִין עֶלְיוֹן׃ אֶזְכּוֹר מַעַלְלֵי־יָהּ כִּי־אֶזְכְּרָה
will I Surely :Jah the will I Most the right the the This my
remember of works remember .High of hand of years ,(is) sickness

7878 5949 646 6467 8605 1897 6382 6924
13 מִקֶּדֶם פִּלְאֶךָ׃ וְהָגִיתִי בְכָל־פָּעֳלֶךָ וּבַעֲלִילוֹתֶיךָ אָשִׂיחָה׃
,muse Your of and Your on I And Your old of
doings works all meditate will .wonders

430 1419 410 4310 1870 6944 430
14
15 אֱלֹהִים בַּקֹּדֶשׁ דַּרְכֶּךָ מִי־אֵל גָּדוֹל כֵּאלֹהִים׃ אַתָּה הָאֵל
the You like great a Who Your holiness in ,God O
God (are) ?God God (is) ;way (is)

1121 5971 2220 1350 5797 5971 3045 6382 6213
16 עֹשֵׂה פֶלֶא הוֹדַעְתָּ בָעַמִּים עֻזֶּךָ׃ גָּאַלְתָּ בִּזְרוֹעַ עַמֶּךָ בְּנֵי־
sons the Your with have You Your the among have You ;wonders who
of ,people arm Your redeemed .strength peoples revealed does

2342 4325 7200 430 4325 7200 5542 3127 3290
17 יַעֲקֹב וְיוֹסֵף סֶלָה׃ רָאוּךָ מַּיִם ׀ אֱלֹהִים רָאוּךָ מַּיִם יָחִילוּ
they the saw ,God O The saw .Selah and Jacob
;trembled ;waters You ,waters You .Joseph

7834 5414 6963 5645 4325 2229 8415 7264 637
18 אַף יִרְגְּזוּ תְהֹמוֹת׃ זֹרְמוּ מַיִם ׀ עָבוֹת קוֹל נָתְנוּ שְׁחָקִים
the gave a The water poured the trembled yea,
;skies voice .clouds out .deeps

1300 215 1534 7482 6963 1980 2687
19 אַף־חֲצָצֶיךָ יִתְהַלָּכוּ׃ קוֹל רַעַמְךָ ׀ בַּגַּלְגַּל הֵאִירוּ בְרָקִים
lightnings up lit the in Your The go will Your even
tempest thunder of voice .forth arrows

4325 7635 1870 3220 776 7493 7264 8398
20 תֵּבֵל רָגְזָה וַתִּרְעַשׁ הָאָרֶץ׃ בַּיָּם דַּרְכֶּךָ וּשְׁבִילְךָ בְּמַיִם
in (was) Your and Your (is) In the and trembled the
waters the path ;way sea the earth quaked ;world

3027 5971 6629 5148 3045 3808 6119 7227
21 רַבִּים וְעִקְּבוֹתֶיךָ לֹא נֹדָעוּ׃ נָחִיתָ כַצֹּאן עַמֶּךָ בְּיַד־
the by Your a like You are not Your and ;great
of hand people flock led .known footsteps

175 4872
מֹשֶׁה וְאַהֲרֹן׃
and Moses
.Aaron

PSAL. LXXVIII עח

PSALM 78

PSALM 78

A Lesson of Asaph.

[1]O my people, listen to my law; bow your ears to the words of my mouth. [2]I will open my mouth in a parable; I will pour forth dark sayings of old, [3]those which we have heard and known, and our fathers have told us. [4]We will not hide *them* from their sons; to declare to the coming generation the praises of Jehovah; yea, His strength and His wonderful works

561 241 5186 8451 5971 238 623 4905
1 מַשְׂכִּיל לְאָסָף הַאֲזִינָה עַמִּי תּוֹרָתִי הַטּוּ אָזְנְכֶם לְאִמְרֵי־
the to ears your bow my to my O ,ear Give .Asaph of ,lesson A
of words ;law ,people

834 6924 2420 5042 6310 4912 6605 6310
2
3 פִי׃ אֶפְתְּחָה בְמָשָׁל פִּי אַבִּיעָה חִידוֹת מִנִּי־קֶדֶם׃ אֲשֶׁר
which ,old of dark pour will I my a in will I my
sayings out ;mouth parable open .mouth

1121 3582 3808 5608 1 3045 8085
4 שָׁמַעְנוּ וַנֵּדָעֵם וַאֲבוֹתֵינוּ סִפְּרוּ־לָנוּ׃ לֹא נְכַחֵד ׀ מִבְּנֵיהֶם
their from will We not .us to have our and and have we
;sons (them) hide told fathers ,them known heard

6381 5807 3068 8416 5608 314 1755
לְדוֹר אַחֲרוֹן מְסַפְּרִים תְּהִלּוֹת יְהוָה וֶעֱזוּזוֹ וְנִפְלְאוֹתָיו
won- His and His and ;Jehovah the declaring following the to
,works derful strength of praises generation

that He has done. 5For he
raised a testimony in Jacob,
and set a law in Israel;
which he commanded our
fathers, to teach them to
their sons; 6so that a
coming generation may
know; sons shall be born,
and they shall rise up and
tell their sons, 7so that they
might set their hope in God,
and not forget the works of
God, but keep His com-
mandments. 8And they
shall not be like their
fathers, a stubborn and
rebellious generation, a
generation that prepared
not its heart; yea, whose
spirit was not faithful with
God. 9The sons of Ephraim
were shooters of bows;
yet turned back in the day
of battle. 10They did not
keep the covenant of God,
and refused to walk in His
law. 11And they forgot His
works, and His wonders
which He had shown them;
12He did wonders before
their fathers in the land of
Egypt, the field of Zoan.
13He divided the sea and
passed them through; and
He caused the waters to
stand in a heap. 14And He
led them by a cloud in the
day, and all the night with a
light of fire. 15He split the
rocks in the wilderness and
made them drink, as *from*
great floods. 16And He
brought streams out of the
rock, and caused waters to
run down like torrents. 17Yet
they sinned still more
against Him, to provoke the
Most High in the desert.
18And they tempted God in
their heart, by asking food
for their souls. 19And they
spoke against God, saying,
Shall God be able to set a
table in the wilderness?
20Behold! He struck the
rock and the waters gushed
out, and the torrents overflowed. Can He also give
bread? Will He provide flesh
for His people? 21So
Jehovah heard and He was
angry; so a fire was kindled
against Jacob, and also
anger went up against

3478 7760 8451 3290 5715 6965 6213 834
5 אֲשֶׁר עָשָׂה׃ וַיָּקֶם עֵדוּת ׀ בְּיַעֲקֹב וְתוֹרָה שָׂם בְּיִשְׂרָאֵל
;Israel in set a and ,Jacob in a He For has He which
law testimony raised .done

3045 1121 3045 1 6680 834
6 אֲשֶׁר צִוָּה אֶת־אֲבוֹתֵינוּ לְהוֹדִיעָם לִבְנֵיהֶם׃ לְמַעַן יֵדְעוּ ׀
may that so their to .them make to our He which
know ;sons known ,fathers commanded

7760 1121 5608 6965 3205 1121 314 1755
7 דּוֹר אַחֲרוֹן בָּנִים יִוָּלֵדוּ יָקֻמוּ וִיסַפְּרוּ לִבְנֵיהֶם׃ וְיָשִׂימוּ
they that so their tell and they (and) be shall sons ;coming a
set may ,sons up rise shall born generation

5341 4687 410 4611 7911 3808 3689 430
בֵּאלֹהִים כִּסְלָם וְלֹא יִשְׁכְּחוּ מַעַלְלֵי־אֵל וּמִצְוֹתָיו יִנְצֹרוּ׃
.keep His but ,God the forget and their God in
commands of works not ,confidence

3820 3559 3808 1755 4784 5637 1755 1961 3808
8 וְלֹא יִהְיוּ ׀ כַּאֲבוֹתָם דּוֹר סוֹרֵר וּמֹרֶה דּוֹר לֹא־הֵכִין לִבּוֹ
its prepared not gen- a and stubborn gen- a their like they And
:heart eration ,rebellious eration ,fathers be shall not

7198 7411 5401 669 1121 7307 410 539 3808
9 וְלֹא־נֶאֶמְנָה אֶת־אֵל רוּחוֹ׃ בְּנֵי־אֶפְרַיִם נוֹשְׁקֵי רוֹמֵי־קֶשֶׁת
;bows shooters were Ephraim The whose God with was and
of armed of sons ,spirit faithful not

8451 430 1285 8104 3808 7128 3117 2015
10 הָפְכוּ בְּיוֹם קְרָב׃ לֹא שָׁמְרוּ בְּרִית אֱלֹהִים וּבְתוֹרָתוֹ
His in and ,God the did They not .battle the in (they yet)
law of covenant keep of day turned

7200 834 6381 5949 7911 3212 3985
11 מֵאֲנוּ לָלֶכֶת׃ וַיִּשְׁכְּחוּ עֲלִילוֹתָיו וְנִפְלְאוֹתָיו אֲשֶׁר הֶרְאָם׃
had He which His and His they And to they
.them shown wonders ,works forgot .walk refused

1234 6814 7704 4714 776 6382 6213 1 5048
12 נֶגֶד אֲבוֹתָם עָשָׂה פֶלֶא בְּאֶרֶץ מִצְרַיִם שְׂדֵה־צֹעַן׃ 13 בָּקַע
He .Zoan the ,Egypt the in wonders He their Before
divided of field of land did fathers

3605 3117 6051 5148 5067 4325 5324 5674 3220
14 יָם וַיַּעֲבִירֵם וַיַּצֶּב־מַיִם כְּמוֹ־נֵד׃ וַיַּנְחֵם בֶּעָנָן יוֹמָם וְכָל־
and by a in He And a in as made He and passed and the
all ,day cloud them led .heap stand waters the ;them through sea

8415 8248 4057 6697 1234 784 216 3915
15 הַלַּיְלָה בְּאוֹר אֵשׁ׃ יְבַקַּע צֻרִים בַּמִּדְבָּר וַיַּשְׁקְ כִּתְהֹמוֹת
(from) as made and the in the He .fire a by the
depths ,drink them wilderness rocks split of light night

3254 4325 5104 3381 5553 5140 3318 7227
16 רַבָּה׃ וַיּוֹצִא נוֹזְלִים מִסָּלַע וַיּוֹרֶד כַּנְּהָרוֹת מָיִם׃ 17 וַיּוֹסִיפוּ
they And .waters like made and the of streams he And .great
added torrents down run ,rock out brought

3824 410 5254 6723 5945 4784 2398 5750
18 עוֹד לַחֲטֹא־לוֹ לַמְרוֹת עֶלְיוֹן בַּצִּיָּה׃ וַיְנַסּוּ־אֵל בִּלְבָבָם
their in God they And the in Most the rebel to against to still
hearts tempted .desert High against ,Him sin

3201 559 430 1696 5315 400 7592
19 לִשְׁאָל־אֹכֶל לְנַפְשָׁם׃ וַיְדַבְּרוּ בֵּאלֹהִים אָמְרוּ הֲיוּכַל
be Shall ,saying against they And their for food by
able ,God spoke .souls asking

4325 2100 6697 5221 2009 4057 7979 6186 410
20 אֵל לַעֲרֹךְ שֻׁלְחָן בַּמִּדְבָּר׃ הֵן הִכָּה־צוּר ׀ וַיָּזוּבוּ מַיִם
the and the He ,Behold the in table a to God
,waters out gushed rock struck ?wilderness arrange

5971 7607 3559 5414 3201 3899 1571 7857 5158
וּנְחָלִים יִשְׁטֹפוּ הֲגַם־לֶחֶם יוּכַל תֵּת אִם־יָכִין שְׁאֵר לְעַמּוֹ׃
His for flesh He Will to He is bread Also were the and
?people provide ?give able .overflowing torrents

637 1571 3290 5400 784 5674 3068 8085 3651
21 לָכֵן ׀ שָׁמַע יְהוָה וַיִּתְעַבָּר וְאֵשׁ נִשְּׂקָה בְיַעֲקֹב וְגַם־אַף
anger and against was a so He and ,Jehovah heard There-
also ,Jacob kindled fire ;cross was fore

Israel, ²²because they did not believe in God, and trusted not in His salvation. ²³And He commanded the fine clouds above; and He opened the doors of the heavens; ²⁴and He rained on them manna to eat; and He gave the grain of the heavens to them. ²⁵Man ate the bread of the mighty; He sent them food to the full. ²⁶He made an east *wind* blow in the heavens; and He led out the south *wind* by His power. ²⁷Yea, He rained flesh on them like dust, and winged birds as the sand of the seas. ²⁸And He made them fall amidst His camp, all around to His tents. ²⁹So they ate and were filled full; for their own lust He brought to them. ³⁰They were not estranged from their lust; their food *was* still in their mouths, ³¹and God's wrath came on them and killed the fattest of them; and He struck down the choice ones of Israel.

³²In all this they sinned still, and did not believe in His wonderful works; ³³and He ended their days in vanity, and their years in sudden terror. ³⁴When He killed them, then they sought Him; and they turned and searched for God. ³⁵So they remembered that God *was* their rock, and the Most High God their redeemer. ³⁶But they flattered Him with their mouth, and with their tongues lied to Him. ³⁷For their heart was not steadfast with Him; and they were not faithful in His covenant. ³⁸But He being merciful atoned for iniquity and did not destroy; and He added to turn away His anger, and did not stir up all his wrath. ³⁹For He remembered that they *were* flesh, a breath passing away, and not returning. ⁴⁰How often they disobeyed Him in the wilderness, angering Him in the desert! ⁴¹Yea, they turned back and tempted God, and pained the Holy One of Israel. ⁴²They did

---

22 עָלָה בְּיִשְׂרָאֵל: כִּי לֹא הֶאֱמִינוּ בֵּאלֹהִים וְלֹא בָטְחוּ

| rose up | against ;Israel | not because | they did believe | ,God in | and not | did trust |
| 5927 | 3478 | 3808 | 539 | 430 | 982 | 3808 |

23 בִּישׁוּעָתוֹ: וַיְצַו שְׁחָקִים מִמָּעַל וְדַלְתֵי שָׁמַיִם פָּתָח:

| His in ;salvation | He commanded | fine clouds | above | the and of doors | the heavens | He ;opened |
| | 6680 | 7834 | 4605 | 1817 | 8064 | 6605 |

24 25 וַיַּמְטֵר עֲלֵיהֶם מָן לֶאֱכֹל וּדְגַן שָׁמַיִם נָתַן לָמוֹ: לֶחֶם

| He rained | on them | manna | ;eat to | the and of grain | the heavens | He gave | them .to | The of bread |
| 4305 | | 4478 | 398 | 1715 | 8064 | 5414 | | 3899 |

26 אַבִּירִים אָכַל אִישׁ צֵידָה שָׁלַח לָהֶם לָשֹׂבַע: יַסַּע קָדִים

| the mighty | eat | ;man | food | He sent | them | to the .full | blow | east an (wind) made He |
| 47 | 398 | 376 | 6720 | 7971 | | 7648 | 5265 | 6921 |

27 בַּשָּׁמָיִם וַיְנַהֵג בְּעֻזּוֹ תֵימָן: וַיַּמְטֵר עֲלֵיהֶם כֶּעָפָר שְׁאֵר

| the in heavens; | He and led out | power His by | the south .(wind) | rained He And | them on | dust like | ,flesh |
| 8064 | 5090 | 5797 | 8486 | 4305 | | 6083 | 7607 |

28 וּכְחוֹל יַמִּים עוֹף כָּנָף: וַיַּפֵּל בְּקֶרֶב מַחֲנֵהוּ סָבִיב

| sand the like and seas of | the birds winged | .fall them made He And | amidst | ,camp His | all around |
| 2344 | 3671 | 5775 | 5307 | 7130 | 4264 | 5439 |

29 לְמִשְׁכְּנֹתָיו: וַיֹּאכְלוּ וַיִּשְׂבְּעוּ מְאֹד וְתַאֲוָתָם יָבִא לָהֶם:

| .tents His to | ate they So | filled and were | ;full | own lust their for | brought He | .them to |
| 4908 | 398 | 7646 | 3966 | 8378 | 935 | |

30 31 לֹא־זָרוּ מִתַּאֲוָתָם עוֹד אָכְלָם בְּפִיהֶם: וְאַף אֱלֹהִים עָלָה

| were estranged ,lust | They from their | yet | food ,mouths | their in | and the wrath | God | came |
| 3808 | 2114 | 8378 | 5750 | 400 | 6310 | 639 | 430 | 5927 |

32 בָהֶם וַיַּהֲרֹג בְּמִשְׁמַנֵּיהֶם וּבַחוּרֵי יִשְׂרָאֵל הִכְרִיעַ: בְּכָל־

| them upon | and killed | fattest the of them | choice ;ones | the and | Israel | struck He down | In all |
| 2026 | 2026 | 4924 | 970 | 3478 | 3766 | 3605 |

33 זֹאת חָטְאוּ־עוֹד וְלֹא הֶאֱמִינוּ בְּנִפְלְאוֹתָיו: וַיְכַל־בַּהֶבֶל

| this | sinned they ,more | still | and | did not believe | His in ;works | wonderful | He And ended | vanity in |
| 2088 | 2398 | 5750 | 3808 | 539 | 6381 | 3615 | 1892 |

34 יְמֵיהֶם וּשְׁנוֹתָם בַּבֶּהָלָה: אִם־הֲרָגָם וּדְרָשׁוּהוּ וְשָׁבוּ

| ,days their | their and | years | in sudden .terror | ,them killed | Him sought ;them | they then | they and turned |
| 3117 | 8141 | 928 | 2026 | 1875 | 7725 |

35 וְזָכְרוּ כִּי־אֱלֹהִים צוּרָם וְאֵל עֶלְיוֹן גֹּאֲלָם:

| .God remembered | that they | God | ,rock | the and | Most High | their .redeemer |
| 7836 | 1410 | 430 | 6697 | 410 | 5945 | 1350 |

36 37 וַיְפַתּוּהוּ בְּפִיהֶם וּבִלְשׁוֹנָם יְכַזְּבוּ־לוֹ: וְלִבָּם לֹא־נָכוֹן

| Him deceived | ,mouth their with | their with and | tongues | .Him to lied | heart their | For was not | steadfast |
| 6601 | 6310 | 3956 | 3576 | 3820 | 3808 | 3559 |

38 עִמּוֹ וְלֹא נֶאֶמְנוּ בִּבְרִיתוֹ: וְהוּא רַחוּם יְכַפֵּר עָוֹן וְלֹא

| ;Him | and with | were | they not faithful | His in .covenant | He But | being merciful | atoned | for iniquity | and not |
| 5973 | 3808 | 539 | 1285 | 7349 | 3722 | 5771 | 3808 |

39 יַשְׁחִית וְהִרְבָּה לְהָשִׁיב אַפּוֹ וְלֹא־יָעִיר כָּל־חֲמָתוֹ: וַיִּזְכֹּר

| destroy did | He And multiplied | away to turn | His anger | and did not up stir | all | .wrath His | He For remembered |
| 7843 | 7235 | 7725 | 639 | 5782 | 3605 | 2534 | 2142 |

40 כִּי־בָשָׂר הֵמָּה רוּחַ הוֹלֵךְ וְלֹא יָשׁוּב: כַּמָּה יַמְרוּהוּ

| that flesh | they (were) | a breath | passing away | and .return | not does | How | they dis-obeyed Him |
| 1320 | 7307 | 3808 | 7725 | 4100 | 4784 |

41 בַמִּדְבָּר יַעֲצִיבוּהוּ בִּישִׁימוֹן: וַיָּשׁוּבוּ וַיְנַסּוּ אֵל וּקְדוֹשׁ

| the in ,wilderness | Him grieved | the in !desert | And they back turned | and they tempted | ,God | Holy and of One |
| 4057 | 6087 | 3452 | 7725 | 5254 | 410 | 6918 |

not remember His hand, on the day He redeemed them from the enemy; [43]who set His signs in Egypt, and His wonders in the field of Zoan. [44]He turned their rivers into blood, also their streams *that* they might not drink. [45]He sent swarms of flies against them, and they devoured them; also frogs, and they destroyed them. [46]He also gave their crops to the stripping locust, and their labor to the locust. [47]He killed their vines with hail, and their sycamore trees with sleet. [48]He gave their cattle up to the hail, and their flocks to bolts of fire. [49]He sent the heat of His anger on them, fury and indignation and distress, a sending angels of evils. [50]He leveled a path for His anger; He did not keep back their soul from death, but gave their life over to the plague. [51]And he struck all the firstborn in Egypt, the firstfruits of strength in the tents of Ham; [52]and He led His people forth like sheep; and He led them like a flock in the wilderness. [53]And he led them on safely, and they did not fear; but the sea flooded over their enemies.

[54]He brought them to the border of His holy place; this mountain *that* His right hand had gained. [55]And He cast out the nations before them; and by a line He made a possession fall to them; and He made the tribes of Israel to live in their tents. [56]Yet they tempted and provoked the most high God; and they did not keep His testimonies; [57]but they turned back and betrayed, like their fathers; they veered aside like a deceitful bow. [58]For they enraged Him with their high places; and they provoked Him to jealousy with their molten images. [59]When God heard, He was angry, and He utterly rejected Israel. [60]And He left the tabernacle of Shiloh; the tent He dwelt

42 ישראל התוו: לא־זכרו את־ידו יום אשר־פדם מני־צר:

the from He which (in) the His did They not .pained Israel
;enemy them redeemed day ,hand remember

43 אשר־שם במצרים אתותיו ומופתיו בשדה־צען:
44 ויהפך

He .Zoan the in His and His Egypt in set who
turned of field wonders signs

45 לדם יאריהם ונזליהם בל־ישתיון: ישלח בהם ערב

fly against sent He they (that) not their also their into
,swarms them .drink might ,streams ;rivers blood

46 ויאכלם וצפרדע ותשחיתם: ויתן לחסיל יבולם ויגיעם

their and their strip- the to also He they and also they and
labor ,crops locust ing gave .them destroyed ,frogs ;them devoured

47 לארבה: יהרג בברד גפנם ושקמותם בחנמל:
48 ויסגר

He And .sleet by their and their with was He the to
up gave trees sycamore ,vines hail killing .locust

49 לברד בעירם ומקניהם לרשפים: ישלח־בם חרון אפו

His the on He the to their and their the to
,anger of heat them sent .bolts flaming flocks ,cattle hail

50 עברה וזעם וצרה משלחת מלאכי רעים: יפלס נתיב

path a He .evils angels deputation a and indig- and fury
leveled of of ,trouble nation

51 לאפו לא־חשך ממות נפשם וחיתם לדבר הסגיר: ויך

He And gave the to their but their from He not His for
struck .over plague life souls death back kept ;anger

52 כל־בכור במצרים ראשית אונים באהלי־חם: ויסע

He then ;Ham the in strength first- the ;Egypt in the all
forth led of tents of fruits firstborn

53 כצאן עמו וינהגם כעדר במדבר: וינחם לבטח ולא

and ;safely He And the in a like He and own His like
not on them led .wilderness flock them led ,people sheep

54 פחדו ואת־אויביהם כסה הים: ויביאם אל־גבול קדשו

holy His the to He And the covered their but did they
;place of border them brought .sea over enemies ,fear

55 הר־זה קנתה ימינו: ויגרש מפניהם גוים ויפילם בחבל

a by made He and the before He And right His had this
line fall them nations them out cast .hand gained mountain

56 נחלה וישכן באהליהם שבטי ישראל: וינסו וימרו

and they And .Israel the their in He and pos- a
provoked tested of tribes tents dwell made .session

57 את־אלהים עליון ועדותיו לא שמרו: ויסגו ויבגדו

and they but did they not His and Most God the
betrayed back turned ;keep testimonies ,High

58 כאבותם נהפכו כקשת רמיה: ויכעיסוהו בבמותם

their by they For .deceitful a like they their like
;places high Him enraged bow veered ;fathers

59 ובפסיליהם יקניאוהו: שמע אלהים ויתעבר וימאס

He and was and God heard provoked they their with
rejected ;cross jealousy to Him images casted

60 מאד בישראל: ויטש משכן שלו אהל שכן באדם:

among He the ,Shiloh taber- the And .Israel utterly
;men in dwelt tent of nacle left He

in among men; 61and delivered His strength into captivity, and His glory into the enemy's hands. 62And He gave His people to the sword; and was angry with His inheritance. 63The fire burned up His young men; and His virgins were not praised. 64His priests fell by the sword; and their widows were not able to weep.

65Then the Lord awoke, as one asleep; like a mighty man rejoicing *with* wine. 66And He drove His enemies backward; He put them to a never-ending shame. 67And He refused the tabernacle of Joseph; and He did not elect the tribe of Ephraim; 68but He chose the tribe of Judah, the Mount Zion which He loved. 69And He built His sanctuary like high places; like the earth He has founded forever. 70He also chose His servant David, and took him from the sheepfolds; 71He brought him in from the suckling *ewes*; He brought him to feed His people Jacob, and His inheritance, Israel. 72And he fed them in the integrity of his heart; and guided them in the skillfulness of his hands.

5971 2719 546 6862/3027 8547 5797 7628 5414
61 62 וַיִּתֵּן לַשְּׁבִי עֻזּוֹ וְתִפְאַרְתּוֹ בְיַד־צָר׃ וַיַּסְגֵּר לַחֶרֶב עַמּוֹ
His the to He and the into His and His into and
,people sword delivered ,enemy's hands glory ,strength captivity gave

3808 1330 784 398 970 5674 5159
63 וּבְנַחֲלָתוֹ הִתְעַבָּר׃ בַּחוּרָיו אָכְלָה־אֵשׁ וּבְתוּלֹתָיו לֹא
not His and The burned young His was His with and
virgins ,fire up men ,cross inheritance

3364 1058 3808 490 5307 2719 3548 1984
64 65 הוּלָּלוּ׃ כֹּהֲנָיו בַּחֶרֶב נָפָלוּ וְאַלְמְנֹתָיו לֹא תִבְכֶּינָה׃ וַיִּקַץ
Then able were not their and ;fell the by His were
awoke .weep to widows sword priests .praised

2781 268 6862 5221 3196 7442 1368 136 3463
66 כְּיָשֵׁן ׀ אֲדֹנָי כְּגִבּוֹר מִתְרוֹנֵן מִיָּיִן׃ וַיַּךְ־צָרָיו אָחוֹר חֶרְפַּת
shame a back- His He and (with) rejoicing a like the one as
;ward enemies beat ;wine man mighty ;Lord asleep

3808 669 7626 3127 168 3985 5414/5769
67 עוֹלָם נָתַן לָמוֹ׃ וַיִּמְאַס בְּאֹהֶל יוֹסֵף וּבְשֵׁבֶט אֶפְרַיִם לֹא
not Ephraim the and ;Joseph taber- the He And them He ever-
of tribe of nacle refused .to put lasting

157 834 6726 2022 3063 7626 977 977
68 בָחָר׃ וַיִּבְחַר אֶת־שֵׁבֶט יְהוּדָה אֶת־הַר צִיּוֹן אֲשֶׁר אָהֵב׃
He which Zion the ,Judah the He But did He
.loved Mount of tribe chose .elect

977 5769 3245 776 4720 7311 3644 1129
69 70 וַיִּבֶן כְּמוֹ־רָמִים מִקְדָּשׁוֹ כְּאֶרֶץ יְסָדָהּ לְעוֹלָם׃ וַיִּבְחַר
also He .forever has He the like His high like He And
chose it founded earth ;sanctuary places built

935 5763 310 6629 4356 3947 5650 1732
71 בְּדָוִד עַבְדּוֹ וַיִּקָּחֵהוּ מִמִּכְלְאֹת צֹאן׃ מֵאַחַר עָלוֹת הֱבִיאוֹ
took He suck- the from ;sheep the from took and His David
him (ewes) ling after of folds him ,servant

3824 8537 7462 5159 3478 5971 3290 7462
72 לִרְעוֹת בְּיַעֲקֹב עַמּוֹ וּבְיִשְׂרָאֵל נַחֲלָתוֹ׃ וַיִּרְעֵם כְּתֹם לְבָבוֹ
his the in he So His and His Jacob feed to
,heart of integrity them fed .inheritance Israel ,people

5148 3709 8394
וּבִתְבוּנוֹת כַּפָּיו יַנְחֵם׃
guided his the in and
.them palms of skillfulness

PSAL. LXXIX עט

PSALM 79

PSALM 79
A Psalm of Asaph.

1O God, the nations have come into Your inheritance; they have defiled Your holy temple; they have laid Jerusalem in heaps. 2They have given the bodies of Your servants as food for the birds of the heavens; the flesh of Your saints to the beasts of the earth. 3They have shed their blood like water all around Jerusalem; and there is no one burying. 4We have become a shame to our neigbors, a scorn and a mockery to those who are around us. 5How long, O Jehovah? Will You be angry with us forever? Shall Your jealousy burn like fire? 6Pour out Your wrath on the nations

2930 5159 1471 935 430 623 4210
1 מִזְמוֹר לְאָסָף אֱלֹהִים בָּאוּ גוֹיִם ׀ בְּנַחֲלָתֶךָ טִמְּאוּ אֶת־
have they Your into the have ,God O of psalm A
defiled ;inheritance nations come .Asaph

5038 5414 5856 3389 7760 6944 1964
2 הֵיכַל קָדְשֶׁךָ שָׂמוּ אֶת־יְרוּשָׁלַםִ לְעִיִּים׃ נָתְנוּ אֶת־נִבְלַת
the have They .heaps in Jerusalem have they Your temple
of corpses given laid ;holy

776 2416 2623 1320 8064 5775 3978 5650
עֲבָדֶיךָ מַאֲכָל לְעוֹף הַשָּׁמָיִם בְּשַׂר חֲסִידֶיךָ לְחַיְתוֹ־אָרֶץ׃
the the to Your the the the food as Your
.earth of beasts saints of flesh ,heavens of birds for servants

1961 6912 369 3389 5439 4325 1818 8210
3 4 שָׁפְכוּ דָמָם ׀ כַּמַּיִם סְבִיבוֹת יְרוּשָׁלָםִ וְאֵין קוֹבֵר׃ הָיִינוּ
have We .burying and ;Jerusalem all like their have They
been is none around water blood shed

3068 5704 5439 7046 3933 7934 2781
5 חֶרְפָּה לִשְׁכֵנֵינוּ לַעַג וָקֶלֶס לִסְבִיבוֹתֵינוּ׃ עַד־מָה יְהוָה
O ,when Until who those to a and a our to shame a
?Jehovah .us around are mockery scorn ,neighbors

2534 8210 7068 784 3644 1197 5331 599
6 תֶּאֱנַף לָנֶצַח תִּבְעַר כְּמוֹ־אֵשׁ קִנְאָתֶךָ׃ שְׁפֹךְ חֲמָתְךָ ׀ אֶל־
to Your Pour Your fire like Shall ?forever You Will
wrath out ?jealousy burn angry be

who have not known You, and on the kingdoms who have not called on Your name. 7For *they have* eaten up Jacob, and laid waste to his dwelling-place. 8O do not remember for us the sins of our first ones; let Your tender mercies meet us speedily, for we have been brought very low. 9Help us, O God of our salvation, for the matter of the glory of Your name; and deliver us and atone for our sins, for Your name's sake.

10Why should the nations say, Where *is* their God? Let Him be known among the nations before our eyes, the avenging of the blood of Your servants *that* has been poured out. 11Let the groaning of the prisoner come before You; according to the greatness of Your arm, preserve the sons of death. 12And reward our neighbors sevenfold, *Give* into their bosom their curse with which they have cursed You, O Lord. 13Then we Your people, and sheep of Your pasture, will give thanks to You forever; we will declare Your praise to all generations.

3808 8034 834 4467 5921 3045 3808 834 1471
הַגּוֹיִם אֲשֶׁר לֹא־יְדָעוּךָ וְעַל־מַמְלָכוֹת אֲשֶׁר בְּשִׁמְךָ לֹא
not Your on who the and have not who the
name kingdoms on You known nations

7 8 2142 408 8074 5116 3290 398 7121
קָרָאוּ׃ כִּי אָכַל אֶת־יַעֲקֹב וְאֶת־נָוֵהוּ הֵשַׁמּוּ׃ אַל־תִּזְכָּר
O not laid hjs and Jacob they For have
remember .waste place dwelling devoured have .called

3966 1809 7356 6923 4118 7223 5771
לָנוּ עֲוֺנֹת רִאשֹׁנִים מַהֵר יְקַדְּמוּנוּ רַחֲמֶיךָ כִּי דַלּוֹנוּ מְאֹד׃
greatly have we For tender Your let speedily first our the for
weakened been .mercies us meet ;fathers of iniquities us

9 3722 5337 8034 3519 1697 3468 430 5826
עָזְרֵנוּ ׀ אֱלֹהֵי יִשְׁעֵנוּ עַל־דְּבַר כְּבוֹד־שְׁמֶךָ וְהַצִּילֵנוּ וְכַפֵּר
and and Your the the for our God O Help
atone us deliver ;name of glory of matter ,salvation of ,us

10 1471 559 4100 8034 4616 2403
עַל־חַטֹּאתֵינוּ לְמַעַן שְׁמֶךָ׃ לָמָּה ׀ יֹאמְרוּ הַגּוֹיִם אַיֵּה
Where the should Why Your for our for
(is) ,nations say .name's sake sins

8210 5650 1818 5360 5869 1471 3045 430
אֱלֹהֵיהֶם יִוָּדַע בַּגּוֹיִם לְעֵינֵינוּ נִקְמַת דַּם־עֲבָדֶיךָ הַשָּׁפוּךְ׃
been has of blood the the our before the in Him Let their
.out poured servants your of avenging ,eyes nations known be ?God

11 8546 1121 3498 2220 1433 615 603 6440 935
תָּבוֹא לְפָנֶיךָ אֶנְקַת אָסִיר כְּגֹדֶל זְרוֹעֲךָ הוֹתֵר בְּנֵי תְמוּתָה׃
.death the preserve Your the by the groan- the before Let
of sons ,arm of greatness ;prisoner of ing You come

12 2778 834 2781 2436 7659 7934 7725
וְהָשֵׁב לִשְׁכֵנֵינוּ שִׁבְעָתַיִם אֶל־חֵיקָם חֶרְפָּתָם אֲשֶׁר חֵרְפוּךָ
re- they with their their into ,sevenfold our And
,You proached which reproach bosom neighbors return

13 5769 3034 4830 6629 5971 136
אֲדֹנָי׃ וַאֲנַחְנוּ עַמְּךָ ׀ וְצֹאן מַרְעִיתֶךָ נוֹדֶה לְּךָ לְעוֹלָם
;forever to give will Your the and Your Then O
You thanks pasture of sheep ,people ,we .Lord

8416 5608 1755 1755
לְדֹר וָדֹר נְסַפֵּר תְּהִלָּתֶךָ׃
Your will we gen- and gen- to
.praise declare eration eration

PSAL. LXXX פ

PSALM 80

PSALM 80

To the chief musician. A Testimony Concerning the Lilies. A Psalm of Asaph.

1Give ear, O Shepherd of Israel, You leading Joseph like a flock; shine forth, You dwelling *between* the cherubs. 2Stir up Your might before Ephraim, and Benjamin, and Manasseh, and come for salvation. 3O God, turn us again, and make Your face shine, and we will be saved! 4O Jehovah, God of Hosts, how long will You smoke against the prayer of Your people? 5You made them eat with the bread of tears; yea, You made them drink with tears a third time. 6You make us a strife for our

1 2 3478 7462 4210 623 5715 7799 5329
לַמְנַצֵּחַ אֶל־שֹׁשַׁנִּים עֵדוּת לְאָסָף מִזְמוֹר׃ רֹעֵה יִשְׂרָאֵל ׀
,Israel O .psalm A .Asaph of A the concern- chief the To
of Shepherd testimony lilies ing musician

3 6440 3313 3742 3427 3127 6629 5090 238
הַאֲזִינָה נֹהֵג כַּצֹּאן יוֹסֵף יֹשֵׁב הַכְּרוּבִים הוֹפִיעָה׃ לִפְנֵי
Before shine the (between) You ;Joseph a like You give
.forth ,cherubim dwell who flock leads who ;ear

3444 3212 1369 5782 4519 1144 669
אֶפְרַיִם ׀ וּבִנְיָמִן וּמְנַשֶּׁה עוֹרְרָה אֶת־גְּבוּרָתֶךָ וּלְכָה לִישֻׁעָתָה
for and Your stir and and Ephraim
salvation come ,might up Manasseh Benjamin

4 5 3068 3467 6440 215 7725 430
לָּנוּ׃ אֱלֹהִים הֲשִׁיבֵנוּ וְהָאֵר פָּנֶיךָ וְנִוָּשֵׁעָה׃ יְהוָה
O will we and Your make and us turn ,God O .us to
Jehovah !saved be ,face shine again

6 398 5971 8605 6225 5704 6635 430
אֱלֹהִים צְבָאוֹת עַד־מָתַי עָשַׁנְתָּ בִּתְפִלַּת עַמֶּךָ׃ הֶאֱכַלְתָּם
made You Your the against You when until ,hosts of God
eat them ?people of prayer smoke will

7 4066 7760 7991 1832 8248 1832 3899
לֶחֶם דִּמְעָה וַתַּשְׁקֵמוֹ בִּדְמָעוֹת שָׁלִישׁ׃ תְּשִׂימֵנוּ מָדוֹן
a make You third a with made You and ;tears the (with)
strife us .time tears drink them of bread

neighbors, and our enemies laugh to themselves. [7]O God of hosts, turn us again, and cause Your face to shine, and we will be saved.

[8]You have led a vine out of Egypt; You have cast out the nations, and have planted it. [9]You cleared before it, and You have rooted its roots; and it has filled the land. [10]The hills were covered *with* its shadow; and its boughs *were as* the great cedars. [11]It was sending its boughs out to the sea, and its branches to the River. [12]Why have You broken down its walls, so that it is plucked by all who pass by the way? [13]A boar out of the forest wastes it,and the beast of the field feeds on it. [14]O God of hosts, we beg You, return! Look down from Heaven and see and visit this vine, [15]and the vineyard which Your right hand has planted, and on the Son You made strong for Yourself. [16]*It is* burned with fire, cut down; they perish at the rebuke of Your face. [17]Let Your hand be on the Man of Your right hand; on the Son of man *whom* You have made strong for Yourself. [18]So we will not backslide from You; make us live, and we will call on Your name.

[19]O Jehovah, God of hosts, turn us again! Cause Your face to shine, and we will be saved.

7725 6635 430 3932 341 7934
8 לשכנינו ואיבינו ילעגו־למו: אלהים צבאות השיבנו
us turn osts God O to laugh our and our for
again of .themselves enemies ;neighbors

1471 1644 5265 4714 1612 3467 6440 215
9 והאר פניך ונושעה: גפן ממצרים תסיע תגרש גוים
the have You have You of out A will we and Your make and
nations out cast ;out led Egypt vine .saved be ;face shine

776 4390 8327 8328 6437 6437 5193
10 ותטעה: פנית לפניה ותשרש שרשיה ותמלא־ארץ:
the it and its have You and before have You have and
.land filled has ;roots rooted ;it cleared .it planted

7105 79 71 1410 730 6057 6738 2022 3680
11
12 כסו הרים צלה וענפיה ארזי־אל: תשלח קציריה עד
to its was It of the (as) its and its (with) The were
boughs sending .God cedars boughs ;shadow hills covered

3105 717 1447 6555 4100 3127 5104 3220
13 ים ואל־נהר יונקותיה: למה פרצת גדריה וארוה כל־
by is it that its You have Why its the and the
all plucked ,walls down broken .branches River to ,sea

7462 7704 2123 3293 2386 3765 1870 5674
14 עברי דרך: יכרסמנה חזיר מיער וזיז שדי ירענה:
feed the and the of out wild A wastes the who
.it on field of movers ,forest boar it .way by pass

1612 6485 7200 8064 5027 7725 6635 430
15 אלהים צבאות שוב נא הבט משמים וראה ופקד גפן
vine and see and from Look we ,return ,hosts God of
visit Heaven down !You beg of

553 1121 5921 3225 5193 834 3657 2063
16 זאת: וכנה אשר־נטעה ימינך ועל־בן אמצתה לך:
for made You the and Your has which and ,this
.Yourself strong son on ,hand right planted shoot the

3027 1961 6 6440 1606 3683 784 8313
17
18 שרפה באש כסוחה מגערת פניך יאבדו: תהי־ידך על־
on Your Let they Your the at cut with is It
hand be .perish face of rebuke ;down ,fire burned

5472 3808 553 120 1121 5921 3225 376
19 איש ימינך על־בן־אדם אמצת לך: ולא־נסוג ממך
from will we So for You man the on Your the
;You backslide not .Yourself ,strengthened of son ,hand right of man

7725 6635 430 3068 7121 8034 2421
20 תחינו ובשמך נקרא: יהוה אלהים צבאות השיבנו
us turn ,hosts of God O will we on and us make
;again Jehovah .call name Your ,live

3467 6440 215
האר פניך ונושעה:
will we and Your make
.saved be ,face shine

PSAL. LXXXI פא

PSALM 81

To the chief musician on Gittith. Of Asaph.

[1]Sing aloud to God our strength; shout for joy to the God of Jacob. [2]Lift up a song, and the timbrel *here*, the pleasing lyre with the harp. [3]Blow the trumpet in the new moon, at the full moon, on our feast day. [4]For this *was* a statute for Israel, an ordinance of the God of Jacob. [5]This He ordained *as* a testimony in Joseph, when He went out

7442 5797 430 7321 623 1665 5921 5329
1
2 למנצח על־הגתית לאסף: הרנינו לאלהים עוזנו הריעו
shout our God to Sing .Asaph Of the on chief the To
joy for ;strength aloud .Gittith musician

5035 5273 3658 8596 2172 5375 3290 430
3 לאלהי יעקב: שאו־זמרה ותנו־תף כנור נעים עם־נבל:
the with pleasing the the and ,song a up Lift .Jacob the to
.harp lyre ,timbrel give of God

3478 2706 2282 3117 3677 7782 2320 8628
4
5 תקעו בחדש שופר בכסה ליום חגנו: כי חק לישראל
Israel for a For our on the at ram's the the in Blow
statute .feast day moon full ,horn moon new

3318 7760 3084 5715 3290 430 4941 2063
6 הוא משפט לאלהי יעקב: עדות ביהוסף שמו בצאתו
He when He in A .Jacob the of ord- an this
out went ,it set Joseph testimony of God inance ,(was)

over the land of Egypt; I heard a lip I did not understand. [6]I removed his shoulder from the burden; his hands were freed from the basket. [7]You called in distress, and I rescued you; I answered you in the secret place of thunder; I tested you at the waters of Meribah. Selah.

[8]O My people, listen, and I will testify against you, whether you will listen to Me: [9]There shall be no strange god among you; nor shall you worship a foreign god—[10]I *am* Jehovah your God, who brought you out from the land of Egypt; open your mouth wide, and I will fill it. [11]But My people would not listen to My voice; and Israel did not consent to Me. [12]So I gave them up to the stubbornness of their own hearts; they walked in their own conceits.

[13]O if My people were hearing Me! *If* Israel had walked in My ways, [14]in a little I would have subdued their enemies, and I would have turned My hand against their foes. [15]The haters of Jehovah will be found liars to Him and their time is forever. [16]Yea, He would make them eat of the fat of the wheat, and I would satisfy you *with* honey out of the rock.

PSALM 82

A Psalm of Asaph

[1]God stands in the company of God; He judges in the midst of the gods. [2]Until when will you judge unjustly and lift up the faces of the wicked? Selah.

[3]Vindicate the poor and fatherless; do justice to the afflicted and needy. [4]Deliver the poor and needy; save from the hand of the wicked. [5]They do not know and do not understand; they walk in darkness; all the foundations of the earth are shaken.

[6]I have said, You *are* gods, and all of you sons

5447 5493 8085 3045 38,08 8193 4714 776 59,21
7 עַל־אֶרֶץ מִצְרָיִם שְׂפַת לֹא־יָדַעְתִּי אֶשְׁמָע׃ הֲסִירוֹתִי מִסֵּבֶל
the from turned I ;heard I did I not lip a ;Egypt the over
burden away understand of land

2502 7121 6864 5674 1731 3709 7926
8 שִׁכְמוֹ כַּפָּיו מִדּוּד תַּעֲבֹרְנָה׃ בַּצָּרָה קָרָאתָ וָאֲחַלְּצֶךָּ
I and You trouble in were the from his his
;you rescued ,called .freed basket palms ;shoulder

8085 55,42 4808 43,25 974 7482 5643 6030
9 אֶעֶנְךָ בְּסֵתֶר רַעַם אֶבְחָנְךָ עַל־מֵי מְרִיבָה סֶלָה׃ שְׁמַע
Listen .Selah .Meribah the at tested I ;thunder the in an- I
of waters you of covert you swered

1961 38,08 8085 518 3478 5749 5971
10 עַמִּי וְאָעִידָה בָּךְ יִשְׂרָאֵל אִם־תִּשְׁמַע־לִי׃ לֹא־יִהְיֶה בְךָ
among There not to will you if ,Israel O against will I and my O
you be shall .Me listen ,you testify ,people

430 3068 5236 410 78,12 38,08 2114 410
11 אֵל זָר וְלֹא תִשְׁתַּחֲוֶה לְאֵל נֵכָר׃ אָנֹכִי ׀ יְהוָה אֱלֹהֶיךָ
your Jehovah (am) I .foreign a to you shall and ;strange a
God god down bow not god

8085 38,08 4390 63,10 7337 4714 776 59,27
12 הַמַּעַלְךָ מֵאֶרֶץ מִצְרָיִם הַרְחֶב־פִּיךָ וַאֲמַלְאֵהוּ׃ וְלֹא־שָׁמַע
did But will I and your open ;Egypt the from brought who
listen not .it fill mouth wide of land up you

8307 5414 14 38,08 3478 6963 5971
13 עַמִּי לְקוֹלִי וְיִשְׂרָאֵל לֹא־אָבָה לִי׃ וָאֲשַׁלְּחֵהוּ בִּשְׁרִירוּת
the to gave I So to did not and My to My
of obstinacy ,up him .Me consent Israel ,voice people

3478 8085 5971 38,63 4156 321,2 3820
14 לִבָּם יֵלְכוּ בְּמוֹעֲצוֹתֵיהֶם׃ לוּ עַמִּי שֹׁמֵעַ לִי יִשְׂרָאֵל
Israel (If) !Me were My if O own their in they their
hearing people .counsels walk ;heart

7725 6862 3665 341 4592 32,12 1870
15 בִּדְרָכַי יְהַלֵּכוּ׃ כִּמְעַט אוֹיְבֵיהֶם אַכְנִיעַ וְעַל־צָרֵיהֶם אָשִׁיב
would I their and would I their little a In would My in
turn foes against .subdue enemies ,walk ways

398 57,69 6256 1961 3584 3068 8130 3027
16
17 יָדִי׃ מְשַׂנְאֵי יְהוָה יְכַחֲשׁוּ־לוֹ וִיהִי עִתָּם לְעוֹלָם׃ וַיַּאֲכִילֵהוּ
would He and —forever their and to be will Jehovah who those My
eat him make time is ,Him liars found hate —hand

7646 1706 6697 2406 2459
מֵחֵלֶב חִטָּה וּמִצּוּר דְּבַשׁ אַשְׂבִּיעֶךָ׃
would I (with) of out and the the of
.you satisfy honey rock the ;wheat of fat

PSAL. LXXXII פב

PSALM 82

430 7310 410 5712 5324 430 623 42,10
1 מִזְמוֹר לְאָסָף אֱלֹהִים נִצָּב בַּעֲדַת־אֵל בְּקֶרֶב אֱלֹהִים
gods the the in ;God the in stands God .Asaph of psalm A
of midst of company

55,42 5375 7563 6440 5766 8199 5704 8199
2 יִשְׁפֹּט׃ עַד־מָתַי תִּשְׁפְּטוּ־עָוֶל וּפְנֵי רְשָׁעִים תִּשְׂאוּ־סֶלָה׃
.Selah ?up lift the and ,unjustly you will when Until He
wicked of faces the judge .judges

3027 34 1800/ 64,03 6663 7326 6041 3490 1800 8199
3
4 שִׁפְטוּ־דַל וְיָתוֹם עָנִי וָרָשׁ הַצְדִּיקוּ׃ פַּלְּטוּ־דַל וְאֶבְיוֹן מִיַּד
from and the Deliver justice do and af- the the and the Vindi-
hand needy poor .to needy flicted ,orphan poor cate

19,80 2825 995 3045/ 38,08 5337 7563
5 רְשָׁעִים הַצִּילוּ׃ לֹא יָדְעוּ ׀ וְלֹא יָבִינוּ בַּחֲשֵׁכָה יִתְהַלָּכוּ
they darkness in they and They not .save the
;walk ;understand not ,know wicked's

1121 430 559 776 4146 4131
6 יִמּוֹטוּ כָּל־מוֹסְדֵי אָרֶץ׃ אֲנִי־אָמַרְתִּי אֱלֹהִים אַתֶּם וּבְנֵי
and You gods have I the foun- the all are
of sons ;(are) ,said ,earth of dations shaken

of the Most High, [7]but you shall die as man, and you shall fall like one of the rulers. [8]Rise, O God; judge the earth; for You shall inherit in all the nations.

PSALM 83

A Song. A Psalm of Asaph.

[1]O God, do not keep silence to Yourself; do not be speechless; yea, do not be still, O God. [2]For lod, Your enemies are roaring; and those who hate You have lifted up *their* head. [3]They take shrewd counsel against Your people; *they* plot against Your hidden ones. [4]They have said, Come, and we will cut them off from being a nation, and, The name of Israel will not be recalled again. [5]For they plotted together *with* one heart; they have cut a covenant against You; [6]*even* the tents of Edom, and of the Ishmaelites; Moab and the Hagarites; [7]Gebal and Ammon, and Amalek; Philistia and the inhabitants of Tyre. [8]Also Assyria has joined with them; they were an arm to the sons of Lot. Selah.

[9]Do to them as *to* Midian, as *to* Sisera, as *to* Jabin at the torrent Kishon. [10]At Endor they were destroyed; the became dung for the ground. [11]Make their nobles as Oreb and Zeeb, and all their princes like Zebah and Zalmunna; [12]who said, Let us take possession *of* God's pastures for ourselves.

[13]O my God, make them as whirling dust, as the stubble before the wind. [14]As the fire burns a forest, and as the flame sets the mountains on fire, [15]so pursue them with Your tempest, and frighten them with Your storm. [16]Fill their faces with shame, and they will seek Your name, O

5307 8269 259 4191 120 403 3605 5945

7 עֶלְיוֹן כֻּלְּכֶם׃ אָכֵן כְּאָדָם תְּמוּתוּן וּכְאַחַד הַשָּׂרִים תִּפֹּלוּ׃

shall you fall | the princes | like and of one | shall you ,die | as man | But | of all .you | Most the ,High

1471 3605 5157 776 8199 430 6965

8 קוּמָה אֱלֹהִים שָׁפְטָה הָאָרֶץ כִּי־אַתָּה תִנְחַל בְּכָל־הַגּוֹיִם׃

the .nations | all in | shall inherit | You for | the ;earth | judge | ,God O | ,Rise

PSAL. LXXXIII פג

PSALM 83

3808 2790 1824 3808 430 623 4210 7892

1 שִׁיר מִזְמוֹר לְאָסָף׃
2 אֱלֹהִים אַל־דֳּמִי־לָךְ אַל־תֶּחֱרַשׁ וְאַל־

and not | be do ;speechless | not ;yourself to | silence keep | do not | ,God O | .Asaph of | psalm a | A ,song

7218 5375 8130 1993 341 410 8252

3 תִּשְׁקֹט אֵל׃ כִּי־הִנֵּה אוֹיְבֶיךָ יֶהֱמָיוּן וּמְשַׂנְאֶיךָ נָשְׂאוּ רֹאשׁ׃

(their) .head | have up lifted | who those and You hate | are ;roaring | Your enemies | ,lo For | .God O | be do ,still

3212 559 6845 3289 5475 6191 5971

4 עַל־עַמְּךָ יַעֲרִימוּ סוֹד וְיִתְיָעֲצוּ עַל־צְפוּנֶיךָ׃
5 אָמְרוּ לְכוּ

,Come | They ,said have | Your .ones hidden | against | they and conspire | ;counsel | They shrewd take | Your against people

3820 3289 5750 3478 8034 2142 3808 1471 3582

6 וְנַכְחִידֵם מִגּוֹי וְלֹא־יִזָּכֵר שֵׁם־יִשְׂרָאֵל עוֹד׃ כִּי נוֹעֲצוּ לֵב

one heart | con- ,spired | they For | .again | Israel | name the | be will recalled | of | and not | a from ,nation | will we and off them cut

4124 3459 123 168 3772 1285 3162

7 יַחְדָּו עָלֶיךָ בְּרִית יִכְרֹתוּ׃ אָהֳלֵי אֱדוֹם וְיִשְׁמְעֵאלִים מוֹאָב

Moab | the of and ;Ishmaelites | Edom | tents the of | they ;cut have | a covenant | against You | to- ;gether

1571 6865 3427 6429 6002 5983 1381 1905

8 וְהַגְרִים׃ גְּבָל וְעַמּוֹן וַעֲמָלֵק פְּלֶשֶׁת עִם־יֹשְׁבֵי צוֹר׃
9 גַּם־

Also | .Tyre of dwellers | the with | Philistia | and ;Amalek | and ,Ammon | ,Gebal | the and ;Hagarites

6213 5542 3876 1121 2220 1961 3867 804

10 אַשּׁוּר נִלְוָה עִמָּם הָיוּ זְרוֹעַ לִבְנֵי־לוֹט סֶלָה׃ עֲשֵׂה־לָהֶם

to them | Do | .Selah | .Lot | the to of sons | an arm | they were | with ;them | has joined | Assyria

5874 8045 7028 5158 2985 5516 4080

11 כְּמִדְיָן כְּסִיסְרָא כְיָבִין בְּנַחַל קִישׁוֹן׃ נִשְׁמְדוּ בְעֵין־דֹּאר

;dor | at En- | were They destroyed | .Kishon | the at torrent | (to) as Jabin | (to) as ,Sisera | (to) as ,Midian

2078 2062 6159 5081 7896 127 1828

12 הָיוּ דֹּמֶן לָאֲדָמָה׃ שִׁיתֵמוֹ נְדִיבֵמוֹ כְּעֹרֵב וְכִזְאֵב וּכְזֶבַח

like and Zebah | and ;Zeeb | like Oreb | their nobles | Make them | the for .ground | dung | they became

4999 3423 559 834 5257 3605 6759

13 וּכְצַלְמֻנָּע כָּל־נְסִיכֵמוֹ׃ אֲשֶׁר אָמְרוּ נִירְשָׁה־לָּנוּ אֵת נְאוֹת

pastures for ourselves | take us Let ,possession | ,said | who | their ;princes | all | and Zalmunnah

784 7307 7179 1534 7896 430 430

14 אֱלֹהִים׃ אֱלֹהַי שִׁיתֵמוֹ כַגַּלְגַּל כְּקַשׁ לִפְנֵי־רוּחַ׃
15 כְּאֵשׁ

the As fire | the .wind | before | the as stubble | whirling as ,dust | make them | my O ,God | .God's

5591 7291 2022 3857 3852 3293 1197

16 תִּבְעַר־יָעַר וּכְלֶהָבָה תְּלַהֵט הָרִים׃ כֵּן תִּרְדְּפֵם בְּסַעֲרֶךָ

Your with ,tempest | pursue them | so | the ,mountains | on sets fire | as and flame the | the ,forest | burns

8034 1245 7036 6440 4390 926 5492

17 וּבְסוּפָתְךָ תְבַהֲלֵם׃ מַלֵּא פְנֵיהֶם קָלוֹן וִיבַקְשׁוּ שִׁמְךָ

Your ,name | they that may seek | ,shame | their faces | Fill with | frighten .them | Your with and storm

Jehovah. 17Let them be ashamed and terrified forever; yea, let them be confounded and perish. 18And let them know—Your name *is* Jehovah—that You alone *are* the Most High over all the earth.

PSALM 84
To the chief musician on Gittith. A Psalm for the sons of Korah

1How lovely *are* Your dwellings, O Jehovah of hosts! 2My soul longs and even faints for the courts of Jehovah; my heart and my flesh cry out for the living God. 3Even the sparrow has found a house, and the swallow a nest for herself, where she may lay her young, *on* Your altars, O Jehovah of hosts, my King and my God.

4Blessed *are* they who dwell in Your house; they will always be praising You. Selah.

5Blessed *is* the man whose strength *is* in You; the highways *are* in their hearts. 6Passing through the valley of weeping, they will make it a fountain; yea, the rain clothes with blessings. 7They go from strength to strength, being seen in Zion before God. 8O Jehovah God of hosts, hear my prayer; give ear, O God of Jacob. Selah.

9Behold, O God, our shield; and look upon the face of Your anointed. 10For a day in Your courts *is* better than a thousand; I have chosen to stand at the threshold in the house of my God, rather than to dwell in the tents of wickedness. 11For Jehovah God *is* a sun and shield; Jehovah will give grace and glory; He will withhold nothing good from those who walk in integrity. 12O Jehovah of hosts, blessed *is* the man who trusts in You!

3045 6 2659 5703 926 954 3068
18 19 יְהוָה׃ יֵבֹשׁוּ וְיִבָּהֲלוּ עֲדֵי־עַד וְיַחְפְּרוּ וְיֹאבֵדוּ׃ וְיֵדְעוּ כִּי־
that let And and them let and ,forever and them Let Jeho- O
know them .perish pale be terrified ashamed be .vah

776 3605 5921 5945 905 3068 8034
אַתָּה שִׁמְךָ יְהוָה לְבַדֶּךָ עֶלְיוֹן עַל־כָּל־הָאָרֶץ׃
the all over the You —Jehovah Your ,You
.earth High Most alone (is) name

PSAL. LXXXIV פד

PSALM 84

3039 4210 7141 1121 1665 5921 4908
1 2 לַמְנַצֵּחַ עַל־הַגִּתִּית לִבְנֵי־קֹרַח מִזְמוֹר׃ מַה־יְּדִידוֹת
lovely How .psalm A Korah the for the on chief the To
(are) of sons .Gittith ,musician

5315 3615 1571 3700 6635 3068 4908
3 מִשְׁכְּנוֹתֶיךָ יְהוָה צְבָאוֹת׃ נִכְסְפָה וְגַם־כָּלְתָה ׀ נַפְשִׁי
My faints and longs .hosts O Your
soul even of Jehovah ,dwellings

6833 2416 410 7442 1320 3820 3068 2691
4 לְחַצְרוֹת יְהוָה לִבִּי וּבְשָׂרִי יְרַנְּנוּ אֶל אֵל־חָי׃ גַּם־צִפּוֹר ׀
the Even .living the to shout my and my ;Jehovah the for
bird God joy for flesh heart of courts

666 7896 1866 7064 1004 4672
מָצְאָה בַיִת וּדְרוֹר ׀ קֵן לָהּ אֲשֶׁר־שָׁתָה אֶפְרֹחֶיהָ אֶת־
her may she where for a the and a has
,young lay herself nest swallow ;house found

3427 835 430 4428 6635 3068 4196
5 מִזְבְּחוֹתֶיךָ יְהוָה צְבָאוֹת מַלְכִּי וֵאלֹהָי׃ אַשְׁרֵי יוֹשְׁבֵי
who they Blessed my and my ,hosts O ,altars Your
in dwell (are) .God king of Jehovah

4546 5797 120 835 5542 1984 5750 1004
6 בֵיתֶךָ עוֹד יְהַלְלוּךָ סֶּלָה׃ אַשְׁרֵי אָדָם עוֹז־לוֹ בָךְ מְסִלּוֹת
the in (is) to strength the Blessed .Selah will they still Your
highways ;You him man (is) .You praise ;house

1293 7896 4599 1057 6010 5674 3824
7 בִּלְבָבָם׃ עֹבְרֵי ׀ בְּעֵמֶק הַבָּכָא מַעְיָן יְשִׁיתוּהוּ גַּם־בְּרָכוֹת
(with) even will they a ;weeping the Passing their in (are)
blessings ;it make fountain of valley through .hearts

430 7200 2428 2428 3212 4175 5844
8 יַעְטֶה מוֹרֶה׃ יֵלְכוּ מֵחַיִל אֶל־חָיִל יֵרָאֶה אֶל־אֱלֹהִים
God before appearing ;strength to from They early the covers
strength go .rain

430 238 8605 8085 6635 430 3068 6726
9 בְּצִיּוֹן׃ יְהוָה אֱלֹהִים צְבָאוֹת שִׁמְעָה תְפִלָּתִי הַאֲזִינָה אֱלֹהֵי
O ear give my hear ,hosts of God O .Zion in
of God ;prayer Jehovah

4899 6440 5027 430 7200 4043 5542 3290
10 יַעֲקֹב סֶלָה׃ מָגִנֵּנוּ רְאֵה אֱלֹהִים וְהַבֵּט פְּנֵי מְשִׁיחֶךָ׃
Your the look and ,God O ,See our .Selah .Jacob
.anointed of face upon shield

430 1004 5605 977 505 2691 3117/2896
11 כִּי טוֹב־יוֹם בַּחֲצֵרֶיךָ מֵאָלֶף בָּחַרְתִּי הִסְתּוֹפֵף בְּבֵית אֱלֹהַי
my the in at stand to have I a than Your in a (is) For
God of house threshold the chosen ;thousand courts day better

2580 430 3068 4043 8121 7562 168 1752
12 מִדּוּר בְּאָהֳלֵי־רֶשַׁע׃ כִּי שֶׁמֶשׁ ׀ וּמָגֵן יְהוָה אֱלֹהִים חֵן
Grace God (is) a and sun a For wicked- the in to than
Jehovah shield .ness of tents dwell

3068 8549 1980 2896/4513 3808 3068 5414 3519
13 וְכָבוֹד יִתֵּן יְהוָה לֹא יִמְנַע־טוֹב לַהֹלְכִים בְּתָמִים׃ יְהוָה
O .integrity in those to with- will He not ;Jehovah will and
of Jehovah walk who good hold give glory

982 120 835 6635
צְבָאוֹת אַשְׁרֵי אָדָם בֹּטֵחַ בָּךְ׃
in who the blessed ,hosts
.You trusts man (is)

PSAL. LXXXV פה

PSALM 85

To the chief musician. A Psalm for the sons of Korah

[1]O Jehovah, You have been gracious to Your land; You have turned back the captivity of Jacob. [2]You have taken away the iniquity of Your people; You covered all of their sins. Selah.

[3]You gathered all of Your wrath; You turned from the heat of Your anger. [4]O God of our salvation, turn us, and break up Your anger with us. [5]Will You be angry with us forever? [6]Will You give us life anew, so that Your people may rejoice in You? [7]Cause us to see Your mercy, O Jehovah, and give us Your salvation.

[8]I will hear what Jehovah God will say; for He will speak peace to His people, and to His saints; but let them not turn again to folly. [9]Surely His salvation *is* near to fearers of Him; for glory to dwell in our land. [10]Mercy and truth have met together; righteousness and peace kissed *each other*. [11]Truth shall sprout out of the earth, and righteousness looks down from Heaven. [12]Yea, Jehovah shall give good, and our land shall give its produce. [13]Righteousness shall go before Him, and shall make a way for His footsteps.

7725 776 3068 7521 4210 7141 1121 5329
1 2 לַמְנַצֵּחַ לִבְנֵי־קֹרַח מִזְמוֹר׃ רָצִיתָ יְהוָה אַרְצֶךָ שַׁבְתָּ
You Your O have You .psalm A Korah the for chief the To
turned ;land ,Jehovah ,favored of sons .musician

5542 2403 3605 3680 5971 5771 5375 3290 7622
3 שְׁבוּת יַעֲקֹב׃ נָשָׂאתָ עֲוֹן עַמֶּךָ כִּסִּיתָ כָל־חַטָּאתָם סֶלָה׃
.Selah their all You Your iniquity You .Jacob cap- the
.sins covered ;people's up lifted of tivity

430 7725 639 2740 7725 5678 622
4 5 אָסַפְתָּ כָל־עֶבְרָתֶךָ הֱשִׁיבוֹתָ מֵחֲרוֹן אַפֶּךָ׃ שׁוּבֵנוּ אֱלֹהֵי
God O Turn Your the from You Your all You
of ,us .anger of heat turned ;wrath gathered

4900 599 5769 3908 6565 3468
6 יִשְׁעֵנוּ וְהָפֵר כַּעַסְךָ עִמָּנוּ׃ הַלְעוֹלָם תֶּאֱנַף־בָּנוּ תִּמְשֹׁךְ
You Will with you Will forever with Your and sal- our
out draw ?us angry be .us anger up break ,vation

8056 5971 2421 7725 3808 1755 1755 639
7 אַפְּךָ לְדֹר וָדֹר׃ הֲלֹא אַתָּה תָּשׁוּב תְּחַיֵּנוּ וְעַמְּךָ יִשְׂמְחוּ
may Your that You Will Will You not gen- and gen- to Your
rejoice people ,us revive ?turn ?eration eration anger

8085 5414 3468 2617 3068 7200
8 9 בָךְ׃ הַרְאֵנוּ יְהוָה חַסְדֶּךָ וְיֶשְׁעֲךָ תִּתֶּן־לָנוּ׃ אֶשְׁמְעָה מַה
what will I to give Your and Your O Show in
hear .us salvation ,mercy ,Jehovah ,us ?You

2623 5971 7965 1696 3068 410 1696
יְדַבֵּר הָאֵל יְהוָה כִּי ׀ יְדַבֵּר שָׁלוֹם אֶל־עַמּוֹ וְאֶל־חֲסִידָיו
His and His to peace will He for ;Jehovah God will
;saints to ,people speak say

3519 7931 3468 3373 7138 389 3690 7725 3808
10 וְאַל־יָשׁוּבוּ לְכִסְלָה׃ אַךְ קָרוֹב לִירֵאָיו יִשְׁעוֹ לִשְׁכֹּן כָּבוֹד
glory to sal- His fearers to (is) Surely .folly to them let but
dwell ,vation Him of near again turn not

571 5401 7965 6664 6298 571 2617 776
11 12 בְּאַרְצֵנוּ׃ חֶסֶד־וֶאֱמֶת נִפְגָּשׁוּ צֶדֶק וְשָׁלוֹם נָשָׁקוּ׃ אֱמֶת
Truth have and righteous- met have and Mercy our in
.kissed peace ness ;together truth .land

5414 3068 1571 8259 8064 6664 6779 776
13 מֵאֶרֶץ תִּצְמָח וְצֶדֶק מִשָּׁמַיִם נִשְׁקָף׃ גַּם־יְהוָה יִתֵּן
shall Jehovah ,Yea looks from righ- and shall of out
give .down Heaven teousness ;sprout earth the

7760 1980 6440 6664 2981 5414 776 2896
14 הַטּוֹב וְאַרְצֵנוּ תִּתֵּן יְבוּלָהּ׃ צֶדֶק לְפָנָיו יְהַלֵּךְ וְיָשֵׂם
shall and shall before Righteous- its shall our and ;good
make ,go Him ness .produce give land

6471 1870
לְדֶרֶךְ פְּעָמָיו׃
His a for
.footsteps way

PSAL. LXXXVI פו

PSALM 86

A Prayer of David.

[1]O Jehovah, bow down Your ear, answer me, for I *am* poor and needy. [2]Keep my soul, for I *am* godly; O You my God, save Your servant who trusts in You. [3]Favor Me, O Lord, for I cry to You daily. [4]Give

34 6041 6030 241 3068 5186 1732 8605
1 תְּפִלָּה לְדָוִד הַטֵּה־יְהוָה אָזְנְךָ עֲנֵנִי כִּי־עָנִי וְאֶבְיוֹן אָנִי׃
I and poor for answer Your O Bow of A
.(am) needy ;me ;ear ,Jehovah ,down .David prayer

430 5650 3462 2623 5315 8104
2 שָׁמְרָה נַפְשִׁי כִּי־חָסִיד אָנִי הוֹשַׁע עַבְדְּךָ אַתָּה אֱלֹהַי
my You O Your Save ;(am) I godly for my Guard
,God ,servant ,soul

3117 3605 7121 136 2603 982
3 הַבּוֹטֵחַ אֵלֶיךָ׃ חָנֵּנִי אֲדֹנָי כִּי־אֵלֶיךָ אֶקְרָא כָּל־הַיּוֹם׃
the all cry I to for O Favor .You in who
.day You ,Lord ,me trusts

joy to the soul of Your servant; for to You, O Lord, I lift up my soul. [5]For You, O Lord, *are* good and ready to forgive; and rich in mercy to all who call on You. [6]O Lord, give ear to my prayer; listen to my voice of supplications. [7]I will call on You in the day of my trouble, for You will answer me. [8]None among the gods *is* like You, O Lord; nor *any* like Your works. [9]All nations whom You have made shall come and worship before You; yea, Lord, *they* shall glorify Your name. [10]For You *are* great, and do wonderful things; You alone *are* God.

[11]Teach me Your way, O Jehovah; I will walk in your truth; unite my heart to fear Your name. [12]With all my heart I will thank You, O Lord my God; and I will glorify Your name forevermore. [13]For Your mercy toward me *is* great; and You have delivered my soul from the lowest Sheol. [14]O God, the proud have risen against me; and the troop of the violent have sought after my life, and have not set You before their eyes. [15]But You, O God, *are* God, full of pity; and gracious, long-suffering and rich in mercy and truth. [16]O turn to me and be gracious to me; give Your strength to Your servant, and save the son of Your handmaid. [17]Show me a token for good, that those who hate me may see and be ashamed, O Jehovah, because You have helped me and comforted me.

PSALM 87

For the Sons of Korah. A Psalm. A Song.

[1]His foundation *is* in the holy mountains. [2]Jehovah loves the gates of Zion more than all the tents of Jacob. [3]Glorious things *are* spoken of you, O city of God. Selah.

5375 5315 136 5650 5315 8056
4 5 שמח נפש עבדך כי־אליך אדני נפשי אשא: כי־אתה
,You For lift I my O to for Your soul the make
up soul ,Lord ,You ,servant of glad

3068 238 7121 3605 2617 7227 5546 2896 136
6 אדני טוב וסלח ורב־חסד לכל־קראיך: האזינה יהוה
O ear Give call who to mercy and and (are) O
,Jehovah ,to ,You on all in rich ,forgiving good ,Lord

7121 6869 3117 8469 6963 7181 8605
7 תפלתי והקשיבה בקול תחנונותי: ביום צרתי אקראך
call will I my the In sup- my the to and my
,You on trouble of day .plications of voice attend ,prayer

4639 369 136 430 3644 369 6030
8 כי תענני: אין־כמוך באלהים | אדני ואין כמעשיך:
Your like and ;Lord O among like None will You for
.works are none ,gods the You (is) .me answer

3513 136 6440 7812 935 6213 834 1471 3605
9 כל־גוים | אשר עשית יבואו | וישתחוו לפניך אדני ויכבדו
shall and O before and shall have You whom nations All
glorify ,Lord ,You worship come made

905 430 6387 6213 1419 8034
10 לשמך: כי־גדול אתה ועשה נפלאות אתה אלהים לבדך:
.alone God You wonderful and You great For Your
(are) ;things do ,(are) .name

3372 3824 3161 571 1980 1870 3068 3384
11 הורני יהוה | דרכך אהלך באמתך יחד לבבי ליראה
fear to my unite Your in will I Your O Teach
heart ;truth walk ;way ,Jehovah ,me

8034 3513 3824 3605 430 136 3034 8034
12 שמך: אודך | אדני אלהי בכל־לבבי ואכבדה שמך
Your will I and my with my O will I Your
name glorify ;heart all ,God Lord ,You thank .name

7585 5315 5337 1419 2617 5769
13 לעולם: כי־חסדך גדול עלי והצלת נפשי משאול
the from my You and toward (is) Your For .forever
Sheol soul saved have ;me great mercy

1245 6184 5712 6965 2086 430 8482
14 תחתיה: אלהים | זדים קמו עלי ועדת עריצים בקשו
have the the and against have the ,God O .lowest
sought violent of troop ;me risen proud

2587 7349 410 136 6440 7760 3808 5315
15 נפשי ולא שמוך לנגדם: ואתה אדני אל־רחום וחנון
and of full (are) O But before have and my
,gracious ,pity ,God ,Lord ,You .themselves You set not ,life

5797 2603 6437 571 2617 7227 639 750
16 ארך אפים ורב־חסד ואמת: פנה אלי וחנני תנה־עזך
Your give and to O and mercy and ,anger long
strength ;me favor ,me turn .truth in rich (before)

2896 226 6213 519 1121 3467 5650
17 לעבדך והושיעה לבן־אמתך: עשה־עמי אות לטובה
for a with Make Your the save and Your to
,good sign me .handmaid of son ;servant

5162 5826 3068 954 8130 7200
ויראו שנאי ויבשו כי־אתה יהוה עזרתני ונחמתני:
com- and have O ,You for be and my shall and
.me forted me helped ,Jehovah ;ashamed haters see

PSAL. LXXXVII פז

PSALM 87

3068 157 6944 2048 3248 7892 4210 7141 1121
1 2 לבני־קרח מזמור שיר יסודתו בהררי־קדש: אהב יהוה
Jehovah loves .holiness the in (is) His A A .Korah the For
of mountains foundation .song .psalm of sons

5892 1696 3513 3290 4908 3605 6726 8179
3 שערי ציון מכל משכנות יעקב: נכבדות מדבר בך עיר
O of are Glorious .Jacob tents the more Zion the
of city ,You spoken things of all than of gates

⁴I will mention Rahab and Babylon to those knowing me. Behold, Philistia and Tyre with Ethiopia; this *man* was born there. ⁵And it shall be said to Zion, A man and a man was born in her; and He, the Highest, will establish her. ⁶Jehovah shall count in recording the peoples: This *man* was born there. Selah.

⁷And the singers, the players of the pipe; all my springs *are* in You.

PSALM 88

A Song. A Psalm for the Sons of Korah, to the Chief Musician on Mahalath, to make humble. A Poem of Heman the Ezrahite.

¹O Jehovah God of my salvation, I have cried in the day, in the night before You. ²Let my prayer come before You; bow down Your ear to my cry. ³For my soul is full with evils; and my life touches Sheol. ⁴I am counted with those who go down to the Pit; I have been like a feeble man, ⁵free among the dead, as pierced ones lying in the grave, whom You remember no more; yea, by Your hand they are cut off. ⁶You have laid me in the lowest pit, in dark places; in the deeps. ⁷Your fury has lain hard upon me, and You afflict *me* with all Your waves. Selah.

⁸You have taken my friends away from me; You have made me a hateful thing to them; *I am* shut up, I cannot go out. ⁹My eye mourns because of affliction; O Jehovah, I have called on You every day; I have spread out my hands to You. ¹⁰For will You do wonders to the dead? Or shall the departed spirits rise *to* thank You? Selah. ¹¹Shall Your mercy be declared in the grave, Your faithfulness amidst ruin? ¹²Shall Your wonders be known in the dark, and

---

4 אֱלֹהִים סֶלָה: | אַזְכִּיר | רַהַב וּבָבֶל לְיֹדְעָי הִנֵּה פְלֶשֶׁת
.God .Selah .will I mention Rahab and Babylon to those knowing me ;behold Philistia

5 וְצוֹר עִם־כּוּשׁ זֶה יֻלַּד־שָׁם: וּלְצִיּוֹן | יֵאָמַר אִישׁ וְאִישׁ
and Tyre with Ethiopia; This was born there. And to Zion A man and man

6 יֻלַּד־בָּהּ וְהוּא יְכוֹנְנֶהָ עֶלְיוֹן: יְהוָה יִסְפֹּר בִּכְתוֹב עַמִּים
was born in her; and He will establish her, the Highest. Jehovah shall count in recording the peoples,

7 זֶה יֻלַּד־שָׁם סֶלָה: וְשָׁרִים כְּחֹלְלִים כָּל־מַעְיָנַי בָּךְ:
this was born there. Selah. And the singers, the players of the pipe; all my springs (are) in You.

PSAL. LXXXVIII פח

PSALM 88

1 שִׁיר מִזְמוֹר לִבְנֵי־קֹרַח לַמְנַצֵּחַ עַל־מָחֲלַת לְעַנּוֹת מַשְׂכִּיל
A song A psalm for the sons of Korah to the chief musician on Mahalath to make humble. A poem teaching

2 לְהֵימָן הָאֶזְרָחִי: יְהוָה אֱלֹהֵי יְשׁוּעָתִי יוֹם־צָעַקְתִּי בַלָּיְלָה
of Heman the Ezrahite. O Jehovah God of my salvation, in the day have I cried in the night

3,4 נֶגְדֶּךָ: תָּבוֹא לְפָנֶיךָ תְּפִלָּתִי הַטֵּה אָזְנְךָ לְרִנָּתִי: כִּי
before You. Let come before You my prayer; bow down Your ear to my cry. For

5 שָׂבְעָה בְרָעוֹת נַפְשִׁי וְחַיַּי לִשְׁאוֹל הִגִּיעוּ: נֶחְשַׁבְתִּי עִם־
full is with evils my soul; and my life to Sheol touches. am I counted with

6 יוֹרְדֵי בוֹר הָיִיתִי כְּגֶבֶר אֵין־אֱיָל: בַּמֵּתִים חָפְשִׁי כְּמוֹ
those go- to the pit; have I been like a man without strength. Among the dead free, as

chlolim piercing ones lying grave in whom not You remember, and they from Your hand

7,8 נִגְזָרוּ: שַׁתַּנִי בְּבוֹר תַּחְתִּיּוֹת בְּמַחֲשַׁכִּים בִּמְצֹלוֹת: עָלַי
are cut off. You have put me in the pit lowest, in dark places, in the deeps. Upon me

9 סָמְכָה חֲמָתֶךָ וְכָל־מִשְׁבָּרֶיךָ עִנִּיתָ סֶלָה: הִרְחַקְתָּ מְיֻדָּעַי
has lain Your fury, and all Your waves You afflict. Selah. You have taken away my friends

10 מִמֶּנִּי שַׁתַּנִי תוֹעֵבוֹת לָמוֹ כָּלֻא וְלֹא אֵצֵא: עֵינִי דָאֲבָה מִנִּי
from me; You have made me a hateful thing to them; (am I) shut up and not will I go out. My eye wastes because

11 עֹנִי קְרָאתִיךָ יְהוָה בְּכָל־יוֹם שִׁטַּחְתִּי אֵלֶיךָ כַפָּי: הֲלַמֵּתִים
of affliction; I called on You, Jehovah, every day; I spread out to You my palms. to the dead For

12 תַּעֲשֶׂה־פֶּלֶא אִם־רְפָאִים יָקוּמוּ יוֹדוּךָ סֶלָה: הַיְסֻפַּר
will You do wonders? Or departed spirits shall rise (and) thank you? Selah. Shall be declared

13 בַקֶּבֶר חַסְדֶּךָ אֱמוּנָתְךָ בָּאֲבַדּוֹן: הֲיִוָּדַע בַּחֹשֶׁךְ פִּלְאֶךָ
in the grave Your mercy; Your faithfulness in ruin? Shall be known in the dark Your wonders,

Your righteousness in the land of forgetfulness? [13]But to You I have cried, O Jehovah; and in the morning my prayer shall go before You. [14]O Jehovah, why do You cast off my soul, do You hide Your face from me? [15]I *am* afflicted and dying from childhood; I suffer Your terrors; I am distracted. [16]Your fierce wrath goes over me; Your terrors have cut me off.

[17]They surrounded me like waters all the day long; they have come together around me. [18]You have taken lover and friend far from me; he who knows me, *into* darkness.

PSALM 89

A Poem of Ethan the Ezrahite.

[1]I will sing *of* the mercies of Jehovah forever; I will declare with my mouth Your faithfulness to all generations. [2]For I have said, Mercy shall be built up forever; You shall establish Your faithfulness in the heavens.

[3]I have cut a covenant with My chosen; I have sworn to David My servant, [4]I will establish Your seed forever, and build up Your throne to all generations. Selah.

[5]And the heavens shall thank Your wonders, O Jehovah; also Your faithfulness in the assembly of the saints. [6]For who in the heaven shall be ranked with Jehovah, *who* among the sons of the mighty is like Jehovah? [7]God is greatly to be feared in the congregation of the saints, and to be adored by all around Him. [8]O Jehovah God of hosts, who *is* a strong Jehovah like You? And Your faithfulness *is* all around You. [9]You rule the pride of the sea; when its waves rise high, You still them. [10]You have broken Rahab in pieces, as one slain; You

7768 3068 5388 776 6666

14 וְצִדְקָתְךָ בְּאֶרֶץ נְשִׁיָּה׃ וַאֲנִי ׀ אֵלֶיךָ יְהוָה שִׁוַּעְתִּי

have ;cried | O ,Jehovah | ,You to | I But | forgetful ?ness | the in land of | Your and righteousness

5640 5315 2186 3068 4100 6923 8605 1242

15 וּבַבֹּקֶר תְּפִלָּתִי תְקַדְּמֶךָּ׃ לָמָה יְהוָה תִּזְנַח נַפְשִׁי תַּסְתִּיר

You do hide | my ;soul | You do off cast | O Jehovah | Why | go shall .You before | my prayer | the in and morning

6323 367 5375 5290 147.8 60~41 6440

16 פָּנֶיךָ מִמֶּנִּי׃ עָנִי אֲנִי וְגֹוֵעַ מִנֹּעַר נָשָׂאתִי אֵמֶיךָ אָפוּנָה׃

am I .perplexed | Your ;terrors | bear I | from ;youth (my) | and (am) I afflicted dying | from ?me | Your face

3605 4325 5437 6789 1161 2740 5674 5921

17 עָלַי עָבְרוּ חֲרוֹנֶיךָ בִּעוּתֶיךָ צִמְּתוּתֻנִי׃
18 סַבּוּנִי כַמַּיִם כָּל־

all | like waters | en- They me circled | cut have .off me | Your terrors | Your ;wrath | passes | Over me

7453 157 7368 3162 5362 3117

19 הַיּוֹם הִקִּיפוּ עָלַי יָחַד׃ הִרְחַקְתָּ מִמֶּנִּי אֹהֵב וָרֵעַ

and ;friend | lover | from me | have You far put | .together | me | have they around gone | the ;day

4285 3045

מְיֻדָּעַי מַחְשָׁךְ׃

(into) .darkness | acquain- my tances

PSAL. LXXXIX פט

PSALM 89

1755 7891 5769 3068 2617 250 387 7919

1 מַשְׂכִּיל לְאֵיתָן הָאֶזְרָחִי׃
2 חַסְדֵי יְהוָה עוֹלָם אָשִׁירָה לְדֹר

gen- eration | to ;(of) | will I sing | forever | Jehovah | the of mercies | the .Ezrahite | of Ethan | teaching A poem

1129 2617 5769 559 6310 530 559 17.55

3 וָדֹר ׀ אוֹדִיעַ אֱמוּנָתְךָ בְּפִי׃ כִּי־אָמַרְתִּי עוֹלָם חֶסֶד יִבָּנֶה

be shall ;up built | Mercy | forever | have I ,said | For | my with .mouth | Your faithfulness | will I declare | gen- and eration

7650 972 1285 3772 530 3559 8064

4 שָׁמַיִם ׀ תָּכִן אֱמוּנָתְךָ בָהֶם׃ כָּרַתִּי בְרִית לִבְחִירִי נִשְׁבַּעְתִּי

have I sworn | My with ;chosen | a covenant | have I cut | in .them | Your faithfulness | will You set | the heavens

1755 1755 1129 2233 3559 5769 5704 5650 1732

5 לְדָוִד עַבְדִּי׃ עַד־עוֹלָם אָכִין זַרְעֶךָ וּבָנִיתִי לְדֹר־וָדוֹר

gen- and eration | to generation | build and up | Your ,seed | will I establish | forever | until | My ;servant | to David

530 637 3068 6382 8064 3034 5542 3678

6 כִּסְאֲךָ סֶלָה׃ וְיוֹדוּ שָׁמַיִם פִּלְאֲךָ יְהוָה אַף־אֱמוּנָתְךָ

Your faithfulness | also | O ;Jehovah | Your ,wonders | the heavens | shall And thank | .Selah | Your .throne

3068 1819 3068 6186 7834 4310 6918 6951

7 בִּקְהַל קְדֹשִׁים׃ כִּי מִי בַשַּׁחַק יַעֲרֹךְ לַיהוָה יִדְמֶה לַיהוָה

to Jehovah | like is | (with) ,Jehovah | be ranked | the in sky | who | For | .saints the | the in of assembly

3372 7227 6918 5475 6206 410 410 1121

8 בִּבְנֵי אֵלִים׃ אֵל נַעֲרָץ בְּסוֹד־קְדֹשִׁים רַבָּה וְנוֹרָא עַל־

by | be to and feared | ;greatly | the saints | the in of council | be to is feared | God | the ?mighty | among of sons the

3050 2626 3644 4310 6635 430 3068 5439 3605

9 כָּל־סְבִיבָיו׃ יְהוָה ׀ אֱלֹהֵי צְבָאוֹת מִי־כָמוֹךָ חֲסִין ׀ יָהּ

?Jah | a strong | like You | who (is) | ,hosts | of God | O Jehovah | around .him | all

5375 3220 1348 4910 5439 530

10 וֶאֱמוּנָתְךָ סְבִיבוֹתֶיךָ׃ אַתָּה מוֹשֵׁל בְּגֵאוּת הַיָּם בְּשׂוֹא

rise when high | the ;sea | the of pride | rule | You | around all (is) .You | Your And faithfulness

2220 7293 2491 1792 7623 1530

11 גַלָּיו אַתָּה תְשַׁבְּחֵם׃ אַתָּה דִכִּאתָ כֶחָלָל רָהַב בִּזְרוֹעַ

arm with of | ;Rahab | one as slain | have crushed | You | .them still | You | its ,waves have scattered Your enemies with Your mighty arm. 11The heavens *are* yours, and the earth *is* Yours—the world and its fullness—You founded them. 12You have created the north and the south; Tabor and Herman rejoice in Your name. 13You have a mighty arm; Your hand is strong, Your right hand is high. 14Justice and righteousness *are* Your throne's foundation; mercy and truth go before Your face. 15Blessed is the people knowing the joyful sound; O Jehovah, they shall walk in the light of Your face. 16They shall rejoice in Your name always; and they are exalted in Your righteousness. 17For You *are* the glory of their strength; and by Your favor You lift up our horn. 18For Jehovah *is* our shield, and the Holy One of Israel our King.

19Then You spoke in a vision to Your holy one; and You said, I have laid help on a mighty one. I have exalted a chosen one from the people. 20I have found My servant David; I have anointed him with My holy oil. 21My hand shall be fixed with him; and My arm shall make him strong. 22An enemy will not exact against him; nor the son of iniquity afflict him. 23And I will beat down his foes before Him, and plague those hating him. 24But My faithfulness and My mercy *is* with him; and his horn shall be exalted in My name. 25And I will set his hand in the sea, and his right hand in the rivers. 26He shall cry to Me, My father You *are* my God, and the rock of my salvation. 27And I will make him My firstborn; higher than the kings of the earth. 28I will keep My mercy for him forever; and My covenant shall hold fast with him. 29And I have established his seed forever, and his throne as the days of the heavens. 30If his children forsake My law and do not walk in My judgments; 31if they profane My

4393 8398 776 637 8064 341 6340 5797
12 עֻזְּךָ פִּזַּרְתָּ אוֹיְבֶיךָ׃ לְךָ שָׁמַיִם אַף־לְךָ אָרֶץ תֵּבֵל וּמְלֹאָהּ
its and the the to also The to Your have You Your
,fulness world —earth You ,heavens You .enemies scattered might

27,68 8396 1254 3225 6828 3245
13 אַתָּה יְסַדְתָּם׃ צָפוֹן וְיָמִין אַתָּה בְרָאתָם תָּבוֹר וְחֶרְמוֹן
and Tabor have You the and The have You
Hermon ;them created south north .them founded

3225 7311 3027 5810 1369 2220 7442 8034
14 בְּשִׁמְךָ יְרַנֵּנוּ׃ לְךָ זְרוֹעַ עִם־גְּבוּרָה תָּעֹז יָדְךָ תָּרוּם יְמִינֶךָ׃
Your high is Your is ;might with an to shout Your at
.hand right ;hand strong arm (is) You ;joy for name

6440 6923 571 2617 3678 4349 4941 6664
15 צֶדֶק וּמִשְׁפָּט מְכוֹן כִּסְאֶךָ חֶסֶד וֶאֱמֶת יְקַדְּמוּ פָנֶיךָ׃
Your go shall and mercy Your foun- the and Righ-
.face before truth ;throne of dation justice teousness

1980 6440 216 30,68 8643 3045 5971 835
16 אַשְׁרֵי הָעָם יוֹדְעֵי תְרוּעָה יְהוָה בְּאוֹר־פָּנֶיךָ יְהַלֵּכוּן׃
shall they Your the in O joyful the who the Blessed
.walk face of light ,Jehovah ;sound know people (is)

8597 7311 6666 3117 3605 1523 8034
17
18 בְּשִׁמְךָ יְגִילוּן כָּל־הַיּוֹם וּבְצִדְקָתְךָ יָרוּמוּ׃ כִּי־תִפְאֶרֶת
the For are they Your in and the all shall They Your in
of glory .exalted righteousness ;day rejoice name

4043 3068 7161 7311 7522 5797
19 עֻזָּמוֹ אָתָּה וּבִרְצוֹנְךָ תָּרִים קַרְנֵנוּ׃ כִּי לַיהוָה מָגִנֵּנוּ
our Jehovah For our You Your by and You their
,shield (is) .horn up lift favor ,(are) strength

559 2623 2377 1696 227 4428 3478 6918
20 וְלִקְדוֹשׁ יִשְׂרָאֵל מַלְכֵּנוּ׃ אָז דִּבַּרְתָּ־בְחָזוֹן לַחֲסִידֶיךָ וַתֹּאמֶר
You and Your to a in You Then .king our Israel the and
said ;one holy vision spoke of One Holy

1732 4672 5971 977 7311 1368 5828 7737
21 שִׁוִּיתִי עֵזֶר עַל־גִּבּוֹר הֲרִימוֹתִי בָחוּר מֵעָם׃ מָצָאתִי דָּוִד
David have I the from chosen a have I mighty a on help have I
found .people one exalted ;one laid

637 3559 3027 834 4886 69,44 8081 5650
22 עַבְדִּי בְּשֶׁמֶן קָדְשִׁי מְשַׁחְתִּיו׃ אֲשֶׁר יָדִי תִּכּוֹן עִמּוֹ אַף־
also with be shall My whom have I My with My
;him fixed hand him anointed holy oil ;servant

6031 38,08 57,66 341 53,78 553 2220
23 זְרוֹעִי תְאַמְּצֶנּוּ׃ לֹא־יַשִּׁא אוֹיֵב בּוֹ וּבֶן־עַוְלָה לֹא יְעַנֶּנּוּ׃
af- shall not iniquity the against An shall not make shall My
.him flict of son ;him enemy exact .strong him arm

2617 530 5061 8130 6862 6440 3807
24
25 וְכַתּוֹתִי מִפָּנָיו צָרָיו וּמְשַׂנְאָיו אֶגּוֹף׃ וֶאֱמוּנָתִי וְחַסְדִּי עִמּוֹ
with My and My But .plague those and his before will I And
;him (is) mercy faithfulness him hating ,foes face his down beat

3225 5104 3027 3220 7760 7161 7311 80,34
26 וּבִשְׁמִי תָּרוּם קַרְנוֹ׃ וְשַׂמְתִּי בַיָּם יָדוֹ וּבַנְּהָרוֹת יְמִינוֹ׃
right his the in and his the in I And his be shall My in and
.hand rivers ,hand sea set will .horn exalted name

1060 637 3444 6697/410 1 7121
27
28 הוּא יִקְרָאֵנִי אָבִי אָתָּה אֵלִי וְצוּר יְשׁוּעָתִי׃ אַף־אָנִי בְּכוֹר
first- I Also my the and my You my cry shall He
born .salvation of rock ,God ,(are) father ,Me to

2617 8104 5769 776 44,28 59,45 5414
29 אֶתְּנֵהוּ עֶלְיוֹן לְמַלְכֵי־אָרֶץ׃ לְעוֹלָם אֶשְׁמוֹר־לוֹ חַסְדִּי
My for will I Forever the the than higher make will
;mercy him keep .earth of kings ;him

8064 3117 3678 2233 5703 7760 539 1285
30 וּבְרִיתִי נֶאֱמֶנֶת לוֹ׃ וְשַׂמְתִּי לָעַד זַרְעוֹ וְכִסְאוֹ כִּימֵי שָׁמָיִם׃
the the as his and his forever I And to (be shall) My and
.heavens of days throne ,seed set have .him confirmed covenant

2708 3212 38,08 4941 8451 1121 5800 518
31
32 אִם־יַעַזְבוּ בָנָיו תּוֹרָתִי וּבְמִשְׁפָּטַי לֹא יֵלֵכוּן׃ אִם־חֻקֹּתַי
My if do not My in and My his forsake If
statutes ,walk judgments ,law children

statutes and do not keep
My commands; 32then I will
visit their transgressions
with the rod, and their sins
with stripes. 33But I will not
annul My mercy from him,
and I will not be false in My
faithfulness. 34I will not
profane My covenant, nor
change what goes from My
lips. 35Once I have sworn
by My holiness; I will not lie
to David. 36His seed shall
be forever, and his throne
as the sun before Me.
37Like the moon it shall be
forever, and a faithful
witness in the sky. Selah.
38But You have cast off
and rejected; You have
been angry with Your
anointed. 39You have
spurned the covenant of
Your servant; You have defiled his crown to the
ground. 40You have broken
down all his walls; You
have set his strongholds *to*
ruin. 41All who pass by the
way plunder him; he is a
reproach to his neighbors.
42You have set up the right
hand of his opposers; You
have made rejoice all his
enemies. 43And You have
turned back the edge of his
sword, and *You* have not
made him stand in battle.
44You have made his glory
cease and have hurled his
throne to the ground. 45You
have shortened the days of
his youth; You have
covered shame over him.
Selah.
46O Jehovah, until when
will You hide Yourself?
Shall Your wrath burn like
fire forever? 47Please remember the time of life; for
what vanity You have
created all the sons of men.
48What man lives and does
not see death? Shall he
deliver his soul from the
hand of Sheol? Selah. 49O
Lord, where *are* Your
former kindnesses, *that*
You swore to David in Your
faithfulness? 50Remember,
O Lord the reproach of Your
servants; my bearing in my

6588 7626 6485 8904 38,08 4687 2490
33 יְחַלֵּלוּ וּמִצְוֺתַי לֹא יִשְׁמֹרוּ׃ וּפָקַדְתִּי בְשֵׁבֶט פִּשְׁעָם
trans- their the with will I then ;keep do not My and they
.gressions rod visit commands ,profane

82.66 3808 6331 38,08 2617 57,71 5061
34 וּבִנְגָעִים עֲוֺנָם׃ וְחַסְדִּי לֹא־אָפִיר מֵעִמּוֹ וְלֹא אֲשַׁקֵּר
will I and with from will I not My But their with and
false be not him annul mercy .iniquities stripes

8138 38,08 819,3 4161 1285 2490 530
35 בֶּאֱמוּנָתִי׃ לֹא־אֲחַלֵּל בְּרִיתִי וּמוֹצָא שְׂפָתַי לֹא אֲשַׁנֶּה׃
will I not My what and My will I not My in
.change lips from goes ,covenant profane .faithfulness

57,69 2233 3576 1732 6944 7650 259
36 37 אַחַת נִשְׁבַּעְתִּי בְקָדְשִׁי אִם־לְדָוִד אֲכַזֵּב׃ זַרְעוֹ לְעוֹלָם
forever His will I to not My by have I Once
seed .lie David ;holiness sworn

7834 5707 5769 3559 3394 5048 8121 3678 1961
38 יִהְיֶה וְכִסְאוֹ כַשֶּׁמֶשׁ נֶגְדִּי׃ כְּיָרֵחַ יִכּוֹן עוֹלָם וְעֵד בַּשַּׁחַק
the in a and ;forever shall it the Like before the as his and shall
sky witness set be moon .Me sun throne ,be

4899 5674 3985 2186 55,42 539
39 נֶאֱמָן סֶלָה׃ וְאַתָּה זָנַחְתָּ וַתִּמְאָס הִתְעַבַּרְתָּ עִם־מְשִׁיחֶךָ׃
Your with have You re- and cast have But .Selah faith-
.anointed cross been (us) jected off You .ful

3605 6555 5145 776 2490 5650 1285 5610
40 41 נֵאַרְתָּה בְּרִית עַבְדֶּךָ חִלַּלְתָּ לָאָרֶץ נִזְרוֹ׃ פָּרַצְתָּ כָל־
all have You his the to have You Your cove- the have You
down broken .crown ground defiled ;servant of nant spurned

1961 1870 5674 8155 4288 4013 7760 1448
42 גְּדֵרֹתָיו שַׂמְתָּ מִבְצָרָיו מְחִתָּה׃ שַׁסֻּהוּ כָּל־עֹבְרֵי דָרֶךְ הָיָה
he the who All plunder (to) his have You his
is ;way by pass him .ruin strongholds set ;walls

341 3605 8056 6862 3225 7311 7934 27,81
43 חֶרְפָּה לִשְׁכֵנָיו׃ הֲרִימוֹתָ יְמִין צָרָיו הִשְׂמַחְתָּ כָּל־אוֹיְבָיו׃
his all have You his right have You his to re- a
.enemies rejoice made ;enemies' hand exalted .neighbors proach

7673 4421 6965 38,08 2719 6697 7725 637
44 45 אַף־תָּשִׁיב צוּר חַרְבּוֹ וְלֹא הֲקֵמֹתוֹ בַּמִּלְחָמָה׃ הִשְׁבַּתָּ
have You .battle in made have and his the have You Truly
cease made stand him not ,sword of edge back turned

5934 3117 7114 4048 776 3678 2892
46 מִטְּהָרוֹ וְכִסְאוֹ לָאָרֶץ מִגַּרְתָּה׃ הִקְצַרְתָּ יְמֵי עֲלוּמָיו
his the have You have the to his and his
;youth of days shortened .hurled ground throne ;lustre

5331 5640 3068 5704 55,42 955 59,21 5844
47 הֶעֱטִיתָ עָלָיו בּוּשָׁה סֶלָה׃ עַד־מָה יְהוָה תִּסָּתֵר לָנֶצַח
?forever You will O ,when Until .Selah .shame him on have You
Yourself hide ,Jehovah covered

7723 2465 3142 2534 784 1197
48 תִּבְעַר כְּמוֹ־אֵשׁ חֲמָתֶךָ׃ זְכָר־אֲנִי מֶה־חָלֶד עַל־מַה־שָּׁוְא
vanity what for time the ,Remember Your fire like Shall
;life of ,please ?wrath burn

4422 4194 38,08 2421 1397 120 1121 1254
49 בָּרָאתָ כָל־בְּנֵי־אָדָם׃ מִי גֶבֶר יִחְיֶה וְלֹא יִרְאֶה־מָּוֶת יְמַלֵּט
he Shall ?death does and lives man What ?men the all You have
deliver see not of sons created

136 7223 2617 55,42 7585 3027 53,15
50 נַפְשׁוֹ מִיַּד־שְׁאוֹל סֶלָה׃ אַיֵּה ׀ חֲסָדֶיךָ הָרִאשֹׁנִים ׀ אֲדֹנָי
,Lord O ,former Your Where .Selah ?Sheol the from his
kindnesses (are) of hand soul

5375 5650 2781 136 21,42 530 17,32 7650
51 נִשְׁבַּעְתָּ לְדָוִד בֶּאֱמוּנָתֶךָ׃ זְכֹר אֲדֹנָי חֶרְפַּת עֲבָדֶיךָ שְׂאֵתִי
my Your re- the ,Lord O ,Remember Your in to You (that)
bearing ;servants of proach ?faithfulness David swore

bosom the insults of the many peoples; [51]*with* which Your enemies have cursed, O Jehovah; *with* which they have cursed the footsteps of Your anointed.

[52]Blessed *be* Jehovah forever. Amen and amen!

PSALM 90

A Prayer of Moses the Man of God.

[1]O Lord, You have been our dwelling-place in all generations. [2]Before the mountains were born, or ever You had formed the earth and the world; even from everlasting to everlasting You *are* God. [3]You turn man to dust, and say, Return, O sons of men. [4]For a thousand years in Your eyes *are* as yesterday when it passes, and *as* a watch in the night. [5]You flooded them away; they are *as* a sleep; in the morning *they are* like grass growing; [6]in the morning it sprouts and shoots up; in the evening it withers and dries up. [7]For we are consumed by Your anger, and we are troubled by Your wrath. [8]You have set our iniquities before You, our secret *sins* in the light of Your face. [9]For all our days pass away in Your wrath; we finish our years like a murmur. [10]The days of our years *are* seventy; and if *any* by strength *live* eighty years, yet their pride *is* labor and vanity; for it soon passes, and we fly away. [11]Who knows the power of Your anger? And as Your fear *is, so is* Your fury. [12]So teach *us* to number our days, so that we may bring a heart of wisdom. [13]Return, O Jehovah! How long? And give pity to Your servants. [14]O satisfy us in the morning with Your mercy, and we will be glad and rejoice all our days. [15]Make us glad according to the days of our affliction, the years in which we have seen evil. [16]Let

834 3068 341 2778 5971 7727 3605 2436
52 בְחֵיקִי כָּל־רַבִּים עַמִּים׃ אֲשֶׁר חֵרְפוּ אוֹיְבֶיךָ ׀ יְהוָה אֲשֶׁר
(with) O Your re- have (with) ;peoples the all my in
which ;Jehovah ,enemies proached which many bosom

543 543 5769 3068 1288 4899 6119 2778
53 חֵרְפוּ עִקְּבוֹת מְשִׁיחֶךָ׃ בָּרוּךְ יְהוָה לְעוֹלָם אָמֵן ׀ וְאָמֵן׃
and amen ;forever Jehovah Blessed Your step the re- they
!amen (be) .anointed of proached

PSAL. XC צ

PSALM 90

1961 4583 136 430 376 4872 8605
1 תְּפִלָּה לְמֹשֶׁה אִישׁ־הָאֱלֹהִים אֲדֹנָי מָעוֹן אַתָּה הָיִיתָ לָּנוּ
us to have You a ,Lord O .God the Moses of A
been habitation of man prayer

8398 776 2342 3205 2022 2962 1755 1755
2 בְּדֹר וָדֹר׃ בְּטֶרֶם ׀ הָרִים יֻלָּדוּ וַתְּחוֹלֵל אֶרֶץ וְתֵבֵל
the and the You or were the Before gen- and gen- in
;world earth to birth gave ,born mountains .eration eration

559 1793 582 7725 410 5769 5704 5769
3 וּמֵעוֹלָם עַד־עוֹלָם אַתָּה אֵל׃ תָּשֵׁב אֱנוֹשׁ עַד־דַּכָּא וַתֹּאמֶר
,say and ,dust to man You .God You to from even
turn (are) everlasting everlasting

865 5869 8141 505 120 1121 7725
4 שׁוּבוּ בְנֵי־אָדָם׃ כִּי אֶלֶף שָׁנִים בְּעֵינֶיךָ כְּיוֹם אֶתְמוֹל כִּי
when yesterday (are) Your in years a For .men O ,Return
as eyes thousand of sons

1242 1961 8142 2229 3915 821 5674
5 יַעֲבֹר וְאַשְׁמוּרָה בַלָּיְלָה׃ זְרַמְתָּם שֵׁנָה יִהְיוּ בַּבֹּקֶר
the in they a (as) flooded You the in a (as) and passes it
morning ;are sleep ;away them night watch by

3001 4135 6153 2498 6692 1242 2498 2682
6 כֶּחָצִיר יַחֲלֹף׃ בַּבֹּקֶר יָצִיץ וְחָלָף לָעֶרֶב יְמוֹלֵל וְיָבֵשׁ׃
and it the in and it the in ;sprouting like
.up dries withers evening ;sprouts blooms morning grass

5048 5771 7896 926 2534 639 3615
7
8 כִּי־כָלִינוּ בְאַפֶּךָ וּבַחֲמָתְךָ נִבְהָלְנוּ׃ שַׁתָּ עֲוֺנֹתֵינוּ לְנֶגְדֶּךָ
before our have You are we by and Your by are we For
,You iniquities set .troubled wrath Your .anger consumed

3615 5678 6437 3117/3605 6440 3974 5956
9 עֲלֻמֵנוּ לִמְאוֹר פָּנֶיךָ׃ כִּי כָל־יָמֵינוּ פָּנוּ בְעֶבְרָתֶךָ כִּלִּינוּ
we Your in pass our all For Your the in our
finish ;wrath away days .face of light secret

518 8141 7657 8141 3117 1899 3644 8141
10 שָׁנֵינוּ כְמוֹ־הֶגֶה׃ יְמֵי־שְׁנוֹתֵינוּ ׀ בָהֶם שִׁבְעִים שָׁנָה וְאִם
and ,years (are) them in ,years our The a like our
if seventy of days .sigh years

2440 1468 205 5999 7296 8141 8084 1369
בִּגְבוּרֹת שְׁמוֹנִים שָׁנָה וְרָהְבָּם עָמָל וָאָוֶן כִּי־גָז חִישׁ
soon it for and (is) their yet ,years (live) by
passes ;vanity labor pride eighty strength

4487 5678 3373 639 5797 3045/4310 5774
11
12 וַנָּעֻפָה׃ מִי־יוֹדֵעַ עֹז אַפֶּךָ וּכְיִרְאָתְךָ עֶבְרָתֶךָ׃ לִמְנוֹת
number to Your (so) Your as And Your the knows Who we and
fury (is) fear ?anger of might .away fly

5704 3068 7725 2451 3824 935 3045 3651 3117
13 יָמֵינוּ כֵּן הוֹדַע וְנָבִא לְבַב חָכְמָה׃ שׁוּבָה יְהוָה עַד־מָתָי
?when until O ,Return .wisdom heart a we that teach There- our
,Jehovah of bring may (us) ,fore days

8056 7442 2617 1242 7646 5650 5162
14 וְהִנָּחֵם עַל־עֲבָדֶיךָ׃ שַׂבְּעֵנוּ בַבֹּקֶר חַסְדֶּךָ וּנְרַנְּנָה וְנִשְׂמְחָה
be and we and Your (with) the in ,O Your to give and
glad rejoice will ,mercy morning us satisfy .servants pity

7951 7200 8141 6037 3117 8056 3117 3605
15 בְּכָל־יָמֵינוּ׃ שַׂמְּחֵנוּ כִּימוֹת עִנִּיתָנוּ שְׁנוֹת רָאִינוּ רָעָה׃
.evil have we the our to according us Make our all in
seen years ,affliction of days the glad .days

Your work appear to Your servants, and Your majesty to their sons. [17]And let the delight of the Lord our God be upon us; and establish the works of our hands upon us; yea, the work of our hands, establish it!

16 17 יראה אל־עבדיך פעלך והדרך על־בניהם׃ ויהי ׀ נעם
5278 1961 1121 1926 6467 5650 7200
the let And their to Your and Your Your to Let
delight be .sons majesty ,work servants appear

אדני אלהינו עלינו ומעשה ידינו כוננה עלינו ומעשה
4639 5921 3559 3027 4639 5921 430 136
the and upon establish our the and upon our the
of work ;us hands of work ;us God's Lord

ידינו כוננהו׃
3559 3027
establish our
!it ,hands

PSALM 91

[1]He who dwells in the secret place of the Most High shall abide *in* the Almighty's shade. [2]I will say to Jehovah: My refuge and my fortress, my God; I will trust in Him. [3]For He delivers you from the fowler's trap, from destruction's plague. [4]With His feathers He will cover you, and under His wings you shall seek refuge; His truth *is* a shield and buckler. [5]You shall not fear the terror of night, of the arrow *that* flies by day; [6]of the plague *that* walks in darkness; of the destruction laying waste at noonday. [7]A thousand shall fall by your side, and ten thousand at your right hand; it shall not come near you. [8]Only with your eyes you shall look, and see the reward of the wicked. [9]Because You, O Jehovah, *are* my refuge; you make the Most High your habitation. [10]No evil shall happen to You, nor shall any plague come near Your tent. [11]For He shall give His angels charge over You, to keep You in all Your ways. [12]They shall bear You up in their palms, that You not dash Your foot on a stone. [13]You shall tread on the lion and adder; the young lion and the serpent You shall trample underfoot. [14]Because he has set his love on Me, therefore I will deliver him; I will set him on high, because he has known My name. [15]He shall call on Me and I will answer him; I *will be* with him in distress; I will rescue him and honor him. [16]I will satisfy him *with* length of days and will make him see My salvation.

PSAL. XCI צא

PSALM 91

1 2 ישב בסתר עליון בצל שדי יתלונן׃ אמר ליהוה מחסי
4268 3068 559 3885 7706 6738 5945 5643 3427
My to will I shall the shade Most the the in who He
refuge :Jehovah say .abide Almighty's High of covert dwells

3 ומצודתי אלהי אבטח־בו׃ כי הוא יצילך מפח יקוש
3353 6341 5337 982 430 4486
the from delivers He For in will I my my and
,fowler's trap you .Him trust ,God ,fortress

4 מדבר הוות׃ באברתו ׀ יסך לך ותחת־כנפיו תחסה
2620 3671 8478 5526 84 1942 1698
shall you His and ,you shall He His with de- from
;refuge seek wings under cover feathers structions plague

5 צנה וסחרה אמתו׃ לא תירא מפחד לילה מחץ יעוף
5774 2671 3915 6343 3372 3808 571 5507 6793
(that) the of night the shall You not His buckler and a
flies arrow of terror fear .truth (is) shield

6 7 יומם׃ מדבר באפל יהלך מקטב ישוד צהרים׃ יפל
5307 6672 7736 6986 1980 652 1698 3119
shall .noon at (that) the of (that) in the of ;day by
fall waste lays destruction ;walks darkness plague

8 מצדך ׀ אלף ורבבה מימינך אליך לא יגש׃ רק בעיניך
5869 7535 5066 3808 413 3225 7233 505 6654
with Only shall it not you your at ten and A your by
eyes your .near come ;hand right thousand ,thousand side

9 תביט ושלמת רשעים תראה׃ כי־אתה יהוה מחסי
4268 3068 3588 7200 7563 8011 5027
my (are) O ,You Because .see wicked the the and shall you
;refuge ,Jehovah of reward ,look

10 עליון שמת מעונך׃ לא־תאנה אליך רעה ונגע לא־יקרב
7126 3808 5061 7451 413 579 3808 4583 7760 5945
shall not and ,Evil you shall not habit- your you Most the
near come plague befall .ation make High

11 באהלך׃ כי מלאכיו יצוה־לך לשמרך בכל־דרכיך׃
1870 3605 8104 6680 4397 168
your all in keep to for will He His For your
.ways you you order angels .tent

12 13 על־כפים ישאונך פן־תגף באבן רגלך׃ על־שחל ופתן
6620 7826 7272 68 5062 5375 3709
and the On your a on you lest shall They their on
adder lion .foot stone dash .up you bear palms

14 תדרך תרמס כפיר ותנין׃ כי בי חשק ואפלטהו אשגבהו
7682 6403 2836 8577 3715 7429 1869
set will I will I has he on Because the and the shall you shall you
.high on him ,him deliver ,love set Me .snake cub lion trample ,tread

15 כי־ידע שמי׃ יקראני ׀ ואענהו עמו אנכי בצרה אחלצהו
2502 6864 6030 7121 8034 3045
will I in I with will I and shall He My he for
him rescue ;distress (be will) him ;him answer ,Me on call .name known has

16 ואכבדהו׃ ארך ימים אשביעהו ואראהו בישועתי׃
3444 7200 7646 3117 753 3513
My will and will I days (with) honor and
.salvation see him make him satisfy of length .him

PSALM 92

A Psalm, A Song for the Sabbath Day.

[1]*It is* good to give thanks to Jehovah, and to sing praises to Your name, O Most High; [2]to make Your mercy known in the morning, and Your faithfulness every night; [3]on the ten *strings*, and on the harp —on the lyre with sounding music. [4]For You have rejoiced me with Your work, O Jehovah; I will shout in the works of Your hands. [5]O Jehovah, Your purposes are very deep. How great are Your works! [6]An animal-like man does not know; a fool does not understand this. [7]When the wicked flourish like grass; and all the evildoers blossom; *it is* for them *to be* destroyed forever. [8]But You, O Jehovah, *are* exalted forever. [9]For, lo, Your enemies, O Jehovah; for, lo, Your enemies shall perish; all the evildoers shall be scattered. [10]But You will lift up my horn as the wild ox, and I will be anointed with fresh oil. [11]And my eye shall look on my enemies; my ears shall hear the evildoers who rise up against me. [12]The righteous shall flourish as the palm tree; he shall grow like a cedar in Lebanon. [13]Those planted in the house of Jehovah, in the courts of our God, shall flourish. [14]They shall bear fruit in old age; they shall be fat and fresh, [15]to declare Jehovah upright, my rock —and in Him *is* no evil.

PSALM 93

[1]Jehovah reigns! He is clothed with majesty; Jehovah is clothed with strength; He girded Himself; and the world is established; it shall not be shaken. [2]Your throne *is* established from then; You Jehovah, the floods have lifted up their voice; the

PSAL. XCII צב

PSALM 92

2167 3068 3034 2896 7676 3117 7892 4210
1 2 מִזְמוֹר שִׁיר לְיוֹם הַשַּׁבָּת׃ טוֹב לְהֹדוֹת לַיהוָה וּלְזַמֵּר
to and | to | give to | (is It) | the | for song A .psalm A
praises sing ,Jehovah thanks good .sabbath day

3915 530 2617 1242 5046 5945 8034
3 לְשִׁמְךָ עֶלְיוֹן׃ לְהַגִּיד בַּבֹּקֶר חַסְדֶּךָ וֶאֱמוּנָתְךָ בַּלֵּילוֹת׃
every Your and Your the in make to Most O Your to
;night faithfulness ,mercy morning known ;High ,name

8056 3658 1902 5035 5921 6218
4 5 עֲלֵי־עָשׂוֹר וַעֲלֵי־נָבֶל עֲלֵי הִגָּיוֹן בְּכִנּוֹר׃ כִּי שִׂמַּחְתַּנִי
have You For the on sounding with the and ten the on
,glad me made .lyre music ,harp on (strings)

3068 4639 1430 7442 3027 4639 6467 3068
6 יְהוָה בְּפָעֳלֶךָ בְּמַעֲשֵׂי יָדֶיךָ אֲרַנֵּן׃ מַה־גָּדְלוּ מַעֲשֶׂיךָ יְהוָה
O Your are How will I Your the in with Jeho- O
,Jehovah ,works great .shout hands of works ;work Your ,vah

3808 3684 3045 3808 1198 376 4284 6009 3966
7 מְאֹד עָמְקוּ מַחְשְׁבֹתֶיךָ׃ אִישׁ־בַּעַר לֹא יֵדָע וּכְסִיל לֹא־
not fool a does not brutish A Your are very
,know man ;thoughts deep

6466 6692 6212 3644 7563 6524 2088 995
8 יָבִין אֶת־זֹאת׃ בִּפְרֹחַ רְשָׁעִים כְּמוֹ עֵשֶׂב וַיָּצִיצוּ כָּל־פֹּעֲלֵי
the all and ;grass like the In .this does
of doers blossom wicked flourishing understand

2009 3068 5769 4791 5703 8045 205
9 10 אָוֶן לְהִשָּׁמְדָם עֲדֵי־עַד׃ וְאַתָּה מָרוֹם לְעֹלָם יְהוָה׃ כִּי הִנֵּה
,lo ,For O ,forever are But .forever (to) them for ;evil
Jehovah exalted ,You destroyed (be)

6466 3605 6504 6 341 2009 3068 341
אֹיְבֶיךָ יְהוָה כִּי־הִנֵּה אֹיְבֶיךָ יֹאבֵדוּ יִתְפָּרְדוּ כָּל־פֹּעֲלֵי
the all be shall shall Your ,lo ,for O Your
of doers scattered ;perish enemies ;Jehovah ,enemies

5869 5027 7488 8081 1101 7161 7214 7311 205
11 12 אָוֶן׃ וַתָּרֶם כִּרְאֵים קַרְנִי בַּלֹּתִי בְּשֶׁמֶן רַעֲנָן׃ וַתַּבֵּט עֵינִי
my shall and .fresh with be will I my the as You But .evil
eye look oil anointed ,horn ox wild up lift will

8558 6662 241 8085 7489 6965 7790
13 בְּשׁוּרָי בַּקָּמִים עָלַי מְרֵעִים תִּשְׁמַעְנָה אָזְנָי׃ צַדִּיק כַּתָּמָר
the as The my hear shall the against rise who my on
tree palm righteous .ears evildoers me up ;enemies

2691 3068 1004 8362 7685 3844 730 6524
14 יִפְרָח כְּאֶרֶז בַּלְּבָנוֹן יִשְׂגֶּה׃ שְׁתוּלִים בְּבֵית יְהוָה בְּחַצְרוֹת
the in ,Jehovah the in Those shall he in a like will
of courts of house planted .grow Lebanon cedar ;flourish

1961 7488 1879 7872 5107 5750 6524 430
15 אֱלֹהֵינוּ יַפְרִיחוּ׃ עוֹד יְנוּבוּן בְּשֵׂיבָה דְּשֵׁנִים וְרַעֲנַנִּים יִהְיוּ׃
they fresh and fat old in shall They still shall ,God our
;be shall ;age fruit bear .flourish

5766 6697 3068 3477 5046
16 לְהַגִּיד כִּי־יָשָׁר יְהוָה צוּרִי וְלֹא־עַלְתָה בּוֹ׃
in (is) evil And my ,Jehovah (is) that to
.Him no !rock upright declare

PSAL. XCIII צג

PSALM 93

3559 241 5797 3068 3847 3847 1348 4427 3068
1 יְהוָה מָלָךְ גֵּאוּת לָבֵשׁ לָבֵשׁ יְהוָה עֹז הִתְאַזָּר אַף־תִּכּוֹן
is ,yea He strength Jeho- clothed is is He majesty ;reigns Jeho-
established ;Himself girded vah with ;with clothed vah

5375 5769 227 3678 3559 4131 1097 8398
2 3 תֵּבֵל בַּל־תִּמּוֹט׃ נָכוֹן כִּסְאֲךָ מֵאָז מֵעוֹלָם אָתָּה׃ נָשְׂאוּ
Have You from from Your (is) shall it not the
up lifted .(are) everlasting ,then throne established ;shaken be ;world

floods have lifted their roaring waves. [4]Jehovah on high *is* mightier than the noise of many waters, *than* the mighty waves of the sea. [5]Your testimonmies are very sure; holiness becomes Your house to length of days, O Jehovah.

1796 5104 5375 6963 5104 5375 3068 5104
נְהָר֨וֹת ׀ יְֽהוָ֗ה נָשְׂא֣וּ נְהָרוֹת֮ קוֹלָ֥ם יִשְׂא֖וּ נְהָר֣וֹת דָּכְיָֽם׃
roar- their the have their the have Jeho- O the
waves ing floods up lifted ;voice floods up lifted ,vah ,floods

4791 117 3220 4867 117 7227 4325 6963
4 מִקֹּל֨וֹת ׀ מַ֤יִם רַבִּ֗ים אַדִּירִ֣ים מִשְׁבְּרֵי־יָ֑ם אַדִּ֖יר בַּמָּר֣וֹם
high on mighty is the breakers mighty the ,many waters than more
;sea of of voices the

3068 6944 4998 1004 3966 539 5713 3068
5 יְהוָֽה׃ עֵֽדֹתֶ֨יךָ ׀ נֶאֶמְנ֬וּ מְאֹ֗ד לְבֵיתְךָ֥ נַאֲוָה־קֹ֑דֶשׁ יְ֝הוָ֗ה
O ,holiness becomes Your ;very are Your .Jehovah
,Jehovah house sure testimonies

3117 753
לְאֹ֣רֶךְ יָמִֽים׃
.days to
of length

PSAL. XCIV צד

PSALM 94

PSALM 94

[1]O Jehovah, God of vengeance, shine forth! [2]Lift up Yourself, O judge of the earth; give a just repayment on the proud. [3]O Jehovah, how long *shall* the wicked exult? [4]They gush; they speak impudent things; all the workers of evil speak proudly. [5]O Jehovah, they crush Your people and afflict Your inheritance. [6]They kill the widow and the stranger, and murder the orphan. [7]Yet they say, The Lord shall not see, nor shall the God of Jacob observe. [8]Understand, you beastly ones among the people; yea, you fools, when will you be wise? [9]He who planted the ear, shall He not hear? He who formed the eye, shall He not see? [10]He who chastises the nations, shall He not punish—He who teaches man knowledge?

[11]Jehovah knows the thoughts of man, that they *are* vain. [12]Blessed is the man You chasten, O Jehovah, You teach him out of Your law; [13]to give him rest from troubled days, until the pit is dug for the wicked. [14]For Jehovah will not leave His people; nor will He forsake His inheritance. [15]For judgment shall turn to righteousness; and all the upright in heart shall follow after it. [16]Who will rise up for Me against the

776 8199 5375 3313 5360 410 3068 5360 410
1 אֵל־נְקָמ֥וֹת יְהוָ֑ה אֵ֖ל נְקָמ֣וֹת הוֹפִֽיעַ׃
2 הִ֭נָּשֵׂא שֹׁפֵ֣ט הָאָ֑רֶץ
the judge O up Lift shine .revenges God Jehovah ,revenges O
;earth of ,yourself !forth of of God

5704 3068 7563 5704 1343 1576 7725
הָשֵׁ֥ב גְּ֝מ֗וּל עַל־גֵּאִֽים׃ 3 עַד־מָתַ֣י רְשָׁעִ֣ים ׀ יְהוָ֑ה עַד־מָ֝תַ֗י
when until O the (shall) when Until the on just a give
Jehovah ,wicked .proud repayment

205 6466 3605 559 6279 1696 5042 5937 7563
4 רְשָׁעִ֣ים יַעֲלֹֽזוּ׃ יַבִּ֣יעוּ יְדַבְּר֣וּ עָתָ֑ק יִ֝תְאַמְּר֗וּ כָּל־פֹּ֥עֲלֵי אָֽוֶן׃
.evil the all speak impudent they They shall the
of workers proudly ;things speak ,sputter ?exult wicked

7523 1616 490 6031 5159 1792 3068 5971
5 עַמְּךָ֣ יְהוָ֣ה יְדַכְּא֑וּ וְֽנַחֲלָתְךָ֥ יְעַנּֽוּ׃
6 אַלְמָנָ֣ה וְגֵ֣ר יַהֲרֹ֑גוּ
;kill they and The .afflict Your and they O Your
alien the widow inheritance ,crush ,Jehovah ,people

430 995 3808 3068/7200 3808 559 2026 3490
7 וִיתוֹמִ֥ים יְרַצֵּֽחוּ׃ וַ֭יֹּאמְרוּ לֹ֣א יִרְאֶה־יָּ֑הּ וְלֹא־יָ֝בִ֗ין אֱלֹהֵ֥י
the shall not ,Jehovah shall Not they Yet they the and
of God ,perceive see ,say .murder orphan

5193 7919 3684 5971 1197 995 3290
8 יַעֲקֹֽב׃ בִּ֭ינוּ בֹּעֲרִ֣ים בָּעָ֑ם וּ֝כְסִילִ֗ים מָתַ֥י תַּשְׂכִּֽילוּ׃
9 הֲ֤נֹטַע
who He you will when you and among you ,Understand .Jacob
planted ?wise be ,fools ;people the brutish

3808 1471 3256 5027 3808/5869 3335 8085 3808/241
10 אֹ֭זֶן הֲלֹ֣א יִשְׁמָ֑ע אִם־יֹ֥צֵֽר עַ֝֗יִן הֲלֹ֣א יַבִּֽיט׃ הֲיֹסֵ֣ר גּ֭וֹיִם הֲלֹ֣א
shall the who He He shall the He Or He shall the
not ,nations chastises ?see not ,eye formed who ?hear not ,ear

120 4284 3045 3068 1847 120 3925 3198
11 י֭וֹכִיחַ הַֽמְלַמֵּ֖ד אָדָ֣ם דָּֽעַת׃ יְֽהוָ֗ה יֹ֭דֵעַ מַחְשְׁב֣וֹת אָדָ֑ם כִּי־
that ,man the knows Jehovah knowl- man who He He
of thoughts ?edge teaches —rebuke

8451 3050 3256 834 1397 835 1892
12 הֵ֥מָּה הָֽבֶל׃ אַשְׁרֵ֤י ׀ הַגֶּ֣בֶר אֲשֶׁר־תְּיַסְּרֶ֣נּוּ יָּ֑הּ וּֽמִתּוֹרָתְךָ֥
Your from O You whom the Blessed .vain they
law ,Jah ,chasten man is (are)

7845 7563 3738 5704/7451 3117 8252 3045
13 תְלַמְּדֶֽנּוּ׃ לְהַשְׁקִ֣יט ל֭וֹ מִ֣ימֵי רָ֑ע עַ֤ד יִכָּרֶ֖ה לָרָשָׁ֣ע שָֽׁחַת׃
.pit the the for dug is until ,evil from to rest give make You
wicked days him ;know him

6664 5800 3808 5159 5971 3068 5203 3808
14 כִּ֤י ׀ לֹא־יִטֹּ֣שׁ יְהוָ֣ה עַמּ֑וֹ וְ֝נַחֲלָת֗וֹ לֹ֣א יַעֲזֹֽב׃
15 כִּֽי־עַד־צֶ֭דֶק
righ- to For He will not His and His Jehovah will not For
teousness .forsake inheritance ;people leave

6965 3820 3477 3605 310 4941 7725
16 יָשׁ֣וּב מִשְׁפָּ֑ט וְ֝אַחֲרָ֗יו כָּל־יִשְׁרֵי־לֵֽב׃ מִֽי־יָק֣וּם לִ֭י עִם־
against for will Who .heart the all it after ;judgment shall
me up rise in upright turn

evildoers? Who will stand for Me against the evil workers? 17 Unless Jehovah *had been* my help almost my soul would have dwelt in silence. 18 If I say, My foot has slipped, O Jehovah, Your mercy has held me up. 19 In the host of my inward thoughts Your comforts delight my soul. 20 Shall the throne of iniquity be allied to You, forming mischief for a statute? 21 They crowd against the soul of the righteous, and they condemn the blood of the innocent. 22 But Jehovah is a stronghold to me; yea, my God is a rock of refuge to me. 23 And he turns back on them their own iniquity, and He will cut them off in their evil. Jehovah our God shall cut them off.

5833 3068 38 84 205 646.6 3320 7489
17 מְרֵעִים מִי־יִתְיַצֵּב לִי עִם־פֹּעֲלֵי אָוֶן׃ לוּלֵי יְהוָה עֶזְרָתָה
(been had) Jehovah Unless ?evil the against for will Who the
help a of workers Me stand ?evildoers

7272 4131 559 518 53 15 1745 7931 4592
18 לִּי כִּמְעַט ׀ שָׁכְנָה דוּמָה נַפְשִׁי׃ אִם־אָמַרְתִּי מָטָה רַגְלִי
My has ,say I If my in would almost for
foot slipped .soul silence dwelt have ,me

8575 7130 8312 7230 5582 30 68 2617
19 חַסְדְּךָ יְהוָה יִסְעָדֵנִי׃ בְּרֹב שַׂרְעַפַּי בְּקִרְבִּי תַּנְחוּמֶיךָ
Your my in my the In held has O Your
comforts midst ,thoughts of host .up me ,Jehovah ,mercy

2206 5999 3335 1942 3678 2266/1961 53 15 8173
20 יְשַׁעַשְׁעוּ נַפְשִׁי׃ הַיְחָבְרְךָ כִּסֵּא הַוּוֹת יֹצֵר עָמָל עֲלֵי־חֹק׃
a for mischief form- iniquity the allied be Shall my delight
?statute ing of throne You to .soul

3068 19 61 7561 5355 1818 6662 53 15 1413
21 22 יָגוֹדּוּ עַל־נֶפֶשׁ צַדִּיק וְדָם נָקִי יַרְשִׁיעוּ׃ וַיְהִי יְהוָה לִי
to Jehovah But con- they the the and the the against They
me is .demn innocent of blood ,righteous of soul crowd

205 5921 77 25 4268 6697 430 4869
23 לְמִשְׂגָּב וֵאלֹהַי לְצוּר מַחְסִי׃ וַיָּשֶׁב עֲלֵיהֶם ׀ אֶת־אוֹנָם
own their upon He And my the is my and a for
;iniquity them back turns .refuge of rock God ,stronghold

430 3068 67 89 3772 7451
וּבְרָעָתָם יַצְמִיתֵם יַצְמִיתֵם יְהוָה אֱלֹהֵינוּ׃
our Jehovah cut shall shall He their in and
.God off them ;off them cut evil

PSAL. XCV צה

PSALM 95

1 O come, let us sing to Jehovah; let us make a joyful noise to the Rock of our salvation. 2 Let us come before His face with praise; let us shout for joy to Him with songs. 3 For Jehovah *is* a great God, and a great King above all gods. 4 The deep places of the earth *are* in His hand; the summits of the mountains also *are* His. 5 The sea *is* His, and He made it; and His hands formed the dry land. 6 O come, let us worship and bow down; let us kneel before Jehovah our Maker. 7 For He *is* our God; and we *are* the people of His pasture, and the sheep of His hand. Today, if you will hear His voice, 8 do not harden your heart as *in* Meribah; as *in* the day of Massah in the wilderness; 9 when your fathers tempted Me, they tested Me and they saw My work. 10 For forty years I was disgusted with this generation; and I said, They *are* a people who err in heart; and, They

6440 6923 3468 6697 7321 3068 7442 32 12
1 2 לְכוּ נְרַנְּנָה לַיהוָה נָרִיעָה לְצוּר יִשְׁעֵנוּ׃ נְקַדְּמָה פָנָיו
His come us Let our the to us let Jeho- to us let O
face before .salvation of Rock shout ;vah joy for sing ,come

141 9 4428 3068 1419 410 7321 21 58 8426
3 בְּתוֹדָה בִּזְמִרוֹת נָרִיעַ לוֹ׃ כִּי אֵל גָּדוֹל יְהוָה וּמֶלֶךְ גָּדוֹל
great a and (is) great God a For to us let with with
king ,Jehovah .Him shout songs ;praise

2022 8443 776 4278 3027 834 430 3605/5921
4 עַל־כָּל־אֱלֹהִים׃ אֲשֶׁר בְּיָדוֹ מֶחְקְרֵי־אָרֶץ וְתוֹעֲפוֹת הָרִים
the the and the deep The in (are) which .gods all above
heights of summits ;earth of places hand His

935 3335 3027 3006 6213 3220 834
5 6 לוֹ׃ אֲשֶׁר־לוֹ הַיָּם וְהוּא עָשָׂהוּ וְיַבֶּשֶׁת יָדָיו יָצָרוּ׃ בֹּאוּ
O .formed His the and made and The to which to
,come hands land dry ;it He ,sea (is) Him .Him

6213 3068 6440 1288 3766 7812
7 נִשְׁתַּחֲוֶה וְנִכְרָעָה נִבְרְכָה לִפְנֵי־יְהוָה עֹשֵׂנוּ׃ כִּי־הוּא
He For our Jehovah before us let bow and us let
(is) .Maker kneel ;down worship

6963 518 3117 3027 6629 4830 5971 430
אֱלֹהֵינוּ וַאֲנַחְנוּ עַם מַרְעִיתוֹ וְצֹאן יָדוֹ הַיּוֹם אִם־בְּקֹלוֹ
His if Today His the and His the we and ,God our
voice .hand of sheep ,pasturing of people (are)

4531 3117 4808 3824 7185 3808 8085
8 תִשְׁמָעוּ׃ אַל־תַּקְשׁוּ לְבַבְכֶם כִּמְרִיבָה כְּיוֹם מַסָּה
Massah in as (in) as your do not will you
of day the ,Meribah hearts harden ,hear

6467 7200 974 1 5254 4057
9 בַּמִּדְבָּר׃ אֲשֶׁר נִסּוּנִי אֲבוֹתֵיכֶם בְּחָנוּנִי גַּם־רָאוּ פָעֳלִי׃
My they and they your tempted when the in
.work saw Me tried ,fathers .Me ;wilderness

38 14 8582 5971 5 59 1755 6962 81 41 705
10 אַרְבָּעִים שָׁנָה ׀ אָקוּט בְּדוֹר וָאֹמַר עַם תֹּעֵי לֵבָב הֵם
They (their) in who a and the with was I years forty (For)
;(are) heart err people ,said ,generation disgusted

do not know My ways, [11]to whom I swore in My anger, They shall not enter into My rest.

935 518 639 7650 834 1870 3045

11 וְהֵם לֹא־יָדְעוּ דְרָכָי׃ אֲשֶׁר־נִשְׁבַּעְתִּי בְאַפִּי אִם־יְבֹאוּן

they If | My in | swore I | to | My | do not | and
enter shall | ,anger | | whom | ,ways | know | they

4496

אֶל־מְנוּחָתִי׃

my into
.rest

PSAL. XCVI צו

PSALM 96

PSALM 96

[1]O sing to Jehovah a new song; sing to Jehovah, all the earth. [2]Sing to Jehovah; bless His name, bear news of His salvation day by day. [3]Tell of His glory among the nations, His wonders among all people. [4]For Jehovah *is* great and greatly to be praised; He *is* to be feared above all gods. [5]For all the gods of the peoples *are* idols; but Jehovah made the heavens. [6]Honor and majesty *are* before Him; strength and beauty *are* in His sanctuary. [7]Give to Jehovah, O families of the people; give to Jehovah glory and might. [8]Give to Jehovah the glory *due* His name; bring an offering and come in to His courts. [9]O worship Jehovah in the beauty of holiness; tremble before Him, all the earth.

[10]Say among the nations, Jehovah reigns; and, The world shall be established, it shall not be moved; He shall judge the peoples in uprightness. [11]Let the heavens be glad, and let the earth rejoice; let the sea roar, and the fullness of it. [12]Let the field be joyful, and all that *is* in it; then the trees of the forest shall rejoice [13]before Jehovah; for He comes; for He comes to judge the earth; He shall judge the world with righteousness, and the people with His truth.

7891 776 3605 3068 7891 2319 7892 3068 7891

1
2 שִׁירוּ לַיהוָה שִׁיר חָדָשׁ שִׁירוּ לַיהוָה כָּל־הָאָרֶץ׃ שִׁירוּ

Sing | the all | to | sing | ;new | song a | to | sing O
.earth | | ,Jehovah | | | | Jehovah |

5608 3444 3117 3117 1319 8034 1288 3068

3 לַיהוָה בָּרְכוּ שְׁמוֹ בַּשְּׂרוּ מִיּוֹם־לְיוֹם יְשׁוּעָתוֹ׃ סַפְּרוּ

Tell | His | day by | day | Bear | His | bless | to
.salvation | | | | of tidings | ;name | | ,Jehovah

3068 1419 6381 5971 854 3519 1471

4 בַגּוֹיִם כְּבוֹדוֹ בְּכָל־הָעַמִּים נִפְלְאוֹתָיו׃ כִּי גָדוֹל יְהוָה

Jehovah | (is) | For | His | the | among | His | among
great | | .wonders | peoples | all | ,glory | nations the |

430 3605 430 3605 5921 3372 3966 1984

5 וּמְהֻלָּל מְאֹד נוֹרָא הוּא עַל־כָּל־אֱלֹהִים׃ כִּי ׀ כָּל־אֱלֹהֵי

the | all | For | .gods | all above | He | be to | ;greatly | be to and
of gods | | | | | (is) | feared | | praised

6440 1926 1935 6213 8064 3068 457 5971

6 הָעַמִּים אֱלִילִים וַיהוָה שָׁמַיִם עָשָׂה׃ הוֹד־וְהָדָר לְפָנָיו

before | and | Honor | .made | the | but | (are) | the
;Him | majesty | | | heavens | Jehovah | ;idols | peoples

3053 5971 4940 3068 3053 4720 8597 5797

7 עֹז וְתִפְאֶרֶת בְּמִקְדָּשׁוֹ׃ הָבוּ לַיהוָה מִשְׁפְּחוֹת עַמִּים הָבוּ

give | the | families O | to | Give | His in (are) | and | strength
;peoples | | of | ,Jehovah | | .sanctuary | beauty |

4503 5375 8034 3519 3068 3053 5797 3519 3068

8 לַיהוָה כָּבוֹד וָעֹז׃ הָבוּ לַיהוָה כְּבוֹד שְׁמוֹ שְׂאוּ־מִנְחָה

an | bring | His | glory the | to | Give | and | glory | to
offering | | ;name | (due) | Jehovah | | .might | | Jehovah

2342 6944 1927 3068 7812 2691 935

9 וּבֹאוּ לְחַצְרוֹתָיו׃ הִשְׁתַּחֲווּ לַיהוָה בְּהַדְרַת־קֹדֶשׁ חִילוּ

tremble | ;holiness | the in | Jehovah | worship O | His into | and
| | of beauty | | | .courts | come

8398 3559 427 1471 559 776 3605 6440

10 מִפָּנָיו כָּל־הָאָרֶץ׃ אִמְרוּ בַגּוֹיִם ׀ יְהוָה מָלָךְ אַף־תִּכּוֹן תֵּבֵל

the | be shall | ,yea | ;reigns Jehovah | among | Say | the | all | before
,world | established | | | ,nations the | | .earth | | ,Him

8056 8064 8056 4339 5971 1777 4131 1097

11 בַּל־תִּמּוֹט יָדִין עַמִּים בְּמֵישָׁרִים׃ יִשְׂמְחוּ הַשָּׁמַיִם וְתָגֵל

let and | the | be Let | in | the | shall He | shall it | not
rejoice | heavens | glad | .uprightness | peoples | judge | ;moved be |

227 834 3605 3605 7704 5937 4393 3220 7481 776

12 הָאָרֶץ יִרְעַם הַיָּם וּמְלֹאוֹ׃ יַעֲלֹז שָׂדַי וְכָל־אֲשֶׁר־בּוֹ אָז

then | in | that | and | the | be Let | its and | the | Let | the
| ;it | (is) | all | field | joyful | .fulness | sea | roar | ;earth

776 8199 935 935 3068 6440 3293 6086 7442

13 יְרַנְּנוּ כָּל־עֲצֵי־יָעַר׃ לִפְנֵי יְהוָה ׀ כִּי בָא כִּי בָא לִשְׁפֹּט הָאָרֶץ

the | judge to | He | for | He | for | ;Jehovah | Before | the | the | all | shall
;earth | | comes | | ;comes | | | | .forest of | trees | | rejoice

530 5971 6664 8398 8199

יִשְׁפֹּט־תֵּבֵל בְּצֶדֶק וְעַמִּים בֶּאֱמוּנָתוֹ׃

His with | the and | with | world the | shall He
.truth | peoples | ,righteousness | | judge

PSAL. XCVII צז

PSALM 97

1 ¹Jehovah reigns; let the earth rejoice; let the multitude of islands be glad. ²Clouds and darkness *are* all around Him; righteousness and judgment *are* the foundation of His throne. ³A fire goes before Him and burns up His enemies all around. ⁴His lightnings lit up the world; the earth saw and trembled. ⁵The mountains melted like wax before the face of Jehovah; before the face of Jehovah of the whole earth. ⁶The heavens declare His righteousness and all the people see His glory. ⁷All who serve graven images are shamed, those who boast themselves in idols; all gods bow down before Him. ⁸Zion heard and was glad; yea, the daughters of Judah rejoiced because of Your judgments, O Jehovah. ⁹For You, Jehovah, *are* exalted above all the earth; You are lifted on high far above all gods. ¹⁰You who love Jehovah, hate evil; He keeps the souls of His saints; He delivers them out of the hand of the wicked. ¹¹Light is sown for the righteous, and gladness for the upright in heart. ¹²Be glad in Jehovah, O righteous ones; give thanks to the memory of His holiness.

1
2 יהוה מלך תגל הארץ ישמחו איים רבים׃ ענן וערפל

and darkness, Clouds; the many islands be let glad; the earth let rejoice; reigns Jehovah

3 סביביו צדק ומשפט מכון כסאו׃ אש לפניו תלך

(are) all around Him; righteousness and judgment (the) basis of His throne. A fire before Him goes,

4 ותלהט סביב צריו׃ האירו ברקיו תבל ראתה ותחל

and burns up around His enemies. lit up His lightnings the world; saw and trembled

5 הארץ׃ הרים כדונג נמסו מלפני יהוה מלפני אדון כל־

the earth. The mountains like wax melted before Jehovah; before the Lord of the whole

6 הארץ׃ הגידו השמים צדקו וראו כל־העמים כבודו׃

the earth. Declare the heavens His righteousness, and see all the peoples His glory.

7 יבשו כל־עבדי פסל המתהללים באלילים השתחוו־לו

are ashamed All who serve graven images, those who boast themselves in idols; bow down before Him

8 כל־אלהים׃ שמעה ותשמח ציון ותגלנה בנות יהודה

all gods. heard and was glad Zion; and rejoiced the daughters of Judah

9 למען משפטיך יהוה׃ כי־אתה יהוה עליון על־כל־

because of Your judgments, O Jehovah. For You, O Jehovah, (are) high above all

10 הארץ מאד נעלית על־כל־אלהים׃ אהבי יהוה שנאו

the earth; for You are exalted above all gods. who You love Jehovah, hate

11 רע שמר נפשות חסידיו מיד רשעים יצילם׃ אור זרע

evil; He keeps the souls of His saints; out of hand of the wicked He delivers them. Light is sown

12 לצדיק ולישרי־לב שמחה׃ שמחו צדיקים ביהוה והודו

for the righteous; and for the upright in heart gladness. Be glad, O righteous ones, in Jehovah; give thanks

לזכר קדשו׃

to the memory of His holiness.

PSAL. XCVIII צח

PSALM 98

A Psalm.

1 ¹O sing to Jehovah a new song; for He has done wondrous things; His right hand and His holy arm has saved Him. ²Jehovah has revealed His salvation; He unveiled His righteousness to the eyes of the nations. ³He has remembered His mercy and His faithfulness to the house of Israel; all the ends of the earth have seen

1 מזמור שירו ליהוה שיר חדש כי־נפלאות עשה הושיעה־

A psalm. O sing to Jehovah a song new; for wondrous things He has done; has saved

2 לו ימינו וזרוע קדשו׃ הודיע יהוה ישועתו לעיני הגוים

Him for His right hand and arm His holy. has made known Jehovah His salvation; to the eyes of the nations

3 גלה צדקתו׃ זכר חסדו ואמונתו לבית ישראל ראו

He revealed His righteousness. He has remembered His mercy, and His faithfulness to the house of Israel; have seen

4 3605 3068 7321 430 3444 776 657 3605
כָּל־אַפְסֵי־אָרֶץ אֵת יְשׁוּעַת אֱלֹהֵינוּ׃ הָרִיעוּ לַיהוָה כָּל־
all to Jehovah Shout joyfully .God our the salvation of the earth the ends of all

5 776 6476 7442 2167 2167 3068 3658 36·58
הָאָרֶץ פִּצְחוּ וְרַנְּנוּ וְזַמֵּרוּ׃ זַמְּרוּ לַיהוָה בְּכִנּוֹר בְּכִנּוֹר
the with lyre the with ;lyre to Jehovah Sing praise sing and .praise and rejoice break out the ;earth

6 6963 2172 2689 6963 7782 7321 6440 44·28
וְקוֹל זִמְרָה׃ בַּחֲצֹצְרוֹת וְקוֹל שׁוֹפָר הָרִיעוּ לִפְנֵי ׀ הַמֶּלֶךְ
king the before shout joyfully ,horn a the and of sound With trumpets .song a the and of voice

7
8 3068 7481 3220 4393 3427 83·98 5104 4222
יְהוָה׃ יִרְעַם הַיָּם וּמְלֹאוֹ תֵּבֵל וְיֹשְׁבֵי בָהּ׃ נְהָרוֹת יִמְחֲאוּ
clap Let the rivers .it in those and live who the ,world its and fulness the sea Let roar .Jehovah

9 3709 3162 2022 7442 6440 30·68 935 8199 776
כַף יַחַד הָרִים יְרַנֵּנוּ׃ לִפְנֵי־יְהוָה כִּי בָא לִשְׁפֹּט הָאָרֶץ
the ;earth judge to He comes for ,Jehovah before shout let joy for the heights to- ;gether (their) hands

8199 8398 6664 59·71 4339
יִשְׁפֹּט־תֵּבֵל בְּצֶדֶק וְעַמִּים בְּמֵישָׁרִים׃
in .uprightness the and peoples with righteousness the world shall He judge

the salvation of our God. 4Make a joyful noise to Jehovah, all the earth; break out and rejoice and sing praise. 5Sing praise to Jehovah with the lyre; with the lyre and the voice of a song. 6With trumpets and the sound of a horn, make a joyful noise before Jehovah the King. 7Let the sea roar, and the fullness of it; the world, and those who live in it. 8Let the rivers clap *their* hands; let the heights shout for joy, 9before the face of Jehovah; for He comes to judge the earth; He shall judge the word with righteousness and the peoples in uprightness.

PSAL. XCIX צט

PSALM 99

1
2 3068 4427 7264 5971 3427 3742 5120 776 3068
יְהוָה מָלָךְ יִרְגְּזוּ עַמִּים יֹשֵׁב כְּרוּבִים תָּנוּט הָאָרֶץ׃ יְהוָה
Jehovah the .earth let shake the (on) ;cherubim (He) sits the ;peoples let tremble ;reigns Jehovah

3 6726 1419 7311 3605 5971 3034 8034 1419
בְּצִיּוֹן גָּדוֹל וְרָם הוּא עַל־כָּל־הָעַמִּים׃ יוֹדוּ שִׁמְךָ גָּדוֹל
great Your ,name They thank shall the .peoples all above He and (is) high (is) ;great Zion in

4 33·72 6918 5797 4428 4941 157 3559
וְנוֹרָא קָדוֹשׁ הוּא׃ וְעֹז מֶלֶךְ מִשְׁפָּט אָהֵב אַתָּה כּוֹנַנְתָּ
have established You ;loved judgment the king's And strength .(is) it holy and ;fearful

5 4339 4941 6666 3290 6213 7311
מֵישָׁרִים מִשְׁפָּט וּצְדָקָה בְּיַעֲקֹב ׀ אַתָּה עָשִׂיתָ׃ רוֹמְמוּ
Exalt .work You Jacob in and righteousness judgment upright- ;ness

6 3068 430 7812 19·16 7·272 6918 4872
יְהוָה אֱלֹהֵינוּ וְהִשְׁתַּחֲווּ לַהֲדֹם רַגְלָיו קָדוֹשׁ הוּא׃ מֹשֶׁה
Moses .(is) He holy His ;foot- stool at worship and our God Jehovah

175 35·48 8050 7121 8034 7121 3068
וְאַהֲרֹן ׀ בְּכֹהֲנָיו וּשְׁמוּאֵל בְּקֹרְאֵי שְׁמוֹ קֹרְאִים אֶל־יְהוָה
,Jehovah to they called His ;name the among callers on and Samuel among (were) ;priests His and Aaron

7 6030 5982 6051 1696 8104 57·13 2706
וְהוּא יַעֲנֵם׃ בְּעַמּוּד עָנָן יְדַבֵּר אֲלֵיהֶם שָׁמְרוּ עֵדֹתָיו וְחֹק
the and law His testimonies they kept ;them to He spoke cloudy the in pillar answered .them and He

8 5414 3068 430 6030 410 5375 1961
נָתַן־לָמוֹ׃ יְהוָה אֱלֹהֵינוּ אַתָּה עֲנִיתָם אֵל נֹשֵׂא הָיִיתָ לָהֶם
to ,them You were who forgives a God answered ;them You ,God our O Jehovah to .them He gave

9 53·58 5949 7311 30·68 430 7812 2022
וְנֹקֵם עַל־עֲלִילוֹתָם׃ רוֹמְמוּ יְהוָה אֱלֹהֵינוּ וְהִשְׁתַּחֲווּ לְהַר
hill at worship and ,God our Jehovah Exalt their .works on and avenging

69·44 6918 3068 430
קָדְשׁוֹ כִּי־קָדוֹשׁ יְהוָה אֱלֹהֵינוּ׃
.God our Jehovah (is) holy for His ;holy

PSALM 99

1Jehovah reigns; let the peoples tremble; *He* sits *upon* the cherubs; let the earth quake. 2Jehovah *is* great in Zion; and He *is* high above all the peoples. 3They shall thank Your great and fearful name; it *is* holy.

4The king's strength also loved judgment; You have established uprightness; You work judgment and righteousness in Jacob. 5Exalt Jehovah our God and worship at His footstool; He *is* holy.

6Moses and Aaron *were* among His priests; and Samuel *was* among those who called on His name; they called to Jehovah, and He answered them. 7He spoke to them in the cloudy pillar; they kept His testimonies and the law that He gave to them. 8You answered them, O Jehovah our God; You were a God who forgives to them, but taking vengeance on their works. 9Exalt Jehovah our God and worship at His holy hill; for Jehovah our God *is* holy.

PSALM 100

A Psalm of Thanksgiving.

[1]Shout joyfully to Jehovah, all you lands. [2]Worship Jehovah with gladness; come before His face with joyful singing. [3]Know that Jehovah, He *is* God; He has made us, and not we ourselves — His people and the sheep of His pasture. [4]Enter into His gates with thanksgiving; *into* His courts with praise; be thankful to Him; bless His name. [5]For Jehovah *is* good; His mercy *is* everlasting, and His faithfulness to generation and generation.

PSALM 101

A Psalm of David.

[1]I will sing of mercy and judgment; to You O Jehovah, I will sing praise. [2]I will behave myself wisely in a perfect way; O when will You come to me? I will walk in the integrity of my heart in the midst of my house. [3]I will set no wicked thing before my eyes; I have hated the work of those who turn aside; it shall not fasten upon me. [4]A perverse heart shall depart from me; I will not know evil. [5]*Whoever* secretly slanders his neighbor, I will cut him off; I will not endure him who has high eyes and a proud heart. [6]My eyes *shall be* on the faithful of the land, so that they may dwell with Me; he who walks in a perfect way shall serve Me. [7]*He* who works falsely shall not live inside my house; he who speaks lies shall not be established before My eyes. [8]In the mornings I will cut off all the wicked of the land; so that I may cut off all the evil workers from the city of Jehovah.

PSAL. C ק

PSALM 100

3068 5647 776 3605 3068 7321 8426 4210
1 2 מִזְמוֹר לְתוֹדָה הָרִיעוּ לַיהוָה כָּל־הָאָרֶץ׃ עִבְדוּ אֶת־יְהוָה
Jehovah Serve the all to Shout thanks- of psalm A
.land ,Jehovah joyfully .giving

430 3068 3045 7445 6440 935 8057
3 בְּשִׂמְחָה בֹּאוּ לְפָנָיו בִּרְנָנָה׃ דְּעוּ כִּי־יְהוָה הוּא אֱלֹהִים
;God (is) He ,Jehovah that Know with His before come with
.singing face ;gladness

8179 935 4830 6629 5971 3808 6213
4 הוּא עָשָׂנוּ וְלֹא אֲנַחְנוּ עַמּוֹ וְצֹאן מַרְעִיתוֹ׃ בֹּאוּ שְׁעָרָיו
His Enter His the and His we and made has He
gates into .pasture of sheep people (ourselves) not ,us

2896 8034 1288 3034 8416 2691 8426
5 בְּתוֹדָה חֲצֵרֹתָיו בִּתְהִלָּה הוֹדוּ לוֹ בָּרְכוּ שְׁמוֹ׃ כִּי־טוֹב
(is) For His bless to be with His (into) with
good .name ,Him thankful ;praise courts ;thanksgiving

530 1755 1755 5704 2617 5769 3068
יְהוָה לְעוֹלָם חַסְדּוֹ וְעַד־דֹּר וָדֹר אֱמוּנָתוֹ׃
faith- His gen- and genera- and His (is) ;Jehovah
.fulness eration tion unto ;mercy everlasting

PSAL. CI קא

PSALM 101

2167 3068 7892 4941 2617 4210 1732
1 לְדָוִד מִזְמוֹר חֶסֶד־וּמִשְׁפָּט אָשִׁירָה לְךָ יְהוָה אֲזַמֵּרָה׃
sing will I O ,You to will I and mercy .psalm A of
praise ,Jehovah ;of sing judgment David

8537 1980 935 8549 1870 7919
2 אַשְׂכִּילָה ׀ בְּדֶרֶךְ תָּמִים מָתַי תָּבוֹא אֵלָי אֶתְהַלֵּךְ בְּתָם־
in walk will I to will when O ;perfect a in act will I
integrity ?me come You way wisely

1100 1697/5869 6440 7896 3808 1004 7130 3824
3 לְבָבִי בְּקֶרֶב בֵּיתִי׃ לֹא־אָשִׁית ׀ לְנֶגֶד עֵינַי דְּבַר־בְּלִיָּעַל
,worthless a my before will I not my the in my
thing eyes set .house of midst ,heart's

5493 6145 3824 1691 3808 8130 7750 6213
4 עֲשֹׂה־סֵטִים שָׂנֵאתִי לֹא יִדְבַּק בִּי׃ לֵבָב עִקֵּשׁ יָסוּר מִמֶּנִּי
from shall perverse A upon shall it not have I the of doing the
;me depart heart .me fasten ;hated aside turning ones

1362 6789 7453 5643 3960 3047/3808 7451
5 רָע לֹא אֵדָע׃ מְלוֹשְׁנִי בַסֵּתֶר ׀ רֵעֵהוּ אוֹתוֹ אַצְמִית גְּבַהּ־
(has who) will I him his secretly (Whoever) will I not evil
high ;off cut ;neighbor slanders .know

776 539 5869 3201 3808 3824 7342 5869
6 עֵינַיִם וּרְחַב לֵבָב אֹתוֹ לֹא אוּכָל׃ עֵינַי ׀ בְּנֶאֶמְנֵי־אֶרֶץ
the on (be shall) My will I not him heart a proud and eyes
,land of faithful the eyes .endure

3427 3808 8334 8549 1870 1980 3421
7 לָשֶׁבֶת עִמָּדִי הֹלֵךְ בְּדֶרֶךְ תָּמִים הוּא יְשָׁרְתֵנִי׃ לֹא־יֵשֵׁב ׀
Shall not minister shall he ,perfect a in who (he) with dwell to
dwell .me to way walks ;me

5869 5048 3559 3808 8267 1696 7423 6213 1004 7130
בְּקֶרֶב בֵּיתִי עֹשֵׂה רְמִיָּה דֹּבֵר שְׁקָרִים לֹא־יִכּוֹן לְנֶגֶד עֵינָי׃
my before shall not lies who ,falsely who (he) my inside
.eyes fixed be speaks works house

3068 5892 3771 776 7563 3605 6789 1242
8 לַבְּקָרִים אַצְמִית כָּל־רִשְׁעֵי־אָרֶץ לְהַכְרִית מֵעִיר־יְהוָה
Jehovah the from cut to the the all will I the In
of city off ;land of wicked off cut mornings

205 6466 3605
כָּל־פֹּעֲלֵי אָוֶן׃
.evil the all
of workers

PSAL. CII קב

PSALM 102

PSALM 102
A prayer of the afflicted,
when he is faint and pours
out his complaint before
the face of Jehovah.

[1]Hear my prayer, O
Jehovah, and let my cry
come to You. [2]Do not hide
Your face from me in the
day of my trouble; bow
down Your ear to me in the
day I call; answer me
quickly. [3]For my days are
finished in smoke, and my
bones glow like a firebrand.
[4]My heart is stricken and
dried like grass, so that I
forget to eat my bread.
[5]Because of the voice of my
sighing, my bones cleave to
my flesh. [6]I am like a
pelican of the wilderness; I
am like an owl of the desert.
[7]I watch and am like a
sparrow alone on the
housetop. [8]My enemies
curse me all the day long;
those who rave against me
have sworn against me.
[9]For I have eaten ashes like
bread, and have mixed my
drink with weeping; [10]be-
cause of Your anger and
Your wrath; for You have
lifted me and cast me
down. [11]My days *are* like
a shadow stretched out,
and I wither like grass.
[12]But You, O Jehovah,
shall dwell forever, and
Your memory to generation
and generation. [13]You shall
arise; have mercy on Zion;
for the time to pity her, yea,
the appointed time has
come. [14]For Your servants
take pleasure in its stones,
and pity its dust. [15]So
nations shall fear the name
of Jehovah, and all the
kings of the earth Your
glory. [16]When Jehovah
shall build up Zion, He shall
appear in His glory. [17]He
will turn to the prayer of the
destitute, and will not
despise their prayer. [18]This
shall be written for the
generation to come; and
people to be created shall
praise Jehovah. [19]For He
has looked down from the
height of His sanctuary;

3068 7879 8210 3068 6440 5848 6041 8605
1 2 תְּפִלָּה לְעָנִי כִי־יַעֲטֹף וְלִפְנֵי יְהוָה יִשְׁפֹּךְ שִׂיחוֹ׃ יְהוָה
.Jehovah his pours Jehovah and is he when the of prayer A
.complaint out before ,faint ,afflicted

6440 5640 935 7775 8605 8085
3 שִׁמְעָה תְפִלָּתִי וְשַׁוְעָתִי אֵלֶיךָ תָבוֹא׃ אַל־תַּסְתֵּר פָּנֶיךָ
Your Do not .come let You to cry my and my hear
face hide ,prayer

6030 4118 7121 3117 241 5186 6862 3117
מִמֶּנִּי בְּיוֹם צַר־לִי הַטֵּה־אֵלַי אָזְנֶךָ בְּיוֹם אֶקְרָא מַהֵר עֲנֵנִי׃
answer quickly ;call I the in Your me to incline to dis- the in from
.me day ear ;me tress of day me

6212 5221 2787 4168 6106 3117 6227 3615
4 5 כִּי־כָלוּ בְעָשָׁן יָמָי וְעַצְמוֹתַי כְּמוֹקֵד נִחָרוּ׃ הוּכָּה כָעֵשֶׂב
like Is are a like my and my in are For
grass stricken .burned hearth bones ,days smoke finished

1692 585 6963 3899 398 7911 3820 3001
6 וַיִּבַשׁ לִבִּי כִּי שָׁכַחְתִּי מֵאֲכֹל לַחְמִי׃ מִקּוֹל אַנְחָתִי דָּבְקָה
clings my of Because my eat to forget I so my and
,sighing of voice the .bread that ,heart up dried

2723 3563 1961 4057 6893 1819 1320 6106
7 עַצְמִי לִבְשָׂרִי׃ דָּמִיתִי לִקְאַת מִדְבָּר הָיִיתִי כְּכוֹס חֳרָבוֹת׃
.desert the an like am I the pelican a am I my to my
of owl ;wilderness of like .flesh bone

2778 3117 3605 1406 909 6833 1961 8245
8 9 שָׁקַדְתִּי וָאֶהְיֶה כְּצִפּוֹר בּוֹדֵד עַל־גָּג׃ כָּל־הַיּוֹם חֵרְפוּנִי
reproach the All a on alone a like am and ,watch I
me day .top house bird

8249 398 3899 665 7650 1984 341
10 אוֹיְבָי מְהוֹלָלַי בִּי נִשְׁבָּעוּ׃ כִּי־אֵפֶר כַּלֶּחֶם אָכָלְתִּי וְשִׁקֻּוַי
my and have I like ashes For have against those my
drink ,eaten bread .sworn me boasting ;enemies

7993 5375 7110 2195 4537 1065
11 בִּבְכִי מָסָכְתִּי׃ מִפְּנֵי־זַעַמְךָ וְקִצְפֶּךָ כִּי נְשָׂאתַנִי וַתַּשְׁלִיכֵנִי׃
cast and have You for Your and Your because have with
.down me me lifted ;wrath anger of ,mixed weeping

5769 3068 3001 6212 5186 6738 3117
12 13 יָמַי כְּצֵל נָטוּי וַאֲנִי כָּעֵשֶׂב אִיבָשׁ׃ וְאַתָּה יְהוָה לְעוֹלָם
forever O ,You But .wither grass as I and drawn as (are) My
,Jehovah ,out shadow a days

6256 6726 7355 6965 1755 1755 2143 3427
14 תֵּשֵׁב וְזִכְרְךָ לְדֹר וָדֹר׃ אַתָּה תָקוּם תְּרַחֵם צִיּוֹן כִּי־עֵת
the for ;Zion have shall You gen- and gen- to Your and shall
time on mercy ;arise .eration eration memory ;dwell

68 5650 7521 4150 935 2603
15 לְחֶנְנָהּ כִּי־בָא מוֹעֵד׃ כִּי־רָצוּ עֲבָדֶיךָ אֶת־אֲבָנֶיהָ וְאֶת־
and ,stones its Your delight For ap- the has for pity to
servants in .time pointed come ,her

776 4428 3605 3068 8034 1471 3372 2603 6083
16 עֲפָרָהּ יְחֹנֵנוּ׃ וְיִירְאוּ גוֹיִם אֶת־שֵׁם יְהוָה וְכָל־מַלְכֵי הָאָרֶץ
the the and ,Jehovah the nations shall So have its (on)
earth of kings all of name fear .favor dust

6437 3519 7200 6726 3068 1129 3519
17 18 אֶת־כְּבוֹדֶךָ׃ כִּי־בָנָה יְהוָה צִיּוֹן נִרְאָה בִּכְבוֹדוֹ׃ פָּנָה אֶל־
to He His in He ,Zion Jehovah builds When Your
turns .glory appears up .glory

1755 2088 3789 8605 959 3808 6199 8605
19 תְּפִלַּת הָעַרְעָר וְלֹא־בָזָה אֶת־תְּפִלָּתָם׃ תִּכָּתֶב זֹאת לְדוֹר
the for This be shall their despises and the the
generation written .prayer not destitute of prayer

6944 4791 8259 3050 1984 1254 5971 314
20 אַחֲרוֹן וְעַם נִבְרָא יְהַלֶּל־יָהּ׃ כִּי־הִשְׁקִיף מִמְּרוֹם קָדְשׁוֹ
His the from looked has He For .Jehovah shall be to and ;next
,sanctuary of height down praise created people

Jehovah looked from Heaven to the earth; [20]to hear the groaning of the prisoner, to set free the sons of death; [21]to declare the name of Jehovah in Zion, and His praise in Jerusalem; [22]when the peoples and the kingdoms are gathered together to serve Jehovah.

[23]He diminished my strength in the way; He shortened my days. [24]I said, O my God, do not take me up in the half of my days; Your years *are* through the generation of generations. [25]You have laid the foundation of the earth of old; and the heavens *are* the work of Your hands. [26]They shall perish, but You shall endure; yea, all of them shall become old like a garment; You shall change them like clothing, and they shall be changed. [27]But You *are* He, and Your years shall not be ended. [28]The sons of Your servants shall dwell; and their seed shall be established before You.

PSALM 103
Of David.

[1]Bless Jehovah, O my soul; and all within me, *bless* His holy name. [2]Bless Jehovah, O my soul, and forget not all His rewards; [3]who forgives all your iniquities; who heals all your diseases; [4]who redeems your life from destruction; who crowns you *with* kindness and tender mercies; [5]who satisfies your desire with good; your youth is renewed like the eagle's.

[6]Jehovah works righteousness and judgments for all the oppressed. [7]He made known His ways to Moses, His acts to the sons of Israel. [8]Jehovah *is* merciful and gracious, slow to anger, and of much mercy. [9]He will not always chasten, nor will He keep His *anger* forever. [10]He has not done to us according to our sins, nor rewarded us according to our iniquities.

6605 615 603 8085 5027 776 8064 3068
21 יְהוָה מִשָּׁמַיִם ׀ אֶל־אֶרֶץ הִבִּיט׃ לִשְׁמֹעַ אֶנְקַת אָסִיר לְפַתֵּחַ
set to free | the ,prisoner's | groaning | hear to | ;looked | the earth | to | from Heaven | Jehovah

33 89 8416 3068 8034 6726 5608 8546 1121
22 בְּנֵי תְמוּתָה׃ לְסַפֵּר בְּצִיּוֹן שֵׁם יְהוָה וּתְהִלָּתוֹ בִּירוּשָׁלָםִ׃
in ,Jerusalem | His and praise | ,Jehovah | the of name | Zion in | to proclaim | ;death | the of sons

6031 3068 5647 4467 3162 5971 6908
23 24 בְּהִקָּבֵץ עַמִּים יַחְדָּו וּמַמְלָכוֹת לַעֲבֹד אֶת־יְהוָה׃ עִנָּה
He lessened | .Jehovah | serve to | and kingdoms | ,together | peoples | are When gathered

3117 2677 5927 410 559 3117 7114 3581 1870
25 בַדֶּרֶךְ כֹּחוֹ קִצַּר יָמָי׃ אֹמַר אֵלִי אַל־תַּעֲלֵנִי בַּחֲצִי יָמָי
my ;days | the in of half | make up go me | do not | my O ,God | ,said I | my .days | He shortened | my ;strength | the in way

3027 4639 3245 776 6440 8141 1755 1755
26 בְּדוֹר דּוֹרִים שְׁנוֹתֶיךָ׃ לְפָנִים הָאָרֶץ יָסַדְתָּ וּמַעֲשֵׂה יָדֶיךָ
Your hands | the and of work | You ;founded | the earth | old Of | Your (are) .years | gen- erations | of | gen- eration | the in

1086 899 3605 5975 6 8064
27 שָׁמָיִם׃ הֵמָּה ׀ יֹאבֵדוּ וְאַתָּה תַעֲמֹד וְכֻלָּם כַּבֶּגֶד יִבְלוּ
shall ;old wax | a as garment | they ,yea all | shall ;stand | You but | shall ,perish | They | the (are) .heavens

8552 3808 8141 2498 2498 3830
28 כַּלְּבוּשׁ תַּחֲלִיפֵם וְיַחֲלֹפוּ׃ וְאַתָּה־הוּא וּשְׁנוֹתֶיךָ לֹא יִתָּמּוּ׃
be shall .ended | not | Your and years | (are) ,He | But You | shall they and .changed be | shall You ;them change | like clothing

3559 6440 2233 7931 5650 1121
29 בְּנֵי־עֲבָדֶיךָ יִשְׁכּוֹנוּ וְזַרְעָם לְפָנֶיךָ יִכּוֹן׃
be shall .established | before You | their and seed | shall ;dwell | Your servants | The of sons

PSAL. CIII קג

PSALM 103

6944 8034 7130 3605 3068 5315 1288 1732
1 לְדָוִד ׀ בָּרְכִי נַפְשִׁי אֶת־יְהוָה וְכָל־קְרָבַי אֶת־שֵׁם קָדְשׁוֹ׃
His .holiness | name the of | within me | and all | ;Jehovah | my O ,soul | ,Bless | Of .David

5545 1576 3605 7911 408 3068 5315 1288
2 3 בָּרְכִי נַפְשִׁי אֶת־יְהוָה וְאַל־תִּשְׁכְּחִי כָּל־גְּמוּלָיו׃ הַסֹּלֵחַ
who forgives | .rewards His | all | do forget | and not | ,Jehovah | my O ,soul | ,Bless

2416 7845 1350 8463 3605 7495 5771 3605
4 לְכָל־עֲוֺנֵכִי הָרֹפֵא לְכָל־תַּחֲלוּאָיְכִי׃ הַגּוֹאֵל מִשַּׁחַת חַיָּיְכִי
your ,life | from ruin | who redeems | your ;diseases | all | who heals | your ,iniquities | all

2318 5716 2896 7646 7356 2617 5850
5 הַמְעַטְּרֵכִי חֶסֶד וְרַחֲמִים׃ הַמַּשְׂבִּיעַ בַּטּוֹב עֶדְיֵךְ תִּתְחַדֵּשׁ
re- is newed | your ;desire | the with good | who satisfies | tender and ;compassion | (with) mercy | crowns who you

3605 4941 3068 6666 6213 5271 5404
6 כַּנֶּשֶׁר נְעוּרָיְכִי׃ עֹשֵׂה צְדָקוֹת יְהוָה וּמִשְׁפָּטִים לְכָל־
all for | judgments and | ,Jehovah | righteous deeds | works | your .youth | the like eagle

5949 3478 1121 4872 1870 3045 6231
7 עֲשׁוּקִים׃ יוֹדִיעַ דְּרָכָיו לְמֹשֶׁה לִבְנֵי יִשְׂרָאֵל עֲלִילוֹתָיו׃
.acts His | Israel | the to of sons | to ,Moses | His ways | made He known | the .oppressed

7378 5331 3808 2617 7227 639 750 3068 2587 7349
8 9 רַחוּם וְחַנּוּן יְהוָה אֶרֶךְ אַפַּיִם וְרַב־חָסֶד׃ לֹא־לָנֶצַח יָרִיב
will He ,strive | always | not | .mercy | and much | anger | slow of | (is) ,Jehovah | and gracious | compas- sionate

5771 3808 6213 2399 3808 5201 5769 3808
10 וְלֹא לְעוֹלָם יִטּוֹר׃ לֹא כַחֲטָאֵינוּ עָשָׂה לָנוּ וְלֹא כַעֲוֺנֹתֵינוּ
our iniquities | and not | .us to | has He done | to according sins our | not | keep .(anger) | forever | nor

11For as the heavens *are* above the earth, *so* is His mercy mighty over those who fear Him. 12As far as the east *is* from the west, *so* far has He removed our transgressions from us. 13As the pity of a father over his sons, *so* Jehovah pities those who fear Him. 14For He knows how we are made, remembering that we *are* dust. 15*As for* man, his days *are* as grass; as the flower of the field, so he flourishes. 16For the wind passes over it, and it is not; and its place never knows it again. 17But the mercy of Jehovah *is* from everlasting, even to everlasting, on those who fear Him; yea, His righteousness *is* to the sons of sons; 18to those who keep His covenant, and to those who remember His commandments, to do them.

19Jehovah has prepared His throne in Heaven; and His kingdom rules over all. 20Bless Jehovah, O angels of His; mighty in strength; doing His word; listening to the voice of His word. 21Bless Jehovah, all His hosts; ministers of His, doing His will. 22Bless Jehovah, all His works in all the places of His dominion; bless Jehovah, O my soul.

2617 1396 776 8064 1364 1580
11 גָּמַל עָלֵינוּ׃ כִּי כִגְבֹהַּ שָׁמַיִם עַל־הָאָרֶץ גָּבַר חַסְדּוֹ עַל־
over His is the above the is as For .us re- has
mercy mighty ,earth heavens high warded

6588 7368 4628 4217 7368 3372
12 יְרֵאָיו׃ כִּרְחֹק מִזְרָח מִמַּעֲרָב הִרְחִיק מִמֶּנּוּ אֶת־פְּשָׁעֵינוּ׃
our from has He the from the far As fearers
.transgressions us far put ,west (is) east (as) .Him of

3045 3373 5921 3068 7355 1121 1 7355
13 14 כְּרַחֵם אָב עַל־בָּנִים רִחַם יְהוָה עַל־יְרֵאָיו׃ כִּי־הוּא יָדַע
knows He For fearers over Jehovah pities (his) over a the As
.Him of ,sons father of pity

6731 3117 2682 582 6083 2142 3336
15 יִצְרֵנוּ זָכוּר כִּי־עָפָר אֲנָחְנוּ׃ אֱנוֹשׁ כֶּחָצִיר יָמָיו כְּצִיץ
as his grass as (for As) we dust that remem- our
flower ;days (are) ,man .(are) bering ;form

5234 3808 369 5674 7307 6692 7704
16 הַשָּׂדֶה כֵּן יָצִיץ׃ כִּי רוּחַ עָבְרָה־בּוֹ וְאֵינֶנּוּ וְלֹא־יַכִּירֶנּוּ
recognizes and it and over passes the For he so ,field the
it not .not is it wind .flourishes

3373 5769 5704 5769 3068 2617 4725 5704
17 עוֹד מְקוֹמוֹ׃ וְחֶסֶד יְהוָה מֵעוֹלָם וְעַד־עוֹלָם עַל־יְרֵאָיו
fearers on ever- even from (is) Jehovah the But .place its again
;Him of lasting to ,everlasting of mercy

6490 2142 1285 8104 1121 1121 6666
18 וְצִדְקָתוֹ לִבְנֵי בָנִים׃ לְשֹׁמְרֵי בְרִיתוֹ וּלְזֹכְרֵי פִקֻּדָיו
His remem- and His those to ;sons the to His and
,precepts bering covenant keeping of sons righteousness

3605 4438 3678 3559 8064 3068 6213
19 לַעֲשׂוֹתָם׃ יְהוָה בַּשָּׁמַיִם הֵכִין כִּסְאוֹ וּמַלְכוּתוֹ בַּכֹּל
over His and His has the in Jehovah .them do to
all kingdom ;throne prepared heavens

8085 1697 6213 3581 1368 4397 3068 1288 4910
20 מָשָׁלָה׃ בָּרֲכוּ יְהוָה מַלְאָכָיו גִּבֹּרֵי כֹחַ עֹשֵׂי דְבָרוֹ לִשְׁמֹעַ
listen to His doing ;strength mighty His O ,Jehovah Bless .rules
,word of ;angels

7522 6213 8334 6635 3605 3068 1288 1697 6963
21 בְּקוֹל דְּבָרוֹ׃ בָּרֲכוּ יְהוָה כָּל־צְבָאָיו מְשָׁרְתָיו עֹשֵׂי רְצוֹנוֹ׃
.will His doing ministers His all ,Jehovah Bless His the to
,His of ,hosts .word of voice

1288 4475 4725 3605 4639 3605 3068 1288
22 בָּרֲכוּ יְהוָה כָּל־מַעֲשָׂיו בְּכָל־מְקֹמוֹת מֶמְשַׁלְתּוֹ בָּרְכִי
bless His the all in His all ,Jehovah Bless
,dominion of places ,works

3068 5315
נַפְשִׁי אֶת־יְהוָה׃
.Jehovah my O
,soul

PSAL. CIV קד

PSALM 104

PSALM 104

1Bless Jehovah, O my soul! O Jehovah my God, You are very great; You have put on honor and majesty, 2covering Yourself *with* light like a cloak, and stretching out the heavens like a curtain; 3who lays beams in the waters *of* His upper rooms; setting thick clouds *as* His chariots; walking on the wings of the wind. 4He makes His angels spirits, His ministers a flaming fire.

1926 1935 3966 1431 430 3068 3068 5315 1288
1 בָּרְכִי נַפְשִׁי אֶת־יְהוָה יְהוָה אֱלֹהַי גָּדַלְתָּ מְּאֹד הוֹד וְהָדָר
and majesty ;very are You my O .Jehovah my O ,Bless
honor great God Jehovah ,soul

3407 806 4 5186 8008 216 5844 3847
2 לָבָשְׁתָּ׃ עֹטֶה־אוֹר כַּשַּׂלְמָה נוֹטֶה שָׁמַיִם כַּיְרִיעָה׃
a like the stretching a like (with) covering have You
;curtain heavens out ;cloak light Yourself ,on put

1980 7398 5645 7760 5944 4325 7136
3 הַמְקָרֶה בַמַּיִם עֲלִיּוֹתָיו הַשָּׂם־עָבִים רְכוּבוֹ הַמְהַלֵּךְ עַל־
on who His (as) thick who His (of) the in lays who
marches ;chariot clouds sets ;rooms upper waters beams

3857 784 8334 7307 4397 6213 7307 3671
4 כַּנְפֵי־רוּחַ׃ עֹשֶׂה מַלְאָכָיו רוּחוֹת מְשָׁרְתָיו אֵשׁ לֹהֵט׃
.flame fire a His ,winds His He the the
of ministers angels makes .wind of wings

5He founded the earth on its
foundations; it shall not be
shaken forever and ever.
6You have covered the deep
as with a robe; the waters
stood above the mountains.
7From Your rebuke, they
flee; from the sound of Your
thunder, they hurry away.
8They go up the mountains;
they go down the valleys to
the place which You
founded for them. 9You
have set a boundary; they
may not pass over; they
shall not return to cover the
earth. 10*He* sends springs
into the valleys; they flow
between the hills; 11they
give drink to every animal of
the field; wild asses break
their thirst; 12over them
the birds of the heavens
dwell; they give voice from
between the branches.
13*He* waters the hills from
His upper rooms; the earth
is satisfied from the fruit of
Your works. 14*He* causes
the grass to grow for the
livestock and plants for the
service of man; to bring
food out of the earth.
15And wine cheers the heart
of man; oil makes *his* face
shine; and bread sustains
the heart of man.
16The trees of Jehovah
are satisfied; the cedars of
Lebanon that He planted;
17there where the birds
nest; the fir trees *are* the
house of the stork; 18high
hills *are* for the wild goats;
rocks *are* a refuge for the
badgers. 19He made the
moon for seasons; the sun
knows its going down.
20You put darkness, and it is
night; in it all the forest
animals creep. 21The
young lions roar for prey,
and to seek their food from
God. 22The sun rises; they
are gathered, and go to
their dens to lie down.
23Man goes out to his work,
and to his labor until the

8415 5703 5769 41,31 1097 4349 776 3245
5 6 יָסַד־אֶרֶץ עַל־מְכוֹנֶיהָ בַּל־תִּמּוֹט עוֹלָם וָעֶד׃ תְּהוֹם
deep The and forever shall it not its on the He
.ever shake ;foundations earth founded

5127 1606 4480 4325 5975 2022 3680 3830
7 כַּלְּבוּשׁ כִּסִּיתוֹ עַל־הָרִים יַעַמְדוּ־מָיִם׃ מִן־גַּעֲרָתְךָ יְנוּסוּן
they Your From the stand the above You a with as
;flee rebuke .waters mountains ;it covered ,garment

1237 3381 2022 5921 2648 7482 6963
8 מִן־קוֹל רַעַמְךָ יֵחָפֵזוּן׃ יַעֲלוּ הָרִים יֵרְדוּ בְקָעוֹת אֶל־
to the down go the up go hurry they Your the from
valleys ;mountains —away thunder of sound

77.25 1097 56 74 1097 7760 1366 3245 2088 472.5
9 מְקוֹם זֶה יָסַדְתָּ לָהֶם׃ גְּבוּל־שַׂמְתָּ בַּל־יַעֲבֹרוּן בַּל־יְשׁוּבוּן
shall they not shall they not You A for You which the
return .over pass ;set have boundary .them founded place

2022 996 5158 4599 797.1 776 3680
10 לְכַסּוֹת הָאָרֶץ׃ הַמְשַׁלֵּחַ מַעְיָנִים בַּנְּחָלִים בֵּין הָרִים
hills the between the into springs sends who ;earth the cover to
;valleys

6772 6501 7665 7704 2416 3604 8248 1980
11 יְהַלֵּכוּן׃ יַשְׁקוּ כָּל־חַיְתוֹ שָׂדָי יִשְׁבְּרוּ פְרָאִים צְמָאָם׃
their wild break the animal every give they ;go they
.thirst asses ;field of to drink

6963 5414 607.3 996 7931 8064 5775
12 עֲלֵיהֶם עוֹף־הַשָּׁמַיִם יִשְׁכּוֹן מִבֵּין עֳפָאיִם יִתְּנוּ־קוֹל׃
.voice they branches from ;dwell the the Over
give between heavens of birds them

776 7646 4639 6529 5944 2022 8248
13 מַשְׁקֶה הָרִים מֵעֲלִיּוֹתָיו מִפְּרִי מַעֲשֶׂיךָ תִּשְׂבַּע הָאָרֶץ׃
—earth the is works Your the from His from the (is He)
satisfied of fruit —rooms upper heights watering

3318 120 5656 6212 929 2682 6779
14 מַצְמִיחַ חָצִיר ׀ לַבְּהֵמָה וְעֵשֶׂב לַעֲבֹדַת הָאָדָם לְהוֹצִיא
bring to ;man the for and the for grass causing
out of service plants ,cattle grow to

6440 6670 582 3824 8056 3196 776 3899
15 לֶחֶם מִן־הָאָרֶץ׃ וְיַיִן ׀ יְשַׂמַּח לְבַב־אֱנוֹשׁ לְהַצְהִיל פָּנִים
(his) make to ,men the cheers And the from food
face shine of heart wine .earth

730 3068 6086 7646 5582 582 3824 3899 8081
16 מִשָּׁמֶן וְלֶחֶם לְבַב־אֱנוֹשׁ יִסְעָד׃ יִשְׂבְּעוּ עֲצֵי יְהוָה אַרְזֵי
cedars ,Jehovah The are .sustains man the and from
of trees satisfied of heart bread ;oil

26.34 7064 6833 8033 834 5193 834 38.44
17 לְבָנוֹן אֲשֶׁר נָטָע׃ אֲשֶׁר־שָׁם צִפֳּרִים יְקַנֵּנוּ חֲסִידָה
,stork the —nest birds there (in) He which Lebanon's
which ;planted

4268 5553 32.77 1364 2022 1004 1265
18 בְּרוֹשִׁים בֵּיתָהּ׃ הָרִים הַגְּבֹהִים לַיְּעֵלִים סְלָעִים מַחְסֶה
refuge a ,rocks the for High mounts her trees fir
;goats wild (are) .house (are)

7896 3996 3045 8121 4150 3394 6213 8227
19 20 לַשְׁפַנִּים׃ עָשָׂה יָרֵחַ לְמוֹעֲדִים שֶׁמֶשׁ יָדַע מְבוֹאוֹ׃ תָּשֶׁת־
put You its knows sun the for the He the for
.down going ;seasons moon made .badgers

3715 3293 2416 3605 74 30 3915 1961 2822
21 חֹשֶׁךְ וִיהִי לָיְלָה בּוֹ־תִרְמֹשׂ כָּל־חַיְתוֹ־יָעַר׃ הַכְּפִירִים
young The the the all creep it in ;night it and dark-
lions .forest of beasts is ness

622 8121 2224 400 410 1245 2964 7580
22 שֹׁאֲגִים לַטָּרֶף וּלְבַקֵּשׁ מֵאֵל אָכְלָם׃ תִּזְרַח הַשֶּׁמֶשׁ יֵאָסֵפוּן
are they ;sun The rises their from to and ,prey for roar
,gathered .food God seek

5704 5656 6467 120 3318 7257 4585
23 וְאֶל־מְעוֹנֹתָם יִרְבָּצוּן׃ יֵצֵא אָדָם לְפָעֳלוֹ וְלַעֲבֹדָתוֹ עֲדֵי־
until to and his to Man goes .down lie their and
service his ,work out dens to

evening.
24 O Jehovah, how many are Your works! You have made all of them in wisdom; the earth is full of Your riches.
25 This *is* the sea, great and wide on both hands; there *are* creeping things even without number; living things, small and great.
26 There the ships go; You made this great sea-animal to play in it.
27 All of them wait for You to give *them* their food in due season.
28 You give to them; they gather; You open Your hand, *and* they are filled with good.
29 You hide Your face, *and* they are troubled; You gather Your breath, *and* they expire and return to their dust.
30 You send out Your Spirit, *and* they are created; and You renew the face of the earth.
31 The glory of Jehovah shall be forever; Jehovah shall rejoice in His works.
32 He looks to the earth, and it trembles; He touches the hills, and they smoke.
33 I will sing to Jehovah during my life; I will sing praise to my God while I exist.
34 My thoughts on Him shall be sweet; I will be glad in Jehovah.
35 Let sinners perish from the earth and let the wicked be no more; bless Jehovah, O my soul; praise Jehovah!

6213 2451 3605 3068 4639 7231 6153
24 עֶרֶב: מָה־רַבּוּ מַעֲשֶׂיךָ | יְהוָה כֻּלָּם בְּחָכְמָה עָשִׂיתָ
have You ;made | wisdom in | of All them | O !Jehovah | Your ,works | many How are | the .evening

8033 3027 7342 1419 3220 2088 7075 776 4390
25 מָלְאָה הָאָרֶץ קִנְיָנֶךָ: זֶה | הַיָּם גָּדוֹל וּרְחַב יָדָיִם שָׁם־
There (are) | both ;hands | and wide | great | sea the | This (is) | Your .possessions | the earth | full is of

591 8033 1419 6996 2416 4557 369 7431
26 רֶמֶשׂ וְאֵין מִסְפָּר חַיּוֹת קְטַנּוֹת עִם־גְּדֹלוֹת: שָׁם אֳנִיּוֹת
ships | There | .great | with | small | living ,things | ;number without | even creeping ,things

7663 3605 7832 3335 2088 3882 3212
27 יְהַלֵּכוּן לִוְיָתָן זֶה־יָצַרְתָּ לְשַׂחֶק־בּוֹ: כֻּלָּם אֵלֶיךָ יְשַׂבֵּרוּן
,wait | for You | of All them | .it in | play to | You this formed | sea- animal | ;ply

7646 3027 6605 3950 5414 6256 400 5414
28 לָתֵת אָכְלָם בְּעִתּוֹ: תִּתֵּן לָהֶם יִלְקֹטוּן תִּפְתַּח יָדְךָ יִשְׂבְּעוּן
are they satisfied | Your ;hand | You open | they ;gather | to ,them | You give | its in .time | their food | give to

6083 1478 7307 622 926 6440 5640 2896
29 טוֹב: תַּסְתִּיר פָּנֶיךָ יִבָּהֵלוּן תֹּסֵף רוּחָם יִגְוָעוּן וְאֶל־עֲפָרָם
their dust | and to | they expire | their ,breath | You gather | are they ;troubled | Your ,face | You hide | (with) .good

1961 127 6440 2318 1254 7307 7971 7725
30 31 יְשׁוּבוּן: תְּשַׁלַּח רוּחֲךָ יִבָּרֵאוּן וּתְחַדֵּשׁ פְּנֵי אֲדָמָה: יְהִי
shall be | the .ground | the of face | You and renew | are they ;created | Your ,Spirit | send You out | .return

776 5027 4639 3068 8056 5769 3068 3519
32 כְבוֹד יְהוָה לְעוֹלָם יִשְׂמַח יְהוָה בְּמַעֲשָׂיו: הַמַּבִּיט לָאָרֶץ
the to earth | looks He | His in .works | Jehovah | shall rejoice | ;forever | Jehovah | The of glory

216 2416 3068 7891 6225 2022 5060 7460
33 וַתִּרְעָד יִגַּע בֶּהָרִים וְיֶעֱשָׁנוּ: אָשִׁירָה לַיהוָה בְּחַיָּי אֲזַמְּרָה
will I praise | during ;life my | to Jehovah | will I sing | they and .smoke | the heights | He touches | it and ;trembles

3068 8056 7879 6149 5750 430
34 לֵאלֹהַי בְּעוֹדִי: יֶעֱרַב עָלָיו שִׂיחִי אָנֹכִי אֶשְׂמַח בַּיהוָה:
in .Jehovah | be will glad | I | my ;meditation | on Him | be Shall sweet | I while .(am) still | my to God

5315 1288 369 5750 7563 776 2400 8552
35 יִתַּמּוּ חַטָּאִים | מִן־הָאָרֶץ וּרְשָׁעִים | עוֹד אֵינָם בָּרְכִי נַפְשִׁי
my O ,soul | ,bless | (may) they ;be not | still | the and ,wicked | the ;earth | from | sinners | May perish

1984 3068
אֶת־יְהוָה הַלְלוּ־יָהּ:
praise !Jehovah | ;Jehovah

PSAL. CV קה

PSALM 105

1 O give thanks to Jehovah; call on His name; make His deeds known among the peoples.
2 Sing to Him; sing praises to Him; tell of all His wonders.
3 Glory in His holy name; let the heart of those who seek Jehovah rejoice.
4 Seek Jehovah and His strength; seek His face without ceasing.
5 Remember His wonders that He has done; His miracles, and the judgments of His mouth,

7891 5949 5971 3045 8034 7121 3068 3034
1 2 הוֹדוּ לַיהוָה קִרְאוּ בִּשְׁמוֹ הוֹדִיעוּ בָעַמִּים עֲלִילוֹתָיו: שִׁירוּ־
Sing | .deeds His | among peoples the | make known | His on ;name | call | to ;Jehovah | Give thanks

6944 8034 1984 6381 3605 7878 2167
3 לוֹ זַמְּרוּ־לוֹ שִׂיחוּ בְּכָל־נִפְלְאוֹתָיו: הִתְהַלְלוּ בְּשֵׁם קָדְשׁוֹ
His ;holiness | the in of name | Glory | His .wonders | all of | tell | to ;Him | Sing praises | to ;Him

6440 1245 5797 3068 1875 3068 1245 3820 8056
4 יִשְׂמַח לֵב | מְבַקְשֵׁי יְהוָה: דִּרְשׁוּ יְהוָה וְעֻזּוֹ בַּקְּשׁוּ פָנָיו
His face | seek | His and ;strength | Jehovah | Seek | .Jehovah | those seek who | the of heart | may rejoice

6310 4941 4159 6213 834 6381 2142 8548
5 תָּמִיד: זִכְרוּ נִפְלְאוֹתָיו אֲשֶׁר־עָשָׂה מֹפְתָיו וּמִשְׁפְּטֵי־פִיו:
His .mouth | the and of judgments | His ;miracles | has He ,done | that | His wonders | Remember | .always

[6]O seed of His servant
Abraham; O sons of Jacob,
His chosen ones. [7]He *is*
Jehovah our God; His
judgments *are* in all the
earth; [8]He has remembered
His covenant forever; the
word He commanded to
a thousand generations;
[9]which He cut with Abraham, and His oath to Isaac;
[10]and He confirmed it to
Jacob for a statute, to Israel
for a perpetual covenant;
[11]saying, To you I will give
the land of Canaan, the lot of
your inheritance; [12]when
they were *a few* men of
number; very few, and
strangers in it. [13]And they
went about from nation to
nation; from *one* kingdom to
another people. [14]He
allowed no man to oppress
them; yea, He reproved
kings for their sakes; [15]*saying*, Touch not My anointed;
and, Do My prophets no
harm. [16]And He called a
famine on the land; He
broke the whole staff of
bread. [17]He sent a man
before them—Joseph, *be-
ing* sold for a slave; [18]they
hurt his feet with chains; his
soul came into iron; [19]until
the time His word came; the
word of Jehovah refined
him; [20]the king, the ruler of
peoples, sent and released
him; even set him free; [21]he
made him lord of his house,
and ruler over all he
owned; [22]to bind his
leaders at his will, and to
teach his elders wisdom.

[23]Israel also came *into*
Egypt, and Jacob sojourned
in the land of Ham. [24]And
He greatly increased His
people, and made them
stronger than their enemies.
[25]He turned their heart to
hate His people, to deal
craftily with His servants.
[26]He sent His servant
Moses; *and* Aaron whom
He had chosen. [27]They put
things of His signs among
them; yea, miracles in the
land of Ham. [28]He sent
darkness and made it dark;

430 3068 972 3290 1121 5650 85 2233
6 7 זרע אברהם עבדו בני יעקב בחיריו׃ הוא יהוה אלהינו
;God our Jehovah He His ,Jacob sons His Abraham Seed
(is) ;ones chosen of ;servant of

6680 1697 1285 5769 2142 4941 776 3605
8 בכל־הארץ משפטיו׃ זכר לעולם בריתו דבר צוה
com- He the His forever has He His (are) the all in
manded word ;covenant remembered ;judgments earth

3446 7621 85 3772 834 1255 505
9 לאלף דור׃ אשר כרת את־אברהם ושבועתו לישחק׃
;Isaac to His and ;Abraham with He which genera- a to
oath cut ,tions thousand

559 5769 1285 3478 2706 3290 5975
10 11 ויעמידה ליעקב לחק לישראל ברית עולם׃ לאמר לך
To ,saying ,perpetual a (for) Israel to a for to He and
you covenant ,statute Jacob it confirmed

4557 4962 1961 5159 2256 3667 776 5414
12 אתן את־ארץ כנען חבל נחלתכם׃ בהיותם מתי מספר
,number (few a) they when your the ,Canaan the will I
of men were ;inheritance of portion of land give

4467 1471 1471 1980 1481 4592
13 כמעט וגרים בה׃ ויתהלכו מגוי אל־גוי מממלכה אל־
to (one) from ;nation to from they and ;it in and very
kingdom nation about went aliens few

4428 5668 3198 6231 120 3240 3808 312 5971
14 עם אחר׃ לא־הניח אדם לעשקם ויוכח עליהם מלכים׃
;kings their for He ,yea oppress to man did He not .another
sakes reproved ;them allow people

7458 7121 7489 408 5030 4899 5060
15 16 אל־תגעו במשיחי ולנביאי אל־תרעו׃ ויקרא רעב על־
on a He And do not My to and My touch Do not
famine called .harm prophets ,anointed

5650 376 6440 7971 7665 3899 4294 3605 776
17 הארץ כל־מטה־לחם שבר׃ שלח לפניהם איש לעבד
a for a before sent He He bread staff the the
slave ,man them .broke of whole ;land

5704 5315 935 1270 7272 3525 6031 3130 4376
18 19 נמכר יוסף׃ ענו בכבל רגליו ברזל באה נפשו׃ עד
until ;soul his came into his with they ;Joseph was
iron ,feet chains hurt sold

5425 4428 7971 6884 3068 565 1697 935 6256
20 עת בא־דברו אמרת יהוה צרפתהו׃ שלח מלך ויתירהו
loosed and The sent refined Jehovah the His came the
;him king .him of word ;word time

3605 4910 1004 113 7760 6605 5971 4910
21 משל עמים ויפתחהו׃ שמו אדון לביתו ומשל בכל־
all over ruler and his of lord made He him set and ,peoples the
,house him .free of ruler

3478 935 2449 2205 5315 8269 631 7075
22 23 קנינו׃ לאסר שריו בנפשו וזקניו יחכם׃ ויבא ישראל
Israel And teach to his and his at his bind to his
came .wisdom elders ,will princes ,property

3966 5971 6509 2526 776 1481 3290 4714
24 מצרים ויעקב גר בארץ־חם׃ ויפר את־עמו מאד
,greatly His He And .Ham the in so- and ,Egypt (to)
people increased of land journed Jacob

5230 5971 8130 3820 2015 6862 6105
25 ויעצמהו מצריו׃ הפך לבם לשנא עמו להתנכל
deal to His hate to their He his than him made and
craftily ,people heart turned .enemies stronger

7760 977 834 175 5650 4872 7971 5650
26 27 בעבדיו׃ שלח משה עבדו אהרן אשר־בחר־בו׃ שמו
They had He whom Aaron His Moses sent He His with
put .chosen ,servant .servants

2821 2822 7971 2526 776 4159 226 1697
28 בם דברי אתותיו ומפתים בארץ חם׃ שלח חשך ויחשך
made and dark- sent He .Ham the in and His things among
;dark it ness of land miracles ,signs of them

and they did not rebel
against His word. 29 He
turned their waters into
blood and killed their fish.
30 The land swarmed with
frogs in the rooms of their
kings. 31 He spoke, and *fly-*
swarms came; *even* gnats in
all their borders. 32 He gave
hail *for* their rain, flaming fire
in their land. 33 He struck
their vines also, and their
fig-trees; and *He* broke the
trees of their borders. 34 He
spoke, and locusts came;
and larvae without number;
35 and they ate up all the
plants in the land; and ate
the fruit of their ground. 36 He
also struck all the firstborn
in their land, the firstfruit of
all their vigor.
37 And He led them out
with silver and gold; and
among their tribes, not one
was stumbling. 38 Egypt
was glad when they went
out, for their dread had
fallen on them. 39 He spread
a cloud for a covering; and
fire to give light *in* the
night. 40 He asked, and He
brought quail; and satisfied
them *with* the food *from* the
heavens. 41 He opened the
rock, and waters gushed
out; they went in the dry
places *like* a river. 42 For He
remembered His holy word,
and His servant Abraham;
43 and He brought His
people out with joy; His
chosen ones with gladness.
44 And He gave to them the
lands of the nations; and
they inherited the labor of
the peoples; 45 so that they
might observe His statutes
and keep His laws. Praise
Jehovah!

4191 1818 4325 2015 1697 4784 3808
29 וְלֹא מָרוּ אֶת־דְּבָרוֹ׃ הָפַךְ אֶת־מֵימֵיהֶם לְדָם וַיָּמֶת
and into waters their He .word His re- they and
killed blood turned belled against not

4428 2315 6854 776 8317 1710
30 אֶת־דְּגָתָם׃ שָׁרַץ אַרְצָם צְפַרְדְּעִים בְּחַדְרֵי מַלְכֵיהֶם׃
.kings their the in frogs (with) Their swarmed .fish their
of rooms land

1259 1653 5414 1366 3605 3654 6157 935 559
31 אָמַר וַיָּבֹא עָרֹב כִּנִּים בְּכָל־גְּבוּלָם׃
32 נָתַן גִּשְׁמֵיהֶם בָּרָד
,hail their He their all in (and) fly and He
rain gave .border gnats ,swarms came spoke

1366 6086 7665 8384 1612 5221 776 3852 784
33 אֵשׁ לֶהָבוֹת בְּאַרְצָם׃ וַיַּךְ גַּפְנָם וּתְאֵנָתָם וַיְשַׁבֵּר עֵץ גְּבוּלָם׃
their the and their and their also He their in flames fire
,border of trees broke ;trees fig ,vines struck .land of

6212 398 4557 369 3218 697 935 559
34 אָמַר וַיָּבֹא אַרְבֶּה וְיֶלֶק וְאֵין מִסְפָּר׃
35 וַיֹּאכַל כָּל־עֵשֶׂב
the all they and ;number without and ,locusts and He
plants ate larvae came ,spoke

776 1060 3605 5221 127 6529 398 776
36 בְּאַרְצָם וַיֹּאכַל פְּרִי אַדְמָתָם׃ וַיַּךְ כָּל־בְּכוֹר בְּאַרְצָם
their in the all also He their the they and their in
,land firstborn struck .ground of fruit ate ;land

7626 369 2091 3701 3318 202 3605 7225
37 רֵאשִׁית לְכָל־אוֹנָם׃ וַיּוֹצִיאֵם בְּכֶסֶף וְזָהָב וְאֵין בִּשְׁבָטָיו
their in and and with led He And their all of first- the
tribes was none ;gold silver out them .vigor fruit

6343 5307 3318 4714 8056 3782
38 כּוֹשֵׁל׃ שָׂמַח מִצְרַיִם בְּצֵאתָם כִּי־נָפַל פַּחְדָּם עֲלֵיהֶם׃
.them on their had for they when Egypt was .stumbling
dread fallen ,out went glad

7958 935 7592 3915 215 784 4539 6051 6566
39 פָּרַשׂ עָנָן לְמָסָךְ וְאֵשׁ לְהָאִיר לָיְלָה׃
40 שָׁאַל וַיָּבֵא שְׂלָו
,quail He and He the (in) give to and a for a He
brought ,asked .night light fire ,covering cloud spread

6723 1980 4325 2100 6697 6605 7646 8064 3899
41 וְלֶחֶם שָׁמַיִם יַשְׂבִּיעֵם׃ פָּתַח צוּר וַיָּזוּבוּ מָיִם הָלְכוּ בַּצִּיּוֹת
the in they ;water and the He satisfied heaven food and
deserts ,went out gushed ,rock opened .them of

5650 85 6944 1697 2142 5104
42 נָהָר׃ כִּי־זָכַר אֶת־דְּבַר קָדְשׁוֹ אֶת־אַבְרָהָם עַבְדּוֹ׃
His Abraham (and) His the He For a (as)
;servant ,holiness of word remembered .river

776 5414 972 7440 8342 5971 3318
43 וַיּוֹצִא עַמּוֹ בְשָׂשׂוֹן בְּרִנָּה אֶת־בְּחִירָיו׃
44 וַיִּתֵּן לָהֶם אַרְצוֹת
the to He And His with with His He and
of lands them gave .chosen gladness ;joy people out led

8451 2706 8104 3423 3816 5999 1471
45 גּוֹיִם וַעֲמַל לְאֻמִּים יִירָשׁוּ׃ בַּעֲבוּר ׀ יִשְׁמְרוּ חֻקָּיו וְתוֹרֹתָיו
His and His might they that they peoples the and ;nations
laws ,statutes observe ;inherited of labor

1984 5341
יִנְצֹרוּ הַלְלוּ־יָהּ׃
praise ;keep
!Jehovah

PSAL. CVI קו

PSALM 106

PSALM 106
1 Praise Jehovah! Give
thanks to Jehovah, for *He is*
good; for His mercy *endures*
forever. 2 Who can express
the mighty deeds of
Jehovah, *or* cause all His
praise to be heard? 3 Blessed
are those who keep

4310 2617 5769 2896 3068 3034 1984
1 הַלְלוּ־יָהּ ׀ הוֹדוּ לַיהוָה כִּי־טוֹב כִּי לְעוֹלָם חַסְדּוֹ׃
2 מִי
Who His forever for (is He) for to give Praise
.mercy (is) ;good ,Jehovah thanks ;Jehovah

8104 835 8416 3605 8085 3068 1369 4448
3 יְמַלֵּל גְּבוּרוֹת יְהוָה יַשְׁמִיעַ כָּל־תְּהִלָּתוֹ׃ אַשְׁרֵי שֹׁמְרֵי
ones the Blessed His all make (or) ,Jehovah mighty the can
keeping (are) ?praise heard of deeds say

judgment; he who does righteousness in every season. [4]Remember me, Jehovah, with the favor of Your people; O visit me with Your salvation, [5]to see the good of Your chosen ones; to rejoice in the joy of Your nation; to glory with Your inheritance.

[6]We have sinned with our fathers; we did iniquity; we did wrong. [7]Our fathers did not understand Your wonders in Egypt; they did not remember Your many mercies; and *they* rebelled at the sea, at the Red Sea. [8]But He saved them for His name's sake, to make known His might. [9]And He rebuked the Red Sea; and it dried up; and He made them go through the depths, *as* through the wilderness. [10]And He saved them from the hand of the hater, and ransomed him from the hand of the enemy; [11]and water covered their enemies; not one of them was left. [12]Then they believed His words; they sang His praise. [13]They hurried *and* forgot His works; they did not wait for His counsel; [14]and they greedily lusted in the wilderness, and tested God in the desert. [15]And He gave their request to them, but sent wasting into their soul. [16]And they were jealous of Moses the saint of Jehovah, in the camp of Aaron; [17]the earth opened up and swallowed Dathan; and covered the company of Abiram. [18]And a fire burned in their company; the flame burned up the wicked.

[19]They made a calf in Horeb, and fell down before the casted image; [20]and they changed their Glory into the image of an ox eating grass. [21]They forgot God their deliverer, doing great things in Egypt; [22]wonders in the land of Ham; awesome things by the Red Sea. [23]And He said to destroy them; except Moses His chosen one

5971 7522 3068 2142 6256 3605 6666 6213 4441
4 מִשְׁפָּט עֹשֵׂה צְדָקָה בְכָל־עֵת׃ זָכְרֵנִי יְהוָה בִּרְצוֹן עַמֶּךָ
Your the with ,Jehovah Remember .time in righteousness he ;judgment
;people of favor me every does who

8056 972 2896 7200 3444 6485
5 פָּקְדֵנִי בִּישׁוּעָתֶךָ׃ לִרְאוֹת ׀ בְּטוֹבַת בְּחִירֶיךָ לִשְׂמֹחַ
to Your good the see to Your with me visit
rejoice ;chosen of ;salvation

1 2398 5159 1984 1471 8057
6 בְּשִׂמְחַת גּוֹיֶךָ לְהִתְהַלֵּל עִם־נַחֲלָתֶךָ׃ חָטָאנוּ עִם־אֲבוֹתֵינוּ
our with have We Your with glory to Your joy the in
;fathers sinned .inheritance ,nation of

6381 7919 3808 4714 1 7561 5753
7 הֶעֱוִינוּ הִרְשָׁעְנוּ׃ אֲבוֹתֵינוּ בְמִצְרַיִם לֹא־הִשְׂכִּילוּ נִפְלְאוֹתֶיךָ
Your did not Egypt in Our did we did we
;wonders understand fathers .wrong ;iniquity

3462 5488 3220 3220 4784 2617 72 30 2142 3808
8 לֹא זָכְרוּ אֶת־רֹב חֲסָדֶיךָ וַיַּמְרוּ עַל־יָם בְּיַם־סוּף׃ וַיּוֹשִׁיעֵם
He But .Reeds the at the at and Your many they not
them saved of Sea ,sea rebelled ,mercies remembered

2717 5488 3220 1605 1369 3045 8034 4616
9 לְמַעַן שְׁמוֹ לְהוֹדִיעַ אֶת־גְּבוּרָתוֹ׃ וַיִּגְעַר בְּיַם־סוּף וַיֶּחֱרָב
it and ,Reeds the He And His make to His the for
;up dried of Sea rebuked .might known ,name of sake

1350 8130 3027 3462 4057 8415 3212
10 וַיּוֹלִיכֵם בַּתְּהֹמוֹת כַּמִּדְבָּר׃ וַיּוֹשִׁיעֵם מִיַּד שׂוֹנֵא וַיִּגְאָלֵם
ran- and the from He And the in (as) the in He and
them somed ,hater's hand them saved .wilderness ,depths go them made

3498 3808 259 6862 4325 3680 341 3027
11 מִיַּד אוֹיֵב׃ וַיְכַסּוּ־מַיִם צָרֵיהֶם אֶחָד מֵהֶם לֹא נוֹתָר׃
was not of one their water and the from
.left them ;enemies covered ;enemy's hand

380 8 4639 7911 4116 8416 7892 1697 539
12 וַיַּאֲמִינוּ בִדְבָרָיו יָשִׁירוּ תְּהִלָּתוֹ׃ מִהֲרוּ שָׁכְחוּ מַעֲשָׂיו לֹא־
13
not His they They His they His they Then
;works forgot ,hurried .praise sang ;words believed

3453 410 5254 4057 8378 183 6098 2442
14 חִכּוּ לַעֲצָתוֹ׃ וַיִּתְאַוּוּ תַאֲוָה בַּמִּדְבָּר וַיְנַסּוּ־אֵל בִּישִׁימוֹן׃
the in God and the in lust a they and His for they
.desert tempted ,wilderness lusted ;counsel waited

1885 7065 5315 7332 7971 7596 5414
15 וַיִּתֵּן לָהֶם שֶׁאֱלָתָם וַיְשַׁלַּח רָזוֹן בְּנַפְשָׁם׃ וַיְקַנְאוּ לְמֹשֶׁה
16
of they And their into wasting but their to He And
Moses jealous were .soul sent ,request them gave

1885 1104 776 6605 3068 6918 175 4264
17 בַּמַּחֲנֶה לְאַהֲרֹן קְדוֹשׁ יְהוָה׃ תִּפְתַּח־אֶרֶץ וַתִּבְלַע דָּתָן
;Dathan and the opened ;Jehovah holy the ,Aaron of the in
swallowed earth of one camp

3852 5712 784 1167 48 5712 3680
18 וַתְּכַס עַל־עֲדַת אֲבִירָם׃ וַתִּבְעַר־אֵשׁ בַּעֲדָתָם לֶהָבָה
the their in a And .Abiram the over and
flame ;company fire burned of company covered

4541 7812 2722 5695 6213 7563 3857
19 תְּלַהֵט רְשָׁעִים׃ יַעֲשׂוּ־עֵגֶל בְּחֹרֵב וַיִּשְׁתַּחֲווּ לְמַסֵּכָה׃
casted the and in calf a They the consumed
;image worshiped ,Horeb made .wicked

410 7911 6213 398 7794 8403 3519 4171
20 וַיָּמִירוּ אֶת־כְּבוֹדָם בְּתַבְנִית שׁוֹר אֹכֵל עֵשֶׂב׃ שָׁכְחוּ אֵל
21
God They .grass eating ox an the into their they And
forgot of image Glory changed

2526 776 6381 4714 1419 6213 3462
22 מוֹשִׁיעָם עֹשֶׂה גְדֹלוֹת בְּמִצְרָיִם׃ נִפְלָאוֹת בְּאֶרֶץ חָם
;Ham the in wonders ,Egypt in great was (who) their
of land things doing ,Deliverer

972 4872 3884 8045 559 5488 3220 3372
23 נוֹרָאוֹת עַל־יַם־סוּף׃ וַיֹּאמֶר לְהַשְׁמִידָם לוּלֵי מֹשֶׁה בְּחִירוֹ
His Moses except destroy to He And .Reeds the by awesome
one chosen ,them said of Sea things

had stood before Him in the breach, to turn away His wrath from destroying *them*. 24 And they despised the pleasant land; they did not believe His word. 25 And they murmured in their tents, not listening to the voice of Jehovah; 26 and He lifted up His hand to them, to make them fall in the wilderness; 27 to make their seed fall also among the nations, and to scatter them in the lands.

28 They also were joined to Baal-peor, and ate the sacrifices of the dead; 29 and provoked *Him* with their deeds; and a plague broke out among them. 30 Then Phinehas stood and intervened; and the plague was stayed; 31 and it was counted to him for righteousness to generation and generation, forever.

32 And they angered *Him* at the waters of Meribah, and it went ill for Moses because of them; 33 for they provoked his spirit, and he spoke rashly with his lips. 34 They did not destroy the peoples, as Jehovah said to them, 35 but mixed with the nations, and learned their works. 36 And they served their idols, and they became a snare to them. 37 Yea, they sacrificed their sons and their daughters to the demons; 38 and they shed innocent blood, the blood of their sons and of their daughters, whom they sacrificed to the idols of Canaan. And the land was defiled with the blood. 39 And they were unclean with their works, and went whoring in their acts. 40 And the anger of Jehovah burned against His people; and He detested His inheritance. 41 And He gave them into the hand of the nations; and those who hated them ruled over them. 42 And their enemies oppressed them; and they were humbled under their hand. 43 Many times He delivered them, but they rebelled in their plans, and sank in their iniquities. 44 And He looked

24
3985 7843 2534 7725 6440 6556 5975
עָמַד בַּפֶּרֶץ לְפָנָיו לְהָשִׁיב חֲמָתוֹ מֵהַשְׁחִית׃ וַיִּמְאֲסוּ
they And destroying from His turn to before the in stood
despised .(them) wrath away ,Him breach

25
3808 1168 7279 1697 539 3808 2532 776
בְּאֶרֶץ חֶמְדָּה לֹא־הֶאֱמִינוּ לִדְבָרוֹ׃ וַיֵּרָגְנוּ בְאָהֳלֵיהֶם לֹא
not their in they And His they not ;pleasant the
;tents murmured .word believed land

26
4057 5307 3027 5375 3068 6963 8085
שָׁמְעוּ בְּקוֹל יְהוָה׃ וַיִּשָּׂא יָדוֹ לָהֶם לְהַפִּיל אוֹתָם בַּמִּדְבָּר׃
the in them cause to to His He and ;Jehovah the to they
,wilderness fall to ,them hand lifted of voice listened

27
28
1187 6775 776 2219 1471 2233 5307
וּלְהַפִּיל זַרְעָם בַּגּוֹיִם וּלְזָרוֹתָם בָּאֲרָצוֹת׃ וַיִּצָּמְדוּ לְבַעַל
Baal- to they And the in to and the among their cause to and
joined were .lands them scatter ;nations seed fall to

29
6555 4611 3707 4191 2077 398 1187
פְּעוֹר וַיֹּאכְלוּ זִבְחֵי מֵתִים׃ וַיַּכְעִיסוּ בְּמַעַלְלֵיהֶם וַתִּפְרָץ־
and their with provoked and the the ate and ,peor
out broke ;deeds (Him) ;dead of sacrifices

30
4046 6113 6419 6372 5975 4046
בָּם מַגֵּפָה׃ וַיַּעֲמֹד פִּינְחָס וַיְפַלֵּל וַתֵּעָצַר הַמַּגֵּפָה׃
;plague the was and and Phinehas Then .plague a among
restrained ;intervened stood them

31
32
4325 7107 5769 5704 1755 1755 6666 2803
וַתֵּחָשֶׁב לוֹ לִצְדָקָה לְדֹר וָדֹר עַד־עוֹלָם׃ וַיַּקְצִיפוּ עַל־מֵי
the at they And .forever gen- and gen- to righ- for to was it and
of waters (Him) angered eration eration teousness him reckoned

33
981 7307 4784 5668 4872 3415 4808
מְרִיבָה וַיֵּרַע לְמֹשֶׁה בַּעֲבוּרָם׃ כִּי־הִמְרוּ אֶת־רוּחוֹ וַיְבַטֵּא
he and spirit his they because their for for it and ,Meribah
rashly spoke provoked ,sakes Moses ill went

34
3068 559 834 5971 8045 3808 8193
בִּשְׂפָתָיו׃ לֹא־הִשְׁמִידוּ אֶת־הָעַמִּים אֲשֶׁר אָמַר יְהוָה
Jehovah said as the did They not his with
,peoples destroy .lips

35
36
5647 4639 3925 1471 6148
לָהֶם׃ וַיִּתְעָרְבוּ בַגּוֹיִם וַיִּלְמְדוּ מַעֲשֵׂיהֶם׃ וַיַּעַבְדוּ אֶת־
they And their and the with but to
served .works learned nations mixed ,them

37
1121 2076 4170 1961 6091
עֲצַבֵּיהֶם וַיִּהְיוּ לָהֶם לְמוֹקֵשׁ׃ וַיִּזְבְּחוּ אֶת־בְּנֵיהֶם וְאֶת־
and sons their they ,Yea .snare a them to and their
sacrificed became ;idols

38
1323 1121 1818 5355 1818 8210 7700 1323
בְּנוֹתֵיהֶם לַשֵּׁדִים׃ וַיִּשְׁפְּכוּ דָם נָקִי דַּם־בְּנֵיהֶם וּבְנוֹתֵיהֶם
their and their the inno- blood they and the to their
,daughters sons of blood ,cent shed ,demons daughters

39
2930 1818 776 2610 3667 6091 2076 834
אֲשֶׁר זִבְּחוּ לַעֲצַבֵּי כְנָעַן וַתֶּחֱנַף הָאָרֶץ בַּדָּמִים׃ וַיִּטְמְאוּ
they So the with the was and ;Canaan the to they whom
unclean were .blood land defiled of idols sacrificed

40
5971 3068 639 2734 4611 2181 4639
בְמַעֲשֵׂיהֶם וַיִּזְנוּ בְּמַעַלְלֵיהֶם׃ וַיִּחַר־אַף יְהוָה בְּעַמּוֹ
against Jehovah the And .acts their in went and their by
;people His of anger burned whoring ,works

41
4910 1471 3027 5414 5159 8581
וַיְתָעֵב אֶת־נַחֲלָתוֹ׃ וַיִּתְּנֵם בְּיַד־גּוֹיִם וַיִּמְשְׁלוּ בָהֶם
over ruled and ,nations the into He And His He and
them of hand them gave .inheritance abhorred

42
43
6471 3027 8478 3665 341 3905 8130
שֹׂנְאֵיהֶם׃ וַיִּלְחָצוּם אוֹיְבֵיהֶם וַיִּכָּנְעוּ תַּחַת יָדָם׃ פְּעָמִים
times their under they and their oppressed And who those
.hand humbled were ,enemies them .them hated

44
7200 5771 4355 6098 4784 5337 7227
רַבּוֹת יַצִּילֵם וְהֵמָּה יַמְרוּ בַעֲצָתָם וַיָּמֹכּוּ בַּעֲוֹנָם׃ וַיַּרְא
He And their in and their in rebelled but He Many
looked .iniquities sank ,counsel they ,them delivered

on their affliction when
He heard their shout;
[45]He remembered *His*
covenant for them and
breathed a sigh accord-
ing to His many mercies.
[46]And He gave them to
tender mercies before
the face of all their
captors.
[47]Save us, O Jehovah
our God, and gather us
from the nations, to give
thanks to Your holy name,
to exult in Your praise.
[48]Blessed *is* Jehovah
God of Israel, from ever-
lasting even to everlast-
ing. And let all the people
say, Amen! Praise
Jehovah!

PSALM 107

[1]Give thanks to Jehovah,
for *He is* good; for His
mercy *endures* forever.
[2]Let the redeemed of
Jehovah say *so*; whom He
redeemed from the hand of
the foe; [3]and gathered
them from the lands; from
east and from west; from
north and from south.
[4]They wandered in the
wilderness, in a desert way;
they found no city of
dwelling; [5]hungry and
thirsty, their soul fainted in
them; [6]and they cried to
Jehovah in their distress;
He delivered them from
their straits. [7]And He
guided them in the right
way; to go to a city of
dwelling. [8]Let them thank
Jehovah *for* His mercy; and
His wonders to the sons of
man. [9]He satisfies the
thirsty soul, and He fills the
hungry soul *with* good.
[10]Those who live in the
darkness, and in the
shadow of death, *being*
prisoners in affliction and
iron—[11]because they re-
belled against the words of
God, and despised the
counsel of the Most High;
—[12]and He humbled their
heart by toil; they stumbled,
and none *were* helping;
[13]and they cried to Jehovah
in their distress; He saved
them out of their distresses;

1285 2142 7440 8085 6862
45 בצר להם בשמעו את־רנתם׃ ויזכר להם בריתו
His for He and ;shout their He when to the on
,covenant them remembered heard them affliction

3605 64 40 7356 5414 2617 72 30 51 62
46 וינחם כרב חסדו׃ ויתן אותם לרחמים לפני כל־
all before tender to them He And His according and
mercies gave .mercies many to ,sighed

1471 6908 430 3068 3467 7617
47 שוביהם׃ הושיענו ׀ יהוה אלהינו וקבצנו מן־הגוים
the from and ;God our O ,us Save their
,nations us gather Jehovah .captors

3068 1288 8416 7623 6944 8034 3034
48 להודות לשם קדשך להשתבח בתהלתך׃ ברוך יהוה ׀
Jehovah Blessed Your in boast to Your the to give to
(is) .praise ,holiness of name thanks

5971 3605 559 5769 5704 5769 3478 430
אלהי ישראל מן־העולם ׀ ועד העולם ואמר כל־העם
the all let and ;everlasting even everlast- from ,Israel of God
,people say to ing

1984 543
אמן הללו־יה׃
Praise !Amen
!Jehovah

PSAL. CVII קז

PSALM 107

3068 1350 559 2617 5769 2896 3068 3034
1
2 הדו ליהוה כי־טוב כי לעולם חסדו׃ יאמרו גאולי יהוה
,Jehovah the say Let His forever for (is He) for to Give
of redeemed (so) .mercy (is) ;good ,Jehovah thanks

4628 4217 6908 776 6862 1350 834
3 אשר גאלם מיד־צר׃ ומארצות קבצם ממזרח וממערב
from and from gathered from and the the from He whom
,west ,east ,them lands ,foe of hand redeemed

3808 4186 5892 1870 3452 4057 8582 3220 6828
4 מצפון ומים׃ תעו במדבר בישימון דרך עיר מושב לא
not dwelling a ;way a in the in They from and from
of city desert ,wilderness wandered .south ,north

6817 5848 53 15 6771 1571 7457 4672
5
6 מצאו׃ רעבים גם־צמאים נפשם בהם תתעטף׃ ויצעקו
they and —fainted them in their ,thirsty and hungry they
cried soul —found

1869 5337 4691 6862 3068
7 אל־יהוה בצר להם ממצוקותיהם יצילם׃ וידריכם
He And delivered He their from to the in Jehovah to
them guided .them straits ;them distress

2617 3068 3034 4186 5892 3212 3477 1870
8 בדרך ישרה ללכת אל־עיר מושב׃ יודו ליהוה חסדו
His (for) Jehovah them Let .dwelling a to go to ;right the in
;mercy thank of city way

5315 8264 5315 7646 120 1121 63 81
9 ונפלאותיו לבני אדם׃ כי־השביע נפש שקקה ונפש
the and ,thirsty the He For .man the to His and
soul soul satisfies of sons wonders

1270 6040 615 6757 2822 3427 2896 4390 74 56
10 רעבה מלא־טוב׃ ישבי חשך וצלמות אסירי עני וברזל׃
and affliction prison- deep in and dark- Those (with) he hungry
—iron of ers ,shadow ness in living .good fills

3820 5999 3665 5006 59 45 6098 410 561 4784
11
12 כי־המרו אמרי־אל ועצת עליון נאצו׃ ויכנע בעמל לבם
their toil by He And .spurned the the and ,God the they for
;heart subdued High Most of counsel of words at rebelled

46 91 6862 3068 2199 5826 369 3782
13 כשלו ואין עזר׃ ויזעקו אל־יהוה בצר להם ממצוקותיהם
their from to the in Jehovah to they and help- was and they
straits ;them distress cried —ing none stumbled

[14]He brought them out from darkness and the shadow of death; and He broke their bands apart. [15]Let them thank Jehovah *for* His mercy, and His wonders to the sons of man. [16]For He has broken the gates of bronze; and He cut bars of iron in two.

[17]Fools are afflicted from the way of their rebellion, and from their iniquities; [18]their soul hates every food; and they touch the gates of death; [19]and they cried to Jehovah in their distress; He saved them from their straits; [20]He sent His word and healed them; and delivered *them* from all their pitfalls. [21]Let them thank Jehovah *for* His mercy, and His wonders to the sons of man. [22]And let them sacrifice the sacrifices of thanksgiving; and recount His works with rejoicing.

[23]They who go down to the sea in ships, who work in the great waters; [24]these see the works of Jehovah, and His wonders in the deep. [25]For He speaks and raises stormy wind, and makes its waves high; [26]they go up to the heavens; they go down *to* the depths; their soul is melted because *they are* in evil; [27]they reel and stagger like a drunken man; and all their wisdom is swallowed up; [28]and they cry to Jehovah in their distress; and He saves them out of their straits. [29]He settles the storm to a whisper, so that its waves are still; [30]and they are glad, because they are quiet; and He led them to their desired haven. [31]Let them thank Jehovah *for* His mercy, and His wonders to the sons of mankind; [32]and exalt Him in the congregation of the people; and praise Him in the seat of the elders.

[33]He sets rivers to a wilderness, and water-springs to thirsty ground; [34]a fruitful land to a salty desert; because of the

14 יושיעם׃ יוציאם מחשך וצלמות ומוסרותיהם ינתק׃
5423 4147 6757 2822 3318 3462
broke He .off | their and bands | deep and ,shadow | from darkness | brought He out them | saved He ;them

15 16 יודו ליהוה חסדו ונפלאותיו לבני אדם׃ כי־שבר דלתות
1817 7665 120 1121 6381 2617 3068 3034
of gates | has He For broken | .man | the to of sons | His and wonders | (for) Jehovah ,mercy His | They thank

17 נחשת ובריחי ברזל גדע׃ אולים מדרך פשעם
6588 1870 191 1438 1270 1280 5178
their revolt | the from of way | ,Fools | cut He .two in | iron | bars and of | ,bronze

18 ומעונתיהם יתענו׃ כל־אכל תתעב נפשם ויגיעו עד
5704 5060 5315 8581 400 3605 6031 5771
to | they and reach | their ;soul | hates | .food every | are ;afflicted | from and ,iniquities their

19 שערי־מות׃ ויזעקו אל־יהוה בצר להם ממצוקותיהם
4691 6862 3068 2199 4194 8179
their from straits | to ;them | the in distress | Jehovah to | they then cried | ;death | the of gates

20 יושיעם׃ ישלח דברו וירפאם וימלט משחיתותם׃
7825 4422 7495 1697 7971 3462
their all from .pit-falls | and delivers | heals and ,them | His word | He sends | saves He ;them

21 22 יודו ליהוה חסדו ונפלאותיו לבני אדם׃ ויזבחו זבחי
2077 2076 120 1121 6381 2617 3068 3034
sacrifices of | And sacrifice they | .man | the to of sons | His and wonders | His (for) ,mercy | Jehovah | They thank

23 תודה ויספרו מעשיו ברנה׃ יורדי הים באניות עשי
6213 591 3220 3381 7440 4639 5608 8426
who do | in ,ships | the sea | who Those to down go | with !rejoicing | His works | and recount | thanks- ,giving

24 מלאכה במים רבים׃ המה ראו מעשי יהוה ונפלאותיו
6381 3068 4639 7200 7227 4325 4399
His and wonders | ,Jehovah | the of works | see | these | ,great | in waters | work

25 במצולה׃ ויאמר ויעמד רוח סערה ותרומם גליו׃
1530 7311 5592 7307 5975 559 4688
its ;waves | it and high makes | ,storm | wind a of | and raises | He For ,speaks | the in .deep

26 יעלו שמים ירדו תהומות נפשם ברעה תתמוגג׃
4127 7451 5315 8415 3381 8064 5927
;melted is | evil in | their soul | the (to) ;depths | go they down | (to) ;heaven | they on go

27 28 יחוגו וינועו כשכור וכל־חכמתם תתבלע׃ ויצעקו אל־
6817 1104 2451 3605 7910 5128 2287
to | they then cry | swallowed is ;up | their wisdom | and all | a like ;drunkard | they stagger | they ;reel

29 יהוה בצר להם וממצקתיהם יוציאם׃ יקם סערה
5592 6965 3318 4691 6862 3068
the storm | He settles | brings He .out them | their from and straits | to ;them | the in distress | Jehovah

30 לדממה ויחשו גליהם׃ וישמחו כי־ישתקו וינחם אל־
5148 8367 8056 1530 2814 1827
to | He so them led | they for ;quiet are | they then ,glad are | its ;waves | that so still are | a to ,whisper

31 מחוז חפצם׃ יודו ליהוה חסדו ונפלאותיו לבני אדם׃
120 1121 6381 2617 3068 3034 2656 4231
.man | the to of sons | His and wonders | His (for) ,mercy | Jehovah | They thank | their .desire of | the haven

32 33 וירוממוהו בקהל עם ובמושב זקנים יהללוהו׃ ישם
7760 1984 2205 4186 5971 6951 7311
sets He | praise .Him | the elders | the in and of seat | the ;people | the in of assembly | exalt And Him

34 נהרות למדבר ומצאי מים לצמאון׃ ארץ פרי למלחה
4420 6529 776 6774 4325 4161 4057 5104
salty to ;desert | fruit | a of land | thirsty to ;ground | water | and of springs | a to ,wilderness | rivers

wickedness of those who live in it. [35]He puts the wilderness into a water-pond; and dry land into water-springs; [36]and He makes the hungry live there, and they may prepare a city of dwelling. [37]And they sow the fields, and plant vineyards, and make fruits of produce. [38]He also blesses them, so that they multiply greatly; and He does not allow their cattle to diminish; [39]but they are diminished and humbled, from coercion, evil and grief. [40]He pours scorn on nobles, and causes them to wander in a desert; there *is* no path. [41]But He raises the poor up from affliction, and He sets families like a flock. [42]The upright shall see and be glad; and all iniquity shuts its mouth. [43]Whoever *is* wise, and will observe these things, they shall discern the mercies of Jehovah.

35 מֵרָעַת יֹשְׁבֵי בָהּ׃ יָשֵׂם מִדְבָּר לַאֲגַם־מַיִם וְאֶרֶץ צִיָּה
6723 776 4325 98 4057 7760 3427 7451
dry | and land | ,water | a to of pool | the wilderness | puts He | .it in | who those dwell | the from of evil

36 לְמֹצָאֵי מָיִם׃ וַיּוֹשֶׁב שָׁם רְעֵבִים וַיְכוֹנְנוּ עִיר מוֹשָׁב׃
4186 5892 3559 7456 8033 3427 4325 4161
.dwelling | a of city | they and prepare | hungry ,ones | there | He and live makes | ;water | to of springs

37 38 וַיִּזְרְעוּ שָׂדוֹת וַיִּטְּעוּ כְרָמִים וַיַּעֲשׂוּ פְּרִי תְבוּאָה׃ וַיְבָרְכֵם
1288 8393 6529 6213 3754 5193 7704 2232
also He ,them blesses | .produce | fruit of | and make | ,vineyards | and plant | fields | they And sow

39 וַיִּרְבּוּ מְאֹד וּבְהֶמְתָּם לֹא יַמְעִיט׃ וַיִּמְעֲטוּ וַיָּשֹׁחוּ מֵעֹצֶר
6115 7817 4591 4591 3808 929 3966 7235
through ,coercion | put ,down | and they but diminish | lets He ;diminish | not | their and cattle | ;greatly | and multiplies

40 רָעָה וְיָגוֹן׃ שֹׁפֵךְ בּוּז עַל־נְדִיבִים וַיַּתְעֵם בְּתֹהוּ לֹא־
3808 8414 8582 5081 937 8210 3015 7451
not | a in ;waste | makes and wander them | ,nobles | on | scorn (is He) pouring | and .grief | evil

41 42 דָּרֶךְ׃ וַיְשַׂגֵּב אֶבְיוֹן מֵעוֹנִי וַיָּשֶׂם כַּצֹּאן מִשְׁפָּחוֹת׃ יִרְאוּ
7200 4940 6629 7760 6040 34 7682 1870
Shall see | .families | a like flock | He and sets | from ;affliction | the needy | set He And high on | a (is) .path

43 יְשָׁרִים וְיִשְׂמָחוּ וְכָל־עַוְלָה קָפְצָה פִּיהָ׃ מִי־חָכָם וְיִשְׁמָר־
8104 2450 6310 7092 5766 3605 8055 3477
will and keep | (is) wise | Who | its .mouth | shuts | wickedness | and all | be and ;glad | the upright

אֵלֶּה וְיִתְבּוֹנְנוּ חַסְדֵי יְהוָה׃
3068 2617 995 428
.Jehovah | the of mercies | they For discern | these ?things

PSAL. CVIII קח

PSALM 108

PSALM 108

A Song or Pasl of David.

[1]O God, my heart is fixed; I will sing; yea, I will sing songs even *with* my glory. [2]Awake, harp and lyre! I will awake early; [3]I will thank You, O Jehovah, among the peoples; and I will sing to You among the nations. [4]For Your mercy *is* great above the heavens; and Your truth *reaches* to the clouds. [5]Be lifted up, O God, above the heavens; and Your glory above all the earth; [6]so that Your beloved may be delivered; save *by* Your right hand and answer me.

[7]God has spoken in His holiness; I will rejoice; I will portion out Shechem; and I will measure out the valley of Succoth. [8]Gilead *is* Mine; *and* Manasseh *is* Mine; and Ephraim *is* the fort *of* My head; Judah *is* My lawgiver; [9]Moab *is* My washpot; I will throw My shoe out over Edom; I will

1 2 שִׁיר מִזְמוֹר לְדָוִד׃ נָכוֹן לִבִּי אֱלֹהִים אָשִׁירָה וַאֲזַמְּרָה
2167 7891 430 3820 3559 1732 4210 7892
will I ,yea songs sing | sing will I | ;God O | My ,heart | is fixed | .David of | psalm A | .song A

3 4 אַף־כְּבוֹדִי׃ עוּרָה הַנֵּבֶל וְכִנּוֹר אָעִירָה שָּׁחַר׃ אוֹדְךָ
3034 7837 5782 3658 5035 5782 3519 637
will I You thank | ;early | will I awake | ;lyre and | harp | ,Awake | (with) .glory my | even

5 בָעַמִּים ׀ יְהוָה וַאֲזַמֶּרְךָ בַּלְאֻמִּים׃ כִּי־גָדוֹל מֵעַל־שָׁמַיִם
8064 5921 1419 3816 2167 3068 5971
the heavens | above | (is) For great | the among .nations | will I and You to sing | ;Jehovah | the among ,peoples

6 חַסְדֶּךָ וְעַד־שְׁחָקִים אֲמִתֶּךָ׃ רוּמָה עַל־שָׁמַיִם אֱלֹהִים
430 8064 7311 571 7834 5704 2617
;God O | the ,heavens | above | lifted Be up | Your .truth | the (is) clouds | even to | Your ;mercy

7 וְעַל כָּל־הָאָרֶץ כְּבוֹדֶךָ׃ לְמַעַן יֵחָלְצוּן יְדִידֶיךָ הוֹשִׁיעָה
3467 3039 2502 3519 776 3605
(by) save | Your ;ones beloved | be may delivered | that so | Your ;glory | the earth | all | and above

8 יְמִינְךָ וַעֲנֵנִי׃ אֱלֹהִים ׀ דִּבֶּר בְּקָדְשׁוֹ אֶעְלֹזָה אֲחַלְּקָה שְׁכֶם
7927 2505 5937 6944 1696 430 6030 3225
;Shechem | will I out portion | will I ;rejoice | His in ;holiness | has spoken | God | answer and .me | Your hand right

9 וְעֵמֶק סֻכּוֹת אֲמַדֵּד׃ לִי גִלְעָד ׀ לִי מְנַשֶּׁה וְאֶפְרַיִם מָעוֹז
4581 669 4519 1568 4058 5523 6010
the (is) fort | and Ephraim | (is) ,Manasseh | to Me | (is) ;Gilead | To Me | will I .out measure | Succoth | the and of valley

10 רֹאשִׁי יְהוּדָה מְחֹקְקִי׃ מוֹאָב ׀ סִיר רַחְצִי עַל־אֱדוֹם
123 7366 5518 4124 2710 3063 7218
Edom | over | My ;washing | pot the of | Moab (is) | My (is) ;lawgiver | Judah | My (of) ;head

shout in triumph over Philistia. [10]Who will lead me into the fortified city? Who will lead me over Edom? [11]O God, have You not cast us off? And, O God, will You not go out with our armies? [12]Give help to us from distress; for the deliverance of man *is* vain. [13]In God we shall do mighty things, for He shall trample our foes.

11 אשליך נעלי עלי פלשת אתרועע: מי יבלני עיר מבצר

the city lead will Who shout will I Philistia over My throw will I
;fortified into me .triumph in ;shoe

12 מי נחני עד־אדום: הלא־אלהים זנחתנו ולא־תצא אלהים

,God O will You And cast You ,God O Have ?Edom over leads who
,out go not ?off us ,not me

13 בצבאתינו: הבה־לנו עזרת מצר ושוא תשועת אדם:

.man the (is) for from help us to Give our with
of deliverance vanity ;distress ?armies

14 באלהים נעשה־חיל והוא יבוס צרינו:

our shall for mighty shall we God In
.foes trample He ,things do

PSAL. CIX קט

PSALM 109

PSALM 109

To the Chief Musician, A Psalm of David.

[1]O God of my praise, do not be silent; [2]for the mouth of the wicked, and the deceitful mouth, are opened against me; they spoke against me *with* a lying tongue. [3]And they hemmed me in *with* words of hatred; and fought against me without a cause. [4]In return for my love, they are my enemies; but I *am in* prayer. [5]And they put on me evil for good; and hatred for my love. [6]Set a wicked man over him; and let a foe stand at his right hand; [7]when he is judged, let him go out wicked; and let his prayer become sin; [8]let his days be few; and let another take his office; [9]let his sons be orphans, and his wife a widow; [10]and let his sons always beg and wander, and seek *food* out of their ruins; [11]let the money-lender lay a snare for all that *is* his; and let strangers plunder his labor; [12]let there be none giving mercy to him; nor *any* to have pity on his orphans; [13]let his posterity be cut off; let their name be blotted out in the following generation; [14]let the iniquity of his fathers be remembered to Jehovah; and let not the sin of his mother be blotted out; [15]let them be always before Jehovah, so that He may cut off the memory of them

1 2 למנצח לדוד מזמור אלהי תהלתי אל־תחרש: כי פי

the For be do not my God O .psalm A of chief the To
of mouth .silent ,praise of David .musician

3 רשע ופי־מרמה עלי פתחו דברו אתי לשון שקר: ודברי

(with) and false- a (with) against they they against mouth the and the
of words .hood of tongue me spoke ;opened me deceit of ,wicked

4 שנאה סבבוני וילחמוני חנם: תחת־אהבתי ישטנוני

are they ,love my Instead without fought and en- They hatred
;foes my of .cause a me against me circled

5 ואני תפלה: וישימו עלי רעה תחת טובה ושנאה תחת

for and ;good for evil me on they And (in) I but
hatred put .prayer (am)

6 אהבתי: הפקד עליו רשע ושטן יעמד על־ימינו:

right his at let a and wicked a over Set .love my
;hand stand foe ,man him

7 8 בהשפטו יצא רשע ותפלתו תהיה לחטאה: יהיו־ימיו

his let ;sin let his and ;wicked him let is he when
days be become prayer forth go ,judged

9 מעטים פקדתו יקח אחר: יהיו־בניו יתומים ואשתו

his and ;orphans his let ;another let his and ;few
wife sons be take office

10 אלמנה: ונוע ינועו בניו ושאלו ודרשו מחרבותיהם:

their of out seek and ,beg and his let and ;widow a
;ruins (food) ,sons wander always

11 12 ינקש נושה לכל־אשר־לו ויבזו זרים יגיעו: אל־יהי־לו

to Let not his strangers let and to that for the lay let
him be .labor plunder ;him (is) all exactor snare a

13 משך חסד ואל־יהי חונן ליתומיו: יהי־אחריתו להכרית

cutting a his Let his on (one) let nor ;mercy giving
;off posterity be .orphans pity having be

14 בדור אחר ימח שמם: יזכר | עון אבתיו אל־יהוה

;Jehovah to his the be Let their be let following the in
fathers of iniquity recalled .name out blotted generation

15 וחטאת אמו אל־תמח: יהיו נגד־יהוה תמיד ויכרת

He that always Jehovah before Let be let not his the and
off cut may be them .out blotted mother of sin

from the earth; [16]because
he did not remember to do
mercy; and persecuted the
poor and needy man; even
to kill the broken-hearted.
[17]Yea, he loved cursing, and
it came to him; he also had
no pleasure in blessing, and
it was far from him. [18]As
he clothed himself with
cursing, as with a robe,
even it came into his
bowels like water, and like
oil into his bones. [19]Let it be
to him as a garment he
wraps in, and for a girdle
that he always girds on.

[20]This *is* the reward of my
foes from Jehovah, and *of*
those who speak evil
against my soul. [21]But You,
O Jehovah the Lord, work
with me for Your name's
sake; deliver me because
Your mercy *is* good. [22]For I
am poor and needy, and my
heart is pierced within me.
[23]As a shadow when it
stretches out, I am gone; I
am shaken off like the
locust. [24]My knees stumble
from fasting, and my flesh
grows lean from fatness.
[25]And I have become a
reproach to them; they
looked at me; they shook
their heads. [26]O Jehovah
my God, help me; save me
according to Your mercy;
[27]and they will know that
this *is* Your hand; that You,
O Jehovah, have done it.
[28]They will curse, but You
will bless; they rise up and
are ashamed; but Your
servant will be glad. [29]Let
those who accuse me be
clothed with shame; and
cover themselves in their
shame as with a robe. [30]I
will greatly thank Jehovah
with my mouth; yea, I will
praise Him in the midst of
the multitude. [31]For He shall
stand at the right hand of
the needy; to save from
those judging his soul.

16 מֵאֶרֶץ זִכְרָם׃ יַעַן אֲשֶׁר לֹא־זָכַר עֲשׂוֹת חָסֶד וַיִּרְדֹּף אִישׁ־

the from earth | their memory | because | did he not remember | do to | ;mercy | and persecuted | the man

17 עָנִי וְאֶבְיוֹן וְנִכְאֵה לֵבָב לְמוֹתֵת׃ וַיֶּאֱהַב קְלָלָה וַתְּבוֹאֵהוּ

poor | and ,needy | and the broken of | heart | .kill to | And he loved | ,cursing | and it came to him

18 וְלֹא־חָפֵץ בִּבְרָכָה וַתִּרְחַק מִמֶּנּוּ׃ וַיִּלְבַּשׁ קְלָלָה כְּמַדּוֹ

And not had he pleasure | in ,blessing | but it was far | from .him | And he put on | cursing | as his robe

19 וַתָּבֹא כַמַּיִם בְּקִרְבּוֹ וְכַשֶּׁמֶן בְּעַצְמוֹתָיו׃ תְּהִי־לוֹ כְּבֶגֶד

and it came | as water | into his ,body | and as oil | into his .bones | Let it be to him | as a garment

20 יַעְטֶה וּלְמֵזַח תָּמִיד יַחְגְּרֶהָ׃ זֹאת פְּעֻלַּת שֹׂטְנַי מֵאֵת יְהוָה

he wraps ,in | and for a belt | always | he girds .on it | This (is) | the reward of | my foes | from ;Jehovah

21 וְהַדֹּבְרִים רָע עַל־נַפְשִׁי׃ וְאַתָּה יְהוִה אֲדֹנָי עֲשֵׂה־אִתִּי

and (of) those who speak | evil | against my .soul | But ,You | O Jehovah | ,Lord | work | with ,me

22 לְמַעַן שְׁמֶךָ כִּי־טוֹב חַסְדְּךָ הַצִּילֵנִי׃ כִּי־עָנִי וְאֶבְיוֹן אָנֹכִי

for Your name's sake; | because good (is) | Your mercy | deliver .me | For poor | and needy | I (am),

23 וְלִבִּי חָלַל בְּקִרְבִּי׃ כְּצֵל־כִּנְטוֹתוֹ נֶהֱלָכְתִּי נִנְעַרְתִּי

and my heart | (is) pierced | within .me | As a shadow | when it stretches out | I am ;gone | I am shaken off

24 25 כָּאַרְבֶּה׃ בִּרְכַּי כָּשְׁלוּ מִצּוֹם וּבְשָׂרִי כָּחַשׁ מִשָּׁמֶן׃ וַאֲנִי

like the .locust | My knees | stumble | from ,fasting | and my flesh | grows lean | from .fatness | And I

26 הָיִיתִי חֶרְפָּה לָהֶם יִרְאוּנִי יְנִיעוּן רֹאשָׁם׃ עָזְרֵנִי יְהוָה

have become | a reproach | to ;them | they saw ;me | they shook | their .heads | Help ,me | O Jehovah

27 אֱלֹהָי הוֹשִׁיעֵנִי כְחַסְדֶּךָ׃ וְיֵדְעוּ כִּי־יָדְךָ זֹּאת אַתָּה יְהוָה

my ;God | save me | by Your ;mercy | and they will know | that Your hand | this ;(is) | (that) ,You | O ,Jehovah

28 עֲשִׂיתָהּ׃ יְקַלְלוּ־הֵמָּה וְאַתָּה תְבָרֵךְ קָמוּ וַיֵּבֹשׁוּ וְעַבְדְּךָ

have .it done | will curse ,They | but You | will I ;bless | they rise ,up | and are ;ashamed | but Your servant

29 30 יִשְׂמָח׃ יִלְבְּשׁוּ שׂוֹטְנַי כְּלִמָּה וְיַעֲטוּ כַמְעִיל בָּשְׁתָּם׃ אוֹדֶה

be will .glad | Let put on | my foes | disgrace | and wrap themselves | as with a robe | in their .shame | I will thank

31 יְהוָה מְאֹד בְּפִי וּבְתוֹךְ רַבִּים אֲהַלְלֶנּוּ׃ כִּי־יַעֲמֹד לִימִין

Jehovah | greatly | with my ;mouth | and in the midst of | many | I will praise .Him | For He shall stand | at right hand

אֶבְיוֹן לְהוֹשִׁיעַ מִשֹּׁפְטֵי נַפְשׁוֹ׃

the ,needy's | to save | from those judging | his .soul

PSAL. CX קי

PSALM 110

A Psalm of David.

[1]A statement of Jehovah
to my Lord: Sit at My right
hand, until I place Your

1 לְדָוִד מִזְמוֹר נְאֻם יְהוָה לַאדֹנִי שֵׁב לִימִינִי עַד־אָשִׁית

of David | A .psalm | A statement | Jehovah | to my :Lord | Sit | at My right ,hand | until | I set enemies *as* Your footstool. [2]Jehovah shall send the rod of Your strength out of Zion; rule in the midst of Your enemies. [3]Your people *shall be* willing in the day of Your power; in the majesties of holiness from the womb of the dawn, to You *is* the dew of Your youth. [4]Jehovah has sworn and will not repent: You *are* a priest forever according to the order of Melchizedek. [5]The Lord at Your right hand shatters kings in the day of His anger. [6]He shall judge among the nations; He shall fill with dead bodies; He shall shatter heads over much land. [7]He shall drink out of the brook on the way; on this account He shall lift up the head.

7287 6726 3068 7971 5797 4294 7272 1916 341

2 אֹיְבֶיךָ הֲדֹם לְרַגְלֶיךָ׃ מַטֵּה עֻזְּךָ יִשְׁלַח יְהוָה מִצִּיּוֹן רְדֵה

rule of out Jehovah shall Your rod The Your for stool a Your
;Zion send strength of .feet enemies

6944 1926 2428 3117 5071 5971 341 7130

3 בְּקֶרֶב אֹיְבֶיךָ׃ עַמְּךָ נְדָבֹת בְּיוֹם חֵילֶךָ בְּהַדְרֵי־קֹדֶשׁ

;holiness the in Your the in (be shall) Your Your the in
of majesties ;might of day willing people .enemies of midst

5162 3808 3068 7650 3208 2919 4891 7355

4 מֵרֶחֶם מִשְׁחָר לְךָ טַל יַלְדֻתֶיךָ׃ נִשְׁבַּע יְהוָה ׀ וְלֹא יִנָּחֵם

will and Jehovah has Your the to ,dawn the the from
;repent not sworn .youth of dew You of womb

136 4442 1700 5921 5769 3548

5 אַתָּה־כֹהֵן לְעוֹלָם עַל־דִּבְרָתִי מַלְכִּי־צֶדֶק׃ אֲדֹנָי עַל־

at Lord The .Melchizedek the according forever a You
of order to priest (are)

1472 4390 1471 7777 4428 639 3117 4272 3225

6 יְמִינְךָ מָחַץ בְּיוֹם־אַפּוֹ מְלָכִים׃ יָדִין בַּגּוֹיִם מָלֵא גְוִיּוֹת

with will He the in shall He .kings His the in shatters Your
;corpses fill ;nations judge anger of day hand right

8354 1870 5158 7227 776 7218 7272

7 מָחַץ רֹאשׁ עַל־אֶרֶץ רַבָּה׃ מִנַּחַל בַּדֶּרֶךְ יִשְׁתֶּה עַל־כֵּן

therefore shall He the in the From .much land over heads will He
;drink way brook shatter

7218 7311

יָרִים רֹאשׁ׃

the shall He
.head up lift

PSAL. CXI קיא

PSALM 111

[1]Praise Jehovah! I will thank Jehovah with all *my* heart; in the council of the upright, and of the assembly. [2]The works of Jehovah *are* great, sought out by all those desiring them. [3]His work *is* honorable and glorious; and His righteousness endures forever. [4]He has made a memorial for His wonders; Jehovah *is* gracious and full of pity. [5]He has given food to those who fear Him; He will always remember His covenant. [6]He has shown to His people the power of His works, to give to them inheritance of the nations. [7]The works of His hands *are* truth and judgment; all His commandments *are* true, [8]standing firm forever and ever; *they are* done in truth and uprightness. [9]He sent redemption to His people; He has commanded His covenant forever; holy and awesome *is* His name. [10]The fear of Jehovah *is* the beginning of wisdom; all who practice them *have* a good understanding; His praise is standing forever!

5712 3477 5475 3824 3605 3068 3034 1984

1 הַלְלוּ יָהּ ׀ אוֹדֶה יְהוָה בְּכָל־לֵבָב בְּסוֹד יְשָׁרִים וְעֵדָה׃

the of and the the in the with Jehovah will I Praise
.assembly ,upright of council ;heart all thank ;Jehovah

1926 1935 2656 3605 1875 3068 4639 1419

2
3 גְּדֹלִים מַעֲשֵׂי יְהוָה דְּרוּשִׁים לְכָל־חֶפְצֵיהֶם׃ הוֹד־וְהָדָר

and Honorable desiring those by out sought ,Jehovah the Great
glorious .them all of works (are)

2587 6381 6213 2143 5703 5975 6666 6467

4 פָּעֳלוֹ וְצִדְקָתוֹ עֹמֶדֶת לָעַד׃ זֵכֶר עָשָׂה לְנִפְלְאוֹתָיו חַנּוּן

gracious His for has He A .forever endures His and His (is)
;wonders made memorial righteousness ,work

3581 1285 5769 2142 3373 5414 2964 3068 7349

5
6 וְרַחוּם יְהוָה׃ טֶרֶף נָתַן לִירֵאָיו יִזְכֹּר לְעוֹלָם בְּרִיתוֹ׃ כֹּחַ

The His to will He His to He Food (is) full and
of power .covenant forever remember ;fearers gave .Jehovah pity of

3027 4639 1471 5159 5414 5971 5046 4639

7 מַעֲשָׂיו הִגִּיד לְעַמּוֹ לָתֵת לָהֶם נַחֲלַת גּוֹיִם׃ מַעֲשֵׂי יָדָיו

His works The the inheritance to give to His to has He His
hands of .nations of them ,people shown works

5769 5703 5564 6490 3605 539 4941 571

8 אֱמֶת וּמִשְׁפָּט נֶאֱמָנִים כָּל־פִּקּוּדָיו׃ סְמוּכִים לָעַד לְעוֹלָם

,ever and forever standing His all (are) true and (are)
firm ,commands ;judgment truth

5769 6680 5971 7971 6304 3477 571 6213

9 עֲשׂוּיִם בֶּאֱמֶת וְיָשָׁר׃ פְּדוּת ׀ שָׁלַח לְעַמּוֹ צִוָּה־לְעוֹלָם

forever has He His to sent He Redemption and truth in being
commanded ;people .uprightness done

3068 3373 2451 7225 8034 3372 6918 1285

10 בְּרִיתוֹ קָדוֹשׁ וְנוֹרָא שְׁמוֹ׃ רֵאשִׁית חָכְמָה ׀ יִרְאַת יְהוָה

;Jehovah the(is) wisdom be- the His (is) and holy His
of fear of ginning .name awesome ;covenant

5703 5975 8416 6213 3605 2896 7922

שֵׂכֶל טוֹב לְכָל־עֹשֵׂיהֶם תְּהִלָּתוֹ עֹמֶדֶת לָעַד׃

!forever is praise His practicing to (is) good under- a
standing ;them all standing

PSAL. CXII קיב

PSALM 112

3966 2654 4687 3068 3372 376 835 3068/1984

1 הללו יה | אשרי-איש ירא את-יהוה במצותיו חפץ מאד:

.greatly he His in ;Jehovah who the Blessed Praise
delights commands fears man (is) !Jehovah

6239 1952 1288 3477 1755 2233 1961 776 1368

2
3 גבור בארץ יהיה זרעו דור ישרים יברך: הון-ועשר

and wealth be shall the gen- the his shall the on Mighty
riches ;blessed upright of eration ;seed be earth

3477 216 2822 2224 5703 5975 6666 1004

4 בביתו וצדקתו עמדת לעד: זרח בחשך אור לישרים

the to Light the in rises .forever is his and his in
;upright darkness standing righteousness ;house

1697 3557 3867 2003 376 2896 6662 7349 2557

5 חנון ורחום וצדיק: טוב-איש חונן ומלוה יכלכל דבריו

his will he and showing a Good and full and (is he)
matters nourish ;lending favor man (is) .righteous ,pity of ,gracious

6662 1961 4131 5769 2143 3808 5769 3588 4941

6 במשפט: כי-לעולם לא-ימוט לזכר עולם יהיה צדיק:

the be shall forever a for will he not forever For with
.righteous memorial ;shaken be .justice

5564 3068 982 3820 3559 3372 3808 7451 8052

7
8 משמועה רעה לא יירא נכון לבו בטח ביהוה: סמוך

(is) in trusting his is will he not Bad news
upheld .Jehovah ,heart fixed .fear

34 5414 6340 6862 7200 5704 3372 3808 3820

9 לבו לא יירא עד אשר-יראה בצריו: פזר | נתן לאביונים

the to has he has He his upon he until shall he not His
;needy given ;scattered .foes looks fear ;heart

7200 7563 3519 7311 7161 5703 5975 6666

10 צדקתו עמדת לעד קרנו תרום בכבוד: רשע יראה |

see shall The .honor with be shall his ;forever is righ- his
wicked exalted horn standing teousness

6 7563 8378 4549 2786 8127 3707

וכעס שניו יחרק ונמס תאות רשעים תאבד:

shall wicked the and shall he his be and
.perish ones of desire ;melt ,gnash teeth ;vexed

PSALM 112

[1]Praise Jehovah! Blessed is the man who fears Jehovah, delighting greatly in His commands. [2]His seed shall be mighty on the earth; the generation of the upright shall be blessed; [3]wealth and riches in his house; and his righteousness is standing forever. [4]Light rises in the darkness to the upright; *he is* gracious and full of pity, and *of* righteousness. [5]Good *is* a man showing favor and lending; he will nourish his matters with equity. [6]For he shall not be shaken forever; the righteous shall be for a memorial forever. [7]He shall not be afraid of evil news; his heart *is* fixed, trusting in Jehovah. [8]His heart *is* upheld; he shall not be afraid *though* he looks on his foes. [9]He has scattered; he has given to the needy; his righteousness endures forever; his horn shall be lifted up with honor. [10]The wicked shall see and be vexed; he shall gnash his teeth and melt; the desire of the wicked shall perish.

PSAL. CXIII קיג

PSALM 113

8034 1961 3068 8034 1984 3068 5650 1984 3068 1984

1
2 הללו יה | הללו עבדי יהוה הללו את-שם יהוה: יהי שם

the Is .Jehovah the praise ,Jehovah servants ,Praise Praise
of name of name of !Jehovah

3996 5704 8121 4217 5769 5704 6258 1288 3068

3 יהוה מברך מעתה ועד-עולם: ממזרח-שמש עד-מבואו

his to sun the the from .forever and from being Jehovah
;going of rising now blessed

8064 5921 3068 1471 3605 5921 7311 3068 8034 1984

4 מהלל שם יהוה: רם על-כל-גוים | יהוה על השמים

the above ,Jehovah nations all above Is .Jehovah the being
heavens high of name praised

8213 3427 1361 430 3068 4310 3519

5
6 כבודו: מי כיהוה אלהינו המגביהי לשבת: המשפילי

humbles who ;dwell to sits who our like Who His
himself high on ,God Jehovah (is) .glory

7311 830 1800 6083 6965 776 8064 7200

7 לראות בשמים ובארץ: מקימי מעפר דל מאשפת ירים

lifts He from and the the from raising in and the in see to
dunghill the ;poor dust up ,earth the heavens

PSALM 113

[1]Praise Jehovah! Praise, O servants of Jehovah; praise the name of Jehovah. [2]Blessed is the name of Jehovah from now on and forever. [3]From the sunrise to its going, the name of Jehovah *is* being praised. [4]Jehovah *is* high above all nations; His glory above the heavens. [5]Who *is* like Jehovah our God? *He* sits on high to dwell! [6]*He* lowers Himself to see in the heavens and in the earth! [7]*He* raises up the poor from the dust; and He lifts the needy out of the dunghill, [8]in order to

make him sit with nobles, with the nobles of his people. [9]He causes the barren to live in the house *as* the joyful mother of sons. Praise Jehovah!

8 אֶבְיוֹן: לְהוֹשִׁיבִי עִם־נְדִיבִים עִם נְדִיבֵי עַמּוֹ: מוֹשִׁיבִי ׀
9

3427 5971 5081 5081 6213 34

to causing dwell | his ,people | the of nobles | with | ;nobles | with | sit him make to | the ,needy

עֲקֶרֶת הַבַּיִת אֵם־הַבָּנִים שְׂמֵחָה הַלְלוּ־יָהּ:

3050 1984 8056 1121 517 1004 6135

Praise !Jah | .joyful | sons | the of mother | the (in) ,house | the barren

PSAL. CXIV קיד

PSALM 114

PSALM 114

[1]When Israel came out of Egypt, the house of Jacob from a people of strange language; [2]Judah became His sanctuary, Israel His kingdom. [3]The sea looked and fled; the Jordan turned back; [4]the mountains skipped like rams; the little hills like lambs! [5]What *ails* you, O sea, that you flee? O Jordan, that you turn back? [6]O mountains, that you skip like rams? O little hills, like lambs? [7]Tremble, O earth, from the face of the Lord, from the face of the God of Jacob; [8]who turned the rock *into* a pool of water; the flint into a fountain of waters.

1 בְּצֵאת יִשְׂרָאֵל מִמִּצְרָיִם בֵּית יַעֲקֹב מֵעַם לֹעֵז: הָיְתָה
2

1961 3937 5971 3920 1004 4714 3478 3318

became | alien speech | a from of people | Jacob | the of house | ,Egypt from | Israel | came When out

3 יְהוּדָה לְקָדְשׁוֹ יִשְׂרָאֵל מַמְשְׁלוֹתָיו: הַיָּם רָאָה וַיָּנֹס הַיַּרְדֵּן

3383 5127 7200 3220 4415 3478 6944 3063

the Jordan | and ;fled | saw | The sea | His .dominion | Israel | His ,sanctuary | Judah

4 יִסֹּב לְאָחוֹר: הֶהָרִים רָקְדוּ כְאֵילִים גְּבָעוֹת כִּבְנֵי־צֹאן:

6629 1121 1389 352 7540 2022 268 5437

a flock | like of sons | hills the | ;rams as | skipped | the mountains | ;back | turned

5 מַה־לְּךָ הַיָּם כִּי תָנוּס הַיַּרְדֵּן תִּסֹּב לְאָחוֹר: הֶהָרִים
6

2022 268 5437 3383 5127 3220

O mountains | ?back | you that turn | O Jordan | ?flee you that | ,sea O | to What ,you (is)

7 תִּרְקְדוּ כְאֵילִים גְּבָעוֹת כִּבְנֵי־צֹאן: מִלִּפְנֵי אָדוֹן חוּלִי

2342 113 6440 6629 1121 1389 352 7540

,tremble | the Lord | From before | a ?flock | sons as of | ,hills O | ?rams as | you that skip

8 אָרֶץ מִלִּפְנֵי אֱלוֹהַּ יַעֲקֹב: הַהֹפְכִי הַצּוּר אֲגַם־מָיִם חַלָּמִישׁ

2496 4325 98 6697 2015 3290 433 6440 776

flint the | ;water (into) of pool a | the rock | who turned | ,Jacob | the of God | from before | O ,earth

לְמַעְיְנוֹ־מָיִם:

4325 4599

.water | a into of spring

PSAL. CXV קטו

PSALM 115

PSALM 115

[1]Not to us, O Jehovah, not to us, but to Your name give glory; for Your mercy; because of Your truth. [2]Why do the nations say, Where *is* their God now? [3]But our God *is* in Heaven; He has done all that He has pleased. [4]Their idols *are* silver and gold, the work of man's hands; [5]they *have* mouths, but they do not speak; they *have* eyes, but they do not see; [6]they *have* ears, but they do not hear; they *have* a nose, but they do not smell; [7]their hands do not feel; their feet do not walk; they do not mutter

1 לֹא לָנוּ ׀ יְהוָה לֹא־לָנוּ כִּי־לְשִׁמְךָ תֵּן כָּבוֹד עַל־חַסְדְּךָ

2617 3519 5414 8034 3808 3068 3808

Your ,mercy | for | ,glory | give | Your to name | but | to ,us | not | O ,Jehovah | to ,us | Not

2 עַל־אֲמִתֶּךָ: לָמָּה יֹאמְרוּ הַגּוֹיִם אַיֵּה־נָא אֱלֹהֵיהֶם:

430 4994 1471 559 4100 571

?God their | now | Where is | the ,nations | say | Why | Your .truth | for

3 וֵאלֹהֵינוּ בַשָּׁמָיִם כֹּל אֲשֶׁר־חָפֵץ עָשָׂה: עֲצַבֵּיהֶם כֶּסֶף
4

3701 6091 6213 2654 834 3605 8064 430

silver | Their (are) idols | has He .done | has He pleased | which | all | the in (is) ;heavens | our But God

5 וְזָהָב מַעֲשֵׂה יְדֵי אָדָם: פֶּה־לָהֶם וְלֹא יְדַבֵּרוּ עֵינַיִם לָהֶם

5869 1696 3808 6310 120 3027 4639 2091

to ,them | eyes (are) | they ;speak | but not | to mouths ,them (are) | ;man | the of hands | work the of | and ,gold

6 וְלֹא יִרְאוּ: אָזְנַיִם לָהֶם וְלֹא יִשְׁמָעוּ אַף לָהֶם וְלֹא יְרִיחוּן:

7306 3808 639 8085 3808 241 7200 3808

they ;smell | but not | to (is) ,them | a nose | they ;hear | but not | to ,them | ears (are) | they ;see | but not

7 יְדֵיהֶם ׀ וְלֹא יְמִישׁוּן רַגְלֵיהֶם וְלֹא יְהַלֵּכוּ לֹא־יֶהְגּוּ

1897 3808 1980 3808 7272 4184 3808 3027

they speak | not | they ;march | but not | their ,feet | they ;feel | but not | their ,hands through their throat. 8The ones who make them are like them, *and* everyone trusting in them.

9O Israel, trust in Jehovah; He *is* their help and their shield. 10O house of Aaron, trust in Jehovah; He *is* their help and their shield. 11You who fear Jehovah, trust in Jehovah; He *is* their help and their shield. 12Jehovah remembers us; He will bless; He will bless the house of Israel; He will bless the house of Aaron; 13He will bless those who fear Jehovah, the small and the great. 14Jehovah will add *more* on you; on you and on your sons. 15You *are* blessed to Jehovah, *who* makes heavens and earth. 16The heavens; the heavens *are* Jehovah's; but He has given the earth to the sons of men. 17The dead do not praise Jehovah; nor all those who go down into silence; 18but we will bless Jehovah, from now on and forever. Praise Jehovah!

8 בִּגְרוֹנָם׃ כְּמוֹהֶם יִהְיוּ עֹשֵׂיהֶם כֹּל אֲשֶׁר־בֹּטֵחַ בָּהֶם׃
9 10 יִשְׂרָאֵל בְּטַח בַּיהוָה עֶזְרָם וּמָגִנָּם הוּא׃ בֵּית אַהֲרֹן
11 בִּטְחוּ בַיהוָה עֶזְרָם וּמָגִנָּם הוּא׃ יִרְאֵי יְהוָה בִּטְחוּ בַיהוָה
12 עֶזְרָם וּמָגִנָּם הוּא׃ יְהוָה זְכָרָנוּ יְבָרֵךְ יְבָרֵךְ אֶת־בֵּית
13 יִשְׂרָאֵל יְבָרֵךְ אֶת־בֵּית אַהֲרֹן׃ יְבָרֵךְ יִרְאֵי יְהוָה הַקְּטַנִּים
14 עִם־הַגְּדֹלִים׃ יֹסֵף יְהוָה עֲלֵיכֶם עֲלֵיכֶם וְעַל־בְּנֵיכֶם׃
15 16 בְּרוּכִים אַתֶּם לַיהוָה עֹשֵׂה שָׁמַיִם וָאָרֶץ׃ הַשָּׁמַיִם שָׁמַיִם
17 לַיהוָה וְהָאָרֶץ נָתַן לִבְנֵי־אָדָם׃ לֹא הַמֵּתִים יְהַלְלוּ־יָהּ
18 וְלֹא כָּל־יֹרְדֵי דוּמָה׃ וַאֲנַחְנוּ נְבָרֵךְ יָהּ מֵעַתָּה וְעַד־
עוֹלָם הַלְלוּ־יָהּ׃

PSAL. CXVI קטז

PSALM 116

1I love Jehovah because He hears my voice *and* my prayers. 2Because He has bowed His ear to me, I will also call in my days. 3The cords of death hemmed me in; and the pains of Sheol found me; I find distress and sorrow; 4then I call on the name of Jehovah: O Jehovah, I beseech You, deliver my soul! 5Jehovah *is* gracious and righteous; yea, our God *is* merciful. 6Jehovah keeps the simple; I was low, but He saved me. 7Return to your rest, O soul; for Jehovah has blessed you. 8For You have delivered my soul from death; my eye from tears,

1 2 אָהַבְתִּי כִּי־יִשְׁמַע יְהוָה אֶת־קוֹלִי תַּחֲנוּנָי׃ כִּי־הִטָּה
3 אָזְנוֹ לִי וּבְיָמַי אֶקְרָא׃ אֲפָפוּנִי חֶבְלֵי־מָוֶת וּמְצָרֵי שְׁאוֹל
4 מְצָאוּנִי צָרָה וְיָגוֹן אֶמְצָא׃ וּבְשֵׁם־יְהוָה אֶקְרָא אָנָּה יְהוָה
5 6 מַלְּטָה נַפְשִׁי׃ חַנּוּן יְהוָה וְצַדִּיק וֵאלֹהֵינוּ מְרַחֵם׃ שֹׁמֵר
7 פְּתָאיִם יְהוָה דַּלֹּתִי וְלִי יְהוֹשִׁיעַ׃ שׁוּבִי נַפְשִׁי לִמְנוּחָיְכִי
8 כִּי־יְהוָה גָּמַל עָלָיְכִי׃ כִּי חִלַּצְתָּ נַפְשִׁי מִמָּוֶת אֶת־עֵינִי

my feet from stumbling. [9]I will walk before the face of Jehovah, in the lands of the living. [10]I believed; so I speak; I was greatly afflicted; [11]I said in my alarm, Every man *is* a liar. [12]What shall I return to Jehovah *for* His benefits to me? [13]I will lift up the cup of salvation, and I will call on the name of Jehovah. [14]I will pay my vows to Jehovah now in the presence of all His people.

[15]Precious in the eyes of Jehovah *is* the death of His saints. [16]O Jehovah, truly I *am* Your servant now; I *am* Your servant, the son of Your handmaid; You have loosed my bonds. [17]I will sacrifice to You the sacrifice of thanks, and will call on the name of Jehovah. [18]I will pay my vows to Jehovah now in the presence of all His people, [19]in the courts of the house of Jehovah; in your midst, O Jerusalem. Praise Jehovah!

776 3068 6440 1980 1762 7272 1832
9 מן־דמעה את־רגלי מדחי: אתהלך לפני יהוה בארצות
in ,Jehovah before will I from foot my ,tears from
of lands walk .stumbling

559 3966 6031 1696 539 2416
10 11 החיים: האמנתי כי אדבר אני עניתי מאד: אני אמרתי
said I ;greatly was I ;speak I so have I the
afflicted ;believed .living

8408 3605 3068 7725 4100 3576 120 3605 2648
12 בחפזי כל־האדם כזב: מה־אשיב ליהוה כל־תגמולוהי
His for to I shall What a (is) man Every my in
benefits all Jehovah return .liar ,alarm

3068 5088 7121 3068 8034 5375 3444 3563
13 14 עלי: כוס־ישועות אשא ובשם יהוה אקרא: נדרי ליהוה
to My will I Jehovah on and will I salvation The to
Jehovah vows .call of name the ,up lift of cup ?me

4194 3068 5869 3368 5971 3605 4994/5048 7999
15 אשלם נגדה־נא לכל־עמו: יקר בעיני יהוה המותה
the (is) Jehovah the in Precious His of ,pray I the in will I
death of eyes .people all ,presence ,pay

519 1121 5650 5650 3068 577 2623
16 לחסידיו: אנה יהוה כי־אני עבדך אני עבדך בן־אמתך
Your son the Your I Your I truly O ,pray I His of
;handmaid of ,servant (am) ;servant (am) ,Jehovah .saints

7121 3068 8034 8426 2077 2076 4147 6605
17 פתחת למוסרי: לך־אזבח זבח תודה ובשם יהוה אקרא:
.call will Jehovah on and ,thanks the will I You To my have You
of name the of sacrifice sacrifice .bonds loosed

1004 2691 5971 3605 4994 5048 7999 3068 5088
18 19 נדרי ליהוה אשלם נגדה־נא לכל־עמו: בחצרות | בית
the the in His of I the in will I to My
of house of courts ,people all ,pray ,presence pay Jehovah vows

1984 3389 8432 3068
יהוה בתוככי ירושלם הללו־יה:
Praise O your in ,Jehovah
!Jah .Jerusalem ,midst

PSAL. CXVII קיז

PSALM 117

PSALM 117

[1]Praise Jehovah, all nations; praise Him, all peoples; [2]for His mercy is mighty over us, and the truth of Jehovah *is* forever. Praise Jehovah!

1396 523 3605 7623 1471 3605 3068 1984
1 2 הללו את־יהוה כל־גוים שבחוהו כל־האמים: כי גבר
is For .peoples all praise ;nations all ,Jehovah Praise
mighty ,Him

1984 5769 3068 571 2617 5921
עלינו | חסדו ואמת־יהוה לעולם הללו־יה:
Praise (is) Jehovah the and His over
!Jah .forever of truth ,mercy us

PSAL. CXVIII קיח

PSALM 118

PSALM 118

[1]Give thanks to Jehovah, for *He is* good; because His mercy *endures* forever. [2]Let Israel say now that His mercy *endures* forever. [3]Let the house of Aaron say now that His mercy *endures* forever. [4]Let those who fear Jehovah say now that His mercy *endures* forever. [5]I called Jehovah from the distress; He answered me in the large place of Jehovah. [6]Jehovah *is* for me; I will not fear; what can

3478 559 2617 5769 2896 3068 3034
1 2 הודו ליהוה כי־טוב כי לעולם חסדו: יאמר־נא ישראל
Israel I Let His (is) for (is He) for to Give
,pray ,say .mercy forever ;good ,Jehovah thanks

2617 5769 175 1004 4994/559 2617 5769
3 כי לעולם חסדו: יאמרו־נא בית־אהרן כי לעולם חסדו:
His (is) that Aaron the I Let His (is) that
.mercy forever of house ,pray ,say .mercy forever

4712 2617 5769 3068 3373 4994 559
4 5 יאמרו־נא יראי יהוה כי לעולם חסדו: מן־המצר
the From His (is) that Jehovah who those I Let
distress .mercy forever fear ,pray ,say

4100 3372 3808 3068 3050 4800 6030 3050 7121
6 קראתי יה ענני במרחב יה: יהוה לי לא אירא מה־
what will I not for Jehovah .Jehovah the in an- He ;Jehovah I
;fear ;me of place large me swered called

man do to me? 7Jehovah *is* for me among those who help me; and I shall see *my desire* on those who hate me. 8*It is* better to take refuge in Jehovah than to trust in man; 9*it is* better to trust in Jehovah than to trust in princes. 10All the nations surround me; but surely I will destroy them in the name of Jehovah. 11They surround me; yea, they surround me; I surely will destroy them in the name of Jehovah. 12They surround me like bees; they are quenched like the fire of thorns; for surely I will cut them off in the name of Jehovah.

13Pushing, you pushed me to fall; but Jehovah helped me. 14Jehovah *is* my strength and my song; and He is my salvation. 15the voice of rejoicing and salvation *is* in the tabernacle of the righteous; the right hand of Jehovah works mightily. 16The right hand of Jehovah is exalted; the right hand of Jehovah acts mightily. 17I shall not die, but I shall live and declare the works of Jehovah. 18Jehovah has grievously chastened me, but He has not given me to death. 19Open the gates of righteousness to me, I will enter into them; I will thank Jehovah! 20This *is* the gate of Jehovah; the righteous shall enter into it. 21I will thank You, for You answered me, and are my salvation.

22The Stone *which* the builders rejected has become the Head of the corner. 23This is from Jehovah, it is marvelous in our eyes. 24This *is* the day Jehovah has made; we will rejoice and be glad in it. 25O Jehovah, I beseech You, cause *us* to prosper now. 26Blessed *is* he who comes in the name of Jehovah; we blessed you from the house of Jehovah. 27Jehovah *is* God, and He gives light to us. Tie the sacrifice with cords, to the horns of the altar. 28You *are*

8130 7200 5826 3068 120 6213
7 יעשה לי אדם: יהוה לי בעזרי ואני אראה בשנאי:
those on shall and my among for Jehovah ?man to do can
.me hating look I ;helpers me (is) me

2620 2896 120 982 3068 2620 2896
8
9 טוב לחסות ביהוה מבטח באדם: טוב לחסות
take to (is It) .man in to than in take to (is It)
refuge better trust Jehovah refuge better

3068 8034 5437 1471/3605 5081 982 3068
10 ביהוה מבטח בנדיבים: כל־גוים סבבוני בשם יהוה
Jehovah the in surround the All .princes in to than in
4135 of name ,me nations trust Jehovah

3068 8034 5437 5437 4135
11 כי אמילם: סבוני גם־סבבוני בשם יהוה כי אמילם:
cut will I surely Jehovah the in they also sur- They cut will I surely
.off them of name ;me surround ,me round .off them

4135 3068 8034 6975 784 1846 1682 5437
12 סבוני כדבורים דעכו כאש קוצים בשם יהוה כי אמילם:
cut will I surely Jehovah the in ;thorns the like are they like sur- They
.off them of name of fire quenched ;bees me round

3050 2176 5797 5826 3068 5307 1760 1760
13
14 דחה דחיתני לנפל ויהוה עזרני: עזי וזמרת יה ויהי־
He and (is) my and My helped has but ,fall to you Pushing
is ;Jah song strength .me Jehovah me pushed

3225 6662 168 3444 7440 6963 3444
15 לי לישועה: קול ׀ רנה וישועה באהלי צדיקים ימין
right the the in (is) and joyful The .salvation to
hand ;righteous of tents salvation shouting of voice me

6213 3068 3225 7426 3068 3225 2428 6213 3068
16 יהוה עשה חיל: ימין יהוה רוממה ימין יהוה עשה
acts Jehovah right the is Jehovah right The .mightily works Jeho-
of hand ;exalted of hand vah's

3256 3050 4639 5608 2421 4191 3808 2428
17
18 חיל: לא אמות כי־אחיה ואספר מעשי יה: יסר
Sorely .Jah the tell and shall I but shall I not .mightily
of works live ,die

935 6664 8179 6605 5414 3808 4194 3050 3256
19 יסרני יה ולמות לא נתנני: פתחו־לי שערי־צדק אבא־
will I righteous- the to Open has He not to but ,Jah chas-
enter .ness of gates me .me given death me tened

935 6662 3068 8179 2088 3050 3034
20 בם אודה יה: זה־השער ליהוה צדיקים יבאו בו:
into shall the of the This .Jehovah will I into
it enter righteous ;Jehovah gate (is) thank .them

1129 3973 68 3444 1961 6030 3034
21
22 אודך כי עניתני ותהי־לי לישועה: אבן מאסו הבונים
the (which) The .salvation to and an- You for will I
builders rejected stone me are me swered ,You thank

6381 2088 1961 3068 6438 7218 1961
23 היתה לראש פנה: מאת יהוה היתה זאת היא נפלאת
marvelous it ;this is Jehovah From the the has
(is) .corner of Head become

8056 1523 3068 6213 3117 2088 5869
24 בעינינו: זה־היום עשה יהוה נגילה ונשמחה בו:
it in be and will we ;Jehovah has the This our in
glad rejoice made day (is) .eyes

1288 4994 6743 3068 577 4994 3467 3068 577
25
26 אנא יהוה הושיעה נא אנא יהוה הצליחה נא: ברוך
Blessed .now to make O beg I ;now save O beg I
(is) prosper ,Jehovah ,You ,Jehovah ,You

3068 410 3068 1004 1288 3068 8034 935
27 הבא בשם יהוה ברכנוכם מבית יהוה: אל ׀ יהוה
(is) God .Jehovah the from blessed we ;Jehovah the in who he
,Jehovah of house you of name comes

410 4196 7161 5704 5688 2282 631 215
28 ויאר לנו אסרו־חג בעבתים עד־קרנות המזבח: אלי
my .altar the the to with the tie ,us to He and
God of horns cords sacrifice light gives

my God, and I will exalt You; My God, I will thank You! 29O give thanks to Jehovah, for He is good; for His mercy *endures* forever.

PSALM 119

Aleth

1Blessed are the upright in the way, who walk in the law of Jehovah. 2Blessed *are* those keeping His testimonies, who seek Him with the whole heart. 3They also do not work evil; they walk in His way. 4You have commanded to carefully keep Your precepts. 5O that my ways were fixed to keep Your statutes! 6Then I shall not be ashamed, when I look to all Your commands. 7I will thank You with integrity of heart, in my learning the judgments of Your righteousness. 8I will keep Your statutes; do not forsake me utterly.

Beth

9By what shall a young man purify his way, to keep *it* according to Your word? 10I have sought You with my whole heart; do not let me wander from Your commands. 11I have hidden You word in my heart, that I might not sin against You. 12Blessed *are* You, O Jehovah; teach me Your statutes. 13I have declared all the judgments of Your mouth with my lips; 14I have rejoiced in the way of Your testimonies as over all riches. 15I will meditate in Your precepts and I will regard Your ways. 16I will delight in Your statutes. I will not forget Your word.

Gimel

17Deal bountifully with Your servant *that* I may live, and I will keep Your word. 18Open my eyes and I will see wonderful things from Your law. 19I *am* an alien in the earth; hide not Your commandments from me. 20My soul is breaking for the

2896 3068 3034 7311 430 3038
29 אַתָּה וְאוֹדֶךָּ אֱלֹהַי אֲרוֹמְמֶךָּ׃ הוֹדוּ לַיהוָה כִּי־טוֹב כִּי
for (is He) for | to | give O | will I | my | will I and | You
;good | Jehovah | thanks | .You exalt | ,God | ;You thank | ,(are)

2617 5769
לְעוֹלָם חַסְדּוֹ׃
His | forever
!mercy | (is)

PSAL. CXIX קיט

PSALM 119

5341 835 3068 8451 1980 1870 8549 835
1 אַשְׁרֵי תְמִימֵי־דָרֶךְ הַהֹלְכִים בְּתוֹרַת יְהוָה׃
2 אַשְׁרֵי נֹצְרֵי
those | Blessed | .Jehovah | the in | walk who | the in | the | Blessed
keeping | (are) | | of law | | ,way | upright | (are)

1870 5766 6466 637 1875 3820 5773
3 עֵדֹתָיו בְּכָל־לֵב יִדְרְשׁוּהוּ׃ אַף לֹא־פָעֲלוּ עַוְלָה בִּדְרָכָיו
His in | ;evil | they do not | Also | seek who | heart | the with | His
way | | practice | | .Him | | whole | ,testimonies

3559 305 3966 8104 6490 6680 1980
4 הָלָכוּ׃ אַתָּה צִוִּיתָה פִקֻּדֶיךָ לִשְׁמֹר מְאֹד׃
5 אַחֲלַי יִכֹּנוּ
were | that O | .carefully | be to | Your | have | You | they
fixed | | | kept | precepts | commanded | | .walk

3605 5027 954 3808 227 2706 8104 1870
6 דְרָכַי לִשְׁמֹר חֻקֶּיךָ׃ אָז לֹא־אֵבוֹשׁ בְּהַבִּיטִי אֶל־כָּל־
all | to | I when | shall I | not | Then | Your | keep to | my
| | look | ashamed be | | | !statutes | | ways

6664 4941 3925 3824 3476 3034 4687
7 מִצְוֹתֶיךָ׃ אוֹדְךָ בְּיֹשֶׁר לֵבָב בְּלָמְדִי מִשְׁפְּטֵי צִדְקֶךָ׃
righ- | Your | judg- | the | my in | ,heart | with | will I | Your
.teousness | | of ments | | learning | of integrity | | You thank | .commands

2135 4100 3966 5704 5800 408 8104 2706
8 אֶת־חֻקֶּיךָ אֶשְׁמֹר אַל־תַּעַזְבֵנִי עַד־מְאֹד׃
9 בַּמֶּה יְזַכֶּה־
shall | By | very | till | do | not | will I | Your
purify | what | .much | | me forsake | | ;keep | statutes

408 1875 3820 3605 1697 8104 734 5288
10 נַּעַר אֶת־אָרְחוֹ לִשְׁמֹר כִּדְבָרֶךָ׃ בְּכָל־לִבִּי דְרַשְׁתִּיךָ אַל־
not | have I | my | With | to according | keep To | his | young a
;You sought | heart | whole | !word Your | (it) | ?path | man

3808 565 6845 3820 4687 7686
11 תַּשְׁגֵּנִי מִמִּצְוֹתֶיךָ׃ בְּלִבִּי צָפַנְתִּי אִמְרָתֶךָ לְמַעַן לֹא
not | that | ,word Your | have I | my In | Your from | let
| | | hidden | heart | !commands | wander me

8193 2706 3925 3068 1288 2398
12 אֶחֱטָא־לָךְ׃ בָּרוּךְ אַתָּה יְהוָה לַמְּדֵנִי חֻקֶּיךָ׃
13 בִּשְׂפָתַי
my With | Your | teach | O | ,You | Blessed | against might I
lips | .statutes | me | ;Jehovah | | (are) | You sin

5927 7797 5715 1870 6310 4941 3605 5608
14 סִפַּרְתִּי כֹּל מִשְׁפְּטֵי־פִיךָ׃ בְּדֶרֶךְ עֵדְוֹתֶיךָ שַׂשְׂתִּי כְּעַל
as | have I | Your | the in | Your | judg- | the all | have I
over | rejoiced | testimonies | of way | ;mouth | of ments | | declared

2708 734 5027 7878 6490 1952
15 כָּל־הוֹן׃ בְּפִקֻּדֶיךָ אָשִׂיחָה וְאַבִּיטָה אֹרְחֹתֶיךָ׃
16 בְּחֻקֹּתֶיךָ
Your In | Your | will I and | will I | Your In | riches all
statutes | .ways | regard | ,meditate | precepts |

2421 5650 1580 1697 7911 3808 8173
17 אֶשְׁתַּעֲשָׁע לֹא אֶשְׁכַּח דְּבָרֶךָ׃ גְּמֹל עַל־עַבְדְּךָ אֶחְיֶה
I (that) | Your | to | Grant | Your | will I | not | delight will I
,live may | servant | | | .word | forget | | ;myself

8451 6381 5027 1540 1697 8104
18 וְאֶשְׁמְרָה דְבָרֶךָ׃ גַּל־עֵינַי וְאַבִּיטָה נִפְלָאוֹת מִתּוֹרָתֶךָ׃
Your of out | wonderful | may I that | my | Open | Your | keep I and
.law | things | behold | ,eyes | | .word |

5315 1638 4687 5640 776 1616
19 גֵּר אָנֹכִי בָאָרֶץ אַל־תַּסְתֵּר מִמֶּנִּי מִצְוֹתֶיךָ׃
20 גָּרְסָה נַפְשִׁי
My | is | Your | from | hide do | not | the in | I | an
soul | crushed | .commands | me | | | ;earth | (am) | alien

longing to Your judgments
in every season. [21]You
have rebuked the proud, the
cursed ones who go astray
from Your commands.
[22]Roll from me reproach
and scorn from me; for I
have kept Your testi-
monies. [23]Princes also sat,
speaking against me; *but*
Your servant meditates on
Your laws. [24]Your testimonies also *are* my delight,
my counselors.

Daleth

[25]My soul clings to the
dust; give me life according
to Your word. [26]I have
declared my ways, and You
answered me; teach me
Your statutes. [27]Make me
understand the way of Your
precepts, and I will meditate on Your wonders.
[28]My soul drops *with* grief;
Lift me up according to Your
word. [29]Remove from me
the way of lying, and favor
me with Your law. [30]I have
chosen the way of truth; I
have held Your judgments
level; [31]I have clung to Your
testimonies; O Jehovah, do
not shame me. [32]I will run
the way of Your commands,
for You shall enlarge my
heart.

He

[33]O Jehovah, teach me
the way of Your statutes,
and I will keep it *to* the
end. [34]Make me under-
stand and I will keep Your
law, and observe it with the
whole heart. [35]Make me
walk in the way of Your
commands, for in it I
delight. [36]Bow my heart to
Your testimonies, and not
to unjust gain. [37]Turn my
eyes from seeing vanity; in
Your way give me life.
[38]Make Your word sure to
Your servant, who *is de-*
voted to Your fear. [39]Turn
away my shame which I
fear; for Your judgments *are*
good. [40]Behold, I have
longed for Your precepts;
grant to me life in Your
righteousness.

Vau

[41]By Your word, accord-
ing to Your salvation, let
Your mercies come to me,
O Jehovah. [42]And I will
answer my reprover a word;
for I trust in Your word.

779 2086 1605 6256 3605 4941 8375
לתאבה אל־משפטיך בכל־עת׃ גערת זדים ארורים 21
cursed the ones | the ,proud | have You rebuked | .season | in every | Your judgments | to | the for longing

5341 5713 937 2764 1556 4687 7686
השגים ממצותיך׃ גל מעלי חרפה ובוז כי עדתיך נצרתי׃ 22
have I .kept | Your testimonies | for and reproach ;scorn | from me | Roll | Your from .commands | go who astray

1571 8451 7878 5650 1696 8269 3427 1571
גם ישבו שרים בי נדברו עבדך ישיח בחקיך׃ גם־ 23 24
Also | Your on .laws | meditates | Your (but) servant | speak- ;ing | against me | princes | sat | Also

5315 6083 1692 6098 582 8191 5713
עדתיך שעשעי אנשי עצתי׃ דבקה לעפר נפשי 25
My ;soul | the to dust | clings | my .counsel | men of | my (are) ,delight | Your testimonies

2706 3925 6030 5608 1870 1697 2421
חיני כדברך׃ דרכי ספרתי ותענני למדני חקיך׃ 26
Your .statutes | teach me | You and ;me answered | have I ,declared | my ways | to according word Your | me give life

1811 6381 7878 995 6490 1870
דרך־פקודיך הבינני ואשיחה בנפלאותיך׃ דלפה 27 28
drops | Your on .wonders | will I and meditate | me Make ;understand | Your precepts | way The of

5493 8267 1697 6965 8424 5315
נפשי מתוגה קימני כדברך׃ דרך־שקר הסר ממני 29
from ,me | Turn | lying | the of way | to according .word Your | strengthen me | (with) ;grief | My soul

7737 4941 977 530 1870 2603 8451
ותורתך חנני׃ דרך־אמונה בחרתי משפטיך שויתי׃ 30
have I ;level held | Your judgments | have I ;chosen | truth | way the of | favor .me | with and law Your

7323 4487 1870 954 3808 3068 5715 1692
דבקתי בעדותיך יהוה אל־תבישני׃ דרך־מצותיך ארוץ 31 32
will I ,run | Your commands | the of way | me put do .shame to | not | O ,Jehovah | Your to ;testimonies | have I clung

5341 2706 1870 3068 3384 3820 7337
כי תרחיב לבי׃ הורני יהוה דרך חקיך ואצרנה 33
will I and it keep | Your ,statutes | the of way | O ,Jehovah | Teach ,me | my .heart | shall You for enlarge

3820 3605 8104 8451 5341 995 6118
עקב׃ הבינני ואצרה תורתך ואשמרנה בכל־לב׃ 34
(my) .heart | with whole | observe and it | Your ;law | will I and keep | me Make understand | the (to) .end

3820/5186 2654 4487 5410 3381
הדריכני בנתיב מצותיך כי־בו חפצתי׃ הט־לבי אל־ 35 36
to | my heart | Bow | !delight I | in for it | Your ,commands | the in of way | to me Cause walk

1870 7723 7200 5869 5674 1215 408 5715
עדותיך ואל אל־בצע׃ העבר עיני מראות שוא בדרכך 37
Your in way | ;vanity | from seeing | my eyes | Turn away | unjust .gain | to | and not | Your ,testimonies

5674 3373 834 565 5650 6965 2421
חיני׃ הקם לעבדך אמרתך אשר ליראתך׃ העבר 38 39
Turn away | to (devoted) .fear Your | who is | Your ,word | Your to servant | Make rise | me give .life

8373 2009 2896 4941 3025 834 2764
חרפתי אשר יגרתי כי משפטיך טובים׃ הנה תאבתי 40
have I longed | ,Behold | (are) .good | Your judgments | for | ;fear I | which | my reproach

3068 2142 935 2421 6666 6480
לפקדיך בצדקתך חיני׃ ויבאני חסדך יהוה 41
O ,Jehovah | Your ,mercies | come Let me to | me give .life | Your in righteousness | Your for ,precepts

982 1697 2778 6030 565 8668
תשועתך כאמרתך׃ ואענה חרפי דבר כי־בטחתי 42
trust I | for | a ;word | my reprover | will I And answer | to according .word Your | Your by ,salvation

43 And do not take the word of truth completely out of my mouth; for I have hoped in Your judgments. 44 And I shall keep Your law continually, forever and ever. 45 And I will walk in a wide space, for I seek Your commands. 46 And I will speak of Your testimonies before kings, and will not be ashamed. 47 And I will delight myself in Your commandments, which I have loved. 48 And I will lift up my hands to Your commandments that I love; and I will meditate on Your statutes.

Zayin

49 Remember the word to Your servant, on which You made me hope. 50 This *is* my comfort in my affliction; for Your word has given me life. 51 The proud have scorned me utterly; I have not veered from Your law. 52 I remembered Your judgments from of old, O Jehovah, and I take comfort. 53 Hot zeal has seized me because of the wicked forsaking Your law. 54 Your statutes have been my songs in the house of my pilgrimages. 55 O Jehovah, I have remembered Your name in the night and have kept Your law. 56 This was done to me, because I kept Your commandments.

Cheth

57 Jehovah *is* my portion; I have said to keep Your words. 58 I entreated Your face with all *my* heart; favor me according to Your word. 59 I mused on my ways and turned my feet to Your testimonies. 60 I hurried and delayed not to keep Your commands. 61 The cords of the wicked encircle me; I have not forgotten Your law. 62 At halves of the night I will rise to give thanks to You because of Your righteous judgments. 63 I *am* a companion of all who fear You; yea, of those who keep your precepts. 64 O Jehovah, the earth is full

4941 3966 571 1697 6310 5337 408 1697
43 בִּדְבָרֶךָ׃ וְאַל־תַּצֵּל מִפִּי דְבַר־אֱמֶת עַד־מְאֹד כִּי לְמִשְׁפָּטֶךָ
Your in for very till truth the my from deliver And Your in
judgments ,much of word mouth not .word

1980 5703 5669 85.48 8451 8104 3176
44 45 יִחָלְתִּי׃ וְאֶשְׁמְרָה תוֹרָתְךָ תָמִיד לְעוֹלָם וָעֶד׃ וְאֶתְהַלְּכָה
will I And and forever continually Your I And have I
walk .ever law keep shall .hoped

5048 5713 1696 1875 6490 7342
46 בָרְחָבָה כִּי פִקֻּדֶיךָ דָרָשְׁתִּי׃ וַאֲדַבְּרָה בְעֵדֹתֶיךָ נֶגֶד
before Your of will I .seek I Your for the in
testimonies speak commands ,wideness

157 834 4487 8173 954 3808 4428
47 מְלָכִים וְלֹא אֵבוֹשׁ׃ וְאֶשְׁתַּעֲשַׁע בְּמִצְוֹתֶיךָ אֲשֶׁר אָהָבְתִּי׃
have I which Your in will I And be will and ,kings
.loved commands myself delight .ashamed not

2706 7878 157 834 4487 3709 5375
48 וְאֶשָּׂא כַפַּי אֶל־מִצְוֹתֶיךָ אֲשֶׁר אָהָבְתִּי וְאָשִׂיחָה בְחֻקֶּיךָ׃
Your on will I and ;love I which Your to my will I and
.statutes meditate commands palms up lift

5165 2088 3176 834 5921 5650 1697 2142
49 50 זְכָר־דָּבָר לְעַבְדֶּךָ עַל אֲשֶׁר יִחַלְתָּנִי׃ זֹאת נֶחָמָתִי
my This made You which on Your to the Remember
comfort (is) .hope me ,servant word

8451 39.66 5704 3887 2086 2421 565 6040
51 בְעָנְיִי כִּי אִמְרָתְךָ חִיָּתְנִי׃ זֵדִים הֱלִיצֻנִי עַד־מְאֹד מִתּוֹרָתְךָ
Your from very till have The given has Your for my in
law ;much me scorned proud .life me word affliction

5162 3068 5769 4941 2142 5186 3808
52 לֹא נָטִיתִי׃ זָכַרְתִּי מִשְׁפָּטֶיךָ מֵעוֹלָם ׀ יְהוָה וָאֶתְנֶחָם׃
take I and O from Your remem- I have I not
.comfort Jehovah old of judgments bered .veered

1961 2158 8451 58.00 7563 270 2152
53 54 זַלְעָפָה אֲחָזַתְנִי מֵרְשָׁעִים עֹזְבֵי תּוֹרָתֶךָ׃ זְמִרוֹת הָיוּ־לִי
to have Songs Your forsaking of because has zeal Hot
me been .law wicked the me seized

8104 3068 8034 3915 2142 4033 1004 27.06
55 חֻקֶּיךָ בְּבֵית מְגוּרָי׃ זָכַרְתִּי בַלַּיְלָה שִׁמְךָ יְהוָה וָאֶשְׁמְרָה
have and O Your the in have I pilgrim- my the in Your
kept ,Jehovah ,name night remembered .ages of house statutes

2506 5341 6480 1961 2088 8451
56 57 תּוֹרָתֶךָ׃ זֹאת הָיְתָה־לִּי כִּי פִקֻּדֶיךָ נָצָרְתִּי׃ חֶלְקִי
my .kept I Your for to was This .law Your
(is) portion commands ,me done

3820 6440 2470 1697 8104 559 3068
58 יְהוָה אָמַרְתִּי לִשְׁמֹר דְּבָרֶיךָ׃ חִלִּיתִי פָנֶיךָ בְכָל־לֵב
(my) with Your I Your keep to have I ;Jehovah
;heart whole face entreated .words said

7272 7725 1870 2803 565 2603
59 חָנֵּנִי כְּאִמְרָתֶךָ׃ חִשַּׁבְתִּי דְרָכָי וָאָשִׁיבָה רַגְלַי אֶל־
to my and my thought I to according favor
feet turned ways on .word Your me

2256 4487 8104 81.04 4102 3808 2363 5713
60 61 עֵדֹתֶיךָ׃ חַשְׁתִּי וְלֹא הִתְמַהְמָהְתִּי לִשְׁמֹר מִצְוֹתֶיךָ׃ חֶבְלֵי
cords The Your keep to delay did and hurried I Your
of .commands not .testimonies

6965 39.15 2666 7911 3808 8451 5749 7563
62 רְשָׁעִים עִוְּדֻנִי תּוֹרָתְךָ לֹא שָׁכָחְתִּי׃ חֲצוֹת־לַיְלָה אָקוּם
will I the halves (At) have I not Your hemmed the
rise night of .forgotten law ;in me wicked

834 36.05 2272 6664 4941 3034
63 לְהוֹדוֹת לָךְ עַל מִשְׁפְּטֵי צִדְקֶךָ׃ חָבֵר אָנִי לְכָל־אֲשֶׁר
who of I com- a Your judgments because to give to
all (am) panion .righteous of You thanks

776 4390 3068 2617 6490 8104 3372
64 יְרֵאוּךָ וּלְשֹׁמְרֵי פִּקּוּדֶיךָ׃ חַסְדְּךָ יְהוָה מָלְאָה הָאָרֶץ
the fills O Your Your of and fear
;earth ,Jehovah ,mercy .precepts keeping those ;You

of Your mercy; teach me
Your statutes.

Teth

[65]You have done good
with Your servant, O
Jehovah, by Your word.
[66]Teach me good judg-
ment and knowledge, for I
have believed Your com-
mands. [67]Before I was
afflicted I went astray; but
now I have kept Your word.
[68]You *are* good and do
good — teach me Your
statutes. [69]The proud have
forged a lie against me; I
will keep Your precepts
with all *my* heart. [70]Their
heart is like fat, without
feeling; I delight in Your
law. [71]For my good I was
afflicted, to learn Your
statutes. [72]The law of Your
mouth *is* better to me than
thousands of gold and
silver.

Jod

[73]Your hands made me
and fixed me; give me
discernment that I may
learn Your commands.
[74]The ones fearing You will
see me and rejoice; for I
hoped in Your word. [75]I
know, O Jehovah, Your
judgments *are* right; and in
fidelity You afflicted me.
[76]Please let Your mercy be
for my comfort, by Your
word to Your servant. [77]Let
Your mercies come to me
that I may live; for Your law
is my delight. [78]Let the
proud be ashamed, for with
lies they perverted me; I will
muse on Your precepts.
[79]Let fearers of You turn to
me, and knowers of Your
testimonies. [80]Let my heart
be blameless in Your
statutes, that I may not be
ashamed.

Kaph

[81]My soul *is* being
consumed for Your salva-
tion; I hope in Your word.
[82]My eyes fail for Your word,
saying, When will You
comfort me? [83]For I am like
a wineskin in the smoke; I
do not forget Your statutes.
[84]As what *are* the days of
Your servant? When will
You execute judgment on
my persecutors? [85]The
proud have dug pits for me
which *are* not according to
Your law. [86]All Your

1697 3068 56 50 6213 2896 3925 2706
65 חֻקֶּיךָ לַמְּדֵנִי׃ טוֹב עָשִׂיתָ עִם־עַבְדְּךָ יְהוָה כִּדְבָרֶךָ׃
to according O Your with You good teach Your
.word Your ,Jehovah ,servant done have .me statutes

2962 539 4687 3925 1847 2940 2898
66 67 טוּב טַעַם וָדַעַת לַמְּדֵנִי כִּי בְמִצְוֹתֶיךָ הֶאֱמָנְתִּי׃ טֶרֶם
Before have I Your for teach and judgment Good
.believed commandments ,me knowledge

2895 8104 565 6258 7683 6031
68 אֶעֱנֶה אֲנִי שֹׁגֵג וְעַתָּה אִמְרָתְךָ שָׁמָרְתִּי׃ טוֹב־אַתָּה
You good have I Your but went I was I
(are) .kept word now ,astray afflicted

3605 2086 8267 2950 2706 3925 2896
69 וּמֵטִיב לַמְּדֵנִי חֻקֶּיךָ׃ טָפְלוּ עָלַי שֶׁקֶר זֵדִים אֲנִי בְּכָל־
with I the lie a against Have Your teach do and
whole ;proud me forged .statutes me ;good

8451 3820 2459 2954 6490 5341 3820
70 לֵב ׀ אֶצֹּר פִּקּוּדֶיךָ׃ טָפַשׁ כַּחֵלֶב לִבָּם אֲנִי תּוֹרָתְךָ
Your (but) Their like without is Your will (my)
law I ;heart fat feeling .precepts keep heart

2896 2706 3925 6031 2896 8170
71 72 שִׁעֲשָׁעְתִּי׃ טוֹב־לִי כִי־עֻנֵּיתִי לְמַעַן אֶלְמַד חֻקֶּיךָ׃ טוֹב־
(is) Your might I that so was I that for (is It) take I
better .statutes learn afflicted me good in delight

3559 6213 3027 3701 2091 505 6310 8451
73 לִי תוֹרַת־פִּיךָ מֵאַלְפֵי זָהָב וָכָסֶף׃ יָדֶיךָ עָשׂוּנִי וַיְכוֹנְנוּנִי
made and have Your and gold thou- than Your The to
;stand me me made hands .silver of sands mouth of law me

8056 7200 3373 4487 3925 995
74 הֲבִינֵנִי וְאֶלְמְדָה מִצְוֹתֶיךָ׃ יְרֵאֶיךָ יִרְאוּנִי וְיִשְׂמָחוּ כִּי
because and see will who They Your may I that me give
;rejoice me You fear .commands learn understanding

530 4941 6664 3068 3045 3171 1697
75 לִדְבָרְךָ יִחָלְתִּי׃ יָדַעְתִּי יְהוָה כִּי־צֶדֶק מִשְׁפָּטֶיךָ וֶאֱמוּנָה
in and Your (are) that O ,know I have I Your for
fidelity ;judgments righteous ,Jehovah .hoped word

935 5650 565 5162 2017 4494/1961 6031
76 77 עִנִּיתָנִי׃ יְהִי־נָא חַסְדְּךָ לְנַחֲמֵנִי כְּאִמְרָתְךָ לְעַבְדֶּךָ׃ יְבֹאוּנִי
come Let Your to to according my for Your beg I Let have You
me to .servant word Your ,comfort mercy ,You be .me afflicted

8267 2086 954 8191 8451 2421 7356
78 רַחֲמֶיךָ וְאֶחְיֶה כִּי־תוֹרָתְךָ שַׁעֲשֻׁעָי׃ יֵבֹשׁוּ זֵדִים כִּי־שֶׁקֶר
lies for the be Let my (is) Your for that so Your
with ,proud ashamed .delight law ;live may I mercies

5713 3045 3373 7725 6490 7878 5791
79 עִוְּתוּנִי אֲנִי אָשִׂיחַ בְּפִקּוּדֶיךָ׃ יָשׁוּבוּ לִי יְרֵאֶיךָ וְיֹדְעֵי עֵדֹתֶיךָ׃
Your ones and fearers to Let Your on will I per- they
.testimonies knowing You of me turn .precepts meditate ;me verted

3615 954 3808 2706 8549 3820
80 81 יְהִי־לִבִּי תָמִים בְּחֻקֶּיךָ לְמַעַן לֹא אֵבוֹשׁ׃ כָּלְתָה
being (is) may I not that so Your in blame- my Let
consumed .ashamed be .statutes less heart be

565 5869 3615 3176 1697 5315 8668
82 לִתְשׁוּעָתְךָ נַפְשִׁי לִדְבָרְךָ יִחָלְתִּי׃ כָּלוּ עֵינַי לְאִמְרָתֶךָ
Your for My fail .hope I Your in My Your for
,word eyes word ;soul salvation

3808 2706 7008 4997 5162 559
83 לֵאמֹר מָתַי תְּנַחֲמֵנִי׃ כִּי־הָיִיתִי כְּנֹאד בְּקִיטוֹר חֻקֶּיךָ לֹא
not Your the in a like am I For You will When ,saying
statutes ;smoke wineskin ?me comfort

4941 7291 6213 5650 3117 4100 7911
84 שָׁכָחְתִּי׃ כַּמָּה יְמֵי־עַבְדֶּךָ מָתַי תַּעֲשֶׂה בְרֹדְפַי מִשְׁפָּט׃
?judgment my on You will When Your the (are) As I do
persecutors execute ?servant of days what .forget

4687 8451 3808 7882 2086 3738
85 86 כָּרוּ־לִי זֵדִים שִׁיחוֹת אֲשֶׁר לֹא כְתוֹרָתֶךָ׃ כָּל־מִצְוֹתֶיךָ
Your All according (are) not which pits The for have
commandments .law Your to proud me dug

commands *are* faithful; they
persecute me *with* lying;
help me! [87]In a little they
had finished me on earth;
but I did not forsake Your
precepts. [88]Give me life
according to Your mercy;
and I will keep the testimonies of Your mouth.

Lamed

[89]Your word is settled in
Heaven forever, O Jehovah.
[90]Your fidelity *is* to every
generation; You founded
the earth, and it stands.
[91]They stand by Your judgments to this day, for all *are*
Your servants. [92]If Your law
had not been my delight,
then I had perished in my
grief. [93]I will never forget
Your precepts; for with
them You gave me life. [94]I
am Yours—save me; for I
have sought Your precepts.
[95]The wicked waited for me,
to destroy me; I will muse
on Your testimonies. [96]I
have seen an end to all
perfection; Your command
is exceedingly broad.

Mem

[97]O how I love Your law!
It is my meditation all day.
[98]You make me wiser than
my enemies by Your com-
mands; for they *are* forever
mine. [99]I have more wisdom than all my teachers;
for Your testimonies *are* a
meditation to me. [100]I
understand more than the
aged, for I keep Your precepts. [101]I have kept my
feet from every evil way, to
keep Your word. [102]I turned
not from Your judgments;
for You have taught me.
[103]How sweet are Your
words to my palate! More
than honey to my mouth!
[104]By Your precepts I know;
so then I hate every false
way.

Nun

[105]Your word *is* a lamp
to my feet and a light to
my path. [106]I have sworn
and I rise to *it*, to keep
Your righteous judg-
ments. [107]I am afflicted
very much; O Jehovah,
give me life by Your word.
[108]Please, O Jehovah, accept the free offering of
my mouth and teach me

776 3615 4592 5826 7291 8267 530
87 אמונה שקר רדפוני עזרני׃ כמעט כלוני בארץ ואני
but on hadThey little a In help per- they (with) (are)
I ;earth .me finished !me ;me secute lying ;faithful

6310 5715 8104 2421 2617 6490 5800 3808
88 לא־עזבתי פקודיך׃ כחסדך חייני ואשמרה עדות פיך׃
Your testi- the will I and me give Your By Your did not
.mouth of mony keep ;life mercy .precepts forsake

530 1755 1755 8064 5324 1697 3068 5769
89
90 לעולם יהוה דברך נצב בשמים׃ לדר ודר אמונתך
Your (is) gen- and gen- to in is Your O ,Forever
;fidelity eration eration .Heaven settled word ,Jehovah

3605 3117 5975 4941 5975 776 3559
91 כוננת ארץ ותעמד׃ למשפטיך עמדו היום כי הכל
all for this to They to according it and the You
;day stand judgments Your ,stands still ,earth founded

5769 6040 6 8191 8451 3884 5650
92
93 עבדיך׃ לולי תורתך שעשעי אז אבדתי בעניי׃ לעולם
Forever my in had I then my (was) Your Unless Your (are)
.grief perished ,delight law .servants

3462 2421 6490 7911 3808
94 לא־אשכח פקודיך כי־בם חייתני׃ לך־אני הושיעני כי
for ,me save I to gave You with for Your will I not
—(am) You .life me them ;precepts forget

995 5713 6 7563 6960 1875 6490
95 פקודיך דרשתי׃ לי קוו רשעים לאבדני עדתיך אתבונן׃
will I Your destroy to The me for have I Your
.consider testimonies ;me wicked waited .sought precepts

39 66 4687 7342 7093 7200 8502/3605
96
97 לכל־תכלה ראיתי קץ רחבה מצותך מאד׃ מה
O exceed- Your (is) an have I perfection to
how .ingly commandment broad ;end seen all

2449 341 7881 3117 3605 8451 157
98 אהבתי תורתך כל־היום היא שיחתי׃ מאיבי תחכמני
make You my than medi- my (is) it the all Your love I
wiser me enemies .tation day !law

7919 3925 3605 5769 4687
99 מצותך כי לעולם היא־לי׃ מכל־מלמדי השכלתי כי
for more have I my than to they forever for Your by
;understanding teachers all .me (are) ;commands

5341 6490 995 2205 7881 5715
100 עדותיך שיחה לי׃ מזקנים אתבונן כי פקודיך נצרתי׃
.keep I Your because under- I the than to a (are) Your
precepts ,more stand ancients .me meditation testimonies

1697 8104 7272 3607 7451 734 3605
101 מכל־ארח רע כלאתי רגלי למען אשמר דברך׃
Your might I that my had I evil way From
.word keep ,feet kept every

2441 4452 3384 5493 3808 4941
102
103 ממשפטיך לא־סרתי כי־אתה הורתני׃ מה־נמלצו לחכי
my to sweet How have You for have I not Your From
palate are .me taught ;turned judgments

8130 995 6490 6310 1706 565
104 אמרתך מדבש לפי׃ מפקודיך אתבונן על־כן שנאתי |
hate I therefore get I Your Through my to than More Your
;understanding precepts !mouth honey !words

5410 216 1697 7272 5216 8267 734 3605
105 כל־ארח שקר׃ נר־לרגלי דברך ואור לנתיבתי׃
my to a and Your my to A .false way every
.path light ,(is) word feet lamp

5704 6031 6664 4941 8104 6965 7650
106
107 נשבעתי ואקימה לשמר משפטי צדקך׃ נעניתי עד
to am I Your judgments to I and have I
afflicted ,righteous observe ,(it) raised sworn

3068 4494/7521 6310 5071 1697 2421 3068 3966
108 מאד יהוה חיני כדברך׃ נדבות פי רצה־נא יהוה
O ,please accept My free Your by me give O very
,Jehovah ,mouth's offering .word life ,Jehovah ;much

Your judgments. [109]My life *is* in my hand continually, yet I do not forget Your law. [110]The wicked have laid a snare for me; yet I do not wander from Your precepts. [111]I have inherited Your testimonies forever; for they *are* the rejoicing of my heart. [112]I have bowed my heart always to do Your statutes to the end.

Samech

[113]I hate the half-hearted; but I love Your law. [114]You *are* my covert and my shield; I hope in Your word. [115]Depart from me, O evildoers, for I will keep my God's commands. [116]Uphold me by Your word, that I may live; and let me not be ashamed of my hope. [117]Hold me up and I will be saved; and I will always look to Your statutes. [118]You have trampled all who go astray from Your statutes; for their deceit is falsehood. [119]*As* dross You have made all the wicked of the earth to cease; so I love Your testimonies. [120]My flesh has shivered because of Your fear; and I have feared Your judgments.

Ayin

[121]I have done the just and right *thing*; do not leave me to my oppressors. [122]Be surety for Your servant for good; let not the proud oppress me. [123]My eyes fail for Your salvation, and for the word of Your righteousness. [124]Deal with Your servant by Your mercy; and teach me Your statutes. [125]I *am* Your servant; make me consider and I will know Your testimonies. [126]*It is* time for Jehovah to work; they have broken Your law. [127]So I have loved Your commands, more than gold, even fine gold. [128]So I count wholly right all the precepts; I have hated every false way.

Pe

[129]Your testimonies *are* wonderful; so my soul keeps them. [130]The entering of Your word gives light, instructing the simple ones.

---

109 וּמִשְׁפָּטֶיךָ לִמְּדֵנִי׃ נַפְשִׁי בְכַפִּי תָמִיד וְתוֹרָתְךָ לֹא שָׁכָחְתִּי
7911 3808 8451 8548 3709 5315 3925 4941
do I not / Your yet / contin- / in (is) / My / teach / Your and
.forget / law ;ually / palm my / life / .me / judgments

110 / 111 נָתְנוּ רְשָׁעִים פַּח לִי וּמִפִּקּוּדֶיךָ לֹא תָעִיתִי׃ נָחַלְתִּי עֵדְוֹתֶיךָ
5715 5157 8581 38.08 64.90 6341 7563 5414
Your have I / do I / not / Your from yet for / a / The / have
testimonies inherited / .wander / precepts / ;me snare wicked / given

112 לְעוֹלָם כִּי־שְׂשׂוֹן לִבִּי׃ נָטִיתִי לִבִּי לַעֲשׂוֹת חֻקֶּיךָ
2706 6213 38.20 5186 38.20 8342 5769
Your do to / my have I / they / my / the for / ;forever
statutes heart bowed / .(are) heart of rejoicing

113 לְעוֹלָם עֵקֶב׃ סֵעֲפִים שָׂנֵאתִי וְתוֹרָתְךָ אָהָבְתִּי
157 8451 8130 5588 6118 5769
.love I / Your but / ,hate I / half- / the to / always
law / hearted / .end

114 / 115 סִתְרִי וּמָגִנִּי אָתָּה לִדְבָרְךָ יִחָלְתִּי׃ סוּרוּ מִמֶּנִּי מְרֵעִים
7489 5493 31.76 1697 4043 5643
O / from / Turn / .hope I / Your in / You my and / my
,evildoers / ,me / away / word / ;(are) shield / covert

116 וְאֶצְּרָה מִצְוֺת אֱלֹהָי׃ סָמְכֵנִי כְאִמְרָתְךָ וְאֶחְיֶה וְאַל־
13808 2421 565 5564 430 4687 5341
and / I that / to according / Uphold / my / com- the / will I for
not ;live may / word Your / me / .God / of mands / keep

117 תְּבִישֵׁנִי מִשִּׂבְרִי׃ סְעָדֵנִי וְאִוָּשֵׁעָה וְאֶשְׁעָה בְחֻקֶּיךָ תָמִיד׃
8548 2706 8159 3467 5582 7664 .559
.always / Your to / I and / will I and / me Hold / my of / be me let
statutes look will / ;saved be / up / .hope / ashamed

118 / 119 סָלִיתָ כָּל־שׁוֹגִים מֵחֻקֶּיךָ כִּי־שֶׁקֶר תַּרְמִיתָם׃ סִיגִים
5509 8640 8267 2706 7686 55.41
(Like) / their / (is) / for / Your from / who all / have You
,dross / .deceit / falsehood / ;statutes astray go / trampled

120 הִשְׁבַּתָּ כָל־רִשְׁעֵי־אָרֶץ לָכֵן אָהָבְתִּי עֵדֹתֶיךָ׃ סָמַר
5568 5913 157 776 7563 3605 7673
has / Your / love I therefore / ;earth the the all have You
shivered .testimonies / of wicked cease made

121 מִפַּחְדְּךָ בְשָׂרִי וּמִמִּשְׁפָּטֶיךָ יָרֵאתִי׃ עָשִׂיתִי מִשְׁפָּט
4941 6213 3372 4941 13.20 6343
(is what) / have I / have I / Your of and / My / of because
just / done / .feared / judgments / ;flesh / fear Your

122 / 123 וָצֶדֶק בַּל־תַּנִּיחֵנִי לְעֹשְׁקָי׃ עֲרֹב עַבְדְּךָ לְטוֹב אַל־יַעַשְׁקֻנִי
6231 13808 2896 5650 6148 6231 3240 6664
let do / not / for / Your for / Be / my to / leave do / not / and
me oppress ;good / servant / surety / .oppressors / me / ;right

123 / 124 זֵדִים׃ עֵינַי כָּלוּ לִישׁוּעָתֶךָ וּלְאִמְרַת צִדְקֶךָ׃ עֲשֵׂה עִם־
6213 6664 565 3444 3615 5869 2086
with / Deal / Your / the for and / Your for / fail / my / the
.righteousness of word / ,salvation / eyes / .proud

125 עַבְדְּךָ כְחַסְדֶּךָ וְחֻקֶּיךָ לַמְּדֵנִי׃ עַבְדְּךָ־אָנִי הֲבִינֵנִי וְאֵדְעָה
3045 995 5650 3925 2706 26.27 5650
I and / me make I / Your by / teach / Your and / Your by / Your
know will consider ;(am) servant / statutes / ;mercy servant

126 / 127 עֵדֹתֶיךָ׃ עֵת לַעֲשׂוֹת לַיהוָה הֵפֵרוּ תּוֹרָתֶךָ׃ עַל־כֵּן
3651 5921 8451 65.65 3068 6213 6256 5713
Therefore / Your / have they / for / work to / (is It) / Your
.law / broken / —Jehovah / time / .testimonies

128 אָהַבְתִּי מִצְוֺתֶיךָ מִזָּהָב וּמִפָּז׃ עַל־כֵּן כָּל־פִּקּוּדֵי כֹל
3605 6490 6337 2091 4687 157
wholly / the / all / Therefore / fine even than more / Your / have I
.precepts ,gold / ,gold / commands / loved

129 יִשָּׁרְתִּי כָּל־אֹרַח שֶׁקֶר שָׂנֵאתִי׃ פְּלָאוֹת עֵדְוֹתֶיךָ
5715 6382 8130 8267 734 13605 3474
Your / (are) / have I / false / way every / count I
.testimonies wonderful / .hated / ;right

130 עַל־כֵּן נְצָרָתַם נַפְשִׁי׃ פֵּתַח־דְּבָרֶיךָ יָאִיר מֵבִין פְּתָיִים׃
6612 995 214 1697 6608 5315 5341
the / instruct- / gives / Your / the / my / keeps therefore
.simple / ing / ,light / word / of entrance .soul / them

131 I opened my mouth and panted; for I longed for Your commands. 132 Turn to me and favor me, as is the way to those who love Your name. 133 Fix my steps in Your word; and let no evil rule over me. 134 Redeem me from the oppression of man; and I will keep Your precepts. 135 Make Your face shine on Your servant, and teach me Your statutes. 136 Rivers of waters run down my eyes for they do not keep Your law.

Tzaddi

137 O Jehovah, You *are* righteous, and Your judgments right. 138 You have enjoined Your testimonies *as* exceedingly righteous and faithful. 139 My zeal has eaten me up for my enemies have forgotten Your word. 140 Your word *is* pure, and Your servant loves it. 141 I *am* small and despised; I do not forget Your precepts. 142 Your righteousness *is an* eternal righteousness; and Your law *is* truth. 143 Distress and anguish have found me; Your commands *are* my delight. 144 The righteousness of Your testimonies *are* everlasting; make me know and I will live.

Qoph

145 I cried with *my* whole heart; O Jehovah, answer me; I will keep Your statutes. 146 I cried to You; save me and I will keep Your testimonies. 147 I go before the dawn of day and cry; I hope in Your word. 148 My eyes go before the *night* watches, to meditate on Your word. 149 Hear my voice by Your mercy, O Jehovah; give me life by Your judgment. 150 The pursuers of mischief draw near; they are far from Your law. 151 You *are* near, O Jehovah, and all Your commands *are* truth. 152 Of old I have known from Your testimonies, for You have founded them forever.

Resh

153 Look on my affliction and deliver me; for I do not forget Your law. 154 Contend

131 132
6437 2968 4687 7602 6473 6310
פי פערתי ואשאפה כי למצותיך יאבתי: פנה־אלי
to Turn .longed I Your for for and I My
me commands ;panted opened mouth

133
565 3559 6471 8034 157 4941 2603
וחנני כמשפט לאהבי שמך: פעמי הכן באמרתך ואל־
and Your in Fix my Your those to the is as and
not ;word steps .name love who manner ;me favor

134
6490 8104 120 6233 6299 205 3605 7980
תשלט־בי כל־און: פדני מעשק אדם ואשמרה פקודיך
Your I and ;man the from Redeem .evil any over let do
.precepts keep will of oppression me me rule

135 136
3381 4325 6388 2706 3925 5650 215 6440
פניך האר בעבדך ולמדני את־חקיך: פלגי־מים ירדו
run water Rivers Your teach and Your on make Your
down of .statutes me ,servant shine face

137
3477 3068 6662 8451 8104 3808 5869
עיני על לא־שמרו תורתך: צדיק אתה יהוה וישר
(are) and O You righteous Your do not because my
right ;Jehovah ,(are) .law keep they ,eyes

138 139
6789 3966 530 5713 6664 6680 4941
משפטיך: צוית צדק עדתיך ואמונה מאד: צמתתני
eaten has exceed- faith- and Your righteous- have You Your
up me .ingly fulness ,testimonies of ness enjoined .judgments

140
3966 565 6884 6862 1697 7911 7068
קנאתי כי־שכחו דבריך צרי: צרופה אמרתך מאד
,very Your pure (is) my Your have for My
word .enemies word forgotten ,zeal

141
7911 3808 6490 959 6810 157 5650
ועבדך אהבה: צעיר אנכי ונבזה פקדיך לא שכחתי:
do I not Your and (am) I small loves Your and
forget precepts ,despised it servant

142 143
4672 4689 6862 571 8451 5769 6666 6664
צדקתך צדק לעולם ותורתך אמת: צר־ומצוק מצאוני
have and Distress (is) Your and ;forever righ- (is) righ- Your
;me found anguish .truth law teousness teousness

144
2421 995 5769 5715 6664 8191 4687
מצותיך שעשעי: צדק עדותיך לעולם הבינני ואחיה:
will I and me make ever- (is) Your right- the my (are) Your
live understand ;lasting testimonies of ness .delight commands

145 146
7121 5341 2706 3068 6030 3820 3605 7121
קראתי בכל־לב ענני יהוה חקיך אצרה: קראתיך
cried I will I Your O answer (my) with cried I
;You to .keep statutes ;Jehovah ,me ;heart whole

147
7768 5399 6923 5713 8104 3462
הושיעני ואשמרה עדתיך: קדמתי בנשף ואשועה
;cry and dawning the go I Your I and me save
day the of before .testimonies keep will

148
565 7878 821 5869 6923 3176 1697
לדברך יחלתי: קדמו עיני אשמרות לשיח באמרתך:
Your in to (night) the My go .hope I Your in
.word meditate ,watches eyes before word

149 150
7291 7126 2421 4941 3068 2617 8085 6963
קולי שמעה כחסדך יהוה כמשפטך חייני: קרבו רדפי
pur- the Draw me give Your by O Your by Hear my
of suers near .life judgment ,Jehovah ,mercy voice

151
4687 3605 3068 7138 7368 8451 2154
זמה מתורתך רחקו: קרוב אתה יהוה וכל־מצותיך
Your and O You near they Your from mis-
commands all ,Jehovah ,(are) .far are law ;chief

152
3245 5769 5713 3045 6924 571
אמת: קדם ידעתי מעדתיך כי לעולם יסדתם:
have You forever for Your from have I Of (are)
.them founded ;testimonies known old .truth

153 154
7379 7378 7911 3808 8451 2502 6040
ראה־עניי וחלצני כי־תורתך לא שכחתי: ריבה ריבי
my Contend do I not Your for and my Look
cause (for) .forget law ;me deliver affliction on

2706 3444 7563 7350 2421 565 1350
וגאלני לאמרתך חיני׃ רחוק מרשעים ישועה כי־חקיך
Your for ;salvation the from Far (is) me give Your by re- and
statutes wicked ,life word ;me deem

7227 2421 4941 3068 7227 7356 1875 3808
156 157 לא דרשו׃ רחמיך רבים ׀ יהוה כמשפטיך חיני׃ רבים
(are) me give to according O (are) Your they do not
many .life judgments Your ;Jehovah ,great mercies .seek

6962 898 7200 5186 3808 5715 6862 7291
158 רדפי וצרי מעדותיך לא נטיתי׃ ראיתי בגדים ואתקוטטה
was and the saw I do I not Your from my and per- My
;grieved traitors .turn testimonies ;enemies secutors

157 6490 7200 8104 3808 565
159 אשר אמרתך לא שמרו׃ ראה כי־פקודיך אהבתי
,love I Your how See they not word Your because
precepts .keep did

3605 5769 571 1697 7218 2421 2617 3068
160 יהוה כחסדך חיני׃ ראש־דברך אמת ולעולם כל־
every and true (is) Your sum The me give Your by O
of one forever word of .life mercy ;Jehovah

6342 1697 2600 7291 8269 6664 4941
161 משפט צדקך׃ שרים רדפוני חנם ומדבריך פחד
has Your at but without per- have Princes Your judgments
feared word ;cause me secuted .righteous

8267 7227 7998 4672 565 7797 3820
162 163 לבי׃ שש אנכי על־אמרתך כמוצא שלל רב׃ שקר
lying .great spoil one as Your at I rejoice my
finds who word .heart

1984 3117 7651 157 8451 8581 8130
164 שנאתי ואתעבה תורתך אהבתי׃ שבע ביום הללתיך
praise I a in Seven .love I Your (but) ;despise and hate I
You day (times) law

369 8451 157 7227 7965 6664 4941
165 על משפטי צדקך׃ שלום רב לאהבי תורתך ואין למו
for and Your those to Great peace Your judgments for
them (is) not ,law love who (is) .righteous

8104 6213 4687 3068 3444 7663 4383
166 167 מכשול׃ שברתי לישועתך יהוה ומצותיך עשיתי׃ שמרה
kept has have I Your and O Your for have I an
.done commands ,Jehovah ,salvation hoped .obstacle

5713 6490 8104 3966 157 5713 5315
168 נפשי עדתיך ואהבם מאד׃ שמרתי פקודיך ועדתיך כי
for Your and Your have I very I and Your My
testimonies precepts kept .much them love ;testimonies soul

1697 3068 7440 7126 5048 1870 3605
169 כל־דרכי נגדך׃ תקרב רנתי לפניך יהוה כדברך
Your by O You to cry my come Let are my all
word ;Jehovah near .You before ways

5042 5337 565 6440 8467 935 995
170 171 הבינני׃ תבוא תחנתי לפניך כאמרתך הצילני׃ תבענה
pour shall deliver to according before my Let me give
forth .me word Your ;You prayer come .wisdom

565 3956 6030 2706 3925 8416 8193
172 שפתי תהלה כי תלמדני חקיך׃ תען לשוני אמרתך כי
for Your My shall Your have You when ,praise My
;word tongue answer .statutes me taught lips

977 6490 5826 3027 6664 4687 3605
173 כל־מצותיך צדק׃ תהי־ידך לעזרני כי פקודיך בחרתי׃
have I Your for help Your Let righ- (are) Your all
.chosen precepts ,me hand .teousness commands

5315 2421 8191 8451 3068 3444 8373
174 תאבתי לישועתך יהוה ותורתך שעשעי׃ תחי־נפשי
my Let my (is) Your and O Your for have I
soul live .delight law ;Jehovah ,salvation longed

for my cause and redeem
me; give me life according
to Your word.
155 Salvation
is far from the wicked; for
they do not seek Your
statutes.
156 O Jehovah,
Your tender mercies *are*
great; give me life according to Your judgments.
157 My persecutors and
enemies *are* many; I do not
turn from Your testimonies.
158 I saw the traitors and was
grieved, because they did
not keep Your word.
159 See
how I love Your precepts, O
Jehovah; give me life
according to Your mercy.
160 The sum of Your word *is*
true; every one of Your
righteous judgments *en-
dures* forever.

Shin

161 Princes have perse-
cuted me without cause;
but my heart has feared at
Your word.
162 I rejoice at
Your word, as one who
finds great spoil.
163 I hate
and despise lying; *but* I love
Your law.
164 I praise You
seven *times* a day because
of Your righteous judg-
ments.
165 Great peace *is* to
those who love Your law,
and there is no stumbling-
block to them.
166 O
Jehovah, I have hoped for
Your salvation, and have
done Your precepts.
167 My
soul has kept Your testi-
monies, and I love them
very much;
168 I have kept
Your commands and Your
testimonies, for all my ways
are before You.

Tau

169 Let my cry come near
You, O Jehovah; give me
wisdom according to Your
word.
170 Let my prayer
come before You; deliver
me according to Your word.
171 My lips shall pour forth
praise when You have
taught me Your statutes.
172 My tongue shall answer
Your word; for all Your
commands *are* righteous-
ness.
173 Let Your hand
help me; for I have chosen
Your precepts.
174 I have
longed for Your salvation, O
Jehovah; and Your law *is*
my delight.
175 Let my soul

live, and it will praise You; and let Your judgments help me. [176]I have gone astray like a lost sheep; seek Your servant; for I do not forget Your commandments.

PSALM 120

A Song of Ascents.

[1]In my distress I cried to Jehovah, and He answered me. [2]O Jehovah, deliver my soul from lying lips, from a deceitful tongue. [3]What shall be given to you, or what shall *one* add to you, O false tongue? [4]Sharp arrows of the mighty, with coals of broom!

[5]Woe is me that I sojourned in Meshech; I dwell with the tents of Kedar! [6]My soul has long dwelt to itself, with him who hates peace. [7]I *am for* peace; but when I speak, they *are* for war.

PSALM 121

A Song of Ascents.

[1]I will lift up my eyes to the hills; where shall my help come from? [2]My help *comes* from Jehovah, the Maker of the heavens and the earth. [3]He will not give your foot to slip; He who keeps you will not slumber. [4]Behold, He who keeps Israel will not slumber nor sleep. [5]Jehovah *is* your keeper; Jehovah *is* your shade on your right hand. [6]The sun shall not strike you by day, nor the moon by night; [7]Jehovah shall keep you from all evil; He shall keep your soul. [8]Jehovah shall keep your going out, and your coming in; from now on and till forever.

1245 6 7716 8582 3826 4941 1984
176 וּתְהַלְלֶךָּ וּמִשְׁפָּטֶךָ יַעְזְרֻנִי׃ תָּעִיתִי כְּשֶׂה אֹבֵד בַּקֵּשׁ
seek ;lost a like sheep have I astray gone help Let .me Your and judgments shall and ;You praise

7911 3808 4687 5650
עַבְדֶּךָ כִּי מִצְוֹתֶיךָ לֹא שָׁכָחְתִּי׃
do I .forget not Your commands for Your ;servant

PSAL. CXX קכ

PSALM 120

3068 6030 7121 6864 3068 4609 7892
1
2 שִׁיר הַמַּעֲלוֹת אֶל־יְהוָה בַּצָּרָתָה לִּי קָרָאתִי וַיַּעֲנֵנִי׃ יְהוָה
Jeho- ,vah O He and .me answered ,cried I me to the in trouble Jehovah To .ascents A of song

5414 7423 3956 8267 8193 5315 5337
3 הַצִּילָה נַפְשִׁי מִשְּׂפַת־שֶׁקֶר מִלָּשׁוֹן רְמִיָּה׃ מַה־יִּתֵּן לְךָ
to ,you given be shall What .deceitful a from tongue ,lying lips from soul my deliver

1513 8150 1368 2671 7423 3956 3254 4100
4 וּמַה־יֹּסִיף לָךְ לָשׁוֹן רְמִיָּה׃ חִצֵּי גִבּוֹר שְׁנוּנִים עִם גַּחֲלֵי
coals of with ,Sharp the mighty arrows of ?false O tongue to ,you (one) shall add or what

6938 168 7931 4902 1481 190 7574
5 רְתָמִים׃ אוֹיָה־לִי כִּי־גַרְתִּי מֶשֶׁךְ שָׁכַנְתִּי עִם־אָהֳלֵי קֵדָר׃
!Kedar the of tents with dwell I ;Meshech I in sojourned that is ,me Woe !broom

7965 7965 8130 5315 7931 7227
6
7 רַבַּת שָׁכְנָה־לָּהּ נַפְשִׁי עִם שׂוֹנֵא שָׁלוֹם׃ אֲנִי־שָׁלוֹם וְכִי
but when ,peace I (for am) .peace him hates who with my soul to itself has dwelt Long

4421 1696
אֲדַבֵּר הֵמָּה לַמִּלְחָמָה׃
.war for they (are) ,speak I

PSAL. CXXI קכא

PSALM 121

5828 935 370 2022 5869 5375 4609 7892
1 שִׁיר לַמַּעֲלוֹת אֶשָּׂא עֵינַי אֶל־הֶהָרִים מֵאַיִן יָבֹא עֶזְרִי׃
my ?help shall come from where the ;hills to my eyes will I up lift .ascents song A of

7272 4131 5414/408 776 8064 6213 3068 5828
2
3 עֶזְרִי מֵעִם יְהוָה עֹשֵׂה שָׁמַיִם וָאָרֶץ׃ אַל־יִתֵּן לַמּוֹט רַגְלֶךָ
your ;foot slip to He will give not the and .earth the heavens of Maker the ,Jehovah (comes) from My help

3478 8104 3462 3808 5123 3808 2009 8104 5123
4 אַל־יָנוּם שֹׁמְרֶךָ׃ הִנֵּה לֹא־יָנוּם וְלֹא יִישָׁן שׁוֹמֵר יִשְׂרָאֵל׃
!Israel who He keeps sleep nor not shall slumber ,Behold who He .you keeps will not slumber

8121 3119 3225 3027 6738 3068 8104 3068
5
6 יְהוָה שֹׁמְרֶךָ יְהוָה צִלְּךָ עַל־יַד יְמִינֶךָ׃ יוֹמָם הַשֶּׁמֶשׁ
sun The day by your .right hand on your shade Jehovah (is) Your ;keeper Jehovah (is)

8104 8104 3068 3915 3394 5221 3808
7 לֹא־יַכֶּכָּה וְיָרֵחַ בַּלָּיְלָה׃ יְהוָה יִשְׁמָרְךָ מִכָּל־רָע יִשְׁמֹר
shall He keep ;evil from all shall you keep Jehovah ;night by the nor moon shall not ,you strike

5769 5704 6258 935 3318 8104 3068 5315
8 אֶת־נַפְשֶׁךָ׃ יְהוָה יִשְׁמָר־צֵאתְךָ וּבוֹאֶךָ מֵעַתָּה וְעַד־עוֹלָם׃
.forever and till from now on your and ;in coming your going out shall keep Jehovah your .soul

PSAL. CXXII קכב

PSALM 122

A Song of Ascents; of David.

1 I was glad when they said to me, Let us go into the house of Jehovah. 2 Our feet shall stand within your gates, O Jerusalem. 3 Jerusalem is built like a city that *is* joined to itself, together. 4 *There* the tribes go up, the tribes of Jehovah; to the testimony of Israel; to give thanks to the name of Jehovah. 5 For the thrones of judgment were established there, the thrones of the house of David. 6 Pray for the peace of Jerusalem; those who love you shall prosper. 7 Peace be within your walls; prosperity in your towers. 8 Because of my brothers and my companions, I will now say, Peace *be* in you. 9 Because of the house of Jehovah, our God, I will seek your good.

1 שִׁיר הַמַּעֲלוֹת לְדָוִד שָׂמַחְתִּי בְּאֹמְרִים לִי בֵּית יְהוָה נֵלֵךְ׃
3212 3068 1004 559 8056 1732 4609 7892
us let Jehovah the to they when was I Of .ascents song A
.into go of house me said glad .David of

2
3 עֹמְדוֹת הָיוּ רַגְלֵינוּ בִּשְׁעָרַיִךְ יְרוּשָׁלִָם׃ יְרוּשָׁלִַם הַבְּנוּיָה
1129 3389 3389 8179 7272 1961 5975
built is Jerusalem O within Our are standing
.Jerusalem ,gates Your feet

4 כְּעִיר שֶׁחֻבְּרָה־לָּהּ יַחְדָּו׃ שֶׁשָּׁם עָלוּ שְׁבָטִים שִׁבְטֵי־יָהּ
3050 7626 7626 5927 3162 2266 5892
,Jah the the up go where ;together to (is) that a like
of tribes ,tribes itself joined city

5 עֵדוּת לְיִשְׂרָאֵל לְהֹדוֹת לְשֵׁם יְהוָה׃ כִּי שָׁמָּה ׀ יָשְׁבוּ
7760 3068 8034 3034 3478 5715
were there For .Jehovah the to give to ,Israel to testi- a
set of name thanks mony

6 כִסְאוֹת לְמִשְׁפָּט כִּסְאוֹת לְבֵית דָּוִד׃ שַׁאֲלוּ שְׁלוֹם יְרוּשָׁלִָם
3389 7965 7592 1732 1004 3678 4941 3678
;Jerusalem the Pray .David the the ,judgment the
of peace for of house of thrones thrones

7 יִשְׁלָיוּ אֹהֲבָיִךְ׃ יְהִי־שָׁלוֹם בְּחֵילֵךְ שַׁלְוָה בְּאַרְמְנוֹתָיִךְ׃
759 7962 2426 7965 157 7951
your in prosperity within peace May who those shall
.towers ,walls your be .you love prosper

8
9 לְמַעַן אַחַי וְרֵעָי אֲדַבְּרָה־נָּא שָׁלוֹם בָּךְ׃ לְמַעַן בֵּית־יְהוָה
3068 1004 4616 7965 4994 1696 7453 251 4616
,Jehovah the Because (be) peace ,now will I my and my Because
of house of .you in say ,companions brothers of

אֱלֹהֵינוּ אֲבַקְשָׁה טוֹב לָךְ׃
2896 1245 430
.your good will I ,God our
seek

PSAL. CXXIII קכג

PSALM 123

A Song of Ascents.

1 I will lift up my eyes on You, O Dweller in Heaven. 2 Behold, as the eyes of servants *look* to the hand of their masters; as the eyes of a maiden to the hand of her mistress; so our eyes *wait* on Jehovah our God, until He shows grace to us. 3 Be gracious to us, O Jehovah; be gracious to us! For we are exceedingly filled with scorn. 4 Our soul is exceedingly filled for itself *with* the contempt of those who are at ease, the scorn of the proud.

1 שִׁיר הַמַּעֲלוֹת אֵלֶיךָ נָשָׂאתִי אֶת־עֵינַי הַיֹּשְׁבִי בַּשָּׁמָיִם׃
8064 3427 5869 5375 4609 7892
the in who You ,eyes my will I You To .ascents A
.heavens dwell up lift of song

2 הִנֵּה כְעֵינֵי עֲבָדִים אֶל־יַד אֲדוֹנֵיהֶם כְּעֵינֵי שִׁפְחָה אֶל־יַד
3027 8198 5869 113 3027 5650 5869 2009
the to maiden a the as their the (look) servants the as ,Behold
of hand of eyes ;masters of hand to of eyes

3 גְּבִרְתָּהּ כֵּן עֵינֵינוּ אֶל־יְהוָה אֱלֹהֵינוּ עַד שֶׁיְּחָנֵּנוּ׃ חָנֵּנוּ יְהוָה
3068 2603 2603 5704 430 3068 5869 1404
O Favor He until our Jehovah (wait) our so her
;Jehovah ,us .us favors God on eyes ,mistress

4 חָנֵּנוּ כִּי־רַב שָׂבַעְנוּ בוּז׃ רַבַּת שָׂבְעָה־לָּהּ נַפְשֵׁנוּ הַלַּעַג
3933 5315 7646 7227 937 7646 7227 2603
the soul Our for is exceedingly .scorn are we exceed- for favor
of contempt itself filled with filled ingly ;us

הַשַּׁאֲנַנִּים הַבּוּז לִגְאֵיוֹנִים׃
3238 939 7600
the the are who those
.proud of scorn ,ease at

PSAL. CXXIV קכד

PSALM 124

A Song of Ascents, of David.

1 Except that *it was* Jehovah who was for us, O

1 שִׁיר הַמַּעֲלוֹת לְדָוִד לוּלֵי יְהוָה שֶׁהָיָה לָנוּ יֹאמַר־נָא
559 1961 3068 3884 1732 4609 7892
O may for who Jehovah Except Of .ascents A
say ,us was that .David of song

2 233 120 6965 1961 3068 38 84 3478
3 יִשְׂרָאֵל׃ לוּלֵא יְהוָה שֶׁהָיָה לָנוּ בְּקוּם עָלֵינוּ אָדָם׃ אֲזַי
then ,men against the in for who Jehovah Except ;Israel
us of rising us was that

4 51,58 7857 4325 233 639 2734 1104 2416
חַיִּים בְּלָעוּנוּ בַּחֲרוֹת אַפָּם בָּנוּ׃ אֲזַי הַמַּיִם שְׁטָפוּנוּ נַחְלָה
the over- had the Then against their glowing had they alive
torrent ;us flowed waters us anger ;us swallowed

5 2121 4325 5315 5921 5674 233 5315 5921 5674
עָבַר עַל־נַפְשֵׁנוּ׃ אֲזַי עָבַר עַל־נַפְשֵׁנוּ הַמַּיִם הַזֵּידוֹנִים׃
.raging waters the soul our over had then ;soul our over had
passed passed

6 6833 5315 8127 2964 5414 3808 3068 1288
7 בָּרוּךְ יְהוָה שֶׁלֹּא נְתָנָנוּ טֶרֶף לְשִׁנֵּיהֶם׃ נַפְשֵׁנוּ כְּצִפּוֹר
a like soul Our their to a (as) give did who Jehovah Blessed
bird teeth prey us not (be)

8 5828 4422 7665 6341 3369 6341 4422
נִמְלְטָה מִפַּח יוֹקְשִׁים הַפַּח נִשְׁבָּר וַאֲנַחְנוּ נִמְלָטְנוּ׃ עֶזְרֵנוּ
Our have we and is the the the from has
help .escaped broken snare ;fowlers of snare escaped

776 8064 6213 3068 8034
בְּשֵׁם יְהוָה עֹשֵׂה שָׁמַיִם וָאָרֶץ׃
.earth and the the Jehovah's in (is)
heavens of Maker name

may Israel say; [2]except that *it was* Jehovah who was for us when men rose up against us, [3]then they would have swallowed us alive, when their anger glowed against us. [4]Then the waters would have flowed over us; the torrent would have covered our soul; [5]then the raging waters would have passed over our soul.

[6]Blessed *be* Jehovah, who did not give us as a prey to their teeth. [7]Our soul has escaped like a bird out of the fowlers' snare; the snare is broken, and we have escaped. [8]Our help *is* in the name of Jehovah, the Maker of the heavens and earth.

PSAL. CXXV קכה

PSALM 125

1 4131 3808 6726 2022 3068 982 46,09 7892
שִׁיר הַמַּעֲלוֹת הַבֹּטְחִים בַּיהוָה כְּהַר־צִיּוֹן לֹא־יִמּוֹט
is it not ;Zion (be shall) in who They .ascents song A
;shaken Mount like Jehovah trust of

2 5439 3068 5439 2022 3389 3427 5769
לְעוֹלָם יֵשֵׁב׃ יְרוּשָׁלַםִ הָרִים סָבִיב לָהּ וַיהוָה סָבִיב
all is and to all are the ,Jerusalem it forever
around Jehovah ;her around mountains .remains

3 5921/7562 7626 5117 3808 3588 5769 5704 6258 5971
לְעַמּוֹ מֵעַתָּה וְעַד־עוֹלָם׃ כִּי לֹא יָנוּחַ שֵׁבֶט הָרֶשַׁע עַל
on wickedness the shall not For .forever and this from His
of rod rest to time people

5766 6662 7971 3808 4618 6662 1486
גּוֹרַל הַצַּדִּיקִים לְמַעַן לֹא־יִשְׁלְחוּ הַצַּדִּיקִים | בְּעַוְלָתָה
iniquity to the put not that the the
righteous forth ;righteous of lot

4 3826 3477 2895 3068 2896 3027
יְדֵיהֶם׃ הֵיטִיבָה יְהוָה לַטּוֹבִים וְלִישָׁרִים בְּלִבּוֹתָם׃
.hearts their in the to and the to O ,good Do their
upright ,good Jehovah .hands

5 79,65 205 6466 3068 3212 6128 5186
וְהַמַּטִּים עֲקַלְקַלּוֹתָם יוֹלִיכֵם יְהוָה אֶת־פֹּעֲלֵי הָאָוֶן שָׁלוֹם
peace ;evil the with Jehovah lead shall crooked their those And
of workers them ,ways incline who

3478 5921
עַל־יִשְׂרָאֵל׃
.Israel (be)
upon

PSALM 125

A Song of Ascents.

[1]They who trust in Jehovah *shall be* like Mount Zion; it is not shaken; it remains forever. [2]The mountains *are* all around Jerusalem; and Jehovah *is* all around His people, from this time and forever. [3]For the scepter of wickedness shall not rest on the lot of the righteous; that the righteous not put forth their hands to evil. [4]Do good, O Jehovah, to the good, and to the upright in their heart. [5]And those who turn aside to their crooked ways, Jehovah shall lead them with the evildoers. Peace be upon Israel.

PSAL. CXXVI

PSALM 126

1 2492 1961 6726 7870 3068 7725 46,09 7892
שִׁיר הַמַּעֲלוֹת בְּשׁוּב יְהוָה אֶת־שִׁיבַת צִיּוֹן הָיִינוּ כְּחֹלְמִים׃
those like we ,Zion the Jehovah When .ascents song A
.dream who were of captivity returned of

2 1430 1471 559 227 7440 3956 6310 7814 4390
אָז יִמָּלֵא שְׂחוֹק פִּינוּ וּלְשׁוֹנֵנוּ רִנָּה אָז יֹאמְרוּ בַגּוֹיִם הִגְדִּיל
great the in they then with our and our laughter was Then
nations said ;shouting tongue ,mouth of full

PSALM 126

A Song of Ascents.

[1]When Jehovah turned back the captivity of Zion, we were like those who dream. [2]Then our mouth was full of laughter, and our tongue *with* joyful shouting; then they said among

the nations, Jehovah *will* work great *things* with these. [3]Jehovah *did* great things to work with us; we are glad. [4]Turn her captivity again, O Jehovah, like the south streams. [5]Those who sow in tears shall reap with joyful shouting. [6]Surely *he who* walks and weeps, bearing a bag of seed, shall come again with joyful shouting, bearing his sheaves.

1961 6213 3068 1430 428 62 13 30 68
3 יְהוָה לַעֲשׂוֹת עִם־אֵלֶּה׃ הִגְדִּיל יְהוָה לַעֲשׂוֹת עִמָּנוּ הָיִינוּ
we are | with ;us | work to | Jehovah | Great things | .these | with | work to | Jehovah

5045 650 7622 3068 7725 8056
4 5 שְׂמֵחִים׃ שׁוּבָה יְהוָה אֶת־שְׁבוּתֵנוּ כַּאֲפִיקִים בַּנֶּגֶב׃
the in .south | the like streams | our ;captivity | O ,Jehovah | Turn ,again | .glad

5375 1058/3212 1980 71 14 7440 18 32 2232
6 הַזֹּרְעִים בְּדִמְעָה בְּרִנָּה יִקְצֹרוּ׃ הָלוֹךְ יֵלֵךְ וּבָכֹה נֹשֵׂא
bearing | and ,weeps | (he) walks | walking | shall ,reap | with shouting | ,tears in | who Those sow

485 53 7 5 7440 935 2233 4901
מֶשֶׁךְ־הַזָּרַע בֹּא־יָבֹא בְרִנָּה נֹשֵׂא אֲלֻמֹּתָיו׃
his .sheaves | bearing | with ,rejoicing | come shall again | the seed | bag a of

PSAL. CXXVII

PSALM 127

PSALM 127

A Song of Ascents for Solomon.

[1]If Jehovah does not build the house, they who build it labor in vain. If Jehovah does not keep the city, the watchman stays awake in vain. [2]*It is* in vain for you to rise early, sit up late, to eat the bread of toils; *for* so He gives His beloved sleep. [3]Lo, children *are* an inheritance of Jehovah; the fruit of the womb *is His* reward. [4]As arrows in the hand of a mighty man, so *are* the sons of the young. [5]Blessed is the man who has filled his quiver with them; they shall not be ashamed, for they shall speak with their enemies in the gate.

7723 1004 1129 3808 3068 518 8010 4609 7892
1 שִׁיר הַמַּעֲלוֹת לִשְׁלֹמֹה אִם־יְהוָה ׀ לֹא־יִבְנֶה בַיִת שָׁוְא
vain in | the ,house | does not build | Jehovah | If | Of .Solomon | .ascents | song A of

8245 7723 5892 8104 3808 3068 518 1129 5998
עָמְלוּ בוֹנָיו בּוֹ אִם־יְהוָה לֹא־יִשְׁמָר־עִיר שָׁוְא ׀ שָׁקַד
stays awake | vain in | the ,city | does not keep | Jehovah | if | ;it in | its builders | labor

3899 398 7925 309 6965 7925 7723 8104
2 שׁוֹמֵר׃ שָׁוְא לָכֶם ׀ מַשְׁכִּימֵי קוּם מְאַחֲרֵי־שֶׁבֶת אֹכְלֵי לֶחֶם
the of bread | to eat | sitting ;up | being of late | ,rising | being of early | for you | (is It) vain | the keeper

1121 3068 5159 2009 8142 3039 5414 6089
3 הָעֲצָבִים כֵּן יִתֵּן לִידִידוֹ שֵׁנָא׃ הִנֵּה נַחֲלַת יְהוָה בָּנִים
(are) ;sons | Jehovah | the of inheritance | ,Lo | .sleep | His to beloved | He gives | (for) so | ;toils

5271 1121 1368 3027 2671 990 6529 79 39
4 שְׂכַר פְּרִי הַבָּטֶן׃ כְּחִצִּים בְּיַד־גִּבּוֹר כֵּן בְּנֵי הַנְּעוּרִים׃
the .young | the of sons | (so) (are) | mighty a ,man's | in hand | arrows As | the .womb | the of fruit | a (is it) ,reward

954 827 43 90 834 1397 835
5 אַשְׁרֵי הַגֶּבֶר אֲשֶׁר מִלֵּא אֶת־אַשְׁפָּתוֹ מֵהֶם לֹא־יֵבֹשׁוּ כִּי־
for shall they not ,ashamed be | with ,them | his quiver | has filled | who | the man | Blessed (is)

8179 341 1696
יְדַבְּרוּ אֶת־אוֹיְבִים בַּשָּׁעַר׃
the in .gate | their enemies | :shall they to speak

PSAL. CXXVIII קכח

PSALM 128

PSALM 128

A Song of Ascents.

[1]Blessed *is* everyone who fears Jehovah, who walks in His ways. [2]For you shall surely eat the labor of your hands; you *shall be* happy, and all *is* good to you. [3]Your wife *shall be* like a fruitful vine by the sides of your house; your sons *shall be* like olive plants around your table. [4]Behold! So shall the man be blessed who fears Jehovah. [5]Jehovah shall bless you out of Zion; and

1870 1980 3068 3373 3605 835 46 09 7892
1 שִׁיר הַמַּעֲלוֹת אַשְׁרֵי כָּל־יְרֵא יְהוָה הַהֹלֵךְ בִּדְרָכָיו׃
His in .ways | who walks | ,Jehovah | who fears | every- one | Blessed (is) | .ascents | song A of

1612 802 2896 835 398 3709 301
2 3 יְגִיעַ כַּפֶּיךָ כִּי תֹאכֵל אַשְׁרֶיךָ וְטוֹב לָךְ׃ אֶשְׁתְּךָ ׀ כְּגֶפֶן
like (be) vine a | Your wife | to .you | and (is) good | (shall) you happy (be) | you ;eat shall | surely | your hands | The of labor

7979 54 39 2132 8363 1121 1004 3411 6500
פֹּרִיָּה בְּיַרְכְּתֵי בֵיתֶךָ בָּנֶיךָ כִּשְׁתִלֵי זֵיתִים סָבִיב לְשֻׁלְחָנֶךָ׃
your .table | around | olive | like plants | your sons | your ;house | the by of sides | fruitful

6726 3068 1288 3068 3373 1397 1288 2009
4 הִנֵּה כִי־כֵן יְבֹרַךְ גָּבֶר יְרֵא יְהוָה׃ יְבָרֶכְךָ יְהוָה מִצִּיּוֹן
of out ;Zion | Jehovah | shall you bless | .Jehovah | who fears | the man | be shall blessed | that so ,Behold

you shall see the good of Jerusalem all the days of your life. [6]Yes, you shall see the sons of your sons. Peace be upon Israel!

6 וּרְאֵה בְּטוּב יְרוּשָׁלָ͏ִם כֹּל יְמֵי חַיֶּיךָ׃ וּרְאֵה־בָנִים לְבָנֶיךָ

1121 1121 7200 2416 3117 3605 3389 2898 7200

your of .sons | the sons | you And see shall | your .life | the of days | all | Jerusalem | the of good | you and see shall

שָׁלוֹם עַל־יִשְׂרָאֵל׃

3478 5921 7965

.Israel | upon | Peace (be)

PSAL. CXXIX קכט

PSALM 129

A Song of Ascents.

[1]Many times they have afflicted me from my youth, let Israel now say; [2]they have afflicted me from my youth many times; yet they have not prevailed over me. [3]The plowers plowed on my back; they made their furrows long. [4]Jehovah *is* righteous; He cuts the cords of the wicked in two. [5]Let them all be ashamed and turned back, those who hate Zion; [6]let them be like the grass on the rooftops, which dries up before it draws out; [7]with which the reaper does not fill his hand; nor the binder of sheaves his bosom.

[8]And those who pass by have never said, The blessing of Jehovah *be* on you; we bless you in the name of Jehovah.

1 שִׁיר הַמַּעֲלוֹת רַבַּת צְרָרוּנִי מִנְּעוּרָי יֹאמַר־נָא יִשְׂרָאֵל׃

3478 4994/559 5271 6031 7227 4609 7892

;Israel | now | let say | my from ,youth | have they me afflicted | Many times | .ascents | song A of

2
3 רַבַּת צְרָרוּנִי מִנְּעוּרָי גַּם לֹא־יָכְלוּ לִי׃ עַל־גַּבִּי חָרְשׁוּ

2790 1354 3201 5271 6887 7227

plowed | my back | On | over .me | they not prevailed have | yet | my from ;youth | have they me afflicted | many times

4 חֹרְשִׁים הֶאֱרִיכוּ לְמַעֲנוֹתָם׃ יְהוָה צַדִּיק קִצֵּץ עֲבוֹת

5688 7112 6662 3068 4618 748 2790

the of cords | cuts He two in | (is) ,righteous | Jehovah | their .furrows | made they long | the ;plowers

5
6 רְשָׁעִים׃ יֵבֹשׁוּ וְיִסֹּגוּ אָחוֹר כֹּל שֹׂנְאֵי צִיּוֹן׃ יִהְיוּ כַּחֲצִיר

2682 1961 6726 8130 3605 268 5472 954 7563

the like on grass | them let be | ;Zion | those hate who | all | ,back | and turned | be Let ashamed | the .wicked

7 גַּגּוֹת שֶׁקַּדְמַת שָׁלַף יָבֵשׁ׃ שֶׁלֹּא מִלֵּא כַפּוֹ קוֹצֵר וְחִצְנוֹ

2683 7114 3709 4390 3808 3001 8025 6927 1406

his nor bosom | the ;reaper | his palm | does fill | with not which | dries ;up | draws it out | which before | the ,roofs

8 מְעַמֵּר׃ וְלֹא אָמְרוּ הָעֹבְרִים בִּרְכַּת־יְהוָה אֲלֵיכֶם בֵּרַכְנוּ

1288 3068 1293 5674 559 3808 6014

we bless | on (be) ;you | Jehovah | The of blessing | who those ;by pass | have said | And not | binder the sheaves of

אֶתְכֶם בְּשֵׁם יְהוָה׃

3068 8034

.Jehovah | the in of name | you

PSAL. CXXX קל

PSALM 130

A Song of Ascents.

[1]Out of the depths I have called You, O Jehovah. [2]Lord, hear my voice; and let Your ears attend to the voice of my prayers. [3]If You will keep iniquities, O Lord, who shall stand? [4]But forgiveness *is* with You, in order that You may be feared. [5]I wait *for* Jehovah; my soul waits, and I hope for His word. [6]My soul *waits* for the Lord more than morning-watchers *who are* watching for the morning. [7]Let Israel hope

1
2 שִׁיר הַמַּעֲלוֹת מִמַּעֲמַקִּים קְרָאתִיךָ יְהוָה׃ אֲדֹנָי שִׁמְעָה

8085 136 3068 7121 4615 4609 7892

hear | ,Lord | O .Jehovah | have I ,You called | of Out depths the | .ascents | song A of

3 בְקוֹלִי תִּהְיֶינָה אָזְנֶיךָ קַשֻּׁבוֹת לְקוֹל תַּחֲנוּנָי׃ אִם־עֲוֺנוֹת

5771 8469 6963 7183 241 1961 6963

iniquities If | my .prayers | the to of voice | attentive | Your ears | be let | my voice

4 תִּשְׁמָר־יָהּ אֲדֹנָי מִי יַעֲמֹד׃ כִּי־עִמְּךָ הַסְּלִיחָה לְמַעַן תִּוָּרֵא׃

3372 5547 5975 136 3050 8104

may You .feared be | that | (is) ,forgiveness | with But You | shall who ?stand | O ,Lord | O Jah | will You ,keep

5
6 קִוִּיתִי יְהוָה קִוְּתָה נַפְשִׁי וְלִדְבָרוֹ הוֹחָלְתִּי׃ נַפְשִׁי לַאדֹנָי

136 5315 3176 1697 5315 6960 3068 6960

the for Lord | soul My (waits) | .hope I | for and word His | my soul | waits | ;Jehovah | wait I (for)

7 מִשֹּׁמְרִים לַבֹּקֶר שֹׁמְרִים לַבֹּקֶר׃ יַחֵל יִשְׂרָאֵל אֶל־יְהוָה

3068 3478 3176 1242 8104 1242 8104

;Jehovah to | Israel | Let hope | the for .morning | watching | the for ,morning | than more watchers to Jehovah; for with Jehovah *is* mercy; and with Him *is* abundant redemption; 8and He shall redeem Israel from all his sins.

8 כי־עם־יהוה החסד והרבה עמו פדות׃ והוא יפדה את־

will redeem He and ;redemption with Him and abundant (is) ;mercy Jehovah with for

ישראל מכל עונתיו׃

his .iniquities all from Israel

PSALM 131

A Song of Ascents. Of David.

1O Jehovah, my heart is not proud; nor have my eyes been lofty; nor have I walked in great things, nor in things too wondrous for me. 2Surely I have set *myself* and have quieted my soul, like one weaned by its mother; my soul on me *is* like one weaned. 3Let Israel hope in Jehovah, from now and till forever.

PSAL. CXXXI קלא

1 שיר המעלות לדוד יהוה לא־גבה לבי ולא־רמו עיני

my ;eyes been lofty have not and ;heart proud my is not O ,Jehovah Of .David .ascents song A of

2 ולא־הלכתי בגדלות ובנפלאות ממני׃ אם־לא שויתי

have I set not If for too .me things in and wondrous great in ;things have I walked and not

3 ודוממתי נפשי כגמל עלי אמו כגמל עלי נפשי׃ יחל

Let hope my (is) .soul upon me the as weaned its ;mother by one like weaned my soul have and quieted

ישראל אל־יהוה מעתה ועד־עולם׃

.forever and till from now Jehovah in Israel

PSALM 132

A Song of Ascents.

1O Jehovah, remember David *with* all his afflictions; 2how he swore to Jehovah; he vowed to the Mighty One of Jacob; 3If I will go into the tent of my house; if I go up on the couch of my bed; 4if I give sleep to my eyes, slumber to my eyelids; 5until I search out a place for Jehovah, dwellings for the Mighty One of Jacob. 6Lo, we have heard of it at Ephratah; we found it in the fields of the forest; 7we will enter into His tabernacles; we will worship at His footstool. 8Arise, O Jehovah, into Your rest; You, and the ark of Your strength; 9let Your priests be clothed with righteousness; and let Your saints shout for joy. 10For Your servant David's sake, do not turn away the face of Your anointed. 11Jehovah has sworn to David *in* truth; He will not turn from it; I will set *one* of the fruit of your body on the throne for you.

PSAL. CXXXII . קלב

1
2 שיר המעלות זכור־יהוה לדוד את כל־ענותו׃ אשר

who his ;afflictions all with for ,David O ,Remember ,Jehovah .ascents song A of

3 נשבע ליהוה נדר לאביר יעקב׃ אם־אבא באהל ביתי

my ,house the into of tent will I go If .Jacob the to of One Mighty he vowed to ;Jehovah swore

4 אם־אעלה על־ערש יצועי׃ אם־אתן שנת לעיני לעפעפי

my to eyelids my to ,eyes sleep give I if ;bed my the on of couch up go I if

5 תנומה׃ עד־אמצא מקום ליהוה משכנות לאביר

the for of One Mighty dwellings for ,Jehovah place a search I out until ;slumber

6 יעקב׃ הנה־שמענוה באפרתה מצאנוה בשדי־יער׃

the ;forest the in of fields found we it at ;Ephratah have we it of heard ,Lo .Jacob

7
8 נבואה למשכנותיו נשתחוה להדם רגליו׃ קומה יהוה

O ,Jehovah ,Arise his .foot- stool at will we worship His into ;dwellings will we enter

9 למנוחתך אתה וארון עזך׃ כהניך ילבשו־צדק וחסידיך

Your and saints righ- ;teousness be let with clothed Your priests Your ;strength of the and Ark You into Your ;rest

10
11 ירננו׃ בעבור דוד עבדך אל־תשב פני משיחך׃ נשבע־

has sworn Your .anointed the of face turn do away not Your ,servant David the of For sake shout .joy for

יהוה לדוד אמת לא־ישוב ממנה מפרי בטנך אשית

will I set your body the Of of fruit .it from will He turn not (in) ;truth to David Jehovah

[12]If your sons will keep My covenant and My testimonies which I will teach them, their sons shall also sit on your throne till forever. [13]Jehovah has chosen Zion; He has desired *it* for His dwelling-place. [14]This *is* My rest till forever; I will dwell here; I have desired it. [15]I will surely bless her food; I will satisfy her poor *with* food. [16]And I will clothe her priests *with* salvation; and her saints shall surely shout. [17]I will make the horn of David to sprout; I have prepared a lamp for My anointed. [18]I will clothe his enemies *with* shame; but his crown shall shine upon him.

3925 2098/5713 1285 1121 8104 518 3678
12 לְכִסֵּא־לָךְ׃ אִם־יִשְׁמְרוּ בָנֶיךָ ׀ בְּרִיתִי וְעֵדֹתִי זוֹ אֲלַמְּדֵם
will I which My and My your will If for the on
,them teach testimonies covenant sons keep .you throne

3068 977 3678 3427 5703/5704 1121 1571
13 גַּם־בְּנֵיהֶם עֲדֵי־עַד יֵשְׁבוּ לְכִסֵּא־לָךְ׃ כִּי־בָחַר יְהוָה
Jehovah has For for the on shall forever till their also
chosen .you throne sit sons

3427 5703/5704 4496 2088 4186 183
14 בְּצִיּוֹן אִוָּהּ לְמוֹשָׁב לוֹ׃ זֹאת־מְנוּחָתִי עֲדֵי־עַד פֹּה אֵשֵׁב
will I here ;forever till my This to a for has He ;Zion
;dwell rest (is) .Him dwelling (it) desired

3899 7646 34 1288 1288 6718 183
15 כִּי אִוִּתִיהָ׃ צֵידָהּ בָּרֵךְ אֲבָרֵךְ אֶבְיוֹנֶיהָ אַשְׂבִּיעַ לָחֶם׃
(with) will I her will I blessing her have I for
.food satisfy poor ;bless food it desired

6779 8033 7442 7442 2623 3468 3847 3548
16
17 וְכֹהֲנֶיהָ אַלְבִּישׁ יֶשַׁע וַחֲסִידֶיהָ רַנֵּן יְרַנֵּנוּ׃ שָׁם ׀ אַצְמִיחַ
make will I There shall shouting her and (with) will I her And
sprout .shout saints ;salvation clothe priests

1322 3847 341 4899 5216 6186 1732 7161
18 קֶרֶן לְדָוִד עָרַכְתִּי נֵר לִמְשִׁיחִי׃ אוֹיְבָיו אַלְבִּישׁ בֹּשֶׁת
(with) will I his My for lamp a have I of the
;shame clothe enemies .anointed prepared ;David horn

5145 6692
וְעָלָיו יָצִיץ נִזְרוֹ׃
his shall upon but
.crown shine him

PSAL. CXXXIII קלג

PSALM 133

A Song of Ascents. Of David.

[1]Behold! How good and how pleasant *is* the living of brothers, even in unity. [2]*It is* like the precious oil on the head, that ran down on the beard; Aaron's beard; going down to the mouth of his garments; [3]like the dew of Hermon coming down on the mountains of Zion; for there Jehovah commanded the blessing: life till everlasting.

251 2416 5273 2896 2009 1732 4609 7892
1 שִׁיר הַמַּעֲלוֹת לְדָוִד הִנֵּה מַה־טּוֹב וּמַה־נָּעִים שֶׁבֶת אַחִים
brothers the (is) pleasant and good How !Behold Of .ascents song A
of living how .David of

2266 2206 5291 3381 7218 5921 2896 8081 3162
2 גַּם־יָחַד׃ כַּשֶּׁמֶן הַטּוֹב ׀ עַל־הָרֹאשׁ יֹרֵד עַל־הַזָּקָן זְקַן
beard the on ran that the on precious like (is It) in even
—beard down ,head oil the !unity

2042 5921 3381 2768 2919 4060 6310 3381 175
3 אַהֲרֹן שֶׁיֹּרֵד עַל־פִּי מִדּוֹתָיו׃ כְּטַל־חֶרְמוֹן שֶׁיֹּרֵד עַל־הַרְרֵי
the on coming Hermon the like his the to going ,Aaron's
of mountains down of dew ;garments of mouth down

5769 5704 2416 1293 3068 6680 8033 6726
צִיּוֹן כִּי שָׁם ׀ צִוָּה יְהוָה אֶת־הַבְּרָכָה חַיִּים עַד־הָעוֹלָם׃
ever- till life the Jehovah com- there for ;Zion
.lasting ;blessing manded

PSAL. CXXXIV קלד

PSALM 134

A Song of Ascents.

[1]Behold, bless Jehovah, all servants of Jehovah; who stand in the house of Jehovah at night. [2]Lift up your hands *in* the holy place, and bless Jehovah. [3]*May* Jehovah bless you out of Zion, *He* who made the heavens and earth.

5975 3068 5650 3068 1288 4609 7892
1 שִׁיר הַמַּעֲלוֹת הִנֵּה ׀ בָּרְכוּ אֶת־יְהוָה כָּל־עַבְדֵי יְהוָה הָעֹמְדִים
who ;Jehovah servants all ,Jehovah bless ,Behold .ascents song A
stand of of

3068 1288 6944 5375 3915 3068 1004
2 בְּבֵית־יְהוָה בַּלֵּילוֹת׃ שְׂאוּ־יְדֵכֶם קֹדֶשׁ וּבָרְכוּ אֶת־יְהוָה׃
.Jehovah and the (in) your Lift at Jehovah the in
bless ,sanctuary hands up .night of house

776 8064 6213 6726 3068 1288
3 יְבָרֶכְךָ יְהוָה מִצִּיּוֹן עֹשֵׂה שָׁמַיִם וָאָרֶץ׃
the and the who (He) of out Jehovah Let
.earth heavens made ,Zion you bless

PSAL. CXXXV קלה

PSALM 135

PSALM 135

[1]Praise Jehovah! Praise the name of Jehovah; sing praise, servants of Jehovah; [2]*those* who stand in the house of Jehovah, in the courts of the house of our God; [3]praise Jehovah! For Jehovah *is* good! Sing praises to His name, for *it is* delightful. [4]For Jehovah has chosen Jacob to Himself—Israel for His special treasure. [5]For I know that Jehovah *is* great, and our Lord *is* above all gods. [6]Every *thing* which Jehovah *was* pleased to do, He did, in the heavens and in the earth; and in the seas and all deep places. [7]He causes the vapors to rise from the end of the earth; He makes lightnings for the rain; He brings the wind out of His storehouses; [8]*He* who struck the firstborn of Egypt, from man to animal; [9]*who* sent signs and wonders into your midst, O Egypt, on Pharaoh and on all his servants; [10]who struck great nations, and killed mighty kings; [11]Sihon king of the Amorites; and Og king of Bashan; and all the kingdoms of Canaan. [12]And He gave their land *as* an inheritance, an inheritance to His people Israel. [13]O Jehovah, Your name *endures* forever; O Jehovah, Your memorial *is* from generation and generation. [14]For Jehovah will judge His people; and He will have pity on His servants.

[15]The idols of the nations *are* silver and gold, the work of men's hands; [16]they *have* mouths, but they say nothing; they *have* eyes, but they see nothing; [17]they *have* ears, but they hear nothing; yea, there is no breath in their mouths. [18]Those who make them are like them, everyone who is trusting in them. [19]Bless Jehovah, O house of

5975 3068 5650 1984 3068 8034 1984 3050/1984
1 2 הַלְלוּיָהּ ׀ הַלְלוּ אֶת־שֵׁם יְהוָה הַלְלוּ עַבְדֵי יְהוָה׃ שֶׁעֹמְדִים
who ;Jehovah the Praise ;Jehovah the Praise Praise
stand of servants of name !Jah

2896 3050 1984 430 1004 2691 3068 1004
3 בְּבֵית יְהוָה בְּחַצְרוֹת בֵּית אֱלֹהֵינוּ׃ הַלְלוּיָהּ כִּי־טוֹב
(is) For praise ;God our the the in ,Jehovah the in
good !Jah of house of courts of house

3478 977 3290 5273 80 34 2167 3068
4 יְהוָה זַמְּרוּ לִשְׁמוֹ כִּי נָעִים׃ כִּי־יַעֲקֹב בָּחַר־לוֹ יָהּ יִשְׂרָאֵל
Israel —Jah for has Jacob For (is it) for His to Sing Jeho-
himself chosen .delightful ,name praises ?vah

3605 113 3068 1419 3045 5459
5 לִסְגֻלָּתוֹ׃ כִּי אֲנִי יָדַעְתִּי כִּי־גָדוֹל יְהוָה וַאֲדֹנֵינוּ מִכָּל־
above (is) our and ,Jehovah (is) that know I For His for
all Lord great ,treasure

3220 776 8064 6213 3068 2654 834 3605 430
6 אֱלֹהִים׃ כֹּל אֲשֶׁר־חָפֵץ יְהוָה עָשָׂה בַּשָּׁמַיִם וּבָאָרֶץ בַּיַּמִּים
in and in and the in He ,Jehovah (was) Every .gods
;seas the ;earth the heavens ;did do to pleased (thing)

4306 1300 776 7097 5387 5927 8415 3605
7 וְכָל־תְּהֹמוֹת׃ מַעֲלֶה נְשִׂאִים מִקְצֵה הָאָרֶץ בְּרָקִים לַמָּטָר
the for lightnings the the from the causes He deep and
rain ;earth of end mists rise to ,places all

4714 1060 5221 214 7307 3318 6213
8 עֹשֶׂה מוֹצֵא־רוּחַ מֵאוֹצְרוֹתָיו׃ שֶׁהִכָּה בְּכוֹרֵי מִצְרָיִם
,Egypt the who (He) His of out wind (He) He
of firstborn struck ;storehouses brings ;makes

4714 8432 4159 226 7971 929 5704 120
9 מֵאָדָם עַד־בְּהֵמָה׃ שָׁלַח ׀ אוֹתֹת וּמֹפְתִים בְּתוֹכֵכִי מִצְרָיִם
,Egypt O your into and signs (who) ;animal to from
,midst wonders sent man

4428 2026 7227 1471 5221 5650 3605 6547
10 בְּפַרְעֹה וּבְכָל־עֲבָדָיו׃ שֶׁהִכָּה גּוֹיִם רַבִּים וְהָרַג מְלָכִים
kings and great nations who his on and on
killed struck ;servants all Pharaoh

3605 1316 4428 5747 567 4428 5511 6099
11 עֲצוּמִים׃ לְסִיחוֹן ׀ מֶלֶךְ הָאֱמֹרִי וּלְעוֹג מֶלֶךְ הַבָּשָׁן וּלְכֹל
and ;Bashan king and the king Sihon :mighty
all to of Og ;Amorites of

5971 3478 5159 5159 776 5414 3667 4467
12 מַמְלְכוֹת כְּנָעַן׃ וְנָתַן אַרְצָם נַחֲלָה נַחֲלָה לְיִשְׂרָאֵל עַמּוֹ׃
His Israel to in- an an (as) their And .Canaan king- the
.people heritance ,inheritance land gave He of doms

3068 1777 1755 1755 2143 3068 5769 8034 3068
13 14 יְהוָה שִׁמְךָ לְעוֹלָם יְהוָה זִכְרְךָ לְדֹר־וָדֹר׃ כִּי־יָדִין יְהוָה
Jehovah will For gen- and gen- from Your O (endures) Your Jeho- O
judge .ation .ation (is) memorial ,Jehovah ;forever name ,vah

4639 2091 3701 1471 6091 5162 5650 5921 5971
15 עַמּוֹ וְעַל־עֲבָדָיו יִתְנֶחָם׃ עֲצַבֵּי הַגּוֹיִם כֶּסֶף וְזָהָב מַעֲשֵׂה
the and (are) the The will He His and His
of work ,gold silver nations of idols .pity have servants on ;people

7200 3808 5869 1696 3808 6310 120 3027
16 יְדֵי אָדָם׃ פֶּה־לָהֶם וְלֹא יְדַבֵּרוּ עֵינַיִם לָהֶם וְלֹא יִרְאוּ׃
they do but to eyes they but they mouths ;men's hands
;see not them (are) ;speak not ,have

3644 6310 7307 3426 637 238 3808 241
17 18 אָזְנַיִם לָהֶם וְלֹא יַאֲזִינוּ אַף אֵין־יֶשׁ־רוּחַ בְּפִיהֶם׃ כְּמוֹהֶם
them Like their in breath there not ,yea do they but to ears
.mouths is ;hear not ,them (are)

1288 3478 1004 982 834 3605 6213
19 יִהְיוּ עֹשֵׂיהֶם כֹּל אֲשֶׁר־בֹּטֵחַ בָּהֶם׃ בֵּית יִשְׂרָאֵל בָּרְכוּ
bless ,Israel house O in is who every who are
of .them trusting one ,them make they

Israel; bless Jehovah, O house of Aaron; [20]bless Jehovah, O house of Levi; you who fear Jehovah, bless Jehovah. [21]Blessed *be* Jehovah out of Zion, *He* who dwells at Jerusalem. Praise Jehovah!

20 אֶת־יְהוָה בֵּית אַהֲרֹן בָּרְכוּ אֶת־יְהוָה׃ בֵּית הַלֵּוִי בָּרְכוּ

3068 1004 175 1288 3068 1004 3881 1288

bless ,Levi house O ;Jehovah bless Aaron O ,Jehovah
of of house

21 אֶת־יְהוָה יִרְאֵי יְהוָה בָּרְכוּ אֶת־יְהוָה׃ בָּרוּךְ יְהוָה מִצִּיּוֹן

3068 3373 3068 1288 3068 1288 3068 6726

of out Jehovah Blessed .Jehovah bless ,Jehovah you ,Jehovah
,Zion (be) fear who

שֹׁכֵן יְרוּשָׁלָ‍ִם הַלְלוּ־יָהּ׃

7931 3389 1984

Praise .Jerusalem who
!Jah at dwells

PSAL. CXXXVI קלו

PSALM 136

PSALM 136

[1]O give thanks to Jehovah, for *He is* good; for His mercy *endures* forever. [2]O give thanks to the God of gods; for His mercy *endures* forever. [3]O give thanks to the Lord of lords; for His mercy *endures* forever; [4]to Him who alone does great wonders; for His mercy *endures* forever; [5]to Him who by wisdom made the heavens; for His mercy *endures* forever; [6]to Him who spread the earth on the waters; for His mercy *endures* forever; [7]to Him who made great lights; for His mercy *endures* forever; [8]the sun to rule by day; for His mercy *endures* forever; [9]the moon and the stars to rule by night; for His mercy *endures* forever; [10]to Him who struck Egypt in her firstborn; for His mercy *endures* forever; [11]and brought Israel out from among them; for His mercy *endures* forever; [12]with a strong hand and a stretched out arm; for His mercy *endures* forever; [13]to Him who divided the Red Sea into parts; for His mercy *endures* forever; [14]and made Israel pass through the middle of it; for His mercy *endures* forever; [15]but shook Pharaoh and his army off in the Red Sea; for His mercy *endures* forever; [16]to Him who led His people in the wilderness; for His mercy *endures* forever; [17]to Him who

1
2 הוֹדוּ לַיהוָה כִּי־טוֹב כִּי לְעוֹלָם חַסְדּוֹ׃ הוֹדוּ לֵאלֹהֵי

3034 3068 2896 5769 2617 3034 430

the to give O His (endures) for (is He) for to give O
of God thanks .mercy forever ;good ,Jehovah thanks

3 הָאֱלֹהִים כִּי לְעוֹלָם חַסְדּוֹ׃ הוֹדוּ לַאֲדֹנֵי הָאֲדֹנִים כִּי

430 5769 2617 3034 113 113

for ,Lords the to give O His (endures) for ;Gods
of Lord thanks .mercy forever

4 לְעוֹלָם חַסְדּוֹ׃ לְעֹשֵׂה נִפְלָאוֹת גְּדֹלוֹת לְבַדּוֹ כִּי לְעוֹלָם

5769 2617 6213 6381 1419 905 5769

(endures) for ;alone great wonders Him To His (endures)
forever does who .mercy forever

5 חַסְדּוֹ׃ לְעֹשֵׂה הַשָּׁמַיִם בִּתְבוּנָה כִּי לְעוֹלָם חַסְדּוֹ׃

2617 6213 8064 8394 5769 2617

His (endures) for by the who Him to His
.mercy forever ,understanding heavens made ;mercy

6
7 לְרֹקַע הָאָרֶץ עַל־הַמָּיִם כִּי לְעוֹלָם חַסְדּוֹ׃ לְעֹשֵׂה אוֹרִים

7554 776 5921 4325 5769 2617 6213 216

lights Him to His (endures) for the above the who Him To
made who ;mercy forever ,waters earth spread

8 גְּדֹלִים כִּי לְעוֹלָם חַסְדּוֹ׃ אֶת־הַשֶּׁמֶשׁ לְמֶמְשֶׁלֶת בַּיּוֹם

1419 5769 2617 8121 4475 3117

;day by rule to sun the His (endures) for ;great
;mercy forever

9 כִּי לְעוֹלָם חַסְדּוֹ׃ אֶת־הַיָּרֵחַ וְכוֹכָבִים לְמֶמְשְׁלוֹת בַּלָּיְלָה

5769 2617 3394 3556 4475 3915

;night by rule to the and the His (endures) for
stars moon ;mercy forever

10 כִּי לְעוֹלָם חַסְדּוֹ׃ לְמַכֵּה מִצְרַיִם בִּבְכוֹרֵיהֶם כִּי לְעוֹלָם

5769 2617 5221 4714 1060 5769

(endures) for their in Egypt who Him to His (endures) for
forever ;firstborn struck ;mercy forever

11
12 חַסְדּוֹ׃ וַיּוֹצֵא יִשְׂרָאֵל מִתּוֹכָם כִּי לְעוֹלָם חַסְדּוֹ׃ בְּיָד

2617 3318 3478 8432 5769 2617 3027

a with His (endures) for from Israel and His
hand ;mercy forever ,them among out brought ;mercy

13 חֲזָקָה וּבִזְרוֹעַ נְטוּיָה כִּי לְעוֹלָם חַסְדּוֹ׃ לְגֹזֵר יַם־סוּף

2389 2220 5186 5769 2617 1504 3220 5488

Reeds the Him to His (endures) for stretched a and strong
of Sea divided who ;mercy forever ;out arm

14 לִגְזָרִים כִּי לְעוֹלָם חַסְדּוֹ׃ וְהֶעֱבִיר יִשְׂרָאֵל בְּתוֹכוֹ כִּי

1506 5769 2617 5674 3478 8432

for middle the Israel made and His (endures) for into
;it of through pass ;mercy forever ;parts

15 לְעוֹלָם חַסְדּוֹ׃ וְנִעֵר פַּרְעֹה וְחֵילוֹ בְיַם־סוּף כִּי לְעוֹלָם

5769 2617 5287 6547 2428 3220 5488 5769

(endures) for ;Reeds the in and Pharaoh but His (endures
forever of Sea army his shook ;mercy forever

16
17 חַסְדּוֹ׃ לְמוֹלִיךְ עַמּוֹ בַּמִּדְבָּר כִּי לְעוֹלָם חַסְדּוֹ׃ לְמַכֵּה

2617 3212 5971 4057 5769 2617 5221

Him to His (endures) for the in His Him to His
struck who ;mercy forever ;wilderness people led who ;mercy

struck great kings; for His mercy *endures* forever; [18]and killed majestic kings; for His mercy *endures* forever; [19]Sihon, king of the Amorites; for His mercy *endures* forever; [20]and Og, the king of Bashan; for His mercy *endures* forever; [21]and gave their land for an inheritance; for His mercy *endures* forever; [22]an inheritance to His servant Israel; for His mercy *endures* forever; [23]who remembered us in our low estate; for His mercy *endures* forever; [24]and has rescued us from our enemies; for His mercy *endures* forever; [25]who gives food to all flesh; for His mercy *endures* forever. [26]O give thanks to the God of Heaven; for His mercy *endures* forever.

117 4428 2026 2617 5769 1419 4428
18 מְלָכִים גְּדֹלִים כִּי לְעוֹלָם חַסְדּוֹ׃ וַיַּהֲרֹג מְלָכִים אַדִּירִים
;majestic kings and killed His ;mercy (endures) forever for ;great kings

2617 5769 567 4428 5511 2617 5769
19
20 כִּי לְעוֹלָם חַסְדּוֹ׃ לְסִיחוֹן מֶלֶךְ הָאֱמֹרִי כִּי לְעוֹלָם חַסְדּוֹ׃
His ;mercy (endures) forever for the ;Amorites king of ,Sihon His ;mercy (endures) forever for

5159 776 5414 2617 5769 1316 4428 5747
21 וּלְעוֹג מֶלֶךְ הַבָּשָׁן כִּי לְעוֹלָם חַסְדּוֹ׃ וְנָתַן אַרְצָם לְנַחֲלָה
an for ;inheritance their land and gave His ;mercy (endures) forever for ;Bashan the ,Og and of king

5769 5650 3478 5159 2617 5769
22 כִּי לְעוֹלָם חַסְדּוֹ׃ נַחֲלָה לְיִשְׂרָאֵל עַבְדּוֹ כִּי לְעוֹלָם
(endures) forever for His ;servant Israel to an inheritance His ;mercy (endures) forever for

6561 2617 5769 2142 8216 2617
23
24 חַסְדּוֹ׃ שֶׁבְּשִׁפְלֵנוּ זָכַר לָנוּ כִּי לְעוֹלָם חַסְדּוֹ׃ וַיִּפְרְקֵנוּ
has and us rescued His ;mercy (endures) forever for ;us remembered our in who estate low His ;mercy

5769 1320/3605 3899 5414 2617 5769 6862
25 מִצָּרֵינוּ כִּי לְעוֹלָם חַסְדּוֹ׃ נֹתֵן לֶחֶם לְכָל־בָּשָׂר כִּי לְעוֹלָם
(endures) forever for ;flesh all to food who gives His ;mercy (endures) forever for our from ;enemies

2617 5769 8064 410 3034 2617
26 חַסְדּוֹ׃ הוֹדוּ לְאֵל הַשָּׁמָיִם כִּי לְעוֹלָם חַסְדּוֹ׃
His .mercy (endures) forever for ;Heaven the to of God give O thanks His ;mercy

PSAL. CXXXVII קלז

PSALM 137

[1]We sat down by the rivers of Babylon; also, we wept when we remembered Zion. [2]We hung our lyres on the willows in its midst. [3]For there our captors asked us the words of a song; yea, our plunderers *asked* joy, *saying*, Sing to us a song of Zion. [4]How shall we sing the song of Jehovah on a foreign soil? [5]If I forget you, O Jerusalem, let my right hand forget; [6]let my tongue cleave to my palate, if I do not remember you—if I do not bring up Jerusalem above the head of my joy. [7]O Jehovah, remember for the sons of Edom the day of Jerusalem; who said, Make it bare! Make it bare, even to its foundation! [8]O daughter of Babylon, O destroyed one! Blessed *is* he who shall repay to you

6726 2142 1058 1571 3427 8033 894 5104
1 עַל נַהֲרוֹת ׀ בָּבֶל שָׁם יָשַׁבְנוּ גַּם־בָּכִינוּ בְּזָכְרֵנוּ אֶת־צִיּוֹן׃
.Zion we when remembered we wept ,also we ;down sat there ,Babylon the of rivers By

7592 8033 3658 8518 8432 6155 5921
2
3 עַל־עֲרָבִים בְּתוֹכָהּ תָּלִינוּ כִּנֹּרוֹתֵינוּ׃ כִּי שָׁם שְׁאֵלוּנוּ
asked us there For our .lyres we hung its in midst the willows On

6726 7892 7891 8057 8437 7892 1697 7617
שׁוֹבֵינוּ דִּבְרֵי־שִׁיר וְתוֹלָלֵינוּ שִׂמְחָה שִׁירוּ לָנוּ מִשִּׁיר צִיּוֹן׃
.Zion song a of to us Sing ,joy (saying) our and plunderers ;song a the of words our captors

7911 518 5236 127 3068 7892 7891
4
5 אֵיךְ נָשִׁיר אֶת־שִׁיר־יְהוָה עַל אַדְמַת נֵכָר׃ אִם־אֶשְׁכָּחֵךְ
forget I .you If ?foreign land a on Jehovah the of song we shall sing How

3808/518 2441 3956 1692 3225 7911 3389
6 יְרוּשָׁלָ͏ִם תִּשְׁכַּח יְמִינִי׃ תִּדְבַּק לְשׁוֹנִי ׀ לְחִכִּי אִם־לֹא
not if my to ,palate my tongue let cleave right my ;hand let forget O ,Jerusalem

8057 7218 5921 3389 5927 3808/518 2142
אֶזְכְּרֵכִי אִם־לֹא אַעֲלֶה אֶת־יְרוּשָׁלַ͏ִם עַל רֹאשׁ שִׂמְחָתִי׃
.joy my the of head above Jerusaelm bring I up not if re- do I —you member

6168 559 3389 3117 123 1121 3068 2142
7 זְכֹר יְהוָה ׀ לִבְנֵי אֱדוֹם אֵת יוֹם יְרוּשָׁלָ͏ִם הָאֹמְרִים עָרוּ
Lay !bare ,said who ;Jerusalem the of day Edom the for of sons O ,Jehovah ,Recall

7999 835 7703 894 1323 3247 5704/6168
8 עָרוּ עַד הַיְסוֹד בָּהּ׃ בַּת־בָּבֶל הַשְּׁדוּדָה אַשְׁרֵי שֶׁיְשַׁלֶּם־
shall who repay he Blessed (is) destroyed O !one ,Babylon O of daughter !its foundation even to Lay ,bare

your reward which you rewarded to us. [9]Blessed *is* he who seizes your little ones and dashes *them* against the stone!

PSALM 138

A Psalm of David.

[1]I will thank You with my whole heart; I will sing praise to You before the gods; [2]I will worship toward Your holy temple; and give thanks to Your name for Your mercy, and for Your truth; for You have magnified Your word above all Your name. [3]You answered me in the day that I cried; You emboldened me in my soul *with* strength. [4]All the kings of the earth shall thank You, O Jehovah; because they have heard the words of Your mouth. [5]Yes, they shall sing in the ways of Jehovah; for the glory of Jehovah *is* great. [6]Though Jehovah *is* high, yet He looks upon the lowly; but the proud He knows from afar. [7]If I walk in the midst of distress, You give me life; You send out Your hand against the wrath of my enemies; and Your right hand delivers me. [8]Jehovah will perfect *His work* in me; O Jehovah, Your mercy *endures* forever; *You will* not forsake the works of Your hands.

PSALM 139

To the chief musician. A Psalm of David.

[1]O Jehovah, You have searched me and known *me*. [2]You know my sitting down, and my rising up; You understand my thought from afar off. [3]You sift my path and my lying down, and are acquainted *with* all my ways. [4]For not a word is on my tongue, but, lo, O Jehovah, You know it all. [5]You have closed me in behind, and in front; and Your hand *is* laid on me.

5210 270 835 7576 1580

9 לך את־גמולך שגמלת לנו׃ אשרי ׀ שיאחז ונפץ את־

and dashes | who he seizes | Blessed (is) | .us to | you which reward did | your reward | to

55,53 5768

עלליך אל־הסלע׃

the .stone | against | your ones little

PSAL. CXXXVIII קלח

PSALM 138

7812 2167 430 5048 38 20 3605 3034 1732

1 לדוד ׀ אודך בכל־לבי נגד אלהים אזמרך׃ אשתחוה
2

will I worship | sing will I ;You to praise | the gods | before | my ;heart | with whole | will I You thank | Of .David

571 2617 80 34 3034 6944 1964

אל־היכל קדשך ואודה את־שמך על־חסדך ועל־אמתך

Your ;truth | and for | Your ,mercy | For | Your .name | give and to thanks | Your ;holy | temple | to- ward

6030 7121 3117 1697 8034 1430

3 כי־הגדלת על־כל־שמך אמרתך׃ ביום קראתי ותענני

an- You ;me swered | ,called I | the In day | Your .word | Your ,name | all above | have You magnified | for

8085 776 4428 3605 3068 3034 5797 5315 7292

4 תרהבני בנפשי עז׃ יודוך יהוה כל־מלכי־ארץ כי־שמעו

they because heard have | the ;earth | the of kings | All ,Jehovah | shall You thank | (with) .strength | my in soul | made You bold me

3068 3519 1419 3068 1870 7891 6310 561

5 אמרי־פיך׃ וישירו בדרכי יהוה כי גדול כבוד יהוה׃

.Jehovah | the of glory | (is) great | for ;Jehovah | the in of ways | they And sing shall | Your .mouth | the of words

3212 3045 4801 1364 7200 8217 3068 7311

6 כי־רם יהוה ושפל יראה וגבה ממרחק ידע׃ אם־אלך
7

walk I | If | He .knows | from afar | the but proud | He ;upon looks | the yet lowly | Jeho- ,vah | is Though exalted

3462 3027 7971 341 639 2421 68 64 7130

בקרב צרה תחיני על אף איבי תשלח ידך ותושיעני

and me delivers | Your ;hand | send You out | my enemies | the against of wrath | give You ;life me | ,distress | the in of midst

4639 5769 2617 3068 1584 3068 3225

8 ימינך׃ יהוה יגמר בעדי יהוה חסדך לעולם מעשי

the of works | (endures) ;forever | Your mercy | O ,Jehovah | ;me in | will perfect | Jehovah | right Your .hand

7503 3808 3027

ידיך אל־תרף׃

do | not .forsake | Your hands

PSAL. CXXXIX קלט

PSALM 139

3045 3045 2713 3068 4210 1732 5329

1 למנצח לדוד מזמור יהוה חקרתני ותדע׃ אתה ידעת
2

know | You | known and .(me) | have You me searched | O ,Jehovah | .psalm A | of .David | chief the To ,musician

2219 7252 734 7350 7454 995 6965 3427

3 שבתי וקומי בנתה לרעי מרחוק׃ ארחי ורבעי זרית

You ;sift | my and down lying | My path | afar from .off | my thought | You understand | my and ;rising | my sitting

3068 2009 3956 4405 369 5532 1870 3605

4 וכל־דרכי הסכנתה׃ כי אין מלה בלשוני הן יהוה

O ,Jehovah | (but) ,lo | my on ,tongue | word a | not is | For | are You .acquainted | my (with) ways | and all

3709 7896 6696 6924 268 3605 3045

5 ידעת כלה׃ אחור וקדם צרתני ותשת עלי כפכה׃

Your .palm | on me | is and laid | have You ;in me closed | in and front | Behind | .all it | You know

[6]*Such* knowledge *is* too wonderful for me; it is set on high; I am not able to *reach* it. [7]Where shall I go from Your Spirit? Or where shall I flee from Your face? [8]If I go up to Heaven, You *are* there; if I make my bed *in* Sheol, behold, You *are there*! [9]*If* I take the wings of the morning, dwelling in the uttermost part of the sea, [10]even there Your hand shall lead me; and Your right hand shall seize me. [11]If I say: Surely the darkness shall fall on me; even the night *shall be* light around me. [12]Even the darkness will not be dark from You, but the night shines as the day; as *is* the darkness, so *is* the light. [13]For You have possessed my inward parts; You wove me in the womb of my mother. [14]I will thank You, for with fearful *things* I am wonderful; Your works *are* marvelous, and my soul knows *it* very well. [15]My bones were not hidden from You when I was made in secret; when I was woven in the depths of the earth. [16]Your eyes saw my embryo; and in Your book all *my members* were written; the days they were formed, and none *was* among them.

[17]And how precious are Your thoughts to me, O God! How great is the sum of them! [18]*If* I should count them, they are more than the sand; when I awake I am still with You. [19]Surely You will slay the wicked, O God; and bloody men, depart from me. [20]Who will maliciously speak against You? Your enemies are lifted up with vanity. [21]O Jehovah, do not I hate those hating You? And am I *not* detesting those rising against You? [22]I hate them *with* a perfect hatred; they have become my enemies.

[23]Search me, O God, and know my heart; try me, and know my thoughts; [24]and see if *any* wicked way *is* in me; and lead me in the way everlasting.

3212 3201 7862 1847 6383
6 7 פְּלִאיָה דַעַת מִמֶּנִּי נִשְׂגְּבָה לֹא־אוּכַל לָהּ׃ אָנָה אֵלֵךְ
shall Where to am I not set is it much too (such) won- (is)
go I .it (reach) able ;high on ;me for knowledge derful

8033 8065 5266 1272 6440 7307
8 מֵרוּחֶךָ וְאָנָה מִפָּנֶיךָ אֶבְרָח׃ אִם־אֶסַּק שָׁמַיִם שָׁם אָתָּה
You there ,Heaven go I If I shall Your from Or Your from
;(are) to up ?flee face where ?Spirit

319 7931 7837 3671 5375 2009 7585 3331
9 וְאַצִּיעָה שְּׁאוֹל הִנֶּךָּ׃ אֶשָּׂא כַנְפֵי־שָׁחַר אֶשְׁכְּנָה בְּאַחֲרִית
ut- the in I if the the I (If) behold ,Sheol make I if
of part most dwell ,morning of wings take I (there are) You in bed my

2822 389 559 3225 270 5148 3027 8033 3220
10 11 יָם׃ גַּם־שָׁם יָדְךָ תַנְחֵנִי וְתֹאחֲזֵנִי יְמִינֶךָ׃ וָאֹמַר אַךְ־חֹשֶׁךְ
the Surely I If right Your shall and shall Your there even the
darkness ,say .hand me seize ;me lead hand ,sea

2821 3808 2822 1157 216 3915 7779
12 יְשׁוּפֵנִי וְלַיְלָה אוֹר בַּעֲדֵנִי׃ גַּם־חֹשֶׁךְ לֹא־יַחְשִׁיךְ מִמֶּךָ
from will not the Even around (be shall) the even fall shall
;You dark be darkness .me light night ,me on

7069 219 2825 214 3117 3915
13 וְלַיְלָה כַּיּוֹם יָאִיר כַּחֲשֵׁיכָה כָּאוֹרָה׃ כִּי־אַתָּה קָנִיתָ
have You For the (is) so the (is) as ;shines the as the but
possessed .light ,darkness day night

6395 3372 3034 517 990 5526 3629
14 כִלְיֹתָי תְּסֻכֵּנִי בְּבֶטֶן אִמִּי׃ אוֹדְךָ עַל כִּי נוֹרָאוֹת נִפְלֵיתִי
am I fearful (with) for will I my the in wove You my
.wonderful things ,You thank .mother of womb me ;reins

6108 3582 3966 3045 5315 4639 6381
15 נִפְלָאִים מַעֲשֶׂיךָ וְנַפְשִׁי יֹדַעַת מְאֹד׃ לֹא־נִכְחַד עָצְמִי
My were not very knows my and Your (are)
bones hidden .well (it) soul ,works marvelous

1564 776 8482 7551 5643 6213
16 מִמֶּךָּ אֲשֶׁר־עֻשֵּׂיתִי בַסֵּתֶר רֻקַּמְתִּי בְּתַחְתִּיּוֹת אָרֶץ׃ גָּלְמִי
My the the in I when in was I when from
embryo .earth of depths woven was ;secret made ,You

259 3808 3335 3117 3789 3605 5612 5921 5869 7200
רָאוּ עֵינֶיךָ וְעַל־סִפְרְךָ כֻּלָּם יִכָּתֵבוּ יָמִים יֻצָּרוּ וְלֹא אֶחָד
one not and were they the were of all Your and Your saw
(was) formed days ;written them book on ;eyes

7218 6105 410 7454 3365 854
17 בָּהֶם׃ וְלִי מַה־יָּקְרוּ רֵעֶיךָ אֵל מֶה עָצְמוּ רָאשֵׁיהֶם׃
sum the great How O Your precious how to And among
!them of is !God ,thoughts are me .them

6991 5750 6974 7235 2344 5608
18 19 אֶסְפְּרֵם מֵחוֹל יִרְבּוּן הֱקִיצֹתִי וְעוֹדִי עִמָּךְ׃ אִם־תִּקְטֹל
will You If with am I I when are they the than should I (If)
,slay .You still ,awake ;more sand ,them count

4209 559 834 5493 1818 582 7563 433
20 אֱלוֹהַּ רָשָׁע וְאַנְשֵׁי דָמִים סוּרוּ מֶנִּי׃ אֲשֶׁר יֹמְרֻךָ לִמְזִמָּה
with speak will Who from turn ,blood men and the ,God O
,malice You against .me away of ;wicked

8618 8130 3068 8130 3808 6145 7723 5375
21 נָשֻׂא לַשָּׁוְא עָרֶיךָ׃ הֲלוֹא־מְשַׂנְאֶיךָ יְהוָה אֶשְׂנָא וּבִתְקוֹמְמֶיךָ
those with And ?hate I O who those not Do Your with lifted are
,You against rising ,Jehovah ,You hate .enemies vanity up

1961 341 8130 8130 8503 6962
22 אֶתְקוֹטָט׃ תַּכְלִית שִׂנְאָה שְׂנֵאתִים לְאוֹיְבִים הָיוּ לִי׃
to they enemies hate I a (with) perfect detesting
.me become have ;them hatred ?am I

518 7200 8312 3045 974 3824 3045 410 2713
23 24 חָקְרֵנִי אֵל וְדַע לְבָבִי בְּחָנֵנִי וְדַע שַׂרְעַפָּי׃ וּרְאֵה אִם־
if see and my and me try my and ,God O Search
,thoughts know ;heart know ,me

5769 1870 5148 6090 1870
דֶּרֶךְ־עֹצֶב בִּי וּנְחֵנִי בְּדֶרֶךְ עוֹלָם׃
ever- the in lead and (is) wicked (any)
.lasting way me ;me in way

PSAL. CXL קמ

PSALM 140

PSALM 140

To the chief musician. A Psalm of David.

[1]O Jehovah, deliver me from the evil man; keep me from the violent man; [2]who devised evil things in the heart; they gather wars all the day. [3]They sharpen their tongues like a snake; adders' poison *is* under their lips, Selah. [4]O Jehovah, keep me from the wicked's hands; keep me from the violent man, who plans to trip up my steps. [5]The proud have hidden cords and a trap for me; they have spread a net by the wayside; they have set snares for me. Selah.

[6]I said to Jehovah, You *are* my God; O Jehovah, hear the voice of my prayers. [7]O Jehovah the Lord, the strength of my salvation, You have covered my head in the day of armor. [8]O Jehovah, do not grant the desires of the wicked; do not promote his plan, *lest* they be exalted. Selah. [9]*As for* the leaders of those around me, let the evil of their own lips cover them. [10]Let burning coals fall on them; let them fall into deep pits, so that they do not rise again. [11]Do not let a man of tongue be established in the earth; evil shall hunt the violent man, thrust upon thrust. [12]I know that Jehovah will maintain the cause of the afflicted, the justice of the poor. [13]Surely the righteous shall give thanks to Your name; the upright shall dwell in Your presence.

376 7451 120 3068 2502 1732 4210 5329
1 2 לַמְנַצֵּחַ מִזְמוֹר לְדָוִד׃ חַלְּצֵנִי יְהוָה מֵאָדָם רָע מֵאִישׁ
the from ;evil the from O Deliver of psalm A chief the To
man man Jehovah ,me .David .musician

1481 3117 3605 3820 7451 2803 834 5341 2555
3 חֲמָסִים תִּנְצְרֵנִי׃ אֲשֶׁר חָשְׁבוּ רָעוֹת בְּלֵב כָּל־יוֹם יָגוּרוּ
they the all the in evil devises who preserve violent
up stir day ;heart things ;me

8478 5919 2534 5175 3956 8150 4421
4 מִלְחָמוֹת׃ שָׁנְנוּ לְשׁוֹנָם כְּמוֹ־נָחָשׁ חֲמַת עַכְשׁוּב תַּחַת
(is) adders' poison a like their They .wars
under ;snake tongues sharpen

2555 376 7563 3027 3068 8104 5542 8193
5 שְׂפָתֵימוֹ סֶלָה׃ שָׁמְרֵנִי יְהוָה ׀ מִידֵי רָשָׁע מֵאִישׁ חֲמָסִים
violent the from the from O Keep .Selah their
man ;wicked's hands ,Jehovah ,me .lips

6341 1343 2934 6471 1760 2803 834 5341
6 תִּנְצְרֵנִי אֲשֶׁר חָשְׁבוּ לִדְחוֹת פְּעָמָי׃ טָמְנוּ־גֵאִים ׀ פַּח לִי
for a The have my trip to plans who preserve
me trap proud hidden .steps up ;me

5542 7896 4170 1870 3027 7568 6566 2256
וַחֲבָלִים פָּרְשׂוּ רֶשֶׁת לְיַד־מַעְגָּל מֹקְשִׁים שָׁתוּ־לִי סֶלָה׃
.Selah for they snares the the by net a have they and
.me set have ;way of side spread ;cords

8469 6963 3068 238 859 410 3068 559
7 אָמַרְתִּי לַיהוָה אֵלִי אָתָּה הַאֲזִינָה יְהוָה קוֹל תַּחֲנוּנָי׃
my the O ,hear You My to said I
prayer of voice Jehovah ;(are) God ,Jehovah

408 5402 3117 7218 5526 3444 5797 136 3068
8 9 יֱהוִה אֲדֹנָי עֹז יְשׁוּעָתִי סַכֹּתָה לְרֹאשִׁי בְּיוֹם נָשֶׁק׃ אַל־
not .armor the in my have You my ,strength the O
of day head covered ,salvation's ,Lord Jehovah

7218 5542 7311 6329 408 2162 7563 3970 3068 5414
10 תִּתֵּן יְהוָה מַאֲוַיֵּי רָשָׁע זְמָמוֹ אַל־תָּפֵק יָרוּמוּ סֶלָה׃ רֹאשׁ
(for As) .Selah they (lest) do not his the desires O Do
of head the .exalted be ,promote plan ;wicked's ,Jehovah ,grant

1513 4131 3680 8193 5999 4524
11 מְסִבָּי עֲמַל שְׂפָתֵימוֹ יְכַסּוּמוֹ׃ יִמִּיטוּ עֲלֵיהֶם גֶּחָלִים
coals them on make cover let their evil the those
fall ;them lips of ,me around

3559 1097 3956 376 6965 3605 4113 5307 784
12 בָּאֵשׁ יַפִּלֵם בְּמַהֲמֹרוֹת בַּל־יָקוּמוּ׃ אִישׁ לָשׁוֹן בַּל־יִכּוֹן
let do not tongue A that not ;pits into make of
fixed be of man .rise shall they fall them fire

6213 3045 4073 6679 7451 2555 376 776
13 בָּאָרֶץ אִישׁ־חָמָס רָע יְצוּדֶנּוּ לְמַדְחֵפֹת׃ יָדַעְתִּי כִּי־יַעֲשֶׂה
will that know I upon thrust shall evil ,violent the the in
maintain .thrust him hunt man ;earth

8034 3034 6662 389 34 4941 6041 1779 3068
14 יְהוָה דִּין עָנִי מִשְׁפַּט אֶבְיֹנִים׃ אַךְ צַדִּיקִים יוֹדוּ לִשְׁמֶךָ
Your to shall righ- the Surely the justice the cause Jeho-
;name thanks give teous .poor's ;afflicted's vah

6440 3477 3427
יֵשְׁבוּ יְשָׁרִים אֶת־פָּנֶיךָ׃
Your the shall
.presence upright in dwell

PSAL. CXLI קמא

PSALM 141

PSALM 141

A Psalm of David.

[1]O Jehovah, I cry to You; hasten to me; hear my voice when I cry to You. [2]Let my

6963 238 2363 7121 3068 1732 4210
1 מִזְמוֹר לְדָוִד יְהוָה קְרָאתִיךָ חוּשָׁה לִּי הַאֲזִינָה קוֹלִי
my ear give to hasten cry I O .David of psalm A
voice to ;me ;You to ,Jehovah

בְּקָרְאִי־לָךְ׃ 2 תִּכּוֹן תְּפִלָּתִי קְטֹרֶת לְפָנֶיךָ מַשְׂאַת כַּפַּי

my lifting the before (as) my be Let to my in
palms of up ;You incense prayer forth set .You calling

3 מִנְחַת־עָרֶב׃ שִׁיתָה יְהוָה שָׁמְרָה לְפִי נִצְּרָה עַל־דַּל

the on keep my to guard a O ,Set .evening the (as)
of door watch ;mouth ,Jehovah sacrifice

4 שְׂפָתָי׃ אַל־תַּט־לִבִּי לְדָבָר ׀ רָע לְהִתְעוֹלֵל עֲלִלוֹת ׀ בְּרֶשַׁע

wick- in deeds practice to ,evil any- to my let Do not .lips my
edness thing heart aside turn

5 אֶת־אִישִׁים פֹּעֲלֵי־אָוֶן וּבַל־אֶלְחַם בְּמַנְעַמֵּיהֶם׃ יֶהֶלְמֵנִי

strike Let their of let do And .evil who men with
me .delicacies eat me not practice

צַדִּיק ׀ חֶסֶד וְיוֹכִיחֵנִי שֶׁמֶן רֹאשׁ אַל־יָנִי רֹאשִׁי כִּי־עוֹד

yet for my let not the (is it) he and a (is it) the
;head refuse ;head of oil ,me rebukes ;mercy ;righteous

6 וּתְפִלָּתִי בְּרָעוֹתֵיהֶם׃ נִשְׁמְטוּ בִידֵי־סֶלַע שֹׁפְטֵיהֶם וְשָׁמְעוּ

shall they their the against been Have against (is) my also
hear ;judges rock down cast .evils their prayer

7 אֲמָרַי כִּי נָעֵמוּ׃ כְּמוֹ פֹלֵחַ וּבֹקֵעַ בָּאָרֶץ נִפְזְרוּ עֲצָמֵינוּ

our are so the rips and one As are they for my
bones scattered ,earth plows when .pleasant ,words

8 לְפִי שְׁאוֹל׃ כִּי אֵלֶיךָ ׀ יְהוָה אֲדֹנָי עֵינָי בְּכָה חָסִיתִי אַל־

not take I in my my O on (are) But .Sheol the at
;refuge You ;eyes ,Lord Jehovah ,You of mouth

9 תְּעַר נַפְשִׁי׃ שָׁמְרֵנִי מִידֵי פַח יָקְשׁוּ לִי וּמֹקְשׁוֹת פֹּעֲלֵי

the the and for they the the from Keep my make do
workers' snares from ,me laid trap of hands me .soul bare

אָוֶן׃ יִפְּלוּ בְמַכְמֹרָיו רְשָׁעִים יַחַד אָנֹכִי עַד־אֶעֱבוֹר׃

shall even I the at the their into Let .evil
.by pass ,time same wicked nets own fall

prayer be set forth before You *as* incense; the lifting up of my palms *as* the evening sacrifice. [3]O Jehovah, set a guard to my mouth; keep watch on the door of my lips. [4]Do not let my heart turn aside to any evil thing, to practice deeds in wickedness with men who do evil; and do not let me eat of their delicacies. [5]Let the righteous strike me; *it is* a mercy; and he *who* rebukes me, *it is* oil of the head; let not my head refuse *it*; for yet my prayer *shall* also *be* against their evils. [6]Their judges have been dashed against the rock; they shall hear my words; for they are pleasant. [7]As when one plows and tears the earth, so our bones are scattered at the mouth of Sheol.

[8]But my eyes *are* on You, O Jehovah, my Lord; in You I take refuge; do not make my soul naked. [9]Keep me from the hands of the trap they laid for me; and from the snares of the workers of evil. [10]Let the wicked fall into their own nets at the same time; I even shall pass by.

PSAL. CXLII קמב

PSALM 142

1 מַשְׂכִּיל לְדָוִד בִּהְיוֹתוֹ בַמְּעָרָה תְפִלָּה׃ 2 קוֹלִי אֶל־יְהוָה

Jehovah to (with) .prayer A the in his in ,David of An
voice my .cave being instruction

3 אֶזְעָק קוֹלִי אֶל־יְהוָה אֶתְחַנָּן׃ אֶשְׁפֹּךְ לְפָנָיו שִׂיחִי צָרָתִי

my my before pour I I Jehovah to (with) ;cried I
trouble ;musing Him out .prayed voice my

4 לְפָנָיו אַגִּיד׃ בְּהִתְעַטֵּף עָלַי ׀ רוּחִי וְאַתָּה יָדַעְתָּ נְתִיבָתִי

my knew then my within When I before
;path You spirit me faints ,declare Him

5 בְּאֹרַח־זוּ אֲהַלֵּךְ טָמְנוּ פַח לִי׃ הַבֵּיט יָמִין ׀ וּרְאֵה וְאֵין

and and the to Look for a have They I (in) the in
none ,see right .me trap hidden .walk which path

6 לִי מַכִּיר אָבַד מָנוֹס מִמֶּנִּי אֵין דּוֹרֵשׁ לְנַפְשִׁי׃ זָעַקְתִּי

cried I my for cares none from escape has is me
soul ;me perished ;recognizing

אֵלֶיךָ יְהוָה אָמַרְתִּי אַתָּה מַחְסִי חֶלְקִי בְּאֶרֶץ הַחַיִּים׃

the the in my my You ,said I O ;You to
.living of land portion ,refuge (are) ;Jehovah

PSALM 142

An Instruction of David, a Prayer when he was in the cave.

[1]I cry to Jehovah *with* my voice; I pray to Jehovah *with* my voice. [2]I pour out my musing before Him; I declare my distress before Him. [3]When my spirit faints within me, then You know my path; they have hidden a snare for me in the path *in* which I walk. [4]I look to the right hand and see, and no one recognizes me; every escape is hidden from me; no one cares for my soul. [5]I cried to You, O Jehovah; I said, You *are* my refuge, my portion in the land of the living.

⁶Give ear to my cry; for I am brought very low; deliver me from those pursuing me, for they are stronger than I. ⁷Cause my soul to go out from prison to give thanks to Your name. The righteous shall surround me, for You shall deal bountifully with me.

7291 5337 3966 1809 7440 7181
7 הַקְשִׁיבָה ׀ אֶל־רִנָּתִי כִּי־דַלּוֹתִי מְאֹד הַצִּילֵנִי מֵרֹדְפַי כִּי
for those from deliver ;very am I for my to heed Give
me pursuing me low brought :cry

8034 3034 5315 4525 3318 553
8 אָמְצוּ מִמֶּנִּי׃ הוֹצִיאָה מִמַּסְגֵּר ׀ נַפְשִׁי לְהוֹדוֹת אֶת־שְׁמֶךָ
Your give to soul my from out Bring .I than are they
;name to thanks prison stronger

1580 6662 3803
בִּי יַכְתִּרוּ צַדִּיקִים כִּי תִגְמֹל עָלָי׃
.me shall You for the shall me
reward ,righteous surround

PSAL. CXLIII קמג

PSALM 143

PSALM 143

A Psalm of David.

¹Hear my prayer, O Jehovah; give ear to my supplications; answer me in Your faithfulness, in Your righteousness; ²and do not enter into judgment with Your servant; for not anyone living is just in Your sight. ³For the enemy has pursued my soul; he has beaten my life to the ground; he has made me dwell in darkness, like the dead of old. ⁴And my spirit within me has fainted; my heart within me is stunned. ⁵I remember the days of old; I meditate on all Your works; I muse on the work of Your hands. ⁶I spread out my hands to You; my soul *thirsts* to You like a thirsty land. Selah.

⁷O Jehovah, answer me quickly; my spirit is failing; do not hide Your face from me, lest I be like the ones who go down to the Pit. ⁸Cause me to hear Your mercy in the morning; for I do trust in You; cause me to know the way I should walk; for I lift up my soul to You. ⁹O Jehovah, deliver me from my enemies; to You I have hidden. ¹⁰Teach me to do Your will; for You *are* my God; Your Spirit *is* good; lead me into the land of justice. ¹¹O Jehovah, because of Your name, make me live; in Your

8469 238 8605 8085 3068 1732 4210
1 מִזְמוֹר לְדָוִד יְהוָה ׀ שְׁמַע תְּפִלָּתִי הַאֲזִינָה אֶל־תַּחֲנוּנַי
my to ear give my hear O .David of psalm A
;supplications ;prayer ,Jehovah

4941 935 408 6666 6030 530
2 בֶּאֱמֻנָתְךָ עֲנֵנִי בְּצִדְקָתֶךָ׃ וְאַל־תָּבוֹא בְמִשְׁפָּט אֶת־
with into do And Your in answer Your in
judgment enter not .righteousness ,me faithfulness

5315 341 7291 2416 3605 6440 6663 3808 5650
3 עַבְדֶּךָ כִּי לֹא־יִצְדַּק לְפָנֶיךָ כָל־חָי׃ כִּי רָדַף אוֹיֵב ׀ נַפְשִׁי
my the has For anyone Your in be shall not for Your
;soul enemy pursued .living sight just ;servant

5769 4191 4285 3427 2416 776 1792
דִּכָּא לָאָרֶץ חַיָּתִי הוֹשִׁיבַנִי בְמַחֲשַׁכִּים כְּמֵתֵי עוֹלָם׃
.old the as ,darkness in made has he my the to has he
of dead dwell me ;life ground crushed

3117 2142 3820 8074 8432 7307 5848
4 וַתִּתְעַטֵּף עָלַי רוּחִי בְּתוֹכִי יִשְׁתּוֹמֵם לִבִּי׃ זָכַרְתִּי יָמִים ׀
5 days the I my stunned is within my within has And
remember ;heart me ;spirit me fainted

6566 7878 3027 4639 6467 3605 1897 6924
6 מִקֶּדֶם הָגִיתִי בְכָל־פָּעֳלֶךָ בְּמַעֲשֵׂה יָדֶיךָ אֲשׂוֹחֵחַ׃ פֵּרַשְׂתִּי
spread I .muse I Your the on Your all on I ;old of
out hands of work ;works meditate

3068 6030 4118 5542 5889 776 5315 3027
7 יָדַי אֵלֶיךָ נַפְשִׁי ׀ כְּאֶרֶץ־עֲיֵפָה לְךָ סֶלָה׃ מַהֵר עֲנֵנִי ׀ יְהוָה
O Answer quickly .Selah (is) weary a like my ;You to my
,Jehovah ,me .You to land soul hands

3383 4911 6440 5640 7307 3615
כָּלְתָה רוּחִי אַל־תַּסְתֵּר פָּנֶיךָ מִמֶּנִּי וְנִמְשַׁלְתִּי עִם־יֹרְדֵי
who those with be I lest from Your do not my is
to down go like ,me face hide ,spirit failing

3045 982 2617 1242 8085 953
8 בוֹר׃ הַשְׁמִיעֵנִי בַבֹּקֶר ׀ חַסְדֶּךָ כִּי־בְךָ בָטָחְתִּי הוֹדִיעֵנִי
me cause do I in for Your the in me Cause the
know to ;trust You ;mercy morning hear to .Pit

341 5337 5315 5375 3212 2098 1870
9 דֶּרֶךְ־זוּ אֵלֵךְ כִּי־אֵלֶיךָ נָשָׂאתִי נַפְשִׁי׃ הַצִּילֵנִי מֵאֹיְבַי ׀
my from Deliver .soul my up lift I You to for should I way the
,enemies me ;walk which

430 7522 6213 3925 3680 3068
10 יְהוָה אֵלֶיךָ כִסִּתִי׃ לַמְּדֵנִי ׀ לַעֲשׂוֹת רְצוֹנֶךָ כִּי־אַתָּה אֱלוֹהָי
my You for Your do to me Teach have I to O
;God (are) ,will .hidden You ,Jehovah

3068 8034 4616 4334 776 5148 2896 7307
11 רוּחֲךָ טוֹבָה תַּנְחֵנִי בְּאֶרֶץ מִישׁוֹר׃ לְמַעַן־שִׁמְךָ יְהוָה
O Your Because .plainness the into lead (is) Your
,Jehovah ,name of of land me ;good Spirit

12 2421 6666 3318 6864 5315 2617 6789
תְּחַיֵּנִי בְּצִדְקָתְךָ | תוֹצִיא מִצָּרָה נַפְשִׁי׃ וּבְחַסְדְּךָ תַּצְמִית
off cut in And .soul my of out bring Your in me make
mercy Your trouble righteousness ;live
3341 6 3605 6887 5315 5650
אֹיְבָי וְהַאֲבַדְתָּ כָּל־צֹרְרֵי נַפְשִׁי כִּי אֲנִי עַבְדֶּךָ׃
Your I for my those all and my
.servant (am) ;soul afflict who destroy ;enemies

PSAL. CXLIV קמד

PSALM 144

1 1732 1288 3068 6697 3925 3027 7128 676
לְדָוִד | בָּרוּךְ יְהוָה | צוּרִי הַמְלַמֵּד יָדַי לַקְרָב אֶצְבְּעוֹתַי
fingers my ,war for my who ;rock my Jehovah Blessed (psalm A)
hands teaches (be) .David of

2 4421 2617 4686 4869 6403 4043
לַמִּלְחָמָה׃ חַסְדִּי וּמְצוּדָתִי מִשְׂגַּבִּי וּמְפַלְטִי־לִי מָגִנִּי וּבוֹ
in and my to and high my my and mercy my ;battle for
Him shield ;me deliverer tower ;fortress

3 2620 7286 5971 8478 3068 4100 120 3045 1121
חָסִיתִי הָרוֹדֵד עַמִּי תַחְתָּי׃ יְהוָה מָה־אָדָם וַתֵּדָעֵהוּ בֶּן־
the You that man what O under my who He take I
of son ,him know (is) ,Jehovah .me people subdues ;refuge

4 582 2803 120 1892 1819 3117 6738 5674
אֱנוֹשׁ וַתְּחַשְּׁבֵהוּ׃ אָדָם לַהֶבֶל דָּמָה יָמָיו כְּצֵל עוֹבֵר׃
that a like his ,like is to Man You that ,man
.passes shadow days vanity ?him esteem

5
6 3068 5186 8064 3381 5060 2022 6225 1299 1300
יְהוָה הַט־שָׁמֶיךָ וְתֵרֵד גַּע בֶּהָרִים וְיֶעֱשָׁנוּ׃ בְּרוֹק בָּרָק
light- Flash they and the touch and Your bow Jeho- O
ning out .smoke shall mountains ;down come heavens down ,vah

7 6327 7971 2671 2000 7971 3027 4791 6475
וּתְפִיצֵם שְׁלַח חִצֶּיךָ וּתְהֻמֵּם׃ שְׁלַח יָדֶיךָ מִמָּרוֹם פְּצֵנִי
rescue from Your Send con- and Your Send scatter and
me ;above hand .them found arrows out ;them

8 5337 4325 7227 3027 1121 5236 834 6310 1696
וְהַצִּילֵנִי מִמַּיִם רַבִּים מִיַּד בְּנֵי נֵכָר׃ אֲשֶׁר פִּיהֶם דִּבֶּר־
have their whose a sons the the from ,great of out deliver and
spoken mouths ,foreigner of of hand waters me

9 7723 3225 3225 8267 430 7892 2319 7891
שָׁוְא וִימִינָם יְמִין שָׁקֶר׃ אֱלֹהִים שִׁיר חָדָשׁ אָשִׁירָה לָּךְ
to will I new song a ,God O .lies a (is) their and ;vanity
;You sing of hand right hand right

10 5035 6218 2167 5414 8668 4428 6475
בְּנֵבֶל עָשׂוֹר אֲזַמְּרָה־לָּךְ׃ הַנּוֹתֵן תְּשׁוּעָה לַמְּלָכִים הַפּוֹצֶה
who ,kings to salvation (You is It) to sing will I ten a on
rescues gives who .You praises strings of harp

11 1732 5650 2719 7451 6475 5337 3027 1121 5236
אֶת־דָּוִד עַבְדּוֹ מֵחֶרֶב רָעָה׃ פְּצֵנִי וְהַצִּילֵנִי מִיַּד בְּנֵי־נֵכָר
of sons the from deliver and Rescue .evil the from His David
,foreigners of hand the me me sword servant

12 834 6310 1696 7723 3225 3225 8267 834 1121
אֲשֶׁר פִּיהֶם דִּבֶּר־שָׁוְא וִימִינָם יְמִין שָׁקֶר׃ אֲשֶׁר בָּנֵינוּ
our That .lies right a (is) their and ;vanity have their whose
sons of hand hand right spoken mouths
5195 1430 5271 1323 2106 2404
כִּנְטִעִים מְגֻדָּלִים בִּנְעוּרֵיהֶם בְּנוֹתֵינוּ כְזָוִיֹּת מְחֻטָּבוֹת
hewn corner-like our (and) their in up grown like (be may)
pillars daughters ;youths plants

13 8403 1964 4200 4393 6329 2177 6629/2177
תַּבְנִית הֵיכָל׃ מְזָוֵינוּ מְלֵאִים מְפִיקִים מִזַּן אֶל־זַן צֹאונֵנוּ
our ;kind to kind furnishing (be may) our (and) ;palace a the like
flocks full storehouses of structure

14 503 7233 2351 441 5445 369
מַאֲלִיפוֹת מְרֻבָּבוֹת בְּחוּצוֹתֵינוּ׃ אַלּוּפֵינוּ מְסֻבָּלִים אֵין
not be may oxen Our our in ten (and) breed may
is ;laden .streets thousands thousands

name, make me live; in Your
righteousness, bring my
soul out of distress. [12]And
in Your mercy cut off my
enemies; and destroy all
those who afflict my soul;
for I *am* Your servant.

PSALM 144
A Psalm of David.

[1]Blessed *be* Jehovah my
rock, who teaches my
hands for war, my fingers
for battle; [2]my mercy and
my fortress; my high tower
and my deliverer; my shield,
and in Him I take refuge; *He*
who humbles my people
under me. [3]O Jehovah,
what *is* man that You know
him; the son of man, that
you esteem him? [4]Man is
like to vanity; his days *are*
like a shadow that passes.
[5]Bow down Your heavens,
O Jehovah; and come
down; touch the moun-
tains and they shall smoke.
[6]Flash out lightning and
scatter them; send out your
arrows and confound them.
[7]Send Your hand from
above; rescue me and
deliver me out of great
waters, from the hand of a
foreigner's sons, [8]whose
mouths have spoken vanity;
and their right hand *is* a
right hand of lies. [9]I will
sing a new song to You, O
God; I will sing praises to
You on a harp of ten strings.
[10]*It is You* who gives
salvation to kings, who
delivers His servant David
from the evil sword.
[11]Rescue me and deliver me
from the foreigner's sons,
those whose mouths have
spoken vanity; and their
right hand *is* a right hand of
lies; [12]so that our sons *may*
be like plants grown up in
their youth; *and* our
daughters like corner-
stones hewn like a palace
building; [13]*and* our storehouses *may be* full, furnishing kind to kind; our flocks
may breed thousands *and*
ten thousands outside;
[14]our oxen *may be* laden;

there is no break and no going out, and no crying in our plazas. 15 Blessed *is* the people that is thus; blessed *is* the people whose God *is* Jehovah!

PSALM 145
A Psalm *of Praise, of David.*

1 I will exalt you, my God, O king; and bless Your name forever and ever. 2 I will bless You every day; and I will praise Your name forever and ever. 3 Jehovah *is* great and to be greatly praised; and to His greatness there *is* no finding out. 4 Generation to generation shall praise Your works; and shall declare Your mighty acts. 5 I will muse on the glorious honor of Your majesty, and the things of Your wonderful works. 6 And they shall speak of the might of Your awesome works; and I will declare Your greatness. 7 They shall express the memory of Your great goodness, and they shall sing of Your righteousness. 8 Jehovah *is* gracious and merciful, long to anger and of great mercy; 9 Jehovah *is* good to all; and His tender mercies *are* over all His works. 10 All Your works shall thank You, O Jehovah; and Your saints shall bless You. 11 They shall speak of the glory of Your kingdom, and talk of Your might; 12 to make Your might known to the sons of men; yea, the glorious majesty of His kingdom. 13 Your kingdom *is* a kingdom to all eternities; and Your rule in all generation and generation. 14 Jehovah upholds all who fall, and raises up all who are bowed down. 15 The eyes of all hope to You; and You give them their food in due time. 16 *You* open Your hand and satisfy the desire of every living thing. 17 Jehovah *is* righteous in all His ways,

5971 835 7339 66.82 369 3318 369 6556
15 פֶּרֶץ וְאֵין יוֹצֵאת וְאֵין צְוָחָה בִּרְחֹבֹתֵינוּ׃ אַשְׁרֵי הָעָם
the Blessed .plazas our in crying and going and a
people (are) no out no ;break

430 3068 59.71 835 3602
שֶׁכָּכָה לּוֹ אַשְׁרֵי הָעָם שֶׁיהוָה אֱלֹהָיו׃
his (is) which (to) the Blessed to which
:God Jehovah people (is) .it thus are

PSAL. CXLV קמה

PSALM 145

5769 8034 1288 4428 430 7311 1732 8416
1 תְּהִלָּה לְדָוִד אֲרוֹמִמְךָ אֱלוֹהַי הַמֶּלֶךְ וַאֲבָרְכָה שִׁמְךָ לְעוֹלָם
forever Your bless and ;King O ,God my will I ,David Of .Praise
name ,You exalt

5703 5769 80.34 1984 1288 3117 3605 5703
2 וָעֶד׃ בְּכָל־יוֹם אֲבָרְכֶךָּ וַאֲהַלְלָה שִׁמְךָ לְעוֹלָם וָעֶד׃
and forever Your praise and will I day In and
.ever name ;You bless every .ever

1755 1755 2714 369 1420 3966 1984 3068 1419
3
4 גָּדוֹל יְהוָה וּמְהֻלָּל מְאֹד וְלִגְדֻלָּתוֹ אֵין חֵקֶר׃ דּוֹר לְדוֹר
to Generation .search a (is) His to and ;greatly to and Jehovah Great
generation not greatness praised be

1697 1935 3519 1926 5046 1369 46.39 7623
5 יְשַׁבַּח מַעֲשֶׂיךָ וּגְבוּרֹתֶיךָ יַגִּידוּ׃ הֲדַר כְּבוֹד הוֹדֶךָ וְדִבְרֵי
the and Your the The shall Your and Your shall
of things ,majesty of glory of honor .declare acts mighty ;works praise

1420 559 3372 5807 7878 6381
6 נִפְלְאוֹתֶיךָ אָשִׂיחָה׃ וֶעֱזוּז נוֹרְאוֹתֶיךָ יֹאמֵרוּ וּגְדוּלֹּתֶיךָ
Your and shall they awesome Your the And will I won- Your
greatness ;speak works of might .upon muse works drous

2587 7442 6666 5042 2898 7227 2143 5608
7
8 אֲסַפְּרֶנָּה׃ זֵכֶר רַב־טוּבְךָ יַבִּיעוּ וְצִדְקָתְךָ יְרַנֵּנוּ׃ חַנּוּן
Gracious shall they Your and shall they Your great The will I
.of sing righteousness ,express goodness of memory .declare

3605 3068 2896 2617 1419 639 750 3068 7349
9 וְרַחוּם יְהוָה אֶרֶךְ אַפַּיִם וּגְדָל־חָסֶד׃ טוֹב־יְהוָה לַכֹּל
;all to (is) good ;mercy of and anger long (is) and
Jehovah great (to) ;Jehovah merciful

2623 4639 3605 3068 3034 4639 3605 73.56
10 וְרַחֲמָיו עַל־כָּל־מַעֲשָׂיו׃ יוֹדוּךָ יְהוָה כָּל־מַעֲשֶׂיךָ וַחֲסִידֶיךָ
Your and Your All O shall His all (are) His and
saints ;works ,Jehovah ,You thank .works over mercies

3045 1696 1369 559 4438 3519 1288
11
12 יְבָרְכוּכָה׃ כְּבוֹד מַלְכוּתְךָ יֹאמֵרוּ וּגְבוּרָתְךָ יְדַבֵּרוּ׃ לְהוֹדִיעַ
make to talk Your and shall They Your the bless shall
known ;of might ,of speak kingdom of glory .You

4438 4438 1926 3519 1369 120 1121
13 לִבְנֵי הָאָדָם גְּבוּרֹתָיו וּכְבוֹד הֲדַר מַלְכוּתוֹ׃ מַלְכוּתְךָ
Your His the the and Your men the to
kingdom .kingdom of majesty of glory ;might of sons

5564 1755 1755 3605 44.75 5769 3605 4438
14 מַלְכוּת כָּל־עֹלָמִים וּמֶמְשַׁלְתְּךָ בְּכָל־דּוֹר וָדֹר׃ סוֹמֵךְ
upholds and genera- all in Your and ;eternities all a (is)
.generation tion rule of kingdom

3605 5869 3721 3605 2210 5307 3605 3068
15 יְהוָה לְכָל־הַנֹּפְלִים וְזוֹקֵף לְכָל־הַכְּפוּפִים׃ עֵינֵי כֹל אֵלֶיךָ
to all The are who all and ;fall who all Jehovah
You of eyes .down bowed up raising

6605 6256 400 5414 7663
16 יְשַׂבֵּרוּ וְאַתָּה נוֹתֵן־לָהֶם אֶת־אָכְלָם בְּעִתּוֹ׃ פּוֹתֵחַ אֶת־
(You) due in their them to give and ;hope
open .time food You

1870 3605 3068 6662 7522 2416 3605 7646 3027
17 יָדֶךָ וּמַשְׂבִּיעַ לְכָל־חַי רָצוֹן׃ צַדִּיק יְהוָה בְּכָל־דְּרָכָיו
His all in Jehovah righteous the living of and Your
,ways (is) desire thing every satisfy hand

and kind in all His works. [18]Jehovah *is* near to all who call on Him, to all those who call on Him in truth. [19]He will fulfill the desire of the ones who fear Him; and He will hear their cry and save them. [20]Jehovah watches over all who love Him; but He destroys all the wicked. [21]My mouth shall speak the praise of Jehovah; and all flesh shall bless His holy name forever and ever.

18 וחסיד בכל־מעשיו׃ קרוב יהוה לכל־קראיו לכל אשר

those all to call who Him on to Jehovah (is) near His .works all in and kind

19 יקראהו באמת׃ רצון־יראיו יעשה ואת־שועתם ישמע

will He hear their cry and will He .do fearers Him of The of desire .truth in call who Him on

20 ויושיעם׃ שומר יהוה את־כל־אהביו ואת כל־הרשעים

the wicked all but love who ;Him all Jehovah watches over save and .them

21 ישמיד׃ תהלת יהוה ידבר־פי ויברך כל־בשר שם

name flesh all bless and My ;mouth shall speak Jehovah the of praise He .destroys

קדשו לעולם ועד׃

and .ever forever His holy

PSAL. CXLVI קמו

PSALM 146

PSALM 146

[1]Praise Jehovah, praise Jehovah, O my soul. [2]While I live I will praise Jehovah; while I have being I will sing praises to my God. [3]Do not trust in princes, in a son of man, for there is no salvation to him. [4]His breath will go out; he returns to the earth; in that day his thoughts perish. [5]Blessed *is he* who *has* the God of Jacob in his help; his hope is on Jehovah his God, [6]who made the heavens and the earth, the seas and all that *is* in them; who keeps truth forever; [7]who executes judgment for the oppressed; who gives food to the hungry; Jehovah sets free the prisoners; [8]Jehovah opens *the eyes* of the blind; Jehovah lifts up those bowed down; Jehovah loves the righteous; [9]Jehovah guards the aliens; He relieves the orphan and the widow, but He warps the way of the wicked.

[10]Jehovah shall reign forever, O Zion, your God from generation and generation. Praise Jehovah!

1 2 הללו־יה הללי נפשי את־יהוה׃ אהללה יהוה בחיי

I while ;live Jehovah will I praise !Jehovah my O ,soul ,praise Praise ;Jah

3 אזמרה לאלהי בעודי׃ אל־תבטחו בנדיבים בבן־אדם ׀

;man a in of son ,princes in trust Do not I while .being have my to God sing will I praises

4 שאין לו תשועה׃ תצא רוחו ישב לאדמתו ביום ההוא

that day in the to ;ground he returns His ;breath will out go .salvation to there for him not is

5 אבדו עשתנתיו׃ אשרי שאל יעקב בעזרו שברו על־

(is) on his hope his in ;help Jacob (has) who of God the Blessed (he is) his .thoughts perish

6 יהוה אלהיו׃ עשה ׀ שמים וארץ את־הים ואת־כל־

all and the seas the and ,earth the heavens who made his ;God Jehovah

7 אשר־בם השמר אמת לעולם׃ עשה משפט ׀ לעשוקים

the for ;oppressed judgment who executes ;forever truth who keeps in ,them is that

8 נתן לחם לרעבים יהוה מתיר אסורים׃ יהוה ׀ פקח

opens (eyes) Jehovah the ;prisoners sets free Jehovah the to ;hungry food who gives

9 עורים יהוה זקף כפופים יהוה אהב צדיקים׃ יהוה ׀ שמר

guards Jehovah the ;righteous loves Jehovah those raises ;down bowed Jehovah the ;blind

10 את־גרים יתום ואלמנה יעודד ודרך רשעים יעות׃ ימלך

shall reign He .warps the wicked the but of way He ;relieves the and widow the orphan ;aliens the

יהוה ׀ לעולם אלהיך ציון לדר ודר הללו־יה׃

Praise !Jah gen- and .eration from generation Zion O your God ;forever Jehovah

PSAL. CXLVII קמז

PSALM 147

PSALM 147

[1]Praise Jehovah; for *it is* good to sing praise to our God; because praise *is* delightful *and* becoming. [2]Jehovah builds up Jerusalem; He gathers the outcasts of Israel. [3]*He* heals the broken-hearted and binds up their sorrows. [4]*He* appoints the number of the stars; He calls to them all by names. [5]Our Lord *is* great and of great might; there is no limit to His understanding. [6]Jehovah relieves the meek; He throws the wicked down to the ground. [7]Sing to Jehovah with thanksgiving; sing praise on the lyre to our God, [8]who covers the heavens with clouds; who prepares rain for the earth; who makes grass to grow *on* the mountains. [9]*He* gives the animals their food, to the young ravens that cry. [10]He takes no delight in the strength of the horse; nor any pleasure in the legs of a man. [11]Jehovah takes pleasure in those who fear Him; those who hope in His mercy. [12]Praise Jehovah, O Jerusalem; praise your God, O Zion. [13]For He has made strong the bars of your gates; He has blessed your sons within you. [14]He makes peace *in* your border, He satisfies you *with* the fat of the wheat. [15]He sends His command out *upon* the earth; His word runs very swiftly; [16]He gives snow like wool; He scatters the white frost like ashes; [17]He casts out His ice like crumbs; who can stand before His cold? [18]He sends out His word and melts them; He causes His wind to blow, and the waters flow. [19]He declares His word to Jacob, His

8416 5000 5273 430 2167 2896 1984
1 הַלְלוּיָהּ | כִּי־טוֹב זַמְּרָה אֱלֹהֵינוּ כִּי־נָעִים נָאוָה תְהִלָּה׃
praise (and) de- because our sing to (is it) for Praise
(is) becoming lightful ;God to praise good ;Jah

7665 7495 3664 3478 1760 3068 3389 1129
2 3 בּוֹנֵה יְרוּשָׁלַםִ יְהוָה נִדְחֵי יִשְׂרָאֵל יְכַנֵּס׃ הָרֹפֵא לִשְׁבוּרֵי
the (He) He Israel the ;Jehovah Jerusalem builds
of broken heals .gathers of outcasts up

3605 3556 4557 4487 6094 2280 3820
4 לֵב וּמְחַבֵּשׁ לְעַצְּבוֹתָם׃ מוֹנֶה מִסְפָּר לַכּוֹכָבִים לְכֻלָּם
them to the of the (He) their and .heart
all ;stars number appoints .sorrows up binds

4557 369 8394 3581 7227 113 1419 7121 8034
5 שֵׁמוֹת יִקְרָא׃ גָּדוֹל אֲדוֹנֵינוּ וְרַב־כֹּחַ לִתְבוּנָתוֹ אֵין מִסְפָּר׃
.numbering not His to ;might and Our great (is) He (by)
is understanding of great Lord .calls names

3068 6030 776 5704 7563 8213 3068 6035 5749
6 7 מְעוֹדֵד עֲנָוִים יְהוָה מַשְׁפִּיל רְשָׁעִים עֲדֵי־אָרֶץ׃ עֱנוּ לַיהוָה
to Sing the to the throws He ;Jehovah the relieves
Jehovah .ground wicked down meek

5645 8064 3680 3658 430 2167 8426
8 בְּתוֹדָה זַמְּרוּ לֵאלֹהֵינוּ בְכִנּוֹר׃ הַמְכַסֶּה שָׁמַיִם | בְּעָבִים
with the (He) the on our to sing with
;clouds heavens covers .lyre God praise ;thanksgiving

929 5414 2682 2022 6779 4306 776 3559
9 הַמֵּכִין לָאָרֶץ מָטָר הַמַּצְמִיחַ הָרִים חָצִיר׃ נוֹתֵן לִבְהֵמָה
the to (He) .grass the (on) makes who ;rain the for who
beasts gives mountain grow to earth prepares

2654 5483 1369 3808 7121 834 6158 1121 3899
10 לַחְמָהּ לִבְנֵי עֹרֵב אֲשֶׁר יִקְרָאוּ׃ לֹא בִגְבוּרַת הַסּוּס יֶחְפָּץ
takes He the the in no .cry that ravens the to their
;delight horse of strength of sons ;food

3373 3068 7521 7521 376 7785 3808
11 לֹא־בְשׁוֹקֵי הָאִישׁ יִרְצֶה׃ רוֹצֶה יְהוָה אֶת־יְרֵאָיו אֶת־
who those Jehovah takes takes He man a the in not
,Him fear in pleasure .pleasure of legs

430 1984 3068 3389 7623 2617 3176
12 הַמְיַחֲלִים לְחַסְדּוֹ׃ שַׁבְּחִי יְרוּשָׁלַםִ אֶת־יְהוָה הַלְלִי אֱלֹהַיִךְ
Your praise ;Jehovah O Shout His in who those
God ,Jerusalem ,praise .mercy hope

7760 7130 1121 1288 8179 1280 2388 6726
13 14 צִיּוֹן׃ כִּי־חִזַּק בְּרִיחֵי שְׁעָרָיִךְ בֵּרַךְ בָּנַיִךְ בְּקִרְבֵּךְ׃ הַשָּׂם־
He within your has He your the He For .Zion O
makes .you sons blessed ;gates of bars strong made

776 565 7971 7646 2406 2459 7965 1366
15 גְּבוּלֵךְ שָׁלוֹם חֵלֶב חִטִּים יַשְׂבִּיעֵךְ׃ הַשֹּׁלֵחַ אִמְרָתוֹ אָרֶץ
the (on) His sends He satisfies He the fat the ,peace your (in)
;earth command out .you wheat of border

665 3713 6785 7950 5414 1697 7323 4120 5704
16 עַד־מְהֵרָה יָרוּץ דְּבָרוֹ׃ הַנֹּתֵן שֶׁלֶג כַּצָּמֶר כְּפוֹר כָּאֵפֶר
like the like snow (He) His runs very until
ashes frost white ;wool gives .word , swiftly

7971 5975 4310 7135 6440 6595 7140 7993 6340
17 18 יְפַזֵּר׃ מַשְׁלִיךְ קַרְחוֹ כְפִתִּים לִפְנֵי קָרָתוֹ מִי יַעֲמֹד׃ יִשְׁלַח
sends He can who His before like His casts He He
out ?stand cold ;crumbs ice out ;scatters

3290 1697 5046 4325 5140 7307 5380 4529 1697
19 דְּבָרוֹ וְיַמְסֵם יַשֵּׁב רוּחוֹ יִזְּלוּ־מָיִם׃ מַגִּיד דְּבָרָיו לְיַעֲקֹב
to His He the and His makes He and His
;Jacob words declares .flow waters ,wind blow ;them melts word

statutes and His judgments
to Israel. [20]He has not done
so with any nation; and they
have not known *His*
judgments. Praise Jehovah!

4941 1471 3605 6213 3808 3478 4941 2706
20 חֻקָּיו וּמִשְׁפָּטָיו לְיִשְׂרָאֵל׃ לֹא־עָשָׂה כֵן ׀ לְכָל־גּוֹי וּמִשְׁפָּטִים
(His) and ;nation with so has He not .Israel to His and His
judgments any done judgments statutes
3050/1984 3045 1097
בַּל־יְדָעוּם הַלְלוּיָהּ׃
Praise they have not
!Jah .known

PSALM CXLVIII קמח

PSALM 148

PSALM 148
[1]Praise Jehovah! Praise
Jehovah from the heavens;
praise Him in the heights.
[2]Praise Him, all His angels;
praise Him, all His hosts.
[3]Praise Him, sun and moon;
praise Him, all you stars of
light. [4]Praise Him, O
heavens of heavens; and O
waters that *are* above the
heavens. [5]Let them praise
the name of Jehovah; for
He commanded, and they
were created. [6]And He
established them forever
and ever; He gave a decree
that they not pass away.
[7]Let the sea-monsters and
all deeps praise Jehovah
from the earth; [8]fire and
hail; snow and smoke;
stormy wind fulfilling His
word; [9]mountains and all
hills; fruitful trees and all
cedars; [10]beasts and all
livestock; creeping things
and birds of the wing;
[11]kings of the earth and all
people; princes and all
judges of the earth; [12]both
young men and virgins too;
old men and youths. [13]Let
them praise the name of
Jehovah; for His name
alone is exalted; His glory *is*
above the earth and
heavens. [14]He also lifts up
the horn of His people, the
praise of all His saints, of
the sons of Israel, a people
near to Him. Praise
Jehovah!

4791 1984 80 64 3068 1984 3050/1984
1 הַלְלוּיָהּ ׀ הַלְלוּ אֶת־יְהוָה מִן־הַשָּׁמַיִם הַלְלוּהוּ בַּמְּרוֹמִים׃
the in praise the from Jehovah Praise Praise
.heights Him ;heavens !Jah
8121 1984 6635 3605 1984 4397 36 05 1984
2 הַלְלוּהוּ כָל־מַלְאָכָיו הַלְלוּהוּ כָּל־צְבָאָו׃
3 הַלְלוּהוּ שֶׁמֶשׁ
sun Praise His all Praise His all Praise
,Him .hosts ,Him .angels ,Him
8064 8064 1984 216 3556 3605 1984 3394
4 וְיָרֵחַ הַלְלוּהוּ כָּל־כּוֹכְבֵי אוֹר׃ הַלְלוּהוּ שְׁמֵי הַשָּׁמָיִם
;heavens O Praise .light stars all praise and
of heaven ,Him of ,Him ;moon
3068 8034 1984 8064 4791 834 4325
5 וְהַמַּיִם אֲשֶׁר ׀ מֵעַל הַשָּׁמָיִם׃ יְהַלְלוּ אֶת־שֵׁם יְהוָה כִּי
for ;Jehovah the them Let the above that and
of name praise .heavens (are) waters
3808 5414 2706 5769 5703 5975 1254 6680
6 הוּא צִוָּה וְנִבְרָאוּ׃ וַיַּעֲמִידֵם לָעַד לְעוֹלָם חָק־נָתַן וְלֹא
and He a and forever made He And they and com- He
not gave decree ;ever stand them .created were manded
8415 3605 85 77 776 3068 1984 5674
7 יַעֲבוֹר׃ הַלְלוּ אֶת־יְהוָה מִן־הָאָרֶץ תַּנִּינִים וְכָל־תְּהֹמוֹת׃
.deeps and sea- the the from Jehovah Let pass will it
all monsters earth praise .away
2022 1697 6213 5592 7307 7008 7950 1259 784
8 אֵשׁ וּבָרָד שֶׁלֶג וְקִיטוֹר רוּחַ סְעָרָה עֹשָׂה דְבָרוֹ׃
9 הֶהָרִים
the His fulfilling stormy wind and snow and Fire
mountains ;word ;smoke ;hail
929 3605 2416 730 36 05 6529 6086 1389 3605
10 וְכָל־גְּבָעוֹת עֵץ פְּרִי וְכָל־אֲרָזִים׃ הַחַיָּה וְכָל־בְּהֵמָה
;cattle and beasts ;cedars and fruit- trees ;hills and
all all all
3605 8269 3816 36 05 776 44 28 3671 6833 7431
11 רֶמֶשׂ וְצִפּוֹר כָּנָף׃ מַלְכֵי־אֶרֶץ וְכָל־לְאֻמִּים שָׂרִים וְכָל־
and princes ;peoples and the kings the and creeping
all all earth of ;wing of bird things
5288 2205 1330 1571 970 776 8199
12 שֹׁפְטֵי אָרֶץ׃ בַּחוּרִים וְגַם־בְּתוּלוֹת זְקֵנִים עִם־נְעָרִים׃
.youths with old ;virgins and men young the judges
men also ;earth of
776 1935 905 8034 7682 3068 8034 1984
13 יְהַלְלוּ ׀ אֶת־שֵׁם יְהוָה כִּי־נִשְׂגָּב שְׁמוֹ לְבַדּוֹ הוֹדוֹ עַל־אֶרֶץ
the (is) His ;alone His is for ;Jehovah the them Let
earth above glory name exalted of name praise
1121 2623 3605 8416 5971 7161 7311 8064
14 וְשָׁמָיִם׃ וַיָּרֶם קֶרֶן ׀ לְעַמּוֹ תְּהִלָּה לְכָל־חֲסִידָיו לִבְנֵי
the of His of the His of the also He and
of sons ,saints all praise ,people horn up lifts .heavens
3050 1984 7138 5971 3478
יִשְׂרָאֵל עַם קְרֹבוֹ הַלְלוּיָהּ׃
Praise to near a ,Israel
!Jah .Him people

PSALM CXLIX קמט

PSALM 149

1 2623 6951 8416 2319 7892 3068 7891 1984
הַלְלוּ יָהּ ׀ שִׁירוּ לַיהוָה שִׁיר חָדָשׁ תְּהִלָּתוֹ בִּקְהַל חֲסִידִים׃
the the in His ,new song a to Sing Praise
.saints of assembly praise Jehovah !Jah

2
3 8034 1984 4428 1523 1121 6726 6213 3478 8056
יִשְׂמַח יִשְׂרָאֵל בְּעֹשָׂיו בְּנֵי־צִיּוֹן יָגִילוּ בְמַלְכָּם׃ יְהַלְלוּ שְׁמוֹ
His them Let their in be Zion the His in Israel Let
name praise .king joyful of sons ,Maker rejoice

4 6286 5971 3068 7521 2167 3658 8596 4234
בְמָחוֹל בְּתֹף וְכִנּוֹר יְזַמְּרוּ־לוֹ׃ כִּי־רוֹצֶה יְהוָה בְּעַמּוֹ יְפָאֵר
He His in Jehovah takes for to them let and the with the in
adorns ;people pleasure .Him praise sing lyre timbrel ;dance

5 4904 7442 3519 2623 5937 3444 6035
עֲנָוִים בִּישׁוּעָה׃ יַעְלְזוּ חֲסִידִים בְּכָבוֹד יְרַנְּנוּ עַל־מִשְׁכְּבוֹתָם׃
their on them let in the Let with the
,beds aloud sing ;glory saints exult .salvation humble

6
7 6213 3027 6374 2719 1627 410 7318
רוֹמְמוֹת אֵל בִּגְרוֹנָם וְחֶרֶב פִּיפִיּוֹת בְּיָדָם׃ לַעֲשׂוֹת
execute to their in two- a and their in God the (and)
;hand edged sword throats; of exaltation

8 2131 4428 631 3816 8433 1471 5360
נְקָמָה בַּגּוֹיִם תּוֹכֵחֹת בַּל־אֻמִּים׃ לֶאְסֹר מַלְכֵיהֶם בְּזִקִּים
with their bind to the on punishment the on ven-
chains kings ;peoples ,nations geance

9 3789 4941 6213 1270 3525 3513
וְנִכְבְּדֵיהֶם בְּכַבְלֵי בַרְזֶל׃ לַעֲשׂוֹת בָּהֶם ׀ מִשְׁפָּט כָּתוּב
;written the on execute to ;iron with their and
judgment them of bands nobles

3050 1984 2623 1926
הָדָר הוּא לְכָל־חֲסִידָיו הַלְלוּ־יָהּ׃
Praise His for this (an)
!Jah .saints all (is) honor

PSALM 149

[1]Praise Jehovah! Sing to Jehovah a new song, His praise in the assembly of the saints. [2]Let Israel rejoice in Him who made him; let the sons of Zion be joyful in their King. [3]Let them praise His name in the dance: let them sing praise to Him with the timbrel and lyre. [4]For Jehovah takes pleasure in His people; He beautifies the meek with salvation. [5]Let the saints be joyful in glory; let them sing aloud on their beds, [6]*and* the exaltation of God *be* in their throat; and a two-edged sword in their hand, [7]to execute vengeance on the nations, punishment on the peoples; [8]to bind their kings with chains and their nobles with iron bands; [9]to execute on them the judgment written; this *is an* honor for all His saints. Praise Jehovah!

PSALM CL קנ

PSALM 150

1
2 1984 5797 7549 1984 6944 410 1984 3050/1984
הַלְלוּ יָהּ ׀ הַלְלוּ־אֵל בְּקָדְשׁוֹ הַלְלוּהוּ בִּרְקִיעַ עֻזּוֹ׃ הַלְלוּהוּ
Praise His the in praise His in God Praise Praise
Him .might of expanse Him ;place holy !Jah

3 7782 8629 1984 1433 7230 1984 1369
בִגְבוּרֹתָיו הַלְלוּהוּ כְּרֹב גֻּדְלוֹ׃ הַלְלוּהוּ בְּתֵקַע שׁוֹפָר
the the with Praise His according Praise mighty His in
;trumpet of sound Him .greatness excellent to Him ;acts

4 1984 4234 8596 1984 3658 5035 1984
הַלְלוּהוּ בְּנֵבֶל וְכִנּוֹר׃ הַלְלוּהוּ בְתֹף וּמָחוֹל הַלְלוּהוּ
praise and the with Praise and the with Praise
Him ;dance timbrel Him .lyre harp Him

5 6767 1984 8088 6767 1984 5748 4482
בְּמִנִּים וְעוּגָב׃ הַלְלוּהוּ בְצִלְצְלֵי־שָׁמַע הַלְלוּהוּ בְּצִלְצְלֵי
the with praise ;loud the on Praise and with
of cymbals Him cymbals Him .pipes strings

6 3050 1984 3050 1984 5397 3605 8643
תְרוּעָה׃ כֹּל הַנְּשָׁמָה תְּהַלֵּל יָהּ הַלְלוּ־יָהּ׃
!Jah Praise .Jah Let that every- .resounding
praise breathes thing

PSALM 150

[1]Praise Jehovah! Praise God in His holy place; praise Him in the expanse of His might. [2]Praise Him in His mighty acts; praise Him according to His excellent greatness. [3]Praise Him with the sound of the trumpet; praise Him with the harp and lyre. [4]Praise Him with the timbrel and dance; praise Him with stringed instruments and pipes. [5]Praise Him on the sounding cymbals; praise Him with the resounding cymbals. [6]Let everything that breathes praise Jehovah. Praise Jehovah!

מִשְׁלֵי

A LITERAL TRANSLATION
OF THE BIBLE
THE BOOK OF PROVERBS

CHAPTER 1

[1]The Proverbs of Solomon, son of David, king of Israel: [2]To know wisdom and instruction; to understand the words of understanding; [3]to receive instruction in prudence, justice, and judgment, and uprightness; [4]to give sense to the simple, knowledge and discretion to the young man—[5]the wise hears and increases learning; and the understanding ones will get wise counsel—[6]to understand a proverb and an enigma; the words of the wise, and their acute sayings.

[7]The fear of Jehovah *is* the beginning of knowledge; fools despise wisdom and instdruction. [8]My son, hear your father's instruction; and do not forsake the teaching of your mother; [9]for they *shall be* an ornament of grace to your head, and chains for your neck. [10]My son, if sinners lure you, do not be willing. [11]If they say, Walk with us, let us lie in wait for blood; let us secretly lurk for the innocent without cause; [12]let us swallow them up alive as Sheol; and whole, as those who go down *into* the Pit, [13]we shall find all precious goods; we shall fill our houses *with* plunder; [14]cast in your lot among us; one purse shall be to all of us. [15]My son, do not walk in the way with them! Hold back your foot from their path; [16]for their feet run to evil and they haste to shed blood. [17]For in vain the net is spread in the sight of every bird. [18]And they lie

LIBER PROVERBIORUM

(THE) BOOK OF PROVERBS

CAPUT. I א

CHAPTER 1

2451 3045 3478 4428 1732 1121 8010 4912
1, 2 מִשְׁלֵי שְׁלֹמֹה בֶן־דָּוִד מֶלֶךְ יִשְׂרָאֵל׃ לָדַעַת חָכְמָה
wisdom know to :Israel king ,David son ,Solomon The
of of of Proverbs

6664 7919 4148 3947 998 561 995 4148
3 וּמוּסָר לְהָבִין אִמְרֵי בִינָה׃ לָקַחַת מוּסַר הַשְׂכֵּל צֶדֶק
right- pru- instruction to under- the under- to in- and
ness dence in receive ;standing of words stand ;struction

1847 5288 6195 6612 5414 4339 4941
4 וּמִשְׁפָּט וּמֵישָׁרִים׃ לָתֵת לִפְתָאיִם עָרְמָה לְנַעַר דַּעַת
knowledge the to ;prudence the to give to and and
man young simple ;uprightness judgment

7069 8458 995 3948 3254 2450 8085 4209
5 וּמְזִמָּה׃ יִשְׁמַע חָכָם וְיוֹסֶף לֶקַח וְנָבוֹן תַּחְבֻּלוֹת יִקְנֶה׃
will wise the and ,learning and The hears dis- and
—get counsel understanding increases wise .cretion

3068 3373 2420 2450 1697 4426 4910 995
6, 7 לְהָבִין מָשָׁל וּמְלִיצָה דִּבְרֵי חֲכָמִים וְחִידֹתָם׃ יִרְאַת יְהוָה
Jehovah The their and the the an and a under- to
of fear .riddles wise of words enigma proverb stand

1121 8085 936 191 4148 2451 1847 7225
8 רֵאשִׁית דָּעַת חָכְמָה וּמוּסָר אֱוִילִים בָּזוּ׃ שְׁמַע בְּנִי
my ,Hear .despise fools and wisdom ;knowledge the (is)
,son instruction of beginning

2580 3880 517 8451 5203 408 1 4148
9 מוּסַר אָבִיךָ וְאַל־תִּטֹּשׁ תּוֹרַת אִמֶּךָ׃ כִּי ׀ לִוְיַת חֵן הֵם
they grace orn- a for your teaching do and your in-
(are) of ament ,mother's forsake not ;father's struction

2400 6601 1121 1621 6060 7218
10 לְרֹאשֶׁךָ וַעֲנָקִים לְגַרְגְּרֹתֶךָ׃ בְּנִי אִם־יְפַתּוּךָ חַטָּאִים אַל־
not ;sinners lure if My your for and your to
you ,son .neck necklaces ,head

5355 6845 1818 693 3212 559 14
11 תֹּבֵא׃ אִם־יֹאמְרוּ לְכָה אִתָּנוּ נֶאֶרְבָה לְדָם נִצְפְּנָה לְנָקִי
the for us let for lie us let with Walk they If be do
innocent lurk ;blood wait in ,us ,say .willing

3605 953 3381 8549 2416 7585 1104 2600
12, 13 חִנָּם׃ נִבְלָעֵם כִּשְׁאוֹל חַיִּים וּתְמִימִים כְּיוֹרְדֵי בוֹר׃ כָּל־
all (into) those as and ;alive Sheol as us let without
.pit the going ,whole them swallow ;cause

8432 5307 1486 7998 1004 4390 4672 3368 1952
14 הוֹן יָקָר נִמְצָא נְמַלֵּא בָתֵּינוּ שָׁלָל׃ גּוֹרָלְךָ תַּפִּיל בְּתוֹכֵנוּ
among Let your (with) our shall we shall We wealth
;us fall lot .spoil houses fill ;find precious

4513 1870 1980 408 1121 3605 1961 259 3599
15 כִּיס אֶחָד יִהְיֶה לְכֻלָּנוּ׃ בְּנִי אַל־תֵּלֵךְ בְּדֶרֶךְ אִתָּם מְנַע
Hold with the in do not My all for shall one purse
back !them way walk ,son .us of be

8210 4116 7323 7451 7272 5410 7272
16 רַגְלְךָ מִנְּתִיבָתָם׃ כִּי רַגְלֵיהֶם לָרַע יָרוּצוּ וִימַהֲרוּ לִשְׁפָּךְ־
to they and ,run evil to their for their from your
shed hasten feet ;path foot

3671 1167 3605 5869 7561 2219 2600 1818
17, 18 דָּם׃ כִּי־חִנָּם מְזֹרָה הָרָשֶׁת בְּעֵינֵי כָּל־בַּעַל כָּנָף׃ וְהֵם
and the lord every the in net the is in For .blood
they .wing of of eyes spread vain

in wait for their own blood; they lurk secretly for their own souls. [19]So are the ways of everyone who gets *unjust* gain; *it* takes away its owner's soul.

[20]Wisdom cries aloud in the plaza; she gives her voice in the square; [21]she calls at the head of gathering places; in the opening of the gates; in the city she utters her words; [22]How long will you love to be simple, you simple ones? And will scorners desire scorn for themselves? And will fools hate knowledge? [23]Turn back at my warning; behold, I will pour out my Spirit to you; I will make my words known to you. [24]Because I have called, and you have refused; I have stretched out a hand, and none inclines; [25]but you have ignored all my counsel; you did not want my warning; [26]I also will laugh in your calamity, I will mock when your dread comes; [27]when your dread comes like a storm; and your calamity arrives like a hurricane; when distress and constraint come on you. [28]Then they shall call on me, and I will not answer; they shall seek me early, but they shall not find me. [29]Instead they hated knowledge and chose not the fear of Jehovah. [30]They did not want my counsel; they despised all my reproof; [31]and they shall eat of the fruit of their own way, and be filled with their own lusts. [32]For the going astray of the simple kills them; and the ease of fools destroys them. [33]But he who listens to me shall live securely, and shall be at ease from the dread of evil.

CHAPTER 2

[1]My son, if you will receive My words and treasure up My commandments with you, [2]so that you attend to

1214 3605 734 3651 5315 6845 693 1818
19 לְדָמָם יֶאֱרֹבוּ יִצְפְּנוּ לְנַפְשֹׁתָם׃ כֵּן אָרְחוֹת כָּל־בֹּצֵעַ
who every gains one | the are of ways | So | their for .souls own | lurk they secretly | in lie ;wait | their for blood own

7339 7442 2351 2454 3947 1167 5315 1215
20 בָּצַע אֶת־נֶפֶשׁ בְּעָלָיו יִקָּח׃ חָכְמוֹת בַּחוּץ תָּרֹנָּה בָּרְחֹבוֹת
the in plaza | cries ;aloud | outside | Wisdom | ,takes he | its owner | soul the of | (unjust) ;gain

5892 8179 6607 7121 1993 7218 6963 5414
21 תִּתֵּן קוֹלָהּ׃ בְּרֹאשׁ הֹמִיּוֹת תִּקְרָא בְּפִתְחֵי שְׁעָרִים בָּעִיר
the in city | the ;gates | the at of opening | she ;calls | commotion places | head At of the | her .voice | she gives

3944 6612 157 6612 5704 559 561
22 אֲמָרֶיהָ תֹאמֵר׃ עַד־מָתַי ׀ פְּתָיִם תְּאֵהֲבוּ פֶתִי וְלֵצִים
And scorners | sim- ?licity | will you love | simple ,ones | ,when Until | she :speaks | her words

8433 7725 1847 8130 3684 2530 3944
23 לָצוֹן חָמְדוּ לָהֶם וּכְסִילִים יִשְׂנְאוּ־דָעַת׃ תָּשׁוּבוּ לְתוֹכַחְתִּי
my at ;warning | Turn back | ?knowledge | will hate | And fools | for ?them | will desire | scorn

3282 1697 3045 7307 5042 2009
24 הִנֵּה אַבִּיעָה לָכֶם רוּחִי אוֹדִיעָה דְבָרַי אֶתְכֶם׃ יַעַן
Because | .you to | my words | will I known make | my ;spirit | you to | will I out pour | ,behold

6098 3605 6544 7181 369 3027 5186 3985 7121
25 קָרָאתִי וַתְּמָאֵנוּ נָטִיתִי יָדִי וְאֵין מַקְשִׁיב׃ וַתִּפְרְעוּ כָל־עֲצָתִי
my ,advice | all | you And ignored | .inclines | yet none | a hand | ex- I tend | you and refused | have I ,called

3932 7832 343 1571 14 3808 8433
26 וְתוֹכַחְתִּי לֹא אֲבִיתֶם׃ גַּם־אֲנִי בְּאֵידְכֶם אֶשְׂחָק אֶלְעַג
will I mock | will ;laugh | your in calamity | I Also | you .wanted | not | my and warning

5492 343 6343 7722 935 6343 935
27 בְּבֹא פַחְדְּכֶם׃ בְּבֹא כְשׁאוה ׀ פַּחְדְּכֶם וְאֵידְכֶם כְּסוּפָה
a like tempest | your and calamity | your ;dread | a like storm | when comes | your ;dread | when comes

6030 3808 7121 227 6695 6864 935 857
28 יֶאֱתֶה בְּבֹא עֲלֵיכֶם צָרָה וְצוּקָה׃ אָז יִקְרָאֻנְנִי וְלֹא אֶעֱנֶה
will I ;answer | and not | shall they me on call | Then | and constraint | distress | upon you | when comes | ;arrives

3068 3373 1847 8130 8478 4672 3808 7836
29 יְשַׁחֲרֻנְנִי וְלֹא יִמְצָאֻנְנִי׃ תַּחַת כִּי־שָׂנְאוּ דָעַת וְיִרְאַת יְהוָה
Jehovah | the and of fear | knowl- ,edge | they hated | Instead | find shall .me | but not | shall they early me seek

398 8433 3605 5006 6098 14 3808 977 3808
30 31 לֹא בָחָרוּ׃ לֹא־אָבוּ לַעֲצָתִי נָאֲצוּ כָּל־תּוֹכַחְתִּי׃ וְיֹאכְלוּ
they and eat shall | my ;reproof | all | they despised | my ;counsel | they wanted | Not | .chose | not

6612 4878 7646 4156 1870 6529
32 מִפְּרִי דַרְכָּם וּמִמֹּעֲצֹתֵיהֶם יִשְׂבָּעוּ׃ כִּי מְשׁוּבַת פְּתָיִם
the simple | going the of astray | For | be .filled | their with and devices own | own their way | the of of fruit

982 7931 8085 6 3684 7962 2026
33 תַּהַרְגֵם וְשַׁלְוַת כְּסִילִים תְּאַבְּדֵם׃ וְשֹׁמֵעַ לִי יִשְׁכָּן־בֶּטַח
,securely shall dwell | to me | one But listening | destroys .them | fools | the and of ease | slays ;them

7451 6343 7599
וְשַׁאֲנַן מִפַּחַד רָעָה׃
evil | the from of fear | shall and ease at be

CAP. II ב

CHAPTER 2

7181 6845 4687 561 3947 518 1121
1 2 בְּנִי אִם־תִּקַּח אֲמָרָי וּמִצְוֹתַי תִּצְפֹּן אִתָּךְ׃ לְהַקְשִׁיב
you that so attend | with ,you | hide | my and commands | my ,treasure | will you receive | if | My ,son

wisdom, you shall extend
your heart to understand-
ing; 3for if you cry for
discernment, lifting up your
voice for understanding; 4if
you seek her as silver, and
search for her as hidden
treasures; 5then you shall
understand the fear of
Jehovah, and find knowl-
edge of God. 6For Jehovah
gives wisdom; out of His
mouth *come* knowledge
and understanding. 7He
lays up sound wisdom for
the upright; *He is* a shield to
the ones who walk in
integrity, 8to guard the
paths of judgment, and He
protects the way of His
saints. 9Then you shall
understand righteousness
and judgment and honesty;
yea, every good path.
10When wisdom enters into
your heart; and knowledge
is pleasing to your soul;
11discretion shall keep you;
understanding shall watch
over you; 12to deliver you
from the evil way; from the
man who speaks perverse
things; 13those who leave
the paths of uprightness to
walk in the ways of dark-
ness; 14who rejoice to do
evil; they delight in the
perversities of the wicked;
15whose paths *are* crooked,
who are devious in their
tracks. 16*These will* deliver
you from the strange
woman, from the foreigner
who flatters *with* her words;
17who forsakes the guide of
her youth, and forgets the
covenant of her God. 18For
her house bows down to
death, and her tracks to the
departed spirits. 19All going in to her do not return;
nor do they reach the ways
of life. 20Then you may
walk in the paths of the
good, and keep the ways of
the righteous. 21For the
upright shall live *in* the land;

7121 998 518 8394 3820 5186 241 2451
3 לַחָכְמָה אָזְנֶךָ תַּטֶּה לִבְּךָ לַתְּבוּנָה׃ כִּי אִם לַבִּינָה תִקְרָא
you under- for if ,for under- to your shall you your to
,cry standing ;standing heart extend ,ear wisdom

4301 3701 1245 518 6963 5414 8394
4 לַתְּבוּנָה תִּתֵּן קוֹלֶךָ׃ אִם־תְּבַקְשֶׁנָּה כַכָּסֶף וְכַמַּטְמוֹנִים
hidden as and as seek you if your lifting under- for
treasures ,silver her ;voice up standing

4672 430 1847 3068 3373 995 227 2664
5 תַּחְפְּשֶׂנָּה׃ אָז תָּבִין יִרְאַת יְהוָה וְדַעַת אֱלֹהִים תִּמְצָא׃
.find God the and ,Jehovah the shall you then search you
of knowledge of fear know ;her for

3477 6845 8394 1847 6310 2451 5414 3068
6
7 כִּי־יְהוָה יִתֵּן חָכְמָה מִפִּיו דַּעַת וּתְבוּנָה׃ וְצָפַן לַיְשָׁרִים
the for He And under- and knowl- His from ,wisdom gives Jehovah For
upright up lays .standing edge (are) mouth

1870 4941 734 5341 8537 1980 4043 8454
8 תּוּשִׁיָּה מָגֵן לְהֹלְכֵי תֹם׃ לִנְצֹר אָרְחוֹת מִשְׁפָּט וְדֶרֶךְ
the and ;judgment the guard to in those for (is He) sound
of way of paths ,integrity walking ,shield a ;wisdom

3605 4339 494 6664 995 8104 2623
9 חֲסִידָו יִשְׁמֹר׃ אָז תָּבִין צֶדֶק וּמִשְׁפָּט וּמֵישָׁרִים כָּל־
every and and righteous- shall you Then He His
,honesty judgment ness understand .guards saints

5276 5315 1847 3820 2451 935 2896 4570
10 מַעְגַּל־טוֹב׃ כִּי־תָבוֹא חָכְמָה בְלִבֶּךָ וְדַעַת לְנַפְשְׁךָ יִנְעָם׃
is your to and your into wisdom enters When .good path
;pleasing soul knowledge ;heart

1870 5337 5341 8394 8104 4209
11
12 מְזִמָּה תִּשְׁמֹר עָלֶיךָ תְּבוּנָה תִנְצְרֶכָּה׃ לְהַצִּילְךָ מִדֶּרֶךְ
the from deliver to watch shall understand- ;you shall dis-
way you you over ing keep cretion

3212 3476 734 5800 8419 1696 376 7451
13 רָע מֵאִישׁ מְדַבֵּר תַּהְפֻּכוֹת׃ הַעֹזְבִים אָרְחוֹת יֹשֶׁר לָלֶכֶת
to upright- paths the ones the perverse speaking the from ;evil
walk ness of leaving ,things man

8419 1523 7451 6213 8056 2822 1870
14 בְּדַרְכֵי־חֹשֶׁךְ׃ הַשְּׂמֵחִים לַעֲשׂוֹת רָע יָגִילוּ בְּתַהְפֻּכוֹת
per- the in they ;evil do to rejoicing ;darkness the in
of versities delight of ways

4570 3868 6141 734 834 7451
15 רָע׃ אֲשֶׁר אָרְחֹתֵיהֶם עִקְּשִׁים וּנְלוֹזִים בְּמַעְגְּלוֹתָם׃
their in (are) and (are) paths whose the
tracks devious ,crooked ;evil

5800 2505 561 5237 2114 802 5337
16
17 לְהַצִּילְךָ מֵאִשָּׁה זָרָה מִנָּכְרִיָּה אֲמָרֶיהָ הֶחֱלִיקָה׃ הַעֹזֶבֶת
who ;flattering her (by) the from ,strange the from will (These)
forsakes words foreigner woman you deliver

7743 7911 430 1285 5271 441
18 אַלּוּף נְעוּרֶיהָ וְאֶת־בְּרִית אֱלֹהֶיהָ שָׁכֵחָה׃ כִּי שָׁחָה אֶל־
to leads For .forgets her the and her the
down God of covenant ,youth of guide

7725 3808 935 3605 4570 7496 1004 4194
19 מָוֶת בֵּיתָהּ וְאֶל־רְפָאִים מַעְגְּלֹתֶיהָ׃ כָּל־בָּאֶיהָ לֹא יְשׁוּבוּן
;return not going All her departed and her death
her to in .tracks spirits to ,house

2896 1870 1980 4616 2416 734 5381 3808
20 וְלֹא יַשִּׂיגוּ אָרְחוֹת חַיִּים׃ לְמַעַן תֵּלֵךְ בְּדֶרֶךְ טוֹבִים
,good the the in may you order In .life paths the they and
of ways walk that of reach not

776 7931 3477 8104 6662 734
21 וְאָרְחוֹת צַדִּיקִים תִּשְׁמֹר׃ כִּי־יְשָׁרִים יִשְׁכְּנוּ־אָרֶץ
the (in) shall the For .keep may the the and
;land dwell upright righteous of paths

and the perfect shall remain
in it. [22]But the wicked shall
be cut off from the earth;
and the transgressors shall
be rooted out of it.

CHAPTER 3

[1]My son, do not forget
my law; but let your heart
keep my commands; [2]for
they shall add length of
days, and long life and
peace to you. [3]Mercy and
truth will not forsake you;
tie them on your neck; write
them on the tablet of your
heart; [4]and you shall find
favor and good understanding in the sight of God and
man. [5]Trust in Jehovah
with all your heart; and lean
not to your own under-
standing. [6]In all your ways
acknowledge Him, and He
shall direct your paths. [7]Do
not be wise in your own
eyes; fear Jehovah and
depart from evil. [8]Healing
shall be to your navel and
marrow to your bones.
[9]Honor Jehovah with your
substance, and with the
firstfruits of all your
increase; [10]and your barns
shall be filled *with* plenty;
and your presses shall burst
with new wine. [11]My son,
do not reject the chastening of Jehovah; and do not
loathe His correction; [12]for
whom Jehovah loves He
corrects, even as a father
the son he loves.

[13]Happy *is* the man who
finds wisdom, and the man
who gets understanding.
[14]For its gain *is* better than
the gain from silver; and its
produce more than fine
gold; [15]she *is* more
precious than rubies; and all
the things you can desire
are not to be compared with
her. [16]Length of days *is* in
her right hand; riches and
honor in her left hand.

898 3772 776 7563 3498 8549

22 וּתְמִימִים יִוָּתְרוּ בָהּ׃ וּרְשָׁעִים מֵאֶרֶץ יִכָּרֵתוּ וּבוֹגְדִים

the and treacherous | be shall ;off cut | the from earth | the But wicked | .it in | shall remain | the and blameless

5255

יִסְּחוּ מִמֶּנָּה׃

from .it | be shall up rooted

CAP. III ג

CHAPTER 3

3117 753 3820 5341 4687 7911 408 8451 1121

1
2 בְּנִי תּוֹרָתִי אַל־תִּשְׁכָּח וּמִצְוֹתַי יִצֹּר לִבֶּךָ׃ כִּי אֹרֶךְ יָמִים

days | length of | for | your ;heart | let guard | my but commands | do ;forget | not | my teaching | My ,son

5800 408 571 2617 3254 7965 2416 8141

3 וּשְׁנוֹת חַיִּים וְשָׁלוֹם יוֹסִיפוּ לָךְ׃ חֶסֶד וֶאֱמֶת אַל־יַעַזְבֻךָ

will you forsake | not | and truth | Mercy | .you to | they add shall | and peace | life | and of years

2580 4672 3820 3871 3789 1621 7194

4 קָשְׁרֵם עַל־גַּרְגְּרוֹתֶיךָ כָּתְבֵם עַל־לוּחַ לִבֶּךָ׃ וּמְצָא־חֵן

favor | and find | your ;heart | the of tablet | on | write them | your ;neck | on | them tie

3605 3068 982 120 430 5869 2896 7922

5 וְשֵׂכֶל טוֹב בְּעֵינֵי אֱלֹהִים וְאָדָם׃ בְּטַח אֶל־יְהוָה בְּכָל־

with all | Jehovah | to | Trust | and .man | God | the in of eyes | good | and wisdom

3045 1870 3605 8172 408 998 3820

6 לִבֶּךָ וְאֶל־בִּינָתְךָ אַל־תִּשָּׁעֵן׃ בְּכָל־דְּרָכֶיךָ דָעֵהוּ וְהוּא

and He | acknowledge ,Him | your ways | all In | do ,lean | not | (own) your understanding | to and | your ;heart

3068 3372 5869 2450 1961 408 734 3474

7 יְיַשֵּׁר אֹרְחֹתֶיךָ׃ אַל־תְּהִי חָכָם בְּעֵינֶיךָ יְרָא אֶת־יְהוָה

Jehovah | fear | your in ;eyes own | wise | be do | Not | your .paths | shall direct

3513 6106 8250 8270 1961 7500 7451 5493

8
9 וְסוּר מֵרָע׃ רִפְאוּת תְּהִי לְשָׁרֶּךָ וְשִׁקּוּי לְעַצְמוֹתֶיךָ׃ כַּבֵּד

Honor | your to .bones | and moisture | your to navel | shall be | Healing | from .evil | and turn

618 4390 8393 3605 7225 1952 3068

10 אֶת־יְהוָה מֵהוֹנֶךָ וּמֵרֵאשִׁית כָּל־תְּבוּאָתֶךָ׃ וְיִמָּלְאוּ אֲסָמֶיךָ

your barns | shall and filled be | your ;produce | all | the from and of firstfruits | your from substance | Jehovah

3985 1121 3068 4148 6555 3342 8492 7647

11 שָׂבָע וְתִירוֹשׁ יְקָבֶיךָ יִפְרֹצוּ׃ מוּסַר יְהוָה בְּנִי אַל־תִּמְאָס

do ;reject do | not | my ,son | ,Jehovah | The of chastening | shall .burst | wine your vats | (with) and wine new | (with) ;plenty

3198 3068 157 834 8433 6973 408

12 וְאַל־תָּקֹץ בְּתוֹכַחְתּוֹ׃ כִּי אֶת אֲשֶׁר־יֶאֱהַב יְהוָה יוֹכִיחַ

He ,corrects | Jehovah | loves | whom | for | His ;correction | do loathe | and not

120 2451 4672 120 835 7521 1121

13 וּכְאָב אֶת־בֵּן יִרְצֶה׃ אַשְׁרֵי אָדָם מָצָא חָכְמָה וְאָדָם

the and man | ,wisdom | finding | the man | Blessed (is) | is he .with pleased | the son | as even father a

2742 3701 5505 5504 2896 8394 6329

14 יָפִיק תְּבוּנָה׃ כִּי טוֹב סַחְרָהּ מִסְּחַר־כָּסֶף וּמֵחָרוּץ

more and gold than | ;silver | the than of gain | its gain | better is | For | understanding getting

7737 3808 2656 3605 6443 3368 8393

15 תְּבוּאָתָהּ׃ יְקָרָה הִיא מִפְּנִיִּים וְכָל־חֲפָצֶיךָ לֹא יִשְׁווּ־בָהּ׃

with her | are likened | not | your all delights | and | than ;jewels | she | (More) precious | .produce its

1870 3519 6239 8040 3225 3117 753

16
17 אֹרֶךְ יָמִים בִּימִינָהּ בִּשְׂמֹאולָהּ עֹשֶׁר וְכָבוֹד׃ דְּרָכֶיהָ

ways Her | and .honor | riches | left her in (hand) | her in (hand)right | days (is) | Length of

[17]Her ways *are* ways of pleasantness, and all her paths peace. [18]She *is* a tree of life to the ones who lay hold on her; and happy *are* the ones holding her fast. [19]Jehovah founded the earth by wisdom; He founded the heavens by understanding; [20]the depths were broken up by His knowledge; and the clouds dropped down the dew. [21]My son, do not let them depart from your eyes; keep sound wisdom and judgment; [22]and they shall be life to your soul, and grace to your neck; [23]then you shall walk in your way safely; and your foot shall not stumble. [24]When you lie down, you shall not dread; yea, you shall lie down and your sleep shall be sweet. [25]Do not be afraid of sudden terror; nor of the destruction of the wicked, when it comes. [26]For Jehovah shall be at your side; and He shall keep your foot from being caught.

[27]Do not withhold good from those to whom it is due, when it is in the power of your hand to do *it*. [28]Do not say to your neighbor, Go and come back again; or, Tomorrow I will give; when you have it beside you. [29]Do not plan evil against your neighbor, since he lives trustingly by you. [30]Do not strive with a man without cause, if he has done you no harm. [31]Do not envy the cruel man, and choose not among all his ways. [32]For the perverse one *is* hateful to Jehovah, but His intimacy *is* with the righteous. [33]The curse of Jehovah *is* in the house of the wicked; but He blesses the abode of the just. [34]Surely He scorns the scorners; but He gives grace to the lowly. [35]The wise inherit honor, but the foolish exalt shame.

2388 2416 6086 7965 5410 3605 5278 1870
18 דרכי־נעם וכל־נתיבותיה שלום׃ עץ־חיים היא למחזיקים
those for she life tree A are her and pleasant- (are)
hold taking (is) of .peace paths all ,ness of ways

3559 776 3245 2451 3068 833 8551
19 בה ותמכיה מאשר׃ יהוה בחכמה יסד־ארץ כונן
He the founded by Jehovah (are) those and on
fixed ;earth wisdom .blessed her holding ;her

7491 7834 1234 8415 1847 8394 8064
20 שמים בתבונה׃ בדעתו תהומות נבקעו ושחקים ירעפו־
dropped the and were the His By under- by the
down clouds ;up broken depths knowledge .standing heavens

1961 4009 8454 5341 5869 3868 1121 2919
21
22 טל׃ בני אל־ילזו מעיניך נצר תשיה ומזמה׃ ויהיו
they and and sound keep your from not let My
be shall ;discretion wisdom ;eyes depart them ,son .dew

1870 982 1980 1621 2580 5315 2416
23 חיים לנפשך וחן לגרגרתיך׃ אז תלך לבטח דרכך
your (in) with shall you Then your to and your to life
;way safety walk .neck grace ,soul

6149 7901 6342 /3808 7901 5061 3808 7272
24 ורגלך לא תגוף׃ אם־תשכב לא־תפחד ושכבת וערבה
shall and you and shall you not ,rest you When shall not your and
sweet be lie shall dread .stumble foot

7563 7722 6597 6343 3372 408 8142
25 שנתך׃ אל־תירא מפחד פתאם ומשאת רשעים כי
for the the of and ,sudden from be do Not your
,wicked of ruin dread afraid .sleep

408 3921 7272 8104 3689 1961 3068 935
26
27 תבא׃ כי־יהוה יהיה בכסלך ושמר רגלך מלכד׃ אל־
Not from your He and your at shall Jehovah For is it
.capture foot keep shall ;loins be .coming

559 408 6213 3027 410 1961 1167 2896 4513
28 תמנע־טוב מבעליו בהיות לאל ידיך לעשות׃ אל־תאמר
do Not do to your the in When its from good do
say .(it) hand of power is it ..owners withhold

2790 408 3426 5414 4279 7725 3212 7453
29 לרעיך לך ושוב ומחר אתן ויש אתך׃ אל־תחרש על־
against do Not with but -will I and and Go your to
plot .you is it ,give tomorrow ,return ,neighbor

120 7378 408 983 3427 7451 7453
30 רעך רעה והוא־יושב לבטח אתך׃ אל־תרוב עם־אדם
a with do Not with securely dwells he and evil your
man strive .you neighbor

408 2555 376 7068 408 7451 1580 3808 518 2600
31 חנם אם־לא גמלך רעה׃ אל־תקנא באיש חמס ואל־
and ,violence against do Not .evil has he not if without
not of man a envy you dealt ,cause

3477 3868 3068 8441 1870 3605 977
32 תבחר בכל־דרכיו׃ כי תועבת יהוה נלוז ואת־ישרים
the with but the (is) Jehovah hateful For his among do
(is) upright devious to .ways all choose

1288 6662 5116 7563 1004 3068 3994 5475
33 סודו׃ מארת יהוה בבית רשע ונוה צדיקים יברך׃
He the the but the on (is) Jehovah The His
.blesses righteous of abode ;wicked's house of curse intimacy

2450 3519 2580 5415 6035 3887 3887
34
35 אם־ללצים הוא־יליץ ולעניים יתן־חן׃ כבוד חכמים
wise the Honor .grace He to yet ,scorns He the at If
gives lowly the scorners

7036 7311 3684 5157
ינחלו וכסילים מרים קלון׃
.shame (are) the but ,inherit
exalting foolish

CHAPTER 4

[1]Sons, hear the instruction of a father; and listen so as to know understanding. [2]For I give you good teaching; do not forsake my law. [3]For I was my father's son, tender, and an only one in the sight of my mother. [4]And he taught me and said to me, Let your heart cling to my words; keep my commands and live. [5]Get wisdom, get understanding; do not forsake and do not turn away from the words of my mouth. [6]Do not forsake her, and she will preserve you; love her, and she will keep you. [7]Wisdom *is* the main thing; get wisdom; and with all your getting, get understanding. [8]Exalt her, and she will lift you up; she shall bring you to honor when you embrace her. [9]She shall give a wreath of grace to your head; she shall shield you with a crown of glory.

[10]O my son, hear and receive my sayings; and the years of your life *shall be* many. [11]I have taught you in the way of wisdom; I have led you in the right tracks; [12]when you go, your tracks shall not be narrowed; and when you run, you shall not stumble. [13]Take fast hold of instruction; do not let her go; keep her, for she *is* your life. [14]Do not enter the path of the wicked; and do not go in the way of evildoers. [15]Avoid it; do not pass by it; turn from it and pass on. [16]For they do not sleep if they have done no evil; and their sleep is taken away unless they cause *some* to fall. [17]For they eat the bread of wickedness, and drink the wine of violence. [18]But the path of the just *is* as a bright light going on and shining till the day is established. [19]The way of the wicked *is* as darkness; they do not know at what they stumble.

CAP. IV ד

CHAPTER 4

3948 998 3045 7181 1 4148 1121 8085
1 2 שמעו בנים מוסר אב והקשיבו לדעת בינה׃ כי לקח
teaching For under- to and a teaching ,sons ,Hear
.standing know listen ,father's

1 1961 1121 5800 8451 5414 2896
3 טוב נתתי לכם תורתי אל־תעזבו׃ כי־בן הייתי לאבי
my to was I son For do not law my ,you to give I good
father .forsake

3820 1697 8551 559 3384 517 6440 3173 7390
4 רך ויחיד לפני אמי׃ ויריני ויאמר לי יתמך־דברי לבך
your to my May to said and he And my before only and ten-
;heart words cling ,me me taught .mother (son) der

7911 998 7069 2451 7069 2421 4687 8104
5 שמר מצותי וחיה׃ קנה חכמה קנה בינה אל־תשכח
do not under- get ,wisdom Get and my keep
,forget ;standing live commands

157 8104 5800 408 6310 561 5186 408
6 ואל־תט מאמרי־פי׃ אל־תעזבה ותשמרך אהבה
love will she and do Not my the from stretch and
her ;you keep her forsake .mouth of words away not

7069 7075 3605 2451 7069 2451 7225 5341
7 ותצרך׃ ראשית חכמה קנה חכמה ובכל־קנינך קנה
get your with and ,wisdom get (is) first The will she and
,getting all ;wisdom thing .you guard

5414 2263 3513 7311 5549 998
8 9 בינה׃ סלסלה ותרוממך תכבדך כי תחבקנה׃ תתן
shall She you when will she will she and Exalt under-
give .her embrace you honor ;up you lift ,her .standing

3947 1121 8085 4042 8597 5850 2580 3880 7218
10 לראשך לוית־חן עטרת תפארת תמגנך׃ שמע בני וקח
and my ,Hear shall she glory crown a ;grace a your to
receive ,son with you shield of of wreath head

3384 2451 1870 2416 8141 7235 561
11 אמרי וירבו לך שנות חיים׃ בדרך חכמה הרתיך
have I wisdom the In .life the to shall and my
;you taught of way of years you many be ;sayings

518 6806 3334 3808 3212 3476 4570 3212
12 הדרכתיך במעגלי־ישר׃ בלכתך לא־יצר צעדך ואם־
and your shall not you When upright- the in made have I
if ,steps narrowed be go .ness of tracks walk you

5341 7503 408 4148 2388 3782 3808 7323
13 תרוץ לא תכשל׃ החזק במוסר אל־תרף נצרה כי־היא
she for keep let do not on Take shall you not you
(is) ,her ;go ;instruction hold .stumble run

7451 1870 833 408 935 408 7563 734 2416
14 חייך׃ בארח רשעים אל־תבא ואל־תאשר בדרך רעים׃
evil the in do and do not the the On your
.ones of way advance not ,enter wicked of path .life

3462 3808 5674 5921 7847 5674 408 6544
15 16 פרעהו אל־תעבר־בו שטה מעליו ועבור׃ כי לא ישנו
they do not For and from turn into do not Ignore
sleep .on pass it upon aside ;it pass ;it

3898 3782 3808 518 8142 1497 7489 3808 518
17 אם־לא ירעו ונגזלה שנתם אם־לא יכשולו׃ כי לחמו
they For cause they not if their is and have they not if
eat .stumble to sleep away taken ;evil done

5051 215 6662 734 8354 2555 3196 7562 3899
18 לחם רשע ויין חמסים ישתו׃ וארח צדיקים כאור נגה
bright as (is) the the But they violence and wicked- the
light a righteous of path .drink of wine ,ness of bread

3045 3808 653 7563 1870 3117 3559 5704 216 1980
19 הולך ואור עד־נכון היום׃ דרך רשעים כאפלה לא ידעו
they not as (is) the The the is till and going
know do ;darkness wicked of way .day established shining

[20]My son, listen to my words; bow your ear to what I say; [21]let them not depart from your eyes; keep them in the center of your heart; [22]for they *are* life to those who find them and healing to all his flesh.

[23]Keep your heart with all diligence, for out of it *are* the issues of life. [24]Turn away from you the crooked mouth and put devious lips far from you. [25]Let your eyes look to the front; and let your eyelids look straight before you. [26]Study the track of your feet and all your ways *will be* established. [27]Do not turn to the right or to the left; turn your foot aside from evil.

20 במה יכשלו׃ בני לדברי הקשיבה לאמרי הט־אזנך׃
241 5186 559 7181 561 1121 3782 4100
your ;ear | bow | what to say I | ;listen | my to words | My ,son | they .stumble | at what

21
22 אל־ילזו מעיניך שמרם בתוך לבבך׃ כי־חיים הם
2416 3824 8432 8104 5869 3212
they (are) | life | for | your ;heart | the in of center | keep them | your from ;eyes | them let not depart

23 למצאיהם ולכל־בשרו מרפא׃ מכל־משמר נצר לבך
3820 5341 4929 3605 4832 1320 3605 4672
your heart | keep | diligence | With all | .healing | his flesh | to and all | who those to them find

24 כי ממנו תוצאות חיים׃ הסר ממך עקשות פה ולזות
3891 6310 6143 5493 2416 8444
and devious | ,mouth | the crooked | from you | turn away | .life | the (are) of issues | of out it | for

25 שפתים הרחק ממך׃ עיניך לנכח יביטו ועפעפיך יישרו
3477 6079 5027 5227 5869 7368 8193
look let straight | your and eyelids | let ;look | the to front | Your eyes | from .you | put far | lips

26
27 נגדך׃ פלס מעגל רגלך וכל־דרכיך יכנו׃ אל־תט־ימין
3225 5186 3559 1870 3605 7272 4570 6424 5048
right | Do not bend | will .set be | your ways | and all | your ,feet | the of track | Ponder | before .you

ושמאול הסר רגלך מרע׃
7451 7272 5493 8040
from .evil | your foot | turn aside | ;left or

CAP. V ה

CHAPTER 5

[1]My son, listen to my wisdom; bow your ear to my understanding [2]in order to keep discretion, that your lips may guard knowledge. [3]For the lips of a strange woman drip honey, and her palate *is* smoother than oil; [4]but afterwards she *is* as bitter as wormwood, sharp as a sword of mouths. [5]Her feet go down *to* death; her steps take hold on Sheol — [6]lest you should meditate on the path of life; her tracks are moveable; you can not know *them*.

[7]Then hear me now, O sons, and do not depart from the words of my mouth. [8]Remove your ways far from her; and do not come near to the door of her house; [9]lest you give your honor to others, and your years to the cruel; [10]that strangers not be filled *with* your strength; and your labors *be* in the house of an alien; [11]and you moan when your end *comes*; when your flesh and muscle

1
2 בני לחכמתי הקשיבה לתבונתי הט־אזנך׃ לשמר
8104 241 5186 8394 7181 2451 1121
keep to | your ;ear | bow | my to understanding | ;listen | my to wisdom | My ,son

3 מזמות ודעת שפתיך ינצרו׃ כי נפת תטפנה שפתי
8193 5197 5317 5341 8193 1847 4209
lips the of | drip | honey | For | may .guard | your lips | and knowledge | discre- ,tion

4 זרה וחלק משמן חכה׃ ואחריתה מרה כלענה חדה
2299 3939 4751 319 2441 8081 2509 2114
sharp | worm- ,wood | as (as is) bitter | after- wards | But she | her (is) .palate | than oil | and smoother | strange a ,woman

5 כחרב פיות׃ רגליה ירדות מות שאול צעדיה יתמכו׃
8551 6806 7585 4194 3381 7272 6310 2719
take .on hold | her steps | Sheol | (to) ;death | down go | Her feet | .mouths | a as of sword

6 ארח חיים פן־תפלס נעו מעגלתיה לא תדע׃
3045 4570 5128 6424 2416 734
can you not (it) know | —tracks her | are moveable | you ponder | lest | —life | The of path

7
8 ועתה בנים שמעו־לי ואל־תסורו מאמרי־פי׃ הרחק
7368 6310 561 5493 3808 8085 1121 6258
Remove far | my .mouth | the from of words | turn away | and not do | ;me hear | O sons | And ,now

9 מעליה דרכך ואל־תקרב אל־פתח ביתה׃ פן־תתן
5414 1004 6607 7126 408 1870
you lest give | her ,house | the of door | to | come do near | and not | your ;ways | from her

10 לאחרים הודך ושנתיך לאכזרי׃ פן־ישבעו זרים כחך
3581 2114 7646 394 8141 1935 312
your ;strength (with) | strangers | filled be | lest | the to ;one cruel | your and years | your ,vigor | others to

11 ועצביך בבית נכרי׃ ונהמת באחריתך בכלות בשרך
1320 3615 319 5098 5237 1004 6089
your flesh | are when consumed | your when (comes) end | you and moan | an alien's | house in | your and toil

lower yourself

are eaten away; [12]and say, How I have hated instruction; and my heart despised correction; [13]and I have not bowed to the voice of my teachers; nor bowed my ears to those instructing me. [14]I was almost in all evil in the midst of the congregation and assembly.

[15]Drink waters out of your own cistern, and running waters out of your own well. [16]Should your overflowing springs be scattered outside, *like* rivers of waters in the streets? [17]Let them be only your own, and not to strangers with you; [18]let your fountains be blessed; and rejoice with the wife of your youth; [19]*she is* a loving deer, a graceful doe; let her breasts satisfy you every time; and always be ravished in her love. [20]And my son, why will you be ravished with a strange woman, and embrace a foreigner's bosom? [21]For the ways of man *are* before the eyes of Jehovah; and He ponders all his tracks. [22]His own iniquities shall take the wicked himself; and he shall be held with the cords of his sin. [23]He shall die without instruction; and in the greatness of his foolishness, he shall go astray.

CHAPTER 6

[1]My son, if you are surety for your friend, *if* you struck your palms with an alien, [2]you are snared with the words of your mouth; you are captured with the words of your own mouth. [3]My son, do this then, and deliver yourself when you come into the palm of your friend: go humble yourself and be bold *to* your friend. [4]Do not give sleep to your eyes, or slumber to your eyelids. [5]Deliver yourself like a gazelle from a hand *of a hunter*, and as a bird from the fowler's hand.

[6]Go to the ant, lazy man; consider her ways and be

12 שארך: ואמרת איך שנאתי מוסר ותוכחת נאץ לבי:
my heart! despised And correction instruction! have I hated How you and say, and muscle.

13 ולא־שמעתי בקול מורי ולמלמדי לא־הטיתי אזני:
my ear. turned not those to and me teaching my teachers the of voice have I heard and not

14 כמעט הייתי בכל־רע בתוך קהל ועדה: שתה־מים
waters Drink con- and gregation. the assembly the in of midst ,evil all in was I a As little

16 מבורך ונזלים מתוך בארך: יפוצו מעינתיך חוצה
outside your springs be Should dispersed own your .well the from of midst flow- and ing waters your from cistern own

17 ברחבות פלגי־מים: יהיו־לך לבדך ואין לזרים אתך:
with .you for strangers and not you ,alone for ,you Let be them ?waters (like) of rivers the in streets

18
19 יהי־מקורך ברוך ושמח מאשת נעוריך: אילת אהבים
,loving (is She) deer a Your .youth the in of wife and rejoice ,blessed your fountain Let be

ויעלת־חן דדיה ירוך בכל־עת באהבתה תשגה תמיד:
.always be ravished her in love ,time every at let you satisfy her breasts grace- ful a and doe

20
21 ולמה תשגה בני בזרה ותחבק חק נכריה: כי נכח
(are) before For a .foreigner's bosom hug and alien an ,woman by son my you will ,ravished be And why

22 עיני יהוה דרכי־איש וכל־מעגלתיו מפלס: עוונותיו
own His iniquities is He .pondering his tracks and all a ,man the of ways Jehovah the of eyes

23 ילכדנו את־הרשע ובחבלי חטאתו יתמך: הוא ימות
shall die He shall he be seized his sin with and of cords the the ;wicked cap- will ture ,him

באין מוסר וברב אולתו ישגה:
goes he astray his folly's in and greatness instruction in of absence

CAP. VI ו

CHAPTER 6

1
2 בני אם־ערבת לרעך תקעת לזר כפיך: נוקשת באמרי־
the with of words are you snared your palms: with alien an you (if) struck your for ;friend are you surety if My son

3 פיך נלכדת באמרי־פיך: עשה־זאת אפוא בני והנצל
save and yourself my ,son ,then this do your ;mouth the with of words are you captured your ,mouth

4 כי באת בכף־רעך לך התרפס ורהב רעיך: אל־תתן
give do Not your .friend be and (to) bold humble yourself ,go your friend of the into palm you when come

5 שנה לעיניך ותנומה לעפעפיך: הנצל כצבי מיד וכצפור
a as and bird a from ;hand a as gazelle Deliver yourself your to .eyelids or slumber your to eyes sleep

6 מיד יקוש: לך־אל־נמלה עצל ראה דרכיה וחכם:
be and ;wise her ways see lazy ;man the ,ant to Go the .fowler's from hand

wise; 7who, having no guide, overseer or ruler, 8provides her bread in the summer; gathers her food in the harvest. 9How long will you lie down, O lazy man? When will you arise out of your sleep? 10A little sleep, a little slumber; a little folding of the hands to lie down; 11so shall your poverty come as one stalking, and your need like an armed man. 12A worthless person, a wicked man, walks with a perverse mouth, 13winking with his eyes; he speaking with his feet; teaching with his fingers; 14perversity *is* in his heart; he is plotting evil at every time, he sends out strife. 15On account of this, calamity shall come suddenly; he is quickly broken and there is no healing. 16These six *things* Jehovah hates; yea, seven are hateful to His soul; 17a proud look, a lying tongue, and hands that shed innocent blood; 18a heart that plots evil plans; feet hurrying to run to mischief; 19a false witness who breathes lies; and he who causes strife among brothers.

20My son, keep your father's commands; and do not forsake the law of your mother. 21Tie them to your heart forever; tie them around your neck. 22When you go, it shall lead you; when you sleep, it shall watch over you; and *when* you awaken, it will meditate *with* you. 23For the commandment *is* a lamp; and the law a light; and reproofs of instruction *are* a way of life; 24to keep you from the evil woman, from the flattery of the tongue of the strange woman. 25Do not lust after her beauty in your heart; and do not let her take you with her eyelids. 26For on account of a woman, a harlot, *a man comes* to the *last* loaf of

---

7/8
103 3899 7019 3559 4910 | 7860 7101 369
אֲשֶׁר אֵין־לָהּ קָצִין שֹׁטֵר וּמֹשֵׁל׃ הָכִין בַּקַּיִץ לַחְמָהּ אָגְרָה
gathers her | the in | provides | or over- | a | to | not | of
,bread | summer | ,ruler | seer | ,leader her | is | whom

9
6965 7901 6102 5704 3978 7102
בַקָּצִיר מַאֲכָלָהּ׃ עַד־מָתַי עָצֵל תִּשְׁכָּב מָתַי תָּקוּם
will you When you will | lazy O | when Until | her | the in
arise ?down lie | man | food | harvest

10
3027 2264 4592 8572 4592 8142 4592 8142
מִשְּׁנָתֶךָ׃ מְעַט שֵׁנוֹת מְעַט תְּנוּמוֹת מְעַט חִבֻּק יָדַיִם
the folding | a | ,slumber | a | ,sleep | A | of out
hands of | little | little | little | ?sleep your

11
120 4043 376 4270 7389 1980 935 7901
לִשְׁכָּב׃ וּבָא־כִמְהַלֵּךְ רֵאשֶׁךָ וּמַחְסֹרְךָ כְּאִישׁ מָגֵן׃ אָדָם
A | a | a as | your and | your | one as | shall so | lie to
man | shield of man | want | ,poverty | stalking | come | ;down

12/13
1100 205 376 6310 6143 1980 7169 5869 4448
בְּלִיַּעַל אִישׁ אָוֶן הוֹלֵךְ עִקְּשׁוּת פֶּה׃ קֹרֵץ בְּעֵינָיו מֹלֵל
speaking with | winking | ,mouth crooked a | walks | ,evil man a | worth-
,eyes his | (with) | of | less

14
7451 2790 3820 8419 676 3384 7272
בְּרַגְלָיו מֹרֶה בְּאֶצְבְּעֹתָיו׃ תַּהְפֻּכוֹת בְּלִבּוֹ חֹרֵשׁ רָע
evil | is he | his in | perverse | his with | teaching his with
plotting | ,heart | (are) things | ;fingers | ,feet

15
6621 343 935 6597 7971 4090 6256
בְּכָל־עֵת מִדְיָנִים יְשַׁלֵּחַ׃ עַל־כֵּן פִּתְאֹם יָבוֹא אֵידוֹ פֶּתַע
quickly | his | shall | suddenly Therefore | sends he | strife | ;time | at
,calamity come | out | every

16
84·44 7651 3068 8130 8337 4832 369 76·65
יִשָּׁבֵר וְאֵין מַרְפֵּא׃ שֶׁשׁ־הֵנָּה שָׂנֵא יְהוָה וְשֶׁבַע תּוֹעֲבוֹת
hateful are | and | ,Jehovah hates | these Six | .healing | is and | is he
to | seven | (things) | not | ,broken

17
5315 5869 7311 3956 8267 1818/8210 3027
נַפְשׁוֹ׃ עֵינַיִם רָמוֹת לְשׁוֹן שָׁקֶר וְיָדַיִם שֹׁפְכוֹת דָּם־נָקִי׃
innocent | shedding | and | lying | a | ,high | eyes | His
blood | hands | tongue | soul

18
7451 7323 41·16 7272 205 4284 2790 3820
לֵב חֹרֵשׁ מַחְשְׁבוֹת אָוֶן רַגְלַיִם מְמַהֲרוֹת לָרוּץ לָרָעָה׃
,evil to | run to | hurrying | feet | ;evil | plans | that
plots heart

19
251 996 40·90 79/71 8267 5701 3577 6315
יָפִיחַ כְּזָבִים עֵד שָׁקֶר וּמְשַׁלֵּחַ מְדָנִים בֵּין אַחִים׃
.brothers between | strife | one and | ,lying | a | ,lies | he
out sending | witness | breathes

20/21
7194 517 8451 5203 1 4687 114 5341
נְצֹר בְּנִי מִצְוַת אָבִיךָ וְאַל־תִּטֹּשׁ תּוֹרַת אִמֶּךָ׃ קָשְׁרֵם
them Tie | your | the | do | and | your | commands my | ,Keep
.mother of law | forsake | not | ;father's | son

22
5148 1980 1621 59/121 6029 8548 3820 59/121
עַל־לִבְּךָ תָמִיד עָנְדֵם עַל־גַּרְגְּרֹתֶךָ׃ בְּהִתְהַלֶּכְךָ תַּנְחֶה
shall it | you When | your | on | bind | con- | your | on
lead | ,go | .neck | them | ,tinually | heart

23
7878 69·74 59/21 8104 7901
אֹתָךְ בְּשָׁכְבְּךָ תִּשְׁמֹר עָלֶיךָ וַהֲקִיצוֹתָ הִיא תְשִׂיחֶךָ׃ כִּי
For | muse shall | (when) and | over | shall it | you when | ;you
(is) | you (with) | ,awaken you | ,you | watch | down lie

24
8104 4148 8433 24·16 1870 216 8451 4687 5216
נֵר מִצְוָה וְתוֹרָה אוֹר וְדֶרֶךְ חַיִּים תּוֹכְחוֹת מוּסָר׃ לִשְׁמָרְךָ
keep to | ;instruction | reproofs | life | the and | a | the and com- the a
you | of | (is) | of way | ;light | law | mand lamp

25
3824 3308 2530 408 5237 3956 2513 7451 802
מֵאֵשֶׁת רָע מֵחֶלְקַת לָשׁוֹן נָכְרִיָּה׃ אַל־תַּחְמֹד יָפְיָהּ בִּלְבָבֶךָ
your in | her | do | Not strange the | tongue the | the from | ,evil the from
;heart | beauty | after lust | .woman | of | smooth | woman

26
3603 21·81 802 2181 6075 3947
וְאַל־תִּקָּחֲךָ בְּעַפְעַפֶּיהָ׃ כִּי בְעַד־אִשָּׁה זוֹנָה עַד־כִּכַּר
(last) the to | a | of behalf on | For | her with | let do | and
of loaf | harlot woman a | .eyelids | you take her | not

bread; and *another* man's
wife will hunt for the
precious soul. 27Can a man
take fire into his bosom and
his clothes not be burned?
28Or can a man walk on hot
coals and his feet not be
burned? 29So *is* he who
goes in to his neighbor's
wife; everyone touching her
shall not be innocent.
30They do not despise a
thief, if he steals to fill his
appetite when he is hungry.
31But *if* he is found, he shall
restore sevenfold; he shall
give all the goods of his
house. 32He who commits
adultery *with* a woman
lacks heart; he who does it
is a destroyer of his own
soul. 33He shall find a
wound and dishonor; and
his shame shall not be
wiped away. 34For jealousy
is the rage of a man, and he
will not spare in the day of
vengeance. 35He will not
lift up the face of every
ransom; nor will he consent
if you multiply the bribes.

27 לָחֶם וְאֵשֶׁת אִישׁ נֶפֶשׁ יְקָרָה תָצוּד׃ הֲיַחְתֶּה אִישׁ אֵשׁ
fire man a take Can hunts precious the (another) and ;bread
up .for soul man's wife

28 בְּחֵיקוֹ וּבְגָדָיו לֹא תִשָּׂרַפְנָה׃ אִם־יְהַלֵּךְ אִישׁ עַל־הַגֶּחָלִים
coals hot on a can Or be not his and his into
man walk ?burned clothes bosom

29 וְרַגְלָיו לֹא תִכָּוֶינָה׃ כֵּן הַבָּא אֶל־אֵשֶׁת רֵעֵהוּ לֹא יִנָּקֶה
be shall not his wife to one So be not his and
innocent ;neighbor's in going (is) ?burned feet

30 כָּל־הַנֹּגֵעַ בָּהּ׃ לֹא־יָבוּזוּ לַגַּנָּב כִּי יִגְנוֹב לְמַלֵּא נַפְשׁוֹ
his satisfy to he when a they not Do .her touch- every-
soul steals thief despise ing one

31 כִּי יִרְעָב׃ וְנִמְצָא יְשַׁלֵּם שִׁבְעָתָיִם אֶת־כָּל־הוֹן בֵּיתוֹ יִתֵּן׃
shall he his the all ,sevenfold shall he (if) but is he when
.give house of goods restore found is he ;hungry

32
33 נֹאֵף אִשָּׁה חֲסַר־לֵב מַשְׁחִית נַפְשׁוֹ הוּא יַעֲשֶׂנָּה׃ נֶגַע
A (who) he own his de- a ;heart lacks a (with) doing one
wound .it does (is) soul of stroyer woman adultery

34 וְקָלוֹן יִמְצָא וְחֶרְפָּתוֹ לֹא תִמָּחֶה׃ כִּי־קִנְאָה חֲמַת־גָּבֶר
a the (is) jealousy For be shall not his and shall he and
;man of rage .away wiped reproach ;find dishonor

35 וְלֹא־יַחְמוֹל בְּיוֹם נָקָם׃ לֹא־יִשָּׂא פְּנֵי כָל־כֹּפֶר וְלֹא־יֹאבֶה
will he and ;ransom every the will he Not venge- the in will he and
consent not of face lift .ance of day spare not

כִּי תַרְבֶּה־שֹׁחַד׃
the you when
.bribes multiply

CAP. VII ז

CHAPTER 7

1My son, keep my words
and store up my commands
within you. 2Keep my
commands and live; and my
law as the pupil of your
eye. 3Tie them on your
fingers; write them on the
tablet of your heart. 4Say
to wisdom, You *are* my
sister; and call understanding *your* kinsman; 5so that
they may keep you from the
strange woman, from the
alien *with* her flattering
words. 6For I looked
through my lattice, at the
window of my house, 7and
I saw among the simple
ones; I observed among the
sons a young man lacking
heart; 8passing through the
street near her corner; and
he went the way to her
house; 9in the twilight, in
the evening; in the black
and darkness of night.
10And, behold, a woman to

CHAPTER 7

1
2 בְּנִי שְׁמֹר אֲמָרָי וּמִצְוֹתַי תִּצְפֹּן אִתָּךְ׃ שְׁמֹר מִצְוֹתַי וֶחְיֵה
and my Keep with treasure my and my keep My
live commands .you commands ,words son

3 וְתוֹרָתִי כְּאִישׁוֹן עֵינֶיךָ׃ קָשְׁרֵם עַל־אֶצְבְּעֹתֶיךָ כָּתְבֵם עַל־
on write your on them Tie your the as my and
them ;fingers .eyes of pupil teaching

4 לוּחַ לִבֶּךָ׃ אֱמֹר לַחָכְמָה אֲחֹתִי אָתְּ וּמֹדָע לַבִּינָה תִקְרָא׃
;call under- to a and you My to Say your tablet
standing kinsman ;(are) sister ,wisdom .heart's

5
6 לִשְׁמָרְךָ מֵאִשָּׁה זָרָה מִנָּכְרִיָּה אֲמָרֶיהָ הֶחֱלִיקָה׃ כִּי
For .smooth her (with) the from ,strange the from keep to
words foreigner woman you

7 בְּחַלּוֹן בֵּיתִי בְּעַד אֶשְׁנַבִּי נִשְׁקָפְתִּי׃ וָאֵרֶא בַפְּתָאיִם אָבִינָה
I the among I and looked I my through my the at
observed ones simple saw ,down lattice house of window

8 בַבָּנִים נַעַר חֲסַר־לֵב׃ עֹבֵר בַּשּׁוּק אֵצֶל פִּנָּהּ וְדֶרֶךְ בֵּיתָהּ
her the and her beside through passing ;heart lacking of among
house to way ;corner street the youth sons the

9
10 יִצְעָד׃ בְּנֶשֶׁף־בְּעֶרֶב יוֹם בְּאִישׁוֹן לַיְלָה וַאֲפֵלָה׃ וְהִנֵּה
And and night the in ,day the at the in he
,behold .darkness of black of evening ,twilight ,walked

meet him, with a harlot's dress, and a guarded heart; [11]she is loud and stubborn; her feet do not stay in her own house. [12]At this time *she* is outside, now in the streets, and *she* lies in wait at every corner; [13]and she seizes him and kisses him; she hardens her face and says to him, [14]Sacrifices of peace offerings *are* on me; today I have paid my vows; [15]so I came out to meet you, earnestly to seek your face; and I have found you. [16]I have spread my couch with coverings; with striped cloths of Egyptian linen. [17]I have sprinkled my bed with myrrh, aloes and cinnamon. [18]Come, let us take our fill of love until the morning; let us delight ourselves with caresses. [19]For my husband *is* not at his house; he is going in the way, far away. [20]He has taken a bag of silver in his hand; at the day of the full moon, he will enter his house. [21]With the sum of her persuasion she turned him aside; with the flattering of her lips, she forced him. [22]He goes after her immediately, as an ox goes to the slaughter; or as one in fetters *goes* to the correction of a fool; [23]until an arrow strikes through his liver; as a bird hastens to the snare, and not knowing that it *is* for his soul.

[24]Now, then, listen to me, O sons; and attend to the words of my mouth; [25]Do not let your heart turn aside to her ways; do not go astray in her paths. [26]For many *are* the wounded she has caused to fall; and plentiful all her slain ones. [27]The ways of Sheol *are* in her house, leading down to the rooms of death.

11
אִשָּׁה לִקְרָאתוֹ שִׁית זוֹנָה וּנְצֻרַת לֵב: הֹמִיָּה הִיא וְסֹרָרֶת

5607	1993	38,20	5341	2181	7897	7125	802
and she stubborn (is)	loud	;heart a and guarded	har- a (with) ,lot's	meet to him	dress	woman	a

12
בְּבֵיתָהּ לֹא־יִשְׁכְּנוּ רַגְלֶיהָ: פַּעַם ׀ בַּחוּץ פַּעַם בָּרְחֹבוֹת

7339	6471	2351	6471	7272	7931	3808	1004
the in streets	now	,outside	now	her ;feet (is she)	do not dwell	her in house own	

13
וְאָצַל כָּל־פִּנָּה תֶּאֱרֹב: וְהֶחֱזִיקָה בּוֹ וְנָשְׁקָה לּוֹ הֵעֵזָה

5810	5401	2388	693	6438	1681
she hardens	;him and kisses	him she and seizes	lies she .wait in	corner every	and at

14
פָּנֶיהָ וַתֹּאמַר לוֹ: זִבְחֵי שְׁלָמִים עָלָי הַיּוֹם שִׁלַּמְתִּי נְדָרָי:

5088	7999	3117	8002	2077	559	644,0
my ;vows	have I repaid	today	are peace ;me on offerings of	Sacrifices of	to says and ,him	her face

15
16
עַל־כֵּן יָצָאתִי לִקְרָאתֶךָ לְשַׁחֵר פָּנֶיךָ וָאֶמְצָאֶךָּ: מַרְבַדִּים

4765	4672	6440	7836	7125	3318
(with) coverings	have I .you found	your face	seek to early	meet to ,you	came I out therefore

17
רָבַדְתִּי עַרְשִׂי חֲטֻבוֹת אֵטוּן מִצְרָיִם: נַפְתִּי מִשְׁכָּבִי מֹר

4753	4904	5130	4714	330	2405	6210	7234
(with) ,myrrh	my bed	have I sprinkled	;Egypt	linen of	striped of cloths	my ,couch	have I spread

18
אֲהָלִים וְקִנָּמוֹן: לְכָה נִרְוֶה דֹדִים עַד־הַבֹּקֶר נִתְעַלְּסָה

5965	1242	5704	1730	7301	3212	7076	174
delight us let ourselves	;morning the until	of loves	us let ,Come	fill our drink	and	.cinnamon	aloes

19
בָּאֲהָבִים: כִּי אֵין הָאִישׁ בְּבֵיתוֹ הָלַךְ בְּדֶרֶךְ מֵרָחוֹק:

7350	1870	1980	1004	376	369	159
far ;off	the in way	is he going	his in ;house	(my) husband	is For not	with .caresses

20
21
צְרוֹר־הַכֶּסֶף לָקַח בְּיָדוֹ לְיוֹם הַכֵּסֶא יָבֹא בֵיתוֹ: הִטַּתּוּ

5186	1004	935	3677	3117	3027	3947	3701	6872
bowed She him	his .house	will he enter	full the moon	the at of day	his in hand	has he taken	silver	bag a of

22
בְּרֹב לִקְחָהּ בְּחֵלֶק שְׂפָתֶיהָ תַּדִּיחֶנּוּ: הוֹלֵךְ אַחֲרֶיהָ פִּתְאֹם

65.97	310	1980	5080	8193	2506	3940	72.30
at ,once	after her	(is He) going .him	she forced	lips her	the with of flattering	per- her suasion of sum	the by

23
כְּשׁוֹר אֶל־טֶבַח יָבוֹא וּכְעֶכֶס אֶל־מוּסַר אֱוִיל: עַד יְפַלַּח

631.98	5704	191	4148	5914	935	2874	7794
strikes until through	a ;fool of	chastise-to ment chained	one as	;goes the slaughter	the to	an as ox	

חֵץ כְּבֵדוֹ כְּמַהֵר צִפּוֹר אֶל־פָּח וְלֹא־יָדַע כִּי־בְנַפְשׁוֹ הוּא:

5315	304.5	38,08	6341	6833	4116	35,16	267H
.(is) it his for soul	that knowing and	the to not ,snare	a	Like his bird's hastening .liver	his	a dart	

24
25
וְעַתָּה בָנִים שִׁמְעוּ־לִי וְהַקְשִׁיבוּ לְאִמְרֵי־פִי: אַל־יֵשְׂטְ

7847	6310	561	7181	8085	1121	6258
do not aside turn	my ;mouth	the to of words	incline	to listen ,me	,sons	And ,now

26
אֶל־דְּרָכֶיהָ לִבֶּךָ אַל־תֵּתַע בִּנְתִיבוֹתֶיהָ: כִּי־רַבִּים חֲלָלִים

2491	7227	5410	8582	3820	1870
the wounded	many (are)	For her .paths	her in go do not astray	your ,heart ways	her to

27
הִפִּילָה וַעֲצֻמִים כָּל־הֲרֻגֶיהָ: דַּרְכֵי שְׁאוֹל בֵּיתָהּ יֹרְדוֹת

3381	1004	7585	1870	2026	36,05	6099	5307
going down	her ,house	Sheol (are)	The of ways	her .ones slain	all	and has she numerous ;fall made	

אֶל־חַדְרֵי־מָוֶת:

4194	2315
.death the	to of rooms

CAP. VIII ח

CHAPTER 8

CHAPTER 8

¹Does not wisdom call? And understanding gives her voice. ²She stands in the head of heights, by the roadside, between the houses of the paths. ³She cries beside the gates; in the entrance to the city; *at* the doors. ⁴I call to you, O men, and my voice *is* to the sons of men. ⁵Understand wisdom, simple ones; and be of an understanding heart, fools. ⁶Hear, for I will speak of excellent things; and from the opening of my lips *shall be* right things. ⁷For my mouth shall speak of truth; and wickedness *is* hateful to my lips. ⁸All the words of my mouth *are* in righteousness; nothing twisted or perverse *is* in them; ⁹they *are* all plain to the understanding one; and right to those who find knowledge. ¹⁰Receive my instruction, and not silver; and knowledge, rather than choice gold. ¹¹For wisdom *is* better than jewels; and all delights cannot be compared to it. ¹²I, wisdom, dwell with sense, and search out knowledge of wise actions. ¹³The fear of Jehovah *is* to hate evil; I hate pride and loftiness, and the evil way, and the perverse mouth. ¹⁴Counsel and sound wisdom are Mine; I *am* understanding; I have strength. ¹⁵By Me kings reign, and princes decree righteousness. ¹⁶Rulers and nobles rule by Me, and all the judges of the earth. ¹⁷I love those who love Me, and those who seek Me early find Me. ¹⁸Riches and honor *are* with Me; enduring wealth and righteousness. ¹⁹My fruit *is* better than gold, yea, than fine gold; and My increase *is* better than the best silver. ²⁰I walk in the path of righteousness, in the midst of the paths of justice;

4791	7218	69,63	5414	83.94		7121	2451	3808

1
2
הֲלֹא־חָכְמָה תִקְרָא וּתְבוּנָה תִתֵּן קוֹלָהּ׃ בְּרֹאשׁ־מְרֹמִים

| high | the on | her | .gives | under- | And | does | wisdom | Not |
| places | of head | ?voice | | standing | | ?call | | |

7176 6310   8179   3027   5324   5410   996   1870 59,21

3
עַל־דֶּרֶךְ בֵּית נְתִיבוֹת נִצָּבָה׃ לְיָד־שְׁעָרִים לְפִי־קָרֶת

the before	the	the At	she	the	between	the	on
,city 6963	,gates	of side	!stands	paths		,way	
	7121	376		7442	6607	3996

4
מְבוֹא פְתָחִים תָּרֹנָּה׃ אֲלֵיכֶם אִישִׁים אֶקְרָא וְקוֹלִי אֶל־

(is)	my	and	;call I	O	,you To	she	the (at)	,entrance
to		voice		,men		.cries	,doors
38 20	995		3684		6195	6612	995	120	1121

5
בְּנֵי אָדָם׃ הָבִינוּ פְתָאִים עָרְמָה וּכְסִילִים הָבִינוּ לֵב׃

(in)	under-	,fools and	;prudence	simple	,Understand	.men	the
!heart	stand			,ones			of sons
571	4339	81,93	4669	1696	5057	8085

6
7
שִׁמְעוּ כִּי־נְגִידִים אֲדַבֵּר וּמִפְתַּח שְׂפָתַי מֵישָׁרִים׃ כִּי־אֱמֶת

truth	For	.things right	my	the from and	will I	excellent for	,Hear
			lips	of opening		speak	things
6310	561	3605 6664	7562	81,93	8441	2441 1897

8
יֶהְגֶּה חִכִּי וְתוֹעֲבַת שְׂפָתַי רֶשַׁע׃ בְּצֶדֶק כָּל־אִמְרֵי־פִי

my words	(are)	righ-	In	wicked-	lips my	and	my	shall
;mouth of	all	teousness	.ness	(is)		to hateful	;palate	utter
3477	995	5228	36,05	6141	16617	369

9
אֵין בָּהֶם נִפְתָּל וְעִקֵּשׁ׃ כֻּלָּם נְכֹחִים לַמֵּבִין וִישָׁרִים

and	the to	(are)	of all	and	twisted	a	in	is
upright	,discerning	straight	them	;crooked	thing	them	not
977	2742	7847	3701 3808	4148	3947	1847	4672

10
לְמֹצְאֵי דָעַת׃ קְחוּ־מוּסָרִי וְאַל־כָּסֶף וְדַעַת מֵחָרוּץ נִבְחָר׃

.choice	than	rather	and	;silver and	my	Receive	knowl-	those to
		gold	knowledge	not	,instruction		.edge	finding
7737	38,08 2656	3605	6443	2451	2896

11
כִּי־טוֹבָה חָכְמָה מִפְּנִינִים וְכָל־חֲפָצִים לֹא יִשְׁווּ־בָהּ׃

com-	be can	not	delights	and	wisdom	better	For
.it to	pared		all	,jewels		(is)	
3373	4672	4209	1847	6195	7931	2451

12
13
אֲנִי־חָכְמָה שָׁכַנְתִּי עָרְמָה וְדַעַת מְזִמּוֹת אֶמְצָא׃ יִרְאַת

The	find I	discretions	knowl- and	;prudence	dwell	,wisdom	I
of fear	.out		edge		(with)	
8130	8419	63.10 7451	1870	13,47/1344 ~7451	8130	~3068

יְהוָה שְׂנֹאת רָע גֵּאָה וְגָאוֹן וְדֶרֶךְ רָע וּפִי תַהְפֻּכוֹת שָׂנֵאתִי׃

.hate I	perverse	and	,evil and	and	pride	;evil	to (is)	Jehovah
		mouth the	way the		loftiness		hate
44,27	44,28	1369	998	8454	6098

14
15
לִי־עֵצָה וְתוּשִׁיָּה אֲנִי בִינָה לִי גְבוּרָה׃ בִּי מְלָכִים יִמְלֹכוּ

reign	kings	By	.strength (is)	to under-	I	sound and (is)	To
		me	;standing (am)	;wisdom counsel me			
8199	3605 50,81	8323	8269	6664	2710	7336

16
וְרוֹזְנִים יְחֹקְקוּ צֶדֶק׃ בִּי שָׂרִים יָשֹׂרוּ וּנְדִיבִים כָּל־שֹׁפְטֵי

judges	the	all	and	,rule	rulers	By	right-	decree	and
of			nobles			me	.eousness		princes
3569	6239	4672	7836	157	157	776

17
18
אָרֶץ׃ אֲנִי אֹהֲבַי אֵהָב וּמְשַׁחֲרַי יִמְצָאֻנְנִי׃ עֹשֶׁר־וְכָבוֹד

and	Riches	find	ones me	,love	those	I	the
honor		.me	seeking		me loving		.earth
8393	6337	2742	6529	2896	6666	62,76 1952

19
אִתִּי הוֹן עָתֵק וּצְדָקָה׃ טוֹב פִּרְיִי מֵחָרוּץ וּמִפָּז וּתְבוּאָתִי

my	and	pure and	gold than	my	Better	and	enduring	with
produce	,gold			fruit	(is)		.righteousness	wealth ,me
5410	8432	1980	6662	734	977	3701

20
מִכֶּסֶף נִבְחָר׃ בְּאֹרַח צְדָקָה אֲהַלֵּךְ בְּתוֹךְ נְתִיבוֹת

| of paths | the among | walk I | righteous- | the In | .choice | than |
| | | | ness | of path | | silver |

21 I cause those who love Me to inherit wealth; and I will fill up their treasuries.
22 Jehovah possessed Me in the beginning of His way, from then, before His works. 23 I was set up from everlasting; from the beginning, before the earth ever was. 24 When there were no depths, I was brought forth; when there were no springs heavy *with* water. 25 Before the mountains were settled; before the hills, I was brought forth; 26 before He had made the earth, and the fields, or the highest part of the dust of the world. 27 When He prepared the heavens, I was there; when He set a circle on the face of the deep; 28 when He set the clouds above; when He made the strong fountains of the deep; 29 when He gave to the sea its limit, that the waters should not go beyond His commands; when He decreed the foundations of the earth; 30 then I was at His side, like a master workman; and I was *His* delights day *by* day, rejoicing before Him at every time; 31 rejoicing in the world, His earth; and My delights *were* with the sons of men.
32 And now listen to Me, O sons; for blessed *are those who* keep My ways. 33 Hear instruction, and be wise, and do not refuse it. 34 Blessed *is* the man listening to Me, watching daily at My gates, waiting at the posts of My doors. 35 For whoever finds Me finds life; and he shall obtain favor from Jehovah. 36 But he who sins against Me does violence to his own soul; all who hate Me love death.

4390 214 3426 157 5157 4941
21 משפט׃ להנחיל אהבי ׀ יש ואצרתיהם אמלא׃
will I / up fill | their and / .storehouses | ;wealth | my / lovers | cause to / inherit to | ,justice

5769 4659 6924 1870 7225 7069 3068
22 יהוה קנני ראשית דרכו קדם מפעליו מאז׃
23 מעולם
From / everlasting | from / then | his / works | before | His / ,way | the in / of beginning | possessed / me | Jeho- / vah

369 234 2 8415 369 776 6924 7218 5258
24 נסכתי מראש מקדמי־ארץ׃ באין־תהמות חוללתי באין
when / no were | I / ,travailed | ,depths | When / no were | the / .earth | ancient from / of times | the from / ,beginning | was I / ;up set

1389 6440 2883 2022 2962 4325 3513 4599
25 מעינות נכבדי־מים׃ בטרם הרים הטבעו לפני גבעות
the / ,hills | before | were / ,sunk | the / mountains | Before | .waters | heavy / with | springs

8398 6083 7218 2351 776 6213 3808/5704 234 2
26 חוללתי׃ עד־לא עשה ארץ וחוצות וראש עפרות תבל׃
the / .world | the / of dust | the and / of head | the and / ,fields | the / earth | had He / made | not While | I / .travailed

553 8415 6440 5921/2329 2710 8033 8064 3559
27
28 בהכינו שמים שם אני בחקו חוג על־פני תהום׃ באמצו
His in / firming | the / ;deep | the / of face | on | a / circle | His in / inscribing | I / ;(was) | there | the / heavens | His In / preparing

2706 3220 7760 8415 5869 5810 4605 7834
29 שחקים ממעל בעזוז עינות תהום׃ בשומו לים ׀ חקו
its / ,limit | for / sea the | His in / setting | the / ;deep | the / of springs | making in / strong | from / ,above | the / clouds

681 1961 776 4146 2706 6310 5674 3808/4325
30 ומים לא יעברו־פיו בחוקו מוסדי ארץ׃ ואהיה אצלו
(at) / ,side His | I and / was | the / ;earth's | found- / ations | His in / decreeing | pass should / ;mouth His | not / over | that / waters the

6256 3605 6440 7832 3117 3117 8191 1961 525
אמון ואהיה שעשעים יום ׀ יום משחקת לפניו בכל־עת׃
.time | at / every | before / Him | rejoicing | (by) / ,day | day | (His) / delights | I and / was | work- a / ;man

120 1121 8191 776 8398 7832
31 משחקת בתבל ארצו ושעשעי את־בני אדם׃
.men | the / of sons | (were) / with | my and / delight | His / earth | the in / world | rejoicing

4148 8085 8104 1870 835 8085 1121 6258
32
33 ועתה בנים שמעו־לי ואשרי דרכי ישמרו׃ שמעו מוסר
instruc- / ,tion | Hear | (who) they / .keep | My / ways | for / (are) blessed | ;Me to | listen | (O) / ,sons | And / ,now

5921 8245 8085 120 835 6544 3808 2449
34 וחכמו ואל־תפרעו׃ אשרי אדם שמע לי לשקד על־
over | to / watch | to / ,me | listening | the / man | Blessed / (is) | do / .ignore | and / not | be and / ,wise

4672 4672 6607 4201 8104 3117 3117 1817
35 דלתתי יום ׀ יום לשמר מזוזת פתחי׃ כי מצאי מצא
finds | one the / me finding | For | my / .doors | the / of posts | guarding | (by) / ,day | day | my / doors

8130 3605 5315 2554 2398 3068 7522 6329 2416
36 חיים ויפק רצון מיהוה׃ וחטאי חמס נפשו כל־משנאי
hating / me | all | own his / ;soul | hurts | sin- / ning | he / Me against | But | from / .Jehovah | favor | he and / obtain shall | ;life

4194 157
אהבו מות׃
.death | love

CAP. IX ט

CHAPTER 9

1 Wisdom has built her house; she has carved out her seven pillars; 2 she has slaughtered her slaughter;

2873 7651 5982 2672 1004 1129 2454
1
2 חכמות בנתה ביתה חצבה עמודיה שבעה׃ טבחה
has She / slaughtered | .seven | her / pillars | has she / carved | her / ;house | has / built | Wisdom

she has mixed her wine; she has also set her table. [3]She has sent out her maidens; she cries on the highest places of the city; [4]The simple one, turn in here; *and to* one lacking heart, she says to him: [5]Come, eat of my bread, and drink of the wine I have mixed. [6]Forsake the foolish, and live; and go in the way of understanding.

[7]He who reproves a scorner gets shame to himself; and he who rebukes a wicked man *gets* his own blot. [8]Do not reprove a scorner, that he not hate you; rebuke a wise man, and he will love you. [9]Give to a wise one, and he will be more wise; teach a just one, and he will increase in learning. [10]The fear of Jehovah *is* the beginning of wisdom; and the knowledge of the Holy Ones *is* understanding. [11]For by Me your days shall be multiplied; and the years of your life shall be increased. [12]If you are wise, you shall be wise for yourself; but *if* you scorn, you alone shall bear *it*. [13]A foolish woman *is* loud; *she is* thoughtlessness; and she knows not what. [14]And she sits at the door of her house, in a seat in the high places of the city; [15]to call those who pass by; who are going straight *on* their ways: [16]The simple one, let him turn in here; and *to the* one lacking heart, she says to him: [17]Stolen waters are sweet, and bread *eaten* in secret is pleasant. [18]But he does not know that the departed spirits *are* there; her guests *are* in the depths of Sheol.

3
5291 7971 7979 6186 637 3196 4537 2874
טִבְחָה מָסְכָה יֵינָהּ אַף עָרְכָה שֻׁלְחָנָהּ׃ שָׁלְחָה נַעֲרֹתֶיהָ
her has She her has she also her has she her
;maidens out sent .table set ;wine mixed ;slaughter

4
3820/2038 5483 6612 7176 47.71 1610 7121
תִּקְרָא עַל־גַּפֵּי מְרֹמֵי קָרֶת׃ מִי־פֶתִי יָסֻר הֵנָּה חֲסַר־לֵב
,heart One ;here turn (is) Who the heights the on she
lacking aside ,simple :city's of tops calls

5
6
5800 4537 3196 83 54 3899 3898 3212 559
אָמְרָה לּוֹ׃ לְכוּ לַחֲמוּ בְלַחְמִי וּשְׁתוּ בְּיַיִן מָסָכְתִּי׃ עִזְבוּ
Forsake have I the of and my of eat ,Come to says she
.mixed wine drink ,bread him

7
7036 3947 3887 3256 998 1870 833 2421 66•12
פְתָאיִם וִחְיוּ וְאִשְׁרוּ בְּדֶרֶךְ בִּינָה׃ יֹסֵר לֵץ לֹקֵחַ לוֹ קָלוֹן
;shame for takes a re- One under- the in and and the
himself scorner buking .standing of way walk ;live simple

8
3198 8130 3887 3198 3808 3971 7563 3198
וּמוֹכִיחַ לְרָשָׁע מוּמוֹ׃ אַל־תּוֹכַח לֵץ פֶּן־יִשְׂנָאֶךָּ הוֹכַח
reprove hate he lest a do Not own his wicked a one and
;you ,scorner reprove .blemish man reproving

9
6662 3045 5750 2449 2450 5414 157 2450
לְחָכָם וְיֶאֱהָבֶךָּ׃ תֵּן לְחָכָם וְיֶחְכַּם־עוֹד הוֹדַע לְצַדִּיק
just a cause to ;more he and a to Give will he and wise a
man know to wise be will ,one wise .you love ,one

10
6918 1847 3068 3373 2451 8462 3948 3254
וְיוֹסֶף לֶקַח׃ תְּחִלַּת חָכְמָה יִרְאַת יְהוָה וְדַעַת קְדֹשִׁים
Holy the the and ,Jehovah the wisdom be- The (to) he and
Ones of knowledge of fear (is) of ginning .learning add will

11
12
2416 8141 3212 3254 3117 7235 998
בִּינָה׃ כִּי־בִי יִרְבּוּ יָמֶיךָ וְיוֹסִיפוּ לְּךָ שְׁנוֹת חַיִּים׃ אִם־
If .life the to shall and your in- shall by For under- (is)
of years you added be ;days crease me .standing

13
3687 802 5375 905 3887 2449 2449
חָכַמְתָּ חָכַמְתָּ לָּךְ וְלַצְתָּ לְבַדְּךָ תִשָּׂא׃ אֵשֶׁת כְּסִילוּת
foolishness A bear shall you you if and for are you are you
(is) of woman .(it) alone ,scorn ;yourself wise ,wise

14
5921 1004 6607 3427 4100 3045 1077 66•15 1993
הֹמִיָּה פְּתַיּוּת וּבַל־יָדְעָה מָּה׃ וְיָשְׁבָה לְפֶתַח בֵּיתָהּ עַל־
on her the at she And .what she and simple making
,house of door sits knows not ;noise

15
3474 1870 5674 7121 7176 4791 36•78
כִּסֵּא מְרֹמֵי קָרֶת׃ לִקְרֹא לְעֹבְרֵי־דָרֶךְ הַמְיַשְּׁרִים
going those the in those to call to the the (in) a
straight ,way passing ,city of heights seat

16
17
4325 559 3820 2638 5493 6612 734
אֹרְחוֹתָם׃ מִי־פֶתִי יָסֻר הֵנָּה וַחֲסַר־לֵב וְאָמְרָה לּוֹ׃ מַיִם־
waters to says she heart one And !here turn (is) Who their (on)
:him lacking aside ,simple :paths

18
7496 3045 3808 5276 5643 3899 4985 1589
גְּנוּבִים יִמְתָּקוּ וְלֶחֶם סְתָרִים יִנְעָם׃ וְלֹא־יָדַע כִּי־רְפָאִים
departed that does he But is (in) and are Stolen
spirits know not .pleasant secret bread ,sweet

7121 7585 6012 8033
שָׁם בְּעִמְקֵי שְׁאוֹל קְרֻאֶיהָ׃
here (are) Sheol the in (are)
.(ones) called of depths ,there

CAP. X י

CHAPTER 10

[1]The proverbs of Solomon: A wise son makes a father rejoice; but the foolish son *is* his mother's sorrow. [2]Treasures of wickedness profit nothing; but righteousness delivers from death. [3]Jehovah will not allow the soul of the

1
517 8424 3684 1121 1 8056 2450 1121 8010 4912
מִשְׁלֵי שְׁלֹמֹה בֵּן חָכָם יְשַׂמַּח־אָב וּבֵן כְּסִיל תּוּגַת אִמּוֹ׃
his sorrow foolish a but a makes wise A :Solomon Proverbs
.mother of (is) .son ,father rejoice son of

2
3
7456 3808 4194 5337 66•66 7562 214 3276 3808
לֹא־יוֹעִילוּ אוֹצְרוֹת רֶשַׁע וּצְדָקָה תַּצִּיל מִמָּוֶת׃ לֹא־יַרְעִיב
allows Not from delivers but ;wickedness treasures do Not
hunger to .death righteousness of profit

righteous to go hungry; but He pushes away the desire of the wicked. [4]He who deals *with* a lazy palm *becomes* poor; but the hand of the hard worker makes *him* rich. [5]He who gathers in summer *is* a prudent son; he who sleeps in harvest *is* a son who causes shame. [6]Blessings *are* on the head of the just; but violence covers the mouth of the wicked. [7]The memory of the just *is* blessed; but the name of the wicked shall rot. [8]The wise in heart accepts commands; but the foolish of lips shall be thrust away. [9]He who walks in integrity walks securely; but he who perverts his way shall be found out. [10]He who winks the eye causes sorrow; but the foolish of lips shall be thrust away. [11]The mouth of the righteous *is* a fountain of life; but violence covers the mouth of the wicked. [12]Hatred stirs up fights; but love covers all transgressions. [13]Wisdom is found in the lips of him who has understanding; but a rod *is waiting* for him who lacks heart. [14]The wise store up knowledge; but the mouth of the foolish *is* near ruin. [15]The rich man's wealth *is* his strong city; the ruin of the poor *is* their poverty.

[16]The labor of the righteous *is* for life; the gain of the wicked *is* for sin. [17]He who heeds instruction *is* in the way of life; but he who refuses reproof is going astray. [18]He who hides hatred *with* lying lips, and he who sends out a slander, he *is* a fool. [19]In the abundance of words, transgression does not cease; but one restraining his lips *is* prudent. [20]The tongue of the just *is as* choice silver; the heart of the wicked *is* as a little. [21]The lips of the righteous feed many; but fools die for lack of heart. [22]The blessing of Jehovah, it makes rich, and he adds no pain with it.

3709 6213 7326 1920 7563 1942 6662 5315 3068
4 יְהוָה נֶפֶשׁ צַדִּיק וְהַוַּת רְשָׁעִים יֶהְדֹּף׃ רָאשׁ עֹשֶׂה כַף־
(with) who he (Becomes) pushes He the but the soul the Jehovah
palm a deals poor .away wicked's desire ;righteous of

7290 7919 1121 7019 103 6238 2742 3027 7423
5 רְמִיָּה וְיַד חָרוּצִים תַּעֲשִׁיר׃ אֹגֵר בַּקַּיִץ בֵּן מַשְׂכִּיל נִרְדָּם
who he ;prudent a (is) in who He makes hard the but ;lazy
sleeps son summer gathers .rich workers' hand

3680 7563 6310 6662 7218 1293 954 1121 7019
6 בַּקָּצִיר בֵּן מֵבִישׁ׃ בְּרָכוֹת לְרֹאשׁ צַדִּיק וּפִי רְשָׁעִים יְכַסֶּה
covers the but the the to Blessings causing a (is) in
wicked's mouth :just of head (are) .shame son harvest

2450 7537 7563 8034 1293 6662 2145 2555
7 8 חָמָס׃ זֵכֶר צַדִּיק לִבְרָכָה וְשֵׁם רְשָׁעִים יִרְקָב׃ חֲכַם־
The shall the the but a for (is) just the The .violence
of wise :rot wicked of name ,blessing of memory

3212 8537 3212 3832 8193 191 4687 3947 3820
9 לֵב יִקַּח מִצְוֹת וֶאֱוִיל שְׂפָתַיִם יִלָּבֵט׃ הוֹלֵךְ בַּתֹּם יֵלֶךְ
walks in who He he shall lips the but com- accepts heart
integrity walks .away thrust of foolish ;mands

191 6094 5414 5869 7169 3045 1870 6140 982
10 בֶּטַח וּמְעַקֵּשׁ דְּרָכָיו יִוָּדֵעַ׃ קֹרֵץ עַיִן יִתֵּן עַצָּבֶת וֶאֱוִיל
the but ,pain gives the One be shall his who he but ;safely
of foolish eye winking .known ways perverts

3680 7563 6310 6662 6310 2416 4726 3832 8193
11 שְׂפָתַיִם יִלָּבֵט׃ מְקוֹר חַיִּים פִּי צַדִּיק וּפִי רְשָׁעִים יְכַסֶּה
covers the but the mouth life foun- A be shall lips
wicked's mouth ;righteous' (is) of tain .away thrust

3680 6588 3605 5921 4090 5782 8130 2555
12 חָמָס׃ שִׂנְאָה תְּעֹרֵר מְדָנִים וְעַל כָּל־פְּשָׁעִים תְּכַסֶּה
covers trans- all but ,strifes stirs Hatred .violence
gressions over up

2638 1460 7626 2451 4672 995 8193 160
13 אַהֲבָה׃ בְּשִׂפְתֵי נָבוֹן תִּמָּצֵא חָכְמָה וְשֵׁבֶט לְגֵו חֲסַר־
one the for a but ;wisdom found is dis- the the On .love
lacking of back (is) rod cerning of lips

1952 7138 4288 191 6310 1847 6845 2450 3820
14 15 לֵב׃ חֲכָמִים יִצְפְּנוּ־דָעַת וּפִי אֱוִיל מְחִתָּה קְרֹבָה׃ הוֹן
Wealth (is) ruin the but knowl- store The .heart
of .near —fool's mouth ;edge up wise

6662 6468 7389 1800 4288 5797 7151 6223
16 עָשִׁיר קִרְיַת עֻזּוֹ מְחִתַּת דַּלִּים רֵישָׁם׃ פְּעֻלַּת צַדִּיק
the The their (is) the ruin the his the (is) rich the
righteous of work .poverty poor of ;strength of city man

4118 8104 2416 734 2403 7563 8393 2416
17 לְחַיִּים תְּבוּאַת רָשָׁע לְחַטָּאת׃ אֹרַח לְחַיִּים שׁוֹמֵר מוּסָר
instruc- one life to the (On) for (is) the gain the for (is)
;tion keeping (is) path .sin wicked of ;life

3318 8267 8193 8130 3680 8582 8433 5800
18 וְעוֹזֵב תּוֹכַחַת מַתְעֶה׃ מְכַסֶּה שִׂנְאָה שִׂפְתֵי־שָׁקֶר וּמוֹצִא
one and false- of lips hatred who He going (is) reproof one but
out sending ,hood (has) hides .astray forsaking

2820 6588 2308 1697 7230 3684 1681
19 דִּבָּה הוּא כְסִיל׃ בְּרֹב דְּבָרִים לֹא יֶחְדַּל־פָּשַׁע וְחֹשֵׂךְ
one but trans- ceases not words abun- In .fool a he slander
restraining ;gression of dance (is)

7563 3820 6662 3956 977 3701 7919 8193
20 שְׂפָתָיו מַשְׂכִּיל׃ כֶּסֶף נִבְחָר לְשׁוֹן צַדִּיק לֵב רְשָׁעִים
the the the the Choice silver prudent (is) lips his
wicked of heart ;just of tongue (is)

3820/2638 191 7227 7462 6662 8193 4592
21 כִּמְעָט׃ שִׂפְתֵי צַדִּיק יִרְעוּ רַבִּים וֶאֱוִילִים בַּחֲסַר־לֵב
heart lack in but ;many feed the lips The a as (is)
of fools righteous of .little

6089 3254 3808 6238 3068 1293 4191
22 יָמוּתוּ׃ בִּרְכַּת יְהוָה הִיא תַעֲשִׁיר וְלֹא יוֹסִף עֶצֶב עִמָּהּ׃
with pain He and makes it Jehovah The .die
.it adds not ;rich of blessing

23 To work out evil devices *is* as laughter to the foolish; so wisdom *is* to a man of understanding. 24 That which the wicked fears shall come upon him; but the desire of the righteous is granted. 25 As the storm passes, so the wicked is not; but the righteous *is* an everlasting foundation. 26 Like vinegar to the teeth, and like smoke to the eyes, so is the lazy one to those who send him. 27 The fear of Jehovah prolongs days; but the years of the wicked shall be cut short. 28 The expectation of the righteous *is* joyful; but the hope of the wicked shall perish. 29 The way of Jehovah *is* strength to the upright; but ruin *is* to workers of iniquity. 30 The righteous shall never be moved; and the wicked shall not dwell in the land. 31 The mouth of the just flourishes *with* wisdom; but the perverse tongue shall be cut off. 32 The lips of the righteous know what is pleasing; but the mouth of the wicked *knows only* perversities.

CHAPTER 11

1 False balances *are* hateful to Jehovah; but a perfect stone His delight. 2 Pride comes—then shame comes — but with the lowly *is* wisdom. 3 The integrity of the upright guides them; but the perversity of traitors will devastate them. 4 Riches do not profit in the day of wrath; but righteousness delivers from death. 5 The righteousness of the perfect shall make his way right; but the wicked shall fall by his own wickedness. 6 The righteousness of the upright shall deliver them; but traitors shall be taken in their lust. 7 In the death of a wicked man, *his* expectation shall perish, and the hope of the unjust shall be lost. 8 The righteous is delivered from distress; and the wicked comes *in* his place. 9 The ungodly is corrupting his neighbor with *his* mouth; but the just

---

4034 8394 376 2451 2154 6213 3684 7814
23 24 כשחוק לכסיל עשות זמה וחכמה לאיש תבונה: מגורת
is What under- the to wis- so evil work to the to laughter As
by feared .standing of man (is) dom ;devices out foolish

5492 5674 5414 6662 8378 935 7563
25 רשע היא תבואנו ותאות צדיקים יתן: כעבור סופה
the passes As is the the but come shall that the
;tempest .given righteous of desire ;him upon ,wicked

6227 8127 2558 5769 3247 6662 7563 369
26 ואין רשע וצדיק יסוד עולם: כחמץ לשנים וכעשן
like and the to Like ever- a (is) the but the is so
smoke ,teeth vinegar .lasting foundation righteous ;wicked not

3117 3254 3068 3373 7971 6102 5869
27 לעינים כן העצל לשלחיו: יראת יהוה תוסיף ימים
;days prolongs Jehovah The those to lazy the so the to
of fear .him sending man (is) ,eyes

8615 8057 6662 8431 7114 7563 8141
28 ושנות רשעים תקצרנה: תוחלת צדיקים שמחה ותקות
the but (is) the hope The be shall the the but
of hope ;joy righteous of .shortened wicked of years

6466 4288 3068 1870 8537 4581 6 7563
29 רשעים תאבד: מעוז לתם דרך יהוה ומחתה לפעלי
to ruin but ,Jehovah way the the to (Is) shall the
of workers of upright strength .perish wicked

776 7931 3808 7563 4131 1077 5769 6662 205
30 און: צדיק לעולם בל ימוט ורשעים לא ישכנו ארץ:
the shall not the but be shall not forever The .evil
.land in dwell wicked ,shaken righteous

6662 8193 3772 8419 3956 2451 5107 6662/6310
31 32 פי צדיק ינוב חכמה ולשון תהפכות תכרת: שפתי צדיק
the lips The be shall perversities the but (with) flour- The mouth
righteous of off cut of tongue ;wisdom ishes righteous'

8419 7563 6310 7522 3045
ידעון רצון ופי רשעים תהפכות:
(only) the but is what know
.perversities ,wicked's mouth ;pleasing

CAP. XI יא

CHAPTER 11

935 7522 8003 68 3068 8441 4820 3976
1 2 מאזני מרמה תועבת יהוה ואבן שלמה רצונו: בא
Comes His (is) perfect but ;Jehovah hateful (are) False balances
.delight stone a to

5148 3477 8538 2451 6800 7036 935 2087
3 זדון ויבא קלון ואת צנועים חכמה: תמת ישרים תנחם
guides the The (is) the but ;shame then ,pride
;them upright of integrity .wisdom humble with comes

6666 5678 3117 1952 3276 3808 7703 898 5557
4 וסלף בוגדים ושדם: לא יועיל הון ביום עברה וצדקה
but ;wrath the in wealth does Not destroys traitors the but
righteousness of day profit them of perversity

5307 7564 1870 3474 8549 6666 4194 5337
5 תציל ממות: צדקת תמים תישר דרכו וברשעתו יפל
falls his by but his makes The righteousness from delivers
wickedness ;way straight perfect's .death

3920 898 1942 5337 3477 6666 7563
6 רשע: צדקת ישרים תצילם ובהות בגדים ילכדו:
be shall .traitors in but delivers the righ- The the
.taken lust (their) ;them upright of teousness .wicked

6 205 8431 8615 6 7563 120 4194
7 במות אדם רשע תאבד תקוה ותוחלת אונים אבדה:
be shall evil the and expect- (his) shall ,wicked a the In
.lost of hope ,ation perish man of death

7843 2611 6310 8478 7563 935 2502 6864 6662
8 9 צדיק מצרה נחלץ ויבא רשע תחתיו: בפה חנף ישחת
ruins un- the the With his (in) the and is from righ- The
godly mouth .place wicked enters ;delivered trouble eous

is delivered by knowledge.
10 When the righteous pros-
pers, the city rejoices; and at
the wicked's perishing *is*
singing. 11 A city is lifted up
by the blessing of the
upright; but by the wicked's
mouth it is overthrown.
12 One despising his friend
lacks heart—but an under-
standing man remains
silent. 13 A slanderer is a
revealer of secrets; but the
faithful of spirit keeps a
matter hidden. 14 Without
guidance the people fall; but
safety *is* in a great counselor. 15 One suffers evil
when he is surety for a
stranger; but one hating
strikers of hands is safe.
16 A gracious woman holds
to honor; and terrifying *men*
hold to riches. 17 A merciful
man does good to his own
soul; but the cruel troubles
his own flesh. 18 The wicked
makes a deceitful wage; but
one sowing righteousness
has a reward of truth. 19 So
righteousness *leads* to life;
but one pursuing evil, to his
death. 20 Hateful to Jehovah
are the perverse hearted;
but His delight *is* the upright
in way. 21 *Though* hand join
to hand, the evil shall not be
innocent; but the righteous
seed escapes. 22 *As* a ring of
gold in a swine's snout, *so is*
a woman *who is* beautiful,
yet turning aside discretion.
23 The desire of the righteous
is only good; the hope of the
wicked *is* wrath. 24 There is
one who scatters yet in-
creases more; but a with-
holder of just due *comes*
only to poverty. 25 The
blessed soul will be made
fat; he who waters will also
drink fully. 26 One holding
back grain, the people curse
him; but a blessing *is* to the
head of one selling grain.
27 He who early *is* seeking
good seeks favor; but one
pursuing evil, it shall come
to him. 28 One trusting in
his riches, he shall fall; but
like a green leaf the
righteous shall sprout.
29 One troubling his house
inherits the wind; and the
fool *is* servant to the wise of

7151 5970 6662 2898 2502 6662 1847 7453
10 רֵעֵהוּ וּבְדַעַת צַדִּיקִים יֵחָלֵצוּ׃ בְּטוּב צַדִּיקִים תַּעֲלֹץ קִרְיָה
the rejoices the When is the by but his
;city ,righteous prosper .delivered righteous knowledge ,friend

6310 7176 7311 3477 1293 7440 7563 6
11 וּבַאֲבֹד רְשָׁעִים רִנָּה׃ בְּבִרְכַּת יְשָׁרִים תָּרוּם קָרֶת וּבְפִי
by but ;city a lifted is the the By (is) the the at and
mouth up upright of blessing .singing wicked of perishing

8384 376 3820 2638 7453 936 2040 7563
12 רְשָׁעִים תֵּהָרֵס׃ בָּז־לְרֵעֵהוּ חֲסַר־לֵב וְאִישׁ תְּבוּנוֹת
understanding but ;heart lacks his One is it the
of man a friend despising .overthrown wicked's

1697 3680 7307 539 5475 1540 7400 1980 2790
13 יַחֲרִישׁ׃ הוֹלֵךְ רָכִיל מְגַלֶּה־סּוֹד וְנֶאֱמַן־רוּחַ מְכַסֶּה דָבָר׃
.matter a keeps faith- the but revealer a is (with) One remains
hidden spirit of ful ,secrets of slander going .silent

7321 7451 3289 7230 8668 5307 8458 369
14 15 בְּאֵין תַּחְבֻּלוֹת יִפָּל־עָם וּתְשׁוּעָה בְּרֹב יוֹעֵץ׃ רַע־יֵרוֹעַ
one Evil .counselor a in but the fall (wise) the In
suffers great (is) safety ;people counsel of absence

8551 2580 802 982 8628 8130 2114 6148
16 כִּי־עָרַב זָר וְשֹׂנֵא תֹקְעִים בּוֹטֵחַ׃ אֵשֶׁת־חֵן תִּתְמֹךְ כָּבוֹד
;honor holds gracious a (is) strikers one but an is he when
to woman safe (hands of) hating ;alien for surety

7607 5916 2617 376 5315 1580 6239 8551 6184
17 וְעָרִיצִים יִתְמְכוּ־עֹשֶׁר׃ גֹּמֵל נַפְשׁוֹ אִישׁ חָסֶד וְעֹכֵר שְׁאֵרוֹ
own his but merciful a his (to) Treats .riches hold terrify- and
flesh troubles man soul own (well) to (men) ing

571 7938 6666 2232 8267 6468 6213 7563 394
18 אַכְזָרִי׃ רָשָׁע עֹשֶׂה פְעֻלַּת־שָׁקֶר וְזֹרֵעַ צְדָקָה שֶׂכֶר אֱמֶת׃
.truth re- a righteous- one but ;falsehood a makes The the
of ward (has) ness sowing of wage wicked .cruel

3068 8441 4194 7451 7291 2416 6666
19 20 כֵּן־צְדָקָה לְחַיִּים וּמְרַדֵּף רָעָה לְמוֹתוֹ׃ תּוֹעֲבַת יְהוָה
Jehovah Hateful his to evil one but (is) righteous- Gen-
(are) to .death own pursuing ;life to ness uine

7451 5352 3808 3027 3027 1870 8549 7522 3820 6141
21 עִקְּשֵׁי־לֵב וּרְצוֹנוֹ תְּמִימֵי דָרֶךְ׃ יָד לְיָד לֹא־יִנָּקֶה רָּע
the be shall not (join) (Though) .way up- the His but ;heart per- the
,one evil innocent hand to hand in right delight of verse

3303 802 2386 639 2091 5141 4422 6662 2233
22 וְזֶרַע צַדִּיקִים נִמְלָט׃ נֶזֶם זָהָב בְּאַף חֲזִיר אִשָּׁה יָפָה
beauti- a (is) a in gold A .escapes the the but
,ful woman ,swine's snout of ring righteous of seed

7563 8615 2896 389 6662 8378 2940 5493
23 וְסָרַת טָעַם׃ תַּאֲוַת צַדִּיקִים אַךְ־טוֹב תִּקְוַת רְשָׁעִים
the the ;good (is) the The discre- turn- even
wicked of hope only righteous of desire .tion aside ing

4270 389 3476 2820 5750 3254 6340 3426 5678
24 עֶבְרָה׃ יֵשׁ מְפַזֵּר וְנוֹסָף עוֹד וְחוֹשֵׂךְ מִיֹּשֶׁר אַךְ־לְמַחְסוֹר׃
to (comes) rightness a but ,more in- yet who one There (is)
poverty only of withholder creases scatters is .wrath

5344 1250 4513 3384 1571 7301 1878 1293 5315
25 26 נֶפֶשׁ־בְּרָכָה תְדֻשָּׁן וּמַרְוֶה גַּם־הוּא יוֹרֶא׃ מֹנֵעַ בָּר יִקְּבֻהוּ
curse grain One drink will he also he and be shall blessing The
him back holding ,fully ,watering ,fat made of soul

7522 1245 2896 7836 7666 7218 1293 3816
27 לְאוֹם וּבְרָכָה לְרֹאשׁ מַשְׁבִּיר׃ שֹׁחֵר טוֹב יְבַקֵּשׁ רָצוֹן
,favor seeks good early One selling one the to a but the
seeking .grain of head blessing ;people

5929 5307 6239 982 935 7451 1875
28 וְדֹרֵשׁ רָעָה תְבוֹאֶנּוּ׃ בּוֹטֵחַ בְּעָשְׁרוֹ הוּא יִפֹּל וְכֶעָלֶה
a like but shall he his in one shall it ,evil one but
leaf green ;fall ,riches trusting ;him to come pursuing

2450 191 5650 7307 5157 1004 5916 6524 6662
29 צַדִּיקִים יִפְרָחוּ׃ עֹכֵר בֵּיתוֹ יִנְחַל־רוּחַ וְעֶבֶד אֱוִיל לַחֲכַם־
the to the a and the inherits his One shall the
of wise fool (is) servant ;wind house troubling .flourish righteous

heart. [30]The fruit of the
righteous *is* a tree of life; and
he who takes souls *is* wise.
[31]Behold, the righteous shall
be rewarded in the earth;
much more the wicked and
the sinner.

CHAPTER 12

[1]Whoever loves instruc-
tion loves knowledge; but
he who hates correction *is*
like a brute animal. [2]The
good obtain grace from
Jehovah; but He will con-
demn a man of wicked
devices. [3]A man shall not
be established by wicked-
ness; but the root of the
righteous shall not be
moved. [4]A woman of virtue
is a crown to her lord; but
one causing shame is like
rottenness in his bones.
[5]The thoughts of the
righteous *are* right; the
counsels of the wicked *are*
deceit. [6]The words of the
wicked ambush *for* blood;
but the mouth of the upright
shall deliver them. [7]Over-
throw the wicked, and they
are not; but the house of the
righteous stands. [8]A man
shall be praised according
to his wisdom; but he who is
of a crooked heart shall be
despised. [9]*He who is*
despised, and *has* a servant, *is* better than one
being honored and lacking
bread. [10]The righteous
knows the life of his animal;
but the mercies of the
wicked *are* cruel. [11]He who
tills his land shall be
satisfied *with* bread; but he
chasing vanities lacks heart.
[12]The wicked desires the
net of evils, but the root *of*
the righteous gives *fruit*.
[13]In the transgression of the
lips *is* the snare of evil; but
the righteous will come out
from distress.

[14]A man shall be satis-
fied with good by the fruit
of the mouth; and the
dealing of man's hands
will return to him. [15]The
way of a fool *is* right in his
own eyes, but one listen-
ing to counsel *is* wise.
[16]A fool's vexation is
known in a day, but the
astute one covers shame.

6662 2009 2450 5315 3947 2416 6086 6662 6529 3820
30 31 לֵב׃ פְּרִי־צַדִּיק עֵץ חַיִּים וְלֹקֵחַ נְפָשׁוֹת חָכָם׃ הֵן צַדִּיק
the ,Behold (is) souls one and ;life tree a the fruit The .heart
righteous .wise taking of (is) just of

2398 7563 637 389 7999 776
בָּאָרֶץ יְשֻׁלָּם אַף כִּי־רָשָׁע וְחוֹטֵא׃
the and the in- also be will the in
.sinner wicked deed repaid earth

CAP. XII יב

CHAPTER 12

6329 2896 1198 8433 8130 1847 157 4148 157
1 2 אֹהֵב מוּסָר אֹהֵב דָּעַת וְשֹׂנֵא תוֹכַחַת בָּעַר׃ טוֹב יָפִיק
obtains The (is) correction one but ;knowledge (is) instruc- One
good .brutish hating loving tion loving

7562 120 3559 7561 4209 376 3068 7522
3 רָצוֹן מֵיְהוָה וְאִישׁ מְזִמּוֹת יַרְשִׁיעַ׃ לֹא־יִכּוֹן אָדָם בְּרֶשַׁע
wick- by a be will Not will He evil a but from favor
;edness man established .condemn plots of man ,Jehovah

7538 1167 5850 2428 802 4131 6662 8328
4 וְשֹׁרֶשׁ צַדִּיקִים בַּל־יִמּוֹט׃ אֵשֶׁת־חַיִל עֲטֶרֶת בַּעְלָהּ וּכְרָקָב
as but her the (is) virtue A will not the the but
rottenness ;lord of crown of woman .totter righteous of root

8458 4941 6662 4284 954 6106
5 בְּעַצְמוֹתָיו מְבִישָׁה׃ מַחְשְׁבוֹת צַדִּיקִים מִשְׁפָּט תַּחְבֻּלוֹת
the (are) the thoughts The one is his in
of counsel ;justice righteous of .shame causing bones

3477 6310 1818 693 7563 1697 4820 7563
6 רְשָׁעִים מִרְמָה׃ דִּבְרֵי רְשָׁעִים אֱרָב־דָּם וּפִי יְשָׁרִים
the but ,blood am- the words The (is) the
upright's mouth (for) bush wicked of .deceit wicked

6310 5975 6662 1004 369 7563 2015 5337
7 8 יַצִּילֵם׃ הָפוֹךְ רְשָׁעִים וְאֵינָם וּבֵית צַדִּיקִים יַעֲמֹד׃ לְפִי
the By .stands the the but they and the Overthrow delivers
of mouth righteous of house ,not are ,wicked .them

7034 2896 937 3830 5953 376 1984 7922
9 שִׂכְלוֹ יְהֻלַּל־אִישׁ וְנַעֲוֵה־לֵב יִהְיֶה לָבוּז׃ טוֹב נִקְלֶה
despised a Better .despised shall heart the but a be shall his
one (is) become of perverse ,man praised prudence

929 5315 6662 3045 3899 2638 3513 5650
10 וְעֶבֶד לוֹ מִמִּתְכַּבֵּד וַחֲסַר־לָחֶם׃ יוֹדֵעַ צַדִּיק נֶפֶשׁ בְּהֶמְתּוֹ
his the the Knows .bread and -honor- one than to a and
,beast of life righteous lacking himself ing him servant

7291 3899 7646 127 5647 394 7563 7356
11 וְרַחֲמֵי רְשָׁעִים אַכְזָרִי׃ עֹבֵד אַדְמָתוֹ יִשְׂבַּע־לָחֶם וּמְרַדֵּף
one but (with) be will his who He (are) the the but
pursuing ,bread satisfied land serves .cruel wicked of mercies

6662 8328 7451 4685 7563 2530 3820 2638 7386
12 רֵיקִים חֲסַר־לֵב׃ חָמַד רָשָׁע מְצוֹד רָעִים וְשֹׁרֶשׁ צַדִּיקִים
the a but evils the the Desires .heart lacks vanities
righteous (to) root of net wicked

6529 6662 6864 3118 7451 4170 8193 6588 5414
13 14 יִתֵּן׃ בְּפֶשַׁע שְׂפָתַיִם מוֹקֵשׁ רָע וַיֵּצֵא מִצָּרָה צַדִּיק׃ מִפְּרִי
the From the from will but;evil snare the the In .gives
of fruit .righteous distress emerge of (is) lips of transgression

191 1870 7725 120 1576 2896 7646 376 6310
15 פִי־אִישׁ יִשְׂבַּע־טוֹב וּגְמוּל יְדֵי־אָדָם יָשׁוּב לוֹ׃ דֶּרֶךְ אֱוִיל
fool a The to will a hands the and (with) is he a mouth
of way .him return man's of dealing ;good satisfied man's

3708 3045 3117 191 2450 6098 8085 5869 3477
16 יָשָׁר בְּעֵינָיו וְשֹׁמֵעַ לְעֵצָה חָכָם׃ אֱוִיל בַּיּוֹם יִוָּדַע כַּעְסוֹ
vex- his is a in fool A (is) to one but his in is
ation known day .wise counsel listening eyes own right

8267 5707 6664 5046 530 6315 6185 7036 3680
17 וְכֹסֶה קָלוֹן עָרוּם׃ יָפִיחַ אֱמוּנָה יַגִּיד צֶדֶק וְעֵד שְׁקָרִים
falsehoods a but right- reveals faith- who He the shame but
of witness ,eousness fulness breathes .astute covers

[17]He who breathes truth reveals righteousness; but a false witness deceit. [18]There is a rash speaking like thrusts of a sword; but the tongue of the wise heals. [19]The lips of truth are established forever; but a lying tongue *is only* while I wink. [20]Deceit *is* in the heart of those who plot evil; but to counselors of peace *is* joy. [21]No trouble shall happen to the just; but the wicked shall be filled with evil. [22]Lying lips *are* hateful to Jehovah; but those who deal faithfulness *are* His delight. [23]A wise man conceals knowledge; but the heart of fools calls out their folly. [24]The hand of the hard worker shall rule; but the idle will become forced labor. [25]Heaviness in a man's heart makes it droop, but a good word makes it glad. [26]The righteous searches out *with* his friend; but the way of the wicked leads them astray. [27]The lazy one does not start after his game; but the wealth of a working man *is* precious. [28]In the way of righteousness *is* life; and in that pathway *is* no death.

4832 2450 3956 2719 4094 981 3426 4820
18 מִרְמָה׃ יֵשׁ בּוֹטֶה כְּמַדְקְרוֹת חָרֶב וּלְשׁוֹן חֲכָמִים מַרְפֵּא׃
(is) the the but a thrusts like rash a There .deceit
.healing wise of tongue ;sword of speaking is

4820 8267 3956 7280 5704 5703 3559 571 8193
19 שְׂפַת־אֱמֶת תִּכּוֹן לָעַד וְעַד־אַרְגִּיעָה לְשׁוֹן שָׁקֶר׃ מִרְמָה
20
Deceit .falsehood a (is) I (only) but .forever are truth The
(is) of tongue wink while established of lips

6662 577 3808 8057 7965 3289 7451 2790 3820
21 בְּלֶב־חֹרְשֵׁי רָע וּלְיֹעֲצֵי שָׁלוֹם שִׂמְחָה׃ לֹא־יְאֻנֶּה לַצַּדִּיק
the to shall Not .joy (is) peace to but ,evil those the in
righteous happen of counselors plotting of heart

8267 8193 3068 8441 7451 4390 7563 205 3605
22 כָּל־אָוֶן וּרְשָׁעִים מָלְאוּ רָע׃ תּוֹעֲבַת יְהוָה שִׂפְתֵי־שָׁקֶר
,falsehood lips Jehovah abomi- An (with) be shall the but every
of to ination .evil filled wicked .trouble

3684 3820 1847 3680 6185 120 7522 530 6213
23 וְעֹשֵׂי אֱמוּנָה רְצוֹנוֹ׃ אָדָם עָרוּם כֹּסֶה דָּעַת וְלֵב כְּסִילִים
fools the but knowl- covers shrewd A His (are) faith- those but
of heart ,edge man .delight fulness do who

4522 1961 7423 4910 2742 3027 200 7121
24 יִקְרָא אִוֶּלֶת׃ יַד־חָרוּצִים תִּמְשׁוֹל וּרְמִיָּה תִּהְיֶה לָמַס׃
forced will re- but shall hard the The .folly calls
.labor become ones miss ,rule workers of hand out

8446 8056 2896 1697 7812 376 3820 1674
26 דְּאָגָה בְלֶב־אִישׁ יַשְׁחֶנָּה וְדָבָר טוֹב יְשַׂמְּחֶנָּה׃ יָתֵר
Searches it makes good a but it makes a in Anxiety
out .glad word ,droop man's heart

7423 2760 3808 8582 7563 1870 6662 7453
27 מֵרֵעֵהוּ צַדִּיק וְדֶרֶךְ רְשָׁעִים תַּתְעֵם׃ לֹא־יַחֲרֹךְ רְמִיָּה
re- the does Not misleads the the but the his (with)
one miss after start .them wicked of way ,righteous friend

1870 2416 6666 734 2742 3368 120 1952 6718
28 צֵידוֹ וְהוֹן־אָדָם יָקָר חָרוּץ׃ בְּאֹרַח־צְדָקָה חַיִּים וְדֶרֶךְ
the and (is) righteousness the In hard a (is) man's but his
of way ,life of path .working precious wealth ;prey

4194 3808 5410
נְתִיבָה אַל־מָוֶת׃
.death (is) (that)
not path

CHAPTER 13

[1]A wise son *hears* his father's instruction; but a scorner does not hear rebuke. [2]From the fruit of his mouth a man eats good; but the desire of the deceiver *is* violence. [3]He who guards his mouth keeps his life; he who opens his lips wide *is* ruined. [4]The sluggard's soul is craving, but *is* not *getting*; but the soul of the hard workers shall be made fat. [5]The righteous hates lying; but the wicked is odious and acts shamefully. [6]Righteousness keeps the upright one in the way; but wickedness overthrows sin. [7]There are *those* who act rich, yet *have* nothing at all; *and those* who act poor, yet *have* great wealth. [8]The ransom of a man's life *are*

CAP. XIII יג

CHAPTER 13

376 6310 6529 1606 8085 3808 3887 1 4148 2450 1121
1 בֵּן חָכָם מוּסַר אָב וְלֵץ לֹא־שָׁמַע גְּעָרָה׃ מִפְּרִי פִי־אִישׁ
2
a mouth the From .rebuke does not a but his instruction wise A
man's of fruit hear scorner ;father's (hears) son

5315 8104 6310 5341 2555 898 5315 2896 398
3 יֹאכַל טוֹב וְנֶפֶשׁ בֹּגְדִים חָמָס׃ נֹצֵר פִּיו שֹׁמֵר נַפְשׁוֹ
his keeps his who He (eats) treach- the the but ,good he
;soul mouth guards violence erous of soul eats

5315 6102 5315 369 183 4288 8193 6589
4 פֹּשֵׂק שְׂפָתָיו מְחִתָּה־לוֹ׃ מִתְאַוָּה וָאַיִן נַפְשׁוֹ עָצֵל וְנֶפֶשׁ
the but the soul the not but ,Craving to ruin his who he
of soul ;lazy of (is getting) .him (is) ,lips wide opens

887 7563 6662 8130 8267 1697 1878 2742
5 חָרֻצִים תְּדֻשָּׁן׃ דְּבַר־שֶׁקֶר יִשְׂנָא צַדִּיק וְרָשָׁע יַבְאִישׁ
is the but the hates false- A be will hard
odious wicked ;righteous hood of word fat made workers

2403 5557 7564 1870 8537 5341 6666 2659
6 וְיַחְפִּיר׃ צְדָקָה תִּצֹּר תָּם־דָּרֶךְ וְרִשְׁעָה תְּסַלֵּף חַטָּאת׃
.sin over- but ,way the guards Righteous- acts and
throws wickedness of perfect ness .shamefully

376 5315 3724 7227 1952 7326 3605 369 6238
7 יֵשׁ מִתְעַשֵּׁר וְאֵין כֹּל מִתְרוֹשֵׁשׁ וְהוֹן רָב׃ כֹּפֶר נֶפֶשׁ־אִישׁ
8
a life The .much but acting one a but acting one There
man's of ransom wealth ,poor ;all not (has) ,rich is

his riches but the poor man
does not hear rebuke. [9]The
light of the righteous rejoices; but the lamp of the
wicked shall be put out.
[10]Argument only comes by
pride; but wisdom *is* with
those who take advice.
[11]Wealth from vanity shall
be diminished; but he who
gathers by labor shall increase. [12]Hope deferred
makes the heart sick; but
desire fulfilled *is* a tree of
life. [13]He who despises the
word shall be destroyed; but
he who fears the command-
ment shall be rewarded.
[14]The law of the wise *is* a
fountain of life, to depart
from the snares of death.
[15]Good sense gives grace;
but the way of the
treacherous *is* continual.
[16]Every prudent one deals
with knowledge; but a fool
lays open *his* foolishness.
[17]A wicked messenger falls
into evil; but a faithful
ambassador *is* healing.
[18]Poverty and shame *shall*
be to him who refuses
instruction; but he who
keeps to correction shall be
honored. [19]The desire
coming to pass is sweet to
the soul; but to depart from
evil is hateful to fools.
[20]He who walks with the
wise shall be wise; but a
feeder of fools shall be
broken. [21]Evil pursues sinners; but the righteous shall
be rewarded *with* good.
[22]A good man leaves an
inheritance to his son's
sons; but the wealth of the
sinner *is* laid up for the
just. [23]The tilled ground of
the poor yields much food;
but without justice, it is
swept away. [24]He who
spares his rod hates his son;
but he who loves him seeks
him *with* correction. [25]The
righteous eats to the satis-
fying of his appetite; but the
belly of the wicked shall
lack.

CHAPTER 14

[1]A wise woman builds her
house, but the foolish pulls
it down with her own hands.
[2]He who walks in his

5216 8056 6662 216 1606 8085 3808 7326 6239
9 עשרו ורש לא־שמע גערה: אור־צדיקים ישמח ונר
but ;rejoices the The .rebuke does not the but his (is)
lamp righteous of light hear poor ,riches

2451 3289 4683 5414 2087 1846 7563
10 רשעים ידעך: רק־בזדון יתן מצה ואת־נועצים חכמה:
(is) those with but ,strife comes by Only put is the
,wisdom counsel taking pride .out wicked's

4900 8431 7235 3027 6908 4591 1892 1952
11
12 הון מהבל ימעט וקבץ על־יד ירבה: תוחלת ממשכה
deferred Hope shall hand by one but will from Wealth
.increase gathering ;dwindle vanity

2252 1697 936 935 8378 2416 6086 3820 2470
13 מחלה לב ועץ חיים תאוה באה: בז לדבר יחבל לו
him- ruins the One .fulfilled (is) life a but the makes
;self word despising desire of tree ;heart sick

5493 2416 4726 2459 8451 7999 4687 3373
14 וירא מצוה הוא ישלם: תורת חכם מקור חיים לסור
turn to ,life a (is) the The be shall he the one but
away of fountain wise of law .rewarded ,command fearing

386 898 1870 2880 2896 7922 4194 4170
15 ממקשי מות: שכל־טוב יתן־חן ודרך בגדים איתן:
con- (is) the but ;grace gives good Pru- .death the from
.tinual traitors of way dence of snares

7513 4397 200 6566 3684 1847 6213 6185 3605
16
17 כל־ערום יעשה בדעת וכסיל יפרש אולת: מלאך רשע
wicked mes- A (his) lays a but with deals shrewd Every
senger .folly open fool ,knowledge (one)

4148 6544 7036 7389 4832 529 6735 7451 5307
18 יפל ברע וציר אמונים מרפא: ריש וקלון פורע מוסר
chastise- one shame and Poverty (is) faith- an but into falls
,ment ignoring (for) ,healing ful envoy ,evil

8441 5315 6149 1961 8378 3513 8433 8104
19 ושמר תוכחת יכבד: תאוה נהיה תערב לנפש ותועבת
is it but the to is so (when) The be shall correction one but
to hateful ,soul sweet comes (it) desire .honored keeping

3684 7462 2449 2450 1980 7451 5493 3684
20 כסילים סור מרע: הלוך את־חכמים וחכם ורעה כסילים
fools a but be shall the with who He from turn to fools
of feeder ,wise wise walks .evil away

2896 7999 6662 7451 7291 2400 7321
21 ירוע: חטאים תרדף רעה ואת־צדיקים ישלם־טוב:
(with) be shall the but ,evil are Sinners suffers
good rewarded righteous by pursued .evil

400 7230 2398 2428 6662 6845 1121 1121 5157 2896
22
23 טוב ינחיל בני־בנים וצפון לצדיק חיל חוטא: רב־אכל
food Much the wealth the for is and (his) sons makes good A
(yields) .sinner's righteous stored ,sons of inherit (man)

8130 7626 2820 4941 3808 5595 3426 7326 5215
24 ניר ראשים ויש נספה בלא משפט: חושך שבטו שונא
is his who He .justice when swept but the fallow
hating rod holds back (is) not away is (it) ,poor's land

990 5315 7648 398 6662 4148 7836 157 1121
25 בנו ואהבו שחרו מוסר: צדיק אכל לשבע נפשו ובטן
the but his satis- to eats The (with) seeks he but his
of belly ,soul's faction righteous .correction him him loving ,son

2637 7563
רשעים תחסר:
shall the
.lack wicked

CAP. XIV יד

CHAPTER 14

1980 2040 3027 200 1004 1129 802 2454
1
2 חכמות נשים בנתה ביתה ואולת בידיה תהרסנו: הולך
One pulls it her with the but her build women Wise
walking .down hands foolish ;house

uprightness fears Jehovah; but the perverse in his ways despises Him. 3A rod of pride *is* in the mouth of a fool; but the lips of the wise shall keep them. 4The stall *is* empty where there *are* no oxen; but much gain *is* by the strength of an ox. 5A faithful witness will not lie; but a false witness breathes lies. 6A scorner seeks wisdom but *finds* it not; yet knowledge *is* swift to the discerning. 7Leave a foolish man, or you will not see the lips of knowledge. 8The wisdom of the wise *is* to understand his way; but the foolishness of fools *is* deceit. 9Fools laugh at guilt-offering; but among the righteous *is* favor. 10The heart knows the bitterness of its soul; and a stranger does not mix in its joy. 11The wicked's house shall be thrown down; but the tent of the upright will flourish. 12There is a way *that seems* right to a man; but the end of it *is* the ways of death. 13Even in laughter the heart is sorrowful; and the end of that joy *is* heaviness. 14The backslider in heart shall be filled with his own ways; but a good man from himself. 15The simple believes everything; but the wise considers his step. 16The wise fears and departs from evil; but the fool rages and is sure. 17He who is short of temper acts foolishly; and a man of *evil* plots is hated. 18The simple inherit foolishness; but the wise are crowned *with* knowledge. 19The evil bow before the good; yea, the wicked at the gates of the just. 20The poor is hated even by his own neighbor; but the rich *has* many friends. 21He who despises his neighbor sins; but he who has mercy on the poor, O how happy *is* he! 22Do not those who think evil go astray? But mercy and truth *will be* to those who think

2415 191 6310 959 1870 38,68 3068 3373 3476
3 בישרו ירא יהוה ונלוז דרכיו בוזהו: בפי־אויל חטר
a (is) a the In depises his in the but ,Jehovah fears up his in
of rod fool of mouth .Him ways perverse rightness

1249 18 504 369 8104 24,50 8193 1346
4 גאוה ושפתי חכמים תשמורם: באין אלפים אבוס בר
(is) the ,cattle Where preserve the the but ;pride
;clean manger no (are) .them wise of lips

6315 3577 38,08 529 5707 7794 3581 83·93 7230
5 ורב־תבואות בכח שור: עד אמונים לא יכזב ויפיח
but will not faithful A .ox an the by increase but
breathes ;lie witness of strength much

7043 995 1847 369 2451 38,87 1245 8267 5707 35·76
6 כזבים עד שקר: בקש־לץ חכמה ואין ודעת לנבון נקל:
is the to but it and ,wisdom A seeks .false a lies
.swift discerning ,knowledge ;not is scorner witness

2451 1847 8193 3045 1077 3684 376 5048 32,12
7 8 לך מנגד לאיש כסיל ובל־ידעת שפתי־דעת: חכמת
The .knowledge the will you or ,foolish man a from Go
of wisdom of lips know not before

38,87 191 4820 3684 200 1870 995 6175
9 ערום הבין דרכו ואולת כסילים מרמה: אולים יליץ
mock Fools .deceit (is) fools the but his discerns the
of folly ;way astute

8057 5315 47·87 3045 38,20 7522 3477 996 816
10 אשם ובין ישרים רצון: לב יודע מרת נפשו ובשמחתו
its in and its bitter- knows The (is) the but at
joy soul of ness heart favor upright among ;guilt

6524 3477 168 8045 7563 1004 2114 6148 3808
11 לא־יתערב זר: בית רשעים ישמד ואהל ישרים יפריח:
will the the but be will The house a does not
flourish upright of tent wasted wicked's .stranger share

1571 4194 1870 319 376 6440 3477 1870 3426
12 13 יש דרך ישר לפני־איש ואחריתה דרכי־מות: גם־
Even .death the its but ,man a before (seeming) a There
of ways (is) end upright way is

1870 8424 8057 319 3820 3510 7814
14 בשחק יכאב־לב ואחריתה שמחה תוגה: מדרכיו
his from (is) joy in and the is in
ways own grief end its ;heart pained laughter

1697 36,05 539 6612 2896 376 3820 5472 7646
15 ישבע סוג לב ומעליו איש טוב: פתי יאמין לכל־דבר
;word every believes The .good man a from but ;heart The be will
simple himself of backslider filled

5674 36·84 7451 5493 3373 2450 838 995 61·85
16 וערום יבין לאשרו: חכם ירא וסר מרע וכסיל מתעבר
passes the but from and fears The .step his watches the but
over foolish ,evil turns wise prudent

8130 420·9 3,76 200 6213 639 7116 982
17 ובוטח: קצר־אפים יעשה אולת ואיש מזמות ישנא:
.hated is (evil) a and ;foolishly acts (to) who He is and
plots of man anger short (is) .bold

7451 7817 1847 3803 6185 200 66·12 5157
18 19 נחלו פתאים אולת וערומים יכתרו דעת: שחו רעים
The will (with) are the but foolish- The inherit
evil bow .knowledge circled prudent ;ness simple

8130 7453 1571 6662 81·79 75·63 2896 6440
20 לפני טובים ורשעים על־שערי צדיק: גם־לרעהו ישנא
is his by Even the the at the and the before
hated neighbor .just of gates wicked ;good

60·35 2603 2398 7453 936 7227 6223 157 7326
21 רש ואהבי עשיר רבים: בז־לרעהו חוטא ומחונן ענוים
the he but ;sins his who He (are) rich the but the
,poor favors who neighbor despises .many of lovers ;poor

2896 2790 571 2617 7451 2790 8582 19,80 835
22 אשריו: הלוא יתעו חרשי רע וחסד ואמת חרשי טוב:
.good devisers truth and But ?evil devisors astray not Do happy
of (follow) mercy of go !he (is)

of good. 23 In all labor there is profit; but the talk of the lips *tends* only to poverty. 24 The crown of the wise *is* their riches *of wisdom*; the foolishness of fools *is* folly. 25 A true witness delivers souls; but a deceitful *witness* speaks lies. 26 In the fear of Jehovah *is* strong trust; and His sons shall have a hiding place. 27 The fear of Jehovah *is* a fountain of life, to turn away from snares of death. 28 In the multitude of people *is* the king's glory; but in the lack of people *is* the ruin of a prince. 29 One slow *to* anger *is* of great understanding; but he who is short of spirit exalts folly. 30 A healthy heart *is* the life of the flesh; but envy *is* the rottenness of the bones. 31 He who oppresses the poor curses his Maker; but he who honors Him has mercy on the needy. 32 The wicked is thrust out in his wickedness; but the righteous *has* hope in his death. 33 Wisdom rests in the heart of the intelligent; and among fools it is revealed. 34 Righteousness exalts a nation; but sin *is* a shame to any people. 35 The king's favor *is* toward a servant who acts prudently; but his wrath takes place *on* one causing shame.

CHAPTER 15

1 A soft answer turns away wrath; but a hurtful word stirs up anger. 2 The tongue of the wise uses knowledge rightly; but the mouth of fools pours out foolishness. 3 The eyes of Jehovah *are* in every place, watching the evil and the good. 4 A wholesome tongue *is* a tree of life; but perverseness in it *is* a break of the spirit. 5 A fool despises his father's instruction; but he keeping correction is sensible. 6 In the house of the righteous *is* much treasure; but in the gain of the wicked *is*

4270 389 8193 1697 4195 1961 6089 3605
23 בְּכָל־עֶצֶב יִהְיֶה מוֹתָר וּדְבַר שְׂפָתַיִם אַךְ לְמַחְסוֹר׃
.poverty to only lips the the but ,profit there toil all In
(tends) of word is

5315 5337 200 3684 200 6239 2450 5850
24
25 עֲטֶרֶת חֲכָמִים עָשְׁרָם אִוֶּלֶת כְּסִילִים אִוֶּלֶת׃ מַצִּיל נְפָשׁוֹת
souls delivers fool- (is) fools The their is wise the The
ishness of folly .riches of crown

5797 4009 3068 3373 4820 3577 6315 571 5707
26 עֵד אֱמֶת וְיָפִחַ כְּזָבִים מִרְמָה׃ בְּיִרְאַת יְהוָה מִבְטַח־עֹז
;strong (is) Jehovah the In deceit(ful) a lies but ;true A
trust of fear .(witness) breathes witness

5493 2416 4726 3068 3373 4268 1961 1121
27 וּלְבָנָיו יִהְיֶה מַחְסֶה׃ יִרְאַת יְהוָה מְקוֹר חַיִּים לָסוּר
turn to ;life a (is) Jehovah fear The hiding a shall to and
away of fountain of .place be sons His

3816 657 4428 1927 5971 7230 4194 4170
28 מִמֹּקְשֵׁי מָוֶת׃ בְּרָב־עָם הַדְרַת־מֶלֶךְ וּבְאֶפֶס לְאֹם
people the in but the (is) people the In .death the from
of lack king's splendor of multitude of snares

7311 7307 7116 8394 7227 639 750 7333 4288
29 מְחִתַּת רָזוֹן׃ אֶרֶךְ אַפַּיִם רַב־תְּבוּנָה וּקְצַר־רוּחַ מֵרִים
exalts of one but under- of (is) (to) One a the (is)
spirit short ;standing great anger long prince of ruin

7068 6106 7537 4832 3820 1320 2416 200
30 אִוֶּלֶת׃ חַיֵּי בְשָׂרִים לֵב מַרְפֵּא וּרְקַב עֲצָמוֹת קִנְאָה׃
(is) bones the the but ;healing A flesh the (is) .folly
jealousy of rottenness of heart (to) life

1760 7451 34 2603 3513 6213 2778 1800 6231
31
32 עֹשֵׁק דָּל חֵרֵף עֹשֵׂהוּ וּמְכַבְּדוֹ חֹנֵן אֶבְיוֹן׃ בְּרָעָתוֹ יִדָּחֶה
thrust (is) his In the favors one but his curses the op- One
out evildoing .needy Him honoring ,Maker poor pressing

7130 2451 5117 995 3820 6662 4194 2620 7563
33 רָשָׁע וְחֹסֶה בְמוֹתוֹ צַדִּיק׃ בְּלֵב נָבוֹן תָּנוּחַ חָכְמָה וּבְקֶרֶב
and ;wisdom rests under the In the his in has but the
among standing heart .righteous death refuge ;wicked

2403 3816 2617 1471 7311 6666 3045 3684
34 כְּסִילִים תִּוָּדֵעַ׃ צְדָקָה תְרוֹמֵם־גּוֹי וְחֶסֶד לְאֻמִּים חַטָּאת׃
.sin (is) to a but a exalts Righteousness made is it fools
peoples shame ;nation .known

954 8478 5678 7919 5650 4428 7522
רְצוֹן־מֶלֶךְ לְעֶבֶד מַשְׂכִּיל וְעֶבְרָתוֹ תִּהְיֶה מֵבִישׁ׃
35 causer a bottoms his but acts who a to (is) The favor
.shame of (on) wrath ;wisely .servant king's

CAP. XV טו

CHAPTER 15

3956 639 5927 6089 1697 2534 7725 7390 4617
1
2 מַעֲנֶה־רַּךְ יָשִׁיב חֵמָה וּדְבַר־עֶצֶב יַעֲלֶה־אָף׃ לְשׁוֹן
The .anger to causes pain a but ;wrath turns soft answer An
tongue up go to of word away

4725 3605 200 5042 3684 6310 1847 3190 2450
3 חֲכָמִים תֵּיטִיב דָּעַת וּפִי כְסִילִים יַבִּיעַ אִוֶּלֶת׃ בְּכָל־מָקוֹם
place In foolish- makes fools' but knowl- makes wise the
every .ness flow mouth ;ledge good

2416 6086 3956 4832 2896 7451 6822 3068 5869
4 עֵינֵי יְהוָה צֹפוֹת רָעִים וְטוֹבִים׃ מַרְפֵּא לָשׁוֹן עֵץ חַיִּים
;life a (is) tongue A the and the watching Jehovah the
of tree healing .good evil (are) of eyes

8104 1 4148 5006 191 7307 7667 5557
5 וְסֶלֶף בָּהּ שֶׁבֶר בְּרוּחַ׃ אֱוִיל יִנְאַץ מוּסַר אָבִיו וְשֹׁמֵר
one but his instruction despises fool A the in a (is) it in but
keeping father's .spirit breaking perversity

7563 8393 7227 2633 6662 1004 6191 8433
6 תּוֹכַחַת יַעְרִם׃ בֵּית צַדִּיק חֹסֶן רָב וּבִתְבוּאַת רָשָׁע
the the in but ;much (is) the (In) is correction
wicked of increase treasure righteous house astute

trouble. [7]The lips of the wise extend knowledge; but the heart of the fool is not so. [8]The sacrifice of the wicked *is* a hateful thing to Jehovah; but the prayer of the upright *is* His delight. [9]The way of the wicked *is* hateful to Jehovah; but He loves him who pursues righteousness. [10]Discipline *is* grievous to him who forsakes the way; he who hates reproof shall die. [11]Hell and destruction *are* before Jehovah; even more the hearts of the sons of men! [12]A scorner loves not one who corrects him; nor will he go to the wise. [13]A joyful heart makes a good face; but by grief of heart the spirit is stricken. [14]The heart of the understanding one seeks knowledge; but the mouth of fools feeds on folly. [15]All the days of the afflicted *are* evil; but gladness of heart is a continual feast. [16]Better *is* a little with the fear of Jehovah than great treasure and tumult with it. [17]Better *is* a dinner of vegetables where love is, than a stalled ox and hatred with it. [18]A furious man stirs up quarreling; but he who is slow to anger calms fighting. [19]The way of the lazy one *is* like a hedge of thorns; but the path of the righteous *is* exalted. [20]A wise son makes a glad father; but a foolish man despises his mother. [21]Foolishness *is* joy to him who lacks understanding; but a man of understanding walks straight. [22]Without counsel, purposes are broken; but by great counselors they rise. [23]A man *has* joy by the answer of his mouth; and how good *is* a word in its season! [24]The path of life *is* upward to the prudent, that he may turn away from Sheol downward. [25]Jehovah will destroy the house of the proud; but He will set up the widow's border. [26]The thoughts of

3651 3808 3684 38 20 1847 2219 2450 8193 5916
7 נעכרת׃ שפתי חכמים יזרו דעת ולב כסילים לא־כן׃
is not fools the but knowl- scatter the lips The is
.so of heart ;edge wise of .trouble

8441 7522 3477 8605 3068 8441 7563 2077
8 9 זבח רשעים תועבת יהוה ותפלת ישרים רצונו׃ תועבת
hateful (is) His (is) the the but ;Jehovah a (is) the sacri-
to .delight upright of prayer to thing hateful wicked's fice

5800 7451 4148 157 6666 7291 7563 1870 3068
10 יהוה דרך רשע ומרדף צדקה יאהב׃ מוסר רע לעזב
one to (is) Instruction He righteous- one but the The Jehovah
forsaking evil .loves ness pursuing ;wicked of way

637 3068 5048 11 7585 4191 8433 8130 734
11 ארח שונא תוכחת ימות׃ שאול ואבדון נגד יהוה אף
even ;Jehovah (are) and Sheol .die shall reproof one the
before destruction hating ;path

2450 3198 3887 157 3808 120 1121 3826
12 כי־לבות בני־אדם׃ לא־יאהב לץ הוכח לו אל־חכמים
the to ;him who one A does not !men sons the the more
wise corrects scorner love of of hearts

5218 7307 3820 6094 6440 3190 8056 3820 3212 3808
13 לא ילך׃ לב שמח ייטב פנים ובעצבת־לב רוח נכאה׃
is the heart by but a makes joyful A he will not
.stricken spirit of pain ;face good heart .go

3117 3605 200 7462 3684 6310 1847 1245 995 3820
14 15 לב נבון יבקש־דעת ופני כסילים ירעה אולת׃ כל־ימי
the All .folly feeds fools the but knowl- seeks the The
of days on of mouth ;edge wise of heart

3373 4592 2896 8548 4960 3820 2896 7451 6041
16 עני רעים וטוב־לב משתה תמיד׃ טוב־מעט ביראת
the with a Better .continual a (is) heart but (are) the
of fear little is feast of goodness ;evil poor

160 3419 737 2896 4103 7227 214 3068
17 יהוה מאוצר רב ומהומה בו׃ טוב ארחת ירק ואהבה־
love and herbs meal a Better with and great than Jehovah
of .it tumult- treasure

4066 1624 2534 376 8130 75 7794 8033
18 שם משור אבוס ושנאה־בו׃ איש חמה יגרה מדון
;strife stirs fury man A with and being than ,there
up of .it hatred stalled oxen

734 2312 4881 6102 1870 7379 8252 639 750
19 וארך אפים ישקיט ריב׃ דרך עצל כמשכת חדק וארח
the but ;thorns like (is) the The .fighting calms anger one but
of path of hedge a lazy of way (to) long

959 120 3684 8056 2450 1121 5549 3477
20 ישרים סללה׃ בן חכם ישמח־אב וכסיל אדם בוזה
despises a but a makes wise A (is) the
man foolish ;father glad son .exalted upright

3212 3474 8394 376 3820 2638 8057 200 517
21 אמו׃ אולת שמחה לחסר־לב ואיש תבונה יישר־לכת׃
.walks straight under- a but ;heart him to (is) Foolishness his
standing of man lacks who joy .mother

8057 6965 3289 7230 5475 369 4284 6565
22 23 הפר מחשבות באין סוד וברב יועצים תקום׃ שמחה
Joy .rise they counselors by but ;counsel without Purposes frus- are
great trated

2416 734 2896 6256 1697 6310 4617 376
24 לאיש במענה־פיו ודבר בעתו מה־טוב׃ ארח חיים
life The good how its in a and his the by to (is)
of path .(is it) ,time word ;mouth of answer man a

1343 1004 4295 7585 5493 7919 4605
25 למעלה למשכיל למען סור משאול מטה׃ בית גאים
the The .below from may he that the to is
proud of house Sheol turn prudent upward

4284 3068 8441 490 1366 5324 3068 5255
26 יסח יהוה ויצב גבול אלמנה׃ תועבת יהוה מחשבות
thoughts The Jehovah (are) the border He but ;Jehovah pulls
of (to) hateful .widow's up sets

the wicked *are* very hateful
to Jehovah; but the words
of pleasantness *are* pure.
27He who is greedy for gain
troubles his own house; but
he who hates bribes shall
live. 28The heart of the
righteous muses *how* to
answer; but the mouth of
the wicked pours out evil
things. 29Jehovah *is* far
from the wicked; but He
hears the prayer of the
righteous. 30The light of
the eyes rejoices the heart;
a good report makes the
bones fat. 31The ear that
hears the reproof of life
shall remain among the
wise. 32He who refuses
instruction despises his
own soul; but he who hears
reproof gets understanding.
33The fear of Jehovah *is*
instruction in wisdom; and
before honor *is* humility.

CHAPTER 16

1The orderings of the
heart *are* for man, and the
answer of the tongue from
Jehovah. 2All the ways of a
man *are* pure in his own
eyes; but Jehovah weighs
the spirits. 3Roll your
works on Jehovah, and your
thoughts shall be blessed.
4Jehovah has made all for
His purpose; yea, even the
wicked for the day of evil.
5Everyone proud in heart *is*
disgusting *to* Jehovah;
though hand *join* in hand,
he shall not be innocent.
6Iniquity is covered by
mercy and truth; and in the
fear of Jehovah, *men* turn
aside from evil. 7When a
man's ways please Jehovah,
He makes even his enemies
to be at peace with him.
8Better *is* a little with
righteousness than great
increase without right. 9A
man's heart plans his way,
but Jehovah fixes his step.
10A godly decision *is* on the
lips of the king; his mouth is
not treacherous in judg-
ment. 11A just scale and
balances *are* to Jehovah; all
the stones of the bag *are*

8130 1215 1214 1004 5916 5278 561 2889 7451
27 רָע וּטְהֹרִים אִמְרֵי־נֹעַם׃ עֹכֵר בֵּיתוֹ בּוֹצֵעַ בָּצַע וְשׂוֹנֵא
he but unjust who he his Troubles pleasant- the but the
hates who gain gains house ness of words(are) pure ;evil

5042 7563 6310 6030 1897 6662 3820 2421 4979
28 מַתָּנֹת יִחְיֶה׃ לֵב צַדִּיק יֶהְגֶּה לַעֲנוֹת וּפִי רְשָׁעִים יַבִּיעַ
makes the the but to studies the heart The shall bribes
flow wicked of mouth ;answer righteous of .live

8085 6662 8605 7563 3068 7350 7451
29 רָעוֹת׃ רָחוֹק יְהוָה מֵרְשָׁעִים וּתְפִלַּת צַדִּיקִים יִשְׁמָע׃
He the the but the from Jehovah far (is) evil
.hears righteous of prayer ;wicked .things

241 6106 1878 2896 8052 3820 8056 5869 3974
30
31 מְאוֹר־עֵינַיִם יְשַׂמַּח־לֵב שְׁמוּעָה טוֹבָה תְּדַשֶּׁן־עָצֶם׃ אֹזֶן
The the makes good report a the rejoices the The
ear bone fat ;heart eyes of light

4148 6544 3885 2450 7130 2416 8433 8085
32 שֹׁמַעַת תּוֹכַחַת חַיִּים בְּקֶרֶב חֲכָמִים תָּלִין׃ פּוֹרֵעַ מוּסָר
correc- who He shall wisdom the in ,life the that
tion ignores .dwell of midst of reproof hears

4148 3068 3373 3820 7069 8433 8085 5315 3988
33 מוֹאֵס נַפְשׁוֹ וְשׁוֹמֵעַ תּוֹכַחַת קוֹנֶה לֵּב׃ יִרְאַת יְהוָה מוּסַר
instruc- Jehovah The .heart gets reproof he but own his despises
in tion of fear hears who ;soul

6038 3519 6440 2451
חָכְמָה וְלִפְנֵי כָבוֹד עֲנָוָה׃
(is) honor and ;wisdom
.humility before

CAP. XVI טז

CHAPTER 16

376 1870 3605 3956 4617 3068 3820 4623 120
1
2 לְאָדָם מַעַרְכֵי־לֵב וּמֵיְהוָה מַעֲנֵה לָשׁוֹן׃ כָּל־דַּרְכֵי־אִישׁ
a the All the the from and the The are for
man of ways .tongue of answer Jehovah ,heart of arrays man

3559 4639 3068 1516 3068 7307 8505 5869 2134
3 זַךְ בְּעֵינָיו וְתֹכֵן רוּחוֹת יְהוָה׃ גֹּל אֶל־יְהוָה מַעֲשֶׂיךָ וְיִכֹּנוּ
shall and your Jehovah on Roll .Jehovah the but his in (are)
set be works spirits weighs ;eyes own pure

3117 7563 1571 4617 3068 6466 3605 4284
4 מַחְשְׁבֹתֶיךָ׃ כֹּל פָּעַל יְהוָה לַמַּעֲנֵהוּ וְגַם־רָשָׁע לְיוֹם
the for the and His for Jehovah has all your
of day wicked even ,purpose made .thoughts

5352 3808 3027 3027 3820 1361 3605 3068 8441 7451
5 רָעָה׃ תּוֹעֲבַת יְהוָה כָּל־גְּבַהּ־לֵב יָד לְיָד לֹא יִנָּקֶה׃
be will he not in hand in proud (is) Jehovah abomi- An .evil
.innocent hand heart everyone to nation

7521 7451 5493 3068 3373 5771 3722 571 2617
6
7 בְּחֶסֶד וֶאֱמֶת יְכֻפַּר עָוֺן וּבְיִרְאַת יְהוָה סוּר מֵרָע׃ בִּרְצוֹת
When from (men) Jehovah in and ;iniquity is and By
please .evil turn of fear the covered truth mercy

4592 2896 7999 341 1571 376 1870 3068
8 יְהוָה דַּרְכֵי־אִישׁ גַּם־אוֹיְבָיו יַשְׁלִם אִתּוֹ׃ טוֹב מְעַט
a Better with makes He his even a ways Jehovah
little (is) .him peace at enemies ,man's

2803 120 3820 4941 1097 8393 7230 6666
9 בִּצְדָקָה מֵרֹב תְּבוּאוֹת בְּלֹא מִשְׁפָּט׃ לֵב אָדָם יְחַשֵּׁב
plans A heart .justice without increase than righ- with
man's much teousness

4941 4428 8193 7081 6806 3559 3068 1870
10 דַּרְכּוֹ וַיהוָה יָכִין צַעֲדוֹ׃ קֶסֶם ׀ עַל־שִׂפְתֵי־מֶלֶךְ בְּמִשְׁפָּט
judg- in the the on (is) godly A his fixes but his
ment ;king of lips decision .step Jehovah ,way

3605 4639 3068 4941 3976 6425 6310 4603 3808
11 לֹא יִמְעַל־פִּיו׃ פֶּלֶס ׀ וּמֹאזְנֵי מִשְׁפָּט לַיהוָה מַעֲשֵׂהוּ כָּל־
(is) His to (are) justice and scale A his trait- (is) not
all work ;Jehovah of balances .mouth orous

His work. [12]*It is* an abomination for kings to commit wickedness; for the throne is made firm by righteousness. [13]Righteous lips *are* the kings' delight; and he speaking uprightly is loved. [14]A king's fury *is as* messengers of death; but a wise man will cover it. [15]In the light of the face of the king *is* life; and his favor *is* like a cloud of the latter rain. [16]How much better to get wisdom than gold! And to get understanding *is* to be chosen above silver. [17]The way of the upright *is* to turn away from evil; he keeping his soul watches his way. [18]Pride *goes* before destruction, and a haughty spirit before a fall. [19]It is better *to be* of a lowly spirit with the poor than to divide the spoil with the proud. [20]He who acts prudently shall find good; and he who trusts in Jehovah, O how happy is he! [21]The wise in heart shall be called prudent; and sweetness of lips increases learning. [22]Prudence *is* a fountain of life to those who own it; but the teaching of fools *is* folly. [23]The heart of the wise makes his mouth prudent and he adds learning on his lips. [24]Pleasant words *are* an overflowing of honey, sweetness to the soul and healing to the bones. [25]There is a way *that seems* right to a man's face, but the end of it is the ways of death. [26]He who labors works for himself; for his mouth urges him on. [27]A worthless man plots evil; and on his lips *it is* like a burning fire.

[28]A perverse man causes strife; and a whisperer separates close friends. [29]A violent man lures his neighbor, and causes him to go in a way *that is* not good. [30]He who shuts his eyes, to plan perverse things; compressing his lips, he brings evil to pass. [31]The gray head *is* a crown

3559 66 66 7562 6213 4428 8441 3599 68
12 אַבְנֵי־כִיס׃ תּוֹעֲבַת מְלָכִים עֲשׂוֹת רֶשַׁע כִּי בִצְדָקָה יִכּוֹן
is set by righteousness for wickedness to commit kings abomination An for of stones the bag the

157 3477 1696 6664 8193 4428 7522 3678
13 כִּסֵּא׃ רְצוֹן מְלָכִים שִׂפְתֵי־צֶדֶק וְדֹבֵר יְשָׁרִים יֶאֱהָב׃
.loved is uprightly he and speaks who ;Righteous lips kings the (are) of delight the .throne

6440 216 3722 2450 376 4194 4397 4428 2534
14 15 חֲמַת־מֶלֶךְ מַלְאֲכֵי־מָוֶת וְאִישׁ חָכָם יְכַפְּרֶנָּה׃ בְּאוֹר־פְּנֵי־
face the In of light will .it cover wise a but man ;death (as is) of messengers A king's fury

2896 4100 2451 7069 4456 5645 7522 2416 4428
16 מֶלֶךְ חַיִּים וּרְצוֹנוֹ כְּעָב מַלְקוֹשׁ׃ קְנֹה־חָכְמָה מַה־טּוֹב
better how much ,wisdom To get latter the .rain a like (is) of cloud his and favor (is) ;life the king's

5493 3477 4546 3701 977 998 7069 2742
17 מֵחָרוּץ וּקְנוֹת בִּינָה נִבְחָר מִכָּסֶף׃ מְסִלַּת יְשָׁרִים סוּר
to (is) turn the upright highway The of above .silver be to chosen understanding to and get than !gold

6440 1347 7667 6440 1870 5341 5315 8104 7451
18 מֵרָע שֹׁמֵר נַפְשׁוֹ נֹצֵר דַּרְכּוֹ׃ לִפְנֵי־שֶׁבֶר גָּאוֹן וְלִפְנֵי
and before Pride ,(goes) destruction before his .way watches his soul who he keeps from ;evil

7998 2505 6035 7307 8217 2896 7307 1363 3783
19 כִשָּׁלוֹן גֹּבַהּ רוּחַ׃ טוֹב שְׁפַל־רוּחַ אֶת־עֲנִיִּים מֵחַלֵּק שָׁלָל
the spoil to than divide the with ,poor of lowness spirit Better is .spirit a haughty stumbling

3068 982 2896 4672 1697 7919 1343
20 אֶת־גֵּאִים׃ מַשְׂכִּיל עַל־דָּבָר יִמְצָא־טוֹב וּבוֹטֵחַ בַּיהוָה
in ,Jehovah he and trusts who ;good shall find a matter on He who prudently acts the .proud with

3948 3254 4986 995 7121 8193 2450 835
21 אַשְׁרָיו׃ לַחֲכַם־לֵב יִקָּרֵא נָבוֹן וּמֶתֶק שְׂפָתַיִם יֹסִיף לֶקַח׃
persuasion. increases lips sweetness of and understanding be shall called heart The in wise is blessed .he

2450 3820 200 191 4148 1167 7922 2416 4726
22 23 מְקוֹר חַיִּים שֵׂכֶל בְּעָלָיו וּמוּסַר אֱוִלִים אִוֶּלֶת׃ לֵב חָכָם
the wise The of heart (is) .folly fools instruction of the but its to ,owners prudence life (is) well A of

561 1706 6688 3948 3254 8193 5921 6310 7919
24 יַשְׂכִּיל פִּיהוּ וְעַל־שְׂפָתָיו יֹסִיף לֶקַח׃ צוּף־דְּבַשׁ אִמְרֵי־
(are) words (with) honey flowing persuasion he adds his lips and on his ,mouth makes prudent

6440 3477 1870 3426 6106 4832 5315 4966 5278
25 נֹעַם מָתוֹק לַנֶּפֶשׁ וּמַרְפֵּא לָעָצֶם׃ יֵשׁ דֶּרֶךְ יָשָׁר לִפְנֵי־
before (seeming) upright a way There is the to .bones and healing the to soul sweetness Pleas- ;ant

404 6310 6001 5998 5315 4194 1870 319 376
26 אִישׁ וְאַחֲרִיתָהּ דַּרְכֵי־מָוֶת׃ נֶפֶשׁ עָמֵל עָמְלָה לּוֹ כִּי־אָכַף
for urges for ;himself labors who labors The soul .death ways the of its but (is) end a ,man

784 8193 7451 3738 1100 376 6310 5921
27 עָלָיו פִּיהוּ׃ אִישׁ בְּלִיַּעַל כֹּרֶה רָעָה וְעַל־שְׂפָתָיו כְּאֵשׁ
like fire a his lips (is it) and on ;evil digs up worthless man A his .mouth on him

441 6504 5372 4066 7971 8419 376 6867
28 צָרָבֶת׃ אִישׁ תַּהְפֻּכוֹת יְשַׁלַּח מָדוֹן וְנִרְגָּן מַפְרִיד אַלּוּף׃
separates .friends a and slanderer ;strife sends out perversities A of man .burning

6095 2896 3808 1870 3212 7453 6601 2555 376
29 30 אִישׁ חָמָס יְפַתֶּה רֵעֵהוּ וְהוֹלִיכוֹ בְּדֶרֶךְ לֹא־טוֹב׃ עֹצֶה
who He shuts .good not a in way makes and go him his ,neighbor lures violence A of man

5850 7451 3615 8193 7169 8419 2803 5869
31 עֵינָיו לַחְשֹׁב תַּהְפֻּכוֹת קֹרֵץ שְׂפָתָיו כִּלָּה רָעָה׃ עֲטֶרֶת
crown A of .evil finishes (in) his ,lips compressing perverse things plan to his eyes

of glory; it is found in the way of righteousness. 32One slow to anger *is* better than the mighty; and he who rules his spirit than he who takes a city. 33The lot is cast into the lap, but all ordering of it *is* from Jehovah.

CHAPTER 17

1Better *is* a dry piece of bread, and quietness with it, than a house full of sacrifices *with* fighting. 2A servant who acts prudently shall rule over a son who causes shame; and *he* shall have part of the inheritance among the brothers. 3The refining pot *is* for silver, and the furnace for gold, but Jehovah tries the hearts. 4An evildoer gives heed to false lips; a liar listens to a tongue of *evil* desire. 5Whoever scorns the poor reviles his Maker; he who rejoices at calamity shall not be innocent. 6Grandsons *are* the crown of old men; and the glory of sons *is* their fathers. 7An arrogant lip *is* not fitting for a fool; much less are lying lips *for* a noble. 8A bribe *is* a precious stone in the eyes of him who possesses it; wherever he turns, he is circumspect. 9He who covers a transgression seeks love; but he who repeats a matter separates friends. 10A reproof enters more into a wise man than a hundred stripes into a fool. 11A rebel seeks evil, so a cruel messenger is sent against him. 12Let a bear bereaved *of her cubs* meet a man, rather than a fool in his foolishness. 13Whoever rewards evil for good, evil shall not depart from his house. 14The beginning of strife *is* like the releasing of water; therefore, leave off fighting before it breaks out. 15He who justifies the wicked, and he who condemns the just, even both

639 750 2896 4672 6666 1870 7872 8597

32 תִּפְאֶרֶת שֵׂיבָה בְּדֶרֶךְ צְדָקָה תִּמָּצֵא׃ טוֹב אֶרֶךְ אַפַּיִם

anger One (is) is it righteous- the in gray a glory
(to) long better .found ness of way head

1486 2904 2436 5892 3920 7307 4910 1368

33 מִגִּבּוֹר וּמֹשֵׁל בְּרוּחוֹ מִלֹּכֵד עִיר׃ בַּחֵיק יוּטַל אֶת־הַגּוֹרָל

,lot The is the into a one than his he and the than
cast bosom .city takes who spirit rules who ;mighty

4941 3605 3068

וּמֵיְהוָה כָּל־מִשְׁפָּטוֹ׃

ordering the (is) from but
.it of all Jehovah

CAP. XVII יז

CHAPTER 17

5650 7378 2077 4393 1004 7962 2720 6595 2896

1
2 טוֹב פַּת חֲרֵבָה וְשַׁלְוָה־בָהּ מִבֵּית מָלֵא זִבְחֵי־רִיב׃ עֶבֶד

A (with) sacri- full a than with and dry piece a Better
servant .strife fices of house ,it quietness bread of (is)

5159 2505 251 8432 954 1121 4910 7919

מַשְׂכִּיל יִמְשֹׁל בְּבֶן־מֵבִישׁ וּבְתוֹךְ אַחִים יַחֲלֹק נַחֲלָה׃

inheri- the shall he the and causes who a over shall acts who
.tance share brothers among ;shame son rule prudently

7181 7489 3068 3826 974 2091 3564 3701 4715

3
4 מַצְרֵף לַכֶּסֶף וְכוּר לַזָּהָב וּבֹחֵן לִבּוֹת יְהוָה׃ מֵרַע מַקְשִׁיב

heeds evil- An .Jehovah the but for the and for The
doer hearts tries ;gold furnace ,silver crucible

2778 7326 3932 1942 3956 238 8267 205 8193

5 עַל־שְׂפַת־אָוֶן שֶׁקֶר מֵזִין עַל־לְשׁוֹן הַוֹּת׃ לֹעֵג לָרָשׁ חֵרֵף

reviles the who He (evil) a to listens a ;false lips
poor mocks .desire of tongue liar

1121 1121 2205 5850 5352 3808 343 8056 6213

6 עֹשֵׂהוּ שָׂמֵחַ לְאֵיד לֹא יִנָּקֶה׃ עֲטֶרֶת זְקֵנִים בְּנֵי בָנִים

,sons of Sons old crown the be shall not at who he his
(is) men of .innocent calamity rejoices ;Maker

637 3499 8193 5036 5000 3808 1121 8597

7 וְתִפְאֶרֶת בָּנִים אֲבוֹתָם׃ לֹא־נָאוָה לְנָבָל שְׂפַת יֶתֶר אַף

much ex- lip A a for is not their sons the and
less cess of fool fitting .fathers of glory

1167 5869 7810 2580 68 8267 8193 5081

8 כִּי־לְנָדִיב שְׂפַת־שָׁקֶר׃ אֶבֶן־חֵן הַשֹּׁחַד בְּעֵינֵי בְעָלָיו אֶל־

to its the in the stone A .lying lips for
,owner of eyes bribe (is) grace of of noble a

8138 160 1245 6588 3680 7919 6437 3605

9 כָּל־אֲשֶׁר יִפְנֶה יַשְׂכִּיל׃ מְכַסֶּה־פֶּשַׁע מְבַקֵּשׁ אַהֲבָה וְשֹׁנֶה

one but ,love seeks trans- who He is he he where every
repeating gression covers prudent turns

3684 5221 995 1606 5181 441 6504 1697

10 בְדָבָר מַפְרִיד אַלּוּף׃ תֵּחַת גְּעָרָה בְמֵבִין מֵהַכּוֹת כְּסִיל

a (into) than more an into A goes friends separates matter a
fool blows one astute rebuke down

6298 7971 394 4397 7451 1245 4805 389 3967

11
12 מֵאָה׃ אַךְ־מְרִי יְבַקֶּשׁ־רָע וּמַלְאָךְ אַכְזָרִי יְשֻׁלַּח־בּוֹ׃ פָּגוֹשׁ

Let against is cruel a so ;evil seeks A only a
meet .him sent messenger rebel hundred

8478 7451 7725 200 3684 408 376 7909 1677

13 דֹּב שַׁכּוּל בְּאִישׁ וְאַל־כְּסִיל בְּאִוַּלְתּוֹ׃ מֵשִׁיב רָעָה תַּחַת

instead evil who He his in fool a and ,man a bereaved a
of returns .foolishness not (cubs of) bear

4066 7225 4325 6362 1004 7451 4185 3808 2896

14 טוֹבָה לֹא־תָמִישׁ רָעָה מִבֵּיתוֹ׃ פּוֹטֵר מַיִם רֵאשִׁית מָדוֹן

strife be- The water the (like) from evil shall not ,good
;(is) of ginning of releasing .house his depart

6662 7561 7563 6663 5203 7378 1566 6440

15 וְלִפְנֵי הִתְגַּלַּע הָרִיב נְטוֹשׁ׃ מַצְדִּיק רָשָׁע וּמַרְשִׁיעַ צַדִּיק

the and the who He for- striving breaks it so
just condemns ,wicked justifies .sake ,out before

of them *are* disgusting to Jehovah. [16]Why *is there* hire in a fool's hand to get wisdom, and there is no heart *for it*. [17]A friend loves at every time; but a brother is born for the time of trouble. [18]A man lacking heart strikes the palm; he pledges in the presence of his friend. [19]He loving strife loves rebellion; he who exalts his door seeks shattering. [20]One crooked of heart does not find good; and he who *is* perverse in his tongue falls into evil. [21]He who fathers a fool has sorrow for it; yea, the father of a fool has no joy. [22]A cheerful heart makes good healing; but a stricken spirit dries the bone. [23]The wicked takes a bribe out of the bosom to stretch the paths of justice.

[24]With the face of the wise *is* wisdom; but a fool's eyes *are* in the ends of the earth. [25]A foolish son *is* a vexation to his father; and bitterness to her who bore him. [26]And it *is* not good to punish the just; to strike leaders for uprightness. [27]He who restrains his words knows knowledge; and a man of understanding *is* of a rare spirit. [28]Even a fool who is silent *is* thought wise, he who shuts his lips *to be* understanding.

CHAPTER 18

[1]He who separates himself seeks *his own* desire; he breaks out against all sound wisdom. [2]A fool has no delight in understanding, but only in uncovering his heart. [3]When the wicked comes, scorn comes, too; and with shame *comes* reproach. [4]The words of a man's mouth *are* like deep waters; the fountain of wisdom *like* a flowing brook. [5]To lift up the face of the wicked *is* not good; *nor* to turn aside the

16 תועבת יהוה גם־שניהם׃ למה־זה מחיר ביד־כסיל

a fool · the in hand of · hire · (is) this · Why · of both them · even ,Jehovah · (are) to hateful

17 לקנות חכמה ולב־אין׃ בכל־עת אהב הרע ואח לצרה

for trouble · a and brother · the friend; · loves · time every · At · is there ?not heart · a and wisdom · to obtain

18 יולד׃ אדם חסר־לב תקע כף ערב ערבה לפני רעהו׃

his .friend · before · a pledge · he pledges · the palm; · strikes · lacking heart · A man · is .born

19 אהב פשע אהב מצה מגביה פתחו מבקש־שבר׃ עקש־

of One crooked · ,shattering · seeks · his door · who he exalts · ;strife · loves · trans-gression · who He loves

21 לב לא ימצא־טוב ונהפך בלשונו יפול ברעה׃ ילד

who He fathers · into .evil · falls · his in tongue · one and perverse · ;good · finds · not heart

22 כסיל לתוגה לו ולא ישמח אבי נבל׃ לב שמח ייטב

makes good · joyful · A heart · .fool a · the of father · will rejoice · and not · for ;it · into grief · fool a (falls)

23 גהה ורוח נכאה תיבש־גרם׃ שחד מחיק רשע יקח

;takes · The wicked · of out bosom the · bribe a · the .bone · dries · stricken · a but spirit · ;healing

24 להטות ארחות משפט׃ את־פני מבין חכמה ועיני כסיל

fool a · the but of eyes · (is) ;wisdom · the wise · the With of face · .justice · paths of · the · to stretch

25
26 בקצה־ארץ׃ כעס לאביו בן כסיל וממר ליולדתו׃ גם

Also · who her to .him bore · and bitterness · ;foolish son · A · his to father · a (is) vexation · the .earth · the in (are) of ends

27 ענוש לצדיק לא־טוב להכות נדיבים על־ישר׃ חושך

who He restrains · upright-.ness for · nobles · strike to · ;good (is) not · just the · to punish

28 אמריו יודע דעת וקר־רוח איש תבונה׃ גם אויל

fool a · Even · under-.standing · a (is) of man · spirit of rare a · and knowl-;edge · knows · his words

מחריש חכם יחשב אטם שפתיו נבון׃

(as) .understanding · lips his · who he shuts · is ;thought · wise · is who silent

CAP. XVIII יח

CHAPTER 18

1
2 לתאוה יבקש נפרד בכל־תושיה יתגלע׃ לא־יחפץ

has delight · not · breaks he .out · sound wisdom · against all · who he ;himself separates · seeks (own his) · To desire

3 כסיל בתבונה כי אם־בהתגלות לבו׃ בבוא רשע בא

comes · the ,wicked · When comes · his .heart · uncov-ering · in · only but · under- ,standing · in · fool A

4 גם־בוז ועם־קלון חרפה׃ מים עמקים דברי פי־איש

a .man's · mouth · the of words · Deep (are) · waters · (comes) .reproach · shame · and with · also ;scorn

5 נחל נבע מקור חכמה׃ שאת פני־רשע לא־טוב להטות

to (nor) bow · (is) not ;good · the wicked · the of face · lift To up · .wisdom · the of fountain · flowing · a is stream righteous in judgment. [6]A fool's lips enter into strife; and his mouth calls for strokes. [7]A fool's mouth *is* his destruction, and his lips *are* a snare of his soul. [8]The words of a talebearer *are* as wounds; yea, they go down *into* the innermost chambers of the belly. [9]And he who is slack in his work, he *is* a brother to a master destroyer. [10]The name of Jehovah *is* a tower of strength; the righteous runs into it, and is set on high. [11]The rich man's wealth *is* his strong city; and as a high wall in his imagination. [12]A man's heart is haughty before shattering; but humility *goes* before honor. [13]If one turns back a matter before he hears, it *is* folly and shame to him. [14]The spirit of a man will nourish his sickness; but who can bear a wounded spirit? [15]The heart of the prudent gets knowledge; and the ear of the wise seeks knowledge. [16]A man's bribe makes room for him and brings him before great men. [17]*He who is* first in his cause *seems* just; *but* his neighbor comes and searches him. [18]The lot causes arguments to cease, and divides between the mighty. [19]An offended brother *is worse* than a fortified city; yea, *their* contentions *are* like the bars of a castle. [20]A man's belly shall be satisfied with the fruit of his mouth; he shall be satisfied *with* the produce of his lips. [21]Death and life *are* in the power of the tongue; and those who love it shall eat its fruit. [22]*Whoever* finds a wife finds good, and gets favor from Jehovah. [23]The poor speak with entreaties, but the rich answer fiercely. [24]A man of friends may be broken up; but there is a Lover who sticks closer than a brother.

4112 6310 7379 935 3684 8193 4941 6662
6 צַדִּיק בַּמִּשְׁפָּט׃ שִׂפְתֵי כְסִיל יָבֹאוּ בְרִיב וּפִיו לְמַהֲלֻמוֹת
for his and into enter fool's A lips in the
strokes mouth ;strife judgment righteous

1697 5315 4170 8193 4288 3684 6310 7121
7 8 יִקְרָא׃ פִּי־כְסִיל מְחִתָּה־לוֹ וּשְׂפָתָיו מוֹקֵשׁ נַפְשׁוֹ׃ דִּבְרֵי
words The his the (are) his and to (is) A mouth .calls
of soul of snare lips him ruin fool's

7503 1571 990 2315 3381 3859 5372
9 נִרְגָּן כְּמִתְלַהֲמִים וְהֵם יָרְדוּ חַדְרֵי־בָטֶן׃ גַּם מִתְרַפֶּה
is who he ,Also the chambers the go and like are a
slack .belly of (into) they ;morsels tasty slanderer

5797 4026 7843 1167 251 4399
10 בִמְלַאכְתּוֹ אָח הוּא לְבַעַל מַשְׁחִית׃ מִגְדַּל־עֹז
tower a destruction a to he (is) his in
strength of of lord a brother ,work

5797 7151 6223 1952 7682 6662 7323 3068 8034
11 שֵׁם יְהוָה בּוֹ־יָרוּץ צַדִּיק וְנִשְׂגָּב׃ הוֹן עָשִׁיר קִרְיַת עֻזּוֹ
his are The riches is and the run into Jehovah The
;strong city man's rich .exalted righteous it ;(is) of name

376 3820 1361 7667 6440 4906 7682 2346
12 וּכְחוֹמָה נִשְׂגָּבָה בְּמַשְׂכִּיתוֹ׃ לִפְנֵי־שֶׁבֶר יִגְבַּהּ לֶב־אִישׁ
a heart is shattering Before his in high a as and
;man's haughty .imagination wall

1931 200 8085 2962 1697 7725 6038 3519 6440
13 וְלִפְנֵי כָבוֹד עֲנָוָה׃ מֵשִׁיב דָּבָר בְּטֶרֶם יִשְׁמָע אִוֶּלֶת הִיא־
(is) it folly he before a who He (goes) honor but
,hears matter returns .humility before

4310 5218 7307 4245 3557 376 7307 3639
14 לוֹ וּכְלִמָּה׃ רוּחַ־אִישׁ יְכַלְכֵּל מַחֲלֵהוּ וְרוּחַ נְכֵאָה מִי
who stricken a but his will a The and to
spirit ;sickness endure man of spirit .shame him

1847 1245 2450 241 1847 7069 995 3820 5375
15 יִשָּׂאֶנָּה׃ לֵב נָבוֹן יִקְנֶה־דָּעַת וְאֹזֶן חֲכָמִים תְּבַקֶּשׁ־דָּעַת׃
.knowledge seeks the the and knowl- gets the The can
wise of ear ,ledge prudent of heart ? it bear

7223 6662 5148 1419 6440 7337 120 4976
16 17 מַתָּן אָדָם יַרְחִיב לוֹ וְלִפְנֵי גְדֹלִים יַנְחֶנּוּ׃ צַדִּיק הָרִאשׁוֹן
first The (seems) leads great and for makes a bribe
just .him (men) before ,him room man's

996 1486 7673 4066 2713 7453 935 7379
18 בְּרִיבוֹ יָבֹא רֵעֵהוּ וַחֲקָרוֹ׃ מִדְיָנִים יַשְׁבִּית הַגּוֹרָל וּבֵין
and The to causes strifes tests and his (but) his in
between ,lot cease .him neighbor comes ;cause

1280 4066 5797 7151 6586 251 6504 6099
19 עֲצוּמִים יַפְרִיד׃ אָח נִפְשָׁע מִקִּרְיַת־עֹז וּמִדְוָנִים כִּבְרִיחַ
the like and of city a offended A .divides the
of bars strifes strength (like is) brother mighty

8193 8393 990 7646 376 6310 6529 759
20 אַרְמוֹן׃ מִפְּרִי פִי־אִישׁ תִּשְׂבַּע בִּטְנוֹ תְּבוּאַת שְׂפָתָיו
lips his the (with) his be shall a mouth the With .citadel a
of produce ;belly satisfied man's of fruit

4672 6529 398 157 3956 3027 2416 4194 7646
21 22 יִשְׂבָּע׃ מָוֶת וְחַיִּים בְּיַד־לָשׁוֹן וְאֹהֲבֶיהָ יֹאכַל פִּרְיָהּ׃ מָצָא
who He its shall those and hand the in life and Death be shall
finds .fruit eat it loving ,tongue the of (are) .satisfied be

7326 1696 8469 3068 7522 6329 2896 4672 802
23 אִשָּׁה מָצָא טוֹב וַיָּפֶק רָצוֹן מֵיְהוָה׃ תַּחֲנוּנִים יְדַבֶּר־רָשׁ
The speak (with) from favor and ,good finds wife a
,poor entreaties Jehovah gets

157 3426 1489 7453 376 5794 6030 6223
24 וְעָשִׁיר יַעֲנֶה עַזּוֹת׃ אִישׁ רֵעִים לְהִתְרֹעֵעַ וְיֵשׁ אֹהֵב
Lover a but be may friends man A .roughly answers the but
is there ;up broken of rich

251 1695
דָּבֵק מֵאָח׃
a than sticks who
.brother closer

CAP. XIX יט

CHAPTER 19

1571 3684 8193 6141 8537 1980 7326 2896
1 2 טוב רש הולך בתמו מעקש שפתיו והוא כסיל: גם
,Also .fool a he and ;lips his one than his in who The (is)
(is) (in) crooked integrity walks poor better
120 200 2398 7272 213 2896 3808 5314 1847 1097
3 בלא־דעת נפש לא־טוב ואץ ברגלים חוטא: אולת אדם
man The .sins (his) with he and (is) not the knowl- with-
of folly feet rushing ;good soul edge out
7227 7453 3254 1952 3820 2196 3068 1870 5557
4 תסלף דרכו ועל־יהוה יזעף לבו: הון יסיף רעים רבים
;many friends adds Wealth his rages Jehovah and his perverts
heart against ;way
3577 6315 5352 3808 8267 5707 6504 7453 1800
5 ודל מרעהו יפרד: עד שקרים לא ינקה ויפיח כזבים
lies a and be shall not falsehoods A is his from the but
of breather clean of witness .separated neighbor poor
4976 376 7453 3605 5081 6440 2470 7227 4422
6 לא ימלט: רבים יחלו פני־נדיב וכל־הרע לאיש מתן:
.gifts a to are and a the will Many shall not
of man friends all noble of face beg .escape
7291 6440 7368 4828 637 3588 8130 7326 251 3605
7 כל אחי־רש | שנאהו אף כי מרעהו רחקו ממנו מרדף
pursues he from have his surely also hate poor a the All
(them) ;him far been friends ;him man of brothers
3808 1992 8104 5315 157 3820 7069 3808 561
8 אמרים לא־המה: קנה־לב אהב נפשו שמר תבונה
under- who he own his loves heart He they (yet) (with)
standing keeps ;soul gets who .are not ,words
6 3577 6315 5352 3808 8267 5707 2896 4672
9 למצא־טוב: עד שקרים לא ינקה ויפיח כזבים יאבד:
shall lies a and be shall not falsehood A .good finds
.perish of breather clean of witness
8269 4910 5650 637 8588 3684 5000 3808
10 לא־נאוה לכסיל תענוג אף כי־לעבד | משל בשרים:
over rule to a for less much ;Luxury a for is not
.rulers servant fool becoming
5097 6588 5674 8597 639 748 120 7922
11 12 שכל אדם האריך אפו ותפארתו עבר על־פשע: נהם
roar a over to (it is) and his makes A dis-
.transgression pass glory ;anger slow man's cretion
1121 1 1942 7522 6212 5921 2919 4428 2197 3715
13 ככפיר זעף מלך וכטל על־עשב רצונו: הות לאביו בן
a (is) his to A his (is) the on as but The rage like (is)
son father ruin .favor grass dew the ;king's lion's a
1 5159 1952 1004 802 1812 2956 1812 3684
14 כסיל ודלף טרד מדיני אשה: בית והון נחלת אבות
;fathers the (are) and House .woman a the never a and ,foolish
of legacy riches of strivings ending dropping
5315 8639 5307 6103 7919 802 3068
15 ומיהוה אשה משכלת: עצלה תפיל תרדמה ונפש
a and deep (into) one makes Laziness acts who woman a from but
soul ;sleep fall prudently (is) Jehovah
1870 959 5315 8104 4687 8104 7456 7423
16 רמיה תרעב: שמר מצוה שמר נפשו בוזה דרכיו
His who he own his keeps the who He be shall idle
ways despises ;soul command keeps .hungry
1121 3256 7999 1576 1800 2603 3068 3867 4191
17 18 יומת: מלוה יהוה חונן דל וגמלו ישלם־לו: יסר בנך
your Chasten to will He his and the one Jehovah Lends shall
,son .him reward dealing poor favoring to .die
2534 1632 5315 5375 408 4191 8615 3426
19 כי־יש תקוה ואל־המיתו אל־תשא נפשך: גרל־חמה
fury great He your lift do not making and ;hope there for
of .soul die him on is

CHAPTER 19

[1]The poor one who walks in his integrity *is* better than he who *is* perverse in his lips, and he *is* a fool. [2]Also, without knowledge the soul *is* not good; and he rushing with *his* feet sins. [3]The foolishness of man perverts his way, and his heart rages against Jehovah. [4]Wealth adds many friends, but the poor *is* separated from his neighbor. [5]A false witness shall not be clean, and a breather of lies shall not escape. [6]Many will beg the face of a noble, and all are friends to a man of gifts. [7]All the brothers of a poor one hate him, and surely his friends have been far from him; he pursues *them with* words, *yet* they are not. [8]A false witness shall not be clean, and a breather of lies shall perish. [10]Luxury is not becoming for a fool; much less for a servant to rule over rulers. [11]A man's discretion makes his anger slow, and *it is* glory to pass over a transgression. [12]The rage *is* like the roar of a lion, but his favor *is* as the dew on the grass. [13]A foolish son *is* a calamity to his father, and the strivings of a woman *are* a never-ending dropping.

[14]House and riches *are* the legacy of fathers, but a woman who acts prudently *is* from Jehovah. [15]Laziness makes one fall into a deep sleep; and an idle soul shall be hungry.[16]He keeping the commandment keeps his own soul; he despising His ways shall die. [17]He having pity on the poor lends to Jehovah, and He will reward his dealing to him. [18]Chasten your son, for there *is* hope; and do not set your soul on making him die. [19]A man great of fury

will have to pay the fine; for
if you deliver *him*, then you
must do it again. [20]Hear
advice and receive instruction, that you may be wise
in your latter end. [21]Many
purposes *are* in a man's
heart; but the counsel of
Jehovah shall stand. [22]The
desire of a man *is* his
kindness; and a poor man *is*
better than a liar. [23]The
fear of Jehovah *tends* to
life; he shall rest satisfied;
he shall not be visited with
evil. [24]A lazy one puts his
hand in a dish, and he will
not return it to his mouth.
[25]Strike a scorner and the
simple will become careful;
reprove a discerner, and he
will discern knowledge.
[26]He who assaults *his* father
chases *his* mother away; he
is a son who causes shame
and brings reproach. [27]My
son, cease to hear the
teaching, *and you will* err
from the words of knowl-
edge. [28]A worthless witness scorns justice; and the
mouth of the wicked
devours evil. [29]Judgments
are prepared for scorners,
and blows for the backs of
fools.

20 — 6901 6098 8085 3254 5750 53 37 6066 5375
נֹשֵׂא עֹנֶשׁ כִּי אִם־תַּצִּיל וְעוֹד תּוֹסִף׃ שְׁמַע עֵצָה וְקַבֵּל
and counsel Hear must you then you if for a will
accept .add again ,(him) deliver ;fine bear

21 — 38 20 4284 7227 319 2449 4148
מוּסָר לְמַעַן תֶּחְכַּם בְּאַחֲרִיתֶךָ׃ רַבּוֹת מַחֲשָׁבוֹת בְּלֶב־
in (are) purposes Many latter your in may you that ,discipline
heart .end wise be

22 — 2896 2617 120 8378 6965 30 68 6098 376
אִישׁ וַעֲצַת יְהוָה הִיא תָקוּם׃ תַּאֲוַת אָדָם חַסְדּוֹ וְטוֹב
(is) and his (is) a The shall it ,Jehovah the but a
better ,mercy man of desire .rise of counsel ;man's

23 — 6485 1077 3885 7649 2416 3068 3373 3577 376 7326
רָשׁ מֵאִישׁ כָּזָב׃ יִרְאַת יְהוָה לְחַיִּים וְשָׂבֵעַ יָלִין בַּל־יִפָּקֵד
be shall he not he and (tends) Jehovah The .lie a a than (be to)
visited .lodges satisfied ;life to of fear of man poor

24 — 7725 3808 6310 1571 6747 3027 6102 2934 7451
רָע׃ טָמַן עָצֵל יָדוֹ בַּצַּלָּחַת גַּם־אֶל־פִּיהוּ לֹא יְשִׁיבֶנָּה׃
will he not his to even a in his lazy A hides (with)
.it return mouth dish hand one .evil

25
26 — 7703 1847 995 995 3198 6191 6612 5221 3887
לֵץ תַּכֶּה וּפֶתִי יַעְרִם וְהוֹכִיחַ לְנָבוֹן יָבִין דָּעַת׃ מְשַׁדֶּד־
who He .knowledge will he dis- a but be will the and Strike a
assaults discern ,cerner reprove ;astute simple scorner

27 — 8085 1127 2308 2659 954 1121 517 1272 1
אָב יַבְרִיחַ אֵם בֵּן מֵבִישׁ וּמַחְפִּיר׃ חֲדַל־בְּנִי לִשְׁמֹעַ
hear to my ,Cease bringing and causing a (his) chases (his)
,son .reproach shame son ,mother away ,father

28 — 6310 4941 3887 1100 5707 1847 561 7686 4148
מוּסָר לִשְׁגוֹת מֵאִמְרֵי־דָעַת׃ עֵד בְּלִיַּעַל יָלִיץ מִשְׁפָּט וּפִי
and ;justice scorns worthless A .knowledge the from to (only) the
mouth witness of words stray ,discipline

29 — 4112 8201 3885 3559 205 1104 7563
רְשָׁעִים יְבַלַּע־אָוֶן׃ נָכוֹנוּ לַלֵּצִים שְׁפָטִים וּמַהֲלֻמוֹת
blows and ,Judgments for are .evil devours the
scorners prepared wicked's

3684 1460
לְגֵו כְּסִילִים׃
.fools the for
of back

CAP. XX כ׳

CHAPTER 20

CHAPTER 20

[1]Wine *is* a mocker;
strong drink *is* noisy; and all
who stray by it are not wise.
[2]The fear of a king *is* as the
roar of a lion; he who stirs
him up to anger wrongs his
own soul. [3]For a man to
cease from strife *is* an
honor; but every fool
exposes himself. [4]The lazy
man will not plow because
of the cold; he begs at
harvest, and nothing is
there. [5]Counsel in a man's
heart *is* like deep water; but
an understanding man will
draw it out. [6]Most men
will proclaim each his own
kindness; but who can find
a faithful man? [7]The just
one walks in his integrity;
blessed *are* his sons after
him! [8]A king who sits on

1
2 — 3715 5099 2449 3808 7686 3605 7941 1993 3196 3887
לֵץ הַיַּיִן הֹמֶה שֵׁכָר וְכָל־שֹׁגֶה בּוֹ לֹא יֶחְכָּם׃ נַהַם כַּכְּפִיר
a like roar A .wise is not by who and strong is ;Wine a
lion it strays each; drink noisy (is) scorner

3 — 7674 376 3519 5315 2398 5674 4428 367
אֵימַת מֶלֶךְ מִתְעַבְּרוֹ חוֹטֵא נַפְשׁוֹ׃ כָּבוֹד לָאִישׁ שֶׁבֶת
To a for an (is) own his sins stirs who he a the (is)
cease man honor .soul against anger to him ;king of dread

4 — 7592 2790 3808 6102 2779 1566 191 3605 7379
מֵרִיב וְכָל־אֱוִיל יִתְגַּלָּע׃ מֵחֹרֶף עָצֵל לֹא יַחֲרֹשׁ ישאל
begs he will not The the after exposes fool but from
;plow lazy autumn .himself every ;strife

5 — 8394 376 376 3820 6098 6013 4325 369 7102
בַּקָּצִיר וָאָיִן׃ מַיִם עֲמֻקִּים עֵצָה בְלֶב־אִישׁ וְאִישׁ תְּבוּנָה
under- a but a in (is) deep Like is but at
standing of man ;man's heart counsel water .nothing ,harvest

6 — 4310 529 376 2617 376 7121 120 7230 1802
יִדְלֶנָּה׃ רָב־אָדָם יִקְרָא אִישׁ חַסְדּוֹ וְאִישׁ אֱמוּנִים מִי
who faithful a but own his each will men Many draw will
man ;kindness proclaim .out it

7
8 — 4428 310 1121 835 6662 8537 1980 4672
יִמְצָא׃ מִתְהַלֵּךְ בְּתֻמּוֹ צַדִּיק אַשְׁרֵי בָנָיו אַחֲרָיו׃ מֶלֶךְ
king A after his blessed The his in walks can
!him sons (are) ;just integrity about .find

the throne of judgment scatters away all evil with his eyes. [9]Who can say, I have cleansed my heart from sin? [10]A stone and a stone, an ephah and an ephah — both *are* hateful to Jehovah. [11]Even a child makes himself known by his acts, whether his work *is* clean or upright. [12]Jehovah has made the hearing ear and the seeing eye, even both of them. [13]Do not love sleep, lest you be dispossessed; open your eyes and be satisfied *with* bread.

[14]Bad! Bad! says the buyer; but when *it is* left to him, then he boasts. [15]There *is* gold and many gems, but the lips of knowledge *are* a rare vessel. [16]Take his garment when he *is* surety *for* an alien, and bind him in pledge for strangers. [17]Bread of falsehood *is* sweet to a man, but afterwards his mouth will be filled *with* gravel. [18]Purposes *are* established in counsel; yea, make war with wise guidance. [19]A revealer of a secret walks about as a gossip; yea, do not meddle with him who opens his lips. [20]He cursing his father or his mother, his lamp shall be put out in blackest darkness. [21]An inheritance gotten hastily in the beginning, even the end of it shall not blessed. [22]Do not say, I will repay evil; wait on Jehovah and He will save you. [23]A stone and a stone *are* hateful to Jehovah, and balances of deceit *are* not good. [24]The steps of a man *are* from Jehovah; and man — what can he discern of his way? [25]*It is* a snare *to* a man to say rashly, A holy thing! and later *he* vows to inquire. [26]A wise king scatters the wicked and turns the wheel over them. [27]The spirit of man *is* the lamp of Jehovah, searching all the chambers of the belly. [28]Mercy and truth

2135 559 4310 7451 3605 5869 2219 1779 3678 3427
9 יוֹשֵׁב עַל־כִּסֵּא־דִין מְזָרֶה בְעֵינָיו כָּל־רָע׃ מִֽי־יֹאמַר זִכִּיתִי
have I can Who .evil all his with scatters judgment the on who
cleansed ,say eyes of throne sits

8441 374 374 68 68 2403 3820
10 לִבִּי טָהַרְתִּי מֵחַטָּאתִי׃ אֶבֶן וָאֶבֶן אֵיפָה וְאֵיפָה תּוֹעֲבַת
(are) an and an a and A my from am I my
to hateful —ephah ephah stone stone ?sin pure ;heart

2134 5288 5234 4611 1571 8147 1571 3068
11 יְהוָה גַּם־שְׁנֵיהֶם׃ גַּם בְּמַעֲלָלָיו יִתְנַכֶּר־נָעַר אִם־זַךְ וְאִם־
or is whether a himself makes his by Even of both even Jeho-
clean lad known acts .them ,vah

8147 1571 6213 3068 7200 5869 8085 241 6467 3477
12 יָשָׁר פָּעֳלוֹ׃ אֹזֶן שֹׁמַעַת וְעַיִן רֹאָה יְהוָה עָשָׂה גַם־שְׁנֵיהֶם׃
both even has Jehovah seeing and hearing The his upright
.them of ,made eye the ear .work

7451 3899 7646 5869 6491 3423 6435 8142 159 408
13
14 אַל־תֶּאֱהַב שֵׁנָה פֶּן־תִּוָּרֵשׁ פְּקַח עֵינֶיךָ שְׂבַע־לָחֶם׃ רַע
!Evil .bread be your open you lest ,sleep Do not
(with) satisfied ,eyes ;dispossessed be love

7230 2091 3426 1984 227 235 7069 559 7451
15 רַע יֹאמַר הַקּוֹנֶה וְאֹזֵל לוֹ אָז יִתְהַלָּל׃ יֵשׁ זָהָב וְרָב־
and gold There he then to when but the says !Evil
many is .boasts him left (is it) ;buyer

2114 6148 899 3947 1847 8193 3366 3627 6443
16 פְּנִינִים וּכְלִי יְקָר שִׂפְתֵי־דָעַת׃ לְקַח־בִּגְדוֹ כִּי־עָרַב זָר
an (for) is he when his Take .knowledge the rare (is) but ;gems
;alien surety garment of lips vessel a

310 8267 3899 376 6156 2254 5237
17 וּבְעַד נָכְרִים חַבְלֵהוּ׃ עָרֵב לָאִישׁ לֶחֶם שָׁקֶר וְאַחַר
but ;falsehood Bread a to (is) him bind strangers and
afterwards of man sweet .pledge in for

8458 3559 6098 4284 2687 6310 4390
18 יִמָּלֵא־פִיהוּ חָצָץ׃ מַחֲשָׁבוֹת בְּעֵצָה תִכּוֹן וּבְתַחְבֻּלוֹת
with and are in Purposes (with) his be shall
guidance wise ;established counsel .gravel mouth filled

8193 6601 7400 1980 5475 1540 4421 6213
19 עֲשֵׂה מִלְחָמָה׃ גּוֹלֶה־סּוֹד הוֹלֵךְ רָכִיל וּלְפֹתֶה שְׂפָתָיו
his him to and a as walks secret a A .war make
lips opens who ;gossip about of revealer

2822 380 5216 1846 517 1 7043 6148 3808
20 לֹא תִתְעָרָב׃ מְקַלֵּל אָבִיו וְאִמּוֹ יִדְעַךְ נֵרוֹ בְּאִישׁוֹן חֹשֶׁךְ׃
.darkness in his be shall his or his who He do not
blackest lamp out put ,mother father curses .meddle

408 1288 3808 319 7223 973 5159
21
22 נַחֲלָה מְבֹחֶלֶת בָּרִאשֹׁנָה וְאַחֲרִיתָהּ לֹא תְבֹרָךְ׃ אַל־
not shall not the but the in gotten in- An
.blessed be it of end —beginning hastily heritance

3068 8441 3462 3068 6960 7451 7999 559
23 תֹּאמַר אֲשַׁלְּמָה־רָע קַוֵּה לַיהוָה וְיֹשַׁע לָךְ׃ תּוֹעֲבַת יְהוָה
Jehovah (are) .you He and on wait ;evil will I ,say Do
to hateful save will Jehovah repay

1397 4703 3068 2896 3808 4820 3976 68 68
24 אֶבֶן וָאָבֶן וּמֹאזְנֵי מִרְמָה לֹא־טוֹב׃ מֵיְהוָה מִצְעֲדֵי־גָבֶר
a The from (are) (are) not deceit and a and A
;man of steps Jehovah .good of balances ;stone stone

310 6944 3216 120 4170 1870 995 4100 120
25 וְאָדָם מַה־יָּבִין דַּרְכּוֹ׃ מוֹקֵשׁ אָדָם יָלַע קֹדֶשׁ וְאַחַר
And holy A say (to) a (to) a (is It) his of can what and
after !thing ,rashly man snare ?way discern he —man

2617 7725 2450 4428 7563 2219 1239 5088
26 נְדָרִים לְבַקֵּר׃ מְזָרֶה רְשָׁעִים מֶלֶךְ חָכָם וַיָּשֶׁב עֲלֵיהֶם
over and ,wise A the scatters inquire to (he)
them turns king wicked vows

2617 990 2315 3605 2664 120 5397 3068 5216 212
27
28 אוֹפָן׃ נֵר יְהוָה נִשְׁמַת אָדָם חֹפֵשׂ כָּל־חַדְרֵי־בָטֶן׃ חֶסֶד
Mercy the the all searching ;man the (is) Jehovah The the
belly of chambers of breath of lamp .wheel

preserve the king, and his throne is upheld by mercy. [29]The glory of young men *is* their vigor; and the honor of old men *is* the gray head. [30]The stripes of a wound cleanse away evil; and strokes the inward parts of the heart.

ואמת יצרו-מלך וסעד בחסד כסאו׃ תפארת בחורים 29

young glory The his by is and the preserve and
:men of .throne mercy upheld ;king truth

כחם והדר זקנים שיבה׃ חברות פצע תמריק ברע 30

against cleanse a Stripes the old the and their
evil away wound of .head gray :men of honor ;vigor

ומכות חדרי-בטן׃

the the and
.heart of chambers strokes

CHAPTER 21

[1]The king's heart *is* in the hand of Jehovah, *as* streams of waters; He turns it wherever He desires. [2]Every way of a man *is* upright in his own eyes; but Jehovah measures the hearts. [3]To do righteousness and justice is to be chosen for Jehovah more than sacrifice. [4]High eyes, a proud heart, *and* the lamp of the wicked, *is* sin. [5]The thoughts of the diligent *tend* only to plenty; but *those of* every hasty one only to poverty. [6]The getting of treasures by a lying tongue *is* a vapor driven by those who seek death. [7]The violence of the wicked ensnares them, because they refuse to do justice. [8]The way of a guilty man *is* perverted; but the pure, his work *is* right. [9]*It is* better to dwell on a corner of a housetop, than *with* a contentious woman, and to share a house. [10]The soul of the wicked desires evil; his neighbor finds no favor in his eyes. [11]The simple is made wise when the scorner is punished; and when the wise is instructed, he receives knowledge. [12]The Righteous One wisely considers the house of the wicked; He overthrows the wicked for his evil. [13]Whoever stops his ears at the cry of the poor, he himself shall also call, and shall not be answered. [14]A gift in secret subdues anger; yea, a bribe in the bosom *quiets* great fury. [15]*It is* joy to the just to do justice; but terror *shall come* to the workers of evil. [16]The man who wanders out

CAP. XXI כא

CHAPTER 21

פלגי-מים לב-מלך ביד-יהוה על-כל-אשר יחפץ יטנו׃ 1

in- He He wherever to ;Jehovah in (is) King's the waters (As)
.it clines ,desires of hand the heart of streams

כל-דרך איש ישר בעיניו ותכן לבות יהוה׃ עשה צדקה 2 3

righteous- To .Jehovah the but his in (is) a way Every
ness do hearts weighs ;eyes own right man of

ומשפט נבחר ליהוה מזבח׃ רום-עינים ורחב-לב נר 4

the ,heart a and ,eyes Exalted than more for be to is and
of lamp proud .sacrifice Jehovah chosen justice

רשעים חטאת׃ מחשבות חרוץ אך-למותר וכל-אץ אך 5

only hasty but (tend) only the The .sin (is) the
one every ;plenty to diligent of plans ,wicked

למחסור׃ פעל אצרות בלשון שקר הבל נדף מבקשי 6

those driven a (is) lying a by treasures The .poverty to
seeking by vapor tongue of getting

מות׃ שד-רשעים יגורם כי מאנו לעשות משפט׃ 7

.justice do to they because ensnares the The .death
refuse ,them wicked of violence

הפכפך דרך איש וזר וזך ישר פעלו׃ טוב לשבת על- 8 9

on dwell to (is It) his (is) upright but ;guilty a the Perverted
better .work ,pure the man of way (is)

פנת-גג מאשת מדונים ובית חבר׃ נפש רשע אותה- 10

desires the The to a and strivings a (with) than corner a
wicked of soul .share house of woman roof a of

רע לא-יחן בעיניו רעהו׃ בענש-לץ יחכם-פתי ובהשכיל 11

is when and the made is the is When his his in finds not ;evil
instructed ;simple wise scorner punished .neighbor eyes favor

לחכם יקח-דעת׃ משכיל צדיק לבית רשע מסלף 12

over- He the the Righteous The wisely .knowledge he the
turns ;wicked of house One considers in takes ,wise

רשעים לרע׃ אטם אזנו מזעקת-דל גם-הוא יקרא ולא 13

and shall he himself also the the at his who He (his) for the
not ,call ,poor of cry ear shuts .evil wicked

יענה׃ מתן בסתר יכפה-אף ושחד בחק חמה עזה׃ 14

.strong wrath the in a and ;anger subdues in A be will
,bosom bribe secret gift .answered

שמחה לצדיק עשות משפט ומחתה לפעלי און׃ אדם 15 16

A .evil the to but ;justice do to the to (It)
man of workers ruin righteous joy is

of the way of prudence shall rest in the congregation of departed spirits. 17A man who loves pleasure *shall be* poor; he who loves wine and oil shall not be rich. 18The wicked *shall be* a ransom for the just; and the treacherous in the place of the upright. 19*It is* better to live in a land of the wilderness than *with* a contentious woman and vexation. 20A desirable treasure and oil *are* in the dwelling of the wise; but a foolish man devours it. 21He who pursues righteousness and mercy finds life, righteousness and honor. 22A wise one ascends the city of the mighty and topples the strength *in which* it trusts. 23Whoever keeps his mouth and his tongue keeps his soul from distresses. 24Proud, haughty scorner *is* his name—he who deals in proud wrath. 25The lust of the lazy man kills him, for his hands have refused to work. 26He lusts with lust all the day long; but the righteous gives and does not withhold. 27The sacrifice of the wicked *is* hateful; how much more *when* he brings it with an evil intent! 28A false witness shall perish; but the man who attends will speak forever. 29A wicked man hardens his face; but the upright sets up his way. 30*There is* no wisdom nor understanding nor counsel before Jehovah. 31The horse *is* made ready for the day of battle; but to Jehovah *belongs* deliverance.

4270 376 5117 7496 6951 7919 1870 8582
17 תּוֹעֶה מִדֶּרֶךְ הַשְׂכֵּל בִּקְהַל רְפָאִים יָנוּחַ׃ אִישׁ מַחְסוֹר
(be shall) A shall departed the in prudence the of out who
poor man .rest spirits of assembly of way wanders

6662 3724 6238 3808/ 808.1 3196 157 8057 157
18 אֹהֵב שִׂמְחָה אֹהֵב יַיִן וָשֶׁמֶן לֹא יַעֲשִׁיר׃ כֹּפֶר לַצַּדִּיק
the for (be shall) be shall not and wine who he ;pleasure who
righteous ransom a .rich oil loves loves

4057 776 3427 2896 898 7477 8478 7563
19 רָשָׁע וְתַחַת יְשָׁרִים בּוֹגֵד׃ טוֹב שֶׁבֶת בְּאֶרֶץ מִדְבָּר
wilderness a in live to (is It) the the in and The
of land better .treacherous upright of place ;wicked

2450 5116 8081 2530 214 3708 4066 802
20 מֵאֵשֶׁת מִדְוָנִים וָכָעַס׃ אוֹצָר ׀ נֶחְמָד וָשֶׁמֶן בִּנְוֵה חָכָם
the in (is) oil and A and strivings a with than
;wise of home the desirable treasure vexation of woman

2416 4672 2617 6666 7291 1104 120 3684
21 וּכְסִיל אָדָם יְבַלְּעֶנּוּ׃ רֹדֵף צְדָקָה וָחָסֶד יִמְצָא חַיִּים
:,life finds and righteousness who He devours a but
mercy pursues .it man foolish

5797 3381 2450 5927 1368 5892 3519 6666
22 צְדָקָה וְכָבוֹד׃ עִיר גִּבֹּרִים עָלָה חָכָם וַיֹּרֶד עֹז
the and wise A makes the city the and righteous-
force down go one up go mighty of honor ness

3093 2086 5315 6864 8104 3956 6310 8104 4009
23 24 מִבְטֶחָה׃ שֹׁמֵר פִּיו וּלְשׁוֹנוֹ שֹׁמֵר מִצָּרוֹת נַפְשׁוֹ׃ זֵד יָהִיר
arro- ,Proud his from keeps his and his who He (which in)
gant .soul distresses tongue mouth keeps .trusts it

4191 6102 8378 2087 5678 6213 8034 3887
25 לֵץ שְׁמוֹ עוֹשֶׂה בְּעֶבְרַת זָדוֹן׃ תַּאֲוַת עָצֵל תְּמִיתֶנּוּ כִּי
for kills lazy the The .pride the in who he his ,scoffer
,him man of lust of wrath deals —name

5414 6662 8378 183 3117 3605 6213 3027 3985
26 מֵאֲנוּ יָדָיו לַעֲשׂוֹת׃ כָּל־הַיּוֹם הִתְאַוָּה תַאֲוָה וְצַדִּיק יִתֵּן
gives the but ;lust lusts he the All .work to his have
righteous with long day hands refused

935 2154 637 8441 7563 2077 2820 3808
27 וְלֹא יַחְשֹׂךְ׃ זֶבַח רְשָׁעִים תּוֹעֵבָה אַף כִּי־בְזִמָּה יְבִיאֶנּוּ׃
brings he an with when much (is) the The .withholds and
!it intent evil more ;hateful wicked of sacrifice not

376 5810 1696 5331 8085 376 6 3577 5707
28 29 עֵד־כְּזָבִים יֹאבֵד וְאִישׁ שׁוֹמֵעַ לָנֶצַח יְדַבֵּר׃ הֵעֵז אִישׁ
A hardens will forever who the but shall false A
man .speak hears man ;perish witness

369 2451 369 1870 3559 3477 6440 7563
30 רָשָׁע בְּפָנָיו וְיָשָׁר הוּא ׀ יָכִין דְּרָכָיו׃ אֵין חָכְמָה וְאֵין
and wisdom There his establishes he the but his wicked
no no is .way ,upright ;face

4421 3117 3559 5483 3068 6440 6098 369 8394
31 תְּבוּנָה וְאֵין עֵצָה לְנֶגֶד יְהוָה׃ סוּס מוּכָן לְיוֹם מִלְחָמָה
;battle the for made is The .Jehovah before counsel and under-
of day ready horse no standing

8668 3068
וְלַיהוָה הַתְּשׁוּעָה׃
(belongs) to but
.deliverance Jehovah

CAP. XXII כב

CHAPTER 22

1A *good* name is to be chosen rather than great riches; rather than silver or gold, favor *is* better. 2The rich and poor meet together; Jehovah *is* the Maker of all of them. 3A sensible one sees the evil and hides himself; but the

CHAPTER 22

6223 2896 2580 2091 3701 7227 6239 8034 977
1 2 נִבְחָר שֵׁם מֵעֹשֶׁר רָב מִכֶּסֶף וּמִזָּהָב חֵן טוֹב׃ עָשִׁיר
The (is) favor ,gold or rather ;great than rather A be to is
rich better silver than riches name chosen

5640 7451 7200 6175 3068 3605 6213 6298 7326
3 וָרָשׁ נִפְגָּשׁוּ עֹשֵׂה כֻלָּם יְהוָה׃ עָרוּם ׀ רָאָה רָעָה וְיִסָּתֵר
hides and the sees sensible A .Jehovah of all the is meet the and
;himself evil one them of Maker :together poor

simple go on and are punished. [4]The reward of humility *is* the fear of Jehovah, riches, and honor, and life. [5]Thorns *and* snares *are* in the way of the perverse; he who keeps his soul shall be far from them. [6]Train up a boy on the opening of his way; even when he is old, he will not turn aside from it. [7]The rich rules over the poor; and the borrower *is* servant to a man who lends. [8]He who sows injustice will reap evil; and the rod of his wrath shall fail. [9]He who has a good eye, he is blessed; for he gives of his bread to the poor. [10]Throw the scorner out and strife shall go out; yea, quarrels and shame shall cease. [11]He who loves pureness of heart, grace *is on* his lips; the king *shall be* his friend. [12]The eyes of Jehovah keep knowledge; and He overthrows the words of the treacherous. [13]The lazy one says, A lion *is* outside! I will be killed in the streets! [14]The mouth of alien women *is* a deep pit; those despised *by* Jehovah shall fall there. [15]Foolishness *is* bound up in the heart of a boy; the rod of correction shall drive it far from him. [16]One oppresses the poor to multiply for himself; another gives to the rich, only *to come* to poverty.

[17]Stretch your ear and hear the words of the wise; and set your heart to My knowledge; [18]for they are pleasant when you keep them within you; they shall all be fixed together on your lips; [19]so that your trust may be in Jehovah, I caused you to know today, even you. [20]Have I not written to you the third *time* with counsels and knowledge; [21]to cause you to know the verity of the words of truth; to return words of truth to those who send you?

[22]Rob not the poor because he *is* poor; and oppress not the afflicted in the gate. [23]For Jehovah

4 ופתיים עברו ונענשו׃ עקב ענוה יראת יהוה עשר וכבוד
the but simple pass on are and .punished The reward humility (is) the of fear Jehovah; riches, and honor,

5 וחיים׃ צנים פחים בדרך עקש שומר נפשו ירחק מהם׃
and life. Thorns, snares (are) in the way of the crooked; he who keeps his soul shall be far from them.

6 חנך לנער על־פי דרכו גם כי־יזקין לא־יסור ממנה׃
Train up a boy on the mouth of his way, even when he is old, not will he turn aside from it.

7 עשיר ברשים ימשול ועבד לוה לאיש מלוה׃
8 זורע
The rich over the poor rules; and the borrower (is) servant to a man who lends. He who sows

9 עולה יקצור־און ושבט עברתו יכלה׃ טוב־עין הוא
injustice shall reap evil, and the rod of his wrath shall cease. The good of eye— He

10 יברך כי־נתן מלחמו לדל׃ גרש לץ ויצא מדון וישבת
is blessed; for he gives of his bread to the poor. Drive out the scorner, and strife shall go out; and shall cease

11 דין וקלון׃ אהב טהור־לב חן שפתיו רעהו מלך׃
12 עיני
quarrels and shame. He who loves pureness of heart, grace (is on) his lips; his friend (shall be) the king. The eyes of

13 יהוה נצרו דעת ויסלף דברי בגד׃ אמר עצל ארי
Jehovah keep knowledge; and He overthrows the words of the sly. The lazy one says, A lion

14 בחוץ בתוך רחבות ארצח׃ שוחה עמקה פי זרות זעום
(is) outside; in the midst of the streets I will be killed. A deep pit (is) the mouth of alien women; those hated

15 יהוה יפול־שם׃ אולת קשורה בלב־נער שבט מוסר
(by) Jehovah shall fall there. Foolishness is bound up in the heart of a boy; the rod of discipline

16 ירחיקנה ממנו׃ עשק דל להרבות לו נתן לעשיר אך
shall drive it far from him. He who oppresses the poor to multiply to him, he gives to the rich, only

17 למחסור׃ הט אזנך ושמע דברי חכמים ולבך תשית
to poverty (come to). Stretch your ear and hear the words of the wise; and your heart apply

18 לדעתי׃ כי־נעים כי־תשמרם בבטנך יכנו יחדו על־
to My knowledge; for (are they) pleasant when you keep them within you; they shall be fixed together on

19 שפתיך׃ להיות ביהוה מבטחך הודעתיך היום אף־
your lips. So that may be in Jehovah your trust, I caused you to know today, even

20 אתה׃ הלא כתבתי לך שלשום במעצות ודעת׃
21 להודיעך
you. Have not I written to you three times with counsels and knowledge; to make you know

קשט אמרי אמת להשיב אמרים אמת לשלחיך׃
the verity of the words of truth; to return words of truth to him who sent you?

22 אל־תגזל־דל כי דל־הוא ואל־תדכא עני בשער׃
23 כי־
Do not rob the poor because he is poor; and not do crush the afflicted in the gate. For

will contend for their cause, and will plunder the soul of their plunderers. ²⁴Do not feed a possessor of anger; and do not go in with a man of fury, ²⁵lest you learn his ways and take a snare for your soul. ²⁶Do not be one of those who strike the palm, those who are sureties for loans. ²⁷If you have nothing to repay, why should he take away your bed from under you? ²⁸Do not move the old landmark which your fathers have set. ²⁹Do you see a man who is prompt in his work? he shall stand before kings; he shall not stand before obscure *men*.

24

7462	408		5315	6906		6906	7379	7378	3068
אַל־תִּתְרַע		וְלָבַע	אֶת־קֹבְעֵיהֶם	נָפֶשׁ׃					
Do not feed		the (in)	plundering	those	will and	plunder	their cause,	con- tends	Jehovah for
			soul	them					

25

502	6435		935	38.08	2.434	376	639	1167
פֶּן־תֶּאֱלַף			אֶת־בַּעַל אַף וְאֶת־אִישׁ חֵמֹת לֹא תָבוֹא׃					
you learn	lest		go do not	fury	a	and	anger	lord a	with of
					of man	with			

26

3709	8628	408		5315		4170	3947	734
אַל־תְּהִי בַתֹּקְעֵי־כָף			אַל־תִּהִי	לְנַפְשֶׁךָ׃				
the those of one	palm	strike who		be	Do not	your for	a	and	his
						soul	snare	take	paths

27

4904		3947	7999	369	518	4859	6148
מִשְׁכָּבְךָ מִתַּחְתֶּיךָ׃		לָמָּה יִקַּח אִם־אֵין־לְךָ לְשַׁלֵּם					
your bed		should take he	why	to	to is	If	.loans	are who for sureties
				repay	you not			

28

2372		1	6213	834	5769	1366	5253	408	8478
חָזִיתָ	אֲבוֹתֶיךָ׃		אֲשֶׁר עָשׂוּ				אַל־תַּסֵּג גְּבוּל עוֹלָם		מִתַּחְתֶּיךָ
you Do see	your fathers.	have	which	set	old	the	Do not move	landmark	under from ?you

29

33.20	1077	3320	4428	6440	4399		4106	376
אִישׁ	מָהִיר	בִּמְלַאכְתּוֹ לִפְנֵי־מְלָכִים יִתְיַצָּב בַּל־יִתְיַצֵּב						
shall he stand	not shall He stand;	kings	before	?work his in	is who prompt		man a

2823	6440
לִפְנֵי חֲשֻׁכִּים׃	
obscure .(men)	before

CAP. XXIII כג
CHAPTER 23

CHAPTER 23

When you sit down to eat with a ruler, look carefully at what *is* before you; ²and put a knife to your throat, if you *are* an owner of an appetite. ³Do not desire his delicacies, for it is the bread of lies. ⁴Do not labor to be rich; cease from your own understanding. ⁵Will your eyes fly on it? And *it* is gone! For surely it makes wings for itself; it flies *into* the heavens like an eagle.

⁶Do not eat the bread of *one having* an evil eye; and do not desire his delicacies; ⁷for as he thinks in his heart, so *is* he! He says to you, Eat and drink—but his heart *is* not with you. ⁸The morsel you have eaten, you shall vomit up and spoil your sweet words. ⁹Do not speak in the ears of a fool, for he will despise the good sense of your words. ¹⁰Do not move the old landmark,

1

6440	834	995	995	4910	3898	3427
כִּי־תֵשֵׁב לִלְחוֹם אֶת־מוֹשֵׁל בִּין תָּבִין אֶת־אֲשֶׁר לְפָנֶיךָ׃						
before (is) you,	what	con- sider	care- fully	ruler a	with	eat to	you When down sit

2 3

183	408		5315	1167	518	3930	7915	7760
וְשַׂמְתָּ שַׂכִּין בְּלֹעֶךָ אִם־בַּעַל נֶפֶשׁ אָתָּה׃	אַל־תִּתְאָו							
Do not desire	you a of (are)	a	if	your to throat,	a knife	put	and
		soul	master					

4

6238	3021	408		3577	3899		4303
לְמַטְעַמֹּתָיו וְהוּא לֶחֶם כְּזָבִים׃	אַל־תִּיגַע לְהַעֲשִׁיר						
be to rich;	Do not labor	not	lies	bread of	it for (is)	his .delicacies

5

6213	6213	369	5869	5774	2308	998
מִבִּינָתְךָ חֲדָל׃	הֲתָעִיף עֵינֶיךָ בּוֹ וְאֵינֶנּוּ כִּי עָשֹׂה יַעֲשֶׂה					
will it make	surely	For (it)	and on	your fly Will	.cease	your from
		!not is	,it	eyes		understanding

6

3899	398	408		8064	5774	5404	3671
לּוֹ כְנָפַיִם כְּנֶשֶׁר וְעוֹף הַשָּׁמָיִם׃	אַל־תִּלְחַם אֶת־לֶחֶם						
bread the of	eat Do not	not	the .heavens	will and into fly	eagle	an like	wings	for itself

7

5315	8176		4303	183	408	5869	7450
רַע עָיִן וְאַל־תִּתְאָו לְמַטְעַמֹּתָיו׃	כִּי כְּמוֹ־שָׁעַר בְּנַפְשׁוֹ						
his in soul,	he as reckons		for	his ;delicacies	do desire	and not	;eye an	evil

8

6595		1077	3820	559	8354	398	6310
כֵּן־הוּא אֱכֹל וּשְׁתֵה יֹאמַר לָךְ וְלִבּוֹ בַּל־עִמָּךְ׃							פִּתְּךָ
Your bit	with (is) not .you	his but heart	to he ;you says	and drink,	Eat	(is) so	!he

9

3684	241		5273	1697	78.43	6958	1398
אָכַלְתָּ תְקִיאֶנָּה וְשִׁחַתָּ דְּבָרֶיךָ הַנְּעִימִים׃ בְּאָזְנֵי כְסִיל							
fool a	the In of ears		.pleasant	your words	and spoil	shall you up vomit	have you ,eaten

10

5769	1366	5253	408	44.05	7922	936	1696	408
אַל־תְּדַבֵּר כִּי־יָבוּז לְשֵׂכֶל מִלֶּיךָ׃	אַל־תַּסֵּג גְּבוּל עוֹלָם							
old	the landmark	Do not move	your .words of	the prudence despise	will he for	do not	,speak

and do not enter into the fields of the fatherless; [11]for their Redeemer is mighty; He will contend for their cause with you. [12]Bring your heart in for instruction, and your ears to the words of knowledge. [13]Do not withhold correction from a boy; for *if* you strike him with the rod, he will not die. [14]You shall beat him with the rod, and you shall deliver him from Sheol. [15]My son, if your heart is wise, my heart shall rejoice, even I. [16]And my reins shall rejoice when your lips speak right things. [17]Do not let your heart envy sinners, but only *be* in the fear of Jehovah all the day. [18]For surely there is a hereafter, and your hope shall not be cut off. [19]My son, hear you, and be wise; and advance your heart in the way. [20]Be not among heavy drinkers of wine, with flesh-gluttons to themselves; [21]for the drunkard and the glutton lose all; and sleepiness shall clothe *one with* rags. [22]Listen to your father, this one fathered you; and do not despise your mother when she is old. [23]Buy the truth, and sell *it* not; *also* wisdom, and instruction and understanding. [24]The father of the righteous shall greatly rejoice; and he who fathers a wise one shall even be glad in him. [25]Your father and your mother shall be glad; and she who bore you shall rejoice. [26]My son, give Me your heart; and let your eyes watch My ways. [27]For a harlot *is* a deep pit, and a strange woman *is* a narrow well. [28]Surely she lies in wait, as for prey; and she increases the treacherous among men.

[29]Who *has* woe; who sorrow? Who *has* contentions; who *has* babbling? Who *has* wounds without cause? Who *has* dullness of eyes? [30]—those who stay long at the wine; those who go to seek mixed wine. [31]Do not look at the wine

11 ובשדי יתומים אל־תבא׃ כי־גאלם חזק הוא־יריב את־
shall He is their for do not the into and
for contend ;mighty Redeemer ;enter fatherless of fields the

12 ריבם אתך׃ הביאה למוסר לבך ואזניך לאמרי־דעת׃
.knowledge the to your and your for Bring with their
of words ears ,heart instruction in .you cause

13 אל־תמנע מנער מוסר כי־תכנו בשבט לא ימות׃
14 אתה
You will he not the with you (if) for correc- a from Do not
.die rod him strike ;tion boy withhold

15 בשבט תכנו ונפשו משאול תציל׃ בני אם־חכם לבך
your is if My shall you from and shall the with
heart wise ,son .deliver Sheol soul his him beat rod

16 ישמח לבי גם־אני׃ ותעלזנה כליותי בדבר שפתיך
your when my shall And .I even my shall
lips speak .reins exult ,heart rejoice

17 מישרים׃ אל־יקנא לבך בחטאים כי אם־ביראת יהוה
Jehovah the in only but against your let Do not right
of fear (be) sinners heart envy .things

18 כל־היום׃ כי אם־יש אחרית ותקותך לא תכרת׃
19 שמע־
Hear be shall not your and -here a there surely For the all
.off cut hope after is .day

20 אתה בני וחכם ואשר בדרך לבך׃ אל־תהי בסבאי־יין
;wine heavy with Do not your the in and be and my ,you
of drinkers be .heart way advance ;wise ,son

21 בזללי בשר למו׃ כי־סבא וזולל יורש וקרעים תלביש
shall (with) and lose the and the For them- to flesh- with
(one) clothe rags ;all glutton drunkard selves gluttons

22 נומה׃ שמע לאביך זה ילדך ואל־תבוז כי־זקנה אמך׃
your is she when do and begot this your to Listen .sleepiness
.mother old despise not ;you one :father

23 אמת קנה ואל־תמכר חכמה ומוסר ובינה׃
24 גיל יגיל
shall greatly under- and and (also) sell do and obtain the
rejoice .standing instruction ,wisdom ;(it) not truth

25 אבי צדיק יולד חכם וישמח־בו׃ ישמח־אביך ואמך
your and your be Let in even shall wise a the and right- the The
;mother father glad .him .glad be one of father ;eous of father

26 ותגל יולדתך׃ תנה־בני לבך לי ועיניך דרכי תצרנה׃
let my your and to your my ,Give who she let and
.watch ways eyes ;me heart ,son .you bore rejoice

27 כי־שוחה עמקה זונה ובאר צרה נכריה׃
28 אף־היא
she surely strange a narrow a and a (is) deep pit a For
woman well ,harlot

29 כחתף תארב ובוגדים באדם תוסף׃ למי אוי למי אבוי
(is) To (is) To she among the and in lies for as
?sorrow whom ?woe whom .increases men treacherous ;wait prey

למי מדונים ׀ למי־שיח למי פצעים חנם למי חכללות
dullness, To without (are) To ?babbling To ;contentions To
of whom ?cause wounds whom whom whom

30 עינים׃ למאחרים על־היין לבאים לחקר ממסך׃
31 אל־
not mixed seek to those the over who Those ?eyes
.wine in go who ;wine long stay

when it is red; when it gives its color in the cup; when it goes *down* smoothly—[32]at its last it bites like a snake, and it stings like a viper. [33]Your eyes shall look on strange women; and your heart shall speak perverse things; [34]yes, you shall be as one who lies down in the middle of the sea; or as he who lies on the top of a mast, [35]*saying,* They struck me! I was not sick! They beat me, *yet* I did not know. When I awaken, I will add *to it,* I will still seek it.

4334 1980 5869 3563 5414 119 3196 7200
תֵּרֶא יַיִן כִּי יִתְאַדָּם כִּי־יִתֵּן בַּכּוֹס עֵינוֹ יִתְהַלֵּךְ בְּמֵישָׁרִים׃
—smoothly it when its the in it when is it when the look Do
(down) goes ;eye cup gives ;red (down) wine at

2114 7200 5869 6567 6848 5391 5175 319
32 33 אַחֲרִיתוֹ כְּנָחָשׁ יִשָּׁךְ וּכְצִפְעֹנִי יַפְרִשׁ׃ עֵינֶיךָ יִרְאוּ זָרוֹת
strange shall Your it like and it a like its at
;women on look eyes stings viper a ;bites snake last

7901 3220 3820 7901 1961 8419 1696 3820
34 וְלִבְּךָ יְדַבֵּר תַּהְפֻּכוֹת׃ וְהָיִיתָ כְּשֹׁכֵב בְּלֶב־יָם וּכְשֹׁכֵב
he as or the the in who one as you And perverse shall your and
lies who ;sea of heart down lies be shall .things speak heart

4100 3045 1077 1986 2470 1077 5221 2260 7218
35 בְּרֹאשׁ חִבֵּל׃ הִכּוּנִי בַל־חָלִיתִי הֲלָמוּנִי בַּל־יָדָעְתִּי מָתַי
When did I not They was I not struck They a the on
.(it) know ;me beat !sick ;me .mast of top

5750 1245 3254 6974
אָקִיץ אוֹסִיף אֲבַקְשֶׁנּוּ עוֹד׃
.still will I will I I will
it seek ,add ,awaken

CAP. XXIV כד

CHAPTER 24

[1]Do not envy evil men, nor desire to be with them. [2]For their heart studies violence, and their lips talk of mischief. [3]Through wisdom a house is built; and it is established by understanding; [4]and by knowledge the rooms shall be filled with all precious and pleasant riches. [5]A wise warrior *is* in strength; yes, a man of knowledge firms up power. [6]For you shall make war for yourself by wise advice; and safety *is* in the great counselor. [7]Wisdom *is* too high for a fool; he does not open his mouth in the gate. [8]He who plots to do evil shall be called a lord of evil plots [9]The plot of foolishness *is* sin; and the scorner *is* hateful to men. [10]*If* you faint in the day of distress, your strength *is* small. [11]If you hold back *to* deliver those being taken to death, and *those* stumbling for killing;—[12]for you say, Behold, we did not know it—does not He who weighs the heart consider? And He who keeps our soul, does He *not* know? And He repays to a man according to his work. [13]My son, eat honey because *it is* good; and the honeycomb *is*

7701 1961 183 408 7451 582 7065 408
1 2 אַל־תְּקַנֵּא בְּאַנְשֵׁי רָעָה וְאַל־תִּתְאָו לִהְיוֹת אִתָּם׃ כִּי־שֹׁד
For with be to do and ,evil men Do not
violence .them desire not of envy

1129 2451 1696 8193 5999 3820 1897
3 יֶהְגֶּה לִבָּם וְעָמָל שִׂפְתֵיהֶם תְּדַבֵּרְנָה׃ בְּחָכְמָה יִבָּנֶה
built is Through .speak lips their and their medi-
wisdom mischief ;heart tates

1952 3605 4390 2315 1847 3559 8394 1004
4 בַּיִת וּבִתְבוּנָה יִתְכּוֹנָן׃ וּבְדַעַת חֲדָרִים יִמָּלְאוּ כָּל־הוֹן
riches all be will the by and is it with and ;house a
with filled rooms knowledge ;established understanding

3581 553 1847 376 5797 1397 5265 3368
5 6 יָקָר וְנָעִים׃ גֶּבֶר־חָכָם בַּעוֹז וְאִישׁ־דַּעַת מְאַמֶּץ־כֹּחַ׃ כִּי
For .might up firms know- and in (is) warrior wise A and precious
ledge of man a ;strength .pleasant

3289 7230 8668 4421 6213 8458
בְתַחְבֻּלוֹת תַּעֲשֶׂה־לְּךָ מִלְחָמָה וּתְשׁוּעָה בְּרֹב יוֹעֵץ׃
coun- by (is) and ;war for shall you wise with
.selor great the deliverance yourself make advice

2803 6310 6605 3808 8179 2454 191 7311
7 8 רָאמוֹת לֶאֱוִיל חָכְמוֹת בַּשַּׁעַר לֹא יִפְתַּח־פִּיהוּ׃ מְחַשֵּׁב
who He his does he not the in ;Wisdom a for too (is)
devises .mouth open gate fool high

8441 2403 200 2154 7121 4209 1167 7489
9 לְהָרֵעַ לוֹ בַּעַל־מְזִמּוֹת יִקְרָאוּ׃ זִמַּת אִוֶּלֶת חַטָּאת וְתוֹעֲבַת
(is) and (is) foolish- The be shall evil lord a to do to
hateful ;sin ness of plot .called plots of .him ,evil

5337 3581 6862 6864 3117 7503 3887 120
10 11 לְאָדָם לֵץ׃ הִתְרַפִּיתָ בְּיוֹם צָרָה צַר כֹּחֶכָה׃ הַצֵּל
Deliver your (is) distress the in you (If) the men to
.strength narrow of day faint .scorner

2009 559 2820 2027 4131 4194 3947
12 לְקֻחִים לַמָּוֶת וּמָטִים לַהֶרֶג אִם־תַּחְשׂוֹךְ׃ כִּי־תֹאמַר הֵן
be- you for hold you unless for those and to being those
,hold ,say .back ;killing stumbling ,death taken

5315 5341 995 3826 8505 3808/2088 3045/3808
לֹא־יָדַעְנוּ זֶה הֲלֹא־תֹכֵן לִבּוֹת הוּא־יָבִין וְנֹצֵר נַפְשְׁךָ הוּא
(Does) your the And consider the He not does ,this did we not
he ,soul of Keeper ?it hearts weighs who know

5317 2896 1706 1121 398 6467 120 7725 3045
13 יֵדָע וְהֵשִׁיב לְאָדָם כְּפָעֳלוֹ׃ אֱכָל־בְּנִי דְבַשׁ כִּי־טוֹב וְנֹפֶת
the and (is it) for honey my ,Eat according a to He And
comb ;good ,son ?work his to man repays ?know

14 מָתוֹק עַל־חִכֶּךָ׃ כֵּן ׀ דְּעֶה חָכְמָה לְנַפְשֶׁךָ אִם־מָצָאתָ

have you when found | to (be) ;soul your | wisdom | knowledge of | so (shall) | your ;palate | on | is sweet

15 וְיֵשׁ אַחֲרִית וְתִקְוָתְךָ לֹא תִכָּרֵת׃ אַל־תֶּאֱרֹב רָשָׁע לִנְוֵה

the at abode | O ,wicked | lie do ,ambush in | not | cut is .off | not | your and hope | here- after | a there that is

16 צַדִּיק אַל־תְּשַׁדֵּד רִבְצוֹ׃ כִּי שֶׁבַע ׀ יִפּוֹל צַדִּיק וָקָם

rises and ;again | just a one | falls | seven (times) | for | resting- his ;place | do violate | not | the ;righteous

17 וּרְשָׁעִים יִכָּשְׁלוּ בְרָעָה׃ בִּנְפֹל אוֹיִבְךָ אַל־תִּשְׂמָח וּבִכָּשְׁלוֹ

when and stumbles he | do ;rejoice | not | your enemy | When falls | into .evil | shall stumble | the but wicked

18 אַל־יָגֵל לִבֶּךָ׃ פֶּן־יִרְאֶה יְהוָה וְרַע בְּעֵינָיו וְהֵשִׁיב מֵעָלָיו

from him | He and away turn | His in ,eyes | (it) and evil (be) | Jehovah | see | lest | your ;heart | let do glad be | not

19 אַפּוֹ׃ אַל־תִּתְחַר בַּמְּרֵעִים אַל־תְּקַנֵּא בָּרְשָׁעִים׃

20 כִּי ׀

for | the ;wicked | do envy | (and) not | of because ,evildoers | glow Do (anger in) | not | His anger

21 לֹא־תִהְיֶה אַחֲרִית לָרָע נֵר רְשָׁעִים יִדְעָךְ׃ יְרָא־אֶת־יְהוָה

,Jehovah | Fear | be shall .out put | the wicked | the of lamp | the to ;evil | here- after | a | there be shall | not

22 בְּנִי וָמֶלֶךְ עִם־שׁוֹנִים אַל־תִּתְעָרָב׃ כִּי־פִתְאֹם יָקוּם אֵידָם

their ;woe | shall rise | suddenly For | .meddle do | not | who those with change | the and ;king | my ,son

23 וּפִיד שְׁנֵיהֶם מִי יוֹדֵעַ׃ גַּם־אֵלֶּה לַחֲכָמִים הַכֵּר־פָּנִים

faces | to know | the for ;wise | these (are) | Also | ?knows who | of both them | the and of ruin

24 בְּמִשְׁפָּט בַּל־טוֹב׃ אֹמֵר לְרָשָׁע צַדִּיק אָתָּה יִקְּבֻהוּ עַמִּים

the ;peoples | shall him curse | you —(are) | righteous | the to —wicked | who He says | (is) | not .good | judgment in

25 יִזְעָמוּהוּ לְאֻמִּים׃ וְלַמּוֹכִיחִים יִנְעָם וַעֲלֵיהֶם תָּבוֹא בִרְכַּת־

blessing a | comes | on and them | is it ;pleasant | those to But rebuke who | the .nations | abhor shall him

26 טוֹב׃ שְׂפָתַיִם יִשָּׁק מֵשִׁיב דְּבָרִים נְכֹחִים׃

27 הָכֵן בַּחוּץ ׀

outside | Prepare | .straight | words | that return | He kiss shall | lips the | .good

28 מְלַאכְתֶּךָ וְעַתְּדָהּ בַּשָּׂדֶה לָךְ אַחַר וּבָנִיתָ בֵיתֶךָ׃ אַל־תְּהִי

Do be | not | your .house | even build | after- ;wards | for ;you | the in ,field | make and ready it | your ;work

29 עֵד־חִנָּם בְּרֵעֶךָ וַהֲפִתִּיתָ בִּשְׂפָתֶיךָ׃ אַל־תֹּאמַר כַּאֲשֶׁר

As | do ,say | not | your with ;lips | or deceive | a against ,neighbor | witness a causelessly

30 עָשָׂה־לִי כֵּן אֶעֱשֶׂה־לּוֹ אָשִׁיב לָאִישׁ כְּפָעֳלוֹ׃ עַל־שְׂדֵה

the over of field | according .work his to | (each) to man | will I repay | to ;him | will I do | so | to ,me | has he done

31 אִישׁ־עָצֵל עָבַרְתִּי וְעַל־כֶּרֶם אָדָם חֲסַר־לֵב׃ וְהִנֵּה עָלָה

was it ,up going | and ,lo | ;heartless | the man | the of vineyard | by and | I ,passed | lazy | the man

כֻלּוֹ ׀ קִמְּשֹׂנִים כָּסּוּ פָנָיו חֲרֻלִּים וְגֶדֶר אֲבָנָיו נֶהֱרָסָה׃

broken was .down | its stone | and wall | ;nettles | sur- its face | had covered | with ;thistles | of all it

sweet to your palate; [14]so *shall* knowledge of wisdom *be* to your soul; when you have found there is a future, and your hope is not cut off. [15]O wicked one, do not lie in ambush against the dwelling of the righteous; do not violate his resting place; [16]for a just one falls seven *times*, and rises up again; but the wicked shall stumble into evil. [17]Do not rejoice when your enemy falls; and do not let your heart be glad when he stumbles; [18]that Jehovah not see and it be evil in His eyes; and He turn away His anger from him. [19]Do not burn *in anger* because of evildoers, and do not envy the wicked; [20]for no hereafter shall be to the evil; the lamp of the wicked will be put out. [21]My son, fear Jehovah and the king; do not meddle with those who change; [22]for their calamity shall rise suddenly; and who knows the ruin of both of them?

[23]These also are for the wise: to know persons in judgment *is* not good; [24]he who says to the wicked, You *are* righteous—the peoples shall curse him; nations shall abhor him. [25]But to those who rebuke, it is pleasant; and a good blessing comes to them. [26]He shall kiss the lips that return right words. [27]Prepare your work outside; and make it fit for yourself in the field; and afterwards build your house. [28]Do not be a witness against your neighbor without cause, or deceive with your lips; [29]do not say, I will do to him as he has done to me; I will repay each according to his work.

[30]I passed over the field of the lazy man, and by the vineyard of the heartless man; [31]and, lo, it was going up, all of it with thistles; nettles had covered its surface and its stone wall was broken

down—[32]then I saw—I set my heart on it—I looked—I received instruction: [33]A little sleep, a little slumber, a little folding of the hands to sleep; [34]so shall your poverty come stalking; and your want like a man *with* a shield.

32 33 8142 4592 4148 3947 7200 3820 7896 2372
וָאֶחֱזֶה אָנֹכִי אָשִׁית לִבִּי רָאִיתִי לָקַחְתִּי מוּסָר׃ מְעַט שֵׁנוֹת
,sleep A :instruction I looked I my set I I And
little received ;heart ;beheld

34 1980 935 7901 3027 2264 4592 8572 4592
מְעַט תְּנוּמוֹת מְעַט ׀ חִבֻּק יָדַיִם לִשְׁכָּב׃ וּבָא־מִתְהַלֵּךְ
walking then lie to the folding a ,slumber little a
about comes ;down hands of little

4043 376 4270 7389
רֵישֶׁךָ וּמַחְסֹרֶיךָ כְּאִישׁ מָגֵן׃
a (with) a like your and your
.shield man want ;poverty

CAP. XXV כה

CHAPTER 25

CHAPTER 25

[1]These *are* the proverbs of Solomon, which the men of Hezekiah king of Judah copied out: [2]The glory of God *is* to conceal a thing; but the glory of kings *is* to search out a matter. [3]The heavens for height; and the earth for depth; but the heart of kings *is* unsearchable. [4]Take away the dross from the silver, and a vessel of the refiner's shall appear. [5]Take away the wicked from before the king; and his throne is established in righteousness. [6]Do not honor yourself before a king; and do not stand in the place of the great. [7]For it is better he shall say to you, Come up here! than that you should be put lower before a noble whom your eyes have seen. [8]Do not hastily go out to fight. What shall you do in the end of it, when your neighbor has put you to shame? [9]Contend for your cause with your neighbor; and do not uncover the secret of another; [10]lest he who hears put you to shame; and your slander have no end. [11]A word rightly spoken *is like* apples of gold in settings of silver. [12]*As* a ring of gold, and an ornament of fine gold, *so is* a wise reprover on a hearing ear. [13]Like the cold of snow in harvest time, *so is* a faithful messenger to those sending him; for he refreshes his master's soul. [14]He who boasts himself of a false gift *is like* clouds and wind, and with no rain.

1 2396 582 6275 834 8010 4912 428 1571
גַּם־אֵלֶּה מִשְׁלֵי שְׁלֹמֹה אֲשֶׁר הֶעְתִּיקוּ אַנְשֵׁי ׀ חִזְקִיָּה
Hezekiah the made which ,Solomon proverbs These also
of men advance of (are)

2 4428 3519 1697 5640 430 3519 3063 4428
מֶלֶךְ־יְהוּדָה׃ כְּבֹד אֱלֹהִים הַסְתֵּר דָּבָר וּכְבֹד מְלָכִים
kings the but a to God the :Judah king
(is) of glory ;matter conceal (is) of glory of

3 369 4428 3820 6011 776 7312 8064 1697 2713
חֲקֹר דָּבָר׃ שָׁמַיִם לָרוּם וָאָרֶץ לָעֹמֶק וְלֵב מְלָכִים אֵין
there kings the but for the and for The a search to
no is of heart ;depth earth ;height heavens .matter out

4 5 7563 1898 3627 6884 3318 3701 5509 1898 2714
חֵקֶר׃ הָגוֹ סִיגִים מִכָּסֶף וַיֵּצֵא לַצֹּרֵף כֶּלִי׃ הָגוֹ רָשָׁע
the Take a the as shall and the from the Take search-
wicked away .vessel refiners out go ,silver dross away .ing

6 4428 6440 1921 408 3678 6664 3559 4428/6440
לִפְנֵי־מֶלֶךְ וְיִכּוֹן בַּצֶּדֶק כִּסְאוֹ׃ אַל־תִּתְהַדַּר לִפְנֵי־מֶלֶךְ
a before honor Do not his righ- in is and a (from)
;king yourself .throne teousness settled ,king before

7 5927 559 2896 5975 408 1419 4725
וּבִמְקוֹם גְּדֹלִים אַל־תַּעֲמֹד׃ כִּי טוֹב אֲמָר־לְךָ עֲלֵה הֵנָּה
!here Come to he is it for do not the the in and
up ,you says better —stand great of place

8 7378 3318 408 5869 7200 834 5081 6440 8213
מֵהַשְׁפִּילְךָ לִפְנֵי נָדִיב אֲשֶׁר רָאוּ עֵינֶיךָ׃ אַל־תֵּצֵא לָרִב
to go Do not your have whom a before be you than
fight out .eyes seen noble lower put

7453 3637 319 6213 4100 6435 4118
מַהֵר פֶּן מַה־תַּעֲשֶׂה בְּאַחֲרִיתָהּ בְּהַכְלִים אֹתְךָ רֵעֶךָ׃
your you has when the in shall what ,lest ;hastily
?neighbor shamed ,it of end do you

9 10 2616 6435 1540 408 312 5475 7453 7378 7379
רִיבְךָ רִיב אֶת־רֵעֶךָ וְסוֹד אַחֵר אַל־תְּגָל׃ פֶּן־יְחַסֶּדְךָ
you put lest do not another the and your with Contend your
shame to ;uncover of secret ;neighbor for cause

11 3701 4906 2091 8598 7725 3808 1681 8085
שֹׁמֵעַ וְדִבָּתְךָ לֹא תָשׁוּב׃ תַּפּוּחֵי זָהָב בְּמַשְׂכִּיּוֹת כָּסֶף
silver settings in gold (Like) returns not your and who he
of of apples report evil ;hears

12 2450 3198 2481 2481 2091 5141 655 1696 1697
דָּבָר דָּבֻר עַל־אָפְנָיו׃ נֶזֶם זָהָב וַחֲלִי־כָתֶם מוֹכִיחַ חָכָם
wise a (so) item an and ,golden a As the at spoken a (is)
reprover gold of ring .time (right) word

13 539 6735 7102 3117 7950 6793 8085 241
עַל־אֹזֶן שֹׁמָעַת׃ כְּצִנַּת־שֶׁלֶג ׀ בְּיוֹם קָצִיר צִיר נֶאֱמָן
faithful a (so) harvest a in snow Like ear an on
messenger of day cold .hearing

14 376 369 1653 5387 5387 7725 113 5315 7971
לְשֹׁלְחָיו וְנֶפֶשׁ אֲדֹנָיו יָשִׁיב׃ נְשִׂיאִים וְרוּחַ וְגֶשֶׁם אַיִן אִישׁ
a (is) (with) but and (Like) makes he his and his to
man ,no rain wind clouds .return master's soul ;senders

[15]In *being* slow to anger, a
ruler is persuaded, and a
soft tongue shatters the
bone. [16]Have you found
honey? Eat *only* your fill, lest
you be satiated, and vomit it
out. [17]Make your foot rare
from your neighbor's house;
lest he be full of you and
hate you. [18]A man who
gives false witness against
his neighbor *is* a maul, and
a sword and a sharp arrow.
[19]Confidence in a treacherous man in time of distress
is like a bad tooth and a
slipping foot. [20]*As* he who
takes away a garment in
cold weather, *and as*
vinegar on soda, *so is* he
who sings songs on an evil
heart. [21]If your hater is
hungry, give him bread to
eat; and if he is thirsty, give
him water to drink; [22]for
you shall heap coals *of fire*
on his head; and Jehovah
shall reward you. [23]The
north wind brings rain; so
does a secret tongue an
angry face. [24]*It is* better to
dwell in the corner of the
housetop, than to share a
house with a contentious
woman. [25]*Like* cold waters
to a weary soul, so *is* a good
report from a far country.
[26]The righteous falling
down before the wicked *is*
like a fouled fountain and a
ruined spring. [27]*It is* not
good to eat much honey;
and to search out their glory
is not glory. [28]A man *to*
whom there is no control to
his spirit *is* like a broken-
down city without a wall.

15 מִתְהַלֵּל בְּמַתַּת־שָׁקֶר׃ בְּאֹרֶךְ אַפַּיִם יְפֻתֶּה קָצִין וְלָשׁוֹן
3956 7101 6601 639 753 8267 4991 1984
a and tongue | a ,ruler | is persuaded | anger to | length In (before) | false- .hood | gift in of | boasting himself

16 רַכָּה תִּשְׁבָּר־גָּרֶם׃ דְּבַשׁ מָצָאתָ אֱכֹל דַּיֶּךָּ פֶּן־תִּשְׂבָּעֶנּוּ
7646 1767 398 4672 1706 1634 7665 7390
be you ,satiated | lest | your fill | Eat (only) | you Have ?found | honey | the .bone | shatters | soft

17 וַהֲקֵאתוֹ׃ הֹקַר רַגְלְךָ מִבֵּית רֵעֶךָ פֶּן־יִשְׂבָּעֲךָ וּשְׂנֵאֶךָ׃
8130 7646 7453 1004 7272 3365 6958
hate and .you | be he you of full | lest | your ,neighbor's | from house | your foot | make rare | vomit and ,out it

18 מֵפִיץ וְחֶרֶב וְחֵץ שָׁנוּן אִישׁ־עֹנֶה בְרֵעֵהוּ עֵד שָׁקֶר׃
19 שֵׁן
8127 8267 5707/7453 6030 376 8150 2671 2719 4650
(Like) tooth a | .false | witness | against neighbor his | who testifies | (is) man | a sharp | and arrow | a and ,sword | A ,maul

20 רָעָה וְרֶגֶל מוּעָדֶת מִבְטָח בּוֹגֵד בְּיוֹם צָרָה׃ מַעֲדֶה־בֶּגֶד
899 5710 6864 3117 898 4009 4154 7272 7465
a garment | one (As) removing | .distress | a in of day | a traitor | trust (is) in | slipping | a and foot | bad

21 בְּיוֹם קָרָה חֹמֶץ עַל־נָתֶר וְשָׁר בַּשִּׁרִים עַל לֶב־רָע׃ אִם־
518 7451/3820 7892 7891 5427 5921/2558 7135 3117
If | ,evil heart | a | on | with songs | one (so) singing | soda on | (as and) vinegar | ,cold | a in day

22 רָעֵב שֹׂנַאֲךָ הַאֲכִלֵהוּ לֶחֶם וְאִם־צָמֵא הַשְׁקֵהוּ מָיִם׃ כִּי
4325 8248 6771 518 3899 398 8130 7456
for | ;water | him gave drink to | is he thirsty | and if | ;bread | him give eat to | your ,hater | is hungry

23 גֶחָלִים אַתָּה חֹתֶה עַל־רֹאשׁוֹ וַיהוָה יְשַׁלֶּם־לָךְ׃ רוּחַ צָפוֹן
6828 7307 7999 3068 7218 5921 2846 1513
north | The wind | .you | shall reward | and Jehovah | his ;head | upon | shall heap | you | coals (fire of)

24 תְּחוֹלֵל גֶּשֶׁם וּפָנִים נִזְעָמִים לְשׁוֹן סָתֶר׃ טוֹב שֶׁבֶת עַל־
5921 3427 2896 5643 3956 2194 6440 1653 2342
on | to dwell | (is It) better | .secret | a (by) tongue | indignant | an and face | ;rain | brings forth

25 פִּנַּת־גָּג מֵאֵשֶׁת מִדְיָנִים וּבֵית חָבֶר׃ מַיִם קָרִים עַל־נֶפֶשׁ
5315 7119 4325 2267 1004 4066 802 1906/6438
soul a | to | cold | (Like) waters | to .share | a and house | strifes | with than of woman a | roof a corner

26 עֲיֵפָה וּשְׁמוּעָה טוֹבָה מֵאֶרֶץ מֶרְחָק׃ מַעְיָן נִרְפָּשׂ וּמָקוֹר
4726 7515 4599 4801 776 2896 8052 5889
a and fountain | fouled | (Like) spring a | .far off | a from country | good | report a (is) | ,weary

27 מָשְׁחָת צַדִּיק מָט לִפְנֵי־רָשָׁע׃ אָכֹל דְּבַשׁ הַרְבּוֹת לֹא־
3808 7235 1706 398 7563 6440 4131 6662 7843
not | much | honey | eat To | the .wicked | before | totter- ing | the (are) righteous | ruined

28 טוֹב וְחֵקֶר כְּבֹדָם כָּבוֹד׃ עִיר פְּרוּצָה אֵין חוֹמָה אִישׁ
376 2346 369 6555 5892 3519 3519 2714 2896
a (is) man | a wall | without | broken down | (Like) city a | (is) .glory | their glory | to and out search | (is) ;good

אֲשֶׁר אֵין מַעְצָר לְרוּחוֹ׃
7307 4623 369 834
his to .spirit | control | there not is | (to) whom

CAP. XXVI כו

CHAPTER 26

CHAPTER 26

[1]As snow in summer, and
as rain in harvest, so honor
is not right for a fool. [2]As
the wandering bird, as the
swallow in its flying, so the
causeless curse shall never
come. [3]A whip for the

1 כַּשֶּׁלֶג בַּקַּיִץ וְכַמָּטָר בַּקָּצִיר כֵּן לֹא־נָאוֶה לִכְסִיל כָּבוֹד׃
3519 3684 5000 3808/3651/7102 4306 7019 7950
.honor | a for fool | (is) right | not | so | in ,harvest | like and rain | in ,summer | Like snow

2 כַּצִּפּוֹר לָנוּד כַּדְּרוֹר לָעוּף כֵּן קִלְלַת חִנָּם לֹא תָבֹא׃
3 שׁוֹט
7752 935 2600 7045 5774 1866 5110 6833
A whip | shall come | not | cause- less | the curse | so | its in ,flying | the as swallow | ,wandering | the As bird

horse; a bridle for the ass;
and a rod for the back of
fools. 4Answer not a fool
according to his foolish-
ness, lest you also become
like him, even you.
5Answer a fool according to
his foolishness, that he not
be wise in his own eyes.
6He that sends a message
by a fool's hand cuts off his
own feet *and* drinks
violence. 7*As* the legs of
the lame *are* weak, *so* a
proverb in the mouth of
fools. 8As he binding a
stone on a sling, so he
giving honor to a fool. 9*As*
a thorn goes up into the
drunkard's hand, so a
proverb in the mouth of
fools. 10Great is the Former
of all things; but he who
hires a fool *is like* one who
hires those passing by.
11As a dog that returns to
his own vomit, *so* a fool
repeats his foolishness.
12Do you see a man wise in
his own eyes? *There is more*
hope for a fool than for
him. 13The lazy one says, A
lion *is* in the way; a lion *is*
between the streets! 14*As*
the door turns on its hinge,
so the lazy one on his bed.
15The lazy one buries his
hand in the dish; he is
weary to bring it back to his
mouth. 16The lazy one *is*
wiser in his own eyes than
seven that return a wise
answer.

17The passer-by en-
raging himself over strife
not his own *is like* one
who grabs the ears of a
dog. 18Like a madman
throwing sparks, arrows
and death, 19so *is* the
man who deceives his
neighbor and says, Am I
not joking? 20The fire
goes out when the wood
ceases; and when there
is no whisperer the strife
grows silent. 21*As* coal to
burning embers, so *is* a
contentious man to
kindle strife. 22A whis-
perer's words *are* like
burns, and they descend
into the chambers of the
heart. 23*As with* silver
dross laid over an

4 לְסּוּס מֶתֶג לַחֲמוֹר וְשֵׁבֶט לְגֵו כְּסִילִים׃ אַל־תַּעַן כְּסִיל
fool a Do not .fools the for a and the for a the for
answer of back rod ;ass bridle ,horse

5 כְּאִוַּלְתּוֹ פֶּן־תִּשְׁוֶה־לּוֹ גַם־אָתָּה׃ עֲנֵה כְסִיל כְּאִוַּלְתּוֹ פֶּן
lest his by a Answer .you even ,him you lest his by
,folly fool like become ,folly

6 יִהְיֶה חָכָם בְּעֵינָיו׃ מְקַצֶּה רַגְלַיִם חָמָס שֹׁתֶה שֹׁלֵחַ
who ,drinks (and) (own his) cuts (He) his in wise may he
sends violence feet off .eyes own be

7 דְּבָרִים בְּיַד־כְּסִיל׃ דַּלְיוּ שֹׁקַיִם מִפִּסֵּחַ וּמָשָׁל בְּפִי
the in a is so the the Weak a by messages
of mouth proverb ,lame of legs (are) .fool's hand

8 כְסִילִים׃ כִּצְרוֹר אֶבֶן בְּמַרְגֵּמָה כֵּן־נוֹתֵן לִכְסִיל כָּבוֹד׃
.honor a to he so a on a who he As .fools
fool gives who ,sling stone binds

9
10 חוֹחַ עָלָה בְיַד־שִׁכּוֹר וּמָשָׁל בְּפִי כְסִילִים׃ רַב מְחוֹלֵל־
Former the Great .fools the in a and the into goes A
of (is) of mouth proverb ,drunkard's hand up thorn

11 כֹּל וְשֹׂכֵר כְּסִיל וְשֹׂכֵר עֹבְרִים׃ כְּכֶלֶב שָׁב עַל־קֵאוֹ כְּסִיל
fool a own its to that As those (like is) ,fool a he but all
,vomit returns dog a .by passing hiring one hires who ;things

12 שׁוֹנֶה בְאִוַּלְתּוֹ׃ רָאִיתָ אִישׁ חָכָם בְּעֵינָיו תִּקְוָה לִכְסִיל
a for (more) his in wise a you Do his with repeats
fool hope ?eyes own man see .foolishness

13
14 מִמֶּנּוּ׃ אָמַר עָצֵל שַׁחַל בַּדָּרֶךְ אֲרִי בֵּין הָרְחֹבוֹת׃ הַדֶּלֶת
the (As) the is a in (is) A The says (for) than
door !streets between lion ;way the lion ,one lazy .him

15 תִּסּוֹב עַל־צִירָהּ וְעָצֵל עַל־מִטָּתוֹ׃ טָמַן עָצֵל יָדוֹ בַּצַּלָּחַת
the in his The buries his on the (so) its on turns
,dish hand one lazy .couch one lazy ,hinge

16 נִלְאָה לַהֲשִׁיבָהּ אֶל־פִּיו׃ חָכָם עָצֵל בְּעֵינָיו מִשִּׁבְעָה מְשִׁיבֵי
that than his in The (is) his to bring to is he
return seven eyes own one lazy wiser .mouth back it weary

17 טָעַם׃ מַחֲזִיק בְּאָזְנֵי־כָלֶב עֹבֵר מִתְעַבֵּר עַל־רִיב לֹּא־לוֹ׃
to not strife over crossing the (is) a the one (Like) wise a
.him (is that) himself by passer ,dog of ears grabs who .answer

18
19 כְּמִתְלַהְלֵהַּ הַיֹּרֶה זִקִּים חִצִּים וָמָוֶת׃ כֵּן־אִישׁ רִמָּה אֶת־
who the so and ,arrows ,sparks who a Like
deceives man (is) .death throws madman

20 רֵעֵהוּ וְאָמַר הֲלֹא־מְשַׂחֵק אָנִי׃ בְּאֶפֶס עֵצִים תִּכְבֶּה־אֵשׁ
the goes ,wood where ?I Am ,says and his
;fire out no is joking not ,neighbor

21 וּבְאֵין נִרְגָּן יִשְׁתֹּק מָדוֹן׃ פֶּחָם לְגֶחָלִים וְעֵצִים לְאֵשׁ
to and to burning (As) the grows whisperer and
,fire wood embers coal .strife silent no where

22 וְאִישׁ מִדְוָנִים לְחַרְחַר־רִיב׃ דִּבְרֵי נִרְגָּן כְּמִתְלַהֲמִים וְהֵם
and like (are) a The .contention to strifes (is) so
they burns whisperer of words kindle of man a

23 יָרְדוּ חַדְרֵי־בָטֶן׃ כֶּסֶף סִיגִים מְצֻפֶּה עַל־חָרֶשׂ שְׂפָתַיִם
(are so) an over laid dross (with As) the the enter
lips ,vessel earthen silver .heart of chambers into

earthen vessel, *so are* burning lips and an evil heart. 24He who hates dissembles with his lips, and in his inner being he lays up deceit; 25when his voice favors, do not believe him, for seven hateful things *are* in his heart. 26*Though his* hatred *is* covered by guile, his evil will be revealed in the assembly. 27He who digs a pit shall fall into it, and he rolling a stone, to him it shall turn back. 28A lying tongue hates the one it crushes, and a flattering mouth works stumbling.

CHAPTER 27

1Do not boast in the day of tomorrow, for you do not know what a day may bring forth. 2Let another praise you, and not your own mouth; *let it be* a stranger, and not your own lips. 3A stone *is* heavy, and sand a burden; but a fool's anger *is* heavier than both. 4Fury *is* fierce, and anger overflows; but who can stand before jealousy? 5Better *is* revealed reproof than secret love. 6Faithful *are* the wounds of a lover; and the kisses of a hated one *are* plentiful. 7One who is full tramples a honeycomb; but to a hungry soul, every bitter thing *is* sweet. 8A man wandering from his place *is like* a bird that wanders from the nest. 9Ointment and perfume give joy to the heart; and one's friend *is* sweet from the counsel of the soul. 10Do not forsake your friend, nor your father's friend; and do not go into your brother's house in the day of your calamity; *for* a near neighbor *is* better than a brother far away. 11My son, become wise and give joy to my heart; so that I may return a word to him that taunts me. 12A sensible man sees the evil and hides himself; the simple go on *and* are

7896 7130 8130 5234 8193 7451 3820 1814
24 דֹּלְקִים וְלֶב־רָע׃ בִּשְׂפָתָו יִנָּכֵר שׂוֹנֵא וּבְקִרְבּוֹ יָשִׁית
lays he | his in and | who He dissembles | with | evil | and | burning
up | being inner | ;hates | lips his | heart a

8441 7651 539 408 6963 2603 4820
25 מִרְמָה׃ כִּי־יְחַנֵּן קוֹלוֹ אַל־תַּאֲמֶן־בּוֹ כִּי שֶׁבַע תּוֹעֵבוֹת
hateful | seven | for | ,him | do | not | his | is when | ;deceit
things | believe | ,voice | gracious

3738 6951 7451 1540 4860 8130 3680 3820
26 27 בְּלִבּוֹ׃ תִּכַּסֶּה שִׂנְאָה בְּמַשָּׁאוֹן תִּגָּלֶה רָעָתוֹ בְקָהָל׃ כֹּרֶה
who He | the in | his | be shall | by | Hatred | is | in (are)
digs | .assembly | evil | revealed | ;guile | covered | .heart his

8130 8267 395 7725 68 1556 5307 7845
28 שַׁחַת בָּהּ יִפֹּל וְגֹלֵל אֶבֶן אֵלָיו תָּשׁוּב׃ לְשׁוֹן־שֶׁקֶר יִשְׂנָא
hates | lying | tongue A | shall it | to | a | he and | shall | into | pit a
.return | him | —stone | rolls who | ;fall | it

4072 6213 2509 6310 1790
דַכָּיו וּפֶה חָלָק יַעֲשֶׂה מִדְחֶה׃
stumbling | works | flattering | a and | it those
mouth | crushes

CAP. XXVII כז

CHAPTER 27

1984 3117 3205 3045 3808 4279 3117 1984 3808
1 2 אַל־תִּתְהַלֵּל בְּיוֹם מָחָר כִּי לֹא־תֵדַע מַה־יֵּלֶד יוֹם׃ יְהַלֶּלְךָ
praise Let | a | may what | do you not | for | to- | the in | boast | Do | not
you | .day | forth bring | know | ,morrow | of day

2344 5192 68 3514 8193 3808 5237 6310 2114
3 זָר וְלֹא־פִיךָ נָכְרִי וְאַל־שְׂפָתֶיךָ׃ כֹּבֶד־אֶבֶן וְנֵטֶל הַחוֹל
;sand | a and | A | (is) | own your | and | one | your | and | an-
burden | stone | heavy | .lips | not | ,foreign | ;mouth | not | ,alien

639 7858 2534 395 8147 3515 191 3708
4 וְכַעַס אֱוִיל כָּבֵד מִשְּׁנֵיהֶם׃ אַכְזְרִיּוּת חֵמָה וְשֶׁטֶף אָף
;anger | is and | Fury | fierce | both than | (is) | fool's a | but
overflowing | (is) | .them of | heavier | vexation

160 1540 8433 2896 7068 6440 5975
5 וּמִי יַעֲמֹד לִפְנֵי קִנְאָה׃ טוֹבָה תּוֹכַחַת מְגֻלָּה מֵאַהֲבָה
love than | revealed | reproof | (is) Better | ?jealousy | before | can | but
stand | who

8130 5390 6280 157 6482 539 5640
6 מְסֻתָּרֶת׃ נֶאֱמָנִים פִּצְעֵי אוֹהֵב וְנַעְתָּרוֹת נְשִׁיקוֹת שׂוֹנֵא׃
hated a | kisses the | (are) but | a | wounds | Faithful | .concealed
one | of | plentiful | lover's | (are)

4966 4751 7456 5315 5317 947 7649 5315
7 נֶפֶשׁ שְׂבֵעָה תָּבוּס נֹפֶת וְנֶפֶשׁ רְעֵבָה כָּל־מַר מָתוֹק׃
(is) | bitter every | ,hungry | (to) but | honey-a | tramples | A | soul
.sweet | thing | soul a | ;comb | sated

8081 4725 5074 376 3651 7064 5074 6833
8 9 כְּצִפּוֹר נוֹדֶדֶת מִן־קִנָּהּ כֵּן־אִישׁ נוֹדֵד מִמְּקוֹמוֹ׃ שֶׁמֶן
Oil | his from | wander- | a | so | its from | wandering | a Like
.place | ing | man | (is) | ,nest | bird

7453 7453 5315 6098 7453 4986 3820/8056 7004
10 וּקְטֹרֶת יְשַׂמַּח־לֵב וּמֶתֶק רֵעֵהוּ מֵעֲצַת־נָפֶשׁ׃ רֵעֲךָ וְרֵעַ
nor | Your | the | the from | one's | (is) and | the | joy give | and
friend | ,friend | .soul | of counsel | friend | sweet | ;heart | to | perfume

2896 343 3117 935 3808 251 1004 5800 1
אָבִיךָ אַל־תַּעֲזֹב וּבֵית אָחִיךָ אַל־תָּבוֹא בְּיוֹם אֵידֶךָ טוֹב
(is for) | your | the in | go do | not | your | and | do | not | your
better | ;calamity | of day | into | brother's | house | ;forsake | ,father's

7725 3820 8056 1121 2450 7350 251 7138 7934
11 שָׁכֵן קָרוֹב מֵאָח רָחוֹק׃ חֲכַם בְּנִי וְשַׂמַּח לִבִּי וְאָשִׁיבָה
I that so | my | give and | my | Be | far | a than | near | a
return may | ;heart | to joy | ,son | ,wise | .away | brother | neighbor

5674 6612 5640 7451 7200 6175 1697 2778
12 חֹרְפִי דָבָר׃ עָרוּם רָאָה רָעָה נִסְתָּר פְּתָאיִם עָבְרוּ
pass | the | hides and | the | sees | sensible a | a | my
on | simple | ;himself | evil | one | .word | reproacher

punished. [13]Take the garment of him who is surety for a stranger; and hold him in pledge *who is surety* for a strange woman. [14]He who rises early in the morning and blesses his friend with a loud voice, it is counted as cursing to him. [15]Drops that never cease on a rainy day, and a contentious woman are alike; [16]he who hides her hides the wind, and his right hand encounters *slippery* oil. [17]Iron sharpens iron; so a man sharpens his friend's face. [18]The keeper of the fig tree eats its fruit; so he keeping his master is honored. [19]As face *reflects* face *in* the water, so the heart of man *reflects* a man. [20]Sheol and destruction are never satisfied; so the eyes of man are never satisfied. [21]The refining pot *tries* silver, and the furnace *tries* gold; but a man *is tried* by the mouth of his praise. [22]If you pound a fool in the mortar with a pestle amidst grain, his foolishness will not turn away from him.

[23]Know well the state of your flock; set your heart on your herds; [24]for wealth *is* not forever; nor the crown from generation *to* generation. [25]When the hay is removed, and the tender grass is seen, and the mountain-plants are taken up, [26]the lambs *will be* for your clothing; and the he-goats the price for a field; [27]and there will be goat's milk enough for your food; for the food of your household, and *for* the life of your maidens.

2254 5237 2114 6148 899 3947 6064

13 נֶעֱנָשׁוּ׃ קַח־בִּגְדוֹ כִּי־עָרַב זָר וּבְעַד נָכְרִיָּה חַבְלֵהוּ׃

him bind .pledge in | strange a woman | and for | a ;stranger | is he for surety | when | his garment | Take | are (and) .punished

2803 7045 7925 1242 1419 6963 7453 1288

14 מְבָרֵךְ רֵעֵהוּ ׀ בְּקוֹל גָּדוֹל בַּבֹּקֶר הַשְׁכֵּים קְלָלָה תֵּחָשֶׁב

be will it as deemed | cursing | rising ,early | the in morning | loud | a with voice | his friend | who He blesses

7737 4066 802 5414 3117 2956 1812

15 לוֹ׃ דֶּלֶף טוֹרֵד בְּיוֹם סַגְרִיר וְאֵשֶׁת מִדְוָנִים נִשְׁתָּוָה׃

are ;alike | strivings | a and of woman | steady ;rain | a on of day | A constant | dripping | to .him

2300 1270 1270 7121 3225 8081 7307/6845 6845

16 17 צֹפְנֶיהָ צָפַן־רוּחַ וְשֶׁמֶן יְמִינוֹ יִקְרָא׃ בַּרְזֶל בְּבַרְזֶל יָחַד

;sharpens | iron on | Iron | .meets | his hand right | and oil | the ;wind | hides | who he her hides

8104 6529 398 8384 5341 7453 6440 2300 376

18 וְאִישׁ יַחַד פְּנֵי־רֵעֵהוּ׃ נֹצֵר תְּאֵנָה יֹאכַל פִּרְיָהּ וְשֹׁמֵר

he and keeps who | its ;fruit | eats | fig a tree | The of keeper | his .friend's | face | sharpens | a and man

120 120 3820 6440 6440 4325 3513 113

19 אֲדֹנָיו יְכֻבָּד׃ כַּמַּיִם הַפָּנִים לַפָּנִים כֵּן לֵב־הָאָדָם לָאָדָם׃

(reflects) .man the | man a | the of heart | so | (reflects) ,face | face | (in) As water the | is .honored | his master

7646 3808 120 5869 7646 3808 10 7585

20 שְׁאוֹל וַאֲבַדּוֹ לֹא תִשְׂבַּעְנָה וְעֵינֵי הָאָדָם לֹא תִשְׂבַּעְנָה׃

are .satisfied | not | man a | the and of eyes | are ;satisfied | not | and destruction | Sheol

3806 4110/6310 376 2091 3564 3701 4715

21 22 מַצְרֵף לַכֶּסֶף וְכוּר לַזָּהָב וְאִישׁ לְפִי מַהֲלָלוֹ׃ אִם־תִּכְתּוֹשׁ

you though pound | his praise | the by of mouth | a but man | for ;gold | the and furnace | for silver | refining The pot

5493 5940 7383 8432 4388 191

אֶת־הָאֱוִיל ׀ בַּמַּכְתֵּשׁ בְּתוֹךְ הָרִיפוֹת בַּעֱלִי לֹא־תָסוּר מֵעָלָיו

from him | will turn | not | a with ,pestle | grain the | amidst | the in mortar | fool a

3808 5739 3820 7896 6629 6440 3045 3045 200

23 24 אִוַּלְתּוֹ׃ יָדֹעַ תֵּדַע פְּנֵי צֹאנֶךָ שִׁית לִבְּךָ לַעֲדָרִים׃ כִּי לֹא

(are) for not | your on ;herds | your heart | set | your flock's | face | Know well | his .folly

7200 2682 1540 1755 1755 5145 2633 5769

25 לְעוֹלָם חֹסֶן וְאִם־נֵזֶר לְדוֹר דּוֹר׃ גָּלָה חָצִיר וְנִרְאָה־

is seen | and | the grass | One moves | gen- (and) eration | genera- to ration | the nor crown | ;strength | forever

4242 3830 3532 2022 6212 622 1877

26 דֶשֶׁא וְנֶאֶסְפוּ עִשְּׂבוֹת הָרִים׃ כְּבָשִׂים לִלְבוּשֶׁךָ וּמְחִיר

a and of price | for (be will) ;clothing your | the lambs | the mountains | the of plants | are and gathered | new the ,grass

1004 3899 3899 5795 2461 1767 6260 7704

27 שָׂדֶה עַתּוּדִים׃ וְדֵי ׀ חֲלֵב עִזִּים לְלַחְמְךָ לְלֶחֶם בֵּיתֶךָ

your ,household | the for of food | your for ,food | goats' | milk | and enough | the ;goats -he | field a

5291 2416

וְחַיִּים לְנַעֲרוֹתֶיךָ׃

your .maidens | for and of lives the

CHAPTER 28

[1]The wicked flee *though* no one *is* pursuing; but the righteous *are* as bold as a lion. [2]Because of transgression *in* a land, it *has* many rulers; but it is prolonged by a discerning man who knows *right*. [3]A poor man that oppresses the

CAP. XXVIII כח

CHAPTER 28

776 6588 982 3775 6662 7563 7291 369 5127

1 2 נָסוּ וְאֵין־רֹדֵף רָשָׁע וְצַדִּיקִים כִּכְפִיר יִבְטָח׃ בְּפֶשַׁע אֶרֶץ

(in) ,land a | trans- gression | By | are .bold | a as lion | the but righteous | The ;wicked | pur- suing | and none | flee

6231 7326 1397 748 3651/3045 995 120 8269 7227

3 רַבִּים שָׂרֶיהָ וּבְאָדָם מֵבִין יֹדֵעַ כֵּן יַאֲרִיךְ׃ גֶּבֶר רָשׁ וְעֹשֵׁק

who oppresses | poor | A man | is it .prolonged | thus | who ,knows | dis- cerning | a by but man | rulers ;(has) it | many

the weak *is like* a sweeping rain that *leaves* no food.
4 Those who forsake the law
praise the wicked; but
those who keep the law
strive with them. 5 Evil men
do not understand justice;
but those seeking Jehovah
understand all. 6 Better *is*
the poor walking in his
integrity than the perverse
of two ways, even *if* he *is*
rich. 7 He who keeps the
law *is* a wise son; but he
who is a feeder of gluttons
shames his father. 8 He
who multiplies his wealth
by interest and usury, *he
shall* gather it for him who
pities the weak. 9 Whoever
turns aside his ear from
hearing the law, even his
prayer *is* an abomination.
10 He who causes the
upright to go astray in an
evil way shall fall into his
own pit; and the blameless
shall inherit good. 11 A rich
man *is* wise in his own
eyes; but the discerning
weak searches him out.

12 When the righteous
rejoice, great *is* the glory;
but when the wicked rise,
a man will be sought.
13 He covering his tres-
passes will not fare well,
but one confessing and
forsaking has pity.
14 Blessed is the man al-
ways dreading *God*! But
the one hardening his
heart falls into evil. 15 The
wicked ruler *is* a roaring
lion, and a ranging bear,
over a weak people. 16 A
ruler lacking understand-
ing even adds oppres-
sions; one hating unjust
gain prolongs days. 17 A
man pressed down with
the blood of a soul shall
flee to the pit; do not let
them uphold him. 18 He
who walks blamelessly
shall be saved; but the
one perverse in his ways
shall fall at once.
19 He who tills his ground
shall have plenty of bread;
but one who pursues
vanities shall be filled
with poverty. 20 A faithful
man shall be full of blessings; but one rushing to
be rich will not be acquitted. 21 To regard faces *is*

7563 1984 8451 5800 3899 369 5502 4306 1800
4 דלים מטר סחף ואין לחם: עזבי תורה יהללו רשע
the praise the Forsakers .food that sweeping a (is) the
;wicked law of no (leaves) rain weak

4941 995 3808 7451 582 1624 8451 8104
5 ושמרי תורה יתגרו בם: אנשי רע לא יבינו משפט
;justice do not Evil men with strive the but
understand .them law of keepers

6141 8537 1980 7326/2896 3605 995 3068 1245
6 ומבקשי יהוה יבינו כל: טוב רש הולך בתמו מעקש
the than his in who the Better .all under- Jehovah those but
of crooked integrity walks poor (is) stand seeking

2151 7462 995 1121 8451 5341 6223 1870
7 דרכים והוא עשיר: נוצר תורה בן מבין ורעה זוללים
gluttons a but ,wise a (is) the who He .rich (if) even two
of feeder son law keeps (is) he ,ways

1800 2603 8636 5392 1952 7235 1 3637
8 יכלים אביו: מרבה הונו בנשך ובתרבית לחונן דלים
the the for by and by his who He his shames
,weak of pitier usury interest wealth increases .father

8441 8605 8451 8085 241 5493 6908
9 יקבצנו: מסיר אזנו משמע תורה גם תפלתו תועבה:
an (is) his even the from his Who He gathers
.abomination prayer ,law hearing ear aside turns .it

8549 5307 7816 7451 1870 3477 7686
10 משגה ישרים בדרך רע בשחותו הוא יפול ותמימים
the and shall he own his into an way in the lead- one
blameless ;fall pit ,evil upright astray ing

2713 995 1800 6223 376 5869 2450 2896 5157
11 ינחלו טוב: חכם בעיניו איש עשיר ודל מבין יחקרנו:
examines dis- the but ;rich A his in (is) .good shall
.him cerning weak man eyes own wise inherit

120 2664 7563 6965 8597 7227 6662 5970
12 בעלץ צדיקים רבה תפארת ובקום רשעים יחפש אדם:
a be will the when but the great the When
.man sought ,wicked rise ;glory (is) ,righteous rejoice

120 835 7355 5800 3034 6743 3808 6588 3680
13
14 מכסה פשעיו לא יצליח ומודה ועזב ירחם: אשרי אדם
the Blessed has and one but fare will not his He
man .pity leaving confessing ,well trespasses covering

1677 5098 738 7451 5307 3820 7185 8548 6342
15 מפחד תמיד ומקשה לבו יפול ברעה: ארי נהם ודב
a and ,roaring A into falls his the but ,always dreading
bear lion .evil heart of hardener (God)

7227 8394 2638 5057 1800 5971 7563 4910 8264
16 שוקק מושל רשע על עם דל: נגיד חסר תבונות ורב
even understand- lacking A .weak a over wicked ruler a charging
adds ing ruler people (is)

1818 6231 *120 3117 748 1215 *8130 4642
17 מעשקות שנא בצע יאריך ימים: אדם עשק בדם
the with pressed man A (his) prolongs unjust one oppressions
of blood down .days gain hating

3467 8549 1980 8551 408 5127 953/5704 5315
18 נפש עד בור ינוס אל יתמכו בו: הולך תמים יושע
be shall blame- who He to them let do shall the to ,soul a
;saved lessly walks him uphold not ;flee pit

3899 7646 127 5647 259 5307 1870 6140
19 ונעקש דרכים יפול באחת: עבד אדמתו ישבע לחם
(with) have shall his who He at shall his the but
bread of plenty ground tills .once fall ways in crooked

213 1293 7227 530 376 7389 7386 7291
20 ומרדף רקים ישבע ריש: איש אמונות רב ברכות ואץ
one but full be shall faithful A sated be shall vanities one but
rushing blessings of man .poverty (with) pursuing

3899 6595 2896 3808 6440 5234 5352 3808 6238
21 להעשיר לא ינקה: הכר פנים לא טוב ועל פת לחם
bread a and (is) not faces To be shall not be to
of piece for ;good regard .acquitted rich

not good; for a man will transgress for a piece of bread. 22A man *with* an evil eye hastens after wealth; but *he* does not know that poverty will come on him. 23He who reproves a man afterwards finds grace; *more* than he who flatters *with* the tongue. 24He who robs his father or his mother, and says, *It is* not a transgression—he shall be a companion to a destroyer. 25The proud in soul stirs up strife; but he who is trusting on Jehovah shall be abundantly satisfied. 26He who trusts in his own heart is a fool; but he who walks in wisdom shall be delivered. 27He who gives to the poor shall not lack; but he who hides his eyes shall have plenty of curses. 28When the wicked rise, a man hides himself; but when they perish, the righteous multiply.

CHAPTER 29

1A man who hardens *his* neck *when* reproved shall be suddenly broken, and there will be no healing. 2When the righteous increase, the people rejoice; but the people sigh when the wicked rule. 3He who loves wisdom gladdens his father; but a feeder of harlots wastes wealth. 4A king establishes a land by justice; but he *taking* bribes tears it down. 5A man who flatters his neighbor spreads a net for his steps. 6A snare *is* in the transgression of an evil man; but the righteous sing and rejoice. 7The righteous attends to the cause of the weak; but the wicked does not discern any knowledge. 8Scornful men puff against a city; but the wise turn away anger. 9*If* a wise man disputes with a foolish man, even he shakes, or laughs; and there is no rest. 10Men of blood hate the blameless; but the upright seek his soul.

2629 3045 3808 5869 7451 376 1952 926 1397 6586
22 יִפְשַׁע־גָּבֶר׃ נִבְהָל לַהוֹן אִישׁ רַע עָיִן וְלֹא־יֵדַע כִּי־חֶסֶר
want that (he) but an man A wealth hastens transgress will
knows not eye evil (with) after .man a

3956 2505 4672 2350 310 120 3198 935
23 יְבֹאֶנּוּ׃ מוֹכִיחַ אָדָם אַחֲרַי חֵן יִמְצָא מִמַּחֲלִיק לָשׁוֹן׃
the (with) he than ;finds (more) after- man a who He come will
.tongue flatters who grace ward reproves him on

7843 376 2272 6588 559 517 1 1497
24 גּוֹזֵל ׀ אָבִיו וְאִמּוֹ וְאֹמֵר אֵין־פָּשַׁע חָבֵר הוּא לְאִישׁ מַשְׁחִית׃
who a to he a a (is it) not and his or his who He
.destroys man (is) partner ;transgression ,says ,mother father robs

3820 982 1878 3068 5921 982 4069 1624 5315 7342
25
26 רְחַב־נֶפֶשׁ יְגָרֶה מָדוֹן וּבוֹטֵחַ עַל־יְהוָה יְדֻשָּׁן׃ בּוֹטֵחַ בְּלִבּוֹ
his in who He be will Jehovah on one but ;strife stirs soul The
heart trusts fat made trusting up of broad

369 7326 5414 4422 2451 1980 3684
27 הוּא כְסִיל וְהוֹלֵךְ בְּחָכְמָה הוּא יִמָּלֵט׃ נוֹתֵן לָרָשׁ אֵין
has the to who He be shall he in he but ;fool a he
no poor gives .delivered ,wisdom walks who (is)

5640 7563 6965 3994 7227 5869 5956 4270
28 מַחְסוֹר וּמַעְלִים עֵינָיו רַב־מְאֵרוֹת׃ בְּקוּם רְשָׁעִים יִסָּתֵר
hides the When .curses (have shall) his who he but ;lack
himself ,wicked rise ,many eyes hides

6662 7235 6 120
אָדָם וּבְאָבְדָם יִרְבּוּ צַדִּיקִים׃
the multiply when but ;man a
.righteous ,perish they

CAP. XXIX כט

CHAPTER 29

4832 369 7665 6621 6203 7185 8433 376
1 אִישׁ תּוֹכָחוֹת מַקְשֶׁה־עֹרֶף פֶּתַע יִשָּׁבֵר וְאֵין מַרְפֵּא׃
.healing not and be shall suddenly (his) who reproofs A
be will shattered neck hardens of man

5971 584 7563 4910 5971 8056 6662 7235
2 בִּרְבוֹת צַדִּיקִים יִשְׂמַח הָעָם וּבִמְשֹׁל רָשָׁע יֵאָנַח עָם׃
the sigh the when but the rejoice the When
.people wicked rule ;people ,righteous increase

1952 6 2181 7462 1 8056 2451 157 376
3 אִישׁ־אֹהֵב חָכְמָה יְשַׂמַּח אָבִיו וְרֹעֶה זוֹנוֹת יְאַבֶּד־הוֹן׃
.wealth wastes harlots a but his gladdens wisdom who man A
of feeder ;father loves

1397 2040 8641 376 776 5915 4941 4428
4
5 מֶלֶךְ בְּמִשְׁפָּט יַעֲמִיד אָרֶץ וְאִישׁ תְּרוּמוֹת יֶהֶרְסֶנָּה׃ גֶּבֶר
man A it tears (taking) a but a establishes by king A
.down bribes man ,land justice

376 6588 6471 6566 7561 7453/5921 2505
6 מַחֲלִיק עַל־רֵעֵהוּ רֶשֶׁת פּוֹרֵשׂ עַל־פְּעָמָיו׃ בְּפֶשַׁע אִישׁ
a trans- By his for spreads net a his on who
man gression .steps ,neighbor flatters

7563 1800 1779 6662 3045 8056 7442 6662 4170 7451
7 רָע מוֹקֵשׁ וְצַדִּיק יָרוּן וְשָׂמֵחַ׃ יֹדֵעַ צַדִּיק דִּין דַּלִּים רָשָׁע
the but the the The knows and sing the but a (is) evil
wicked ;weak of plea righteous .rejoice righteous snare

7725 2450 7151 6315 3944 582 1847 995 3808
8 לֹא־יָבִין דָּעַת׃ אַנְשֵׁי לָצוֹן יָפִיחוּ קִרְיָה וַחֲכָמִים יָשִׁיבוּ
turn the but ;city a puff scorn Men .knowledge do not
away wise against of discern

369 7832 7264 191 376 8199 2450 376 639
9 אָף׃ אִישׁ־חָכָם נִשְׁפָּט אֶת־אִישׁ אֱוִיל וְרָגַז וְשָׂחַק וְאֵין
and or he even ,foolish a with disputes wise a (If) .anger
no is laughs shakes man man

5315 1245 3477 8535 8130 1818 582 5183
10 נָחַת׃ אַנְשֵׁי דָמִים יִשְׂנְאוּ־תָם וִישָׁרִים יְבַקְשׁוּ נַפְשׁוֹ׃
his seek the but the hate blood Men .rest
.soul upright ;blameless of

¹¹A fool brings out all of his spirit, but holding back, the wise quiets it. ¹²To a ruler who listens to lying words, all his ministers *are* wicked. ¹³The poor and the injurious man meet together; *but* Jehovah enlightens both their eyes. ¹⁴A king that judges the weak truly shall have his throne established forever. ¹⁵The rod and reproof give wisdom; but a youth sent off *is* a cause of shame to his mother. ¹⁶When the wicked are multiplied, transgression increases; but the righteous shall see their fall. ¹⁷Correct your son, and you will get rest; and it will give delight to your soul. ¹⁸Where there is no vision, the people are let loose; but blessed is he, the keeper of the law. ¹⁹A servant is not corrected by words; though he discerns, there is no answer. ²⁰Do you see a man hasty in his words? *There is* more hope for a fool than of him. ²¹He pampering his servant from youth, he shall also afterwards be *his* successor. ²²An angry man stirs up contention; and a furious one abounds in transgression. ²³The pride of man brings him low; but the humble of spirit takes hold of honor. ²⁴He who shares with a thief hates his soul; he hears an oath, but does not tell *it*. ²⁵The fear of man brings a snare; but trusting Jehovah is set on high. ²⁶Many seek the face of the ruler; but the judgment of each man *is* from Jehovah. ²⁷An unjust man *is* an abomination to the righteous; and the upright of way *are* an abomination to the wicked.

CHAPTER 30

¹The words of Agur the son of Jakeh, the burden: The man spoke to Ithiel, *even* to Ithiel and Ucal,

---

11 כׇל־רוּחוֹ יוֹצִיא כְסִיל וְחׇכׇם בְּאָחוֹר יְשַׁבְּחֶנׇּה׃ **12** מֹשֵׁל

4910		7623	268	2450	3684	3318	7307	36,05
ruler A	.it quiets	holding	the	but	wise	fool A	brings	his all
		back					out	spirit of

13 רָשׁ וְאִישׁ

376 7326	7563	8334	3605	8267	1697	5921	7181
a and The	(are)	his	all	,lying	word a	to	who
of man poor	.wicked	ministers					listens

14 שׁוֹפֵט

8199	4428	3068	8147	5869	215	6298	8501
who	king A	.Jehovah	of both the	(but)	meet	injuries	together
judges				of eyes enlightens			them

15 בֶּאֱמֶת דַּלִּים כִּסְאוֹ לָעַד יִכּוֹן שֵׁבֶט וְתוֹכַחַת יִתֵּן חׇכְמׇה

2459	5414	8433	7626	3559	5703	3678	1800	571
;wisdom	give	and	The	be shall	forever	his	the	with
		reproof	rod	established		throne	weak	truth

16 וְנַעַר מְשֻׁלָּח מֵבִישׁ אִמּוֹ׃ בִּרְבוֹת רְשָׁעִים יִרְבֶּה־פָּשַׁע

6588	7235	7563	7235	517	957	7971	5288
trans-	increases	the	are When	his	causes	sent	a but
gression		,wicked	multiplied	.mother	to shame	off	youth

17 וְצַדִּיקִים בְּמַפַּלְתָּם יִרְאוּ׃ יַסֵּר בִּנְךָ וִינִיחֶךָ וְיִתֵּן מַעֲדַנִּים

45-74	5414	5117	1121	3256	7200	4658	6662
delight	it and	you and	your	Correct	shall	their	the but
	give will	rest get	son		.see	fall	righteous

18 לְנַפְשֶׁךָ׃ בְּאֵין חׇזוֹן יִפׇּרַע עׇם וְשֹׁמֵר תּוֹרׇה אַשְׁרֵהוּ׃

835	8451	8104	5971	6544	2377	369	5315
blessed	the	the And	the	let are	,vision	Where	your to
!he is	law	of keeper	people	loose		no is	.soul

19 בִּדְבׇרִים לֹא־יִוׇּסֶר עׇבֶד כִּי־יׇבִין וְאֵין מַעֲנֶה

376	23.72	4617	369	995	5650	3256	1870
a	you Do	.answer	no is	,discerns	he though	A	by
man			there			servant corrected	words

20 אֵין

5650	5290	6445	3684	8615	1697	213

21 בִּדְבׇרׇיו תִּקְוׇה לִכְסִיל מִמֶּנּוּ׃ מְפַנֵּק מִנֹּעַר עַבְדּוֹ

	his	from	who He	than	a for	More	his in	hasty
	servant	youth	pampers	!him of	fool	hope	?words	

22 וְאַחֲרִיתוֹ יִהְיֶה מׇנוֹן׃ אִישׁ־אַף יְגׇרֶה מׇדוֹן וּבַעַל חֵמׇה

2534	1167	4066	1624	639	3.76	4497	1961	319
fury of	a and	conten-	stirs	anger A	(his)	he shall	his in	also
	master	,tion	up		of man	.successor	be	days after

23 רַב־פׇּשַׁע׃ גַּאֲוַת אׇדׇם תַּשְׁפִּילֶנּוּ וּשְׁפַל־רוּחַ יִתְמֹךְ כׇּבוֹד׃

3519	8551	7307	8217	8213	120	1347	6588	7227
.honor	takes	spirit	the but	brings	man	The	trans-	abounds
		of hold	of humble	;low him		of pride	gression	in

24 חוֹלֵק עִם־גַּנׇּב שׂוֹנֵא נַפְשׁוֹ אׇלׇה יִשְׁמַע וְלֹא יַגִּיד׃ **25**

2731	5046	3808	8085	422	5315	8130	1590	2505
fear The	does	but	he	an	his	hates	a with	who He
of	.(it) tell	not	,hears	oath	;soul		thief	shares

26 אׇדׇם יִתֵּן מוֹקֵשׁ וּבוֹטֵחַ בַּיהוׇה יְשֻׂגׇּב׃ רַבִּים מְבַקְשִׁים

1245	7227	76.82	3068	982	4170	5414	120
seeking	are Many	set is	in	he but	;snare a	brings	man
		.high on	Jehovah	trusts who			

27 פְנֵי־מוֹשֵׁל וּמֵיְהוׇה מִשְׁפַּט־אִישׁ׃ תּוֹעֲבַת צַדִּיקִים אִישׁ

376	6662	8441	376	4941	3068	4910	6440
A.	the	hateful (is)	each	the (is)	from but	the	the
man	righteous	to		.man of judgment	Jehovah	ruler of	face

עׇוֶל וְתוֹעֲבַת רׇשׇׁע יְשַׁר־דׇּרֶךְ׃

1870	3477	756.3	8441	5766
.way	the	the	,(is) and	;unjust
	upright	wicked	to hateful	

CAP. XXX ל

CHAPTER 30

1 דִּבְרֵי ׀ אׇגוּר בִּן־יׇקֶה הַמַּשָּׂא נְאֻם הַגֶּבֶר לְאִיתִיאֵל לְאִיתִיאֵל וְאֻכׇל

384	384	1397	5002	4853	33.48/1121	94	1697
to (even)	to	the	Spoke	the	33.48/1121	94	The
Ithiel	,Ithiel	man		.burden	of son	of son Agur	of words

saying, 2Surely I *am more* brutish than anyone; and I do not have the understanding of a man.
3I have not learned wisdom, but I do know the knowledge of holiness.
4Who has gone up *to* Heaven, and come down? Who has gathered the wind in His fists? Who has bound the waters in *His* garments? Who has made all the ends of the earth to rise? What *is* His name, and what *is* His Son's name? Surely you know.
5Every word of God *is* tested; He *is* a shield to those who seek refuge in Him.
6Do not add to His words, that He not reprove you, and you be found a liar.
7I have asked two *things* from You: Do not hold back from me before I die;
8Remove vanity and a lying word far from me; do not give me poverty or riches; tear my portion of bread,
9that I not become full and deceive, and say, Who *is* Jehovah? Or that I not become poor and steal, and violate the name of my God.
10Do not slander a servant to his master, that he not curse you, and you be found guilty.
11A generation curses its father, and does not bless its mother;
12a generation pure in its own eyes, and yet not washed from its own filth.
13*There is* a generation, O how lofty *are* its eyes! And its eyelids are lifted up;
14a generation whose teeth *are like* swords; and its jaw teeth *like* knives, to devour the poor from the earth, and the needy from *among* men.
15The leech *has* two daughters *crying,* Give! Give! Three things *are* not satisfied; four never have said, Enough!
16Sheol; and the barren womb; the earth not filled *with* water; and the fire, never said, Enough!
17The eye that mocks its father, and despises to obey its mother, the ravens of the

2 3808 120 998 3808 376 1198 401
3 ואכל: כי בער אנכי מאיש ולא־בינת אדם לי: ולא־
not And to (is) a under- the and than (am) I (more) Surely and
me man of standing not man any brutish :Ucal

4 3381 8064 5927 4310 3045 6918 1847 2451 3925
למדתי חכמה ודעת קדשים אדע: מי עלה־שמים | וירד
come and Heaven has Who I do holiness the but ,wisdom have I
?down (to) up gone .know of knowledge learned

6965 4310 8071 4325 6887 4310 2651 7307 622 4310
מי אסף־רוח | בחפניו מי צרר־מים | בשמלה מי הקים
made Who the in the has Who His in the has Who
rise ?garment waters bound ?fists wind gathered

5 3605 3045 1121 8034 4100 8034 4100 776 657 3605
כל־אפסי־ארץ מה־שמו ומה־שם־בנו כי תדע: כל־
Every you Surely His name And His What the the all
!know ?Son's (is) what ?name (is) ?earth of ends

6 3254 408 2620 4043 6884 433 565
אמרת אלוה צרופה מגן הוא לחסים בו: אל־תוסף
Do not in seekers to He a is God word
add .Him refuge of (is) shield ;tested of

7 7592 8147 3576 3198 1697
על־דבריו פן־יוכיח בך ונכזבת: שתים שאלתי
have I Two be you and ,you He lest His to
asked things .liar a found reprove ,words

8 3577/1697 7723 4191 2962 4513 408
מאתך אל־תמנע ממני בטרם אמות: שוא | ודבר־כזב
a the and vanity :die I before from hold do not from
lie of word me back ;You

2706 3899 2963 5414 6239 7389 7368
הרחק ממני ראש ועשר אל־תתן־לי הטריפני לחם חקי:
my of tear to do not and poverty from remove
;portion bread me for ;me give riches ;me far

9 1589 3423 3068 4310 559 3584 7646
פן אשבע | וכחשתי ואמרתי מי יהוה ופן־אורש וגנבתי
and become Or ?Jehovah Who and ,deceive and become I lest
,steal poor I lest is ,say ,full

10 113 5650 3960 3808 430 8034 8610
ותפשתי שם אלהי: אל־תלשן עבד אל־אדנו פן
lest his to a Do not my the and
,master servant slander .God of name violate

11 1288 3808 517 7043 1 1755 816 7043
יקללך ואשמת: דור אביו יקלל ואת־אמו לא יברך:
does not its and its gene- A be you and curse he
;bless mother ,curses father ration ,guilty held ,you

12 13 5869 7311 1755 7364 3808 6675 5869 2889 1755
דור טהור בעיניו ומצאתו לא רחץ: דור מה־רמו עיניו
its lofty O genera- A is not from and its in pure genera-
!eyes (are) how tion washed filth its !eyes own tion

14 4973 3979 8127 2719 1755 5375 6079
ועפעפיו ינשאו: דור | חרבות שניו ומאכלות מתלעתיו
jaw its and its swords genera- A lifted are its and
,teeth knives ,teeth (are) tion .up eyelids

15 5936 120 6041 776 6041 398
לאכל עניים מארץ ואביונים מאדם: לעלוקה |
leech The To among from the and the from the to
(are) .men needy ,earth poor devour

702 7646 3808 7969 3053 3053 1323 8147
שתי בנות הב | הב שלוש הנה לא תשבענה ארבע לא־
not four ;satisfied not they Three !Give !Give daughters two
(are) (things) (crying)

16 784 4325 7646 3808 776 7356 6115 7585 1952 559
אמרו הון: שאול ועצר רחם ארץ לא־שבעה מים ואש
the and ;water filled not the the and Sheol !Enough have
fire (with) earth ;womb barren ,said

17 5365 517 3349 936 1 3932 5869 1952 559
לא־אמרה הון: עין | תלעג לאב ותבוז ליקהת־אם יקרוה
shall (his) to and (his) that The !Enough has not
it pick ,mother obey despises ,father mocks eye ,said

valley shall pick it out; the sons of the eagle shall eat it.
[18]Three *things are* too wonderful for me; yea, I do not know the way of four:
[19]The way of an eagle in the heavens; the way of a snake on a rock; the way of a ship in the heart of the sea; and the way of a man with a virgin.
[20]So *is* the way of an adulterous woman: She eats, and wipes her mouth, and says, I have done no evil.
[21]The earth quakes under three *things*; yea, it is not able to bear up under four:
[22]Under a servant when he reigns; and a fool when he is filled with food;
[23]under a hated one when she is married; under a handmaid when she is heir to her mistress.
[24]Four *things are* little on the earth, but they *are* the wise ones of those made wise:
[25]The ants *are* a people not strong, yet they prepare their food in summer;
[26]the rock-badgers *are* not a powerful people, yet they make their houses in the rock;
[27]the locusts have no king, yet they go out in a swarm, all of them;
[28]the lizard you can take with the hands, yet it *is* in king's palaces.
[29]There are three *things* that go well in a march; yea, four that go well in walking:
[30]a lion is mighty among beasts, and he does not turn away from facing all;
[31]one girded in loins; and a he-goat; and a king *when his* army *is* with him.
[32]If you have been foolish in lifting yourself up; or if you have thought evil, *lay your* hand on your mouth!
[33]Surely, the squeezing of milk brings curds; and the squeezing of the nose brings blood; so the squeezing of wrath brings out strife.

18 עֹרְבֵי־נַחַל וְיֹאכְלוּהָ בְנֵי־נָשֶׁר׃ שְׁלֹשָׁה הֵמָּה נִפְלְאוּ
too wonderful they (are) Three (things) .eagle the of sons the shall eat it and the valley of; the ravens

19 מִמֶּנִּי וְאַרְבָּעָ לֹא יְדַעְתִּים׃ דֶּרֶךְ הַנֶּשֶׁר ׀ בַּשָּׁמַיִם דֶּרֶךְ
the of way the in ;heavens an eagle the :of way know I not four and ,me for

נָחָשׁ עֲלֵי־צוּר דֶּרֶךְ־אֳנִיָּה בְלֶב־יָם וְדֶרֶךְ גֶּבֶר בְּעַלְמָה׃
a with virgin a man the and of way the ;sea the in of heart ship a the of way ;rock a on a snake

20 כֵּן ׀ דֶּרֶךְ אִשָּׁה מְנָאָפֶת אָכְלָה וּמָחֲתָה פִיהָ וְאָמְרָה לֹא־
not ,says and her mouth and wipes she eats ;adulterous woman a the of way So (is)

21 פָעַלְתִּי אָוֶן׃ תַּחַת שָׁלוֹשׁ רָגְזָה אֶרֶץ וְתַחַת אַרְבַּע
four and under the ;earth quakes three (things) Under (any) .evil have I done

22 לֹא־תוּכַל שְׂאֵת׃ תַּחַת עֶבֶד כִּי יִמְלוֹךְ וְנָבָל כִּי יִשְׂבַּע־
is he with filled when a and fool he ;reigns when a servant :under bear to up is it able not

23 לָחֶם׃ תַּחַת שְׂנוּאָה כִּי תִבָּעֵל וְשִׁפְחָה כִּי־תִירַשׁ גְּבִרְתָּהּ׃
her .mistress is she to heir when a and handmaid is she ;married when hated a one under ;food

24 אַרְבָּעָה הֵם קְטַנֵּי־אָרֶץ וְהֵמָּה חֲכָמִים מְחֻכָּמִים׃
those :wise made wise the of ones but (are) they the ,earth little on they (are) Four (things)

25 הַנְּמָלִים עַם לֹא־עָז וַיָּכִינוּ בַקַּיִץ לַחְמָם׃
26 שְׁפַנִּים עַם לֹא־
not a (are) people rock-the badgers their ;food in summer yet prepare they strong not a people ants the (are)

27 עָצוּם וַיָּשִׂימוּ בַסֶּלַע בֵּיתָם׃ מֶלֶךְ אֵין לָאַרְבֶּה וַיֵּצֵא חֹצֵץ
a in swarm they yet ,out go the to ,locusts not is king a their ;house the in rock they yet make ,mighty

28 כֻּלּוֹ׃ שְׂמָמִית בְּיָדַיִם תְּתַפֵּשׂ וְהִיא בְּהֵיכְלֵי מֶלֶךְ׃
the king's palaces in it and (is) can you take the with hands The lizard of all .them

29 שְׁלֹשָׁה הֵמָּה מֵיטִיבֵי צָעַד וְאַרְבָּעָה מֵיטִבֵי לָכֶת׃
30 לַיִשׁ
lion a (is) in ;walking go that well four and a in ,march go that well They (are) three (things)

31 גִּבּוֹר בַּבְּהֵמָה וְלֹא־יָשׁוּב מִפְּנֵי־כֹל׃ זַרְזִיר מָתְנַיִם אוֹ־תָיִשׁ
the ;he goat and loins the in girded one ;all from facing turns he away and not among ,beasts mighty

32 וּמֶלֶךְ אַלְקוּם עִמּוֹ׃ אִם־נָבַלְתָּ בְהִתְנַשֵּׂא וְאִם־זַמּוֹתָ יָד
(lay) hand you ;plot or if lifting in ;yourself have you foolish been If with him (is) (his when) army a and king

33 לְפֶה׃ כִּי מִיץ חָלָב יוֹצִיא חֶמְאָה וּמִיץ־אַף יוֹצִיא דָם וּמִיץ
and squeeze ;blood out comes the nose and squeeze ;curds out comes ,milk squeeze ,For (your) on !mouth

אַפַּיִם יוֹצִיא רִיב׃
.strife brings it forth wrath

CAP. XXXI לא

CHAPTER 31

[1]The words of king Lemuel, the burden that his mother taught him: [2]What, my son? And what, the son of my womb? And what, the son of my vows? [3]Do not give your strength to women, or your ways to that which wipes out kings. [4]*It is* not for kings, O Lemuel; *it is* not for kings to drink wine; nor for princes to lust for fermented drink; [5]that they not drink and forget what is decreed, and pervert the right of the afflicted ones. [6]Give fermented drink to one perishing, and wine to the bitter of soul; [7]let him drink and forget his poverty, and remember his misery no more. [8]Open your mouth for the dumb, in the cause of all the sons of the fatherless. [9]Open your mouth; judge righteously, and defend the poor and needy.

[10]Who can find an able woman? For her value *is* far above jewels. [11]The heart of her husband trusts in her, so that he has no lack *of* gain. [12]She deals good with him, and not evil, all the days of her life. [13]She seeks wool and flax, and she works *with* her palms *with* delight. [14]She is like the merchant-ships; she brings in her food from afar. [15]She also rises while *it is* still night, and gives game to her household, and an order to her maidens. [16]She has examined a field, and takes it; she plants a vineyard from the fruit of her hands. [17]She has girded her loins with strength, and has made her arms strong. [18]She tastes whether her gain *is* good; her lamp does not go out by night. [19]She has sent forth her hands on the distaff, and her palms have held the spindle. [20]She spreads out her palms to the poor; yea, she reaches out her hands to the needy. [21]She is not

CHAPTER 31

1121/4100 517 3256 48 53 44 28 3927 16 97
1 2 דִּבְרֵי לְמוּאֵל מֶלֶךְ מַשָּׂא אֲשֶׁר־יִסְּרַתּוּ אִמּוֹ׃ מַה־בְּרִי
my What his taught that the ,King Lemuel The
?son .mother him burden of words

2428 802 5414 408 5088 1121 4100 990 1121 4100
3 וּמַה־בַּר־בִּטְנִי וּמֶה בַּר־נְדָרָי׃ אַל־תִּתֵּן לַנָּשִׁים חֵילֶךָ
your to Do not my the And my the And
,might women give ?vows of son ,what ?womb of son ,what

4428 408 3927 4428 408 4428 4229 1870
4 וּדְרָכֶיךָ לַמְחוֹת מְלָכִין׃ אַל לַמְלָכִים לְמוֹאֵל אַל לַמְלָכִים
for (is it) O for (is it) .kings that to your or
kings not ,Lemuel ,kings not out wiping ways

2710 7911 8354 7941 176 7336 335 3196/8354
5 שְׁתוֹ־יָיִן וּלְרוֹזְנִים אֵו שֵׁכָר׃ פֶּן־יִשְׁתֶּה וְיִשְׁכַּח מְחֻקָּק
is what and they lest strong lust to princes nor ,wine to
decreed forget drink ;drink for for drink

5315 4751 3191 6 7941 6040 1121 3605/1779 81 38
6 וִישַׁנֶּה דִּין כָּל־בְּנֵי־עֹנִי׃ תְּנוּ־שֵׁכָר לְאוֹבֵד וְיַיִן לְמָרֵי נָפֶשׁ׃
;soul the to and one to strong Give the sons the the and
of bitter wine perishing drink .afflicted of of right pervert

6310/6605 5750 2142 38 08 5999 7389 7911 8354
7 8 יִשְׁתֶּה וְיִשְׁכַּח רִישׁוֹ וַעֲמָלוֹ לֹא יִזְכָּר־עוֹד׃ פְּתַח־פִּיךָ
your Open .more remember not his and his and him let
mouth misery ,poverty forget drink

1777 6664 8199 6310 6605 2475 1121 3605 1779 483
9 לְאִלֵּם אֶל־דִּין כָּל־בְּנֵי חֲלוֹף׃ פְּתַח־פִּיךָ שְׁפָט־צֶדֶק וְדִין
and righ- judge your Open father- the all the to the for
defend teously ;mouth .less sons of cause ,dumb

6443 7350 4672 4310 2428 802 34 6041
10 עָנִי וְאֶבְיוֹן׃ אֵשֶׁת־חַיִל מִי יִמְצָא וְרָחֹק מִפְּנִינִים
above (is) And can who able An and the
gems far ?find woman .needy poor

1580 2637 3808 7998 1167 3820 982 4377
11 12 מִכְרָהּ׃ בָּטַח בָּהּ לֵב בַּעְלָהּ וְשָׁלָל לֹא יֶחְסָר׃ גְּמָלַתְהוּ
to deals She has he no that so Her heart in trusts her
him .lack gain (of) ,husband's her .value

6213 6593 6785 1875 2416 3117 3605/7451/3808 2896
13 טוֹב וְלֹא־רָע כֹּל יְמֵי חַיֶּיהָ׃ דָּרְשָׁה צֶמֶר וּפִשְׁתִּים וַתַּעַשׂ
she and and wool She her the all ,evil and good
works ;flax seeks .life of days not

3899 935 4801 5503 591 3709 2656
14 בְּחֵפֶץ כַּפֶּיהָ׃ הָיְתָה כָּאֳנִיּוֹת סוֹחֵר מִמֶּרְחָק תָּבִיא לַחְמָהּ׃
her she from ;merchant the like She (with) (with)
.food in brings afar . ships is .palms her delight

5291 2706 1004 2964 5414 3915 5750 6965
15 וַתָּקָם ׀ בְּעוֹד לַיְלָה וַתִּתֵּן טֶרֶף לְבֵיתָהּ וְחֹק לְנַעֲרֹתֶיהָ׃
her to a and her to game and ,night while also She
.maidens decree ,household gives still (is it) rises

3754 5193 3709 6529 3947 7704 2161
16 זָמְמָה שָׂדֶה וַתִּקָּחֵהוּ מִפְּרִי כַפֶּיהָ נָטְעָ כָּרֶם׃
a she her the from and a has She
.vineyard plants palms of fruit ;it takes field examined

5504 2896 2938 2220 553 4975 5797 2296
17 18 חָגְרָה בְעוֹז מָתְנֶיהָ וַתְּאַמֵּץ זְרוֹעֹתֶיהָ׃ טָעֲמָה כִּי־טוֹב סַחְרָהּ
her whether She her has and her with has She
;gain good (is) tastes .arms strengthened ,loins strength girded

3709 3601 7971 3027 5216 3915 3518 3808
19 לֹא־יִכְבֶּה בַלַּיְל נֵרָהּ׃ יָדֶיהָ שִׁלְּחָה בַכִּישׁוֹר וְכַפֶּיהָ
her and the on has She her her by go does not
palms distaff forth sent hands .lamp night out

34 7971 3027 6041 6566 3709 6418 8551
20 תָּמְכוּ פָלֶךְ׃ כַּפָּהּ פָּרְשָׂה לֶעָנִי וְיָדֶיהָ שִׁלְּחָה לָאֶבְיוֹן׃
the to she her and the to She her the have
.needy reaches hands ;poor spreads palms spindle held

afraid of the snow for her household; for all her household *are* clothed *with* scarlet. 22She makes herself ornamental coverings; her clothing *is* fine linen and purple. 23Her husband is known in the gates, when he sits with the elders of the land. 24She makes fine linen garments, and sells; and she delivers belts to the merchant. 25Strength and dignity *are* her clothing; and she shall rejoice at the day to come. 26She opens her mouth in wisdom, and the law of kindness *is* on her tongue. 27She watches the ways of her household, and does not eat the bread of idleness. 28Her children rise up and call her blessed; her husband *also*, for he praises her: 29many *are* the daughters who work ably, but you rise above them all!

30Favor *is* deceitful, and beauty *is* vain; *but* a woman who fears Jehovah, she shall be praised. 31Give her of the fruit of her hands, and let her works praise her in the gates.

8144 3847 1004 3605 7950 1004 3372 3808
21 לֹא־תִירָא לְבֵיתָהּ מִשָּׁלֶג כִּי כָל־בֵּיתָהּ לָבֻשׁ שָׁנִים׃
,scarlet clothed are her all for the of her for is She not
(with) household ;snow household afraid.

8179 3045 3830 713 8336 6213 4765
22 מַרְבַדִּים עָשְׂתָה־לָּהּ שֵׁשׁ וְאַרְגָּמָן לְבוּשָׁהּ׃
23 נוֹדָע בַּשְּׁעָרִים
the in is clothing her and fine her to She coverings
gates known (is) purple linen ;self makes

2289 4376 6213 5466 776 2205 3427 1167
24 בַּעְלָהּ בְּשִׁבְתּוֹ עִם־זִקְנֵי־אָרֶץ׃ סָדִין עָשְׂתָה וַתִּמְכֹּר וַחֲגוֹר
and and She linen the the with he when Her
belts ;sells ,makes garments .land of elders sits ,husband

314 3117 7832 3830 1926 5797 3669 5414
25 נָתְנָה לַכְּנַעֲנִי׃ עֹז־וְהָדָר לְבוּשָׁהּ וַתִּשְׂחַק לְיוֹם אַחֲרוֹן׃
to the at she and her (are) and Strength the to she
.come day laughs ;clothing dignity .merchant gives

6822 3956 2617 8451 2451 6605 6310
26 פִּיהָ פָּתְחָה בְחָכְמָה וְתוֹרַת־חֶסֶד עַל־לְשׁוֹנָהּ׃
27 צוֹפִיָּה
She her (is) kindness the and in She her
watches ,tongue on of law wisdom opens mouth

1121 6965 398 3808 6104 3899 1004 1979
28 הֲלִיכוֹת בֵּיתָהּ וְלֶחֶם עַצְלוּת לֹא תֹאכֵל׃ קָמוּ בָנֶיהָ
Her rise does she not idleness the and her the
children up .eat of bread household of ways

59 27 2428 6213 1323 7227 1984 1167 833
29 וַיְאַשְּׁרוּהָ בַּעְלָהּ וַיְהַלְלָהּ׃ רַבּוֹת בָּנוֹת עָשׂוּ חָיִל וְאַתְּ עָלִית
rise but ,ably who the Many he for her her call and
you work daughters (are) .her praises ,husband ;blessed

3068 3373 802 3308 1892 2580 8267 3605 5921
30 עַל־כֻּלָּנָה׃ שֶׁקֶר הַחֵן וְהֶבֶל הַיֹּפִי אִשָּׁה יִרְאַת־יְהוָה הִיא
she ,Jehovah who a beauty and Charm deceitful of all over
fears woman ,(is) vain (is) them

4639 8179 1984 3027 6529 5414 1984
31 תִתְהַלָּל׃ תְּנוּ־לָהּ מִפְּרִי יָדֶיהָ וִיהַלְלוּהָ בַשְּׁעָרִים מַעֲשֶׂיהָ׃
her the in let and her the from to Give be shall
.works gates her praise ;hands of fruit her .praised

קהלת

LIBER ECCLESIASTAE

(THE) BOOK OF ECCLESIASTES

CAPUT. I א

CHAPTER 1

A LITERAL TRANSLATION
OF THE BIBLE

THE BOOK OF
ECCLESIASTES

CHAPTER 1

[1]The words of the Preacher, the son of David, king in Jerusalem: [2]Vanity of vanities, says the Preacher, vanity of vanities! All *is* vanity! [3]What *is* the profit to a man in all his labor which he labors under the sun? [4]A generation passes away, and *another* generation comes; but the earth stands forever. [5]The sun also arises, and the sun goes hurrying to its place; it arises there *again*. [6]The wind goes toward the south, and turning around to the north; the wind is going around and around. And the wind returns on its circuits. [7]All the rivers are going to the sea; yet the sea is not full. To the place where the rivers are going, there they *are* returning to go *again*. [8]All words are wearisome; a man is not able to utter *it*. The eye is not satisfied to see, nor is the ear filled from hearing. [9]That which has been, it is that which shall be. And that which has been done, it *is* that which will be done. And there is no new *thing* under the sun. [10]Is there a thing *of* which one might say, See this, it *is* new. It has already been for the ages which were before us. [11]*There is* no memory of former *things*, and also there is no memory for them of *things* which will be afterward; with those who will be at the last.

18,92 1892 3389 44:28 1732/1121 6953 1697
1 2 דִּבְרֵי קֹהֶלֶת בֶּן־דָּוִד מֶלֶךְ בִּירוּשָׁלִָם׃ הֲבֵל הֲבָלִים
,vanities Vanity in king ,David the the The
of .Jerusalem of son ,Preacher of words

120 3504 1892 3605 1892 1892 69 53 559
3 אָמַר קֹהֶלֶת הֲבֵל הֲבָלִים הַכֹּל הָבֶל׃ מַה־יִּתְרוֹן לָאָדָם
a to (the) What !vanity All !vanities vanity the says
man profit (is) (is) of ,Preacher

935 1755 1980 1755 8121 8478 5998 5999 36:05
4 בְּכָל־עֲמָלוֹ שֶׁיַּעֲמֹל תַּחַת הַשָּׁמֶשׁ׃ דּוֹר הֹלֵךְ וְדוֹר בָּא
comes a and goes A ?sun the under he which his in
generation generation labors labor all

8121 935 8121 2224 5975 57 69 776
5 וְהָאָרֶץ לְעוֹלָם עֹמָדֶת׃ וְזָרַח הַשֶּׁמֶשׁ וּבָא הַשֶּׁמֶשׁ וְאֶל־
and ,sun the and ,sun the And .stands forever the but
to goes arises earth

5437 1864 1980 8033 2224 7602 4725
6 מְקוֹמוֹ שׁוֹאֵף זוֹרֵחַ הוּא שָׁם׃ הוֹלֵךְ אֶל־דָּרוֹם וְסוֹבֵב
turn- and the toward Going there it arises ;panting its
around ing ,south .(again) place

7725 5439 59121 73:07 19,80 5439 5439 6828
אֶל־צָפוֹן סוֹבֵב ׀ סֹבֵב הוֹלֵךְ הָרוּחַ וְעַל־סְבִיבֹתָיו שָׁב
returns its and the is (and) going the to
circuits on ;wind going ,around around ;north

4393 369 3220 32:20 1980 5158/ 3605 7307
7 הָרוּחַ׃ כָּל־הַנְּחָלִים הֹלְכִים אֶל־הַיָּם וְהַיָּם אֵינֶנּוּ מָלֵא
.full is it the yet the to are the All the
not sea ;sea going torrents .wind

3605 1980 7725 8033 1980 5158 4725
8 אֶל־מְקוֹם שֶׁהַנְּחָלִים הֹלְכִים שָׁם הֵם שָׁבִים לָלָכֶת׃ כָּל־
All go to returning they there are where the To
.(again) (are) ,going torrents place

5869 7646 3808 1696 376 3201 3023 1697
הַדְּבָרִים יְגֵעִים לֹא־יוּכַל אִישׁ לְדַבֵּר לֹא־תִשְׂבַּע עַיִן
The is not say to a is not (are) words
eye satisfied .(it) man able ;wearisome

1961 1961 8085 241 43,90 38,08 7200
9 לִרְאוֹת וְלֹא־תִמָּלֵא אֹזֶן מִשְּׁמֹעַ׃ מַה־שֶּׁהָיָה הוּא שֶׁיִּהְיֶה
which that it which That from the is and ,see to
;be will (is) ,been has .hearing ear filled not

8121 8478 2319 3605 369 6213 6213
וּמַה־שֶּׁנַּעֲשָׂה הוּא שֶׁיֵּעָשֶׂה וְאֵין כָּל־חָדָשׁ תַּחַת הַשָּׁמֶשׁ׃
.sun the under new any not So which that it has which and
(thing) is .done be will (is) ,done been that

5769 1961 3528 2319 2088/7200 559 1697
10 יֵשׁ דָּבָר שֶׁיֹּאמַר רְאֵה־זֶה חָדָשׁ הוּא כְּבָר הָיָה לְעֹלָמִים
ages the for has it Already ?(is) it new ,this See one which a Is
,been ,say might thing there

310 7223 2146 369 6440 1961 834
11 אֲשֶׁר הָיָה מִלְּפָנֵנוּ׃ אֵין זִכְרוֹן לָרִאשֹׁנִים וְגַם לָאַחֲרֹנִים
after of and former of memory There .us before were which
(things) also ,(things) no is

314 1961 21:46 1961 38,08 1961
שֶׁיִּהְיוּ לֹא־יִהְיֶה לָהֶם זִכָּרוֹן עִם שֶׁיִּהְיוּ לָאַחֲרֹנָה׃
.afterwards who those with re-a for be shall not which
be will membrance them ;be will

¹²I the Preacher was king over Israel in Jerusalem. ¹³And I gave my heart to seek and to investigate by wisdom concerning all which is done under the heavens. It *is* an evil task God has given to the sons of men, to be afflicted by it. ¹⁴I have seen all the works which are done under the sun; and, behold, all is vanity and striving *after* wind. ¹⁵What is crooked is not able to be put straight, and *what is* lacking is not able to be weighed out. ¹⁶I spoke with my heart, saying, Behold, I have become great and have increased wisdom over all who have been before me over Jerusalem. Yea, my heart has seen abundance of wisdom and knowledge. ¹⁷And I gave my heart to know wisdom and to know madness and folly. I know that this also *is* striving *after* wind. ¹⁸For in much wisdom *is* much grief; and he increasing knowledge increases pain.

12 | 5414 וְנָתַ֣תִּי : 3389 בִּירוּשָׁלָ֑͏ִם 3478 עַל־יִשְׂרָאֵ֖ל 59,21 44,28 מֶ֥לֶךְ 1961 הָיִ֥יתִי 69,53 קֹהֶ֗לֶת אֲנִ֣י

13

I And .Jerusalem in Israel over king was the I gave Preacher

8478 834 36;05 24:51 8441 1875 3820
אֶת־לִבִּ֗י לִדְר֤וֹשׁ וְלָתוּר֙ בַּֽחָכְמָ֔ה עַ֛ל כָּל־אֲשֶׁ֥ר נַעֲשָׂ֖ה תַּ֣חַת 6213

under done is which all con- by to and seek to my
cerning wisdom investigate heart

6031 120 1121 430,1 5414 7451 6045 8064
הַשָּׁמָ֑יִם ה֣וּא ׀ עִנְיַ֣ן רָ֗ע נָתַ֧ן אֱלֹהִ֛ים לִבְנֵ֥י הָאָדָ֖ם לַעֲנ֥וֹת

be to men the to God has evil task a it the
afflicted of sons given (is) ;heavens

2009 8121 8478 6213 4639 3605 7200
14 בּֽוֹ : רָאִ֙יתִי֙ אֶֽת־כָּל־הַֽמַּעֲשִׂ֔ים שֶֽׁנַּעֲשׂ֖וּ תַּ֣חַת הַשָּׁ֑מֶשׁ וְהִנֵּ֥ה 2009

and ,sun the under are which the all have I .it by
,behold done works seen

2642 8626 3201 3808 5791 7307 7467 1892 3605
15 הַכֹּ֖ל הֶ֥בֶל וּרְע֥וּת ר֖וּחַ : מְעֻוָּ֖ת לֹא־יוּכַ֣ל לִתְקֹ֑ן וְחֶסְר֖וֹן

(what) and put be to is not is What (after) and vanity all
lacking ,straight able crooked wind striving (is)

20,09 559: 13820 1696 4487 3201
16 לֹא־יוּכַ֣ל לְהִמָּנֽוֹת : דִּבַּ֙רְתִּי֩ אֲנִ֨י עִם־לִבִּ֤י לֵאמֹר֙ אֲנִ֣י הִנֵּ֨ה

,behold ,I ,saying my with I spoke be to is not
heart .counted able

59,21 6440;1 1961 834 36;05 5921 24:51 3254 1430
הִגְדַּ֣לְתִּי וְהוֹסַ֔פְתִּי חָכְמָ֔ה עַ֥ל כָּל־אֲשֶׁר־הָיָ֛ה לְפָנַ֖י עַל־

over before have who all over wisdom and be- have
me been great come

3820 5414 1847 2451 7227 7200 3820 3389
17 יְרֽוּשָׁלָ֑͏ִם וְלִבִּ֛י רָאָ֥ה הַרְבֵּ֖ה חָכְמָ֥ה וָדָֽעַת : וָאֶתְּנָ֤ה לִבִּ֙י

my I And and wisdom abundance has my and ;Jerusalem
heart gave .knowledge of seen heart

2088/1571 3045; 55;31 1948 3045 2451 3045
לָדַ֣עַת חָכְמָ֗ה וְדַ֙עַת֙ הֽוֹלֵל֣וֹת וְשִׂכְל֔וּת יָדַ֕עְתִּי שֶׁגַּם־זֶ֥ה ה֖וּא

it ,this that know I ;folly and madness to and wisdom know to
(is) also know

3254 1847 3254 3708/7235 2451 7227 7307 7475
18 רַעְי֥וֹן ר֖וּחַ : כִּ֛י בְּרֹ֥ב חָכְמָ֖ה רָב־כָּ֑עַס וְיוֹסִ֥יף דַּ֖עַת יוֹסִ֥יף

increases knowl- he and ;grief much wisdom in For .wind striving
,edge increases who (is) much (after)

4341
מַכְאֽוֹב :

.pain

CAP. II ב

CHAPTER 2

¹I said in my heart, Come now, I will test you with mirth. Therefore, consider with goodness. And behold, this also *is* vanity. ²I said of laughter, *It is* madness, and of mirth, What does it do? ³I sought in my heart *how* to drag my flesh with wine, and leading my heart in wisdom; and to lay hold on folly, until I might see where the good for the sons of men *is, that* which they should do under the heavens the number of

2896 7200 8057. 5254 4994/3212 3820 559
1 אָמַ֤רְתִּי אֲנִי֙ בְּלִבִּ֔י לְכָה־נָּ֛א אֲנַסְּכָ֥ה בְשִׂמְחָ֖ה וּרְאֵ֣ה בְט֑וֹב

with And with will I ,now Come my in I said
goodness see .mirth you test ,heart

8057. 1984 559 7814. 1892 2009
2 וְהִנֵּ֥ה גַם־ה֖וּא הָֽבֶל : לִשְׂח֖וֹק אָמַ֣רְתִּי מְהוֹלָ֑ל וּלְשִׂמְחָ֖ה

of and is It ,said I of .vanity this ,also and
,mirth ,madness laughter (is) behold

39;2,0 1320 3196 4900 3820 8446 6213 2090
3 מַה־זֹּ֥ה עֹשָֽׂה : תַּ֣רְתִּי בְלִבִּ֞י לִמְשׁ֥וֹךְ בַּיַּ֖יִן אֶת־בְּשָׂרִ֑י וְלִבִּ֤י

my and my with to (how) my with and I does this What
heart flesh wine drag heart explored ?accomplish

5090 2451 270 5531 5704 5090
נֹהֵ֣ג בַּֽחָכְמָ֔ה וְלֶאֱחֹ֖ז בְּסִכְל֑וּת עַ֣ד ׀ אֲשֶׁר־אֶרְאֶ֗ה אֵי־זֶ֤ה 72.00

where might I until folly on to and in leading
see hold lay wisdom

3117 4557 80:64 8478 6213 120 1121 2896
ט֣וֹב לִבְנֵ֣י הָאָדָ֗ם אֲשֶׁ֤ר יַעֲשׂוּ֙ תַּ֣חַת הַשָּׁמַ֔יִם מִסְפַּ֖ר יְמֵ֥י

days the the under they which ,men the for the
of of number heavens do should of sons good

days of their life. [4]I made my works great — I built houses for myself; I planted vineyards for myself; [5]I made gardens and parks for myself, and I planted trees in them, of every fruit; [6]I made pools of water for myself, to water from them the forest shooting forth trees; [7]I bought slaves and slavegirls; and I had sons of slavegirls; the slaves of the house were mine. Also livestock, a herd and a great flock were mine, above all that were in Jerusalem before me. [8]I also gathered to me silver and gold, and the treasure of kings and of provinces. I made ready male singers and female singers for myself, and the delights of the sons of men, a concubine, and concubines. [9]And I became great and increased more than all who were before me in Jerusalem; also my wisdom stayed with me. [10]And all that my eyes desired, I did not set aside from them; I withheld not my heart from all mirth; for my heart rejoiced from all my labor; and this was my part from all my labor. [11]Then I faced on all my works that my hands had done, and on the labor that I had labored to do. And, lo, all *is* vanity and striving *after* wind, and there *is* no profit under the sun.

[12]And I turned to behold wisdom, and madness, and folly. For what *can* a man *do* who comes after the king, when they have already done it? [13]Then I saw that there is advantage to wisdom above folly, even as light *has* advantage over darkness. [14]The wise man's eyes *are* in his head; but the fool walks in darkness; and I also know that one event happens with all of them.

4 חייהם׃ הגדלתי מעשי בניתי לי בתים נטעתי לי כרמים׃
.vineyards for myself I planted ,houses for myself I built my .works I made great their .life

5 עשיתי לי גנות ופרדסים ונטעתי בהם עץ כל־פרי׃
.fruit every of tree a in them I and planted ;parks and gardens for myself I made

6 עשיתי לי ברכות מים להשקות מהם יער צומח עצים׃
.trees shooting forth the forest from them to water ,water of pools for myself I made

7 קניתי עבדים ושפחות ובני־בית היה לי גם מקנה בקר
a herd property of Also to .me were the house and sons of women slaves and men slaves I bought

8 וצאן הרבה היה לי מכל שהיו לפני בירושלם׃ כנסתי
I gathered in .Jerusalem before me that were above all to me was great a and flock

לי גם־כסף וזהב וסגלת מלכים והמדינות עשיתי לי
for myself I provided the and .provinces kings the and of treasure and ,gold silver also for myself

9 שרים ושרות ותענגות בני האדם שדה ושדות׃ וגדלתי
be- great I Then came con- .cubines and con- a cubine ,men the of sons the and of pleasures and women ,singers men singers

והוספתי מכל שהיה לפני בירושלם אף חכמתי עמדה
stood my wisdom also in ,Jerusalem before me who were more than all and increased

10 לי׃ וכל אשר שאלו עיני לא אצלתי מהם לא־מנעתי
did I withhold not from .them set did I aside not my ,eyes asked that And all by .me

את־לבי מכל־שמחה כי־לבי שמח מכל־עמלי וזה־היה
was and this my ,labor from all rejoiced my heart for ;mirth from all heart my

11 חלקי מכל־עמלי׃ ופניתי אני בכל־מעשי שעשו ידי
my ,hands which had done my works all on I Then faced my .labor from all my part

ובעמל שעמלתי לעשות והנה הכל הבל ורעות רוח
(after) wind and striving vanity all (was) and ,behold :do to had I that labored on and the labor

12 ואין יתרון תחת השמש׃ ופניתי אני לראות חכמה
,wisdom to see I And turned .sun the under profit and is not

והוללות וסכלות כי ׀ מה האדם שיבוא אחרי המלך
,king the after who comes the (do) man what (will) for ,folly and and ,madness

13 את אשר־כבר עשוהו׃ וראיתי אני שיש יתרון לחכמה
to wisdom advantage that is there I saw Then have they ?it done already when

14 מן־הסכלות כיתרון האור מן־החשך׃ החכם עיניו בראשו
in (are) ;head his his eyes wise The ,man .darkness (has) above light the as advantage ,folly above

והכסיל בחשך הולך וידעתי גם־אני שמקרה אחד יקרה
happens one that event I also know and ;walks in darkness the but fool

[15]And I said in my heart, As the event of the stupid one, even *so* it will happen to me; and why then was I more wise? Then I said in my heart that this also *is* vanity. [16]For there is not a memory of the wise *more than* with the fool forever; in that already the days to come will be forgotten. And how does the wise die above the fool? [17]So then I hated life; because the work that is done under the sun *is* evil to me; for all *is* vanity and striving *after* wind.

[18]Yes, I hated all my labor that I labored under the sun, that I must leave it to the man who will be after me. [19]And who knows *if* he will be a wise man or a fool? Yet he shall rule among all my labor *in* which I labored, and acted wisely under the sun. This *is* also vanity. [20]And I turned to make my heart despair over all the labor which I labored under the sun. [21]When there is a man whose labor *is* with wisdom, and with knowledge, and with advantage; yet he shall give it to a man who has not labored with it, *for* his share; this also *is* vanity and a great evil.

[22]For what is there for man in all his labor, and in striving of his heart, which he has labored under the sun? [23]For all his days *are* pains, and his task is grief; his heart does not even take rest in the night. Even this also *is* vanity. [24]Is it not good that he should eat and drink and make his soul see good in his labor? This I also saw, that it *was* from the hand of God. [25]For who can

1571 3684 4745 3820 559 227 3605
15 אֶת־כֻּלָּם׃ וְאָמַרְתִּי אֲנִי בְּלִבִּי כְּמִקְרֵה הַכְּסִיל גַּם־אֲנִי
to even ,fool the the like my in I said Then of all with
me (so) of event heart .them

2088/1571 3820 1696 3148 227 2449 4100 7136
יִקְרֵנִי וְלָמָּה חָכַמְתִּי אֲנִי אָז יֹתֵר וְדִבַּרְתִּי בְלִבִּי שֶׁגַּם־זֶה
this that my in I Then ?more then I was why And will it
also heart said wise meet

3528 5769 3684 5973 2450 2146 369 1892
16 הָבֶל׃ כִּי אֵין זִכְרוֹן לֶחָכָם עִם־הַכְּסִיל לְעוֹלָם בְּשֶׁכְּבָר
that in ,forever the (more any) the of a not For (is)
already fool with (than) wise memory is .vanity

3684 2450 4191 79:11 3605 935 3117
הַיָּמִים הַבָּאִים הַכֹּל נִשְׁכָּח וְאֵיךְ יָמוּת הֶחָכָם עִם־הַכְּסִיל׃
!fool the with the does and be will all are which the
wise die how ,forgotten coming days

8478 6213 4139 7451 24:16 8130
17 וְשָׂנֵאתִי אֶת־הַחַיִּים כִּי רַע עָלַי הַמַּעֲשֶׂה שֶׁנַּעֲשָׂה תַּחַת
under is that work the me on (is) because ,life Therefore
done evil hated I

3605 8130 7307 7469 1892 3605 8121
18 הַשָּׁמֶשׁ כִּי־הַכֹּל הֶבֶל וּרְעוּת רוּחַ׃ וְשָׂנֵאתִי אֲנִי אֶת־כָּל־
all I Thus (after) and vanity all for ;sun the
hated wind striving (is)

1961 120 32:40 8121 8478 6001 5999
עֲמָלִי שֶׁאֲנִי עָמֵל תַּחַת הַשָּׁמֶשׁ שֶׁאַנִּיחֶנּוּ לָאָדָם שֶׁיִּהְיֶה
will that the to I that ,sun the under had which my
be man it leave must labored I labor

3605 7980 55:30 176 1961 2450 3045 4310 310
19 אַחֲרָי׃ וּמִי יוֹדֵעַ הֶחָכָם יִהְיֶה אוֹ סָכָל וְיִשְׁלַט בְּכָל־
among he Yet ?fool a or will he wise the knows And after
all rule shall be man (whether) who .me

1892 1571 8121 8478 2449 5999
עֲמָלִי שֶׁעָמַלְתִּי וְשֶׁחָכַמְתִּי תַּחַת הַשָּׁמֶשׁ גַּם־זֶה הָבֶל׃
.vanity this also ;sun the under acted and which (in) my
(is) wisely labored I labor

8478 5998 59:99 3605 5921 3820 2976 5437
20 וְסַבּוֹתִי אֲנִי לְיַאֵשׁ אֶת־לִבִּי עַל כָּל־הֶעָמָל שֶׁעָמַלְתִּי תַּחַת
under I which the all over my cause to I And
labored labor heart .despair to turned

3788 1847 2451 5999 120 3426 8121
21 הַשָּׁמֶשׁ׃ כִּי־יֵשׁ אָדָם שֶׁעֲמָלוֹ בְּחָכְמָה וּבְדַעַת וּבְכִשְׁרוֹן
with and with and with (is) whose man a there When .sun the
;success ,knowledge ,wisdom labor is

7451 1892 1571 2506 5414 5998 3808 120
וּלְאָדָם שֶׁלֹּא עָמַל־בּוֹ יִתְּנֶנּוּ חֶלְקוֹ גַּם־זֶה הֶבֶל וְרָעָה
evil and vanity this also his shall he with has who to yet
(is) share ,it give ,it labored not man a

1931 38 20 7475 5999 3605 120 19:33 7227
22 רַבָּה׃ כִּי מֶה־הֹוֶה לָאָדָם בְּכָל־עֲמָלוֹ וּבְרַעְיוֹן לִבּוֹ שֶׁהוּא
which his in and his all in for is what For .great a
he ,heart of striving the ,labor man there

6045 3708 4341 3117 3605 8121 8478 6001
23 עָמֵל תַּחַת הַשָּׁמֶשׁ׃ כִּי כָל־יָמָיו מַכְאֹבִים וָכַעַס עִנְיָנוֹ
his and pains (are) his all For ?sun the under has
;task grief days labored

2896 1892 2088/1571/38:20 7901 39:15 1571
24 גַּם־בַּלַּיְלָה לֹא־שָׁכַב לִבּוֹ גַּם־זֶה הֶבֶל הוּא׃ אֵין־טוֹב
good Is .(is) it vanity ,this Even his lie does not the in even
not it .heart down night

1571 5999 2896 5315 3318 83:54 398 120
בָּאָדָם שֶׁיֹּאכַל וְשָׁתָה וְהֶרְאָה אֶת־נַפְשׁוֹ טוֹב בַּעֲמָלוֹ גַּם־
Also his in good soul his cause and and he that a with
?labor see to ,drink eat should man

4310 398 4310 430 3027 7200 2090
25 זֹה רָאִיתִי אָנִי כִּי מִיַּד הָאֱלֹהִים הִיא׃ כִּי מִי יֹאכַל וּמִי
or can who For it God the from that I saw this
who eat .(was) of hand

26 יָחוּשׁ חוּץ מִמֶּנִּי׃ כִּי לְאָדָם שֶׁטּוֹב לְפָנָיו נָתַן חָכְמָה וָדַעַת

1847 2451 5414 6440 2896 120 2351 2363

and knowledge | wisdom | He gives | before Him, | (is) who good | a to man | For | from Me? | -out side | can enjoy-

וְשִׂמְחָה וְלַחוֹטֶא נָתַן עִנְיָן לֶאֱסֹף וְלִכְנוֹס לָתֵת לְטוֹב

2896 5414 3664 622 6045 5414 2398 8057

the to one good | give to | and collecting | of gathering | the task | He gives | the to but sinner | ,joy and

לִפְנֵי הָאֱלֹהִים גַּם־זֶה הֶבֶל וּרְעוּת רוּחַ׃

7307 7469 1892 2088/1571/430 6440

(after) wind | and striving | vanity | this Also (is) | .God | before

eat, or who can enjoy, apart from me? [26]For *God* gives wisdom, and knowledge and joy to a man who *is* good in His sight. But to the sinner He gives the task of gathering and collecting, to give to *him who is* good before God. This also *is* vanity and striving *after* wind.

CAP. III ג

CHAPTER 3

1 לַכֹּל זְמָן וְעֵת לְכָל־חֵפֶץ תַּחַת הַשָּׁמָיִם׃

8064 8478 2656 6256 2165 3605

the heavens: | under | purpose for every | a and time | set a time | all To (is)

2 עֵת לָלֶדֶת וְעֵת לָמוּת

3205 6256 | 4191 6256

a time bear to | a and time ;die to

עֵת לָטַעַת וְעֵת לַעֲקוֹר נָטוּעַ׃

5193 6256 | 6131 5193 6256

a time plant to | a and time uproot to | what is planted;

3 עֵת לַהֲרוֹג וְעֵת לִרְפּוֹא

2026 6256 | 7495 6256

a time kill to | a and time ;heal to

עֵת לִפְרוֹץ וְעֵת לִבְנוֹת׃

6555 6256 | 1129 6256

a time to tear down | a and time build to ;up

4 עֵת לִבְכּוֹת וְעֵת לִשְׂחוֹק

1058 6256 | 7832 6256

a time weep to | a and time ;laugh to

עֵת סְפוֹד וְעֵת רְקוֹד׃

5594 6256 | 7540 6256

a time wail to | a and time ;dance to

5 עֵת לְהַשְׁלִיךְ אֲבָנִים וְעֵת כְּנוֹס אֲבָנִים

7993 68 6256 | 3664 68 6256

a time throw to away stones | a and time gather to ;stones

עֵת לַחֲבוֹק וְעֵת לִרְחֹק מֵחַבֵּק׃

2263 6256 | 7368 2263 6256

a time to embrace | a and time refrain to from ;embracing

6 עֵת לְבַקֵּשׁ וְעֵת לְאַבֵּד

1245 6256 | 6 6256

a time seek to | a and time let to perish

עֵת לִשְׁמוֹר וְעֵת לְהַשְׁלִיךְ׃

8104 6256 | 7993 6256

a time keep to | a and time throw to ;away

7 עֵת לִקְרוֹעַ וְעֵת לִתְפּוֹר

7167 6256 | 8609 6256

a time tear to | a and time sew to ,together

עֵת לַחֲשׁוֹת וְעֵת לְדַבֵּר׃

2814 6256 | 1696 6256

a time be to silent | a and time ;speak to

CHAPTER 3

[1]To all *there is* an appointed time, even a time for every purpose under the heavens — [2]a time to be born, and a time to die — a time to plant, and a time to pull up what is planted —[3]a time to kill, and a time to heal — a time to tear down, and a time to build up—[4]a time to weep, and a time to laugh — a time to mourn, and a time to dance—[5]a time to throw away stones, and a time to gather stones — a time to embrace, and a time to refrain from embracing —[6]a time to seek, and a time to give up as lost — a time to keep, and a time to throw away—[7]a time to tear, and a time to sew together—a time to keep silence, and a time to speak — [8]a time to

love, and a time to hate—a time of war, and a time of peace.

9What profit does he who works have in that in which he labors? 10I have seen the task which God has given to the sons of men, to be humbled by it. 11He has made everything beautiful in its time. Also, He has set eternity in their heart, without which man cannot find out the work that God makes from the beginning and to the end. 12I know that *there is* no good in them, but for *a man* to rejoice to do good in his life. 13And also every man that eats and drinks, and sees good in his labor, it *is* the gift of God. 14I know that whatever God does, it shall be forever; nothing is to be added to it, and nothing is to diminish from it. And God does *it* so that they fear before Him. 15That which has been, it already is; and that which *is* to be, *it* already has been. And God seeks what has gone by.

16And again I saw under the sun the place of justice: wickedness *is* there; and the place of righteousness, wickedness *is* there. 17I said in my heart, God shall judge the righteous and the wicked; for *there is* a time there for every purpose and for every work.

18I said in my heart concerning the matter of the sons of men, that God may test them and see that they by themselves *are* beasts.

8130 6256 157 6256
8 עת לאהב ועת לשנא
;hate to a and time love to a time

7965 6256 4421 6256
עת מלחמה ועת שלום׃
.peace a and of time war a of time

6045 7200 6001 834 6213 3504 4100
9 מה־יתרון העושה באשר הוא עמל׃ 10 ראיתי את־הענין
task the have I seen ?labors he that in which who he works advantage What (has)

3605 6031 120 1121 430 5414 834
אשר נתן אלהים לבני האדם לענות בו׃ 11 את־הכל
everything .it by be to humbled ,men the to of sons God has given which

834 1097 3820 5414 5769 1571 6256 3303 6213
עשה יפה בעתו גם את־העלם נתן בלבם מבלי אשר
which without their in heart He set has eternity Also its in .time beautiful has He made

7218 430 6213 4639 120 4672/3808
לא־ימצא האדם את־המעשה אשר־עשה האלהים מראש
the from beginning God makes that the work man can out find not

6213 8056 2896 369 3045 5490
ועד־סוף׃ 12 ידעתי כי אין טוב בם כי אם־לשמוח ולעשות
do to rejoice to except in them good not is that know I the .end even to

2896 7200 8354 398 120 3605 2416 2896
טוב בחייו׃ 13 וגם כל־האדם שיאכל ושתה וראה טוב
good and sees and ,drinks that eats man every and also his in ,life good

6213 3605 3045 430 4991 5999 3605
בכל־עמלו מתת אלהים היא׃ 14 ידעתי כי כל־אשר יעשה
does which all that know I .(is) it God the of gift his ,labor all in

369 3254 369 5769 1961 430
האלהים הוא יהיה לעולם עליו אין להוסיף וממנו אין
not is and it from be to ,added not is it to ;forever be shall it ,God

3528 1961 6440 3372 6213 430 1639
לגרע והאלהים עשה שיראו מלפניו׃ 15 מה־שהיה כבר
already which That ,been has before .Him that so fear they does (it) for God to ,diminish

7291 1245 430 1961 3528 1961 834
הוא ואשר להיות כבר היה והאלהים יבקש את־נרדף׃
is what .pursued seeks God for has ,been already ,be will that and which it ,(is)

7562 8033 4941 4725 8121 8478 7200 5750
16 ועוד ראיתי תחת השמש מקום המשפט שמה הרשע
wicked- ;ness there (is) justice the of place ;sun the under saw I And again

6662 3820 559 7562 8033 6664 4725
ומקום הצדק שמה הרשע׃ 17 אמרתי אני בלבי את־הצדיק
The righteous my in .heart I said .wickedness there (is) righteous- ness the and of place

3605 2656 6256 430 8199 7563
ואת־הרשע ישפט האלהים כי־עת לכל־חפץ ועל כל־
every and for purpose for every (is) for time a ;God shall judge the wicked and

120 1121 1697 3820 559 8033 4639
המעשה שם׃ 18 אמרתי אני בלבי על־דברת בני האדם
,men the of sons the of matter concern- ing my in heart I said .there work

1992 929 7200 430 1305
לברם האלהים ולראות שהם־בהמה המה להם׃ 19 כי
For by .themselves they (are) beasts that they in and see to order ,God may that them test

[19]For that which happens *to* the sons of men, and that which happens *to* beasts; even one event *is* to them. As this *one* dies, so that *one* dies; yea, one breath *is* to all; so that there is to the man no advantage over the beast; for all *is* vanity. [20]All go to one place; all are of the dust, and all return to the dust. [21]Who knows the spirit of the sons of man, *whether* it goes upward; and the spirit of the beast, *whether* it goes downward to the earth? [22]Therefore, I have seen that nothing is better than that the man should rejoice in his works; for that *is* his portion; for who can bring him to see what shall be after him?

מִקְרֶה בְנֵי־הָאָדָם וּמִקְרֶה הַבְּהֵמָה וּמִקְרֶה אֶחָד לָהֶם
4745 929 4745 120 1121 4745
to ;them | one | even event | ;beasts | the and of event | men | the of sons | the of event

כְּמוֹת זֶה כֵּן מוֹת זֶה וְרוּחַ אֶחָד לַכֹּל וּמוֹתַר הָאָדָם מִן
120 4195 3605 259 7307 2088 4194 2088 4194
over | man the | that so advantage | ,all to | one | even breath | ;this dies | so | ,this | dies as

20 הַבְּהֵמָה אָיִן כִּי הַכֹּל הָבֶל׃ הַכֹּל הוֹלֵךְ אֶל־מָקוֹם אֶחָד
259 4725 1980 3605 259 1892 369 929
;one | place | to | go | All | .vanity | all (is) | for | is ,not | beast the

21 הַכֹּל הָיָה מִן־הֶעָפָר וְהַכֹּל שָׁב אֶל־הֶעָפָר׃ מִי יוֹדֵעַ רוּחַ
7307 3045 4310 6083 7725 3605 6083 1961 3605
the of spirit | knows | Who | .dust the | to | return | all and | ,dust the | of | are | all

בְּנֵי הָאָדָם הָעֹלָה הִיא לְמָעְלָה וְרוּחַ הַבְּהֵמָה הַיֹּרֶדֶת
3381 929 7307 4605 5927 120 1121
(whether) descends | beast the | the and of spirit | ,upward | it | (whether) ascends | man | the of sons

22 הִיא לְמַטָּה לָאָרֶץ׃ וְרָאִיתִי כִּי אֵין טוֹב מֵאֲשֶׁר יִשְׂמַח
8056 2896 369 7200 776 4295
should rejoice | than that | better nothing is | there that | Therefore seen have I | the to .earth | downward | it

הָאָדָם בְּמַעֲשָׂיו כִּי־הוּא חֶלְקוֹ כִּי מִי יְבִיאֶנּוּ לִרְאוֹת בְּמֶה
7200 935 4310 2506 4639 120
what | see to | can him bring | who for | his ;portion | that (is) | for | his in ,works own | the man

שֶׁיִּהְיֶה אַחֲרָיו׃
310 1961
after ?him | shall be

CAP. IV ד

CHAPTER 4

CHAPTER 4

[1]So I returned and considered all the oppressions that are done under the sun. And behold the tears of those who were oppressed, and they had no comforter! And at the hand of those who oppressed them *was* power; but there was no comforter to them. [2]Therefore, I commended the dead who already have died, more than the living who *are* alive until now. [3]Yea, better than both *is he* who has not yet been, who has not seen the evil work that is done under the sun.

[4]And I considered every labor, and every advantage of the work, that it is the envy of a man against his neighbor; this *is* also vanity and striving *after* wind.

[5]The fool folds his hands

1 וְשַׁבְתִּי אֲנִי וָאֶרְאֶה אֶת־כָּל־הָעֲשֻׁקִים אֲשֶׁר נַעֲשִׂים תַּחַת
8478 6213 6217 3605 7200 7725
under | done are | that | the oppressions | all | saw and | I | So returned

הַשָּׁמֶשׁ וְהִנֵּה דִּמְעַת הָעֲשֻׁקִים וְאֵין לָהֶם מְנַחֵם וּמִיַּד
3027 5162 369 6231 1832 2009 8121
at and hand | who one ;comforts | for them | and is not | who those oppressed are | tears the of | And ,behold | .sun the

2 עֹשְׁקֵיהֶם כֹּחַ וְאֵין לָהֶם מְנַחֵם׃ וְשַׁבֵּחַ אֲנִי אֶת־הַמֵּתִים
4191 7623 5162 369 3581 6231
the dead | I | And commended | who one .comforts | to them was not | but power | (was) | their oppressors'

3 שֶׁכְּבָר מֵתוּ מִן־הַחַיִּים אֲשֶׁר הֵמָּה חַיִּים עֲדֶנָה׃ וְטוֹב
2896 5750 2416 834 2416 4191 3528
But better | .still | alive | they (are) | which | the living | more than | have ,died | who already

מִשְּׁנֵיהֶם אֵת אֲשֶׁר־עֲדֶן לֹא הָיָה אֲשֶׁר לֹא־רָאָה אֶת־
7200 3808 834 1961 3808 5704 834 8147
has seen | not | who | has ,been | not | to up now | (that is) which | ,both than them of

4 הַמַּעֲשֶׂה הָרָע אֲשֶׁר נַעֲשָׂה תַּחַת הַשָּׁמֶשׁ׃ וְרָאִיתִי אֲנִי
7200 8121 8478 6213 7451 4639
I | saw And | .sun the | under | done is | that | evil | work the

אֶת־כָּל־עָמָל וְאֵת כָּל־כִּשְׁרוֹן הַמַּעֲשֶׂה כִּי הִיא קִנְאַת־אִישׁ
376 7068 4639 3788 5999 3605
a man | envy the of | it (is) | that | ,work the | success of | every | and | labor all

5 מֵרֵעֵהוּ גַּם־זֶה הֶבֶל וּרְעוּת רוּחַ׃ הַכְּסִיל חֹבֵק אֶת־יָדָיו
3027 2263 3684 7307 7469 1892 2088/1571 7453
his hands | folds | fool The | .wind | and (after) striving | vanity | this also (is) | his against ;neighbor

together and eats his own flesh. ⁶Better *is* a palm filled *with* rest, than two fists *with* labor and striving *after* wind.

⁷Then I returned and saw vanity under the sun. ⁸There is one *alone*, and there is not a second; yea, he has neither son nor brother; and there is no end to all his labor; even his eyes are not satisfied with riches; and *he* says, For whom do I labor, and take good from my soul? This *is* also vanity. Yes, it *is* an evil task.

⁹Two *are* better than one; because they have a good reward for their labor. ¹⁰For if they fall, this one will lift up his fellow. But woe to him, the one that falls, and there is not another to lift him up. ¹¹Also if two lie *together*, then they *have* warmth; but for one, how is he warm? ¹²And if one overthrows him, two shall withstand him; and a threefold cord is not quickly torn apart. ¹³A poor and a wise child *is* better than the old and stupid king, who does not know to be warned any more. ¹⁴For from the house of the imprisoned he goes forth to reign, although in his kingdom he was born poor. ¹⁵I saw all the living who walk about under the sun, with the second child who shall stand up in his place. ¹⁶*There is* no end to all the people, to all who have been before them; they also who come after shall not rejoice with him. Surely this *is* also vanity and striving *after* wind.

CHAPTER 5

¹Guard your feet when you go to the house of God, and draw near to hear, more than to give a sacrifice, *as do* the fools. For they do not know that they are doing

6 וְאָכַל אֶת־בְּשָׂרוֹ׃ טוֹב מְלֹא כַף נָחַת מִמְּלֹא חָפְנַיִם עָמָל
(with) two than (with) a filled Better own his and
labor fists filled rest palm (is) flesh eats

7 וּרְעוּת רוּחַ׃ וְשַׁבְתִּי אֲנִי וָאֶרְאֶה הֶבֶל תַּחַת הַשָּׁמֶשׁ׃ יֵשׁ
8 There the under vanity saw and I Then (after) and
is sun returned wind striving

אֶחָד וְאֵין שֵׁנִי גַּם בֵּן וָאָח אֵין־לוֹ וְאֵין קֵץ לְכָל־עֲמָלוֹ גַּם
even his to an and to not a and a also a and one
:labor all end is not him is brother son ,second is not

עֵינָיו לֹא־תִשְׂבַּע עֹשֶׁר וּלְמִי אֲנִי עָמֵל וּמְחַסֵּר אֶת־נַפְשִׁי
soul my and and do I for and ;riches are not his
deprive labor whom with satisfied eyes

9 מְטוֹבָה גַּם־זֶה הֶבֶל וְעִנְיַן רָע הוּא׃ טוֹבִים הַשְּׁנַיִם מִן
than Two better .(is) it evil a and vanity This also from
(are) task (is) ?good

10 הָאֶחָד אֲשֶׁר יֵשׁ־לָהֶם שָׂכָר טוֹב בַּעֲמָלָם׃ כִּי אִם־יִפֹּלוּ
they if For their with good a to there because ,one
fall .labor reward them is

הָאֶחָד יָקִים אֶת־חֲבֵרוֹ וְאִילוֹ הָאֶחָד שֶׁיִּפּוֹל וְאֵין שֵׁנִי
a and that one the woe but his cause will the
second is not falls ,companion rise to one
;him to

11 לַהֲקִימוֹ׃ גַּם אִם־יִשְׁכְּבוּ שְׁנַיִם וְחַם לָהֶם וּלְאֶחָד אֵיךְ
how for but to then ,two lie if ,Again make to
(alone) one ;them warmth together rise him

12 יֵחָם׃ וְאִם־יִתְקְפוֹ הָאֶחָד הַשְּׁנַיִם יַעַמְדוּ נֶגְדּוֹ וְהַחוּט
the And before shall two the ,one over-shall And he is
cord him stand him power if ?warm

13 הַמְשֻׁלָּשׁ לֹא בִמְהֵרָה יִנָּתֵק׃ טוֹב יֶלֶד מִסְכֵּן וְחָכָם מִמֶּלֶךְ
the than and poor a Better torn is quickly not threefold
king ,wise child (is) .apart

14 זָקֵן וּכְסִיל אֲשֶׁר לֹא־יָדַע לְהִזָּהֵר עוֹד׃ כִּי־מִבֵּית הַסּוּרִים
the the from For any to (how) does not who and old
imprisoned of house .more warned be know foolish

15 יָצָא לִמְלֹךְ כִּי גַּם בְּמַלְכוּתוֹ נוֹלַד רָשׁ׃ רָאִיתִי אֶת־כָּל־
all saw I .poor was he his in although be to king
born kingdom ;goes

הַחַיִּים הַמְהַלְּכִים תַּחַת הַשָּׁמֶשׁ עִם הַיֶּלֶד הַשֵּׁנִי אֲשֶׁר
who second the with sun the under walk who the
child living

16 יַעֲמֹד תַּחְתָּיו׃ אֵין־קֵץ לְכָל־הָעָם לְכֹל אֲשֶׁר־הָיָה לִפְנֵיהֶם
before have who all to the to end There of instead stands
;them been people all no is him

גַּם הָאַחֲרוֹנִים לֹא יִשְׂמְחוּ־בוֹ כִּי־גַם־זֶה הֶבֶל וְרַעְיוֹן רוּחַ׃
.wind and vanity this also Surely with shall not later the also
after striving (is) .him rejoice ones

17 שְׁמֹר רַגְלְךָ כַּאֲשֶׁר תֵּלֵךְ אֶל־בֵּית הָאֱלֹהִים וְקָרוֹב לִשְׁמֹעַ
,hear to draw and ,God the to you when your Guard
near of house go feet

מִתֵּת הַכְּסִילִים זָבַח כִּי־אֵינָם יוֹדְעִים לַעֲשׂוֹת רָע׃
.evil they that do they for a the (like) than
do know not ,sacrifice fools give to

evil. [2]Do not be hasty *with* your mouth, and do not let your heart hurry to bring forth a word before God. For God *is* in Heaven, and you *are* on earth; therefore, let your words be few. [3]For the dream comes through the greatness of the task; and the voice of the fool *is* known by the multitude of words. [4]When you vow a vow to God, do not wait to fulfill it. For *He* has no pleasure in fools. Fulfill that which you have vowed. [5]*It is* better that you should not vow, than that you should vow and not fulfill it. [6]Do not allow your mouth to cause your flesh to sin; do not say before the angel that it *was* an error. Why should God be angry over your voice, and destroy the works of your hands? [7]For in the multitude of dreams, both words and vanities abound; but fear God. [8]If you see the oppression of the poor, or the removing of justice and righteousness in the province, do not be amazed at the purpose. For a high one over a high one is watching; and high ones *are* over them.

[9]And the advantage of a land, it *is* among all; *even* a king has a field being tilled. [10]He who loves silver will not be satisfied with silver; and he who loves abundance not *with* gain. This *is* also vanity. [11]When the good multiplies, those who eat it multiply; then what profit *is it* to its owners, except to see *it* with his eyes? [12]The sleep of the laboring man *is* sweet, whether he eats little or much. But the abundance of the rich will not allow him to sleep. [13]There is a painful evil

CAP. V ה

CHAPTER 5

6440 1697 3318 4116 3820 6310 926 408
1 אַל־תְּבַהֵל עַל־פִּיךָ וְלִבְּךָ אַל־יְמַהֵר לְהוֹצִיא דָבָר לִפְנֵי
before a word bring forth to hurry do not your heart and your mouth, with be hasty Do not

3651 5921 776 5921 8064 430 430
הָאֱלֹהִים כִּי הָאֱלֹהִים בַּשָּׁמַיִם וְאַתָּה עַל־הָאָרֶץ עַל־כֵּן
therefore the ;earth on (are) and you Heaven in God (is) for —God

3684 6963 6045 7230 2472 935 4592 1697 1961
2 יִהְיוּ דְבָרֶיךָ מְעַטִּים׃ כִּי בָּא הַחֲלוֹם בְּרֹב עִנְיָן וְקוֹל כְּסִיל
fool's a voice and ; the task the of greatness by the dream comes For .few your words let be

7999 309 408 430 5088/5087 834 1697 7230
3 בְּרֹב דְּבָרִים׃ כַּאֲשֶׁר תִּדֹּר נֶדֶר לֵאלֹהִים אַל־תְּאַחֵר לְשַׁלְּמוֹ
fulfill to ,it do delay not ,God to vow a you vow When .words the by of greatness

2896 79 99 5087 834 3684 2656 369
4 כִּי אֵין חֵפֶץ בַּכְּסִילִים אֵת אֲשֶׁר־תִּדֹּר שַׁלֵּם׃ טוֹב אֲשֶׁר
that (is It) better fulfill .(it) have you ,vowed that which ;fools in pleasure He has for no

2398 6310 5414 408 7999 3808 5087 5087 3808
5 לֹא־תִדֹּר מִשֶּׁתִּדּוֹר וְלֹא תְשַׁלֵּם׃ אַל־תִּתֵּן אֶת־פִּיךָ לַחֲטִיא
cause to sin to your mouth Do give not fulfill .(it) and you not that than you vow should not ,vow should

7684 4397 6440 559 408 1320
אֶת־בְּשָׂרֶךָ וְאַל־תֹּאמַר לִפְנֵי הַמַּלְאָךְ כִּי שְׁגָגָה הִיא לָמָּה
Why it .(was) an error that the angel before do say and not your ;flesh

7230 3027 4639 2254 6963 430 7107
6 יִקְצֹף הָאֱלֹהִים עַל־קוֹלֶךָ וְחִבֵּל אֶת־מַעֲשֵׂה יָדֶיךָ׃ כִּי בְרֹב
the in of host For your ?hands the of works and destroy your voice at God should angry be

3372 430 7235 1697 1892 2472
חֲלֹמוֹת וַהֲבָלִים וּדְבָרִים הַרְבֵּה כִּי אֶת־הָאֱלֹהִים יְרָא׃
.fear God but ;abound words and both vanities dreams

408 4082 7200 6664 4941 1499 7326 6233
7 אִם־עֹשֶׁק רָשׁ וְגֵזֶל מִשְׁפָּט וָצֶדֶק תִּרְאֶה בַמְּדִינָה אַל־
not the in ,province you see and righteousness justice the or of removing the poor op- the of pression If

5921 1364 8104 1364 2656 8539
תִּתְמַהּ עַל־הַחֵפֶץ כִּי גָבֹהַּ מֵעַל גָּבֹהַּ שֹׁמֵר וּגְבֹהִים עֲלֵיהֶם׃
over .them (are) high ones and ,watching is high a one over high a one for the ,reason at be do amazed

3808 3701 157 5647 7704 4428 3605 776 3504
8 וְיִתְרוֹן אֶרֶץ בַּכֹּל הִיא מֶלֶךְ לְשָׂדֶה נֶעֱבָד׃
9 אֹהֵב כֶּסֶף לֹא־
not silver who loves He being .tilled a field has a king ;(is) it in all ,land a the of advantage And

1892 2088/1571 8393 3808 1995 157 3701 7646
יִשְׂבַּע כֶּסֶף וּמִי־אֹהֵב בֶּהָמוֹן לֹא תְבוּאָה גַּם־זֶה הָבֶל׃
.vanity this (is) Also (with) ?gain not abundance he and loves who ,silver be will with satisfied

1167 3788 4100 398 7231 2896 7235
10 בִּרְבוֹת הַטּוֹבָה רַבּוּ אוֹכְלֶיהָ וּמַה־כִּשְׁרוֹן לִבְעָלֶיהָ כִּי
its to owners profit (it is) then what who those ;it devour increase the ,thing good When increases

4592 518 5647 8142 4966 5869 7200
11 אִם־רְאִית עֵינָיו׃ מְתוּקָה שְׁנַת הָעֹבֵד אִם־מְעַט וְאִם־
or little whether the ,man laboring sleep the of (is) sweet his ?eyes with to see (it) except

3426 3462 3240 369 6223 7646 398 7235
12 הַרְבֵּה יֹאכֵל וְהַשָּׂבָע לֶעָשִׁיר אֵינֶנּוּ מַנִּיחַ לוֹ לִישׁוֹן׃ יֵשׁ
There is to .sleep him will allow not the of rich the but abundance ;eats he much

which I have seen under the sun: riches being kept for their owner to his evil; [14]but those riches perish by an evil use; and he fathers a son, and nothing *is* in his hand. [15]As he came forth from his mother's womb naked, he shall return to go as he came. And from his labor he may not carry anything that may go in his hand. [16]And this also *is* a painful evil, *that in* all, as he came, so shall he go. And what profit *is* to him who has labored for the wind? [17]Also all his days he eats in darkness, and with much grief, *along with* his sickness and wrath.

[18]See what I have seen: *It is* good *and* beautiful to eat and to drink and to see good in all his labor that he labors under the sun, the number of the days of his life which God gives to him — for it is his portion. [19]Also every man to whom God has given riches and treasures, and gives him power to eat of it, and to take his share, and to rejoice in his labor—this *is* the gift of God. [20]For he shall not much remember the days of his life, because God answers *him* in the joy of his heart.

1167 8104 6239 8121 8478 7200 2470 7451
רָעָה חוֹלָה רָאִיתִי תַּחַת הַשָּׁמֶשׁ עֹשֶׁר שָׁמוּר לִבְעָלָיו
its for kept riches ;sun the under I (which) a evil
owner seen have sickly

369 11:21 3205 7451 6045 6239 6 7451
13 לְרָעָתוֹ: וְאָבַד הָעֹשֶׁר הַהוּא בְּעִנְיַן רָע וְהוֹלִיד בֵּן וְאֵין
and ,son a he and ,evil an by those riches but his to
is not fathers task perish .evil

3212 7725 6174 517 990 3318 3972 3027
14 בְּיָדוֹ מְאוּמָה: כַּאֲשֶׁר יָצָא מִבֶּטֶן אִמּוֹ עָרוֹם יָשׁוּב לָלֶכֶת
go to he ,naked his from he As .anything his in
return shall mother's womb forth came hand

2090 3027 32 1 2 5999 5375/3808 3972 935
15 כְּשֶׁבָּא וּמְאוּמָה לֹא־יִשָּׂא בַעֲמָלוֹ שֶׁיֹּלֵךְ בְּיָדוֹ: וְגַם־זֹה
this And his in may that his in may he not and he as
(is) also .hand go toil carry anything ;came

5998 3504 32 12 935 5980 3605 2470/7451
רָעָה חוֹלָה כָּל־עֻמַּת שֶׁבָּא כֵּן יֵלֵךְ וּמַה־יִּתְרוֹן לוֹ שֶׁיַּעֲמֹל
has who to profit And shall so he as (in) a evil
labored him what .go he came all ,sickly

2483 7235 3707 398 28 22 3117 3605 7307
16 לָרוּחַ: גַּם כָּל־יָמָיו בַּחֹשֶׁךְ יֹאכֵל וְכָעַס הַרְבֵּה וְחָלְיוֹ
his and ,much with he in his all Also the for
sickness grief ,eats darkness days ?wind

398 3303 2896 7200 7110
17 וָקָצֶף: הִנֵּה אֲשֶׁר־רָאִיתִי אָנִי טוֹב אֲשֶׁר־יָפֶה לֶאֱכוֹל
eat to (is it) that (is It) .I seen have what Behold and
beautiful good .wrath

8121 8478 6001 5998 3605 2896 7200 8354
וְלִשְׁתּוֹת וְלִרְאוֹת טוֹבָה בְּכָל־עֲמָלוֹ ׀ שֶׁיַּעֲמֹל תַּחַת־הַשֶּׁמֶשׁ
sun the under he that his in good to and to and
labors labor all see drink

2506 430 5414 834 2416/3117 4557
מִסְפַּר יְמֵי־חַיָּו אֲשֶׁר־נָתַן־לוֹ הָאֱלֹהִים כִּי־הוּא חֶלְקוֹ:
his it for —God to gives which his the the
.portion (is) him life of days of number

5233 6239 430 5414 834 120 3605 1571
18 גַּם כָּל־הָאָדָם אֲשֶׁר נָתַן־לוֹ הָאֱלֹהִים עֹשֶׁר וּנְכָסִים
and riches God to has whom man every Also
,treasures him given

6001 8056 2506 5375 398 7980
וְהִשְׁלִיטוֹ לֶאֱכֹל מִמֶּנּוּ וְלָשֵׂאת אֶת־חֶלְקוֹ וְלִשְׂמֹחַ בַּעֲמָלוֹ
his in to and his to and it of eat to him gives and
—labor rejoice ,portion take power

2416 3117 21 42 72 35 38 08 430 4991/2090
19 זֹה מַתַּת אֱלֹהִים הִיא: כִּי לֹא הַרְבֵּה יִזְכֹּר אֶת־יְמֵי חַיָּיו
his the shall he much not For .(is) it .God the this
;life of days remember of gift

38 20 8057 6031 430
כִּי הָאֱלֹהִים מַעֲנֶה בְּשִׂמְחַת לִבּוֹ:
his the in to causes God for
.heart of joy respond

CAP. VI ו

CHAPTER 6

CHAPTER 6

[1]There is an evil that I have seen under the sun, and it *is* great among men: [2]A man to whom God has given riches, and wealth, and honor, so that he lacks nothing for his soul of all that he desires; yet God does not give him the

120 5921 7227 8121 8478 7200 834 74 51 3426
1 יֵשׁ רָעָה אֲשֶׁר רָאִיתִי תַּחַת הַשָּׁמֶשׁ וְרַבָּה הִיא עַל־הָאָדָם:
—men upon (is) it and ,sun the under have I which an There
great seen evil is

369 35 19 5233 6239 430 5414 834 376
2 אִישׁ אֲשֶׁר יִתֶּן־לוֹ הָאֱלֹהִים עֹשֶׁר וּנְכָסִים וְכָבוֹד וְאֵינֶנּוּ
that so and and ,riches God to has whom a
nothing ,honor treasures him given man

430 7980 183 3 605 53 15 2638
חָסֵר לְנַפְשׁוֹ ׀ מִכֹּל אֲשֶׁר־יִתְאַוֶּה וְלֹא־יַשְׁלִיטֶנּוּ הָאֱלֹהִים
God give does yet he that all of his for he
power him not ,desires soul lacks

power to eat of it, but a stranger eats it — this *is* vanity, and it is an evil disease. [3]If a man fathers a hundred *children*, and lives many years, and the days of his years are many, and his soul is not satisfied from the good, and also there is no burial for him; I say, a miscarriage *is* better than he. [4]For he comes in with vanity, and goes out in darkness; his name shall be covered in darkness. [5]Also he has not seen nor known the sun; this *one* has more rest than that *one*. [6]Yea, though he lives twice a thousand years, yet he has seen no good. Do not all go to one place? [7]All the labor of man *is* for his mouth, and yet the soul is not filled. [8]For what *is* the advantage to the wise more than the fool? What *gain* to the poor who knows *how* to walk before the living? [9]Better *is* the sight of the eyes than the wandering of the soul. This *is* also vanity and striving *after* wind. [10]That which has been is named already, and it is known that he *is* man; and he is not able to contend with Him who is stronger than he.

[11]For there are many things that increase vanity, *and* what *is* the advantage to man? [12]For who knows what *is* good for man in *this* life, the number of the days of his vain life? Even he makes them like the shadow. For who can tell a man what shall be after him under the sun?

7451 2483 1892 2088 398 5237 376 398
לֶאֱכֹל מִמֶּנּוּ כִּי אִישׁ נָכְרִי יֹאכְלֶנּוּ זֶה הֶבֶל וָחֳלִי רָע הוּא׃
.(is) it an and ,vanity this eats foreign a but ,it of eat to
evil disease (is) —it man

3 3426 7227 2421 7227 8141 3967 376 3205
אִם־יוֹלִיד אִישׁ מֵאָה וְשָׁנִים רַבּוֹת יִחְיֶה וְרַב ׀ שֶׁיִּהְיוּ
that so ,lives many and hundred a a fathers If
are many years (children) man

3808 6900 2896 7646 3808 5315 8141 3117
יְמֵי־שָׁנָיו וְנַפְשׁוֹ לֹא־תִשְׂבַּע מִן־הַטּוֹבָה וְגַם־קְבוּרָה לֹא־
not burial and the from is not his and his the
also ,good satisfied soul ,years of days

4 2822 935 1892 5309 2896 559 1961
הָיְתָה לּוֹ אָמַרְתִּי טוֹב מִמֶּנּוּ הַנָּפֶל׃ כִּי־בַהֶבֶל בָּא וּבַחֹשֶׁךְ
in and he with For the than (is) ,say I for is
darkness enters vanity .miscarriage he better ,him

5 3045 3808 7200 3808 8121 3680 8034 2822 3212
יֵלֵךְ וּבַחֹשֶׁךְ שְׁמוֹ יְכֻסֶּה׃ גַּם־שֶׁמֶשׁ לֹא־רָאָה וְלֹא יָדָע
has and has he not sun the Also be shall his in and he
;known not seen .covered name darkness ,goes

6 2896 6471 8141 505 2421 432 2088 2088 5183
נַחַת לָזֶה מִזֶּה׃ וְאִלּוּ חָיָה אֶלֶף שָׁנִים פַּעֲמַיִם וְטוֹבָה
good yet ,twice years a he if Even than to more
thousand lives .this this (is) rest

7 120 5999 3212 3605 259 4725 3808 7200 3808
לֹא רָאָה הֲלֹא אֶל־מָקוֹם אֶחָד הַכֹּל הוֹלֵךְ׃ כָּל־עֲמַל הָאָדָם
(is) man the All ?go all one place to (do) he not
of labor not —seen has

8 2450 3148/4100 4390 3808 5315 1571 6310
לְפִיהוּ וְגַם־הַנֶּפֶשׁ לֹא תִמָּלֵא׃ כִּי מַה־יּוֹתֵר לֶחָכָם מִן־
more the to advantage what For .filled is not soul the and his for
than wise yet ,mouth

9 4758 2896 2416 5048 1980 3045 6041 4100 3684
הַכְּסִיל מַה־לֶּעָנִי יוֹדֵעַ לַהֲלֹךְ נֶגֶד הַחַיִּים׃ טוֹב מַרְאֵה
the Better the before (how) knowing the to what ;fool the
of sight (is) ?living walk to poor

10 1961 4100 7307 7469 1892 2088/1571 5315 1981 5869
עֵינַיִם מֵהֲלָךְ־נָפֶשׁ גַּם־זֶה הֶבֶל וּרְעוּת רוּחַ׃ מַה־שֶּׁהָיָה
Whatever (after) and vanity this Also the the than eyes the
been has wind striving (is) .soul of wandering

1777 3201 3808 120 3045 8034 7121 3528
כְּבָר נִקְרָא שְׁמוֹ וְנוֹדָע אֲשֶׁר־הוּא אָדָם וְלֹא־יוּכַל לָדִין
to is he and ;man he that it and its was already
contend able not (is) known is ,name called

11 1892 7235 7235 1697 3426 8623
עִם שֶׁהַתַּקִּיף מִמֶּנּוּ׃ כִּי יֵשׁ־דְּבָרִים הַרְבֵּה מַרְבִּים הָבֶל
,vanity that many things there Since than that Him with
increase are .he stronger is

12 2416 120 2896 4100 3045/4310 120 3148
מַה־יֹּתֵר לָאָדָם׃ כִּי מִי־יוֹדֵעַ מַה־טּוֹב לָאָדָם בַּחַיִּים
(this) in man for (is) what knows who For ?man to the what
,life good advantage (is)

120 5046 6738 6213 1892 2416 4557
מִסְפַּר יְמֵי־חַיֵּי הֶבְלוֹ וְיַעֲשֵׂם כַּצֵּל אֲשֶׁר מִי־יַגִּיד לָאָדָם
man a can who For the as he and his life the the
tell .shadow them does ;vain of days of number

8121 8478 310 1961 4100
מַה־יִּהְיֶה אַחֲרָיו תַּחַת הַשָּׁמֶשׁ׃
?sun the under after shall what
him be

CHAPTER 7

[1]A *good* name *is* better than good ointment; and the day of death than the day of one's birth.

[2]*It is* better to go to the

CAP. VII ז

CHAPTER 7

1 2 2896 3205 3117 4194 3117 2896 8081 8034 2896
טוֹב שֵׁם מִשֶּׁמֶן טוֹב וְיוֹם הַמָּוֶת מִיּוֹם הִוָּלְדוֹ׃ טוֹב
(is It) one's the than death the and ,good than (good) a Better
better .birth of day of day oil name (is)

house of mourning than to go to the house of feasting; for it *is* the end of every man; and the living will lay *it* to his heart. [3]Vexation *is* better than laughter; for by the sadness of the face the heart is made good. [4]The heart of the wise *is* in the house of mourning; but the heart of the stupid one *is* in the house of mirth. [5]*It is* better to hear the rebuke of the wise, than for a man to hear the song of the fool. [6]For as the crackling of thorns under a pot, so *is* the laughter of the stupid one. And this also *is* vanity.

[7]For oppression makes a wise man mad; and a bribe destroys the heart. [8]Better *is* the end of a thing than its beginning; the patient in spirit *is* better than the the proud in spirit. [9]Do not be hasty in your spirit to be vexed; for vexation rests in the bosom of fools. [10]Do not say, Why was *it* that the former days were better than these? For you do not ask from wisdom concerning this.

[11]Wisdom *is* good with an inheritance; yea, a gain to those who see the sun. [12]For wisdom *is* in a shadow; *and* silver *is* in a shadow; but the excellency of knowledge is *that* wisdom gives life to those who have it. [13]Consider the work of God: for who can make that straight which He has bent? [14]In the good day, be in good *spirit*, but also consider in the evil day, *that* God has made one along with the other, so that man should not find anything after him. [15]All *things* I have seen in the days of my vanity; there is a just *man* who perishes in his righteousness, and there is a wicked one who prolongs *his life* in his evil.

4960 1004 3212 60 1004 3212
לָלֶכֶת אֶל־בֵּית־אֵבֶל מִלֶּכֶת אֶל־בֵּית מִשְׁתֶּה בַּאֲשֶׁר הוּא
that because ,feasting the to to than mourn- the to go to
(is) of house go ing of house

7814 3708 3190 3820 5414 2416 120 36 105 5490
3 סוֹף כָּל־הָאָדָם וְהַחַי יִתֵּן אֶל־לִבּוֹ׃ טוֹב כַּעַס מִשְּׂחוֹק
than Vexation (is) his to will the and ;man every the
,laughter better .heart (it) lay living of end

38 120 60 1004 2450 38 120 38 120 2896 6440 7455
4 כִּי־בְרֹעַ פָּנִים יִיטַב לֵב׃ לֵב חֲכָמִים בְּבֵית אֵבֶל וְלֵב
the but mourn- the in the The the made is the the by for
of heart ,ing of house (is) wise of heart .heart good face of sadness

376 2450 1606 8085 2896 8057 1004 3684
5 כְּסִילִים בְּבֵית שִׂמְחָה׃ טוֹב לִשְׁמֹעַ גַּעֲרַת חָכָם מֵאִישׁ
a than the the hear to (is It) .mirth the in fools
man wise of rebuke better of house (is)

3651 5518 8478 5518 6963 3684 7892 8085
6 שֹׁמֵעַ שִׁיר כְּסִילִים׃ כִּי כְקוֹל הַסִּירִים תַּחַת הַסִּיר כֵּן
so ,pot a under thorns the like For .fools the hearing
(is) of sound of song

2459 1984 62 33 1892 2088/1571 3684 7814
7 שְׂחֹק הַכְּסִיל וְגַם־זֶה הָבֶל׃ כִּי הָעֹשֶׁק יְהוֹלֵל חָכָם
wise a makes oppression For .vanity this and the the
;man mad (is) also ;fool of laughter

2896 7225 1697 319 2896 4979 3820 6
8 וִיאַבֵּד אֶת־לֵב מַתָּנָה׃ טוֹב אַחֲרִית דָּבָר מֵרֵאשִׁיתוֹ טוֹב
better its than a end the Better .bribe a the and
is ;beginning thing of (is(heart destroys

3707 7307 926 408 7307 1362 7307 750
9 אֶרֶךְ־רוּחַ מִגְּבַהּ־רוּחַ׃ אַל־תְּבַהֵל בְּרוּחֲךָ לִכְעוֹס כִּי
for be to your in be Do not .spirit the than spirit the
,angry spirit hasty in proud of long

3117 1961 4310 559 408 5117 3684 2436 3708
10 כַעַס בְּחֵיק כְּסִילִים יָנוּחַ׃ אַל־תֹּאמַר מֶה הָיָה שֶׁהַיָּמִים
the that was Why ,say Do not .rests fools the in vex-
days it of bosom ation

7592 2451 38 108 428 2896 1961 7223
הָרִאשֹׁנִים הָיוּ טוֹבִים מֵאֵלֶּה כִּי לֹא מֵחָכְמָה שָׁאַלְתָּ עַל־
to as you do from not For than better were former
ask wisdom ?these

8121 7200 3148 5159 2451 2896 2088
11 זֶה׃ טוֹבָה חָכְמָה עִם־נַחֲלָה וְיֹתֵר לְרֹאֵי הַשָּׁמֶשׁ׃ כִּי
12 For .sun the those to an and an with Wisdom (is) .this
see who advantage inheritance good

2421 2451 1847 3504 3701 6738 2451 6738
בְּצֵל הַחָכְמָה בְּצֵל הַכָּסֶף וְיִתְרוֹן דַּעַת הַחָכְמָה תְּחַיֶּה
gives (that is) knowledge the but (is) a in (and) (is) a in
to life wisdom of profit ,silver shadow wisdom shadow

86 26 3201 4310 430 46 39 7200 1167
13 בְעָלֶיהָ׃ רְאֵה אֶת־מַעֲשֵׂה הָאֱלֹהִים כִּי מִי יוּכַל לְתַקֵּן
to able is who For ;God the Consider its
straighten of work .possessors

7200 7451 3117 28 96 1961 2896 3117 5791 834
14 אֵת אֲשֶׁר עִוְּתוֹ׃ בְּיוֹם טוֹבָה הֱיֵה בְטוֹב וּבְיוֹם רָעָה רְאֵה
consider evil in but good in be good the On has He that
day the (.spirit) day ?bent which

3808 17 00 59 21 430 6213 2088 59 80 1571
גַּם אֶת־זֶה לְעֻמַּת־זֶה עָשָׂה הָאֱלֹהִים עַל־דִּבְרַת שֶׁלֹּא
that the upon God has this along this ,also
not ,matter made with

3117 7200 3605 3972 310 120 4672
15 יִמְצָא הָאָדָם אַחֲרָיו מְאוּמָה׃ אֶת־הַכֹּל רָאִיתִי בִּימֵי
the in- have I All .anything after man should
of days seen (things) him find

7451 748 7563 3426 6664 6 6662 3426 1892
הֶבְלִי יֵשׁ צַדִּיק אֹבֵד בְּצִדְקוֹ וְיֵשׁ רָשָׁע מַאֲרִיךְ בְּרָעָתוֹ׃
his in pro- who wicked a and righ- his in who just a there my
.evilness (life) longs man is there teousness perishes man is vanity

16 Do not be *too* much righteous, nor make yourself overly wise; why destroy yourself? 17 Do not be very wicked, and do not be a fool; why should you die *and it* not your time? 18 *It is* good that you grasp this; yea, also from this do not let your hand rest. For he fearing God shall come out with all of them. 19 Wisdom makes the wise stronger than ten rulers who are in the city. 20 For *there is* a not a just man on the earth who does good, and does not sin. 21 Also, do not give your heart to all the words they speak, that you not hear your servant cursing you. 22 For also your own heart knows that you yourself have also cursed others many times. 23 All this I have tested by wisdom: I said, I will be wise; but it *was* far from me. 24 That which is far off and exceeding deep, who can find it out? 25 And I turned my heart about, to know, and to search, and to seek out wisdom, and the reason *of things*, and to know the wickedness of folly, and the foolishness of madness: 26 and I found more bitter than death the woman whose heart *is* snares and nets; her hands *are like* bands. He who is good before God shall escape from her; but the sinner shall be captured by her. 27 Behold, I have found this, says the Preacher, *counting* one by one to find out the sum; 28 that my soul still seeks, but I have not found; one man among a thousand I have found, but a woman among all those I have not found. 29 Behold, this only I have

8074 4310 3148 2449 408 7235 6662 1961 408
16 אַל־תְּהִי צַדִּיק הַרְבֵּה וְאַל־תִּתְחַכַּם יוֹתֵר לָמָּה תִּשּׁוֹמֵם׃
destroy ,yourself - why ;overly make wise yourself and not much righteous Be not

6256 3808 4191 4100 5530 1961 408 7235 7561 408
17 אַל־תִּרְשַׁע הַרְבֵּה וְאַל־תְּהִי סָכָל לָמָּה תָמוּת בְּלֹא עִתֶּךָ׃
your ?time (it and) not should die you why —fool a be and not much be do wicked not

3373 3027 3240 2088 1571 270 2896
18 טוֹב אֲשֶׁר תֶּאֱחֹז בָּזֶה וְגַם־מִזֶּה אַל־תַּנַּח אֶת־יָדֶךָ כִּי־יְרֵא
who he For fears your .hand do rest let not from this and also this you grasp should that (is it) good

6235 2450 5810 2451 3605 3318 430
19 אֱלֹהִים יֵצֵא אֶת־כֻּלָּם׃ הַחָכְמָה תָּעֹז לֶחָכָם מֵעֲשָׂרָה
than ten the wise makes stronger Wisdom of all .them with shall forth come God

834 776 6662 369 120 5892 1961 834 7989
20 שַׁלִּיטִים אֲשֶׁר הָיוּ בָּעִיר׃ כִּי אָדָם אֵין צַדִּיק בָּאָרֶץ אֲשֶׁר
who the on earth righteous there not is a man For the in .city are who rulers

1696 834 1697 3605 1571 2398 3808 2896 6213
21 יַעֲשֶׂה־טּוֹב וְלֹא יֶחֱטָא׃ גַּם לְכָל־הַדְּבָרִים אֲשֶׁר יְדַבֵּרוּ
they speak which the words to all Also does .sin and not good does

7043 5650 6213 3808 3820 5414 408
22 אַל־תִּתֵּן לִבֶּךָ אֲשֶׁר לֹא־תִשְׁמַע אֶת־עַבְדְּךָ מְקַלְלֶךָ׃ כִּי
For cursing .you your servant you hear may not that your heart do give not

312 7043 1571 3820 3045 7227 6471 1571
גַּם־פְּעָמִים רַבּוֹת יָדַע לִבֶּךָ אֲשֶׁר גַּם־אַתְּ קִלַּלְתָּ אֲחֵרִים׃
.others have cursed you also that your heart knows many times also

7350 2449 559 2451 5254 2090 3605
23 כָּל־זֹה נִסִּיתִי בַחָכְמָה אָמַרְתִּי אֶחְכָּמָה וְהִיא רְחוֹקָה
far (was) it but be will I ;wise said I :wisdom by have I tested this All

5437 4672 4310 6013 6013 1961 4100 7350
24 25 מִמֶּנִּי׃ רָחוֹק מַה־שֶּׁהָיָה וְעָמֹק ׀ עָמֹק מִי יִמְצָאֶנּוּ׃ סַבּוֹתִי
turned about find can ?it who exceeding and ,deep Whatever is off far from .me

3045 2808 2451 1245 8446 3045 3820 589
אֲנִי וְלִבִּי לָדַעַת וְלָתוּר וּבַקֵּשׁ חָכְמָה וְחֶשְׁבּוֹן וְלָדַעַת
to and know the and reckoning wisdom to and seek to and investigate know to my even heart I

4194 4753 4672 1948 5531 3689 7562
26 רֶשַׁע כֶּסֶל וְהַסִּכְלוּת הוֹלֵלוֹת׃ וּמוֹצֶא אֲנִי מַר מִמָּוֶת
than death more bitter I And found .madness the and of foolishness ,folly wick- of edness the

612 3820 2764 4685 834 802
אֶת־הָאִשָּׁה אֲשֶׁר־הִיא מְצוֹדִים וַחֲרָמִים לִבָּהּ אֲסוּרִים
(are and) bonds her heart (for) nets and snares she (has) of whom woman the

3920 2398 4422 430 6440 2896 3027
יָדֶיהָ טוֹב לִפְנֵי הָאֱלֹהִים יִמָּלֵט מִמֶּנָּה וְחוֹטֵא יִלָּכֶד בָּהּ׃
.her by be will captured the but sinner from ,her shall escape God before good A man her .hands

4672 259 259 6953 559 4672 2088 2009
27 רְאֵה זֶה מָצָאתִי אָמְרָה קֹהֶלֶת אַחַת לְאַחַת לִמְצֹא
to out find one by one (adding) the ,Preacher says have I found this ,Behold

259 120/4672 3808 5315 1245 5750 2808
28 חֶשְׁבּוֹן׃ אֲשֶׁר עוֹד־בִּקְשָׁה נַפְשִׁי וְלֹא מָצָאתִי אָדָם אֶחָד
one man have I :found but not ,soul my seeks still that the ;sum

905 4672 3808 428 3605 802 4672 505
29 מֵאֶלֶף מָצָאתִי וְאִשָּׁה בְכָל־אֵלֶּה לֹא מָצָאתִי׃ לְבַד רְאֵה־
Behold only have I .found not these among all a but woman have I ,found a among thousand

found, that God has made man upright, but they have sought out many inventions.

CHAPTER 8

1 Who *is* as the wise? And who knows the meaning of a thing? A man's wisdom makes his face shine, and the strength of his face is changed. 2 I *say*, Keep the king's word, even on the matter of the oath of God; 3 do not be hasty to go from before him. Do not take a stand in an evil thing; for he does whatever he pleases. 4 Because the king's word *is* that which has power; who then will say to him, What are your doing? 5 Whoever keeps the command shall know no evil thing. A wise man's heart knows both time and judgment. 6 Because there is a time and judgment to every purpose, in *this* the evil of man *is* great upon him. 7 For he does not know what shall be. For who can tell him when it shall be? 8 Man is not a ruler over the spirit, to restrain the spirit; nor has he power in the day of death. And *there is* no discharge in *that* war, nor shall wickedness deliver its possessors.

9 All this I have seen. I gave my heart to every work that is done under the sun. *There is* a time *in* which a man rules over a man for his evil. 10 And so I saw the wicked buried; and they came and went from the holy place; and were forgotten in the city, *these* things that they had done. This *is* also vanity.

11 Where sentence *on* an

3477 120 430 6213 4672 2088
זה מצאתי אשר עשה האלהים את־האדם ישר והמה
they but ,upright man God has made that have I ,found this

7227 2810 1245
בקשו חשבנות רבים׃
.many inventions have out sought

CAP. VIII ח

CHAPTER 8

1 64:40 215 120 2451 1697 6592 3045 4310 24:50 4310
מי כהחכם ומי יודע פשר דבר חכמת אדם תאיר פניו
his ,face makes shine A man's wisdom ?thing a of inter- pretation the knows who or the like ,man wise Who (is)

2 7621 1700 59:21 81:04 44 28 6310 *8132 6440 57,97
ועז פניו ישנא׃ אני פי־מלך שמר ועל דברת שבועת
the of oath the of matter even on ,Keep the king's mouth I ,(say) is .changed face his and strength

3 7451 1697 59.75 408 1980 6440 926 408 430
אלהים׃ אל־תבהל מפניו תלך אל־תעמד בדבר רע
;evil a with matter do stand not ;go to his from presence be Do hasty not .God

4 4310 7983 4428 1697 6213 2654 36,05
כי כל־אשר יחפץ יעשה׃ באשר דבר־מלך שלטון ומי
who then which that ,power has the (is) king the of word Because .does he he pleases that all for

5 6256 7451 1697 3045 38.08 4687 8104 6213 4100 559
יאמר־לו מה־תעשה׃ שומר מצוה לא ידע דבר רע ועת
both time ;evil a thing shall know not the command Whoever keeps you are ?doing What to ,him will say

6 4941 6256 34.26 2656 3605 2450 38 20 3045 49:41
ומשפט ידע לב חכם׃ כי לכל־חפץ יש עת ומשפט
and ,judgment a time there is purpose to every Because wise a .man's heart knows and judgment

7 1961 4100 3045 369 59 21 7227 120 7451
כי־רעת האדם רבה עליו׃ כי־איננו ידע מה־שיהיה כי
for shall be what does know he not For upon .him (is) great man the for of evil

8 36,07 73 07 78,89 120 369 5046 4310 19:61
כאשר יהיה מי יגיד לו׃ אין אדם שליט ברוח לכלוא
to restrain the ,spirit over ruler a man Not is to him can tell who shall it be when

4917 369 4194 3117 79 83 369 7307
את־הרוח ואין שלטון ביום המות ואין משלחת
discharge and is not ;death the in of day which that power has and is not the ;spirit

9 7200 2088 3605 11 67 75 62 4422 38 08 4421
במלחמה ולא־ימלט רשע את־בעליו׃ את־כל־זה ראיתי
have I ,seen this All its .possessors wicked- ness shall deliver and not the in ;war

6256 8121 8478 6213 4639 36 05 3820 5414
ונתון את־לבי לכל־מעשה אשר נעשה תחת השמש עת
(a is) time ;sun the under done is that work to every my heart and gave

10 75 63 7200 3651 74 51 120 120 79 80 8.34
אשר שלט האדם באדם לרע לו׃ ובכן ראיתי רשעים
the wicked saw I in And this to .him for evil man a man rules over (in) which

5892 7911 1980 6918 4725 935 69 12
קברים ובאו וממקום קדוש יהלכו וישתכחו בעיר אשר
(these) ,things the in ,city and were forgotten ,went holy from and place the they and came ,buried

11 4639 6599 6213 369 1892 2088/1571 6213
כן־עשו גם־זה הבל׃ אשר אין־נעשה פתגם מעשה
a work (on) a sentence is executed not Where .vanity this also (is) they thus had —done

evil work is not executed speedily, on account of this the heart of the sons of men is fully set in them to do evil.

12 Though a sinner does evil a hundred *times*, and *his days* are prolonged to him, yet surely I know that it shall be well to those who fear God, who fear before Him. 13 But it shall not be well for the wicked; and he shall not lengthen *his* days like a shadow; because he does not fear before God. 14 There is a vanity which is done on the earth: There are just *men* to whom it happens according to the work of the wicked; and there are wicked men to whom it happens according to the work of the righteous — I said that this also *is* vanity. 15 Then I praised mirth, because nothing is good for man under the sun except to eat, and to drink and to be glad. For that shall go with him in his labor for the days of his life which God gives him under the sun.

16 When I gave my heart to know wisdom, and to see the business that is done on the earth—for even by day and by night he does not see sleep in his eyes— 17 then I looked at all the work of God, that a man cannot find out the work that is done under the sun; because though a man labors to seek *it* out, yet he shall not find it. And even if the wise speaks of knowing, he shall not be able to find *it*.

6213 120 1121 38,20 4390 4120 7451
הָרָעָה מְהֵרָה עַל־כֵּן מָלֵא לֵב בְּנֵי־הָאָדָם בָּהֶם לַעֲשׂוֹת
do to in men the the is therefore ,speedily evil
them of sons of heart filled

3045 1571 748 3967 7451 6213 2398 7451
12 רָע׃ אֲשֶׁר חֹטֶא עֹשֶׂה רָע מְאַת וּמַאֲרִיךְ לוֹ כִּי גַם־יוֹדֵעַ
know also yet to (days) and a evil does sinner a Though .evil
him long are (times) hundred

6440 3372 834 430 3373 2896 1961
אָנִי אֲשֶׁר יִהְיֶה־טּוֹב לְיִרְאֵי הָאֱלֹהִים אֲשֶׁר יִירְאוּ מִלְּפָנָיו׃
before fear who ,God those with well will it that I
,Him fear who be

6738 3117 748 3808 7563 1961 3808 2896
13 וְטוֹב לֹא־יִהְיֶה לָרָשָׁע וְלֹא־יַאֲרִיךְ יָמִים כַּצֵּל אֲשֶׁר אֵינֶנּוּ
he because a like (his) shall he and the for will it not But
not ;shadow days lengthen not ,wicked be well

776 5921 6213 1892/3426 430 6440 3373
14 יָרֵא מִלִּפְנֵי אֱלֹהִים׃ יֶשׁ־הֶבֶל אֲשֶׁר נַעֲשָׂה עַל־הָאָרֶץ
the on , done is which a There .God before does
;earth vanity is fear

7563 4639 5060 834 6662 3426
אֲשֶׁר ׀ יֵשׁ צַדִּיקִים אֲשֶׁר מַגִּיעַ אֲלֵהֶם כְּמַעֲשֵׂה הָרְשָׁעִים
the according it whom just there that
.wicked's works to them touches men are

559 6662 4639 5060 6213 3426
וְיֵשׁ רְשָׁעִים שֶׁמַּגִּיעַ אֲלֵהֶם כְּמַעֲשֵׂה הַצַּדִּיקִים אָמַרְתִּי
said I the according to whom to wicked And
.righteous' works to them touches it men are there

369 8087 7623 1892 1571
15 שֶׁגַּם־זֶה הָבֶל׃ וְשִׁבַּחְתִּי אֲנִי אֶת־הַשִּׂמְחָה אֲשֶׁר אֵין
not because ,mirth I Then .vanity this that
is commended (is) also

8056 8354 398 81:21 8478 120 2896
טוֹב לָאָדָם תַּחַת הַשֶּׁמֶשׁ כִּי אִם־לֶאֱכוֹל וְלִשְׁתּוֹת וְלִשְׂמוֹחַ
to and to and eat to except sun the under for good
,rejoice drink man

8478 430 5414 834 2416 3117 5999 3867
וְהוּא יִלְוֶנּוּ בַעֲמָלוֹ יְמֵי חַיָּיו אֲשֶׁר־נָתַן־לוֹ הָאֱלֹהִים תַּחַת
under God to gives which his the his in lodges for
him life of days labor him with that

7200 2451 3045 3820 5414 8121
16 הַשָּׁמֶשׁ׃ כַּאֲשֶׁר נָתַתִּי אֶת־לִבִּי לָדַעַת חָכְמָה וְלִרְאוֹת
to and ,wisdom know to my gave I When .sun the
see heart

3915 3117 1571 776 5921 6213 834 6045
אֶת־הָעִנְיָן אֲשֶׁר נַעֲשָׂה עַל־הָאָרֶץ כִּי גַם בַּיּוֹם וּבַלַּיְלָה
by and by even for the on done is which the
night day -earth task

430 4639 3605 7200 7200 5869 8142
17 שֵׁנָה בְּעֵינָיו אֵינֶנּוּ רֹאֶה׃ וְרָאִיתִי אֶת־כָּל־מַעֲשֵׂה הָאֱלֹהִים
,God the all I then —sees he his in sleep
of work saw not eyes

6213 4639 4672 120 3201 3808
כִּי לֹא יוּכַל הָאָדָם לִמְצוֹא אֶת־הַמַּעֲשֶׂה אֲשֶׁר נַעֲשָׂה
done is that work the find to man able is not that
out

4672 3808 1245 120 5998 7945 8121 8478
תַּחַת־הַשֶּׁמֶשׁ בְּשֶׁל אֲשֶׁר יַעֲמֹל הָאָדָם לְבַקֵּשׁ וְלֹא יִמְצָא
he will yet seek to man labors which for the under
.(it) find not out (it) that ,sun

4672 3201 3808 3045 2450 559 518
וְגַם אִם־יֹאמַר הֶחָכָם לָדַעַת לֹא יוּכַל לִמְצֹא׃
find to is he (yet) of wise the speaks if And
.(it) able not ,(it) knowing man even

CHAPTER 9

[1]For all this I gave to heart, even to explain all this, that the righteous and the wise and their works *are* in the hand of God. Whether love or hatred, man does not know all *that is* before them. [2]All *happens* alike to all; one event to the righteous, and to the wicked; to the good, and to the clean; and to the unclean; to him who sacrifices, and to him who does not sacrifice. As *is* the good, so *is* the sinner; he who swears is as *he* that fears an oath. [3]This *is* an evil among all *things* that are done under the sun, that *there is* one event to all. Yea, also the heart of the sons of men is full of evil, and madness *is* in their heart throughout their lives; and after that, *they go* to the dead. [4]For to whoever is chosen to all the living, there is hope. For a living dog *is* better than a dead lion. [4]For the living know that they shall die; but the dead do not know anything; nor do they have any more a reward; for their memory is forgotten. [6]Also their love, their hatred, and their envy has now perished; nor do they any longer have a part forever in all that is done under the sun.

[7]Go, eat your bread with joy, and drink your wine with a merry heart, for God now is pleased with your works. [8]Let your garments be white at every time; and let your head lack no ointment. [9]Look *on* life with the wife whom you

CAP. IX ט

CHAPTER 9

2088/3605 952 38 20 5414 2088 3605

1 כִּי אֶת־כָּל־זֶה נָתַתִּי אֶל־לִבִּי וְלָבוּר אֶת־כָּל־זֶה אֲשֶׁר

that ,this all to even my to gave I this all For
explain ,heart in

160 1571 430 3027 5652 2450 6662

הַצַּדִּיקִים וְהַחֲכָמִים וַעֲבָדֵיהֶם בְּיַד הָאֱלֹהִים גַּם־אַהֲבָה

love Also .God the in their and the and the
of hand (are) works ,wise ,righteous

36 05 6440 3605 120 3045 369 8130

2 גַּם־שִׂנְאָה אֵין יוֹדֵעַ הָאָדָם הַכֹּל לִפְנֵיהֶם׃ הַכֹּל כַּאֲשֶׁר

that All before all men do not ,hatred also
(happens) .them (is that) know

2931 2889 2896 7563 6662 259 3605

לַכֹּל מִקְרֶה אֶחָד לַצַּדִּיק וְלָרָשָׁע לַטּוֹב וְלַטָּהוֹר וְלַטָּמֵא

to and to and the to the to and the to one event (is)
,unclean the ,clean the ,good ;wicked ,righteous (is) ;all to

7650 2398 2896 2076 834 369 08 2076

וְלַזֹּבֵחַ וְלַאֲשֶׁר אֵינֶנּוּ זֹבֵחַ כַּטּוֹב כַּחֹטֶא הַנִּשְׁבָּע כַּאֲשֶׁר

as the the so the as sacri- not is to and the to
whom swearer ;sinner good ;ficing him to whom ,sacrificer

8121 8478 6213 3605 7451 2088 3373 7621

3 שְׁבוּעָה יָרֵא׃ זֶה רָע בְּכֹל אֲשֶׁר־נַעֲשָׂה תַּחַת הַשָּׁמֶשׁ

,sun the under (is that among an This oath an
done all evil (is) fears

1948 7451 1439 120 1121/ 3820 3605 259 4745

כִּי־מִקְרֶה אֶחָד לַכֹּל וְגַם לֵב בְּנֵי־הָאָדָם מָלֵא־רָע וְהוֹלֵלוֹת

and ;evil is men the the and to one event that
madness of full of sons of heart also ;all (is)

977 4310 4191 3212 310 2416 38 34

4 בִּלְבָבָם בְּחַיֵּיהֶם וְאַחֲרָיו אֶל־הַמֵּתִים׃ כִּי־מִי אֲשֶׁר יְבֻחַר

is whoever For the (go they) after and throughout their in
chosen .dead to that ,lives their heart

2896 2416 36 61 986 3426 2416 36 05

אֶל כָּל־הַחַיִּים יֵשׁ בִּטָּחוֹן כִּי־לְכֶלֶב חַי הוּא טוֹב מִן

than better it living a for —hope there the all to
(is) dog is ,living

369 4191 4191 3045 2416 4191 738

5 הָאַרְיֵה הַמֵּת׃ כִּי הַחַיִּים יוֹדְעִים שֶׁיָּמֻתוּ וְהַמֵּתִים אֵינָם

they the but they that know the For .dead lion a
not ,dead ;die will living

2143 7911 79 3 9 5704 369 3972 3045

יוֹדְעִים מְאוּמָה וְאֵין־עוֹד לָהֶם שָׂכָר כִּי נִשְׁכַּח זִכְרָם׃

their is for a for any and anything do
.memory forgotten ,reward them more is not know

25 06 6 2528 7068 8130 1571 160

6 גַּם אַהֲבָתָם גַּם־שִׂנְאָתָם גַּם־קִנְאָתָם כְּבָר אָבָדָה וְחֵלֶק

a and has already their and their and their Also
part ;perished envy hatred love

8121 8478 6213 3605 57 69 5704 369

אֵין־לָהֶם עוֹד לְעוֹלָם בְּכֹל אֲשֶׁר־נַעֲשָׂה תַּחַת הַשָּׁמֶשׁ׃

.sun the under done is that all in forever any for not
more them is

3528 3196 2896 38 20 8354 38 99 8057 398 32 12

7 לֵךְ אֱכֹל בְּשִׂמְחָה לַחְמֶךָ וּשְׁתֵה בְלֶב־טוֹב יֵינֶךָ כִּי כְבָר

already for your good a with and your with eat ,Go
,wine heart drink ,bread joy

3836 899 1961 62 56 3605 4639 430 7521

8 רָצָה הָאֱלֹהִים אֶת־מַעֲשֶׂיךָ׃ בְּכָל־עֵת יִהְיוּ בְגָדֶיךָ לְבָנִים

;white your be let time At your with God is
garments every .works pleased

802 2416 7200 2637 408 7218 59 21 8081

9 וְשֶׁמֶן עַל־רֹאשְׁךָ אַל־יֶחְסָר׃ רְאֵה חַיִּים עִם־אִשָּׁה אֲשֶׁר

whom the with life Look be let not your upon and
wife (upon) .lacking head oil

love all the days of your life of your vanity, which He gave you under the sun, all the days of your vanity. For that is your share in this life, and in your labor which you labor under the sun.

[10]All that your hand finds to do, do it with your strength. For there is no work, or planning, or knowledge, or wisdom, in Sheol, there where you go.

[11]I returned and saw under the sun that the race is not to the swift, nor the battle to the mighty; nor even bread to the wise; nor even riches to the men of discernment; nor even favor to knowing men — for time and occurrence happen to

them all. [12]For man also does not know his time. As the fish that are taken in the evil net; and as the birds that are caught in the trap; like them are the sons of men snared in an evil time, when it falls suddenly on them. [13]This wisdom I saw also under the sun, and it is great to me: [14]There was a little city, and few men in it. And a great king came against it, and besieged it, and built huge siege-works against it. [15]And there was found in it a poor wise man, and he by his wisdom saved the city. Yet no man remembered that poor man! [16]And I said, Wisdom is better than strength; but the poor man's wisdom is despised, and his words are not heard.

[17]The words of wise men are heard in quiet, more than the cry of one who rules among fools. [18]Wisdom is better than weapons

---

אָהַבְתָּ כָל־יְמֵי חַיֵּי הֶבְלֶךָ אֲשֶׁר נָתַן־לְךָ תַּחַת הַשֶּׁמֶשׁ כֹּל
3605 8121 | 8478 | 5414 834 | 1892 2416 3117 3605 157
all ;sun the under to He which your the the all you / you given has vanity of life of days love

יְמֵי הֶבְלֶךָ כִּי הוּא חֶלְקְךָ בַּחַיִּים וּבַעֲמָלְךָ אֲשֶׁר־אַתָּה עָמֵל
6001 | 834 | 5999 | 24:16 | 25:06 | 18:92 3117
labor you which in and life in your that for your the / labor your share (is) —vanity of days

10 תַּחַת הַשָּׁמֶשׁ: כֹּל אֲשֶׁר תִּמְצָא יָדְךָ לַעֲשׂוֹת בְּכֹחֲךָ עֲשֵׂה
358.1 6213 3027 4672 3605 81.21 8478
;(it) do (all) with do to your finds that All .sun the under / strength your hand

כִּי אֵין מַעֲשֶׂה וְחֶשְׁבּוֹן וְדַעַת וְחָכְמָה בִּשְׁאוֹל אֲשֶׁר אַתָּה
75:85 2451 1847 2808 4639 369
you where ,Sheol in or or or ,work not for / ,wisdom ,knowledge ,planning is

11 הֹלֵךְ שָׁמָּה: שַׁבְתִּי וְרָאֹה תַחַת־הַשֶּׁמֶשׁ כִּי לֹא לַקַּלִּים
7031 3808 81.21 8478 72.00 7725 8033 19.80
the to not that sun the under and I .there go / swift

הַמֵּרוֹץ וְלֹא לַגִּבּוֹרִים הַמִּלְחָמָה וְגַם לֹא לַחֲכָמִים לֶחֶם
3899 2450 38:08 1571 44:21 1368 3808 47:93
(is) the to not and the (is) the to and the (is) / ,bread wise even ,battle mighty not ,race

וְגַם לֹא לַנְּבֹנִים עֹשֶׁר וְגַם לֹא לַיֹּדְעִים חֵן כִּי־עֵת וָפֶגַע
6294 6256 2580 3045 38:08 1571 6239 995 38:08
oc- and time for ;favor men to not and ,riches astute to not and / currence skill of even men even

12 יִקְרֶה אֶת־כֻּלָּם: כִּי גַם לֹא־יֵדַע הָאָדָם אֶת־עִתּוֹ כַּדָּגִים
1709 62:56 120 30:45 38:08 7136
the as his man does not also For them to happen / fish ,time ,know .all

שֶׁנֶּאֱחָזִים בִּמְצוֹדָה רָעָה וְכַצִּפֳּרִים הָאֲחֻזוֹת בַּפָּח כָּהֵם
19:92 6341 270 68:33 74:51 4685 270
like the in are that the as and ,evil the in are that / them ;trap seized birds net seized

יוּקָשִׁים בְּנֵי הָאָדָם לְעֵת רָעָה כְּשֶׁתִּפּוֹל עֲלֵיהֶם פִּתְאֹם:
6597 5921 5307 74:51 62:56 120: 1121 3369
.suddenly upon it when an time in men the are / them falls ,evil of sons snared

13 גַּם־זֹה רָאִיתִי חָכְמָה תַּחַת הַשֶּׁמֶשׁ וּגְדוֹלָה הִיא אֵלָי:
1419 8121 8478 2451 7200 20:90
:me to (is) it great and ,sun the under (as) saw I this Also / wisdom

14 עִיר קְטַנָּה וַאֲנָשִׁים בָּהּ מְעָט וּבָא־אֵלֶיהָ מֶלֶךְ גָּדוֹל וְסָבַב
5437 1419 4428 935 4592 582 66:96 5892
en- and great a against and ;few it in men and ,little A / circled king it came city

15 אֹתָהּ וּבָנָה עָלֶיהָ מְצוֹדִים גְּדֹלִים: וּמָצָא בָהּ אִישׁ מִסְכֵּן
4542 376 4672 1419 4685 1129
poor a it in was and ;huge siegeworks against and ,it built / man found it

חָכָם וּמִלַּט־הוּא אֶת־הָעִיר בְּחָכְמָתוֹ וְאָדָם לֹא זָכַר אֶת־
214:2 38:08 120 2451 5892 4422 24:50
remem- not yet his by the he and ;wise / bered man —wisdom city delivered

16 הָאִישׁ הַמִּסְכֵּן הַהוּא: וְאָמַרְתִּי אָנִי טוֹבָה חָכְמָה מִגְּבוּרָה
1369 2451 2896 559 4542 376
than Wisdom better ,I said And !that poor man / ;strength (is)

17 וְחָכְמַת הַמִּסְכֵּן בְּזוּיָה וּדְבָרָיו אֵינָם נִשְׁמָעִים: דִּבְרֵי
1697 8085 369 1697 959 4542 2451
The .heard are they his and is poor the but / of words not words ,despised man's wisdom

18 חֲכָמִים בְּנַחַת נִשְׁמָעִים מִזַּעֲקַת מוֹשֵׁל בַּכְּסִילִים: טוֹבָה
2896 36:84 491.0 2201 8085 5183 2450
better among who one than more are quiet in wise / .fools rules of cry the ;heard men

of conflict; but one sinner destroys much good.

CHAPTER 10

[1]*As* dead flies cause the perfumer's ointment to stink *and* ferment; *so* a little foolishness is *more* rare than wisdom *and* than honor. [2]The heart of the wise *is* toward his right, but the fool's heart toward his left. [3]And also, in the way in which a stupid one walks, his heart fails, and he says to all *that* he *is* a fool. [4]If the spirit of the ruler rises up against you, do not leave your place; for composure quiets great offenses. [5]There is an evil I have seen under the sun, sins which come from the face of the ruler: [6]folly is set in many high *positions*, and many rich men sit in low *situations*. [7]I have seen slaves on horses, and rulers walking as slaves on the earth.

[8]He who digs a pit may fall into it; and one breaking a wall, a snake may bite him. [9]Whoever removes stones may be hurt with them; he who splits trees may be endangered by them. [10]If the iron is blunt, and he does not whet the edges, then he must put more strength to *it*. But wisdom *is* an advantage giving success. [11]If the snake will bite without charming, then there *is* no advantage to a master of tongue. [12]The words of a wise mouth *are* grace, but the lips of a stupid one swallow him; [13]the beginning of the words of his mouth *is* foolishness; and the end of his mouth *is* evil madness. [14]Yet the stupid one makes many words; a man knows not what they shall be; and what shall be after him, who can tell him?

חָכְמָה מִכְּלֵי קְרָב וְחוֹטֶא אֶחָד יְאַבֵּד טוֹבָה הַרְבֵּה׃

.much good destroys one but (hostile) than Wisdom
sinner ,conflict of weapons (is)

CAP. X י

CHAPTER 10

1 זְבוּבֵי מָוֶת יַבְאִישׁ יַבִּיעַ שֶׁמֶן רוֹקֵחַ יָקָר מֵחָכְמָה מִכָּבוֹד

than than (more) the ,oil (and) make of Flies
,honor ,wisdom rare ,perfumer's ferment stink death

2 3 סִכְלוּת מְעָט׃ לֵב חָכָם לִימִינוֹ וְלֵב כְּסִיל לִשְׂמֹאלוֹ׃ וְגַם־

And toward fool's a but toward the The .little a folly (is)
also .left his (is) heart right his (is) wise of heart

בַּדֶּרֶךְ כְּשֶׁהַסָּכָל הֹלֵךְ לִבּוֹ חָסֵר וְאָמַר לַכֹּל סָכָל הוּא׃

fool a all to he and is his ,walks which in the in
.(is) he that says ;lacking heart fool the way

4 אִם־רוּחַ הַמּוֹשֵׁל תַּעֲלֶה עָלֶיךָ מְקוֹמְךָ אַל־תַּנַּח כִּי מַרְפֵּא

com- for do not your against up rises ruler the the If
posure ,leave place ,you of spirit

5 יַנִּיחַ חֲטָאִים גְּדוֹלִים׃ יֵשׁ רָעָה רָאִיתִי תַּחַת הַשָּׁמֶשׁ

,sun the under have I evil an There .great offenses quiets
seen is

6 כִּשְׁגָגָה שֶׁיֹּצָא מִלִּפְנֵי הַשַּׁלִּיט׃ נִתַּן הַסֶּכֶל בַּמְּרוֹמִים

high in folly Is .ruler's the from which an like
(positions) given presence comes error

7 רַבִּים וַעֲשִׁירִים בַּשֵּׁפֶל יֵשֵׁבוּ׃ רָאִיתִי עֲבָדִים עַל־סוּסִים

,horses on slaves have I .sit humble in rich and ,many
seen (situations) men

8 וְשָׂרִים הֹלְכִים כַּעֲבָדִים עַל־הָאָרֶץ׃ חֹפֵר גּוּמָּץ בּוֹ יִפּוֹל

may into ,pit a who He the on slaves as walking and
;fall it digs .earth rulers

9 וּפֹרֵץ גָּדֵר יִשְּׁכֶנּוּ נָחָשׁ׃ מַסִּיעַ אֲבָנִים יֵעָצֵב בָּהֶם בּוֹקֵעַ

who he by be may stones who He .snake a may ,wall a one and
splits ;them hurt quarries him bite breaking

10 עֵצִים יִסָּכֶן בָּם׃ אִם־קֵהָה הַבַּרְזֶל וְהוּא לֹא־פָנִים קִלְקַל

does the not he and the is If by be may trees
,whet faces ,iron blunt .them endangered

11 וַחֲיָלִים יְגַבֵּר וְיִתְרוֹן הַכְשֵׁיר חָכְמָה׃ אִם־יִשֹּׁךְ הַנָּחָשׁ

the will If (is) giving an but must he more then
snake bite .wisdom success advantage ,exert strength

12 בְּלוֹא־לָחַשׁ וְאֵין יִתְרוֹן לְבַעַל הַלָּשׁוֹן׃ דִּבְרֵי פִי־חָכָם חֵן

grace wise a The the a to advantage then ,charming with-
(are) mouth of words .tongue of master no out

13 וְשִׂפְתוֹת כְּסִיל תְּבַלְּעֶנּוּ׃ תְּחִלַּת דִּבְרֵי־פִיהוּ סִכְלוּת וְאַחֲרִית

the and (is) his the be- the swallow fool a the but
of end ,folly mouth of words of ginning .him of lips

14 פִּיהוּ הוֹלֵלוּת רָעָה׃ וְהַסָּכָל יַרְבֶּה דְבָרִים לֹא־יֵדַע הָאָדָם

man does not ;words makes the Yet .evil (is) his
know many fool madness mouth

15 מַה־שֶּׁיִּהְיֶה וַאֲשֶׁר יִהְיֶה מֵאַחֲרָיו מִי יַגִּיד לוֹ׃ עֲמַל

The to can who after be shall and ;be shall what
of labor ?him tell ,him what

[15]The labor of the fools wearies him, because he does not know *how* to go to the city.
[16]Woe to you, O land, when your king *is* a boy, and your leaders eat in the morning. [17]Blessed *are* you, O land, when your king *is* the son of nobles, and your leaders eat in *due* time; in strength, and not in drinking. [18]The framework tumbles through indolence; and through lowering of hands, the house leaks. [19]Bread is made for laughter, and wine gladdens life; but silver answers all *things*. [20]Also, do not curse a king in your thought; and do not curse the rich in your bedrooms; for a bird of the heavens may carry the voice; yea, the lord of wings may tell the matter.

337 5892 3212 3045 3808 3021 3684
16 הכסילים תיגענו אשר לא־ידע ללכת אל־עיר׃ אי־לך
to Woe the to to (how) he not because wearies fools
,you .city go know does him

776 835 398 1242 8269 5288 4428 776
17 ארץ שמלכך נער ושריך בבקר יאכלו׃ אשריך ארץ
O Blessed .eat the in your and a (is) when O
,land you (are) morning officials lad king your ,land

8358 3808 1369 398 6256 8269 2715 1121 4428
שמלכך בן־חורים ושריך בעת יאכלו בגבורה ולא בשתי׃
for and for ,eat due in your and ,nobles a your when
drinking not ,strength time officials of son (is) king

1004 1811 3027 8220 4716 4355 6103
18 בעצלתים ימך המקרה ובשפלות ידים ידלף הבית׃
the leaks hands through and the sinks Through
.house of lowering rafter indolence

6030 3701 2416 8056 3196 3899 6213 7814
19 לשחוק עשים לחם ויין ישמח חיים והכסף יענה את־
answers but ,life gladdens and Bread is for
silver wine prepared laughter

3808 4904 2315 7043 408 4428 4093 1571 3605
20 הכל׃ גם במדעך מלך אל־תקלל ובחדרי משכבך אל־
not your in and do not king a your in Also all
bed of rooms ;curse thought .(things)

3671 1167 6963 3212 8064 5775 6223 7043
תקלל עשיר כי עוף השמים יוליך את־הקול ובעל הכנפים
wings the and the may the a for rich a do
of lord ,voice carry heavens of bird ;man curse

1697 5046
יגיד דבר׃
the may
.matter tell

CAP. XI יא

CHAPTER 11

CHAPTER 11
[1]Send out your bread on the face of the waters, for you shall find it in many days. [2]Give a share to seven, or even to eight; for you do not know what evil may be on the earth. [3]If the clouds are full of rain, they empty on the earth. And if the tree falls in the south, or in the north, *in the* place where the tree falls, there it shall be. [4]He who watches the wind shall not sow. And he who looks at the clouds shall not reap. [5]As you do not know what *is* the way of the wind, *as* the bones in the pregnant woman's womb, even so you do not know the works of God who makes all. [6]Sow your seed in the morning, and do not rest your hand until evening; for you do not

4672 3117 7230 4325 6440 3899 7971
1 שלח לחמך על־פני המים כי־ברב הימים תמצאנו׃
will you days in for the the on your Send
.it find many ,waters of surface bread out

2451 1961 4100 3045 3808 8083 1571 7651 2506/5414
2 תן־חלק לשבעה וגם לשמונה כי לא תדע מה־יהיה רעה
evil may what you not for ;eight to or ;seven to a Give
be know do even share

7324 776 5921 1653 5645 4390 776 5921
3 על־הארץ׃ אם־ימלאו העבים גשם על־הארץ יריקו
they the on ,rain the full are If the on
;empty earth of clouds .earth

8033 6086 5307 4725 6828 518 1864 6086 5307 518
ואם־יפול עץ בדרום ואם בצפון מקום שיפול העץ שם
there the where (the in) the to or the to the falls and
,tree falls place ,north if ,south tree if

7114 3808 5645 7200 2232 3808 7307 8104 1933
4 יהוא׃ שמר רוח לא יזרע וראה בעבים לא יקצור׃
shall not the at he and shall not the who He shall it
.reap clouds looks who ;sow wind watches .be

4390 990 6106 7307 1870 4100 3045 369
5 כאשר אינך יודע מה־דרך הרוח כעצמים בבטן המלאה
pregnant the the in the (as) the the what do you As
,woman of womb bones ,wind of way (is) know not

6213 834 430 4639 3045 3808
ככה לא תדע את־מעשה האלהים אשר יעשה את־
makes who God the you do not even
of work know so

369 3027 3240 408 6153 2233 2232 1242 3605
6 הכל׃ בבקר זרע את־זרעך ולערב אל־תנח ידך כי אינך
you for your let do not until and your sow the In all
not ;hand rest evening ,seed morning .(things)

know what shall be blessed, this or that; or whether they both *shall be* good as one.

7Truly, also the light *is* sweet; yea, *it is* good for the eyes to behold the sun. 8But if the man lives many years, let him rejoice in them all, and remember the days of darkness; for they shall be many. All that may come *is* vanity.

9Rejoice, O young man, in your youth. And make your heart glad in the days of your youth, and walk in the ways of your heart, and in the sight of your eyes—but know that for all these *things* God will bring you into judgment. 10So then remove vexation from your heart, and put away evil from your flesh. For childhood and prime *of life are* vanity.

2896 259 8147 518 2088 2088 3787 335 3045
יודע אי זה יכשר הזה או־זה ואם־שניהם כאחד טובים:
(be will) one as they or —this or (either) shall this where do
.good both whether this succeed know

7
8 518 8121 7200 5869 2896 216 4966
ומתוק האור וטוב לעינים לראות את־השמש: כי אם־
if but ;sun the see to the for and the (is) Also
eyes good (is it) light sweet

3117 2142 8056 3605 120 2421 7235 8141
שנים הרבה יחיה האדם בכלם ישמח ויזכר את־ימי
the and him let them in ,man the lives many years
of days remember rejoice all

9 970 8056 1892 935 3605 1961 7235 2822
החשך כי־הרבה יהיו כל־שבא הבל: שמח בחור
young O ,Rejoice (is) that all they many for ,darkness
man .vanity come may ;be shall

1870 1980 979 3117 3820 2875 3208
בילדותך ויטיבך לבך בימי בחורותך והלך בדרכי
the in and your the in your make and your in
of ways walk ,youth of days heart good childhood

430 935 428 3605 3045 5869 4758 3820
לבך ובמראי עיניך ודע כי על־כל־אלה יביאך האלהים
God will these all for that but your the in and your
you bring (things) know ;eyes of sight ,heart

10 1320 7451 5671 3823 3708 5493 4941
במשפט: והסר כעס מלבך והעבר רעה מבשרך כי־
for your from evil make and your from vexa- Therefore into
;flesh pass ,heart tion remove .judgment

1892 7839 3208
הילדות והשחרות הבל:
(are) prime and childhood
.vanity life of

CAP. XII יב

CHAPTER 12

CHAPTER 12

1Remember now your Creator in the days of your youth, while the evil days do not come, or the years draw near when you shall say, I have no pleasure in them; 2while not *yet* the sun, or the light, or the moon, or the stars, are darkened, or the clouds return after rain; 3in the day when the housekeepers shall tremble, and the strong men are bowed, and the grinders cease because they are few; and those looking out the windows are darkened; 4and the doors shall be shut in the streets, when the sound of the mill is low, and one rises up at the voice of a bird, and all the daughters of music are silenced; 5also they shall be afraid of a high place, and terrors in the way; and the almond tree shall blossom, and the locust makes himself a burden; and desire breaks

1 3117 935 3808 5704 979 3117 1254 2142
וזכר את־בוראיך בימי בחורתיך עד אשר לא־יבאו ימי
the do not that So your the in your Remember
of days come long ,youth of days Creator now

2 2656 369 559 834 8141 5060 7451
הרעה והגיעו שנים אשר תאמר אין־לי בהם חפץ: עד
So .pleasure in for Not you when the and the
long them me is ,say shall years strike ,evil

7725 3556 3394 216 8121 2821 3808 834
אשר לא־תחשך השמש והאור והירח והכוכבים ושבו
or the or the or the or sun the are not that
return ,stars ,moon ,light darkened

3 5791 1004 8104 2111 3117 1653 310 5645
העבים אחר הגשם: ביום שיזעו שמרי הבית והתעותו
will and the the when the in ;rain the after the
bend ;house of guards trembles day clouds

7200 2821 4591 3588 2912 988 2428 582
אנשי החיל ובטלו הטחנות כי מעטו וחשכו הראות
who they are and they because the will and ;valor men the
out look darkened ;few are grinders idle be of

4 6965 2913 6963 8217 7784 1817 5462 699
בארבות: וסגרו דלתים בשוק בשפל קול הטחנה ויקום
one and ;grinding the is when the in the are and the
arises of sound low ,streets doors shut ;windows

5 3372 1364 1571 7892 1323 3605 7817 6833 6963
לקול הצפור וישחו כל־בנות השיר: גם מגבה יראו
are they a of ,Also the the all are and the the at
;afraid place high .song of daughters silenced ;bird of sound

6565 2284 5445 8247 5006 1870 2849
וחתחתים בדרך וינאץ השקד ויסתבל החגב ותפר
and the -him makes and almond the and the along and
breaks ;locust burden a self ,tree blooms ;way terrors

— because man goes to his eternal home; and the mourners go about in the street—[6]while the silver cord is not *yet* loosed, or the golden bowl is crushed, or the pitcher is shattered at the fountain, or the wheel broken at the cistern — [7]then the dust shall return to the earth as it was, and the spirit shall return to God who gave it.

[8]Vanity of vanities, says the preacher, all *is* vanity. [9]And more than that, the Preacher *was* wise; he still taught the people knowledge. Yes, he listened, and looked, *and* set in order many proverbs. [10]The Preacher sought to find out pleasing words; and words of truth rightly written. [11]The words of the wise *are* as goads; yea, as nails driven by the masters of collections, they *are* given from one Shepherd. [12]And more than these, my son, be warned: The making of many books has no end, and much study *is* the weariness of the flesh.

[13]Let us hear the conclusion of the whole matter: Fear God, and keep His commandments; for this *applies to* every man. [14]For God shall bring every work into judgment, with all that is hidden, whether *it is* good, or whether *it is* evil.

7784 5437 5769 1004 120 1980 35
הָאֲבִיּוֹנָה כִּי־הֹלֵךְ הָאָדָם אֶל־בֵּית עוֹלָמוֹ וְסָבְבוּ בַשּׁוּק
the in street | go and about | his ;eternity | house of | the to | man | is because going | ;desire

6 15:43 7533 3701 2256 7368 38:08 5594
הַסֹּפְדִים׃ עַד אֲשֶׁר לֹא־יֵרָחֵק חֶבֶל הַכֶּסֶף וְתָרֻץ גֻּלַּת
the bowl | is or crushed | the ,silver | cord | is removed | not | Before | the .mourners

953 1534 7533 40:02 3537 7665 2091
הַזָּהָב וְתִשָּׁבֶר כַּד עַל־הַמַּבּוּעַ וְנָרֹץ הַגַּלְגַּל אֶל־הַבּוֹר׃
the .cistern | at | the wheel | is or crushed | the ,spring | at | the pitcher | is or shattered | ,golden

7 430 7725 7307 1961 776 5921 6083 7725
וְיָשֹׁב הֶעָפָר עַל־הָאָרֶץ כְּשֶׁהָיָה וְהָרוּחַ תָּשׁוּב אֶל־הָאֱלֹהִים
God | to | shall return | the and spirit | it as ;was | the earth | on | the dust | will then return

8 1892 3605 6953 559 1892 1892 5414 834
אֲשֶׁר נְתָנָהּ׃ הֲבֵל הֲבָלִים אָמַר הַקּוֹהֶלֶת הַכֹּל הָבֶל׃
.vanity | (is) all | the ;Preacher | says | ,vanities of | Vanity | .it gave | who

9 238 5971 1847/3925 3148 2450 6953
וְיֹתֵר שֶׁהָיָה קֹהֶלֶת חָכָם עוֹד לִמַּד־דַּעַת אֶת־הָעָם וְאִזֵּן
gave and ,ear | the ,people | knowledge | he taught | still more | ;wise | the Preacher | than that | And more

10 1697 4672 6953 1245 7235 4912 8626 2713
וְחִקֵּר תִּקֵּן מְשָׁלִים הַרְבֵּה׃ בִּקֵּשׁ קֹהֶלֶת לִמְצֹא דִּבְרֵי־
words of | find to out | The Preacher | sought | .many | proverbs | set (and) order in | and ;sought

11 1861 2450 1697 571 1697 3476 3789 2656
חֵפֶץ וְכָתוּב יֹשֶׁר דִּבְרֵי אֱמֶת׃ דִּבְרֵי חֲכָמִים כַּדָּרְבֹנוֹת
like (are) ;ox-goads | wise the | The words of | .truth | words of | upright | and written | ,delight

12 3148 259 7462 5414 627 1167 5193 4930
וּכְמַשְׂמְרוֹת נְטוּעִים בַּעֲלֵי אֲסֻפּוֹת נִתְּנוּ מֵרֹעֶה אֶחָד׃ וְיֹתֵר
And more | .one | from Shepherd | are they given | ;collections | the of masters | driven (are) in | nails as and

3854 7093 369 7235 5612 6213 2094 1121 1992
מֵהֵמָּה בְּנִי הִזָּהֵר עֲשׂוֹת סְפָרִים הַרְבֵּה אֵין קֵץ וְלַהַג
and study | an ;end | has not | many | books | the of making | be warned | my ,son | than ,these

13 430 8085 3605 1697 5490 1320 3024 7235
הַרְבֵּה יְגִעַת בָּשָׂר׃ סוֹף דָּבָר הַכֹּל נִשְׁמָע אֶת־הָאֱלֹהִים
God | us let .hear | whole | the matter | The end of | the .flesh | weariness of | much (is)

14 3605 120 3605 8104 4687 3372
יְרָא וְאֶת־מִצְוֺתָיו שְׁמוֹר כִּי־זֶה כָּל־הָאָדָם׃ כִּי אֶת־כָּל־
every | For | .man | every | this for (to applies) | —keep | His and commandments | ,Fear

2896 5956 3605 4941 935 430 4639
מַעֲשֶׂה הָאֱלֹהִים יָבִא בְמִשְׁפָּט עַל כָּל־נֶעְלָם אִם־טוֹב
(is it) ,good | whether | that ,hidden is | all | with | into ,judgment | shall bring | God | work

7451 518
וְאִם־רָע׃
(is it) .evil | or whether

שיר השירים

CANTICUM CANTICORUM

(THE) SONG OF SONGS

CAPUT. I א

CHAPTER 1

A LITERAL TRANSLATION
OF THE BIBLE

THE SONG OF SOLOMON

CHAPTER 1

[1]The song of songs which *is* Solomon's. [2]Let Him kiss me with the kisses of His mouth; for Your loves *are* better than wine. [3]For Your ointments *have* a lovely fragrance; Your name is *as* ointment poured out; therefore the virgins love You. [4]Draw me; we will run after You. The King has brought me *into* His chambers. We will be glad and rejoice in You; we will remember Your loves more than wine; the upright love You. [5]I *am* black, but comely, O daughters of Jerusalem, like the tents of Kedar, like the curtains of Solomon. [6]Do not look at me, that I *am* black, that the sun has looked on me. My mother's sons were angry with me; they made me the keeper of the vineyards; *but* my own vineyard I have not kept. [7]Tell me, *You* whom my soul loves, where do You feed; where do You lie down at noon? For why should I be as one who is veiled beside the flocks of Your companions?

[8]If you yourself do not know, most beautiful among women, go in the footsteps of the flock. And feed your kids beside the tents of the shepherds. [9]O my love, I have compared you to My mares in Pharaoh's chariots. [10]Your cheeks *are* lovely with ornaments, your neck with chains *of gold*. [11]We will make you ornaments of gold with studs of silver. [12]While the King is in His circle, my spikenard gives

6310 5390 5401 8010 834 7891 7891
1 2 שיר השירים אשר לשלמה: ישקני מנשיקות פיהו כי־
for His the with Him Let .Solomon's which ,songs The
;mouth of kisses me kiss (is) of song
8034 7324 8081 2896 8081 7381 3196 1730 2896
3 טובים דדיך מיין: לריח שמניך טובים שמן תורק שמך
Your poured oint- (are) Your a For than Your (are)
;name (is)out ment ;good ointments fragrance .wine love better
935 7323 310 4900 157 5959
4 על־כן עלמות אהבוך: משכני אחריך נרוצה הביאני
brought has will we after Draw love the therefore
me into ;run You ,me .You virgins
3196 1730 2142 8056 1523 2315 4428
המלך חדריו נגילה ונשמחה בך נזכירה דדיך מיין
above Your will we in rejoice and will we His the
;wine loves remember ;You glad be ;chambers King
3389 1323 5000 7838 157 4339
5 מישרים אהבוך: שחורה אני ונאוה בנות ירושלם
,Jerusalem O but ,(am) I Black love they the
of daughters comely you upright
7840 7200 8010 3407 6938 168
6 כאהלי קדר כיריעות שלמה: אל־תראוני שאני שחרחרת
,black that look do Not .Solomon the like ,Kedar the like
,(am) I ,me at of curtains of tents
5201 7760 2787 517 1121 8121 7805
ששזפתני השמש בני אמי נחרו־בי שמני נטרה את־
keeper they with were my The ;sun the has that
of me made ;me angry mother of sons me on looked
157 5046 5201 3808 3754 3754
7 הכרמים כרמי שלי לא נטרתי: הגידה לי שאהבה
loves whom to Tell have I not which my (but) the
,me .kept me to is vineyard ,vineyards
1961 4100 6672 7257 349 7462 349 5315
נפשי איכה תרעה איכה תרביץ בצהרים שלמה אהיה
should For ?noon at You do Where You do where my
be I down lie ?feed soul
802 3303 3045 3808 2272 5739 5844
8 כעטיה על עדרי חבריך: אם־לא תדעי לך היפה בנשים
among most your- you not If Your the beside one as
women beautiful ,self know ?companions of flocks veiled
4908 1429 7462 6629 6119
צאי־לך בעקבי הצאן ורעי את־גדיתיך על משכנות
dwellings the beside your and the the in your- go
of kids feed ,flock of footsteps self out
4998 7472 1819 6547 7393 5484 7462
9 10 הרעים: לססתי ברכבי פרעה דמיתיך רעיתי: נאוו
Lovely My O have I Pharoah's among my To the
(are) ,love ,You compared chariots mares .shepherds
6213 2091 8447 2737 6677 8447 3895
11 לחייך בתרים צוארך בחרוזים: תורי זהב נעשה־לך
for will we gold Orna- strings with your with your
,you make of ments (beads of) neck ,ornaments cheeks
7381 5414 5373 4524 4428 5704 3701 5351
12 עם נקדות הכסף: עד־שהמלך במסבו נרדי נתן ריחו:
its gives my his in the While .silver studs with
.fragrance spikenard ,circle (is) King of

its fragrance. [13]A bundle of myrrh *is* my Beloved to me. *He* shall lodge between my breasts. [14]My Beloved is to me *like* a cluster of henna in the vineyards of Engedi. [15]Behold, you *are* beautiful, my love. Behold, you *are* beautiful; your eyes *as* doves'. [16]Behold, you *are* beautiful, my Beloved; yea, pleasant. Also our couch *is* green. [17]The beams of our house *are* cedars; our rafters are of firs.

1730 3724 811 38 85 7699 996 1730 4753 6872
13 14 צְרוֹר הַמֹּר ׀ דּוֹדִי לִי בֵּין שָׁדַי יָלִין׃ אֶשְׁכֹּל הַכֹּפֶר ׀ דּוֹדִי
my henna cluster A shall He my between to my (is) myrrh A
Beloved (is) of .lie breasts ,me Beloved of bundle

3178 3303 2009 7472 3302 2009 5872 3754
15 לִי בְּכַרְמֵי עֵין גֶּדִי׃ הִנָּךְ יָפָה רַעְיָתִי הִנָּךְ יָפָה עֵינַיִךְ יוֹנִים׃
.dove's your are ,behold my are Behold .Engedi the in to
eyes ;beautiful you ;love ,beautiful you of vineyards ,me

1004 6982 7488 6210 637 5273 637 1730 5303 2009
16 17 הִנְּךָ יָפֶה דוֹדִי אַף נָעִים אַף־עַרְשֵׂנוּ רַעֲנָנָה׃ קֹרוֹת בָּתֵּינוּ
our The .green is our Also .pleasant ,yea my are ,Behold
houses of beams couch ,Beloved ,beautiful you

1266 7351 730
אֲרָזִים רָחִיטֵנוּ בְּרוֹתִים׃
.firs of our (and) (are)
rafters ,cedars

CAP. II ב

CHAPTER 2

[1]I *am* a rose of Sharon, a lily of the valleys. [2]As a lily among thorns, so *is* My love among the daughters. [3]As the apple among the trees of the forest, so *is* my Beloved among the sons. I delighted in His shadow, and I sat down; and His fruit *was* sweet to my taste. [4]He brought me to the house of wine, and His banner over me *was* love. [5]Feed me with raisin cakes, refresh me with apples—for I am sick *with* love. [6]His left hand *is* under my head, and His right hand embraces me. [7]I adjure you by the gazelles, and by the does of the field, O daughters of Jerusalem, that you do not stir up and do not awaken the Beloved until it pleases.

[8]The voice of my Beloved! Behold, He comes leaping on the mountains, skipping on the hills. [9]My Beloved is likened to a gazelle, or to a young deer, the stag. Behold, *He* stands behind our wall, looking from the windows, peering from the lattice. [10]My Beloved answered and said to me, Arouse yourself, My love, My beautiful one, and come away. [11]For, behold, the winter has passed, the rain has passed, it goes to

996 7799 6010 7799 8289 2261
1 2 אֲנִי חֲבַצֶּלֶת הַשָּׁרוֹן שׁוֹשַׁנַּת הָעֲמָקִים׃ כְּשׁוֹשַׁנָּה בֵּין
among a As the of lily a plain the a I
lily .valleys Sharon of of rose (am)

3651 3293 6086 8598 1323 996 7472 3651 2336
3 הַחוֹחִים כֵּן רַעְיָתִי בֵּין הַבָּנוֹת׃ כְּתַפּוּחַ בַּעֲצֵי הַיַּעַר כֵּן
so the the in the As the among my so ,thorns
(is) ,forest of trees apple .daughters love (is)

2441 4966 6529 3427 2530 6738 1121 1730
דּוֹדִי בֵּין הַבָּנִים בְּצִלּוֹ חִמַּדְתִּי וְיָשַׁבְתִּי וּפִרְיוֹ מָתוֹק לְחִכִּי׃
my to (was) His and I and I His in the among my
.palate sweet fruit ;down sat ,delighted shadow ;sons Beloved

809 5564 160 1714 3196 1004 935
4 5 הֱבִיאַנִי אֶל־בֵּית הַיָּיִן וְדִגְלוֹ עָלַי אַהֲבָה׃ סַמְּכוּנִי בָּאֲשִׁישׁוֹת
with me Feed (was) over His and the house a to He
,raisin-cakes .love me banner ,wine of me brought

8478 8040 160 2470 8598 7502
רַפְּדוּנִי בַּתַּפּוּחִים כִּי־חוֹלַת אַהֲבָה אָנִי׃ שְׂמֹאלוֹ תַּחַת
(is) left His I love sick for with sustain
under hand .(am) with —apples me

3389 1323 7650 2263 3225 7218
6 7 לְרֹאשִׁי וִימִינוֹ תְּחַבְּקֵנִי׃ הִשְׁבַּעְתִּי אֶתְכֶם בְּנוֹת יְרוּשָׁלִַם
,Jerusalem O ,you charge I embraces His and my
of daughters .me hand right ,head

5782 5782 7704 355 176 6643
בִּצְבָאוֹת אוֹ בְּאַיְלוֹת הַשָּׂדֶה אִם־תָּעִירוּ ׀ וְאִם־תְּעוֹרְרוּ
awaken you and you that ,field the the by or the by
not that up stir not of does gazelles

1801 935 2009 1730 6963 2654 5704 160
8 אֶת־הָאַהֲבָה עַד שֶׁתֶּחְפָּץ׃ קוֹל דּוֹדִי הִנֵּה־זֶה בָּא מְדַלֵּג
leaping He this Be- my The .pleases it until the
comes ,hold !Beloved of voice Beloved

176 6643 1730 1819 1389 5921 7092 2022
9 עַל־הֶהָרִים מְקַפֵּץ עַל־הַגְּבָעוֹת׃ דּוֹמֶה דוֹדִי לִצְבִי אוֹ
or a to my Is .hills the on skipping the on
gazelle Beloved likened ,mountains

76 88 3796 310 5975 2009 354 6082
לְעֹפֶר הָאַיָּלִים הִנֵּה־זֶה עוֹמֵד אַחַר כָּתְלֵנוּ מַשְׁגִּיחַ מִן
from looking our behind standing this ,Behold the a to
,wall :one .stag ,deer young

6965 559 1730 6030 2762 6692 2474
10 הַחַלֹּנוֹת מֵצִיץ מִן־הַחֲרַכִּים׃ עָנָה דוֹדִי וְאָמַר לִי קוּמִי
Rise to said and my Answered the from blooming the
up ,me Beloved .lattice ,windows

1653 5674 5638 2009 3212 3303 7472
11 לָךְ רַעְיָתִי יָפָתִי וּלְכִי־לָךְ׃ כִּי־הִנֵּה הַסְּתָו עָבָר הַגֶּשֶׁם
rain the has the behold ,For your- and beau- My My your-
,passed winter .self come ,one tiful ,love ,self

itself. [12]The flowers appear on the earth; the time of singing has come; and the voice of the turtle-dove is heard in our land. [13]The fig-tree spices her unripe figs, and the vines give a fragrance *by* the blossom. Arise, My love; come, My beautiful one, and come yourself. [14]O My dove, in the clefts of the rock, in the secrecy of the steep place, let Me see your form. Let Me hear your voice; for your voice *is* sweet, and your form *is* beautiful. [15]Take for us the foxes, the little foxes that spoil the vines; and our vineyards *have* blossoms.

[16]My Beloved *is* mine, and I *am* His. He feeds among the lilies. [17]Until when does the day blow, and the shadows flee away? Turn, my Beloved, and be like a gazelle, or a young deer, the stag, on the cleft mountains.

6963 5060 2158 6256 776 7200 5339 1980 2498
12 חָלַף הָלַךְ לוֹ׃ הַנִּצָּנִים נִרְאוּ בָאָרֶץ עֵת הַזָּמִיר הִגִּיעַ וְקוֹל
the and has the the the on appear The to it has
of voice ;come singing of time ;earth flowers .itself goes ,passed

1612 6291 2590 8384 776 8085 8449
13 הַתּוֹר נִשְׁמַע בְּאַרְצֵנוּ׃ הַתְּאֵנָה חָנְטָה פַגֶּיהָ וְהַגְּפָנִים
the and unripe her spices fig The our in heard is the
vines ,figs tree .land turtle-dove

3128 3212 3303 7472 3212 6965 7381 5414 5563
14 סְמָדַר נָתְנוּ רֵיחַ קוּמִי לָכִי רַעְיָתִי יָפָתִי וּלְכִי־לָךְ׃ יוֹנָתִי
my O your- and beau- My My ,come ,Arise a give the (by)
,dove .self come tiful ,love .fragrance blossom

4758 7200 4095 5643 5553 2288
בְּחַגְוֵי הַסֶּלַע בְּסֵתֶר הַמַּדְרֵגָה הַרְאִינִי אֶת־מַרְאַיִךְ
your Me make steep the the in ,rock the the in
.form see place of secrecy of clefts

270 5000 4758 6156 6963 6963 8085
15 הַשְׁמִיעִינִי אֶת־קוֹלֵךְ כִּי־קוֹלֵךְ עָרֵב וּמַרְאֵיךְ נָאוֶה׃ אֶחֱזוּ־
Take (is) your and (is) your for your Me Let
.comely form ,sweet voice ;voice hear

3754 3754 2254 6996 7776 7776
לָנוּ שׁוּעָלִים שׁוּעָלִים קְטַנִּים מְחַבְּלִים כְּרָמִים וּכְרָמֵינוּ
our and the spoiling little foxes the ,foxes the for
vineyards ;vineyards us

6315 5704 7799 7462 1730 5563
16 17 סְמָדַר׃ דּוֹדִי לִי וַאֲנִי לוֹ הָרֹעֶה בַּשּׁוֹשַׁנִּים׃ עַד שֶׁיָּפוּחַ
when Until among He to I and (is) Be- My (have)
blows .lilies the feeds ;him (am) ,me to loved . blossoms

6082 176 6643 1730 1819 5437 6752 5127 3117
הַיּוֹם וְנָסוּ הַצְּלָלִים סֹב דְּמֵה־לְךָ דוֹדִי לִצְבִי אוֹ לְעֹפֶר
young a or a my to like be ,turn the and the
,deer gazelle ,Beloved ,Yourself ;shadows flee ,day

1335 2022 5921 354
הָאַיָּלִים עַל־הָרֵי בָתֶר׃
cleft the on ,stag the
mountains

CAP. III ג

CHAPTER 3

CHAPTER 3

[1]By night on my bed I sought *Him* whom my soul loves. I sought Him, but I did not find Him. [2]I will rise now and go about in the city, in the streets and in the broad places. I will seek *Him* whom my soul loves. I sought Him, but I did not find Him. [3]The watchmen going about in the city found me. *I said*, Have you seen *Him* my soul loves? [4]When I had passed on from them, *it was* a little while until I found *Him* whom my soul loves. I seized Him, and I did not let Him go, until I had brought Him into my mother's house, and into the room of her who conceived me. [5]I adjure you, O daughters of

1245 5315 157 1245 3915 4904 5921
1 עַל־מִשְׁכָּבִי בַּלֵּילוֹת בִּקַּשְׁתִּי אֵת שֶׁאָהֲבָה נַפְשִׁי בִּקַּשְׁתִּיו
sought I my whom (Him) sought I night by my On
;Him ;soul loved bed

7784 5892 5437 4994 6965 4672 3808
2 וְלֹא מְצָאתִיו׃ אָקוּמָה נָּא וַאֲסוֹבְבָה בָעִיר בַּשְּׁוָקִים
the in the in go I and ,now will I did I but
streets ,city about rise .Him find not

3808 1245 5315 157 1245 7339
וּבָרְחֹבוֹת אֲבַקְשָׁה אֵת שֶׁאָהֲבָה נַפְשִׁי בִּקַּשְׁתִּיו וְלֹא
but sought I my whom (Him) will I the in and
not ,Him ;soul loves seek ;places broad

5892 5437 8104 4672 4672
3 מְצָאתִיו׃ מְצָאוּנִי הַשֹּׁמְרִים הַסֹּבְבִים בָּעִיר אֵת
the in going (those) The me found find did I
:city about ,watchmen .Him

5704 5674 4592 7200 5315 157
4 שֶׁאָהֲבָה נַפְשִׁי רְאִיתֶם׃ כִּמְעַט שֶׁעָבַרְתִּי מֵהֶם עַד
until from had I when little A you Have soul my (Him)
,them passed while ?seen loves whom

7503 3808 270 5315 157 4672
שֶׁמָּצָאתִי אֵת שֶׁאָהֲבָה נַפְשִׁי אֲחַזְתִּיו וְלֹא אַרְפֶּנּוּ עַד־
until Him let I and seized I my whom (Him) found I
,go not ,Him ;soul loves

7650 2029 2315 517 1004 935
5 שֶׁהֲבֵיאתִיו אֶל־בֵּית אִמִּי וְאֶל־חֶדֶר הוֹרָתִי׃ הִשְׁבַּעְתִּי
charge I who her the and my house into brought had I
.me conceived of room into ,mother's Him

Jerusalem, by the gazelles and by the does of the field, that you do not stir up, even not stir up the Beloved until it pleases.

6 Who *is* this who comes up out of the wilderness like pillars of smoke, perfumed with myrrh and frankincense, from all powders of the merchant? 7 Behold his bed, Solomon's! Sixty mighty men *are* around it, of the mighty men of Israel. 8 They all hold the sword, instructed in war; each man *has* his sword on his thigh from dread in the night. 9 King Solomon made himself a litter-bed of the trees of Lebanon. 10 He made its poles of silver; its back *of* gold; its seat *of* purple; its middle was paved *with* love by the daughters of Jerusalem. 11 Go forth, O daughters of Zion, and see king Solomon with the crown *with* which his mother crowned him on his wedding day, even on the day of the gladness of his heart.

518 7704 355 176 6643 3389 1323
אֶתְכֶם בְּנוֹת יְרוּשָׁלִַם בִּצְבָאוֹת אוֹ בְּאַיְלוֹת הַשָּׂדֶה אִם־
that ,field the the by or the by ,Jerusalem O ,you
not of does gazelles of daughters

6 2088 4310 2654 5704 160 5782 5782
תָּעִירוּ וְאִם־תְּעוֹרְרוּ אֶת־הָאַהֲבָה עַד שֶׁתֶּחְפָּץ׃ מִי זֹאת
(is) Who .pleases it until the you ,yea stir you
this Beloved up stir not up

3605 3828 4753 6999 6227 8490 4057 5927
עֹלָה מִן־הַמִּדְבָּר כְּתִימֲרוֹת עָשָׁן מְקֻטֶּרֶת מוֹר וּלְבוֹנָה מִכֹּל
from and myrrh burned ,smoke like the of out coming
all ,frankincense with of pillars wilderness up

7 5439 1368 8346 8010 4296 2009 7402 81
אַבְקַת רוֹכֵל׃ הִנֵּה מִטָּתוֹ שֶׁלִּשְׁלֹמֹה שִׁשִּׁים גִּבֹּרִים סָבִיב
(are) mighty sixty is which his Behold the powders
around men ;Solomon's ,bed ?merchant of

8 4421 3925 2719 270 3605 3478 1368
לָהּ מִגִּבֹּרֵי יִשְׂרָאֵל׃ כֻּלָּם אֲחֻזֵי חֶרֶב מְלֻמְּדֵי מִלְחָמָה
;battle instructed ,swords hold They .Israel's mighty of ,it
in all men

9 6213 668 3915 6343 3409 2719 376
אִישׁ חַרְבּוֹ עַל־יְרֵכוֹ מִפַּחַד בַּלֵּילוֹת׃ אַפִּרְיוֹן עָשָׂה לוֹ
for made A the in from his on his (has) a
him palanquin .night dread thigh sword man

10 7507 3701 6213 5982 3844 6086 8010 4428
הַמֶּלֶךְ שְׁלֹמֹה מֵעֲצֵי הַלְּבָנוֹן׃ עַמּוּדָיו עָשָׂה כֶסֶף רְפִידָתוֹ
its of he poles The .Lebanon the of Solomon King
support ,silver made it of of trees

3389 1323 160 7528 8432 713 4817 2091
זָהָב מֶרְכָּבוֹ אַרְגָּמָן תּוֹכוֹ רָצוּף אַהֲבָה מִבְּנוֹת יְרוּשָׁלִָם׃
.Jerusalem the by (in) was its (of) its (of)
of daughters ,love paved middle ;purple seat ,gold

11 5849 5850 8010 4428 6726 1323 7200 3318
צְאֶינָה וּרְאֶינָה בְּנוֹת צִיּוֹן בַּמֶּלֶךְ שְׁלֹמֹה בָּעֲטָרָה שֶׁעִטְּרָה־
which (with) the with Solomon King ,Zion O ,see and out Go
crowned crown of daughters

3820 8057 3117 2861 3117 517
לּוֹ אִמּוֹ בְּיוֹם חֲתֻנָּתוֹ וּבְיוֹם שִׂמְחַת לִבּוֹ׃
his gladness the on even his the on his him
.heart of of day the ;wedding of day mother

CAP. IV ד

CHAPTER 4

CHAPTER 4

1 Behold, you *are* beautiful, My love. Behold, you *are* beautiful; your eyes *are as* doves' from behind your veil. Your hair *is* like a flock of goats which lie down from Mount Gilead. 2 Your teeth *are* like a flock of shorn *sheep* which come up from the washing-place; of which all of them *are* bearing twins; and barrenness is not among them. 3 Your lips *are* like a cord of scarlet, and your speech *is* becoming; your temples *are* like a piece of pomegranate behind your veil. 4 Your neck *is* like the tower of David, built for an armory; a thousand bucklers hang on it, all the shields of the mighty men. 5 Your two

1 6777 1157 3128 5869 3303 2009 7472 3303 2009
הִנָּךְ יָפָה רַעְיָתִי הִנָּךְ יָפָה עֵינַיִךְ יוֹנִים מִבַּעַד לְצַמָּתֵךְ
your from doves' Your (are) ,Behold My (are) Behold
;veil behind eyes !beautiful you !love ,beautiful ,you

2 5739 8127 1568 2022 1570 5795 5739 8181
שַׂעְרֵךְ כְּעֵדֶר הָעִזִּים שֶׁגָּלְשׁוּ מֵהַר גִּלְעָד׃ שִׁנַּיִךְ כְּעֵדֶר
a as Your .Gilead from which goats like (is) your
of flock teeth Mount recline of flock a hair

7909 8382 3605 7367 5927 7094
הַקְּצוּבוֹת שֶׁעָלוּ מִן־הָרַחְצָה שֶׁכֻּלָּם מַתְאִימוֹת וְשַׁכֻּלָה
barren- and bearing (are) which the from come which shorn
ness ;twins all they ;washing-place up (sheep)

3 6400 5000 4057 8193 8144 2339 854 369
אֵין בָּהֶם׃ כְּחוּט הַשָּׁנִי שִׂפְתֹתַיִךְ וּמִדְבָּרֵיךְ נָאוֶה כְּפֶלַח
a as (is) your and your scarlet a As among not
of piece comely speech ;lips of cord ;them is

4 1129 6677 1732 4026 6777 1157 7541 7416
הָרִמּוֹן רַקָּתֵךְ מִבַּעַד לְצַמָּתֵךְ׃ כְּמִגְדַּל דָּוִיד צַוָּארֵךְ בָּנוּי
built your (is) David the As your from your pome- a
,neck of tower .veil behind temples granate

5 1368 7982 3605 8518 4043 505 8530
לְתַלְפִּיּוֹת אֶלֶף הַמָּגֵן תָּלוּי עָלָיו כֹּל שִׁלְטֵי הַגִּבֹּרִים׃
mighty the shields all ;it on hang shields a an for
.men of thousand ,armory

breasts *are* like two fawns, twins of a gazelle feeding among the lilies. 6Until when the day blows, and the shadows flee away, I myself will go to the mountain of myrrh, and to the hills of frankincense. 7You *are* all beautiful, My love. There is no blemish on you.

8Come with Me from Lebanon, *My* spouse; with Me from Lebanon. Look from the top of Amana, from the top of Shenir and Hermon, from the lions' dens, from the mountains of the leopards. 9You have ravished My heart, My sister, *My* spouse; you have ravished My heart with one of your eyes, with one chain of your neck. 10How beautiful *are* your loves, My sister, *My* spouse! How *much* better *are* your loves than wine, and the scent of your ointments than all spices! 11Your lips, *My* spouse, drip *like* the honeycomb; honey and milk *are* under your tongue. And the scents of your garments *are* like the scent of Lebanon.

12A locked garden *is* My sister, *My* spouse; a rock heap locked up, a sealed fountain. 13 Your plants *are* an orchard of pomegranates with excellent fruits, with henna *and* spikenard; 14spikenard and saffron, calamus and cinnamon; with all trees of frankincense, myrrh and aloes; with all the chief balsam spices; 15a fountain of gardens, a well of living waters; even flowings from Lebanon. 16Awake, north *wind*; yea, come, south *wind*; blow on my garden; let its spices flow out. Let my Beloved come into His garden, and eat its excellent fruits.

CHAPTER 5

1I have come into My garden, My sister, *My* spouse; I have gathered My myrrh with My spice. I have

---

7799 7462 6646 8388 6082 8147 7699 8147
5 שְׁנֵי שָׁדַיִךְ כִּשְׁנֵי עֳפָרִים תְּאוֹמֵי צְבִיָּה הָרוֹעִים בַּשּׁוֹשַׁנִּים׃
the among feeding a of twins ,fawns like (are) Your two
.lilies ,gazelle two breasts

475:3 2022 32 12 6752 5127 3117: 63 15 5704
6 עַד שֶׁיָּפוּחַ הַיּוֹם וְנָסוּ הַצְּלָלִים אֵלֶךְ לִי אֶל־הַר הַמּוֹר
myrrh the to my- will I the flee and the when Until
of mountain self go ,shadows ,day blows

369 3971 :7472 3303 3605 3828 1389
7 וְאֶל־גִּבְעַת הַלְּבוֹנָה׃ כֻּלָּךְ יָפָה רַעְיָתִי וּמוּם אֵין בָּךְ׃
8 אִתִּי
With on is a and My ,beautiful You .frankincense the and
Me .you not blemish ;love all (are) of hills to

549 7218 7784 935 3844 3618 3844
מִלְּבָנוֹן כַּלָּה אִתִּי מִלְּבָנוֹן תָּבוֹאִי תָּשׁוּרִי ׀ מֵרֹאשׁ אֲמָנָה
,Amana the from look ;come from with (My) from
of top Lebanon Me ,spouse Lebanon

5246 2042 :738 4585 :2768 8149 7218
מֵרֹאשׁ שְׂנִיר וְחֶרְמוֹן מִמְּעֹנוֹת אֲרָיוֹת מֵהַרְרֵי נְמֵרִים׃
the the from ,lions' the from and Shenir the from
.leopards of mountains dens ,Hermon of top

6060 259 :5869 259 38 23 3618 269 3823
9 לִבַּבְתִּנִי אֲחֹתִי כַלָּה לִבַּבְתִּינִי בְּאַחַד מֵעֵינַיִךְ בְּאַחַד עֲנָק
chain with your of with have you (My) My ravished You
one ,eyes one heart My ravished ,spouse ,sister ,heart My

3196 1730. 2895 36 18 269 1730. 3303 6677
10 מִצַּוְּרֹנָיִךְ׃ מַה־יָּפוּ דֹדַיִךְ אֲחֹתִי כַלָּה מַה־טֹּבוּ דֹדַיִךְ מִיַּיִן
than your better How (My) My your fair How your of
,wine loves (are) much) !spouse ,sister loves (are) .neck

36 18 8143 5197. 5317 1314 3605 8081 7381
11 וְרֵיחַ שְׁמָנַיִךְ מִכָּל־בְּשָׂמִים׃ נֹפֶת תִּטֹּפְנָה שִׂפְתוֹתַיִךְ כַּלָּה
(My) your (so) the As balsam- than your the and
;spouse ,lips drips honeycomb !spices all ointments of scent

3844 7381 8008 7381 39 56 8478 2461 1706
דְּבַשׁ וְחָלָב תַּחַת לְשׁוֹנֵךְ וְרֵיחַ שַׂלְמֹתַיִךְ כְּרֵיחַ לְבָנוֹן׃
.Lebanon the like outer your the and your (are) and honey
of scent garments of scent ;tongue under milk

7973 2856 4599 5274 15 30 36 18 269 5274 1588
12 גַּן ׀ נָעוּל אֲחֹתִי כַלָּה גַּל נָעוּל מַעְיָן חָתוּם׃
13 שְׁלָחַיִךְ
Your .sealed a locked rock a (My) My (is) locked A
(are) plants fountain ;up heap ;spouse ,sister up garden

5373 5373 3724 4022 6529 7416 6508
14 פַּרְדֵּס רִמּוֹנִים עִם פְּרִי מְגָדִים כְּפָרִים עִם־נְרָדִים׃ נֵרְד
spike- ;spikenard with henna ;excellent fruits with pome- orchard an
nard ,granates of

174 4753 3828 6086 3605 7076 7070 3750
וְכַרְכֹּם קָנֶה וְקִנָּמוֹן עִם כָּל־עֲצֵי לְבוֹנָה מֹר וַאֲהָלוֹת עִם
with and myrrh frankin- trees all with and calamus and
aloes ;cense of ,cinnamon ;saffron

5140 2416 4325 875 1588: 4599 1314 7218 3605
15 כָּל־רָאשֵׁי בְשָׂמִים׃ מַעְיַן גַּנִּים בְּאֵר מַיִם חַיִּים וְנֹזְלִים
even ,living waters a ,gardens a balsam the all
flowings of well of fountain spices chief

1314 5140 1588 6315 :8486 935 6828 5782 3844
16 מִן־לְבָנוֹן׃ עוּרִי צָפוֹן וּבוֹאִי תֵימָן הָפִיחִי גַנִּי יִזְּלוּ בְשָׂמָיו
its let my blow south and north ,Awaken from
.spices flow ,garden on ;(wind) ,come ,(wind) .Lebanon

4022 6529 398 1588 1730 935
יָבֹא דוֹדִי לְגַנּוֹ וְיֹאכַל פְּרִי מְגָדָיו׃
its fruits eat and His into Be- my Let
.excellent ,garden loved come

CAP. V ה

CHAPTER 5

398 1313 4753 717 3618 269 1588 935
1 בָּאתִי לְגַנִּי אֲחֹתִי כַלָּה אָרִיתִי מוֹרִי עִם־בְּשָׂמִי אָכַלְתִּי
have I My with My have I (My) My My to have I
eaten ;spice myrrh gathered ,spouse ,sister ,garden come

eaten My honeycomb with My honey; I have drunk My wine with My milk. Eat and drink, O friends; yea, drink fully, beloved ones.

[2]I sleep, but my heart is awake. *It is* the sound of my Beloved that knocks, *saying*, Open to Me, My sister, My love, My dove, My undefiled. For My head is filled with dew, My locks with the drops of the night. [3]I have stripped off My coat; how shall I put it on? I have washed My feet; how shall I defile them? [4]My Beloved sent His hand from the opening, and my inner being sighed for Him. [5]I rose up to open to my Beloved, and my hands dripped with myrrh, and my fingers flowing *with* myrrh on the handles of the bolt. [6]I opened to my Beloved; but my Beloved had left; He passed on. My soul went out when He spoke; I sought Him, but I could not find Him. I called Him, but He did not answer me. [7]The watchmen who went about the city found me *and* struck me; they wounded me; the keepers of the walls lifted my veil from me. [8]I adjure you, O daughters of Jerusalem, if you find my Beloved, what do you tell Him? That I am sick *with* love.

[9]What *is* your Beloved more than *another* Beloved, most beautiful among women? What *is* your Beloved more than *another* Beloved, that you adjure us so? [10]My Beloved *is* bright and ruddy, standing out among ten thousand. [11]His head *is like* refined gold; His locks *are* bushy *and* black as a raven. [12]His eyes *are* as *the eyes* of doves on the rivers of waters, washed with milk, sitting on a setting. [13]His cheeks *are* like a bed of spices, a raised bed of aromatic herbs. His lips are *like* lilies dropping

יערי עם־דבשי שתיתי ייני עם־חלבי אכלו רעים שתו
2 ושכרו דודים: אני ישנה ולבי ער קול ׀ דודי דופק
פתחי־לי אחתי רעיתי יונתי תמתי שראשי נמלא־טל
3 קוצותי רסיסי לילה: פשטתי את־כתנתי איככה אלבשנה
4 רחצתי את־רגלי איככה אטנפם: דודי שלח ידו מן
5 החור ומעי המו עליו: קמתי אני לפתח לדודי וידי
6 נטפו־מור ואצבעתי מור עבר על כפות המנעול: פתחתי
אני לדודי ודודי חמק עבר נפשי יצאה בדברו בקשתיהו
7 ולא מצאתיהו קראתיו ולא ענני: מצאני השמרים
הסבבים בעיר הכוני פצעוני נשאו את־רדידי מעלי
8 שמרי החמות: השבעתי אתכם בנות ירושלם אם־
9 תמצאו את־דודי מה־תגידו לו שחולת אהבה אני: מה־
דודך מדוד היפה בנשים מה־דודך מדוד שככה
10 11 השבעתנו: דודי צח ואדום דגול מרבבה: ראשו כתם
12 פז קוצותיו תלתלים שחרות כעורב: עיניו כיונים על־
13 אפיקי מים רחצות בחלב ישבות על־מלאת: לחיו
כערוגת הבשם מגדלות מרקחים שפתותיו שושנים

flowing myrrh. [14]His hands *are like* rings of gold filled with jewels; His body an ivory plate overlaid with sapphires. [15]His legs *are like* pillars of marble founded on bases of fine gold; His appearance *is like* Lebanon, excellent as the cedars. [16]His mouth *is* most sweet; and He *is* altogether lovely. This *is* my Beloved, and this *is* my Friend, O daughters of Jerusalem.

14 נטפות מור עבר׃ ידיו גלילי זהב ממלאים בתרשיש
with ;jewels — filled — gold — (as are) rings — His hands — .flowing myrrh — dropping

15 מעיו עשת שן מעלפת ספירים׃ שוקיו עמודי שש
,marble — (as) of pillars — legs His — ;sapphires — overlaid with — ,ivory — a of plate — His body

מיסדים על־אדני־פז מראהו כלבנון בחור כארזים׃
the as ;cedars — choice — (as) ,Lebanon — His appearance — fine ;gold — bases of — on — founded

16 חכו ממתקים וכלו מחמדים זה דודי וזה רעי בנות
daugh- of ters — O — my ,Friend — and this — my ,Beloved — this (is) — ;desirable — all and Him of — most (is) ;sweet — His mouth

ירושלם׃
.Jerusalem

CAP. VI ו

CHAPTER 6

[1]Where has your Beloved gone, most beautiful among women? Where has your Beloved turned? For we seek Him along with you. [2]My Beloved has gone down to His garden, to the terraces of spices, to feed in the gardens, and to gather lilies. [3]I *am* my Beloved's, and my Beloved *is* mine. He feeds among the lilies.

[4]O my love, you *are* as beautiful as Tirzah, as lovely as Jerusalem, awesome as bannered armies. [5]Turn away your eyes from Me, because they have overcome Me. Your hair *is* like a flock of goats that recline from Gilead. [6]Your teeth *are* like a flock of ewes which come up from the washing-place, bearing twins; and barrenness is not among them. [7]Your temples behind your veil *are* like a piece of pomegranate. [8]Sixty of them *are* queens, and eighty concubines, and virgins without number. [9]*But* My dove, My perfect one is one *alone*. She *is* the *only* one to her mother; she is the choice of the one who bore her. The daughters saw her and called her blessed; the queens and the concubines *saw her*, and they praised her.

[10]Who *is* she *who* looks down like the dawn,

1 אנה הלך דודך היפה בנשים אנה פנה דודך ונבקשנו
we for Him seek — your ?Beloved — has faced — Where — among ?women — most beautiful — your ,Beloved — gone has — Where

2 עמך׃ דודי ירד לגנו לערוגות הבשם לרעות בגנים
the in ,gardens — feed to — balsam-spices — the to of beds — His to ,garden — went down — My Beloved — with .you

3 וללקט שושנים׃ אני לדודי ודודי לי הרעה בשושנים׃
the among .lilies — He feeds — to (is) ;me — my and Beloved — my to ,Beloved — I (am) — .lilies — to and gather

4 יפה את רעיתי כתרצה נאוה כירושלם אימה כנדגלות׃
bannered as .armies — awesome — as Jerusalem — comely — as ,Tirzah — My O ,love — you are — Beauti-ful

5 הסבי עיניך מנגדי שהם הרהיבני שערך כעדר העזים
goats — a like of flock — your (is) hair — disturb ;Me — because they — from .Me — your eyes — Turn away

6 שגלשו מן־הגלעד׃ שניך כעדר הרחלים שעלו מן
from — which up come — ewes — like (are) of flock a — Your teeth — .Gilead — from — which reclines

7 הרחצה שכלם מתאימות ושכלה אין בהם׃ כפלח
a Like of piece — among .them — is not — a and one barren — bearing ,twins — all (are) them of — which — the ;washing

8 הרמון רקתך מבעד לצמתך׃ ששים המה מלכות ושמנים
and eighty — ,queens — them are — of Sixty — your .veil — from behind — your (are) temples — pome-granate

9 פילגשים ועלמות אין מספר׃ אחת היא יונתי תמתי
per- fect ;one — My ,dove — she (is) — ,One (only) — .number — without — and virgins — ,concubines

אחת היא לאמה ברה היא ליולדתה ראוה בנות
the daughters — her saw — the to one who bore ;her — she (is) — the choice — her to ;mother — she (is) — the one

10 ויאשרוה מלכות ופילגשים ויהללוה׃ מי־זאת הנשקפה
looks who down — (is) Who ,this — they and .her praised — the and ;concubines — the queens — blessed and ,her

beautiful as the moon, clear as the sun, awesome as bannered *armies*.

[11]I went down to the garden of nut-trees, to see the fruits of the ravine, to see whether the vine flowered *and* the pomegranates budded. [12]I did not know, *but* my soul set me *on* the chariots of My princely people. [13]Return, return, O Shulamite! Return, return, that we may gaze upon you. What will you see in the Shulamite? As it were the dance of two *army* camps.

CHAPTER 7

[1]How beautiful are your steps in sandals, O prince's daughter! The curves of your thighs *are* like jewels, the work of an artisan's hands. [2]Your navel *is like* a round goblet; it lacks not mixed wine. Your belly *is like* a heap of wheat set about with lilies. [3]Your two breasts *are like* two fawns, twins of a gazelle. [4]Your neck *is like* an ivory tower; your eyes *like* the fish-pools in Heshbon by the gate of Bath-rabbim. Your nose *is like* a tower of Lebanon, peering toward the face of Damascus. [5]Your head *is like* Carmel on you, and the hair of your head *like* purple; the King *is* held captive in its tresses. [6]How beautiful and how pleasant are you in delights, O love! [7]Your stature is likened to a palm-tree, and your breasts to clusters of grapes. [8]I said, I will go up *in* the palm-tree; I will take hold of its stalk. And please let your breasts be like clusters of the vine, and the scent of your nose like apples, [9]and the roof of your mouth like the best wine going down smoothly, for my Beloved, flowing

1713 3662 25:35 1249 38:42 3303 7827
כמו־שחר יפה כלבנה ברה כחמה אימה כנדגלות׃
bannered as ?(armies) | awesome | the as ,sun | pure | the as ,moon | fair | the | as ,dawn

6524 7200 5158 3 7200 3381 93 1594
11 אל־גנת אגוז ירדתי לראות באבי הנחל לראות הפרחה
whether blossomed | see to | the ,ravine | the of fruits | see to | went I ,down | nut trees | the To of garden

4818 7760 5315 3045 3808 7416 5132 1612
12 הגפן הנצו הרמנים׃ לא ידעתי נפשי שמתני מרכבות
the (on) of chariots | set me | (but) soul my | ,knew I | Not | the pomegranate | (and) budded | the vine

5081 5971
עמי נדיב׃
.princely | My people

CAP. VII ז

CHAPTER 7

2372 2372 7725 7725 7759 7725 7725
1 שובי שובי השולמית שובי שובי ונחזה־בך מה־תחזו
will see you | What | upon you | we that gaze may | ,return !you | ,Return | O !Shulamite | ,return | ,Return

5275 6471 3303 4264 4246 7759
2 בשולמית כמחלת המחנים׃ מה־יפו פעמיך בנעלים
,sandals in | your footsteps | beautiful How are | (army) two camps | the As of dance | the in ?Shulamite

542 3027 4639 2481 3644 3409 2542 5081 1323
בת־נדיב חמוקי ירכיך כמו חלאים מעשה ידי אמן׃
art- an ;isan's | hands | the of work | ,jewels | (are) like | your thighs | the of curves | ;prince's | O daughter

2406 6194 990 4197 2637 408 5469 101 8326
3 שררך אגן הסהר אל־יחסר המזג בטנך ערמת חטים
wheat | a (as) of heap | your belly | mixed ;wine | lacks it | not | ,round | a (as) goblet | your navel

6646 8380 6082 8147 7699 8147 7799 5473
4 סוגה בשושנים׃ שני שדיך כשני עפרים תאמי צביה׃
;gazelle a | twins of | ,fawns | like two | your breasts | two | with ;lilies | hedged about

1337 8179 2809 1395 5869 8127 4026 6677
5 צוארך כמגדל השן עיניך ברכות בחשבון על־שער בת־
Bath- | the of gate | by | in ,Heshbon | the (as) fish-pools | your eyes | ;ivory | a (as) of tower | your neck

7218 1834 6440 6822 3844 4026 639 7227
6 רבים אפך כמגדל הלבנון צופה פני דמשק׃ ראשך
your head | ;Damascus | the of face | peering toward | ,Lebanon | a (as) of tower | your nose | ;rabbim

7298 631 4428 713 7218 1803 3759
עליך ככרמל ודלת ראשך כארגמן מלך אסור ברהטים׃
(its) .tresses | in | held (is) captive | the King | like ;purple | your head | the and of hair | (as) ,Carmel | on you

6967 2088 8588 160 5276 3303
7 8 מה־יפית ומה־נעמת אהבה בתענוגים׃ זאת קומתך
your stature | This | !delights in | ,love O | pleasant ,you are | and how | How beautiful

8558 5927 559 811 7699 8558 1819
9 דמתה לתמר ושדיך לאשכלות׃ אמרתי אעלה בתמר
the (in) ;tree palm | go will I up | ,said I | clusters .grapes of | to | your and breasts | palm a to ,tree | liken- is ed

7381 5577 1612 811 7699 4994 1961 5577 270
אחזה בסנסניו ויהיו־נא שדיך כאשכלות הגפן וריח
the and of scent | the ,vine | like of clusters | your breasts | please and be let | its of ;stalk | will I hold take

4339 1730 1980 2896 3196 2441 8598 639
10 אפך כתפוחים׃ וחכך כיין הטוב הולך לדודי למישרים
,uprightly | my for Beloved | going down | the best | like wine | your and palate | like ;apples | your nose

softly *over* the lips of sleeping ones.
10 I *am* my Beloved's, and His desire *is* toward me. 11 Come, my Beloved, let us go forth into the field; let us stay in the villages. 12 Let us rise up early to the vineyards; let us see if the vine flowers *and* the blossom opens, *and* the pomegranates bud forth. There I will give my loves to You. 13 The love-apples give a scent, and over our doors *are* all excellent *fruits*; new, also old, I have laid up for You, my Beloved.

CHAPTER 8

1 Who can give You to me, as *my* brother, who sucked the breasts of my mother? *When* I find You outside, I would kiss You. They also would not despise me. 2 I would lead You; I would bring You into my mother's house; You would teach me; I would cause You to drink the spiced wine from the juice of my pomegranate. 3 His left hand *would be* under my head, and His right *hand* embracing me. 4 I adjure you, O daughters of Jerusalem; why should you stir up or why should you awaken *my* love until it pleases? 5 Who *is* this that comes up from the wilderness, leaning on her Beloved? I awakened you under the apple-tree; there your mother travailed with you; there she travailed; she bore you.
6 Set me as a seal on Your heart, as a seal on Your arm. For love *is* strong as death; jealousy *is* cruel as Sheol; its flames *are* flames of fire, a flame of Jehovah. 7 Many waters cannot quench love, nor will the rivers overflow it. If a man would give all the wealth of his house for love, they surely would despise him.

1730 32 12 8669 :1730 3463 8193 1680
11 12 דּוֹבֵב שִׂפְתֵי יְשֵׁנִים׃ אֲנִי לְדוֹדִי וְעָלַי תְּשׁוּקָתוֹ׃ לְכָה דוֹדִי
my ,Come desire His and my (am) I sleeping (over) flowing
,Beloved .(is) me toward ,Beloved's .ones lips softly

7200 37:54 7925 3723 3885 77:04 3318
13 נֵצֵא הַשָּׂדֶה נָלִינָה בַּכְּפָרִים׃ נַשְׁכִּימָה לַכְּרָמִים נִרְאֶה
us let the to rise us Let the in us let the to us let
see ;vineyards early up .villages lodge ;field out go

5414 8033 7416 5132 :5563 6605 16 12 6524 518
אִם־פָּרְחָה הַגֶּפֶן פִּתַּח הַסְּמָדַר הֵנֵצוּ הָרִמּוֹנִים שָׁם אֶתֵּן
will I there pome- the (and) the (whether) the flowers if
give ;granates forth bud ,blossom opens ,vine

40:22 36:05 6607 5921 7381 1736 1730
14 אֶת־דֹּדַי לָךְ׃ הַדּוּדָאִים נָתְנוּ־רֵיחַ וְעַל־פְּתָחֵינוּ כָּל־מְגָדִים
excellent (are) our and a give love- The to my
;fruits all doors over ,scent apples .You loves

6845 1730 3465 2319
חֲדָשִׁים גַּם־יְשָׁנִים דּוֹדִי צָפַנְתִּי לָךְ׃
for have I my ,old also ,new
.You up laid ,Beloved

CAP. VIII ח

CHAPTER 8

:5401 2351 4672 517 7699 3243 251 5414 4310
1 מִי יִתֶּנְךָ כְּאָח לִי יוֹנֵק שְׁדֵי אִמִּי אֶמְצָאֲךָ בַחוּץ אֶשָּׁקְךָ
would I ,outside I (If) my the sucking to as can Who
;You kiss You find !mother of breasts ,me brother You give

3925 517 1004 935 5090 936 3808 1571
2 גַּם לֹא־יָבוּזוּ לִי׃ אֶנְהָגֲךָ אֲבִיאֲךָ אֶל־בֵּית אִמִּי תְּלַמְּדֵנִי
would You my house to would I would I .me they not ,also
;me instruct ;mother's You bring ,You lead despise would

:7218 8478 8040 74:16 6071 7544 3196 8248
3 אַשְׁקְךָ מִיַּיִן הָרֶקַח מֵעֲסִיס רִמֹּנִי׃ שְׂמֹאלוֹ תַּחַת רֹאשִׁי
my (be would) left His pome- my the from the wine make would I
,head under hand .granate of juice spiced drink You

5782 4100 3389 1323 7650 2263 3225
4 וִימִינוֹ תְּחַבְּקֵנִי׃ הִשְׁבַּעְתִּי אֶתְכֶם בְּנוֹת יְרוּשָׁלִָם מַה־תָּעִירוּ
you why ,Jerusalem O ,you charge I embraces His and
up stir should of daughters .me right

5 9,27 4310 2654 5704 160 5782 4100
5 וּמַה־תְּעֹרְרוּ אֶת־הָאַהֲבָה עַד שֶׁתֶּחְפָּץ׃ מִי זֹאת עֹלָה
coming (is) Who .pleases it until love (my) you should or
up this awaken why

:5782 85 98 8478 1730 59,21 7514 4057
מִן־הַמִּדְבָּר מִתְרַפֶּקֶת עַל־דּוֹדָהּ תַּחַת הַתַּפּוּחַ עוֹרַרְתִּיךָ
awoke I the Under her on leaning the from
;you apple-tree ?Beloved ,wilderness

2368 77 60 3205 2754 8033 517: 2354 8033
6 שָׁמָּה חִבְּלַתְךָ אִמֶּךָ שָׁמָּה חִבְּלָה יְלָדַתְךָ׃ שִׂימֵנִי כַחוֹתָם
a as me Set she she there your travailed there
seal .you bore ,travailed ;mother you with

7181 :160 41 94 5794 :2220 5921 2368 3820
עַל־לִבֶּךָ כַּחוֹתָם עַל־זְרוֹעֶךָ כִּי־עַזָּה כַמָּוֶת אַהֲבָה קָשָׁה
(is) ,love as (is) for Your upon a as Your upon
cruel death strong ;arm seal ,heart

7227 4325 7957 784 75,65 7563 7068 7585
7 כִשְׁאוֹל קִנְאָה רְשָׁפֶיהָ רִשְׁפֵּי אֵשׁ שַׁלְהֶבֶתְיָה׃ מַיִם רַבִּים
Many waters of flame a ,fire (are) flames its ;jealousy as
.Jehovah of flames Sheol

518 7857 38 08 5104 :160 3518 3201 38 08
לֹא יוּכְלוּ לְכַבּוֹת אֶת־הָאַהֲבָה וּנְהָרוֹת לֹא יִשְׁטְפוּהָ אִם־
if over- will I not the and ,love quench to are not
;it flow rivers able

269 936 936 160 1004 1952 3605 37 6 5414
8 יִתֵּן אִישׁ אֶת־כָּל־הוֹן בֵּיתוֹ בָּאַהֲבָה בּוֹז יָבוּזוּ לוֹ׃ אָחוֹת
sister A .him they de- ,love for his the all a would
despise spising house of wealth man give

8We have a little sister, and she has no breasts. What shall we do for our sister in the day *in* which she shall be spoken for? 9If she *is* a wall, we will build a turret of silver on her. And if she *is* a door, we will enclose her *with* boards of cedar. 10I *was* a wall, and my breasts like towers; then I was in His eyes as one finding peace.

11Solomon had a vineyard in Baal-hamon. He let the vineyard out to keepers; for its fruit everyone was to bring a thousand of silver. 12My vineyard which *is* mine *is* before me; the thousand *is* for you, O Solomon, and two hundred for the keepers of its fruit. 13You who dwell in the gardens, the companions *are* listening to your voice; cause me to hear *it*. 14Hurry, my Beloved, and be like a gazelle, or a young deer, the stag, on the mountains of spices.

3117		:269		6213 4100		369	7699	66:96	
לָ֖נוּ קְטַנָּ֔ה וְשָׁדַ֖יִם אֵ֣ין לָ֑הּ מַֽה־נַּעֲשֶׂה֙ לַאֲחֹתֵ֔נוּ בַּיּ֖וֹם									
the in	our for	shall	what	to	are	and	,little	to (is)	
day	sister	do we	;her	not	breasts			us	

9 | 3701 | 2918 | 59;21 | 1129 | | 2346 | 518 | 1696 | |

אִם־חוֹמָ֣ה הִ֔יא נִבְנֶ֥ה עָלֶ֖יהָ טִ֣ירַת כָּ֑סֶף

;silver　a　her on　will we she　wall a　If　for he that
　　　of turret　on　build　(is)　　　?her spoken has

10 | 7699 | 23:46 | 730 | 38-9;1 | 59 ;21 | 6696 | 1817 |

וְאִם־דֶּ֣לֶת הִ֔יא נָצ֥וּר עָלֶ֖יהָ ל֣וּחַ אָ֑רֶז: אֲנִ֣י חוֹמָ֔ה וְשָׁדַ֖י

and ,wall a (was) I .cedar boards upon will we she a and
breasts my　of　her　enclose　(is)　door　if

11 | 1961 | 3754 | 7965 | 4672 | 5869 | 1961 | 227 | 4026 |

כַּמִּגְדָּל֑וֹת אָ֧ז הָיִ֛יתִי בְעֵינָ֖יו כְּמוֹצְאֵ֥ת שָׁלֽוֹם: כֶּ֣רֶם הָיָ֤ה

was A .peace one as His in I then ;towers like
vineyard finding eyes became

| 935 | 3.76 | 5201 | 3754 | 5414 | 1174 | 1174 | 8010 |

לִשְׁלֹמֹה֙ בְּבַ֣עַל הָמ֔וֹן נָתַ֥ן אֶת־הַכֶּ֖רֶם לַנֹּטְרִ֑ים אִ֛ישׁ יָבִ֥א

to was (each)· to the gave he ;hamor Baal- at to
bring man ;keepers vineyard Solomon

12 | 8010;1 | 505 | 6440 | 3754 | 3701 | 505 | 6529 |

בְּפִרְי֖וֹ אֶ֥לֶף כָּֽסֶף: כַּרְמִ֥י שֶׁלִּ֖י לְפָנָ֑י הָאֶ֤לֶף לְךָ֙ שְׁלֹמֹ֔ה

O for (is) the be- (is) which My .silver a its for
,Solomon ,you thousand ;me fore ,me to (is) vineyard of thousand fruit

13 | 2272 | 15-88 | 3427 | 6529 | 5201 | 3967 |

וּמָאתַ֖יִם לַנֹּטְרִ֣ים אֶת־פִּרְי֑וֹ הַיּוֹשֶׁ֣בֶת בַּגַּנִּ֗ים חֲבֵרִ֛ים

the the in who You .fruit its the for two and
companions ,gardens dwell of keepers hundred

14 | 6643 | 1819 | 1730 | 1272 | 8085 | 69 ;63 | 7181 |

מַקְשִׁיבִ֥ים לְקוֹלֵ֖ךְ הַשְׁמִיעִֽנִי: בְּרַ֣ח ׀ דּוֹדִ֗י וּֽדְמֵה־לְךָ֤ לִצְבִי֙

a be and my ,Flee to me cause your for listening (are)
gazelle like ,Beloved (it) hear ;voice

| 1314 | 2022 | 5921 | :354 | 6082 | 176 |

א֚וֹ לְעֹ֣פֶר הָֽאַיָּלִ֔ים עַ֖ל הָ֥רֵי בְשָׂמִֽים:

balsam- the on the young a or
spices of mountains stag ,deer

ישעיה

LIBER JESAIAE

(THE) BOOK OF ISAIAH

CAPUT. I א

CHAPTER 1

A LITERAL TRANSLATION OF THE BIBLE

THE BOOK OF ISAIAH

CHAPTER 1

[1]The vision of Isaiah the son of Amoz, which he saw concerning Judah and Jerusalem in the days of Uzziah, Jotham, Ahaz *and* Hezekiah, kings of Judah.
[2]Hear, O heavens, and listen, O earth! For Jehovah has spoken: I have nursed and brought up sons, but they have rebelled against Me. [3]The ox knows his owner, and the ass his master's manger, *but* Israel does not know; My people have not understood.
[4]Woe, sinful nation, a people heavy *with* iniquity, a seed of evildoers, sons who corrupt! They have forsaken Jehovah; they have scorned the Holy One of Israel. They *are* estranged backward.

[5]Why will you be beaten any more? Will you continue the revolt? The whole head is sick, and the whole heart is faint. [6]From the sole of the foot to the head, no soundness is in it; *only* a wound and a stripe and a fresh blow; they have not been closed, nor bound up; nor was it softened with oil. [7]Your land *is* a desolation; your cities burned with fire. Foreigners devour your land before you; and *it is* desolation, as overthrown by foreigners.
[8]And the daughter of Zion is left a booth in a vineyard, like a hut in a cucumber field, like a besieged city. [9]Except Jehovah of hosts had left a survivor for us, a few, we would be as Sodom; we would become as Gomorrah.

3389 3063 23:72 834 531 1121 3470 2377

1 חֲזוֹן יְשַׁעְיָהוּ בֶן־אָמוֹץ אֲשֶׁר חָזָה עַל־יְהוּדָה וִירוּשָׁלָ‍ִם

and Jerusalem | Judah | concerning | saw he | which | ,Amoz | the of son | Isaiah | The of vision

806 4 8034 3063 44 28 3169 271 3147 5818 31 17

2 בִּימֵי עֻזִּיָּהוּ יוֹתָם אָחָז יְחִזְקִיָּהוּ מַלְכֵי יְהוּדָה׃ שִׁמְעוּ שָׁמַיִם

O ,heavens | ,Hear | .Judah | kings of | (and) ,Hezekiah | ,Ahaz | ,Jotham | ,Uzziah | the in of days

7311 14 30 1121 1696 3068 776 238

וְהַאֲזִינִי אֶרֶץ כִּי יְהוָה דִּבֵּר בָּנִים גִּדַּלְתִּי וְרוֹמַמְתִּי וְהֵם

but they | brought and ,up | have I reared | sons | has :spoken | Jehovah | For | O !earth | give and ,ear

3478 1167 18 2543 7069 7794 3045 4784

3 פָּשְׁעוּ בִי׃ יָדַע שׁוֹר קֹנֵהוּ וַחֲמוֹר אֵבוּס בְּעָלָיו יִשְׂרָאֵל

(but) Israel | his ,master's | manger | the and ass | his owner | The ox | knows | against .Me | have rebelled

57:71 3515 5971 2398 1471 1945 995 38 08 5971 30:45 38 08

4 לֹא יָדַע עַמִּי לֹא הִתְבּוֹנָן׃ הוֹי ׀ גּוֹי חֹטֵא עַם כֶּבֶד עָוֺן

iniquity | heavy (with) | a people | ,sinful nation | Woe | have .understood | not | My people | does ;know | not

853 5006 3063/853 5800 7843 1121 74 89 2233

זֶרַע מְרֵעִים בָּנִים מַשְׁחִיתִים עָזְבוּ אֶת־יְהוָה נִאֲצוּ אֶת־

have they spurned | ,Jehovah | have They forsaken | who !corrupt | sons | evil ,doers | seed a of

5627 3254 5704 5221 4100 268 2114 3478 6918

5 קְדוֹשׁ יִשְׂרָאֵל נָזֹרוּ אָחוֹר׃ עַל־מֶה תֻכּוּ עוֹד תּוֹסִיפוּ סָרָה

the ?revolt | you Will continue | any ?more | you will be beaten | Why | back- .ward | they away turned | ,Israel | Holy the of One

7218 7272 3709 1742 3824 2483 7218 3605

6 כָּל־רֹאשׁ לָחֳלִי וְכָל־לֵבָב דַּוָּי׃ מִכַּף־רֶגֶל וְעַד־רֹאשׁ

the head | to | the foot | From of sole | .faint is | heart | and the all | ,sick is | head | All the

38 08 2115 2961 4347 2250 6482 4974 369

אֵין־בּוֹ מְתֹם פֶּצַע וְחַבּוּרָה וּמַכָּה טְרִיָּה לֹא־זֹרוּ וְלֹא

nor | have they not ,closed been | ;fresh a blow and | and stripe a | (only) wound a | sound- ;ness | in it | not is

8313 5892 8077 776 8081 7401 38 08 2280

7 חֻבָּשׁוּ וְלֹא רֻכְּכָה בַּשָּׁמֶן׃ אַרְצְכֶם שְׁמָמָה עָרֵיכֶם שְׂרֻפוֹת

burned with | your cities | a (is) ;desolation | Your land | with .oil | it was softened | nor | bound ,up

8077 398 2114 5048 127 784

אֵשׁ אַדְמַתְכֶם לְנֶגְדְּכֶם זָרִים אֹכְלִים אֹתָהּ וּשְׁמָמָה

(is it) and desolation | it | devour | foreigners | before you | your land | ;fire

4412 3754 5521 6726 1323 3498 2114 4114

8 כְּמַהְפֵּכַת זָרִים׃ וְנוֹתְרָה בַת־צִיּוֹן כְּסֻכָּה בְכָרֶם כִּמְלוּנָה

a like hut | a in ,vineyard | a like booth | Zion the of daughter | left is And | foreigners | over- as by thrown

3498 6635 3068 3884 5341 5892 4750

9 בְמִקְשָׁה כְּעִיר נְצוּרָה׃ לוּלֵי יְהוָה צְבָאוֹת הוֹתִיר לָנוּ

for us | had left | hosts | Jehovah of | Except | .besieged | a like city | a in ,garden

8085 1819 6017 1961 5967 4592 8300

10 שָׂרִיד כִּמְעָט כִּסְדֹם הָיִינוּ לַעֲמֹרָה דָּמִינוּ׃ שִׁמְעוּ

Hear | would we become | as Gomorrah | we ;be would | as Sodom | ,few a | a ;survivor

[10]Hear the word of Jehovah, rulers of Sodom. Listen to the law of our God, people of Gomorrah. [11]What *good* to Me *are* your many sacrifices, says Jehovah? I am full of burnt offerings of rams, and the fat of fattened cattle, and the blood of bulls; nor do I delight in the blood of lambs and he-goats. [12]When you come to see My face, who has required this at your hand, to trample My courts? [13]Do not add to bringing vain sacrifice; it *is* hateful incense to Me. I cannot endure the new moon and sabbath, the calling of meeting, and the evil assembly. [14]My soul hates your new moons and your appointed feasts. They are a burden to Me. I am weary of bearing them. [15]And when you spread out your hands, I will hide My eyes from you. Yea, when you multiply prayer, I will not hear. Your hands are full of blood. [16]Wash yourselves, purify yourselves. Put away the evil of your doings from My sight; stop doing evil. [17]Learn to do good; seek justice; reprove the oppressor; judge the orphan; strive for the widow.

[18]Come now and let us reason together, says Jehovah: Though your sins are as scarlet, they shall be white as snow; though they are red as the crimson, they shall be like wool. [19]If you are willing and hear, you shall eat the good of the land. [20]But if you refuse and rebel, you shall be devoured *with* the sword; for the mouth of Jehovah has spoken.

[21]O how the faithful city has become a harlot! *She was* full of justice; righteousness lodged in it — but now, murderers! [22]Your silver has become dross; your wine is diluted

דְּבַר־יְהוָה קְצִינֵי סְדֹם הַאֲזִינוּ תּוֹרַת אֱלֹהֵינוּ עַם עֲמֹרָה׃
!Gomorrah O ,God our the listen ;Sodom O ,Jehovah the
of people of law to of rulers of word

11 לָמָּה־לִּי רֹב־זִבְחֵיכֶם יֹאמַר יְהוָה שָׂבַעְתִּי עֹלוֹת אֵילִים
,rams burnt am I ?Jehovah says your many to What
of offerings of full ,sacrifices Me (use)

וְחֵלֶב מְרִיאִים וְדַם פָּרִים וּכְבָשִׂים וְעַתּוּדִים לֹא חָפָצְתִּי׃
I do not and and ;bulls the and fattened the and
.in delight he-goats lambs of blood ,cattle of fat

12 כִּי תָבֹאוּ לֵרָאוֹת פָּנָי מִי־בִקֵּשׁ זֹאת מִיֶּדְכֶם רְמֹס חֲצֵרָי׃
My to your from this has who My see to you When
?courts trample ,hand required ,face come

13 לֹא תוֹסִיפוּ הָבִיא מִנְחַת־שָׁוְא קְטֹרֶת תּוֹעֵבָה הִיא לִי
to it abomination incense ;vain sacrifice to do Not
;Me (is) bringing add

14 חֹדֶשׁ וְשַׁבָּת קְרֹא מִקְרָא לֹא־אוּכַל אָוֶן וַעֲצָרָה׃ חָדְשֵׁיכֶם
new Your the and ,evil can I not ;meeting the and new the
moons .assembly endure to going ,sabbath moon

וּמוֹעֲדֵיכֶם שָׂנְאָה נַפְשִׁי הָיוּ עָלַי לָטֹרַח נִלְאֵיתִי נְשֹׂא׃
bearing am I a upon They My hates your and
.(them) of tired ;burden Me are .soul feasts appointed

15 וּבְפָרִשְׂכֶם כַּפֵּיכֶם אַעְלִים עֵינַי מִכֶּם גַּם כִּי־תַרְבּוּ תְפִלָּה
,prayer you when also from my will I your you when So
multiply ;you eyes hide hands out spread

16 אֵינֶנִּי שֹׁמֵעַ יְדֵיכֶם דָּמִים מָלֵאוּ׃ רַחֲצוּ הִזַּכּוּ הָסִירוּ רֹעַ
the remove purify wash full are blood Your will I
of evil ;yourselves ,yourselves of palms .hear not

17 מַעַלְלֵיכֶם מִנֶּגֶד עֵינָי חִדְלוּ הָרֵעַ׃ לִמְדוּ הֵיטֵב דִּרְשׁוּ
seek do to Learn doing cease My from your
;good .evil ;eyes before doings

מִשְׁפָּט אַשְּׁרוּ חָמוֹץ שִׁפְטוּ יָתוֹם רִיבוּ אַלְמָנָה׃
the contend the judge the reprove ,justice
.widow for ,orphan ;oppressor

18 לְכוּ־נָא וְנִוָּכְחָה יֹאמַר יְהוָה אִם־יִהְיוּ חֲטָאֵיכֶם כַּשָּׁנִים
,scarlet as sins your are though ;Jehovah says us let and ,now Come
,right be

19 כַּשֶּׁלֶג יַלְבִּינוּ אִם־יַאְדִּימוּ כַתּוֹלָע כַּצֶּמֶר יִהְיוּ׃ אִם־תֹּאבוּ
are you If they like the as they though shall they as
willing !be shall wool ,crimson red are ;white be snow

20 וּשְׁמַעְתֶּם טוּב הָאָרֶץ תֹּאכֵלוּ׃ וְאִם־תְּמָאֲנוּ וּמְרִיתֶם
,rebel and you if But shall you the the and
refuse .eat land of good ,hear

21 חֶרֶב תְּאֻכְּלוּ כִּי פִּי יְהוָה דִּבֵּר׃ אֵיכָה הָיְתָה
has How has Jehovah the for be shall you the (by)
become .spoken of mouth devoured sword

לְזוֹנָה קִרְיָה נֶאֱמָנָה מְלֵאֲתִי מִשְׁפָּט צֶדֶק יָלִין בָּהּ וְעַתָּה
but in lodged righ- ;justice (was She) !faithful the harlot a
now —her teousness of full city

22 מְרַצְּחִים׃ כַּסְפֵּךְ הָיָה לְסִיגִים סָבְאֵךְ מָהוּל בַּמָּיִם׃
with is your ;dross has Your !murderers
.water diluted liquor become silver

with water. ²³Your princes *are* rebellious and companions of thieves. Everyone loves a bribe, and is pursuing rewards. They do not judge the orphan, nor does the cause of the widow come to them, ²⁴and says the Lord, Jehovah of hosts, the mighty One of Israel, Alas! I will be eased of My foes, and avenge Myself of My enemies. ²⁵And I will return My hand on you, and refine your dross, as *with* lye, and take away all your alloy. ²⁶And I will return your judges as at the first; and your advisors, as at the beginning; then you shall be called the city of righteousness, a faithful town. ²⁷Zion shall be redeemed with justice, and her returning ones with righteousness. ²⁸And the ruin of the transgressors and of the sinners *shall be* together. And those who forsake Jehovah shall be consumed. ²⁹For they shall be ashamed of the trees which you lusted after; and you shall be ashamed of the gardens that you have chosen. ³⁰For you shall be like a tree whose leaf fades, and like a garden that has no water in it. ³¹And the strong shall be for tow, and his work for a spark; and they shall burn both together; and no one shall quench *them*.

23
שָׂרַ֣יִךְ סוֹרְרִ֗ים וְחַבְרֵי֙ גַּנָּבִ֔ים כֻּלּוֹ֙ אֹהֵ֣ב שֹׁ֔חַד וְרֹדֵ֖ף
Your rulers | are rebellious | and companions | of thieves; | every one | loves | a bribe, | com- | and is | panions | seeking

שַׁלְמֹנִ֑ים יָת֤וֹם לֹ֣א יִשְׁפֹּ֔טוּ וְרִ֥יב אַלְמָנָ֖ה לֹֽא־יָב֥וֹא אֲלֵיהֶֽם׃
gifts; | the | orphan | do they | not | judge, | and the | of cause | widow | does | not | come | to them.

24 לָכֵ֗ן נְאֻ֤ם הָֽאָדוֹן֙ יְהוָ֣ה צְבָא֔וֹת אֲבִ֖יר יִשְׂרָאֵ֑ל ה֣וֹי אֶנָּחֵ֣ם
Therefore | states | the Lord, | Jehovah | of hosts, | the One Mighty | of Israel, | Alas, | I will eased be

25 מִצָּרַ֔י וְאִנָּקְמָ֖ה מֵאוֹיְבָֽי׃ וְאָשִׁ֤יבָה יָדִי֙ עָלַ֔יִךְ וְאֶצְרֹ֥ף כַּבֹּ֖ר
of My | foes, | and avenge | Myself | My of | enemies. | And I will | my | hand | upon | you, | and | refine | as lye | return | (with)

26 סִיגָ֑יִךְ וְאָסִ֖ירָה כָּל־בְּדִילָֽיִךְ׃ וְאָשִׁ֤יבָה שֹׁפְטַ֙יִךְ֙ כְּבָרִ֣אשֹׁנָ֔ה
your | dross, | and | turn | all | your alloy. | And I | will | your judges, | as at | first the | away

וְיֹעֲצַ֖יִךְ כְּבַתְּחִלָּ֑ה אַחֲרֵי־כֵ֗ן יִקָּ֤רֵא לָךְ֙ עִ֣יר הַצֶּ֔דֶק קִרְיָ֖ה
your | advisors, | beginning; | as at the | afterwards | shall it | be | to | you | city a | of | righteous- | town a | ness,

27 **28** נֶאֱמָנָֽה׃ צִיּ֖וֹן בְּמִשְׁפָּ֣ט תִּפָּדֶ֑ה וְשָׁבֶ֖יהָ בִּצְדָקָֽה׃ וְשֶׁ֧בֶר
faithful. | Zion | with | justice | redeemed | be shall | and returnees | her | with | righteousness. | And crushing of

29 פֹּשְׁעִ֛ים וְחַטָּאִ֖ים יַחְדָּ֑ו וְעֹזְבֵ֥י יְהוָ֖ה יִכְל֑וּ כִּ֣י יֵבֹ֗שׁוּ
trans- | gressors | and | sinners | together, | and those who | forsake | Jehovah | shall be | consumed. | For | shall they | ashamed be

מֵאֵילִים֙ אֲשֶׁ֣ר חֲמַדְתֶּ֔ם וְתַחְפְּר֖וּ מֵהַגַּנּ֥וֹת אֲשֶׁ֥ר בְּחַרְתֶּֽם׃
the of | trees | which | you | desired | and | ashamed be | the of | gardens | that | you | have | chosen.

30 כִּ֣י תִהְי֔וּ כְּאֵלָ֖ה נֹבֶ֣לֶת עָלֶ֑הָ וּֽכְגַנָּ֔ה אֲשֶׁר־מַ֖יִם אֵ֥ין לָֽהּ׃
For | be shall | you | a like | tree | whose | fades | leaf, | and like | garden a | which | (in) | water | not | for | is | it.

31 וְהָיָ֤ה הֶחָסֹן֙ לִנְעֹ֔רֶת וּפֹעֲל֖וֹ לְנִיצ֑וֹץ וּבָעֲר֧וּ שְׁנֵיהֶ֛ם יַחְדָּ֖ו
And | be will | the | strong | for tow, | and | his | work | for a | spark; | and they | both | together,

וְאֵ֥ין מְכַבֶּֽה׃
and | none | quench | (them) shall.

CHAPTER 2

¹The word that Isaiah the son of Amoz saw concerning Judah and Jerusalem: ²And it shall be in the last days, the mountain of the house of Jehovah shall be established in the top of the mountains, and shall be exalted above the hills; and all nations shall flow into it. ³And many people shall go and say, Come and let us go up to the mount of Jehovah, to the house of the God of

1 הַדָּבָר֙ אֲשֶׁ֣ר חָזָ֔ה יְשַׁעְיָ֖הוּ בֶּן־אָמ֑וֹץ עַל־יְהוּדָ֖ה וִירוּשָׁלִָֽם׃
The | word | that | saw | Isaiah, | son | of | Amoz, | con- | cerning | Judah | and | Jerusalem.

2 וְהָיָ֣ה ׀ בְּאַחֲרִ֣ית הַיָּמִ֗ים נָכ֨וֹן יִֽהְיֶ֜ה הַ֤ר בֵּית־יְהוָה֙ בְּרֹ֣אשׁ
And | be will | it | in | the | last | days the | estab- | lished | be shall | mountain | of house | Jehovah's | in | top of

הֶהָרִ֔ים וְנִשָּׂ֖א מִגְּבָע֑וֹת וְנָהֲר֥וּ אֵלָ֖יו כָּל־הַגּוֹיִֽם׃
the | mountains, | and | exalted | the above | hills; | and | flow | it to | all | nations. | And will | go

3 וְהָֽלְכ֞וּ עַמִּ֣ים רַבִּ֗ים וְאָמְרוּ֙ לְכ֣וּ ׀ וְנַעֲלֶ֣ה אֶל־הַר־יְהוָ֗ה אֶל־בֵּ֚ית
many | peoples | and | say, | Come, | and let | us go | up | to | the | mount | of | Jehovah, | to | the house

Jacob. And He will teach from His ways, and we will walk in His paths. For out of Zion the Law will go forth, and the word of Jehovah from Jerusalem. 4And He shall judge among the nations and shall rebuke many people. And they shall beat their swords into plowshares, and their spears into pruning-hooks. Nation shall not lift up sword against nation, nor shall they learn war any more. 5O house of Jacob, come and let us walk in the light of Jehovah. 6For You have forsaken Your people, the house of Jacob, because they are filled from the east, and *are* fortune-tellers like the Philistines. And they clap *hands* with children of foreigners. 7And his land is filled *with* silver and gold. There is no end of his treasures. And his land is full of horses; his chariots also do not have an end. 8And his land is full of idols; they worship the work of their own hands, that which their own fingers have made. 9And man bowed down; and man was humbled, but You do not lift them up. 10Enter into the rock and hide in the dust from fear of Jehovah, and from the glory of His majesty. 11The lofty eyes of man shall be humbled, and the pride of men shall be bowed down; but Jehovah, He alone, will be exalted in that day. 12For the day of Jehovah of hosts *shall be* on all the proud and lofty ones, and on all that is lifted up; and it will be abased; 13and against all Lebanon's cedars, high and lifted up; and against all the oaks of Bashan; 14and against all the high mountains; and against all the lifted up hills; 15and against every tall tower; and against every fortified wall; 16and against all the ships of Tarshish;

6726 734 3212 1870 3 384 3290 430
אֱלֹהֵי יַעֲקֹב וְיֹרֵנוּ מִדְּרָכָיו וְנֵלְכָה בְּאֹרְחֹתָיו כִּי מִצִּיּוֹן
of out Zion | for | His in ,paths | we and walk will | His from ,ways | He and teach will | ,Jacob | the of God

4
1471 996 8199 3389 3068 1697 8451 3318
תֵּצֵא תוֹרָה וּדְבַר־יְהוָה מִירוּשָׁלָםִ׃ וְשָׁפַט בֵּין הַגּוֹיִם
the ,nations | among | He And judge shall | from .Jerusalem | Jehovah's and word | ,law the | go will forth

2595 855 2719 3807 7227 5971 3198
וְהוֹכִיחַ לְעַמִּים רַבִּים וְכִתְּתוּ חַרְבוֹתָם לְאִתִּים וַחֲנִיתוֹתֵיהֶם
their and spears | into ,plowshares | their swords | they And beat shall | .many | peoples | shall and rebuke

5750 3925 3808 2719 1471 1471 5375 3808 4211
לְמַזְמֵרוֹת לֹא־יִשָּׂא גוֹי אֶל־גּוֹי חֶרֶב וְלֹא־יִלְמְדוּ עוֹד
any more | they shall learn | nor | ,sword | nation against nation | lift shall not up | pruning into ;knives

5
6
3068 216 3212 3212 3290 1004 4421
מִלְחָמָה׃ בֵּית יַעֲקֹב לְכוּ וְנֵלְכָה בְּאוֹר יְהוָה׃ כִּי
For .Jehovah | the in of light | let and walk us | Come | ,Jacob | O of house | .war

6430 6049 6924 4390 3290 1004 5971 5203
נָטַשְׁתָּה עַמְּךָ בֵּית יַעֲקֹב כִּי מָלְאוּ מִקֶּדֶם וְעֹנְנִים כַּפְּלִשְׁתִּים
the like ;Philistines | (are) and soothsayers | from ,east the | are they filled | for | ,Jacob | the of house | Your ,people | have You forsaken

7
369 2091 3701 776 4390 5606 5237 3206
וּבְיַלְדֵי נָכְרִים יַשְׂפִּיקוּ׃ וַתִּמָּלֵא אַרְצוֹ כֶּסֶף וְזָהָב וְאֵין
not and is | and ,gold | (with) silver | his land | is And filled | clap they .(hands their) | foreigners | with and of children

4818 7097 369 5483 776 4390 214 7097
קֵצֶה לְאֹצְרֹתָיו וַתִּמָּלֵא אַרְצוֹ סוּסִים וְאֵין קֵצֶה לְמַרְכְּבֹתָיו׃
his to .chariots | an end | and is not | (with) ,horses | his land | is and filled | his to ,treasures | an end

8
6213 834 7812 3027 4639 457 776 4390
וַתִּמָּלֵא אַרְצוֹ אֱלִילִים לְמַעֲשֵׂה יָדָיו יִשְׁתַּחֲווּ לַאֲשֶׁר עָשׂוּ
have made | that which | he ,worships | his hands | work the of | (with) ;idols | his land | is And filled

9
5375 376 8213 120 7817 676
אֶצְבְּעֹתָיו׃ וַיִּשַּׁח אָדָם וַיִּשְׁפַּל־אִישׁ וְאַל־תִּשָּׂא לָהֶם׃
.them | You up lift | but not | ,man | was and humbled | ,man | was and down bowed | own his .fingers

10
1347 1926 3068 6343 6440 6083 2934 6697 935
בּוֹא בַצּוּר וְהִטָּמֵן בֶּעָפָר מִפְּנֵי פַּחַד יְהוָה וּמֵהֲדַר גְּאֹנוֹ׃
His ,majesty's | from and glory | ,Jehovah | fear the of | from before | the in dust | and hide | the into rock | Enter

11
3068 7682 582 7312 7817 8213 120 1365 5869
עֵינֵי גַּבְהוּת אָדָם שָׁפֵל וְשַׁח רוּם אֲנָשִׁים וְנִשְׂגַּב יְהוָה
Jehovah | will but exalted be | ,men | the of pride | and bowed | be will ,humbled | man's | haughtiness | the of eyes

12
3605 6635 3068 3117 3117 905
לְבַדּוֹ בַּיּוֹם הַהוּא׃ כִּי יוֹם לַיהוָה צְבָאוֹת עַל כָּל־
all | against (be will) | hosts | Jehovah of | the of day | For | .that | day in | He alone

13
3844 730 3605 8213 5375 3605 7311 1343
גֵּאֶה וָרָם וְעַל כָּל־נִשָּׂא וְשָׁפֵל׃ וְעַל כָּל־אַרְזֵי הַלְּבָנוֹן
,Lebanon | the of cedars | all | and against | will it and ;abased be | ever | is that all ,lifted | and lofty and against ;ones | the proud

14
2022 3605 1316/437 3605 5375 7311
הָרָמִים וְהַנִּשָּׂאִים וְעַל כָּל־אַלּוֹנֵי הַבָּשָׁן׃ וְעַל כָּל־הֶהָרִים
the mountains | all | and against | ;Bashan | the of oaks | all | and against | lifted and ;up | high

15
1364 4026 5375 1389 3605 5921 7311
הָרָמִים וְעַל כָּל־הַגְּבָעוֹת הַנִּשָּׂאוֹת׃ וְעַל כָּל־מִגְדָּל גָּבֹהַּ
;tall | tower every | and against | ;up lifted | the hills | all | and against | ;high

16
3605 5921 8659 591 3605 5921 1219 2346
וְעַל כָּל־חוֹמָה בְצוּרָה׃ וְעַל כָּל־אֳנִיּוֹת תַּרְשִׁישׁ וְעַל כָּל־
all | and against | ;Tarshish | the of ships | all | and against | ;fortified | wall every | and against

and on all pleasurable craft. 17 And the pride of man shall be humbled; and the loftiness of men shall be abased; and Jehovah alone will be exalted in that day. 18 And the idols shall completely vanish. 19 And they shall go into the caves of the rocks, and into the holes of the earth, for fear of Jehovah, and from the glory of His majesty; when He rises up to make the earth quake. 20 In that day a man shall throw his silver and his golden idols which they made for him to worship, to the hole of the burrower and to the bats; 21 to go into the crevices of the rocks, and into the clefts of the cliffs, from the dread of Jehovah, and from the glory of His majesty; when He rises up to make the earth quake.

22 Cease yourself from man, whose breath *is* in his nostril, for in what is he to be esteemed?

582 7312 8213 120 1365 7817 2532 7914
17 שְׂכִיּוֹת הַחֶמְדָּה׃ וְשַׁח גַּבְהוּת הָאָדָם וְשָׁפֵל רוּם אֲנָשִׁים
;men's lofti- will and ,man's pride be will And .desirable the
ness abased be humbled craft

2498 3632 457 3117 905 3068 7682
18 וְנִשְׂגַּב יְהוָה לְבַדּוֹ בַּיּוֹם הַהוּא׃ וְהָאֱלִילִים כָּלִיל יַחֲלֹף׃
will completely the And .that day in alone Jehovah will and
.vanish idols exalted be

3068 6343 6440 6083 5157 6697 4247 935
19 וּבָאוּ בִּמְעָרוֹת צֻרִים וּבִמְחִלּוֹת עָפָר מִפְּנֵי פַּחַד יְהוָה
Jehovah the from the into and the the into they And
of fear before dust of holes the ,rocks of caves go shall

7993 3117 776 6206 6965 1347 1926
20 וּמֵהֲדַר גְּאוֹנוֹ בְּקוּמוֹ לַעֲרֹץ הָאָרֶץ׃ בַּיּוֹם הַהוּא יַשְׁלִיךְ
shall that day In the make to He when His from and
throw .earth tremble arises ;majesty's glory

6213 834 2091 457 3701 457 120
הָאָדָם אֵת אֱלִילֵי כַסְפּוֹ וְאֵת אֱלִילֵי זְהָבוֹ אֲשֶׁר עָשׂוּ־לוֹ
for they which his idols and his of idols man
him made ,gold of ,silver

5366 935 5847 6512 2661 7812
21 לְהִשְׁתַּחֲוֹת לַחְפֹּר פֵּרוֹת וְלָעֲטַלֵּפִים׃ לָבוֹא בְּנִקְרוֹת
the into go to to and burrowers the to ,worship to
of crevices ,bats the

1347 1926 3068 6343 6440 5553 5585 6697
הַצֻּרִים וּבִסְעִפֵי הַסְּלָעִים מִפְּנֵי פַּחַד יְהוָה וּמֵהֲדַר גְּאוֹנוֹ
His from and Jehovah the from ,cliffs the into and the
,majesty's glory of dread before of clefts the ,rocks

5397 120 2308 776 6206 6965
22 בְּקוּמוֹ לַעֲרֹץ הָאָרֶץ׃ חִדְלוּ לָכֶם מִן־הָאָדָם אֲשֶׁר נְשָׁמָה
breath whose man from your- Cease the make to He when
(is) self .earth tremble arises

2803 4100 639
בְּאַפּוֹ כִּי־בַמֶּה נֶחְשָׁב הוּא׃
.he be to is in for his in
esteemed what ,nostril

CAP. III ג

CHAPTER 3

1 For, behold, the Lord, Jehovah of hosts, takes away the stay and the staff from Jerusalem and from Judah; the whole stay of bread and the whole stay of water; 2 the mighty man, and the man of war, the judge and the prophet; and the diviner and the elder; 3 the commander of fifty; and the exalted of face; the counselor and the skilled craftsman; and the expert enchanter. 4 And I will give young boys *to be* their rulers, and caprices shall rule over them. 5 And the people shall be crushed, man against man, and a man on his neighbor. The child will be insolent against the elder, and the despised against the honorable. 6 When a man shall take hold of his brother, *at* his father's house, *saying*, A cloak! Come, you be a ruler

3063 3389 5493 6635 3068 113 2009
1 כִּי הִנֵּה הָאָדוֹן יְהוָה צְבָאוֹת מֵסִיר מִירוּשָׁלַםִ וּמִיהוּדָה
from and from (is) hosts Jehovah the ,behold For
Judah Jerusalem turning of Lord

1368 4325 4937 3605 3899 4937 4938 4937
2 מַשְׁעֵן וּמַשְׁעֵנָה כֹּל מִשְׁעַן־לֶחֶם וְכֹל מִשְׁעַן־מָיִם׃ גִּבּוֹר
the ;water stay and bread stay the the and the
mighty of whole the of whole ,staff stay

2572 8269 2205 7080 5030 8199 4421 376
3 וְאִישׁ מִלְחָמָה שׁוֹפֵט וְנָבִיא וְקֹסֵם וְזָקֵן׃ שַׂר־חֲמִשִּׁים
,fifty com- the the and the the and the ;war the and
of mander ;elder diviner ;prophet judge of man

5414 3908 995 2791 2450 3289 6440 5375
4 וּנְשׂוּא פָנִים וְיוֹעֵץ וַחֲכַם חֲרָשִׁים וּנְבוֹן לָחַשׁ׃ וְנָתַתִּי
I And .enchanter the and ,craftsmen the and the and of the and
give will expert skilled counselor ,face exalted

376 5971 5065 4910 8586 8269 5288
5 נְעָרִים שָׂרֵיהֶם וְתַעֲלוּלִים יִמְשְׁלוּ־בָם׃ וְנִגַּשׂ הָעָם אִישׁ
man the will And over shall and (be to) young
,people oppress .them rule caprices rulers their boys

3513 7034 2205 5288 7292 7453 376 376
בְּאִישׁ וְאִישׁ בְּרֵעֵהוּ יִרְהֲבוּ הַנַּעַר בַּזָּקֵן וְהַנִּקְלֶה בַּנִּכְבָּד׃
the against the and against the be will his on and against
.honorable despised elder the boy insolent ;neighbor man a ,man

7101 3212 8071 1004 251 376 8610
6 כִּי־יִתְפֹּשׂ אִישׁ בְּאָחִיו בֵּית אָבִיו שִׂמְלָה לְכָה קָצִין
a ,Come ,(saying) his (at) his of a shall When
ruler !cloak A ,father's house brother man hold take

for us; let this ruin *be* under your hand— [7]in that day he shall swear, saying, I will not be one who binds up; for there is no bread nor a cloak in my house; you shall not make me a ruler of the people. [8]For Jerusalem has stumbled, and Judah has fallen; because their tongue and their deeds toward Jehovah *are* to rebel against the eyes of His glory. [9]The look of their faces answers against them; they have declared their sin like Sodom; they do not hide *it*. Woe to their soul! For they have dealt evil to themselves.

[10]Say to the righteous that *it is* well; for they shall eat of the fruit of their doings. [11]Woe to the wicked! *It shall be* ill; for the reward of his hand is done to him. [12]*As for* My people, children *are* their oppressors, and women rule over him. O My people, your rulers cause *you* to go astray, and they swallow the way of your paths.

[13]Jehovah stands up to plead His cause, and stands up to judge the peoples. [14]Jehovah will enter into judgment with the elders of His people, and their kings. For you have eaten up the vineyard, the plunder of the poor *is* in your houses. [15]What do you *mean that* you crush My people, and grind the faces of the poor, says the Lord, Jehovah of hosts? [16]And Jehovah says, Because the daughters of Zion are proud, and walk with stretched out necks and wanton eyes, walking and mincing *as* they go, and make a tinkling with their feet; [17]therefore, Jehovah will make the crown of the daughter of Zion scabby; and Jehovah will lay their secret parts bare. [18]In that day the Lord will take away the beauty of the ankle-bracelets, and the head-bands, and the crescents, [19]the pendants, and the

---

7

3117	5375	3027	8478	4384	1961
day in	will He up lift	your hand.	under	this ruin and	for us be shall you

369 3899	369	1004	228:0	1961 38:08 559	
and ,bread	not	in for	who one will I not ,saying ,that house my ;up binds be		

8

3063 3389	378:2	5971 7101 7760	38:08 807.1
and ,Jerusalem has For the ruler shall you not ;cloak a Judah stumbled .people's me appoint			

3519	5869	4784	3068	4611	3956	5307
His the rebel to Jehovah toward their and their because has glory .of eyes against (are) deeds tongue ,fallen						

9

3808	5046	5467	2403	6030	6440	1971
not have they like their and against answers their The ;declared Sodom sin ,them faces of look						

10

6662	559	7451	1550	5315	188	3582
that the Tell levil them- to they for their to Woe they righteous selves dealt have ,soul .(it) hide						

11

1576	7451	7563	188	398	4611	6529	2896
the for ;evil the to Woe will they their the for (is it) of doing ,wicked .eat deeds of fruit ,well							

12

5971	4910	802	5953	5065	5971	6213	3027
My O over rule and (are) their My to be will his people .him women ,children oppressors people .him done hand							

13

7378	5324	11041	734	1870	8582:	833
to Stands they your the and (you) make your contend up .swallow paths of way ,stray leaders						

14

2205	935	4941	3068	5971	1777	5975	3068
the with will into Jehovah the to and ,Jehovah of elders enter judgment .peoples judge up stands							

1004	6041	1500 3754	1197	8269	5971
your in (is) the the the have for their and His .houses poor of spoil ;vineyard burned you ,rulers people					

15

3068	1.36	5002	2912	6041	6440	5971	1792
Jehovah the declares ,grind the the and My You (is) What of Lord poor of faces ,people crush ?you to							

16

67 :26	1323	1361	3282	3068	559	6635
,Zion the proud are Because ,Jehovah said And ?hosts of daughters						

3212	2952	19 ;80	5869	8265	16 :27 51 ;86	3212
they (as) and walking ,eyes with and ,necks with walk and ;go mincing wanton out stretched						

17

3068	6726 1323	6936	136	5596	5913	7272
and ;Zion the crown the the will so a making with and Jehovah of daughter of Lord scabby make ;tinkling feet their						

18

8599	136	5493	3117	6168	6596
the the will that day In lay will their of beauty Lord turn .bare shame					

19

8285	5188	7720	7636	5914
the and the the and the and the bracelets ,pendants ,crescents headbands ,anklets				

bracelets, and the veils; [20]the headdresses, and the leg ornaments, and the sashes, and the houses of the soul, and the amulets; [21]the rings and nose jewels; [22]the festal apparel and the outer garments; and the mantles, and the purses; [23]the mirrors and the fine linen; and the turbans and the veils. [24]And it shall be, instead of a smell of perfume, there shall be an odor of decay. And instead of a sash, a rope. And instead of well-set hair, baldness. And instead of a rich robe, a girding of sackcloth; burning instead of beauty. [25]Your men shall fall by the sword, and your mighty in the war. [26]And her gates shall lament and mourn; and she shall sit bare on the ground.

CHAPTER 4

[1]And in that day seven women shall take hold of one man, saying, We will eat our own bread and wear our own clothing, only let your name be called on us; collect our shame. [2]In that day the branch of Jehovah will be beautiful and glorious, and the fruit of the earth for pride and for glory for the survivors of Israel. [3]And it shall be, he remaining in Zion, and he who is left in Jerusalem, shall be called holy, every one who is written among the living in Jerusalem; [4]when the Lord shall have washed away the filth of the daughters of Zion, and the blood of Jerusalem shall have been rinsed away from its midst by a spirit of judgment, and by a spirit of burning. [5]Then Jehovah will create a cloud and smoke by day, and the shining of a flaming fire by night, for over all the site of

5315 1004 7196 6807 6287 7478
20 וְהָרְעָלוֹת׃ הַפְּאֵרִים וְהַצְּעָדוֹת וְהַקִּשֻּׁרִים וּבָתֵּי הַנֶּפֶשׁ
the ,soul | the and of houses | the and sashes | ankle the and bracelets | the head-dresses | the and ;veils

4595 42 54 639 5141 2885 3908
21 22 וְהַלְּחָשִׁים׃ הַטַּבָּעוֹת וְנִזְמֵי הָאָף׃ הַמַּחֲלָצוֹת וְהַמַּעֲטָפוֹת
outer the and ,garments | festal the ,clothing | the ;nose | the and of rings | the rings | the and ;amulets

6797 5466 1549 2754 4304
23 וְהַמִּטְפָּחוֹת וְהַחֲרִיטִים׃ הַגִּלְיֹנִים וְהַסְּדִינִים וְהַצְּנִיפוֹת
the and turbans | linen the and garments | the mirrors | the and ;purses | the and mantles

2290 8478 1961 4716 1314 8478 1961 7289
24 וְהָרְדִידִים׃ וְהָיָה תַחַת בֹּשֶׂם מַק יִהְיֶה וְתַחַת חֲגוֹרָה
sash a of instead | and ;be | shall there smell a decay of | per- fume | instead of | it And be will | the and .veils

4228 2290 8478 7142 4748 4639 8478 5364
נִקְפָּה וְתַחַת מַעֲשֶׂה מִקְשֶׁה קָרְחָה וְתַחַת פְּתִיגִיל מַחֲגֹרֶת
girding a of | rich a robe | and of instead | ;baldness | well-set ,hair | the of work | and of instead | ,rope a

4421 1369 5307 2719 4962 3308 8478 3587 8242
25 שַׂק כִּי־תַחַת יֹפִי׃ מְתַיִךְ בַּחֶרֶב יִפֹּלוּ וּגְבוּרָתֵךְ בַּמִּלְחָמָה׃
the in .battle | your and ones mighty | will ,fall | the by sword | Your men | .beauty | instead of | a scar; | sack- cloth

3427 776 5352 6607 56 578
26 וְאָנוּ וְאָבְלוּ פְּתָחֶיהָ וְנִקָּתָה לָאָרֶץ תֵּשֵׁב׃
shall she .sit | the on ground | bare and | her :gates | and mourn | shall and lament

CAP. IV ד

CHAPTER 4

559 3117 259 376 802 7651 2388
1 וְהֶחֱזִיקוּ שֶׁבַע נָשִׁים בְּאִישׁ אֶחָד בַּיּוֹם הַהוּא לֵאמֹר
,saying | ,that | day in | one | man of | women | seven | shall And of hold take

622 5921 8034 7121 7535 3847 8071 398 3899
לַחְמֵנוּ נֹאכֵל וְשִׂמְלָתֵנוּ נִלְבָּשׁ רַק יִקָּרֵא שִׁמְךָ עָלֵינוּ אֱסֹף
collect | upon ;us | your name | be let called | only | will we ,wear | own our clothing | and will We ,eat | own our bread

3519 6643 30:68 6780 1961 3117 2781
2 חֶרְפָּתֵנוּ׃ בַּיּוֹם הַהוּא יִהְיֶה צֶמַח יְהוָה לִצְבִי וּלְכָבוֹד
and ,glorious | beautiful | Jehovah | the of branch | be will | .,that | day In | our .shame

1961 3478 6413 8597 1347 776 6529
3 וּפְרִי הָאָרֶץ לְגָאוֹן וּלְתִפְאֶרֶת לִפְלֵיטַת יִשְׂרָאֵל׃ וְהָיָה
it And be shall | .Israel | the for of survivors | for and glory | for pride | the earth | the and of fruit

3605 559 6918 3389 3498 6726 7604
הַנִּשְׁאָר בְּצִיּוֹן וְהַנּוֹתָר בִּירוּשָׁלַםִ קָדוֹשׁ יֵאָמֶר לוֹ כָּל־
every one | of —him | will it said be | (is He) holy | in ,Jerusalem | he and left is who | ,Zion in | who him remains

6675 136 7364 3389 2416 3789
4 הַכָּתוּב לַחַיִּים בִּירוּשָׁלָםִ׃ אִם רָחַץ אֲדֹנָי אֵת צֹאַת
the of filth | the Lord | have shall away washed | when | in ;Jerusalem | the among living | are who written

4941 7307 7130 1740 3389 1818 67:26 1323
בְּנוֹת־צִיּוֹן וְאֶת־דְּמֵי יְרוּשָׁלַםִ יָדִיחַ מִקִּרְבָּהּ בְּרוּחַ מִשְׁפָּט
,judgment a by of spirit | its from midst | have shall away rinsed | Jerusalem | the of blood | and | ,Zion the of daughters

5921 67:26/2022 4349 3605 3068 1254 1197 7307
5 וּבְרוּחַ בָּעֵר׃ וּבָרָא יְהוָה עַל כָּל־מְכוֹן הַר־צִיּוֹן וְעַל־
and over | ,Zion mount | the of site | all | over Jehovah | Then create will | .burning | a by and of spirit

5921 39:15 3852 784 5051 62:27 3119 6051 4744
מִקְרָאֶהָ עָנָן יוֹמָם וְעָשָׁן וְנֹגַהּ אֵשׁ לֶהָבָה לָיְלָה כִּי עַל־
over | for | by ;night | flaming | fire a | the and of shining | and ,smoke | day by | a cloud | her ,assemblies

Mount Zion, and over her assemblies; for over all the glory *will be* a canopy. [6]And there shall be a booth for a shade by day from the heat, and for a refuge, and for a hiding-place from storm and rain.

CHAPTER 5

[1]Now I will sing to my Beloved a song of my Beloved concerning His vineyard: My Beloved has a vineyard in a fruitful horn. [2]And He dug it, and cleared it of stones, and planted it *with* the choicest vine, and built a tower in its midst, and also hewed out a wine vat in it. And He waited for *it* to produce grapes, but it produced rotten grapes. [3]And now, O people of Jerusalem and men of Judah, I ask you, judge between Me and My vineyard. [4]What more could have been done to My vineyard that I have not done in it? Who knows? I waited *for it* to yield grapes, but it yielded rotten grapes. [5]And now I will make known to you what I will do then to My vineyard. I will take away its hedge, and it will be burned. I will breach its wall, and it will become a trampling-ground. [6]And I will lay it waste; it shall not be pruned nor hoed; but briers and thorns shall come up. And I will command the clouds from raining rain on it. [7]For the vineyard of Jehovah of hosts *is* the house of Israel, and the man of Judah *is* His delightful plant. And He waited for justice, but behold, bloodshed; for righteousness, but behold, a cry!

[8]Woe *to* those touching house to house, bringing near field to field until no end of space, and you are made to dwell alone in the middle of the land! [9]Jehovah of hosts *has sworn* in my ears, If not, many houses shall be a

6 כָּל־כָּבוֹד חֻפָּה׃ וְסֻכָּה תִּהְיֶה לְצֵל־יוֹמָם מֵחֹרֶב וּלְמַחְסֶה

a for and the from by a for there a And canopy a the all
,refuge ,heat day shadow be shall booth .(be will) glory

וּלְמִסְתּוֹר מִזֶּרֶם וּמִמָּטָר׃

.rain and from a for and
storm place hiding

CAP. V ה

CHAPTER 5

1 אָשִׁירָה נָּא לִידִידִי שִׁירַת דּוֹדִי לְכַרְמוֹ כֶּרֶם הָיָה לִידִידִי

my to there a His about my song a my to now will I
Beloved was vineyard :vineyard Beloved of Beloved sing

2 בְּקֶרֶן בֶּן־שָׁמֶן׃ וַיְעַזְּקֵהוּ וַיְסַקְּלֵהוּ וַיִּטָּעֵהוּ שֹׂרֵק וַיִּבֶן

and choicest the planted and cleared and he And .fatness a a in
built vine (with) it stones of it it digged of son horn

מִגְדָּל בְּתוֹכוֹ וְגַם־יֶקֶב חָצֵב בּוֹ וַיְקַו לַעֲשׂוֹת עֲנָבִים וַיַּעַשׂ

it but ,grapes (it for) he And in hewed a and its in a
produced produce to waited .it out vat wine also ,midst tower

3 בְּאֻשִׁים׃ וְעַתָּה יוֹשֵׁב יְרוּשָׁלִַם וְאִישׁ יְהוּדָה שִׁפְטוּ־נָא

ask I judge ,Judah and ,Jerusalem inhab- O And rotten
you of men of itants now .grapes

4 בֵּינִי וּבֵין כַּרְמִי׃ מַה־לַּעֲשׂוֹת עוֹד לְכַרְמִי וְלֹא עָשִׂיתִי בּוֹ

in have I that my to more be could What My and between
?it done not vineyard done ,vineyard Me

5 מַדּוּעַ קִוֵּיתִי לַעֲשׂוֹת עֲנָבִים וַיַּעַשׂ בְּאֻשִׁים׃ וְעַתָּה אוֹדִיעָה־

make will I now And rotten it but grapes to (it for) I Who
know you ?grapes produced produce waited ?knows

נָּא אֶתְכֶם אֵת אֲשֶׁר־אֲנִי עֹשֶׂה לְכַרְמִי הָסֵר מְשׂוּכָּתוֹ

hedge its will I My to do will I what you now
remove ;vineyard

6 וְהָיָה לְבָעֵר פָּרֹץ גְּדֵרוֹ וְהָיָה לְמִרְמָס׃ וַאֲשִׁיתֵהוּ בָתָה

;waste will I And trampling a will it and its will I ;burned it and
it lay .ground become wall breach be will

לֹא יִזָּמֵר וְלֹא יֵעָדֵר וְעָלָה שָׁמִיר וָשָׁיִת וְעַל הֶעָבִים אֲצַוֶּה

will I the and and briers shall but hoed nor shall it not
command clouds on ;thorns up come pruned be

7 מֵהַמְטִיר עָלָיו מָטָר׃ כִּי כֶרֶם יְהוָה צְבָאוֹת בֵּית יִשְׂרָאֵל

,Israel the hosts Jehovah the For .rain it on from
of house (is) of of vineyard raining

וְאִישׁ יְהוּדָה נְטַע שַׁעֲשׁוּעָיו וַיְקַו לְמִשְׁפָּט וְהִנֵּה מִשְׂפָּח

bloodshed but for He and His plants the Judah the and
,behold justice waited ;delight of (is) of man

8 לִצְדָקָה וְהִנֵּה צְעָקָה׃ הוֹי מַגִּיעֵי בַיִת בְּבַיִת שָׂדֶה

field to house Those Woe !cry a but righ- for
,house touching (to) ,behold teousness

בְשָׂדֶה יַקְרִיבוּ עַד אֶפֶס מָקוֹם וְהוּשַׁבְתֶּם לְבַדְּכֶם בְּקֶרֶב

the in alone are you and ,space the until they field to
of midst dwell to made of end near bring

9 הָאָרֶץ׃ בְּאָזְנָי יְהוָה צְבָאוֹת אִם־לֹא בָּתִּים רַבִּים לְשַׁמָּה

waste a many houses Surely hosts Jehovah my In the
.(sworn has) of ears !land

waste, big and beautiful *ones* without inhabitant. [10]Yea, ten acres of vineyard shall yield one bath, and the seed of a homer shall yield an ephah. [11]Woe *to* those who rise early in the morning to go after fermented drink, tarrying in the twilight *while* wine inflames them! [12]And the lyre and the harp, the timbrel and flute, and wine are *at* their feasts; but they do not regard the work of Jehovah; yea, they do not see the work of His hands. [13]For this My people go into exile without knowledge, and his men of glory *into* famine; and their multitude is parched with thirst. [14]So Sheol has enlarged its appetite, and opened its mouth without measure, and her glory and her multitude, and her uproar, he who exults in her, shall come down *in it*. [15]And man is bowed down, and man is humbled, and the eyes of the proud are humbled. [16]But Jehovah of hosts is exalted in judgment, and God the Holy One is proven holy in righteousness. [17]Then the lambs shall feed as *in* their pasture, and strangers shall eat the waste places of the fatlings.

[18]Woe *to* those who draw iniquity with cords of vanity, and sin as *with* ropes of a cart; [19]who say, Let Him hurry and hasten His work, so that we may see; and let the purpose of the Holy One of Israel draw near and come, so that we may know! [20]Woe *to* those who say to evil, good; and to good, evil; who put darkness for light, and light for darkness; who put bitter for sweet, and sweet for bitter! [21]Woe *to* those wise in their own eyes, and discerning in their own sight! [22]Woe *to* those mighty to drink wine, and brave men to mix fermented drink; who justify the wicked for a

---

10 יִֽהְיוּ גְּדֹלִים וְטוֹבִים מֵאֵין יוֹשֵׁב: כִּי עֲשֶׂרֶת צִמְדֵּי־כֶרֶם
vineyard | acres of | ten | For | a | without | and | big | shall become
.resident | | | | .beautiful

11 יַעֲשׂוּ בַּת אֶחָת וְזֶרַע חֹמֶר יַעֲשֶׂה אֵיפָה: הוֹי
Woe | an | shall | a | the and | homer | of seed | one | bath | shall yield
(to) | ephah | yield

11 מַשְׁכִּימֵי בַבֹּקֶר שֵׁכָר יִרְדֹּפוּ מְאַחֲרֵי בַנֶּשֶׁף יַיִן יַדְלִיקֵם:
inflames (while) | the in | tarrying | (to) | fermented | the in | who those
.them | wine | twilight | | pursue | drink | morning | early rise

12 וְהָיָה כִנּוֹר וָנֶבֶל תֹּף וְחָלִיל וְיַיִן מִשְׁתֵּיהֶם וְאֵת פֹּעַל יְהוָה
Jeho- | work | but | their(at) | and | and | timbrel | and | lyre | And
vah's | | | feasts | wine | flute | | harp, | are

13 לֹא יַבִּיטוּ וּמַעֲשֵׂה יָדָיו לֹא רָאוּ: לָכֵן גָּלָה עַמִּי מִבְּלִי־
without | My | into | go | Therefore | they | not | His | the and | do they | not
people | exile | .see do | hands | of work | ,regard

14 דָעַת וּכְבוֹדוֹ מְתֵי רָעָב וַהֲמוֹנוֹ צִחֵה צָמָא: לָכֵן הִרְחִיבָה
has | Therefore | .thirst | is | their and | ,famine | men | his and | knowl-
enlarged | | with parched | multitude | | | (is) glory | edge

15 שְׁאוֹל נַפְשָׁהּ וּפָעֲרָה פִיהָ לִבְלִי־חֹק וְיָרַד הֲדָרָהּ וַהֲמוֹנָהּ
her and | her | will and | mea- | without | its | and | its | Sheol
multitude | glory | descend | sure | | mouth | opened | appetite

וּשְׁאוֹנָהּ וְעָלֵז בָּהּ: וַיִּשַּׁח אָדָם וַיִּשְׁפַּל־אִישׁ וְעֵינֵי גְבֹהִים
the | the and | man | is and | ,man | is | And | .her in | he and | her and
| the | proud | of eyes | | | humbled | down bowed | exults who | uproar

16 תִּשְׁפַּלְנָה: וַיִּגְבַּהּ יְהוָה צְבָאוֹת בַּמִּשְׁפָּט וְהָאֵל הַקָּדוֹשׁ
the | and | in | hosts | Jehovah | is But | are
One Holy | God | ,judgment | | | exalted | .humbled

17 נִקְדָּשׁ בִּצְדָקָה: וְרָעוּ כְבָשִׂים כְּדָבְרָם וְחָרְבוֹת מֵחִים
the | waste the | and | (in) as | lambs the | Then | righteous- | in | proven is
fatlings | of places | pasture | their | | feed shall | .ness | | holy

18 גָּרִים יֹאכֵלוּ: הוֹי מֹשְׁכֵי הֶעָוֹן בְּחַבְלֵי הַשָּׁוְא
.vanity | with | iniquity | those | Woe | | shall | strangers
| of cords | | draw who | (to) | | | .eat

19 וְכַעֲבוֹת הָעֲגָלָה חַטָּאָה: הָאֹמְרִים יְמַהֵר יָחִישָׁה מַעֲשֵׂהוּ
His | and | Him let | Who | .sin | cart a | (with) as | and
.work | hasten | hurry | say | | | | of ropes

לְמַעַן נִרְאֶה וְתִקְרַב וְתָבוֹאָה עֲצַת קְדוֹשׁ יִשְׂרָאֵל וְנֵדָעָה:
we that so | Israel | holy the | the | let and | let And | may we | that so
.know may | of One | of purpose | come | near draw | .(it) see

20 הוֹי הָאֹמְרִים לָרַע טוֹב וְלַטּוֹב רָע שָׂמִים חֹשֶׁךְ
darkness | who | ;evil | to and | good | ,evil | to those | Woe
| say who | put | | ,good | | | (to)

לְאוֹר וְאוֹר לְחֹשֶׁךְ שָׂמִים מַר לְמָתוֹק וּמָתוֹק לְמָר:
for | sweet and | for | bitter | put who | for | and | for
lbitter | | sweet | | ;darkness | light | light | light

21 **22** הוֹי חֲכָמִים בְּעֵינֵיהֶם וְנֶגֶד פְּנֵיהֶם נְבֹנִים: הוֹי גִּבּוֹרִים
those | Woe | .discerning | own their | and | their | in | those | Woe
mighty | (to) | | faces | before | eyes own | | wise | (to)

23 לִשְׁתּוֹת יָיִן וְאַנְשֵׁי־חַיִל לִמְסֹךְ שֵׁכָר: מַצְדִּיקֵי רָשָׁע עֵקֶב
for | the | who those | fermented | mix to | valor | and | ,wine | drink to
| wicked | justify | ,drink | | | of men

bribe, and turning aside the righteousness of the righteous from him! 24So, as the tongue of fire devours the stubble, and the flame burns up the chaff; their root shall be like rottenness, and their blossom shall go up like dust, because they have cast away the law of Jehovah of hosts; and despised the word of the Holy One of Israel. 25On account of this the anger of Jehovah is kindled on His people, and He has stretched out His hand against them, and has struck them; and the mountains quaked, and their dead bodies were as filth in the midst of the streets. In all this His anger does not turn away, but His hand is stretched out still.

26And He will lift up a banner to distant nations, and will hiss to them from the ends of the earth; and, behold, it shall come *with* swift speed! 27None *shall be* weary nor stumble among them; none will slumber nor sleep; nor shall the waistcloth of their loins be opened, nor the thong of their sandals broken; whose arrows *are* sharp, and all their bows bent; their horses' hooves shall appear as flint, and their wheels like a hurricane. 29Their roaring *shall be* like a lion; they shall roar like young lions. Yea, they roar and seize the prey, and carry *it* away; and no one shall deliver. 30And in that day they shall roar against them like the roaring of the sea; when one looks to the land, and lo, darkness! Distress! And light shall be darkened by its clouds.

CHAPTER 6

1In the year that king Uzziah died, then I saw the Lord sitting on a throne, high and lifted up. And His train filled the temple. 2Above it stood the seraphs.

24
717 9 | 398 | 36 51 | 5493 | 6662 | 6666 | 7810
לָכֵן כֶּאֱכֹל קַשׁ ... יָסִירוּ מִמֶּנּוּ׃ ... צַדִּיקִים ... צִדְקַת ... שֹׁחַד
the / as / Therefore / stubble devours / from / turn / the / and the / ,bribe a / him! / aside / righteous / of righteousness

6525 | 19:61 | 4716 | 83 28 | 75 03 | 3852 | 28 42 | 784 | 3956
לָשׁוֹן אֵשׁ וַחֲשַׁשׁ לֶהָבָה יִרְפֶּה שָׁרְשָׁם כָּמָק יֶהֱוָה וּפִרְחָם
their and / shall / like / their / ,falls / the (in) / dry and / ,fire / the
blossom / be / rottenness / root / flame / grass / of tongue

663 5 | 3068 | 8451 | 3973 | 59 21 | 80
כְּאָבָק יַעֲלֶה כִּי מָאֲסוּ אֵת תּוֹרַת יֶהֱוָה צְבָאוֹת וְאֵת
and / ;hosts / Jehovah / the / have they / for / shall / like
of law / rejected / up go / dust

25
5971 | 3068/639 | 2734 | 5006 | 3478 | 6918 | 565
אָמְרַת קְדוֹשׁ־יִשְׂרָאֵל נִאֵצוּ׃ עַל־כֵּן חָרָה אַף־יֶהֱוָה בְּעַמּוֹ
His on / Jehovah the / is / Therefore / .despised / Israel / Holy the / the
,people / of anger kindled / of One / of word

5478 | 5038 | 1961 | 20:22 | 7264 | 52·21 | 3027 | 5186
וַיֵּט יָדוֹ עָלָיו וַיַּכֵּהוּ וַיִּרְגְּזוּ הֶהָרִים וַתְּהִי נִבְלָתָם כַּסּוּחָה
like / their / and / the / and struck and / against His / He and
offal / corpses / were / mountains quaked / ;him / ;him / hand / sent

5186 | 3027 | 5750 | 639 | 7725 | 3808 | 13605 | 2351 | 7130
בְּקֶרֶב חוּצוֹת בְּכָל־זֹאת לֹא־שָׁב אַפּוֹ וְעוֹד יָדוֹ נְטוּיָה
stretched / is His / but / His / returns / not / this / In / the / the
.out / hand / still / ,anger / all / .streets / of midst

26
2009 | 776 | 7097 | 8319 | 7350 | 1471 | 5251 | 5375
וְנָשָׂא־נֵס לַגּוֹיִם מֵרָחוֹק וְשָׁרַק לוֹ מִקְצֵה הָאָרֶץ וְהִנֵּה
and / the / the / from / and / from / the to / a / He And
behold / ;earth / of end / it / whistle / ,afar / nations / banner raise will

38·08 | 5123 | 38·08 | 3782/369 | 5889 | 369 | 935 | 7031 | 4120
מְהֵרָה קַל יָבוֹא׃ אֵין־עָיֵף וְאֵין־כּוֹשֵׁל בּוֹ לֹא יָנוּם וְלֹא
nor / will one / not / in / stumbles and / weary / None / will it / quick / (with)
slumber / ;it / none / (is) / .come / speed

27
52 75 | 8288 | 5423 | 38·08 | 12504 | 232 | 6605 | 34 · 62
יִישָׁן וְלֹא נִפְתַּח אֵזוֹר חֲלָצָיו וְלֹא נִתַּק שְׂרוֹךְ נְעָלָיו׃
its / thong the / be will / and / its / waist the- / be shall / nor / ;sleep
;sandals / of / broken / not / ;loins / of cloth / opened

28
5483 | 6541 | 1869 | 7198 | 36 105 | 8150 | 2671 | 834
אֲשֶׁר חִצָּיו שְׁנוּנִים וְכָל־קַשְּׁתֹתָיו דְּרֻכוֹת פַּרְסוֹת סוּסָיו
its / hooves / ;bent / bows its / and / are / its / of
horses' / all / ,sharpened / arrows / which

29
75 80 | 3833 | 7580 | 5492 | 15 ·34 | 2803 | 6862
כַּצַּר נֶחְשָׁבוּ וְגַלְגִּלָּיו כַּסּוּפָה׃ שְׁאָגָה לוֹ כַּלָּבִיא וְשָׁאַג
it and / like (is) / Its / roaring / a like / its and / ,seem / like
roar will / ,lion a / .windstorm / wheels / flint

30
5098 | 5337 | 369 | 6403 | 2966 | 290 | 5098 | 3715
כַּכְּפִירִים וְיִנְהֹם וְיֹאחֵז טֶרֶף וְיַפְלִיט וְאֵין מַצִּיל׃ וְיִנְהֹם
it And / shall / and carries and / (its) / seizes and / it for / young like
roar will / .deliver / none / ,away (it) / ,prey / roars / lions

6862 | 2822 | 2009 | 776 | 5027 | 3220 | 5100 | 3117 | 59 121
עָלָיו בַּיּוֹם הַהוּא כְּנַהֲמַת־יָם וְנִבַּט לָאָרֶץ וְהִנֵּה־חֹשֶׁךְ צַר
dis- / ,darkness and / the to / one when / the / the like / ,that / day in / over
!tress / ,lo / ,land / looks / ;sea / of roaring / it

6183 | 2821 | 216
וָאוֹר חָשַׁךְ בַּעֲרִיפֶיהָ׃
its by / is / And
.clouds / darkened / light

CAP. VI ו

CHAPTER 6

1
3678 | 3427 | 136 | 853 | 7200 | 5818 | 44 128 | 4194 | 8141
בִּשְׁנַת־מוֹת הַמֶּלֶךְ עֻזִּיָּהוּ וָאֶרְאֶה אֶת־אֲדֹנָי יֹשֵׁב עַל־כִּסֵּא
a / on / sitting / the / I then / ,Uzziah / King / the / the In
,throne / Lord / saw / of death / of year

2
5975 | 831 4 | 1964 | 853 | 4393 | 7757 | 5375 | 7311
רָם וְנִשָּׂא וְשׁוּלָיו מְלֵאִים אֶת־הַהֵיכָל׃ שְׂרָפִים עֹמְדִים
stood / Seraphim / the / filled / His and / and / high
.temple / train / up lifted

Each one had six wings; with two he covered his face; and with two he covered his feet; and with two he flew. [3]And one cried to the other and said, Holy, holy, holy *is* Jehovah of hosts; all the earth *is* full *of* His glory! [4]And the doorposts shook from the voice of the one who cried; and the house was filled with smoke. [5]Then I said, Woe is me! For I am cut off; for I *am* a man of unclean lips, and I live amongst a people of unclean lips; for my eyes have seen the King, Jehovah of hosts. [6]Then one of the seraphs flew to me *with* a live coal in his hand, snatched with tongs from the altar. [7]And he touched *it* on my mouth, and said, See, this has touched your lips; and your iniquity is taken away, and your sin is covered. [8]And I heard the voice of Jehovah, saying, Whom shall I send, and who will go for Us? Then I said, I *am* here. Send me! [9]And He said, Go and tell this people, Hearing you hear, but do not understand; and seeing you see, but do not know. [10]Make the heart of this people fat, and make his ears heavy, and shut his eyes, that he not see with his eyes, and hear with his ears, and understand with his heart, and turn and one heals him. [11]Then I said, How long, O Lord? And He said, Until cities lie desolate without inhabitant, and the houses without man, and the land is laid waste, a desolation; [12]and *until* Jehovah has sent mankind far away, and the desolation in the midst of the land *is* great. [13]But yet a tenth *shall be* in it, and it shall

3680 8147 259 3671 8337 3671 8337 460 5
ממעל לו שש כנפים שש כנפים לאחד בשתים | יכסה
he two with each to wings six ,wings six ;Him above
covered one

2088 7121 5774 8147 7272 3680 8147 6440
3 פניו ובשתים יכסה רגליו ובשתים יעופף: וקרא זה
this And .flew he with and his he with and his
cried two ,feet covered two ,face

4393 6635 3068 6918 6918 6918 559
אל־זה ואמר קדוש | קדוש | קדוש יהוה צבאות מלא
(is) ;hosts Jehovah (is) holy ,holy ,Holy ,said and this to
full of

7121 6963 5592 520 5128 3519 776 3605
4 כל־הארץ כבודו: וינעו אמות הספים מקול הקורא
one the the from the the And His (of) the all
called who of voice threshold of posts shook !glory earth

2931 376 1820 188 559 6227 4390 1004
5 והבית ימלא עשן: ואמר אוי־לי כי־נדמיתי כי איש טמא־
unclean a for am I for to Woe I Then .smoke was the and
of man ,off cut ,me said with filled house

3427 8193 2930 5971 8432 8193
שפתים אנכי ובתוך עם־טמא שפתים אנכי ישב כי את־
for ,live I lips unclean a and ,(am) I lips
of people amongst

8314 259 5774 5869 7200 6635 3068 4428
6 המלך יהוה צבאות ראו עיני: ויעף אלי אחד מן־השרפים
the of one to Then my have ,hosts Jehovah the
seraphim me flew .eyes seen of ,King

63 10 5060 4196 3947 44 57 7531 3027
7 ובידו רצפה במלקחים לקח מעל המזבח: ויגע על־פי
my on And the from taken with burning a in and
mouth it touched .altar tongs coal hand his

3722 2403 5771 5493 8193 5060 2009 559
ויאמר הנה נגע זה על־שפתיך וסר עונך וחטאתך תכפר:
is your and your is and your on this has ,See ,said and
.covered sin ,iniquity removed ,lips touched

32 12 4310 79 71 4310 559 136 6913 8085
8 ואשמע את־קול אדני אמר את־מי אשלח ומי ילך־לנו
for will and I shall Whom ,saying the the I And
?Us go who send ,Lord of voice heard

8085 2088 5971 559 32 12 559 7971 559
9 ואמר הנני שלחני: ויאמר לך ואמרת לעם הזה שמעו
Hear ,this people tell and Go He And Send Here I Then
,said !me ,I (am) ,said

5971/3820 8080 3045 3808 7200 995 408 8085
10 שמוע ואל־תבינו וראו ראו ואל־תדעו: השמן לב־העם
people the Make do but seeing and under- do but hearing
of heart fat .know not see ;stand not

241 5869 7200 8173 5869 3511 241 20 88
הזה ואזניו הכבד ועיניו השע פן־יראה בעיניו ובאזניו
with and with he lest ,shut his and make his and ,this
ears his eyes his see eyes ,heavy ears

136 5704 559 7495 7725 995 3824 8085
11 ישמע ולבבו יבין ושב ורפא לו: ואמר עד־מתי אדני
O Until I Then .him one and and under with and ,hear
?Lord ,when ,said heals turn ,stand heart his

369 1004 3427 369 5892 75 82 5704 559
ויאמר עד אשר אם־שאו ערים מאין יושב ובתים מאין
without the even inhabi- without cities lie might that Until He And
houses ,tant desolate ,said

120 3068 7368 8077 7582 127 120
12 אדם והאדמה תשאה שממה: ורחק יהוה את־האדם
,mankind Jehovah has And a (for) laid the and ,man
away far sent .desolation waste land

7725 6224 5750 776 7130 8077 7227
13 ורבה העזובה בקרב הארץ: ועוד בה עשריה ושבה
will it and (be will) it in But the the in the great and
return ;tenth a yet .land of midst desolation (is)

return and be consumed
like the terebinth and like
the oak that in being felled
yet has its stump—the holy
seed *is* its stump.

4673 7995 834 437 424 1197 1961
וְהָיְתָה לְבָעֵר כָּאֵלָה וְכָאַלּוֹן אֲשֶׁר בְּשַׁלֶּכֶת מַצֶּבֶת בָּם
of the (have) being in which like and the like burned it and
;them stump felled oak the terebinth be shall

4673 6944 2233
זֶרַע קֹדֶשׁ מַצַּבְתָּהּ׃
.stump its holy the
(is) seed

CAP. VII ז

CHAPTER 7

CHAPTER 7
[1]And it happened in the
days of Ahaz the son of
Jotham, the son of Uzziah,
king of Judah, Rezin the
king of Syria, and Pekah the
son of Remaliah, king of
Israel, went up to Jeru-
salem to a war against it,
but were not able to do
battle against it. [2]And the
house of David was told,
saying, Syria is allied with
Ephraim, and his heart and
the heart of his people
shook, as the trees of the
forest shake from the wind.
[3]And Jehovah said to
Isaiah, Go out to meet Ahaz,
you and your son Shear-
jashub, at the end of the
conduit of the upper pool,
to the highway of the
Fuller's Field. [4]And say to
him, Be on guard and be
calm. Do not fear nor be
timid of heart because of
the two tails of these
smoking firebrands, be-
cause of the fierce anger of
Rezin and Syria, and of the
son of Remaliah. [5]Because
Syria, Ephraim, and the son
of Remaliah have plotted
evil against you, saying,
[6]Let us go up against Judah
and make her to dread, and
break her for ourselves, and
set a king in her midst, the
son of Tabeal. [7]So says the
Lord Jehovah, It shall not
rise, nor shall it happen.
[8]For the head of Syria *is*
Damascus, and the head of
Damascus *is* Rezin; and
within sixty-five years
Ephraim shall be broken
from *being* a people. [9]And

1
7526 5927 3063 4428 5818 3147 271 3117 1961
וַיְהִי בִּימֵי אָחָז בֶּן־יוֹתָם בֶּן־עֻזִּיָּהוּ מֶלֶךְ יְהוּדָה עָלָה רְצִין
Rezin went ,Judah king Uzziah the ,Jotham the Ahaz the in it And
up of of son of son of days was

3389 3478 4428 7425 1121 6492 758 4428
מֶלֶךְ־אֲרָם וּפֶקַח בֶּן־רְמַלְיָהוּ מֶלֶךְ־יִשְׂרָאֵל יְרוּשָׁלַםִ
to ,Israel king ,Remaliah the and ,Aram the
Jerusalem of of son Pekah of king

2
1732 1004 5046 3898 3201 3808 4421
לַמִּלְחָמָה עָלֶיהָ וְלֹא יָכֹל לְהִלָּחֵם עָלֶיהָ׃ וַיֻּגַּד לְבֵית דָּוִד
,David the to it And against do to were but against war a to
of house told was .it battle able not ;it

5128 5971 3824 3824 5128 669 5921 758 5117 559
לֵאמֹר נָחָה אֲרָם עַל־אֶפְרָיִם וַיָּנַע לְבָבוֹ וּלְבַב עַמּוֹ כְּנוֹעַ
as his the and his And .Ephraim upon Aram is ,saying
shake people of heart ,heart shook resting

3
3318 3470 3068 559 7307 3293/6086
עֲצֵי־יַעַר מִפְּנֵי־רוּחַ׃ וַיֹּאמֶר יְהוָה אֶל־יְשַׁעְיָהוּ צֵא־
Go ,Isaiah to Jehovah Then the from the the
out said .wind forest of trees

8585 7097 1121 7610 7605 271 7125
נָא לִקְרַאת אָחָז אַתָּה וּשְׁאָר יָשׁוּב בְּנֶךָ אֶל־קְצֵה תְּעָלַת
the end the to your and you ,Ahaz meet to now
of conduit of ,son jashub Shear-

4
559 3526 7704 4546 5945 1295
הַבְּרֵכָה הָעֶלְיוֹנָה אֶל־מְסִלַּת שְׂדֵה כוֹבֵס׃ וְאָמַרְתָּ אֵלָיו
to say And .fuller's the the to upper pool the
,him field of highway

2180 8147 7401 3824 3372 408 8252 8104
הִשָּׁמֵר וְהַשְׁקֵט אַל־תִּירָא וּלְבָבְךָ אַל־יֵרַךְ מִשְּׁנֵי זַנְבוֹת
tails , because be let not your and do and be and Take
of two the of timid heart ,fear not ;calm heed

1121 758 7526 639 2750 428 6226 181
הָאוּדִים הָעֲשֵׁנִים הָאֵלֶּה בָּחֳרִי־אַף רְצִין וַאֲרָם וּבֶן־
the and and Rezin the of because ,these smoking firebrands
of son ,Aram of anger of heat the

5
7425 1121 669 7451 758 3289 7425
רְמַלְיָהוּ׃ יַעַן כִּי־יָעַץ עָלֶיךָ אֲרָם רָעָה אֶפְרַיִם וּבֶן־רְמַלְיָהוּ
,Remaliah the and ,Ephraim ,evil Aram against has Because .Remaliah
of son you plotted

6
4427 1234 6973 3063 5927 559
לֵאמֹר׃ נַעֲלֶה בִיהוּדָה וּנְקִיצֶנָּה וְנַבְקִעֶנָּה אֵלֵינוּ וְנַמְלִיךְ
cause and for break and make and against us Let ,saying
reign to ;ourselves her ,hated her Judah up go

7
3068 136 559 3541 2870 8432 4428
מֶלֶךְ בְּתוֹכָהּ אֵת בֶּן־טָבְאַל׃ כֹּה אָמַר אֲדֹנָי יְהוִה
,Jehovah the says Thus .Tabeal the her in king a
Lord of son ,midst

8
7218 1834 758 7218 1961 3808 6965 3808
לֹא תָקוּם וְלֹא תִהְיֶה׃ כִּי רֹאשׁ אֲרָם דַּמֶּשֶׂק וְרֹאשׁ
the and (is) Aram the For it shall nor will it not
of head Damascus of head .be ,rise

5971 669 2865 8141 2568 8346 7526 1834
דַּמֶּשֶׂק רְצִין וּבְעוֹד שִׁשִּׁים וְחָמֵשׁ שָׁנָה יֵחַת אֶפְרַיִם מֵעָם׃
from Ephraim be shall years and sixty and (is) Damascus
.people a broken five within ;Rezin

the head of Ephraim *is* Samaria, and the head of Samaria *is* Remaliah's son. If you will not believe, surely you will not be established.

10And Jehovah spoke again to Ahaz, saying, 11Ask a sign from Jehovah your God; make deep the request, or make *it* high above. 12But Ahaz said, I will not ask, nor will I tempt Jehovah. 13And He said, Hear now, O house of David, is it too little that you weary men, but will you also weary my God? 14So, The Lord Himself will give you a sign: Behold! The virgin is with child, and shall bring forth a son; and she shall call His name Immanuel. 15He shall eat curds and honey until He knows to refuse the evil and choose the good. 16For before the boy shall know to refuse the evil and choose the good, the land that you hate will be forsaken before both her kings. 17Jehovah shall bring the king of Assyria on you, and on your people, and on your father's house, days which have not come since the days Ephraim turned aside from Judah. 18And it shall be, in that day Jehovah shall hiss for the fly that *is* in the end of the rivers of Egypt, and for the bee that *is* in the land of Assyria. 19And they shall come, and they shall all rest in the steep ravines, and in the clefts of the rocks, and in all the thorn bushes, and in all the pastures. 20In that day the Lord will shave with a razor that is hired, beyond the River, by the king of Assyria, the head, and the hair of the feet, and also it

3808 518 7425 1121 8111 7218 8111 1669 7218
9 וראש אפרים שמרון וראש שמרון בן־רמליהו אם לא
not If .Remaliah's (is) Samaria the and (is) Ephraim the And
son of head Samaria of head

271 1696 3068 3254 539 3808 539
10 תאמינו כי לא תאמנו׃ ויוסף יהוה דבר אל־אחז
,Ahaz to spoke Jehovah And be will you not surely will you
again .established ,believe

7592 6009 430 3068 226 7592 559
11 לאמר׃ שאל־לך אות מעם יהוה אלהיך העמק שאלה
the make your Jehovah from sign a for Ask ,saying
request deep ;God yourself

5254 3808 7592 271 559 4605 1361 176
12 או הגבה למעלה׃ ויאמר אחז לא־אשאל ולא־אנסה
will I not will I not ,Ahaz said But .above make or
test ,ask high

3811 4592 1732 1004 4994 8085 559 3068 853
13 את־יהוה׃ ויאמר שמעו־נא בית דוד המעט מכם הלאות
weary to for (it Is) ,David O ,now Hear he Then .Jehovah
you little too of house ,said

136 5414 430 1571 3811 582
14 אנשים כי תלאו גם את־אלהי׃ לכן יתן אדני הוא לכם
to Himself the shall Therefore my also will you that ,men
you Lord give ?God weary

410 6005 8034 7121 1121 3205 2030 5959 2009 226
אות הנה העלמה הרה וילדת בן וקראת שמו עמנו אל׃
.Immanuel His she and a bear and will the ,behold a
name call will ,son conceive virgin ,sign

2896 977 7451 3988 3045 398 1706 2529
15 חמאה ודבש יאכל לדעתו מאוס ברע ובחור בטוב׃
,good the and the to he when shall He and curds
choose evil refuse knows ,eat honey

5800 2896 977 7451 3988 5288 3045 2962
16 כי בטרם ידע הנער מאס ברע ובחר בטוב תעזב
be will ,good the and the to the shall before For
forsaken choose evil reject boy know

3068 935 4428 8147 6440 6973 127
17 האדמה אשר־אתה קץ מפני שני מלכיה׃ יביא יהוה
Jehovah shall her both before hate you that the
bring .kings land

935 3808 834 3117 1 1004 5921 5971 5921 5921
עליך ועל־עמך ועל־בית אביך ימים אשר לא־באו
have not which days your house and your and on
come ,father's on ,people on you

804 4428 3063 5493 669 3117
למיום סור־אפרים מעל יהודה את מלך אשור׃
.Assyria the ,Judah from Ephraim turned the since
of king aside day

2975 7097 2070 3068 8319 3117 1961
18 והיה ביום ההוא ישרק יהוה לזבוב אשר בקצה יארי
the the at that the for Jehovah will ,that day in it And
of rivers of end (is) fly whistle be shall

3605 5117 935 804 776 1682 4714
19 מצרים ולדבורה אשר בארץ אשור׃ ובאו ונחו כלם
of all and they And .Assyria the in that for and ,Egypt
them rest ,come shall of land (is) bee the

3605 5285 3605 5553 5357 1327 5158
בנחלי הבתות ובנקיקי הסלעים ובכל הנעצוצים ובכל
and thorn the and the in and ,steep the in
all in bushes all in ,rocks of clefts ravines

7917 8593 136 1548 3117 5097
20 הנהללים׃ ביום ההוא יגלח אדני בתער השכירה
is that a with the will that day In the
,hired razor Lord shave pastures

1571 7272 8181 7218 804 4428 5104 5676
בעברי נהר במלך אשור את־הראש ושער הרגלים וגם
and the the and the ,Assyria the by the beyond
also ;feet of hair ,head of king ,River

shall sweep away the beard. [21]And it shall be in that day, a man shall keep alive a heifer of the herd, and two sheep. [22]And it shall be, he shall eat curds from the plenty of milk-making; for everyone who is left in the land shall eat curds and honey. [23]And it shall be in that day, every place where there were a thousand vines *worth* a thousand pieces of silver, *it* shall be for briers and thorns. [24]With arrows and with the bow, he shall come there; because all the land shall be briers and thorns. [25]And all the hills which were hoed with the hoe, you shall not come there for fear of briers and thorns; but it shall be for the sending out of the ox, and for trampling of sheep.

5697 376 2421 3117 1961 5595 2206
21 אֶת־הַזָּקָן תִּסְפֶּה׃ וְהָיָה בַּיּוֹם הַהוּא יְחַיֶּה־אִישׁ עֶגְלַת
heifer a of | a man | shall alive keep | ,that | day in | it And be will | shall it .away sweep | the beard

2529 398 2461 6213 7230 1961 6629/8147 1241
22 בָּקָר וּשְׁתֵּי־צֹאן׃ וְהָיָה מֵרֹב עֲשׂוֹת חָלָב יֹאכַל חֶמְאָה
;curds | he eat shall | milk | making | the from of plenty | it and ,be will | ;sheep | and two | the ,herd

1961 776 7130 3498 398 1706 2529
23 כִּי־חֶמְאָה וּדְבַשׁ יֹאכַל כָּל־הַנּוֹתָר בְּקֶרֶב הָאָרֶץ׃ וְהָיָה
it And be will | the .land | the in of midst | is who left | every- one | shall eat | and honey | curds | for

1612 505 8033 4725 3605 1961 3117
בַּיּוֹם הַהוּא יִהְיֶה כָל־מָקוֹם אֲשֶׁר יִהְיֶה־שָּׁם אֶלֶף גֶּפֶן
vines | a thousand | there | is | where | place | every | will it ,be | ,that | day in

935 7198 2671 1961 7898 8068 3701 505
24 בְּאֶלֶף כֶּסֶף לַשָּׁמִיר וְלַשַּׁיִת יִהְיֶה׃ בַּחִצִּים וּבַקֶּשֶׁת יָבוֹא
shall he come | with and bow the | the arrows | With | shall it .be | the and thorns | the for briars | silver (pieces) | a (worth) thousand

2022 3605 776 3605 1961 7898 8068 8033
25 שָׁמָּה כִּי־שָׁמִיר וָשַׁיִת תִּהְיֶה כָל־הָאָרֶץ׃ וְכֹל הֶהָרִים
the mountains | And all | the .land | all | shall be | and thorns | briars because | ,there

7898 8068 3373 8033 935 5737 4576 834
אֲשֶׁר בַּמַּעְדֵּר יֵעָדֵרוּן לֹא־תָבוֹא שָׁמָּה יִרְאַת שָׁמִיר וָשָׁיִת
and ;thorns | briars | (for) of fear | ,there | you come shall | not | were ,hoed | the with hoe | which

7716 4823 7794 4916 1961
וְהָיָה לְמִשְׁלַח שׁוֹר וּלְמִרְמַס שֶׂה׃
.sheep | for and of trampling | ,ox the | for sending | it but be shall

CAP. VIII ח

CHAPTER 8

CHAPTER 8

[1]And Jehovah said to me, Take a big tablet and write in it with a man's pen: Make haste *to* plunder! Hasten to the prey! [2]And I took to myself faithful witnesses to record, Uriah the priest, and Zechariah the son of Jeberechiah. [3]And I drew near the prophetess. And she conceived, and bore a son. Then Jehovah said to me, Call his name, Maher-shalal-hash-baz. [4]For before the boy knows to cry, My father, or, My mother, the riches of Damascus and the plunder of Samaria shall be taken away before the king of Assyria.

[5]Jehovah also spoke to me again, saying, [6]Because this people has refused the waters of Shiloah that flow softly, and rejoices in Rezin

2747 3789 1419 1549 3947 3068 559
1 וַיֹּאמֶר יְהוָה אֵלַי קַח־לְךָ גִּלָּיוֹן גָּדוֹל וּכְתֹב עָלָיו בְּחֶרֶט
the with of pen | it on | and write | big | a tablet | to Take you | ,me to Jehovah said And

539 5707 5749 957 2363 7998 4116 582
2 אֱנוֹשׁ לְמַהֵר שָׁלָל חָשׁ בַּז׃ וְאָעִידָה לִּי עֵדִים נֶאֱמָנִים
,faithful | witnesses | for me | took I And record to | the !spoil | hurry | ;plunder to | make To (to) haste | ;man a

7126 3000 1121 2148 3548 223
3 אֵת אוּרִיָּה הַכֹּהֵן וְאֶת־זְכַרְיָהוּ בֶּן יְבֶרֶכְיָהוּ׃ וָאֶקְרַב אֶל
to | I And near drew | .Jeberechiah | the of son | Zechariah | and | the priest | Uriah

4118 8034 7121 3068 559 1121 3205 2029 5031
הַנְּבִיאָה וַתַּהַר וַתֵּלֶד בֵּן וַיֹּאמֶר יְהוָה אֵלַי קְרָא שְׁמוֹ מַהֵר
Maher- | his name | Call | ,me to | Jehovah | then said | a ;son | and bore | she and conceived | the ,prophetess

5375 517 1 7121 5288 3045 2962 957 2363 7998
4 שָׁלָל חָשׁ בַּז׃ כִּי בְּטֶרֶם יֵדַע הַנַּעַר קְרֹא אָבִי וְאִמִּי יִשָּׂא
be will taken | my and ,mother | My ,father | to ,cry | the boy | knows | before | For | .baz | hash- | shalal-

804 4428 6440 8111 7998 1834 2428
אֶת־חֵיל דַּמֶּשֶׂק וְאֵת שְׁלַל שֹׁמְרוֹן לִפְנֵי מֶלֶךְ אַשּׁוּר׃
.Assyria | the of king | before | Samaria | the of plunder | and | Damascus | the of riches

2088 5971 3973 3286 559 5750 1696 3068 3254
5 וַיֹּסֶף יְהוָה דַּבֵּר אֵלַי עוֹד לֵאמֹר׃
6 יַעַן כִּי מָאַס הָעָם הַזֶּה
this | people | has rejected | Because | ,saying | ,still | me to | spoke | Jehovah | And more

1121 7526 4885 328 1980 7975 4325
אֵת מֵי הַשִּׁלֹחַ הַהֹלְכִים לְאַט וּמְשׂוֹשׂ אֶת־רְצִין וּבֶן
the and of son | Rezin | rejoices and in | ,gently | which flow | Shiloah | the of waters

and Remaliah's son, [7]Behold, therefore the Lord also brings on them the channels of the River, mighty and many: the king of Assyria and all his glory. And he shall come up over all its channels, and go over all its banks. [8]And he shall pass through Judah; He shall overflow and go over. He shall reach to the neck; and his wings will be stretching out, filling the breadth of your land, O Immanuel. [9]O peoples, suffer evil, and be broken! And listen, all from the far places of the earth; gird yourselves, and be broken. Gird yourselves and be broken! [10]Counsel a counsel, and it is frustrated; speak a word, and it shall not rise; for God *is* with us.

[11]For so Jehovah spoke to me with a strong hand, and taught me against walking in the way of this people, saying, [12]Do not say, A conspiracy, to everything of which this people says, A conspiracy! And do not fear its fear, and do not dread. [13]Sanctify Jehovah of hosts Himself, and let Him *be* your fear; and let Him *be* your dread. [14]And He shall be for a sanctuary, and for a stone of stumbling, and for a rock of falling to the two houses of Israel; for a trap and for a snare to the dweller of Jerusalem. [15]And many among them shall stumble and fall, and be broken, and be snared, and be taken. [16]Bind up the testimony, seal the law among My disciples. [17]And I will wait on Jehovah, who hides His face from the house of Jacob; and I will look for Him. [18]Behold, I and the children whom Jehovah has given to me *are* for signs and wonders in Israel from Jehovah of hosts, who dwells in Mount Zion.

7 רמליהו׃ ולכן הנה אדני מעלה עליהם את־מי הנהר
the River of channels the them on brings up the Lord ,behold And ,therefore .Remaliah

העצומים והרבים את־מלך אשור ואת־כל־כבודו ועלה
will it And up go his .glory all and Assyria king the of and many powerful

8 על־כל־אפיקיו והלך על־כל־גדותיו׃ וחלף ביהודה
through ;Judah he and pass shall its ;banks all over go and its channels all over

שטף ועבר עד־צואר יגיע והיה מטות כנפיו מלא־רחב
the of breadth filling his wings stretching out and be will shall he ;reach the neck to go and ;over shall he overflow

9 ארצך עמנו אל׃ רעו עמים וחתו והאזינו כל
all and listen be and ,broken O ,peoples Suffer ,evil .Immanuel Your ,land

10 מרחקי־ארץ התאזרו וחתו התאזרו וחתו׃ עצו עצה
a ,plan Counsel be and !broken gird yourselves be and ;broken gird yourselves the ;earth far from of places

11 ותפר דברו דבר ולא יקום כי עמנו אל׃ כי
For (is) .God with us for shall it :rise and not ,word a speak is it and ;broken

כה אמר יהוה אלי כחזקת היד ויסרני מלכת בדרך
the in of way against walking taught and me the ,hand the of strength me to Jehovah spoke thus

12 העם־הזה לאמר׃ לא־תאמרון קשר לכל אשר־יאמר
says of which every- thing to A conspiracy ,say Do not ,saying ,this people

העם הזה קשר ואת־מוראו לא־תיראו ולא תעריצו׃
.dread do not and ,fear do not dread its And A !conspiracy ,this people

13 את־יהוה צבאות אתו תקדישו והוא מוראכם והוא
and He fear your ,(be will) and He ,sanctify Him ,hosts of Jehovah

14 מערצכם׃ והיה למקדש ולאבן נגף ולצור מכשול לשני
the to two falling a and of rock stumb- ling a and of stone a ,sanctuary He And become shall .dread your

15 בתי ישראל לפח ולמוקש ליושב ירושלם׃ וכשלו בם
among them shall And stumble .Jerusalem the to of dweller a and snare a for trap ,Israel houses of

16 רבים ונפלו ונשברו ונוקשו ונלכדו׃ צור תעודה
the ,testimony Bind up be and .taken be and snared be and ,broken and ,fall ,many

17 חתום תורה בלמדי׃ וחכיתי ליהוה המסתיר פניו מבית
the from of house His face who hides for ,Jehovah will I And wait my among .disciples the law seal

18 יעקב וקויתי־לו׃ הנה אנכי והילדים אשר נתן־לי יהוה
Jehovah to me has given whom the and children I ,Behold .Him will I and for look ;Jacob

לאתות ולמופתים בישראל מעם יהוה צבאות השכן
who dwells ,hosts Jehovah of from Israel in and wonders for (are) signs

[19]And when they say to you, Seek to those who have familiar spirits, and to wizards who peep and mutter; should not a people seek to its God, *than* for the living to *seek* to the dead? [20]To the law and to the testimony! If they do not speak according to this word, *it is* because there is no dawn to them! [21]And they shall pass through it, hard-pressed and hungry. And it shall be, they shall be hungry; he will rave and curse his king and his God, and face upward. [22]And they shall look to the land. And, behold, trouble and darkness and gloom of anguish; and *they* are driven *to* darkness.

CHAPTER 9

[1]Yet there shall not be gloom for which anguish *is* to her; as *in* the former time *when* He degraded the land of Zebulun, and the land of Naphtali, so afterwards He will glorify the way of the sea, beyond the Jordan, Galilee of the nations: [2]The people who walk in darkness have seen a great light. The ones who dwell in the land of the shadow of death —Light has shone on them. [3]You have multiplied the nation; You have increased the joy. They rejoice before You as in the joy of harvest, as *men* shout when they divide the plunder. [4]For You have broken his burdensome yoke and the staff of his shoulder, the rod of his taskmaster, as *in* the day of Midian. [5]For every boot of the trampler *is* with commotion, and a coat rolled in blood shall be burning fuel for the fire. [6]For a Child is born; to us a Son is given; and the government is on His shoulder; and His name is called

178 1875 559 6726 2022
19 בְּהַר צִיּוֹן׃ וְכִי־יֹאמְרוּ אֲלֵיכֶם דִּרְשׁוּ אֶל־הָאֹבוֹת וְאֶל־
to and the to Seek ,you to they And .Zion in
mediums say when Mount

1875 430 5971 3808 1897 6850 3049
הַיִּדְּעֹנִים הַמְצַפְצְפִים וְהַמַּהְגִּים הֲלוֹא־עַם אֶל־אֱלֹהָיו יִדְרֹשׁ
seek God its to a should and who the
people not —mutter peep wizards

559 3808/518 8584 8451 4191 2418
20 בְּעַד הַחַיִּים אֶל־הַמֵּתִים׃ לְתוֹרָה וְלִתְעוּדָה אִם־לֹא יֹאמְרוּ
do they not If the to and the To the to the (than)
speak !testimony law ?dead (seek) living for

7457 7185 5674 7837 369 1697
21 כַּדָּבָר הַזֶּה אֲשֶׁר אֵין־לוֹ שָׁחַר׃ וְעָבַר בָּהּ נִקְשֶׁה וְרָעֵב
and hard through they And .dawn to not then ,this according
.hungry pressed it pass shall them is word to

6437 430 4428 7043 7107 7456 1961
וְהָיָה כִי־יִרְעַב וְהִתְקַצַּף וְקִלֵּל בְּמַלְכּוֹ וּבֵאלֹהָיו וּפָנָה
and his and his and will he shall they that it And
face God king curse rave hungry be be shall

6695 4588 2825 6864 2009 5027 776 4605
22 לְמָעְלָה׃ וְאֶל־אֶרֶץ יַבִּיט וְהִנֵּה צָרָה וַחֲשֵׁכָה מְעוּף צוּקָה
anguish gloom and ,distress ,and they the And .upward
of ,darkness ,behold ;look shall land to

6256 4164 834 4155 3808 5080 653
23 וַאֲפֵלָה מְנֻדָּח׃ כִּי לֹא מוּעָף לַאֲשֶׁר מוּצָק לָהּ כָּעֵת
the As .her to anguish for (be shall) not Yet are (they) (to) and
time (was) which gloom .driven darkness

314 5320 776 2074 776 7043 7223
הָרִאשׁוֹן הֵקַל אַרְצָה זְבֻלוּן וְאַרְצָה נַפְתָּלִי וְהָאַחֲרוֹן
after- so ,Naphtali the and Zebulun land the He former the
wards of land of degraded (when)

1471 1551 3383 5676 3220 1870 3513
הִכְבִּיד דֶּרֶךְ הַיָּם עֵבֶר הַיַּרְדֵּן גְּלִיל הַגּוֹיִם׃
the Galilee the beyond the the will He
.nations of ,Jordan ,sea of way glorify

CAP. IX ט

CHAPTER 9

6757 776 3427 1419 216 7200 2822 1980 5971
1 הָעָם הַהֹלְכִים בַּחֹשֶׁךְ רָאוּ אוֹר גָּדוֹל יֹשְׁבֵי בְּאֶרֶץ צַלְמָוֶת
death- the in who they ;great a have in who The
;shadow of land dwell light seen darkness walk people

8057 1430 3808 1471 7235 5050 216
2 אוֹר נָגַהּ עֲלֵיהֶם׃ הִרְבִּיתָ הַגּוֹי לֹא הִגְדַּלְתָּ הַשִּׂמְחָה
.joy the have You not the have You on has light
increased ;nation multiplied .them shone

7998 2505 1523 7102/ 8057 6440 8056
שָׂמְחוּ לְפָנֶיךָ כְּשִׂמְחַת בַּקָּצִיר כַּאֲשֶׁר יָגִילוּ בְּחַלְּקָם שָׁלָל׃
.spoil they when the as as the in they before They
divide rejoicing ;harvest exult ,You rejoice

2865 5065 7626 7926 4294 5448 5923
3 כִּי ׀ אֶת־עֹל סֻבֳּלוֹ וְאֵת מַטֵּה שִׁכְמוֹ שֵׁבֶט הַנֹּגֵשׂ בּוֹ הַחִתֹּתָ
have you ,him him rod the his the and his yoke the For
,broken oppressing of ,shoulder of staff burden of

1556 8071 7494 5430 5431 3605 4080 3117
4 כְּיוֹם מִדְיָן׃ כִּי כָל־סְאוֹן סֹאֵן בְּרַעַשׁ וְשִׂמְלָה מְגוֹלָלָה
rolled a and with (is) the boot every For .Midian the as
coat ,shaking trampler of of day

3205 2206 784 3980 8316 1961 1818
5 בְּדָמִים וְהָיְתָה לִשְׂרֵפָה מַאֲכֹלֶת אֵשׁ׃ כִּי־יֶלֶד יֻלַּד־לָנוּ
;us to is a For the fuel burning for even shall it in
born child .fire for become blood

6382 8034 7121 7926 4951 1961 5414 1121
בֵּן נִתַּן־לָנוּ וַתְּהִי הַמִּשְׂרָה עַל־שִׁכְמוֹ וַיִּקְרָא שְׁמוֹ פֶּלֶא
wonder- His is and His on the is and to is a
,ful name called ;shoulder government ;us given son

Wonderful, Counselor, the mighty God, the everlasting Father, the Prince of Peace. 7There is no end to the increase of *His* government and of peace on the throne of David, and on His kingdom, to order it, and to sustain it with justice and with righteousness, from now and forever. The zeal of Jehovah of hosts will do this.

8The Lord sent a word into Jacob, and it has fallen into Israel. 9And all the people shall know — Ephraim and the inhabitants of Samaria, who say in pride and greatness of heart, 10Bricks have fallen, but we will build *with* cut stones; the sycamores are cut down, but we will use cedars instead. 11And Jehovah will set up Rezin's foes against him, and spur on his enemies; 12Syria in front, and the Philistines behind; and they shall devour Israel with all the mouth. In all this His anger does not turn away, but His hand *is* still stretched out. 13For the people do not turn to Him who strikes them, and they do not seek Jehovah of hosts. 14And Jehovah will cut off from Israel head and tail, branch and rush, *in* one day. 15The elder and the exalted of face; he *is* the head. And the prophet who teaches lies; he *is* the tail. 16For this people's leaders led *them* astray, and its guided ones *are* swallowed up. 17For this the Lord shall not rejoice over their young men, nor have pity on their orphans and widows—for everyone is a hypocrite and an evildoer; and every mouth speaks foolishness. In all this His anger does not turn away, but His hand *is* still stretched out.

18For wickedness burns like a fire; it shall devour the briers and thorns and shall kindle the thickets of the

4951 4766 79,65 8269 5702 1 1368 410 3289
6 יוֹעֵץ אֵל גִּבּוֹר אֲבִי־עַד שַׂר־שָׁלוֹם׃ לְםַרְבֵּה הַמִּשְׂרָה
the government | the To of increase | .peace | Prince | Everlasting ,Father | ,Mighty God the | Coun- selor

3559 4467 5921 1732 3678 7093 79,65
וּלְשָׁלוֹם אֵין־קֵץ עַל־כִּסֵּא דָוִד וְעַל־מַמְלַכְתּוֹ לְהָכִין אֹתָהּ
it | order to | His ,kingdom | and on | ,David | the of throne | on ,end there no is | of and peace

3068 7068 5769 6258 6666 4941 5582
וּלְסַעֲדָהּ בְּמִשְׁפָּט וּבִצְדָקָה מֵעַתָּה וְעַד־עוֹלָם קִנְאַת יְהוָה
Jehovah of | The of zeal | .forever | and | from now | with and righteousness | with justice | to and it sustain

3290 136 79,71 1697 2088 62,13 6635
7 צְבָאוֹת תַּעֲשֶׂה־זֹּאת׃ דָּבָר שָׁלַח אֲדֹנָי בְּיַעֲקֹב
,Jacob into | the Lord | sent | word A | .this | will do | hosts

8111 3427 669 3605 5971 3045 3478 5307
8 וְנָפַל בְּיִשְׂרָאֵל׃ וְיָדְעוּ הָעָם כֻּלּוֹ אֶפְרַיִם וְיוֹשֵׁב שֹׁמְרוֹן
,Samaria | the and of inhabitants | Ephraim | all ,it of | the ,people | shall And know | .Israel into | it and fallen has

1129 1496 5307 3843 559 3822 14,33 1346
9 בְּגַאֲוָה וּבְגֹדֶל לֵבָב לֵאמֹר׃ לְבֵנִים נָפָלוּ וְגָזִית נִבְנֶה
will we ;build | (with) but stones cut | have fallen | Bricks | ,saying | ,heart | and of greatness | pride in

7526 6862 3068 7682 2498 730 14,38 8256
10 שִׁקְמִים גֻּדָּעוּ וַאֲרָזִים נַחֲלִיף׃ וַיְשַׂגֵּב יְהוָה אֶת־צָרֵי רְצִין
Rezin | foes the of | Jehovah | has And up set | will we .substitute | but cedars | cut are ,down | syca- mores

268 6430 6924 758 5526 341
11 עָלָיו וְאֶת־אֹיְבָיו יְסַכְסֵךְ׃ אֲרָם מִקֶּדֶם וּפְלִשְׁתִּים מֵאָחוֹר
—behind | the and Philistines | front in | Syria | :on spurs | his enemies | and against him

5750 639 7725/38,08 2088/3605 6310 3605 3478 398
וַיֹּאכְלוּ אֶת־יִשְׂרָאֵל בְּכָל־פֶּה בְּכָל־זֹאת לֹא־שָׁב אַפּוֹ וְעוֹד
but still | His ,anger | returns not | this all | In | the .mouth | with all | Israel | they and devour

6635 3068 5221 5704 7725/38,08 5971 5186 3027
12 יָדוֹ נְטוּיָה׃ וְהָעָם לֹא־שָׁב עַד־הַמַּכֵּהוּ וְאֶת־יְהוָה צְבָאוֹת
hosts | Jehovah of | and | who Him ,them strikes | to | do return | not | the For people | stretched (is) ,out | His hand

3712 2180 7218 3478 3068 3772 1875 38,08
13 לֹא דָרָשׁוּ׃ וַיַּכְרֵת יְהוָה מִיִּשְׂרָאֵל רֹאשׁ וְזָנָב כִּפָּה
branch | and ,tail | head | from Israel | Jehovah | will And off cut | do they .seek | not

5030 7218 1931 6440 5375 2205 259 3117 100
14 וְאַגְמוֹן יוֹם אֶחָד׃ זָקֵן וּנְשׂוּא־פָנִים הוּא הָרֹאשׁ וְנָבִיא
the and prophet | the ;head | he (is) | ,face | and of lifted | The elder | .one | day in | and ,rush

8582 2088 5971 833 1961 2180 1931 8267 3384
15 מוֹרֶה־שֶּׁקֶר הוּא הַזָּנָב׃ וַיִּהְיוּ מְאַשְּׁרֵי הָעָם־הַזֶּה מַתְעִים
led astray | this | people | leaders the of | And are | the .tail | he (is) | ,lying | teaching

136 8056 38,08 970 59,21 1104 833
16 וּמְאֻשָּׁרָיו מְבֻלָּעִים׃ עַל־כֵּן עַל־בַּחוּרָיו לֹא־יִשְׂמַח ׀ אֲדֹנָי
the ,Lord | shall rejoice | not | their men young | over | ,Therefore | (are) .swallowed | its and ones guided

74,89 2611 3605 7355 38,08 490 3490
וְאֶת־יְתֹמָיו וְאֶת־אַלְמְנֹתָיו לֹא יְרַחֵם כִּי כֻלּוֹ חָנֵף וּמֵרַע
an and ,evildoer | (is) profane | every- one | for | will He ,pity | not | widows their | and | their orphans | and

3027 5750 639 7725 2088/3605 50,39 1696 6310 3605
וְכָל־פֶּה דֹּבֵר נְבָלָה בְּכָל־זֹאת לֹא־שָׁב אַפּוֹ וְעוֹד יָדוֹ
His hand | but still | His ,anger | returns not | this | all In | foolish- .ness | speaks | mouth and every

3341 398 7898 8086 7564 784 1197 5186
17 נְטוּיָה׃ כִּי־בָעֲרָה כָאֵשׁ רִשְׁעָה שָׁמִיר וָשַׁיִת תֹּאכֵל וַתִּצַּת
it and kindles | shall it devour | and thorns | briars | wicked- ;ness | a like fire | burns | For | out- (is) .stretched

forest; and they shall roll upward, like the going up of smoke. ¹⁹The land is scorched by the wrath of Jehovah of hosts, and the people shall be as the fuel of the fire; no man shall spare his brother. ²⁰And *he shall* cut off on the right hand, yet be hungry. And he shall eat on the left, but not be satisfied. Each man shall eat the flesh of his own arm; ²¹Manasseh, Ephraim; and Ephraim, Manasseh— together they are against Judah. In all this His anger does not turn away, but His hand *is* still stretched out.

18

3068	5678		6227	1348	55	3293:	5442
Jehovah	the By		.smoke	a as	they and	up roll	the thickets the
of	of wrath	3980		of column		,up roll	,forest of

	376	784:		5971	1961	776	6272	6635
to	man	the	fuel as	the	and	the	is	hosts
	;fire	of		people	is	;land	scorched	

19

8040		398	74:57	3225	5921/1604	2550	38.08	251
,left the	on	he and	is and	the	on he And	shall they	not	his
	eats		;hungry	hand right	off cuts	.spare		,brother

20

	669		4519		398	22.20	1320	376	7646	38:08
;Ephraim	,Manasseh	shall	own his	each	are they	but
			.eat	arm	of flesh	man	;satisfied	not

3808	-2088	3605	3063		3162	4519	669
not	,this	In	.Judah	against	they together	;Manasseh	and
	all				(are)		,Ephraim

	5186	3027	5750	:639 7725
stretched	is His	but	His returns
.out	hand	still	,anger

CAP. X ʼ

CHAPTER 10

CHAPTER 10

¹Woe to those who decree decrees of injustice, and writers *who* write toil; ²to keep back the poor from judgment, and to steal justice from the poor of My people; that widows may be their prey; that they may rob orphans. ³And what will you do in the day of visitation and of destruction? It comes from far away. To whom will you flee for help? And where will you leave your glory? ⁴Surely, he will grovel under the prisoners, and they will fall under the slain. In all this His anger does not turn away, but His hand *is* still stretched out.

⁵Woe *to* Assyria, the rod of My anger! And My fury is the staff in their hand. ⁶I will send him against an ungodly nation, and against the people of My wrath. I will command him to plunder plunder, and to strip off spoil, and to trample them like the mud of the streets. ⁷Yet he does not purpose this, nor does his heart think so. For it *is* in his heart to destroy, and to cut off not a few nations. ⁸For he says, Are not my

1
2

5186		3789	5999	3789		205	2711	2710		1945
keep to	(who)	toil	and	in-	justice of	who those	decree	Woe
back	,write		writers	justice of		decree	to

490	1961	5971	6041	4941	14:917	1800:	1779
widows	may that	My the from	justice	to and	the	from
	be	,people of poor		away take	,poor	judgment

3

7722	648.6	3117:	6213	4100	962	3490	:7998
of and	visita-	the in	will	And	they orphans	and	their
—ruin	,tion	of day	do you	what	!plunder		,spoil

3519	5800	58:33	5127/43:10	935	4801
your	you will	And	for	you shall	whom To	it	far from
?glory	leave	where	?help	flee	?comes	away

4

2088	3605	5307	2026	8478	615:	8478	3766	11 :15
,this	all	In	they	the	and	the	under	will he	Surely
			fall will	slain	under	,prisoners		grovel

5

7626	804	9145		5286	3027	5750	:639 7725
the	,Assyria	Woe	stretched	is His	but	His returns not
of rod		to	.out	hand	still	,anger

6

5971 5921		2611	1471	2195	3027		4294	639
the on even	will I	profane	Against	My	their in	it	the and	My
of people	;him send	nation a	.fury	,hand	(is)	,staff	,anger

2563	4823	7760	957	9162	:7998	7997	6680	5678
the like	tram- a	to and	,spoil to and	,plunder	to	will I	My
of mud	pling	them make	spoil		plunder	,him order	wrath

7

	2803	3651	3808	3824	18 :19		2351
for	does	so not	his and	does	so not	Yet	the
;think			heart	,intend		he	.streets

8

559	4592	38.08	1471	3772	38:22	8045
he	For	.few a	not	nations	to and	to
,says					off cut	destroy
					,heart his	

commanders all like kings?
9Is not Calno like Carchemish? Is Hamath not like Arpad? Is Samaria not like Damascus? 10As my hand has found the kingdoms of the idols—for their carved images *excelled* Jerusalem's and Samaria's — 11shall I not do to Jerusalem and her idols as I have done to Samaria and her idols? 12And it will be, when the Lord has broken off all His work on Mount Zion and on Jerusalem, I will visit on the fruit of the proud heart of the king of Assyria, and on the glory of his lofty eyes. 13For he says, I have worked by the strength of my hand and by my wisdom; for I am wise. And I take away the borders of peoples, and have robbed their treasures. And like a mighty one, I subdue inhabitants. 14And my hand has found the riches of the people. Like a nest, I also have gathered all the earth, as forsaken eggs are gathered. And there was not one moving a wing, or opening a mouth, or one chirping.

15Shall the axe glorify itself over him chopping with it? Or shall the saw magnify itself over him moving it? As *if* a rod *could* wave those who lift it. As *if* a staff *could* raise *what is* not wood! 16Therefore, the Lord, Jehovah of hosts, shall send leanness among his fat ones. And under His glory *He* will kindle a burning like the burning of fire. 17And the light of Israel shall be for a fire, and His Holy One for a flame—and it shall burn and devour his thorns and briers in one day. 18And He shall consume the glory of his forest and his fruitful field, even from soul to flesh; and it shall be as a sick man melts away. 19And the rest of the trees of the forest

9 הֲלֹא שָׂרַי יַחְדָּו מְלָכִים׃ הֲלֹא כְּכַרְכְּמִישׁ כַּלְנוֹ אִם־לֹא
(is) not Or ?Calno like Carchemish Is not ?kings together my captains Are not

10 כְּאַרְפַּד חֲמָת אִם־לֹא כְדַמֶּשֶׂק שֹׁמְרוֹן׃ כַּאֲשֶׁר מָצְאָה
found has As ?Samaria like Damascus (is) not Or ?Hamath like Arpad

יָדִי לְמַמְלְכֹת הָאֱלִיל וּפְסִילֵיהֶם מִירוּשָׁלִַם וּמִשֹּׁמְרוֹן׃
than and ,Samaria than (more were) Jerusalem their and images carved the ,idols the to of kingdoms My hand

11 הֲלֹא כַּאֲשֶׁר עָשִׂיתִי לְשֹׁמְרוֹן וְלֶאֱלִילֶיהָ כֵּן אֶעֱשֶׂה
do I so to and ,idols her Samaria to have I done as should not

12 לִירוּשָׁלִַם וְלַעֲצַבֶּיהָ׃ וְהָיָה כִּי־יְבַצַּע אֲדֹנָי אֶת־כָּל־
all the Lord has when off broken it And ,be will her to and ?idols to Jerusalem

מַעֲשֵׂהוּ בְּהַר צִיּוֹן וּבִירוּשָׁלִָם אֶפְקֹד עַל־פְּרִי־גֹדֶל לְבַב
heart of greatness of the on of fruit will I visit on and Jerusalem Zion on Mount His work

13 מֶלֶךְ־אַשּׁוּר וְעַל־תִּפְאֶרֶת רוּם עֵינָיו׃ כִּי אָמַר בְּכֹחַ יָדִי
my hand's By might he ,says For his .eyes high (of) the glory and on ,Assyria the of king

עָשִׂיתִי וּבְחָכְמָתִי כִּי נְבֻנוֹתִי וְאָסִיר ׀ גְּבֻלֹת עַמִּים וַעֲתוּדֹתֵיהֶם
their and treasures ,peoples of borders I And away take am I astute for my by and wisdom have I ,worked

14 שׁוֹשֵׂתִי וְאוֹרִיד כַּאבִּיר יוֹשְׁבִים׃ וַתִּמְצָא כַקֵּן ׀ יָדִי לְחֵיל
the of riches my hand a like nest has And found .inhabitants a as one mighty I and subdue have ;robbed

הָעַמִּים וְכֶאֱסֹף בֵּיצִים עֲזֻבוֹת כָּל־הָאָרֶץ אֲנִי אָסָפְתִּי וְלֹא
and not have ;gathered I the earth all ,forsaken eggs as and gathers one the ;peoples

15 הָיָה נֹדֵד כָּנָף וּפֹצֶה פֶה וּמְצַפְצֵף׃ הֲיִתְפָּאֵר הַגַּרְזֶן עַל
over the axe glorify Shall itself one or .chirping a ,mouth or opening ,wing a moving one there was

הַחֹצֵב בּוֹ אִם־יִתְגַּדֵּל הַמַּשּׂוֹר עַל־מְנִיפוֹ כְּהָנִיף שֵׁבֶט
rod's a As waving him over ?it moving saw the shall Or itself magnify with him ?it chopping

16 אֶת־מְרִימָיו כְּהָרִים מַטֶּה לֹא־עֵץ׃ לָכֵן יְשַׁלַּח הָאָדוֹן
the ,Lord shall send Therefore (is) (what) !wood not a staff's As raising who those ?it lift

יְהוָה צְבָאוֹת בְּמִשְׁמַנָּיו רָזוֹן וְתַחַת כְּבֹדוֹ יֵקַד יְקֹד כִּיקוֹד
burn- of ing like a ,burning will burn His glory and under ;leanness his among ones fat ,hosts Jehovah of

17 אֵשׁ׃ וְהָיָה אוֹר־יִשְׂרָאֵל לְאֵשׁ וּקְדוֹשׁוֹ לְלֶהָבָה וּבָעֲרָה
it and burn shall a for ;flame His and One Holy a for ,fire Israel the of light shall And be .fire

18 וְאָכְלָה שִׁיתוֹ וּשְׁמִירוֹ בְּיוֹם אֶחָד׃ וּכְבוֹד יַעְרוֹ וְכַרְמִלּוֹ
his and ,field fruitful his forest the And of glory .one day in his and briars his thorns and devour

19 מִנֶּפֶשׁ וְעַד־בָּשָׂר יְכַלֶּה וְהָיָה כִּמְסֹס נֹסֵס׃ וּשְׁאָר עֵץ
the of trees the And of rest sick a .man melts as away it and be shall will He ;consume flesh even to from soul

shall be few, so that a boy might write them.
[20]And it shall be in that day, the remnant of Israel, and the escaped ones from the house of Jacob, shall not any more lean on him who struck him. But *they* will truly lean on Jehovah, the Holy One of Israel. [21]The remnant shall return, the remnant of Jacob, to the mighty God. [22]For though Your people Israel is like the sand of the sea, *only* a remnant of it shall return; a determined end, overflowing *with* righteousness. [23]For the Lord Jehovah of hosts is making a full end, even ordained, in the midst of all the land. [24]Therefore, the Lord Jehovah of hosts says this: O My people who dwell *in* Zion, do not fear Assyria. He shall strike you with the rod, and he shall lift up his staff against you in the way of Egypt. [25]But yet a little while, and the fury is finished; and My anger *shall be* over their destruction. [26]And Jehovah of hosts shall stir up a whip on him according to the striking of Midian at the rock Oreb; and as His rod *was* on the sea, and He lifted it up in the way of Egypt. [27]And it shall be in that day, his burden shall turn away from on your shoulder, and his yoke from your neck; and the yoke shall be destroyed because of the anointing. [28]He has come to Aiath; he has passed to Migron; he has left his baggage at Michmash. [29]They have crossed the ford; they have bedded down at Geba; Ramah is afraid; Gibeah of Saul has fled.

[30]Daughter of ruins, shriek *with* your voice, bow, Laishah, afflicted of Anathoth. [31]Madmenah wanders; Gebim's inhabitants take refuge. [32]Yet he remains in Nob today; *he*

3117 1961 3789 5288 1961 4557 3293
20 והיה ביום ההוא | יערו מספר יהיו ונער יכתבם׃
,that day in it And be will write could a even shall few his
.them boy ;be forest

8172 3290 1004 6413 3478 7605 5750 3254 3808
לא־יוסיף עוד שאר ישראל ופליטת בית־יעקב להשען
lean to Jacob the the and Israel the more shall not
of house of escaped of remnant add

7605 571 3478 6918 3068 8172 5221
21 על־מכהו ונשען על־יהוה קדוש ישראל באמת׃ שאר
A .truth in ,Israel Holy the ,Jehovah on will but his on
remnant of One lean ,striker

5971 1961 518 1368 410 3290 7605 7725
22 ישוב שאר יעקב אל־אל גבור׃ כי אם־יהיה עמך
Your is though For .mighty the to ,Jacob rem- the shall
people God of nant ,return

7857 2782 3631 7725 7605 32:20 2344 3478
ישראל כחול הים שאר ישוב בו כליון חרוץ שוטף
over- ,decisive end a of shall a (only) the the like Israel
flowing ;it return remnant ,sea of sand

6213 66:35 3068 136 2782 3617 6666
23 צדקה׃ כי כלה ונחרצה אדני יהוה צבאות עשה
makes hosts Jehovah the and full a For (with)
of Lord ,ordained end ,righteousness

3068 136 559 776 3605 7130
24 בקרב כל־הארץ׃ לכן כה־אמר אדני יהוה
Jehovah the says thus ,Therefore the all the in
of Lord .land of midst

5221 7626 804 6726 3427 5971 3372 408 6635
צבאות אל־תירא עמי ישב ציון מאשור בשבט יככה
shall he the With !Assyria ,Zion who my O Do not ,hosts
,you strike rod (in) dwell people ,fear

4592 5750 4714 1870 5375 4294
25 ומטהו ישא עליך בדרך מצרים׃ כי־עוד מעט
little a yet But .Egypt the in against shall he his and
of way ,you up lift staff

3068 5782 8399 639 2195 3615 4213
26 מזער וכלה זעם ואפי על־תבליתם׃ ועורר עליו יהוה
Jehovah on shall And their over My and ,fury is and very
of him up stir .destruction anger finished

32:20 4294 6159 6697 4080 4347 7752 6635
צבאות שוט כמכת מדין בצור עורב ומטהו על־הים
the (was) (as) and ;Oreb the at Midian the as whip a hosts
;sea on rod His rock of striking

5448 5493 3117 1961 4714 1870 5375
27 ונשאו בדרך מצרים׃ והיה | ביום ההוא יסור סבלו
his shall ,that day in shall it And .Egypt the in he and
burden turn be of way it lifted

8081 6440 2254 5923 6677 5921 5923 7926 5921
מעל שכמך ועלו מעל צוארך וחבל על מפני־שמן׃
.fatness because the shall and your from his and your from
of yoke destroyed be ;neck on yoke ,shoulder on

5674 3627 6485 4363 4051 5674 5857 935
28 29 בא על־עית עבר במגרון למכמש יפקיד כליו׃ עברו
They his left he at into he ;Aiath on He
crossed .baggage Michmash ;Migron passed came

5127 7586 1387 74:14 2729 4411 1387 4569
מעברה גבע מלון לנו חרדה הרמה גבעת שאול נסה׃
has Saul Gibeah ;Ramah is to a Geba the
.fled of terrified ;them lodging (was) ;ford

5074 6068 6041 3919 7181 1530 1323 6963 6670
30 31 צהלי קולך בת־גלים הקשיבי לישה עניה ענתות׃ נדדה
wanders .Anathoth af- ;Laishah bow ;heaps daughter your Shriek
of flicted (ear your) of ,voice with

5975 50.11 31.17 5750 5736 1356 3427 4088
32 מדמנה ישבי הגבים העיזו׃ עוד היום בנב לעמד
(he) in today Yet take Gebim the ;Madmenah
;remains Nob .refuge of dwellers

will shake his hand *against* the mount of the daughter of Zion, the hill of Jerusalem. 33Behold, the Lord, Jehovah of hosts, shall lop the bough of terror! And the lofty ones shall be cut down, and the proud shall be humbled. 34And He shall cut down the thickets of the forest with iron, and Lebanon shall fall by a mighty one.

CHAPTER 11

1And a Shoot goes out from the stump of Jesse, and a Branch will bear fruit out of his roots. 2And the Spirit of Jehovah shall rest on Him; *He will have* the spirit of wisdom and understanding, the spirit of counsel and power, the spirit of knowledge and of the fear of Jehovah. 3And He is made to breathe in the fear of Jehovah. But He shall not judge by the seeing of His eyes, nor decide by the hearing of His ears. 4But He shall judge the poor in righteousness, and shall decide rightly for the meek of the earth. And He shall strike the earth with the rod of His mouth, and He shall slay the wicked with the breath of His lips. 5And righteousness shall be the encircler of His thighs, and faithfulness the encircler of His loins. 6And the wolf shall live with the lamb; and the leopard shall lie with the kid; and the calf and the young lion and the fatling together; and a little boy leads them. 7The cow and the bear shall feed, their young shall lie together; and the lion shall eat straw like the ox. 8And the infant shall play on the hole of the asp; yea, the weaned child shall put his hand on the viper's den. 9They shall not do evil, nor destroy in all My holy mountain. For the earth shall be full of the knowledge of Jehovah, as the waters cover the sea.
10And it shall be in that

---

713 2009 3389 1389 67:26/100-4 2022 3027 5130

33 יְנֹפֵף יָדוֹ הַר בֵּית־צִיּוֹן גִּבְעַת יְרוּשָׁלִָם׃ הִנֵּה הָאָדוֹן

the ,Behold .Jerusalem the ,Zion's daugh- (at) his he

,Lord of hill ter's mount hand shakes

143 8 6967 7311 4637 6288 5586 66:35 3068

יְהוָה צְבָאוֹת מְסָעֵף פֻּארָה בְּמַעֲרָצָה וְרָמֵי הַקּוֹמָה גְּדֻעִים

be shall high and with the lop shall ,hosts Jehovah

,down cut height of ones ,terror bough off of

3844 1270 3293 5442 5362 8213 1364

34 וְהַגְּבֹהִים יִשְׁפָּלוּ׃ וְנִקַּף סִבְכֵי הַיַּעַר בַּבַּרְזֶל וְהַלְּבָנוֹן

and with the the he And be shall the and

Lebanon ,iron forest of thickets cut shall .lowered ones lofty

5307 117

בְּאַדִּיר יִפּוֹל׃

shall a by

.fall one mighty

CAP. XI א

CHAPTER 11

59 21 5117 6509 8328 5342 3448 1503 2415 3318

1 וְיָצָא חֹטֶר מִגֵּזַע יִשָׁי וְנֵצֶר מִשָּׁרָשָׁיו יִפְרֶה׃ וְנָחָה עָלָיו

2

on shall And bear will of out a and ,Jesse the from a And

Him rest .fruit roots his branch of stump shoot out goes

1847 7307 1369 6098 7307 998 2451 7307 3068 7307

רוּחַ יְהוָה רוּחַ חָכְמָה וּבִינָה רוּחַ עֵצָה וּגְבוּרָה רוּחַ דַּעַת

knowl- the and counsel the and wisdom the ;Jehovah the

edge of spirit ;might of spirit ;understanding of spirit of Spirit

5869 4758 3808 3068 3373 7306 3068 3373

3 וְיִרְאַת יְהוָה׃ וַהֲרִיחוֹ בְּיִרְאַת יְהוָה וְלֹא־לְמַרְאֵה עֵינָיו

His the by But .Jehovah the in is He and ;Jehovah the and

eyes of seeing not of fear breathe to made of fear

1800 6664 8199 3198 241 4926 3808 8199

4 יִשְׁפּוֹט וְלֹא־לְמִשְׁמַע אָזְנָיו יוֹכִיחַ׃ וְשָׁפַט בְּצֶדֶק דַּלִּים

poor the righ- in He But .decide His the by and shall He

teousness judge shall ears of hearing not ,judge

7307 63:10 7626 776 5221 776 6035 43.34 3198

וְהוֹכִיחַ בְּמִישׁוֹר לְעַנְוֵי־אָרֶץ וְהִכָּה־אֶרֶץ בְּשֵׁבֶט פִּיו וּבְרוּחַ

with and His with the He And the the for with shall and

breath mouth's rod earth strikes earth of meek rightness decide

530 4975 232 6664 1961 7563 4191 8193

5 שְׂפָתָיו יָמִית רָשָׁע׃ וְהָיָה צֶדֶק אֵזוֹר מָתְנָיו וְהָאֱמוּנָה

and His the righteous- And the shall He lips' His

faithfulness thighs of band ness be shall .wicked kill

5695 7257 1423 5246 3532 2061 1481 2504 232

6 אֵזוֹר חֲלָצָיו׃ וְגָר זְאֵב עִם־כֶּבֶשׂ וְנָמֵר עִם־גְּדִי יִרְבָּץ וְעֵגֶל

the and shall the with the and the with the And .loins His the

calf ;lie kid leopard ;lamb wolf stay shall of band

7462 1677 6510 5090 6996 5288 3162 4806 3715

7 וּכְפִיר וּמְרִיא יַחְדָּו וְנַעַר קָטֹן נֹהֵג בָּם׃ וּפָרָה וָדֹב תִּרְעֶינָה

shall the and And .them leads little a and ;together the and the and

feed bear cow the boy fatling cub lion

81 73 8401 398 1241 738 3206 7257 3162

8 יַחְדָּו יִרְבְּצוּ יַלְדֵיהֶן וְאַרְיֵה כַּבָּקָר יֹאכַל־תֶּבֶן׃ וְשִׁעֲשַׁע

shall And .straw shall the like the and their shall together

play eat ox lion ;young lie

3808 1911 3027 1580 6848 3975 6620 23.52 3243

יוֹנֵק עַל־חֻר פָּתֶן וְעַל מְאוּרַת צִפְעוֹנִי גָּמוּל יָדוֹ הָדָה׃ לֹא

not shall his weaned a the den the and the the over suck-a

put hand child ,viper of on ;snake of hole ling

1844 776 4390 6944 2022 3605 7843 3808 7489

9 יָרֵעוּ וְלֹא־יַשְׁחִיתוּ בְּכָל־הַר קָדְשִׁי כִּי־מָלְאָה הָאָרֶץ דֵּעָה

of the be shall for My mountain in they and They

knowing earth full ;holy all destroy not evil do

3117 1961 3680 3220 4325 3068

10 אֶת־יְהוָה כַּמַּיִם לַיָּם מְכַסִּים׃ וְהָיָה בַּיּוֹם הַהוּא

,that day in it And .cover the the as Jehovah

be will sea waters

day, the Root of Jesse stands as a banner of peoples; nations shall seek to Him; and His resting place shall be glory.
11 And it shall be in that day, the Lord shall again set His hand, the second time, to recover the remnant of His people that remains, from Assyria, and from Egypt, and from Pathros, and from Ethiopia, and from Persia, and from Shinar, and from Hamath, and from the coasts of the sea.
12 And He shall lift up a banner for the nations, and shall gather the outcasts of Israel, and gather those dispersed from Judah, from the four wings of the earth.
13 And the envy of Ephraim shall turn off; and Judah's foes shall be cut off. Ephraim shall not envy Judah, and Judah shall not trouble Ephraim.
14 But they shall fly onto the shoulder of the Philistines to the west; they shall plunder the sons of the east, the stretching of the hand on Edom and Moab and the sons of Ammon; *they will* obey them.
15 And Jehovah shall utterly destroy the tongue of the sea of Egypt; and with His scorching wind He shall wave His hand over the River, and shall strike it into seven torrents, and make one tread *it* with shoes.
16 And there shall be a highway for the remnant of His people, those left from Assyria, as it was to Israel in the day when he came up out of the land of Egypt.

שרש ישי אשר עמד לנס עמים אליו גוים ידרשו והיתה

shall and shall nations to ;peoples a as stands that Jesse the
be ;seek Him of banner (is it) of root

11 מנחתו כבוד׃ והיה ביום ההוא יוסיף אדני

the shall ,that day in it And .glory resting His
Lord add be shall place

שנית ידו לקנות את־שאר עמו אשר ישאר מאשור

from remains that His the obtain to His second the
,Assyria ,people of remnant hand time

וממצרים ומפתרוס ומכוש ומעילם ומשנער ומחמת

from and from and from and from and from and from and
Hamath ,Shinar ,Persia ,Ethiopia ,Pathros ,Egypt

12 ומאיי הים׃ ונשא נס לגוים ואסף נדחי ישראל ונפצות

those and ;Israel out- the shall and the for a He And the from and
of dispersed of casts gather ,nations banner lift shall .sea of coasts

13 יהודה יקבץ מארבע כנפות הארץ׃ וסרה קנאת אפרים

;Ephraim the shall And the wings the from shall And Judah
of envy off turn .earth of four aside turn

וצררי יהודה יכרתו אפרים לא־יקנא את־יהודה ויהודה

and ,Judah shall not Ephraim be shall Judah and
Judah envy —off cut of foes

14 לא־יצר את־אפרים׃ ועפו בכתף פלשתים ימה יחדו

together the to the (on) the onto they But .Ephraim shall not
;west Philistines shoulder fly shall trouble

יבזו את־בני־קדם אדום ומואב משלוח ידם ובני עמון

Am- the and their stretch- the and Edom the the shall they
mon of sons ,hand of ing ,Moab ;east of sons spoil

15 משמעתם׃ והחרים יהוה את לשון ים־מצרים והניף

He and ;Egypt the the Jehovah shall And obeying
wave shall of sea of tongue destroy utterly .them

ידו על־הנהר בעים רוחו והכהו לשבעה נחלים והדריך

make and ,torrents seven into shall and His the in the over His
(it) tread (one) it strike ,wind of heat ,river hand

16 בנעלים׃ והיתה מסלה לשאר עמו אשר ישאר מאשור

from remains which His the for a there And with
,Assyria ,people of remnant highway be shall .shoes the

כאשר היתה לישראל ביום עלתו מארץ מצרים׃

.Egypt the from his the in Israel to was it as
of land up going of day

CAP. XII יב

CHAPTER 12

1 And in that day you shall say, O Jehovah, I will thank You. Though You were angry with me, turn away Your anger and You shall comfort me.
2 Behold, God is my salvation! I will trust and not be afraid, for my strength and song *is* Jah Jehovah; yea, He has become my salvation.
3 And you shall draw waters out of

1 ואמרת ביום ההוא אודך יהוה כי אנפת בי ישב אפך

Your turns with were You though Jeho- will I ,that day in you And
anger away ;me angry ,vah You thank say shall

2 ותנחמני׃ הנה אל ישועתי אבטח ולא אפחד כי עזי

my for be and will I my God ,Behold shall You and
strength ,afraid not trust !salvation (is) .me comfort

3 וזמרת יה יהוה ויהי־לי לישועה׃ ושאבתם־מים

water you And .salvation to He and ;Jehovah Jah (my) and
draw shall me became (is) song

4 the wells of salvation with joy. [4]And in that day you shall say, Praise Jehovah! Call on His name; declare His doings among the peoples; make mention that His name is exalted.
5 [5]Sing *to* Jehovah, for He has done majestically; this *is* known in all the earth.
6 [6]Cry and shout, O dweller of Zion! For great *is* the Holy One of Israel in your midst.

3034 3117 559 3444 4599 8342
4 בששון ממעיני הישועה: ואמרתם ביום ההוא הודו
Thank ,that day in you And .salvation the of out with
say shall of wells joy

2142 5949 5971 3045 8034 7121 3068
ליהוה קראו בשמו הודיעו בעמים עלילתיו הזכירו כי
that make His the among make His on Call !Jehovah
mention ;doings peoples known ;name

2088 3045 6213 1348 30:68 2167 8034 7682
5 נשגב שמו: זמרו יהוה כי גאות עשה מידעת זאת
this (is) has He majesti- for (to) Sing His is
known ;done cally Jehovah praise .name exalted

7130 1419 6726 3427 74.42 6670 776 3605
6 בכל־הארץ: צהלי ורני יושבת ציון כי־גדול בקרבך
your in great For !Zion dweller and Cry the in
midst of ,shout .earth all

3478 6918
קדוש ישראל:
.Israel the (is)
of One Holy

CAP. XIII יג

CHAPTER 13

CHAPTER 13

1 [1]The burden of Babylon which Isaiah the son of Amoz saw:
2 [2]Lift up a banner on a bare mountain; make the voice rise to them; wave the hand that they may enter the gates of nobles.
3 [3]I have commanded My holy ones; I have also called My warriors for My anger, those who rejoice in My highness.
4 [4]The noise of a multitude in the mountains, as of a great people! A noise of tumult of the kingdoms of nations gathered together; Jehovah of hosts is calling up an army for the battle.
5 [5]They come from a distant land, from the end of the heavens, Jehovah and the weapons of His wrath, to destroy all the land.
6 [6]Howl! For the day of Jehovah *is* at hand. It shall come as a destruction from the Almighty.
7 [7]On account of this all hands shall droop, and every heart of man shall melt;
8 [8]and they shall be afraid. Pangs and sorrows shall take hold of them; they shall be in pain like a woman bearing; they shall be amazed, each man to his neighbor; faces of flames *shall be* their faces.
9 [9]Behold, the day of Jehovah comes, cruel and *with* wrath and fierce anger, to lay the land waste. And He shall destroy its sinners

8192 2022 531 1121 3470 23:72 834 884 4853
1 משא בבל אשר חזה ישעיהו בן־אמוץ: על הר־נשפה
2 bare a on :Amoz the Isaiah saw which ,Babylon The
mountain of son of burden

5081 6607 935 30:27 5130 6963 7311 52:51/5375
שאו־נס הרימו קול להם הניפו יד ויבאו פתחי נדיבים:
.nobles the they that the wave to the Make a up Lift
of gates enter may hand ;them voice rise .banner

1346 5947 639 1368 7121 1571 69.42 6680
3 אני צויתי למקדשי גם קראתי גבורי לאפי עליזי גאותי:
My rejoicers My for My have I also holy My have I
.pride of ,anger warriors called ;ones commanded

4467 7588 6965 7227 5971 1823 2022 1995 6963
4 קול המון בהרים דמות עם־רב קול שאון ממלכות
kingdoms tumult A !great a like- the the in mul- a The
of of noise people of ness ;mountains titude of noise

4421 6635 6485 66:35 3068 622 1471
גוים נאספים יהוה צבאות מפקד צבא מלחמה:
.battle an is hosts Jehovah —assembled nations
of army mustering of

2195 3627 3068 8064 7093 4801 776 935
5 באים מארץ מרחק מקצה השמים יהוה וכלי זעמו
His and Jehovah the the from ,distant a from Are
,wrath of weapons ,heavens of end land coming

7.7.01 3068 3117 7138 3213 776 3605 2254
6 לחבל כל־הארץ: הילילו כי קרוב יום יהוה כשד
as ;Jehovah the (is) For !Howl the all to
destruction of day near .land destroy

582 3824 3605 7503 3027 3605 935 7706
7 משדי יבוא: על־כן כל־ידים תרפינה וכל־לבב אנוש
man heart and shall hands all ,Therefore shall it the from
of every droop .come Almighty

376 2342 32:05 270 2256 6735 926 4549
8 ימס: ונבהלו צירים וחבלים יאחזון כיולדה יחילון איש
a shall they giv- one as shall and pangs shall they and shall
man ;pain in be birth ing ;them seize sorrows ;afraid be ;melt

9 35 3068 3117 2009 6440 3851 6440 8539 74 53
9 אל־רעהו יתמהו פני להבים פניהם: הנה יום־יהוה בא
,comes Jeho- the ,Behold their flames faces shall they his to
vay of day .faces (be will) of ;amazed be ,neighbor

2400 80 47 776 776.0 639 2740 5678 394
אכזרי ועברה וחרון אף לשום הארץ לשמה וחטאיה
its And .waste the lay to ,anger and and ,cruel
sinners land of heat wrath

out of it. [10]For the stars of the heavens and their constellations shall not give light; the sun shall be darkened in its going forth, and the moon shall not reflect its light. [11]And I will visit evil on the world, and their iniquity on the wicked. And I will cause the arrogance of the proud to cease; and I will humble the pride of tyrants.

[12]I will make a man more rare than fine gold; even a man more than the carvings of Ophir. [13]So I will shake the heavens, and the earth shall move out of its place, in the wrath of Jehovah of hosts, and in the day of His fierce anger. [14]And it shall be as a gazelle driven away, and as a sheep no one gathers; each man shall look to his own people, and each one shall flee to his land. [15]Everyone who is found shall be pierced through; yea, everyone who is caught shall fall by the sword. [16]And their children shall be dashed in pieces before their eyes; their houses shall be robbed, and their wives raped. [17]Behold, I stir up the Medes against them, who shall not value silver. And they shall not delight in gold. [18]And bows shall also smash the young men to pieces; and they shall have no pity on the fruit of the womb; their eye shall not spare sons. [19]And Babylon, the glory of the kingdoms, the beauty of the pride of the Chaldeans, shall be as when God overthrew Sodom and Gomorrah. [20]It shall never be inhabited forever, nor shall it be lived in from generation to generation. And the Arabian shall not pitch a tent there, nor shall the shepherds make *flocks* lie down there. [21]But the desert creatures shall lie there; and their houses shall be full of howling creatures; and daughters of

1984 3808 3684 80 64 3556 8045
10 יַשְׁמִיד מִמֶּנָּה׃ כִּי־כוֹכְבֵי הַשָּׁמַיִם וּכְסִילֵיהֶם לֹא יָהֵלּוּ
shall not their and the the For of out shall He
shine constellations heavens of stars .it destroy

6485 216 5050/3808 3394 3318 8121 2821 216
11 אוֹרָם חָשַׁךְ הַשֶּׁמֶשׁ בְּצֵאתוֹ וְיָרֵחַ לֹא־יַגִּיהַּ אוֹרוֹ׃ וּפָקַדְתִּי
will I And its shall not the and its in the is their
visit .light reflect moon ;forth going sun dark ;light

2086 1347 7673 577.1 7563 5921 74:51 8398
עַל־תֵּבֵל רָעָה וְעַל־רְשָׁעִים עֲוֹנָם וְהִשְׁבַּתִּי גְּאוֹן זֵדִים
proud arro- the will I And their the and ,evil the on
,ones of gance cease make .iniquity wicked on world

3800 120 6337 582 3365 8213 6184 1346
12 וְגַאֲוַת עָרִיצִים אַשְׁפִּיל׃ אוֹקִיר אֱנוֹשׁ מִפָּז וְאָדָם מִכֶּתֶם
fine than a and than man a make will I will I tyrants the and
of gold man ;gold rare more ,low bring of pride

4725 776 7493 7264 8064 211
13 אוֹפִיר׃ עַל־כֵּן שָׁמַיִם אַרְגִּיז וְתִרְעַשׁ הָאָרֶץ מִמְּקוֹמָהּ
its of out the shall and will I the ,Therefore .Ophir
,place earth move ,shake heavens

6643 1961 639 2740 3117 6635 3068 5678
14 בְּעֶבְרַת יְהוָה צְבָאוֹת וּבְיוֹם חֲרוֹן אַפּוֹ׃ וְהָיָה כִּצְבִי
a as it And His the in and ,hosts Jehovah the in
gazelle be shall .anger of heat of day the of of wrath

376 6437 5971 376 6908 369 6629 50:80
מֻדָּח וּכְצֹאן וְאֵין מְקַבֵּץ אִישׁ אֶל־עַמּוֹ יִפְנוּ וְאִישׁ
each and they his to each ;gathers and as and ;chased
.one ,look shall people man none sheep a

5307 5595 3605 1856 4672 36 05 5127 776
15 אֶל־אַרְצוֹ יָנוּסוּ׃ כָּל־הַנִּמְצָא יִדָּקֵר וְכָל־הַנִּסְפֶּה יִפּוֹל
shall is who and be shall is who Everyone they his to
fall caught everyone ;pierced found .flee shall land

802 1004 8155 5869 7376 5768 2719
16 בֶחָרֶב׃ וְעֹלְלֵיהֶם יְרֻטְּשׁוּ לְעֵינֵיהֶם יִשַּׁסּוּ בָּתֵּיהֶם וּנְשֵׁיהֶם
their and their be shall their before be shall their And the by
wives ;houses robbed ;eyes dashed children .sword

3808 3701 834 4074 5782 2009 7693
17 תִּשָּׁגַלְנָה׃ הִנְנִי מֵעִיר עֲלֵיהֶם אֶת־מָדָי אֲשֶׁר־כֶּסֶף לֹא
not silver who the against stir ,Behold .raped
,Medes them up I

7376 5288 7198 2654 3808 2091 2803
18 יַחְשֹׁבוּ וְזָהָב לֹא יַחְפְּצוּ־בוֹ׃ וּקְשָׁתוֹת נְעָרִים תְּרַטַּשְׁנָה
dash shall young bows And in shall not and shall
;pieces to men .it delight gold ,reckon

1961 5869 2347/3808 1121 7355 3808 990 6529
19 וּפְרִי־בֶטֶן לֹא יְרַחֵמוּ עַל־בָּנִים לֹא־תָחוּס עֵינָם׃ וְהָיְתָה
shall And their shall not sons on shall they not the the and
be .eye spare ;pity womb of fruit

4114 3778 1347 8597 4467 6643 894
בָבֶל צְבִי מַמְלָכוֹת תִּפְאֶרֶת גְּאוֹן כַּשְׂדִּים כְּמַהְפֵּכַת
when as the pride the the ,kingdoms the ,Babylon
overthrew ,Chaldeans of of beauty of glory

7931 3808 5331 3427 3808 6017 5467 430
20 אֱלֹהִים אֶת־סְדֹם וְאֶת־עֲמֹרָה׃ לֹא־תֵשֵׁב לָנֶצַח וְלֹא תִשְׁכֹּן
be it shall and ,forever shall It not .Gomorrah and Sodom God
in lived not inhabited be

8033 7257 3808 7462 61:63 8033 167 3808 1755 1755 5704
עַד־דּוֹר וָדוֹר וְלֹא־יַהֵל שָׁם עֲרָבִי וְרֹעִים לֹא־יַרְבִּצוּ שָׁם׃
.there make shall not and the there shall And gen- and genera- to
lie (flocks) shepherds ,Arabian tent pitch not .eration tion

1323 8033 7931 255 1004 4390 672:8 8033 7257
21 וְרָבְצוּ־שָׁם צִיִּים וּמָלְאוּ בָתֵּיהֶם אֹחִים וְשָׁכְנוּ שָׁם בְּנוֹת
daughters there and howling of their shall And desert there shall But
of dwell shall ,creatures houses full be .creatures lie

ostriches shall dwell there; and he-goats shall skip there. 22And hyenas shall cry along with his widows; and jackals in palaces of delight. Yea, her time to come *is* near, and her days shall not be prolonged.

CHAPTER 14

1For Jehovah will have pity on Jacob, and will yet choose among Israel, and set them in their own land. And the stranger shall be joined to them; and they shall cling to the house of Jacob. 2And the peoples shall take them and bring them to their own place. And the house of Israel shall possess them in the land of Jehovah for slaves and slavegirls. And they shall be captives of their captors; and they shall rule over their oppressors. 3And it shall be, in the day that Jehovah shall give you rest from your sorrow, and from your trouble, and from the hard bondage which was pressed on you, 4you shall take up this proverb against the king of Babylon, and say: How the exactor, the gold gatherer, has ceased! 5Jehovah has broken the rod of the wicked, the staff of rulers, 6who struck the peoples in wrath, a blow without turning away, ruling the nations in anger, *dealing out* persecution without restraint. 7All the earth is at rest, quiet; they break forth into singing. 8Yea, the firtrees rejoice over you; the cedars of Lebanon *say,* Since you have lain down, no woodcutter will come up against us.

9Sheol from below is stirred for you, to meet you at your coming; it stirs up the departed spirits for you, all the he-goats of the earth. It has raised all the kings of the nations from their thrones. 10All of them shall answer and say to you, Are

8577 490 338 6030 8033 7540 8163 32:84
22 יַעֲנָה וּשְׂעִירִים יְרַקְּדוּ־שָׁם׃ וְעָנָה אִיִּים בְּאַלְמְנוֹתָיו וְתַנִּים
and jackals his with ,widows hyenas And cry shall .there shall skip he- goats and ;ostriches
4900 38:08 3117 62:56 935 71:38 602:7 1964
בְּהֵיכְלֵי עֹנֶג וְקָרוֹב לָבוֹא עִתָּהּ וְיָמֶיהָ לֹא יִמָּשֵׁכוּ׃
be shall .prolonged not her and days her (is) ,time to come and near ,delight in of palaces

CAP. XIV יד

CHAPTER 14

3240 34:78 5750 977 3290 30 68 7355
1 כִּי יְרַחֵם יְהוָה אֶת־יַעֲקֹב וּבָחַר עוֹד בְּיִשְׂרָאֵל וְהִנִּיחָם
give and rest them among ,Israel yet will and choose ,Jacob on Jehovah have will For pity
3290 1004 5596 1616 38:67 127
עַל־אַדְמָתָם וְנִלְוָה הַגֵּר עֲלֵיהֶם וְנִסְפְּחוּ עַל־בֵּית יַעֲקֹב׃
.Jacob the of house to they and cling shall ;them to the alien shall And be joined their .land on
1004 5157 4725 935 5971 3947
2 וּלְקָחוּם עַמִּים וֶהֱבִיאוּם אֶל־מְקוֹמָם וְהִתְנַחֲלוּם בֵּית־
the of house shall And them possess their .place to bring and them peoples shall And them take
7617 1961 8198 5650 30:68 127 347:8
יִשְׂרָאֵל עַל אַדְמַת יְהוָה לַעֲבָדִים וְלִשְׁפָחוֹת וְהָיוּ שֹׁבִים
cap- tives they and be shall slave- and ,girls for slaves Jehovah land the of on Israel
3068 51:17 3117 19:61 5065 7287 7617
3 וְהָיָה בְּיוֹם הָנִיחַ יְהוָה לְשֹׁבֵיהֶם וְרָדוּ בְּנֹגְשֵׂיהֶם׃
Jehovah shall rest give the in day it And be shall their over .oppressors they and .rule shall their of ;captors
5647 834 71:86 5656 7267 6090
לְךָ מֵעָצְבְּךָ וּמֵרָגְזֶךָ וּמִן־הָעֲבֹדָה הַקָּשָׁה אֲשֶׁר עֻבַּד־בָּךְ׃
on ;you was pressed which ,hard the bondage and from from and ,trouble your your from ,toil to you
7673 349 559 884 4428 2088 4912 5375
4 וְנָשָׂאתָ הַמָּשָׁל הַזֶּה עַל־מֶלֶךְ בָּבֶל וְאָמָרְתָּ אֵיךְ שָׁבַת
has ceased How ,say and ,Babylon the of king against this proverb will you and up take
7626 7563 4294 3068 7665 4062 7673 506 5
5 נֹגֵשׂ שָׁבְתָה מַדְהֵבָה׃ שָׁבַר יְהוָה מַטֵּה רְשָׁעִים שֵׁבֶט
staff the of the ,wicked the of rod Jehovah Has broken gold the !gatherer has ceased the ;exactor
7287 5627 1115 4347 56:78 5971 4347 49 10
6 מֹשְׁלִים׃ מַכֶּה עַמִּים בְּעֶבְרָה מַכַּת בִּלְתִּי סָרָה רֹדֶה
ruling turning ;away without blow a —wrath in peoples striking ,rulers
776 36 05 8252 5117 2820 1097 4783 1471 639
7 בָאַף גּוֹיִם מֻרְדָּף בְּלִי חָשָׂךְ׃ נָחָה שָׁקְטָה כָּל־הָאָרֶץ
the ;earth All (and) quiet at is rest .restraint without perse- cution ;nations in anger
3844 730 8056 1265 1571 7440 6476
8 פָּצְחוּ רִנָּה׃ גַּם־בְּרוֹשִׁים שָׂמְחוּ לְךָ אַרְזֵי לְבָנוֹן מֵאָז
Since Lebanon (say) the of cedars over ;you rejoice fir trees ,Yea .singing break they into out
7264 7585 3772 5927 38 08 7901
9 שָׁכַבְתָּ לֹא־יַעֲלֶה הַכֹּרֵת עָלֵינוּ׃ שְׁאוֹל מִתַּחַת רָגְזָה לְךָ
for ,you is stirred from below Sheol against .us wood- cutter the will up come not have you ,down lain
6965 776 6260 3605 7496 57 82 935 7125
לִקְרַאת בּוֹאֶךָ עוֹרֵר לְךָ רְפָאִים כָּל־עַתּוּדֵי אָרֶץ הֵקִים
has It raised the .earth he- of goats the all departed spirits for you it up stirs your ;coming meet to
1571 559 6030 3605 1471 44 28 3605 3678
10 מִכִּסְאוֹתָם כֹּל מַלְכֵי גוֹיִם׃ כֻּלָּם יַעֲנוּ וְיֹאמְרוּ אֵלֶיךָ גַּם־
Also to ,you say and shall answer All them of the .nations the of kings all their from thrones

you also made as weak as we? Are you likened to us? 11 Your majesty is lowered into Sheol; the noise of your harps. The maggot is spread under you; yea, the worms cover you. 12 O shining star, son of the morning, how you have fallen from the heavens! You weakening the nations, you are cut down to the ground. 13 For you have said in your heart, I will go up *to* the heavens; I will raise my throne above the stars of God, and I will sit in the mount of meeting, in the sides of the north. 14 I will rise over the heights of the clouds; I will be compared to the Most High. 15 Yet you shall be brought out to Sheol, to the sides of the Pit. 16 They that see you shall stare and closely watch you, *saying*, Is this the man who made the earth tremble, shaking kingdoms, 17 making the world like a wilderness, and who tore down its cities—he did not open a house *for* his prisoners? 18 All kings of nations, all of them lie in glory, each man in his house. 19 But you are thrown from your grave *like* a despised branch, *like* the covering of the slain, those pierced by the sword, those who go down into the stones of the Pit, like a dead body trampled under foot.

20 You shall not be united with them in burial, because you ruined your land; you have slain your people; the seed of evildoers shall never be named. 21 Prepare for the slaughter of his sons, for the iniquity of their fathers; that they may not rise and possess the land, and fill the face of the earth *with* cities. 22 For I will rise against them, says Jehovah of hosts, and cut off the name and remnant, the son and grandson, from Babylon, declares Jehovah. 23 I will make it a possession of the hedgehog, and pools of water; and I will sweep it

1347 7585 3381 4911 2470
11 אַתָּה חֻלֵּיתָ כָמוֹנוּ אֵלֵינוּ נִמְשָׁלְתָּ׃ הוּרַד שְׁאוֹל גְּאוֹנֶךָ
Your into goes are you us To we as made are you
,majesty Sheol down !likened !(are) weak

349 8438 4374 7415 3311 8478 5035 1998
12 הֶמְיַת נְבָלֶיךָ תַּחְתֶּיךָ יֻצַּע רִמָּה וּמְכַסֶּיךָ תּוֹלֵעָה׃ אֵיךְ
How .worms cover and the is Under your noise the
you ,maggot spread you .harps of

2522 776 1438 7837 1121 1966 8064 5307
נָפַלְתָּ מִשָּׁמַיִם הֵילֵל בֶּן־שָׁחַר נִגְדַּעְתָּ לָאָרֶץ חוֹלֵשׁ עַל־
on who the to are You the son shining O the from have you
weakens ,ground down cut !morning of ,star ,heavens fallen

4605 5927 8064 3824 559 1471
13 גּוֹיִם׃ וְאַתָּה אָמַרְתָּ בִלְבָבְךָ הַשָּׁמַיִם אֶעֱלֶה מִמַּעַל
above will I the (to) your in have For the
;up go heavens ,heart said you nations

3411 4150 2022 3427 3678 7311 410 3556
לְכוֹכְבֵי־אֵל אָרִים כִּסְאִי וְאֵשֵׁב בְּהַר־מוֹעֵד בְּיַרְכְּתֵי
the in ,meeting the on I And my will I God the
of sides of mount sit will .throne raise of stars

389 5945 1819 5645 1116 5921 5927 6828
14 15 צָפוֹן׃ אֶעֱלֶה עַל־בָּמֳתֵי עָב אֶדַּמֶּה לְעֶלְיוֹן׃ אַךְ אֶל־
to Yet the to be will I ;clouds the over will I the
.High Most likened of heights up go .north

7688 7200 935 3411 3381 7585
16 שְׁאוֹל תּוּרָד אֶל־יַרְכְּתֵי־בוֹר׃ רֹאֶיךָ אֵלֶיךָ יַשְׁגִּיחוּ אֵלֶיךָ
at shall at who They the the to shall you Sheol
you ,stare you you see .Pit of sides ,down go

4467 7493 776 7264 376 2088 995
יִתְבּוֹנָנוּ הֲזֶה הָאִישׁ מַרְגִּיז הָאָרֶץ מַרְעִישׁ מַמְלָכוֹת׃
;kingdoms shaking the making the Is shall
earth tremble man this ,ponder

1004 6605 3808 615 2040 5892 4057 8398 7760
17 שָׂם תֵּבֵל כַּמִּדְבָּר וְעָרָיו הָרָס אֲסִירָיו לֹא־פָתַח בָּיְתָה׃
a he not his tore its and a like the setting
?house opened prisoners ,down cities ;desert world

1004 376 3519 7901 3605 4428 1471 3605
18 19 כָּל־מַלְכֵי גוֹיִם כֻּלָּם שָׁכְבוּ בְכָבוֹד אִישׁ בְּבֵיתוֹ׃ וְאַתָּה
you But his in each ,glory in lie all ,nations kings All
.house man them of of

2716 2944 2026 3830 8581 5342 6913 7993
הָשְׁלַכְתָּ מִקִּבְרְךָ כְּנֵצֶר נִתְעָב לְבוּשׁ הֲרֻגִים מְטֹעֲנֵי חָרֶב
the those ,slain the (as) ;despised a like your from are
,sword by pierced of covering branch grave thrown

6900 3161 3808 947 6297 953 68 3381
20 יוֹרְדֵי אֶל־אַבְנֵי־בוֹר כְּפֶגֶר מוּבָס׃ לֹא־תֵחַד אִתָּם בִּקְבוּרָה
;burial in with shall You not .trampled a as ,Pit the the in- who those
them united be corpse of stones to down go

2233 5769 7121 3808 2026 5971 7843 776
כִּי־אַרְצְךָ שִׁחַתָּ עַמְּךָ הָרַגְתָּ לֹא־יִקָּרֵא לְעוֹלָם זֶרַע
the forever be let not have you your you your because
of seed called ;slain people ;ruined land

6965 1077 1 5771 4293 1121 3559 7489
21 מְרֵעִים׃ הָכִינוּ לְבָנָיו מַטְבֵּחַ בַּעֲוֹן אֲבוֹתָם בַּל־יָקֻמוּ
them let not their for ,slaughter for Prepare !evildoers
rise ,fathers' iniquity sons his

5002 6965 6145 8398 6440 4390 776 3423
22 וְיָרְשׁוּ אָרֶץ וּמָלְאוּ פְנֵי־תֵבֵל עָרִים׃ וְקַמְתִּי עֲלֵיהֶם נְאֻם
states against I For (with) the the and the and
,them rise will cities earth of face fill ,land possess

5002 5220 5209 7605 8034 884 3772 6635 3068
יְהוָה צְבָאוֹת וְהִכְרַתִּי לְבָבֶל שֵׁם וּשְׁאָר וְנִין וָנֶכֶד נְאֻם־
states and son and and name from cut and ,hosts Jehovah
,posterity ,remnant Babylon off of

2894 4325 98 7090 4180 7760 3068
23 יְהוָה׃ וְשַׂמְתִּיהָ לְמוֹרַשׁ קִפֹּד וְאַגְמֵי־מָיִם וְטֵאטֵאתִיהָ
will I and ;water and the pos- a will I .Jehovah
it sweep of pools ,hedgehog of session it make

with the broom of ruin, says Jehovah of hosts.

[24]Jehovah of hosts has sworn, saying, Surely as I have thought, so it shall be; and as I have purposed, it shall rise up; [25]to break Assyria in My land, and trample him on My mountains. Then his yoke shall depart from them, and his burden shall depart from his shoulders. [26]This *is* the purpose that is purposed on all the earth; and this the hand that is stretched out on all the nations. [27]For Jehovah of hosts has purposed. And who shall reverse *it*? And His hand is stretched out. Who shall turn it back?

[28]This burden was in the year king Ahaz died: [29]Do not rejoice, O Philistia, all of you, for the rod of your striking is broken, because a viper comes forth from the root of a snake, and his fruit *shall be* a fiery flying serpent. [30]And the firstborn of the poor shall eat; and the needy shall lie down in safety; and I will kill your root with famine; and it shall kill your remnant. [31]Howl, O gate! Cry, O city! Philistia *is* melted away, all of you. For a smoke comes from the north, and not one is alone in his ranks. [32]What then shall one answer to the messengers of the nation? That Jehovah has founded Zion, and the poor of His people shall trust in it.

3068 7650 6635 3068 5002 8045 4292

24 בְּמַטְאֲטֵא הַשְׁמֵד נְאֻם יְהוָה צְבָאוֹת׃ נִשְׁבַּע יְהוָה

Jehovah has .hosts Jehovah states ,ruin the with
of sworn of of broom

1961 3651 1819 3808 518 559 6635

צְבָאוֹת לֵאמֹר אִם־לֹא כַּאֲשֶׁר דִּמִּיתִי כֵּן הָיָתָה וְכַאֲשֶׁר

as and ,is it so have I as ,Surely ,saying ,hosts
,thought

2022 776 804 7665 6965 3289

25 יָעַצְתִּי הִיא תָקוּם׃ לִשְׁבֹּר אַשּׁוּר בְּאַרְצִי וְעַל־הָרַי

My on and My in Assyria break to shall it have I
mountains ,land ;rise ,purposed

5493 7926 5448 5923 5493 947

אֲבוּסֶנּוּ וְסָר מֵעֲלֵיהֶם עֻלּוֹ וְסֻבֳּלוֹ מֵעַל שִׁכְמוֹ יָסוּר׃

shall his from his and his from Then trample will I
go shoulders burden yoke them depart shall.him

5186 3027 2088 776 3605 6098 6098 2088

26 זֹאת הָעֵצָה הַיְּעוּצָה עַל־כָּל־הָאָרֶץ וְזֹאת הַיָּד הַנְּטוּיָה

is that the and the all on is that the This
out stretched hand this ;earth purposed purpose (is)

3027 6565 4310 3289 6635 3068 1471 3605

27 עַל־כָּל־הַגּוֹיִם׃ כִּי־יְהוָה צְבָאוֹת יָעָץ וּמִי יָפֵר וְיָדוֹ

And shall who and ,purposes hosts Jehovah For the all on
hand His ?reverse of .nations

271 4428 4194 8141 7725 4310 5186

28 הַנְּטוּיָה וּמִי יְשִׁיבֶנָּה׃ בִּשְׁנַת־מוֹת הַמֶּלֶךְ אָחָז

,Ahaz King the the In turn shall and ex- is
of death of year ?back it who tended

7665 3605 6429 8055 408 2088 4853 1961

29 הָיָה הַמַּשָּׂא הַזֶּה׃ אַל־תִּשְׂמְחִי פְלֶשֶׁת כֻּלֵּךְ כִּי נִשְׁבַּר

is for of all O Do not :this burden was
broken ,you ,Philistia ,rejoice

8314 6529 6848 3318 5175 8328 5221 7626

שֵׁבֶט מַכֵּךְ כִּי־מִשֹּׁרֶשׁ נָחָשׁ יֵצֵא צֶפַע וּפִרְיוֹ שָׂרָף

fiery a his and a comes a the from for your the
serpent fruit ;viper forth snake of root ,striking of rod

7257 982 34 1800 1060 7462 5774

30 מְעוֹפֵף׃ וְרָעוּ בְּכוֹרֵי דַלִּים וְאֶבְיוֹנִים לָבֶטַח יִרְבָּצוּ

shall safety in the and the the shall And .flying
;down lie needy ;poor of firstborn feed

8179 3213 2026 7611 8328 7458 4191

31 וְהֵמַתִּי בָרָעָב שָׁרְשֵׁךְ וּשְׁאֵרִיתֵךְ יַהֲרֹג׃ הֵילִילִי שַׁעַר

O ,Howl shall it your and your with will I and
!gate .kill remnant ,root famine slay

909 369 935 6227 6828 3605 6429 4127 5892 2199

זַעֲקִי־עִיר נָמוֹג פְּלֶשֶׁת כֻּלֵּךְ כִּי מִצָּפוֹן עָשָׁן בָּא וְאֵין בּוֹדֵד

is and ,comes a the from for of all (is) Melted O ,Cry
isolated none smoke north ,you ,Philistia away !city

6726 3245 3068 1471 4397 6030 4100 4151

32 בְּמוֹעָדָיו׃ וּמַה־יַּעֲנֶה מַלְאֲכֵי־גוֹי כִּי יְהוָה יִסַּד צִיּוֹן וּבָהּ

and ,Zion has Jehovah That the mes- the shall what And his in
it in founded ?nation of sengers answer he .ranks

5971 6041 2620

יֶחֱסוּ עֲנִיֵּי עַמּוֹ׃

His the shall
.people of poor trust

CAP. XV טו

CHAPTER 15

CHAPTER 15

[1]The burden of Moab: Because Ar of Moab is laid waste; it is cut off; because in a night Kir of Moab is laid waste; it is cut off. [2]One goes up to the house, even to Dibon, the high places, to

3915 1820 4124 6144 7703 3915 4124 4853

1 מַשָּׂא מוֹאָב כִּי בְּלֵיל שֻׁדַּד עָר מוֹאָב נִדְמָה כִּי בְּלֵיל

a in that is it ,Moab Ar laid is a in that :Moab The
night ;off cut of waste night of burden

1065 1116 1769 1004 5927 1820 4124 7024 7703

2 שֻׁדַּד קִיר־מוֹאָב נִדְמָה׃ עָלָה הַבַּיִת וְדִיבֹן הַבָּמוֹת לְבֶכִי

for high the (to) even the to One is it ,Moab Kir laid is
.weeping ,places ,Dibon ,house up goes .destroyed of waste

weep. Moab shall howl over Nebo and over Medeba; all its heads *shall be* bald, every beard shorn. [3]They shall dress with sackcloth in the streets; everyone shall howl on their housetops and in their plazas, melting in tears. [4]And Heshbon and Elealeh shall cry; their voice shall be heard as far as Jahaz; so the warriors of Moab shall shout; his life *is* broken to him. [5]My heart shall cry to Moab; her fugitives to Zoar, a heifer of three years; he goes up the ascent of Luhith, with weeping, for *in* the way of Horonaim they shall raise up a cry of ruin. [6]For Nimrim's waters are desolations; for the hay is dried up; the grass fails; there is not a green thing.

[7]Therefore, one made up the remainder and their store, over the torrent of the willows they shall carry them. [8]For the cry has gone around the border of Moab, its howling even to Eglaim; yea, its howling even to Beer-elim. [9]For the waters of Dimon are full of blood; for I will put on Dimon more *things*, for the escaped ot Moab —a lion, even for the remnant of the land.

3605 71:42 7218 3605 3213 4124 4311 5921 5015
עַל־נְבוֹ וְעַל מֵידְבָא מוֹאָב יְיֵלִיל בְּכָל־רֹאשָׁיו קָרְחָה כָּל־
every (is) its all on shall Moab Medeba and Nebo over
;baldness heads ,howl over

3 7339 1406 82 42 2296 2351 1438 2206
זָקָן גְּרוּעָה׃ בְּחוּצֹתָיו חָגְרוּ שָׂק עַל־גַּגּוֹתֶיהָ וּבִרְחֹבֹתֶיהָ
its in and its on sack- they its In .shorn is beard
squares housetops ;cloth don shall streets

4 3096 5704 500 2809 2199 1065 3381 3213 3605
כֻּלֹּה יְיֵלִיל יֹרֵד בַּבֶּכִי׃ וַתִּזְעַק חֶשְׁבּוֹן וְאֶלְעָלֵה עַד־יַהַץ
Jahaz as and Heshbon And in going shall every-
as far ;Elealeh cries .weeping down ,howl one

3415 5315 732:1 4124 2502 6963 8085
נִשְׁמַע קוֹלָם עַל־כֵּן חֲלֻצֵי מוֹאָב יָרִיעוּ נַפְשׁוֹ יָרְעָה לּוֹ׃
to (is) his shall Moab war- the therefore their is
.him broken life ;shout of riors ;voice heard

5 7992 56 97 6820 5704 1280 2199 4124 3820
לִבִּי לְמוֹאָב יִזְעָק בְּרִיחֶהָ עַד־צֹעַר עֶגְלַת שְׁלִשִׁיָּה כִּי ׀
for years three a ,Zoar (are) her shall Moab to My
;old of heifer to fugitives ;cry heart

2201 2273 1870 5927 1065 3872 4608
מַעֲלֵה הַלּוּחִית בִּבְכִי יַעֲלֶה־בּוֹ כִּי דֶּרֶךְ חוֹרֹנַיִם זַעֲקַת־
cry a Horonaim the (in) for ;it in he with ,Luhith the
of of way up goes weeping of ascent

6 2682 3001 1961 4923 5249 4325 5782 7667
שֶׁבֶר יְעֹעֵרוּ׃ כִּי־מֵי נִמְרִים מְשַׁמּוֹת יִהְיוּ כִּי־יָבֵשׁ חָצִיר
the is for ;are desolations Nimrim the For shall they ruin
;hay up dried of waters .up raise

7 64:86 62 13 3502 1961 3808 3418 1817 3615
כָּלָה דֶשֶׁא יֶרֶק לֹא הָיָה׃ עַל־כֵּן יִתְרָה עָשָׂה וּפְקֻדָּתָם
their and one the Therefore there not green a the fails
,store ,made remainder .is thing ;grass

8 1366 2201 5362 5375 6155 5158
עַל נַחַל הָעֲרָבִים יִשָּׂאוּם׃ כִּי־הִקִּיפָה הַזְּעָקָה אֶת־גְּבוּל
the cry the gone has For shall they the the over
of border around .them carry willows of torrent

9 4325 3215 879 3215 97 5704 4124
מוֹאָב עַד־אֶגְלַיִם יִלְלָתָהּ וּבְאֵר אֵילִים יִלְלָתָהּ׃ כִּי מֵי
the For its Elim even and its Eglaim even ,Moab
of waters .howling Beer- to ;howling to

6413 3254 1775 7896 1818 4390 1775
דִּימוֹן מָלְאוּ דָם כִּי־אָשִׁית עַל־דִּימוֹן נוֹסָפוֹת לִפְלֵיטַת
the for more Dimon on will I for ;blood are Dimon
of escaped ,(things) put of full

127 7611 738 4124
מוֹאָב אַרְיֵה וְלִשְׁאֵרִית אֲדָמָה׃
the the for and ,lion a ,Moab
.land of remnant

CAP. XVI טז

CHAPTER 16

CHAPTER 16

[1]Send a lamb to the ruler of the land, from the rock of the desert to the mount of the daughter of Zion. [2]For it is as a fleeing bird cast out of the nest; the daughters of Moab shall be *at* the fords of Arnon. [3]Take counsel; do judgment; make your shadow as the night in midday; hide the outcasts; do not uncover the fugitive! [4]Let My outcasts tarry with

1 6726 1323 2022 4057 5553 776 4910 3733 7971
שִׁלְחוּ־כַר מֹשֵׁל־אֶרֶץ מִסֶּלַע מִדְבָּרָה אֶל־הַר בַּת־צִיּוֹן׃
Zion's the to the (in) from the of the to a Send
.daughter of mount wilderness Sela ,land ruler lamb

2 4569 41:24 13 23 1961 79:71 7064 5074 57:75 1961
וְהָיָה כְעוֹף־נוֹדֵד קֵן מְשֻׁלָּח תִּהְיֶינָה בְּנוֹת מוֹאָב מַעְבָּרוֹת
the (at) Moab the be shall cast a ,fleeing a as it For
fords of daughters ;out nest bird is

3 6738 39 15 7896 6415 6213 6098 935 769
לְאַרְנוֹן׃ הָבִיאוּ עֵצָה עֲשׂוּ פְלִילָה שִׁיתִי כַלַּיִל צִלֵּךְ
your the as make ;judgment do ;counsel Take of
shadow night ,Arnon

4 1481 1540 408 5074 50:80 5640 6672 8432
בְּתוֹךְ צָהֳרַיִם סַתְּרִי נִדָּחִים נֹדֵד אַל־תְּגַלִּי׃ יָגוּרוּ בָךְ
with Let do not the the hide ;midday the in
you tarry !uncover fugitive ;outcasts of midst

you, Moab. Be a hiding-place to them from the face of the destroyer. For the exactor has ceased, destruction has failed; the trampler is ended out of the land. [5]And in mercy the throne shall be founded; and *he* shall sit on it in truth in the tabernacle of David, judging and seeking justice, and swift in righteousness.

[6]We have heard of the pride of Moab, very proud; of his pride, his arrogance, and his rage; not so *are* his babblings. [7]So Moab shall howl for Moab; everyone shall howl; you shall moan for the raisin-cakes of Kirhareseth; surely they are stricken. [8]For the fields of Heshbon droop, the vine of Sibmah. The masters of the nations have crushed its choice plants—they have come to Jazer; they wander *in* the desert; her branches are spread out; they have crossed the sea. [9]On account of this the vine of Sibmah will weep with the weeping of Jazer; I will drench you with my tears, O Heshbon and Elealeh; for shouting has fallen on your fruit and on your harvest. [10]And gladness and joy is gathered up from the fruitful field; and there is no singing and no shouting in the vineyards; the treaders shall not tread out wine in the presses; I have made the exultation to cease. [11]For this reason my belly shall sound like a harp for Moab, and my inward parts for Kir-haresh. [12]And it shall be, when it is seen that Moab shall be wearied on the high place, then he shall come to his shrine to pray, and he shall not be able. [13]This *is* the word that Jehovah had spoken to Moab from that time. [14]But now Jehovah has spoken, saying, Within three years, as the years of a hireling, then the glory of Moab will be abased, with all the great host; and the remnant *shall be* few; small, not mighty.

16:5 And in mercy shall the throne be established; and he shall sit on it in truth in the tent of David, judging and seeking justice, and swift in righteousness.

5643 1933 8552 5080
My outcasts; be a hiding place to them from the face of the destroyer. For the has ceased, ex-actor

36:15 7701 8552 7429 776 3559 26:17 36:78
has failed; destruc-tion is ended trampler the out of the land.

And established be the throne in mercy; and he shall sit on it in truth in the tent of David, judging and justice, and seeking in swift righteousness.

6 We have heard the pride of Moab the very proud —his pride, and his arrogance, and his rage; so not his babblings.

7 So shall howl Moab for Moab, shall howl it all; for the foundations of Kir-hareseth shall you moan; surely they are smitten.

8 For the fields of Heshbon droop, the vine of Sibmah. The masters of the nations have crushed its choice plants—to Jazer they come, they wander the desert; her branches are spread out, they have crossed the sea.

9 Therefore will weep with the weeping of Jazer the vine of Sibmah; I will drench you with my tears, Heshbon and Elealeh; for on your fruit and on your harvest shouting has fallen.

10 And is gathered up gladness and joy from the fruitful field; and not singing and not shout-ing; in the vineyards in the wine presses not shall tread the treader; shouting I have made to cease.

11 Therefore my belly for Moab like the harp shall sound; and my inward parts for Kir-haresh.

12 And it shall be, when it is seen that Moab shall be wearied on the high place, then shall come he to his sacred place to pray, but not shall he be able.

13 This (is) the word which Jehovah had spoken to Moab from that time.

14 But now has Jehovah spoken, saying, Within three years, as the years of a hireling, then will the glory of Moab be abased, with all the host; and the remnant small, not mighty.

CAP. XVII יז

CHAPTER 17

CHAPTER 17

[1]The burden of Damascus: Behold, Damascus is taken away from *being* a city, and it shall be a ruined heap. [2]The cities of Aroer are forsaken; now they are for flocks; they lie down and no one terrifies *them*. [3]And the fortress shall cease from Ephraim; and the kingdom from Damascus and the rest of Syria. They shall be as the glory of the sons of Israel, declares Jehovah of hosts.

[4]And it shall be in that day, Jacob's glory shall be made thin, and the fatness of his flesh shall be made lean. [5]And it shall be as the reaping of the harvest grain, and his arm reaps the ears. And it shall be as he who gathers ears in the Valley of the Giants. [6]Yet gleaning grapes shall be left in it, as the shaking of an olive tree; two *or* three ripe olives in the top of the uppermost branch; four *or* five in the fruit-tree branches, declares Jehovah God of Israel.

[7]In that day a man shall gaze to his Maker; and his eyes shall look to the Holy One of Israel. [8]And he shall not gaze to the altars, work of his hands; and he will not see what his fingers have made, even the Asherim, and the sun-pillars. [9]In that day his fortified cities shall be as a thing left in the forest, or the branch that they leave, from before the sons of Israel. And it will become a desolation. [10]Because you have forgotten the God of your salvation, and you did not remember the Rock of your strength, therefore you shall plant pleasing plants, and shall sow it a foreign shoot. [11]In the day of your planting you

4596 1961 5892 5493 1834 2009 1834 4853

1 מַשָּׂא דַּמָּשֶׂק הִנֵּה דַמֶּשֶׂק מוּסָר מֵעִיר וְהָיְתָה מְעִי

heap a | it and be shall | (being) city a | from turned away | is Damascus | ,Behold | Damas- cus | the of burden

369 7257 1961 5739 6177 5892 5800 4654

2 מַפָּלָה׃ עֲזֻבוֹת עָרֵי עֲרֹעֵר לַעֲדָרִים תִּהְיֶינָה וְרָבְצוּ וְאֵין

and none | they and down lie | ;are they | for flocks | ;Aroer | The of cities | are forsaken | .ruined

1834 4467 669 4013 7673 2729

3 מַחֲרִיד׃ וְנִשְׁבַּת מִבְצָר מֵאֶפְרַיִם וּמַמְלָכָה מִדַּמֶּשֶׂק

from Damascus | the and kingdom | from ,Ephraim | the fortress | shall And cease | terrifies .(them)

6635 3068 5002 1961 3478 1121 3519 758 7605

וּשְׁאָר אֲרָם כִּכְבוֹד בְּנֵי־יִשְׂרָאֵל יִהְיוּ נְאֻם יְהוָה צְבָאוֹת׃

.hosts | Jehovah of | states | they ,be shall | Israel | the of sons | the As of glory | .Syria | the and of rest

4924 3290 3519 1809 3117 1961

4 וְהָיָה בַּיּוֹם הַהוּא יִדַּל כְּבוֹד יַעֲקֹב וּמִשְׁמַן

the and of fatness | ,Jacob | the of glory | be shall weak made | ,that | day in | it And be shall

7641 2220 7054 7102 622 1961 7329 1320

5 בְּשָׂרוֹ יֵרָזֶה׃ וְהָיָה כֶּאֱסֹף קָצִיר קָמָה וּזְרֹעוֹ שִׁבֳּלִים

ears the | his and arm | the ,grain | the ,harvest | the as of reaping | it And be shall | be shall .lean made | his flesh

7604 7497 6010 7641 3950 1961 7114

6 יִקְצוֹר וְהָיָה כִּמְלַקֵּט שִׁבֳּלִים בְּעֵמֶק רְפָאִים׃ וְנִשְׁאַר־בּוֹ

it in | shall Yet left be | .Rephaim | the in of valley | ears | who he as gathers | it and be shall | ;reaps

534 7218 1620 7969 8147 2132 5362 5955

עוֹלֵלֹת כְּנֹקֶף זַיִת שְׁנַיִם שְׁלֹשָׁה גַּרְגְּרִים בְּרֹאשׁ אָמִיר

high a ,branch | the in of top | ripe olives | (or) three | two | olive an —tree | the as of shaking | ,gleanings

430 3068 5002 6509 5585 2568 702

אַרְבָּעָה חֲמִשָּׁה בִּסְעִפֶיהָ פֹּרִיָּה נְאֻם־יְהוָה אֱלֹהֵי

God of | Jehovah | states | the (of) ,tree fruit | branches in its | five (or) | four

5869 6213 120 8159 3117 3478

7 יִשְׂרָאֵל׃ בַּיּוֹם הַהוּא יִשְׁעֶה הָאָדָם עַל־עֹשֵׂהוּ וְעֵינָיו אֶל־

to | his and eyes | his ;Maker | on | man a | shall gaze | that | day In | .Israel

4196 8159 3808 7200 3478 6918

8 קְדוֹשׁ יִשְׂרָאֵל תִּרְאֶינָה׃ וְלֹא יִשְׁעֶה אֶל־הַמִּזְבְּחוֹת

the ,altars | to | shall he gaze | And not | shall .look | Israel | Holy the of One

842 7200 3808 676 6213 834 3027 4639

מַעֲשֵׂה יָדָיו וַאֲשֶׁר עָשׂוּ אֶצְבְּעֹתָיו לֹא יִרְאֶה וְהָאֲשֵׁרִים

the Asherim | even | will he ,see | not | his fingers | have made | and what | his ;hands | the of work

5800 4581 5892 1961 3117 2553

9 וְהָחַמָּנִים׃ בַּיּוֹם הַהוּא יִהְיוּ ׀ עָרֵי מָעֻזּוֹ כַּעֲזוּבַת

thing a as in left | his fortified | cities | shall be | that | day In | the and .sun-pillars

1961 3478 1121 6440 5800 834 534 2793

הַחֹרֶשׁ וְהָאָמִיר אֲשֶׁר עָזְבוּ מִפְּנֵי בְּנֵי יִשְׂרָאֵל וְהָיְתָה

it and be will | ;Israel | the of sons | from before | they ,leave | that | the or branch | the forest

2142 3808 4581 6697 3468 430 7911 8077

10 שְׁמָמָה׃ כִּי שָׁכַחַתְּ אֱלֹהֵי יִשְׁעֵךְ וְצוּר מָעֻזֵּךְ לֹא זָכָרְתְּ

did you remember | not | your strength | the and of Rock | your ;salvation | God the of | have you forgotten | Because | deso- a .lation

3117 2232 2114 2156 5282 5194 5193

11 עַל־כֵּן תִּטְּעִי נִטְעֵי נַעֲמָנִים וּזְמֹרַת זָר תִּזְרָעֶנּוּ׃ בְּיוֹם

the In of day | shall you .it sow | foreign- ness | a and of shoot | ,pleasantness | plants of | you plant shall | Therefore fence it in; in the morning you make your seed sprout; the crop *is* a heap in the day of sickness and incurable pain. [12]Woe *to* the multitude of many peoples; they roar like the roar of seas; and the crash of nations *is* like the crash like the crash of mighty waters! [13]Nations shall crash like the crashing of many waters, but He rebukes it, and it flees far away; yea, *it* is driven like the chaff of mountains before the wind, and like a rolling thing before a tempest. [14]At the time of evening, behold, terror! Before *it is* morning, it shall not be. This *is* the portion of those robbing us, and the lot of those plundering us.

3117 7102 5067 6524 2233 1242 7735 5194
נִטְעֵךְ תְּשַׂגְשֵׂגִי וּבַבֹּקֶר זַרְעֵךְ תַּפְרִיחִי נֵד קָצִיר בְּיוֹם
the in the (is) a make you your the in fence you your
of day crop heap ;sprout seed morning ,in it planting

1993 7227 5971 1995 1945 605 3511 2470
12 נַחֲלָה וּכְאֵב אָנוּשׁ׃ הוֹי הֲמוֹן עַמִּים רַבִּים כַּהֲמוֹת
the like ;many peoples mul- the Woe .incurable and sick-
of roar of titude (to) pain ness

7588 3524 4325 7588 3816 7588 1993 3220
יַמִּים יֶהֱמָיוּן וּשְׁאוֹן לְאֻמִּים כִּשְׁאוֹן מַיִם כַּבִּירִים יִשָּׁאוּן׃
they mighty waters the like ;nations the and they seas
!crash of crash of crash ;roar

4801 5127 1605 7588 7227 4325 7588 3816
13 לְאֻמִּים כִּשְׁאוֹן מַיִם רַבִּים יִשָּׁאוּן וְגָעַר בּוֹ וְנָס מִמֶּרְחָק
far it and ,it He but ;crash many waters the like Nations
;away flees rebukes of crashing

6256 5492 6440 1534 7307 6440 2022 4671 7291
14 וְרֻדַּף כְּמֹץ הָרִים לִפְנֵי־רוּחַ וּכְגַלְגַּל לִפְנֵי סוּפָה׃ לְעֵת
the At a before a like and the before mountains the like is and
of time .tempest thing rolling ,wind of chaff chased

8154 2506 2088 369 1242 6440 1091 2009 6153
עֶרֶב וְהִנֵּה בַלָּהָה בְּטֶרֶם בֹּקֶר אֵינֶנּוּ זֶה חֵלֶק שׁוֹסֵינוּ
our the This shall it (is it) Before !terror ,and ,evening
,robbers of portion (is) .be not ,morning ,behold

962 1486
וְגוֹרָל לְבֹזְזֵינוּ׃
our of the and
.plunderers lot

CHAPTER 18

[1]Woe *to the* land of whirring of wings, which *is* beyond the rivers of Ethiopia; [2]which sends envoys by the sea, even in ships of papyrus on the face of the waters. Go, swift messengers, to a nation tall and smooth, to a dreadful people from it, and onwards; and a nation stalwart and trampling down, whose land the rivers have divided! [3]All you inhabitants of the world and dwellers of the earth, you will see as one lifts a banner *on the* peaks. And you will hear as the blowing of a ram's horn. [4]For so Jehovah said to me, I will rest, and I will watch in My dwelling; as the glowing heat on light; as the cloud of dew in the heat of harvest. [5]For before the harvest, when the bud is perfect, and the sour grape is ripening in the flower, then He will cut off the sprigs with pruning knives, and cut down and take away the branches. [6]They shall be left together to the birds of the hills, and to

CAP. XVIII יח

CHAPTER 18

7971 3568 5104 5676 834 3471 6767 776 1945
1 הוֹי אֶרֶץ צִלְצַל כְּנָפָיִם אֲשֶׁר מֵעֵבֶר לְנַהֲרֵי־כוּשׁ׃ הַשֹּׁלֵחַ
2
which ,Ethiopia the from which ,wings whirring the Woe
sends of rivers beyond (is) of of land (to)

7031 4397 3212 4325 6440 1573 3627 6735 3220
בַּיָּם צִירִים וּבִכְלֵי־גֹמֶא עַל־פְּנֵי־מַיִם לְכוּ מַלְאָכִים קַלִּים
,swift messengers ,Go the the on papyrus in even ,envoys the by
:waters of face of ships sea

1973 3372 5971 4803 4900 1471
אֶל־גּוֹי מְמֻשָּׁךְ וּמוֹרָט אֶל־עַם נוֹרָא מִן־הוּא וָהָלְאָה גּוֹי
a and ,it from ,dreadful a to and tall a to
nation ,onwards people ,smooth nation

8398 7931 3605 776 5704 958 834 4001 6978
3 קַו־קָו וּמְבוּסָה אֲשֶׁר־בָּזְאוּ נְהָרִים אַרְצוֹ׃ כָּל־יֹשְׁבֵי תֵבֵל
the inhabitants All its the have of tramp- and mighty
world of !land rivers divided whom ,down ling

8085 7782 8628 7200 2022 5251 5375 776 3427
וְשֹׁכְנֵי אָרֶץ כִּנְשֹׂא־נֵס הָרִים תִּרְאוּ וְכִתְקֹעַ שׁוֹפָר תִּשְׁמָעוּ׃
will you a the as and will you (the on) a one as the and
.hear ,trumpet of blowing ;see peaks flag lifts earth of dwellers

4349 5027 8252 3068 559 3541
4 כִּי כֹה אָמַר יְהוָה אֵלַי אֶשְׁקוֹטָה וְאַבִּיטָה בִמְכוֹנִי
My in will I and will I to Jehovah said so For
dwelling watch rest ,me

7102 6440 7102 2527 2919 5645 216 6703 2527
5 כְּחֹם צַח עֲלֵי־אוֹר כְּעָב טַל בְּחֹם קָצִיר׃ כִּי־לִפְנֵי קָצִיר
the before For .harvest the in dew the as ;light upon glow- the as
harvest of heat of cloud ing heat

2150 3772 5328 1961 1580 1155 6525 8552
כְּתָם־פֶּרַח וּבֹסֶר גֹּמֵל יִהְיֶה נִצָּה וְכָרַת הַזַּלְזַלִּים
the will He then the (in) is ripening the and the is when
sprigs off cut ,flower grape sour ,bud perfect

5861 3162 5800 8456 5493 5189 4211
6 בַּמַּזְמֵרוֹת וְאֶת־הַנְּטִישׁוֹת הֵסִיר הֵתַז׃ יֵעָזְבוּ יַחְדָּו לְעֵיט
the to together They cut take the and the with
of birds left be shall .down ,away branches ;knives pruning

the birds of the hills, and to the beasts of the earth. And the birds shall summer on them, and every beast of the earth shall winter on them.
7Then shall be brought in that time a present to Jehovah of hosts *from* a tall and smooth people, and a dreadful people, from it and onward; a stalwart and trampling nation whose land the rivers have divided, to the place of the name of Jehovah of hosts: Mount Zion.

776 929 3605 5861 6972 776 929 2022
הָרִים וּלְבֶהֱמַת הָאָרֶץ וְקָץ עָלָיו הָעַיִט וְכָל־בֶּהֱמַת הָאָרֶץ
the earth | beast of | and every | the birds, | on them | shall summer | and the earth; | to beasts of | and mountains,

6635 3068 7862 2986 6256 2778
7 עָלָיו תֶּחֱרָף׃ בָּעֵת הַהִיא יוּבַל־שַׁי לַיהוָה צְבָאוֹת
hosts of | Jehovah to | a present | be brought shall | that | In time | shall winter. | on them

6978 1471 1973 3372 5971 4803 4900 5971
עַם מְמֻשָּׁךְ וּמוֹרָט וּמֵעַם נוֹרָא מִן־הוּא וָהָלְאָה גּוֹי ׀ קַו
migh- | a nation | and onward; | it from | dreadful | from and people a | and smooth, | tall | a (from) people

3068 8034 4725 776 5104 958 834 4001 6957
קָו וּמְבוּסָה אֲשֶׁר בָּזְאוּ נְהָרִים אַרְצוֹ אֶל־מְקוֹם שֵׁם־יְהוָה
Jehovah of | the name of | the place | to | its land, | rivers | have divided | of whom | and trampling, | ty

6726 2022 6635
צְבָאוֹת הַר־צִיּוֹן׃
.Zion Mount —hosts

CHAPTER 19

1The burden of Egypt: Behold! Jehovah rides on a light cloud and comes into Egypt. And the idols of Egypt shall tremble from before Him; and the heart of Egypt shall melt in its midst. 2And I will stir up Egypt*ians* against Egypt*ians*; and they each man shall fight against his brother; and each against his neighbor; city against city, kingdom against kingdom. 3And the spirit of *the* Egypt shall be empty in its midst; and I will swallow its counsel And they shall seek to idols, and to the enchanters, and to the mediums, and to the future-tellers. 4And I will shut up Egypt into the hand of cruel lords; and a fierce king shall rule them, declares the Lord, Jehovah of hosts. 5And the waters shall dry up from the sea, and the river shall fail and dry up. 6And rivers shall be fouled; and the Nile of Egypt will languish and dry up; the reed and the rush shall decay. 7Bare places *shall be* at the Nile, by the mouth of the Nile, and everything sown *by* the Nile shall dry up, driven away, and be no more. 8The fishermen shall mourn; and all who cast a hook into the Nile shall wail; and those who spread nets on the

CAP. XIX יט

CHAPTER 19

4714 935 7031 5645 7392 3068 2009 4714 4853
1 מַשָּׂא מִצְרָיִם הִנֵּה יְהוָה רֹכֵב עַל־עָב קַל וּבָא מִצְרַיִם
.Egypt | and enters | light, | a cloud | on | rides | Jehovah | Behold, | Egypt: | The burden of

7130 4549 4714 3824 6440 4714 457 5128
וְנָעוּ אֱלִילֵי מִצְרַיִם מִפָּנָיו וּלְבַב מִצְרַיִם יִמַּס בְּקִרְבּוֹ׃
its in midst. | shall melt | Egypt | the and heart of | be- from fore Him; | Egypt | the idols of | shall And tremble

376 251 376 3898 4714 4714 5526
2 וְסִכְסַכְתִּי מִצְרַיִם בְּמִצְרַיִם וְנִלְחֲמוּ אִישׁ בְּאָחִיו וְאִישׁ
and each | against brother his, | each man | they and fight will, | against Egypt, | Egypt | will I And up stir

7307 1238 4467 4467 5892 5892 7453
3 בְּרֵעֵהוּ עִיר בְּעִיר מַמְלָכָה בְּמַמְלָכָה׃ וְנָבְקָה רוּחַ־
the of spirit | will And be empty | against kingdom. | kingdom | against city, | city | his against neighbor;

4714 457 1875 1104 6098 7130 4714
מִצְרַיִם בְּקִרְבּוֹ וַעֲצָתוֹ אֲבַלֵּעַ וְדָרְשׁוּ אֶל־הָאֱלִילִים וְאֶל־
and to | idols, the | to | they And seek shall | will I swallow, | its and counsel | its in midst, | Egypt

4714 853 5534 3049 178 328
4 הָאִטִּים וְאֶל־הָאֹבוֹת וְאֶל־הַיִּדְּעֹנִים׃ וְסִכַּרְתִּי אֶת־מִצְרַיִם
Egypt | will I And up shut | future the tellers. | and to | the mediums, | and to | the enchanters,

3068 136 5002 4910 5794 4428 7186 113 3027
בְּיַד אֲדֹנִים קָשֶׁה וּמֶלֶךְ עַז יִמְשָׁל־בָּם נְאֻם הָאָדוֹן יְהוָה
Jehovah of | the Lord | states, | them | shall rule | fierce | a and king | cruel; | lords | the into of hand

2186 5405 2717 5104 3220 4325 3001 6635
5 צְבָאוֹת׃ וְנִשְּׁתוּ־מַיִם מֵהַיָּם וְנָהָר יֶחֱרַב וְיָבֵשׁ׃ וְהֶאֶזְנִיחוּ
6
be will And fouled | and up dry. | shall fail | the and river | from sea the, | the waters | shall And up dry | .hosts

6169 7060 5488 7070 4692 2975 2717 1809 5104
7 נְהָרוֹת דָּלְלוּ וְחָרְבוּ יְאֹרֵי מָצוֹר קָנֶה וָסוּף קָמֵלוּ׃ עָרוֹת
Bare places | shall decay. | and rush | the reed | Egypt; | the of Nile | and dry | will languish | rivers;

369 5068 3001 2233 2975 3605 2975 6310 2975
עַל־יְאוֹר עַל־פִּי יְאוֹר וְכֹל מִזְרַע יְאוֹר יִיבַשׁ נִדַּף וְאֵינֶנּוּ׃
be and more no. | driven away, | shall up dry | the Nile | sown (by) | every and thing | the mouth by Nile's, | the Nile | at

6566 2443 2975 7993 3605 578 1771 56
8 וְאָנוּ הַדַּיָּגִים וְאָבְלוּ כָּל־מַשְׁלִיכֵי בַיְאוֹר חַכָּה וּפֹרְשֵׂי
those and spread who | hook a; | the into Nile | who cast | all | shall and wail | the fishermen; | shall And mourn

surface of the waters shall
droop. 9And the workers in
fine flax, and the weavers of
white cloth are ashamed.
10And her supports shall be
crushed; and all who make
wages *shall be* sad of soul.
11Surely the rulers of Zoan
are fools; the advice of
Pharaoh's wise counselors
has become stupid. How
can you say to Pharaoh, I
am the son of wise ones,
the son of kings of old?
12Where *are* your wise ones
now? Yea, let them tell you
now, that they may know
what Jehovah of hosts has
planned against Egypt.
13The rulers of Zoan are
fools; the rulers of Noph are
deceived; they also have
led Egypt astray, the cornerstone of her tribes.
14Jehovah has mixed a
perverse spirit in her midst;
and they led astray Egypt in
all his work; as a drunkard
strays in his vomit. 15And
Egypt shall have no work
that the head or the tail, the
branch or rush, may do.
16In that day Egypt shall be
like women; and it will
tremble and dread from
before the shaking of the
hand of Jehovah of hosts,
which He shakes over it.
17And the land of Judah
shall be a terror to Egypt;
everyone who mentions it
shall dread to it, from before
the purpose of Jehovah of
hosts, which He purposes
against it. 18In that day five
cities in the land of Egypt
shall speak the language of
Canaan, and swear to
Jehovah of hosts. One shall
be called, City of Ruin.
19Then an altar to Jehovah
shall be in the midst of the
land of Egypt, and a pillar to

9 6593 5647 954 535 4325 6440 4365
מִכְמֹרֶת עַל־פְּנֵי־מַיִם אֻמְלָלוּ׃ וּבֹשׁוּ עֹבְדֵי פִשְׁתִּים
flax the are and shall waters the on nets
in workers ashamed .droop of surface

10 6213 3605 1792 8356 2355 707 8305
שְׂרִיקוֹת וְאֹרְגִים חוֹרָי׃ וְהָיוּ שָׁתֹתֶיהָ מְדֻכָּאִים כָּל־עֹשֵׂי
who and ,crushed her shall And white and ,combed
make all supports be .cloth of weavers

11 6:547 6098 2450 6814 8269 191 389 53.15 99 7938
שֶׂכֶר אַגְמֵי־נָפֶשׁ׃ אַךְ־אֱוִלִים שָׂרֵי צֹעַן חַכְמֵי יֹעֲצֵי פַרְעֹה
;Pharaoh's coun- the ,Zoan the (are) Surely .soul sad wages
selors of wise of chiefs fools of

1121 2450 1121 6547: 559 349 1197 3289
עֵצָה נִבְעָרָה אֵיךְ תֹּאמְרוּ אֶל־פַּרְעֹה בֶּן־חֲכָמִים אֲנִי בֶּן־
the I wise the ,Pharaoh to you can How become has (their)
of son ,(am) ones of son say .brutish advice

12 4100 3045 4994 3046 2450 645 335 6924 4428
מַלְכֵי־קֶדֶם׃ אַיָּם אֵפוֹא חֲכָמֶיךָ וְיַגִּידוּ נָא לָךְ וְיֵדְעוּ מַה־
what they that ;you now let And wise your then Where ?old kings
know may tell them ?ones (are) of

13 8269 5377 68:14 8269 2973 4714 6635 3068 3289
יָּעַץ יְהוָה צְבָאוֹת עַל־מִצְרָיִם׃ נוֹאֲלוּ שָׂרֵי צֹעַן נִשְּׁאוּ שָׂרֵי
the are ;Zoan The are .Egypt against hosts Jehovah has
of chiefs deceived of chiefs fools of planned

14 7130 4537 3068 7626 6438 4714 8582 5297
נֹף הִתְעוּ אֶת־מִצְרַיִם פִּנַּת שְׁבָטֶיהָ׃ יְהוָה מָסַךְ בְּקִרְבָּהּ
her in has Jehovah her the ,Egypt have they ;Noph
midst mixed tribes of cornerstone astray led

8582 4639 3605 47:14 8582 5773 7307
רוּחַ עִוְעִים וְהִתְעוּ אֶת־מִצְרַיִם בְּכָל־מַעֲשֵׂהוּ כְּהִתָּעוֹת
strays as his all in Egypt they and perverse a
—work astray led spirit

15 6213 834 4639 4714 1961 38:08 6992 7910
שִׁכּוֹר בְּקִיאוֹ׃ וְלֹא־יִהְיֶה לְמִצְרַיִם מַעֲשֶׂה אֲשֶׁר יַעֲשֶׂה
may which ,work Egypt to shall And his in a
do be not .vomit drunkard

16 4714 1961 3117 100 3712 2180 7218
רֹאשׁ וְזָנָב כִּפָּה וְאַגְמוֹן׃ בַּיּוֹם הַהוּא יִהְיֶה מִצְרַיִם
Egypt shall that day In .rush or branch or head
be ,tail

834 6635 3068 3027 8573 6440 6342 2729 802
כַּנָּשִׁים וְחָרַד ׀ וּפָחַד מִפְּנֵי תְּנוּפַת יַד־יְהוָה צְבָאוֹת אֲשֶׁר־
which ,hosts Jehovah the the be- from and will it and like
of of hand of shaking fore dread tremble ;women

17 2283 147:14 3063 127 1961 5921 5130
הוּא מֵנִיף עָלָיו׃ וְהָיְתָה אַדְמַת יְהוּדָה לְמִצְרַיִם לְחָגָּא
;terror a Egypt to Judah the shall And .it over shakes He
of land become

3068 3289 6440 6342 2142 834 3605
כֹּל אֲשֶׁר יַזְכִּיר אֹתָהּ אֵלָיו יִפְחָד מִפְּנֵי עֲצַת יְהוָה
Jehovah the from shall it to it mentions who every
of of purpose before ,dread one

18 1961 3117 6098 834 6635
צְבָאוֹת אֲשֶׁר־הוּא יוֹעֵץ עָלָיו׃ בַּיּוֹם הַהוּא יִהְיוּ
shall that day In against purposes He which ,hosts
be .it

7650 3667 8193 1696 47:14 776 5892 2568
חָמֵשׁ עָרִים בְּאֶרֶץ מִצְרַיִם מְדַבְּרוֹת שְׂפַת כְּנַעַן וְנִשְׁבָּעוֹת
and Canaan the speaking Egypt the in cities five
swearing of lip of land

19 3117 259 559 2041 5869 6635 3068
לַיהוָה צְבָאוֹת עִיר הַהֶרֶס יֵאָמֵר לְאֶחָת׃ בַּיּוֹם
day In .one to be shall it ,ruin city ;hosts to
called of of Jehovah

681 4676 4714 776 8432 3068 4196 1961
הַהוּא יִהְיֶה מִזְבֵּחַ לַיהוָה בְּתוֹךְ אֶרֶץ מִצְרַיִם וּמַצֵּבָה אֵצֶל־
beside a and ,Egypt the the in to an shall that
pillar of land of midst Jehovah altar be

776 6635 3068 5707 226 1961 3068 1366
20 גְּבוּלָהּ לַיהוָה׃ וְהָיָה לְאוֹת וּלְעֵד לַיהוָה צְבָאוֹת בְּאֶרֶץ
the in of land | hosts | to of Jehovah | a for and witness | a for ,sign | it And be shall | to Jehovah | its border

7971 3905 6440 3068 6817 4714
מִצְרַיִם כִּי־יִצְעֲקוּ אֶל־יְהוָה מִפְּנֵי לֹחֲצִים וְיִשְׁלַח לָהֶם
to them | He and send will | ,oppressors | because of | Jeho-vah | to | will they for out cry | ;Egypt

4714 3045 47:14 3068 3045 5337 7227 3462
21 מוֹשִׁיעַ וָרָב וְהִצִּילָם׃ וְנוֹדַע יְהוָה לְמִצְרַיִם וְיָדְעוּ מִצְרַיִם
Egypt | and know shall | ,Egypt to | Jehovah shall And known be | .them save shall and | a and ,one great | a ,savior

3068 5088 5087 4503 2077 5647 3117 3068
אֶת־יְהוָה בַּיּוֹם הַהוּא וְעָבְדוּ זֶבַח וּמִנְחָה וְנָדְרוּ־נֵדֶר לַיהוָה
to Jehovah | a vow | and vow | food and ;offering | sacrifice | and offer shall | ;that | day in | Jehovah

3068 5704 7725 7495 5061 4714 3068 5061 7999
22 וְשִׁלֵּמוּ׃ וְנָגַף יְהוָה אֶת־מִצְרַיִם נָגֹף וְרָפוֹא וְשָׁבוּ עַד־יְהוָה
,Jehovah to they and return shall | and striking ;healing | ,Egypt | Jehovah shall And strike | re- and .(it) pay

4546 1961 3117 7495 6279
23 וְנֶעְתַּר לָהֶם וּרְפָאָם׃ בַּיּוֹם הַהוּא תִּהְיֶה מְסִלָּה
a highway | shall be | that | day In | shall and .them heal | them | He and hear shall

804 4714 4714 804 935 804 4714
מִמִּצְרַיִם אַשּׁוּרָה וּבָא אַשּׁוּר בְּמִצְרַיִם וּמִצְרַיִם בְּאַשּׁוּר
into ;Assyria | and Egypt | ;Egypt into | Assyria shall and come | to ;Assyria | of out Egypt

3478 1961 3117 804 4714 5647
24 וְעָבְדוּ מִצְרַיִם אֶת־אַשּׁוּר׃ בַּיּוֹם הַהוּא יִהְיֶה יִשְׂרָאֵל
Israel | be shall | that | day In | .Assyria | Egypt | shall and serve

834 776 7130 1293 804 4714 7992
25 שְׁלִישִׁיָּה לְמִצְרַיִם וּלְאַשּׁוּר בְּרָכָה בְּקֶרֶב הָאָרֶץ׃ אֲשֶׁר
whom | the ,earth | the in of midst | a blessing | with and ,Assyria | with Egypt | third the

3027 4639 4714 5971 1288 559 6635 3068 1288
בֵּרְכוֹ יְהוָה צְבָאוֹת לֵאמֹר בָּרוּךְ עַמִּי מִצְרַיִם וּמַעֲשֵׂה יָדַי
My hands | the and of work | ,Egypt | My people | Blessed (be) | ,saying | ,hosts | Jehovah of | He blesses

3478 5159 804
אַשּׁוּר וְנַחֲלָתִי יִשְׂרָאֵל׃
.Israel | My and inheritance | ,Assyria

Jehovah at its border.
[20]And it shall be for a sign and for a witness to Jehovah of hosts in the land of Egypt. For they shall cry to Jehovah because of the oppressors; and He shall send them a deliverer, even a great one; and will deliver them.
[21]And Jehovah shall be known to Egypt, Egypt shall know Jehovah in that day. And *they* shall offer sacrifice and offering, and vow a vow to Jehovah, and repay *it*.
[22]And Jehovah shall strike Egypt. He shall strike and heal. Then they shall return to Jehovah, and He shall hear them, and shall heal them.
[23]In that day there shall be a highway out of Egypt to Assyria. And Assyria shall come into Egypt; and Egypt into Assyria; and Egypt shall serve Assyria.
[24]In that day Israel shall be the third with Egypt and with Assyria, a blessing in the midst of the earth,
[25]whom Jehovah of hosts shall bless, saying, Blessed *be* My people Egypt, and Assyria, the work of My hands, and Israel My inheritance.

CAP. XX כ

CHAPTER 20

804 4428 5623 7971 795 8661 935 8141
1 בִּשְׁנַת בֹּא תַרְתָּן אַשְׁדּוֹדָה בִּשְׁלֹחַ אֹתוֹ סַרְגוֹן מֶלֶךְ אַשּׁוּר
,Assyria | the of king | Sargon | him | when sent | to ,Ashdod | Tartan | came | the In year

3027 3068 1696 6256 3920 795 3898
2 וַיִּלָּחֶם בְּאַשְׁדּוֹד וַיִּלְכְּדָהּ׃ בָּעֵת הַהִיא דִּבֶּר יְהוָה בְּיַד
the by of hand | Jehovah | spoke | that | time at | took and it | against ,Ashdod | and fought

49:75 8242 6605 559 531 1121 3470
יְשַׁעְיָהוּ בֶן־אָמוֹץ לֵאמֹר לֵךְ וּפִתַּחְתָּ הַשַּׂק מֵעַל מָתְנֶיךָ
your ,loins | from | the sackcloth | and loose | ,Go | ,saying | ,Amoz | the of son | Isaiah

3182 6174 1980 6213 7272 2502 5275
וְנַעַלְךָ תַחֲלֹץ מֵעַל רַגְלֶךָ וַיַּעַשׂ כֵּן הָלֹךְ עָרוֹם וְיָחֵף׃
and .barefoot | naked | walking | ,so | and did he | your ;foot | from | take off | your and shoe

7969 3182 6174 3470 5650 1980 30:68 559
3 וַיֹּאמֶר יְהוָה כַּאֲשֶׁר הָלַךְ עַבְדִּי יְשַׁעְיָהוּ עָרוֹם וְיָחֵף שָׁלֹשׁ
three | and ,barefoot | naked | Isaiah | My servant | has walked | Just as | ,Jehovah | And said

CHAPTER 20
[1]In the year Tartan came to Ashdod, when Sargon the king of Assyria sent him, and fought against Ashdod, and took it;
[2]at that time Jehovah spoke by Isaiah the son of Amoz, saying, Go and loosen the sackcloth from your loins, and take your shoe off from your foot. And he did so, walking naked and barefoot.
[3]And Jehovah said, Just as My servant Isaiah has walked naked and barefoot three

4 years — a sign and a
wonder on Egypt and on
Ethiopia —[4]so shall the
king of Assyria lead away
the captives of Egypt and
the exiles of Ethiopia,
young and old; naked and
barefoot, and with un-
5 covered buttocks; *to* the
nakedness of Egypt. [5]And
they shall be afraid and
ashamed of their hope
6 Ethiopia, and of their
glory, Egypt. [6]And he
who lives in this coast
shall say in that day,
Behold, this *has become*
of our hope *to* which we
fled for help there, to be
delivered from before the
king of Assyria; and, How
shall we escape?

CHAPTER 21

1 [1]The burden of the
desert of the sea: As
tempests in the Negeb
pass, it comes from the
2 desert, from a dreadful
land. [2]A harsh vision is
revealed to me; the de-
ceiver deceives and the
3 plunderer plunders. Go
up, O Elam! Besiege, O
Media! I have caused all
her sighing to cease.
[3]Because of this my loins
are filled *with* pain; pangs
have taken hold on me
like the pangs of a travail-
4 ing woman. I am bowed
from hearing; I am
troubled from seeing. [4]My
heart wanders; terror
5 overwhelms me; He has
turned the twilight of my
pleasure into trembling.
6 [5]Arrange the table; watch
in the watchtower; eat,
drink; rise up, rulers, *and*
anoint the shield. [6]For so
7 the Lord has said to me:
Go, station a watchman;
he will declare what he
sees. [7]And he sees a
chariot, a pair of horse-
men; a chariot of an ass; a
chariot of a camel; and let
him attend attentively,
8 very attentively. [8]And he
cried, A lion! My lord, I
always stand on my

44,28 5090 3568 4714 4159 226 8141
שנים אות ומופת על־מצרים ועל־כוש׃ כן ינהג מלך
king the shall so —Ethiopia and Egypt on a and a —years
of away lead on wonder sign

6174 2205 5288 3568 1546 4714 7628 804
אשור את־שבי מצרים ואת־גלות כוש נערים וזקנים ערום
naked and young ,Ethiopia exiles and Egypt the Assyria
—old of of captives

5 4007 3568 954 2865 4714 6172 8357 2834 3182
ויחף וחשופי שת ערות מצרים׃ וחתו ובשו מכוש מבטם
their of be and they And .Egypt's (to) but- un- and and
,hope Ethiopia ashamed fear shall nakedness tocks covered barefoot

6 3117 2088 339 3427 559 8597 4714
וממצרים תפארתם׃ ואמר ישב האי הזה ביום ההוא
,that day in this coast that he And their Egypt and
in dwells say shall .glory of

44,28 6440 5337 58:33 8033/5127 834 40.07 3541 2009
הנה־כה מבטנו אשר־נסנו שם לעזרה להנצל מפני מלך
the be- from be to for there we (to) our of thus ,Behold
of king fore delivered ,help fled which hope (become has)

4422 349 804
אשור ואיך נמלט אנחנו׃
?we shall and ;Assyria
escape how

CAP. XXI כא

CHAPTER 21

1 776 935 4057 2498 5045 5492 3220 4057 4853
משא מדבר־ים כסופות בנגב לחלוף ממדבר בא מארץ
a from it the from ,pass the in as the desert the The
land ,comes desert Negeb tempests :sea of of burden

2 77:03 7703 898 898 5046 7186 2380 3372
נוראה׃ חזות קשה הגד־לי הבוגד בוגד והשודד שודד
.spoils the and de- the to is harsh A .dreadful
4390 spoiler ,ceives deceiver :me revealed vision

3 7673 585 3605 40:74 6690 5867 5927
עלי עילם צורי מדי כל־אנחתה השבתי׃ על־כן מלאו
are There- caused I her All O ,Besiege O Go
filled fore .cease to sighing !Media !Elam ,up

8085 5753 3205 6735 270 6735 23:42 4975
מתני חלחלה צירים אחזוני כצירי יולדה נעויתי משמע
from am I travailing a like seized pangs (with) my
;hearing bowed .woman of pangs ,me ;pain loins

4 5399 1200 6427 38:24 8582 7200 926
נבהלתי מראות׃ תעה לבבי פלצות בעתתני את נשף
twi- the overwhelms terror My wanders from am I
of light ;me ;heart .seeing ,troubled

5 398 6820 6823 7979 61,86 2731 8033 28 37
חשקי שם לי לחרדה׃ ערך השלחן צפה הצפית אכול
,eat the watch the Arrange into to has He my
,watchtower ;table trembling me turned pleasure

6 559 4043 4886 8269 6965 83 54
שתה קומו השרים משחו מגן׃ כי כה אמר אלי
to has so For the (and) ,chiefs ,arise ;drink
me said .shield anoint

7 7393 7200 5046 7200 68:22 5975 32,12 136
אדני לך העמד המצפה אשר יראה יגיד׃ וראה רכב
a he And him let he what the station ,Go the
,chariot sees .declare sees ;watchman ,Lord

7227 7181 7181 1581 7393 2543 7393 6571 6776
צמד פרשים רכב חמור רכב גמל והקשיב קשב רב־
very atten him let a a ,ass an a ,horsemen pair a
tively attend ;camel of chariot of chariot of

8 8548 5975 136 4707 5921 738 7121 7187
קשב׃ ויקרא אריה על־מצפה אדני אנכי עמד תמיד
always stand I my the On a (as) he And atten-
,Lord ,watchtower ,lion ,cried .tively

9 יוֹמָם וְעַל־מִשְׁמַרְתִּי אָנֹכִי נִצָּב כָּל־הַלֵּילוֹת׃ וְהִנֵּה־זֶה בָא
comes ,this ,And behold the night all stationed am I my post and at by ;day
רֶכֶב אִישׁ צֶמֶד פָּרָשִׁים וַיַּעַן וַיֹּאמֶר נָפְלָה נָפְלָה בָּבֶל
!Babylon has fallen Has ,fallen ,said and And answered .horses pair a of a ,man of a chariot
10 וְכָל־פְּסִילֵי אֱלֹהֶיהָ שִׁבַּר לָאָרֶץ׃ מְדֻשָׁתִי וּבֶן־גָּרְנִי אֲשֶׁר
That which my !floor the and of son my O ,threshed the to .earth has he shattered gods her cut the of images And all
שָׁמַעְתִּי מֵאֵת יְהוָה צְבָאוֹת אֱלֹהֵי יִשְׂרָאֵל הִגַּדְתִּי לָכֶם׃
.you to have I told ,Israel the of God ,hosts Jehovah from of have I heard
11 מַשָּׂא דּוּמָה אֵלַי קֹרֵא מִשֵּׂעִיר שֹׁמֵר מַה־מִלַּיְלָה שֹׁמֵר
Watch- ,man the of ?night what Watch- ,man from ,Seir (He) calls To me ;Dumah The of burden
12 מַה־מִלֵּיל׃ אָמַר שֹׁמֵר אָתָא בֹקֶר וְגַם־לָיְלָה אִם־תִּבְעָיוּן
would you ,inquire if ;night and also ,Morning comes The ,watchman says the of ?night what
13 בְּעָיוּ שֻׁבוּ אֵתָיוּ׃ מַשָּׂא בַּעְרָב בַּיַּעַר בַּעְרַב תָּלִינוּ
shall you ,stay Arabia the In of forest .Arabia The of burden !Come !Return in- .quire
14 אֹרְחוֹת דְּדָנִים׃ לִקְרַאת צָמֵא הֵתָיוּ מַיִם יֹשְׁבֵי אֶרֶץ תֵּימָא
;Tema the of land the of people water bring the thirsty meet To .Dedanites caravans of
15 בְּלַחְמוֹ קִדְּמוּ נֹדֵד׃ כִּי־מִפְּנֵי חֲרָבוֹת נָדָדוּ מִפְּנֵי ׀ חֶרֶב
the sword from before they ,fled swords from before For the .fugitive meet his with bread
נְטוּשָׁה וּמִפְּנֵי קֶשֶׁת דְּרוּכָה וּמִפְּנֵי כֹּבֶד מִלְחָמָה׃
.battle the of press from and before ,bent the bow from and before ;drawn
16 כִּי־כֹה אָמַר אֲדֹנָי אֵלַי בְּעוֹד שָׁנָה כִּשְׁנֵי שָׂכִיר וְכָלָה כָּל־
all be shall ended a ,hireling the as of years ,year a Within to ,me the Lord has said thus For
17 כְּבוֹד קֵדָר׃ וּשְׁאָר מִסְפַּר־קֶשֶׁת גִּבּוֹרֵי בְנֵי־קֵדָר יִמְעָטוּ
be shall ;few ,Kedar the of sons warriors of the ,archers of number the and of rest ;Kedar the of glory
כִּי יְהוָה אֱלֹהֵי־יִשְׂרָאֵל דִּבֵּר׃
has .spoken Israel God of Jehovah for

CAP. XXII כב

CHAPTER 22

1 מַשָּׂא גֵּיא חִזָּיוֹן מַה־לָּךְ אֵפוֹא כִּי־עָלִית כֻּלָּךְ לַגַּגּוֹת׃
the to ?housetops all you have up gone that ,now to What you (is) :vision valley the of The of burden
2 תְּשֻׁאוֹת ׀ מְלֵאָה עִיר הוֹמִיָּה קִרְיָה עַלִּיזָה חֲלָלַיִךְ לֹא
not your ones slain ,joyous city the ,noisy the city fill Crashings
3 חַלְלֵי־חֶרֶב וְלֹא מֵתֵי מִלְחָמָה׃ כָּל־קְצִינַיִךְ נָדְדוּ־יַחַד
together fled your rulers All .battle dead in and not the ,sword slain are by

watchtower by day; and I am stationed at my post all the nights. [9]And, behold, here comes a chariot of a man, a pair of horses. And he answered and said, Babylon has fallen, has fallen! And He has smashed the cut images of her gods to the earth. [10]O my threshing, and the grain of my floor! That which I have heard of Jehovah of hosts, the God of Israel, I have told to you.

[11]The burden of Dumah: *He* calls to me out of Seir, Watchman, what of the night? Watchman, what of the night? [12]The watchman says, The morning comes, and also night. If you would inquire, inquire. Come! Return!

[13]The burden of Arabia: You shall stay in the forest of Arabia, O traveling companies of Dedanites. [14]The people of the land of Tema bring water to him who is thirsty; *they went* to meet the fugitive with his bread. [15]For they fled from before swords, from the drawn sword, and from the bent bow, and from the press of battle. [16]For so the Lord has said to me, Within a year, as the years of a hireling, all the glory of Kedar shall be ended, [17]and the rest of the number of the archers, the warriors of the sons of Kedar, shall be few. For Jehovah God of Israel has spoken.

CHAPTER 22

[1]The burden of the valley of vision: What *ails* you now, that you have gone up to the housetops? [2]Crashings fill the noisy city, the joyous city. Your slain ones are not slain by the sword, nor dead in battle. [3]All your rulers fled together; *they*

מקשת אסרו כל-נמצאיך אסרו יחדו מרחוק ברחו:
4 על-כן אמרתי שעו מני אמרר בבכי אל-תאיצו לנחמני
5 על-שד בת-עמי: כי יום מהומה ומבוסה ומבוכה
לאדני יהוה צבאות בגיא חזיון מקרקר קר ושוע אל-
6 ההר: ועילם נשא אשפה ברכב אדם פרשים וקיר
7 ערה מגן: ויהי מבחר-עמקיך מלאו רכב והפרשים
8 שת שתו השערה: ויגל את מסך יהודה ותבט ביום
9 ההוא אל-נשק בית היער: ואת בקיעי עיר-דוד ראיתם
10 כי-רבו ותקבצו את-מי הברכה התחתונה: ואת-בתי
11 ירושלם ספרתם ותתצו הבתים לבצר החומה: ומקוה
עשיתם בין החמתים למי הברכה הישנה ולא הבטתם
12 אל-עשיה ויצרה מרחוק לא ראיתם: ויקרא אדני יהוה
צבאות ביום ההוא לבכי ולמספד ולקרחה ולחגר שק:
13 והנה ששון ושמחה הרג בקר ושחט צאן אכל בשר
14 ושתות יין אכול ושתו כי מחר נמות: ונגלה באזני יהוה
צבאות אם-יכפר העון הזה לכם עד-תמתון אמר אדני
15 יהוה צבאות: כה אמר אדני יהוה צבאות לך-בא

were bound without the bow; all found in you were bound together; they have fled from afar. 4Therefore, I said, Look away from me; I will weep bitterly; do not hurry to comfort me over the ruin of the daughter of my people. 5for it *is* a day of trouble, and of trampling down, and of perplexity, by the Lord Jehovah of hosts in the valley of vision; digging down a wall, and crying to the mountain. 6And Persia carried the quiver with a chariot of a man *and* horsemen; and Kir uncovered the shield. 7And it happened; your choicest valleys were full of chariots; and the horsemen surely set in order at the gate. 8And he removed Judah's covering; and you looked in that day to the armor of the house of the forest. 9You have also seen the breaks in the city of David, that they are many; and you gathered the waters of the lower pool. 10And you have counted the houses of Jerusalem; and you broke down the houses to fortify the wall. 11And you made a reservoir between the walls, for the water of the old pool. But you have not looked to its Maker, nor did you see its Former from long ago. 12And in that day the Lord Jehovah of hosts called to weeping and mourning; and to baldness, and to girding with sackcloth.

13Then, lo, joy and gladness, slaying oxen and slaughtering sheep; eating flesh and drinking wine, *saying*, Eat and drink, for tomorrow we die! 14And Jehovah of hosts revealed in my ears, Surely this iniquity shall not be covered for you until you die, says the Lord Jehovah of hosts.

15So says the Lord Jehovah of hosts, Go! Go to

this treasurer, to Shebna who *is* over the house. [16]What *is* to you here? And who *is* here to you, that you have carved a tomb for yourself here, *as one* having cut out his tomb on high, having carved out a home for himself in the rock? [17]Behold, Jehovah hurls you *with* a hurling, O man, and grasps you *with* a grasping. [18]Whirling, He will whirl you like a ball, into a land wide of hands. You shall die there, and there *are* the chariots of your glory, the shame of your lord's house. [19]And I will drive you from your position; and he will pull you from your station. [20]And in that day it shall be, even I will call to My servant Eliakim the son of Hilkiah. [21]And I will clothe him with your robe, and will fasten your sash on him. And I will give your authority into his hand. And he shall be a father to the inhabitants of Jerusalem and to the house of Judah. [22]And the key of the house of David I will lay on his shoulder, so that he opens, and no one shuts; and he shuts, and no one opens. [23]And I will drive him *as* a nail in a sure place; and he shall be for a glorious throne to his father's house. [24]And they shall hang on him all the glory of his father's house, the offspring and the offshoots, all small vessels, from vessels of cups even to all vessels of jars. [25]In that day, says Jehovah of hosts, the nail that is driven in the sure place shall be removed, and be cut down, and fall. And the burden that *was* on it shall be cut off. Jehovah has spoken.

4100 1004 5921 834 7644 2088 5532
16 אל־הסכן הזה על־שבנא אשר על־הבית׃ מה־לך פה
?here to What the over who ,Shebna to ,this steward to
you (is) ,house (is)

6913 4791 2672 6913 6311 2672 4310
ומי־לך פה כי־חצבת לך פה קבר חצבי מרום קברו
his on hewing a here for have you that ,here to And
,tomb high ,tomb yourself carved you (is) who

29 25 2904 3068 2009 4808 5553 2710
17 חקקי בסלע משכן לו׃ הנה יהוה מטלטלך טלטלה
a (with) you hurls Jehovah ,Behold for a the in carving
,hurling ?himself dwelling rock

776 1754 6801 6800 6800 5844 5844 1397
18 גבר ועטך עטה׃ צנוף יצנפך צנפה כדור אל־ארץ
a into a like a (with) will He ,Surely a (with) and O
land ball whirling you whirl .grasping you grasps ,man

7036 3519 4818 8033 4191 8033 3027 7342
רחבת ידים שמה תמות ושמה מרכבות כבודך קלון
the your chariots the and you There .hands wide
of shamed ,glory of (are) there ,die shall of

2040 4612 4673 1920 113 1004
19 בית אדניך׃ והדפתיך ממצבך וממעמדך יהרסך׃
will he from and your from will I And your the
.you pull station your ;position you drive .lord of house

2518 1121 471 5650 7121 3117 1961
20 והיה ביום ההוא וקראתי לעבדי לאליקים בן־חלקיהו׃
.Hilkiah the Eliakim to My to I that ,that day in it and
of son ,servant call will be shall

4475 2388 73 3801 3847
21 והלבשתיו כתנתך ואבנטך אחזקנו וממשלתך
your and fasten will your and your (with) will I And
authority ;him on sash robe him clothe

3063 1004 3089 3427 1961 3027 5414
אתן בידו והיה לאב ליושב ירושלם ולבית יהודה׃
.Judah to and Jerusalem the to a he And his into will I
of house the of dwellers father be shall .hand give

5462 5462 369 6605 7926 5921 1732 1004 4668 5414
22 ונתתי מפתח בית־דוד על־שכמו ופתח ואין סגר וסגר
he and ;shuts and he that his on David the key the I And
,shuts none opens ;shoulder of house of give will

3519 3678 1961 539 4725 3489 8628 6605 369
23 ואין פתח׃ ותקעתיו יתד במקום נאמן והיה לכסא כבוד
glorious a for he and ;sure a in a (as) will I And .opens and
throne be shall place nail him drive none

6631 1 1004 3519 3605 8518 1004
24 לבית אביו׃ ותלו עליו כל ׀ כבוד בית־אביו הצאצאים
the his house the all on they And his to
offspring ,father's of glory him hang shall .father's house

3627 3605 5704 101 3627 6996 3627 3605 6849
והצפעות כל כלי הקטן מכלי האגנות ועד כל־כלי
vessels all even cups from ,smallness vessels all the and
of to of vessels of ,offshoots

34:89 4185 6635 3068 5002 3117 5035
25 הנבלים׃ ביום ההוא נאם יהוה צבאות תמוש היתד
the be shall ,hosts Jehovah states ,that day In .jars
nail removed of

4853 1438 5307 3772 539 4725 8628
התקועה במקום נאמן ונגדעה ונפלה ונכרת המשא אשר־
that the shall And and be and ,sure the in is that
burden off cut be .fall ,down cut place driven

1696 3068 5921
עליה כי יהוה דבר׃
has Jehovah for on (was)
.spoken ,it

CHAPTER 23

[1]The burden of Tyre: Howl, ships of Tarshish! For it is ruined, without house, without entrance. It is revealed to them from the land of Chittim. [2]Be still, inhabitants of the coast, merchant of Sidon crossing the sea; they have filled you. [3]And by great waters, the seed of Sihor and the harvest of the river Nile *was* her revenue; and she a mart of nations. [4]Be ashamed, Sidon, for the sea has spoken, the strength of the sea, saying, I have not travailed, nor brought forth, I have not nourished young men *nor* raised up virgins. [5]As the report comes to Egypt, so they shall be grieved *at* the report of Tyre. [6]Pass over Tarshish; howl, people of the coast! [7]Is this your exulting *city* from days of her old age? Her own feet carry it far away to stay. [8]Who has purposed this against Tyre, the crowning *city*, whose merchants *are* rulers, whose traders *are* the honored of the earth? [9]Jehovah of hosts has purposed it, to stain the pride of all glory, to bring all the honored of the earth into contempt.

[10]Pass through your land as the Nile, O daughter of Tarshish; there is no more strength. [11]He stretched His hand over the sea; He shook kingdoms; Jehovah has made a decree against the merchant *city*, to destroy its forts. [12]And He said, You shall rejoice no more, oppressed one, virgin daughter of Sidon. Arise, cross over to Chittim, even there is no rest to you. [13]Behold, the land of the Chaldeans! This people did not exist! Assyria founded it for those who live in the desert. They set up their siege-towers; they stripped its palaces. They made it a

CAP. XXIII כג

CHAPTER 23

935 1004 7703 8659 591 3213 6865 4853
1 משא צר הילילו ׀ אניות תרשיש כי־שדד מבית מבוא
without without is it For !Tarshish ships ,Howl :Tyre The
.entrance ,house ,ruined of of burden

5671 6721 5503 339 3427 1826 1540 3794 776
2 מארץ כתים נגלה־למו׃ דמו ישבי אי סחר צידון עבר
cross- ,Sidon Trader the residents Be to is it Kittim the From
ing of ,coast of ,silent .them revealed of land

8393 2975 7102 7883 2233 7227 4325 4390 3220
3 ים מלאוך׃ ובמים רבים זרע שחר קציר יאור תבואתה
her (was) the the ,Sihor seed ,great by And have they the
;revenue Nile of harvest of waters .you filled ;sea

559 3220 4581 3220 559 6721 954 1471 5505 1961
4 ותהי סחר גוים׃ בושי צידון כי אמר ים מעוז הים לאמר
,saying the the the has for ,Sidon Be .nations the she and
,sea of strength ,sea said ,ashamed of mart was

7311 970 1430 3808 3205 2342 3808
לא־חלתי ולא־ילדתי ולא גדלתי בחורים רוממתי
(nor) young have I not brought nor have I not
up raised ,men nourished ;forth travailed

5674 6865 8088 2342 4714 8088 1330
5 בתולות׃ כאשר שמע למצרים יחילו כשמע צר׃ עברו
6
Pass .Tyre the at will they to (comes) the When .virgins
,over of report pained be ,Egypt report

6924 3117 5947 339 3427 3213 8659
7 תרשישה הילילו ישבי אי׃ הזאת לכם עליזה מימי־קדם
old from exult- the to Is the dwellers ,howl ;Tarshish
of days ,(city) ing you this !coast of

6865 3289 4310 1481 7350 7272 2986 6927
8 קדמתה יבלוה רגליה מרחוק לגור׃ מי יעץ זאת על־צר
,Tyre on this has Who to far feet Her carry ?age her
purposed .stay away her

3068 776 3513 3667 8269 5503 5849
9 המעטירה אשר סחריה שרים כנעניה נכבדי־ארץ׃ יהוה
Jehovah the (are) whose (are) merchants whose crowning the
of ?earth of weighty traders ,chiefs ,(city)

3513 3605 7043 6643 3605/1347 2490 3289 6635
צבאות יעצה לחלל גאון כל־צבי להקל כל־נכבדי־
the all bring to ,glory all the stain to pur- hosts
of weighty contempt into of pride ,it posed

4206 369 8659 1323 2975 776 5674 776
ארץ׃ עברי ארצך כיאר בת־תרשיש אין מזח 10
girdle there ;Tarshish daughter the as your Pass the
no is of ,Nile land through .earth

6680 3068 4467 7264 3220 5921 5186 3027 5750
עוד׃ ידו נטה על־הים הרגיז ממלכות יהוה צוה אל־ 11
against has Jehovah ;kingdoms He the over He His any
decreed shook ;sea stretched hand .more

5937 5750 3254 3808 559 4581 8045 3667
כנען לשמד מעזניה׃ ויאמר לא־תוסיפי עוד לעלוז 12
,rejoice more shall You not he And .forts its to ,Canaan
again ,said destroy

8033 1571 5674 6965 3794 6721 1330 6231
המעשקה בתולת בת־צידון כתיים קומי עברי גם־שם
there even cross ,Arise to .Sidon daughter ,virgin oppressed
;over Kittim of

804 1961 3808 5971 3778 776 2009 5117/3808
לא־ינוח לך׃ הן ׀ ארץ כשדים זה העם לא היה אשור 13
Assyria did not people This the the ,Behold to is not
;exist !Chaldeans of land .you rest

7760 759 6209 969 6965 6728 3245
יסדה לציים הקימו בחיניו עוררו ארמנותיה שמה
they its they siege- their They desert for founded
it made ;palaces stripped ;towers up set !creatures it

ruin. [14]Howl, ships of Tarshish! For your fortress is ruined. [15]And it shall be in that day that Tyre shall be forgotten seventy years, according to the days of one king. At the end of seventy years, it will be as the song of a harlot to Tyre. [16]Take a harp; go about the city, O forgotten harlot. Do well to play; make many songs, that you may be remembered. [17]And it will be, after the end of seventy years, Jehovah will visit Tyre; and she shall return to her hire, and will fornicate with all the kingdoms of the earth, on the face of the ground. [18]And her goods and her wages shall be holiness to Jehovah; it shall not be hoarded nor stored; for her goods shall be for those who dwell before Jehovah, to eat enough, and for a choice covering.

4581 7703 8659 591 3213 4654
14 למפלה׃ הילילו אניות תרשיש כי שדד מעזכן׃
your is For !Tarshish ships ,Howl a for
.fortress ruined of .ruin

4428 3117 81:41 7657 6865 7911 3117 1961
15 והיה ביום ההוא ונשכחת צר שבעים שנה כימי מלך
king the as ,years seventy Tyre shall that ,that day in it And
of days forgotten be be shall

3947 2181 7892 6865 1961 8141 7657 7093 259
16 אחד מקץ שבעים שנה יהיה לצר כשירת הזונה׃ קחי
Take the the as to will it ,years seventy the At .one
.harlot of song Tyre be of end

7892 7235 5059 3190 7911 2181 5892 5437 3658
כנור סבי עיר זונה נשכחה היטיבי נגן הרבי־שיר למען
that ,songs make to Do !forgotten O the go a
many ;play well harlot ,city about ,harp

6865 3068 6485 81.41 7657 7093 1961 2142
17 תזכרי׃ והיה מקץ ׀ שבעים שנה יפקד יהוה את־צר
:;Tyre Jehovah will ,years seventy the at it And be may you
visit of end be will .remembered

6440 5921 776 4467 3605 2181 868 7725
ושבה לאתננה וזנתה את־כל־ממלכות הארץ על־פני
the on the the all with will and her to she and
of face ,earth of kingdoms fornicate hire return shall

686 3808 3068 6944 868 5504 1961 127
18 האדמה׃ והיה סחרה ואתננה קדש ליהוה לא יאצר
shall It not to holy her and her shall And the
hoarded be .Jehovah wages traffic be .ground

398 5504 1961 3068 6440 3427 2630 3808
ולא יחסן כי לישבים לפני יהוה יהיה סחרה לאכל
eat to traffic her be shall Jehovah before those to for ,stored nor
dwell who

6266 4374 7654
לשבעה ולמכסה עתיק׃
.choice for and to
covering a sufficiency

CAP. XXIV כד

CHAPTER 24

CHAPTER 24

[1]Lo, Jehovah empties the land and makes it bare, and distorts its face, and scatters its inhabitants. [2]And as *it is* with the people, so with the priest; as with the servant, so with the master; as with the maid, so with her mistress; as with the buyer, so with the seller; as with the lender, so with the borrower; as with the creditor, so with the debtor. [3]The land shall completely be emptied and utterly stripped, for Jehovah has spoken this word.

[4]The land mourns *and* languishes; the world droops *and* languishes; the proud people of the earth droop. [5]And the earth is profaned under its inhabitants, because they transgress laws *and* violate a statute, and break the everlasting covenant. [6]On account of this a curse has

6327 6440 5753 1110 776 1238 3068 2009
1 הנה יהוה בוקק הארץ ובולקה ועוה פניה והפיץ
and its and makes and the empties Jehovah Be-
scatters ,face distorts waste it ,land ,hold

1404 8198 113 5650 3548 5971 1961 3427
2 ישביה׃ והיה כעם ככהן כעבד כאדניו כשפחה כגברתה
her so the as his so the as the so the as it And in- its
;mistress ,maid ;master ,servant ;priest ,people is .habitants

5378 5383 3867 3867 4376 7069
כקונה כמוכר כמלוה כלוה כנשה כאשר נשא בו׃
with the so the as the so the as the so the as
.him debtor ,creditor ;borrower ,lender ;seller ,buyer

1696 3068 962 962 776 1238 1238
3 הבוק ׀ תבוק הארץ והבוז ׀ תבוז כי יהוה דבר את־
has Jehovah for ;stripped and The be shall com-
spoken utterly ,land emptied pletely

8398 5034 535 776 5034 56 2088 1697
4 הדבר הזה׃ אבלה נבלה הארץ אמללה נבלה תבל
the lan- (and) droops the (and) Mourns .this word
;world guishes ,land languishes

3427 8478 2610 776 776 4791 535
5 אמללו מרום עם־הארץ׃ והארץ חנפה תחת ישביה
its under is the And the the proud the droop
inhabitants profaned earth .earth of people of

422 5769 1285 6565 2706 2498 8451 5674
6 כי־עברו תורת חלפו חק הפרו ברית עולם׃ על־כן אלה
a Therefore ever- the and a violate ,laws they for
curse .lasting covenant break ,statute transgress

devoured the land; and they
who live in it are held guilty.
For this the dwellers of the
land are consumed, and
few men are left. 7The new
wine has failed; the vine
droops; all the merry-
hearted sigh. 8The joy of
timbrels ceases; the noise
of those who revel ends;
the joy of the harp ceases.
9They shall not drink wine
with a song; fermented
drink shall be bitter to those
who drink it. 10The city of
shame is broken down;
every house is shut, that no
one may enter. 11A crying
over the wine *is* in the
streets; all joy is darkened;
the gladness in the land is
carried away. 12Desolation
is remaining in the city, and
a ruin; the gate is battered.
13For it is thus in the midst
of the land, among the
peoples, *it shall be* as the
shaking of an olive tree, and
as gleanings when the
grape harvest is com-
pleted. 14They lift up their
voice; they sing for the
majesty of Jehovah; they
cry aloud from the sea.
15On account of this, glorify
Jehovah in the east, the
name of Jehovah God of
Israel, in the coasts of the
sea. 16We have heard songs
from the end of the earth,
Honor to the Righteous. But
I said, Leanness to me!
Leanness to me! Woe to
me! Traitors betray, even
perfidy; traitors betray!
17Dread, and the pit, and
a snare *are* upon you,
dweller of the earth. 18And
it shall be, he who flees
from the sound of dread
shall fall into the pit. And he
who comes up out of the
middle of the pit shall be
taken in the snare. For the
windows from on high are
opened, and the earth's
foundations quake. 19The
earth is breaking, breaking!
The earth is crashing,
crashing! The earth is tottering, tottering. 20The earth
is staggering, staggering,
like a drunkard! And it rocks
to and fro like a hut. And its
trespass is heavy on it; and

776 3427 2787 3651 5921 3427 816 776 398
אָכְלָה אֶרֶץ וַיֶּאְשְׁמוּ יֹשְׁבֵי בָהּ עַל־כֵּן חָרוּ יֹשְׁבֵי אֶרֶץ
the land, the dwellers of are burned Therefore .it in who they live are held guilty and ;land the devours

7
584 1412 535 8492 56 4213 582 7604
וְנִשְׁאַר אֱנוֹשׁ מִזְעָר׃ אָבַל תִּירוֹשׁ אֻמְלְלָה־גָפֶן נֶאֶנְחוּ
sigh the vine, droops new The ;wine mourns .few men re- maining and

8
5947 7588 2308 8596 4885 7673 3820 8056 3605
כָּל־שִׂמְחֵי־לֵב׃ שָׁבַת מְשׂוֹשׂ תֻּפִּים חָדַל שְׁאוֹן עַלִּיזִים
;revelers the of noise ceases the timbrels The of joy ceases .heart the of merry all

9
8354 7941 4843/3196/8354 3808 7892 3658 4885 7673
שָׁבַת מְשׂוֹשׂ כִּנּוֹר׃ בַּשִּׁיר לֹא יִשְׁתּוּ־יָיִן יֵמַר שֵׁכָר לְשֹׁתָיו׃
its to .drinkers strong drink is bitter ;wine they not drink shall With song the the .harp the of joy ceases

10
11
3196 5921 6682 935 1004 3605 5462 8414 7151 7664
נִשְׁבְּרָה קִרְיַת־תֹּהוּ סֻגַּר כָּל־בַּיִת מִבּוֹא׃ צְוָחָה עַל־הַיַּיִן
the over wine crying A from .entering house every is shut ;emptiness the of city broken Is down

12
7604 776 4885 1540 8057 3605 6150 2351
בַּחוּצוֹת עָרְבָה כָּל־שִׂמְחָה גָּלָה מְשׂוֹשׂ הָאָרֶץ׃ נִשְׁאַר
is remaining the .land the in gladness is exiled ;joy all dark- ened is the in (is) ;streets

13
7130 1961 3541 8179 3807 7591 8047 5892
בָּעִיר שַׁמָּה וּשְׁאִיָּה יֻכַּת־שָׁעַר׃ כִּי כֹה יִהְיֶה בְּקֶרֶב
the in of midst is it thus For the .gate is battered a and ,ruin deso- ,lation the in city

1208 3615 5955 2132 5363 5971 8432 776
הָאָרֶץ בְּתוֹךְ הָעַמִּים כְּנֹקֶף זַיִת כְּעוֹלֵלֹת אִם־כָּלָה בָצִיר׃
grape the .harvest is ended when glean- ings as an tree olive the as of shaking the ,peoples among the ,land

14
15
3220 6670 3068 1347 7442 6963 5375
הֵמָּה יִשְׂאוּ קוֹלָם יָרֹנּוּ בִּגְאוֹן יְהוָה צָהֲלוּ מִיָּם׃ עַל־כֵּן
Therefore from .sea the cry they aloud Jehovah the for of majesty they ;sing their ,voice lift up They

3478 430 3068 8034 3220 339 3068 3513 217
בָּאֻרִים כַּבְּדוּ יְהוָה בְּאִיֵּי הַיָּם שֵׁם יְהוָה אֱלֹהֵי יִשְׂרָאֵל׃
.Israel God of Jehovah the of name the ,sea the in of coasts ;Jehovah glorify the in east

16
559 6662 6643 8085 2158 776 3671
מִכְּנַף הָאָרֶץ זְמִרֹת שָׁמַעְנוּ צְבִי לַצַּדִּיק וָאֹמַר
I But ,said the to .Righteous Honor have we ,heard songs the earth the From of wing

898 898 879 898/898 188 7334 7334
רָזִי־לִי רָזִי־לִי אוֹי לִי בֹּגְדִים בָּגָדוּ וּבֶגֶד בּוֹגְדִים בָּגָדוּ׃
.betray traitors even ;perfidy ,betray Traitors to !me Woe to !me Lean- ness to !Me Lean- ness

17
18
6963 5127 1961 776 3427 6341 6354 6343
פַּחַד וָפַחַת וָפָח עָלֶיךָ יוֹשֵׁב הָאָרֶץ׃ וְהָיָה הַנָּס מִקּוֹל
the from of sound who he flees it And be will the .earth dweller of (are) ,you on and snare and pit Dread

6341 3920 6354 8432 5927 6354 5307 6343
הַפַּחַד יִפֹּל אֶל־הַפַּחַת וְהָעוֹלֶה מִתּוֹךְ הַפַּחַת יִלָּכֵד בַּפָּח
the in .snare be shall taken the pit of out of midst the who he And up comes the .pit into shall fall dread

19
7489 776 4146 7493 6605 4791 699
כִּי־אֲרֻבּוֹת מִמָּרוֹם נִפְתָּחוּ וַיִּרְעֲשׁוּ מוֹסְדֵי אָרֶץ׃ רֹעָה
,Breaking the earth's foundations and quake are ,opened on from high the windows For

4131 4131 776 6565 6565 776 7489
הִתְרֹעֲעָה הָאָרֶץ פּוֹר הִתְפּוֹרְרָה אֶרֶץ מוֹט הִתְמוֹטְטָה
is tottering Totter- ,ing the !earth is crashing ,Crashing the !earth breaking is itself

20
3520 4412 5110 7910 776 5128 5128 776
אָרֶץ׃ נוֹעַ תָּנוּעַ אֶרֶץ כַּשִּׁכּוֹר וְהִתְנוֹדְדָה כַּמְּלוּנָה וְכָבַד
is And heavy a like hut rocks it And fro and to a like !drunkard the ,earth stag- gering is Stag- ,gering the !earth

it shall fall, and not rise again. [21]And it shall be in that day, Jehovah shall punish the army of the high place on high, and on the kings of the land on the land. [22]And they will be gathered, a gathering of prisoners in a dungeon. And they shall be shut up in a prison; and after many days they will be visited. [23]Then the moon shall blush, and the sun shall be ashamed, when Jehovah of hosts shall reign in Mount Zion and in Jerusalem; and before His elders *is His* glory.

3117 1961 6965 3254 3808 5307 6588 5921
עָלֶיהָ פִּשְׁעָהּ וְנָפְלָה וְלֹא־תֹסִיף קוּם׃ וְהָיָה בַּיּוֹם הַהוּא 21
,that day in it And .rise shall and it and its it on
be shall again not fall shall ;trespass

127 4428 5921 4791 4791 6635 3068 6485
יִפְקֹד יְהוָה עַל־צְבָא הַמָּרוֹם בַּמָּרוֹם וְעַל־מַלְכֵי הָאֲדָמָה
the kings the and the in high the the on Jehovah shall
land of on ,place high place of army visit

5462 953 615 622 626 127
עַל־הָאֲדָמָה׃ וְאֻסְּפוּ אֲסֵפָה אַסִּיר עַל־בּוֹר וְסֻגְּרוּ עַל־ 22
in be will and a in prisoners gather- a will they And the on
up shut ,dungeon of ing gathered be land

954 3842 2659 6485 3117 7230 4525
מַסְגֵּר וּמֵרֹב יָמִים יִפָּקֵדוּ׃ וְחָפְרָה הַלְּבָנָה וּבוֹשָׁה 23
be will and the will Then be will they days after and a
ashamed ,moon blush .visited many ;prison

5048 3389 6726 2022 6635 3068 4427 2535
הַחַמָּה כִּי־מָלַךְ יְהוָה צְבָאוֹת בְּהַר צִיּוֹן וּבִירוּשָׁלַםִ וְנֶגֶד
and in and ,Zion in hosts Jehovah reigns for ,sun the
before ,Jerusalem Mount of

3519 2205
זְקֵנָיו כָּבוֹד׃
(His is) His
.glory elders

CAP. XXV כה

CHAPTER 25

CHAPTER 25

[1]O Jehovah, You *are* my God. I will exalt You; I will thank Your name; for You have done a wonderful thing: counsels from afar; faithful faithfulness. [2]Because You have made a heap from a city, a fortified city into a ruin; a citadel of foreigners not *to be* a city, not to be built, to forever. [3]For this the mighty people glorify You, the city of the ruthless nations shall fear You. [4]For You are a stronghold to the poor, a stronghold to the needy in his distress, a refuge from storm, a shadow from heat; because the breath of the ruthless *is* like a storm *against* a wall. [5]You shall lay low the noise of foreigners, like the heat in a dry place, the heat with the shadow of cloud; the shouting of the terrifying ones shall be laid low. [6]And Jehovah of hosts shall make a feast of fat things for all the peoples in this mountain; a feast of wine on the lees, of fat things full of marrow, refined wine on the lees. [7]And He will destroy in this mountain the face of the covering which covers all people, and the

6382 6213 8034 3034 7311 430 3068
יְהוָה אֱלֹהַי אַתָּה אֲרוֹמִמְךָ אוֹדֶה שִׁמְךָ כִּי עָשִׂיתָ פֶּלֶא 1
a have You for Your will I exalt will I You my ,Jehovah
,wonder done ,name thank .You !(are) God

7151 1530 5892 7760 544 530 7350 6098
עֵצוֹת מֵרָחוֹק אֱמוּנָה אֹמֶן׃ כִּי שַׂמְתָּ מֵעִיר לַגָּל קִרְיָה 2
city a a to a from have You For .faithful faithful- from counsels
,heap city made ness ,afar

1129 3808 5769 5892 2114 759 4654 1219
בְּצוּרָה לְמַפֵּלָה אַרְמוֹן זָרִים מֵעִיר לְעוֹלָם לֹא יִבָּנֶה׃ עַל־ 3
There may it not to a not for- citadel a ;ruin a into fortified
.built be forever ;city eigners of

1961 3372 6184 1471 7151 5704 3513
כֵּן יְכַבְּדוּךָ עַם־עָז קִרְיַת גּוֹיִם עָרִיצִים יִירָאוּךָ׃ כִּי־הָיִיתָ 4
You For fear shall ruthless nations the ;might peo- glorify fore
are .You of city of ple You

2721 6738 2230 4268 6862 34 4581 1800 4581
מָעוֹז לַדָּל מָעוֹז לָאֶבְיוֹן בַּצַּר־לוֹ מַחְסֶה מִזֶּרֶם צֵל מֵחֹרֶב
from a from refuge a to the in the to a the to a
,heat shadow ,storm ,him distress ,needy fort ,poor fort

2114 7588 6724 2721 7023 2230 6185 7307
כִּי רוּחַ עָרִיצִים כְּזֶרֶם קִיר׃ כְּחֹרֶב בְּצָיוֹן שְׁאוֹן זָרִים 5
for- the dry a in Like (against) like (is) ruth- the the for
eigners of noise ,place heat .wall a storm a less of breath

6213 6030 6185 2158 5645 6738 3771 3665
תַּכְנִיעַ חֹרֶב בְּצֵל עָב זְמִיר עָרִיצִים יַעֲנֶה׃ וְעָשָׂה 6
shall And be shall the the ,cloud the by (as) shall You
make .humbled ruthless of song of shadow heat ,low lay

8081 4960 2022 5971 3605 6635 3068
יְהוָה צְבָאוֹת לְכָל־הָעַמִּים בָּהָר הַזֶּה מִשְׁתֵּה שְׁמָנִים
fat a this in the for hosts Jehovah
,things of feast mountain peoples all of

1104 2212 8105 4229 8081 8105 4960
מִשְׁתֵּה שְׁמָנִים שְׁמָרִים שְׁמָנִים מְמֻחָיִם שְׁמָרִים מְזֻקָּקִים׃ וּבִלַּע 7
He And .refined on wine of full fat on wine feast a
swallow will lees the ,marrow things ,lees the of

4541 5971 3605 5921 5259 3875/6440 2088 2022
בָּהָר הַזֶּה פְּנֵי־הַלּוֹט ׀ הַלּוֹט עַל־כָּל־הָעַמִּים וְהַמַּסֵּכָה
the and the all over which the the this in
veil ,peoples covers covering of face mountain

veil that is woven over all nations. [8]He will swallow up death in victory! And the Lord Jehovah will wipe away tears from all faces. And He shall reprove the reproach of His people from all the earth; for Jehovah has spoken. [9]And one shall say in that day, Behold, this *is* our God; we have waited for Him, and He will save us. This *is* Jehovah; we have waited for Him; we will be glad and rejoice in His salvation. [10]For the hand of Jehovah shall rest in this mountain; and Moab shall be trampled under Him, even as straw *is* trampled in the water of a dung pit. [11]And He shall spread His hands in his midst, as he who swims strokes to swim. And He shall lay low his pride with the skill of His hands. [12]And He shall bow down the fortress of the height of your walls; *He will* lay low, touch to the earth, even to the dust.

136 4229 5331 4194 1104 1471 3605 5921 5259
8 הַסֻּכָה עַל־כָּל־הַגּוֹיִם׃ בִּלַּע הַמָּוֶת לָנֶצַח וּמָחָה אֲדֹנָי
the will And !forever death will He the all over is that
Lord away wipe up swallow .nations woven

3605 5493 5971 2781 6440 3605 1832 3068
יְהוִה דִּמְעָה מֵעַל כָּל־פָּנִים וְחֶרְפַּת עַמּוֹ יָסִיר מֵעַל כָּל־
all from will He His the And .faces all from tears Jehovah
remove people of reproach

2009 3117 559 1696 3068 776
9 הָאָרֶץ כִּי יְהוָה דִּבֵּר׃ וְאָמַר בַּיּוֹם הַהוּא הִנֵּה
,Behold ,that day in one And has Jehovah for the
say shall .spoken —earth

1523 6960 3068 2088 3462 6960 2088 430
אֱלֹהֵינוּ זֶה קִוִּינוּ לוֹ וְיוֹשִׁיעֵנוּ זֶה יְהוָה קִוִּינוּ לוֹ נָגִילָה
will we for have we ;Jehovah This He and for have we this our
glad be ;Him waited (is) .us save will ,Him waited ;(is) God

1758 2088 2022 3068 3027 5117 3444 8056
10 וְנִשְׂמְחָה בִּישׁוּעָתוֹ׃ כִּי־תָנוּחַ יַד־יְהוָה בָּהָר הַזֶּה וְנָדוֹשׁ
shall and ;this in Jehovah the shall For His in rejoice and
trampled be mountain of hand rest .salvation

3027 6566 4087 1119 4963 1758 8478 4124
11 מוֹאָב תַּחְתָּיו כְּהִדּוּשׁ מַתְבֵּן בְּמֵי מַדְמֵנָה׃ וּפֵרַשׂ יָדָיו
His He And dung a the in straw is as under Moab
hands spread shall .pit of water trampled ,Him

1376 8213 7811 7811 6566 7130
בְּקִרְבּוֹ כַּאֲשֶׁר יְפָרֵשׂ הַשֹּׂחֶה לִשְׂחוֹת וְהִשְׁפִּיל גַּאֲוָתוֹ עִם
with his He And .swim to the spreads as its in
pride low lay shall swimmer ,midst

5060 8213 7817 2346 4869 4013 3027 698
12 אָרְבּוֹת יָדָיו׃ וּמִבְצַר מִשְׂגַּב חוֹמֹתֶיךָ הֵשַׁח הִשְׁפִּיל הִגִּיעַ
strike ,low lay will He your the the And His the
down ,down bow walls of height of fortress .hands of skill

6083 776
לָאָרֶץ עַד־עָפָר׃
the even the to
.dust to ,earth

CAP. XXVI כו

CHAPTER 26

CHAPTER 26

[1]In that day this song shall be sung in the land of Judah: A strong city *is* ours; He sets up salvation *as our* walls and rampart. [2]Open the gates, and the righteous nation shall come in, keeping faithfulness. [3]You will keep in perfect peace the mind stayed *on You*, for he trusts in You. [4]Trust in Jehovah forever, for in Jah Jehovah *is* everlasting strength. [5]For He bows the dwellers on high; He lays low the lofty city; He lays it low to the ground; He makes it touch even to the dust. [6]The foot shall trample it, the feet of the poor, steps of the weak. [7]The path for the just *is* uprightness. Upright One, level the track of the just.

5797 5872 3063 776 7892 7891 2088 3117
1 בַּיּוֹם הַהוּא יוּשַׁר הַשִּׁיר־הַזֶּה בְּאֶרֶץ יְהוּדָה עִיר עָז־לָנוּ
(is) strong A :Judah the in this song be shall that day In
;us to city of land sung be

6662 935 8179 6605 2426 2346 7896 3444
2 יְשׁוּעָה יָשִׁית חוֹמוֹת וָחֵל׃ פִּתְחוּ שְׁעָרִים וְיָבֹא גוֹי־צַדִּיק
,righteous a may that the Open and (our as) He salvation
nation come ,gates .rampart walls sets

982 7965 7965 5341 5564 3336 529 8104
3 שֹׁמֵר אֱמֻנִים׃ יֵצֶר סָמוּךְ תִּצֹּר שָׁלוֹם ׀ שָׁלוֹם כִּי בְךָ בָּטוּחַ׃
he in for ;peace (in) will You stayed the faithful- keeping
.trusts You ,peace keep You on mind .ness

5769 6697 3068 3050 5702 3068 982
4 בִּטְחוּ בַיהוָה עֲדֵי־עַד כִּי בְּיָהּ יְהוָה צוּר עוֹלָמִים׃ כִּי
5
For .everlasting (is) Jehovah in for ,forever in Trust
Rock a Jah Jehovah

5704 8213 8213 7682 7151 4791 3427 7817
הֵשַׁח יֹשְׁבֵי מָרוֹם קִרְיָה נִשְׂגָּבָה יַשְׁפִּילֶנָּה יַשְׁפִּילָהּ עַד־
to lays He lays He lofty the ;high on the He
,low it ,low it city dwellers bows

6471 6041 7272 7272 7429 6083 5060 776
6 אֶרֶץ יַגִּיעֶנָּה עַד־עָפָר׃ תִּרְמְסֶנָּה רָגֶל רַגְלֵי עָנִי פַּעֲמֵי
steps the feet The shall the even makes He the
of poor of —foot it trample .dust to touch it ;ground

6424 6662 4570 3477 4339 6662 734 1800
דַלִּים׃ אֹרַח לַצַּדִּיק מֵישָׁרִים יָשָׁר מַעְגַּל צַדִּיק תְּפַלֵּס׃
make the the Upright (is) the for The the
.level just of track ,One ;uprightness just path .weak

8Yea, Jehovah, *in* the path of Your judgments we awaited You; for Your name and for Your memory *is* the desire of our soul. 9*With* my soul I desire You in the night; yea, *with* my spirit within me I diligently seek You. For when Your judgments *are* in the earth, the inhabitants of the world learn righteousness.

10The wicked finds favor; he does not learn righteousness; he deals perversely in the land of honesty, and does not see the majesty of Jehovah. 11Jehovah, Your hand is high; they do not see; they see, and are ashamed of the zeal of the people. Yea, the fire of Your foes devours them. 12You will ordain peace for us; for also You have worked all our works for us. 13Jehovah our God, masters beside You have governed us; only in You we will mention Your name. 14Dead ones do not live; departed spirits do not rise; because of this You visited and destroyed them, and caused all memory of them to perish. 15You have added to the nation, Jehovah; You have added to the nation, You are glorified; You have extended all the ends of the land. 16Jehovah, they visited You in distress; they poured out a whisper; Your chastening *was* to them. 17As a pregnant woman draws near to bear, she writhes *and* cries out in her pangs. So are we before You, Jehovah. 18We conceived; we writhe; as it were, we gave birth *to* wind. We have not worked salvation *for* the earth; and the world's inhabitants have not fallen. 19Your dead ones shall live, my dead body; they shall rise up. Awake and sing, dust-dwellers; for the dew of lights *is* your dew; and the earth shall cast out departed spirits. 20Come, My people, go in your rooms and shut your doors behind you. Hide *for* a little moment, until the fury passes. 21For, behold,

8

8378	2143	8034	6960	3068	4941		734	637
the (is) Your for	and Your for	awaited we	,Jehovah	Your	the (in)	,Yea
of desire memory	memory	name ;You		judgments	of path	

9

7836	7130	5307	39 15		183	53.15	53 1 5
You seek I	within (with)	,yea	the in	desire I	(With)	(our)
;diligently	me spirit my		;night	You soul my	.soul

10

3605	8398	3427 3925	6664	776	49 41	
finds	the inhab-	the learn	righ-	to (are)	Your	when for
favor .world	of itants	teousness ,earth the	judgments

1348	7200	1077 5765	5228	776	6664	3925 10 77	7563
the	sees	and deals he honesty	,perversely	of land	righ-	he not	;wicked
of majesty	not			.teousness	learns	The wicked

11

7068	954	2372	2372	1077	3027 7311	3068	3068
zeal the	are and	they	they	not	Your is ,Jehovah	.Jehovah
of	of ashamed	see	;see		;hand high

12

7965	82.39	3068	398	6862	.784/637	5971
peace	will You ,Jehovah	devours	Your	the ,Yea the
	ordain	them	foes of fire	;people

13

430	3068	64 66	44.39	3605	1571
Our Jehovah	for	have You	our	all also for	for
,God	.us	worked	works	;us

14

1077 4191	8034	42	905	2108	113	1166
not Dead	Your	we in	only	beside	masters gov-	have
ones	.name	mention You	;You	us erned

3605	6	80 45	6485	6965	1077 7496	2421
all	caused and	destroyed and	You	there-	do not departed	do
perish to	them	visited	fore	,arise	spirits	;live

15

7368	3513	1471	3254	30 68	1 1471 3254	2143
have You	are You	the to	have You	Jeho-	the to have You	of memory
extended	;glorified	,nation added	;vah	,nation added	.them

3908	6694	6485	6862	3068	776 7099	3605
a	they	visited they	in	,Jehovah	the the	all
;whisper poured	;You	distress		.land of ends

16

2199	2342	3205	7126	2030	3644	4148
(and)	she	give to	draws	woman a	As	to (was) Your
cries	writhes	,birth	near	child with	.them chastening

17

320 5	3644	23 42	2030	3068	6440	1961 3651	2256
gave we	it as	we con-	We	,Jehovah	be-	from we	so	her in
birth	,were	,ceived		;You fore are		,pangs

18

2421	8398	3427	5307	1077	776	6213	1077	3444	7307
shall	the inhabi-	the have	and the (for)	have we	not	Salvation (to)	.wind
live	,world of tants	fallen	not	,earth	worked

19

2.19	2919	6083	7931	7442	6974	6965	50 38	4191
lights	the for	the dwellers	and	awake	shall they	dead my	Your
(is)	of dew	,dust of	,sing	;arise	,body	,ones dead

20

2315	935	5971	3212	5307	7496	776	29 19
your	enter My	,Come	make shall	departed	the and	your
rooms	,people	.fall	spirits	.earth	;dew

2195	5674	5704	7281	4592	2247	1157	18 17	54 62
.fury	passes	until	,moment	a as	hide	behind	your	and
	over		little			;you	doors	shut

Jehovah comes out of His place to visit his iniquity on the dweller of the earth. The earth shall also reveal her blood, and shall no more cover over her slain ones.

CHAPTER 27

[1]In that day Jehovah will visit the sea-monster, the fleeing serpent, with His fierce and great and strong sword, even on the sea-monster, the twisting serpent. And He will slay the monster which *is* in the sea. [2]In that day *will be* a vineyard of delight; sing to it; [3]I, Jehovah, keep it; I will water it *every* moment, that no one punish it; I will guard it night and day. [4]Fury is not in Me. Who will give Me briers *and* thorns in the battle? I will step through it; I would burn it at once. [5]Or will he lay hold of My strength that he may make peace with Me? Let him make peace with Me. [6]Those who come to Jacob, He shall make take root. Israel shall blossom and bud and fill the face of the world *with* fruit. [7]*As* the striking of His striker, did He strike him? Or as the slaying of His slain, is he slain? [8]You will contend with her by driving her away, by sending her away. He shall take away by His harsh wind, in the day of the east wind. [9]By this, then, the iniquity of Jacob will be covered, and this *is* all the fruit, to take away his sin; when he makes all the stones of the altar as chalkstones that are beaten in pieces; Asherim and sun-pillars shall not rise. [10]For the fortified city *shall be* lonely, a forsaken pasture, and left like a wilderness. The calf shall feed there, and he shall lie there, and eat up its branches. [11]When its boughs dry up, they are broken off. Women

5921 776 3427 5771 6485 4725 3318 3068 2009
21 כִּי־הִנֵּה יְהוָה יֹצֵא מִמְּקוֹמוֹ לִפְקֹד עֲוֺן יֹשֵׁב־הָאָרֶץ עָלָיו
on of dweller the in- the visit to His from comes Jehovah be- ,For
;him earth the of iquity place forth ,hold
2026 5750 3680 3808 1818 776 1540
וְגִלְּתָה הָאָרֶץ אֶת־דָּמֶיהָ וְלֹא־תְכַסֶּה עוֹד עַל־הֲרוּגֶיהָ׃
her over more shall and her the shall also
.slain cover not ,blood earth reveal

CAP. XXVII כז

CHAPTER 27

2389 1419 7186 2719 3068 6485 3117
1 בַּיּוֹם הַהוּא יִפְקֹד יְהוָה בְּחַרְבּוֹ הַקָּשָׁה וְהַגְּדוֹלָה וְהַחֲזָקָה
and and fierce His with Jehovah shall that day In
strong great sword visit
2026 6129 5175 3882 1281 5175 3882
עַל לִוְיָתָן נָחָשׁ בָּרִחַ וְעַל לִוְיָתָן נָחָשׁ עֲקַלָּתוֹן וְהָרַג אֶת־
He and ;twisting the sea the even ,fleeing the sea the on
slay shall serpent ,monster on serpent ,monster
6031 2531 3754 3117 3220 834 8577
2 הַתַּנִּין אֲשֶׁר בַּיָּם׃ בַּיּוֹם הַהוּא כֶּרֶם חֶמֶר עַנּוּ־לָהּ׃
to sing ,delight vine- a that day In the in which the
;it of yard .sea (is) monster
3915 6485 6435 8248 7281 5341 3068
3 אֲנִי יְהוָה נֹצְרָהּ לִרְגָעִים אַשְׁקֶנָּה פֶּן יִפְקֹד עָלֶיהָ לַיְלָה
night ,it on one lest water I (every) keep Jehovah I
visit ;it moment ;it
4421 7898 8068 5414 4310 369 2534 5341 3117
4 וָיוֹם אֶצֳּרֶנָּה׃ חֵמָה אֵין לִי מִי־יִתְּנֵנִי שָׁמִיר שַׁיִת בַּמִּלְחָמָה
the in (and) briars will Who to is Fury guard I and
?battle thorns Me give .Me not .it day
7965 6213 4581 2388 3162 6702 6585
5 אֶפְשְׂעָה בָהּ אֲצִיתֶנָּה יָּחַד׃ אוֹ יַחֲזֵק בְּמָעוּזִּי יַעֲשֶׂה שָׁלוֹם
peace he that My of he will Or at would I through would I
make may strength hold take .once it burn ;it step
6524 6692 3290 8327 935 6213 7965
6 לִי שָׁלוֹם יַעֲשֶׂה־לִּי׃ הַבָּאִים יַשְׁרֵשׁ יַעֲקֹב יָצִיץ וּפָרַח
and shall ;Jacob take will the (In) with him let Peace with
bud blossom root (days) coming .Me make ;Me
4347 4347 8570 8398 6440 4390 3478
7 יִשְׂרָאֵל וּמָלְאוּ פְנֵי־תֵבֵל תְּנוּבָה׃ הַכְּמַכַּת מַכֵּהוּ
His the (As) (with) the the they and Israel
striker of striking .fruit world of face fill will
7378 7971 5433 2026 2026 2027 5221
8 הִכָּהוּ אִם־כְּהֶרֶג הֲרֻגָיו הֹרָג׃ בְּסַאסְּאָה בְּשַׁלְחָהּ תְּרִיבֶנָּה
contend You sending by driving By he is His the as Or He did
.her with away her ,away her ?slain slain of slaying ?him strike
5771 3722 2063 3651 6921 3117 7186 7307 1898
9 הָגָה בְּרוּחוֹ הַקָּשָׁה בְּיוֹם קָדִים׃ לָכֵן בְּזֹאת יְכֻפַּר עֲוֺן
in- the be will by Then east the in ,harsh His by shall He
of iquity covered this .wind of day wind remove
4196 68 3605 7760 2403 5493 6529 3605 2088 3290
יַעֲקֹב וְזֶה כָּל־פְּרִי הָסִר חַטָּאתוֹ בְּשׂוּמוֹ ׀ כָּל־אַבְנֵי מִזְבֵּחַ
the the all he when ;sin his turn to the all and ;Jacob
altar of stones sets away fruit (is) this
5892 2553 842 6965 3808 5210 1615 68
10 כְּאַבְנֵי־גִר מְנֻפָּצוֹת לֹא־יָקֻמוּ אֲשֵׁרִים וְחַמָּנִים׃ כִּי עִיר
the For sun- and Asherim shall not beaten chalk as
city .pillars rise ,pieces in of stones
5695 7462 8033 4057 5800 7971 5116 910 1219
בְּצוּרָה בָּדָד נָוֶה מְשֻׁלָּח וְנֶעֱזָב כַּמִּדְבָּר שָׁם יִרְעֶה עֵגֶל
the shall There the like for- and left a ,lonely fortified
,calf feed .wilderness saken alone pasture (be will)
7665 7102 3001 5585 3615 7257 8033
11 וְשָׁם יִרְבַּץ וְכִלָּה סְעִפֶיהָ׃ בִּיבֹשׁ קְצִירָהּ תִּשָּׁבַרְנָה
are they its When its eat and shall he and
.off broken ,boughs up dry .branches up lie there

shall come and burn them, for it *is* a people with no understanding. On account of this His Maker shall not pity him, and His Former will not favor him. [12]And it shall be in that day, Jehovah shall thresh from the channel of the River to the torrent of Egypt; and you shall be gathered one *by* one, sons of Israel. [13]And it shall be in that day, the great trumpet shall be blown; and those perishing in the land of Assyria and the outcasts in the land of Egypt shall come, and shall worship Jehovah in the holy mountain in Jerusalem.

998 3808 215 935 802
נָשִׁים בָּאוֹת מְאִירוֹת אוֹתָהּ כִּי לֹא עַם־בִּינוֹת הוּא עַל־כֵּן
There- it discern- a not for ,them (and) come Women
,fore .(is) ment of people burn

3117 1961 2603 3808 3335 6213 7355 3808
12 לֹא־יְרַחֲמֶנּוּ עֹשֵׂהוּ וְיֹצְרוֹ לֹא יְחֻנֶּנּוּ׃ וְהָיָה בַּיּוֹם
day in it And show will not his and his pity shall not
be shall .favor him Former ,Maker him

4714 5158 5704 5104 7641 3068 2251
הַהוּא יַחְבֹּט יְהוָה מִשִּׁבֹּלֶת הַנָּהָר עַד־נַחַל מִצְרַיִם וְאַתֶּם
and ;Egypt the to the the from Jehovah shall ,that
you of torrent River of stream thresh

3117 1961 3478 1121 259 259 3950
13 תְּלֻקְּטוּ לְאַחַד אֶחָד בְּנֵי יִשְׂרָאֵל׃ וְהָיָה בַּיּוֹם הַהוּא
,that day in it And .Israel sons (by) one be shall
be shall of one gathered

5080 804 776 6 935 1419 7782 8628
יִתָּקַע בְּשׁוֹפָר גָּדוֹל וּבָאוּ הָאֹבְדִים בְּאֶרֶץ אַשּׁוּר וְהַנִּדָּחִים
the and ,Assyria the in those shall and ,great a be shall
outcasts of land perishing come trumpet blown

3389 6944 2022 3068 7812 4714 776
בְּאֶרֶץ מִצְרָיִם וְהִשְׁתַּחֲווּ לַיהוָה בְּהַר הַקֹּדֶשׁ בִּירוּשָׁלִָם׃
.Jerusalem in holiness the in Jehovah shall and ,Egypt the in
of mountain worship of land

CAP. XXVIII כח

CHAPTER 28

CHAPTER 28

[1]Woe *to* the crown of pride of the drunkards of Ephraim, whose glorious beauty is a fading flower on the head of the fat valley of those who are overcome with wine! [2]Behold, the Lord *is* a mighty and strong one; like a hailstorm, a destroying storm; like a flood of mighty waters overflowing; He sets down to the earth *by* hand. [3]The crown of pride of the drunkards of Ephraim shall be trampled down. [4]And the glorious beauty which is on the head of the fat valley shall be a fading flower, like the first ripe fig before summer which the seeing one sees; while it *is* yet in his hand, he swallows it. [5]In that day Jehovah of hosts shall become a crown of glory and a diadem of beauty to the rest of His people; [6]and a spirit of justice to him who sits on the judgment *seat*; and for might to those turning back the battle toward the gate. [7]But they also have gone astray by wine, and have erred through fermented drink; priest and prophet have erred through fermented drink; they have been swallowed by wine;

8597 6643 3034 6731 669 7910 1348 5850 1945
1 הוֹי עֲטֶרֶת גֵּאוּת שִׁכֹּרֵי אֶפְרַיִם וְצִיץ נֹבֵל צְבִי תִפְאַרְתּוֹ
,beauty his the ,fading the and ,Ephraim the pride the Woe
of glory flower of drunkards of of crown (to)

533 2389 2009 3196 1986 8081 1516 5892 5921 834
2 אֲשֶׁר עַל־רֹאשׁ גֵּיא־שְׁמָנִים הֲלוּמֵי יָיִן׃ הִנֵּה חָזָק וְאַמִּץ
and might ,Behold !wine those ,fatness the the on which
strength by smitten of valley of head (is)

7857 3524 4325 2230 6987 8178 1259 2230 136
לַאדֹנָי כְּזֶרֶם בָּרָד שַׂעַר קָטֶב כְּזֶרֶם מַיִם כַּבִּירִים שֹׁטְפִים
over- mighty waters a like destruc- a ,hail a like to (are)
;flowing of storm ;tion of storm of storm ,Lord the

7910 1348 5850 7429 7272 3027 776 3240
3 הִנִּיחַ לָאָרֶץ בְּיָד׃ בְּרַגְלַיִם תֵּרָמַסְנָה עֲטֶרֶת גֵּאוּת שִׁכּוֹרֵי
drunk- the the the be shall feet By with the to sets He
of ards of pride of crown trampled .hand earth down

7218 5921 834 8597 6643 5034 6733 1961 669
4 אֶפְרָיִם׃ וְהָיְתָה צִיצַת נֹבֵל צְבִי תִפְאַרְתּוֹ אֲשֶׁר עַל־רֹאשׁ
the on which ,beauty his the ,fading the shall And .Ephraim
of head (is) of glory flower be

7200 7200 834 7019 6440 1061 8081 1516
גֵּיא שְׁמָנִים כְּבִכּוּרָהּ בְּטֶרֶם קַיִץ אֲשֶׁר יִרְאֶה הָרֹאֶה
one the sees which ,summer before the like ;fatness the
seeing fig early of valley

1961 3117 1104 3709 5750
5 אוֹתָהּ בְּעוֹדָהּ בְּכַפּוֹ יִבְלָעֶנָּה׃ בַּיּוֹם הַהוּא יִהְיֶה
shall that day In swallows he his in yet while :it
become it palm (is) it

7605 8597 6843 6643 5850 6635 3068
יְהוָה צְבָאוֹת לַעֲטֶרֶת צְבִי וְלִצְפִירַת תִּפְאָרָה לִשְׁאָר
the to beauty a for and glory a hosts Jehovah
of rest of diadem of crown of

1369 4941 3427 4941 7307 5971
6 עַמּוֹ׃ וּלְרוּחַ מִשְׁפָּט לַיּוֹשֵׁב עַל־הַמִּשְׁפָּט וְלִגְבוּרָה
might for and the over him to justice a and His
judgment sits who of spirit ;people

8582 7941 7686 3196 428 1571 8179 4421 7725
7 מְשִׁיבֵי מִלְחָמָה שָׁעְרָה׃ וְגַם־אֵלֶּה בַּיַּיִן שָׁגוּ וּבַשֵּׁכָר תָּעוּ
stray- by and have by these But toward battle the those to
.ed liquor ,erred wine also .gate the back turning

they strayed from fermented drink; they err in seeing; they stumble in judgment; [8]for all tables are full of vomit *and* filth, without *a clean* place.

[9]Whom shall He teach knowledge? And *to* whom shall He explain the message? Those weaned from milk, those moving from breasts? [10]For precept *must be* on precept, precept on precept; line on line, line on line; here a little, there a little. [11]For with stammering lip and another tongue, He will speak to this people; [12]to whom He said, This *is* the rest; cause the weary to rest. Also, This *is* the repose. But they willed not to hear. [13]Yet the word of Jehovah was to them, precept on precept, precept on precept; line on line, line on line; here a little, there a little; that they might go, and stumble, and be broken, and snared, and taken [14]So hear the word of Jehovah, scornful men, rulers of this people in Jerusalem. [15]Because you have said, We have cut a covenant with death; and, We have made a vision with Sheol—when the overwhelming rod passes through, it will not come to us, for we have made the lie our refuge, and we have hidden in falsehood. [16]So, the Lord Jehovah says this: Behold, I place in Zion a Stone for a foundation, a tried Stone, a precious Cornerstone, a sure Foundation; he who believes shall not make haste. [17]And I will lay justice for a line, and righteousness for a plummet; and the hail shall sweep away the refuge of the lie; and the waters shall overflow the hiding place. [18]And your covenant with death shall be covered; and your vision

7686 7941 8582 3196 1104 79 41 7686 5030 3548
כֹּהֵן וְנָבִיא שָׁגוּ בַשֵּׁכָר נִבְלְעוּ מִן־הַיַּיִן תָּעוּ מִן־הַשֵּׁכָר שָׁגוּ
they ;liquor from they ,wine from are they by have and Priest / err stray swallowed ;liquor erred prophet

6675 6892 43 90 79 79 36 05 6417 6328 7203
8 בָּרֹאֶה פָּקוּ פְּלִילִיָּה׃ כִּי כָּל־שֻׁלְחָנוֹת מָלְאוּ קִיא צֹאָה
;filth vomit are tables all For in they in / (and) of full .judgment stumble ;seeing

8052 995 4310 18:44 3384 4310 4725 1097
9 בְּלִי מָקוֹם׃ אֶת־מִי יוֹרֶה דֵעָה וְאֶת־מִי יָבִין שְׁמוּעָה
the He shall whom And knowl- shall Whom (clean a) with- / ?message explain ?edge teach He .place out

6957 66 73/6673 6673 6673 7699 6267 2461 1580
10 גְּמוּלֵי מֵחָלָב עַתִּיקֵי מִשָּׁדָיִם׃ כִּי צַו לָצָו צַו לָצָו קַו
line on rule on rule For from those from Those / ;rule ;rule (is) ?breasts moving ,milk weaned

3956 81:93 39 34 8033 2191 8033 2191 6957 6957 6957
11 לָקָו קַו לָקָו זְעֵיר שָׁם זְעֵיר שָׁם׃ כִּי בְּלַעֲגֵי שָׂפָה וּבְלָשׁוֹן
with and ,lip with For .there a ,there a on line on / tongue of stammering little little ;line ,line

2088 559 834 2088 5971 1696 312
12 אַחֶרֶת יְדַבֵּר אֶל־הָעָם הַזֶּה׃ אֲשֶׁר אָמַר אֲלֵיהֶם זֹאת
This to said He (of) ;this people to will He another / (is) ,them whom speak

8085 38 08 4774 2088 5889 5117 4496
הַמְּנוּחָה הָנִיחוּ לֶעָיֵף וְזֹאת הַמַּרְגֵּעָה וְלֹא אָבוּא שְׁמוֹעַ׃
.hear to they But the this and the cause the / willed not .repose (is) ;weary rest to ,rest

6957 6957 69 57/6957 66 73/6673 6673 6673 3068 1697 19 61
13 וְהָיָה לָהֶם דְּבַר־יְהוָה צַו לָצָו צַו לָצָו קַו לָקָו קַו לָקָו
on line on line on rule on rule ,Jehovah the to was Yet / ;line ;line ;rule ;rule of word them

76 65 268 378 2 3212 8033 2191 8033 2191
זְעֵיר שָׁם זְעֵיר שָׁם לְמַעַן יֵלְכוּ וְכָשְׁלוּ אָחוֹר וְנִשְׁבָּרוּ
be and back- and they that ;there a ;there a / broken ward stumble ,go might little little

3944 582 3068 1697 8085 3920 3369
14 וְנוֹקְשׁוּ וְנִלְכָּדוּ׃ לָכֵן שִׁמְעוּ דְבַר־יְהוָה אַנְשֵׁי לָצוֹן
,scorn men ,Jehovah the hear ,Therefore and and / of of word .taken snared

3772 559 3389 834 20:88 5971 4910
15 מֹשְׁלֵי הָעָם הַזֶּה אֲשֶׁר בִּירוּשָׁלִָם׃ כִּי אֲמַרְתֶּם כָּרַתְנוּ
have We have you Because .Jerusalem in who ,this people rulers / cut ,said (are) of

7857 7752 2374 6213 7585 41:94 1285
בְרִית אֶת־מָוֶת וְעִם־שְׁאוֹל עָשִׂינוּ חֹזֶה שׁוֹט שׁוֹטֵף כִּי־
when over- the a have Sheol and ,death with cove- a / whelming whip ,vision made with nant

5640 8267 4268 3577 7760 935 3808 5674
יַעֲבֹר לֹא יְבוֹאֵנוּ כִּי שַׂמְנוּ כָזָב מַחְסֵנוּ וּבַשֶּׁקֶר נִסְתָּרְנוּ׃
have we in and our lie the we for shall it not passes it / .hidden falsehood ,refuge made have ,us to come ,through

68 68 6726 3245 2009 30:68 1 36 559
16 לָכֵן כֹּה אָמַר אֲדֹנָי יְהוִה הִנְנִי יִסַּד בְּצִיּוֹן אָבֶן אֶבֶן
a a in lay Behold ,Jehovah the says thus ,Therefore / stone ,stone Zion I Lord

7760 23 63 38 08 539 32 45 4143 3368 6438 976
17 בֹּחַן פִּנַּת יִקְרַת מוּסָד מוּסָּד הַמַּאֲמִין לֹא יָחִישׁ׃ וְשַׂמְתִּי
I And shall not who he ;founded foun- a ,precious a ,tried / put will .hurry believes dation cornerstone

35 77 4268 1259 3261 4949 6666 6957 4941
מִשְׁפָּט לְקָו וּצְדָקָה לְמִשְׁקָלֶת וְיָעָה בָרָד מַחְסֵה כָזָב
the the hail shall and a for righ- and a for justice / ;lie of refuge away sweep ;plummet teousness ,line

2380 4194 1285 3722 7857 4325 5643
18 וְסֵתֶר מַיִם יִשְׁטֹפוּ׃ וְכֻפַּר בְּרִיתְכֶם אֶת־מָוֶת וְחָזוּתְכֶם
your and ;death with your will And shall waters the and / vision covenant covered be .overflow place hiding

with Sheol shall not rise up. When the overwhelming whip passes through, then you shall be for a trampling to it. [19]As often as it passes, it shall take you; for morning by morning it shall pass; and by day and by night, it shall only be a terror to understand the message. [20]For the bed is shorter than one can stretch himself on; and the cover is narrower than one can wrap himself in. [21]For Jehovah shall rise up, as at Mount Perazim; He shall be stirred as in the Gibeon Valley; to do His work, His strange work; and to perform His task, His foreign task. [22]So, then, do not be mockers, that your bonds not be made strong. For I have heard from the Lord Jehovah of hosts that a full end *is* decreed on all the earth.

[23]Listen and hear My voice; pay attention and hear My word: [24]Does the plowman plow all day to sow? Does he open and break the clods of his ground? [25]When he has leveled its surface, does he not strew black cummin, and scatter cummin, and place wheat in rows, and barley *in its* place, and spelt *in* its border? [26]And He instructs him for the right; his God teaches him. [27]For black cummin is not threshed with the sledge; nor is a cartwheel turned on cummin. But black cummin is beaten out with the staff, and cummin with the rod. [28]Bread is crushed, but not always does one thresh it *with* threshing; and he drives the wheel of his cart; and his horses do not beat it small. [29]This also comes from Jehovah of hosts, doing wonders in counsel, making sound wisdom great.

אֶת־שְׁאוֹל לֹא תָקוּם שׁוֹט שׁוֹטֵף כִּי יַעֲבֹר וִהְיִיתֶם לוֹ
to you then passes When over- the shall not Sheol with
it be shall ,through whelming whip .arise

19 לְמִרְמָס׃ מִדֵּי עָבְרוֹ יִקַּח אֶתְכֶם כִּי־בַבֹּקֶר בַּבֹּקֶר יַעֲבֹר
shall it the in the in for ;you shall it it often As a for
.pass morning ,morning take ,passes as .trampling

20 בַּיּוֹם וּבַלָּיְלָה וְהָיָה רַק־זְוָעָה הָבִין שְׁמוּעָה׃ כִּי־קָצַר
is For the to a only it and in and the In
shorter .message discern terror be shall ,night the day

21 הַמַּצָּע מֵהִשְׂתָּרֵעַ וְהַמַּסֵּכָה צָרָה כְּהִתְכַּנֵּס׃ כִּי כְהַר־
as For oneself than (too) the and oneself than the
Mount .in wrap can narrow cover ,on stretch can bed

פְּרָצִים יָקוּם יְהוָה כְּעֵמֶק בְּגִבְעוֹן יִרְגָּז לַעֲשׂוֹת מַעֲשֵׂהוּ
His do to shall He in the as ;Jehovah shall ,Perazim
;work stirred be Gibeon valley up rise

22 זָר מַעֲשֵׂהוּ וְלַעֲבֹד עֲבֹדָתוֹ נָכְרִיָּה עֲבֹדָתוֹ׃ וְעַתָּה אַל־
not And His foreign His to and His strange
now .task (is) ,task perform ;work (is)

תִּתְלוֹצָצוּ פֶּן־יֶחְזְקוּ מוֹסְרֵיכֶם כִּי־כָלָה וְנֶחֱרָצָה שָׁמַעְתִּי
have I (is) even full a For your be lest be do
heard ,decreed end .bonds strengthened ;mockers

23 מֵאֵת אֲדֹנָי יְהוִה צְבָאוֹת עַל־כָּל־הָאָרֶץ׃ הַאֲזִינוּ
Listen the all on ,hosts Jehovah the from
.earth of Lord

24 וְשִׁמְעוּ קוֹלִי הַקְשִׁיבוּ וְשִׁמְעוּ אִמְרָתִי׃ הֲכֹל הַיּוֹם יַחֲרֹשׁ
plow the Does my hear and pay my hear and
day all :word attention ;voice

25 הַחֹרֵשׁ לִזְרֹעַ יְפַתַּח וִישַׂדֵּד אַדְמָתוֹ׃ הֲלוֹא אִם־שִׁוָּה
has he when Does his break and Does ?sow to the
leveled not ?ground of clods the open he plowman

פָנֶיהָ וְהֵפִיץ קֶצַח וְכַמֹּן יִזְרֹק וְשָׂם חִטָּה שׂוֹרָה וּשְׂעֹרָה
and ,rows in wheat and ,scatter and black then its
barley place cummin ,cummin strew ,surface

26 נִסְמָן וְכֻסֶּמֶת גְּבֻלָתוֹ׃ וְיִסְּרוֹ לַמִּשְׁפָּט אֱלֹהָיו יוֹרֶנּוּ׃
teaches his the for He And its (in) and (its in)
.him God ;right him instructs ?border spelt ,place

27 כִּי לֹא בֶחָרוּץ יוּדַשׁ קֶצַח וְאוֹפַן עֲגָלָה עַל־כַּמֹּן יוּסָּב כִּי
but turned is on cart a a nor black is the with not For
cummin of wheel ,cummin threshed sledge

28 בַמַּטֶּה יֵחָבֶט קֶצַח וְכַמֹּן בַּשָּׁבֶט׃ לֶחֶם יוּדָק כִּי לֹא
not but is Bread the with and black beaten is the with
crushed .rod cummin ,cummin out staff

לָנֶצַח אָדוֹשׁ יְדוּשֶׁנּוּ וְהָמַם גַּלְגַּל עֶגְלָתוֹ וּפָרָשָׁיו לֹא
not his and his wheel the he and one threshing always
horses ,cart of drives ,it threshes

29 יְדֻקֶּנּוּ׃ גַּם־זֹאת מֵעִם יְהוָה צְבָאוֹת יָצָאָה הִפְלִא עֵצָה
,counsel doing comes hosts Jehovah from this Also beat do
in wonders ,forth of small it

הִגְדִּיל תּוּשִׁיָּה׃
sound making
.wisdom great

CHAPTER 29

[1]Woe *to* Ariel, to Ariel, the city *where* David camped. Add year on year; let feasts run their circle. [2]Then I will compress Ariel, and there shall be mourning and sorrow; and it shall be to Me as Ariel. [3]And I will camp as a circle on you, and will lay siege-work on you; and I will raise up ramparts on you. [4]And you shall be brought low; you shall speak from the ground; and your speech shall be bowed down; and your voice shall be from the ground, like a spiritist; and your speech shall chirp out of the dust. [5]And the host of your strangers shall be as fine powder, and as chaff passing, the host of terrifying ones; and it will be suddenly, instantly; [6]you shall be visited from Jehovah of hosts; with thunder and earthquake, and great noise, tempest and storm, and flame of devouring fire. [7]And the multitude of all the nations who fight against Ariel, even all battling her and compressing her and her stronghold, shall be like a dream of a night vision. [8]It shall even be as when a hungry one dreams; and, behold, he is eating; but when he awakes, his soul is empty. Or *it shall be* as when a thirsty one dreams; and, behold, he is drinking; but when he awakes, he is faint, and his soul is longing. So shall be the multitude of all the nations who fight against Mount Zion.

[9]Wait and wonder! Blind yourselves, and be blind! They are drunk, but not *with* wine! They stagger, but not *with* fermented drink! [10]For Jehovah has poured out on you the spirit of deep sleep, and has closed your eyes. He has covered the prophets and your heads,

CAP. XXIX כט

CHAPTER 29

8141 8141 5595 1732 2583 7151 740 740 1945
1 הוֹי אֲרִיאֵל אֲרִיאֵל קִרְיַת חָנָה דָוִד סְפוּ שָׁנָה עַל־שָׁנָה
;year on year Add !David camped the ,Ariel ,Ariel Woe
(where) city (to)

592 8386 1961 740 6693 5362 2282
2 חַגִּים יִנְקֹפוּ׃ וַהֲצִיקוֹתִי לַאֲרִיאֵל וְהָיְתָה תַאֲנִיָּה וַאֲנִיָּה
and mourning there and ,Ariel will I Then run let feasts
;sorrow be shall compress .circle their

6696 1754 2583 740 1961
3 וְהָיְתָה לִּי כַּאֲרִיאֵל׃ וְחָנִיתִי כַדּוּר עָלַיִךְ וְצַרְתִּי עָלַיִךְ
on will and on a as I And .Ariel as to it and
you besiege ,you circle camp will Me be shall

1696 776 8213 4694 6965 4674
4 מֻצָּב וַהֲקִמֹתִי עָלַיִךְ מְצֻרֹת׃ וְשָׁפַלְתְּ מֵאֶרֶץ תְּדַבֵּרִי
shall you the from shall you And .ramparts on will I and siege-
,speak ground ;abased be you up lift ;work

6083 6963 776 178 1961 565 7817 6083
וּמֵעָפָר תִּשַּׁח אִמְרָתֵךְ וְהָיָה כְּאוֹב מֵאֶרֶץ קוֹלֵךְ וּמֵעָפָר
from and your the from a as shall And your be shall from and
dust the ;voice ground spiritist be .speech bowed dust the

4671 2114 1995 1851 80 1961 6850 565
5 אִמְרָתֵךְ תְּצַפְצֵף׃ וְהָיָה כְּאָבָק דַּק הֲמוֹן זָרָיִךְ וּכְמֹץ
as and your host the fine powder as shall And shall your
chaff ,strangers of be ,chirp speech

3068 6597 6521 1961 6184 1995 5674
6 עֹבֵר הֲמוֹן עָרִיצִים וְהָיָה לְפֶתַע פִּתְאֹם׃ מֵעִם יְהוָה
Jehovah from —instantly ,suddenly it and terrible the ,passing
of be will —ones of host

5592 5492 1419 6963 7494 7482 6485 6635
צְבָאוֹת תִּפָּקֵד בְּרַעַם וּבְרַעַשׁ וְקוֹל גָּדוֹל סוּפָה וּסְעָרָה
and tempest ,great and with and with shall you hosts
storm noise ,earthquake ,thunder :visited be

3605 1995 3915 2377 2472 1961 398 784 3851
7 וְלַהַב אֵשׁ אוֹכֵלָה׃ וְהָיָה כַּחֲלוֹם חֲזוֹן לַיְלָה הֲמוֹן כָּל־
all the night a a as shall And .devouring fire and
of multitude of vision ,dream be of flame

6693 4686 6638 3605 740 6633 1471
הַגּוֹיִם הַצֹּבְאִים עַל־אֲרִיאֵל וְכָל־צֹבֶיהָ וּמְצֹדָתָהּ וְהַמְּצִיקִים
and her and fighting even ,Ariel against who the
compressing ,stronghold her all fight nations

6974 398 2009 7457 2492 1961
8 לָהּ׃ וְהָיָה כַּאֲשֶׁר יַחֲלֹם הָרָעֵב וְהִנֵּה אוֹכֵל וְהֵקִיץ
he but is he ,and hungry a dreams when as it And .her
awakes —eating ,behold ;one be will

6974 8354 2009 6771 2492 5315 7386
וְרֵקָה נַפְשׁוֹ וְכַאֲשֶׁר יַחֲלֹם הַצָּמֵא וְהִנֵּה שֹׁתֶה וְהֵקִיץ
he but is he ,and thirsty a dreams as or his is and
awakes —drinking ,behold ;one when ;soul empty

6633 1471 3605 1995 1961 8264 5315 5889 2009
וְהִנֵּה עָיֵף וְנַפְשׁוֹ שׁוֹקֵקָה כֵּן יִהְיֶה הֲמוֹן כָּל־הַגּוֹיִם הַצֹּבְאִים
who the all the shall So is his and is he and
fight nations of host be .longing soul faint behold

8173 8173 8539 4102 6726 2022
9 עַל־הַר צִיּוֹן׃ הִתְמַהְמְהוּ וּתְמָהוּ הִשְׁתַּעַשְׁעוּ וָשֹׁעוּ
be and Blind and Wait .Zion Mount on
!blind yourselves !wonder

7307 3068 5921 5258 7941 3808/5128 3196 3808 7937
10 שָׁכְרוּ וְלֹא־יַיִן נָעוּ וְלֹא שֵׁכָר׃ כִּי־נָסַךְ עֲלֵיכֶם יְהוָה רוּחַ
a Jehovah you on has For (with) but They (with) but are They
of spirit out poured .liquor not ,slip !wine not ,drunk

7218 5030 5869 6105 8639
תַּרְדֵּמָה וַיְעַצֵּם אֶת־עֵינֵיכֶם אֶת־הַנְּבִאִים וְאֶת־רָאשֵׁיכֶם
,heads your and the your has and deep
prophets ;eyes closed ,sleep

the seers. [11]And the whole vision to you *is* like the words of a sealed book which they give to one knowing books, saying, Please read this. Then he says, I am not able, for it *is* sealed. [12]And the book is given to one who does not know books, saying, Please read this. Then he says, I do not know books. [13]And the Lord says, Because this people draws near with its mouth, and they honor Me with its lips; but its heart *is* far from Me; and their fear of Me *is* taught *by* the command *of* men; [14]so, behold, I am adding to do the wonders with this people; the wonder, even a wonder. For the wisdom of his wise ones shall perish, and the wit of his witty ones shall be hidden. [15]Woe *to* those who go deep to hide *their* purpose from Jehovah; yea, their works are in the dark; and they say, Who sees us? And, Who knows us? [16]O your perversity! Shall the former be counted as the clay? For shall the work of its maker say, He did not make me? Or shall the thing formed say to him who formed it, He does not understand? [17]Is it not yet a little while, and Lebanon shall be turned into a fruitful field; and the fruitful field shall be counted for the forest?

[18]And in that day the deaf shall hear the words of a book; and the eyes of the blind shall see out of their gloom and out of darkness. [19]And the humble ones shall increase joy in Jehovah, and the poor among men shall rejoice in the Holy One of Israel. [20]For the terrible one is brought to nothing; and the scorner is ended; and all that watch for evil are cut off; [21]those who make a man sin by a word, even laying a trap for the reprover in the gate; and turn aside

11 הַחֹזִים כִּסָּה׃ וַתְּהִי לָכֶם חָזוּת הַכֹּל כְּדִבְרֵי הַסֵּפֶר
book the | the like of words | the whole | vision | you to | has And been | has He covered | the seers

הֶחָתוּם אֲשֶׁר־יִתְּנוּ אֹתוֹ אֶל־יוֹדֵעַ הַסֵּפֶר לֵאמֹר קְרָא־נָא
Read, please | saying | books | one knowing | to | it | they give | which | sealed

12 זֶה וְאָמַר לֹא אוּכַל כִּי חָתוּם הוּא׃ וְנִתַּן הַסֵּפֶר עַל אֲשֶׁר
one who | to | the book | is And given | it (is) | sealed | for | am I able | not | then says he | this

לֹא־יָדַע סֵפֶר לֵאמֹר קְרָא־נָא זֶה וְאָמַר לֹא יָדַעְתִּי סֵפֶר׃
books | do I know | not | he then says | this | please Read | saying | books | does not know

13 וַיֹּאמֶר אֲדֹנָי יַעַן כִּי נִגַּשׁ הָעָם הַזֶּה בְּפִיו וּבִשְׂפָתָיו
with and lips its | its with mouth | this | people | draws near | Because | the Lord | says And

כִּבְּדוּנִי וְלִבּוֹ רִחַק מִמֶּנִּי וַתְּהִי יִרְאָתָם אֹתִי מִצְוַת אֲנָשִׁים
(by) men | the command | Me | their of fear | and is | from Me | far (is) | its but heart | they honor Me

14 מְלֻמָּדָה׃ לָכֵן הִנְנִי יוֹסִף לְהַפְלִיא אֶת־הָעָם־הַזֶּה הַפְלֵא
the wonder | this people | with | do to wonders | adding | am I | behold | therefore | taught

וָפֶלֶא וְאָבְדָה חָכְמַת חֲכָמָיו וּבִינַת נְבֹנָיו תִּסְתַּתָּר׃
be shall hidden | his witty ones | the and of wit | wise his ones | the of wisdom | shall For perish | a even wonder

15 הוֹי הַמַּעֲמִיקִים מֵיהוָה לַסְתִּר עֵצָה וְהָיָה בְמַחְשָׁךְ
the in dark | and are | (their) counsel | hide to | from Jehovah | who those deep go | Woe (to)

16 מַעֲשֵׂיהֶם וַיֹּאמְרוּ מִי רֹאֵנוּ וּמִי יֹדְעֵנוּ׃ הַפְכְּכֶם אִם־
Shall | your O perversity! | knows us? | And who | sees us? | Who | they and say | their works

כְּחֹמֶר הַיֹּצֵר יֵחָשֵׁב כִּי־יֹאמַר מַעֲשֶׂה לְעֹשֵׂהוּ לֹא עָשָׂנִי
did He make me? | not | its to maker | is what made | shall say | that | be counted | the former | the as clay

17 וְיֵצֶר אָמַר לְיֹצְרוֹ לֹא הֵבִין׃ הֲלוֹא־עוֹד מְעַט מִזְעָר וְשָׁב
shall and return | a bit | little a | yet | it Is not | under-stands? | He | not | its to former | say | is what formed | Or

18 לְבָנוֹן לַכַּרְמֶל וְהַכַּרְמֶל לַיַּעַר יֵחָשֵׁב׃ וְשָׁמְעוּ בַיּוֹם
day in | shall And hear | be reckoned? | the for forest | fruit-ful field | the and | fruitful the field | Lebanon

הַהוּא הַחֵרְשִׁים דִּבְרֵי־סֵפֶר וּמֵאֹפֶל וּמֵחֹשֶׁךְ עֵינֵי עִוְרִים
blind ones | the of eyes | from and darkness | from and gloom | book a | the of words | deaf the | that

19 תִּרְאֶינָה׃ וְיָסְפוּ עֲנָוִים בַּיהוָה שִׂמְחָה וְאֶבְיוֹנֵי אָדָם
men | the and of poor | (have) joy | in Jehovah | humble ones | shall And increase | shall see

20 בִּקְדוֹשׁ יִשְׂרָאֵל יָגִילוּ׃ כִּי־אָפֵס עָרִיץ וְכָלָה לֵץ וְנִכְרְתוּ
are and off cut | the scorner | is and ended | the ruthless | ceases | For | shall rejoice | Israel | the in of One Holy

21 כָּל־שֹׁקְדֵי אָוֶן׃ מַחֲטִיאֵי אָדָם בְּדָבָר וְלַמּוֹכִיחַ בַּשַּׁעַר
the in gate | for even reprover the | a by word | man a | those sin making | evil | watching for | all

the just for a worthless thing. [22]So Jehovah says this: *He* who redeemed Abraham, as to the house of Jacob: Jacob shall not be ashamed now, nor shall his face become pale now. [23]But when he sees his children in his midst, the work of My hands, they shall sanctify My name. They shall sanctify the Holy One of Jacob, and shall fear the God of Israel. [24]Those who erred in spirit shall come to understanding, and those who murmured shall learn the teaching.

3068 559 3541, 3651. 6662 8414 5186 6983
22 לָכֵן כֹּה־אָמַר יְהוָה אֶל־ יִקְשׁוּן וַיַּטּוּ בַתֹּהוּ צַדִּיק׃
to Jehovah says thus ,Therefore the empty by and they
.righteous (pleas) turn ,ensnare

3290 954 6258 3808 85 6299 834 3290 1004
בֵּית יַעֲקֹב אֲשֶׁר פָּדָה אֶת־אַבְרָהָם לֹא־עַתָּה יֵבוֹשׁ יַעֲקֹב
,Jacob shall now Not :Abraham redeemed (He) ,Jacob the
ashamed be who of house

3027 4639 3206 7200 3588 2357 6440 6258 3808
23 וְלֹא עַתָּה פָּנָיו יֶחֱוָרוּ׃ כִּי בִרְאֹתוֹ יְלָדָיו מַעֲשֵׂה יָדַי
My the his he when Because turn shall his now and
,hands of work ,children sees .pale face not

32 :90 6918 6942 8034 6942 7130
בְּקִרְבּוֹ יַקְדִּישׁוּ שְׁמִי וְהִקְדִּישׁוּ אֶת־קְדוֹשׁ יַעֲקֹב וְאֶת־
and ,Jacob Holy the will they and My shall they his in
of One sanctify ;name sanctify ,midst

7279 998 7307 8582 3045 6206 3478 430
24 אֱלֹהֵי יִשְׂרָאֵל יַעֲרִיצוּ׃ וְיָדְעוּ תֹעֵי־רוּחַ בִּינָה וְרוֹגְנִים
and discern- spirit wan- shall And shall they Israel the
murmurers ,ment of derers know .fear of God

3948 3925
יִלְמְדוּ־לֶקַח׃
.teaching shall
learn

CAP. XXX ל

CHAPTER 30

CHAPTER 30

[1]Woe *to* rebellious sons, declares Jehovah, to make counsel, but not from Me; and to weave a covering web, but not *of* My Spirit, in order to add sin on sin; [2]who set out to go down *to* Egypt, but have not asked *at* My mouth, to take refuge in the stronghold of Pharaoh, and to trust in the shadow of Egypt. [3]And the stronghold of Pharaoh shall become a shame to you; and relying on the shadow of Egypt *shall be* a disgrace. [4]For his rulers were in Zoan, and his ambassadors reached *to* Hanes. [5]Every one is ashamed over a people who do not profit them; *they are* not for a help, and not for profiting, but for a shame; yea, also for a reproach.

[6]The burden of the beasts of the south: Into the land of trouble and constraint. The lioness and the lion *are* from them; the viper and fiery flying serpent — they carry their riches on the shoulders of young asses, and their treasures on the hump of camels, to a people who cannot profit *them*. [7]And Egypt; vainly and

5258 3808 6098 6213 3068 5002 5637 1121 1945
1 הוֹי בָּנִים סוֹרְרִים נְאֻם־יְהוָה לַעֲשׂוֹת עֵצָה וְלֹא מִנִּי וְלִנְסֹךְ
to and from but ,counsel make to ,Jehovah states ,rebellious sons Woe
weave ;Me not (to)

2403 2399 5595 3616 7307 3808 4541
מַסֵּכָה וְלֹא רוּחִי לְמַעַן סְפוֹת חַטָּאת עַל־חַטָּאת׃
;sin on sin add to order in My (by) but a
,Spirit not ,web

4581 5810 7592 3808 6310 4714 3381 1980
2 הַהֹלְכִים לָרֶדֶת מִצְרַיִם וּפִי לֹא שָׁאָלוּ לָעוֹז בְּמָעוֹז
strong- in take to they not My but (to) go to set who
hold refuge ,asked mouth ,Egypt down out

6547 4581 1961 4714 6738 2620 132:2
3 פַּרְעֹה וְלַחְסוֹת בְּצֵל מִצְרָיִם׃ וְהָיָה לָכֶם מָעוֹז פַּרְעֹה
Pharaoh's strong- you to shall And .Egypt the in to and ,Pharaoh's
hold become of shadow trust

6814 1961 3639 4714 6738 2623 1322
4 לְבֹשֶׁת וְהֶחָסוּת בְּצֵל־מִצְרַיִם לִכְלִמָּה׃ כִּי־הָיוּ בְצֹעַן
in were For .disgrace a Egypt the in trust and ,shame a
Zoan of shadow

3808 5971 3001 3605 5060 2609 4397 8269
5 שָׂרָיו וּמַלְאָכָיו חָנֵס יַגִּיעוּ׃ כֹּל הִבְאִישׁ עַל־עַם לֹא־
not a over is Every .reached (to) his and his
people ashamed one Hanes ambassadors ,chiefs

2781 1571 1322 3276 3808 5828 3808 3276
יוֹעִילוּ לָמוֹ לֹא לְעֵזֶר וְלֹא לְהוֹעִיל כִּי לְבֹשֶׁת וְגַם־לְחֶרְפָּה׃
a for and a for but for and a for not ,them do who
.reproach also shame ,profiting not ,help profit

3918 3833 6685 6864 776 5045 929 4853
6 מַשָּׂא בַּהֲמוֹת נֶגֶב בְּאֶרֶץ צָרָה וְצוּקָה לָבִיא וָלַיִשׁ
the and the con- and distress the in the beasts the The
lion lioness ;straint of land :Negeb of of burden

2428 5985 3801 5375 5774 8314 660
מֵהֶם אֶפְעֶה וְשָׂרָף מְעוֹפֵף יִשְׂאוּ עַל־כֶּתֶף עֲיָרִים חֵילֵהֶם
their young the on they —flying fiery and viper from (are)
,riches asses of shoulder up lift serpent ,them

4714 3276 3808 5971 214 1581 1707
7 וְעַל־דַּבֶּשֶׁת גְּמַלִּים אוֹצְרוֹתָם עַל־עַם לֹא יוֹעִילוּ׃ וּמִצְרַיִם
even can who not a to their camels the and
;Egypt ,profit people ,treasures of hump on

emptily they help. So I have called to this: Their strength *is* to sit still.
8 Now come, write it before them on a tablet, and note it on a book, so that it may be for the latter day, until forever; 9 that this is a rebellious people, lying sons; sons who are not willing to hear the law of Jehovah; 10 who say to the seers, Do not see; and to visioners, Do not have a vision for right things *to* us; speak smooth things to us; have a vision of trifles. 11 Turn aside from the way; stretch from the path; cause the Holy One of Israel to cease from before us. 12 For this reason, so says the Holy One of Israel, Because of your rejection of this word, and your trust in oppression and perversity, even resting on it; 13 so this iniquity shall be to you as a broken *section* falling, like the bulging out of a high wall, the breaking of which comes suddenly, in an instant. 14 And its smashing *is* as the smashing of a potter's vessel; *when* broken in pieces, he has no pity; for in its breaking there is not found a sherd to carry fire from the hearth, nor to skim water from a well. 15 For so says the Lord Jehovah, the Holy One of Israel, In returning and rest you shall be saved; and in quietness and hope shall be your strength. But you were not willing. 16 For you said, No! For we will flee on horse*back*. Therefore, you shall flee. Also, *you say*, We will ride on swift ones. On account of this, those who pursue you shall be swift. 17 One thousand *shall flee* at the rebuke of one. You shall flee from the rebuke of five, until you are left like a pole on the top of the mountain, and like a sign on a hill.

7674 7293 2063 7121 5826 7385 1892
הבל וריק יעזרו לכן קראתי לזאת רהב הם שבת׃
sit to | Their strength | to | have I | Therefore | they | and | vainly
.still | (is) | ,this | called | .help | emptily

1961 2710 5612 3871 3789 935 6258
8 עתה בוא כתבה על־לוח אתם ועל־ספר חקה ותהי
it that inscribe | a | and | before | a | on | write | ,come | ,Now
be may ,it | book | on ,them | tablet | it

3586 1129 4805 5971 5703/5704/5769 314 3117
9 ליום אחרון לעד עד־עולם׃ כי עם מרי הוא בנים כחשים
,lying | sons | this | rebel- | a | for | :forever | until | ,forever | latter | the for
,(is) | lious | people | day

2374 559 834 3068 8451 8085 14 3808 1121
10 בנים לא־אבו שמוע תורת יהוה׃ אשר אמרו לראים
the to | say | who | ,Jehovah | the | hear to | are who not | sons
,seers | of law | willing

2513 1696 5228 2372 38.08 32:74 7200 3808
לא תראו ולחזים לא־תחזו־לנו נכחות דברו־לנו חלקות
smooth | to | speak | right | for | have Do | not | to and | ;See | not
,things | us | ;things | us | vision a | ,visioners

7673 734 5186 1870 5493 2372 4123
11 חזו מהתלות׃ סורו מני־דרך הטו מני־ארח השביתו
to cause | the | from stretch | the from | turn | a have | trifles
cease | ;path | ;way | aside | of vision

34:78 6918 559 3478 6918 6440
12 מפנינו את־קדוש ישראל׃ לכן כה אמר קדוש ישראל
,Israel | Holy the | says thus | ,Therefore | .Israel | Holy the | from
of One | of One | us before

8172 3868 6233 982 2088 1697 3973
יען מאסכם בדבר הזה ותבטחו בעשק ונלוז ותשענו
and | and | in | you and | ,this | word of | your | Because
rely | ,perversity | oppression | trust | rejection | of

2346 1158 53:07 6556 20:88 5771 1961
13 עליו׃ לכן יהיה לכם העון הזה כפרץ נפל נבעה בחומה
a in | bulging | ,falling | a as | this iniquity | to | shall therefore | ;it on
wall | out | breach | you | be

7667 7665 7667 935 6621 6597 834 7682
14 נשגבה אשר־פתאם לפתע יבוא שברה׃ ושברה כשבר
(is) as | its And | its | comes | an in | ,suddenly | which | made
smashing | smashing | .smashing | ,instant | ,high

2789 7667 4672 38.08 2550 38.08 3807 3335 5035
נבל יוצרים כתות לא יחמל ולא־ימצא במכתתו חרש
a | its in | there | and | has he | not | (when) | a | vessel the
sherd | breaking | found is | not | ;pity | ,broken | ;potter's | of

3541 1360 4325 2834 33:44 7.84 2846
15 לחתות אש מיקוד ולחשף מים מגבא׃ כי כה־
thus | For | from | water | to or | the from | fire | take to
.pool a | skim | ,hearth | up

3467 5183 7729 3478 6918 30:68 136 559
אמר אדני יהוה־קדוש ישראל בשובה ונחת תושעון
shall you | and | In | ,Israel | Holy the | ,Jehovah | the | says
;saved be | rest | returning | of One | Lord

559 14 3808 1369 1961 985 8252
16 בהשקט ובבטחה תהיה גבורתכם ולא אביתם׃ ותאמרו
you But | were you | But | your | shall | in and | in and
,said | .willing | not | .might | be | trust | quietness

3651 5921 7392 7031 5127 5127 5483 38.08
לא־כי על־סוס ננוס על־כן תנוסון ועל־קל נרכב על־כן
Therefore | shall we | the | ,Also | you | Therefore | we | horse | on | For | !No
.ride | swift | on | flee shall | flee will

1606 259 1606 259 505 7291 7043
17 יקלו רדפיכם׃ אלף אחד מפני גערת אחד מפני גערת
the | from | ;one | the | (flee shall) | One thousand | your | be shall
of rebuke | of rebuke | from | pursuers | swift

5251 20:22 7218 86.50 3498 5704 5127 2568
חמשה תנסו עד אם־נותרתם כתרן על־ראש ההר וכנס
as and | the | the | on | the as | are you | until | you | five
sign a | ,mount | of top | pole | left | ,flee shall

18 And so Jehovah waits to be gracious to you. And for this He is exalted to have mercy on you; for Jehovah *is* a God of justice. Blessed *are* all who wait for Him.
19 For the people shall live in Zion, at Jerusalem; you shall surely cry no more. He surely will be gracious to you at the sound of your cry. When He hears, He will answer you.
20 And the Lord gives you the bread of adversity, and the water of affliction; but your teachers shall not be hidden any more; but your eyes shall be to see your teachers.
21 And your ears shall hear a word behind you, saying, this is the way, walk in it, when you go right, or when you go left.
22 And you shall defile the covering of your carved images of silver; and the covering of your molten images of gold. You shall cast them out like a menstruous cloth; you shall say to it, Go away!
23 Then He shall give rain *for* your seed, with which you sow the ground. And the bread of the produce of the earth also shall be fat and plentiful. In that day your livestock shall feed *in* a pasture made wide.
24 Also, the oxen and the young asses that till the ground shall eat seasoned fodder which one winnows with the shovel and with the fork.
25 And on every high mountain, and on every high hill, shall be rivulets lifted up, streams of water, in a day of great slaying, when towers fall.
26 And the moonlight shall be like the light of the sun. And the sun's light shall be sevenfold, as the light of seven days, in the day of binding up, Jehovah *binding* the break of His people, and healing the wound of His blow.
27 Behold, the name of Jehovah comes from afar; His anger burns; and

7311 :2603 3068 2442 1389
18 על־הגבעה׃ ולכן יחכה יהוה לחננכם ולכן ירום
is He high | And therefore | gracious be to you to | Jehovah | waits | And therefore | .hill the | on

2442 3605 835 3068 4941 430 7355
לרחמכם כי־אלהי משפט יהוה אשרי כל־חוכי לו׃
for .Him | who wait | all | blessed (are) | (is) ;Jehovah | justice | a of God | for | mercy have to ,you on

2603 1058 3808 3389 3427 6726 5971
19 כי־עם בציון ישב בירושלם בכו לא־תבכה חנון
Surely | you .weep will | not | surely | ;Jerusalem in | shall live | Zion in | the For people

3899 136 5414 6030 8085 2199 6963 2603
20 יחנך לקול זעקך כשמעתו ענך׃ ונתן לכם אדני לחם
bread of | the Lord | you to | And gives | will He .you answer | He when ,hears | your ;cry | the at of sound | favors He ,you

7200 5869 1961 3381 5750 3670 3808 3906 4325 6862
צר ומים לחץ ולא־יכנף עוד מוריך והיו עיניך ראות
to see | your eyes | but be shall | your ,teachers | any more | be shall hidden | but not | oppres- ,sion of | and water | afflic- tion

2088 559 310 1697 241 3384
21 את־מוריך׃ ואזניך תשמענה דבר מאחריך לאמר זה
This (is) | ,saying | from ,you behind | word a | hear shall | your And ears | your .teachers

2930 8041 541 3212 1870
22 הדרך לכו בו כי תאמינו וכי תשמאילו׃ וטמאתם את־
you And defile shall | go you .left | or when | go you right | when | in walk ;it | ,way the

3644 2219 2091 4541 642 3701 6456 6826
צפוי פסילי כספך ואת־אפדת מסכת זהבך תזרם כמו
like | will you them strew | your ;gold | casted the of image | the of case | and | your ,silver | carved of images | the of case

2232 834 4306 5414 559 3318 1739
23 דוה צא תאמר לו׃ ונתן מטר זרעך אשר־תזרע את־
you sow | (with) which | your ,seed | rain (for) | He Then give shall | .it to | shall you say | Go ,away | filthy a ;rag

7462 8082 1879 1961 127 8393 3899 127
האדמה ולחם תבואת האדמה והיה דשן ושמן ירעה׃
shall feed | and ;fertile | fat | shall even be | the ground | produce of | the the of bread | and | the ;ground

5647 5895 504 7337 3733 3117 4735
24 מקניך ביום ההוא כר נרחב׃ והאלפים והעירים עבדי
serving | the and asses | the Also oxen | made .wide | a (in) pasture | that | day in | your livestock

4214 7371 2219 834 398 2548 1098 127
האדמה בליל חמיץ יאכלו אשר־זרה ברחת ובמזרה׃
with and .fork the | the with shovel | one winnows | which | shall ,eat | seasoned | fodder | the ground

6388 5375 1389 3605 1364 2022 3605 1961
25 והיה ׀ על־כל־הר גבה ועל כל־גבעה נשאה פלגים
,rivulets | lifted ,up | hill | every | and on | high | moun- tain | every on | And be shall

216 1961 4026 5307 7227 2027 3117 4325 2988
26 יבלי־מים ביום הרג רב בנפל מגדלים׃ והיה אור־
light | shall And be | .towers | when fall | ,great | slaying | a in of day | water | streams of

216 7659 1961 8121 216 2535 216 3842
הלבנה כאור החמה ואור החמה יהיה שבעתים כאור
the as of light | ,sevenfold | be shall | —sun s the | and light | ;sun the | the like of light | the moon

4273 5971 7667 3068 2280 3117 3117 7651
שבעת הימים ביום חבש יהוה את־שבר עמו ומחץ
the and of wound | His ,people | the of break | Jehovah | binding up | the in of day | ,days | seven

1197 4801 935 3068 8034 2009 7495 4347
27 מכתו ירפא׃ הנה שם־יהוה בא ממרחק בער
burns | from ;afar | comes | Jehovah the of name | ,Behold | .heals | His blow

that which rises heavy; His lips are full of fury, and His tongue like a devouring fire. [28]And like an overflowing torrent, His breath shall divide to the neck, to sift nations in the sieve of vanity, and a misleading bridle on the jaws of the peoples. [29]The song shall be to you, as the night when a feast is sanctified, and gladness of heart; as one going with the flute, to come into the mount of Jehovah, to the Rock of Israel. [30]And Jehovah shall make the majesty of His voice heard; and He shows the coming down of His arm with raging anger and flame of consuming fire, cloudburst and storm, and hailstones. [31]For by the voice of Jehovah Assyria is crushed; with the rod He strikes. [32]And every passage of the appointed staff that Jehovah causes to rest on him will be with timbrels and with harps. He fights with her in brandishing battles. [33]For Topheth is ordained from yesterday. Also, it *is* prepared for the king; He deepened; He widened its pyre; *He* makes great *with* fire and wood. The breath of Jehovah burns in it like a torrent of brimstone.

אַפּוֹ וְכֹבֶד מַשָּׂאָה שְׂפָתָיו מָלְאוּ זַעַם וּלְשׁוֹנוֹ כְּאֵשׁ אֹכָלֶת׃
.devouring a like fire His and tongue ,fury full are of His lips (which that) and ;rises heavy His ;anger

28 וְרוּחוֹ כְּנַחַל שׁוֹטֵף עַד־צַוָּאר יֶחֱצֶה לַהֲנָפָה גוֹיִם בְּנָפַת
the in of sieve nations sift to shall He ,divide the neck to over- flowing a like torrent His And breath

29 שָׁוְא וְרֶסֶן מַתְעֶה עַל לְחָיֵי עַמִּים׃ הַשִּׁיר יִהְיֶה לָכֶם
,you to shall be song the ,peoples the of jaws on misleading a and bridle ,vanity

כְּלֵיל הִתְקַדֶּשׁ־חָג וְשִׂמְחַת לֵבָב כַּהוֹלֵךְ בֶּחָלִיל לָבוֹא
to come the with flute one as going ,heart glad- of ness and ,feast a is sanctified night the as when

30 בְהַר־יְהוָה אֶל־צוּר יִשְׂרָאֵל׃ וְהִשְׁמִיעַ יְהוָה אֶת־הוֹד
the of majesty Jehovah shall And heard make .Israel the of Rock to ,Jehovah the into of mount

קוֹלוֹ וְנַחַת זְרוֹעוֹ יַרְאֶה בְּזַעַף אַף וְלַהַב אֵשׁ אוֹכֵלָה נֶפֶץ
cloud- burst con- ;suming fire and of flame ,anger with raging ,shows He His arm the and of descent His ;voice

31 וָזֶרֶם וְאֶבֶן בָּרָד׃ כִּי־מִקּוֹל יְהוָה יֵחַת אַשּׁוּר בַּשֵּׁבֶט יַכֶּה׃
He .strikes the with rod ;Assyria is crushed Jehovah the by of voice For .hail and of stones and storm

32 וְהָיָה כֹּל מַעֲבַר מַטֵּה מוּסָדָה אֲשֶׁר יָנִיחַ יְהוָה עָלָיו
on him Jehovah causes rest to that appoint- ment the of staff passage of every And be will

33 בְּתֻפִּים וּבְכִנֹּרוֹת וּבְמִלְחֲמוֹת תְּנוּפָה נִלְחַם־בָּהּ׃ כִּי־
For with .her He fights brandishing in And of battles with and .harps with timbrels

עָרוּךְ מֵאֶתְמוּל תָּפְתֶּה גַּם־הוּא לַמֶּלֶךְ הוּכָן הֶעְמִיק הִרְחִב
He ;widened He ;deepened ;prepared the for king it (is) ,Also .Topheth from yesterday is ordained

מְדֻרָתָהּ אֵשׁ וְעֵצִים הַרְבֵּה נִשְׁמַת יְהוָה כְּנַחַל גָּפְרִית
brimstone a like of torrent Jehovah The of breath makes !great wood and (with) fire pyre its

בֹּעֲרָה בָּהּ׃
.it in burns

CAP. XXXI לא

CHAPTER 31

1 הוֹי הַיֹּרְדִים מִצְרַיִם לְעֶזְרָה וְעַל־סוּסִים יִשָּׁעֵנוּ וַיִּבְטְחוּ עַל־
on trust and they lean horses and on ,help for (to) Egypt who those down go Woe (to)

רֶכֶב כִּי רָב וְעַל פָּרָשִׁים כִּי־עָצְמוּ מְאֹד וְלֹא שָׁעוּ עַל־
to they gaze but not ;very they because are strong ,horsemen and on (is it) for ;great char- ,iotry

2 קְדוֹשׁ יִשְׂרָאֵל וְאֶת־יְהוָה לֹא דָרָשׁוּ׃ וְגַם־הוּא חָכָם וַיָּבֵא
and brings wise He (is) And also .seek not Jehovah and ,Israel Holy the of One

רָע וְאֶת־דְּבָרָיו לֹא הֵסִיר וְקָם עַל־בֵּית מְרֵעִים וְעַל־עֶזְרַת
help the of and against evil- doers the against of house but rises turns ,aside not His words and ,evil

CHAPTER 31

[1]Woe *to* those who go down *to* Egypt for help; and lean on horses, and trust on chariotry, because *it is* great; and in horsemen because they are very strong! But they do not look to the Holy One of Israel, nor seek Jehovah. [2]And He also *is* wise, and brings evil, and will not turn aside His words, but will rise against the house of evildoers, and against the help of those

who work iniquity. ³And
Egypt *is* a man, and not
God. And their horses *are*
flesh, and not spirit. And
Jehovah stretches out His
hand, and both he who
helps shall fall, and he who
is helped shall fall; and they
shall all cease together. ⁴For so Jehovah has said to
me: As the lion roars, even
the young lion on his prey
when the multitude of
shepherds are gathered
against him, he will not fear
their voice, nor fret himself
because of their noise. So
Jehovah of hosts shall
come down to fight on
Mount Zion, and on its
hill. ⁵As birds that fly, so
Jehovah of hosts will shield
over Jerusalem, shielding
and delivering, and passing
over, He will save *it*.

⁶Turn back to *Him*
against whom you have
made a deep revolt, sons of
Israel. ⁷For in that day each
shall despise his silver idols
and his golden idols, which
your hands have made for
you — a sin. ⁸Then Assyria
shall fall by a sword, not *of*
man; yea, a sword, not *of*
man, shall devour him. For
he shall flee from the
sword, and his young men
shall become forced labor.
⁹And his rock will pass
away from fear; and his
commanders shall tremble
at the banner, declares
Jehovah, whose fire is in
Zion, and His furnace in
Jerusalem.

CHAPTER 32

¹Behold, a king shall
reign in righteousness, and
princes shall rule in judgment. ²And a man shall be
as a hiding-place from the
wind; as a shelter from the
tempest; as streams of
water in a dry place; like the
shadow of a great rock in a
weary land. ³And the eyes
of those that see shall not
be dim, and the ears of

ISAIAH 31:3

וּמִצְרַיִם אָדָם וְלֹא־אֵל וְסוּסֵיהֶם בָּשָׂר וְלֹא פֹֿעֲלֵי אָוֶן:
Now Egypt a (is) and not God, and their horses flesh and not workers iniquity.
3808 120 4714 205 6466
1320 5483 410 3808

רוּחַ וַיהוָה יַטֶּה יָדוֹ וְכָשַׁל עוֹזֵר וְנָפַל עָזֻר וְיַחְדָּו כֻּלָּם
spirit. And Jehovah stretches out His hand, and the helper will stumble, and fall the will and together all
36 05 3162 5307 5826 37 82 30 27 5186 30 68 7307

יִכְלָיוּן: כִּי כֹה אָמַר־יְהוָה אֵלַי כַּאֲשֶׁר יֶהְגֶּה הָאַרְיֵה
will cease. For thus has said Jehovah to me As roars the lion,
738 1897 3068 559 3541 3615

וְהַכְּפִיר עַל־טַרְפּוֹ אֲשֶׁר יִקָּרֵא עָלָיו מְלֹא רֹעִים מְקוֹלָם
lion young on his prey when called him a band of shepherds, their voice
6963 7462 4393 834 7121 2966 3715

לֹא יֵחָת וּמֵהֲמוֹנָם לֹא יַעֲנֶה כֵּן יֵרֵד יְהוָה צְבָאוֹת לִצְבֹּא
not he fears and their noise himself frets not So shall descend Jehovah of hosts to fight
6633 66 35 3068 3381 6031 1995 28 65 3808

עַל־הַר־צִיּוֹן וְעַל־גִּבְעָתָהּ: כְּצִפֳּרִים עָפוֹת כֵּן יָגֵן יְהוָה
on Mount Zion and its hill. As birds fly, so will shield Jehovah
3068 1598 5774 6833 1389 6726 2022

צְבָאוֹת עַל־יְרוּשָׁלַ͏ִם גָּנוֹן וְהִצִּיל פָּסֹחַ וְהִמְלִיט: שׁוּבוּ
of hosts over Jerusalem shielding and delivering passing over He will save. Turn back
7725 4422 6452 5337 1598 3389 6635

לַאֲשֶׁר הֶעְמִיקוּ סָרָה בְּנֵי יִשְׂרָאֵל: כִּי בַּיּוֹם הַהוּא יִמְאָסוּן
to whom (at) made deep revolt sons of Israel. For in day that shall reject
39 73 3117 3478 1121 5627 6009 834

אִישׁ אֱלִילֵי כַסְפּוֹ וֶאֱלִילֵי זְהָבוֹ אֲשֶׁר עָשׂוּ לָכֶם יְדֵיכֶם
each man the idols of his silver and the idols of his gold which have made you for your hands—
3027 6213 834 2091 457 3701 1457 3 76

חֵטְא: וְנָפַל אַשּׁוּר בְּחֶרֶב לֹא־אִישׁ וְחֶרֶב לֹא־אָדָם תֹּאכְלֶנּוּ
a sin. Then shall fall Assyria by a sword not man (of) and a sword not man (of) shall devour him.
1398 120 3808 2719 376 3808 2719 1804 5307 2399

וְנָס לוֹ מִפְּנֵי־חֶרֶב וּבַחוּרָיו לָמַס יִהְיוּ: וְסַלְעוֹ מִמָּגוֹר
And he for him shall flee from fear sword and his young men labor forced shall become. And his rock from fear
4032 5553 1961 4522 970 2719 5127

יַעֲבוֹר וְחַתּוּ מִנֵּס שָׂרָיו נְאֻם־יְהוָה אֲשֶׁר־אוּר לוֹ בְּצִיּוֹן
pass away and tremble at the banner his chiefs Jehovah states whose fire Him to (is) in Zion,
6726 2865 5251 8269 5002 3068 834 217 6726

וְתַנּוּר לוֹ בִּירוּשָׁלָ͏ִם:
and a furnace Him to in Jerusalem.
8574 133 89

CAP. XXXII לב

CHAPTER 32

הֵן לְצֶדֶק יִמְלָךְ־מֶלֶךְ וּלְשָׂרִים לְמִשְׁפָּט יָשֹׂרוּ: וְהָיָה־אִישׁ
Behold in righteousness shall reign a king, and princes for justice they shall rule. And shall be a man
376 1961 8323 4941 8269 4428 4427 6664 2009

כְּמַחֲבֵא־רוּחַ וְסֵתֶר זָרֶם כְּפַלְגֵי־מַיִם בְּצָיוֹן כְּצֵל סֶלַע
as a hiding place from wind and covert storm as streams of water in a dry place like shadow rock a
55 53 6738 6 724 4325 6388 2230 5643 7307 4224

כָּבֵד בְּאֶרֶץ עֲיֵפָה: וְלֹא תִשְׁעֶינָה עֵינֵי רֹאִים וְאָזְנֵי שֹׁמְעִים
heavy in a land weary. And not shall gaze the eyes of those seeing, and the ears of those hearing
8085 241 7200 5869 8159 3808 5889 776 3515

those who hear shall listen.
4And the heart of the rash
shall discern knowledge;
and the tongue of those
that stutter shall hurry to
speak clear things. 5The
fool shall no more be called
noble, and a miser will not
be said *to be* generous.
6For the fool will speak
foolishness, and his heart
will work iniquity, to do
ungodliness; and *he* will
utter error against Jehovah,
to make the hungry soul
empty; and he causes drink
to fail the thirsty. 7And the
weapons of the miser *are*
evil; he devises wicked
plots to destroy the poor
with lying words, even the
needy when he speaks
right. 8But the noble one
devises noble things; and
he shall rise by noble
things.
9O women who are at
ease, rise up. Hear my
voice; confident daughters,
listen to my word. 10You
will shake for days on a
year, confident women;for
the vintage fails; the harvest
shall not come. 11Tremble,
women at ease; shake,
confident women; strip and
make yourselves bare, and
bind on *sackcloth* on *your*
loins; 12be wailing over
breasts, over pleasant fields,
over the fruitful vine.
13Thorns *and* briers shall
spring up on the land of My
people; even over all the
houses of joy in the jubilant
city, 14because the palace
is forsaken; the crowd of
the city is forsaken; mound
and tower are instead
caves, until forever; a joy of
wild asses; pasture for
flocks; 15until is poured out
on us the Spirit from on
high, and the wilderness
becomes a fruitful field; and
the fruitful field is reckoned
as a forest. 16Then justice
shall dwell in the wilderness, and righteousness
shall dwell in the fruitful
field. 17And the work of
righteousness shall be
peace; and the service of
righteousness shall be

4116 5926 3956 1847 995 4116 3824 7181
4 תִּקְשַׁבְנָה׃ וּלְבַב נִמְהָרִים יָבִין לָדָעַת וּלְשׁוֹן עִלְּגִים תְּמַהֵר
shall stutterers the and ;knowl- will rash the And shall
hurry of tongue edge discern ones of heart .listen

3808 3596 5081 5036 5750 7121 3808 6703 1696
5 לְדַבֵּר צָחוֹת׃ לֹא־יִקָּרֵא עוֹד לְנָבָל נָדִיב וּלְכִילַי לֹא
not a and ,noble fool a more shall Not clear speak to
miser called be .things

6213 205 6213 3820 1696 5039 5036 7771 559
6 יֵאָמֵר שׁוֹעַ׃ כִּי נָבָל נְבָלָה יְדַבֵּר וְלִבּוֹ יַעֲשֶׂה־אָוֶן לַעֲשׂוֹת
do to iniq- works and ,speaks foolish- the For .generous be will
,uity heart his ness fool said

4945 7457 5315 7324 8442 3068 1696 2612
חֹנֶף וּלְדַבֵּר אֶל־יְהוָה תּוֹעָה לְהָרִיק נֶפֶשׁ רָעֵב וּמַשְׁקֶה
drink and the the make to ,error Jeho- against to and ungod-
of ;hungry of soul empty vah speak liness

2254 3289 2154 7451 3627 3596 2637 6771
7 צָמֵא יַחְסִיר׃ וְכֵלַי כֵּלָיו רָעִים הוּא זִמּוֹת יָעָץ לְחַבֵּל
to ,devises wicked he (are) his the And causes he the
destroy schemes ;evil weapons ,miser .fail to thirsty

5081 5081 4941 34 1696 8267 561 6035
8 עֲנָוִים בְּאִמְרֵי־שֶׁקֶר וּבְדַבֵּר אֶבְיוֹן מִשְׁפָּט׃ וְנָדִיב נְדִיבוֹת
noble the But .justice the when even ,lying with af- the
things noble needy speaks of words flicted

6965 7600 802 6965 5081 3289
9 יָעָץ וְהוּא עַל־נְדִיבוֹת יָקוּם׃ נָשִׁים שַׁאֲנַנּוֹת קֹמְנָה
!up rise are who O .rises noble by and de-
,ease at women things he ;vises

3117 565 238 982 1323 6963 8085
10 שְׁמַעְנָה קוֹלִי בָּנוֹת בֹּטְחוֹת הַאְזֵנָּה אִמְרָתִי׃ יָמִים עַל־
on Days .word my listen ;confident daughters my Hear
to ,voice

935 1097 625 1208 3615 982 7264 8141
שָׁנָה תִּרְגַּזְנָה בֹּטְחוֹת כִּי כָּלָה בָצִיר אֹסֶף בְּלִי יָבוֹא׃
shall not the the fails for confident will you a
,come harvest ;vintage ,women ,quake year

2290 6209 6584 982 7264 7600 2729
11 חִרְדוּ שַׁאֲנַנּוֹת רְגָזָה בֹּטְחוֹת פְּשֹׁטָה וְעֹרָה וַחֲגוֹרָה עַל־
on bind and make and strip confident ,quake women ,Tremble
(sackcloth) ,bare you ;women ,ease at

6509 1612 2531 7704 5594 7699 2504
12 חֲלָצָיִם׃ עַל־שָׁדַיִם סֹפְדִים עַל־שְׂדֵי־חֶמֶד עַל־גֶּפֶן פֹּרִיָּה׃
.fruitful the over pleasant- fields over be breasts over (your)
vine ,ness of ,wailing ;loins

4885 1004 3605 5927 8068 6975 5971 127 5921
13 עַל אַדְמַת עַמִּי קוֹץ שָׁמִיר תַּעֲלֶה כִּי עַל־כָּל־בָּתֵּי מָשׂוֹשׂ
,joy houses all over even shall (and) thorns my the On
of ;up go briars people of ground

975 6076 5800 5892 1995 5203 759 5947 7151
14 קִרְיָה עַלִּיזָה׃ כִּי־אַרְמוֹן נֻטָּשׁ הֲמוֹן עִיר עֻזָּב עֹפֶל וָבַחַן
and mound for- is the the is palace the For .jubilant city the
tower ;saken city of crowd ;left

5739 4829 6501 4885 5769 5704 4631 1961
הָיָה בְעַד מְעָרוֹת עַד־עוֹלָם מְשׂוֹשׂ פְּרָאִים מִרְעֵה עֲדָרִים׃
,flocks pasture wild joy a ,forever till caves instead are
for ;asses of

3759 3759 4057 1961 4791 7307 6168 5704
15 עַד־יֵעָרֶה עָלֵינוּ רוּחַ מִמָּרוֹם וְהָיָה מִדְבָּר לַכַּרְמֶל וְכַרְמֶל
the and fruitful a wilder- the and on from the upon poured is until
field fruitful ;field ness becomes ,high Spirit us out

3759 6666 4941 4057 3427 2803 3293
16 לַיַּעַר יֵחָשֵׁב׃ וְשָׁכַן בַּמִּדְבָּר מִשְׁפָּט וּצְדָקָה בַּכַּרְמֶל
fruit- the in and ,justice the in shall Then is a as
field ful righteousness wilderness dwell .reckoned forest

8252 6666 5656 7965 6666 4639 1961 3427
17 תֵּשֵׁב׃ וְהָיָה מַעֲשֵׂה הַצְּדָקָה שָׁלוֹם וַעֲבֹדַת הַצְּדָקָה הַשְׁקֵט
quietness righteous- the and ;peace righteous- the shall And shall
ness of service ness of work be .dwell

quietness and hope forever. [18]And My people shall live in a peaceful home, and in safe dwellings, and in secure resting places. [19]Though it hails when the forest *is* felled, and the city is laid low, [20]blessed *are* you who sow beside all waters, who send out the foot of the ox and the ass.

4908 79 65 5116 5971 3427 5769 5704 982
18 ובמשכנות שלום בנוה עמי וישב: עד-עולם ובטח
in and of dwellings ,peace of home a in My people shall And dwell .forever till and trust

8218 3293 3381 1258 7600 4496 40:09
19 ובשפלה היער ברדת וברד שאננות: ובמנוחת מבטחים
the in and place low the ,forest (is) when felled Though hails it .secure resting and places in ,safety

7272 7971 4325 3605 2232 835 5892 8213
20 רגל- משלחי על-כל-מים זרעי אשריכם העיר: תשפל
the of foot send who out ,waters all beside who sow blessed you (are) the ,city laid is low

2543 7794
והחמור: השור
the and .ass the ox

CAP. XXXIII לג

CHAPTER 33

CHAPTER 33

[1]Woe *to* the destroyer, and you not being destroyed; and *to* the betrayer, though they did not betray you! When you finish destroying, you will be destroyed; when you stop betraying, they will betray you. [2]O Jehovah, be gracious to us. We have hoped in You; be their arm in the mornings, our salvation also in time of distress. [3]At the sound of the tumult, the peoples fled; at Your exaltation, nations scattered. [4]And Your prey shall be gathered *as* the stripping locust gathers; as locusts run to and fro, he also runs about on it. [5]Jehovah is exalted; for *He* lives on high; He has filled Zion *with* justice and righteousness. [6]And He will be the security of your times, strength of salvation, wisdom, and knowledge; the fear of Jehovah *is* His treasure. [7]Behold, their heroes cry outside; the envoys of peace shall weep bitterly. [8]The highways are deserted; the path-crosser ceases. He has broken the covenant; he has rejected cities; he has not respected man. [9]The land mourns *and* droops; Lebanon is ashamed; Sharon withers like a wilderness; Bashan is shaken out; also Carmel. [10]Now I will rise up, says Jehovah. Now I will be exalted; now I will be lifted up. [11]You shall conceive

8552 898 3808 898 77:03 3808 77.03 1945
1 כהתמך בך ולא-בגדו ובוגד שדוד לא ואתה שודד הוי
you As finish !you they and betrayed not and ,betrayer being not ;destroyed you and the ,destroyer Woe (to)

2603 3068 898 898 5239 7703 7703
2 חננו יהוה :יבגדו-בך לבגד כנלתך תושד שודד
favor ,us O ,Jehovah .you they betray shall ,betraying you as stop be will you ;destroyed destroy- ,ing

6864 6256 3444 637 12:42 2220 1961 6960
בעת צרה: אף-ישועתנו לבקרים זרעם היה קוינו לך
.distress of time in our salvation also the in ,mornings their arm be have we ;hoped in You

622 1471 5311 7427 5971 5074 19:95 6963
3 ואסף :גוים נפצו מרוממתך עמים נדדו המון מקול
4
shall And gathered be .nations scat- tered Your at exaltation ;peoples fled tumult the At of sound

76.82 8264 1357 4944 2425 625 7998
5 נשגב :בו שקק גבים כמשק החסיל אסף שללכם
is exalted on .it runs he about ,locusts to run as fro and strip- the ;locust ing (as) gathers your prey

1961 6666 4941 67:26 4390 4791 7931 30:68
6 והיה :וצדקה משפט ציון מלא מרום שכן כי יהוה
He And be will righ- and .teousness (with) justice Zion has He filled on ;high (He) lives for ,Jehovah

3068 3373 1847 2451 3444 26 33 6256 530
היא יהוה יראת ודעת חכמת ישועת חסן עתיך אמונת
it (is) ,Jehovah the of fear and ;knowledge ,wisdom ,salvation wealth of your ,times the of security

7965 4397 2351 6817 691 2009 214
7 שלום מלאכי חצה צעקו אראלם הן :אוצרו
peace the of envoys ;outside cry their heroes ,Behold His .treasure

1285 6565 734 5674 7673 4546 8074 1058 4751
8 ברית הפר ארח עבר שבת מסלות נשמו :יבכיון מר
the ;covenant has He broken ;path- crosser the ceases ;highways are deserted shall .weep bitterly

2659 776 535 56 582 2803 38.08 5892 3973
9 החפיר ארץ אמללה אבל :אנוש חשב לא ערים מאס
is ashamed the ;land (and) droops Mourns .man he respected not ;cities has he rejected

3760 13.16 5287 61:60 8289 1961 70.60 3844
וכרמל: בשן ונער כערבה השרון היה קמל לבנון
and .Carmel ,Bashan is and out shaken a like ,desert Sharon Is wither- ing ,Lebanon

2029 5375 6258 73 11 6258 3068 559 6965
10 11 תהרו :אנשא עתה ארומם עתה יהוה יאמר אקום עתה
shall You conceive be will I .up lifted now be will I ;exalted Now ;Jehovah says will I ,up rise Now

chaff; you shall bear stubble; your fiery breath shall devour you. ¹²And peoples shall be *as* burnings of lime; *as* thorns cut away, they shall be burned in fire. ¹³Distant ones, hear what I have done; and you near ones, know My might.

¹⁴The sinners of Zion are afraid; terror has seized profane ones; who of us shall tarry *with* consuming fire? Who of us shall tarry with everlasting burnings? ¹⁵He who walks righteously and speaks uprightly; he who despises the gain of oppressions, who shakes his hands free from taking the bribe, who stops his ear from hearing of blood, and shuts his eyes from looking at evil—¹⁶he shall live *on* high; strongholds of rocks *will be* his retreat; his bread shall be given; his waters are faithful. ¹⁷Your eyes shall see the king in his beauty; they shall see a land that is very far off. ¹⁸Your heart shall ponder terror: Where *is* the scribe? Where *is* the weigher? Where *is* he who counted the towers? ¹⁹You shall not see the fierce people, from hearing a people of a difficult lip, *of* a foreign tongue *that* none understands. ²⁰Behold, Zion, the city of our appointed meetings! Your eyes shall see Jerusalem, a quiet home, a tent *that* shall not be moved; its stakes shall not be pulled up forever, nor shall any of its cords be pulled off. ²¹But majestic Jehovah *will place* there for us a place of rivers *and* streams, broad on both hands; a ship with oars shall not go in it, and a majestic boat shall not pass through it. ²²For Jehovah *is* our judge; Jehovah *is* our lawgiver; Jehovah *is* our king; He will save us. ²³Your ropes are loosened; they do not hold the base of

---

Interlinear (Hebrew right-to-left with English glosses and Strong's numbers):

12 — 2842 05 32 7179 7307 • 7179 784 398 1961 5971
חֲשַׁשׁ תֵּלְדוּ קַשׁ רוּחֲכֶם אֵשׁ תֹּאכַלְכֶם ... וְהָיוּ עַמִּים
;chaff — you — -stubble your — -breath, fire a — shall devour you, be shall — And peoples

13 — 8085 3341 784 3683 6975 7875 4855
שִׁמְעוּ מִשְׂרְפוֹת שִׂיד קוֹצִים כְּסוּחִים בָּאֵשׁ יִצַּתּוּ
,Hear — burnings of — lime — thorns — cut — fire in shall they — burned be. away

14 — 6726 6342 1369 7138 3045 6213 834 7350
פָּחֲדוּ בְצִיּוֹן גְּבוּרָתִי קְרוֹבִים וּדְעוּ עָשִׂיתִי אֲשֶׁר רְחוֹקִים
in Zion Are afraid — My might — near ones — and know — have I ;done — what — distant ones

398 784 1481 4310 2611 7461 270 2400
חַטָּאִים אָחֲזָה רְעָדָה חֲנֵפִים מִי יָגוּר לָנוּ אֵשׁ אוֹכֵלָה
;sinners — has seized — terror — profane ,ones — who — shall tarry us — of (with) consuming? fire

15 — 4339 1696 6666 1980 5769 4168 1481
מֵישָׁרִים וְדֹבֵר צְדָקוֹת הֹלֵךְ עוֹלָם מִי־יָגוּר לָנוּ
right things — and speaks — righteously — who He walks — for-ever? — burnings (with) — of us tarry — shall Who

241 8551 3709 5287 4642 1215 3973
מֹאֵס בְּבֶצַע מַעֲשַׁקּוֹת נֹעֵר כַּפָּיו מִתְּמֹךְ בַּשֹּׁחַד אֹטֵם אָזְנוֹ
his ear — who stops — the ,bribe — from taking — his palms — who shakes — ,oppressions gain — of who he rejects

16 — 4791 7451 7200 5869 1818 8085
מִשְּׁמֹעַ דָּמִים וְעֹצֵם עֵינָיו מֵרְאוֹת בְּרָע הוּא מְרוֹמִים
high (on) places — He .evil at — from looking — his eyes — and shuts — ,blood — of hearing

539 4325 54:14 3899 4869 5553 4679 79:31
יִשְׁכֹּן מְצָדוֹת סְלָעִים מִשְׂגַּבּוֹ לַחְמוֹ נִתָּן מֵימָיו נֶאֱמָנִים
faith-ful are — his waters — be shall His bread; given — his .retreat — rocks — Strongholds (be will) — be shall of !live

17 — 3820 4801 776 7200 5869 2372 3308 44:28
מֶלֶךְ בְּיָפְיוֹ תֶּחֱזֶינָה עֵינֶיךָ אֶרֶץ מַרְחַקִּים לָבֶךְ
Your heart — off far .places — a of land — shall they see — your ;eyes — shall behold — his in beauty — The king

18 — 40:26 5608 8254 5608 367 1897
לִבְּךָ יֶהְגֶּה אֵימָה אַיֵּה סֹפֵר אַיֵּה שֹׁקֵל אַיֵּה סֹפֵר אֶת־הַמִּגְדָּלִים
the ?towers — who he Where counted (is) — the Where ?weigher (is) — the Where ?scribe (is) — .terror shall ponder

19 — 39:32 8085 8193 6012 5971 7200 3808 3267 5971
אֶת־עַם נוֹעָז לֹא תִרְאֶה עַם עִמְקֵי שָׂפָה מִשְּׁמוֹעַ נִלְעַג
foreign of — from ;hearing — lip of — difficult people — a ;see — shall you people — not — fierce — The

20 — 7200 5869 4150 7151 6726 67:26 2372 998 369 3956
חֲזֵה צִיּוֹן קִרְיַת מוֹעֲדֵנוּ עֵינֶיךָ תִרְאֶינָה
shall see — Your eyes — set our meetings of — the city — ,Zion hold — Be-under- (which) stands none — ,tongue

5331 3489 5265 1077 6813 1077 168 7600 5116 3389
יְרוּשָׁלִַם נָוֶה שַׁאֲנָן אֹהֶל בַּל־יִצְעָן בַּל־יִסַּע יְתֵדֹתָיו לָנֶצַח
for-ever — its stakes — be shall not up pulled — be shall not ,removed — tent a — ,quiet home — a — ,Jerusalem

21 — 3068 117 80:33 5423 36:05 22:56 36:05
וְכָל־חֲבָלָיו בַּל־יִנָּתֵקוּ כִּי אִם־שָׁם אַדִּיר יְהוָה לָנוּ
for us (be will) — Jehovah ma-jestic — -jestic there — But — be shall — not .off torn — its cords — and all

788:5 590 1980 1077 3027 7342 2975 5104 4725
מְקוֹם־נְהָרִים יְאֹרִים רַחֲבֵי יָדָיִם בַּל־תֵּלֶךְ בּוֹ אֳנִי־שַׁיִט
;oars ship a with it — in shall go — not — both ;hands — broad on — (and) ,streams — ,rivers of place a

22 — 2710 3068 81:99 3068 5674 38:08 117 6716
וְצִי אַדִּיר לֹא יַעַבְרֶנּוּ כִּי יְהוָה שֹׁפְטֵנוּ יְהוָה מְחֹקְקֵנוּ
our ;lawgiver (is) — Jehovah our ;judge (is) — Jehovah For — pass shall .it through — not — majestic and boat a

23 — 3653 2388 1077 2256 5203 3467 44:28 3068
יְהוָה מַלְכֵּנוּ הוּא יוֹשִׁיעֵנוּ נִטְּשׁוּ חֲבָלָיִךְ בַּל־יְחַזְּקוּ כֵן
the of base — they hold — not — Your ;ropes — are loosened — save will .us — He — our ;king — Jehovah (is)

their mast; they could not spread the sail. Then the prey of much plunder shall be divided; the lame shall seize on the spoil. [24]And an inhabitant, the people who live in it, shall not say, I am sick; iniquity is taken away.

תָּרְנָם בַּל־פָּרְשׂוּ נֵס אָז חֻלַּק עַד־שָׁלָל מַרְבֶּה פִּסְחִים בָּזְזוּ

spoil the ;much plunder the shall Then the they not their
lame of prey divided sail spread ;mast

24 בַז׃ וּבַל־יֹאמַר שָׁכֵן חָלִיתִי הָעָם הַיֹּשֵׁב בָּהּ נְשֻׂא עָוֺן׃

ini- taken is in who the am I inhabi- shall And the
.quity away ;it live people ;sick ,tant say not .spoil

CAP. XXXIV לד

CHAPTER 34

1 קִרְבוּ גוֹיִם לִשְׁמֹעַ וּלְאֻמִּים הַקְשִׁיבוּ תִּשְׁמַע הָאָרֶץ וּמְלֹאָהּ

its and the Let !listen and ;hear to nations Come
,fullness ,earth hear ,peoples ,near

2 תֵּבֵל וְכָל־צֶאֱצָאֶיהָ׃ כִּי קֶצֶף לַיהוָה עַל־כָּל־הַגּוֹיִם וְחֵמָה

and the all (is) to wrath For its and the
fury ,nations on Jehovah .offspring all world

3 עַל־כָּל־צְבָאָם הֶחֱרִימָם נְתָנָם לַטָּבַח׃ וְחַלְלֵיהֶם יֻשְׁלָכוּ

be shall their And to gave He de- has He their all on
;out cast slain .slaughter them ;them voted ;army

4 וּפִגְרֵיהֶם יַעֲלֶה בָאְשָׁם וְנָמַסּוּ הָרִים מִדָּמָם׃ וְנָמַקּוּ כָּל־

all shall And their with moun- shall and their shall (from) and
dissolved be .blood tains melt ;stench rise carcases their

צְבָא הַשָּׁמַיִם וְנָגֹלּוּ כַסֵּפֶר הַשָּׁמָיִם וְכָל־צְבָאָם יִבּוֹל כִּנְבֹל

as shall their then the a like shall and the the
droops, ,droop host all ;heavens scroll rolled be ;heavens of host

5 עָלֶה מִגֶּפֶן וּכְנֹבֶלֶת מִתְּאֵנָה׃ כִּי־רִוְּתָה בַשָּׁמַיִם חַרְבִּי

My the in is For a from the as and the off leaf a
.sword heavens drenched .tree fig drooping ;vine

6 הִנֵּה עַל־אֱדוֹם תֵּרֵד וְעַל־עַם חֶרְמִי לְמִשְׁפָּט׃ חֶרֶב

A for My the and shall it Edom on Be-
sword .judgment ,ban of people on ;descend ,hold

לַיהוָה מָלְאָה דָם הֻדַּשְּׁנָה מֵחֵלֶב מִדַּם כָּרִים וְעַתּוּדִים

and lambs the with with is it (with) is it to (is)
,goats of blood ,fatness fat made ;blood filled ;Jehovah

מֵחֵלֶב כִּלְיוֹת אֵילִים כִּי זֶבַח לַיהוָה בְּבָצְרָה וְטֶבַח גָּדוֹל

great a and in to sac- a for —rams inward the the with
slaughter ,Bozrah Jehovah (is) rifice of parts of fat

7 בְּאֶרֶץ אֱדוֹם׃ וְיָרְדוּ רְאֵמִים עִמָּם וּפָרִים עִם־אַבִּירִים

strong with and with wild shall And .Edom the in
,(bulls) bullocks ,them oxen down come of land

8 וְרִוְּתָה אַרְצָם מִדָּם וַעֲפָרָם מֵחֵלֶב יְדֻשָּׁן׃ כִּי יוֹם נָקָם

ven- the For made with their and with their is and
geance of day .fat fatness dust ,blood land drenched

9 לַיהוָה שְׁנַת שִׁלּוּמִים לְרִיב צִיּוֹן׃ וְנֶהֶפְכוּ נְחָלֶיהָ לְזֶפֶת

to its shall And .Zion the for repay- the to (is)
,pitch torrents turned be of cause ments of year ,Jehovah

10 וַעֲפָרָהּ לְגָפְרִית וְהָיְתָה אַרְצָהּ לְזֶפֶת בֹּעֵרָה׃ לַיְלָה וְיוֹמָם

day or Night .burning pitch land its shall and brim- to its and
become ,stone dust

לֹא תִכְבֶּה לְעוֹלָם יַעֲלֶה עֲשָׁנָהּ מִדּוֹר לָדוֹר תֶּחֱרָב לְנֵצַח

forever shall it gen- to From .smoke its shall forever shall it not
;waste lie eration generation arise ;out put be

CHAPTER 34

[1]Nations, come near to hear; and peoples, listen! Let the earth hear, and its fullness, the world and all its offspring. [2]For the wrath of Jehovah *is* on all the nations, and fury on all their army; He has devoted them; He gave them to slaughter. [3]And their slain shall be thrown out; and the stench from their carcases shall rise; and the mountains shall be melted with their blood. [4]And all the host of the heavens shall be dissolved, and the heavens shall be rolled together like a scroll ; then all their host shall droop, as a leaf drooping from the vine, and as the drooping from a fig-tree. [5]For My sword is drenched in the heavens. Behold, it shall come down on Edom, and on the people of My curse, for judgment. [6]A sword *is* to Jehovah; it is filled *with* blood; it is made fat with fatness, with the blood of lambs and goats, with the fat of the kidneys of rams. For Jehovah *has* a sacrifice in Bozrah, and a great slaughter in the land of Edom. [7]And wild oxen shall come down with them, and bullocks with strong *bulls*; and their land is drenched with blood, and their dust made fat with fatness. [8]For the day of vengeance *is* to Jehovah, the year of repayments for Zion's cause. [9]And its torrents shall be turned to pitch, and its dust to brimstone; and its land shall become burning pitch. [10]It shall not be put out night or day; its smoke shall rise forever. From generation to generation, it shall lie

waste; no one shall pass through it forever and forever. ¹¹But the owl and the hedgehog shall possess it; and the eared owl and the raven shall live in it. And He shall stretch out on it the line of shame, and the stones of emptiness. ¹²They shall call its nobles to a kingdom, but none shall be there; and all her rulers shall be nothing. ¹³And thorns shall grow in her palaces, nettles and thistles in its fortresses; and it shall be a home for jackals, a court for daughters of ostriches. ¹⁴The wild beasts of the desert shall also meet with the howling beasts; and the shaggy goat shall cry to his fellow. The screech owl shall also settle there, and find a place of rest for herself. ¹⁵The snake shall nest there, and shall lay, and hatch, and shall gather in her shadow. Vultures shall also be gathered together, each with its mate.

¹⁶Search and read from the book of Jehovah —not one of these misses, each not lacking her mate; for He has commanded my mouth, and by His Spirit He has assembled them. ¹⁷And He has made fall a lot for them, and His hand divided it to them by line. They shall possess it till forever, from generation to generation they shall live in it.

11

6158	3244	70:90	6893	1342 3	5674	369	53:31
וְיַנְשׁוֹף	וְקִפֹּד	קָאַת	וִירֵשׁוּהָ	בָּהּ׃	עֹבֵר	אֵין	נְצָחִים
and raven	eared and owl	and owl; hedgehog	owl	shall But it possess	through passes .it	no one forever	(and)

12

369	2715	922	8414	6957	5186	7931
even none	Its nobles	.emptiness	and shame-ness	of line	it on He And stretch shall .it	in shall live

13

1759	59:27	657	1961	8269	3605	44101	8033
her (in) palaces	shall And go up	.nothing shall be	her	and chiefs all	they a (to) call shall kingdom	(are) there

2681	8:577	5116	1961	4013	2336	7057	55:18
a court	,jackals a for home be shall	it and	its in ;fortresses	and	nettles	,thorns	thistles

14

7453	8163	:338	6728	.6298	3284	1323
his fellow	to the goat shaggy	the and ;howlers	the with creatures	desert shall meet	Also .ostriches	for of daughters

15

8033	4494	4672	3917	7280	8033 389	7121
There	place a .rest of	for herself and find	screech the ,owl	shall settle	there Also	shall .call

6908	8033 389	6738	1716	1234	4422	7091	7077
be shall assembled	there Also	her in .shadow	shall and gather	and ,hatch	shall and ,lay	,snake	shall nest

16

71:21	3068	5612	1875	7468	802	1772
and —read	Jehovah the of book	the from Search	her (with) .mate	each	,hawks

6310	6485	38:108	7468	802	5737	38:08	200:7	259
my for ,mouth	lack-:ing	not	her mate	each	does -miss	not these	of	one

17

148:6	5307	6908	7307	66:80
,lot a for them	made has He And fall	has them assembled	He His and ,Spirit	has He ,commanded

1755	1755	3423	5769 5704 6957	2505	3027
gen- and eration	gen- to eration	shall they ,it possess	forever Till	a by line them	to divided has His and it hand

7931
in shall they .it live

CHAPTER 35

¹The wilderness and dry land shall rejoice for them; and the desert shall exult and bloom like the crocus. ²Blooming, it shall bloom and exult, even with joy and singing. Lebanon's glory shall be given to it, the honor of Carmel and Sharon; they shall see the glory of Jehovah, the majesty of our God. ³Make the weak hands strong, and firm up the feeble knees. ⁴Say to those of a hasty

1

2261	6524	6160	1523	6723	4057	7797
the like .crocus	and bloom	the desert	shall and exult	dry and ;land	wilder,ness	joy Shall them for

2

5414	3844	3519	7891	1525 637	15:23	65:24	65:24
to shall ,it given be	Lebanon	The of glory	and .singing joy	(with) also	and ,exult	shall it bloom	Surely

430	1926	3068	3519	7200	8289	3760	1926
.God our	the of honor	,Jehovah	the of glory	shall see	They .Sharon	and Carmel	the of honor

3 / 4

559	553	378:2	1290	7504	3027	2388
Say	firm .up	stumbling	the and knees	,sinking hands	the	Stengthen

heart, Be strong! Do not fear! Behold, your God will come *with* vengeance; with the full dealing of God, He will come and save you. [5]Then the eyes of the blind shall be opened, and the ears of the deaf opened. [6]Then the lame shall leap like a deer, and the tongue of the dumb shall sing. For waters shall break out in the wilderness, and streams in the desert. [7]And the mirage shall become a pool, and the thirsty land shall become springs of waters, in the home of jackals, in its lair, and a place for the reed and rush.

[8]And a highway shall be there, and a way, and it shall be called, The Way of Holiness. The unclean shall not pass over it. And it *is* for them, the wayfaring one; yea, fools shall not go astray. [9]No lion shall be there; and no violent beast shall go up on it; it shall not be found there. But redeemed ones shall walk there. [10]And the ransomed of Jehovah shall return and enter Zion, with singing and everlasting joy on their head; gladness and joy shall reach *them*; and sorrow and sighing shall flee.

935 5359 430 2009 3372 2388 3820 4116
לְנִמְהֲרֵי־לֵב חִזְקוּ אַל־תִּירָאוּ הִנֵּה אֱלֹהֵיכֶם נָקָם יָבוֹא
will (with) your ,Behold !Fear not Be ,heart the to
;come vengeance God !strong of hasty

5 5787 5869 6491 227 3467 935 430 1576
גְּמוּל אֱלֹהִים הוּא יָבוֹא וְיֹשַׁעֲכֶם׃ אָז תִּפָּקַחְנָה עֵינֵי עִוְרִים
the the be shall Then save and will He ,God full the
,blind of eyes opened ,you come of dealing

6 3956 7442 64:55 354 1801 227 6605 2795 241
וְאָזְנֵי חֵרְשִׁים תִּפָּתַחְנָה׃ אָז יְדַלֵּג כָּאַיָּל פִּסֵּחַ וְתָרֹן לְשׁוֹן
the shall and the a like shall Then be shall deaf the the and
of tongue sing ,lame deer leap .opened of ears

7 1961 6160 5158 4325 4057 1234 483
אִלֵּם כִּי־נִבְקְעוּ בַמִּדְבָּר מַיִם וּנְחָלִים בָּעֲרָבָה׃ וְהָיָה
shall And the in and ,waters the in shall For the
become .desert torrents wilderness out break .dumb

72:58 8577 5116 4325 4002 6774 98 8273
הַשָּׁרָב לַאֲגַם וְצִמָּאוֹן לְמַבּוּעֵי מָיִם בִּנְוֵה תַנִּים רִבְצָהּ
rest- its ,jackals the in ;water of springs the and ,pool a parched the
;place ing of home land thirsty ground

8 6944 1870 1870 4547 8033/1961 1573 7070 2682
חָצִיר לְקָנֶה וָגֹמֶא׃ וְהָיָה־שָׁם מַסְלוּל וָדֶרֶךְ וְדֶרֶךְ הַקֹּדֶשׁ
Holiness the and a and a there And and ,reed for ,grass
of Way ,way ,highway be shall .rush

191 1870 1980 2931 5674 3808 7121
יִקָּרֵא לָהּ לֹא־יַעַבְרֶנּוּ טָמֵא וְהוּא־לָמוֹ הֹלֵךְ דֶּרֶךְ וֶאֱוִילִים
fools and the the for And the pass shall Not .it to shall
.way of goer ;them (is) it .unclean .it over called be

9 5921 3605 2416 6530 738 8033 1961 3808 8582 3808
לֹא יִתְעוּ׃ לֹא־יִהְיֶה שָׁם אַרְיֵה וּפְרִיץ חַיּוֹת בַּל־יַעֲלֶנָּה
go shall not beasts a and ,lion a there shall Not go shall not
;it on up of one violent be .astray

10 935 7725 3068 6299 1350 1980 8033 4672 3808
לֹא תִמָּצֵא שָׁם וְהָלְכוּ גְּאוּלִים׃ וּפְדוּיֵי יְהוָה יְשֻׁבוּן וּבָאוּ
and shall Jehovah the And redeemed shall But .there shall it not
enter return of ransomed .ones walk found be

5381 8057 8342 7218 5769 8057 7440 6726
צִיּוֹן בְּרִנָּה וְשִׂמְחַת עוֹלָם עַל־רֹאשָׁם שָׂשׂוֹן וְשִׂמְחָה יַשִּׂיגוּ
shall and gladness their on ever- joy and with Zion
reach joy ,head lasting singing
.(them)

585 3015 5127
וְנָסוּ יָגוֹן וַאֲנָחָה׃
and sorrow And
.sighing flee shall

CAP. XXXVI לו

CHAPTER 36

CHAPTER 36

[1]And it happened in the fourteenth year of king Hezekiah, Sennacherib, king of Assyria, came against all the fortified cities of Judah, and took them. [2]And the king of Assyria sent the chief of the cupbearers from Lachish to Jerusalem, to king Hezekiah, with a heavy army. And he stood by the conduit of the upper pool, in the highway of the Fuller's Field. [3]And Eliakim, Hilkiah's son,

1 5576 5927 2396 4428 8141 6240 702 1961
וַיְהִי בְּאַרְבַּע עֶשְׂרֵה שָׁנָה לַמֶּלֶךְ חִזְקִיָּהוּ עָלָה סַנְחֵרִיב
Sennacherib came ,Hezekiah King of year the in it And
up fourteenth ,was

2 7971 8610 1219 3063 5892 3605 804 4428
מֶלֶךְ־אַשּׁוּר עַל כָּל־עָרֵי יְהוּדָה הַבְּצֻרוֹת וַיִּתְפְּשֵׂם׃ וַיִּשְׁלַח
sent And took and ,fortified Judah the all against Assyria king
.them of cities of

4428 3389 3923 7262 804 4428
מֶלֶךְ־אַשּׁוּר ׀ אֶת־רַבְשָׁקֵה מִלָּכִישׁ יְרוּשָׁלַיְמָה אֶל־הַמֶּלֶךְ
King to to from Rabshakeh Assyria the
Jerusalem Lachish of king

5945 1295 8585 5975 3515 2426 2396
חִזְקִיָּהוּ בְּחֵיל כָּבֵד וַיַּעֲמֹד בִּתְעָלַת הַבְּרֵכָה הָעֶלְיוֹנָה
,upper pool the the by he And .heavy with Hezekiah
of conduit stood army a

3 834 2518 1121 471 3318 3526 7704 4546
בִּמְסִלַּת שְׂדֵה כוֹבֵס׃ וַיֵּצֵא אֵלָיו אֶלְיָקִים בֶּן־חִלְקִיָּהוּ אֲשֶׁר
who ,Hilkiah son ,Eliakim to Then the field the in
(was) of him out came .fuller's of highway

who *was* over the house, and Shebna the scribe, and Asaph's son Joah, the recorder, came out to him. [4]And the chief of the cupbearers said to them, Say now to Hezekiah, The great king says this, the king of Assyria, What trust *is* this in which you trust? [5]I say, *Are* only words of the lips counsel and strength for war? Now, in whom have you trusted that you rebelled against me? [6]Behold, you trust on the staff of this broken reed, on Egypt—which *if* a man leans on it, it goes into his palm and pierces it—so is Pharaoh king of Egypt to all who trust in him. [7]But if you say to me, We trust in Jehovah our God; is it not He whose high places and altars Hezekiah has removed? And He said to Judah and Jerusalem, You shall worship before this altar. [8]Now, then, exchange pledges with my master the king of Assyria, and I will give you two thousand horses, if you are able to set riders on them. [9]How then will you turn away the face of one commander of the least of my master's servants, and put your trust in Egypt for chariotry and horsemen?

[10]And now have I come up against this land to destroy it without Jehovah? Jehovah said to me, Go up to this land and destroy it. [11]And Eliakim and Shebna and Joah said to the chief of the cupbearers, Please speak to your servants *in* Aramaic, for we hear. But do not speak to

4 עַל־הַבַּיִת וְשֶׁבְנָא הַסֹּפֵר וְיוֹאָח בֶּן־אָסָף הַמַּזְכִּיר׃ וַיֹּאמֶר
559 2142 623 1121 3098 5608 7644 1004
And said | the .recorder | Asaph | son of | and Joah | the ,scribe | and Shebna | the ,house | over

אֲלֵיהֶם רַבְשָׁקֵה אִמְרוּ־נָא אֶל־חִזְקִיָּהוּ כֹּה־אָמַר הַמֶּלֶךְ
4428 559 3541 2396 4994 559 7262
king the | says | Thus | ,Hezekiah | to | now | Say | ,Rabshakeh | them to

הַגָּדוֹל מֶלֶךְ אַשּׁוּר מָה הַבִּטָּחוֹן הַזֶּה אֲשֶׁר בָּטָחְתָּ׃
982 834 2088 986 4100 804 4428 1419
?trust you | which | this | trust (is) | What | ,Assyria | the of king | ,great

5 אָמַרְתִּי אַךְ־דְּבַר־שְׂפָתַיִם עֵצָה וּגְבוּרָה לַמִּלְחָמָה עַתָּה
6258 4421 1368 6098 8193 1697 389 559
Now | the ?battle for | and might | counsel | ,lips | words of | (Are) only | ,say I

6 עַל־מִי בָטַחְתָּ כִּי מָרַדְתָּ בִּי׃ הִנֵּה בָטַחְתָּ עַל־מִשְׁעֶנֶת
4938 982 2009 4775 982 4310
the of staff | on | you trust | ,Behold | against ?me | have you rebelled | that | you have trusted | whom on

הַקָּנֶה הָרָצוּץ הַזֶּה עַל־מִצְרַיִם אֲשֶׁר יִסָּמֵךְ אִישׁ עָלָיו וּבָא
935 3,76 5564 834 4714 2088 7533 7070
then comes it | ,it on | a man | (if) leans | ,which | —Egypt | on | ,this | broken | reed

בְכַפּוֹ וּנְקָבָהּ כֵּן פַּרְעֹה מֶלֶךְ־מִצְרַיִם לְכָל־הַבֹּטְחִים עָלָיו׃
982 3605 4714 4428 6547 5344 3709
on .him | who trust | all to | Egypt | king of | Pharaoh | So (is) | and .it pierces | his into palm

7 וְכִי־תֹאמַר אֵלַי אֶל־יְהוָה אֱלֹהֵינוּ בָּטָחְנוּ הֲלוֹא הוּא אֲשֶׁר
3808 834 982 430 3068 559
of whom | He | it Is not | we :trust | God our | Jehovah in | ,me to | you say | But if

הֵסִיר חִזְקִיָּהוּ אֶת־בָּמֹתָיו וְאֶת־מִזְבְּחֹתָיו וַיֹּאמֶר לִיהוּדָה
3063 559 4196 1116 2396 5493
Judah to | he And said | ?altars His | and | high His places | Hezekiah | has removed

8 וְלִירוּשָׁלִַם לִפְנֵי הַמִּזְבֵּחַ הַזֶּה תִּשְׁתַּחֲווּ׃ וְעַתָּה הִתְעָרֶב
6148 6258 7812 2088 4196 6440 3389
exchange ,pledges | Now ,then | shall you !worship | this | altar | Before | to and Jerusalem

נָא אֶת־אֲדֹנִי הַמֶּלֶךְ אַשּׁוּר וְאֶתְּנָה לְךָ אַלְפַּיִם סוּסִים אִם־
518 54:83 505 5414 804 4428 113 4994
if | ,horses | two thousand | to you | I and give will | ,Assyria | the of king | my lord | with | I ,pray

9 תּוּכַל לָתֶת לְךָ רֹכְבִים עֲלֵיהֶם׃ וְאֵיךְ תָּשִׁיב אֵת פְּנֵי
6440 7725 349 7392 5414 3201
the of face | you will away turn | How then | .them on | riders | for you | set to | are you able

פַּחַת אַחַד עַבְדֵי אֲדֹנִי הַקְּטַנִּים וַתִּבְטַח לְךָ עַל־מִצְרַיִם
4714 982 6996 113 5650 259 6346
Egypt | on | for you | trust and | ,least the | my master's | servants | one | governor of

10 לָרֶכֶב וּלְפָרָשִׁים׃ וְעַתָּה הֲמִבַּלְעֲדֵי יְהוָה עָלִיתִי עַל־
5927 3068 1107 6258 6571 7393
against | I have up come | Jehovah | without | ,now And | and ?horsemen | for chariotry

הָאָרֶץ הַזֹּאת לְהַשְׁחִיתָהּ יְהוָה אָמַר אֵלַי עֲלֵה אֶל־הָאָרֶץ
776 5927 559 3068 7843 2088 776
land | to | up Go | to me | said | Jehovah | destroy to ?it | this | land

11 הַזֹּאת וְהַשְׁחִיתָהּ׃ וַיֹּאמֶר אֶלְיָקִים וְשֶׁבְנָא וְיוֹאָח אֶל־
3098 7644 471 559 7843 2088
to | and Joah | and Shebna | Eliakim | Then said | destroy and .it | this

רַבְשָׁקֵה דַּבֶּר־נָא אֶל־עֲבָדֶיךָ אֲרָמִית כִּי שֹׁמְעִים אֲנָחְנוּ
8085 3066 5650 4994 1696 7262
.we | hear | for | ,Aramaic in | your servants | to | ,please | ,Speak | Rab- ,shakeh

us *in* Judean, in the ears of the people on the wall. [12]But the chief of the cupbearers said, Has my master sent me to your master and to you to speak these words? Is it not on the men who sit on the wall, to eat their own dung, and to drink the water of their feet with you? [13]And the chief of the cupbearers stood and cried with a loud voice *in* Judean, and said, Hear the words of the great king, the king of Assyria. [14]So says the king, Do not let Hezekiah deceive you, for he will not be able to save you. [15]And let not Hezekiah make you trust in Jehovah, saying, Jehovah will surely save us; this city shall not be delivered into the hand of the king of Assyria. [16]Do not listen to Hezekiah. For the king of Assyria says this, Make peace with me and come out to me. Then let each eat *of* his own vine, and each of his own fig-tree, and each drink the waters *of* his own well, [17]until I come and take you to a land like your own land, a land of grain and new wine, a land of bread and vineyards. [18]*Let* not Hezekiah persuade you, saying, Jehovah will deliver us. Have the gods of the nations delivered a man of his land from the king of Assyria's hand? [19]Where *are* the gods of Hamath, and Arpad? Where are the gods of Sepharvaim? And when have they delivered out of my hand? [20]Who among all the gods of these lands has delivered their land out of

2346 834 5971 241 3064 1696 408
וְאַל־תְּדַבֵּר אֵלֵינוּ יְהוּדִית בְּאָזְנֵי הָעָם אֲשֶׁר עַל־הַחוֹמָה׃
the on who the the in in us to do But
.wall (are) people of ears ,Judean speak not

1696 113 7971 113 7262 559
12 וַיֹּאמֶר רַבְשָׁקֵה הַאֶל אֲדֹנֶיךָ וְאֵלֶיךָ שְׁלָחַנִי אֲדֹנִי לְדַבֵּר
to my sent to and your Has ,Rabshakeh But
speak master me you master to said

5921 3427 582 3808 428 1697
אֶת־הַדְּבָרִים הָאֵלֶּה הֲלֹא עַל־הָאֲנָשִׁים הַיֹּשְׁבִים עַל־
on sit who men the on it Is ?these words
not

7890 8354 2716 398 2346
הַחוֹמָה לֶאֱכֹל אֶת־חֲרָאֵיהֶם וְלִשְׁתּוֹת אֶת־שֵׁינֵיהֶם עִמָּכֶם׃
with their of water to and own their eat to the
?you feet drink dung ,wall

8085 559 3066 1419 6963 7121 7262 5975
13 וַיַּעֲמֹד רַבְשָׁקֵה וַיִּקְרָא בְקוֹל־גָּדוֹל יְהוּדִית וַיֹּאמֶר שִׁמְעוּ
Hear ,said and (in) loud a with and Rabshakeh Then
Judean voice called stood

4428 559 3541 804 4428 1419 4428 1697
14 אֶת־דִּבְרֵי הַמֶּלֶךְ הַגָּדוֹל מֶלֶךְ אַשּׁוּר׃ כֹּה אָמַר הַמֶּלֶךְ
,king the says Thus .Assyria the ,great king the the
of king of words

5337 3201 3808 2396 5377 408
15 אַל־יַשִּׁא לָכֶם חִזְקִיָּהוּ כִּי לֹא־יוּכַל לְהַצִּיל אֶתְכֶם׃ וְאַל־
And .you save to will He not for ,Hezekiah you let Do not
not able be deceive

3068 5337 559 3068 2396 982
יַבְטַח אֶתְכֶם חִזְקִיָּהוּ אֶל־יְהוָה לֵאמֹר הַצֵּל יַצִּילֵנוּ יְהוָה
,Jehovah will Surely ,saying ,Jehovah in Hezekiah you let
us save trust make

8085 408 804 4428 3027 2088 5892 5414 3808
16 לֹא תִנָּתֵן הָעִיר הַזֹּאת בְּיַד מֶלֶךְ אַשּׁוּר׃ אַל־תִּשְׁמְעוּ
do Not .Assyria the the into this city be shall not
listen of king of hand delivered

1293 6213 804 4428 559 2396
אֶל־חִזְקִיָּהוּ כִּי כֹה אָמַר הַמֶּלֶךְ אַשּׁוּר עֲשׂוּ־אִתִּי בְרָכָה
a with Make ,Assyria the says thus for ;Hezekiah to
,blessing me of king

4325 376 8354 8384 1612 376 398 3318
וּצְאוּ אֵלַי וְאִכְלוּ אִישׁ־גַּפְנוֹ וְאִישׁ תְּאֵנָתוֹ וּשְׁתוּ אִישׁ מֵי־
the each and his (of) and his (of) each let then ;me to and
of waters drink ,tree fig each ,vine man eat out come

776 776 776 3947 935 5704 953
17 בוֹרוֹ׃ עַד־בֹּאִי וְלָקַחְתִּי אֶתְכֶם אֶל־אֶרֶץ כְּאַרְצְכֶם אֶרֶץ
a your like a to you take and I until his
of land ,land own land come ,well

2396 5496 6435 3754 3899 776 8492 1715
18 דָּגָן וְתִירוֹשׁ אֶרֶץ לֶחֶם וּכְרָמִים׃ פֶּן־יַסִּית אֶתְכֶם חִזְקִיָּהוּ
,Hezekiah you persuade Lest and bread land a new and grain
.vineyards of ,wine

776 376 1471 430 5337 3068 3068 559
לֵאמֹר יְהוָה יַצִּילֵנוּ הַהִצִּילוּ אֱלֹהֵי הַגּוֹיִם אִישׁ אֶת־אַרְצוֹ
his man a the gods the Have deliver will Jehovah ,saying
land of nations of delivered .us

430 335 774 2574 430 335 804 4428 3027
19 מִיַּד מֶלֶךְ אַשּׁוּר׃ אַיֵּה אֱלֹהֵי חֲמָת וְאַרְפָּד אַיֵּה אֱלֹהֵי
the Where and Hamath the Where ?Assyria's the from
of gods (are) ?Arpad of gods (are) of king hand

430 3605 4310 3027 8111 5337 5617
20 סְפַרְוָיִם וְכִי־הִצִּילוּ אֶת־שֹׁמְרוֹן מִיָּדִי׃ מִי בְּכָל־אֱלֹהֵי
the among Who my from Samaria they have And Shephar-
of gods all (is) ?hand delivered when ?vaim

5337 3027 776 5337 834 428 776
הָאֲרָצוֹת הָאֵלֶּה אֲשֶׁר־הִצִּילוּ אֶת־אַרְצָם מִיָּדִי כִּי־יַצִּיל
should that from their has that ,these lands
deliver ,hand my land delivered

my hand, that Jehovah should keep Jerusalem out of my hand?

21But they were silent, and did not answer him a word; for this was the king's order, saying, Do not answer him. 22And Eliakim, Hilkiah's son who *was* over the house, and Shebna the scribe, and Asaph's son Joah, the recorder, came to Hezekiah *with their* garments torn. And *they* reported to him the words of the chief of cupbearers.

1697 6030 3808 2790 3027 3389 3068
21 יְהוָה אֶת־יְרוּשָׁלִַם מִיָּדִי׃ וַיַּחֲרִישׁוּ וְלֹא־עָנוּ אֹתוֹ דָּבָר
a him answered and they But my from Jerusalem Jehovah
,word not ,quiet were ?hand

471 935 6030 3808 559 4428 4687
22 כִּי־מִצְוַת הַמֶּלֶךְ הִיא לֵאמֹר לֹא תַעֲנֻהוּ׃ וַיָּבֹא אֶלְיָקִים
Eliakim Then Answer not ,saying it the command for
came .him (was) king's

1121 3098 5608 7644 1004 834 2518 1121
בֶּן־חִלְקִיָּהוּ אֲשֶׁר־עַל־הַבַּיִת וְשֶׁבְנָא הַסֹּפֵר וְיוֹאָח בֶּן
son and the and the over who ,Hilkiah son
of Joah scribe Shebna ,house (was) of

5046 899 7167 2396 2142 623
אָסָף הַמַּזְכִּיר אֶל־חִזְקִיָּהוּ קְרוּעֵי בְגָדִים וַיַּגִּידוּ לוֹ אֵת
to and ,garments (with) ,Hezekiah to the ,Asaph
him reported torn recorder

7262 1697
דִּבְרֵי רַבְשָׁקֵה׃
.Rabshakeh's words

CAP. XXXVII לז

CHAPTER 37

CHAPTER 37

1And it happened when king Hezekiah heard, he tore his garments and was covered with sackcloth. And he went into the house of Jehovah. 2And he sent Eliakim, who *was* over the house, and Shebna the scribe, and the elders of the priests, covered with sackcloth, to Isaiah the prophet, the son of Amoz. 3And they said to him, So says Hezekiah, This day *is* a day of trouble, and reproach, and contempt. For sons have come to the breach, and there is no strength to give birth. 4It may be Jehovah your God will hear the words of the chief of the cupbearers, whom his master the king of Assyria has sent to reproach the living God, and rebuke against the words which Jehovah your God has heard. And you shall lift up prayer for the remnant that is found.

5So the servants of king Hezekiah came to Isaiah. 6And Isaiah said to them, You shall say this to your master, So says Jehovah: Do not fear the words

8242 3680 899 7167 2396 4428 8085 1961
1 וַיְהִי כִּשְׁמֹעַ הַמֶּלֶךְ חִזְקִיָּהוּ וַיִּקְרַע אֶת־בְּגָדָיו וַיִּתְכַּס בַּשָּׂק
with was and his he that ,Hezekiah King when And
,sackcloth covered garments tore heard ,was it

1004 834 471 7971 3068 1004 935
2 וַיָּבֹא בֵּית יְהוָה׃ וַיִּשְׁלַח אֶת־אֶלְיָקִים אֲשֶׁר־עַל־הַבַּיִת
the over who ,Eliakim he And .Jehovah the he and
,house (was) sent of house entered

8242 3680 3548 2205 5608 7644
וְאֵת ׀ שֶׁבְנָא הַסּוֹפֵר וְאֵת זִקְנֵי הַכֹּהֲנִים מִתְכַּסִּים בַּשַּׂקִּים
with covered the the and the Shebna and
,sackcloth priests of elders ,scribe

559 3541 559 5030 531 1121 3470
3 אֶל־יְשַׁעְיָהוּ בֶן־אָמוֹץ הַנָּבִיא׃ וַיֹּאמְרוּ אֵלָיו כֹּה אָמַר
says Thus ,him to they And the ,Amoz the Isaiah to
said .prophet of son

1121 935 2088 3117 5007 8433 6864 3117 2396
חִזְקִיָּהוּ יוֹם־צָרָה וְתוֹכֵחָה וּנְאָצָה הַיּוֹם הַזֶּה כִּי־בָאוּ בָנִים
sons have For !this (is) and and trouble A ,Hezekiah
come day ,contempt reproach of day

430 3068 8085 3205 369 3581 4866 5704
4 עַד־מַשְׁבֵּר וְכֹחַ אַיִן לְלֵדָה׃ אוּלַי יִשְׁמַע יְהוָה אֱלֹהֶיךָ
your Jehovah will may it give to not and the to
God hear be .birth is strength ;breach

2778 113 804 4428 7971 834 7262 1697
אֵת ׀ דִּבְרֵי רַבְשָׁקֵה אֲשֶׁר שְׁלָחוֹ מֶלֶךְ־אַשּׁוּר ׀ אֲדֹנָיו לְחָרֵף
to his Assyria the has whom Rabshakeh the
reproach ,master of king ,him sent of words

430 3068 8085 834 1697 3198 2416 430
אֱלֹהִים חַי וְהוֹכִיחַ בַּדְּבָרִים אֲשֶׁר שָׁמַע יְהוָה אֱלֹהֶיךָ
your Jehovah has which the against and living the
God heard words rebuke God

5650 935 4672 7611 5704 8605 5375
5 וְנָשָׂאתָ תְפִלָּה בְּעַד הַשְּׁאֵרִית הַנִּמְצָאָה׃ וַיָּבֹאוּ עַבְדֵי
the So is that the for prayer you and
of servants came .found remnant up lift shall

3541 3470 430 559 3470 2396 4428
6 הַמֶּלֶךְ חִזְקִיָּהוּ אֶל־יְשַׁעְיָהוּ׃ וַיֹּאמֶר אֲלֵיהֶם יְשַׁעְיָהוּ כֹּה
Thus ,Isaiah them to said And .Isaiah to Hezekiah King

6440 3372 408 3068 559 3541 113 559
תֹאמְרוּן אֶל־אֲדֹנֵיכֶם כֹּה ׀ אָמַר יְהוָה אַל־תִּירָא מִפְּנֵי
from Do not ,Jehovah says Thus your to shall you
before fear ,master say

which you have heard, with which the followers of the king of Assyria have blasphemed Me. [7]Behold, I will send a spirit into him, and he shall hear a rumor, and return to his own land. And I will cause him to fall by the sword in his own land.

[8]So the chief of the cupbearers returned and found the king of Assyria warring against Libnah; for he had heard that he had set out from Lachish. [9]And he heard about Tirhakah *the* king of Ethiopia, saying, He has come out to fight with you. And he heard and sent messengers to Hezekiah, saying, [10]So you shall say to Hezekiah, king of Judah, saying, Do not let your God in whom you trust deceive you, saying, Jerusalem shall not be delivered into the king of Assyria's hand. [11]Behold, you have heard what the kings of Assyria have done to all lands, to destroy them utterly. And shall you be saved? [12]Have the gods of the nations saved those whom my fathers have destroyed, Gozan, and Haran, and Rezeph, and the sons of Eden in Telassar? [13]Where *is* Hamath's king, and Arpad's king, and the king of the city of Sepharvaim, Hena, and Ivah?

[14]And Hezekiah received the letter from the hand of the couriers, and read it. Then Hezekiah went up *to* the house of Jehovah and spread it before Jehovah. [15]And Hezekiah prayed to Jehovah, saying, [16]O Jehovah of hosts, God of Israel, who dwells *between* the cherubs, You *are* He, God, You alone to all the kingdoms of the earth. You have made the heavens and

804 4428 5288 1442 834 8085 834 1697
הַדְּבָרִים אֲשֶׁר שָׁמַעְתָּ אֲשֶׁר גִּדְּפוּ נַעֲרֵי מֶלֶךְ־אַשּׁוּר אוֹתִי׃
.Me Assyria the of king the of boys blasphemed with which have you heard which words the

5307 776 7725 8052 8085 7307 5414 2009
7 הִנְנִי נוֹתֵן בּוֹ רוּחַ וְשָׁמַע שְׁמוּעָה וְשָׁב אֶל־אַרְצוֹ וְהִפַּלְתִּיו
will I And fall him make his .land to and return ,report a he and hear shall a into ;spirit him give ,Behold I

804 4428 4672 7262 7725 776 2719
8 בַּחֶרֶב בְּאַרְצוֹ׃ וַיָּשָׁב רַבְשָׁקֵה וַיִּמְצָא אֶת־מֶלֶךְ אַשּׁוּר
Assyria the of king and found Rabshakeh So returned his in .land the by sword

8085 3923 5265 8085 3841 3898
9 נִלְחָם עַל־לִבְנָה כִּי שָׁמַע כִּי נָסַע מִלָּכִישׁ׃ וַיִּשְׁמַע עַל־
about he And heard from .Lachish had he out set that had he heard for ;Libnah against fighting

7971 8085 3898 3318/559 3568 4428 8640
תִּרְהָקָה מֶלֶךְ־כּוּשׁ לֵאמֹר יָצָא לְהִלָּחֵם אִתָּךְ וַיִּשְׁמַע וַיִּשְׁלַח
sent and he And heard with .you fight to has He out come ,saying ,Ethiopia king of Tirhakah

2396 559 559 2396 4397
10 מַלְאָכִים אֶל־חִזְקִיָּהוּ לֵאמֹר׃ כֹּה תֹאמְרוּן אֶל־חִזְקִיָּהוּ
Hezekiah to shall you say So ,saying ,Hezekiah to messengers

982 834 430 5377 408 559 3063 4428
מֶלֶךְ־יְהוּדָה לֵאמֹר אַל־יַשִּׁאֲךָ אֱלֹהֶיךָ אֲשֶׁר אַתָּה בּוֹטֵחַ
trust you whom your God let Do you deceive not ,saying ,Judah King of

2009 804 4428 3027 3389 5414 3808 559
11 בּוֹ לֵאמֹר לֹא תִנָּתֵן יְרוּשָׁלַםִ בְּיַד מֶלֶךְ אַשּׁוּר׃ הִנֵּה
,Behold .Assyria's the of king into hand Jerusalem be shall delivered Not ,saying in ,Him

776 3605 804 4428 6213 834 8085
אַתָּה שָׁמַעְתָּ אֲשֶׁר עָשׂוּ מַלְכֵי אַשּׁוּר לְכָל־הָאֲרָצוֹת
the ,lands to all Assyria the of kings have done what have heard you

1471 430 5337 5337 2763
12 לְהַחֲרִימָם וְאַתָּה תִּנָּצֵל׃ הַהִצִּילוּ אוֹתָם אֱלֹהֵי הַגּוֹיִם
the nations the of gods ,them Have delivered shall ?delivered be you and to utterly ;them destroy

5729 1121 7530 2771 1470 1 7843 834
אֲשֶׁר־הִשְׁחִיתוּ אֲבוֹתַי אֶת־גּוֹזָן וְאֶת־חָרָן וְרֶצֶף וּבְנֵי־עֶדֶן
Eden of and sons the and Rezeph Haran and Gozan my :fathers have destroyed whom

5892 4428 774 4428 2574 4428 8515 834
13 אֲשֶׁר בִּתְלַשָּׂר׃ אַיֵּה מֶלֶךְ־חֲמָת וּמֶלֶךְ אַרְפָּד וּמֶלֶךְ לָעִיר
the of city the and king ,Arpad the And of king ?Hamath the of king Where (is) in ?Telassar who (were)

3027 5612 2396 3947 5755 2012 5617
14 סְפַרְוָיִם הֵנַע וְעִוָּה׃ וַיִּקַּח חִזְקִיָּהוּ אֶת־הַסְּפָרִים מִיַּד
the from of hand the letters Hezekiah And received and ?Ivah ,Hena Sepharvaim

2396 6566 3068 1004 5927 7121 4397
הַמַּלְאָכִים וַיִּקְרָאֵהוּ וַיַּעַל בֵּית יְהוָה וַיִּפְרְשֵׂהוּ חִזְקִיָּהוּ
Hezekiah spread and it ,Jehovah the of house (to) he And up went read and .it the ,messengers

3068 559 3068 2396 6419 3028 6440
15
16 לִפְנֵי יְהוָה׃ וַיִּתְפַּלֵּל חִזְקִיָּהוּ אֶל־יְהוָה לֵאמֹר׃ יְהוָה
Jehovah of ,saying ,Jehovah to Hezekiah And prayed .Jehovah before

430 3742 3427 3478 430 6635
צְבָאוֹת אֱלֹהֵי יִשְׂרָאֵל יֹשֵׁב הַכְּרֻבִים אַתָּה־הוּא הָאֱלֹהִים
,God He You (are) the ,cherubs dwelling (between) ,Israel God of ,hosts

8065 6213 776 4467 3605 905
לְבַדְּךָ לְכֹל מַמְלְכוֹת הָאָרֶץ אַתָּה עָשִׂיתָ אֶת־הַשָּׁמַיִם
the heavens have made You the :earth the of kingdoms all to You ,alone

the earth. 17 Bow down Your ear, O Jehovah, and hear. Open Your eye, O Jehovah, and see; and hear all the words of Sennacherib which he has sent, to reproach the living God. 18 Truly, O Jehovah, the kings of Assyria have crushed all the lands, and their land, 19 and have given their gods into the fire—for they *were* not gods, only the work of men's hands, wood and stone; so they have destroyed them. 20 And now, O Jehovah our God, save us from his hand, so that all the kingdoms of the earth may know that You *are* Jehovah, You alone.

21 And Isaiah the son of Amoz sent to Hezekiah, saying, So says Jehovah, God of Israel, Because you have prayed to Me against Sennacherib *the* king of Assyria, 22 this *is* the word Jehovah has spoken about him: The virgin, the daughter of Zion, has despised you, laughing you to scorn; the daughter of Jerusalem has shaken the head behind you. 23 Whom have you mocked and reviled? And against whom have you lifted your voice, and lifted your eyes on high? Against the Holy One of Israel! 24 By your servants, you have mocked the Lord, and said, By my many chariots I have come up *to* the tops of mountains, the sides of Lebanon; and I will cut down its tall cedars, its choice fir trees; and I will go to its greatest height, the forest of its fruitful field. 25 I have dug and drunk water; and I have dried up the streams of Egypt with the sole of my feet.

26 Have you not heard it from afar? I made it from days of old, even I formed it.

5869 3068 6491 8085 241 3068 5186 776
17 וְאֶת־הָאָרֶץ׃ הַטֵּה יְהוָה ׀ אָזְנְךָ וּשְׁמָע פְּקַח יְהוָה עֵינְךָ
Your O ,open and Your O ,Incline the and
,eye ,Jehovah ;hear ear ,Jehovah .earth

2778 7971 834 5576 1697 3605 8085 7200
וּרְאֵה וּשְׁמַע אֵת כָּל־דִּבְרֵי סַנְחֵרִיב אֲשֶׁר שָׁלַח לְחָרֵף
to has he which Sennacherib the all and and
reproach sent of words hear ;see

3605 804 4428 2717 3068 551 2416 430
18 אֱלֹהִים חָי׃ אָמְנָם יְהוָה הֶחֱרִיבוּ מַלְכֵי אַשּׁוּר אֶת־כָּל־
all Assyria the laid have O ,Truly .living the
of kings waste ,Jehovah God

3808 784 430 5414 776 776
19 הָאֲרָצוֹת וְאֶת־אַרְצָם׃ וְנָתֹן אֶת־אֱלֹהֵיהֶם בָּאֵשׁ כִּי לֹא
not for into their have And their and the
—fire the gods given .land ,lands

6 68 6086 120 3027 4639 430
אֱלֹהִים הֵמָּה כִּי אִם־מַעֲשֵׂה יְדֵי־אָדָם עֵץ וָאֶבֶן וַיְאַבְּדוּם׃
they so and wood ,man the the only but they gods
.them destroyed ;stone of hands of work ,(were)

4467 3605 3045 3027 3467 430 3068 6258
20 וְעַתָּה יְהוָה אֱלֹהֵינוּ הוֹשִׁיעֵנוּ מִיָּדוֹ וְיֵדְעוּ כָּל־מַמְלְכוֹת
kingdoms the all that so his from save our O And
of know may ,hand us ,God Jehovah ,now

531 1121 3470 7971 905 3068 776
21 הָאָרֶץ כִּי־אַתָּה יְהוָה לְבַדֶּךָ׃ וַיִּשְׁלַח יְשַׁעְיָהוּ בֶן־אָמוֹץ
Amoz the Isaiah sent And You ,Jehovah You that the
of son .alone (are) earth

834 3478 430 3068 559 559 2396
אֶל־חִזְקִיָּהוּ לֵאמֹר כֹּה־אָמַר יְהוָה אֱלֹהֵי יִשְׂרָאֵל אֲשֶׁר
Because .Israel God Jehovah says Thus ,saying Hezekiah to
of

834 1697/2088 804 4428 5576 6419
22 הִתְפַּלַּלְתָּ אֵלַי אֶל־סַנְחֵרִיב מֶלֶךְ אַשּׁוּר׃ זֶה הַדָּבָר אֲשֶׁר־
which the this ,Assyria king Sennacherib about to have you
word (is) of Me prayed

6726/1323 1330 3932 959 3068 1696
דִּבֶּר יְהוָה עָלָיו בָּזָה לְךָ לָעֲגָה לְךָ בְּתוּלַת בַּת־צִיּוֹן
;Zion the the ,you laughing ,you Has against Jehovah has
of daughter ,virgin scorn to despised :him spoken

2778 2778 4310 3389 1323 5128 7218 310
23 אַחֲרֶיךָ רֹאשׁ הֵנִיעָה בַּת יְרוּשָׁלִָם׃ אֶת־מִי חֵרַפְתָּ וְגִדַּפְתָּ
and you have Whom .Jerusalem the has (her) behind
?reviled mocked of daughter shaken head you

6918 5869 4791 5375 6963 7311 4310
וְעַל־מִי הֲרִימוֹתָה קּוֹל וַתִּשָּׂא מָרוֹם עֵינֶיךָ אֶל־קְדוֹשׁ
Holy the Against your on and your have you whom And
of One ?eyes high lifted ,voice raised against

7393 7230 559 136 2778 5650 3027 3478
24 יִשְׂרָאֵל׃ בְּיַד עֲבָדֶיךָ חֵרַפְתָּ ׀ אֲדֹנָי וַתֹּאמֶר בְּרֹב רִכְבִּי
my By and the have you your the By !Israel
chariots many said Lord mocked servants of hand

730 6967 3772 3844 3411 2022 4791 5927
אֲנִי עָלִיתִי מְרוֹם הָרִים יַרְכְּתֵי לְבָנוֹן וְאֶכְרֹת קוֹמַת אֲרָזָיו
its tall I and ;Lebanon the ,mountains the (to) have I
,cedars down cut of sides of height up come

3759 3293 7093 2022 935 1265 4005
25 מִבְחַר בְּרֹשָׁיו וְאָבוֹא מְרוֹם קִצּוֹ יַעַר כַּרְמִלּוֹ׃ אֲנִי
I fruit- its the its the (to) I and fir its choice the
.field ful of forest ,end of height go will ;trees of

4692 2975 3605 6471 3709 2717 4325 8354 6979
קַרְתִּי וְשָׁתִיתִי מָיִם וְאַחְרִב בְּכַף־פְּעָמַי כֹּל יְאֹרֵי מָצוֹר׃
.Egypt the all my the with have and ,water drunk and have
of streams feet of sole up dried dug

3335 6924 3117 6213 7350 8085 3808
26 הֲלוֹא־שָׁמַעְתָּ לְמֵרָחוֹק אוֹתָהּ עָשִׂיתִי מִימֵי קֶדֶם וִיצַרְתִּיהָ
I even old from made I it ?afar from heard you not Have
?it formed of days

Now I have caused it to come, and you are to cause to crash fortified cities *into* heaps, ruins.
27And their inhabitants were short of hand, dismayed and ashamed. They were as the field grass and the green herbs; *like* the grass of the housetops, even blasted before it has risen.
28But I know your sitting down, and your going out, and your coming in, and your raging against Me.
29Because of your raging against Me, and your arrogance has come up to My ears; and I will put My hook in your nose, and My bridle in your lips; and I will turn you back by the way you came in.

30And this *shall be* the sign to you: You shall eat self-sown grain *this* year; and the second year, that which springs up; and in the third year you shall sow and reap, and plant vineyards, and eat their fruit.
31The remnant of the house of Judah that has escaped shall again take root downward, and it makes fruit upward.
32For a remnant shall go out of Jerusalem, and the escaped ones out of Mount Zion; the zeal of Jehovah of hosts shall do this.
33So Jehovah says this to the king of Assyria, He shall not come into this city, nor shoot an arrow there, nor come before it *with* a shield, nor pour out a siege-mound on it.
34He shall return by the same way that he came in, and he shall not come into this city, says Jehovah.
35For I will defend over this city to save it, for My own sake, and for My servant David's sake.

36Then the Angel of Jehovah went out and struck a hundred and eighty-five thousand in the camp of Assyria. And they rose early in the morning; and, behold! They *were* all dead corpses.
37And Sennacherib, king of Assyria,

1219 5892 5327 1530 7582 1961 935 6528
עתה הבאתיה ותהי להשאות גלים נצים ערים בצרות׃
.fortified cities ,ruins (into) cause to you and caused have I Now
heaps crash to are come to it

27 1877 3419 7704 6212 1961 954 2865 3027 7116 3427
וישביהן קצרי־יד חתו ובשו היו עשב שדה וירק דשא
,herb the and the grass They and were hand of short their So
green field of were ,ashamed ,dismayed inhabitants

28 935 3318 3427 7054 6440 7709 1406 2682
חציר גגות ושדמה לפני קמה׃ ושבתך וצאתך ובואך
your and your and your But has it before and house- (like)
,coming going sitting .risen blasted ,tops of grass

29 7600 7264 7264 3045
ידעתי ואת התרגזך אלי׃ יען התרגזך אלי ושאננך
your and against your Because against your and ,know I
complacency ,Me raging of .me raging

7725 8193 4965 639 2397 7760 241 5927
עלה באזני ושמתי חחי באפך ומתגי בשפתיך והשיבתיך
will I and your in My and your in My therefore My in has
back you turn ;lips bridle nose hook put will I ,ears up come

30 5599 8141 398 226 2088 935 834 1870
בדרך אשר־באת בה׃ וזה־לך האות אכול השנה ספיח
self-sown (this) eat the to And in you which the by
;grain year :sign you (is) this .it came way

7114 2232 7992 8141 7823 8145 8141
ובשנה השנית שחיס ובשנה השלישית זרעו וקצרו
,reap and sow third in and which that second in and
year the ;up springs year the

31 3063 1004 6413 3254 6529 398 3754 5193
ונטעו כרמים ואכול פרים׃ ויספה פליטת בית־יהודה
Judah the the shall And their eat and vineyards and
of house of escaped add .fruit plant

32 3389 4605 6529 6213 4295 8328 7604
הנשארה שרש למטה ועשה פרי למעלה׃ כי מירושלם
of out For .upward fruit it and down- root that
Jerusalem makes ,ward remains

6635 3068 7068 6726 2022 6413 7611 3318
תצא שארית ופליטה מהר ציון קנאת יהוה צבאות
hosts Jehovah the :Zion of out the and a shall
of of zeal Mount escaped ,remnant out go

33 804 4428 3068 559 3651 2088 6213
תעשה־זאת׃ לכן כה־אמר יהוה אל־מלך אשור
,Assyria the to Jehovah says thus ,Therefore .this shall
of king do

6923 3808 2671 8033 3384 3808 2088 5892 935/3808
לא יבוא אל־העיר הזאת ולא־יורה שם חץ ולא־יקדמנה
come will and an there shoot and ,this city into shall He not
it before not ,arrow not come

34 7725 935 834 1870 5550 5927 8210 3808 4043
מגן ולא־ישפך עליה סללה׃ בדרך אשר־בא בה ישוב
shall He in he that the By seige- a upon will he and a
;return it came way mound it out pour not ,shield

35 5892 1598 3068 5002 935 3808 2088 5892
ואל־העיר הזאת לא יבוא נאם־יהוה׃ וגנותי על־העיר
city over I For .Jehovah states shall he not this city and
defend will ,come into

36 4397 3318 5650 1732 4616 4616 3467 2088
הזאת להושיעה למעני ולמען דוד עבדי׃ ויצא | מלאך
the went Then My David for and My for save to ,this
of angel out .servant of sake the sake ,it

505 2568 8084 3967 804 4264 5221 3068
יהוה ויכה במחנה אשור מאה ושמנים וחמשה אלף
.thousand five and and a Assyria the in and Jehovah
eighty hundred of camp struck

37 7971 5265 4191 6297 3605 2009 1242 7925
וישכימו בבקר והנה כלם פגרים מתים׃ ויסע וילך
and set So .dead (were) they and the in they And
went out corpses all ,behold ,morning early rose

set out, and went and returned; and he lived at Nineveh. [38]And it happened *as* he was worshiping *in* the house of his god Nisroch, even his sons Adrammelech and Sharezer struck him with the sword. And they escaped *into* the land of Ararat. And his son Esarhaddon reigned in his place.

1961 5210 3427 804 44:28 5576 7725
38 וַיָּשָׁב סַנְחֵרִיב מֶלֶךְ־אַשּׁוּר וַיֵּשֶׁב בְּנִינְוֵה׃ וַיְהִי הוּא
he And in he and ,Assyria the Sennacherib and
,was it .Nineveh lived of king ,returned

1121 8272 1146 430 5268 1004 7812
מִשְׁתַּחֲוֶה בֵּית ׀ נִסְרֹךְ אֱלֹהָיו וְאַדְרַמֶּלֶךְ וְשַׂרְאֶצֶר בָּנָיו
his and and his Nisroch the (in) was
,sons ,Sharezer Adrammelech ,god of house worshiping

634 4427 780 776 4422 2719 5221
הִכֻּהוּ בַחֶרֶב וְהֵמָּה נִמְלְטוּ אֶרֶץ אֲרָרָט וַיִּמְלֹךְ אֵסַר־חַדֹּן
Esarhaddon And .Ararat the (to) escaped And the with struck
reigned of land they .sword him

8478 1121
בְּנוֹ תַּחְתָּיו׃
his in his
.place son

CAP. XXXVIII לח

CHAPTER 38

CHAPTER 38

[1]In those days Hezekiah was sick to death. And Isaiah the son of Amoz, the prophet, came to him and said to him, So says Jehovah, Command your house, for you are dying, and shall not live. [2]And Hezekiah turned his face to the wall and prayed to Jehovah, [3]and said, O Jehovah, I beg You to remember now that I have walked before You in truth and with a whole heart; and I have done *that which is* good in Your eyes. And Hezekiah wept *with* a great weeping. [4]Then the word of Jehovah was to Isaiah, saying, [5]Go and say to Hezekiah, So says Jehovah the God of your father David, I have heard your prayer; I have seen your tears. Behold, I will add fifteen years to your days. [6]And I will deliver you and this city out of the king of Assyria's palm. And I will shield over this city. [7]So this *shall be* the sign to you from Jehovah, that Jehovah shall do this thing that He has spoken: [8]Behold, I will bring back the shadow of the steps which has gone

34:70 935 4194 2396 24:70 3117
1 בַּיָּמִים הָהֵם חָלָה חִזְקִיָּהוּ לָמוּת וַיָּבוֹא אֵלָיו יְשַׁעְיָהוּ
Isaiah to And .death to Hezekiah was those in And
him came sick days

10:04 6680 3068 559 559 5030 531 1121
בֶּן־אָמוֹץ הַנָּבִיא וַיֹּאמֶר אֵלָיו כֹּה־אָמַר יְהוָה צַו לְבֵיתֶךָ
your Com- ,Jehovah says Thus to he and the ,Amoz the
,house mand ,him said ,prophet of son

7023 6440 2396 5432 2421 38:08 4191
2 כִּי מֵת אַתָּה וְלֹא תִחְיֶה׃ וַיַּסֵּב חִזְקִיָּהוּ פָּנָיו אֶל־הַקִּיר
the to his Hezekiah Then shall and ,you are for
,wall face turned .live not dying

2142 3068 577 559 3068 6419
3 וַיִּתְפַּלֵּל אֶל־יְהוָה׃ וַיֹּאמַר אָנָּה יְהוָה זְכָר־נָא אֵת אֲשֶׁר
that ,now re- ,Jehovah beg I ,said and ,Jehovah to and
member ,You prayed

6213 5869 2896 3820 571 6440 1980
הִתְהַלַּכְתִּי לְפָנֶיךָ בֶּאֱמֶת וּבְלֵב שָׁלֵם וְהַטּוֹב בְּעֵינֶיךָ עָשִׂיתִי
have I Your in and ,whole with and truth in before have I
.done eyes good the heart a You about walked

3470 30:68 1697 1961 1419 1065 2396 1058
4 וַיֵּבְךְּ חִזְקִיָּהוּ בְּכִי גָדוֹל׃ וַיְהִי דְּבַר־יְהוָה אֶל־יְשַׁעְיָהוּ
,Isaiah to Jehovah the Then .great a Hezekiah And
of word was weeping wept

430 3068 559 3541 23:96 559 1980 559
5 לֵאמֹר׃ הָלוֹךְ וְאָמַרְתָּ אֶל־חִזְקִיָּהוּ כֹּה־אָמַר יְהוָה אֱלֹהֵי
the Jehovah says Thus ,Hezekian to say and Go ,saying
of God

2009 1832 7200 8605 8085 1 1732
דָּוִד אָבִיךָ שָׁמַעְתִּי אֶת־תְּפִלָּתֶךָ רָאִיתִי אֶת־דִּמְעָתֶךָ הִנְנִי
Behold your have I your have I your David
I .tears seen ;prayer heard ,father

804 44:28 3709 8141 624 0 2568 31:17 3254
6 יוֹסִף עַל־יָמֶיךָ חֲמֵשׁ עֶשְׂרֵה שָׁנָה׃ וּמִכַּף מֶלֶךְ־אַשּׁוּר
Assyria the from And .years fifteen your to will
of king of palm the days add

1961 5892 5921 1598 2088 5892 5337
7 אַצִּילְךָ וְאֵת הָעִיר הַזֹּאת וְגַנּוֹתִי עַל־הָעִיר הַזֹּאת׃ וְזֶה
this And .this city over I And .this city and will I
(be shall) defend will you deliver

2088 1697 3068 6213 3068 226
לְּךָ הָאוֹת מֵאֵת יְהוָה אֲשֶׁר יַעֲשֶׂה יְהוָה אֶת־הַדָּבָר הַזֶּה
this thing Jehovah do will that Jehovah from sign the to
you

3381 834 4609 6738 7725 2009 1696
8 אֲשֶׁר דִּבֵּר׃ הִנְנִי מֵשִׁיב אֶת־צֵל הַמַּעֲלוֹת אֲשֶׁר יָרְדָה
gone has which the the bring ,Behold has He which
down ,steps of shadow back I :spoken

down in the steps of Ahaz with the sun, backward ten steps. And the sun went back ten steps, by the steps which it had gone down!

[9]The writing of Hezekiah king of Judah when he was sick and had revived from his illness: [10]I said in the pause of my days, Let me go to the gates of Sheol; I am deprived of the rest of my years. [11]I said, I shall not see Jah Jehovah in the land of the living; I shall not still look on man with the dwellers of the death-rest. [12]My generation *is* departed and removed from me like a shepherd's tent; I have cut off my life like the weaver; He cuts off me from the loom. From day to night You make an end of me. [13]I smoothed *my soul* until morning. Like a lion, so He shatters all my bones. From day until night You make an end of me. [14]Like a twittering swallow, so I chatter; I moan as the dove; my eyes look weakly to the heights, O Jehovah; it presses down to me; be surety for me!

[15]What shall I say? For He speaks to me, and He has acted. I shall go softly all my years over the bitterness of my soul. [16]O Lord, on them they live, and for all in them *is* the life of my spirit. And You heal me, and make me live. [17]Behold, for peace *was* bitter to me, *most* bitter; but You loved my soul from the pit of destruction; You have cast all my sins behind Your back. [18]For Sheol cannot thank You; death *cannot* praise You; the ones going down to the Pit cannot hope for Your truth. [19]The living, the living *is* the one thanking You; as I *do* today. The father makes known Your truth to *his* sons. [20]For Jehovah *is* for my salvation; and we will play my songs on stringed instruments all the days of our life, at the house of Jehovah.

1821 7725 4609 6235 322 8121 271 4609
בְּמַעֲלוֹת אָחָז בַּשֶּׁמֶשׁ אֲחֹרַנִּית עֶשֶׂר מַעֲלוֹת וַתָּשָׁב הַשֶּׁמֶשׁ
the went So .steps ten backward the with Ahaz the in
sun back ,sun of steps

9 2396 4385 3381 834 4609 4609 6235
עֶשֶׂר מַעֲלוֹת בַּמַּעֲלוֹת אֲשֶׁר יָרָדָה׃ מִכְתָּב לְחִזְקִיָּהוּ
of The had it which the by ,steps ten
Hezekiah writing .down gone steps

10 3117 1804 559 2483 2421 2470 3063 4428
מֶלֶךְ־יְהוּדָה בַּחֲלֹתוֹ וַיְחִי מֵחָלְיוֹ׃ אֲנִי אָמַרְתִּי בִּדְמִי יָמַי
my the in said I his from had and he when ,Judah king
,days of pause :illness revived sick was of

11 3808 559 8141 3499 6485 7585 8179 3212
אֵלֵכָה בְּשַׁעֲרֵי שְׁאוֹל פֻּקַּדְתִּי יֶתֶר שְׁנוֹתָי׃ אָמַרְתִּי לֹא־
not ,said I my the de- am I ;Sheol the to me Let
.years of rest of prived of gates go

3427 5750 120 5027 3808 2416 776 3050/3050 7200
אֶרְאֶה יָהּ יָהּ בְּאֶרֶץ הַחַיִּים לֹא־אַבִּיט אָדָם עוֹד עִם־יוֹשְׁבֵי
the with still man shall I not the the in Jehovah Jah shall I
of dwellers on look ;living of land see

12 707 7088 7473 168 1540 5265 1755 2309
חָדֶל׃ דּוֹרִי נִסַּע וְנִגְלָה מִנִּי כְּאֹהֶל רֹעִי קִפַּדְתִּי כָאֹרֵג
the like have I ;shepherd's like from and de- is My death- the
weaver off cut tent a ,me removed parted age rest

13 5704 7737 7999 3915 5704 3117 1214 1803 2416
חַיַּי מִדַּלָּה יְבַצְּעֵנִי מִיּוֹם עַד־לַיְלָה תַּשְׁלִימֵנִי׃ שִׁוִּיתִי עַד־
until smoothed I an make You night to from cuts He the From my
(soul my) .me of end day ;off me loom .life

3915 5704 6106 3605 7665 3651 738 1242
בֹּקֶר כָּאֲרִי כֵּן יְשַׁבֵּר כָּל־עַצְמוֹתָי מִיּוֹם עַד־לַיְלָה
night until From my all He so Like .morning
day .bones shatters ,lion a

14 5869 1809/3128 1897 6850 5693 5483 7999
תַּשְׁלִימֵנִי׃ כְּסוּס עָגוּר כֵּן אֲצַפְצֵף אֶהְגֶּה כַּיּוֹנָה דַּלּוּ עֵינַי
my look the as I ;chatter I so twitter- a Like an make You
eyes weakly ;dove moan ,ing swallow .me of end

15 559 1696 4100 6148 6234 3068 4791
לַמָּרוֹם יְהוָה עָשְׁקָה־לִּי עָרְבֵנִי׃ מָה־אֲדַבֵּר וְאָמַר־לִי
to He For shall What surety be to presses it O the to
,me speaks ?say I .me for ;me down ,Jehovah .heights

16 136 5315 4751 5921 8141 3605 1718 6213
וְהוּא עָשָׂה אֶדַּדֶּה כָל־שְׁנוֹתַי עַל־מַר נַפְשִׁי׃ אֲדֹנָי עֲלֵיהֶם
them on O my bit- the over my all shall I has and
,Lord .soul of terness years softly go .acted He

17 7965 2009 2421 2492 7307/2416 3605 2416
יִחְיוּ וּלְכָל־בָּהֶן חַיֵּי רוּחִי וְתַחֲלִימֵנִי וְהַחֲיֵנִי׃ הִנֵּה לְשָׁלוֹם
for ,Behold make and You And my the (is) in for and they
peace .live me ,me heal .spirit of life them all ,live

7993 1097 7845 5315 2836 4751 4843
מַר־לִי מָר וְאַתָּה חָשַׁקְתָּ נַפְשִׁי מִשַּׁחַת בְּלִי כִּי־הִשְׁלַכְתָּ
have You for de- the from soul my loved but (yea) to (was)
cast ,struction of pit You ;bitter,me bitter

18 1984 4194 3034 7585 3808 2399 3605 1458 310
אַחֲרֵי גֵוְךָ כָּל־חֲטָאָי׃ כִּי־לֹא שְׁאוֹל תּוֹדֶךָּ מָוֶת יְהַלְלֶךָּ
praise (nor) thank can Sheol not For my all Your be-
;You death ,You .sins back hind

19 3034 2416/2416 571 953 3381 7663 3808
לֹא־יְשַׂבְּרוּ יוֹרְדֵי־בוֹר אֶל־אֲמִתֶּךָ׃ חַי חַי הוּא יוֹדֶךָ כָּמוֹנִי
I as thanking (is) the The Your for the going they can not
,You he living ,living .truth Pit to down hope

20 5058 3462 3068 571 3045 1121 1 3117
הַיּוֹם אָב לְבָנִים יוֹדִיעַ אֶל־אֲמִתֶּךָ׃ יְהוָה לְהוֹשִׁיעֵנִי וּנְגִנוֹתַי
therefore my for (is) Jehovah Your about makes (his) to The .today
songs my ;salvation .truth known sons father

21 5375 3470 559 3068 1004 2416 3117 3605/5059
נְנַגֵּן כָּל־יְמֵי חַיֵּינוּ עַל־בֵּית יְהוָה׃ וַיֹּאמֶר יְשַׁעְיָהוּ יִשְׂאוּ
Let .Isaiah said And .Jehovah the at our the all will we
bear them of house ,life of days play

[21]For Isaiah had said, Let them take a cake of figs and rub it on the ulcer, and he will live. [22]And Hezekiah said, What *is* the sign that I will go up to the house of Jehovah?

2396 559 2421 7822 4799 8384 1690
22 דְּבֶלֶת תְּאֵנִים וְיִמְרְחוּ עַל־הַשְּׁחִין וְיֶחִי׃ וַיֹּאמֶר חִזְקִיָּהוּ
,Hezekiah said And he that the on rub and figs cake a
.live may ,boil (it) of

3068 1004 5927 226 4100
מָה אוֹת כִּי אֶעֱלֶה בֵּית יְהוָה׃
?Jehovah the shall I that the What
of house (to) up go sign (is)

CAP. XXXIX לט

CHAPTER 39

[1]At that time Merodach-baladan, the son of Baladan, king of Babylon, sent letters and a present to Hezekiah—for he had heard that he was ill, and was strengthened. [2]And Hezekiah was glad because of them and let them see the house of his treasure, the silver, and the gold, and the spices, and the good oil, and all his weapons, and all that was found in his treasuries — there was nothing in his house or in all his kingdom that Hezekiah did not make them see. [3]And Isaiah the prophet came to King Hezekiah and said to him, What did these men say? And from where did they come to you? And Hezekiah said, They have come from a distant land to me, from Babylon. [4]Then he said, What have they seen in your house? And Hezekiah said, They have seen all that *is* in my house; there is not a thing among my treasures that I have not made them see. [5]And Isaiah said to Hezekiah, Hear the word of Jehovah of hosts:

884 4428 1081 1121 4757 7971 6256
1 בָּעֵת הַהִוא שָׁלַח מְרֹאדַךְ בַּלְאֲדָן בֶּן־בַּלְאֲדָן מֶלֶךְ־בָּבֶל
,Babylon king ,Baladan the baladan Merodach- sent that At
of of son time

2388 2470 8085 2396 4503 5612
סְפָרִים וּמִנְחָה אֶל־חִזְקִיָּהוּ וַיִּשְׁמַע כִּי חָלָה וַיֶּחֱזָק׃
was and was he that he for —Hezekiah to a and letters
strong made ill heard had present

3701 5238 1004 7200 2396 8056
2 וַיִּשְׂמַח עֲלֵיהֶם חִזְקִיָּהוּ וַיַּרְאֵם אֶת־בֵּית נְכֹתֹה אֶת־הַכֶּסֶף
,silver the his the let he and .Hezekiah because was And
,treasure of house see them them of glad

3605 2896 8081 1314 2091
וְאֶת־הַזָּהָב וְאֶת־הַבְּשָׂמִים וְאֵת ׀ הַשֶּׁמֶן הַטּוֹב וְאֵת כָּל־
all and ,good oil the and the and the and
,spices ,gold

1697 1961 3808 214 4672 3605 3627 1004
בֵּית כֵּלָיו וְאֵת כָּל־אֲשֶׁר נִמְצָא בְּאוֹצְרֹתָיו לֹא־הָיָה דָבָר
a there not his in was that all and his the
thing was ;treasuries found weapons of house

935 4475 3605 1004 2396 7200 3808 834
3 אֲשֶׁר לֹא־הֶרְאָם חִזְקִיָּהוּ בְּבֵיתוֹ וּבְכָל־מֶמְשַׁלְתּוֹ׃ וַיָּבֹא
Then his in or his in Hezekiah made not which
came .kingdom all house see them

559 4100 559 2396 4428 5030 3470
יְשַׁעְיָהוּ הַנָּבִיא אֶל־הַמֶּלֶךְ חִזְקִיָּהוּ וַיֹּאמֶר אֵלָיו מָה־אָמְרוּ ׀
did What to said and ,Hezekiah King to the Isaiah
say ,him prophet

776 2396 559 935 370 428 582
הָאֲנָשִׁים הָאֵלֶּה וּמֵאַיִן יָבֹאוּ אֵלֶיךָ וַיֹּאמֶר חִזְקִיָּהוּ מֵאֶרֶץ
a from ,Hezekiah said And to they did And ?these men
land ?you come where from

559 1004 7200 4100 559 884 935 7350
4 רְחוֹקָה בָּאוּ אֵלַי מִבָּבֶל׃ וַיֹּאמֶר מָה רָאוּ בְּבֵיתֶךָ וַיֹּאמֶר
And your in have What he Then from to they distant
said ?house seen they ,said .Babylon ,me came

1697 1961 3808 7200 1004 3605 2396
חִזְקִיָּהוּ אֵת כָּל־אֲשֶׁר בְּבֵיתִי רָאוּ לֹא־הָיָה דָבָר אֲשֶׁר
that thing a there not they my in that All ,Hezekiah
is ;seen have house (is)

8085 2396 3470 559 214 7200 3808
5 לֹא־הִרְאִיתִים בְּאוֹצְרֹתָי׃ וַיֹּאמֶר יְשַׁעְיָהוּ אֶל־חִזְקִיָּהוּ שְׁמַע
Hear ,Hezekiah to Isaiah Then my among made have I not
said .treasures see them

[6]Behold, days come when all that *is* in your house, even what your fathers have treasured up until now, shall be carried to Babylon; nothing shall be left, says Jehovah. [7]And they shall take of your sons who shall issue from you, which you shall father, and they shall

3605 5375 935 3117 2009 6635 3068 1697
6 דְּבַר־יְהוָה צְבָאוֹת׃ הִנֵּה יָמִים בָּאִים וְנִשָּׂא ׀ כָּל־אֲשֶׁר
that all shall when ,come days ,Behold :hosts Jehovah the
(is) carried be of of word

3498 884 2088 3117 5704 1 686 1004
בְּבֵיתֶךָ וַאֲשֶׁר אָצְרוּ אֲבֹתֶיךָ עַד־הַיּוֹם הַזֶּה בָּבֶל לֹא־יִוָּתֵר
shall not (to) ,this day until your trea- have even your in
left be ;Babylon fathers up sured what ;house

3205 834 3318 1121 3068 559 1697
7 דָּבָר אָמַר יְהוָה׃ וּמִבָּנֶיךָ אֲשֶׁר יֵצְאוּ מִמְּךָ אֲשֶׁר תּוֹלִיד
shall you whom from go shall who your And .Jehovah says a
father ,you forth sons ,thing

be eunuchs in the palace of
the king of Babylon.
[8]Then Hezekiah said to
Isaiah, The word of
Jehovah that you have said
is good. And he said, For
there shall be peace and
truth in my days.

2396 559 884 44,28 1964 56:31 1961 3947
8 יקחו והיו סריסים בהיכל מלך בבל׃ ויאמר חזקיהו
Hezekiah Then .Babylon the the in eunuchs they and they
said of king of palace be shall ;take shall

1961 559 1696 3068 1697 2896 3470
אל־ישעיהו טוב דבר־יהוה אשר דברת ויאמר כי יהיה
there For he And have you that Jehovah the Good ,Isaiah to
be will ,said .spoken of word (is)

3117 571 7965
שלום ואמת בימי׃
my in and peace
.days truth

CAP. XL מ

CHAPTER 40

CHAPTER 40

[1]Comfort, O comfort My
people, says your God.
[2]Speak lovingly to the heart
of Jerusalem — yea, cry to
her that her warfare is done,
that her iniquity is
pardoned; for she has taken
from the hand of Jehovah
double for all her sins.
[3]The voice of him who cries
in the wilderness: Prepare
the way of Jehovah; make
straight in the desert a
highway for our God. [4]Every
valley shall be exalted, and
every mountain and hill
shall be made low; and the
knoll shall be a level place,
and the rough places a
plain. [5]And the glory of
Jehovah shall be revealed,
and all flesh shall see *it* together, for the mouth of
Jehovah has spoken. [6]A
voice said, Cry! And he said,
What shall I cry? All flesh is
grass, and all its grace as the
flower of the field! [7]The
grass withers; the flower
fades; because the Spirit of
Jehovah blows on it. Surely
the people *is* grass. [8]The
grass withers; the flower
fades; but the word of our
God shall rise forever. [9]You
who bring good news to
Zion, go up for yourself on
the high mountain, bringer
of good news to Zion. Lift up
your voice with strength,
bringer of good news to
Jerusalem. Lift up; do not
fear. Say to the cities of
Judah, Behold! Your God!
[10]Behold, the Lord Jehovah
will come with strength, and
His arm rules for Him.

3389 3820 1696 430 559 5971 5162 5162
1 2 נחמו נחמו עמי יאמר אלהיכם׃ דברו על־לב ירושלם
,Jerusalem the to Speak .God your says My comfort Com-
of heart ,people ,fort

3947 577,1 7521 66:35 43:90 7121
וקראו אליה כי מלאה צבאה כי נרצה עונה כי לקחה
has she for her par- is that her ful- is that ,her to call and
taken ;iniquity doned ,warfare filled

4057 71:21 6963 2403 36 05 37:18 30:68 3027
3 מיד יהוה כפלים בכל־חטאתיה׃ קול קורא במדבר
the in him The .sins her all for double Jehovah's from
,wilderness crying of voice hand

1516 3605 430 4546 61:60 3474 3068 1870 6437
4 פנו דרך יהוה ישרו בערבה מסלה לאלהינו׃ כל־גיא
valley Every our for a the in make ;Jehovah the Pre-
.God highway desert straight of way pare

4334 6121 1961 8213 1389 2022 3605 53:75
ינשא וכל־הר וגבעה ישפלו והיה העקב למישור
level a steep the shall and be shall hill and moun- and be shall
,place ground become ;low made tain every ,up lifted

1320 3605 7200 3068 3519 1540 1237 7406
5 והרכסים לבקעה׃ ונגלה כבוד יהוה וראו כל־בשר
flesh all shall and ,Jehovah the shall And .plain a the and
see of glory revealed be places rough

4100 559 71:21 559 6963 1696 3068 6310 31:62
6 יחדו כי פי יהוה דבר׃ קול אמר קרא ואמר מה
What he And !Cry ,said A has Jehovah the for to-
,said voice .spoken of mouth ,gether

3001 7704 6731 2617 3605 26:82 1320 3605 7121
7 אקרא כל־הבשר חציר וכל־חסדו כציץ השדה׃ יבש
Dries the the as its and ,grass flesh All I shall
up !field of flower grace all (is) ?cry

5971 2682 403 5380 3068 7307 6731 5034 2682
חציר נבל ציץ כי רוח יהוה נשבה בו אכן חציר העם׃
the (is) surely on blows Jehovah the for the fades the
.people grass ;it of breath ;flower ,grass

57:69 6965 430 1697 6731 5034 2682 30:01
8 יבש חציר נבל ציץ ודבר אלהינו יקום לעולם׃
.forever shall God our the but the fades the Dries
rise of word ,flower ;grass up

6963 3581 7311 6726 1319 59:27 13:64 59:21
9 על הר־גבה עלי־לך מבשרת ציון הרימי בכח קולך
your with Lift .Zion of bringer up Go high the On
,voice strength up to tidings .yourself for mountain

30:63 5892 559 3372 408 7311 3389 1319
מבשרת ירושלם הרימי אל־תיראי אמרי לערי יהודה
,Judah the to Say .fear do not ;up Lift .Jerusalem of bringer
of cities to tidings

4910 2220 935 2389 3068 136 20:09 430
10 הנה אלהיכם׃ הנה אדני יהוה בחזק יבוא וזרעו משלה
rules His and will with Jehovah the ,Behold !God your ,Behold
arm ,come strength Lord

Behold, His reward *is* with Him, and His wage before Him. [11]He shall feed His flock like a shepherd; He shall gather lambs with His arm; and in His bosom carry *them*; those with young He will lead. [12]Who has measured in His palm the waters and the heavens by a span meted out; and enclosed in the measure the dust of the earth, and weighed in the balance the mountains, and the hills in the scales? [13]Who has meted out the Spirit of Jehovah, or a man His counsel taught Him? [14]With whom did He take counsel, and who trained Him and taught Him in the path of justice; and taught Him knowledge, and made known to Him the way of discernment? [15]Lo, nations *are* as a drop from a bucket, and are reckoned as dust of the scales. Lo, He takes up coasts as a little thing. [16]And Lebanon is not enough to burn, nor are its beasts enough *for* a burnt offering. [17]All the nations *are* as nothing before Him; to Him they are reckoned less than nothing and emptiness.

[18]And to whom will you liken God? Or what likeness will you array to Him? [19]The craftsman pours out the carved image, the smelter spreads it with gold; and he casts the chains of silver. [20]He *too* poor for *that* offering chooses a tree that will not rot; he seeks a skilled artisan for him, to prepare a carved image that will not be shaken. [21]Have you not known? Have you not heard? Was it not told to you from the beginning? Did you not discern *from* the foundations of the earth? [22]He who sits on the circle of the earth, even its dwellers *are* like grasshoppers; He who stretches the heavens like a curtain, and spreads them like a tent to live in; [23]who gives potentates into nothing— He makes judges of the earth as nothing. [24]Yes, they

---

11　74:62　5739　7462　6440　6468　7939　2009

יִרְעֶה עֶדְרוֹ כְּרֹעֶה לְפָנָיו וּפְעֻלָּתוֹ אִתּוֹ הִנֵּה לוֹ

shall He His a Like before His and with (is) His Be- for
feed flock shepherd Him wage Him reward hold Him

12　4310　5095　57:163　5375　2436　2922:　6908　2220

יְנַהֵל עָלוֹת יִשָּׂא וּבְחֵיקוֹ טְלָאִים יְקַבֵּץ בִּזְרֹעוֹ מִ

Who will He those carry His in and ,lambs shall He His with
it lead young with ;(them) bosom gather arm

6083　79:91　3557　85:05　2239　80:64　4325：　40:58

עָפָר בְּשָׁלִשׁ וְכָל תִּכֵּן בְּזֶרֶת וְשָׁמַיִם מַיִם בְּשָׁעֳלוֹ מָדַד

the the in en- and meted the by the and the his in has
of dust measure closed ;out span heavens ,waters hand measured

13　8505　6425　1389　20:22　39:76　8254　776

מִרְתְּכָן בְּמֹאזְנַיִם וּגְבָעוֹת הָרִים בַּפֶּלֶס וְשָׁקַל הָאָרֶץ

has Who ?scales in the and the the in and the
out meted hills mounts balance weighed ,earth

14　995:　3289　4310　3045　6098　376　30:68　7307

וִיבִינֵהוּ נוֹעָץ אִישׁ וְאֶת עֲצָתוֹ אִישׁ אֶת תִּכֵּן יְהוָה רוּחַ אֶת

who and He took whom With taught His a or ,Jehovah the
Him trained counsel Him counsel man of Spirit

995　1870　1847：　3925　4941　734　3045

תְּבוּנוֹת וְדֶרֶךְ דַּעַת וַיְלַמְּדֵהוּ מִשְׁפָּט בְּאֹרַח וַיְלַמְּדֵהוּ

discernment the and knowl- taught and ;justice the in taught and
of way ,edge Him of path Him

15　2803　3976　7834　1805　4752　1471　3045

הֵן נֶחְשָׁבוּ מֹאזְנַיִם וּכְשַׁחַק מִדְּלִי כְּמַר גּוֹיִם הֵן יֹדִיעֶנּוּ

,Lo are scales the as and a from a like nations ,Lo known made
.reckoned of dust ,bucket drop (are) ?Him to

16　1767/369　24:16　1197　1767　369　38:44　5190　1851　339

דֵּי חַיָּתוֹ וְאֵין בָּעֵר דֵּי אֵין וּלְבָנוֹן יִטּוֹל כַּדַּק אִיִּים

enough are its and to enough is And takes He a as coasts
(for) not beasts ;burn not Lebanon .up thing little

17　2803　8414　657　5048　369　1471　3605　5930

נֶחְשְׁבוּ וָתֹהוּ מֵאֶפֶס נֶגְדּוֹ כְּאַיִן הַגּוֹיִם כָּל עוֹלָה:

are they and than less before as (are) the All burnt a
reckoned emptiness nothing ,Him nothing nations .offering

18
19　6459　6186　1823　4100　410　1819　4310

הַפָּסֶל תַּעַרְכוּ לוֹ וּמַה דְּמוּת תְּדַמְּיוּן אֵל וְאֶל לוֹ:

carved The to you will likeness Or ?God you will whom And to
image ?Him array what liken to .Him

6884　3701　7577　7554　2091　6884　2796　5058

צוֹרֵף כֶּסֶף וּרְתֻקוֹת יְרַקְּעֶנּוּ בַּזָּהָב וְצֹרֵף חָרָשׁ נָסַךְ

he silver chains and spreads the with the and the pours
.casts of ;it gold smelter ;craftsman out

20　12,45　2450　2796　977　7537　6086　86:21　5533

יְבַקֶּשׁ לוֹ חָכָם חָרָשׁ יִבְחָר יִרְקַב לֹא עֵץ תְּרוּמָה הַמְסֻכָּן

he skilled crafts- a ;chooses that not (that) (too) He
seeks man rot will tree ,offering for poor

21　8085　38:08　3045　38:08　4131　38:08　6459　3559

תִּשְׁמָעוּ הֲלוֹא תֵּדְעוּ הֲלוֹא יִמּוֹט לֹא פֶּסֶל לְהָכִין לוֹ

you Have you Have will that carved a to for
?heard not ?known not .shaken be not ;image prepare him

776　4146　995　38:08　5046　38:08

הָאָרֶץ מוֹסְדוֹת הֲבִינֹתֶם הֲלוֹא לָכֶם הֻגַּד הֲלוֹא מֵרֹאשׁ הַגַּד

the the (from) discern you Did ?you to the from it Was
?earth of foundations not beginning told not

22　1852　5186　2284　3427　776　2329　3427

כַּדֹּק הַנֹּטֶה וְיֹשְׁבֶיהָ הָאָרֶץ חוּג עַל הַיֹּשֵׁב

the like who He like (are) its even the the over who He
curtain stretches ;grasshoppers dwellers ,earth of circle sits

8199　369　7336　5414　3427　168　4969　8064

שָׁפְטֵי לְאַיִן רוֹזְנִים הַנּוֹתֵן לָשָׁבֶת כָּאֹהֶל וַיִּמְתָּחֵם שָׁמַיִם

judges into poten- who live to a like spreads and
of ;nothing tates gives ;in tent them ,heavens

24　1077　637　22:32　637　5193　1077　637　6213　8414　796

בָל אַף בַּל נִטָּעוּ אַף בַּל עָשָׂה כַּתֹּהוּ אֶרֶץ

not ,yes they not ,yes shall they not ,Yes He as the
;sown are ;planted be .makes nothing earth

shall not be planted; yes, they are not sown; yes, their stem *is* not taking root in the earth. And He blows on them also, and they wither, and the tempest shall take them away like stubble.

25And to whom will you liken Me, or am I equaled, says the Holy One? 26Lift up your eyes on high and see: Who has created these, bringing out their host by number? By greatness of vigor and might of power He calls them all by name — not one is lacking. 27Why will you say, O Jacob, and speak, O Israel: My way is hidden from Jehovah, and, My judgment shall pass over from my God. 28Or have you not heard? Jehovah, the everlasting God, the Creator of the ends of the earth; He is not faint, nor grow weary; there is no searching to His understanding. 29*He* gives power to the faint, and to him with no vigor He increases might. 30Even youths are faint and fatigued; and young men surely shall stumble; but the ones waiting for Jehovah shall renew power; they shall go up *with* wings as the eagles; they shall run and not be weary; they shall walk and not be faint!

7179 5592 3001 5398 1571 1503 776 8327
שֹׁרֵשׁ בָּאָרֶץ גִּזְעָם וְגַם נָשַׁף בָּהֶם וַיִּבָשׁוּ וּסְעָרָה כַּקַּשׁ
like stubble | the and tempest | they and ;wither | on ,them | He blows | And also | their .stem | the in earth | taking root

25
26
5375 6918 559 7737 1819 4310 5375
תִּשָּׂאֵם׃ וְאֶל־מִי תְדַמְּיוּנִי וְאֶשְׁוֶה יֹאמַר קָדוֹשׁ׃ שְׂאוּ
Lift up | Holy the ?One | says | I am or ,equaled | you will ,Me liken | whom And to | take shall .away them

6635 4557 3318 428 1254 4310 7200 5869 4791
מָרוֹם עֵינֵיכֶם וּרְאוּ מִי־בָרָא אֵלֶּה הַמּוֹצִיא בְמִסְפָּר צְבָאָם
their ?host | by number | bringing out | ,these | has who created | and :see | your eyes | on high

3808 376 3581 533 202 7230 7121 8034 3605
לְכֻלָּם בְּשֵׁם יִקְרָא מֵרֹב אוֹנִים וְאַמִּיץ כֹּחַ אִישׁ לֹא
not | one ;power | and of mighty | vigor | great- by of ness | He ,calls | by name | them to all

27
5640 3478 1696 3290 559 4100 5737
נֶעְדָּר׃ לָמָּה תֹאמַר יַעֲקֹב וּתְדַבֵּר יִשְׂרָאֵל נִסְתְּרָה
Is hidden | ,Israel O | ,speak and | O ;Jacob | you will ,say | Why | is .lacking

28
3045 3808 5674 4941 430 3068 1870
דַרְכִּי מֵיְהוָה וּמֵאֱלֹהַי מִשְׁפָּטִי יַעֲבוֹר׃ הֲלוֹא יָדַעְתָּ אִם
Or | you ?known | Have not | pass shall ?over | my judgment | from and God my | from ,Jehovah | my way

3808 776 7098 1254 3068 5769 430 8085 3808
לֹא שָׁמַעְתָּ אֱלֹהֵי עוֹלָם | יְהוָה בּוֹרֵא קְצוֹת הָאָרֶץ לֹא
not | the ,earth | the of ends | the of Creator | Jehovah ,(is) | ever- lasting | The God | you have ?heard | not

29
369 3581 3287 5414 8394 2714 369 3025 3286
יִיעַף וְלֹא יִיגָע אֵין חֵקֶר לִתְבוּנָתוֹ׃ נֹתֵן לַיָּעֵף כֹּחַ וּלְאֵין
him and no with | ;power | the to faint | (He) gives | His to .understanding | search- ing | not is | grows ,weary | and not | is He faint

30
970 3021 5288 3286 7235 6109 202
אוֹנִים עָצְמָה יַרְבֶּה׃ וְיִעֲפוּ נְעָרִים וְיִגָעוּ וּבַחוּרִים כָּשׁוֹל
surely | young and men | and ;fatigued | youths | are Even faint | He .increases | might | ,vigor

31
7323 5404 83 5927 3581 2498 3068 6960 3782
יִכָּשֵׁלוּ׃ וְקוֹיֵ יְהוָה יַחֲלִיפוּ כֹחַ יַעֲלוּ אֵבֶר כַּנְּשָׁרִים יָרוּצוּ
they run shall | the as ;eagles | (with) wings | they up go shall | ;power | shall renew | Jehovah | but for waiters | shall ;stumble

3286 3808 3212 3808
וְלֹא יִיגָעוּ יֵלְכוּ וְלֹא יִיעָפוּ׃
.faint be not | and walk | they shall | be ;weary | and not

CAP. XLI מא

CHAPTER 41

1Be quiet before Me, O coasts; and let peoples renew their power. They come near; then they speak: Let us draw near together for judgment. 2Who raised up the righteous one from the east? He called him to His foot; He gives nations before him, and subdues kings; He gives *them* as dust *to* his sword, as driven stubble *to* his bow; 3He pursues them; he passes on in peace; he does not go *by* the way with his feet. 4Who has planned and done *it*, calling forth the generations from the beginning? I Jehovah *am* the first and the

1
1696 227 5066 3581 2498 3816 339 2790
הַחֲרִישׁוּ אֵלַי אִיִּים וּלְאֻמִּים יַחֲלִיפוּ כֹחַ יִגְּשׁוּ אָז יְדַבֵּרוּ
they ;speak | then | They .near come | ,power | shall renew | and peoples | O :coasts | before ,Me | Be quiet

2
7121 6664 4217 5782 4310 7126 4941 3162
יַחְדָּו לַמִּשְׁפָּט נִקְרָבָה׃ מִי הֵעִיר מִמִּזְרָח צֶדֶק יִקְרָאֵהוּ
called He Him | the ?Righteous | the from east | raised up | Who | us let .near draw | for judgment | to- gether

7179 2719 6083 5414 7287 4428 1471 6440 5414 7272
לְרַגְלוֹ יִתֵּן לְפָנָיו גּוֹיִם וּמְלָכִים יַרְדְּ יִתֵּן כֶּעָפָר חַרְבּוֹ כְּקַשׁ
as stubble | His (to) ,sword | dust as | He gives | sub- .dues | kings and | ,nations | before Him | He gives | His to ?foot

3
935 3808 7272 934 7965 5674 7291 7198 5086
נִדָּף קַשְׁתּוֹ׃ יִרְדְּפֵם יַעֲבוֹר שָׁלוֹם אֹרַח בְּרַגְלָיו לֹא יָבוֹא׃
he goes | not | His with feet | (by) way the | in ;peace | passes He on | pur- He ;them sues | His to .bow | driven

4
7218 3069 7223 1755 7121 6213 6466/4310
מִי־פָעַל וְעָשָׂה קֹרֵא הַדֹּרוֹת מֵרֹאשׁ אֲנִי יְהוָה רִאשׁוֹן
the first | Jehovah I | the from ?beginning | genera- tions | the calling forth | and ,(it) done | has appointed | Who

the last; I *am* He. ⁵The coasts have seen and fear; the ends of the earth tremble; they have drawn near; yea, they come. ⁶Each man helps his neighbor, and says to his brother, Be strong. ⁷So the carver strengthens the refiner; and he smoothing *with* the hammer, him who struck the anvil, saying of the soldering, It *is* good. And he made it strong with nails—it will not totter.

⁸But you, Israel *are* My servant; Jacob whom I have chosen; the seed of My friend Abraham; ⁹whom I have made strong from the ends of the earth, and called you from its sides; and I said to you, You *are* My servant. I chose you, and have not rejected *you*. ¹⁰Do not fear, for I *am* with you; do not gaze about, for I *am* your God; I make you strong; yea, I help you; yea, I uphold you with the right hand of My righteousness. ¹¹Behold, all who are provoked with you shall be ashamed and confounded; they shall be as nothing, and they who fight with you shall perish. ¹²You shall seek them and shall not find them; men of your strife shall be as nothing, even men of your battle as ceasing. ¹³For I, Jehovah your God am making strong your right hand; who says to you, Do not fear; I will help you. ¹⁴Fear not, worm of Jacob, men of Israel; I will help you; states Jehovah, and your Redeemer, the Holy One of Israel. ¹⁵Behold! I have made you a new sharp threshing instrument, a master of mouths; you shall thresh mountains and beat them small, and shall make hills like the chaff. ¹⁶You shall fan them, and the wind will carry them away; and the tempest will scatter them. And you will rejoice in Jehovah; you shall glory

---

5
776	7098	3372	339	7200			314	
וַיִּירָ֖אוּ קְצ֥וֹת הָאָ֑רֶץ			אִיִּ֣ים רָא֤וּ		אֶת־אַחֲרֹנִ֖ים אָֽנִי־הֽוּא׃			
the earth	the of ends	;fear and	the coasts	seen	Have	.He	I (am)	;last the and

6
559	251	5826	7753	376	376	857	7126	2729
יֹאמַ֥ר וּלְאָחִ֖יו יַעְזֹ֑רוּ אֶת־רֵעֵ֙הוּ֙ אִ֣ישׁ							קָרֵ֔בוּ חָֽרְד֖וּ	
,says	to and ,helps brother his	his neighbor	Each man	they and they ;came near drew	;tremble

7
1986	6360	25,105	6884	2796	2388	2388
מַכֶּֽה־פָּ֔עַם מַחֲלִ֣יק פָּטִ֔ישׁ אֶת־צֹרֵ֔ף חָרָשׁ֙ וַיְחַזֵּ֤ק						חֲזָ֑ק׃
who him struck	,hammer the smoothing he	(with)	,refiner	the artisan strengthens	the So	Be .strong

4131	38,08	4548	2388	2896	1694	559	6471
יִמּֽוֹט׃ לֹ֥א בְּמַסְמְרִ֖ים וַֽיְחַזְּקֵ֥הוּ ה֑וּא ט֣וֹב לַדֶּ֖בֶק אֹמֵ֥ר							
will it not	with ,nails	made it strong	it And	(is) .good	the of ,soldering	,saying	,anvil .totter

8
2233	977	834	3290	5650	3478
זֶ֖רַע בְּחַרְתִּ֑יךָ אֲשֶׁ֣ר יַעֲקֹ֔ב עַבְדִּ֔י וְאַתָּה֙ יִשְׂרָאֵ֣ל					
the seed of	have I ,chosen	whom	,Jacob	My (are) ,servant	Israel O But ,you

9
1678	776	7098	2388	834	157	85
וּמֵאֲצִילֶ֖יהָ הָאָ֔רֶץ מִקְצ֣וֹת הֶחֱזַקְתִּ֙יךָ֙ אֲשֶׁ֤ר אֹֽהֲבִ֑י אַבְרָהָ֖ם						
from and sides its	the earth	the from of ends	have I strong made	whom	My ,friend	Abraham

3973	38,08	977	5650	559	7121
מְאַסְתִּֽיךָ׃ וְלֹ֥א בְחַרְתִּ֖יךָ עַבְדִּי־אַ֛תָּה לְךָ֤ וָאֹ֣מַר קְרָאתִ֑יךָ					
have .rejected	and not ,you	chose I	you My (are) servant	to I and ,you said	;you called

10
553	430	8159	3372	1408
אֲמִצְתִּ֖יךָ אֱלֹהֶ֑יךָ כִֽי־אֲנִ֣י אֱלֹהֶ֔יךָ אַל־תִּשְׁתָּע֙ אָ֔נִי כִֽי־עִמְּךָ֣ אַל־תִּירָא֙				
make I ;strong you	your ;God	I for (am)	your ,about God	gaze do not	I with ;(am) you	for ,fear do Not ;fear

11
1639	954	6664	3225	8551	637	5826
וְיִכָּלְמ֔וּ יֵבֹ֣שׁוּ הֵ֚ן צִדְקִֽי׃ בִּימִ֥ין תְּמַכְתִּ֖יךָ אַף־עֲזַרְתִּ֑יךָ						אַ֖ף
and humiliated	be shall ,ashamed	,Lo	My right ,just hand	uphold I you	,yea help I ;you	,yea

7379	582	6	369	1961	2734	36,105
רִיבֶֽךָ׃ אַנְשֵׁ֥י כְּאַ֖יִן וְיֹאבְד֥וּ בָ֑ךְ יִֽהְי֖וּ הַנֶּחֱרִ֣ים כֹּ֤ל						
con- your tention of	men	shall and ;nothing be	as shall they perish	with ;you be	are who provoked	all

12
657	369	1961	4695	582	46:72	1245
וּכְאֶ֥פֶס כְּאַ֛יִן יִהְי֥וּ מַצָּתֶ֖ךָ אַנְשֵׁ֥י תִמְצָאֵ֑ם וְלֹ֣א תְּבַקְשֵׁם֙						
as even	as ceasing	shall be ,nothing	your strife of	your men	find shall and ;them	You shall them seek not

13
3225	2388	430	3068	4421	582
יְמִינֶ֑ךָ מַחֲזִ֣יק אֱלֹהֶ֖יךָ יְהוָ֥ה אֲנִ֛י כִּ֗י מִלְחַמְתֶּֽךָ׃ אַנְשֵׁ֖י					
your ,hand right	making am strong	your God	Jehovah	I For	your .battle	men of

14
8433	3372	5826	3372	1408	559
תּוֹלַ֥עַת אַל־תִּֽירְאִ֖י עֲזַרְתִּ֑יךָ אֲנִ֖י אַל־תִּירְאִ֛י לְךָ֥ הָאֹמֵ֣ר					
worm of	Do not ,fear	help will I .you	I	Do not ,fear to	who says

6918	1350	3068/5002	5826	3478	4962	3290
קְד֥וֹשׁ וְגֹאֲלֵ֖ךְ נְאֻם־יְהוָ֑ה עֲזַרְתִּ֜יךְ אֲנִ֧י יִשְׂרָאֵ֔ל מְתֵ֣י יַעֲקֹב֙						
Holy the your and of One ,Redeemer	,Jehovah states	help will I you	;Israel men of	,Jacob

15
6374	11,167	2319	2742	4173	7760	2009	3478
פִּֽיפִיּ֑וֹת בַּ֣עַל חָדָ֖שׁ חָר֥וּץ לְמוֹרַ֔ג שַׂמְתִּ֙יךְ֙ הִנֵּ֥ה יִשְׂרָאֵֽל׃							
;mouths	a ,master of	,new	sharp	threshing a instrument	made I you	,Behold	.Israel

16
7307	2219	7760	4671	1389	1852	2022	1758
וְר֖וּחַ תִּזְרֵ֥ם כַּמֹּ֥ץ תָּשִׂ֑ים וּגְבָע֖וֹת וְתָדֹ֔ק הָרִ֣ים תָּד֤וּשׁ							
and shall You wind ,them winnow	shall .make	the as chaff	;crush	hills and	and mountains shall you ,thresh

6918	3068	1523	6258	6327	5592	5375
בִּקְד֥וֹשׁ בַּֽיהוָ֖ה תָּגִ֑יל וְאַתָּ֕ה אֹתָ֑ם תָּפִ֖יץ וּסְעָרָ֥ה תִּשָּׂאֵ֔ם						
the in of One Holy	in ;Jehovah	shall you rejoice	And	.them	will a and scatter tempest	carry shall ;away them

in the Holy One of Israel. **17**The poor and the needy seek water, and there is none; their tongue is parched for thirst — I, Jehovah will hear them; the God of Israel will not leave them. **18**I will open rivers in bare places, and fountains in the midst of valleys; I will make the desert for a pool of water, and the dry land springs of water. **19**I will plant cedar in the wilderness, acacia, and myrtle, and the oil-tree; I will set fir, pine and boxwood together in the desert; **20**so that they may see, and know, and consider, and understand together, that the hand of Jehovah has done this; and the Holy One of Israel has created it.

21Bring your cause, says Jehovah; let your strong *reasons* come near, says the King of Jacob. **22**Let them draw near and tell us what shall happen; the former things, let them reveal what they *are*, that we may set our heart and know their end; or declare to us the coming things. **23**Reveal the coming things hereafter, so that we may know that you *are* gods. Yea, do good, or do evil, that we may gaze and see together. **24**Behold, you *are* of nothing; and your work of nothing; he who chooses you *is* an abomination. **25**I have raised up *one* from the north; and he shall come from the east; he will call on My name. And he shall come *upon* rulers as *on* mortar, and as a potter tramples clay. **26**Who has declared from the beginning, that we may know; and beforetime, that we may say, He is right? Yea, no one declares; yea, no one proclaims; yea, there is no one who hears your words. **27**At first to Zion, *I*

17

3478	8597		6041	34	1245
Israel	shall you	The	and the	the	seek
	.glory	poor	needy		

4325	369	3956	6772	5405	3068	589	430
,water	is not	tongue	their	is	for	I	the answer will Jehovah
			thirst	—parched		of God	,them

18

3478	08	38	5800	6605	5921	8205	5104	8432
,Israel	not	will	leave will I	open	on	bare	,rivers	the in
			.them	will	places			of midst

1237	4599	7760	4057	98	25	43	776	6763	4161
valleys	,fountains	will I	the	a for	water	,land	the and	dry	springs for
		make	desert	pool of			water		of

19

4325	5414	4057	730	7848	1918	6086	8081	7760
,water	will I	the in	,acacia	cedar	and	and	;oil	will I
	give	wilderness			,myrtle	of tree		set

20

6160	1265	8410	8391	3162	7200	3045
the in	,fir	,elm	box- and	;together	they	and
desert			wood		see may	,know

7760	7919	3162	3027	3068	6213	853	6918
con- and	under- and	to-	the	Jehovah	has	;this	the and
sider	stand	.gether	of hand		done		of One Holy

21

3478	1254	7126	7379	559	3068	50
Israel	created has	Bring	your	says	;Jehovah	come let
	.it	near	;cause			near

22

6110	559	44	28	3290	5066	5046
strong your	says	the	Jacob	them Let	and	us to tell and
.(reasons)		King of				near draw

7136	7223	4100	5046	7760	3820	3045
shall	former the	what they	them let	we that	our	and
;happen	—things	(are)	,reveal	set may	heart	know

23

319	176	935	5046	46	50	854	268
their	or	coming the	declare	Reveal	coming the	here-
;end		things	.us to		things	,after

3045	637	9	748	3190	430	8159	7200
know may	that we	,Yes	do	do or	gods	we that	and
	that	(are)	good	evil			see

24

3162	2009	369	6467	8441	977
to-	Be-	you	of	your and	who he
.gether	hold	(are)	nothing;	work	chooses

	5782	6828	857	4217	8121	7121	8034
have I	from (one)	he and	from	the	the	will he	My on
raised up	;north the	come shall	of rising	sun		call	.name

25

935	5461	2563	3335	7429	2916	5046
come shall	rulers	(on)	as mortar	and	as	And he
	(on)	clay	potter a	trample	;clay	has declared

26

369	8085	637	369	8085	561	559	6440	6662
not	;proclaims	,yea	hears not	,yea	your	say may	before and	(is He)
(one)			(one)		.words		time from	?right

637	5046	3045
,yea	;declares not	know may
	(one)	,beginning

27

2009	6726	7223
,Behold	to	first At
.Zion	.Zion	

say, Behold! Behold them! **28** And I will give to Jerusalem one bearing tidings. **28**But I saw, and there was not a man; and of these, there **29** was not a counselor, that I may ask them, and they could answer a word. **29**Behold, they *are* all evil; their works *are* nothing; their images *are* wind and vanity.

CHAPTER 42

1Behold My Servant; I will uphold Him; My Elect *in whom* My soul delights! I **1** have put My Spirit on Him; He shall bring forth justice to the nations. **2**He shall **2** not cry, nor lift up, nor cause His voice to be heard in the street. **3**A bruised reed He **3** shall not break, and a smoking wick He shall not quench; He shall bring forth justice to truth. **4**He shall **4** not fail nor be crushed until He has set justice in the earth; and the coasts shall wait for His law. **5**So says **5** Jehovah God, creating the heavens and stretching them out; spreading out the earth and its offspring, giving breath to the people on it, and spirit to those walking in it. **6**I, Jehovah, have called You in **6** righteousness, and will hold Your hand, and will keep You, and give You for a covenant of the people, for a Light of the nations; **7**to open blind eyes, to deliver the prisoner from the prison; those who sit in darkness from the prison. **7** **8**I *am* Jehovah; that is My name; and I will not give My **8** glory to another, nor My praise to engraved images. **9**Behold, the former things have come to pass, and I declare new things — be- **9** fore they happen, I cause you to hear.

10Sing a new song to Jehovah; His praise from the end of the earth, you who go to sea, and all that is **10**

ISAIAH 41:28 (interlinear)

2009	3389		1319	5414	7200	369	376	376	428
behold	to And		bearing one	will I	,saw	and	a	of and	
!them	Jerusalem		tidings .give		was not ;man	I But	,these		

369	3289	7592		1697	7725		1697	13605	205	657
not	coun- a	them ask		they and	answer could		.word a	all	;evil	nothing
was	selor	may I that					,Behold	they	(are)	(are)

4639	7307	8441	5262
their	and wind		their (are)
;works	vanity	casted	images.

CAP. XLII מב

CHAPTER 42

2009	5650	8551		973	7521	5315	5414	7307	5921
My Behold	servant,	support		,elect	delights	,soul	have I	Spirit	on
					My	!soul given	My	;Him	Him

4941	1471	3318		6817	53.75	38.08	8085
justice	the to	shall He		shall He	and	lift	to cause
	nations	.forth bring		not ,out cry	not	,up	heard be not

2351	6963	7533	7070	7665		6594	3544	3808
the in	His	bruised	A	not		,break	wick	not
street	.voice	reed		shall He		a and	dim	growing

3518	571	3318		4941	3543	38.08	7533	5704
it quench	truth to	shall He		.justice	not	dim grow	be	until
		forth bring			shall He	and	,crushed	

760	776	4941	8451	339	13176		559
the in	has He	;justice	and law	the	shall		says Thus
earth	set		His	coasts	.wait		

410	30.68	1254		80.64	7554	51.86	776	6631
God	Jehovah	creating		the	spreading stretch- and	the	776	its and
				heavens	them out	,out	earth	,offspring

5414	5397	5971	5921		7307	1980		3068
giving	breath	the to	it on		and	those to		Jehovah I
		people	,it in		spirit	who walk		.it in

7121	2388	2388	3027		3027	5341	5414	1285	5971
called have	righ- in		Your		will and	will and	give	of nant	the cove- a for
You	teousness,		;hand		hold	keep You,	You		people,

216	1471		6495	5869	5787	3318	4525	615
a for	.nations		To	eyes	,blind	deliver to	prison	the
of light			open					;prisoner from

1004	36.08	3427	2822		3069	8034	3519
the from	sit in	those who	,darkness		Jehovah I	My	My and
house of	straint				(am)	;name	glory

312	38.08	54.14	8416	6456		722.3	933
to	will I not	My and	praise	to images.		,things	former The
another	,give	praise		carved			,behold have

2319	5046	2962	6779		8085
new and	declare I	before	;forth		.you
things		they spring			cause I hear to

7891	3068	7892	23:19	8416		7097	776	3381	3220
,Sing	to	a song	;new	His		from	the	go down	the to
	Jehovah			praise		of end	,earth	who	,sea

in it; the coasts and their
people. [11]Let the wilderness and its cities lift up, the
villages where Kedar lives.
Let the dwellers of the rock
sing; let them shout from
the top of the mountains.
[12]They give glory to
Jehovah and declare His
praise in the islands.
[13]Jehovah shall go out as a
giant; and He shall stir up
His zeal like a warrior; He
shall cry, yea, roar on His
enemies; He shall act
mightily. [14]I have forever
kept silence; I have been
quiet and refrained Myself; I
will groan like a woman in
travail; I will pant and gasp
at once. [15]I will make
mountains and hills be-
come a waste, and dry up all
their plants. And I will make
the rivers coastlands, and I
will dry up pools. [16]And I
will lead the blind by a way
they knew not; I will lead
them in paths they never
knew; I will make darkness
into light before them, and
crooked places a level
place—I do these things to
them and do not forsake
them; [17]they are turned
back; they are ashamed
with shame, those trusting
in the carved image, who
say to cast images, You *are*
our gods. [18]O deaf ones,
hear! And O blind ones,
look to see! [19]Who *is* blind
but My servant? Or deaf, as
My messenger whom I
send? Who *is* blind as he
who is at peace, and blind
as Jehovah's servant? [20]You
see many things, but do not
observe; *your* ears *are*
open, but not any hears.
[21]Jehovah is delighted for
His righteousness' sake; He
will magnify the Law and
make *it* honorable.

[22]But it *is* a people
robbed and spoiled; they
shall all be snared in holes;
they were hidden in prison-
houses. They were for spoil,
and no one delivers; a prey,
and no one says, Return!
[23]Who among you will hear
this, will listen and hear for
the time to come? [24]Who

11
3427 2691 5892 4057 5375 3427 339 4393
וּמְלֹאוֹ אִיִּים וְיֹשְׁבֵיהֶם׃ יִשְׂאוּ מִדְבָּר וְעָרָיו חֲצֵרִים תֵּשֵׁב
(where) the its and the lift Let their and coasts its and
lives villages ,cities wilderness up .inhabitants ,fulness

12
3068 7760 6681 2022 7218 5553 3427 7442 6938
קֵדָר יָרֹנּוּ יֹשְׁבֵי סֶלַע מֵרֹאשׁ הָרִים יִצְוָחוּ׃ יָשִׂימוּ לַיהוָה
to They them let the from ;Sela the Let .Kedar
Jehovah give .shout mountains of top of dwellers sing

13
376 3318 4421 3068 5046 339 8416 3519
כָּבוֹד וּתְהִלָּתוֹ בָּאִיִּים יַגִּידוּ׃ יְהוָה כַּגִּבּוֹר יֵצֵא כְּאִישׁ
a as goes a as Jehovah they the in His and ,glory
of man ;out warrior .declare coasts praise

1368 341 5921 6873 637 7321 7068 5782 4421
מִלְחָמוֹת יָעִיר קִנְאָה יָרִיעַ אַף־יַצְרִיחַ עַל־אֹיְבָיו יִתְגַּבָּר׃
act will He His on ;roar ,yea will He (His) He battles
.mightily enemies ,shout ;zeal up stirs

14
5395 6463 3205 662 2814 5769 2790
הֶחֱשֵׁיתִי מֵעוֹלָם אַחֲרִישׁ אֶתְאַפָּק כַּיּוֹלֵדָה אֶפְעֶה אֶשֹּׁם
will I will I woman a like refrained I was I from have I
,pant ,groan travail in ;Myself ,quiet , forever silence kept

15
3001 6212 3605 1389 2022 2717 3162 7602
וְאֶשְׁאַף יָחַד׃ אַחֲרִיב הָרִים וּגְבָעוֹת וְכָל־עֶשְׂבָּם אוֹבִישׁ
dry their and ,hills and mountains will I at will and
.up plants all waste lay .once gasp

16
5787 3212 3001 98 339 5104 7760
וְשַׂמְתִּי נְהָרוֹת לָאִיִּים וַאֲגַמִּים אוֹבִישׁ׃ וְהוֹלַכְתִּי עִוְרִים
blind will I And will I pools and for rivers I And
ones walk make .up dry , coastlands make will

4285 7760 3381 3045 5410 3045 3808 1870
בְּדֶרֶךְ לֹא יָדָעוּ בִּנְתִיבוֹת לֹא־יָדְעוּ אַדְרִיכֵם אָשִׂים מַחְשָׁךְ
darkness will I will I they not in and they not a by
put ;go make knew paths ;knew way

6213 1697 418 4334 4625 216 6440
לִפְנֵיהֶם לָאוֹר וּמַעֲקַשִּׁים לְמִישׁוֹר אֵלֶּה הַדְּבָרִים עֲשִׂיתִם
to do I things these level a crooked and into before
them —place places ,light them

17
6459 982 1322 954 268 5493 5800 3808
וְלֹא עֲזַבְתִּים׃ נָסֹגוּ אָחוֹר יֵבֹשׁוּ בֹשֶׁת הַבֹּטְחִים בַּפָּסֶל
cut the in those (with) are they ,back are they forsake and
,image trusting ,shame ashamed turned ;them not

18
8085 2795 930 4541 559
הָאֹמְרִים לְמַסֵּכָה אַתֶּם אֱלֹהֵינוּ׃ הַחֵרְשִׁים שְׁמָעוּ
!hear deaf O our You cast to say who
,ones .gods (are) , images

19
2795 5650 5787 7200 5027 5787
וְהַעִוְרִים הַבִּיטוּ לִרְאוֹת׃ מִי עִוֵּר כִּי אִם־עַבְדִּי וְחֵרֵשׁ
Or My except (is) Who !see to look O And
,deaf ?servant blind ,ones blind

3068 5650 5787 7999 5787 4310 7971 4397
כְּמַלְאָכִי אֶשְׁלָח מִי עִוֵּר כִּמְשֻׁלָּם וְעִוֵּר כְּעֶבֶד יְהוָה׃
?Jehovah's as and who he as (is) Who (whom) My as
servant blind ,peace at is blind ?send I messenger

20
21
3068 8085 3808 241 6491 8104 7227 7200
רָאוֹת רַבּוֹת וְלֹא תִשְׁמֹר פָּקוֹחַ אָזְנַיִם וְלֹא יִשְׁמָע׃ יְהוָה
Jehovah any but (your) open ,keep do but many You
.hears not ,ears (are) not ,things see

22
962 142 8451 1430 6664 4616 2654
חָפֵץ לְמַעַן צִדְקוֹ יַגְדִּיל תּוֹרָה וְיַאְדִּיר׃ וְהוּא עַם־בָּזוּז
robbed a it But make and the will He righ- His for de- is
people (is) .honorable (it) Law magnify ;teousness' sake lighted

957 2244 3608 1004 3605 2352 6351 8154
וְשָׁסוּי הָפֵחַ בַּחוּרִים כֻּלָּם וּבְבָתֵּי כְלָאִים הָחְבָּאוּ הָיוּ לָבַז
for They were they re- in and of all ,holes in ensnared and
,spoil were .hidden ;straint of houses ,them ;spoiled

23
2088 238 854 4310 7725 559 4933 5337 369
וְאֵין מַצִּיל מְשִׁסָּה וְאֵין־אֹמֵר הָשַׁב׃ מִי בָכֶם יַאֲזִין זֹאת
?this will among Who !Return ,says and ,prey a ;delivers and
hear you none none

Left column

gave Jacob to the plunderer, and Israel to the robbers? Did not Jehovah, He against whom we have sinned? For they willed not to walk in His ways, and they did not obey His law. [25] Therefore He has poured on him the fury of His anger, and the strength of battle; and it has set him on fire all around, yet he did not know; and it burned him, yet he did not lay *it* on *his* heart.

CHAPTER 43

[1] But now so says Jehovah who formed you, O Jacob; and He who made you, O Israel: Fear not, for I have redeemed you; I called you by your name; you *are* Mine. [2] When you pass through the waters, I will be with you; and through the rivers, they shall not overflow you. When you walk in the fire, you shall not be burned, nor shall the flame kindle on you. [3] For I *am* Jehovah your God, the Holy One of Israel, your Savior. I gave Egypt *for* your atonement; Ethiopia and Seba instead of you. [4] Since you were precious in My eyes, you are honored, and I love you; and I give men instead of you; and peoples instead of your soul. [5] Fear not, for I *am* with you; I will bring your seed from the sunrise; and I will gather you from the sunset. [6] I will say to the north, Give up! And to the south, Do not hold back! Bring My sons from afar, and bring My daughters from the ends of the earth; [7] everyone who is called by My name, and I have created him for My glory; I have formed him; yea, *I have* made him. [8] Bring out the blind people, yet there are eyes; and the deaf, yet there *are* ears to him. [9] Let all the

Interlinear column

24

יַקְשִׁיב וְיִשְׁמַע לָאָחוֹר: 5414 מִי־נָתַן לִמְשׁוֹסָה יַעֲקֹב וְיִשְׂרָאֵל
7181 8085   268   לְמְשׁוֹסָה 4882 3290   3478
will He | hear and | the for | Who gave | the to | plunderer | ;Jacob | and
incline (ears) | | .come to time | | | | | Israel

לִכְזוּ הֲלוֹא יְהוָה זוּ חָטָאנוּ לוֹ וְלֹא־אָבוּ בִּדְרָכָיו הָלוֹךְ
962   3068 3808 2098 2398   14   1870   1980
Did | Jeho- | of | whom vah | we | against | For | they | His in | to
not | ?robbers | | | sinned | ?Him | willed | not | ways | walk

וְלֹא שָׁמְעוּ בְּתוֹרָתוֹ: וַיִּשְׁפֹּךְ עָלָיו חֵמָה אַפּוֹ
8085 3808   8451   8210   5921   2534   639 5809
and | did they | .law His | He So | on | the | His | and
not | obey | | poured | him | fury of | anger, | of force

25 וְעֱזוּז

מִלְחָמָה וַתְּלַהֲטֵהוּ מִסָּבִיב וְלֹא יָדַע וַתִּבְעַר־בּוֹ וְלֹא־
4421 3857   5439   3045 1197   38:08
;battle | set has it and | ;around | yet | ;know | it and | but
| fire on him | | not | did he | burned | not , him | among

יָשִׂים עַל־לֵב:
7760 38 120
did he | (his) on
(it) lay | .heart

CHAPTER 43

1 וְעַתָּה כֹּה־אָמַר יְהוָה בֹּרַאֲךָ יַעֲקֹב וְיֹצֶרְךָ יִשְׂרָאֵל אַל־
62 58 559 3541.   3068 1254   32:90   3335   3478   38:08
But | says thus | Jehovah | who | ;Jacob | who and | ;Israel | not
,now | | | created | | formed you, |

2 תִּירָא כִּי גְאַלְתִּיךָ קָרָאתִי בְשִׁמְךָ לִי־אָתָּה: כִּי־תַעֲבֹר
3372 .1350   7121   8034   5674
,Fear | for | re-have I | called | your by | to | you When
| | ;you deemed | (you) | ;name | Me (are) | pass

בַּמַּיִם אִתְּךָ אָנִי וּבַנְּהָרוֹת לֹא יִשְׁטְפוּךָ כִּי־תֵלֵךְ בְּמוֹ־אֵשׁ
4325   784   5104   3808   7857   1980
the | in | you when | shall they | not | through and | I | with through
,fire | walk | ;you overflow | | rivers the | ;(am) | you | waters the

3 לֹא תִכָּוֶה וְלֶהָבָה לֹא תִבְעַר־בָּךְ: כִּי אֲנִי יְהוָה אֱלֹהֶיךָ
35 54   3852   38:08   1197   3068   430:
your | Jehovah | I | For | on | shall | not | the and | shall you | not
,God | (am) | | | ;you | kindle | | flame | ;burned be

קְדוֹשׁ יִשְׂרָאֵל מוֹשִׁיעֶךָ נָתַתִּי כָפְרְךָ מִצְרַיִם כּוּשׁ וּסְבָא
6918 3478   3462   5414   3724 4714: 3568 5434
Holy the | ,Israel | your | gave I | your (for) | ;Egypt | Ethiopia | and
of One | | ;Savior | | atonement | | | Seba

4 תַּחְתֶּיךָ: מֵאֲשֶׁר יָקַרְתָּ בְעֵינַי נִכְבַּדְתָּ וַאֲנִי אֲהַבְתִּיךָ וְאֶתֵּן
8478   3365   5869   3513   157   5414
of instead | Since | precious | My in | were you | I and | I | I and
.you | | eyes, | honored, | | love ,you | give

5 אָדָם תַּחְתֶּיךָ וּלְאֻמִּים תַּחַת נַפְשֶׁךָ: אַל־תִּירָא כִּי־אִתְּךָ
120   8478: 3816   8478   5315   3372
men | of instead | and | instead | ;soul your | not | with for
,you | | peoples of | | | ,Fear | you

6 אָנִי מִמִּזְרָח אָבִיא זַרְעֶךָ וּמִמַּעֲרָב אֲקַבְּצֶךָ: אֹמַר לַצָּפוֹן
4217   935 2233   4628   6908   559. 6828
I | the from | will I | your | the from | will I | the to | will I
;(am) | sunrise | bring | ,seed | sunset | gather you. | north | say

7 תְּנִי וּלְתֵימָן אַל־תִּכְלָאִי בָּנַי מֵרָחוֹק וּבְנוֹתַי מִקְצֵה
8486 7428 3607   935   1121   7350: 1323 7097
Give | to and | not | My | from | My and | from
!up | ,south the | !back | sons | afar, | daughters | the from of end

הָאָרֶץ: כֹּל הַנִּקְרָא בִשְׁמִי וְלִכְבוֹדִי בְּרָאתִיו יְצַרְתִּיו אַף־
776 3605 13.   8034   3519   1254   3335 637
the | everyone | called | ;name My | for and | I created | I formed | ,yea
:earth | who is | | | ,glory My | ;him | ;him

8 עֲשִׂיתִיו: הוֹצִיא עַם־עִוֵּר וְעֵינַיִם יֵשׁ וְחֵרְשִׁים וְאָזְנַיִם לָמוֹ:
6213   3318   5869   5787   3426   2795   241
made | Bring | blind the | yet | there | yet | the and | to
.him | out | people | eyes | ;are | there | ,deaf | .him (are) ears

nations be assembled, and let the peoples be gathered. Who among them can declare this and cause us to hear former things? Let them give their witnesses, that they may be justified. Or let them hear and say, *It is* true. 10You *are* My witnesses, says Jehovah; and My servant whom I have chosen; that you may know and believe Me, and understand that I *am* He. Before Me there was no god formed; nor shall *any* be after Me. 11I, I *am* Jehovah; and there is no Savior besides Me. 12I declared, and I saved, and I proclaimed; and there is no strange *god* among you. And you *are* My witnesses, says Jehovah, and I *am* God. 13Yea, from this day I *am* He, and no one delivers from My hand. I will work, and who will reverse it?

14So says Jehovah, your Redeemer, the Holy One of Israel: For your sake I have sent to Babylon, and have brought down *as* fugitives all of them, even the Chaldeans, whose shout is in the ships. 15I *am* Jehovah, your Holy One, the Creator of Israel, your King. 16So says Jehovah, who makes a way in the sea, and a path in mighty waters; 17who brings out chariot and horse, force and power; they shall lie down together; they shall not rise; they are put out; they are snuffed out like the wick.

18Do not remember former things, nor consider the things of old. 19Behold, I will do a new thing; now it shall sprout. Shall you not know it? I will even make a way in the wilderness; rivers in the desert. 20The beast of the field shall honor Me, jackals and daughters of ostriches; because I give waters in the wilderness, rivers in the desert, to give drink to My people, My chosen. 21This people *that* I formed for Myself shall

2088 5046 854 4310 3816 622 31 62 6908 1471 3605
9 כָּל־הַגּוֹיִם נִקְבְּצוּ יַחְדָּו וְיֵאָסְפוּ לְאֻמִּים מִי בָהֶם יַגִּיד זֹאת
,this can among Who .peoples are and ,together are the All
declare them assembled gathered nations

559 8085 666:3 5707 5414 8085 7223
וְרִאשֹׁנוֹת יַשְׁמִיעֻנוּ יִתְּנוּ עֵדֵיהֶם וְיִצְדָּקוּ וְיִשְׁמְעוּ וְיֹאמְרוּ
,say and let and be and their them Let us cause former and
hear them ;justified ;witnesses give ?hear to things

977 5650 3068/5002 5707 571
10 אֱמֶת׃ אַתֶּם עֵדַי נְאֻם־יְהוָה וְעַבְדִּי אֲשֶׁר בָּחָרְתִּי לְמַעַן
that have I whom My and ,Jehovah states My You (is It)
chosen servant ,witnesses (are) .true

410 3335 64 40 995 539 3045
תֵּדְעוּ וְתַאֲמִינוּ לִי וְתָבִינוּ כִּי־אֲנִי הוּא לְפָנַי לֹא־נוֹצַר אֵל
a was not Before .He I that and ,Me and may you
.god formed Me (am) discern believe know

1107 369 3068 1961 3808 310
11 וְאַחֲרַי לֹא יִהְיֶה׃ אָנֹכִי אָנֹכִי יְהוָה וְאֵין מִבַּלְעָדַי
besides and ;Jehovah I ,I shall not And
Me is not (am) .be (any) Me after

2114/854 369 8085 3467 5046 3462
12 מוֹשִׁיעַ׃ אָנֹכִי הִגַּדְתִּי וְהוֹשַׁעְתִּי וְהִשְׁמַעְתִּי וְאֵין בָּכֶם זָר
an among and pro- I and I and ,declared I .Savior a
alien you is not ;claimed saved

369 3117 410 3068 5002 5707 6258
13 וְאַתֶּם עֵדַי נְאֻם־יְהוָה וַאֲנִי־אֵל׃ גַּם־מִיּוֹם אֲנִי הוּא וְאֵין
and ,He I from ,Also .God I and ;Jehovah states My you and
none (am) day (this) (am) ,witnesses (are)

1350 3068 559 3541 7725 4310 6466 5337 3027
14 מִיָּדִי מַצִּיל אֶפְעַל וּמִי יְשִׁיבֶנָּה׃ כֹּה־אָמַר יְהוָה גֹּאַלְכֶם
your Jehovah says Thus reverse will and will I .delivers from
Redeemer ?it who work hand My

1281 3381 894 7971 4616 3478 6918
קְדוֹשׁ יִשְׂרָאֵל לְמַעַנְכֶם שִׁלַּחְתִּי בָבֶלָה וְהוֹרַדְתִּי בָרִיחִים
(as) brought and to have I your For ,Israel Holy the
fugitives down Babylon sent sake of One

1254 6918 3068 7440 591 3778 3605
15 כֻּלָּם וְכַשְׂדִּים בָּאֳנִיּוֹת רִנָּתָם׃ אֲנִי יְהוָה קְדוֹשְׁכֶם בּוֹרֵא
the Holy your ,Jehovah I shout their the in even of all
of Creator ,One (am) .joy of of ships Chaldeans ,them

1870 3220 5414 3068 559 3541 4428 3478
16 יִשְׂרָאֵל מַלְכְּכֶם׃ כֹּה אָמַר יְהוָה הַנּוֹתֵן בַּיָּם דָּרֶךְ
,way a the in who ,Jehovah says Thus .King your ,Israel
sea puts

3162 5808 2428 5483 7393 3318 5410 5794 4325
17 וּבְמַיִם עַזִּים נְתִיבָה׃ הַמּוֹצִיא רֶכֶב־וָסוּס חַיִל וְעִזּוּז יַחְדָּו
to- and force and chariot brings who ,path a mighty in and
gether ;power ,horse out waters

7223 2142 408 3518 6594 1846 6965 7901
18 יִשְׁכְּבוּ בַּל־יָקוּמוּ דָּעֲכוּ כַּפִּשְׁתָּה כָבוּ׃ אַל־תִּזְכְּרוּ רִאשֹׁנוֹת
former Do not are they the like are they they not shall they
;things remember .out snuffed wick ;quenched ;rise shall ;down lie

6779 6258 2319 6213 2009 995 408 6931
19 וְקַדְמֹנִיּוֹת אַל־תִּתְבֹּנָנוּ׃ הִנְנִי עֹשֶׂה חֲדָשָׁה עַתָּה תִצְמָח
shall it now new a do ,Behold ,consider do not things or
;sprout ;thing I .old of

5104 3452 1870 4057 7760 637 3045 3808
הֲלוֹא תֵדָעוּהָ אַף אָשִׂים בַּמִּדְבָּר דֶּרֶךְ בִּישִׁמוֹן נְהָרוֹת׃
.rivers the in ;way a the in will I ,Yea know you shall
desert wilderness make ?it not

4057 5414 3286 1323 8577 7704 2416 3513
20 תְּכַבְּדֵנִי חַיַּת הַשָּׂדֶה תַּנִּים וּבְנוֹת יַעֲנָה כִּי־נָתַתִּי בַמִּדְבָּר
the in I because the dau- and jackals the the honor shall
wilderness give ;ostriches of ghters ,field of beast Me

3335 2098 972 5971 8248 3452 5104 4325
21 מַיִם נְהָרוֹת בִּישִׁימֹן לְהַשְׁקוֹת עַמִּי בְחִירִי׃ עַם־זוּ יָצַרְתִּי
I This My My give to the in rivers ,waters
formed people .chosen ,people drink to ,desert

22 3021 3290 7121 38,08 5608 8416
לי תהלתי יספרו: ולא־אתי קראת יעקב כי־יגעת בי
of are you for ;Jacob you Me But will they My for
,Me weary ,called not .tell praise ;Me

23 3513 38,08 2077 5930 77,16 935 3478
ישראל: לא־הביאת לי שה עלתיך וזבחיך לא כבדתני
honored not your even burnt your lamb, to have you Not .Israel
.Me sacrifices ,offerings of Me brought

24 7069 3808 3828 3021 38,08 45,03 56,47 3808
לא העבדתיך במנחה ולא הוגעתיך בלבונה: לא־קנית
You not with wearied and food a with you caused I Not
bought .frankincense you not ,offering serve to

5647 389 7301 38,08 2077 2459 70,70 3701
לי בכסף קנה וחלב זבחיך לא הרויתני אך העבדתני
made you but filled you not your (with) and cala- with for
serve Me only ;Me sacrifices of fat ,mus silver Me

25 4229 5771 3021 2403
בחטאותיך הוגעתני בעונתיך: אנכי אנכי הוא מחה
blotting He I ,I your by wearied you your by
out (am) .iniquities Me ;sins

26 8199 21,42 2142 38,08 2403 4616 6588
פשעיך למעני וחטאתיך לא אזכר: הזכירני נשפטה
us let Remind will I not your and My for your
judge ,Me .remember sins ,sake trespasses

27 2398 7223 1 6663 5608 3162
יחד ספר אתה למען תצדק: אביך הראשון חטא
,sinned first Your may you that (for) sum to-
father .justified be ,yourself up ;gether

28 2764 5414 6,9,44 82,69 2490 6586 3887
ומליציך פשעו בי: ואחלל שרי קדש ואתנה לחרם
the to will and the the will I So against trans- your and
devotion give ,sanctuary of chiefs defile .Me gressed interpreters

1421 3478 32,90
יעקב וישראל לגדופים:
to and ,Jacob
.blasphemies Israel

declare My praise. [22]But you have not called on Me, Jacob; but you have been weary of Me, Israel. [23]You have not brought Me the lamb of your burnt offerings; even your sacrifices have not honored Me. I have not caused you to serve with an offering, nor wearied you with incense. [24]You have not bought calamus for Me with silver, nor have you filled Me *with* fat of your sacrifices; but you made Me serve by your sins; you wearied Me by your iniquities. [25]I *am* He who blots out your trespasses for My sake; and I will not remember your sins. [26]Cause Me to remember; let us enter into judgment together; sum up *for* yourself, that you may be justified. [27]Your first father sinned, and your interpreters transgressed against Me. [28]And I will defile the rulers of the sanctuary, and will give Jacob to the curse, and Israel to reviling.

CAP. XLIV מד

CHAPTER 44

1
2 559 977 3478 5650 3290 8085 6258
ועתה שמע יעקב עבדי וישראל בחרתי בו: כה־אמר
says Thus :him have I Israel and My Jacob ,listen And
chosen ;servant now

32,90 5650 3372 5826 990 3335 6213 3068
יהוה עשך ויצרך מבטן יעזרך אל־תירא עבדי יעקב
;Jacob My ,fear do not helps He the from your and your Jehovah
servant ,you ,womb Former Maker

3 5921 5140 67,71 5921 43,25 3332 977 3484
וישרון בחרתי בו: כי אצק־מים על־צמא ונזלים על־
on and thirsty a on water will I For .him have I and
floods ,place pour chosen ,Jeshurun

4 6779 6631 59,21 1293 22,33 59,21 7307 33,32 300,6
יבשה אצק רוחי על־זרעך וברכתי על־צאצאיך: וצמחו
they And your on My and your on My will I dry
sprout shall .offspring blessing seed spirit pour ;ground

5 3068 559 2088 4325 2988 6155 268 996
בבין חציר כערבים על־יבלי־מים: זה יאמר ליהוה
To shall This .water streams by as ,grass as
Jehovah ,say one of willows among

8085 30,68 3027 3789 3290 8085 7121
אני וזה יקרא בשם־יעקב וזה יכתב ידו ליהוה ובשם
the by and For his shall and ,Jacob the by shall and I
of name ,Jehovah ,hand write this of name call this ;(am)

6 135,0 347,8 44,28 3068 559 3655 3478
ישראל יכנה: כה־אמר יהוה מלך־ישראל וגאלו
his and ,Israel the Jehovah says Thus be shall Israel
,Redeemer of King .named

CHAPTER 44

[1]And now listen, My servant Jacob, and Israel *whom* I have chosen. [2]So says Jehovah, your Maker and your Former from the womb. He helps you. Do not fear, My servant Jacob; and you, Jeshurun *whom* I have chosen. [3]For I will pour water on a thirsty place, and floods on the dry ground. I will pour My Spirit on your seed, and My blessing on your offspring. [4]And they shall sprout as among grass, as willows by streams of water. [5]One shall say, I *am* Jehovah's; and another will call by the name of Jacob; and this *one* shall write with his hand, For Jehovah; and be named by the name of Israel.

[6]So says Jehovah, the King of Israel, and his Redeemer, Jehovah of

hosts: I *am* the First and I am the Last; and there is no God except Me. [7]And who, as I, shall call, and shall declare this, and set it in order before Me, since I placed the people of old? And *as to* things to come, even which shall come, let them declare concerning them. [8]Do not dread, nor be afraid. Have I not declared and made you hear since then? So you *are* My witnesses: Is there a God besides Me? Yea, there is none. I have not known a Rock.

[9]Those who form a carved image are all of them vanity. And their delights do not profit; and they *are* their own witnesses. They do not see, nor know, that they may be ashamed. [10]Who has formed a god, or poured out an image, to no profit? [11]Behold, all his companions shall be ashamed; and the craftsmen, they *are* from men. They shall assemble, all of them shall stand; they shall dread; they shall be ashamed together. [12]He carves iron with a tool; he works in the coals and forms it with hammers, and works it with his powerful arm; then he is hungry, and has no strength; he drinks no water and is weary. [13]He fashions wood, and stretches a line; he marks it with a stylus; he shapes it with the carving tool; and he marks it with a compass. And he makes it according to the figure of a man, as the beauty of a man, to sit *in the* house. [14]He cuts down cedars and takes cypress and oak, and he makes the trees of the forest strong for him. He plants a laurel, and rain makes *it* grow. [15]And it shall be for a man to burn; yea, he takes of them and is warmed; and he kindles *it* and bakes bread. Yea, he makes a god and worships; he makes a carved image and bows to it. [16]He burns half of it in the fire; he eats flesh on half of it; he roasts

יְהוָה צְבָאוֹת אֲנִי רִאשׁוֹן וַאֲנִי אַחֲרוֹן וּמִבַּלְעָדַי אֵין אֱלֹהִים׃
,God there except and the I and the I :hosts Jehovah
no is Me ,last (am) first (am) of

7 וּמִי־כָמוֹנִי יִקְרָא וְיַגִּידֶהָ וְיַעְרְכֶהָ לִי מִשּׂוּמִי עַם־עוֹלָם
.old the I since before it set and and Let ?I as (is) And
of people placed ,Me order in it declare call him who

8 וְאֹתִיּוֹת וַאֲשֶׁר תָּבֹאנָה יַגִּידוּ לָמוֹ׃ אַל־תִּפְחֲדוּ וְאַל־
and Do not about them let shall ,yea things And
not ,dread .them declare ,come which ;come to

תִּרְהוּ הֲלֹא מֵאָז הִשְׁמַעְתִּיךָ וְהִגַּדְתִּי וְאַתֶּם עֵדָי הֲיֵשׁ
Is My (are) And and you made I since Have be
there :witnesses you ?declared hear then not .afraid

9 אֱלוֹהַּ מִבַּלְעָדַי וְאֵין צוּר בַּל־יָדָעְתִּי׃ יֹצְרֵי־פֶסֶל כֻּלָּם
of all carved a Those have I not A ,Yea beside God a
them ,image forming .known rock .(is) none ?Me

תֹּהוּ וַחֲמוּדֵיהֶם בַּל־יוֹעִילוּ וְעֵדֵיהֶם הֵמָּה בַּל־יִרְאוּ וּבַל־
and do not they their and do not their And (are)
not ,see witnesses ;profit delights .vanity

10 יֵדְעוּ לְמַעַן יֵבֹשׁוּ׃ מִי־יָצַר אֵל וּפֶסֶל נָסָךְ לְבִלְתִּי הוֹעִיל׃
?profit no to poured an or a has Who may they that do
,out image ,god formed .ashamed be ,know

11 הֵן כָּל־חֲבֵרָיו יֵבֹשׁוּ וְחָרָשִׁים הֵמָּה מֵאָדָם יִתְקַבְּצוּ כֻלָּם
of all them let from they the and be shall his all Be-
them ,assemble ;men (are) ,artisans ,ashamed companions ,hold

12 יַעַמְדוּ יִפְחֲדוּ יֵבֹשׁוּ יָחַד׃ חָרַשׁ בַּרְזֶל מַעֲצָד וּפָעַל
and (with) iron He .together are they they let
works ,tool a engraves ashamed ,dread ;stand

בַּפֶּחָם וּבַמַּקָּבוֹת יִצְּרֵהוּ וַיִּפְעָלֵהוּ בִּזְרוֹעַ כֹּחוֹ גַּם־רָעֵב
is he and his the with and forms with and the in
,hungry ;strength of arm it works ,it hammers the ,coals

13 וְאֵין כֹּחַ לֹא־שָׁתָה מַיִם וַיִּיעָף׃ חָרַשׁ עֵצִים נָטָה קָו
a he ,wood He is and ,water he not ;strength and
;line stretches carves .weary drinks is not

יְתָאֲרֵהוּ בַשֶּׂרֶד יַעֲשֵׂהוּ בַּמַּקְצֻעוֹת וּבַמְּחוּגָה יְתָאֳרֵהוּ
marks he with and carving the with he the with marks he
.it compass a ,tools it makes ;stylus it

וַיַּעֲשֵׂהוּ כְּתַבְנִית אִישׁ כְּתִפְאֶרֶת אָדָם לָשֶׁבֶת בָּיִת׃
(the in) to ,man a the as ,man a the as he And
.house sit of beauty of figure it makes

14 לִכְרָת־לוֹ אֲרָזִים וַיִּקַּח תִּרְזָה וְאַלּוֹן וַיְאַמֶּץ־לוֹ בַּעֲצֵי־יָעַר
the the in for he and and cypress and ,cedars for cuts (He)
;forest of trees him strengthens ;oak takes he him down

15 נָטַע אֹרֶן וְגֶשֶׁם יְגַדֵּל׃ וְהָיָה לְאָדָם לְבָעֵר וַיִּקַּח מֵהֶם
of he and ;burn to a for it And (it) makes and a he
them takes man be shall .grow rain ,laurel plants

וַיָּחָם אַף־יַשִּׂיק וְאָפָה לָחֶם אַף־יִפְעַל־אֵל וַיִּשְׁתָּחוּ עָשָׂהוּ
makes he and god a he ,Yea .bread and he ,yea is and
it ;worships makes bakes ,kindles ;warmed

16 פֶסֶל וַיִּסְגָּד־לָמוֹ׃ חֶצְיוֹ שָׂרַף בְּמוֹ־אֵשׁ עַל־חֶצְיוֹ בָּשָׂר
flesh half on the in he Half .it to and carved a
it of ;fire burns it of bows ,image

roast, and is satisfied. Then he warms himself and says, Ah, I am warm; I have seen the fire. [17]And he makes a god of the rest, his carved image; he bows to it and worships, and prays to it, and says, Deliver me, for you *are* my god.

[18]They do not know, nor discern; for He has smeared their eyes from seeing, their hearts from understanding. [19]And not one turns back to his heart, nor has knowledge nor discernment to say, I have burned half of it in the fire; and I also have baked bread on its coals. I have roasted flesh and have eaten it; and I have made the rest of it into an idol. Shall I bow to a product of a tree? [20]Feeding on ashes, a deceived heart turns him aside, and he does not deliver his soul, nor say, Is there not a lie in my right hand?

[21]Remember these, O Jacob, and Israel. For you *are* My servant; I have formed you; you *are* My servant, O Israel; you shall not forget Me. [22]I have blotted out your transgressions like a thick cloud; and your sins like a cloud. Return to Me, for I have redeemed you. [23]Sing, O heavens, for Jehovah has done *it*. Shout, O lower parts of the earth; burst forth into praise, O mountains. O forest and every tree in it, *sing praise*, because Jehovah has redeemed Jacob, and glorifies Himself in Israel. [24]So says Jehovah, your Redeemer and your Former from the womb; I *am* Jehovah who makes all things; stretching out the heavens; I alone, spreading out the earth. Who *was* with Me, [25]frustrating the signs of liars; yea, He makes diviners mad; turning wise ones backward, and making their knowledge foolish. [26]He confirms the word of His servant, and completes the counsel of His messengers.

יֹאכַל יִצְלֶה צָלִי וְיִשְׂבָּע אַף־יָחֹם וְיֹאמַר הֶאָח חַמּוֹתִי
רָאִיתִי אוּר׃ 17 וּשְׁאֵרִיתוֹ לְאֵל עָשָׂה לְפִסְלוֹ יִסְגָּד־לוֹ
וְיִשְׁתַּחוּ וְיִתְפַּלֵּל אֵלָיו וְיֹאמַר הַצִּילֵנִי כִּי אֵלִי אָתָּה׃ 18 לֹא
יָדְעוּ וְלֹא יָבִינוּ כִּי טַח מֵרְאוֹת עֵינֵיהֶם מֵהַשְׂכִּיל לִבֹּתָם׃
19 וְלֹא־יָשִׁיב אֶל־לִבּוֹ וְלֹא דַעַת וְלֹא־תְבוּנָה לֵאמֹר חֶצְיוֹ
שָׂרַפְתִּי בְמוֹ־אֵשׁ וְאַף אָפִיתִי עַל־גֶּחָלָיו לֶחֶם אֶצְלֶה
בָשָׂר וְאֹכֵל וְיִתְרוֹ לְתוֹעֵבָה אֶעֱשֶׂה לְבוּל עֵץ אֶסְגּוֹד׃
20 רֹעֶה אֵפֶר לֵב הוּתַל הִטָּהוּ וְלֹא־יַצִּיל אֶת־נַפְשׁוֹ וְלֹא
יֹאמַר הֲלוֹא־שֶׁקֶר בִּימִינִי׃ 21 זְכָר־אֵלֶּה יַעֲקֹב וְיִשְׂרָאֵל
כִּי עַבְדִּי־אָתָּה יְצַרְתִּיךָ עֶבֶד־לִי אַתָּה יִשְׂרָאֵל לֹא תִנָּשֵׁנִי׃
22 מָחִיתִי כָעָב פְּשָׁעֶיךָ וְכֶעָנָן חַטֹּאותֶיךָ שׁוּבָה אֵלַי כִּי גְאַלְתִּיךָ׃
23 רָנּוּ שָׁמַיִם כִּי־עָשָׂה יְהוָה הָרִיעוּ תַּחְתִּיּוֹת אָרֶץ פִּצְחוּ
הָרִים רִנָּה יַעַר וְכָל־עֵץ בּוֹ כִּי־גָאַל יְהוָה יַעֲקֹב וּבְיִשְׂרָאֵל
יִתְפָּאָר׃ 24 כֹּה־אָמַר יְהוָה גֹּאֲלֶךָ וְיֹצֶרְךָ מִבָּטֶן אָנֹכִי יְהוָה
עֹשֶׂה כֹּל נֹטֶה שָׁמַיִם לְבַדִּי רֹקַע הָאָרֶץ מִי אִתִּי׃ 25 מֵפֵר
אֹתוֹת בַּדִּים וְקֹסְמִים יְהוֹלֵל מֵשִׁיב חֲכָמִים אָחוֹר
וְדַעְתָּם יְסַכֵּל׃ 26 מֵקִים דְּבַר עַבְדּוֹ וַעֲצַת מַלְאָכָיו יַשְׁלִים

He says to Jerusalem, You will be peopled; and to the cities of Judah, You shall be built; and, I will raise up its ruins. [27]*He* says to the deep, Be a waste! And I will dry up your rivers! [28]*He* says to Cyrus, *You are* My shepherd; and he shall fulfill all My will, even to say to Jerusalem, You shall be built; and to the temple, You shall be set up.

2723 1129 3063 5892 3427 3389 559
הָאֹמֵר לִירוּשָׁלִַם תּוּשָׁב וּלְעָרֵי יְהוּדָה תִּבָּנֶינָה וְחָרְבוֹתֶיהָ
its and wastes | shall you ;built be | ,Judah's cities | to and | be will You ,peopled | to ,Jerusalem | Who says

27 28 559 3001 5104 2717 6683 559 6965
אֲקוֹמֵם׃ הָאֹמֵר לַצּוּלָה חֳרָבִי וְנַהֲרֹתַיִךְ אוֹבִישׁ׃ הָאֹמֵר
Who says | will I .up dry | your And rivers | a Be !waste | the to ,deep | Who says | will I .up raise

1129 3389 559 7999 2656 7466 3566
לְכוֹרֶשׁ רֹעִי וְכָל־חֶפְצִי יַשְׁלִם וְלֵאמֹר לִירוּשָׁלִַם תִּבָּנֶה
be will You ;built | to ,Jerusalem | to even say | shall he ,complete | My pleasure | and all | My ,Cyrus to ,shepherd

3245 1964
וְהֵיכָל תִּוָּסֵד׃
shall You .founded be | the (to) and , temple

CAP. XLV מה

CHAPTER 45

CHAPTER 45

[1]So says Jehovah to His anointed, to Cyrus, whom I have seized by his right hand, to subdue nations before him. Yea, I will open the loins of kings, to open the two-leaved doors before him, and the gates shall not be shut. [2]I will go before you and make hills level; I will tear apart the bronze doors, and cut the iron bars in two. [3]And I will give you the treasures of darkness, even treasures in secret places, that you may know that I *am* Jehovah, who calls you by your name, the God of Israel. [4]For My servant Jacob's sake, and *for* Israel My chosen, I even call you by your name. I name you, but you do not know Me. [5]I *am* Jehovah, and there *is* none else; there is no God except Me. I will clothe you, though you do not know Me, [6]that they may know from the sunrise, and to the sunset, that there *is* none besides Me; I *am* Jehovah, and there *is* none else; [7]forming light, and creating darkness; making peace, and creating evil — I, Jehovah, do all these things.
[8]Drop down from above, O heavens; and let the cloud pour down righteousness. Let the earth open and let salvation bear fruit;

1 3225 2388 834 3566 4899 3068 559 3541
כֹּה־אָמַר יְהוָה לִמְשִׁיחוֹ לְכוֹרֶשׁ אֲשֶׁר־הֶחֱזַקְתִּי בִימִינוֹ
his by ,hand right | have I seized | whom | ,Cyrus to | His to ,anointed | Jehovah | says Thus

6440 6605 6605 4428 4975 1471 6440 7286
לְרַד־לְפָנָיו גּוֹיִם וּמָתְנֵי מְלָכִים אֲפַתֵּחַ לִפְתֹּחַ לְפָנָיו
before him | open to | will I ,open | kings | the yea of loins | ;nations | before him | to subdue

2 1921 3212 6440 5462 3808 8179 1817
דְּלָתַיִם וּשְׁעָרִים לֹא יִסָּגֵרוּ׃ אֲנִי לְפָנֶיךָ אֵלֵךְ וַהֲדוּרִים
and swells | will ,go | before you | I | shall .shut be | not | the and gates | leaved-two ;doors

3 5414 1438 1270 1280 7665 5178 1817 3474
אֲיַשֵּׁר דַּלְתוֹת נְחוּשָׁה אֲשַׁבֵּר וּבְרִיחֵי בַרְזֶל אֲגַדֵּעַ׃ וְנָתַתִּי
I And give | cut .apart | iron | bars and of | will I apart break | bronze | doors of | make ;level

3045 4565 4301 2822 214
לְךָ אוֹצְרוֹת חֹשֶׁךְ וּמַטְמֻנֵי מִסְתָּרִים לְמַעַן תֵּדַע כִּי־אֲנִי
I (am) | that you know may | that | secret ,places | riches and of | ,darkness | treasures of | to you

4 3290 5650 4616 3478 430 8034 7121 3068
יְהוָה הַקּוֹרֵא בְשִׁמְךָ אֱלֹהֵי יִשְׂרָאֵל׃ לְמַעַן עַבְדִּי יַעֲקֹב
,Jacob | My servant | the For of sake | .Israel | the of God | your by ,name | who (you) calls | ,Jehovah

3045 3808 3655 8034 7121 972 3478
וְיִשְׂרָאֵל בְּחִירִי וָאֶקְרָא לְךָ בִּשְׁמֶךָ אֲכַנְּךָ וְלֹא יְדַעְתָּנִי׃
know you .Me | but not | name I ,you | your by .name | you | I even call | My ,elect | Israel and

5 3045 241 430 369 2108 5750 369 3068
אֲנִי יְהוָה וְאֵין עוֹד זוּלָתִי אֵין אֱלֹהִים אֲאַזֶּרְךָ וְלֹא יְדַעְתָּנִי׃
know you ,Me | though not | will I ,you clothe | .God | there no is | except Me | any ,more | and none | ,Jehovah | I (am)

6 1107 657 4628 8121 4217 3045
לְמַעַן יֵדְעוּ מִמִּזְרַח־שֶׁמֶשׁ וּמִמַּעֲרָבָה כִּי־אֶפֶס בִּלְעָדָי
besides ;Me | none that (is) | the to and sunset | the sun | the from of rising | may they know | that

7 7965 6213 2822 1254 216 3335 5750 369 3068
אֲנִי יְהוָה וְאֵין עוֹד׃ יוֹצֵר אוֹר וּבוֹרֵא חֹשֶׁךְ עֹשֶׂה שָׁלוֹם
peace | making | ;darkness | and creating | light Forming | any !more | and none | Jeho- | I (am)

8 7491 428 3605 6213 3068 7451 1254
וּבוֹרֵא רָע אֲנִי יְהוָה עֹשֶׂה כָל־אֵלֶּה׃ הַרְעִיפוּ
Drop ,down | these .things | all | do | ,Jehovah | ,I | ;evil | and creating

3468 6509 776 6605 6664 5140 7834 4605 8064
שָׁמַיִם מִמַּעַל וּשְׁחָקִים יִזְּלוּ־צֶדֶק תִּפְתַּח־אֶרֶץ וְיִפְרוּ־יֶשַׁע
salva- tion | let and fruit bear | the ,earth | let open | righ- ;teousness | pour let | and clouds | from ;above | O ,heavens

and let righteousness sprout together — I, Jehovah have created it. [9]Woe *to* him who fights with his Former! A potsherd among the potsherds of the earth! Shall the clay say to its former, What are you making? Or *does* your work *say*, He *has* no hands? [10]Woe *to* him who says to a father, What are you fathering? Or to the woman, What are you laboring over?

[11]So says Jehovah, the Holy One of Israel, and his Former, Do you ask Me the things to come? Do you give command to Me about My sons, and about the work of My hands? [12]I have made the earth, and created man on it. I stretched out the heavens *with* My hands; and I have set all their host in order. [13]I raised him up in righteousness, and have made straight all his ways. He shall build My city, and he will release My captives; not for price, nor for reward, says Jehovah of hosts.

[14]So says Jehovah, The labor of Egypt, and the goods of Ethiopia, and of the Sabeans, men of stature, shall come to you; and they shall be yours. They shall come after you; they shall cross in chains; and they shall bow to you; they shall plead to you. Surely God *is* in you, and there *is* none else, no *other* God.

[15]Truly, You *are* a God who hides Himself, O God of Israel, the Savior. [16]They shall be ashamed, and also are disgraced, all of them. Together they go into disgrace, carvers of images. [17]Israel is saved in Jehovah *with* everlasting salvation. You shall not be ashamed nor disgraced to the forevers of eternity.

[18]For so says Jehovah, Creator of the heavens; He *is* God, forming the earth and making it; He makes it stand, not creating it empty, *but* forming it to be

9 וּצְדָקָה תַצְמִיחַ יַחַד אֲנִי יְהוָה בְּרָאתִיו׃ הוֹי רָב
who him Woe have Jehovah I ;together make it let righ- and
strives (to) .it created sprout teousness

אֶת־יֹצְרוֹ חֶרֶשׂ אֶת־חַרְשֵׂי אֲדָמָה הֲיֹאמַר חֹמֶר לְיֹצְרוֹ
its to clay Shall the pot- the among A his with
,former say !earth of sherds potsherd !Former

10 מַה־תַּעֲשֶׂה וּפָעָלְךָ אֵין־יָדַיִם לוֹ׃ הוֹי אֹמֵר לְאָב
a to him Woe to hands No your Or you are What
,father says who (to) ?him (are) ,work ?making

11 מַה־תּוֹלִיד וּלְאִשָּׁה מַה־תְּחִילִין׃ כֹּה־אָמַר יְהוָה קְדוֹשׁ
Holy the ,Jehovah says Thus you are What a to Or you are What
of One ?over laboring ,woman ?fathering

יִשְׂרָאֵל וְיֹצְרוֹ הָאֹתִיּוֹת שְׁאָלוּנִי עַל־בָּנַי וְעַל־פֹּעַל יָדַי
My the and My about you Do things the his and Israel
hands of work about ;sons ?Me ask come to ,Former

12 תְּצַוֻּנִי׃ אָנֹכִי עָשִׂיתִי אֶרֶץ וְאָדָם עָלֶיהָ בָרָאתִי אֲנִי יָדַי
(with) I created it on and the have I com- you do
hands My man ,earth made ?Me mand

13 נָטוּ שָׁמַיִם וְכָל־צְבָאָם צִוֵּיתִי׃ אָנֹכִי הַעִירֹתִהוּ בְצֶדֶק וְכָל־
and righ- in raised I have I their and the stretched
all ,teousness up him .ordered host all ;heavens out

דְּרָכָיו אֲיַשֵּׁר הוּא־יִבְנֶה עִירִי וְגָלוּתִי יְשַׁלֵּחַ לֹא בִמְחִיר
for not will he My and My shall He made his
,price ;release captives ,city build .straight ways

14 וְלֹא בְשֹׁחַד אָמַר יְהוָה צְבָאוֹת׃ כֹּה ׀ אָמַר יְהוָה
,Jehovah says Thus .hosts Jehovah says for and
of ,reward not

יְגִיעַ מִצְרַיִם וּסְחַר־כּוּשׁ וּסְבָאִים אַנְשֵׁי מִדָּה עָלַיִךְ יַעֲבֹרוּ
shall to ,stature men of and ,Ethiopia the and ,Egypt The
,cross you of Sabeans the of goods of labor

וְלָךְ יִהְיוּ אַחֲרַיִךְ יֵלֵכוּ בַּזִּקִּים יַעֲבֹרוּ וְאֵלַיִךְ יִשְׁתַּחֲווּ אֵלַיִךְ
you to they to and shall they in shall they after shall they and
;bow shall you ;cross chains ;come you ;be you to

15 יִתְפַּלָּלוּ אַךְ בָּךְ אֵל וְאֵין עוֹד אֶפֶס אֱלֹהִים׃ אָכֵן אַתָּה אֵל
a You Truly .God no any is and God in ,Surely shall they
God (are) (other) ,more not ;(is) you .plead

16 מִסְתַּתֵּר אֱלֹהֵי יִשְׂרָאֵל מוֹשִׁיעַ׃ בּוֹשׁוּ וְגַם־נִכְלְמוּ כֻּלָּם
of all dis- are and are They the ,Israel the hiding
;them ,graced also ,ashamed .Savior of God ,Himself

17 יַחְדָּו הָלְכוּ בַכְּלִמָּה חָרָשֵׁי צִירִים׃ יִשְׂרָאֵל נוֹשַׁע בַּיהוָה
in saved is Israel .images carvers into go they to-
,Jehovah of ,disgrace gether

תְּשׁוּעַת עוֹלָמִים לֹא־תֵבֹשׁוּ וְלֹא־תִכָּלְמוּ עַד־עוֹלְמֵי עַד׃
of for- the to be shall and shall You not .everlasting (with)
.eternity evers disgraced not ashamed be salvation

18 כִּי כֹה אָמַר־יְהוָה בּוֹרֵא הַשָּׁמַיִם הוּא הָאֱלֹהִים
;God (is) He the Creator ,Jehovah says thus For
,heavens of

יֹצֵר הָאָרֶץ וְעֹשָׂהּ הוּא כוֹנְנָהּ לֹא־תֹהוּ בְרָאָהּ לָשֶׁבֶת
be to creating empty not establishes He mak- and the forming
inhabited ,it ;it ;it ing earth

inhabited. I *am* Jehovah, and there *is* none else. [19]I
have not spoken in secret,
in a dark place of the earth. I
did not say to Jacob's seed,
Seek Me in vain. I Jehovah
speak righteousness, declaring right things.
[20]Gather yourselves and
come; draw near together,
escaped ones of the
nations; the ones who set
up the wood of their carved
image, and the ones who
pray to a god *who* cannot
save—they know nothing
—[21]declare and bring near;
yea, let them consult together. Who has revealed
this of old; who has told it
from then? Is it not I,
Jehovah? And there *is* no
God other than Me; a just
God and a Savior; there is
none except Me. [22]Turn to
Me and be saved, all the
ends of the earth; for I *am*
God, and there *is* no other.
[23]I have sworn by Myself,
the word has gone out of
My mouth *in* righteousness,
and shall not return, that to
Me every knee shall bow,
every tongue shall swear;
[24]he shall say, Only in
Jehovah do I have
righteousness and strength;
to Him he comes; and they
are ashamed, all who are
angry with Him. [25]In
Jehovah all of the seed of
Israel shall be justified, and
shall glory.

19 4725 1696 5643 38:08 5750 369 3068 3335
יְצָרָהּ אֲנִי יְהוָה וְאֵין עוֹד׃ לֹא בַסֵּתֶר דִּבַּרְתִּי בִּמְקוֹם
a in of place | have I ,spoken | in secret | Not | any .more | and none | Jeho- vah (am) | I | forming :it

3068 1245 8414 3290 2233 559 38:08/2822 776
אֶרֶץ חֹשֶׁךְ לֹא אָמַרְתִּי לְזֶרַע יַעֲקֹב תֹּהוּ בַקְּשׁוּנִי אֲנִי יְהוָה
Jehovah I | Seek ;Me | vain in | ,Jacob | the to of seed | did I say | not | ;dark | the earth

20 3162 5066 935 6908 4339 5046 6664 1696
דֹּבֵר צֶדֶק מַגִּיד מֵישָׁרִים׃ הִקָּבְצוּ וָבֹאוּ הִתְנַגְּשׁוּ יַחְדָּו
,together | draw near | and come | Gather yourselves | right .things | declaring | righ- ,teousness | speak

6419 6459 6086 5375 3045 3808 1471 6412
פְּלִיטֵי הַגּוֹיִם לֹא יָדְעוּ הַנֹּשְׂאִים אֶת־עֵץ פִּסְלָם וּמִתְפַּלְלִים
those and pray who | their ,image | the of wood | who those up lift | they know | not | the ;nations | escaped of ones

21 4310 3162 3289 637 5066 5046 3467 38:08 410
אֶל־אֵל לֹא יוֹשִׁיעַ׃ הַגִּידוּ וְהַגִּישׁוּ אַף יִוָּעֲצוּ יַחְדָּו מִי
Who | to- .gether | them let consult | ,yea | bring and ;near (it) | Declare | (who) .saves | not | a god | to

369 3068 5046 6924 2088 8085
הִשְׁמִיעַ זֹאת מִקֶּדֶם מֵאָז הִגִּידָהּ הֲלוֹא אֲנִי יְהוָה וְאֵין
And not | ?Jehovah | ,I | it not | Is | told has ?it | from then | from ,old of | this | has revealed

22 6437 2108 369 34:67 6662 410 11:07 430 5750
עוֹד אֱלֹהִים מִבַּלְעָדַי אֵל־צַדִּיק וּמוֹשִׁיעַ אַיִן זוּלָתִי׃ פְּנוּ
Turn | except .Me | none is | a and —Savior | just | a God | beside —Me | a God | any more

23 5750 369 410 776 657 36:05 3467
אֵלַי וְהִוָּשְׁעוּ כָּל־אַפְסֵי־אָרֶץ כִּי אֲנִי־אֵל וְאֵין עוֹד׃ בִּי
By Myself | any .more | and none | ,God I (am) | for | the earth | the of ends | all | be and saved | to Me

3766 7725 38:08 1697 6666 6310 33:18 7650
נִשְׁבַּעְתִּי יָצָא מִפִּי צְדָקָה דָּבָר וְלֹא יָשׁוּב כִּי־לִי תִּכְרַע
shall bow | to that Me | shall ;return | and not | the ,word | righ- teousness | (in) My mouth | from gone | has | have I ;sworn

24 6666 559 3068 389 3956 3605/7650 1290
כָּל־בֶּרֶךְ תִּשָּׁבַע כָּל־לָשׁוֹן׃ אַךְ בַּיהוָה לִי אָמַר צְדָקוֹת
righ- teousness | he says | (is) ,me to | in Jehovah | Only | .tongue every | shall swear | ,knee every

25 6663 3068 2734 3605 954 935 5797
וָעֹז עָדָיו יָבוֹא וְיֵבֹשׁוּ כֹּל הַנֶּחֱרִים בּוֹ׃ בַּיהוָה יִצְדְּקוּ
be shall justified | In Jehovah | with .Him | are who angry | all | they and ashamed are | he ,comes | to Him;strength | and

3478 2233 3605 8597
וְיִתְהַלְלוּ כָּל־זֶרַע יִשְׂרָאֵל׃
.Israel | the of seed | all | shall and glory

CAP. XLVI מו

CHAPTER 46

CHAPTER 46

[1]Bel has bowed; Nebo
stoops; their idols are for
the beast, and for the cattle;
your things carried are
loads; a burden for the
weary. [2]They stoop; they
bow together; they are not
able to deliver the burden;
and their soul has gone into
captivity. [3]Listen to me, O
house of Jacob, and all the
remnant of the house of
Israel; who are borne from

1 929 2416 6097 1961 50:15 7164 1078 3766
כָּרַע בֵּל קֹרֵס נְבוֹ הָיוּ עֲצַבֵּיהֶם לַחַיָּה וְלַבְּהֵמָה
for and ;cattle the | the for beast | their idols | are | ;Nebo | stoops | ,Bel | has bowed

2 38:08 3162 3766 7164 5889 4853 6006 5385
נְשֻׂאֹתֵיכֶם עֲמוּסוֹת מַשָּׂא לַעֲיֵפָה׃ קָרְסוּ כָרְעוּ יַחְדָּו לֹא
not ;together | they bow | They ,stoop | the for .weary | a burden | (are) ;loads | things your carried

3 8085 1980 7628 5315 4853 44:22 3201
יָכְלוּ מַלֵּט מַשָּׂא וְנַפְשָׁם בַּשְּׁבִי הָלָכָה׃ שִׁמְעוּ
Listen | has .gone | into captivity | their and soul | the ;burden | to rescue | are they able

6006 3478 1004 7611 36:05 3290/1004
אֵלַי בֵּית יַעֲקֹב וְכָל־שְׁאֵרִית בֵּית יִשְׂרָאֵל הָעֲמֻסִים מִנִּי־
from | are who borne | ,Israel | the of house | rem- of nant | the all | and | ,Jacob | house of | to Me

the belly, who are lifted from the womb: [4]Even to old age I *am* He; and I will bear to gray hair; I made, and I will carry; and I will bear and deliver.

[5]To whom will you compare Me and make Me equal; and compare Me, that we may be alike? [6]Those who lavish gold out of the bag, and weigh silver on the measure; they hire a refiner and he makes it a god. They fall down; yea, they worship. [7]They carry it on the shoulder; they bear it and set it in its place, and it stands; it shall not move from its place. Yes, he cries to it, but it does not answer, it does not save him from his distress. [8]Remember this and be a man; return *it* on *your* heart, transgressors. [9]Remember former things from forever, for I am God, and no one else *is* God, even none like Me, [10]declaring the end from the beginning, and from the past those things which were not done, saying, My purpose shall rise; and, I will do all My desire; [11]calling a bird of prey from the sunrise, the man of My counsel from a far off land. Yes, I have spoken; yes, I will cause it to come; I have formed; yes, I will do it.

[12]Listen to Me, mighty ones of heart who are far from righteousness: I bring near My righteousness; it shall not be far off, and My salvation shall not wait; I will place salvation in Zion, My glory for Israel.

7872 2209 5704 7356 5375 990
4 בטן הנשאים מני-רחם: ועד-זקנה אני הוא ועד-שיבה
gray hair and to ;He I (am) old age Even to the from !womb are who lifted the ,belly

44122 5445 53 75 6213 5445
אני אסבל אני עשיתי ואני אשא ואני אסבל ואמלט:
and .rescue will bear and I will carry I and ,made I will ;bear I

2107 1819 4911 7737 1819 4310
5 למי תדמיוני ותשוו ותמשלוני ונדמה: הזלים
Those lavishing may we that ?alike be compare and Me make and ;equal Me you will ,Me liken To whom

6213 6884 7936 8254 7070 3701 5599 2091
6 זהב מכיס וכסף בקנה ישקלו ישכרו צורף ויעשהו
he and it makes re- a ,finer they hire ;weigh the on rod cane even silver of out ,bag a gold

3240 5445 3801 5921 5375 7812 5456 410
7 אל יסגדו אף-ישתחוו: ישאהו על-כתף יסבלהו ויניחהו
rest and it bear they it the ;shoulder on They it carry they .worship yea they ;down bow ;god a

3808 6817 637 4185 3808 4725 5975 8478
תחתיו ויעמד ממקומו לא ימיש אף-יצעק אליו ולא
but not ,it to he cries ,Yes shall it .depart not its from place it and ;stands its in ,place

377 2142 3467 3808 6864 6030
8 יענה מצרתו לא יושיענו: זכרו-זאת והתאששו
a be and ;man this Remember saves it .him not his from distress it ,answers

5769 7223 2142 3820 6586 7725
9 השיבו פושעים על-לב: זכרו ראשנות מעולם כי אנכי
I (am) for from .forever former things Remember (your) on ;heart ;transgressors return .(it)

7225 5046 3644 657 430 5750 369 410
10 אל ואין עוד אלהים ואפס כמוני: מגיד מראשית
the from beginning declaring ,Me like even none ,God any more and none ; God

3605 6965 6098 559 6213 834 6924 319
אחרית ומקדם אשר לא-נעשו אמר עצתי תקום וכל-
and all shall ,rise My purpose ,saying were ,done not things which from and past the the ,end

376 4801 776 5861 4217 7121 6213 2656
11 חפצי אעשה: קרא ממזרח עיט מארץ מרחק איש
the of man far off from land a bird a ,prey of the from sunrise calling will I ;do My desire

6213 637 3335 935 637 1696 637 6098
עצתו אף-דברתי אף-אביאנה יצרתי אף-אעשנה:
do will I .it ,yes have I ,formed will I ;it bring ,yes have I ;spoken ,Yes My purpose

6666 7126 6666 7350 3820 47 8085
12 13 שמעו אלי אבירי לב הרחוקים מצדקה: קרבתי צדקתי
righ- My ;teousness bring I near from :righteousness are who far heart mighty of ones to ,Me Listen

8668 5414 309 3808 8668 7368
לא תרחק ותשועתי לא תאחר ונתתי בציון תשועה
,salvation Zion in will I place shall ,wait not My and salvation shall it ,off far be not

8597 3478
לישראל תפארתי:
.glory My Israel for

CAP. XLVII מז

CHAPTER 47

CHAPTER 47

[1]Go down and sit on the dust, O virgin daughter of Babylon; sit on the earth; a throne is not *to* the

369 776 3427 884/1323 1330 6083 3427 3381
1 רדי ושבי על-עפר בתולת בת-בבל שבי-לארץ אין
not is the on ;ground sit ;Baby- lon daughter of O virgin the ,dust on sit and Go down

daughter of the Chaldeans; for they shall not again call you tender and delicate. 2Take millstones and grind meal; uncover your veil; strip off the skirt; uncover the leg; pass over rivers. 3Your nakedness shall be uncovered; yea, your shame shall be seen—I will take vengeance and I will not meet a man. 4Our Redeemer; Jehovah of hosts *is* His name, the Holy One of Israel. 5Sit *in* silence, and go into darkness, O daughter of the Chaldeans, for they shall no more call you the mistress of kingdoms.

6I was angry with My people; I defiled My inheritance and gave them into your hand. You gave them no mercy; you made very heavy your yoke on the aged. 7And you said, I shall be a mistress forever; until you did not set these things on your heart, and not did remember its end. 8Now, then, hear this, O pleasure seeker, who lives carelessly; who says in her heart, I *am*, and none else *is*; I shall not sit *as* a widow, nor shall I know the loss of children. 9But these two things shall suddenly come to you, in one day: loss of children, and widowhood; as complete they come on you, for your many sorceries, for the multitude of your great spells. 10For you trusted in your wickedness; you said, No one sees me. Your wisdom and your knowledge, it leads you away, and you said in your heart, I *am* and none else *is*. 11For this, evil shall come on you; you shall not know its origin. And mischief shall fall on you; you shall not be able to cover it. And ruin shall come on you suddenly, you shall not know. 12Stand now among your spells, and

6028 7390 7121 3254 38,08 3778 1323 3678
כִּסֵּא בַּת־כַּשְׂדִּים כִּי לֹא תוֹסִיפִי יִקְרְאוּ־לָךְ רַכָּה וַעֲנֻגָּה׃
and tender you they shall not for the daughter a
.delicate call again ;Chaldeans of ,throne

7785 1540 7640 2834 6776 1540 7058 2912 7347 3947
2 קְחִי רֵחַיִם וְטַחֲנִי קָמַח גַּלִּי צַמָּתֵךְ חֶשְׂפִּי־שֹׁבֶל גַּלִּי־שׁוֹק
the uncover the strip your un- ;meal and mill Take
;leg ;skirt off ;veil cover grind stones

394 7 7535 2781 7200 1571 61 72 1540 5104 5674
3 עִבְרִי נְהָרוֹת׃ תִּגָּל עֶרְוָתֵךְ גַּם תֵּרָאֶה חֶרְפָּתֵךְ נָקָם אֶקָּח
will I venge- your be shall also Your be shall ,rivers pass
,take ance ;shame seen ;nakedness uncovered over

6718 8034 6635 3068 1350 120 6293 38,08
4 וְלֹא אֶפְגַּע אָדָם׃ גֹּאֲלֵנוּ יְהוָה צְבָאוֹת שְׁמוֹ קְדוֹשׁ
Holy the His (is) hosts Jehovah Our .man a will I and
of One ,name of ,Redeemer meet not

38,08 3778 28 22 935 1748 3427 3478
5 יִשְׂרָאֵל׃ שְׁבִי דוּמָם וּבֹאִי בַחֹשֶׁךְ בַּת־כַּשְׂדִּים כִּי לֹא
not for the daughter into go and (in) Sit .Israel
Chaldeans of darkness silence

5971 5921 7107 4467 1404 7121 3254
6 תוֹסִיפִי יִקְרְאוּ־לָךְ גְּבֶרֶת מַמְלָכוֹת׃ קָצַפְתִּי עַל־עַמִּי
My over was I .kingdoms mistress you they shall
;people angry of call again

5921 7356 7760 3027 5414 5159 2490
חִלַּלְתִּי נַחֲלָתִי וָאֶתְּנֵם בְּיָדֵךְ לֹא־שַׂמְתְּ לָהֶם רַחֲמִים עַל־
on compas- to You not your into and inheri- My I
;sion them gave .hand them gave tance defiled

1404 1961 5769 559 39 66 5923 3513 2205
7 זָקֵן הִכְבַּדְתְּ עֻלֵּךְ מְאֹד׃ וַתֹּאמְרִי לְעוֹלָם אֶהְיֶה גְבָרֶת
a shall I forever you And .very your you made the
;mistress be ,said yoke heavy aged

319 2142 38,08 3820 428 7760 3808 5704
עַד לֹא־שַׂמְתְּ אֵלֶּה עַל־לִבֵּךְ לֹא זָכַרְתְּ אַחֲרִיתָהּ׃
.end its you not your on these you not until
remembered ;heart things set

38 24 559 982 3427 5719 2088 8085 6258
8 וְעַתָּה שִׁמְעִי־זֹאת עֲדִינָה הַיּוֹשֶׁבֶת לָבֶטַח הָאֹמְרָה בִּלְבָבָהּ
her in says who ;securely who sensual ,this hear No
,heart lives ,one ,then

7908 3045 38,08 490 3427 5750 657
אֲנִי וְאַפְסִי עוֹד לֹא אֵשֵׁב אַלְמָנָה וְלֹא אֵדַע שְׁכוֹל׃
of loss shall I and a (as) shall I not any is and I
.children know not ,widow sit ;more none (am)

489 7908 259 3117 7281 428/8147 935
9 וְתָבֹאנָה לָּךְ שְׁתֵּי־אֵלֶּה רֶגַע בְּיוֹם אֶחָד שְׁכוֹל וְאַלְמֹן
and of loss :one day in ,suddenly these two to shall But
;widowhood children things you come

3966 2267 6109 3785 7230 935 8537
כְּתֻמָּם בָּאוּ עָלַיִךְ בְּרֹב כְּשָׁפַיִךְ בְּעָצְמַת חֲבָרַיִךְ מְאֹד׃
.great your the for your for ,you on they com- as
spells of power sorceries many come plete

1847 2451 7200 369 559 7451 982
10 וַתִּבְטְחִי בְרָעָתֵךְ אָמַרְתְּ אֵין רֹאָנִי חָכְמָתֵךְ וְדַעְתֵּךְ הִיא
it your and your sees no you your in you For
,knowledge wisdom ;me one said ;evil trusted

935 5750 657 3820 7725
11 שׁוֹבְבָתֶךְ וַתֹּאמְרִי בְלִבֵּךְ אֲנִי וְאַפְסִי עוֹד׃ וּבָא עָלַיִךְ
you on shall But any and I your in you and you leads
come more none (am) heart said ;away

3722 3201 38,08 1943 5921 5307 7837 3045 7451
רָעָה לֹא תֵדְעִי שַׁחְרָהּ וְתִפֹּל עָלַיִךְ הֹוָה לֹא תוּכְלִי כַּפְּרָהּ
to shall you not mis- you on and its shall you not ;evil
.it cover able be ;chief fall shall ;origin know

22 67 4994/5975 3045 38,08 7722 6597 935
12 וְתָבֹא עָלַיִךְ פִּתְאֹם שׁוֹאָה לֹא תֵדָעִי׃ עִמְדִי־נָא בַחֲבָרַיִךְ
among now Stand shall you not ;ruin suddenly on shall And
.spells your .know you come

with your many sorceries, in which you have wearied yourself since your youth—perhaps you will be able to profit; perhaps you may cause quaking. [13]You are exhausted by your many plans; let those dividing the heavens stand up now and save you, the gazers into the stars, making known what is coming on you into the new moons. [14]Behold, they are as stubble; the fire burns them; they shall not save their soul from the flame's hand; there is no coal to warm them; nor fire, to sit before it. [15]So they are to you with whom you have labored, your traders from your youth; each one wanders to his own way; no one saves you.

7230 3785 834 3021 5271 194 3201 3276
וּבְרֹב כְּשָׁפַיִךְ בַּאֲשֶׁר יָגַעַתְּ מִנְּעוּרָיִךְ אוּלַי תּוּכְלִי הוֹעִיל
with and many, your sorceries, which in, you labored, your from youth;, perhaps, will you able be, to profit;

13 194 6206 3811 7230 6098 5975 3467
אוּלַי תַּעֲרוֹצִי׃ נִלְאֵית בְּרֹב עֲצָתָיִךְ יַעַמְדוּ־נָא וְיוֹשִׁיעֻךְ
perhaps may you cause quaking, are You exhausted, by many, your plans;, let up stand, now, save and you.

1895 8064 2374 3556 3045 2320
הֹבְרֵו שָׁמַיִם הַחֹזִים בַּכּוֹכָבִים מוֹדִיעִם לֶחֳדָשִׁים מֵאֲשֶׁר
those dividing, the heavens, the gazers, the into stars, making known, the into new moons, from what

14 935 1961 7179 784 8313 5337
יָבֹאוּ עָלָיִךְ׃ הִנֵּה הָיוּ כְקַשׁ אֵשׁ שְׂרָפָתַם לֹא־יַצִּילוּ אֶת־
are coming, on you., Behold, they are, as stubble, the fire, burns them;, shall they not save

5315 3027 3852 369 1513 2552 217 3427 5048
נַפְשָׁם מִיַּד לֶהָבָה אֵין־גַּחֶלֶת לַחְמָם אוּר לָשֶׁבֶת נֶגְדּוֹ׃
their soul, the from of hand, the flame;, there no is, coal, to warm them, (nor) fire, to sit, before it.

15 834 3021 5503 5271 376 5676
כֵּן הָיוּ־לָךְ אֲשֶׁר יָגָעַתְּ סֹחֲרַיִךְ מִנְּעוּרַיִךְ אִישׁ לְעֶבְרוֹ
So, they are to you, (with) whom, you labored,, your traders, your from youth;, each man, his to own side

8582 369 3462
תָּעוּ אֵין מוֹשִׁיעֵךְ׃
they wander;, none, saves you.

CAP. XLVIII מח

CHAPTER 48

CHAPTER 48

[1]Hear this, O house of Jacob, who are called by the name of Israel, and have come out from the waters of Judah, who swear by Jehovah's name and profess by the God of Israel—not in truth or in righteousness. [2]For they are called of the holy city, and rest themselves on the God of Israel; Jehovah of hosts *is* His name. [3]I have foretold the former things from then; and they went out of My mouth; and I made them hear; suddenly I acted, and they came about. [4]Because I knew that you *are* hard, and your neck is a sinew of iron, and your brow brass. [5]And I declared to you from then; before it came I made you hear, lest you should say, My idol did them; and my image and my casted image commanded them. [6]You heard; see it all; and will you not declare? I made you hear new things from now, even hidden things,

1 8085 2088 1004 3290 7121 8034 3478 4325
שִׁמְעוּ־זֹאת בֵּית־יַעֲקֹב הַנִּקְרָאִים בְּשֵׁם יִשְׂרָאֵל וּמִמֵּי
Hear, this,, house of, Jacob,, who are called, the by of name, Israel,, from and waters

3063 3318 7650 8034 3068 430 3478
יְהוּדָה יָצָאוּ הַנִּשְׁבָּעִים ׀ בְּשֵׁם יְהוָה וּבֵאלֹהֵי יִשְׂרָאֵל
Judah's, have come out;, swear who, the by of name, Jehovah,, by and the of God, Israel

2 2142 3808 571 3808 6666 5892 6944 7121
יַזְכִּירוּ לֹא בֶאֱמֶת וְלֹא בִצְדָקָה׃ כִּי־מֵעִיר הַקֹּדֶשׁ נִקְרָאוּ
mention—, not, truth in, and not, in righteousness., For from city, the holy, are they called,

5921 430 3478 5564 3068 6635 8034
וְעַל־אֱלֹהֵי יִשְׂרָאֵל נִסְמָכוּ יְהוָה צְבָאוֹת שְׁמוֹ׃
and on the of God, Israel, support themselves;, Jehovah, of hosts, His (is) name.

3 7223 227 5046 6310 3318 8085 6597
הָרִאשֹׁנוֹת מֵאָז הִגַּדְתִּי וּמִפִּי יָצְאוּ וְאַשְׁמִיעֵם פִּתְאֹם
The former things, from then, have I foretold;, from and my mouth, they went out;, made I and hear them, suddenly

4 6213 935 1847 7186 1517 1270 6203
עָשִׂיתִי וַתָּבֹאנָה׃ מִדַּעְתִּי כִּי קָשֶׁה אָתָּה וְגִיד בַּרְזֶל עָרְפֶּךָ
I acted;, they and came about., Because knew I, that, hard, you (are)—, a and sinew of, iron, (is) your neck.

5 4696 5154 5046 227 2962 935 8085
וּמִצְחֲךָ נְחוּשָׁה׃ וָאַגִּיד לְךָ מֵאָז בְּטֶרֶם תָּבוֹא הִשְׁמַעְתִּיךָ
your and brow (is), brass., I And declared, to you, from then;, before, it came, I made you hear

6 559 6090 6213 6459 5262 6680 8085 2372
פֶּן־תֹּאמַר עָצְבִּי עָשָׂם וּפִסְלִי וְנִסְכִּי צִוָּם׃ שָׁמַעְתָּ חֲזֵה
lest you should say, My idol, did them;, my and image, my and casted image, commanded them., You heard,, behold

3808 5046 8085 2319 6258 5341
כֻּלָּהּ וְאַתֶּם הֲלוֹא תַגִּידוּ הִשְׁמַעְתִּיךָ חֲדָשׁוֹת מֵעַתָּה וּנְצֻרוֹת
all of it;, you and, will not, you declare?, made I hear you, new things, from now,, even hidden things,

and you did not know them. [7]They are created now, and not from then; even before today, but you did not hear them; lest you should say, See, I knew them. [8]Yea, you did not hear; yea, you did not know; yea, from then your ear was not opened; for I know you surely will betray and trespass, from the womb it was called to you. [9]For My name's sake I will put off My anger; and for My praise I will hold back for you, so as not to cut you off. [10]Behold, I have refined you, but not with silver; I have chosen you in the furnace of affliction. [11]For My sake, for My sake, I will act; for how is it defiled? And I will not give My glory to another.

[12]Listen to Me, O Jacob, and Israel My called: I *am* He; I *am* the first; I surely *am* the last. [13]My hand surely founded earth, and My right hand has stretched out the heavens; I called, they stood up together. [14]All of you gather and hear: Who among them has declared these things? Jehovah has loved him. He will do His pleasure on Babylon; yea, His arm *shall be on* the Chaldeans. [15]I, I have spoken; yea, I have called him, I brought him, and he causes his way to prosper. [16]Come near to me; hear this: I have not spoken in secret from the beginning. From its being, I *was* there; and now the Lord Jehovah, and His spirit, has sent Me. [17]So says Jehovah, your Redeemer, the Holy One of Israel, I *am* Jehovah your God, who teaches you to profit, who leads you in the way you should go. [18]Oh that you had listened to My commands! Then your peace would have been like the river, and your righteousness like the waves of the sea. [19]And your seed would have been like the sand, and your offspring like its grains; his name would not have been cut off

8085 38,08 3117/6440 1254 6258 3045 38,08
7 ולא ידעתם׃ עתה נבראו ולא מאז ולפני־יום ולא שמעתם
heard you but ,today even from and are they Now knew you and
;them not before ,then not created them not

3045 38,08/1571 8085 3045 2009 559
8 פן־תאמר הנה ידעתין׃ גם לא־שמעת גם לא ידעת גם
,yea did you not ,yea did you not ,Yea knew I ,Behold you lest
;know ;hear .them ,say should

990 6586 898 898 3045 241 6605 38,08 227
מאז לא־פתחה אזנך כי ידעתי בגוד תבגוד ופשע מבטן
the from and will you surely know I for your was not from
womb,trespass betray ;ear opened then

24113 84,16 639 748 8034 4616 7121
9 קרא לך׃ למען שמי אאריך אפי ותהלתי אחטם־לך
for will I for and My will I My For to was it
,you back hold praise My ,anger off put name's sake .you called

977 3701 38,08 6884 2009 3772 1097
10 לבלתי הכריתך׃ הנה צרפתיך ולא בכסף בחרתיך
have I with but have I ,Behold cut to as so
you chosen ;silver not ,you refined .off you not

312 3519 2490 6213 4616 4616 6040 3564
11 בכור עני׃ למעני למעני אעשה כי־איך יחל וכבודי לאחר
to My And it is how For will I My for My for,affliction the in
another glory ?defiled ,act sake ,sake of furnace

7121 3478 32,90 8085 5414/3808
12 לא־אתן׃ שמע אלי יעקב וישראל מקראי אני־הוא
,He I My Israel and O to Listen will I not
(am) :called ,Jacob ,Me .give

3225 776 3245 3027/637 314 637 72,23
13 אני ראשון אף אני אחרון׃ אף־ידי יסדה ארץ וימיני
My and the founded My Sure the I surely ;first the I
hand right ;earth hand ly .last (am) (am)

36,05 6908 3162 5975 7121 8064 2946
14 טפחה שמים קרא אני אליהם יעמדו יחדו׃ הקבצו כלכם
of all Gather .together they ,them to I called the stretched
you up stood ;heavens out

2656 6213 157 3068 428 5046 854 4310 80,85
ושמעו מי בהם הגיד את־אלה יהוה אהבו יעשה חפצו
His will He has Jehovah these has among Who and
pleasure do ;him loved ?things declared them ,hear

935 7121 637 1696 3778 2220 884
15 בבבל וזרעו כשדים׃ אני אני דברתי אף־קראתיו הביאתיו
brought I have I ,yea have I ,I the (on) His and on
him ;him called ;spoken .Chaldeans arm ;Babylon

5643 72,18 38,08 2088 8085 7126 1870 6743
16 והצליח דרכו׃ קרבו אלי שמעו־זאת לא מראש בסתר
in the from not ;this hear to Come .way his makes he and
secret beginning ;me near succeed

7971 3068 136 6258 8033 1961 6256 1696
דברתי מעת היותה שם אני ועתה אדני יהוה שלחני
sent has Jehovah the and I there ,being its the From have I
,me Lord now ;(was) of time spoken

3068 3478 6918 1350 3068 559 35,41 7307
17 ורוחו׃ כה־אמר יהוה גאלך קדוש ישראל אני יהוה
Jehovah I ,Israel Holy the your Jehovah says Thus His and
(am) of One ,Redeemer .Spirit

3863 1980 1870 1869 3276 3925 430
18 אלהיך מלמדך להועיל מדריכך בדרך תלך׃ לוא
Oh should you the in leading ,profit to teaching your
that go way you you ,God

3220 1530 6666 7965 5104 1961 4687 7181
הקשבת למצותי ויהי כנהר שלומך וצדקתך כגלי הים׃
the the as your and your the like Then My to had you
.sea of waves righteousness ,peace river been had !commands listened

380,8 3772 4579 4578 6621 22,33 2344 1961
19 ויהי כחול זרעך וצאצאי מעיך כמעותיו לא־יכרת ולא
and be would not its like your the and your the like And
not ,off cut ,belly bowels of offspring ,seed sand been had

nor destroyed from My presence. [20]Go out of Babylon; flee from the Chaldeans. Tell this with the voice of rejoicing; let this be heard, let it go out to the end of the earth; say, Jehovah has redeemed His servant Jacob. [21]And they did not thirst; He led them in the deserts; He made waters flow out of rock for them. And He cut open the rock and the water gushed out. [22]There is no peace, says Jehovah, to the wicked.

20 ישמד שמו מלפני׃ צאו מבבל ברחו מכשדים

the from flee from out Go before from his destroyed
.Chaldeans ;Babylon .Me name

בקול רנה הגידו השמיעו זאת הוציאוה עד־קצה הארץ

the the to go it let ,this be let tell rejoicing the with
;earth of end out heard ;(this) of voice

21 אמרו גאל יהוה עבדו יעקב׃ ולא צמאו בחרבות הוליכם

led He the in they And .Jacob His Jehovah has ,Say
;them deserts ;thirsted not servant redeemed

22 מים מצור הזיל למו ויבקע־צור ויזבו מים׃ אין שלום

,peace There ;water and ,rock the He And for He from water
no is out gushed split .them flow made rock

אמר יהוה לרשעים׃

the to ,Jehovah says
.wicked

CAP. XLIX מט

CHAPTER 49

CHAPTER 49

[1]Coasts, hear Me; and you people from afar, prick up *your ear*. Jehovah called Me from the womb; He mentioned My name from My mother's belly. [2]And He made My mouth like a sharp sword; He hid Me in the shadow of His hand, and made Me a polished arrow; He hid Me in His quiver; [3]and said to Me, You are My servant, Israel, You in whom I shall be glorified. [4]Then I said, I have labored in vain; I have spent My strength for nothing, and in vain; yet surely My judgment *is* with Jehovah, and My work with My God. [5]And now, says Jehovah who formed Me from the womb to be His servant, to bring Jacob back to Him: Though Israel is not gathered, yet I am honored in the eye of Jehovah, and My God is My strength. [6]And He said, it is *too* little that You should be My servant to raise up the tribes of Jacob, and to restore the preserved ones of Israel; I will also give You for a light of the nations, *that You may* be My salvation to the end of the earth. [7]So says Jehovah, the Redeemer of Israel, His Holy One, to the despised

1 שמעו איים אלי והקשיבו לאמים מרחוק יהוה מבטן

the from Jehovah from peoples the up prick to ,coasts ,Hear
womb ;afar ,ear .Me

2 קראני ממעי אמי הזכיר שמי׃ וישם פי כחרב חדה

;sharp a like My He And My men- He My from called
sword mouth made .name tioned mother's belly ;Me

בצל ידו החביאני וישימני לחץ ברור באשפתו הסתירני׃

hid He His in ;polished a for made and hid He His in
.Me quiver arrow Me ,Me hand's shadow

3
4 ויאמר לי עבדי־אתה ישראל אשר־בך אתפאר׃ ואני

Then be shall I in whom ,Israel You My to He And
I .glorified You .(are) servant ,Me said

אמרתי לריק יגעתי לתהו והבל כחי כליתי אכן משפטי

My yet have I My in and for have I for ,said
judgment surely ;spent strength ,vain nothing ;labored nothing

5 את־יהוה ופעלתי את־אלהי׃ ועתה | אמר יהוה

,Jehovah says And My with My and ,Jehovah (is)
,now .God work with

יצרי מבטן לעבד לו לשובב יעקב אליו וישראל לא

not Though to Jacob bring to to (be) to the from My
Israel :Him back ,Him servant ,womb Former

6 יאסף ואכבד בעיני יהוה ואלהי היה עזי׃ ויאמר נקל

is It He And My is My and ,Jehovah the in am I yet is
trifling ,said .strength God of eyes honored ,gathered

מהיותך לי עבד להקים את־שבטי יעקב ונצירי ישראל

Israel the and ,Jacob the raise to a to You that
of preserved of tribes up ,servant Me be should

להשיב ונתתיך לאור גוים להיות ישועתי עד־קצה

the to My be to ,nations a for also will I .restore to
of end salvation of light You give

7 הארץ׃ כה אמר־יהוה גאל ישראל קדושו לבזה

the to Holy His ,Israel the Jehovah says Thus the
of despised ,One of Redeemer .earth

of soul, to the hated of the
nation, the servant of rulers,
Kings shall see and rise up;
and chiefs shall worship;
because of Jehovah who is
faithful, and the Holy One of
Israel; and He chose You.
[8]So says Jehovah: In a
favorable time I have
answered You, and in a day
of salvation I have helped
You. And I will preserve
You, and give You for a
covenant of the people; to
establish the earth, to cause
to inherit the desolated in-
heritances; [9]to say to the
prisoners, Go out! To those
who are in darkness, Show
yourselves! They shall feed
in the ways, and their pastures shall be in all high
places. [10]They shall not
hunger nor thirst; and the
heat and sun shall not strike
them. For He who has
mercy on them shall lead
them; and He shall guide
them by the springs of
water. [11]And I will make all
My mountains a way, and
My highways shall be set on
high. [12]Behold, these shall
come from afar; and, lo,
these from the north and
from the west; and these
from the land of Sinim.
[13]Sing, O heavens; and be
joyful, O earth; break out
into singing, O mountains.
For Jehovah has comforted
His people and will have
pity on His afflicted. [14]But
Zion said, Jehovah has
forsaken me, and, My Lord
has forgotten me. [15]Can a
woman forget her suckling
child, from pitying the son of
her womb? Yes, these may
forget, yet I will surely not
forget you. [16]Behold, I have
carved you on the palms of
My hands; your walls *are*
always before Me. [17]Your
sons hurry; those destroying you and ruining you
shall go out from you. [18]Lift
up your eyes all around and
see! They all gather *and*
come to you. *As* I live, says
Jehovah, you shall surely
wear all of them as an
ornament, and bind them
on as a bride. [19]For your
wastes and your deserted
places, and your land of
ruins shall even now be too

8269 6965 7200 44 28 49 10 5650 1471 85 81 5315
נֶפֶשׁ לִמְתָעֵב גּוֹי לְעֶבֶד מֹשְׁלִים מְלָכִים יִרְאוּ וָקָמוּ שָׂרִים
chiefs and shall Kings ,rulers the the the to ,soul
;up rise see of servant ,nation of hated
977 3478 6918 539 834 3068 4616 7812
וְיִשְׁתַּחֲווּ לְמַעַן יְהוָה אֲשֶׁר נֶאֱמָן קְדֹשׁ יִשְׂרָאֵל וַיִּבְחָרֶךָּ׃
He and ,Israel Holy the is who Jehovah the for shall
You chose of One ,faithful of sake ,worship
3444 3117 60 30 7522 6256 3068 559 3541
8 כֹּה אָמַר יְהוָה בְּעֵת רָצוֹן עֲנִיתִיךָ וּבְיוֹם יְשׁוּעָה
salvation in and replied I favor- a In ,Jehovah says Thus
of day a ,You to able time
5157 776 6965 5971 1285 5414 5341 5826
עֲזַרְתִּיךָ וְאֶצָּרְךָ וְאֶתֶּנְךָ לִבְרִית עָם לְהָקִים אֶרֶץ לְהַנְחִיל
cause to the estab- to the a for give and will I And helped I
inherit to ,earth lish ,people of covenant You You keep .You
28 22 3318 631 559 8074 51 59
9 נְחָלוֹת שֹׁמֵמוֹת׃ לֵאמֹר לַאֲסוּרִים צֵאוּ לַאֲשֶׁר בַּחֹשֶׁךְ
dark- in those to Go the to saying desolated inherit-
.ness ;out ,prisoners ances
74 56 38 08 4830 8205 3605 74 62 1870 1540
10 הִגָּלוּ עַל־דְּרָכִים יִרְעוּ וּבְכָל־שְׁפָיִים מַרְעִיתָם׃ לֹא יִרְעָבוּ
shall They not their bare and shall they the By Show
hunger .pastures heights all in ,feed ways !yourselves
5090 7355 8121 8273 5221 38 08 6770
וְלֹא יִצְמָאוּ וְלֹא־יַכֵּם שָׁרָב וָשָׁמֶשׁ כִּי־מְרַחֲמָם יְנַהֲגֵם
lead shall who He For .sun and heat shall and ;thirst and
;them them pities them strike not not
4546 1870 2022 3605 7760 5095 4325 4002
11 וְעַל־מַבּוּעֵי מַיִם יְנַהֲלֵם׃ וְשַׂמְתִּי כָל־הָרַי לַדָּרֶךְ וּמְסִלֹּתַי
My and ,way a My all I And guide shall water springs and
highways mountains make will .them of by
3220 6828 2009 935 7350 428 2009 7311
12 יְרֻמוּן׃ הִנֵּה־אֵלֶּה מֵרָחוֹק יָבֹאוּ וְהִנֵּה־אֵלֶּה מִצָּפוֹן וּמִיָּם
from and from these and shall from these ,Behold be shall
;west north ,behold ;come afar .high
2022 6476 776 1523 8064 7442 5515 776 428
13 וְאֵלֶּה מֵאֶרֶץ סִינִים׃ רָנּוּ שָׁמַיִם וְגִילִי אָרֶץ יִפְצְחוּ הָרִים
O ,break O be and O ,Sing .Sinim the from and
mountains ;earth ,joyful ,heavens of land these
6726 559 7355 6041 59 71 3068 5162 7440
14 רִנָּה כִּי־נִחַם יְהוָה עַמּוֹ וַעֲנִיָּו יְרַחֵם׃ וַתֹּאמֶר צִיּוֹן
,Zion said But will He His and His Jehovah has for (into)
.pity afflicted ,people comforted ;singing
7355 5764 802 7911 7911 136 3068 5800
15 עֲזָבַנִי יְהוָה וַאדֹנָי שְׁכֵחָנִי׃ הֲתִשְׁכַּח אִשָּׁה עוּלָהּ מֵרַחֵם
from suckling her a forget Can forgot my and ,Jehovah for-
pitying ,child woman .me Lord me sook
5921 7911 38 08 7911 428 990 1121
16 בֶּן־בִּטְנָהּ גַּם־אֵלֶּה תִשְׁכַּחְנָה וְאָנֹכִי לֹא אֶשְׁכָּחֵךְ׃ הֵן עַל־
on ,Behold will not yet may these ,Yes her the
.you forget I ,forget ?womb of son
2040 1121 4116 8548 5048 2346 2710 3709
17 כַּפַּיִם חַקֹּתִיךְ חוֹמֹתַיִךְ נֶגְדִּי תָּמִיד׃ מִהֲרוּ בָּנָיִךְ מְהָרְסַיִךְ
de- those Your hurry .always (are) your have I My
you stroying ;sons Me before walls ;you carved palms
3605 7200 58 69 5439 53 75 3318 2717
18 וּמַחֲרִבַיִךְ מִמֵּךְ יֵצֵאוּ׃ שְׂאִי־סָבִיב עֵינַיִךְ וּרְאִי כֻּלָּם
They and your all Lift shall from ruining and
all !see eyes around up .out go you ,you
3847 5716 3605 3068/5002 2416 935 6908
נִקְבְּצוּ בָאוּ־לָךְ חַי־אָנִי נְאֻם־יְהוָה כִּי כֻלָּם כָּעֲדִי תִלְבָּשִׁי
shall you an as them surely ,Jehovah states I (As) to (and) gather
wear ornament all ,live .you come
2035 776 8074 2723 3618 7194
19 וּתְקַשְּׁרִים כַּכַּלָּה׃ כִּי חָרְבֹתַיִךְ וְשֹׁמְמֹתַיִךְ וְאֶרֶץ הֲרִסֻתֵךְ
de- your and your and your For a as bind and
structions of land ,ruins wastes .bride on them

20 narrow to live *there*; and they who swallow you shall be broad. [20]The sons of your bereavement shall yet say in your ears, The place *is* too narrow for me; come near so that I may live. [21]Then you shall say in your heart, Who has borne these to me, for I *am* bereaved and desolate, turned aside and an exile; who then has brought up these? Behold, I was left alone. Where *do* these *come from*? [22]So says the Lord Jehovah, Behold, I will lift up My hand to the nations, and will set up My banner to peoples. And they shall bring your sons in the bosom, and your daughters shall be carried on the shoulder. [23]And kings shall be your nursing fathers, and their queens your nurses. They shall bow to you, faces *down to* the earth, and lick up the dust of your feet. And you shall know that I *am* Jehovah, by whom they who wait for Me shall not be ashamed. [24]Shall the booty be taken from the warrior, or the righteous captive escape? [25]But so says Jehovah, Even the captives of the warrior shall be taken, and the booty of the terrifying ones shall be delivered. For I will strive with him who contends with you; and I will save your sons. [26]And those who oppress you, I will feed with their own flesh: and they shall be drunk by their own blood, as with fresh wine. And all flesh shall know that I Jehovah *am* your Savior and your Redeemer, the mighty One of Jacob.

20 כִּי עַתָּה תֵּצְרִי מִיּוֹשֵׁב וְרָחֲקוּ מְבַלְּעָיִךְ׃ עוֹד יֹאמְרוּ בְאָזְנַיִךְ
your in ears / shall say / Yet / who those swallow you. / shall and wide be / live to (there); / be shall narrow too / now / for
21 בְּנֵי שִׁכֻּלָיִךְ צַר־לִי הַמָּקוֹם גְּשָׁה־לִּי וְאֵשֵׁבָה׃ וְאָמַרְתְּ
you Then say shall / I that dwell may / for me / come near / the (is) place; / for Too me narrow / bereave- your ment, / the of sons
בִּלְבָבֵךְ מִי יָלַד־לִי אֶת־אֵלֶּה וַאֲנִי שְׁכוּלָה וְגַלְמוּדָה גֹּלָה
an exile / and barren, / bereaved / I For (am) / these? / to me / has borne / Who / your in heart,
וְסוּרָה וְאֵלֶּה מִי גִדֵּל הֵן אֲנִי נִשְׁאַרְתִּי לְבַדִּי אֵלֶּה אֵיפֹה
(from) where / These, / alone. I / left was, / I / Lo, / has brought up? / who these, / and turned and aside;
22 הֵם׃ כֹּה־אָמַר אֲדֹנָי יְהוִה הִנֵּה אֶשָּׂא אֶל־גּוֹיִם יָדִי
My hand, / the to nations / will I lift up / Behold, / Jehovah, the Lord / says Thus / (are) they?
וְאֶל־עַמִּים אָרִים נִסִּי וְהֵבִיאוּ בָנַיִךְ בְּחֹצֶן וּבְנֹתַיִךְ עַל־כָּתֵף
the shoulder / on / your and daughters / the in bosom; / your sons / they And bring shall / My banner. / will set up / peoples and to
23 תִּנָּשֶׂאנָה׃ וְהָיוּ מְלָכִים אֹמְנַיִךְ וְשָׂרוֹתֵיהֶם מֵינִיקֹתַיִךְ אַפַּיִם
faces (toward) / your nurses; / their and princesses / nursing your fathers, / kings / And be shall / be shall carried.
אֶרֶץ יִשְׁתַּחֲווּ לָךְ וַעֲפַר רַגְלַיִךְ יְלַחֵכוּ וְיָדַעַתְּ כִּי־אֲנִי יְהוָה
Jehovah, / I (am) / that / you And know shall / lick up. / your feet / the and of dust / to you / they bow shall / the earth
24 אֲשֶׁר לֹא־יֵבֹשׁוּ קֹוָי׃ הֲיֻקַּח מִגִּבּוֹר מַלְקוֹחַ וְאִם־שְׁבִי
the captive / or / booty, / a from warrior / be Shall taken / waiting those Me. for / be shall not ashamed / by whom
25 צַדִּיק יִמָּלֵט׃ כִּי־כֹה ׀ אָמַר יְהוָה גַּם־שְׁבִי גִבּוֹר יֻקָּח
be shall taken, / the warrior's / captive Even / Jehovah, / says / thus For / escape? / righteous
וּמַלְקוֹחַ עָרִיץ יִמָּלֵט וְאֶת־יְרִיבֵךְ אָנֹכִי אָרִיב וְאֶת־בָּנַיִךְ
your sons / and / will strive; / I / your striver / And with / shall escape. / terri- fying ones / the / booty and of
26 אָנֹכִי אוֹשִׁיעַ׃ וְהַאֲכַלְתִּי אֶת־מוֹנַיִךְ אֶת־בְּשָׂרָם וְכֶעָסִיס
as fresh wine / and / own their flesh; / who those you oppress / will I And feed / will save. / I
דָּמָם יִשְׁכָּרוּן וְיָדְעוּ כָל־בָּשָׂר כִּי אֲנִי יְהוָה מוֹשִׁיעֵךְ וְגֹאֲלֵךְ
your and Redeemer, / your Savior / Jehovah / I (am) / that / flesh / all shall And know / shall they drunk. be / their blood
אֲבִיר יַעֲקֹב׃
Jacob. / the One Mighty of

CAP. L נ

CHAPTER 50

[1]So says Jehovah, Where *is* the scroll of your mother's divorce whom I have put away? Or who of My creditors that I have sold you to him? Behold, you were sold for your

1 כֹּה ׀ אָמַר יְהוָה אֵי זֶה סֵפֶר כְּרִיתוּת אִמְּכֶם אֲשֶׁר שִׁלַּחְתִּיהָ
have I put away? / whom / your mother, / divorce of / scroll the of / Where (is) / Jeho- vah, / says / Thus
אוֹ מִי מִנּוֹשַׁי אֲשֶׁר־מָכַרְתִּי אֶתְכֶם לוֹ הֵן בַּעֲוֹנֹתֵיכֶם
your for iniquities / Behold, / to him? / you / have I sold / that / My of creditors / who / Or

iniquities, and your
mother was put away for
your trespasses. 2 Who
knows why I have come,
and no one *is here*? I
called, and not one an-
swered. Is My hand truly
cut short from ransom? Or
is there not power in Me
to deliver? Behold, at My
rebuke I dry up the sea; I
make rivers a wilderness;
their fish stink because of
no water, and die in thirst.
3 I clothe the heavens
with blackness, and sackcloth sets their covering.
4 The Lord Jehovah has
given to Me the tongue of
taught ones, to know, to
help the weary *with a*
word. He arouses in the
morning; He arouses the
ear to Me, to hear as the
learned. 5 The Lord Jeho-
vah has opened My ear
and I did not rebel; I did
not turn away backwards.
6 I gave My back to
strikers, and My cheeks
to pluckers; I did not hide
My face from shame and
spitting. 7 And the Lord
Jehovah will help Me. On
account of this I was not
ashamed. On account of
this I set My face like flint,
and I know that I shall not
be ashamed. 8 My Justi-
fier *is* near. Who will contend with Me? Let us
stand up together; who *is*
master of My judgment?
Let him come near to Me.
9 Behold, the Lord Jeho-
vah will help Me; who *is*
the one who will con-
demn Me? Behold, like a
garment they shall wear
out; the moth shall eat
them.
10 Who among you fears
Jehovah, obeying the
voice of His servant, who
walks *in* darkness, and no
light is in him? Let him
trust in the name of
Jehovah, and lean on his
God. 11 Behold, all of you
who kindle fire, who are
encircled *by* sparks; walk

2 נִמְכַּרְתֶּם וּבְפִשְׁעֵיכֶם שֻׁלְּחָה אִמְּכֶם׃ מַדּוּעַ בָּאתִי וְאֵין
and no | have I come | knows why | Who | your .mother | put was away | your for and trespasses | were you ,sold

אִישׁ קָרָאתִי וְאֵין עוֹנֶה הֲקָצוֹר קָצְרָה יָדִי מִפְּדוּת וְאִם־
Or | from ?ransom | My ,hand | cut is short | Cutting ,short | answer- .ed | and none | ,called I | one ?(here is)

אֵין־בִּי כֹחַ לְהַצִּיל הֵן בְּגַעֲרָתִי אַחֲרִיב יָם אָשִׂים נְהָרוֹת
rivers | make I | the ;sea | dry I up | My at rebuke | ,Behold | ?deliver to | power in Me | is not

3 מִדְבָּר תִּבְאַשׁ דְּגָתָם מֵאֵין מַיִם וְתָמֹת בַּצָּמָא׃ אַלְבִּישׁ
clothe I | .thirst in | die and | ,water no | because of | their fish | stink | wil- a ;derness

4 שָׁמַיִם קַדְרוּת וְשַׂק אָשִׂים כְּסוּתָם׃ אֲדֹנָי יְהוִה נָתַן
has given | Jehovah | The Lord | their .covering | make | and sackcloth | black- ness | (with) the heavens

לִי לְשׁוֹן לִמּוּדִים לָדַעַת לָעוּת אֶת־יָעֵף דָּבָר יָעִיר ׀ בַּבֹּקֶר
the in ,morning | He arouses | a (with) ;word | the weary | help to | ;know to | taught ,ones | the of tongue | to Me

5 בַּבֹּקֶר יָעִיר לִי אֹזֶן לִשְׁמֹעַ כַּלִּמּוּדִים׃ אֲדֹנָי יְהוִה פָּתַח
has opened | Jehovah | The Lord | the as taught | hear to | the ,ear | to Me | He arouses | the in morning

6 לִי אֹזֶן וְאָנֹכִי לֹא מָרִיתִי אָחוֹר לֹא נְסוּגֹתִי׃ גֵּוִי נָתַתִּי
gave I | My back | turned I away | not | backwards | did ,rebel | not | I and | the ,ear | to Me

לְמַכִּים וּלְחָיַי לְמֹרְטִים פָּנַי לֹא הִסְתַּרְתִּי מִכְּלִמּוֹת וָרֹק׃
and .spitting | from shame | did I hide | not | My face | ;pluckers to | My and cheeks | to ;strikers

7 וַאדֹנָי יְהוִה יַעֲזָר־לִי עַל־כֵּן לֹא נִכְלָמְתִּי עַל־כֵּן שַׂמְתִּי
have I set | therefore | was I ;ashamed | not | therefore | ,Me | will help | Jehovah | the And Lord

8 פָּנַי כַּחַלָּמִישׁ וָאֵדַע כִּי־לֹא אֵבוֹשׁ׃ קָרוֹב מַצְדִּיקִי מִי־
who | My ;justifier | Near (is) | shall I .ashamed be | not that | I and know | like ,flint | My face

9 יָרִיב אִתִּי נַעַמְדָה יָּחַד מִי־בַעַל מִשְׁפָּטִי יִגַּשׁ אֵלָי׃ הֵן
,Lo | .Me to | him Let near come | My ?judgment | master of | who (is) | to- ;gether | us Let stand | with ?Me | will contend

אֲדֹנָי יְהוִה יַעֲזָר־לִי מִי־הוּא יַרְשִׁיעֵנִי הֵן כֻּלָּם כַּבֶּגֶד יִבְלוּ
shall ;out wear | a like garment | they all | ,Lo | will condemn ?Me | He who (is) | who ;Me | will help | Jehovah | the Lord

10 עָשׁ יֹאכְלֵם׃ מִי בָכֶם יְרֵא יְהוָה שֹׁמֵעַ בְּקוֹל עַבְדּוֹ
His ,servant | the of voice | obeying | ,Jehovah | fears | among you | Who | eat shall .them | the moth

אֲשֶׁר ׀ הָלַךְ חֲשֵׁכִים וְאֵין נֹגַהּ לוֹ יִבְטַח בְּשֵׁם יְהוָה וְיִשָּׁעֵן
and lean | ,Jehovah | the of name | in trust | him Let | to ?him | light and no (is) | (in) ,darkness | walks | who

11 בֵּאלֹהָיו׃ הֵן כֻּלְּכֶם קֹדְחֵי אֵשׁ מְאַזְּרֵי זִיקוֹת לְכוּ ׀
walk | (by) ;sparks | are who surrounded | ,fire | who kindle | of all you | ,Behold | his on .God

in the light of your fire and in the sparks you are burning. This shall be to you from My hand; you shall lie down in pain.

2088 1961 3027 1197 2131 784 217
בְּאוּר אֶשְׁכֶם וּבְזִיקוֹת בִּעַרְתֶּם מִיָּדִי הָיְתָה־זֹּאת לָכֶם
,you to | this | shall be | My From hand | are you .burning | in and sparks the | your ,fire | the in of light

7901 4620
לְמַעֲצֵבָה תִּשְׁכָּבוּן׃
shall you .down lie | in pain

CAP. LI נא

CHAPTER 51

CHAPTER 51

[1]Hear Me, pursuers of righteousness, seekers of Jehovah: Look to the rock from which you were cut, and to the hollow of the pit from which you were dug. [2]Look to your father Abraham, and to Sarah who bore you. For *he being but* one I called him, and blessed him and increased him. [3]For Jehovah comforts Zion. He comforts all her desolations, and He makes her wilderness like Eden, and her desert like the garden of Jehovah; joy and gladness shall be found in it, thanksgiving and the voice of singing praise.

[4]Hear Me, My people; yea, give ear to Me, My nation. For a law shall go out from Me, and My justice I will make rest as light to peoples. [5]My righteousness *is* near; My salvation went out; and My arms shall judge peoples; coasts shall wait on Me, and they shall hope on My arm. [6]Lift up your eyes to the heavens, and look to the earth beneath; for the heavens vanish like smoke, and the earth shall wear out like a garment; and its inhabitants shall die in the same way. but My salvation shall be forever, and My righteousness shall not be broken. [7]Hear Me, knowers of righteousness, the people of My law in their heart; do not fear the reproach of man, and do not be bowed from their blasphemings. [8]For the moth shall eat them like a garment; yea, the mothworm shall eat them

1
6697 5027 3068 1245 6664 7291 8085
שִׁמְעוּ אֵלַי רֹדְפֵי צֶדֶק מְבַקְשֵׁי יְהוָה הַבִּיטוּ אֶל־צוּר
the rock | to | Look | :Jehovah seekers of | righ- ,teousness | pursuers of | ,me | Hear

2
85 5027 5365 953 4718 2672
חֻצַּבְתֶּם וְאֶל־מַקֶּבֶת בּוֹר נֻקַּרְתֶּם׃ הַבִּיטוּ אֶל־אַבְרָהָם
Abraham | to | Look | which from .dug were you | the pit | the of hollow | and to | which from ,cut were you

1288 7121 259 2342 8283 1
אֲבִיכֶם וְאֶל־שָׂרָה תְּחוֹלֶלְכֶם כִּי־אֶחָד קְרָאתִיו וַאֲבָרְכֵהוּ
blessed and ,him | called I ,him | (being) one | for | bore who ;you | Sarah | and to | your ,father

3
6213 2723 3605 5162 6726 3068 5162 7235
וְאַרְבֵּהוּ׃ כִּי־נִחַם יְהוָה צִיּוֹן נִחַם כָּל־חָרְבֹתֶיהָ וַיָּשֶׂם
He and makes | her ,desolations | all | He comforts | .Zion | Jehovah | comforts For | in- and .him creased

4672 8057 8342 3068 1588 6160 5731 4057
מִדְבָּרָהּ כְּעֵדֶן וְעַרְבָתָהּ כְּגַן־יְהוָה שָׂשׂוֹן וְשִׂמְחָה יִמָּצֵא
be shall found | and gladness | joy | ;Jehovah's like garden | her and desert | like Eden | her wilderness

4
3816 5971 7181 2172 6963 8426
בָהּ תּוֹדָה וְקוֹל זִמְרָה׃ הַקְשִׁיבוּ אֵלַי עַמִּי וּלְאוּמִּי
My and ,nation | My ;people | ,Me to | Listen | singing .praise | the and of voice | thanks- giving | ,it in

5971 216 4941 3318 8451 238
אֵלַי הַאֲזִינוּ כִּי תוֹרָה מֵאִתִּי תֵצֵא וּמִשְׁפָּטִי לְאוֹר עַמִּים
peoples | light as to | My and justice | shall ,out go | from Me | law a | For | give .ear | to Me

5
8199 5971 2220 3468 3318 6664 7138 7280
אַרְגִּיעַ׃ קָרוֹב צִדְקִי יָצָא יִשְׁעִי וּזְרֹעַי עַמִּים יִשְׁפֹּטוּ אֵלַי
on Me | shall ;judge | peoples | My and arms | My ;salvation | went out | righ- My ;teousness | Near (is) | will I rest make

6
5869 8064 5375 3176 2220 6960 339
אִיִּים יְקַוּוּ וְאֶל־זְרֹעִי יְיַחֵלוּן׃ שְׂאוּ לַשָּׁמַיִם עֵינֵיכֶם
,eyes your | the to heavens | Lift up | shall they hope | My arm | and on | shall ,wait | coasts

776 4414 6227 8064 8478 776 5027
וְהַבִּיטוּ אֶל־הָאָרֶץ מִתַּחַת כִּי־שָׁמַיִם כֶּעָשָׁן נִמְלָחוּ וְהָאָרֶץ
the and earth | ,vanish | like smoke | the heavens | for | from ;beneath | the earth | to | look and

5769 3444 4191 3644 3427 1086 899
כַּבֶּגֶד תִּבְלֶה וְיֹשְׁבֶיהָ כְּמוֹ־כֵן יְמוּתוּן וִישׁוּעָתִי לְעוֹלָם
forever | My But salvation | .die shall | like in manner | its and dwellers | shall ;out wear | a like garment

7
6664 3045 8085 2865 3808 6666 1961
תִּהְיֶה וְצִדְקָתִי לֹא תֵחָת׃ שִׁמְעוּ אֵלַי יֹדְעֵי צֶדֶק
righ- ,teousness | knowers of | to ,Me | Listen | be shall .broken | not | My and ,righteousness | ;be shall

3808 1421 582 2781 3372 3820 8451 5971
עַם תּוֹרָתִי בְלִבָּם אַל־תִּירְאוּ חֶרְפַּת אֱנוֹשׁ וּמִגִּדֻּפֹתָם אַל־
not | their from and blasphemings | ,man | the of reproach | fear Do | not | their in .heart | law My | the of people

8
6666 5580 398 6785 6211 398 899 2865
תֵּחָתּוּ׃ כִּי כַבֶּגֶד יֹאכְלֵם עָשׁ וְכַצֶּמֶר יֹאכְלֵם סָס וְצִדְקָתִי
righ- eousness | My But | he mothworm | eat shall them | like and wool | the ,moth | eat shall them | a like garment | For | be do .bowed

like wool. But My righteousness shall be forever, and My salvation generation to generation. 9Awake! Awake! Put on strength, arm of Jehovah. Awake, as in days of old, everlasting generations. Was it not You cutting in pieces Rahab, piercing the sea-monster? 10Was it not You drying up the sea, the waters of the great deep, who made the depths of the sea a way for the redeemed to pass? 11Yea, the ransomed of Jehovah shall return and come *to* Zion with singing, and everlasting joy *shall be* on their head; gladness and joy shall overtake; sorrow and sighing shall flee.

12I, I *am* He comforting you. Who *are* you, that you should fear from man? He shall die! And from the son of man? He *is* given *as* grass. 13And you forget your Maker Jehovah, who stretched out the heavens and founded the earth. And you dread continually, every day, from the fury of the oppressor, since he was ready to destroy. And where *is* the fury of the oppressor? 14Bowed he hurries to be freed, and not *that* he die in the pit, and not *that* he lack his bread. 15But I *am* Jehovah your God, stirring up the sea and *making* its waves roar; Jehovah of hosts *is* His name. 16And I have put My words in your mouth, and covered you in the shade of My hand, to plant the heavens and found the earth, and to say to Zion, You are My people.

17Awake! Awake! Rise up, O Jerusalem, who drank the cup of His fury from the hand of Jehovah; you drank the bowl of the cup of reeling; you fully drained *it*. 18No guide *is* for her among all the sons she has borne; and none takes her by the hand of all the sons she made to grow.

9 לְעוֹלָם תִּהְיֶה וִישׁוּעָתִי לְדוֹר דּוֹרִים׃ עוּרִי עוּרִי לִבְשִׁי
on Put !Awake !Awake gene- to gene- My and shall forever
of ration ration salvation ,be

עֹז זְרוֹעַ יְהוָה עוּרִי כִּימֵי קֶדֶם דֹּרוֹת עוֹלָמִים הֲלוֹא אַתְּ־
You it Was .everlasting genera- ,old days as ,Awake Je- arm
not tions of .hovah's ,strength

10 הִיא הַמַּחְצֶבֶת רַהַב מְחוֹלֶלֶת תַּנִּין׃ הֲלוֹא אַתְּ־הִיא
which ,You it Was sea- the piercing ,Rahab in cutting which
(was) not ?monster pieces (was)

הַמַּחֲרֶבֶת יָם מֵי תְּהוֹם רַבָּה הַשָּׂמָה מַעֲמַקֵּי־יָם דָּרֶךְ
a the the which ,great the the the one the
way sea of depths made deep of waters ,sea up drying

11 לַעֲבֹר גְּאוּלִים׃ וּפְדוּיֵי יְהוָה יְשׁוּבוּן וּבָאוּ צִיּוֹן בְּרִנָּה
with (to) and shall Jehovah the And the to
,singing Zion come return of ransomed ?redeemed pass

וְשִׂמְחַת עוֹלָם עַל־רֹאשָׁם שָׂשׂוֹן וְשִׂמְחָה יַשִּׂיגוּן נָסוּ יָגוֹן
sor- shall shall joy and gladness their (be shall) ever- joy and
row flee ;overtake ;head on lasting

12 וַאֲנָחָה׃ אָנֹכִי אָנֹכִי הוּא מְנַחֶמְכֶם מִי־אַתְּ וַתִּירְאִי
you that ,you Who comforting ,He (am) I ,I and
fear should (are) you .sighing

13 מֵאֱנוֹשׁ יָמוּת וּמִבֶּן־אָדָם חָצִיר יִנָּתֵן׃ וַתִּשְׁכַּח יְהוָה עֹשֶׂךָ
your Jehovah you And is He (As) ?man from Or He from
,Maker forget given grass of son the !die shall ?man

נֹטֶה שָׁמַיִם וְיֹסֵד אָרֶץ וַתְּפַחֵד תָּמִיד כָּל־הַיּוֹם מִפְּנֵי חֲמַת
the from ,day every ,always you And the and hea- the who
of fury dread .earth founded vens stretched

14 הַמֵּצִיק כַּאֲשֶׁר כּוֹנֵן לְהַשְׁחִית וְאַיֵּה חֲמַת הַמֵּצִיק׃ מִהַר
He the the where And to was he since the
hurries ?oppressor of fury (is) .destroy ready ,oppressor

15 צֹעֶה לְהִפָּתֵחַ וְלֹא־יָמוּת לַשַּׁחַת וְלֹא יֶחְסַר לַחְמוֹ׃ וְאָנֹכִי
I But his that and the in he(that) and be to ,bowed
(am) .bread lacks he not ,pit die not ,freed

יְהוָה אֱלֹהֶיךָ רֹגַע הַיָּם וַיֶּהֱמוּ גַּלָּיו יְהוָה צְבָאוֹת שְׁמוֹ׃
His hosts Jehovah its and the stirring your Jehovah
.name (is) of ;waves roar ,sea up ,God

16 וָאָשִׂם דְּבָרַי בְּפִיךָ וּבְצֵל יָדִי כִּסִּיתִיךָ לִנְטֹעַ שָׁמַיִם וְלִיסֹד
and the plant to covered My the in and your in My I And
found heavens ,you hand of shade ,mouth words put have

17 אֶרֶץ וְלֵאמֹר לְצִיּוֹן עַמִּי־אָתָּה׃ הִתְעוֹרְרִי הִתְעוֹרְרִי
!Awake !Awake you My to and the
.(are) people ,Zion say to ,earth

קוּמִי יְרוּשָׁלַםִ אֲשֶׁר שָׁתִית מִיַּד יְהוָה אֶת־כּוֹס חֲמָתוֹ
;fury His cup the Jehovah the from drank who O Rise
of of hand ,Jerusalem up

18 אֶת־קֻבַּעַת כּוֹס הַתַּרְעֵלָה שָׁתִית מָצִית׃ אֵין־מְנַהֵל לָהּ
for guide No fully you you reeling the the
her (is) .drained ,drank of cup of bowl

מִכָּל־בָּנִים יָלָדָה וְאֵין מַחֲזִיק בְּיָדָהּ מִכָּל־הַבָּנִים גִּדֵּלָה׃
she sons the all of by her takes and has she the among
.grow made —hand the none ;borne sons all

[19]Those two things came to you; who shall wail for you? Ruin and shattering and famine and the sword — who *but* I shall comfort you? [20]Your sons have fainted; they lie at the head of all the streets, like an antelope *in* a net, filled with the fury of Jehovah, the rebuke of your God. [21]So hear this now, afflicted one, and drunken, but not from wine: [22]So says your Lord Jehovah and your God, He strives *for* His people. Behold, I have taken the cup of reeling out of your hand, the bowl of the cup of My fury; you shall not yet again drink it. [23]But I will put it into the hand of your oppressor, who have said to your soul, Bow down that we may cross and put your back as the ground, and as the street to those who cross.

CHAPTER 52

[1]Awake! Awake! Put on your strength, Zion; put on your beautiful robes, O Jerusalem, the holy city. For never again shall come to you uncircumcised and unclean ones. [2]Shake yourself from the dust; rise up! Sit, Jerusalem. Free yourself from your neckbands, O captive daughter of Zion. [3]For so says the Lord Jehovah: You *were* sold for nothing, and you shall not be redeemed with silver. [4]For so says the Lord Jehovah: My people went down at the first *into* Egypt, to reside there, and without cause Assyria oppressed him. [5]Now, then, what *is* to Me here, declares Jehovah? For My people is taken away for nothing. Those ruling him howl, declares Jehovah. And My name is despised continually, every day. [6]So My people shall know My name. So *it shall be* in

7458 7667 7701 5110 7122 8147
19 שְׁתַּיִם הֵנָּה קֹרְאֹתַיִךְ מִי יָנוּד לָךְ הַשֹּׁד וְהַשֶּׁבֶר וְהָרָעָב
and and ,Ruin for shall who came Those two
,famine ,shattering ?you bewail ;you to things

2351 3605 7218 7901 5968 1121 5162 4310 2719
20 וְהַחֶרֶב מִי אֲנַחֲמֵךְ׃ בָּנַיִךְ עֻלְּפוּ שָׁכְבוּ בְּרֹאשׁ כָּל־חוּצוֹת
the all the at they have Your shall I who the and
,streets of head lie ;fainted sons ?you comfort (but) —sword

3651 430 1606 3068 2534 4393 4364 8377
21 כְּתוֹא מִכְמָר הַמְלֵאִים חֲמַת־יְהוָה גַּעֲרַת אֱלֹהָיִךְ׃ לָכֵן
There- your the ,Jehovah the filled a (in) an like
fore .God of rebuke of fury with ,net antelope

113 559/35.41 3196 3808 7937 6041 2088 4994 8085
22 שִׁמְעִי־נָא זֹאת עֲנִיָּה וּשְׁכֻרַת וְלֹא מִיָּיִן׃ כֹּה־אָמַר אֲדֹנַיִךְ
your says Thus from but and afflicted ,this now hear
Lord :wine not ,drunken ,one

3563 3027 3947 2009 5971/7378 430 3068
יְהוָה וֵאלֹהַיִךְ יָרִיב עַמּוֹ הִנֵּה לָקַחְתִּי מִיָּדֵךְ אֶת־כּוֹס
cup the of out have I ,Behold His He your and ,Jehovah
of ,hand your taken .people (for) strives :God

8354 3254 3808 2534 3563 6907 8653
הַתַּרְעֵלָה אֶת־קֻבַּעַת כּוֹס חֲמָתִי לֹא־תוֹסִיפִי לִשְׁתּוֹתָהּ
it drink shall you not My the bowl the ,reeling
again ;fury of cup of

5674 7812 5315 559 3013 3027 7760 5750
23 עוֹד׃ וְשַׂמְתִּיהָ בְּיַד־מוֹגַיִךְ אֲשֶׁר־אָמְרוּ לְנַפְשֵׁךְ שְׁחִי וְנַעֲבֹרָה
we that Bow your to have who your into will I But any
;cross may ,down ,soul said ,oppressor's hand it put .more

5674 2351 1460 776 7760
וַתָּשִׂימִי כָאָרֶץ גֵּוֵךְ וְכַחוּץ לַעֹבְרִים׃
those to as and your the as and
.cross who ,street the ,back ground put

CAP. LII נב

CHAPTER 52

3389 8597 899 3847 6726 5797 3847/5782 5782
1 עוּרִי עוּרִי לִבְשִׁי עֻזֵּךְ צִיּוֹן לִבְשִׁי ׀ בִּגְדֵי תִפְאַרְתֵּךְ יְרוּשָׁלַםִ
,Jerusalem your robes on put ;Zion your Put !Awake !Awake
,beauty of ,strength on

5287 2931 6189 5750 935 3054 3808 6944 5892
2 עִיר הַקֹּדֶשׁ כִּי לֹא יוֹסִיף יָבֹא־בָךְ עוֹד עָרֵל וְטָמֵא׃ הִתְנַעֲרִי
Shake and uncir- more to come shall not for the city
yourself .unclean cumcised you ,again ,holy

7628 6677 4147 6605 3389 6965 6083
מֵעָפָר קוּמִי שְּׁבִי יְרוּשָׁלָםִ הִתְפַּתְּחִו מוֹסְרֵי צַוָּארֵךְ שְׁבִיָּה
O your the your- Free !Jerusalem ,Sit rise the from
captive ,neck of bands from self !up ;dust

3808 4376 2600 3068 559 3541 6726/1323
3 בַּת־צִיּוֹן׃ כִּי־כֹה אָמַר יְהוָה חִנָּם נִמְכַּרְתֶּם וְלֹא
and you were for ;Jehovah says thus For .Zion daugh-
not ,sold nothing of ter

3381 4714 3068 1136 559 3541 1350 3701
4 בְכֶסֶף תִּגָּאֵלוּ׃ כִּי כֹה אָמַר אֲדֹנָי יְהוִה מִצְרַיִם יָרַד־
went (to) ;Jehovah the says thus For shall you with
down Egypt Lord .redeemed be silver

4100 6258 6231 657 804 8033 1481 7223 5971
5 עַמִּי בָרִאשֹׁנָה לָגוּר שָׁם וְאַשּׁוּר בְּאֶפֶס עֲשָׁקוֹ׃ וְעַתָּה מַה־
what Now oppressed without and ,there to the at My
(is) ,then .him cause Assyria sojourn ,first people

5002 3213 4910 2600 5971 3947 3068 5002
לִּי־פֹה נְאֻם־יְהוָה כִּי־לֻקַּח עַמִּי חִנָּם מֹשְׁלָו יְהֵילִילוּ נְאֻם־
states ,howl His for My taken is For ,Jehovah states ?here to
rulers .nothing people away Me

3651 8034 5971 3045 5006 8034 3117 3605 8548 3068
6 יְהוָה וְתָמִיד כָּל־הַיּוֹם שְׁמִי מִנֹּאָץ׃ לָכֵן יֵדַע עַמִּי שְׁמִי לָכֵן
there- My My shall There- is My day every And .Jehovah
fore ;name people know ,fore .despised name continually

4998 2009 1696 3117
7 בַּיּוֹם הַהוּא כִּי־אֲנִי־הוּא הַמְדַבֵּר הִנֵּנִי׃ מַה־נָּאווּ עַל־
on beauti- How Behold who He I for ;that day in
are ful !Me ;speaks (am)

8085 2896 1319 7965 8085 1319 7272 2022
הֶהָרִים רַגְלֵי מְבַשֵּׂר מַשְׁמִיעַ שָׁלוֹם מְבַשֵּׂר טוֹב מַשְׁמִיעַ
making of bringing ,peace making bring- him the moun- the
heard ,good tidings heard .tidings ing of feet tains

6963 5375 6822 6963 430 4427 6726 559 3444
8 יְשׁוּעָה אֹמֵר לְצִיּוֹן מָלַךְ אֱלֹהָיִךְ׃ קוֹל צֹפַיִךְ נָשְׂאוּ קוֹל
the they your The Your reigns to saying salva-
voice lift ,watchmen of voice !God ,Zion ,tion

7442 6476 6726 3068 7725 7200 5869 5869 7442 3162
9 יַחְדָּו יְרַנֵּנוּ כִּי עַיִן בְּעַיִן יִרְאוּ בְּשׁוּב יְהוָה צִיּוֹן׃ פִּצְחוּ רַנְּנוּ
sing Break .Zion Jehovah when they to eye For sing they to-
,out back brings see shall eye .aloud ,gether

3389 6476 6726 3068 5162 3389 2723 3162
יַחְדָּו חָרְבוֹת יְרוּשָׁלָ͏ִם כִּי־נִחַם יְהוָה עַמּוֹ גָּאַל יְרוּשָׁלָ͏ִם׃
.Jerusalem has He His Jehovah com- for ;Jerusalem waste to-
redeemed ;people forts of places ,gether

3605 7200 1471 3605 5869 6944 2220 3068 2834
10 חָשַׂף יְהוָה אֶת־זְרוֹעַ קָדְשׁוֹ לְעֵינֵי כָּל־הַגּוֹיִם וְרָאוּ כָּל־
all shall and the all the in His arm the Jehovah has
see ;nations of eyes holiness of bared

3318 5493 5493 430 3444 776 657
11 אַפְסֵי־אָרֶץ אֵת יְשׁוּעַת אֱלֹהֵינוּ׃ סוּרוּ סוּרוּ צְאוּ מִשָּׁם
from Go Turn Turn .God our sal- the the the
!there out !aside !aside of vation earth of ends

3808 3068 3627 5375 1305 8432 3318 5060 2931
12 טָמֵא אַל־תִּגָּעוּ צְאוּ מִתּוֹכָהּ הִבָּרוּ נֹשְׂאֵי כְּלֵי יְהוָה׃ כִּי לֹא
not For .Jehovah the bearers purify her from Go !touch not The
of vessels of yourself ,midst out unclean

3068 6440 1980 1980 3808 4499 3318 2649
בְחִפָּזוֹן תֵּצֵאוּ וּבִמְנוּסָה לֹא תֵלֵכוּן כִּי־הֹלֵךְ לִפְנֵיכֶם יְהוָה
,Jehovah before is for will not in and shall you with
you going ,go you flight ,out go haste

7311 5650 7919 2009 3478 430 622
13 וּמְאַסִּפְכֶם אֱלֹהֵי יִשְׂרָאֵל׃ הִנֵּה יַשְׂכִּיל עַבְדִּי יָרוּם
shall He My rule shall ,Behold .Israel the and
exalted be ;servant wisely of God you gathers

4893 7227 8074 3966 1361 5375
14 וְנִשָּׂא וְגָבַהּ מְאֹד׃ כַּאֲשֶׁר שָׁמְמוּ עָלֶיךָ רַבִּים כֵּן־מִשְׁחַת
disfig- the so —many over were as Just .very be and and
urement You astonished high up lifted

7227 1471 5137 120 1121 8392 4756 376
15 מֵאִישׁ מַרְאֵהוּ וְתֹאֲרוֹ מִבְּנֵי אָדָם׃ כֵּן יַזֶּה גּוֹיִם רַבִּים עָלָיו
At .many nations He So —man from his and ap- His from
Him from sprinkles of sons form pearance man

7200 5608 3808 834 6310 4428 7092
יִקְפְּצוּ מְלָכִים פִּיהֶם כִּי אֲשֶׁר לֹא־סֻפַּר לָהֶם רָאוּ וַאֲשֶׁר
and will they to was not that for their kings shall
what ;see them told which ;mouth shut

995 8085 3808
לֹא־שָׁמְעוּ הִתְבּוֹנָנוּ׃
will they they not
.understand heard

CAP. LIII נג

CHAPTER 53

5927 1540 4310 3068 2220 8052 539 4310
1 2 מִי הֶאֱמִין לִשְׁמֻעָתֵנוּ וּזְרוֹעַ יְהוָה עַל־מִי נִגְלָתָה׃ וַיַּעַל
He For is whom to Jehovah the And our has Who
up comes ?revealed of arm ?report believed

1926 3808 8389 3808 6723 776 8328 6440 3126
כַּיּוֹנֵק לְפָנָיו וְכַשֹּׁרֶשׁ מֵאֶרֶץ צִיָּה לֹא־תֹאַר לוֹ וְלֹא הָדָר
,majesty and to form a Not .dry of out as and before a as
(is) not ,Him (is) ground root a ,Him shoot

that day; for I *am* He who
speaks. Behold Me!
7How beautiful on the
mountains are the feet of
him bringing tidings,
making peace heard,
bringing good news,
making heard salvation;
saying to Zion, Your God
reigns! 8The voice of your
watchmen, they lift the
voice together, they sing
aloud. For they shall see
eye to eye when Jehovah
brings back Zion. 9Break
out, sing together, waste
places of Jerusalem; for
Jehovah comforts His
people; He has re-
deemed Jerusalem. 10Je-
hovah has bared His holy
arm in the eyes of all the
nations; and all the ends
of the earth shall see the
salvation of our God.
11Turn! Turn! Go out from
there! Touch not the un-
clean! Go out of her
midst, purify yourself,
bearers of the vessels of
Jehovah. 12For you shall
not go out with haste, nor
will you go in flight; for
Jehovah is going before
you, and the God of Israel
gathers you.
13Behold, My Servant
shall rule wisely; he shall
be exalted and lifted up
and be very high. 14Just
as many were aston-
ished over You — so
much was the disfigure-
ment from man, His ap-
pearance and His form
from sons of mankind —
15so He sprinkles from
many nations. At Him,
kings shall shut their
mouths; for they will see
that which was not told
to them; yea, what they
had not heard, they will
understand.

CHAPTER 53
1Who has believed our
report? And to whom is
the arm of Jehovah re-
vealed? 2For He comes
up before Him as a tender
plant, and as a root
out of dry ground.
He *has* no form nor

that we should see Him; nor form that we should desire Him. [3]*He is* despised and abandoned of men, a Man of pains, and acquainted with sickness. And as *if* hiding *our* faces from Him, He being despised, and we did not value Him. [4]Surely He has borne our sicknesses, and He carried our pain; yet we esteemed Him plagued, smitten by God, and afflicted. [5]But He was wounded for our transgressions; *He was* bruised for our iniquities; the chastisement of our peace *was* on Him; and with His wounds we ourselves are healed. [6]All we like sheep have gone astray; we have each one turned to his own way; and Jehovah made meet in Him the iniquity of all of us. [7]He was oppressed, and He was afflicted, but He did not open His mouth. He was led as a lamb to the slaughter; and as a ewe before her shearers is dumb, so He opened not His mouth. [8]He was taken from prison and from justice; and who shall consider His generation? For He was cut off out of the land of the living; from the transgression of My people, the stroke *was* to Him. [9]And He put His grave with the wicked; and with a rich *man* in His death; although He had done no violence, and deceit *was* not in His mouth. [10]But Jehovah pleased to crush Him, to make Him sick, *so that* If He should put His soul *as* a guilt offering, He shall see *His* seed; He shall prolong *His* days; and the will of Jehovah shall prosper in His hand. [11]He shall see *the fruit* of the travail of His soul; He shall be fully satisfied. By His knowledge shall My righteous Servant justify for many, and He shall bear their iniquities. [12]Because of this I will divide to Him with the great, and with the strong He shall divide the spoil; because He poured out His soul to death; and He was counted with transgressors; and He bore the sin of many, and interceded for transgressors.

376 376 2310 959 2530 4758 3808 7200
3 וְנִרְאֵהוּ וְלֹא־מַרְאֶה וְנֶחְמְדֵהוּ׃ נִבְזֶה וַחֲדַל אִישִׁים אִישׁ
a ,men ab- and despised should we that ap- an not and we that
of man of andoned :him desire pearance ;Him see should

3808 959 6440 5640 2483 3045 4341
מַכְאֹבוֹת וִידוּעַ חֹלִי וּכְמַסְתֵּר פָּנִים מִמֶּנּוּ נִבְזֶה וְלֹא
and being from faces as And sick- known and
not despised ;Him of hiding nesses of pains

5445 4341 5375 2483 403 2803
4 חֲשַׁבְנֻהוּ׃ אָכֵן חֳלָיֵנוּ הוּא נָשָׂא וּמַכְאֹבֵינוּ סְבָלָם וַאֲנַחְנוּ
we but carried He pains our and has He sick- our Surely did we
;them borne ness .Him value

6588 2490 6031 430 5221 5060 2803
5 חֲשַׁבְנֻהוּ נָגוּעַ מֻכֵּה אֱלֹהִים וּמְעֻנֶּה׃ וְהוּא מְחֹלָל מִפְּשָׁעֵנוּ
our for was He But and ,God struck ,plagued esteem-
,transgressions pierced .afflicted by Him ed

7495 2250 7965 4148 5771 1792
מְדֻכָּא מֵעֲוֺנֹתֵינוּ מוּסַר שְׁלוֹמֵנוּ עָלָיו וּבַחֲבֻרָתוֹ נִרְפָּא־
are we with and on (was) our chastise- the our for crushed
healed wounds His ;Him peace of ment ;iniquities

6293 3068 6437 1870 376 8582 6629
6 לָנוּ׃ כֻּלָּנוּ כַּצֹּאן תָּעִינוּ אִישׁ לְדַרְכּוֹ פָּנִינוּ וַיהוָה הִפְגִּיעַ
made has and have we his to each go like All our-
meet Jehovah ;turned way man ;astray sheep we .selves

7716 6310 6605 3808 6031 5065 3605 5771
7 בּוֹ אֵת עֲוֺן כֻּלָּנוּ׃ נִגַּשׂ וְהוּא נַעֲנֶה וְלֹא יִפְתַּח־פִּיו כַּשֶּׂה
a As His did He but was He and was He .all us the in
lamb .mouth open not ;afflicted ,oppressed of iniquity Him

6310 6605 3808 481 1494 6440 7353 2986 2874
לַטֶּבַח יוּבָל וּכְרָחֵל לִפְנֵי גֹזְזֶיהָ נֶאֱלָמָה וְלֹא יִפְתַּח פִּיו׃
His He so is her before as and was He the to
.mouth opens not ,dumb shearers ewe an ;led slaughter

776 1504 7878 4310 1755 3947 4941 6115
8 מֵעֹצֶר וּמִמִּשְׁפָּט לֻקָּח וְאֶת־דּוֹרוֹ מִי יְשׂוֹחֵחַ כִּי נִגְזַר מֵאֶרֶץ
the from was He For shall who His and was He from and From
of land off cut ?consider generation ;taken justice prison

6913 7563 5414 5061 5971 6588 2416
9 חַיִּים מִפֶּשַׁע עַמִּי נֶגַע לָמוֹ׃ וַיִּתֵּן אֶת־רְשָׁעִים קִבְרוֹ וְאֶת־
and His the with He And to (was) the My tres- the from the
with ,grave wicked put .Him stroke people of pass ;living

3068 6310 4820 3808 6213 2555 3808 4194 6223
10 עָשִׁיר בְּמֹתָיו עַל לֹא־חָמָס עָשָׂה וְלֹא מִרְמָה בְּפִיו׃ וַיהוָה
But His in deceit and had He violence not though His in rich a
Jehovah .mouth (was) not ,done ;death (man)

748 2233 7200 5315 816 7760 2470 1792 2656
חָפֵץ דַּכְּאוֹ הֶחֱלִי אִם־תָּשִׂים אָשָׁם נַפְשׁוֹ יִרְאֶה זֶרַע יַאֲרִיךְ
shall He ,seed He His guilt a He If make to to pleased
prolong see shall ,soul offering put shall sick Him ,Him crush

7646 7200 5315 5999 6743 3027 3068 2656 3117
11 יָמִים וְחֵפֶץ יְהוָה בְּיָדוֹ יִצְלָח׃ מֵעֲמַל נַפְשׁוֹ יִרְאֶה יִשְׂבָּע
shall He shall He His the Of shall His in Jehovah the and days
.satisfied be ;see soul of travail .prosper hand of pleasure

5445 5771 7227 5650 6662 6663 1847
בְּדַעְתּוֹ יַצְדִּיק צַדִּיק עַבְדִּי לָרַבִּים וַעֲוֺנֹתָם הוּא יִסְבֹּל׃
shall He their and ,many for My righteous shall His By
.bear iniquities servant justify knowledge

8478 7998 2505 6099 7227 2505 3651
12 לָכֵן אֲחַלֶּק־לוֹ בָרַבִּים וְאֶת־עֲצוּמִים יְחַלֵּק שָׁלָל תַּחַת
be- ,spoil shall He the and the with to will I There-
divide strong with ,great Him divide ,fore

2399 4487 4487 5315 4194 6168 834
אֲשֶׁר הֶעֱרָה לַמָּוֶת נַפְשׁוֹ וְאֶת־פֹּשְׁעִים נִמְנָה וְהוּא חֵטְא־
the He and was trans- and His death to poured He cause
of sin ;counted gressors with ;soul out

6293 6586 5375 7227
רַבִּים נָשָׂא וְלַפֹּשְׁעִים יַפְגִּיעַ׃
made for and ,bore many
.intercession transgressors

CAP. LIV נד

CHAPTER 54

CHAPTER 54

[1]Rejoice, unfruitful one that never bore; break out a song and shout, *you* who never travailed. For the sons of the desolate one *are* more than the sons of the married woman, says Jehovah. [2]Make the place of your tent larger, and let them stretch out the curtains of your dwellings. Do not spare, lengthen your cords and strengthen your stakes. [3]For you shall break forth *on* the right hand and *on* the left. And your seed shall possess nations, and people will inhabit ruined cities. [4]Do not fear, for you shall not be ashamed, nor shall you be disgraced, for you shall not be wounded. For you shall forget the shame of your youth, and you shall not remember the reproach of your widowhood any more. [5]For your Maker *is* your husband; Jehovah of hosts *is* His name; and your Redeemer *is* the Holy One of Israel; He is called the God of all the earth. [6]For Jehovah has called you as a woman forsaken and grieved in spirit, even a wife of young men when she is rejected, says your God. [7]For a little moment I have left you, but I will gather you with great pityings. [8]In a flood of wrath I hid My face from you *for* a moment; but I will have pity on you with everlasting kindness, says Jehovah your Redeemer. [9]For this *is* the waters of Noah to Me; *for as* I swore *to refrain* from passing over the waters of Noah over the earth again, so I have sworn from being angry with you and rebuking you. [10]For the mountains shall depart and the hills be removed, but My mercy shall not depart from you; nor shall the covenant of My peace be removed, says Jehovah who has pity on you.

[11]Afflicted one, storm-tossed, and not comforted!

2342 3808 6670 7440 6476 3205 3808 6135 7442
1 רָנִּי עֲקָרָה לֹא יָלָדָה פִּצְחִי רִנָּה וְצַהֲלִי לֹא־חָלָה כִּי־
For who (you) not and song a break that not barren Re-
.travailed shout out ;bore ,one ,joice

7337 3068 559 1166 1121 8074 1121 7227
2 רַבִּים בְּנֵי־שׁוֹמֵמָה מִבְּנֵי בְעוּלָה אָמַר יְהוָה׃ הַרְחִיבִי ׀
Make .Jehovah says the the than the the (are)
larger ,married of sons desolate of sons more

748 2820 408 5186 4908 3407 168 4725
מְקוֹם אָהֳלֵךְ וִירִיעוֹת מִשְׁכְּנוֹתַיִךְ יַטּוּ אַל־תַּחְשֹׂכִי הַאֲרִיכִי
lengthen do not stretch your the and ,tent your the
;spare ;out dwellings of curtains of place

2233 6555 8040 3225 2388 3489 3407
3 מֵיתָרַיִךְ וִיתֵדֹתַיִךְ חַזֵּקִי׃ כִּי־יָמִין וּשְׂמֹאול תִּפְרֹצִי וְזַרְעֵךְ
your And shall you the and the (on) For .strengthen your and your
seed .forth break left right stakes cords

3808 3372 408 3427 8074 5892 3423 1471
4 גּוֹיִם יִירָשׁ וְעָרִים נְשַׁמּוֹת יוֹשִׁיבוּ׃ אַל־תִּירְאִי כִּי־לֹא
not for Do not indwell will ruined and shall nations
,fear .people cities ,possess

5934 1322 2659 3637 408 1322
תֵבוֹשִׁי וְאַל־תִּכָּלְמִי כִּי־לֹא תַחְפִּירִי כִּי בֹשֶׁת עֲלוּמַיִךְ
your the For shall you not for you shall and be shall you
youth of shame ;wounded be .abashed be not ,ashamed

1166 5750 2142 3808 491 2781 7911
5 תִּשְׁכָּחִי וְחֶרְפַּת אַלְמְנוּתַיִךְ לֹא תִזְכְּרִי־עוֹד׃ כִּי בֹעֲלַיִךְ
your For any shall you not your the and shall you
husband .more remember widowhood of reproach ,forget

3605 430 3478 6918 1350 6635 3068 6213
עֹשַׂיִךְ יְהוָה צְבָאוֹת שְׁמוֹ וְגֹאֲלֵךְ קְדוֹשׁ יִשְׂרָאֵל אֱלֹהֵי כָל־
all the ;Israel the (is) your and His Hosts Jehovah your (is)
of God of One Holy Redeemer ;name (is) of ,Maker

7121 7307 6087 5800 802 7121 776
6 הָאָרֶץ יִקָּרֵא׃ כִּי־כְאִשָּׁה עֲזוּבָה וַעֲצוּבַת רוּחַ קְרָאָךְ
has spirit grieved and forsaken a as For is He the
you called in woman .called earth

6996 7281 430 559 3985 5271 802 3068
7 יְהוָה וְאֵשֶׁת נְעוּרִים כִּי תִמָּאֵס אָמַר אֱלֹהָיִךְ׃ בְּרֶגַע קָטֹן
little a For your says is she when young a even ,Jehovah
moment .God ,rejected men of wife

5646 7110 82 41 6908 3478 7356 5800
8 עֲזַבְתִּיךְ וּבְרַחֲמִים גְּדֹלִים אֲקַבְּצֵךְ׃ בְּשֶׁצֶף קֶצֶף הִסְתַּרְתִּי
hid I wrath a In will I great with but have I
of flood ,you gather compassion ,you left

3068 1350 559 7355 5769 2617 72 81/6440
פָנַי רֶגַע מִמֵּךְ וּבְחֶסֶד עוֹלָם רִחַמְתִּיךְ אָמַר גֹּאֲלֵךְ יְהוָה׃
.Jehovah your says have will I ever- with but from a My
Redeemer ,you on pity lasting mercy ;you moment face

5750 5146 4325 5674 7650 834 2088 5146 4325
9 כִּי־מֵי נֹחַ זֹאת לִי אֲשֶׁר נִשְׁבַּעְתִּי מֵעֲבֹר מֵי־נֹחַ עוֹד
again Noah the from swore I which to this Noah the For
of waters crossing Me (is) of waters

2022 1605 1107 7650 776
10 עַל־הָאָרֶץ כֵּן נִשְׁבַּעְתִּי מִקְּצֹף עָלַיִךְ וּמִגְּעָר־בָּךְ׃ כִּי הֶהָרִים
the For .you from and with being from have I so the over
mountains rebuking you angry sworn ,earth

1285 4185 3808 854 2617 4131 1389 4185
יָמוּשׁוּ וְהַגְּבָעוֹת תְּמוּטֶינָה וְחַסְדִּי מֵאִתֵּךְ לֹא־יָמוּשׁ וּבְרִית
the and shall not from My but be the and shall
of covenant ,depart you mercy ,removed hills depart

5590 6041 3068 7355 559 4131 3808 7965
11 שְׁלוֹמִי לֹא תָמוּט אָמַר מְרַחֲמֵךְ יְהוָה׃ עֲנִיָּה סֹעֲרָה
storm Afflicted .Jehovah pity having says be shall not My
,tossed ,one you on ,removed peace

Behold, I stretch out your stones among antimony, and lay your foundations with sapphires. 12 And I will make your battlements of ruby, and your gates carbuncle stones, and all your borders pleasing stones; 13 and all your sons *will be* taught of Jehovah; and the peace of your sons *will be* great. 14 You shall be established in righteousness; *you shall* be far from oppression, for you shall not fear; and from terror, for it shall not come near you. 15 Behold, they shall surely gather, but not from Me. Who has gathered against you? By you he shall fall. 16 Behold, I have created the smith who blows the coal in the fire, and who brings out a weapon for his work; and I have created the waster to destroy. 17 Every weapon formed against you shall not prosper, and every tongue that shall rise against you in judgment, you shall condemn. This *is* the inheritance of the servants of Jehovah, and their righteousness *is* from Me, says Jehovah.

לֹא נֻחָמָה הִנֵּה אָנֹכִי מַרְבִּיץ בַּפּוּךְ אֲבָנַיִךְ וִיסַדְתִּיךְ
your lay and / foundations — your stones — among antimony — stretch out — I — ,Behold — comforted — not

12 בַּסַּפִּירִים׃ וְשַׂמְתִּי כַּדְכֹד שִׁמְשֹׁתַיִךְ וּשְׁעָרַיִךְ לְאַבְנֵי אֶקְדָּח
carbuncle — stones — your and gates — your battlements — ruby of — I And make will — among .sapphires

13 וְכָל־גְּבוּלֵךְ לְאַבְנֵי־חֵפֶץ׃ וְכָל־בָּנַיִךְ לִמּוּדֵי יְהוָה וְרַב
and great — ;Jehovah — taught of — your sons — and all — ;delight — stones of — your border — and all

14 שְׁלוֹם בָּנָיִךְ׃ בִּצְדָקָה תִּכּוֹנָנִי רַחֲקִי מֵעֹשֶׁק כִּי־לֹא תִירָאִי
shall you ;fear — not — for — from oppression — far be — shall you ;set be — righteousness — In — your .sons — the (is) of peace

15 וּמִמְּחִתָּה כִּי לֹא־תִקְרַב אֵלָיִךְ׃ הֵן גּוֹר יָגוּר אֶפֶס מֵאוֹתִי
from .Me — not but — they surely gather will — Behold — .you to — shall it near come — not — for — from and ,terror

16 מִי־גָר אִתָּךְ עָלַיִךְ יִפּוֹל׃ הֵן אָנֹכִי בָּרָאתִי חָרָשׁ נֹפֵחַ
blowing — the ,smith — have created — I — ,Behold — shall he .fall — By you — against ?you — has Who gathered

בְּאֵשׁ פֶּחָם וּמוֹצִיא כְלִי לְמַעֲשֵׂהוּ וְאָנֹכִי בָּרָאתִי מַשְׁחִית
waster the — have created — I and — his for ;work — a weapon — bring-and out ing — ,coal — the in of fire

17 לְחַבֵּל׃ כָּל־כְּלִי יוּצַר עָלַיִךְ לֹא יִצְלָח וְכָל־לָשׁוֹן תָּקוּם
shall that arise — tongue and every — shall ,prosper — not — against you — formed — weapon Every — to .destroy

אִתָּךְ לַמִּשְׁפָּט תַּרְשִׁיעִי זֹאת נַחֲלַת עַבְדֵי יְהוָה וְצִדְקָתָם
their and righteousness — ,Jehovah — the of servants — inheri- of tance — the (is) — This — shall you .condemn — in judgment — against you

מֵאִתִּי נְאֻם־יְהוָה׃
.Jehovah — states — from ,Me

CAP. LV נה

CHAPTER 55

CHAPTER 55

1 Ho, everyone who thirsts, come to the water; and he who *has* no money, come buy grain and eat. Yes, come buy grain, wine and milk without silver and with no price. 2 Why do you weigh out silver for *that which is* not bread, and your labor for *that which* never satisfies? Listen carefully to Me and eat that which is good; and let your soul delight itself in fatness. 3 Bend you ear and come to Me; hear, and your soul shall live; and I will cut a covenant everlasting with you, the faithful mercies of David. 4 Behold, I gave Him a witness to peoples, a

1 הוֹי כָּל־צָמֵא לְכוּ לַמַּיִם וַאֲשֶׁר אֵין־לוֹ כָּסֶף לְכוּ שִׁבְרוּ
,buy grain — ,come — (is) silver — to not him — he and who — the to ;water — come — who ,thirsts — every one — ,Ho

וֶאֱכֹלוּ וּלְכוּ שִׁבְרוּ בְּלוֹא־כֶסֶף וּבְלוֹא מְחִיר יַיִן וְחָלָב׃
and .milk — wine — ,price — and without — silver without — buy grain — ,yes come — ;eat and

2 לָמָּה תִשְׁקְלוּ־כֶסֶף בְּלוֹא־לֶחֶם וִיגִיעֲכֶם בְּלוֹא לְשָׂבְעָה
satis- to ?faction — (what) for not (is) — your and labor — ,bread (what) for not (is) — silver — you do out weigh — Why

שִׁמְעוּ שָׁמוֹעַ אֵלַי וְאִכְלוּ־טוֹב וְתִתְעַנַּג בַּדֶּשֶׁן נַפְשְׁכֶם׃
.soul your — fatness in — let and itself delight — the good — eat and — ,Me to — care- fully — Listen

3 הַטּוּ אָזְנְכֶם וּלְכוּ אֵלַי שִׁמְעוּ וּתְחִי נַפְשְׁכֶם וְאֶכְרְתָה
will I and cut — ;soul your — shall and live — ,hear — ;Me to — and come — your ear — Incline

4 לָכֶם בְּרִית עוֹלָם חַסְדֵי דָוִד הַנֶּאֱמָנִים׃ הֵן עֵד לְאוּמִּים
peoples to — a (as) witness — ,Lo — faithful the — David — mercies of — ever- ,lasting — a covenant — with you

Leader and Commander of peoples. [5]Behold You shall call a nation You do not know; yea, a nation that does not know You shall run to You, because of Jehovah Your God, and for the Holy One of Israel; for He has glorified You.

[6]Seek Jehovah while He may be found; call on Him while He is near. [7]Let the wicked forsake his way and the vain man his thoughts; and let him return to Jehovah, and He will have mercy on him—and to our God, for He will abundantly pardon. [8]For My thoughts *are* not your thoughts; nor *are* your ways My ways, says Jehovah. [9]For as the heavens are high from the earth, so My ways are high from your ways, and My thoughts from your thoughts. [10]For as the rain and the snow goes down from the heavens and do not return there, but waters the earth and makes it bring forth and bud, and give seed to the sower and bread to the eater — [11]so shall My word be, which goes out of My mouth; it shall not return to Me void, but it shall accomplish that which I please, and it shall prosper in what I sent it *to do*! [12]For you shall go out with joy and be led out with peace. The mountains and the hills shall break out into song before you, and all the trees of the field shall clap the palm. [13]Instead of the thorn-bush, the fir-tree shall come up; instead of the brier, the myrtle shall come up; and it shall be for a name to Jehovah, for an everlasting sign that shall not be cut off.

1471 7121 3045 3808 1471 2009 3816 6680 5057 5414
5 נְתַתִּיו נָגִיד וּמְצַוֵּה לְאֻמִּים׃ הֵן גּוֹי לֹא־תֵדַע תִּקְרָא וְגוֹי
a and shall You You not a ,Lo .peoples Com- and a gave I
nation ;call know do nation of mander Leader Him

3478 6918 430 3068 4616 7323 3045 3808
לֹא־יְדָעוּךָ אֵלֶיךָ יָרוּצוּ לְמַעַן יְהוָה אֱלֹהֶיךָ וְלִקְדוֹשׁ יִשְׂרָאֵל
;Israel the for and your Jehovah because shall to that not
of One Holy ,God of ;run You ,You knows

1961 7121 4672 3068 1875 6286
6 כִּי פֵאֲרָךְ׃ דִּרְשׁוּ יְהוָה בְּהִמָּצְאוֹ קְרָאֻהוּ בִּהְיוֹתוֹ
He while on call He while Jehovah Seek has He for
is Him ;found be may .You glorified

7725 4284 369 376 1870 7563 5800 7138
7 קָרוֹב׃ יַעֲזֹב רָשָׁע דַּרְכּוֹ וְאִישׁ אָוֶן מַחְשְׁבֹתָיו וְיָשֹׁב אֶל־
to let and His vanity the and his the Let .near
return him ;thoughts of man ,way wicked forsake

3808 5545 7235 430 7355 3068
8 יְהוָה וִירַחֲמֵהוּ וְאֶל־אֱלֹהֵינוּ כִּי־יַרְבֶּה לִסְלוֹחַ׃ כִּי לֹא
not For .pardon to will He for our to and may He that Jeho-
(are) multiply ,God ;him pity ,vah

3068 5002 1870 1870 3808 4284 4284
מַחְשְׁבוֹתַי מַחְשְׁבוֹתֵיכֶם וְלֹא דַרְכֵיכֶם דְּרָכָי נְאֻם יְהוָה׃
.Jehovah states My ways your and your My
,ways (are) not ;thoughts thoughts

1870 1870 1361 776 8064 1361
9 כִּי־גָבְהוּ שָׁמַיִם מֵאָרֶץ כֵּן גָּבְהוּ דְרָכַי מִדַּרְכֵיכֶם
your from My are so the from the are For
,ways ways high ,earth heavens high (as)

7950 1653 4284 4284
10 וּמַחְשְׁבֹתַי מִמַּחְשְׁבֹתֵיכֶם׃ כִּי כַּאֲשֶׁר יֵרֵד הַגֶּשֶׁם וְהַשֶּׁלֶג
and the goes as For your from My and
snow the rain down .thoughts thoughts

776 7301 7925 3808 8033 8064
מִן־הַשָּׁמַיִם וְשָׁמָּה לֹא יָשׁוּב כִּי אִם־הִרְוָה אֶת־הָאָרֶץ
the it ex- do not to and the from
earth waters cept ,return there ,heavens

1961 398 3899 2232 2233 5414 6779 3205
11 וְהוֹלִידָהּ וְהִצְמִיחָהּ וְנָתַן זֶרַע לַזֹּרֵעַ וְלֶחֶם לָאֹכֵל׃ כֵּן יִהְיֶה
shall so the to and the to seed and and it makes and
be —eater bread sower give ,sprout forth bring

6213 7387 7725 3808 6310 3318 834 1697
דְבָרִי אֲשֶׁר יֵצֵא מִפִּי לֹא־יָשׁוּב אֵלַי רֵיקָם כִּי אִם־עָשָׂה
do shall it ex- ,void Me to shall it not My of goes that My
cept return ;mouth out word

8057 7971 834 6743 2654 834
12 אֶת־אֲשֶׁר חָפַצְתִּי וְהִצְלִיחַ אֲשֶׁר שְׁלַחְתִּיו׃ כִּי־בְשִׂמְחָה
with For .it sent I what in shall it and ;please I that
joy prosper which

6440 6476 1389 2022 2986 7965 3318
תֵצֵאוּ וּבְשָׁלוֹם תּוּבָלוּן הֶהָרִים וְהַגְּבָעוֹת יִפְצְחוּ לִפְנֵיכֶם
before break shall the and the ;led be with and shall you
you out hills mountains peace ,out go

5927 5285 8478 3709 4222 7704 6086 3605 7440
13 רִנָּה וְכָל־עֲצֵי הַשָּׂדֶה יִמְחֲאוּ־כָף׃ תַּחַת הַנַּעֲצוּץ יַעֲלֶה
shall thorn- the Instead (the) shall the the and (into)
up go bush of palm clap field of trees all ;song

226 8034 3068 1961 1918 5927 5636 8478 1265
בְרוֹשׁ תַּחַת הַסִּרְפַּד יַעֲלֶה הֲדַס וְהָיָה לַיהוָה לְשֵׁם לְאוֹת
a for a for to it and the shall the instead fir- the
sign ;name Jehovah be shall ;myrtle up go ,brier of ;tree

3772 3808 5769
עוֹלָם לֹא יִכָּרֵת׃
shall that not ever-
off cut be lasting

CAP. LVI נו

CHAPTER 56

CHAPTER 56

¹So says Jehovah: Keep justice and do righteousness, for My salvation *is* near to come, and My righteousness to be revealed. ²Blessed *is* the man who does this, and the son of man who lays hold on it; keeping sabbath, from defiling it; and keeping his hand from doing every evil. ³And do not let the son of the foreigner speak, he who joins himself to Jehovah, saying, Jehovah surely separates me from His people; and not do let the eunuch say, Behold, I *am* a dried tree. ⁴For so says Jehovah to the eunuchs who keep My sabbaths and choose things I am pleased with, and take hold of My covenant: ⁵I even will give to them in My house and in My walls a hand and a name better than sons and than daughters; I will give them an everlasting name, which shall not be cut off. ⁶And the sons of the alien who join themselves on Jehovah to serve Him, and to love Jehovah's name, to be His servants, everyone who keeps from defiling the sabbath, and takes hold of My covenant: ⁷even them I will bring to My holy mount and make them joyful in My house of prayer. Their burnt offerings and their sacrifices *shall be* accepted on My altar, for My house shall be called a house of prayer for all the peoples, ⁸states the Lord Jehovah, who gathers the outcasts of Israel, I will yet gather beside him his gathered ones. ⁹All beasts of the field come to devour, all beasts in the forest! ¹⁰His watchmen *are* blind; they all do not know

1 כֹּה אָמַר יְהֹוָה שִׁמְרוּ מִשְׁפָּט וַעֲשׂוּ צְדָקָה כִּי־קְרוֹבָה
near   for   righ- do and   justice Keep :Jehovah says Thus
(is)   eousness

2 יְשׁוּעָתִי לָבוֹא וְצִדְקָתִי לְהִגָּלוֹת: אַשְׁרֵי אֱנוֹשׁ יַעֲשֶׂה־
does who man the Blessed   be to   My and   ,come to   My
(is)   .revealed righteousness   salvation

זֹּאת וּבֶן־אָדָם יַחֲזִיק בָּהּ שֹׁמֵר שַׁבָּת מֵחַלְּלוֹ וְשֹׁמֵר יָדוֹ
his and   from   ,sabbath keeping ;it on who   man the and ,this
hand keeping   ,it defiling   holds   of son

3 מֵעֲשׂוֹת כָּל־רָע: וְאַל־יֹאמַר בֶּן־הַנֵּכָר הַנִּלְוָה אֶל־יְהֹוָה
,Jehovah to who   the   son   let do And   .evil every from
            himself joins foreigner of speak not   doing

לֵאמֹר הַבְדֵּל יַבְדִּילַנִי יְהֹוָה מֵעַל עַמּוֹ וְאַל־יֹאמַר הַסָּרִיס
the let do and   His from Jehovah separates Surely ,saying
,eunuch say   not ;people   me

4 הֵן אֲנִי עֵץ יָבֵשׁ: כִּי־כֹה אָמַר יְהֹוָה לַסָּרִיסִים אֲשֶׁר
who   the to   Jehovah says thus For   dried   a I Be-
         eunuchs   up   tree (am) ,hold

יִשְׁמְרוּ אֶת־שַׁבְּתוֹתַי וּבָחֲרוּ בַּאֲשֶׁר חָפָצְתִּי וּמַחֲזִיקִים
take and   am I   things and   My   keep
hold   pleased which with choose sabbaths

5 בִּבְרִיתִי: וְנָתַתִּי לָהֶם בְּבֵיתִי וּבְחוֹמֹתַי יָד וָשֵׁם טוֹב
better a and   a   in and   My in them to even I My of
name   hand   walls My house give will :covenant

מִבָּנִים וּמִבָּנוֹת שֵׁם עוֹלָם אֶתֶּן־לוֹ אֲשֶׁר לֹא יִכָּרֵת:
be shall not which to will I ever- a   than and than
.off cut   them give lasting name .daughters sons

6 וּבְנֵי הַנֵּכָר הַנִּלְוִים עַל־יְהֹוָה לְשָׁרְתוֹ וּלְאַהֲבָה אֶת־שֵׁם
the to and serve to Jehovah on join who the the And
of name love ,Him   themselves   alien of sons

יְהֹוָה לִהְיוֹת לוֹ לַעֲבָדִים כָּל־שֹׁמֵר שַׁבָּת מֵחַלְּלוֹ וּמַחֲזִיקִים
takes and from ,sabbath who every ,servants to be- to Jehovah
hold ,it defiling keeps one   Him come

7 בִּבְרִיתִי: וַהֲבִיאוֹתִים אֶל־הַר קָדְשִׁי וְשִׂמַּחְתִּים בְּבֵית
in   make and   My Mount to will I even My of
of house joyful them ,holy   them bring   .covenant

תְּפִלָּתִי עוֹלוֹתֵיהֶם וְזִבְחֵיהֶם לְרָצוֹן עַל־מִזְבְּחִי כִּי בֵיתִי
My   for My on for (are) their and burnt Their My
house ,altar My   acceptance sacrifices offerings .prayer

8 בֵּית־תְּפִלָּה יִקָּרֵא לְכָל־הָעַמִּים: נְאֻם אֲדֹנָי יְהֹוָה מְקַבֵּץ
gather- ,Jehovah the states the all for be shall prayer a
ing   Lord   ,peoples   called   of house

9 נִדְחֵי יִשְׂרָאֵל עוֹד אֲקַבֵּץ עָלָיו לְנִקְבָּצָיו: כֹּל חַיְתוֹ שָׂדַי
the beasts All   his to upon will I yet ,Israel out- the
       ,field of .ones gathered him gather   of casts

10 אֵתָיוּ לֶאֱכֹל כָּל־חַיְתוֹ בַּיָּעַר: צֹפָו עִוְרִים כֻּלָּם לֹא
not they (are) His   the in   beasts all ,eat to come
    all ;blind watchmen   !forest

are all dumb dogs, they cannot bark, dreaming, lying down, loving to slumber; [11]yea, dogs greedy of soul; they do not know satisfaction. And they *are* shepherds; they know not discernment; they all look to their own way, each one for his own gain, from his own end, *saying*: [12]Come, and let me bring wine, and let us gulp down fermented drink; and tomorrow shall be as this day, great, exceedingly abundant.

ידעו כלם כלבים אלמים לא יוכלו לנבח הזים שכבים
lying ,down ,dreaming ,bark to they able are not ,dumb dogs (are) they all ;know
11 אהבי לנום׃ והכלבים עזי־נפש לא ידעו שבעה והמה
And (are) they .satisfaction know they not ;soul strong of dogs And (are) to .slumber loving
רעים לא ידעו הבין כלם לדרכם פנו איש לבצעו
own his ,gain for each man ,look their to way they all ;discern- ment know they not shep- ;herds
12 מקצהו׃ אתיו אקחה־יין ונסבאה שכר והיה כזה יום
day as this shall and be fermented ;drink let and gulp us ,wine me let take ,Come his from :end
מחר גדול יתר מאד׃
.very abun- dantly ,great to- ,morrow

CAP. LVII נז

CHAPTER 57

[1]The righteous one perishes, and no one lays *it* on *his* heart; and merciful men are gathered, with none discerning that the righteous is gathered from the face of evil. [2]He shall enter peace; they shall rest on their beds, walking *in* his uprightness. [3]But you, draw near here, sons of the sorceress, seed of the adulterer and the harlot. [4]On whom are you making sport? On whom do you make a wide mouth and draw out the tongue? Are you not children of transgression, a lying seed, [5]being inflamed with idols under every green tree, slaughtering the children in the torrent-beds, under the clefts of the rocks? [6]Your portion *is* in the smoothnesses of the torrent; they, they *are* your lot; even to them you have poured a drink offering; you have offered a food offering. Should I be consoled over these? [7]You have set your bed on a high and lofty mountain; yea, you went up to sacrifice a sacrifice. [8]And you have set up your memorial behind the door and the post. For you uncovered yourself from Me and went up; you spread your bed; and you cut

1 הצדיק אבד ואין איש שם על־לב ואנשי־חסד נאספים
are gathered mercy of men and (his) on ;heart lays (it) man and no ,perishes righ- teous The one
2 באין מבין כי־מפני הרעה נאסף הצדיק׃ יבוא שלום
;peace shall He enter .righteous the is gathered evil the from of face that dis- cerning with none
3 ינוחו על־משכבותם הלך נכחו׃ ואתם קרבו־הנה
,here draw near But ,you up- his .rightness walking (in) their ,couches on they rest shall
4 בני עננה זרע מנאף ותזנה׃ על־מי תתענגו על־מי
whom On you are ?sport making whom On the and .harlot the adulterer seed of ,sorceress the sons of
תרחיבו פה תאריכו לשון הלוא־אתם ילדי־פשע זרע
a of seed transgres- ,sion children of you Are not the ?tongue draw and out a mouth make you do wide
5 שקר׃ הנחמים באלים תחת כל־עץ רענן שחטי הילדים
the children slaugh- tering ,green tree every under with idols being inflamed false- ,hood
6 בנחלים תחת סעפי הסלעים׃ בחלקי־נחל חלקך הם
,they your (is) ;portion torrent's the in smoothnesses ?rocks the the of clefts under the in tor- rent ,beds
הם גורלך גם־להם שפכת נסך העלית מנחה העל
Over food a .offering have you offered drink a ;offering have you poured to even them your (are) ;lot they
7 אלה אנחם׃ על הר־גבה ונשא שמת משכבך גם־
also your couch have you set and lofty high a mountain On be I should ?consoled these
8 שם עלית לזבח זבח׃ ואחר הדלת והמזוזה שמת
have you up set the and post door the And behind a .sacrifice to sacrifice went you up there
זכרונך כי מאתי גלית ותעלי הרחבת משכבך ותכרת־
cut you and (covenant) your ;couch en- you larged and ;up went you uncovered from Me For your .memorial

9 לך מהם אהבת משכבם יד חזית׃ ותשרי למלך
the to you And you a (at) their you from for
king went .looked hand ;couch loved ;them you
בשמן ותרבי רקחיך ותשלחי ציריך עד־מרחק ותשפילי
lowered and far mes- your you And your and with
yourself ,away sengers sent .perfume multiplied ,oil
10 עד־שאול׃ ברב דרכך יגעת לא אמרת נואש חית
life The ! Despair you not you your the In .Sheol to
of said ;labored way of length
11 ידך מצאת על־כן לא חלית׃ ואת־מי דאגת ותיראי כי
For and you have whom And were you not therefore you your
?feared ,dreaded .sick ;found hand
תכזבי ואותי לא זכרת לא־שמת על־לבך הלא אני
Have your on laid not have not Me and have you
I not .heart (it) ,remembered lied
12 מחשה ומעלם ואותי לא תיראי׃ אני אגיד צדקתך
righ- your will I have you not Me and from even been
teousness reveal ?feared forever ,silent
13 ואת־מעשיך ולא יועילוך׃ בזעקך יצילך קבוציך ואת־
but your let When will they and your and
gathering you deliver ,cry you .you benefit not ,works
כלם ישא־רוח יקח־הבל והחוסה בי ינחל־ארץ ויירש
and the shall in who he But .vanity takes the bear shall of all
possess land inherit Me refuge takes (them) ;wind away them
14 הר־קדשי׃ ואמר סלו־סלו פנו־דרך הרימו מכשול
stumb- the make the Clear Raise Raise He And My moun-
block ling rise !way !up !up say shall .holy tain
15 מדרך עמי׃ כי כה אמר רם ונשא שכן עד וקדוש
and ,eternity who and the says thus For My the from
(is) Holy inhabits One lofty high .people of way
שמו מרום וקדוש אשכון ואת־דכא ושפל־רוח להחיות
make to ;spirit and the even dwell I holy and The His
live of humble contrite with ,in place high :name
16 רוח שפלים ולהחיות לב נדכאים׃ כי לא לעולם אריב
will I forever not For contrite the to and humble the
,contend ,ones of heart revive ones of spirit
ולא לנצח אקצוף כי־רוח מלפני יעטוף ונשמות אני
I the even be would be- from the for will I always and
breaths ,faint me fore spirit ;angry be not
17 עשיתי׃ בעון בצעו קצפתי ואכהו הסתר ואקצף וילך
he yet was and hid I struck and was I his the For have
,went ;angry Myself ;him angry gain of iniquity .made
18 שובב בדרך לבו׃ דרכיו ראיתי וארפאהו ואנחהו ואשלם
and will and will I but have I His his the in returning
restore him lead ,him heal seen ways .heart of way
19 נחמים לו ולאבליו׃ בורא ניב שפתים שלום שלום
,peace ,peace ;lips the the (I) his to and to com-
of fruit create .mourners him forting
20 לרחוק ולקרוב אמר יהוה ורפאתיו׃ והרשעים כים
the like the But will I and ,Jehovah says the to and far the to
sea (are) wicked him heal ,near off

covenant with them; you loved their couch; at a hand you looked. 9And you went to the king with oil and multiplied your perfume. And you sent your messengers far away, and lowered *yourself* to Sheol. 10You were wearied in the length of your way; you did not say, Despair! You found the life of your hand, so you were not sick. 11And whom have you dreaded and feared? You have lied and have not remembered Me, not laying *it* on your heart. Have I not been silent, even from forever, and you have not feared Me? 12I will reveal your righteousness and your works, and they will not benefit you. 13When you cry, let your gathering deliver you; but the wind shall bear away all of them; vanity takes *them*. But he who takes refuge in Me shall inherit the land and possess My holy mountain.

14And he shall say, Raise up! Raise up! Clear the way! Make the stumbling block rise from the way of My people. 15For so says the high and lofty One who inhabits eternity, and His name is Holy: I dwell in the high and holy place, even with the contrite and humble of spirit; to make live the spirit of the humble and to revive the heart of the contrite ones. 16For I will not contend forever, nor will I always be angry, for the spirit would faint before Me, even the breaths I have made. 17For I was angry and struck him for the iniquity of his gain; I hid Myself and was angry; yet he went, turning in his heart's way. 18His ways I have seen, but I will heal him, and will lead him and restore comforting to him and to his mourners. 19I create the fruit of the lips: peace, peace, to the ones far off and near, says Jehovah — and I will heal him. 20But the wicked are like the troubled sea, which

Left column (English text)

which cannot be quiet, and its waves cast up mire and dirt. ²¹There is no peace to the wicked, says my God.

CHAPTER 58

¹Call out with the throat! Do not spare. Lift up your voice like the trumpet! And show My people their rebellion, and their sins to the house of Jacob. ²Yet they seek Me day by day, and desire knowledge of My ways. As a nation that has done right, and not forsaking the judgment of their God, they ask Me about judgments of righteousness; they desire to draw near to God. ³They say, Why have we fasted, and You did not see? We have afflicted our soul, and You did not acknowledge. Behold, on the day of your fast you find pleasure; and you drive all your laborers hard. ⁴Look! You fast for strife, and for debate, and to strike with the fist of wickedness. Do not fast as today, to sound your voice in the high place. ⁵Is this like the fast I will choose, a day for a man to afflict his soul? To bow his head down like a bulrush, and he spreads sackcloth and ashes? Will you call to this as a fast, and a day of delight to Jehovah? ⁶Is this not the fast I have chosen: to open bands of wickedness, to undo thongs of the yoke, and to let the oppressed ones go free; even that you pull off every yoke? ⁷Is it not to break your bread to the hungry, that you should bring the wandering poor home? When will you see the naked and cover him; and you will not hide yourself from your flesh? ⁸Then your light shall break as the dawn, and your healing

Right column (interlinear)

21

369	2916	7516	4325	1644	3201	38,08	8252	1644

נִגְרָשׁ כִּי הַשֶּׁקֶט לֹא יוּכַל וַיִּגְרְשׁוּ מֵימָיו רֶפֶשׁ וָטִיט׃ אֵין

There and | mire | its | cast and | is not | (be) | which | driven
no is .dirt | | waters | up | ,able | quiet | |

7563	559	7965

שָׁלוֹם אָמַר אֱלֹהַי לָרְשָׁעִים׃

the to | my | says | ,peace
.wicked ,God

CAP. LVIII　נח

CHAPTER 58

1

5971	5046	6963	7311	7782	2820	408	1627	7121

קְרָא בְגָרוֹן אַל־תַּחְשֹׂךְ כַּשּׁוֹפָר הָרֵם קוֹלֶךָ וְהַגֵּד לְעַמִּי

My to | And | your | up lift | the like | do | not | the with | Call
people show | voice | | trumpet | spare | | throat | out
| lvoice | | | | :spare | | ,throat |

2

1875	3117	3117	2403		3290	1004	65 88

פִּשְׁעָם וּלְבֵית יַעֲקֹב חַטֹּאתָם׃ וְאוֹתִי יוֹם יוֹם יִדְרֹשׁוּן

they | day | day | Yet | .sins their | Jacob the to and | their
,seek | (by) | me | | | of house | ,trespass

4941	6213	6664	834	14,71	2654	1870	1847

וְדַעַת דְּרָכַי יֶחְפָּצוּן כְּגוֹי אֲשֶׁר־צְדָקָה עָשָׂה וּמִשְׁפַּט

the and | has | right- | that | a As | desire | My knowl- and
of judgment ,done | eousness | | nation | | ways | of edge

430	7132	6666	4941	7592	5800	38,08	430

אֱלֹהָיו לֹא עָזָב יִשְׁאָלוּנִי מִשְׁפְּטֵי־צֶדֶק קִרְבַת אֱלֹהִים

God | draw to | righteous- | judgments | ask | for- | not | their
| to near | ness of | Me of | Me of | sake | | God

3

3045	38,08	5315	6031	7200	38,08	6684	4100	2654

לָמָּה צַּמְנוּ וְלֹא רָאִיתָ עִנִּינוּ נַפְשֵׁנוּ וְלֹא תֵדָע

did You and | our | We | did You | and | we have | (say They) | they
?know not | soul | afflicted | ?see | not | fasted | | Why desire

4

2009	50,65	6092	3605	2656	4672	6685	3117	2009

הֵן בְּיוֹם צֹמְכֶם תִּמְצְאוּ־חֵפֶץ וְכָל־עַצְּבֵיכֶם תִּנְגֹּשׂוּ׃

!Look | you | your | and | ;pleasure | you | your | the on Be-
| .hard drive | toilers | all | | find | fast | of day ,hold

6684	38,08	7562	106	5221	6684	14683	7379

לְרִיב וּמַצָּה תָּצוּמוּ וּלְהַכּוֹת בְּאֶגְרֹף רֶשַׁע לֹא־תָצוּמוּ

Do | not | wicked- | the with | to and | you | and | for
fast | | .ness | of fist | strike | ,fast | debate | strife

5

977	6685	1961	6963	4791	8085	3117

כַיּוֹם לְהַשְׁמִיעַ בַּמָּרוֹם קוֹלְכֶם׃ הֲכָזֶה יִהְיֶה צוֹם אֶבְחָרֵהוּ

will I | the | is | l.ike | your | the in | make to | as
,choose | fast | this | .voice | height | heard | ,today

665	8242	7218	100	3721	53,15	120	6031	3117

יוֹם עַנּוֹת אָדָם נַפְשׁוֹ הֲלָכֹף כְּאַגְמֹן רֹאשׁוֹ וְשַׂק וָאֵפֶר

and | and | ,head his | a like | bow To | his | man a | to | a
ashes sackcloth | | bulrush | down | ?soul | | afflict day

6

2088	3808	3068	7522	3117	6685	7121	20,88	3331

יָצִיעַ הֲלָזֶה תִּקְרָא־צוֹם וְיוֹם רָצוֹן לַיהוָה׃ הֲלוֹא זֶה

this | not Is | to | delight | a and | fast a | you Will | this to | he
?Jehovah | | of day | | call | | ?spreads

4133	92	5425	7562	2784	6605	997	6685

צוֹם אֶבְחָרֵהוּ פַּתֵּחַ חַרְצֻבּוֹת רֶשַׁע הַתֵּר אֲגֻדּוֹת מוֹטָה

the | thongs | of | undo | wicked- | bands | open to | have I | the
yoke | of | | .ness | of | | :chosen | fast

7

6536	3808	5423	4133	3605	2670	7533	7971

וְשַׁלַּח רְצוּצִים חָפְשִׁים וְכָל־מוֹטָה תְּנַתֵּקוּ׃ הֲלוֹא פָרֹס

to | it Is | you that | yoke | and | ,free | oppressed | to and
break | not | ?off pull | every | | | ones | go let

6174	7200	1004	935	4788	6041	3899	7457

לָרָעֵב לַחְמֶךָ וַעֲנִיִּים מְרוּדִים תָּבִיא בָיִת כִּי־תִרְאֶה עָרֹם

the | will you | when | (your) should you | wander- | the that | your | the to
,naked | see | ?house (to) bring | ing | poor | ,bread | hungry

8

210	7837	1234	227	5956	38,08	1320	3680

וְכִסִּיתוֹ וּמִבְּשָׂרְךָ לֹא תִתְעַלָּם׃ אָז יִבָּקַע כַּשַּׁחַר אוֹרֶךָ

your | the as | shall | Then | will you | not | from and | cover and
,light | dawn | break | | ?yourself hide | | flesh your | ,him

3068 3519 66,64 6440 1980 6779 4120 724
וארכתך מהרה תצמח והלך לפניך צדקך כבוד יהוה
Jehovah the righ- your before shall and shall quickly your and
of glory ;teousness you go ;up spring healing

2009 559 7768 6030 3068 7121 227 622
9 יאספך: אז תקרא ויהוה יענה תשוע ויאמר הנני אם־
If Here He and shall you shall and shall you Then gather shall
.(am) I say shall ,cry ;answer Jehovah call .you

6329 205 1696 676 7971 41:33 8432 5493
10 תסיר מתוכך מוטה שלח אצבע ודבר־און: ותפק
if and ;vanity the and the send- yoke the your from turn you
out let you of speaking finger out ing midst away

2:16 2822 2224 7646 6031 5315 531:5 7457
לרעב נפשך ונפש נענה תשביע וזרח בחשך אורך
your the in then ,satisfy afflicted the and your the to
light darkness rise shall soul ,soul hungry

6710 764 6 8548 3068 5148 6672 653
11 ואפלתך כצהרים: ונחך יהוה תמיד והשביע בצחצחות
dry in and ,always Jehovah shall And the as your and
places satisfy you guide .noonday gloom

834 432:5 4161 73:02 1588 19:61 2502 6106 531:5
נפשך ועצמתיך יחליץ והיית כגן רוה וכמוצא מים אשר
which ,water like and ,watered like you And brace your and your
of spring a garden a be shall .up bones ,soul

1755 4146 5769 2723 1129 4325 3576 3808
12 לא־יכזבו מימיו: ובנו ממך חרבות עולם מוסדי דור־
genera- foun- the forever the (those) shall And its prove do not
and tion of dations of wastes you from build .waters false

3427 5410 7725 6556 1443 7121 6965 1755
ודור תקומם וקרא לך גדר פרץ משובב נתיבות לשבת:
live to paths restorer the repair- to one and shall you gene-
in of ,breach of er ,you call will ;rear ration

7121 69 44 3117 2656 621 3 72:72 7676 7725
13 אם־תשיב משבת רגלך עשות חפצך ביום קדשי וקראת
and My day on you what do to your the from turn you If
call ;holy please foot sabbath away

18:70 62 13 3513 35:13 3068 6918 6027 76 76
לשבת ענג לקדוש יהוה מכבד וכבדתו מעשות דרכיך
own your from away shall and glori- Jehovah the to de- a the
,ways doing it glorify fied of holiness ,light sabbath

7392 3068 6026 227 1697 1696 2656 4672
14 ממצוא חפצך ודבר דבר: אז תתענג על־יהוה והרכבתיך
will I And .Jehovah on shall you then (your) or own your from
ride you make yourself delight ;word speaking ,pleasure finding

6310 1 3 290 5159 398 776 1116
על־במותי ארץ והאכלתיך נחלת יעקב אביך כי פי
the for your Jacob the (with) make and the high the on
of mouth ,father of inheritance eat you ,earth of places

1696 3068
יהוה דבר:
has Jehovah
.spoken

shall spring up quickly; and your righteousness shall go before you; the glory of Jehovah shall gather you. [9]Then you shall call, and Jehovah will answer; you shall cry, and He shall say, Here I *am*. If you put the yoke away from among you, the pointing of the finger, and the speaking of vanity; [10]and if you let out your soul to the hungry, and satisfy the afflicted soul; then your light shall rise in the darkness, and your gloom *shall be* as the noonday. [11]And Jehovah shall always guide you, and satisfy your soul in dry places, and support your bones. And you shall be like a watered garden, and like a spring of water whose waters do not fail. [12]And those who come of you shall build the old ruins; you shall rear the foundations of many generations; and you shall be called, The repairer of the breach, the restorer of paths to live in.

[13]If you turn your foot away *because of* the sabbath, *from* doing what you please on My holy day, and call the sabbath a delight, glorified to the holiness of Jehovah; and shall glorify it, away from doing your own ways, from finding your own pleasure or speaking *your* word; [14]then you shall delight yourself in Jehovah. And I will cause you to ride on the heights of the earth, and make you eat *with* the inheritance of your father Jacob. For the mouth of Jehovah has spoken.

CAP. LIX נט

CHAPTER 59

8085 241 3513 3808 3467 3068 3027 7114 3808 2005
1 הן לא־קצרה יד־יהוה מהושיע ולא־כבדה אזנו משמוע:
from His is and from Jehovah the is not Be-
.hearing ear heavy not ,saving of hand shortened ,hold

430 996 996 914 1961 5771
2 כי אם־עונתיכם היו מבדלים בינכם לבין אלהיכם
,God your and between separating are your Except
you iniquities

3709 8085 6440 5640 2403
3 וחטאותיכם הסתירו פנים מכם משמוע: כי כפיכם
your For from from (His) have your and
palms .hearing ,you face hidden sins

CHAPTER 59

[1]Behold, the hand of Jehovah is not shortened from saving; nor is His ear heavy from hearing. [2]But your iniquities are coming between you and your God; and your sins have hidden *His* face from you, from hearing. [3]For your hands are

defiled by blood; yea, your fingers with iniquity. Your lips have spoken falsehood; your tongue murmurs perverseness. ⁴No one calls for righteousness; and no one judges with truth. Trusting emptiness, and speaking vanity, they conceive mischief, and give birth to evil. ⁵They hatch adders' eggs, and weave the spider's web; he who eats their eggs dies; and that which is crushed hatches out a viper. ⁶Their webs shall not become clothing, nor shall they cover themselves with their works. Their works *are* works of evil, and the act of violence *is* in their palms. ⁷Their feet run to evil, and they hurry to pour out innocent blood. Thoughts of iniquity are their thoughts; wasting and ruin *are* in their tracks. ⁸They do not know the way of peace; and no justice is in their tracks. They have made crooked paths for themselves; everyone going in them does not know peace.

⁹For this reason justice is far from us; and righteousness does not overtake us. We wait for light, but, behold, dimness; for brightness, but we walk in gloom. ¹⁰We grope *for* the wall like the blind, and we grope as if *we had* no eyes; we stumble at noonday as in the twilight; in deserted places like the dead. ¹¹We all of us roar like bears, and we moan sadly like doves. We look for justice, but *there is* none; for salvation, *but* it is far from us. ¹²For our trespasses are multiplied before You, and our sins testify against us. For our transgressions *are* with us, and we know our iniquities; ¹³transgressing and lying against Jehovah, and departing from our God; speaking oppression and revolt, conceiving and

---

4 גֹאֲלוּ בַדָּם וְאֶצְבְּעוֹתֵיכֶם בֶּעָוֹן שִׂפְתוֹתֵיכֶם דִּבְּרוּ־שֶׁקֶר
false- have lips Your with your and by are
hood spoken iniquity fingers blood defiled

לְשׁוֹנְכֶם עַוְלָה תֶהְגֶּה אֵין־קֹרֵא בְצֶדֶק וְאֵין נִשְׁפָּט
judges and for calls No murmurs perverse- your
none righteousness one ness tongue

5 בָּאֱמוּנָה בָּטוֹחַ עַל־תֹּהוּ וְדַבֶּר־שָׁוְא הָרוֹ עָמָל וְהוֹלֵיד אָוֶן
evil give and mis- they vanity and in trusting with
to birth chief conceive speaking emptiness truth

בֵּיצֵי צִפְעוֹנִי בִּקֵּעוּ וְקוּרֵי עַכָּבִישׁ יֶאֱרֹגוּ הָאֹכֵל מִבֵּיצֵיהֶם
their of who he weave the webs and they the the Eggs
eggs eats spider of hatch adder of

6 יָמוּת וְהַזּוּרֶה תִּבָּקַע אֶפְעֶה קוּרֵיהֶם לֹא־יִהְיוּ לְבֶגֶד וְלֹא
and clothing shall not Their viper a hatches what and dies
not become webs out crushed is

יִתְכַּסּוּ בְּמַעֲשֵׂיהֶם מַעֲשֵׂיהֶם מַעֲשֵׂי־אָוֶן וּפֹעַל חָמָס
violence the and evil (are) works their their with shall they
of act of works works themselves cover

7 בְּכַפֵּיהֶם רַגְלֵיהֶם לָרַע יָרֻצוּ וִימַהֲרוּ לִשְׁפֹּךְ דָּם נָקִי
inno- blood pour to they and run evil to Their their in (is)
cent out hurry feet palms

8 מַחְשְׁבֹתֵיהֶם מַחְשְׁבוֹת אָוֶן שֹׁד וָשֶׁבֶר בִּמְסִלּוֹתָם דֶּרֶךְ
The their in (are) and wast iniq- (are) thoughts their
of way tracks ruin ing uity of thoughts

שָׁלוֹם לֹא יָדָעוּ וְאֵין מִשְׁפָּט בְּמַעְגְּלוֹתָם נְתִיבוֹתֵיהֶם עִקְּשׁוּ
made they paths their their in (is) justice and they not peace
crooked tracks know no

לָהֶם כֹּל דֹּרֵךְ בָּהּ לֹא יָדַע שָׁלוֹם׃ עַל־כֵּן רָחַק מִשְׁפָּט
justice far is Therefore peace knows not it in going every- for
one them

9 מִמֶּנּוּ וְלֹא תַשִּׂיגֵנוּ צְדָקָה נְקַוֶּה לָאוֹר וְהִנֵּה־חֹשֶׁךְ לִנְגֹהוֹת
bright- for darkness but for we righ- overtakes and from
ness behold light wait eousness us not us

10 בָּאֲפֵלוֹת נְהַלֵּךְ׃ נְגַשְׁשָׁה כַעִוְרִים קִיר וּכְאֵין עֵינַיִם
eyes as and the (for) the like grope We walk we in but
no (having) wall blind gloom

11 נְגַשְׁשָׁה כָּשַׁלְנוּ בַצָּהֳרַיִם כַּנֶּשֶׁף בָּאַשְׁמַנִּים כַּמֵּתִים׃
the as fatness the in as the in we grope we
dead twilight noonday stumble

נֶהֱמֶה כַדֻּבִּים כֻּלָּנוּ וְכַיּוֹנִים הָגֹה נֶהְגֶּה נְקַוֶּה לַמִּשְׁפָּט
for we we sadly like and us of all like We
justice wait moan doves bears roar

12 וְאֵין לִישׁוּעָה רָחֲקָה מִמֶּנּוּ כִּי־רַבּוּ פְשָׁעֵינוּ נֶגְדֶּךָ וְחַטֹּאתֵינוּ
our and before tres- our multi- For from is it for but
sins You passes plied are us far salvation none

עָנְתָה בָּנוּ כִּי־פְשָׁעֵינוּ אִתָּנוּ וַעֲוֹנֹתֵינוּ יְדַעֲנוּם׃ פָּשֹׁעַ וְכַחֵשׁ
and trans- know we our and (are) our For against testify
lying gressing them iniquities us with transgressions us

13 בַּיהֹוָה וְנָסוֹג מֵאַחַר אֱלֹהֵינוּ דַּבֶּר־עֹשֶׁק וְסָרָה הֹרוֹ וְהֹגוֹ
and conceiv- and oppression speak- God our from and against
murmuring ing revolt ing after departing Jehovah

murmuring words of falsehood from the heart. 14And justice is driven back; and righteousness stands far off; for truth stumbles in the plaza, and right is not able to enter.

15And the truth is lacking; and whoever turns from evil makes himself a prey. And Jehovah saw; and it was evil in His eyes, that there was no justice. 16And He saw that there was no man, and He was astonished that there was no intercessor. And His own arm saved for Him; and His righteousness sustained Him. 17For He put on righteousness like armor, and a helmet of salvation on His head. And He put on robes of vengeance *as* clothing; and He put on zeal like a mantle. 18According to works, so He will repay; fury to His foes; recompense to His foes; He will repay recompense to the coasts. 19So they shall fear Jehovah's name from the sunset, and His glory from the sunrise. When the foe comes like a flood, the Spirit of Jehovah shall cause him to flee. 20And the Redeemer comes to Zion, and to those in Jacob who turn from transgression, declares Jehovah.

21As for Me, this *is* My covenant with them, says Jehovah: My Spirit who is on you, and My words which I have put in your mouth, shall not depart out of your mouth, or out of the mouth of your seed, or out of the mouth of your seed's seed, from now on and forever, says Jehovah.

7350 6666 49:41 268 5253 8267 1697 38:20
14 מלב דברי־שקר׃ והסג אחור משפט וצדקה מרחוק
off far and ;justice back is And .falsehood words from
righteousness driven of heart the

935 3201 380,8 5228 571: 7339 378 2 5975
תעמד כי־כשלה ברחוב אמת ונכחה לא־תוכל לבוא׃
.enter to able is not and ,truth the in stumbles for ;stands
right plaza

3415 3068 7200 7997 7451 5493 5737: 571 1961
15 ותהי האמת נעדרת וסר מרע משתולל וירא יהוה וירע
it and Jehovah And himself makes from he and ;lacking truth the is And
evil was saw prey a evil turns who

8074 376 369 7200 4941 369 5869
16 בעיניו כי־אין משפט׃ וירא כי־אין איש וישתומם כי־
that was He and ,man there that He And .justice there that His in
astonished no was saw no was eyes

3847 5564 6666 2220 3467 5293 369
17 אין מפגיע ותושע לו זרעו וצדקתו היא סמכתהו׃ וילבש
He And sustained it His and His for and inter- an not
on put .Him ,righteousness ;arm Him saved ,cessor was

5359 899/3847 72.18 3444 3553 8302 6666
צדקה כשרין וכובע ישועה בראשו וילבש בגדי נקם
ven- of robes He And His on salvation a and like righ-
,geance on put .head of helmet ,armor teousness

79.99 4399 7068 4598 5844 8516
18 תלבשת ויעט כמעיל קנאה׃ כעל גמלות כעל ישלם
will He so (their) According .zeal a like He and (as)
;repay ,works to mantle on put ;clothing

3372 7999 1578 339 341 1576 68:62 2534
19 חמה לצריו גמול לאיביו לאיים גמול ישלם׃ וייראו
they So will He recom- the to His to recom- His to fury
fear shall .repay pence coasts ;enemies pence ;foes

935 3519 8121 4217 30:68 8034 4628
ממערב את־שם יהוה וממזרח־שמש את־כבודו כי־יבוא
comes When His the from and ,Jehovah the the from
.glory sun of rising the of name sunset

7725 13:50 6726 935 5127 3068 7307 6862 5104
20 כנהר צר רוח יהוה נססה בו׃ ובא לציון גואל ולשבי
re- to and Re- the Zion to And against shall Jeho- the the a like
turnees deemer comes .him flee make vah of Spirit ,foe flood

559 1285 2088 3068 5002 3290 6588
21 פשע ביעקב נאם יהוה׃ ואני זאת בריתי אותם אמר
says with My this for As .Jehovah states ,Jacob in tres- from
,them covenant (is) ,Me pass

3808 6310 7760 834 1697 834 7307 30:68
יהוה רוחי אשר עליך ודברי אשר־שמתי בפיך לא־
not your in have I that My and on who My ;Jehovah
mouth put words ,you (is) Spirit

30:68 559 2233 6310 2233 6310 6310 4185
ימושו מפיך ומפי זרעך ומפי זרע זרעך אמר יהוה
,Jehovah says your seed the or your the or your from shall
,seed's of mouth ,seed of mouth ,mouth depart

5769 5704 6258
מעתה ועד־עולם׃
.forever and from
till now

CAP. LX ס

CHAPTER 60

CHAPTER 60

1Arise, shine; for your light has come, and the glory of Jehovah has risen on you! 2For behold, the darkness shall cover the earth, and gross darkness *the* peoples. But Jehovah shall rise on you, and His

2224 3068 3519 216 935 215 6965
1 קומי אורי כי־בא אורך וכבוד יהוה עליך זרח׃ כי־
2
For has on Jehovah the and your has for ;shine ,Arise
.risen you of glory ,light come

3068 2224 3816 6205 776 3680 2822 2009
הנה החשך יכסה־ארץ וערפל לאמים ועליך יזרח יהוה
,Jehovah shall on But .peoples gross and the shall the ,behold
rise you darkness ,earth cover darkness

glory shall be seen on you. 3And nations shall walk to your light, and kings to the brilliance of your dawning. 4Lift up your eyes all around and see; they are all assembling; they are coming to you. Your sons shall come from far away and your daughters shall be supported on the side. 5Then you shall fear and be bright; and your heart shall dread and swell. For the abundance of the sea shall be turned to you; the force of nations shall come to you. 6A host of camels shall cover you, young camels of Midian and Ephah. All of them shall come from Sheba; they shall carry gold and incense; and they shall proclaim the praises of Jehovah. 7All the flocks of Kedar shall be gathered to you; rams of Nebaioth shall serve you; they shall come up for acceptance *on* My altar; and I will glorify the house of My glory. 8Who *are* these who fly like a cloud, and with the doves to their windows? 9For the coasts shall wait for Me, and the ships of Tarshish at the first, to bring your sons from far away, their silver and their gold to them, to the name of Jehovah your God, and to the Holy One of Israel, because He has glorified you.

10And the sons of the stranger shall build your walls, and their kings shall serve you. For I struck you in My wrath, but I pitied you in My favor. 11So your gates shall be always open; they shall not be shut day or night, so that men may bring to you the force of nations, and that their kings may be led. 12For the nations and the kingdom that will not serve you shall perish; yea, the nations shall be utterly destroyed. 13The glory of Lebanon shall come to you: the juniper, the box-tree, and the cypress together, to beautify the place of My sanctuary; yea, I will glorify the place of

3 וּכְבוֹדוֹ עָלַיִךְ יֵרָאֶה׃ וְהָלְכוּ גוֹיִם לְאוֹרֵךְ וּמְלָכִים לְנֹגַהּ
the to kings and your to nations shall And shall you on His and
of brilliance ,light walk .seen be glory

4 זַרְחֵךְ׃ שְׂאִי־סָבִיב עֵינַיִךְ וּרְאִי כֻּלָּם נִקְבְּצוּ בָאוּ־לָךְ
to they are of all ;see and your all Lift your
.you come gathered them eyes around up .rising

5 בָּנַיִךְ מֵרָחוֹק יָבֹאוּ וּבְנֹתַיִךְ עַל־צַד תֵּאָמַנָה׃ אָז תִּרְאִי
you Then be shall the on your and shall far from Your
fear shall .supported side daughters ,come away sons

וְנָהַרְתְּ וּפָחַד וְרָחַב לְבָבֵךְ כִּי־יֵהָפֵךְ עָלַיִךְ הֲמוֹן יָם חֵיל
the the abun- you to be shall for your and shall and will and
wealth sea's dance turned ;heart swell dread ;bright be

6 גּוֹיִם יָבֹאוּ לָךְ׃ שִׁפְעַת גְּמַלִּים תְּכַסֵּךְ בִּכְרֵי מִדְיָן וְעֵיפָה
and Midian young shall camels mul- A to shall of
.Ephah of camels ,you cover of titude .you come nations

כֻּלָּם מִשְּׁבָא יָבֹאוּ זָהָב וּלְבוֹנָה יִשָּׂאוּ וּתְהִלֹּת יְהוָה
Jehovah the and shall they and gold shall from of All
of praises ;carry incense ;come Sheba them

7 יְבַשֵּׂרוּ׃ כָּל־צֹאן קֵדָר יִקָּבְצוּ לָךְ אֵילֵי נְבָיוֹת יְשָׁרְתוּנֶךְ
minister shall Nebaioth rams to be shall Kedar the All shall they
.you to of ;you gathered of flocks .proclaim

8 יַעֲלוּ עַל־רָצוֹן מִזְבְּחִי וּבֵית תִּפְאַרְתִּי אֲפָאֵר׃ מִי־אֵלֶּה
?these Who will I My the and My (on) for shall they
(are) .beautify beauty of house ,altar acceptance up come

9 כָּעָב תְּעוּפֶינָה וְכַיּוֹנִים אֶל־אֲרֻבֹּתֵיהֶם׃ כִּי־לִי ׀ אִיִּים יְקַוּוּ
shall the for Because their to with and ,fly they a Like
,wait coasts Me .windows doves the cloud

וָאֳנִיּוֹת תַּרְשִׁישׁ בָּרִאשֹׁנָה לְהָבִיא בָנַיִךְ מֵרָחוֹק כַּסְפָּם
their far from your bring to the at Tarshish the and
silver —away sons ,first of ships

וּזְהָבָם אִתָּם לְשֵׁם יְהוָה אֱלֹהַיִךְ וְלִקְדוֹשׁ יִשְׂרָאֵל כִּי
for ;Israel the to and your Jehovah the to with their and
of One Holy ,God of name —them gold

10 פֵּאֲרָךְ׃ וּבָנוּ בְנֵי־נֵכָר חֹמֹתַיִךְ וּמַלְכֵיהֶם יְשָׁרְתוּנֶךְ כִּי
For minister shall their and your the the will And beau- He
.you to kings ,walls stranger of sons build .you tified

11 בְקִצְפִּי הִכִּיתִיךְ וּבִרְצוֹנִי רִחַמְתִּיךְ׃ וּפִתְּחוּ שְׁעָרַיִךְ תָּמִיד
;always your shall And pitied I My in but struck I My in
gates open be .you favor ,you wrath

יוֹמָם וָלַיְלָה לֹא יִסָּגֵרוּ לְהָבִיא אֵלַיִךְ חֵיל גּוֹיִם וּמַלְכֵיהֶם
their and ,nations the you to bring to they not or day
kings of wealth ;shut be shall night

12 נְהוּגִים׃ כִּי־הַגּוֹי וְהַמַּמְלָכָה אֲשֶׁר לֹא־יַעַבְדוּךְ יֹאבֵדוּ
shall they serve will not that the and the For be may
;perish ,you kingdom nation .led

13 וְהַגּוֹיִם חָרֹב יֶחֱרָבוּ׃ כְּבוֹד הַלְּבָנוֹן אֵלַיִךְ יָבוֹא בְּרוֹשׁ
the shall you to Lebanon The be shall utterly the even
juniper ;come of glory .destroyed nations

תִּדְהָר וּתְאַשּׁוּר יַחְדָּו לְפָאֵר מְקוֹם מִקְדָּשִׁי וּמְקוֹם רַגְלַי
My the and My the to ,together the and the
feet of place ;sanctuary of place beautify cypress box-tree

My feet. ¹⁴Also the sons of your afflicters shall come bowing to you. And all who despised you shall fall at the soles of your feet. And they shall call you, The City of Jehovah, the Zion of the Holy One of Israel. ¹⁵Instead of your being forsaken and hated, so that no one passes through, I will make you for everlasting majesty, a joy of many generations. ¹⁶You shall also suck the milk of nations, and you shall suck the breast of kings. And you shall know that I, Jehovah, *am* your Savior and your Redeemer, the mighty One of Jacob. ¹⁷Instead of bronze, I will bring gold; and instead of iron, I will bring silver. And instead of timber, bronze; and instead of stones, iron. And I will make your governors peace, and your exactors righteousness. ¹⁸Violence shall not still be heard in your land, or wasting and ruin within your borders; but you shall call your walls, Salvation, and your gates, Praise. ¹⁹The sun shall not still be your light by day, or the brightness of the moon give you light; but Jehovah shall be for everlasting light to you, and your God for your beauty. ²⁰Your sun shall not set any more; and your moon shall not withdraw; for Jehovah will become your everlasting light; and the days of your mourning shall end. ²¹And your people *shall* all *be* righteous; they shall possess the earth forever, a branch of My planting, a work of My hands, to beautify Myself. ²²A little one shall become a thousand, and a small one a strong nation. I, Jehovah, will hasten it in its time.

---

14 at shall and your the bowing you to shall Also will I
down fall ;afflicters of sons come .glorify

Holy the the ,Jehovah the ,you they and who all your the
of One of Zion of City call shall ;you despised feet of soles

15 will I passes and and forsaken your Instead .Israel
you make ,through none ,hated being of

16 the and ;nations the you And gen- and gene- joy a ever- for
of breast of milk suck will eration ration of ,lasting majesty

mighty the your and your Jehovah I that you And shall you kings
of One ,Redeemer Savior (am) know shall .suck

17 will I iron and ;gold will I bronze Instead .Jacob
bring of instead bring of

I And .iron ,stones and ;bronze ,timber and ;silver
make will of instead of instead

18 violence still shall Not .righteousness your and ,peace your
heard be exactors governors

your salvation you but your in ruin or wasting your in
,walls call shall ;borders ,land

19 by for sun the any to shall Not .Praise your and
,day light more you be .gates

ever- light for Jehovah to But to shall not the bright- the
;lasting you be shall you light give moon of ness

20 not your and your any shall Not your for your and
moon ;sun more set .beauty God

your the shall and ever- light to will Jehovah for shall
mourning of days end ,lasting you become ;withdraw

21 work a My branch the shall they forever (be shall) of all your And
of planting's earth possess ;righteous them ,people

I —strong a for a and a for shall little A beautify to My
nation one small ;thousand become one .Myself ,hands

hasten will its in Jehovah
.it time

CAP. LXI סא

CHAPTER 61

[1]The Spirit of the Lord
Jehovah *is* on Me, because
Jehovah has anointed Me
to preach the gospel to the
meek. He has sent Me to
bind up the brokenhearted,
to proclaim liberty to
captives, and complete
opening to the bound ones;
[2]to proclaim the acceptable
year of Jehovah, and the
day of vengeance of our
God; to comfort all who
mourn; [3]to appoint to
those who mourn in Zion,
to give them beauty instead
of ashes, the oil of joy
instead of mourning, the
mantle of praise instead of
the spirit of infirmity; so that
one calls them trees of
righteousness, the planting
of Jehovah, in order to
beautify Himself.

[4]And they shall build old
ruins; they shall raise up
former desolations; and
they shall restore the waste
cities, ruins of generations
and generations. [5]And
strangers shall stand and
feed your flocks, and the
sons of strangers *shall be*
your plowmen and your
vinedressers. [6]But you shall
be called, Priests of
Jehovah; it will be said of
you, Ministers of God. You
shall eat the riches of the
nations, and you shall revel
in their glory. [7]Instead of
your shame and disgrace,
double. They rejoice *in* their
portion; for they shall
possess a second time in
their land; everlasting joy
shall be theirs. [8]For I,
Jehovah, love judgment,
hating plunder in burnt-
offering. And I will give their
work in truth; and I will cut
an everlasting covenant for
them. [9]And their seed shall
be known among the
nations, and their offspring
among the peoples; all who
see them shall acknowl-
edge them, that they *are* the
seed *that* Jehovah has
blessed.

[10]I will greatly rejoice in
Jehovah. My soul shall be
joyful in my God. For He

CHAPTER 61

6035 1319 3068 4886 3068 136 7307
1 רוּחַ אֲדֹנָי יְהוִה עָלָי יַעַן מָשַׁח יְהוָה אֹתִי לְבַשֵּׂר עֲנָוִים
the preach to Me Jehovah has for (is) Jehovah the The
.meek to news good anointed ;Me on Lord of Spirit

1865 7617 7121 38 20 7665 2280 7971
שְׁלָחַנִי לַחֲבֹשׁ לְנִשְׁבְּרֵי־לֵב לִקְרֹא לִשְׁבוּיִם דְּרוֹר
,liberty to to ,heart the bind to has He
captives proclaim of broken up Me sent

5359 3117 3068 7522 8141 7121 6495 631
2 וְלַאֲסוּרִים פְּקַח־קוֹחַ׃ לִקְרֹא שְׁנַת־רָצוֹן לַיהוָה וְיוֹם נָקָם
ven- the and of accept- the pro- to complete the to and
geance of day ,Jehovah ance of year claim ;opening ones bound

5414 57 6726 57 7760 57 3605 5162 430
3 לֵאלֹהֵינוּ לְנַחֵם כָּל־אֲבֵלִים׃ לָשׂוּם ׀ לַאֲבֵלֵי צִיּוֹן לָתֵת
to ,Zion the to appoint to ;mourners all to our of
give of mourners comfort ;God

4594 60 8478 8342 8081 665 8478 6287
לָהֶם פְּאֵר תַּחַת אֵפֶר שֶׁמֶן שָׂשׂוֹן תַּחַת אֵבֶל מַעֲטֵה
the ,mourning instead joy the ,ashes instead beauty to
of mantle of of oil of them

4302 6664 352 7121 3544 7307 8478 8416
תְהִלָּה תַּחַת רוּחַ כֵּהָה וְקֹרָא לָהֶם אֵילֵי הַצֶּדֶק מַטַּע
plant- righteous- trees ,them (one) that in- the instead praise
of ing ,ness of calls ;firmity of spirit of

7223 8074 5769 2723 1129 6286 3068
4 יְהוָה לְהִתְפָּאֵר׃ וּבָנוּ חָרְבוֹת עוֹלָם שֹׁמְמוֹת רִאשֹׁנִים
former desolations ;forever ruins they And beautify to Jeho-
times of of build shall .Himself ,vah

5975 1755 1755 8074 2721 5892 2318 6965
5 יְקוֹמֵמוּ וְחִדְּשׁוּ עָרֵי חֹרֶב שֹׁמְמוֹת דּוֹר וָדוֹר׃ וְעָמְדוּ
shall And gen- and gene- ruins ,waste cities they and shall they
stand .eration ration of of restore shall ;up raise

3755 406 5236 1121 6629 7462 2114
6 זָרִים וְרָעוּ צֹאנְכֶם וּבְנֵי נֵכָר אִכָּרֵיכֶם וְכֹרְמֵיכֶם׃ וְאַתֶּם
But your and your (be shall) an and your and strangers
you .vinedressers plowmen alien's sons ;flocks feed

1471 2428 559 430 8334 7121 3068 3548
כֹּהֲנֵי יְהוָה תִּקָּרֵאוּ מְשָׁרְתֵי אֱלֹהֵינוּ יֵאָמֵר לָכֶם חֵיל גּוֹיִם
na- Riches .you of will it our Ministers be shall Jehovah Priests
tions of said be God of ;called of

3639 3519 3235 8478 1322 4932 3519 398
7 תֹּאכֵלוּ וּבִכְבוֹדָם תִּתְיַמָּרוּ׃ תַּחַת בָּשְׁתְּכֶם מִשְׁנֶה וּכְלִמָּה
dis- and ;double your Instead shall you their in and shall you
;grace ,shame of .boast glory ,eat

1961 5769 8057 3423 4932 776 3651 2506 7442
יָרֹנּוּ חֶלְקָם לָכֵן בְּאַרְצָם מִשְׁנֶה יִירָשׁוּ שִׂמְחַת עוֹלָם תִּהְיֶה
shall forever joy shall they second a their in there- your (in) they
be ;possess time land fore ;portion rejoice

5414 5930 1498 8130 4941 157 3068
8 לָהֶם׃ כִּי אֲנִי יְהוָה אֹהֵב מִשְׁפָּט שֹׂנֵא גָזֵל בְּעוֹלָה וְנָתַתִּי
I And burnt a in plunder hating ,judg- love Jehovah I For to
give will offering ,ment .them

1471 3045 3772 5769 1285 571 6468
9 פְעֻלָּתָם בֶּאֱמֶת וּבְרִית עוֹלָם אֶכְרוֹת לָהֶם׃ וְנוֹדַע בַּגּוֹיִם
the in shall And for will I ever- a and in their
nations known be .them cut lasting covenant ;truth work

5234 7200 3605 5971 8432 6631 2233
זַרְעָם וְצֶאֱצָאֵיהֶם בְּתוֹךְ הָעַמִּים כָּל־רֹאֵיהֶם יַכִּירוּם כִּי
them ac- shall seeing all the the in their and their
that knowledge them ;peoples of midst offspring ,seed

5315 1523 3068 7797 7797 3068 1288 2233
10 הֵם זֶרַע בֵּרַךְ יְהוָה׃ שׂוֹשׂ אָשִׂישׂ בַּיהוָה תָּגֵל נַפְשִׁי
my let in will I greatly .Jehovah has the they
soul exult ;Jehovah rejoice blessed seed (are)

clothed me *with* garments of salvation; He put on me the robe of righteousness, even as a bridegroom is adorned *with his* ornament, and as the bride wears her jewels. [11]For as the earth gives causes to go out her buds, and as a garden causes that which is sown to grow, so the Lord Jehovah will make righteousness and praise to grow before all the nations.

2860 3276 6666 4598 3468 899 3847 430
באלהי כי הלבישני בגדי־ישע מעיל צדקה יעטני כחתן
a as , put He righteous- the salva- (with) clothed He for my in
groom. ;me on ness of robe ;tion of garments me ;God

67:80 3318 776 36 27 5710 3618 62:87 3547
11 יכהן פאר וככלה תעדה כליה׃ כי כארץ תוציא צמחה
,buds her comes the as For her wears as and (his) on puts
with out earth .jewels bride the ,ornaments

:8416 6666 6779 3068 136 6779 2221 1593
וכגנה זרועיה תצמיח כן ׀ אדני יהוה יצמיח צדקה ותהלה
and righteous- makes Jehovah the so makes which that a as and
praise ness grow Lord ,grow sown is garden

1471 36 05 5048
נגד כל־הגוים׃
the all before
.nations

CAP. LXII סב

CHAPTER 62

[1]For Zion's sake, I will not be silent; and for Jerusalem's sake, I will not rest; until her righteousness goes forth as brightness, and her salvation as a burning lamp. [2]And nations shall see your righteousness, and all kings your glory. And you shall be called by a new name which the mouth of Jehovah shall name. [3]You also shall be a crown of beauty in the hand of Jehovah, and a royal diadem in the palm of your God. [4]You no longer shall be called Forsaken; nor shall your land any longer be called Desolate. But you shall be called, My Delight *is* in Her; and your land, Married. For Jehovah delights in you, and your land is married. [5]For as a young man marries a virgin, *so* shall your sons marry you. And as a bridegroom rejoices over the bride, *so* your God shall rejoice over you.

[6]I have set watchmen on your walls, O Jerusalem. All the day and all the night they shall not always be silent; you who remember Jehovah, do not let a pause be to you. [7]And give no pause to Him until He sets up and makes Jerusalem a praise in the earth. [8]Jehovah has sworn by His right hand, and by the might of His arm: Surely I will no

5704 8252 3808 3389 4616 2814 3808 6726 4616
1 למען ציון לא אחשה ולמען ירושלם לא אשקוט עד
until will I not Jerusalem's for and be will I not Zion's For
;rest sake ;silent sake

1471 7200 1197 3940 3444 66 64 50 51 3318
2 יצא כנגה צדקה וישועתה כלפיד יבער׃ וראו גוים
nations And .burning a as her and righ- her as goes
see shall torch salvation ,teousness brightness forth

6310 834 2319 8034 7121 3519 4428 36 05 66:64
צדקך וכל־מלכים כבודך וקרא לך שם חדש אשר פי
the which ,new a you (one) and your kings all and your
of mouth name calls ;glory ,righteousness

67 97 3068 3027 8597 5850 1961 5344 3068
3 יהוה יקבנו׃ והיית עטרת תפארת ביד־יהוה וצניף
a and ,Jehovah the in beauty crown a shall You shall Jehovah
of diadem of hand of be also .designate

776 5800 5750 559 3808 430 3709 44 10
4 מלוכה בכף־אלהיך׃ לא־יאמר לך עוד עזובה ולארצך
your and ;Forsaken any to you be shall Not your the in royalty
land ,more said .God of palm

776 2656 7121 80:77 5750 559 3808
לא־יאמר עוד שממה כי לך יקרא חפצי־בה ולארצך
your and in (is) My be shall you but ;Desolate any be shall not
,land ;her delight ,called ,longer called

970 1166 1166 776 3068 2654 1166
5 בעולה כי־חפץ יהוה בך וארצך תבעל׃ כי־יבעל בחור
young a marries For be shall your and in Jehovah delights for ;Married
man (as) .married land ,you

7797 3618 2860 4885 1121 1166 1330
בתולה יבעלוך בניך ומשוש חתן על־כלה ישיש עליך
over shall (so) the over bride- a as and your shall (so) a
you rejoice ,bride groom rejoices ;sons you marry ,virgin

3117 3605 8104 6485 3389 2346 5921 430
6 אלהיך׃ על־חומתיך ירושלם הפקדתי שמרים כל־היום
the all ;watchmen have I O your On your
day set ,Jerusalem ,walls .God

1824 3068 2142 2814 38 08 8548 3915 36 05
וכל־הלילה תמיד לא יחשו המזכרים את־יהוה אל־דמי
a not let ,Jehovah who you shall they not ;always the and
pause be remember ;silent be ,night all

3389 7760 5704 3559/5704 1824 5414 408
7 לכם׃ ואל־תתנו דמי לו עד־יכונן ועד־ישים את־ירושלם
Jerusalem He and He until to a give And to
makes until establishes him pause not .you

5414 518 5797 2220 3225 3068 7650 776 8416
8 תהלה בארץ׃ נשבע יהוה בימינו ובזרוע עזו אם־אתן
I If His by and His by Jehovah has the in praise a
give will ;might of arm the hand right sworn .earth

longer give your grain *as* food for your enemies; and the sons of a stranger shall not drink your new wine for which you have labored. ⁹But those who have gathered it shall eat it, and praise Jehovah. And they who have collected it shall drink it in My holy courts. ¹⁰Pass! Pass through the gates; prepare the way of the people! Raise up! Raise up the highway; clear *it* from stones; lift up a banner over the peoples. ¹¹Behold, Jehovah has made *it* heard to the end of the earth. Say to the daughter of Zion, Behold, your salvation comes! Behold, His reward *is* with Him and His work before His face. ¹²And they shall call them, The Holy People, the Redeemed of Jehovah. And to you it shall be called, Sought Out, a City Not Forsaken.

אֶת־דְּגָנֵךְ עוֹד מַאֲכָל לְאֹיְבָיִךְ וְאִם־יִשְׁתּוּ בְנֵי־נֵכָר תִּירוֹשֵׁךְ

8492	5236 1121	518	341		3978	5750	1715	
new your wine	a sons stranger of	shall drink	and if	(as) ;enemies	food	longer	your grain	

אֲשֶׁר יָגַעַתְּ בּוֹ׃ כִּי מְאַסְפָיו יֹאכְלֻהוּ וְהִלְלוּ אֶת־יְהוָה

3068	1984	398	622		3021	834
;Jehovah	shall and praise	shall it eat	its gatherers	For .it	.for have you labored	which

וּמְקַבְּצָיו יִשְׁתֻּהוּ בְּחַצְרוֹת קָדְשִׁי׃

81;79	5674 5674	6944 2691	8354	6908
through Pass !Pass	My courts in	.holiness of	shall it drink	its and collectors

עִבְרוּ עִבְרוּ בַּשְּׁעָרִים פַּנּוּ דֶּרֶךְ הָעָם סֹלּוּ סֹלּוּ הַמְסִלָּה סַקְּלוּ מֵאֶבֶן הָרִימוּ נֵס

5251 7311	68	5619	4546	5549 5971	1870 6437		
a up lift banner	from ;stones	clear (it)	the ;highway	Raise Raise up !up	the the !people of way pare		

עַל־הָעַמִּים׃ הִנֵּה יְהוָה הִשְׁמִיעַ אֶל־קְצֵה הָאָרֶץ אִמְרוּ

559	776	7097	80 185	30 68	2009	5971
say	the earth of	the end	to made has heard (it)	Jehovah ,Behold	the over peoples	

לְבַת־צִיּוֹן הִנֵּה יִשְׁעֵךְ בָּא הִנֵּה שְׂכָרוֹ אִתּוֹ וּפְעֻלָּתוֹ לְפָנָיו׃

6440	6468	7939 2009	935 3468	2009	67;26 1323		
before .Him	His and work ,Him	with (is) His reward	Be .comes your salvation	,Behold	,Zion the to of daughter		

וְקָרְאוּ לָהֶם עַם־הַקֹּדֶשׁ גְּאוּלֵי יְהוָה וְלָךְ יִקָּרֵא דְרוּשָׁה

1875	7121	3068	1350	69 44 5971	7121	
Sought ,out	shall it to And ,called be you	.Jehovah	the of redeemed	,holy The people	them they And call shall	

עִיר לֹא נֶעֱזָבָה׃

5800	38;08 5892	
.forsaken	not	a city

CAP. LXIII   סג

CHAPTER 63

CHAPTER 63

¹Who *is* this who comes from Edom *with* dyed garments from Bozrah, this One adorned in His clothing, inclining in His great power? It is I, speaking in righteousness, mighty to save! ²Why *is* Your clothing red, and Your garments like one who treads in the winepress? ³I have trodden the winepress, I alone, and no man of the peoples *was* with Me. And I will tread them in My anger, and trample them in My fury; and their juice shall be spattered on My garments; and I will pollute all My clothes. ⁴For the day of vengeance *is* in My heart, and the year of My redeemed has come. ⁵And I looked, and no one *was* helping. And I wondered that no one *was* upholding. Then My own arm saved for Me, and My fury upheld Me. ⁶And I trod down the people in My anger, and made them drunk in My fury. And I

מִי־זֶה בָּא מֵאֱדוֹם חֲמוּץ בְּגָדִים מִבָּצְרָה זֶה הָדוּר

1921	2088	1224	899	2556	123	935	2088 4310
adorned	this	from Bozrah	garments	(with) dyed	from Edom	coming	this Who (is)

בִּלְבוּשׁוֹ צֹעֶה בְּרֹב כֹּחוֹ אֲנִי מְדַבֵּר בִּצְדָקָה רַב לְהוֹשִׁיעַ׃

3467	7230	6666	1696	35 81 7 227	6808	3 830
!save to	great	righ- ,teousness	in speaking (is It)	His power great	in inclining ?	His in clothing

מַדּוּעַ אָדֹם לִלְבוּשֶׁךָ וּבְגָדֶיךָ כְּדֹרֵךְ בְּגַת׃

1869	6333	16 60	1869	899		3045
have I wine- The ,trodden	the in press ?winepress	the one like treading garments	your and ,clothing	Your red	(is) knows Who why	

פּוּרָה דָּרַכְתִּי לְבַדִּי וּמֵעַמִּים אֵין־אִישׁ אִתִּי וְאֶדְרְכֵם בְּאַפִּי וְאֶרְמְסֵם

7429	1869	376 369	5971	905		
trample and them	My in anger	man no of and them tread .Me	peoples the	,alone My and Me in with (was) My (is) alone		

בַּחֲמָתִי וְיֵז נִצְחָם עַל־בְּגָדַי וְכָל־מַלְבּוּשַׁי אֶגְאָלְתִּי׃ כִּי

1351	4403	3605	899	5332	5137	2534
For	will I .pollute	My clothes all	and ;garments	My on juice spatter	their will and	My in fury

יוֹם נָקָם בְּלִבִּי וּשְׁנַת גְּאוּלַי בָּאָה׃ וְאַבִּיט וְאֵין עֹזֵר

5826	369	5027	935	1350	8141	38;20 5359 3117
help- ,ling	and none	I And .looked	has .come	redeemed of	year ,heart My	ven- the geance of day

וְאֶשְׁתּוֹמֵם וְאֵין סוֹמֵךְ וַתּוֹשַׁע לִי זְרֹעִי וַחֲמָתִי הִיא

2534	2220	3467	5564	369	8074	
it My and ,fury	My arm	My own Me.	Then saved	uphold- .ing (was)	that none	was I And astonished

סְמָכָתְנִי׃ וְאָבוּס עַמִּים בְּאַפִּי וַאֲשַׁכְּרֵם בַּחֲמָתִי וְאוֹרִיד

3381	2534	7937	639	5971	947	5564
I and poured	My in ,fury	made and drunk them	My in ,anger	peoples	I And trod	upheld .Me

poured their juice to the
earth.
7 I will mention the
mercies of Jehovah, the
praises of Jehovah, according to all that Jehovah has
benefited us, and the great
good to the house of Israel,
by which He benefited
them according to His
mercies, and according to
the multitude of His loving-
kindness. 8 For He said,
Surely they *are* My people,
sons that do not lie, and He
is their Savior. 9 In all their
affliction, *He was* not a foe;
and the Angel of His face
saved them. In His love and
in His pity He redeemed
them. And He bore them,
and carried them all the
days of old. 10 But they rebelled, and provoked His
Holy Spirit, so He was
turned *to be* their enemy;
He fought against them.
11 Then His people remem-
bered the days past *of*
Moses, *saying*, Where *is* He
who brought *us* up from the
sea with the shepherd of
His flock. Where *is* He who
put His Holy Spirit within
him; 12 who led them by
Moses' right hand, with His
glorious arm, dividing the
water before them, to make
for Him an everlasting
name? 13 *He* led them
through the deeps; like the
horse in the wilderness,
they did not stumble. 14 As
the cattle go down into the
valley, the Spirit of Jehovah
caused him to rest; so You
led Your people, to make a
glorious name for Yourself.
15 Look down from
Heaven, and peer from the
place of Your holiness and
your glory. Where *is* Your
zeal and Your might? The
stirring of Your affections
and Your mercies toward
me, are they held back?
16 For You *are* our Father,
though Abraham does not
know us, and Israel does
not acknowledge us; You,
Jehovah, *are* our Father, our
Redeemer; Your name *is*
from everlasting.
17 O Jehovah, why do You
make us wander from Your
ways? You harden our heart

3068 8416 2142 3068 2617 5332 776
7 לָאָרֶץ נִצְחָם׃ חַסְדֵי יְהוָה ׀ אַזְכִּיר תְּהִלֹּת יְהוָה
.Jehovah the will I Jehovah The their the to
of praises ,mention of mercies juice earth

834 34:78 1004 2898 7227 3068 1580 834 3605
כְּעַל כֹּל אֲשֶׁר־גְּמָלָנוּ יְהוָה וְרַב־טוּב לְבֵית יִשְׂרָאֵל אֲשֶׁר
which ,Israel the to good and ,Jehovah bene- has that all accord-
of house great the us fitted to ing

5971 389 559 2617 7227 7356 1580
8 גְּמָלָם כְּרַחֲמָיו וּכְרֹב חֲסָדָיו׃ וַיֹּאמֶר אַךְ־עַמִּי הֵמָּה
they My Surely He For loving- His by and His by bene- He
,(are) people ,said .kindness much mercies them fitted

3808 6864 3605 3467 1961 8266 38:08 1121
9 בָּנִים לֹא יְשַׁקֵּרוּ וַיְהִי לָהֶם לְמוֹשִׁיעַ׃ בְּכָל־צָרָתָם ׀ לֹא
not their all In .Savior a to He and that not sons
(was He) affliction them became ;lie do

1350 2551 160 34:67 6440 43:97 6862
צָר וּמַלְאַךְ פָּנָיו הוֹשִׁיעָם בְּאַהֲבָתוֹ וּבְחֶמְלָתוֹ הוּא גְאָלָם
redeemed He His in and His in saved His the and a
.them pity love ;them face of Angel ;foe

6087 4784 5769 3117 3605 5375 5190
10 וַיְנַטְּלֵם וַיְנַשְּׂאֵם כָּל־יְמֵי עוֹלָם׃ וְהֵמָּה מָרוּ וְעִצְּבוּ אֶת־
and rebelled But .forever the all carried and He And
provoked they of days them them bore

2142 3898 341 2015 69:44 7307
11 רוּחַ קָדְשׁוֹ וַיֵּהָפֵךְ לָהֶם לְאוֹיֵב הוּא נִלְחַם־בָּם׃ וַיִּזְכֹּר
Then against fought He (be to) to He so His Spirit
remembered .them ;enemy an them turned was ,Holy

66:29 74:62 32:20 5927 5971 4872 5769 3117
יְמֵי־עוֹלָם מֹשֶׁה עַמּוֹ אַיֵּה ׀ הַמַּעֲלֵם מִיָּם אֵת רֹעֵה צֹאנוֹ
His shep- the with from who He Where His (of) ,forever the
?flock of herd sea the up brought (is) :people Moses of days

48:72 3225 3212 6944 7307 7130 7760
12 אַיֵּה הַשָּׂם בְּקִרְבּוֹ אֶת־רוּחַ קָדְשׁוֹ׃ מוֹלִיךְ לִימִין מֹשֶׁה
,Moses' by leading His Spirit within who He Where
hand right ;holy him put (is)

5769 8034 6213 64:40 4325 1234 8597 2220
זְרוֹעַ תִּפְאַרְתּוֹ בּוֹקֵעַ מַיִם מִפְּנֵיהֶם לַעֲשׂוֹת לוֹ שֵׁם עוֹלָם׃
ever- a for to before the dividing His the
,lasting name Him make ,them water ,beauty of arm

929 3782 38:08 4057 5483 8415 3212
13 14 מוֹלִיכָם בַּתְּהֹמוֹת כַּסּוּס בַּמִּדְבָּר לֹא יִכָּשֵׁלוּ׃ כַּבְּהֵמָה
the As did they not the in the like the through leading
cattle .stumble wilderness horse ,deeps them

6213 5971 5090 5117 3068 7307 33:81 1237
בַּבִּקְעָה תֵרֵד רוּחַ יְהוָה תְּנִיחֶנּוּ כֵּן נִהַגְתָּ עַמְּךָ לַעֲשׂוֹת
make to Your You so him caused Jehovah the goes the into
,people led ,rest to of Spirit .down valley

6944 2073 72:00 80:64 5027 8597 8034
15 לְךָ שֵׁם תִּפְאָרֶת׃ הַבֵּט מִשָּׁמַיִם וּרְאֵה מִזְּבֻל קָדְשְׁךָ
Your the from see and from Look .beauty a for
holiness of place ,Heaven of name You

7356 4578 1995 1368 7068 8597
וְתִפְאַרְתֶּךָ אַיֵּה קִנְאָתְךָ וּגְבוּרֹתֶךָ הֲמוֹן מֵעֶיךָ וְרַחֲמֶיךָ
Your and Your The Your and Your where your and
mercies affections of stirring ?might zeal (is) —beauty

3045 38:08 85 662
16 אֵלַי הִתְאַפָּקוּ׃ כִּי־אַתָּה אָבִינוּ כִּי אַבְרָהָם לֹא יְדָעָנוּ
knows not Abraham though our You For they are toward
us ,Father (are) ?back held ,me

5764 1350 3068 5234 38:08 34:78
וְיִשְׂרָאֵל לֹא יַכִּירָנוּ אַתָּה יְהוָה אָבִינוּ גֹּאֲלֵנוּ מֵעוֹלָם
ever- from our our Jehovah You acknowledge not Israel and
lasting ;Redeemer ,Father (are) ;us

3373 3820 7188 18:70 3068 8582 4100 8034
17 שְׁמֶךָ׃ לָמָּה תַתְעֵנוּ יְהוָה מִדְּרָכֶיךָ תַּקְשִׁיחַ לִבֵּנוּ מִיִּרְאָתֶךָ
from our harden You Your from ,Jehovah You do Why Your (is)
?fear Your heart ;ways ,wander us make .name

from Your fear. For Your servants' sake, return the tribes of Your inheritance. 18For a little *while* Your holy people possessed *it*. Our enemies have trampled Your sanctuary. 19We are of old; You never ruled over them. Your name was never called on them.

CHAPTER 64

1Oh that You would tear the heavens *and* come down, *that* mountains would quake before You. 2As the brushwood fire burns, fire causes water to boil, make known Your name to Your foes, *that* nations might tremble before You. 3When You did terrifying things which we did not look for, You came down; mountains flowed down before You. 4And from forever they have not heard; they did not give ear. Eye has not seen a God except You, who works for him who waits for Him. 5You meet him who rejoices and works righteousness; they recall You in Your ways. Behold, You were angry, for we sinned. In them *is* eternity, we shall be saved. 6But we are all as the unclean thing, and all our righteousnesses *are* as a filthy cloth. And we all fade as a leaf, and like the wind our iniquities take us away. 7And there is not one who calls on Your name, who stirs himself up to take hold of You. For You have hidden Your face from us, and have melted us away into the hand of our iniquities.

8But now, Jehovah, You *are* our Father; we *are* the clay, and You are our Former; and we all *are* Your handiwork. 9Do not be vehemently angry, Jehovah, and do not remember iniquity forever. Behold! Look, please; all of us *are* Your people. 10Your holy cities are a wilderness; Zion *is* a wilderness; Jerusalem *is* a desolation. 11The house

5971 3425 4705 5159 7626 5650 4616 7725
18 שוב למען עבדיך שבטי נחלתך: למצער ירשו עם-
people possessed (it) | a For little | Your .inheritance | the of tribes | Your ,servants' | for sake | ,Return

4910 3808 5769 1961 4720 947 6862 6944
19 קדשך צרינו בוססו מקדשך: היינו מעולם לא-משלת
You ruled | not | from ;forever | are We | Your .sanctuary | have trampled | foes our | Your ;holy

3381 8064 7167 3863 5921 8034 7121 3808
בם לא-נקרא שמך עליהם לוא-קרעת שמים ירדת
come (and) ;down | the heavens | You tear | O would that | .them on | Your name | was called | not over ;them

2151 2022 6440
מפניך הרים נזלו:
would .quake | mountains | from You before

CAP. LXIV סד

CHAPTER 64

6862 8034 3045 784 1158 4325 2003 784 6919
1 כקדח אש המסים מים תבעה-אש להודיע שמך לצריך
Your to ;foes | Your name | make to known | —fire | causes boil to | water | brush- ,wood | the fire | As burns

3381 6960 3808 3372 6213 7264 1471 6440
2 מפניך גוים ירגזו: בעשותך נוראות לא נקוה ירדת
came You ;down | we expected | not | terrifying things | You When did | might .tremble | nations | before ,You

5869 238 3808 8085 3808 5769 2151 2022 6440
3 מפניך הרים נזלו: ומעולם לא-שמעו לא האזינו עין
eye | they ;ear gave | not | have they ,heard | not | from And forever | flowed .down | mountains | before You

6293 2442 6213 2108 430 7200 3808
4 לא-ראתה אלהים זולתך יעשה למחכה-לו: פגעת את-
You met | for .Him | him for waits who | who works | except ,You | God a | has seen | not

2398 7107 2142 1870 6664 6213 7797
שש ועשה צדק בדרכיך יזכרוך הן-אתה קצפת ונחטא
we for .sinned | were ,angry | You Be- ,hold | remem- they .You ber | Your in ways | righ- ;teousness | and who him works rejoices

3605 5708 899 3605 2931 3467 5769
5 בהם עולם ונושע: ונהי כטמא כלנו וכבגד עדים כל-
(are) all | filthy | as and garment a | of all us | un- the as ,thing clean | we But are | shall we and .saved be | (is) ,eternity | In them

369 5375 7307 5771 3605 5929 5034 6666
6 צדקתינו ונבל כעלה כלנו ועוננו כרוח ישאנו: ואין
And none is | us take .away | the like ,wind | our and ,iniquities | all us of | a as ,leaf | we And fade | righ- our teousnesses

4480 6440 5641 2388 5782 8034 7121
קורא בשמך מתעורר להחזיק בך כי-הסתרת פניך ממנו
from ,us | Your face | have You For hidden | of .You | take to hold | stirring himself up | Your on ,name | calling

2563 3068 6258 5771 3027 4127
7 ותמוגנו ביד-עוננו: ועתה יהוה אבינו אתה אנחנו החמר
the clay | we (are) | You ;(are) | our Father | ,Jehovah | But now | hand the into ,iniquities of | have and us melted

3966 5704 3068 7107 408 3605 3027 4639 3335
8 ואתה יצרנו ומעשה ידך כלנו: אל-תקצף יהוה עד-מאד
an ,extreme | to | ,Jehovah | be angry | Do not | all we .(are) | Your hand | the and of work | our ;Former | You and (are)

6944 5892 3605 5971 4994 5027 5771 2142 5703 408
9 ואל-לעד תזכר עון הן הבט-נא עמך כלנו: ערי קדשך
Your holy | cities | of all ;(are) us | Your people | ,please | ,look | ,Lo | ini- .quity | do remember | forever | and not

1004 8077 3389 1961 3657 6726 4057
10 היו מדבר ציון מדבר היתה ירושלם שממה: בית
The of house | deso- a lation | Jerusalem | is | wilder- a ;ness | Zion (is) | wilder- a .ness | are

of our holiness and our beauty, where our fathers praised You, has become a burning of fire; and all our pleasant things have become a ruin. [12]Will You restrain Yourself over these things, Jehovah? Will you be silent and sorely afflict us?

11

8316	1961	1	1984	85,97	6944
קָדְשֵׁנוּ וְתִפְאַרְתֵּנוּ אֲשֶׁר הִלְלוּךָ אֲבֹתֵינוּ הָיָה לִשְׂרֵפַת					
burning a of	has become	our fathers	praised You	where	our and ,beauty	our holiness

661	1428	5921	2723	1961	4261	36,05	78,4
אֵשׁ וְכָל־מַחֲמַדֵּינוּ הָיָה לְחָרְבָּה: הַעַל־אֵלֶּה תִתְאַפַּק							
re- You will these Over ,Yourself strain things			.ruin a	have become	pleasant our things	and all	;fire

3966	6031	28,14	3068
יְהוָה תֶּחֱשֶׁה וּתְעַנֵּנוּ עַד־מְאֹד:			
?vehemently afflict and You Will us silent be		Jeho- ?vah

CAP. LXV   סה

CHAPTER 65

CHAPTER 65

[1]I have been sought, not by those who asked. I have been found, not by those who sought Me. To a nation not calling on My name, I said, Behold Me! Behold Me! [2]I have spread out My hands all the day long to a rebellious people who walk *in* the way not good, after their own thoughts; [3]a people who continually provoke Me to My face; who sacrifice in gardens, and burn incense on the bricks; [4]who sit among the graves and lodge in the towers; who eat swine's flesh, and broth of unclean things *in* their pots; [5]who say, Keep to yourself! Do not come near me, for I am holier than you! These *are* a smoke in My nose, a fire burning all the day. [6]Behold! It is written before Me: I will not be silent, except I repay; yea, I will repay to their bosom, [7]your iniquities and the iniquities of your fathers together, says Jehovah; *they* that burned incense on the mountains, and have blasphemed Me on the hills. And I will measure their former work into their bosom. [8]So says Jehovah: As the new wine is found in the cluster, and one says, Do not destroy it, for a blessing *is* in it; so I will do for the sake of My servants, not to destroy the whole. [9]And I will bring forth a seed out of

1

2009	559	1245	38,08	4672	7592	3808	1875
נִדְרַשְׁתִּי לְלוֹא שָׁאָלוּ נִמְצֵאתִי לְלֹא בִקְשֻׁנִי אָמַרְתִּי הִנֵּנִי							
Behold ,said I !Me	who those not .Me sought	have I of found been	who those not ;asked	have I of sought been		

2

3117	3605/3027	6566	8034	7121	38,08	1471
הִנֵּנִי אֶל־גּוֹי לֹא־קֹרָא בִשְׁמִי: פֵּרַשְׂתִּי יָדַי כָּל־הַיּוֹם אֶל						
to the all My have I My on calling not a to Behold day hands out spread .name nation ,Me						

4284	310	28,96	3808	1870	1980	5637	5971
עַם סוֹרֵר הַהֹלְכִים הַדֶּרֶךְ לֹא־טוֹב אַחַר מַחְשְׁבֹתֵיהֶם:							
own their after ,good not the (in) walk who rebellious a ,thoughts way people							

3

6999	15,93	2076	8543	6440	3707	59,71
הָעָם הַמַּכְעִסִים אֹתִי עַל־פָּנַי תָּמִיד זֹבְחִים בַּגַּנּוֹת וּמְקַטְּרִים						
burning and in sacrificing contin- My to Me who a incense ,gardens ,ually face provoke people						

4

1398	3885	5341	6913	3427	3843	59,21
עַל־הַלְּבֵנִים: הַיֹּשְׁבִים בַּקְּבָרִים וּבַנְּצוּרִים יָלִינוּ הָאֹכְלִים						
eat who they watch in and the among sit who ,bricks the on ,sleep towers ,graves						

5

7126	559	3627	62,92	6564	23,86	1320
בְּשַׂר הַחֲזִיר וּפְרַק פִּגֻּלִים כְּלֵיהֶם: הָאֹמְרִים קְרַב אֵלֶיךָ						
to Draw ,say who their (in) unclean broth and ,swine flesh !yourself near ;vessels things of of						

3344	7,84	6,39	6227	1428	6942	5066
אַל־תִּגַּשׁ־בִּי כִּי קְדַשְׁתִּיךָ אֵלֶּה עָשָׁן בְּאַפִּי אֵשׁ יֹקֶדֶת						
burning fire a My in a These holier am I for to come not nose smoke (are) !you than ,me near						

6

7999	2814	38,08	64,40	3789	2009	3117/36,05
כָּל־הַיּוֹם: הִנֵּה כְתוּבָה לְפָנָי לֹא אֶחֱשֶׂה כִּי אִם־שִׁלַּמְתִּי						
;repay I except will I not before is It !Behold the all ,silent be :Me written .day						

7

559	3162	1	57,71	5771	2436	7725
וְשִׁלַּמְתִּי אֶל־חֵיקָם: עֲוֹנֹתֵיכֶם וַעֲוֹנֹת אֲבוֹתֵיכֶם יַחְדָּו אָמַר						
says ,together your the and your their to I and fathers of iniquities iniquities ,bosom repay will						

4058	2778	1389	59,21	20,22	59,21	6999	30,68
יְהוָה אֲשֶׁר קִטְּרוּ עַל־הֶהָרִים וְעַל־הַגְּבָעוֹת חֵרְפוּנִי וּמַדֹּתִי							
I And blasphemed the on and the on burned that Jeho- mete will .Me hills ,mountains incense vah							

8

3068	559	3541	2436	59,21	7223	64,68
פְעֻלָּתָם רִאשֹׁנָה עַל־חֵיקָם: כֹּה אָמַר יְהוָה כַּאֲשֶׁר						
As ,Jehovah says Thus their upon former their .bosom work						

1293	78,43	559	811	8492	4672
יִמָּצֵא הַתִּירוֹשׁ בָּאֶשְׁכּוֹל וְאָמַר אַל־תַּשְׁחִיתֵהוּ כִּי בְרָכָה					
a for destroy Do not one and the in new the is blessing ,it ,says ,cluster wine found					

9

3318	3605	7843	5650	4616	6213	3651
בּוֹ כֵּן אֶעֱשֶׂה לְמַעַן עֲבָדַי לְבִלְתִּי הַשְׁחִית הַכֹּל: וְהוֹצֵאתִי						
will I And the to not in My for will I so (is) forth bring .whole destroy order ,servants sake do ,it in						

Jacob, and out of Judah one to inherit My mountains. And My chosen one shall inherit, and My servants shall live there. 10And Sharon shall be a fold of flocks; and the valley of Achor a resting place of herds for My people who have sought Me. 11But you *are* those who forsake Jehovah, who forget My holy mountain; who array a table for Fortune, and who fill mixed wine for Fate. 12And I will number you to the sword; and you shall all bow down to the slaughter; because I called and you did not answer. I spoke, and you did not hear; and you did the evil in My eyes; and you chose that in which I had no pleasure. 13So the Lord Jehovah says this: Behold, My servants shall eat, but you shall be hungry. Behold, My servants shall drink, but you shall be thirsty. Behold, My servants shall rejoice, but you shall be ashamed. 14Behold, My servants shall sing for joy of heart, but you shall cry from heartbreak, and howl from breaking of spirit. 15And you shall leave your name for a curse to My chosen. And the Lord Jehovah shall kill you; and He shall call His servants by another name. 16*He* who blesses himself in the earth shall bless himself in the God of truth. And he who swears in the earth shall swear by the God of truth; because the former distresses are forgotten; and because they are hidden from My eyes.

17For, behold, I create new heavens and new earth. And the things before shall not be recalled, and shall not go up on the heart. 18However, be glad and rejoice forever in what I create. For, behold, I create

מיעקב זרע ומיהודה יורש הרי וירשוה בחירי ועבדי
10 ישכנו־שמה׃ והיה השרון לנוה־צאן ועמק עכור לרבץ
11 בקר לעמי אשר דרשוני׃ ואתם עזבי יהוה השכחים
את־הר קדשי הערכים לגד שלחן והממלאים למני
12 ממסך׃ ומניתי אתכם לחרב וכלכם לטבח תכרעו
יען קראתי ולא עניתם דברתי ולא שמעתם ותעשו הרע
13 בעיני ובאשר לא־חפצתי בחרתם׃ לכן כה־אמר
אדני יהוה הנה עבדי יאכלו ואתם תרעבו הנה עבדי
ישתו ואתם תצמאו הנה עבדי ישמחו ואתם תבשו׃
14 הנה עבדי ירנו מטוב לב ואתם תצעקו מכאב לב
15 ומשבר רוח תילילו׃ והנחתם שמכם לשבועה לבחירי
16 והמיתך אדני יהוה ולעבדיו יקרא שם אחר׃ אשר
המתברך בארץ יתברך באלהי אמן והנשבע בארץ
ישבע באלהי אמן כי נשכחו הצרות הראשנות וכי
17 נסתרו מעיני׃ כי־הנני בורא שמים חדשים וארץ חדשה
18 ולא תזכרנה הראשנות ולא תעלינה על־לב׃ כי־אם־
שישו וגילו עדי־עד אשר אני בורא כי הנני בורא את־

Jerusalem a rejoicing, and
her people a joy. [19]And I
will rejoice in Jerusalem,
and joy in My people. And
the voice of weeping and
the voice of crying shall no
longer be heard in her.
[20]There shall not still be an
infant of days, or an old man
that has not filled his days.
For the youth shall die the
son of a hundred years, but
the sinner the son of a
hundred years shall be
accursed. [21]And they shall
build houses and live *in
them*; and they shall plant
vineyards and eat their fruit.
[22]They shall not build, and
another live *in them*; they
shall not plant, and another
eat. For like the days of the
tree *are* the days of My
people; and My elect shall
grow old *to* the work of their
hands. [23]They shall not
labor in vain, nor bring forth
for terror. For they are the
seed of the beloved ones of
Jehovah, and their offspring
with them. [24]And it will be,
before they call, I will
answer. While they are
speaking, then I will hear.
[25]The wolf and the lamb
shall feed as one; and the
lion shall eat straw like the
ox. And dust *is* the food of
the snake. They shall not do
evil nor destroy in all My
holy mountain, says
Jehovah.

7797 3389 15 23 4885 5971 15 25 33 89
19 יְרוּשָׁלַםִ גִּילָה וְעַמָּהּ מָשׂוֹשׂ׃ וְגַלְתִּי בִירוּשָׁלַםִ וְשַׂשְׂתִּי
joy and | in | I And | .joy a | her and | a | Jerusalem
,Jerusalem | rejoice will | people | ,rejoicing

3808 2201 6963 1065 6963 5750 8085 38 08 5971
20 בְעַמִּי וְלֹא־יִשָּׁמַע בָּהּ עוֹד קוֹל בְּכִי וְקוֹל זְעָקָה׃ לֹא־
Not | crying | the and | weep- | the | any | her in | shall | And | My in
.out | of voice | ing | of voice | more | heard be | not | .people

3117 43 90 3 808 834 2205 3117 5764/5750 1961
יִהְיֶה מִשָּׁם עוֹד עוּל יָמִים וְזָקֵן אֲשֶׁר לֹא־יְמַלֵּא אֶת־יָמָיו
;days his | has | not | who | an or | ,days | suck- a | any | there | shall
filled | man old | of ling | more | be

8141 3967/1121 2398 4191 8141 3967/1121 5288
כִּי הַנַּעַר בֶּן־מֵאָה שָׁנָה יָמוּת וְהַחוֹטֶא בֶּן־מֵאָה שָׁנָה
years | -hun a | the | the But | shall | years | a | the | the | for
dred | of son | sinner | .die | hundred | of son | boy

6529 398 3754 5193 3427 1004 1129 7043
21 יְקֻלָּל׃ וּבָנוּ בָתִּים וְיָשָׁבוּ וְנָטְעוּ כְרָמִים וְאָכְלוּ פִּרְיָם׃
their | eat and | vineyards | they and | live and | houses | they And | be shall
.fruit | plant shall | ;(them in) | build shall | .accursed

6086 3117 398 312 5193 38 08 34 27 312 1129
22 לֹא יִבְנוּ וְאַחֵר יֵשֵׁב לֹא יִטְּעוּ וְאַחֵר יֹאכֵל כִּי־כִימֵי הָעֵץ
the | the like | For | .eat | and shall | they | not | live | and | they | Not
tree | of days | another | plant | ;(them in) | another | build shall

7385 3121 38 08 972 1086 3027 4639 59 71 3117
23 יְמֵי עַמִּי וּמַעֲשֵׂה יְדֵיהֶם יְבַלּוּ בְחִירָי׃ לֹא יִיגְעוּ לָרִיק
in | they | Not | .elect My | grow shall | their | the and | My | the (are)
,vain | labor shall | (to) old | hands | of work | ;people | of days

6631 3068 1288 2233 928 32 05 38 08
וְלֹא יֵלְדוּ לַבֶּהָלָה כִּי זֶרַע בְּרוּכֵי יְהוָה הֵמָּה וְצֶאֱצָאֵיהֶם
their and | they | Jehovah's | blessed | the | for | for | bring | and
offspring | ,are | ones | of seed | ;terror | forth | not

1696 5750 6030 7121 2962 1961
24 אִתָּם׃ וְהָיָה טֶרֶם־יִקְרָאוּ וַאֲנִי אֶעֱנֶה עוֹד הֵם מְדַבְּרִים
are | they | while | will | I | they | before | it And | with
speaking | ;answer | ,call | be will | .them

398 1241 738 259 7462 2924 20 61 8085
25 וַאֲנִי אֶשְׁמָע׃ זְאֵב וְטָלֶה יִרְעוּ כְאֶחָד וְאַרְיֵה כַּבָּקָר יֹאכַל־
shall | the like | the and | ,one as | shall | the and | The | .hear will | then
eat | ox | lion | feed | lamb | wolf | I

2022 3605 7843 38 08 7489 3899 6083 5175 8401
תֶּבֶן וְנָחָשׁ עָפָר לַחְמוֹ לֹא־יָרֵעוּ וְלֹא־יַשְׁחִיתוּ בְּכָל־הַר
moun- | in | destroy | and | they Not | .food its | dust | the and | ;straw
tain | all | not | ,evil do shall | ,snake

3068 559 6944
קָדְשִׁי אָמַר יְהוָה׃
.Jehovah | says | My
,holy

CAP. LXVI סו

CHAPTER 66

CHAPTER 66
[1]So says Jehovah:
Heaven *is* My throne, and
earth the footstool of My
feet. Where then *is* the
house that you build for Me?
And where then *is* the place
of My rest? [2]And My hand
has made all these things,
even all these things exist,
declares Jehovah. But I will
look toward this one, to the
afflicted, and *the* contrite of
spirit, even trembling at My
word.
[3]He who kills an ox *is as if*
he struck a man; he who

227 7272 1916 776 3678 8064 3068 559 3541
1 כֹּה אָמַר יְהוָה הַשָּׁמַיִם כִּסְאִי וְהָאָרֶץ הֲדֹם רַגְלָי אֵי־זֶה
then Where | My | the | and | My | Heaven | :Jehovah | says | Thus
(is) 428 | .feet | of stool | earth | ,throne | (is)

3605 4496 4725 227 1129 1004
2 בַיִת אֲשֶׁר תִּבְנוּ־לִי וְאֵי־זֶה מָקוֹם מְנוּחָתִי׃ וְאֶת־כָּל־אֵלֶּה
these | all | And | ?rest My | the | then And | for you | that | the
things | (of) place | (is) where | ?Me build | house

50 27 3068 5002 428 3605 1961 6213 3027
יָדִי עָשָׂתָה וַיִּהְיוּ כָל־אֵלֶּה נְאֻם־יְהוָה וְאֶל־זֶה אַבִּיט אֶל־
to | will I | this But | .Jehovah | states | these all | and | has | My
,look | one to | ,things | exist | ,made | hand

376 5221 7794 7819 1697 2730 7307 6041
3 עָנִי וּנְכֵה־רוּחַ וְחָרֵד עַל־דְּבָרִי׃ שׁוֹחֵט הַשּׁוֹר מַכֵּה־אִישׁ
a | he(as is) | ,ox the | He | My | at | and | ,spirit | con- and | the
;man striking | slaughtering | .word | trembling | of trite | afflicted

sacrifices a lamb *is as if* he broke a dog's neck; he who offers a present *as if it were* swine's blood; he who marks incense *is if* he blessed an idol. Yea, they have chosen their way, and their soul delights in their abominations. [4]I also will choose their vexations; and I will bring their fears to them; because I called, and no one answered; I spoke, and they did not hear; but they did the evil in My eyes, and chose that in which I had no pleasure.

[5]Hear the word of Jehovah, those who tremble at His word. Your brothers who hate you, who drive you out for My name's sake, have said, Jehovah is glorified. But He shall appear in your joy, and they shall be ashamed. [6]A roaring sound from the city! A sound from the temple! *It is* the sound of Jehovah repaying recompense to His enemies.

[7]Before she travailed, she brought forth; before pain came to her, she delivered a male child. [8]Who has heard *anything* like this? Who has seen *things* like these? Shall the earth be brought forth *in* one day? Shall a nation be born *in* one step? For Zion travailed *and* also brought forth her sons. [9]Shall I bring to the birth, and not cause to bring forth? says Jehovah. Surely I cause birth, and hold back, says your God.

[10]Rejoice with Jerusalem, and be glad with her, all who love her. Rejoice a rejoicing with her, all who mourn for her; [11]that you may suck and be satisfied with her comforting breasts; that you may milk out and delight yourselves with the fullness of her glory. [12]for so says Jehovah: Behold, I stretch out peace to her like a river, and glory of nations like an overflowing torrent. And You shall suck; you

זֹבֵחַ הַשֶּׂה עֹרֵף כֶּלֶב מַעֲלֵה מִנְחָה דַּם־חֲזִיר מַזְכִּיר
he marking ;swine (as) of blood a present he offering ;dog's a breaking neck the lamb sacri- he ficing
לְבֹנָה מְבָרֵךְ אָוֶן גַּם־הֵמָּה בָּחֲרוּ בְּדַרְכֵיהֶם וּבְשִׁקּוּצֵיהֶם
their in and abominations way their have chosen they ,also an evil— (as) blessing ,incense
4 נַפְשָׁם חָפֵצָה׃ גַּם־אֲנִי אֶבְחַר בְּתַעֲלֻלֵיהֶם וּמְגוּרֹתָם אָבִיא
will I bring their and fears ,vexations their will choose I Also .delights their soul
לָהֶם יַעַן קָרָאתִי וְאֵין עוֹנֶה דִּבַּרְתִּי וְלֹא שָׁמֵעוּ וַיַּעֲשׂוּ הָרַע
the evil they did but they ;hear did and not ,spoke I (one) ;answered and not ,called I because to ,them
5 בְּעֵינַי וּבַאֲשֶׁר לֹא־חָפַצְתִּי בָּחָרוּ׃ שִׁמְעוּ דְּבַר־יְהוָה
,Jehovah the of word Hear they .chose had I in pleasure not that and which My in ,eyes
הַחֲרֵדִים אֶל־דְּבָרוֹ אָמְרוּ אֲחֵיכֶם שֹׂנְאֵיכֶם מְנַדֵּיכֶם לְמַעַן
for sake driving out you hating ,you Your brothers have said His :word at who those tremble
6 שְׁמִי יִכְבַּד יְהוָה וְנֵרְאֶה בְשִׂמְחַתְכֶם וְהֵם יֵבֹשׁוּ׃ קוֹל
sound A of be shall .ashamed and they your in ,joy He But shall appear !Jehovah is glorified My ,name's
שָׁאוֹן מֵעִיר קוֹל מֵהֵיכָל קוֹל יְהוָה מְשַׁלֵּם גְּמוּל לְאֹיְבָיו׃
His to .enemies recom- pence repaying Jehovah the of sound the from ,temple a sound from ,city the roaring
7 בְּטֶרֶם תָּחִיל יָלָדָה בְּטֶרֶם יָבוֹא חֵבֶל לָהּ וְהִמְלִיטָה
she then delivered to ,her pain came before gave she ;birth she ,travailed Before
8 זָכָר׃ מִי־שָׁמַע כָּזֹאת מִי רָאָה כָּאֵלֶּה הֲיוּחַל אֶרֶץ בְּיוֹם
day in the earth Shall travail ?these like has seen Who like ?this has heard Who .male a
אֶחָד אִם־יִוָּלֵד גּוֹי פַּעַם אֶחָת כִּי־חָלָה גַּם־יָלְדָה צִיּוֹן אֶת־
Zion brought forth also travailed For one (in) step a nation be Shall born ?one
9 בָּנֶיהָ׃ הַאֲנִי אַשְׁבִּיר וְלֹא אוֹלִיד יֹאמַר יְהוָה אִם־אֲנִי
I Sure- ly .Jehovah says to cause ?forth bring and not to bring birth the Shall I her .sons
10 הַמּוֹלִיד וְעָצַרְתִּי אָמַר אֱלֹהָיִךְ׃ שִׂמְחוּ אֶת־יְרוּשָׁלַם
,Jerusalem with Rejoice God your says and ,restrain cause ,birth
וְגִילוּ בָהּ כָּל־אֹהֲבֶיהָ שִׂישׂוּ אִתָּהּ מָשׂוֹשׂ כָּל־הַמִּתְאַבְּלִים
who mourn all a ,rejoicing with her Rejoice who .her love all with ,her be and glad
11 עָלֶיהָ׃ לְמַעַן תִּינְקוּ וּשְׂבַעְתֶּם מִשֹּׁד תַּנְחֻמֶיהָ לְמַעַן תָּמֹצּוּ
may you out drain that her ,comforts the with of breast be and satisfied may you suck that for ;her
12 וְהִתְעַנַּגְתֶּם מִזִּיז כְּבוֹדָהּ׃ כִּי־כֹה ׀ אָמַר יְהוָה הִנְנִי
,Behold I Jeho- :vah says thus For her .glory the with of fullness delight and yourselves
נֹטֶה־אֵלֶיהָ כְּנָהָר שָׁלוֹם וּכְנַחַל שׁוֹטֵף כְּבוֹד גּוֹיִם וִינַקְתֶּם
you And ;suck shall .nations glory of over flowing like and torrent a ,peace a like river her to hold out

shall be carried on the side and be dandled on knees. 13 As a man whom his mother comforts, so I will comfort you. And you shall be comforted in Jerusalem. 14 And you will see, and your heart shall rejoice; and your bones shall flourish like the grass. And the hand of Jehovah shall be known toward His servants, and He shall be indignant with His enemies.

15 For, behold, Jehovah will come with fire, and His chariots like the tempest, to return His wrath in fury, and His rebuke in flames of fire. 16 For by fire and by His sword Jehovah will execute judgment with all flesh; and the slain of Jehovah shall be many. 17 Those who sanctify themselves, and purify themselves to the gardens, *each* one in the midst, eaters of swine's flesh, and the hateful thing, and the mouse—*these* are cut off together, says Jehovah.

18 for I *know* their works and their thoughts; it comes to gather all the nations and the tongues; and they shall come and see My glory. 19 And I will set a sign among them, and I will send those who escape from them to the nations of Tarshish, Pul, and Lud, drawers of the bow; to Tubal and Javan, to the far away coasts that have not heard My fame nor seen My glory. And they shall declare My glory among the nations. 20 And they shall bring all your brothers out of all nations, an offering to Jehovah, on horses, and in chariots, and in litters, and on mules, and on camels, to My holy mountain Jersualem, says Jehovah; as the sons of Israel bring the offering in a clean vessel *to* the house of Jehovah. 21 And I will also

---

517 3761 8173 1290 5375 6654

13 עַל־צַד תִּנָּשֵׂאוּ וְעַל־בִּרְכַּיִם תְּשָׁעֳשָׁעוּ׃ כְּאִישׁ אֲשֶׁר אִמּוֹ

his mother whom a As man be shall you .dandled knees and on shall you carried be the side on

5162 3389 5162 5162

14 תְּנַחֲמֶנּוּ כֵּן אָנֹכִי אֲנַחֶמְכֶם וּבִירוּשָׁלִַם תְּנֻחָמוּ׃ וּרְאִיתֶם

you And ,see will shall you .comforted be in and Jerusalem comfort will ;you I so comforts ,him

3068 6524 1877 6106 3820 7797

וְשָׂשׂ לִבְּכֶם וְעַצְמוֹתֵיכֶם כַּדֶּשֶׁא תִפְרַחְנָה וְנוֹדְעָה יַד־יְהוָה

Jehovah the of hand shall And known be shall .sprout the like grass your and bones your ,heart shall and rejoice

935 784 3068 341 2194 5650

15 אֶת־עֲבָדָיו וְזָעַם אֶת־אֹיְבָיו׃ כִּי־הִנֵּה יְהוָה בָּאֵשׁ יָבוֹא

will ,come with fire Jehovah ,behold ,For His .enemies (over) He and rage shall His ,servants toward

3851 1606 639 2534 4818 5492

וְכַסּוּפָה מַרְכְּבֹתָיו לְהָשִׁיב בְּחֵמָה אַפּוֹ וְגַעֲרָתוֹ בְּלַהֲבֵי־

flames in of His and rebuke His ,wrath fury in bring to back His ,chariots the like and tempest

7231 1320 2719 3068 784 784

16 אֵשׁ׃ כִּי בָאֵשׁ יְהוָה נִשְׁפָּט וּבְחַרְבּוֹ אֶת־כָּל־בָּשָׂר וְרַבּוּ

shall and many be ;flesh all with with and sword His will ,judge Jehovah by fire For .fire

310 2891 6942 3068 2491

17 חַלְלֵי יְהוָה׃ הַמִּתְקַדְּשִׁים וְהַמִּטַּהֲרִים אֶל־הַגַּנּוֹת אַחַר

behind the ,gardens to purify and themselves sanctify who Those themselves .Jehovah the of slain

3162 5909 8263 2386 1320 398 8432 259

אַחַד בַּתָּוֶךְ אֹכְלֵי בְּשַׂר הַחֲזִיר וְהַשֶּׁקֶץ וְהָעַכְבָּר יַחְדָּו

together the and —mouse the and ,thing hateful ,swine the flesh of eaters of the in midst (each) one

935 4284 4639 3068 5486

18 יָסֻפוּ נְאֻם־יְהוָה׃ וְאָנֹכִי מַעֲשֵׂיהֶם וּמַחְשְׁבֹתֵיהֶם בָּאָה

it comes their and —thoughts works their For (know) I .Jehovah states are they ,off cut

3519 935 3956 1471 6908

לְקַבֵּץ אֶת־כָּל־הַגּוֹיִם וְהַלְּשֹׁנוֹת וּבָאוּ וְרָאוּ אֶת־כְּבוֹדִי׃

.glory My see and they and come shall the and ,tongues the nations all to gather

1471 6412 226 7760

19 וְשַׂמְתִּי בָהֶם אוֹת וְשִׁלַּחְתִּי מֵהֶם ׀ פְּלֵיטִים אֶל־הַגּוֹיִם

the :nations to who those escape from them I and send will a ,sign among them I And set will

7350 339 3120 8422 7198 4900 3865 6322 8659

תַּרְשִׁישׁ פּוּל וְלוּד מֹשְׁכֵי קֶשֶׁת תֻּבַל וְיָוָן הָאִיִּים הָרְחֹקִים

far ,away the to coasts and ,Javan to Tubal the drawers ,bow of and ,Lud ,Put ,Tarshish

5046 3519 8088 8085

אֲשֶׁר לֹא־שָׁמְעוּ אֶת־שִׁמְעִי וְלֹא־רָאוּ אֶת־כְּבוֹדִי וְהִגִּידוּ

they And declare shall My .glory have seen and not My ,fame have heard not that

1471 251 935 1471 3519

20 אֶת־כְּבוֹדִי בַּגּוֹיִם׃ וְהֵבִיאוּ אֶת־כָּל־אֲחֵיכֶם ׀ מִכָּל־הַגּוֹיִם ׀

the ,nations of out all your brothers all they And bring shall among .nations the My glory

3753 6632 7393 5483 3068 4503

מִנְחָה ׀ לַיהוָה בַּסּוּסִים וּבָרֶכֶב וּבַצַּבִּים וּבַפְּרָדִים

on and ,mules in and ,wagons in and ,chariots ,horses on to ,Jehovah food— a offering

935 3068 559 3389 6944 3753

וּבַכִּרְכָּרוֹת עַל הַר קָדְשִׁי יְרוּשָׁלִַם אָמַר יְהוָה כַּאֲשֶׁר יָבִיאוּ

bring as ,Jehovah says ,Jerusalem My holy moun- tain to on and ,dromedaries

3068 1004 2889 3627 4503 3478 1121

21 בְנֵי יִשְׂרָאֵל אֶת־הַמִּנְחָה בִּכְלִי טָהוֹר בֵּית יְהוָה׃ וְגַם־

And also .Jehovah the of house (to) clean a in vessel food— the offering Israel the of sons also take some of them for the priests, for the Levites, says Jehovah.

[22]For as the new heavens and the new earth which I will make stand before Me, states Jehovah, so shall your seed and your name stand. [23]And it will be, from new moon to its new moon, and from sabbath to its sabbath, all flesh shall come to worship before Me, says Jehovah. [24]And they shall go out and see the dead bodies of the men who have transgressed against Me, for their worm shall not die, nor shall their fire be put out, and they shall be an object of disgust to all flesh.

8064 3068 559 3881 3548 3947

22 מֵהֶם אֶקַּח לַכֹּהֲנִים לַלְוִיִּם אָמַר יְהוָה׃ כִּי כַאֲשֶׁר הַשָּׁמַיִם

the heavens | as | For | .Jehovah | says | the for ,Levites | the for ,priests | will I take them of | some

6440 5975 6213 834 2319 776 2319

הַחֲדָשִׁים וְהָאָרֶץ הַחֲדָשָׁה אֲשֶׁר אֲנִי עֹשֶׂה עֹמְדִים לְפָנַי

before ,Me | stand | ,make | I | which | ,new | the and earth | new

2320 2320 1961 8034 2233 5975 3068 5002

23 נְאֻם־יְהוָה כֵּן יַעֲמֹד זַרְעֲכֶם וְשִׁמְכֶם׃ וְהָיָה מִדֵּי־חֹדֶשׁ בְּחָדְשׁוֹ

its to ,moon | new moon | from | it And be will | your and ,name | your seed | shall stand | so | Jehovah | states

559 6440 7812 1320 3605 935 7676 7676 1767

וּמִדֵּי שַׁבָּת בְּשַׁבַּתּוֹ יָבוֹא כָל־בָּשָׂר לְהִשְׁתַּחֲוֹת לְפָנַי אָמַר

says | before Me | worship to | flesh | all | shall come | its to ,sabbath | sabbath | and from

8438 6586 582 6297 7200 3318 3068

24 יְהוָה׃ וְיָצְאוּ וְרָאוּ בְּפִגְרֵי הָאֲנָשִׁים הַפֹּשְׁעִים בִּי כִּי תוֹלַעְתָּם

their worm | for against .Me | have who transgressed | the men | dead the of bodies | and ,see | they And out go shall | Jehovah.

1320 3605 1860 1961 3518 3808 784 4191 3808

לֹא תָמוּת וְאִשָּׁם לֹא תִכְבֶּה וְהָיוּ דֵרָאוֹן לְכָל־בָּשָׂר׃

flesh | all to | an abhorrence | they and be shall | be shall not ;out put | their and fire | shall ,die | not

A LITERAL TRANSLATION
OF THE BIBLE
THE BOOK OF
JEREMIAH

CHAPTER 1

[1]The words of Jeremiah the son of Hilkiah, *one* of the priests who *resided* in Anathoth in the land of Benjamin, [2]*to* whom the word of Jehovah came in the days of Josiah the son of Amon, king of Judah, in the thirteenth year of his reign. [3]It also came in the days of Jehoiakim the son of Josiah, king of Judah, to the end of the eleventh year of Zedekiah the son of Josiah, king of Judah, to the exile of Jerusalem in the fifth month. [4]Then the word of Jehovah was to me, saying, [5]Before I formed you in the belly, I knew you; and before you came out of the womb, I set you apart. I gave you a *as* prophet to the nations. [6]Then I said, Ah, Lord Jehovah! Behold, I do not know how to speak; for I *am* a boy.

[7]But Jehovah said to me, Do not say, I *am* a boy; for you shall go to all that I shall send you. And whatever I command you, you shall speak. [8]Do not be afraid of their faces, for I *am* with you to deliver you, says Jehovah. [9]Then Jehovah put out His hand and touched my mouth. And Jehovah said to me, Behold, I have put My words in your mouth. [10]Behold, I have today appointed you over the nations and over the kingdoms, to root out,

יִרְמְיָה

LIBER JEREMIAE

(THE) BOOK OF JEREMIAH

CAPUT. I א

CHAPTER 1

6068 834 3548 2518 1121 3414 1697
1 דִּבְרֵי יִרְמְיָהוּ בֶּן־חִלְקִיָּהוּ מִן־הַכֹּהֲנִים אֲשֶׁר בַּעֲנָתוֹת
in who the (one) ,Hilkiah the Jeremiah The
Anathoth (were) priests of of son of words

2977 3117 3068 1697 1961 834 1144 776
2 בְּאֶרֶץ בִּנְיָמִן׃ אֲשֶׁר הָיָה דְבַר־יְהוָה אֵלָיו בִּימֵי יֹאשִׁיָּהוּ
Josiah the in to Jehovah the came whom ,Benjamin the in
of days him of word of land

1961 4427 8141 6240 7969 3063 4428 526 1121
3 בֶן־אָמוֹן מֶלֶךְ יְהוּדָה בִּשְׁלֹשׁ־עֶשְׂרֵה שָׁנָה לְמָלְכוֹ׃ וַיְהִי
it Also his of year the in ,Judah king ,Amon the
came .reign thirteenth of of son

6249 8552/5704 3063 4428 2977 1121 3079 3117
בִּימֵי יְהוֹיָקִים בֶּן־יֹאשִׁיָּהוּ מֶלֶךְ יְהוּדָה עַד־תֹּם עַשְׁתֵּי־
eleventh the until ,Judah king ,Judah the Jehoiakim the in
of end of of son of days

1540 3063 4428 2977 1121 6667 8141 6240
עֶשְׂרֵה שָׁנָה לְצִדְקִיָּהוּ בֶן־יֹאשִׁיָּהוּ מֶלֶךְ יְהוּדָה עַד־גְּלוֹת
the to ,Judah king ,Josiah the of the
of exile of of son Zedekiah year

3068 1697 1961 2549 2320 3389
4 יְרוּשָׁלַםִ בַּחֹדֶשׁ הַחֲמִישִׁי׃ וַיְהִי דְבַר־יְהוָה אֵלַי
to Jehovah the it And .fifth the in Jerusalem
,me of word ,was month

3318 2962 3045 990 3335 2962 559
5 לֵאמֹר׃ בְּטֶרֶם אֶצָּרְךָ בַבֶּטֶן יְדַעְתִּיךָ וּבְטֶרֶם תֵּצֵא
you and knew I the in formed I Before :saying
out came before ,you belly ,you

162 559 5414 1471 5030 6942 7358
6 מֵרֶחֶם הִקְדַּשְׁתִּיךָ נָבִיא לַגּוֹיִם נְתַתִּיךָ׃ וָאֹמַר אֲהָהּ
,Alas I Then ap- I the to a consecrated I the of
said .you pointed nations prophet ;you womb

559 5288 1696 3045 3808 2009 3068 136
7 אֲדֹנָי יְהוִה הִנֵּה לֹא־יָדַעְתִּי דַּבֵּר כִּי־נַעַר אָנֹכִי׃ וַיֹּאמֶר
But .(am) I a for to do I not ,Behold !Jehovah Lord
said boy ,speak how know

7971 3605 5288 559 3808 3068
יְהוָה אֵלַי אַל־תֹּאמַר נַעַר אָנֹכִי כִּי עַל־כָּל־אֲשֶׁר אֶשְׁלָחֲךָ
send I that all to for ;(am) I a do not to Jehovah
,you boy ,say ,me

6440 3372 3808 1696 6680 1980
8 תֵּלֵךְ וְאֵת כָּל־אֲשֶׁר אֲצַוְּךָ תְּדַבֵּר׃ אַל־תִּירָא מִפְּנֵיהֶם
their of be do Not will you com- I what ever And you
faces afraid .speak ,you mand .go shall

3027 3068 7971 3068 5002 5337
9 כִּי־אִתְּךָ אֲנִי לְהַצִּלֶךָ נְאֻם־יְהוָה׃ וַיִּשְׁלַח יְהוָה אֶת־יָדוֹ
His Jehovah Then .Jehovah says deliver to I with for
hand forth put ,you ,(am) you

6310 1697 5414 2009 3068 559 6310 5060
וַיַּגַּע עַל־פִּי וַיֹּאמֶר יְהוָה אֵלַי הִנֵּה נָתַתִּי דְבָרַי בְּפִיךָ׃
your in My have I ,Behold to Jehovah and my on and
.mouth words put ,me said ;mouth touched

4467 5921 1471 5921 2088 3117 6485 7200
10 רְאֵה הִפְקַדְתִּיךָ ׀ הַיּוֹם הַזֶּה עַל־הַגּוֹיִם וְעַל־הַמַּמְלָכוֹת
the and the over this day have I ,See
kingdoms over nations you appointed

and to tear down, and to destroy, and to throw down, to build, and to plant.

11 And was the word of Jehovah to me, saying, Jeremiah, what do you see? And I said, I see an almond rod. 12 Then Jehovah said to me, You have seen well; for I will watch over My word to perform it. 13 And the word of Jehovah came to me the second time, saying, What do you see? And I said, I see a boiling pot; and its face *is* from the face of the north. 14 And Jehovah said to me, Out of the north evil will be set loose on all the inhabitants of the land. 15 For, behold, I will call all the families of the kingdoms of the north, declares Jehovah. And they shall come, and they shall each one set his throne at the entrance of the gates of Jerusalem, and all against its walls all around, and against the cities of Judah. 16 And I will pronounce My judgments against them regarding all their evil, *those* who have forsaken Me, and have burned incense to other gods, and have worshiped the works of their hands.

17 And you must gird up your loins, and rise up, and speak to them all that I command you. Do not be terrified before their faces, that I not prostrate you before them. 18 For, behold, today I have made you a fortified city, and an iron pillar, and bronze walls against the whole land, against the kings of Judah, against her princes, against her priests, and to the people of the land. 19 And they shall fight against you; but they shall not overcome you. For I am with you to deliver you, declares Jehovah.

5193 1129 2040 6 5422 5428
לנתוש ולנתוץ ולהאביד ולהרוס לבנות ולנטוע׃
to and ,build to to and to and to and to
.plant ,down throw destroy ,down tear ,uproot

559 3414 7200 4100 559 3068/1697 1961
11 ויהי דבר־יהוה אלי לאמר מה־אתה ראה ירמיהו ואמר
I And ?Jeremiah do you What ,saying to Jehovah the And
,said ,see me of word came

7200 3190 3068 559 7200 8247 4731
12 מקל שקד אני ראה׃ ויאמר יהוה אלי היטבת לראות
;seen have You to Jehovah Then .see I an rod
well ,me said almond

3068 1697 1961 6213 1697 5921 8245
13 כי־שקד אני על־דברי לעשתו׃ ויהי דבר־יהוה
Jehovah the And perform to My over I will for
of word came .it word watch

5301 5518 559 7200 4100 559 8145
אלי שנית לאמר מה אתה ראה ואמר סיר נפוח אני
I boiling pot a I And do you What ,saying second the to
,said ?see (time) me

6605 6828 3068 559 6828 6440 6440 7200
14 ראה ופניו מפני צפונה׃ ויאמר יהוה אלי מצפון תפתח
be will From to Jehovah Then .north the the from its and ,see
loosed north the ,me said of face (is) face

3605 7121 2009 776 3427 3605 5921 7451
15 הרעה על כל־ישבי הארץ׃ כי | הנני קרא לכל־
all call will I ,lo For the the all on evil
.land of inhabitants

376 5414 935 3068/5002 6828 4467 4940
משפחות ממלכות צפונה נאם־יהוה ובאו ונתנו איש
each will and they and ;Jehovah declares the king- the the
man set come will ,north of doms of families

5439 2346 3605 5921 3389 8179 6607 3678
כסאו פתח | שערי ירושלם ועל כל־חומתיה סביב ועל
and around its all and ,Jerusalem the the at his
against walls against of gates of entrance throne

7451 3605 5921 853 4941 1696 3063 5892 3605
16 כל־ערי יהודה׃ ודברתי משפטי אותם על כל־רעתם
their all re- against My I And .Judah the all
,evilness garding them judgments utter will of cities

4639 7812 312 430 6999 5800 834
אשר עזבוני ויקטרו לאלהים אחרים וישתחוו למעשי
the have and ,other gods to burned and for- have who
of works worshiped incense Me saken

853 413 1696 6965 4975 247 859 3027
17 ידיהם׃ ואתה תאזר מתניך וקמת ודברת אליהם את
them to and and your up gird Now their
speak ,arise ,loins you .hands

2865 6440 2865 408 6680 595 834 3605
כל־אשר אנכי אצוך אל־תחת מפניהם פן־אחתך
prostrate I lest before be do not command I that all
you ,them terrified ,you

5982 4013 5892 3117 5414 2009 589 6440
18 לפניהם׃ ואני הנה נתתיך היום לעיר מבצר ולעמוד
and ,fortified city a today have ,behold For before
pillar you made ,I .them

8269 3063 4428 776 3605 5921 5178 2346 1270
ברזל ולחמות נחשת על־כל־הארץ למלכי יהודה לשריה
against ,Judah the against the whole against bronze and an
,rulers her of kings ,land walls ,iron

3588 3201 3808 413 3898 776 5971 3548
19 לכהניה ולעם הארץ׃ ונלחמו אליך ולא־יוכלו לך כי־
For .you will they but against they And the to and against
overcome not ,you fight will .land's people priests her

5337 3068 5002 589 854
אתך אני נאם־יהוה להצילך׃
deliver to ,Jehovah declares I with
.you ,(am) you

CAP. II. ב

CHAPTER 2

3389 241 7121 19‥80 559 3068 1697 1961
1 2 ויהי דבר־יהוה אלי לאמר׃ הלך וקראת באזני ירושלם
,Jerusalem the in of ears and cry Go ,saying to me Jehovah the of word And came

160 52:71 2617 2142 30:68 559 3541 559.
לאמר כה אמר יהוה זכרתי לך חסד נעוריך אהבת
the of love your ,youth the of kindness ,you re- member I ,Jehovah says Thus ,saying

6944 2232 38:08 776 40:59 310 3212 3623
3 כלולתיך לכתך אחרי במדבר בארץ לא זרועה׃ קדש
Holy (was) .sown not a in land the in ,wilderness after Me your going your ,espousals

7451 816 398 3605 8393 7225 30:68 3478
ישראל ליהוה ראשית תבואתה כל־אכליו יאשמו רעה
evil become ;guilty that it devour all His ;increase first- the of fruits to ,Jehovah Israel

1004 3068 1697 8085 3068 5002 935
4 תבא אליהם נאם־יהוה׃ שמעו דבר־יהוה בית
O of house ,Jehovah the of word Hear .Jehovah declares on ,them shall come

4100 3068 559 35:41 3478 1004 4940 36:05 32:90
5 יעקב וכל־משפחות בית ישראל׃ כה אמר יהוה מה־
What :Jehovah says Thus .Israel the of house the of families and all ,Jacob

310 32:12 7368 5766 4672
מצאו אבותיכם בי עול כי רחקו מעלי וילכו אחרי
after have and walked from ,Me they far went that in- iquity in Me your fathers have found

776 5927 30:68 559 38:08 1891 1892
6 ההבל ויהבלו׃ ולא אמרו איה יהוה המעלה אתנו מארץ
the from of land us who up brought Jehovah Where (is) did ,say they not And ?vain become have and vanity

7745 6160 776 40:57 3212 4714
מצרים המוליך אתנו במדבר בארץ ערבה ושוחה
of and ;pits deserts a in of land the in ,wilderness us who led ,Egypt

3427 3808 376 5674 776 6757 6723 776
בארץ ציה וצלמות בארץ לא־עבר בה איש ולא־ישב
has lived and not a ,man through it has passed not a in land deep and ;darkness drought a in of land

6529 398 3759 776 935 120
7 אדם שם׃ ואביא אתכם אל־ארץ הכרמל לאכל פריה
its fruit eat to plentiful a land into you I And brought ?there a man

8441 7760 5159 776 2930 935 2898
וטובה ותבאו ותטמאו את־ארצי ונחלתי שמתם לתועבה׃
an .abomination made My inheritance and My ,land you and defiled entered you its and goodness

304:5 38:08 8451 8610 30:68 559 38:08 3548
8 הכהנים לא אמרו איה יהוה ותפשי התורה לא ידעוני
knew .Me not the law they And handle who ?Jehovah Where (is) did ,say not The priests

3808 310 1168 5012 5030 6586 7462
והרעים פשעו בי והנביאים נבאו בבעל ואחרי לא־
not things and after ,Baal by proph- esied the and prophets against ;Me rebelled the And shepherds

1121 3068 5002 7378 5750 1980 3276
9 יועלו הלכו׃ לכן עד אריב אתכם נאם־יהוה ואת־בני
the of sons and with ;Jehovah says with ,you will I contend still Therefore they .went profit- able

7971 6933 7200 3794 339 5674 7378 1121
10 בניכם אריב׃ כי עברו איי כתיים וראו וקדר שלחו
send ,to and Kedar and ,see Kittim the of coasts cross to over For will I .contend your sons

CHAPTER 2

[1]And was the word of Jehovah to me, saying, [2]Go and cry in the ears of Jerusalem, saying, So says Jehovah, I remember you, the kindness of your youth, the love of your espousals, your going after Me in the wilderness, in a land not sown. [3]Israel was holy to Jehovah, the firstfruits of His increase. All that devour him become guilty; evil shall come on them, declares Jehovah. [4]Hear the word of Jehovah, O house of Jacob, and all the families of the house of Israel.

[5]So says Jehovah, What iniquity have your fathers found in Me, that they went far from Me, and have walked after vanity, and have become vain? [6]Nor did they say, Where *is* Jehovah who brought us up out of the land of Egypt, who led us in the wilderness; in a land of deserts and of pits; in a dry land, and death-shade; in a land that no man has passed through, and not a man has lived there? [7]And I brought you into a plentiful land, to eat its fruit and its goodness. But when you went in, you defiled My land, and made My inheritance an abomination. [8]The priests did not say, Where *is* Jehovah? And they who handle the law did not know Me. And the shepherds rebelled against Me; and the prophets prophesied by Baal, and went after things not profitable.

[9]Therefore, I will contend with you, says Jehovah, and I will contend with your sons' sons. [10]For go to the isles of Chittim and see; and send to Kedar; and carefully

consider and see if there is *any* like this. [11]Has a nation changed *its* gods; and they *were* not gods? But My people have changed their Glory without it having profit. [12]Be amazed at this, O heavens, and be horrified; be completely desolated, declares Jehovah. [13]For My people have committed two evils: they have forsaken Me, the Fountain of living waters, to hew out cisterns for themselves, broken cisterns that can hold no water.

[14]*Is* Israel a servant? Or *is* he a servant of the house? Why has he become a prey? [15]The young lions roared against him; they gave their voice. And they made his land a waste; his cities are burned, without inhabitant. [16]Also the sons of Noph and Tahpanhes have fed on your crown. [17]Have you not done this to yourself, by your forsaking Jehovah your God, when He led you by the way? [18]And now what *is* for you toward the way of Egypt, to drink the waters of Sihor? Or what for you toward Assyria, to drink the waters of the River? [19]Your own evil shall teach you, and your apostasies shall reprove you. Know, then, and see that *is* evil and bitter your forsaking Jehovah your God; and My fear *is* not in you, declares the Lord Jehovah of Hosts.

[20]For long ago you broke your yoke *and* tore up your bonds. And you said, I will not transgress — when on every high hill and under every green tree you lay down *like* a harlot. [21]Yet I planted you a choice vine, wholly a true seed. How then have you turned into the deteriorating *shoots* of an alien vine to Me? [22]Though you wash yourself with potash, and

430 1471 3235 2088 1961 7200 3966 995
11 וְהִתְבּוֹנְנוּ מְאֹד וּרְאוּ הֵן הָיְתָה כָּזֹאת׃ הַהֵימִיר גּוֹי אֱלֹהִים
(its) a Has like there if and care- and
,gods nation changed .this (any) is see fully consider

8074 3276 1097 3519 4171 5971 430 3808
12 וְהֵמָּה לֹא אֱלֹהִים וְעַמִּי הֵמִיר כְּבוֹדוֹ בְּלוֹא יוֹעִיל׃ שֹׁמּוּ
Be having it without their have My But ?gods (were) and
,amazed .profit Glory changed people not they

8147 3068 5002 3966 2717 8175 2088 8064
13 שָׁמַיִם עַל־זֹאת וְשַׂעֲרוּ חָרְבוּ מְאֹד נְאֻם־יְהוָה׃ כִּי־שְׁתַּיִם
two For .Jehovah de- ,utterly be be and ,this at O
clares desolated ;horrified ,heavens

2672 2416 4325 4726 5800 5971 6213 7451
רָעוֹת עָשָׂה עַמִּי אֹתִי עָזְבוּ מְקוֹר ׀ מַיִם חַיִּים לַחְצֹב
to ,living waters foun- the have they Me My have evils
out hew of tain ,forsaken :people committed

4325 3557 3808 7665 877 877
לָהֶם בֹּארוֹת בֹּארֹת נִשְׁבָּרִים אֲשֶׁר לֹא־יָכִלוּ הַמָּיִם׃
.water can not that broken cisterns ;cisterns for
hold themselves

957 1961 4069 1004 3211 3478 5650
14 הַעֶבֶד יִשְׂרָאֵל אִם־יְלִיד בַּיִת הוּא מַדּוּעַ הָיָה לָבַז׃
a he has Why (is) the a Or ?Israel a (Is)
?prey become ?he house of servant .servant

5892 8047 776 7896 6963 5414 3715 7580
15 עָלָיו יִשְׁאֲגוּ כְפִרִים נָתְנוּ קוֹלָם וַיָּשִׁיתוּ אַרְצוֹ לְשַׁמָּה עָרָיו
his ;waste a his they and their they young the roared Against
cities land made ;voice gave ;lions him

6936 7462 8471 5297/1121 3427 1097 3341
16 נִצְּתָה מִבְּלִי יֹשֵׁב׃ גַּם־בְּנֵי־נֹף וְתַחְפַּנֵס יִרְעוּךְ קָדְקֹד׃
your on fed have and Noph the Also inhabi- without are
.crown Tahpanhes of sons .tant burned

6256 430 3068 5800 6213 2088
17 הֲלוֹא־זֹאת תַּעֲשֶׂה־לָּךְ עָזְבֵךְ אֶת־יְהוָה אֱלֹהַיִךְ בְּעֵת
the at your Jehovah your by to you Have this not
time God forsaking yourself done

8354 4714 1870 4100 6258 1870 3212
18 מוֹלִכֵךְ בַּדָּרֶךְ׃ וְעַתָּה מַה־לָּךְ לְדֶרֶךְ מִצְרַיִם לִשְׁתּוֹת
drink to ,Egypt toward for what And the by led He
of way the you (is) ,now ?way you

3259 5104 4325 8354 804 1870 4100 7883 4325
19 מֵי שִׁחוֹר וּמַה־לָּךְ לְדֶרֶךְ אַשּׁוּר לִשְׁתּוֹת מֵי נָהָר׃ תְּיַסְּרֵךְ
teach will the the drink to ,Assyria toward for Or ?Sihor the
you ?River of waters of way the you what of waters

5800 4751 7451 7200 3045 3198 4878 7451
רָעָתֵךְ וּמְשֻׁבוֹתַיִךְ תּוֹכִחֻךְ וּדְעִי וּרְאִי כִּי־רַע וָמָר עָזְבֵךְ
your and evil that and Therefore re- will your and own Your
forsaking bitter (is) see know .you prove apostasies ,evil

3068 136/5002 6345 3808 430 3068
אֶת־יְהוָה אֱלֹהָיִךְ וְלֹא פַחְדָּתִי אֵלַיִךְ נְאֻם־אֲדֹנָי יְהוִה
Jehovah the declares in (is) My and your Jehovah
of Lord ,you fear not ,God

4147 5423 5923 7665 5769 6635
20 צְבָאוֹת׃ כִּי מֵעוֹלָם שָׁבַרְתִּי עֻלֵּךְ נִתַּקְתִּי מוֹסְרוֹתַיִךְ
your tore (and) your broke you long For .Hosts
;bonds up yoke ago

3605 8478 1364 1389 3605 5921 5674 3808 559
וַתֹּאמְרִי לֹא אֶעֱבוֹד כִּי עַל־כָּל־גִּבְעָה גְּבֹהָה וְתַחַת כָּל
every and high hill every on for will I not you but
under by pass ,said

2233 3605 8321 5193 2181 6808 7488/6086
21 עֵץ רַעֲנָן אַתְּ צֹעָה זֹנָה׃ וְאָנֹכִי נְטַעְתִּיךְ שׂוֹרֵק כֻּלֹּה זֶרַע
a wholly choice a planted Yet a (like) lay you green tree
seed ,vine you I .harlot down

3526 5237 1612 5494 2015 571
22 אֱמֶת וְאֵיךְ נֶהְפַּכְתְּ לִי סוּרֵי הַגֶּפֶן נָכְרִיָּה׃ כִּי אִם־תְּכַבְּסִי
wash you Though ?foreign vine a the for have you How .true
yourself of shoots Me into turned then

multiply soap for yourself, your iniquity *is* multiply soal for yourself, your iniquity *is* stained befoe Me, states the Lord Jehovah. [23]How can you say, I am not defiled; I have not gone after Baals? See your way in the valley; know what you have done! *You are* a swift camel crossing her ways, [24]a wild ass used to the wilderness; in the desire of her passion she sniffs at the wind; *in* her time who can turn her away? All those who seek her will not tire themselves; in her month they will find her. [25]Withhold your foot from *being* bare, and your throat from thirst. But you said, It is hopeless! No! For I love strangers, and after them I will go. [26]As the thief is ashamed when he is found, so is the house of Israel ashamed; they, their kings, their princes, and their priests, and their prophets; [27]saying to a tree, You *are* my father; and to a stone, You gave us birth. For they turned *their* back to Me, and not the face. But in the time of their evil, they will say, Arise, and save us! [28]But where *are* your gods that you have made for yourselves? Let them arise, if they can save you in the time of your evil; for *according to* the number of your cities are your gods, O Judah. [29]Why do you contend with Me? All of you, you have rebelled against Me, says Jehovah. [30]In vain I have stricken your sons; they received no correction. Your own sword has devoured your prophets, like a destroying lion.

[31]O generation, see the word of Jehovah. Have I been a wilderness to Israel, or a land of darkness? Why do My people say, We roam; we will come no more to You. [32]Can a virgin forget her finery, a bride her

בנתר ותרבי-לך ברית נכתם עונך לפני נאם אדני
the Lord declares ,Me before your iniquity (is) stained ,soap your-self for multiply and with ,potash
23 יהוה: איך תאמרי לא נטמאתי אחרי הבעלים לא
not Baals after am I ;defiled not you can say How .Jehovah
הלכתי ראי דרכך בגיא דעי מה עשית בכרה קלה
swift camel a (are You) have you !done what Know the in !valley your way See have I !gone
24 משרכת דרכיה: פרא למד מדבר באות נפשו שאפה
she sniffs at her passion the in desire of the ,wilderness used to wild a ass her ,ways crossing
רוח תאנתה מי ישיבנה כל-מבקשיה לא ייעפו בחדשה
her in month tire will not ;themselves who those her seek All turn can ?away her who her (in) time the ;wind
25 ימצאונה: מנעי רגלך מיחף וגורנך מצמאה ותאמרי
you but said from ;thirst your and throat from ,bare (being) your foot Withhold will they .her find
26 נואש לוא כי-אהבתי זרים ואחריהם אלך: כבשת גנב
the thief is As ashamed will I .go after and them ,strangers love I For !No is It !hopeless
כי ימצא כן הבישו בית ישראל המה מלכיהם שריהם
their ,rulers their ,kings ,they ;Israel the of house is ashamed so is he ,found when
27 וכהניהם ונביאיהם: אמרים לעץ אבי אתה ולאבן את
You to and ,stone a You ;(are) my father a to ,tree say who their and ,prophets their and ,priests
ילדתני כי-פנו אלי ערף ולא פנים ובעת רעתם יאמרו
will they ,say their evil in But of time the (their) .face and not (their) ,back to Me they For turned gave we .birth
28 קומה והושיענו: ואיה אלהיך אשר עשית לך יקומו
them Let ,arise for ?you have you made that your gods where But (are) save and .us Rise up
אם-יושיעוך בעת רעתך כי מספר עריך היו אלהיך יהודה:
O .Judah your ,gods (so) are your ,cities the (as) for of number your ;evil the in of time can they you save if
29 30 למה תריבו אלי כלכם פשעתם בי נאם-יהוה: לשוא
In vain .Jehovah says against ,Me have you rebelled of All ,you with ?me you do contend Why
הכיתי את-בניכם מוסר לא לקחו אכלה חרבכם
own Your sword has devoured they .took not correction your ;sons have I struck
31 נביאיכם כאריה משחית: הדור אתם ראו דבר-יהוה
.Jehovah the of word see you gen- O ,eration .destroying a like lion your ,prophets
המדבר הייתי לישראל אם ארץ מאפליה מדוע אמרו
do say Why ?darkness a of land or Israel to Have been I wilder- a ness
32 עמי רדנו לוא-נבוא עוד אליך: התשכח בתולה עדיה
her ,finery virgin a Can forget ?You to more we come will not roam We ;(freely) My ,people

attire? Yet My people have forgotten Me days without number. 33What? Do you trim your ways to seek love? For this reason you have even taught the evil women your ways. 34Also on your skirts is found the blood of the souls of the poor innocents; you did not find them breaking in, but on all these. 35Yet you say, Because I am innocent, surely His anger shall turn from me. Behold, I will judge with you, because you say, I have not sinned. 36Why do you go about so much to change your way? You also shall be ashamed of Egypt, as you were ashamed of Assyria. 37Yes, you shall go out from this *place*, and your hands on your head. For Jehovah has rejected those in whom you trust, and you will not prosper by them.

3190 4100 4557 369 3117 7911 5971 7196 3618
33 כַּלָּה קִשֻּׁרֶיהָ וְעַמִּי שְׁכֵחוּנִי יָמִים אֵין מִסְפָּר׃ מַה־תֵּיטִבִי
you do trim What .number with- out days for- gotten have Me My people Yet her ?attire a (or) bride
3925 7451 1571 160 1245 1870
דַּרְכֵּךְ לְבַקֵּשׁ אַהֲבָה לָכֵן גַּם אֶת־הָרָעוֹת לִמַּדְתִּי אֶת־
have you taught evil the women even There- fore !love seek to your way
5355 34 5315 1818 4672 3671 1571 1870
34 דְּרָכָיִךְ׃ גַּם בִּכְנָפַיִךְ נִמְצְאוּ דַּם נַפְשׁוֹת אֶבְיוֹנִים נְקִיִּים
;innocents poor the lives the of the blood found is your on skirts Also your .ways
3588 559 428 3605/5921 4672 4290 3808
35 לֹא־בַמַּחְתֶּרֶת מְצָאתִים כִּי עַל־כָּל־אֵלֶּה׃ וַתֹּאמְרִי כִּי
Be- cause you Yet ,say .these all on but did you ,them find breaking in not
559 8199 2009 639 7725 5352
נִקֵּיתִי אַךְ שָׁב אַפּוֹ מִמֶּנִּי הִנְנִי נִשְׁפָּט אוֹתָךְ עַל־אָמְרֵךְ
you say because with ,you will judge Behold I from .me His anger shall turn surely am I ,innocent
4714 1571 1870 8138 3966 235 4100 2398 3808
36 לֹא חָטָאתִי׃ מַה־תֵּזְלִי מְאֹד לְשַׁנּוֹת אֶת־דַּרְכֵּךְ גַּם מִמִּצְרַיִם
Egypt of Also your ?way change to so much you do Why about go have I .sinned not
3027 3318 1571 804 954 954
37 תֵּבֹשִׁי כַּאֲשֶׁר בֹּשְׁתְּ מֵאַשּׁוּר׃ גַּם מֵאֵת זֶה תֵּצְאִי וְיָדַיִךְ
your hands and will you ,out go this (place) from Even of .Assyria were you ashamed as be will you ashamed
6743 3808 4009 3068 3973 7218 5921
עַל־רֹאשֵׁךְ כִּי־מָאַס יְהוָה בְּמִבְטַחַיִךְ וְלֹא תַצְלִיחִי לָהֶם׃
by .them will you prosper and not whom in those ;trust you Jehovah has rejected for your ;head on

CAP. III ג

CHAPTER 3

CHAPTER 3

1*They* say, If a man puts away his wife, and she goes from him and will be for another man, will he return to her again? Would not that land be greatly defiled? But you play the harlot with many lovers; yet *would* you come back to Me? says Jehovah. 2Lift up your eyes on the bare heights and see. Where have you not been lain with? By the highways you have sat for them, like an Arab in the wilderness. And you have defiled the land with your fornications and with your evil. 3And the showers are withheld, and there has been no latter rain. And the forehead of a woman, a whore, was *on* you; you refused to be ashamed. 4Have you not just now called to Me, *saying*, My father, You *are* the friend of my youth? 5Will He keep His anger forever? Or will He guard *it* to the end? Behold, you have spoken,

1961 1980 802 376 7971 559
1 לֵאמֹר הֵן יְשַׁלַּח אִישׁ אֶת־אִשְׁתּוֹ וְהָלְכָה מֵאִתּוֹ וְהָיְתָה
will and be from him she and goes his ,wife man a go lets if ,Saying
776 2610 2610 5750 7725 312 376
לְאִישׁ־אַחֵר הֲיָשׁוּב אֵלֶיהָ עוֹד הֲלוֹא חָנוֹף תֶּחֱנַף הָאָרֶץ
land be Would defiled greatly not ?again her to he will return ,another for man
5375 3068 5002 7725 7227 7453 2181
2 הַהִיא וְאַתְּ זָנִית רֵעִים רַבִּים וְשׁוֹב אֵלַי נְאֻם־יְהוָה׃ שְׂאִי
Lift up .Jehovah says to ?Me you yet return ,many com- panions whore with But you ?that
3427 1870 7693 3808 375 7200 8205 5869
עֵינַיִךְ עַל־שְׁפָיִם וּרְאִי אֵיפֹה לֹא שֻׁגַּלְתְּ עַל־דְּרָכִים יָשַׁבְתְּ
have you sat the highways By ?with lain been you have not Where and ;see bare the ,heights on your eyes
7451 2184 776 2610 4057 6163
לָהֶם כַּעֲרָבִי בַּמִּדְבָּר וַתַּחֲנִיפִי אֶרֶץ בִּזְנוּתַיִךְ וּבְרָעָתֵךְ׃
your and .evilness your with fornications the land you And defiled have the in .wilderness an like Arab for ,them
1961 2181 802 4696 1961 3808 4456 7241 4513
3 וַיִּמָּנְעוּ רְבִבִים וּמַלְקוֹשׁ לוֹא הָיָה וּמֵצַח אִשָּׁה זוֹנָה הָיָה
there was a ,harlot a ,woman And forehead has .been not the late rain and ,showers the are So withheld
441 7121 6258 3637 3980
4 לָךְ מֵאַנְתְּ הִכָּלֵם׃ הֲלוֹא מֵעַתָּה קָרָאתִי לִי אָבִי אַלּוּף
the friend of My ,father to ,Me you Have called just now not • be to .ashamed you refused to ;you
1696 2009 5331 8104 5769 5201 5271
5 נְעֻרַי אָתָּה׃ הֲיִנְטֹר לְעוֹלָם אִם־יִשְׁמֹר לָנֶצַח הִנֵּה דִבַּרְתְּ
have you spoken ,Behold the to ?end He will (it) guard or ,forever He Will anger His keep You ?(are) my youth

and you have done *all* the evil things that you could. [6]Jehovah also said to me in the days of Josiah the king, Have you seen what the apostate Israel has done? She has gone up on every high hill and under every green tree, and has fornicated there. [7]And after she has done all these, will she return to Me? But she did not return. And her treacherous sister Judah saw. [8]And I saw, when for all the causes *for* which the apostate Israel committed adultery I sent her away and gave a writ of divorce to her. Yet her treacherous sister Judah did not fear, but she went and whored, she also. [9]And it happened, from the folly of her whoredom she defiled the land, and fornicated with stones and with trees. [10]And yet for all this her treacherous sister Judah has not turned to Me with her whole heart, but with falsehood, says Jehovah. [11]And Jehovah said to me, the apostate Israel has justified herself more than treacherous Judah.

[12]Go and cry these words toward the north, and say, Return, O backsliding Israel, says Jehovah. I will not cause My face to fall on you; for I *am* merciful, says Jehovah; I will not keep *anger* forever. [13]Only acknowledge your iniquity, that you have rebelled against Jehovah your God and have scattered your ways to the strangers under every green tree. And you have not obeyed My voice, says Jehovah. [14]Return, O apostate sons, declares Jehovah; for I am Lord over

3117 3068 559 3201 7451 6213
6 וַיֹּאמֶר יְהוָה אֵלַי בִּימֵי ... וַתַּעֲשִׂי הָרָעוֹת וַתּוּכָל׃
the in of days | to me | Jehovah | Now said | you that .could | the (all) things evil | you and done have

3478 4818 6213 7200 4428 2977
יֹאשִׁיָּהוּ הַמֶּלֶךְ הַרָאִית אֲשֶׁר עָשְׂתָה מְשֻׁבָה יִשְׂרָאֵל
?Israel | the apostate | done has | what | you Have seen | ,king the | Josiah

2181 7488 6086 8478 1364 2022 3605 5921 1980
הֹלְכָה הִיא עַל־כָּל־הַר גָּבֹהַּ וְאֶל־תַּחַת כָּל־עֵץ רַעֲנָן וַתִּזְנִי־
for- and nicated | ,green | tree every | under | and high | hill | every | on | She | went up

3808 7725 428 3605 6213 310 559
7 שָׁם׃ וָאֹמַר אַחֲרֵי עֲשׂוֹתָהּ אֶת־כָּל־אֵלֶּה אֵלַי תָּשׁוּב וְלֹא
but not | will she ;return | to Me | these all ,(things) | has she done | After | I And ,said | .there

3605 7200 3063 269 901 7200 7725
8 שָׁבָה וַתִּרְאֶה בָּגוֹדָה אֲחוֹתָהּ יְהוּדָה׃ וָאֵרֶא כִּי עַל־כָּל־
all | for | When | I And :saw | .Judah | her sister | treacherous | and (it) saw | did she ,return

5414 7971 3478 4878 5003 182
אֹדוֹת אֲשֶׁר נִאֲפָה מְשֻׁבָה יִשְׂרָאֵל שִׁלַּחְתִּיהָ וָאֶתֵּן אֶת־
and gave | sent I away her | ,Israel | the apostate | committed adultery | (for) which | the causes

269 3063 898 3372 3808 3748 5612
סֵפֶר כְּרִיתֻתֶיהָ אֵלֶיהָ וְלֹא יָרְאָה בֹּגֵדָה יְהוּדָה אֲחוֹתָהּ
her ,sister | Judah | treacherous | did fear | yet not | ,her to | her divorce | writ a of

776 2610 2184 6963 1961 1571 2181 1980
9 וַתֵּלֶךְ וַתִּזֶן גַּם־הִיא׃ וְהָיָה מִקֹּל זְנוּתָהּ וַתֶּחֱנַף אֶת־הָאָרֶץ
the land | she defiled | her harlotry's | from folly | it And ,was | .she also | and ,whored | she but went

7725 3808 3605 6086 68 5003
10 וַתִּנְאַף אֶת־הָאֶבֶן וְאֶת־הָעֵץ׃ וְגַם־בְּכָל־זֹאת לֹא־שָׁבָה אֵלַי
to Me | has turned | not | this | for all | And yet | .trees | and | stones with | for- and nicated

5002 8267 3820 3605 3063 269 901
בָּגוֹדָה אֲחוֹתָהּ יְהוּדָה בְּכָל־לִבָּהּ כִּי אִם־בְּשֶׁקֶר נְאֻם־
says | with ,falsehood | but | her ,heart | with whole | Judah | her sister | treach- erous

4878 6663 3068 559 3068
11 יְהוָה׃ וַיֹּאמֶר יְהוָה אֵלַי צִדְּקָה נַפְשָׁהּ מְשֻׁבָה
the apostate | herself | Has justified | ,me to | Jehovah | And said | .Jehovah

428 1697 7121 1980 3068 898 3478
12 יִשְׂרָאֵל מִבֹּגֵדָה יְהוּדָה׃ הָלֹךְ וְקָרָאתָ אֶת־הַדְּבָרִים הָאֵלֶּה
these | words | cry and | Go | .Judah | than more treacherous | Israel

5307 3068 5002 3478 4878 7725 559 6828
צָפוֹנָה וְאָמַרְתָּ שׁוּבָה מְשֻׁבָה יִשְׂרָאֵל נְאֻם־יְהוָה לוֹא־אַפִּיל
will I make fall | not | ;Jehovah | says | ,Israel | O apostate | ,Return | ,say and | north- ward

389 5769 5201 3808 3068/5002 2623 6440
13 פָּנַי בָּכֶם כִּי־חָסִיד אֲנִי נְאֻם־יְהוָה לֹא אֶטּוֹר לְעוֹלָם׃ אַךְ
Only | .forever | will I keep anger | not | ;Jehovah says | I (am) | merci- full | for | on ;you | My face

1870 6340 6586 430 3068 5771 3045
דְּעִי עֲוֹנֵךְ כִּי בַּיהוָה אֱלֹהַיִךְ פָּשַׁעַתְּ וַתְּפַזְּרִי אֶת־דְּרָכַיִךְ
your ways | have and scattered | have you rebelled | your God | against Jehovah | that | your ,iniquity | know

3068 5002 8085 3808 6963 7488 6086 8478 2114
לַזָּרִים תַּחַת כָּל־עֵץ רַעֲנָן וּבְקוֹלִי לֹא־שְׁמַעְתֶּם נְאֻם־יְהוָה׃
.Jehovah | says | have you ,obeyed | not | My And voice | .green | tree every | under | the to strangers

1166 3068 5002 7726 1121 7725
14 שׁוּבוּ בָנִים שׁוֹבָבִים נְאֻם־יְהוָה כִּי אָנֹכִי בָּעַלְתִּי בָכֶם
over you | lord am | I | for | ;Jehovah says | ,apostate | sons O | Turn back

you. And I will take you, one
from a city, and two from a
family, and I will bring you
to Zion. 15And I will give
you shepherds according to
My heart, who will feed you
with knowledge and understanding. 16And it will be,
when you multiply and
increase in the land in those
days, says Jehovah, they
will no longer say, The ark
of the covenant of Jehovah!
Nor shall it come to the
heart, nor shall they
remember it; nor shall they
miss *it*; nor shall it be made
any more. 17At that time
they shall call Jerusalem
the throne of Jehovah. And
all nations shall be
gathered to it, to the name
of Jehovah, to Jerusalem.
And they shall not walk any
more after the stubborn-
ness of their evil heart.
18In those days the house of
Judah shall walk with the
house of Israel, and they
shall come together out of
the land of the north, to the
land that I have given for an
inheritance to your fathers.
19But I said, How *gladly*
would I put you among the
sons, and give you a
pleasant land, a beautiful
inheritance *among* the
multitudes of nations! And I
said, You shall call Me, My
Father; and *you* shall not
turn away from Me.
20Surely *as* a wife
treacherously departs from
her lover, so you have dealt
treacherously with Me, O
house of Israel, declares
Jehovah. 21A voice was
heard weeping on the bare
heights, pleadings of the
sons of Israel; for they have
perverted their way; they
have forgotten Jehovah
their God. 22Return, O
apostate sons; I will heal
your apostasies. Behold,
we come to You, for You *are*
Jehovah our God. 23Truly,
for delusion *comes* from the
hills, tumult *on* the
mountains. Truly, in
Jehovah our God *is* the
salvation of Israel. 24For the

935 4940 81 47 5892 259 3947
וְלָקַחְתִּי אֶתְכֶם אֶחָד מֵעִיר וּשְׁנַיִם מִמִּשְׁפָּחָה וְהֵבֵאתִי
I and a from two and a from one ,you I And
bring will ,family city take will

1844 7462 3820 7462 5414 6726
15 אֶתְכֶם צִיּוֹן׃ וְנָתַתִּי לָכֶם רֹעִים כְּלִבִּי וְרָעוּ אֶתְכֶם דֵּעָה
(with) you they and My as shepherds you I And to you
knowledge feed will ,heart give will ,Zion

3117 776 6509 7235 1961 7919
16 וְהַשְׂכֵּיל׃ וְהָיָה כִּי תִרְבּוּ וּפְרִיתֶם בָּאָרֶץ בַּיָּמִים הָהֵמָּה
,those days in the in are and you when it And under- and
land fruitful multiply be will .standing

5927/3808 3068 1285 727 5750 559 3808 3068/5002
נְאֻם־יְהוָה לֹא־יֹאמְרוּ עוֹד אֲרוֹן בְּרִית יְהוָה וְלֹא יַעֲלֶה עַל־
to it will and ,Jehovah cove- the The ,still they not ,Jehovah says
come not of nant of ark say will

6256 5750 6213 3808 6485 3808 2142 3808 3820
17 לֵב וְלֹא יִזְכְּרוּ־בוֹ וְלֹא יִפְקֹדוּ וְלֹא יֵעָשֶׂה עוֹד׃ בָּעֵת הַהִיא
that At .again it will nor miss nor ;it they will nor the
time made be (it) remember heart

8034 1471 3605 6960 3068 3678 3389 7121
יִקְרְאוּ לִירוּשָׁלִַם כִּסֵּא יְהוָה וְנִקְווּ אֵלֶיהָ כָל־הַגּוֹיִם לְשֵׁם
the to ,nations all it to be will And Jeho- the Jerusalem they
of name gathered .vah of throne call will

7451 3820 8307 310 5750 3212 3808 3389 3068
יְהוָה לִירוּשָׁלִָם וְלֹא־יֵלְכוּ עוֹד אַחֲרֵי שְׁרִרוּת לִבָּם הָרָע׃
.evil their stub- the after any shall they and to ,Jehovah
heart of bornness more walk not ;Jerusalem

935 3478 1004 3063 1004 3212 3117
18 בַּיָּמִים הָהֵמָּה יֵלְכוּ בֵית־יְהוּדָה עַל־בֵּית יִשְׂרָאֵל וְיָבֹאוּ
they and ,Israel the with Judah the shall those days In
come will of house of house walk

51 57 776 6828 776 3162
יַחְדָּו מֵאֶרֶץ צָפוֹן עַל־הָאָרֶץ אֲשֶׁר הִנְחַלְתִּי אֶת־
a as gave I that the to the the from to-
to heritage land north of land gether

5414 11:21 7896 559 1
19 אֲבוֹתֵיכֶם׃ וְאָנֹכִי אָמַרְתִּי אֵיךְ אֲשִׁיתֵךְ בַּבָּנִים וְאֶתֶּן־לָךְ
you and among would I How ,said I Then your
give sons (My) you set (gladly) .fathers

7121 1 559 1471 6635 6643 5159 2532 776
אֶרֶץ חֶמְדָּה נַחֲלַת צְבִי צִבְאוֹת גּוֹיִם וָאֹמַר אָבִי תִּקְרְאִי־
shall You My I And !nations (among) beautiful a ,pleasant a
call Father ,said of hosts the inheritance land

898 7453 802 898 403 7725 3808 310
20 לִי וּמֵאַחֲרַי לֹא תָשׁוּבוּ׃ אָכֵן בָּגְדָה אִשָּׁה מֵרֵעָהּ כֵּן בְּגַדְתֶּם
have you so her from a treacherously Surely turn not from and ,Me
betrayed ,companion wife departs (as) .away Me following

1065 80 85 8205 5921 6963 3068 5002 3478 1004
21 בִּי בֵּית יִשְׂרָאֵל נְאֻם־יְהוָה׃ קוֹל עַל־שְׁפָיִים נִשְׁמָע בְּכִי
weep- was bare the on A .Jehovah says ,Israel O ,Me
,ing ,heard heights voice of house

3068 7911 1870 5753 3478 1121 8469
תַּחֲנוּנֵי בְּנֵי יִשְׂרָאֵל כִּי הֶעֱוּוּ אֶת־דַּרְכָּם שָׁכְחוּ אֶת־יְהוָה
Jehovah have they their have they for ,Israel the pleadings
forgotten ,way perverted of sons of

2009 4878 7495 7726 1121 7725 430
22 אֱלֹהֵיהֶם׃ שׁוּבוּ בָּנִים שׁוֹבָבִים אֶרְפָּה מְשׁוּבֹתֵיכֶם הִנְנוּ
,Behold your will I ,apostate O Return their
we .apostasies heal sons .God

1389 8267 403 430 3068 859
אָתָנוּ לָךְ כִּי אַתָּה יְהוָה אֱלֹהֵינוּ׃ אָכֵן לַשֶּׁקֶר מִגְּבָעוֹת
from (comes) for ,Truly !God our Jehovah You for to come
,hills the delusion (are) ;You

3478 8668 430 3068 403 2022 1995
23 הָמוֹן הָרִים אָכֵן בַּיהוָה אֱלֹהֵינוּ תְּשׁוּעַת יִשְׂרָאֵל׃
.Israel the (is) God our in truly the (on) tumult
of salvation Jehovah ;mountains

shameful thing has eaten up the labor of our fathers from our youth, their flocks and their herds, their sons and their daughters. [25]We lie down in our shame, and our confusion covers us. For we have sinned against Jehovah our God, we and our fathers, from our youth even to this day. And we have not obeyed the voice of Jehovah our God.

24 וְהַבֹּשֶׁת אָכְלָה אֶת־יְגִיעַ אֲבוֹתֵינוּ מִנְּעוּרֵינוּ אֶת־צֹאנָם
their flocks | our from youth | our fathers | the of labor | has devoured | the But idol shameful

25 וְאֶת־בְּקָרָם אֶת־בְּנֵיהֶם וְאֶת־בְּנוֹתֵיהֶם׃ נִשְׁכְּבָה בְּבָשְׁתֵּנוּ
our in shame | us Let down lie | their daughters | and | their sons | their herds | and

וּתְכַסֵּנוּ כְּלִמָּתֵנוּ כִּי לַיהוָה אֱלֹהֵינוּ חָטָאנוּ אֲנַחְנוּ
we | have we sinned | God our | against Jehovah | for | our disgrace | let and us cover

וַאֲבוֹתֵינוּ מִנְּעוּרֵינוּ וְעַד־הַיּוֹם הַזֶּה וְלֹא שָׁמַעְנוּ בְּקוֹל
the of voice | have we obeyed | And not | this | day | even to | our from youth | our and fathers

יְהוָה אֱלֹהֵינוּ׃
our God | Jehovah

CAP. IV. ד

CHAPTER 4

CHAPTER 4

[1]If you will return, O Israel, says Jehovah, return to Me. And if you will put away your hateful idols out of My face, and will not waver, [2]and you will swear, *As* Jehovah lives, in truth, in justice, and in righteousness; even the nations shall bless themselves in Him, and in Him they will glory.

[3]For so says Jehovah to the men of Judah and to Jerusalem, Break up your fallow ground, and do not sow to the thorns. [4]Circumcise yourselves to Jehovah, and take away the foreskin of your heart, O men of Judah and inhabitants of Jerusalem; that My fury not go forth like fire and burn, so that no one can put it out; because of the evil of your doings. [5]Declare in Judah, and sound out in Jerusalem; and say, Blow the ram's horn in the land. Cry the end, and say, Assemble yourselves and go into the fortified cities. [6]Lift up a banner toward Zion; flee for safety and do not wait. For I will bring evil from the north, and a great ruin. [7]The lion has come up from his thicket, and a destroyer of nations has set

1 אִם־תָּשׁוּב יִשְׂרָאֵל ׀ נְאֻם־יְהוָה אֵלַי תָּשׁוּב וְאִם־תָּסִיר
will you remove | And if | return | to Me | Jehovah says | Israel O | will you return | If

2 שִׁקּוּצֶיךָ מִפָּנַי וְלֹא תָנוּד׃ וְנִשְׁבַּעְתָּ חַי־יְהוָה בֶּאֱמֶת
truth in | Jehovah | (As) lives | you and swear will | will waver | and not | My from face | hateful your idols

בְּמִשְׁפָּט וּבִצְדָקָה וְהִתְבָּרְכוּ בוֹ גּוֹיִם וּבוֹ יִתְהַלָּלוּ׃
will they glory | in and Him | the nations | in Him | bless will then themselves | in and righteousness | justice in

3 כִּי־כֹה ׀ אָמַר יְהוָה לְאִישׁ יְהוּדָה וְלִירוּשָׁלִַם נִירוּ לָכֶם
your | Break up | to and Jerusalem | Judah | the to of man | Jehovah says | thus | For

4 נִיר וְאַל־תִּזְרְעוּ אֶל־קֹצִים׃ הִמֹּלוּ לַיהוָה וְהָסִרוּ עָרְלוֹת
fore- the of skin | and remove | to Jehovah | Circumcise yourselves | the thorns | to | do sow | and fallow not ground

לְבַבְכֶם אִישׁ יְהוּדָה וְיֹשְׁבֵי יְרוּשָׁלִָם פֶּן־תֵּצֵא כָאֵשׁ
like fire | goes lest forth | Jerusalem | inhab- and of itants | Judah | men O of | your heart

5 חֲמָתִי וּבָעֲרָה וְאֵין מְכַבֶּה מִפְּנֵי רֹעַ מַעַלְלֵיכֶם׃ הַגִּידוּ
Declare | your doings | the because of evil of | can (it) quench | that so none | and burn | My wrath

בִיהוּדָה וּבִירוּשָׁלִַם הַשְׁמִיעוּ וְאִמְרוּ וְתִקְעוּ שׁוֹפָר בָּאָרֶץ
the in land | ram's the horn | Blow | say and | (it) made heard | in and Jerusalem | Judah in

קִרְאוּ מַלְאוּ וְאִמְרוּ הֵאָסְפוּ וְנָבוֹאָה אֶל־עָרֵי הַמִּבְצָר׃
fortification | cities into of | let and go us | Assemble yourselves | say and | end the | Cry

6 שְׂאוּ־נֵס צִיּוֹנָה הָעִיזוּ אַל־תַּעֲמֹדוּ כִּי רָעָה אָנֹכִי מֵבִיא
will bring | I | evil | for | do stand | not | be strong | toward Zion banner | a | lift up

7 מִצָּפוֹן וְשֶׁבֶר גָּדוֹל׃ עָלָה אַרְיֵה מִסֻּבְּכוֹ וּמַשְׁחִית גּוֹיִם
nations | a and of destroyer | his from thicket | The lion | has up come | great | a even smashing | the from north

out. He has left his place to make your land a waste. Your cities will fall into ruins without inhabitant. [8]Clothe yourselves with sackcloth for this, wail and howl. For the fierce anger of Jehovah has not turned back from us. [9]And it will be on that day, says Jehovah, the king's heart and the heart of the rulers shall fail. And the priests shall be amazed; and the prophets shall be astounded. [10]Then I said, Ah, Lord Jehovah! Surely You have greatly deceived this people and Jerusalem, saying, You shall have peace; but the sword reaches to the soul. [11]At that time it shall be said to this people and to Jerusalem, A hot wind *from* the bare hills in the desert toward the daughter of My people, not to sift nor to cleanse! [12]A wind more full than these shall come for Me; now I also will utter judgments against them. [13]Behold, he shall come up like clouds, and his chariots like a tempest. His horses are swifter than eagles. Woe to us, for we are plundered!

[14]O Jerusalem, cleanse your heart from evil so that you may be saved. How long will your vain thoughts lodge within you? [15]For a voice declares from Dan and proclaims wickedness from Mount Ephraim. [16]Tell *it* to the nations: Behold, proclaim against Jerusalem! Besiegers are going to come from a distant land, and *they* will set their voice against the cities of Judah. [17]Like watchmen of a field, they are against her all around, because she rebelled against Me declares Jehovah. [18]Your way and your doings have done these things to you; this is your evil, because it is bitter, because it reaches to your heart.

נָסַע יָצָא מִמְּקֹמוֹ לָשׂוּם אַרְצֵךְ לְשַׁמָּה עָרַיִךְ תִּצֶּינָה
in fall will Your .waste a your make to his from has he has
ruins cities land place gone ;out set

8 מֵאֵין יוֹשֵׁב׃ עַל־זֹאת חִגְרוּ שַׂקִּים סִפְדוּ וְהֵילִילוּ כִּי לֹא־
not for and wail sack- put this For inhabi- with-
;howl ;cloth on .tant out

9 שָׁב חֲרוֹן אַף־יְהוָה מִמֶּנּוּ׃ וְהָיָה בַיּוֹם־הַהוּא נְאֻם־יְהוָה
,Jehovah says ,that day on it And from Jehovah's anger the has
be will .us of glow turned

יֹאבַד לֵב־הַמֶּלֶךְ וְלֵב הַשָּׂרִים וְנָשַׁמּוּ הַכֹּהֲנִים וְהַנְּבִאִים
the and the be will and the the and the heart shall
prophets ;priests stunned ,officials of heart ,king's fail

10 יִתְמָהוּ׃ וָאֹמַר אֲהָהּ ׀ אֲדֹנָי יְהוִה אָכֵן הַשֵּׁא הִשֵּׁאתָ לָעָם
people have you utterly Surely !Jehovah Lord ,Ah I Then be will
deceived ,said .astounded

הַזֶּה וְלִירוּשָׁלִַם לֵאמֹר שָׁלוֹם יִהְיֶה לָכֶם וְנָגְעָה חֶרֶב עַד־
to the but to shall Peace ;saying and this
sword touches ,you be ,Jerusalem

11 הַנָּפֶשׁ׃ בָּעֵת הַהִיא יֵאָמֵר לָעָם־הַזֶּה וְלִירוּשָׁלִַם רוּחַ צַח
hot A to and this to will it that At the
(from) wind ,Jerusalem people said be time .soul

שְׁפָיִם בַּמִּדְבָּר דֶּרֶךְ בַּת־עַמִּי לוֹא לִזְרוֹת וְלוֹא לְהָבַר׃
to nor to not My the toward the in bare the
!cleanse winnow —people of daughter desert heights

12 רוּחַ מָלֵא מֵאֵלֶּה יָבוֹא לִי עַתָּה גַּם־אֲנִי אֲדַבֵּר מִשְׁפָּטִים
judgments will I also Now for shall than more A
utter .Me come these full wind

13 אוֹתָם׃ הִנֵּה ׀ כַּעֲנָנִים יַעֲלֶה וְכַסּוּפָה מַרְכְּבוֹתָיו קַלּוּ
are his a like and will he like ,Behold against
swifter ;chariots windstorm ,up come clouds .them

14 מִנְּשָׁרִים סוּסָיו אוֹי לָנוּ כִּי שֻׁדָּדְנוּ׃ כַּבְּסִי מֵרָעָה לִבֵּךְ
your evil from Wash are we for to Woe his than
,heart !devastated ,us .horses eagles

יְרוּשָׁלִַם לְמַעַן תִּוָּשֵׁעִי עַד־מָתַי תָּלִין בְּקִרְבֵּךְ מַחְשְׁבוֹת
thoughts within will long How may you that so O
of you lodge .saved be ,Jerusalem

15 אוֹנֵךְ׃ כִּי קוֹל מַגִּיד מִדָּן וּמַשְׁמִיעַ אָוֶן מֵהַר אֶפְרָיִם׃
.Ephraim from wicked- and from declares a For your
Mount ness proclaims ,Dan voice ?vanity

16 הַזְכִּירוּ לַגּוֹיִם הִנֵּה הַשְׁמִיעוּ עַל־יְרוּשָׁלִַם נֹצְרִים בָּאִים
are beseigers ,Jerusalem against proclaim ,Behold the to Mention
coming :nations (it)

17 מֵאֶרֶץ הַמֶּרְחָק וַיִּתְּנוּ עַל־עָרֵי יְהוּדָה קוֹלָם׃ כְּשֹׁמְרֵי שָׂדַי
a watch- Like their Judah the against and ,distant from
field of men .voice of cities set will land a

18 הָיוּ עָלֶיהָ מִסָּבִיב כִּי־אֹתִי מָרָתָה נְאֻם־יְהוָה׃ דַּרְכֵּךְ
Your .Jehovah says has she against because all against they
way .rebelled Me ,around her are

וּמַעֲלָלַיִךְ עָשׂוֹ אֵלֶּה לָךְ זֹאת רָעָתֵךְ כִּי מָר כִּי נָגַע עַד־
to it for (is it) for your this to these have your and
reaches ,bitter evil (is) ;you things done doings

¹⁹My bowels, my bowels! I convulse in pain. O walls of my heart! My heart is restless within me. I cannot be silent, for I have heard. O my soul, the sound of the ram's horn, the alarm of war! ²⁰Ruin on ruin has been called; for the whole land is laid waste. Suddenly my tents are laid waste, my curtains *in* a moment. ²¹How long must I see the banner *and* hear the sound of the ram's horn? ²²For My people *are* foolish. They do not know Me. They *are* stupid children, and they have no understanding. They *are* wise to do evil, but they do not know to do good. ²³I looked on the earth, and, behold, *it was* without form and void; and to the heavens, and they *had* no light. ²⁴I looked on the mountains, and, be-hold, they quaked. And all the hills were shaken. ²⁵I looked, and, behold, there was no man; and all the birds of the skies had fled. ²⁶I looked, and, behold, the fruitful place *was* a wilder-ness, and all its cities were broken down before the face of Jehovah, before His glowing anger. ²⁷For so Jehovah has said, The whole land shall be a desolation; yet I will not make a full end. ²⁸The earth shall mourn for this, and the heavens above shall grow black; because I have spoken; I have pur-posed, and I will not re-pent, nor will I turn back from it. ²⁹Every city shall flee from the sound of the horsemen and the shoot-ers of the bow. They shall go into thickets and will climb up among the rocks. All the city is aban-doned, and not a man shall live in them. ³⁰And you, O desolate one, what will you do? Though you dress with crimson, though you put on ornaments of gold; though you make

---

19
מֵעַי | מֵעַי | אוֹחִילָה קִירוֹת לִבִּי הֹמֶה־לִּי
within me / is restless / My / walls / O / writhe I / My / My / your
me / restless / !heart / of / pain in / !bowels / !bowels / .heart

לִבִּי לֹא אַחֲרִישׁ כִּי קוֹל שׁוֹפָר שָׁמַעְתְּ נַפְשִׁי תְּרוּעַת
the / my / O / ram's- the / for / can I / not / My
of alarm / ,soul / .heard / horn / of sound / ,silent be / / .heart

20
שֶׁבֶר עַל־שֶׁבֶר נִקְרָא כִּי־שֻׁדְּדָה כָּל־הָאָרֶץ
the whole / is / for / ,out call / ruin / upon / Ruin / !war
;land / devastated

21
פִּתְאֹם שֻׁדְּדוּ אֹהָלַי רֶגַע יְרִיעֹתָי עַד־מָתַי אֶרְאֶה־נֵּס
the / I must / long How / my / a (in) / my / are / suddenly
banner / see / .curtains / moment ,tents / devastated

22
אֶשְׁמְעָה קוֹל שׁוֹפָר כִּי | אֱוִיל עַמִּי אוֹתִי לֹא יָדָעוּ
they / not / Me / My / (are) For / ram's the / the / (and)
know / .people / foolish / ?horn / of sound / hear

בָּנִים סְכָלִים הֵמָּה וְלֹא נְבוֹנִים הֵמָּה חֲכָמִים הֵמָּה לְהָרַע
do to / they / wise / ;they / have / and / they / stupid children
,evil / (are) / / understanding not / (are)

23
רָאִיתִי אֶת־הָאָרֶץ וְהִנֵּה־תֹהוּ וָבֹהוּ וְאֶל־הַשָּׁמַיִם וְלֹא יָדָעוּ
and / (was it) and / the / looked I / do they / not / do to but
;void / formless / ,lo / ,earth / on / .know / good

24
רָאִיתִי הֶהָרִים וְהִנֵּה רֹעֲשִׁים וְכָל־הַגְּבָעוֹת הִתְקַלְקָלוּ
they / and / the / looked I / their (gave) and / none / the / and
,quaked / ,lo / mountains / on / light / ,heavens / to

25
רָאִיתִי וְהִנֵּה אֵין הָאָדָם וְכָל־
and / ,man / there / and / ,looked I / were / the / and
all / no was / ,lo / / .shaken / hills / all

26
עוֹף הַשָּׁמַיִם נָדָדוּ רָאִיתִי וְהִנֵּה הַכַּרְמֶל הַמִּדְבָּר וְכָל־
and / a (was) / fruitful the / and / ,looked I / had / the / and
all / ,wilderness / land / ,lo / .fled / skies / of birds

27
עָרָיו נִתְּצוּ מִפְּנֵי יְהוָה מִפְּנֵי חֲרוֹן אַפּוֹ כִּי־כֹה אָמַר
has / thus For / His / the / before / Jehovah / the at / broken / its
said / / .anger of glow / of face / / cities

יְהוָה שְׁמָמָה תִהְיֶה כָל־הָאָרֶץ וְכָלָה לֹא אֶעֱשֶׂה:
will I / not / a but / the / whole / shall / a / ,Jehovah
.make / end full / ,land / be / desolation

28
עַל־זֹאת תֶּאֱבַל הָאָרֶץ וְקָדְרוּ הַשָּׁמַיִם מִמָּעַל עַל כִּי־
because / ;above / the / grow and / the / shall / this / For
heavens / dark / ,earth / mourn

29
דִּבַּרְתִּי זַמֹּתִי וְלֹא נִחַמְתִּי וְלֹא־אָשׁוּב מִמֶּנָּה: מִקּוֹל
the / From / from / I will / nor / will I / and / have I / and
of sound / / .it / back turn / ,repent / not ,purposed / ,spoken

פָּרָשׁ וְרֹמֵה קֶשֶׁת בָּרְחָה כָּל־הָעִיר בָּאוּ בֶּעָבִים וּבַכֵּפִים
among and / into / They / .city every / shall / the / the and / horse-
rocks the / ,thickets / go shall / / flee / bow of shooters / men

30
עָזוּבָה כָּל־הָעִיר וְאֵין־יוֹשֵׁב בָּהֶן אִישׁ: וְאַתִּי שָׁדוּד
desolate O / And / a / in / shall / and / is / city the / All / go
,one / you / .man / them / live / not / ,abandoned / .up

מַה־תַּעֲשִׂי כִּי־תִלְבְּשִׁי שָׁנִי כִּי־תַעְדִּי עֲדִי־זָהָב כִּי־תִקְרְעִי
you though / gold orna- / you though / crim- / you Though / will / what
enlarge / of ments / on put / ,son / with dress / ?do you

large your eyes with paint, you beautify yourself in vain; lovers despise you; they will seek your life.
[31]for I have heard a voice like a woman in labor, the anguish as one bearing her first child, the voice of Zion's daughter gasping and spreading her palms, *saying,* Woe to me now, for my soul faints because of murderers.

CHAPTER 5

[1]Roam around in Jerusalem's streets, and see now, and know, and seek in her plazas, if you can find a man, if there is one who does justice, who seeks truth; and I will pardon her.
[2]And though they say, *As* Jehovah lives, surely they swear falsely. [3]O Jehovah, are not Your eyes for the truth? You struck them, but they felt no pain. You consumed them; they refused to take correction; they made their faces harder than rock; they have refused to return. [4]So I said, Surely they *are* poor; they *are* foolish; for they do not know the way of Jehovah, the ordinance of their God. [5]I will go up for myself, to the great men, and will speak to them. For they have known the way of Jehovah, the judgment of their God. Surely these have joined in breaking the yoke; they have torn off the bonds. [6]On account of this a lion out of the forest shall strike them; a wolf of the desert shall destroy them; a leopard is watching over their cities. Everyone who goes out from them shall be torn in pieces, because their transgressions are many; their apostasies are multiplied.
[7]Why should I pardon you for this? Your sons have forsaken Me and have sworn by *those who are* no gods. When I adjured them, they then committed adultery and gathered themselves by troops in a harlot's house. [8]They were *like* lusty, well-fed stallions in

---

1245 5315 5689 3973 3303 7723 5869 6320
בַפּוּךְ עֵינַיִךְ לַשָּׁוְא תִּתְיַפִּי מָאֲסוּ־בָךְ עֹגְבִים נַפְשֵׁךְ יְבַקֵּשׁוּ׃
will they your ,lovers you despise beautify in your with
seek life ,yourself vain ,eyes paint

6726 1323 6963 :1069 6864 8085 2470 6963
31 כִּי קוֹל כְּחוֹלָה שָׁמַעְתִּי צָרָה כְּמַבְכִּירָה קוֹל בַּת־צִיּוֹן
Zion the voice the bearing one as the have I woman a like a For
of daughter of ,child first her anguish ,heard labor in voice

2026 5315 5888 4994/188 3709 6566 3306
תִּתְיַפֵּחַ תְּפָרֵשׂ כַּפֶּיהָ אוֹי־נָא לִי כִּי־עָיְפָה נַפְשִׁי לְהֹרְגִים׃
of because my faints for to now Woe her and ,gasping
.murderers soul ,me (is) ,palms spreading

CAP. V ה

CHAPTER 5

7739 1245 3045 7200 3389 2351 7751
1 שׁוֹטְטוּ בְּחוּצוֹת יְרוּשָׁלַםִ וּרְאוּ־נָא וּדְעוּ וּבַקְשׁוּ בִרְחוֹבוֹתֶיהָ
open her in and and ,now and ,Jerusalem the in Roam
squares seek know see of streets around

530 1245 4941 6213 3426/518 376 4672 518
אִם־תִּמְצְאוּ אִישׁ אִם־יֵשׁ עֹשֶׂה מִשְׁפָּט מְבַקֵּשׁ אֱמוּנָה
,truth who ,justice who one there if ,man a can you if
seeks does is find

7650 8267 3651 559 3068/2416 5545
2 וְאֶסְלַח לָהּ׃ וְאִם חַי־יְהוָה יֹאמֵרוּ לָכֵן לַשֶּׁקֶר יִשָּׁבֵעוּ׃
they falsely surely they ,Jehovah (As) And .her will I and
.swear say lives lives ,though pardon

3615 2342/3808 5221 530 3808 5869 3068
3 יְהוָה עֵינֶיךָ הֲלוֹא לֶאֱמוּנָה הִכִּיתָה אֹתָם וְלֹא־חָלוּ כִּלִּיתָם
con- you felt they but them You faith- for (they) are Your O
;them sumed .pain not struck ?fulness not ;eyes ,Jehovah

7725 3985 5553 6440 2388 4148 3947 3985
4 מֵאֲנוּ קַחַת מוּסָר חִזְּקוּ פְנֵיהֶם מִסֶּלַע מֵאֲנוּ לָשׁוּב׃ וַאֲנִי
Then to have they than their made they cor- take to they
I .return refused ;rock faces harder ;rection refused

3068 1870 3045 3808 2973 1800 389
אָמַרְתִּי אַךְ דַּלִּים הֵם נוֹאֲלוּ כִּי לֹא יָדְעוּ דֶּרֶךְ יְהוָה
,Jehovah the do they not for are they they poor Surely ,said
of way know ,foolish (are)

1696 1419 3212 430 4941
5 מִשְׁפַּט אֱלֹהֵיהֶם׃ אֵלְכָה־לִּי אֶל־הַגְּדֹלִים וַאֲדַבְּרָה אוֹתָם
them will and great the to for will I their ordi- the
to speak men myself up go .God of nance

3162 389 430 4941 3068 1870 3045
כִּי הֵמָּה יָדְעוּ דֶּרֶךְ יְהוָה מִשְׁפַּט אֱלֹהֵיהֶם אַךְ הֵמָּה יַחְדָּו
to- they Surely their ordi- the Jehovah the have they For
gether .God of nance of way known

2061 3293 738 5221 4147 5423 5923 7605
6 שָׁבְרוּ עֹל נִתְּקוּ מוֹסֵרוֹת׃ עַל־כֵּן הִכָּם אַרְיֵה מִיַּעַר זְאֵב
wolf a from lion a will Therefore the have they the have
of forest the them smite !bonds burst ;yoke broken

2007 3318 3605 5892 5921 8245 5246 7703 6160
עֲרָבוֹת יְשָׁדְדֵם נָמֵר שֹׁקֵד עַל־עָרֵיהֶם כָּל־הַיּוֹצֵא מֵהֵנָּה
from goes who Every their over is a destroy will the
them out one .cities watching leopard ,them deserts

2063 335 4878 6105 6588 7231 2963
7 יִטָּרֵף כִּי רַבּוּ פִּשְׁעֵיהֶם עָצְמוּ מְשֻׁבוֹתֵיהֶם׃ אֵי לָזֹאת
for Why their are their are be- be will
this .apostasies numerous ;apostasies many cause torn

7650 430 3808 7650 5800 1121 5545
אֶסְלוֹחַ־לָךְ בָּנַיִךְ עֲזָבוּנִי וַיִּשָּׁבְעוּ בְּלֹא אֱלֹהִים וָאַשְׂבִּעַ
I When .gods -non by have and for- have Your ?You should I
adjured sworn Me saken sons pardon

7904 2109 5483 1413 2181 1004 5003
8 אוֹתָם וַיִּנְאָפוּ וּבֵית זוֹנָה יִתְגֹּדָדוּ׃ סוּסִים מְיֻזָּנִים מַשְׁכִּים
well-fed lusty stallions they a and they then ;them
.to thronged harlot's house ;adultery did

the morning, every one neighing after the wife of his neighbor. [9]Shall I not judge for these *things*? says Jehovah. And shall not My soul be avenged on such a nation as this?

[10]Go up on her vine rows and destroy; but do not make a full end. Take away her branches, for they *are* not Jehovah's. [11]For the house of Israel and the house of Judah have been very devious with Me, declares Jehovah. [12]They have lied against Jehovah and said, *It is* not He; and, No evil shall come on us; and, We shall not see sword or famine. [13]And the prophets shall become wind, and the word *is* not in them; so it shall be done to them. [14]So Jehovah God of hosts says this: Because you spoke this word, behold, I will make My words fire in your mouth, and this people wood; and it shall consume them. [15]Behold, I will bring a nation on you from far away, O house of Israel, declares Jehovah. It *is* an enduring nation; it *is* an ancient nation, a nation whose language you do not know, nor understand what they say. [16]Their quiver *is* as an open grave; they *are* all mighty men. [17]And they will eat up your harvest and your food; and they will eat up your sons and your daughters; they shall eat up your flocks and your herds; they shall eat up your vines and your fig-trees. One shall beat down your fortified cities with the sword, those in which you trust. [18]Yet even in those days, declares Jehovah, I will not make a full end with you.

[19]And it will be, when you shall say, Why does Jehovah our God do all these *things* to us? Then you shall answer them, Just

6485 3808 428 6670 7453 802 376 1961
9 הָיוּ אִישׁ אֶל־אֵשֶׁת רֵעֵהוּ יִצְהָלוּ׃ הַעַל־אֵלֶּה לוֹא־אֶפְקֹד
I shall not these For .neighing his wife to each they
,punish things neighbor's ;were

5315 5358 3808 2088 834 1471 3068 5002
נְאֻם־יְהוָה וְאִם בְּגוֹי אֲשֶׁר כָּזֶה לֹא תִתְנַקֵּם נַפְשִׁי׃
My take will not like that a on And ?Jehovah says
?soul vengeance ,this (is) nation

5189 5493 408 3615 7843 82 84 5927
10 עֲלוּ בְשָׁרוֹתֶיהָ וְשַׁחֵתוּ וְכָלָה אַל־תַּעֲשׂוּ הָסִירוּ נְטִישׁוֹתֶיהָ
her turn do not full but and her against Go
,branches away ;make destruction ;destroy vine-rows up

3478 1004 898 898 3068 3808
11 כִּי לוֹא לַיהוָה הֵמָּה׃ כִּי בָגוֹד בָּגְדוּ בִּי בֵּית יִשְׂרָאֵל
Israel the with have they very For they Jehovah's not for
of house Me devious been .(are)

3808 559 3068 3584 3068 5002 3063 1004
12 וּבֵית יְהוּדָה נְאֻם־יְהוָה׃ כִּחֲשׁוּ בַּיהוָה וַיֹּאמְרוּ לוֹא־הוּא
He not ,said and against have They .Jehovah says ,Judah the and
(is) Jehovah lied of house

5030 7200 3808 7450 2719 7451 5921 935 3808
13 וְלֹא־תָבוֹא עָלֵינוּ רָעָה וְחֶרֶב וְרָעָב לוֹא נִרְאֶה׃ וְהַנְּבִיאִים
the And will we not and and ;evil upon will and
prophets .see famine sword us come not

6213 369 1697 7307 1961
14 יִהְיוּ לְרוּחַ וְהַדִּבֵּר אֵין בָּהֶם כֹּה יֵעָשֶׂה לָהֶם׃ לָכֵן
Therefore to will it thus in is the and ,wind will
.them done be ;them not word become

2088 1697 1696 6635 430 3068 559 3541
כֹּה־אָמַר יְהוָה אֱלֹהֵי צְבָאוֹת יַעַן דַּבֶּרְכֶם אֶת־הַדָּבָר הַזֶּה
,this word you Because :hosts God Jehovah says thus
spoke of

398 6086 2088 5971 784 6310 1697 5414 2009
הִנְנִי נֹתֵן דְּבָרַי בְּפִיךָ לְאֵשׁ וְהָעָם הַזֶּה עֵצִים וַאֲכָלָתַם׃
will it and ,wood ,this and ,fire your in My will ,behold
.them devour people mouth words make

3068 5002 3478 1004 4801 1471 5921 935
15 הִנְנִי מֵבִיא עֲלֵיכֶם גּוֹי מִמֶּרְחָק בֵּית יִשְׂרָאֵל נְאֻם־יְהוָה
.Jehovah says ,Israel O from a you on will ,Lo
of house ,afar nation bring I

3808 3956 3045 3808 1471 1931 5769 1471 1931 386 1471
גּוֹי אֵיתָן הוּא גּוֹי מֵעוֹלָם הוּא גּוֹי לֹא־תֵדַע לְשֹׁנוֹ וְלֹא
nor whose do you not a ,(is) it of from a (is) it enduring An
,language know nation old nation nation

1368 3605 6605 6913 827 1696 4100 8085
16 תִשְׁמַע מַה־יְדַבֵּר׃ אַשְׁפָּתוֹ כְּקֶבֶר פָּתוּחַ כֻּלָּם גִּבּוֹרִים׃
mighty (are) of all an like (is) Their they what under-
.men them ;open grave quiver .say stand

6629 398 1323 1121 398 3899 7105 398
17 וְאָכַל קְצִירְךָ וְלַחְמֶךָ יֹאכְלוּ בָּנֶיךָ וּבְנוֹתֶיךָ יֹאכַל צֹאנְךָ
your will they your and your will they your and your they And
flocks devour ;daughters sons devour ;food harvest devour will

834 4013 5892 7567 8384 1612 398 1241
וּבְקָרֶךָ יֹאכַל גַּפְנְךָ וּתְאֵנָתֶךָ יְרֹשֵׁשׁ עָרֵי מִבְצָרֶיךָ אֲשֶׁר
which your cities will one your and your will they your and
fortified down beat ;trees fig vines devour ,herds

3068 5002 3117 1571 7719 2007 982
18 אַתָּה בֹּטֵחַ בָּהֵנָּה בֶּחָרֶב׃ וְגַם בַּיָּמִים הָהֵמָּה נְאֻם־יְהוָה
,Jehovah says ,those days in Yet the with those in trust you
even .sword

6213 4100 8478 559 1961 3615 6213 3808
19 לֹא־אֶעֱשֶׂה אִתְּכֶם כָּלָה׃ וְהָיָה כִּי תֹאמְרוּ תַּחַת מֶה עָשָׂה
does Why shall you when And com- a you will I not
do ,say be will it .end plete make

559 428 3605 430 3068
יְהוָה אֱלֹהֵינוּ לָנוּ אֶת־כָּל־אֵלֶּה וְאָמַרְתָּ אֲלֵיהֶם כַּאֲשֶׁר
as Just ,them to you Then these all us to our Jehovah
say ?(things) God

as you have forsaken Me, and served foreign gods in your land, so you shall serve strangers in a land *that is* not yours.
20Declare this in the house of Jacob, and cry it in Judah, saying,
21Now hear this, O foolish people, even without heart; who have eyes and do not see; who have ears, and do not hear;
22do you not fear Me? declares Jehovah. Will you not tremble before My face, that I have placed the sand *as* the boundary for the sea *by* a never-ending decree, so that it cannot cross over it? And though they toss themselves, yet they cannot prevail; though its waves roar, yet they cannot cross over it.
23But to this people there is a revolting and a rebellious heart; they have turned, and are gone.
24And they do not say in their heart, Let us now fear Jehovah our God, who gives both the former and the latter rain in its season; He keeps for us the appointed weeks of the harvest.

25Your iniquities have turned away these *things*, and your sins have withheld good from you.
26For among My people are found wicked ones; they lie in wait, as one who sets snares; they set a trap; they catch men.
27Like a cage full of birds, so their houses are full of treachery; On account of this they have become great and grown rich.
28They have become fat; they shine. Yes, they pass over the deeds of the evil; they do not plead the cause, the cause of the orphan, that they may prosper; and they do not vindicate the right of the needy.
29Shall I not visit for these things? declares Jehovah. Shall not My soul be avenged on such a nation as this?

30An astounding and horrible thing has happened in the land.
31The prophets prophesy falsely,

עֲזַבְתֶּם אוֹתִי וַתַּעַבְדוּ אֱלֹהֵי נֵכָר בְּאַרְצְכֶם כֵּן תַּעַבְדוּ
shall you serve so your in ,land foreign gods and served Me have you forsaken

20 זָרִים בְּאֶרֶץ לֹא לָכֶם׃ הַגִּידוּ זֹאת בְּבֵית יַעֲקֹב
,Jacob the in of house this Declare to .you not (belonging) a in land strangers

21 וְהַשְׁמִיעוּהָ בִיהוּדָה לֵאמֹר׃ שִׁמְעוּ־נָא זֹאת עַם־סָכָל
foolish O people ,this now Hear ,saying ,Judah in proclaim it

וְאֵין לֵב עֵינַיִם לָהֶם וְלֹא יִרְאוּ אָזְנַיִם לָהֶם וְלֹא יִשְׁמָעוּ׃
they do .hear but not to ,them ears (are) they do ;see but not to ,them eyes (are) ;heart and without

22 הַאוֹתִי לֹא־תִירָאוּ נְאֻם־יְהוָה אִם מִפָּנַי לֹא תָחִילוּ אֲשֶׁר־
that you will tremble not from face My Or .Jehovah says you Do ?fear not Me

שַׂמְתִּי חוֹל גְּבוּל לַיָּם חָק־עוֹלָם וְלֹא יַעַבְרֶנְהוּ וַיִּתְגָּעֲשׁוּ
they though fall and rise can it ;it over cross that so not eternal an ,decree the for sea the (as) boundary the sand have I placed

23 וְלֹא יוּכָלוּ וְהָמוּ גַלָּיו וְלֹא יַעַבְרֻנְהוּ׃ וְלָעָם הַזֶּה הָיָה
there is this people to But can they .it over cross yet not its waves Though roar can they .prevail yet not

24 לֵב סוֹרֵר וּמוֹרֶה סָרוּ וַיֵּלֵכוּ׃ וְלוֹא־אָמְרוּ בִלְבָבָם נִירָא
us Let fear their in heart they say do And not gone and .away they turned have rebel- ;lious and stubborn a heart

נָא אֶת־יְהוָה אֱלֹהֵינוּ הַנֹּתֵן גֶּשֶׁם יֹרֶה וּמַלְקוֹשׁ בְּעִתּוֹ
its in ;time and latter both former the rain who gives our ,God Jehovah now

25 שְׁבֻעֹת חֻקּוֹת קָצִיר יִשְׁמָר־לָנוּ׃ עֲוֺנוֹתֵיכֶם הִטּוּ־אֵלֶּה
these ,(things) have away turned iniquities Your for .us He keeps the harvest the of appointed weeks

26 וְחַטֹּאותֵיכֶם מָנְעוּ הַטּוֹב מִכֶּם׃ כִּי־נִמְצְאוּ בְעַמִּי רְשָׁעִים
wicked ;ones My among people are found For from .you good have withheld your and sins

יָשׁוּר כְּשַׁךְ יְקוּשִׁים הִצִּיבוּ מַשְׁחִית אֲנָשִׁים יִלְכֹּדוּ׃
they .catch men ;trap a set they ;fowlers the like of crouching lie they ,wait in

27 כִּכְלוּב מָלֵא עוֹף כֵּן בָּתֵּיהֶם מְלֵאִים מִרְמָה עַל־כֵּן גָּדְלוּ
have they great become there- fore ;treachery filled are with their houses so ,birds full of a Like birdcage

28 וַיַּעֲשִׁירוּ׃ שָׁמְנוּ עָשְׁתוּ גַּם עָבְרוּ דִבְרֵי־רָע דִּין לֹא־דָנוּ
they not ,plead do the cause the ;evil the of deeds pass they over Also they .shine have they ,fat become grown and .rich

29 דִּין יָתוֹם וְיַצְלִיחוּ וּמִשְׁפַּט אֶבְיוֹנִים לֹא שָׁפָטוּ׃ הַעַל־
For do they .vindicate not poor the the and of right they that prosper may the or- ,phan of cause the

אֵלֶּה לֹא־אֶפְקֹד נְאֻם־יְהוָה אִם בְּגוֹי אֲשֶׁר־כָּזֶה לֹא תִתְנַקֵּם
be shall avenged not like this that (is) a on nation Or .Jehovah says I shall ?punish not these things

30
31 נַפְשִׁי׃ שַׁמָּה וְשַׁעֲרוּרָה נִהְיְתָה בָּאָרֶץ׃ הַנְּבִאִים
The prophets the in .land has happened horrible and thing An appalling My ?soul

and the priests bear rule by their hands; and My people love *it* so. And what will you do at the end of it?

CHAPTER 6

[1]O sons of Benjamin, take refuge to flee out of the midst of Jerusalem. And blow the ram's horn in Tekoa; and set up a signal over Beth-haccerem. For evil appears out of the north, and great destruction. [2]I will destroy the daughter of Zion, the beautiful and tender one. [3]The shepherds with their flocks shall come to her; they shall pitch tents on her all around. They shall each one feed *in* his hand. [4]Consecrate war against her; rise up and let us go up at noon. Woe to us! For the day wanes; for the shadows of the evening are stretched out. [5]Rise up and let us go up by night, and let us destroy her palaces.

[6]For so Jehovah of hosts has said, Cut down her trees and pour out a mound against Jerusalem. She *is* the city to be visited; in her midst *is* oppression, all of her. [7]As a cistern keeps fresh its waters, so she keeps fresh her evil. Violence and destruction are heard in her; sickness and wounds *are* continually before My face. [8]O Jerusalem, be taught, lest My soul be alienated from you; lest I make you a ruin, a land not inhabited.

[9]So says Jehovah of hosts, they shall thoroughly glean the remnant of Israel like a vine. Turn back your hand, as a grape gatherer over the tendrils. [10]To whom shall I speak and give warning, that they may hear? Behold, their ear *is* not circumcised and they

157 5971 :3027 7287 3548 8267 5012
נבאו בשקר והכהנים ירדו על־ידיהם ועמי אהבו כן
.so love (it) My people and ,hands their own according to rule the priests and ,falsely prophesy

319 6213 4100
ומה־תעשו לאחריתה׃
?it of end the at will do they But what

CAP. VI ו

CHAPTER 6

1 7782 8628 8620 :3389 7130 1144 1121 5756
העזו ׀ בני בנימן מקרב ירושלם ובתקוע תקעו שופר
ram's the blow in And .Jerusalem the from ,Benjamin O Take
horn Tekoa of midst of sons ,refuge

6828 8259 7451 4864 5375 3754 1004
ועל־בית הכרם שאו משאת כי רעה נשקפה מצפון
the from looks evil for ;signal a raise haccerem Beth- and
,north down over

2
3 6726 1004 1820 6026 5116 1419 7667
ושבר גדול׃ הנוה והמענגה דמיתי בת־ציון׃ אליה
her To .Zion daugh- the will I delicate and The .great a even
of ter ,destroy one beautiful shattering

376 7462 5439 168 8628 5739 7462 935
יבאו רעים ועדריהם תקעו עליה אהלים סביב רעו איש
each They all tents upon shall they their with the shall
man feed shall .around her pitch ;flock shepherds come

4 188 6672 5927 6965 4421 6942 3027
את־ידו׃ קדשו עליה מלחמה קומו ונעלה בצהרים אוי
Woe at let and ,arise ;war against Consecrate his (in)
.noon up go us her .hand

5 5927 6965 6153 6752 5186 3117 6437
לנו כי־פנה היום כי־ינטו צללי־ערב׃ קומו ונעלה
let and Arise .evening the are for ;day the declines for to
up go us of shadows out stretched ,us

6 3068 559 3541 759 7843 3915
בלילה ונשחיתה ארמנותיה׃ כי כה אמר יהוה
Jehovah has thus For .palaces her and by
of said destroy night

5892 5550 3389 8210 6097 3772 :6635
צבאות כרתו עצה ושפכו על־ירושלם סללה היא העיר
the She siege a Jerusalem against and her Cut ,hosts
city (is) ;mound pour trees down

7 935 6979 4325 6979 7130 6233 3605 6485
הפקד כלה עשק בקרבה׃ כהקיר בור מימיה כן הקרה
keeps she so its a keeps As her in (is) of all be to
fresh ,waters cistern fresh .midst oppression her ;punished

4347 2483 8548 6440 8085 7701 2555 7451
רעתה חמס ושד ישמע בה על־פני תמיד חלי ומכה׃
and sickness (are) my before in are and Violence her
.wounds continually face ;her heard destruction .evilness

8 :8077 7760 6435 5315 3363 6435 :3389 3256
הוסרי ירושלם פן־תקע נפשי ממך פן־אשימך שממה
a make I lest from My be lest O Be
desolation you ;you soul alienated .Jerusalem ,taught

9 5953 6635 3068 559 3541 3427 3808 776
ארץ לוא נושבה׃ כה אמר יהוה צבאות עולל
thoroughly ,hosts Jehovah says Thus .inhabited not a
of land

1219 3027 7725 3478 7611 1612 5953
יעוללו כגפן שארית ישראל השב ידך כבוצר על־
over grape a as your bring ;Israel rem- the a as will they
gatherer hand back of nant vine glean

10 6189 2009 8085 5749 1696 4310 5552
סלסלות׃ על־מי אדברה ואעידה וישמעו הנה ערלה
un- (is) ,Behold they that give and I shall whom To the
circumcised ?hear may warning speak .tendrils

cannot listen. Behold, the word of Jehovah is a reproach to them. They have no delight in it. 11 And I am full of the fury of Jehovah; I am weary with holding in. Pour it out on the child in the street, and on the circle of the young men together. For even the husband with the wife shall be taken, the elder with fullness of days. 12 And their houses shall be turned to others, fields and wives together. For I will stretch out My hand on the inhabitants of the land, declares Jehovah. 13 For everyone from the least of them even to the greatest of them cuts off a profit; and from the prophet even to the priest everyone deals falsely. 14 They have also healed the break of My people slightly, saying, Peace, peace; when there is no peace. 15 Were they ashamed when they made an abomination? They were not at all ashamed, nor did they know to blush. So they shall fall among those who fall. At the time I visit them, they shall be cast down, says Jehovah. 16 So says Jehovah, Stand by the ways and see; and ask for the old paths where the good way *is*, and walk in it; and you shall find rest for your souls. But they said, We will not walk *in it*.

17 Also I set watchmen over you, *saying*, Listen to the sound of the ram's horn. But they said, We will not listen. 18 So hear, O nations; and know, O congregation, that which is *coming* on them. 19 Hear, O earth; behold, I will bring evil on this people, the fruit of their thoughts. For they have not listened to My words, and My law, they also rejected it. 20 Why *is* to Me, frankincense coming from

אָזְנָם וְלֹא יוּכְלוּ לְהַקְשִׁיב הִנֵּה דְבַר־יְהוָה הָיָה לָהֶם
to them is Jehovah the word of ,Behold .listen to are they able and not their ,ear

11 לְחֶרְפָּה לֹא יַחְפְּצוּ־בוֹ׃ וְאֵת חֲמַת יְהוָה ׀ מָלֵאתִי נִלְאֵיתִי
am I tired of am I ;full Jehovah the wrath of Therefore with .it in have they delight no a ,reproach

הָכִיל שְׁפֹךְ עַל־עוֹלָל בַּחוּץ וְעַל סוֹד בַּחוּרִים יַחְדָּו כִּי־
for ;together young the men the circle of and on the in ,street the child on Pour out (it) holding .in (it)

12 גַּם־אִישׁ עִם־אִשָּׁה יִלָּכֵדוּ זָקֵן עִם־מְלֵא יָמִים׃ וְנָסַבּוּ
will And turned be .days fullness of with the elder be shall ,taken the wife and the husband even

בָתֵּיהֶם לַאֲחֵרִים שָׂדוֹת וְנָשִׁים יַחְדָּו כִּי־אַטֶּה אֶת־יָדִי
My hand will I out stretch for ;together and wives fields ,others to their house

13 עַל־יֹשְׁבֵי הָאָרֶץ נְאֻם־יְהוָה׃ כִּי מִקְּטַנָּם וְעַד־גְּדוֹלָם
their greatest even to their least from For .Jehovah says the ,land the of inhabitants against

כֻּלּוֹ בֹּצֵעַ בָּצַע וּמִנָּבִיא וְעַד־כֹּהֵן כֻּלּוֹ עֹשֶׂה שָּׁקֶר׃
.falsely deals every one the priest even to from and prophet the a ;profit cuts off every one

14 וַיְרַפְּאוּ אֶת־שֶׁבֶר עַמִּי עַל־נְקַלָּה לֵאמֹר שָׁלוֹם ׀ שָׁלוֹם
;peace ,Peace ,saying ,lightly My people fracture of the they Also healed have

15 וְאֵין שָׁלוֹם׃ הֹבִשׁוּ כִּי־תוֹעֵבָה עָשׂוּ גַּם־בּוֹשׁ לֹא־יֵבוֹשׁוּ
were They ;ashamed not at all even they ?made an abomination when they Were ashamed .peace no is there when

גַּם־הַכְלִים לֹא יָדָעוּ לָכֵן יִפְּלוּ בַנֹּפְלִים בְּעֵת־פְּקַדְתִּים
punish I them the at time those among ;fall who they fall shall So they .know do not blush to also

16 יִכָּשְׁלוּ אָמַר יְהוָה׃ כֹּה אָמַר יְהוָה עִמְדוּ עַל־דְּרָכִים
the ways by Stand ,Jehovah says Thus .Jehovah says be will they ,ashamed

וּרְאוּ וְשַׁאֲלוּ ׀ לִנְתִבוֹת עוֹלָם אֵי־זֶה דֶרֶךְ הַטּוֹב וּלְכוּ־בָהּ
in ;it and walk the ,good way where (is) ,ancient the for paths ask and and ,see

17 וּמִצְאוּ מַרְגּוֹעַ לְנַפְשְׁכֶם וַיֹּאמְרוּ לֹא נֵלֵךְ׃ וַהֲקִמֹתִי
I Also set will we .(it in) walk Not they ,said But your for .souls rest a you and will find

עֲלֵיכֶם צֹפִים הַקְשִׁיבוּ לְקוֹל שׁוֹפָר וַיֹּאמְרוּ לֹא נַקְשִׁיב׃
will We ,listen not they But ,said ram's the ,horn the to of sound ,(saying) Listen watch- ,men over you

18 19 לָכֵן שִׁמְעוּ הַגּוֹיִם וּדְעִי עֵדָה אֶת־אֲשֶׁר־בָּם׃ שִׁמְעִי הָאָרֶץ
O ;earth ,Hear on .them what (coming is) con- O ,gregation and ,know O ,nations ,hear there- fore

הִנֵּה אָנֹכִי מֵבִיא רָעָה אֶל־הָעָם הַזֶּה פְּרִי מַחְשְׁבוֹתָם כִּי
for their ;thoughts the of fruit ,this people on evil will bring I ,Behold

20 עַל־דְּבָרַי לֹא הִקְשִׁיבוּ וְתוֹרָתִי וַיִּמְאֲסוּ־בָהּ׃ לָמָּה־זֶּה לִי
to Me this Why .it they also rejected My and law have they ,listened not My words to

Sheba, and the good cane from a far land? Your burnt offerings *are* not for acceptance, nor *are* your sacrifices sweet to Me. 21 So Jehovah says this, Behold, I am giving stumbling-blocks to this people; and the fathers and the sons together shall stumble on them; *a* neighbor and his friend shall perish. 22 So says Jehovah, Behold, a people comes from the north country; and a great nation shall be stirred from the sides of the earth. 23 They shall lay hold on bow and javelin; they are cruel and have no mercy. Their voice roars like the sea; and they ride on horses, arrayed like a man for the battle against you, O daughter of Zion. 24 We have heard the rumor of it. Our hands have dropped down; anguish has seized us, pain like a travailing woman. 25 Do not go out into the field, or walk by the way; because of the sword of the enemy, *and* terror from every side.

26 O daughter of my people, put on sackcloth and roll in ashes. Make mourning for yourself, *as for* an only son, most bitter mourning—for the ravager shall suddenly come on us. 27 I have set you up *as* assayer, an examiner among My people, that you may know, and examine their way. 28 They are all rebellious revolters, goers of slander. All of them *are as* bronze and iron; they are corrupters. 29 The bellows blow; the lead is consumed from the fire; the refiner refines in vain; for the evil is not separated. 30 *Men* will call them reprobate silver, for Jehovah has rejected them.

5930 4801 776 2896 7070 935 7614 3828
לְבוֹנָה מִשְּׁבָא תָבוֹא וְקָנֶה הַטּוֹב מֵאֶרֶץ מֶרְחָק עֹלוֹתֵיכֶם
burnt Your ?far a from good the and does from frankin-
offerings land cane ,come Sheba cense

21 3068 559 3651 6149 3808 2077 7522 3808
לֹא לְרָצוֹן וְזִבְחֵיכֶם לֹא־עָרְבוּ לִי׃ לָכֵן כֹּה אָמַר יְהוָה
,Jehovah says thus Therefore to are not your and ac- for (are)
.Me pleasing sacrifices ,ceptance not

1121 1 3782 4383 2088 5971 5414 2009
הִנְנִי נֹתֵן אֶל־הָעָם הַזֶּה מִכְשֹׁלִים וְכָשְׁלוּ בָם אָבוֹת וּבָנִים
and fathers on will and stumbling this people to am ,Behold
sons them stumble ,blocks giving I

22 5971 2009 3068 559 6 7453 7934 3162
יַחְדָּו שָׁכֵן וְרֵעוֹ יֹאבֵדוּ׃ כֹּה אָמַר יְהוָה הִנֵּה עַם
a ,Behold ,Jehovah says Thus shall his and neigh- to-
people .perish friend bor ;gether

23 7198 776 3411 5782 1419 1471 6828 776 935
בָּא מֵאֶרֶץ צָפוֹן וְגוֹי גָּדוֹל יֵעוֹר מִיַּרְכְּתֵי־אָרֶץ׃ קֶשֶׁת
Bow the the from be will great a and the from come
.earth of parts remote up stirred nation ,north country

1993 3220 6963 7355 3808 394 2388 3591
וְכִידוֹן יַחֲזִיקוּ אַכְזָרִי הוּא וְלֹא יְרַחֵמוּ קוֹלָם כַּיָּם יֶהֱמֶה
;roars the like Their have and they cruel will they and
sea voice .mercy no (are) ,on hold lay javelin

1323 4421 376 6186 7392 5483
וְעַל־סוּסִים יִרְכָּבוּ עָרוּךְ כְּאִישׁ לַמִּלְחָמָה עָלַיִךְ בַּת־
daugh- O against the for a as arrayed they horses and
of ter you battle man ,ride on

24 2427 2388 6864 3027 7503 8089 8085 6726
צִיּוֹן׃ שָׁמַעְנוּ אֶת־שָׁמְעוֹ רָפוּ יָדֵינוּ צָרָה הֶחֱזִקַתְנוּ חִיל
pain seized has anguish our have ,report its have We !Zion
,us ;hands dropped heard

25 2719 1980 408 1870 7704 3318 408 3205
כַּיּוֹלֵדָה׃ אַל־תֵּצְאוּ הַשָּׂדֶה וּבַדֶּרֶךְ אַל־תֵּלֵכוּ כִּי חֶרֶב
the because do not by or the go do Not tra- a like
sword of ,walk way the ,field into out .woman vailing

26 665 6428 8242/2296 5971 1004 5439 4032 341
לְאֹיֵב מָגוֹר מִסָּבִיב׃ בַּת־עַמִּי חִגְרִי־שָׂק וְהִתְפַּלְּשִׁי בָאֵפֶר
the in roll and sack- put my daugh- O all from (and) the of
;ashes cloth on ,people of ter .around terror ,enemy

935 6597 8653 4553 6213 3173 60
אֵבֶל יָחִיד עֲשִׂי לָךְ מִסְפַּד תַּמְרוּרִים כִּי פִתְאֹם יָבֹא
shall suddenly for ,bitterness mourning for make only an the
come of ,yourself (son) of mourning

27 974 3045 4013 5971 5414 969 7703
הַשֹּׁדֵד עָלֵינוּ׃ בָּחוֹן נְתַתִּיךָ בְעַמִּי מִבְצָר וְתֵדַע וּבָחַנְתָּ
and you that a (and) My among have I an upon the
test know may ,tester people you set assayer .us destroyer

28 1270 5178 7400 1980 5637 5493 3605 1870
אֶת־דַּרְכָּם׃ כֻּלָּם סָרֵי סוֹרְרִים הֹלְכֵי רָכִיל נְחֹשֶׁת וּבַרְזֶל
iron and Bronze .slander goers rebellious the (are) of All their
(are) of ,ones of revolters them .way

29 7723 5777 8552 800 4647 2787 7843 3605
כֻּלָּם מַשְׁחִיתִים הֵמָּה׃ נָחַר מַפֻּחַ מֵאֵשׁ תַּם עֹפָרֶת לַשָּׁוְא
in the comes from The blow they corrupters of all
vain ;lead whole fire the bellows .(are) ;them

30 7121 3988 3701 5423 3808 7451 6884 6884
צָרַף צָרוֹף וְרָעִים לֹא נִתָּקוּ׃ כֶּסֶף נִמְאָס קָרְאוּ לָהֶם כִּי־
for ,them they Refuse silver is not the for re- he
call separated evil ,fining refines

3068 3973
מָאַס יְהוָה בָּהֶם׃
.them Jehovah has
rejected

CAP. VII

CHAPTER 7

CHAPTER 7

[1]The word that was to Jeremiah from Jehovah, saying, [2]Stand in the gate of the house of Jehovah and call out this word there, and say, Hear the word of Jehovah, all Judah entering at these gates to worship Jehovah. [3]So says Jehovah of hosts, the God of Israel, Amend your ways and your doings, and I will let you dwell in this place. [4]Do not trust yourself to lying words, saying, The temple of Jehovah! The temple of Jehovah! This *is* the temple of Jehovah!

[5]For if you thoroughly amend your ways and your doings; if you truly practice justice between a man and his neighbor; [6]*if* you do not oppress the stranger, the orphan, and the widow; and do not shed innocent blood in this place; or walk after other gods to your hurt; [7]then I will let you dwell in this place, in the land that I gave to your fathers, from forever and to forever.

[8]Behold, you trust for yourself on lying words without being of use. [9]Will you steal, murder, and commit adultery, and swear falsely, and burn incense to Baal, and walk after other gods whom you do not know; [10]and *then* come and stand before Me in this house on which My name is called, and say, We are delivered in order to do all

5975 559 3068 341:4 1961 834 1697
1 2 הַדָּבָר אֲשֶׁר־הָיָה אֶל־יִרְמְיָהוּ מֵאֵת יְהוָה לֵאמֹר׃ עֲמֹד
Stand ,saying ,Jehovah from Jeremiah to came that The word

559 2088 1697 8033 7121 3068 1004 8179
בְּשַׁעַר בֵּית יְהוָה וְקָרָאתָ שָּׁם אֶת־הַדָּבָר הַזֶּה וְאָמַרְתָּ
,say and ,this word there and Jehovah's house the in
out call of gate

428 8179 935 3063 3605 3068 1697 8085
שִׁמְעוּ דְבַר־יְהוָה כָּל־יְהוּדָה הַבָּאִים בַּשְּׁעָרִים הָאֵלֶּה
these gates at enter who ,Judah all ,Jehovah the Hear
in of word

3478 430 6635 3068 559 3068 7812
3 לְהִשְׁתַּחֲוֹת לַיהוָה׃ כֹּה־אָמַר יְהוָה צְבָאוֹת אֱלֹהֵי יִשְׂרָאֵל
,Israel the ,hosts Jehovah says Thus .Jehovah to
of God of worship

4725 7931 4611 1870 3190
הֵיטִיבוּ דַרְכֵיכֶם וּמַעַלְלֵיכֶם וַאֲשַׁכְּנָה אֶתְכֶם בַּמָּקוֹם
place in you will I and your and ways your Amend
dwell let ,doings

1964 559 8267 1697 982 408 2088
4 הַזֶּה׃ אַל־תִּבְטְחוּ לָכֶם אֶל־דִּבְרֵי הַשֶּׁקֶר לֵאמֹר הֵיכַל
The ,saying the words to yourself Do not .this
of temple ,lie of trust

3190 518 3068 1964 3:068 1964 3068
5 יְהוָה הֵיכַל יְהוָה הֵיכַל יְהוָה הֵמָּה׃ כִּי אִם־הֵיטֵיב
thoroughly if For that Jehovah the ,Jehovah the ,Jehovah
.(is) of temple of temple

6213 6213 518 4611 1870 3190
תֵּיטִיבוּ אֶת־דַּרְכֵיכֶם וְאֶת־מַעַלְלֵיכֶם אִם־עָשׂוֹ תַעֲשׂוּ
you indeed if your and your you
practice ;doings ways amend

6213 3808 490 3490 1616 7453 996 376 996 4941
6 מִשְׁפָּט בֵּין אִישׁ וּבֵין רֵעֵהוּ׃ גֵּר יָתוֹם וְאַלְמָנָה לֹא תַעֲשֹׁקוּ
do you not the and the the (if) his and a be- justice
,oppress widow ,orphan ,stranger ;neighbor man tween

312 430 310 2088 4725 8210 408 53:55 1818
וְדָם נָקִי אַל־תִּשְׁפְּכוּ בַּמָּקוֹם הַזֶּה וְאַחֲרֵי אֱלֹהִים אֲחֵרִים
other gods or ,this place in do not inno- and
after shed cent blood

2088 4725 7931 7451 1980 3808
7 לֹא תֵלְכוּ לְרַע לָכֶם׃ וְשִׁכַּנְתִּי אֶתְכֶם בַּמָּקוֹם הַזֶּה
,this place in you will I then —your to do you not
dwell let hurt go

5769 5704 5769 1 5414 834 776
בָּאָרֶץ אֲשֶׁר נָתַתִּי לַאֲבוֹתֵיכֶם לְמִן־עוֹלָם וְעַד־עוֹלָם׃
.forever even forever from your to I , that the in
to ,fathers gave land

3276 1097 8267 1697 982 2009
8 הִנֵּה אַתֶּם בֹּטְחִים לָכֶם עַל־דִּבְרֵי הַשָּׁקֶר לְבִלְתִּי הוֹעִיל׃
of being without the words upon for are you ,Behold
.use lie of yourself trusting

1168 6999 8267 7650 50:03 7523 1589
9 הֲגָנֹב ׀ רָצֹחַ וְנָאֹף וְהִשָּׁבֵעַ לַשֶּׁקֶר וְקַטֵּר לַבָּעַל וְהָלֹךְ
and ,Baal to burn and ,falsely and com- and murder you Will
walk incense swear ,adultery mit ,steal

5975 935 3045 3808 834 312 430 310
10 אַחֲרֵי אֱלֹהִים אֲחֵרִים אֲשֶׁר לֹא־יְדַעְתֶּם׃ וּבָאתֶם וַעֲמַדְתֶּם
and then and do you not that other gods after
stand come ,know

53•37 559 8034 7121 834 2088 1004 64:40
לְפָנַי בַּבַּיִת הַזֶּה אֲשֶׁר נִקְרָא־שְׁמִי עָלָיו וַאֲמַרְתֶּם נִצַּלְנוּ
are We ,say and upon My been has which this in before
delivered it name called house Me

those detestable things. [11]Has this house on which My name is called become a den of violent ones in your eyes? Behold, even I have seen, declares Jehovah. [12]But go now to My place which *was* in Shiloh, where I made My name dwell at the first, and see what I did to it for the wickedness of My people Israel. [13]And now, because you have done all these works, says Jehovah; and I spoke to you, rising up early and speaking, but you did not hear; yea, I called you, but you did not answer. [14]And I will do to the house on which My name is called, in which you are trusting, and to the place which I gave to you and to your fathers, as I have done to Shiloh. [15]And I will cast you out from My face, as I cast out all your brothers, all the seed of Ephraim. [16]And you, do not pray for this people; do not lift up cry or prayer for them; do not intercede with Me, for I do not hear you.

[17]Do you not see what they are doing in the cities of Judah, and in the streets of Jerusalem? [18]The sons gather wood, and the fathers kindle the fire, and the women knead dough, to make cakes to the queen of heaven, and to pour out drink offerings to other gods, that they may provoke Me. [19]Do they provoke Me, says Jehovah? *Is it* not themselves, to the

---

11 למען עשות את כל־התועבת האלה׃ המערת פרצים
6530 4631 428 8441 3605 6213 4616
violent ones | of den a | ?those | abominations all | do to | in order

היה הבית הזה אשר־נקרא שמי־עליו בעיניכם גם אנכי
1571 5869 8034 7121 834 2088 1004 1961
I | even | your in ?eyes | upon it | My name | been has called | which | this | house | Has become

12 הנה ראיתי נאם־יהוה׃ כי לכו־נא אל־מקומי אשר
834 4725 4994 3212 3068 5002 7200 2009
which (was) | My place | to | now | go | But | .Jehovah | says | have ,seen | Behold

בשילו אשר שכנתי שמי שם בראשונה וראו את אשר־
834 7200 7223 8033 8034 7931 834 7887
what | and see | the at ,first | there | My name | made I dwell | where | in ,Shiloh

13 עשיתי לו מפני רעת עמי ישראל׃ ועתה יען עשותכם
6213 3282 6258 3478 5971 7451 6213
have you done | because | And ,now | .Israel | My people | the of evil | because of | to it | did I

את־כל־המעשים האלה נאם־יהוה ואדבר אליכם השכם
7925 1696 3068 5002 428 4639 3605
up rising early | ,you to | I and spoke | ,Jehovah says | ,these | works | all

14 ודבר ולא שמעתם ואקרא אתכם ולא עניתם׃ ועשיתי
6213 6030 3808 7121 8085 3808 1696
I therefore do will | did you —answer | but not | ,you | I and called | did you —hear | but not | and ,speaking

לבית ׀ אשר נקרא־שמי עליו אשר אתם בטחים בו
982 834 5921 8034 7121 834 1004
in ,it | are trusting | you | which | upon ,it | My name | been has called | which | the to house

ולמקום אשר־נתתי לכם ולאבותיכם כאשר עשיתי
6213 5414 834 4725
have I done | as | your to and ,fathers | you to | gave I | which | the to and place

15 לשלו׃ והשלכתי אתכם מעל פני כאשר השלכתי את־
7993 6440 7993 7887
cast I away | as | My face | from | you | cast will I And away | to .Shiloh

16 כל־אחיכם את כל־זרע אפרים׃ ואתה אל־תתפלל ׀
6419 408 669 2233 3605 251 3605
pray do | not | ,you And | .Ephraim | seed of | the whole | your ,brothers | all

בעד־העם הזה ואל־תשא בעדם רנה ותפלה ואל־תפגע־
6293 408 8605 7440 1157 5375 408 2088 5971 1157
do intercede | and not | or ,prayer | cry | for them | lift do up | and not | ;this | people | for

17 בי כי־אינני שמע אתך׃ האינך ראה מה המה עשים
6213 4100 7200 369 8085 369
are doing | they | what | Do see | you not | .you | do hear | I not | for | with ,Me

18 בערי יהודה ובחצות ירושלם׃ הבנים מלקטים עצים
6086 3950 1121 3389 2351 3063 5892
wood | gather | The sons | ?Jerusalem | the in and of streets | Judah | the in of cities

והאבות מבערים את־האש והנשים לשות בצק לעשות
6213 1217 3888 802 784 1197 1
to make | dough | knead | the and women | the ,fire | kindle | the and fathers

כונים למלכת השמים והסך נסכים לאלהים אחרים
312 430 5262 5258 8064 4446 3561
,other | gods to | drink offerings | to and out pour | ,heaven | the for of queen | cakes

19 למען הכעסני׃ האתי הם מכעסים נאם־יהוה הלוא
3808 3068 5002 3707 3707
(it Is) not | Jehovah | says | Do ,vex | they | Me | may they .Me vex | that

shame of their own faces? [20]So the Lord Jehovah says this: Behold, My anger and My fury will be poured out on this place; on man and on animal; and on the trees of the field; and on the fruit of the ground. And it will burn, and will not be put out.

[21]So says Jehovah of hosts, the God of Israel. Add your burnt offerings to your sacrifices, and eat flesh. [22]For I did not speak to your fathers, nor command them in the day that I brought them out from the land of Egypt, concerning matters of burnt offerings and sacrifices. [23]But I commanded them this thing, saying, Obey My voice, and I will be your God, and you shall be My people. Also, Walk in all the ways that I have commanded you, so that it may be well with you. [24]But they did not listen nor bow their ear. But *they* walked in *their own* plans, in the stubbornness of their evil heart, and went backward, and not forward. [25]Since the day that your fathers came out of the land of Egypt until this day I have even sent to you all My servants, the prophets, daily rising up early, and sending. [26]Yet they did not listen to Me nor bow their ear, but stiffened their neck; they did more evil than their fathers. [27]And you shall speak all these words to them, but they will not listen to you. And you will call to them, but they will not answer you. [28]But you shall say to them, This *is* the nation that does not obey

20 אֹתָם לְמַעַן בֹּשֶׁת פְּנֵיהֶם׃ לָכֵן כֹּה־אָמַר ׀ אֲדֹנָי
the Lord says thus Therefore own their faces? the of shame to themselves
יְהוִה הִנֵּה אַפִּי וַחֲמָתִי נִתֶּכֶת אֶל־הַמָּקוֹם הַזֶּה עַל־הָאָדָם
man on ,this place on be will out poured My and wrath My ,Behold anger Jehovah
וְעַל־הַבְּהֵמָה וְעַל־עֵץ הַשָּׂדֶה וְעַל־פְּרִי הָאֲדָמָה וּבָעֲרָה
it And burn will the ground the of fruit and on the ;field the of trees and on ;animal and on
21 וְלֹא תִכְבֶּה׃ כֹּה אָמַר יְהוָה צְבָאוֹת אֱלֹהֵי יִשְׂרָאֵל
,Israel the of God hosts Jehovah of says Thus be quenched and not
22 עֹלוֹתֵיכֶם סְפוּ עַל־זִבְחֵיכֶם וְאִכְלוּ בָשָׂר׃ כִּי לֹא־דִבַּרְתִּי
did I speak not For .flesh eat and your sacrifices to Add burnt your .offerings
אֶת־אֲבוֹתֵיכֶם וְלֹא צִוִּיתִים בְּיוֹם הוֹצִיא אוֹתָם מֵאֶרֶץ
the from of land them brought I out the in day command them nor your ,fathers with
23 מִצְרָיִם עַל־דִּבְרֵי עוֹלָה וָזָבַח׃ כִּי אִם־אֶת־הַדָּבָר הַזֶּה
this thing But or .sacrifices burnt offering the about of matters ,Egypt
צִוִּיתִי אוֹתָם לֵאמֹר שִׁמְעוּ בְקוֹלִי וְהָיִיתִי לָכֶם לֵאלֹהִים
,God for to you I and be will My voice Obey ,saying ,them com- I manded
וְאַתֶּם תִּהְיוּ־לִי לְעָם וַהֲלַכְתֶּם בְּכָל־הַדֶּרֶךְ אֲשֶׁר אֲצַוֶּה
have I commanded that the way in all ,and Walk a for ,people to Me will be and you
24 אֶתְכֶם לְמַעַן יִיטַב לָכֶם׃ וְלֹא שָׁמְעוּ וְלֹא־הִטּוּ אֶת־אָזְנָם
their ,ear incline nor did they listen But not with .you may it well be so that ,you
וַיֵּלְכוּ בְּמֹעֵצוֹת בִּשְׁרִרוּת לִבָּם הָרָע וַיִּהְיוּ לְאָחוֹר וְלֹא
and not back- ward they and went ,evil their heart the in of stubbornness (their) in plans (own) but walked
25 לְפָנִים׃ לְמִן־הַיּוֹם אֲשֶׁר יָצְאוּ אֲבוֹתֵיכֶם מֵאֶרֶץ מִצְרַיִם
Egypt the out of land your fathers came out that the Since day .forward
עַד הַיּוֹם הַזֶּה וָאֶשְׁלַח אֲלֵיכֶם אֶת־כָּל־עֲבָדַי הַנְּבִיאִים
the ,prophets My servants all to you have I sent even ,this day until
26 יוֹם הַשְׁכֵּם וְשָׁלֹחַ׃ וְלוֹא שָׁמְעוּ אֵלַי וְלֹא הִטּוּ אֶת־אָזְנָם
their ,ear incline nor to ,Me they listened Yet not and .sending up rising early daily
27 וַיַּקְשׁוּ אֶת־עָרְפָּם הֵרֵעוּ מֵאֲבוֹתָם׃ וְדִבַּרְתָּ אֲלֵיהֶם אֶת־
them to you So shall speak their than .fathers did they more evil their ;neck stif- fened but
כָּל־הַדְּבָרִים הָאֵלֶּה וְלֹא יִשְׁמְעוּ אֵלֶיךָ וְקָרָאתָ אֲלֵיהֶם
,them to you And will call to .you will they listen but not ,these words all
28 וְלֹא יַעֲנוּכָה׃ וְאָמַרְתָּ אֲלֵיהֶם זֶה הַגּוֹי אֲשֶׁר לוֹא־שָׁמְעוּ
does obey not which the nation This (is) ,them to you But shall say will they .you answer but not

the voice of Jehovah their God, nor receive instruction. Truth has perished, and it is cut off from their mouth. [29]Cut off and throw away your crown. And take up a dirge on the heights. For Jehovah has rejected and forsaken the generation of His wrath. [30]For the sons of Judah have done evil in My eyes, says Jehovah. They have set their idols in the house on which is called My name, in order to defile it. [31]They have built the high places of Tophet, which is in the valley of the son of Hinnom, to burn their sons and their daughters in the fire; which I did not command, nor did it come into My heart.

[32]So, behold, the days come, declares Jehovah, when it shall no more be called Tophet, or the valley of the son of Hinnom, but the Valley of Slaughter. For they shall bury in Tophet, from lack of a place. [33]And the bodies of this people shall be food for the birds of the heavens, and for the beasts of the earth; and no one shall frighten *them* away. [34]Then I will cause the voice of gladness to cease from the cities of Judah, and from the streets of Jerusalem; even the voice of joy, and the voice of the bridegroom, and the voice of the bride. For the land shall become a waste.

530 6 4148 3947 38 08 430 3068 6963
בְּקוֹל יְהוָה אֱלֹהָיו וְלֹא לָקְחוּ מוּסָר אָבְדָה הָאֱמוּנָה
truth has ;instruction receive nor their Jehovah the
perished ,God of voice

29 5375 79 93 5145 1494 6310 3772
וְנִכְרְתָה מִפִּיהֶם׃ גָּזִּי נִזְרֵךְ וְהַשְׁלִיכִי וּשְׂאִי עַל־
on and throw and your Cut their from is it and
up take ,away (it) crown off .mouth off cut

30 5678 1755 5 203 3068 3973 7015 8205
שְׁפָיִם קִינָה כִּי מָאַס יְהוָה וַיִּטֹּשׁ אֶת־דּוֹר עֶבְרָתוֹ׃ כִּי־
For His gen- the and Jehovah has For a the
wrath of eration forsaken rejected .dirge heights

8251 7760 3068 5002 5869 7451 3063 1121 6213
עָשׂוּ בְנֵי־יְהוּדָה הָרַע בְּעֵינַי נְאֻם־יְהוָה שָׂמוּ שִׁקּוּצֵיהֶם
abomin- their They ;Jehovah says My in evil Judah the have
idols able set have ,eyes of sons done

31 8612 1116 1129 2930 5921 8034 7121 834 1004
בַּבַּיִת אֲשֶׁר־נִקְרָא־שְׁמִי עָלָיו לְטַמְּאוֹ׃ וּבָנוּ בָּמוֹת הַתֹּפֶת
Tophet high the They defile to upon My been has which the in
of places built have .it ,it name called house

784 1323 1121 8313 20 11 1121 1516 834
אֲשֶׁר בְּגֵיא בֶן־הִנֹּם לִשְׂרֹף אֶת־בְּנֵיהֶם וְאֶת־בְּנֹתֵיהֶם בָּאֵשׁ
the in their and their burn to Hinnom the the in which
;fire daughters sons of son of valley (is)

32 3117 2009 3820 38 08 6680 38 08 834
אֲשֶׁר לֹא צִוִּיתִי וְלֹא עָלְתָה עַל־לִבִּי׃ לָכֵן הִנֵּה־יָמִים
the ,behold ,Therefore My into it did nor did I not which
days .heart come ,command

2011 1121 8612 5750 559 3808 3068 5002 935
בָּאִים נְאֻם־יְהוָה וְלֹא־יֵאָמֵר עוֹד הַתֹּפֶת וְגֵיא בֶן־הִנֹּם
,Hinnom the the or ,Tophet still will it that ,Jehovah says ,come
of son of valley called be not

33 19 61 4725 369 8612 6912 2028 1516
כִּי אִם־גֵּיא הַהֲרֵגָה וְקָבְרוּ בְתֹפֶת מֵאֵין מָקוֹם׃ וְהָיְתָה
will And .place a from in they for the valley but
be of lack Tophet bury will ,slaughter of

776 929 8064 5775 39 78 2088 5971 50 38
נִבְלַת הָעָם הַזֶּה לְמַאֲכָל לְעוֹף הַשָּׁמַיִם וּלְבֶהֱמַת הָאָרֶץ
the for and ,sky the the for food this people the
;earth of beasts the of birds of bodies

34 3389 2351 30 63 5892 7673 2729 369
וְאֵין מַחֲרִיד׃ וְהִשְׁבַּתִּי ׀ מֵעָרֵי יְהוּדָה וּמֵחֻצוֹת יְרוּשָׁלַםִ
Jerusalem from and Judah the from will I Then frighten will and
of streets the of cities cease make .away none

2723 36 18 6963 2860 6963 80 57 6963 8342 6963
קוֹל שָׂשׂוֹן וְקוֹל שִׂמְחָה קוֹל חָתָן וְקוֹל כַּלָּה כִּי לְחָרְבָּה
waste a for ,bride the and bride- the ,joy the and glad- the
of voice ,groom of voice of voice ;ness of voice

776 1961
תִּהְיֶה הָאָרֶץ׃
the will
.land become

CAP. VIII ח

CHAPTER 8

CHAPTER 8

[1]At that time, declares Jehovah, they will bring out the bones of the kings of Judah, and the bones of its rulers, and the bones of the priests, and the bones of the prophets, and the bones of the inhabitants of Jerusalem, out of their graves. [2]And they shall

1 3063 4428 6106 6 3068 5002 6256
בָּעֵת הַהִיא נְאֻם־יְהוָה וְיוֹצִיאוּ אֶת־עַצְמוֹת מַלְכֵי־יְהוּדָה
,Judah the the shall they ,Jehovah says ,that At
of kings of bones out bring time

6106 3548 6106 8269 6106
וְאֶת־עַצְמוֹת שָׂרָיו וְאֶת־עַצְמוֹת הַכֹּהֲנִים וְאֵת ׀ עַצְמוֹת
the and the the and its the and
of bones ,priests of bones officials of bones

2 7849 6913 3389 3421 6106 5030
הַנְּבִיאִים וְאֵת עַצְמוֹת יוֹשְׁבֵי־יְרוּשָׁלַםִ מִקִּבְרֵיהֶם׃ וּשְׁטָחוּם
they and their from ,Jerusalem in- the the and the
spread will ;graves of habitants of bones ;prophets

spread them before the sun, and the moon, and all the host of the heavens whom they have loved, and whom they have served, and after whom they have walked, and whom they have sought, and whom they have worshiped. They shall not be gathered, or buried; they shall be dung on the face of the ground.
3And death shall be chosen rather than life by all the rest of those who remain of this evil family, who remain there in all the places where I have driven them, says Jehovah of hosts.
4And you shall say to them, So says Jehovah, Shall they fall, and not rise up? Or shall one turn away, and not return?
5Why has this people, Jerusalem, turned away *to* a never-ending apostasy? They hold fast to deceit; they refuse to return.
6I listened and heard; they did not speak so. No man repented because of this evil, saying, What have I done? Everyone turned in their own courses, as a horse rushes into the battle.
7Also the stork in the heavens knows her seasons; and the turtle-dove, and the swallow, and the thrush observe the time of their coming. But My people do not know the judgment of Jehovah.
8How do you say, We *are* wise, and the law of Jehovah *is* with us? Behold, the lying pen of the scribes has certainly worked deceit.
9The wise are ashamed; they are terrified, and are captured. Behold, they have rejected the word of Jehovah; and what wisdom *is* theirs?
10So I will give their wives to others, their fields to those who shall inherit. For everyone from the least even to the greatest cuts off a profit.

לַשֶּׁמֶשׁ וְלַיָּרֵחַ וּלְכֹל צְבָא הַשָּׁמַיִם אֲשֶׁר אֲהֵבוּם וַאֲשֶׁר
and whom | have they them loved | whom | the heavens | the of host | to and all | to and moon the | the to sun

עֲבָדוּם וַאֲשֶׁר הָלְכוּ אַחֲרֵיהֶם וַאֲשֶׁר דְּרָשׁוּם וַאֲשֶׁר
and whom | have they them sought | and whom | after them | have they walked | and whom | have they them served

הִשְׁתַּחֲווּ לָהֶם לֹא יֵאָסְפוּ וְלֹא יִקָּבֵרוּ לְדֹמֶן עַל־פְּנֵי הָאֲדָמָה
the ground | the of face | on dung | for ;buried | nor | will They not gathered be | .them | have they worshipped

3 יִהְיוּ׃ וְנִבְחַר מָוֶת מֵחַיִּים לְכֹל הַשְּׁאֵרִית הַנִּשְׁאָרִים מִן
from | who those left are | rem- the of nant | all by | rather life than | death | be will And chosen | they .be will

הַמִּשְׁפָּחָה הָרָעָה הַזֹּאת בְּכָל־הַמְּקֹמוֹת הַנִּשְׁאָרִים אֲשֶׁר
where | who remain | the places | all in | ,this | evil | family

4 הִדַּחְתִּים שָׁם נְאֻם יְהוָה צְבָאוֹת׃ וְאָמַרְתָּ אֲלֵיהֶם כֹּה
Thus | ,them to | you And say shall | .hosts | Jehovah of | says | ,there | have I them driven

5 אָמַר יְהוָה הֲיִפְּלוּ וְלֹא יָקוּמוּ אִם־יָשׁוּב וְלֹא יָשׁוּב׃ מַדּוּעַ
Why | ?return | and not | one does Or away turn | ?arise | and not | they Do fall | ;Jehovah | says

שׁוֹבְבָה הָעָם הַזֶּה יְרוּשָׁלַםִ מְשֻׁבָה נִצַּחַת הֶחֱזִיקוּ בַּתַּרְמִית
to ;deceit | hold They fast | ?perpetual | a apostasy | ,Jerusalem | ,this | people | turned has away

6 מֵאֲנוּ לָשׁוּב׃ הִקְשַׁבְתִּי וָאֶשְׁמָע לוֹא־כֵן יְדַבֵּרוּ אֵין אִישׁ
man | no | did they ;speak | so not | and ;heard | listened I | to .return | they refuse

נִחָם עַל־רָעָתוֹ לֵאמֹר מֶה עָשִׂיתִי כֻּלֹּה שָׁב בִּמְרוּצוֹתָם
own their courses | turned in | Every one | I have ?done | What | ,saying | his ,evil | because of | re- pented

7 כְּסוּס שׁוֹטֵף בַּמִּלְחָמָה׃ גַּם־חֲסִידָה בַשָּׁמַיִם יָדְעָה
knows | the in skies | the stork | Also | the into .battle | rushes | a like horse

מוֹעֲדֶיהָ וְתֹר וְסוּס וְעָגוּר שָׁמְרוּ אֶת־עֵת בֹּאָנָה וְעַמִּי
My but people | their ;coming | the of time | observe | the and thrush | the and swift | the and turtle-dove | her ;seasons

8 לֹא יָדְעוּ אֵת מִשְׁפַּט יְהוָה׃ אֵיכָה תֹאמְרוּ חֲכָמִים אֲנַחְנוּ
We (are) | wise | you do ,say | How | .Jehovah | the of judgment | do know | not

וְתוֹרַת יְהוָה אִתָּנוּ אָכֵן הִנֵּה לַשֶּׁקֶר עָשָׂה עֵט שֶׁקֶר
the of lie | the of pen | has practiced | deceit | ,Lo ;certainly | with ?us | Jehovah (is) | the and of law

9 סֹפְרִים׃ הֹבִשׁוּ חֲכָמִים חַתּוּ וַיִּלָּכֵדוּ הִנֵּה בִדְבַר־יְהוָה
Jehovah | the of word | ,lo | are and ;captured | are they terrified | The ;wise | put are shame to | the .scribes

10 מָאָסוּ וְחָכְמַת־מֶה לָהֶם׃ לָכֵן אֶתֵּן אֶת־נְשֵׁיהֶם לַאֲחֵרִים
,others to | their wives | will I give | There- fore | ?theirs | what (is) | and wisdom | have they ;rejected

שְׂדוֹתֵיהֶם לְיוֹרְשִׁים כִּי מִקָּטֹן וְעַד־גָּדוֹל כֻּלֹּה בֹּצֵעַ בָּצַע
a ;profit | cuts off | every one | the greatest | even to | the from least | for | the to ,possessors | their fields

From the prophet even to the priest, everyone deals falsely. [11]For they have healed the hurt of the daughter of My people slightly, saying, Peace, peace; when there is no peace. [12]Were they ashamed when they had done hateful things? They were not even at all ashamed, nor did they know how to blush. So they shall fall among those who fall. In the time of their punishment, they will stumble, says Jehovah.

[13]I will utterly consume them, says Jehovah. No grapes will be on the vine, or figs on the fig-tree; even the leaf withers. And I will give to them those who pass over them. [14]Why do we sit still? Gather yourselves, and let us enter into the fortified cities; and let us stand still there. For Jehovah our God has made us stand still there, and *He* has made us drink poisonous water, because we have sinned against Jehovah. [15]We looked for peace, but no good *came*; for a time of healing, but, behold, terror! [16]The snorting of his horses was heard from Dan; all the land trembles at the sound of the neighing of his stallions. For they come and devour the land and its fullness, the city and those who live in it. [17]For, behold, I will send serpents among you, vipers *for* which there is no charm; and they will bite you, says Jehovah.

[18]I suffer from desolation; my heart *is* sick within me, beyond grief. [19]Behold, the voice of the cry of the daughter of my people from a distant land! Is not Jehovah in Zion? Or is not her king in her? Why have they provoked Me with their carved images, with foreign vanities? [20]Harvest has passed; the summer has ended; and we are not delivered. [21]For the breaking of the daughter of my people, I am broken. I mourn; horror has taken hold on me. [22]Is there no balm in Gilead? Is there no

11 מִנָּבִיא וְעַד־כֹּהֵן כֻּלֹּה עֹשֶׂה שֶּׁקֶר: וַיְרַפְּאוּ אֶת־שֶׁבֶר בַּת־

| the from | the even | the | priest | every | deals | falsely. | And | they | the | of fracture | the daugh-ter of |
| prophet | | priest | to | one | | | | | healed | | |

12 עַמִּי עַל־נְקַלָּה לֵאמֹר שָׁלוֹם שָׁלוֹם וְאֵין שָׁלוֹם: הֹבִשׁוּ

| My | slightly, | saying, | Peace, | peace, | when | no | peace. | Were they |
| people | | | | | there is | | | ashamed |

כִּי תוֹעֵבָה עָשׂוּ גַּם־בּוֹשׁ לֹא־יֵבֹשׁוּ וְהִכָּלֵם לֹא יָדָעוּ לָכֵן

| when | an | abomination made | they | even | not | ashamed; | blush | how to | They | did not | there-fore |
| | | | | | at all | | | | know they | | |

יִפְּלוּ בַנֹּפְלִים בְּעֵת פְּקֻדָּתָם יִכָּשְׁלוּ אָמַר יְהוָה:

| they | among who fall | the in | their | punishment of time; | stumble | will they | says | Jehovah. |
| shall fall | | those | | | | | | |

13 אָסֹף אֲסִיפֵם נְאֻם־יְהוָה אֵין עֲנָבִים בַּגֶּפֶן וְאֵין תְּאֵנִים

| I utterly | take will | away I | says Jehovah; | not | grapes | the on | nor | the on | figs |
| | | | | | | vine | | fig | |

14 בַּתְּאֵנָה וְהֶעָלֶה נָבֵל וָאֶתֵּן לָהֶם יַעַבְרוּם: עַל־מָה אֲנַחְנוּ

| the on | the even | withers; | I and will give | to | them | who those | pass over them. | Why | we |
| fig tree | leaf | | | them | | | | | |

יֹשְׁבִים הֵאָסְפוּ וְנָבוֹא אֶל־עָרֵי הַמִּבְצָר וְנִדְּמָה־שָּׁם כִּי יְהוָה

| sit do | Gather | let and | cities into | the | fortified, | let and | there; | for | Jehovah |
| still? | yourselves | enter us | | | | perish us | | | |

15 אֱלֹהֵינוּ הֲדִמָּנוּ וַיַּשְׁקֵנוּ מֵי־רֹאשׁ כִּי חָטָאנוּ לַיהוָה:

| our | has let and perish us, | made and us drink | waters poison | for | have we sinned | against Jehovah. |
| God | | | of | | | |

16 לְשָׁלוֹם וְאֵין טוֹב לְעֵת מַרְפֵּא וְהִנֵּה בְעָתָה: מִדָּן נִשְׁמַע

| for | no (came) | good | a for | healing, | but, | behold, | terror! | From Dan | has heard |
| peace | | | time of | | | | | | |

נַחְרַת סוּסָיו מִקּוֹל מִצְהֲלוֹת אַבִּירָיו רָעֲשָׁה כָּל־הָאָרֶץ

| the snort-ing | his horses; | the from sound of | the neighing of | his stallions | quakes | the all | the land. |

17 וַיָּבוֹאוּ וַיֹּאכְלוּ אֶרֶץ וּמְלוֹאָהּ עִיר וְיֹשְׁבֵי בָהּ: כִּי הִנְנִי מְשַׁלֵּחַ

| they For come | and devour | the land | and its fullness, | the city | and who dwell | in it. | For, | behold I | will send |

בָּכֶם נְחָשִׁים צִפְעֹנִים אֲשֶׁר אֵין־לָהֶם לָחַשׁ וְנִשְּׁכוּ אֶתְכֶם

| among you | serpents, | vipers | which | not there | for them | a charm; | will and bite them | you, |

18 נְאֻם־יְהוָה: מַבְלִיגִיתִי עֲלֵי יָגוֹן עָלַי לִבִּי דַוָּי:
19

| says Jehovah. | From | I suffer desolation, | be-yond | grief | me | within | my heart | (is) | Behold |
| | | | | | | | sick. | | |

הִנֵּה־קוֹל שַׁוְעַת בַּת־עַמִּי מֵאֶרֶץ מַרְחַקִּים הַיהוָה אֵין בְּצִיּוֹן אִם־

| the voice the | the cry | the daugh-ter of people | a from | distant: | Is Jehovah | not | in Zion? | Or |
| | of | | land | | | | | |

מַלְכָּהּ אֵין בָּהּ מַדּוּעַ הִכְעִסוּנִי בִּפְסִלֵיהֶם בְּהַבְלֵי נֵכָר:

| her | is | not | her? her in | Why | Me provoked they have | their with images graven, | vanities with | foreign? |
| king | | | | | | | | |

20 עָבַר קָצִיר כָּלָה קָיִץ וַאֲנַחְנוּ לוֹא נוֹשָׁעְנוּ: עַל־שֶׁבֶר בַּת־
21

| has passed, | Harvest | has ended, | the summer | are and | not | saved. | the Because | of breaking of | the daugh-ter of |
| | | | | we | | | | | |

22 עַמִּי הָשְׁבָּרְתִּי קָדַרְתִּי שַׁמָּה הֶחֱזִקָתְנִי: הַצֳרִי אֵין בְּגִלְעָד

| my | am I | I mourn; | horror | hold on has me. | Is balm | no there | in Gilead? |
| people | broken. | | | | | | |

healer there? Why then has the healing of my people not come?

CHAPTER 9

[1]Oh that my head were waters, and my eyes a fountain of tears, that I might weep day and night for the slain of the daughter of my people! [2]Oh that I had a lodging place for travelers in the wilderness, that I might leave my people and go away from them! For they are all adulterers, an assembly of treacherous ones. [3]And they bend their tongues; their bow *is* a lie. And they are not mighty for the truth on the earth; for they go from evil to evil. They do not know Me, says Jehovah. [4]Let everyone be on guard against his neighbor, and do not trust any brother. For every brother will supplant, and every neighbor will walk as a slanderer. [5]And everyone will deceive his neighbor; and they will not speak the truth. They have taught their tongue to speak lies; they weary themselves to commit iniquity. [6]Your home *is* in the midst of deceit; through deceit they refuse to know Me, says Jehovah. [7]For this reason, so says Jehovah of hosts, Behold, I will refine them and test them. What *else* can I do because of the daughter of My people? [8]Their tongue *is* a murdering arrow; it speaks deceit; *one* speaks peace with his neighbor, with his mouth, but in his heart he sets his ambush.

[9]Shall I not visit them for these *things*? says Jehovah. Or shall not My soul be avenged on such a nation as this? [10]I will take up a weeping and a wailing for

5971 1323 724 5927 3808 4069 8033 369 7495
אִם־רֹפֵא אֵין שָׁם כִּי מַדּוּעַ לֹא עָלְתָה אֲרֻכַת בַּת־עַמִּי׃
my daugh- the the has not Why then ?there is healer Or
?people of ter of healing come no there

3915 3117 1058 1832 4726 5869 4325 7218 1961
23 מִי־יִתֵּן רֹאשִׁי מַיִם וְעֵינִי מְקוֹר דִּמְעָה וְאֶבְכֶּה יוֹמָם וָלַיְלָה
and day I that ,tears foun- a and ,waters my that O
night for weep might of tain eyes my head were

5971 1323 2490
אֵת חַלְלֵי בַת־עַמִּי׃
my daugh- the the
.people of ter of slain

CAP. IX ט

CHAPTER 9

3212 5971 5800 732 4411 4057 1961
1 מִי־יִתְּנֵנִי בַמִּדְבָּר מְלוֹן אֹרְחִים וְאֶעֶזְבָה אֶת־עַמִּי וְאֵלְכָה
go and my I that ,travelers lodging a the in that O
away people leave might of wilderness had I

1869 898 6116 5003 3605
2 מֵאִתָּם כִּי כֻלָּם מְנָאֲפִים עֲצֶרֶת בֹּגְדִים׃ וַיַּדְרְכוּ אֶת־
they And treacherous assembly an are of all For from
bend .men of adulterers them !them

7451 776 1396 530 3808 8267 7198 3956
לְשׁוֹנָם קַשְׁתָּם שֶׁקֶר וְלֹא לֶאֱמוּנָה גָּבְרוּ בָאָרֶץ כִּי מֵרָעָה
from for the on are they the for and ,lie a their their
evil ;earth mighty truth not (is) bow ,tongues

376 3068 5002 3045 3808 3318 7451
3 אֶל־רָעָה ׀ יָצָאוּ וְאֹתִי לֹא־יָדָעוּ נְאֻם־יְהוָה׃ אִישׁ
Every .Jehovah says they not and they evil to
man ,know do Me go

6117 251 3605 982 408 251 3605 8104 7453
מֵרֵעֵהוּ הִשָּׁמֵרוּ וְעַל־כָּל־אָח אַל־תִּבְטָחוּ כִּי כָל־אָח עָקוֹב
surely brother every For do not brother any and be let his against
!trust ,guarded neighbor

571 2048 7453 376 1980 7400 7453 3605 6117
4 יַעְקֹב וְכָל־רֵעַ רָכִיל יַהֲלֹךְ׃ וְאִישׁ בְּרֵעֵהוּ יְהָתֵלּוּ וֶאֱמֶת
the and will his every and goes a neighbor and will
truth ,deceive neighbor man ,as about slanderer every ,supplant

3427 3811 5753 8267 1696 3956 3925 1696 3808
5 לֹא יְדַבֵּרוּ לִמְּדוּ לְשׁוֹנָם דַּבֶּר־שֶׁקֶר הַעֲוֵה נִלְאוּ׃ שִׁבְתְּךָ
Your tired they do to ;lies to their have they will they not
dwelling ,themselves iniquity speak tongue taught ;speak

3068 5002 3045 3985 4820 4820 8432
בְּתוֹךְ מִרְמָה בְּמִרְמָה מֵאֲנוּ דַעַת־אוֹתִי נְאֻם־יְהוָה׃
.Jehovah says ,Me to they through ;deceit the in (is)
know refuse deceit of midst

974 6884 2009 6635 3068 559
6 לָכֵן כֹּה אָמַר יְהוָה צְבָאוֹת הִנְנִי צוֹרְפָם וּבְחַנְתִּים כִּי־
for test and refine will ,Behold ,hosts Jehovah says thus There-
,them them I of fore

4820 3956 7929 2671 5971 1323 6440 6213 349
7 אֵיךְ אֶעֱשֶׂה מִפְּנֵי בַּת־עַמִּי׃ חֵץ שׁוֹחֵט לְשׁוֹנָם מִרְמָה
deceit their slaughtering A My daugh- the for I can what
;tongue (is) arrow ?people of ter do (else)

696 7760 7130 1696 7453 7965 6310 1696
דִּבֵּר בְּפִיו שָׁלוֹם אֶת־רֵעֵהוּ יְדַבֵּר וּבְקִרְבּוֹ יָשִׂים אָרְבּוֹ׃
his he his in but one his with peace his with it
.ambush sets midst ,speaks neighbor mouth ;speaks

2088 834 1471 3068 5002 64 3808 428
8 הַעַל־אֵלֶּה לֹא־אֶפְקָד־בָּם נְאֻם־יְהוָה אִם בְּגוֹי אֲשֶׁר־כָּזֶה
as such a on Or ?Jehovah says ,them I shall not these For
this nation punish (things)

5091 1065 5375 2022 5315 5358 3808
9 לֹא תִתְנַקֵּם נַפְשִׁי׃ עַל־הֶהָרִים אֶשָּׂא בְכִי וָנֶהִי וְעַל־
and a and a will I the For My be shall not
for ,wailing weeping up take mountains ?soul avenged

the mountains, and a mourning for the pastures of the wilderness; because they are burned up, without a man passing through; yea, they do not hear the voice of cattle. From the fowl of the heavens, and to the beast, they have fled; they are gone. ¹¹And I will make Jerusalem ruins, a den of jackals; and I will make the cities of Judah a desolation without inhabitant.

¹²Who is the wise man that can understand this? And he to whom the mouth of Jehovah has spoken, that he may declare it? Why does the land perish? It is burned up like the wilderness, so that no one passes through. ¹³And Jehovah says, because they have forsaken My law which I set before them, and have not heard My voice, and have not walked in it; ¹⁴but have walked after the stubbornness of their own heart, and after the Baals, which their fathers taught them; ¹⁵so Jehovah of hosts, the God of Israel, says this: Behold, I will feed them, this people with wormwood, and make them drink water of poison. ¹⁶I will also scatter them among the nations which they have not known, nor their fathers. And I will send the sword after them until I have consumed them.

¹⁷So says Jehovah of hosts, Think carefully, and call for the wailers, that they may come. And send for the wise women, that they may come. ¹⁸And let them make haste and take up a lament over us, so that our eyes may run down with tears, and waters flow from our eyelids. ¹⁹For the voice of lament is heard from Zion. How we are ravaged! We are greatly ashamed because we have forsaken the land; because they have thrown down our dwellings. ²⁰Yet hear the

---

4999	4057		7015	3341	1097	376		5674	3808	8085
the pas-	the wil-	a	;dirge	for	up burned	are they	without	man	a	and passing	they hear
ture	derness of torage								not ;through	

10

6963	4735	5775	8064		5704	929		5892	5074	1980	5414
of voice	of	the	From	the	to	the	have they	;fled	are they	And	I
	cattle	of bird	the From	skies	to	beast	even	;fled	gone		will make

3389		15 30	4583	8577		5892	3063	6213		859
Jerusalem	a heap a	ruins of	,jackals	a den	and	the	Judah	will I		
				of		of cities		make		

11

8077	1097	3427		4310	376	2450	995	
deso- a	without	.inhabitant	the	Who	wise	can that		
lation			man (is)			understand		

776	1696	6310	3068	5046		4100	6	776
?this	And	has	the	of mouth	Jehovah the	to	he that	Why	does	the
								?land perish

12

3341	4057	1097	5674		559	3068	5800
burned	wilderness	none	that	passes		And	says	Jeho-	Be-	have they
is it	the		;through				vah	cause	forsaken

8451	834	5414	6440	38 08	8085	3808	6963	38 08
My	which	set I	before	not	have	and	My	and
law			,them		heard	not	,voice	not

19 80	5927	301	8307	3820	310	1168
have	;it in	walked	after	of	heart	own their	and	,Baals the
			bornness	stub-				

13

834	8451	1	3925	3068	6635
which	taught	their	;fathers	says thus	therefore	,hosts Jehovah	of
	them						

14

430	3478	2009	398	5971	2088	3939
the	,Israel	I	make will	,people	this	worm-
of God		,Behold	eat			wood,

6327	1471	834	3808	3045
them scatter	nations the	which	not	have
	among			,known

8248	7219 4325		559	3068	6635
make and	.poison waters		Thus	says	Jehovah	,hosts
drink them	of					of

15

7971	310	2719		5704	36 15
send will	them	after	the	until	have I
		,sword			consumed

		559	3068	6635	7121	995
.them		Thus	says	Jehovah	,hosts	Consider	and
				of		call

16

6969		935		2450	79 71	935
the for		that they	,send	wise the	and	that they
wailers		come may		women	to	;come may

4116	5375	59 21	5091	3381	2450	1832
them let And	up	us	over	a	that so	(with)	eyes our
haste make	take and		lament		down run may	,tears	

17

6079	51 40	4325	6963	5091	3381	8085	6726	7703
our and	flow	.waters	For	of voice	is lament	heard	,Zion	How	are we
eyelids									!devastated

18

	954	3966	5800	776	7993	3427	4908
But	,greatly are We	for	have we	the	for	have they	our	But
	ashamed		left	;land		down thrown	.dwellings	

19

word of Jehovah, O women; and let your ear receive the word of His mouth; and teach your daughters a lament; and each one her neighbor a dirge. [21]For death has come into our windows, entering into our fortified palaces, to cut off the children from the street, *the* young men from the plazas. [22]Speak, So says Jehovah, Even the bodies of men shall fall as dung on the open field, and as the fallen grain after the reaper; and no one shall gather *them*.

[23]So says Jehovah, Do not let the wise glory in his wisdom; and do not let the mighty glory in his might; do not let the rich glory in his riches; [24]but let him who glories glory in this, that *he* understands and knows Me, that I *am* Jehovah, doing kindness, justice and righteousness in the earth; for I delight in these, says Jehovah.

[25]Behold, the days come, says Jehovah, that I will punish all the circumcised with foreskin: [26]Egypt, and Judah, and Edom, and the sons of Ammon, and Moab, and all those trimmed on the edges *of their beards*, who dwell in the wilderness. For all the nations *are* uncircumcised, and all the house of Israel—those uncircumcised of heart.

3925 6310 241 3941 3068 1697 802 8085
שִׁמַעְנָה נָשִׁים דְּבַר־יְהוָה וְתִקַּח אָזְנְכֶם דְּבַר־פִּיו וְלַמֵּדְנָה
and His the your let and ,Jehovah the O ,hear
teach ,mouth of word ear receive of word ,women

2474 41 94 5927 7065 7468 802 5091 1323
20 בְנֹתֵיכֶם נֶהִי וְאִשָּׁה רְעוּתָהּ קִינָה׃ כִּי־עָלָה מָוֶת בְּחַלּוֹנֵינוּ
our through death has For .dirge a her and a your
windows up come neighbor each ,lament daughters

7339 970 2351 5768 3772 759 935
בָּא בְּאַרְמְנוֹתֵינוּ לְהַכְרִית עוֹלָל מִחוּץ בַּחוּרִים מֵרְחֹבוֹת׃
the from (the and) the from the cast to our into enter-
.squares open men young ,street children off palaces fortified ing

6440 5921 18 28 120 5038 5307 30 68 5002 35 41 16 96
21 דַּבֵּר כֹּה נְאֻם־יְהוָה וְנָפְלָה נִבְלַת הָאָדָם כְּדֹמֶן עַל־פְּנֵי
the on dung as men the will Even ,Jehovah says thus ,Speak
of face of bodies fall

559 622 369 7114 310 5995 7704
22 הַשָּׂדֶה וּכְעָמִיר מֵאַחֲרֵי הַקֹּצֵר וְאֵין מְאַסֵּף׃ כֹּה ׀ אָמַר
says Thus gather will and the after like and the
.(them) .none ,reaper swath the ,field

1368 8597 408 2451 2450 8597 408 3068
יְהוָה אַל־יִתְהַלֵּל חָכָם בְּחָכְמָתוֹ וְאַל־יִתְהַלֵּל הַגִּבּוֹר
the let do and his in the let Do not ,Jehovah
mighty glory not wisdom man wise glory

1984 2088 6239 6223 8597 408 1369
23 בִּגְבוּרָתוֹ אַל־יִתְהַלֵּל עָשִׁיר בְּעָשְׁרוֹ׃ כִּי אִם־בְּזֹאת יִתְהַלֵּל
let this in but his in the let do not his in
glory —riches rich glory ,might

4941 2617 6213 30 68 30 45 7919 1984
הַמִּתְהַלֵּל הַשְׂכֵּל וְיָדֹעַ אוֹתִי כִּי אֲנִי יְהוָה עֹשֶׂה חֶסֶד מִשְׁפָּט
,justice kind- doing ,Jehovah I that ,Me and he (that) who him
,ness (am) knows understands ,glories

2009 3068 5002 2654 428 776 6666
24 וּצְדָקָה בָּאָרֶץ כִּי־בְאֵלֶּה חָפַצְתִּי נְאֻם־יְהוָה׃ הִנֵּה
Behold .Jehovah says I in for the in righ- and
,delight these —earth teousness

6190 4135 3605 5921 6485 3068 5002 935 3117
25 יָמִים בָּאִים נְאֻם־יְהוָה וּפָקַדְתִּי עַל־כָּל־מוּל בְּעָרְלָה׃ עַל־
with the all I that ,Jehovah says ,come the
—foreskin circumcised punish will days

4124 5783 1121 123 30 63 4714
מִצְרַיִם וְעַל־יְהוּדָה וְעַל־אֱדוֹם וְעַל־בְּנֵי עַמּוֹן וְעַל־מוֹאָב
,Moab and ,Ammon the and ,Edom and ,Judah and Egypt
of sons

61 89 1471 3605 4057 3427 62 85 7112 36 05
וְעַל כָּל־קְצוּצֵי פֵאָה הַיֹּשְׁבִים בַּמִּדְבָּר כִּי כָל־הַגּוֹיִם עֲרֵלִים
uncir- (are) the all for the in who the those all and
cumcised nations ,wilderness dwell ,edges on trimmed

38 20 6189 3478 1004 3605
וְכָל־בֵּית יִשְׂרָאֵל עַרְלֵי־לֵב׃
.heart those Israel the and
of uncircumcised of house all

CAP. X

CHAPTER 10

CHAPTER 10

[1]Hear the word which Jehovah speaks to you, O house of Israel. [2]So says Jehovah, You shall not be goaded to the way of the nations; and do not be terrified at the signs of the heavens; for the nations are terrified at them. [3]For the ordinances of the people

3478 1004 3068 1696 834 1697 8085
1 שִׁמְעוּ אֶת־הַדָּבָר אֲשֶׁר דִּבֶּר יְהוָה עֲלֵיכֶם בֵּית יִשְׂרָאֵל׃
.Israel O ,you to Jehovah speaks which the Hear
of house word

226 3925 3808 1471 1870 30 68 559
2 כֹּה ׀ אָמַר יְהוָה אֶל־דֶּרֶךְ הַגּוֹיִם אַל־תִּלְמָדוּ וּמֵאֹתוֹת
the by and shall you not the the to ,Jehovah says Thus
of signs ,goaded be ,nations of way

2708 1992 1471 2865 2865 408 8064
3 הַשָּׁמַיִם אַל־תֵּחָתּוּ כִּי־יֵחַתּוּ הַגּוֹיִם מֵהֵמָּה׃ כִּי־חֻקּוֹת
the For .them by the are for be do not the
of statutes nations terrified ,terrified heavens

are vanity; for one cuts a
tree out of the forest with
the axe, the work of the
hands of the craftsman.
[4]They adorn it with silver
and with gold; they fasten
them with nails and ham-
mers, so that it will not
wobble. [5]They *are* like a
rounded post, and they
cannot speak. The must
surely be lifted, because
they cannot walk. Do not be
afraid of them; for they
cannot do evil nor good; it is
not with them. [6]There is
none like You, O Jehovah;
You *are* great, and Your
name *is* great in might.
[7]Who would not fear You, O
King of nations? For it is
fitting to You, because
among all the wise of the
nations, and in all their
kingdoms, there is none
like You. [8]But they are at
once foolish and animal-
like; *their* tree *is* an
instruction of vanities.
[9]Silver beaten into plates
is brought from Tarshish,
and gold from Uphaz, the
work of the craftsman and
the hands of the goldsmith.
Violet and purple *is* their
clothing; they *are* all the
works of skillful ones.
[10]But Jehovah *is* the true
God, He *is* the living God,
and the everlasting King. At
His wrath the earth shall
tremble, and the nations
shall not be able to stand
His indignation. [11]So you
shall say to them, The gods
who have not made the
heavens and the earth, they
shall perish from the earth,
and from under these
heavens. [12]*It is* He who
made the earth by His
power; who established the
world by His wisdom, and
who stretched out the
heavens by His under-
standing. [13]When He utters
His voice, *there is* a noise of
waters in the heavens. He
causes the vapors to go up
from the ends of the earth;
He makes lightnings for the
rain, and brings forth the
wind out of His store-
houses. [14]Every man is
stupid from *lack of*

העמים הבל הוא כי עץ מיער כרתו מעשה ידי חרש
of hands the | the | one | the from | a | for | it | vanity | the
craftsman the | of work | ,cuts | forest | tree | ,(is) | —people

4 במעצד׃ בכסף ובזהב ייפהו במסמרות ובמקבות
with and | with | They | with and | with | the with
hammers | nails | ,it adorn | gold | silver | axe

5 יחזקום ולוא יפיק׃ כתמר מקשה המה ולא ידברו
can they | and | they | rounded | a Like | will it | that so | they
;speak | not | ,(are) | post | .wobble | not them | fasten

נשוא ינשוא כי לא יצעדו אל תיראו מהם כי לא ירעו
can they | not for | of | be Do | not | can they | not for | must they surely
evil do | ;them | afraid | .walk | lifted be

6 וגם היטיב אין אותם׃ מאין כמוך יהוה גדול
great | O | like | There | with | is it | do | and
;Jehovah | ,You | none is | .them | not | ;good | not

7 אתה וגדול שמך בגבורה׃ מי לא יראך מלך הגוים
?nations | O | would | not Who | .might in | Your (is) | and | You
of King | You fear | name | great | ,(are)

כי לך יאתה כי בכל חכמי הגוים ובכל מלכותם מאין
there | their | in and | the | wise the among | for | is it | for | For
none is | ,kingdoms | all | ,nations | of men | all | ,fitting | You

8 כמוך׃ ובאחת יבערו ויכסלו מוסר הבלים עץ הוא׃
(is) | (their) | vanities | in- an | and | are they | And | like
tree | of struction | ;foolish | stupid | altogether | .You

9 כסף מרקע מתרשיש יובא וזהב מאופז מעשה חרש
the | work the | from | and | is | from | beaten | silver
,craftsman | of | ,Uphaz | gold | ,brought | Tarshish | plates into

וידי צורף תכלת וארגמן לבושם מעשה חכמים כלם׃
of all | skillful | the | their (is) | and | violet | the | the and
.them | ones | of work | ,clothing | purple | ,goldsmith of hands

10 ויהוה אלהים אמת הוא אלהים חיים ומלך עולם מקצפו
His At | ever- | the and | ,living | the | He | ;true | the (is) | But
wrath | .lasting | king | God | (is) | God | Jehovah

11 תרעש הארץ ולא יכלו גוים זעמו׃ כדנה תאמרון
shall you | Like | His | the | can | and | the | shall
say | .indignation | nations | endure not | ,earth | quake

להום אלהיא די שמיא וארקא לא עבדו יאבדו מארעא
the from | shall they | have | not | the and | the | who | The | to
earth | perish | ,made | earth | heavens | gods | ,them

12 ומן תחות שמיא אלה׃ עשה ארץ בכחו מכין
es- who | His by | the | He (is It) | .these | heavens | under | and
tablished | ;power | earth | made who | from

13 תבל בחכמתו ובתבונתו נטה שמים׃ לקול תתו המון
tumult a | His | the At | .heavens the | has | His by and | His by | the
of | giving | of sound | out stretched | understanding | ,wisdom | world

מים בשמים ויעלה נשאים מקצה ארץ ברקים למטר
the for | lightning | the | the from | mists the | causes He | the in | waters
rain | ;earth | of end | ascend to | ;heavens | (is)

14 עשה ויוצא רוח מאצרתיו׃ נבער כל אדם מדעת
(of lack) from | man Every | is | His from | the | and | He
;knowledge | stupid | .storehouses | wind forth brings | ,makes

knowledge; every refiner is is put to shame by the carved image; for his molten image *is* a lie, and no breath *is* in them. [15]They are vanity, the work of delusion. In the time of their judgment, they shall perish. [16]The Portion of Jacob *is* not like these. For He *is* the Former of all things; and Israel *is* the tribe of His inheritance; Jehovah of hosts *is* His name.

[17]Gather up your bundle from the ground, you who live under the siege. [18]For so says Jehovah, Behold, I will sling out the dwellers of the land at this time, and will distress them, so that they may find *Me.*

[19]Woe *to* me for my breaking! My wound is grievous; but I said, Truly this *is* a malady, and I must bear it. [20]My tent is ravaged, and all my cords are broken; my sons went away from me and they are not. *There is* no stretching out my tent any more, or setting up my curtains. [21]For the pastors have become stupid, and they have not sought Jehovah; therefore, they shall not be blessed, and all their flock shall be scattered. [22]Behold, the sound of a report! It comes, and a great commotion from the land of the north, to make the cities of Judah a desolation, a den of jackals.

[23]O Jehovah, I know that his way does not *belong* to man; *it is* not in man who walks to direct his steps. [24]O Jehovah, correct me; only with judgment, not in Your anger, that You do not bring me to nothing. [25]Pour out Your fury on the nations who do not know You, and on the families who do not call on Your name. For they have eaten up Jacob; and they have devoured him, and have destroyed him, and have made his dwelling-place desolate.

הֹבִישׁ כָּל־צוֹרֵף מִפָּסֶל כִּי שֶׁקֶר נִסְכּוֹ וְלֹא־רוּחַ בָּם׃
in (is) breath and his a (is) for the by every put is / .them no ,image molten lie ;image graven refiner shame to

15 הֶבֶל הֵמָּה מַעֲשֵׂה תַּעְתֻּעִים בְּעֵת פְּקֻדָּתָם יֹאבֵדוּ׃
16 לֹא־
Not will they their the in ,mockery the They vanity / .perish punishment of time of work (are)

כְאֵלֶּה חֵלֶק יַעֲקֹב כִּי־יוֹצֵר הַכֹּל הוּא וְיִשְׂרָאֵל שֵׁבֶט
the (is) Israel and He all the for ,Jacob the these like / of tribe ;(is) of Former of Portion (is)

נַחֲלָתוֹ יְהוָה צְבָאוֹת שְׁמוֹ׃
17 אִסְפִּי מֵאֶרֶץ כִּנְעָתֵךְ
your the from Gather His hosts Jehovah in- His / bundle ground up .name (is) of ,heritance

יֹשֶׁבֶת בַּמָּצוֹר׃
18 כִּי־כֹה אָמַר יְהוָה הִנְנִי קוֹלֵעַ
will ,Behold ,Jehovah says thus For under who you / out sling I .seige dwell

אֶת־יוֹשְׁבֵי הָאָרֶץ בַּפַּעַם הַזֹּאת וַהֲצֵרוֹתִי לָהֶם לְמַעַן יִמְצָאוּ׃
may they so them will and ,this time at the inhab- the / .(Me) find that distress land of itants

19 אוֹי לִי עַל־שִׁבְרִי נַחְלָה מַכָּתִי וַאֲנִי אָמַרְתִּי אַךְ
Truly ,said but My is my for to Woe / I ;wound grievous !breaking me

20 זֶה חֳלִי וְאֶשָּׂאֶנּוּ׃ אָהֳלִי שֻׁדָּד וְכָל־מֵיתָרַי נִתָּקוּ בָּנַי יְצָאֻנִי
have my are my and is My must I and a this / ,me left sons ;broken cords all ,destroyed tent .it bear sickness (is)

21 וְאֵינָם אֵין־נֹטֶה עוֹד אָהֳלִי וּמֵקִים יְרִיעוֹתָי׃ כִּי נִבְעֲרוּ
be- have For my setting or my any stretch- Not they and / stupid come .curtains up ,tent more out ing is .not are

הָרֹעִים וְאֶת־יְהוָה לֹא דָרָשׁוּ עַל־כֵּן לֹא הִשְׂכִּילוּ וְכָל־
and will they not therefore have they not Jehovah and the / all ,succeed ;sought ,shepherds

22 מַרְעִיתָם נְפוֹצָה׃ קוֹל שְׁמוּעָה הִנֵּה בָאָה וְרַעַשׁ גָּדוֹל
great a and it ,Behold !report a The is their / commotion ,comes of sound .scattered flock

מֵאֶרֶץ צָפוֹן לָשׂוּם אֶת־עָרֵי יְהוּדָה שְׁמָמָה מְעוֹן תַּנִּים׃
.jackals den a a Judah the make to the the from / of ,desolation of cities ,north of land

23 יָדַעְתִּי יְהוָה כִּי לֹא לָאָדָם דַּרְכּוֹ לֹא־לְאִישׁ הֹלֵךְ וְהָכִין
he that who to (is it) ,way his to (belongs) that O ,know I / direct walks man not man not ,Jehovah

24 אֶת־צַעֲדוֹ׃ יַסְּרֵנִי יְהוָה אַךְ־בְּמִשְׁפָּט אַל־בְּאַפְּךָ פֶּן־
lest Your in not with only O Correct his / ,anger ,judgment ,Jehovah me .steps

25 תַּמְעִטֵנִי׃ שְׁפֹךְ חֲמָתְךָ עַל־הַגּוֹיִם אֲשֶׁר לֹא־יְדָעוּךָ וְעַל
and do not who the on Your Pour bring You / on ,You know nations wrath out .nothing to me

מִשְׁפָּחוֹת אֲשֶׁר בְּשִׁמְךָ לֹא קָרָאוּ כִּי־אָכְלוּ אֶת־יַעֲקֹב
;Jacob have they For do not Your on who families / devoured .call name

וַאֲכָלֻהוּ וַיְכַלֻּהוּ וְאֶת־נָוֵהוּ הֵשַׁמּוּ׃
made have his and con- and de- they and / .desolate dwelling him sumed him voured

CAP. XI יא

CHAPTER 11

8085 559 3068 3414 1961 1697

1 הַדָּבָר אֲשֶׁר־הָיָה אֶל־יִרְמְיָהוּ מֵאֵת יְהוָה לֵאמֹר׃ 2 שִׁמְעוּ

Hear ,saying ,Jehovah from Jeremiah to came that The word

3063 376 1696 2088 1285 1697

אֶת־דִּבְרֵי הַבְּרִית הַזֹּאת וְדִבַּרְתֶּם אֶל־אִישׁ יְהוּדָה וְעַל־

and to Judah the of men to speak and this covenant the of words

430 3068 559 559 3389 3427

3 יֹשְׁבֵי יְרוּשָׁלִָם׃ וְאָמַרְתָּ אֲלֵיהֶם כֹּה־אָמַר יְהוָה אֱלֹהֵי

the of God ,Jehovah says Thus ,them to say and ;Jerusalem in- the of habitants

1285 1697 8085 3808 834 376 779 3478

יִשְׂרָאֵל אָרוּר הָאִישׁ אֲשֶׁר לֹא יִשְׁמַע אֶת־דִּבְרֵי הַבְּרִית

covenant the of words does not obey who the man Cursed (is) ,Israel

3318 3117 1 6680 834 2088

4 הַזֹּאת׃ אֲשֶׁר צִוִּיתִי אֶת־אֲבוֹתֵיכֶם בְּיוֹם הוֹצִיאִי־אוֹתָם

them brought I out the in day your fathers com- I manded which this

6213 6963 8085 559 1270 3564 4714 776

מֵאֶרֶץ־מִצְרַיִם מִכּוּר הַבַּרְזֶל לֵאמֹר שִׁמְעוּ בְקוֹלִי וַעֲשִׂיתֶם

do and My voice Obey ,saying ,iron the from furnace ,Egypt the from of land

5971 1961 6680 3605

אוֹתָם כְּכֹל אֲשֶׁר־אֲצַוֶּה אֶתְכֶם וִהְיִיתֶם לִי לְעָם וְאָנֹכִי

I and a for ,people to Me you So be will .you com- I mand that according all to them

834 7621 6965 4616 430 1961

5 אֶהְיֶה לָכֶם לֵאלֹהִים׃ לְמַעַן הָקִים אֶת־הַשְּׁבוּעָה אֲשֶׁר־

which the oath to establish order in ,God for to you shall be

1706 2461 2100 776 5414 1 7650

נִשְׁבַּעְתִּי לַאֲבוֹתֵיכֶם לָתֵת לָהֶם אֶרֶץ זָבַת חָלָב וּדְבָשׁ

and ,honey milk flowing with a land to them give to your to fathers swore I

3068 559 3068 543 559 6030 2088 3117

6 כַּיּוֹם הַזֶּה וָאַעַן וָאֹמַר אָמֵן ׀ יְהוָה׃ וַיֹּאמֶר יְהוָה

Jehovah Then said O .Jehovah ,Amen ,said and I Then answered .this (is it) as day

2351 3063 5892 428 1697 3605 7121

אֵלַי קְרָא אֶת־כָּל־הַדְּבָרִים הָאֵלֶּה בְּעָרֵי יְהוּדָה וּבְחֻצוֹת

in and of streets the Judah the in of cities these words all Proclaim to ,Me

6213 1285 1697 8085 559 3389

יְרוּשָׁלִַם לֵאמֹר שִׁמְעוּ אֶת־דִּבְרֵי הַבְּרִית הַזֹּאת וַעֲשִׂיתֶם

do and this covenant the of words Hear ,saying ,Jerusalem

5927 3117 1 5749 5749

7 אוֹתָם׃ כִּי הָעֵד הַעִדֹתִי בַּאֲבוֹתֵיכֶם בְּיוֹם הַעֲלוֹתִי אוֹתָם

them brought I up the in day your fathers I admonished solemnly For .them

8085 559 5749 7925 2088 3117 5704 4714 776

מֵאֶרֶץ מִצְרַיִם וְעַד־הַיּוֹם הַזֶּה הַשְׁכֵּם וְהָעֵד לֵאמֹר שִׁמְעוּ

Obey ,saying and ,admonishing rising early ,this day to ,Egypt of out of land the

376 3212 241 5186 3808 8085 3808 6963

8 בְּקוֹלִי׃ וְלֹא שָׁמְעוּ וְלֹא־הִטּוּ אֶת־אָזְנָם וַיֵּלְכוּ אִישׁ

each man but walked their ,ear incline nor did they obey Yet not My .voice

1285 1697 3605 5921 935 7451 3820 8307

בִּשְׁרִירוּת לִבָּם הָרָע וָאָבִיא עֲלֵיהֶם אֶת־כָּל־דִּבְרֵי הַבְּרִית־

covenant the of words all them on I So bring will .evil their heart stub- the in of bornness

CHAPTER 11

[1]the word that came to Jeremiah from Jehovah, saying, [2]Hear the words of this covenant, and speak to the men of Judah and to the inhabitants of Jerusalem; [3]and say to them, So says Jehovah, the God of Israel, Cursed *is* the man who does not obey the words of this covenant, [4]which I commanded your fathers in the day I brought them out of the land of Egypt, from the iron furnace, saying, Obey My voice, and do them according to all that I command you, so that you shall be My people, and I will be your God; [5]in order to establish the oath which I swore to your fathers, to give them a land flowing with milk and honey, as *it is* this day. Then I answered and said, Amen, O Jehovah.

[6]And Jehovah said to me, Declare all these words in the cities of Judah, and in the streets of Jerusalem, saying, Hear the words of this covenant and do them. [7]For I solemnly warned your fathers in the day I brought them up out of the land of Egypt, to this day, rising early and warning, saying, Obey My voice. [8]Yet they did not obey, nor bow down their ear, but each one walked in the stubbornness of their evil heart. And I will bring on them all the words of this covenant,

which I commanded *them* to do; but they did not do. [9]And Jehovah said to me, A plot is found among the men of Judah, and among the inhabitants of Jerusalem. [10]They have turned back to the iniquities of their forefathers, who refused to hear My words. And they went after other gods to serve them. The house of Israel and the house of Judah have broken My covenant which I cut with their fathers.

[11]So Jehovah says this: Behold, I will bring evil on them, from which they shall not be able to escape. And though they cry to Me, I will not listen to them. [12]Then the cities of Judah and the inhabitants of Jerusalem shall go and cry to the gods to whom they burned incense. But they not at all are able to save them in the time of their trouble. [13]For *according to* the number of your cities were your gods, O Judah; yea, *according to* the number of the streets of Jerusalem you have set up altars to *that* shameful thing, altars to burn incense to Baal. [14]And you, do not pray for this people; and do not lift up a cry or prayer for them. For I will not hear in the time they cry to Me for their trouble. [15]What *is to* My beloved in My house, *since* she has committed her many evils? And has the holy flesh caused your evil to pass from you? *How* then do you exult? [16]Jehovah called your name, a green olive tree, fair, *with* fine fruit. With the sound of a great storm, He has set fire to it, and its branches are

3068 559 6213 3808 6213 6680 834 2088
9 הַזֹּאת אֲשֶׁר־צִוִּיתִי לַעֲשׂוֹת וְלֹא עָשׂוּ׃ וַיֹּאמֶר יְהוָה
Jehovah said And they but ;do to com- I which ,this
.do did not manded

7725 3389 3427 3063 376 7195 4672
10 אֵלַי נִמְצָא־קֶשֶׁר בְּאִישׁ יְהוּדָה וּבְיֹשְׁבֵי יְרוּשָׁלָםִ׃ שָׁבוּ
have They .Jerusalem the and ,Judah among plot A is to
returned of inhabitants of men the found ,me

8085 3985 834 7223 1 5771
עַל־עֲוֺנֹת אֲבוֹתָם הָרִאשֹׁנִים אֲשֶׁר מֵאֲנוּ לִשְׁמוֹעַ אֶת־
hear to refused who former their the to
fathers of iniquities

6565 5647 312 430 310 1980 1697
דְּבָרַי וְהֵמָּה הָלְכוּ אַחֲרֵי אֱלֹהִים אֲחֵרִים לְעָבְדָם הֵפֵרוּ
have serve to other gods after went and My
broken .them they ,words

3772 834 1285 3063 1004 3478 1004
בֵית־יִשְׂרָאֵל וּבֵית יְהוּדָה אֶת־בְּרִיתִי אֲשֶׁר כָּרַתִּי אֶת־
with cut I which My Judah the and Israel The
covenant of house of house

935 3068 559 3541
11 אֲבוֹתָם׃ לָכֵן כֹּה אָמַר יְהוָה הִנְנִי מֵבִיא אֲלֵיהֶם
them on will Behold ,Jehovah says thus Therefore their
bring I .fathers

3808 2199 3318 3201 3808 834 7451
רָעָה אֲשֶׁר לֹא־יוּכְלוּ לָצֵאת מִמֶּנָּה וְזָעֲקוּ אֵלַי וְלֹא
not to (if) And from go to will they not which ,evil
,Me cry they ;it forth able be

3389 3427 3063 5892 1980 8085
12 אֶשְׁמַע אֲלֵיהֶם׃ וְהָלְכוּ עָרֵי יְהוּדָה וְיֹשְׁבֵי יְרוּשָׁלַםִ
Jerusalem the and Judah the shall Then .them to will I
of inhabitants of cities go listen

3808 6999 430 2199
וְזָעֲקוּ אֶל־הָאֱלֹהִים אֲשֶׁר הֵם מְקַטְּרִים לָהֶם וְהוֹשֵׁעַ לֹא־
not at But .them to burned they whom the to and
all incense gods cry

430 1961 5892 4557 7451 6256 3467
13 יוֹשִׁיעוּ לָהֶם בְּעֵת רָעָתָם׃ כִּי מִסְפַּר עָרֶיךָ הָיוּ אֱלֹהֶיךָ
your (so) your the (as) For their the in them can they
,gods were ,cities of number .trouble of time save

1322 4196 7760 3389 2351 4557 3063
יְהוּדָה וּמִסְפַּר חֻצוֹת יְרוּשָׁלַםִ שַׂמְתֶּם מִזְבְּחוֹת לַבֹּשֶׁת
the to altars have you ,Jerusalem the the (as) and O
,thing shameful up set of streets of number ;Judah

6419 408 1168 6999 4196
14 מִזְבְּחוֹת לְקַטֵּר לַבָּעַל׃ וְאַתָּה אַל־תִּתְפַּלֵּל בְּעַד־
for do not ,you And .Baal to burn to altars
pray incense

8085 8605 7440 5375 3808 5971
הָעָם הַזֶּה וְאַל־תִּשָּׂא בַעֲדָם רִנָּה וּתְפִלָּה כִּי ׀ אֵינֶנִּי שֹׁמֵעַ
will I for or cry a for lift do and ,this people
hear not ,prayer them up not

1004 3039 4100 7451 7121 6256
15 בְּעֵת קָרְאָם אֵלַי בְּעַד רָעָתָם׃ מֶה לִידִידִי בְּבֵיתִי
My in My to What their for to they the in
,house beloved (belongs) .trouble Me cry time

5674 6944 1320 7227 4209 6213
עֲשׂוֹתָהּ הַמְזִמָּתָה הָרַבִּים וּבְשַׂר־קֹדֶשׁ יַעַבְרוּ מֵעָלָיִךְ כִּי
but from has holy the And .many her she (since)
you away passed flesh evils done has

3068 7121 8389 6529 3303 7488 2132 5937 227 7451
16 רָעָתֵכִי אָז תַּעֲלֹזִי׃ זַיִת רַעֲנָן יְפֵה פְרִי־תֹאַר קָרָא יְהוָה
Jehovah called ,fine (with) ,fair ,green A you do (How) your
fruit tree olive ;exult then ?evil

1808 7451 784 3341 1419 1999 6963 8034
שְׁמֵךְ לְקוֹל ׀ הֲמוּלָּה גְדֹלָה הִצִּית אֵשׁ עָלֶיהָ וְרָעוּ דָּלִיּוֹתָיו׃
its are and ,it to fire has He great storm the with your
.branches bad set of sound ;name

worthless. [17]And Jehovah of hosts who planted you has spoken evil against you, because of the evil of the house of Israel and of the house of Judah, which they have done to themselves, to provoke Me to anger, by burning incense to Baal.

[18]And Jehovah made me know. And I knew. Then You showed me their doings. [19]And I was like a docile lamb being brought to the slaughter; and I did not know that they had plotted schemes against me, *saying*, Let us destroy the tree with its fruit; and let us cut him off from the land of the living, so that his name may be remembered no more. [20]But, O Jehovah of hosts who judges with righteousness, who tries the reins and the heart, let me see Your vengeance on them. For to You I have laid open my cause. [21]For this reason, so says Jehovah concerning the men of Anathoth who seek your life, saying, Do not prophesy in the name of Jehovah, that you do not die by our hand. [22]So Jehovah of hosts says this: Behold, I will punish them. The young men shall die by the sword; their sons and their daughters shall die by famine; [23]and there shall be no survivor of them, for I will bring evil on the men of Anathoth, *even* the year of their punishment.

7451	1558	7451	1696	5193	6635	3068	17

וַיהוָה צְבָאוֹת הַנּוֹטֵעַ אוֹתָךְ דִּבֶּר עָלַיִךְ רָעָה בִּגְלַל רָעַת

the because ,evil against has you who hosts Jeho- And
of evil of you spoken planted of vah

בֵּית־יִשְׂרָאֵל וּבֵית יְהוּדָה אֲשֶׁר עָשׂוּ לָהֶם לְהַכְעִסֵנִי לְקַטֵּר

burn- by Me vex to them- to they which ,Judah the and Israel the
incense ing ,anger to selves done have of house of house

לַבָּעַל: [18]וַיהוָה הוֹדִיעַנִי וָאֵדָעָה אָז הִרְאִיתַנִי מַעַלְלֵיהֶם:

their showed You then I and informed And .Baal to
.doings me ;knew ,me Jehovah

[19]וַאֲנִי כְּכֶבֶשׂ אַלּוּף יוּבַל לִטְבוֹחַ וְלֹא־יָדַעְתִּי כִּי־עָלַי

against that did I and know the to being docile a like I And
me ;slaughter brought lamb (was)

חָשְׁבוּ מַחֲשָׁבוֹת נַשְׁחִיתָה עֵץ בְּלַחְמוֹ וְנִכְרְתֶנּוּ מֵאֶרֶץ

the from us let and its with the us Let schemes had they
of land off him cut ,food tree destroy ,(saying) plotted

חַיִּים וּשְׁמוֹ לֹא־יִזָּכֵר עוֹד: [20]וַיהוָה צְבָאוֹת שֹׁפֵט

who hosts O ,But .still be may not his that the
with judges of Jehovah remembered name ,living

צֶדֶק בֹּחֵן כְּלָיוֹת וָלֵב אֶרְאֶה נִקְמָתְךָ מֵהֶם כִּי אֵלֶיךָ גִּלִּיתִי

have I to for on Your me let see ,heart kidneys tries who righ-
revealed you ,them vengeance teousness

אֶת־רִיבִי: [21]לָכֵן כֹּה־אָמַר יְהוָה עַל־אַנְשֵׁי עֲנָתוֹת

,Anathoth the about Jehovah says thus Therefore .cause my
of men

הַמְבַקְשִׁים אֶת־נַפְשְׁךָ לֵאמֹר לֹא תִנָּבֵא בְּשֵׁם יְהוָה וְלֹא

that ,Jehovah the in Do not ,saying your who
not of name prophesy ,life seek

תָמוּת בְּיָדֵנוּ: [22]לָכֵן כֹּה אָמַר יְהוָה צְבָאוֹת הִנְנִי פֹקֵד

will ,Behold ,hosts Jehovah says thus Therefore our by you
punish I .hand die might

עֲלֵיהֶם הַבַּחוּרִים יָמֻתוּ בַחֶרֶב בְּנֵיהֶם וּבְנוֹתֵיהֶם יָמֻתוּ

shall their and their the by shall young the them
die daughters sons ;sword die men

בָּרָעָב: [23]וּשְׁאֵרִית לֹא תִהְיֶה לָהֶם כִּי־אָבִיא רָעָה אֶל־אַנְשֵׁי

the on evil will I for of will not a and by
of men bring ,them be remnant ;famine

עֲנָתוֹת שְׁנַת פְּקֻדָּתָם:

their the —Anathoth
.punishment of year

CAP. XII יב

CHAPTER 12

CHAPTER 12

[1]Righteous *are* You, O Jehovah, when I complain, yet let me speak with You *of Your* O Jehovah; yet let me speak *with You of Your* judgments. Why does the way of the wicked prosper? *Why* are all *those* at ease who deal treacherously? [2]You planted them; yea, they take root; they grow; they even make fruit. You *are* near in their mouth, and

צַדִּיק אַתָּה יְהוָה כִּי אָרִיב אֵלֶיךָ אַךְ מִשְׁפָּטִים אֲדַבֵּר

would I (Your about) indeed to might I that O You righteous
speak judgments ;You complain ,Jehovah ,(are)

אוֹתָךְ מַדּוּעַ דֶּרֶךְ רְשָׁעִים צָלֵחָה שָׁלוּ כָּל־בֹּגְדֵי בָגֶד:

treach- who all at (Why) does the the Why with
.erously deal ease ?prosper wicked of way .You

נְטַעְתָּם גַּם־שֹׁרָשׁוּ יֵלְכוּ גַּם־עָשׂוּ פֶרִי קָרוֹב אַתָּה בְּפִיהֶם

their in You near .fruit they even they they also planted You
,mouth (are) make ,grow ;root take ,them

far from their reins. 3 But You know me, O Jehovah. You have seen me and tried my heart toward You. Pull them out like sheep for the slaughter, and devote them to the day of slaughter. 4 How long shall the land mourn, and the grass of every field wither from the evil of those who dwell in it? The beasts and the birds are swept away, because they said, He will not see our last end.

5 If you have run with footmen, and they wore you out, then how can you compete with horses? And if you feel secure in the land of peace, then how will you do in the swelling of Jordan? 6 For even your brothers and the house of your father, even they have dealt treacherously with you; even they have fully called after you. Do not believe them, though they speak good things to you.

7 I have forsaken My house; I have left My inheritance. I have given the beloved of My soul into the hand of her enemies. 8 My inheritance has become as a lion in the forest to Me; she gave out her voice against Me; on account of this I hated her. 9 My inheritance *is like* a speckled bird to Me; the birds all around are against her. Come, gather all the beasts of the field, bring them to devour. 10 Many shepherds have destroyed My vineyard; they have trampled My portion under foot; they have made My pleasant portion a desolate wilderness. 11 One has made it desolate; it mourns to Me; the whole land is made desolate, but no man lays *it* to heart. 12 The ravagers have come on all bare heights through the wilderness; for the sword of Jehovah devours from *one* end of the land even to the *other* end of the land. There

974 72:00 30:45 3068 3629 7350
3 ורחוק מכליותיהם׃ ואתה יהוה ידעתני תראני ובחנת
and have You know O ,you But their from far but
tested me seen ;me ,Jehovah .reins

7819 3117 694.2 2428 6629 5423 38 20
לבי אתך התקם כצאן לטבחה והקדשם ליום הרגה׃
.slaughter the for con- and the for like Separate toward my
of day them secrate ,slaughter sheep them .You heart

3001 7704 36 05 6212 776 56 5704
4 עד־מתי תאבל הארץ ועשב כל־השדה ייבש
,wither field every the and the shall How
of grass ,land mourn long

7200 3808 559 5975 929 5595 3427 7451
מרעת ישבי־בה ספתה בהמות ועוף כי אמרו לא יראה
will He not they for the and The swept are ?it in those the from
see ,said ,birds beasts away dwell who of evil

2734 3811 7323 7273 379
5 את־אחריתנו׃ כי את־רגלים ׀ רצתה וילאוך ואיך תתחרה
you can then they and have you footmen with If last our
compete how ,you wearied ,run .end

62.13 982 7965 776 5483
את־הסוסים ובארץ שלום אתה בוטח ואיך תעשה
you will then feel you peace in if And ?horses with
do how ,secure of land the

898 1571 1004 251 3383 1347
6 בגאון הירדן׃ כי גם־אחיך ובית־אביך גם־המה בגדו
be- have they even your the and your even For the the in
trayed ,father of house brothers ?Jordan of swelling

1696 539 408 43 93 310 7121 1571
בך גם־המה קראו אחריך מלא אל־תאמן בם כי־ידברו
they though ,them Do not .fully after have they even ,you
speak believe you called

5159 5203 10:04 5800 2896
7 אליך טובות׃ עזבתי את־ביתי נטשתי את־נחלתי
My have I My have I good to
.inheritance left ;house forsaken .things you

5159 1961 341 3709 53.15 3033 5414
8 נתתי את־ידדות נפשי בכף איביה׃ היתה־לי נחלתי
in- My to has her the into My the have I
heritance Me become .enemies of palm soul of beloved given

58 61 8130 3651 5921 6963 5414 3293 738
9 כאריה ביער נתנה עלי בקולה על־כן שנאתיה׃ העיט
the (Like) hated I therefore her against she the in a like
bird .her ;voice Me out gave forest lion

2416 622 3212 5439 5861 5159 6641
צבוע נחלתי לי העיט סביב עליה לכו אספו כל־חית
the all gather ,Go against all (are) the (is) in- My speckled
of beasts .her around birds ;Me to heritance

947 3754 7843 7227 7462 402 857 77.04
10 השדה התיו לאכלה׃ רעים רבים שחתו כרמי בססו
they My have Many shepherds .devour to bring the
trod ,vineyard destroyed them ,field

8077 4057 2532 2513 5414 2513
את־חלקתי נתנו את־חלקת חמדתי למדבר שממה׃
.desolate wilder- a My portion have they My
ness pleasant made ;portion

776 36 05 6213 8077 56 80 76 7760
11 שמה לשממה אבלה עלי שממה נשמה כל־הארץ כי
but the whole is desolate to it deso- a has One
,land made ,Me mourns ,lation it made

770:3 935 4057 8205 3605 5921 38 20 77 60 376 369
12 אין איש שם על־לב׃ על־כל־שפים במדבר באו שדדים
;destroyers have the in the all On .heart to lays man no
come wilderness heights (it)

369 776 7097 776 7097 398 3068 2719
כי חרב ליהוה אכלה מקצה־ארץ ועד־קצה הארץ אין
not the the even the (one) from devours of the for
;land of end (other) to land of end Jehovah sword

is no peace for any flesh. [13]They have sown wheat, but they have reaped thorns. They are worn out, but they do not profit. And they shall be ashamed of your harvests, because of the glow of the anger of Jehovah.

[14]So says Jehovah against all my evil neighbors who touch the inheritance which I have caused My people Israel to inherit: Behold, I will tear them from their land, and I will tear the house of Judah from among them. [15]And it shall be, after I have torn them out, I will return and have pity on them, and will bring them again, each man to his inheritance, and each man to his land. [16]And it shall be, if they will carefully learn the ways of My people, to swear by My name, *As* Jehovah lives—as they taught My people to swear by Baal—then they will be built in the midst of My people. [17]But if they will not obey, then I will tear and destroy that nation, says Jehovah.

2470 7114 6975 2406 2232 1320 3605 7965
13 שָׁלוֹם לְכָל־בָּשָׂר׃ זָרְעוּ חִטִּים וְקֹצִים קָצָרוּ נֶחְלוּ
are they have but ,wheat They .flesh for peace
exhausted ;reaped thorns sown have any

3068 639 2740 8393 954 3276 3808
לֹא יוֹעִלוּ וּבֹשׁוּ מִתְּבוּאֹתֵיכֶם מֵחֲרוֹן אַף־יְהוָה׃
Jeho- anger of because your of are they and they but
.vah's of glow the ,harvests ashamed ;profit not

5159 5060 7451 7934 3605 5921 3068 559 3541
14 כֹּה ׀ אָמַר יְהוָה עַל־כָּל־שְׁכֵנַי הָרָעִים הַנֹּגְעִים בַּנַּחֲלָה
the who evil my all against Jeho- says Thus
inheritance touch neighbors vah

5428 3478 5971 5157 834
אֲשֶׁר־הִנְחַלְתִּי אֶת־עַמִּי אֶת־יִשְׂרָאֵל הִנְנִי נֹתְשָׁם מֵעַל
from will I ,Behold :Israel My have I which
them tear I people inherit to caused

310 1961 8432 5428 3063 1004 127
15 אַדְמָתָם וְאֶת־בֵּית יְהוּדָה אֶתּוֹשׁ מִתּוֹכָם׃ וְהָיָה אַחֲרֵי
after it And their from will I Judah the and their
be will .midst tear of house ,land

5159 376 7725 7355 7725 5428
נָתְשִׁי אוֹתָם אָשׁוּב וְרִחַמְתִּים וַהֲשִׁבֹתִים אִישׁ לְנַחֲלָתוֹ
his to each bring will and pity have and will I ,them have I
inheritance man ,back them them on return out torn

7650 5971 1870 3925 3925 518 1961 776 582
16 וְאִישׁ לְאַרְצוֹ׃ וְהָיָה אִם־לָמֹד יִלְמְדוּ אֶת־דַּרְכֵי עַמִּי לְהִשָּׁבֵעַ
swear to My the will they diligently if it And his to and
,people of ways learn ,be will .land man each

1129 1168 7650 5971 3925 3068 2416 8035
בִּשְׁמִי חַי־יְהוָה כַּאֲשֶׁר לִמְּדוּ אֶת־עַמִּי לְהִשָּׁבֵעַ בַּבָּעַל וְנִבְנוּ
they so ;Baal by to My they as ;Jehovah (as) My by
built be will swear people taught lives ,name

5428 1471 5428 8085 3808 518 5971 8432
17 בְּתוֹךְ עַמִּי׃ וְאִם לֹא יִשְׁמָעוּ וְנָתַשְׁתִּי אֶת־הַגּוֹי הַהוּא נָתוֹשׁ
tear ,that nation I then they not But My the in
out tear will ,obey will if .people of midst

3068 5002 6
וְאַבֵּד נְאֻם־יְהוָה׃
.Jehovah says and
,(it) destroy

CAP. XIII יג

CHAPTER 13

CHAPTER 13

[1]So says Jehovah to me, Go and buy for yourself a linen band, and put it on your loins, and do not put it in water. [2]So I bought a band according to the word of Jehovah, and put *it* on my loins. [3]And the word of Jehovah came to me a second time, saying, [4]Take the band that you bought, which *is* on your loins, and rise up; go to Euphrates and hide it there in the cleft of the rock. [5]So I went and hid it by Euphrates, as Jehovah commanded me.

7760 6593 232 7069 1980 3068 559 3541
1 כֹּה־אָמַר יְהוָה אֵלַי הָלוֹךְ וְקָנִיתָ לְּךָ אֵזוֹר פִּשְׁתִּים וְשַׂמְתּוֹ
put and linen band a for and Go ,me to Jehovah says Thus
it yourself buy

1697 232 7069 935 3808 4325 4975 5921
2 עַל־מָתְנֶיךָ וּבַמַּיִם לֹא תְבִאֵהוּ׃ וָאֶקְנֶה אֶת־הָאֵזוֹר כִּדְבַר
according the I So put do not in and your on
word to band bought .it water loins

8145 3068 1697 1961 4975 7760 3068
3 יְהוָה וָאָשִׂם עַל־מָתְנָי׃ וַיְהִי דְבַר־יְהוָה אֵלַי שֵׁנִית
second a to Jehovah the And my on put and Jeho-
time me of word came .loins (it) vah's

4975 5921 834 7069 834 232 3947 559
4 לֵאמֹר׃ קַח אֶת־הָאֵזוֹר אֲשֶׁר קָנִיתָ אֲשֶׁר עַל־מָתְנֶיךָ
your on which you which the Take ,saying
,loins (is) bought band

3212 5553 5357 8033 2934 6578 6965
5 וְקוּם לֵךְ פְּרָתָה וְטָמְנֵהוּ שָׁם בִּנְקִיק הַסָּלַע׃ וָאֵלֵךְ
I And .rock the the in there hide and to go and
went of cleft it Euphrates ,arise

1961 3068 6680 6578 2934
6 וָאֶטְמְנֵהוּ בִּפְרָת כַּאֲשֶׁר צִוָּה יְהוָה אוֹתִי׃ וַיְהִי
it And .me Jehovah com- as by hid and
was manded ,Euphrates it

[6]And it happened at the end of many days, Jehovah said to me, Rise up, go to Euphrates and take the band from there, which I commanded you to hide there. [7]Then I went to Euphrates and dug, and I took the band from the place, there where I had hidden it. And behold, the band was rotted; it was not useful for anything. [8]Then the word of Jehovah came to me, saying, [9]So says Jehovah, So I will spoil the pride of Judah, and the great pride of Jerusalem. [10]This evil people, who refuse to hear My words, who walk in the stubbornness of their heart, and walk after other gods, to serve them and to worship them, shall even be like this girdle; which is not useful for anything. [11]For as this girdle holds fast to the loins of a man, so I have caused the whole house of Israel and the whole house of Judah to cling to Me, says Jehovah; to be to Me for a people, and for a name, and for praise, and for glory; but they would not listen.

[12]So you will speak to them this word: So says Jehovah, God of Israel, Every skin shall be filled with wine. And they shall say to you, Do we not know full well that every skin shall be filled with wine? [13]Then you shall say to them, So says Jehovah, Behold, I will fill all the inhabitants of this land, even the kings that sit on David's throne, and the priests, and the prophets, and all the inhabitants of

3947 6578 32:12 6965 3068 559 7227 3117 7093
מִקֵּץ יָמִים רַבִּים וַיֹּאמֶר יְהוָה אֵלַי קוּם לֵךְ פְּרָתָה וְקַח
and take | to Euphrates | go | ,Arise | ,me to Jehovah | said | ,many | days | the at of end

6578 32:12 8033 2934 6680 834 232 8033
7 מִשָּׁם אֶת־הָאֵזוֹר אֲשֶׁר צִוִּיתִךָ לְטָמְנוֹ־שָׁם׃ וָאֵלֵךְ פְּרָתָה
to Euphrates | I Then went | .there | hide to | com- you manded | which I | the band | from there

8033 2934 4725 232 3947 2658
וָאֶחְפֹּר וָאֶקַּח אֶת־הָאֵזוֹר מִן־הַמָּקוֹם אֲשֶׁר־טְמַנְתִּיו שָׁמָּה
there | had I it hidden | where | the place | from | the band | I and took | ,dug and

1697 1961 3605 6743 3808 232 7843 2009
8 וְהִנֵּה נִשְׁחַת הָאֵזוֹר לֹא יִצְלַח לַכֹּל׃ וַיְהִי דְבַר־
the of word | Then came | any- .thing | for | was it useful | not | the band | was rotted | And ,behold

7843 3068 559 3541 559 3068
9 יְהוָה אֵלַי לֵאמֹר׃ כֹּה אָמַר יְהוָה כָּכָה אַשְׁחִית אֶת־
will I ruin | so | ,Jehovah says | Thus | ,saying | ,me to Jehovah

7451 2088 5971 7227 3389 1347 3063 1347
10 גְּאוֹן יְהוּדָה וְאֶת־גְּאוֹן יְרוּשָׁלִַם הָרָב׃ הָעָם הַזֶּה הָרָע
evil | This | people | .great | Jerusalem | the and of pride | Judah | the of pride

3820 8307 1980 1697 8085 3987
הַמֵּאֲנִים ׀ לִשְׁמוֹעַ אֶת־דְּבָרַי הַהֹלְכִים בִּשְׁרִרוּת לִבָּם
their heart | stub- the in of bornness | who walk | My ,words | hear to | who refuse

7812 5647 312 430 310 3212
וַיֵּלְכוּ אַחֲרֵי אֱלֹהִים אֲחֵרִים לְעָבְדָם וּלְהִשְׁתַּחֲוֹת לָהֶם
,them | to and worship | serve to them | other | gods | after | and walk

1692 3605 6743 3808 834 2088 232 1961
11 וִיהִי כָּאֵזוֹר הַזֶּה אֲשֶׁר לֹא־יִצְלַח לַכֹּל׃ כִּי כַּאֲשֶׁר יִדְבַּק
clings | as | For | for .anything | is useful | not | which | this | like band | even be will

1004 3605 1692 376 4975 232
הָאֵזוֹר אֶל־מָתְנֵי אִישׁ כֵּן הִדְבַּקְתִּי אֵלַי אֶת־כָּל־בֵּית
house of | the whole | Me to | made I cling | so | ,man a | the of loins | to | the band

5971 1961 3068 5002 3063 1004 3605 3478
יִשְׂרָאֵל וְאֶת־כָּל־בֵּית יְהוּדָה נְאֻם־יְהוָה לִהְיוֹת לִי לְעָם
a for ,people | to Me | be to | ,Jehovah says | ,Judah | house of | the and whole | Israel

559 8085 3808 8597 8416 8034
12 וּלְשֵׁם וְלִתְהִלָּה וּלְתִפְאָרֶת וְלֹא שָׁמֵעוּ׃ וְאָמַרְתָּ אֲלֵיהֶם
them to | you So speak will | would they .listen | but not | for and ;glory | for and ,praise | for and ,name a

5035 3605 3478 430 3068 559 3541 2088 1697
אֶת־הַדָּבָר הַזֶּה כֹּה־אָמַר יְהוָה אֱלֹהֵי יִשְׂרָאֵל כָּל־נֵבֶל
skin | Every | ,Israel | God of | Jehovah | says | Thus | :this | word

4390 5035 3605 3045 3808 3045 559 3196 4390
יִמָּלֵא יָיִן וְאָמְרוּ אֵלֶיךָ הֲיָדֹעַ לֹא נֵדַע כִּי־כָל־נֵבֶל יִמָּלֵא
be will with filled | skin | every that | we Do not know | very well | ,you to | they And say will | .wine | be will with filled

4390 3068 559 3541 3196
13 יָיִן׃ וְאָמַרְתָּ אֲלֵיהֶם כֹּה־אָמַר יְהוָה הִנְנִי מְמַלֵּא
fill will with | ,Behold I | ,Jehovah | says | thus | ,them to | you Then say will | ?wine

1732 3427 4428 2088 776 3427
אֶת־כָּל־יֹשְׁבֵי הָאָרֶץ הַזֹּאת וְאֶת־הַמְּלָכִים הַיֹּשְׁבִים לְדָוִד
for David | that sit | the kings | even | ,this | the land | inhab- the all of itants

3427 3605 5030 3548 3678/5921
עַל־כִּסְאוֹ וְאֶת־הַכֹּהֲנִים וְאֶת־הַנְּבִיאִים וְאֵת כָּל־יֹשְׁבֵי
the of inhabitants | all | and | the ,prophets | and | the ,priests | and | his ,throne | upon

Jerusalem, with drunken-
ness. 14And I will smash
them one against another,
even the fathers and the
sons together, declares
Jehovah; I will not pity, nor
spare, nor have compas-
sion, *to keep them* from
their destruction.
15Hear and give ear; do
not be proud; for Jehovah
has spoken. 16Give glory to
Jehovah your God, before
He brings darkness, and
before your feet stumble on
the dark mountains. Yea,
while you look for light, He
puts it into death-shade,
setting up deep gloom.
17But if you will not hear it,
my soul shall weep in secret
places for *your* pride. And
my eye shall bitterly weep
and run down with tears,
because Jehovah's flock
was captured. 18Say to the
king and to the queen
mother, Humble yourselves,
sit down. For the crown of
your glory will come down
from your head-places.
19The cities of the south
have been shut up, and
none are opening. Judah
has been exiled; all of it has
been peacefully exiled.
20Lift up your eyes and
behold those who come
from the north. Where *is* the
flock *that* was given to you,
your beautiful flock? 21What
will you say when He visits
you? For you taught them *to
be* rulers over you for a
head. Do not pangs seize
you, like a woman in travail?
22And if you say in your
heart, Why do these things
come upon me? *It is* be-
cause of the greatness of
your iniquity; your skirts are
bared; your heels suffer
violence. 23Can the Ethi-
opian change his skin, or
the leopard his spots? *Then*
you also may do good, who
are accustomed to doing
evil. 24And I will scatter
them as the stubble that
passes away to the wilderness wind. 25This *is* your
lot, the share of your
measure from Me, declares
Jehovah; because you have

1121 1 251 376 5310 7943 3389
14 ירושלם שכרון׃ ונפצתים איש אל־אחיו והאבות והבנים
the and the even his against man will I And drunken- ,Jerusalem
sons fathers brother them smash .ness
7355 2347 2550 3808 3068 5002 3162
יחדו נאם־יהוה לא־אחמול ולא־אחוס ולא ארחם
have nor ,spare nor will I not ;Jehovah says ,together
,compassion pity
1697 3068 1361 3808 238 8085 7843
15 מהשחיתם׃ שמעו והאזינו אל־תגבהו כי יהוה דבר׃
has Jehovah for be not give and Hear their from
.spoken ,proud ,ear .destruction
5061 2962 2821 2962 3519 430 3068 5414
16 תנו ליהוה אלהיכם כבוד בטרם יחשך ובטרם יתנגפו
stumble and brings He before glory your to Give
before darkness God Jehovah
6757 7760 216 6960 5399 2022 5921 7272
רגליכם על־הרי נשף וקויתם לאור ושמה לצלמות
into puts He for while and dark- the on your
,death-shade it ,light wait you ;ness of mountains feet
1058 4565 8085 3808 518 6205 7896
17 ישית לערפל׃ ואם לא תשמעוה במסתרים תבכה־
shall secret in will you not But deep (and)
weep places ,it to listen if .gloom up sets
7617 1830 5869 3381 1832 1830 1466 5315
נפשי מפני גוה ודמע תדמע ותרד עיני דמעה כי נשבה
was for (with) my run and shed and (such) for my
seized ,tears eye down tears bitterly ,pride soul
3427 8213 1377 4428 559 3068 5739
18 עדר יהוה׃ אמר למלך ולגבירה השפילו שבו
sit Humble the to and the to Say .Jehovah's flock
;down ,yourselves ,mother queen king
5462 5045 5892 8597 5850 4761 3381
19 כי ירד מראשתיכם עטרת תפארתכם׃ ערי הנגב סגרו
been have the The your the your from will for
,up shut south of cities .glory of crown head-places descend
7965 1540 3605 3063 1540 6605 369
ואין פתח הגלת יהודה כלה הגלת שלומים׃
.peacefully been has of all ;Judah been has are and
exiled it exiled opening none
6629 5414 5739 6828 935 7200 5869 5375
20 שאי עיניכם וראי הבאים מצפון איה העדר נתן־לך צאן
flock to (that) the where the from those and your Lift
,you given was flock (is) ;north come who behold eyes up
3925 6485 559 4100 8597
21 תפארתך׃ מה־תאמרי כי־יפקד עליך ואת למדת אתם
them taught For ?you He when you will What your
you visits say ?beautiful
3205 802 3644 270 2256 7218 441 5921
עליך אלפים לראש הלוא חבלים יאחזוך כמו אשת לדה׃
?bearing a like seize Will birth not a for chieftains (be to)
woman you pangs !head you over
1540 5771 7230 428 7125 4100 3824 559
22 וכי תאמרי בלבבך מדוע קראני אלה ברב עונך נגלו
are your Great these hap- have Why your in you And
bared ;iniquity ?things me to pened ,heart say if
2272 5246 5785 3569 2015 6119 2554 7757
23 שוליך נחמסו עקביך׃ היהפך כושי עורו ונמר חברברתיו
his the or his the Can your suffer your
?spots leopard ,skin Ethiopian change .heels violence ;skirts
5674 7179 6327 7489 3928 3190 3201 1571
24 גם־אתם תוכלו להיטיב למדי הרע׃ ואפיצם כקש עובר
passing the as will I So doing are who do may you (Then)
away stubble them scatter .evil to accustomed ,good also
3068 5002 4055 4490 1486 4057 7307
25 לרוח מדבר׃ זה גורלך מנת־מדיך מאתי נאם־יהוה אשר
because ;Jehovah says from your the your This wilder- the the to
,Me measure of portion ,lot (is) .ness of wind

forgotten Me, and have trusted in falsehood. 26So I also have stripped off your skirts over your face, that your shame may appear. 27I have seen your adulteries, and your neighings, the plot of your infidelity, your abominations on the hills, in the fields. Woe to you, O Jerusalem! Will you not be made clean? How long *will it* still *be*?

5921 77 57 2834 8267 982 7911
26 שְׁכַחַתְּ אוֹתִי וַתִּבְטְחִי בַּשָּׁקֶר׃ וְגַם־אֲנִי חָשַׂפְתִּי שׁוּלַיִךְ עַל־
over your have I also So in and Me have you
skirts off stripped .falsehood trusted forgotten

5921 2184 2154 4684 5004 7036 7200 6440
27 פָּנָיִךְ וְנִרְאָה קְלוֹנֵךְ׃ נִאֻפַיִךְ וּמִצְהֲלוֹתַיִךְ זִמַּת זְנוּתֵךְ עַל־
on your the your and your your may and your
infidelity of plot ;neighings ,adulteries ,shame seen be face

2891 3808 3389 188 8251 7200 7704 1389
גְּבָעוֹת בַּשָּׂדֶה רָאִיתִי שִׁקּוּצָיִךְ אוֹי לָךְ יְרוּשָׁלַםִ לֹא תִטְהֲרִי
you Will not O to Woe your have I in the the
?clean be !Jerusalem you .abominations ,seen field hills

5750 310
אַחֲרֵי מָתַי עֹד׃
?still how After
long

CAP. XIV יד

CHAPTER 14

CHAPTER 14

1That which came, the word of Jehovah to Jeremiah, concerning the matter of droughts. 2Judah mourns, and her gates droop. They put on mourning for the land, and the cry of Jerusalem has gone up. 3And their nobles have sent their little ones for water; they came to the cisterns; they found no water. They returned with their vessels empty; they were ashamed and confounded, and covered their head. 4Because the ground was cracked, for there was no rain in the land; the plowmen were ashamed; they covered their head. 5For even the doe calved in the field, and forsook *it*, because there was no grass. 6And the wild asses stood in the high places; they snuffed up the wind like jackals; their eyes failed because *there was* no grass.

7O Jehovah, though our iniquities testify against us, act for Your name's sake; for our apostasies are many; we have sinned against You. 8O Hope of Israel, its Savior in time of distress, why should You be as an alien in the land, and as a traveler turning in to lodge? 9Why should You be as a man stunned, as one mighty, yet cannot save? Yet You, O Jehovah *are* in our midst, and Your

1226 1697 3414 3068 1697 1961 834
1 אֲשֶׁר הָיָה דְבַר־יְהוָה אֶל־יִרְמְיָהוּ עַל־דִּבְרֵי הַבַּצָּרוֹת׃
:droughts the con- Jeremiah to Jehovah the came That
of matter cerning of word (as) which

6682 776 6937 535 8179 3063 56
2 אָבְלָה יְהוּדָה וּשְׁעָרֶיהָ אֻמְלְלוּ קָדְרוּ לָאָרֶץ וְצִוְחַת
the and the for on put They .languish her and Judah mourns
of cry ,land ashes gates

935 4325 6810 7971 117 5927 3389
3 יְרוּשָׁלַםִ עָלָתָה׃ וְאַדִּרֵיהֶם שָׁלְחוּ צְעוֹרֵיהֶם לַמָּיִם בָּאוּ
they for little their have their And gone has Jerusalem
came ;water ones sent nobles .up

3637 954 7387 3627 7725 4325 4672 1356
עַל־גֵּבִים לֹא־מָצְאוּ מַיִם שָׁבוּ כְלֵיהֶם רֵיקָם בֹּשׁוּ וְהָכְלְמוּ
and were they ;empty their They .water they no the to
,blushed ashamed vessels ,returned found ;cisterns

1653 1961 3808 2865 127 7218 2645
4 וְחָפוּ רֹאשָׁם׃ בַּעֲבוּר הָאֲדָמָה חַתָּה כִּי לֹא־הָיָה גֶשֶׁם
rain there no for is the Because their and
was ,shattered ground .head covered

7704 365 7218 2645 4060 954 776
5 בָּאָרֶץ בֹּשׁוּ אִכָּרִים חָפוּ רֹאשָׁם׃ כִּי גַם־אַיֶּלֶת בַּשָּׂדֶה
the in the even For their they plow- the were the in
field doe .head covered ;men ashamed ;land

8205 5921 6501 1877 1961 5800 3205
6 יָלְדָה וְעָזוֹב כִּי לֹא־הָיָה דֶּשֶׁא׃ וּפְרָאִים עָמְדוּ עַל־שְׁפָיִם
the on stood the And .grass there no for and gave
;heights asses wild was (it) abandoned birth

5771 6212 369 5869 3615 8577 7307 7602
7 שָׁאֲפוּ רוּחַ כַּתַּנִּים כָּלוּ עֵינֵיהֶם כִּי־אֵין עֵשֶׂב׃ אִם־עֲוֺנֵינוּ
our Though .grass there for their failed like the they
iniquities no was eyes ;jackals wind up snuffed

4878 7231 8034 4616 6213 3068 6030
עָנוּ בָנוּ יְהוָה עֲשֵׂה לְמַעַן שְׁמֶךָ כִּי־רַבּוּ מְשׁוּבֹתֵינוּ לְךָ
against our are for Your for act O against testi-
You ;apostasies many ;name's sake ,Jehovah ,us fy

1961 4100 6864 6256 3467 3478 4723 2398
8 חָטָאנוּ׃ מִקְוֵה יִשְׂרָאֵל מוֹשִׁיעוֹ בְּעֵת צָרָה לָמָּה תִהְיֶה
should why ,distress in its ,Israel O have we
be You of time Savior of Hope .sinned

1724 376 1961 4100 3885 5186 732 776 1616
9 כְּגֵר בָּאָרֶץ וּכְאֹרֵחַ נָטָה לָלוּן׃ לָמָּה תִהְיֶה כְּאִישׁ נִדְהָם
,stunned a like should Why to who a as or the in a as
man be You ?lodge in turns traveler ,land stranger

8034 3068 7130 3467 3201 3808 1368
כְּגִבּוֹר לֹא־יוּכַל לְהוֹשִׁיעַ וְאַתָּה בְקִרְבֵּנוּ יְהוָה וְשִׁמְךָ
Your and O our in (are) Yet ?save who not one as
name ,Jehovah ,midst You can ,mighty

name is called on us. Do not leave us.

[10]So says Jehovah to this people: So they have loved to wander; they have not restrained their feet; therefore Jehovah does not accept them. He will now remember their iniquity, and punish their sins. [11]Then Jehovah said to me, Do not pray for good for this people. [12]When they fast, I will not listen to their cry; and when they offer burnt offering and grain offering, I will not accept them. But I will consume them by the sword, and by famine, and by the plague.

[13]Then I said, Ah, O Lord Jehovah! Behold, the prophets are saying to them, You shall not see the sword, nor shall you have famine; but I will give you true peace in this place. [14]And Jehovah said to me, The prophets prophesy lies in My name. I did not send them, and I have not commanded them; nor did I speak to them. They prophesy to you a false vision, and a worthless divination, and the deceit of their heart. [15]So Jehovah says this concerning the prophets who prophesy in My name, and I did not send them; yet they say, Sword and famine shall not be in this land: By sword and famine those prophets shall be consumed. [16]And the people to whom they prophesy shall be cast out in the streets of Jerusalem, because of the famine and the sword. And none will bury them; *either* them, their wives, or their sons, or their daughters. For I will pour their evil on them.

[17]And you shall speak this word to them: Let my

עָלֵינוּ נִקְרָא אַל־תַּנִּחֵנוּ׃ 10 כֹּה־אָמַר יְהוָה לָעָם הַזֶּה
,this to Jehovah says Thus leave do not is upon
people .us ;called us

כֵּן אָהֲבוּ לָנוּעַ רַגְלֵיהֶם לֹא חָשָׂכוּ וַיהוָה לֹא רָצָם עַתָּה
now does not therefore have they not their to have they So
;them accept Jehovah ;restrained feet ;wander loved

11 יִזְכֹּר עֲוֺנָם וְיִפְקֹד חַטֹּאתָם׃ וַיֹּאמֶר יְהוָה אֵלָי
.me to Jehovah .sins their and their re- will He
said punish iniquities member

12 אַל־תִּתְפַּלֵּל בְּעַד־הָעָם הַזֶּה לְטוֹבָה׃ כִּי יָצֻמוּ אֵינֶנִּי שֹׁמֵעַ
will I they When for this people for Do not
listen not ,fast .good pray

אֶל־רִנָּתָם וְכִי יַעֲלוּ עֹלָה וּמִנְחָה אֵינֶנִּי רֹצָם כִּי בַּחֶרֶב
the by but will not I grain and burnt they and their to
sword ;them accept ,offering offering offer when ;cry

13 וּבָרָעָב וּבַדֶּבֶר אָנֹכִי מְכַלֶּה אוֹתָם׃ וָאֹמַר אֲהָהּ ׀ אֲדֹנָי
O ,Ah I Then .them will I by and by and
Lord ,said consume plague the ,famine

יְהוִה הִנֵּה הַנְּבִאִים אֹמְרִים לָהֶם לֹא־תִרְאוּ חֶרֶב וְרָעָב
and the you not ,them to are the Behold Jeho-
famine ,sword see shall saying prophets vah

לֹא־יִהְיֶה לָכֶם כִּי־שְׁלוֹם אֱמֶת אֶתֵּן לָכֶם בַּמָּקוֹם הַזֶּה׃
.this place in you to will I true peace but for will not
give you be

14 וַיֹּאמֶר יְהוָה אֵלַי שֶׁקֶר הַנְּבִאִים נִבְּאִים בִּשְׁמִי
My in prophesy The lies ,me to Jehovah said And
.name prophets

לֹא שְׁלַחְתִּים וְלֹא צִוִּיתִים וְלֹא דִבַּרְתִּי אֲלֵיהֶם חֲזוֹן שֶׁקֶר
,false a ;them to I did nor have I and did I not
vision speak ,them commanded not them send

וְקֶסֶם וֶאֱלוּל וְתַרְמוּת לִבָּם הֵמָּה מִתְנַבְּאִים לָכֶם׃
.you to are they their the and worthless a and
prophesying heart of deceit divination

15 לָכֵן כֹּה־אָמַר יְהוָה עַל־הַנְּבִאִים הַנִּבְּאִים בִּשְׁמִי וַאֲנִי לֹא־
not and My in who the con- Jehovah says thus There-
I ,name prophesy prophets cerning fore

שְׁלַחְתִּים וְהֵמָּה אֹמְרִים חֶרֶב וְרָעָב לֹא יִהְיֶה בָּאָרֶץ הַזֹּאת
:this in shall not and Sword ,say yet send did
land be famine they ;them

16 בַּחֶרֶב וּבָרָעָב יִתַּמּוּ הַנְּבִאִים הָהֵמָּה׃ וְהָעָם אֲשֶׁר־הֵמָּה
they whom the And .those prophets be shall and by
people consumed famine sword

נִבְּאִים לָהֶם יִהְיוּ מֻשְׁלָכִים בְּחֻצוֹת יְרוּשָׁלַםִ מִפְּנֵי ׀ הָרָעָב
the because Jerusalem the into cast will to prophesy
famine of of streets out be them

וְהַחֶרֶב וְאֵין מְקַבֵּר לָהֵמָּה הֵמָּה נְשֵׁיהֶם וּבְנֵיהֶם וּבְנֹתֵיהֶם
their and their and their ,them ,them will And the and
;daughters ,sons ,wives bury none ,sword

17 וְשָׁפַכְתִּי עֲלֵיהֶם אֶת־רָעָתָם׃ וְאָמַרְתָּ אֲלֵיהֶם אֶת־הַדָּבָר
word them to you So .evil their them on will I for
speak shall out pour

eyes run down with tears night and day, and do not let them cease. For the virgin daughter of my people is broken with a great break, *with* a very grievous blow. [18]If I go out into the field, then I see those killed with the sword. And if I enter into the city, then, behold, pollutions of famine! Yes, both the prophet and the priest have gone up into a land that they do not know. [19]Have You completely rejected Judah? Or has Your soul hated Zion? Why have You stricken us, and no healing *is* for us? *We* looked for peace, but no good *came;* and for a healing time, but, behold, terror! [20]We acknowledge our wickedness, O Jehovah, the iniquity of our fathers; for we have sinned against You. [21]For Your name's sake, do not spurn *us;* do not dishonor the throne of Your glory. Remember, *and* do not break Your covenant with us. [22]Among the vanities of the nations, are there *any* who make rain fall? Or can the heavens give showers? *Is* it not You, O Jehovah our God? Then we will wait for You; for You do all these *things.*

1820 3808 3119 3915 1832 5869 3381 2088
הַזֶּה תֵּרַדְנָה עֵינַי דִּמְעָה לַיְלָה וְיוֹמָם וְאַל־תִּדְמֶינָה כִּי
for let do and ,day and night (with) my run Let :this
,cease them not tears eyes down

3966 2470 4347 5971/1323 1330 7667 1419 7665
שֶׁבֶר גָּדוֹל נִשְׁבְּרָה בְּתוּלַת בַּת־עַמִּי מַכָּה נַחְלָה מְאֹד׃
.very grievous a My daughter the is great (with)
blow people of virgin broken break a

5892 935 518 2719 2491 2009 7704 3318 518
אִם־יָצָאתִי הַשָּׂדֶה וְהִנֵּה חַלְלֵי־חֶרֶב וְאִם בָּאתִי הָעִיר
the enter I And the those then ,field the go I If
,city into if !sword with pierced behold in out

18 776 5503 3548 5030 7458 2491
וְהִנֵּה תַּחֲלוּאֵי רָעָב כִּי גַם־נָבִיא גַם־כֹּהֵן סָחֲרוּ אֶל־אֶרֶץ
a to have the and the both For !famine diseases than
land traveled priest prophet of ,behold

19 6726 3063 3973 3973 3045 3808
וְלֹא יָדָעוּ׃ הֲמָאֹס מָאַסְתָּ אֶת־יְהוּדָה אִם־בְּצִיּוֹן
Zion Or ?Judah You Have utterly do they that
rejected .know not

7965 6960 4832 369 5221 4100 5315 1602
גָּעֲלָה נַפְשֶׁךָ מַדּוּעַ הִכִּיתָנוּ וְאֵין לָנוּ מַרְפֵּא קַוֵּה לְשָׁלוֹם
for We ?healing for and you have Why Your has
,peace waited us is not us struck ?soul abhorred

20 7562 3068 3045 1205 2009 4832 6256 2896 369
וְאֵין טוֹב וּלְעֵת מַרְפֵּא וְהִנֵּה בְעָתָה׃ יָדַעְנוּ יְהוָה רִשְׁעֵנוּ
wick- our O We !terror but ,healing a for and good but
,edness ,Jehovah ,know ,behold of time (came) nothing

21 8034 4616 5006 2398 1 5771
עֲוֹן אֲבוֹתֵינוּ כִּי חָטָאנוּ לָךְ׃ אַל־תִּנְאַץ לְמַעַן שִׁמְךָ
Your for Do not against have we for our ini- the
;name's sake spurn ,You sinned ,fathers of quity

1285 6565 2142 3519 3678 5034 408
אַל־תְּנַבֵּל כִּסֵּא כְבוֹדֶךָ זְכֹר אַל־תָּפֵר בְּרִיתְךָ אִתָּנוּ׃
with Your do not Remem- Your the do not
.us covenant break ,ber .glory of throne dishonor

22 7241 5414 8064 1652 1471 1892 3426
הֲיֵשׁ בְּהַבְלֵי הַגּוֹיִם מַגְשִׁמִים וְאִם־הַשָּׁמַיִם יִתְּנוּ רְבִבִים
?showers can the Or who those the the among Are
grant heavens ?fall rain make nations of vanities there

6213 6960 430 3068
הֲלֹא אַתָּה־הוּא יְהוָה אֱלֹהֵינוּ וּנְקַוֶּה־לָּךְ כִּי־אַתָּה עָשִׂיתָ
do You for for Therefore our O (Is) You not
;You wait will we ?God Jehovah it

428 3605
אֶת־כָּל־אֵלֶּה׃
these all
.(things)

CAP. XV טו

CHAPTER 15

[1]Then Jehovah said to me, Though Moses and Samuel stood before Me, My soul *could* not *be* toward this people. Send *them* out from before My face; yea, let them go out. [2]And it will be, if they say to you, Where shall we go? Then you will tell them, So says Jehovah, Those who *are* for death, go to death; and those for the sword, to the sword; and those for the famine, to the famine;

1 369 6440 8050 4872 5975 3068 559
וַיֹּאמֶר יְהוָה אֵלַי אִם־יַעֲמֹד מֹשֶׁה וּשְׁמוּאֵל לְפָנַי אֵין
(could) before and Moses stood Though to Jehovah Then
not Me Samuel ,me said

2 1961 3318 6440 7971 2088 5971 5315
נַפְשִׁי אֶל־הָעָם הַזֶּה שַׁלַּח מֵעַל־פָּנַי וְיֵצֵאוּ׃ וְהָיָה כִּי
when it And let and My (them) Send .this people (turn) My
be will .out go them face from away toward soul

3068 559 3541 559 3318 575 559
יֹאמְרוּ אֵלֶיךָ אָנָה נֵצֵא וְאָמַרְתָּ אֲלֵיהֶם כֹּה־אָמַר יְהוָה
:Jehovah says Thus ,them to you Then shall Where to shall they
say will ?go we ,you say

7458 2719 2719 4194 4194
אֲשֶׁר לַמָּוֶת לַמָּוֶת וַאֲשֶׁר לַחֶרֶב לַחֶרֶב וַאֲשֶׁר לָרָעָב
the for and the to the for and to (go) for (are) those
,famine those ,sword ,sword those ;death ,death who

and those for the captivity, to the captivity. [3]And I will set over them four kinds, says Jehovah: the sword to kill, and the dogs to drag off, and the birds of the heavens and the beasts of the earth to devour and destroy. [4]And I will cause them to be a terror to all the kingdoms of the earth, because of Manasseh, the son of Hezekiah, king of Judah; for what he did in Jerusalem.

[5]For who shall have pity on you, O Jerusalem? Or who shall weep over you? Or who shall turn aside to ask your welfare? [6]You have forsaken Me, says Jehovah; you have gone backward; therefore, I will stretch out My hand against you and destroy you; I am weary of repenting. [7]And I will sift them with a fork in the gates of the land; I will bereave; I will destroy My people, *for* they do not turn from their ways. [8]Their widows are more numerous about Me than the sand of the seas; I have brought for them a ravager at noonday against the mother of a young man; I caused anguish and terror to fall on her suddenly. [9]She who bore seven *now* languishes; she has breathed out her life; her sun has gone down while *it was* still day. She has been ashamed and humiliated; and I will deliver the rest of them to the sword before their enemies, declares Jehovah.

[10]Woe to me, my mother, that you have borne me, a man of strife, and a man of contention to the whole earth! I have not loaned, nor have they loaned to me; *yet* everyone curses me. [11]Jehovah said, Truly I will free you for good. Truly I will cause the enemy to entreat you in the time of evil and in

3 לָרָעָב וַאֲשֶׁר לַשְּׁבִי לַשֶּׁבִי׃ וּפָקַדְתִּי עֲלֵיהֶם אַרְבַּע
four over them will I And appoint the to .captivity the for ,captivity and those the to ;famine
מִשְׁפָּחוֹת נְאֻם־יְהוָה אֶת־הַחֶרֶב לַהֲרֹג וְאֶת־הַכְּלָבִים
dogs the and ,kill to sword the :Jehovah says kinds (doom of)
לִסְחֹב וְאֶת־עוֹף הַשָּׁמַיִם וְאֶת־בֶּהֱמַת הָאָרֶץ לֶאֱכֹל
devour to the earth the of beasts and the heavens the of birds and drag to ,off
4 וּלְהַשְׁחִית׃ וּנְתַתִּים לְזוּעָה לְכֹל מַמְלְכוֹת הָאָרֶץ בִּגְלַל
because of the ,earth king- of doms the all to terror a will I And them make to and .destroy
מְנַשֶּׁה בֶּן־יְחִזְקִיָּהוּ מֶלֶךְ יְהוּדָה עַל אֲשֶׁר־עָשָׂה בִּירוּשָׁלָםִ׃
in .Jerusalem did he what for ,Judah king of ,Hezekiah the of son Manas- ,seh
5 כִּי מִי־יַחְמֹל עָלַיִךְ יְרוּשָׁלַםִ וּמִי יָנוּד לָךְ וּמִי יָסוּר
turn will aside Or who for ;you will lament Or who O ?Jerusalem ,you on shall who pity have For
6 לִשְׁאֹל לְשָׁלֹם לָךְ׃ אַתְּ נָטַשְׁתְּ אֹתִי נְאֻם־יְהוָה אָחוֹר
back- ward ;Jehovah says ,Me have forsaken You ?your welfare ask to about
תֵּלֵכִי וָאַט אֶת־יָדִי עָלַיִךְ וָאַשְׁחִיתֵךְ נִלְאֵיתִי הִנָּחֵם׃
.repenting am I of weary and ;you destroy against you My hand will I so extend have you ;gone
7 וָאֶזְרֵם בְּמִזְרֶה בְּשַׁעֲרֵי הָאָרֶץ שִׁכַּלְתִּי אִבַּדְתִּי אֶת־עַמִּי
My ;people make perish will I ,bereave the ;land the in of gates a with fork will I And them winnow
8 מִדַּרְכֵיהֶם לוֹא שָׁבוּ׃ עָצְמוּ־לִי אַלְמְנוֹתָו מֵחוֹל יַמִּים
the ;seas the than of sand Their widows about Me more are numerous they .turn do not from (for) way their
הֵבֵאתִי לָהֶם עַל־אֵם בָּחוּר שֹׁדֵד בַּצָּהֳרַיִם הִפַּלְתִּי עָלֶיהָ
on her made I fall at ;noonday a destroyer young a ,man of a mother against for ,them have I brought
9 פִּתְאֹם עִיר וּבֶהָלוֹת׃ אֻמְלְלָה יֹלֶדֶת הַשִּׁבְעָה נָפְחָה נַפְשָׁהּ
;life her has she out breathed ,seven who She bore languishes and .terror anguish sud- ,denly
בָּאָה שִׁמְשָׁהּ בְּעֹד יוֹמָם בּוֹשָׁה וְחָפֵרָה וּשְׁאֵרִיתָם לַחֶרֶב
the to sword their remnant and ;humiliated and was she ashamed ;day while yet (was it) her sun has gone
10 אֶתֵּן לִפְנֵי אֹיְבֵיהֶם נְאֻם־יְהוָה׃ אוֹי־לִי אִמִּי כִּי
that my ,mother to Woe ,me .Jehovah says their ,enemies before will I deliver
יְלִדְתִּנִי אִישׁ רִיב וְאִישׁ מָדוֹן לְכָל־הָאָרֶץ לֹא־נָשִׁיתִי וְלֹא־
nor have I ,loaned not the ,land all to con- tention a and of man ,strife a of man have you me borne
11 נָשׁוּ־בִי כֻּלֹּה מְקַלְלַונִי׃ אָמַר יְהוָה אִם־לֹא שֵׁרִותִךָ לְטוֹב
for .good will I you free Truly ,Jehovah Said curses .me (yet) everyone ,me to have loaned they
אִם־לוֹא הִפְגַּעְתִּי בְךָ בְּעֵת רָעָה וּבְעֵת צָרָה אֶת־הָאֹיֵב׃
the .enemy distress a of time in and evil a of time in you cause will I entreat to Truly

the time of distress. 12 Can one break iron, iron or bronze from the north? 13 Your wealth and your treasures I will give for prey, not for price, but for all your sins, even in all your borders. 14 And I will make *you* pass with your enemies into a land you do not know. For a fire has been kindled in My anger; it shall burn against you.

15 O Jehovah, You know. Remember me and visit me, and take vengeance for me on those who seek to hurt me. Do not take me away in Your long-suffering; know that I bear reproach for You. 16 Your words were found, and I ate them; and Your word was to me the joy and gladness of my heart; for I am called by Your name, O Jehovah, God of hosts. 17 I did not sit in the circle of merrymakers, nor exult; I sat alone, because of Your hand; for You have filled me with indignation. 18 Why has my pain been without end, and my wound incurable, refusing to be healed? You surely are to me like a false stream *whose* waters cannot be trusted.

19 So Jehovah says this: If you return, then I will bring you again; you shall stand before Me. And if you take the precious from the worthless, you shall be as My mouth. Let them turn back to you, but do not return to them. 20 And I will make you a fortified wall of bronze to this people. And they shall fight against you, but they shall not overcome you; for I *am* with you to save you and to deliver you, says Jehovah. 21 And I will deliver you out of the hand of the wicked, and I will redeem you from the palm of the evil ones.

214 2428 5178 6828 1270 1270 7489
12 13 הירע ברזל ברזל מצפון ונחשת׃ חילך ואוצרותיך
your and treasures | Your wealth | or ?bronze | the from north | iron | ,iron | one Can break

1366 3605 2403 3605 4242 3808 957
לבז אתן לא במחיר ובכל־חטאותיך ובכל־גבוליך׃
your .borders | in even all | your sins | for but all | a for ,price | not will I give | for prey

6919 784 3045 3808 776 341 5674
14 והעברתי את־איביך בארץ לא ידעת כי־אש קדחה
been has kindled | a fire | for | do you ;know | (which) not | a into land | your enemies | with | will I And pass (you) make

2142 3068 3045 3344 639
15 באפי עליכם תוקד׃ אתה ידעת יהוה זכרני
Remember me | O .Jehovah | ,know | You | will it .burn | against you | My in ;anger

3045 3947 639 750 408 7291 5358 6485
ופקדני והנקם לי מרדפי אל־לארך אפך תקחני דע
know (that) | take Do ;away me | Your anger | the for of length | not | my on .persecutors | for me | take and vengeance | visit ,me

1697 1961 398 1697 4672 2781 5375
16 שאתי עליך חרפה׃ נמצאו דבריך ואכלם ויהי דבריך
Your words | and were | I and ,them ate | Your words | were found | .reproach | for You | bear I

3068 5921 8034 7121 3824 8057 8342
לי לששון ולשמחת לבבי כי־נקרא שמך עלי יהוה
O ,Jehovah | upon me | Your name | is called | for | my ;heart | glad- of ness | and the joy | to me

5937 7832 5475 3427 3808 6635 430
17 אלהי צבאות׃ לא־ישבתי בסוד־משחקים ואעלז מפני
because of | nor ;exult | merry- makers | the in of circle | did I sit | not | .hosts | God of

5331 3511 1961 4100 4390 2195 3427 910 3027
18 ידך בדד ישבתי כי־זעם מלאתני׃ למה היה כאבי נצח
con- ,tinual | my pain | has been | Why | have You .with me filled | indig- nation | for | ;sat I | alone | Your hand

4325 391 7495 3985 605 4347
ומכתי אנושה מאנה הרפא היו תהיה לי כמו אכזב מים
(whose) waters | false a ,stream | to me | You are | Surely | be to ?healed | refusing | ,incurable | my and wound

7725 7725 3068 559 3541 539 3808
19 לא נאמנו׃ לכן כה־אמר יהוה אם־תשוב ואשיבך
will I then ;you restore | you return | if | ,Jehovah | says thus | Therefore | be can .trusted | not

7725 1961 6310 1251 3368 3318 518 5975 6440
לפני תעמד ואם־תוציא יקר מזולל כפי תהיה ישבו המה
They | may turn | will you .be | My as mouth | the from worthless | the precious | bring you out | And if | will you .stand | before Me

2346 2088 5971 5414 7725 3808
20 אליך ואתה לא־תשוב אליהם׃ ונתתיך לעם הזה לחומת
a of wall | this | to people | will I And you make | .them to | do turn | not | but | ,you to you

3201 3808 3898 1219 5178
21 נחשת בצורה ונלחמו אליך ולא־יוכלו לך כי־אתך אני
I ,(am) | with you | for | against ,you | will prevail | but not | against ,you | they And will fight | .fortified | bronze

7451 3027 5337 3068 5002 5337 3467
להושיעך ולהצילך נאם־יהוה׃ והצלתיך מיד רעים
the ,evil | the from of hand | will I And you deliver | .Jehovah | says | to and ,you deliver | save to you

6184 3709 6299
ופדתיך מכף עריצים׃
the .tyrants | the from of palm | will I and you redeem

CAP. XVI טז

CHAPTER 16

[1]The word of Jehovah was to me, saying, [2]You shall not take a wife for yourself, nor shall you have sons or daughters in this place. [3]For so says Jehovah concerning the sons and concerning the daughters who are born in this place, and concerning their mothers who bore them, and concerning their fathers who fathered them in this land: [4]They shall die from deaths of diseases; they shall not be mourned, nor shall they be buried; they shall be as dung on the face of the earth. And they shall be consumed by the sword and by famine; and their bodies shall be food for the birds of the heavens, and for the beasts of the earth. [5]For so says Jehovah, Do not enter into the house of mourning; do not go to weep or moan for them. For I have taken away My peace with loving-kindness and compassions from this people, says Jehovah. [6]Both the great and the small shall die in this land. They shall not be buried, nor shall *men* mourn for them, nor cut himself, nor make himself bald for them. [7]Nor shall *men* break for them in mourning, to comfort him for the dead. Nor shall *they* give them the cup of comfort to drink for one's father or one's mother.

[8]Also, you shall not go into the house of feasting, to sit with them to eat and drink. [9]For so says Jehovah of hosts, the God of Israel: Behold, I will cause to cease out of this place, *before* your eyes, and in your days, the voice of joy, and the voice of gladness,

CHAPTER 16

3808 802 3947 38 08 559 3068 1697 1961
1 2 וַיְהִי דְבַר־יְהוָה אֵלַי לֵאמֹר׃ לֹא־תִקַּח לְךָ אִשָּׁה וְלֹא־
nor ,wife a for shall you not ,saying to Jehovah the Also
yourself take ,me of word came

559 2088 4725 1323: 1121 1961
3 יִהְיוּ לְךָ בָּנִים וּבָנוֹת בַּמָּקוֹם הַזֶּה׃ כִּי־כֹה ׀ אָמַר
says thus For .this place in or sons for will
daughters you be there

2088 4725 3209 1323: 1121 30 68
יְהוָה עַל־הַבָּנִים וְעַל־הַבָּנוֹת הַיִּלּוֹדִים בַּמָּקוֹם הַזֶּה וְעַל־
and ,this place in are who the con- and the con- Jehovah
to as born daughters cerning sons cerning

776 3205 3205 517
אִמֹּתָם הַיֹּלְדוֹת אוֹתָם וְעַל־אֲבוֹתָם הַמּוֹלִדִים אוֹתָם בָּאָרֶץ
in them who their and ;them bore who their
land 3808 fathered fathers concerning mothers

6912: 5594 38 08 4191: 8463 4463 2088
4 הַזֹּאת׃ מְמוֹתֵי תַחֲלֻאִים יָמֻתוּ לֹא יִסָּפְדוּ וְלֹא יִקָּבֵרוּ
they will nor be will they not will they diseases from ;this
;buried be mourned ;die of deaths

1961 3615 7458 2719 1961 127 6440 1828
לְדֹמֶן עַל־פְּנֵי הָאֲדָמָה יִהְיוּ וּבַחֶרֶב וּבָרָעָב יִכְלוּ וְהָיְתָה
will and will they by and the by and they the the on as
be .end famine the sword ;be shall earth of face dung

776 929 8064 5775 3978 5038
נִבְלָתָם לְמַאֲכָל לְעוֹף הַשָּׁמַיִם וּלְבֶהֱמַת הָאָרֶץ׃
the the for and the the for food their
.earth of beasts heavens of birds bodies

1980 408 4798 1004 935 408 3068 559 3541
5 כִּי־כֹה ׀ אָמַר יְהוָה אַל־תָּבוֹא בֵּית מַרְזֵחַ וְאַל־תֵּלֵךְ
do and ;mourning the do not ,Jehovah says thus For
go not of house into enter

5971 7965 622 5110 408 5594:
לִסְפּוֹד וְאַל־תָּנֹד לָהֶם כִּי־אָסַפְתִּי אֶת־שְׁלוֹמִי מֵאֵת הָעָם
people from peace My have I for for moan nor to
collected ,them lament

1419 4191 7356 2617 3068 5002 2088
6 הַזֶּה נְאֻם־יְהוָה אֶת־הַחֶסֶד וְאֶת־הָרַחֲמִים׃ וּמֵתוּ גְדֹלִים
the Both .compassions and loving with ,Jehovah says ,this
great die will kindness

3808 5594 3808 6912 3808 2088 776 6996
וּקְטַנִּים בָּאָרֶץ הַזֹּאת לֹא יִקָּבֵרוּ וְלֹא־יִסְפְּדוּ לָהֶם וְלֹא
nor for will they nor will they not ;this in the and
,them mourn buried be land small

60 6536 3808 7139 3808 1413
7 יִתְגֹּדַד וְלֹא יִקָּרֵחַ לָהֶם׃ וְלֹא־יִפְרְסוּ לָהֶם עַל־אֵבֶל
,mourning in for they will Nor for him- shave nor cut
them (bread) break .them bald self ,himself

5162: 3563 8248 3808 4191 5162
לְנַחֲמוֹ עַל־מֵת וְלֹא־יַשְׁקוּ אוֹתָם כּוֹס תַּנְחוּמִים עַל־אָבִיו
one's for consolation the them they will Nor the for com- to
father of cup drink to give .dead him fort

398 3427 935 3808 4960 1004 517
8 וְעַל־אִמּוֹ׃ וּבֵית־מִשְׁתֶּה לֹא־תָבוֹא לָשֶׁבֶת אוֹתָם לֶאֱכֹל
eat to with sit to will you not feasting the Also one's or
them ,enter of house .mother for

3478 430 6635 3068 559 8354
9 וְלִשְׁתּוֹת׃ כִּי כֹה אָמַר יְהוָה צְבָאוֹת אֱלֹהֵי יִשְׂרָאֵל
:Israel the ,hosts Jehovah says thus For to and
of God of .drink

6963 3117 5869 2088 4725 7673 2005
הִנְנִי מַשְׁבִּית מִן־הַמָּקוֹם הַזֶּה לְעֵינֵיכֶם וּבִימֵיכֶם קוֹל
the your in and your for this place from cause will ,Behold
of voice days eyes cease to I

the voice of the bridegroom and the voice of the bride.
[10]And it shall be, when you declare to this people all these words, they will say to you, Why has Jehovah pronounced all this great evil against us? Or what *is* our perversity, or what our sin that we have sinned against Jehovah our God? [11]Then you shall say to them, Because your fathers have forsaken Me, declares Jehovah, and have walked after other gods, and have served them, and have worshiped them, and have forsaken Me, and have not kept My law. [12]And you have done more evil than your fathers. For, behold, you each one walk after the stubbornness of his evil heart, without listening to Me, [13]even I will cast you out of this land, into a land that you do not know, you nor your fathers. And there you shall serve other gods day and night; where I will not grant you favor.

[14]So, behold, the days come, declares Jehovah, that it shall no more be said, *As* Jehovah lives who brought up the sons of Israel out of the land of Egypt—[15]but rather, *As* Jehovah lives who brought up the sons of Israel from the land of the north, and from all the lands, there where He had driven them. And I will bring them again into their land that I gave to their fathers.

[16]Behold, I will send for many fishermen, declares Jehovah, and they shall fish them. And after this I will send for many hunters, and

5046 1961 3618 6963 2860 6963 8057 6963 8342
10 ששון וקול שמחה קול חתן וקול כלה׃ והיה כי תגיד
you when it And the the and the the (and) glad- the and joy
declare be will .bride of voice bridgroom of voice ness of voice

559 428 1697 3605 2088 5971
לעם הזה את כל־הדברים האלה ואמרו אליך על־
you to they that ,these words all thus to
say will people

4100 2088 1419 7451 3605 3068 1696 4100
מה דבר יהוה עלינו את כל־הרעה הגדולה הזאת ומה
Or ?this great evil all against Jehovah has Why
(is) what us pronounced

559 430 3068 2398 834 2403 4100 5771
11 עוננו ומה חטאתנו אשר חטאנו ליהוה אלהינו׃ ואמרת
you Then ?God our against have we that sin our what or our
say shall Jehovah sinned (is) ,perversity

3212 3068 5002 1 5800 834
אליהם על אשר־עזבו אבותיכם אותי נאם־יהוה וילכו
have and ,Jehovah says ,Me your have Because ,them to
walked fathers forsaken

5800 7812 5647 312 430 310
אחרי אלהים אחרים ויעבדום וישתחוו להם ואתי עזבו
have they but ,them have and have and ,other gods after
,forsaken Me worshipped ,them served

1 6213 7489 8104 3808 8451
12 ואת־תורתי לא שמרו׃ ואתם הרעתם לעשות מאבותיכם
your than done have And have not My and
,fathers evil more you .kept law

1097 7451 3820 8307 310 376 1980 2009
והנכם הלכים איש אחרי שררות לבו־הרע לבלתי
without evil his stub- the after each are be- for
heart of bornness man walking you hold

2088 776 2904 8085
13 שמע אלי׃ והטלתי אתכם מעל הארץ הזאת על־
into this land of out you therefore ;me hearing
hurl will I

8033 5647 3045 3808 834 776
הארץ אשר לא ידעתם אתם ואבותיכם ועבדתם־שם
there you and your nor you do you not that a
serve will fathers ,know land

5414 3808 834 3915 3119 312 430
את־אלהים אחרים יומם ולילה אשר לא־אתן לכם
you will I not where and day other gods
grant ;night

559 3808 3068 5002 935 3117 2009 3651 2594
14 חנינה׃ לכן הנה־ימים באים נאם־יהוה ולא־יאמר
will it that ,Jehovah says ,come the ,behold ,Therefore .favor
said be not days

4714 776 3478 1121 5927 834 3068 2416 5750
עוד חי־יהוה אשר העלה את־בני ישראל מארץ מצרים׃
Egypt of out Israel the brought who Jeho- (As) ,more
of land the of sons up .vah lives

6828 776 3478 1121 5927 834 3068 2416
15 כי אם־חי־יהוה אשר העלה את־בני ישראל מארץ צפון
the the from Israel the brought who ,Jehovah (As) but
,north of land of sons up lives,rather

7725 8033 5080 834 776 3605
ומכל הארצות אשר הדיחם שמה והשבתים על־
into will I And .there had He where the from and
back them bring them banished lands all

7971 2005 1 5414 834 127
16 אדמתם אשר נתתי לאבותם׃ הנני שלח
will ,Behold their to gave I that their
send I .fathers land

7227 7971 310 1770 3068 5002 7227 1771
לדוגים רבים נאם־יהוה ודיגום ואחרי־כן אשלח לרבים
for will I after and they and ,Jehovah says ,many fisher- for
many send this ;them fish will men

they will hunt them, from every mountain, and from every hill, and out of the clefts of the rocks. [17]For My eyes *are* on all their ways; they are not hidden from My face; their iniquity is not hidden from My eyes. [18]And first I will twice repay their iniquity and their sin, because they have defiled My land with the bodies of their hateful things. Yea, their hateful idols have filled My inheritance. [19]O Jehovah, my strength and my fortress, and my refuge in the day of affliction, the nations shall come to You from the ends of the earth, and say, Our fathers have inherited only lies, vanity, and there is no profit in them. [20]Can a man make gods to himself? But they *are* not gods! [21]Therefore, behold, I will make them know; this time I will cause them to know My hand and My might; and they shall know that My name *is* Jehovah.

5357 1389 3605 2022 3605 6679 6719
צַיָּדִים וְצָדוּם מֵעַל כָּל־הַר וּמֵעַל כָּל־גִּבְעָה וּמִנְּקִיקֵי
from and ,hill every and moun- every from they and ,hunters
of clefts the from ,tain them hunt will

17 6440 5640 3808 1870 3605 5892 5553
הַסְּלָעִים׃ כִּי עֵינַי עַל־כָּל־דַּרְכֵיהֶם לֹא נִסְתְּרוּ מִלְּפָנָי
My from are they not their all (are) My For the
face hidden ;ways on eyes .rocks

18 4932 7223 7999 5869 5048 5771 6845 3808
וְלֹא־נִצְפַּן עֲוֹנָם מִנֶּגֶד עֵינָי׃ וְשִׁלַּמְתִּי רִאשׁוֹנָה מִשְׁנֵה
double first will I And My from their is not
repay .eyes iniquity hidden

8251 5038 776 2490 2403 5771
עֲוֹנָם וְחַטָּאתָם עַל חַלְּלָם אֶת־אַרְצִי בְּנִבְלַת שִׁקּוּצֵיהֶם
abomin- their the with My have they for their and their
;idols able of bodies ,land defiled ,sin iniquity

19 4581 5797 3068 5159 4390 8441
וְתוֹעֲבוֹתֵיהֶם מָלְאוּ אֶת־נַחֲלָתִי׃ יְהוָה עֻזִּי וּמָעֻזִּי
my and my Jehovah O My have their ,yea
stronghold strength .inheritance filled abominations

559 776 657 935 1471 6864 3117 4499
וּמְנוּסִי בְּיוֹם צָרָה אֵלֶיךָ גּוֹיִם יָבֹאוּ מֵאַפְסֵי־אָרֶץ וְיֹאמְרוּ
,say and the the from shall the to ,distress the in my and
,earth of ends come nations You of day refuge

20 6213 3276 369 1892 1 5157 8267 389
אַךְ־שֶׁקֶר נָחֲלוּ אֲבוֹתֵינוּ הֶבֶל וְאֵין־בָּם מוֹעִיל׃ הֲיַעֲשֶׂה־
make Can .profit in and ,vanity our have lies Only
them is not ,fathers inherited

21 3045 2005 3651 430 3808 430 120
לוֹ אָדָם אֱלֹהִים וְהֵמָּה לֹא אֱלֹהִים׃ לָכֵן הִנְנִי מוֹדִיעָם
make will behold Therefore !gods not they But ?gods man a for
—know them I (are) himself

3045 1369 3027 3045 2088 6471
בַּפַּעַם הַזֹּאת אוֹדִיעֵם אֶת־יָדִי וְאֶת־גְּבוּרָתִי וְיָדְעוּ כִּי
that they and My and My make will I this time
know will ;might hand know them

3068 8034
שְׁמִי יְהוָה׃
.Jehovah My
(is) name

CAP. XVII יז

CHAPTER 17

CHAPTER 17

[1]The sin of Judah is engraved with an iron pen. *It is* carved on the tablet of their heart with the point of a diamond, and on the horns of your altars; [2]*even* while their sons remember their altars and their Asherahs by the green trees on the high hills. [3]O My mountain in the field! I will give your wealth, all your treasures, for prey; your high places for sin throughout all your borders. [4]And you, even through yourself, will let drop from your inheritance which I gave you; and I will cause you to serve your enemies in a land which you do not

1 2790 8068 6856 1270 5842 3789 3063 2403
חַטַּאת יְהוּדָה כְּתוּבָה בְּעֵט בַּרְזֶל בְּצִפֹּרֶן שָׁמִיר חֲרוּשָׁה
is it a the with ;iron an with is Judah The
engraved ;diamond of point stylus written of sin

2 1121 2142 4196 7161 3820 3871
עַל־לוּחַ לִבָּם וּלְקַרְנוֹת מִזְבְּחוֹתֵיכֶם׃ כִּזְכֹּר בְּנֵיהֶם
their while Your the on and their the on
sons remember —altars of horns ,heart of tablet

1364 1389 7488 6086 842 4196
מִזְבְּחוֹתָם וַאֲשֵׁרֵיהֶם עַל־עֵץ רַעֲנָן עַל גְּבָעוֹת הַגְּבֹהוֹת׃
the hills on green the by their and their
.high trees Asherahs altars

3 1116 5414 957 214 3605 2428 7704 2042
הֲרָרִי בַּשָּׂדֶה חֵילְךָ כָּל־אוֹצְרוֹתֶיךָ לָבַז אֶתֵּן בָּמֹתֶיךָ
high your will I for your all your the in My O
places ,give prey treasures ,wealth ,field mountain

4 834 5159 8058 1366 3605 2403
בְּחַטָּאת בְּכָל־גְּבוּלֶיךָ׃ וְשָׁמַטְתָּה וּבְךָ מִנַּחֲלָתְךָ אֲשֶׁר
which your from by even will you And your throughout sin for
inheritance yourself drop let .borders all

3045 3808 834 776 341 5647 5414
נָתַתִּי לָךְ וְהַעֲבַדְתִּיךָ אֶת־אֹיְבֶיךָ בָּאָרֶץ אֲשֶׁר לֹא־יָדָעְתָּ
do you not which the in your will I and to gave I
;know land enemies serve you make ;you

know; for you have kindled a fire in My anger; it will burn forever.
[5]So says Jehovah, Cursed is the man who trusts in man, and who makes flesh his arm; and who turns aside his heart from Jehovah. [6]For he shall be like a juniper in the desert, and shall not see when good comes. But he shall live in parched places in the wilderness, *in* a salt land that is not inhabited.
[7]Blessed is the man who trusts in Jehovah, and Jehovah is his trust. [8]For he shall be like a tree planted by the waters; *it* sends out its roots by the stream, and will not fear when the heat comes; but its foliage will be green; and it is not worried in the year of drouth; nor will it cease from producing fruit.
[9]The heart *is* deceitful above all things, and it is incurable; who can know it? [10]I, Jehovah, search the heart; I try the reins, even to give to each man according to his ways, according to the fruit of his doings. [11]*As* a partridge broods and does not hatch, *so is* he who makes riches, and not by right; it will leave him in the middle of his days, and in his end he will be a fool.
[12]A glorious high throne from the beginning *is* the place of our sanctuary. [13]O Jehovah, the Hope of Israel, all who forsake You shall be ashamed. Those who depart from Me shall be written in the earth, because they have forsaken Jehovah, the Fountain of living waters. [14]Heal me, O Jehovah, and I will be healed; save me, and I will be saved; for You *are* my praise.
[15]Behold, they say to me, Where *is* the word of Jehovah? Let it come now. [16]And I have not hurried away from shepherding after You; nor have I desired the woeful day. You surely

559 3344 5769 5704 639 6919 784
5 כִּי־אֵשׁ קְדַחְתֶּם בְּאַפִּי עַד־עוֹלָם תּוּקָד׃ כֹּה ׀ אָמַר
says Thus will it forever My in have you a for
.burn ;anger kindled fire

2220 1320 7760 120 982 834 1397 779 3068
יְהוָה אָרוּר הַגֶּבֶר אֲשֶׁר יִבְטַח בָּאָדָם וְשָׂם בָּשָׂר זְרֹעוֹ
his flesh and man in trusts who the Cursed Jeho-
,arm makes man is .vah

7200 3808 6160 6199 1961 3820 5493 3068
6 וּמִן־יְהוָה יָסוּר לִבּוֹ׃ וְהָיָה כְּעַרְעָר בָּעֲרָבָה וְלֹא יִרְאֶה
shall and the in a like he For his turns Jehovah and
see not ,desert juniper be will .heart aside from

3808 4420 776 4057 7788 7931 2896 935
כִּי־יָבוֹא טוֹב וְשָׁכַן חֲרֵרִים בַּמִּדְבָּר אֶרֶץ מְלֵחָה וְלֹא
that ,salt a (in) the in dried the will but ,good comes
not land ,wilderness places in live when

1961 3068 982 834 1397 1288 3427
7 תֵשֵׁב׃ בָּרוּךְ הַגֶּבֶר אֲשֶׁר יִבְטַח בַּיהוָה וְהָיָה
is and in trusts who the Blessed in- is
,Jehovah man is .habited

3105 4325 8362 6086 1961 4009 3068
8 יְהוָה מִבְטַחוֹ׃ וְהָיָה כְּעֵץ ׀ שָׁתוּל עַל־מַיִם וְעַל־יוּבַל
the and the by planted a like he For his Jehovah
stream by waters tree be will .trust

7488 5929 1961 2527 935 3372 3808 8328 7971
יְשַׁלַּח שָׁרָשָׁיו וְלֹא יִרְאֶ כִּי־יָבֹא חֹם וְהָיָה עָלֵהוּ רַעֲנָן
—green its will for ,heat comes when will and its sends
foliage be fear not ;roots out

6121 6529 6213 4185 3808 1672 3808 1226 8141
9 וּבִשְׁנַת בַּצֹּרֶת לֹא יִדְאָג וְלֹא יָמִישׁ מֵעֲשׂוֹת פֶּרִי׃ עָקֹב
Deceitful .fruit from he will nor is he not drought the in and
(is) producing cease ,worried of year

974 3820 2713 3068 3045 4310 605 3605 3820
10 הַלֵּב מִכֹּל וְאָנֻשׁ הוּא מִי יֵדָעֶנּוּ׃ אֲנִי יְהוָה חֹקֵר לֵב בֹּחֵן
I the search ,Jehovah I can who ;it is and above the
test ,heart ?it know incurable all heart

7124 4611 6529 1870 376 5414 3629
11 כְּלָיוֹת וְלָתֵת לְאִישׁ כִּדְרָכָו כִּפְרִי מַעֲלָלָיו׃ קֹרֵא
a (As) .doings his according according each to to even the
partridge of fruit the to ,ways his to man give kidneys

5800 3117 2677 4941 3808 6239 6213 3205 3808 1716
דָגַר וְלֹא יָלָד עֹשֶׂה עֹשֶׁר וְלֹא בְמִשְׁפָּט בַּחֲצִי יָמָו יַעַזְבֶנּוּ
will it his the in with but riches he (is so) does and broods
,him leave days of middle ;justice not makes who ,hatch not

4725 7223 4791 3519 3678 5036 1961 319
12 וּבְאַחֲרִיתוֹ יִהְיֶה נָבָל׃ כִּסֵּא כָבוֹד מָרוֹם מֵרִאשׁוֹן מְקוֹם
the (is) the from high glorious A .fool a will he at and
of place beginning throne be end his

3249 954 5800 3605 3068 3478 4723 4720
13 מִקְדָּשֵׁנוּ׃ מִקְוֵה יִשְׂרָאֵל יְהוָה כָּל־עֹזְבֶיךָ יֵבֹשׁוּ יְסוּרַי
leav- Those be will who all O ,Israel the our
Me ing .ashamed You forsake ,Jehovah of hope .sanctuary

3068 2416 4325 4726 5800 3789 776
בָּאָרֶץ יִכָּתֵבוּ כִּי עָזְבוּ מְקוֹר מַיִם־חַיִּים אֶת־יְהוָה׃
.Jehovah ,living waters the have they for be will the in
of Fountain forsaken ,written earth

8416 3467 3467 7495 3068 7495
14 רְפָאֵנִי יְהוָה וְאֵרָפֵא הוֹשִׁיעֵנִי וְאִוָּשֵׁעָה כִּי תְהִלָּתִי אָתָּה׃
You my for will I and save be will I and O Heal
.(are) praise ;saved be me ;healed ,Jehovah ,me

4994 935 3068 1697 346 559 2009
15 הִנֵּה־הֵמָּה אֹמְרִים אֵלַי אַיֵּה דְבַר־יְהוָה יָבוֹא נָא׃ וַאֲנִי
16
And !now it Let ?Jehovah the Where to say they ,Behold
I come of word (is) ,me

183 3808 605 3117 310 7462 213 3808
לֹא־אַצְתִּי ׀ מֵרֹעֶה אַחֲרֶיךָ וְיוֹם אָנוּשׁ לֹא הִתְאַוֵּיתִי אַתָּה
You I have not woefull the after from have not
;desired day ;You shepherding away hurried

know *that* the going forth of my lips was before Your face. [17]Do not be a terror to me; You *are* my refuge in the day of evil. [18]Let those who persecute me be ashamed, but do not let me be ashamed. Let them be terrified; but do not let me be terrified. Bring on them the day of evil, and break them *with* double breaking.

[19]So said Jehovah to me, Go and stand in the gate of the sons of the people, *that* by which the kings of Judah come in, and by which they go out, and in all the gates of Jerusalem. [20]And say to them, Hear the word of Jehovah, kings of Judah, and all Judah, and all the residents of Jerusalem who enter in by these gates. [21]So says Jehovah, Take heed for the sake of your lives, and do not carry a burden on the sabbath day, nor bring *it* in by the gates of Jerusalem. [22]And do not carry a burden from your houses on the sabbath day, nor do any work, but keep the sabbath day holy, as I commanded your fathers. [23]But they did not obey or bow down their ear, but they made their neck stiff, not to hear, nor to take instruction. [24]And it shall be, if you carefully listen to me, says Jehovah, to bring in no burden through the gates of this city on the sabbath day, but keep the sabbath day holy, to do no work in it, [25]then kings and rulers sitting on the throne of David shall enter into the gates of this city,

---

17

3045	4161	8:193	5048	6440	1961	408	1961
the know	of forth going	my lips	before	Your face	.was	Do not be	to me	;terror a

18

4268	3117	7451	954	7291	954	408	954
my refuge	(are) You	the in	of day	.evil	be Let ashamed	secutors per- my	not	but	me let ;ashamed

2865	408	2665	935	3117	7451	935	51:74	4932
them be let	terrified	not	terrified them be let ;them	Bring	on	the	of day them	evil, and (with) and double

19

7670	7665		559	30:68	1980	5975
breaking	break .them		Thus said Jehovah to me, Go	and stand

8179	1121	5971	834	935	44:28	3063	834
the in	of gate	the of sons	,people of	which	enter	it by	the of kings	,Judah	and which

20

3318	8179	3389	559	3605	8085
go out they	,it the in and	of gates all	.Jerusalem	And say	,them to	Hear

3389	3427	3605	3063	3605	3063	44:28	30:68	1697
Jerusalem	inhab- the and	of itants all	,Judah	and	,Judah	kings	Jehovah the	of word

21

8104	30:68	559		428	8179	935
Take heed	,Jehovah	says	Thus	!these	by in	who enter

935	7676	3117	4853	5375	408	5315
bring nor (them)	the ,Sabbath	day on	a burden	do carry	and not	of sake the for ,lives your

22

8179	3389	4853	3318	3808	3389	8179
day on your from houses	a burden	carry do out	And not	.Jerusalem	the by in of gates

7676	3117	6942	6213	38:108	4399	3605	7676
the ,Sabbath	the day	keep but holy	,do	not	work	and	the ,Sabbath

23

6680		8085	3808	3808	5186
I commanded	as	incline	nor did they obey	But not	your ,fathers

241	71:85	6203	11115	8085	11:15	3947
their ,ear	they but stiffened	their ,neck	to not hear	to nor obey	take

24

4748	1961	8085		8085	5002	3068	11:15
instruc- .tion	it And ,be will	carefully if listen Me,		you	to	says	,Jehovah	to not

935	48:53	8179	5892	2088	3117	7676	6942
bring	a through of gates the burden	city	this	on day	,Sabbath	keep but holy

25

3117	76:76	11115	6213	3605	4399	935
day	the Sabbath	to not do	it in	any	,work	will then enter

8179	5892	2088	4428	8269	3427	3678
of gates	the into	city	this	kings	and rulers	sitting on	the of throne

riding on chariots and on horses; they, and their rulers, the men of Judah, and the inhabitants of Jerusalem. And this city will be inhabited forever. [26]And they will come from the cities of Judah, and from the places about Jerusalem, and from the land of Benjamin, and from the lowland, and from the mountains, and from the south, bringing burnt offerings, and sacrifices, and grain offerings, and incense, and bringing sacrifices of thanksgiving to the house of Jehovah. [27]But if you will not listen to Me to keep the sabbath day holy, and not to carry a burden and enter at the gates of Jerusalem on the sabbath day, then I will kindle a fire in her gates. And it shall devour the palaces of Jerusalem; yea, it shall not be put out.

3063 376 8269 5483 7393 7392 1732
דָּוִד רֹכְבִים בָּרֶכֶב וּבַסּוּסִים הֵמָּה וְשָׂרֵיהֶם אִישׁ יְהוּדָה
,Judah the their and ,they on and chariots in riding David
of men ,rulers horses

5892 935 5769 2088 5892 3427 3389 2427
26 וְיֹשְׁבֵי יְרוּשָׁלָם וְיָשְׁבָה הָעִיר הַזֹּאת לְעוֹלָם׃ וּבָאוּ מֵעָרֵי־
the from they And .forever this city will and ,Jerusalem the and
of cities come will inhabited be of inhabitants

8219 1144 776 3389 5439 3063
יְהוּדָה וּמִסְּבִיבוֹת יְרוּשָׁלַםִ וּמֵאֶרֶץ בִּנְיָמִן וּמִן־הַשְּׁפֵלָה
the and ,Benjamin from and ,Jerusalem the from and ,Judah
Shephelah from of land the around places

3828 4503 2077 5930 935 5045 2022
וּמִן־הָהָר וּמִן־הַנֶּגֶב מְבִאִים עֹלָה וְזֶבַח וּמִנְחָה וּלְבוֹנָה
frank- and grain and and burnt bringing the and moun- the and
,incense ,offerings sacrifices offerings ,south from ,tains from

6942 8085 3808 518 3068 1004 8426 935
27 וּמְבִאֵי תוֹדָה בֵּית יְהוָה׃ וְאִם־לֹא תִשְׁמְעוּ אֵלַי לְקַדֵּשׁ אֶת־
keep to to will you not But .Jehovah's house thank bear- and
holy ,Me listen if offerings to ing

3389 8179 935 4853 5375 1115 7676 3117
יוֹם הַשַּׁבָּת וּלְבִלְתִּי שְׂאֵת מַשָּׂא וּבֹא בְּשַׁעֲרֵי יְרוּשָׁלָם
Jerusalem the at and a carry not and the day
of gates enter ,burden to Sabbath

3389 759 398 8179 784 3341 7676 3117
בְּיוֹם הַשַּׁבָּת וְהִצַּתִּי אֵשׁ בִּשְׁעָרֶיהָ וְאָכְלָה אַרְמְנוֹת יְרוּשָׁלָם
,Jerusalem the it and her in fire a I then the day on
of palaces devour will ;gates kindle will —Sabbath

3518 3808
וְלֹא תִכְבֶּה׃
be and
.quenched not

CAP. XVIII יח

CHAPTER 18

CHAPTER 18

[1]The word which was to Jeremiah from Jehovah, saying, [2]Rise up and go down to the potter's house, and there I will cause you to hear My words. [3]Then I went down to the potter's house, and behold, he was working a work on the wheel. [4]And the vessel that he made in clay was ruined in the hand of the potter. And returning, he made it, another vessel, as it seemed good in the potter's eyes to make *it*. [5]And the word of Jehovah was to me, saying, [6]O house of Israel, Am I not able to do to you as did this potter? declares Jehovah. Behold, as the clay in the potter's hand, so *are* you in My hand, O house of Israel. [7]The instant I speak concerning a

6965 559 3068 3414 1961 834 1697
1
2 הַדָּבָר אֲשֶׁר הָיָה אֶל־יִרְמְיָהוּ מֵאֵת יְהוָה לֵאמֹר׃ קוּם
Arise ,saying ,Jehovah from Jeremiah to came which The
word

3381 1697 8085 8033 3335 1004 3381
3 וְיָרַדְתָּ בֵּית הַיּוֹצֵר וְשָׁמָּה אַשְׁמִיעֲךָ אֶת־דְּבָרָי׃ וָאֵרֵד
went I So My cause will I and the house go and
to down .words hear to you there ,potter's to down

7843 70 4399 6213 2009 3335 1004
4 בֵּית הַיּוֹצֵר וְהִנֵּהוּ עֹשֶׂה מְלָאכָה עַל־הָאָבְנָיִם׃ וְנִשְׁחַת
was And the on work a was be- and the house
ruined .wheel working he ,hold ;potter's

6213 7725 3335 3027 2563 6213 834 3627
הַכְּלִי אֲשֶׁר הוּא עֹשֶׂה בַּחֹמֶר בְּיַד הַיּוֹצֵר וְשָׁב וַיַּעֲשֵׂהוּ
made he going and the the in clay in made he that the
,it back ;potter of hand vessel

1961 6213 3335 5869 3474 312 3627
5 כְּלִי אַחֵר כַּאֲשֶׁר יָשַׁר בְּעֵינֵי הַיּוֹצֵר לַעֲשׂוֹת׃ וַיְהִי
Then make to the the in it as ,another vessel
came .(it) potter of eyes good seemed

6213 3201 3808 2088 3335 559 3068 1697
6 דְבַר־יְהוָה אֵלַי לֵאמוֹר׃ הֲכַיּוֹצֵר הַזֶּה לֹא־אוּכַל לַעֲשׂוֹת
do to I Am not this like ,saying ,me to Jehovah the
able (did) potter of word

3335 3027 2563 2009 3068 5002 3478 1004
לָכֶם בֵּית יִשְׂרָאֵל נְאֻם־יְהוָה הִנֵּה כַחֹמֶר בְּיַד הַיּוֹצֵר
the in the as ,Behold .Jehovah says ?Israel house O to
,potter's hand clay of ,you

1471 1696 7281 3478 1004 3027
7 כֵּן־אַתֶּם בְּיָדִי בֵּית יִשְׂרָאֵל׃ רֶגַע אֲדַבֵּר עַל־גּוֹי
a con- speak I The .Israel house O My in (are) so
,nation cerning instant of ,hand you

nation, and concerning a kingdom, to pluck up, or to break down, or to destroy; [8]if that nation against whom I have spoken will turn from their evil, I will repent of the evil that I thought to do to it. [9]And the instant I speak concerning a nation, and concerning a kingdom, to build and to plant *it;* [10]if it does evil in My eye, not to obey My voice, then I will repent of the good which I had said to do good to it.

[11]Now, then, please speak to the men of Judah, and to the inhabitants of Jerusalem, saying, So says Jehovah, Behold, I am forming evil against you, and devising a plan against you. Now each one turn from his evil way, and make your ways and your doings good. [12]And they say, It is hopeless. For we will walk after our own thoughts, and we will each one do *according to* the stubbornness of his evil heart. [13]So Jehovah says this: Ask now among the nations. Who has heard *things* like these? The virgin of Israel has done a very horrible thing.

[14]Does the snow of Lebanon cease from the rock of the field? Or are the cold flowing waters that come from another place uprooted? [15]But My people have forgotten Me; they have burned incense to vain idols; and they have caused them to stumble in their ways, *from* the old paths, to walk *in* bypaths, not *on* the highway; [16]to make their land a desolation, a hissing forever. Everyone who passes by will be amazed, and will shake his head. [17]I will scatter them like an east wind before the enemy; I will make them see the back, and not the

1471 7725 6 5422 5428 4467
8 וְעַל־מַמְלָכָה לִנְתוֹשׁ וְלִנְתוֹץ וּלְהַאֲבִיד׃ וְשָׁב הַגּוֹי הַהוּא
that nation will if cause to and to and uproot to a con- or
turn perish to (it) ,break kingdom cerning

834 7451 5162 5921 1696 834 7451
מֵרָעָתוֹ אֲשֶׁר דִּבַּרְתִּי עָלָיו וְנִחַמְתִּי עַל־הָרָעָה אֲשֶׁר
that the of will I against have I whom its from
evil repent ,it spoken evil

1471 1696 7281 6213 2803
9 חָשַׁבְתִּי לַעֲשׂוֹת לוֹ׃ וְרֶגַע אֲדַבֵּר עַל־גּוֹי וְעַל־
con- or a concern- speak I the But .it to do to thought I
cerning ,nation ing instant

5869 7451 6213 5193 1129 4467
10 מַמְלָכָה לִבְנוֹת וְלִנְטוֹעַ׃ וְעָשָׂה הָרָעָה בְּעֵינַי לְבִלְתִּי
to not My in evil it if to or build to ,kingdom a
,eye does ,(it) plant

3190 559 834 2896 5162 6963 8085
שְׁמֹעַ בְּקוֹלִי וְנִחַמְתִּי עַל־הַטּוֹבָה אֲשֶׁר אָמַרְתִּי לְהֵיטִיב
do to had I which the of I then My obey
to good said good repent will ,voice

3389 3427 3063 376 4994 559 6258
11 אוֹתוֹ׃ וְעַתָּה אֱמָר־נָא אֶל־אִישׁ־יְהוּדָה וְעַל־יוֹשְׁבֵי יְרוּשָׁלַםִ
,Jerusalem inhab- the and ,Judah the to please speak Now .it
of itants to of men ,then

7451 3335 2009 3068 559 3541 559
לֵאמֹר כֹּה אָמַר יְהוָה הִנֵּה אָנֹכִי יוֹצֵר עֲלֵיכֶם רָעָה
evil against am I ,Behold ,Jehovah says Thus ,saying
you forming

7451 1870 376 4994 7725 4284 2803
וְחֹשֵׁב עֲלֵיכֶם מַחֲשָׁבָה שׁוּבוּ נָא אִישׁ מִדַּרְכּוֹ הָרָעָה
evil his from each now turn ;plan a against and
way man you devising

310 2976 559 4611 1870 3190
12 וְהֵיטִיבוּ דַרְכֵיכֶם וּמַעַלְלֵיכֶם׃ וְאָמְרוּ נוֹאָשׁ כִּי־אַחֲרֵי
after For is It they But your and ways your make and
!hopeless ,say .doings good

6213 7451 3820 8307 376 3212 4284
מַחְשְׁבוֹתֵינוּ נֵלֵךְ וְאִישׁ שְׁרִרוּת לִבּוֹ־הָרָע נַעֲשֶׂה׃
will we evil his stub- the each and will we own our
.do heart of bornness man ,walk thoughts

428 8085 4310 1471 4994 7592 3068 559 3541
13 לָכֵן כֹּה אָמַר יְהוָה שַׁאֲלוּ־נָא בַּגּוֹיִם מִי שָׁמַע כָּאֵלֶּה
like has who the among now Ask ,Jehovah says thus There-
?these heard ,nations fore

7704 6697 5800 3478 1330 3966 6213 8186
14 שַׁעֲרֻרִת עָשְׂתָה מְאֹד בְּתוּלַת יִשְׂרָאֵל׃ הֲיַעֲזֹב מִצּוּר שָׂדַי
the the from Does .Israel The done has something
field of rock forsake of virgin horrible

5140 7119 2114 4325 5428 3844 7950
15 שֶׁלֶג לְבָנוֹן אִם־יִנָּתְשׁוּ מַיִם זָרִים קָרִים נוֹזְלִים׃ כִּי־
But ?flowing cold foreign the are Or ?Lebanon the
waters uprooted of snow

7635 1870 3782 6999 7723 5971 7911
שְׁכֵחֻנִי עַמִּי לַשָּׁוְא יְקַטֵּרוּ וַיַּכְשִׁלוּם בְּדַרְכֵיהֶם שְׁבִילֵי
the (from) their in made they and burn they vain to My forgot
paths ways stumble them ;incense idols ,people Me

776 7760 5549 3808 1870 5410 3212 5769
16 עוֹלָם לָלֶכֶת נְתִיבוֹת דֶּרֶךְ לֹא סְלוּלָה׃ לָשׂוּם אַרְצָם
their make to (the on) not a of (on) walk to ,old
land ;highway way paths

7218 5110 8074 5674 3605 5769 8292 8047
לְשַׁמָּה שְׁרוּקֹת עוֹלָם כֹּל עוֹבֵר עָלֶיהָ יִשֹּׁם וְיָנִיד בְּרֹאשׁוֹ׃
his will and be will it by who All perpet- a a
.head shake horrified pass ual hissing ,horror

7200 6440 3808 6203 341 6440 6327 6921 7307
17 כְּרוּחַ־קָדִים אֲפִיצֵם לִפְנֵי אוֹיֵב עֹרֶף וְלֹא־פָנִים אַרְאֵם
will I (My) and (My) the before will I east an Like
.them show face not back ;enemy them scatter wind

face, in the day of their calamity.

¹⁸Then they said, Come and let us plot schemes against Jeremiah. For the law shall not perish from the priest, nor counsel from the wise, nor word from the prophet. Come and let us strike him with the tongue, and let us not listen to any of his words. ¹⁹O Jehovah, pay attention to me, and listen to the voice of my foes. ²⁰Should evil be repaid for good? For they have dug a pit for my soul. Remember, I stood before You to speak good concerning them, to turn Your wrath from them. ²¹So give their sons to the famine, and give them over to the hand of the sword. And let their wives be bereaved, and widows. And let their men be the slain of death, their young men those struck by the sword in battle. ²²Let a cry be heard from their houses when You suddenly bring a raiding party on them. For they have dug a pit to seize me, and have hidden snares for my feet. ²³Yet, O Jehovah, You know all their counsel to death against me. Do not atone for their iniquity, nor blot out their sin from Your face; but let them be those made to stumble before You; deal with them in the time of Your anger.

CHAPTER 19

¹So says Jehovah, Go and buy a potter's earthen jar, and *gather* from the elders of the people, and from the elders of the priests. ²And go out to the valley of the son of Hinnom by the entry of Potsherd Gate. And there declare the words that I will speak to

---

18

3414	2803	3212	559	343 3117
וַיֹּאמְרוּ לְכוּ וְנַחְשְׁבָה עַל־יִרְמְיָהוּ				בְּיוֹם אֵידָם׃
Jeremiah against us let and Come they Then .said				their the in .calamity of day

| 1697 24:50 6098 3548 8451 6 3808 4284 |
| מַחֲשָׁבוֹת כִּי לֹא־תֹאבַד תּוֹרָה מִכֹּהֵן וְעֵצָה מֵחָכָם וְדָבָר |
| nor the from nor the from the shall not for ;schemes word ,wise counsel ,priest law perish |

| 1697 3605 7181 408 3956 5221 3212 5030 |
| מִנָּבִיא לְכוּ וְנַכֵּהוּ בַלָּשׁוֹן וְאַל־נַקְשִׁיבָה אֶל־כָּל־דְּבָרָיו׃ |
| his any to us let and the with us let and Come the from .words of listen not tongue him strike .prophet |

19 / 20

| 8478 799.9 3401 6963 7181 3068 7181 |
| הַקְשִׁיבָה יְהֹוָה אֵלָי וּשְׁמַע לְקוֹל יְרִיבָי׃ |
| for be Should adver- my the and ,me to O Pay saries of voice to attend Jehovah attention |

| 6440 5975 2142 5315 7745 3738 74:51 2896 |
| מוּבָה רָעָה כִּי־כָרוּ שׁוּחָה לְנַפְשִׁי זְכֹר עָמְדִי לְפָנֶיךָ |
| before stood I ,Remember my for pit a they For ?evil good You .soul dug have |

| 2534 7725 2896 1696 |
| לְדַבֵּר עֲלֵיהֶם טוֹבָה לְהָשִׁיב אֶת־חֲמָתְךָ מֵהֶם׃ |
| from Your turn to ,good concerning speak to .them wrath them |

21

| 1961 2719 3027 5064 74.58 1121 5414 36.51 |
| לָכֵן תֵּן אֶת־בְּנֵיהֶם לָרָעָב וְהַגִּרֵם עַל־יְדֵי־חֶרֶב וְתִהְיֶנָה |
| let And the the over give and the to their give There- be .sword of hand to them famine sons ,fore |

| 4194 2026 1961 582 490 7909 802 |
| נְשֵׁיהֶם שַׁכֻּלוֹת וְאַלְמָנוֹת וְאַנְשֵׁיהֶם יִהְיוּ הֲרֻגֵי מָוֶת |
| ;death the be let their and and ,bereaved their of slain men ;widows wives |

22

| 10:04 2201 8085 4421 2719 5221 970 |
| בַּחוּרֵיהֶם מֻכֵּי־חֶרֶב בַּמִּלְחָמָה׃ תִּשָּׁמַע זְעָקָה מִבָּתֵּיהֶם |
| their from cry a be Let .battle in the those young their ,houses heard sword by struck men |

| 392:0 774.5 3738 6597 1416 935 |
| כִּי־תָבִיא עֲלֵיהֶם גְּדוּד פִּתְאֹם כִּי־כָרוּ שׁוּחָה לְלָכְדֵנִי |
| capture to pit a they For .suddenly raiding a them on you when me dug have party bring |

23

| 6098 3605 3045 3068 7272 2934 6341 |
| וּפַחִים טָמְנוּ לְרַגְלָי׃ וְאַתָּה יְהֹוָה יָדַעְתָּ אֶת־כָּל־עֲצָתָם |
| their all know O Yet my for have and counsel Jehovah ,You feet hidden snares |

| 408 6440 2403 5771 3722 408 4194 |
| עָלַי לַמָּוֶת אַל־תְּכַפֵּר עַל־עֲוֺנָם וְחַטָּאתָם מִלְּפָנֶיךָ אַל־ |
| not Your from their or their for do not to against presence sin ;iniquity atone ;death me |

| 6.213 639 6256 6440 1378.2 1961 4229 |
| תֶּמְחִי וְיִהְיוּ מֻכְשָׁלִים לְפָנֶיךָ בְּעֵת אַפְּךָ עֲשֵׂה בָהֶם׃ |
| with deal Your the in before made those let and blot do .them anger of time ,You stumble to be them ,out |

CAP. XIX יט

CHAPTER 19

1

| 59:71 2204 2790 3335 1228 7069 1980 3:068 559 |
| כֹּה אָמַר יְהֹוָה הָלוֹךְ וְקָנִיתָ בַקְבֻּק יוֹצֵר חָרֶשׂ וּמִזִּקְנֵי הָעָם |
| the from and ,earthen a jar buy and Go ,Jehovah says Thus ,people of elders the potter's |

2

| 8179 6607 834 2:011/1121/1516 3318 3548 2205 |
| וּמִזִּקְנֵי הַכֹּהֲנִים׃ וְיָצָאתָ אֶל־גֵּיא בֶן־הִנֹּם אֲשֶׁר פֶּתַח שַׁעַר |
| Gate the by which ,Hinnom the the to go And the from and of entry (is) of son of valley out .priests of elders the |

| 1696 834 1697 8033.0 7121 2777 |
| הַחַרְסִית וְקָרָאתָ שָּׁם אֶת־הַדְּבָרִים אֲשֶׁר־אֲדַבֵּר אֵלֶיךָ׃ |
| .you to will I that the there and Potsherd speak words proclaim |

you. And say, Hear the word of Jehovah, O kings of Judah, and inhabitants of Jerusalem. So says Jehovah of hosts, the God of Israel: Behold, I will bring evil on this place *by* which all who hear it will *have* tingling ears. [4]Because they have forsaken Me, and have estranged this place and have burned incense in it to other gods whom neither they nor their fathers have known, nor the kings of Judah; and have filled this place with the blood of innocents. [5]They have also built the high places of Baal, to burn their sons with fire *for* burnt offerings to Baal, which I never commanded nor spoke, nor did *it* come into My heart. [6]So, behold, the days come, says Jehovah, that this place shall be no more called Tophet, or the valley of the son of Hinnom, but Valley of Slaughter. [7]And I will make the counsel of Judah and Jerusalem come to nothing in this place. And I will cause them to fall by the sword before their enemies, and by the hand of those who seek their life. And I will give their dead bodies for food to the birds of the heavens, and for the animals of the earth. [8]And I will make this city a waste and a hissing. Everyone who passes by shall be amazed and shall hiss because of all its plagues. [9]And I will cause them to eat the flesh of their sons, and the flesh of their daughters; and they shall each one eat the flesh of his friend in the siege and distress with which their enemies and those who seek their life shall distress them.

[10]Then you shall break the jar before the eyes of

3389 3427 30:63 44:28 3068 1697 8085 559
3 וְאָמַרְתָּ שִׁמְעוּ דְבַר־יְהוָה מַלְכֵי יְהוּדָה וְיֹשְׁבֵי יְרוּשָׁלִָם
.Jerusalem inhab- and Judah kings ,Jehovah the Hear ,say And
of itants of of word

7451 935 2005 34:78 430 66:35 3068 559
כֹּה־אָמַר יְהוָה צְבָאוֹת אֱלֹהֵי יִשְׂרָאֵל הִנְנִי מֵבִיא רָעָה
evil will ,Behold ,Israel the hosts Jehovah says Thus
bring I of God of

241 6750 8085 3605 834 20:88 4725
4 עַל־הַמָּקוֹם הַזֶּה אֲשֶׁר כָּל־שֹׁמְעָהּ תִּצַּלְנָה אָזְנָיו׃ יַעַן ׀
Because his tingle will who all which this place on
.ears it hears

430 6999 2088 4725 5234 58:00 834
אֲשֶׁר עֲזָבֻנִי וַיְנַכְּרוּ אֶת־הַמָּקוֹם הַזֶּה וַיְקַטְּרוּ־בוֹ לֵאלֹהִים
gods to it in have and ,this place have and have they
incense burned estranged Me forsaken

3063 4428 1 3045 3808 834 312
אֲחֵרִים אֲשֶׁר לֹא־יְדָעוּם הֵמָּה וַאֲבוֹתֵיהֶם וּמַלְכֵי יְהוּדָה
;Judah the nor their nor they have neither whom other
of kings ,fathers known

1168 1116 11:29 5355 1818 2088 4725 43:90
5 וּמָלְאוּ אֶת־הַמָּקוֹם הַזֶּה דַּם נְקִיִּם׃ וּבָנוּ אֶת־בָּמוֹת הַבַּעַל
,Baal high the have They inno- the this place have and
of places built also .cents of blood with filled

6680/ 38:08 834 1168 5930 784 1121 83:13
לִשְׂרֹף אֶת־בְּנֵיהֶם בָּאֵשׁ עֹלוֹת לַבָּעַל אֲשֶׁר לֹא־צִוִּיתִי
com- I never which ,Baal to burnt (as) with their burn to
manded offerings fire sons

3117 2009 3820 5927 3808 1696 3808
6 וְלֹא דִבַּרְתִּי וְלֹא עָלְתָה עַל־לִבִּי׃ לָכֵן הִנֵּה־יָמִים
the ,behold Therefore My into it did nor ,spoke nor
days .heart up come

1516 8612 5750 2088 4725 7121 3808 3068 5002 935
בָּאִים נְאֻם־יְהוָה וְלֹא־יִקָּרֵא לַמָּקוֹם הַזֶּה עוֹד הַתֹּפֶת וְגֵיא
the or ,Tophet more this place be will that ,Jehovah says ,come
of valley called not

3063 6098 1238 2028 1516 2011 1121
7 בֶן־הִנֹּם כִּי אִם־גֵּיא הַהֲרֵגָה׃ וּבַקֹּתִי אֶת־עֲצַת יְהוּדָה
Judah counsel the will I And .Slaughter Valley ,but ,Hinnom the
of void make of of son

341 6440 2719 5307 20:88 4725 33:89
וִירוּשָׁלִַם בַּמָּקוֹם הַזֶּה וְהִפַּלְתִּים בַּחֶרֶב לִפְנֵי אֹיְבֵיהֶם
their before the by will I and ,this place in and
,enemies sword fall them make Jerusalem

5775 39:78 5038 5414 5315 1245 3027
וּבְיַד מְבַקְשֵׁי נַפְשָׁם וְנָתַתִּי אֶת־נִבְלָתָם לְמַאֲכָל לְעוֹף
the to food for dead their I And their who those by and
of birds bodies give will .life seek of hand the

2088 5892 7760 776 929 8064
8 הַשָּׁמַיִם וּלְבֶהֱמַת הָאָרֶץ׃ וְשַׂמְתִּי אֶת־הָעִיר הַזֹּאת
this city I And the the to and ,sky the
make will .earth of animals

3605 8319 8074 5674 3605 8322 8047
לְשַׁמָּה וְלִשְׁרֵקָה כֹּל עֹבֵר עָלֶיהָ יִשֹּׁם וְיִשְׁרֹק עַל־כָּל־
all because will and be will it by who All a and horror a
of hiss horrified pass .hissing

1323 1320 1121 1320 398 4347
9 מַכּוֹתֶהָ׃ וְהַאֲכַלְתִּים אֶת־בְּשַׂר בְּנֵיהֶם וְאֵת בְּשַׂר בְּנֹתֵיהֶם
their the and their the will I And its
,daughters of flesh sons of flesh eat them make .plagues

6693 834 4689 4692 398 7453 1320 376
וְאִישׁ בְּשַׂר־רֵעֵהוּ יֹאכֵלוּ בְּמָצוֹר וּבְמָצוֹק אֲשֶׁר יָצִיקוּ
will which the in and the in eat will his the and
oppress distress ,siege friend of flesh each

5869 1228 7665 5315 1245 341
10 לָהֶם אֹיְבֵיהֶם וּמְבַקְשֵׁי נַפְשָׁם׃ וְשָׁבַרְתָּ הַבַּקְבֻּק לְעֵינֵי
before jar the you Then .life their those and their them
of eyes the break shall seek who enemies

the men who go with you, [11]and shall say to them, So says Jehovah of hosts, Even so I will break this people and this city, as *one* breaks the potter's vessel that cannot be healed again. And they shall bury in Tophet, since no place is *left* to bury. [12]I will do this to this place, says Jehovah, and to its inhabitants, and make this place as Tophet. [13]And the houses of Jerusalem, and the houses of the kings of Judah, shall be defiled as the place of Tophet; because of all the roofs of the houses on *which* they have burned incense to all the host of the heavens, and have poured out drink offerings to other gods.

[14]Then Jeremiah came from Tophet, there where Jehovah had sent him to prophesy. And he stood in the court of the house of Jehovah, and *he* said to all the people, [15]So says Jehovah of hosts, the God of Israel: Behold, I will bring to this city, and on all its towns, all the evil that I have spoken against it, because they have stiffened their necks in order not to hear My words.

559 3541 559 1980 582
11 הָאֲנָשִׁים הַהֹלְכִים אוֹתָךְ׃ וְאָמַרְתָּ אֲלֵיהֶם כֹּה־אָמַר
says Thus ,them to shall and say with ,you go who the men

2088 5892 2088 5971 76 65 3602 6635 3068
יְהוָה צְבָאוֹת כָּכָה אֶשְׁבֹּר אֶת־הָעָם הַזֶּה וְאֶת־הָעִיר הַזֹּאת
this city and this people will I break So ,hosts Jehovah of

7495 3201 3808 834 3335 3627 7665
כַּאֲשֶׁר יִשְׁבֹּר אֶת־כְּלִי הַיּוֹצֵר אֲשֶׁר לֹא־יוּכַל לְהֵרָפֵה
be mended can not that the potter's vessel one breaks as

6213 6912 4725 369 6912 8612 5750
12 עוֹד וּבְתֹפֶת יִקְבְּרוּ מֵאֵין מָקוֹם לִקְבּוֹר׃ כֵּן־אֶעֱשֶׂה
I will do This .bury to place there is no since they bury shall in And Tophet .again

2088 5892 5414 3427 3068 5002 2088 4725
לַמָּקוֹם הַזֶּה נְאֻם־יְהוָה וּלְיוֹשְׁבָיו וְלָתֵת אֶת־הָעִיר הַזֹּאת
this city and make its to and inhabitants ,Jehovah says ,this place to

4725 3063 4428 1004 3389 1004 1961 8612
13 כְּתֹפֶת׃ וְהָיוּ בָּתֵּי יְרוּשָׁלַםִ וּבָתֵּי מַלְכֵי יְהוּדָה כִּמְקוֹם
the like of place ,Judah the of kings the and of houses ,Jerusalem the of houses And be shall as .Tophet

1406 6999 834 1004 3605 2931 8612
הַתֹּפֶת הַטְּמֵאִים לְכֹל הַבָּתִּים אֲשֶׁר קִטְּרוּ עַל־גַּגֹּתֵיהֶם
their roofs on have they incense burned which the houses because all of ,defiled Tophet

312 430 5262 5258 8064 6635 3605
לְכֹל צְבָא הַשָּׁמַיִם וְהַסֵּךְ נְסָכִים לֵאלֹהִים אֲחֵרִים׃
.other gods to drink offerings have and out poured ;heaven the of host all to

5012 8033 3068 7971 834 8612 3414 935
14 וַיָּבֹא יִרְמְיָהוּ מֵהַתֹּפֶת אֲשֶׁר שְׁלָחוֹ יְהוָה שָׁם לְהִנָּבֵא
to .prophesy there Jehovah had him sent where from ,Tophet Jeremiah Then came

559 5971 3605 559 3068 1004 2691 5975
15 וַיַּעֲמֹד בַּחֲצַר בֵּית־יְהוָה וַיֹּאמֶר אֶל־כָּל־הָעָם׃ כֹּה־אָמַר
says Thus the ,people all to said and Jehovah's house the of court in he And stood

2088 5892 935 2005 3478 430 6635 3068
יְהוָה צְבָאוֹת אֱלֹהֵי יִשְׂרָאֵל הִנְנִי מֵבִיא אֶל־הָעִיר הַזֹּאת
this city to will I bring ,Behold :Israel the of God ,hosts Jehovah of

1696 834 7451 3605 5892 3605
וְעַל־כָּל־עָרֶיהָ אֵת כָּל־הָרָעָה אֲשֶׁר דִּבַּרְתִּי עָלֶיהָ כִּי
for against ,it have I spoken that the evil all its towns all and on

1697 8085 1115 6203 7185
הִקְשׁוּ אֶת־עָרְפָּם לְבִלְתִּי שְׁמוֹעַ אֶת־דְּבָרָי׃
My .words hear not to their neck have they stiffened

CAP. XX כ

CHAPTER 20

CHAPTER 20

[1]When Pashur the son of Immer the priest —he also *was* chief officer in the house of Jehovah—heard Jeremiah prophesying these things, [2]then Pashur struck Jeremiah the prophet, and put him in the stocks that *were* in the upper Benjamin

1004 5057 6496 3548 559 1121 6583 8085
1 וַיִּשְׁמַע פַּשְׁחוּר בֶּן־אִמֵּר הַכֹּהֵן וְהוּא־פָקִיד נָגִיד בְּבֵית
the in of house chief (was) officer he also the ,priest Immer the of son Pashur When heard

6583 5221 428 1697 5012 3414 3068
יְהוָה אֶת־יִרְמְיָהוּ נִבָּא אֶת־הַדְּבָרִים הָאֵלֶּה׃ וַיַּכֶּה פַּשְׁחוּר
Pashur then struck ,these things prophe- sying Jeremiah Jehovah

8179 834 4115 5414 5030 3414
2 אֵת יִרְמְיָהוּ הַנָּבִיא וַיִּתֵּן אֹתוֹ עַל־הַמַּהְפֶּכֶת אֲשֶׁר בְּשַׁעַר
in Gate that (were) the stocks in him and put the ,prophet Jeremiah

Gate, which *was* by the house of Jehovah. [3]And it was on the next day that Pashur released Jeremiah from the stocks. Then Jeremiah said to him, Jehovah has not called your name Pashur, but Terror from all around. [4]For so says Jehovah, Behold, I will make you a terror to yourself, and to all your friends. And they shall fall by the sword of their enemies, and your eyes shall see. And I will give all Judah into the hand of the king of Babylon, and he will exile them into Babylon, and kill them with the sword. [5]And I will give all the wealth of this city, and all its produce, and all its precious things, and all the treasures of the kings of Judah, *even* I will give *them* into the hand of their enemies; who will strip them and take them, and carry them to Babylon. [6]And you, Pashur, and all who live in your house, shall go into captivity. And you shall come to Babylon; and you shall die there; and you shall be buried there; you and all your friends to whom you have prophesied lies.

[7]O Jehovah, You have deceived me; yea, I was deceived. You are stronger than I, and You have prevailed. I am in derision all the day; everyone laughs at me. [8]For whenever I speak, I cry out, I proclaim violence and ruin; for the word of Jehovah has been to me a reproach and derision all the day. [9]Then I said, I will not mention Him or speak any more in His name. But *His word* was in my heart like a burning fire shut up in my bones; and I was weary of holding in; and I could not prevail.

[10]For I heard the slanders of many. Terror is all around! Expose! Yea, let us expose him! Every man of my peace

3318 4283 1961 3068 1004 834 5945 1144
3 בנימן העליון אשר בבית יהוה: ויהי ממחרת ויצא
that released | the on day next | it And was | .Jehovah | the by of house | which (was) | the upper | Benjamin

3414 559 4115 3414 6583
פשחור את־ירמיהו מן־המהפכת ויאמר אליו ירמיהו
,Jeremiah | him to | Then said | the .stocks | from | Jeremiah | Pashur

5439 4032 8034 3068 7121 6583 3808
לא פשחור קרא יהוה שמך כי אם־מגור מסביב:
all from .around | terror | but | your ,name | Jehovah | has called | Pashur | not

157 3605 4032 5414 2005 3068 559
4 כי־כה אמר יהוה הנני נתנך למגור לך ולכל־אהביך
your .friends | to and all | to yourself | terror a | will I make you | Behold | ,Jehovah | says | thus For

5414 3063 3605 7200 5869 341 2719 5307
ונפלו בחרב איביהם ועיניך ראות ואת־כל־יהודה אתן
will I give | Judah | all and | shall ;see | your and eyes | their ,enemies | the by of sword | they And fall will

5414 2719 5221 884 1540 884 4428 3027
5 ביד מלך־בבל והגלם בבלה והכם בחרב: ונתתי את־
I And give will I | the with .sword | strike and them | into Babylon | will he and them exile | ,Babylon | the of king | the into of hand

3366 3605 3018 3605 2088 5892 2633 3605
כל־חסן העיר הזאת ואת־כל־יגיעה ואת־כל־יקרה ואת
and | precious ;things | its | all and | its ,produce | all and | ,this | city | the of wealth | all

3947 962 341 3027 5414 3063 4428 214 3605
כל־אוצרות מלכי יהודה אתן ביד איביהם ובזזום ולקחום
take and them | will who them strip | their ,enemies' | into hand | will I give | Judah | the of king | the of treasures | all

1980 1004 3427 3605 6583 859 884 935
6 והביאום בבלה: ואתה פשחור וכל ישבי ביתך תלכו
shall go | your in ,house | who live | and all | ,Pashur | And ,you | to .Babylon | bring and them

3605 6912 8033 4191 8033 935 884 7628
בשבי ובבל תבוא ושם תמות ושם תקבר אתה וכל־
and all | you | shall you ,buried be | and there | shall you ,die | and there | shall you enter | And Babylon | into .captivity

3068 6601 8267 5012 834 157
7 אהביך אשר־נבאת להם בשקר: פתיתני יהוה
O ,Jehovah | have You me deceived | .lies | them to | have you prophesied | whom | your friends

3932 3605 3117 3605 7814 1961 3201 2388 6601
ואפת חזקתני ותוכל הייתי לשחוק כל־היום כלה לעג
mocks | every one | the ;day | all | laughing- stock a | am I | have and .prevailed I | are You than stronger | was I and .deceived

3068 7121 7701 2555 2199 1696 1767
8 לי: כי־מדי אדבר אזעק חמס ושד אקרא כי־היה
has been | For | I .proclaim | and ruin | violence | cry I out | ,speak I | when- ever | For | .me

3808 559 3117 3605 7047 2781 3068 1697
9 דבר־יהוה לי לחרפה ולקלס כל־היום: ואמרתי לא־
not | I Then ,said | the .day | all | and derision | a reproach | to me | Jehovah | the of word

1197 784 3820 1961 8034 5750 1696 3808 2142
אזכרנו ולא־אדבר עוד בשמו והיה בלבי כאש בערת
burning | a like flame | my in heart | it But was | His in .name | any more | speak | or | will I Him mention

8085 3201 3808 3557 3811 6106 6113
10 עצר בעצמתי ונלאיתי כלכל ולא אוכל: כי שמעתי
heard I | For | was I .able | and not | holding (it) | was I and of weary | my in ,bones | shut up

7965 582 3605 5046 5046 5439 4032 7227 1681
דבת רבים מגור מסביב הגידו ונגידנו כל אנוש שלומי
my peace | man of | Every | us let ,Yea !him expose | !Expose | all ;around | Terror (is) | ,many | the of rumor

watching for my fall,
Perhaps he will be lured
away, and we shall prevail
against him; and we shall
take revenge on him. [11]But
Jehovah *is* with me like a
mighty, awesome one. On
account of this my perse-
cutors shall stumble, and
will not prevail. And they
shall be greatly ashamed.
For they have not acted
wisely; *they are* an everlasting disgrace that will
not be forgotten. [12]But, O
Jehovah of hosts, who tries
the righteous, *who* sees the
reins and the heart, let me
see Your vengeance on
them; for I have revealed my
cause to You. [13]Sing to
Jehovah; praise Jehovah;
for He has delivered the
soul of the poor from the
hand of evildoers.
[14]Cursed *is* the day in
which I was born; let not the
day in which my mother
bore me be blessed.
[15]Cursed *is* the man who
brought news to my father,
saying, A man child is born
to you; making him very
glad. [16]And let that man
be as the cities which
Jehovah overthrew, and did
not repent. And let him hear
a cry in the morning, and
the shouting at noontime;
[17]because he did not kill me
from the womb; and that my
mother would have been
my grave, and her womb
always great *with me*.
[18]Why did I come forth from
the womb to see toil and
sorrow, and my days
consumed in shame?

CHAPTER 21
[1]The word which was to
Jeremiah from Jehovah,
when king Zedekiah sent
Pashur the son of Melchiah,
and Zephaniah the son of
Maaseiah the priest, to him,
saying, [2]I beg you, inquire
of Jehovah for us. For

5360 3947 3201 6601 194 67 63 8104
שֹׁמְרֵי צַלְעִי אוּלַי יְפֻתֶּה וְנוּכְלָה לוֹ וְנִקְחָה נִקְמָתֵנוּ מִמֶּנּוּ׃
on our and against we and be will he (saying) my watching
.him revenge take him prevail will ,lured Perhaps ,fall for

3201 3808 3782 7291 618:4 1368 3068
11 וַיהוָה אוֹתִי כְּגִבּוֹר עָרִיץ עַל־כֵּן רֹדְפַי יִכָּשְׁלוּ וְלֹא יֻכָלוּ
will and will per- my Therefore awesome a like with (is) But
;prevail not ,stumble secutors .one mighty me Jehovah

7911 38:08 5769 36:39 7919 38:08 3966 954
בֹּשׁוּ מְאֹד כִּי־לֹא הִשְׂכִּילוּ כְּלִמַּת עוֹלָם לֹא תִשָּׁכֵחַ׃
will that not ever- an have they not for ,greatly will they
.forgotten be lasting disgrace ;wisely acted ashamed be

5360 7200 38:20 3629 7200 666:2 974 6635 3068
12 וַיהוָה צְבָאוֹת בֹּחֵן צַדִּיק רֹאֶה כְלָיוֹת וָלֵב אֶרְאֶה נִקְמָתְךָ
Your me let the and the (and) the who hosts O But
vengeance see ;heart reins sees righteous tests of Jehovah

1984 3068 7891 7379 1540
13 מֵהֶם כִּי אֵלֶיךָ גִּלִּיתִי אֶת־רִיבִי׃ שִׁירוּ לַיהוָה הַלְלוּ
praise to Sing my have I to for on
,Jehovah .cause revealed You ,them

7489 3027 34 53,15 5337 3068
אֶת־יְהוָה כִּי הִצִּיל אֶת־נֶפֶשׁ אֶבְיוֹן מִיַּד מְרֵעִים׃
.evildoers the from the the has He for ,Jehovah
of hand poor of soul delivered

1408 517 3205 834 3117 3205 834 3117 779
14 אָרוּר הַיּוֹם אֲשֶׁר יֻלַּדְתִּי בּוֹ יוֹם אֲשֶׁר־יְלָדַתְנִי אִמִּי אַל־
not my bore which the ;it in was I which the Cursed
mother me day born day (is)

3205 559 1319 834 376 779 1288 1961
15 יְהִי בָרוּךְ׃ אָרוּר הָאִישׁ אֲשֶׁר בִּשַּׂר אֶת־אָבִי לֵאמֹר יֻלַּד־
is ,saying my brought who the Cursed .blessed let
born ,father to news man (is) be

5892 376 1961 8056 8056 2145 1121
16 לְךָ בֵּן זָכָר שַׂמֵּחַ שִׂמְּחָהוּ׃ וְהָיָה הָאִישׁ הַהוּא כֶּעָרִים
the like that man let And making very ,male a to
cities be .glad him child you

8643 1242 2201 8085 5162 38:08 3068 2015 834
אֲשֶׁר־הָפַךְ יְהוָה וְלֹא נִחָם וְשָׁמַע זְעָקָה בַּבֹּקֶר וּתְרוּעָה
the and the in cry a let and did and ,Jehovah over- which
shouting ,morning hear him ,repent not threw

517 1961 7356 4191 3808 834 6672 6256
17 בְּעֵת צָהֳרָיִם׃ אֲשֶׁר לֹא־מוֹתְתַנִי מֵרָחֶם וַתְּהִי־לִי אִמִּי
my for would so the from did he not because ;noon the at
mother me been have ;womb me kill of time

7200 3318 7356 2088/4100 5769 2030 7356 6913
18 קִבְרִי וְרַחְמָה הֲרַת עוֹלָם׃ לָמָּה זֶּה מֵרֶחֶם יָצָאתִי לִרְאוֹת
see to did I the from Why .ever great her and my
forth come womb womb ,grave

3117 1322 3615 3015 5999
עָמָל וְיָגוֹן וַיִּכְלוּ בְּבֹשֶׁת יָמָי׃
my in and and toil
?days shame consumed ,torment

CAP. XXI כא

CHAPTER 21

79.71 3068 3414 1961 834 1697
1 הַדָּבָר אֲשֶׁר־הָיָה אֶל־יִרְמְיָהוּ מֵאֵת יְהוָה בִּשְׁלֹחַ אֵלָיו
to when ,Jehovah from Jeremiah to came which The
him sent word

1121 6846 44:41 1121 6583 66 77 4428
הַמֶּלֶךְ צִדְקִיָּהוּ אֶת־פַּשְׁחוּר בֶּן־מַלְכִּיָּה וְאֶת־צְפַנְיָה בֶן־
the Zephaniah and ,Melchiah the Pashur Zedekiah King
of son of son

3068 11:57 4994 1875 559 35 48 46 41
2 מַעֲשֵׂיָה הַכֹּהֵן לֵאמֹר׃ דְּרָשׁ־נָא בַעֲדֵנוּ אֶת־יְהוָה כִּי
for ,Jehovah us for now Inquire ,saying the Maaseiah
of ,priest

us. For Nebuchadnezzar king of Babylon *is* warring against us. It may be Jehovah will deal with us according to all His wonderful works, that he may go up from us.

[3]And Jeremiah said to them, You shall say this to Zedekiah, [4]So says Jehovah, the God of Israel: Behold, I will turn back the weapons of war that *are* in your hand, with which you fight against the king of Babylon, and *against* the Chaldeans who besiege you outside the wall. And I will gather them together in the middle of the city. [5]And I Myself will fight against you with an outstretched arm and with a strong arm, even in anger, and in fury, and in great wrath. [6]And I will strike the people of this city, both man and beast. They shall die of a great plague. [7]And afterward, says Jehovah, I will deliver Zedekiah king of Judah, and his servants, and the people, and those who remain in this city, from the plague, from the sword, and from the famine, into the hand of Nebuchadnezzar king of Babylon,and into the hand of their enemies, and into the hand of those who seek their life. And he shall strike them with the mouth of the sword; he shall not spare them, nor have pity, nor have compassion.

[8]And you shall say to this people, So says Jehovah, Behold, I set before you the way of life, and the way of death. [9]He who remains in this city shall die by the sword, and by the famine, and by the plague. But he who goes out and falls to the Chaldeans who are besieging you, he shall live;

3068 62 13 194 3898 884 4428 5019
נְבוּכַדְרֶאצַּר מֶלֶךְ־בָּבֶל נִלְחָם עָלֵינוּ אוּלַי יַעֲשֶׂה יְהוָה
Jehovah will Perhaps against is Babylon king Nebuchadnezzar
deal .us warring of

3 3414 559 5927 63:81 3605
אוֹתָנוּ כְּכָל־נִפְלְאֹתָיו וְיַעֲלֶה מֵעָלֵינוּ׃ וַיֹּאמֶר יִרְמְיָהוּ
Jeremiah Then from he that wonder- His according with
said .us up go may ,works ful all to us

4 430 3068 559 3541 6677 559
אֲלֵיהֶם כֹּה תֹאמְרֻן אֶל־צִדְקִיָּהוּ׃ כֹּה־אָמַר יְהוָה אֱלֹהֵי
the Jehovah says Thus ,Zedekiah to shall you Thus to
of God say ,them

834 3027 834 4421 3627 5437 2005 3478
יִשְׂרָאֵל הִנְנִי מֵסֵב אֶת־כְּלֵי הַמִּלְחָמָה אֲשֶׁר בְּיֶדְכֶם אֲשֶׁר
which your in that war the turn will ,Behold :Israel
,hand (are) of weapons back I

6696 3778 884 4428 3898
אַתֶּם נִלְחָמִים בָּם אֶת־מֶלֶךְ בָּבֶל וְאֶת־הַכַּשְׂדִּים הַצָּרִים
who the and ,Babylon the with fight you
besiege Chaldeans of king them against

5892 8432 622 2346 2351
עֲלֵיכֶם מִחוּץ לַחוֹמָה וְאָסַפְתִּי אוֹתָם אֶל־תּוֹךְ הָעִיר
city the to them will I And the outside you
of midst gather .wall

5 2389 2220 5186 3027 3898 2088
הַזֹּאת׃ וְנִלְחַמְתִּי אֲנִי אִתְּכֶם בְּיָד נְטוּיָה וּבִזְרוֹעַ חֲזָקָה
strong with and stretched with against Myself will I And .this
arm a out hand a you fight

6 5892 3427 5221 1419 7110 2534 639
וּבְאַף וּבְחֵמָה וּבְקֶצֶף גָּדוֹל׃ וְהִכֵּיתִי אֶת־יוֹשְׁבֵי הָעִיר
city inhab- the I And .great in and in and in even
of itants strike will rage ,wrath anger

4191 1419 1698 929 120 2088
הַזֹּאת וְאֶת־הָאָדָם וְאֶת־הַבְּהֵמָה בְּדֶבֶר גָּדוֹל יָמֻתוּ׃
will they great a by ;beast and man both ,this
.die plague

7 3063 4428 6677 5414 3068 5002 310
וְאַחֲרֵי־כֵן נְאֻם־יְהוָה אֶתֵּן אֶת־צִדְקִיָּהוּ מֶלֶךְ־יְהוּדָה וְאֶת־
and ,Judah king Zedekiah will I ,Jehovah says Then
of deliver ,afterwards

1698 2088 5892 7604 5971 5650
עֲבָדָיו וְאֶת־הָעָם וְאֶת־הַנִּשְׁאָרִים בָּעִיר הַזֹּאת מִן־הַדֶּבֶר
the from ,this city in who those and the and his
,plague remain people servants

3027 884 4428 5019 3027 7458 2719
מִן־הַחֶרֶב וּמִן־הָרָעָב בְּיַד נְבוּכַדְרֶאצַּר מֶלֶךְ־בָּבֶל וּבְיַד
into and ,Babylon king Nebuchadnezzar into the and the from
hand of of hand the ,famine from ,sword

2347 3808 2719 6310 5221 5315 1245 3027 341
אֹיְבֵיהֶם וּבְיַד מְבַקְשֵׁי נַפְשָׁם וְהִכָּם לְפִי־חֶרֶב לֹא־יָחוּס
will he not the with will he And their who those into and your
spare ;sword's edge them strike .life seek of hand the ,enemies'

8 559 2088 5971 7355 3808 2550 3808
עֲלֵיהֶם וְלֹא יַחְמֹל וְלֹא יְרַחֵם׃ וְאֶל־הָעָם הַזֶּה תֹּאמַר
shall you this people And have nor have nor ,them
,say to .compassion pity

2416 1870 6440 5414 2005 3068 559
כֹּה אָמַר יְהוָה הִנְנִי נֹתֵן לִפְנֵיכֶם אֶת־דֶּרֶךְ הַחַיִּים וְאֶת־
and life the before set ,Behold ,Jehovah says Thus
of way you I

9 7458 2719 4191 2088 5892 3427 4194 1870
דֶּרֶךְ הַמָּוֶת׃ הַיֹּשֵׁב בָּעִיר הַזֹּאת יָמוּת בַּחֶרֶב וּבָרָעָב
by and the by shall this city in who He .death the
,famine the ,sword die dwells of ways

2421 6696 3778 5307 3318 1698
וּבַדָּבֶר וְהַיּוֹצֵא וְנָפַל עַל־הַכַּשְׂדִּים הַצָּרִים עֲלֵיכֶם יִחְיֶה
shall he ,you are who the to and who he But by and
,live besieging Chaldeans falls out goes .plague the

for evil, and not for good, says Jehovah. It shall be given into the hand of the king of Babylon, and he shall burn it with fire.

[11]And concerning the house of the king of Judah, *say*, Hear the word of Jehovah, [12]O house of David, so says Jehovah: Do justice in the morning, and deliver the plundered one out of the hand of the oppressor, that My fury not go out like fire, and burn so that none can put *it* out, because of the evil of your doings. [13]Behold, I *am* against you, O dweller of the valley, rock of the plain, says Jehovah; those who say, Who can come down against us? Or who can enter our dwellings? [14]But I will punish you according to the fruit of your doings, says Jehovah. And I will kindle a fire in its forest; and it shall devour all things around it.

2008 5892 6440 7760 7998 5315 1961
10 וְהָיְתָה־לּוֹ נַפְשׁוֹ לְשָׁלָל׃ כִּי שַׂמְתִּי פָנַי בָּעִיר הַזֹּאת
this against city / My face / have I set / For / a for prize / his life / to him / and be shall

8313 5414 884 4428 3027 3068 5002 2896 3808 7451
לְרָעָה וְלֹא לְטוֹבָה נְאֻם־יְהוָה בְּיַד מֶלֶךְ־בָּבֶל תִּנָּתֵן וּשְׂרָפָהּ
will he burn it / and given be / will it / Babylon / the of king / Into hand the / ,Jehovah / says / for good / and not / for ,evil

1732 1004 3068 1697 8085 3063 4428 1004 784
11 12 בָּאֵשׁ׃ וּלְבֵית מֶלֶךְ יְהוּדָה שִׁמְעוּ דְבַר־יְהוָה׃ בֵּית דָּוִד
,David O of house / :Jehovah / the of word / ,(say) Hear / ,Judah / the of king / the to of house / And with .fire

6231 3027 1491 5337 4941 1242 1777 3068 559
כֹּה אָמַר יְהוָה דִּינוּ לַבֹּקֶר מִשְׁפָּט וְהַצִּילוּ גָזוּל מִיַּד עוֹשֵׁק
op- ,pressor's / the from hand / the robbed / and deliver / ,justice / the for morning / Do justice / :Jehovah / says / thus

7451 3518 369 1197 2534 784 3318 6435
פֶּן־תֵּצֵא כָאֵשׁ חֲמָתִי וּבָעֲרָה וְאֵין מְכַבֶּה מִפְּנֵי רֹעַ
the of evil / because of / can (it) quench / that so none / and ,burn / My wrath / like fire / go forth / lest

5002 4334 6697 6010 3427 2005 4611
13 מַעַלְלֵיהֶם׃ הִנְנִי אֵלַיִךְ יֹשֶׁבֶת הָעֵמֶק צוּר הַמִּישֹׁר נְאֻם־
says / the ,plain / rock of / the ,valley / dweller O of / against ,Behold ,you (am) I / your .doings

4585 935 4310 5181 559 3068
יְהוָה הָאֹמְרִים מִי־יֵחַת עָלֵינוּ וּמִי יָבוֹא בִּמְעוֹנוֹתֵינוּ׃
our into .dwellings / can enter / Or who / against ?us / can Who down come / who those ,say / ,Jehovah

784 3341 3068 5002 4611 6529 6485
14 וּפָקַדְתִּי עֲלֵיכֶם כִּפְרִי מַעַלְלֵיכֶם נְאֻם־יְהוָה וְהִצַּתִּי אֵשׁ
a fire / will I and kindle / ;Jehovah / says / your ,doings / to according of fruit the / you / will I But punish

5439 3605 398 3293
בְּיַעְרָהּ וְאָכְלָה כָּל־סְבִיבֶיהָ׃
around .it / all things / may it that devour / its in ,forest

CAP. XXII כב

CHAPTER 22

CHAPTER 22

[1]So says Jehovah, Go down to the house of the king of Judah and speak this word there, [2]and say, Hear the word of Jehovah, O king of Judah, who sits on the throne of David, you and your servants, and your people who enter in by these gates. [3]So says Jehovah, Do justice and righteousness, and deliver the one robbed from the oppressor's hand. And do not oppress the alien, the widow, or the orphan, and do not do violence nor shed innocent blood in this place. [4]For if you indeed do this thing, then there shall enter in by the gates of this house kings sitting on the

8033 1696 3063 4428 1004 3381 3068 559 3541
1 כֹּה אָמַר יְהוָה רֵד בֵּית־מֶלֶךְ יְהוּדָה וְדִבַּרְתָּ שָּׁם אֶת־
there / and speak / ,Judah / the of king / the of house / down to / Go / Jeho- ,vah / says / Thus

3427 3063 4428 3068 1697 8085 559 2088 1697
2 הַדָּבָר הַזֶּה׃ וְאָמַרְתָּ שְׁמַע דְּבַר־יְהוָה מֶלֶךְ יְהוּדָה הַיֹּשֵׁב
who sits / ,Judah / O of king / ,Jehovah / the of word / Hear / ,say and / ;this / word

8179 935 5971 5650 859 1732 3678
עַל־כִּסֵּא דָוִד אַתָּה וַעֲבָדֶיךָ וְעַמְּךָ הַבָּאִים בַּשְּׁעָרִים
gates by / enter who in / your and people / your and ,servants / you / ,David / the on of throne

5337 6666 4941 6213 3068 559 428
3 הָאֵלֶּה׃ כֹּה אָמַר יְהוָה עֲשׂוּ מִשְׁפָּט וּצְדָקָה וְהַצִּילוּ
and deliver / and ,righteousness / justice / Do / ,Jehovah / says / Thus / .these

2554 408 3238 408 490 3490 1616 6216 3027 1497
גָזוּל מִיַּד עָשׁוֹק וְגֵר יָתוֹם וְאַלְמָנָה אַל־תֹּנוּ אַל־תַּחְמֹסוּ
do ,violence / nor / do ,oppress / not / the or ,widow / or- phan / the ,stranger / the with / op- ,pressor's / (his) from hand / the robbed

6213 6213 518 2088 4725 8210 408 5355 1818
4 וְדָם נָקִי אַל־תִּשְׁפְּכוּ בַּמָּקוֹם הַזֶּה׃ כִּי אִם־עָשׂוֹ תַּעֲשׂוּ
you do / indeed / if / For / .this / place in / shed do / not / inno- cent / and blood

3427 4428 2088 1004 8179 935 2088 1697
אֶת־הַדָּבָר הַזֶּה וּבָאוּ בְשַׁעֲרֵי הַבַּיִת הַזֶּה מְלָכִים יֹשְׁבִים
sitting / kings / this / house / the by of gates / will then enter / ,this / thing

the throne of David, riding on chariots and on horses, he and his servants and his people. [5]But if you will not hear these words, I swear by Myself, says Jehovah, that this house shall become a ruin. [6]For so says Jehovah concerning the king of Judah's house, You *are* Gilead to Me, the head of Lebanon; yet surely I will make you a wilderness, cities not inhabited. [7]And I will consecrate destroyers against you, each one with his weapons; and they will cut down your choice cedars, and make *them* fall into the fire. [8]And many nations shall pass by this city; and they shall each say to one another, Why has Jehovah done this to this great city? [9]Then they will answer, Because they have forsaken the covenant of Jehovah their God, and worshiped other gods, and served them.

[10]Weep not for the dead, nor moan for him; weep bitterly for him who goes away, for he shall return no more, nor see the land of his birth. [11]For so says Jehovah concerning Shallum the son of Josiah king of Judah, who reigned in his father Josiah's place, who went forth from this place, he shall not return there any more. [12]But he shall die there in the place where they have exiled him, and he will see this land no more.

[13]Woe *to* him who builds his house without righteousness, and his upper rooms without justice; his neighbor serves without pay, and he does not give him his work; [14]who says, I will build myself a wide

5971 5650 5483 7393 7392 3678 17,32
לְדָוִד עַל־כִּסְאוֹ רֹכְבִים בָּרֶכֶב וּבַסּוּסִים הוּא וְעַבְדוֹ וְעַמּוֹ׃
his and his and he on and on riding his on of
.people servants ,horses chariots ,throne David

5002 7650 428 1697 8085 3808 518
5 וְאִם לֹא תִשְׁמְעוּ אֶת־הַדְּבָרִים הָאֵלֶּה בִּי נִשְׁבַּעְתִּי נְאֻם
says swear I by ,these words will you not But
Myself obey if

559 2088 1004 1961 2723 30,68
6 יְהוָה כִּי־לְחָרְבָּה יִהְיֶה הַבַּיִת הַזֶּה׃ כִּי־כֹה ׀ אָמַר
says thus For .this house shall ruin a that ,Jehovah
become

3844 7218 1568 3063 4428 1004 3068
יְהוָה עַל־בֵּית מֶלֶךְ יְהוּדָה גִּלְעָד אַתָּה לִי רֹאשׁ הַלְּבָנוֹן
;Lebanon the to You (like) ,Judah the the about Jehovah
of head ,Me (are) Gilead of king of house

694,2 3427 38,08 5892 40,57 7896 38,08 518
7 אִם־לֹא אֲשִׁיתְךָ מִדְבָּר עָרִים לֹא נוֹשָׁבָה׃ וְקִדַּשְׁתִּי עָלֶיךָ
against will I And are not cities wilder- a will I yet
you consecrate .inhabited (which) ,ness you make surely

5307 730 4005 3772 3627 376 7843
מַשְׁחִתִים אִישׁ וְכֵלָיו וְכָרְתוּ מִבְחַר אֲרָזֶיךָ וְהִפִּילוּ עַל־
into made and your the will and his with each ,destroyers
fall cedars of best down cut weapons man

376 559 2088 5892 7227 1471 5674 784
8 הָאֵשׁ׃ וְעָבְרוּ גּוֹיִם רַבִּים עַל הָעִיר הַזֹּאת וְאָמְרוּ אִישׁ
each they and ,this city by many nations will And the
man say will pass .fire

2088 1419 5892 3068 62,13 4100 7453
אֶל־רֵעֵהוּ עַל־מֶה עָשָׂה יְהוָה כָּכָה לָעִיר הַגְּדוֹלָה הַזֹּאת׃
?this great city to thus ,Jehovah has Why his to
done ,companion

7812 430 3068 1285 5800 834 559
וְאָמְרוּ עַל אֲשֶׁר עָזְבוּ אֶת־בְּרִית יְהוָה אֱלֹהֵיהֶם וַיִּשְׁתַּחֲווּ
and their Jehovah the have they Because they Then
worshiped ,God of covenant forsaken ,say will

408 4191 1058 408 5647 312 430
10 לֵאלֹהִים אֲחֵרִים וַיַּעַבְדוּם׃ אַל־תִּבְכּוּ לְמֵת וְאַל־
nor the for Do not served and other gods
,dead weep .them

7200 5750 7725 3808 1980 1059 1058 5110
תָּנֻדוּ לוֹ בְּכוּ בָכוֹ לַהֹלֵךְ כִּי לֹא יָשׁוּב עוֹד וְרָאָה אֶת־
nor any will he not for him for bitterly weep for lament
see ,more return ,away goes who ;him

297,7 1121 7967 3068 559 4138 776
11 אֶרֶץ מוֹלַדְתּוֹ׃ כִּי־כֹה אָמַר־יְהוָה אֶל־שַׁלֻּם בֶּן־יֹאשִׁיָּהוּ
Josiah the Shallum con- Jehovah says thus For his the
of son cerning .birth of land

3318 834 1 2977 8478 4427 30,63 4428
מֶלֶךְ יְהוּדָה הַמֹּלֵךְ תַּחַת יֹאשִׁיָּהוּ אָבִיו אֲשֶׁר יָצָא מִן
from went who his Josiah the in who ,Judah king
forth ,father of place reigned of

1540 834 4725 5750 8033 7725 3808 2088 4725
12 הַמָּקוֹם הַזֶּה לֹא־יָשׁוּב שָׁם עוֹד׃ כִּי בִּמְקוֹם אֲשֶׁר־הִגְלוּ
have they where the in But any there will he not ;this place
exiled place .more return

5750 7200 38,08 2088 776 4191 8033
אֹתוֹ שָׁם יָמוּת וְאֶת־הָאָרֶץ הַזֹּאת לֹא־יִרְאֶה עוֹד׃
.more will he no this land and will he there ,him
see ,die

174 53 4941 1097 5944 6664 1097 1004 1129 1945
13 הוֹי בֹּנֶה בֵיתוֹ בְּלֹא־צֶדֶק וַעֲלִיּוֹתָיו בְּלֹא מִשְׁפָּט בְּרֵעֵהוּ
his ,justice without his and without his who him Woe
neighbor roof-rooms righteousness house builds (to)

1004 1129 559 5414 38,08 646,7 26,00 5647
14 יַעֲבֹד חִנָּם וּפֹעֲלוֹ לֹא יִתֶּן־לוֹ׃ הָאֹמֵר אֶבְנֶה־לִּי בֵּית
a my- will I ,says who to he not his and for serves
house self build ,him give does work ,nothing

house and large upper rooms, and who cuts out windows for it, and covers with cedar, and paints with vermilion.
15 Do you reign, because you lust to excel in cedar? Did not your father eat and drink and do justice and righteousness? Then *it was* well for him.
16 He judged the cause of the poor and needy; then *it was* well. Was this not to know Me, says Jehovah?
17 But your eyes and your heart *lust for* nothing but your unjust gain, and to shed innocent blood, and oppression, and to do violence.
18 So Jehovah says this concerning Jehoiakim the son of Josiah king of Judah, They shall not mourn for him, *saying* Ah, my brother! Or, Ah, sister! They shall not mourn for him, *saying*, Ah, lord! Or, Ah, his glory!
19 He shall be buried *with* the burial of an ass, drawn beyond the gates of Jerusalem, and thrown out.

20 Go up to Lebanon and cry. And lift up your voice in Bashan, and cry out from Abarim; for all your lovers are destroyed.
21 I spoke to you in your ease, but you said, I will not hear. This *has been* your way from your youth, for you have not obeyed My voice.
22 The wind shall rule all your shepherds, and your lovers shall go into captivity. Surely then you will be ashamed and humiliated for all your wickedness.
23 O dweller in Lebanon, nested in the cedars, how you will supplicate when pangs come to you, the pain as one giving birth!
24 *As* I live, says Jehovah, though Coniah the son of Jehoiakim king of Judah were the signet on My right hand, yet I would tear you out of there!
25 And I will give you into the hand

4886 730 5603 2470 7167 7304 5944 4060
מדות ועליות מרוחים וקרע לו חלוני וספון בארז ומשוח
and paints with cedar and covered its windows it for cut out and ,large upper rooms and spacious

15
3808 730 2734 4427 8350
בששר׃ התמלך כי אתה מתחרה בארז אביך הלוא
nor your father in ?cedar to lust excel you because you Do reign with .vermilion

16
1779 1777 2896 227 6666 4941 6213 8354 398
אכל ושתה ועשה משפט וצדקה אז טוב לו׃ דן דין
cause of the He judged for .him was it well ,Then and ?righteousness justice do and drink and Did eat

17
3068 5002 1847 3808 2896 227 34 6041
עני ואביון אז טוב הלא־היא הדעת אתי נאם־יהוה׃ כי
But ?Jehovah says ,Me know to that (Was) not (was it) .well then and ;needy the poor

8210 5355 1818 1215 3820 5869 369
אין עיניך ולבך כי אם־על־בצעך ועל דם־הנקי לשפוך
,shed to inno- cent blood and your ,gain unjust except your heart and your eyes (want) nothing

18
559 3541 6213 4835 6233
ועל־העשק ועל־המרוצה לעשות׃ לכן כה־אמר
says thus Therefore .do to extortion and oppression and

5594 3808 3063 4428 2977 1121 3079 3068
יהוה אל־יהויקים בן־יאשיהו מלך יהודה לא־יספדו לו
for ,him will they mourn not ,Judah king of Josiah the of son Jehoiakim con- cerning Jeho- vah

1935 1945 113 1945 5594 3808 269 1945 251 1945
הוי אחי והוי אחות לא־יספדו לו הוי אדון והוי הדה׃
his .splendor ,or Alas !lord ,(saying) ,Alas for him They mourn not will !sister ,or Alas my !brother ,(saying) ,Alas

19
8179 1973 7993 5498 6912 2543 6900
קבורת חמור יקבר סחוב והשלך מהלאה לשערי
the of gates beyond thrown and out dragged off will he ;buried be ass an the (With) of burial

20
6963 5414 1316 6817 3844 5927 3389
ירושלם׃ עלי הלבנון וצעקי ובבשן תני קולך
your ;voice lift up in and Bashan cry and ,out Lebanon Go to up .Jerusalem

21
1696 157 3605 7665 5682 6817
וצעקי מעברים כי נשברו כל־מאהביך׃ דברתי אליך
you to spoke I your .lovers all are crushed for from ,Abarim cry and ,out

3808 5271 1870 2088 8085 3808 559 7962
בשלותיך אמרת לא אשמע זה דרכך מנעוריך כי לא־
not for your from ,youth your way this (been has) will I ;listen not you (but) ,said your in ,prosperity

22
7628 157 7307 7462 7462 3605 6963 8085
שמעת בקולי׃ כל־רעיך תרעה־רוח ומאהביך בשבי
into captivity your and lovers the ,wind will rule your shepherds All My .voice have you obeyed

23
3844 3427 7451 3605 3637 954 227 3212
ילכו כי אז תבשי ונכלמת מכל רעתך׃ ישבתי בלבנון
in ,Lebanon O dweller your wickedness all for and humiliated be will you ashamed then Surely will .go

3205 2427 2256 935 2589 4100 730 7077
מקננתי בארזים מה־נחנת בבא־לך חבלים חיל כילדה׃
giv- !birth one as ing the pain ,pangs to you when come will you supplicate how the in ,cedars nested

24
4428 3079 1121 3659 1961 3068 5002 2416
חי־אני נאם־יהוה כי אם־יהיה כניהו בן־יהויקים מלך
king of Jehoiakim the of son Coniah were though ,Jehovah says ,I (As) live

25
5414 5423 8033 3225 3027 2368 3063
יהודה חותם על־יד ימיני כי משם אתקנך׃ ונתתיך
will I and you give tear would I ;away you from there yet My ,right hand on the ring signet Judah

of those who seek your life,
and into the hand *of
those* whose face you
are dreading, even into
the hand of Nebuchad-
nezzar king of Babylon, and
into the hand of the
Chaldeans. [26]And I will
cast you and your mother
who bore you into another
land where you *were* not
born there, and there you
will die. [27]But concerning
the land which they lift up
with their soul to return
there, they shall not re-
turn there. [28]*Is* this man
Coniah a despised broken
jar? Or a vessel *in which is*
no pleasure? Why are they
hurled, he and his seed,
and thrown into the land
which they did not know?
[29]O earth, earth, earth!
Hear the word of Jehovah!
[30]Jehovah says this: Write
this man childless, a man
who will not prosper in
his days. For not one of
his seed will prosper, a
man sitting on the throne
of David and ruling any
more in Judah.

26

3027	6440	3026	834	3027	5315	1245	3027
בְּיַד	מְבַקְשֵׁי	נַפְשֶׁךָ	וּבְיַד־אֲשֶׁר־אַתָּה	יָגוֹר	מִפְּנֵיהֶם		וּבְיַד

even / before / are / you / those into and / your / who those / into
hand into / ,them / dreading / whom of hand the / ,life / seek / of hand the

2904	3778	3027	884	44.28	5019
וְהִטַּלְתִּי אֹתְךָ			וּבְיַד הַכַּשְׂדִּים:	מֶלֶךְ־בָּבֶל	נְבוּכַדְרֶאצַּר

you / I And / the / the into ,Babylon of king / Nebuchad-
hurl will / Chaldeans' / hand / nezzar's

3205	3808	834	312	776	3205	834	517
וְאֶת־אִמְּךָ	אֲשֶׁר	יְלָדַתְךָ	עַל הָאָרֶץ אַחֶרֶת אֲשֶׁר	לֹא־יֻלַּדְתֶּם			

were you / not where / another / land / into / bore / who / your and
born / you / mother

27

5375	834	776	4191	8033	8033
שָׁם וְשָׁם תָּמוּתוּ:	וְעַל־הָאָרֶץ	אֲשֶׁר	הֵם מְנַשְּׂאִים אֶת־		

with / up lift / they / which / the / But / will you / and / ,there
land / for as / .die / there

28

5210	959	6089	7725	38.08	8033	8033	7725	5315
נַפְשָׁם לָשׁוּב שָׁם שָׁמָּה לֹא יָשׁוּבוּ:	הָעֶצֶב נִבְזֶה נָפוּץ							

shat- / despised / a (Is) / shall they / not / ,there ,there / return to / their
tered / jar / .return / soul

2904	4069	2656	369	3627	3659	2088	376
הָאִישׁ הַזֶּה כָּנְיָהוּ אִם־כְּלִי אֵין חֵפֶץ בּוֹ מַדּוּעַ הוּטֲלוּ הוּא							

he / are / Why / in pleasure / not / a / or / ,Coniah / this / man
hurled / ?it / is vessel

29

776	776	776	3045	38.08	834	776	799 3	22:33
וְזַרְעוֹ וְהֻשְׁלְכוּ עַל־הָאָרֶץ אֲשֶׁר לֹא־יָדָעוּ: אֶרֶץ אֶרֶץ אָרֶץ								

learth / ,earth / O / did they / not / which / the / into / and / his and
,earth / ?know / land / thrown / ,seed

30

2088	376	3068	559	3789	3068	1697	8085
שִׁמְעוּ דְּבַר־יְהוָה: כֹּה אָמַר יְהוָה כִּתְבוּ אֶת־הָאִישׁ הַזֶּה							

this / man / Write ,Jehovah says This / !Jehovah the / of word
Hear

376	2233	6743	3808	3117	6743	3808	1377	6185
עֲרִירִי גֶּבֶר לֹא־יִצְלַח בְּיָמָיו כִּי לֹא יִצְלַח מִזַּרְעוֹ אִישׁ								

a / his from / will one not For / his in / will who not / man a / child-
man / ,seed / succeed / ,days / will prosper / .less

3063	5750	4910	17:32	3678	3427
יֹשֵׁב עַל־כִּסֵּא דָוִד וּמֹשֵׁל עוֹד בִּיהוּדָה:					

.Judah in / any / and / David / the / on sitting
more / ruling / of throne

CAP. XXIII כג

CHAPTER 23

CHAPTER 23

[1]Woe *to* shepherds who
destroy and scatter the
sheep of My pasture, de-
clares Jehovah. [2]So
Jehovah the God of Israel
says this against the
shepherds who shepherd
My people: You have scat-
tered My flock, and have
driven them away, and have
not visited them. Behold, I
will visit on you the evil of
your doings, says Jehovah.
[3]And I will gather the
remnant of My flock out of
all the lands where I have
driven them there, and will
bring them again to their
fold. And they shall be
fruitful and multiply. [4]And I
will raise up shepherds over

1

3068	5002	4830	6629	6327	6	7462	1945
הוֹי רֹעִים מְאַבְּדִים וּמְפִצִים אֶת־צֹאן מַרְעִיתִי נְאֻם־יְהוָה:							

.Jehovah says / My the / and / who / the / Woe
,pasture / of sheep / scatter / destroy / shepherds (to)

2

7462	7462	3478	1430	3068	559
לָכֵן כֹּה־אָמַר יְהוָה אֱלֹהֵי יִשְׂרָאֵל עַל־הָרֹעִים הָרֹעִים					

are who / the / against / Israel / the / Jehovah / says thus / There-
shepherding shepherds / of God / fore

6485	38.08	50:80	6629	63.27	5971
אֶת־עַמִּי אַתֶּם הֲפִצֹתֶם אֶת־צֹאנִי וַתַּדִּחוּם וְלֹא פְקַדְתֶּם					

have / and / driven and / My / have / You / my
visited / not / away them / flock / scattered / :people

3068	5002	4611	7455	6485	2005
אֹתָם הִנְנִי פֹקֵד עֲלֵיכֶם אֶת־רֹעַ מַעַלְלֵיכֶם נְאֻם־יְהוָה:					

.Jehovah says / Your / the / upon / will ,Behold / .them
,doings / of evil / you / visit

3

5080	834	776	3605	66.29	7611	6908
וַאֲנִי אֲקַבֵּץ אֶת־שְׁאֵרִית צֹאנִי מִכֹּל הָאֲרָצוֹת אֲשֶׁר־הִדַּחְתִּי						

have I / where / the / from / My / the / will / And
driven / lands / all / flock of remnant / gather / I

4

6965	7235	6509	5116	7725	8033
אֹתָם שָׁם וַהֲשִׁבֹתִי אֶתְהֶן עַל־נְוֵהֶן וּפָרוּ וְרָבוּ: וַהֲקִמֹתִי					

will I And / and they and / their / to them / will and / there / them
up set / .multiply / bear will / ;fold / back bring

them who will tend them. And they will fear no more, nor be terrified; nor will they be missing *anything*, says Jehovah.

5 Behold, the days come, says Jehovah, that I will raise to David a righteous Branch, and a King shall reign and act wisely, and shall do justice and righteousness in the earth. 6 In His days Judah shall be saved, and Israel shall dwell safely. And this is His name *by* which He shall be called, Jehovah our Righteousness. 7 Therefore, behold, the days come, says Jehovah, that they shall no more say, As Jehovah lives, who brought the sons of Israel up out of the land of Egypt; 8 but, As Jehovah lives, who brought up and led the house of Israel out of the land of the north, and from all the lands where I have driven them there. And they shall dwell on their own land.

9 My heart within me is broken concerning the prophets; all my bones shake. I am like a drunken man, and like a man passed out by wine, because of Jehovah, and because of the words of His holiness. 10 For the land is full of adulterers. For the land mourns because of a curse; the pastures of the wilderness are dried up, and their way is evil, and their might *is* not right. 11 For both prophet and priest are ungodly; yea, I have found their evil in My house, says Jehovah. 12 So their way shall be to them as slippery places in the darkness; they shall be driven out and fall by it. For I will bring evil on them, *even* the year of their visitation, says Jehovah.

13 And I have seen frivolity among the prophets of Samaria; they prophesied by

---

עֲלֵיהֶם רֹעִים וְלֹא־יִירְאוּ עוֹד וְלֹא־יֵחַתּוּ וְלֹא יִפָּקֵדוּ

6485   3808   2865   3808/5750   3372   3808   7462   7462

they will not   be   nor   again will they   and   will who shep- over
,missing be   ,terrified   fear   not   ,them tend herds   them

נְאֻם־יְהוָה: הִנֵּה יָמִים בָּאִים נְאֻם־יְהוָה וַהֲקִמֹתִי

6965   3068   5002   935   3117   2009   3068   5002

will I that   Jehovah says   ,come   the   ,Behold   .Jehovah says
up set   days

לְדָוִד צֶמַח צַדִּיק וּמָלַךְ מֶלֶךְ וְהִשְׂכִּיל וְעָשָׂה מִשְׁפָּט

4941   6213   7919   4428   4427   6662   6780   1732

justice   will and   act and   a   shall and ,righteous   a   for
  do   ,wisely   King   reign   Branch   David

וּצְדָקָה בָּאָרֶץ: בְּיָמָיו תִּוָּשַׁע יְהוּדָה וְיִשְׂרָאֵל יִשְׁכֹּן לָבֶטַח

982   7931   3478   3063   3467   3117   776   6666

.safely   shall and   ,Judah be will   His In   the in   righ- and
  dwell   Israel   saved   ,days   .earth   teousness

וְזֶה־שְּׁמוֹ אֲשֶׁר־יִקְרְאוֹ יְהוָה צִדְקֵנוּ: לָכֵן הִנֵּה־יָמִים

3117   2009   6666   3068   7121   834   8034   2088

the ,behold ,Therefore   our   Jehovah will He   (by)   His this And
days   .Righteousness   :called be   which   (is)

בָּאִים נְאֻם־יְהוָה וְלֹא־יֹאמְרוּ עוֹד חַי־יְהוָה אֲשֶׁר הֶעֱלָה

5927   834   3068/2416   5750   559   3808   3068   5002   935

brought   who   Jehovah (As) ,more they   that   Jehovah says   ,come
up   lives   say shall   no

אֶת־בְּנֵי יִשְׂרָאֵל מֵאֶרֶץ מִצְרָיִם: כִּי אִם־חַי־יְהוָה אֲשֶׁר

834   3068   2416   4714   776   3478   1121

who   Jehovah   (As)   ,but   ;Egypt   the them   Israel   the
  lives   of land   of sons

הֶעֱלָה וַאֲשֶׁר הֵבִיא אֶת־זֶרַע בֵּית יִשְׂרָאֵל מֵאֶרֶץ צָפוֹנָה

6828   776   3478   1004   2233   935   834   5927

the   the from   Israel   the   the   led   and   brought
,north   of land   of house   of seed   up

וּמִכֹּל הָאֲרָצוֹת אֲשֶׁר הִדַּחְתִּים שָׁם וְיָשְׁבוּ עַל־אַדְמָתָם:

127   3427   8033   5080   834   776   3605

own their   upon they And   .there   have I   where   the   from and
.land   dwell will   them driven   lands   all

לַנְּבִאִים נִשְׁבַּר לִבִּי בְּקִרְבִּי רָחֲפוּ כָּל־עַצְמוֹתַי

6106   3605   7363   7130   3820   7665   5030

my   all   shake   my in   my   is   Concerning
.bones   ,midst   heart   broken ,prophets the

הָיִיתִי כְּאִישׁ שִׁכּוֹר וּכְגֶבֶר עֲבָרוֹ יָיִן מִפְּנֵי יְהוָה וּמִפְּנֵי

6440   3068   6440   3196   5674   1397   7910   376   1961

and   Jehovah before   ,wine passed like and   ,drunken a like   am I
before   by out   man a   man

דִּבְרֵי קָדְשׁוֹ: כִּי מְנָאֲפִים מָלְאָה הָאָרֶץ כִּי־מִפְּנֵי אָלָה

1422   776   4390   5003   6944   1697

a   because For   the   full is   adulterers For   His
,curse   of   .land   of   .holiness   of words

אָבְלָה הָאָרֶץ יָבְשׁוּ נְאוֹת מִדְבָּר וַתְּהִי מְרוּצָתָם רָעָה

74:51   4794   1961   4057   4999   3001   776   56

,evil   their   is and   wil- the   pas- the   are   the   mourns
  course   ,derness of   tures up dried   ;land

וּגְבוּרָתָם לֹא־כֵן: כִּי־גַם־נָבִיא גַם־כֹּהֵן חָנֵפוּ גַּם־בְּבֵיתִי

1004   1571   2610   3548   1571   5030   1571   3808   1369

My in even   are   priest and prophet both For   .right not   their and
house   ;ungodly   (is) might

מָצָאתִי רָעָתָם נְאֻם־יְהוָה: לָכֵן יִהְיֶה דַרְכָּם לָהֶם

1870   1961   3068   5002   7451

for   their   shall Therefore   .Jehovah says   their   have I
them   way   be   ,evilness   found

כַּחֲלַקְלַקּוֹת בָּאֲפֵלָה יִדַּחוּ וְנָפְלוּ בָהּ כִּי־אָבִיא עֲלֵיהֶם

935   5307   1760   653   2519

on   will I For   .it by   and be will they   the in   slipperi- like
them   bring   fall   out driven ;darkness   ness

רָעָה שְׁנַת פְּקֻדָּתָם נְאֻם־יְהוָה: וּבִנְבִיאֵי שֹׁמְרוֹן

8111   5030   3068   5002   6486   8141   7451

Samaria among And   .Jehovah says   their   the   ,evil
of prophets the   ,punishment of year

Baal, and caused My people Israel to go astray. [14]I have also seen a horrible thing among the prophets of Jerusalem; they commit adultery and walk in falsehood. And they make the hands of evildoers strong, so that not a man returns from his evil. They are all of them like Sodom to Me, and her inhabitants *are* like Gomorrah. [15]So Jehovah of hosts says this concerning the prophets: Behold, I will feed them wormwood, and make them drink poisonous water; for ungodliness has gone forth from the prophets of Jerusalem into all the land. [16]So says Jehovah of hosts, do not listen to the words of the prophets who prophesy to you; they make you vain; they speak a vision of their own heart, not out of the mouth of Jehovah. [17]They say to those who despise Me, Jehovah has said, You shall have peace. And they say to everyone who walks in the stubbornness of his own heart, Evil shall not come on you. [18]For who has stood in the counsel of Jehovah, and has seen and heard His word? Who has listened to His word, and heard? [19]Behold, the tempest of Jehovah has gone forth in fury, even a whirling tempest. It will whirl on the head of the wicked. [20]The anger of Jehovah shall not turn back until He has executed, and until He has set up the purposes of His heart. In latter days you shall understand it perfectly. [21]I have not sent the prophets, yet they ran; I have not spoken to them, yet they prophesied. [22]But if they had stood in My counsel, and had caused My people to hear My words, then they would have turned them

3478 5971 8582 1168 5012 2613 7200
רָאִיתִי תִפְלָה הִנַּבְּאוּ בַבַּעַל וַיַּתְעוּ אֶת־עַמִּי אֶת־יִשְׂרָאֵל׃
.Israel My and Baal by they ,frivolity have I
people mislead prophesied seen

1980 5003 8186 7200 3389 5030
14 וּבִנְבִאֵי יְרוּשָׁלִַם רָאִיתִי שַׁעֲרוּרָה נָאוֹף וְהָלֹךְ
and commit they horrible a have I Jerusalem's among Also
walk adultery :thing seen prophets

1961 7451 376 7725 1115 7489 3027 2388 8267
בַּשֶּׁקֶר וְחִזְּקוּ יְדֵי מְרֵעִים לְבִלְתִּי־שָׁבוּ אִישׁ מֵרָעָתוֹ הָיוּ־
They his from a does that so evil- the they and false- in
are ,evilness man return not ,doers of hands strengthen ,hood

559 6017 3427 5467 3605
15 לִי כֻלָּם כִּסְדֹם וְיֹשְׁבֶיהָ כַּעֲמֹרָה׃ לָכֵן כֹּה־אָמַר
says thus Therefore like her and like of all to
.Gomorrah inhabitants Sodom them Me

3939 398 2005 5030 6635 3068
יְהוָה צְבָאוֹת עַל־הַנְּבִאִים הִנְנִי מַאֲכִיל אוֹתָם לַעֲנָה
worm- them feed will ,Behold the con- hosts Jehovah
,wood I :prophets cerning of

2613 3318 3389 5030 7219 4325 8248
וְהִשְׁקִתִים מֵי־רֹאשׁ כִּי מֵאֵת נְבִיאֵי יְרוּשָׁלִַם יָצְאָה חֲנֻפָּה
ungodli- has Jerusalem the from for ;poison the make and
ness out gone of prophets of water drink them

8085 408 6635 3068 559 776 3605
16 לְכָל־הָאָרֶץ׃ כֹּה־אָמַר יְהוָה צְבָאוֹת אַל־תִּשְׁמְעוּ
Do not ,hosts Jehovah says Thus the into
listen of .land all

1891 5012 5030 1697
עַל־דִּבְרֵי הַנְּבִאִים הַנִּבְּאִים לָכֶם מַהְבִּלִים הֵמָּה אֶתְכֶם
;you they to cause ,you to who the the to
vain become prophesy prophets of words

5006 559 559 3068 6310 3808 1696 3820 2377
17 חֲזוֹן לִבָּם יְדַבֵּרוּ לֹא מִפִּי יְהוָה׃ אֹמְרִים אָמוֹר לִמְנַאֲצַי
those to continually They .Jehovah's from not they their a
,Me spurn who say mouth ,speak heart of vision

3820 8307 1980 3605 1961 7965 3068 1696
דִּבֶּר יְהוָה שָׁלוֹם יִהְיֶה לָכֶם וְכֹל הֹלֵךְ בִּשְׁרִרוּת לִבּוֹ
own his stub- the in who And !you to shall Peace ,Jehovah has
,heart of bornness walks everyone be said

3068 5475 5975 4310 7451 935 3808 559
18 אָמְרוּ לֹא־תָבוֹא עֲלֵיכֶם רָעָה׃ כִּי מִי עָמַד בְּסוֹד יְהוָה
Jehovah the in has who For !Evil you on will not they
of council stood come ,say

8085 697 7181 4310 1697 8085 7200
וְיֵרֶא וְיִשְׁמַע אֶת־דְּבָרוֹ מִי־הִקְשִׁיב דְּבָרִי וַיִּשְׁמָע׃
and His has Who His and has and
?heard word to listened ?word heard seen

7218 2342 5591 3318 2534 3068 5591 2009
19 הִנֵּה ׀ סַעֲרַת יְהוָה חֵמָה יָצְאָה וְסַעַר מִתְחוֹלֵל עַל רֹאשׁ
the on ;whirling a even gone has (in) Jehovah the ,Behold
of head tempest forth ,wrath of tempest

6965 5704 6213 5704 3068 639 7725 3808 2342 7563
20 רְשָׁעִים יָחוּל׃ לֹא יָשׁוּב אַף־יְהוָה עַד־עֲשֹׂתוֹ וְעַד־הֲקִימוֹ
has He and has He until ,Jehovah The will not will it the
up set until ,executed of anger back turn .whirl wicked

3808 998 995 3117 319 3820 4209
21 מְזִמּוֹת לִבּוֹ בְּאַחֲרִית הַיָּמִים תִּתְבּוֹנְנוּ בָהּ בִּינָה׃ לֹא־
not (with) it will you days in his pur- the
.understanding understand latter ;heart of poses

1696 3808 7323 5030 7971
שָׁלַחְתִּי אֶת־הַנְּבִאִים וְהֵם רָצוּ לֹא־דִבַּרְתִּי אֲלֵיהֶם וְהֵם
yet ,them to have I not ;ran yet the have I
they spoken they ;prophets sent

7725 5971 1697 8085 5475 5975 518 5012
22 נִבָּאוּ׃ וְאִם־עָמְדוּ בְּסוֹדִי וְיַשְׁמִעוּ דְבָרַי אֶת־עַמִּי וִישִׁבוּם
had they then My My had they then My in had they But prophe-
them turned ,people words hear made counsel stood if .sied

from their evil way, and from
the evil of their doings.
23*Am* I a God near by, says
Jehovah, and not a God from
afar? 24Or can anyone hide
himself in secret places so
that I do not see him, says
Jehovah? Do I not fill
Heaven and earth, says
Jehovah? 25I have heard
what the prophets said,
those who prophesy lies in
My name, saying, I have
dreamed, I have dreamed.
26How long is *this* there in
the heart of the prophets,
the prophets of lies; yea, the
prophets of the deceit of
their own heart? 27*They* plot
to cause My people to forget
My name by their dreams
which they tell, each one to
his neighbor, even as their
fathers have forgotten My
name for Baal. 28The
prophet who has a dream,
let him tell a dream. And he
who has My word, let him
speak My word faithfully.
What *has* the straw to *do*
with the grain, declares
Jehovah? 29Is not My word
thus like fire, says Jehovah,
and like a hammer which
breaks a rock in pieces?
30So Jehovah declares,
Behold, I *am* against the
prophets who steal My
words, each one from his
neighbor. 31Jehovah says,
Behold, I *am* against the
prophets who use their
tongues and say, *He* says.
32Jehovah declares, Behold,
I *am* against those who
prophesy false dreams, and
tell them, and cause My
people to go astray by their
lies, and by their frivolity. Yet
I did not send them, nor
command them. And they
will not profit this people at
all, declares Jehovah.

33And when this people,
or the prophet, or a priest,
shall ask you, saying, What
is the burden of Jehovah?

23 מדרכם הרע ומרע מעלליהם: האלהי מקרב
near from by | God a | their .doings | from and of evil the | evil | their from way

24 אני נאם־יהוה ולא אלהי מרחק: אם־יסתר איש
a man | hide can himself | Or | from .afar | God a | and not | ,Jehovah | says | I (am)

במסתרים ואני לא־אראנו נאם־יהוה הלוא את־השמים
the heavens | not | ?Jehovah | says | see do him | not I | that so | hiding in places

25 ואת־הארץ אני מלא נאם־יהוה: שמעתי את אשר
what | have I heard | ?Jehovah | says | ,fill Do | I | the earth | and

אמרו הנבאים הנבאים בשמי שקר לאמר חלמתי
have I ,dreamed | ,saying | ,lies | My in name | who prophesy | the ,prophets | said

26 חלמתי: עד־מתי היש בלב הנבאים נבאי השקר ונביאי
and of prophets | ,lies | prophets of | the ,prophets | the in of heart | is there | when Until | have I .dreamed

27 תרמת לבם: החשבים להשכיח את־עמי שמי בחלומתם
their by dreams | My name | My people | make to forget | (They) plan | own their ?heart | the of deceit

אשר יספרו איש לרעהו כאשר שכחו אבותם את־שמי
My name | their fathers | have forgotten | as | his to ;neighbor | each man | they tell | which

28 בבעל: הנביא אשר־אתו חלום יספר חלום ואשר דברי
My word | he but who | (his) ,dream | him let tell | a (has) ,dream | with him | who | The prophet | for !Baal

אתו ידבר דברי אמת מה־לתבן את־הבר נאם־יהוה:
?Jehovah | says | the ,grain | with | the to straw | What (is) | faith- .fully | My word | him let speak | (has) him with

29 הלוא כה דברי כאש נאם־יהוה וכפטיש יפצץ סלע:
?rock a | which shatters | a like and hammer | ,Jehovah | says | like ,fire | My word | thus | (Is) not

30 לכן הנני על־הנבאים נאם־יהוה מגנבי דברי איש מאת
from | each man | My ,words | who steal | ,Jehovah | says | the ,prophets | against | ,behold (am) I | There- ,fore

31 רעהו: הנני על־הנבאים נאם־יהוה הלקחים לשונם
their tongue | take who | ,Jehovah | says | the prophets | against | ,behold am I | his ;neighbor

32 וינאמו נאם: הנני על־נבאי חלמות שקר נאם־יהוה
,Jehovah | says | ,false | dreams | those against prophecy who | ,Behold (am) I | (Jehovah) ,says | and declare

ויספרום ויתעו את־עמי בשקריהם ובפחזותם ואנכי לא־
not | yet I | their by and ;frivolity | their by ,lies | My people | lead and astray | tell and ,them

שלחתים ולא צויתים והועיל לא־יועילו לעם־הזה נאם־
says | ,this people | they profit will | not | at and all | command ;them | nor | send did them

33 יהוה: וכי־ישאלך העם הזה או־הנביא או־כהן לאמר
,saying | a ,priest | or | the prophet | or | ,this | people | shall you ask | And when | .Jehovah

מַה־מַּשָּׂא יְהוָה וְאָמַרְתָּ אֲלֵיהֶם אֶת־מַה־מַּשָּׂא וְנָטַשְׁתִּי

even will I abandon ?burden What ,them to you Then say shall ?Jehovah the of burden What (is)

34 אֶתְכֶם נְאֻם־יְהוָה׃ וְהַנָּבִיא וְהַכֹּהֵן וְהָעָם אֲשֶׁר יֹאמַר מַשָּׂא

The of burden ,say shall who the people and the ,priest and the ,prophet And .Jehovah declares ,you

35 יְהוָה וּפָקַדְתִּי עַל־הָאִישׁ הַהוּא וְעַל־בֵּיתוֹ׃ כֹּה תֹאמְרוּ

shall you say So his .house and that man will I punish even ,Jehovah

אִישׁ עַל־רֵעֵהוּ וְאִישׁ אֶל־אָחִיו מֶה־עָנָה יְהוָה וּמַה־דִּבֶּר

has spoken And what ?Jehovah has answered What his ,brother to each man ask his ,companion to each man

36 יְהוָה׃ וּמַשָּׂא יְהוָה לֹא תִזְכְּרוּ־עוֹד כִּי הַמַּשָּׂא יִהְיֶה לְאִישׁ

each man for will be the burden for ;again will you mention not Jehovah the of burden And ?Jehovah

דְּבָרוֹ וַהֲפַכְתֶּם אֶת־דִּבְרֵי אֱלֹהִים חַיִּים יְהוָה צְבָאוֹת

hosts Jehovah of the ,living God the of words have you perverted for own his word

37 אֱלֹהֵינוּ׃ כֹּה תֹאמַר אֶל־הַנָּבִיא מֶה־עָנָךְ יְהוָה וּמַה־דִּבֶּר

has spoken And what ?Jehovah you answered has What the ,prophet to shall you say Thus .God our

38 יְהוָה׃ וְאִם־מַשָּׂא יְהוָה תֹּאמֵרוּ לָכֵן כֹּה אָמַר יְהוָה יַעַן

Be- cause ,Jehovah says thus There- fore ,say you —Jehovah the of burden And —if ?Jehovah

אֲמָרְכֶם אֶת־הַדָּבָר הַזֶּה מַשָּׂא יְהוָה וָאֶשְׁלַח אֲלֵיכֶם

you to I when sent have —Jehovah the of burden —this word say you

39 לֵאמֹר לֹא תֹאמְרוּ מַשָּׂא יְהוָה׃ לָכֵן הִנְנִי וְנָשִׁיתִי אֶתְכֶם

you even will I forget ,behold ,I there- fore ;Jehovah the of burden shall you —say not ,saying

נָשֹׂא וְנָטַשְׁתִּי אֶתְכֶם וְאֶת־הָעִיר אֲשֶׁר־נָתַתִּי לָכֶם

you to gave I that the city and ,you cast off and ,surely

40 וְלַאֲבוֹתֵיכֶם מֵעַל פָּנָי׃ וְנָתַתִּי עֲלֵיכֶם חֶרְפַּת עוֹלָם וּכְלִמּוּת

and disgrace ever- ,lasting an reproach you on I And put will My .face away from your to and fathers

עוֹלָם אֲשֶׁר לֹא תִשָּׁכֵחַ׃

be will .forgotten not which per- petual

You shall then say to them, What burden? I will even forsake you, declares Jehovah. [34]And the prophet, and the priest, and the people who shall say, The burden of Jehovah—I will even punish that man and his house. [35]So you shall say each one to his neighbor, and each one to his brother, What has Jehovah answered? And what has Jehovah spoken? [36]And you shall not mention the burden of Jehovah again; for each man's word shall be his burden. For you have perverted the words of the living God, of Jehovah of hosts, our God.

[37]So you shall say to the prophet, What has Jehovah answered you? And what has Jehovah spoken? [38]But if you say, The burden of Jehovah, therefore so says Jehovah: Because you say this word, the burden of Jehovah; and I have sent to you saying, You shall not say, The burden of Jehovah; [39]therefore, behold, I, even I will, utterly forget you, and I will cast off you and the city that I gave to you and your fathers, away from My face. [40]And I will bring an everlasting reproach on you, and never-ending shame, which shall not be forgotten.

CAP. XXIV כד

CHAPTER 24

1 הֶרְאַנִי יְהוָה וְהִנֵּה שְׁנֵי דּוּדָאֵי תְאֵנִים מוּעָדִים לִפְנֵי הֵיכַל

the of temple before set figs baskets of two and ,behold Jehovah showed me

יְהוָה אַחֲרֵי הַגְלוֹת נְבוּכַדְרֶאצַּר מֶלֶךְ־בָּבֶל אֶת־יְכָנְיָהוּ

Jeconiah Babylon king of Nebuchadnezzar had exiled after ,Jehovah

בֶּן־יְהוֹיָקִים מֶלֶךְ־יְהוּדָה וְאֶת־שָׂרֵי יְהוּדָה וְאֶת־הֶחָרָשׁ

the craftsmen with ,Judah the of rulers and ,Judah king of Jehoiakim the of son

CHAPTER 24

[1]Jehovah caused me to see; and, behold, two baskets of figs set before the temple of Jehovah, after Nebuchadnezzar king of Babylon had exiled Jeconiah the son of Jehoiakim king of Judah, and the rulers of Judah, and the craftsmen,

and the smiths from Jerusalem, and had brought them to Babylon. [2]One basket *had* very good figs, like first-ripe figs. And the other basket *had* very bad figs which could not be eaten from *their* badness. [3]And Jehovah said to me, What do you see, Jeremiah? And I said, Figs. The good figs are very good, and the bad are very bad, so that they cannot be eaten from *their* badness.

[4]Again the word of Jehovah was to me, saying, [5]So says Jehovah, the God of Israel, Like these good figs, so I will acknowledge the exiles of Judah whom I have sent out of this place *into* the land of the Chaldeans for good. [6]For I will set My eyes on them for good, and I will bring them again to this land. And I will build them and not tear down; and I will plant them, and will not pluck up. [7]And I will give them a heart to know Me, that I *am* Jehovah. And they shall be My people, and I will be their God. For they shall return to Me with their whole heart.

[8]And like the bad figs which cannot be eaten from badness, so says Jehovah: So I shall make Zedekiah the king of Judah, and his rulers, and the remnant of Jerusalem who remain in this land, and those who dwell in the land of Egypt; [9]I will even make them a horror among all the kingdoms of the earth for evil, for a reproach, and a proverb, a gibe, and a curse, there in all

8384 259 1731 884 935 3389 4525
2 וְאֶת־הַמַּסְגֵּר מִירוּשָׁלַםִ וַיְבִאֵם בָּבֶל׃ הַדּוּד אֶחָד תְּאֵנִים
(had) One basket .Babylon had and from the and
figs to them brought ,Jerusalem smiths

7451 8384 259 1731 1073 8384 3966 2896
טֹבוֹת מְאֹד כִּתְאֵנֵי הַבַּכֻּרוֹת וְהַדּוּד אֶחָד תְּאֵנִים רָעוֹת
bad (had) other the but ,first-ripe like ,very good
figs basket figs

3068 559 7455 398 3808 834 3966
3 מְאֹד אֲשֶׁר לֹא־תֵאָכַלְנָה מֵרֹעַ׃ וַיֹּאמֶר יְהוָה אֵלַי
to Jehovah Then (their) from be could not which ,very
,me said .badness eaten

2896 8384 8384 559 3414 7200 4100
מָה־אַתָּה רֹאֶה יִרְמְיָהוּ וָאֹמַר תְּאֵנִים הַתְּאֵנִים הַטֹּבוֹת
good the —figs I And ?Jeremiah ,see do you What
figs ,said

398 3808 3966 7451 7451 3966 2896
טֹבוֹת מְאֹד וְהָרָעוֹת רָעוֹת מְאֹד אֲשֶׁר לֹא־תֵאָכַלְנָה
can they not that so ,very (are) the but ,very (are)
eaten be bad bad good

559 3541 559 3068 1697 1961 7455
4 מֵרֹעַ׃ וַיְהִי דְבַר־יְהוָה אֵלַי לֵאמֹר׃ כֹּה־אָמַר
5
says Thus ,saying to Jehovah the Again from
,me of word came .badness

5234 428 2896 8384 3478 430 3068
יְהוָה אֱלֹהֵי יִשְׂרָאֵל כַּתְּאֵנִים הַטֹּבוֹת הָאֵלֶּה כֵּן אַכִּיר אֶת־
will I so ,these good Like :Israel the Jehovah
acknowledge figs of God

3778 776 2088 4725 7971 834 3063 1546
גָּלוּת יְהוּדָה אֲשֶׁר שִׁלַּחְתִּי מִן־הַמָּקוֹם הַזֶּה אֶרֶץ כַּשְׂדִּים
the the this place out have I whom ,Judah the
Chaldeans of land (to) of sent of exiles

7725 2896 5869 7760 2896
6 לְטוֹבָה׃ וְשַׂמְתִּי עֵינִי עֲלֵיהֶם לְטוֹבָה וַהֲשִׁבֹתִים עַל־
to will I and ,good for them on My I For .good for
back them bring eyes set will

5428 3808 5193 2040 3808 1129 2088 776
הָאָרֶץ הַזֹּאת וּבְנִיתִים וְלֹא אֶהֱרֹס וּנְטַעְתִּים וְלֹא אֶתּוֹשׁ׃
.uproot and will I and tear and will I And .this land
not ,them plant ;down not them build

5971 1961 3068 3045 3820 5414
7 וְנָתַתִּי לָהֶם לֵב לָדַעַת אֹתִי כִּי אֲנִי יְהוָה וְהָיוּ־לִי לְעָם
a for to they and Jeho- I that ,Me know to a them to I And
people Me be will ;vah (am) heart give will

3820 3605 7725 430 1961
וְאָנֹכִי אֶהְיֶה לָהֶם לֵאלֹהִים כִּי־יָשֻׁבוּ אֵלַי בְּכָל־לִבָּם׃
their with to will they for ;God for them to will I and
.heart whole Me return be

7455 398 834 7451 8384
8 וְכַתְּאֵנִים הָרָעוֹת אֲשֶׁר לֹא־תֵאָכַלְנָה מֵרֹעַ כִּי־
for from be can not which bad like And
,badness ,eaten figs the

3063 4428 6667 5414 3068 559 3541
כֹה אָמַר יְהוָה כֵּן אֶתֵּן אֶת־צִדְקִיָּהוּ מֶלֶךְ־יְהוּדָה וְאֶת־
and ,Judah the Zedekiah will I So ,Jehovah says thus
of king make

2088 776 7604 3389 7611 8269
שָׂרָיו וְאֵת שְׁאֵרִית יְרוּשָׁלַםִ הַנִּשְׁאָרִים בָּאָרֶץ הַזֹּאת
,this in are who Jerusalem the and his
land left of remnant rulers

3605 7451 2189 5414 4714 776 3427
9 וְהַיֹּשְׁבִים בְּאֶרֶץ מִצְרָיִם׃ וּנְתַתִּים לְזַוְעָה לְרָעָה לְכֹל
all to evil for an for even will I —Egypt the in those and
agitation them make of land dwell who

3605 7045 8148 4912 2781 776 4467
מַמְלְכוֹת הָאָרֶץ לְחֶרְפָּה וּלְמָשָׁל לִשְׁנִינָה וְלִקְלָלָה בְּכָל־
all in a and a for a and a for the king- the
,curse gibe ,proverb reproach ,earth of doms

places where I will drive them. [10]And I will send the sword, the famine, and the plague among them until they are destroyed from on the land that I gave to them and to their fathers.

10 2719 7971 8033 5080 4725
הַמְּקֹמוֹת אֲשֶׁר־אַדִּיחֵם שָׁם׃ וְשִׁלַּחְתִּי בָם אֶת־הַחֶרֶב
the ,sword among them I And send will .there will I them drive where the places

5414 127 5921 8552/5704/1698 7458
אֶת־הָרָעָב וְאֶת־הַדֶּבֶר עַד־תֻּמָּם מֵעַל הָאֲדָמָה אֲשֶׁר־נָתַתִּי
gave I that the land from upon are they destroyed until the plague and the ,famine

1
לָהֶם וְלַאֲבוֹתֵיהֶם׃
to and .fathers their to them

CAP. XXV כה

CHAPTER 25

CHAPTER 25

[1]The word that was to Jeremiah concerning all the people of Judah in the fourth year of Jehoiakim the son of Josiah king of Judah. It *was* the first year of Nebuchadnezzar king of Babylon. [2]*This* Jeremiah the prophet spoke to all the people of Judah and to all the inhabitants of Jerusalem, saying, [3]From the thirteenth year of Josiah the son of Amon, king of Judah, even to this day, this twenty-three years, the word of Jehovah has come to me, and I have spoken to you, rising up early and speaking; but you have not listened. [4]And Jehovah has sent to you all His servants the prophets, rising early and sending, but you have not listened nor bowed your ear to hear, [5]saying, Now turn each one from his evil way, and from the evil of your doings, and live on the land which Jehovah has given to you and to your fathers from forever even to forever. [6]And do not go after other gods to serve them, and to worship them, and do not provoke Me to anger with the works of your hands; and

1 8141 3063 5971/3605/5921 3414 1961 1697
הַדָּבָר אֲשֶׁר־הָיָה עַל־יִרְמְיָהוּ עַל־כָּל־עַם יְהוּדָה בַּשָּׁנָה
the in year Judah the of people all con- cerning Jeremiah to came that The word

8141 3068 4428 2977 1121 3079 7243
הָרְבִעִית לִיהוֹיָקִים בֶּן־יֹאשִׁיָּהוּ מֶלֶךְ יְהוּדָה הִיא הַשָּׁנָה
the year it (was) ,Judah king of Josiah the of son of Jehoiakim fourth

2 3414 1696 834 894 4428 5019 7224
הָרִאשֹׁנִית לִנְבוּכַדְרֶאצַּר מֶלֶךְ בָּבֶל׃ אֲשֶׁר דִּבֶּר יִרְמְיָהוּ
Jeremiah spoke which ;Babylon king of Nebuchadnezzar of first

559 3389 3427 3605 3063 5971 3605 5921 5030
הַנָּבִיא עַל־כָּל־עַם יְהוּדָה וְאֶל כָּל־יֹשְׁבֵי יְרוּשָׁלִַם לֵאמֹר׃
,saying ,Jerusalem the of inhabitants all to and Judah the of people all to the prophet

3 3063 4428 526/1121 2977 8141 6240 7969
מִשְּׁלֹשׁ עֶשְׂרֵה שָׁנָה לְיֹאשִׁיָּהוּ בֶן־אָמוֹן מֶלֶךְ יְהוּדָה
,Judah king of ,Amon the of son Josiah of year the thirteenth From

3068 1697 1961 8141 6242 7969 2088 2088 3117 5704
וְעַד ׀ הַיּוֹם הַזֶּה זֶה שָׁלֹשׁ וְעֶשְׂרִים שָׁנָה הָיָה דְבַר־יְהוָה
Jehovah the of word has come ,years and twenty three this ,this day even to

4 7971 8085 3808 1696 7925 1696
אֵלַי וָאֲדַבֵּר אֲלֵיכֶם אַשְׁכֵּים וְדַבֵּר וְלֹא שְׁמַעְתֶּם׃ וְשָׁלַח
has And sent have you .listened but not ,speaking and up rising early ,you to have I and spoken to ,me

3808 7971 7925 5630 5650 3605 3068
יְהוָה אֲלֵיכֶם אֶת־כָּל־עֲבָדָיו הַנְּבִאִים הַשְׁכֵּם וְשָׁלֹחַ וְלֹא
but not and ;sending rising early the ,prophets His servants all you to Jehovah

5 7725 559 8085 241 5186 3808 8085
שְׁמַעְתֶּם וְלֹא־הִטִּיתֶם אֶת־אָזְנְכֶם לִשְׁמֹעַ׃ לֵאמֹר שׁוּבוּ
turn saying ,hear to ear your inclined nor have you ,listened

5921 3427 4611 7455 7451 1870 376 4994
נָא אִישׁ מִדַּרְכּוֹ הָרָעָה וּמֵרֹעַ מַעַלְלֵיכֶם וּשְׁבוּ עַל־
upon and dwell your ,doings from and of evil the ,evil his from way each man ,now

5769 1 3068 5414 834 127
הָאֲדָמָה אֲשֶׁר נָתַן יְהוָה לָכֶם וְלַאֲבוֹתֵיכֶם לְמִן־עוֹלָם
forever from your to and fathers to you Jehovah has given which the land

6 5647 312 430 310 1980 408 5769/5704
וְעַד־עוֹלָם׃ וְאַל־תֵּלְכוּ אַחֲרֵי אֱלֹהִים אֲחֵרִים לְעָבְדָם
serve to them other gods after go do And not .forever even to

3808 3027 4639 3707 3808 7812
וּלְהִשְׁתַּחֲוֹת לָהֶם וְלֹא־תַכְעִיסוּ אוֹתִי בְּמַעֲשֵׂה יְדֵיכֶם וְלֹא
and not your ;hands the with of works Me provoke do anger to and not ,them to and worship

I will do you no harm. **7**Yet you have not listened to Me, says Jehovah, so that you might provoke Me to anger with the works of your hands; for harm to you.

8So Jehovah of hosts says this: Because you have not heard My words, **9**behold, I will send and take all the families of the north, says Jehovah, and Nebuchadnezzar the king of Babylon, My servant; and I will bring them against this land, and against its inhabitants, and against all these nations all around. And I will completely destroy them, and make them a horror, and a hissing, and everlasting ruins. **10**And I will take from them the voice of rejoicing, and the voice of gladness, the voice of the bridegroom, and the voice of the bride, the sound of the millstones, and the light of the lamp. **11**And this whole land shall be a waste and a horror; and these nations shall serve the king of Babylon seventy years.

12And it shall be, when seventy years are fulfilled, I will punish the king of Babylon and that nation, and the land of the Chaldeans, for their iniquity, declares Jehovah; and I will make it everlasting ruins. **13**And I will bring on that land all My words which I have spoken against it, all that is written in this book which Jeremiah has prophesied against all the nations. **14**For many nations and great kings will lay service on them, even they. And I will repay them according to their deeds, and according to the work of their own hands.

15For so says Jehovah, the God of Israel, to me. Take the wine cup of this wrath

---

7

```
· 3707        3068 5002      8085       38 ,08         7489
אָרַע לָכֶם: וְלֹא־שְׁמַעְתֶּם אֵלַי נְאֻם־יְהוָה לְמַעַן הַכְעִסֵנִי
might you that so ,Jehovah says to   have you Yet .you to will I
Me provoke                    ,Me   listened not    harm do
```

8

```
6635 3068    559    3541                 7451 3027      4639
בְּמַעֲשֵׂה יְדֵיכֶם לְרַע לָכֶם: לָכֵן כֹּה אָמַר יְהוָה צְבָאוֹת
,hosts Jehovah says thus Therefore to  for   your   the with
  of                         .you  harm hands of work
```

9

```
Q 3947       79 71  2005   1697        8085  38 08
יַעַן אֲשֶׁר לֹא־שְׁמַעְתֶּם אֶת־דְּבָרָי: הִנְנִי שֹׁלֵחַ וְלָקַחְתִּי
take and will ,behold My    have you not Because
  send  I       ,words   heard
```

```
44 28      5019       3068 5002        4940       3605
אֶת־כָּל־מִשְׁפְּחוֹת צָפוֹן נְאֻם־יְהוָה וְאֶל־נְבוּכַדְרֶאצַּר מֶלֶךְ
the  Nebuchadnezzar even ,Jehovah says  the    the    all
of king                     north of families
```

```
34:27                208.8 776    935        5650    884
בָּבֶל עַבְדִּי וַהֲבִאֹתִים עַל־הָאָרֶץ הַזֹּאת וְעַל־יֹשְׁבֶיהָ וְעַל
and inhabi- its and  ,this   land against will I and  a and
against ,tants against    them bring ;servant My ,Babylon
```

```
8047        7760    2763    5439        1428 1471 36 05
כָּל־הַגּוֹיִם הָאֵלֶּה סָבִיב וְהַחֲרַמְתִּים וְשַׂמְתִּים לְשַׁמָּה
horror a  make and  utterly will I and all    these  nations all
  them          them destroy ,around
```

10

```
8342    6963    6        57 69      2723          83:22
וְלִשְׁרֵקָה וּלְחָרְבוֹת עוֹלָם: וְהַאֲבַדְתִּי מֵהֶם קוֹל שָׂשׂוֹן
joy  the  from  will I And  ever-   ruins and   hissing
of voice them perish to cause .lasting
```

```
5216 216    7347    6963    36 18  6963    2860    6963  8057   6963
וְקוֹל שִׂמְחָה קוֹל חָתָן וְקוֹל כַּלָּה קוֹל רֵחַיִם וְאוֹר נֵר:
the  and  the  and  the  and  the  voice  gladness the and
.lamp's light millstones of ,bride's voice ,bridegroom's  of voice
```

11

```
1471     5647       8047      2723      2088     776  36 05   1961
וְהָיְתָה כָּל־הָאָרֶץ הַזֹּאת לְחָרְבָּה לְשַׁמָּה וְעָבְדוּ הַגּוֹיִם
nations will and  a and  a     this   land whole will And
   serve  ;horror ,waste              be
```

12

```
4376     1961    8141   7657    884    44 28   428
הָאֵלֶּה אֶת־מֶלֶךְ בָּבֶל שִׁבְעִים שָׁנָה: וְהָיָה כִמְלֹאות
are when  it And  .years seventy  Babylon  the   these
fulfilled ,be will                    of king
```

```
5002      14 71   884  44 28       6485  81 41    7657
שִׁבְעִים שָׁנָה אֶפְקֹד עַל־מֶלֶךְ־בָּבֶל וְעַל־הַגּוֹי הַהוּא נְאֻם־
says ,that nation and Baby-  the   will I  ,years seventy
            lon of king  punish
```

```
8077       77 60   3778      776      5771      3068
יְהוָה אֶת־עֲוֹנָם וְעַל־אֶרֶץ כַּשְׂדִּים וְשַׂמְתִּי אֹתוֹ לְשִׁמְמוֹת
ruins  it  I and  the  the  the  their (for) Jeho-
make will ,Chaldeans of land  iniquity ,vah
```

13

```
834    1697    3605       776  59 21     935
עוֹלָם: וְהֵבֵאֹתִי עַל־הָאָרֶץ הַהִיא אֶת־כָּל־דְּבָרַי אֲשֶׁר
which  My    all    that    land    on  will I And  ever-
   words                            bring  .lasting
```

```
5012      1696           5612   3789  36 05
דִּבַּרְתִּי עָלֶיהָ אֵת כָּל־הַכָּתוּב בַּסֵּפֶר הַזֶּה אֲשֶׁר־נִבָּא
has  which this  book in  is that  all   against  have I
prophesied           written         it      spoken
```

14

```
7227 1471     1571 5647       1471 36 05        3414
יִרְמְיָהוּ עַל־כָּל־הַגּוֹיִם: כִּי עָבְדוּ־בָם גַּם־הֵמָּה גּוֹיִם רַבִּים
many nations ,they even will them on For  the  all against Jere-
    service lay ·        ,nations           miah
```

```
3027    4639    6467          7999         1419  44 28
וּמְלָכִים גְּדוֹלִים וְשִׁלַּמְתִּי לָהֶם כְּפָעֳלָם וּכְמַעֲשֵׂה יְדֵיהֶם:
their according and to according them will I And  .great  and
.hands of work the to  deeds their  repay          kings
```

15

```
3947     3478   430     3068    559  3541
כִּי כֹה אָמַר יְהוָה אֱלֹהֵי יִשְׂרָאֵל אֵלַי קַח אֶת־
Take ,me to Israel  the   Jehovah says thus For
           of God
```

from My hand, and cause all
the nations to whom I shall
send you to drink it. [16]And
they shall drink, and reel to
and fro, and be maddened,
because of the sword that I
will send among them.
[17]Then I took the cup from
Jehovah's hand, and made
all the nations drink, *those* to
whom Jehovah had sent
me: [18]Jerusalem, and the
cities of Judah, and their
kings, and their rulers, to
make them a ruin, a horror,
a hissing, and a curse, as *it
is* this day; [19]Pharaoh, king
of Egypt, and his servants,
and his rulers, and all his
people; [20]and all the mixed
people; and all the kings of
the land of Uz; and all the
kings of the land of the
Philistines, and Ashkelon,
and Gaza, and Ekron, and
the remnant of Ashdod;
[21]Edom; and Moab; and the
sons of Ammon; [22]and all
the kings of Tyre; and all the
kings of Sidon; and the
coastal kings which *are*
beyond the sea; [23]Dedan;
and Tema; and Buz; and all
who cut the corners *of their
beards*; [24]and all the kings
of Arabia; and all the kings
of the mixed people who
dwell in the desert; [25]and
all the kings of Zimri; and all
the kings of Elam; and all
the kings of Media; [26]and all
the kings of the north, far
and near; each one to his
brother; and all the kingdoms of the world which
are on the face of the earth;

כּוֹס הַיַּיִן הַחֵמָה הַזֹּאת מִיָּדִי וְהִשְׁקִיתָה אֹתוֹ אֶת־כָּל־
all it cause and drink to My from hand this wrath wine the of the of cup

16 הַגּוֹיִם אֲשֶׁר אָנֹכִי שֹׁלֵחַ אוֹתְךָ אֲלֵיהֶם׃ וְשָׁתוּ וְהִתְגֹּעֲשׁוּ
reel and fro and to they And ,drink shall .them to you shall send I whom the nations

17 וְהִתְהֹלָלוּ מִפְּנֵי הַחֶרֶב אֲשֶׁר אָנֹכִי שֹׁלֵחַ בֵּינֹתָם׃ וָאֶקַּח
I Then took among .them will send I that the sword because of go and mad

אֶת־הַכּוֹס מִיַּד יְהוָה וָאַשְׁקֶה אֶת־כָּל־הַגּוֹיִם אֲשֶׁר־שְׁלָחַנִי
sent had me whom the nations all make and drink to ,Jehovah's from hand the cup

18 יְהוָה אֲלֵיהֶם׃ אֶת־יְרוּשָׁלִַם וְאֶת־עָרֵי יְהוּדָה וְאֶת־מַלְכֶיהָ
her kings and ,Judah the of cities and Jerusalem :them to Jehovah

אֶת־שָׂרֶיהָ לָתֵת אֹתָם לְחָרְבָּה לְשַׁמָּה לִשְׁרֵקָה וְלִקְלָלָה
a and ,curse ,hissing a horror a waste a them make to her (and) ;rulers

19 כַּיּוֹם הַזֶּה׃ אֶת־פַּרְעֹה מֶלֶךְ־מִצְרַיִם וְאֶת־עֲבָדָיו וְאֶת־
and his servants and ,Egypt king of Pharaoh ;this (is it) as day

20 שָׂרָיו וְאֵת כָּל־עַמּוֹ׃ וְאֵת כָּל־הָעֶרֶב וְאֵת כָּל־מַלְכֵי אֶרֶץ
the of land kings the of all and mixed the ;people all and his ;people all and his ;rulers

הָעוּץ וְאֵת כָּל־מַלְכֵי אֶרֶץ פְּלִשְׁתִּים וְאֶת־אַשְׁקְלוֹן וְאֶת־
and ,Ashkelon and the ,Philistines the of land kings the of all and ;Uz

21 עַזָּה וְאֶת־עֶקְרוֹן וְאֵת שְׁאֵרִית אַשְׁדּוֹד׃ אֶת־אֱדוֹם וְאֶת־
and ,Edom ;Ashdod the of remnant and ,Ekron and ,Gaza

22 מוֹאָב וְאֶת־בְּנֵי עַמּוֹן׃ וְאֵת כָּל־מַלְכֵי־צֹר וְאֵת כָּל־מַלְכֵי
the of kings all and ;Tyre the of kings all and ;Ammon the of sons and ;Moab

23 צִידוֹן וְאֵת מַלְכֵי הָאִי אֲשֶׁר בְּעֵבֶר הַיָּם׃ אֶת־דְּדָן וְאֶת־
and Dedan ;sea the beyond which (are) the coasts the of kings and ;Sidon

24 תֵּימָא וְאֶת־בּוּז וְאֵת כָּל־קְצוּצֵי פֵאָה׃ וְאֵת כָּל־מַלְכֵי
the of kings all and the ;edges who trim all and ,Buz and ,Tema

25 עֲרָב וְאֵת כָּל־מַלְכֵי הָעֶרֶב הַשֹּׁכְנִים בַּמִּדְבָּר׃ וְאֵת ׀ כָּל־
all and the in ;desert who dwell mixed the people the of kings all and ;Arabia

מַלְכֵי זִמְרִי וְאֵת כָּל־מַלְכֵי עֵילָם וְאֵת כָּל־מַלְכֵי מָדָי׃
;Media the of kings all and ;Elam the of kings all and ;Zimri the of kings

26 וְאֵת ׀ כָּל־מַלְכֵי הַצָּפוֹן הַקְּרֹבִים וְהָרְחֹקִים אִישׁ אֶל־
to each man ,far and near ,north the the of kings all and

אָחִיו וְאֵת כָּל־הַמַּמְלְכוֹת הָאָרֶץ אֲשֶׁר עַל־פְּנֵי הָאֲדָמָה
.earth the the of face on which (are) the world of kingdoms the all and his ,brother

the king of Sheshach shall
drink after them.
27So you shall say to
them, So says Jehovah of
hosts, the God of Israel:
Drink, and be drunk, and
vomit, and fall, and do not
rise up, because of the
sword which I will send
among you. 28And it shall
be, if they refuse to take the
cup from your hand to drink,
then you shall say to them,
So says Jehovah of hosts,
You shall certainly drink.
29For, behold, I begin to
bring evil on the city on
which is called My name.
and shall you be found
entirely without guilt? You
shall not be without guilt.
For I will call for a sword on
all the inhabitants of the
earth, declares Jehovah of
hosts. 30Now you prophesy
against them all these
words, and say to them,
Jehovah shall roar from on
high, and utter His voice
from His holy habitation; He
shall mightily roar over His
dwelling place. He answers
with a shout, like those who
tread out *the grapes*,
against all the inhabitants
of the earth. 31A roaring
will go to the ends of the
earth; for Jehovah has a
controversy with the
nations. He will enter into
judgment with all flesh; He
will give the wicked to the
sword, declares Jehovah.
3So says Jehovah of hosts,
Behold, evil is going from
nation to nation, and a great
tempest shall be stirred up
from the corners of the
earth. 33And the slain of
Jehovah shall be at that day
from *one* end of the earth
even to the *other* end of the
earth; they shall not be
mourned, nor gathered, nor
buried; they shall be *as*
dung on the face of the
earth.

34Howl, O shepherds;
and cry; and roll, O leaders
of the flock. For the days of

27 ומלך ששך ישתה אחריהם׃ ואמרת אליהם כה־אמר
559 559 310 8354 8347 44,28
says thus ,them to you So after shall Sheshach the and
say will .them drink of king

יהוה צבאות אלהי ישראל שתו ושכרו וקיו ונפלו ולא
3808 5307 7006 7937 8354 3478 430 6635 3068
and and and be and ,Drink ,Israel the ,hosts Jehovah
not ,fail ,vomit ,drunk of God of

28 תקומו מפני החרב אשר אנכי שלח ביניכם׃ והיה כי
1961 996 7971 834 2719 6965
if it And among will - I which the because ;rise
,be will .you send sword of

ימאנו לקחת־הכוס מידך לשתות ואמרת אליהם כה
3541 559 8354 3027 3563 3947 3985
Thus ,them to you then ,drink to from the take to they
say will hand your cup refuse

29 אמר יהוה צבאות שתו תשתו׃ כי הנה בעיר אשר
834 5892 2009 8354 8354 6635 3068 559
which the in ,lo ,For shall You surely ,hosts Jehovah says
city .drink of

נקרא־שמי עליה אנכי מחל להרע ואתם הנקה תנקו
5352 5352 7489 2490 5921 8034 7121
be shall entirely and bring to begin I upon My been has
?guiltless you ,evil ,it name called

לא תנקו כי חרב אני קרא על־כל־ישבי הארץ נאם
5002 776 3427 3605 7121 2719 5352 3808
says the inhabi- the all against am I a for will You not
,earth of tants calling sword ,guiltless be

30 יהוה צבאות׃ ואתה תנבא אליהם את כל־הדברים
1697 3605 5012 6258 6635 3068
words all against prophesy Therefore .hosts Jehovah
them you of

האלה ואמרת אליהם יהוה ממרום ישאג וממעון קדשו
6944 4583 7580 4791 3068 559 428
His from and shall from Jehovah ,them to say and ,these
holy habitation ,roar high on

יתן קולו שאג ישאג על־נוהו הידד כדרכים יענה אל
6030 1869 1959 5116 7580 7580 6963 5414
against He those like a (with) His over will He mightily His utter
answers tread who shout ;dwelling-place roar ,voice

31 כל־ישבי הארץ׃ בא שאון עד־קצה הארץ כי ריב
7379 776 7097 5704 7588 935 776 3427 3605
a for the the to A go will the in- the all
quarrel ,earth of end roaring .earth of habitants

ליהוה בגוים נשפט הוא לכל־בשר הרשעים נתנם לחרב
2719 5414 7563 1320 3605 8199 1471 3068
the to will He The .flesh with He into enter the with (to is)
,sword put wicked all (will) judgment ,nations Jehovah

32 נאם־יהוה׃ כה אמר יהוה צבאות הנה רעה יצאת
3318 7451 2009 6635 3068 559 3541 3068 5002
going is evil ,Behold ,hosts Jehovah says Thus .Jehovah says
forth of

33 מגוי אל־גוי וסער גדול יעור מירכתי־ארץ׃ והיו חללי
2491 1961 776 3411 5782 1419 5591 1471 1471
the shall And the the from be will great a and ,nation to from
of slain be .earth of corners stirred tempest nation

יהוה ביום ההוא מקצה הארץ ועד־קצה הארץ לא
3808 776 7097 5704 776 7097 1931 3117 3068
not the (other) the even the (one) from that on Jehovah
;earth of end to earth of end day

יספדו ולא יאספו ולא יקברו לדמן על־פני האדמה יהיו׃
1961 127 6440 5921 1828 6912 3808 622 5594
they the the on as ;buried nor ,gathered nor will they
.be shall ground of face dung ,mourned be

34 הילילו הרעים וזעקו והתפלשו אדירי הצאן כי־מלאו
4390 6629 117 6428 2199 7462 3213
are For the leaders O roll and ;cry and shep- O ,Howl
full .flock of ,herds

your slaughter and of your scatterings are fulfilled; and you shall fall like a desirable vessel. [35]And refuge has perished from the shepherds, and escape from the leaders of the flock. [36]The sound of the cry of the shepherds, and the howling from the leaders of the flock! For Jehovah is spoiling their pasture. [37]And the peaceful folds are devastated, because of the glow of the anger of Jehovah. [38]Like the young lion, He has left His den; for their land is a waste because of the oppressor's burning *anger*, and because of His glowing anger.

6 2532 3627 5307 8600 2873 3117
35 יְמֵיכֶם לִטְבוֹחַ וּתְפוֹצוֹתִיכֶם וּנְפַלְתֶּם כִּכְלִי חֶמְדָּה׃ וְאָבַד
has And .desirable a like you and your and for your
perished vessel fall will ,dispersions ,slaughtering days

6818 6963 6629 117 6413 7462 4499
36 מָנוֹס מִן־הָרֹעִים וּפְלֵיטָה מֵאַדִּירֵי הַצֹּאן׃ קוֹל צַעֲקַת
the The the the from and the from refuge
of cry of sound .flock of leaders escape ,shepherds

4830 3068 7703 6629 117 3215 7462
הָרֹעִים וִילְלַת אַדִּירֵי הַצֹּאן כִּי־שֹׁדֵד יְהוָה אֶת־מַרְעִיתָם׃
their Jehovah is For the the the and shep- the
.pasture destroying !flock of leaders of wailing ,herds

3715 5800 3068 639 2740 7965 4830 1826
37 וְנָדַמּוּ נְאוֹת הַשָּׁלוֹם מִפְּנֵי חֲרוֹן אַף־יְהוָה׃
38 עָזַב כַּכְּפִיר
the like has He Jehovah's anger the because the folds are And
lion young left of glow of ,peaceful devastated

6440 3238 2740 6440 8047 776 1961 5520
סֻכּוֹ כִּי־הָיְתָה אַרְצָם לְשַׁמָּה מִפְּנֵי חֲרוֹן הַיּוֹנָה וּמִפְּנֵי
be- and op- the the because waste a their is for his
of cause pressor of glow of land ;den

639 2740
חֲרוֹן אַפּוֹ׃
His the
.anger of glow

CAP. XXVI כו

CHAPTER 26

CHAPTER 26

[1]In the beginning of the reign of Jehoiakim the son of Josiah, king of Judah, this word came from Jehovah, saying, [2]So says Jehovah, Stand in the court of the house of Jehovah and speak to all the cities of Judah which come to worship in the house of Jehovah, all the words that I command you to speak to them. Do not keep back a word. [3]It may be that they will listen, and each man turn from his evil way, that I may repent of the evil which I plan to do to them because of the evil of their doings. [4]And you shall say to them, So says Jehovah, If you will not listen to Me, to walk in My law which I have set before you, [5]to listen to the words of My servants the prophets whom I am sending to you; even rising up early and sending—but you have not listened — [6]then I will make this house like Shiloh, and will make

1961 3063 4428 2977 1121 3079 4468 7225
1 בְּרֵאשִׁית מַמְלְכוּת יְהוֹיָקִים בֶּן־יֹאשִׁיָּהוּ מֶלֶךְ יְהוּדָה הָיָה
came ,Judah king Josiah the Jehoiakim the the In
of of son of reign of beginning

5975 3068 559 3541 559 3068 2088 1697
2 הַדָּבָר הַזֶּה מֵאֵת יְהוָה לֵאמֹר׃ כֹּה ׀ אָמַר יְהוָה עֲמֹד
Stand ,Jehovah says Thus ,saying ,Jehovah from this word

935 3063 5892 3605 1696 3068/1004 2691
בַּחֲצַר בֵּית־יְהוָה וְדִבַּרְתָּ עַל־כָּל־עָרֵי יְהוּדָה הַבָּאִים
which Judah the all to speak and ,Jehovah's house the in
come of cities of court

1696 6680 1697 3605 3068 1004 7812
לְהִשְׁתַּחֲוֺת בֵּית־יְהוָה אֵת כָּל־הַדְּבָרִים אֲשֶׁר צִוִּיתִיךָ לְדַבֵּר
speak to com- I that the all ,Jehovah the worship to
you mand words of house at

1870 376 7725 8085 194 1697 1639 408
3 אֲלֵיהֶם אַל־תִּגְרַע דָּבָר׃ אוּלַי יִשְׁמְעוּ וְיָשֻׁבוּ אִישׁ מִדַּרְכּוֹ
.his from each and will they Perhaps .word a do not to
way man turn listen diminish them

6213 2803 834 7451 5162 7455
הָרָעָה וְנִחַמְתִּי אֶל־הָרָעָה אֲשֶׁר אָנֹכִי חֹשֵׁב לַעֲשׂוֹת לָהֶם
them to do to am I which the towards may I that ,evil
planning evil repent

3068 559 3541 559 4611 7451 6440
4 מִפְּנֵי רֹעַ מַעַלְלֵיהֶם׃ וְאָמַרְתָּ אֲלֵיהֶם כֹּה אָמַר יְהוָה
:Jehovah says Thus ,them to you And their the because
say shall .doings of evil of

6440 5414 834 8451 3212 8085 3808 518
אִם־לֹא תִשְׁמְעוּ אֵלַי לָלֶכֶת בְּתוֹרָתִי אֲשֶׁר נָתַתִּי לִפְנֵיכֶם׃
before have I which My in walk to to will you not If
,you set law ,Me listen

7971 834 5030 5650 1697 8085
5 לִשְׁמֹעַ עַל־דִּבְרֵי עֲבָדַי הַנְּבִאִים אֲשֶׁר אָנֹכִי שֹׁלֵחַ אֲלֵיכֶם
,you to am I whom the My the to listen to
sending prophets servants of words

2088 1004 5414 8085 3808 7971 7925
6 וְהַשְׁכֵּם וְשָׁלֹחַ וְלֹא שְׁמַעְתֶּם׃ וְנָתַתִּי אֶת־הַבַּיִת הַזֶּה
this house I then have you but send- and rising even
make will —listened not (them) ing early up

this city a curse to all the nations of the earth.

7And the priests and the prophets and all the people heard Jeremiah speaking these words in the house of Jehovah. 8And it happened when Jeremiah had made an end of speaking all that Jehovah had commanded him to speak to all the people, the priests and the prophets and all the people seized him, saying, You shall surely die. 9Why have you prophesied in the name of Jehovah, saying, This house shall be like Shiloh, and this city shall be wasted, without inhabitant? And all the people were gathered against Jeremiah in the house of Jehovah.

10When the rulers of Judah heard these things, then they came up from the king's house to the house of Jehovah. And *they* sat down in the entrance of the New Gate of Jehovah. 11And the priests and the prophets spoke to the rulers, and to all the people, saying, *Let* a death sentence *be* for this man, for he has prophesied against this city, as you have heard with your ears.

12Then Jeremiah spoke to all the rulers and to all the people, saying, Jehovah sent me to prophesy against this house and against this city all the words that you have heard. 13So now make good your ways and your doings, and obey the voice of Jehovah your God; and Jehovah will repent toward the evil that He has spoken against you. 14As for me, behold, I *am* in your hands; do with me as *seems* good and right to

776 1471 3605 7045 5414 2088 5892 7887
כְּשִׁלֹה וְאֶת־הָעִיר הַזֹּאתָה אֶתֵּן לִקְלָלָה לְכֹל גּוֹיֵ הָאָרֶץ׃
the .earth | the of nations | all to | curse a | will I make | this | city | and | like ,Shiloh

7 3414 5971/3605 5030 3548 8085
וַיִּשְׁמְעוּ הַכֹּהֲנִים וְהַנְּבִאִים וְכָל־הָעָם אֶת־יִרְמְיָהוּ
Jeremiah | the people | and all | the and prophets | the priests | heard And

8 3615 1961 3068 1004 428 1697 1696
מְדַבֵּר אֶת־הַדְּבָרִים הָאֵלֶּה בְּבֵית יְהוָה׃ וַיְהִי ׀ כְּכַלּוֹת
when finished | Now ,was it | .Jehovah | the in of house | these | words | speaking

3605 1696 3068 6680 3605 1696 3414
יִרְמְיָהוּ לְדַבֵּר אֵת כָּל־אֲשֶׁר־צִוָּה יְהוָה לְדַבֵּר אֶל־כָּל־
all | to | speak to | Jehovah | com- (him) manded | had that | all | speaking | Jere- miah

559 5971/3605 5030 3548 8610 5971
הָעָם וַיִּתְפְּשׂוּ אֹתוֹ הַכֹּהֲנִים וְהַנְּבִאִים וְכָל־הָעָם לֵאמֹר
,saying | the ,people | and all | the and prophets | the priests | him | seized | the ,people

9 1961 7887 559 3068 8034 5012 4100 4191 4191
מוֹת תָּמוּת׃ מַדּוּעַ נִבֵּיתָ בְשֵׁם־יְהוָה לֵאמֹר כְּשִׁלוֹ יִהְיֶה
shall be | Like Shiloh | ,saying | ,Jehovah | the in of name | you have prophesied | Why | shall you .die | Surely

3605 6950 3428 369 2717 2088 5892 1004
הַבַּיִת הַזֶּה וְהָעִיר הַזֹּאת תֶּחֱרַב מֵאֵין יוֹשֵׁב וַיִּקָּהֵל כָּל־
all | were And gathered | inhabi- ?tant | without | be will desolate | this | and city | ,this | house

10 3063 8269 8085 3068 1004 3414 5971
הָעָם אֶל־יִרְמְיָהוּ בְּבֵית יְהוָה׃ וַיִּשְׁמְעוּ ׀ שָׂרֵי יְהוּדָה אֵת
Judah | the of rulers | heard When | .Jehovah | the in of house | Jeremiah against | the people

7760 3068 1004 4428 1004 5927 418 1697
הַדְּבָרִים הָאֵלֶּה וַיַּעֲלוּ מִבֵּית־הַמֶּלֶךְ בֵּית יְהוָה וַיֵּשְׁבוּ
sat and | Jehovah | the (to) of house | the king's | from house | they then up came | ,these | things

11 5030 3548 559 2319 3068 8179 6607
בְּפֶתַח שַׁעַר־יְהוָה הֶחָדָשׁ׃ וַיֹּאמְרוּ הַכֹּהֲנִים וְהַנְּבִאִים
the and prophets | priests the | spoke And | .New | (house) Jehovah's | the of Gate | the in of entrance

376 4194 4941 559 5971 3605 8269
אֶל־הַשָּׂרִים וְאֶל־כָּל־הָעָם לֵאמֹר מִשְׁפַּט־מָוֶת לָאִישׁ הַזֶּה
,this | for man | a death | (be Let) of sentence | ,saying | the ,people | all | and to | the rulers | to

241 8085 2088 5012
כִּי נִבָּא אֶל־הָעִיר הַזֹּאת כַּאֲשֶׁר שְׁמַעְתֶּם בְּאָזְנֵיכֶם׃
your with .ears | have you heard | as | ,this | city | against | has he prophesied | for

12 3068 559 5971/3605 8269 3605 3414 559
וַיֹּאמֶר יִרְמְיָהוּ אֶל־כָּל־הַשָּׂרִים וְאֶל־כָּל־הָעָם לֵאמֹר יְהוָה
Jehovah | ,saying | the ,people | all | and to | the rulers | all | to | Jeremiah | Then spoke

3605 2088 5892 1004 5012 7971
שְׁלָחַנִי לְהִנָּבֵא אֶל־הַבַּיִת הַזֶּה וְאֶל־הָעִיר הַזֹּאת אֵת כָּל־
all | this | city | and against | this | house against | to prophesy | me sent

13 4611 1870 3190 6258 11 1697
הַדְּבָרִים אֲשֶׁר שְׁמַעְתֶּם׃ וְעַתָּה הֵיטִיבוּ דַרְכֵיכֶם וּמַעַלְלֵיכֶם
your and .doings | your ways | make good | Therefore ,now | have you .heard | that | the words

7451 3068 5162 430 3068 6963 8085
וְשִׁמְעוּ בְּקוֹל יְהוָה אֱלֹהֵיכֶם וְיִנָּחֵם יְהוָה אֶל־הָרָעָה אֲשֶׁר
that | the evil | toward | Jeho- vah | will and repent | your ;God | Jehovah | the of voice | and obey

14 3477 2896 6213 3027 2005 1696
דִּבֶּר עֲלֵיכֶם׃ וַאֲנִי הִנְנִי בְיֶדְכֶם עֲשׂוּ־לִי כַּטּוֹב וְכַיָּשָׁר
and right | (seems) as good | to me | do | your in ;hands | ,behold (am) I | for As ,me | against You | has He spoken

you. [15]But know for certain that if you put me to death, you shall surely bring innocent blood on yourselves, and on this city, and on its inhabitants. For truly Jehovah has sent me to you, to speak all these words in your ears.

[16]Then the rulers, and all the people, said to the priests and to the prophets, There *is* not a sentence of death for this man; for he has spoken to us in the name of Jehovah our God. [17]Then some of the elders of the land rose up and spoke to all the assembly of the people, saying, [18]Micah of Moresheth prophesied in the days of Hezekiah king of Judah. And he spoke to all the people of Judah, saying, So says Jehovah of hosts: Zion shall be plowed *like* a field, and Jerusalem shall become heaps, and the mountain of the house like the high places of a forest. [19]Did Hezekiah king of Judah and all Judah indeed put him to death? Did he not fear Jehovah, and entreat the face of Jehovah; and *did not* Jehovah repent of the evil which He had spoken against them? So we are doing great evil against our souls. [20]And there was also a man who prophesied in the name of Jehovah, Urijah the son of Shemaiah of Kirjath-jearim, who prophesied against this city and against this land according to the words of Jeremiah. [21]And when Jehoiakim the king, with all his mighty men, and all the rulers, heard his words, the king tried to put him to death. But Urijah heard, and he was afraid, and fled, and

4194 518 3045 3045 389 5869
15 בְּעֵינֵיכֶם׃ אַךְ ׀ יָדֹעַ תֵּדְעוּ כִּי אִם־מְמִתִים אַתֶּם אֹתִי כִּי־
surely ,me you to put death if that know certain for Only your in .eyes

3427 2088 5892 5414 5355 1818
דָם נָקִי אַתֶּם נֹתְנִים עֲלֵיכֶם וְאֶל־הָעִיר הַזֹּאת וְאֶל־יֹשְׁבֶיהָ
inhabi- .tants its on and ,this city and on your- ,selves on shall bring you inno- cent blood

3605 241 1696 3068 7971 571
כִּי בֶאֱמֶת שְׁלָחַנִי יְהוָה עֲלֵיכֶם לְדַבֵּר בְּאָזְנֵיכֶם אֵת כָּל־
all your in ears speak to you to Jehovah sent has me truly For

3548 5971 3605 8269 559 428 1697
16 הַדְּבָרִים הָאֵלֶּה׃ וַיֹּאמְרוּ הַשָּׂרִים וְכָל־הָעָם אֶל־הַכֹּהֲנִים
the priests to the people and all the rulers Then said .these words

3068 8034 4194 4941 2088 376 369 5030
וְאֶל־הַנְּבִיאִים אֵין־לָאִישׁ הַזֶּה מִשְׁפַּט־מָוֶת כִּי בְּשֵׁם יְהוָה
Jehovah the of name in for ,death sen- of tence a this man for Not (is) the .prophets and to

559 776 2201 582 6965 1696 430
17 אֱלֹהֵינוּ דִּבֶּר אֵלֵינוּ׃ וַיָּקֻמוּ אֲנָשִׁים מִזִּקְנֵי הָאָרֶץ וַיֹּאמְרוּ
and spoke the land the from of elders men Then up rose !us to has he spoken God our

5012 1961 4183 4318 559 5971 6951 3605
18 אֶל־כָּל־קְהַל הָעָם לֵאמֹר׃ מִיכָה הַמּוֹרַשְׁתִּי הָיָה נִבָּא
proph- esying was the Morasthite Micah ,saying the ,people of the assembly all to

559 3063 5971 3605 559 3063 4428 2396 3117
בִּימֵי חִזְקִיָּהוּ מֶלֶךְ־יְהוּדָה וַיֹּאמֶר אֶל־כָּל־עַם יְהוּדָה לֵאמֹר
,saying ,Judah the of people all to he and spoke ,Judah king of Hezekiah the in of days

5856 3389 2790 7704 6726 6635 3068 559 3541
כֹּה־אָמַר ׀ יְהוָה צְבָאוֹת צִיּוֹן שָׂדֶה תֵחָרֵשׁ וִירוּשָׁלַיִם עִיִּים
heap a ruins of and Jerusalem be will ,plowed a (like) field Zion :hosts of Jehovah says Thus

3293 1116 1004 2022 1961
19 תִּהְיֶה וְהַר הַבַּיִת לְבָמוֹת יָעַר׃ הֶהָמֵת הֱמִתֻהוּ חִזְקִיָּהוּ
Hezekiah put Did death to him indeed a .forest high the (as) of places the house of and the mountain be- will ,come

2470 3068 3373 3063 3605 3063 4428
מֶלֶךְ־יְהוּדָה וְכָל־יְהוּדָה הֲלֹא יָרֵא אֶת־יְהוָה וַיְחַל אֶת־
and entreat Jehovah he Did fear not ?Judah and all Judah king of

1696 834 7451 3068 5162 3068 6440
פְּנֵי יְהוָה וַיִּנָּחֶם יְהוָה אֶל־הָרָעָה אֲשֶׁר־דִּבֶּר עֲלֵיהֶם
against ?them had He spoken which the evil toward Jehovah and repented ;Jehovah the of face

1961 376 5315 1419 7451 6213 587
20 וַאֲנַחְנוּ עֹשִׂים רָעָה גְדוֹלָה עַל־נַפְשׁוֹתֵינוּ׃ וְגַם־אִישׁ הָיָה
there was a man And also .souls our against great evil are doing we So

7157 8098 1121 223 3068 8034 5012
מִתְנַבֵּא בְּשֵׁם יְהוָה אוּרִיָּהוּ בֶּן־שְׁמַעְיָהוּ מִקִּרְיַת הַיְּעָרִים
,jearim Kirjath- at Shemaiah the of son Urijah ,Jehovah the in of name proph- who esied

1697 3605 2088 776 2088 5892 5012
וַיִּנָּבֵא עַל־הָעִיר הַזֹּאת וְעַל־הָאָרֶץ הַזֹּאת כְּכֹל דִּבְרֵי
the of words according all to this land and against ,this city against who prophesied

8269 3605 1368 3605 3079 4428 8085 3414
21 יִרְמְיָהוּ׃ וַיִּשְׁמַע הַמֶּלֶךְ יְהוֹיָקִים וְכָל־גִּבּוֹרָיו וְכָל־הַשָּׂרִים
the rulers and all mighty his ,men and all ,Jehoiakim the king when And heard .Jeremiah

3372 223 8085 4191 4428 1245 1697
אֶת־דְּבָרָיו וַיְבַקֵּשׁ הַמֶּלֶךְ הֲמִיתוֹ וַיִּשְׁמַע אוּרִיָּהוּ וַיִּרָא
was and ,afraid ,Urijah But (it) heard execute to .him king the then sought his ,words

went to Egypt. 22And Jehoiakim the king sent men to Egypt, Elnathan the son of Achbor, and men with him into Egypt. 23And they brought Urijah out of Egypt, and brought him to Jehoiakim the king, who struck him with the sword, and threw his dead body into the graves of the sons of the people. 24However, the hand of Ahikam the son of Shaphan was with Jeremiah, that they should not give him into the hand of the people to put him to death.

582 3079 4428 7971 4714 935 1272
22 וַיִּבְרַח וַיָּבֹא מִצְרָיִם׃ וַיִּשְׁלַח הַמֶּלֶךְ יְהוֹיָקִים אֲנָשִׁים
men Jehoiakim King sent And .Egypt went and and
to to fled

4714 582 5907 1121 494 471
מִצְרָיִם אֶת־אֶלְנָתָן בֶּן־עַכְבּוֹר וַאֲנָשִׁים אִתּוֹ אֶל־מִצְרָיִם׃
.Egypt into with and ,Achbor the Elnathan —Egypt
him men of son

3079 4428 935 4714 223 3318
23 וַיּוֹצִיאוּ אֶת־אוּרִיָּהוּ מִמִּצְרַיִם וַיְבִאֻהוּ אֶל־הַמֶּלֶךְ יְהוֹיָקִים
,Jehoiakim King to brought and from Urijah they And
him Egypt out brought

5971 1121 6913 5038 7993 2719 5221
24 וַיַּכֵּהוּ בֶּחָרֶב וַיַּשְׁלֵךְ אֶת־נִבְלָתוֹ אֶל־קִבְרֵי בְּנֵי הָעָם׃ אַךְ
But the the the into dead his and the with who
.people of sons of graves body threw sword him struck

5414 3414 1961 8227 1121 296 3027
יַד אֲחִיקָם בֶּן־שָׁפָן הָיְתָה אֶת־יִרְמְיָהוּ לְבִלְתִּי תֶּת־אֹתוֹ
him to not ,Jeremiah with was Shaphan the Ahikam the
give of son — of hand

4191 5971 3027
בְיַד־הָעָם לַהֲמִיתוֹ׃
him put to the the into
.death to people of hand

CAP. XXVII כז

CHAPTER 27

CHAPTER 27

1In the beginning of the reign of Jehoiakim the son of Josiah king of Judah, this word was to Jeremiah from Jehovah, saying, 2So says Jehovah to me, Make bonds and yokes for yourself, and put them on your neck. 3And send them to the king of Edom, and to the king of Moab, and to the king of the sons of Ammon, and to the king of Tyre, and to the king of Sidon, by the hand of the messengers who came to Jerusalem to Zedekiah king of Judah. 4And command them to *go to* their masters, saying, So says Jehovah of hosts, the God of Israel: So you shall say to your masters, 5I have made the earth, the man, and the animals that are on the face of the earth, by My great power, and by My outstretched arm; and I have given it to whom it seemed right in My eyes. 6And now I have given all these

1961 3063 4428 2977 1121 3079 4467 7225
1 בְּרֵאשִׁית מַמְלֶכֶת יְהוֹיָקִים בֶּן־יֹאשִׁיָּהוּ מֶלֶךְ יְהוּדָה הָיָה
came ,Judah king Josiah the Jehoiakim reign the the In
of of son of of beginning

559 3541 559 3068 3414 2088 1697
2 הַדָּבָר הַזֶּה אֶל־יִרְמְיָה מֵאֵת יְהוָה לֵאמֹר׃ כֹּה־אָמַר
says Thus ,saying ,Jehovah from Jeremiah to this word

6677 5921 5414 4133 4147 6213 3068
יְהוָה אֵלַי עֲשֵׂה לְךָ מוֹסֵרוֹת וּמֹטוֹת וּנְתַתָּם עַל־צַוָּארֶךָ׃
your on put and and bonds for Make to Jehovah
.neck them yokes yourself ,me

1121 4428 4124 4428 123 4428 7971
3 וְשִׁלַּחְתָּם אֶל־מֶלֶךְ אֱדוֹם וְאֶל־מֶלֶךְ מוֹאָב וְאֶל־מֶלֶךְ בְּנֵי
the king the and ,Moab the and Edom the to And
of sons of to of king to of king them send

935 4397 3027 6721 4428 6865 4428 5983
עַמּוֹן וְאֶל־מֶלֶךְ צֹר וְאֶל־מֶלֶךְ צִידוֹן בְּיַד מַלְאָכִים הַבָּאִים
who mes- the the by ,Sidon the and ,Tyre the and Am-
to came sengers of hand of king to of king to ,mon

6680 3063 4428 6667 3389
4 יְרוּשָׁלַםִ אֶל־צִדְקִיָּהוּ מֶלֶךְ יְהוּדָה׃ וְצִוִּיתָ אֹתָם אֶל־
(go to) them And .Judah king Zedekiah to Jerusalem
to command of

3478 430 6635 3068 559 3541 559 113
אֲדֹנֵיהֶם לֵאמֹר כֹּה־אָמַר יְהוָה צְבָאוֹת אֱלֹהֵי יִשְׂרָאֵל כֹּה
Thus :Israel the hosts Jehovah says Thus ,saying their
of God of masters

120 776 6213 113 559
5 תֹאמְרוּ אֶל־אֲדֹנֵיכֶם׃ אָנֹכִי עָשִׂיתִי אֶת־הָאָרֶץ אֶת־הָאָדָם
,man the have I your to shall you
earth made ,masters say

2220 1419 3581 776 6440 929
וְאֶת־הַבְּהֵמָה אֲשֶׁר עַל־פְּנֵי הָאָרֶץ בְּכֹחִי הַגָּדוֹל וּבִזְרוֹעִי
by and ,great My by the the on that the and
arm My power ,earth of face (are) animals

5414 6258 5869 3474 5414 5186
6 הַנְּטוּיָה וּנְתַתִּיהָ לַאֲשֶׁר יָשַׁר בְּעֵינָי׃ וְעַתָּה אָנֹכִי נָתַתִּי
have I And My in seemed it to have and out-
given ,now eyes right whom it given ,stretched

lands into the hand of Nebuchadnezzar the king of Babylon, My servant. And I have also given him the beast of the field to serve
7 him. [7]And all nations shall serve him, and his son, and his son's son, until the time of his own land comes, and his *time*; and many nations and great kings shall make
8 him a slave. [8]And it shall be, the nation and kingdom which will not serve him, Nebuchadnezzar the king of Babylon, and that will not put its neck in the yoke of the king of Babylon, I will punish that nation, says Jehovah, with the sword, and with the famine, and with the plague, until I have destroyed them by his
9 hand. [9]As for you, do not listen to your prophets, or to your fortune-tellers, or to your dreams, or to your conjurers, or to your sorcerers, those who speak to you, saying, You shall not serve the king of Babylon.
10 [10]For they prophesy a lie to you, to remove you far from your land, that I should drive you out, and you should
11 perish. [11]But the nation that will bring its neck into the yoke of the king of Babylon, and serve him, I will leave it on its own land, says Jehovah; and *it* will till it and live in it.

12 [12]I also spoke to Zedekiah king of Judah according to all these words, saying, Bring your necks into the king of Babylon's yoke, and serve him and his people, and live.
13 [13]Why will you die, you and your people, by the sword, by the famine, and by the plague, as Jehovah has

884 4428 5019 3027 428 776 3605
אֶת־כָּל־הָאֲרָצוֹת הָאֵלֶּה בְּיַד נְבוּכַדְנֶאצַּר מֶלֶךְ־בָּבֶל
,Babylon the of king Nebuchadnezzar the into of hand these lands all

5647 5647 5414 7704 2416 1571 5650
7 עַבְדִּי וְגַם אֶת־חַיַּת הַשָּׂדֶה נָתַתִּי לוֹ לְעָבְדוֹ׃ וְעָבְדוּ אֹתוֹ
him shall And serve serve to .him to him have I given the field the of beast And also My .servant

1571 776 935 5704 1121 1121 1121 1471
כָּל־הַגּוֹיִם וְאֶת־בְּנוֹ וְאֶת־בֶּן־בְּנוֹ עַד בֹּא־עֵת אַרְצוֹ גַּם־
Also own his .land the of time comes until his son's son and his ,son and ,nations all

1471 1961 1419 4428 7227 1471 5647
8 הוּא וְעָבְדוּ בוֹ גּוֹיִם רַבִּים וּמְלָכִים גְּדֹלִים׃ וְהָיָה הַגּוֹי
the nation it And ,be will .great and kings many nations him will and ,him enslave

4428 5019 5647 834 4467
וְהַמַּמְלָכָה אֲשֶׁר לֹא־יַעַבְדוּ אֹתוֹ אֶת־נְבוּכַדְנֶאצַּר מֶלֶךְ
the of king Nebuchadnezzar ,him will serve not which the and kingdom

884 4428 5923 6677 5414 3808 884
בָּבֶל וְאֵת אֲשֶׁר לֹא־יִתֵּן אֶת־צַוָּארוֹ בְּעֹל מֶלֶךְ בָּבֶל
,Babylon the of king the in of yoke its neck will put not that and ,Babylon

3068 5002 1471 6485 1698 7458 2719
בַּחֶרֶב וּבָרָעָב וּבַדֶּבֶר אֶפְקֹד עַל־הַגּוֹי הַהוּא נְאֻם־יְהוָה
,Jehovah says ,that nation will I punish with and plague the with and the famine the with sword

5030 8085 408 3027 8552 5704
9 עַד־תֻּמִּי אֹתָם בְּיָדוֹ׃ וְאַתֶּם אַל־תִּשְׁמְעוּ אֶל־נְבִיאֵיכֶם
your ,prophets to listen do not for As ,you his by .hand them have I until destroyed

3786 6049 2472 7080
וְאֶל־קֹסְמֵיכֶם וְאֶל־חֲלֹמֹתֵיכֶם וְאֶל־עֹנְנֵיכֶם וְאֶל־כַּשָּׁפֵיכֶם
your sorcerers to or your conjurers to or ,dreams your to or your diviners to or

4428 5647 3808 559 559 834
אֲשֶׁר־הֵם אֹמְרִים אֲלֵיכֶם לֵאמֹר לֹא תַעַבְדוּ אֶת־מֶלֶךְ
the of king shall you serve Not ,saying ,you to speak they who

7368 5012 8267 884
10 בָּבֶל׃ כִּי שֶׁקֶר הֵם נִבְּאִים לָכֶם לְמַעַן הַרְחִיק אֶתְכֶם
you remove far order in to ,you to prophesy they lie a For .Babylon

1471 6 5080 127
11 מֵעַל אַדְמַתְכֶם וְהִדַּחְתִּי אֶתְכֶם וַאֲבַדְתֶּם׃ וְהַגּוֹי אֲשֶׁר
that the But nation will and .perish you you will I and out drive your land from

5921 3240 5647 884 4428 5923 6677 935
יָבִיא אֶת־צַוָּארוֹ בְּעֹל מֶלֶךְ־בָּבֶל וַעֲבָדוֹ וְהִנַּחְתִּיו עַל־
on will I it leave serve and ,him Babylon the of king the into of yoke neck its will bring

4428 6667 3427 5647 3068 5002 127
12 אַדְמָתוֹ נְאֻם־יְהוָה וַעֲבָדָהּ וְיָשַׁב בָּהּ׃ וְאֶל־צִדְקִיָּה מֶלֶךְ־
king of Zedekiah Also to .it in and live will and it till ;Jehovah says ,land its

935 559 428 1697 3605 1696 3063
יְהוּדָה דִּבַּרְתִּי כְּכָל־הַדְּבָרִים הָאֵלֶּה לֵאמֹר הָבִיאוּ אֶת־
Bring ,saying ,these words according all to spoke I Judah

4100 2421 5971 5647 884 4428 5923 6677
13 צַוְּארֵיכֶם בְּעֹל ׀ מֶלֶךְ בָּבֶל וְעִבְדוּ אֹתוֹ וְעַמּוֹ וִחְיוּ׃ לָמָּה
Why and .live his and ,people him serve and Babylon the of king the into of yoke your necks

1696 1698 7458 2719 5971 4191
תָמוּתוּ אַתָּה וְעַמְּךָ בַּחֶרֶב בָּרָעָב וּבַדֶּבֶר כַּאֲשֶׁר דִּבֶּר
has spoken as by and plague the the by famine the by ,sword your and ,people you you will ,die

spoken against the nation that will not serve the king of Babylon? [14]So then do not listen to the words of the prophets who speak to you, saying, You shall not serve the king of Babylon; for they prophesy a lie to you. [15]For I have not sent them, says Jehovah. Yet they prophesy a lie in My name, so that I might drive you out, and that you might perish, you and the prophets who prophesy to you. [16]Also I spoke to the priests and to all this people, saying, So says Jehovah, Do not listen to the words of your prophets who prophesy to you, saying, Behold, the vessels of the house of Jehovah shall now be quickly brought again from Babylon. For they prophesy a lie to you. [17]Do not listen to them. Serve the king of Babylon, and live. Why should this city be a waste? [18]But if they *are* prophets, and if the word of Jehovah is with them, let them now intercede with Jehovah of hosts that the vessels which are left in the house of Jehovah, and in the house of the king of Judah, and at Jerusalem, may not go to Babylon.

[19]For so says Jehovah of hosts concerning the pillars, and concerning the sea, and concerning the bases, and concerning the rest of the vessels which remain in this city, [20]which Nebuchadnezzar king of Babylon did not take when he exiled Jeconiah the son of Jehoiakim king of Judah from Jerusalem to Babylon, and all the nobles of Judah

14 יְהוָה אֶל־הַגּוֹי אֲשֶׁר לֹא־יַעֲבֹד אֶת־מֶלֶךְ בָּבֶל׃ וְאַל־
Therefore not Baby-?lon the of king will serve not that the nation against Jehovah

תִּשְׁמְעוּ אֶל־דִּבְרֵי הַנְּבִאִים הָאֹמְרִים אֲלֵיכֶם לֵאמֹר לֹא
not ,saying ,you to speak who the prophets the of words to listen do

15 תַעַבְדוּ אֶת־מֶלֶךְ בָּבֶל כִּי שֶׁקֶר הֵם נִבְּאִים לָכֶם׃ כִּי לֹא
not For .you to prophesy they lie a for ;Babylon the of king shall You serve

שְׁלַחְתִּים נְאֻם־יְהוָה וְהֵם נִבְּאִים בִּשְׁמִי לַשָּׁקֶר לְמַעַן
so that ,lie a My in name prophesy Yet they .Jehovah says have I ,them sent

הַדִּיחִי אֶתְכֶם וַאֲבַדְתֶּם אַתֶּם וְהַנְּבִאִים הַנִּבְּאִים לָכֶם׃
.you to who prophesy the and prophets you you that and ,perish may ,you might I out drive

16 וְאֶל־הַכֹּהֲנִים וְאֶל־כָּל־הָעָם הַזֶּה דִּבַּרְתִּי לֵאמֹר כֹּה אָמַר
says Thus ,saying ,spoke I this people all and to the priests Also to

יְהוָה אַל־תִּשְׁמְעוּ אֶל־דִּבְרֵי נְבִיאֵיכֶם הַנִּבְּאִים לָכֶם לֵאמֹר
,saying you to who prophesy your prophets the of words to listen do Not Jeho-,vah

הִנֵּה כְלֵי בֵית־יְהוָה מוּשָׁבִים מִבָּבֶלָה עַתָּה מְהֵרָה כִּי שֶׁקֶר
lie a for ,quickly now from Babylon be will back brought Jehovah the of house the of vessels ,Behold

17 הֵמָּה נִבְּאִים לָכֶם׃ אַל־תִּשְׁמְעוּ אֲלֵיהֶם עִבְדוּ אֶת־מֶלֶךְ
the of king Serve .them to Do listen not .you to prophesy they

18 בָּבֶל וִחְיוּ לָמָּה תִהְיֶה הָעִיר הַזֹּאת חָרְבָּה׃ וְאִם־נְבִאִים
prophets But if .waste a this city should be Why and Babylon .live

הֵם וְאִם־יֵשׁ דְּבַר־יְהוָה אִתָּם יִפְגְּעוּ־נָא בַּיהוָה צְבָאוֹת
hosts with of Jehovah now them let intercede with ,them Jehovah the of word is if and they (are)

לְבִלְתִּי־בֹאוּ הַכֵּלִים ׀ הַנּוֹתָרִים בְּבֵית־יְהוָה וּבֵית מֶלֶךְ
the of king the in and of house ,Jehovah the in of house are that left the vessels may go that not

19 יְהוּדָה וּבִירוּשָׁלִַם בָּבֶלָה׃ כִּי כֹה אָמַר יְהוָה צְבָאוֹת
hosts Jehovah of says thus For to .Babylon at and ,Jerusalem ,Judah

אֶל־הָעַמֻּדִים וְעַל־הַיָּם וְעַל־הַמְּכֹנוֹת וְעַל יֶתֶר הַכֵּלִים
the vessels the of rest con- and cerning the ,bases con- and cerning the ,sea con- and cerning the ,pillars concern-ing

20 הַנּוֹתָרִים בָּעִיר הַזֹּאת׃ אֲשֶׁר לֹא־לְקָחָם נְבוּכַדְנֶאצַּר
Nebuchadnezzar did take not which ;this city in are which left

מֶלֶךְ בָּבֶל בַּגְלוֹתוֹ אֶת־יְכוֹנְיָה בֶן־יְהוֹיָקִים מֶלֶךְ־יְהוּדָה
Judah king of Jehoiakim the of son Jeconiah he when exile into took Babylon king of

מִירוּשָׁלִַם בָּבֶלָה וְאֵת כָּל־חֹרֵי יְהוּדָה וִירוּשָׁלִָם׃
and .Jerusalem Judah the of nobles all and to ,Babylon from Jerusalem

and Jerusalem. [21]For so says Jehovah of hosts, the God of Israel, concerning the vessels that remain in the house of Jehovah, and the house of the king of Judah, and Jerusalem: [22]They shall be carried to Babylon, and they shall be there until the day I visit them, says Jehovah. Then I will bring them up and give them back to this place.

3627 3478 430 6635 3068 559 3541
21 כִּי כֹה אָמַר יְהוָה צְבָאוֹת אֱלֹהֵי יִשְׂרָאֵל עַל־הַכֵּלִים
the concern- ,Israel the hosts Jehovah says thus For
vessels ing of God of

884 3089 3063 4428 1004 3068 1004 3498
22 הַנּוֹתָרִים בֵּית יְהוָה וּבֵית מֶלֶךְ־יְהוּדָה וִירוּשָׁלִָם׃ בָּבֶלָה
To and ,Judah the the and Jehovah the are that
Babylon :Jerusalem of king of house of house in left

5927 3068 5002 6485 3117 5704 1961 8033 935
יוּבָאוּ וְשָׁמָּה יִהְיוּ עַד יוֹם פָּקְדִי אֹתָם נְאֻם־יְהוָה וְהַעֲלִיתִים
will I and ;Jehovah says ,them visit I the until they and be will they
up them bring day be shall there ,brought

2088 4725 7725
וַהֲשִׁבֹתִים אֶל־הַמָּקוֹם הַזֶּה׃
.this place to restore and
them

CAP. XXVIII כח

CHAPTER 28

CHAPTER 28

[1]And it happened in that year, in the beginning of the reign of Zedekiah king of Judah, in the fourth year, in the fifth month, Hananiah the son of Azur the prophet, of Gibeon, spoke to me in the house of Jehovah, for the eyes of the priests and of all the people, saying, [2]So says Jehovah of hosts, the God of Israel, saying, I have broken the yoke of the king of Babylon. [3]Within two years I will again bring into this place all the vessels of the house of Jehovah which Nebuchadnezzar king of Babylon took away from this place and carried to Babylon. [4]And I will bring again to this place Jeconiah the son of Jehoiakim king of Judah, with all the exiles of Judah who went into Babylon, declares Jehovah. For I will break the yoke of the king of Babylon.

[5]Then the prophet Jeremiah said to the prophet Hananiah for the eyes of the priests, and for the eyes of all the people who stood in the house of Jehovah, [6]even the prophet Jeremiah said, Amen! May Jehovah

4428 6667 4467 7225 8141 1961
1 וַיְהִי ׀ בַּשָּׁנָה הַהִיא בְּרֵאשִׁית מַמְלֶכֶת צִדְקִיָּה מֶלֶךְ־
king Zedekiah the the in that year in it And
of of reign of beginning was

2608 559 2549 2320 7243 8141 3063
יְהוּדָה בַּשָּׁנַת הָרְבִעִית בַּחֹדֶשׁ הַחֲמִישִׁי אָמַר אֵלַי חֲנַנְיָה
Hananiah to spoke ,fifth the in ,fourth the in ,Judah
me month year

3548 5869 3068 1004 1391 834 5030 5809 1121
בֶּן־עַזּוּר הַנָּבִיא אֲשֶׁר מִגִּבְעוֹן בְּבֵית יְהוָה לְעֵינֵי הַכֹּהֲנִים
the the for ,Jehovah the in from who the Azur the
priests of eyes of house ,Gibeon (was) ,prophet of son

3478 430 6635 3068 559 559 5971 3605
2 וְכָל־הָעָם לֵאמֹר׃ כֹּה־אָמַר יְהוָה צְבָאוֹת אֱלֹהֵי יִשְׂרָאֵל
,Israel the hosts Jehovah says Thus ,saying the and
of God of ,people all

3117 8141 884 4428 5923 7665 559
3 לֵאמֹר שָׁבַרְתִּי אֶת־עֹל מֶלֶךְ בָּבֶל׃ בְּעוֹד ׀ שְׁנָתַיִם יָמִים
days two Within .Babylon the the have I ,saying
of years of king of yoke broken

834 3068 1004 3627 2088 4725 7725
אֲנִי מֵשִׁיב אֶל־הַמָּקוֹם הַזֶּה אֶת־כָּל־כְּלֵי בֵּית יְהוָה אֲשֶׁר
which ,Jehovah the the all this place to bring will I
of house of vessels back

935 2088 4725 884 4428 5019 3947
לָקַח נְבוּכַדְנֶאצַּר מֶלֶךְ־בָּבֶל מִן־הַמָּקוֹם הַזֶּה וַיְבִיאֵם
carried and this place from Babylon king Nebuchadnezzar took
to them of away

1546 3605 3063 4428 3079 1121 3204 884
4 בָּבֶל׃ וְאֶת־יְכָנְיָה בֶן־יְהוֹיָקִים מֶלֶךְ־יְהוּדָה וְאֶת־כָּל־גָּלוּת
the all with ,Judah king Jehoiakim the Jeconiah And .Babylon
of exiles of of son

5002 2088 4725 7725 589 935 3063
יְהוּדָה הַבָּאִים בָּבֶלָה אֲנִי מֵשִׁיב אֶל־הַמָּקוֹם הַזֶּה נְאֻם־
says ,this place to bring will I to who Judah
back Babylon went

3414 559 884 4428 5923 7665 3068
5 יְהוָה כִּי אֶשְׁבֹּר אֶת־עֹל מֶלֶךְ בָּבֶל׃ וַיֹּאמֶר יִרְמְיָה
Jeremiah Then .Babylon the the will I For .Jehovah
said of king of yoke break

5971 3605 5869 3548 5869 5030 2608 5030
הַנָּבִיא אֶל־חֲנַנְיָה הַנָּבִיא לְעֵינֵי הַכֹּהֲנִים וּלְעֵינֵי כָּל־הָעָם
the all for and the the for the Hananiah to the
people of eyes the priests of eyes prophet prophet

543 5030 3414 559 3068 1004 5975
6 הָעֹמְדִים בְּבֵית יְהוָה׃ וַיֹּאמֶר יִרְמְיָה הַנָּבִיא אָמֵן כֵּן
So !Amen the Jeremiah said and ;Jehovah the in who
,prophet of house stood

do *so*; may Jehovah confirm your words which you have prophesied, to bring again the vessels of the house of Jehovah, and all the exiles, from Babylon into this place. ⁷But hear now this word that I speak in your ears and in the ears of all the people: ⁸The prophets who have been before me and before you from times past prophesied against many lands and against great kingdoms; of war, and of evil, and of plague. ⁹*As for* the prophet who prophesies of peace, when the word of the prophet shall come to pass, the prophet shall be known *as one* whom Jehovah has truly sent him.

¹⁰Then Hananiah the prophet took the yoke from the prophet Jeremiah's neck and broke it. ¹¹And Hananiah spoke for the eyes of the people saying, So says Jehovah, Even so I will break the yoke of Nebuchadnezzar king of Babylon from the neck of all nations within the time of two years. And the prophet Jeremiah went his way.

¹²Then the word of Jehovah was to Jeremiah, after Hananiah the prophet had broken the yoke from the neck of the prophet Jeremiah, saying, ¹³Go and tell Hananiah, saying, So says Jehovah, You have broken yokes of wood, but you shall make instead of them yokes of iron. ¹⁴For so says Jehovah of hosts, the God of Israel: I have put a yoke of iron on the neck of all these nations to serve Nebuchadnezzar king of Babylon. And they shall serve him. And I have given

---

7725	5012	834	1697	3068	6965	3068	6213
bring to back	have you prophesied	which	your words	Jehovah	May establish	Jehovah	may do

7

2088	4725	884	1473	3605	3068/1004	3627
But .this place into	from the Babylon	the exiles	and	all	Jehovah the the	of house of vessels

241	241	1696	2088	1697	4994/8085
in and your in of ears the ears	speak	I	that	this word	now hear

8

5769	6440	6440	1961	5030	5971/3605
antiquity from	and before you before me	were	who	the the prophets	the all ;people

4421	1419/4467	7227	776	4421
,war of	;great kingdoms	and ,many	lands against	prophe- sied

9

1697	935	7965	5012	834	5030	1698	7451
the comes when of word pass to	,peace	prophesies	who	The prophet	of and .plague	of and ,evil

10

2608	3947	571	3068	7971	834	3045
Hana- niah	Then took	.truly	Jehovah	has him sent	(one as) whom	the be will known ,prophet

7665	5030	3414	6677	41:33	5030
and .it broke	the prophet	the Jeremiah's	neck	from the yoke	the prophet

11

3068	559	559	5971/3605	5869 2608	559
Even ,Jehovah says so	Thus ,saying	the ,people	all of eyes	the for Hananiah	And said

8141	884	4428	5019	5923	7665
two of years	within	Babylon king of	Nebuchadnezzar	the of yoke	will I break

1870	5030	3414	3212	1471/3605	6677	3117
.way his	the prophet	Jeremiah	Then went	.nations all	of neck	the from days

12

2608	1665	310	3414	3068	1697	1961
Hana- niah	had broken	after	,Jeremiah	to Jehovah	the of word	Then came

559	5030	3414	6677	4133	5030
,saying	the ,prophet	Jeremiah	the of neck	from the yoke	the prophet

13

6086	4133	3068	2608	559	1980
wood yokes	,Jehovah says of	Thus ,saying	,Hananiah to	say and	Go

14

3068	559	1270	4133	8478	6213	7665
Jehovah says of	thus	For .iron	yokes of	of instead them	you have make will	You ,broken

3605	6677/5921	5414	1270	5923	3478	430	6635
all	the of neck	on have I put	iron	a of yoke	,Israel	the of God	,hosts

5647	884	4428	5019	5647	428	6635
they and .him serve will	;Babylon king of	Nebuchadnezzar	serve to	,these	nations

him the beasts of the field also.
[15]Then the prophet Jeremiah said to Hananiah the prophet, Hear now, Hananiah, Jehovah has not sent you, but you have made this people trust in a lie. [16]So Jehovah says this: Behold, I send you away from the face of the earth. You shall die this year, because you have spoken apostasy against Jehovah. [17]And Hananiah died the same year in the seventh month.

15
5030 3414 559 5414 7704 2416 1571
וְגַם אֶת־חַיַּת הַשָּׂדֶה נָתַתִּי לוֹ׃ וַיֹּאמֶר יִרְמְיָה הַנָּבִיא
the prophet | Jeremiah | Then said | to .him | have I given | the field | the of beasts | And also

30:68 7971 38:08 2608 4994/8085 5030 2608
אֶל־חֲנַנְיָה הַנָּבִיא שְׁמַע־נָא חֲנַנְיָה לֹא־שְׁלָחֲךָ יְהוָה וְאַתָּה
but you | ,Jehovah | has you sent | not ,Hananiah | ,now Hear | the ,prophet | Hananiah to

16
3068 559 2088 8267 2088 5971 982
הִבְטַחְתָּ אֶת־הָעָם הַזֶּה עַל־שָׁקֶר׃ לָכֵן כֹּה אָמַר יְהוָה
,Jehovah | says | this Therefore | .lie a | in | this | people | made have trust

4191: 8141 127 6440 :79:71 2005
הִנְנִי מְשַׁלֵּחֲךָ מֵעַל פְּנֵי הָאֲדָמָה הַשָּׁנָה אַתָּה מֵת כִּי
for | shall ,die | you | This year | the .earth | the of face | from | you send away | ,Behold I

17
8141 5030 2608 4191 3068 1696 5627
סָרָה דִבַּרְתָּ אֶל־יְהוָה׃ וַיָּמָת חֲנַנְיָה הַנָּבִיא בַּשָּׁנָה הַהִיא
that | year in | the prophet | Hananiah | So died | .Jehovah against | have you spoken | apos- tasy

7637 2320
בַּחֹדֶשׁ הַשְּׁבִיעִי׃
.seventh | the in month

CAP. XXIX כט

CHAPTER 29

CHAPTER 29
[1]And these *are* the words of the letter that Jeremiah the prophet sent from Jerusalem to the rest of the elders of the exile, and to the priests, and to the prophets, and to all the people whom Nebuchadnezzar had exiled from Jerusalem to Babylon — [2]after Jeconiah the king, and the queen-mother, and the eunuchs, the rulers of Judah and Jerusalem, and the craftsmen, and the smiths, went out from Jerusalem —[3]*He sent* by the hand of Elasah the son of Shaphan, and Gemariah the son of Hilkiah, whom Zedekiah king of Judah sent to Babylon to Nebuchadnezzar king of Babylon, saying, [4]So says Jehovah of hosts, the God of Israel, to all the exiles whom I have caused to be exiled from Jerusalem to Babylon: [5]Build houses, and live; and plant gardens, and eat their fruit; [6]Take wives, and father sons and daughters. And take wives for your sons; and give your

1
3389 5030 3414 79:71 5612: 1697 428
וְאֵלֶּה דִּבְרֵי הַסֵּפֶר אֲשֶׁר שָׁלַח יִרְמְיָה הַנָּבִיא מִירוּשָׁלָ͏ִם
from Jerusalem | the prophet | Jeremiah | sent | that | letter the | words the of (are) | Now these

5030 3548 1473 2205 3499
אֶל־יֶתֶר זִקְנֵי הַגּוֹלָה וְאֶל־הַכֹּהֲנִים וְאֶל־הַנְּבִיאִים וְאֶל־
to and | the ,prophets | and to | the ,priests | and to | the exile | the of elders | rest the of | to

884 3389 5019 15 40 59:71 3605
כָּל־הָעָם אֲשֶׁר הֶגְלָה נְבוּכַדְנֶאצַּר מִירוּשָׁלַ͏ִם בָּבֶלָה׃
to —Babylon | from Jerusalem | Nebuchadnezzar | had deported | whom | the people | all

2
3063 8269 5631 1377 44 28 3204 3318 310
אַחֲרֵי צֵאת יְכָנְיָה־הַמֶּלֶךְ וְהַגְּבִירָה וְהַסָּרִיסִים שָׂרֵי יְהוּדָה
Judah | the and of leaders | the and eunuchs | the and ,mother queen | the ,king | Jeconiah | went out | after

3
1121 501 3027 3389 4525 2796 3389
וִירוּשָׁלַ͏ִם וְהֶחָרָשׁ וְהַמַּסְגֵּר מִירוּשָׁלָ͏ִם׃ בְּיַד אֶלְעָשָׂה בֶן־
the of son | Elasah | the by of hand | from —Jerusalem | the and smiths | the and ,craftsmen | and ,Jerusalem

30 63 44 28 6667 79 71 2518 1121 1587 :8227
שָׁפָן וּגְמַרְיָה בֶּן־חִלְקִיָּה אֲשֶׁר שָׁלַח צִדְקִיָּה מֶלֶךְ־יְהוּדָה
Judah | king of | Zedekiah | sent | whom | ,Hilkiah | the of son Gemariah | and ,Shaphan

4
559 35 41 559 884 884 44 28 5019
אֶל־נְבוּכַדְנֶאצַּר מֶלֶךְ־בָּבֶל בָּבֶלָה לֵאמֹר׃ כֹּה אָמַר
says | Thus | ,saying | to ,Babylon | Babylon | king of | Nebuchadnezzar | to

15 40 834 1473 36 05 3478 430 6635 3068
יְהוָה צְבָאוֹת אֱלֹהֵי יִשְׂרָאֵל לְכָל־הַגּוֹלָה אֲשֶׁר־הִגְלֵיתִי
sent I into exile | whom | the exiles | to all | ,Israel | the of God | ,hosts | Jehovah of

5
398 1593 5193 3427 1004 1129 884 338 9
מִירוּשָׁלַ͏ִם בָּבֶלָה׃ בְּנוּ בָתִּים וְשֵׁבוּ וְנִטְעוּ גַנּוֹת וְאִכְלוּ
and eat | gardens | and plant | ;live and | houses | Build | to :Babylon | from Jerusalem

6
11 21 39 47 1323 1121 32 05 802 3947 6529
אֶת־פִּרְיָן׃ קְחוּ נָשִׁים וְהוֹלִידוּ בָּנִים וּבָנוֹת וּקְחוּ לִבְנֵיכֶם
your for sons | And take | and .daughters | sons | and father | ,wives | Take | their .fruit

daughters to husbands, that
they may bear sons and
daughters, and multiply
there, and do not become
few. 7And seek the peace
of the city there, where I
have caused you to be
exiled. And pray to Jehovah
for it; for in its peace you
shall have peace.
8For so says Jehovah of
hosts, the God of Israel: Do
not let your prophets and
your fortune-tellers in your
midst deceive you. And do
not listen to your dreams
which you dream. 9For they
prophesy falsely to you in
My name. I have not sent
them, declares Jehovah.
10For so says Jehovah,
When according to My
mouth seventy years have
been fulfilled for Babylon, I
will visit you and confirm
My good word to you, to
bring you back to this place.
11For I know the purposes
which I am purposing for
you, declares Jehovah;
purposes of peace, and not
for evil; to give you a future
and a hope. 12Then you
shall call on Me, and you
shall go and pray to Me, and
I will listen to you. 13And
you shall seek and find Me,
when you search for Me
with all your heart. 14And I
will be found by you, says
Jehovah. And I will turn
away your captivity, and I
will gather you from all the
nations, and from all the
places, there where I have
driven you, says Jehovah.
And I will bring you again

1323 1121 3205 582 5414 1323 802
נָשִׁים וְאֶת־בְּנוֹתֵיכֶם תְּנוּ לַאֲנָשִׁים וְתֵלַדְנָה בָּנִים וּבָנוֹת
and sons they that husbands to give your and ,wives
,daughters bear may daughters

5892 7965 1875 4591 408 7235
7 וּרְבוּ־שָׁם וְאַל־תִּמְעָטוּ׃ וְדִרְשׁוּ אֶת־שְׁלוֹם הָעִיר אֲשֶׁר
where the the seek And become and ,there and
city of peace .few not multiply

3068 6419 8033 1540
הִגְלֵיתִי אֶתְכֶם שָׁמָּה וְהִתְפַּלְלוּ בַעֲדָהּ אֶל־יְהוָה כִּי
for ,Jehovah to it for and ,there you sent have I
pray exile into

3068 559 3541 7965 1961 7965
8 בִשְׁלוֹמָהּ יִהְיֶה לָכֶם שָׁלוֹם׃ כִּי כֹה אָמַר יְהוָה
Jehovah says thus For .peace for there its in
of you be will peace

834 5030 5377 3478 430 6635
צְבָאוֹת אֱלֹהֵי יִשְׂרָאֵל אַל־יַשִּׁיאוּ לָכֶם נְבִיאֵיכֶם אֲשֶׁר־
who your you let Do not :Israel the hosts
(are) prophets deceive of God

834 2472 8085 408 7080 7130
בְּקִרְבְּכֶם וְקֹסְמֵיכֶם וְאַל־תִּשְׁמְעוּ אֶל־חֲלֹמֹתֵיכֶם אֲשֶׁר
which your to do and your and your in
dreams listen not ,diviners midst

3808 8034 5012 8267 2492
9 אַתֶּם מַחְלְמִים׃ כִּי בְשֶׁקֶר הֵם נִבְּאִים לָכֶם בִּשְׁמִי לֹא
not My in to prophesy they falsely For .dream you
;name you

6310 3068 559 3541 3068 5002 7971
10 שְׁלַחְתִּים נְאֻם־יְהוָה׃ כִּי־כֹה אָמַר יְהוָה כִּי לְפִי
My as When Jeho- says thus For .Jehovah says have I
mouth ,vah them sent

6965 6485 8141 7657 884 4376
מְלֹאת לְבָבֶל שִׁבְעִים שָׁנָה אֶפְקֹד אֶתְכֶם וַהֲקִמֹתִי עֲלֵיכֶם
for and you will I ,years seventy for been have
you establish visit Babylon fulfilled

2088 4725 7725 2896 1697
11 אֶת־דְּבָרִי הַטּוֹב לְהָשִׁיב אֶתְכֶם אֶל־הַמָּקוֹם הַזֶּה׃ כִּי
For .this place to you bring to good word My
back

5002 2803 4284 3045
אָנֹכִי יָדַעְתִּי אֶת־הַמַּחֲשָׁבֹת אֲשֶׁר אָנֹכִי חֹשֵׁב עֲלֵיכֶם נְאֻם־
says for am I which purposes the know I
,you planning

319 5414 7451 3808 7965 4284 3068
יְהוָה מַחְשְׁבוֹת שָׁלוֹם וְלֹא לְרָעָה לָתֵת לָכֶם אַחֲרִית
future a you give to ,evil for and peace of purposes ;Jehovah
not

8085 6419 1980 7121 8615
12 וְתִקְוָה׃ וּקְרָאתֶם אֹתִי וַהֲלַכְתֶּם וְהִתְפַּלַּלְתֶּם אֵלָי וְשָׁמַעְתִּי
will I and to pray and and Me you Then a and
listen ,Me come upon call will .hope

3605 1875 4672 1245
13 אֲלֵיכֶם׃ וּבִקַּשְׁתֶּם אֹתִי וּמְצָאתֶם כִּי תִדְרְשֻׁנִי בְּכָל־
with seek you when find and Me you And to
all Me (Me) seek will .you

7622 7725 3068 5002 4672 3824
14 לְבַבְכֶם׃ וְנִמְצֵאתִי לָכֶם נְאֻם־יְהוָה וְשַׁבְתִּי אֶת־שְׁבִיתְכֶם
your I And .Jehovah says by will I And your
,captivity turn will ,you found be .heart

5080 4725 3605 1471 3605 6908
וְקִבַּצְתִּי אֶתְכֶם מִכָּל־הַגּוֹיִם וּמִכָּל־הַמְּקוֹמוֹת אֲשֶׁר הִדַּחְתִּי
have I where the and the from you will I and
driven places all from ;nations all gather

834 4725 7725 3068 5002 8033
אֶתְכֶם שָׁם נְאֻם־יְהוָה וַהֲשִׁבֹתִי אֶתְכֶם אֶל־הַמָּקוֹם אֲשֶׁר־
which the to you will I and ,Jehovah says there you
place back bring

15 הגליתי אתכם משם: כי אמרתם הקים לנו יהוה
Jehovah for raised has have you Because from you sent I
us up ,said .there exile into

16 נבאים בבלה: כי־כה ׀ אמר יהוה אל־המלך
the to Jehovah says thus for in prophets
king —Babylon

היושב אל־כסא דוד ואל־כל־העם היושב בעיר הזאת
,this city in who the all and ,David the on who
dwell people to of throne sits

17 אחיכם אשר לא־יצאו אתכם בגולה: כה אמר
says thus into with have not who your
—exile you out gone brothers

יהוה צבאות הנני משלח בם את־החרב את־הרעב
the the on am ,Behold ,hosts Jehovah
,famine ,sword them sending I of

ואת־הדבר ונתתי אותם כתאנים השערים אשר לא־
not which offensive figs like them will and the and
make ,plague

18 תאכלנה מרע: ורדפתי אחריהם בחרב ברעב ובדבר
with and the with the with them will I And from be can
,plague the ,famine ,sword pursue .badness eaten

ונתתים לזועה לכל ׀ ממלכות הארץ לאלה ולשמה
a and a for the the all to an will I and
horror ,curse earth of kingdoms agitation them make

19 ולשרקה ולחרפה בכל־הגוים אשר־הדחתים שם: תחת
because ;there have I where the among a and a and
them driven nations all reproach ,hissing

אשר־לא־שמעו אל־דברי נאם־יהוה אשר שלחתי
sent I which ,Jehovah says My to have they not
,words listened

אליהם את־עבדי הנבאים השכם ושלח ולא שמעתם
would you but and up rising the My with them to
listen not ,sending early ,prophets servants

20 נאם־יהוה: ואתם שמעו דבר־יהוה כל־הגולה אשר
whom the all ,Jehovah the hear Therefore .Jehovah says
exiles of word you

21 שלחתי מירושלם בבלה: כה־אמר יהוה צבאות
hosts Jehovah says Thus to from have I
of ;Babylon Jerusalem sent

אלהי ישראל אל־אחאב בן־קוליה ואל־צדקיהו בן
the Zedekiah con- and ,Kolaiah the Ahab con- Israel the
of son cerning of son cerning of God

מעשיה הנבאים לכם בשמי שקר הנני ׀ נתן אתם ביד
the into them will ,Behold :lie a My in to who ,Maaseiah
of hand. deliver I name you prophesy

22 נבוכדראצר מלך־בבל והכם לעיניכם: ולקח מהם
from will And your before he and ,Babylon king Nebuchadnezzar
them taken be .eyes them strike will of

קללה לכל גלות יהודה אשר בבבל לאמר ישמך יהוה
Jehovah May ,saying in who Judah the for curse a
you make ,Babylon (are) of exiles all

into the place from which I sent you into exile from there.

[15]Because you have said, Jehovah has raised up for us prophets in Babylon— [16]for so says Jehovah to the king who sits on the throne of David, and to all the people who live in this city, your brothers who have not gone out with you into exile— [17]so says Jehovah of hosts, Behold, I am sending on them the sword, the famine, and the plague, and will make them like worthless figs which cannot be eaten from badness. [18]And I will pursue them with the sword, with the famine, and with the plague. And I will make them an agitation to all the kingdoms of the earth, to be a curse, and a terror, and a hissing, and a reproach among all the nations, there where I have driven them. [19]For they have not listened to My words, says Jehovah, which I sent to them by My servants the prophets, rising up early and sending; but you would not hear, declares Jehovah.

[20]Now you hear the word of Jehovah, all you exiles whom I have sent from Jerusalem to Babylon; [21]so says Jehovah of hosts, the God of Israel concerning Ahab the son of Kolaiah, and concerning Zedekiah the son of Maaseiah, who prophesy a lie to you in My name: Behold, I will deliver them into the hand of Nebuchadnezzar king of Babylon, and he shall strike them before your eyes. [22]And a curse shall be taken up from them for all the exiles of Judah who *are* in Babylon, saying, May Jehovah make you like

Zedekiah and like Ahab, whom the king of Babylon roasted in the fire, [23]because they have committed disgraceful folly in Israel, and have committed adultery with their neighbor's wives, and have spoken a lying word in My name, which I have not commanded them; for I *am* He who knows, and a witness, says Jehovah.

[24]You shall also speak to Shemaiah the Nehelamite, saying, [25]So says Jehovah of hosts, the God of Israel, saying, Because you have sent letters in your name to all the people in Jerusalem, and to Zephaniah the son of Maaseiah the priest, and to all the priests, saying, [26]Jehovah has made you priest instead of Jehoiada the priest, to be officers *in* the house of Jehovah, over every madman who prophesies, that you should put him into the stocks and into the *torture* collar. [27]Now, therefore, why have you not reproved Jeremiah the Anathothite, who prophesies to you? [28]For this cause he sent to us *in* Babylon, saying, This *captivity* is long; build houses and live; and plant gardens and eat their fruit. [29]And Zephaniah the priest read this letter in the ears of Jeremiah the prophet.

[30]Then the word of Jehovah was to Jeremiah, saying, [31]Send to all the exiles, saying, So says Jehovah concerning Shemaiah the Nehelamite: Because Shemaiah has prophesied to you, and I did not send him; and he caused you to trust in a lie; [32]So Jehovah says this: Behold, I will punish Shemaiah

784 884 44 28 7033 834 256 6677
23 כְּצִדְקִיָּהוּ וּכְאֶחָב אֲשֶׁר־קָלָם מֶלֶךְ־בָּבֶל בָּאֵשׁ׃ יַעַן אֲשֶׁר
because the in Babylon the roasted whom like and like
,fire of king them Ahab Zedekiah

1697 1696 74:53 802 5003 3478 5039 6213
עָשׂוּ נְבָלָה בְּיִשְׂרָאֵל וַיְנַאֲפוּ אֶת־נְשֵׁי רֵעֵיהֶם וַיְדַבְּרוּ דָבָר
a have and their wives with have and ,Israel in disgraceful they
word spoken ,neighbor's adultery committed folly done have

5002 5707 3045 6680 3808 8267 8034
בִּשְׁמִי שֶׁקֶר אֲשֶׁר לוֹא צִוִּיתִם וְאָנֹכִי הַוּיֹדֵעַ וָעֵד נְאֻם־
says a and who He I and com- have I not which ,lying My in
,witness ,knows (am) ;them manded name

3541 559 559 5161 8098 3068
24
25 יְהוָה׃ וְאֶל־שְׁמַעְיָהוּ הַנֶּחֱלָמִי תֹּאמַר לֵאמֹר׃ כֹּה
Thus ,saying shall you the Shemaiah Also .Jehovah
,speak Nehelamite to

559 3478 430 6635 3068 559
אָמַר יְהוָה צְבָאוֹת אֱלֹהֵי יִשְׂרָאֵל לֵאמֹר יַעַן אֲשֶׁר אַתָּה
you Because ,saying ,Israel the ,hosts Jehovah says
of God of

3389 834 5971 3605 56:12 8034 7971
שָׁלַחְתָּ בְשִׁמְכָה סְפָרִים אֶל־כָּל־הָעָם אֲשֶׁר בִּירוּשָׁלַםִ
in who the all to letters your in have
,Jerusalem (are) people name sent

559 3548 3605 3548 4641 1121 6846
וְאֶל־צְפַנְיָה בֶן־מַעֲשֵׂיָה הַכֹּהֵן וְאֶל־כָּל־הַכֹּהֲנִים לֵאמֹר׃
,saying the all and the Maaseiah the Zephaniah and
,priests to ,priest of son to

1004 6496 1961 3548 3077 8478 3548 5414 3068
26 יְהוָה נְתָנְךָ כֹהֵן תַּחַת יְהוֹיָדָע הַכֹּהֵן לִהְיוֹת פְּקִדִים בֵּית
the officers be to the Jehoiada instead priest has Jehovah
of house (in) ,priest of you made

4115 5414 5012 7696 376 3605 3068
יְהוָה לְכָל־אִישׁ מְשֻׁגָּע וּמִתְנַבֵּא וְנָתַתָּה אֹתוֹ אֶל־הַמַּהְפֶּכֶת
the into him you that who raving man over ,Jehovah
stocks put ,prophesies every

6069 3414 1605 3808 4100 6258 6729
27 וְאֶל־הַצִּינֹק׃ וְעַתָּה לָמָּה לֹא גָעַרְתָּ בְּיִרְמְיָהוּ הָעַנְּתֹתִי
the Jeremiah you have not why Now the and
,Anathothite reproved therefore .collar into

752 559 884 7971 5012
28 הַמִּתְנַבֵּא לָכֶם׃ כִּי עַל־כֵּן שָׁלַח אֵלֵינוּ בָּבֶל לֵאמֹר אֲרֻכָּה
long ,saying (in) us to he therefore For to who
Babylon sent ?you prophesies

6529 398 1593 5193 3427 1004 1129 1931
הִיא בְּנוּ בָתִּים וְשֵׁבוּ וְנִטְעוּ גַנּוֹת וְאִכְלוּ אֶת־פְּרִיהֶן׃
their and gardens and and houses Build It
.fruit eat plant ,dwell .(be will)

3414 241 2088 5612 3548 6846 7121
29 וַיִּקְרָא צְפַנְיָה הַכֹּהֵן אֶת־הַסֵּפֶר הַזֶּה בְּאָזְנֵי יִרְמְיָהוּ
Jeremiah the in this letter the Zephaniah And
of ears priest read

559 3414 3068 1697 1961 5030
30 הַנָּבִיא׃ וַיְהִי דְּבַר־יְהוָה אֶל־יִרְמְיָהוּ לֵאמֹר׃
,saying ,Jeremiah to Jehovah the Then the
of word came .prophet

8098 3068 559 3541 559 1473/3605 7971
31 שְׁלַח עַל־כָּל־הַגּוֹלָה לֵאמֹר כֹּה אָמַר יְהוָה אֶל־שְׁמַעְיָה
Shemaiah con- Jehovah says Thus ,saying the all to Send
cerning exiles

7971 3808 8098 5012 5161
הַנֶּחֱלָמִי יַעַן אֲשֶׁר נִבָּא לָכֶם שְׁמַעְיָה וַאֲנִי לֹא שְׁלַחְתִּיו
send did not and ,Shemaiah to prophesied Because the
,him I you :Nehelamite

6485 2005 3068 559 3541 8267 982
32 וַיַּבְטַח אֶתְכֶם עַל־שָׁקֶר׃ לָכֵן כֹּה־אָמַר יְהוָה הִנְנִי פֹקֵד
will ,Behold ,Jehovah says thus therefore ,lie a in you he and
punish I trust to caused

the Nehelamite and his seed. There shall not be to him a man living among this people; nor shall he behold the good which I shall do for My people, says Jehovah, because he has uttered rebellion against Jehovah.

3427 376 1961 3808 2233 5161 8098
עַל־שְׁמַעְיָה הַנֶּחֱלָמִי וְעַל־זַרְעוֹ לֹא־יִהְיֶה לוֹ אִישׁ ׀ יוֹשֵׁב ׀
living a man to him shall be not his ,seed and the Nehelamite Shemaiah

5971 6213 834 2896 7200 3808 5971 8432
בְּתוֹךְ־הָעָם הַזֶּה וְלֹא־יִרְאֶה בַטּוֹב אֲשֶׁר־אֲנִי עֹשֶׂה־לְעַמִּי
My people for will do I which the good he will see nor ;this people the in of midst

3068 1696 5627 3068 5002
נְאֻם־יְהוָה כִּי־סָרָה דִבֶּר עַל־יְהוָה׃
.Jehovah against he has spoken apostasy for ,Jehovah says

CAP. XXX ל

CHAPTER 30

[1]The word that was to Jeremiah from Jehovah, saying, [2]So says Jehovah, God of Israel, saying, Write for yourself all the words that I have spoken to you in a book. [3]For, lo, the days come, says Jehovah, that I will turn the captivity of My people Israel and Judah, says Jehovah; and I will cause them to return to the land that I gave to their fathers, and they shall possess it.

[4]And these *are* the words that Jehovah spoke concerning Israel and concerning Judah: [5]For so says Jehovah, We have heard a sound of trembling, of dread, and not of peace. [6]Ask now and see whether a man is giving birth? Why do I see every man *with* his hands on his loins, like a woman in travail, and all faces are turned to paleness? [7]Alas! For that day *is* great, for none *is* like it. And it *is* a time of Jacob's trouble. But he will be saved out of it. [8]For it shall be in that day, says Jehovah of hosts, I will break his yoke from your neck, and I will burst your bonds. And strangers will not again enslave him; [9]but they shall serve Jehovah their God, and David their King, whom I will raise up to them.

CHAPTER 30

1 3541 559 3068 3414 1961 1697
2 הַדָּבָר אֲשֶׁר־הָיָה אֶל־יִרְמְיָהוּ מֵאֵת יְהוָה לֵאמֹר׃ כֹּה
Thus ,saying ,Jehovah from Jeremiah to came that The word

1697 3605 3789 559 3478 430 3068 559
אָמַר יְהוָה אֱלֹהֵי יִשְׂרָאֵל לֵאמֹר כְּתָב־לְךָ אֵת כָּל־הַדְּבָרִים
the words all for Write yourself ,saying ,Israel the of God Jehovah says

3 559 935 3117 5612 1696
אֲשֶׁר־דִּבַּרְתִּי אֵלֶיךָ אֶל־סֵפֶר׃ כִּי הִנֵּה יָמִים בָּאִים נְאֻם־
says ,come the days ,lo ,For .book a in you to have I spoken that

3068 559 3063 3478 5971 7622 7725 3068
יְהוָה וְשַׁבְתִּי אֶת־שְׁבוּת עַמִּי יִשְׂרָאֵל וִיהוּדָה אָמַר יְהוָה
,Jehovah says Judah and Israel My people of the captivity I that will turn ,Jehovah

3423 1 5414 776 7725
וַהֲשִׁבֹתִים אֶל־הָאָרֶץ אֲשֶׁר־נָתַתִּי לַאֲבוֹתָם וִירֵשׁוּהָ׃
shall they and .it possess their to fathers gave I that the land to bring will I and back them

4 3063 3478 3068 1696 1697 428
וְאֵלֶּה הַדְּבָרִים אֲשֶׁר דִּבֶּר יְהוָה אֶל־יִשְׂרָאֵל וְאֶל־יְהוּדָה׃
,Judah and Israel con- cerning Jehovah spoke that the words And (are) these

5 7965 369 6343 8085 2731 6963 3068 559
כִּי־כֹה אָמַר יְהוָה קוֹל חֲרָדָה שָׁמָעְנוּ פַּחַד וְאֵין שָׁלוֹם׃
.peace and of not of ,dread have we ,heard trembling A of sound ,Jehovah says thus for

6 3027 1397 3605/7200 4100 2145 3205 518 7200 4994/7592
שַׁאֲלוּ־נָא וּרְאוּ אִם־יֹלֵד זָכָר מַדּוּעַ רָאִיתִי כָל־גֶּבֶר יָדָיו
his hands (with) man every I do see Why a ?male giving is birth if and ,see now Ask

7 1945 3420 6440 3605 2015 3205 2504 5921
עַל־חֲלָצָיו כַּיּוֹלֵדָה וְנֶהֶפְכוּ כָל־פָּנִים לְיֵרָקוֹן׃ הוֹי כִּי
For !Alas to .paleness faces all have and turned woman a bearing like his ,loins on

3290 6864 6256 369 3117 1419
גָדוֹל הַיּוֹם הַהוּא מֵאַיִן כָּמֹהוּ וְעֵת־צָרָה הִיא לְיַעֲקֹב וּמִמֶּנָּה
from but it for ;Jacob it (is) distress a and of time like ,it because none (is) ,that day (is) great

8 7665 6635 3068 5002 3117 1961 3467
יִוָּשֵׁעַ׃ וְהָיָה בַיּוֹם הַהוּא נְאֻם ׀ יְהוָה צְבָאוֹת אֶשְׁבֹּר
will I break ,hosts Jehovah of says ,that day in it And be will will he saved be

5750 5647 3808 5423 4147 6677 5921 5923
עֻלּוֹ מֵעַל צַוָּארֶךָ וּמוֹסְרוֹתֶיךָ אֲנַתֵּק וְלֹא־יַעַבְדוּ־בוֹ עוֹד
again him will enslave And not will I burst your and bonds your ,neck from upon his yoke

9 834 4428/1732 430 3068 5647 2114
זָרִים׃ וְעָבְדוּ אֵת יְהוָה אֱלֹהֵיהֶם וְאֵת דָּוִד מַלְכָּם אֲשֶׁר
whom their ,king David and their God Jehovah they but serve shall ,strangers

10 And you, O My servant Jacob, do not fear, says Jehovah. Do not be terrified, O Israel. For, lo, I will save you from afar, and your seed from the land of their captivity. And Jacob shall return, and have quiet, and be untroubled, and no one will make *him* afraid. 11 For I *am* with you, says Jehovah, to save you. Though I make a full end among all nations where I have scattered you, yet I will not make a full end with you. But I will correct you justly, and I will not leave you unpunished. 12 For so says Jehovah, Your break cannot be cured; your wound is grievous. 13 There is no one to plead your cause, for *your* ulcer there are *no* healing medicines for you. 14 All your lovers have forgotten you; they do not seek you. For I have wounded you with the wound of an enemy, with the chastisement of a cruel one; because of the greatness of your iniquity. Your sins are many; 15 Why do you cry out over your crushing? Your pain is incurable, for the greatness of your iniquity; your sins are many; *so* I have done these things to you. 16 So all those who devour you shall be devoured. And all your enemies, every one of them, shall go into captivity. And they who rob you shall be *given* for plunder; and all who strip you, I will give to *be* stripped. 17 For I will give health back to you; and I will heal you of your wounds, says Jehovah; because they called you, Outcast; *saying,* This *is* Zion; no one is seeking for her.

18 So says Jehovah, Behold I will turn the captivity of Jacob's tents and will have mercy on his dwelling places. And the city shall be built on her ruin-heap; and the palace shall remain on its own place. 19 And out of them shall come thanksgiving, and the voice of

3068 5002 3290 5650 3372 408 6258 6965
10 אָקִים לָהֶם׃ וְאַתָּה אַל־תִּירָא עַבְדִּי יַעֲקֹב נְאֻם־יְהוָה
;Jehovah says ,Jacob My O do not Now for will I
servant ,fear ,you them up raise

2233 7350 3467 2005 3478 2865 408
וְאַל־תֵּחַת יִשְׂרָאֵל כִּי הִנְנִי מוֹשִׁיעֲךָ מֵרָחוֹק וְאֶת־זַרְעֲךָ
your and from save will I ,lo for ;Israel O be do not
seed ,afar you terrified

2729 369 7599 8252 3290 7725 7628 776
מֵאֶרֶץ שִׁבְיָם וְשָׁב יַעֲקֹב וְשָׁקַט וְשַׁאֲנַן וְאֵין מַחֲרִיד׃
make will and be and have and Jacob will And their the from
.afraid (him) none untroubled quiet return .captivity of land

3611 6213 3467 3068 5002
11 כִּי־אִתְּךָ אֲנִי נְאֻם־יְהוָה לְהוֹשִׁיעֶךָ כִּי אֶעֱשֶׂה כָלָה בְּכָל־
among a will I for ,you save to ,Jehovah says I with For
all destruction make ,(am) you

3615 6213 3808 389 8033 6327 1471
הַגּוֹיִם ׀ אֲשֶׁר הֲפִצוֹתִיךָ שָּׁם אַךְ אֹתְךָ לֹא־אֶעֱשֶׂה כָלָה
complete a will I not with only there have I where the
,end make you you scattered nations

559 3541 5352 3808 5352 4941 3256
12 וְיִסַּרְתִּיךָ לַמִּשְׁפָּט וְנַקֵּה לֹא אֲנַקֶּךָּ׃ כִּי כֹה אָמַר
says thus For leave will I not and justly will I but
.unpunished you entirely you chasten

4205 1779 7777 4347 2470 7667 605 3068
13 יְהוָה אָנוּשׁ לְשִׁבְרֵךְ נַחְלָה מַכָּתֵךְ׃ אֵין־דָּן דִּינֵךְ לְמָזוֹר
(your) for your to There your is Your is Jehovah
ulcer ,cause plead none is .wound grievous ,fracture incurable

3808 7911 157 3605 369 8585 7499
14 רְפֻאוֹת תְּעָלָה אֵין לָךְ׃ כָּל־מְאַהֲבַיִךְ שְׁכֵחוּךְ אוֹתָךְ לֹא
not you for- have your All for there healing (no)
;you gotten lovers .you is ,medicines

5771 7230 394 4148 5221 341 4347 1875
יִדְרֹשׁוּ כִּי מַכַּת אוֹיֵב הִכִּיתִיךְ מוּסַר אַכְזָרִי עַל רֹב עֲוֺנֵךְ
your great- for foe a chas- the have I an the (with) for do they
;iniquity's ness of tisement ,you struck enemy of wound ,seek

4341 605 7667 2199/4100 2403 6105
15 עָצְמוּ חַטֹּאתָיִךְ׃ מַה־תִּזְעַק עַל־שִׁבְרֵךְ אָנוּשׁ מַכְאֹבֵךְ
your is your for you do Why your are
pain incurable ,crushing out cry .sins many

3651 428 6213 2403 6105 5771 7230
16 עַל ׀ רֹב עֲוֺנֵךְ עָצְמוּ חַטֹּאתָיִךְ עָשִׂיתִי אֵלֶּה לָךְ׃ לָכֵן
Therefore to these I (so) your are in- your the for
.you things done have sins many ,iquity of greatness

8154 1961 3212 7628 3605 6862 3605 398 398/3605
כָּל־אֹכְלַיִךְ יֵאָכֵלוּ וְכָל־צָרַיִךְ כֻּלָּם בַּשְּׁבִי יֵלֵכוּ וְהָיוּ שֹׁאסַיִךְ
your will And shall into of all your and be will who those all
plunderers be .go captivity ,them ,foes all ;devoured you devour

724 5927 957 5414 962 3605 4933
17 לִמְשִׁסָּה וְכָל־בֹּזְזַיִךְ אֶתֵּן לָבַז׃ כִּי אַעֲלֶה אֲרֻכָה לָךְ
for healing will I For for will I your and for
you up bring .spoil give spoilers all ,plunder

6726 7121 5080 3068 5002 7495 4347
וּמִמַּכּוֹתַיִךְ אֶרְפָּאֵךְ נְאֻם־יְהוָה כִּי נִדָּחָה קָרְאוּ לָךְ צִיּוֹן
Zion you they an for ;Jehovah says will I from and
(saying) called outcast you heal wounds your

7725/2005 3068 559 3541 369 1875
18 הִיא דֹּרֵשׁ אֵין לָהּ׃ כֹּה ׀ אָמַר יְהוָה הִנְנִי־שָׁב
will ,Behold ,Jehovah says Thus .her no is This
turn I one seeking ,(is)

5921 5892 1129 7355 4908 3290 168 7622
שְׁבוּת אָהֳלֵי יַעֲקוֹב וּמִשְׁכְּנֹתָיו אֲרַחֵם וְנִבְנְתָה עִיר עַל־
on the shall And have will I dwell- his and Jacob's tents cap- the
city built be .on mercy places ing of tivity

6963 8426 3318 3427 4941 5921 759 8510
19 תִּלָּהּ וְאַרְמוֹן עַל־מִשְׁפָּטוֹ יֵשֵׁב׃ וְיָצָא מֵהֶם תּוֹדָה וְקוֹל
the and thanks- from shall And shall own its on its and its
of voice ,giving them forth go .remain place palace ruin

those who are merry. And I will multiply them, and they shall be not few. I also will honor them, and they shall not be small. ²⁰Also, his sons shall be as before, and his assembly shall be made to stand before Me; and I will punish all who oppress them. ²¹And his leader shall be from him, and his ruler shall come from among him. And I will cause him to draw near, and he shall approach Me. For who is he who pledged his heart to come near to Me, says Jehovah? ²²And you shall be My people; and I will be your God. ²³Behold, the tempest of Jehovah: fury goes forth; a sweeping tempest; it shall swirl on the head of the wicked. ²⁴The fierce anger of Jehovah shall not turn back until He has finished, and until He has fulfilled the intentions of His heart. In latter days you will understand it.

CHAPTER 31

¹At that time, says Jehovah, I will be the God of all the families of Israel, and they shall be My people. ²So says Jehovah, The people, the survivors of the sword, have found grace in the wilderness—Israel—when I go to give rest to him. ³Jehovah has appeared to me from far away, saying, Yes, I have loved you with an everlasting love! Therefore, with loving-kindness I have drawn you. ⁴Again I will build you, and you shall be built again, O virgin of Israel. You will again adorn your tambourines, and go forth in the dance of merry ones. ⁵You shall yet plant vineyards on the mountains of Samaria, the planters shall plant, and shall treat them as common. ⁶For there shall be a day when the watchmen on Mount Ephraim shall call out, Arise and let us go up to Zion, to

20

7832		7235	38,08		4591	3513	3,808	6819
who those	will I And	will I	and	will they	will I also	and	will they
.merry are	them multiply	,them	few be	;them honor	,not	and	.light be

3605	5712		6440	3559	6485	3605
1961 1121	6924	5712	6440	3559	6485	3605
all	will I and	be will	before	.established ,Me	will I and	And his
punish	his and	as	assembly ,before	sons	be will

21

3905	19,61	117	49.10	7130	3318	7126	5414
will I And	come will	his from	his and	from	his	And his
,near him bring	.forth	midst	ruler	,him	leader	be will .oppressors

22

5066		43 10		6149	38 20	5066	5002
says	to	come to	his	gives who	he	who For	.Me he and
	,Me	near	heart	pledge	(is)	approach Me

3068	1961	5971	1961	430
.God for	you to	be will	I and	a for	to	you And ?Jehovah
		,people Me	be will

23

2009	5592	3,068	2534	33,18	5591	1641	5921	7218
,Behold	the	;Jehovah	wrath	goes	a	;sweeping	on	the
of tempest	the			,forth	tempest			of head

24

7563	12342		38,08	7725	2740	30,68	639	5704	62,13	5704
the	will it	not	back	The turn	anger	Jeho-	until	has He	and
wicked	.swirl		.will	of glow	,vah's		,performed	until

25

6865	4209	38 20	319	3117	995	6256
has He	the	His	in	the	.it will you	At
established	of plans	,heart	latter	days	understand	time

1961	3068/5002	430	36,05	4940	3478
will I	,Jehovah says	that
be			God for	all to	the	,Israel
				of families

5971	1961
a for	to	will	and
.people	Me	be	they

CAP. XXXI   לֹא

CHAPTER 31

1

3541	559	30,68	4672	2 580	40:57	5971	8300	2719	19,80
Thus	,Jehovah says	have	grace	in	the	the	the	sur- the	I when
		found	wilderness	,people	the	vivors of	,sword	go will

2

7280	3478	73:50	3068	7200	160	5769
give to	.Israel	from	Jehovah	has	to	yea, with	ever-
,rest him		away far		appeared	me, love an	lasting

3

157:	5921	3651	4900	2617	5750	1129	11:29
have I	,you loved	therefore	drawn have I	loving-	Again	will I and	will you and
		with you	kindness		.you build	,rebuilt be

4

1330	3478	5750	5710	8596:	3318	14234	7822
of	virgin O	.Israel	again You will	your	will You	again .Israel	who those
			put on	tambourines	forth	of dance	.merry make

5

5750	5193	3754	2022	8111	5193	5193	2490
again you will	vineyards	on the	;Samaria	will	the	treat and
plant		of mountains	plant	,planters	the	.common as

31:17	7121	5341	2022	669	6965	5927	67:26
For	a there	(when) shall the	on	,Ephraim	,Arise	let and	Zion
be will	day	out call	Mount	watchmen		to up go

Jehovah our God. [7]For so
says Jehovah, Sing with
gladness for Jacob, and
shout among the chief of
the nations. Cry out, give
praise and say, O Jehovah,
save Your people, the remnant of Israel. [8]Behold I will
bring them from the north
country, and gather them
from the corners of the
earth. Among them the
blind, and the lame, the
pregnant one, and the
travailing one together, a
great company shall return
here. [9]They shall come
with weeping, and I will
lead them with prayers. I
will cause them to walk by
rivers of waters, in a right
way; they will not stumble
in it. For I am a father to
Israel, and Ephraim *is* My
firstborn.

[10]Hear the word of
Jehovah, O nations, and declare in the coasts far away.
And say, He who scattered
Israel will gather him and
keep him, as a shepherd his
flock. [11]For Jehovah has
redeemed Jacob, and ran-
somed him from the hand of
the one stronger than he.
[12]And they shall come and
sing in the height of Zion,
and be radiant over the
goodness of Jehovah, for
grain, and for wine, and for
oil, and for the sons of the
flock and the herd. And
their life shall be as a
watered garden; and they
shall not pine away any
more at all. [13]Then the
virgin shall rejoice in the
dance, both young men and
elders together. For I will
turn their mourning into joy,
and will comfort them and
make them rejoice from
their affliction. [14]And I will
fill the soul of the priests
with fatness, and My
people will be satisfied
with My goodness, de-
clares Jehovah.

[15]So says Jehovah, A
voice was heard in Ramah,
wailing, bitter weeping;
Rachel weeping for her
sons; she refuses to be
comforted for her sons, for

6 אֶל־יְהוָה אֱלֹהֵינוּ׃ כִּי־כֹה ׀ אָמַר יְהוָה רָנּוּ לְיַעֲקֹב
for Sing ,Jehovah says thus For our Jehovah to
Jacob !God

שִׂמְחָה וְצַהֲלוּ בְּרֹאשׁ הַגּוֹיִם הַשְׁמִיעוּ הַלְלוּ וְאִמְרוּ הוֹשַׁע
,Save ,say and give ,proclaim the the among and (with)
praise ;nations of chief shout ,gladness

7 יְהוָה אֶת־עַמְּךָ אֵת שְׁאֵרִית יִשְׂרָאֵל׃ הִנְנִי מֵבִיא אוֹתָם
them will I ,Behold .Israel the Your O
bring of remnant ,people Jehovah

מֵאֶרֶץ צָפוֹן וְקִבַּצְתִּים מִיַּרְכְּתֵי־אָרֶץ בָּם עִוֵּר וּפִסֵּחַ הָרָה
one the the and the among the re- the from gather and north the from
pregnant ,lame blind them ,earth of parts mote them country

8 וְיֹלֶדֶת יַחְדָּו קָהָל גָּדוֹל יָשׁוּבוּ הֵנָּה׃ בִּבְכִי יָבֹאוּ וּבְתַחֲנוּנִים
with and shall they With .here shall great a along tra- the and
supplications ;come weeping return company ;(with) one vailing

אוֹבִילֵם אוֹלִיכֵם אֶל־נַחֲלֵי מַיִם בְּדֶרֶךְ יָשָׁר לֹא יִכָּשְׁלוּ
will they not ;right a in ,water torrents by make will I will I
stumble way of walk them ;them lead

9 בָּהּ כִּי־הָיִיתִי לְיִשְׂרָאֵל לְאָב וְאֶפְרַיִם בְּכֹרִי הוּא׃ שִׁמְעוּ
Hear .(is) he My and ,father a Israel to am I for ;it on
firstborn Ephraim

דְבַר־יְהוָה גּוֹיִם וְהַגִּידוּ בָאִיִּים מִמֶּרְחָק וְאִמְרוּ מְזָרֵה
who He ,say And far from the in declare and O ,Jehovah the
scattered .away coasts (it) ,nations of word

10 יִשְׂרָאֵל יְקַבְּצֶנּוּ וּשְׁמָרוֹ כְּרֹעֶה עֶדְרוֹ׃ כִּי־פָדָה יְהוָה אֶת־
Jehovah has For his a as keep and gather will Israel
redeemed .flock shepherd ,him him

11 יַעֲקֹב וּגְאָלוֹ מִיַּד חָזָק מִמֶּנּוּ׃ וּבָאוּ וְרִנְּנוּ בִמְרוֹם־צִיּוֹן
Zion the in and they And than one the from saved and Jacob
of height sing come will .he stronger of hand him

וְנָהֲרוּ אֶל־טוּב יְהוָה עַל־דָּגָן וְעַל־תִּירֹשׁ וְעַל־יִצְהָר וְעַל־
and ,oil and new and grain for ,Jehovah the over be and
for for ,wine for of goodness radiant

בְּנֵי־צֹאן וּבָקָר וְהָיְתָה נַפְשָׁם כְּגַן רָוֶה וְלֹא־יוֹסִיפוּ לְדַאֲבָה
to will they and ;watered as their shall And the and the the
languish continue not garden a life be .herd flock of sons

12 עוֹד׃ אָז תִּשְׂמַח בְּתוּלָה בְּמָחוֹל וּבַחֻרִים וּזְקֵנִים יַחְדָּו
to- and young both the in the shall Then any
gether elders men ,dance virgin rejoice .more

וְהָפַכְתִּי אֶבְלָם לְשָׂשׂוֹן וְנִחַמְתִּים וְשִׂמַּחְתִּים מִיגוֹנָם׃
their from make and will I and ,joy into their will I For
.trouble rejoice them them comfort mourning turn

13 וְרִוֵּיתִי נֶפֶשׁ הַכֹּהֲנִים דָּשֶׁן וְעַמִּי אֶת־טוּבִי יִשְׂבָּעוּ נְאֻם־
says be will My with My and ,fatness the the will I And
,satisfied goodness people priests of soul with fill

14 יְהוָה׃ כֹּה ׀ אָמַר יְהוָה קוֹל בְּרָמָה נִשְׁמָע נְהִי בְּכִי
and wailing was in A ,Jehovah says Thus .Jehovah
weeping ,heard Ramah voice

תַּמְרוּרִים רָחֵל מְבַכָּה עַל־בָּנֶיהָ מֵאֲנָה לְהִנָּחֵם עַל־בָּנֶיהָ
,sons her for be to she her for weeping ,Rachel ;bitter
comforted refuses ,sons

they are not.
[16]So says Jehovah, Hold back your voice from weeping, and your eyes from tears. For there will be a reward for your work, says Jehovah; and they shall come again from the land of the enemy. [17]And there is hope for your future, says Jehovah, that *your* sons will come again to their own territory.
[18]I have surely heard Ephraim moaning over himself, *saying*, You have chastised me, and I was chastised, as a bull not broken in. Turn me, and I shall be turned; for You *are* Jehovah my God. [19]For after I had turned away, I repented; and after I was taught, I slapped on *my* thigh. I was ashamed; yea, I even blushed, because I bore the disgrace of my youth. [20]Is Ephraim My dear son? Or *is he* a delightful child? For as often as I spoke against him, I earnestly remember him still. So My bowels groan for him; I will surely have pity on him, declares Jehovah.
[21]Set up roadmarks for yourself; make sign posts for yourself. Set your heart toward the highway, *even* the way you went. Turn again, O virgin of Israel; turn again to these cities of yours. [22]How long will you turn to and fro, O faithless daughter? For Jehovah has created a new thing in the land. a woman shall enclose a man. [23]So says Jehovah of hosts, the God of Israel: Again they will speak this word in the land of Judah, and in its cities, when I turn again their captivity, *saying*, Jehovah bless you, O home of righteousness, O holy mountain! [24]And Judah and all its cities shall live in it together, the farmers and those who travel with flocks. [25]For I satisfy the

5869 1065 6963 4513 3068 559 3541 369
15 כי איננו׃ כה | אמר יהוה מנעי קולך מבכי ועיניך
your and from your Hold ,Jehovah says Thus they for
eyes weeping voice back .not are

776 7725 3068 5002 6468 7939 3426 1832
מדמעה כי יש שכר לפעלתך נאם־יהוה ושבו מארץ
the from they and ;Jehovah says your for a there For from
of land return will ,work reward be will .tears

1121 7725 3068 5002 319 8615 3426 341
16 אויב׃ ויש־תקוה לאחריתך נאם־יהוה ושבו בנים
(your) will that ,Jehovah says your for hope And the
sons return ,future is there .enemy

3256 3256 5110 669 8085 8085 1366
17 לגבולם׃ שמוע שמעתי אפרים מתנודד יסרתני ואוסר
was I and chas- You bemoaning Ephraim have I Surely their to
chastised ,me tened :himself heard .territory

430 3068 7725 7725 3925 3808 6499
כעגל לא למד השבני ואשובה כי אתה יהוה אלהי׃
My Jehovah You for will I and me turn ;trained not a as
.God (are) ;turned be ,back calf bull

3409 5606 3045 310 5162 7725 310
18 כי־אחרי שובי נחמתי ואחרי הודעי ספקתי על־ירך
(my) on slapped I was I and I turned I after For
.thigh ,instructed after ;repented ,away

3357 1121 5271 2781 5375 3637 1571 954
19 בשתי וגם־נכלמתי כי נשאתי חרפת נעורי׃ הבן יקיר
dear (Is) my re- the bore I for ,humiliated and was I
son .youth of proach also ,ashamed

2142 1696 1767 8191 3206 669
לי אפרים אם ילד שעשעים כי־מדי דברי בו זכר
surely against I as For ?delight child a Or ?Ephraim My
,him spoke as often of (he is)

5002 7355 7355 4578 1993 5750 2142
אזכרנו עוד על־כן המו מעי לו רחם ארחמנו נאם־
says have will I surely for My groan therefore ;still remem- I
,him on pity ;him bowels him ber

7896 8564 7790 6725 5324 3068
20 יהוה׃ הציבי לך צינים שמי לך תמרורים שתי
Set .posts sign for make road- for up Set .Jehovah
yourself ,marks yourself

7725 3478 1330 7725 1980 1870 4546 3820
לבך למסלה דרך הלכתי שובי בתולת ישראל שבי
return ,Israel O ,Return you way the the to your
of virgin .went ,highway heart

7728 1323 2559 5704 428 5892
21 אל־עריך אלה׃ עד־מתי תתחמקין הבת השובבה כי־
For .faithless O turn you will when Until .these your to
daughter ,fro and to cities

1397 5437 5347 776 2319 3068 1254
ברא יהוה חדשה בארץ נקבה תסובב גבר׃
.man a shall woman a the in new a Jehovah has
encircle ;land thing created

559 5750 3478 430 6635 3068 559 3541
22 כה־אמר יהוה צבאות אלהי ישראל עוד יאמרו את־
will they Again :Israel the ,hosts Jehovah says Thus
speak of God of

7622 7725 5892 3063 776 2088 1697
הדבר הזה בארץ יהודה ובעריו בשובי את־שבותם
their I when in and Judah the in this word
;captivity turn ,cities its of land

3063 3427 6944 2022 6664 5116 3068 1288
23 יברכך יהוה נוה־צדק הר הקדש׃ וישבו בה יהודה
Judah it in Then .holiness mount O of abode O,Jehovah bless
dwell will of righteousness you

5315 7301 5739 5265 406 3162 5892 3605
24 וכל־עריו יחדו אכרים ונסעו בעדר׃ כי הרויתי נפש
the satisfy I For with they and the ,together its and
soul .flocks travel who farmers cities all

weary soul, and I have filled every sorrowful soul. ²⁶On this I awoke, and looked up; and my sleep was sweet to me.

²⁷Behold, the days come, says Jehovah, even I will sow the house of Israel and the house of Judah with the seed of man, and the seed of animal. ²⁸And it shall be, as I have watched over them to pluck up, and to break down, and to throw down, and to destroy, and to bring calamity; so I will watch over them to build, and to plant, says Jehovah. ²⁹In those days they shall not any more say, The fathers have eaten sour grapes, and the teeth of the sons are dull. ³⁰But every man will die in his iniquity. Every man who eats the sour grapes, his teeth will be dull.

³¹Behold, the days come, says Jehovah, that I will cut a new covenant with the house of Israel, and with the house of Judah, ³²not according to the covenant that I cut with their fathers in the day I took *them* by the hand to bring them out of the land of Egypt—which covenant of Mine they broke, although I was a husband to them, says Jehovah— ³³but this *shall be* the covenant that I will cut with the house of Israel: After those days, declares Jehovah, I will put My law in their inward parts, and I will write it on their hearts; and I will be their God, and they shall be My people. ³⁴And they shall no longer each man teach his neighbor, and each man his brother, saying, Know Jehovah. For they shall all know Me, from the least of them even to the greatest of them, declares Jehovah. For I will forgive their

---

25
7200 ... 6974 ... 2088 ... 5921 ... 4390 ... 1669 ... 5315 ... 3605 ... 5889
and looked / awoke I / this / Upon / .fill I / who / soul / every / ,weary / languishes

26
3068 ... 5002 ... 935 ... 3117 ... 2009 ... 6149 ... 8142
,Jehovah says / ,come / the / ,Behold / .me to / was / my and / days / sweet / sleep

27
2233 ... 120 ... 2233 ... 3063 ... 1004 ... 3478 ... 1004 ... 2232
the and / man (with) / Judah / the and / Israel / the / I when / of seed / of seed / of house / of house / sow will

28
5422 ... 5428 ... 5921 ... 8245 ... 1961 ... 929
to and uproot to / over / have I / as / it And / .beast / down tear / them / watched / be will

5193 ... 1129 ... 5921 ... 8245 ... 7489 ... 6 ... 2040
to and / ,build to / over / will I so / bring to and / ,calamity / destroy / to and / ,plant / them / watch / demolish

29
398 ... 5750 ... 559 ... 3808 ... 3117 ... 3068 ... 5002
have / the / any / they / not / those / days In / .Jehovah says / eaten / fathers / ,more say shall

30
3605 ... 4191 ... 5771 ... 6949 ... 1121 ... 8127 ... 1155
Every / will / his in / every / But / .dull are / sons' the / and / sour / die / iniquity / man / teeth / grapes

935 ... 3117 ... 2009 ... 8127 ... 6949 ... 1155 ... 398 ... 120
,come / the / ,Behold / his / dull be will / sour the / who / man / days / .teeth / ,grapes / eats

31
1285 ... 3063 ... 1004 ... 3478 ... 1004 ... 3772 ... 3068 ... 5002
a / Judah / the and / Israel / the / that / .Jehovah says / covenant / of house with / of house / cut will

3117 ... 3772 ... 1285 ... 3808 ... 2319
the in / their / with / cut I / that / the like / not / ,new / day / fathers / covenant

32
6565 ... 834 ... 4714 ... 776 ... 3318 ... 3027 ... 2388
broke / they / which / ,Egypt / the from / bring to / their by / took I / of land / out them / hand / them

1285 ... 2088 ... 3068/5002 ... 1166 ... 1285
the / this / But .Jehovah says / to / a was / although / My / covenant (is) / ,them husband / I / ,covenant

5002 ... 3117 ... 310 ... 3478 ... 1004 ... 3772
says / ,those / days / After / :Israel / the / with / cut I that / of house

33
1961 ... 3789 ... 3820 ... 8451 ... 5414 ... 3068
I and / their and / their in / law My / will I / ,Jehovah / be will / ;it write / heart / upon / ,parts inward / put

376/5750 ... 3925 ... 3808 ... 5971 ... 1961 ... 430
each again / will they / And / a for / to / will / they and / ,God for / to / man / teach / not / .people / Me / be / them

34
3605 ... 3068 ... 3045/559 ... 251 ... 376
of all for / ;Jehovah / Know / ,saying / his / each and / his / them / ,brother / man / neighbor

5545 ... 3068/5002 ... 1419 ... 6996 ... 3045
will I / For / .Jehovah says / their / even / their from / ,Me / shall / forgive / greatest / to / least / know

iniquity, and I will remember their sins no more. [35]So says Jehovah, who gives the sun for a light by day, the laws of the moon, and the stars for a light by night; who stirs up the sea so that its waves roar—Jehovah of hosts *is* His name — [36]if these ordinances depart from before Me, says Jehovah, the seed of Israel also shall cease from being a nation before Me forever. [37]So says Jehovah, If the heavens above can be measured, and the foundations of the earth below can be searched out, I will also reject all the seed of Israel for all that they have done, declares Jehovah.

[38]Behold, the days come, says Jehovah, that the city will be built to Jehovah, from the Tower of Hananeel to the Corner Gate. [39]And the measuring line shall yet go before it to the hill Gareb, and shall go around to Goath. [40]And the whole valley of the dead bodies, and the ashes, and all the fields to the brook Kidron, to the corner of the Horse Gate east, *shall be* holy to Jehovah. It shall not be torn up, nor thrown down, any more forever.

34 3068 559 3541 5750 2142 3808 2403 5771
לַעֲוֺנָם וּלְחַטָּאתָם לֹא אֶזְכָּר־עוֹד׃ כֹּה ׀ אָמַר יְהוָה
,Jehovah says Thus .again will I remember not their and sins their ,iniquity

3915 216 3556 3394 2708 3119 216 8121 5414
נֹתֵן שֶׁמֶשׁ לְאוֹר יוֹמָם חֻקֹּת יָרֵחַ וְכוֹכָבִים לְאוֹר לָיְלָה
;night by a for light the and stars the ,moon the of laws day by a for light the sun who gives

35 4185 8034 6635 3068 1530 1993 3220 7280
רֹגַע הַיָּם וַיֶּהֱמוּ גַלָּיו יְהוָה צְבָאוֹת שְׁמוֹ׃ אִם־יָמֻשׁוּ
depart If His .name (is) hosts Jehovah of its —waves that so roar the sea who up stirs

7673 3478 2233 1571/3068 5002 6440 428 2708
הַחֻקִּים הָאֵלֶּה מִלְּפָנַי נְאֻם־יְהוָה גַּם זֶרַע יִשְׂרָאֵל יִשְׁבְּתוּ
shall cease Israel the of seed also ,Jehovah says from Me before these ordinances

36 518 3068 559 3541 3117 3605 6440 1471 1961
מִהְיוֹת גּוֹי לְפָנַי כָּל־הַיָּמִים׃ כֹּה ׀ אָמַר יְהוָה אִם־
If ,Jehovah says Thus .days the all before Me a nation from being

1571 4295 776 4146 2706 4605 8064 4058
יִמַּדּוּ שָׁמַיִם מִלְמַעְלָה וְיֵחָקְרוּ מוֹסְדֵי־אֶרֶץ לְמָטָּה גַּם־
also ,below the earth foun- of dations the be can searched out and be ,above the heavens be can measured

5002 6213 3605 3478 2233 3605 3973
אֲנִי אֶמְאַס בְּכָל־זֶרַע יִשְׂרָאֵל עַל־כָּל־אֲשֶׁר עָשׂוּ נְאֻם־
says have they ,done that all for Israel the of seed all will reject I

37 5892 1129 3068 5002 935 3117 2009 3068
יְהוָה׃ הִנֵּה יָמִים ° נְאֻם־יְהוָה וְנִבְנְתָה הָעִיר
the city will that built be Jehovah says,come the days ,Behold .Jehovah

38 6957/5750 3318 6438 8179 2606 4026 3068
לַיהוָה מִמִּגְדַּל חֲנַנְאֵל עַד־שַׁעַר הַפִּנָּה׃ וְיָצָא עוֹד קָוֶה
line yet will And out go the .Corner Gate to Hananeel the from of Tower to Jehovah

39 6010 3605 1601 5437 1619 1389 5048 4060
הַמִּדָּה נֶגְדּוֹ עַל גִּבְעַת גָּרֵב וְנָסַב גֹּעָתָה׃ וְכָל־הָעֵמֶק
the of valley And whole toward .Goath turn and Gareb hill the to before it the measuring

6438 6939 5158 7709 3605 1880 6297
הַפְּגָרִים ׀ וְהַדֶּשֶׁן וְכָל־הַשְּׁרֵמוֹת עַד־נַחַל קִדְרוֹן עַד־פִּנַּת
the of corner to ,Kidron the torrent to the fields and all the and ,ashes dead the ,bodies

2040 3808 5428 3068 6944 4217 5483 8179
שַׁעַר הַסּוּסִים מִזְרָחָה קֹדֶשׁ לַיהוָה לֹא־יִנָּתֵשׁ וְלֹא־יֵהָרֵס
demol- ished nor be will It up torn not to .Jehovah (be will) holy ,east the Horse Gate

5769 5750
עוֹד לְעוֹלָם׃
.forever any more

CAP. XXXII לב

CHAPTER 32

CHAPTER 32

[1]The word which came to Jeremiah from Jehovah in the tenth year of Zedekiah king of Judah, which *was* the eighteenth year of Nebuchadnezzar. [2]For then the king of Babylon's army was besieging Jerusalem. And

1 6224 8141 3068 3414 1961 1697
הַדָּבָר אֲשֶׁר־הָיָה אֶל־יִרְמְיָהוּ מֵאֵת יְהוָה בִּשְׁנַת הָעֲשִׂרִית
tenth the in year Jehovah from Jeremiah to came that The word

8141 6240 8083 8141 3063 4428 6667
לְצִדְקִיָּהוּ מֶלֶךְ יְהוּדָה הִיא הַשָּׁנָה שְׁמֹנֶה־עֶשְׂרֵה שָׁנָה
year eighteenth ,year the which (was) ,Judah king of of Zedekiah

2 3389 6696 894 4428 2428 227 5019
לִנְבוּכַדְרֶאצַּר׃ וְאָז חֵיל מֶלֶךְ בָּבֶל צָרִים עַל־יְרוּשָׁלָםִ
.Jerusalem was besieging Babylon of king the of army the For then of .Nebuchadnezzar

Jeremiah the prophet was shut in the court of the guard, which *was* in the king of Judah's house. 3For Zedekiah king of Judah had shut him up, saying, Why do you prophesy and say, So says Jehovah, Behold, I will give this city into the hand of the king of Babylon, and he will take it. 4And Zedekiah king of Judah shall not escape out of the hand of the Chaldeans, but shall surely be delivered into the hand of the king of Babylon; and he will speak with him mouth to mouth, and will see his eyes with his eyes. 5And he shall lead Zedekiah into Babylon, and there he shall be until I visit him, says Jehovah. Though you fight with the Chaldeans, you shall not succeed.

6And Jeremiah said, The word of Jehovah was to me, saying, 7Behold, Hanameel the son of Shallum, your uncle, shall come to you, saying, Buy my field in Anathoth for yourself; for the right to redeem *is* yours, to buy *it*. 8So Hanameel, my uncle's son, came to me in the court of the guard, according to the word of Jehovah, and said to me, Please buy my field in Anathoth, which *is* in the land of Benjamin; for the right of inheritance *is* yours, and the right of redemption *is* yours. Buy *it* for yourself. Then I knew that this *was* the word of Jehovah. 9And I bought the field in Anathoth from my uncle's son, Hanameel, and weighed him the silver, seventeen shekels *of* silver. 10And I wrote it in the document, and sealed *it*, and called witnesses, and weighed

1004 834 43:07 2691 3607 1961 50 30 3414
וְיִרְמְיָהוּ הַנָּבִיא הָיָה כָלוּא בַּחֲצַר הַמַּטָּרָה אֲשֶׁר בֵּית־
the (in) which the the in up shut was the And
of house (was) ,guard of court prophet Jeremiah

559 3063 4428 6677 3607 3063 4428
3 מֶלֶךְ יְהוּדָה׃ אֲשֶׁר כְּלָאוֹ צִדְקִיָּהוּ מֶלֶךְ־יְהוּדָה לֵאמֹר
,saying ,Judah king Zedekiah shut had For .Judah the
of up him of king

5414 2005 3068 559 35 41 559 50 12 4100
מַדּוּעַ אַתָּה נִבָּא לֵאמֹר כֹּה אָמַר יְהוָה הִנְנִי נֹתֵן אֶת־
will ,Behold ,Jehovah says Thus ,saying do you Why
give I ,prophesy

4428 6677 3920 884 4428 3027 2088 5892
4 הָעִיר הַזֹּאת בְּיַד מֶלֶךְ־בָּבֶל וּלְכָדָהּ׃ וְצִדְקִיָּהוּ מֶלֶךְ
king and will he and ,Babylon the the into this city
of Zedekiah ;it take of king of hand

4428 3027 5414 5414 3778 3027 4422 3808 3063
יְהוּדָה לֹא יִמָּלֵט מִיַּד הַכַּשְׂדִּים כִּי־הִנָּתֹן יִנָּתֵן בְּיַד מֶלֶךְ־
the the into will surely but the the from shall not Judah
of king of hand given be ,Chaldeans of hand escape

884 7200 5869 5869 63:10 6310 1696 884
5 בָּבֶל וְדִבֶּר־פִּיו עִם־פִּיו וְעֵינָיו אֶת־עֵינָו תִּרְאֶינָה׃ וּבָבֶל
into and ;see and his with his and his with his he and ,Babylon
Babylon eyes eyes ,mouth mouth speak will

3068 5002 6485 19 61 6677 32 12
יוֹלִךְ אֶת־צִדְקִיָּהוּ וְשָׁם יִהְיֶה עַד־פָּקְדִי אֹתוֹ נְאֻם־יְהוָה
;Jehovah says ,him visit I until shall he and ,Zedekiah will he
be there lead

559 6743 3808 3778 3898
6 כִּי תִלָּחֲמוּ אֶת־הַכַּשְׂדִּים לֹא תַצְלִיחוּ׃ וַיֹּאמֶר
said And shall you not the with you though
.suceed Chaldeans fight

1121 2601 2009 559 3068 1697 1961 3414
7 יִרְמְיָהוּ הָיָה דְּבַר־יְהוָה אֵלַי לֵאמֹר׃ הִנֵּה חֲנַמְאֵל בֶּן
the Hanameel ,Behold ,saying ,me to Jehovah The came ,Jeremiah
of son of word

834 7704 7069 559 935 1730 7967
שַׁלֻּם דֹּדְךָ בָּא אֵלֶיךָ לֵאמֹר קְנֵה לְךָ אֶת־שָׂדִי אֲשֶׁר
which my for Buy ,saying ,you to shall your Shallum
(is) field yourself come uncle

2601 935 7069 1353 4911 6068
8 בַּעֲנָתוֹת כִּי לְךָ מִשְׁפַּט הַגְּאֻלָּה לִקְנוֹת׃ וַיָּבֹא אֵלַי חֲנַמְאֵל
Hanameel to So buy to ,redemption the (is) to for in
me came .(it) of right you ;Anathoth

7069 559 4307 2691 3068 1697 1730/1121
בֶּן־דֹּדִי כִּדְבַר יְהוָה אֶל־חֲצַר הַמַּטָּרָה וַיֹּאמֶר אֵלַי קְנֵה
Buy ,me to said and ,guard the the to ,Jehovah's according of son
of court word to ,uncle my

1144 776 834 6068 834 7704 4994
נָא אֶת־שָׂדִי אֲשֶׁר־בַּעֲנָתוֹת אֲשֶׁר ׀ בְּאֶרֶץ בִּנְיָמִין כִּי לְךָ
to for ,Benjamin the in which in which my please
you of land (is) ,Anathoth (is) field

1697 30 45 7069 1353 3425 4941
מִשְׁפַּט הַיְרֻשָּׁה וּלְךָ הַגְּאֻלָּה קְנֵה־לָךְ וָאֵדַע כִּי דְבַר־
the that I Then for Buy right the to and ,possession the (is)
of word knew .yourself (it) .redemption of you of right

1730/1121 2601 7704 7069 3069
9 יְהוָה הוּא׃ וָאֶקְנֶה אֶת־הַשָּׂדֶה מֵאֵת חֲנַמְאֵל בֶּן־דֹּדִי
my son Hanameel from the I And that Jehovah
uncle's field bought .(was)

8255 7651 3701 82.54 60 68
אֲשֶׁר בַּעֲנָתוֹת וָאֶשְׁקֲלָה־לּוֹ אֶת־הַכֶּסֶף שִׁבְעָה שְׁקָלִים
shekels seven the for and in that
,silver him weighed ,Anathoth (was)

5707 5749 28 56 5612 3789 3701 6235
10 וַעֲשָׂרָה הַכָּסֶף׃ וָאֶכְתֹּב בַּסֵּפֶר וָאֶחְתֹּם וָאָעֵד עֵדִים
,witnesses and sealed and the in I And .silver (of) ten and
called .(it) book (it) wrote

the silver on the scales.
[11]So I took the document of the purchase, that which was sealed according to the law and the statutes, and the open copy. [12]And I gave the purchase document to Baruch the son of Neriah, the son of Maaseiah, before the eyes of my uncle's son Hanameel, and before the eyes of the witnesses who wrote in the purchase document before the eyes of all the Jews who sat in the court of the guard.
[13]And I commanded Baruch before their eyes, saying, [14]So says Jehovah of hosts, the God of Israel: Take these books, the purchase document, the one sealed, and the open book, and put them in an earthen vessel so that they may stand many days. [15]For so says Jehovah of hosts, the God of Israel: Houses and fields and vineyards will again be bought in this land.

[16]And after I gave the document of the purchase to Baruch the son of Neriah, I prayed to Jehovah, saying, [17]Ah, Lord Jehovah! You have made the heavens and the earth by Your great power and Your outstretched arm; not any thing is too difficult for You; [18]who acts with loving-kindness to thousands, and repays the iniquity of the fathers into the bosom of their sons after them. The great, the mighty God, Jehovah of hosts, *is* His name, [19]great in counsel and mighty in work; for Your eyes are open on all the ways of the sons of men, to give to each man according to his ways,

4736 5612 3947 3976 3701 8254
11 וָאֶשְׁקֹל הַכֶּסֶף בְּמֹאזְנָיִם׃ וָאֶקַּח אֶת־סֵפֶר הַמִּקְנָה אֶת־
the the I So the on the did
,purchase of document took .scales silver weighed

5612 5414 1540 2706 6680 2856
12 הֶחָתוּם הַמִּצְוָה וְהַחֻקִּים וְאֶת־הַגָּלוּי׃ וָאֶתֵּן אֶת־הַסֵּפֶר
the I And open the and the and (containing) which that
of document gave .copy statutes command the sealed was

1730 2601 5869 4271/1121 5374/1121 1263 4736
הַמִּקְנָה אֶל־בָּרוּךְ בֶּן־נֵרִיָּה בֶּן־מַחְסֵיָה לְעֵינֵי חֲנַמְאֵל דֹּדִי
my ,Hanameel before ,Maaseiah the ,Neriah the Baruch to the
(son) uncle's of eyes the of son of son purchase

3064 3605 5869 4736 5612 3789 5707 5869
וּלְעֵינֵי הָעֵדִים הַכֹּתְבִים בְּסֵפֶר הַמִּקְנָה לְעֵינֵי כָּל־הַיְּהוּדִים
the all the before the the in who the before and
Jews of eyes ,purchase of document wrote witnesses of eyes the

5869 1263 6680 4307 2691 3427
13 הַיֹּשְׁבִים בַּחֲצַר הַמַּטָּרָה׃ וָאֲצַוֶּה אֶת־בָּרוּךְ לְעֵינֵיהֶם
before Baruch I And .guard the the in sat who
eyes their commanded of court

3947 3478 430 6635 3068 559 3541 559
14 לֵאמֹר׃ כֹּה־אָמַר יְהוָה צְבָאוֹת אֱלֹהֵי יִשְׂרָאֵל לָקוֹחַ אֶת־
Take :Israel the hosts Jehovah says Thus ,saying
of God of

2856 2088 4736 5612 428 5612
הַסְּפָרִים הָאֵלֶּה אֵת סֵפֶר הַמִּקְנָה הַזֶּה וְאֵת הֶחָתוּם וְאֵת
and the both ,this purchase the ,these documents
one sealed of document

3117 5975 2789 3627 5414 2088 1540 5612
סֵפֶר הַגָּלוּי הַזֶּה וּנְתַתָּם בִּכְלִי־חָרֶשׂ לְמַעַן יַעַמְדוּ יָמִים
days may they that so an in put and this open docu-
stand earthen vessel them ment

3478 430 6635 3068 559 3541 7227
15 רַבִּים׃ כִּי כֹה אָמַר יְהוָה צְבָאוֹת אֱלֹהֵי יִשְׂרָאֵל
:Israel the ,hosts Jehovah says thus For .many
of God of

776 3754 7704 1004 7069 5750
עוֹד יִקָּנוּ בָתִּים וְשָׂדוֹת וּכְרָמִים בָּאָרֶץ הַזֹּאת׃
.this in and and houses be will Again
land vineyards fields bought

1263 4736 5612 5414 310 3068 6419
16 וָאֶתְפַּלֵּל אֶל־יְהוָה אַחֲרֵי תִתִּי אֶת־סֵפֶר הַמִּקְנָה אֶל־בָּרוּךְ
Baruch to the the gave I after Jehovah to I And
purchase of document prayed

6213 2009 3068 136 162 559 5374/1121
17 בֶּן־נֵרִיָּה לֵאמֹר׃ אֲהָהּ אֲדֹנָי יְהוִה הִנֵּה ׀ אַתָּה עָשִׂיתָ
have You ,Behold !Jehovah Lord Ah ,saying ,Neriah the
made of son

5186 2220 1419 3581 776 8064
אֶת־הַשָּׁמַיִם וְאֶת־הָאָרֶץ בְּכֹחֲךָ הַגָּדוֹל וּבִזְרֹעֲךָ הַנְּטוּיָה
stretched Your and great Your by the and the
out arm power earth heavens

7999 505 2617 6213 1697 3605 6381 3808
18 לֹא־יִפָּלֵא מִמְּךָ כָּל־דָּבָר׃ עֹשֶׂה חֶסֶד לַאֲלָפִים וּמְשַׁלֵּם
and for loving who ,thing any for too is not
repays ,thousands kindness exercises You difficult

1368 1419 410 310 1121 2436 1 5771
עֲוֹן אָבוֹת אֶל־חֵיק בְּנֵיהֶם אַחֲרֵיהֶם הָאֵל הַגָּדוֹל הַגִּבּוֹר
,mighty ,great the after their the into the ini- the
God ,them sons of bosom fathers of quity

5950 7227 6098 1419 8034 6635 3068
19 יְהוָה צְבָאוֹת שְׁמוֹ׃ גְּדֹל הָעֵצָה וְרַב הָעֲלִילִיָּה אֲשֶׁר
for ;deed and ,counsel great His hosts Jehovah
in great in ;name (is) of

1870 376 5414 120 1121 1870 3605 5921 6491 5869
עֵינֶיךָ פְּקֻחוֹת עַל־כָּל־דַּרְכֵי בְּנֵי אָדָם לָתֵת לְאִישׁ כִּדְרָכָיו
to according to give to ,men the the all on are Your
ways his man each of sons of ways open eyes

and according to the fruit of his doings. 20For You have set signs and wonders in the land of Egypt until this day, and in Israel, and among men; and You have made a name for Yourself, as at this day. 21And *You* have brought Your people Israel out of the land of Egypt with signs, and with wonders, and with a strong hand, and with an outstretched arm, and with great terror. 22And You have given them this land which You swore to their fathers, to give to them a land flowing with milk and honey. 23And they came in and possessed it, but they did not obey Your voice, nor did they walk in Your law. They have not done all that You commanded them to do; so You have caused all this evil to meet them. 24Behold, the siege-mounds have come to the city, to capture it. And the city is given into the hand of the Chaldeans who fight against it, because of the sword, and the famine, and the plague. And what You have spoken has happened. And, behold, You see *it*. 25And You have said to me, O Lord Jehovah, Buy for yourself the field with silver, and call witnesses; for the city is given into the hand of the Chaldeans.

26And the word of Jehovah was to Jeremiah, saying, 27Behold, I *am* Jehovah, the God of all flesh. Is anything too difficult for Me? 28So Jehovah says this: Behold, I will give this city into the hand of the Chaldeans, and into the hand of Nebuchadnezzar, king of Babylon, and he shall take it. 29And the Chaldeans who fight against this city shall enter and set this city *on* fire, and

4714 776 4159 226 7760 4611 6529
20 וְכִפְרִי מַעֲלָלָיו׃ אֲשֶׁר־שַׂמְתָּ אֹתוֹת וּמֹפְתִים בְּאֶרֶץ־מִצְרַיִם
Egypt the in and signs have You For his to according
of land wonders set .doings of fruit the

3117 8034 6213 120 3478 2088 3117/5704
עַד־הַיּוֹם הַזֶּה וּבְיִשְׂרָאֵל וּבָאָדָם וַתַּעֲשֶׂה־לְּךָ שֵׁם כַּיּוֹם
at as ,name a for You and among and in and ,this day until
day Yourself made have ;men Israel

226 4714 776 3478 5971 3318 2088
21 הַזֶּה׃ וַתֹּצֵא אֶת־עַמְּךָ אֶת־יִשְׂרָאֵל מֵאֶרֶץ מִצְרָיִם בְּאֹתוֹת
with ,Egypt the from Israel Your have and ,this
,signs of land people out brought

1419 4172 5186 248 2389 3027 4159
וּבְמוֹפְתִים וּבְיָד חֲזָקָה וּבְאֶזְרוֹעַ נְטוּיָה וּבְמוֹרָא גָּדוֹל׃
.great with and stretched with and ,strong with and with and
terror ,out arm an hand a ,wonders

5414 1 7650 834 776 5414
22 וַתִּתֵּן לָהֶם אֶת־הָאָרֶץ הַזֹּאת אֲשֶׁר־נִשְׁבַּעְתָּ לַאֲבוֹתָם לָתֵת
give to their to You which ,this land to You And
fathers swore them gave

3808 3423 935 1706 2461 2100 776
23 לָהֶם אֶרֶץ זָבַת חָלָב וּדְבָשׁ׃ וַיָּבֹאוּ וַיִּרְשׁוּ אֹתָהּ וְלֹא־
but ,it and they And and milk flowing a to
not possessed in came .honey with land ,them

6680 3605 1980 3808 8451 6963 8085
שָׁמְעוּ בְקוֹלֶךָ וּבְתוֹרוֹתֶךָ לֹא־הָלָכוּ אֵת כָּל־אֲשֶׁר צִוִּיתָה
You that all they not Your in and Your did they
commanded ;walk did law ,voice obey

7451 3605 7125 6213 3808 6213
לָהֶם לַעֲשׂוֹת לֹא עָשׂוּ וַתַּקְרֵא אֹתָם אֵת כָּל־הָרָעָה
evil all them You and have they not do to to
meet to made ;done them

5414 5892 3920 5892 935 5550 2009 2088
24 הַזֹּאת׃ הִנֵּה הַסֹּלְלוֹת בָּאוּ הָעִיר לְלָכְדָהּ וְהָעִיר נִתְּנָה
is the and capture to ,city the have siege the ,Behold .this
given city ,it to come mounds

1698 7458 2719 6440 3898 3778 3027
בְּיַד הַכַּשְׂדִּים הַנִּלְחָמִים עָלֶיהָ מִפְּנֵי הַחֶרֶב וְהָרָעָב וְהַדָּבֶר
the and the and the because against who the the into
.plague ,famine sword of ,it fight Chaldeans of hand

136 559 7200 1961 1696
25 וַאֲשֶׁר דִּבַּרְתָּ הָיָה וְהִנְּךָ רֹאֶה׃ וְאַתָּה אָמַרְתָּ אֵלַי אֲדֹנָי
O to said have You And see ,lo and has have You And
Lord ,Me .(it) You ,happened spoken what

5414 5892 5707 5749 3701 7704 7069 3068
יְהוִה קְנֵה־לְךָ הַשָּׂדֶה בַּכֶּסֶף וְהָעֵד עֵדִים וְהָעִיר נִתְּנָה
given is the for ,witnesses call and with the for Buy ,Jehovah
city silver field yourself

559 3414 3068/1697 1961 3778 3027
26 בְּיַד הַכַּשְׂדִּים׃ וַיְהִי דְּבַר־יְהוָה אֶל־יִרְמְיָהוּ לֵאמֹר׃
,saying ,Jeremiah to Jehovah the Then the the into
of word came .Chaldeans of hand

1697 3605 6381 430 1320 3605 3068 2088
27 הִנֵּה אֲנִי יְהוָה אֱלֹהֵי כָּל־בָּשָׂר הֲמִמֶּנִּי יִפָּלֵא כָּל־דָּבָר׃
?thing any too Is for .flesh all the ,Jehovah I ,Behold
difficult Me of God (am)

3027 2088 5892 5414 2005 3068 559 3541 3651
28 לָכֵן כֹּה אָמַר יְהוָה הִנְנִי נֹתֵן אֶת־הָעִיר הַזֹּאת בְּיַד
the into this city will ,Behold :Jehovah says thus There-
of hand give I fore

935 3920 884 4428 5019 3027 3778
29 הַכַּשְׂדִּים וּבְיַד נְבוּכַדְרֶאצַּר מֶלֶךְ־בָּבֶל וּלְכָדָהּ׃ וּבָאוּ
will And will he and ,Babylon king Nebuchadnezzar into and the
enter .it take will of of hand the ,Chaldeans

5892 3341 2088 5892 3898 3778
הַכַּשְׂדִּים הַנִּלְחָמִים עַל־הָעִיר הַזֹּאת וְהִצִּיתוּ אֶת־הָעִיר
city set and this city against fight who the
Chaldeans

burn it, with the houses where they offered incense on their roofs to Baal, and poured out drink offerings to other gods, to provoke Me to anger. ³⁰For the sons of Israel and the sons of Judah have only done evil in My eyes from their youth. For the sons of Israel have only provoked Me to anger with the work of their hands, declares Jehovah. ³¹For this city has been to Me a cause of My anger and My wrath from the day that they built it even to this day; that I should remove it from My face; ³²because of all the evil of the sons of Israel and of the sons of Judah which they have done to provoke Me to anger; they, their kings, their rulers, their priests, their prophets, and the men of Judah, and the inhabitants of Jerusalem. ³³And they have turned the back to Me, and not the face; though I taught them, rising up early and teaching, yet they have not listened to receive instruction. ³⁴But they set their idols in the house on which My name is called, to defile it. ³⁵And they built the high places of Baal which are in the valley of the son of Hinnom, to cause their sons and their daughters to pass through the fire to Molech; which I did not command them, nor did it come into My heart, that they should do this detestable thing, to cause Judah to sin.

³⁶And now, therefore, so says Jehovah, God of Israel, concerning this city, of which you say, It is given into the hand of the king of Babylon by the sword, and by the famine, and by the plague; ³⁷Behold, I will gather them out of all the

---

30

הַזֹּאת בָּאֵשׁ וְשָׂרְפוּ וְאֵת הַבָּתִּים אֲשֶׁר קִטְּרוּ עַל־גַּגּוֹתֵיהֶם

this / with fire / burn / and / the houses / where / they offered / incense / on / their roofs

לַבַּעַל וְהִסִּכוּ נְסָכִים לֵאלֹהִים אֲחֵרִים לְמַעַן הַכְעִסֵנִי׃

to Baal, / and poured out / drink offerings / to gods / other, / in order to / provoke Me to anger

כִּי־הָיוּ בְנֵי־יִשְׂרָאֵל וּבְנֵי יְהוּדָה אַךְ עֹשִׂים הָרַע בְּעֵינַי

For / have / the sons of Israel / and the sons of / Judah / only / done / the evil / in My eyes

31

מִנְּעֻרֹתֵיהֶם כִּי בְנֵי־יִשְׂרָאֵל אַךְ מַכְעִסִים אֹתִי בְּמַעֲשֵׂה

their youth, / For / the sons of Israel / only / provoked / Me / with the work of

יְדֵיהֶם נְאֻם־יְהוָה׃ כִּי עַל־אַפִּי וְעַל־חֲמָתִי הָיְתָה לִּי

their hands, / says Jehovah. / For / (a) cause / My anger / and / My wrath / has been / to Me

הָעִיר הַזֹּאת לְמִן־הַיּוֹם אֲשֶׁר בָּנוּ אוֹתָהּ וְעַד הַיּוֹם הַזֶּה

the city / this / from / the day / that / built / it / and / even / to / day / this;

32

לַהֲסִירָהּ מֵעַל פָּנָי׃ עַל כָּל־רָעַת בְּנֵי־יִשְׂרָאֵל וּבְנֵי יְהוּדָה

that I should / remove it / from / My face; / because / all / the evil of / the sons of Israel / and the sons of / Judah,

אֲשֶׁר עָשׂוּ לְהַכְעִסֵנִי הֵמָּה מַלְכֵיהֶם שָׂרֵיהֶם כֹּהֲנֵיהֶם

which / they / done / to provoke Me to anger; / they, / their kings, / their rulers, / their priests,

33

וּנְבִיאֵיהֶם וְאִישׁ יְהוּדָה וְיֹשְׁבֵי יְרוּשָׁלִָם׃ וַיִּפְנוּ אֵלַי עֹרֶף

their prophets, / and men of / Judah, / and the inhabitants of / Jerusalem. / And have turned / to Me / back,

וְלֹא פָנִים וְלַמֵּד אֹתָם הַשְׁכֵּם וְלַמֵּד וְאֵינָם שֹׁמְעִים לָקַחַת

and not / face; / though taught I / them / rising up early / and teaching, / yet have not / they / listened / to receive

34

מוּסָר׃ וַיָּשִׂימוּ שִׁקּוּצֵיהֶם בַּבַּיִת אֲשֶׁר־נִקְרָא שְׁמִי־עָלָיו

instruction. / But / set / they / their idols / in the / house / which / has been / called / My name / upon

35

לְטַמְּאוֹ׃ וַיִּבְנוּ אֶת־בָּמוֹת הַבַּעַל אֲשֶׁר בְּגֵיא בֶן־הִנֹּם

to defile / it. / And / built they / the high places of / Baal / which / (are) in / the valley / of son of / Hinnom,

לְהַעֲבִיר אֶת־בְּנֵיהֶם וְאֶת־בְּנוֹתֵיהֶם לַמֹּלֶךְ אֲשֶׁר לֹא

to make / pass through / (fire) / their sons / and / their daughters / to Molech— / which / not

צִוִּיתִים וְלֹא עָלְתָה עַל־לִבִּי לַעֲשׂוֹת הַתּוֹעֵבָה הַזֹּאת לְמַעַן

did I command them, / nor / come / did it / into / My heart, / that they should do / abomination / this, / in order to

36

הַחֲטִי אֶת־יְהוּדָה׃ וְעַתָּה לָכֵן כֹּה־אָמַר יְהוָה אֱלֹהֵי

cause / to sin / Judah. / And / now / therefore / thus / says / Jehovah, / the God of

יִשְׂרָאֵל אֶל־הָעִיר הַזֹּאת אֲשֶׁר אַתֶּם אֹמְרִים נִתְּנָה בְּיַד

Israel, / concerning / the city / this / which / you / say, / is given / into the hand of

37

מֶלֶךְ־בָּבֶל בַּחֶרֶב וּבָרָעָב וּבַדָּבֶר׃ הִנְנִי מְקַבְּצָם מִכָּל

the king of Babylon / by the sword / and by the famine / and by the plague: / Behold, / will / I gather them / out of all lands, there where I have driven them in My anger, and in My fury, and in great indignation. And I will bring them again to this place, and I will cause them to live in safety. [38]And they shall be My people, and I will be their God. [39]And I will give them one heart and one way, that they may fear Me all the days, for good to them and to their sons after them. [40]And I will cut an everlasting covenant with them, that I will not turn away from them, to do good to them. But I will put My fear in their heart, that they shall not depart from Me. [41]And I will rejoice over them, to do good to them; and I will truly plant them in this land with all My heart and with all My soul. [42]For so says Jehovah: As I have brought this great evil on this people, so I will bring on them all the good that I am speaking to them.

הָאֲרָצוֹת אֲשֶׁר הִדַּחְתִּים שָׁם בְּאַפִּי וּבַחֲמָתִי וּבְקֶצֶף גָּדוֹל
.great in and indignation | in and fury My | My in ,anger | ,there | have I them driven | where | the lands

38 וַהֲשִׁבֹתִים אֶל־הַמָּקוֹם הַזֶּה וְהֹשַׁבְתִּים לָבֶטַח׃ וְהָיוּ לִי
to they And Me be will | in .safety | make and dwell them | this | place | to | bring will I And back them

39 לְעָם וַאֲנִי אֶהְיֶה לָהֶם לֵאלֹהִים׃ וְנָתַתִּי לָהֶם לֵב אֶחָד
one | heart | to them | I And give will | .God for | to them | will be | and I | a for ,people

וְדֶרֶךְ אֶחָד לְיִרְאָה אוֹתִי כָּל־הַיָּמִים לְטוֹב לָהֶם וְלִבְנֵיהֶם
to and sons their | to them | for ,good | the days | all | Me | they that fear may | ,one | and way

40 אַחֲרֵיהֶם׃ וְכָרַתִּי לָהֶם בְּרִית עוֹלָם אֲשֶׁר לֹא־אָשׁוּב
will I away turn | not | that | ever-lasting | an covenant | for them | I And cut will | after .them

מֵאַחֲרֵיהֶם לְהֵיטִיבִי אוֹתָם וְאֶת־יִרְאָתִי אֶתֵּן בִּלְבָבָם
their in heart | will I put | My fear | But | .them | do to good | from them

41 לְבִלְתִּי סוּר מֵעָלָי׃ וְשַׂשְׂתִּי עֲלֵיהֶם לְהֵטִיב אוֹתָם וּנְטַעְתִּים
will I and them plant | ,them | do to good | over them | will I And rejoice | from .Me | shall they depart | that not

42 בָּאָרֶץ הַזֹּאת בֶּאֱמֶת בְּכָל־לִבִּי וּבְכָל־נַפְשִׁי׃ כִּי
For | My .soul | and all with | My ,heart | with all | ,truly | this | in land

כֹּה אָמַר יְהוָה כַּאֲשֶׁר הֵבֵאתִי אֶל־הָעָם הַזֶּה אֵת כָּל־
all | this | people | on | have I brought | As | :Jehovah says | thus

הָרָעָה הַגְּדוֹלָה הַזֹּאת כֵּן אָנֹכִי מֵבִיא עֲלֵיהֶם אֶת־כָּל־
all | them on | will bring | I | so | ,this | great | evil

[43]And fields will be bought in this land, of which you say, It *is* a desolation, without man or beast; it has been given into the hand of the Chaldeans. [44]Men shall buy fields for silver, and write in a document, and seal *it*, and call witnesses in the land of Benjamin, and in the places around Jerusalem, and in the cities of Judah, and in the cities of the mountains, and in the cities of the lowland, and in the cities of the Negeb. For I will cause their captivity to return, says Jehovah.

43 הַטּוֹבָה אֲשֶׁר אָנֹכִי דֹּבֵר עֲלֵיהֶם׃ וְנִקְנָה הַשָּׂדֶה בָּאָרֶץ
in land | fields | will And bought be | .them to | am speaking | I | that | the good

הַזֹּאת אֲשֶׁר ׀ אַתֶּם אֹמְרִים שְׁמָמָה הִיא מֵאֵין אָדָם וּבְהֵמָה
;beast or | man | without | (is) it | A desolation | ,say | you | of which | ,this

44 נִתְּנָה בְּיַד הַכַּשְׂדִּים׃ שָׂדוֹת בַּכֶּסֶף יִקְנוּ וְכָתוֹב בַּסֵּפֶר ׀
a in ,document | write and (it) | men ,buy will | For silver | fields | the .Chaldeans' | into hand | is it given

וְחָתוֹם וְהָעֵד עֵדִים בְּאֶרֶץ בִּנְיָמִן וּבִסְבִיבֵי יְרוּשָׁלִַם וּבְעָרֵי
in and cities | ,Jerusalem | the in and around places | ,Benjamin | the in of land | witnesses | and call | and it seal

יְהוּדָה וּבְעָרֵי הָהָר וּבְעָרֵי הַשְּׁפֵלָה וּבְעָרֵי הַנֶּגֶב כִּי־אָשִׁיב
will I back bring | for ,Negeb | the of cities | in and the | the of ,Lowland | in and cities | the ,mountain | in and cities | ,Judah's

אֶת־שְׁבוּתָם נְאֻם־יְהוָה׃
.Jehovah | says | their ,captivity

CAP. XXXIII לג

CHAPTER 33

CHAPTER 33
1And the word of
Jehovah was to Jeremi-
ah the second time, while
he was still shut up in the
court of the guard, saying,
2So says Jehovah the
Maker of it, Jehovah who
formed it in order to
establish it; Jehovah *is*
His name: 3Call to Me,
and I will answer you and
tell you great and inscrut-
able things; you do not
know them. 4For so says
Jehovah, the God of
Israel, Concerning the
houses of this city, and
concerning the houses of
the kings of Judah, which
are broken down *to de-*
fend against the siege-
mounds, and against the
sword, 5they come to
fight with the Chaldeans,
and to fill them with the
dead bodies of men
whom I have struck in My
anger and in My wrath;
and for whom I have hid-
den My face from this
city, because of all their
evil. 6Behold, I will bring
health and healing to it,
and I will heal them and
reveal to them the abun-
dance of peace and truth.
7And I will cause the captivity of Judah and the
captivity of Israel to return, and will build them,
as at the first. 8And I will
cleanse them from all
their iniquity which they
have sinned against Me;
and I will pardon all their
iniquities which they
have sinned against Me,
and which they have
rebelled against Me.

9And it shall be a name
of joy to Me, a praise and
a glory to all the nations
of the earth, which shall
hear all the good that I do
for them. And they shall
fear and tremble for all
the goodness and for all
the peace that I do
for it. 10So says
Jehovah, In this place

CHAPTER 33

6113 5750 8145 3414 3068 1697 1961
1 וַיְהִי דְבַר־יְהוָה אֶל־יִרְמְיָהוּ שֵׁנִית וְהוּא עוֹדֶנּוּ עָצוּר
was still while the Jeremiah to Jehovah the Then
up shut he ,time second of word came

3335 3068 6213 3068 559/3541 559 4307 2691
2 בַּחֲצַר הַמַּטָּרָה לֵאמֹר׃ כֹּה־אָמַר יְהוָה עֹשָׂהּ יְהוָה יוֹצֵר
who Jehovah its Jehovah says Thus ,saying guard the the in
formed ,Maker of court

5047 6030 7121 8034 3068 3559
3 אוֹתָהּ לַהֲכִינָהּ יְהוָה שְׁמוֹ׃ קְרָא אֵלַי וְאֶעֱנֶךָּ וְאַגִּידָה
will and will I and to Call His Jehovah to order in it
tell you answer Me .name (is) ;it establish

3068 559 3541 3045 3808 1219 1419
4 לְךָ גְּדֹלוֹת וּבְצֻרוֹת לֹא יְדַעְתָּם׃ כִּי כֹה אָמַר יְהוָה
Jehovah says thus For do you not inscrut- and ,great you
.them know ,things able

3063 4428 1004 2088 5892 1004 3478 430
אֱלֹהֵי יִשְׂרָאֵל עַל־בָּתֵּי הָעִיר הַזֹּאת וְעַל־בָּתֵּי מַלְכֵי יְהוּדָה
,Judah kings the the and ,this city the con- ,Israel the
of of houses concerning of houses cerning of God

3898 935 2719 5550 5422
5 הַנְּתֻצִים אֶל־הַסֹּלְלוֹת וְאֶל־הֶחָרֶב׃ בָּאִים לְהִלָּחֵם אֶת־
with fight to They the and siege the against are which
come .sword against ,mounds down broken

639 5221 120 6297 4390 3778
הַכַּשְׂדִּים וּלְמַלְאָם אֶת־פִּגְרֵי הָאָדָם אֲשֶׁר הִכֵּיתִי בְאַפִּי
My in have I that men dead the with fill to and the
anger struck of bodies them ,Chaldeans

3605 5892 6440 5640 2534
וּבַחֲמָתִי וַאֲשֶׁר הִסְתַּרְתִּי פָנַי מֵהָעִיר הַזֹּאת עַל כָּל־
all because ,this from My have I and My and
of city face hidden ,wrath

1540 7495 4832 724 5927 2009 7451
6 רָעָתָם׃ הִנְנִי מַעֲלֶה־לָּהּ אֲרֻכָה וּמַרְפֵּא וּרְפָאתִים וְגִלֵּיתִי
and will I and and health it to will ,Behold their
reveal them heal ,healing up bring I .evil

3063 7622 7725 571 7965 6283
7 לָהֶם עֲתֶרֶת שָׁלוֹם וֶאֱמֶת׃ וַהֲשִׁבֹתִי אֶת־שְׁבוּת יְהוּדָה
Judah the will I And and peace the them to
of captivity back bring .truth of abundance

2891 7223 1129 3478 7622
8 וְאֵת שְׁבוּת יִשְׂרָאֵל וּבְנִתִים כְּבָרִאשֹׁנָה׃ וְטִהַרְתִּים מִכָּל־
from will I And the at as will and ,Israel the and
them cleanse .first ,them build of captivity

834 5771 3605 5545 2398 834 5771
עֲוֺנָם אֲשֶׁר חָטְאוּ־לִי וְסָלַחְתִּי לְכוֹל־עֲוֺנוֹתֵיהֶם אֲשֶׁר
which their all will I and against they which their
iniquities pardon ,Me sinned have iniquity

8416 8342 8034 1961 6586 834 2398
9 חָטְאוּ־לִי וַאֲשֶׁר פָּשְׁעוּ בִי׃ וְהָיְתָה לִּי לְשֵׁם שָׂשׂוֹן לִתְהִלָּה
praise a ,joy a to it And against have they and against they
of name Me be will .Me rebelled which Me ,sinned have

2896 3605 8085 834 776 1471 3605 8597
וּלְתִפְאֶרֶת לְכֹל גּוֹיֵי הָאָרֶץ אֲשֶׁר יִשְׁמְעוּ אֶת־כָּל־הַטּוֹבָה
the all shall which the the all to a and
good hear ,earth of nations glory

2896 3605 7264 6342 6213
אֲשֶׁר אָנֹכִי עֹשֶׂה אֹתָם וּפָחֲדוּ וְרָגְזוּ עַל כָּל־הַטּוֹבָה וְעַל
and the all for and they and ,them for do I that
goodness tremble fear will

559 3541 6213 7965 3605
10 כָּל־הַשָּׁלוֹם אֲשֶׁר אָנֹכִי עֹשֶׂה לָּהּ׃ כֹּה | אָמַר
says Thus .it for do I that peace the all

which you say *shall be* a desert without man and without beast, in the cities of Judah, and in the streets of Jerusalem, that are desolate, without man, without inhabitant and without beast; [11]There shall be heard again the voice of joy, and the voice of gladness, the voice of the bridegroom, and the voice of the bride, the voice of those saying, Praise Jehovah of hosts, for Jehovah *is* good, for His mercy *endures* forever; those who shall bring the sacrifice of thanksgiving into the house of Jehovah. For I will bring back the captivity of the land, as at the first, says Jehovah. [12]So says Jehovah of hosts, Again in this place *which is* a waste without man or even beast, and in all its cities *shall be* a home of shepherds causing flocks to lie down. [13]In the cities of the mountains, in the cities of the lowland, and in the cities of the Negeb, and in the land of Benjamin, and in the places around Jerusalem, and in the cities of Judah, the flocks shall pass again under the hands of him who tallies, says Jehovah.

[14]Behold, the days come, says Jehovah, that I will establish the good thing which I have spoken to the house of Israel and to the house of Judah. [15]In those days and at that time I will cause a Branch of righteousness to grow up to David. And He will do judgment and righteousness in the land. [16]In those days Judah shall be saved, and Jerusalem shall dwell in safety. And this is the name that shall be called on her: Jehovah our righteousness. [17]For so says Jehovah, David shall not have cut off a man to sit

יְהוָה עוֹד יִשָּׁמַע בַּמָּקוֹם־הַזֶּה אֲשֶׁר אַתֶּם אֹמְרִים חָרֵב
a waste ,say you which this in place will there be heard Again Jehovah

הוּא מֵאֵין אָדָם וּמֵאֵין בְּהֵמָה בְּעָרֵי יְהוּדָה וּבְחֻצוֹת
the in and of streets ,Judah the in of cities ,beast and without man without it (is)

יְרוּשָׁלִַם הַנְשַׁמּוֹת מֵאֵין אָדָם וּמֵאֵין יוֹשֵׁב וּמֵאֵין בְּהֵמָה׃
—beast and without inhabi- ,tant and without ,man without are that desolate Jerusalem

11 קוֹל שָׂשׂוֹן וְקוֹל שִׂמְחָה קוֹל חָתָן וְקוֹל כַּלָּה קוֹל אֹמְרִים
those ,saying the of voice the ,bride the and of voice the voice the groom the ,gladness of the and of voice joy the of voice

הוֹדוּ אֶת־יְהוָה צְבָאוֹת כִּי־טוֹב יְהוָה כִּי־לְעוֹלָם חַסְדּוֹ
His ,mercy (endures) forever for Jehovah (is) good for ,hosts Jehovah of Praise

מְבִאִים תּוֹדָה בֵּית יְהוָה כִּי־אָשִׁיב אֶת־שְׁבוּת־הָאָרֶץ
the land the of captivity will I back bring For Jeho- ,vah's house sacrifice a thanksgiving of who into those bring

12 כָּבָרִאשֹׁנָה אָמַר יְהוָה׃ כֹּה אָמַר יְהוָה צְבָאוֹת
:hosts Jehovah of says Thus .Jehovah says the at as ,first

עוֹד יִהְיֶה ׀ בַּמָּקוֹם הַזֶּה הֶחָרֵב מֵאֵין־אָדָם וְעַד־בְּהֵמָה
;beast or even man with- out the waste ,this place in shall be Again

13 וּבְכָל־עָרָיו נְוֵה רֹעִים מַרְבִּצִים צֹאן׃ בְּעָרֵי הָהָר בְּעָרֵי
the in of cities moun- ,tain the in of cities In (their) .flocks to causing down lie shepherds an of abode its cities in and all

הַשְּׁפֵלָה וּבְעָרֵי הַנֶּגֶב וּבְאֶרֶץ בִּנְיָמִן וּבִסְבִיבֵי יְרוּשָׁלִַם
,Jerusalem the in and around places ,Benjamin in and of land the ,Negeb the in and of cities the Lowland

וּבְעָרֵי יְהוּדָה עֹד תַּעֲבֹרְנָה הַצֹּאן עַל־יְדֵי מוֹנֶה אָמַר
says who him (them) counts the under of hands the flocks shall pass again ,Judah the in and of cities

14 יְהוָה׃ הִנֵּה יָמִים בָּאִים נְאֻם־יְהוָה וַהֲקִמֹתִי אֶת־
will I that establish ,Jehovah says ,come the days ,Behold .Jehovah

הַדָּבָר הַטּוֹב אֲשֶׁר דִּבַּרְתִּי אֶל־בֵּית יִשְׂרָאֵל וְעַל־בֵּית
the and of house to Israel the of house to have I spoken which good the thing

15 יְהוּדָה׃ בַּיָּמִים הָהֵם וּבָעֵת הַהִיא אַצְמִיחַ לְדָוִד צֶמַח
branch a of to David make will I up grow ,that at and time ,those days In .Judah

16 צְדָקָה וְעָשָׂה מִשְׁפָּט וּצְדָקָה בָּאָרֶץ׃ בַּיָּמִים הָהֵם תִּוָּשַׁע
be will saved these days In the in .land righ- and teousness judgment will He and execute righ- ,teousness

יְהוּדָה וִירוּשָׁלִַם תִּשְׁכּוֹן לָבֶטַח וְזֶה אֲשֶׁר־יִקְרָא־לָהּ
,her call will one (name the) which (is) this and safety in shall dwell and Jerusalem ,Judah

17 יְהוָה ׀ צִדְקֵנוּ׃ כִּי־כֹה אָמַר יְהוָה לֹא־יִכָּרֵת לְדָוִד
David to be will off cut Not Jehovah says thus For our .righteousness Jehovah

on the throne of the house of Israel. [18]And for the Levitical priests, they shall not have a man cut off before Me to offer burnt offerings, and to kindle grain offerings, and to do sacrifice continually.

[19]And the word of Jehovah was to Jeremiah, saying, [20]So says Jehovah, If you can break My covenant of the day, and My covenant of the night, and there should not be day and night in their time, [21]*then* My covenant with My servant David may also be broken, that he should not have a son to reign on his throne; and with the Levitical priests, My ministers. [22]As the host of the heavens cannot be numbered, nor the sand of the sea measured, so I will multiply the seed of My servant David, and the Levites who minister to Me. [23]And the word of Jehovah came to Jeremiah, saying, [24]Have you not observed what these people have spoken, saying, The two families that Jehovah has chosen, He has also rejected them? And they despise My people, no more to be a nation before them. [25]So says Jehovah, If My covenant *is* not *with* day and night, *and if* I have not appointed the ordinances of the heavens and earth,

[26]then I also will reject the seed of Jacob, and My servant David, not to take of his seed *to be* rulers over the seed of Abraham, Isaac, and Jacob. For I will bring back their captivity, and have pity on them.

18 אִישׁ יֹשֵׁב עַל־כִּסֵּא בֵית־יִשְׂרָאֵל׃ וְלַכֹּהֲנִים הַלְוִיִּם לֹא

not Levitical the for and priests ;Israel the of house the of throne on sitting man a

יִכָּרֵת אִישׁ מִלְּפָנַי מַעֲלֶה עוֹלָה וּמַקְטִיר מִנְחָה וְעֹשֶׂה

and perform grain ,offerings make to and smoke burnt ,offerings offering before Me man a be will off cut

19 זֶבַח כָּל־הַיָּמִים׃ וַיְהִי דְּבַר־יְהוָה אֶל־יִרְמְיָהוּ לֵאמוֹר׃

,saying ,Jeremiah to Jehovah the of word And came .days the all sacri- fice

כֹּה אָמַר יְהוָה אִם־תָּפֵרוּ אֶת־בְּרִיתִי הַיּוֹם וְאֶת־בְּרִיתִי

cove- My of nant and the day cove- My of nant can you break If :Jehovah says Thus

20 הַלַּיְלָה וּלְבִלְתִּי הֱיוֹת יוֹמָם־וָלַיְלָה בְּעִתָּם׃ גַּם־בְּרִיתִי
21

My covenant (then) also their in ,time and night day there be should that not the ,night

תֻּפַר אֶת־דָּוִד עַבְדִּי מִהְיוֹת־לוֹ בֵן מֹלֵךְ עַל־כִּסְאוֹ וְאֶת־

and with his ,throne on reigning a son to should that him be not My ,servant David with be may broken

22 הַלְוִיִּם הַכֹּהֲנִים מְשָׁרְתָי׃ אֲשֶׁר לֹא־יִסָּפֵר צְבָא הַשָּׁמַיִם

,heaven the of host be can counted not As My .ministers the ,priests Levitical

וְלֹא יִמַּד חוֹל הַיָּם כֵּן אַרְבֶּה אֶת־זֶרַע דָּוִד עַבְדִּי וְאֶת־

and My ,servant David the of seed will I multiply so the ,sea the measured of sand nor

23 הַלְוִיִּם מְשָׁרְתֵי אֹתִי׃ וַיְהִי דְּבַר־יְהוָה אֶל־יִרְמְיָהוּ

,Jeremiah to Jehovah the of word And came .Me minister who to the Levites

24 לֵאמֹר׃ הֲלוֹא רָאִיתָ מָה־הָעָם הַזֶּה דִּבְּרוּ לֵאמֹר שְׁתֵּי

two ,saying have ,spoken these peoples what you Have seen not ,saying

הַמִּשְׁפָּחוֹת אֲשֶׁר בָּחַר יְהוָה בָּהֶם וַיִּמְאָסֵם וְאֶת־עַמִּי

My people And also He has ?them rejected ,them Jehovah has chosen which The families

25 יִנְאָצוּן מִהְיוֹת עוֹד גּוֹי לִפְנֵיהֶם׃ כֹּה אָמַר יְהוָה

:Jehovah says Thus before .them a nation yet to be not they disdain

אִם־לֹא בְרִיתִי יוֹמָם וָלַיְלָה חֻקּוֹת שָׁמַיִם וָאָרֶץ לֹא־

not and earth heaven ordi- the of nances and ,night (with) day My covenant (is) not If

26 שָׂמְתִּי׃ גַּם־זֶרַע יַעֲקוֹב וְדָוִד עַבְדִּי אֶמְאַס מִקַּחַת מִזַּרְעוֹ

his from seed not take to will I ,reject My servant and David Jacob the of seed then also have I ,appointed

מֹשְׁלִים אֶל־זֶרַע אַבְרָהָם יִשְׂחָק וְיַעֲקֹב כִּי־אָשׁוּב אֶת־

will I back bring For and .Jacob ,Isaac ,Abraham the of seed over rulers

שְׁבוּתָם וְרִחַמְתִּים׃

compassion have and .them on their captivity

CAP. XXXIV לד

CHAPTER 34

5019 3068 3414 1961 834 1697
1 הדבר אשר היה אל ירמיהו מאת יהוה ונבוכדראצר
when and Jehovah from Jeremiah to came which The
Nebuchadnezzar word
44,75 9776 4467 3605 2428,3605 884 44,28
מלך בבל וכל חילו וכל ממלכות ארץ ממשלת ידו
his because the the and his and ,Babylon king
hand rules ,earth of kingdoms all ,army all of
559 5892 3605 3389 3898 5971 3605
וכל העמים נלחמים על ירושלם ועל כל עריה לאמר:
saying its all and Jerusalem against fought the and
,cities against ,peoples all
6677 559 1980 3478 430 3068 559 3541
2 כה אמר יהוה אלהי ישראל הלך ואמרת אל צדקיהו
Zedekiah to speak and Go :Israel the Jehovah says Thus
of God
5414 2005 3068 559 3541 559 3063 44,28
מלך יהודה ואמרת אליו כה אמר יהוה הנני נתן את
will ,Behold ,Jehovah says Thus to say and Judah king
give I ,him of
3808 784 8313 8 :84 44,28 3027 2088 5892
3 העיר הזאת ביד מלך בבל ושרפה באש: ואתה לא
not And with will he and ,Babylon the the into this city
you .fire it burn of king of hand
5869 5869 5414 3027 8610 86,10 30,27 4422
תמלט מידו כי תפש תתפש ובידו תנתן ועיניך את עיני
the your And .given into and will you surely for his from will
of eyes eyes hand his ,seized be ,hand escape
935 884 1696 6310 6310 7200 884 44,28
מלך בבל תראינה ופיהו את פיך ידבר ובבל תבוא:
will you and will he your with his and ,see will Babylon the
.to go Babylon ;speak mouth mouth of king
3068 559 3541 3063 44,28 6677 30:68 1697 8085 5750
4 אך שמע דבר יהוה צדקיהו מלך יהודה כה אמר יהוה
Jehovah says Thus :Judah king O ,Jehovah the hear Yet
of Zedekiah of word
4955 4191 7965 2719 4191 38,08
5 עליך לא תמות בחרב: בשלום תמות ובמשרפות
the as and shall you peace In the by shall You not of
spices of burnings ;die .sword die .you
8313 6440 1961 834 7223 4428
אבותיך המלכים הראשנים אשר היו לפניך כן ישרפו
shall they so before were which former the your (for)
burn ,you kings ,fathers
3068 5002 1696 1697 5594 113 1945
לך והוי אדון יספדו לך כי דבר אני דברתי נאם יהוה:
.Jehovah says have I the For for will They and for
,spoken word .you lament ,lord (saying) ,you
,Ah
3063 44,28 6677 50:30 3414 1696
6 וידבר ירמיהו הנביא אל צדקיהו מלך יהודה
Judah king Zedekiah to the Jeremiah Then
of prophet spoke
884 44,28 2428 3389 428 1697 36,05
7 את כל הדברים האלה בירושלם: וחיל מלך בבל
Babylon the the when in these words all
of king of army ,Jerusalem
3498 3063 5892 3605 3389 3898
נלחמים על ירושלם ועל כל ערי יהודה הנותרות אל
against were that Judah the all and Jerusalem against fought
;left of cities against
5892 3063 5892 7604 58:25 3923
לכיש ואל עזקה כי הנה נשארו בערי יהודה ערי
cities Judah among remained those for ;Azekah and ,Lachish
of cities the against

CHAPTER 34

[1]The word which came to Jeremiah from Jehovah when Nebuchadnezzar king of Babylon and all his army, and all the kingdoms of the earth—because his hand rules—and all the peoples fought against Jerusalem, and against all its cities, saying, [2]So says Jehovah, the God of Israel: Go and speak to Zedekiah king of Judah, and tell him, So says Jehovah, Behold, I will give this city into the hand of the king of Babylon, and he shall burn it with fire. [3]And you shall not escape out of his hand, but shall surely be captured and delivered into his hand. And your eyes shall behold the eyes of the king of Babylon, and he shall speak, his mouth with your mouth; and you shall go to Babylon.

[4]Yet hear the word of Jehovah, O Zedekiah king of Judah: So says Jehovah concerning you, You shall not die by the sword. [5]You shall die in peace; and as the burnings of spices *for* your fathers, the former kings who were before you, so they shall burn spices for you, *saying,* Ah, lord! They will wail for you. For I have spoken the word, says Jehovah. [6]Then Jeremiah the prophet spoke all these words to Zedekiah king of Judah in Jerusalem, [7]when the king of Babylon's army fought against Jerusalem and against all the cities of Judah that remained; against Lachish, and against Azekah; for these fortified cities remained of the cities of Judah.

[8]The word that was to Jeremiah from Jehovah after king Zedekiah had cut a covenant with all the people in Jerusalem, to proclaim liberty to them, [9]that each man should release his male slave, and each man his slavegirl; *if* a Hebrew man or a Hebrew woman, *to go* free, that not *any* should enslave a Jew, a man, his brother among them. [10]And all the rulers obeyed, and all the people who had entered into the covenant allowed *them to* go free, each man his male slave, and each man his slavegirl; so that not *any* should enslave among them any more; and they obeyed and let *them* go. [11]But afterward they turned and made return the male slaves and the slavegirls whom they sent away. And they subjected them for male slaves and for slavegirls. [12]For this reason the word of Jehovah came to Jeremiah from Jehovah, saying, [13]So says Jehovah, the God of Israel: I cut a covenant with your fathers in the day I brought them forth out of the land of Egypt, out of the house of slavery, saying, [14]At the end of seven years each man should let go his brother *who is* a Hebrew, who has been sold to him. When he has served you six years, you shall let him go free from you. But your fathers did not listen to Me, nor bow down their ear.

[15]And you had turned today, and you did right in My eyes, to call for liberty, each man to his neighbor. And you cut a covenant before Me in the house on which is called My name. [16]But you turned and profaned My

8 מִבְצָר׃ הַדָּבָר אֲשֶׁר־הָיָה אֶל־יִרְמְיָהוּ מֵאֵת יְהוָה
,Jehovah from Jeremiah to came that The word .fortified

אַחֲרֵי כְּרֹת הַמֶּלֶךְ צִדְקִיָּהוּ בְּרִית אֶת־כָּל־הָעָם אֲשֶׁר
who (were) the people all with a covenant Zedekiah King cut had after

9 בִּירוּשָׁלִַם לִקְרֹא לָהֶם דְּרוֹר׃ לְשַׁלַּח אִישׁ אֶת־עַבְדּוֹ
male his slave each man should that go let ,liberty them to to proclaim in ,Jerusalem

וְאִישׁ אֶת־שִׁפְחָתוֹ הָעִבְרִי וְהָעִבְרִיָּה חָפְשִׁים לְבִלְתִּי עֲבָד־
should enslave that not ,free Hebrew a and woman Hebrew a man female his slave each and man

10 בָּם בִּיהוּדִי אָחִיהוּ אִישׁ׃ וַיִּשְׁמְעוּ כָל־הַשָּׂרִים וְכָל־הָעָם
the people and all the rulers all obeyed And .man a his brother Jew a among them

אֲשֶׁר־בָּאוּ בַבְּרִית לְשַׁלַּח אִישׁ אֶת־עַבְדּוֹ וְאִישׁ אֶת־
each and man male his slave man each let to go the into covenant had entered who

שִׁפְחָתוֹ חָפְשִׁים לְבִלְתִּי עֲבָד־בָּם עוֹד וַיִּשְׁמְעוּ וַיְשַׁלֵּחוּ׃
let and .go (them) they and obeyed ,again among might one so them enslave not that ,free female his slave

11 וַיָּשׁוּבוּ אַחֲרֵי־כֵן וַיָּשִׁבוּ אֶת־הָעֲבָדִים וְאֶת־הַשְּׁפָחוֹת
female the slaves and male the slaves made and return afterward they But turned

אֲשֶׁר שִׁלְּחוּ חָפְשִׁים וַיִּכְבִּישׁוּם לַעֲבָדִים וְלִשְׁפָחוֹת׃
for and .slaves female male for slaves they And them subjected .free sent they away whom

12 וַיְהִי דְבַר־יְהוָה אֶל־יִרְמְיָהוּ מֵאֵת יְהוָה לֵאמֹר׃
13 כֹּה־אָמַר
says Thus ,saying ,Jehovah from Jeremiah to Jehovah the of word came There- fore

יְהוָה אֱלֹהֵי יִשְׂרָאֵל אָנֹכִי כָּרַתִּי בְרִית אֶת־אֲבוֹתֵיכֶם בְּיוֹם
the in day your fathers with a covenant cut I :Israel the of God ,Jehovah

14 הוֹצִאִי אוֹתָם מֵאֶרֶץ מִצְרַיִם מִבֵּית עֲבָדִים לֵאמֹר׃ מִקֵּץ
the At of end ,saying ,slavery the of out of house ,Egypt the from of land them brought I out

שֶׁבַע שָׁנִים תְּשַׁלְּחוּ אִישׁ אֶת־אָחִיו הָעִבְרִי אֲשֶׁר־יִמָּכֵר
been has sold who Hebrew a his brother each man should go let years seven

לְךָ וַעֲבָדְךָ שֵׁשׁ שָׁנִים וְשִׁלַּחְתּוֹ חָפְשִׁי מֵעִמָּךְ וְלֹא־שָׁמְעוּ
did listen But not from .you free shall you then go him let ,years six he When you serves to .him

15 אֲבוֹתֵיכֶם אֵלַי וְלֹא הִטּוּ אֶת־אָזְנָם׃ וַתָּשֻׁבוּ אַתֶּם הַיּוֹם
,today you And turned their .ear incline nor to Me your fathers

וַתַּעֲשׂוּ אֶת־הַיָּשָׁר בְּעֵינַי לִקְרֹא דְרוֹר אִישׁ לְרֵעֵהוּ וַתִּכְרְתוּ
you and cut his to ,neighbor each man liberty to proclaim My in eyes right did and

16 בְרִית לְפָנַי בַּבַּיִת אֲשֶׁר־נִקְרָא שְׁמִי עָלָיו׃ וַתָּשֻׁבוּ וַתְּחַלְּלוּ
and profaned you but turned upon ,it My name been has which called the in house before Me a covenant

name, and each man caused his slave, and each man his slavegirl to return whom you had sent away according to their desire. And *you* subjected them to be slaves and slavegirls to you.
17 So Jehovah says this: You have not listened to Me, to call for liberty, each man to his brother, and each man to his neighbor. Behold, I call for freedom to you, says Jehovah: to the sword, to the plague, and to the famine. And I will cause you to be a horror to all the kingdoms of the earth.

18 And I will give the men who have transgressed My covenant, who have not stood on the words of the covenant which they have cut with Me *when they* cut the calf in two, and passed between its parts;
19 the rulers of Judah, and the rulers of Jerusalem, the eunuchs, and the priests, and all the people of the land who passed between the parts of the calf;
20 I will even give them into the hand of their enemies, and into the hand of those seeking their life. And their dead bodies shall be for food to the birds of the heavens, and to the beasts of the earth.
21 And I will give Zedekiah king of Judah, and his rulers, into the hand of their enemies, and into the hand of those seeking their life, even into the hand of the king of Babylon's army that has withdrawn from you.
22 Behold, I will command and cause them to return to this city, says Jehovah. And they shall fight against it, and take it, and burn it with fire. And I will make the cities of Judah a ruin, without a soul to live in it.

אֶת־שְׁמִי וַתָּשִׁבוּ אִישׁ אֶת־עַבְדּוֹ וְאִישׁ אֶת־שִׁפְחָתוֹ אֲשֶׁר
whom female his slave each and man male his ,slave each man made and return My ,name

שִׁלַּחְתֶּם חָפְשִׁים לְנַפְשָׁם וַתִּכְבְּשׁוּ אֹתָם לִהְיוֹת לָכֶם
you to be to them you and subjected to according ;desire their free had you out sent

17 לַעֲבָדִים וְלִשְׁפָחוֹת׃ לָכֵן כֹּה־אָמַר יְהוָה אַתֶּם
You ;Jehovah says thus Therefore for and .slave female male for slaves

לֹא־שְׁמַעְתֶּם אֵלַי לִקְרֹא דְרוֹר אִישׁ לְאָחִיו וְאִישׁ לְרֵעֵהוּ
his to neighbor each and man his to brother each man ,liberty to proclaim to Me have listened not

הִנְנִי קֹרֵא לָכֶם דְּרוֹר נְאֻם־יְהוָה אֶל־הַחֶרֶב אֶל־הַדֶּבֶר
the ,plague to the ,sword to :Jehovah says ,liberty you to proclaim Be- I ,hold

וְאֶל־הָרָעָב וְנָתַתִּי אֶתְכֶם לְזַעֲוָה לְכֹל מַמְלְכוֹת הָאָרֶץ׃
the .earth the of kingdoms all to terror a you will I and make the ,famine and to

18 וְנָתַתִּי אֶת־הָאֲנָשִׁים הָעֹבְרִים אֶת־בְּרִתִי אֲשֶׁר לֹא־הֵקִימוּ
have up raised not who My ,covenant have who transgressed the men I And give will

אֶת־דִּבְרֵי הַבְּרִית אֲשֶׁר כָּרְתוּ לְפָנַי הָעֵגֶל אֲשֶׁר כָּרְתוּ
they cut which the calf bull before ,Me have they cut which the covenant the of words

19 לִשְׁנַיִם וַיַּעַבְרוּ בֵּין בְּתָרָיו׃ שָׂרֵי יְהוּדָה וְשָׂרֵי יְרוּשָׁלַםִ
,Jerusalem the and of rulers ,Judah the of rulers its —pieces between and passed into two

הַסָּרִסִים וְהַכֹּהֲנִים וְכֹל עַם הָאָרֶץ הָעֹבְרִים בֵּין בִּתְרֵי
the of pieces between who passed the land the of people and all the and ,priests the ,eunuchs

20 הָעֵגֶל׃ וְנָתַתִּי אוֹתָם בְּיַד אֹיְבֵיהֶם וּבְיַד מְבַקְשֵׁי נַפְשָׁם
their .life who those seek into and of hand the their ,enemies the into of hand them will I give even bull the ;calf

וְהָיְתָה נִבְלָתָם לְמַאֲכָל לְעוֹף הַשָּׁמַיִם וּלְבֶהֱמַת הָאָרֶץ׃
the .earth the for and of beasts the sky the for of birds food for their bodies dead will And be

21 וְאֶת־צִדְקִיָּהוּ מֶלֶךְ־יְהוּדָה וְאֶת־שָׂרָיו אֶתֵּן בְּיַד אֹיְבֵיהֶם
their enemies' into hand will I give his rulers and Judah king of Zedekiah And

וּבְיַד מְבַקְשֵׁי נַפְשָׁם וּבְיַד חֵיל מֶלֶךְ בָּבֶל הָעֹלִים מֵעֲלֵיכֶם׃
from .you has that withdrawn Babylon's the of king of army the into and of hand their ,life who those seek into and of hand the

22 הִנְנִי מְצַוֶּה נְאֻם־יְהוָה וַהֲשִׁבֹתִים אֶל־הָעִיר הַזֹּאת וְנִלְחֲמוּ
they And fight will .this city to bring and back them ,Jehovah says will ,Behold I command

עָלֶיהָ וּלְכָדוּהָ וּשְׂרָפֻהָ בָאֵשׁ וְאֶת־עָרֵי יְהוּדָה אֶתֵּן שְׁמָמָה
deso- a ,lation will I give Judah the And of cities with .fire burn and it and ,it capture against ,it

מֵאֵין יֹשֵׁב׃
.inhabitant with- out

CAP. XXXV לה

CHAPTER 35

[1]The word which came to Jeremiah from Jehovah in the days of Jehoiakim, the son of Josiah, king of Judah, saying, [2]Go to the house of the Rechabites and speak to them, and bring them to the house of Jehovah, into one of the rooms; and give them wine to drink. [3]Then I took Jaazaniah the son of Jeremiah, the son of Habazziniah, and his brothers, and all his sons, and the whole house of the Rechabites. [4]And I brought them into the house of Jehovah, into the room of the sons of Hanan, the son of Igdaliah, a man of God, which *was* near the room of the rulers, above the room of Maaseiah the son of Shallum, the keeper of the threshold. [5]And I set bowls and cups full of wine before the sons of the house of the Rechabites. And I said to them, Drink wine. [6]But they said, We will not drink wine, for Jonadab, the son of Rechab our father, commanded us, saying, You shall not drink wine, you nor your sons forever.

[7]And you shall not build a house, nor sow seed, nor plant a vineyard, nor shall there be *anything* to you; but all your days you shall live in tents, so that you may live many days on the face of the land where you are staying. [8]And we have obeyed the voice of Jonadab, the son of Rechab our father, to all that he commanded us, to drink no wine all our days, we, our wives, our sons, and our daughters; [9]nor to build

CHAPTER 35

3079 3117 3068 3414 1961 834 1697
1 הַדָּבָר אֲשֶׁר־הָיָה אֶל־יִרְמְיָהוּ מֵאֵת יְהוָה בִּימֵי יְהוֹיָקִים
Jehoiakim the in Jehovah from Jeremiah to came which The
of days word

7397 1004 1980 559 3063 4428 2977 1121
2 בֶּן־יֹאשִׁיָּהוּ מֶלֶךְ יְהוּדָה לֵאמֹר׃ הָלוֹךְ אֶל־בֵּית הָרֵכָבִים
the the to Go ,saying ,Judah king Josiah the
Rechabites of house of of son

3957 259 3068 1004 935 1696
וְדִבַּרְתָּ אוֹתָם וַהֲבִאוֹתָם בֵּית יְהוָה אֶל־אַחַת הַלְּשָׁכוֹת
the one into ,Jehovah the bring and them and
;rooms of of house into them to speak

1121 3414 2970 3947 3196 8248
3 וְהִשְׁקִיתָ אוֹתָם יָיִן׃ וָאֶקַּח אֶת־יַאֲזַנְיָה בֶן־יִרְמְיָהוּ בֶּן־
the ,Jeremiah the Jaazaniah I Then .wine them give and
of son of son took drink to

7397 1004 3605 1121 3605 251 2262
חֲבַצִּנְיָה וְאֶת־אֶחָיו וְאֶת־כָּל־בָּנָיו וְאֵת כָּל־בֵּית הָרֵכָבִים׃
the house the and his all and his and Haba-
.Rechabites of whole ,sons ,brothers ,ziniah

3012 1121 2605 1121 3957 3068 1004 935
4 וָאָבִא אֹתָם בֵּית יְהוָה אֶל־לִשְׁכַּת בְּנֵי חָנָן בֶּן־יִגְדַּלְיָהוּ
,Igdaliah the Hanan the the into ,Jehovah the them I And
of son of sons of room of house into brought

4605 834 8269 3957 681 430 376
אִישׁ הָאֱלֹהִים אֲשֶׁר־אֵצֶל לִשְׁכַּת הַשָּׂרִים אֲשֶׁר מִמַּעַל
above which the the near which ,God man a
(was) ,rulers of room (was) of

1121 6440 5414 5592 8104 7967 4641 3957
5 לְלִשְׁכַּת מַעֲשֵׂיָהוּ בֶן־שַׁלֻּם שֹׁמֵר הַסַּף׃ וָאֶתֵּן לִפְנֵי בְּנֵי
the before Then the the ,Shallum the Maaseiah room the
of sons set I .threshold of keeper of son of

8354 559 3563 3196/4393 1375 7391 1004
בֵית־הָרֵכָבִים גְּבִעִים מְלֵאִים יַיִן וְכֹסוֹת וָאֹמַר אֲלֵיהֶם שְׁתוּ־
Drink ,them to I and and wine of full bowls the the
said ;cups Rechabites of house

6680 1 7394 1121 3122 3196/8354 559 3196
6 יָיִן׃ וַיֹּאמְרוּ לֹא נִשְׁתֶּה־יָּיִן כִּי יוֹנָדָב בֶּן־רֵכָב אָבִינוּ צִוָּה
com- father our Rechab the Jonadab for ,wine will We not they But !wine
manded of son drink ,said

1004 5769/5704 1121 3196/8354 559
7 עָלֵינוּ לֵאמֹר לֹא תִשְׁתּוּ־יַיִן אַתֶּם וּבְנֵיכֶם עַד־עוֹלָם׃ וּבַיִת
a And .forever your nor you ,wine You not ,saying ,us
house sons drink shall

1961 3808 5193 3808 3754 2232 3808 2233 1129 3808
לֹא־תִבְנוּ וְזֶרַע לֹא־תִזְרָעוּ וְכֶרֶם לֹא־תִטָּעוּ וְלֹא יִהְיֶה לָכֶם
you to shall and you not a and shall you not and shall you not
(anything) be not ,plant shall vineyard ;sow seed ,build

7227 3117 2421 3117 3605 3427 168
כִּי בָּאֳהָלִים תֵּשְׁבוּ כָּל־יְמֵיכֶם לְמַעַן תִּחְיוּ יָמִים רַבִּים
many days may you so your all shall you tents in but
live that ,days live

6963 8085 8033 1481 127 6440 5921
8 עַל־פְּנֵי הָאֲדָמָה אֲשֶׁר אַתֶּם גָּרִים שָׁם׃ וַנִּשְׁמַע בְּקוֹל
the have we So .there are you where the the on
of voice obeyed sojourning land of face

8354 6680 3605 1 7394/1121 3082
יְהוֹנָדָב בֶּן־רֵכָב אָבִינוּ לְכֹל אֲשֶׁר צִוָּנוּ לְבִלְתִּי שְׁתוֹת־
drink to com- he that all to our Rechab the Jonadab
not ,us manded ,father of son

1129 1323 1121 802 3117 3605 3196
9 יַיִן כָּל־יָמֵינוּ אֲנַחְנוּ נָשֵׁינוּ בָּנֵינוּ וּבְנֹתֵינוּ׃ וּלְבִלְתִּי בְּנוֹת
built to and our and our our ,we our all wine
not ;daughters ,sons ,wives ,days

houses for us for our dwelling; nor do we have a vineyard, or field, or seed; [10]but we live in tents, and have obeyed and done according to all that Jonadab our father commanded us. [11]But it happened when Nebuchadnezzar king of Babylon came up against the land, then we said, Come, and let us go to Jerusalem, because of the army of the Chaldeans, and because of the army of the Syrians. And we live in Jerusalem.

[12]Then the word of Jehovah was to Jeremiah, saying, [13]So says Jehovah of hosts, the God of Israel: Go and tell the men of Judah and the people of Jerusalem, Will you not receive instruction, to listen to My words? says Jehovah. [14]The words of Jonadab the son of Rechab, in which he commanded his sons not to drink wine, are done. And to this day they do not drink but obey their father's command. But I have spoken to you, rising early and speaking; and you did not listen to Me. [15]I have also sent to you all My servants the prophets, rising up early and sending, saying, Each man now return from his evil way, and amend your doings, and do not go after other gods to serve them; and you shall live in the land which I have given to you and to your fathers. But you have not bowed your ear, nor listened to Me. [16]Because the sons of Jonadab, the son of Rechab, have stood on the command of their father which he gave them, but this people has not listened to Me, [17]so

10
3427 1961 38,08 2233 7704 3754 3427 1004
בָּתִּים לְשִׁבְתֵּנוּ וְכֶרֶם וְשָׂדֶה וָזֶרַע לֹא יִהְיֶה־לָּנוּ : וַנֵּשֶׁב
we And .us to there not ,seed or or a and our for houses
dwell is ,field vineyard ,dwelling

11
1961 1 3122 6680 ,3605 6213: 8085 168
בָּאֹהָלִים וַנִּשְׁמַע וַנַּעַשׂ כְּכֹל אֲשֶׁר־צִוָּנוּ יוֹנָדָב אָבִינוּ : וַיְהִי
it But our Jonadab com- that according and have and in
,was .father us manded all to done obeyed ,tents

935 559 776 884/ 44,28 5019 6927
בַּעֲלוֹת נְבוּכַדְרֶאצַּר מֶלֶךְ־בָּבֶל אֶל־הָאָרֶץ וַנֹּאמֶר בֹּאוּ
Come we then the against Babylon king Nebuchadnezzar when
,said ,land of up came

3427 758 2428 6440 3778 2428 ,6440 ,3389 935
וְנָבוֹא יְרוּשָׁלִַם מִפְּנֵי חֵיל הַכַּשְׂדִּים וּמִפְּנֵי חֵיל אֲרָם וַנֵּשֶׁב
we so ,Aram the be- and the the because Jerusalem let and
dwell of army of cause of Chaldeans of army of to go us

12
559 3414 3068 1697 1961 3389
בִּירוּשָׁלִָם : וַיְהִי דְּבַר־יְהוָה אֶל־יִרְמְיָהוּ לֵאמֹר :
:saying ,Jeremiah to Jehovah the Then in
of word came .Jerusalem

13
376 559 1980 ,3478 430 6635 3068 559
כֹּה־אָמַר יְהוָה צְבָאוֹת אֱלֹהֵי יִשְׂרָאֵל הָלֹךְ וְאָמַרְתָּ לְאִישׁ
the to say and Go :Israel the hosts Jehovah says Thus
of men of God of

8085 4148 3947 3389 3427 3063
יְהוּדָה וּלְיוֹשְׁבֵי יְרוּשָׁלִָם הֲלוֹא תִקְחוּ מוּסָר לִשְׁמֹעַ אֶל־
to listen to instruc- you Will not :Jerusalem the and Judah
tion receive of inhabitants

14
834 7394 1121 3082 1697 69,65 3068 5002 1697
דְּבָרַי נְאֻם־יְהוָה הוּקַם אֶת־דִּבְרֵי יְהוֹנָדָב בֶּן־רֵכָב אֲשֶׁר־
(in) ,Rechab the Jonadab The carried are ?Jehovah says My
which of son out of words

2088 3117 5704 8354 38,08 31,96/8,354 1121 6680
צִוָּה אֶת־בָּנָיו לְבִלְתִּי שְׁתוֹת־יַיִן וְלֹא שָׁתוּ עַד־הַיּוֹם הַזֶּה
,this day to do they So .wine drink not to his he
drink not sons commanded

7925 1696 1 4687 8085
כִּי שָׁמְעוּ אֵת מִצְוַת אֲבִיהֶם וְאָנֹכִי דִּבַּרְתִּי אֲלֵיכֶם הַשְׁכֵּם
up rising ,you to have I But their command obey but
early spoken .father's

15
5650 3605 7971 8085 38,08 16,96
וְדַבֵּר וְלֹא שְׁמַעְתֶּם אֵלָי : וָאֶשְׁלַח אֲלֵיכֶם אֶת־כָּל־עֲבָדַי
My all you to I Also .Me to did you but and
servants sent listen not ,speaking

1870 376 4994/7725 559 79,71 7925 5030
הַנְּבִיאִים הַשְׁכֵּם וְשָׁלֹחַ לֵאמֹר שֻׁבוּ־נָא אִישׁ מִדַּרְכּוֹ
his from each now Return ,saying and up rising the
way man ,sending early ,prophets

430 310 1408 4611 3190 7451
הָרָעָה וְהֵיטִיבוּ מַעַלְלֵיכֶם וְאַל־תֵּלְכוּ אַחֲרֵי אֱלֹהִים
gods after go do and your amend and evil
not ,doings

5414 834 127 3427 5647 312
אֲחֵרִים לְעָבְדָם וּשְׁבוּ אֶל־הָאֲדָמָה אֲשֶׁר־נָתַתִּי לָכֶם
you to have I which the in dwell and serve to other
given land ,them

8085 38,08 241 5186 38,08 1
וְלַאֲבֹתֵיכֶם וְלֹא הִטִּיתֶם אֶת־אָזְנְכֶם וְלֹא שְׁמַעְתֶּם אֵלָי :
.Me to listened nor ear your have you But your to and
inclined not .fathers

16
834 1 4687 73,94/1121 3082 11,21 6965 3588
כִּי הֵקִימוּ בְּנֵי יְהוֹנָדָב בֶּן־רֵכָב אֶת־מִצְוַת אֲבִיהֶם אֲשֶׁר
which their com- the Rechab the Jonadab the have Because
father of mand of son of sons up raised

17
30,68 559/3541/3651 8085 38,08 5971 6680
צִוָּם וְהָעָם הַזֶּה לֹא שָׁמְעוּ אֵלָי : לָכֵן כֹּה־אָמַר יְהוָה
Jehovah says thus therefore ;Me to has not this but gave he
listened people ;them

Jehovah, God of hosts, the God of Israel, says this: Behold, I will bring on Judah and on all the people of Jerusalem all the evil that I have spoken against them; because I have spoken to them, but they did not listen. Yea, I have called to them, but they did not answer.

[18]And Jeremiah said to the house of the Rechabites, So says Jehovah of hosts, the God of Israel: Because you have obeyed your father Jonadab's command, and have kept all his commands, and have done according to all that he has commanded you, [19]so Jehovah of hosts, the God of Israel, says this: Jonadab, the son of Rechab, shall not have a man cut off *from* standing before Me all the days.

3063 935 2005 3478 430 6635 430
אֱלֹהֵי צְבָאוֹת אֱלֹהֵי יִשְׂרָאֵל הִנְנִי מֵבִיא אֶל־יְהוּדָה וְאֶל
and Judah on will ,Behold :Israel the ,hosts God
on bring I of God of

1696 74:51 36:05 3389 3427 3605
כָּל־יוֹשְׁבֵי יְרוּשָׁלִַם אֵת כָּל־הָרָעָה אֲשֶׁר דִּבַּרְתִּי עֲלֵיהֶם
against have I that the all Jerusalem the all
;them spoken evil of inhabitants

6030 38:08 7121 80:85 38:08 1696
יַעַן דִּבַּרְתִּי אֲלֵיהֶם וְלֹא שָׁמֵעוּ וָאֶקְרָא לָהֶם וְלֹא עָנוּ׃
did they but to have I and they but ,them to spoke I be-
.answer not ,them called listen did not .cause

6635 3068 559 3541 3414 559 7397 1004
18 וּלְבֵית הָרֵכָבִים אָמַר יִרְמְיָהוּ כֹּה־אָמַר יְהוָה צְבָאוֹת
hosts Jehovah says Thus ,Jeremiah said the to And
of Rechabites of house the

1 3082 4682 80:85 834 3478 430
אֱלֹהֵי יִשְׂרָאֵל יַעַן אֲשֶׁר שְׁמַעְתֶּם עַל־מִצְוַת יְהוֹנָדָב אֲבִיכֶם
your Jonadab the have you Because ,Israel the
,father of command obeyed of God

6180 3605 6213 4687 36:05 8104
וַתִּשְׁמְרוּ אֶת־כָּל־מִצְוֹתָיו וַתַּעֲשׂוּ כְּכֹל אֲשֶׁר־צִוָּה אֶתְכֶם׃
;you has he that according have and his all have and
commanded all to done commands kept

376 37 72/38:08 3478 430 6635 3068 559 3541
19 לָכֵן כֹּה אָמַר יְהוָה צְבָאוֹת אֱלֹהֵי יִשְׂרָאֵל לֹא־יִכָּרֵת אִישׁ
man a be shall Not ,Israel the ,hosts Jehovah says thus so
off cut of God of

3117 36:05 6440 5975 7394 1121 3122
לְיוֹנָדָב בֶּן־רֵכָב עֹמֵד לְפָנַי כָּל־הַיָּמִים׃
.days the all before stand Rechab the to
Me ing of son Jonadab

CAP. XXXVI לו

CHAPTER 36

CHAPTER 36

[1]And in the fourth year of Jehoiakim the son of Josiah, king of Judah, this word was to Jeremiah from Jehovah, saying, [2]Take a roll of a book for yourself, and write in it all the words that I have spoken to you against Israel, and against Judah, and against all the nations, from the day I spoke to you, from the days of Josiah even to this day. [3]It may be the house of Judah will hear all the evil which I plan to do to them, that they may each man turn from his evil way, and I may forgive their iniquity and their sin. [4]Then Jeremiah called Baruch, the son of Neriah. And Baruch

3063 4428 2977 1121 3079 72:43 8141 1961
1 וַיְהִי בַּשָּׁנָה הָרְבִיעִת לִיהוֹיָקִים בֶּן־יֹאשִׁיָּהוּ מֶלֶךְ יְהוּדָה
,Judah king Josiah the of fourth the in And
of of son Jehoiakim year was it

3947 559 3068 3414 2088 1697 1961
2 הָיָה הַדָּבָר הַזֶּה אֶל־יִרְמְיָהוּ מֵאֵת יְהוָה לֵאמֹר׃ קַח־לְךָ
for Take ,saying ,Jehovah from Jeremiah to this word came
yourself

1696 834 1697 36:05 3789 5612 4039
מְגִלַּת־סֵפֶר וְכָתַבְתָּ אֵלֶיהָ אֵת כָּל־הַדְּבָרִים אֲשֶׁר דִּבַּרְתִּי
have I which the all it in write and book a a
spoken words of scroll

1696 3117 1471 36:05 3063 3478
אֵלֶיךָ עַל־יִשְׂרָאֵל וְעַל־יְהוּדָה וְעַל־כָּל־הַגּוֹיִם מִיּוֹם דִּבַּרְתִּי
spoke I from the all and ,Judah and ,Israel against you to
day the ,nations against against

1004 8085 194 2088 3117 5704 2977 3117
3 אֵלֶיךָ מִימֵי יֹאשִׁיָּהוּ וְעַד הַיּוֹם הַזֶּה׃ אוּלַי יִשְׁמְעוּ בֵּית
house the will Perhaps .this day to even ,Josiah the from you to
of hear of days

62:13 2803 834 77:51 36:05 3063
יְהוּדָה אֵת כָּל־הָרָעָה אֲשֶׁר אָנֹכִי חֹשֵׁב לַעֲשׂוֹת לָהֶם
,them to do to plan I which evil the all Judah

5771 5545 74:51 1870 376 7725 4616
לְמַעַן יָשׁוּבוּ אִישׁ מִדַּרְכּוֹ הָרָעָה וְסָלַחְתִּי לַעֲוֺנָם
their will I then ;evil his from each may they so
iniquity forgive way man turn that

5374 1121 1263 34:14 7121 2403
4 וּלְחַטָּאתָם׃ וַיִּקְרָא יִרְמְיָהוּ אֶת־בָּרוּךְ בֶּן־נֵרִיָּה
.Neriah the Baruch Jeremiah Then their and
of son called .sin

wrote from the mouth of Jeremiah, all the words of Jehovah that He had spoken to him, on a roll of a book. [5]And Jeremiah commanded Baruch, saying, I am shut up; I cannot go to the house of Jehovah; [6]so you go and read in the roll the words of Jehovah that you have written from my mouth, *in* the house of Jehovah, in the ears of the people on the fasting day. And also you shall read them in the ears of all Judah who come out from their cities. [7]Perhaps their pleading will fall before Jehovah, and each man will turn from his evil way. For great *is* the anger and the wrath that Jehovah has spoken against this people.

[8]And Baruch, the son of Neriah, did according to all that Jeremiah the prophet commanded him, reading in the book the words of Jehovah *in* the house of Jehovah. [9]And it happened in the fifth year of Jehoiakim, the son of Josiah, king of Judah, in the ninth month, they called a fast before Jehovah, to all the people of Jerusalem, and to all the people who came from the cities of Judah to Jerusalem. [10]And Baruch read in the book the words of Jeremiah, *in* the house of Jehovah, in the room of Gemariah, the son of Shaphan the scribe, in the upper court, at the entrance to the New Gate of the house of Jehovah, in the ears of all the people.

[11]When Micaiah, the son of Gemariah, the son of Shaphan, had heard all the words of Jehovah out of the book, [12]then he went down into the king's house, into the scribe's room. And, behold, all the rulers were sitting there, Elishama the

ויכתב ברוך מפי ירמיהו את כל־דברי יהוה אשר־דבר
had he spoken | that | Jehovah | the of words | all | Jeremiah | the from of mouth | Baruch | And wrote

5 אליו על־מגלת־ספר׃ ויצוה ירמיהו את־ברוך לאמר
,saying | Baruch | Jeremiah | And commanded | .book a | the of scroll | on | ,him to

6 אני עצור לא אוכל לבוא בית יהוה׃ ובאת אתה וקראת
and read | you | go So | .Jehovah | the of house | go to | am I able | not | ;up shut | am I

במגלה אשר־כתבת מפי את־דברי יהוה באזני העם
the people | the in of ears | Jehovah | the of words | my from ,mouth | have you written | that | the in scroll

בית יהוה ביום צום וגם באזני כל־יהודה הבאים
who come | Judah | all | the in of ears | And also | .fasting | the on of day | Jehovah's | (in) house

7 מעריהם תקראם׃ אולי תפל תחנתם לפני יהוה וישבו
will and turn | ,Jehovah before | their supplication | fall will | Perhaps | shall you .them read | their from cities

איש מדרכו הרעה כי־גדול האף והחמה אשר־דבר
has spoken | that | the and wrath | the anger | great (is) | For | .evil | his from way | each man

8 יהוה אל־העם הזה׃ ויעש ברוך בן־נריה ככל אשר־
that | according all to | Neriah the of son | Baruch | did And | .this | people against | Jehovah

צוהו ירמיהו הנביא לקרא בספר דברי יהוה בית
(in) house | Jehovah | the of words | the in book | read to | the ,prophet | Jeremiah | com-him manded

9 יהוה׃ ויהי בשנה החמשית ליהויקים בן־יאשיהו
Josiah | the of son | of Jehoiakim | fifth | the in year | it And ,was | .Jehovah's

מלך־יהודה בחדש התשעי קראו צום לפני יהוה כל־
all (to) | Jehovah before | a fast | they proclaimed | ,ninth | the in month | ,Judah | king of

העם בירושלם וכל־העם הבאים מערי יהודה בירושלם׃
.Jerusalem to | Judah | the from of cities | who came | the people | and all | in ,Jerusalem | the people

10 ויקרא ברוך בספר את־דברי ירמיהו בית יהוה בלשכת
the in of room | ,Jehovah's | (in) house | Jeremiah | the of words | the in book | Baruch | Then read

גמריהו בן־שפן הספר בחצר העליון פתח שער בית־
the of house | Gate the | the (at) of entrance | ,upper | the in court | the scribe | Shaphan the of son | Gemariah

11 יהוה החדש באזני כל־העם׃ וישמע מכיהו בן־גמריהו
.Gemariah the of son | Micaiah | When heard had | the .people | all | the in of ears | New • | Jehovah

12 בן־שפן את־כל־דברי יהוה מעל־הספר׃ וירד בית־
house | he then to down went | ,book the | from | Jehovah | the of words | all | ,Shaphan the of son

המלך על־לשכת הספר והנה־שם כל־השרים ישבים
were sitting | the rulers | all | there | And ,behold | the .scribe's | room | into | the king's

scribe, and Delaiah the son of Shemaiah, and Elnathan the son of Achbor, and Gemariah, the son of Shaphan, and Zedekiah, the son of Hananiah, and all the rulers. [13]And Micaiah declared to them all the words that he had heard when Baruch read the book in the ears of the people. [14]And all the rulers sent Jehudi, the son of Nethaniah, the son of Shelemiah, the son of Cushi, to Baruch, saying, Take the roll in your hand, which you have read in the ears of the people, and come. So Baruch, the son of Neriah, took the roll in his hand and came to them. [15]And they said to him, Sit down now and read it in our ears. So Baruch read in their ears. [16]And it happened, when they had heard all the words, they turned each man to his companion in fear. And *they* said to Baruch, We will surely tell all these words to the king. [17]And they asked Baruch, saying, Tell us now, how did you write all these words? From his mouth? [18]And Baruch said to them, He spoke all these words to me from his mouth, and I wrote with ink on the book. [19]And the rulers said to Baruch, Go, hide yourselves, you and Jeremiah; and do not let any man know where you are.

[20]And they went in to the king, into the court. But they laid up the roll in the room of Elishama the scribe. And *they* told all the words in the ear of the king. [21]And the king sent Jehudi to take the

אֱלִישָׁמָע הַסֹּפֵר וּדְלָיָהוּ בֶן־שְׁמַעְיָהוּ וְאֶלְנָתָן בֶּן־עַכְבּוֹר
,Achbor the of son / and Elnathan / ,Shemaiah the of son / and Delaiah / the ,scribe / Elishama

13 וּגְמַרְיָהוּ בֶן־שָׁפָן וְצִדְקִיָּהוּ בֶן־חֲנַנְיָהוּ וְכָל־הַשָּׂרִים׃ וַיַּגֵּד
Then declared / the rulers. / and all / ,Hananiah the of son / and Zedekiah / ,Shephan the of son / and Gemariah

לָהֶם מִיכָיְהוּ אֵת כָּל־הַדְּבָרִים אֲשֶׁר שָׁמֵעַ בִּקְרֹא בָרוּךְ
Baruch / when read / had he heard / that / the words / all / Micaiah / to them

14 בַּסֵּפֶר בְּאָזְנֵי הָעָם׃ וַיִּשְׁלְחוּ כָל־הַשָּׂרִים אֶל־בָּרוּךְ אֶת־
Baruch / to / the rulers / all / sent And / the .people / the in of ears / the book

יְהוּדִי בֶּן־נְתַנְיָהוּ בֶּן־שֶׁלֶמְיָהוּ בֶן־כּוּשִׁי לֵאמֹר הַמְּגִלָּה
scroll the / ,saying / ,Cushi the of son / ,Shelemiah the of son / ,Nethaniah the of son / Jehudi

אֲשֶׁר קָרָאתָ בָּהּ בְּאָזְנֵי הָעָם קָחֶנָּה בְיָדְךָ וָלֵךְ וַיִּקַּח
So took / and .come / your in ,hand / it take / the ,people / the in of ears / ,it in / have you read / which

15 בָּרוּךְ בֶּן־נֵרִיָּהוּ אֶת־הַמְּגִלָּה בְּיָדוֹ וַיָּבֹא אֲלֵיהֶם׃ וַיֹּאמְרוּ
they And said / .them to / and came / his in hand / scroll the / Neriah / the of son / Baruch

אֵלָיו שֵׁב־נָא וּקְרָאֶנָּה בְּאָזְנֵינוּ וַיִּקְרָא בָרוּךְ בְּאָזְנֵיהֶם׃
.ears their in / Baruch / read So / .ears our in / and it read / now Sit down / ,him to

16 וַיְהִי כְּשָׁמְעָם אֶת־כָּל־הַדְּבָרִים פָּחֲדוּ אִישׁ אֶל־רֵעֵהוּ
his companion / to / each man / turned they fear in / the ,words / all / they when heard had / it And was

וַיֹּאמְרוּ אֶל־בָּרוּךְ הַגֵּיד נַגִּיד לַמֶּלֶךְ אֵת כָּל־הַדְּבָרִים
words / all / the to king / will We tell / surely / ,Baruch to / said and

17 הָאֵלֶּה׃ וְאֶת־בָּרוּךְ שָׁאֲלוּ לֵאמֹר הַגֶּד־נָא לָנוּ אֵיךְ כָּתַבְתָּ
you did write / how / to ,us / now Tell / ,saying / they ,asked / Baruch / And / .these

18 אֶת־כָּל־הַדְּבָרִים הָאֵלֶּה מִפִּיו׃ וַיֹּאמֶר לָהֶם בָּרוּךְ מִפִּיו
From mouth his / ,Baruch / to them / Then said / From ?mouth his / ?these / words / all

יִקְרָא אֵלַי אֵת כָּל־הַדְּבָרִים הָאֵלֶּה וַאֲנִי כֹּתֵב עַל־הַסֵּפֶר
book the / on / wrote / I and / ,these / words / all / me to / he read

19 בַּדְּיוֹ׃ וַיֹּאמְרוּ הַשָּׂרִים אֶל־בָּרוּךְ לֵךְ הִסָּתֵר אַתָּה
you / hide ,yourself / Go / ,Baruch / to / rulers the / Then said / with .ink

20 וְיִרְמְיָהוּ וְאִישׁ אַל־יֵדַע אֵיפֹה אַתֶּם׃ וַיָּבֹאוּ אֶל־הַמֶּלֶךְ
king the / to / they And in went / you .(are) / where / let do not know / a and man / and ,Jeremiah

חָצֵרָה וְאֶת־הַמְּגִלָּה הִפְקִדוּ בְּלִשְׁכַּת אֱלִישָׁמָע הַסֹּפֵר
the ,scribe / Elishama / the in of room / left they / the scroll / but / the into ,court

21 וַיַּגִּידוּ בְּאָזְנֵי הַמֶּלֶךְ אֵת כָּל־הַדְּבָרִים׃ וַיִּשְׁלַח הַמֶּלֶךְ
king the / sent So / .words the / all / king the / the in of ears / they and told

roll. And he took it out of the room of Elishama the scribe. And Jehudi read it in the king's ears, and in the ears of all the rulers who stood beside the king.
22And the king was sitting *in* the winter house in the ninth month, and with the burning fire-pan before him.
23And it happened, when Jehudi had read three or four leaves, he cut it with the scribe's knife and threw *it* into the fire that *was* in the fire-pan, until all the roll was burned up in the fire that *was* in the fire-pan.
24Yet the king and all his servants who heard these words were not afraid, nor did they tear their garments.
25But Elnathan, and Delaiah, and Gemariah had pleaded with the king that he should not burn the roll, but he would not listen to them.

26And the king commanded Jerahmeel, the son of the king, and Seraiah, the son of Azriel, and Shelemiah, the son of Abdeel, to seize Baruch the scribe and Jeremiah the prophet. But Jehovah hid them.

27Then the word of Jehovah was to Jeremiah, after the king had burned the roll, and the words which Baruch wrote from the mouth of Jeremiah, saying,
28Take for yourself another roll, and write on it all the former words that were in the first roll, which Jehoiakim the king of Judah has burned.
29And

---

476 3957 3947 4039 3065

אֶת־יְהוּדִי לָקַחַת אֶת־הַמְּגִלָּה וַיִּקָּחֶהָ מִלִּשְׁכַּת אֱלִישָׁמָע

Elishama the from of room | he And it took | .scroll the | take to | Jehudi

8269 3605 241 4428 241 3065 7121 5608

הַסֹּפֵר וַיִּקְרָאֶהָ יְהוּדִי בְּאָזְנֵי הַמֶּלֶךְ וּבְאָזְנֵי כָּל־הַשָּׂרִים

rulers the | all | the in and of ears | ,king the | the in of ears | Jehudi | read And it | the .scribe

22 2320 2779 1004 3427 4428 4428 5921 5975

הָעֹמְדִים מֵעַל הַמֶּלֶךְ׃ וְהַמֶּלֶךְ יוֹשֵׁב בֵּית הַחֹרֶף בַּחֹדֶשׁ

the in month | the ,winter | (in) house | was sitting | the Now king | .king the | beside | stood who

23 3065 7121 1961 1197 6440 254 8671

הַתְּשִׁיעִי וְאֶת־הָאָח לְפָנָיו מְבֹעָרֶת׃ וַיְהִי ׀ כִּקְרוֹא יְהוּדִי

Jehudi | had when read | And was it | .burning | before him | the brazier | and with | ,ninth

7969 1817 702 7167 8593 5608 7993

שָׁלֹשׁ דְּלָתוֹת וְאַרְבָּעָה יִקְרָעֶהָ בְּתַעַר הַסֹּפֵר וְהַשְׁלֵךְ

threw and (it) | the scribe's | with knife | tore he it | ,four or | leaves | three

784 4039 3605 8552 254 784

אֶל־הָאֵשׁ אֲשֶׁר אֶל־הָאָח עַד־תֹּם כָּל־הַמְּגִלָּה עַל־הָאֵשׁ

the fire | in | scroll the | all | was until consumed | the ,brazier | in | that (was) | the fire | into

24 899 7167 3808 6342 3808 254

אֲשֶׁר עַל־הָאָח׃ וְלֹא פָחֲדוּ וְלֹא קָרְעוּ אֶת־בִּגְדֵיהֶם

their garments | they did tear | nor | were ,afraid | Yet not | .brazier the in | that (was)

428 1697 3605 8085 5650 3605 4428

הַמֶּלֶךְ וְכָל־עֲבָדָיו הַשֹּׁמְעִים אֵת כָּל־הַדְּבָרִים הָאֵלֶּה׃

.these | words | all | heard who | his servants | and all | king the

25 8313 4428 6293 1587 1806 494

וְגַם אֶלְנָתָן וּדְלָיָהוּ וּגְמַרְיָהוּ הִפְגִּעוּ בַמֶּלֶךְ לְבִלְתִּי שְׂרֹף

should he burn | that not | the with king | had pleaded | and Gemariah | and Delaiah | Elnathan But

26 4428 6680 8085 3808 4039

אֶת־הַמְּגִלָּה וְלֹא שָׁמַע אֲלֵיהֶם׃ וַיְצַוֶּה הַמֶּלֶךְ אֶת־

king the | And commanded | .them to | would he listen | but not | the ,scroll

8018 5837/1121 8304 4428 1121 3396

יְרַחְמְאֵל בֶּן־הַמֶּלֶךְ וְאֶת־שְׂרָיָהוּ בֶן־עַזְרִיאֵל וְאֶת־שֶׁלֶמְיָהוּ

Shelemiah | and | ,Azriel | the of son | Seraiah | and | king the | the of son | Jerameel

5030 3414 5608 1263 3947 5655/1121

בֶּן־עַבְדְּאֵל לָקַחַת אֶת־בָּרוּךְ הַסֹּפֵר וְאֵת יִרְמְיָהוּ הַנָּבִא

the ;prophet | Jeremiah | and | the scribe | Baruch | seize to | Abdeel | the of son

27 310 3414 3068 1697 1961 3068 5640

וַיַּסְתִּרֵם יְהוָה׃ וַיְהִי דְבַר־יְהוָה אֶל־יִרְמְיָהוּ אַחֲרֵי ׀

after | ,Jeremiah | to | Jehovah | the of word | Then came | .Jehovah | hid but them

3789 834 1697 4039 4428 8313

שְׂרֹף הַמֶּלֶךְ אֶת־הַמְּגִלָּה וְאֶת־הַדְּבָרִים אֲשֶׁר כָּתַב

wrote | which | words the | and | ,scroll the | king the | had burned

28 312 4039 3947 7725 559 3414 6310 1263

בָּרוּךְ מִפִּי יִרְמְיָהוּ לֵאמֹר׃ שׁוּב קַח־לְךָ מְגִלָּה אַחֶרֶת

another | scroll | for Take yourself | again | ,saying | ,Jeremiah's | from mouth | Baruch

1961 834 7223 1697 3605 5921 3789

וּכְתֹב עָלֶיהָ אֵת כָּל־הַדְּבָרִים הָרִאשֹׁנִים אֲשֶׁר הָיוּ עַל־

in | were | that | former | words the | all | it upon | and write

3063 4428 3079 8313 834 7223 4039

הַמְּגִלָּה הָרִאשֹׁנָה אֲשֶׁר שָׂרַף יְהוֹיָקִים מֶלֶךְ־יְהוּדָה׃

.Judah | the of king | Jehoiakim | has burned | which | ,former | scroll the you shall say to Jehoiakim the king of Judah, So says Jehovah, You have burned this roll, saying, Why have you written on it, saying, The king of Babylon shall surely come and destroy this land, and shall cause man and beast to cease from there? [30]Therefore, so says Jehovah of Jehoiakim, king of Judah: There shall not be *one* to him to sit on the throne of David; and his dead body shall be cast out in the day to the heat, and in the night to the frost. [31]And I will punish him and his seed and his servants for their sin. And I will bring on them, and on the people of Jerusalem, and on the men of Judah, all the evil that I have spoken against them. But they did not listen.

[32]Then Jeremiah took another roll, and gave it to Baruch the scribe, the son of Neriah, who wrote in it from the mouth of Jeremiah, all the words of the book which Jehoiakim, king of Judah, had burned in the fire. And many words like them were added to them.

3068 559 3541 559 3063 44,28 3079

29 וְעַל־יְהוֹיָקִים מֶלֶךְ־יְהוּדָה תֹאמַר כֹּה אָמַר יְהוָה אַתָּה

You :Jehovah says Thus shall you Judah the Jehoiakim And
,say of king to

5921 3789 4100 559 2088 4039 8313

שָׂרַפְתָּ אֶת־הַמְּגִלָּה הַזֹּאת לֵאמֹר מַדּוּעַ כָּתַבְתָּ עָלֶיהָ

it on you have Why ,saying ,this roll have
written burned

2088 776 7843 884 44,28 935 935 559

לֵאמֹר בֹּא־יָבוֹא מֶלֶךְ־בָּבֶל וְהִשְׁחִית אֶת־הָאָרֶץ הַזֹּאת

,this land and Babylon The shall surely ,saying
destroy of king come

3068 559 3541 3651 929 120 7673

30 וְהִשְׁבִּית מִמֶּנָּה אָדָם וּבְהֵמָה׃ לָכֵן כֹּה־אָמַר יְהוָה

Jehovah says thus Therefore ?beast and man from will and
there cease make

3678 5921/3427 1961 38,08 2977 44,28 3079

עַל־יְהוֹיָקִים מֶלֶךְ יְהוּדָה לֹא־יִהְיֶה־לּוֹ יוֹשֵׁב עַל־כִּסֵּא

the on sit to to shall Not :Judah king Jehoiakim of
of throne him be (any) of

3915 7140 3117 2721 7993 1961 5038 1732

דָוִד וְנִבְלָתוֹ תִּהְיֶה מֻשְׁלֶכֶת לַחֹרֶב בַּיּוֹם וְלַקֶּרַח בַּלָּיְלָה׃

the in to and the in the to out cast shall His And .David
.night frost the ,day heat be body dead

935 5771 5650 2233 6485

31 וּפָקַדְתִּי עָלָיו וְעַל־זַרְעוֹ וְעַל־עֲבָדָיו אֶת־עֲוֺנָם וְהֵבֵאתִי

I And their (for) his and seed his and him will I And
bring will .iniquity servants punish

3605 3063 376 408 3389 3427 5921

עֲלֵיהֶם וְעַל־יֹשְׁבֵי יְרוּשָׁלַםִ וְאֶל־אִישׁ יְהוּדָה אֵת כָּל־

all ,Judah the and ,Jerusalem the and them on
of men on of people on

3414 8085 38,08 1696 7451

32 הָרָעָה אֲשֶׁר־דִּבַּרְתִּי אֲלֵיהֶם וְלֹא שָׁמֵעוּ׃ וְיִרְמְיָהוּ

Then did they But against have I that evil the
Jeremiah .listen not .them spoken

5008 5374/1121 1263 5414 312 4039 3947

לָקַח ׀ מְגִלָּה אַחֶרֶת וַיִּתְּנָהּ אֶל־בָּרוּךְ בֶּן־נֵרִיָּהוּ הַסֹּפֵר

the ,Neriah the ,Baruch to gave and another roll took
,scribe of son it

5612 1697 3605 3414 6310 5921 3789

וַיִּכְתֹּב עָלֶיהָ מִפִּי יִרְמְיָהוּ אֵת כָּל־דִּבְרֵי הַסֵּפֶר אֲשֶׁר

which book the the all Jeremiah from it on who
of words mouth the wrote

1697 3254 784 3063 44,28 3079 8363

שָׂרַף יְהוֹיָקִים מֶלֶךְ־יְהוּדָה בָּאֵשׁ וְעוֹד נוֹסַף עֲלֵיהֶם דְּבָרִים

words them to were And the in Judah king Jehoiakim had
added again .fire of burned

1992 7227

רַבִּים כָּהֵמָּה׃

like many
.them

CAP. XXXVII לז

CHAPTER 37

CHAPTER 37

[1]And king Zedekiah, the son of Josiah, reigned instead of Coniah, the son of Jehoiakim, whom Nebuchadnezzar, king of Babylon, made king in the land of Judah. [2]But not he, nor his servants, nor the people of the land, listened to the words of Jehovah which He

3079 1121 3659 8478 2977 1121 6677 44,28 44,27

1 וַיִּמְלָךְ־מֶלֶךְ צִדְקִיָּהוּ בֶּן־יֹאשִׁיָּהוּ תַּחַת כָּנְיָהוּ בֶּן־יְהוֹיָקִים

,Jehoiakim the Coniah instead Josiah the Zedekiah King And
of son of of son reigned

3808 3063 776 884 44,28 5019 4428

2 אֲשֶׁר הִמְלִיךְ נְבוּכַדְרֶאצַּר מֶלֶךְ־בָּבֶל בְּאֶרֶץ יְהוּדָה׃ וְלֹא

But .Judah the in Babylon king Nebuchadnezzar made whom
not of land of king

834 3068 1697 776 5650 8085

שָׁמַע הוּא וַעֲבָדָיו וְעַם הָאָרֶץ אֶל־דִּבְרֵי יְהוָה אֲשֶׁר

which Jehovah the to the the nor his nor he listened
of words land of people servants

spoke by Jeremiah the prophet. 3And Zedekiah the king sent Jehucal, the son of Shelemiah, and Zephaniah, the son of Maaseiah the priest, to Jeremiah the prophet, saying, Pray now for us to Jehovah our God. 4And Jeremiah came in and went out among the people, for they had not put him into prison. 5And Pharaoh's army had come forth out of Egypt. And when the Chaldeans who besieged Jerusalem heard news of them, they departed from Jerusalem.

6And the word of Jehovah was to the prophet Jeremiah, saying, 7So says Jehovah, the God of Israel, You shall say this to the king of Judah who sent you to Me to inquire of Me: Behold, Pharaoh's army, which has come out to help you, shall return to Egypt, into their own land. 8And the Chaldeans shall come again and fight against this city, and capture it, and burn it with fire. 9So says Jehovah, Do not deceive yourselves, saying, The Chaldeans will surely leave us; for they shall not leave. 10For though you had stricken the entire army of the Chaldeans who fight against you, and *only* wounded men remained among them, *yet* they would rise up, each man in his tent, and burn this city with fire.

11And it happened, when the army of the Chaldeans departed from Jerusalem because of Pharaoh's army, 12then Jeremiah went out of Jerusalem, to go into the land of Benjamin, to receive

3 דִּבֶּר בְּיַד־יִרְמְיָהוּ הַנָּבִיא׃ וַיִּשְׁלַח הַמֶּלֶךְ צִדְקִיָּהוּ אֶת־
6677 4428 7971 5030 3414 3027 1696
Zedekiah King the And sent the prophet Jeremiah the by of hand He spoke

יְהוּכַל בֶּן־שֶׁלֶמְיָה וְאֶת־צְפַנְיָהוּ בֶן־מַעֲשֵׂיָה הַכֹּהֵן אֶל־
3548 4641 1121 6846 8018 1121 3081
to the priest Maaseiah the son of Zephaniah and ,Shelemiah the son of Jehucal

יִרְמְיָהוּ הַנָּבִיא לֵאמֹר הִתְפַּלֶּל־נָא בַעֲדֵנוּ אֶל־יְהוָה
3068 4994 6419 559 5030 3414
Jehovah to us for now Pray ,saying the prophet Jeremiah

4 אֱלֹהֵינוּ׃ וְיִרְמְיָהוּ בָּא וְיֹצֵא בְּתוֹךְ הָעָם וְלֹא־נָתְנוּ אֹתוֹ
5414 3808 5971 8432 3318 935 3414 430
him they put had not for the people among went and came out Now in Jeremiah .God our

5 בֵּית הַכְּלִיא׃ וְחֵיל פַּרְעֹה יָצָא מִמִּצְרָיִם וַיִּשְׁמְעוּ
8085 4714 3318 6547 2428 3628 1004
when And heard .Egypt of had out come Pharaoh's army Then .prison a in of house

הַכַּשְׂדִּים הַצָּרִים עַל־יְרוּשָׁלַםִ אֶת־שִׁמְעָם וַיֵּעָלוּ מֵעַל
5927 8088 3389 6696 3778
from they departed of news ,them Jerusalem who besieged the Chaldeans

6 יְרוּשָׁלָםִ׃ וַיְהִי דְּבַר־יְהוָה אֶל־יִרְמְיָהוּ הַנָּבִיא
5030 3414 3068 1697 1961 3389
the ,prophet Jeremiah to Jehovah the of word Then came .Jerusalem

7 לֵאמֹר׃ כֹּה־אָמַר יְהוָה אֱלֹהֵי יִשְׂרָאֵל כֹּה תֹאמְרוּ אֶל־
559 3541 3478 430 3068 559 3541 559
to shall you say This :Israel the of God ,Jehovah says Thus ,saying

מֶלֶךְ יְהוּדָה הַשֹּׁלֵחַ אֶתְכֶם אֵלַי לְדָרְשֵׁנִי הִנֵּה ׀ חֵיל
2428 2009 1875 7971 3063 4428
army ,Behold inquire to :Me of Me to you sent who ,Judah the of king

8 פַּרְעֹה הַיֹּצֵא לָכֶם לְעֶזְרָה שָׁב לְאַרְצוֹ מִצְרָיִם׃ וְשָׁבוּ
7725 4714 776 7725 5833 3318 6547
shall And return of .Egypt his to land own shall return ,help to you to which out came Pharaoh's

הַכַּשְׂדִּים וְנִלְחֲמוּ עַל־הָעִיר הַזֹּאת וּלְכָדֻהָ וּשְׂרָפֻהָ בָאֵשׁ׃
784 8313 3920 2088 5892 3898 3778
with .fire burn and it take and ,it ,this city against and fight the Chaldeans

9 כֹּה אָמַר יְהוָה אַל־תַּשִּׁאוּ נַפְשֹׁתֵיכֶם לֵאמֹר הָלֹךְ
1980 559 5377 408 3068 559 3541
Surely ,saying ,yourselves Do deceive not ,Jehovah says Thus

10 יֵלְכוּ מֵעָלֵינוּ הַכַּשְׂדִּים כִּי לֹא יֵלֵכוּ׃ כִּי אִם־הִכִּיתֶם כָּל־
3605 5221 3212 3778 3212
the whole had you struck though For shall they not leave for the ;Chaldeans from us will leave

חֵיל כַּשְׂדִּים הַנִּלְחָמִים אִתְּכֶם וְנִשְׁאֲרוּ־בָם אֲנָשִׁים
582 7604 3898 3778 2428
men among them there and remained against ,you fight who the Chaldeans army of

מְדֻקָּרִים אִישׁ בְּאָהֳלוֹ יָקוּמוּ וְשָׂרְפוּ אֶת־הָעִיר הַזֹּאת
2088 5892 8313 6965 168 376 1856
this city burn and would they rise up his in ,tent each man ,wounded

11 בָּאֵשׁ׃ וְהָיָה בְּהֵעָלוֹת חֵיל הַכַּשְׂדִּים מֵעַל יְרוּשָׁלָםִ מִפְּנֵי
6440 3389 3778 2428 5927 1961 784
because of ,Jerusalem from Chaldeans the of army left when it And ,was with .fire

12 חֵיל פַּרְעֹה׃ וַיֵּצֵא יִרְמְיָהוּ מִירוּשָׁלַםִ לָלֶכֶת אֶרֶץ
776 3212 3389 3414 3318 6547 2428
the of land go to (into) of Jerusalem Jeremiah Then out went .Pharaoh's army

a portion from there in the midst of the people. [13]And it happened, he *being* in the gate of Benjamin, a captain of the guard *was* there, and his name *was* Irijah, the son of Shelemiah, the son of Hananiah. And he seized Jeremiah the prophet, saying, You are falling to the Chaldeans. [14]And Jeremiah said, A lie! I am not falling to the Chaldeans. But he did not listen to him. And Irijah took Jeremiah and brought him to the rulers. [15]And the rulers were angry with Jeremiah, and struck him, and put him in the prison-house, the house of Jonathan the scribe. For they had made it into a prison-house.

[16]When Jeremiah had gone into the house of the pit, and into the cells, then Jeremiah remained there many days. [17]And Zedekiah the king sent and took him out. And the king asked him secretly in his house, and said, Is there word from Jehovah? And Jeremiah said, There is. For He said, You shall be delivered into the hand of the king of Babylon. [18]And Jeremiah said to king Zedekiah, What have I sinned against you, or against your servants, or against this people, that you have put me into the house of the prison? [19]Where now *are* your prophets who prophesied to you, saying, The king of Babylon will not come against you or against this land? [20]And please hear, O my lord the king, I beg you, let my plea fall before you, and do not make me return to the house of Jonathan the scribe, that I not die there. [21]And Zedekiah the king commanded, and they committed Jeremiah into

1144 8179 1961 5971 8432 2505 1144
13 בִנְיָמִן לַחֲלִק מִשָּׁם בְּתוֹךְ הָעָם׃ וַיְהִי־הוּא בְּשַׁעַר בִּנְיָמִן
,Benjamin the in (as) it And the the in from receive to Benja-
of gate (was) he ,was .people of midst there portion a ,min

2608 1121 8018 1121 3376 8034 6488 1167 8033
וְשָׁם בַּעַל פְּקִדֻת וּשְׁמוֹ יִרְאִיָּיה בֶּן־שֶׁלֶמְיָה בֶּן־חֲנַנְיָה
,Hananiah the ,Shelemiah the Irijah his and the cap- a and
of son of son name guard of tain there

3778 559 5030 3414 8610
וַיִּתְפֹּשׂ אֶת־יִרְמְיָהוּ הַנָּבִיא לֵאמֹר אֶל־הַכַּשְׂדִּים אַתָּה
You the to ,saying the Jeremiah he And
Chaldeans ,prophet seized

3808 3778 5307 369 8267 3414 559 5307
14 נֹפֵל׃ וַיֹּאמֶר יִרְמְיָהוּ שֶׁקֶר אֵינֶנִּי נֹפֵל עַל־הַכַּשְׂדִּים וְלֹא
But the to am I not !lie A ,Jeremiah Then are
not .Chaldeans falling said .falling

8269 935 3414 3376 8610 8085
שָׁמַע אֵלָיו וַיִּתְפֹּשׂ יִרְאִיָּיה בְּיִרְמְיָהוּ וַיְבִאֵהוּ אֶל־הַשָּׂרִים׃
the to brought and Jeremiah Irijah seized so to did he
.rulers him ;him listen

1004 5414 5221 3414 8269 7107
15 וַיִּקְצְפוּ הַשָּׂרִים עַל־יִרְמְיָהוּ וְהִכּוּ אֹתוֹ וְנָתְנוּ אוֹתוֹ בֵּית
the (in) him put and ,him and Jeremiah with the were And
of house struck rulers angry

3608 1004 6213 5608 3083 1004 612
הָאֵסוּר בֵּית יְהוֹנָתָן הַסֹּפֵר כִּי־אֹתוֹ עָשׂוּ לְבֵית הַכֶּלֶא׃
.prison a into they it For the Jonathan the (in) prison
of house made had .scribe of house

8033 3427 2588 953 1004 3414 935
16 כִּי בָא יִרְמְיָהוּ אֶל־בֵּית הַבּוֹר וְאֶל־הַחֲנֻיוֹת וַיֵּשֶׁב־שָׁם
there then the and pit the the into Jeremiah had When
remained ,cells into of house entered

3947 6677 4428 7971 7227 3117 3414
17 יִרְמְיָהוּ יָמִים רַבִּים׃ וַיִּשְׁלַח הַמֶּלֶךְ צִדְקִיָּהוּ וַיִּקָּחֵהוּ
took and Zedekiah king the sent And .many days Jeremiah
.out him

1697 3426 559 5643 1004 4428 7592
וַיִּשְׁאָלֵהוּ הַמֶּלֶךְ בְּבֵיתוֹ בַּסֵּתֶר וַיֹּאמֶר הֲיֵשׁ דָּבָר מֵאֵת
from word Is ,said and secretly his in king the asked And
there house him

5414 884 4428 3027 559 3426 3414 559 3068
יְהוָה וַיֹּאמֶר יִרְמְיָהוּ יֵשׁ וַיֹּאמֶר בְּיַד־מֶלֶךְ בָּבֶל תִּנָּתֵן׃
shall you Baby- the Into He For There ,Jeremiah said And Jeho-
.given be lon's of king hand ,said .is ?vah

2398 4100 6677 4428 3414 559
18 וַיֹּאמֶר יִרְמְיָהוּ אֶל־הַמֶּלֶךְ צִדְקִיָּהוּ מֶה חָטָאתִי לְךָ
against have I What ,Zedekiah King to Jeremiah said And
,you sinned

3608 1004 5414 2088 5971 5650
וְלַעֲבָדֶיךָ וְלָעָם הַזֶּה כִּי־נְתַתֶּם אוֹתִי אֶל־בֵּית הַכֶּלֶא׃
?prison the in me you that ,this against or against or
of house put have people ,servants Your

4428 935 559 5012 5030 346
19 וְאַיֵּו נְבִיאֵיכֶם אֲשֶׁר־נִבְּאוּ לָכֶם לֵאמֹר לֹא־יָבֹא מֶלֶךְ
The shall not ,saying ,you to prophesied who your Where
of king come prophets (are) now

113 4994/8085 6258 2088 776 884
20 בָּבֶל עֲלֵיכֶם וְעַל הָאָרֶץ הַזֹּאת׃ וְעַתָּה שְׁמַע־נָא אֲדֹנִי
my O beg I ,hear Therefore ?this land or against Baby-
lord you now against you lon

3083 1004 7725 408 6440 8467 4994 5307 4428
הַמֶּלֶךְ תִּפָּל־נָא תְחִנָּתִי לְפָנֶיךָ וְאַל־תְּשִׁבֵנִי בֵּית יְהוֹנָתָן
Jonathan the me make do and before plea my please let ,king the
of house to return not ,you fall

6485 6677 4428 6680 8033 4191 5608
21 הַסֹּפֵר וְלֹא אָמוּת שָׁם׃ וַיְצַוֶּה הַמֶּלֶךְ צִדְקִיָּהוּ וַיַּפְקִדוּ
they and ,Zedekiah the Then .there die I lest the
committed king commanded ,scribe

the court of the guardhouse, and that they should give him a piece of bread out of the baker's street daily, until all the bread of the city was gone. And Jeremiah remained in the court of the guardhouse.

3117 3899 3603 5414 4307 2691 3414

אֶת־יִרְמְיָהוּ בַּחֲצַר הַמַּטָּרָה וְנָתֹן לוֹ כִכַּר־לֶחֶם לַיּוֹם

daily bread a of piece to him they gave and guard- the house, the into of court Jeremiah

3414 3427 5892 3899 3605 8552/5704 2351

מִחוּץ הָאֹפִים עַד־תֹּם כָּל־הַלֶּחֶם מִן־הָעִיר וַיֵּשֶׁב יִרְמְיָהוּ

Jeremiah And remained .city the of the bread all was gone until the ,bakers' of out street

4307 2691

בַּחֲצַר הַמַּטָּרָה׃

guard- the .house the in of court

CAP. XXXVIII לח

CHAPTER 38

[1]And Shephatiah the son of Mattan, and Gedeliah the son of Pashur, and Jucal, the son of Shelemiah, and Pashur, the son of Melchiah, heard the words that Jeremiah had spoken to all the people, saying, [2]So says Jehovah, He who remains in this city shall die by the sword, by the famine, and by the plague. But he who goes forth to the Chaldeans shall live; and his life shall be a prize; and he shall live. [3]So says Jehovah, This city shall surely be given into the hand of the king of Babylon's army, and he shall capture it. [4]And the rulers said to the king, Please let this man be put to death. For in this way he weakens the hands of the men of war who remain in this city, and the hands of all the people, in speaking these words to them. For this man does not seek the peace of this people, but the evil. [5]And Zedekiah the king said, Behold, he *is* in your hand. For the king cannot do anything against you. [6]And they took Jeremiah and threw him into the pit of Malchiah, the king's son, which *was* in the court of the guardhouse. And they let Jeremiah down

1121 3116 6583 1121 1436 4977 1121 8203 8085

1 וַיִּשְׁמַע שְׁפַטְיָה בֶן־מַתָּן וּגְדַלְיָהוּ בֶּן־פַּשְׁחוּר וְיוּכַל בֶּן־

the of son and Jucal ,Pashhur the of son and Gedaliah ,Mattan the of son Shephatiah And heard

3414 1697 4441 1121 6583 8018

שֶׁלֶמְיָהוּ וּפַשְׁחוּר בֶּן־מַלְכִּיָּה אֶת־הַדְּבָרִים אֲשֶׁר יִרְמְיָהוּ

Jeremiah that the words Malchiah the of son and Pashhur ,Shelemiah

5892 3427 3068 559 3541 559 5971 3605 1696

2 מְדַבֵּר אֶל־כָּל־הָעָם לֵאמֹר׃ כֹּה אָמַר יְהוָה הַיֹּשֵׁב בָּעִיר

city in who remains He ,Jehovah says Thus ,saying the ,people all to had spoken

3778 3318 1698 7458 2719 4191 2088

הַזֹּאת יָמוּת בַּחֶרֶב בָּרָעָב וּבַדָּבֶר וְהַיֹּצֵא אֶל־הַכַּשְׂדִּים

the Chaldeans to he But out going the by and .plague the by ,famine the by ,sword shall die this

3068 559 3541 2425 7998 5315 1961 2421

3 יְחְיֶה וְהָיְתָה־לּוֹ נַפְשׁוֹ לְשָׁלָל וָחָי׃ כֹּה אָמַר יְהוָה

:Jehovah says Thus he and .live shall a as ,prize his life to him shall and be shall ;live

3920 884 4428 2428 3027 2088 5892 5414

הִנָּתֹן תִּנָּתֵן הָעִיר הַזֹּאת בְּיַד חֵיל מֶלֶךְ־בָּבֶל וּלְכָדָהּ׃

he and .it take shall Babylon's the of king army the into of hand this city shall given be Surely

2088 376 4994 4191 4428 8269 559

4 וַיֹּאמְרוּ הַשָּׂרִים אֶל־הַמֶּלֶךְ יוּמַת נָא אֶת־הָאִישׁ הַזֶּה כִּי

For .this man Please be let executed ,king the to rulers the Therefore said

7604 4421 582 3027 7503 3652

עַל־כֵּן הוּא־מְרַפֵּא אֶת־יְדֵי אַנְשֵׁי הַמִּלְחָמָה הַנִּשְׁאָרִים ׀

who remain war the men of the of hands weakens he this in way

1697 1696 5971 3605/3027 5892

בָּעִיר הַזֹּאת וְאֵת יְדֵי כָל־הָעָם לְדַבֵּר אֲלֵיהֶם כַּדְּבָרִים

words them to in speaking the ,people all the of hands and ,this city in

2088 5971 7965 1875 369 376 428

הָאֵלֶּה כִּי ׀ הָאִישׁ הַזֶּה אֵינֶנּוּ דֹרֵשׁ לְשָׁלוֹם לָעָם הַזֶּה כִּי

but ,this of people peace the seek does not this man for ;these

3027 2009 6667 4428 559 7451

5 אִם־לְרָעָה׃ וַיֹּאמֶר הַמֶּלֶךְ צִדְקִיָּהוּ הִנֵּה־הוּא בְּיֶדְכֶם כִּי־

For your in .hand he (is) ,Behold ,Zedekiah ,king the Then said .evil the

7993 3414 3947 1697 3201 4428 369

6 אֵין הַמֶּלֶךְ יוּכַל אֶתְכֶם דָּבָר׃ וַיִּקְחוּ אֶת־יִרְמְיָהוּ וַיַּשְׁלִכוּ

and threw Jeremiah Then took they (any) .thing against you able is to do king the not

4307 2691 834 4428 1121 4441 953

אֹתוֹ אֶל־הַבּוֹר ׀ מַלְכִּיָּהוּ בֶן־הַמֶּלֶךְ אֲשֶׁר בַּחֲצַר הַמַּטָּרָה

guard- the house the in of court which (was) the ,king the of son Malchiah the of pit into him with ropes; but no water was in the pit, only mud. So Jeremiah sank into the mud.

[7]And Ebed-melech, the Ethiopian man, of the eunuchs which *were* in the king's house, heard that they had put Jeremiah into the pit — the king then sitting in the gate of Benjamin— [8]Ebed-melech went out of the king's house and spoke to the king, saying, [9]My lord the king, these men have done evil in all that they have done to Jeremiah the prophet, whom they have thrown into the pit. And he has died in his place because of the famine; for there is no more food in the city. [10]And the king commanded Ebed-melech the Ethiopian, saying, Take in your hand thirty men from here, and lift Jeremiah the prophet out of the pit before he dies.

[11]And Ebed-melech took the men in his hand, and went into the king's house, to under the treasury. And he took worn-out clothes, and worn-out rags from there, and let them down by ropes into the pit to Jeremiah. [12]And Ebed-melech the Ethiopian said to Jeremiah, Now put *these* old worn out clothes and rags under your armpits, under the ropes. And Jeremiah did so. [13]And they drew up Jeremiah with ropes, and took him out of the pit. And Jeremiah lived in the court of the guard-house.

[14]Then Zedekiah the king sent and took Jeremiah the

43 25 953 2256 3414 79 71
וַיְשַׁלְּחוּ אֶת־יִרְמְיָהוּ בַּחֲבָלִים וּבַבּוֹר אֵין־מַיִם כִּי אִם־
only ,water not in and with Jeremiah they And
was pit the ,ropes down let

3569 56 63 8085 2916 3414 2883 2916
7 טִיט וַיִּטְבַּע יִרְמְיָהוּ בַּטִּיט׃ וַיִּשְׁמַע עֶבֶד־מֶלֶךְ הַכּוּשִׁי
the ,melech Ebed- And the into Jeremiah sank So .mud
Ethiopian heard .mud

3414 5414 44 28 1004 56 31 376
אִישׁ סָרִיס וְהוּא בְּבֵית הַמֶּלֶךְ כִּי־נָתְנוּ אֶת־יִרְמְיָהוּ אֶל־
into Jeremiah they that the in which the man
put had ,king's house (was) eunuchs of

1004 56 63 3318 1144 8179 3427 44 28 953
8 הַבּוֹר וְהַמֶּלֶךְ יוֹשֵׁב בְּשַׁעַר בִּנְיָמִן׃ וַיֵּצֵא עֶבֶד־מֶלֶךְ מִבֵּית
of melech Ebed- and ;Benjamin the in sitting the and ;pit the
house out went of gate king

74 89 44 28 113 559 44 28 1696 44 28
9 הַמֶּלֶךְ וַיְדַבֵּר אֶל־הַמֶּלֶךְ לֵאמֹר׃ אֲדֹנִי הַמֶּלֶךְ הֵרֵעוּ
done have the My ,saying ,king the to and the
evil ,king lord 428 spoke king's

50 30 3414 6213 36 105 582
הָאֲנָשִׁים הָאֵלֶּה אֵת כָּל־אֲשֶׁר עָשׂוּ לְיִרְמְיָהוּ הַנָּבִיא
the to have they that in these men
,prophet Jeremiah done all

7458 6440 8478 4191 953 7993 834
אֵת אֲשֶׁר־הִשְׁלִיכוּ אֶל־הַבּוֹר וַיָּמָת תַּחְתָּיו מִפְּנֵי הָרָעָב
the because his in he And the into have they whom
,famine of place died has .pit thrown

5663 44 28 6680 5892 5750 3899 369
10 כִּי אֵין הַלֶּחֶם עוֹד בָּעִיר׃ וַיְצַוֶּה הַמֶּלֶךְ אֵת עֶבֶד־מֶלֶךְ
melech Ebed- king the Then the in more food there for
commanded .city no is

59 27 582 7970 3027 3947 559 3569
הַכּוּשִׁי לֵאמֹר קַח בְּיָדְךָ מִזֶּה שְׁלֹשִׁים אֲנָשִׁים וְהַעֲלִיתָ
lift and ,men thirty from your in Take ,saying the
up here hand ,Ethiopian

5663 3947 4191 2962 953 5030 3414
11 אֶת־יִרְמְיָהוּ הַנָּבִיא מִן־הַבּוֹר בְּטֶרֶם יָמוּת׃ וַיִּקַּח עֶבֶד
Ebed- So .dies he before the out the Jeremiah
took pit of prophet

8478 44 28 1004 935 30 27 582 5663
מֶלֶךְ אֶת־הָאֲנָשִׁים בְּיָדוֹ וַיָּבֹא בֵית־הַמֶּלֶךְ אֶל־תַּחַת
under to the house went and his in the melech
king's into hand men

4418 1094 5499 1094 8033 3947 214
הָאוֹצָר וַיִּקַּח מִשָּׁם בְּלוֹיֵ הַסְּחָבוֹת וּבְלוֹיֵ מְלָחִים
rags and clothes worn from he And the
out worn out there took .treasury

5663 559 2256 953 3414 797 1
12 וַיְשַׁלְּחֵם אֶל־יִרְמְיָהוּ אֶל־הַבּוֹר בַּחֲבָלִים׃ וַיֹּאמֶר עֶבֶד
Ebed- said And .ropes by the into Jeremiah to let and
pit down them

5499 1094 4994 7760 3414 35 69 56 63
מֶלֶךְ הַכּוּשִׁי אֶל־יִרְמְיָהוּ שִׂים נָא בְּלוֹאֵי הַסְּחָבוֹת
clothes (these) now Put .Jeremiah to the melech
out worn Ethiopian

6213 2256 8478 3027 679 8478 4418
וְהַמְּלָחִים תַּחַת אַצִּלוֹת יָדֶיךָ מִתַּחַת לַחֲבָלִים וַיַּעַשׂ
And the under your arm- the under rags and
did ,ropes ,hands of pits

5927 2256 3414 4900 3651 3414
13 יִרְמְיָהוּ כֵּן׃ וַיִּמְשְׁכוּ אֶת־יִרְמְיָהוּ בַּחֲבָלִים וַיַּעֲלוּ אֹתוֹ
him took and with Jeremiah they So .so Jeremiah
out ropes up drew

44 28 7971 4307 2691 3414 3427 953
14 מִן־הַבּוֹר וַיֵּשֶׁב יִרְמְיָהוּ בַּחֲצַר הַמַּטָּרָה׃ וַיִּשְׁלַח הַמֶּלֶךְ
the Then guard- the the in Jeremiah And the of
king sent .house of court dwelt .pit

prophet to him, into the third entrance that is in the house of Jehovah. And the king said to Jeremiah, I will ask you one thing; do not hide a thing from me.
15And Jeremiah said to Zedekiah, If I declare *it* to you, will you not surely put me to death? And if I counsel you, you will not listen to me.
16And Zedekiah the king swore secretly to Jeremiah, saying, *As* Jehovah lives, who made us this soul, I will not put you to death, nor will I give you into the hand of these men who seek your life.
17Then Jeremiah said to Zedekiah, So says Jehovah, the God of hosts, the God of Israel: If you will surely go out to the king of Babylon's rulers, then your soul shall live, and this city shall not be burned with fire. And you and your house shall live.
18But if you will not go out to the king of Babylon's rulers, then this city shall be given into the hands of the Chaldeans, and they shall burn it with fire. And you shall not escape out of their hand.
19And Zedekiah the king said to Jeremiah, I am afraid of the Jews who have fallen to the Chaldeans, lest they deliver me into their hand, and they abuse me.
20But Jeremiah said, They will not deliver *you*. I beg you, obey the voice of Jehovah which I speak to you, and it will be well to you, and your soul will live.
21But if you refuse to go out, this *is* the word Jehovah

צִדְקִיָּהוּ וַיִּקַּח אֶת־יִרְמְיָהוּ הַנָּבִיא אֵלָיו אֶל־מָבוֹא הַשְּׁלִישִׁי
the third | entrance into | to him | the prophet | Jeremiah | and took | Zedekiah

אֲשֶׁר בְּבֵית יְהוָה וַיֹּאמֶר הַמֶּלֶךְ אֶל־יִרְמְיָהוּ שֹׁאֵל אֲנִי
I will ask | ,Jeremiah | to | king the | said And | .Jehovah | the in of house | that (is)

15 אֹתְךָ דָּבָר אַל־תְּכַחֵד מִמֶּנִּי דָּבָר׃ וַיֹּאמֶר יִרְמְיָהוּ אֶל־
to | Jeremiah | said Then | (any) .thing | from me | hide do | not | (one) ;thing | you

צִדְקִיָּהוּ כִּי אַגִּיד לְךָ הֲלוֹא הָמֵת תְּמִיתֵנִי וְכִי אִיעָצְךָ
counsel I ,you | And if | you will ?me execute | surely | not | to ,you | declare I (it) | If | ,Zedekiah

16 לֹא תִשְׁמַע אֵלָי׃ וַיִּשָּׁבַע הַמֶּלֶךְ צִדְקִיָּהוּ אֶל־יִרְמְיָהוּ
Jeremiah | to | Zedekiah | king the | And swore | .me to | will you listen | not

בַּסֵּתֶר לֵאמֹר חַי־יְהוָה אֵת אֲשֶׁר עָשָׂה־לָנוּ אֶת־הַנֶּפֶשׁ
soul | for us | made | who | ,Jehovah (As) lives | ,saying | ,secretly

הַזֹּאת אִם־אֲמִיתֶךָ וְאִם־אֶתֶּנְךָ בְּיַד הָאֲנָשִׁים הָאֵלֶּה אֲשֶׁר
who | these | men | the into of hand | will I you give not | and | will I you execute | not | ,this

17 מְבַקְשִׁים אֶת־נַפְשֶׁךָ׃ וַיֹּאמֶר יִרְמְיָהוּ אֶל־צִדְקִיָּהוּ
,Zedekiah | to | Jeremiah | said Then | .life your | seek

כֹּה־אָמַר יְהוָה אֱלֹהֵי צְבָאוֹת אֱלֹהֵי יִשְׂרָאֵל אִם־יָצֹא תֵצֵא
will you surely out go | If | :Israel | the of God | ,hosts | the of God | ,Jehovah | says Thus

אֶל־שָׂרֵי מֶלֶךְ־בָּבֶל וְחָיְתָה נַפְשֶׁךָ וְהָעִיר הַזֹּאת לֹא תִשָּׂרֵף
shall burned be | not | this | city and | your ,soul | shall then live | Baby- ,lon's | the of king | princes to

18 בָּאֵשׁ וְחָיִתָה אַתָּה וּבֵיתֶךָ׃ וְאִם לֹא־תֵצֵא אֶל־שָׂרֵי מֶלֶךְ
the of king | princes | to | will you out go | not | But if | your and .house | you | shall and live | with ;fire

בָּבֶל וְנִתְּנָה הָעִיר הַזֹּאת בְּיַד הַכַּשְׂדִּים וּשְׂרָפוּהָ בָּאֵשׁ
with ,fire | they and it burn shall | the ,Chaldeans | the into of hands | this | city | shall then given be | Baby- ,lon's

19 וְאַתָּה לֹא־תִמָּלֵט מִיָּדָם׃ וַיֹּאמֶר הַמֶּלֶךְ צִדְקִיָּהוּ
Zedekiah | king the | said And | of out .hand their | shall escape | not | you and

אֶל־יִרְמְיָהוּ אֲנִי דֹאֵג אֶת־הַיְּהוּדִים אֲשֶׁר נָפְלוּ אֶל־
to | have fallen | who | the Jews | am of afraid | I | ,Jeremiah | to

20 הַכַּשְׂדִּים פֶּן־יִתְּנוּ אֹתִי בְּיָדָם וְהִתְעַלְּלוּ־בִי׃ וַיֹּאמֶר
said But | .me | they and abuse | their into ,hand | me | they lest deliver | the ,Chaldeans

יִרְמְיָהוּ לֹא יִתֵּנוּ שְׁמַע־נָא בְּקוֹל יְהוָה לַאֲשֶׁר אֲנִי דֹּבֵר
am speaking | I | which | Jehovah | the of voice | please obey | They ; give shall | not | Jere- ,miah

21 אֵלֶיךָ וְיִיטַב לְךָ וּתְחִי נַפְשֶׁךָ׃ וְאִם־מָאֵן אַתָּה לָצֵאת זֶה
this (is) | go to ,out | you | refuse | But if | your .soul | will and live | with it and ,you well be will | ;you to

has made me see: [22]Even, behold, all the women who are left in the king of Judah's house shall be brought out to the king of Babylon's rulers. And they will say, Your friends have seduced you, and have prevailed against you. Your feet have sunk in the mire; they have turned back. [23]And they shall bring out all your wives, and your sons, to the Chaldeans. And you shall not escape out of their hand, but shall be taken by the hand of the king of Babylon. And you shall cause this city to be burned with fire.

[24]Then Zedekiah said to Jeremiah, Let no man know of these words, and you shall not die. [25]But if the rulers hear that I have talked with you, and they come to you and say to you, Tell us now what you said to the king; do not hide it from us, and we will not put you to death; also, what did the king say to you; [26]then you shall say to them, I was presenting my plea before the king, that he would not return me to the house of Jonathan to die there. [27]And all the rulers came to Jeremiah and asked him. And he told them according to all these words that the king had commanded. And they were quiet with him, because the matter was not heard. [28]And Jeremiah lived in the court of the guard-house until the day Jerusalem was captured. And he was *there* when Jerusalem was captured.

7604 834 802 3605 2009 3068 7200 834 1697
22 הַדָּבָר אֲשֶׁר הִרְאַנִי יְהוָה׃ וְהִנֵּה כָל־הַנָּשִׁים אֲשֶׁר נִשְׁאֲרוּ
left are who the all And :Jehovah has which the
women ;behold me shown word

884 4428 8269 3318 3063 4428 559
בְּבֵית מֶלֶךְ־יְהוּדָה מוּצָאוֹת אֶל־שָׂרֵי מֶלֶךְ בָּבֶל וְהֵנָּה
and ,Babylon's the princes to be shall Judah's the in
they of king out brought of king house

7272 1206 2883 7965 582 3201 5496 559
אֹמְרוֹת הִסִּיתוּךָ וְיָכְלוּ לְךָ אַנְשֵׁי שְׁלֹמֶךָ הָטְבְּעוּ בַבֹּץ רַגְלֶךָ
Your the in have your The against have and have shall
feet mire sunk ;peace of men you prevailed seduced ,say

3318 1121 802 3605 268 5472
23 נָסֹגוּ אָחוֹר׃ וְאֶת־כָּל־נָשֶׁיךָ וְאֶת־בָּנֶיךָ מוֹצִאִים אֶל־
to shall they your and your all And .back they and
out bring sons wives turned

884 4428 3027 3027 4422 3808 3778
הַכַּשְׂדִּים וְאַתָּה לֹא־תִמָּלֵט מִיָּדָם כִּי בְיַד מֶלֶךְ־בָּבֶל
Babylon the the by but of out shall not And the
of king of hand hand their escape you .Chaldeans

559 784 8313 2088 5892 8610
24 תִּתָּפֵשׂ וְאֶת־הָעִיר הַזֹּאת תִּשְׂרֹף בָּאֵשׁ׃ וַיֹּאמֶר
Then with be shall this city And be shall
said .fire burned seized

3808 428 1697 3045 408 376 3414 6667
צִדְקִיָּהוּ אֶל־יִרְמְיָהוּ אִישׁ אַל־יֵדַע בַּדְּבָרִים־הָאֵלֶּה וְלֹא
and ,these of Let not a ,Jeremiah to Zedekiah
not words know man

935 1696 8269 8085 4191
25 תָמוּת׃ וְכִי־יִשְׁמְעוּ הַשָּׂרִים כִּי־דִבַּרְתִּי אִתָּךְ וּבָאוּ אֵלֶיךָ
to they and with have I that the hear But shall you
you come ,you talked rulers if .die

408 4428 1696 4100 4994 5046 559
וְאָמְרוּ אֵלֶיךָ הַגִּידָה־נָּא לָנוּ מַה־דִּבַּרְתָּ אֶל־הַמֶּלֶךְ אַל־
not the to you what us now Tell ,you to say and
;king said

559 4428 1696 4100 4191 3808 3584
26 תְּכַחֵד מִמֶּנּוּ וְלֹא נְמִיתֶךָ וּמַה־דִּבֶּר אֵלֶיךָ הַמֶּלֶךְ׃ וְאָמַרְתָּ
you then the you to said also will we and from hide do
say shall ;king what ;kill you not ,us (it)

7725 4428 6440 8467 5307
אֲלֵיהֶם מַפִּיל־אֲנִי תְחִנָּתִי לִפְנֵי הַמֶּלֶךְ לְבִלְתִּי הֲשִׁיבֵנִי
would he not that ,king the before my I was ,them to
to me return plea presenting

8269 3605 935 8033 4191 3083 1004
27 בֵּית יְהוֹנָתָן לָמוּת שָׁם׃ וַיָּבֹאוּ כָל־הַשָּׂרִים אֶל־
to the all Then .there die to Jonathan's house
rulers came

428 1697 3605 5046 7592 3414
יִרְמְיָהוּ וַיִּשְׁאֲלוּ אֹתוֹ וַיַּגֵּד לָהֶם כְּכָל־הַדְּבָרִים הָאֵלֶּה אֲשֶׁר
that these words according them he And .him and Jeremiah
all to told asked

3427 1697 8085 3808 2790 4428 6680
28 צִוָּה הַמֶּלֶךְ וַיַּחֲרִשׁוּ מִמֶּנּוּ כִּי לֹא־נִשְׁמַע הַדָּבָר׃ וַיֵּשֶׁב
So the was not for with they And the had
lived .matter heard ;him quiet were .king ordered

3389 3920 3117/5704 4307 2691 3414
יִרְמְיָהוּ בַּחֲצַר הַמַּטָּרָה עַד־יוֹם אֲשֶׁר־נִלְכְּדָה יְרוּשָׁלָםִ
;Jerusalem was the until guard- the the in Jeremiah
captured day house of court

3389 3920 1961
וְהָיָה כַּאֲשֶׁר נִלְכְּדָה יְרוּשָׁלָםִ׃
.Jerusalem was when he and
captured (present) was

CHAPTER 39

[1]In the ninth year of Zedekiah king of Judah, in the tenth month, Nebuchadnezzar king of Babylon and all his army went up against Jerusalem, and they besieged it. [2]In the eleventh year of Zedekiah, in the fourth month, the ninth of the month, the city was breached. [3]And all the rulers of the king of Babylon went in and sat in the middle gate: Nergal-sharezer; Samgar-nebo; Sarcechim, chief of the eunuchs; Nergal-sharezer; Rab-mag; and all the rest of the rulers of the king of Babylon.

[4]And it happened when Zedekiah the king of Judah and all the men of war saw them, they fled and went out from the city by night, the way of the king's garden, by the gate between the two walls. And he went the way of the Arabah. [5]But the Chaldean army ran after them and overtook Zedekiah in the Arabah of Jericho. And they took him and made him go up to Nebuchadnezzar king of Babylon, *to* Riblah in the land of Hamath, where he spoke judgment on him. [6]And the king of Babylon slaughtered the sons of Zedekiah before his eyes at Riblah. Also the king of Babylon slaughtered all the rulers of Judah. [7]And he blinded the eyes of Zedekiah and bound him in bronze fetters, to make him go to Babylon.

[8]And the Chaldeans burned the king's house and the houses of the people with fire. And *they* broke down the walls of

CAP. XXXIX לט

CHAPTER 39

6224 2320 3063 4428 6677 8671 8141
1 בִּשְׁנָה הַתְּשִׁעִית לְצִדְקִיָּהוּ מֶלֶךְ־יְהוּדָה בַּחֹדֶשׁ הָעֲשִׂרִי
,tenth | the in month | ,Judah | king of | Zedekiah of | ninth | the In year

6696 3389 2428 3605 884 4428 5019 935
בָּא נְבוּכַדְרֶאצַּר מֶלֶךְ־בָּבֶל וְכָל־חֵילוֹ אֶל־יְרוּשָׁלַםִ וַיָּצֻרוּ
they and besieged | Jeru- ,salem | against | his army | and all | Babylon | king of | Nebuchadnezzar | came

7243 2320 6677 8141 6240 6249
2 עָלֶיהָ׃ בְּעַשְׁתֵּי־עֶשְׂרֵה שָׁנָה לְצִדְקִיָּהוּ בַּחֹדֶשׁ הָרְבִיעִי
,fourth | the in month | of ,Zedekiah | year | the In eleventh | .it

8269 3605/935 5892 1234 2320 8672
3 בְּתִשְׁעָה לַחֹדֶשׁ הָבְקְעָה הָעִיר׃ וַיָּבֹאוּ כֹּל שָׂרֵי
the of rulers | all | And in came | .city the | was breached | the of ,month | the ninth

5562 5371 8432 8179 3427 884 4428
מֶלֶךְ־בָּבֶל וַיֵּשְׁבוּ בְּשַׁעַר הַתָּוֶךְ נֵרְגַל שַׂרְאֶצֶר סַמְגַּר־נְבוֹ
nebo Samgar- | ,sharezer Nergal- | the :middle | gate in | and sat | Babylon | the of king

7611 3605 7248 5371 5631 7227 8310
שַׂרְסְכִים רַב־סָרִיס נֵרְגַל שַׂרְאֶצֶר רַב־מָג וְכָל־שְׁאֵרִית
the of rest | and all | mag Rab- | ,sharezer Nergal- | the ,eunuchs | chief of | ,Sarsechim

3063 4428 6677 7200 1961 884 4428 8269
4 שָׂרֵי מֶלֶךְ־בָּבֶל׃ וַיְהִי כַּאֲשֶׁר רָאָם צִדְקִיָּהוּ מֶלֶךְ־יְהוּדָה
Judah | king of | Zedekiah | saw them | when ,was | it And | .Babylon | the of king | the of rulers

1870 5892 3915 3318 1272 4421 582 3605
וְכֹל אַנְשֵׁי הַמִּלְחָמָה וַיִּבְרְחוּ וַיֵּצְאוּ לַיְלָה מִן־הָעִיר דֶּרֶךְ
the (by) of way | the from ,city | by night | went and out | they ,fled | the ,war | men of | and all

6160 1870 3318 2346 996 8179 4428 1588
גַּן הַמֶּלֶךְ בְּשַׁעַר בֵּין הַחֹמֹתָיִם וַיֵּצֵא דֶּרֶךְ הָעֲרָבָה׃
the .Arabah | the (by) of way | And went he | two the .walls | between | the by gate | the ,king's | garden

6160 6677 5381 310 3778 2428 7291
5 וַיִּרְדְּפוּ חֵיל־כַּשְׂדִּים אַחֲרֵיהֶם וַיַּשִּׂגוּ אֶת־צִדְקִיָּהוּ בְּעַרְבוֹת
the in of Arabah | Zedekiah | and overtook | after them | the Chaldeans | the of army | But pursued

884 4428 5019 5927 3947 3405
יְרֵחוֹ וַיִּקְחוּ אֹתוֹ וַיַּעֲלֻהוּ אֶל־נְבוּכַדְרֶאצַּר מֶלֶךְ־בָּבֶל
,Babylon | king of | Nebuchadnezzar | to | brought and up him | ,him | they And took | Jeri- .cho

7819 4941 1696 2574 776 7247
6 רִבְלָתָה בְּאֶרֶץ חֲמָת וַיְדַבֵּר אִתּוֹ מִשְׁפָּטִים׃ וַיִּשְׁחַט
And slaughtered | .judgment | him on | he where spoke | ,Hamath | the in of land | (to) Riblah

2715 5869 7247 6677 1121 884 4428
מֶלֶךְ בָּבֶל אֶת־בְּנֵי צִדְקִיָּהוּ בְּרִבְלָה לְעֵינָיו וְאֵת כָּל־חֹרֵי
the of rulers | all | Also | before .eyes his | Riblah at | Zedekiah | the of sons | Babylon | the of king

631 5786 6677 5892 884 4428 7819 3063
7 יְהוּדָה שָׁחַט מֶלֶךְ בָּבֶל׃ וְאֶת־עֵינֵי צִדְקִיָּהוּ עִוֵּר וַיַּאַסְרֵהוּ
bound and him | he ,blinded | Zedekiah | the of eyes | And | .Babylon | the of king | killed | Judah

1004 4428 1004 884 935 5178
8 בַּנְחֻשְׁתַּיִם לָבִיא אֹתוֹ בָּבֶלָה׃ וְאֶת־בֵּית הַמֶּלֶךְ וְאֶת־בֵּית
the of houses | and | the king's | house | And | to .Babylon | him carry to | bronze in ,fetters

5422 3389 2346 784 3778 8313
הָעָם שָׂרְפוּ הַכַּשְׂדִּים בָּאֵשׁ וְאֶת־חוֹמוֹת יְרוּשָׁלַםִ נָתָצוּ׃
broke .down | Jerusalem | the of walls | and | with ,fire | the Chaldeans | burned | the people

Jerusalem.
[9]Then Nebuzar-adan the chief of the executioners deported *to* Babylon the rest of the people who remained in the city, and those who fell away, who fell to him with the rest of the people who remained. [10]But Nebuzar-adan, the chief of the executioners, left *some* of the poor people, who had not a thing *belonging* to them, in the land of Judah, and gave to them vineyards and fields on that day.
[11]And Nebuchadnezzar king of Babylon gave an order concerning Jeremiah to the chief of the executioners, Nebuzar-adan, saying, [12]Take him, and set your eyes on him. But do not do any evil to him. But do with him even as he shall say to you. [13]And Nebuzar-adan, the chief of the executioners, and Nebushasban, chief of the eunuchs, and Nergal-sharezer, Rabmag, and all the king of Babylon's leaders sent; [14]they even sent and took Jeremiah out of the court of the guardhouse. And they gave him to Gedaliah, the son of Ahikam, the son of Shaphan, to take him to the house. And he lived among the people.

[15]And the word of Jehovah was to Jeremiah while he was shut up in the court of the guardhouse, saying, [16]Go and speak to Ebed-melech the Ethiopian, saying, So says Jehovah of hosts, the God of Israel: Behold, I am bringing My words on this city for evil, and not for good. And they shall be before you in that day. [17]But I will deliver you in that day, declares Jehovah. And you shall not be given into the hand of the men, of those whom you fear. [18]For I will surely

4307 834 5307 5892 7604 5971 3499 227
9 וְאֵת יֶתֶר הָעָם הַנִּשְׁאָרִים בָּעִיר וְאֶת־הַנֹּפְלִים אֲשֶׁר נָפְלוּ
fell who who those and the in who the the Then
,away fell ,city remained people of rest
2876 7227 5018 1540 7604 5971 3499
עָלָיו וְאֵת יֶתֶר הָעָם הַנִּשְׁאָרִים הֶגְלָה נְבוּזַרְאֲדָן רַב־טַבָּחִים
the of chief the Nebuzar- deported who the the and to
,executioners adan remained people of rest ,him
7604 3972 369 834 1800 5971 884
10 בָּבֶל׃ וּמִן־הָעָם הַדַּלִּים אֲשֶׁר אֵין־לָהֶם מְאוּמָה הִשְׁאִיר
left ,thing a to was who ,poor the But (to)
them not people of .Babylon
3754 5414 3063 776 2876 7227 5018
נְבוּזַרְאֲדָן רַב־טַבָּחִים בְּאֶרֶץ יְהוּדָה וַיִּתֵּן לָהֶם כְּרָמִים
vineyards to and ,Judah the in the of chief the Nebuzar-
them gave of land ,executioners adan
884 4428 5019 6680 3117 3010
11 וִיגֵבִים בַּיּוֹם הַהוּא׃ וַיְצַו נְבוּכַדְרֶאצַּר מֶלֶךְ־בָּבֶל עַל־
con- Babylon king Nebuchadnezzar gave And that day on and
cerning of order an fields
5869 3947 559 2876 7227 5018 3027 3414
12 יִרְמְיָהוּ בְּיַד נְבוּזַרְאֲדָן רַב־טַבָּחִים לֵאמֹר׃ קָחֶנּוּ וְעֵינֶיךָ
your and Take ,saying the of chief the Nebuzar- the by Jeremiah
eyes him executioners adan of hand
1696 7451 3972 6213 408 7760
שִׂים עָלָיו וְאַל־תַּעַשׂ לוֹ מְאוּמָה רָּע כִּי אִם כַּאֲשֶׁר יְדַבֵּר
shall he as even But .evil anything to do and on set
say him not him
2876 7227 5018 7971 6213 3651
13 אֵלֶיךָ כֵּן עֲשֵׂה עִמּוֹ׃ וַיִּשְׁלַח נְבוּזַרְאֲדָן רַב־טַבָּחִים
the of chief the Nebuzar- sent And with do thus ,you to
executioners adan 5371 .him
4428 7227 3605 7248/7227 5631 7227 5021
וּנְבוּשַׁזְבָּן רַב־סָרִיס וְנֵרְגַל שַׂר־אֶצֶר רַב־מָג וְכֹל רַבֵּי מֶלֶךְ־
the leaders and mag Rab- ,sharezer and the chief Nebu- and
of king of all Nergal- ,eunuchs of shasban
5414 4307 2691 3414 3947 7971 884
14 בָּבֶל׃ וַיִּשְׁלְחוּ וַיִּקְחוּ אֶת־יִרְמְיָהוּ מֵחֲצַר הַמַּטָּרָה וַיִּתְּנוּ
they And guard- the of out Jeremiah took and they and ,Babylon
gave .house of court the sent
1004 3318 8227/1121/296/1121 1436
אֹתוֹ אֶל־גְּדַלְיָהוּ בֶּן־אֲחִיקָם בֶּן־שָׁפָן לְהוֹצִאֵהוּ אֶל־הַבָּיִת
the to take to ,Shaphan the ,Ahikam the Gedaliah to him
.house him of son of son
3068 1697 1961 3414 5971 8432 3427
15 וַיֵּשֶׁב בְּתוֹךְ הָעָם׃ וְאֶל־יִרְמְיָהוּ הָיָה דְבַר־יְהוָה
,Jehovah the came Jeremiah to And the among he So
of word .people lived
5663 1696 1980 559 4307 2691 6113 1961
16 בִּהְיֹתוֹ עָצוּר בַּחֲצַר הַמַּטָּרָה לֵאמֹר׃ הָלוֹךְ וְאָמַרְתָּ לְעֶבֶד־
Ebed- to and Go ,saying guard- the the in shut while
speak house of court up was he
3478 430 6635 3068 559 559 3569 5663
מֶלֶךְ הַכּוּשִׁי לֵאמֹר כֹּה־אָמַר יְהוָה צְבָאוֹת אֱלֹהֵי יִשְׂרָאֵל
:Israel the ,hosts Jehovah says Thus ,saying the melech
of God of ,Ethiopian
2896 3808 7451 2088 5892 1697 935 2005
הִנְנִי מֵבִי אֶת־דְּבָרַי אֶל־הָעִיר הַזֹּאת לְרָעָה וְלֹא לְטוֹבָה
for and for this city on My am ,Behold
;good not ,evil words bringing I
3068 5002 3117 5337 3117 6440 1961
17 וְהָיוּ לְפָנֶיךָ בַּיּוֹם הַהוּא׃ וְהִצַּלְתִּיךָ בַיּוֹם־הַהוּא נְאֻם־יְהוָה
.Jehovah says ,that day in will I But .that in before they and
you deliver day you be shall
3025 834 582 3027 5414 3808
18 וְלֹא תִנָּתֵן בְּיַד הָאֲנָשִׁים אֲשֶׁר־אַתָּה יָגוֹר מִפְּנֵיהֶם׃ כִּי
For .them of fear you whom ,men the the into shall you And
of hand given be not

deliver you, and you shall not fall by the sword; but your life shall be as a prize to you, because you put your trust in Me, says Jehovah.

CHAPTER 40

[1]*This is* the word that was to Jeremiah from Jehovah, after Nebuzar-adan, the chief of the executioners, had sent him from Ramah, when he had taken him, and he was bound in chains among all the captives of Jerusalem and Judah, who were being exiled to Babylon. [2]And the chief of the executioners took Jeremiah and said to him, Jehovah your God has spoken this evil against this place. [3]And Jehovah has brought *it*, and has done according as He said; because you have sinned against Jehovah, and have not obeyed His voice, and this thing has come on you. [4]And now, behold, I set you free today from the chains which *are* on your hand. If it *is* good in your eyes to come with me into Babylon, come. And I will set my eye on you. But if it *is* evil in your eyes to come with me into Babylon, stay. Behold, all the land *is* before you, to go to the right and good, go there[5]—and while he had not yet returned—Or go back to Gedaliah, the son of Ahikam, the son of Shaphan, whom the king of Babylon has appointed over the cities of Judah, and live with him among the people. Or to all *that is* right in your eyes to go, go. And the chief of the executioners gave him ration and a

7998 5315 1961 5307 3808 2719 4422
מַלֵּט אֲמַלֶּטְךָ וּבַחֶרֶב לֹא תִפֹּל וְהָיְתָה לְךָ נַפְשְׁךָ לְשָׁלָל
a as prize, your life to you shall be but fall shall, not you by sword the and, deliver you will I surely

3068 5002 982 3588
כִּי־בָטַחְתָּ בִּי נְאֻם־יְהוָה׃
Jehovah. says in Me have you trusted be- cause

Cap. XL. מ

CHAPTER 40

79,71 310 3068 3414 1961 834 1697
1 הַדָּבָר אֲשֶׁר־הָיָה אֶל־יִרְמְיָהוּ מֵאֵת יְהוָה אַחַר ׀ שַׁלַּח
had sent after Jehovah, from Jeremiah to came which The word

3947 7414 2876 7227 5018
אֹתוֹ נְבוּזַרְאֲדָן רַב־טַבָּחִים מִן־הָרָמָה בְּקַחְתּוֹ אֹתוֹ וְהוּא־
and he ;him he when taken had Ramah, from the of chief the executioners Nebuzar-adan him

1546 3063 3389 1540 3605 8432 246 628
אָסוּר בָּאזִקִּים בְּתוֹךְ כָּל־גָּלוּת יְרוּשָׁלִַם וִיהוּדָה הַמֻּגְלִים
were who exiled being and Judah Jerusalem the of captives all among chains in, was bound

3068 559 3414 2876 7227 3947 884
2 בָּבֶלָה׃ וַיִּקַּח רַב־טַבָּחִים לְיִרְמְיָהוּ וַיֹּאמֶר אֵלָיו יְהוָה
Jehovah to him, said and Jeremiah the of chief the executioners And took to Babylon.

935 2088 4725 7451 1696 430
3 אֱלֹהֶיךָ דִּבֶּר אֶת־הָרָעָה הַזֹּאת אֶל־הַמָּקוֹם הַזֶּה׃ וַיָּבֵא
has And (it) brought this. place against this evil has spoken your God

8085 3808 3068 2398 3588 1696 3068 6213
וַיַּעַשׂ יְהוָה כַּאֲשֶׁר דִּבֵּר כִּי־חֲטָאתֶם לַיהוָה וְלֹא־שְׁמַעְתֶּם
have obeyed and not against Jehovah, have you sinned be- cause has He ;said according as Jeho- vah has and done

31,17 6605 2009 6258 2088 1697 1961 6963
4 בְּקוֹלוֹ וְהָיָה לָכֶם דָּבָר הַזֶּה׃ וְעַתָּה הִנֵּה פִתַּחְתִּיךָ הַיּוֹם
today you set I free behold, And now this. thing you on therefore His voice, has come

935 5869 2896 3027 5921 834 246
מִן־הָאזִקִּים אֲשֶׁר עַל־יָדֶךָ אִם־טוֹב בְּעֵינֶיךָ לָבוֹא אִתִּי
with me to come your in eyes good If your on hands. which (were) the chains from

935 5869 7451/518 5869 935 884
בָבֶל בֹּא וְאָשִׂים אֶת־עֵינִי עָלֶיךָ וְאִם־רַע בְּעֵינֶיךָ לָבוֹא־
go to your in eyes evil But if you. on eye my I And will set come. into Babylon,

2896 413 6440 776 3605 2308 884
אִתִּי בָבֶל חֲדָל רְאֵה כָּל־הָאָרֶץ לְפָנֶיךָ אֶל־טוֹב וְאֶל־
and to good to before (is) you, the land all Behold, stay. into Babylon, with me

7725 7725 5750 8033 3212 5892 3477
5 הַיָּשָׁר בְּעֵינֶיךָ לָלֶכֶת שָׁמָּה לֵךְ׃ וְעוֹדֶנּוּ לֹא־יָשׁוּב וְשֻׁבָה
go Or back had he returned— not yet while and —go there go to, your in eyes the right

884/4428 6485 834 8227/1121 296/1121 1436
אֶל־גְּדַלְיָה בֶן־אֲחִיקָם בֶּן־שָׁפָן אֲשֶׁר הִפְקִיד מֶלֶךְ־בָּבֶל
Babylon the of king has appointed whom Shaphan, the of son Ahikam the of son Gedaliah to

3477 3605 176 5971 8432 3427 3063 5892
בְּעָרֵי יְהוּדָה וְשֵׁב אִתּוֹ בְּתוֹךְ הָעָם אוֹ אֶל־כָּל־הַיָּשָׁר
(is that) right all to Or the people. among with him and live Judah, the over of cities

4864 737 2876 7227 5414 3212/3212 5892
בְּעֵינֶיךָ לָלֶכֶת לֵךְ וַיִּתֶּן־לוֹ רַב־טַבָּחִים אֲרֻחָה וּמַשְׂאֵת
a and reward, ration the of chief the executioners to him So gave go. go to, your in eyes

reward, and sent him away. [6]Then Jeremiah went to Gedaliah, the son of Ahikam, at Mizpah, and lived with him among the people who were left in the land.

[7]And when all the commanders of the army who *were* in the field, they and their men, heard that the king of Babylon had appointed Gedaliah, the son of Ahikam, over the land, and had appointed with him men, and women, and children, and of the poor of the land, of those who were not exiled to Babylon, [8]then they came to Gedaliah, to Mizpah, even Ishmael, the son of Nethaniah, and Johanan, and Jonathan, the sons of Kareah; and Seraiah, the son of Tanhumeth; and the sons of Ephai of Netopha; and Jezaniah, the son of the Maachathite; they and their men. [9]And Gedaliah, the son of Ahikam, the son of Shaphan, swore to them and to their men, saying, Do not fear to serve the Chaldeans. Live in the land, and serve the king of Babylon, and it shall be well with you. [10]*As for* me, behold, I will live at Mizpah to stand before the Chaldeans who have come to us. But you go gather wine, and the harvest, and oil, and put *them* in your vessels, and live in your cities that you have taken.

[11]Also when all the Jews that *were* in Moab and among the sons of Ammon, and in Edom, and who *were* in all the lands, heard that the king of Babylon had given a remnant of Judah, and that he had set over them Gedeliah the son of Ahikan, the son of Shaphan, —[12]even all the Jews returned out of all places where they were driven, and came ot the land

4708 296/1121 14 36 3414 935 7971
6 וַיְשַׁלְּחֵהוּ׃ וַיָּבֹא יִרְמְיָהוּ אֶל־גְּדַלְיָה בֶן־אֲחִיקָם הַמִּצְפָּתָה
of Ahikam the Gedaliah to Jeremiah Then sent and
,Mizpah of son went .away him

8085 776 7604 5971 8432 3427
7 וַיֵּשֶׁב אִתּוֹ בְּתוֹךְ הָעָם הַנִּשְׁאָרִים בָּאָרֶץ׃ וַיִּשְׁמְעוּ
when And the in were who the among with and
heard .land left people him lived

6485 582 7704 834 2428 8269
כָל־שָׂרֵי הַחֲיָלִים אֲשֶׁר בַּשָּׂדֶה הֵמָּה וְאַנְשֵׁיהֶם כִּי־הִפְקִיד
had that their and they the in who the the all
appointed ,men ,field (were) armies of rulers

6485 776 296/1121 1436 884 4428
מֶלֶךְ־בָּבֶל אֶת־גְּדַלְיָהוּ בֶּן־אֲחִיקָם בָּאָרֶץ וְכִי ׀ הִפְקִיד
had and the over Ahikam the Gedaliah Babylon the
appointed land of son of king

1540 834 776 1803 2945 802 582
אִתּוֹ אֲנָשִׁים וְנָשִׁים וָטָף וּמִדַּלַּת הָאָרֶץ מֵאֲשֶׁר לֹא־הָגְלוּ
were not those of the of and and and ,men with
exiled who land poor the children women him

5418 1121 3458 4708 14 36 935 884
8 בָּבֶלָה׃ וַיָּבֹאוּ אֶל־גְּדַלְיָה הַמִּצְפָּתָה וְיִשְׁמָעֵאל בֶּן־נְתַנְיָהוּ
,Nethaniah the even ,Mizpah to Gedaliah to they to
of son Ishmael came ;Babylon

5778 1121 8576 1121 8304 7143 1121 3126 3110
וְיוֹחָנָן וְיוֹנָתָן בְּנֵי־קָרֵחַ וּשְׂרָיָה בֶן־תַּנְחֻמֶת וּבְנֵי ׀ עֵיפַי (עוֹפַי)
Ephai the and ,Tanhumeth the and ,Kareah the and and
of sons of son Seraiah of sons Jonathan ,Johanan

7650 582 4602 1121 3153 5199
9 הַנְּטֹפָתִי וִיזַנְיָהוּ בֶּן־הַמַּעֲכָתִי הֵמָּה וְאַנְשֵׁיהֶם׃ וַיִּשָּׁבַע
And their and they the the and of
swore 559 .men ,Maachathite of son Jezaniah ,Netopha

582 8227/1121 296 1121 1436
לָהֶם גְּדַלְיָהוּ בֶן־אֲחִיקָם בֶּן־שָׁפָן וּלְאַנְשֵׁיהֶם לֵאמֹר אַל־
not ,saying to and Shaphan the Ahikam the Gedaliah to
,men their of son of son them

4428 5647 776 3427 3778 5647 3372
תִּירְאוּ מֵעֲבוֹד הַכַּשְׂדִּים שְׁבוּ בָאָרֶץ וְעִבְדוּ אֶת־מֶלֶךְ
king the and the in Live the serve to fear Do
of serve land .Chaldeans

5975 4708 3427 2005 3190 884
10 בָּבֶל וְיִיטַב לָכֶם׃ וַאֲנִי הִנְנִי יֹשֵׁב בַּמִּצְפָּה לַעֲמֹד
stand to Mizpah at will ,behold (for As) with will it and Baby-
live I ,me .you well be ,lon

7019 3196 622 935 834 3778 6440
לִפְנֵי הַכַּשְׂדִּים אֲשֶׁר יָבֹאוּ אֵלֵינוּ וְאַתֶּם אִסְפוּ יַיִן וְקַיִץ
the and wine (go) you But .us to have who the before
,harvest gather come ,Chaldeans

1571 8610 5892 3427 3627 7760 8081
11 וְשֶׁמֶן וְשִׂמוּ בִּכְלֵיכֶם וּשְׁבוּ בְּעָרֵיכֶם אֲשֶׁר־תְּפַשְׂתֶּם׃ וְגַם
Also have you that your in live and your put and and
when .seized cities ,vessels in (them) ,oil

834 123 5983/1121 4124 3064 3605
כָּל־הַיְּהוּדִים אֲשֶׁר־בְּמוֹאָב ׀ וּבִבְנֵי־עַמּוֹן וּבֶאֱדוֹם וַאֲשֶׁר
who and in and sons the and in that the all
(were) ;Edom Ammon of Moab (were) Jews

3063 7611 884 4428 5414 8085 776 3605
בְּכָל־הָאֲרָצוֹת שָׁמְעוּ כִּי־נָתַן ׀ מֶלֶךְ־בָּבֶל שְׁאֵרִית לִיהוּדָה
of a Babylon the had that heard the all in
,Judah remnant of king given lands

8227 1121 296 1121 1436 5921 6485
וְכִי הִפְקִיד עֲלֵיהֶם אֶת־גְּדַלְיָהוּ בֶּן־אֲחִיקָם בֶּן־שָׁפָן׃
—Shaphan the Ahikam the Gedaliah over had he and
of son of son them appointed that

935 5080 4725 3605 3064 3605 7725
12 וַיָּשֻׁבוּ כָל־הַיְּהוּדִים מִכָּל־הַמְּקֹמוֹת אֲשֶׁר נִדְּחוּ־שָׁם וַיָּבֹאוּ
and there had they where places out the all even
to came ,driven been all of Jews returned

of Judah, to Gedaliah, to Mizpah, and gathered wine and the harvest *in* great abundance.

13And Johanan, the son of Kareah, and all the commanders of the army that *were* in the field, came to Gedaliah, to Mizpah. 14And *they* said to him, You certainly know that Baalis, the king of the sons of Ammon, has sent Ishmael, the son of Nethaniah, to strike your soul. But Gedaliah, the son of Ahikam, did not believe them. 15And Johanan, the son of Kareah, spoke to Gedaliah in Mispah secretly, saying, Please let me go, and I will strike Ishmael, the son of Nethaniah, and a man shall not know. Why should he strike your soul, and all the Jews who are gathered to you be scattered; and the remnant of Judah perish? 16But Gedaliah, the son of Ahikam, said to Johanan, the son of Kareah, You shall not do this thing. For you speak falsely concerning Ishmael.

ארץ־יהודה אל־גדליהו המצפתה ויאספו יין וקיץ

the harvest and wine and gathered ,Mizpah to ,Gedaliah to ,Judah the of land

13 הרבה מאד׃ ויוחנן בן־קרח וכל־שרי החילים אשר

that (were) army the the of captains and all Kareah the of son And Johanan .great (in) abundance

14 בשדה באו אל־גדליהו המצפתה׃ ויאמרו אליו הידע

Certainly to him they And said .Mizpah to Gedaliah to came the in field

תדע כי בעלים ׀ מלך בני־עמון שלח את־ישמעאל בן

the of son Ishmael has sent Ammon the of sons king the Baalis that you know

נתניה להכתך נפש ולא־האמין להם גדליהו בן־אחיקם׃

.Ahikam the of son Gedaliah them did believe But not .soul your strike to Nethaniah

15 ויוחנן בן־קרח אמר אל־גדליהו בסתר במצפה לאמר

,saying ,Mizpah in secretly Gedaliah to spoke Kareah the of son Then Johanan

אלכה נא ואכה את־ישמעאל בן־נתניה ואיש לא ידע

shall not .know a and man ,Nethaniah the of son Ishmael I And will strike .Please me let go

למה יכה נפש ונפצו כל־יהודה הנקבצים אליך ואבדה

and perish ,you to are who gathered the Jews all should and be scattered soul your he strike Why does

16 שארית יהודה׃ ויאמר גדליהו בן־אחיקם אל־יוחנן

Johanan to Ahikam the of son Gedaliah said But ?Judah the rem- of nant

בן־קרח אל־תעש את־הדבר הזה כי־שקר אתה דבר

speak you falsely for ,this thing shall you not do ,Kareah the of son

אל־ישמעאל׃

.Ishmael con- cerning

CAP. XLI. מא

CHAPTER 41

CHAPTER 41

1And it happened, in the seventh month Ishmael, the son of Nethaniah, the son of Elishama, of the royal seed, and of the chief ones of the king, and ten men with him, came to Gedaliah, the son of Ahikam, to Mizpah. And they ate bread together there in Mizpah. 2And Ishmael, the son of Nethaniah, rose up, and the ten men who were with him, and struck Gedaliah, the son of Ahikam, the son of Shaphan, with the sword.

1 ויהי בחדש השביעי בא ישמעאל בן־נתניה בן־אלישמע

Elishama the of son Nethaniah the of son Ishmael came ,seventh the in month it And was

מזרע המלוכה ורבי המלך ועשרה אנשים אתו אל־

to with him men ten and the ,king the of and chief ones ,royal the of seed

גדליהו בן־אחיקם המצפתה ויאכלו שם לחם יחדו

to- gether food there they And ate .Mizpah to ,Ahikam the of son Gedaliah

2 במצפה׃ ויקם ישמעאל בן־נתניה ועשרת האנשים ׀

men the ten and ,Nethaniah the of son Ishamel Then arose .Mizpah in

אשר־היו אתו ויכו את־גדליהו בן־אחיקם בן־שפן בחרב

the with .sword Shaphan the of son Ahikam the of son Gedaliah and struck with ,him were who

And they killed him whom the king of Babylon had appointed over the land. [3]Ishmael also struck all the Jews who were with him, with Gedaliah at Mizpah, and the Chaldeans who were found there, the men of war. [4]And it happened, the second day after he had killed Gedaliah; and no one knew; [5]men from Shechem came from Shiloh, and from Samaria, eighty men, *having their* beards shaved, and their clothes torn, and having cut themselves, and *with* offerings and incense in their hand, to bring to the house of Jehovah. [6]And Ishmael, the son of Nethaniah, went out from Mizpah to meet them, walking as he walked and weeping. And it happened, as he met them, he said to them, Come to Gedaliah, the son of Ahikam. [7]And when they came into the middle of the city, Ishmael, the son of Nethaniah, killed them, he and the men with him, *throwing them* into the middle of the pit.

[8]But ten men were found among them who said to Ishmael, Do not kill us, for we have treasures in the field, *of* wheat, and barley, and oil, and honey. So he held back, not killing them with their brothers. [9]And the pit there, *in* which Ishmael had thrown all the dead bodies of the men, whom he had struck because of Gedaliah, *was* the one which Asa the king had made from the face of Baasha, king of Israel. Ishmael, the son of Nethaniah, filled it with the slain. [10]And Ishmael took captive all the rest of the people who *were* in Mizpah, the king's daughters, and all the

3605 1571 776 884 44:28 6485 834 4191
3 וימת אתו אשר־הפקיד מלך־בבל בארץ׃ ואת כל־
all Also the over Babylon the ap- had whom him they And
.land of king pointed killed

47:09 1436 1961 834 3064
היהודים אשר־היו אתו את־גדליהו במצפה ואת־
and ,Mizpah at Gedaliah with with were who the
,him Jews

5221 42:21 582 4672 834 3778
הכשדים אשר נמצאו־שם את אנשי המלחמה הכה
struck the of men ,there were who the
,war found Chaldeans

38:08 376 1436 4191 8145 3117 1961 3458
4 ישמעאל׃ ויהי ביום השני להמית את־גדליהו ואיש לא
not and ,Gedaliah he after second the on And .Ishmael
man a killed had day ,was it

376 8084 8111 7887 7927 582 935 3045
5 ידע׃ ויבאו אנשים משכם משלו ומשמרון שמנים איש
,men eighty from and from from men came —knew
,Samaria ,Shiloh Shechem

30:27 3828 4503 1413 899 7167 2206 1548
מגלחי זקן וקרעי בגדים ומתגדדים ומנחה ולבונה בידם
their in and (with) and having and (their) and (their) (with)
,hand incense offerings ,themselves cut ,clothes torn ,beards shaved

7125 5418 345 3318 3068 1004 935
6 להביא בית יהוה׃ ויצא ישמעאל בן־נתניה לקראתם
meet to Nethaniah the Ishmael went And .Jehovah the bring to
them of son forth of house to (them)

559 6298 1961 1058 19:80 19:80 47:09
מן־המצפה הלך הלך ובכה ויהי כפגש אתם ויאמר
said he ,them he as it And and he as walking ,Mizpah from
met ,was .weeping walked

935 296 1121 1436 935
7 אליהם באו אל־גדליהו בן־אחיקם׃ ויהי כבואם אל־
into they when And .Ahikam the Gedaliah to Come ,them to
came of son

953 8432 4518 3458 7919 5892 8432
תוך העיר וישחטם ישמעאל בן־נתניה אל־תוך הבור
,pit the the into ;Nethaniah the Ishmael killed ,city the the
of middle of son them of middle

4672 582 6235 834 582
8 הוא והאנשים אשר־אתו׃ ועשרה אנשים נמצאו־בם
among were men ten But with who the and he
;them found .him (were) men

4301 3426 41:91 408 3458 559
ויאמרו אל־ישמעאל אל־תמיתנו כי־יש־לנו מטמנים
treasures us to there for kill Do not ,Ishmael to they and
is us said

4191 38:08 2308 1706 8081 8184 2406 77:04
בשדה חטים ושערים ושמן ודבש ויחדל ולא המיתם
kill did and he So and ,oil and and (of) the in
them not ,back held .honey ,barley ,wheat ,field

3458 8033 7993 953 251 8432
9 בתוך אחיהם׃ והבור אשר השליך שם ישמעאל את ׀
Ishmael there had where the And their with
thrown pit .brothers

834 1436 3588 5221 834 582 6293
כל־פגרי האנשים אשר הכה ביד־גדליהו הוא אשר
which (was) ,Gedaliah because had he whom men the dead the all
one the of struck of bodies

4390 3478 44:28 1201 6440 609 44:28 6213
עשה המלך אסא מפני בעשא מלך־ישראל אתו מלא
filled it ;Israel king Baasha before Asa the had
with of of face the king made

3605 3458 7617 2491 4518 3458
10 ישמעאל בן־נתניהו חללים׃ וישב ׀ ישמעאל את־כל־
all Ishmael took Then .slain the Nethaniah the Ishmael
captive of son

people who stayed in Mizpah, whom Nebuzar-adan, the chief of the executioners, had entrusted to Gedaliah, the son of Ahikam. And Ishmael, the son of Nethaniah, carried them away captive, and went to go over to the sons of Ammon.
[11]But when Johanan, the son of Kareah, and all the army commanders with him, heard of all the evil that Ishmael, the son of Nethaniah, had done, [12]then they took all the men and went to fight with Ishmael, the son of Nethaniah. And they found him by the great waters that *are* in Gibeon.

[13]And it happened when all the people who *were* with Ishmael saw Johanan, the son of Kareah, and all the army commanders with him, then they were glad.
[14]And all the people that Ishmael had taken captive from Mizpah turned around and came back, and went to Johanan, the son of Kareah.
[15]But Ishmael, the son of Nethaniah, escaped from Johanan with eight men, and went to the the sons of Ammon.
[16]Then Johanan, the son of Kareah, and all the army commanders with him, took all the remnant of the people, whom he had recovered from Ishmael, the son of Nethaniah, from Mizpah — after he had killed Gedaliah, the son of Ahikam — mighty men of war, and the women, and the children, and the eunuchs, whom he had brought again from Gibeon.
[17]And they departed and lived in the inn of Chimham, which is by Bethlehem, to go to enter Egypt,

3605 4428 1323 4709 834 5971 7611
שארית העם אשר במצפה את־בנות המלך ואת־כל־
all and the daughters ,Mizpah in who the rest the
,king's (were) people of

7227 5018 6485 834 4709 7604 5971
העם הנשארים במצפה אשר הפקיד נבוזראדן רב־
the Nebuzar-adan com- had whom ,Mizpah in were who the
of chief to mitted left people

1121 3458 7617 296 1121 1436 2876
טבחים את־גדליהו בן־אחיקם וישבם ישמעאל בן־
the Ishmael took And .Ahikam the Gedaliah the
of son captive of son executioners

71:43 3110 8085 5983 1121 5674 3212 45:18
11 נתניה וילך לעבר אל־בני עמון: וישמע יוחנן בן־קרח
Kareah the Johanan when But ,Ammon the to go to and Nethaniah
of son heard of sons over went

6213 7451/3605 2428 8269
וכל־שרי החילים אשר אתו את כל־הרעה אשר עשה
had that the all of with who the cap- the and
done evil ,him (were) army of tains all

3898 3212 582 3605 3947 4518 3458
12 ישמעאל בן־נתניה: ויקחו את־כל־האנשים וילכו להלחם
fight to and the all then ,Nethaniah the Ishmael
went men took they of son

7227 4325 4672 4518 3458
עם־ישמעאל בן־נתניה וימצאו אתו אל־מים רבים אשר
that great the by him they And .Nethaniah the Ishmael with
(are) waters found of son

3458 834 5971 3605 7200 1961 1391
13 בגבעון: ויהי כראות כל־העם אשר את־ישמעאל את־
Ishmael with who the all when And in
(were) people saw ,was it .Gibeon

8056 834 2428 82 69 71:43 3110
יוחנן בן־קרח ואת כל־שרי החילים אשר אתו וישמחו:
they then with who the the all and ,Kareah the Johanan
.glad were ,him (were) army of captains of son

7725 4709 3458 7617 5971 3605 5437
14 ויסבו כל־העם אשר־שבה ישמעאל מן־המצפה וישבו
and Mizpah from Ishmael taken had that the all turned And
back came captive people around

4422 4518 3458 7143 3110 32:12
15 וילכו אל־יוחנן בן־קרח: וישמעאל בן־נתניה נמלט
escaped Nethaniah the But .Kareah the Johanan to and
of son Ishmael of son went

3947 5983 1121 32:12 3110 582 8083
16 בשמנה אנשים מפני יוחנן וילך אל־בני עמון: ויקח
Then .Ammon the to and ,Johanan from ,men with
took of sons went eight

3605 2428 8269 71:43 3110
יוחנן בן־קרח וכל־שרי החילים אשר־אתו את כל־
all with that the cap- the and Kareah the Johanan
him (were) army of tains all of son

4518 3458 7725 834 5971 7611
שארית העם אשר השיב מאת ישמעאל בן־נתניה מן
from ,Nethaniah the Ishmael from had he whom the rem- the
of son recovered people of nant

582 1397 296/1121 14:36 52:21 310 4709
המצפה אחר הכה את־גדליה בן־אחיקם גברים אנשי
men mighty ,Ahikam the Gedaliah had he after —Mizpah
of of son struck

1391 7725 834 5631 2945 802 44:21
המלחמה ונשים וטף וסרסים אשר השיב מגבעון:
from had he whom the and the and the and ,war
.Gibeon again brought ,eunuchs ,children ,women

3212 1035 1035 681 834 3643 1678 3427 3212
17 וילכו וישבו בגרות כמוהם אשר־אצל בית לחם ללכת
go to ,Bethlehem by which ,Chimham the in and they And
(is) of inn lived left

¹⁸because of the Chaldeans; for they were afraid of them, because Ishmael, the son of Nethaniah, had struck Gedaliah, the son of Ahikam, whom the king of Babylon had appointed in the land.

18

5221	3588		3372		:3778	١6440	4714	935
לָבוֹא מִצְרָיִם׃	מִפְּנֵי הַכַּשְׂדִּים כִּי יָרְאוּ מִפְּנֵיהֶם כִּי־הִכָּה						
had	because	of	were they	For	the	because	,Egypt	to
struck	,them		afraid		.Chaldeans	of		enter

6485		:296/1121	4518	3458
יִשְׁמָעֵאל בֶּן־נְתַנְיָה אֶת־גְּדַלְיָהוּ בֶּן־אֲחִיקָם אֲשֶׁר־הִפְקִיד				
had	whom	,Ahikam the	Gedaliah	Nethaniah the	Ishmael
appointed		of son		of son

776	١884	44 ١28
מֶלֶךְ־בָּבֶל בָּאָרֶץ׃		
the in	Babylon	the
.land		of king

CAP. XLII. מב

CHAPTER 42

CHAPTER 42

¹And all the army commanders, and Johanan, the son of Kareah, and Jezaniah, the son of Hoshaiah, and all the people, from the least even to the greatest, came near. ²And *they* said to Jeremiah the prophet, We beg you, let our plea fall before you; and pray for us to Jehovah your God, for all this remnant, for we are left *but* a few of many, as your eyes see us; ³that Jehovah your God may show us the way in which we may walk, and the thing that we may do. ⁴Then Jeremiah the prophet said to them, I have heard. Behold, I will pray to Jehovah your God according to your words; and it shall be, all the word Jehovah shall answer, I will declare to you. I will not keep back a thing from you. ⁵And they said to Jeremiah, Let Jehovah be a true and faithful witness between us if not according to all things Jehovah your God shall send you to us, so we will do. ⁶Whether *it is* good, or whether evil, we will obey the voice of Jehovah your God, to whom we send you; so that it may be well with us when we obey the voice of Jehovah our God.

1

1955	١1121	3153	71 :43/1121	١3110	2428:		8269	١5066
וַיִּגְּשׁוּ כָּל־שָׂרֵי הַחֲיָלִים וְיוֹחָנָן בֶּן־קָרֵחַ וִיזַנְיָה בֶּן־הוֹשַׁעְיָה								
,Hoshaiah the	and	,Kareah the	and	,army the	the	all	Then
	of son	Jezaniah	of son	Johanan		of captains	near came

2

50 ,30	3414			١559	١1418	5704	6996	5971	١3605
וְכָל־הָעָם מִקָּטֹן וְעַד־גָּדוֹל׃ וַיֹּאמְרוּ אֶל־יִרְמְיָהוּ הַנָּבִיא									
the	Jeremiah	to	said and	the	even	from the	least	people	all
,prophet				,greatest		to			

1430	3068		6440:		8467	15307
תִּפָּל־נָא תְחִנָּתֵנוּ לְפָנֶיךָ וְהִתְפַּלֵּל בַּעֲדֵנוּ אֶל־יְהוָה אֱלֹהֶיךָ						
your	Jehovah	to	us for	pray and	before	now Let
,God					you	fall
					plea	

72 :35	١4592	7604	2088	7611	36 ١05
בְּעַד כָּל־הַשְּׁאֵרִית הַזֹּאת כִּי־נִשְׁאַרְנוּ מְעַט מֵהַרְבֵּה כַּאֲשֶׁר					
as	,many of	(but)	are we	for	,this	remnant	all	for
		few a		left				

3

1870		430:		3068	5046		7200	5869
עֵינֶיךָ׃ וְיַגֶּד־לָנוּ יְהוָה אֱלֹהֶיךָ אֶת־הַדֶּרֶךְ								
the		your	Jehovah	to	may that	,us	see	your
way		God		us	show			eyes

4

		559		6213	1697		19 ١80	834
אֲשֶׁר נֵלֶךְ־בָּהּ וְאֶת־הַדָּבָר אֲשֶׁר נַעֲשֶׂה׃ וַיֹּאמֶר אֲלֵיהֶם								
them to	said Then	.do may we	that	thing the	and	,in	may we	which
								walk

430		3068		6499	2005	8085:		5030	3414
יִרְמְיָהוּ הַנָּבִיא שָׁמַעְתִּי הִנְנִי מִתְפַּלֵּל אֶל־יְהוָה אֱלֹהֵיכֶם									
your		Jehovah	to	pray will	,Behold	have I	the	Jeremiah
God						.heard	prophet	

5046		3068		6030 834		1697	:3605 19 ١61	1697
כְּדִבְרֵיכֶם וְהָיָה כָּל־הַדָּבָר אֲשֶׁר־יַעֲנֶה יְהוָה אֶתְכֶם אַגִּיד								
will I	,you	Jehovah	shall	which	the	all	it and	to according
declare			answer		word		,be shall	,words your

5

1961	3414		559		1697		4513	38 ١08
לָכֶם לֹא־אֶמְנַע מִכֶּם דָּבָר׃ וְהֵמָּה אָמְרוּ אֶל־יִרְמְיָהוּ יְהִי								
Let	,Jeremiah	to	said	Then	a	from	will I	not	to
be			they		,thing	you	back keep	,you

834 ٠	1697	؟ ٠3605	38 ١08	539	5707 996:		١3068
יְהוָה בָּנוּ לְעֵד אֱמֶת וְנֶאֱמָן אִם־לֹא כְּכָל־הַדָּבָר אֲשֶׁר							
which	things according	not if	and	true	a	between	Jeho-
	all to		,faithful		witness	us	vah

6

518	2896 518		6213	3651		430:	3068	797١1
יִשְׁלָחֲךָ יְהוָה אֱלֹהֵינוּ אֵלֵינוּ כֵּן נַעֲשֶׂה׃ אִם־טוֹב וְאִם־								
or	(is it) Whether	shall we	so	,us to	your	Jehovah	shall
whether	,good	.do			God		you send

	7971		580	834	430:	3068	١6963	7451:
רָע בְּקוֹל ׀ יְהוָה אֱלֹהֵינוּ אֲשֶׁר אֲנוּ שֹׁלְחִים אֹתְךָ אֵלָיו								
to	you	send	we	whom	,God our	Jehovah	the	(is it)
Him							of voice	,evil

3068	١6963	80 ١85:		3190		8085
נִשְׁמָע לְמַעַן אֲשֶׁר יִיטַב־לָנוּ כִּי נִשְׁמַע בְּקוֹל יְהוָה						
Jehovah	the	obey we	when	with	may it	that so	will we
	of voice			us	well be		;obey

[7]And it happened, at the end of ten days the word of Jehovah was to Jeremiah. [8]And he called Johanan, the son of Kareah, and all the army commanders with him, and all the people, from the least even to the greatest. [9]And *he* said to them, So says Jehovah, the God of Israel, to whom you sent me to cause to fall your petition before Him: [10]If you will still remain in this land, then I will build you up, and will not tear *you* down. And I will plant you, and will not pluck *you* up. For I repent as to the evil that I have done to you. [11]Do not be afraid of the king of Babylon, of whom you are afraid. Do not be afraid of his face, declares Jehovah; for I *am* with you to save you and to deliver you from his hand. [12]And I will give mercies on you, so that he will pity you, and cause you to return to your own land.

[13]But if you say, We will not live in this land, or obey the voice of Jehovah your God, [14]saying, No, but we will go into the land of Egypt, where we shall see no war or hear the sound of the trumpet. And we will not hunger for bread, and there we will live. [15]Then hear now the word of Jehovah, O remnant of Judah, So says Jehovah of hosts, the God of Israel: If you surely set your faces to go into Egypt, and go to live there, [16]then it shall be, the sword which you feared

7 3068 1697 1961 3117 6235 7093 19,61 430
אֱלֹהֵינוּ׃ וַיְהִי מִקֵּץ עֲשֶׂרֶת יָמִים וַיְהִי דְבַר־יְהוָה
Jehovah | the word of | came | days | ten | the end at | it And ,was | .God our

8 8269 3605 7143 1121 3110 7121 3414
אֶל־יִרְמְיָהוּ׃ וַיִּקְרָא אֶל־יוֹחָנָן בֶּן־קָרֵחַ וְאֶל כָּל־שָׂרֵי
the of captains | all | to and | ,Kareah the of son | Johanan to | he Then called | .Jeremiah to

9 559 1419 5704 6996 5971/3605 2428
הַחֲיָלִים אֲשֶׁר אִתּוֹ וּלְכָל־הָעָם לְמִקָּטֹן וְעַד־גָּדוֹל׃ וַיֹּאמֶר
he And said | the .greatest | even to | the from least | the people | and all | with ,him | that (were) | the army

7971 834 3478 430 3068 559 3541
אֲלֵיהֶם כֹּה־אָמַר יְהוָה אֱלֹהֵי יִשְׂרָאֵל אֲשֶׁר שְׁלַחְתֶּם אֹתִי
me | you sent | whom | ,Israel | the of God | ,Jehovah | says Thus | ,them to

10 776 772,5 7725 6440 8467 5307
אֵלָיו לְהַפִּיל תְּחִנַּתְכֶם לְפָנָיו׃ אִם־שׁוֹב תֵּשְׁבוּ בָּאָרֶץ
in land | will you remain | still | If | before :Him | your petition | cause to fall to | to Him

38,08 5193 20:40 38,08 1129 2088
הַזֹּאת וּבָנִיתִי אֶתְכֶם וְלֹא אֶהֱרֹס וְנָטַעְתִּי אֶתְכֶם וְלֹא
and not | you | will I and plant | tear ;down | and not | you | will I then up build | ,this

11 621,3 7451 5162 5428
אֶתּוֹשׁ כִּי נִחַמְתִּי אֶל־הָרָעָה אֲשֶׁר עָשִׂיתִי לָכֶם׃ אַל־
not | .you to | have I done | that | evil the | to | repent I | For | pluck .up

408 6440 834 884 44,28 6440 3372
תִּירְאוּ מִפְּנֵי מֶלֶךְ בָּבֶל אֲשֶׁר־אַתֶּם יְרֵאִים מִפָּנָיו אַל־
not | of .him | are afraid | you | whom | ,Babylon | the of king | before .face his | be Do afraid

3467 30,68 5002 6440 3372
תִּירְאוּ מִמֶּנּוּ נְאֻם־יְהוָה כִּי־אִתְּכֶם אֲנִי לְהוֹשִׁיעַ אֶתְכֶם
you | save to | (am) I | with you | for | ;Jehovah says | ,him of | be Do afraid

12 7355 7356 5414 3027 5337
וּלְהַצִּיל אֶתְכֶם מִיָּדוֹ׃ וְאֶתֵּן לָכֶם רַחֲמִים וְרִחַם אֶתְכֶם
you | he and pity will | mercies | you on | I And give will | his from .hand | you | to and deliver

13 3427 559 127 7725
וְהֵשִׁיב אֶתְכֶם אֶל־אַדְמַתְכֶם׃ וְאִם־אֹמְרִים אַתֶּם לֹא נֵשֵׁב
will we not live | ,you | say | if But | .land own your | to | you | cause and return to

14 559 430 3068 6963 80,85 776
בָּאָרֶץ הַזֹּאת לְבִלְתִּי שְׁמֹעַ בְּקוֹל יְהוָה אֱלֹהֵיכֶם׃ לֵאמֹר
,saying | ,God our | Jehovah | the of voice | obey | or | ,this | in land

6963 44:21 7200 38,08 935 4714 776 38,08
לֹא כִּי אֶרֶץ מִצְרַיִם נָבוֹא אֲשֶׁר לֹא־נִרְאֶה מִלְחָמָה וְקוֹל
the and of sound | war | will we not see | where | will we ,into go | Egypt | the of land | but | ,No

15 62,58 3427 8033 7456 3808 3899 8085 38,08 7782
שׁוֹפָר לֹא נִשְׁמָע וְלַלֶּחֶם לֹא־נִרְעָב וְשָׁם נֵשֵׁב׃ וְעַתָּה
And now | will we .live | and there | will we ;hunger | not | for and bread | will we ;hear | not | ram's the horn

3068 559 35,41 3063 7611 3068 1697 8085 3651
לָכֵן שִׁמְעוּ דְבַר־יְהוָה שְׁאֵרִית יְהוּדָה כֹּה־אָמַר יְהוָה
Jehovah of | says Thus | ,Judah | O of remnant | ,Jehovah | the of word | hear | there- fore

935 6440 7760 7760 518 34,78 430 6635
צְבָאוֹת אֱלֹהֵי יִשְׂרָאֵל אִם־אַתֶּם שׂוֹם תְּשִׂמוּן פְּנֵיכֶם לָבֹא
go to into | your faces | set | surely | you | If | :Israel | the of God | ,hosts

16 834 2719 1961 8033 1481 935 4714
מִצְרַיִם וּבָאתֶם לָגוּר שָׁם׃ וְהָיְתָה הַחֶרֶב אֲשֶׁר אַתֶּם
you | which | the sword | it then ,be will | ,there | and sojourn | you and go | ,Egypt

shall overtake you there in the land of Egypt. And the famine which you were anxious about shall cling to you there *in* Egypt; and you shall die there. 17So *it* shall be to all the men who have set their faces to go into Egypt to reside there. They shall die by the sword, by the famine, and by the plague. And none of them shall remain or escape from the evil that I will bring on them. 18For so says Jehovah of hosts, the God of Israel, As My anger and My fury has flowed out upon the people of Jerusalem, so shall My fury flow out on you when you enter Egypt. And you shall be a curse, and a horror, and a shame, and a reproach; and you shall not see this place any more. 19Jehovah has spoken concerning you, O remnant of Judah. Do not go into Egypt. Know that I have surely testified against you today. 20For you used deceit against your souls when you sent me to Jehovah your God, saying, Pray for us to Jehovah our God; and according to all that Jehovah our God shall say, so declare to us, and we will do *it*. 21And I have declared *it* to you this day; but you have not obeyed the voice of Jehovah your God, or anything for which He has sent me to you. 22And for this reason, know certainly that you shall die by the sword, by the famine, and by the plague in the place where you desire to go to sojourn.

7458 4714 776 5381 8033 1672
יְרֵאִים מִמֶּנָּה שָׁם תַּשִּׂיג אֶתְכֶם בְּאֶרֶץ מִצְרָיִם וְהָרָעָב
the and famine ;Egypt the in of land you shall overtake there from feared

4714 310 1692 8033 3373 834
אֲשֶׁר־אַתֶּם ׀ דֹּאֲגִים מִמֶּנּוּ שָׁם יִדְבַּק אַחֲרֵיכֶם מִצְרַיִם
,Egypt (in) you to shall cling there about were anxious you which

6440 7760 582 3605 1961 4191 8033
17 וְשָׁם תָּמֻתוּ׃ וְיִהְיוּ כָל־הָאֲנָשִׁים אֲשֶׁר־שָׂמוּ אֶת־פְּנֵיהֶם
their faces have set who the men all it And ,be will shall you .die and there

1697 7458 2719 4191 1481 4714 935
לָבוֹא מִצְרַיִם לָגוּר שָׁם יָמוּתוּ בַּחֶרֶב בָּרָעָב וּבַדָּבֶר וְלֹא
and none the by and ;plague the by ,famine the by ,sword they die shall ,there to sojourn Egypt go to into

935 7451 6440 6412 8300 1961
יִהְיֶה לָהֶם שָׂרִיד וּפָלִיט מִפְּנֵי הָרָעָה אֲשֶׁר אֲנִי מֵבִיא
will bring I that evil the from or escape remain of them shall

3478 430 6635 3068 559 5921
18 עֲלֵיהֶם׃ כִּי כֹה אָמַר יְהוָה צְבָאוֹת אֱלֹהֵי יִשְׂרָאֵל כַּאֲשֶׁר
As :Israel the of God ,hosts Jehovah of says thus For .them on

2534 5413 3651 3389 5971 3427 2534 639 5413
נִתַּךְ אַפִּי וַחֲמָתִי עַל־יֹשְׁבֵי יְרוּשָׁלִַם כֵּן תִּתַּךְ חֲמָתִי
My fury shall flow so ,Jerusalem the of people on My and fury My anger has flowed

7045 8047 423 1961 4714 935 5921
עֲלֵיכֶם בְּבֹאֲכֶם מִצְרַיִם וִהְיִיתֶם לְאָלָה וּלְשַׁמָּה וְלִקְלָלָה
a and ,shame a and ,horror ,curse a you And become shall .Egypt you when enter you on

3068 1696 2088 4725 5750 7200 2781
19 וּלְחֶרְפָּה וְלֹא־תִרְאוּ עוֹד אֶת־הַמָּקוֹם הַזֶּה׃ דִּבֶּר יְהוָה
Jehovah has spoken .this place again you see shall and not a and ;reproach

3045 3045 4714 935 3063 7611
עֲלֵיכֶם שְׁאֵרִית יְהוּדָה אַל־תָּבֹאוּ מִצְרַיִם יָדֹעַ תֵּדְעוּ כִּי
that know Surely .Egypt go Do into not .Judah O of remnant about ,you

5315 8582 3117 5749
20 הַעִידֹתִי בָכֶם הַיּוֹם׃ כִּי הִתְעֵתֶים בְּנַפְשׁוֹתֵיכֶם כִּי־אַתֶּם
you when against souls your used you deceit For .today against you have I testified

6419 559 430 3068 7971
שְׁלַחְתֶּם אֹתִי אֶל־יְהוָה אֱלֹהֵיכֶם לֵאמֹר הִתְפַּלֵּל בַּעֲדֵנוּ
us for Pray ,saying ,God your Jehovah to me sent

430 3068 559 3605 430 3068
אֶל־יְהוָה אֱלֹהֵינוּ וּכְכֹל אֲשֶׁר יֹאמַר יְהוָה אֱלֹהֵינוּ כֵּן
so ,God our Jehovah say shall that accord- and all to ing ;God our Jehovah to

6963 8085 3808 3117 5046 6213 5046
21 הַגֶּד־לָנוּ וְעָשִׂינוּ׃ וָאַגִּד לָכֶם הַיּוֹם וְלֹא שְׁמַעְתֶּם בְּקוֹל
the of voice have you obeyed but not this ;day to you have I And declared we and .(it) do will to declare ,us

3045 6258 7971 834 3605 430 3068
22 יְהוָה אֱלֹהֵיכֶם וּלְכֹל אֲשֶׁר־שְׁלָחַנִי אֲלֵיכֶם׃ וְעַתָּה יָדֹעַ
surely Now therefore .you to has He me sent (for) which or anything ,God your Jehovah

4725 4191 1698 7458 2719 3045
תֵּדְעוּ כִּי בַּחֶרֶב בָּרָעָב וּבַדֶּבֶר תָּמוּתוּ בַּמָּקוֹם אֲשֶׁר
where the in place shall you die the by and plague the by ,famine the by ,sword that know

8033 1481 935 2654
חֲפַצְתֶּם לָבוֹא לָגוּר שָׁם׃
.there to sojourn go to desire you

CAP. XLIII מג

CHAPTER 43

CHAPTER 43

[1]And it happened, when Jeremiah had finished speaking to all the people all the words of Jehovah their God, for which Jehovah their God had sent him to them—all these words— [2]Azariah, the son of Hoshaiah, and Johanan, the son of Kareah, and all the proud men, then spoke, saying to Jeremiah, You speak falsely. Jehovah our God has not sent you to say, Do not go to Egypt, to sojourn there. [3]But Baruch, the son of Neriah, sets you against us, to deliver us into the hand of the Chaldeans, that they might put us to death, or exile us to Babylon. [4]And Johanan, the son of Kareah, and all the army commanders, and all the people, did not obey the voice of Jehovah, to live in the land of Judah. [5]But Johanan, the son of Kareah, and all the army commanders, took all the remnant of Judah who had returned from all the nations where they had been driven, to sojourn in the land of Judah; [6]men, women, and children, and the king's daughters, and every person that Nebuzaradan, the chief of the executioners, had left with Gedaliah, the son of Ahikam, the son of Shaphan. Also *they took* Jeremiah the prophet, and Baruch, the son of Neriah. [7]And they came into the land of Egypt, for they did not obey the voice of Jehovah. And they came to Tahpanhes.

[8]And the word of Jehovah was to Jeremiah in

1697 3605 5971 3605 1696 3414 3615 1961
1 וַיְהִי כְּכַלּוֹת יִרְמְיָהוּ לְדַבֵּר אֶל־כָּל־הָעָם אֶת־כָּל־דִּבְרֵי
the all the all to speaking Jeremiah had when it And
of words people finished ,was

430 3068 7971 834 430 3068
יְהוָה אֱלֹהֵיהֶם אֲשֶׁר שְׁלָחוֹ יְהוָה אֱלֹהֵיהֶם אֲלֵיהֶם אֵת
—them to their Jehovah had (for) their Jehovah
God him sent which ,God

1955 1121 5838 559 428 1697 3605
2 כָּל־הַדְּבָרִים הָאֵלֶּה׃ וַיֹּאמֶר עֲזַרְיָה בֶן־הוֹשַׁעְיָה
Hoshaiah the Azariah spoke —these words all
of son

3414 559 2086 582 3605 7143/1121 3110
וְיוֹחָנָן בֶּן־קָרֵחַ וְכָל־הָאֲנָשִׁים הַזֵּדִים אֹמְרִים אֶל־יִרְמְיָהוּ
,Jeremiah to saying ,proud men the all and ,Kareah the and
of son Johanan

3808 559 430 3068 7971 3808 3478 8267
שֶׁקֶר אַתָּה מְדַבֵּר לֹא שְׁלָחֲךָ יְהוָה אֱלֹהֵינוּ לֵאמֹר לֹא־
not ,say to God our Jehovah sent has not !speak You falsely
you

5491 5374/1121 1263 8033 1481 4714 935
3 תָבֹאוּ מִצְרַיִם לָגוּר שָׁם׃ כִּי בָּרוּךְ בֶּן־נֵרִיָּה מַסִּית אֹתְךָ
you is Neriah the Baruch But .there to Egypt Do
inciting of son sojourn go to

1540 4191 3778 3027 5414 4616
בָּנוּ לְמַעַן תֵּת אֹתָנוּ בְיַד־הַכַּשְׂדִּים לְהָמִית אֹתָנוּ וּלְהַגְלוֹת
to and us put to the the into us deliver to against
exile death to ,Chaldeans of hand ,us

2428 8269 7143 3110 8085 3808 894
4 אֹתָנוּ בָּבֶל׃ וְלֹא־שָׁמַע יוֹחָנָן בֶּן־קָרֵחַ וְכָל־שָׂרֵי הַחֲיָלִים
the cap- the and Kareah the Johanan did So to us
,army of tains all of son obey not .Babylon

3110 3947 3063 776 3427 3068 6963 5971/3605
5 וְכָל־הָעָם בְּקוֹל יְהוָה לָשֶׁבֶת בְּאֶרֶץ יְהוּדָה׃ וַיִּקַּח יוֹחָנָן
Johanan But .Judah the in live to ,Jehovah the the and
took of land of voice people all

834 3063 7611 2428 8269 7123/1121
בֶּן־קָרֵחַ וְכָל־שָׂרֵי הַחֲיָלִים אֵת כָּל־שְׁאֵרִית יְהוּדָה אֲשֶׁר־
who Judah the all army the cap- the and ,Kareah the
of remnant of tains all of son

3063 776 1481 5080 1471 3605 7725
שָׁבוּ מִכָּל־הַגּוֹיִם אֲשֶׁר נִדְּחוּ־שָׁם לָגוּר בְּאֶרֶץ יְהוּדָה׃
—Judah the in to there had they where the from re- had
of land driven been nations all turned

4428 1323 2945 802 1397
6 אֶת־הַגְּבָרִים וְאֶת־הַנָּשִׁים וְאֶת־הַטַּף וְאֶת־בְּנוֹת הַמֶּלֶךְ
the daughters and ,children and ,women and ,men
,king's

2876 7227 5018 3240 5315 3605
וְאֵת כָּל־הַנֶּפֶשׁ אֲשֶׁר הִנִּיחַ נְבוּזַרְאֲדָן רַב־טַבָּחִים אֶת־
with the of chief the Nebuzar- left had that person every and
executioners adan

5030 3414 8227 1121 296 1121 1436
גְּדַלְיָהוּ בֶּן־אֲחִיקָם בֶּן־שָׁפָן וְאֵת יִרְמְיָהוּ הַנָּבִיא וְאֶת־
and the Jeremiah and ,Shaphan the Ahikam the Gedaliah
,prophet of son of son

6963 8085 3808 4714 776 935 5374 1121 1263
7 בָּרוּךְ בֶּן־נֵרִיָּהוּ׃ וַיָּבֹאוּ אֶרֶץ מִצְרַיִם כִּי לֹא שָׁמְעוּ בְּקוֹל
the they not for ,Egypt the they And .Neriah the Baruch
of voice obey did of land into came of son

3068 1697 1961 8471 935 3068
8 יְהוָה וַיָּבֹאוּ עַד־תַּחְפַּנְחֵס׃ וַיְהִי דְבַר־יְהוָה אֶל־
to Jehovah the Then .Tahpanhes to they And Jeho-
of word came came .vah

Tahpanhes, saying, [9]Take great stones to your hand, and hide them in the mortar in the brickwork which *is* at the entrance to Pharaoh's house in Tahpanhes, in the sight of the men of Judah. [10]And say to them, So says Jehovah of hosts, the God of Israel, Behold I will send and take Nebuchadnezzar, the king of Babylon, My servant, and will set his throne on these stones that I have hidden. And he shall spread his royal pavilion over them. [11]And when he comes, he shall strike the land of Egypt. And whoever *is* for death *shall go* to death; and whoever *is* for captivity, *shall go* into captivity; and whoever *is* for the sword, to the sword. [12]And I will kindle a fire in the houses of the gods of Egypt. And he shall burn them, and take them captive. And he shall adorn himself with the land of Egypt, as a shepherd covers himself with his robe. And he shall go forth from there in peace. [13]He shall also break the obelisks of The House of the Sun which *is* in the land of Egypt; and he shall burn the houses of the gods of the Egyptians with fire.

9 ירמיהו בתחפנחס לאמר: קח בידך אבנים גדלות

,great stones your in Take ,saying in Jeremiah
hand Tahpanhes

וטמנתם במלט במלבן אשר בפתח בית־פרעה

Pharaoh's house the at which the in the in hide and
to entrance (is) brickwork mortar them

10 בתחפנחס לעיני אנשים יהודים: ואמרת אליהם כה־

Thus ,them to say And .Judah of men the the in in
of sight ,Tahpanhes

אמר יהוה צבאות אלהי ישראל הנני שלח ולקחתי את־

take and will Behold ,Israel the hosts Jehovah says
send I of God of

נבוכדראצר מלך־בבל עבדי ושמתי כסאו ממעל

on his will and My ,Babylon king Nebuchadnezzar
throne set ,servant of

לאבנים האלה אשר טמנתי ונטה את־שפרורו עליהם:

over his he And have I that these stones
.them pavillion spread shall .hidden

11 ובאה והכה את־ארץ מצרים אשר למות למות ואשר

and (go shall) for Whoever :Egypt the shall He when And
whoever ,death to death (is) of land strike comes he

12 לשבי לשבי ואשר לחרב לחרב: והצתי אש בבתי

the in fire a I And the to the for and into cap- for
of houses kindle will .sword ,sword whoever ;captivity tivity

אלהי מצרים ושרפם ושבם ועטה את־ארץ מצרים

,Egypt the will he and seize and will he and ,Egypt the
of land adorn ,them ,them burn of gods

13 כאשר־יעטה הרעה את־בגדו ויצא משם בשלום: ושבר

shall He .peace in from he and his with shep- a covers as
break also there go shall ;robe herd himself

את־מצבות בית שמש אשר בארץ מצרים ואת־בתי

the and ;Egypt the in which sun the the the
of houses of land (is) of house of obelisks

אלהי מצרים ישרף באש:

with shall he the the
.fire burn Egyptians of gods

CAP. XLIV. מד

CHAPTER 44

CHAPTER 44

[1]The word which was to Jeremiah concerning all the Jews who were living in the land of Egypt, those living at Migdol, and at Tahpanhes, and at Noph, and in the land of Pathros, saying, [2]So says Jehovah of hosts, the God of Israel, You have seen all the evil that I have brought on Jerusalem, and

1 הדבר אשר־היה אל־ירמיהו אל כל־היהודים הישבים

were who the all con- Jeremiah to came that The
living Jews cerning word

בארץ מצרים הישבים במגדל ובתחפנחס ובנף ובארץ

the in and at and at and ,Migdol at those ,Egypt the in
of land ,Noph ,Tahpanhes living of land

2 פתרוס לאמר: כה־אמר יהוה צבאות אלהי ישראל

:Israel God the ,hosts Jehovah says Thus ,saying ,Pathros
of of

אתם ראיתם את כל־הרעה אשר הבאתי על־ירושלם

,Jerusalem on have I that evil the all have You
brought seen

on all the cities of Judah. And, behold! This day *they* are a ruin, and no one lives in them; 3 because of the evil which they have done, by provoking Me to anger, by going to burn incense, by serving other gods that they did not know; they, you, nor your fathers. 4 However, I sent to you all my servants the prophets, rising early and sending, saying, Oh, do not commit this abominable thing which I hate! 5 But they did not listen, nor bow their ear, to turn from their evil, not to burn incense to other gods. 6 For this reason My fury and My anger were poured out and was kindled in the cities of Judah, and in the streets of Jerusalem. And they are wasted *and* deserted as this day. 7 And now so says Jehovah, the God of hosts, the God of Israel: Why do you commit great evil against your souls, to cut off from you man and woman, child and suckling, out of Judah, not leaving to yourselves a remnant; 8 to provoke Me to wrath with the works of your hands, burning incense to other gods in the land of Egypt, there where you have gone to sojourn, that I might cut you off, and that you might be a curse and a reproach among all the nations of the earth?

9 Have you forgotten the evil of your fathers, and the evil of the kings of Judah, and the evil of his wives, and your own evil, and the evil of your wives, which they have committed in the land of Judah and in the streets

369 2088 3117 2723 2009 3063 5892 3605 5921
וְעַל כָּל־עָרֵי יְהוּדָה וְהִנָּם חָרְבָּה הַיּוֹם הַזֶּה וְאֵין בָּהֶם
them in no one and ,This day ruin a And !behold .Judah the of cities all and on

3
6999 3212 3707 6213 834 7451 6440 3427
יֹשֵׁב׃ מִפְּנֵי רָעָתָם אֲשֶׁר עָשׂוּ לְהַכְעִסֵנִי לָלֶכֶת לְקַטֵּר
burn to ,incense by going provoking anger to Me by they have done which evil the because of ;lives

3045 3808 834 312 430 5647
לַעֲבֹד לֵאלֹהִים אֲחֵרִים אֲשֶׁר לֹא יְדָעוּם הֵמָּה אַתֶּם
,you ,they did they —know not that other gods by serving

4
7925 5030 5650 3605 7971 1
וַאֲבֹתֵיכֶם׃ וָאֶשְׁלַח אֲלֵיכֶם אֶת־כָּל־עֲבָדַי הַנְּבִיאִים הַשְׁכֵּים
rising early the ,prophets My servants all you to However sent I your nor .fathers

834 8441 6213 4994 408 559 7971
וְשָׁלֹחַ לֵאמֹר אַל־נָא תַעֲשׂוּ אֵת דְּבַר־הַתֹּעֵבָה הַזֹּאת אֲשֶׁר
which this abominable thing do commit Oh not ,saying and. ,sending

5
7451 7725 241 5186 8085 3808 8130
שָׂנֵאתִי׃ וְלֹא שָׁמְעוּ וְלֹא־הִטּוּ אֶת־אָזְנָם לָשׁוּב מֵרָעָתָם
their ,evil from turn to their ear bow nor did they ,listen But not !hate I

6
1197 639 2534 5413 312 430 6999
לְבִלְתִּי קַטֵּר לֵאלֹהִים אֲחֵרִים׃ וַתִּתַּךְ חֲמָתִי וְאַפִּי וַתִּבְעַר
was kindled and My ,anger My fury and was poured out So .other gods to burn incense to not

8071 2723 1961 3389 2351 3063 5892
בְּעָרֵי יְהוּדָה וּבְחֻצוֹת יְרוּשָׁלִַם וַתִּהְיֶינָה לְחָרְבָּה לִשְׁמָמָה
(and) deserted wasted they are And .Jerusalem of streets the in and Judah the in of cities

7
6635 430 3068 559 3541 6258 2088 3117
כַּיּוֹם הַזֶּה׃ וְעַתָּה כֹּה־אָמַר יְהוָה אֱלֹהֵי צְבָאוֹת
,hosts the of God Jehovah says thus And now .this day as

1419 7451 6213 4100 3478 430
אֱלֹהֵי יִשְׂרָאֵל לָמָּה אַתֶּם עֹשִׂים רָעָה גְדוֹלָה אֶל־
against great evil do commit you Why :Israel the of God

8432 3243 5768 802 376 3772 5315
נַפְשֹׁתֵכֶם לְהַכְרִית לָכֶם אִישׁ־וְאִשָּׁה עוֹלֵל וְיוֹנֵק מִתּוֹךְ
out of and ,suckling child and ,woman man from you cut to off your ,souls

8
4639 3707 7611 3498 3063
יְהוּדָה לְבִלְתִּי הוֹתִיר לָכֶם שְׁאֵרִית׃ לְהַכְעִסֵנִי בְּמַעֲשֵׂי
the with of works provoke to wrath to Me a ;remnant your- selves to leaving not ,Judah

4714 776 312 430 6999 3027
יְדֵיכֶם לְקַטֵּר לֵאלֹהִים אֲחֵרִים בְּאֶרֶץ מִצְרַיִם אֲשֶׁר־אַתֶּם
you where Egypt the in of land other gods to burn to incense your ,hands

1961 4616 3772 8033 1481 935
בָּאִים לָגוּר שָׁם לְמַעַן הַכְרִית לָכֶם וּלְמַעַן הֱיוֹתְכֶם
might you be and that ,you might I cut off that ,there to sojourn have gone

9
7451 7911 776 1471 3605 2781 7045
לִקְלָלָה וּלְחֶרְפָּה בְּכֹל גּוֹיֵי הָאָרֶץ׃ הֲשְׁכַחְתֶּם אֶת־רָעוֹת
the of evilness you Have forgotten the ?earth the of nations among all a and reproach curse a

802 7451 3063 4428 7451 1
אֲבוֹתֵיכֶם וְאֶת־רָעוֹת ׀ מַלְכֵי יְהוּדָה וְאֵת רָעוֹת נָשָׁיו
his ,wives evilness the of and ,Judah the of kings evilness the of and your ,fathers

3063 776 6213 834 802 7451 7451
וְאֵת רָעֹתֵיכֶם וְאֵת רָעֹת נְשֵׁיכֶם אֲשֶׁר עָשׂוּ בְּאֶרֶץ יְהוּדָה
Judah the in of land they have done which your ,wives the and of wickedness own your ,evilness and

of Jerusalem? ¹⁰They are not crushed to this day, nor have they feared, nor walked in My law, nor in My statutes which I have set before you and before your fathers.

¹¹So Jehovah of hosts the God of Israel says this: Behold, I will set My face against you for evil, and to cut off all Judah. ¹²And I will take the remnant of Judah who have set their faces to go into the land of Egypt, to reside there; and they shall all be consumed and fall in the land of Egypt. They shall be consumed by the sword, by the famine. They shall die, from the least even to the greatest, by the sword, and by the famine, and they shall be a curse, a horror, and a shame, and a reproach. ¹³For I will punish those who dwell in the land of Egypt, as I have punished Jerusalem, by the sword, by the famine, and by the plague; ¹⁴so that none of the remnant of Judah which has gone into the land of Egypt, to reside there, will be an escaped one, or a survivor, or return to the land of Judah to which they are lifting up their soul, to return to live there. For not one shall return, except those who escape.

¹⁵Then all the men who knew that their wives had burned incense to other gods, and all the women who stood by, a great assembly, even all the people who lived in the land of Egypt, in Pathros, answered Jeremiah, saying, ¹⁶As for the word that you have spoken to us in the name of Jehovah, we will not listen to you. ¹⁷But we

10

3372	3808	2088	3117	5704	1792	3808		3389	2351
יִרְאוּ	וְלֹא	הַזֶּה	הַיּוֹם	עַד	דֻּכְּאוּ	לֹא	יְרוּשָׁלָ͏ִם:	וּבְחֻצֹת
have they and	not	this	day	to	are They	not	?Jerusalem	the in and
feared,					crushed			of streets

6440	6440	5414	834	2708	8451	1980
וְלִפְנֵי	לִפְנֵיכֶם	נָתַתִּי	אֲשֶׁר	וּבְחֻקֹּתַי	בְתוֹרָתִי	הָלְכוּ וְלֹא
and before	before	set I	which	my in and	My in	walked and
before	you			statutes not	law,	not

11

430	6635	3068	559/35,41				1
אֱלֹהֵי	צְבָאוֹת	יְהוָה	כֹּה־אָמַר	לָכֵן	אֲבֹתֵיכֶם:
the	hosts,	Jehovah	says thus	Therefore	your
of God					fathers.

3063	3605	3772	7451	6440	7760	2005	347,8
יִשְׂרָאֵל	הִנְנִי	שָׂם	פָּנַי	בָּכֶם	לְרָעָה	וּלְהַכְרִית	אֶת־כָּל־יְהוּדָה:
Israel,	Behold, I	set	face	you	against	My will,	Judah.
				for	evil,	to and	all
							off cut

12

3947		7611	3063	834	7760	6440	935
וְלָקַחְתִּי	אֶת־שְׁאֵרִית	יְהוּדָה	אֲשֶׁר־שָׂמוּ	פְנֵיהֶם	לָבוֹא
I And	the	of remnant	Judah	who	set	faces	go to
take will					have		into

776	4714	5307	776	3605	8552	7760	1481
אֶרֶץ־מִצְרַיִם	לָגוּר	שָׁם	וְתַמּוּ	כֹל	בְּאֶרֶץ	מִצְרַיִם	יִפֹּלוּ
the	Egypt	to	there,	cease will	all	the in	Egypt
of land			sojourn			of land	they
							fall shall

2719	7458	8552	6996	5704	1419	2719	7458	4191
בַּחֶרֶב	בָּרָעָב	יִתַּמּוּ	מִקָּטֹן	וְעַד־גָּדוֹל	בַּחֶרֶב	וּבָרָעָב	יָמֻתוּ
the by	the by	cease will	from	even	the by	the by and	die shall
sword,	famine,		least,	greatest	sword	famine	they

13

1961	422	7045	80,47	8047	7046	2781	6485
וְהָיוּ	לְאָלָה	וּלְשַׁמָּה	וְלִקְלָלָה	וּלְחֶרְפָּה:	וּפָקַדְתִּי	עַל־
be shall And	a they	curse, a	horror, a	shame,	a and	reproach.	For I punish

3427	776	4714	6485	834	6485	3389
הַיּוֹשְׁבִים	בְּאֶרֶץ	מִצְרַיִם	כַּאֲשֶׁר	פָּקַדְתִּי	עַל־יְרוּשָׁלָ͏ִם
who those	the in	Egypt,	as	have I	Jerusalem,
live	of land			punished	

14

2719	7458	1481	8033	1698	3808	6412	8300	7611
בַּחֶרֶב	וּבָרָעָב	וּבַדָּבֶר:	וְלֹא	יִהְיֶה	פָּלִיט	וְשָׂרִיד	לִשְׁאֵרִית
the by	the by and	the by and	and	be will	es- an	a or	the for
sword,	famine,	plague;	not		caped	survivor,	of remnant

3063	935	1481	8033	776	4714	7725	776
יְהוּדָה	הַבָּאִים	לָגוּר־שָׁם	בְּאֶרֶץ	מִצְרַיִם	וְלָשׁוּב	אֶרֶץ
Judah,	which has	sojourn	there	the in	Egypt	or return	the
	gone,	to		of land		to	of land

8033	3427	7725	5315	5375	834	3063
יְהוּדָה	אֲשֶׁר־הֵמָּה	מְנַשְּׂאִים	אֶת־נַפְשָׁם	לָשׁוּב	לָשֶׁבֶת	שָׁם
Judah	which	up lifting	soul,	are	their	return to	dwell to	there.
	they (to)						

15

3808	7725	6405	34,14	6030
כִּי	לֹא־יָשׁוּבוּ	כִּי אִם־פְּלֵטִים:	וַיַּעֲנוּ	אֶת־יִרְמְיָהוּ
For	none shall	except	who those	Then	Jeremiah,
	return		escape.	answered

430	802	6999	3045	582	36,05
כָל־הָאֲנָשִׁים	הַיֹּדְעִים	כִּי־מְקַטְּרוֹת	נְשֵׁיהֶם	לֵאלֹהִים
all	men the	who knew	that had	burned	their	gods to
			incense	wives	

312	3605	802	5975	6951	1419	3605	5971
אֲחֵרִים	וְכָל־הַנָּשִׁים	הָעֹמְדוֹת	קָהָל	גָּדוֹל	וְכָל־הָעָם
other,	and	women	who stood	assembly,	a	the	even	people
	all		by,		great,		all

16

3427	776	4714	6624	559	1697	834
הַיֹּשְׁבִים	בְּאֶרֶץ־מִצְרַיִם	בְּפַתְרוֹס	לֵאמֹר:	הַדָּבָר	אֲשֶׁר
who	the in	Egypt	in	saying,	(to As)	which
lived	of land		Pathros,		word the

17

1696	8034	3068	369	8085	6213
דִּבַּרְתָּ	אֵלֵינוּ	בְּשֵׁם	יְהוָה	אֵינֶנּוּ	שֹׁמְעִים	אֵלֶיךָ:	כִּי עָשֹׂה
have you	us to	the in	Jehovah,	will we	listen	.you to	But	cer-
spoken		of name		not				tainly

will certainly do whatever thing goes out of own mouth, to burn incense to the queen of heaven, and to pour out drink offerings to her, as we have done, we and our fathers, our kings, and our rulers, in the cities of Judah and in the streets of Jerusalem. And we had plenty of food, and were well, and saw no evil. [18]But when we stopped burning incense to the queen of heaven, and pouring out drink offerings to her, we have lacked all *things*, and have been devoured by the sword and by the famine. [19]And when we burned incense to the queen of heaven, and poured out drink offerings to her, did we make her cakes to worship her, and pour out drink offerings to her, without our men?

[20]Then Jeremiah said to all the people; to the men, and to the women, and to all the people who were answering: [21]The incense that you burned in the cities of Judah and in the streets of Jerusalem, you, and your fathers, your kings, and your rulers, and the people of the land, did not Jehovah remember them? Yea, it came into His heart. [22]And Jehovah could no longer bear because of the evil of your doings, because of the detestable things you have committed. For this reason your land is a waste, and a horror, and a curse, without inhabitant, as this day. [23]Because you have burned incense, and because you have sinned against Jehovah, and have not obeyed the voice of Jehovah, in His law, or in His statutes; and *because* you did not walk in His testimonies; therefore this evil has happened to you,

4446 6999 6310 3318 1697 3605 6213
נַעֲשֶׂה אֶת־כָּל־הַדָּבָר ׀ אֲשֶׁר־יָצָא מִפִּינוּ לְקַטֵּר לִמְלֶכֶת
the to of queen / burn to incense / our of ,mouth / goes out / that / thing / every / will we do

1 6213 5262 5258 8064
הַשָּׁמַיִם וְהַסֵּיךְ־לָהּ נְסָכִים כַּאֲשֶׁר עָשִׂינוּ אֲנַחְנוּ וַאֲבֹתֵינוּ
our and ,fathers / ,we / have we ,done / as / drink ,offerings / to her / to and out pour / ,heaven

7646 3389 7351 3063 5892 8269 4428
מְלָכֵינוּ וְשָׂרֵינוּ בְּעָרֵי יְהוּדָה וּבְחֻצוֹת יְרוּשָׁלַם וַנִּשְׂבַּע
had we and of plenty / ;Jerusalem / the in and of streets / ,Judah / the in of cities / our and princes / our ,kings

2308 7200 3808 7451 2896 1961 3899
18 לֶחֶם וַנִּהְיֶה טוֹבִים וְרָעָה לֹא רָאִינוּ׃ וּמִן־אָז חָדַלְנוּ
we stopped / then And from / .see did / not / evil and / ,well / and were / ,bread

3605 2637 5262 5258 8064 4446 6999
לְקַטֵּר לִמְלֶכֶת הַשָּׁמַיִם וְהַסֵּךְ־לָהּ נְסָכִים חָסַרְנוּ כֹל
all ;(things) / have we lacked / drink ,offerings / her to / and out poured / ,heaven / the to of queen / burning incense

4446 6999 8552 7458 2719
19 וּבַחֶרֶב וּבָרָעָב תָּמְנוּ׃ וְכִי־אֲנַחְנוּ מְקַטְּרִים לִמְלֶכֶת
the to of queen / burned incense / we / And when / been have .devoured / by and famine the / by and ,sword the

6213 582 1107 5262 5258 8064
הַשָּׁמַיִם וּלְהַסֵּךְ לָהּ נְסָכִים הֲמִבַּלְעֲדֵי אֲנָשֵׁינוּ עָשִׂינוּ לָהּ
to her / we did make / our men / without / drink ,offerings / to her / poured and out / heaven

3414 559 5262 5258 6089 3561
20 כַּוָּנִים לְהַעֲצִבָה וְהַסֵּךְ לָהּ נְסָכִים׃ וַיֹּאמֶר יִרְמְיָהוּ
Jeremiah / said Then / drink ?offerings / her to / and out pour / make to an image / cakes

6030 5971 3605 802 1397 5971 3605
אֶל־כָּל־הָעָם עַל־הַגְּבָרִים וְעַל־הַנָּשִׁים וְעַל־כָּל־הָעָם הָעֹנִים
were who answering / the people / all / and to / the ,women / and to / the men / to / the —people / all / to

5892 6999 7002 559 1696
21 אֹתוֹ דָּבָר לֵאמֹר׃ הֲלוֹא אֶת־הַקִּטֵּר אֲשֶׁר קִטַּרְתֶּם בְּעָרֵי
the in of cities / you burned / that / the incense / Did not / ,saying / ,word a / him

8269 4428 1 3389 2351 3063
יְהוּדָה וּבְחֻצוֹת יְרוּשָׁלִַם אַתֶּם וַאֲבוֹתֵיכֶם מַלְכֵיכֶם וְשָׂרֵיכֶם
your and ,princes / your ,kings / your and ,fathers / ,you / ,Jerusalem / the in and of streets / Judah

3201/3808 3820 5927 3068 2142 776 5971
22 וְעַם הָאָרֶץ אֹתָם זָכַר יְהוָה וַתַּעֲלֶה עַל־לִבּוֹ׃ וְלֹא־יוּכַל
could / And not / His .heart / into / it And came / ?Jehovah / re- membered / them / the ,land / the and of people

834 8441 6440 4611 7451 5375 5750 3068
יְהוָה עוֹד לָשֵׂאת מִפְּנֵי רֹעַ מַעַלְלֵיכֶם מִפְּנֵי הַתּוֹעֵבֹת אֲשֶׁר
which / the abominations / because of / your ,doings / the because of evil of / up lift / still / Jehovah

369 7045 8047 2723 776 1961 6213
עֲשִׂיתֶם וַתְּהִי אַרְצְכֶם לְחָרְבָּה וּלְשַׁמָּה וְלִקְלָלָה מֵאֵין
without / a and ,curse / a and ,horror / ,waste a / your land / Therefore is / have you .done

2398 6999 6440 2088 3117 3427
23 יוֹשֵׁב כְּהַיּוֹם הַזֶּה׃ מִפְּנֵי אֲשֶׁר קִטַּרְתֶּם וַאֲשֶׁר חֲטָאתֶם
have you sinned / and because / have you ,incense burned / Because / .this / day as / inhabi- ,tant

2708 8451 3068 6963 8085 3808 3068
לַיהוָה וְלֹא שְׁמַעְתֶּם בְּקוֹל יְהוָה וּבְתֹרָתוֹ וּבְחֻקֹּתָיו
His in or ,statutes / His in ,law / ,Jehovah / the of voice / have obeyed / and not / against ,Jehovah

2088 7451 7125 1980 3808 5775
וּבְעֵדְוֹתָיו לֹא הֲלַכְתֶּם עַל־כֵּן קָרָאת אֶתְכֶם הָרָעָה הַזֹּאת
,this / evil / you / hap- has to pened / therefore / you ,walked / not / His in and testimonies

as *at* this day.

[24]Jeremiah also said to all the people, and to all the women, Hear the word of Jehovah, all Judah in the land of Egypt; [25]so says Jehovah of hosts, the God of Israel, saying: You and your wives have both spoken with your mouths, and fulfilled with your hands, saying, We will surely fulfill our vows that we have vowed, to burn incense to the queen of heaven, and to pour out drink offerings to her. You certainly do perform your vows, and certainly make stand your vows. [26]So hear the word of Jehovah, all Judah who reside in the land of Egypt: Behold, I have sworn by My great name, says Jehovah, that My name shall no more be named in the mouth of any man of Judah in all the land of Egypt, saying, The Lord Jehovah lives. [27]Behold, I will watch over them for evil, and not for good; and all the men of Judah in the land of Egypt shall be destroyed by the sword, and by the famine, until they come to an end. [28]And he who escapes the sword shall return out of the land of Egypt to the land of Judah, few in number. And all the remnant of Judah who have gone into the land of Egypt, to reside there, shall know whose word shall stand, theirs or Mine.

[29]And this *shall be* a sign to you, says Jehovah, that I will punish you in this place, so that you may know that My words shall surely stand against you for evil: [30]So says Jehovah, Behold, I am giving Pharaoh-hophra,

3605 5971 3605 3414 559 2088 3117
24 כַּיּוֹם הַזֶּה׃ וַיֹּאמֶר יִרְמְיָהוּ אֶל־כָּל־הָעָם וְאֶל כָּל־
all and to the people all to Jeremiah Also said .this (at) as day

4714 776 834 3063 3605 3068 1697 8085 802
הַנָּשִׁים שִׁמְעוּ דְּבַר־יְהוָה כָּל־יְהוּדָה אֲשֶׁר בְּאֶרֶץ מִצְרָיִם׃
,Egypt the in of land who (are) Judah all ,Jehovah the of word Hear the ,women

559 3478 430 6635 3068 559 3541
25 כֹּה־אָמַר יְהוָה־צְבָאוֹת אֱלֹהֵי יִשְׂרָאֵל לֵאמֹר אַתֶּם
You :saying ,Israel the of God hosts of Jehovah says Thus

6213 559 4390 3027 6310 1696 802
וּנְשֵׁיכֶם וַתְּדַבֵּרְנָה בְּפִיכֶם וּבִידֵיכֶם מִלֵּאתֶם ׀ לֵאמֹר עָשֹׂה
Surely ,saying ,fulfilled with and hands your your with mouths both have spoken your and wives

8064 4446 6999 5087 5088 6213
נַעֲשֶׂה אֶת־נְדָרֵינוּ אֲשֶׁר נָדַרְנוּ לְקַטֵּר לִמְלֶכֶת הַשָּׁמָיִם
,heaven the to of queen burn to incense have we ,vowed that our vows will we fulfill

6213 5088 6965 6965 5262 5258
וּלְהַסֵּךְ לָהּ נְסָכִים הָקֵים תָּקִימְנָה אֶת־נִדְרֵיכֶם וְעָשֹׂה
and surely your vows you raise Surely drink .offerings her to to and out pour

3063 3605 3068/1697 8085 3651 5088 6213
26 תַּעֲשֶׂינָה אֶת־נִדְרֵיכֶם׃ לָכֵן שִׁמְעוּ דְבַר־יְהוָה כָּל־יְהוּדָה
Judah all ,Jehovah the of word hear ,Therefore your .vows perform

559 1419 8034 7650 2005 4714 776 3427
הַיֹּשְׁבִים בְּאֶרֶץ מִצְרַיִם הִנְנִי נִשְׁבַּעְתִּי בִּשְׁמִי הַגָּדוֹל אָמַר
says ,great My by name have sworn ,Behold I ;Egypt the in of land who sojourns

3063 376 3605 6310 7121 8034 5750 518 1961 3068
יְהוָה אִם־יִהְיֶה עוֹד שְׁמִי נִקְרָא ׀ בְּפִי ׀ כָּל־אִישׁ יְהוּדָה
,Judah man of any the in of mouth named My name more will (that) be no Jeho- ,vah

5921 8245 2005 4714 776 3605 3068 136/2416 559
27 אֹמֵר חַי־אֲדֹנָי יְהוִה בְּכָל־אֶרֶץ מִצְרָיִם׃ הִנְנִי שֹׁקֵד עֲלֵיהֶם
over them am watching ,Behold I .Egypt the of land in all ,Jehovah The Lord lives ,saying

776 3063 376 3605 8552 2896 3808 7451
לְרָעָה וְלֹא לְטוֹבָה וְתַמּוּ כָל־אִישׁ יְהוּדָה אֲשֶׁר בְּאֶרֶץ
the in of land who (are) Judah the of men all will and cease for ;good and not for ,evil

7725 2719 6412 8552 3615/5704 7458 2719 4714
28 מִצְרַיִם בַּחֶרֶב וּבָרָעָב עַד־כְּלוֹתָם׃ וּפְלִיטֵי חֶרֶב יְשֻׁבוּן
shall return the sword who he escapes And come they .end until an to the by and ,famine the by sword ,Egypt

7611 3605 3045 4557 4962 3063 776 4714 776
מִן־אֶרֶץ מִצְרַיִם אֶרֶץ יְהוּדָה מְתֵי מִסְפָּר וְיָדְעוּ כָּל־שְׁאֵרִית
the of remnant all shall And know .number men of Judah the to of land Egypt the of out of land

6965 4310/1697 8033 1481 4714 776 935 3063
יְהוּדָה הַבָּאִים לְאֶרֶץ־מִצְרַיִם לָגוּר שָׁם דְּבַר־מִי יָקוּם
shall ,stand word whose there to sojourn Egypt the into of land have who gone Judah

6485 3068 5002 226
29 מִמֶּנִּי וּמֵהֶם׃ וְזֹאת־לָכֶם הָאוֹת נְאֻם־יְהוָה כִּי־פֹקֵד אֲנִי
am I that punishing ,Jehovah states the ,sign you to this And (be shall) or .theirs Mine

1697 6965 6965 3045 2088 4725
עֲלֵיכֶם בַּמָּקוֹם הַזֶּה לְמַעַן תֵּדְעוּ כִּי קוֹם יָקוּמוּ דְבָרַי
My words shall rise surely that may you know so that ,this place in you

6548 5414 2005 3068 559 3541 7451
30 עֲלֵיכֶם לְרָעָה׃ כֹּה ׀ אָמַר יְהוָה הִנְנִי נֹתֵן אֶת־פַּרְעֹה
Pharaoh- am giving Behold I ,Jehovah says Thus .evil for against you

king of Egypt, into the hand of his enemies, and into the hand of those who seek his soul, even as I gave Zedekiah, king of Judah, into the hand of Nebuchadnezzar, the king of Babylon, his enemy that sought his soul.

5315 1245 3027 341 3027 4714 4428 6548
חָפְרַע מֶלֶךְ־מִצְרַיִם בְּיַד אֹיְבָיו וּבְיַד מְבַקְשֵׁי נַפְשׁוֹ כַּאֲשֶׁר
as ,soul his seekers of into and of hand the his ,enemies the into of hand Egypt king of Hophra

4428 5019 3027 3063/4428 6667 5414
נָתַתִּי אֶת־צִדְקִיָּהוּ מֶלֶךְ־יְהוּדָה בְּיַד נְבוּכַדְרֶאצַּר מֶלֶךְ
king of Nebuchadnezzar the into of hand Judah king of Zedekiah gave I

5315 1245 341 894
בָּבֶל אֹיְבוֹ וּמְבַקֵּשׁ נַפְשׁוֹ׃
his .soul that sought his ,Babylon enemy

CAP. XLV מה

CHAPTER 45

CHAPTER 45

[1]The word that Jeremiah the prophet spoke to Baruch, the son of Neriah, when he had written these words in a book from the mouth of Jeremiah, in the fourth year of Jehoiakim, the son of Josiah, king of Judah, saying, [2]So says Jehovah, the God of Israel, to you, O Baruch: [3]You said, Woe is me now, for Jehovah has added grief to my pain; I fainted in my sighing, and I find no rest.

[4]So you shall say to him, Jehovah says this: Behold, I am tearing down what I have built; and I am pulling up what I have planted, even all the land itself to Me. [5]And do you seek great things for yourself? Do not seek *them*. For, behold, I will bring evil on all flesh, declares Jehovah. But I will give your soul to you for a prize, there on all the places where you go.

5374/1121 1263 5030 3414 1696 1697
1 הַדָּבָר אֲשֶׁר דִּבֶּר יִרְמְיָהוּ הַנָּבִיא אֶל־בָּרוּךְ בֶּן־נֵרִיָּה
,Neriah the of son Baruch to the prophet Jeremiah spoke that The word

8141 3414 6310 5612 428 1697 3789
בְּכָתְבוֹ אֶת־הַדְּבָרִים הָאֵלֶּה עַל־סֵפֶר מִפִּי יִרְמְיָהוּ בַּשָּׁנָה
the year in ,Jeremiah the of mouth from a book in these words he when written had

3541 559 3063 4428 2977 1121 3079 7243
2 הָרְבִעִית לִיהוֹיָקִים בֶּן־יֹאשִׁיָּהוּ מֶלֶךְ יְהוּדָה לֵאמֹר׃ כֹּה
Thus ,saying ,Judah of king Josiah the of son of Jehoiakim fourth

4994/188 559 1263 3478 430 3068 559
3 אָמַר יְהוָה אֱלֹהֵי יִשְׂרָאֵל עָלֶיךָ בָּרוּךְ׃ אָמַרְתָּ אוֹי־נָא לִי
to .me now Woe (is) You ,said O :Baruch ,you to Israel the of God Jehovah says

3808 4496 585 3021 4341 3015 3068 3254
כִּי־יָסַף יְהוָה יָגוֹן עַל־מַכְאֹבִי יָגַעְתִּי בְּאַנְחָתִי וּמְנוּחָה לֹא
not rest and my in ;groaning fainted I my ;pain to grief Jehovah has for added

834 2009 3068 559 3541 413 559 3541 4672
4 מָצָאתִי׃ כֹּה ׀ תֹאמַר אֵלָיו כֹּה אָמַר יְהוָה הִנֵּה אֲשֶׁר
that which ,Behold ,Jehovah says Thus to ,him shall you say So .find I

776 3605 5428 5193 834 2040 1129
בָּנִיתִי אֲנִי הֹרֵס וְאֵת אֲשֶׁר־נָטַעְתִּי אֲנִי נֹתֵשׁ וְאֶת־כָּל־הָאָרֶץ
the land all even am I ;up pulling have I ,planted that and which and tear- ;down ing am I have I built

935 2005 1245 1419 1245
5 לִי־הִיא׃ וְאַתָּה תְּבַקֶּשׁ־לְךָ גְדֹלוֹת אַל־תְּבַקֵּשׁ כִּי הִנְנִי מֵבִיא
am bringing ,behold I for ;(them) seek Do not great ?things for seek do yourself And you .itself to Me

7998 5315 5414 3068 5002 1320 3605 5921 7451
רָעָה עַל־כָּל־בָּשָׂר נְאֻם יְהוָה וְנָתַתִּי לְךָ אֶת־נַפְשְׁךָ לְשָׁלָל
a as ,prize your soul to you I But will give .Jehovah states ,flesh all on evil

8033 1980 4725 3605 5921
עַל כָּל־הַמְּקֹמוֹת אֲשֶׁר תֵּלֶךְ־שָׁם׃
.there you go where the places all on

CAP. XLVI מו

CHAPTER 46

CHAPTER 46

[1]The word of Jehovah which was to Jeremiah the prophet against the nations; [2]against Egypt; against the army of Pharaoh-necho, king of Egypt, which was by the

1471 5030 3414 3068 1697 1961 834
1 אֲשֶׁר הָיָה דְבַר־יְהוָה אֶל־יִרְמְיָהוּ הַנָּבִיא עַל־הַגּוֹיִם׃
the ;nations against the prophet Jeremiah to Jehovah The of word came which

1961 834 4714 4428 6549 6549 2428 4714
2 לְמִצְרַיִם עַל־חֵיל פַּרְעֹה נְכוֹ מֶלֶךְ מִצְרַיִם אֲשֶׁר־הָיָה עַל־
by was which Egypt king of Necho Pharaoh- the of army against against ,Egypt

river Euphrates in Carchemish, which Nebuchadnezzar, the king of Babylon, struck in the fourth year of Jehoiakim, the son of Josiah, king of Judah: ³Set in order the buckler and shield, and draw near to battle. ⁴Harness the horses, and get up, O horsemen. Yea, stand with helmets, polish the spears, put on coats of mail. ⁵Why have I seen? They *are* afraid *and* turned backward. And their mighty ones are beaten down, and have fled *for* refuge, and do not look back. Terror *is* all around, says Jehovah. ⁶Do not let the swift flee away, nor the mighty man escape. They stumbled and fell to the north, by the side of the river Euphrates. ⁷Who is this rising up like the Nile, whose waters surge about like the rivers? ⁸Egypt rises up like the Nile, and *his* waters surge about like the rivers. And he says, I will go up *and* will cover the earth; I will destroy the city and its people. ⁹Come up, horses; and rage, chariots! And let the mighty men come forth, the Ethiopians and the Libyans who handle the shield; and the Lydians who handle *and* tread the bow. ¹⁰For this *is* the day of the Lord Jehovah of hosts, a day of vengeance, that He may avenge Himself of His foes. And the sword shall devour, and be sated, and made drunk with their blood, for a sacrifice *is* to the Lord Jehovah of hosts in the north country by the river Euphrates. ¹¹Go up into Gilead and take balm, O virgin daughter of Egypt; in vain you shall use many remedies; healing is not for you. ¹²The nations have heard of your shame, and your cry has filled the land. For the mighty man has stumbled against the mighty; they have fallen together, both of them.

¹³The word spoken by Jehovah to Jeremiah the

46:3

884	44 128	5019	5221	834	3751	6578 5104
נְהַר־פְּרָת	בְּכַרְכְּמִשׁ	אֲשֶׁר	הִכָּה	נְבוּכַדְרֶאצַּר	מֶלֶךְ־בָּבֶל	
Babylon king	Nebuchadnezzar struck	which	in	Euphrates the river

,Babylon king Nebuchadnezzar struck which in ,Carchemish of Euphrates the river

6186	3063 44 128	2977	1121	3079	7243 8141
בִּשְׁנַת הָרְבִיעִית	לִיהוֹיָקִים בֶּן־יֹאשִׁיָּהוּ	מֶלֶךְ יְהוּדָה: עִרְכוּ			

3 in Set :Judah king Josiah the of the year in
order of of son Jehoiakim fourth

657 1	5927	5483	631	4421	6793 4043
מָגֵן וְצִנָּה	וּגְשׁוּ	לַמִּלְחָמָה:	אִסְרוּ הַסּוּסִים	וַעֲלוּ הַפָּרָשִׁים	

4 O get and the Harness .battle for draw and and the
;horsemen up horses near ,shield buckler

4100	5630	3847	74 :20	4838	3553	3320
וְהִתְיַצְּבוּ בְּכוֹבָעִים	מָרְקוּ הָרְמָחִים	לִבְשׁוּ הַסִּרְיֹנֹת:	מַדּוּעַ			

5 Why of coats on put ;spears the polish with stand and
,mail ;helmets

4499	3807	1368	268	5472	2844	7200
רָאִיתִי הֵמָּה חַתִּים נְסֹגִים אָחוֹר וְגִבּוֹרֵיהֶם יֻכַּתּוּ וּמָנוֹס						

(for) and are their And back- (and) afraid they I have
refuge crushed ones mighty ?ward turned (are) seen

7031	5127	3068 5002	5439	4032	6437 38 :08 5127
נָסוּ וְלֹא הִפְנוּ מָגוֹר מִסָּבִיב נְאֻם־יְהוָה: אַל־יָנוּס הַקַּל					

6 the let Do not .Jehovah states all terror look do and have
,swift flee around (is) ,back not ,fled

5307	1378.2	65 :78 5104	3027	6829	1368 44 122 3808
וְאַל־יִמָּלֵט הַגִּבּוֹר צָפוֹנָה עַל־יַד נְהַר־פְּרָת כָּשְׁלוּ וְנָפָלוּ:					

.fell and they Euphrates the the by the to the let do and
stumbled river of side north ;mighty escape not

2975	4714	4325	1607	51 :04	59 :27 29 :75 4310
מִי־זֶה כַּיְאֹר יַעֲלֶה כַּנְּהָרוֹת יִתְגָּעֲשׁוּ מֵימָיו: מִצְרַיִם כַּיְאֹר					

7, 8 like Egypt whose surge the like rising the like this Who
Nile the ?waters about rivers ;up Nile (is)

776	3680	5927	559	4325	1607 5104 59 :27
יַעֲלֶה וְכַנְּהָרוֹת יִתְגָּעֲשׁוּ מָיִם וַיֹּאמֶר אַעֲלֶה אֲכַסֶּה־אֶרֶץ					

the (and) will I he and (his) surge like and rises
;earth cover up go says ;waters about rivers the ;up

7393	1984	5483	59 :27	3427	5892	6
אֹבִידָה עִיר וְיֹשְׁבֵי בָהּ: עֲלוּ הַסּוּסִים וְהִתְהֹלְלוּ הָרֶכֶב						

9 !chariots ,rage and ;horses Come .it in the and the will I
,up dwellers city destroy

8610	3866	40 :43	6316	1368	3318
וְיֵצְאוּ הַגִּבּוֹרִים כּוּשׁ וּפוּט תֹּפְשֵׂי מָגֵן וְלוּדִים תֹּפְשֵׂי דֹּרְכֵי					

(and) who the and the who and the mighty the let And
bend handle Lydians ,shield handle Libyans Ethiopians men out come

5358	5360	3117	6635	3068	136	3117	7198
קָשֶׁת: וְהַיּוֹם הַהוּא לַאדֹנָי יְהוִה צְבָאוֹת יוֹם נְקָמָה לְהִנָּקֵם							

10 avenge to venge- day a ;hosts Jehovah to (is) that day For .bow the
Himself of ;ance of the Lord the

136	2077	1818	7301	76 :46	27 :09 398	68 :62
מִצָּרָיו וְאָכְלָה חֶרֶב וְשָׂבְעָה וְרָוְתָה מִדָּמָם כִּי זֶבַח לַאדֹנָי						

the to sac- a for their with made and be and the shall And His of
Lord (is) rifice ;blood drunk sated ,sword devour .foes

3947	15 :68	5927	6578	5104	6 828	776	6635	3068
יְהוִה צְבָאוֹת בְּאֶרֶץ צָפוֹן אֶל־נְהַר־פְּרָת: עֲלִי גִלְעָד וּקְחִי								

11 and (into) up Go .Euphrates the by north the in hosts Jehovah
take Gilead river of land of

369	8585	74 :99	7235	7723	4714	1323	1330	68 :75
צֳרִי בְּתוּלַת בַּת־מִצְרָיִם לַשָּׁוְא הִרְבֵּיתְ רְפֻאֹת תְּעָלָה אֵין								

not healing ;remedies you shall vain in ;Egypt daughter virgin O ,balm
many use of

1368	776	4390	6682	7036	1471	8085
לָךְ: שָׁמְעוּ גוֹיִם קְלוֹנֵךְ וְצִוְחָתֵךְ מָלְאָה הָאָרֶץ כִּי־גִבּוֹר						

12 the For the has your and your (of) The have for
mighty .land filled cry ,shame nations heard .you

1696	1697	8147	5307	3162	37 :82 1318
בְּגִבּוֹר כָּשָׁלוּ יַחְדָּו נָפְלוּ שְׁנֵיהֶם: הַדָּבָר אֲשֶׁר דִּבֶּר					

13 spoke that The of both they together has the against
word .them ;fallen have ;stumbled mighty

prophet, of the coming of
Nebuchadnezzar, the king
of Babylon, to strike the
land of Egypt. [14]Declare *it*
in Egypt, and make it heard
in Migdol, and make it
heard in Noph and in
Tahpanhes; say, Stand fast
and get yourself ready, for
the sword shall devour all
around you. [15]Why is your
mighty one swept away? He
did not stand because
Jehovah thrust him down.
[16]He made many stumble;
yea, one fell on his neighbor. And they said, Arise,
and let us go again to our
own people, and to the land
of our birth, away from the
oppressing sword. [17]They
cried there, Pharaoh, king
of Egypt, *is* a noise; he has
passed the chosen time.
[18]*As* I live, says the King
whose name *is* Jehovah of
hosts, Surely as Tabor *is*
among the mountains, and
as Carmel is by the sea, he
shall come. [19]O daughter
dwelling in Egypt, get ready
to go into captivity. For
Noph shall be a waste, and
set afire, without inhabitant. [20]Egypt *is* a beautiful
heifer, but a stinger surely
comes out of the north.
[21]Also her hired ones *are* in
the midst of her like calves
of the stall; for they also
have turned back, fleeing
together. They did not
stand because the day of
their calamity had come on
them, the time of their
punishment. [22]Its sound *is*
like a serpent's going, for
they shall go in force, and
come against her with axes,
like woodcutters. [23]They
have cut down her forest,
says Jehovah, though it
cannot be searched; be-
cause they are more than
the locusts, and there is no
number to them. [24]The
daughter of Egypt shall be
ashamed. She shall be
delivered into the hand of
the people of the north.
[25]Jehovah of hosts, the God
of Israel, says, Behold, I am
punishing the multitudes of

884 4428 5019 935 5030 3414 3068
יְהוָה אֶל־יִרְמְיָהוּ הַנָּבִיא לָבוֹא נְבוּכַדְרֶאצַּר מֶלֶךְ בָּבֶל
Babylon king Nebuchadnezzar the of the Jeremiah to Jehovah
of of coming ,prophet

8085 4714 5046 4714 776 5221
14 לְהַכּוֹת אֶת־אֶרֶץ מִצְרָיִם׃ הַגִּידוּ בְמִצְרַיִם וְהַשְׁמִיעוּ
make and ,Egypt in Proclaim .Egypt the strike to
heard it (it) of land

3559 3220 559 8471 5297 8085 4024
בְמִגְדּוֹל וְהַשְׁמִיעוּ בְנֹף וּבְתַחְפַּנְחֵס אִמְרוּ הִתְיַצֵּב וְהָכֵן
pre- and Stand ,say in and in make and ;Migdol in
pare fast ;Tahpanhes Noph heard (it)

3808 47 5502 4100 5439 2719 398
15 לָךְ כִּי־אָכְלָה חֶרֶב סְבִיבֶיךָ׃ מַדּוּעַ נִסְחַף אַבִּירֶיךָ לֹא
not your swept is Why around all the shall for your-
?one mighty away you sword devour self

7453 376 5307 3782 7235 1920 3068 3588/5975
עָמַד כִּי יְהוָה הֲדָפוֹ׃ הִרְבָּה כּוֹשֵׁל גַּם־נָפַל אִישׁ אֶל־רֵעֵהוּ
his on one fell ,yea ,stumble made He thrust Jehovah be- He
.neighbor many .down him cause ,stood

6440 4138 776 5971 7725 6965 559
16 וַיֹּאמְרוּ קוּמָה ׀ וְנָשֻׁבָה אֶל־עַמֵּנוּ וְאֶל־אֶרֶץ מוֹלַדְתֵּנוּ מִפְּנֵי
away our the and our to let and ,Arise they And
from ,birth of land to ,people return us ,said

5674 7588 4714 4428 6547 8033 7121 3238 2719
17 חֶרֶב הַיּוֹנָה׃ קָרְאוּ שָׁם פַּרְעֹה מֶלֶךְ־מִצְרַיִם שָׁאוֹן הֶעֱבִיר
has he a (is) Egypt king Pharaoh ,there They the sword
passed ;noise of cried .oppressing

8396 8034 6635 3068 4428 5002 2416 4150
18 הַמּוֹעֵד׃ חַי־אָנִי נְאֻם־הַמֶּלֶךְ יְהוָה צְבָאוֹת שְׁמוֹ כִּי כְּתָבוֹר
as Surely whose hosts Jehovah the states I (As) chosen the
Tabor (is) name of ,king ,live .time

3427 6213 1473 3627 935 3220 3760 2022
19 בֶּהָרִים וּכְכַרְמֶל בַּיָּם יָבוֹא׃ כְּלֵי גוֹלָה עֲשִׂי לָךְ יוֹשֶׁבֶת
dwelling for Prepare exile vessels shall he by (is) as and the in (is)
in ,yourself of .come ,sea the Carmel ,mountains

3427 369 3341 1961 8047 5297 4714 1323
בַּת־מִצְרָיִם כִּי־נֹף לְשַׁמָּה תִהְיֶה וְנִצְּתָה מֵאֵין יוֹשֵׁב׃
a without and shall waste a Noph for ,Egypt O
.dweller burned become daughter

7916 1571 935 935 6828 7171 4714 3304 5697
20
21 עֶגְלָה יְפֵה־פִיָּה מִצְרָיִם קֶרֶץ מִצָּפוֹן בָּא בָא׃ גַּם־שְׂכִרֶיהָ
her Also .comes surely the from a (but) Egypt a heifer
mercenaries north stinger ,(is) beautiful

3808 3162 5127 6437 1571 4770 5695 7130
בְקִרְבָּהּ כְּעֶגְלֵי מַרְבֵּק כִּי־גַם־הֵמָּה הִפְנוּ נָסוּ יַחְדָּיו לֹא
not ;together fleeing have they also for ;stall the like her in
,turned of calves midst

5175 6963 6486 6256 5921 935 343 3117/3588 5975
22 עָמָדוּ כִּי יוֹם אֵידָם בָּא עֲלֵיהֶם עֵת פְּקֻדָּתָם׃ קוֹלָהּ כַּנָּחָשׁ
a like Its their the upon has their the because they
snake's sound .punishment of time ,them come calamity of day ,stood

6086 2404 935 7134 3212 2428 3212
יֵלֵךְ כִּי־בְחַיִל יֵלֵכוּ וּבְקַרְדֻּמּוֹת בָּאוּ לָהּ כְּחֹטְבֵי עֵצִים׃
.wood like against come with and shall they in for ;going
of cutters her axes ;go force

697 7231 3588 2713 3808 3068 5002 3293 3772
23 כָּרְתוּ יַעְרָהּ נְאֻם־יְהוָה כִּי לֹא יֵחָקֵר כִּי רַבּוּ מֵאַרְבֶּה
the than are they be- be can it not though ,Jehovah states her cut They
locusts more cause —searched ,forests down

5971 3027 5414 4714 1323 3001 4557 369
24 וְאֵין לָהֶם מִסְפָּר׃ הֹבִישָׁה בַּת־מִצְרָיִם נִתְּנָה בְּיַד עַם־
people the into shall She ;Egypt The be shall (a by) them to and
of hand given be of daughter ashamed .number not is

6485 2005 3478 430 6635 3068 559 6828
25 צָפוֹן׃ אָמַר יְהוָה צְבָאוֹת אֱלֹהֵי יִשְׂרָאֵל הִנְנִי פוֹקֵד אֶל־
to pun- am ,Behold :Israel the ,hosts Jehovah says the
ishing I of God of .north

4428 430 4714 6547 5011 528
אָמוֹן מִנֹּא וְעַל־פַּרְעֹה וְעַל־מִצְרַיִם וְעַל־אֱלֹהֶיהָ וְעַל־מְלָכֶיהָ
her kings | and | her gods | with | ,Egypt | and Pharaoh | and ,No | mul-titude | the of

26 53:15 1245 3027 54.14 982 6547
וְעַל־פַּרְעֹה וְעַל הַבֹּטְחִים בּוֹ׃ וּנְתַתִּים בְּיַד מְבַקְשֵׁי נַפְשָׁם
their ,lives | seekers of | the into of hand | will I and them give | in ;him | who those trust | and Pharaoh even

793.1 310 5650 3027 884 44:28 5019 3027
וּבְיַד נְבוּכַדְרֶאצַּר מֶלֶךְ־בָּבֶל וּבְיַד עֲבָדָיו וְאַחֲרֵי־כֵן תִּשְׁכֹּן
be will it inhabited | And afterward | his .servant's | into and hand | ,Babylon king of | ,Nebuchadnezzar's | and hand into

27 3290 5650 3372 408 3068 5002 6924 3117
כִּימֵי־קֶדֶם נְאֻם־יְהוָה׃ וְאַתָּה אַל־תִּירָא עַבְדִּי יַעֲקֹב
,Jacob | My O servant | do ,fear | not | ,you But | .Jehovah states | ,old | the as of days

2233 7350 3467 2005 3478 2865 408
וְאַל־תֵּחַת יִשְׂרָאֵל כִּי הִנְנִי מוֹשִׁעֲךָ מֵרָחוֹק וְאֶת־זַרְעֲךָ
your seed | and | afar from ,off | saving am you | ,behold I | For | .Israel O | be afraid | and not

28 2729 369 7599 8252 3290 7725 7628 776
מֵאֶרֶץ שִׁבְיָם וְשָׁב יַעֲקוֹב וְשָׁקַט וְשַׁאֲנַן וְאֵין מַחֲרִיד׃ אַתָּה
You | make shall afraid | and not | at and ,ease | be and rest in | Jacob | shall and return | their ;exile | the from of land

6213 3068 5002 3290 5650 3372 408
אַל־תִּירָא עַבְדִּי יַעֲקֹב נְאֻם־יְהוָה כִּי אִתְּךָ אָנִי כִּי אֶעֱשֶׂה
will I make | for | I. (am) | with you | for | ,Jehovah states | ,Jacob | My O servant | shall ,fear | not

6213 3808 8033 5080 1471 3605 3617
כָלָה בְּכָל־הַגּוֹיִם ׀ אֲשֶׁר הִדַּחְתִּיךָ שָׁמָּה וְאֹתְךָ לֹא־אֶעֱשֶׂה
will I make | not | (of) But you | .there | have I you driven | where | the nations | of all | full a end

5352 3808/5352 49:41 3256 3615
כָלָה וְיִסַּרְתִּיךָ לַמִּשְׁפָּט וְנַקֵּה לֹא אֲנַקֶּךָּ׃
leave I will .unpunished you | not by and means no | justly | correct but you | full a ;end

No, and Pharaoh, and Egypt, with her gods and her kings, even Pharaoh and those who trust in him. [26]And I will deliver them into the hand of those who seek their lives, and into the hand of Nebuchadnezzar, the king of Babylon, and into the hand of his servants. And afterward it will be inhabited, as in the days of old, declares Jehovah.

[27]But you, do not fear, O My servant Jacob; and do not be afraid, O Israel. For, behold, I am saving you from afar off, and your seed from the land of their exile. And Jacob shall return and be in rest and at ease, and none shall make afraid. [28]You shall not fear, O Jacob My servant, says Jehovah, for I *am* with you. For I will make a full end of all the nations there where I have driven you. But I will not make a full end *of* you, but *I will* correct you justly, and by no means will I leave you unpunished.

CAP. XLVII מז

CHAPTER 47

1 6430 5030 3414 3068 1697 1961 834
אֲשֶׁר הָיָה דְבַר־יְהוָה אֶל־יִרְמְיָהוּ הַנָּבִיא אֶל־פְּלִשְׁתִּים
the ,Philistines | against | the prophet | Jeremiah | to | Jehovah The of word | came | which

2 4325 3068 559 3541 5804 6547 5221 2962
בְּטֶרֶם יַכֶּה פַרְעֹה אֶת־עַזָּה׃ כֹּה ׀ אָמַר יְהוָה הִנֵּה־מַיִם
waters Behold | Jeho- ,vah | says | Thus | .Gaza | Pharaoh | struck | before

5892 4393 776 7857 78:57 5158 1961 6828 5927
עֹלִים מִצָּפוֹן וְהָיוּ לְנַחַל שׁוֹטֵף וְיִשְׁטְפוּ אֶרֶץ וּמְלוֹאָהּ עִיר
the ,city | its and ;fulness | the land | shall and overflow | over- ,flowing | an torrent | a | and become | of out north the | rise up

3 6963 776 3427 3605 3213 120 2199 3427
וְיֹשְׁבֵי בָהּ וְזָעֲקוּ הָאָדָם וְהֵילִל כֹּל יוֹשֵׁב הָאָרֶץ׃ מִקּוֹל
the At of noise | the .land's | inhabi- tants | all | shall and wail | the ,men | Then cry shall | .it in | and dwellers

1534 1995 7393 7491 47 6541 8161
שַׁעֲטַת פַּרְסוֹת אַבִּירָיו מֵרַעַשׁ לְרִכְבּוֹ הֲמוֹן גַּלְגִּלָּיו לֹא־
not | his ;wheels | rumb- the of ling | his of ,chariots | the at rushing | strong his ;ones | hoofs the of | stamp- the of ing

4 7703 935 3117 3027 7510 1121 6437
הִפְנוּ אָבוֹת אֶל־בָּנִים מֵרִפְיוֹן יָדָיִם׃ עַל־הַיּוֹם הַבָּא לִשְׁדוֹד
to destroy | that comes | the day | because of | ;hands of despair | from | (their) ,sons | to | the fathers | shall back look

5826 8300 3605 6721 6865 3772 64:30 36:05
אֶת־כָּל־פְּלִשְׁתִּים לְהַכְרִית לְצֹר וּלְצִידוֹן כֹּל שָׂרִיד עֹזֵר
who .helps | survivor | every | and Sidon | from Tyre | cut to off | the ;Philistines | all

CHAPTER 47

[1]The word of Jehovah that was to Jeremiah the prophet against the Philistines, before Pharaoh struck Gaza. [2]So says Jehovah, Behold, waters rise up out of the north, and shall become an overflowing torrent. And *it* shall overflow the land and all its fullness; the city, and those who dwell in it. Then the men shall cry, and all the people of the land shall wail. [3]At the noise of the stamping of the hooves of his strong *horses*, at the rushing of his chariots, the rumbling of his wheels, the fathers shall not look back to *their* sons, because of feebleness of hands; [4]because of the day that comes to destroy all the Philistines; to cut off from Tyre and Sidon every survivor who helps. For

Jehovah will plunder the Philistines, the rest of the coast of Caphtor. [5]Baldness has come on Gaza; Ashkelon is silenced. O remnant of their valley, until when will you cut yourself? [6]O sword of Jehovah, until when will you not be quiet? Put yourself into your sheath; rest, and be still. [7]How can you be quiet, since Jehovah has given it a command? He has set it there against Ashkelon, and against the seashore.

CHAPTER 48

[1]So says Jehovah of hosts, the God of Israel, against Moab: Woe to Nebo, for it is ravaged! Kiriathaim is put to shame *and* captured. The fortress is put to shame and razed. [2]Moab shall not still be praised. In Heshbon they have plotted evil against it, *saying*, Come and let us cut it off as a nation. And you shall be silenced, O madmen; a sword will go after you. [3]A voice of crying from Horonaim; plundering and great ruin! [4]Moab is broken up; her little ones have caused a cry to be heard. [5]For in the ascent to Luhith, they shall go up with great weeping. For in the descent to Horonaim, the enemies have heard a cry of ruin. [6]Flee! Save your lives, and be like a naked thing in the wilderness.

[7]For because you have trusted in your works, and in your treasures, you shall also be captured. And Chemosh shall go into exile; both his priests and his rulers. [8]And a plunderer shall come on every city, and no city shall escape. Also the valley shall perish, and the plain shall be destroyed, as Jehovah has spoken. [9]Give wings to

935 3731 339 7611 6430 3068 7701
כִּי־שֹׁדֵד יְהוָה אֶת־פְּלִשְׁתִּים שְׁאֵרִית אִי כַפְתּוֹר׃ בָּאָה
has .Caphtor the rem- the the Jehovah is For
come of coast of nant ,Philistines destroying

5704 6010 7611 831 1820 5804 7142
5 קָרְחָה אֶל־עַזָּה נִדְמְתָה אַשְׁקְלוֹן שְׁאֵרִית עִמְקָם עַד־מָתַי
when until their remnant O Ashkelon is ;Gaza on Baldness
,valley of silenced

622 8252 3808 5704 3068 2719 1945 1413
6 תִּתְגּוֹדָדִי׃ הוֹי חֶרֶב לַיהוָה עַד־אָנָה לֹא תִשְׁקֹטִי הֵאָסְפִי
Put you will not when until of sword O cut you will
yourself ?quiet be ,Jehovah ?yourself

6680 3068 8252 1826 7280 8593
7 אֶל־תַּעְרֵךְ הֵרָגְעִי וָדֹמִּי׃ אֵיךְ תִּשְׁקֹטִי וַיהוָה צִוָּה־לָהּ אֶל־
Against com- has since you can How be and rest Your into
?it manded Jehovah ,quiet be .still ;sheath

3259 8033 3220 2348 831
אַשְׁקְלוֹן וְאֶל־חוֹף הַיָּם שָׁם יְעָדָהּ׃
has He there the shore and Ashkelon
.it set ,sea against

CAP. XLVIII מח

CHAPTER 48

5015 1946 3478 430 6635 3068 559 3541 4124
1 לְמוֹאָב כֹּה־אָמַר יְהוָה צְבָאוֹת אֱלֹהֵי יִשְׂרָאֵל הוֹי אֶל־נְבוֹ
,Nebo to Woe :Israel the hosts Jehovah says thus Against
of God of ,Moab

4869 954 7156 3920 3001 7703
כִּי שֻׁדְּדָה הֹבִישָׁה נִלְכְּדָה קִרְיָתָיִם הֹבִישָׁה הַמִּשְׂגָּב
the to put is ;Kiriathaim (and) to put is is it for
fortress shame seized shame ;ravaged

7451 2803 2809 4124 8416 5750/369 2865
2 וָחָתָּה׃ אֵין עוֹד תְּהִלַּת מוֹאָב בְּחֶשְׁבּוֹן חָשְׁבוּ עָלֶיהָ רָעָה
,evil against have they in ;Moab praise more There and
it plotted Heshbon of no be shall .razed

2719 1980 310 1826 4086 1571 1471 3772 3212
לְכוּ וְנַכְרִיתֶנָּה מִגּוֹי גַּם־מַדְמֵן תִּדֹּמִּי אַחֲרַיִךְ תֵּלֶךְ חָרֶב׃
.sword a will after be shall you O And a as us let and (saying)
go you ;silenced ,Madmen .nation off it cut Come

4124 7665 1419 7667 7701 2773 6818 6963
3
4 קוֹל צְעָקָה מֵחֹרֹנָיִם שֹׁד וָשֶׁבֶר גָּדוֹל׃ נִשְׁבְּרָה מוֹאָב
;Moab broken is !great and plunder- from crying A
ruin ing ,Horonaim of voice

5927 1065 3872 4608 6810 2201 8085
5 הִשְׁמִיעוּ זְעָקָה צְעוֹרֶיהָ׃ כִּי מַעֲלֵה הַלֻּחוֹת בִּבְכִי יַעֲלֶה־
shall they with Luhith the (in) For little her cry a caused have
up go weeping to ascent .ones heard be to

5127 8085 7667 6818 6862 2773 4174 1065
6 בֶּכִי כִּי בְּמוֹרַד חוֹרֹנַיִם צָרֵי צַעֲקַת־שֶׁבֶר שָׁמֵעוּ׃ נֻסוּ
!Flee have ruin a the ,Horonaim the in for weep-
.heard of cry enemies to descent ;ing

982 4057 6176 1961 5315 4422
7 מַלְּטוּ נַפְשְׁכֶם וְתִהְיֶינָה כַּעֲרוֹעֵר בַּמִּדְבָּר׃ כִּי יַעַן בִּטְחֵךְ
you be- For the in a like be and your Save
trust cause .wilderness thing naked ,lives

1473 3645 3318 3920 214 4639
בְּמַעֲשַׂיִךְ וּבְאוֹצְרוֹתַיִךְ גַּם־אַתְּ תִּלָּכֵדִי וְיָצָא כְמִישׁ בַּגּוֹלָה
into Chemosh And be shall you also your in and your in
;exile go shall .seized ,treasures works

4422 3808 5892/589 2 3605 7703 935 3162 8269 3548
8 כֹּהֲנָיו וְשָׂרָיו יַחְדָּו׃ וְיָבֹא שֹׁדֵד אֶל־כָּל־עִיר וְעִיר לֹא תִמָּלֵט
shall no and ,city every to a shall And .together and his
.escape city spoiler come rulers his priests

6731/5414 3068 559 4334 8045 6010 6
9 וְאָבַד הָעֵמֶק וְנִשְׁמַד הַמִּישֹׁר אֲשֶׁר אָמַר יְהוָה׃ תְּנוּ־צִיץ
wings Give .Jehovah has as the be shall and the shall Also
spoken ,plain destroyed ,valley perish

Moab, for it will fly away;
and its cities shall be a
desert, without an inhabitant in them. 10Cursed *is*
he who does the work of
Jehovah deceitfully; and
cursed he keeping his
sword from blood.
11Moab has been at ease
from his youth; and he
has settled on his lees
and has not been emptied
from vessel to vessel. He
has not gone into exile.
So his taste remains in
him, and his scent is not
changed. 12So, behold,
the days come, states
Jehovah, that I will send
pourers to him, who shall
pour him off, and will
empty his vessels, and
break their jars in pieces.
13And Moab shall be
ashamed of Chemosh, as
the house of Israel was
ashamed of their confi-
dence *in* Bethel. 14How
do you say, We *are*
mighty and strong men
for war? 15Moab is
ravaged, and her cities
have come up. And his
chosen young men have
gone down to the
slaughter, says the King
whose name *is* Jehovah
of hosts
16The calamity of Moab
is near to come, and his
evil hurries fast. 17All
who are around him,
mourn for him. And all
who know his name, say,
How the strong staff is
broken, the beautiful rod!
18O dweller, daughter of
Dibon, come down from
glory and sit in thirst. For
a ravager of Moab shall
come on you; he has
ruined your strongholds.
19O dweller of Aroer,
stand by the way and
watch. Ask him who flees,
and her who escapes;
say, What has happened?
20Moab is put to shame,
for it is razed. Wail and
cry! Tell it in Arnon that
Moab is ravaged. 21And
judgment has come to
the plain land, to Holon,
and to Jahazah and to Me-
phaath, 22and on Dibon;

3427 369 1961 8047 5892 3318 5323 4124
לְמוֹאָב כִּי נָצֹא תֵּצֵא וְעָרֶיהָ לְשַׁמָּה תִהְיֶינָה מֵאֵין יוֹשֵׁב
a without shall desert a its And .away will it for to
dweller ,become cities fly Moab

10 2719 4513 779 7423 3068 4399 6213 779 2004
בָּהֵן׃ אָרוּר עֹשֶׂה מְלֶאכֶת יְהוָה רְמִיָּה וְאָרוּר מֹנֵעַ חַרְבּוֹ
his who he and deceit Jehovah the who he Cursed in
sword keeps (is) cursed ;fully of work does (is) .them

11 3808 8105 8252 5271 4124 7599 1818
מִדָּם׃ שַׁאֲנַן מוֹאָב מִנְּעוּרָיו וְשֹׁקֵט הוּא אֶל־שְׁמָרָיו וְלֹא
and his on he has and his from Moab been has from
not ,lees settled ,youth ease at .blood

2940 5975 1980 3808 1473 3627 3627 7324
הוּרַק מִכְּלִי אֶל־כֶּלִי וּבַגּוֹלָה לֹא הָלָךְ עַל־כֵּן עָמַד טַעְמוֹ
his remains So has he not into and ;vessel to from been has
taste .gone exile vessel emptied

12 3068 5002 935 3117 2009 4171 3808 7381
בּוֹ וְרֵיחוֹ לֹא נָמָר׃ לָכֵן הִנֵּה־יָמִים בָּאִים נְאֻם־יְהוָה
,Jehovah states ,come the behold Therefore is not his and in
days .changed scent ,him

5210 5035 7324 3627 6898 6808 7971
וְשִׁלַּחְתִּי־לוֹ צֹעִים וְצֵעֻהוּ וְכֵלָיו יָרִיקוּ וְנִבְלֵיהֶם יְנַפֵּצוּ׃
break their and shall his and will who pourers to will I that
.pieces in jars ;empty vessels ,off him pour him send

13 410 1008 3478 1004 954 3645 4124 954
וּבֹשׁ מוֹאָב מִכְּמוֹשׁ כַּאֲשֶׁר־בֹּשׁוּ בֵּית יִשְׂרָאֵל מִבֵּית אֵל
of Israel the was as of Moab will And
Bethel of house ashamed ,Chemosh ashamed be

14 4421 3428 582 1368 559 4009
מִבְטֶחָם׃ אֵיךְ תֹּאמְרוּ גִּבּוֹרִים אֲנָחְנוּ וְאַנְשֵׁי־חַיִל לַמִּלְחָמָה׃
the for strong and We mighty you do How their
?war men (are) ,say .confidence

15 5002 2874 3381 970 4005 5927 5892 4124 7703
שֻׁדַּד מוֹאָב וְעָרֶיהָ עָלָה וּמִבְחַר בַּחוּרָיו יָרְדוּ לַטָּבַח נְאֻם־
states the to have young his And have her and ,Moab is
,slaughter gone men chosen .up come cities ravaged

16 7451 935 4124 343 7138 8034 6635 3068 4428
הַמֶּלֶךְ יְהוָה צְבָאוֹת שְׁמוֹ׃ קָרוֹב אֵיד־מוֹאָב לָבוֹא וְרָעָתוֹ
his and to Moab The (is) whose hosts Jehovah the
evil ,come of calamity near .(is) name of ,king

17 559 8034 3045 3605 5439 3605 5110 3966 4116
מִהֲרָה מְאֹד׃ נֻדוּ לוֹ כָּל־סְבִיבָיו וְכֹל יֹדְעֵי שְׁמוֹ אִמְרוּ
,say his who And are who all for Mourn .fast hurries
,name know all .him around ,him

18 3427 3519 3381 8597 4731 5797/4294 7665 349
אֵיכָה נִשְׁבַּר מַטֵּה־עֹז מַקֵּל תִּפְאָרָה׃ רְדִי מִכָּבוֹד וּשְׁבִי
and from Come !beautiful the ,strong the is How
sit glory down rod staff broken

7843 5927 4124 7703 1769 1323 3427 6772
בַצָּמָא יֹשֶׁבֶת בַּת־דִּיבוֹן כִּי־שֹׁדֵד מוֹאָב עָלָה בָךְ שִׁחֵת
has he upon shall Moab plun- a For .Dibon daughter O ,thirst in
ruined ;you come of derer of ,dweller

19 5127 7592 6177 3427 6822 5975 1870 4013
מִבְצָרָיִךְ׃ אֶל־דֶּרֶךְ עִמְדִי וְצַפִּי יוֹשֶׁבֶת עֲרוֹעֵר שַׁאֲלִי־נָס
him Ask .Aroer dweller O and Stand the by strong- your
flees who of ,watch way .holds

20 3213 2865 4124 3001 1961 4100 559 4422
וְנִמְלָטָה אִמְרִי מַה־נִּהְיָתָה׃ הֹבִישׁ מוֹאָב כִּי־חַתָּה הֵילִילוּ
Wail is it for ,Moab to put is has What ,say her and
.razed shame ?happened ;escapes who

21 935 4941 4124 7703 769 5046 2199
וּזְעָקוּ הַגִּידוּ בְאַרְנוֹן כִּי שֻׁדַּד מוֹאָב׃ וּמִשְׁפָּט בָּא אֶל־
to has And .Moab is that in Tell and
come judgment ravaged Arnon (it) !cry

22 5921 4158 5921 3096 2473 4334 776
אֶרֶץ הַמִּישֹׁר אֶל־חֹלוֹן וְאֶל־יַהְצָה וְעַל־מוֹפָעַת׃ וְעַל־
on and ;Mephaath and ;Jahazah and Holon to the country
on to ;plain

and on Nebo; and on Beth-diblathaim; [23]and on Kiriathaim; and on Beth-gamul; and on Beth-meon; [24]and on Kerioth; and on Bozrah; and on all the cities of the land of Moab, far and near. [25]The horn of Moab is cut off, and his arm is broken, says Jehovah.

[26]Make him drunk, for he magnified himself against Jehovah. Moab also shall wallow in his vomit, and he also shall be a mockery. [27]For was not Israel a mockery to you? Was he found among thieves? For ever since you spoke of him, you skipped for joy. [28]Dwellers of Moab, leave the cities, and live in the rock, and be like the dove who makes her nest in the sides of the mouth of the pit. [29]We have heard the pride of Moab; he is exceeding proud; His loftiness, and his pride, and his arrogance, and his elevated heart. [30]I have known, declares Jehovah, his wrath; and it *is* not so; his boast, they have not done so. [31]On account of this I will wail for Moab, and I will cry out for all Moab; *and* he shall mourn for the men of Kirheres.

[32]O vine of Sibmah, I will weep for you more than the weeping of Jazer. Your plants have crossed the sea; they reach to the sea of Jazer. A ravager has fallen on your harvest, and on your grape crop. [33]And joy and gladness is taken from the plentiful field, and from the land of Moab. And I have caused wine to cease from the winepresses; none shall tread *the grapes* with shouting; *their* shouting *shall be* no shouting. [34]From the city of Heshbon to Elealeh, to Jahaz, they have given their voice; from Zoar to Horonaim, *like* a heifer three years old; for the waters of Nimrim also shall be desolate. [35]Also I will cause him who offers in the high places to cease in Moab, says Jehovah; and

1014 7156 5921 =1015= 5921 5015 1769
23 דיבון ועל־נבו ועל־בית דבלתים: ועל קריתים ועל־בית
Beth- and ;Kiriathaim and ;diblathaim Beth- and ;Nebo and ;Dibon
on on on on
3605 1224 7152 1010 1010 5921 1014
24 גמול ועל־בית מעון: ועל־קריות ועל־בצרה ועל כל־
all and ;Bozrah and ;Kerioth and ;meon Beth- and ;gamul
on on on on
41:24 7161 1438 7138 7350 4124 776 5892
25 ערי ארץ מואב הרחקות והקרבות: נגדעה קרן מואב
,Moab The off cut is .near and far ,Moab the cities the
of horn of land of
1431 3068 7937 3068 1571 7665 22:20
26 וזרעו נשברה נאם יהוה: השכירהו כי על־יהוה הגדיל
he Jehovah against for him Make .Jehovah states is his and
.boasted .drunk ,broken arm
38:08 1571 78:14 1961 6892 4124 5606
27 וספק מואב בקיאו והיה לשחק גם־הוא: ואם ׀ לוא
not For .he also a shall and his in Moab also shall
mockery be vomit wallow
1767 4672 1590 34:78 1961 7814
השחק היה לך ישראל אם־בגנבים נמצאה כי־מדי
ever For he Was among ?Israel to was a
since ?found thieves you mockery
4124 3427 55:53 3427 5892 5800 5110 1696
28 דבריך בו תתנודד: עזבו ערים ושכנו בסלע ישבי מואב
;Moab dwellers the in and the Leave skipped you of spoke you
of ,rock dwell cities .joy for ,him
4124 1347 8085 6354 6310 5676 7077 31:38 1961
29 והיו כיונה תקנן בעברי פי־פחת: שמענו גאון־מואב
;Moab the have We .pit the the the in making the like and
of pride heard of mouth of sides nest her dove be
5002 3045 3820 7312 1347 1346 1363 39:66 1343
30 גאה מאד גבהו וגאונו וגאותו ורם לבו: אני ידעתי נאם
states have I his and his and his and His exceed- proud
,known .heart high arrogance pride ,loftiness .ing
4124 6213 3651/3 808 907 3651 3808 5678 30:68
31 יהוה עברתו ולא־כן בדיו לא־כן עשו: על־כן על־מואב
Moab for Therefore they so not his (is it) and wrath his Jeho-
.done have ,boast ;so not vah
1897 7025 582 2199 36:05 4124 321:3
איליל ולמואב כלה אזעק אל־אנשי קיר־חרש יהגה:
shall he Kirheres the (and) will I all for and will I
.mourn of men for ,out cry Moab ,wail
3220 5674 5189 764.3 1612 1058 3270 1065
32 מבכי יעזר אבכה־לך הגפן שבמה נטישתיך עברו ים
the have your ;Sibmah O for will I ,Jazer's weep-
;sea crossed plants of vine ,you weep ing
622 5307/7703 1208 5927 7019 5060 3270 3220
33 עד ים יעזר נגעו על־קיצך ועל־בצירך שדד נפל: ונאספה
is And has a your and your on they Jazer the to
taken .fallen ravager crop grape on harvest .reach of sea
7673 3342 3196 4124 776 3759 1524 8057
שמחה וגיל מכרמל ומארץ מואב ויין מיקבים השבתי
made I the from And .Moab from and the from glad- and joy
;cease to winepresses wine of land the field fruitful ness
5704 2308 2201 1959 3808 1959 19:59 1869 38:08
34 לא־ידרך הידד הידד לא הידד: מזעקת חשבון עד
to Heshbon the From .shouting not shout- the with shall not
of cry (be shall) ing ;shouting tread
56 197 2773 6820 69 1:63 5414 3096 500
אלעלה עד־יהץ נתנו קולם מצער עד־חרנים עגלת
a ,Horonaim to from their have they ,Jahaz to ,Elealeh
heifer Zoar ;voice given
4124 7673 1961 4923 5249 4325 7992
35 שלשיה כי גם־מי נמרים למשמות יהיו: והשבתי למואב
Moab will I And shall desolate Nimrim the also for years three
cease make .become of waters ;old

he who burns incense to his gods. [36]On account of this my heart shall mourn for Moab, like flutes; and my heart shall sound like flutes for the men of Kirheres, because the riches that he has gotten have perished. [37]For every head shall be bald, and every beard clipped. On all the hands *shall be* cuttings, and sackcloth on the loins. [38]On all Moab's housetops, and in its streets, *is* wailing for all. For I have broken Moab like a vessel; no pleasure is in it, says Jehovah. [39]They shall howl, *saying*, How it is broken down! How has Moab turned *his* back *in* shame! So Moab shall be a mockery, and a terror to all those around him. [40]For so says Jehovah: Behold, he shall fly like an eagle, and shall spread his wings toward Moab. [41]Kerioth is captured, and the strongholds are seized; and the mighty men's hearts in Moab shall be at that day like the heart of a woman in *her* pangs. [42]And Moab shall be destroyed from *being* a people, because he has magnified *himself* against Jehovah. [43]Fear, and the pit, and the snare, *shall be* on you, O dweller of Moab, declares Jehovah. [44]He who flees from the dread shall fall into the pit. And he who gets up out of the pit shall be taken in the snare. For I will bring it on Moab, the year of their punishment, declares Jehovah.

[45]Those who fled stood powerless in the shadow of Heshbon, for a fire shall come out of Heshbon, and a flame out of the midst of Sihon, and shall devour the temples of Moab, and the crown of the head of the sons of tumult. [46]Woe to you, Moab! The people of Chemosh have perished; for your sons are taken away into exile, and your daughters into exile.

36 נְאֻם־יְהוָה מַעֲלֶה בָמָה וּמַקְטִיר לֵאלֹהָיו׃ עַל־כֵּן לִבִּי
my heart Therefore his to gods. who he and incense burns the (in) places high who he offers, Jehovah states
לְמוֹאָב כַּחֲלִלִים יֶהֱמֶה וְלִבִּי אֶל־אַנְשֵׁי קִיר־חֶרֶשׂ
Kirheres the of men for my and heart shall mourn, like flutes for Moab
37 כַּחֲלִילִים יֶהֱמֶה עַל־כֵּן יִתְרַת עָשָׂה אָבָדוּ׃ כִּי כָל־רֹאשׁ
head every For have perished. has he gotten the riches because shall sound, like flutes
קָרְחָה וְכָל־זָקָן גְּרֻעָה עַל כָּל־יָדַיִם גְּדֻדֹת וְעַל־מָתְנַיִם
the loins and on (be shall) gashes, the hands all On .clipped beard and every (be shall) bald
38 שָׂק׃ עַל כָּל־גַּגּוֹת מוֹאָב וּבִרְחֹבֹתֶיהָ כֻּלֹּה מִסְפֵּד כִּי
For (is there) wailing. (for) all its in and streets, Moab, the all of housetops On sack- cloth.
39 שָׁבַרְתִּי אֶת־מוֹאָב כִּכְלִי אֵין־חֵפֶץ בּוֹ נְאֻם־יְהוָה׃ אֵיךְ
How .Jehovah states in it, pleasure there no is a like vessel; Moab have I broken
חַתָּה הֵילִילוּ אֵיךְ הִפְנָה־עֹרֶף מוֹאָב בּוֹשׁ וְהָיָה מוֹאָב
Moab shall So become (in) !shame Moab (his) back has turned How shall they !howl is it broken!
40 לִשְׂחֹק וְלִמְחִתָּה לְכָל־סְבִיבָיו׃ כִּי־כֹה אָמַר יְהוָה
:Jehovah says thus For those .him around all to a and terror a mockery
41 הִנֵּה כַנֶּשֶׁר יִדְאֶה וּפָרַשׂ כְּנָפָיו אֶל־מוֹאָב׃ נִלְכְּדָה הַקְּרִיּוֹת
,Kerioth is captured .Moab toward his wings and spread shall he fly an like eagle Be- hold
וְהַמְּצָדוֹת נִתְפָּשָׂה וְהָיָה לֵב גִּבּוֹרֵי מוֹאָב בַּיּוֹם הַהוּא כְּלֵב
the like of heart that day of Moab the hearts of mighty and be shall are ;seized the and strongholds
42 אִשָּׁה מְצֵרָה׃ וְנִשְׁמַד מוֹאָב מֵעָם כִּי עַל־יְהוָה הִגְדִּיל׃
has he .magnified Jehovah against be- cause from people a Moab be shall And destroyed (her) .pangs woman a in
43 פַּחַד וָפַחַת וָפָח עָלֶיךָ יוֹשֵׁב מוֹאָב נְאֻם־יְהוָה׃
44 הַנִּיס מִפְּנֵי
from who He flees .Jehovah states ,Moab O of dweller (be shall) ,you on and the snare the and ,pit ,Dread
הַפַּחַד יִפֹּל אֶל־הַפַּחַת וְהָעֹלֶה מִן־הַפַּחַת יִלָּכֵד בַּפָּח
the in ;snare be shall taken the pit out of who he and up gets the ;pit into shall fall dread the
45 כִּי־אָבִיא אֵלֶיהָ אֶל־מוֹאָב שְׁנַת פְּקֻדָּתָם נְאֻם־יְהוָה׃ בְּצֵל
the In of shadow .Jehovah states their ,punishment year the of ,Moab on ,it on will I bring for
חֶשְׁבּוֹן עָמְדוּ מִכֹּחַ נָסִים כִּי־אֵשׁ יֵצֵא מֵחֶשְׁבּוֹן וְלֶהָבָה מִבֵּין
from midst a and flame from ,Heshbon shall issue fire a for those ;fled who power- less stood Heshbon
46 סִיחוֹן וַתֹּאכַל פְּאַת מוֹאָב וְקָדְקֹד בְּנֵי שָׁאוֹן׃ אוֹי־לְךָ מוֹאָב
!Moab to ,you Woe .tumult the of sons the and of crown Moab the of temples shall and devour ;Sihon's
אָבַד עַם־כְּמוֹשׁ כִּי־לֻקְּחוּ בָנֶיךָ בַּשֶּׁבִי וּבְנֹתֶיךָ בַּשִּׁבְיָה׃
into .exile your and daughters into ,exile your sons taken are away for ;Chemosh The of people have perished

[47]But I will restore the prisoners of Moab in the end of the days, declares Jehovah. So far *is* the judgment of Moab.

47 וְשַׁבְתִּי שְׁבוּת־מוֹאָב בְּאַחֲרִית הַיָּמִים נְאֻם־יְהוָה עַד־הֵנָּה
3068 5002 3117 319 4124 7622 7725
thus far ;Jehovah states the the in Moab pri- the I But
,days of end of soners restore will

מִשְׁפַּט מוֹאָב׃
4124 4941
.Moab the (is)
of judgment

CAP. XLIX מט

CHAPTER 49

CHAPTER 49

[1]So says Jehovah to the sons of Ammon: Has Israel no sons? Or has he no heir? Why does their king inherit Gad, and his people dwell in its cities? [2]So, behold, the days come, declares Jehovah, that I will cause a shout of war to be heard in Rabbah of the sons of Ammon. And it shall be a heap, a ruin; and her daughter villages shall be burned with fire. Then Israel shall inherit his inheritance, says Jehovah. [3]Wail, O Heshbon, for Ai is spoiled! Cry, daughters of Rabbah; gird yourselves with sackcloth; mourn; and run to and fro in the walls. For their king shall go into exile, his priests and his rulers together. [4]Why do you glory in your valleys, your flowing valley, O backsliding daughter? She trusted in her treasures, *saying*, Who shall come to me? [5]Behold, I will bring a dread on you, declares Jehovah of hosts, from all those who are around you. And you shall be driven out, each man before him. And there shall be none to gather up the runaways. [6]And after this I will bring again the prisoners of the sons of Ammon, declares Jehovah.

[7]So says Jehovah of hosts concerning Edom: Is wisdom no more in Teman? Has counsel perished from the prudent? Has their wisdom vanished? [8]Flee, turn back, go deep to dwell,

1 לִבְנֵי עַמּוֹן כֹּה אָמַר יְהוָה הֲבָנִים אֵין לְיִשְׂרָאֵל אִם־
3478 369 1121 3068 559 3541 5983 1121
Or ?Israel to Are sons ,Jehovah says Thus :Ammon the To
no there of sons

יוֹרֵשׁ אֵין לוֹ מַדּוּעַ יָרַשׁ מַלְכָּם אֶת־גָּד וְעַמּוֹ בְּעָרָיו יָשָׁב׃
3427 5892 5971 1410 4428 3423 4100 369 3423
?dwell its in his and ,Gad their does Why to not heir
cities people king inherit ?him is

2 לָכֵן הִנֵּה יָמִים בָּאִים נְאֻם־יְהוָה וְהִשְׁמַעְתִּי אֶל־רַבַּת
7237 8085 3068 5002 935 3117 2009 3651
Rabbah against will I that ,Jehovah states ,come the ,behold There-
of heard make days fore

בְּנֵי־עַמּוֹן תְּרוּעַת מִלְחָמָה וְהָיְתָה לְתֵל שְׁמָמָה וּבְנֹתֶיהָ
1323 8077 8510 1961 4421 8643 5983/1121
her and ;ruin a ,heap a shall it and ;war shout a Ammon the
towns daughter become of of sons

בָּאֵשׁ תִּצַּתְנָה וְיָרַשׁ יִשְׂרָאֵל אֶת־יֹרְשָׁיו אָמַר יְהוָה׃
3068 559 3423 3478 3423 3341 784
.Jehovah says his Israel will and be shall with
,inheritance inherit ,burned fire

3 הֵילִילִי חֶשְׁבּוֹן כִּי שֻׁדְּדָה־עַי צְעַקְנָה בְּנוֹת רַבָּה חֲגֹרְנָה
2296 7237 1323 6818 5857 7703 2809 3213
on gird ;Rabbah daughters ,Cry !Ai is for O ,Wail
of ravaged ,Heshbon

שַׂקִּים סְפֹדְנָה וְהִתְשׁוֹטַטְנָה בַּגְּדֵרוֹת כִּי מַלְכָּם בַּגּוֹלָה
1473 4428 1448 7751 5594 8242
into their for the in to run and ,mourn sack-
exile king ;walls fro and ;cloth

4 יֵלֵךְ כֹּהֲנָיו וְשָׂרָיו יַחְדָּיו׃ מַה־תִּתְהַלְלִי בָּעֲמָקִים זָב
2100 6010 1984 4100 3162 8269 3548 3212
flow- in you do Why .together his and his shall
ing ,valleys glory princes priests ,go

עִמְקֵךְ הַבַּת הַשּׁוֹבֵבָה הַבֹּטְחָה בְּאֹצְרֹתֶיהָ מִי יָבוֹא אֵלָי׃
935 4310 214 982 7728 1323 6010
to shall Who her in She .backsliding O your
?me come ,treasures trusted daughter ,valley

5 הִנְנִי מֵבִיא עָלַיִךְ פַּחַד נְאֻם־אֲדֹנָי יְהוִה צְבָאוֹת מִכָּל־
3605 6635 3069 136 5002 6343 935 2005
from ,hosts Jehovah the states a on will ,Behold
all of Lord dread you bring I

6 סְבִיבָיִךְ וְנִדַּחְתֶּם אִישׁ לְפָנָיו וְאֵין מְקַבֵּץ לַנֹּדֵד׃ וְאַחֲרֵי־
310 5074 6908 369 6440 376 5080 5439
And the gather to and before each will you And around
after .runaways is not ,him one out driven be .you

7 כֵן אָשִׁיב אֶת־שְׁבוּת בְּנֵי־עַמּוֹן נְאֻם־יְהוָה׃ לֶאֱדוֹם
123 3068 5002 5983 1121 7622 7725
Concerning .Jehovah states ,Ammon the the will I this
,Edom of sons of prisoners restore

כֹּה אָמַר יְהוָה צְבָאוֹת הַאֵין עוֹד חָכְמָה בְּתֵימָן אָבְדָה
6 8487 2451 5750 369 6635 3068 559 3541
Has ?Teman in wisdom more no Is :hosts Jehovah says thus
perished of

8 עֵצָה מִבָּנִים נִסְרְחָה חָכְמָתָם׃ נֻסוּ הָפְנוּ הֶעְמִיקוּ לָשֶׁבֶת
3427 6009 6437 5127 2451 5628 995 6098
,dwell to deep go turn ,Flee their Has the from counsel
,back ?wisdom vanished ?prudent

O people of Dedan. For I
will bring the calamity of
Esau on him *in* the time I
will visit him. 9If the grape
gatherers come to you,
would they not leave
gleanings? If thieves *come*
by night, will they ruin *more*
than enough for them?
10But I have stripped Esau; I
have uncovered his secret
places, and he shall not be
able to hide himself. His
seed is ravaged, also his
brothers and his neigh-
bors; and he is not.
11Leave your orphans; I
will keep *them* alive; and let
your widows trust in Me.
12For so says Jehovah:
Behold, those whose judg-
ment was not to drink of the
cup have surely drunk. And
are you to be entirely
acquitted? You shall not be
acquitted, but you shall
surely drink. 13For I have
sworn by Myself, declares
Jehovah, that Bozrah shall
become a ruin, a reproach, a
waste, and a curse. And all
its cities shall be wastes
forever. 14I have heard a
message from Jehovah,
and a herald is sent to the
nations: Gather together
and come against her, and
rise up to the battle. 15For,
behold, I will make you
small among the nations,
despised among men.
16Your fearfulness has deceived you, the pride of your
heart, you who live in the
clefts of the rock, who hold
the height of the hill.
Though you should make
your nest as high as the
eagle, I will bring you down
from there, declares
Jehovah. 17And Edom shall
be a ruin; everyone who
goes by it shall be amazed,
and shall hiss at all its
plagues. 18As in the overthrow of Sodom and Go-
morrah, and its neighbor,
declares Jehovah, no man
shall remain there; a son of
man shall not live in it.
19Behold, he shall come
up like a lion from the
swelling of Jordan against

518 6485 6056 935 6215 343 1719 3427
9 יֹשְׁבֵי דְּדָן כִּי אֵיד עֵשָׂו הֵבֵאתִי עָלָיו עֵת פְּקַדְתִּיו׃ אִם־
If punish I the (in) on will I Esau the for ,Dedan resi-
.him time him bring of calamity of dents

39,15 1590 518 5955 7604 38,08 935 1219
בֹּצְרִים בָּאוּ לָךְ לֹא יַשְׁאִרוּ עוֹלֵלוֹת אִם־גַּנָּבִים בַּלַּיְלָה
by (come) thieves If ?gleanings would not to come grape- the
,night leave they ,you gatherers

1540 6215 2834 1267
10 הִשְׁחִיתוּ דַיָּם׃ כִּי־אֲנִי חָשַׂפְתִּי אֶת־עֵשָׂו גִּלֵּיתִי אֶת־
have I ;Esau have I But their they will
uncovered stripped ?sufficiency destroy

7934 251 2233 7703 3201 38,08 2254 7943 4565
מִסְתָּרָיו וְנֶחְבָּה לֹא יוּכָל שֻׁדַּד זַרְעוֹ וְאֶחָיו וּשְׁכֵנָיו
his and his also His is shall he not to and secret his
;neighbors brothers ,seed ravaged ,able be himself hide ,places

982 490 2421 3490 5800 369
11 וְאֵינֶנּוּ׃ עָזְבָה יְתֹמֶיךָ אֲנִי אֲחַיֶּה וְאַלְמְנוֹתֶיךָ עָלַי תִּבְטָחוּ׃
.trust let on your and keep will I your Leave is he and
Me widows ;alive ,orphans .not

4941 369 834 2009 30,68 559 3541
12 כִּי־כֹה ׀ אָמַר יְהוָה הִנֵּה אֲשֶׁר־אֵין מִשְׁפָּטָם
judgment was whose ,Behold ,Jehovah says thus For
not

38,08 5352 53,52 83,54 8354 3563 8354
לִשְׁתּוֹת הַכּוֹס שָׁתוֹ יִשְׁתּוּ וְאַתָּה הוּא נָקֹה תִּנָּקֶה לֹא
not be to entirely are And they surely ,cup the drink to
?acquitted you .drank

3068 5002 7650 8354 8354 53:52
13 תִנָּקֶה כִּי שָׁתֹה תִּשְׁתֶּה׃ כִּי בִי נִשְׁבַּעְתִּי נְאֻם־יְהוָה כִּי־
that ,Jehovah states have I by For shall you surely but shall you
,sworn Myself .drink ,acquitted be

5892 3605 1224 1961 704,5 2717 2781 8047
לְשַׁמָּה לְחֶרְפָּה לְחֹרֶב וְלִקְלָלָה תִּהְיֶה בָצְרָה וְכָל־עָרֶיהָ
its And .Bozrah shall a and ,waste a a ,horror a
cities all become curse ,reproach

30,68 8085 8052 5769 2721 1961
14 תִהְיֶינָה לְחָרְבוֹת עוֹלָם׃ שְׁמוּעָה שָׁמַעְתִּי מֵאֵת יְהוָה
,Jehovah from have I message a .forever wastes become shall
heard

4421 6965 935 6908 79,71 1471 6735
וְצִיר בַּגּוֹיִם שָׁלוּחַ הִתְקַבְּצוּ וּבֹאוּ עָלֶיהָ וְקוּמוּ לַמִּלְחָמָה׃
the for and against and Gather ;sent is the to a and
.battle up rise ,her come together nations herald

5377 8606 120 959 1471 5414 6946
15 16 כִּי־הִנֵּה קָטֹן נְתַתִּיךָ בַּגּוֹיִם בָּזוּי בָּאָדָם׃ תִּפְלַצְתְּךָ הִשִּׁיא
has Your among despised among made I small ,lo For
deceived dreadfulness .men ,nations the you

1389 4791 8610 55:53 2288 7931 3820 2087
אֹתָךְ זְדוֹן לִבֶּךָ שֹׁכְנִי בְּחַגְוֵי הַסֶּלַע תֹּפְשִׂי מְרוֹם גִּבְעָה
the the hold who ,rock the the in who you your the ,you
.hill of height of clefts live ,heart of pride

1961 3068 5002 3381 8033 70:64 540.4 1361
17 כִּי־תַגְבִּיהַּ כַּנֶּשֶׁר קִנֶּךָ מִשָּׁם אוֹרִידְךָ נְאֻם־יְהוָה׃ וְהָיְתָה
And .Jehovah states bring will I from your the as you Though
be shall ,down you there ,nest eagle high make

4347 3605 8319 80.74 5674 3605 8047 123
אֱדוֹם לְשַׁמָּה כֹּל עֹבֵר עָלֶיהָ יִשֹּׁם וְיִשְׁרֹק עַל־כָּל־מַכּוֹתֶהָ׃
its all at shall and be shall by who every ;horror a Edom
.plagues hiss amazed it passes one

8033 342.7 3069 559 7934 6017 54.67 4114
18 כְּמַהְפֵּכַת סְדֹם וַעֲמֹרָה וּשְׁכֵנֶיהָ אָמַר יְהוָה לֹא־יֵשֵׁב שָׁם
there shall not ,Jehovah says its and and Sodom over- the As
dwell ,neighbor Gomorrah of throw

1347 59,27 738 2009 120 1121 1481 38,08 37.6
19 אִישׁ וְלֹא־יָגוּר בָּהּ בֶּן־אָדָם׃ הִנֵּה כְּאַרְיֵה יַעֲלֶה מִגְּאוֹן
the from shall he a like Behold .man a it in shall not ;man
of pride up come lion of son sojourn

the home of the strong. But I will suddenly make him run away from it. And who is *the* chosen *one* I shall appoint over it? For who *is* like Me? And who will summon Me? And who then *is* a shepherd who will stand before Me? [20]So then, hear the counsel of Jehovah which He has planned against Edom, and His purposes which He has purposed against the inhabitants of Teman: Surely they shall drag them, the least of the flock. Surely He shall make their pastures desolate over them. [21]The earth is shaken at the noise of their fall. When *they* cried, the noise of it was heard in the Red Sea. [22]Behold, he shall come up and fly like the eagle, and spread his wings over Bozrah. And at that day the heart of the mighty men of Edom shall be like the heart of a woman in her pangs.

[23]Regarding Damascus: Hamath and Arpad are put to shame, for they have heard bad news; they are melted; anxiety *is* in the sea; it cannot be quiet. [24]Damascus has become feeble; she has turned to flee, and trembling has seized *her*; anguish and sorrows have taken her like a woman in labor. [25]How is the city of praise not forsaken, the town of my joy! [26]So her young men shall fall in her streets, and all the men of war shall be silenced in that day, declares Jehovah of hosts. [27]And I will kindle a fire in the wall of Damascus; and it shall burn up the palaces of Ben-hadad.

[28]So says Jehovah concerning Kedar, and concerning the kingdoms of Hazor, which Nebuchadnezzar, the king of Babylon, struck: Rise and go to Kedar, and strip the men

4310 7323 7280 386 5116 3383
הַיַּרְדֵּן אֶל־נְוֵה אֵיתָן כִּי־אַרְגִּיעָה אֲרִיצֶנּוּ מֵעָלֶיהָ וּמִי
And from away him make will I but the the against Jordan
(is) who .it run suddenly ;strong of pasture

74:62 227 32:59 4310 36 44 4310 6485 977
בָחוּר אֵלֶיהָ אֶפְקֹד כִּי מִי כָמוֹנִי וּמִי יֹעִידֶנִּי וּמִי־זֶה רֹעֶה
a then And sum- will And like who For shall I over chosen
shepherd (is) who ?Me mon who ?Me (is) .appoint it

20 3289 834 3068/6098 8085 6440 5975 834
אֲשֶׁר יַעֲמֹד לְפָנָי׃ לָכֵן שִׁמְעוּ עֲצַת־יְהוָה אֲשֶׁר יָעַץ אֶל־
against has He which Jehovah the hear Therefore before shall who
planned of counsel ?Me stand

3808 518 8487 3427 2803 834 42:84 123
אֱדוֹם וּמַחְשְׁבוֹתָיו אֲשֶׁר חָשַׁב אֶל־יֹשְׁבֵי תֵימָן אִם־לֹא
Surely :Teman the against has He which His and ;Edom
of dwellers purposed purposes

5116 5921 8074 38 08 518 66:29 6810 5498
יִסְחָבוּם צְעִירֵי הַצֹּאן אִם־לֹא־יַשִּׁים עֲלֵיהֶם נְוֵהֶם׃
their over shall He Surely the least the shall they
.pastures them desolate make .flock of ;them drag

21 8085 5488 3220 6818 776 7493 5307 6963
מִקּוֹל נִפְלָם רָעֲשָׁה הָאָרֶץ צְעָקָה בְּיַם־סוּף נִשְׁמַע
was Reeds the in they (when) the shaken is their the at
heard of Sea cried ;earth fall of noise

22 5921 3671 6566 16:75 5927 5404 2009 6963
קוֹלָהּ׃ הִנֵּה כַנֶּשֶׁר יַעֲלֶה וְיִדְאֶה וְיִפְרֹשׂ כְּנָפָיו עַל־
over his and ,fly and shall he the like ,Behold its
wings spread up come eagle .noise

802 38 20 3117 123 1368 3820 1961 1224
בָּצְרָה וְהָיָה לֵב גִּבּוֹרֵי אֱדוֹם בַּיּוֹם הַהוּא כְּלֵב אִשָּׁה
a the like that day at Edom mighty the the And .Bozrah
woman of heart of men of heart be shall

23 8052 774 2574 953 18:34 6887
מְצֵרָה׃ לְדַמֶּשֶׂק בּוֹשָׁה חֲמָת וְאַרְפָּד כִּי־שְׁמֻעָה
news for and Hamath put are Concerning her in
,Arpad shame to :Damascus .pangs

24 7503 3201 38 08 8252 16 74 3220 41 27 8085 7451
רָעָה שָׁמְעוּ נָמֹגוּ בַּיָּם דְּאָגָה הַשְׁקֵט לֹא יוּכָל׃ רָפְתָה
become has is it not be to (is there) the in are they they bad
feeble able quiet ;anxiety ,sea ;melted ;heard have

2256 6864 2380 7374 5127 6437 1834
דַמֶּשֶׂק הִפְנְתָה לָנוּס וְרֶטֶט הֶחֱזִיקָה צָרָה וַחֲבָלִים
pangs and distress has and ,flee to has she ;Damascus
;(her) seized trembling turned

25 7151 8416 5892 5800 38 08 3205 270
אֲחָזַתָּה כַּיּוֹלֵדָה׃ אֵיךְ לֹא־עֻזְּבָה עִיר תְּהִלָּה קִרְיַת
the ,praise the is not How woman a as taken have
of town of city forsaken .labor in her

26 582 3605 7339 970 5307 3651 4885
מְשׂוֹשִׂי׃ לָכֵן יִפְּלוּ בַחוּרֶיהָ בִּרְחֹבֹתֶיהָ וְכָל־אַנְשֵׁי
men and her in young her shall Therefore !joy my
of all ,streets men fall

27 3341 6635 3068 5002 3117 1826 4421
הַמִּלְחָמָה יִדַּמּוּ בַּיּוֹם הַהוּא נְאֻם יְהוָה צְבָאוֹת׃ וְהִצַּתִּי
will I And .hosts Jehovah states ,that day in be shall the
kindle of silenced war

1130 1121 759 398 1834 2346 784
אֵשׁ בְּחוֹמַת דַּמָּשֶׂק וְאָכְלָה אַרְמְנוֹת בֶּן־הֲדָד׃
.hadad Ben- the shall it and ,Damascus the in fire a
of palaces up burn of wall

28 4428 5019 5221 834 2674 4467 6938
לְקֵדָר ׀ וּלְמַמְלְכוֹת חָצוֹר אֲשֶׁר הִכָּה נְבוּכַדְרֶאצַּור מֶלֶךְ־
king Nebuchadnezzar struck which Hazor concerning and Concerning
of of kingdoms the ,Kedar

1121 7703 69:38 5927 6965 3068 559 3541 8 84
בָּבֶל כֹּה אָמַר יְהוָה קוּמוּ עֲלוּ אֶל־קֵדָר וְשָׁדְדוּ אֶת־בְּנֵי־
of sons the ravage and ,Kedar to up Go ,Arise :Jehovah says So Baby-
.lon

of the east. [29]They shall take their tents and their flocks. They shall take their curtains, and all their vessels, and their camels, to themselves. And they shall cry to them, Fear *is* all around.

[30]Flee, go far away, go deep to dwell, O inhabitants of Hazor, declares Jehovah. For Nebuchadnezzer, the king of Babylon, has taken counsel against you, and has plotted a scheme against you. [31]Rise up, go up to the nation at ease, who dwells securely, declares Jehovah; neither gates nor bars *are* on it; and they dwell alone. [32]And their camels shall be a prize, and the multitude of their cattle a prey. And I will scatter them to all winds, those who cut the corners. And I will bring their calamity from all sides of it, says Jehovah. [33]And Hazor shall be a dwelling for jackals, a ruin forever. No man shall live there, nor *any* son of man stay in it.

[34]The word of Jehovah that came to Jeremiah the prophet against Elam, in the beginning of the reign of Zedekiah, king of Judah, saying, [35]So says Jehovah of hosts, Behold I will break the bow of Elam, the chief of their might. [36]And I will bring the four winds from the four ends of the heavens on Elam, and will scatter them toward all those winds. And there shall be no nation where the outcasts of Elam shall not come. [37]And I will cause Elam to be afraid before their enemies, and before those who seek their life. And I will bring evil on them, the burning of My anger, declares Jehovah. And I will send the sword

29 קֶדֶם׃ אָהֳלֵיהֶם וְצֹאנָם יִקָּחוּ יְרִיעוֹתֵיהֶם וְכָל־כְּלֵיהֶם

their and their They their and their the
vessels all curtains ;take shall flocks tents .east

30 וּגְמַלֵּיהֶם יִשְׂאוּ לָהֶם וְקָרְאוּ עֲלֵיהֶם מָגוֹר מִסָּבִיב׃ נֻסוּ

,Flee all Fear ,them to they And them- to they their and
!around (is) cry shall .selves take shall camels

נֻדוּ מְאֹד הֶעְמִיקוּ לָשֶׁבֶת יֹשְׁבֵי חָצוֹר נְאֻם־יְהוָה כִּי־

For .Jehovah states ,Hazor O ,dwell to deep go ,far go
of dwellers away

יָעַץ עֲלֵיכֶם נְבוּכַדְרֶאצַּר מֶלֶךְ־בָּבֶל עֵצָה וְחָשַׁב עֲלֵיהֶם

against has and counsel Babylon king Nebuchadnezzar against has
you plotted of you planned

31 מַחֲשָׁבָה׃ קוּמוּ עֲלוּ אֶל־גּוֹי שְׁלֵיו יוֹשֵׁב לָבֶטַח נְאֻם־יְהוָה

,Jehovah states ,securely who at the to up go ,Arise .scheme a
dwells ease nation

32 לֹא־דְלָתַיִם וְלֹא־בְרִיחַ לוֹ בָּדָד יִשְׁכֹּנוּ׃ וְהָיוּ גְמַלֵּיהֶם

their shall And they alone (are) bars nor gates not
camels become .dwell ;it to

לָבַז וַהֲמוֹן מִקְנֵיהֶם לְשָׁלָל וְזֵרִתִים לְכָל־רוּחַ קְצוּצֵי פֵאָה

the those ,winds to will I And .spoil a their mul- the and a
.corners cut who all them scatter cattle of titude ,prize

33 וּמִכָּל־עֲבָרָיו אָבִיא אֶת־אֵידָם נְאֻם־יְהוָה׃ וְהָיְתָה חָצוֹר

Hazor And .Jehovah states their will I sides from And
be shall ,calamity bring it of all

לִמְעוֹן תַּנִּים שְׁמָמָה עַד־עוֹלָם לֹא־יֵשֵׁב שָׁם אִישׁ וְלֹא־

nor ,man A there shall not .forever until ruin a ,jackals dwell- a
live for ing

34 יָגוּר בָּהּ בֶּן־אָדָם׃ אֲשֶׁר הָיָה דְבַר־יְהוָה אֶל־

to Jehovah The came which .man (any) it in so-
of word of son journ

יִרְמְיָהוּ הַנָּבִיא אֶל־עֵילָם בְּרֵאשִׁית מַלְכוּת צִדְקִיָּה מֶלֶךְ־

king Zedekiah the the in Elam against the Jeremiah
of of reign of beginning prophet

35 יְהוּדָה לֵאמֹר׃ כֹּה אָמַר יְהוָה צְבָאוֹת הִנְנִי שֹׁבֵר אֶת־

am ,Behold :hosts Jehovah says Thus ,saying ,Judah
breaking I of

36 קֶשֶׁת עֵילָם רֵאשִׁית גְּבוּרָתָם׃ וְהֵבֵאתִי אֶל־עֵילָם אַרְבַּע

the Elam on will I And their the ,Elam the
four bring .might of first of bow

רוּחוֹת מֵאַרְבַּע קְצוֹת הַשָּׁמַיִם וְזֵרִתִים לְכֹל הָרֻחוֹת

winds toward will and the of ends the from winds
all them scatter ,heavens four

הָאֵלֶּה וְלֹא־יִהְיֶה הַגּוֹי אֲשֶׁר לֹא־יָבוֹא שָׁם נִדְּחֵי עוֹלָם׃

.Elam out- the there shall not where a shall And .these
of casts come nation be not

37 וְהַחְתַּתִּי אֶת־עֵילָם לִפְנֵי אֹיְבֵיהֶם וְלִפְנֵי ׀ מְבַקְשֵׁי נַפְשָׁם

their those and their before Elam I And
.life seek who before enemies terrify will

וְהֵבֵאתִי עֲלֵיהֶם ׀ רָעָה אֶת־חֲרוֹן אַפִּי נְאֻם־יְהוָה וְשִׁלַּחְתִּי

will I And .Jehovah states My the ,evil them on I And
send ,anger of burning bring will

after them until I have
destroyed them. [38]And I
will set My throne in Elam,
and will destroy the king
and the rulers from there,
declares Jehovah. [39]But it
shall happen in the latter
days; I will bring again the
prisoners of Elam, declares
Jehovah.

CHAPTER 50

[1]The word that Jehovah
spoke against Babylon,
against the land of the
Chaldeans by Jeremiah the
prophet: [2]Declare among
the nations, and cause
them to hear, and lift up a
banner. Cause them to hear;
do not hide it; say, Babylon
is captured; Bel is put to
shame; Merodach is broken
in pieces; her images are
put to shame; her idols are
broken in pieces. [3]For a
nation comes up against
her from the north, which
shall make her land a
desert. Yea, no one shall
dwell in it. They shall flee;
they shall depart; both man
and animal.

[4]In these days, and at that
time, the sons of Israel shall
come, declares Jehovah;
they and the sons of Judah
together; going and weep-
ing; they shall go and seek
Jehovah their God. [5]They
shall ask the way *to* Zion
with their faces *pointing*
there, saying, Come and let
us join ourselves to
Jehovah *in* an everlasting
covenant never *to be*
forgotten. [6]My people are
lost sheep; their shepherds
have caused them to go
astray; they turned them
away *on* the mountains;
they have gone from moun-
tain to hill; they have
forgotten their resting
place. [7]All who have found
them have devoured them.
And their enemies said, We
are not guilty, because they
have sinned against
Jehovah, the habitation
of righteousness, and
Jehovah, their fathers'
hope. [8]Flee from the midst
of Babylon; and go out of

3678 7760 3615 5704 2719 310
38 אַחֲרֵיהֶם אֶת־הַחֶרֶב עַד כַּלּוֹתִי אוֹתָם׃ וְשַׂמְתִּי כִסְאִי
My will I And .them have I until the after
throne set consumed sword them

1961 3068 5002 8269 4428 8033 6 5769
39 בְּעֵילָם וְהַאֲבַדְתִּי מִשָּׁם מֶלֶךְ וְשָׂרִים נְאֻם־יְהוָה׃ וְהָיָה ׀
it And .Jehovah states the and the from will and Elam in
,be will ,rulers king there destroy

3068 5002 5769 7622 7725 3117 319
בְּאַחֲרִית הַיָּמִים אָשׁוּב אֶת־שְׁבִית עֵילָם נְאֻם־יְהוָה׃
.Jehovah states ,Elam the will I ,days the latter in
of prisoners restore

CAP. L נ

CHAPTER 50

3027 3778 776 884 3068 1696 1697
1 הַדָּבָר אֲשֶׁר דִּבֶּר יְהוָה אֶל־בָּבֶל אֶל־אֶרֶץ כַּשְׂדִּים בְּיַד
the by the the against ,Babylon against Jeho- spoke that The
of hand ,Chaldeans of land vah word

8085 :5251/5375 8085 1471 5046 5030 3414
2 יִרְמְיָהוּ הַנָּבִיא׃ הַגִּידוּ בַגּוֹיִם וְהַשְׁמִיעוּ וּשְׂאוּ־נֵס הַשְׁמִיעוּ
(them) make a lift and make and the in Declare the Jeremiah
;hear ,banner up ;hear (them) nations :prophet

4781 2865 1078 3001 884 3920 559 3582 408
אַל־תְּכַחֵדוּ אִמְרוּ נִלְכְּדָה בָבֶל הֹבִישׁ בֵּל חַת מְרֹדָךְ
;Mero- broken is ;Bel put is ;Babylon is ,say hide do not
;dach pieces in shame to seized ;it

6828 1471 5927 1544 2865 :6091 3001
3 הֹבִישׁוּ עֲצַבֶּיהָ חַתּוּ גִּלּוּלֶיהָ׃ כִּי עָלָה עָלֶיהָ גּוֹי מִצָּפוֹן
the from a against comes For .idols her broken and her put and
,north nation her up pieces in ;images shame to

120 3427 1961 3808 8047 776 7896
הוּא־יָשִׁית אֶת־אַרְצָהּ לְשַׁמָּה וְלֹא־יִהְיֶה יוֹשֵׁב בָּהּ מֵאָדָם
both ;it in dwell shall no and ;horror a her shall which
man one land make

5002 6256 3117 1980 5110 929
4 וְעַד־בְּהֵמָה נָדוּ הָלָכוּ׃ בַּיָּמִים הָהֵמָּה וּבָעֵת הַהִיא נְאֻם־
states that at and ,these days In will they will ,animal and
time .depart ,flee

1058 1980 3162 3063 1121 3478 1121 935 3068
יְהוָה יָבֹאוּ בְנֵי־יִשְׂרָאֵל הֵמָּה וּבְנֵי־יְהוּדָה יַחְדָּו הָלוֹךְ וּבָכוֹ
and going to- Judah the and they ,Israel the shall ,Jehovah
weeping ;gether of sons of sons come

2008 1870 7592 6726 1245 430 3068 3212
5 יֵלֵכוּ וְאֶת־יְהוָה אֱלֹהֵיהֶם יְבַקֵּשׁוּ׃ צִיּוֹן יִשְׁאָלוּ דֶּרֶךְ הֵנָּה
there the shall They (to) shall they their Jehovah and they
way of ask Zion .seek God ,go shall

7911 3808 5769 1285 3068 3867 935 6440
פְּנֵיהֶם בֹּאוּ וְנִלְווּ אֶל־יְהוָה בְּרִית עוֹלָם לֹא תִשָּׁכֵחַ׃
(be to) not ever- an (in) Jehovah to let and (saying) (with)
.forgotten lasting covenant join us ,Come ,faces their

2022 7726 2022 :8582 7462 5971 1961 6 6629
6 צֹאן אֹבְדוֹת הָיוּ עַמִּי רֹעֵיהֶם הִתְעוּם הָרִים שׁוֹבְבִים מֵהַר
from turned they the (on) them led have their My are Lost sheep
mountain ;away them mountain ;astray shepherds ;people

:398 4672 7258 7911 1980 1389
7 אֶל־גִּבְעָה הָלָכוּ שָׁכְחוּ רִבְצָם׃ כָּל־מוֹצְאֵיהֶם אֲכָלוּם
de- have have who All resting their have they they hill to
;them voured them found .place forgotten ,gone have

5116 3068 2398 816 3808 559 6862
וְצָרֵיהֶם אָמְרוּ לֹא נֶאְשָׁם תַּחַת אֲשֶׁר חָטְאוּ לַיהוָה נְוֵה־
hab- the against have they whereas are We not ,said their and
of itations Jehovah sinned ;guilty enemies

776 :884 8432 5110 3068 1 4723 6664
8 צֶדֶק וּמִקְוֵה אֲבוֹתֵיהֶם יְהוָה׃ נֻדוּ מִתּוֹךְ בָּבֶל וּמֵאֶרֶץ
the from ,Baby- from Flee .Jehovah their hope and righ-
of land ,lon's midst ,fathers' ,teousness

the land of the Chaldeans; and be as the he-goats before the flocks.

9For, behold, I am stirring up and bringing up a company of great nations from a northern land against Babylon. And they shall set themselves in order against her. She shall be captured there; their arrows *shall be* as *those* of a mighty, skillful man; they shall not return empty. 10And Chaldea shall be a prize; all who plunder her shall be satisfied, declares Jehovah. 11Because you rejoice; because you exult, O destroyers of My inheritance; because you are fat like the heifer *in* grass, and neigh like strong ones; 12your mother shall be deeply ashamed; she who bore you shall turn pale. Behold, the last of the nations *shall be* a wilderness, a dry land, and a desert. 13Because of the wrath of Jehovah, it shall not be inhabited; but all of it shall be a waste; everyone who goes by Babylon shall be amazed and hiss at all her plagues. 14Put yourselves in order against Babylon all around. All you who tread a bow, shoot at her. Do not spare arrows, for she has sinned against Jehovah. 15Shout against her all around. She has given her hand; her foundations have fallen; her walls have been thrown down; for it *is* the vengeance of Jehovah. Take vengeance on her. As she has done, do to her. 16Cut off the sower from Babylon, and the one who handles the sickle in the time of harvest. They shall turn from a sword of the oppressor, each one to his people. And they shall flee, each one to his own land.

17Israel is a scattered sheep, driven away *by* lions. First, the king of Assyria devoured him. And last, this king Nebuchadnezzar of Babylon crunched *his bones*. 18So Jehovah of hosts, the God of Israel,

2009 6629 6440 6260 1961 3318 3778
9 כשדים יצאו והיו כעתודים לפני־צאן: כי הנה אנכי
I ,lo For the before the as and go the
flocks he-goats be ,forth Chaldeans

6828 776 1368 1471 6951 884 5927 5782
מעיר ומעלה על־בבל קהל־גוים גדלים מארץ צפון
a from great nations a Baby- against bring and am
,northern land of company lon up arousing

7725 3808 7919 1397 2671 3920 8033 6186
וערכו לה משם תלכד חציו כגבור משכיל לא ישוב
will they not skillful a as their shall She from against they and
return man mighty arrows captured be there .her array will

5002 7646 7997 3605 7998 3778 1961 7387
10 ריקם: והיתה כשדים לשלל כל־שלליה ישבעו נאם
states be shall who all ;prize a Chaldea shall And .empty
,satisfied her plunder become

6335 5159 8154 5937 8056 3068
11 יהוה: כי תשמחי כי תעלזי שסי נחלתי כי תפושי
are you because My spoilers you because you Because .Jehovah
fat ;inheritance of ,exult ,rejoice

3966 517 953 47 6670 1877 5697
12 כעגלה דשה ותצהלי כאברים: בושה אמכם מאד
;greatly your be shall strong like neigh and (in) the like
mother ashamed ,ones ,grass heifer

6160 6723 4057 1471 319 2009 3205 2659
חפרה יולדתכם הנה אחרית גוים מדבר ציה וערבה:
a and dry a a (be shall) the last the ,Behold who she turn shall
.desert land ,wildness nations of .bore you pale

5674 3605 3605 8074 1961 3427 3808 3068 7110
13 מקצף יהוה לא תשב והיתה שממה כלה כל עבר על־
by who every of all ,waste a it but will it not Jehovah's Because
passes one ;it be will in lived be wrath of

884 6186 4347 3605 8319 8077 884
14 בבל ישם וישרק על־כל־מכותיה: ערכו על־בבל
Baby- against Array her all at shall and be shall Babylon yourselves .plagues hiss ,amazed lon

2671 2550 3034 7198 1869 3605 5439
סביב כל־דרכי קשת ידו אליה אל־תחמלו אל־חץ כי
for ;arrows do not ;her at shout ;bow a you all all
spare tread who ,around

5307 3027 5414 5439 3321 2398 3068
15 ליהוה חטאה: הריעו עליה סביב נתנה ידה נפלו
have her has She all against Shout has she against
fallen ;hand given ,around her .sinned Jehovah

5358 3068 5360 2346 2040 803
אשויתיה נהרסו חומותיה כי נקמת יהוה היא הנקמו
Take it Jehovah the for her been have her
vengeance .(is) of vengeance ;walls down thrown ;pillars

8610 884 2232 3772 6213
16 בה כאשר עשתה עשו־לה: כרתו זורע מבבל ותפש
him and from the off Cut .her to do has she As on
using Babylon sower ,done .her

6437 5971 376 3238 2719 6440 7102 6256 4038
מגל בעת קציר מפני חרב היונה איש אל־עמו יפנו
shall they his to each the sword a from .harvest the in the
;turn people one ,oppressor of before of time sickle

5080 738 3478 6340 7716 5127 776 376
17 ואיש לארצו ינוסו: שה פזורה ישראל אריות הדיחו
driven lions (by) Israel scattered a shall his to each and
.away ,(is) sheep :flee land one

5019 6105 314 2088 804 4428 398 7223
הראשון אכלו מלך אשור וזה האחרון עצמו נבוכדראצר
Nebuchadnezzar crunched last and ;Assyria the devoured The
bones (bones his) this of king ,first

430 6635 3068 559 3541 3651 884 4428
18 מלך בבל: לכן כה־אמר יהוה צבאות אלהי
the ,hosts Jehovah says thus Therefore .Babylon king
of God of of

says this: Behold, I am punishing the king of Babylon and his land, as I have punished the king of Assyria. [19]And I will again bring Israel to his home, and he shall feed on Carmel and Bashan; and his soul shall be satisfied on Mount Ephraim and Gilead. [20]In those days, and at that time, declares Jehovah, the iniquity of Israel shall not be sought for, and it is not; and the sins of Judah, and they shall not be found; for I will pardon those whom I leave as a remnant.

[21]Go up against the land of Merathaim, against it and against the inhabitants of Pekod. Waste and destroy after them, says Jehovah, and do according to all that I have commanded you. [22]A sound of battle *is* in the land, and of great ruin. [23]How the hammer of all the earth is cut off and broken! How Babylon has become a ruin among the nations! [24]I have laid a trap for you, and you also are captured, Babylon; and you did not know. You were found, and also caught, because you stirred up yourself against Jehovah. [25]Jehovah has opened His armory, and has brought out the weapons of His fury. For this *is* a work of Jehovah, God of hosts, in the land of the Chaldeans. [26]Come up against her from the end; open her granaries; pile her up as heaps and utterly destroy her. Do not let a remnant be left to her. [27]Put the sword to all her bulls; let them go down to the slaughter. Woe to them! For their day has come, the time of their punishment. [28]The voice of those who flee and escape out of the land of Babylon, to declare in Zion the vengeance of Jehovah our God, the vengeance of

776 884 4428 6485 2005 3478
ישראל הנני פקד אל־מלך בבל ואל־ארצו כאשר
as his and Babylon the am ,Behold :Israel
;land of king punishing I

19 5116 3478 7725 804 4428 6485
פקדתי אל־מלך אשור: ושבתי את־ישראל אל־נוהו
his to Israel will I And .Assyria the I
,pasture again bring of king punished

7646 1568 669 2022 1316 3760 7462
ורעה הכרמל והבשן ובהר אפרים והגלעד תשבע
be shall and Ephraim on and and Carmel will he and
satisfied Gilead Mount ,Bashan on feed

20 1245 3068/5002 6256 3117 5315
נפשו: בימים ההם ובעת ההיא נאם־יהוה יבקש את־
be shall ,Jehovah states ,that at and ,those days In his
for sought time .soul

4672 3808 3063 2403 369 3478 5771
עון ישראל ואיננו ואת־חטאת יהודה ולא תמצאינה כי
for shall they and ,Judah the and it and Israel's ini-
;found be not of sins ;not is quity

21 5927 4850 776 7604 834 5545
אסלח לאשר אשאיר: על־הארץ מרתים עלה
up go ,Merathaim the Against as leave I those will I
of land .remnant a whom pardon

3068 5002 310 2763 2717 6489 3427
עליה ואל־יושבי פקוד חרב והחרם אחריהם נאם־יהוה
;Jehovah states after and waste ;Pekod the and against
,them destroy of dwellers against ;it

22 7667 776 4421 6963 6680 3605 6213
ועשה ככל אשר צויתיך: קול מלחמה בארץ ושבר
a and in (is) battle A com- have I that according do and
ruin ,land the of sound .you manded all to

23 1961 776 3605 6360 7665 1438 1419
גדול: איך נגדע וישבר פטיש כל־הארץ איך היתה
has How the all the and cut is How .great
become !earth of hammer broken off

24 88:4 3920 1571 3369 1471 884 8047
לשמה בבל בגוים: יקשתי לך וגם־נלכדת בבל ואת
and ;Babylon are you and for have I the among Babylon horror a
you ,captured also ,you trap a laid !nations

1624 3068 3588 8610 1571 4672 3045 3808
לא ידעת נמצאת וגם־נתפשת כי ביהוה התגרית:
stirred you against because ,caught and were you did not
.yourself up Jehovah also found ;know

25 4399 2195 3627 3318 214 3068 6605
פתח יהוה את־אוצרו ויוצא את־כלי זעמו כי־מלאכה
work a For His the has and his Jehovah has
.fury of weapons out brought armory opened

26 7093 935 3778 776 6635 3068 136
היא לאדני יהוה צבאות בארץ כשדים: באו־לה מקץ
from against Come the the in hosts Jehovah the of this
;end the her .Chaldeans of land of Lord (is)

1961 408 2763 6194 3644 5549 3965 6605
פתחו מאבסיה סלוה כמו־ערמים והחרימוה אל־תהי־
be Let not completely and ,heaps like pile her open
.her destroy up her ;granaries

27 1945 2874 3381 6499 3605 2717 7611
לה שארית: חרבו כל־פריה ירדו לטבח הוי עליהם
!them to Woe the to them let her all to Put a to
.slaughter down go ;bulls sword the .remnant her

28 776 6405 5127 6963 6486 6256 3117 935
כי־בא יומם עת פקדתם: קול נסים ופלטים מארץ
the from and those The their time the their has For
of land escape flee who of voice .punishment of ,day come

1964 5360 430 3068 5360 6726 5046 884
בבל להגיד בציון את־נקמת יהוה אלהינו נקמת היכלו:
His venge- the our Jehovah venge- the in to ,Babylon
.temple of ance ,God of ance Zion declare

His temple. 29Make the archers hear against Babylon. All you who tread a bow, camp against it all around. Let none of them escape. Repay her according to her work, according to all that she has done, do to her. For she has been proud against Jehovah, against the Holy One of Israel. 30So her young men shall fall in the streets, and all her men of war shall be silenced in that day, declares Jehovah. 31Behold, I *am* against you, O proud one, says the Lord Jehovah of hosts; for your day has come, the time I will punish you. 32And the proud one shall stumble and fall, and none shall raise him up. And I will kindle a fire in his cities, and it shall burn up everything all around him.

33So says Jehovah of hosts, The sons of Israel and the sons of Judah are oppressed together. Yea, all who captured them held them fast; they refused to let them go. 34Their Redeemer *is* strong; Jehovah of hosts is His name. He shall surely plead their cause, so that He may give rest to the land, and make to tremble the dwellers of Babylon.

35A sword *is* on the Chaldeans, declares Jehovah; and on the dwellers of Babylon, and on her rulers, and on her wise men. 36A sword *is* on the liars, and they shall become fools; a sword *is* on her mighty men, and they shall be broken. 37A sword *is* on his horses and his chariots, and to all the mixed people in her midst. And they shall become *as* women. A sword *is* to her treasuries, and they shall be robbed. 38A drought *is* on her waters, and they shall be dried up. For it *is* the land of idols, and they boast themselves in idols. 39So, the beasts of the desert shall dwell *there* with jackals; and the daughters of the ostrich shall dwell in

29 הַשְׁמִיעוּ אֶל־בָּבֶל | רַבִּים כָּל־דֹּרְכֵי קֶשֶׁת חֲנוּ עָלֶיהָ
2583 7198 1869 3605 7228 884 8085
against it | camp | ,bow a | who you All tread | the .archers | Baby- against lon | Make hear

סָבִיב אַל־יְהִי־ פְּלֵיטָה שַׁלְּמוּ־לָהּ כְּפָעֳלָהּ כְּכֹל אֲשֶׁר
3605 6467 7999 64:13 408 54:39
that according all to | according ;work her to | her Repay | .escape | of let not them (any) | all ;around

עָשְׂתָה עֲשׂוּ־לָהּ כִּי אֶל־יְהוָה זָדָה אֶל־קְדוֹשׁ יִשְׂרָאֵל׃
3478 6918 2102 3068 6213 6213
.Israel | the of One Holy | against | has she ,proud been | Jehovah | against For | to .her | do | has she done

30 לָכֵן יִפְּלוּ בַחוּרֶיהָ בִּרְחֹבֹתֶיהָ וְכָל־אַנְשֵׁי מִלְחַמְתָּהּ יִדַּמּוּ
1826 4421 582 3605 7339 970 5307/3651
be shall silenced | war her | men of | and all | the in ,streets | young her men | shall fall | There- fore

31 בַּיּוֹם הַהוּא נְאֻם־יְהוָה׃ הִנְנִי אֵלֶיךָ זָדוֹן נְאֻם־אֲדֹנָי
136 2087 2009 3068 5002 3117
the Lord | proud O ,one | against ,you | ,Behold (am) I | .Jehovah | states | ,that | day in

32 יְהוִה צְבָאוֹת כִּי בָא יוֹמְךָ עֵת פְּקַדְתִּיךָ׃ וְכָשַׁל זָדוֹן
2087 3782 6485 6256 3117 935 6635 3068
the one proud | shall stumble | And | punish will I .you | the time | your ,day | has come | for | ,hosts | Jehovah of

וְנָפַל וְאֵין לוֹ מֵקִים וְהִצַּתִּי אֵשׁ בְּעָרָיו וְאָכְלָה כָּל־
3605 398 5892 784 3341 6965 369 5307
every- thing | shall devour | his in ,cities | fire a | will I And kindle | shall .up lift | him none | and | and ,fall

33 סְבִיבֹתָיו׃ כֹּה אָמַר יְהוָה צְבָאוֹת עֲשׁוּקִים בְּנֵי־
1121 6231 6635 3068 559 3541 5439
The of sons | are oppressed | :hosts of | Jehovah | says | Thus | around all .him

יִשְׂרָאֵל וּבְנֵי־יְהוּדָה יַחְדָּו וְכָל־שֹׁבֵיהֶם הֶחֱזִיקוּ בָם מֵאֲנוּ
3985 2388 7617 3605 3162 3063 1121 3478
they refused | ;them | held fast | cap- tured them | who all and | to- ;gether | Judah | the and of sons | ,Israel

34 שַׁלְּחָם׃ גֹּאֲלָם | חָזָק יְהוָה צְבָאוֹת שְׁמוֹ רִיב יָרִיב אֶת־
7378 7378 8034 6635 3068 2389 1350 7971
will He surely plead | His (is) ;name | hosts of | Jehovah | (is) ,strong | Their Redeemer | let to .go them

35 רִיבָם לְמַעַן הִרְגִּיעַ אֶת־הָאָרֶץ וְהִרְגִּיז לְיֹשְׁבֵי בָבֶל׃ חֶרֶב
2719 884 3427 7264 776 2280 7379
A sword | .Babylon | the to of residents | make and tremble | the ,land | give may He to rest | so that | their ,cause

עַל־כַּשְׂדִּים נְאֻם־יְהוָה וְאֶל־יֹשְׁבֵי בָבֶל וְאֶל־שָׂרֶיהָ וְאֶל־
8269 88:4 3427 3068 5002 3778 5921
and to | her ,,rulers | and to | ,Babylon | resi- the of dents | and to | ,Jehovah | states | the ,Chaldeans | (is) on

36 חֲכָמֶיהָ׃ חֶרֶב אֶל־הַבַּדִּים וְנֹאָלוּ חֶרֶב אֶל־גִּבּוֹרֶיהָ וָחָתּוּ׃
2865 1368 2719 2973 3901 2719 2450
they and .broken are | mighty her ,men | (is) to | a sword | they and ;fools be will | the ,liars | (is) to | A sword | wise her .men

37 חֶרֶב אֶל־סוּסָיו וְאֶל־רִכְבּוֹ וְאֶל־כָּל־הָעֶרֶב אֲשֶׁר בְּתוֹכָהּ
8432 834 6153 3605 7393 5483 2719
her in ;midst | who (are) | mixed the people | all | and to | his ,chariots | and to | his horses | (is) to | A sword

38 וְהָיוּ לְנָשִׁים חֶרֶב אֶל־אוֹצְרֹתֶיהָ וּבֻזָּזוּ׃ חֹרֶב אֶל־מֵימֶיהָ
4325 2721 962 214 2719 802 1961
her ;waters | (is) to | A drought | shall they and .robbed be | her ,treasuries | (is) to | sword a | ;women | they and shall become

39 וְיָבֵשׁוּ כִּי אֶרֶץ פְּסִלִים הִיא וּבָאֵימִים יִתְהֹלָלוּ׃ לָכֵן יֵשְׁבוּ
3427 1984 367 6459 776 3001
shall dwell | Therefore | boast they .themselves | in and idols | ,(is) it | idols | the of land | For | they and will .up dry

צִיִּים אֶת־אִיִּים וְיָשְׁבוּ בָהּ בְּנוֹת יַעֲנָה וְלֹא־תֵשֵׁב עוֹד
5750 3427 3284 1323 7931 339 6728
again | shall dwell | And not | the .ostrich of | daugh- ters | the in her | shall and dwell | ;jackals with | desert creatures

her again. And it shall not again have anyone *in it* forever; it shall not be lived in until generation and generation. [40]As God overthrew Sodom and Gomorrah, and their neighbors, declares Jehovah, *so* no man shall live there, nor shall a son of man stay in it.

[41]Behold, a people shall come from the north, and a great nation; and many kings shall be stirred up from the farthest parts of the earth. [42]They lay hold of a bow and a spear; they *shall be* cruel and will show no mercy. Their voice shall roar like the sea; and arrayed like a man for the battle, they shall ride on horses against you, O daughter of Babylon. [43]The king of Babylon has heard their report, and his hands became feeble; anguish took hold of him, pangs like *those of* a woman in labor.

[44]Behold, he shall come up like a lion from the swelling of Jordan, against the home of the strong. But I will make them suddenly run away from it; and who is a chosen *one* I will appoint over it? For who is like Me? And who will summon Me? And who *is* a shepherd who will stand before Me? [45]So hear the counsel of Jehovah that He has planned against Babylon; and His purposes which He has purposed against the land of the Chaldeans: Surely *they* shall drag them, the least of the flock; surely He will make *their* pasture desolate over them. [46]At the sound of the capture of Babylon, the earth shall tremble; and a cry is heard among the nations.

430 4114 1755 1755 5704 3427 3808 5331
40 לָנֶצַח וְלֹא תִשְׁכּוֹן עַד־דּוֹר וָדוֹר׃ כְּמַהְפֵּכַת אֱלֹהִים אֶת־
God As overthrew gene- .ration and genera- tion until shall it be lived in and not ;forever

8033 3427 3808 3068 5002 7934 6017 5467
סְדֹם וְאֶת־עֲמֹרָה וְאֶת־שְׁכֵנֶיהָ נְאֻם־יְהוָה לֹא־יֵשֵׁב שָׁם
there shall dwell not ,Jehovah states their ,neighbors and Gomorrah and Sodom

1471 6828 935 5971 2009 120 1121 1481 3808 376
41 אִישׁ וְלֹא־יָגוּר בָּהּ בֶּן־אָדָם׃ הִנֵּה עַם בָּא מִצָּפוֹן וְגוֹי
a nation and the ,north from coming is a people ,Behold .man son a of it in shall sojourn and not ;man a

3541 7198 776 3411 5782 7227 4428 1419
42 גָּדוֹל וּמְלָכִים רַבִּים יֵעֹרוּ מִיַּרְכְּתֵי־אָרֶץ׃ קֶשֶׁת וְכִידֹן
and spear bow a the .earth the from far parts of be shall aroused many and kings ,great

5921 1993 3220 6963 7355 3808 394 2388
יַחֲזִיקוּ אַכְזָרִי הֵמָּה וְלֹא יְרַחֵמוּ קוֹלָם כַּיָּם יֶהֱמֶה וְעַל־
and on shall ,roar the sea like their voice show ;mercy shall and not they (be shall) cruel lay ;of hold They

884 1323 4421 376 6186 7392 5483
סוּסִים יִרְכָּבוּ עָרוּךְ כְּאִישׁ לַמִּלְחָמָה עָלַיִךְ בַּת־בָּבֶל׃
.Babylon O of daughter against ,you the for battle a like man arrayed shall they ,ride horses

2388 6864 3027 7503 8088 884 4428 8085
43 שָׁמַע מֶלֶךְ־בָּבֶל אֶת־שִׁמְעָם וְרָפוּ יָדָיו צָרָה הֶחֱזִיקַתְהוּ
hold took ,him of anguish his ;hands hang limp their ,report Babylon The of king has heard

5116 3383 1347 5927 738 2009 3205 2427
44 חִיל כַּיּוֹלֵדָה׃ הִנֵּה כְּאַרְיֵה יַעֲלֶה מִגְּאוֹן הַיַּרְדֵּן אֶל־נְוֵה
the of pasture to ,Jordan the from of pride shall he up come a like lion ,Behold woman a as .labor in pangs

6485 977 4310 7323 7280 386
אֵיתָן כִּי־אַרְגִּיעָה אֲרִיצֵם מֵעָלֶיהָ וּמִי בָחוּר אֵלֶיהָ אֶפְקֹד
will I .appoint over it chosen a one and who away ;it from them make run will I suddenly For the .strong

6440 5975 834 7462 2088/4310 3259 4310 3644 4310
כִּי מִי כָמוֹנִי וּמִי יוֹעִדֶנִּי וּמִי־זֶה רֹעֶה אֲשֶׁר יַעֲמֹד לְפָנָי׃
before ?Me will stand who shepherd this (is) who And sum- ?Me mon will And who like ?Me who (is) For

4284 884 3289 3068 6098 8085
45 לָכֵן שִׁמְעוּ עֲצַת־יְהוָה אֲשֶׁר יָעַץ אֶל־בָּבֶל וּמַחְשְׁבוֹתָיו
His and purposes ,Babylon against has He planned that Jehovah the of counsel hear There- fore

6810 5498 3808/518 3778 776 2803 834
אֲשֶׁר חָשַׁב אֶל־אֶרֶץ כַּשְׂדִּים אִם־לֹא יִסְחָבוּם צְעִירֵי
the of least drag shall ,them ,surely the ;Chaldeans the against of land has He purposed which

884 8610 6963 5116 5921 8074 3808 518 6629
46 הַצֹּאן אִם־לֹא יַשִּׁים עֲלֵיהֶם נְוֵהֶם׃ מִקּוֹל נִתְפְּשָׂה בָבֶל
,Babylon the of of capture the At sound (their) .pasture over them will He make desolate surely the ;flock

8085 1471 2201 776 7493
נִרְעֲשָׁה הָאָרֶץ וּזְעָקָה בַּגּוֹיִם נִשְׁמָע׃
is .heard the among nations a and cry the ,earth shall tremble

CAP. LI נא

CHAPTER 51

CHAPTER 51

[1]So says Jehovah, Behold, I am arousing a destroying wind against Babylon, and against those dwelling in the heart of My foes. [2]And I will send foreigners to Babylon, who shall empty

6965 3820 3427 884 5782 2005 3068 559 3541
1 כֹּה אָמַר יְהוָה הִנְנִי מֵעִיר עַל־בָּבֶל וְאֶל־יֹשְׁבֵי לֵב קָמָי
my foes in of heart those living and against Babylon against am arousing ,Behold I ,Jehovah says Thus

1238 2219 2114 884 7971 7843 7307
2 רוּחַ מַשְׁחִית׃ וְשִׁלַּחְתִּי לְבָבֶל זָרִים וְזֵרוּהָ וִיבֹקְקוּ אֶת־
will and empty will who her sift aliens to Babylon I And send will .destroying a wind

her and shall empty her land. For in the day of evil, they shall be against her all around. ³Do not let the treader fully tread his bow, nor lift himself up in his armor. And do not spare her young men; utterly destroy all her army.   ⁴So the slain shall fall in the land of the Chaldeans; yea, thrust through in her streets. ⁵For neither Israel nor Judah has been forsaken by his God, by Jehovah of hosts, though their land was filled with guilt against the Holy One of Israel. ⁶Flee out of the middle of Babylon; yea, each man deliver his soul. Do not be silenced in her iniquity; for the time of the vengeance of Jehovah *is here*; He will give her a just reward. ⁷Babylon *was* a golden cup in the hand of Jehovah, making all the earth drunk. The nations have drunk of her wine; therefore the nations are rage. ⁸Suddenly Babylon has fallen, and it is broken. Wail for her; take balm for her pain; if perhaps she may be healed. ⁹We would have healed Babylon, but she is not healed. Forsake her, and let us go, each one into his own country. For her judgment reaches to the heavens, and is lifted up to the skies. ¹⁰Jehovah has brought forth our righteousness; come and let us declare in Zion the work of Jehovah our God.

¹¹Purify the arrows; fill the shields; Jehovah has aroused the spirit of the kings of the Medes. For His plan *is* against Babylon, to destroy *it*; because it *is* the vengeance of Jehovah, the vengeance of His temple. ¹²Set up the banner to the walls of Babylon; make the watch strong; set up the watches; prepare the ambushes. For Jehovah has both planned and has done

3
1869• 1869 7451 3117 5439 1961 776
אַרְצָהּ כִּי־הָיוּ עָלֶיהָ מִסָּבִיב בְּיוֹם רָעָה:
tread fully Not .evil the in all against they For her
let of day around her be shall .land

:970 408 2550 1408 5630 5927/408• 71:98 1869
הַדֹּרֵךְ קַשְׁתּוֹ וְאַל־יִתְעַל בְּסִרְיֹנוֹ וְאַל־תַּחְמְלוּ אֶל־בַּחֻרֶיהָ
young her do And his in him- lift nor his the
:men spare not .armor self ,bow treader

4
1856 3778 776 2491 5307 6635 2963
הַחֲרִימוּ כָּל־צְבָאָהּ: וְנָפְלוּ חֲלָלִים בְּאֶרֶץ כַּשְׂדִּים וּמְדֻקָּרִים
pierced and the the in the Thus her all utterly
through Chaldeans of land slain fall shall .hosts destroy

5
:1430 3063 3478 4891 3808 2351
בְּחוּצֹתֶיהָ: כִּי לֹא־אַלְמָן יִשְׂרָאֵל וִיהוּדָה מֵאֱלֹהָיו
his by Judah or Israel been has not For her in
.God widowed .streets

3478 6918 816 4390 776 6635 3068
מִיהוה צְבָאוֹת כִּי אַרְצָם מָלְאָה אָשָׁם מִקְּדוֹשׁ יִשְׂרָאֵל:
.Israel the against guilt filled was their though ,hosts Jeho- by
of One Holy with land vah of

6
9 57,71 1826 408 53:15 376 14422 8•84 8432 5127
נֻסוּ מִתּוֹךְ בָּבֶל וּמַלְּטוּ אִישׁ נַפְשׁוֹ אַל־תִּדַּמּוּ בַּעֲוֺנָהּ כִּי
for her in be do not his each and ,Babylon the from Flee
;iniquity silenced ;soul man deliver of midst

7
2071 3563 7999 15:76 3:068 5360 6256
עֵת נְקָמָה הִיא לַיהוה גְּמוּל הוּא מְשַׁלֵּם לָהּ: כּוֹס־זָהָב
golden A .her to will He just a Jehovah's it vengeance the
cup render reward (is) of time

14:71 8354 3196 776 36105 7937 3068 3027 884
בָּבֶל בְּיַד־יהוה מְשַׁכֶּרֶת כָּל־הָאָרֶץ מִיֵּינָהּ שָׁתוּ גוֹיִם עַל־
The have her of the all making ,Jehovah the in (was).
;nations drunk wine .earth drunk of hand Babylon

8
3213 7665 884 5307 6597 1471 11884 3651
כֵּן יִתְהֹלְלוּ גוֹיִם: פִּתְאֹם נָפְלָה בָבֶל וַתִּשָּׁבֵר הֵילִילוּ
Wail is it and ,Babylon has Suddenly the rage there-
.broken fallen .nations fore

9
884 7495 7495 194 43:41 6875 3947
עָלֶיהָ קְחוּ צֳרִי לְמַכְאוֹבָהּ אוּלַי תֵּרָפֵא: רִפִּאנוּ אֶת־בָּבֶל
,Babylon would We may she if her for balm take for
healed have .healed be perhaps ;pain ;her

180614 5060 776 376 3212 58n00 7495• 3808
וְלֹא נִרְפָּתָה עִזְבוּהָ וְנֵלֵךְ אִישׁ לְאַרְצוֹ כִּי־נָגַע אֶל־הַשָּׁמַיִם
the to reaches for his into each let and Forsake is she but
heavens ;country own one ,go us her .healed not

10
6666 3068 3318 7834 5704 5375 4941
מִשְׁפָּטָהּ וְנִשָּׂא עַד־שְׁחָקִים: הוֹצִיא יהוה אֶת־צִדְקֹתֵינוּ
our Jehovah brought has the to is and her
:righteousness forth .skies up lifted ,judgment

11
1305 430 3068 4639 6:726 5-608 935
בֹּאוּ וּנְסַפְּרָה בְצִיּוֹן אֶת־מַעֲשֵׂה יהוה אֱלֹהֵינוּ: הָבֵרוּ
Purify .God our Jehovah the Zion in let and come
of work declare us

40:74 44:28 17307 30-68 5782 14390 ~ 2671
הַחִצִּים מִלְאוּ הַשְּׁלָטִים הֵעִיר יהוה אֶת־רוּחַ מַלְכֵי מָדַי
the the spirit the Jehovah has the fill ;arrows
.Medes of kings of aroused ;shields

5360 3068 5360 7843 4209 884
כִּי־עַל־בָּבֶל מְזִמָּתוֹ לְהַשְׁחִיתָהּ כִּי־נִקְמַת יהוה הִיא נִקְמַת
ven- the ,(is) it Jehovah the because destroy to His Baby- against For
of geance of vengeance ;(it) plan lon (is)

12
6965 49:29 2388 52:51 5375 8814 2346 1964
הֵיכָלוֹ: אֶל־חוֹמֹת בָּבֶל שְׂאוּ־נֵס הַחֲזִיקוּ הַמִּשְׁמָר הָקִימוּ
up set the make the Set Babylon the to His
.watch strong ;banner up of walls .temple

:: 6213/1571 3068 2161 1571 693 3559 8104:
שֹׁמְרִים הָכִינוּ הָאֹרְבִים כִּי־גַם־זָמַם יהוה גַּם־עָשָׂה אֵת
done and Jehovah has both For the prepare the
planned .ambushes ;watches

that which He spoke
against the people of Babylon. [13]O you who live by
many waters, rich in
treasures, your end has
come, the measure of your
unjust gain. [14]Jehovah of
hosts has sworn by Himself,
saying, Surely I will fill you
with men as with locusts;
and they shall lift up a shout
against you. [15]He has
made the earth by His
power; He has established
the world by His wisdom,
and stretched out the
heavens by His under-
standing. [16]When He gives
His voice, a multitude of
waters is in the heavens;
and He causes the mists to
ascend from the end of the
earth. He makes lightnings
for rain, and brings forth the
wind out of His treasuries.
[17]Every man is brutish in
knowledge; every refiner is
put to shame by idols. For
his molten image *is* a lie,
and no breath *is* in them.
[18]They *are* vanity, the work
of errors; in the time of their
punishment they shall
perish. [19]The Portion of
Jacob *is* not like them; for
He *is* the Former of all
things, and the rod of His
inheritance; Jehovah of
hosts, *is* His name. [20]You
are My war club *and*
weapons of war; for with
you I will shatter nations,
and with you I will destroy
kingdoms. [21]And with you I
will shatter the horse and
his rider; and with you I will
shatter the chariot and his
charioteer. [22]And I will shatter man and woman with
you; and with you I will
shatter old and young; and
with you I will shatter the
young man and the girl.
[23]And I will shatter the
shepherd and his flock with
you. And I will shatter the
farmer and his team with
you; and with you I will
shatter heads and rulers.

[24]And I will give to Babylon, and to all the people of
Chaldea all the evil that they
have done in Zion, before
your eyes, declares Jeho-
vah. [25]Behold, I *am* against
you, O destroying mountain
declares Jehovah, who

7227 7227 4325 7931 884 7931 1696 834
13 אֲשֶׁר־דִּבֶּר אֶל־יֹשְׁבֵי בָּבֶל׃ שֹׁכַנְתְּי עַל־מַיִם רַבִּים רַבַּת
rich ,many waters by you O .Babylon in- the against He that
in live who of habitants spoke which

6635 3068 7650 1215 520 7093 935 214
14 אוֹצָרֹת בָּא קִצֵּךְ אַמַּת בִּצְעֵךְ׃ נִשְׁבַּע יְהוָה צְבָאוֹת בְּנַפְשׁוֹ
by hosts Jehovah Has unjust your the your has ,treasures
,Himself of sworn .gain of measure ,end come

6213 1959 6030 3218 120 4390
15 כִּי אִם־מִלֵּאתִיךְ אָדָם כַּיֶּלֶק וְעָנוּ עָלַיִךְ הֵידָד׃ עֹשֵׂה
has He .shout a against they and with as men fill will I Surely
made you lift will locusts with you

8064 5186 8394 2451 8398 3559 3581 776
אֶרֶץ בְּכֹחוֹ מֵכִין תֵּבֵל בְּחָכְמָתוֹ וּבִתְבוּנָתוֹ נָטָה שָׁמָיִם׃
the stretched His by and His by the He His by the
.heavens out understanding ,wisdom world established ;power earth

776 7097 5387 5927 8064 4325 1995 5414 6963
16 לְקוֹל תִּתּוֹ הֲמוֹן מַיִם בַּשָּׁמַיִם וַיַּעַל נְשִׂאִים מִקְצֵה־אָרֶץ
the the from the He and the in waters mul- a He (His) When
;earth of end mists up go makes ,heavens (is) of titude ,gives voice

3605 1197 214 7307 3318 6213 4306 130
17 בְּרָקִים לַמָּטָר עָשָׂה וַיּוֹצֵא רוּחַ מֵאֹצְרֹתָיו׃ נִבְעַר כָּל־
Every is His of out the brings and He rain for lightnings
brutish .treasuries wind forth makes

3808 5262 8262 6459 6884 3605 3001 1847 120
אָדָם מִדַּעַת הֹבִישׁ כָּל־צוֹרֵף מִפָּסֶל כִּי שֶׁקֶר נִסְכּוֹ וְלֹא־
and molten his a (is) for ;idols by refiner every put is in man
is not ,image lie shame to ;knowledge

6 6486 6256 8595 4639 1892 7307
18 רוּחַ בָּם׃ הֶבֶל הֵמָּה מַעֲשֵׂה תַּעְתֻּעִים בְּעֵת פְּקֻדָּתָם יֹאבֵדוּ׃
shall they their the in ;errors work a They vanity in breath
.perish punishment of time of ,(are) .them

5159 7626 3605 3335 3290 2506 428 3808
19 לֹא־כְאֵלֶּה חֵלֶק יַעֲקוֹב כִּי־יוֹצֵר הַכֹּל הוּא וְשֵׁבֶט נַחֲלָתוֹ
in- His the and He all the for ;Jacob The like (is) not
;heritance of rod ,(is) things of Former of portion them

4421 3627 4667 8034 6635 3068
20 יְהוָה צְבָאוֹת שְׁמוֹ׃ מַפֵּץ־אַתָּה לִי כְּלֵי מִלְחָמָה
;war (and) Me to You a His (is) hosts Jehovah
of weapons (are) war-club .name of

5310 4467 7843 1471 5310
21 וְנִפַּצְתִּי בְךָ גּוֹיִם וְהִשְׁחַתִּי בְךָ מַמְלָכוֹת׃ וְנִפַּצְתִּי בְךָ
with will I And ..kingdoms with will I and ,nations with will I for
you shatter you destroy you shatter

376 5310 7393 5310 7392 5483
22 סוּס וְרֹכְבוֹ וְנִפַּצְתִּי בְךָ רֶכֶב וְרֹכְבוֹ׃ וְנִפַּצְתִּי בְךָ אִישׁ
man with will I And his and the with will I and his and the
you shatter .charioteer chariot you shatter ;rider horse

1330 970 5310 5288 2205 5310 802
וְאִשָּׁה וְנִפַּצְתִּי בְךָ זָקֵן וָנָעַר וְנִפַּצְתִּי בְךָ בָּחוּר וּבְתוּלָה׃
the and young the with will I and and old with will I and and
.virgin man you shatter ,young you shatter ;woman

5310 6776 406 5310 5739 7462 5310
23 וְנִפַּצְתִּי בְךָ רֹעֶה וְעֶדְרוֹ וְנִפַּצְתִּי בְךָ אִכָּר וְצִמְדּוֹ וְנִפַּצְתִּי
will I and his and the with will I And his and the with will I And
shatter ;team farmer you shatter .flock shepherd you shatter

3778 3427 3605 894 7999 5461 6346
24 בְךָ פַּחוֹת וּסְגָנִים׃ וְשִׁלַּמְתִּי לְבָבֶל וּלְכֹל יוֹשְׁבֵי כַשְׂדִּים
Chaldea the to and to will I And and governors with
of dwellers all Babylon repay .rulers you

3068 5002 5869 6726 6213 834 7451 3605
אֵת כָּל־רָעָתָם אֲשֶׁר־עָשׂוּ בְצִיּוֹן לְעֵינֵיכֶם נְאֻם יְהוָה׃
.Jehovah states before Zion in they that their all
eyes your done have evil

7843 3068 5002 4889 2022 2005
25 הִנְנִי אֵלֶיךָ הַר הַמַּשְׁחִית נְאֻם־יְהוָה הַמַּשְׁחִית
destroy who ,Jehovah states ,destroying O against ,Behold
mountain ,you (am) I

destroys all the earth. And I will stretch out My hand on you, and will roll you down from the rocks; and I will make you a burned mountain. [26]And they shall not take a stone from you for a corner, or a stone for foundations; but you shall be a waste forever, says Jehovah. [27]Set up a banner in the land; blow a trumpet among the nations; consecrate nations against her. Make hear the kingdoms of Ararat, Minni, and Ashkenaz together against her; set a marshal against her. Cause the horses to come up like rough locusts. [28]Consecrate nations against her, with the kings of the Medes, her governors and all her rulers, and all the land of his dominion. [29]And the land shall tremble and writhe in pain. For every purpose of Jehovah shall be done against Babylon, to make the land of Babylon a desert without inhabitant.

[30]The mighty men of Babylon have stopped fighting; they have dwelt in strongholds; their might has withered; they became *as* women; they have burned their houses; her bars are broken. [31]A runner shall run to meet a runner, and a herald to meet a herald, to announce to the king of Babylon that his city is captured from end *to end*; [32]and that the fords are captured. And they have burned the reeds with fire, and the men of war are terrified. [33]For so says Jehovah of hosts, the God of Israel: The daughter of Babylon *is* like a grain-floor; *it is* time to tread her. Yet a little while, and the time of her harvest shall come.

[34]Nebuchadnezzar, the king of Babylon, has devoured us. He has crushed us. He has made us an empty vessel. He has swallowed us like a jackal. He has filled his belly with delicacies. He has thrown

26

אֶת־כָּל־הָאָרֶץ וְנָטִיתִי אֶת־יָדִי עָלֶיךָ וְגִלְגַּלְתִּיךָ מִן־הַסְּלָעִים
3605 776 5186 3027 5927 1556 5553
all the .earth out stretch will I And My hand on you you down roll and from the ;rocks

וּנְתַתִּיךָ לְהַר שְׂרֵפָה׃ וְלֹא־יִקְחוּ מִמְּךָ אֶבֶן לְפִנָּה וְאֶבֶן
5414 2022 8316 08. 38 3947 68 38:64 68
and you make will I a mountain a .burned And not shall take they from you a stone a for a corner a or stone

27

לְמוֹסָדוֹת כִּי־שִׁמְמוֹת עוֹלָם תִּהְיֶה נְאֻם־יְהוָה׃ שְׂאוּ־נֵס
4146 8077 5769 1961 3068 5251
for ;foundations but a waste forever be shall you .Jehovah states Set up a banner

בָּאָרֶץ תִּקְעוּ שׁוֹפָר בַּגּוֹיִם קַדְּשׁוּ עָלֶיהָ גּוֹיִם הַשְׁמִיעוּ
776 8628 7782 1471 6942 1471 8085
the in ;land blow a horn ram's among .nations against consecrate her against .nations Call

עָלֶיהָ מַמְלְכוֹת אֲרָרַט מִנִּי וְאַשְׁכְּנָז פִּקְדוּ עָלֶיהָ טִפְסָר
4467 780 4508 813 6485 29:51
against her king- the of doms ,Ararat ,Minni and ;Ashkenaz appoint against her ;marshal a

28

הַעֲלוּ־סוּס כְּיֶלֶק סָמָר׃ קַדְּשׁוּ עָלֶיהָ גּוֹיִם אֶת־מַלְכֵי מָדַי
5927 3218 5569 6942 1471 3605 4428 4074
up come to cause horses as the .rough Consecrate against her nations with the kings Medes, the the of

אֶת־פַּחוֹתֶיהָ וְאֶת־כָּל־סְגָנֶיהָ וְאֵת כָּל־אֶרֶץ מֶמְשַׁלְתּוֹ׃
6346 5461 3605 776 4475
her governors ,rulers all her and all land of the .dominion his

29

וַתִּרְעַשׁ הָאָרֶץ וַתָּחֹל כִּי קָמָה עַל־בָּבֶל מַחְשְׁבוֹת יְהוָה
7493 776 2342 6965 894 4284 68:30
tremble shall And land writhes stand ,writhes shall for Baby- against the Baby-lon of purposes ,Jehovah

30

לָשׂוּם אֶת־אֶרֶץ בָּבֶל לְשַׁמָּה מֵאֵין יוֹשֵׁב׃ חָדְלוּ גִבּוֹרֵי
7760 776 894 8047 369 3427 2308 1368
to make of land Babylon a desert without a .dweller stopped have mighty The of men

בָּבֶל לְהִלָּחֵם יָשְׁבוּ בַּמְּצָדוֹת נָשְׁתָה גְבוּרָתָם הָיוּ לְנָשִׁים
894 3898 3427 679: 5405 1369 1961 802
Baby- lon ,fighting have they ,strong in holds, withered has their ;might became they ;women

31

הִצִּיתוּ מִשְׁכְּנוֹתֶיהָ נִשְׁבְּרוּ בְרִיחֶיהָ׃ רָץ לִקְרַאת־רָץ יָרוּץ
3341 4908 7665 1280 7323 7125 7323
burned are her ;dwellings broken are her .bars A runner runner to meet a shall run, runner

וּמַגִּיד לִקְרַאת מַגִּיד לְהַגִּיד לְמֶלֶךְ בָּבֶל כִּי־נִלְכְּדָה עִירוֹ
5046 7125 5046 5046 4428 894 3920 5892
and a herald meet to a herald announce to a to king of Babylon that is captured his city

32

מִקָּצֶה׃ וְהַמַּעְבָּרוֹת נִתְפָּשׂוּ וְאֶת־הָאֲגַמִּים שָׂרְפוּ בָאֵשׁ
7097 4569 :8610 98 8313 784
end from .(end) to fords and that the ;seized are reeds the burned have they with .fire

33

וְאַנְשֵׁי הַמִּלְחָמָה נִבְהָלוּ׃ כִּי כֹה אָמַר יְהוָה צְבָאוֹת
582 4421 926 3541 559 3068 6635
the and of men war are .terrified For thus says Jehovah of hosts

אֱלֹהֵי יִשְׂרָאֵל בַּת־בָּבֶל כְּגֹרֶן עֵת הַדְרִיכָהּ עוֹד מְעַט וּבָאָה
430 3478 1323/884 16:37 6256 1869 5750 4592 935
the of God of Israel the :Babylon of daughter ;grain-floor a as (is) time to trample ,her while, little and shall come

34

אֲכָלָנוּ הֲמָמָנוּ נְבוּכַדְרֶאצַּר מֶלֶךְ בָּבֶל הִצִּיגָנוּ
6256 7102 5019 44:28 884
the a harvest of time of her .us crushed us ,us devoured has Nebuchadnezzar king Babylon of .Babylon

הִצִּיגָנוּ כְּלִי רִיק בְּלָעָנוּ כַּתַּנִּין מִלָּא כְרֵשׂוֹ מֵעֲדָנָי הֱדִיחָנוּ׃
3322 3627 7385/1104 8577 4390 3770 5730 1740
He set us an vessel empty .us swallowed us ;jackal a like He has filled belly his with ;delicacies has he .out me cast has he

me out. [35]The violence done to me and to my flesh *is* on Babylon, the dweller in Zion shall say. And Jerusalem shall say, My blood shall be on the inhabitants of Chaldea. [36]So Jehovah says this:: Behold, I will strive for you and take vengeance for you. And I will dry up her sea, and make her well dry. [37]And Babylon shall become heaps, a home for jackals, a horror and a hissing, without an inhabitant. [38]They shall roar together like lions; they shall growl like lions' cubs. [39]In their heat I will make their feasts, and I will make them drunk so that they rejoice and sleep a never-ending sleep, and never awaken, says Jehovah. [40]I shall bring them down like lambs to the slaughter, like rams with he-goats. [41]How Sheshach is captured! And how the praise of all the earth is seized! How Babylon has become a ruin among the nations! [42]The sea has come up over Babylon; she is covered with the multitude of its waves. [43]Her cities have become a ruin, a dry land and a wilderness, a land in which no man dwells; nor does *any* son of man pass by it. [44]And I will punish Bel in Babylon; and I will bring forth out of his mouth that which he has swallowed up. And the nations shall not flow together any more to him; yea, the wall of Babylon shall fall.

[45]My people, go out of her midst; and each man deliver his soul from the fierce anger of Jehovah. [46]And that your heart not faint, and you fear the report that shall be heard in the land, the report shall come in a year. And after that the report shall come in *another* year; and there shall be violence in the land, ruler against ruler. [47]So behold,

3427 1818 6726 3427 559 884 7607 2555
35 חֲמָסִי וּשְׁאֵרִי עַל־בָּבֶל תֹּאמַר יֹשֶׁבֶת צִיּוֹן וְדָמִי אֶל־יֹשְׁבֵי
resi- (is) my and ;Zion the say shall —Babylon (is) to that My
dents to blood in dweller on flesh my ,violence
30:68 559 338.9 559 37:78
36 כַּשְׂדִּים תֹּאמַר יְרוּשָׁלִָם׃ לָכֵן כֹּה אָמַר יְהוָה
,Jehovah says thus Therefore .Jerusalem say shall ,Chaldea's
2717 5360 5358 7379 7378 2005
הִנְנִי־רָב אֶת־רִיבֵךְ וְנִקַּמְתִּי אֶת־נִקְמָתֵךְ וְהַחֲרַבְתִּי אֶת־
will I and your for and your I Behold
up dry ;vengeance avenge cause for contend
4583 1530 884 1961 4726 3001 3220
37 יַמָּהּ וְהֹבַשְׁתִּי אֶת־מְקוֹרָהּ׃ וְהָיְתָה בָבֶל ׀ לְגַלִּים ׀ מְעוֹן
haunt a ,heaps Babylon shall And .well her make and her
for become dry sea
7380 3715 3162 3427 369 8322 8047 8577
38 תַּנִּים שַׁמָּה וּשְׁרֵקָה מֵאֵין יוֹשֵׁב׃ יַחְדָּו כַּכְּפִרִים יִשְׁאָגוּ
shall They like together a without a and horror a ,jackals
;roar lions .dweller ,hissing
4960 7896 2527 738 1484 5286
39 נָעֲרוּ כְּגוֹרֵי אֲרָיוֹת׃ בְּחֻמָּם אָשִׁית אֶת־מִשְׁתֵּיהֶם
their will I their In .lions' like shall they
.feasts make heat cubs growl
5002 6974 3808 5769 8142 3462 5937 4616 7937
וְהִשְׁכַּרְתִּים לְמַעַן יַעֲלֹזוּ וְיָשְׁנוּ שְׁנַת־עוֹלָם וְלֹא יָקִיצוּ נְאֻם
states ,awaken and never- a and they that so make will I And
not ,ending sleep sleep rejoice drunk them
6260 5973 352 2873 3733 3381 3068
40 יְהוָה׃ אוֹרִידֵם כְּכָרִים לִטְבוֹחַ כְּאֵילִים עִם־עַתּוּדִים׃
.he-goats with like the for like bring will I .Jehovah
rams ,slaughter lambs down them
1961 349 776 3605 8416 8610 8357 3920 349
41 אֵיךְ נִלְכְּדָה שֵׁשַׁךְ וַתִּתָּפֵשׂ תְּהִלַּת כָּל־הָאָרֶץ אֵיךְ הָיְתָה
has How the all the how And !Sheshach cap- is How
become !earth of praise seized is tured
1530 1995 3220 884 5927 1471 884 8047
42 לְשַׁמָּה בָּבֶל בַּגּוֹיִם׃ עָלָה עַל־בָּבֶל הַיָּם בַּהֲמוֹן גַּלָּיו
its the with the Babylon over Has the among Babylon ruin a
waves of host ;sea up come !nations
3808 776 6160 6723 776 8047 5892 1961 3680
43 נִכְסָתָה׃ הָיוּ עָרֶיהָ לְשַׁמָּה אֶרֶץ צִיָּה וַעֲרָבָה אֶרֶץ לֹא־
not land a a and ,dry land a ,ruin a Her have is she
,desert cities become .covered
6485 120 1121 2004 5674 3808 376 3605 3427
44 יֵשֵׁב בָּהֵן כָּל־אִישׁ וְלֹא־יַעֲבֹר בָּהֵן בֶּן־אָדָם׃ וּפָקַדְתִּי
will I And .man (any) it by does and ;man any in dwells
punish of son pass not which
5102 3808 6310 1105 3318 884 1078
עַל־בֵּל בְּבָבֶל וְהֹצֵאתִי אֶת־בִּלְעוֹ מִפִּיו וְלֹא־יִנְהֲרוּ אֵלָיו
to shall And his from has he (what) will I and in Bel
him flow not .mouth swallowed out bring ,Babylon
4422 5971 8432 3318 5307 884 2346 1571 1471 5750
45 עוֹד גּוֹיִם גַּם־חוֹמַת בָּבֶל נָפָלָה׃ צְאוּ מִתּוֹכָהּ עַמִּי וּמַלְּטוּ
and My her of out Go shall Babylon the even the still
deliver ;people midst .fall of wall ,nations
3824 7401 6435 3068 639 2740 5315 376
46 אִישׁ אֶת־נַפְשׁוֹ מֵחֲרוֹן אַף־יְהוָה׃ וּפֶן־יֵרַךְ לְבַבְכֶם
your faint And .Jehovah anger the from his each
heart lest of burning soul man
8052 8141 935 776 8085 8052 3372
וְתִירְאוּ בַּשְּׁמוּעָה הַנִּשְׁמַעַת בָּאָרֶץ וּבָא בַשָּׁנָה הַשְּׁמוּעָה
the a in and the in shall that the you and
,report year come ;land heard be .report fear
4910 4910 776 2555 8052 8141 310
וְאַחֲרָיו בַּשָּׁנָה הַשְּׁמוּעָה וְחָמָס בָּאָרֶץ מֹשֵׁל עַל־מֹשֵׁל׃
.ruler against ruler the in and the a in after and
,land violence ;report year that

the days come that I will punish on the idols of Babylon. And all her land shall be put to shame, and all her slain shall fall in her midst. [48]Then the heavens and the earth, and all that *is* in them, shall shout for Babylon; for the plunderers shall come to her from the north, says Jehovah. [49]As Babylon is to fall for the slain of Israel, so for Babylon the slain of all the earth shall fall. [50]You who have escaped the sword, go away. Do not stand still. Remember Jehovah afar off, and let Jerusalem come into your heart. [51]We have turned pale because we have heard reproach; dishonor has covered our faces; for foreigners have come into the holy places of the house of Jehovah. [52]So, behold, the days are coming, says Jehovah, that I will punish on her idols; and through all her land the wounded shall groan. [53]Though Babylon should mount up to the heavens, and though she should fortify her strong height, plunderers shall come from Me to her, declares Jehovah. [54]A sound of a cry from Babylon, and great ruin from the land of Chaldeans! [55]For Jehovah is stripping Babylon, and the great voice will perish out of her. And her waves will roar like many waters; the noise of their voice is given. [56]Because the plunderer is coming on her, on Babylon, and her mighty men are captured; their bows are shattered; for Jehovah the God of recompenses shall surely repay. [57]And I will make her rulers drunk, and her wise ones, her governors and her rulers, and her mighty men; and they shall sleep a never-ending sleep, and not awaken, says the King whose name *is* Jehovah of hosts.

47 לָכֵן הִנֵּה יָמִים בָּאִים וּפָקַדְתִּי עַל־פְּסִילֵי בָבֶל וְכָל־אַרְצָהּ
her land | And all | .Babylon the of idols | on | will I that punish | come | the days | ,behold | There-fore

48 תֵּבוֹשׁ וְכָל־חֲלָלֶיהָ יִפְּלוּ בְּתוֹכָהּ׃ וְרִנְּנוּ עַל־בָּבֶל שָׁמַיִם
the heavens | Babylon over | will And shout | her in .midst | shall fall | her slain | and all | be shall ,shamed

וָאָרֶץ וְכֹל אֲשֶׁר בָּהֶם כִּי מִצָּפוֹן יָבוֹא־לָהּ הַשּׁוֹדְדִים
the ,plunderers | to her | shall come | the from north | for | in ;them | that (is) | and all | the and ,earth

49 נְאֻם־יְהוָה׃ גַּם־בָּבֶל לִנְפֹּל חַלְלֵי יִשְׂרָאֵל גַּם־לְבָבֶל
for Babylon | so | ,Israel | the (for) of slain | to is fall | Babylon As | .Jehovah | states

50 נָפְלוּ חַלְלֵי כָל־הָאָרֶץ׃ פְּלֵטִים מֵחֶרֶב הִלְכוּ אַל־תַּעֲמֹדוּ
stand .still | do not | go ,away | the ,sword | who You escaped have | the .earth | all | the of slain | shall fall

זִכְרוּ מֵרָחוֹק אֶת־יְהוָה וִירוּשָׁלַםִ תַּעֲלֶה עַל־לְבַבְכֶם׃
your heart | into | let come | and Jerusalem | ,Jehovah | afar off | Remember

51 בֹּשְׁנוּ כִּי־שָׁמַעְנוּ חֶרְפָּה כִּסְּתָה כְלִמָּה פָּנֵינוּ כִּי בָּאוּ זָרִים
aliens | have come | for | our ;faces | dishonor | has covered | ;reproach | have we heard | be-cause | We blush

52 עַל־מִקְדְּשֵׁי בֵּית יְהוָה׃ לָכֵן הִנֵּה־יָמִים בָּאִים נְאֻם־
states | are ,coming | the days | ,behold | Therefore | .Jehovah's house | holy the of places | into

53 יְהוָה וּפָקַדְתִּי עַל־פְּסִילֶיהָ וּבְכָל־אַרְצָהּ יֶאֱנֹק חָלָל׃ כִּי־
Though | the .wounded | shall groan | her land | and all through | ,idols | on | will I that punish | Jeho-,vah

תַעֲלֶה בָבֶל הַשָּׁמַיִם וְכִי תְבַצֵּר מְרוֹם עֻזָּהּ מֵאִתִּי יָבֹאוּ
shall come | from Me | her ,strong | height | should she fortify | and though | the ,heavens | Babylon | should to ascend

54 שֹׁדְדִים לָהּ נְאֻם־יְהוָה׃ קוֹל זְעָקָה מִבָּבֶל וְשֶׁבֶר גָּדוֹל
great | and ruin | from ,Babylon | cry a | A of sound | .Jehovah states | to ,her | ravagers

55 מֵאֶרֶץ כַּשְׂדִּים׃ כִּי־שֹׁדֵד יְהוָה אֶת־בָּבֶל וְאִבַּד מִמֶּנָּה
from her | will and perish | Babylon | Jehovah | is ravaging | because | the ,Chaldeans | the from of land

קוֹל גָּדוֹל וְהָמוּ גַלֵּיהֶם כְּמַיִם רַבִּים נִתַּן שְׁאוֹן קוֹלָם׃
their .voice | the of noise | is given | ,many | like waters | their waves | will And roar | .great | the voice

56 כִּי בָא עָלֶיהָ עַל־בָּבֶל שׁוֹדֵד וְנִלְכְּדוּ גִּבּוֹרֶיהָ חִתְּתָה
are shattered | mighty her ;men | is and capturing | the ,ravager | ,Babylon on | ,her on | has come | Be-cause

57 קַשְּׁתוֹתָם כִּי אֵל גְּמֻלוֹת יְהוָה שַׁלֵּם יְשַׁלֵּם׃ וְהִשְׁכַּרְתִּי
will I And make drunk | will .repay | surely | ,Jehovah | .vengeance | the of God | for | their ,bows

שָׂרֶיהָ וַחֲכָמֶיהָ פַּחוֹתֶיהָ וּסְגָנֶיהָ וְגִבּוֹרֶיהָ וְיָשְׁנוּ שְׁנַת־עוֹלָם
never-ending | a sleep | they And sleep shall | her mighty .men | and her ,rulers | her governors | wise her ,ones | and | her ,princes

58 וְלֹא יָקִיצוּ נְאֻם־הַמֶּלֶךְ יְהוָה צְבָאוֹת שְׁמוֹ׃ כֹּה־
Thus | whose .(is) name | hosts | Jehovah of | the ,King | states | awaken | and not

[58]So says Jehovah of hosts, The broad walls of Babylon shall be utterly laid bare, and her high gates shall be burned with fire. And the peoples shall labor as for vanity; and the peoples as for fire; and they shall be weary.

[59]The word which Jeremiah the prophet commanded Seraiah, the son of Neriah, the son of Maaseiah, when he went with Zedekiah, the king of Judah, *to* Babylon, in the fourth year of his reign. And Seraiah *was* chief quartermaster. [60]So Jeremiah wrote in a book all the evil that should come on Babylon, all these words that are written against Babylon. [61]And Jeremiah said to Seraiah, When you come to Babylon and shall see and shall cry all these words, [62]then you shall say, O Jehovah, You have spoken against this place to cut it off, so that no dweller shall be in it, from man to animal, but it shall be a ruin forever. [63]And it shall be, when you have finished crying this book, you shall tie a stone to it and throw it into the middle of the Euphrates. [64]And you shall say, In this way Babylon shall sink, and shall not rise from the evil that I am bringing on her. And they shall be weary. So far are the words of Jeremiah.

אָמַר יְהוָה צְבָאוֹת חֹמוֹת בָּבֶל הָרְחָבָה עַרְעֵר תִּתְעַרְעָר
be shall completely broad Babylon the ;hosts Jehovah says / ,bare laid of walls of

וּשְׁעָרֶיהָ הַגְּבֹהִים בָּאֵשׁ יִצַּתּוּ וְיָגְעוּ עַמִּים בְּדֵי־רִיק וּלְאֻמִּים
the and ,vanity as the shall and shall with high her and / peoples for peoples labor ;burned be fire gates

59 בְּדֵי־אֵשׁ וְיָעֵפוּ׃ הַדָּבָר אֲשֶׁר־צִוָּה ׀ יִרְמְיָהוּ הַנָּבִיא
the Jeremiah com- which The they and ,fire as / prophet manded word .weary be shall for

אֶת־שְׂרָיָה בֶן־נֵרִיָּה בֶּן־מַחְסֵיָה בְּלֶכְתּוֹ אֶת־צִדְקִיָּהוּ
Zedekiah with he when ,Maasaiah the Neriah the Seraiah / went of son of son

מֶלֶךְ־יְהוּדָה בָּבֶל בִּשְׁנַת הָרְבִעִית לְמָלְכוֹ וּשְׂרָיָה שַׂר
chief And his of the year in (into) Judah king / quarter- ,Seraiah .reign fourth Babylon of

60 מְנוּחָה׃ וַיִּכְתֹּב יִרְמְיָהוּ אֵת כָּל־הָרָעָה אֲשֶׁר־תָּבוֹא אֶל־
to should that the all Jeremiah So .master / come evil wrote

בָּבֶל אֶל־סֵפֶר אֶחָד אֵת כָּל־הַדְּבָרִים הָאֵלֶּה הַכְּתֻבִים
are that these words all ;one book in Baby- / written lon

61 אֶל־בָּבֶל׃ וַיֹּאמֶר יִרְמְיָהוּ אֶל־שְׂרָיָה כְּבֹאֲךָ בָבֶל וְרָאִיתָ
shall and Baby- you When ,Seraiah to Jeremiah said And Baby- against / see to come .lon

62 וְקָרָאתָ אֵת כָּל־הַדְּבָרִים הָאֵלֶּה׃ וְאָמַרְתָּ יְהוָה אַתָּה
You O you then ,these words all shall and / Jehovah ,say shall call

דִבַּרְתָּ אֶל־הַמָּקוֹם הַזֶּה לְהַכְרִיתוֹ לְבִלְתִּי הֱיוֹת־בּוֹ יוֹשֵׁב
a it in shall that so cut to ,this place about have / ,dweller be not ,off it spoken

63 לְמֵאָדָם וְעַד־בְּהֵמָה כִּי־שִׁמְמוֹת עוֹלָם תִּהְיֶה׃ וְהָיָה
it And shall it forever ruin a but ,beast to even from / be will .be man

כְּכַלֹּתְךָ לִקְרֹא אֶת־הַסֵּפֶר הַזֶּה תִּקְשֹׁר עָלָיו אֶבֶן
a it to shall you ,this book calling you when / stone tie out finish

64 וְהִשְׁלַכְתּוֹ אֶל־תּוֹךְ פְּרָת׃ וְאָמַרְתָּ כָּכָה תִּשְׁקַע בָּבֶל וְלֹא־
and ,Babylon shall this In you And the the into throw and / not sink way ,say shall .Euphrates of middle it

תָקוּם מִפְּנֵי הָרָעָה אֲשֶׁר אָנֹכִי מֵבִיא עָלֶיהָ וְיָעֵפוּ עַד־הֵנָּה
far thus they And .it on am I that the from shall / (are) .weary be shall bringing evil rise

דִּבְרֵי יִרְמְיָהוּ׃
.Jeremiah the / of words

CAP. LII נב

CHAPTER 52

CHAPTER 52

[1]Zedekiah *was* a son of twenty-one years when he began to reign, and he

1 בֶּן־עֶשְׂרִים וְאַחַת שָׁנָה צִדְקִיָּהוּ בְמָלְכוֹ וְאַחַת עֶשְׂרֵה
and he when ,Zedekiah ,years one twenty A / eleven ,king became of son

reigned eleven years in Jerusalem. And his the name of his mother was Hamutal, the daughter of Jeremiah of Libnah.
2 And he did evil in the eyes of Jehovah, according to all that Jehoiakim had done.
3 For it was because of the anger of Jehovah in Jerusalem and Judah that Zedekiah rebelled against the king of Babylon, until *Jehovah* had cast them out from his face.
4 And in the ninth year of his reign, in the tenth month, in the tenth *day* of the month, king Nebuchadnezzar of Babylon came, he and all his army against Jerusalem, and pitched against it, and built a siege-wall against it all around.
5 And the city came under siege until the eleventh year of king Zedekiah.
6 And in the fourth month, in the ninth of the month, the famine was severe in the city, so that there was no food for the people of the land.
7 Then the city was breached, and all the men of war fled, and went out of the city by night by the way of the gate between the two walls, which was by the king's garden—and the Chaldeans *lay* all around the city—and they went by the way of the Arabah.
8 But the army of the Chaldeans pursued the king, and overtook Zedekiah in the Arabah of Jericho. And all his army was scattered from him.
9 And they took the king and carried him up to the king of Babylon, to Riblah in the land of Hamath, where he gave judgments against him.
10 And the king of Babylon slaughtered the sons of Zedekiah before his eyes. He also slaughtered all the rulers of Judah in Riblah.
11 And he blinded

שָׁנָה מָלַךְ בִּירוּשָׁלָם וְשֵׁם אִמּוֹ חֲמִיטַל בַּת־יִרְמְיָהוּ
Jeremiah the of daughter Hamutal (was) mother's his name And in Jerusalem he reigned years

2 מִלִּבְנָה׃ וַיַּעַשׂ הָרַע בְּעֵינֵי יְהוָה כְּכֹל אֲשֶׁר־עָשָׂה יְהוֹיָקִים׃
.Jehoiakim had done that all according to Jehovah the of eyes in evil he did And .Libnah of

3 כִּי ׀ עַל־אַף יְהוָה הָיְתָה בִּירוּשָׁלַם וִיהוּדָה עַד־הִשְׁלִיכוֹ
had He cast until and —Judah in Jerusalem was it ,Jehovah's anger because of For

4 אוֹתָם מֵעַל פָּנָיו וַיִּמְרֹד צִדְקִיָּהוּ בְּמֶלֶךְ בָּבֶל׃ וַיְהִי
it was And .Babylon against of king the Zedekiah And rebelled His .presence of out them

בַשָּׁנָה הַתְּשִׁעִית לְמָלְכוֹ בַּחֹדֶשׁ הָעֲשִׂירִי בֶּעָשׂוֹר לַחֹדֶשׁ
the of ,month the in (day) tenth ,tenth the in month his of ,reign ninth the in year

בָּא נְבוּכַדְרֶאצַּר מֶלֶךְ־בָּבֶל הוּא וְכָל־חֵילוֹ עַל־יְרוּשָׁלִַם
.Jerusalem against his ,army and all he ,Babylon king of Nebuchadnezzar .came

5 וַיַּחֲנוּ עָלֶיהָ וַיִּבְנוּ עָלֶיהָ דָּיֵק סָבִיב׃ וַתָּבֹא הָעִיר בַּמָּצוֹר
under siege city the So came all .around siege-wall a against it and built against ,it and pitched

6 עַד עַשְׁתֵּי עֶשְׂרֵה שָׁנָה לַמֶּלֶךְ צִדְקִיָּהוּ׃ בַּחֹדֶשׁ הָרְבִיעִי
,fourth in And month the .Zedekiah King of year the eleventh until

בְּתִשְׁעָה לַחֹדֶשׁ וַיֶּחֱזַק הָרָעָב בָּעִיר וְלֹא־הָיָה לֶחֶם לְעַם
the for of people food there was and not the in ,city the famine was severe the of ,month the in ninth

7 הָאָרֶץ׃ וַתִּבָּקַע הָעִיר וְכָל־אַנְשֵׁי הַמִּלְחָמָה יִבְרְחוּ וַיֵּצְאוּ
and went out fled war the men of and all the ,city was Then breached the .land

מֵהָעִיר לַיְלָה דֶּרֶךְ שַׁעַר בֵּין־הַחֹמֹתַיִם אֲשֶׁר עַל־גַּן הַמֶּלֶךְ
the .king's garden by which (was) two the ,walls between the gate the by of way by night the of city

8 וְכַשְׂדִּים עַל־הָעִיר סָבִיב וַיֵּלְכוּ דֶּרֶךְ הָעֲרָבָה׃ וַיִּרְדְּפוּ
But pursued the .Arabah the by of way they and went all ,around the city around (lay) the Now Chaldeans

חֵיל־כַּשְׂדִּים אַחֲרֵי הַמֶּלֶךְ וַיַּשִּׂיגוּ אֶת־צִדְקִיָּהוּ בְּעַרְבֹת
the in of Arabah Zedekiah and overtook king the after the Chaldeans the of army

9 יְרֵחוֹ וְכָל־חֵילוֹ נָפֹצוּ מֵעָלָיו׃ וַיִּתְפְּשׂוּ אֶת־הַמֶּלֶךְ וַיַּעֲלוּ
and bore the king they Then seized from .him was scattered his army And all .Jericho

אֹתוֹ אֶל־מֶלֶךְ בָּבֶל רִבְלָתָה בְּאֶרֶץ חֲמָת וַיְדַבֵּר אִתּוֹ
against him he where spoke ,Hamath the in of land to Riblah ,Babylon the to of king him

10 מִשְׁפָּטִים׃ וַיִּשְׁחַט מֶלֶךְ־בָּבֶל אֶת־בְּנֵי צִדְקִיָּהוּ לְעֵינָיו וְגַם
And also before .eyes his Zedekiah the of sons Babylon the of king slew And .judgments

11 אֶת־כָּל־שָׂרֵי יְהוּדָה שָׁחַט בְּרִבְלָתָה׃ וְאֶת־עֵינֵי צִדְקִיָּהוּ
Zedekiah the of eyes Then .Riblah in slew he Judah the of rulers all

the eyes of Zedekiah. And the king of Babylon bound him in bronze fetters and carried him to Babylon. And he put him in prison until the day of his death.

[12]And in the fifth month, in the tenth of the month, which *was* the nineteenth year of king Nebuchadnezzar of Babylon, Nebuzar-adan, the chief of the executioners, who stood before the king of Babylon, came into Jerusalem. [13]And *he* burned the house of Jehovah, and the king's house. And he burned all the houses of Jerusalem with fire, and all the houses of the great ones. [14]And all the army of the Chaldeans with the chief of the executioners broke down all the walls of Jerusalem all around. [15]Then Nebuzar-adan, the chief of the executioners, exiled *some* the poor of the people, and the rest of the people who remained in the city, and those who fell away, who fell to the king of Babylon, and the rest of the multitude. [16]But Nebuzar-adan, the chief of the executioners, left *some* of the poor of the land for vinedressers and for farmers. [17]Also the Chaldeans broke the pillars of bronze that *were* in the house of Jehovah, and the bases, and the bronze sea that *was* in the house of Jehovah, and carried all the bronze from them to Babylon. [18]They also took away the pots, and the shovels, and the snuffers, and the bowls, and the spoons, and all the vessels of bronze with which they served. [19]And the chief of the executioners took away the basins, and the firepans, and the bowls, and the pots, the lampstands, and

884 884 44 28 935 5178 631 5786
עור ויאסרהו בנחשתים ויבאהו מלך־בבל בבלה
to Babylon the carried and bronze with bound And he
.Babylon of king him fetters him .blinded

2549 23 20 4194 3117 5704 6486 1004 5414
12 ויתנהו בבית־הפקדת עד־יום מותו: ובחדש החמישי
,fifth in And his the till prison a in he And
month the .death of day of house him put

44 28 8141 6240 8672 8141 2320 6218
בעשור לחדש היא שנת תשע־עשרה שנה למלך
King of year nineteenth the which the of the in
year (was) month tenth

5975 2876 7227 5018 935 884 44 28 5019
נבוכדראצר מלך־בבל בא נבוזראדן רב־טבחים עמד
who the chief Nebuzar- came ,Babylon king Nebuchadnezzar
stood executioners of adan of

3068 1004 8313 3389 884 44 28 6440
13 לפני מלך־בבל בירושלם: וישרף את־בית־יהוה ואת־
and ,Jehovah the he And into Babylon the before
of house burned .Jerusalem of king

1419 1004 3605 3389 1004 3605 4428 1004
בית המלך ואת כל־בתי ירושלם ואת־כל־בית הגדול
great the the all and Jerusalem the all And the house
ones of houses of houses .king's

2428 3605 5422 5439 3389 2346 3605 784 8313
14 שרף באש: ואת־כל־חמות ירושלם סביב נתצו כל־חיל
the all broke all Jerusalem the all And with he
of army down around of walls .fire burned

3499 5971 1803 2876 7227 834 3778
15 כשדים אשר את־רב־טבחים: ומדלות העם ואת־יתר
the and the the of And the chief with who the
of rest people of poor executioners of (were) Chaldeans

4428 5307 834 5307 5892 7604 5971
העם הנשארים בעיר ואת־הנפלים אשר נפלו אל־מלך
the to fell who who those and the in who the
of king ,away fell ,city remained people

2876 7227 5018 1540 527 3499 884
בבל ואת יתר האמון הגלה נבוזראדן רב־טבחים:
the chief Nebuzar-adan exiled the rest the and ;Babylon
executioners of multitude of

3755 2876 7227 5018 7604 776 1803
16 ומדלות הארץ השאיר נבוזראדן רב־טבחים לכרמים
for the chief Nebuzar-adan left the the of But
vinedressers executioners of land of poor

3068 1004 834 5178 5982 3009
וליגבים: ואת־עמודי הנחשת אשר לבית־יהוה ואת־
and ,Jehovah the in that bronze the Also for and
of house (were) of pillars .farmers

3778 7665 3068 1004 834 5178 3220 4350
17 המכנות ואת־ים הנחשת אשר בבית־יהוה שברו כשד־
the broke ,Jehovah's in that the sea and the
,Chaldeans house (were) bronze ,stands

3276 5518 884 5178 3605 5375
וישאו את־כל־נחשתם בבלה: ואת־הסירות ואת־היעים
the and the Also to their all and
,shovels pots .Babylon bronze carried

3627 3605 3709 4219 4212
18 ואת־המזמרות ואת־המזרקת ואת־הכפות ואת כל־כלי
vessels all and the and the and the and
of ,spoons ,bowls snuffers

5592 3947 8334 834 5178
הנחשת אשר־ישרתו בהם לקחו: ואת־הספים ואת־
and the And they with they which bronze
,basins .took ,them served

4501 5518 4219 4289
19 המחתות ואת־המזרקות ואת־הסירות ואת־המנרות ואת־
and the and the and the and the
,lampstands ,pots ,bowls ;firepans

the spoons, and the cups—
what *was* gold, *in* gold; and
what *was* silver, *in* silver—
20 the two pillars, one sea,
and twelve bronze bulls
that *were* under the bases,
which king Solomon had
made in the house of
Jehovah. The weight of the
bronze of all these vessels
was not *known*. 21 And the
pillars, the height of one
pillar *was* eighteen cubits.
And a line of twelve cubits
went around it, and its
thickness *was* four fingers.
It was hollow. 22 And a
capital of bronze *was* on it.
And the height of one
capital *was* five cubits, with
network and pomegranates
on the capitals all around,
all of bronze. And like these
was the second pillar, and
the pomegranates. 23 And
there were ninety-six
pomegranates on a side; all
the pomegranates on the
network *were* a hundred all
around.

24 And the chief of the
executioners took Serai-
ah the head priest, and
Zephaniah the second
priest, and the three
keepers of the threshold.
25 He also took out of the
city oen eunuch who was
in charge of the men of
war, and seven men who
saw the face of the king,
who were found in the
city, and the scribe of the
chief of the army, who
called up the people of
the land, who were found
in the middle of the city.
26 And Nebuzar-adan, the
chief of the executioners,
took them and brought
them to the king of Baby-
lon, to Riblah. 27 And the
king of Babylon struck
them and slaughtered
them in Riblah, in the

3701 3701 834 2091 2091 834 4518 3709
הַכַּפּוֹת וְאֶת־הַמְּנַקִּיּוֹת אֲשֶׁר זָהָב זָהָב וַאֲשֶׁר־כֶּסֶף כָּסֶף
(in) silver and (in) gold what the and the
;silver (was) what ;gold (was) ;cups ,spoons

1241 259 3220 8147 5982 2876 7227 3947
20 לָקַח רַב־טַבָּחִים׃ הָעַמּוּדִים | שְׁנַיִם הַיָּם אֶחָד וְהַבָּקָר
and ,one sea ,two pillars the the cap- the took
bulls away

4428 6213 834 4350 8478 834 5178 6240 8147
שְׁנֵים־עָשָׂר נְחֹשֶׁת אֲשֶׁר־תַּחַת הַמְּכֹנוֹת אֲשֶׁר עָשָׂה הַמֶּלֶךְ
King the had which the under that bronze twelve
made ,stands (were)

3627 3605 5178 4948 1961 3808 3068 1004 8010
שְׁלֹמֹה לְבֵית יְהוָה לֹא־הָיָה מִשְׁקָל לִנְחֻשְׁתָּם כָּל־הַכֵּלִים
vessels all bronze the the was not ;Jehovah the for Solomon
of of weight (known) of house

5982 6967 520 6240 8083 5982 428
21 הָאֵלֶּה׃ וְהָעַמּוּדִים שְׁמֹנֶה עֶשְׂרֵה אַמָּה קוֹמָה הָעַמֻּד
the the (was) cubits eighteen (to as) And .these
pillar of height ,pillars the

702 5672 5437 520 6240 8147 2339 259
הָאֶחָד וְחוּט שְׁתֵּים־עֶשְׂרֵה אַמָּה יְסֻבֶּנּוּ וְעָבְיוֹ אַרְבַּע
four its and went cubits twelve a And .one
thickness ,it around of line

3805 6967 5178 3805 5014 676
22 אֶצְבָּעוֹת נָבוּב׃ וְכֹתֶרֶת עָלָיו נְחֹשֶׁת וְקוֹמַת הַכֹּתֶרֶת
capital the And (of) (was) a And (was it) ;fingers
of height .bronze it on capital .hollow

5439 3805 7416 7639 520 2568 259
הָאַחַת חָמֵשׁ אַמּוֹת וּשְׂבָכָה וְרִמּוֹנִים עַל־הַכּוֹתֶרֶת סָבִיב
all the on pome- and with ,cubits (was) one
;around capital granates network five

741:6 1961 7416 8145 5982 428 5178 3605
23 הַכֹּל נְחֹשֶׁת וְכָאֵלֶּה לָעַמּוּד הַשֵּׁנִי וְרִמּוֹנִים׃ וַיִּהְיוּ הָרִמֹּנִים
pome- there And the and second the (was) And .bronze of all
granates were .pomegranates pillar these like

7639 3967 7416 3605 7307 8337 8673
תִּשְׁעִים וְשִׁשָּׁה רוּחָה כָּל־הָרִמּוֹנִים מֵאָה עַל־הַשְּׂבָכָה
the on a (were) the all a on six ninety-
network hundred pomegranates ,side

7218 3548 8304 2876 7227 3947 5439
24 סָבִיב׃ וַיִּקַּח רַב־טַבָּחִים אֶת־שְׂרָיָה כֹּהֵן הָרֹאשׁ וְאֶת־
and ,head the priest Seraiah the chief And all
executioners of took .around

5892 5592 8104 7969 4932 3548 3947
25 צְפַנְיָה כֹּהֵן הַמִּשְׁנֶה וְאֶת־שְׁלֹשֶׁת שֹׁמְרֵי הַסַּף׃ וּמִן־הָעִיר
the Also the keepers three and the priest Zepha-
city of out .threshold of ,second niah

4421 582 6496 1961 834 259 5631 3947
לָקַח סָרִיס אֶחָד אֲשֶׁר־הָיָה פָקִיד | עַל־אַנְשֵׁי הַמִּלְחָמָה
;war the men of in was who one eunuch he
of charge took

5892 4672 834 4428 6440 7200 582 7651
וְשִׁבְעָה אֲנָשִׁים מֵרֹאֵי פְנֵי־הַמֶּלֶךְ אֲשֶׁר־נִמְצְאוּ בָעִיר וְאֵת
and the in were who the the who men and
;city found king of face saw seven

376 8346 776 5971 6633 6635 8269 5608
סֹפֵר שַׂר הַצָּבָא הַמַּצְבִּא אֶת־עַם הָאָרֶץ וְשִׁשִּׁים אִישׁ
men and the the who the the scribe
sixty ;land of people mustered ,army of chief of

5018 3947 5892 8432 4672 776 5971
26 מֵעַם הָאָרֶץ הַנִּמְצְאִים בְּתוֹךְ הָעִיר׃ וַיִּקַּח אוֹתָם נְבוּזַרְאֲדָן
Nebuzar-adan them And the the in were who the the of
took .city of middle found land of people

5221 7247 894 4428 3212 2876 7227
27 רַב־טַבָּחִים וַיֹּלֶךְ אוֹתָם אֶל־מֶלֶךְ בָּבֶל רִבְלָתָה׃ וַיַּכֶּה
And .Riblah to Babylon the to them and the chief
struck of king brought executioners of

land of Hamath. And Judah was exiled from off his land.

28 This is the people whom Nebuchadnezzar exiled: In the seventh year, three thousand and twenty-three Jews;
29 in the eighteenth year of Nebuchadnezzar, eight hundred thirty-two souls from Jerusalem;
30 in the twenty-third year of Nebuchadnezzar, Nebuzar-adan, the chief of the executioners, exiled seven hundred forty-five souls of the Jews. All the souls *were* four thousand and six hundred.
31 And it happened in the thirty-seventh year of the exile of Jehoiachin, king of Judah, in the twelfth month, in the twenty-fifth of the month, Evil-merodach, king of Babylon, in the year of his reign lifted up the head of Jehoiachin, king of Judah, and brought him from the prison house.
32 And he spoke good to him, and set his throne above the throne of the kings who *were* with him in Babylon.
33 And he changed his prison garments, and he ate bread before his face continually all the days of his life.
34 And his allowance in continual allowance was given to him from the king of Babylon, the matter of a day in its day, until the day of his death, all the days of his life.

3063 1540 2574 776 7247 4191 884 44:28
אוֹתָם מֶלֶךְ בָּבֶל וַיְמִתֵם בְּרִבְלָה בְּאֶרֶץ חֲמָת וַיִּגֶל יְהוּדָה
Judah / was exiled and / Ha- math / the in land of / Riblah in / slew and them / Babylon / the of king / them

8141 5019 1540 834 59:71 2088 127
28 מֵעַל אַדְמָתוֹ׃ זֶה הָעָם אֲשֶׁר הֶגְלָה נְבוּכַדְרֶאצַּר בִּשְׁנַת־
the in year / :Nebuchadnezzar / exiled / whom / the people / This (is) / his .land / from off

8141 7969 6242 505 7969 30:64 7651
29 שֶׁבַע יְהוּדִים שְׁלֹשֶׁת אֲלָפִים וְעֶשְׂרִים וּשְׁלֹשָׁה׃ בִּשְׁנַת
the in year / ;three / and twenty- / thousand / three / Jews / ,seventh

3967 8083 5315 3389 5019 6240 8083
שְׁמוֹנֶה עֶשְׂרֵה לִנְבוּכַדְרֶאצַּר מִירוּשָׁלִַם נֶפֶשׁ שְׁמֹנֶה מֵאוֹת
hundred / eight / souls / from Jerusalem / of Nebuchadnezzar / teenth / eigh-

5019 6242 7969 8141 8147 7970
30 שְׁלֹשִׁים וּשְׁנָיִם׃ בִּשְׁנַת שָׁלֹשׁ וְעֶשְׂרִים לִנְבוּכַדְרֶאצַּר
of Nebuchadnezzar / and twentieth / three / the in year / ;two / thirty-

3967 7651 5315 30:64 28:76 7227 5018 1540
הֶגְלָה נְבוּזַרְאֲדָן רַב־טַבָּחִים יְהוּדִים נֶפֶשׁ שְׁבַע מֵאוֹת
hundred / seven / souls / the Jews / the executioners / chief of / Nebuzar- adan / exiled

3967 8337 505 702 5315 3605 2568 705
אַרְבָּעִים וַחֲמִשָּׁה כָּל־נֶפֶשׁ אַרְבַּעַת אֲלָפִים וְשֵׁשׁ מֵאוֹת׃
.hundred / and six / thousand / four / souls (were) / all the / ;five / forty-

44:28 3078 1546 81:41 7651 7970
31 וַיְהִי בִשְׁלֹשִׁים וָשֶׁבַע שָׁנָה לְגָלוּת יְהוֹיָכִן מֶלֶךְ־
king / Jehoichim / the of of exile / year / seventh / the in thirty- / And ,was it

5375 2320 2568 6242 2320 6240 8147 30:63
יְהוּדָה בִּשְׁנֵים עָשָׂר חֹדֶשׁ בְּעֶשְׂרִים וַחֲמִשָּׁה לַחֹדֶשׁ נָשָׂא
lifted up / the of month / fifth / the in twenty- / ,month / the in twelfth / of Judah

3078 7218 4:43 5869 884 44:28 192
אֱוִיל מְרֹדַךְ מֶלֶךְ בָּבֶל בִּשְׁנַת מַלְכֻתוֹ אֶת־רֹאשׁ יְהוֹיָכִין
Jehoiachin / head the of / his of reign / the in year / Babylon / king of / Merodach / Evil-

2896 1696 3628 1004 3318 30:63 44:28
32 מֶלֶךְ־יְהוּדָה וַיֹּצֵא אֹתוֹ מִבֵּית הַכְּלִיא׃ וַיְדַבֵּר אִתּוֹ טֹבוֹת
good / to him / he And spoke / .prison- / the from house / him / and brought / Judah / king of

884 834 4428 3678 4605 3678 5414
וַיִּתֵּן אֶת־כִּסְאוֹ מִמַּעַל לְכִסֵּא מְלָכִים אֲשֶׁר אִתּוֹ בְּבָבֶל׃
in .Babylon / with him / who (were) / the of kings / the throne / above / his throne / and set

3117 3605 8548 6440 3899 398 3608 899 81:38
33 וְשִׁנָּה אֵת בִּגְדֵי כִלְאוֹ וְאָכַל לֶחֶם לְפָנָיו תָּמִיד כָּל־יְמֵי
the days / all / continually / before face his / bread / he and ate / prison / gar- ments / his / he And changed

884 44:28 5414 85:48 737 737 241:6
34 חַיָּו׃ וַאֲרֻחָתוֹ אֲרֻחַת תָּמִיד נִתְּנָה־לּוֹ מֵאֵת מֶלֶךְ־בָּבֶל
of Babylon / the king / from / to him / was given / continual / an allowance / his And allowance / his of life

2416 3117 3605 4194 3117 5704 3117 3117 1697
דְּבַר־יוֹם בְּיוֹמוֹ עַד־יוֹם מוֹתוֹ כֹּל יְמֵי חַיָּו׃
his of .life / the days / all / his of death / the until day / its in day / day a / the of matter

איכה

LIBER THRENORUM

(THE) BOOK OF LAMENTATIONS

CAPUT. I א

CHAPTER 1

A LITERAL TRANSLATION OF THE BIBLE

THE BOOK OF LAMENTATIONS

CHAPTER 1

[1]How alone sits the city *that was* full of people! She has become like a widow, great among the nations; a noblewoman among the provinces has become a payer of tribute. [2]She bitterly weeps in the night, and her tears *are* on her cheeks; she has no comforter among all her lovers. All her friends dealt deceit with her; they became enemies to her.

[3]Judah went captive from affliction, and from great slavery. She dwells among the nations; she finds no rest. All her pursuers have overtaken her between the straits. [4]The roads of Zion *are* in mourning without *any* going to the appointed *feasts*. All her gates are deserted; her priests sigh; her virgins are afflicted; and she *is in* bitterness. [5]Her foes have become as chief; her haters are at ease. For Jehovah has afflicted her for the multitude of her trespasses. Her children have gone, captive before the foe. [6]And from the daughter of Zion all her splendor has departed. Her rulers have become like bucks; they find no pasture; and they have gone without strength before the pursuer. [7]Jerusalem remembers all her desirable things which were from previous days, when her people fell into the hand of the foe; and there is no ally for her. The foes saw her; they laughed at her annihilations.

[8]Jerusalem has grievously sinned; on account of this she has been removed; all

490 1961 5971 7227 5892 910 3427
1 איכה | ישבה בדד העיר רבתי עם היתה כאלמנה
a like has She !people full the alone sits How
;widow become of city

1058 1058 4522 1961 4082 8282 1471 7227
2 רבתי בגוים שרתי במדינות היתה למס׃ בכו תבכה
she bitterly tribute a has the among noble- a the among (one)
weeps ;payer become ,provinces woman nations great

157 3605 5162 369 3895 5921 1832 3915
בלילה ודמעתה על לחיה אין־לה מנחם מכל־אהביה
her of out com- a to not her (are) her and the in
;lovers all forter her is ;cheeks on tears ,night

6040 3063 1540 341 1961 898 7453 3605
3 כל־רעיה בגדו בה היו לה לאיבים׃ גלתה יהודה מעני
from Judah went .haters to they with dealt her all
affliction captive her became ;her deceit in friends

3605 4494 4672 3808 1471 3427 5656 7230
ומרב עבדה היא ישבה בגוים לא מצאה מנוח כל־
all ;rest she not the among dwells she ;slavery from and
finds nations great

1097 657 6726 1870 4712 996 5381 7291
4 רדפיה השיגוה בין המצרים׃ דרכי ציון אבלות מבלי
with- in (are) Zion The .straits the be- over- have pur- her
out mourning of roads tween her taken suers

1330 584 3548 8074 8179 3605 4150 935
באי מועד כל־שעריה שוממין כהניה נאנחים בתולתיה
her are her (are) her all set (any)
virgins ;groaning priests ;desolate gates ;(feasts) to going

7951 341 7218 6862 1961 4843 3013
5 נוגות והיא מר־לה׃ היו צריה לראש איביה שלו כי־
for are her ;chief as Her have (in is) and (are)
,ease at haters foes become .bitterness she ,afflicted

6862 6440 7628 5768 6588 7230 3013 3068
יהוה הוגה על רב־פשעיה עולליה הלכו שבי לפני־צר׃
the before captive have her tres- her the for has Jehovah
.foe gone children ;passes of many her afflicted

4672 3808 354 8269 1926 3605 6726 1323 3318
6 ויצא מבת־ציון כל־הדרה היו שריה כאילים לא־מצאו
they not like her have her all Zion the from has And
find ;bucks rulers become ,splendor of daughter out gone

3117 3389 2142 7291 6440 1097 3212 4829
7 מרעה וילכו בלא־כח לפני רודף׃ זכרה ירושלם ימי
(in) Jerusalem remem- the before strength with- and ,pasture
of days bers ,pursuer out go they

5307 6924 3117 1961 834 4262 3605 4788 6040
עניה ומרודיה כל מחמדיה אשר היו מימי קדם בנפל
the in previous from were which desirable her all her and af- her
of falling days things ,wanderings fliction

7832 6862 7200 5826 369 6862 3027 5971
עמה ביד־צר ואין עוזר לה ראוה צרים שחקו על־
at .they ;foes the saw for (any) is and foes's into her
laughed her her ally not hand the people

3605 1961 5206 3389 2398 2399 4868
8 משבתה׃ חטא חטאה ירושלם על־כן לנידה היתה כל־
all has one as therefore ,Jerusalem has utterly her
;become defiled sinned .cessations

the ones knowing her despise her, for they saw her nakedness. Also, she groans and turns backward. 9Her uncleanness *is* in her skirts; she did not remember her end, and has gone down astoundingly. There is no comforter for her. O Jehovah, behold my affliction, for the enemy has magnified *himself*. 10The enemy has spread out his hand on all her desirable things. Indeed, she has seen the nations enter into her holy place, whom You commanded *that* they not enter into Your congregation. 11All her people sigh from seeking bread. They gave their desirable things for food to revive the soul. See, O Jehovah, and look on *me*, for I have become vile.

12*Is it* nothing to you, all you who pass by? Behold, and see if there is any sorrow like my sorrow which is done to me, with which Jehovah has afflicted *me* in the day of His burning anger. 13From on high He has sent fire into my bones, and subdued it. He spread a net for my feet; He has turned me back; He gave me desolation; all the days *I* faint. 14The yoke of my transgressions is bound by His hand; they intertwine; they rise on my neck. He caused my strength to falter; the Lord gave me into *their* hands. I am not able to rise. 15The Lord has trampled all my mighty ones in my midst; He called a gathering against me to crush my young men. *As* a winepress, the Lord trod the virgin daughter of Judah. 16I weep for these; my eye, my eye runs down *with* water, because far from me is a comforter reviving my soul. My sons are desolate because the enemy prevails. 17Zion spreads forth her hands; not *one is* comforting to me; Jehovah has commanded about Jacob

7725 584 6172 7200 2107 3513
מְכַבְּדֶיהָ הִזִּילוּהָ כִּי־רָאוּ עֶרְוָתָהּ גַּם־הִיא נֶאֶנְחָה וַתָּשָׁב
turns and groans she also her they for despise knowing ones
;nakedness saw ,her her

9 3381 319 2142 3808 7757 2932 268
אָחוֹר׃ טֻמְאָתָהּ בְּשׁוּלֶיהָ לֹא זָכְרָה אַחֲרִיתָהּ וַתֵּרֶד
has and ,end her did she not her in (is) un- Her .backward
down gone remember ,skirts cleanness

341 1430 6040 3068 7200 5162 369 6382
פְּלָאִים אֵין מְנַחֵם לָהּ רְאֵה יְהוָה אֶת־עָנְיִי כִּי הִגְדִּיל אוֹיֵב׃
the magnified for my O ,See for comforter is astound-
.hater ,affliction ,Jehovah .her no ;ingly

10 4720 935 1471 7200 4261 3605 5921 6862 6566 3027
יָדוֹ פָּרַשׂ צָר עַל כָּל־מַחֲמַדֶּיהָ כִּי־רָאֲתָה גוֹיִם בָּאוּ מִקְדָּשָׁהּ
holy her enter the has she in- desirable her all on The spread his
,place nations seen deed ;things foe out hand

11 584 5971 3605 6951 935 3808 6680 834
אֲשֶׁר צִוִּיתָה לֹא־יָבֹאוּ בַקָּהָל לָךְ׃ כָּל־עַמָּהּ נֶאֱנָחִים
,groan her All of the in they not You which
people .You assembly enter commanded

5315 7725 400 4262 5414 3899 1245
מְבַקְּשִׁים לֶחֶם נָתְנוּ מַחֲמוֹדֵּיהֶם בְּאֹכֶל לְהָשִׁיב נָפֶשׁ
the for for desirable their they bread seeking from
.soul reviving food things gave

12 3605 2151 1961 5027 3068 7200
רְאֵה יְהוָה וְהַבִּיטָה כִּי הָיִיתִי זוֹלֵלָה׃ לוֹא אֲלֵיכֶם כָּל־
all ,you to (it Is) .vile have I for ,look and O ,See
nothing become ,Jehovah

834 4341 4341 3426 518 7200 5027 1870 5674
עֹבְרֵי דֶרֶךְ הַבִּיטוּ וּרְאוּ אִם־יֵשׁ מַכְאוֹב כְּמַכְאֹבִי אֲשֶׁר
which my like sorrow there if and Look the passing
,sorrow is see ?way by

13 4791 639 2740 3117 3068 3013 834 5953
עוֹלַל לִי אֲשֶׁר הוֹגָה יְהוָה בְּיוֹם חֲרוֹן אַפּוֹ׃ מִמָּרוֹם
on From His burning the in Jehovah has which to is
high .anger of day afflicted ,me done

7725 7272 7561 6566 7287 6106 784 7971
שָׁלַח־אֵשׁ בְּעַצְמֹתַי וַיִּרְדֶּנָּה פָּרַשׂ רֶשֶׁת לְרַגְלַי הֱשִׁיבַנִי
has He my for net a He subdued and my into fire He
me turned ,feet spread ;it ,bones sent

14 6588 5923 8244 1739 3117 3605 8074 5414 268
אָחוֹר נְתָנַנִי שֹׁמֵמָה כָּל־הַיּוֹם דָּוָה׃ נִשְׂקַד עֹל פְּשָׁעַי
tres- my The is .faint the all ,desolation He ,back
passes of yoke bound days me gave

136 5414 3581 3782 6677 5921 5927 8276 3027
בְּיָדוֹ יִשְׂתָּרְגוּ עָלוּ עַל־צַוָּארִי הִכְשִׁיל כֹּחִי נְתָנַנִי אֲדֹנָי
the gave my made He my on they inter- they His by
Lord me ;strength falter ,neck rise ,twine ;hand

15 7121 7130 136 47 3605 5541 6965 3201 3808 3027
בִּידֵי לֹא־אוּכַל קוּם׃ סִלָּה כָל־אַבִּירַי ׀ אֲדֹנָי בְּקִרְבִּי קָרָא
He my in the mighty my all Has .rise to am I not into
called ;midst Lord ones trampled able ;hands

1323 1330 136 1869 1660 970 7665 4150 5921
עָלַי מוֹעֵד לִשְׁבֹּר בַּחוּרָי גַּת דָּרַךְ אֲדֹנָי לִבְתוּלַת בַּת־
daughter the the trod a (as) my crush to meet- a against
of virgin Lord ;winepress ;men young ing me

16 4325 3381 5869 5869 1058 589 428 5921 3063
יְהוּדָה׃ עַל־אֵלֶּה ׀ אֲנִי בוֹכִיָּה עֵינִי ׀ עֵינִי יֹרְדָה מַּיִם כִּי־
for (with) runs my my ;weep I these On .Judah
water down eye ,eye of account

1396 8074 1121 1961 5315 7725 5162 4480 7368
רָחַק מִמֶּנִּי מְנַחֵם מֵשִׁיב נַפְשִׁי הָיוּ בָנַי שׁוֹמֵמִים כִּי גָבַר
pre- for ,desolated my are my reviving a from is
vails sons ;soul comforter me far

17 3290 3068 6680 5162 369 3027 6726 6566 341
אוֹיֵב׃ פֵּרְשָׂה צִיּוֹן בְּיָדֶיהָ אֵין מְנַחֵם לָהּ צִוָּה יְהוָה לְיַעֲקֹב
about Jehovah or- to com- (one) is her Zion spreads the
Jacob dered ;me forting not hands .hater

that his enemies *should be* all around him. Jerusalem has become as an impure thing among them.

[18]Jehovah *is* righteous, for I rebelled against His mouth. I beseech you, all peoples, hear and see my sorrow. My virgins and my young men went into exile.

[19]I called for my lovers; they deceived me; my priests and my elders expired in the city while they sought food for them to bring back their life.

[20]Behold, O Jehovah, for I *am* distressed. My inward parts ferment; my heart is overturned within me; for I have grievously rebelled. On the outside the sword bereaves; in the house *it is* as death. [21]They hear that I sigh; *there is* no comforter to me. All my enemies have heard my evil; they rejoice that You have done *it*. You will bring the day *that* You have called, and they shall be like me. [22]Let all their wickedness come before You; and do to them as You have done to me for all my transgressions. For my sighs are many, and my heart *is* faint.

CHAPTER 2

[1]How the Lord has clouded over the daughter of Zion in His anger! He cast down the beauty of Israel from the heavens *to the* earth, and did not remember His footstool in the day of His wrath. [2]The Lord swallowed up all of Jacob's dwelling-places, *and* did not pity. In His wrath He has thrown down the strongholds of the daughter of Judah. He made *them* touch to the earth; He has defiled the kingdom and its rulers. [3]He cut off all the horn of Israel in hot anger. He has turned back His right hand from the face of the haters, and He burned in Jacob as a flaming fire; it consumes all around. [4]He

18 סְבִיבָיו צָרָיו הָיְתָה יְרוּשָׁלִַם לְנִדָּה בֵּינֵיהֶם׃ צַדִּיק הוּא
(is) Righteous among them an impurity Jerusalem has become ;foes his around him
יְהוָה כִּי־פִיהוּ מָרִיתִי שִׁמְעוּ־נָא כָל־עַמִּים וּרְאוּ מַכְאֹבִי
my .sorrow and see peoples all ,please ,hear rebelled I ;against His for mouth ,Jehovah
19 בְּתוּלֹתַי וּבַחוּרַי הָלְכוּ בַשֶּׁבִי׃ קָרָאתִי לַמְאַהֲבַי הֵמָּה
they my to ,lovers called I into .exile went my and men young virgins My
רִמּוּנִי כֹּהֲנַי וּזְקֵנַי בָּעִיר גָּוָעוּ כִּי־בִקְשׁוּ אֹכֶל לָמוֹ וְיָשִׁיבוּ
they back that bring for them food they sought for ex- ;pired the in city my and elders my priests deceived ;me
20 אֶת־נַפְשָׁם׃ רְאֵה יְהוָה כִּי־צַר־לִי מֵעַי חֳמַרְמָרוּ נֶהְפַּךְ
turned is over ,ferment My innards to distress ;me for O Jehovah ,See their soul
לִבִּי בְּקִרְבִּי כִּי מָרוֹ מָרִיתִי מִחוּץ שִׁכְּלָה־חֶרֶב בַּבַּיִת
the in house the ,sword bereaves outside ;rebelled I utterly for within ,me my heart
21 כַּמָּוֶת׃ שָׁמְעוּ כִּי נֶאֱנָחָה אָנִי אֵין מְנַחֵם לִי כָּל־אֹיְבַי
my haters all for ,me com- forter a not is ;I groan for They ,hear as (is it) .death
שָׁמְעוּ רָעָתִי שָׂשׂוּ כִּי אַתָּה עָשִׂיתָ הֵבֵאתָ יוֹם־קָרָאתָ וְיִהְיוּ
they and be shall have You ,called the day will You bring ;(this) have done You that they rejoice ,evil my have heard
22 כָמוֹנִי׃ תָּבֹא כָל־רָעָתָם לְפָנֶיךָ וְעוֹלֵל לָמוֹ כַּאֲשֶׁר עוֹלַלְתָּ
have You done as to them do and before ,You their evil all Let come like .me
לִי עַל כָּל־פְּשָׁעַי כִּי־רַבּוֹת אַנְחֹתַי וְלִבִּי דַוָּי׃
.faint my and heart my groans are many for my ;trespasses all for to me

CAP. II ב

CHAPTER 2

1 אֵיכָה יָעִיב בְּאַפּוֹ ׀ אֲדֹנָי אֶת־בַּת־צִיּוֹן הִשְׁלִיךְ מִשָּׁמַיִם
the from heavens cast He !Zion the of daughter the Lord His in anger has clouded How
אֶרֶץ תִּפְאֶרֶת יִשְׂרָאֵל וְלֹא־זָכַר הֲדֹם־רַגְלָיו בְּיוֹם אַפּוֹ׃
His .anger the in of day His foot the of stool remem- bered and not ,Israel the of beauty (the to) earth
2 בִּלַּע אֲדֹנָי לֹא חָמַל אֵת כָּל־נְאוֹת יַעֲקֹב הָרַס בְּעֶבְרָתוֹ
His in wrath He destroyed ;Jacob the of abodes all pitied not The Lord swallowed up
מִבְצְרֵי בַת־יְהוּדָה הִגִּיעַ לָאָרֶץ חִלֵּל מַמְלָכָה וְשָׂרֶיהָ׃
its and ;rulers the kingdom has He defiled the to ;earth made He touch ;Judah the of daughter strong- the of holds
3 גָּדַע בָּחֳרִי־אַף כֹּל קֶרֶן יִשְׂרָאֵל הֵשִׁיב אָחוֹר יְמִינוֹ מִפְּנֵי
the from of face His hand right back has He turned ;Israel the of horn all anger in of heat cut He off
4 אוֹיֵב וַיִּבְעַר בְּיַעֲקֹב כְּאֵשׁ לֶהָבָה אָכְלָה סָבִיב׃ דָּרַךְ
He trod all .around con- sumes it ;flame a as of fire Jacob in He and burned the ;haters

trod His bow like an enemy,
and set His right hand like a
foe; and killed all *who were*
desirable to the eye in the
tent of the daughter of Zion.
He poured out His fury like
fire. [5]The Lord was like an
enemy; He swallowed up
Israel; He swallowed up all
his palaces *and* destroyed
his strongholds; and He
increased mourning and
weeping in the daughter of
Judah. [6]And He violated
his booth like a garden *and*
destroyed his meeting-
places. Jehovah made
meeting-places and sab-
baths forgotten in Zion; and
He rejected king and priest
in the fury of His anger.
[7]The Lord has cast off His
altar; He rejected His holy
place; He has delivered the
walls of her palaces into the
hater's hand; they gave a
noise in Jehovah's house,
as a day of meeting.
[8]Jehovah willed to destroy
the wall of the daughter of
Zion; He has stretched out a
line; He has not withdrawn
His hand from swallowing;
and He made rampart and
wall lament; they languish
together. [9]Her gates have
sunk in the ground; He has
dispersed and shattered her
bars. Her kings and her
rulers *are* among the
nations. The law is not. Also
her prophets have not
found a vision from
Jehovah.

[10]They sit on the ground;
the elders of Zion's daughters are silent; they send up
dust on their heads, they
gird on sackcloths. The
virgins of Jerusalem let
their heads hang to the
ground. [11]And my eyes *are*
at an end with tears; my
inward parts ferment; my
liver is poured on the
ground for the ruin of the
daughter of my people; in
the fainting of children and
babies in city's plazas.
[12]They say to their mothers,
Where *are* grain and wine?
In their fainting *they are* like
the wounded in the plazas
of the city, in their pouring
out their lives to their
mothers' bosom. [13]What
can I testify for you? What
will I compare to you,

קַשְׁתּוֹ כְּאוֹיֵב נִצָּב יְמִינוֹ כְּצָר וַיַּהֲרֹג כֹּל מַחֲמַדֵּי־עָיִן בְּאֹהֶל
the in the desirable all and like right His set a like His
of tent eye to (these) killed ,foe a hand hater bow

5 בַּת־צִיּוֹן שָׁפַךְ כָּאֵשׁ חֲמָתוֹ׃ הָיָה אֲדֹנָי ׀ כְּאוֹיֵב בִּלַּע
He a like The was His a like He ;Zion the
swallowed ,hater Lord .fury fire out poured of daughter

יִשְׂרָאֵל בִּלַּע כָּל־אַרְמְנוֹתֶיהָ שִׁחֵת מִבְצָרָיו וַיֶּרֶב בְּבַת־
in He and strong- his destroyed ,palaces his all He ,Israel
daughter increased ;holds swallowed

6 יְהוּדָה תַּאֲנִיָּה וַאֲנִיָּה׃ וַיַּחְמֹס כַּגַּן שֻׂכּוֹ שִׁחֵת מֹעֲדוֹ שִׁכַּח
made His destroyed His a like He And and mourning Judah's
forget ;meetings ,booth garden violated .weeping

יְהוָה ׀ בְּצִיּוֹן מוֹעֵד וְשַׁבָּת וַיִּנְאַץ בְּזַעַם־אַפּוֹ מֶלֶךְ וְכֹהֵן׃
and king His the in He and and meeting in Jehovah
.priest anger of fury rejected ,sabbaths places Zion

7 זָנַח אֲדֹנָי ׀ מִזְבְּחוֹ נִאֵר מִקְדָּשׁוֹ הִסְגִּיר בְּיַד־אוֹיֵב חוֹמֹת
walls the the into has He holy His re- He His The has
of hater's hand delivered ,place jected ,altar Lord off cast

8 אַרְמְנוֹתֶיהָ קוֹל נָתְנוּ בְּבֵית־יְהוָה כְּיוֹם מוֹעֵד׃ חָשַׁב
Deter- .meeting a as Jehovah the in they a ;palaces her
mined of day of house gave noise

יְהוָה ׀ לְהַשְׁחִית חוֹמַת בַּת־צִיּוֹן נָטָה קָו לֹא־הֵשִׁיב יָדוֹ
His has He not a He ;Zion's daugh- the destroy to Jehovah
hand returned ,line stretched ter of wall

9 מִבַּלֵּעַ וַיַּאֲבֶל־חֵל וְחוֹמָה יַחְדָּו אֻמְלָלוּ׃ טָבְעוּ בָאָרֶץ
the in Have they together and ram- made He and from
earth sunk .languish ,wall part lament ;swallowing

שְׁעָרֶיהָ אִבַּד וְשִׁבַּר בְּרִיחֶיהָ מַלְכָּהּ וְשָׂרֶיהָ בַגּוֹיִם אֵין
is the among her and her ;bars her and dis- He her
not :nations (are) rulers kings shattered persed ;gates

10 תּוֹרָה גַּם־נְבִיאֶיהָ לֹא־מָצְאוּ חָזוֹן מֵיְהוָה׃ יֵשְׁבוּ לָאָרֶץ
the on They from a have not her also the
,ground sit .Jehovah vision found prophets ;law

יִדְּמוּ זִקְנֵי בַת־צִיּוֹן הֶעֱלוּ עָפָר עַל־רֹאשָׁם חָגְרוּ שַׂקִּים
sack- they their on dust they ,Zion's daugh- the are
;cloths on gird ,head up send ter of elders silent

11 הוֹרִידוּ לָאָרֶץ רֹאשָׁן בְּתוּלֹת יְרוּשָׁלִָם׃ כָּלוּ בַדְּמָעוֹת
tears with at And .Jerusalem virgins the their the to let
end an of heads ground hang

עֵינַי חֳמַרְמְרוּ מֵעַי נִשְׁפַּךְ לָאָרֶץ כְּבֵדִי עַל־שֶׁבֶר בַּת־
daughter the for my the on is my ferment my
of ruin ,liver ground poured bowels ,eyes

12 עַמִּי בֵּעָטֵף עוֹלֵל וְיוֹנֵק בִּרְחֹבוֹת קִרְיָה׃ לְאִמֹּתָם יֹאמְרוּ
they their To the the in and children the in my
,say mothers .city of plazas sucklings of fainting ;people's

אַיֵּה דָּגָן וָיָיִן בְּהִתְעַטְּפָם כֶּחָלָל בִּרְחֹבוֹת עִיר בְּהִשְׁתַּפֵּךְ
their in the the in the like their In and grain Where
out pouring ,city of plazas wounded fainting ?wine (are)

13 נַפְשָׁם אֶל־חֵיק אִמֹּתָם׃ מָה־אֲעִידֵךְ מָה אֲדַמֶּה־לָּךְ הַבַּת
O to I shall What I can What their the to their
daughter ,you compare ?you for testify .mothers of bosom lives

O daughter of Jerusalem? What shall I equate to you, that I may comfort you, O virgin daughter of Zion? For your crushing *is* great like the sea; who can heal you?
14Your prophets have seen false and foolish things for you, and they have not disclosed your iniquity, to turn away your captivity; but they envisioned burdens of falsehood and seductions for you.
15All who pass by clap their hands at you. They hiss and wag their head at the daughter of Jerusalem, *saying, Is* this the city which they called the perfection of beauty, the joy of all the earth? 16All your enemies have opened their mouth against you; they hiss and gnash the teeth; they say, We have swallowed *her* up. Certainly this is the day that we looked for; we have found; we have seen.
17Jehovah has done what He has purposed; He fulfilled His word which he commanded from days of old. He has dashed, and not pitied. And He made the hater glad over you; He raised the horn of your foes.
18Their heart cried to the Lord, O wall of the daughter of Zion, let tears run down like a torrent by day and night; give yourself no relief; let not the daughter of your eye rest. 19Rise up, cry out in the night, at the beginning of the watches pour out your heart like water before the face of Jehovah. Lift up your hands toward Him for the life of your children *who are* faint with hunger at the head of every street.
20Behold, O Jehovah, and consider to whom You have done this. Shall women eat their fruit, children of tender care? Should priest and prophet be killed in the holy place of the Lord? 21Young and old lie on the ground of the plazas; my virgins and my young men have fallen by the sword. You have killed *them* in the day of Your

יְרוּשָׁלַ͏ִם מָה אֲשַׁוֶּה־לָּךְ וַאֲנַחֲמֵךְ בְּתוּלַת בַּת־צִיּוֹן כִּי־גָדוֹל
great For ?Zion daughter of virgin O may I that you comfort to you equate I shall What ?Jerusalem's
14 כַּיָּם שִׁבְרֵךְ מִי יִרְפָּא־לָךְ׃ נְבִיאַיִךְ חָזוּ לָךְ שָׁוְא וְתָפֵל
and folly false-hood for you visioned Your prophets ?you heal can who your (is) crushing like sea the
וְלֹא־גִלּוּ עַל־עֲוֺנֵךְ לְהָשִׁיב שְׁבִיתֵךְ וַיֶּחֱזוּ לָךְ מַשְׂאוֹת שָׁוְא
false-hood burdens of for you they visioned and your ;captivity turn back to your about ,iniquity dis-closed and not
15 וּמַדּוּחִים׃ סָפְקוּ עָלַיִךְ כַּפַּיִם כָּל־עֹבְרֵי דֶרֶךְ שָׁרְקוּ וַיָּנִעוּ
and wag they hiss the ,way passing by all their palms you at Clap and .seductions
רֹאשָׁם עַל־בַּת יְרוּשָׁלָ͏ִם הֲזֹאת הָעִיר שֶׁיֹּאמְרוּ כְּלִילַת יֹפִי
,beauty perfection of the they called which the city (Is) this :Jerusalem the of daughter at their head
16 מָשׂוֹשׂ לְכָל־הָאָרֶץ׃ פָּצוּ עָלַיִךְ פִּיהֶם כָּל־אוֹיְבַיִךְ שָׁרְקוּ
they hiss your ,haters all their mouth against you Have opened ?earth the all of joy the
וַיַּחַרְקוּ־שֵׁן אָמְרוּ בִּלָּעְנוּ אַךְ זֶה הַיּוֹם שֶׁקִּוִּינֻהוּ מָצָאנוּ
have we ,found which for ;waited we the day this (is) Surely have We !up swallowed ,say they the ;teeth and gnash
17 רָאִינוּ׃ עָשָׂה יְהוָה אֲשֶׁר זָמָם בִּצַּע אֶמְרָתוֹ אֲשֶׁר צִוָּה
He commanded which word His He fulfilled He ,planned which (that) Jehovah has done have we .(it) seen
מִימֵי־קֶדֶם הָרַס וְלֹא חָמָל וַיְשַׂמַּח עָלַיִךְ אוֹיֵב הֵרִים קֶרֶן
the of horn He raised the ,hater over you He made and glad ;pitied and not has He dashed .antiquity from of days
18 צָרָיִךְ׃ צָעַק לִבָּם אֶל־אֲדֹנָי חוֹמַת בַּת־צִיּוֹן הוֹרִידִי כַנַּחַל
a like torrent out go let Zion's daughter of wall O ;Lord the to Their heart cried your .foes
דִּמְעָה יוֹמָם וָלַיְלָה אַל־תִּתְּנִי פוּגַת לָךְ אַל־תִּדֹּם בַּת־
the of daughter rest let not to ,yourself relief give do not and ,night day by tears
19 עֵינֵךְ׃ קוּמִי רֹנִּי בַלַּיְלָה לְרֹאשׁ אַשְׁמֻרוֹת שִׁפְכִי כַמַּיִם
like waters out pour ;watches the the at of head the in night cry out ,Arise your .eye
לִבֵּךְ נֹכַח פְּנֵי אֲדֹנָי שְׂאִי אֵלָיו כַּפַּיִךְ עַל־נֶפֶשׁ עוֹלָלַיִךְ
your children the of life for your palms to Him lift up the ;Lord the of face before your heart
20 הָעֲטוּפִים בְּרָעָב בְּרֹאשׁ כָּל־חוּצוֹת׃ רְאֵה יְהוָה וְהַבִּיטָה
!look and O ,Jehovah ,See open .place every the at of head with hunger (are who) faint
לְמִי עוֹלַלְתָּ כֹּה אִם־תֹּאכַלְנָה נָשִׁים פִּרְיָם עֹלֲלֵי טִפֻּחִים
tender ?care children of their ,fruit women Should eat ?thus You have done To whom
21 אִם־יֵהָרֵג בְּמִקְדַּשׁ אֲדֹנָי כֹּהֵן וְנָבִיא׃ שָׁכְבוּ לָאָרֶץ חוּצוֹת
open the places of the on ground Lie down and ?prophet priest the Lord the in of place holy be Should killed
נַעַר וְזָקֵן בְּתוּלֹתַי וּבַחוּרַי נָפְלוּ בֶחָרֶב הָרַגְתָּ בְּיוֹם אַפֶּךָ
Your ,anger the in of day You have killed the by ;sword have fallen my and youth choice my virgins and young ;old

anger; You have killed;
You have not pitied. [22]You
have called my terrors all
around, as in a day of
appointment, and there
was not an escaped one
or a survivor in the day of
the anger of Jehovah.
Those whom I have
nursed and multiplied,
my enemy has consumed.

CHAPTER 3

[1]I the man have seen
affliction by the rod of His
wrath. [2]He led me and
made *me* go in darkness
and not light. [3]Surely He
turned against me; He
turns His hand all the
day. [4]He has wasted my
flesh and my skin. He has
shattered my bones. [5]He
built against me and has
put around *me* bitterness
and hardship. [6]He has
made me live in dark
places like the dead of
old. [7]He walled around
me and I cannot go out;
He has made heavy my
bronze *chain*. [8]Also when
I cry out and shout for
help, He shuts out my
prayer. [9]He walled up my
ways with cut stone; my
paths *are* crooked. [10]He
was a bear lying in wait
for me, a lion in a covert.
[11]He has deflected my
ways and torn me to
pieces; He made me des-
olate. [12]He has trod His
bow and set me up as a
mark for the arrow.

[13]He made enter into
my inward parts the sons
of His quiver. [14]I was a
mockery to all my people,
their song all the day.
[15]He has filled me with
bitterness *and* made me
drunk *with* wormwood.
[16]And He broke my teeth
with gravel; He has cov-
ered me in the ashes.
[17]And You cast off my
soul from peace; I have
forgotten goodness.
[18]And I said, My strength
and my hope *is* gone from
Jehovah.

[19]Remember my afflic-
tion and my roaming, *as*
wormwood and bitter-
ness. [20]My soul vividly remembers and bows down

3808 5439 4032 4150 3117 7121 2550 3808 2873
22 טָבַחְתָּ לֹא חָמָלְתָּ׃ תִּקְרָא כְיוֹם מוֹעֵד מְגוּרַי מִסָּבִיב וְלֹא
and ,around all my appointed in as have You have You not have You
not terrors meeting of day a called !pitied ,killed

7235 2946 834 8300 6412 3068 639 3117 1961
הָיָה בְּיוֹם אַף־יְהוָה פָּלִיט וְשָׂרִיד אֲשֶׁר־טִפַּחְתִּי וְרִבִּיתִי
and have I Whom a or an Jehovah the the in was
,multiplied nursed ;survivor escapee of anger of day

3615 341
אֹיְבִי כִלָּם׃
con- has my
!(them) sumed enemy

CAP. III ג

CHAPTER 3

32:12 5090 5678 7626 6040 7200 1397
1 אֲנִי הַגֶּבֶר רָאָה עֳנִי בְּשֵׁבֶט עֶבְרָתוֹ׃
2 אוֹתִי נָהַג וַיֹּלַךְ
made and He me His of the by afflic- have man the I
go (me) led .wrath rod tion seen

3117 3605/3027 2015 7725 389 216 38:08 2822
3 חֹשֶׁךְ וְלֹא־אוֹר׃ אַךְ בִּי יָשֻׁב יַהֲפֹךְ יָדוֹ כָּל־הַיּוֹם׃
the all His He He against Surely .light and in
.day hand turns ;turned me not darkness

7219 5362 1129 6106 7665 5785 1320 1086
4 בִּלָּה בְשָׂרִי וְעוֹרִי שִׁבַּר עַצְמוֹתָי׃
5 בָּנָה עָלַי וַיַּקַּף רֹאשׁ
bitter- put has and against He .bones my has He my and flesh my has He
ness (me) around me built shattered ;skin wasted

1443 5769 3427 4285 8513
6 וּתְלָאָה׃ בְּמַחֲשַׁכִּים הוֹשִׁיבַנִי כְּמֵתֵי עוֹלָם׃
7 גָּדַר
He .old the like made has He places dark In and
walled of dead live me .hardship

7768 2199 1571 5178 3513 3318 3808
8 בַּעֲדִי וְלֹא אֵצֵא הִכְבִּיד נְחָשְׁתִּי׃ גַּם כִּי אֶזְעַק וַאֲשַׁוֵּעַ
shout and cry I when Also bronze my has He can I and around
,help for out .(chain) heavy made ;out go not ,me

1677 5753 5410 1496 1870 1443 8605 5640
9 שָׂתַם תְּפִלָּתִי׃ גָּדַר דְּרָכַי בְּגָזִית נְתִיבֹתַי עִוָּה׃
10 דֹּב
bear A .crooked paths my cut with ways my has He my shuts He
(are) ,stone up walled .prayer out

6582 5493 1870 4565 738 693
11 אֹרֵב הוּא לִי אֲרִיה בְּמִסְתָּרִים׃ דְּרָכַי סוֹרֵר וַיְפַשְּׁחֵנִי
me torn and has He ways My secret in lion a to He lying
,pieces to deflected .places ,me (was) wait in

2671 4307 53:24 7198 1869 8074 7760
12 שָׂמַנִי שֹׁמֵם׃ דָּרַךְ קַשְׁתּוֹ וַיַּצִּיבֵנִי כַּמַּטָּרָא לַחֵץ׃
the for mark a as set and bow His has He .desolate He
.arrow up me trod me made

5971 3605 7814 1961 827 1121 3629 935
13 הֵבִיא בְּכִלְיוֹתָי בְּנֵי אַשְׁפָּתוֹ׃
14 הָיִיתִי שְׂחֹק לְכָל־עַמִּי
my all to a was I .quiver His the my into made He
,people mockery of sons parts inward enter

3939 7301 4844 7646 3117 3605 5058
15 נְגִינָתָם כָּל־הַיּוֹם׃ הִשְׂבִּיעַנִי בַמְּרוֹרִים הִרְוַנִי לַעֲנָה׃
worm- (with) made (He) bit- with has He the all their
.wood drunk me ,terness me filled .day song

5315 7965 2186 665 37:30 81:27 2687 1638
16 וַיַּגְרֵס בֶּחָצָץ שִׁנָּי הִכְפִּישַׁנִי בָּאֵפֶר׃
17 וַתִּזְנַח מִשָּׁלוֹם נַפְשִׁי
my from You And the in has He my with He And
;soul peace off cast .ashes me covered teeth gravel broke

3068 8431 5331 6 559 2898 5382
18 נָשִׁיתִי טוֹבָה׃ וָאֹמַר אָבַד נִצְחִי וְתוֹחַלְתִּי מֵיְהוָה׃
from my and my is Gone I And .goodness have I
.Jehovah hope strength ,said forgotten

7743 2142 2142 7219 3939 4788 6040 2142
19 זְכָר־עָנְיִי וּמְרוּדִי לַעֲנָה וָרֹאשׁ׃
20 זָכוֹר תִּזְכּוֹר וְתָשִׁיחַ עָלַי
upon bows and remembers Vividly and wormwood my and my Remem-
me down .bitterness ,roaming affliction ber

upon me. [21]I recall this to
my heart, so I hope.
[22]*It is by* the kindness of
Jehovah that we are not
destroyed, for His mercies
never fail. [23]*They are* new
every morning; great *is* Your
faithfulness [24]Jehovah *is*
my portion, says my soul;
therefore I will hope in Him.
[25]Jehovah *is* good to those
who wait for Him, to the
soul seeking Him. [26]*It is*
good that *a man* hopes for
the salvation of Jehovah,
even in silence. [27]*It is* good
for a man that he bear the
yoke in his youth. [28]He sits
alone and is silent, because
He laid *it* on him. [29]He puts
his mouth in the dust, if
perhaps there is hope.
[30]He gives *his* cheek to Him
who strikes him; he is filled
with reproach. [31]For the
Lord will not cast off forever; [32]for though He causes
grief, He will have pity
according to the multitude
of His kindnesses. [33]For He
does not afflict from His
heart, nor does He grieve
the sons of men. [34]To crush
all the prisoners of earth
under His feet; [35]to turn
aside the judgment of a
man before the face of the
Most High; [36]to pervert a
man in his cause; *this* the
Lord does not see.
[37]Who *is* this speaking,
and it occurs *when* the Lord
does not command *it*?
[38]The evil and the good do
not come out of the mouth
of the Most High. [39]What?
Should mankind complain,
a living man, because of his
sins? [40]Let us search and try
our ways, and turn again to
Jehovah. [41]Let us lift up
our hearts *and* palms to
God in Heaven. [42]We have
trespassed and have re-
belled. You have not for-
given. [43]You have wrapped
Yourself with anger and
pursued us; You have slain;
You have not pitied. [44]You
have wrapped *Yourself* with
a cloud from *any* prayer
passing through. [45]You

26•17 3176 3820 7725 2088 5315
21 22 נַפְשִׁי׃ זֹאת אָשִׁיב אֶל־לִבִּי עַל־כֵּן אוֹחִיל׃ חַסְדֵי
kind- (By) .hope I therefore my to bring I This my
nesses ,heart back .soul

1242 2319 7356 36:15 38:08 8552 :• 380:8 3068
23 יְהוָה כִּי לֹא־תָמְנוּ כִּי לֹא־כָלוּ רַחֲמָיו׃ חֲדָשִׁים לַבְּקָרִים
by new His are not for are we not that Jeho-
;mornings (they are) ;mercies ended ,consumed (is it) vah's

3176 5315 559 3068 2506 530 7227
24 רַבָּה אֱמוּנָתֶךָ׃ חֶלְקִי יְהוָה אָמְרָה נַפְשִׁי עַל־כֵּן אוֹחִיל
shall I therefore my says ,Jehovah My faith- Your great
hope ,soul (is) portion .fulness (is)

2342 2896 1875 53:15 :69:60 3068 2896
25 26 לוֹ׃ טוֹב יְהוָה לְקֹוָו לְנֶפֶשׁ תִּדְרְשֶׁנּוּ׃ טוֹב וְיָחִיל
he that (is It) seeks (that) the to those to Jehovah Good for
hopes good .Him soul ,Him awaiting (is) .Him

5271 5923 5375 1397 2896 3068 8668 17:48
27 וְדוּמָם לִתְשׁוּעַת יְהוָה׃ טוֹב לַגֶּבֶר כִּי־יִשָּׂא עֹל בִּנְעוּרָיו׃
his in a he that a for (is It) .Jehovah the for (in) even
.youth yoke bear man good of salvation silence

194 6310 6083 5414 5190 18:26 910 3427
28 29 יֵשֵׁב בָּדָד וְיִדֹּם כִּי נָטַל עָלָיו׃ יִתֵּן בֶּעָפָר פִּיהוּ אוּלַי
perhaps his the in He upon He for is and alone He
,mouth dust puts .him (it) laid ,silent sits

3808 2781 7646 3895 5221 5414 8615 3426
30 31 יֵשׁ תִּקְוָה׃ יִתֵּן לְמַכֵּהוּ לֶחִי יִשְׂבַּע בְּחֶרְפָּה׃ כִּי לֹא
not For with is He his his to He .hope there
.reproach filled ,cheek smiter gives is

•2617 7230 7355 30:13 518 136 5769 2186
32 33 יִזְנַח לְעוֹלָם אֲדֹנָי׃ כִּי אִם־הוֹגָה וְרִחַם כְּרֹב חֲסָדָו׃ כִּי
For kind- His the as will He causes He if For the forever will
.nesses of many pity have ,grief .Lord off cast

:7272 8478 1792 376 1121 3013 :3820 6031 38:08
34 לֹא עִנָּה מִלִּבּוֹ וַיַּגֶּה בְּנֵי־אִישׁ׃ לְדַכֵּא תַּחַת רַגְלָיו
His under To .man the nor His from He not
feet crush of sons grieves ,heart afflicts

59:45 6440 5048 1397• 4941 5186 776 615 3610:5
35 כֹּל אֲסִירֵי אָרֶץ׃ לְהַטּוֹת מִשְׁפַּט־גָּבֶר נֶגֶד פְּנֵי עֶלְיוֹן׃
Most the the before man a the turn to ;earth the all
,High of face of justice aside of prisoners

559 2088 4310 7200 38:08 136 :7379 120 5791•
36 37 לְעַוֵּת אָדָם בְּרִיבוֹ אֲדֹנָי לֹא רָאָה׃ מִי זֶה אָמַר
(who) this Who does not the his in a to
,speaks (is) .see Lord :cause man pervert

2896 1451 33:18 38:08 5945 6310 6680 38:08 136 1961
38 וַתֶּהִי אֲדֹנָי לֹא צִוָּה׃ מִפִּי עֶלְיוֹן לֹא תֵצֵא הָרָעוֹת וְהַטּוֹב׃
the and evil the goes not Most the From com- not the it and
?good out High's mouth ?manding Lord ,occurs

2664 •2399 1391 24:16 120 596 4100
39 40 מַה־יִּתְאוֹנֵן אָדָם חָי גֶּבֶר עַל־חֲטָאָו׃ נַחְפְּשָׂה
us Let his because ,man living man- Should ?What
search ?sins of ,kind complain

38 24 5375 3068 5704 7725 2713 1870
41 דְּרָכֵינוּ וְנַחְקֹרָה וְנָשׁוּבָה עַד־יְהוָה׃ נִשָּׂא לְבָבֵנוּ אֶל־
(and) hearts our Let .Jehovah to return and examine and our
lift us ,(them) ways

3808 4784 6586 5168 8064 410 3709•
42 כַּפַּיִם אֶל־אֵל בַּשָּׁמָיִם׃ נַחְנוּ פָשַׁעְנוּ וּמָרִינוּ אַתָּה לֹא
not ,You and have We .Heaven in God to palms
,rebelled transgressed

2550 38:08 2026 72:91 639 5526 5545
43 סָלָחְתָּ׃ סַכֹּתָה בָאַף וַתִּרְדְּפֵנוּ הָרַגְתָּ לֹא חָמָלְתָּ׃
have You not have You pur- and with have You have You
.pitied ,slain ;us sued anger Yourself wrapped .forgiven

7760 3985 5501 8605 5674 6051 5526
44 45 סַכֹּתָה בֶעָנָן לָךְ מֵעֲבוֹר תְּפִלָּה׃ סְחִי וּמָאוֹס תְּשִׂימֵנוּ
have You and Sweepings (any) passing from for a with have You
,us made garbage .prayer through ,You cloud covered

have made us *as* the
sweepings and garbage in
the midst of the peoples.
[46]All our enemies have
opened their mouths
against us. [47]Dread and a
pit have come to us, shame
and ruin. [48]Streams of
water run down my eye, for
the ruin of the daughter of
my people. [49]My eye flows
out and does not cease,
from there being no inter-
mission, [50]until Jehovah
shall look down and see
from heaven. [51]My eye
pains my soul from all the
daughters of my city. [52]My
haters have hunted me,
like a bird, in vain. [53]They
have cut off my life in
the pit, and threw stones at
me. [54]Waters flowed over
my head; I said, I am cut off.
[55]I called on Your name, O
Jehovah, out of the lowest
pit. [56]You have heard my
voice; do not hide Your ear
at my relief, at my cry for
help. [57]You drew near in
the day I called on You; You
said, Do not fear. [58]O Lord,
You strove for the causes of
my soul; You redeemed my
life. [59]O Jehovah, You have
seen my wrong; judge my
cause. [60]You have seen all
their vengeance, all their
plots against me.
[61]You have heard their
reproach, O Jehovah, all
their plots against me,
[62]the lips of those rising
against me, and their
scheming against me all the
day. [63]Behold their sitting
down and their rising up; I
am their song. [64]You will
return them a recompense,
O Jehovah, according to
the work of their hands.
[65]You will give them dullness of heart, Your curse on
them. [66]Pursue and destroy
them in anger from under
the heavens of Jehovah.

46 47
6343 341 3605 6310 6475 5971 7130
בְּקֶרֶב הָעַמִּים׃ פָּצוּ עָלֵינוּ פִּיהֶם כָּל־אֹיְבֵינוּ׃ פַּחַד
Dread our all their against Have the the in
.enemies mouths us opened .peoples of midst

48
5869 3381 432 5 6388 7667 7612 1961 6354
וָפַחַת הָיָה לָנוּ הַשֵּׁאת וְהַשָּׁבֶר׃ פַּלְגֵי־מַיִם תֵּרַד עֵינִי
my out go waters Streams .ruin and devas- ,us to is a and
eye of of tation pit

49
369 1820 3808 5064 5869 5971 1323 7667
עַל־שֶׁבֶר בַּת־עַמִּי׃ עֵינִי נִגְּרָה וְלֹא תִדְמֶה מֵאֵין
from ,ceases and flows My my daugh- the the for
being not not out eye .people of ter of ruin

50 51
5953 5869 8064 3068 7200 8259 5704 2014
הֲפֻגוֹת׃ עַד־יַשְׁקִיף וְיֵרֶא יְהוָה מִשָּׁמָיִם׃ עֵינִי עוֹלְלָה
treats My the from Jehovah and shall until (any)
severely eye .heavens see down look ,stopping

52
341 6833 6679 6679 5892 1323 3605 5315
לְנַפְשִׁי מִכֹּל בְּנוֹת עִירִי׃ צוֹד צָדוּנִי כַּצִּפּוֹר אֹיְבַי
my a like have Surely my daugh- the from my to
haters bird me hunted .city of ters all ,soul

53 54
5921 4325 6687 68 3034 2416 953 6789 2600
חִנָּם׃ צָמְתוּ בַבּוֹר חַיָּי וַיַּדּוּ־אֶבֶן בִּי׃ צָפוּ־מַיִם עַל־
upon Waters over- .me at threw and my the in have They in
flowed stones life pit off cut .vain

55
953 3068 8034 7121 1504 559 7218
רֹאשִׁי אָמַרְתִּי נִגְזָרְתִּי׃ קָרָאתִי שִׁמְךָ יְהוָה מִבּוֹר
the from O Your called I am I ,said I my
pit ,Jehovah ,name .off cut ;head

56
7775 7309 241 5956 408 8085 6963 8482
תַּחְתִּיּוֹת׃ קוֹלִי שָׁמָעְתָּ אַל־תַּעְלֵם אָזְנְךָ לְרַוְחָתִי לְשַׁוְעָתִי׃
cry my at my at Your do not have You My .lowest
.help for ,relief ear hide ;heard voice

57 58
136 7378 3372 408 559 7121 3117 7126
קָרַבְתָּ בְּיוֹם אֶקְרָאֶךָּ אָמַרְתָּ אַל־תִּירָא׃ רַבְתָּ אֲדֹנָי
O You !Fear not You called I the in came You
,Lord for contended ,said ;You day near

59
8199 5792 3068 7200 2416 1350 5315 7379
רִיבֵי נַפְשִׁי גָּאַלְתָּ חַיָּי׃ רָאִיתָה יְהוָה עַוָּתָתִי שָׁפְטָה
judge my O have You my You my causes the
;wrong ,Jehovah ,seen .life redeemed ,soul of

60
4284 3605 5360 3605 7200 4941
מִשְׁפָּטִי׃ רָאִיתָה כָּל־נִקְמָתָם כָּל־מַחְשְׁבֹתָם לִי׃
against plots their all their all have You my
.me ,vengeance seen .cause

61 62
6965 8193 4284 3605 3068 2781 8085
שָׁמַעְתָּ חֶרְפָּתָם יְהוָה כָּל־מַחְשְׁבֹתָם עָלָי׃ שִׂפְתֵי קָמַי
my lips the against plots their all O their have You
,uprisers of ,me ,Jehovah ,reproach heard

63
5027 7012 3427 3117 3605 1902
וְהֶגְיוֹנָם עָלַי כָּל־הַיּוֹם׃ שִׁבְתָּם וְקִימָתָם הַבִּיטָה אֲנִי
I ;at look their and Their the all against their and
(am) rising sitting .day me scheming

64
3027 4639 3068 1576 7725 4485
מַנְגִּינָתָם׃ תָּשִׁיב לָהֶם גְּמוּל יְהוָה כְּמַעֲשֵׂה יְדֵיהֶם׃
their the to as O a to will You .song their
;hands of work ,Jehovah ,reward them return

65 66
8045 639 7291 8381 3820 4044 5414
תִּתֵּן לָהֶם מְגִנַּת־לֵב תַּאֲלָתְךָ לָהֶם׃ תִּרְדֹּף בְּאַף וְתַשְׁמִידֵם
destroy and in Pursue to your ,heart insolence to will You
them anger .them curse of them give

3068 8064 8478
מִתַּחַת שְׁמֵי יְהוָה׃
.Jehovah the from
of heavens under

CHAPTER 4

[1]How the fine gold dims, the good gold is changed! The stones of the sanctuary are poured out at the head of every street. [2]The precious sons of Zion are weighed against pure gold — how they are counted as earthen vessels, the work of a potter's hand! [3]Even the jackals draw out the breast; they suckle their young; *but* the daughter of my people *is* cruel, like the ostriches in the wilderness. [4]The nursling's tongue cleaves to his palate in thirst; the sucklings ask bread; there is no breaking for them. [5]The eaters of delicacies are desolate in the streets; those reared on scarlet embrace dunghills. [6]And the iniquity of the daughter of my people is heaped more than Sodom's sin, overthrown as *in* a moment, and no hands spun on her. [7]Her Nazarites *were* purer than snow, whiter than milk; they *were* redder *of* bone than corals; their cuttings as lapis lazuli, *azure-blue*. [8]Their appearance *is* darker than soot; they are not recognized in the streets; their skin has shriveled on their bones; it is dried up; it has become like wood. [9]Better are the ones slain by the sword than the ones slain by hunger, those who flow away, pierced because the produce of my fields *failed*. [10]The pitying women's hands have boiled their own children; they became their food in the ruin of the daughter of my people. [11]Jehovah has fulfilled His fury; He has poured out His fierce anger and has kindled a fire in Zion; and it has eaten its foundations. [12]The kings of the earth and all the world's inhabitants would not have believed that the foe and the hater would go into Jerusalem's gates. [13]Because of the sins of her

CAP. IV ד

CHAPTER 4

68 8210 2896 3800 8132 2091 6004
1 אֵיכָה יוּעַם זָהָב יִשְׁנֶא הַכֶּתֶם הַטּוֹב תִּשְׁתַּפֵּכְנָה אַבְנֵי־
the poured Are !good fine the is the dims How
of stones out gold changed ,gold

5537 3368 6726 1121 2351 3605 7218 6944
2 קֹדֶשׁ בְּרֹאשׁ כָּל־חוּצוֹת׃ בְּנֵי צִיּוֹן הַיְקָרִים הַמְסֻלָּאִים
are precious Zion The .street every the at the
weighed of sons of head sanctuary

1571 3335 3027 4639 2789 2803 6337
3 בַּפָּז אֵיכָה נֶחְשְׁבוּ לְנִבְלֵי־חֶרֶשׂ מַעֲשֵׂה יְדֵי יוֹצֵר׃ גַּם־
Even !potter a the work the earthen as are they How against
of hands of vessels reckoned :gold pure

3283 393 5971 1323 1482 3243 7699 2502 8577
תַּנִּין חָלְצוּ שַׁד הֵינִיקוּ גּוּרֵיהֶן בַּת־עַמִּי לְאַכְזָר כִּי עֵנִים
the like (become has) my daugh- their they the draw jackals
ostriches ,cruel people's ter ;young suckle ,breast out

7592 5768 6772 2441 3243 3956 1692 4057
4 בַּמִּדְבָּר׃ דָּבַק לְשׁוֹן יוֹנֵק אֶל־חִכּוֹ בַּצָּמָא עוֹלָלִים שָׁאֲלוּ
ask young the in his to the tongue the Clings the in
children ;thirst palate nursling of .wilderness

2351 8074 4574 398 369 6566 3899
5 לֶחֶם פֹּרֵשׂ אֵין לָהֶם׃ הָאֹכְלִים לְמַעֲדַנִּים נָשַׁמּוּ בַּחוּצוֹת
the in are delicacies ones The for not ;bread
;streets desolate eating .them is breaking

5971 1323/5771 1430 830 2263 8438 539
6 הָאֱמֻנִים עֲלֵי תוֹלָע חִבְּקוּ אַשְׁפַּתּוֹת׃ וַיִּגְדַּל עֲוֺן בַּת־עַמִּי
my daugh- ini- is And .dunghills embrace scarlet on ones the
people's ter quity heaped raised

3027 2342 3808 7281 2015 5467 2403
מֵחַטַּאת סְדֹם הַהֲפוּכָה כְמוֹ־רָגַע וְלֹא־חָלוּ בָהּ יָדָיִם׃
.hands on were and a (in) as (was which) ,Sodom the than
her spun not ,moment overthrown of sin

5601 6443 6106 119 2461 6705 7950 5139 2141
7 זַכּוּ נְזִירֶיהָ מִשֶּׁלֶג צַחוּ מֵחָלָב אָדְמוּ עֶצֶם מִפְּנִינִים סַפִּיר
lapis than (of) were they than whiter than Her were
lazuli ,corals bone redder ;milk ,snow Nazarites purer

6821 2351 5234 3808 8389 7815 2821 1508
8 גִּזְרָתָם׃ חָשַׁךְ מִשְּׁחוֹר תָּאֳרָם לֹא נִכְּרוּ בַּחוּצוֹת צָפַד
has the in are they not their soot than Is their
shriveled ;streets recognized ;appearance darker .cuttings

2719 2491 2896 6086 1961 3001 6106 5785
9 עוֹרָם עַל־עַצְמָם יָבֵשׁ הָיָה כָעֵץ׃ טוֹבִים הָיוּ חַלְלֵי־חֶרֶב
the ones are Better like has it is it their on their
sword by killed .wood become ,up dried bones skin

3027 7704 8570 1856 2100 1992 7458 2491
10 מֵחַלְלֵי רָעָב שֶׁהֵם יָזוּבוּ מְדֻקָּרִים מִתְּנוּבֹת שָׂדָי׃ יְדֵי
The my of because pierced flow who ,hunger ones than
hands .fields of produce the ,(away) by killed

7667 1262 3206 1310 7362 802
נָשִׁים רַחֲמָנִיּוֹת בִּשְּׁלוּ יַלְדֵיהֶן הָיוּ לְבָרוֹת לָמוֹ בְּשֶׁבֶר
the in to food they own their have com- women's
of ruin them become ;children boiled passionate

3341 639 2740 8210 2534 3068 3615 5971 1323
11 בַּת־עַמִּי׃ כִּלָּה יְהוָה אֶת־חֲמָתוֹ שָׁפַךְ חֲרוֹן אַפּוֹ וַיַּצֶּת־
has and His fierce has He His Jehovah has my daughter
kindled ;anger out poured ,fury completed .people's

3605/776 4428 539 3808 3247 398 6726 784
12 אֵשׁ בְּצִיּוֹן וַתֹּאכַל יְסוֹדֹתֶיהָ׃ לֹא הֶאֱמִינוּ מַלְכֵי־אֶרֶץ וְכֹל
and the the have would Not its has it and in a
all earth of kings believed .foundations devoured ,Zion fire

2403 3389 8179 341 6862 935 8398 3427
13 יֹשְׁבֵי תֵבֵל כִּי יָבֹא צַר וְאוֹיֵב בְּשַׁעֲרֵי יְרוּשָׁלִָם׃ מֵחַטֹּאת
of Because .Jerusalem the in the and the would that the the
of sins the of gates enemy foe go world of dwellers

prophets *and* the iniquities of her priests, shedding the blood of the just in her midst; [14]they reeled blind in the streets; they are defiled with blood, so that not *any* are able to touch their clothes. [15]They cried to them, Depart! Unclean! Depart, depart! Touch not! Indeed they fled and reeled; they said among the nations, They will not continue to stay there. [16]The face of Jehovah has shared them out; He will not continue to look on them; they did not lift up the faces of the priests; they did not favor the elders. [17]While we are, our eyes fail for our help *is* vain. In our watching, we have watched for a nation; it does not save. [18]They hunted our steps from going in our streets; our end was near; our days were fulfilled, for our end had come. [19]Our pursuers were swifter than the eagles of the heavens; they hotly pursued us on the mountains; they lay in wait for us in the wilderness. [20]The breath of our nostrils, the anointed of Jehovah, was captured in their pits; *of* whom we said, In his shadow we shall live among the nations.

[21]Rejoice and be glad, O daughter of Edom living in the land of Uz; the cup also shall pass through to you; you shall be drunken and shall make yourself naked.

[22]The punishment of your iniquity *is* fulfilled, O daughter of Zion; He will exile you no more. He will visit your iniquity, daughter of Edom; He will expose your sins.

נְבִיאֶיהָ עֲוֺנוֹת כֹּהֲנֶיהָ הַשֹּׁפְכִים בְּקִרְבָּהּ דַּם צַדִּיקִים׃ נָעוּ 14

they the blood her in shedding her ini- the her
reeled righteous of midst ,priests of quities ,prophets

עִוְרִים בַּחוּצוֹת נְגֹאֲלוּ בַּדָּם בְּלֹא יוּכְלוּ יִגְּעוּ בִּלְבֻשֵׁיהֶם׃

their touch (any) are so with are they the in blind
.clothing to able not ,blood defiled ;streets

15 סוּרוּ טָמֵא קָרְאוּ לָמוֹ סוּרוּ סוּרוּ אַל־תִּגָּעוּ כִּי נָצוּ גַּם־

also they In !Touch not Turn Turn to they !Unclean Turn
fled deed away away ,them called away

16 נָעוּ אָמְרוּ בַּגּוֹיִם לֹא יוֹסִפוּ לָגוּר׃ פְּנֵי יְהוָה חִלְּקָם לֹא

not appor- has Jeho- The live to will they Not among they ;reeled
;them tioned vah of face .there continue ,nations said

יוֹסִיף לְהַבִּיטָם פְּנֵי כֹהֲנִים לֹא נָשָׂאוּ זְקֵנִים לֹא חָנָנוּ׃

they not the they not the the on look to will He
.favored elders ,rejected priests of face ;them continue

17 עוֹדֵינָה תִּכְלֶינָה עֵינֵינוּ אֶל־עֶזְרָתֵנוּ הָבֶל בְּצִפִּיָּתֵנוּ צִפִּינוּ

have we our in ;vain help our for our fail While
watched watching eyes ,are we

18 אֶל־גּוֹי לֹא יוֹשִׁעַ׃ צָדוּ צְעָדֵינוּ מִלֶּכֶת בִּרְחֹבֹתֵינוּ קָרַב

came open our in from our They .saves it not a for
near ;places going steps hunted —nation

19 קִצֵּנוּ מָלְאוּ יָמֵינוּ כִּי־בָא קִצֵּנוּ׃ קַלִּים הָיוּ רֹדְפֵינוּ מִנִּשְׁרֵי

the than our were Swifter our had for our were our
of eagles pursuers .end come ,days fulfilled end

20 שָׁמָיִם עַל־הֶהָרִים דְּלָקֻנוּ בַּמִּדְבָּר אָרְבוּ לָנוּ׃ רוּחַ אַפֵּינוּ

our The .us for lay they the in hotly they the on the
,nostrils of breath wait in wilderness ,us pursued mountains ;heavens

מְשִׁיחַ יְהוָה נִלְכַּד בִּשְׁחִיתוֹתָם אֲשֶׁר אָמַרְנוּ בְּצִלּוֹ נִחְיֶה

shall we his In ,said we (of) their in was ,Jehovah the
live shadow whom ,pits captured of anointed

21 בַגּוֹיִם׃ שִׂישִׂי וְשִׂמְחִי בַּת־אֱדוֹם יוֹשַׁבְתִּי בְּאֶרֶץ עוּץ

;Uz the in living ,Edom daughter be and Rejoice the among
of land of ,glad .nations

22 גַּם־עָלַיִךְ תַּעֲבָר־כּוֹס תִּשְׁכְּרִי וְתִתְעָרִי׃ תַּם־עֲוֺנֵךְ בַּת־

daughter of end The make and shall you the shall to also
of ,iniquity your .naked yourself drunken be ;cup pass you

צִיּוֹן לֹא יוֹסִיף לְהַגְלוֹתֵךְ פָּקַד עֲוֺנֵךְ בַּת־אֱדוֹם גִּלָּה עַל־

will He ,Edom daughter your will He ;exile to shall He not ,Zion
expose of ,iniquity visit you continue

חַטֹּאתָיִךְ׃

.sins your

CAP. V ה

CHAPTER 5

זְכֹר יְהוָה מֶה־הָיָה לָנוּ הַבִּיט וּרְאֵה אֶת־חֶרְפָּתֵנוּ׃ 1

.shame our see and look ,us to has what O Remem
upon become ,Jehovah .ber

2 נַחֲלָתֵנוּ נֶהֶפְכָה לְזָרִים בָּתֵּינוּ לְנָכְרִים׃
3 יְתוֹמִים הָיִינוּ

,are We orphans to our to been has in- Our
.foreigners houses ,strangers turned heritance

CHAPTER 5

[1]Remember, O Jehovah, what has been to us; observe and see our shame. [2]Our inheritance has turned to aliens; our houses to foreigners. [3]We are orphans; there is no father;

our mothers *are* as widows.
4 We have drunk our water for silver; our wood comes for a price.
5 We are pursued on our necks; we grow weary; rest is not given to us.
6 We have given the hand to Egypt, *to* Assyria, to be satisfied with bread.
7 Our fathers have sinned, and they are no more; we have borne their iniquities.
8 Servants rule over us; there is no rescuer from their hand.
9 We bring in our bread with our souls, because of the sword of the wilderness.
10 Our skin is hot like an oven because of the fever heat of famine.
11 They raped the women in Zion, virgins in the cities of Judah.
12 Rulers were hanged by their hand; the faces of the elders were not honored.
13 They took the young men to grind, and the youths stumbled at the wood.
14 The elders have ceased from the gate; the young men from their music.
15 The joy of our heart has ceased; our dance has turned into mourning.
16 The crown has fallen from our head. Woe now to us! For we have sinned.
17 Our heart is faint for this; our eyes are dim for these *things*.
18 On the mountain of Zion which *is* laid waste, the foxes walk about on it.
19 You, O Jehovah, remain forever; Your throne to generation and generation.
20 Why do You forget us forever *and* forsake us the length of days?
21 Return us to You, O Jehovah, and we shall turn; renew our days as of old,
22 unless You have utterly rejected us; You are very angry against us.

4
6086 8354 3701 490 517 1 369
אין אב אמתינו כאלמנות: מימינו בכסף שתינו עצינו
our have we for Our like (are) our a not
wood ,drunk silver water .widows mothers' ;father is

5
5117 3808 3021 7291 6677 935 4242
במחיר יבאו: על צוארנו נרדפנו יגענו לא הונח לנו:
to rest is not grow we are we our On .comes a for
.us given ,weary ;pursued necks price

6
7
2398 3899 7646 804 3027 5414 4713
מצרים נתנו יד אשור לשבע לחם: אבתינו חטאו
have our (with) be to the to the have we the (To)
,sinned fathers ,bread satisfied Assyrian ,hand given Egyptians

8
6561 4910 5650 5445 5771 369
אינם אנחנו עונתיהם סבלנו: עבדים משלו בנו פרק
rescuer over rule Servants have their we they and
,us .borne iniquities ;not are

9
4057 2719 6440 3899 935 5315 3027 369
אין מידם: בנפשנו נביא לחמנו מפני חרב המדבר:
the the the from our bring we our With their from not
.wilderness of sword of face bread in souls .hand is

10
11
6726 802 7458 2152 6440 3648 8574 5785
עורנו כתנור נכמרו מפני זלעפות רעב: נשים בציון
Zion in The .famine fever the because burned is like Our
women of heat of ,black oven an skin

12
2205 6440 8518 3027 8269 3063 5892 1330 6031
ענו בתלת בערי יהודה: שרים בידם נתלו פני זקנים
the the were their by Rulers .Judah the in virgins they
elders of faces ,hanged hands of cities ,raped

13
3782 6086 5288 5375 2911 970 1921 3808
לא נהדרו: בחורים טחון נשאו ונערים בעץ כשלו:
.stumbled the at the and ,lifted hand the young The were not
wood youths mill men .honored

14
15
4885 7673 5058 970 7673 8179 2205
זקנים משער שבתו בחורים מנגינתם: שבת משוש
The has their from young the have the from The
of joy ceased .music men ,ceased gate elders

16
188 7218 5850 5307 4234 60 2015 3820
לבנו נהפך לאבל מחולנו: נפלה עטרת ראשנו אוי
woe ;head our The has .dance our to has our
crown from fallen mourning turned ,heart

17
2821 428 5921 1739 1961 2088 2398 4994
נא לנו כי חטאנו: על זה היה דוה לבנו על אלה חשכו
dim these for our faint is this For have we For to now
(things) ,heart .sinned !us

18
19
1980 7776 8074 6726 2022 5869
עינינו: על הר ציון ששמם שועלים הלכו בו: אתה
,You on walk foxes laid ,Zion the On our
.it about ,waste of mount .eyes

20
5331 4100 1755 1755 3678 3427 5769 3068
יהוה לעולם תשב כסאך לדר ודור: למה לנצח
for Why gen- and gen- to Your ,remain forever O
ever .eration eration throne ,Jehovah

21
3068 7725 3117 753 5800 7911
תשכחנו תעזבנו לארך ימים: השיבנו יהוה אליך
,You to O ,us Return ?days the forsake You do
,Jehovah of length us ,us forget

22
7107 3973 3985 6924 3117 2318 7725
ונשובה חדש ימינו כקדם: כי אם מאס מאסתנו קצפת
are You have You utterly unless of as our renew we and
angry ,us rejected ,old days ;return shall

3966 5704
עלינו עד מאד:
very to against
.much us

יחזקאל

LIBER EZECHIELIS

(THE) BOOK OF EZEKIEL

CAPUT. I א

CHAPTER 1

A LITERAL TRANSLATION OF THE BIBLE

THE BOOK OF EZEKIEL

CHAPTER 1

[1]And it happened in the thirtieth year, in the fourth *month*, in the fifth of the month, as I *was* among the captives by the river Chebar, the heavens *were* opened and I saw visions of God. [2]On the fifth of the month, the fifth year of the captivity of Jehoiachin the king, [3]the word of Jehovah coming became the word of Jehovah to Ezekiel, the son of Buzi the priest in the land of the Chaldeans, by the river Chebar. And there the hand of Jehovah was on him.

[4]And I looked, and behold! A windstorm came out of the north, a great cloud and a fire flashing itself, and a brightness to it all around and out of its midst, like the color of polished bronze out of the midst of the fire. [5]Also from its midst *came* the likeness of four living creatures. And this *was* how they looked: they *had* the likeness of a man, [6]and four faces *were* to each, and four wings to each of them; [7]and their feet *were* straight feet; and the sole of their feet like the sole of a calf's foot; and they sparkled like the color of burnished copper. [8]And the hands of a man *extended* from under their wings on their four sides; and their faces and their wings *were* to the four of them, [9]joining each one to the other *by* their wings. They did not turn in their going; each one went toward the front of their face. [10]And the likeness of their faces: the face of a man, and the face of a lion,

8432 2320 2568 7243 8141 7970 1961
1 וַיְהִי בִּשְׁלֹשִׁים שָׁנָה בָּרְבִיעִי בַּחֲמִשָּׁה לַחֹדֶשׁ וַאֲנִי בְתוֹךְ־
among I as the of fifth the in the in ,year the in Now
(was) ,month (day) (month) fourth thirtieth ,was it

4759 7200 8064 6605 3529 5104 1473
הַגּוֹלָה עַל־נְהַר־כְּבָר נִפְתְּחוּ הַשָּׁמַיִם וָאֶרְאֶה מַרְאוֹת
visions saw I and the were ,Chebar river the by the
heavens opened captives

1546 2549 8141 2320 2568 430
2 אֱלֹהִים׃ בַּחֲמִשָּׁה לַחֹדֶשׁ הִיא הַשָּׁנָה הַחֲמִישִׁית לְגָלוּת
the of fifth the year the it the of the On .God of
of captivity (was) ,month fifth

941 1121 3168 3068 1697 1961 1961 3112 4428
3 הַמֶּלֶךְ יוֹיָכִין׃ הָיֹה הָיָה דְבַר־יְהוָה אֶל־יְחֶזְקֵאל בֶּן־בּוּזִי
,Buzi the ,Ezekiel to Jehovah the became becoming Jehoia- the
of son of word ,chim king

3027 8033 5921 1961 3529 5104 3778 776 3548
הַכֹּהֵן בְּאֶרֶץ כַּשְׂדִּים עַל־נְהַר־כְּבָר וַתְּהִי עָלָיו שָׁם יַד־
the there upon And .Chebar river the by the the in the
of hand him was Chaldeans of land priest

1419 6051 6828 935 5591 7307 2009 7200 3068
4 יְהוָה׃ וָאֵרֶא וְהִנֵּה רוּחַ סְעָרָה בָּאָה מִן־הַצָּפוֹן עָנָן גָּדוֹל
,great a the out came storm wind a and I And .Jehovah
cloud ,north of of ,behold ,looked

2830 5869 8432 5439 5051 3948 784
וְאֵשׁ מִתְלַקַּחַת וְנֹגַהּ לוֹ סָבִיב וּמִתּוֹכָהּ כְּעֵין הַחַשְׁמַל
polished the like of out and all to a and flashing a and
bronze of color ,midst its ,around it brightness ,itself fire

4758 2416 702 1823 8432 784 8432
5 מִתּוֹךְ הָאֵשׁ׃ וּמִתּוֹכָהּ דְּמוּת אַרְבַּע חַיּוֹת וְזֶה מַרְאֵיהֶן
how (was) And living four the its from Also the the of out
;looked they this .creatures of likeness (came) midst .fire of middle

3671 702 259 6440 702 2007 120 1823
6 דְּמוּת אָדָם לָהֵנָּה׃ וְאַרְבָּעָה פָנִים לְאֶחָת וְאַרְבַּע כְּנָפַיִם
wings four and ,each to faces four and to (was) man a the
;them of likeness

3709 7272 3709 3477 7272 7272 259
7 לְאַחַת לָהֶם׃ וְרַגְלֵיהֶם רֶגֶל יְשָׁרָה וְכַף רַגְלֵיהֶם כְּכַף
the like their the and straight- feet their and ;them of each to
of sole (was) feet of sole ;ness of (were) feet

8478 120 3027 7044 5178 5869 5340 5695 7272
8 רֶגֶל עֵגֶל וְנֹצְצִים כְּעֵין נְחֹשֶׁת קָלָל׃ וִידֵי אָדָם מִתַּחַת
from a the And .burnished the like they and a the
under man of hands copper of color sparkled ;calf of foot

702 3671 6440 7253 702 5921 3671
כַּנְפֵיהֶם עַל אַרְבַּעַת רִבְעֵיהֶם וּפְנֵיהֶם וְכַנְפֵיהֶם לְאַרְבַּעְתָּם׃
the to (were) their and their and their four the on wings their
,them of four wings faces ;sides of

3212 5437 3808 3671 269 802 2266
9 חֹבְרֹת אִשָּׁה אֶל־אֲחוֹתָהּ כַּנְפֵיהֶם לֹא־יִסַּבּוּ בְלֶכְתָּן
their in did they Not their other the to each joining
;going turn .wings one

6440 120 6440 6440 1823 3212 6440 5676 376
10 אִישׁ אֶל־עֵבֶר פָּנָיו יֵלֵכוּ׃ וּדְמוּת פְּנֵיהֶם פְּנֵי אָדָם וּפְנֵי
the and a face the their the And they their the toward each
of face ,man of ,faces of likeness .went face of front one

on the right *side* to the four of them; and the face of an ox on the left *side* to the four of them; and the face of an eagle to the four of them. 11So their faces *were*. And their wings were spread upward; to each, the two *wings of* each one were joined; and two *wings* covering their bodies. 12And each went toward the front of their faces. To where the spirit was to go, there they went; they did not turn in their going. 13And the likeness of the living creatures: they appeared like coals of burning fire; like the appearance of torches. It *was* continually circling among the living creatures. And the fire *was* bright, and out of the fire went forth lightning. 14And the living creatures kept running and returning, like the appearance of a flash of lightning.

15And I looked at the living creatures, and, behold, one wheel *was* on the earth beside the living creatures, with the four of its faces. 16The appearance of the wheels, and their workmanship *was* like the color of beryl; and the one likeness *was* to the four of them. And their appearance and their workmanship was like the wheel in the middle of the wheel. 17On the four of their sides, in their going they went; they did not turn in their going. 18And their rims, they *were* even high, even awesome they *were*. And their rims *were* full of eyes all around the four of them. 19And in the going of the living creatures the wheels went beside them; and in the lifting up of the living creatures from on the earth, the wheels were lifted up. 20Where on the spirit was to go, there they went; there the spirit *was* to go, and the wheels were lifted up along with them. For the spirit of the living creature *was* in the wheels. 21In their going, these went; and in

אַרְיֵה אֶל־הַיָּמִין לְאַרְבַּעְתָּם וּפְנֵי־שׁוֹר מֵהַשְּׂמֹאול

left (side) the on an ox the and of face of four the to ;them right (side) the on ,lion a

11 לְאַרְבַּעְתָּן וּפְנֵי־נֶשֶׁר לְאַרְבַּעְתָּן׃ וּפְנֵיהֶם וְכַנְפֵיהֶם פְּרֻדוֹת

were spread their And wings their so .(were) faces of four the to .them an the and of face eagle of four the to ;them

מִלְמָעְלָה לְאִישׁ שְׁתַּיִם חֹבְרוֹת אִישׁ וּשְׁתַּיִם מְכַסּוֹת אֵת

covering two and (wings) (of) ,one each joined were two the (wings) each to ;upward

12 גְּוִיֹּתֵיהֶנָה׃ וְאִישׁ אֶל־עֵבֶר פָּנָיו יֵלֵכוּ אֶל אֲשֶׁר יִהְיֶה־

was where To .went their faces the toward of front each And .bodies their

13 שָׁמָּה הָרוּחַ לָלֶכֶת יֵלֵכוּ לֹא יִסַּבּוּ בְּלֶכְתָּן׃ וּדְמוּת הַחַיּוֹת

living the the And ,creatures of likeness their in .going did they turn not they ;went ,go to the spirit there

מַרְאֵיהֶם כְּגַחֲלֵי־אֵשׁ בֹּעֲרוֹת כְּמַרְאֵה הַלַּפִּדִים הִיא

It (was) .torches the like (and) of appearance ,burning fire like of coals they appeared

מִתְהַלֶּכֶת בֵּין הַחַיּוֹת וְנֹגַהּ לָאֵשׁ וּמִן־הָאֵשׁ יוֹצֵא בָרָק׃

.lightning went forth the fire and of out (was) fire the bright And living the .creatures among continually circling

14 וְהַחַיּוֹת רָצוֹא וָשׁוֹב כְּמַרְאֵה הַבָּזָק׃
15 וָאֵרֶא הַחַיּוֹת וְהִנֵּה

and behold living the ,creatures I And looked at of flash a .lightning ap- the like of pearance re- and ,turning kept living the And running creatures

16 אוֹפַן אֶחָד בָּאָרֶץ אֵצֶל הַחַיּוֹת לְאַרְבַּעַת פָּנָיו׃ מַרְאֵה

ap- the of pearance its .faces the with of four living the ,creatures beside the on earth one (was) wheel

הָאוֹפַנִּים וּמַעֲשֵׂיהֶם כְּעֵין תַּרְשִׁישׁ וּדְמוּת אֶחָד לְאַרְבַּעְתָּן

four the to .them of one (was) the and likeness ,beryl the like of color their and workmanship wheels The

וּמַרְאֵיהֶם וּמַעֲשֵׂיהֶם כַּאֲשֶׁר יִהְיֶה הָאוֹפַן בְּתוֹךְ הָאוֹפָן׃

.wheel the the in of middle wheel the was like their and workmanship their And appearance

17 עַל־אַרְבַּעַת רִבְעֵיהֶן בְּלֶכְתָּם יֵלֵכוּ לֹא יִסַּבּוּ בְּלֶכְתָּן׃

their in .going did they turn not they ;went their In going their .sides of four the On

18 וְגַבֵּיהֶן וְגֹבַהּ לָהֶם וְיִרְאָה לָהֶם וְגַבֹּתָם מְלֵאֹת עֵינַיִם

eyes (were) of full their and rims to ;them even awesome to them even high their And ,rims

19 סָבִיב לְאַרְבַּעְתָּן׃ וּבְלֶכֶת הַחַיּוֹת יֵלְכוּ הָאוֹפַנִּים אֶצְלָם

beside ;them wheels the went living the ,creatures in And of going the four the .them of all around

20 וּבְהִנָּשֵׂא הַחַיּוֹת מֵעַל הָאָרֶץ יִנָּשְׂאוּ הָאוֹפַנִּים׃ עַל אֲשֶׁר

upon where- ;wheels the were up lifted the ,earth from living the upon creatures the in and of up lifting

יִהְיֶה־שָּׁם הָרוּחַ לָלֶכֶת יֵלֵכוּ שָׁמָּה הָרוּחַ לָלֶכֶת וְהָאוֹפַנִּים

the and wheels ;go to (their) spirit there they ;went ,go to the spirit there was

21 יִנָּשְׂאוּ לְעֻמָּתָם כִּי רוּחַ הַחַיָּה בָּאוֹפַנִּים׃ בְּלֶכְתָּם יֵלֵכוּ

these ;went their In going in (was) .wheels the living the creature the of spirit For with along .them were up lifted their standing still, these stood still. And in their being lifted up from on the earth, the wheels were lifted up along with them. For the spirit of the living creature *was* in the wheels.

[22]And a likeness *was* over the heads of the living creature, an expanse like the color of awesome crystal stretched out over their heads from above. [23]And under the expanse their wings *were* straight, the one toward the other; to each, two *wings* covering on this side, and to each two covering on that *side of* their bodies. [24]And I heard the sound of their wings like the sound of great waters; like the voice of the Almighty. In their going *was* the sound of tumult like the sound of an army. In their standing still they let down their wings.

[25]And there was a voice from on the expanse which *was* over their heads, looking like a sapphire stone, the likeness of a throne. And on the likeness of the throne *was* a likeness on it from above, looking like a man. [27]And I saw *Him* looking like the color of polished bronze *with* fire within it all around. From the likeness of His loins and upward, and from the likeness of His loins downward, I saw *Him* looking like fire, and brightness to it all around. [28]As the appearance of the bow that is in the cloud in the day of the rain, so the brightness appeared all around. This *was* the appearance of the likeness of the glory of Jehovah. And I saw; and I fell on my face, and I heard a voice of One speaking.

---

212 5375 776 5375 5975 5975
ובעמדם יעמדו ובהנשאם מעל הארץ ינשאו האופנים
wheels the were ,earth the from their in And these their in and
up lifted upon lifted being .still stood ,still standing

22 7218 1823 212 2416 7307 5980
לעמתם כי רוח החיה באופנים: ודמות על־ראשי
the over a And the in (was) living the the For with along
of heads (was) likeness .wheels creature of spirit .them

7218 5186 3372 7140 5869 7549 2416
החיה רקיע כעין הקרח הנורא נטוי על־ראשיהם
heads their over stretched ,awesome crystal the like an living the
out of color ,expanse creature

23 802 3477 3671 7549 8478 4605
מלמעלה: ותחת הרקיע כנפיהם ישרות אשה אל־
toward one the (were) wings their the And .above from
,straight expanse under

3680 8147 376 2007 3680 8147 376 269
אחותה לאיש שתים מכסות להנה ולאיש שתים מכסות
covering two to and this on covering two each to .other the
(wings) each ,(side) (wings)

24 6963 3671 6963 8085 1472 2007
להנה את גויתיהם: ואשמע את־קול כנפיהם כקול
the like their sound the I And .bodies their (of) that on
of sound ,wings of heard (side)

4264 6963 1999 6963 3212 7706 6963 7227 4325
מים רבים כקול־שדי בלכתם קול המלה כקול מחנה
an the like tumult the their In the the like ;great waters
.army of sound of sound going .Almighty of voice

25 834 7549 6963 1961 3671 7503 5975
בעמדם תרפינה כנפיהן: ויהי־קול מעל לרקיע אשר
that the from a there And their let they their In
(was) expanse upon voice was .wings down ,still standing

26 7549 4605 3671 7503 5975 7218
על־ראשם בעמדם תרפינה כנפיהן: וממעל לרקיע
the from And .wings their they (and) their In their over
expanse above down let still standing .heads

3678 1823 5601 68 4758 7218 834
אשר על־ראשם כמראה אבן־ספיר דמות כסא ועל
And a like- the ,sapphire a looking their over that
on .throne of ness (was) of stone like heads (was)

27 7200 4605 120 4758 1823 3678 1823
דמות הכסא דמות כמראה אדם עליו מלמעלה: וארא
I And .above from it on man a appear- in a (was) the like- the
,(Him) saw like ance likeness throne of ness

4975 4758 5439 1004 784 4758 2830 5869
כעין חשמל כמראה־אש בית־לה סביב ממראה מתניו
His the From all it within fire looking polished the like
loins of likeness .around like bronze of color

5051 784 4758 7200 4295 4975 4758 4605
ולמעלה וממראה מתניו ולמטה ראיתי כמראה־אש ונגה
and ,fire looking saw I and His the from and and
brightness like ,(Him) ,downward loins of likeness ,upward

28 1653 3117 6051 1961 834 7198 4758 5439
לו סביב: כמראה הקשת אשר יהיה בענן ביום הגשם
,rain the the in the in is that bow the ap- the As all to
of day cloud of pearance .around it

3068 3519 1823 4758 2088 5439 5051 4758
כן מראה הנגה סביב הוא מראה דמות כבוד־יהוה
.Jehovah the like- the ap- the This all the appeared so
. of glory of ness of pearance (was) .around brightness

1696 6963 8085 6440 5307 7200
ואראה ואפל על־פני ואשמע קול מדבר:
One a I and my on I even (when) And
.speaking of voice heard ,face fell ,saw I

CAP. II ב

CHAPTER 2

1 2 935 1696 72:72 5921/5975 120 1121 559
וַיֹּאמֶר אֵלַי בֶּן־אָדָם עֲמֹד עַל־רַגְלֶיךָ וַאֲדַבֵּר אֹתָךְ׃ וַתָּבֹא
And .you to I and your on stand of Son ,me to He And
entered speak will feet ,man said

8085 7272 5975 1696 7307
בִּי רוּחַ כַּאֲשֶׁר דִּבֶּר אֵלַי וַתַּעֲמִדֵנִי עַל־רַגְלָי וָאֶשְׁמַע אֵת
I and my on made He and to He as the into
heard ,feet stand me me spoke Spirit me

3 7971 1201/1121 559 1696
מִדַּבֵּר אֵלָי׃ וַיֹּאמֶר אֵלַי בֶּן־אָדָם שׁוֹלֵחַ אֲנִי אוֹתְךָ
you I am ,man of Son to He And .me to Him
sending ,me said speaking

4775 834 4775 1471 3478 1121
אֶל־בְּנֵי יִשְׂרָאֵל אֶל־גּוֹיִם הַמּוֹרְדִים אֲשֶׁר מָרְדוּ־בִי הֵמָּה
they against have who rebelling the the to ,Israel the to
;Me rebelled ones ,nations of sons

4 6440 7186 1121 2088 3117 6106 6586
וַאֲבוֹתָם פָּשְׁעוּ בִי עַד־עֶצֶם הַיּוֹם הַזֶּה׃ וְהַבָּנִים קְשֵׁי פָנִים
of (are) the And .this day the to against trans- their and
face stiff sons ,Me gressed fathers

3541 559 7971 3820 2389
וְחִזְקֵי־לֵב אֲנִי שׁוֹלֵחַ אוֹתְךָ אֲלֵיהֶם וְאָמַרְתָּ אֲלֵיהֶם כֹּה
Thus ,them to you And .them to you am I ;heart and
say shall sending of hard

5 1004 2308 518 8085 3068 136 559
אָמַר אֲדֹנָי יְהוִה׃ וְהֵמָּה אִם־יִשְׁמְעוּ וְאִם־יֶחְדָּלוּ כִּי בֵּית
a for will they or they whether And .Jehovah the says
of house —stop whether hear will ,they Lord

6 120 1121 8432 1961 5030 3045 4805
מְרִי הֵמָּה וְיָדְעוּ כִּי־נָבִיא הָיָה בְתוֹכָם׃ וְאַתָּה בֶן־אָדָם
,man Son ,you And among has a that they but they rebel-
of .them been prophet know shall (are) lion

5544 5621 3372 1697 3372
אַל־תִּירָא מֵהֶם וּמִדִּבְרֵיהֶם אַל־תִּירָא כִּי סָרָבִים וְסַלּוֹנִים
thorns and briers though be do Not their of and of be do not
,afraid .words them afraid

3372 408 1697 3427 6137
אוֹתָךְ וְאֶל־עַקְרַבִּים אַתָּה יוֹשֵׁב מִדִּבְרֵיהֶם אַל־תִּירָא
be do Not their of are you scorpions and with (are)
;afraid words .living among ,you

7 1697 1696 4805 1004 2865 6440
וּמִפְּנֵיהֶם אַל־תֵּחָת כִּי בֵּית מְרִי הֵמָּה׃ וְדִבַּרְתָּ אֶת־דְּבָרַי
words My you And they of a though be do not their by even
speak shall .(are) rebellion house frightened .faces

4805 2308 518 8085 518
אֲלֵיהֶם אִם־יִשְׁמְעוּ וְאִם־יֶחְדָּלוּ כִּי מְרִי הֵמָּה׃
they rebellious for will they or will they whether to
.(are) ;stop whether hear ,them

8 1961 408 1696 8085 120/1121
וְאַתָּה בֶן־אָדָם שְׁמַע אֵת אֲשֶׁר־אֲנִי מְדַבֵּר אֵלֶיךָ אַל־תְּהִי־
be do Not .you to am I what hear of son But
saying ,man ,you

5414 398/6310 6475 4805 1004 4805
מֶרִי כְּבֵית הַמֶּרִי פְּצֵה פִיךָ וֶאֱכֹל אֵת אֲשֶׁר־אֲנִי נֹתֵן אֵלֶיךָ׃
.you to am I what eat and your open ;rebellion like rebellious
giving mouth of house (that)

9 10 6566 5612 4039 2009 7971 3027 2009 7200
וָאֶרְאֶה וְהִנֵּה־יָד שְׁלוּחָה אֵלָי וְהִנֵּה־בוֹ מְגִלַּת־סֵפֶר׃ וַיִּפְרֹשׂ
He And a a (was) in and to was a and I And
spread .book of roll it ,behold ;me extended hand ,behold ;looked

CHAPTER 2

[1]And He said to me, Son of man, stand on your feet, and I will speak to you. [2]And the Spirit entered into me as He spoke to me; and He made me stand on my feet; and I heard Him speaking to me. [3]And He said to me, Son of man, I am sending you to the sons of Israel, to the nations, the rebelling ones who have rebelled against Me; they and their fathers have transgressed against Me to this day. [4]And the sons *are* stiff of face and hard of heart; I am sending you to them. And you shall say to them, So says the Lord Jehovah. [5]And they, whether they will hear, or whether they will forbear—for they are a rebellious house — yea, they shall know that a prophet has been among them.

[6]And you, son of man, do not be afraid of them and of their words. Do not be afraid, though briers and thorns *are* with you, and *though* you are living among scorpions. Do not be afraid of their words; and do not be frightened by their faces, though they *are* a house of rebellion. [7]And you shall speak My words to them, whether they will hear, or whether they will forbear; for they *are* rebellious.

[8]But you, son of man, hear what I am saying to you. Do not be like *that* rebellious house of rebellion. Open your mouth and eat what I am giving to you. [9]And I looked; and behold, a hand was extended to me. And behold, a roll of a book *was* in it. [10]And He spread it

before me; and it was written on the face and the back. And written on it *were* weepings, and mourning, and woe.

7015 3789 268 6440 3789 6440
אוֹתָהּ לְפָנַי וְהִיא כְתוּבָה פָּנִים וְאָחוֹר וְכָתוּב אֵלֶיהָ קִנִים
(were) ,weepings | it on | and written | the and ,back | the on face | was written | it and | before ;me | it

1958 1899
וָהֶגֶה וָהִי׃
and .woe | and mourning

CAP. III. ג

CHAPTER 3

CHAPTER 3

[1]And He said to me, Son of man, eat what you find. Eat this roll, and go speak to the house of Israel. [2]So I opened my mouth, and He made me eat that roll. [3]And He said to me, Son of man, make your belly eat, and fill your bowels with the roll, this that I give to you. And I ate; and it was in my mouth like honey for sweetness.

[4]And He said to me, Son of man, Go! Come to the house of Israel and speak with My words to them. [5]For you are not sent to a people of deep lip and hardness of tongue, *but* to the house of Israel; [6]not to many peoples of deep lip and of a hard tongue, whose words you cannot hear. If rather I had sent you to them, they would have listened to you. [7]But the house of Israel is not willing to listen to you, for they are not willing to listen to Me; for all the house of Israel *are* strong of forehead and hard of heart. [8]Behold, I have made your face strong over against their faces, and your forehead strong over against their foreheads. [9]I have made your forehead as an adamant harder than flint. Do not fear them. And do not be bowed down by their faces, though they *are*

398 398 4672 834 120 1121 559
1 וַיֹּאמֶר אֵלַי בֶּן־אָדָם אֵת אֲשֶׁר־תִּמְצָא אֱכוֹל אֱכוֹל אֶת־
Eat | .eat | find you | what | ,man | Son of | ,me to | He And said

6605 3478 1004 1696 3212 2088 4039
2 הַמְּגִלָּה הַזֹּאת וְלֵךְ דַּבֵּר אֶל־בֵּית יִשְׂרָאֵל׃ וָאֶפְתַּח אֶת־
I So opened | .Israel | the of house | to | speak | and ,go | ,this | roll the

120 1121 559 2088 4039 398 6310
3 פִּי וַיַּאֲכִלֵנִי אֵת הַמְּגִלָּה הַזֹּאת׃ וַיֹּאמֶר אֵלַי בֶּן־אָדָם
,man | Son of | ,me to | He And said | .that | roll the | He and eat me made | my mouth

2088 4039 4390 4578 398 990
בִּטְנְךָ תַאֲכֵל וּמֵעֶיךָ תְמַלֵּא אֵת הַמְּגִלָּה הַזֹּאת אֲשֶׁר אֲנִי
I | that | this | ,roll the | with | fill | your and bowels | cause ,eat to | your belly

559 4966 1706 6310 1961 398 5414
4 נֹתֵן אֵלֶיךָ וָאֹכְלָה וַתְּהִי בְּפִי כִּדְבַשׁ לְמָתוֹק׃ וַיֹּאמֶר
He And said | for .sweetness | like honey | my in mouth | it and was | I And ;ate | to you | give

1697 1696 3478 1004 935 120/1121
אֵלַי בֶּן־אָדָם לֶךְ־בֹּא אֶל־בֵּית יִשְׂרָאֵל וְדִבַּרְתָּ בִדְבָרַי
My with words | speak and | Israel | the of house | to | !Go Come | ,man | Son of | ,me to

3956 3515 8193 6012 5971 3808
5 אֲלֵיהֶם׃ כִּי לֹא אֶל־עַם עִמְקֵי שָׂפָה וְכִבְדֵי לָשׁוֹן אַתָּה
you | tongue | hard- of ness | and | lip | deep of | a people | to | not | For | .them to

8193 6012 722 7 5971 3808 3478 1004 7971
6 שָׁלוּחַ אֶל־בֵּית יִשְׂרָאֵל׃ לֹא ׀ אֶל־עַמִּים רַבִּים עִמְקֵי שָׂפָה
lip | of deep | many | peoples | to | not | ;Israel | the of house | (but) to | are ,sent

3808 518 1697 8085 3808 3956 3515
וְכִבְדֵי לָשׁוֹן אֲשֶׁר לֹא־תִשְׁמַע דִּבְרֵיהֶם אִם־לֹא אֲלֵיהֶם
them to | rather If | .words | can you hear | not | that | tongue | of and hard a

14 3808 3478 1004 8085 7971
7 שְׁלַחְתִּיךָ הֵמָּה יִשְׁמְעוּ אֵלֶיךָ׃ וּבֵית יִשְׂרָאֵל לֹא יֹאבוּ
is willing | not | Israel | the But of house | to .you | have would listened | they | had I ,you sent

3478 1004 8085 14 8085
לִשְׁמֹעַ אֵלֶיךָ כִּי־אֵינָם אֹבִים לִשְׁמֹעַ אֵלַי כִּי כָּל־בֵּית יִשְׂרָאֵל
,Israel | the of house | all | for ;Me | to listen | are willing | not they | for | to ,you | listen to

2389 6440 5414 2009 3820 7186 4696 2389
8 חִזְקֵי־מֵצַח וּקְשֵׁי־לֵב הֵמָּה׃ הִנֵּה נָתַתִּי אֶת־פָּנֶיךָ חֲזָקִים
strong | your face | have I made | ,Behold | they .(are) | heart | and of hard | fore- —head | strong of

8068 4696 5980 2389 4696 6440 5980
9 לְעֻמַּת פְּנֵיהֶם וְאֶת־מִצְחֲךָ חָזָק לְעֻמַּת מִצְחָם׃ כְּשָׁמִיר
an as adamant | their ;foreheads | over against | strong | your forehead | and | their faces | over against

2865 3808 3372 4696 5414 6864 2389
חָזָק מִצֹּר נָתַתִּי מִצְחֶךָ לֹא־תִירָא אוֹתָם וְלֹא־תֵחַת
be do frightened | And not | .them | fear do | Not | your .forehead | have I made | than flint | harder

a house of rebellion. 10And
He said to me, Son of man,
all My words which I speak
to you, receive into your
heart, and hear with your
ears. 11And go! Come to
the exiles, to the sons of
your people, and speak to
them, and say to them, So
says the Lord Jehovah—
whether they will hear, or
whether they will forbear.
12And the Spirit lifted me
up, and I heard behind me a
sound of a great tumult,
saying, Blessed *be* the glory
of Jehovah from His place;
13and the sound of the
wings of the living creatures
touching each one to the
other; and the sound of the
wheels along with them;
and the sound of a great
tumult. 14So the Spirit lifted
me up and took me, and I
went bitterly in the heat of
my spirit; but the hand of
Jehovah was strong upon
me.
15Then I came to the
exiles at Tel-at-abib, those
dwelling by the river
Chebar. And I sat there
where they were sitting. I
also dwelt there seven
days, being benumbed
among them. 16And it
happened at the end of the
seven days; even it happened
that the word of
Jehovah was to me, saying,
17Son of man, I have made
you a watchman for the
house of Israel. And hear
the word of My mouth, and
warn them from Me. 18In
My saying to the wicked,
Surely you shall die; and
you do not warn him, and
you do not speak to warn
the wicked from his wicked
way, to save his life; he, the
wicked, shall die in his
iniquity. But I will require his
blood at your hand. 19And
you, because you have
warned the wicked, and he
does not turn from his
wickedness or from his
way, he, the wicked, shall

10 מפניהם כי בית מרי המה׃ ויאמר אלי בן־אדם
,man Son of ,me to He And said they rebellion a though their by (are) of house faces

את־כל־דברי אשר אדבר אליך קח בלבבך ובאזניך
with and ears your your into heart receive to you speak I which My all words

11 שמע׃ ולך בא אל־הגולה אל־בני עמך ודברת אליהם
,them to speak and your the to ,people of sons the ,exiles to Come And !go .hear

ואמרת אליהם כה אמר אדני יהוה אם־ישמעו ואם־
or whether they whether hear will —Jehovah the Lord says Thus ,them to say and

12 יחדלו׃ ותשאני רוח ואשמע אחרי קול רעש גדול
,great tumult a a of sound behind me I and heard the ,Spirit lifted And me will they .stop

13 ברוך כבוד־יהוה ממקומו׃ וקול כנפי החיות משיקות
touching living the creatures the of wings the and of sound His from ;place Jehovah the of glory (saying) (be) Blessed

אשה אל־אחותה וקול האופנים לעמתם וקול רעש
a tumult the and of sound with along ,them wheels the the and of sound the other to each one

14 גדול׃ ורוח נשאתני ותקחני ואלך מר בחמת רוחי
my ;spirit the in of heat bitterly I and went took and ,me me lifted the So Spirit .great

15 ויד־יהוה עלי חזקה׃ ואבוא אל־הגולה תל אביב
,aviv Tel- at the ,exiles to I Then came was .strong on me Jehovah the but of hand

הישבים אל־נהר־כבר ואשר המה יושבים שם ואשב
also I dwelt ;there were dwelling they I And sat .Chebar the river by those dwelling

16 שם שבעת ימים משמים בתוכם׃ ויהי מקצה
the at of end it And ,was among .them being appalled days seven there

17 שבעת ימים ויהי דבר־יהוה אלי לאמר׃ בן
Son of ,saying ,me to Jehovah the of word and ,was it ;days seven the

אדם צפה נתתיך לבית ישראל ושמעת מפי דבר
the word My of mouth hear And .Israel the for of house have I you made a watchman ,man

18 והזהרת אותם ממני׃ באמרי לרשע מות תמות ולא
and not shall you —die Surely the to ,wicked My In saying from .Me them warn and

הזהרתו ולא דברת להזהיר רשע מדרכו הרשעה
,wicked the (way) his from ,way the wicked warn to you speak and not warn you ;him

19 להחיתו הוא רשע בעונו ימות ודמו מידך אבקש׃ ואתה
,you And will I .require your at hand his but blood shall ;die his in iniquity the wicked he save to —life his

כי־הזהרת רשע ולא־שב מרשעו ומדרכו הרשעה הוא
he wicked the from or ,way his his from wickedness he turns and not the ,wicked have you warned be- cause

die in his iniquity, but you
have delivered your soul.
[20]And when the righteous
turns from his righteous-
ness, and does injustice,
and I lay a stumbling-block
before him, he shall die.
Since you have not warned
him, he shall die in his sin,
and his righteousness
which he has done shall not
be remembered; but I will
require his blood at your
hand. [21]But you, because
you warned him, the
righteous, so that the
righteous should not sin,
and he does not sin, he
shall surely live because he
is warned; and you have
delivered your soul.
[22]And the hand of
Jehovah was on me there.
And He said to me, Rise up,
go forth into the plain, and I
will speak with you there.
[23]And I rose up and went
forth into the plain. And,
behold, there the glory of
Jehovah was standing, like
the glory which I saw by the
river Chebar. And I fell on
my face. [24]And the Spirit
entered into me, and stood
me on my feet, and spoke
with me. And He said to me,
Come, shut yourself within
your house. [25]But you, son
of man, behold, they shall
put on you cords, and shall
bind you with them; and
you shall not go out among
them. [26]And I will make
your tongue cling to your
palate; and you shall be
dumb; and there shall not
be to them a reproving man.
For they *are* a rebellious
house. [27]But in My
speaking with you, I will
open your mouth, and you
shall say to them, So says
the Lord Jehovah: He who
hears, let him hear; and he
who stops, let him stop. For
they *are* a rebellious house.

6662 7725 53,37 5315 4191 5771
20 בַּעֲוֺנוֹ יָמוּת וְאַתָּה אֶת־נַפְשְׁךָ הִצַּלְתָּ׃ וּבְשׁוּב צַדִּיק
the when And have soul your you but shall his in
righteous turns .delivered ;die iniquity

4191 6440 4383 5414 5766 6213 6664
מִצִּדְקוֹ וְעָשָׂה עָוֶל וְנָתַתִּי מִכְשׁוֹל לְפָנָיו הוּא יָמוּת כִּי
Since shall he before stumbling- a I and in- and his from
.die him block lay justice does righteousness

834 6666 2142 3808 4191 2403 2094 3808
לֹא הִזְהַרְתּוֹ בְּחַטָּאתוֹ יָמוּת וְלֹא תִזָּכַרְןָ צִדְקֹתוֹ אֲשֶׁר
which his be shall and shall he his in have you not
righteousness remembered not ,die sin ,him warned

6662 2094 1245 3027 1818 6213
21 עָשָׂה וְדָמוֹ מִיָּדְךָ אֲבַקֵּשׁ׃ וְאַתָּה כִּי הִזְהַרְתּוֹ צַדִּיק לְבִלְתִּי
that so the warned you because But will I your at his but has he
not ,righteous ,him ,require ,hand blood ;done

2094 2421 2421 2398 6662 2398
חֲטֹא צַדִּיק וְהוּא לֹא־חָטָא חָיוֹ יִחְיֶה כִּי נִזְהָר וְאַתָּה
you and is he because shall he living does not he and the should
,warned ,live sin ,righteous sin

559 3068 3027 8033 5921 1961 5337 5315
22 אֶת־נַפְשְׁךָ הִצַּלְתָּ׃ וַתְּהִי עָלַי שָׁם יַד־יְהוָה וַיֹּאמֶר
He And .Jehovah the there on And have soul your
said of hand me was .delivered

6965 1696 1237 3318/6965
23 אֵלַי קוּם צֵא אֶל־הַבִּקְעָה וְשָׁם אֲדַבֵּר אוֹתָךְ׃ וָאָקוּם
I And with will I and plain the into go Arise to
arose .you speak there forth me

3519 5975 3068 3519 8033 2009 1237 3318
וָאֵצֵא אֶל־הַבִּקְעָה וְהִנֵּה־שָׁם כְּבוֹד־יְהוָה עֹמֵד כַּכָּבוֹד
the like was Jehovah the there and the into went and
glory standing of glory behold ;plain forth

7307 935 6440 5307 3529 5104 7200 834
24 אֲשֶׁר רָאִיתִי עַל־נְהַר־כְּבָר וָאֶפֹּל עַל־פָּנָי׃ וַתָּבֹא־בִי רוּחַ
the into And my on I And .Chebar the by saw I which
Spirit me entered .face fell river

5462 935 559 1696 7272 5975
וַתַּעֲמִדֵנִי עַל־רַגְלָי וַיְדַבֵּר אֹתִי וַיֹּאמֶר אֵלַי בֹּא הִסָּגֵר
shut ,Come ,me to He And with and my on stood and
yourself said .me spoke feet me

5688 5921 5414 120 1121 1004 8432
25 בְּתוֹךְ בֵּיתֶךָ׃ וְאַתָּה בֶן־אָדָם הִנֵּה נָתְנוּ עָלֶיךָ עֲבוֹתִים
cords upon they ,behold ,man son But your within
you put shall of ,you !house

1692 3956 8432 3318 3808 631
26 וַאֲסָרוּךָ בָּהֶם וְלֹא תֵצֵא בְּתוֹכָם׃ וּלְשׁוֹנְךָ אַדְבִּיק אֶל־
to make will I your And among shall you and with shall and
cling tongue .them out go not ,them you bind

4805 1004 3198 376 1961 3808 481 2441
חִכֶּךָ וְנֶאֱלַמְתָּ וְלֹא־תִהְיֶה לָהֶם לְאִישׁ מוֹכִיחַ כִּי בֵּית מְרִי
rebel- a for reproving man a them to shall and shall you and your
lious house be not ;dumb be ,palate

559 6310 6605 854 1696
27 הֵמָּה׃ וּבְדַבְּרִי אוֹתְךָ אֶפְתַּח אֶת־פִּיךָ וְאָמַרְתָּ אֲלֵיהֶם
,them to you and your will I with My in But they
say shall ,mouth open ,you speaking .(are)

2308 2308 8085 8085 3068 136 559 3541
כֹּה אָמַר אֲדֹנָי יְהוִה הַשֹּׁמֵעַ ׀ יִשְׁמָע וְהֶחָדֵל ׀ יֶחְדָּל כִּי
for him let he and him let who He :Jehovah the says Thus
;stop stops who ;hear ,hears Lord

4805 1004
בֵּית מְרִי הֵמָּה׃
they rebellion a
.(are) of house

CHAPTER 4

[1]And you, son of man, take a brick to yourself, and lay it before you, and engrave on it a city — Jerusalem. [2]And lay a siege on it, and build a fort on it, and pour out a rampart on it. And place a camp on it, and set battering rams all around on it. [3]And you, take a griddle of iron to yourself, and place it *as a* wall of iron between you and the city. And place your face against it; and it shall be under siege, and thrust upon it. It is a sign to the house of Israel.

[4]And you, lie down on your left side, and lay the iniquity of the house of Israel on it. The number of the days that you shall lie down on it, you shall bear their iniquity. [5]For I have laid on you the years of their iniquity, according to the number of days: three hundred and ninety days. And you shall bear the house of Israel's iniquity. [6]And when you complete them, even lie on your right side, the second. And you shall bear the house of Judah's iniquity forty days, a day for a year. I have set it for you, a day for a year. [7]And you shall set your face toward the siege of Jerusalem, and your arm bared; and you shall prophesy over it. [8]And, behold, I will put cords on you, and you cannot turn from your side to your *other* side, until you have completed the days of your siege. [9]And you, take to yourself wheat, and barley, and beans, and lentils, and millet, and spelt, and place them in a single

---

CAP. IV. ד

CHAPTER 4

2710	6440		5414	58:43	3947	120 1121	
and engrave	before you	it	lay and	a brick	to take yourself	,man son of	And ,you

וְאַתָּה בֶן־אָדָם קַח־לְךָ לְבֵנָה וְנָתַתָּה אוֹתָהּ לְפָנֶיךָ וְחַקּוֹתָ

| 1129 | 4692 | 5921 | 54:14 | | 3389 | 5892 |
| and build | ,siege a | upon it | lay And | | .Jerusalem | a ,city upon it |

עָלֶיהָ אֶת־יְרוּשָׁלָ͏ִם: וְנָתַתָּה עָלֶיהָ מָצוֹר וּבָנִיתָ

| 4264 | 59:21 | 5414 | 5550 | 8210 | 17:85 |
| ,camp a | upon it | Also place | .ramp a | upon it | poured and out | ,fort a upon it |

עָלֶיהָ דָּיֵק וְשָׁפַכְתָּ עָלֶיהָ סֹלְלָה וְנָתַתָּה עָלֶיהָ מַחֲנוֹת

| 1270 | 4227 | 3947 | 5439 | 3733 | 59:21 | 7760 |
| iron | griddle a of | to take yourself | ,you And | all .around | battering rams | upon it | set and |

וְשִׂים־עָלֶיהָ כָּרִים סָבִיב: וְאַתָּה קַח־לְךָ מַחֲבַת בַּרְזֶל

| 3559 | 5892 | 996 | 996 | 1270 | 7023 | 5414 |
| make And ready | the .city between | and between you | iron (as) | of wall a | it | place and |

וְנָתַתָּה אוֹתָהּ קִיר בַּרְזֶל בֵּינְךָ וּבֵין הָעִיר וַהֲכִינֹתָה אֶת־

| 1004 | 226 | 6696 | 4692 | 1961 | 6440 |
| the to of house | .It sign a | upon and thrust | under siege | It and shall be | against your face |

פָּנֶיךָ אֵלֶיהָ וְהָיְתָה בַמָּצוֹר וְצַרְתָּ עָלֶיהָ אוֹת הִיא לְבֵית

| 7760 | 8042 | 6654 | 7901 | 3478 |
| lay and | ,left the | your side | on lie | And ,you down | .Israel |

יִשְׂרָאֵל: וְאַתָּה שְׁכַב עַל־צִדְּךָ הַשְּׂמָאלִי וְשַׂמְתָּ אֶת־

| 59:21 | 7901 | 3117 | 4587 | 3478 | 1004 | 5771 |
| ,it on shall you down lie | that | days the of number | the ;it on | Israel house the of | the the of iniquity |

עֲוֹן בֵּית־יִשְׂרָאֵל עָלָיו מִסְפַּר הַיָּמִים אֲשֶׁר תִּשְׁכַּב עָלָיו

| 4557 | 5771 | 5414 | 5771 | 5375 |
| the by of number | their ,iniquity | the on of years | have you laid | For I | their .iniquity | shall you bear |

תִּשָּׂא אֶת־עֲוֹנָם: וַאֲנִי נָתַתִּי לְךָ אֶת־שְׁנֵי עֲוֹנָם לְמִסְפַּר

| 3478 | 1004/57:71 | 5375 | 3117 | 8673 | 3967 | 79:69 | 3117 |
| .Israel's | the iniquity of house | So .days you bear shall | day | ninety | hundred three | ,days |

יָמִים שְׁלֹשׁ־מֵאוֹת וְתִשְׁעִים יוֹם וְנָשָׂאתָ עֲוֹן בֵּית־יִשְׂרָאֵל:

| 5375 | 81:45 | 3227 | 6654 | 7901 | 428 | 36:15 |
| you and bear shall | the ;second | right the side | your on even | lie | ,them | when And complete you |

וְכִלִּיתָ אֶת־אֵלֶּה וְשָׁכַבְתָּ עַל־צִדְּךָ הַיְמָנִי שֵׁנִית וְנָשָׂאתָ

| 8141 | 3117 | 8141 | 3117 | 3117 | 705 | 3063 | 1004 | 5771 |
| a for ,year | a day | a for —year | a day | —days | forty | Judah's | the of house | iniquity |

אֶת־עֲוֹן בֵּית־יְהוּדָה אַרְבָּעִים יוֹם יוֹם לַשָּׁנָה יוֹם לַשָּׁנָה

| 2834 | 22:20 | 6440 | 3559 | 3389 | 4692 | 5414 |
| ,bared | your and arm | your ,face set | shall you | Jerusalem | the of siege toward | And .you | have I it set |

נְתַתִּיו לָךְ: וְאֶל־מְצוֹר יְרוּשָׁלַ͏ִם תָּכִין פָּנֶיךָ וּזְרֹעֲךָ חֲשׂוּפָה

| 2015 | 38:08 | 5688 | 59:21 | 5414 | 2009 | 5012 |
| can you turn | and not | ,cords | upon you | will I | place ,behold | upon .it prophesy shall | you and |

וְנִבֵּאתָ עָלֶיהָ: וְהִנֵּה נָתַתִּי עָלַיִךָ עֲבוֹתִים וְלֹא־תֵהָפֵךְ

| 3947 | 4692 | 3117 | 3615 | 5704 | 66:54 | 6654 |
| for take And yourself | ,you | your | the of days | have you until | your completed side (other) | to your from side |

מִצִּדְּךָ אֶל־צִדְּךָ עַד־כַּלּוֹתְךָ יְמֵי מְצוּרֶךָ: וְאַתָּה קַח־לְךָ

| 5414 | 3698 | 17:64 | 5742 | 6321 | 8184 | 24:06 |
| them | place and | spelt and | and | ,lentils and | and | and | ,wheat |

חִטִּין וּשְׂעֹרִים וּפוֹל וַעֲדָשִׁים וְדֹחַן וְכֻסְּמִים וְנָתַתָּה אוֹתָם

| | |
| ,millet | ,beans ,barley |

vessel; and prepare them for yourself into bread; *to* the number of days that you are lying on your side. You shall eat it three hundred and ninety days. [10]And your food which you shall eat *shall be* by weight, twenty shekels a day. From time to time you shall eat it. [11]And you shall drink water by measure, the sixth part of a hin. From time to time you shall drink. [12]And you shall eat cakes of barley; and you shall bake it with dung of the excrement of man, in their sight. [13]And Jehovah said, Even so the sons of Israel shall eat their defiled bread among the nations there where I will drive them. [14]Then I said, Ah, Lord Jehovah! Behold, my soul has not been defiled. I have not even eaten a carcase, or a torn animal, from my youth even until now. And unclean flesh has not come into my mouth. [15]Then He said to me, See, I have given to you the dung of cattle in place of the dung of man. And you shall prepare bread over it.

[16]And He said to me, Son of man, behold, I am breaking the staff of bread in Jerusalem. And they shall eat bread by weight, and with anxiety. And they shall drink water by measure, and in horror, [17]because they will lack bread and water, and each one be horrified with his brother. And *they* will waste away in their iniquity.

CHAPTER 5
[1]And you, son of man, take to yourself a sharp sword, the razor of a barber. Take it to

---

בִּכְלִי אֶחָד וְעָשִׂיתָ אוֹתָם לְךָ לְלֶחֶם מִסְפַּר הַיָּמִים אֲשֶׁר
that   days   the (to)   into   for them   and   single   a in
of number ;bread yourself prepare vessel
3117   4557   3899   6213   259   3627

אַתָּה שׁוֹכֵב עַל־צִדְּךָ שְׁלֹשׁ־מֵאוֹת וְתִשְׁעִים יוֹם תֹּאכְלֶנּוּ:
shall you   ,days ninety and   hundred three   your   on   are   you
.it eat   ,side   lying
398   3117 8673   3967 79.69   6654   7901

10 וּמַאֲכָלְךָ אֲשֶׁר תֹּאכְלֶנּוּ בְּמִשְׁקוֹל עֶשְׂרִים שֶׁקֶל לַיּוֹם מֵעֵת
from   ;day a shekels twenty   weight by   shall you which   your And
time   (be shall)   it eat   food
6256 3117   8255 6242   49.46   398 834   3978

11 עַד־עֵת תֹּאכְלֶנּוּ: וּמַיִם בִּמְשׂוּרָה תִּשְׁתֶּה שִׁשִּׁית הַהִין
;hin a sixth the shall you   measure by   And   shall you   time to
of part   ,drink   water   .it eat
1969 8345   8354   4884   4325   398 5703/5704

12 מֵעֵת עַד־עֵת תִּשְׁתֶּה: וְעֻגַת שְׂעֹרִים תֹּאכְלֶנָּה וְהִיא בְּגֶלְלֵי
with   it and   shall you   ,barley   a And   shall you   time to   from
of dung   .it eat   of cake   .drink   time
1561   398 8184 5692   8354   6256   6256

13 צֵאַת הָאָדָם תְּעֻגֶנָה לְעֵינֵיהֶם: וַיֹּאמֶר יְהוָה כָּכָה
Even   ,Jehovah said And   their in   shall you   man   ex- the
so   .sight   ,it bake   of crement
5080   30:68   5869   5746   120:   6627

יֹאכְלוּ בְנֵי־יִשְׂרָאֵל אֶת־לַחְמָם טָמֵא בַּגּוֹיִם אֲשֶׁר אַדִּיחֵם
will I   where   among   defiled   their   Israel   the   shall
them drive   nations the   bread   of sons   eat
5080   14:71   2931 3899   3478.1121   398

14 שָׁם: וָאֹמַר אֲהָהּ אֲדֹנָי יְהוִה הִנֵּה נַפְשִׁי לֹא מְטֻמָּאָה
been has   not   my   ,Behold !Jehovah Lord   ,Ah   I Then   .there
.defiled   soul   said
2930   38.08 53.15   2009 30:68   136   162   5.59 8033

וּנְבֵלָה וּטְרֵפָה לֹא־אָכַלְתִּי מִנְּעוּרַי וְעַד־עַתָּה וְלֹא־בָא
has   And   .now even   my from   have I   not   torn a or   a Even
come not   until   ,youth   eaten   animal   carcase
935   6258 5704   5271   398   38.08   2966   5038

15 בְּפִי בְּשַׂר פִּגּוּל: וַיֹּאמֶר אֵלַי רְאֵה נָתַתִּי לְךָ אֶת־
to   have I   ,See   to   He Then   .unclean   flesh my into
you   given   ,me   said   mouth
5414   72.00   559   6292   1320 6310

צְפוּעֵי הַבָּקָר תַּחַת גֶּלְלֵי הָאָדָם וְעָשִׂיתָ אֶת־לַחְמְךָ עֲלֵיהֶם:
over   your   you and   ;man dung the   in   cattle   dung the
.it   bread   prepare shall   of   of place   of
5921   3899   62.13 120   1561 8478 12:41 6832

16 וַיֹּאמֶר אֵלַי בֶּן־אָדָם הִנְנִי שֹׁבֵר מַטֵּה־לֶחֶם בִּירוּשָׁלַ͏ִם
.Jerusalem in   bread   the   am   Behold   man Son   ,me to He And
of staff breaking   of   said
3389   3899 4294 7665   2005 120 1121   559

וְאָכְלוּ־לֶחֶם בְּמִשְׁקָל וּבִדְאָגָה וּמַיִם בִּמְשׂוּרָה וּבְשִׂמָּמוֹן
in and   ,measure by   And   with and   weight by   bread they And
horror   water   .anxiety   eat shall
8078   4884   4325   1674   4948   3899   398

17 יִשְׁתּוּ: לְמַעַן יַחְסְרוּ לֶחֶם וָמָיִם וְנָשַׁמּוּ אִישׁ וְאָחִיו
his with   each   be and   and   bread   will they   because shall they
,brother   one   appalled ,water   lack   .drink
251   376   8074   4325 3899   2637   4616   8354

וְנָמַקּוּ בַּעֲוֹנָם:
their in   will and
.iniquity away waste
5771
4743

CAP. V ה

CHAPTER 5

1 וְאַתָּה בֶן־אָדָם קַח־לְךָ חֶרֶב חַדָּה תַּעַר הַגַּלָּבִים תִּקָּחֶנָּה
it take   ;barber a   the   ,sharp sword a   to take   ,man son ,you And
of razor   yourself   of
3947   1534   8593 22.99 2719   3947 120 1121

yourself, and make it pass
over your head and over
your beard. And take to
yourself scales to weigh,
and to divide them out.
[2]You shall burn a third part
in the fire in the midst of the
city, when the days of the
siege are fulfilled. And you
shall take the third part *and*
beat with a sword all around
it. And you shall scatter the
third part into the wind; and
I will draw out a sword after
them. [3]Also you shall take
from there a few in number,
and bind them in your
skirts. [4]And take from them
again, and throw them into
the middle of the fire; and
burn them in the fire. From
it shall come forth a fire into
all the house of Israel.
[5]So says the Lord
Jehovah: This *is* Jerusalem. I have set her in the
midst of the nations; and all
around her *are* the lands.
[6]And she has changed My
judgments for wickedness
more than the nations; and
defiled My laws more than
the lands that *are* all around
her. For they have rejected
My judgments and My
laws; they have not walked
in them. [7]So the Lord
Jehovah says this: Because
you raged more than the
nations that *are* all around
you, not having gone on in
My laws, and not having
done My judgments; and
you have not done according to the judgments of the
nations that *are* all around
you; [8]so Lord Jehovah says
this: behold, I, even I *am*
against you, and will
execute judgments in your
midst in the sight of the
nations. [9]And I will do in
you that which I have not
done, and which I will not
do the like again, for all your
abominations. [10]So the

3976 3947 2206 7218 5674
לְךָ וְהַעֲבַרְתָּ עַל־רֹאשְׁךָ וְעַל־זְקָנֶךָ וְלָקַחְתָּ לְךָ מֹאזְנֵי
scales to take And your and your over make and to
yourself .beard over head pass it yourself

5892 8432 1197 217 7992 2505 4948
2 מִשְׁקָל וְחִלַּקְתָּם׃ שְׁלִשִׁית בָּאוּר תַּבְעִיר בְּתוֹךְ הָעִיר
the the in shall you ,the in third a divide and weigh to
city of midst burn fire part out them

2719 5221 7992 3947 4692 3117 4376
כִּמְלֹאת יְמֵי הַמָּצוֹר וְלָקַחְתָּ אֶת־הַשְּׁלִשִׁית תַּכֶּה בַחֶרֶב
a with beat third the you and the the are when
sword (and) part take shall ;siege of days fulfilled

310 7324 2719 7307 2219 7992 5439
סְבִיבוֹתֶיהָ וְהַשְּׁלִשִׁית תִּזְרֶה לָרוּחַ וְחֶרֶב אָרִיק אַחֲרֵיהֶם׃
.them after will I a and the into shall you the and around all
out draw sword ,wind scatter part third ;it

3671 6696 4557 4592 3947
3 4 וְלָקַחְתָּ מִשָּׁם מְעַט בְּמִסְפָּר וְצַרְתָּ אוֹתָם בִּכְנָפֶיךָ׃ וּמֵהֶם
of And your in them bind and ,number in few a from you Also
them .skirts there take shall

8313 784 8432 7993 3947/5740
עוֹד תִּקָּח וְהִשְׁלַכְתָּ אוֹתָם אֶל־תּוֹךְ הָאֵשׁ וְשָׂרַפְתָּ אֹתָם
them burn and the the into them throw and ,take again
fire of middle

559 3541 3478 1004 3605 784 3318 784
5 בָּאֵשׁ מִמֶּנּוּ תֵצֵא־אֵשׁ אֶל־כָּל־בֵּית יִשְׂרָאֵל׃ כֹּה אָמַר
says Thus .Israel the all into a come shall (for) the in
of house fire forth it from ;fire

5439 7760 1471 8432 3389 3068 136
אֲדֹנָי יְהוִה זֹאת יְרוּשָׁלַםִ בְּתוֹךְ הַגּוֹיִם שַׂמְתִּיהָ וּסְבִיבוֹתֶיהָ
around all and have I the the in .Jerusalem This :Jehovah the
her her set nations of middle (is) Lord

1471 7564 4941 4171 776
6 אֲרָצוֹת׃ וַתֶּמֶר אֶת־מִשְׁפָּטַי לְרִשְׁעָה מִן־הַגּוֹיִם וְאֶת־
and the more for My she And the
,nations than wickedness judgments changed has .lands

3988 4941 5439 776 2708
חֻקּוֹתַי מִן־הָאֲרָצוֹת אֲשֶׁר סְבִיבוֹתֶיהָ כִּי בְמִשְׁפָּטַי מָאָסוּ
have they My for around all that the more My
rejected judgments ;her (are) lands than laws

3068 136 559 3541 1980 2708
7 וְחֻקּוֹתַי לֹא־הָלְכוּ בָהֶם׃ לָכֵן כֹּה־אָמַר אֲדֹנָי יְהוִה
:Jehovah the says thus Therefore in have they not My and
Lord .them walked ;laws

3808 2708 5439 1471 1995
יַעַן הֲמָנְכֶם מִן־הַגּוֹיִם אֲשֶׁר סְבִיבוֹתֵיכֶם בְּחֻקּוֹתַי לֹא
not in (and) around all that the more you Because
laws My ,you (are) nations than multiplied

1471 4941 6213 3808 4941 1980
הֲלַכְתֶּם וְאֶת־מִשְׁפָּטַי לֹא עֲשִׂיתֶם וּכְמִשְׁפְּטֵי הַגּוֹיִם אֲשֶׁר
that the the as and have not My and have
(are) nations of judgments ,performed judgments ,walked

3068 136 559 3541 6213 3808 5439
8 סְבִיבוֹתֵיכֶם לֹא עֲשִׂיתֶם׃ לָכֵן כֹּה אָמַר אֲדֹנָי יְהוִה
,Jehovah the says thus ,therefore have you not around all
Lord ;done you

1471 5869 4941 8432 6213 1571 2005
הִנְנִי עָלַיִךְ גַּם־אָנִי וְעָשִׂיתִי בְתוֹכֵךְ מִשְׁפָּטִים לְעֵינֵי הַגּוֹיִם׃
the the in judgments your in will and ,I even (am) ,Behold
.nations of sight midst execute ,you against ,I

6213 3808 834 6213 834 6213
9 וְעָשִׂיתִי בָךְ אֵת אֲשֶׁר לֹא־עָשִׂיתִי וְאֵת אֲשֶׁר־לֹא־אֶעֱשֶׂה
will I not which and have I not that in I And
do ,done which you do will

398 3651 8441 3605 3282 5750 3644
10 כָּמֹהוּ עוֹד יַעַן כָּל־תּוֹעֲבֹתָיִךְ׃ לָכֵן אָבוֹת יֹאכְלוּ
shall the ,Therefore your all for ,again like the
eat fathers .abominations it of

fathers shall eat the sons in your midst; and the sons shall eat their fathers. And I will execute judgments against you, and I will scatter the whole remnant of you into every wind. [11]Therefore, as I live, says the Lord Jehovah, Surely because you have defiled My sanctuary with all your idolatries and with all your abominations, so I also will withdraw. And My eye shall not spare, and I will not have pity.

[12]A third part of you shall die by the plague, and shall be consumed by the famine in your midst. And a third part shall fall by the sword all around you; and a third part I will scatter into every wind; and I will draw out a sword after them. [13]And My anger shall be spent, and I will make My fury rest on them, and I will be eased. And they shall know that I, Jehovah, have spoken in My zeal, in My fulfilling My fury among them. [14]And I will make you into a waste and a reproach among the nations that are around you; in the eyes of all who pass by. [15]And it shall be a reproach and a taunt, an example and a wonder, to the nations whcih are all around you, when I shall execute against you judgments in anger and in fury and in rebukes among them. I, Jehovah, have spoken it. [16]When I shall send the arrows of evil famine among them, which shall be for ruin, for which I will send them to destroy you; even I will increase the famine on you, and break the staff of bread to you. [17]Yea, I will send famine and evil beasts on you; and you will be bereaved. And pestilence and blood shall pass among you; and I shall bring a sword on you. I, Jehovah, have spoken.

1121	84:32	1121	398	1	6213	8201.
the	sons	in	the	and	shall	their	I And	judgments against
בָּנִ֣ים	בְּתוֹכֵ֔ךְ	וּבָנִ֖ים	יֹאכְל֣וּ	אֲבוֹתָ֑ם	וְעָשִׂ֤יתִי	בָ֨ךְ֙ שְׁפָטִ֔ים

| the | sons | midst, | the and | eat | sons | fathers, | do will | you |

3219	3605	7611	1360 5	7307	36:51	2416	~5002
וְזֵרִיתִ֥י	אֶת־כָּל־שְׁאֵרִיתֵ֖ךְ	לְכָל־ר֑וּחַ	לָכֵ֤ן חַי־אָ֨נִי֙	נְאֻ֗ם
scatter will	of remnant the whole	wind into	Therefore, live I	(as) says

.136	3068	518	38:08	47.20	2930	3605	8251
אֲדֹנָ֣י	יְהוִ֔ה	אִם־לֹ֗א	יַ֚עַן	אֶת־מִקְדָּשִׁ֣י	טִמֵּ֔את	בְּכָל־שִׁקּוּצַ֖יִךְ
the Lord	Jehovah,	Surely	because	sanctuary My	defiled have you	with your idolatries all

3605	8441	1571	1639	38:08	2347	5869
וּבְכָל־תּוֹעֲבֹתָ֑יִךְ	וְגַם־אֲנִ֗י	אֶגְרַ֛ע	וְלֹא־תָח֥וֹס	עֵינִ֖י	וְגַם־אֲנִ֥י
abominations your and with	also I so	will I draw.	not spare shall	eye My	And (you) I

3808	2550	7992	1698	4191	7458	3615
לֹ֥א	אֶחְמֽוֹל׃ 12	שְׁלִשִׁיתֵ֞ךְ	בַּדֶּ֤בֶר	יָמ֨וּתוּ֙	וּבָרָעָ֣ב	יִכְל֣וּ
not	pity. A third	you of part	plague the by	die shall,	famine and by	consumed be shall

8432	5439	2719	5307	2719	7992
בְּתוֹכֵ֔ךְ	וְהַשְּׁלִשִׁית֙	בַּחֶ֣רֶב	יִפְּל֣וּ	סְבִיבוֹתָ֑יִךְ	וְהַשְּׁלִישִׁ֨ית
midst. your in	part third And	sword the by	fall shall	you, around	part a and third

1360 5	7307	32:19	2719	7324	310	3615	.639	51,17
לְכָל־ר֣וּחַ	אֱזָרֶ֔ה	וְחֶ֖רֶב	אָרִ֣יק	אַחֲרֵיהֶֽם׃	וְכָלָ֣ה	אַפִּ֗י	וַהֲנִחֹתִ֤י
wind into	scatter will I and	sword a	out draw will I	.them after	spent be shall anger My	So will I and rest make

2534	5162	3045	3068	30:68	1696	7068
חֲמָתִ֥י	בָּ֔ם	וְהִנֶּחַמְתִּי֒	וְֽיָדְע֗וּ	כִּֽי־אֲנִ֤י	יְהוָה֙	דִּבַּ֔רְתִּי	בְּקִנְאָתִ֑י
fury My	them, on	be eased will I and	know shall they And	that I	Jehovah	spoken have	zeal, My in

3615	2534	5414	2723	2781	1471
בְּכַלּוֹתִ֥י	חֲמָתִ֖י	בָּֽם׃	וְאֶתְּנֵךְ֙	לְחָרְבָּ֣ה	וּלְחֶרְפָּ֔ה	בַּגּוֹיִ֖ם
fulfilling My in	fury My	them, on	will I And	waste into a	reproach a and	nations the among

5439	5869	36:05	5674	19 /61	2781	1422
אֲשֶׁ֣ר	סְבִיבוֹתָ֑יִךְ	לְעֵינֵ֖י	כָּל־עוֹבֵֽר׃	וְֽהָיְתָ֨ה	חֶרְפָּ֤ה וּגְדוּפָה֙
that (are)	you, around	eyes of the in	.by pass who all	it So be shall	reproach a and taunt a

4148	49.23	1471	834	5439	.6213
מוּסָ֣ר	וּמְשַׁמָּ֔ה	לַגּוֹיִ֖ם	אֲשֶׁ֣ר	סְבִיבוֹתָ֑יִךְ	בַּעֲשׂוֹתִי֩	בָ֨ךְ
example an	wonder a and	nations the to	which (are)	you, around	when I shall	you against

8201.	639	2534	8433	3068	1696
שְׁפָטִ֜ים	בְּאַ֤ף	וּבְחֵמָה֙	וּבְתֹכְח֣וֹת	חֵמָ֔ה אֲנִ֥י	יְהוָ֖ה	דִּבַּֽרְתִּי׃
judgments in	anger in	fury and in	rebukes in and	them. fury (among) I	Jehovah	spoken (it). have

7971.	2671	74:58	7451	834	1961	4889.
בְּשַׁלְּחִ֣י	אֶת־חִצֵּי֩	הָרָעָ֨ב הָרָעִ֤ים	בָּהֶם֙	אֲשֶׁ֣ר הָי֣וּ	לְמַשְׁחִ֔ית
send shall I When	of arrows the	famine evil	them, against	which shall be	ruin, for

5921.	3254	7458	7843	7971.	834
אֲשֶׁר־אֲשַׁלַּ֥ח	אוֹתָ֖ם	לְשַׁחֶתְכֶ֑ם	וְרָעָ֗ב אֹסֵ֤ף	עֲלֵיכֶ֔ם
you upon will I the and	destroy to them;	them will I for which	famine increase	you, upon

2476	74:58	7971	3899.	4294	7665
וְשָׁבַרְתִּ֥י	לָכֶ֖ם	מַטֵּה־לָֽחֶם׃	וְשִׁלַּחְתִּ֣י	עֲלֵיכֶ֡ם	רָעָ֣ב וְחַיָּ֣ה
and famine	you on	I, yea	bread the	of staff	you to	break and beasts

935	2719.	5674	1818	1198	7921.	7451.
רָעָ֣ה וְשִׁכְּלֻ֗ךְ	וְדֶ֤בֶר וָדָם֙	יַעֲבָר־בָּ֔ךְ	וְחֶ֖רֶב	אָבִ֣יא עָלָ֑יִךְ	אֲנִ֖י
I	upon shall I	a and	among shall	and	and will you and, evil
.you bring sword you; pass blood pestilence ;bereft be

1696	3068
יְהוָ֖ה	דִּבַּֽרְתִּי׃
have Jehovah	.spoken

CAP. VI ו

CHAPTER 6

1 2 וַיְהִי דְבַר־יְהוָה אֵלַי לֵאמֹר׃ בֶּן־אָדָם שִׂים פָּנֶיךָ אֶל־הָרֵי

the towards your set ,man Son ,saying ,me to Jehovah the it And of mountains face of of word (was)

3 יִשְׂרָאֵל וְהִנָּבֵא אֲלֵיהֶם׃ וְאָמַרְתָּ הָרֵי יִשְׂרָאֵל שִׁמְעוּ דְּבַר

word the hear ,Israel Mountains ,say And against and ,Israel of of .them prophesy

אֲדֹנָי יְהוִה כֹּה־אָמַר אֲדֹנָי יְהוִה לֶהָרִים וְלַגְּבָעוֹת לָאֲפִיקִים

the to the to and the to Jehovah the says Thus :Jehovah the ravines ,hills ,mountains Lord Lord

וְלַגֵּאָיוֹת הִנְנִי אֲנִי מֵבִיא עֲלֵיכֶם חֶרֶב וְאִבַּדְתִּי בָּמוֹתֵיכֶם׃

high your I and a you upon will I ,Behold to and places destroy will ,sword bring :valleys the

4 וְנָשַׁמּוּ מִזְבְּחוֹתֵיכֶם וְנִשְׁבְּרוּ חַמָּנֵיכֶם וְהִפַּלְתִּי חַלְלֵיכֶם

slain your will I And your shall and ,altars your shall And fall to cause .pillars broken be ruined be

5 לִפְנֵי גִּלּוּלֵיכֶם׃ וְנָתַתִּי אֶת־פִּגְרֵי בְּנֵי יִשְׂרָאֵל לִפְנֵי גִּלּוּלֵיהֶם

their before Israel the dead the I And .idols your before ;idols of sons of bodies put will

6 וְזֵרִיתִי אֶת־עַצְמוֹתֵיכֶם סְבִיבוֹת מִזְבְּחוֹתֵיכֶם׃ בְּכֹל

all In .altars your around bones your I and scatter will

מוֹשְׁבוֹתֵיכֶם הֶעָרִים תֶּחֱרַבְנָה וְהַבָּמוֹת תִּישָׁמְנָה לְמַעַן

that so be shall the and be shall cities the dwelling- your ,deserted places high ,waste laid places

יֶחֶרְבוּ וְיֶאְשְׁמוּ מִזְבְּחוֹתֵיכֶם וְנִשְׁבְּרוּ וְנִשְׁבְּתוּ גִּלּוּלֵיכֶם

,idols your brought and be may and ,altars your become and be may end an to broken guilty waste laid

7 וְנִגְדְּעוּ חַמָּנֵיכֶם וְנִמְחוּ מַעֲשֵׂיכֶם׃ וְנָפַל חָלָל בְּתוֹכְכֶם

your in the And .works your and pillars your may and ,midst slain fall shall out wiped down cut be

8 וִידַעְתֶּם כִּי־אֲנִי יְהוָה׃ וְהוֹתַרְתִּי בִּהְיוֹת לָכֶם פְּלִיטֵי חֶרֶב

the escapees you to that so will I Yet .Jehovah I that you and sword of be may excess an leave (am) know shall

9 בַּגּוֹיִם בְּהִזָּרוֹתֵיכֶם בָּאֲרָצוֹת׃ וְזָכְרוּ פְלִיטֵיכֶם אוֹתִי בַּגּוֹיִם

among Me your shall And the among your in the among nations the escapees remember .lands scattering ,nations

אֲשֶׁר נִשְׁבּוּ־שָׁם אֲשֶׁר נִשְׁבַּרְתִּי אֶת־לִבָּם הַזּוֹנֶה אֲשֶׁר

which whoring their (by) was I because be will they where heart broken ,captive made

סָר מֵעָלַי וְאֵת עֵינֵיהֶם הַזֹּנוֹת אַחֲרֵי גִּלּוּלֵיהֶם וְנָקֹטּוּ

they And their after go which their and from has loathe shall .idols whoring eyes by ,Me turned

בִּפְנֵיהֶם אֶל־הָרָעוֹת אֲשֶׁר עָשׂוּ לְכֹל תּוֹעֲבֹתֵיהֶם׃ וְיָדְעוּ 10

they And their all in they which the for their against know shall .abominations done have evils faces

כִּי־אֲנִי יְהוָה לֹא אֶל־חִנָּם דִּבַּרְתִּי לַעֲשׂוֹת לָהֶם הָרָעָה

evil to do to have I vain in not ;Jehovah I that them said (am)

CHAPTER 6

[1]And it happened, the word of Jehovah was to me, saying, [2]Son of man, set your face towards the mountains of Israel, and prophesy against them. [3]And say, Mountains of Israel, hear the word of the Lord Jehovah: So says the Lord Jehovah to the mountains, and to the hills, to the ravines, and to the valleys, Behold, I will bring a sword on you, and I will destroy your high places. [4]And your altars shall be ruined, and your pillars shall be broken. And I will make fall your slain before your idols. [5]And I will put the dead bodies of the sons of Israel before their idols; and I will scatter your bones around your altars. [6]In all your dwelling-places the cities shall be laid waste, and the high places shall be deserted; so that your altars may be laid waste and become guilty; and your idols may be broken and brought to an end; and your pillars may be cut down, and your works wiped out. [7]And the slain shall fall in your midst; and you shall know that I *am* Jehovah.

[8]Yet I will leave a remainder, so that may be *left* to you those who escape the sword among the nations, in your scattering among the lands. [9]And those who escape shall remember Me among the nations where they will be made captive, because I was broken *by* their whoring heart which has turned away from Me, and by their whoring eyes which go after their idols. And they shall loathe against their faces for the evils which they have done in all their abominations. [10]And they shall know that I *am* Jehovah; not in vain have I said to do this evil to them.

11So says the Lord Jehovah: Strike with your hand, and stamp with your foot, and say, Alas for all the evil abominations of the house of Israel! For they shall fall by the sword, by the famine, and by the plague. **12**He who is far off shall die by the plague; and he who is near shall fall by the sword; and he who remains and is besieged shall die by the famine. So I will fulfill My fury on them. **13**And you shall know that I *am* Jehovah when their slain shall be in the midst of their idols all around their altars, on every high hill, in all the tops of the mountains, and under every green tree, and under every leafy oak; the place where they offered there a soothing aroma to all their idols. **14**And I will stretch out My hand on them and make the land a desolation, even more desolate than the desert toward Diblath, in all their dwelling-places. And they shall know that I *am* Jehovah.

2088		559	.3068 136	52\21	⸢3709	7554	
11 כֹּה־אָמַר אֲדֹנָי יְהוִֹה הַכֵּה בְכַפְּךָ וּרְקַע							
.this		Thus says	the Jehovah: Strike	with hand your	and stamp		
.Lord							

7272 | 559 | 253 | 3605 | 8441 | 7451 | 1004 | 3478
בְּרַגְלְךָ וֶאֱמָר־אָח אֶל כָּל־תּוֹעֲבוֹת רָעוֹת בֵּית יִשְׂרָאֵל
with your ,foot | ,say and Alas | for all | the abomina- tions | the evil | of house of | Israel!

2719 | 7458 | 1698 | 7350 | 1698 | 4191.
12 אֲשֶׁר כְּחֶרֶב בְּרָעָב וּבַדֶּבֶר יִפֹּלוּ: הָרָחוֹק בַּדֶּבֶר יָמוּת
For | the by sword | the by plague | He who | shall they fall | by and ,plague the | is off far | shall .die

7138 | 2719 | 530:7 | 7458 | 7604 | 5341 | 4191 | 3615
וְהַקָּרוֹב בַּחֶרֶב יִפּוֹל וְהַנִּשְׁאָר וְהַנָּצוּר בְּרָעָב יָמוּת וְכִלֵּיתִי
and he | who near is | shall fall | the by sword | he and remains who | and besieged | the by famine | shall .die | So I fulfill will

2534 | | | | | | 8432 2491:
חֲמָתִי בָּם: וִידַעְתֶּם כִּי־אֲנִי יְהוָֹה בִּהְיוֹת חַלְלֵיהֶם בְּתוֹךְ
My fury | on .them | And you know shall | that I (am) | ,Jehovah | when shall be | their slain | shall the in of midst

3045 | 154:4 | 5439 | 4196 | 3605 | 13\89 | 73\11 | 3605
גִּלּוּלֵיהֶם סְבִיבוֹת מִזְבְּחוֹתֵיהֶם אֶל כָּל־גִּבְעָה רָמָה בְּכֹל
their idols | all around | their altars | on every | hill | ,high | in all

7218 | 2022 | 8478 | 3605 6086 | 7488 | 8478 | 3605 424 | 56:87
13 רָאשֵׁי הֶהָרִים וְתַחַת כָּל־עֵץ רַעֲנָן וְתַחַת כָּל־אֵלָה עֲבֻתָּה
the | the ,mountains of tops | and under | every green tree | ,green | and under | oak every | ,leafy

4725 | 5414 | 7381 | 52:07 | 360:5 | 1544 | 5186
14 מְקוֹם אֲשֶׁר נָתְנוּ־שָׁם רֵיחַ נִיחֹחַ לְכֹל גִּלּוּלֵיהֶם: וְנָטִיתִי
the place | where they offered | there | an soothing aroma | to all | their .idols | So I stretch out will

3027 | 5921 | 5414 | | 8077 | 776 | 4923 | 4057
אֶת־יָדִי עֲלֵיהֶם וְנָתַתִּי אֶת־הָאָרֶץ שְׁמָמָה וּמְשַׁמָּה מִמִּדְבַּר
My hand | upon them and | make | the land | ,desolation | a more even desolate, | than the desert

3068 | 3045 | 4186 | 1689
דִּבְלָתָה בְּכֹל מוֹשְׁבוֹתֵיהֶם וְיָדְעוּ כִּי־אֲנִי יְהוָֹה:
,Diblath | all in | their dwelling- places. | And they know shall (am) | I that | .Jehovah

CAP. VII ז

CHAPTER 7

CHAPTER 7
1And it happened, the word of Jehovah was to me, saying, **2**And you, son of man, so says the Lord Jehovah to the land of Israel: An end! The end has come on the four corners of the land. **3**The end *is* now on you, and I will send My anger on you, and will judge you according to your ways, and will lay on you all your abominations. **4**And My eye shall not spare you, and I will not have pity. But I will lay your ways on you, and your abominations shall be in your midst; and you shall know that I *am* Jehovah.

1961 | 1697 | 3068 | | 1121 | 120: | 559
1 וַיְהִי דְבַר־יְהוָֹה אֵלַי לֵאמֹר: וְאַתָּה בֶן־אָדָם כֹּה־אָמַר
it And was | the of word | Jehovah | ,me to | ,saying | And ,you | son man of | Thus says

136 | 3068 | 127 | 3478 | 7093 | 935 | 776 | 5921 702
2 אֲדֹנָי יְהוִֹה לְאַדְמַת יִשְׂרָאֵל קֵץ בָּא הַקֵּץ עַל־אַרְבַּעַת
the Lord | Jehovah | the to of land | :Israel | An end | has come | The end | on the four

3671 | 776 | 6258 | 7093 | 5921 | 7971 | 639 | ⸢
3 כַּנְפוֹת הָאָרֶץ: עַתָּה הַקֵּץ עָלַיִךְ וְשִׁלַּחְתִּי אַפִּי בָּךְ
corners of | the .land | Now | end (is) | the ,you on | send will | anger My | you on

8199 | 1870 | 5414 | 3605 | 1870 | 8441 | 108\38
4 וּשְׁפַטְתִּיךְ כִּדְרָכָיִךְ וְנָתַתִּי עָלַיִךְ אֵת כָּל־תּוֹעֲבוֹתָיִךְ: וְלֹא
and I judge you | to according ways your | and lay will | upon you | all | .abominations your | And not

2347 | 5869 | 5921 | 3808 | 2550 | 3588 | 1870 | 5921 | 59\21 1870 | 54·14
5 תָחוֹס עֵינִי עָלַיִךְ וְלֹא אֶחְמוֹל כִּי דְרָכַיִךְ עָלַיִךְ אֶתֵּן
shall My spare eye | ,you upon | not pity have | and | will I | ,But your ways | upon you | will I .lay

8441 | 1961 | 8432 | 3045 | 3605 | 3068
וְתוֹעֲבוֹתַיִךְ בְּתוֹכֵךְ תִּהְיֶין וִידַעְתֶּם כִּי־אֲנִי יְהוָֹה:
and abominations your | your in midst | ;be shall | you and know shall | I that (am) | .Jehovah

[5]So says the Lord
Jehovah: An evil! An only
evil! Behold, it has come!
[6]An end has come; the end
has come! It has awakened
against you; behold, it has
come! [7]The encirclement
has come to you, O
dwellers of the land. The
time has come; the day of
tumult is near, and not a
shout of the hills. [8]Now I
will soon pour out My fury
on you, and fulfill My anger
on you. And I will judge you
according to your ways, and
will put on you all your
abominations. [9]And My
eye shall not spare, and I
will not have pity; I will put
on you according to your
ways, and your abomina-
tions that are in your midst.
And you shall know that I
am Jehovah who strikes.
[10]Behold the day! Be-
hold, it has come; the
encirclement has gone out;
the rod has blossomed;
pride has budded.
[11]Violence has risen for a
rod of wickedness. None of
them *shall remain*, even
none of their multitude, and
none of their riches, and
none eminent among them.
[12]The time has come; the
day has arrived. Do not let
the buyer rejoice, and do
not let the sellers mourn; for
wrath *is* on all her multitude. [13]For the seller shall
not return to that which is
sold, although they still are
among the living—for the
vision *is* to all her multitude;
and a man shall not return
to his iniquity; his life shall
not hold strong. [14]They
have blown the trumpet,
even to make all ready. But
no one goes to the battle;
for My wrath *is* on all her
multitude. [15]The sword *is*
outside, and the plague,
and the famine *are* inside.
He who *is* in the field shall
die with the sword; and he
who *is* in the city, famine
and plague shall devour
him.
[16]But *if* their fugitives
shall escape, then *they*
shall be on the mountains
like doves of the valleys, all
of them mourning, each for

5 6 7093 935 2009 7451 259 7451 3068 136 559 3541
כה אמר אדני יהוה רעה אחת רעה הנה באה׃ קץ
An has it ,Behold !evil an An :Jehovah the says Thus
end !come only :evil Lord

7 6843 935 935 2009 6974 7093 935 935
בא בא הקץ הקיץ אליך הנה באה׃ באה הצפירה
encircle- the Has has it ,behold against has It the has has
ment come .come you awakened .end come ,come

1906 4103 3117 7138 6256 935 776 3427
אליך יושב הארץ בא העת קרוב היום מהומה ולא הד
a and tumult day the is the Has the O ,you to
of shout not of near ,time come .land of dwellers

8 639 3615 2534 8210 7138 6258 2022
הרים׃ עתה מקרוב אשפוך חמתי עליך וכליתי אפי בך
on My and ,you on My will I soon Now the
.you anger fulfill fury out pour .hills

9 3808 8441 3605 5414 1870 8199
ושפטתיך כדרכיך ונתתי עליך את כל תועבותיך׃ ולא
And your all you on and to according will I And
not .abominations put will ways your you judge

8441 5414 5921 1870 2550 3808 5869 2347
תחוס עיני ולא אחמול כדרכיך עליך אתן ותועבותיך
your and will I you on to according will I and My shall
abominations ,put ways your ;pity have not ,eye spare

10 3117 2009 5221 3068 3045 1961 8432
בתוכך תהיין וידעתם כי אני יהוה מכה׃ הנה היום
the Behold who Jehovah I that you And that your in
!day .strikes (am) know shall .are midst

11 2555 2087 6524 4294 6692 6843 3318 935 2009
הנה באה יצאה הצפרה צץ המטה פרח הזדון׃ החמס
Violence .pride has ;rod the has the gone has has it ,Behold
budded blossomed ;circling out ;come

1992 3808 1995 3808 7562 4294 6965
קם למטה רשע לא מהם ולא מהמונם ולא מהמהם
their of and their of and them of None wicked- a for has
riches none ;multitude none (;remain shall) .ness of rod risen

12 8056 408 7069 3117 5060 6256 935 1992 5089
ולא נה בהם׃ בא העת הגיע היום הקונה אל ישמח
Let not the the has The has among none and
,rejoice buyer .day arrived ;time come .them eminent

13 4376 4995 3605 2740 56 4376
והמוכר אל יתאבל כי חרון אל כל המונה׃ כי המוכר
the For her all on wrath for let not the and
seller .multitude (is) ;mourn sellers

3605 2377 2416 5750 7725 3808 4465
אל הממכר לא ישוב ועוד בחיים חיתם כי חזון אל כל
all to the for they among although shall not which that to
vision living the still ,return sold is

14 8628 2388 2416 5771 376 7725 3808 1995
המונה לא ישוב ואיש בעונו חיתו לא יתחזקו׃ תקעו
have They hold shall not his his in a and shall not her
blown .strong life iniquity man return multitude

2740 4421 1980 369 3605 3559 8628
בתקוע והכין הכל ואין הלך למלחמה כי חרוני אל
on My for ,battle the to goes but ;all to even the
(is) wrath none ready make ,trumpet

15 834 1004 7458 1698 2351 2719 1995
כל המונה׃ החרב בחוץ והדבר והרעב מבית אשר
He (are) the and the and (is) The her all
(is) who ,inside famine plague ,outside sword .multitude

398 1698 7458 5892 834 4191 2719 7704
בשדה בחרב ימות ואשר בעיר רעב ודבר יאכלנו׃
devour shall and (the) the in he and shall the with the in
.him plague famine city (is) who ;die sword field

16 1993 3605 1516 3123 2022 1961 6412 6403
ופלטו פליטיהם והיו אל ההרים כיוני הגאיות כלם המות
,mourning of all the like the on then their (if) But
them ,valleys of doves mountains be shall fugitives escape

his iniquity. 17All hands
shall be feeble, and all
knees shall go *as* water.
18They shall also gird *on*
sackcloth, and trembling
shall cover them. And
shame *shall be* on all faces,
and baldness on all heads.
19They shall throw their
silver in the streets, and
their gold shall be an
impure thing. Their silver
and their gold shall not be
able to deliver them in the
day of the wrath of Jehovah.
They shall not satisfy their
soul, and they shall not fill
their bowels; for their
iniquity has become a
stumbling-block for *them*.
20And the beauty of His
ornament, He set it in
majesty. But they made it
the images of their abominations, and of their hateful
things. Therefore, I have put
it to them as an impure
thing. 21And I will also
give it into the hand of the
strangers for a prize; and to
the wicked of the earth for a
spoil; and they shall defile
it. 22I also will turn My
face from them, and they
shall defile My hidden
place. And violent ones
shall enter into it and defile
it.

23Make the chain; for the
land is full of bloody
judgments, and the city is
full of violence. 24And I
will bring the evil of the
nations, and they shall
possess their houses. And I
will make cease the pomp
of the strong ones; and their
holy places shall be defiled.
25Anguish comes! And they
shall seek peace, but none
shall be. 26Disaster on
disaster shall come, and
rumor to rumor shall be.
And they shall seek a vision
from the prophet; but the
law shall perish from the
priest, and counsel from the
elders. 27The king shall
mourn, and the ruler shall
be clothed with despair.
And the hands of the
people of the land shall be
terrified. According to their
way, I will do to them; and
according to their judg-
ments, I will judge them.
And they shall know that I
am Jehovah.

4325 1980 1290 3605 7503 3027 3605 5771 376
17 אִישׁ בַּעֲוֺנוֹ׃ כָּל־הַיָּדַיִם תִּרְפֶּינָה וְכָל־בִּרְכַּיִם תֵּלַכְנָה מָּיִם׃
.water shall knees and be shall hands All his for each
(as) go all feeble .iniquity

995 6440 3605 6427 3680 8242 2296
18 וְחָגְרוּ שַׂקִּים וְכִסְּתָה אוֹתָם פַּלָּצוּת וְאֶל כָּל־פָּנִים בּוּשָׁה
shame faces all and ;trembling them shall and sack- also They
(be shall) on cover ,cloth gird shall

2091 7993 2351 3701 7142 7218 3605
19 וּבְכָל־רָאשֵׁיהֶם קָרְחָה׃ כַּסְפָּם בַּחוּצוֹת יַשְׁלִיכוּ וּזְהָבָם
their and shall They the in their .baldness their on and
gold ,throw streets silver heads all

5678 3117 5337 3201 3808 2091 3701 1961 5079
לְנִדָּה יִהְיֶה כַּסְפָּם וּזְהָבָם לֹא־יוּכַל לְהַצִּילָם בְּיוֹם עֶבְרַת
the the in deliver to be shall not their and Their shall impure an
of wrath of day them able gold silver .be thing

4383 4390 3808 4578 7646 3808 5315 3068
יְהוָה נַפְשָׁם לֹא יְשַׂבֵּעוּ וּמֵעֵיהֶם לֹא יְמַלֵּאוּ כִּי־מִכְשׁוֹל
stum- a for shall they not their and shall They not their .Jehovah
block bling ,fill bowels satisfy soul

8441 6754 7760 1347 5716 6643 1961 5771
20 עֲוֺנָם הָיָה׃ וּצְבִי עֶדְיוֹ לְגָאוֹן שָׂמָהוּ וְצַלְמֵי תוֹעֲבֹתָם
their the But set He in his the And has in- their
abominations of images .it majesty ,ornament of beauty .become quity

5414 5079 5414 6213 8251
21 שִׁקּוּצֵיהֶם עָשׂוּ בוֹ עַל־כֵּן נְתַתִּיו לָהֶם לְנִדָּה׃ וּנְתַתִּיו
will I And an as to have I therefore with they their of and
it give .thing impure them it put ;it made things hateful

5437 2490 7998 776 7563 957 2114 3027
22 בְּיַד־הַזָּרִים לָבַז וּלְרִשְׁעֵי הָאָרֶץ לְשָׁלָל וְחִלְּלוּהָ׃ וַהֲסִבּוֹתִי
will I shall they and a for the the to and a for the the into
turn also .it defile ,spoil earth of wicked ,prize strangers of hand

2490 6530 935 6845 2490 6440
פָנַי מֵהֶם וְחִלְּלוּ אֶת־צְפוּנִי וּבָאוּ־בָהּ פָּרִיצִים וְחִלְּלוּהָ׃
defile and violent into shall and hidden My they and from My
.it ones it enter ;(place) defile shall ,them face

4390 5892 1818 4941 4390 776 7569 6213
23 עֲשֵׂה הָרַתּוֹק כִּי הָאָרֶץ מָלְאָה מִשְׁפַּט דָּמִים וְהָעִיר מָלְאָה
full is the and ,bloody of full is the for the Make
city judgments land ;chain

7673 1004 3423 1471 7451 935 2555
24 חָמָס׃ וְהֵבֵאתִי רָעֵי גוֹיִם וְיָרְשׁוּ אֶת־בָּתֵּיהֶם וְהִשְׁבַּתִּי
will I And .houses their they and the the will I And of
cease make possess shall ,nations of evil come make .violence

7965 1245 935 7089 6942 2490 5794 1347
25 גְּאוֹן עַזִּים וְנִחֲלוּ מְקַדְשֵׁיהֶם׃ קְפָדָה־בָא וּבִקְשׁוּ שָׁלוֹם
,peace they and ;comes Anguish holy their be shall and the the
seek shall .places defiled ;strong of pomp

1961 8052 8052 935 1943 1943 369
26 וָאָיִן׃ הֹוָה עַל־הֹוָה תָּבוֹא וּשְׁמֻעָה אֶל־שְׁמוּעָה תִּהְיֶה
.be shall rumor to rumor and shall disaster upon Disaster but
,come .none

2205 6098 3548 6 8451 5030 2377 1245
וּבִקְשׁוּ חָזוֹן מִנָּבִיא וְתוֹרָה תֹּאבַד מִכֹּהֵן וְעֵצָה מִזְּקֵנִים׃
the from and the from shall the but the from a they And
.elders counsel ,priest perish law ;prophet vision seek shall

776 5971 3027 8077 3847 5387 56 4428
27 הַמֶּלֶךְ יִתְאַבָּל וְנָשִׂיא יִלְבַּשׁ שְׁמָמָה וִידֵי עַם־הָאָרֶץ
land the the the and with be shall the and shall king The
of people of hands ,despair clothed prince ,mourn

8199 4941 6213 1870 926
תִּבָּהַלְנָה מִדַּרְכָּם אֶעֱשֶׂה אוֹתָם וּבְמִשְׁפְּטֵיהֶם אֶשְׁפְּטֵם
will I to according and ,them to will I to according be shall
;them judge judgments their do way their .terrified

3068 3045
וְיָדְעוּ כִּי־אֲנִי יְהוָה׃
.Jehovah I that they and
(am) know shall

CAP. VIII ח

CHAPTER 8

CHAPTER 8

¹And it was in the sixth year, in the sixth *month*, on the fifth of the month, I was sitting in my house. And the elders of Judah were sitting before me. And the hand of the Lord Jehovah fell on me there. ²And I looked, and behold, a likeness as the look of fire; from the appearance of His loins and downward, *like* fire. And from His loins and upward, as the look of brightness, like the color of polished bronze. ³And He put forth the form of a hand, and took me by a lock of my head. And the Spirit lifted me up between the earth and the heavens, and brought me to Jerusalem—in the visions of God—to the opening of the inner gate facing north, where there *was* a seat of the image of jealousy, which causes jealousy. ⁴And, behold! The glory of the God of Israel *was* there, like the appearance which I saw in the plain.

⁵And He said to me, Son of man, lift up your eyes now *to* the way of the north. So I lifted up my eyes the way of the north; and, behold, from the north, at the gate of the altar, this *was the* image of jealousy at the entrance. ⁶And He said to me, Son of man, do you see what they are doing, the great abominations which the house of Israel is doing here, that I should be far from My sanctuary? But you turn again; you shall see greater abominations. ⁷And He brought me to the opening of the court. And I looked, and, behold, a single hole in the wall. ⁸And He said to me, Son of man, dig now in the wall. And I dug in the wall, and, behold, an

1 וַיְהִי ׀ בַּשָּׁנָה הַשִּׁשִׁית בַּחֲמִשָּׁה לַחֹדֶשׁ אֲנִי יֹשֵׁב
1961 / 8141 / 8345 / 8345 / 2568 / 2320 / 3427
was / I / the of the / on / the in / the / year in / it And
sitting / ,month / fifth / ,(month) sixth / ,sixth / was

בְּבֵיתִי וְזִקְנֵי יְהוּדָה יוֹשְׁבִים לְפָנָי וַתִּפֹּל עָלַי שָׁם יַד
1004 / 2205 / 3063 / 3427 / 6440 / 15307 / 3027
the there / on / fell and / before / were / Judah / the and / my in
of hand / me / ,me / sitting / of elders / ;house

2 אֲדֹנָי יְהֹוִה: וָאֶרְאֶה וְהִנֵּה דְמוּת כְּמַרְאֵה־אֵשׁ מִמַּרְאֵה
136 / 3068 / 7200 / 2009 / 1823 / 4758 / 784 / 4758
ap- the from / ,fire / the as / a / and / I Then / .Jehovah / the
of pearance / of look / likeness / ,behold / ,looked / Lord

מָתְנָיו וּלְמַטָּה אֵשׁ וּמִמָּתְנָיו וּלְמַעְלָה כְּמַרְאֵה־זֹהַר כְּעֵין
4975 / 4975 / 4295 / 46105 / 4758 / 20,96 / 5869
the like / bright- the as / and / from and / (like) and / His
of color / ,ness / of look / ,upward / loins His / ;fire / downward / loins

3 הַחַשְׁמַלָה: וַיִּשְׁלַח תַּבְנִית יָד וַיִּקָּחֵנִי בְּצִיצִת רֹאשִׁי וַתִּשָּׂא
28,30 / 17971 / 8403 / 3027 / 3747 / 6734 / 72,18 / 5375
And / my / a by / took and / a / the / He And / polished
up lifted / head of / lock / me / ,hand of form / forth put / .metal

אֹתִי רוּחַ ׀ בֵּין־הָאָרֶץ וּבֵין הַשָּׁמַיִם וַתָּבֵא אֹתִי יְרוּשָׁלְַמָה
7307 / 996 / 776 / 8064 / 935 / 3389
to / me and / the / and / the between / the / me
Jerusalem / brought / ,heavens / between / earth / the / Spirit

בְּמַרְאוֹת אֱלֹהִים אֶל־פֶּתַח שַׁעַר הַפְּנִימִית הַפּוֹנֶה צָפוֹנָה
4759 / 430 / 6605 / 8179 / 6442 / 6437 / 6828
,north / facing / inner the / gate / the / to / ,God / the in
of opening / of visions

4 אֲשֶׁר־שָׁם מוֹשַׁב סֵמֶל הַקִּנְאָה הַמַּקְנֶה: וְהִנֵּה־שָׁם כְּבוֹד
8033 / 4186 / 15566 / 7068 / 7069 / 2009 / 8033 / 3519
the / (was) / ,And / causes which / jealousy / the / seat the / there where
of glory / there / ,behold / .jealousy / of image / of / (was)

5 אֱלֹהֵי יִשְׂרָאֵל כַּמַּרְאֶה אֲשֶׁר רָאִיתִי בַּבִּקְעָה: וַיֹּאמֶר אֵלַי
430 / 13478 / 1237 / 834 / 7200 / 1237 / 559
to / He Then / the in / saw I / which / the as / ,Israel / the
,me / said / .plain / appearance / of God

בֶּן־אָדָם שָׂא־נָא עֵינֶיךָ דֶּרֶךְ צָפוֹנָה וָאֶשָּׂא עֵינַי דֶּרֶךְ
1121 / 120 / 5375 / 4994 / 5869 / 1870 / 6828 / 5375 / 5869 / 1870
the (to) my / I So / .northward / the (to) / your / now lift / ,man / Son
way / eyes up lifted / way / eyes / up / of

צָפוֹנָה וְהִנֵּה מִצָּפוֹן לְשַׁעַר הַמִּזְבֵּחַ סֵמֶל הַקִּנְאָה הַזֶּה
6828 / 2009 / 6828 / 8179 / 4196 / 15566 / 7268
this / jealousy / image / ,altar the / the at / the from / and / ,northward
(was) / of / north / ,behold

6 בַּבִּאָה: וַיֹּאמֶר אֵלַי בֶּן־אָדָם הֲרֹאֶה אַתָּה מָה הֵם עֹשִׂים
872 / 559 / 120 / 1121 / 7200 / 4100 / 6213
are / what / you / do / ,man / Son / to / He And / the at
,doing / they / see / of / ,me / said / .entrance

תּוֹעֵבוֹת גְּדֹלוֹת אֲשֶׁר בֵּית־יִשְׂרָאֵל ׀ עֹשִׂים פֹּה לְרָחֳקָה
8441 / 1419 / 834 / 1004 / 13478 / 62,13 / 7368
I that / ,here / is / Israel / the / which / the / abominations
far be should / doing / of house / great

7 מֵעַל מִקְדָּשִׁי וְעוֹד תָּשׁוּב תִּרְאֶה תּוֹעֵבוֹת גְּדֹלוֹת: וַיָּבֵא
4720 / 5750 / 7725 / 7200 / 8441 / 1419 / 935
He And / !greater abominations / shall you / you / But / My / from
brought / see / ;return / still / ?sanctuary

אֹתִי אֶל־פֶּתַח הֶחָצֵר וָאֶרְאֶה וְהִנֵּה חֹר־אֶחָד בַּקִּיר:
6607 / 2691 / 7200 / 2009 / 2356 / 259 / 7023
the in / single a / and / I and / ,looked / the / the / to / me
.wall / hole / ,behold / ;court / of opening

8 וַיֹּאמֶר אֵלַי בֶּן־אָדָם חֲתָר־נָא בַקִּיר וָאֶחְתֹּר בַּקִּיר וְהִנֵּה
559 / 1121 / 120 / 2864 / 4994 / 7023 / 28,75 / 7023 / 2009
and / the in / I And / the in / now dig / ,man / Son / to / He Then
,behold / wall / dug / .wall / of / ,me / said

opening! [9]And He said to me, Go in and see the evil abominations that they are doing here. [10]And I went in and saw. And, behold, every form of creeping thing, and hateful beast, and all the idols of the house of Israel were carved on the wall round *and* round. [11]And seventy men of the elders of the house of Israel, and Jaazaniah, the son of Shaphan, standing among them. *These* were standing among them, and each man with his censer in his hand; and the odor of the cloud of incense *was* rising. [12]And He said to me, Son of man, have you seen what the elders of the house of Israel are doing in the dark, each man in the rooms of his image? For they are saying, Jehovah does not see us; Jehovah has forsaken the earth.

[13]And He said to me, You turn again, you shall see greater abominations that they are doing. [14]And He brought me to the opening of the gate of the house of Jehovah, toward the north. And, behold, women were sitting there, weeping for Tammuz. [15]And He said to me, Have you seen, son of man? Yet turn again; you shall see greater abominations than these. [16]And he brought me into the inner court of the house of Jehovah. And, behold, at the opening of the temple of Jehovah, between the porch and the altar *were* about twenty-five men *with* their backs to the temple of Jehovah, and their faces eastward. And they bowed themselves eastward to the sun. [17]And He said to me, Son of man, have you seen? Is it nothing to the house of

7451 8441 7200 935 559 259 6607
9 פֶּתַח אֶחָד׃ וַיֹּאמֶר אֵלַי בֹּא וּרְאֵה אֶת־הַתּוֹעֵבוֹת הָרָעוֹת
evil the abominations see and Go ,me to He And .an opening
in said

8403 3605 2009 7200 935 6213
10 אֲשֶׁר הֵם עֹשִׂים פֹּה׃ וָאָבוֹא וָאֶרְאֶה וְהִנֵּה כָל־תַּבְנִית
form every And .saw and I So .here are they that
of ,behold in went doing

5921 2707 3478 1004 1544 8263 929 7431
רֶמֶשׂ וּבְהֵמָה שֶׁקֶץ וְכָל־גִּלּוּלֵי בֵּית יִשְׂרָאֵל מְחֻקֶּה עַל־
on were ,Israel the the and ,hateful and creeping
carved of house of idols all beast .thing

3478 1004 2205 376 7657 5439 5439 7023
11 הַקִּיר סָבִיב ׀ סָבִיב׃ וְשִׁבְעִים אִישׁ מִזִּקְנֵי בֵית־יִשְׂרָאֵל
,Israel the the of men And (and) round the
of house of elders seventy .round wall

376 64 40 5975 8432 5975 8227/1121 2970
וְיַאֲזַנְיָהוּ בֶן־שָׁפָן עֹמֵד בְּתוֹכָם עֹמְדִים לִפְנֵיהֶם וְאִישׁ
each and before were among standing ,Shaphan the and
man ,them standing —them of son —Jaazaniah

559 5927 7004 6051 6282 3027 4730
12 מִקְטַרְתּוֹ בְּיָדוֹ וַעֲתַר עֲנַן־הַקְּטֹרֶת עֹלֶה׃ וַיֹּאמֶר אֵלַי
,me to He Then .rising incense the the and his in censer his
said of cloud of odor ,hand

2822 6213 3478 1004 2205 120/1121 7200
הֲרָאִיתָ בֶן־אָדָם אֲשֶׁר זִקְנֵי בֵית־יִשְׂרָאֵל עֹשִׂים בַּחֹשֶׁךְ
the in are Israel the the what ,man Son you have
,dark doing of house of elders of ,seen

7200 3068 369 559 4906 2315 376
אִישׁ בְּחַדְרֵי מַשְׂכִּיתוֹ כִּי אֹמְרִים אֵין יְהוָה רֹאֶה אֹתָנוּ
;us see Jehovah does are they For ?image his the in each
not ,saying of rooms man

7200 7725 5750 559 776 3068 5800
13 עָזַב יְהוָה אֶת־הָאָרֶץ׃ וַיֹּאמֶר אֵלָי עוֹד תָּשׁוּב תִּרְאֶה
shall you you Still ,me to He And the Jehovah has
see ;return said .earth forsaken

6605 935 6213 834 1419 8441
14 תּוֹעֵבוֹת גְּדֹלוֹת אֲשֶׁר־הֵמָּה עֹשִׂים׃ וַיָּבֵא אֹתִי אֶל־פֶּתַח
the to me He And are they which greater abomina-
of opening brought .doing tions

802 8033 2009 6828 834 3068/1004 8179
שַׁעַר בֵּית־יְהוָה אֲשֶׁר אֶל־הַצָּפוֹנָה וְהִנֵּה־שָׁם הַנָּשִׁים
women there ,And the toward which .Jehovah the the
,behold .north (was) of house of gate

120 1121 7200 559 8542 1058 3427
15 יֹשְׁבוֹת מְבַכּוֹת אֶת־הַתַּמּוּז׃ וַיֹּאמֶר אֵלַי הֲרָאִיתָ בֶן־אָדָם
?man son you Have to He And for weeping were
of ,seen ,me said .Tammuz ,sitting

935 428 1419 8441 7200 7725 5750
16 עוֹד תָּשׁוּב תִּרְאֶה תּוֹעֵבוֹת גְּדֹלוֹת מֵאֵלֶּה׃ וַיָּבֵא אֹתִי אֶל־
into me He And than greater abominations \you you Still
brought .these see shall ,return

996 3068 1964 6607 2009 6442 3068/1004 2691
חֲצַר בֵּית־יְהוָה הַפְּנִימִית וְהִנֵּה־פֶתַח הֵיכַל יְהוָה בֵּין
be- ,Jehovah the the at and ,inner the Jehovah's house the
tween of temple of opening ,behold of court

268 376 2568 6242 4196 996 197
הָאוּלָם וּבֵין הַמִּזְבֵּחַ כְּעֶשְׂרִים וַחֲמִשָּׁה אִישׁ אֲחֹרֵיהֶם
their men five and about (were) the and the
backs (with) twenty ,altar between porch

6924 7812 6924 6440 3068 1964
אֶל־הֵיכַל יְהוָה וּפְנֵיהֶם קֵדְמָה וְהֵמָּה מִשְׁתַּחֲוִיתֶם קֵדְמָה
eastward bowed and ;eastward their and Jehovah the to
themselves they faces of temple

3063 1004 7043 120 1121 7200 559 8121
17 לַשָּׁמֶשׁ׃ וַיֹּאמֶר אֵלַי הֲרָאִיתָ בֶן־אָדָם הֲנָקֵל לְבֵית יְהוּדָה
Judah the to it Is ?man son you Have ,me to He And the to
of house nothing of ,seen said sun

Judah from doing the abominations which they do here? For they have filled the land *with* violence, and have returned to provoke Me to anger. And, behold, they are putting the branch to their nose! [18]And I also will deal with fury; My eye shall not spare, and I will not have pity. And though they cry in My ears *with* a loud voice, I will not hear them.

מַעֲשׂוֹת אֶת־הַתּוֹעֵבוֹת אֲשֶׁר עָשׂוּ־פֹה כִּי־מָלְאוּ אֶת־הָאָרֶץ

the land | have they filled | For | ?here they do | which | the abominations | from doing

חָמָס וַיָּשֻׁבוּ לְהַכְעִיסֵנִי וְהִנָּם שֹׁלְחִים אֶת־הַזְּמוֹרָה אֶל־

to | branch the | are they putting | And ,behold | provoke to .anger to Me | have and returned | (with) violence

18 אַפָּם׃ וְגַם־אֲנִי אֶעֱשֶׂה בְחֵמָה לֹא־תָחוֹס עֵינִי וְלֹא אֶחְמֹל

will I .pity have | And not | My .eye | shall spare | not | with ;fury | will deal | I So also | their .nose

וְקָרְאוּ בְאָזְנַי קוֹל גָּדוֹל וְלֹא אֶשְׁמַע אוֹתָם׃

.them | will I hear | not then | ,loud | (with) voice a | My in ears | though And cry they

CAP. IX ט

CHAPTER 9

[1]And He cried in my ears *with* a loud voice, saying, Let the overseers of the city draw near, even each *with* his destroying weapon in his hand. [2]And, behold, six men were coming from the way of the Upper Gate, which faces north. And each *had* his shattering weapon in his hand. And one man among them was clothed in linen, and an ink horn of a scribe at his loins. And they went in and stood beside the bronze altar. [3]And the glory of the God of Israel had gone on, from on the cherub, where it was on it, to the threshold of the house. And He called to the man clothed in linen, *with* the ink horn of a scribe at his loins. [4]And Jehovah said to him, Pass through in the midst of the city, in the midst of Jerusalem, and mark a mark on the foreheads of the men who are groaning and are mourning over all the abominations that are done in her midst. [5]And He said to those in my hearing, Pass over in the city after him, and strike. Do not let your eye spare, and do not have pity. [6]Slay old *men*, choice men, and virgins, and children, and women; slay to destruction.

1 וַיִּקְרָא בְאָזְנַי קוֹל גָּדוֹל לֵאמֹר קָרְבוּ פְּקֻדּוֹת הָעִיר וְאִישׁ

even each | the ,city | over- seers of | the near draw | Let | ,saying | ,loud | (with) voice a | my in ears | He And cried

2 כְּלִי מַשְׁחֵתוֹ בְּיָדוֹ׃ וְהִנֵּה שִׁשָּׁה אֲנָשִׁים בָּאִים ׀ מִדֶּרֶךְ

the from of way | were coming | men | six | And ,behold | his in .hand | his destroying | weapon

שַׁעַר הָעֶלְיוֹן אֲשֶׁר ׀ מָפְנֶה צָפוֹנָה וְאִישׁ כְּלִי מַפָּצוֹ בְּיָדוֹ

his in .hand | his shattering | weapon | and each | ,north | faces | which | the Upper | Gate

וְאִישׁ־אֶחָד בְּתוֹכָם לָבֻשׁ בַּדִּים וְקֶסֶת הַסֹּפֵר בְּמָתְנָיו

his at .loins | a scribe's | an and ink horn | in ,linen | was clothed | among them | one | And man

3 וַיָּבֹאוּ וַיַּעַמְדוּ אֵצֶל מִזְבַּח הַנְּחֹשֶׁת׃ וּכְבוֹד ׀ אֱלֹהֵי יִשְׂרָאֵל

Israel | God the of | the And of glory | .bronze | the altar | beside | and stood | they And in went

נַעֲלָה מֵעַל הַכְּרוּב אֲשֶׁר הָיָה עָלָיו אֶל מִפְתַּן הַבָּיִת

the .house's | threshold | to | upon ,it | was it | where | the cherub | from upon | had on gone

וַיִּקְרָא אֶל־הָאִישׁ הַלָּבֻשׁ הַבַּדִּים אֲשֶׁר קֶסֶת הַסֹּפֵר

scribe's | the inkhorn | who (had) | ,linen in | clothed | the man | to | He And called

4 בְּמָתְנָיו׃ וַיֹּאמֶר יְהוָה אֵלוֹ עֲבֹר בְּתוֹךְ הָעִיר בְּתוֹךְ

the in of midst | the ,city | the in of midst | Pass through | to ,him | Jehovah | said And | his at .loins

יְרוּשָׁלַםִ וְהִתְוִיתָ תָּו עַל־מִצְחוֹת הָאֲנָשִׁים הַנֶּאֱנָחִים

are who groaning | men the | the of foreheads | on | a mark | and mark | ,Jerusalem

5 וְהַנֶּאֱנָקִים עַל כָּל־הַתּוֹעֵבוֹת הַנַּעֲשׂוֹת בְּתוֹכָהּ׃ וּלְאֵלֶּה

to And those | her in .midst | are that done | the abominations | all of | over | are and mourning

אָמַר בְּאָזְנַי עִבְרוּ בָעִיר אַחֲרָיו וְהַכּוּ עַל־תָּחֹס עֵינֵיכֶם

eye your | Let not spare | and .strike | after him | the in city | Pass over | my in hearing | He said

6 וְאַל־תַּחְמֹלוּ׃ זָקֵן בָּחוּר וּבְתוּלָה וְטַף וְנָשִׁים תַּהַרְגוּ

slay | and ;women | and ,children | ,virgins and | choice ,men | Old | have do .pity | and not

But to every man who has the mark on him, do not come near. And begin from My sanctuary. And they began with the old men who *were* before the house. [7]And He said to them, Defile the house and fill the courts *with* the slain. Go forth! And they went out and killed in the city.

[8]And it happened as they struck, and I remained; *even* I; then I fell on my face and I cried out and said, Ah, Lord Jehovah! Will You destroy all the remnant of Israel in Your pouring out of Your fury on Jerusalem? [9]And He said to me, The iniquity of the house of Israel and of Judah is very great; and the land is filled *with* blood; and the city is full of perversity. For they say, Jehovah has forsaken the land; and, Jehovah does not see. [10]And even I, My eye does not spare, and I will not have pity. I will put their way on their head. [11]And, behold, the man clothed with linen, *with* the ink horn at his loins, reported the matter, saying, I have done as You commanded me.

CHAPTER 10
[1]And I looked. And, behold, in the expanse that *was* over the head of the cherubs appeared the look of the form of a throne, like a sapphire stone, above them. [2]And He spoke to the man clothed *with* linen, and said, Go in among the wheels, under the cherub, and fill your hands with coals of fire from between

---

							4889
5066	408	8420		376	36,05		
לְמַשְׁחִית	וְעַל־כָּל־אִישׁ אֲשֶׁר־עָלָיו הַתָּו אַל־תִּגַּשׁוּ						
to	But	every	man	who	on	the	come do not
.destruction			has	him	mark	.near	

1004	6440	834		22,05	582	24-90	2490	4720
וּמִמִּקְדָּשִׁי תָּחֵלוּ וַיָּחֵלוּ בָּאֲנָשִׁים הַזְּקֵנִים אֲשֶׁר לִפְנֵי הַבָּיִת׃								
from And	sanctuary My	.begin	began	they And	the with men	old	who	before	the house.

7 | 2691 | 1004 | 4390 | 559 |
| הֲלָלִים צְאוּ וְיָצְאוּ וְהִכּוּ בָעִיר׃ | | | |
| He And said | ,them to | Defile | ,house the | fill and | courts the | .house |

8 | 7604 | 5221 | 1961 | 5892 | 5221 | 3318 | 3318 | 2491 |
| וְנִשְׁאַר כְּהַכּוֹתָם וַיִּדִי וַיֵּצְאוּ צְאוּ בָעִיר׃ | | | | | | | |
| And I remained | they as struck | And was it | the in city | killed | they And out went | !forth | the (with) slain |

7843	3068	136	162	559	2199	6440	5307
וָאֶפְּלָה עַל־פָּנַי וָאֶזְעַק וָאֹמַר אֲהָהּ אֲדֹנָי יְהוִה הֲמַשְׁחִית							
destroy Will	!Jehovah	Lord	,Ah	and	,cried	face	I and my on I and ;I fell	.said

2534	8210	3478	7611	36,05
אַתָּה אֵת כָּל־שְׁאֵרִית יִשְׂרָאֵל בְּשָׁפְכְּךָ אֶת־חֲמָתְךָ עַל־				
on	Your fury	Your in out pouring	Israel	the all	You	of remnant

9 | 1419 | 3063 | 3478 | 1004 | 5771 | 559 | 3389 |
| יְרוּשָׁלָ͏ִם׃ וַיֹּאמֶר אֵלַי עֲוֹן בֵּית־יִשְׂרָאֵל וִיהוּדָה גָּדוֹל | | | | | | |
| (is) great | and Judah's | Israel's of house | The iniquity | to me | He And said | ?Jerusalem |

4297	4390	5892	776	43,90	3966	3966
בִּמְאֹד מְאֹד וַתִּמָּלֵא הָאָרֶץ דָּמִים וְהָעִיר מֻטֶּה כִּי						
For per-	full is	the and city	the (with) blood	is and land	filled	,much very in

10 | 1571 | 7200 | 3068 | 369 | 776 | 3068 | 5800 | 559 |
| אָמְרוּ עָזַב יְהוָה אֶת־הָאָרֶץ וְאֵין יְהוָה רֹאֶה׃ וְגַם־אֲנִי | | | | | | | |
| ,I | And even | does Jehovah | see not | and the | ,land | Jehovah | forsaken | they say | .versity |

11 | 20,09 | 5414 | 7218 | 1870 | 2550 | 38,08 | 5869 | 2347 |
| לֹא־תָחוֹס עֵינִי וְלֹא אֶחְמֹל דַּרְכָּם בְּרֹאשָׁם נָתָתִּי וְהִנֵּה | | | | | | | |
| And ,behold | will I put | their on head | their way | I will ;pity have not | and | My eye | does not spare |

1697	7725	708,3	4975	7083	906	38,47	376
הָאִישׁ לְבֻשׁ הַבַּדִּים אֲשֶׁר הַקֶּסֶת בְּמָתְנָיו מֵשִׁיב דָּבָר							
the ,matter	reported	his at ,loins	the inkhorn	who (had)	,linen	clothed with	the man

6680	6213	559
לֵאמֹר עָשִׂיתִי כַּאֲשֶׁר צִוִּיתָנִי׃		
have You	as	have I	,saying
.me commanded		done

CAP. X ׳

CHAPTER 10

1 | 68 | 3742 | 7218 | 59,21 | 7549 | 2009 | 7200 |
| וָאֶרְאֶה וְהִנֵּה אֶל־הָרָקִיעַ אֲשֶׁר עַל־רֹאשׁ הַכְּרֻבִים כְּאֶבֶן | | | | | | |
| a like stone | the the ,cherubim | over of head | that (was) | in and expanse | and ,behold | I and looked |

2 | 559 | 5921 | 7200 | 3678 | 1823 | 4758 | 5601 |
| סַפִּיר כְּמַרְאֵה דְּמוּת כִּסֵּא נִרְאָה עֲלֵיהֶם׃ וַיֹּאמֶר אֶל־ | | | | | | |
| to | He And spoke | above .them | appeared | a ,throne | the of form | the the as look | sapphire |

1534	996	935	559	906	38,47	376
הָאִישׁ לְבֻשׁ הַבַּדִּים וַיֹּאמֶר בֹּא אֶל־בֵּינוֹת לַגַּלְגַּל						
the ,wheels	among in	to	Go ,said and	,linen	clothed (with)	man the

996	784	1513	2651	4390	374,2	8478
אֶל־תַּחַת לַכְּרוּב וּמַלֵּא חָפְנֶיךָ גַחֲלֵי־אֵשׁ מִבֵּינוֹת						
from between	fire of	coals	hands your with	fill and	the ,cherub	under to

the cherubs; and sprinkle
on the city. And he went in
before me. 3And the
cherubs were standing on
the right side of the house
when he, the man, went in.
And the cloud filled the
inner court. 4And the
glory of Jehovah rose from
the cherub, over the
threshold of the house. And
the house was filled with
the cloud; and the court
was full of the radiance of
the glory of Jehovah. 5And
the sound of the wings of
cherubs was heard over the
outer court, as the voice of
God Almighty when He
speaks. 6And it happened,
when He had commanded
the man clothed *with* linen,
saying, Take fire from
between the wheels, from
between the cherubs; then
he went and stood beside
the wheels. 7And *one*
cherub stretched out his
hand from between the
cherubs, to the fire that *was*
between the cherubs. And
he lifted and put *it* into the
hands of the one clothed
with linen. And he took *it*
and went out.

8And the form of a man's
hand was seen under the
wings of the cherubs. 9And
I looked, and, behold, the
four wheels *were* beside
the cherubs; one wheel
beside one cherub, one
wheel beside one cherub.
And the look of the wheels
was like the color of a stone
of Tarshish. 10And their
appearance *was* as one, the
four of them; as if the wheel
were in the midst of the
wheel. 11In their going on
their four sides, they went.
They did not turn in their
going; for *to* the place
where the head faces, after
it they went. They did not
turn in their going. 12And

5975 3742 5869 935 5892 2236 3742
3 לַכְּרֻבִים וּזְרֹק עַל־הָעִיר וַיָּבֹא לְעֵינָי׃ וְהַכְּרֻבִים עֹמְדִים
were standing / the And cherubim / before .me / he And in went / the upon .city / and sprinkle / the ,cherubim

2691 4390 6051 376 935 1004 3225
מִימִין לַבַּיִת בְּבֹאוֹ הָאִישׁ וְהֶעָנָן מָלֵא אֶת־הֶחָצֵר
the court / filled / the and cloud / the ;man / he when ,in went / the house / right the on of side

4670 5921 3742 5921 3068 3519 7311 6442
4 הַפְּנִימִית׃ וַיָּרָם כְּבוֹד־יְהוָה מֵעַל הַכְּרוּב עַל מִפְתַּן
thres- of hold / the over / the ,cherub / from upon / Jehovah / the of glory / And arose / .inner

5051 4390 2691 6051 1004 4390 1004
הַבָּיִת וַיִּמָּלֵא הַבַּיִת אֶת־הֶעָנָן וְהֶחָצֵר מָלְאָה אֶת־נֹגַהּ
the with of radiance / full was of / the and court / the with ,cloud / the house / was And filled / the .house

2691 5704 8085 3742 3671 6963 3068 3519
5 כְּבוֹד יְהוָה׃ וְקוֹל כַּנְפֵי הַכְּרוּבִים נִשְׁמַע עַד הֶחָצֵר
the court / to / was heard / cherubim / wings / the And of sound / .Jehovah's glory

376 6680 1696 7706 410 6963 2435
6 הַחִיצֹנָה כְּקוֹל אֵל־שַׁדַּי בְּדַבְּרוֹ׃ וַיְהִי בְּצַוֺּתוֹ אֶת־הָאִישׁ
the man / He when commanded / it And was / He when .speaks / Almighty God of voice the / as / outer

996 1534 996 784 3947 559 906 3847
לְבֻשׁ־הַבַּדִּים לֵאמֹר קַח אֵשׁ מִבֵּינוֹת לַגַּלְגַּל מִבֵּינוֹת
from between / the ,wheels / from between / fire / Take / ,saying / ,linen / clothed with

3742 7971 212 681 5975 935 3742
7 לַכְּרוּבִים וַיָּבֹא וַיַּעֲמֹד אֵצֶל הָאוֹפָן׃ וַיִּשְׁלַח הַכְּרוּב אֶת־
(one) cherub / And out stretched / the .wheel / beside / and stood / he then went / the ,cherubim

3742 996 784 3742 996 3027
יָדוֹ מִבֵּינוֹת לַכְּרוּבִים אֶל־הָאֵשׁ אֲשֶׁר בֵּינוֹת הַכְּרֻבִים
the .cherubim / between / that (was) / the fire / to / the cherubim / from between / his hand

7200 3318 3947 906 3847 2651 5414 5375
8 וַיִּשָּׂא וַיִּתֵּן אֶל־חָפְנֵי לְבֻשׁ הַבַּדִּים וַיִּקַּח וַיֵּצֵא׃ וַיֵּרָא
was And seen / went and .out / He And (it) took / .linen / one the with clothed / the of hands / into / and he And (it) put lifted

2009 7200 3671 8478 120 1121 8403 3742
9 לַכְּרֻבִים תַּבְנִית יַד־אָדָם תַּחַת כַּנְפֵיהֶם׃ וָאֶרְאֶה וְהִנֵּה
and ,behold / I And ,looked / their .wings / under / man's a hand / the of form / the in cherubim

3742 681 259 212 3742 681 212 702
אַרְבָּעָה אוֹפַנִּים אֵצֶל הַכְּרוּבִים אוֹפַן אֶחָד אֵצֶל הַכְּרוּב
cherub / beside / one (was) / wheel / the ,cherubim / beside / wheels / four the

212 4758 259 3742 681 259 212 259
אֶחָד וְאוֹפַן אֶחָד אֵצֶל הַכְּרוּב אֶחָד וּמַרְאֵה הָאוֹפַנִּים
the wheels / the and of look / ;one / cherub / beside / one / and wheel / ,one

702 259 1823 4758 8658 68 5869
10 כְּעֵין אֶבֶן תַּרְשִׁישׁ׃ וּמַרְאֵיהֶם דְּמוּת אֶחָד לְאַרְבַּעְתָּם
four the .them of / one / (was) like / their And appearance / Tarshish / stone a of / the like of color

702 3212 212 8432 212 1961
11 כַּאֲשֶׁר יִהְיֶה הָאוֹפַן בְּתוֹךְ הָאוֹפָן׃ בְּלֶכְתָּם אֶל־אַרְבַּעַת
four / on / their In going / the .wheel / the in of midst / the wheel / were / if as

6437 4725 3212 5437 3808 3212 7253
רִבְעֵיהֶם יֵלֵכוּ לֹא יִסַּבּוּ בְּלֶכְתָּם כִּי הַמָּקוֹם אֲשֶׁר־יִפְנֶה
faces where / the (to) place / for / their in ;going / they turn did / Not / they .went / their sides

1320 3605 3212 5437 3808 3212 310 7218
12 הָרֹאשׁ אַחֲרָיו יֵלֵכוּ לֹא יִסַּבּוּ בְּלֶכְתָּם׃ וְכָל־בְּשָׂרָם
their flesh / And all / their in .going / they turn did / Not / they .went / after it / the ,head

their whole body, and their backs, and their hands, and their wings, and the wheels, were full of eyes all around; *even* their wheels which the four of them had. 13As for the wheels, it was cried to them in my hearing, Whirling Wheel! 14And four faces *were* to each. The first face *was* the face of a cherub; and the second face the face of a man; and the third the face of a lion; and the fourth the face of an eagle. 15And the cherubs rose up. This *is* the living creature that I saw by the river Chebar.

16And in the going of the cherubs, the wheels went beside them. And when the cherubs lifted their wings to soar from the earth, the wheels did not turn from beside them, even they. 17When they stood still, *these* stood still. And when they rose up, *these also* lifted up. For the spirit of the living creature *was* in them. 18And the glory of Jehovah went from the threshold of the house and stood over the cherubs. 19And the cherubs lifted their wings and rose up from the earth in my sight. When they went out, the wheels also *were* with them. And he stood at the door of the gate of the house of Jehovah, the eastern *gate*. And the glory of the God of Israel *was* over them from above. 20This *is* the living creature that I saw under the God of Israel by the river Chebar; and I knew that they *were* cherubs. 21Four, *even* four faces *are* to each; and four wings to each. And the form of a man's hands *was* under their wings. 22And the form of their faces, they *are* the faces that I saw by the

5439 5869 4393 212 3671 3027 1354
וְגַבֵּהֶם וִידֵיהֶם וְכַנְפֵיהֶם וְהָאוֹפַנִּים מְלֵאִים עֵינַיִם סָבִיב
all eyes were the and their and their and their and
,around of full wheels ,wings ,hands ,backs

241 1534 7121 212 212 702
13 לְאַרְבַּעְתָּם אוֹפַנֵּיהֶם׃ לָאוֹפַנִּים לָהֶם קוֹרָא הַגַּלְגַּל בְּאָזְנָי׃
my in whirling was it to for As their four the which
.hearing ,wheel ,cried them wheels the ,wheels had them of

8145 6440 3742 6440 259 6440 259 6440 702
14 וְאַרְבָּעָה פָנִים לְאֶחָד פְּנֵי הָאֶחָד פְּנֵי הַכְּרוּב וּפְנֵי הַשֵּׁנִי
the and ,cherub's the The face to faces four And
second face face (was) first ,each (were)

7426 5404 7243 738 6440 7992 120 6440
15 פְּנֵי אָדָם וְהַשְּׁלִישִׁי פְּנֵי אַרְיֵה וְהָרְבִיעִי פְּנֵי־נָשֶׁר׃ וַיֵּרֹמּוּ
And .eagle's an the and ,lion's a the and a (was)
arose face (was) fourth face (was) third ,man's face

3212 3529 5104 7200 2416 2088 3742
16 הַכְּרוּבִים הִיא הַחַיָּה אֲשֶׁר רָאִיתִי בִּנְהַר־כְּבָר׃ וּבְלֶכֶת
in And .Chebar the by saw I that living the This the
going river creature (is) .cherubim

3742 5375 681 212 3212 3742
הַכְּרוּבִים יֵלְכוּ הָאוֹפַנִּים אֶצְלָם וּבִשְׂאֵת הַכְּרוּבִים אֶת־
the when and beside the went the
cherubim lifted ,them wheels ,cherubim

1992 212 5437 3808 776 5921 7311 3671
כַּנְפֵיהֶם לָרוּם מֵעַל הָאָרֶץ לֹא־יִסַּבּוּ הָאוֹפַנִּים גַּם־הֵם
also the did not the from soar to their
they ,wheels turn ,earth upon wings

7307 7426 7311 5975 5975 681
17 מֵאֶצְלָם׃ בְּעָמְדָם יַעֲמֹדוּ וּבְרוֹמָם יֵרוֹמּוּ אוֹתָם כִּי רוּחַ
the For themselves (these) when and stood they When beside from
of spirit .(also) lifted rose they ,still ,still stood .them

5975 1004 4670 5921 3068 3519 3318 2416
18 הַחַיָּה בָּהֶם׃ וַיֵּצֵא כְּבוֹד יְהוָה מֵעַל מִפְתַּן הַבָּיִת וַיַּעֲמֹד
and the thres- the from Jehovah the And in (was) living the
stood house of hold upon of glory went .them creature

7426 3671 3742 5375 3742 5921
19 עַל־הַכְּרוּבִים׃ וַיִּשְׂאוּ הַכְּרוּבִים אֶת־כַּנְפֵיהֶם וַיֵּרוֹמּוּ
and their the And the over
rose wings cherubim lifted .cherubim

5975 5980 212 3318 5869 776
מִן־הָאָרֶץ לְעֵינַי בְּצֵאתָם וְהָאוֹפַנִּים לְעֻמָּתָם וַיַּעֲמֹד
he and with wheels the they When my in the from
stood ,them (were) also ,out went .sight earth

3478 430 3519 6931 3068 1004 8179 6607
פֶּתַח שַׁעַר בֵּית־יְהוָה הַקַּדְמוֹנִי וּכְבוֹד אֱלֹהֵי־יִשְׂרָאֵל
Israel the the And the ,Jehovah's house the the at
(was) of God of glory .eastern of gate of door

430 8478 7200 2416 4605 5921
20 עֲלֵיהֶם מִלְמָעְלָה׃ הִיא הַחַיָּה אֲשֶׁר רָאִיתִי תַּחַת אֱלֹהֵי־
God the under saw I that living the This from over
of creature (is) .above them

702 3742 3045 3529 5104 3478
21 יִשְׂרָאֵל בִּנְהַר־כְּבָר וָאֵדַע כִּי כְרוּבִים הֵמָּה׃ אַרְבָּעָה
,Four they cherubim that I and ,Chebar the by Israel
.(were) knew river

3027 1823 259 3671 702 259 6440 702
אַרְבָּעָה פָנִים לְאֶחָד וְאַרְבַּע כְּנָפַיִם לְאֶחָד וּדְמוּת יְדֵי
hands the And to wings four and ,each to faces four (even)
of form .each (are)

6440 1992 6440 1823 3671 8478 120
22 אָדָם תַּחַת כַּנְפֵיהֶם׃ וּדְמוּת פְּנֵיהֶם הֵמָּה הַפָּנִים אֲשֶׁר
that the they their the And their (was) a
faces (are) ,faces of form .wings under man's

river Chebar, their appearances, even theirs. They each went straight forward.

CHAPTER 11

[1]And the Spirit lifted me up and brought me to the eastern gate of the house of Jehovah, the *gate* which faces eastward. And, behold, at the opening of the gate *were* twenty-five men. And I saw among them Jaazaniah the son of Azzur, and Pelatiah, the son of Benaiah, leaders of the people. [2]And He said to me, Son of man, these *are* the men who plot evil and advise wicked advice in this city; [3]who say, It is not near; let us build houses; she *is* the pot and we *are* the flesh. [4]Therefore, prophesy against them; prophesy, son of man! [5]And the Spirit of Jehovah fell on me and said to me, Speak, So says Jehovah: So you have said, house of Israel; for I Myself know the elevations of your spirit. [6]You have multiplied your slain in this city, and you have filled her streets *with* the slain. [7]Therefore, so says the Lord Jehovah: Your slain whom you have laid in her midst, they *are* the flesh, and she *is* the pot. But I will bring you forth out of her midst. [8]You have feared the sword; but I will bring a sword on you, says the Lord Jehovah. [9]And I will bring you out of her midst, and will give you into the hand of strangers. And I will execute judgments against you. [10]You shall

5676 376 4758 35:29 5104 7200
רָאִיתִי עַל־נְהַר כְּבָר מַרְאֵיהֶם וְאוֹתָם אִישׁ אֶל־עֵבֶר
straight each even their ,Chebar the by saw I
;theirs appearances river

32:12 6440
פָּנָיו יֵלֵכוּ׃
they forward
.went

CAP. XI יא

CHAPTER 11

6931 3068 1004 8179 935 7307 5375
1 וַתִּשָּׂא אֹתִי רוּחַ וַתָּבֵא אֹתִי אֶל־שַׁעַר בֵּית־יְהוָה הַקַּדְמוֹנִי
the Jehovah's house the to me and the me And
,eastern of gate brought Spirit lifted

376 2568 6242 8179 6607 2009 6921 6437
הַפּוֹנֶה קָדִימָה וְהִנֵּה בְּפֶתַח הַשַּׁעַר עֶשְׂרִים וַחֲמִשָּׁה אִישׁ
—men five and twenty the the at And .eastward which
gate of opening ,behold faces

1121 6410 5809/1121 2970 8432 7200
וָאֶרְאֶה בְתוֹכָם אֶת־יַאֲזַנְיָה בֶן־עַזֻּר וְאֶת־פְּלַטְיָהוּ בֶן
the Pelatiah and Azzur the Jaazaniah among I And
of son of son them saw

428 120 1121 559 5971 8269 1141
2 בְּנָיָהוּ שָׂרֵי הָעָם׃ וַיֹּאמֶר אֵלַי בֶּן־אָדָם אֵלֶּה
these ,man Son ,me to he And the chiefs ,Benaiah
(are) of said .people of

2088 5892 7451/6098 3289 205 2803 582
הָאֲנָשִׁים הַחֹשְׁבִים אָוֶן וְהַיֹּעֲצִים עֲצַת־רָע בָּעִיר הַזֹּאת׃
,this in wicked advice and evil plot who men the
city advise

55:18 1004 1129 7138 38:08 559
3 הָאֹמְרִים לֹא בְקָרוֹב בְּנוֹת בָּתִּים הִיא הַסִּיר וַאֲנַחְנוּ
we and the She houses us let is it Not ,say who
(are) pot (is) build ;near

5307 120 1121 5012 5012 36:51 1320
4 5 הַבָּשָׂר׃ לָכֵן הִנָּבֵא עֲלֵיהֶם הִנָּבֵא בֶּן־אָדָם׃ וַתִּפֹּל עָלַי
on And !man son ,prophesy against prophesy There- the
me fell of ;them fore flesh

559 3651 3068 559 3541 5.59 559 3068 7307
רוּחַ יְהוָה וַיֹּאמֶר אֵלַי אֱמֹר כֹּה־אָמַר יְהוָה כֵּן אֲמַרְתֶּם
have you Thus ,Jehovah says Thus :Speak to said and Jehovah the
,said ,me of Spirit

7235 3045 7307 4609 3478 1004
6 בֵּית יִשְׂרָאֵל וּמַעֲלוֹת רוּחֲכֶם אֲנִי יְדַעְתִּיהָ׃ הִרְבֵּיתֶם
have You .it know I your the for ;Israel house
multiplied myself spirit of steps of

3541 2491 2351 4390 2088 5892 2491
7 חַלְלֵיכֶם בָּעִיר הַזֹּאת וּמִלֵּאתֶם חוּצֹתֶיהָ חָלָל׃ לָכֵן כֹּה
thus There- the (with) her you and ,this city in your
fore .slain streets filled have slain

84:32 7760 834 2491 3068 136 559
אָמַר אֲדֹנָי יְהוִה חַלְלֵיכֶם אֲשֶׁר שַׂמְתֶּם בְּתוֹכָהּ הֵמָּה
They her in have you whom Your :Jehovah the says
(are) ,midst laid slain Lord

3372 2719 8432 3318 5518 1320
8 הַבָּשָׂר וְהִיא הַסִּיר וְאֶתְכֶם הוֹצִיא מִתּוֹכָהּ׃ חֶרֶב יְרֵאתֶם
have You the of out will I you But the and the
,feared sword .midst her forth bring .pot (is) she ,flesh

3318 3068 136 5002 935 2719
9 וְחֶרֶב אָבִיא עֲלֵיכֶם נְאֻם אֲדֹנָי יְהוִה׃ וְהוֹצֵאתִי אֶתְכֶם
you I And .Jehovah the says upon will I a But
bring will Lord ,you bring sword

8201 6213 2914 3027 5414 8432
מִתּוֹכָהּ וְנָתַתִּי אֶתְכֶם בְּיַד־זָרִים וְעָשִׂיתִי בָכֶם שְׁפָטִים׃
.judgments against I and ,strangers' into you and of out
you make will hand give midst her

fall by the sword. I will judge you to the border of Israel, and you shall know that I *am* Jehovah. [11]This *city* shall not be for a pot to you, nor shall you be in its midst for flesh. [12]I will judge you to the border of Israel, and you shall know that I *am* Jehovah, in whose statutes you have not walked; yea, you have not done My judgments. Yea, as the judgments of the nations who are around you, you have done.

[13]And it happened when I prophesied, Pelatiah, the son of Benaiah, died. Then I fell on my face and cried with a loud voice, and said, Ah, Lord Jehovah! Will you make an full end *of* the remnant of Israel? [14]And the word of Jehovah *came* to me, saying, [15]Son of man, your brothers, the redemption-men, your brothers and all the house of Israel that have *heard* the inhabitants of Jerusalem saying to all of them, Go far away from Jehovah; this land is given to us for a possession. [16]Because of this say, So says the Lord Jehovah: Though I have sent them far off among the nations, and though I scattered them among the lands; yet I was to them as a little sanctuary in the countries there where they had gone. [17]Therefore say, So says the Lord Jehovah: I shall gather you from the peoples, and assemble you out of the lands, in those where you were scattered; and I shall give to you the land of Israel. [18]And they will come there, and they will remove all its hateful things and all its abominations from it. [19]And I shall give to them one

3045 8199 3478 1366 5307 2719
10 בַּחֶרֶב תִּפֹּלוּ עַל־גְּבוּל יִשְׂרָאֵל אֶשְׁפּוֹט אֶתְכֶם וִידַעְתֶּם
you and know shall | ,you | will I judge | Israel | the of border | to | shall you .fall | the by sword

1961 5518 1961 38:08 2088 3068
11 כִּי־אֲנִי יְהוָה׃ הִיא לֹא־תִהְיֶה לָכֶם לְסִיר וְאַתֶּם תִּהְיוּ
be shall | nor you | a for ,pot | you to | be shall not | This (city) | .Jehovah | I that (am)

3045 8199 3478 1366 13:20 8432
12 בְּתוֹכָהּ לְבָשָׂר אֶל־גְּבוּל יִשְׂרָאֵל אֶשְׁפֹּט אֶתְכֶם׃ וִידַעְתֶּם
you and know shall | ,you | will I judge | Israel | the of border | To | for .flesh | its in midst

380:8 4941 19:80 38:08 2706 834 30:68
כִּי־אֲנִי יְהוָה אֲשֶׁר בְּחֻקַּי לֹא הֲלַכְתֶּם וּמִשְׁפָּטַי לֹא
not | My and judgments | have you ,walked | not | My in statutes | of —Jehovah whom | I that (am)

1961 6213 5439 834 1471 4942 6213
13 עֲשִׂיתֶם וּכְמִשְׁפְּטֵי הַגּוֹיִם אֲשֶׁר סְבִיבוֹתֵיכֶם עֲשִׂיתֶם׃ וַיְהִי
And was it | have you .done | around ,you | are all | who | the nations | the as of judgments | and | have you ,done

6963 2199 6440 5307 4191 1141 1121 6410 5012
כְּהִנָּבְאִי וּפְלַטְיָהוּ בֶן־בְּנָיָה מֵת וָאֶפֹּל עַל־פָּנַי וָאֶזְעַק קוֹל
a with voice | and cried | my on face | I Then fell | .died | Benaiah | the of son | he Pelatiah (was) | I when ,prophesied

7611 6213 3615 3068 136 162 559 1419
גָּדוֹל וָאֹמַר אֲהָהּ אֲדֹנָי יְהוִה כָּלָה אַתָּה עֹשֶׂה אֵת שְׁאֵרִית
the (of) of remnant | Will make | You | an end | !Jehovah | Lord | Ah | ,said and | ,loud

120 1121 559 3068 1697 1961 3478
14 15 יִשְׂרָאֵל׃ וַיְהִי דְבַר־יְהוָה אֵלַי לֵאמֹר׃ בֶּן־אָדָם
,man | Son of | ,saying | to ,me | Jehovah | the of word | And was | ?Israel

834 36:05 3478 1004 3605 1353 582 251 251
אַחֶיךָ אַחֶיךָ אַנְשֵׁי גְאֻלָּתֶךָ וְכָל־בֵּית יִשְׂרָאֵל כֻּלֹּה אֲשֶׁר
whom | of all | Israel | the of house | and all | your redemption | men the of | your ,brothers | your ,brothers

2088 30:68 7368 3389 3427 559
אָמְרוּ לָהֶם יֹשְׁבֵי יְרוּשָׁלַם רַחֲקוּ מֵעַל יְהוָה לָנוּ הִיא
this | us to | Jehovah | from | far Go away | ,Jerusalem | the of dwellers | to them | have said

136 559 3541/559 3651 4181 776 5414
16 נִתְּנָה הָאָרֶץ לְמוֹרָשָׁה׃ לָכֵן אֱמֹר כֹּה אָמַר אֲדֹנָי
the Lord | says | Thus | ,say Therefore | a for .possession | land | is given

776 6327 14:71 7368 3068
יְהוִה כִּי הִרְחַקְתִּים בַּגּוֹיִם וְכִי הֲפִיצוֹתִים בָּאֲרָצוֹת וָאֱהִי
I yet was | the among ;lands | scattered I them | and though | among ,nations the | sent have I Though far off them | Jeho- :vah

36:51 8033 935 834 776 45:92 4720
17 לָהֶם לְמִקְדָּשׁ מְעַט בָּאֲרָצוֹת אֲשֶׁר־בָּאוּ שָׁם׃ לָכֵן
Therefore | .there | they gone had | where | the in countries | little | a as sanctuary | to them

5971 6908 3068 136 559 559
אֱמֹר כֹּה־אָמַר אֲדֹנָי יְהוִה וְקִבַּצְתִּי אֶתְכֶם מִן־הָעַמִּים
the peoples | from | you | shall I gather | :Jehovah the Lord | says Thus | ,say

5414 6327 776 622
וְאָסַפְתִּי אֶתְכֶם מִן־הָאֲרָצוֹת אֲשֶׁר נְפֹצוֹתֶם בָּהֶם וְנָתַתִּי
I and give shall | in ,them | were you scattered | where | the lands | out of | you | and assemble

5493 8033 935 3478 127
18 לָכֶם אֶת־אַדְמַת יִשְׂרָאֵל׃ וּבָאוּ־שָׁמָּה וְהֵסִירוּ אֶת־
they and remove will | ,there | they And come will | .Israel | the of land | you to

5414 8441 3605 8251 36:05
19 כָּל־שִׁקּוּצֶיהָ וְאֶת־כָּל־תּוֹעֲבוֹתֶיהָ מִמֶּנָּה׃ וְנָתַתִּי לָהֶם
to them | I And give shall | .it from | its abominations | all | and | hateful its things | all

heart, and I will put a new
spirit within you. And I will
remove the stony heart out
of their flesh, and will give
them a heart of flesh, [20]so
that they may walk in My
statutes and keep My judgments, and do them. And
they shall be to Me for a
people, and I will be to
them for God. [21]And *as* to
those whose heart is going
toward their hateful things,
and their heart is going *after*
their disgusting idols, I
will give their way on
their heads, declares the
Lord Jehovah.
[22]Then the cherubs lifted
up their wings, and the
wheels *were* beside them.
And the glory of the God of
Israel *was* over them from
above. [23]And the glory of
Jehovah went up from the
midst of the city and stood
on the mountain which *is*
on the east of the city.
[24]And the Spirit lifted me
up and brought me into
Chaldea, to the exiles, in a
vision by the Spirit of God.
And the vision that I had
seen went up from me.
[25]And I spoke to the exiles
all the things which
Jehovah had shown me.

68 38 20 549 3 7130 5414 2319 7307 259 3820
לֵב אֶחָד וְרוּחַ חֲדָשָׁה אֶתֵּן בְּקִרְבְּכֶם וַהֲסִרֹתִי לֵב הָאֶבֶן
stony the shall I And within will I new a and ,one heart
heart remove .you put spirit

32 12 2708 1320 38 20 5414 1320
20 מִבְּשָׂרָם וְנָתַתִּי לָהֶם לֵב בָּשָׂר׃ לְמַעַן בְּחֻקֹּתַי יֵלֵכוּ וְאֶת־
and they My in that so ,flesh a them will and of out
walk may statutes of heart give ,flesh their

1961 5971 1961 8104 4941
מִשְׁפָּטַי יִשְׁמְרוּ וְעָשׂוּ אֹתָם וְהָיוּ־לִי לְעָם וַאֲנִי אֶהְיֶה לָהֶם
to be will I and a for to And .them do and ,keep judg- My
them ,people Me be shall they ments

1980 3820 8441 8051 38 20 430
21 לֵאלֹהִים׃ וְאֶל־לֵב שִׁקּוּצֵיהֶם וְתוֹעֲבוֹתֵיהֶם לִבָּם הֹלֵךְ
is their their (after) and hateful their the to And God for
;going heart idols disgusting ;things of heart

3742 5375 3068 136 5002 5414 7218 1870
22 דַּרְכָּם בְּרֹאשָׁם נָתַתִּי נְאֻם אֲדֹנָי יְהוִה׃ וַיִּשְׂאוּ הַכְּרוּבִים
the Then .Jehovah the states will I their on their
cherubim up lifted Lord ,give heads way

3478 430 3519 5980 212 3671
אֶת־כַּנְפֵיהֶם וְהָאוֹפַנִּים לְעֻמָּתָם וּכְבוֹד אֱלֹהֵי־יִשְׂרָאֵל
Israel the the And beside the and their
(was) of God of glory .them wheels wings

5975 5892 8432 3068 3519 5927 4605 5921
23 עֲלֵיהֶם מִלְמָעְלָה׃ וַיַּעַל כְּבוֹד יְהוָה מֵעַל תּוֹךְ הָעִיר וַיַּעֲמֹד
and the the from Jehovah the And .above from over
stood city of midst of glory up went them

935 5375 7307 5892 6924 834 2022 5921
24 עַל־הָהָר אֲשֶׁר מִקֶּדֶם לָעִיר׃ וְרוּחַ נְשָׂאַתְנִי וַתְּבִיאֵנִי
brought and me lifted the And the of the on which the on
me Spirit .city east (is) mountain

5927 430 7307 4758 1473 3778
כַּשְׂדִּימָה אֶל־הַגּוֹלָה בַּמַּרְאֶה בְּרוּחַ אֱלֹהִים וַיַּעַל מֵעָלַי
from So .God the by a in the to ,Chaldea into
me up went of Spirit vision ,exiles

1697 3605 1473 1697 7200 4758
25 הַמַּרְאֶה אֲשֶׁר רָאִיתִי׃ וָאֲדַבֵּר אֶל־הַגּוֹלָה אֵת כָּל־דִּבְרֵי
the all the to I And had I that the
of things exiles spoke .seen vision

7200 834 3068
יְהוָה אֲשֶׁר הֶרְאָנִי׃
had He which Jehovah
.me shown

CAP. XII יב

CHAPTER 12

CHAPTER 12
[1]And the word of
Jehovah *came* to me, saying, [2]Son of man, you
dwell in the midst of a
rebellious house. *They* have
eyes to see, but they do not
see; they have ears to hear,
but they do not hear; for
they *are* a rebellious house.
[3]And you, son of man,
prepare for yourself vessels
for exile, and go into exile
by day in their sight. And
you shall be exiled from
your place to another place
in their sight. Perhaps they
will see that they *are* a

4805 1004 8432 120 1121 559 3068 1697 1961
1
2 וַיְהִי דְבַר־יְהוָה אֵלַי לֵאמֹר׃ בֶּן־אָדָם בְּתוֹךְ בֵּית־הַמֶּרִי
a house the in ,man of Son ,saying ,me to Jehovah the And
rebellious of midst of word was

241 7200 3808 7200 5869 3427
אַתָּה יֹשֵׁב אֲשֶׁר עֵינַיִם לָהֶם לִרְאוֹת וְלֹא רָאוּ אָזְנַיִם לָהֶם
to ears they and see to to eyes who ,dwell you
them (are) ;see not them (are)

1121 4805 1004 8085 3808 8085
3 לִשְׁמֹעַ וְלֹא שָׁמֵעוּ כִּי בֵּית מְרִי הֵם׃ וְאַתָּה בֶן־
son ,you And they a house for they and ,hear to
of .(are) rebellious ,hear not

1540 5869 3119 1473 1473 3627 6213 120
אָדָם עֲשֵׂה לְךָ כְּלֵי גוֹלָה וּגְלֵה יוֹמָם לְעֵינֵיהֶם וְגָלִיתָ
you And their in day by go and ,exile vessels for prepare ,man
exiled be shall .sight exile into for yourself

1004 7200 194 1540 312 4725 4725
מִמְּקוֹמְךָ אֶל־מָקוֹם אַחֵר לְעֵינֵיהֶם אוּלַי יִרְאוּ כִּי בֵּית
house that they Perhaps their in another place to your from
,see will .sight place

rebellious house. 4And you
shall bring forth your
vessels, as vessels for exile,
by day in their sight. And
you shall go forth at evening
in their sight, as those
going into exile. 5In their
sight dig for yourself
through the wall, and carry
out through it. 6In their
sight you shall carry on the
shoulder; in the dark, carry
out. You shall cover your
face, so that you do not see
the ground; for I have set
you as a wonder to the
house of Israel. 7And I did
so, as I was commanded. I
brought forth my vessel, as
vessels for exile, by day.
And in the evening I dug by
hand for myself through the
wall. I brought *it* out in the
dark; I carried on *my*
shoulder in their sight.
8And in the morning the
word of Jehovah *came* to
me, saying, 9Son of man,
Has not the house of Israel
that rebellious house, said
to you, What are you doing?
10Say to them, So says the
Lord Jehovah: This burden
is to the prince in Jerusalem, and to all the house
of Israel who *are* among
them. 11Say, I *am* your
wonder. As I have done, so
it shall be done to them.
They shall go into exile, into
captivity. 12And the prince
who *is* among them shall
carry on *his* shoulder in the
dark, and go forth through
the wall. They shall dig to
bring out by it. He shall
cover his face so that he
does not look with the eye
on the earth. 13And I will
spread My net on him, and
he shall be taken in My
snare. And I will bring him
to Babylon, the land of the
Chaldeans. Yet he will not
see it; and he shall die
there. 14And all who *are*
around him, his help and all
his bands, I will scatter to

5869 3119 1473 3627 3627 3318 4805
4 מרי המה: והוצאת כליך ככלי גולה יומם לעיניהם
their in day by ,exile as your shall you Then they re- a
.sight for vessels ,vessels forth bring .(are) bellious

5869 1473 4161 5869 6153 3318
5 ואתה תצא בערב לעיניהם כמוצאי גולה: לעיניהם
their In .exile those as their in at go shall you And
sight into going ,sight evening forth

5375 3801 5869 3318 7023 2864
6 חתר־לך בקיר והוצאת בו: לעיניהם על־כתף תשא
shall you the on their In through carry and through for Dig
;carry shoulder sight .it out ,wall the you

776 7200 3808 3680 6440 3318 5939
בעלטה תוציא פניך תכסה ולא תראה את־הארץ כי
for ,ground the see you so shall you Your carry the in
not that cover face .out (it) dark

3627 6680 6213 3478 1004 5414 4159
7 מופת נתתיך לבית ישראל: ואעש כן כאשר צויתי כלי
My was I as ,so I And .Israel the to have I a as
vessel .commanded did of house you set wonder

3027 7023 2864 6153 3119 1473 3627 3318
הוצאתי ככלי גולה יומם ובערב חתרתי־לי בקיר ביד
by through for dug I the in and by ,exile vessels as brought I
.hand wall the me evening ;day for ,forth

1961 5869 5375 3801 3318 5939
8 בעלטה הוצאתי על־כתף נשאתי לעיניהם: ויהי
And their in carried I (my) on brought I the in
was .sight (it) shoulder .out (it) dark

559 3808 120 1121 559 1242 3068 1697
9 דבר־יהוה אלי בבקר לאמר: בן־אדם הלא אמרו אליך
you to said Has man Son ,saying the in to Jehovah the
not of morning me of word

559 6213 4100 4805 1004 3478 1004
10 בית ישראל בית המרי מה אתה עשה: אמר אליהם
,them to Say ?doing are you What ,rebellious the ,Israel the
house of house

3389 2088 4853 5387 3068 136 559 3541
כה אמר אדני יהוה הנשיא המשא הזה בירושלם
Jerusalem in This burden the :Jehovah Lord the says So
(to is) prince

4159 559 8432 834 3478 1004 3605
11 וכל־בית ישראל אשר־המה בתוכם: אמר אני מופתכם
your I ,Say among they who Israel the and
.wonder (am) .them (are) of house all

3212 7628 1473 6213 3651 6213
כאשר עשיתי כן יעשה להם בגולה בשבי ילכו:
They into into to shall it so have I As
.go shall ,captivity ,exile .them done be ,done

7023 3318 5939 5375 3801 8432 834 5387
12 והנשיא אשר־בתוכם אל־כתף ישא בעלטה ויצא בקיר
through go and ,dark the in shall (his) on among who the And
wall the forth carry shoulder them (is) prince

5869 7200 3808 3282 3680 6440 3318 2864
יחתרו להוציא בו פניו יכסה יען אשר לא־יראה לעין
the with does not so shall He his by bring to They
eye look that cover face .it out dig shall

8610 7561 6566 776
13 הוא את־הארץ: ופרשתי את־רשתי עליו ונתפש
he and ,him on net My will I the (on) (is) he
taken be shall spread also .earth

3808 6258 3778 776 894 935 4486
במצודתי והבאתי אתו בבלה ארץ כשדים ואותה לא־
not it Yet the the to him I And My in
.Chaldeans of land ,Babylon bring will .snare

102 3605 5828 5439 3605 4191 8033 7200
14 יראה ושם ימות: וכל אשר סביבתיו עזרה וכל־אגפיו
his all and his around who And shall he and will he
,bands all ,help him (are) .die there .see

every wind; and I will draw out a sword after them. 15And they shall know that I *am* Jehovah when I shall scatter them among the nations and disperse them in the lands. 16But I will leave of them a number of men, from the sword, from the famine, and from the plague, so that they may declare all their abominations among the nations, there where they go. And they shall know that I *am* Jehovah.

17And the word of Jehovah was to me, saying, 18Son of man, eat your bread with quaking and drink your water with trembling and anxiety. 19And say to the people of the land, So says the Lord Jehovah to the dwellers of Jerusalem, to the land of Israel: They shall eat their bread with anxiety and drink their water with horror, so that her land may be desolated of her fullness, because of the violence of all those who live in her. 20And the cities that have people shall be laid waste, and the land shall be desolate. And You shall know that I *am* Jehovah.

21And the word of Jehovah was to me, saying, 22Son of man, what *is* this proverb to you on the land of Israel, saying, The days are long, and every vision shall perish? 23Therefore, tell them, So says the Lord Jehovah: I will make this proverb cease, and they shall not use it again in Israel. However, say to them, The days draw near, and the matter of every vision. 24For there shall not again be every vain vision, nor slippery divination, within the house of Israel.

3045 310 7324 2719 7307 3605 2219
15 אֱזָרֶה לְכָל־רוּחַ וְחֶרֶב אָרִיק אַחֲרֵיהֶם׃ וְיָדְעוּ כִּי־אֲנִי
I that they And .them after will I a and ;wind to will I
(am) know shall out draw sword every scatter

776 2219 1471 6327 3068
יְהוָה בַּהֲפִיצִי אוֹתָם בַּגּוֹיִם וְזֵרִיתִי אוֹתָם בָּאֲרָצוֹת׃
the in them and the among them I when ,Jehovah
.lands scatter nations scatter shall

1698 7450 2719 4557 582 3498
16 וְהוֹתַרְתִּי מֵהֶם אַנְשֵׁי מִסְפָּר מֵחֶרֶב מֵרָעָב וּמִדָּבֶר לְמַעַן
so from and the from the from a men of will I But
that ,plague the ,famine ,sword of number of them leave

3045 8033 935 834 1471 8441 3605 5608
יְסַפְּרוּ אֶת־כָּל־תּוֹעֲבוֹתֵיהֶם בַּגּוֹיִם אֲשֶׁר־בָּאוּ שָׁם וְיָדְעוּ
they And .there they where the among their all may they
know shall go nations abominations declare

1121 559 3068 1697 1961 3068
17
18 כִּי־אֲנִי יְהוָה׃ וַיְהִי דְבַר־יְהוָה אֵלַי לֵאמֹר׃ בֶּן
Son ,saying ,me to Jehovah the And .Jehovah I that
of of word was (am)

8354 1674 7269 4325 398 7494 3899 120
אָדָם לַחְמְךָ בְּרַעַשׁ תֹּאכֵל וּמֵימֶיךָ בְּרָגְזָה וּבִדְאָגָה תִּשְׁתֶּה׃
.drink with and with your and eat with your ,man
anxiety trembling water quaking bread

3427 3068 136 559 776 5971 559
19 וְאָמַרְתָּ אֶל־עַם הָאָרֶץ כֹּה־אָמַר אֲדֹנָי יְהוִה לְיוֹשְׁבֵי
the to Jehovah the says Thus the the to say And
of dwellers Lord :land of people

398 1674 3899 3478 127 3389
יְרוּשָׁלִַם אֶל־אַדְמַת יִשְׂרָאֵל לַחְמָם בִּדְאָגָה יֹאכֵלוּ
They with their :Israel the to ,Jerusalem
eat shall anxiety bread of land

4393 776 3456 8354 8078 4325
וּמֵימֵיהֶם בְּשִׁמָּמוֹן יִשְׁתּוּ לְמַעַן תֵּשַׁם אַרְצָהּ מִמְּלֹאָהּ
her of her be may that so ,drink with their and
fulness land desolated horror water

2717 5971 5892 3427 3605 2555
20 מֵחֲמַס כָּל־הַיֹּשְׁבִים בָּהּ׃ וְהֶעָרִים הַנּוֹשָׁבוֹת תֶּחֱרַבְנָה
be shall have that the And in who those all of because
,waste laid people cities .her live of violence the

1961 3068 3045 1961 8077 776
21 וְהָאָרֶץ שְׁמָמָה תִהְיֶה וִידַעְתֶּם כִּי־אֲנִי יְהוָה׃ וַיְהִי
And .Jehovah I that you And shall desolate the and
was (am) know shall .be land

2088 4912 120/1121 559 3068 1697
22 דְבַר־יְהוָה אֵלַי לֵאמֹר׃ בֶּן־אָדָם מָה־הַמָּשָׁל הַזֶּה לָכֶם
you to this proverb what ,man Son ,saying to Jehovah the
(is) of ,me of word

2377 3605 3117 748 559 559 3478 127
עַל־אַדְמַת יִשְׂרָאֵל לֵאמֹר יַאַרְכוּ הַיָּמִים וְאָבַד כָּל־חָזוֹן׃
?vision every and days The are ,saying ,Israel the on
perish shall long of land

7673 3068 136 559/3541 559
23 לָכֵן אֱמֹר אֲלֵיהֶם כֹּה־אָמַר אֲדֹנָי יְהוִה הִשְׁבַּתִּי אֶת־
make will I :Jehovah the says Thus ,them tell There-
cease to Lord fore

1696 3478 5750 4911 3808 2088 4912
הַמָּשָׁל הַזֶּה וְלֹא־יִמְשְׁלוּ אֹתוֹ עוֹד בְּיִשְׂרָאֵל כִּי אִם־דַּבֵּר
say ,however ;Israel in still it shall they and ,this proverb
use not

5750 1961 3808 2377 3605 1697 3117 7126
אֲלֵיהֶם קָרְבוּ הַיָּמִים וּדְבַר כָּל־חָזוֹן׃ כִּי לֹא יִהְיֶה עוֹד
24
still shall there not For .vision every the and The draw ,them to
be of matter ,days near

3478 1004 8432 2509 4738 7723 2377 3605
25 כָּל־חֲזוֹן שָׁוְא וּמִקְסַם חָלָק בְּתוֹךְ בֵּית יִשְׂרָאֵל׃ כִּי אֲנִי
,I For .Israel the within slippery nor vain vision every
of house divination

[25]For I, Jehovah, will speak. The word which I shall speak shall be done; it shall not be delayed again. For in your days, O house of rebellion, I will say the word and will do it, declares the Lord Jehovah.

[26]And the word of Jehovah was to me, saying, [27]Son of man, behold, the house of Israel *is* saying, The vision that he *is* seeing *is* for many days, and he prophesies for times far off. [28]Therefore, say to them, So says the Lord Jehovah: Not any of My words will be delayed any longer. What I have spoken, *that* word shall be done, declares the Lord Jehovah.

4900 38,08 6213 1697 1696 834 1697 3068
יְהוָה אֲדַבֵּר אֵת אֲשֶׁר אֲדַבֵּר דָּבָר וְיֵעָשֶׂה לֹא תִמָּשֵׁךְ
be shall it not be shall the shall I (and) will ,Jehovah
out drawn ,done thing speak what ,speak

5002 6.213 1697 1696 4805 1004 3117 5750
עוֹד כִּי בִימֵיכֶם בֵּית הַמֶּרִי אֲדַבֵּר דָּבָר וַעֲשִׂיתִיו נְאֻם
states will and the will I ,rebellious O your in for ;still
,it do word say house ,days

26
27 120 1121 559 3068 1697 1961 3068 136
אֲדֹנָי יְהוִה׃ וַיְהִי דְבַר־יְהוָה אֵלַי לֵאמֹר׃ בֶּן־אָדָם
,man Son ,saying to Jehovah the And .Jehovah the
of ,me of word was Lord

3117 2088 834 2377 559 3478 1004 2009
הִנֵּה בֵית־יִשְׂרָאֵל אֹמְרִים הֶחָזוֹן אֲשֶׁר־הוּא חֹזֶה לְיָמִים
for (is) is he that The ,saying ;Israel the ,behold
days seeing vision of house

28 35.41 559 5012 7350 6256 7227
רַבִּים וּלְעִתִּים רְחוֹקוֹת הוּא נִבָּא׃ לָכֵן אֱמֹר אֲלֵיהֶם כֹּה
Thus to say Therefore proph- he off far for and ,many
,them esies times

1696 834 1697 3605 5750 4900 38.08 3068 136 559
אָמַר אֲדֹנָי יְהוִה לֹא־תִמָּשֵׁךְ עוֹד כָּל־דְּבָרָי אֲשֶׁר אֲדַבֵּר
have I what My any any be will Not :Jehovah the says
,spoken ;words of longer out drawn Lord

3068 136 5002 6213 1697
דָּבָר וְיֵעָשֶׂה נְאֻם אֲדֹנָי יְהוִה׃
.Jehovah the states shall (that)
Lord ,done be word

CAP. XIII. יג

CHAPTER 13

[1]And the word of Jehovah *came* to me, saying, [2]Son of man, prophesy against the prophets of Israel who prophesy. And say to those who prophesy out of their own heart, Hear the word of Jehovah: [3]So says the Lord Jehovah, Woe to the foolish prophets who walk after their own spirit, and have seen nothing! [4]O Israel, your prophets are like foxes in the deserts. [5]You have not gone up into the breaks, nor built a wall around the house of Israel, that it might stand in the battle, in the day of Jehovah. [6]They have seen vanity and lying divination, saying, Jehovah declares! And Jehovah has not sent them; but they hoped to confirm *their* word. [7]Did you not see a vain vision and speak a lying divination? Yet *you* say, Jehovah declares; though I have not spoken.

1
2 5030 5012 120 1121 559 3068 1697 1961
וַיְהִי דְבַר־יְהוָה אֵלַי לֵאמֹר׃ בֶּן־אָדָם הִנָּבֵא אֶל־נְבִיאֵי
the against prophesy ,man Son ,saying ,me to Jehovah the And
of prophets of of word was

1697 8085 3820 5012 559 5012 3478
יִשְׂרָאֵל הַנִּבָּאִים וְאָמַרְתָּ לִנְבִיאֵי מִלִּבָּם שִׁמְעוּ דְּבַר־
the Hear their of out those to say And who Israel
of word ,heart own prophesy who .prophesy

3 5036 5030 1945 3068 136 559 3068
יְהוָה׃ כֹּה אָמַר אֲדֹנָי יְהוִה הוֹי עַל־הַנְּבִיאִים הַנְּבָלִים
foolish the prophets to Woe ,Jehovah the says Thus :Jehovah
Lord

4 2723 7776 7200 1115 7307 310 1980 834
אֲשֶׁר הֹלְכִים אַחַר רוּחָם וּלְבִלְתִּי רָאוּ׃ כְּשֻׁעָלִים בָּחֳרָבוֹת
the in foxes like have and own their after walk who
deserts !seen nothing spirit

5 1447 1443 6556 6927 3808 3478 5030
נְבִיאֶיךָ יִשְׂרָאֵל הָיוּ׃ לֹא עֲלִיתֶם בַּפְּרָצוֹת וַתִּגְדְּרוּ גָדֵר
wall a built nor the into have You not .are ,Israel O your
,breaks up gone prophets

6 7723 2372 3068 3117 4421 5975 3478 1004
עַל־בֵּית יִשְׂרָאֵל לַעֲמֹד בַּמִּלְחָמָה בְּיוֹם יְהוָה׃ חָזוּ שָׁוְא
vanity They .Jehovah the in the in it that ,Israel the around
seen have of day battle stand might of house

3176 7971 3808 3068 5002 559 3577 7081
וְקֶסֶם כָּזָב הָאֹמְרִים נְאֻם־יְהוָה וַיהוָה לֹא שְׁלָחָם וְיִחֲלוּ
they but sent has not And .Jehovah states ,saying ,lying and
hoped ;them Jehovah divination

7 3577 4738 2372 7723 4236 3808 1697 6965
לְקַיֵּם דָּבָר׃ הֲלוֹא מַחֲזֵה־שָׁוְא חֲזִיתֶם וּמִקְסַם כָּזָב
lying a and see you vain vision a Did (their) to
divination not .word confirm

1696 3808 3068 5002 559 559
אֲמַרְתֶּם וְאֹמְרִים נְאֻם־יְהוָה וַאֲנִי לֹא דִבַּרְתִּי׃
have not though ,Jehovah states (you) yet speak
?spoken I ,say

[8]Therefore, so says the Lord Jehovah: Because you have spoken vanity and have seen a lie, therefore, behold, I *am* against you, declares the Lord Jehovah. [9]And My hand shall be against the prophets who see vanity, and who divine a lie. They shall not be in the council of My people, and they shall not be written in the writing of the house of Israel; and they shall not enter into the land of Israel. And you shall know that I *am* the Lord Jehovah.

[10]Because, even because they made My people go astray, saying, Peace—and there was no peace—and he builds a wall, and, behold, *others* daubed it *with* lime. [11]Say to those daubing *with* lime, Yea, it will fall; there will be a flooding rain; and you, O hailstones, shall fall; and a raging wind shall break. [12]And, behold, when the wall has fallen, it shall not be said to you, Where *is* the daubing with which you have daubed?

[13]Therefore, So says the Lord Jehovah: I will even break in My fury *with* a raging wind. And there shall be a flooding rain in My anger, and hailstones in fury, to consume it. [14]And I will break down the wall that you have daubed *with* lime, and touch it to the ground; yea, I will bare its base. And it shall fall, and you will be consumed in its midst. And you shall know that I *am* Jehovah. [15]And I will fulfill My wrath in the wall, and in those who daubed it *with* lime. And I will say to you, The wall is not; and, Those who daubed *are* not —[16]the prophets of Israel who prophesy *as* to Jerusalem, and who see visions of peace for her; and there is no peace—declares the Lord Jehovah.

[17]And you, son of man,

3577 2372 7723 1696 3282 3068 136 559
8 לָכֵן כֹּה אָמַר אֲדֹנָי יְהוִה יַעַן דַּבֶּרְכֶם שָׁוְא וַחֲזִיתֶם כָּזָב
,lie a | and seen | vanity | have you spoken | Be-cause | :Jehovah | the Lord | says | thus | There-fore

3027 1961 3068 136 5002 2009
9 לָכֵן הִנְנִי אֲלֵיכֶם נְאֻם אֲדֹנָי יְהוִה׃ וְהָיְתָה יָדִי אֶל־
against | My hand | And be shall | .Jehovah | the Lord | states | against you | behold (am) I | there-fore

1961 3808 5971 5480 3577 7080 7723 2376 5030
הַנְּבִאִים הַחֹזִים שָׁוְא וְהַקֹּסְמִים כָּזָב בְּסוֹד עַמִּי לֹא־יִהְיוּ
they be shall | not | My people | the of council In | !lie a | who and divine | vanity | see who | the prophets

3808 3478 127 3789 3808 3478 1004 3791
וּבִכְתָב בֵּית־יִשְׂרָאֵל לֹא יִכָּתֵבוּ וְאֶל־אַדְמַת יִשְׂרָאֵל לֹא
not | Israel | the of land | and into | shall they ,written be | not | Israel | the of house | the in and of writing

2937 3282 3282 3068 136 3045 935
10 יָבֹאוּ וִידַעְתֶּם כִּי־אֲנִי אֲדֹנָי יְהוִה׃ יַעַן וּבְיַעַן הִטְעוּ אֶת־
they stray made | even because | ,Because | .Jehovah | the Lord | I that (am) | you And know shall | shall .enter they

2902 2009 2434 1129 7965 369 7965 559 5971
עַמִּי לֵאמֹר שָׁלוֹם וְאֵין שָׁלוֹם וְהוּא בֹּנֶה חַיִץ וְהִנָּם טָחִים
(others) daubed | and ,behold | wall a | builds | and he | —peace | and no was there | —Peace | ,saying | My ,people

7857 1653 1961 5307 8602 2902 559 8602
11 אֹתוֹ תָּפֵל׃ אֱמֹר אֶל־טָחֵי תָפֵל וְיִפֹּל הָיָה ׀ גֶּשֶׁם שׁוֹטֵף
a ;flooding | rain | be will | ;fall will | it ,Yea | (with) ,lime | those daubing | to | Say | (with) .lime | it

1234 5592 7307 5307 417 68 859
וְאַתֵּנָה אַבְנֵי אֶלְגָּבִישׁ תִּפֹּלְנָה וְרוּחַ סְעָרוֹת תְּבַקֵּעַ׃
shall .break | raging | a and wind | shall ;fall | ,hail | O of stones | ,you and

834 2915 559 3808 7023 5307 2009
12 וְהִנֵּה נָפַל הַקִּיר הֲלוֹא יֵאָמֵר אֲלֵיכֶם אַיֵּה הַטִּיחַ אֲשֶׁר
with which | the daubing | Where (is) | ,you to | said be | it shall not | the wall | having fallen | ,And lo

7307 1234 3068 136 559 2902
13 טַחְתֶּם׃ לָכֵן כֹּה אָמַר אֲדֹנָי יְהוִה וּבִקַּעְתִּי רוּחַ
a (with) wind | will I break even | :Jehovah | the Lord | says | thus | Therefore | have you ?daubed

417 68 1961 639 7857 1653 2534 5591
סְעָרוֹת בַּחֲמָתִי וְגֶשֶׁם שֹׁטֵף בְּאַפִּי יִהְיֶה וְאַבְנֵי אֶלְגָּבִישׁ
hail | and of stones | there ;be shall | My in anger | a flooding | a And rain | My in fury | raging

8602 2902 834 7023 2040 3617 2534
14 בְּחֵמָה לְכַלָּה׃ וְהָרַסְתִּי אֶת־הַקִּיר אֲשֶׁר־טַחְתֶּם תָּפֵל
(with) ,lime | have you daubed | that | the wall | will I So down break | con- to .it sume | (My) in fury

8432 3615 5307 3247 1540 776 5060
וְהִגַּעְתִּיהוּ אֶל־הָאָרֶץ וְנִגְלָה יְסֹדוֹ וְנָפְלָה וּכְלִיתֶם בְּתוֹכָהּ
its in ;midst | will you and consumed be | it And fall shall | its .base | I and bare will | the ;ground | to | it touch and

2902 7023 2534 3615 3068 3045
15 וִידַעְתֶּם כִּי־אֲנִי יְהוָה׃ וְכִלֵּיתִי אֶת־חֲמָתִי בַּקִּיר וּבַטָּחִים
those in and daubed who | the in wall | My wrath | I So fulfill will | .Jehovah | I that (am) | you and know shall

5030 2902 369 7023 369 559 8602
16 אֹתוֹ תָּפֵל וְאֹמַר לָכֶם אֵין הַקִּיר וְאֵין הַטָּחִים אֹתוֹ׃ נְבִיאֵי
the of prophets | —it | who those daubed | and (are) not | the ,wall | Is not | ,you to | will and say | (with) ;lime | it

7965 2377 2376 3389 5012 3478
יִשְׂרָאֵל הַנִּבְּאִים אֶל־יְרוּשָׁלִַם וְהַחֹזִים לָהּ חֲזוֹן שָׁלֹם
,peace | visions of | for her | who and see | ,Jerusalem | (as) to | who prophesy | Israel

7760 120 1121 3068 136 5002 7965 369
17 וְאֵין שָׁלֹם נְאֻם אֲדֹנָי יְהוִה׃ וְאַתָּה בֶן־אָדָם שִׂים
set | ,man of | son | ,you And | .Jehovah | the Lord | states | ,peace | and no is there

פָּנֶיךָ אֶל־בְּנוֹת עַמְּךָ הַמִּתְנַבְּאוֹת מִלִּבְּהֶן וְהִנָּבֵא עֲלֵיהֶן׃
against and of out prophesy who your the against your
,them prophesy ;heart their ,people of daughters face

18 וְאָמַרְתָּ כֹּה־אָמַר ׀ אֲדֹנָי יְהוִה הוֹי לִמְתַפְּרוֹת כְּסָתוֹת
bands those to Woe :Jehovah the says Thus ,say and
sewing Lord

עַל ׀ כָּל־אַצִּילֵי יָדַי וְעֹשׂוֹת הַמִּסְפָּחוֹת עַל־רֹאשׁ כָּל־
every the for veils long and my joints all to
of head make ,hands of

קוֹמָה לְצוֹדֵד נְפָשׁוֹת הַנְּפָשׁוֹת תְּצוֹדֵדְנָה לְעַמִּי וּנְפָשׁוֹת
the and My of you will The !souls hunt to (of man)
souls ,people hunt souls ,stature

19 לָכֶנָה תְחַיֶּינָה׃ וַתְּחַלֶּלְנָה אֹתִי אֶל־עַמִּי בְּשַׁעֲלֵי שְׂעֹרִים
barley hand- for My among Me will you And you will your- for
of fuls people profane ?alive save selves

וּבִפְתוֹתֵי לֶחֶם לְהָמִית נְפָשׁוֹת אֲשֶׁר לֹא־תְמוּתֶנָה וּלְחַיּוֹת
to and ,die should not that souls the put to ,bread for and
alive save death to of bits

נְפָשׁוֹת אֲשֶׁר לֹא־תִחְיֶינָה בְּכַזֶּבְכֶם לְעַמִּי שֹׁמְעֵי כָזָב׃
.lies who My to your by should not that souls the
to listen people lying ,live

20 לָכֵן כֹּה־אָמַר ׀ אֲדֹנָי יְהוִה הִנְנִי אֶל־כִּסְּתוֹתֵיכֶנָה
your against ,Behold :Jehovah the says thus Therefore
bands (am) I Lord

אֲשֶׁר אַתֵּנָה מְצֹדְדוֹת שָׁם אֶת־הַנְּפָשׁוֹת לְפֹרְחוֹת וְקָרַעְתִּי
I And make to souls the there are you with
tear will .fly (them) hunting which

אֹתָם מֵעַל זְרוֹעֹתֵיכֶם וְשִׁלַּחְתִּי אֶת־הַנְּפָשׁוֹת אֲשֶׁר אַתֶּם
you which ,souls the will and arms your from them
out send

21 מְצֹדְדוֹת אֶת־נְפָשִׁים לְפֹרְחֹת׃ וְקָרַעְתִּי אֶת־מִסְפְּחֹתֵיכֶם
veils long your I Also make to souls are
tear will .fly hunting

וְהִצַּלְתִּי אֶת־עַמִּי מִיֶּדְכֶן וְלֹא־יִהְיוּ עוֹד בְּיֶדְכֶן לִמְצוּדָה
be to your in yet they and of out My and
.hunted hand be shall not ,hand your people deliver

22 וִידַעְתֶּן כִּי־אֲנִי יְהוָה׃ יַעַן הַכְאוֹת לֵב־צַדִּיק שֶׁקֶר וַאֲנִי לֹא
not and (with) the the have you Be- .Jehovah I that you And
,lies righteous of heart saddened cause (am) know shall

הִכְאַבְתִּיו וּלְחַזֵּק יְדֵי רָשָׁע לְבִלְתִּי־שׁוּב מִדַּרְכּוֹ הָרָע
, evil his from he that so the the have and made have I
way turn should not ,wicked of hands .strong made ;sad him

23 לְהַחֲיֹתוֹ׃ לָכֵן שָׁוְא לֹא תֶחֱזֶינָה וְקֶסֶם לֹא־תִקְסַמְנָה עוֹד
.any shall you not and shall you not vanity Therefore keep to
divine divination see .alive him

וְהִצַּלְתִּי אֶת־עַמִּי מִיֶּדְכֶן וִידַעְתֶּן כִּי־אֲנִי יְהוָה׃
.Jehovah I that you and of out My will I And
(am) know shall ;hand your people deliver

set your face against the daughters of your people, who prophesy out of their heart; and prophesy against them, 18 and say, So says the Lord Jehovah: Woe to those sewing bands to all joints of my hands, and make long veils for the head of every *man of* stature, to hunt souls! Will you hunt the souls of My people; and will you save alive the souls for yourselves? 19 And will you profane Me among My people for handfuls of barley, and for bits of bread, to put to death the souls that should not die, and to save alive the souls that should not live; by your lying to My people who listen to lies?

20 Therefore, so says the Lord Jehovah: Behold, I *am* against your bands with which you are hunting the souls there, to make *them* fly. And I will tear them from your arms, and will send out the souls, souls which you are hunting, to make *them* fly. 21 Also I will tear your long veils and deliver My people out of your hand. And they shall not again be in your hand to be hunted. And you shall know that I *am* Jehovah. 22 Because you have saddened the heart of the righteous *with* lies, and I have not made him sad; and have made the hands of the wicked strong, so that he should not turn from his evil way, to keep him alive; 23 therefore, you shall not see vanity; and you shall not divine any divination. And I will deliver My people out of your hand. And you shall know that I *am* Jehovah.

CHAPTER 14

[1]And the men of the elders of Israel came to me, and sat before me. [2]And the word of Jehovah came to me, saying, [3]Son of man, these men have set up their idols in their hearts, and have put the stumbling-block of their iniquity before their faces. Should I at all be sought by them?

[4]Therefore, speak to them and say to them, So says the Lord Jehovah: Every man of the house of Israel who sets up his idols in his heart, and puts the stumbling-block of his iniquity before his face, and comes to the prophet; I, Jehovah, will answer him in it by the host of his idols; [5]so that I may capture the house of Israel in their own heart, who are estranged from Me by their idols, all of them.

[6]Therefore, say to the house of Israel, So says the Lord Jehovah: Turn, and be turned from your idols, and from all your abominations turn away your faces. [7]For every man of the house of Israel, or of the alien who sojourns in Israel, who is separated from after Me, and sets up his idols in his heart, and puts the stumbling-block of his iniquity before his face, and comes to the prophet to inquire of him concerning Me — I, Jehovah, will answer him Myself. [8]And I will set My face against that man, and I will make him desolate for a sign and for proverbs. And I will cut him off from the midst of My people. And you shall know that I *am* Jehovah.

CAP. XIV יד

CHAPTER 14

1 2 וַיָּבוֹא אֵלַי אֲנָשִׁים מִזִּקְנֵי יִשְׂרָאֵל וַיֵּשְׁבוּ לְפָנָי׃ וַיְהִי
And came / before me / sat and / Israel / the of elders / men / to me / Then came

3 דְבַר־יְהוָה אֵלַי לֵאמֹר׃ בֶּן־אָדָם הָאֲנָשִׁים הָאֵלֶּה הֶעֱלוּ
have set up / these / men / ,man Son of / ,saying / ,me to / Jehovah / the of word

גִלּוּלֵיהֶם עַל־לִבָּם וּמִכְשׁוֹל עֲוֺנָם נָתְנוּ נֹכַח פְּנֵיהֶם הַאִדָּרֹשׁ
all At / their faces / before / put / their iniquity / the and of stumblingblock / ,hearts their / in idols their

4 אִדָּרֵשׁ לָהֶם׃ לָכֵן דַּבֵּר־אוֹתָם וְאָמַרְתָּ אֲלֵיהֶם
,them to / say and / them / speak to / Therefore / by ?them / I should sought be

כֹּה־אָמַר ׀ אֲדֹנָי יְהוִה אִישׁ אִישׁ מִבֵּית יִשְׂרָאֵל אֲשֶׁר
who / Israel / the of house / man / Every / :Jehovah / the Lord / says Thus

יַעֲלֶה אֶת־גִּלּוּלָיו אֶל־לִבּוֹ וּמִכְשׁוֹל עֲוֺנוֹ יָשִׂים נֹכַח פָּנָיו
his ,face / before / puts / his iniquity / stum-the and of blingblock / his heart / in / idols his / up sets

וּבָא אֶל־הַנָּבִיא אֲנִי יְהוָה נַעֲנֵיתִי לוֹ בָהּ בְּרֹב גִּלּוּלָיו׃
;idols his / the by of host / it in / him / will answer / Jehovah / I / the ;prophet / to / and comes

5 לְמַעַן תְּפֹשׂ אֶת־בֵּית־יִשְׂרָאֵל בְּלִבָּם אֲשֶׁר נָזֹרוּ מֵעָלַי
from Me / are estranged / who / their in heart own / Israel / the of house / may I capture / that so

6 בְּגִלּוּלֵיהֶם כֻּלָּם׃ לָכֵן אֱמֹר ׀ אֶל־בֵּית יִשְׂרָאֵל
,Israel / the of house / to / say / Therefore / of all .them / their by idols

כֹּה אָמַר אֲדֹנָי יְהוִה שׁוּבוּ וְהָשִׁיבוּ מֵעַל גִּלּוּלֵיכֶם וּמֵעַל
and from / ,idols your / from / be and turned / ,Turn / :Jehovah / the Lord / says Thus

7 כָּל־תּוֹעֲבֹתֵיכֶם הָשִׁיבוּ פְנֵיכֶם׃ כִּי אִישׁ אִישׁ מִבֵּית
the of of house / man / every / For / .faces your / away turn / your abominations / all

יִשְׂרָאֵל וּמֵהַגֵּר אֲשֶׁר־יָגוּר בְּיִשְׂרָאֵל וְיִנָּזֵר מֵאַחֲרַי וְיַעַל
and go makes / after from ;Me / is who separated / ,Israel in / sojourns who / of or alien the / ,Israel

גִּלּוּלָיו אֶל־לִבּוֹ וּמִכְשׁוֹל עֲוֺנוֹ יָשִׂים נֹכַח פָּנָיו וּבָא אֶל־
to / and comes / his ,face / before / puts / his iniquity / stum-the and of blingblock / his ,heart / in / idols his

8 הַנָּבִיא לִדְרָשׁ־לוֹ בִי אֲנִי יְהוָה נַעֲנֶה־לּוֹ בִּי׃ וְנָתַתִּי פָנַי
My face / I And set will / My- .self / him / will answer / ,Jehovah / ,I / of ;Me / him / seek to / the prophet

בָּאִישׁ הַהוּא וַהֲשִׁמֹתִיהוּ לְאוֹת וְלִמְשָׁלִים וְהִכְרַתִּיו
will I and off him cut / for and ,proverbs / a for sign / make will I and desolate him / that / against man

9 מִתּוֹךְ עַמִּי וִידַעְתֶּם כִּי־אֲנִי יְהוָה׃ וְהַנָּבִיא כִי־יְפֻתֶּה
is he if deceived / the And prophet / .Jehovah / I (am) / that / you and know shall / My ;people / the from of midst

9And the prophet, if he is deceived, and he speaks a word, I, Jehovah, have deceived that prophet. And I will stretch out My hand on him and will destroy him from the midst of My people Israel. 10And they shall bear their iniquity. As the iniquity of the inquirer, so the iniquity of the prophet shall be. 11So that the house of Israel may not stray any more from after Me, and not be defiled again with all their transgressions; but they are to Me for a people, and I will be to them for God, declares the Lord Jehovah.

12And the word of Jehovah was to me, saying, 13Son of man, when a land sins against Me by traitorous betraying, then I will stretch out My hand on it, and will shatter the staff of bread to it, and I will send famine on it. And I will cut off from it man and beast. 14And though these three men were in its midst, Noah, Daniel, and Job; by their righteousness they should deliver only their souls, declares the Lord Jehovah. 15If I make evil beasts go through the land, and they bereave it, and it is desolate, so that no one would go through because of the beasts; 16though these three men were in its midst, as I live, declares the Lord Jehovah, they would deliver neither sons nor daughters; they would only deliver themselves; but the land would be desolate. 17Or if I bring a sword on that land and say, Let a sword go through the land, and I will cut off man and beast from it; 18even though these three men were in its midst, as I live, declares the Lord Jehovah, they should not deliver sons or daughters, but they only would deliver themselves. 19Or if I send a

---

1696   16 97   3068   6601   5030   5186

וְהַנָּבִיא כִי־יְפֻתֶּה וְדִבֶּר דָּבָר אֲנִי יְהוָה פִּתֵּיתִי אֵת הַנָּבִיא הַהוּא וְנָטִיתִי אֶת־

he and speaks   a   I, Jehovah   have   prophet   that,   I and
word   deceived   will stretch out

3027   8045   8432   5971   3478   53 75   5771

10   יָדִי עָלָיו וְהִשְׁמַדְתִּיו מִתּוֹךְ עַמִּי יִשְׂרָאֵל: וְנָשְׂאוּ עֲוֺנָם

My   on   him   will and   the   My   of midst   .Israel   And   they   their
hand   him   destroy   from   people   shall bear   iniquity;

5771   1875   5771   5030   1961   4616   38 08   8582   5750   1004

11   כַּעֲוֺן הַדֹּרֵשׁ כַּעֲוֺן הַנָּבִיא יִהְיֶה: לְמַעַן לֹא־יִתְעוּ עוֹד בֵּית־

the as   of iniquity   the   the so   in- the   shall   that So   not   may   any   the
of   quirer,   iniquity   of prophet   be.   stray   more   house

5971   1961   3478   310   3808   2930   5750   3605   6588   1961

יִשְׂרָאֵל מֵאַחֲרַי וְלֹא־יִטַּמְּאוּ עוֹד בְּכָל־פִּשְׁעֵיהֶם וְהָיוּ־

Israel   from   not   defiled   and   be   again   with   their   transgressions,   but   to
after Me,   they are   Me

3068   136   5002   430   1961   5971

לִי לְעָם וַאֲנִי אֶהְיֶה לָהֶם לֵאלֹהִים נְאֻם אֲדֹנָי יְהוִה:

.Jehovah   the   states   ,God   for   to   will   and   a   for
Lord   them   be   I   ,people

1961   1697   3068   559   1121   120   776   2398

12   וַיְהִי דְבַר־יְהוָה אֵלַי לֵאמֹר: בֶּן־אָדָם אֶרֶץ כִּי תֶחֱטָא־לִי
13

against   it   when   a   ,man   Son   ,saying   to   Jehovah   the   And
Me   sins   ,land   of   me   of word   was

4603   4604   5186   3027   5921   7665   4294   3899

לְמַעַל־מַעַל וְנָטִיתִי יָדִי עָלֶיהָ וְשָׁבַרְתִּי לָהּ מַטֵּה־לָחֶם

bread   the   it to   will and   it on   My   will I then   traitorous by
of staff   shatter   hand   out stretch   ,betraying

7971   7458   3772   120   929   1961

14   וְהִשְׁלַחְתִּי־בָהּ רָעָב וְהִכְרַתִּי מִמֶּנָּה אָדָם וּבְהֵמָה: וְהָיוּ

And   .beast   and   man   from   will I And   .famine   on   will and
were   it   off cut   it   send

7969   582   84:32   4 28   5146   1840   347

שְׁלֹשֶׁת הָאֲנָשִׁים הָאֵלֶּה בְּתוֹכָהּ נֹחַ דָּנִאֵל וְאִיּוֹב הֵמָּה

they   Job and   Daniel   ,Noah   its in   these   men   three
     ,midst

6666   5337   5315   3068   136   5002   7451   2416

15   בְצִדְקָתָם יְנַצְּלוּ נַפְשָׁם נְאֻם אֲדֹנָי יְהוִה: לוּ־חַיָּה רָעָה

evil   beasts If   .Jehovah   the   states   their (only)   should   their by
Lord   ,souls   deliver   righteousness

5674   776   7921   1961   8077   1097   56:74   6440

אַעֲבִיר בָּאָרֶץ וְשִׁכְּלָתָּה וְהָיְתָה שְׁמָמָה מִבְּלִי עוֹבֵר מִפְּנֵי

because   would   that so   ,desolate   is it and   they and   the   pass make I
of   pass   one no   ,it bereave   ,land   through

2416   7969   582   428   8432   2416   5002   136

16   הַחַיָּה: שְׁלֹשֶׁת הָאֲנָשִׁים הָאֵלֶּה בְּתוֹכָהּ חַי־אָנִי נְאֻם אֲדֹנָי

the   states   ,I (as)   its in   these   ,men   (if even)   the
Lord   live   ,midst   (were)   three   ;beasts

3068   1121   1323   5337   905   53:37   776

יְהוָה אִם־בָּנִים וְאִם־בָּנוֹת יַצִּילוּ הֵמָּה לְבַדָּם יִנָּצֵלוּ וְהָאָרֶץ

the but   would   only   they   would they   daugh-   nor   sons   neither   Jeho-
land   ,deliver   themselves   ;deliver   ters   .vah

1961   8077   2719   935   776   559

17   תִהְיֶה שְׁמָמָה: אוֹ חֶרֶב אָבִיא עַל־הָאָרֶץ הַהִיא וְאָמַרְתִּי

,say and   that   land   on   bring I   sword a   Or   .desolate   would
(if)   be

7969   5674   776   3772   120   929   2719

18   חֶרֶב תַּעֲבֹר בָּאָרֶץ וְהִכְרַתִּי מִמֶּנָּה אָדָם וּבְהֵמָה: וּשְׁלֹשֶׁת

(if) even   ;beast   and   man   from   will I and   the   pass Let   a
three   it   off cut   ,land   through   sword

582   428   8432   2416   5002   136   3068   3808   5337

הָאֲנָשִׁים הָאֵלֶּה בְּתוֹכָהּ חַי־אָנִי נְאֻם אֲדֹנָי יְהוִה לֹא יַצִּילוּ

they   not   ,Jehovah   the   states   I (as)   its in   these   men
deliver should   Lord   live   ,midst   (were)

1121   1323   5337   905   5337   1698   7797:1

19   בָּנִים וּבָנוֹת כִּי הֵם לְבַדָּם יִנָּצֵלוּ: אוֹ דֶּבֶר אֲשַׁלַּח אֶל־

into   send I   a   Or   would   only   they   but   or   sons
plague (if)   .deliver   themselves   ,daughters

plague into that land, and pour out My fury on it in blood, to cut off from it man and beast; [20]even *though* Noah, Daniel, and Job *were* in its midst, *as* I live, declares the Lord Jehovah, they would deliver neither son nor daughter; they by their righteousness would deliver *only* their souls.

[21]For so says the Lord Jehovah, How much more when the four of My evil judgments: sword, and famine, and evil beast, and plague, I send on Jerusalem, to cut off from it man and beast! [22]Yet, behold, there shall be left in it escaping ones that shall be led out, sons and daughters. Behold, they shall come to you, and you shall see their way and their doings. And you will be comforted for the evil which I have brought against Jerusalem, *for* all which I have brought upon it. [23]And they will comfort you when you see their way and their doings. And you will know that not in vain I have done all that I did in it, declares the Lord Jehovah.

3772 18:18 2534 8210 776
הָאָרֶץ הַהִיא וְשָׁפַכְתִּי חֲמָתִי עָלֶיהָ בְּדָם לְהַכְרִית מִמֶּנָּה
from it | cut to off | in ,blood | it on | My fury | pour and out | that | land

5002 2416 8432 347 1840 5146 929 120
20 אָדָם וּבְהֵמָה׃ וְנֹחַ דָּנִאֵל וְאִיּוֹב בְּתוֹכָהּ חַי־אָנִי נְאֻם
states | I (as) live | in (were) ,midst its | Job and | Daniel | (if) even ,Noah | ;beast and | man

5337 6666 5337 1323 1121 3068 136
אֲדֹנָי יְהוִה אִם־בֵּן אִם־בַּת יַצִּילוּ הֵמָּה בְצִדְקָתָם יַצִּילוּ
would deliver | their by righteousness | they would ;deliver | they | daughter | nor son | neither | Jehovah | the Lord

702 637 3068 136 559 5315
21 נַפְשָׁם׃ כִּי כֹה אָמַר אֲדֹנָי יְהוִה אַף כִּי־אַרְבַּעַת
of four the | when | How more much | ,Jehovah | the Lord | says | thus | For | their (only) .souls

7971 1698 7451 2416 7458 2719 7451 4941
שְׁפָטַי ׀ הָרָעִים חֶרֶב וְרָעָב וְחַיָּה רָעָה וָדֶבֶר שִׁלַּחְתִּי
send I | and ,plague | ,evil | and beast | and ,famine | ,sword | :evil | My judgments

2009 929 120 3772 3389
22 אֶל־יְרוּשָׁלִָם לְהַכְרִית מִמֶּנָּה אָדָם וּבְהֵמָה׃ וְהִנֵּה
Yet ,behold | !beast and | man | from it | cut to off | ,Jerusalem | on

3318 2009 1323 1121 3318 6413 3498
נוֹתְרָה־בָּהּ פְּלֵטָה הַמּוּצָאִים בָּנִים וּבָנוֹת הִנָּם יוֹצְאִים
come shall out | ,Behold they | and daughters | sons | shall that ,out led be | escaping ones | in it | shall there left be

5162 5949 1870 7200
אֲלֵיכֶם וּרְאִיתֶם אֶת־דַּרְכָּם וְאֶת־עֲלִילוֹתָם וְנִחַמְתֶּם עַל־
for | will you and comforted be | their ;doings | and | way their | you and see shall | ,you to

935 834 3605 3389 935 834 7451
הָרָעָה אֲשֶׁר הֵבֵאתִי עַל־יְרוּשָׁלִַם אֵת כָּל־אֲשֶׁר הֵבֵאתִי
have I brought | which | all | (for) | ,Jerusalem against | have I brought | which | the evil

5949 1870 7200 5162
23 עָלֶיהָ׃ וְנִחֲמוּ אֶתְכֶם כִּי־תִרְאוּ אֶת־דַּרְכָּם וְאֶת־עֲלִילוֹתָם
their ,doings | and | their way | you when see | you | they And comfort will | upon .it

5002 6213 834 3605 6213 2600 3808 3045
וִידַעְתֶּם כִּי לֹא חִנָּם עָשִׂיתִי אֵת כָּל־אֲשֶׁר־עָשִׂיתִי בָהּ נְאֻם
states | in ,it | did I | that | all | have I done | in vain | not | that | you and know will

3068 136
אֲדֹנָי יְהוִה׃
.Jehovah | the Lord

CAP. XV טו

CHAPTER 15

CHAPTER 15

[1]And the word of Jehovah was to me, saying, [2]Son of man, how is the vine tree more than any *other* tree, *or than* a branch that is among the trees of the forest? [3]Shall wood be taken from it to do work? Or will *men* take from it *for* a peg to hang every vessel on it? [4]Behold, it is put in the fire for fuel. Both its ends

6086 1961 4100 120 1121 559 3068 1697 1961
1
2 וַיְהִי דְבַר־יְהוָה אֵלַי לֵאמֹר׃ בֶּן־אָדָם מַה־יִּהְיֶה עֵץ
the tree | is | How | ,man | Son of | ,saying | ,me to | Jehovah | the of word | And was

3947 3293 6086 1961 834 2156 6086 3605 1612
3 הַגֶּפֶן מִכָּל־עֵץ הַזְּמוֹרָה אֲשֶׁר הָיָה בַּעֲצֵי הַיָּעַר׃ הֲיֻקַּח
be Shall taken | the ?forest | the among of trees | is | that | (than or) branch a | ,tree | more any than | vine

8518 3489 3947 4399 6213 6086
מִמֶּנּוּ עֵץ לַעֲשׂוֹת לִמְלָאכָה אִם־יִקְחוּ מִמֶּנּוּ יָתֵד לִתְלוֹת
hang to | peg a | it from | will take | Or (men) | ?work | do to | wood | from it

7098 8147 402 5414 784 2009 3627 3605
4 עָלָיו כָּל־כֶּלִי׃ הִנֵּה לָאֵשׁ נִתַּן לְאָכְלָה אֵת שְׁנֵי קְצוֹתָיו
ends its | Both | .fuel for | is it put | the in fire | ,Behold | ?vessel | every | it on

the fire devours, and its middle is charred. Will it prosper for work? [5]Behold, when it was whole it was not made for work. How much less when the fire has devoured it, and it is charred? Shall it yet be made to work?

[6]So the Lord Jehovah says this: As the vine tree among the trees of the forest, which I have given to the fire for fuel, so I will give the dwellers of Jerualem. [7]And I will set my face against them. They shall go out from the fire, and the fire shall devour them. And you shall know that I *am* Jehovah when I set My face against them. [8]And I will give the land *to be* desolate, because they have committed a treacherous act, declares the Lord Jehovah.

1961 2009 4399 6743 27:87 8432 784 398
5 אכלה האש ותוכו נחר היצלח למלאכה: הנה בהיותו
when was it ,Behold ?work for it will prosper is .charred its and middle The ,fire devours

2287 398 784 637 4399 6213 38:08 85:09
תמים לא יעשה למלאכה אף כי־אש אכלתהו ויחר
is it and !charred de- ,it voured has the fire when How less much .work for was it made not ,whole

3068 136 559 4399 5750 6213
6 ונעשה עוד למלאכה: לכן כה אמר אדני יהוה
,Jehovah the Lord says thus Therefore ?work for any longer it Shall made be

402 784 5414 834 3293 6086 1612 6086
כאשר עץ־הגפן בעץ היער אשר־נתתיו לאש לאכלה
,fuel for the to fire have I it given which the ,forest the in of trees vine the tree As

784 64:40 5414 33.89 3427 54:14
7 כן נתתי את־ישבי ירושלם: ונתתי את־פני בהם מהאש
the From fire against .them My face I And place will .Jerusalem the of dwellers will I give so

77.60 3068 3045 398 784 33:18
יצאו והאש תאכלם וידעתם כי־אני יהוה בשומי את־
I when set Jehovah I that (am) you And know shall devour shall .them the and fire they ,out go shall

5002 4604 4603 3282 8077 776 5414 6440
8 פני בהם: ונתתי את־הארץ שממה יען מעלו מעל נאם
states be- ,trayed have they slyly be- cause (be to) ,desolate the land I And give will against .them My face

3068 136
אדני יהוה:
.Jehovah the Lord

CAP. XVI טז

CHAPTER 16

CHAPTER 16

[1]And the word of Jehovah was to me, saying, [2]Son of man, cause Jerusalem to know her abominations; [3]and say, So says the Lord Jehovah to Jerusalem: Your origin and your birth *is* of the land of Canaan. Your father *was* an Amorite, and your mother a Hittite. [4]As for your birth, in the day you were born your navel was not cut, and you were not washed with water to cleanse *you*. And you were not salted; and you were not at all swaddled. [5]An eye did not have pity on you, to do to you one of these, to have compassion on you. But you were thrown into the face of the field; for your person was loathed in the day you were born. [6]And *when* I passed by you and saw you squirming in your

3389 3045 120 1121 559 3068 1697 1961
1
2 ויהי דבר־יהוה אלי לאמר: בן־אדם הודע את־ירושלם
Jerusalem cause know to ,man Son of ,saying ,me to Jehovah the of word And was

3389 3068 136 559 559 8441
3 את־תועבתיה: ואמרת כה־אמר אדני יהוה לירושלם
:Jerusalem to Jehovah the Lord says Thus ,say and her .abominations

517 559 1 3669 776 4138 4351
מכרתיך ומלדתיך מארץ הכנעני אביך האמרי ואמך
your and mother an (was) ,Amorite Your father .Canaan of (are) of land the your and birth Your origin

8270 3772 38.08 3205 3117 4138 2850
4 חתית: ומולדותיך ביום הולדת אתך לא־כרת שרך
your ,navel was cut not ,you were born the in day your for As ,birth a .Hittite

2853 4414 3808 4414 4935 7364 3808 4325
ובמים לא־רחצת למשעי והמלח לא המלחת והחתל
all at and were you ,salted not all at and cleanse to ;(you) were you washed not with and water

428 259 6213 5869 2347 3808 2853 38.08
5 לא חתלת: לא־חסה עליך עין לעשות לך אחת מאלה
,these of one to you do to an eye you on did Not pity have were you .swaddled not

3117 5315 1604 7704 6440 7993 2550
לחמלה עליך ותשלכי אל־פני השדה בגעל נפשך ביום
the in day your soul with of loathing the ,field the into of face you But thrown were .you on have to compassion

1818 947 72:00 5674 3205
6 הלדת אתך: ואעבר עליך ואראך מתבוססת בדמיך
your in .blood squirming saw and you by you (when) And passed I .you were born

blood, I said to you in your blood, Live! Yea, I said to you in your blood, Live!

[7]As a myriad, as the field shoot I have made you; and you are grown, and are great; and you come *in* the finest ornaments. Your breasts are formed, and hair is grown; yet you *were* naked and bare. [8]And I passed by you, and I looked on you, and, behold, your time *was* the time of love. And I spread My skirt over you, and covered your nakedness. And I swore to you and entered into a covenant with you, declares the Lord Jehovah. And you became Mine. [9]And I washed you with water; I washed away your blood from you; and I anointed you with oil. [10]And I dressed you *with* embroidered work, and I shod you *with* dugong *sandals*. And I wrapped you *in* fine linen, and I covered you *with* silk. [11]And I adorned you *with* ornaments, and I put bracelets on your hands, and a chain on your neck. [12]And I put a ring on your nose, and earrings on your ears, and a crown of beauty on your head. [13]And you were adorned with gold and silver. And your clothing *was* fine linen and silk and embroidered work. Fine flour and honey and oil you ate. And you were very, very beautiful. And you advanced to regal estate. [14]And your name went out among the nations, because of your beauty; for it *was* perfect by My splendor which I had set on you, declares the Lord Jehovah.

[15]But you trusted in your beauty, and played the harlot because of your name, and poured out your fornications on all who passed by—it was to him! [16]And you took from your clothes and made for you high places of various colors, and whored on them; *such as* had not come, nor shall be. [17]And you have taken beautiful things of My gold and of My silver, which I had given to you, and made images of

6780 7233 2421 1818 559 2421 1818 559
7 וָאֹמַר לָךְ בְּדָמַיִךְ חֲיִי וָאֹמַר לָךְ בְּדָמַיִךְ חֲיִי׃ רְבָבָה כְּצֶמַח
the as a As .Live your in to I ,Yea !Live your in to said I
of shoot ,myriad ,blood you said ,blood you

7699 5716 5716 935 1430 7235 5414 7704
הַשָּׂדֶה נְתַתִּיךְ וַתִּרְבִּי וַתִּגְדְּלִי וַתָּבֹאִי בַּעֲדִי עֲדָיִים שָׁדַיִם
Breasts .ornaments the you and are and you and have I the
finest ,come ,great ,grown are ,you made field

7200 5674 6181 5903 6779 8181 3559
8 נָכֹנוּ וּשְׂעָרֵךְ צִמֵּחַ וְאַתְּ עֵרֹם וְעֶרְיָה׃ וָאֶעֱבֹר עָלַיִךְ וָאֶרְאֵךְ
looked and by I And and (were) and is your and are
,you on you passed .bare naked you ;grown hair ,formed

6172 3680 3671 6566 1733 6256 6256 2009
וְהִנֵּה עִתֵּךְ עֵת דֹּדִים וָאֶפְרֹשׂ כְּנָפִי עָלַיִךְ וָאֲכַסֶּה עֶרְוָתֵךְ
your and you over My I And .love (was) your and
.nakedness covered skirt spread of time the time ,behold

1961 3068 136 5002 1285 935 7650
וָאֶשָּׁבַע לָךְ וָאָבוֹא בִבְרִית אֹתָךְ נְאֻם אֲדֹנָי יֱהוִה וַתִּהְיִי
you and ,Jehovah the states with a into and to I And
became Lord you covenant entered you swore

8081 5480 1818 7857 4325 7364
9 לִי׃ וָאֶרְחָצֵךְ בַּמַּיִם וָאֶשְׁטֹף דָּמַיִךְ מֵעָלָיִךְ וָאֲסֻכֵךְ בַּשָּׁמֶן׃
.oil with I and from your washed I with I And .Mine
you anointed ,you blood away .water you washed

3680 8336 2280 8476 5274 7553 3847
10 וָאַלְבִּישֵׁךְ רִקְמָה וָאֶנְעֲלֵךְ תָּחַשׁ וָאֶחְבְּשֵׁךְ בַּשֵּׁשׁ וַאֲכַסֵּךְ
I and fine (in) I And (with) I and em- (with) clothed I And
you covered ,linen you wrapped ,dugong you shod work broidered you

7242 3027 6781 5414 5716 5710 4897
11 מֶשִׁי׃ וָאֶעְדֵּךְ עֶדִי וָאֶתְּנָה צְמִידִים עַל־יָדַיִךְ וְרָבִיד עַל
on a and your on bracelets I and (with) also I (with)
chain ,hands put ornaments you adorned .silk

5850 241 5694 639 5141 5414 1627
12 גְּרוֹנֵךְ׃ וָאֶתֵּן נֶזֶם עַל־אַפֵּךְ וַעֲגִילִים עַל־אָזְנָיִךְ וַעֲטֶרֶת
a and your on and your on ring a I And your
crown ,ears earrings ,nose put .neck

4897 8336 4403 3701 2091 5710 7218 8597
13 תִּפְאֶרֶת בְּרֹאשֵׁךְ׃ וַתַּעְדִּי זָהָב וָכֶסֶף וּמַלְבּוּשֵׁךְ שֵׁשִׁי וָמֶשִׁי
and fine your And and with you And your on beauty of
silk linen (was) clothing .silver gold adorned were .head

3966 3966 3303 398 8081 1706 5560 7553
וְרִקְמָה סֹלֶת וּדְבַשׁ וָשֶׁמֶן אָכָלְתִּי וַתִּיפִי בִּמְאֹד מְאֹד
,very very you And .ate you oil and and Fine em- and
beautiful were honey flour .work broidered

3632 3308 1471 8034 3318 1410 6743
14 וַתִּצְלְחִי לִמְלוּכָה׃ וַיֵּצֵא לָךְ שֵׁם בַּגּוֹיִם בְּיָפְיֵךְ כִּי כָּלִיל
(was) for of because among name your And regal to you and
perfect ;beauty your ,nations the out went .estate advanced

3068 136 5002 7760 834 1926
הוּא בַּהֲדָרִי אֲשֶׁר־שַׂמְתִּי עָלַיִךְ נְאֻם אֲדֹנָי יֱהוִה׃
.Jehovah the states ,you on set had I which My by it
Lord splendor

8457 8210 8034 2181 3308 982
15 וַתִּבְטְחִי בְיָפְיֵךְ וַתִּזְנִי עַל־שְׁמֵךְ וַתִּשְׁפְּכִי אֶת־תַּזְנוּתַיִךְ
your poured and your because played and your in you But
fornications out ,name of harlot the beauty trusted

1116 6213 899 3947 1961 5674 3605
16 עַל־כָּל־עוֹבֵר לוֹ־יֶהִי׃ וַתִּקְחִי מִבְּגָדַיִךְ וַתַּעֲשִׂי־לָךְ בָּמוֹת
high for and your from you And it to passed all on
places you made clothes took .was him —by who

3627 3947 3068 3808 935 3808 2181 2921
17 טְלֻאוֹת וַתִּזְנִי עֲלֵיהֶם לֹא בָאוֹת וְלֹא יִהְיֶה׃ וַתִּקְחִי כְּלֵי
things have You shall and (Such) not .them on played and vari- of
of taken also .be not come have harlot the ,colors ous

6213 5414 834 3701 2091 3308
תִפְאַרְתֵּךְ מִזְּהָבִי וּמִכַּסְפִּי אֲשֶׁר נָתַתִּי לָךְ וַתַּעֲשִׂי־לָךְ
to and ,you had I which of and My of ,beauty
yourself made given ,silver My gold

males, and whored with
them. [18]And *you* took your
embroidered clothes and
covered them; and My oil
and My incense you have
given to their face. [19]Also
My food which I gave you,
fine flour and oil and honey
which I fed you, you have
given it to their face for a
soothing aroma. And it
happened, declares the
Lord Jehovah. [20]And you
have taken your sons and
your daughters, whom you
have borne to Me, and you
gave these to them for food.
Are your fornications small?
[21]You have slaughtered My
sons, and gave them, to
cause these to pass through
the fire for them.
[22]And *in* all your
abominations and your
fornications you have not
remembered the days of
your youth, when you were
naked and bare; you were
trampled in your blood.
[23]Woe, woe to you, says the
Lord Jehovah! *For* it
happened, after all your
evil, [24]that you have also
built yourself a mound, and
you have made yourself a
high place in every open
place. [25]At the head of
every highway you have
built your high place, and
have made your beauty
despised. And *you* have
parted your feet to all who
passed by, and have multiplied your fornications.
[26]You have whored with the
sons of Egypt, your neighbors, great of flesh, and
have multiplied your fornications to provoke Me to
anger. [27]And behold, I have
stretched out My hand over
you, and I drew back your
portion. And I gave you to
the will of those hating you,
the daughters of the
Philistines, who are
ashamed of your wicked
way. [28]You have whored
with the sons of Assyria,
your being satisfied; yea,
you whored and yet you
were not satisfied. [29]And
your whoredom *is* idol-
atry in the land of Canaan,
to the Chaldean, and yet
you were not satisfied
with this.

3680 7553 899 3947 2181 2145 67,54
18 צַלְמֵי זָכָר וַתִּזְנִי־בָם׃ וַתִּקְחִי אֶת־בִּגְדֵי רִקְמָתֵךְ וַתְּכַסִּים
covered and your clothes took and with and males images
,them embroidered them whored of

54 14 834 3899 6440 5414 7004 8081
19 וְשַׁמְנִי וּקְטָרְתִּי נָתַתְּ לִפְנֵיהֶם׃ וְלַחְמִי אֲשֶׁר־נָתַתִּי לָךְ
,you I which My Also their to have you My and My and
gave food .face given incense oil

7381 6440 5414 398 1706 8081 5560
סֹלֶת וָשֶׁמֶן וּדְבַשׁ הֶאֱכַלְתִּיךְ וּנְתַתִּיהוּ לִפְנֵיהֶם לְרֵיחַ
an for their to have you ,you fed I honey and and fine
aroma face it given which oil flour

1323 1121 3947 3068 136 5002 1961 5207
20 נִיחֹחַ וַיֶּהִי נְאֻם אֲדֹנָי יְהוִה׃ וַתִּקְחִי אֶת־בָּנַיִךְ וְאֶת־בְּנוֹתַיִךְ
your and sons your you And .Jehovah the states it And sooth-
,daughters taken have Lord was .ing

8457 4592 398 2076 3205 834
אֲשֶׁר יָלַדְתְּ לִי וַתִּזְבָּחִים לָהֶם לֶאֱכוֹל הַמְעַט מִתַּזְנֻתֵךְ׃
your Are .food for to you and to have you whom
?fornications small them these gave Me borne

5674 54:14 1121 7919
21
22 וַתִּשְׁחֲטִי אֶת־בָּנַי וַתִּתְּנִים בְּהַעֲבִיר אוֹתָם לָהֶם׃ וְאֵת
And for these to cause to gave and sons My have You
(in) .them through pass ,them slaughtered

1961 5271 3117 2142 38:08 8457 8441 3605
כָּל־תּוֹעֲבֹתַיִךְ וְתַזְנֻתַיִךְ לֹא זָכַרְתְּ אֶת־יְמֵי נְעוּרָיִךְ בִּהְיוֹתֵךְ
you when your the have you not your and your all
were ,youth of days remembered fornications abominations

3605 310 1961 1961 1818 947 6181 5903
23 עֵירֹם וְעֶרְיָה מִתְבּוֹסֶסֶת בְּדָמֵךְ הָיִית׃ וַיְהִי אַחֲרֵי כָּל־
all after And you your in squirming (and) and naked
,was it .were blood bare

6213 7354 1129 3068 136 5002 188 188 7451
24 רָעָתֵךְ אוֹי אוֹי לָךְ נְאֻם אֲדֹנָי יְהוִה׃ וַתִּבְנִי־לָךְ גָּב וַתַּעֲשִׂי־
you and a your- have you !Jehovah the says to woe ,woe your
made have mound self built also Lord ,you —evil

7413 1129 1870 7218 3605 7339 3605 7413
25 לָךְ רָמָה בְּכָל־רְחוֹב׃ אֶל־כָּל־רֹאשׁ דֶּרֶךְ בָּנִית רָמָתֵךְ
high your You the head every At open in high a your-
place built have highway of place every place self

7235 5674 3605 7272 6589 3308 8581
וַתְּתַעֲבִי אֶת־יָפְיֵךְ וַתְּפַשְּׂקִי אֶת־רַגְלַיִךְ לְכָל־עוֹבֵר וַתַּרְבִּי
have and who all to your have and your have and
multiplied ,by passed feet parted ,beauty despised made

1320 1432 7934 4714 1121 2181 8457
26 אֶת־תַּזְנוּתָךְ׃ וַתִּזְנִי אֶל־בְּנֵי־מִצְרַיִם שְׁכֵנַיִךְ גִּדְלֵי בָשָׂר
,flesh great your ,Egypt the with have You your
of ,neighbors of sons whored .fornications

3027 5186 2009 3707 8457 7235
27 וַתַּרְבִּי אֶת־תַּזְנֻתֵךְ לְהַכְעִיסֵנִי׃ וְהִנֵּה נָטִיתִי יָדִי עָלַיִךְ
over My have I —Behold provoke to your have and
you hand out stretched .anger to Me fornication multiplied

6430 1323 8130 5315 5414 2706 1639
וָאֶגְרַע חֻקֵּךְ וָאֶתְּנֵךְ בְּנֶפֶשׁ שֹׂנְאוֹתַיִךְ בְּנוֹת פְּלִשְׁתִּים
the daugh- the who those the to I and your I and
,Philistines of ters ,you hate of will you gave share back drew

1115 804 1121 2181 2154 1870 3637
28 הַנִּכְלָמוֹת מִדַּרְכֵּךְ זִמָּה׃ וַתִּזְנִי אֶל־בְּנֵי אַשּׁוּר מִבִּלְתִּי
without Assyria the with have You .wicked way your are who
of sons whored of ashamed

2181 8457 7654 3808 1571 2181 7646
29 שָׂבְעָתֵךְ וַתִּזְנִים וְגַם לֹא שָׂבָעַתְּ׃ וַתַּרְבִּי אֶת־תַּזְנוּתֵךְ אֶל־
in (is) your And were you not and you,Yea being your
whoredom idolatry .satisfied yet whored .satisfied

535 7646 3808 2063 1571 3778 3667 776
30 אֶרֶץ כְּנַעַן כַּשְׂדִּימָה וְגַם־בְּזֹאת לֹא שָׂבָעַתְּ׃ מָה אֲמֻלָה
weak How were you not with and (to) Canaan the
(is) .satisfied ,this yet ,Chaldean of land

30How weak is your heart, declares the Lord Jehovah, since you do all these, the work of a woman, an overbearing harlot; 31in that you built your mound in the head of every highway, and you make your high place in every open place; yet you have not been as a harlot, even scorning wages. 32Like the adulterous wife — instead of her husband, she takes strangers—33they give a gift to all harlots, but you give your gifts to all your lovers, and bribe them to come to you from all around, for your fornication. 34And in you was the opposite from those women, in your fornications, since no one whores after you, and in your giving wages, and hire is not given to you. In this you are opposite.

35Therefore, O harlot, hear the word of Jehovah, 36So says the Lord Jehovah: Because your lewdness was poured out, and your nakedness was bared in your fornications with your lovers, and with the idols of your abominations, and by the blood of your sons whom you gave to them; 37therefore, behold, I will gather all your lovers with whom you have been pleased, even all whom you have loved, with all whom you have hated; I will even gather them against you from all around, and will uncover your nakedness to them; yea, they will see all your nakedness. 38And I will judge you with judgments of adulteresses, and with shedders of blood. And I will give you blood of fury and jealousy. 39And I will give you into their hand, and they will tear down your mound, and will demolish your high places. They shall also strip you of your clothes, and shall take your beautiful things, and leave you naked and bare. 40And they will raise against you a company, and they shall

---

31

4639	428	3605	6213	3068	136	5002	38:26
מַעֲשֵׂה	אֵלֶּה־כָּל־אֶת	בַּעֲשׂוֹתֵךְ	יְהוָה	אֲדֹנָי	נְאֻם	לִבָּתֵךְ
the of work	these (things),	all	you do	since	Jehovah	the Lord	the states	your heart

7413	1870	3605	7218	1354	1129	802	2181	79186
וְרָמָתֵךְ	דֶּרֶךְ כָּל־בְּרֹאשׁ	גַּבֵּךְ	בִּבְנוֹתֵךְ	שַׁלָּטֶת	זוֹנָה	אִשָּׁה
your high- place	high- way,	every	the in	of head	your	you built	mound	that in	an	harlot —overbearing, woman

32

802	868	70:46	2181	1961/3808	7339	3605	6213
הָאִשָּׁה	אֶתְנָן לְקֻלָּם כּוֹנָה לֹא־וְהָיִיתְ רְחוֹב בְּכָל־עֲשֹׂתֵךְ
The wife	.wages scorn to	a as	have you yet	.harlot been	not	place every open	in you make

33

5414	2181	360:5	2114	3947	376	8478	5003
יִתְּנוּ זוֹנוֹת־לְכָל־ זָרִים־אֶת תִּקַּח אִישָׁהּ תַּחַת הַמְּנָאֶפֶת
they give	harlots all	To	strangers!	she takes	her husband	instead of	adulterous,

7809	157	36:05	50:83	5414	5078
אוֹתָם וַתְּשַׁחֲדִי־ מְאַהֲבַיִךְ־לְכָל־ אֶתְנְנַיִךְ־אֶת נָתַתְּ וְאַתְּ נֵדֶה
them	bribe and	your lovers	all to	gifts your	give but a you, gift

34

802	2016	1961	8457	5439	935
מִן־הֵפֶךְ בָךְ־וַיְהִי כְתַזְנוּתַיִךְ מִסָּבִיב אֵלַיִךְ לְבוֹא
(those) women	from the opposite you	in And was	your fornication for	all from around	to come

5414	38:08	868	8457	310	21·81/38.08
לָךְ־נִתַּן וְאֶתְנָן אֶתְנָן וּבְכַתֵּךְ לֹא זוֹנָה אַחֲרַיִךְ וְאַחֲרַיִךְ כְּתַזְנוּתֵךְ
is given	not and	wages,	giving you	in and	whores none	that for	you after fornications, your in

35
36

3541	3068	1697	8085	218:1	36:51	2016	1961
כֹּה־ יְהוָה־דְּבַר שִׁמְעִי זוֹנָה לָכֵן הֵפֶךְ־לְהִיּוֹת לָךְ וּתְהִי
Thus	.Jehovah the of word	the hear	O	harlot, fore	There-	.opposite thus	to	are you you,

36

6172	1540	5178	8210	3282	30:68	136	559
עֶרְוָתֵךְ וַתִּגָּלֶה נְחֻשְׁתֵּךְ הִשָּׁפֵךְ יַעַן יְהוָה אֲדֹנָי אָמַר
naked- your was and ness,	bared	your lewdness	poured was out	Be- cause	:Jehovah the Lord	says

1818	84:41	1544:3605	157	8457
וְכִדְמֵי תּוֹעֲבוֹתַיִךְ גִּלּוּלֵי־כָל־וְעַל מְאַהֲבַיִךְ־עַל כְּתַזְנוּתַיִךְ
the by and of blood	your abominations of	idols all and	your lovers with	your in fornications

37

157	3605	6908	2005	5414	834	1121
מְאַהֲבַיִךְ־כָּל־אֶת מְקַבֵּץ הִנְנִי לָכֵן לָהֶם נָתַתָּ אֲשֶׁר בָּנַיִךְ
your lovers	all	will behold there-	to you	gave ;them	whom your sons

834	3605	157	834	3605	6149	834
אֲשֶׁר כָּל־עַל אָהַבְתָּ אֲשֶׁר־כָּל־וְאֵת עֲלֵיהֶם עָרַבְתְּ אֲשֶׁר
whom	all with	have you loved,	whom all	even ,them with	have you pleased been	whom

38

6172	15:40	54:39	5437	6908	8130
אֵלֵהֶם עֶרְוָתֵךְ וְגִלֵּיתִי עָלַיִךְ מִסָּבִיב אֹתָם וְקִבַּצְתִּי שָׂנֵאת
them to	your nakedness	will and uncover	against you	all from around	them even	will I gather	have you —hated

8210	5003	4941	8199	6172	3605	7200
וְשָׁפַכְתִּי נֹאֲפוֹת מִשְׁפְּטֵי וּשְׁפַטְתִּיךְ עֶרְוָתֵךְ־כָּל־אֶת וְרָאוּ
and shedders of	adulteresses judg- of ments	with	will I And you judge	your all .nakedness	they and see will

39

5375	30·27	32·40	7068	2534	1818	5414	1818
הָרְסוּ בְיָדָם אֹתָךְ וְנָתַתִּי וְקִנְאָה חֵמָה דַּם הֵם וְנָתַתִּיךְ דָּם
they and raise-will their into hand	you	will I And give	and .jealousy	fury	blood of	I will And .blood you give will

3627	3947	899	6584	7413	5422	1354
כְלֵי וְלָקְחוּ בְּגָדַיִךְ אוֹתָךְ וְהִפְשִׁיטוּ רָמָתֵךְ וְנָתְצוּ גַּבֵּךְ
things shall and take	your of clothes,	you	shall They strip also	high your will and	places demolish mound your

40

7275	69:51	5927	6181	5903	3240	8597
וְרָגְמוּ קָהָל עָלַיִךְ וְהֶעֱלוּ וְעֶרְיָה עֵירֹם וְהִנִּיחוּךְ תִּפְאַרְתֵּךְ
they and stone shall	a .company	against they And you raise will	and .bare	naked	leave and you	your beautiful

stone you with stones, and cut you with their swords. [41]And they shall burn your houses with fire, and make judgments against you in the sight of many women. And I will make you stop whoring; and also, you shall not give hire again. [42]So I will make My fury to rest against you, and My jealousy shall depart from you. And I will be quiet, and will not be angry any more. [43]Because you have not remembered the days of your youth, but have troubled Me in all these; so, behold, I also will give your way back on your head, declares the Lord Jehovah. And you shall not commit the wickedness above all your abominations.

[44]Behold, all who use proverbs shall use *this* proverb against you, saying, As the mother, *so is* the daughter. [45]You *are* your mother's daughter, who despises her husband and her sons. And you *are* the sister of your sisters, who despise their husbands and their sons. Your mother *was* a Hittite, and your father *was* an Amorite. [46]And your older sister *is* Samaria; she and her daughters who are dwelling on your left. And your younger sister from you, who dwells on the right, *is* Sodom, and her daughters. [47]Yet you have not walked in their ways, nor have done according to their abominations. As *if it were* only a little *thing*, you were even more corrupted than they in all your ways. [48]As I live, declares the Lord Jehovah, your sister Sodom, she and her daughters have not done as you and your daughters have done. [49]Behold, this was the iniquity of your sister Sodom: pride, fullness of bread, and abundance of idleness was in her and her daughters; and she did not strengthen the hand of the poor and needy. [50]Also they were haughty, and did abomination before My face. And I

41
with / your / they And / their / with / cut and / with / you
.fire / houses / burn shall / .swords / you / stones
784 / 1004 / 8313 / 2719 / 1333 / 68

;whoring / will I and / ,many / women / the in / judgments / against / and
.stop you make / of sight / you make
2181 / 7673 / 7727 / 802 / 5869 / 82:01 / 6213

42
My shall and / against / My / will I So / .again shall you not / wages / and
jealousy / turn / you / fury / rest to make / give / also
7068 / 5493 / 2534 / 51.17 / 5750 / 5414 / 3808 / 868 / 1571

43
have you not / Because .still be / will / and / will I and / from
remembered / angry / not / quiet be / .you
2142 / 3808 / 834 / 3282 / 5750 / 3707 / 38.08 / 8252

your ,behold also so / ;these / all in / Me have but / your / the
way / troubled / youth / of days
1870 / 1887 / 1571 / 428 / 3605 / 21 / 5271 / 3117

above / the / shall you And / .Jehovah the / states give will / (your) on
wickedness / commit / not / Lord / (back) / head
21:54 / 6213 / 38.08 / 3068 / 136 / 5002 / 5414 / 7:21.8 / 4911 / 3605 / 2009 / 844.1 / 36.05

44
the As / ,saying / use shall / against / use who / all Behold / your / all
,mother / proverb (this) / you / proverbs / .abominations
517 / 559 / 49.11 / 1121 / 376 / 1602 / 157 / 1323 / 1323

45
your / the And / her and / her / who / You your daughter / her (so)
sisters / of sister / .sons / husband despises / (are) mother's / .daughter
269 / 269 / 1121 / 376 / 1602 / 157 / 1323 / 1323 / 1323

an / your and / a / Your / their and / their / despise who / you
.Amorite / father / ,Hittite / mother / .sons / husbands / (are)
567 / 2850 / 517 / 1121 / 582 / 834

46
on / are who / her and / she / (is) / older / your And
dwelling / daughters / ,Samaria / sister
3427 / 1323 / 8111 / 1419 / 269

(is) / ,right your / dwells who / from / younger / your and / ;left your
Sodom / on / ,you / sister
5467 / 3225 / 3427 / 6996 / 269 / 8040

47
have / their by / nor / have you / their in / Yet / her and
.done / abominations / ,walked / ways / not / .daughters
6213 / 8441 / 1980 / 1870 / 38.08 / 1323

more were you And / only (if) / as
they than corrupted / little
5002 / 2416 / 1870 / 3605 / 2004 / 7843 / 6985 / 4592

48
states / I As / .ways your / all in / more were you And / only (if) / as
live / they than corrupted / little

as / her nor / she / your / Sodom / has / not / .Jehovah the
,daughters / sister / done / Lord
1323 / 269 / 5467 / 6213 / 518 / 30:68 / 136

49
,pride / your / Sodom the / was / ,this ,Behold / your and / you have you
,sister / of iniquity / .daughters / .done
13:47 / 269 / 5467 / 5771 / 19:61 / 2088 / 2009 / 1323 / 6213

the and / her and / in / was / idleness / and / bread / fulness
poor hand / ;daughters / her / of abundance / of
6041 / 3027 / 1323 / 1961 / 82.52 / 7962 / 3899 / 7653

50
before / abomination / did and / they And / did she / not / the and
.Me / haughty were / .strengthen / needy's
6440 / 8441 / 6213 / 2388 / 38.08 / 34 / 1361

turned them away as I saw *fit*.
[51]And Samaria has not sinned as *much as* half your sins; but you have multiplied your abominations more than they, and have justified your sisters in all your abominations which you have done. [52]And you who have judged your sisters, bear your shame, by your sins which you abominably did, more than they. They are more righteous than you. And also you be ashamed, and bear your shame, since you have justified your sisters. [53]When I shall return their captivity, the captivity of Sodom and her daughters, and the captivity of Samaria and her daughters, then *also* the captivity of your captivity in their midst. [54]So that you may bear your shame and may blush from all that you have done, since you are a comfort to them. [55]When your sisters, Sodom and her daughters, shall return to their former state, and Samaria and her daughters shall return to their former state, then you and your daughters shall return to your former state. [56]For your sister Sodom was not to be heard from your mouth in the day of your pride, [57]before your evil was uncovered, as at the time of the reproach of Syria's daughters, and all the ones around her; the daughters of the Philistines who hated you from all around. [58]You are bearing your wickedness and your abominations, declares Jehovah. [59]For so says the Lord Jehovah: I will even deal with you as you have done, who have despised the oath in breaking the covenant.

[60]But I will remember My covenant with you in the days of your youth, and I will raise up to you an everlasting covenant. [61]Then you shall remember your ways and be ashamed,

3808 2403 2677 8111 7200 5493
51 וָאָסִיר אֶתְהֶן כַּאֲשֶׁר רָאִיתִי׃ וְשֹׁמְרוֹן כַּחֲצִי חַטֹּאתַיִךְ לֹא
not sins your half of as Samaria And saw I (fit). as them I And away turned

269 6663 2007 8441 7235 2398
חָטָאָה וַתַּרְבִּי אֶת־תּוֹעֲבוֹתַיִךְ מֵהֵנָּה וַתְּצַדְּקִי אֶת־אֲחוֹתֵךְ
sisters your have and justified more ,they than your abominations have you but multiplied has ,sinned

834 3639 5375 1571 6213 834 8441 3605
52 בְּכָל־תּוֹעֲבֹתַיִךְ אֲשֶׁר עָשִׂיתִי׃ גַּם־אַתְּ ׀ שְׂאִי כְלִמָּתֵךְ אֲשֶׁר
in that your shame bear you Also have you .done which your abominations by all

6663 2004 8581 834 2403 269 6419
פִּלַּלְתְּ לַאֲחוֹתֵךְ בְּחַטֹּאתַיִךְ אֲשֶׁר־הִתְעַבְתְּ מֵהֵן תִּצְדַּקְנָה
more are They righteous more .they than did you abominably which your by sins your for ,sisters have you pleaded

269 6663 3639 5375 954 1571
מִמֵּךְ וְגַם־אַתְּ בּוֹשִׁי וּשְׂאִי כְלִמָּתֵךְ בְּצַדֶּקְתֵּךְ אַחְיוֹתֵךְ׃
your .sisters have you since justified your ,shame bear and be ashamed you And also than .you

7622 1323 5467 7622 7622 7725
53 וְשַׁבְתִּי אֶת־שְׁבִיתְהֶן אֶת־שְׁבִית סְדֹם וּבְנוֹתֶיהָ וְאֶת־שְׁבִית
the of captivity and her and ,daughters Sodom the of captivity their ,captivity I When return shall

5375 8432 7622 7622 1323 8111
54 שֹׁמְרוֹן וּבְנוֹתֶיהָ וּשְׁבִית שְׁבִיתַיִךְ בְּתוֹכָהְנָה׃ לְמַעַן תִּשְׂאִי
may you bear So that their in .midst cap- your tivity the then of captivity her and ,daughters Samaria

269 5162 6213 834 3605 3639 3637
55 כְלִמָּתֵךְ וְנִכְלַמְתְּ מִכֹּל אֲשֶׁר עָשִׂית בְּנַחֲמֵךְ אֹתָן׃ וַאֲחוֹתַיִךְ
your When ,sisters to .them you since comfort a are have you ,done that from all may and blush your shame

7725 1323 8111 6927 7725 1323 5467
סְדֹם וּבְנוֹתֶיהָ תָּשֹׁבְןָ לְקַדְמָתָן וְשֹׁמְרוֹן וּבְנוֹתֶיהָ תָּשֹׁבְןָ
shall return her and daughters and Samaria their to ,state former shall return her and ,daughters Sodom

1961 3808 6927 7725 1323 6927
56 לְקַדְמָתָן וְאַתְּ וּבְנוֹתַיִךְ תְּשֻׁבֶינָה לְקַדְמַתְכֶן׃ וְלוֹא הָיְתָה
was For not former your to .state shall return your and daughters then you their to ,state former

1540 2962 1347 3117 6310 8052 269 5467
57 סְדֹם אֲחוֹתֵךְ לִשְׁמוּעָה בְּפִיךְ בְּיוֹם גְּאוֹנָיִךְ׃ בְּטֶרֶם תִּגָּלֶה
was uncovered before ,pride your the in of day from mouth your be to heard your sister Sodom

1323 5439 3605 758 1323 2781 6256 7451
רָעָתֵךְ כְּמוֹ עֵת חֶרְפַּת בְּנוֹת־אֲרָם וְכָל־סְבִיבוֹתֶיהָ בְּנוֹת
daugh- ters those ;her around of and all ,Syria of daughters the reproach of the of time the at as your ,evil

2154 5439 7590 6430
58 פְּלִשְׁתִּים הַשָּׁאטוֹת אוֹתָךְ מִסָּבִיב׃ אֶת־זִמָּתֵךְ וְאֶת־
and your wickedness all from .around you hated who the ,Philistines

559 3068 5002 5375 8441
59 תּוֹעֲבוֹתַיִךְ אַתְּ נְשָׂאתִים נְאֻם יְהוָה׃ כִּי כֹה אָמַר
says thus For .Jehovah states are ,bearing You your abominations

422 959 834 6213 6213 3068 136
אֲדֹנָי יְהוִה וְעָשִׂיתִי אוֹתָךְ כַּאֲשֶׁר עָשִׂית אֲשֶׁר־בָּזִית אָלָה
the oath have despised who have you ,done as with you will I deal even :Jehovah the Lord

5271 3117 1285 2142 1285 6565
60 לְהָפֵר בְּרִית׃ וְזָכַרְתִּי אֲנִי אֶת־בְּרִיתִי אוֹתָךְ בִּימֵי נְעוּרָיִךְ
your ,youth the in of days with you My covenant I will But remember the .covenant in breaking

3637 1870 2142 5769 1285 6965
61 וַהֲקִמוֹתִי לָךְ בְּרִית עוֹלָם׃ וְזָכַרְתְּ אֶת־דְּרָכַיִךְ וְנִכְלַמְתְּ
be and ,ashamed ways your you Then remember shall ever- .lasting a covenant to you will I and up raise

when you shall receive your sisters, the older than you to the younger than you. And I will give them to you for daughters, but not by your covenant. [62]And I, *even* I, will raise up My covenant with you. And you shall know that I *am* Jehovah; [63]so that you may remember and be ashamed, and will not any more open your mouth, because of your shame—when I am covered for you for all that you have done, declares the Lord Jehovah.

6996 1419 269 3947
בְּקַחְתֵּךְ אֶת־אֲחוֹתַיִךְ הַגְּדֹלוֹת מִמֵּךְ אֶל־הַקְּטַנּוֹת מִמֵּךְ
than younger the to than ,older the ,sisters your you when
.you you receive shall

6965 1285 38 08 1323 5414
62 וְנָתַתִּי אֶתְהֶן לָךְ לְבָנוֹת וְלֹא מִבְּרִיתֵךְ׃ וַהֲקִימוֹתִי אֲנִי
I will I And your by but for to them I And
,up raise .covenant not ,daughters you give will

954 2142 4616 3068 3045 1285
63 אֶת־בְּרִיתִי אִתָּךְ וְיָדַעַתְּ כִּי־אֲנִי יְהוָה׃ לְמַעַן תִּזְכְּרִי וָבֹשְׁתְּ
be and may you so ;Jehovah I that you And with My
,ashamed remember that (am) know shall .you covenant

3722 3639 6440 6310 6610 5750 1961/3808
וְלֹא יִהְיֶה־לָּךְ עוֹד פִּתְחוֹן פֶּה מִפְּנֵי כְּלִמָּתֵךְ בְּכַפְּרִי־לָךְ
for am I when your because (your) to ,still to will and
you covered humiliation of mouth open you be not

3068 136 5002 6213 834 3605
לְכָל־אֲשֶׁר עָשִׂית נְאֻם אֲדֹנָי יְהוִה׃
.Jehovah the states you that all for
Lord ,done have

CAP. XVII יז

CHAPTER 17

[1]And the word of Jehovah was to me, saying, [2]Son of man, put forth a riddle and speak a parable to the house of Israel. [3]And say, So says the Lord Jehovah: A great eagle came to Lebanon, *one with* great wings, long of pinion, full of feathers, having different colors to him. And *he* took the top of the cedar. [4]He plucked off the first of its young twigs and brought it into a land of traders. He set it in a city of merchants. [5]He also took of the seed of the land and planted it in a field of seed. He took *it* by great waters; he set it *as* a willow. [6]And it sprouted and became a spreading low vine; *and it* turned its branches to face toward him; and its roots were under him. So it became a vine and made branches, and sent out boughs. [7]Also there was another great eagle *with* great wings and many feathers. And, behold, this vine bent its roots toward him, and sent out its branches to him, to water it,

4911 2420 2330 120 1121 559 3068 1697 1961
1 וַיְהִי דְבַר־יְהוָה אֵלַי לֵאמֹר׃
2 בֶּן־אָדָם חוּד חִידָה וּמְשֹׁל
and riddle a put ,man Son ,saying to Jehovah the And
speak forth of ,me of word was

4912 136 559 3541 559 3478 1004 4912
3 מָשָׁל אֶל־בֵּית יִשְׂרָאֵל׃ וְאָמַרְתָּ כֹּה־אָמַר ׀ אֲדֹנָי יְהוִה
:Jehovah the says Thus ,say And .Israel the to a
Lord of house parable

5133 4390 83 750 3671 1419 1419 5404
הַנֶּשֶׁר הַגָּדוֹל גְּדוֹל הַכְּנָפַיִם אֶרֶךְ הָאֵבֶר מָלֵא הַנּוֹצָה
,feathers (and) pinion long ,wings (with) great An
of full of great eagle

730 6788 3947 3844 935 7553 834
אֲשֶׁר־לוֹ הָרִקְמָה בָּא אֶל־הַלְּבָנוֹן וַיִּקַּח אֶת־צַמֶּרֶת הָאָרֶז׃
the of top the and Lebanon to came different to which
.cedar took ,colors him was

5892 3667 776 935 6998 3242 7218
4 אֵת רֹאשׁ יְנִיקוֹתָיו קָטָף וַיְבִיאֵהוּ אֶל־אֶרֶץ כְּנַעַן בְּעִיר
a In of a into brought and He young its the
of city traders land it off plucked twigs of chief

2233 7704 5414 776 2233 3947 7760 7402
5 רֹכְלִים שָׂמוֹ׃ וַיִּקַּח מִזֶּרַע הָאָרֶץ וַיִּתְּנֵהוּ בִּשְׂדֵה־זָרַע
.seed a in planted and the the of also He set he merchants
of field it land of seed took .it

1612 1961 6779 7760 6851 7227 4325 3947
6 קָח עַל־מַיִם רַבִּים צַפְצָפָה שָׂמוֹ׃ וַיִּצְמַח וַיְהִי לְגֶפֶן
a and it And set he a (as) ;great waters by He
vine became sprouted .it willow (it) took

8478 8328 1808 6437 6967 8217 5628
סֹרַחַת שִׁפְלַת קוֹמָה לִפְנוֹת דָּלִיּוֹתָיו אֵלָיו וְשָׁרָשָׁיו תַּחְתָּיו
under its and toward its to (and) (of) low spread-
him roots ,him branches face turned ,(stature) ,ing

5404 1961 6288 7971 905 6213 1612 1961 1961
7 יִהְיוּ וַתְּהִי לְגֶפֶן וַתַּעַשׂ בַּדִּים וַתְּשַׁלַּח פֹּארוֹת׃ וַיְהִי נֶשֶׁר
eagle Also .boughs sent and branches and a it So .were
was out made vine became

2088 1612 2009 5132 7227 3671 1419 1419 259
אֶחָד גָּדוֹל גְּדוֹל כְּנָפַיִם וְרַב נוֹצָה וְהִנֵּה הַגֶּפֶן הַזֹּאת
this vine And .feathers and wings (with) great another
behold many great

8248 7971 1808 8328 3719
כָּפְנָה שָׁרָשֶׁיהָ עָלָיו וְדָלִיּוֹתָיו שִׁלְחָה־לּוֹ לְהַשְׁקוֹת אוֹתָהּ
,it water to to sent its and toward roots its bent
,him out branches him

away from the beds of its planting. [8]It was planted in a good field by great waters, to make branches, and to bear fruit; to be a splendid vine. [9]Say, So says the Lord Jehovah: Shall it prosper? Shall he not pull up its roots and cut off its fruit, and wither it? All the leaves of its sprouting shall wither, and not with great arm, nor by many people *shall any* raise it by its roots. [10]And, behold, being planted, shall it prosper? Shall it not utterly wither when the east wind touches it? It shall wither in the beds *where* it sprouted.

[11]And the word of Jehovah was to me, saying, [12]Say now to the rebellious house, Do you not know what these *mean*? *But* speak, Behold, the king of Babylon has come to Jerusalem, and has taken its king and its rulers, and has brought them to himself at Babylon. [13]And he took of the royal seed, and has cut with him a covenant, and made him enter into an oath. And he took the mighty of the land, [14]that the kingdom might be low, that it might not lift itself up; to keep its covenant, that it might stand. [15]But he rebelled against him in sending his messengers to Egypt, to give horses and many people to him. Shall he prosper? Shall he who does these *things* escape? Or shall he break the covenant, and be delivered? [16]*As* I live, declares the Lord Jehovah, Surely, in the place of the king who made him king, whose oath he despised and whose covenant he broke, he shall die there with him, in the midst of Babylon. [17]And Pharaoh shall not work for him with great army or great

7227 4325 2896 7704 4302 6170
8 מֵעֲרֻגוֹת מַטָּעָהּ׃ אֶל־שָׂדֶה טּוֹב אֶל־מַיִם רַבִּים הִיא
it great waters by good field a In its from away
.planting of beds the

155 1612 1961 6529 5375 6057 6213 8382
שְׁתוּלָה לַעֲשׂוֹת עָנָף וְלָשֵׂאת פֶּרִי לִהְיוֹת לְגֶפֶן אַדָּרֶת׃
.splendid vine a be to ,fruit to and ,branches to was
bear make ,planted

8328 3808 6743 3068 136 559 559
9 אֱמֹר כֹּה אָמַר אֲדֹנָי יְהוִה תִּצְלָח הֲלוֹא אֶת־שָׁרָשֶׁיהָ
roots its Shall it Shall :Jehovah the says Thus ,Say
not he ?prosper Lord

3001 6780 2964 3605 3001 7082 6529 5423
יְנַתֵּק וְאֶת־פִּרְיָהּ ׀ יְקוֹסֵס וְיָבֵשׁ כָּל־טַרְפֵּי צִמְחָהּ תִּיבָשׁ
shall its the All and ,off cut fruit its and up pull
,wither sprouting of leaves ?it wither

8328 5375 7227 5971 1419 2220 3808
וְלֹא־בִזְרֹעַ גְּדוֹלָה וּבְעַם־רָב לְמַשְׂאוֹת אוֹתָהּ מִשָּׁרָשֶׁיהָ׃
.roots its by it raise to ,many by nor ,great with and
people arm not

3001 6921 7307 5060 3808 6743 8382 2009
10 וְהִנֵּה שְׁתוּלָה הֲתִצְלָח הֲלֹא כְגַעַת בָּהּ רוּחַ הַקָּדִים תִּיבַשׁ
wither east the it when Shall it shall being And
wind touches not it ?prosper ,planted ,behold

3068 1697 1961 3001 6780 6170 3001
11 יָבֹשׁ עַל־עֲרֻגֹת צִמְחָהּ תִּיבָשׁ׃ וַיְהִי דְבַר־יְהוָה
Jehovah the And shall it it (where) the In ?utterly
of word came .wither sprouted beds

4100 3045 3808 4805 1004 4994 559 559
12 אֵלַי לֵאמֹר׃ אֱמָר־נָא לְבֵית הַמֶּרִי הֲלֹא יְדַעְתֶּם מָה־
what know you Do :rebellious the to now Say ,saying ,me to
not house

4428 3947 3389 894 4428 935 2009 559 428
אֵלֶּה אֱמֹר הִנֵּה־בָא מֶלֶךְ־בָּבֶל יְרוּשָׁלַםִ וַיִּקַּח אֶת־מַלְכָּהּ
king its has and to Babylon the has ,Behold :Speak these
taken Jerusalem of king come ?(mean)

4410 2233 3947 894 935 8269
13 וְאֶת־שָׂרֶיהָ וַיָּבֵא אוֹתָם אֵלָיו בָּבֶלָה׃ וַיִּקַּח מִזֶּרַע הַמְּלוּכָה
royal the of he And at to them and its and
seed took .Babylon himself brought rulers

3947 776 352 422 935 1285 3772
וַיִּכְרֹת אִתּוֹ בְּרִית וַיָּבֵא אֹתוֹ בְּאָלָה וְאֶת־אֵילֵי הָאָרֶץ לָקָח׃
took he the the And an into him made and a with has and
land of mighty .oath enter covenant him cut

8104 5375 1115 8217 4467 1961
14 לִהְיוֹת מַמְלָכָה שְׁפָלָה לְבִלְתִּי הִתְנַשֵּׂא לִשְׁמֹר אֶת־
keep to might it not ,low the that so
;itself lift that kingdom be might

4714 4397 7971 4775 5975 1285
15 בְּרִיתוֹ לְעָמְדָהּ׃ וַיִּמְרָד־בּוֹ לִשְׁלֹחַ מַלְאָכָיו מִצְרַיִם
,Egypt to his in against he But might it that its
messengers sending him rebelled .stand ,covenant

428 6213 4422 6743 7227 5971 5483 5414
לָתֶת־לוֹ סוּסִים וְעַם־רָב הֲיִצְלָח הֲיִמָּלֵט הָעֹשֵׂה אֵלֶּה
these who he Shall he Shall .many and horses to to
?(things) does escape ?prosper people him give

3808 3068 136 5002 2416 4422 1285 6565
16 וְהֵפֵר בְּרִית וְנִמְלָט׃ חַי־אָנִי נְאֻם אֲדֹנָי יְהוִה אִם־לֹא
Surely ,Jehovah the states (As) be and the shall Or
Lord I live ?delivered covenant break he

834 422 959 834 4427 4428 4725
בִּמְקוֹם הַמֶּלֶךְ הַמַּמְלִיךְ אֹתוֹ אֲשֶׁר בָּזָה אֶת־אָלָתוֹ וַאֲשֶׁר
of and his he of ,him made who king the the in
whom oath despised whom king of place

1419 2428 3808 4191 894 8432 1285 6565
17 הֵפֵר אֶת־בְּרִיתוֹ אִתּוֹ בְתוֹךְ־בָּבֶל יָמוּת׃ וְלֹא בְחַיִל גָּדוֹל
great with And shall he Babylon the in with his he
army not .die of midst him ;covenant broke

company, in the war by pouring out mounds and building siege walls to cut off many souls. [18]And he has despised the oath by breaking the covenant. And, behold, he had given his hand, and he has done all these *things*. He shall not escape.

[19]Therefore, so says the Lord Jehovah: *As* I live, surely My oath that he has despised, and My covenant that he has broken, I will even give it on his head. [20]And I will spread My net over him, and he shall be taken in My snare; and I will bring him to Babylon. And I will judge him there with his treason which he has betrayed against Me. [21]And all his fugitives shall fall by the sword, with all his bands; and those who remain shall be scattered to every wind. And you shall know that I, Jehovah, have spoken. [22]So says the Lord Jehovah: I will also take, *even* I, of the top of the highest cedar, and will set *it*; I will crop off a tender one from the first of its young twigs; and I will plant *it* on a high and lofty mountain, *even* I. [23]I will plant it in a high mountain of Israel. And it will bear boughs and produce fruit, and will become a majestic cedar. And every bird of every wing shall dwell under it; they shall dwell in the shadow of its branches. [24]And all the trees of the field shall know that I, Jehovah, have brought down the high tree, *and* have exalted the low tree; *and* have dried up the green tree; and have made the dry tree flourish. I, Jehovah, have spoken and acted.

5550 8210 44 :21 6547 621 3 7227 6951
וּבְקָהָל רָב יַעֲשֶׂה אוֹתוֹ פַרְעֹה בַּמִּלְחָמָה בִּשְׁפֹּךְ סֹלְלָה
mounds pouring by the in Pharaoh for shall great and
out ,war him work company

6565 422 959 7227 5315 3772 1785 1129
18 וּבִבְנוֹת דָּיֵק לְהַכְרִית נְפָשׁוֹת רַבּוֹת׃ וּבָזָה אָלָה לְהָפֵר
break- by the he And .many souls off cut to siege and
ing oath despised has walls building

4422 3808 6213 428 6213 3027 5414 2009 1285
בְּרִית וְהִנֵּה נָתַן יָדוֹ וְכָל־אֵלֶּה עָשָׂה לֹא יִמָּלֵט׃
shall he not has he these and his had he and cove- the
.escape ,done all ,hand given ,behold ,nant

959 834 3808 422 2416 3068 136 559
19 לָכֵן כֹּה־אָמַר אֲדֹנָי יְהוִה חַי־אָנִי אִם־לֹא אָלָתִי אֲשֶׁר בָּזָה
has he that My surely (As) :Jehovah the says thus There-
,despised oath I live Lord fore

:75 61 6566 7218 5414 6331 834 1285
20 וּבְרִיתִי אֲשֶׁר הֵפִיר וּנְתַתִּיו בְּרֹאשׁוֹ׃ וּפָרַשְׂתִּי עָלָיו רִשְׁתִּי
,net My on will I And his on even will I has he that My and
him spread .head it give ,broken covenant

8033 8199 884 935 4486 8610
וְנִתְפַּשׂ בִּמְצוּדָתִי וַהֲבִיאוֹתִיהוּ בָבֶלָה וְנִשְׁפַּטְתִּי אִתּוֹ שָׁם
there him will I and to will I and My in shall he and
,judge ,Babylon him bring ,snare taken be

102 3605 4015 3605 4604 834 4603
21 מַעֲלוֹ אֲשֶׁר מָעַל־בִּי׃ וְאֵת כָּל־מִבְרָחָו בְּכָל־אֲגַפָּיו
his with his all And against has he which his with
bands all fugitives .Me betrayed treason

30 45 6566 7307 3605 7604 5307 2719
בַּחֶרֶב יִפֹּלוּ וְהַנִּשְׁאָרִים לְכָל־רוּחַ יִפָּרֵשׂוּ וִידַעְתֶּם כִּי אֲנִי
,I that you And be shall wind to those and shall the by
know shall .scattered every remain who ,fall sword

3947 3068 136 559 1696 3068
22 יְהוָה דִּבַּרְתִּי׃ כֹּה אָמַר אֲדֹנָי יְהוִה וְלָקַחְתִּי אָנִי
,I also will I :Jehovah the says Thus have ,Jehovah
,take Lord .spoken

6998 7390 3127 7218 5414 7311 730 6788
מִצַּמֶּרֶת הָאֶרֶז הָרָמָה וְנָתָתִּי מֵרֹאשׁ יֹנְקוֹתָיו רַךְ אֶקְטֹף
will I tender a young its the from will and highest the the of
,off crop one twigs of chief ;(it) set cedar of top

3478 4791 2022 8524 1364 2022 8362
23 וְשָׁתַלְתִּי אָנִי עַל הַר־גָּבֹהַּ וְתָלוּל׃ בְּהַר מְרוֹם יִשְׂרָאֵל
Israel ,high a in .lofty and high a on I will and
of mountain mountain (it) plant

7931 117 730 1961 6529 6213 6057 5375 8362
אֶשְׁתֳּלֶנּוּ וְנָשָׂא עָנָף וְעָשָׂה פֶרִי וְהָיָה לְאֶרֶז אַדִּיר וְשָׁכְנוּ
shall And .majestic a and ,fruit and boughs it And will I
dwell cedar become produce bear will .it plant

3045 7931 1808 6738 3671 3605 6833 3605 8478
24 תַחְתָּיו כֹּל צִפּוֹר כָּל־כָּנָף בְּצֵל דָּלִיּוֹתָיו תִּשְׁכֹּנָּה׃ וְיָדְעוּ
shall And shall they its the in ;wing every bird every it under
know .dwell branches of shadow of

1361 1364 6086 8213 3068 77 04 6086 3605
כָּל־עֲצֵי הַשָּׂדֶה כִּי אֲנִי יְהוָה הִשְׁפַּלְתִּי עֵץ גָּבֹהַּ הִגְבַּהְתִּי
have ,high the brought have ,Jehovah ,I that the the all
exalted tree down field of trees

3068 3002 6086 6524 389 2 6086 3001 8217 6086
עֵץ שָׁפָל הוֹבַשְׁתִּי עֵץ לָח וְהִפְרַחְתִּי עֵץ יָבֵשׁ אֲנִי יְהוָה
,Jehovah I .dry the have and ,green the dried have ,low the
tree flourish made tree up tree

6213 1696
דִּבַּרְתִּי וְעָשִׂיתִי׃
have and have
.acted spoken

CHAPTER 18

[1]And the word of Jehovah was to me, saying, [2]What *is it* to you that you use this proverb concerning the land of Israel, saying, The fathers have eaten sour grapes, and the teeth of the sons are dull. [3]*As* I live, declares the Lord Jehovah, There is not any longer *occasion* to you to use this proverb in Israel. [4]Behold, they *are* all My souls. As the soul of the father, also the soul of the son; they *are* Mine. The soul that sins, it shall die.

[5]But a man that is righteous and does that which is just and right; [6]who has not eaten on the mountains; and his eyes *have* not lifted up to the idols of the house of Israel; and has not defiled his neighbor's wife; and has not come near to a menstruating woman; [7]and has not oppressed a man; he returns his pledge to the debtor; *and* has not robbed by robbery; has given his bread to the hungry; and he has covered the naked *with* clothing; [8]he has not loaned on interest, and he has not taken increase; he has kept his hand from injustice, having done true justice between man and man; [9]he has walked in My statutes, and has kept My judgments to deal truly — he *is* righteous; surely he shall live, declares the Lord Jehovah.

[10]And if he fathers a son who is violent, who sheds blood, and does to a brother *any* of these— [11]even he does not any of these: that also he has eaten on the mountains, and has defiled his neighbor's wife; [12]he has oppressed the poor and needy; thieving, he stole; *he* has not returned the

CAP. XVIII יח

CHAPTER 18

4911 4100 559 3068 1697 1961
1 2 וַיְהִי דְבַר־יְהוָה אֵלַי לֵאמֹר׃ מַה־לָּכֶם אַתֶּם מֹשְׁלִים אֶת־
use you to What ,saying ,me to Jehovah the And
that you (it is) of word was

1155 398 559 3478 127 2088 4912
הַמָּשָׁל הַזֶּה עַל־אַדְמַת יִשְׂרָאֵל לֵאמֹר אָבוֹת יֹאכְלוּ בֹסֶר
sour have The ,saying ,Israel the con- this proverb
grapes eaten fathers of land cerning

1961 518 3068 136 5002 2416 6949 1121 8127
3 וְשִׁנֵּי הַבָּנִים תִּקְהֶינָה׃ חַי־אָנִי נְאֻם אֲדֹנָי יְהוִה אִם־יִהְיֶה
there not ,Jehovah the states As ?dull are the the and
is Lord I live sons of teeth

5315 3605 3478 2088 4912 4911 5750
4 לָכֶם עוֹד מְשֹׁל הַמָּשָׁל הַזֶּה בְּיִשְׂרָאֵל׃ הֵן כָּל־הַנְּפָשׁוֹת
the all ,Behold .Israel in this proverb use to any to
souls longer you

2398 5315 1121 5315 1 5315
לִי הֵנָּה כְּנֶפֶשׁ הָאָב וּכְנֶפֶשׁ הַבֵּן לִי־הֵנָּה הַנֶּפֶשׁ הַחֹטֵאת
,sins that the they to the the also the the As they to
soul ;(are) me son of soul ,father of soul .(are) Me

6666 4941 6213 6662 1961 376 4191
5 הִיא תָמוּת׃ וְאִישׁ כִּי־יִהְיֶה צַדִּיק וְעָשָׂה מִשְׁפָּט וּצְדָקָה׃
and which that and righteous is that a But shall it
;right just is does man .die

1004 1544 5375 3808 5869 398 3808 2022
6 אֶל־הֶהָרִים לֹא אָכָל וְעֵינָיו לֹא נָשָׂא אֶל־גִּלּוּלֵי בֵּית
the idols the to has not his and has not the on
of house of up lifted eyes eaten mountains

3808 5079 802 2930 3808 7453 802 3478
יִשְׂרָאֵל וְאֶת־אֵשֶׁת רֵעֵהוּ לֹא טִמֵּא וְאֶל־אִשָּׁה נִדָּה לֹא
not men- woman a and has not his wife and ;Israel
struating to ;defiled neighbor's

1497 3808 1500 7725 2326 2258 3238 3808 376 7126
7 יִקְרָב׃ וְאִישׁ לֹא יוֹנֶה חֲבֹלָתוֹ חוֹב יָשִׁיב גְּזֵלָה לֹא יִגְזֹל
has not by re- he the (to) his (but) has not a and come has
,robbed robbery ;turns debtor pledge ,pressed man ;near

5414 3808 5392 899 3680 5903 5414 7457 3899
8 לַחְמוֹ לְרָעֵב יִתֵּן וְעֵירֹם יְכַסֶּה־בָּגֶד׃ בַּנֶּשֶׁךְ לֹא־יִתֵּן
has he not on (with) has he the and has the to his (but)
lent interest ;clothing covered naked given hungry bread

6213 571 4941 3027 7725 5766 3947 3808 8636
וְתַרְבִּית לֹא יִקָּח מֵעָוֶל יָשִׁיב יָדוֹ מִשְׁפַּט אֱמֶת יַעֲשֶׂה
has true justice his has he from has he not and
done ;hand kept injustice ;taken increase

6213 8104 4941 1980 2708 376 376 996
9 בֵּין אִישׁ לְאִישׁ׃ בְּחֻקּוֹתַי יְהַלֵּךְ וּמִשְׁפָּטַי שָׁמַר לַעֲשׂוֹת
deal to has My and has My in and man be-
kept judgments walked statutes ;man tween

1121 3205 3068 136 5002 2421 2421 6662 571
10 אֱמֶת צַדִּיק הוּא חָיֹה יִחְיֶה נְאֻם אֲדֹנָי יְהוִה׃ וְהוֹלִיד בֵּן
a if And .Jehovah the states he surely he righteous —truly
son fathers he Lord live shall (is)

428 259 251 6213 1818 8210 6530
11 פָּרִיץ שֹׁפֵךְ דָּם וְעָשָׂה אָח מֵאַחַד מֵאֵלֶּה׃ וְהוּא אֶת־
(if) even ;these of from a does and ,blood who is who
he one ,brother (to) sheds ,violent

802 398 2022 1571 6213 3808 428 3605
כָּל־אֵלֶּה לֹא עָשָׂה כִּי גַם אֶל־הֶהָרִים אָכַל וְאֶת־אֵשֶׁת
wife and has he the on also that does not these any
;eaten mountains ;(himself) of

7725 3808 2258 1497 1500 3238 34 6041 2930 7453
12 רֵעֵהוּ טִמֵּא׃ עָנִי וְאֶבְיוֹן הוֹנָה גְּזֵלוֹת גָּזָל חֲבֹל לֹא יָשִׁיב
has not the he Thieving has he the and the has his
;returned pledge ;stole .pressed needy poor defiled neighbor's

pledge; and has lifted up his eyes to the idols; he has committed abomination; [13]he has loaned on interest and has taken increase; shall he also live? He shall not live. He has done all these abominations; he shall surely die; his blood shall be on him.

[14]Now, behold, *if* he fathers a son who sees all his father's sins which he has done, and sees, and does not do like them— [15]*he* has not eaten on the mountains, and has not lifted up his eyes to the idols of the house of Israel; has not defiled his neighbor's wife; [16]and has not oppressed a man; has not withheld the pledge; and has not robbed by robbery—he has given his bread to the hungry, and he has covered the naked *with* clothes; [17]has withdrawn his hand from the poor; and has not received interest and increase; *he* has done My judgments, has walked in My statutes—he shall not die for the iniquity of his father. He shall surely live. [18]His father, because he did extortion, robbed *his* brother by robbery, and did what is not good among his people, behold, even he shall die in his iniquity.

[19]Yet you say, Why? Does not the son bear the iniquity of the father? When the son has done justice and righteousness; he has kept all My statutes, and has done them; surely he shall live. [20]The soul that sins, it shall die. A son shall not bear the iniquity of the father. And a father shall not bear the iniquity of the son. The righteousness of the righteous shall be upon him; and the wickedness of the wicked shall be on him.

[21]But the wicked, if he will turn from all his sins which he has done, and keep all My statutes, and do justice and righteousness, surely he shall live; he shall

---

13 וְאֶל־הַגִּלּוּלִים נָשָׂא עֵינָיו תּוֹעֵבָה עָשָׂה בְּנֶשֶׁךְ נָתַן

| and to | the idols | has lifted up | his eyes | abomination | has committed; | on interest | has lent |

וְתַרְבִּית לָקַח וָחָי לֹא יִחְיֶה אֵת כָּל־הַתּוֹעֵבוֹת הָאֵלֶּה

| increase | taken, | also live? | shall He | not | he shall | has | all | abominations | these |

14 עָשָׂה מוֹת יוּמָת דָּמָיו בּוֹ יִהְיֶה וְהִנֵּה הוֹלִיד בֵּן וַיַּרְא

| done; | die | shall he surely | his blood | on him | shall be; | Now behold, | he (if) | fathers | a son | who sees |

אֶת־כָּל־חַטֹּאת אָבִיו אֲשֶׁר עָשָׂה וַיִּרְאֶ וְלֹא יַעֲשֶׂה כָּהֵן

| all | sins | his father's | which | has done, | and sees, | and not | do | them; | like |

15 עַל־הֶהָרִים לֹא אָכַל וְעֵינָיו לֹא נָשָׂא אֶל־גִּלּוּלֵי בֵּית

| on | mountains | not | has eaten; | his and eyes | not | has | to | the idols | of house |

יִשְׂרָאֵל אֶת־אֵשֶׁת רֵעֵהוּ לֹא טִמֵּא וְאִישׁ לֹא הוֹנָה חֲבֹל

| Israel; | wife | his neighbor's | not | has defiled; | a and man | not | has pressed; | a pledge |

לֹא חָבָל וּגְזֵלָה לֹא גָזָל לַחְמוֹ לָרָעֵב יִתֵּן וְעֵרוֹם כִּסָּה

| not | has withheld | by robbery | not | has robbed; | his bread | to the hungry | has given | the and naked | has he covered |

17 בֶּעָנִי הֵשִׁיב יָדוֹ נֶשֶׁךְ וְתַרְבִּית לֹא לָקַח מִשְׁפָּטַי

| (with) the poor | has withdrawn | his hand; | interest | and increase | not | has received; | My judgments |

עָשָׂה בְּחֻקֹּתַי הָלַךְ הוּא לֹא יָמוּת בַּעֲוֺן אָבִיו חָיֹה יִחְיֶה

| has done; | My in statutes | has walked; | he | not | die | for the iniquity | his father | surely | shall he live. |

18 אָבִיו כִּי־עָשַׁק עֹשֶׁק גָּזַל גֵּזֶל אָח וַאֲשֶׁר לֹא־טוֹב עָשָׂה

| His father, | because he did | extortion, | robbed | by robbery | brother, | and what | is not good | did |

בְּתוֹךְ עַמָּיו וְהִנֵּה־מֵת בַּעֲוֺנוֹ וַאֲמַרְתֶּם מַדּוּעַ לֹא־נָשָׂא

| among | his people, | behold, even he | in his iniquity. | Yet you say, | Why? | Does not | bear |

19 הַבֵּן בַּעֲוֺן הָאָב וְהַבֵּן מִשְׁפָּט וּצְדָקָה עָשָׂה אֵת כָּל־חֻקּוֹתַי

| the son | the iniquity | the father? | When the son | justice | and righteousness | has done, | | all | My statutes |

20 שָׁמַר וַיַּעֲשֶׂה אֹתָם חָיֹה יִחְיֶה הַנֶּפֶשׁ הַחֹטֵאת הִיא תָמוּת

| has kept, | and has | them; | surely | shall he live. | The soul | that sins, | it | shall die. |

בֵּן לֹא־יִשָּׂא בַּעֲוֺן הָאָב וְאָב לֹא יִשָּׂא בַּעֲוֺן הַבֵּן צִדְקַת

| A son | shall not | bear | the iniquity | the father, | and a | shall not | bear | the iniquity | of the son. | The righteousness |

הַצַּדִּיק עָלָיו תִּהְיֶה וְרִשְׁעַת יָרָשָׁע עָלָיו תִּהְיֶה

| the righteous | on him | shall be, | and the wickedness | wicked | on him | shall be. |

21 וְהָרָשָׁע כִּי יָשׁוּב מִכָּל־חַטֹּאתוֹ אֲשֶׁר עָשָׂה וְשָׁמַר אֶת־

| the But wicked, | if | will he turn | from his sins | which | has he done, | and keep | |

כָּל־חֻקּוֹתַי וְעָשָׂה מִשְׁפָּט וּצְדָקָה חָיֹה יִחְיֶה לֹא יָמוּת

| all | My statutes, | and do | justice | and righteousness, | surely | shall he live, | not | shall he die. |

not die. [22]All his transgressions that he has done, they shall not be mentioned to him—in his righteousness which he has done, he shall live.

[23]Do I actually desire the death of the wicked? declares the Lord Jehovah. Is it not that he should turn from his ways and live? [24]But when the righteous turns from his righteousness, and does injustice; according to all the abominations that the wicked do, he does; shall he live? All his righteousness that he has done shall not be remembered in his treason that he has betrayed, and in his sin that he has sinned—in them he shall die.

[25]Yet you say, The way of the Lord is not fair. Hear now, O house of Israel. Is My way not fair? Are your ways not unfair? [26]When a righteous one turns from his righteousness and does injustice, and dies in them; he shall die for his injustice which he has done. [27]And when the wicked turns from his wickedness that he has done, and does justice and righteousness, he shall keep his soul alive. [28]Because he considers and turns from all his transgressions that he has done, surely he shall live; he shall not die. [29]Yet the house of Israel says, The way of the Lord is not fair. Are My ways not fair, O house of Israel? Is it not your ways that are not fair? [30]So I will judge you, each man by his ways, O house of Israel, declares the Lord Jehovah. Turn and be made to turn from all your transgressions, and iniquity shall not be a stumbling-block to you. [31]Cast away all your transgressions from you by which you have transgressed in them; and make for yourselves a new heart and a new spirit; for

22 כל-פשעיו אשר עשה לא יזכרו לו בצדקתו אשר-עשה
23 יחיה: החפץ אחפץ מות רשע נאם אדני יהוה הלוא
24 בשובו מדרכיו וחיה: ובשוב צדיק מצדקתו
ועשה עול ככל התועבות אשר-עשה הרשע יעשה וחי
כל-צדקתו אשר-עשה לא תזכרנה במעלו אשר-מעל
25 ובחטאתו אשר-חטא בם ימות: ואמרתם לא יתכן דרך
אדני שמעו-נא בית ישראל הדרכי לא יתכן הלא
26 דרכיכם לא יתכנו: בשוב-צדיק מצדקתו ועשה עול
27 ומת עליהם בעולו אשר-עשה ימות: ובשוב רשע
מרשעתו אשר עשה ויעש משפט וצדקה הוא את-נפשו
28 יחיה: ויראה וישוב מכל-פשעיו אשר עשה חיו יחיה
29 לא ימות: ואמרו בית ישראל לא יתכן דרך אדני
הדרכי לא יתכנו בית ישראל הלא דרכיכם לא יתכן:
30 לכן איש כדרכיו אשפט אתכם בית ישראל נאם אדני
יהוה שובו והשיבו מכל-פשעיכם ולא-יהיה לכם
31 למכשול עון: השליכו מעליכם את-כל-פשעיכם אשר
פשעתם בם ועשו לכם לב חדש ורוח חדשה ולמה

why will you die, O house of Israel? [32]For I do not have pleasure in the death of him who dies, declares the Lord Jehovah. So turn and live.

136 5002 41:91 4194 2654 38:08 3478 1004 4191

32 תְּמֻתוּ בֵּית יִשְׂרָאֵל׃ כִּי לֹא אֶחְפֹּץ בְּמוֹת הַמֵּת נְאֻם אֲדֹנָי

the states who him the in have I do not For ?Israel O you will
Lord ,dies of death pleasure of house ,die

2421 7725 3068

יְהוִה וְהָשִׁיבוּ וִחְיוּ׃

.live and So .Jehovah
turn

CAP. XIX יט

CHAPTER 19

CHAPTER 19

[1]And you take up a lament for the rulers of Israel, [2]and say, What *is* your mother? A lioness; she lay down among lions; among young lions she multiplied her cubs. [3]And she raised one of her cubs; he became a young lion, and learned to tear the prey; he ate men. [4]And the nations heard of him. He was taken in their pit, and they brought him in chains to the land of Egypt. [5]And when she saw that she had waited, *and* her hope had been lost, then she took another of her cubs *and* made him a young lion. [6]And he went about among the lions. He became a young lion, and learned to tear the prey; he ate men. [7]And he knew his widows, and he laid their cities waste; and the land and its fullness were desolated from the sound of his roaring. [8]Then the nations set against him on every side from the provinces, and spread their net over him; he was taken in their pit. [9]And they put him in a cage in chains, and brought him to the king of Babylon. They brought him into hunting nets, so that his voice should not any longer be heard on the mountains of Israel.

[10]Your mother *is* like a vine in your blood, planted by the waters. She was fruitful and full of branches because of many waters. [11]And there *were* rods to her, strong for the scepters of rulers; and her stature was exalted among the thick branches. And it was seen in her height, with the

517 559 3478 5387 7015 5375 6258

1
2 וְאַתָּה שָׂא קִינָה אֶל־נְשִׂיאֵי יִשְׂרָאֵל׃ וְאָמַרְתָּ מָה אִמְּךָ

your What ,say and ,Israel the for a take And
?mother (is) of rulers lament up you

1482 7235 3715 8432 7257 738 996 38:33

לְבִיָּא בֵּין אֲרָיוֹת רָבָצָה בְּתוֹךְ כְּפִרִים רִבְּתָה גוּרֶיהָ׃

her she young among She lions among A
.cubs multiplied lions ;down lay .lioness

120 2964 2963 3920 1961 3715 1482 259 5927

3 וַתַּעַל אֶחָד מִגֻּרֶיהָ כְּפִיר הָיָה וַיִּלְמַד לִטְרָף־טֶרֶף אָדָם

men the tear to and he young a her of one she And
;prey learned became lion ;cubs raised

2397 935 8610 7845 1471 8085 398

4 אָכָל׃ וַיִּשְׁמְעוּ אֵלָיו גּוֹיִם בְּשַׁחְתָּם נִתְפָּשׂ וַיְבִאֻהוּ בַחַחִים

in they and was He their In the of heard Also he
chains him brought ,taken pit .nations him .ate

3947 8615 6 3176 7200 4714 776

5 אֶל־אֶרֶץ מִצְרָיִם׃ וַתֵּרֶא כִּי נוֹחֲלָה אָבְדָה תִּקְוָתָהּ וַתִּקַּח

she then her had (and) had she that when And .Egypt the to
took ,hope lost been waited saw she of land

3715 738 8432 1980 7760 3715 1482 259

6 אֶחָד מִגֻּרֶיהָ כְּפִיר שָׂמָתְהוּ׃ וַיִּתְהַלֵּךְ בְּתוֹךְ־אֲרָיוֹת כְּפִיר

young a the among he And .him made a (and) her of another
lion .lions about walked lion young cubs

490 3045 398 120 2964 2963 3920 1961

7 הָיָה וַיִּלְמַד לִטְרָף־טֶרֶף אָדָם אָכָל׃ וַיֵּדַע אַלְמְנוֹתָיו

,widows his he And .ate he men ;prey the tear to and be- he
knew learned came

5414 7581 6963 4393 776 3456 2717 5892

8 וְעָרֵיהֶם הֶחֱרִיב וַתֵּשַׁם אֶרֶץ וּמְלֹאָהּ מִקּוֹל שַׁאֲגָתוֹ׃ וַיִּתְּנוּ

Then his the from its and the were and laid he their and
set .roaring of sound fulness land desolated ,waste cities

7845 7561 6566 4082 5439 1471

עָלָיו גּוֹיִם סָבִיב מִמְּדִינוֹת וַיִּפְרְשׂוּ עָלָיו רִשְׁתָּם בְּשַׁחְתָּם

their in ;net their over and the from every on the against
pit him spread ,provinces side nations him

1884 4428 935 2397 5414 5414 8610

9 נִתְפָּשׂ׃ וַיִּתְּנֻהוּ בַסּוּגַר בַּחַחִים וַיְבִאֻהוּ אֶל־מֶלֶךְ בָּבֶל

.Babylon the to brought and in a in they And was he
of king him chains cage him put .taken

2022 5750 6963 8085 3808 4616 4685 935

יְבִאֻהוּ בַּמְּצֹדוֹת לְמַעַן לֹא־יִשָּׁמַע קוֹלוֹ עוֹד אֶל־הָרֵי

the on any his be should not so hunting into They
of mountains longer voice heard that nets him brought

6509 8362 4325 1818 1612 517 3478

10 יִשְׂרָאֵל׃ אִמְּךָ כַגֶּפֶן בְּדָמְךָ עַל־מַיִם שְׁתוּלָה פֹּרִיָּה

was She .planted the by your in a like Your .Israel
fruitful waters ,blood vine (is) mother

7626 5794 4294 1961 7227 4325 1961 6058

11 וַעֲנֵפָה הָיְתָה מִמַּיִם רַבִּים׃ וַיִּהְיוּ־לָהּ מַטּוֹת עֹז אֶל־שִׁבְטֵי

the for strong ,rods her to And .many because was full and
of scepters was waters of branches of

7230 1363 7200 5688 996 6967 1361 4910

מֹשְׁלִים וַתִּגְבַּהּ קוֹמָתוֹ עַל־בֵּין עֲבֹתִים וַיֵּרָא בְגָבְהוֹ בְּרֹב

the with her in it And thick the among its was and ;rulers
of many height seen was .branches stature exalted

multitude of her branches. [12]But she was plucked in fury. She was thrown to the ground, and the east wind dried up her fruit. Her strong rods were torn away and withered; the fire burned her. [13]And now she is planted in the wilderness, in a dry and thirsty ground. [14]And fire has gone out from a rod of her branches; it consumed her fruit, and there is not a strong rod in her *to be* a scepter to rule. It *is* a lament, and has become a lament.

3001 6921 7307 7993 776 2534 5428 1808
12 דָּלִיֹּתָיו׃ וַתֻּתַּשׁ בְּחֵמָה לָאָרֶץ הֻשְׁלָכָה וְרוּחַ הַקָּדִים הוֹבִישׁ
dried up. east wind the and was She thrown the to ground .fury in she But plucked was its branches
6258 398 784 5797 4294 3001 6561 6529
13 פִּרְיָהּ הִתְפָּרְקוּ וְיָבֵשׁוּ מַטֵּה עֻזָּהּ אֵשׁ אֲכָלָתְהוּ׃ וְעַתָּה
And now .it burned the fire Her ;strong rods and withered torn were away her .fruit
4294 784 3318 6772 6723 776 4057 8362
14 שְׁתוּלָה בַמִּדְבָּר בְּאֶרֶץ צִיָּה וְצָמָא׃ וַתֵּצֵא אֵשׁ מִמַּטֵּה
a from of rod fire has And out gone and .thirsty dry a in ground the in ,wilderness is she planted
4910 7626 5797 4294 1961 3808 398 6529 905
בַדֶּיהָ פִּרְיָהּ אָכָלָה וְלֹא־הָיָה בָהּ מַטֵּה־עֹז שֵׁבֶט לִמְשׁוֹל
.rule to a (be to) scepter strong rod a in her is and not it consumed her fruit her ,branches
7015 1961 7015
קִינָה הִיא וַתְּהִי לְקִינָה׃
.lament a has and become It ,(is) a lament

CAP. XX כ

CHAPTER 20

CHAPTER 20

[1]And it was in the seventh year, in the fifth *month*, the tenth of the month, men came from the elders of Israel to inquire *of* Jehovah, and sat before me. [2]And the word of Jehovah was to me, saying, [3]Son of man, speak to the elders of Israel and say to them, So says the Lord Jehovah: Have you come to inquire *of* Me? *As* I live, declares the Lord Jehovah, I will not be inquired of by you. [4]Will you judge them; will you judge, son of man? Cause them to know the abominations of their fathers.

[5]And say to them, So says the Lord Jehovah: In the day I chose Israel, and lifted My hand to the seed of the house of Jacob—and I was made known to them in the land of Egypt—when I lifted up My hand to them, saying, I *am* Jehovah your God; [6]in that day I lifted up My hand to them to bring them out from the land of Egypt into a land that I had searched out for them, flowing *with* milk and honey, the glory *of* it *is* to all

935 2320 6218 2549 7637 8141 1961
1 וַיְהִי ׀ בַּשָּׁנָה הַשְּׁבִיעִית בַּחֲמִשִׁי בֶּעָשׂוֹר לַחֹדֶשׁ בָּאוּ
came the of ,month tenth the (month) fifth the in ,seventh the in year And was it
6440 3427 3068 1875 3478 2205 582
אֲנָשִׁים מִזִּקְנֵי יִשְׂרָאֵל לִדְרֹשׁ אֶת־יְהוָה וַיֵּשְׁבוּ לְפָנָי׃
before .me sat and (of) Jehovah inquire to Israel from of elders the men
2205 1696 120 1121 559 3068 1697 1961
2 וַיְהִי דְבַר־יְהוָה אֵלַי לֵאמֹר׃
3 בֶּן־אָדָם דַּבֵּר אֶת־זִקְנֵי
the of elders speak to ,man Son of ,saying to ,me Jehovah the of word Then was
1875 3068 136 559 559 3478
יִשְׂרָאֵל וְאָמַרְתָּ אֲלֵהֶם כֹּה אָמַר אֲדֹנָי יְהוִה הֲלִדְרֹשׁ
to Have inquire :Jehovah the Lord says Thus ,them to say and Israel
136 5002 1875 2416 935
אֹתִי אַתֶּם בָּאִים חַי־אָנִי אִם־אִדָּרֵשׁ לָכֶם נְאֻם אֲדֹנָי
the Lord states by ,you be will I of inquired not (As) ,I live ?come You (of) Me
8441 120 1121 8199 8199 3068
4 יְהוִה׃ הֲתִשְׁפֹּט אֹתָם הֲתִשְׁפּוֹט בֶּן־אָדָם אֶת־תּוֹעֲבֹת
abomi- the of nations ?man son of you will ,judge ,them you Will judge .Jehovah
3068 136 559 3541 559 3045
5 אֲבוֹתָם הוֹדִיעֵם׃ וְאָמַרְתָּ אֲלֵיהֶם כֹּה־אָמַר אֲדֹנָי יְהוִה
:Jehovah the Lord says Thus ,them to say And them cause .know to their fathers
3045 3290 1004 2233 3027 5375 3478 977 3117
בְּיוֹם בָּחֳרִי בְיִשְׂרָאֵל וָאֶשָּׂא יָדִי לְזֶרַע בֵּית יַעֲקֹב וָאִוָּדַע
was I and known made ,Jacob the of house the to of seed My hand and lifted Israel I that chose the In day
3068 559 3027 5375 4714 776
לָהֶם בְּאֶרֶץ מִצְרָיִם וָאֶשָּׂא יָדִי לָהֶם לֵאמֹר אֲנִי יְהוָה
Jehovah I (am) ,saying ,them to My hand I when up lifted ;Egypt the in of land to them
776 3318 3027 5375 3117 430
6 אֱלֹהֵיכֶם׃ בַּיּוֹם הַהוּא נָשָׂאתִי יָדִי לָהֶם לְהוֹצִיאָם מֵאֶרֶץ
the from of land bring to out them to them My hand lifted I up that day in ;God your
6643 1706 2461 2100 8446 834 776 4714
מִצְרָיִם אֶל־אֶרֶץ אֲשֶׁר־תַּרְתִּי לָהֶם זָבַת חָלָב וּדְבַשׁ צְבִי
the glory and ,honey (with) milk flowing for ,them had I out searched that a land into Egypt

lands; [7]then I said to them, let each man cast away the filthy idols of his eyes, and do not defile yourselves with the idols of Egypt; I *am* Jehovah your God. [8]But they rebelled against Me, and would not listen to Me. They did not each man throw away the filthy idols of their eyes, and they did not forsake the idols of Egypt. Then I said, I will pour out My fury against them, to fulfill My anger against them in the midst of the land of Egypt. [9]But I worked for My name's sake, that it should not be profaned in the eyes of the nations among whom they *were, for* I made Myself known to them in their eyes, by bringing them out of the land of Egypt.

[10]So I made them leave from the land of Egypt, and brought them into the wilderness. [11]And I gave them My statutes, and I made them know My judgments, which *if* a man does them, he will even live by them. [12]And I also gave them My sabbaths to be a sign between Me and them, that *they* might know that I *am* Jehovah, who sets them apart. [13]But the house of Israel rebelled against Me in the wilderness; they did not walk in My statutes, and they despised My judgments; which *if* a man does them he will even live by them. And they greatly profaned My sabbaths. Then I said, *I* will pour out My fury on them in the wilderness, to consume them. [14]But I worked for My name's sake, that it should not be profaned in the eyes of the nations, *before* whom I brought them out, in their eyes. [15]And I also lifted up My hand to them in the wilderness, that *I* would not bring them into the land which I had given, flowing

7 הִיא לְכָל־הָאֲרָצוֹת׃ וָאֹמַר אֲלֵהֶם אִישׁ שִׁקּוּצֵי עֵינָיו
his eyes | filthy the of idols | each man | ,them to | I then said | ,lands | to all | (is) it

הַשְׁלִיכוּ וּבְגִלּוּלֵי מִצְרַיִם אַל־תִּטַּמָּאוּ אֲנִי יְהוָה אֱלֹהֵיכֶם׃
.God your | Jehovah | I (am) | defile do .yourselves | not | Egypt | with and of idols the | cast Let ,away

8 וַיַּמְרוּ־בִי וְלֹא אָבוּ לִשְׁמֹעַ אֵלַי אִישׁ אֶת־שִׁקּוּצֵי עֵינֵיהֶם
their eyes | filthy the of idols | each man | .Me to | listen to | would and ,not | against they But ,Me rebelled

לֹא הִשְׁלִיכוּ וְאֶת־גִּלּוּלֵי מִצְרַיִם לֹא עָזָבוּ וָאֹמַר לִשְׁפֹּךְ
will (I) out pour | I Then ,said | they .forsake did | not | Egypt | the of idols | and | did They ,away throw | not

חֲמָתִי עֲלֵיהֶם לְכַלּוֹת אַפִּי בָּהֶם בְּתוֹךְ אֶרֶץ מִצְרָיִם׃
.Egypt | the of land | the in of middle | against them | My anger | fulfill to | against them | My fury

9 וָאַעַשׂ לְמַעַן שְׁמִי לְבִלְתִּי הֵחֵל לְעֵינֵי הַגּוֹיִם אֲשֶׁר־הֵמָּה
they (were) | of whom | the nations | the in eyes | be should it profaned | that not | My name | the for of sake | I But worked

בְתוֹכָם אֲשֶׁר נוֹדַעְתִּי אֲלֵיהֶם לְעֵינֵיהֶם לְהוֹצִיאָם מֵאֶרֶץ
the of of land | bringing by out them | ,eyes their in | them to | made I known Myself | whom of | among ,them

10 מִצְרָיִם׃ וָאוֹצִיאֵם מֵאֶרֶץ מִצְרַיִם וָאֲבִאֵם אֶל־הַמִּדְבָּר׃
the .wilderness | into | brought and them | Egypt | the from of land | made I So leave them | .Egypt

11 וָאֶתֵּן לָהֶם אֶת־חֻקּוֹתַי וְאֶת־מִשְׁפָּטַי הוֹדַעְתִּי אוֹתָם אֲשֶׁר
which | ,them | made I know | My judgments | and | My ,statutes | them | I And gave

12 יַעֲשֶׂה אוֹתָם הָאָדָם וָחַי בָּהֶם׃ וְגַם אֶת־שַׁבְּתוֹתַי נָתַתִּי
gave I | My sabbaths | And also | .them by | will he live even | ,man | them | (if) does

לָהֶם לִהְיוֹת לְאוֹת בֵּינִי וּבֵינֵיהֶם לָדַעַת כִּי אֲנִי יְהוָה
Jehovah | I (am) | that | (they) that know might | and ,them | between Me | sign a | be to | to them

13 מְקַדְּשָׁם׃ וַיַּמְרוּ־בִי בֵית־יִשְׂרָאֵל בַּמִּדְבָּר בְּחֻקּוֹתַי לֹא
not | My in statutes | the in ;wilderness | Israel | the of house | against Me | But rebelled | sets who .apart them

הָלָכוּ וְאֶת־מִשְׁפָּטַי מָאָסוּ אֲשֶׁר יַעֲשֶׂה אֹתָם הָאָדָם וָחַי
will he live even | ,man a | them | (if) does | which | they —despised | My judgments | and | did they walk

בָּהֶם וְאֶת־שַׁבְּתֹתַי חִלְּלוּ מְאֹד וָאֹמַר לִשְׁפֹּךְ חֲמָתִי עֲלֵיהֶם
them on | My fury | will (I) out pour | I Then ,said | .greatly | they profaned | My sabbaths | And | by .them

14 בַּמִּדְבָּר לְכַלֹּתָם׃ וָאַעַשׂ לְמַעַן שְׁמִי לְבִלְתִּי הֵחֵל לְעֵינֵי
the in of eyes | be should it profaned | that not | My ,name | the for of sake | I But worked | destroy to .them | the in ,wilderness

15 הַגּוֹיִם אֲשֶׁר הוֹצֵאתִים לְעֵינֵיהֶם׃ וְגַם־אֲנִי נָשָׂאתִי יָדִי
My hand | lifted up | I And also | .eyes their in | brought I out them | of whom | the nations

לָהֶם בַּמִּדְבָּר לְבִלְתִּי הָבִיא אוֹתָם אֶל־הָאָרֶץ אֲשֶׁר־נָתַתִּי
had I ,(them) given | which | the land | into | them | would (I) bring | that not | the in ,wilderness | to them

with milk and honey—it *is* the glory to all the lands; [16]because they despised My judgments, and they did not walk in My statutes; and they profaned My sabbaths; for their heart went after their idols. [17]And My eye spared them, from destroying them; and I did not make an end of them in the wilderness. [18]But I said to their sons in the wilderness, Do not walk in the statutes of your fathers, and do not keep their judgments; and do not defile yourselves with their idols. [19]I *am* Jehovah your God. Walk in My statutes, and keep My judgments, and do them. [20]And keep My sabbaths holy; and they shall be a sign between Me and you, that *you* may know that I *am* Jehovah your God.

[21]But the sons rebelled against Me; they did not walk in My statutes, and they did not keep My judgments, to do them; which *if* a man does them, he shall live by them. They profaned My sabbaths. Then I said *I* would pour out My fury on them, to fulfill My anger against them in the wilderness. [22]But I withdrew My hand and acted for My name's sake, that it should not be profaned in the eyes of the nations, from whom I brought them out in their eyes. [23]And I lifted up My hand to them in the wilderness, to scatter them among the nations and sow them among the lands, [24]because they had not done My judgments, and had despised My statutes, and had profaned My sabbaths; and their eyes were after their fathers' idols. [25]Also I gave them statutes not good, and

16 זבת חלב ודבש צבי היא לכל־הארצות׃ יען במשפטי
My judgments because the ;lands all to (is) it the glory and ,honey (with) flowing milk
מאסו ואת־חקותי לא־הלכו בהם ואת־שבתותי חללו כי
for they ,profaned My sabbaths and in ,them walked not My statutes and they despised
17 אחרי גלוליהם לבם הלך׃ ותחס עיני עליהם משחתם
destroy- ;them from ing them My eye And spared .went their heart their idols after
18 ולא־עשיתי אותם כלה במדבר׃ ואמר אל־בניהם
their sons to I But said the in .wilderness end an of them did I make and not
במדבר בחוקי אבותיכם אל־תלכו ואת־משפטיהם
their judgments and Do ;walk not your fathers the in of statutes the in ,wilderness
19 אל־תשמרו ובגלוליהם אל־תטמאו׃ אני יהוה אלהיכם
.God your Jehovah I (am) defile do .yourselves not with and idols their ;keep do not
20 בחקותי לכו ואת־משפטי שמרו ועשו אתם׃ ואת־
and ,them do and ,keep My judgments and Walk My in statutes
שבתותי קדשו והיו לאות ביני וביניכם לדעת כי אני
I (am) that (you) that know may ,you and between Me sign a they and be shall keep ;holy My sabbaths
21 יהוה אלהיכם׃ וימרו־בי הבנים בחקותי לא־הלכו ואת־
and They ,walk did not My in statutes the .sons against Me But rebelled .God your Jehovah
משפטי לא־שמרו לעשות אותם אשר יעשה אותם
them (if) does ,which —them do to they ,keep did not My judgments
האדם וחי בהם את־שבתותי חללו ואמר לשפך חמתי
My fury would (I) out pour I Then said they .profaned My sabbaths by ,them shall he live ,man a
22 עליהם לכלות אפי בם במדבר׃ והשבתי את־ידי ואעש
and acted My hand I But withdrew the in .wilderness against them My anger fulfill to on ,them
למען שמי לבלתי החל לעיני הגוים אשר־הוצאתי
brought I out from whom the nations the in of sight be should it profaned that not My name the for of sake
23 אותם לעיניהם׃ גם־אני נשאתי את־ידי להם במדבר
the in wilderness them to My hand lifted up I Also their in .sight them
24 להפיץ אתם בגוים ולזרות אותם בארצות׃ יען משפטי
My judgments because the among ,lands them and sow among nations the them to scatter
לא־עשו וחקותי מאסו ואת־שבתותי חללו ואחרי גלולי
idols and after had ,profaned My sabbaths and had ,despised My and statutes they not ,done had
25 אבותם היו עיניהם׃ וגם־אני נתתי להם חקים לא
not statutes them gave I Therefore their .eyes were their fathers'

judgments by which they could not live. [26]And I defiled them by their own gifts, by making all that open the womb to cross *the fire*, so that I might waste them; to the end that they might know that I *am* Jehovah.

[27]Therefore, speak to the house of Israel, son of man, and say to them, So says the Lord Jehovah: Yet in this your fathers have blasphemed Me, by trespassing a trespass against Me. [28]When I had brought them into the land *for* which I lifted up My hand, to give it to them, then they saw every high hill, and every leafy tree; and they offered their sacrifices there. And they gave their provoking offering there. They also made their soothing aroma there, and poured out their drink offerings there. [29]Then I said to them, What *is* the high place to which you go there? And its name is called High Place to this day. [30]For this reason, say to the house of Israel, So says the Lord Jehovah: Are you being defiled in the way of your fathers? And do you go whoring after their filthy idols? [31]For when you lift up your gifts, when you pass your sons through the fire, you defile yourselves with all your idols, even to *this* day. And I will not be inquired of by you, O house of Israel. *As* I live, declares the Lord Jehovah, I will not be inquired of by you. [32]And what comes up on your spirit shall surely not occur, that you say, We will be like the nations, like the families of the lands, to serve wood and stone. [33]*As* I live, says the Lord Jehovah, Surely with a

4979 2930 2421 3808 4941 2896
26 טוֹבִים וּמִשְׁפָּטִים לֹא יִחְיוּ בָּהֶם׃ וָאֲטַמֵּא אוֹתָם בְּמַתְּנוֹתָם
their by them have I And by they not and ,good
,gifts own defiled .them live could judgments

3045 834 4616 8074 4616 7356 6363 3605 5674
בְּהַעֲבִיר כָּל־פֶּטֶר רָחַם לְמַעַן אֲשִׁמֵּם לְמַעַן אֲשֶׁר יֵדְעוּ
they that the to might I that so the that all to making by
,know end ,them waste ,womb open (fire the) cross

120 1121 3478 1004 1696 3068 834
27 אֲשֶׁר אֲנִי יְהוָה׃ לָכֵן דַּבֵּר אֶל־בֵּית יִשְׂרָאֵל בֶּן־אָדָם
,man son ,Israel the to speak Therefore ,Jehovah I that
of of house (am)

1442 2088 5750 3068 136 559 559
וְאָמַרְתָּ אֲלֵיהֶם כֹּה אָמַר אֲדֹנָי יְהוָה עוֹד זֹאת גִּדְּפוּ אוֹתִי
Me have this in Yet :Jehovah the says Thus ,them to say and
blasphemed Lord

834 776 935 4604 4603 1
28 אֲבוֹתֵיכֶם בְּמַעֲלָם בִּי מָעַל׃ וָאָבִיאֵם אֶל־הָאָרֶץ אֲשֶׁר
(for) the into had I When tres- a against tres- by fathers your
which land them brought .pass Me passing

7311 1389 3605 7200 5414 3027 5375
נָשָׂאתִי אֶת־יָדִי לָתֵת אוֹתָהּ לָהֶם וַיִּרְאוּ כָל־גִּבְעָה רָמָה
,high hill every then ,them to it give to My lifted I
saw they hand up

3708 8033 5414 2076 8033 2076 5687 6086 3605
וְכָל־עֵץ עָבֹת וַיִּזְבְּחוּ־שָׁם אֶת־זִבְחֵיהֶם וַיִּתְּנוּ־שָׁם כַּעַס
pro- there they And their there they And !leafy tree and
voking gave .sacrifices offered every

5262 8033 5258 5207 7381 8033 7760 7133
קָרְבָּנָם וַיָּשִׂימוּ שָׁם רֵיחַ נִיחוֹחֵיהֶם וַיַּסִּיכוּ שָׁם אֶת־נִסְכֵּיהֶם׃
drink their there and their aroma there also They their
.offerings out poured soothing made .offering

7121 8033 935 834 1116 4100 559
29 וָאֹמַר אֲלֵהֶם מָה הַבָּמָה אֲשֶׁר־אַתֶּם הַבָּאִים שָׁם וַיִּקָּרֵא
is And ?there go you to high the What ,them to I Then
called which place (is) said

1004 559 3651 2088 3117 5704 1116 8034
30 שְׁמָהּ בָּמָה עַד הַיּוֹם הַזֶּה׃ לָכֵן אֱמֹר ׀ אֶל־בֵּית
the to say Therefore .this day to High its
of house Place name

1 1870 3068 136 559 3478
יִשְׂרָאֵל כֹּה אָמַר אֲדֹנָי יְהוָה הַבְדֶרֶךְ אֲבוֹתֵיכֶם אַתֶּם
are your the In :Jehovah the says Thus ,Israel
you fathers of way Lord

4979 5375 2181 8251 310 2930
31 נִטְמְאִים וְאַחֲרֵי שִׁקּוּצֵיהֶם אַתֶּם זֹנִים׃ וּבִשְׂאֵת מַתְּנֹתֵיכֶם
,gifts your when For go you do filthy their And being
up lift you ?whoring idols after ?defiled

5704 1544 3605 2930 784 1121 5674
בְּהַעֲבִיר בְּנֵיכֶם בָּאֵשׁ אַתֶּם נִטְמְאִים לְכָל־גִּלּוּלֵיכֶם עַד־
even your with defile you the your make you when
to idols all yourselves ,fire sons through pass

136 5002 2416 3478 1004 1875 3117
הַיּוֹם וַאֲנִי אִדָּרֵשׁ לָכֶם בֵּית יִשְׂרָאֵל חַי־אָנִי נְאֻם אֲדֹנָי
the states (As) ?Israel O by be shall And (this)
Lord ,I live of house ,you of inquired I .day

3808 7307 5927 1875 3068
32 יְהוָה אִם־אִדָּרֵשׁ לָכֶם׃ וְהָעֹלָה עַל־רוּחֲכֶם הָיוֹ לֹא
not surely your on what And .you by be will I not ,Jehovah
spirit up comes of inquired

4940 1471 1961 559 834 1961
תִהְיֶה אֲשֶׁר ׀ אַתֶּם אֹמְרִים נִהְיֶה כַגּוֹיִם כְּמִשְׁפְּחוֹת
the like the like We ,say you that ,be shall
of families ,nations be will

3068 136 5002 2416 68 6086 8334 776
33 הָאֲרָצוֹת לְשָׁרֵת עֵץ וָאָבֶן׃ חַי־אָנִי נְאֻם אֲדֹנָי יְהוָה אִם־
sure ,Jehovah the says (As) and wood serve to the
Lord ,I live .stone ,lands

mighty hand, and with an outstretched arm, and with fury poured out, I will reign over you. 34And I will bring you out from the peoples, and gather you from the lands in which you are scattered among them; with a mighty hand, and with an outstretched arm, and with fury poured out. 35And I will bring you into the wilderness of the peoples; and I will be judging with you there face to face. 36Just as I was judging your fathers in the wilderness of the land of Egypt, so I will be judging you, declares the Lord Jehovah. 37And I will cause you to pass under the rod, and I will bring you into the bond of the covenant. 38And I will purge from among you the rebels and the transgressors against Me. I will bring them out of the land where they sojourn. And they shall not enter into the land of Israel. And you shall know that I *am* Jehovah.

39And you, O house of Israel, so says the Lord Jehovah: *Every* man go, serve his idols, even hereafter, if you will not listen to Me. But you will not still profane My holy name with your gifts and with your idols. 40For in My holy mountain in the mountain height *of* Israel, declares the Lord Jehovah, all the house of Israel shall serve Me there; all of them in the land. There I will accept them; and there I will seek your heave offerings, and the firstfruits of your offerings, with all your holy things. 41I will accept you with a soothing aroma, when I bring you from the peoples and gather you

לא ביד חזקה ובזרוע נטויה ובחמה שפוכה אמלוך

will I reign | poured ,out | with and fury | stretched out | with and arm an | mighty | a with hand | ly

34 עליכם: והוצאתי אתכם מן־העמים וקבצתי אתכם מן

from | you | gather and | the peoples | from | you | will I And out bring | over .you

הארצות אשר נפוצותם בם ביד חזקה ובזרוע נטויה

stretched out | with and arm an | mighty | a with hand | among ,them | are you scattered | which in | the lands

35 ובחמה שפוכה: והבאתי אתכם אל־מדבר העמים

the peoples | the of wilderness | into | you | I And bring will | poured .out | with and fury

36 ונשפטתי אתכם שם פנים אל־פנים: כאשר נשפטתי

was I judging | as Just | .face to | face | there | you with | will I and judging be

את־אבותיכם במדבר ארץ מצרים כן אשפט אתכם

,you | be will I judging | so | ,Egypt | the of land | the in of wilderness | your fathers

37 נאם אדני יהוה: והעברתי אתכם תחת השבט והבאתי

will I and bring | ,rod the | under | you | will I And pass to cause | .Jehovah | the Lord | states

38 אתכם במסרת הברית: וברותי מכם המרדים והפושעים

the and transgressors | ;rebels the | from you among | I And purge will | the .covenant | the into of bond | you

בי מארץ מגוריהם אוציא אותם ואל־אדמת ישראל

Israel | the of land | And to | .them | will I bring | they where sojourn | of out land the | against ;Me

39 לא יבוא וידעתם כי־אני יהוה: ואתם בית־ישראל כה־

Thus | ,Israel | O of house | And ,you | .Jehovah | I that (am) | you And know shall | they .enter shall | not

אמר אדני יהוה איש גלוליו לכו עבדו ואחר אם־אינכם

will you not | if | and hereafter | (and) ,serve | go | his idols | (Every) man | :Jehovah | the Lord | says

שמעים אלי ואת־שם קדשי לא תחללו־עוד במתנותיכם

your with gifts | still will you profane | not | My holy | name But | .Me to | listen

40 ובגלוליכם: כי בהר־קדשי בהר מרום ישראל נאם

states | ;Israel | height (of) | the in mountain | My ,holy | in mountain | For | with and .idols your

אדני יהוה שם יעבדני כל־בית ישראל כלה בארץ שם

There | the in .land | of all him | ,Israel | the of house | all | shall Me serve | there ,Jehovah | the Lord

ארצם ושם אדרוש את־תרומתיכם ואת־ראשית

the of firstfruits | and | your offerings heave | will I seek | and there | ac- ,them | will I cept

41 משאותיכם בכל־קדשיכם: בריח ניחח ארצה

will I accept | soothing | an with aroma | holy your .things | with all | your offerings

אתכם בהוציאי אתכם מן־העמים וקבצתי אתכם מן

from | you | gather and | the peoples | from | you | I when out bring | ,you from the lands where you have been scattered in them. And I will be sanctified among you in the eyes of the nations. [42]And you shall know that I *am* Jehovah, when I bring you into the land of Israel, to the land *for* which I lifted up My hand to give it to your fathers. [43]And you shall remember there your ways and all your deeds by which you have been defiled in them. And you will hate yourselves to your faces for all your evils which you have done. [44]And you shall know that I *am* Jehovah, when I have worked with you for My name's sake; *and* not by your evil ways, nor by your corrupt deeds, O house of Israel, declares the Lord Jehovah.

1471 5869 6942 6327 834 776
הָאֲרָצוֹת אֲשֶׁר נְפֹצֹתֶם בָּם וְנִקְדַּשְׁתִּי בָכֶם לְעֵינֵי הַגּוֹיִם׃
the the in among will I And in have you where the
.nations of eyes you sanctified be .them scattered been lands

3478 127 935 3068 3045
42 וִידַעְתֶּם כִּי־אֲנִי יְהוָה בַּהֲבִיאִי אֶתְכֶם אֶל־אַדְמַת יִשְׂרָאֵל
,Israel the into you I when ,Jehovah I that you And
of land bring (am) know shall

5414 3027 5375 834 776
אֶל־הָאָרֶץ אֲשֶׁר נָשָׂאתִי אֶת־יָדִי לָתֵת אוֹתָהּ לַאֲבוֹתֵיכֶם׃
your to it give to My lifted I (for) the to
.fathers hand up which land

834 5949 3605 1870 8033 2142
43 וּזְכַרְתֶּם־שָׁם אֶת־דַּרְכֵיכֶם וְאֵת כָּל־עֲלִילוֹתֵיכֶם אֲשֶׁר
by deeds your all and ways your there you And
which remember shall

834 7451 3605 6440 6962 2930
נִטְמֵאתֶם בָּם וּנְקֹטֹתֶם בִּפְנֵיכֶם בְּכָל־רָעוֹתֵיכֶם אֲשֶׁר
which your for your to will you And in been have you
evils all faces yourselves hate ,them defiled

4616 6213 3068 3045 6213
44 עֲשִׂיתֶם׃ וִידַעְתֶּם כִּי־אֲנִי יְהוָה בַּעֲשׂוֹתִי אִתְּכֶם לְמַעַן
the for with I when Jehovah I that you And have you
of sake you worked have (am) know shall .done

1004 7843 5949 7451 1870 3808 8034
שְׁמִי לֹא כְדַרְכֵיכֶם הָרָעִים וְכַעֲלִילוֹתֵיכֶם הַנִּשְׁחָתוֹת בֵּית
O ,corrupt your by nor ,evil your by not My
of house deeds ways ,name

3068 136 5002 3478
יִשְׂרָאֵל נְאֻם אֲדֹנָי יְהוִה׃
.Jehovah the states ,Israel
Lord

[45]And the word of Jehovah was to me, saying, [46]Son of man, set your face the way of the south, and drop *a word* toward the south, and prophesy against the forest of the field of the Negeb. [3]And say to the forest of the Negeb, Hear the word of Jehovah: So says the Lord Jehovah, Behold, I will kindle a fire in you, and it will eat up among you every moist tree and every dry tree. The glowing of the flame shall not be put out. And by it shall be scorched all the faces from the Negeb to the north. [48]And all flesh shall see that I, Jehovah, have kindled it; it shall not be put out. [49]And I said, Ah, Lord Jehovah! They are saying of me, Does he not speak in parables?

CHAPTER 21

[1]And the word of Jehovah was to me, saying, [2]Son of man, set your face

CAP. XXI כא

CHAPTER 21

1870 6440 7760 120 1121 559 3068 1697 1961
1
2 וַיְהִי דְבַר־יְהוָה אֵלַי לֵאמֹר׃ בֶּן־אָדָם שִׂים פָּנֶיךָ דֶּרֶךְ
the your set ,man Son ,saying to Jehovah the And
of way face of ,me of word was

5045 7704 3293 5012 5045 5197 8486
תֵּימָנָה וְהַטֵּף אֶל־דָּרוֹם וְהִנָּבֵא אֶל־יַעַר הַשָּׂדֶה נֶגֶב׃
the field the the against and the to drop and the
,Negeb of of forest prophesy ,south (word a) south

3068 136 559 3068 1697 8085 5045 3293 559
3 וְאָמַרְתָּ לְיַעַר הַנֶּגֶב שְׁמַע דְּבַר־יְהוָה כֹּה־אָמַר אֲדֹנָי יְהוִה
:Jehovah the says Thus .Jehovah the Hear the the to say And
Lord of word Negeb of forest

3002 6086 3605 3892 6086 3605 398 784 3341 2005
הִנְנִי מַצִּית־בְּךָ אֵשׁ וְאָכְלָה בְךָ כָל־עֵץ־לַח וְכָל־עֵץ יָבֵשׁ
.dry tree and moist tree every among it and ,fire a in will ,Behold
every you up eat will you kindle I

5045 6440 3605 6866 5957 3852 3518 3808
לֹא־תִכְבֶּה לַהֶבֶת שַׁלְהֶבֶת וְנִצְרְבוּ־בָהּ כָּל־פָּנִים מִנֶּגֶב
the from the all it by be shall and the the be shall Not
Negeb faces scorched ;flame of glowing out put

3518 3808 1197 3068 1320 3605 7200 6828
4 צָפוֹנָה׃ וְרָאוּ כָּל־בָּשָׂר כִּי אֲנִי יְהוָה בִּעַרְתִּיהָ לֹא תִכְבֶּה׃
be shall It not have ,Jehovah ,I that flesh all And the to
.out put .it kindled see shall .north

4911 3808 559 3068 136 162 559
5 וָאֹמַר אֲהָהּ אֲדֹנָי יְהוִה הֵמָּה אֹמְרִים לִי הֲלֹא מְמַשֵּׁל
speak Does of are They !Jehovah Lord ,Ah I Then
not ,me saying ,said

1121 559 3068 1697 1961 4912
6
7 מְשָׁלִים הוּא׃ וַיְהִי דְבַר־יְהוָה אֵלַי לֵאמֹר׃ בֶּן
Son ,saying to Jehovah the And ?he in
of ,me of word was parables

against Jerusalem and drop *a word* toward the holy places, and prophesy against the land of Israel. [3]And say to the land of Israel, So says Jehovah: Behold, I *am* against you and will draw out My sword from its sheath, and *I* will cut off from you the righteous and the wicked. [4]Since, then, I will cut off the righteous and the wicked from you, Therefore, My sword shall be drawn from its sheath against all flesh, from the Negeb to the north. [5]And all flesh shall know that I, Jehovah, have drawn out My sword from its sheath; it shall not return any more. [6]And you, son of man, groan with the breaking of your loins; and groan with bitterness before their eyes. [7]And it will be, when they say to you, For what do you groan? Then you shall say, Because of the news that is coming; and every heart will melt; and all hands will become feeble; and every spirit will faint; and all knees will flow *as* water. Behold, it comes; and it shall be, declares the Lord Jehovah.

[8]And the word of Jehovah was to me, saying, [9]Son of man, prophesy and say, So says the Lord; Say, A sword! A sword is sharpened, and also is polished! [10]It is sharpened in order to slaughter; *for* a slaughter. It is polished so that there may be a flash to it. Or shall we rejoice? You are despising the rod of My Son, *as if it were* every tree. [11]And He has given it to be polished, to be taken by the hand. The sword, it is sharpened, and it is polished, to give it into the hand of the slayer. [12]Cry out and howl, son of man. For it shall be on My people. It

5012 4720 5197 3389 6440 77 60 120
אָדָם שִׂים פָּנֶיךָ אֶל־יְרוּשָׁלִַם וְהַטֵּף אֶל־מִקְדָּשִׁים וְהִנָּבֵא
and holy the toward drop and Jerusalem against your set ,man
prophesy ,places (word a) face

559 35 41 3478 127 559 3478 127
8 אֶל־אַדְמַת יִשְׂרָאֵל׃ וְאָמַרְתָּ לְאַדְמַת יִשְׂרָאֵל כֹּה אָמַר
says Thus ,Israel the to say And .Israel the against
of land of land

3772 8593 2719 3318 2005 3068
יְהוָה הִנְנִי אֵלַיִךְ וְהוֹצֵאתִי חַרְבִּי מִתַּעְרָהּ וְהִכְרַתִּי מִמֵּךְ
from will and its from My will and against ,Behold Jeho-
you off cut sheath sword out draw you (am) I :vah

7451 6664 3772 3282 7563 6664
9 צַדִּיק וְרָשָׁע׃ יַעַן אֲשֶׁר־הִכְרַתִּי מִמֵּךְ צַדִּיק וְרָשָׁע לָכֵן
there- the and the from will I Since the and the
fore ,wicked righteous you off cut that .wicked righteous

3045 6828 5045 1320 3605 8593 2719 3318
10 תֵּצֵא חַרְבִּי מִתַּעְרָהּ אֶל־כָּל־בָּשָׂר מִנֶּגֶב צָפוֹן׃ וְיָדְעוּ
will and the to the from flesh all against its from My be shall
know ,north Negeb sheath sword drawn

7725 38 08 8593 2719 3318 3068 1320
כָּל־בָּשָׂר כִּי אֲנִי יְהוָה הוֹצֵאתִי חַרְבִּי מִתַּעְרָהּ לֹא תָשׁוּב
shall It not its from My have ,Jehovah ,I that flesh all
return .sheath sword out drawn

4975 7670 584 120 1121 5750
11 עוֹד׃ וְאַתָּה בֶן־אָדָם הֵאָנַח בְּשִׁבְרוֹן מָתְנַיִם
(your) the with groan ,man son ,you And any
;loins of breaking of .more

559 1961 5869 584 4814
12 וּבִמְרִירוּת תֵּאָנַח לְעֵינֵיהֶם׃ וְהָיָה כִּי־יֹאמְרוּ אֵלֶיךָ עַל־
For ,you to they when it And their before groan with and
say ,be will .eyes bitterness

3605 4549 935 8052 559 584 4100
מָה אַתָּה נֶאֱנָח וְאָמַרְתָּ אֶל־שְׁמוּעָה כִי־בָאָה וְנָמֵס כָּל־
every will and is that the Because You Then do you what
melt ;coming news of ,say shall ?groan

3212 1290 3605 73 07 3605 3543 3027 7503 3820
לֵב וְרָפוּ כָל־יָדַיִם וְכִהֲתָה כָל־רוּחַ וְכָל־בִּרְכַּיִם תֵּלַכְנָה
will knees and ,spirit every will and ,hands all will and ,heart
flow all faint feeble be

1961 3068 136 5002 1961 935 2009 4325
13 מַּיִם הִנֵּה בָאָה וְנִהְיָתָה נְאֻם אֲדֹנָי יְהוִה׃ וַיְהִי
And .Jehovah the states it and it ,Behold (as)
was Lord ,be shall ,comes .water

559 3541 5012 120 1121 559 3068 1697
14 דְבַר־יְהוָה אֵלַי לֵאמֹר׃ בֶּן־אָדָם הִנָּבֵא וְאָמַרְתָּ כֹּה אָמַר
says Thus ,say and prophesy ,man Son ,saying to Jehovah the
of ,me of word

2874 4616 4803 1571 2300 2719 2719 559 136
15 אֲדֹנָי אֱמֹר חֶרֶב חֶרֶב הוּחַדָּה וְגַם־מְרוּטָה׃ לְמַעַן טְבֹחַ
to as So !polished and is A A ,Say the
;slaughter also sharpened sword !sword .Lord

7626 7797 176 4803 1300 1961 4616 2300 2873
טֶבַח הוּחַדָּה לְמַעַן הֱיֵה־לָהּ בָּרָק מֹרָטָּה אוֹ נָשִׂישׂ שֵׁבֶט
The we shall Or is it flash a to there that so is it a (for)
of rod ?rejoice .polished it be may ;sharpened slaughter

3709 8610 4803 5414 6086 3973 1121
16 בְּנִי מֹאֶסֶת כָּל־עֵץ׃ וַיִּתֵּן אֹתָהּ לְמָרְטָה לִתְפֹּשׂ בַּכָּף
the by be to be to it He And !tree every are you My
.palm taken polished given has ,despising son

2026 3027 5414 4803 2719 2300
הִיא הוּחַדָּה חֶרֶב וְהִיא מֹרָטָּה לָתֵת אוֹתָהּ בְּיַד־הוֹרֵג׃
the the into it give to is it and the is it
.slayer of hand ,polished ,sword ,sharpened

3605 5971 1961 120 1121 3213 2199
17 זְעַק וְהֵילֵל בֶּן־אָדָם כִּי־הִיא הָיְתָה בְעַמִּי הִיא בְּכָל־
all on It My on be shall it For .man son ,howl and Cry
(be shall) .people of out

shall be on all the rulers of Israel; they are thrown to the sword with My people; therefore, slap your thigh. [13]Because *it is* a test; and what if even the despising rod shall not be? declares the Lord Jehovah. [14]And you, son of man, prophesy and strike palm to palm. And let the sword be doubled the third time, the sword of the slain. It *is* the sword of the slain, the great one that surrounds them; [15]so that *their* heart may melt, and many stumble at all their gates. I have given the threatening sword. Ah! It is made like lightning; it is wrapped for a slaughter. [16]Sharpen yourself on the right! Set yourself on the left, wherever your face is appointed. [17]And also I, I will strike My palm to My palm, and I will cause My fury to rest. I, Jehovah, have spoken.

[18]And the word of Jehovah was to me, saying, [19]And you, son of man, set for yourself two ways, that the sword of the king of Babylon may come. Both of them shall come out from one land. And create a hand at the head of the way to the city; create it. [20]You shall set a way that the sword may enter *into* Rabbah of the sons of Ammon, and *into* Judah, into fortified Jerusalem. [21]For the king of Babylon shall stand at the mother of the way, at the head of the two ways to practice divination. He shall shake arrows; he shall ask household idols; he shall look at the liver. [22]At his right shall be the divining *for* Jerusalem, to set battering rams, to open the mouth in the slaughter, to lift up the voice with shouting; to set battering rams against the gates; to pour out a

5606 3651 5971 1961 2719 413 4048 3478 5387
נשיאי ישראל מגורי אל־חרב היו את־עמי לכן ספק
slap therefore My with They the to thrown .Israel the
people are sword of rulers

1961 3808 3973 7626 1571 974 3409
18 אל־ירך׃ כי בחן ומה אם־גם־שבט מאסת לא יהיה
,be shall not despising the even if and (is it) Because your
rod what ;test a .thigh

3709 5221 5012/120 1121 3068 136 5002
19 נאם אדני יהוה׃ ואתה בן־אדם הנבא והך כף
(your) and prophesy ,man son ,you And ?Jehovah the states
palm strike of Lord

2719 2491 2719 7992 2719 3717 3709
אל־כף ותכפל חרב שלישתה חרב חללים היא חרב
the It .slain the the third the the be let And .palm to
of sword (is) of sword ,time sword doubled

7235 3820 4127 4616 2314 1419 2491
20 חלל הגדול החדרת להם׃ למען למוג לב והרבה
many and (their) may that so ,them which great the the
,heart melt surrounds one ,slain

253 2719 19 5414 8779 3605 3782
המכשלים על כל־שעריהם נתתי אבחת־חרב אח
!Ah .sword the have I their all at stumble
threatening given .gates

7760 3231 2300 2874 4593 1300 6213
21 עשויה לברק מעטה לטבח׃ התאחדי הימיני השימי
Set the on Sharpen a for is it like is It
yourself !right yourself .slaughter wrapped ,lightning made

3709 3709 5221 1571 3259 6440 575 8041
22 השמילי אנה פניך מעדות׃ וגם־אני אכה כפי אל־כפי
My to My will I also And is your where- on
palm palm strike I .appointed face ever ,left The

3068 1697 1961 1696 3068 2534 5117
23 והנחתי חמתי אני יהוה דברתי׃ ויהי דבר־יהוה
Jehovah the And have Jehovah I My will I and
of word was .spoken .fury rest to cause

1870 8147 7760 120 1121 559
24 אלי לאמר׃ ואתה בן־אדם שים־לך שנים דרכים
ways two for set ,man son ,you And ,saying ,me to
yourself of

1254 3027 8147 3318 259 776 884 4428 2719 935
לבוא חרב מלך־בבל מארץ אחד יצאו שניהם ויד ברא
create a And of Both shall one from .Babylon the the may that
hand .them out come land of king of sword come

2719 935 7760 1870 1254 5892 1870 7218
25 בראש־דרך עיר ברא׃ דרך תשים לבוא חרב את
(into) the may that shall You a create the the the at
sword enter set way .it ,city of way of head

5975 1219 3389 3063 5983/1121 7237
26 רבת בני־עמון ואת־יהודה בירושלם בצורה׃ כי־עמד
shall For .fortified into (into) and Ammon the Rabbah
stand Jerusalem ,Judah of sons of

7080 1870 8147 7218 1870 517 894 4428
מלך־בבל אל־אם הדרך בראש שני הדרכים לקסם־
to ways the the at the the at Babylon the
practice two of head ,way of mother of king

3225 3516 8655 7592 2671 7043 7081
27 קסם קלקל בחצים שאל בתרפים ראה בכבד׃ בימינו
his At the at shall he household shall he ;arrows shall He divina-
right .liver look ;idols ask shake .tion

7524 6310 6605 3733 7760 3389 7081 1961
היה הקסם ירושלם לשום כרים לפתח פה ברצח
the in the open to battering set to (for) the shall
,slaughter mouth ,rams ,Jerusalem divining be

8210 8179 3733 7760 8643 6963 7311
להרים קול בתרועה לשום כרים על־שערים לשפך
pour to the against battering set to with the lift to
out ,gates rams ,shouting voice up

mound, and to build a siege wall. ²³And it shall be to them an empty divining in their sight, those who have sworn oaths to them. But he will remember iniquity, that they may be taken. ²⁴So the Lord Jehovah says this: Because you made remembrance of your iniquity, in that your transgressions are uncovered, so that your sins are seen in all your deeds— because you have been remembered, you shall be taken with the palm. ²⁵And you, O slain, wicked prince of Israel, of whom has come his day in the time of iniquity of the end. ²⁶So says the Lord Jehovah: Remove the diadem and lift off the crown. This *shall* not *be as* this *was*. Lift up the low one, and make the high one low. ²⁷Ruin, ruin, ruin, I will appoint it! Also this shall not be until the coming of Him to whom is the right; and I will give it.

²⁸And you, son of man, prophesy and say, So says the Lord Jehovah concerning the sons of Ammon, and as to their shame; even say: The sword, the sword is drawn; *it is* polished for slaughter to make an end, so that *it may be* like lightning; ²⁹while they see vain visions for you; while they divine a lie to you, to put you on the necks of the slain of the wicked, *of* whom their day has come, in the time of iniquity *it shall have* an end. ³⁰Return it to its sheath. In the place where you were created, in the land of your origin, I will judge you. ³¹And I will pour out on you My disgust — with the fire of My wrath I will blow against you, and give you into the hand of

28
: 5869 / ‌7723 / ‌7080 / ‌1961 / 1785 / 1129 / 5550
סֹלְלָה לִבְנוֹת דָּיֵק : וְהָיָה לָהֶם כְּקֶסָם־שָׁוְא בְּעֵינֵיהֶם
siege- a mound / to and build / siege a wall. / it And shall be / them to / an divining / empty / their in sight,

7650 / 7621 / ‌3771 / 2142 / 8610
שְׁבֻעֵי שְׁבֻעוֹת לָהֶם וְהוּא־מַזְכִּיר עָוֹן לְהִתָּפֵשׂ :
who those / have sworn / oaths / them to. / But he / will remember / iniquity, / may they that be taken.

29 1541 / 57:71. / ‌2142 / 3282 / ‌3068 / 136 / ‌559/3541
לָכֵן כֹּה־אָמַר אֲדֹנָי יְהוִה יַעַן הַזְכַּרְכֶם עֲוֹנְכֶם בְּהִגָּלוֹת
There- fore / says thus / Lord / the :vah / Jeho- Because you made / remembrance of iniquity, / your in that are / uncovered

6588 / ‌7200 / ‌2403 / 3605 / ‌5949 / 3282
פִּשְׁעֵיכֶם לְהֵרָאוֹת חַטֹּאותֵיכֶם בְּכָל עֲלִילוֹתֵיכֶם יַעַן
your trans- gressions / that so seen are / sins your / all in / deeds, your / be- cause

30 5387 / 7563 / ‌2491 / 8610 / 3709 / ‌2142
הִזָּכֶרְכֶם בַּכַּף תִּתָּפֵשׂוּ : וְאַתָּה חָלָל רָשָׁע נְשִׂיא
have you / been recalled / palm the with / you shall be taken. / And you, / O slain, / wicked / prince of

3478 / ‌935 / 31:17 / 6256 / 7093/5771 / ‌559 / 3541
יִשְׂרָאֵל אֲשֶׁר־בָּא יוֹמוֹ בְּעֵת עֲוֹן קֵץ : כֹּה אָמַר
Israel, / whom / of has / come / his / day / time the in / of quity / ini- the / end. / Thus / says

136 / 3068 / ‌5493 / 4701 / 7311 / 5850 / 2063. / ‌3808 / 2068:
אֲדֹנָי יְהוִה הָסִיר הַמִּצְנֶפֶת וְהָרִים הָעֲטָרָה זֹאת לֹא־זֹאת
Lord / the :Jehovah / Remove / diadem / off the lift / and crown. / the This / (was) / not This / (as) this

32 8213 / 13:61 / 1364 / 8217 / 5654 / 5654 / ‌5654 / 7760
הַשָּׁפָל הַגְבֵּהַּ וְהַגָּבֹהַ הַשְׁפִּיל : עַוָּה עַוָּה עַוָּה אֲשִׂימֶנָּה
one / low the / up Lift / one high / the and / one low. / Ruin, / ruin, / ruin, / I will set it!

2062/1571 / ‌3808 / 19:61 / 935 / ‌5414 / 4941
גַּם־זֹאת לֹא הָיָה עַד־בֹּא אֲשֶׁר־לוֹ הַמִּשְׁפָּט וּנְתַתִּיו
Also this / not / be / shall / until the / coming of / whom to / Him is; / right the / and will I give it.

33 1121 / 5983 / ‌120. / 5012 / 559 / 3541 / ‌559 / 136 / 30:68
וְאַתָּה בֶן־אָדָם הִנָּבֵא וְאָמַרְתָּ כֹּה אָמַר אֲדֹנָי יְהוִה אֶל־
And you, / of son / ,man / prophesy / ,say and / Thus / says / the / Lord / Jehovah / concern- ing

4803 / 3615 / ‌1300 / 2372 / 7723. / ‌7080
בְּנֵי עַמּוֹן וְאֶל־חֶרְפָּתָם וְאָמַרְתָּ חֶרֶב חֶרֶב פְּתוּחָה לְטֶבַח
of sons / ,Ammon and / as to / their ,shame / :say and / The ,sword / sword / drawn is; / for slaughter

2874 / ‌6605 / 2719 / 2719 / 559 / 2781
מְרוּטָה לְהָכִיל לְמַעַן בָּרָק : בַּחֲזוֹת לָךְ שָׁוְא בִּקְסָם־
polished / an end / make to / so that / it (is) / lightning (like) / they while / see visions / for you, / ,vain / they while / divine

34 7080 / 7723 / ‌2372 / 1300 / 3615 / 4803
3577 / ‌4725 / 2491 / 6677 / 7563 / 935
לָךְ לָתֵת אוֹתָךְ אֶל־צַוְּארֵי חַלְלֵי רְשָׁעִים אֲשֶׁר־בָּא
you / lie, a / to / place to / you / on / the / of necks / the / slain / the / wicked / whom / has come

35 3117: / ‌6256 / 5771 / 7093 / ‌7725 / 8593 / 4725 / 7563 / ‌2491
יוֹמָם בְּעֵת עֲוֹן קֵץ : הָשֵׁב אֶל־תַּעְרָהּ בִּמְקוֹם אֲשֶׁר
their / day / time of / in the / iniquity / an end. / Return (it) / to its / .sheath / In / place / the / where

1254 / ‌776 / 4351 / ‌8199 / 8210
נִבְרֵאתָ בְּאֶרֶץ מְכֻרוֹתַיִךְ אֶשְׁפֹּט אֹתָךְ : וְשָׁפַכְתִּי עָלַיִךְ
were you / created, / of land / the in / your origin, / will I / judge / .you / And will I / pour out / you on

582 / ‌3027 / 5414. / ‌5678 / 6315 / ‌784 / 21:95
זַעְמִי בְּאֵשׁ עֶבְרָתִי אָפִיחַ עָלַיִךְ וּנְתַתִּיךְ בְּיַד אֲנָשִׁים
My / disgust; / of fire / the with / My / wrath / will I / blow / against you, / and will I give you / into / hand the / of / men

burning men, skilled in destruction. 32You shall be to the fire for food. Your blood shall be in the midst of the land. You shall not be remembered. For I, Jehovah, have spoken.

CHAPTER 22

1And the word of Jehovah was to me, saying, 2And you, son of man, will you judge; will you judge the bloody city? Then cause her to know all her abominations. 3Then you shall say, So says the Lord Jehovah: The city sheds blood in her midst, that her time may come; and makes idols against herself, to defile *herself*. 4By your blood which you have shed, you are guilty; and by your idols which you have made, you are defiled. And your days *are* brought near, and have come to your years. On account of this I have made you a reproach to the nations, and a mocking to all the lands. 5Those who are near, and those who are far from you, shall mock against you, O defiled of name, abounding in tumult. 6Behold, the rulers of Israel, each man by his might, have been in you to enter in *and* shed blood. 7In you they have despised father and mother. In your midst they have dealt with the alien by oppression. In you they oppressed the widow and the orphan. 8You have despised My holy things, and have profaned My sabbaths. 9In you are men of slander, in order to shed blood; and in you they eat on the mountains; in your midst they do unchaste acts. 10In you he has uncovered the nakedness of the father; in you they humbled the defiled *by her* impurity. 11And a man has done abomination with his neighbor's wife; and a man has defiled his daughter-in-law in unchaste acts; and a

1961 1818 402 1961 784 4889 2796 1197

37 בְּעֵרִים חָרָשֵׁי מַשְׁחִית: לָאֵשׁ תִּהְיֶה לְאָכְלָה דָּמֵךְ יִהְיֶה

shall be | Your blood | for food | shall be | You the to fire | destruction. | skilled in | burning,

1696 3068 2142 3808 776 8432

בְּתוֹךְ הָאָרֶץ לֹא תִזָּכֵרִי כִּי אֲנִי יְהוָה דִּבַּרְתִּי:

have spoken. | Jehovah | I | For | shall You remembered be | not | the land. | the in of midst

CAP. XXII כב

CHAPTER 22

8199 120 1121 559 3068 1697 1961

1
2 וַיְהִי דְבַר־יְהוָה אֵלַי לֵאמֹר: וְאַתָּה בֶן־אָדָם הֲתִשְׁפֹּט

you will judge | man, son of | you And, | saying, | me to, | Jehovah | the of word | And was

8441 3605 3045 1818 5892 8199

הֲתִשְׁפֹּט אֶת־עִיר הַדָּמִים וְהוֹדַעְתָּהּ אֵת כָּל־תּוֹעֲבוֹתֶיהָ:

her abominations. | all | cause Then know to her | ?bloody | the city | you will judge

8432 1818 8210 5892 3068 136 559 3541 559

3 וְאָמַרְתָּ כֹּה אָמַר אֲדֹנָי יְהוִה עִיר שֹׁפֶכֶת דָּם בְּתוֹכָהּ

her in midst, | blood | sheds | The city | :Jehovah | the Lord | says | Thus | you Then say shall,

834 1818 2930 1544 6213 6258 935

4 לָבוֹא עִתָּהּ וְעָשְׂתָה גִלּוּלִים עָלֶיהָ לְטָמְאָה: בְּדָמֵךְ אֲשֶׁר

which | your By blood | defile to (herself). | against herself | idols | and makes | her time, | may that come

7126 2930 6213 834 1544 816 8210

שָׁפַכְתְּ אָשַׁמְתְּ וּבְגִלּוּלַיִךְ אֲשֶׁר־עָשִׂית טָמֵאת וַתַּקְרִיבִי

brought And near | are you defiled. | have you made | which | by and idols your | are you ;guilty | have you shed

1471 2781 5414 3651/5921 8141 935 3117

יָמַיִךְ וַתָּבוֹא עַד־שְׁנוֹתַיִךְ עַל־כֵּן נְתַתִּיךְ חֶרְפָּה לַגּוֹיִם

the to nations | a reproach | have I you made | Therefore | your years. | to | have and come | your days,

7046 7350 7138 776 3605 7048

5 וְקַלָּסָה לְכָל־הָאֲרָצוֹת: הַקְּרֹבוֹת וְהָרְחֹקוֹת מִמֵּךְ יִתְקַלְּסוּ־

shall mock | from you, | those and far are who | who Those near are, | the lands. | all to | a and mocking

3478 5387 2009 4103 7227 8034 2931

6 בָךְ טְמֵאַת הַשֵּׁם רַבַּת הַמְּהוּמָה: הִנֵּה נְשִׂיאֵי יִשְׂרָאֵל

Israel, | the of rulers | Behold, | tumult. | abounding in | name, | de- O of filed | against you,

7043 517 1 1818 8210 4616 1961 2220 376

7 אִישׁ לִזְרֹעוֹ הָיוּ בָךְ לְמַעַן שְׁפָךְ־דָּם: אָב וָאֵם הֵקַלּוּ בָךְ

In you. | have they despised | and father mother | blood. | shed | in to order | in you | has been | his by arm | each man

6944 3238 490 3490 8432 6233 6213 1616

8 לַגֵּר עָשׂוּ בַעֹשֶׁק בְּתוֹכֵךְ יָתוֹם וְאַלְמָנָה הוֹנוּ בָךְ: קָדָשַׁי

holy My things | In you. | op- they pressed | the and widow, | the orphan | your In midst. | by oppression | have they dealt | with alien the

4616 1961 7400 582 2490 7676 959

9 בָּזִית וְאֶת־שַׁבְּתֹתַי חִלָּלְתְּ: אַנְשֵׁי רָכִיל הָיוּ בָךְ לְמַעַן

order in to | In you | are | slander of men | have profaned | My sabbaths | and have you despised

6172 8432 6213 2154 398 2022 1818 8210

10 שְׁפָךְ־דָּם וְאֶל־הֶהָרִים אָכְלוּ בָךְ זִמָּה עָשׂוּ בְתוֹכֵךְ: עֶרְוַת־

naked- of ness | the | your in midst. | they do | unchaste acts | in ;you | they eat | the mountains | and on | ;blood shed

802 376 6031 5079 2931 1540

11 אָב גִּלָּה־בָךְ טְמֵאַת הַנִּדָּה עִנּוּ־בָךְ: וְאִישׁ | אֶת־אֵשֶׁת

wife | with | a And man | in you. | they humbled | (her) impurity | defiled (by) the | In ;you | un- has he covered | the father

376 2154 2930 3618 376 8441 6213 7453

רֵעֵהוּ עָשָׂה תּוֹעֵבָה וְאִישׁ אֶת־כַּלָּתוֹ טִמֵּא בְזִמָּה וְאִישׁ

a and man | un- in chaste acts | has defiled | his daughter-in-law | a and man | abomina- ;tion | has done | his neighbor's man has humbled within you his sister, his father's daughter. ¹²In you they have taken bribes, in order to shed blood. You have taken interest and increase; and you have gained by extortion of your neighbor; and you have forgotten Me, declares the Lord Jehovah.

¹³And behold, I have struck My palm against your unjust gain which you have made, and at your blood which has been in your midst. ¹⁴Can your heart stand, or can your hands be strong, in the days that I shall deal with you? I, Jehovah, have spoken, and I will act. ¹⁵And I will scatter you among the nations, and sow you in the lands, and I will destroy your uncleanness out of you. ¹⁶And you will be profaned in you in the sight of the nations, and you shall know that I am Jehovah.

¹⁷And the word of Jehovah was to me, saying, ¹⁸Son of man,, the house of Israel has become dross to Me. All of them are bronze and tin, and iron and lead, in the middle of the furnace; they are the dross of silver. ¹⁹So the Lord Jehovah says this: Because all of you have become for dross, therefore, behold I will gather you into the midst of Jerusalem. ²⁰As they gather silver, and bronze, and iron, and lead, and tin, into the middle of the furnace, to blow the fire on it to melt it; so I will gather you in My anger and in My fury; and I will leave you there, and melt you. ²¹And I will collect you and blow on you in the fire of My wrath; and you shall be melted in its midst. ²²As silver is melted in the midst of the furnace, so you shall be melted in its midst. And you shall know that I, Jehovah, have poured out My fury on you.

²³And the word of Jehovah was to me, saying,

12
את־אחתו בת־אביו עניבך : שחד לקחרבך למען
order in | In have they | bribes | in has | his daughter | his
to | you taken | .you humbled | father's | ,sister
4616 | 3947 7810 | 6033 | 1 1323 | 269

שפידם נשך ותרבית לקחת ותבצעי רעיך בעשק ואתי
and | by | your (of) | you and | have You | and | interest | .blood shed
Me | ,extortion | neighbor | gained have | ,taken | increase
6231 | 7453 | 1214 | 3947 | 8636 | 5392 | 1818/8210

13
שכחת נאם אדני יהוה: והנה הכיתי כפי אל־בצעך
your against | My | have I | And | .Jehovah the | states have you
gain unjust | palm | struck | behold | Lord | ,forgotten
1215 | 3709 5221 | 2009 | 3068 136 | 5002 7911

14
אשר עשית ועל־דמך אשר היו בתוכך: היעמד לבך
your | Can | your in | has | which | your | and have you | which
,heart | stand | .midst | been | blood | at | ,made
834 | 6213 5975 | 8432 | 1961 834 | 18:18 | 6213
אם־תחזקנה ידיך לימים אשר אני עשה אותך אני
I | with | shall | that | the in | your | be can | or
?you | deal | I | | days | ,hands | strong
2388 | | 3117 | | 6213 | |

15
יהוה דברתי ועשיתי: והפיצותי אותך בגוים וזריתך
you | sow and the | among | you | will I And | will and | have | Jehovah
nations | scatter | | .act | spoken
3068 1696 | 6213 | 6327 | | 14:71 2219

16
בארצות והתמתי טמאתך ממך: ונחלת בך לעיני גוים
,nations of | sight you | profaned be | .you | uncleanness | destroy | the in
the the in | in will you And | of out | your | will and | ,lands
776 8552 | 2932 | 5157 | | 5869 1471

17
וידעת כי־אני יהוה: ויהי דבר־יהוה אלי לאמר:
,saying | to | Jehovah the | And | .Jehovah | I that | you and
,me | | of word | was | | (am) | know shall
3045 | | 3068 1961 1697 | 559 | | 3068

18
בן־אדם היו־לי בית־ישראל לסוג כלם נחשת ובדיל
,tin and | (are) | All | for | Israel | the | to has | ,man Son
,bronze | them of | .dross | | of house | Me become | of
1121 | 120 | 3478 | 5509 | 1004 | 1961 | 5178 | 913

19
וברזל ועופרת בתוך כור סיגים כסף היו: לכן כה
thus There- | they | silver | the the | the in | ,lead and | and
,fore | are | | of dross | ;furnace of middle | | ,iron
3651 3541 | 1961 | 3701 | 5509 | 3564 | 8432 | 57 1270
אמר אדני יהוה יען היות כלכם לסגים לכן הנני קבץ
will ,behold there- | for | all you | have | Be- | :Jehovah the | says
gather I | ,fore | dross | | become cause | Lord
6908 2005 | | 5509 | 3605 | 1961 3282 | 30:68 136 | 559

20
אתכם אל־תוך ירושלם: קבצת כסף ונחשת וברזל
,iron and | and | ,silver | (they As) | .Jerusalem | the into | you
| bronze | | gather | | of midst
1270 | | 3701 | 6910 | 3389 | 8432
ועופרת ובדיל אל־תוך כור לפחת־עליו אש להנתך
;melt | the to | it on | blow to | the | the into | tin and | ,lead and
,(it) | fire | | | | furnace of midst
5413 784 | 5921 5301 | 3564 | 8432 | 913 | 5777

21
כן אקבץ באפי ובחמתי והנחתי והתכתי אתכם: וכנסתי
will I And | .you | melt and | will I and | in and | in | will I | so
collect | | (you) leave | | ,fury My | anger | (you) gather
3664 | | 5413 | 3240 | 2534 | 639 | 622
אתכם ונפחתי עליכם באש עברתי ונתכתם בתוכה:
the in | shall you and | My | the in | you on | blow and | you
.it of midst | melted be | ,wrath | | | |
8432 | 5413 | 5678 | 784 | 5301

22
כהתוך כסף בתוך כור כן תתכו בתוכה וידעתם כי־
that | you And | its in | shall you | so | the | the in | silver | is As
know shall | .midst | melted be | ,furnace of midst | | melted
3045 | | 8432 | 2046 | 3651 3564 | 8432 | 3701 | 2046

23
אני יהוה שפכתי חמתי עליכם: ויהי דבר־יהוה
Jehovah the | And | .you on | My | have | Jehovah | I
of word | was | | fury | out poured |
3068 | 1697 1961 | 2534 | 8210 | 3068

24 Son of man, speak to her: You *are* a land, she *is* not being cleansed; you are not rained on in the day of disgust. 25 A plot *by* her prophets *is* in her midst, like a roaring lion tearing prey. They have devoured souls; and they have taken the riches and gems; they multiplied her widows in her midst. 26 Her priests have violated My law and have profaned My holy things; they have not divided between the holy and the common; and between the unclean and clean they have not taught; and they have hidden their eyes from My sabbaths; and I am profaned among them. 27 Her rulers in her midst *are* like wolves tearing prey, to shed blood, to destroy souls, in order to gain unjust gain. 28 And her prophets have daubed themselves *with* lime, seeing empty visions, and divining to them lies, saying, So says the Lord Jehovah, when Jehovah has not spoken. 29 The people of the land have used oppression and practiced robbery; and they troubled the poor and the needy; and *they* have oppressed the alien without justice. 30 And I sought among them a man to wall up a wall, and stand in the breach before Me for the land, that I should not destroy it; but I found not. 31 So I have poured out on them My disgust, with the fire of My wrath I consumed them; I have given their way on their heads, states the Lord Jehovah.

CHAPTER 23

1 And the word of Jehovah was to me, saying, 2 Son of man, there were two women, daughters of one mother. 3 And they played the harlot in Egypt; in their youth they whored

2891 38 08 776 559 120 1121 559
24 אֵלַי לֵאמֹר׃ בֶּן־אָדָם אֱמָר־לָהּ אַתְּ אֶרֶץ לֹא מְטֹהָרָה
being not a You to say ,man Son ,saying to
cleansed land (are) :her of ,me

738 8432 5030 7195 2195 3117 1656 38 08
25 הִיא לֹא גֻשְׁמָהּ בְּיוֹם זָעַם׃ קֶשֶׁר נְבִיאֶיהָ בְּתוֹכָהּ כַּאֲרִי
a like her in (is) her (by) .plot A .disgust the in are you not she
lion ,midst prophets of day on rained ,(is)

490 3947 3366 2633 398 53 15 2964 2963 7580
שׁוֹאֵג טֹרֵף טָרֶף נֶפֶשׁ אָכָלוּ חֹסֶן וִיקָר יִקָּחוּ אַלְמְנוֹתֶיהָ
widows her have they and the have They souls .prey tearing roaring
;taken gems riches ;devoured

996 6944 2490 8451 2554 3548 8432 7235
26 הִרְבּוּ בְתוֹכָהּ׃ כֹּהֲנֶיהָ חָמְסוּ תוֹרָתִי וַיְחַלְּלוּ קָדָשַׁי בֵּין
be- holy My have and law My have Her her in they
tween ;things profaned violated priests .midst multiplied

3045 38 08 2389 2931 996 914 38 08 2455 6944
קֹדֶשׁ לְחֹל לֹא הִבְדִּילוּ וּבֵין־הַטָּמֵא לְטָהוֹר לֹא הוֹדִיעוּ
have they not the and the and have they not the and the
;taught clean unclean between ,divided common holy

7130 8269 8432 2490 5869 5956 7676
27 וּמִשַּׁבְּתוֹתַי הֶעְלִימוּ עֵינֵיהֶם וָאֵחַל בְּתוֹכָם׃ שָׂרֶיהָ בְקִרְבָּהּ
her in Her among am I and their have they My from and
midst rulers .them profaned ,eyes hidden sabbaths

4616 5315 6 1818/8210 2964 2963 2061
כִּזְאֵבִים טֹרְפֵי טָרֶף לִשְׁפָּךְ־דָּם לְאַבֵּד נְפָשׁוֹת לְמַעַן
in ,souls to ,blood to ,prey tearing like (are)
to order destroy shed wolves

7080 7723 2374 86 02 2902 50 30 1215 1214
28 בְּצֹעַ בָּצַע׃ וּנְבִיאֶיהָ טָחוּ לָהֶם תָּפֵל חֹזִים שָׁוְא וְקֹסְמִים
and empty seeing (with) them- have her And unjust gain
divining visions ,slime selves daubed prophets .gain

1696 38 08 3068 3068 136 559 3541 559 35 77
לָהֶם כָּזָב אֹמְרִים כֹּה אָמַר אֲדֹנָי יֱהוִה וַיהוָה לֹא דִבֵּר׃
has not when ,Jehovah the says Thus ,saying ,lies to
.spoken Jehovah Lord them

32 38 34 6041 1498 1497 6233 6233 776 5971
29 עַם הָאָרֶץ עָשְׁקוּ עֹשֶׁק וְגָזְלוּ גָּזֵל וְעָנִי וְאֶבְיוֹן הוֹנוּ וְאֶת־
and they the and and ;robbery and oppression have the The
;troubled needy poor the practiced used land of people

1447 376 1245 4941 1097 6231 1616
30 הַגֵּר עָשְׁקוּ בְּלֹא מִשְׁפָּט׃ וָאֲבַקֵּשׁ מֵהֶם אִישׁ גֹּדֵר־גָּדֵר
wall a to a among I And .justice without have the
wall man them sought oppressed alien

4672 38 08 7843 1115 776 6440 6556 5975
וְעֹמֵד בַּפֶּרֶץ לְפָנַי בְּעַד הָאָרֶץ לְבִלְתִּי שַׁחֲתָהּ וְלֹא מָצָאתִי׃
.found I but should I not that the for before the in and
not ;it destroy ,land Me breach stand

7218 1870 3615 5678 784 21 95 8210
31 וָאֶשְׁפֹּךְ עֲלֵיהֶם זַעְמִי בְּאֵשׁ עֶבְרָתִי כִּלִּיתִים דַּרְכָּם בְּרֹאשָׁם
their on their con- I My the with My on have I Thus
heads way ;them sumed wrath of fire disgust them out poured

3068 136 5002 5414
נָתַתִּי נְאֻם אֲדֹנָי יֱהוִה׃
.Jehovah the states have I
Lord ,given

CAP. XXIII כג

CHAPTER 23

1323 802 8147 120 1121 559 3068 1697 1961
1
2 וַיְהִי דְבַר־יְהוָה אֵלַי לֵאמֹר׃ בֶּן־אָדָם שְׁתַּיִם נָשִׁים בְּנוֹת
daughters ,women two ,man Son ,saying to Jehovah the And
of of ,me of word was

8033 2181 5221 4714 2181 1961 259 517
3 אֵם־אַחַת הָיוּ׃ וַתִּזְנֶינָה בְמִצְרַיִם בִּנְעוּרֵיהֶן זָנוּ שָׁמָּה
there they their in ;Egypt in they And there ,one mother
,whored youth whored .were

there; their breasts were
handled, and there their
virgin nipples were
squeezed. [4]And their
names *were* Oholah, the
oldest; and Oholibah, her
sister. And they were Mine,
and they bore sons and
daughters. And their names:
Samaria *is* Oholah, and
Jerusalem *is* Oholibah.
[5]And Oholah whored under
Me. And she lusted after her
lovers, to Assyrian neighbors, [6]clothed with purple,
governors and rulers, all of
them desirable young men;
horsemen riding horses.
[7]And she bestowed her
harlotries on them, the
choice sons of Assyria, *with*
all of them, and with all
whom she lusted after; she
defiled herself with all their
idols. [8]And she did not
leave her fornications from
Egypt; for they lay with her
in her youth, and they
squeezed her virgin nipples,
and poured their fornica-
tions on her. [9]Therefore I
have given her into the
hand of her lovers, into the
hand of the sons of Assyria
on whom she lusted.
[10]They uncovered her
nakedness. They took her
sons and her daughters.
And they killed her with the
sword. And she became
notorious among women;
and they executed judg-
ments on her.

[11]And her sister Oholibah
saw; and she was more
corrupt in her lust than she;
and her fornications were
greater than her sister's.
[12]She lusted to the sons of
Assyria, neighboring gov-
ernors and rulers clothed
most perfectly; horsemen
riding horses, all of them
desirable young men.
[13]Then I saw that she was
defiled; one way *was* to
both of them. [14]And she
added to her fornications.
And she saw men carved on
the wall—images of the
Chaldeans engraved with

170 8034 1331 1717 6213 8033 7699 4600
4 מֹעֲכוּ שְׁדֵיהֶן וְשָׁם עִשּׂוּ דַּדֵּי בְּתוּלֵיהֶן׃ וּשְׁמוֹתָן אָהֳלָה
,Oholah their And their nipples were and their were
(were) names .virgin squeezed there ,breasts handled

1121 3205 1961 269 172 1419
הַגְּדוֹלָה וְאָהֳלִיבָה אֲחוֹתָהּ וַתִּהְיֶינָה לִי וַתֵּלַדְנָה בָּנִים
sons they and ,Mine they And .sister her and the
bore were ,Oholibah ;oldest

2181 172 3389 170 8111 8034 1323
5 וּבָנוֹת וּשְׁמוֹתָן שֹׁמְרוֹן אָהֳלָה וִירוּשָׁלַם אָהֳלִיבָה׃ וַתִּזֶן
And .Oholibah (is) and ,Oholah Samaria their And and
whored Jerusalem (is) :names .daughters

7138 804 157 5689 8478 170
אָהֳלָה תַּחְתָּי וַתַּעְגַּב עַל־מְאַהֲבֶיהָ אֶל־אַשּׁוּר קְרוֹבִים׃
,nearby Assyria to her after she And under Oholah
,lovers lusted .Me

6571 3605 2531 970 5461 6346 8504 3847
6 לְבֻשֵׁי תְכֵלֶת פַּחוֹת וּסְגָנִים בַּחוּרֵי חֶמֶד כֻּלָּם פָּרָשִׁים
horsemen of all desirable young and governors ,purple clothed
,them men ,rulers with

804 1121 4005 5921 8457 5414 5483 7392
7 רֹכְבֵי סוּסִים׃ וַתִּתֵּן תַּזְנוּתֶיהָ עֲלֵיהֶם מִבְחַר בְּנֵי־אַשּׁוּר
,Assyria sons the ,them on her she And .horses riding
of choice harlotries gave

2930 1544 3605 5689 834 3605 3605
8 כֻּלָּם וּבְכֹל אֲשֶׁר־עָגְבָה בְּכָל־גִּלּוּלֵיהֶם נִטְמָאָה׃ וְאֶת־
And defiled she their with she whom with and all (with)
.herself idols all lusted all them of

5271 7901 5800 3808 4714 8457
תַּזְנוּתֶיהָ מִמִּצְרַיִם לֹא עָזָבָה כִּי אוֹתָהּ שָׁכְבוּ בִנְעוּרֶיהָ
her in they with for did she not from forni- her
,youth lay her ;leave Egypt catnions

3651 8457 8210 1331 1717 6213
9 וְהֵמָּה עִשּׂוּ דַּדֵּי בְתוּלֶיהָ וַיִּשְׁפְּכוּ תַזְנוּתָם עָלֶיהָ׃ לָכֵן
Therefore on their poured and her nipples squeezed and
.her fornications virgin they

5291 5689 804 1121 3027 157 3027 5414
נְתַתִּיהָ בְּיַד־מְאַהֲבֶיהָ בְּיַד בְּנֵי אַשּׁוּר אֲשֶׁר עָגְבָה עֲלֵיהֶם׃
.them on she whom Assyria the the into her the into have I
lusted of sons of hand ,lovers of hand her given

2719 3947 1323 1121 6172 1540
10 הֵמָּה גִּלּוּ עֶרְוָתָהּ בָּנֶיהָ וּבְנוֹתֶיהָ לָקָחוּ וְאוֹתָהּ בַּחֶרֶב
the with her and They her and her her uncovered They
sword ,took daughters sons .nakedness

269 7200 6213 8196 802 8034 1961 2026
11 הָרָגוּ וַתְּהִי־שֵׁם לַנָּשִׁים וּשְׁפוּטִים עָשׂוּ בָהּ׃ וַתֵּרֶא אֲחוֹתָהּ
her saw And on they and among notor- she And they
sister .her executed judgments ,women ious became .killed

1419 2183 5691 7843 172
אָהֳלִיבָה וַתַּשְׁחֵת עַגְבָתָהּ מִמֶּנָּה וְאֶת־תַּזְנוּתֶיהָ מִזְּנוּנֵי
were fornications her and than her in was she and ,Oholibah
than greater ,she lust corrupt more

7138 5467 6346 5689 804 1121 269
12 אֲחוֹתָהּ׃ אֶל־בְּנֵי אַשּׁוּר עָגָבָה פַּחוֹת וּסְגָנִים קְרֹבִים
,nearby and governors she Assyria the To her
rulers ,lusted of sons .sister's

3605 2531 970 5483 7392 6571 4358 3847
לְבֻשֵׁי מִכְלוֹל פָּרָשִׁים רֹכְבֵי סוּסִים בַּחוּרֵי חֶמֶד כֻּלָּם׃
of all desirable young ,horses riding horsemen most clothed
.them men ,perfectly

8457 3254 8147 259 1870 2930 7200
13
14 וָאֵרֶא כִּי נִטְמָאָה דֶּרֶךְ אֶחָד לִשְׁתֵּיהֶן׃ וַתּוֹסֶף אֶל־תַּזְנוּתֶיהָ
her to she And of both to one way was she that I Then
.fornications added .them (was) ;defiled saw

2710 3778 6754 7023 2707 582 7200
וַתֵּרֶא אַנְשֵׁי מְחֻקֶּה עַל־הַקִּיר צַלְמֵי כַשְׂדִּיים חֲקֻקִים
engraved the images the on carved men she And
Chaldeans of —wall saw

red color; [15]girded with girdles on their loins; with overflowing turbans on their heads, the look of rulers, all of them, like the sons of Babylon *in* Chaldea, the land of their birth—
[16]and she lusted after them, to the look of her eyes, and sent messengers to them into Chaldea. [17]And the sons of Babylon came to her, to the bed of love; and they defiled her with their fornications. And she was defiled with them, and her soul was alienated from them. [18]And she uncovered her fornications and uncovered her nakedness. Then My soul was alienated from her, just as My soul was alienated from her sister. [19]And she multiplied her fornications to recall the days of her youth, in which she had whored in the land of Egypt. [20]And she lusted on their lovers of whom the flesh of asses resembles their flesh; and *as* the issue of horses their issue. [21]So you longed for the wickedness of your youth, when *they* squeezed your nipples from Egypt, for the sake of the breasts of your youth.
[22]So, O Oholibah, the Lord Jehovah says this: Behold, I will arouse your lovers against you, from whom your soul is alienated. And I will bring them against you from all around, [23]Babylon's sons and all the Chaldeans, Pekod, and Shoa, and Koa, all the sons of Assyria with them — desirable young men, governors and rulers, all of them; third heads and called ones; all of them riding horses. [24]And they shall come against you *with* weapons, chariots, and wheels, and with a group of peoples; buckler and shield and helmet shall set against you all around. And I will give before them judgment,

15 בְּשָׁשַׁר׃ חֲגוֹרֵי אֵזוֹר בְּמָתְנֵיהֶם סְרוּחֵי טְבוּלִים בְּרָאשֵׁיהֶם
their on turbans over-with their on with girded red with
,heads flowing ,loins girdles ;color
מַרְאֵה שָׁלִשִׁים כֻּלָּם דְּמוּת בְּנֵי־בָבֶל כַּשְׂדִּים אֶרֶץ
the ,Chaldea Babylon the like of all ,rulers look the
of land (in) of sons ,them of
16 מוֹלַדְתָּם׃ וַתַּעְגַּב עֲלֵיהֶם לְמַרְאֵה עֵינֶיהָ וַתִּשְׁלַח מַלְאָכִים
messengers sent and her the to after she and their
eyes of look ,them lusted —birth
17 אֲלֵיהֶם כַּשְׂדִּימָה׃ וַיָּבֹאוּ אֵלֶיהָ בְנֵי־בָבֶל לְמִשְׁכַּב דֹּדִים
,love (her) to Babylon the her to And into them to
of bed of sons came .Chaldea
וַיְטַמְּאוּ אוֹתָהּ בְּתַזְנוּתָם וַתִּטְמָא־בָם וַתֵּקַע נַפְשָׁהּ מֵהֶם׃
from her was and with she And their with her they and
.them soul alienated ,them defiled was .fornications defiled
18 וַתְּגַל תַּזְנוּתֶיהָ וַתְּגַל אֶת־עֶרְוָתָהּ וַתֵּקַע נַפְשִׁי מֵעָלֶיהָ
on from My was Then her and forni- her she And
her soul alienated .nakedness uncovered cations uncovered
19 כַּאֲשֶׁר נָקְעָה נַפְשִׁי מֵעַל אֲחוֹתָהּ׃ וַתַּרְבֶּה אֶת־תַּזְנוּתֶיהָ
her she And her from My was as just
fornications multiplied .sister upon soul alienated
20 לִזְכֹּר אֶת־יְמֵי נְעוּרֶיהָ אֲשֶׁר זָנְתָה בְּאֶרֶץ מִצְרָיִם׃ וַתַּעְגְּבָה
she And .Egypt the in had she in her the to
lusted of land whored which youth of days recall
עַל פִּלַגְשֵׁיהֶם אֲשֶׁר בְּשַׂר חֲמוֹרִים בְּשָׂרָם וְזִרְמַת סוּסִים
horses (as) and their asses flesh the of their on
of issue the ;flesh resembles of whom ,lovers
21 זִרְמָתָם׃ וַתִּפְקְדִי אֵת זִמַּת נְעוּרָיִךְ בַּעְשׂוֹת מִמִּצְרַיִם
from (they) when your wicked- the you So their
Egypt worked ,youth of ness for longed .issue
22 דַּדַּיִךְ לְמַעַן שְׁדֵי נְעוּרָיִךְ׃ לָכֵן אָהֳלִיבָה כֹּה־אָמַר
says thus O ,Therefore your the the for your
,Oholibah .youth of breasts of sake nipples
אֲדֹנָי יְהוִה הִנְנִי מֵעִיר אֶת־מְאַהֲבַיִךְ עָלַיִךְ אֵת אֲשֶׁר־נָקְעָה
is of against your will ,Behold :Jehovah the
alienated whom you lovers arouse I Lord
23 נַפְשֵׁךְ מֵהֶם וַהֲבֵאתִים עָלַיִךְ מִסָּבִיב׃ בְּנֵי בָבֶל וְכָל־
and ,Babylon the all from against will I And from your
all of sons .around you them bring .them soul
כַּשְׂדִּים פְּקוֹד וְשׁוֹעַ וְקוֹעַ כָּל־בְּנֵי אַשּׁוּר אוֹתָם בַּחוּרֵי
young with Assyria the all and and ,Pekod the
men —them of sons ,Koa ,Shoa ,Chaldeans
חֶמֶד פַּחוֹת וּסְגָנִים כֻּלָּם שָׁלִשִׁים וּקְרוּאִים רֹכְבֵי סוּסִים
horses riding called and third of all and governors de-
,ones heads ,them ,rulers ,sirable
24 כֻּלָּם׃ וּבָאוּ עָלַיִךְ הֹצֶן רֶכֶב וְגַלְגַּל וּבִקְהַל עַמִּים צִנָּה
buck- ;peoples with and and ,chariots (with) against they And of all
ler of group a wheels ,weapons you come shall .them
וּמָגֵן וְקוֹבַע יָשִׂימוּ עָלַיִךְ סָבִיב וְנָתַתִּי לִפְנֵיהֶם מִשְׁפָּט
,judgment before I And all against shall and and
them give will .around you set helmet shield

and they will judge you by their judgments. [25]And I will give My jealousy against you, and they will deal with you in fury. Your nose and your ears they will take, and the rest of you shall fall by the sword. They will take your sons and your daughters, and the rest of you shall be devoured by the fire. [26]And they will strip you *of* your clothes, and take the articles of your beauty. [27]And I will make cease your wickedness from you, and your fornication from the land of Egypt; and you shall not lift up your eyes to them; and Egypt shall not be remembered by you any more.

[28]For so says the Lord Jehovah: Behold, I will give you in the hand of those whom you hate, in the hand of whom your soul was alienated from them. [29]And they shall deal with you in hatred, and take all your wealth, and shall leave you naked and bare. And the nudity of your adulteries will be bared, even your lewdness and your fornications. [30]These things will be done to you because you have whored after the nations, because that you are defiled with their idols. [31]You have walked in the way of your sister, and I will give her cup into your hand. [32]So says the Lord Jehovah: You shall drink your sister's cup deep and wide; you shall be laughed at and mocked; for it holds much. [33]*In* drunkenness and sorrow you are filled, the cup of horror and ruin, the cup of your sister Samaria. [34]And you shall drink it and drain *it*. And you shall break its fragments, and tear off your breasts. For I have spoken, declares the Lord Jehovah. [35]So the Lord Jehovah says this: Because you have forgotten Me and cast Me behind your back, so also you bear your wickedness and

25 וּשְׁפָטוּךְ בְּמִשְׁפְּטֵיהֶם׃ וְנָתַתִּי קִנְאָתִי בָּךְ וְעָשׂוּ אוֹתָךְ
you they and against My I And their by will they and / with deal will ,you jealousy give will .judgments you judge
בְּחֵמָה אַפֵּךְ וְאָזְנַיִךְ יָסִירוּ וְאַחֲרִיתֵךְ בַּחֶרֶב תִּפּוֹל הֵמָּה
They shall the by rest the and will they your and Your .fury in / .fall sword you of ,take ears nose
26 בָּנַיִךְ וּבְנוֹתַיִךְ יִקָּחוּ וְאַחֲרִיתֵךְ תֵּאָכֵל בָּאֵשׁ׃ וְהִפְשִׁיטוּךְ
will they And the by be shall rest the and turn will your and your / you strip .fire devoured you of ,away daughters sons
27 אֶת־בְּגָדַיִךְ וְלָקְחוּ כְּלֵי תִפְאַרְתֵּךְ׃ וְהִשְׁבַּתִּי זִמָּתֵךְ מִמֵּךְ
from your will I And your of articles the take and your (of) / ,you wickedness cease make .beauty clothes
וְאֶת־זְנוּתֵךְ מֵאֶרֶץ מִצְרָיִם וְלֹא־תִשְׂאִי עֵינַיִךְ אֲלֵיהֶם
them to your you shall and ,Egypt the from your and / eyes up lift not of land fornication
28 וּמִצְרַיִם לֹא תִזְכְּרִי־עוֹד׃ כִּי כֹה אָמַר אֲדֹנָי יֱהוִה
:Jehovah the says thus For any shall you not and / Lord .more remember Egypt
הִנְנִי נֹתְנָךְ בְּיַד אֲשֶׁר שָׂנֵאת בְּיַד אֲשֶׁר־נָקְעָה נַפְשֵׁךְ מֵהֶם׃
from your was of the in you those the in will ,Behold / .them soul alienated whom hand ,hate whom of hand you give I
29 וְעָשׂוּ אוֹתָךְ בְּשִׂנְאָה וְלָקְחוּ כָּל־יְגִיעֵךְ וַעֲזָבוּךְ עֵירֹם
naked shall and your all shall and hatred in with they And / you leave wealth take you deal shall
30 וְעֶרְיָה וְנִגְלָה עֶרְוַת זְנוּנַיִךְ וְזִמָּתֵךְ וְתַזְנוּתָיִךְ׃ עָשֹׂה אֵלֶּה
These be will your and your even adul- your the will And and / things done .fornications lewdness ,teries of nudity bared be .bare
לָךְ בִּזְנוֹתֵךְ אַחֲרֵי גוֹיִם עַל אֲשֶׁר־נִטְמֵאת בְּגִלּוּלֵיהֶם׃
their with are you that because the after you because to / .idols defiled ,nations whored have you
31 בְּדֶרֶךְ אֲחוֹתֵךְ הָלָכְתְּ וְנָתַתִּי כוֹסָהּ בְּיָדֵךְ׃
32 כֹּה אָמַר
says Thus your into her I and have You your the in / .hand cup give will ,walked sister of way
אֲדֹנָי יֱהוִה כּוֹס אֲחוֹתֵךְ תִּשְׁתִּי הָעֲמֻקָּה וְהָרְחָבָה תִּהְיֶה
shall you ;wide and deep shall You your cup :Jehovah the / be drink sister's Lord
33 לִצְחֹק וּלְלַעַג מִרְבָּה לְהָכִיל׃ שִׁכָּרוֹן וְיָגוֹן תִּמָּלֵאִי כּוֹס
the are you and (With) it for much and laughed / of cup filled ,sorrow drunkenness .holds ;mocked at
34 שַׁמָּה וּשְׁמָמָה כּוֹס אֲחוֹתֵךְ שֹׁמְרוֹן׃ וְשָׁתִית אוֹתָהּ וּמָצִית
drain and it you And .Samaria your cup the ,ruin and horror / .(it) drink shall sister of
וְאֶת־חֲרָשֶׂיהָ תְּגָרֵמִי וְשָׁדַיִךְ תְּנַתֵּקִי כִּי אֲנִי דִבַּרְתִּי נְאֻם
states have I For .off tear your and shall you its And / ,spoken breasts ,break fragments
35 אֲדֹנָי יֱהוִה׃ לָכֵן כֹּה אָמַר אֲדֹנָי יֱהוִה יַעַן שָׁכַחַתְּ
have you Be- :Jehovah the says thus Therefore .Jehovah the / forgotten cause Lord Lord
אוֹתִי וַתַּשְׁלִיכִי אוֹתִי אַחֲרֵי גַוֵּךְ וְגַם־אַתְּ שְׂאִי זִמָּתֵךְ וְאֶת־
and your bear you thus your behind Me cast and Me / wickedness also ,back

your adulteries.
[36]And Jehovah said to me, Son of man, will you judge Oholah and Oholibah? Then declare to them their abominations. [37]For they did adultery, and blood *is* on their hands. And they did adultery with their idols, and even their sons whom they bore to Me they make pass to them, to be devoured. [38]Even still they have done this to Me: They have defiled My sanctuary in that day, and have profaned My sabbaths. [39]And when they had slain their sons to their idols, then they came into My sanctuary in that day to profane it. And, lo, this they have done in the midst of My house. [40]Furthermore, they have sent for men to come from a distance, of whom a messenger was sent to them. And behold, they came, for whom you washed, painted your eyes, and were adorned *with* gems; [41]and you sat on a glorious bed, and a table arranged before it, and My incense and My oil you set on it. [42]And the sound of a crowd at ease *was* with her; and drunkards from the wilderness *were* brought with the men of the host of mankind; and they put bracelets on their hands, and crowns of beauty on their heads. [43]Then I said about the one worn *in* adulteries, Will they now whore with her, and she *with them*? [44]And they went in to her, as *they* go in to a woman of harlotry, so they went in to Oholah and to Oholibah, the wicked women.
[45]And *as* righteous men they shall judge them *with* the judgment of adulteresses, and the judgment of women who shed blood; because they *are* adulteresses, and blood *is* in their hands. [46]For so says

36 תזנותיך׃ ויאמר יהוה אלי בן־אדם התשפוט את־
you will ,man Son to Jehovah said And your
judge of ,me .adulteries

37 אהלה ואת־אהליבה והגד להן את תועבותיהן׃ כי
For their to Then ?Oholibah and Oholah
.abominations them declare

נאפו ודם בידיהן ואת־גלוליהן נאפו וגם את־בניהן אשר
whom their and did they their And their in and did they
.sons even adultery idols with .hands (is) blood adultery

38 ילדו־לי העבירו להם לאכלה׃ עוד זאת עשו לי טמאו
have They to they this Even be to to make they to they
defiled :Me done have still .devoured them pass ,Me bore

39 את־מקדשי ביום ההוא ואת־שבתותי חללו׃ ובשחטם
they when And have My and that day in My
slain had ,profaned sabbaths sanctuary

את־בניהם לגלוליהם ויבאו אל־מקדשי ביום ההוא
that day in My into they then their to their
sanctuary came ,idols sons

40 לחללו והנה־כה עשו בתוך ביתי׃ ואף כי תשלחנה
have they ,Furthermore My the in they this And pro- to
sent .house of midst done have ,lo .it fane

לאנשים באים ממרחק אשר מלאך שלוח אליהם
.them to sent was a of a from come to men for
messenger whom ,distance

41 והנה־באו לאשר רחצת כחלת עיניך ועדית עדי׃ וישבת
you and (with) were and your painted you for they And
sat ;gems adorned eyes ,washed whom ,came ,behold

על־מטה כבודה ושלחן ערוך לפניה וקטרתי ושמני
My and My and before arranged a and ,glorious a bed on
oil incense ,it table

42 שמת עליה׃ וקול המון שלו בה ואל־אנשים מרב
the of the and (was) ease at a the And .it on set you
of host men with ;her with crowd of sound

אדם מובאים סובאים ממדבר ויתנו צמידים אל־ידיהן
their on bracelets they and the from drunkards were man-
hands put ,wilderness brought kind

43 ועטרת תפארת על־ראשיהן׃ ואמר לבלה נאופים עת
now (in) the about I Then their on beauty and
,adulteries worn one said .heads of crowns

44 יזנה תזנותיה והיא׃ ויבוא אליה כבוא אל־אשה זונה
;harlotry a to (they) as ,her to they And she and whore will
of woman in go in went ?(them with) her with they

45 כן באו אל־אהלה ואל־אהליבה אשת הזמה׃ ואנשים
(as) And .wicked the ,Oholibah and Oholah to they so
men women to in went

צדיקם המה ישפטו אותהם משפט נאפות ומשפט
the and ,adulteresses the (with) them shall they ,righteous
of judgment of judgment judge

46 שפכות דם כי נאפת הנה ודם בידיהן׃ כי כה אמר
says thus For their in and they adulteresses be- ;blood women
.hands (is) blood ,(are) cause shed who

the Lord Jehovah: Bring up on them an assembly, and give them to terror and plunder. **47**And the assembly shall stone them *with* stones, and cut them down with their swords. They shall slay their sons and their daughters, and they shall burn their houses with fire. **48**So I will make cease wickedness out of the land, that all the women may be taught, even not to do according to your wickedness. **49**And they shall put your wickedness on you, and you shall bear the sins of your idols. And you shall know that I *am* the Lord Jehovah.

957　2189　　5414　69:51　　　5927　3068　136

אֲדֹנָי יְהוִֹה הַעֲלֵה עֲלֵיהֶם קָהָל וְנָתֹן אֶתְהֶן לְזַעֲוָה וְלָבַז׃

to and | terror | to | them | and | an | them on | Bring | :Jehovah | the
.plunder | | give | | assembly | | | up | | Lord

47
1121　　　2719　　　　1254　69:51　68　　　7275
וְרָגְמוּ עֲלֵיהֶם אֶבֶן קָהָל וּבָרֵא אוֹתְהֶן בְּחַרְבוֹתָם בְּנֵיהֶם

their | their with | them | cut and | the | (with) | them shall | And
sons | .swords | | down | assembly | stones | | stone

48
2154　7673　　　　831:3　　784　7004　20:26　1323
וּבְנוֹתֵיהֶם יַהֲרֹגוּ וּבָתֵּיהֶן בָּאֵשׁ יִשְׂרֹפוּ׃ וְהִשְׁבַּתִּי זִמָּה מִן

out wicked- | will I So | shall they | with | their and | They | their and
of ness | cease make | .burn | fire | houses | ,slay shall | daughters

49
5414　2154　　6313　38:108　802　36:05　3256　776
הָאָרֶץ וְנִוַּסְּרוּ כָּל־הַנָּשִׁים וְלֹא תַעֲשֶׂינָה כְּזִמַּתְכֶנָה׃ וְנָתְנוּ

they And | to according | do to | and | the | all | may that | the
put shall | .wickedness your | | not | women | | taught be | ,land

3045　　5375　1544　2399　5921　2154
זִמַּתְכֶנָה עֲלֵיכֶן וַחֲטָאֵי גִלּוּלֵיכֶן תִּשֶּׂאינָה וִידַעְתֶּם כִּי אֲנִי

I | that | you And | shall you | your | the and | on | your
(am) | know shall | .bear | idols | of sins | ,you | wickedness

3068　136
אֲדֹנָי יְהוִֹה׃

.Jehovah | the
Lord

CAP. XXIV כד

CHAPTER 24

CHAPTER 24
1And the word of Jehovah was to me, in the ninth year, in the tenth month, in the tenth *day* of the month, saying, **2**Son of man, write for yourself the name of the day, this very day; the king of Babylon has leaned toward Jerusalem in this very day. **3**And parable a parable to the house of rebellion, and say to them, So says the Lord Jehovah: Set on the pot! Set on, and also pour water in it. **4**Gather its pieces *into* it, every good piece, the thigh and the shoulder. Fill *it with* choice bones; **5**take the choice of the flock and also pile the bones under it; boiling make it boil; also let them seethe its bones in it.

1
6224　2320　8671　8141　3068　1697　1961
וַיְהִי דְבַר־יְהוָה אֵלַי בַּשָּׁנָה הַתְּשִׁיעִית בַּחֹדֶשׁ הָעֲשִׂירִי

,tenth | the in | ,ninth | the in | me | Jehovah | of word | And
| month | | year | to | | | was

2
3117　8034　3789　120　1121　559　2320　6218
בֶּעָשׂוֹר לַחֹדֶשׁ לֵאמֹר׃ בֶּן־אָדָם כְּתָב־לְךָ אֶת־שֵׁם הַיּוֹם

the | the | for | write | ,man Son | ,saying | the of | the in
;day | of name | yourself | | of | | ,month (day) | tenth

6106　3389　884　44:28　5564　2088　3117　6106
אֶת־עֶצֶם הַיּוֹם הַזֶּה סָמַךְ מֶלֶךְ־בָּבֶל אֶל־יְרוּשָׁלַ͏ִם בְּעֶצֶם

very | in | Jerusalem | to- | Babylon | the | has | :this | day | very
| | | ward | of king | | leaned

3
559　491:1　48:05　1004　4911　2088　3117
הַיּוֹם הַזֶּה׃ וּמְשֹׁל אֶל־בֵּית־הַמֶּרִי מָשָׁל וְאָמַרְתָּ אֲלֵיהֶם

,them to | say and | a | rebellious | the to | parable And | .this | day
| | parable | house | | | day

4
4325　3332　82:39　5518　8239　3068　136　559　3541
כֹּה אָמַר אֲדֹנָי יְהוִֹה שְׁפֹת הַסִּיר שְׁפֹת וְגַם־יְצֹק בּוֹ מָיִם׃

.water | in | pour and | Set | the | Set | :Jehovah | the | says | Thus
| it | also | ,on (it) | .pot | on | | Lord

6106　4005　3801　3409　2896　5409　54:09　600
אֱסֹף נְתָחֶיהָ אֵלֶיהָ כָּל־נֵתַח טוֹב יָרֵךְ וְכָתֵף מִבְחַר עֲצָמִים

bones | the | the and | the | ,good | piece | every | ,it into | its | Gather
| choice | .shoulder | thigh | | | | | pieces

5
8478　6106　1754　1571　3947　6629　4005　43:90
מַלֵּא׃ מִבְחַר הַצֹּאן לָקוֹחַ וְגַם דּוּר הָעֲצָמִים תַּחְתֶּיהָ

;it under | bones the | pile | and | Take | the | the | Fill
| | | | also | flock | of choice | .(with it)

3541　3651　8432　6106　131:0　7571　7571
רַתַּח רְתָחֶיהָ גַּם־בָּשְׁלוּ עֲצָמֶיהָ בְּתוֹכָהּ׃ לָכֵן כֹּה

thus Therefore | .it | in | bones its | them let also | it make | boiling
| | | seethe | .boil | | |

6
2457　834　5518　1818　5892　188　30:68　136　559
אָמַר אֲדֹנָי יְהוִֹה אוֹי עִיר הַדָּמִים סִיר אֲשֶׁר חֶלְאָתָה בָהּ

,it in | rust | whose | the to | the | city | Woe | :Jehovah | the | says
(is) | | pot | ,bloody | | to | | Lord

3318　54:09　5409　3318　38:08　2457
וְחֶלְאָתָהּ לֹא יָצְאָה מִמֶּנָּה לִנְתָחֶיהָ לִנְתָחֶיהָ הוֹצִיאָהּ׃

Bring | piece by | piece | !it of | has | not | its and
,out it | | | out gone | | | rust

6So the Lord Jehovah says this: Woe to the bloody city, to the pot whose rust *is* in it, and its rust has not gone out of it! Bring it out piece by piece.

Let not a lot fall on it. [7]For
her blood is in her midst;
she set it on a shining rock.
She did not pour it on the
ground, to cover it *with*
dust. [8]In order to cause fury
to come up to take
vengeance, I have put her
blood on a shining rock,
that it should not be
covered. [9]So the Lord
Jehovah says this: Woe to
the bloody city! I also shall
heap on the pile. [10]And
kindle the fire on the wood,
complete the flesh, and mix
in the spice; and let the
bones be burned. [11]Then
make it stand on its coals
empty, so that it may be hot,
and its bronze may glow,
and its defilement be
melted in its midst, *that* its
rust may be consumed.
[12]She is wearied with toil,
and the increase of her rust
did not go out; her rust *will
be* in the fire. [13]In your
defilement *is* wickedness.
Because I have cleaned
you, yet you are not clean;
you shall not be cleansed
from your defilement any
more until I have made
cease My fury on you. [14]I,
Jehovah, have spoken, it
shall come, and I will do *it*. I
will not let go, and I will not
spare; I will not pity. By our
ways and by your doings
they shall judge you,
declares the Lord Jehovah.

[15]And the word of
Jehovah was to me, say-
ing, [16]Son of man, behold, I
am taking from you the
desire of your eyes with a
blow. Yet you shall not wail,
and not weep, and your
tears shall not come.
[17]Groan, *but* be silent; do
not make a mourning *for* the
dead. Bind your turban on
you, and put your shoes on
your feet, and do not cover
over the mustache; and do
not eat the bread of men.

6706 1961 8432 1818 1486 59 21 5351
7 לֹא־נָפַל עָלֶיהָ גּוֹרָל׃ כִּי דָמָהּ בְּתוֹכָהּ הָיָה עַל־צְחִיחַ
a on ;is her in her For .lot a it on let not
shining midst blood fall

6083 3680 776 59 21 8210 38 08 7760 55 53
סֶלַע שָׂמָתְהוּ לֹא שְׁפָכַתְהוּ עַל־הָאָרֶץ לְכַסּוֹת עָלָיו עָפָר׃
(with) it cover to the on did She not set she rock
dust ,ground it pour .it

55 53 6706 1818 5414 53 58 5358 2534 5927
8 לְהַעֲלוֹת חֵמָה לִנְקֹם נָקָם נָתַתִּי אֶת־דָּמָהּ עַל־צְחִיחַ סָלַע
,rock a on her have I ven- take to fury cause to
shining blood put ,geance up come to

5892 188 30 68 136 559 3541 3680 1115
9 לְבִלְתִּי הִכָּסוֹת׃ לָכֵן כֹּה אָמַר אֲדֹנָי יְהוִה אוֹי עִיר
city Woe :Jehovah the says thus Therefore be should it not that
to Lord .covered

1814 6086 7235 4071 1430 1571 1818
10 הַדָּמִים גַּם־אֲנִי אַגְדִּיל הַמְּדוּרָה׃ הַרְבֵּה הָעֵצִים הַדְלֵק
kindle, wood the heap And .pile the heap shall I also the
on on bloody

2787 6106 4841 7543 1320 8552 784
הָאֵשׁ הָתֵם הַבָּשָׂר וְהַרְקַח הַמֶּרְקָחָה וְהָעֲצָמוֹת יֵחָרוּ׃
be let the and ;spice the mix and the complete the
.burned bones in ,flesh ,fire

51 78 2787 31 79 4616 7386 1513 59 21 5975
11 וְהַעֲמִידֶהָ עַל־גֶּחָלֶיהָ רֵקָה לְמַעַן תֵּחַם וְחָרָה נְחֻשְׁתָּהּ
,bronze its may and may it so ,empty its on make Then
glow ,hot be that coals stand it

38 11 8383 2457 8552 29 32 8432 5413
12 וְנִתְּכָה בְתוֹכָהּ טֻמְאָתָהּ תִּתֹּם חֶלְאָתָהּ׃ תְּאֻנִים הֶלְאָת
is She with .rust its may (that) defile- its its in may and
,wearied toil consumed be ;ment midst melted be

2932 2457 784 2457 7227 3318 38 08
13 וְלֹא־תֵצֵא מִמֶּנָּה רַבַּת חֶלְאָתָהּ בְּאֵשׁ חֶלְאָתָהּ׃ בְּטֻמְאָתֵךְ
your In rust her the in ;rust her in- the from go did and
(is) defilement .(be will) fire crease her out not

57 50 2891 36 08 2932 2891 38 08 2891 3282 2154
זִמָּה יַעַן טִהַרְתִּיךְ וְלֹא טָהַרְתְּ מִטֻּמְאָתֵךְ לֹא תִטְהֲרִי־עוֹד
any shall you not your from you are yet have I Be- wicked-
more cleansed be defilement ,clean not ,you cleaned cause .ness

6213 935 1696 3068 2534 5117
14 עַד־הֲנִיחִי אֶת־חֲמָתִי בָּךְ׃ אֲנִי יְהוָה דִּבַּרְתִּי בָּאָה וְעָשִׂיתִי
will I and shall It have Jehovah I on My have I until
.(it) do ,come .spoken .you fury cease made

5949 1870 5162 38 08 2347 6544
לֹא־אֶפְרַע וְלֹא־אָחוּס וְלֹא אֶנָּחֵם כִּדְרָכַיִךְ וְכַעֲלִילוֹתַיִךְ
your by and your By will I not will I and will I not
,doings ways .pity ;spare not go let

559 3068 1697 1961 3068 136 5002 8199
15 שְׁפָטוּךְ נְאֻם אֲדֹנָי יְהוִה׃ וַיְהִי דְבַר־יְהוָה אֵלַי לֵאמֹר׃
,saying to Jehovah the And .Jehovah the states shall they
,me of word was Lord you judge

3808 4046 5869 4261 3947 2005/120 1121
16 בֶּן־אָדָם הִנְנִי לֹקֵחַ מִמְּךָ אֶת־מַחְמַד עֵינֶיךָ בְּמַגֵּפָה וְלֹא
Yet a with your the from am ,behold ,man Son
not .blow eyes of desire you taking I of

1826 602 1832 935 38 08 1058 38 08 5594
17 תִסְפֹּד וְלֹא תִבְכֶּה וְלוֹא תָבוֹא דִּמְעָתֶךָ׃ הֵאָנֵק דֹּם
Be Groan .tears your shall and ,weep and shall you
.silent ,(silently) come not not ,wail

7760 5275 59 21 2280 6287 6213 38 08 60 4191
מֵתִים אֵבֶל לֹא־תַעֲשֶׂה פְּאֵרְךָ חֲבוֹשׁ עָלֶיךָ וּנְעָלֶיךָ תָּשִׂים
put your and on Bind your make do not a the (for)
shoes ,you turban .(them for) mourning dead

398 38 08 582 3899 82 22 5844 7272
בְּרַגְלֶיךָ וְלֹא תַעְטֶה עַל־שָׂפָם וְלֶחֶם אֲנָשִׁים לֹא תֹאכֵל׃
.eat do not men the and the over do and your on
of bread ,mustache cover not ,feet

18 So I spoke to the people in the morning. And my wife died in the evening. And I did in the morning as I was commanded. 19 And the people said to me, Will you not tell us what these things *are* to us, that you are doing? 20 Then I said to them, the word of Jehovah was to me, saying, 21 Speak to the house of Israel, So says the Lord Jehovah: Behold, I will profane My sanctuary, the pride of your strength, the desire of your eyes, and that which your soul pities. And your sons and your daughters, whom you have forsaken, shall fall by the sword. 22 And you shall do as I have done. You shall not cover over the mustache, and you shall not eat the bread of men. 23 And your turbans *shall be* on your heads, and your shoes on your feet. You shall not wail nor weep; but you shall rot away in your iniquities, and each man groan to his brother. 24 So Ezekiel is for a sign to you. As all that he has done, you shall do. And when it comes, then you shall know that I *am* the Lord Jehovah.

25 And you, son of man, will *it* not *be* on the day *when* I take from them their strength, the joy of their beauty, the desire of their eyes, and the lifting up of their soul—their sons and their daughters? 26 He will come in that day, he who escaped to you, to cause *you* to hear *with your* ears. 27 In that day your mouth shall be opened to the escaped one, and you shall speak and not be dumb any longer. And you shall be to them a sign, and they shall know that I *am* Jehovah.

6213 6153 802 4191 1242 5971 1696
18 וָאֲדַבֵּר אֶל־הָעָם בַּבֹּקֶר וַתָּמָת אִשְׁתִּי בָעֶרֶב וָאַעַשׂ
I and did | the in ,evening | wife my | died And | the in .morning | the people | to | I So spoke

5046 3808 5971 559 6680 1242
19 בַבֹּקֶר כַּאֲשֶׁר צֻוֵּיתִי׃ וַיֹּאמְרוּ אֵלַי הָעָם הֲלֹא־תַגִּיד לָנוּ
us | you tell | Will not | the ,people | to me | said And | was I .commanded | as | the in morning

3068 1697 559 6213 428/4100
20 מָה־אֵלֶּה לָנוּ כִּי אַתָּה עֹשֶׂה׃ וָאֹמַר אֲלֵיהֶם דְּבַר־יְהוָה
Jehovah | the of word | ,them to | I Then said | are ?doing | you | that | to us | these (are) things | what

136 559 3541 3478 1004 559 559 1961
21 הָיָה אֵלַי לֵאמֹר׃ אֱמֹר ׀ לְבֵית יִשְׂרָאֵל כֹּה־אָמַר אֲדֹנָי
the Lord | says Thus | ,Israel | the to of house | Speak | ,saying | ,me to | was

5869 4261 5797 1347 4720 2490 2005 3068
יֱהוִה הִנְנִי מְחַלֵּל אֶת־מִקְדָּשִׁי גְּאוֹן עֻזְּכֶם מַחְמַד עֵינֵיכֶם
,eyes your | desire the of | your ,strength | the of pride | My sanctuary | will profane | ,Behold I | Jeho- :vah

2719 5800 834 1323 1121 5315 4263
וּמַחְמַל נַפְשְׁכֶם וּבְנֵיכֶם וּבְנוֹתֵיכֶם אֲשֶׁר עֲזַבְתֶּם בַּחֶרֶב
the by sword | have you forsaken | whom | your and daughters | your And sons | .soul your | that and pities which

3899 5844 3808 8222 5921 6213 6213 5307
22 יִפֹּלוּ׃ וַעֲשִׂיתֶם כַּאֲשֶׁר עָשִׂיתִי עַל־שָׂפָם לֹא תַעְטוּ וְלֶחֶם
the and of bread | shall you ,cover | not | the mustache | On | have I .done | as | you And do shall | shall .fall

5275 7218 5921 6287 398 3808 582
23 אֲנָשִׁים לֹא תֹאכֵלוּ׃ וּפְאֵרֵכֶם עַל־רָאשֵׁיכֶם וְנַעֲלֵיכֶם
your and shoes | your heads | on | your And (be shall) turbans | shall you .eat | not | men

5771 4743 1058 3808 5594 7272
בְּרַגְלֵיכֶם לֹא תִסְפְּדוּ וְלֹא תִבְכּוּ וּנְמַקֹּתֶם בַּעֲוֹנֹתֵיכֶם
your in iniquities | shall you but away rot | ;weep | and not | shall You wail | not | your on .feet

2
4159 3168 1961 251 376 5098
24 וְנְהַמְתֶּם אִישׁ אֶל־אָחִיו׃ וְהָיָה יְחֶזְקֵאל לָכֶם לְמוֹפֵת
a for .sign | you to | Ezekiel | is So | his .brother | to | each man | groan and

136 3045 935 6213 6213 3605
כְּכֹל אֲשֶׁר־עָשָׂה תַּעֲשׂוּ בְּבֹאָהּ וִידַעְתֶּם כִּי אֲנִי אֲדֹנָי
the Lord | I (am) | that | you then know shall | when And ;comes it | shall you .do | has he ,done | that | all As

3947 3117 120 1121 3068
25 יֱהוִה׃ וְאַתָּה בֶן־אָדָם הֲלוֹא בְּיוֹם קַחְתִּי מֵהֶם אֶת־
from them | (when) take I | the on day | (it) will (be) not | ,man | son of | ,you And | .Jehovah

4853 5869 4261 8597 4885 4581
מָעוּזָּם מְשׂוֹשׂ תִּפְאַרְתָּם אֶת־מַחְמַד עֵינֵיהֶם וְאֶת־מַשָּׂא
the of up lifting | and | ,eyes their | the of desire | ,beauty their | joy the of | their ,strength

6412 935 1931 3117 1323 1121 5315
26 נַפְשָׁם בְּנֵיהֶם וּבְנוֹתֵיהֶם׃ בַּיּוֹם הַהוּא יָבוֹא הַפָּלִיט אֵלֶיךָ
,you to | who escaped | he will come | it be | (that) In day | their and daughters | their sons | their ,soul

6412 6310 6605 3117 241 2045
27 לְהַשְׁמָעוּת אָזְנָיִם׃ בַּיּוֹם הַהוּא יִפָּתַח פִּיךָ אֶת־הַפָּלִיט
the to ,one escaped | your mouth | be shall opened | that | day In | (your with) .ears | cause to hear to (you)

3045 4159 1961 5750 481 3808 1696
וּתְדַבֵּר וְלֹא תֵאָלֵם עוֹד וְהָיִיתָ לָהֶם לְמוֹפֵת וְיָדְעוּ כִּי־
that | they and know shall | ,sign a | them to | you And be shall | any .longer | be dumb | and not | you and speak shall

3068
אֲנִי יְהוָה׃
.Jehovah | I (am)

CAP. XXV כה

CHAPTER 25

CHAPTER 25

1And the word of Jehovah was to me, saying, 2Son of man, set your face against the sons of Ammon and prophesy against them. 3And say to the sons of Ammon, Hear the word of the Lord Jehovah. So says the Lord Jehovah: Because you have said, Aha! against My sanctuary, when it was profaned, and against the land of Israel when it was ruined, and against the house of Judah when they went into exile; 4therefore, behold, I will give you to the sons of the east for a possession. And they shall set their camp sites among you, and put among you their dwellings. They shall eat your fruit, and they shall drink your milk. 5And I will give Rabbah for a pasture *for* camels, and the sons of Ammon for a resting place *for* flocks. And you shall know Jehovah. 6For so says the Lord Jehovah: Because you have clapped the hand, and you stamped the foot, and rejoiced with all your spite in *your* soul against the land of Israel; 7so, behold, I will stretch out My hand on you and will give you as a prize to the nations. And I will cut you off from the peoples, and I will make you perish from the lands. I will destroy you. And you shall know that I *am* Jehovah.

8So says the Lord Jehovah: Because Moab and Seir say, Behold, the house of Judah *is* like all the nations; 9so, behold, I will open the side of Moab from the cities, from his cities, from his borders, the glory of the land: Beth-jeshimoth, Baalmeon, and Kiriathaim.

1121 6440 7760 12,0/ 1121 559 3068 1697 1961
1 2 וַיְהִי דְבַר־יְהוָה אֵלַי לֵאמֹר׃ בֶּן־אָדָם שִׂים פָּנֶיךָ אֶל־בְּנֵי
the against your set ,man Son ,saying to Jehovah the And
of sons face of ,me of word was

1697 8085 59:83 1121 559 5012 5983
3 עַמּוֹן וְהִנָּבֵא עֲלֵיהֶם׃ וְאָמַרְתָּ לִבְנֵי עַמּוֹן שִׁמְעוּ דְּבַר־
the Hear ,Ammon the to say And against and Ammon
of word of sons .them prophesy

1889 559 3282 3068 .136 559 3541. 3068 .136
אֲדֹנָי יְהוִה כֹּה־אָמַר אֲדֹנָי יְהוִה יַעַן אָמְרֵךְ הֶאָח אֶל־
against ,Aha have you Be- :Jehovah the says Thus .Jehovah the
,said cause Lord Lord

1004 8074 8378 127 2490 4720
מִקְדָּשִׁי כִי־נִחָל וְאֶל־אַדְמַת יִשְׂרָאֵל כִּי נָשַׁמָּה וְאֶל־בֵּית
the and was it when Israel the and was it when My
of house against ,ruined of land against ,profaned sanctuary

6924 1121 5414 2005 1473 1980 3063
4 יְהוּדָה כִּי הָלְכוּ בַּגּוֹלָה׃ לָכֵן הִנְנִי נֹתְנָךְ לִבְנֵי־קֶדֶם
the the to will ,behold ,therefore into they when Judah
east of sons you give I ;exile went

4908 5414 2918 3427 4181
לְמוֹרָשָׁה וְיִשְּׁבוּ טִירוֹתֵיהֶם בָּךְ וְנָתְנוּ בָךְ מִשְׁכְּנֵיהֶם
their among and among their they And a for
.dwellings you put you sites camp set shall .possession

7237 5414 2461 8354 6529 398
5 הֵמָּה יֹאכְלוּ פִרְיֵךְ וְהֵמָּה יִשְׁתּוּ חֲלָבֵךְ׃ וְנָתַתִּי אֶת־רַבָּה
Rabbah I And your shall and your shall They
give will .milk drink they ,fruit eat

3045 6629 4769 5983 1121 1581 5116
לִנְוֵה גְמַלִּים וְאֶת־בְּנֵי עַמּוֹן לְמִרְבַּץ־צֹאן וִידַעְתֶּם כִּי־אֲנִי
I that you And (for) resting a for Ammon the and (for) a for
(am) know shall .flocks place of sons ,camels pasture

3027 4222 3282 3068 136 559 3541 3068
6 יְהוָה׃ כִּי כֹה אָמַר אֲדֹנָי יְהוִה יַעַן מַחְאֲךָ יָד
(your) have you Be- :Jehovah the says thus For .Jehovah
hand clapped cause Lord

127 5315 7589 8056 7272 7554
וְרַקְעֲךָ בְּרֶגֶל וַתִּשְׂמַח בְּכָל־שָׁאטְךָ בְּנֶפֶשׁ אֶל־אַדְמַת
the against (your) in your with and (your) you and
of land soul spite all rejoiced ,foot stamped

897 5414 5921 3027 5186 2005 3478
7 יִשְׂרָאֵל׃ לָכֵן הִנְנִי נָטִיתִי אֶת־יָדִי עָלֶיךָ וּנְתַתִּיךָ לְבַג
a as will and on My will ,Behold ,therefore ;Israel
prize you give you hand out stretch I

776 6 5971 3772 1471
לַגּוֹיִם וְהִכְרַתִּיךָ מִן־הָעַמִּים וְהַאֲבַדְתִּיךָ מִן־הָאֲרָצוֹת
the from will I and the from will I And the to
.lands perish you make peoples off you cut .nations

136 559 3541 3068 3045 8045
8 אַשְׁמִידְךָ וְיָדַעְתָּ כִּי־אֲנִי יְהוָה׃ כֹּה אָמַר אֲדֹנָי
the says Thus .Jehovah I that you and will I
Lord (am) know shall ,you destroy

1004 1471 3605 2009 8165 4124 559 3068
יְהוִה יַעַן אֲמֹר מוֹאָב וְשֵׂעִיר הִנֵּה כְּכָל־הַגּוֹיִם בֵּית
the (is) the like ,Behold ,Seir and Moab say Be- :Jehovah
of house nations all cause

5892 5892 4124 3801 6605 2005 3651 3063
9 יְהוּדָה׃ לָכֵן הִנְנִי פֹתֵחַ אֶת־כֶּתֶף מוֹאָב מֵהֶעָרִים מֵעָרָיו
his from the from Moab the will ,behold there- ;Judah
cities ,cities of side open I ,fore

7156 =1186= =1020= 776 6643 7097
מִקָּצֵהוּ צְבִי אֶרֶץ בֵּית הַיְשִׁימֹת בַּעַל מְעוֹן וְקִרְיָתָמָה׃
and meon Baal- ,jeshimoth Beth- the the his from
,Kiriathaim ;land of glory ,borders

Left column (English translation)

[10]To the sons of the east, with the sons of Ammon, even I will give it for a possession so that the sons of Ammon may not be remembered among the nations. [11]And I will execute on Moab judgments. And they shall know that I *am* Jehovah.

[12]So says the Lord Jehovah: Because Edom has acted by taking vengeance against the house of Judah, and they are very guilty, and are avenged on them; [13]so the Lord Jehovah says this: I will stretch My hand on Edom and will cut off from it man and beast; and I will lay it waste, from Teman even to Dedan they shall fall by the sword. [14]And I will put My vengeance on Edom by the hand of My people Israel. And they shall do in Edom as *is* My anger, and as *is* My fury. And they shall know My vengeance, declares the Lord Jehovah.

[15]So says the Lord Jehovah: Because the Philistines have acted in vengeance, and have taken vengeance with spite in *their* soul, to destroy *with* perpetual enmity; [16]so the Lord Jehovah says this: Behold, I will stretch My hand on the Philistines, and I will cut off the Cherethim, and will detroy the rest of the coast of the sea. [17]And I will execute on them great vengeances, with rebukes of fury. And when I put My vengeance on them, they will know that I *am* Jehovah.

Interlinear

10
3808 לֹא — not | 4616 לְמַעַן — that so | 4181 לְמוֹרָשָׁה — a for possession | 5414 וּנְתַתִּיהָ — will I And it give | 5983 עַמּוֹן — Ammon | 1121 עַל־בְּנֵי — the with of sons | 6924 קֶדֶם — the east | 1121 לִבְנֵי־ — the to of sons

11
3045 וְיָדְעוּ — they And know shall | 8201 שְׁפָטִים — judgments | 6213 אֶעֱשֶׂה — execute | 4124 וּבְמוֹאָב — on And Moab | 1471 גּוֹיִם — nations | 5983/1121 בְּנֵי־עַמּוֹן — the among Ammon of sons | 2142 תִזָּכֵר — the be may recalled

12
123 אֱדוֹם — Edom | 6213 עֲשׂוֹת — has acted | 3282 יַעַן — Be- cause | 3068 יְהוִה — :Jehovah the Lord | 136 אֲדֹנָי — the says | 559 אָמַר — says | 35.41 כֹּה — Thus | 3068 יְהוִה — .Jehovah | כִּי־אֲנִי — I that (am) | 5358 נָקָם — by taking | 5359 לִבֵית — the against | 3063 יְהוּדָה — Judah | 1004 וַיֶּאְשְׁמוּ — they and guilty are | 816 אָשׁוֹם — very | 816 וְנִקְמוּ — are and avenged | 5358 בָהֶם — ;them on

13
3772 וְהִכְרַתִּי — will and off cut | 123 אֱדוֹם — Edom on | 59,21 עַל־אֱדוֹם — My | 3027 יָדִי — will I hand stretch | 5186 וְנָטִתִי — :Jehovah the Lord | 3068 יְהוִה — the says | 136 אֲדֹנָי — says | 559 אָמַר — thus ,there- | 35.41 כֹּה — fore | לָכֵן — | 120 אָדָם — man | 929 וּבְהֵמָה — ;beast and | 5414 וּנְתַתִּיהָ — will I and it lay | 2723 חָרְבָּה — ,waste | 8482 מִתֵּימָן — from Teman | 1719 וּדְדָנֶה — to even Dedan | 2719 בַּחֶרֶב — the by sword | 5307 יִפֹּלוּ — .fall

14
5414 וְנָתַתִּי — I And put will | 5360 אֶת־נִקְמָתִי — ven- geance | 123 בֶּאֱדוֹם — Edom on | 3027 בְּיַד — My the by hand | 5971 עַמִּי — people | 3478 יִשְׂרָאֵל — ,Israel | 6213 וְעָשׂוּ — they And do shall | 123 בֶאֱדוֹם — in Edom | 639 כְּאַפִּי — My (is) as anger | 2534 וְכַחֲמָתִי — My (is) as and fury | 3045 וְיָדְעוּ — they And know shall | 5360 אֶת־נִקְמָתִי — ven- My ,geance | 5002 נְאֻם — states | 136 אֲדֹנָי — the Lord | 3068 יְהוִה — .Jehovah

15
3282 יַעַן — Be- cause | 6213 עֲשׂוֹת — have acted | 6430 פְּלִשְׁתִּים — Philistines | 5360 בִּנְקָמָה — in ;vengeance | 3068 יְהוִה — :Jehovah the Lord | 136 אֲדֹנָי — the says | 559 אָמַר — says | 35.41 כֹּה — Thus

16
3947 וְנִקְמוּ — have and taken | 5359 נָקָם — vengeance | 7589 בִּשְׁאָט — with spite | 5315 בְּנֶפֶשׁ — (their) in soul | 4889 לְמַשְׁחִית — destroy to (with) | 342 אֵיבַת — enmity | 5769 עוֹלָם — per- ,petual | לָכֵן — therefore | 3772 וְהִכְרַתִּי — will I and off cut | 6430 פְּלִשְׁתִּים — the Philistines | 3027 יָדִי — on My hand | 5186 נֹטֶה — will I stretch | 2005 הִנְנִי — Behold | 3068 יְהוִה — :Jehovah the Lord | 136 אֲדֹנָי — the says | 559 אָמַר — says | 35.41 כֹּה — thus

17
3772 אֶת־כְּרֵתִים — Cherethim | 6213 וְהַאֲבַדְתִּי — will and destroy | 319 שְׁאֵרִית — of rest | 2548 חוֹף — coast the | 3220 הַיָּם — .sea of | 6213 וְעָשִׂיתִי — on will I And them execute | בָם — | 5414 נְקָמוֹת — ven- geances | 3068 גְּדֹלוֹת — great | בְּתוֹכְחוֹת — with of rebukes | 2534 חֵמָה — fury | 3045 וְיָדְעוּ — they And know will | 136 כִּי־אֲנִי — that they (am) | 3068 יְהוִה — ,Jehovah | 1419 בְּתִתִּי — I when put | 5360 אֶת־נִקְמָתִי — My vengeance | בָם — on .them

---

CAP. XXVI כו

CHAPTER 26

CHAPTER 26

[1]And it was, in the eleventh year, in the first of the month, the word of Jehovah was to me, saying, [2]Son of man, because Tyre has said against Jerusalem,

1
3068 יְהוָה — Jehovah the | 1697 דְּבַר־ — of word | 1961 הָיָה — was the | 2320 לַחֹדֶשׁ — the of month | 259 בְּאֶחָד — the in first | 8141 שָׁנָה — ,year | 6240 עֶשְׂרֵה — eleventh | 6249 בְּעַשְׁתֵּי — the in | 1961 וַיְהִי — it And ,was

2
3389 עַל־יְרוּשָׁלַם — ,Jerusalem against | 6865 צֹר — Tyre | 559 אֲשֶׁר־אָמְרָה — has that because said | 3282 יַעַן — that of | 120 בֶּן־אָדָם — ,man Son of | 1121 — | 559 לֵאמֹר — ,saying | אֵלַי — to ,me

Aha! She is shattered, the
doors of the peoples; she
has turned to me; I shall be
filled; she is laid waste.
3 So the Lord Jehovah says
this: Behold, I *am* against
you, O Tyre. And I will cause
to come up against you
many nations, as the sea
causes its waves to come
up. 4 And they shall destroy
the walls of Tyre, and break
down her towers. I will also
scrape her dust from her,
and make her like a shining
rock. 5 It shall be a spreading place for nets in the
midst of the sea. For I have
spoken, declares the Lord
Jehovah. And she shall be a
spoil to the nations. 6 And
her daughters who *are* in
the field shall be killed by
the sword; and they shall
know that I *am* Jehovah.
7 For so says the Lord
Jehovah: Behold, I will
bring from the north Nebuchadnezzar king of Baby-
lon, a king of kings, on Tyre,
with horses, and with
chariots, and with a
company of horsemen,
even many people. 8 He
shall kill your daughters in
the field with the sword.
And he shall make siege
walls against you, and pour
out against you a mound;
and raise a buckler against
you. 9 And he will set the
blow of his ram against your
walls; and he shall break
down your towers with his
axes. 10 From the multitude
of his horses, their dust
shall cover you. From the
sound of the horsemen, and
the wheels, and chariots,
your walls shall shake;
when he enters your gates,
as *men* enter a city that is
breached. 11 With the hoofs
of his horses he will trample
all your streets. He shall kill
your people by the sword,
and the pillars of your
strength shall go down to
the ground. 12 And they shall
plunder your wealth, and
rob your merchandise. And
they shall raze your walls,
and and destroy your
desirable houses. And they
shall set your stones, and
your timbers, and your dust
in the midst of the water.

2717 4390 5437 5971 1817 7665 1889
האח נשברה דלתות העמים נסבה אלי אמלאה החרבה׃
is she shall I to has she the the is she !Aha
.waste laid ;filled be ;me turned ;peoples of doors ,shattered

5927 68.65 2005 30:68 136 559 35 41
3 לכן כה אמר אדני יהוה הנני עליך צר והעליתי עליך
against will I And O against ,Behold :Jehovah the says thus There-
you up bring Tyre ,you (am) I Lord fore

68.65 2346 7843 15 20 3220 59:27 722:7 1471
4 גוים רבים כהעלות הים לגליו׃ ושחתו חמות צר
Tyre the they And .waves its the to causes ,many nations
of walls destroy shall sea up come

6706 5414 6083 5500 40:26 2040
והרסו מגדליה וסחיתי עפרה ממנה ונתתי אותה לצחיח
a like her make and from her will I her break and
shining her dust scrape also .towers down

1696 32:20 8432 1961 2764 4894 5 5:53
5 סלע׃ משטח חרמים תהיה בתוך הים כי אני דברתי
have I For the the in shall It nets spreading a .rock
,spoken .sea of midst be for place

77:04 834 1323 1471 957 1961 3068 136 5002
6 נאם אדני יהוה והיתה לבז לגוים׃ ובנותיה אשר בשדה
the in who her And the to spoil a she And .Jehovah the states
field (are) daughters .nations be shall Lord

559 35 41 3068 3045 2026 2719
7 בחרב תהרגנה וידעו כי־אני יהוה׃ כי כה אמר
says thus For .Jehovah I that they and be shall the by
(am) know shall ;killed sword

884 44:28 5019 6865 935 2005 :3068 .136
אדני יהוה הנני מביא אל־צר נבוכדראצר מלך־בבל
,Babylon king Nebuchadnezzar Tyre on will ,Behold :Jehovah the
of bring I Lord

5971 6951 6571 7393 5483 4428 44:28 6828
מצפון מלך מלכים בסוס וברכב ובפרשים וקהל ועם־
even a with and with and with ,kings king a the from
people ,company horsemen ,chariots ,horses of north

8210 1785 5414 2026 2719 7704 1323 7227
8 רב׃ בנותיך בשדה בחרב יהרג ונתן עליך דיק ושפך
and siege against he And shall He the with the in your .many
cast ,walls you make shall .kill sword field daughters

2346 5414 6904 4239 6793 6965 5550
9 עליך סללה והקים עליך צנה׃ ומחי קבלו יתן בחמותיך
your against will he his the And a against and ,mound a against
,walls set ram of blow .buckler you raise you

84 3680 5483 8229 2719 54:22 4026
10 ומגדלתיך יתץ בחרבותיו׃ משפעת סוסיו יכסך אבקם
their shall his the From his with shall he your and
.dust you cover ,horses of plenty .axes down break towers

935 2346 7493 7393 1534 6571 6963
מקול פרש וגלגל ורכב תרעשנה חומותיך בבאו
he when ,walls your shake shall and the and the the From
enters ,chariots ,wheels ,horsemen of sound

7429 5483 6541 1234 5892 3996 8179
11 בשעריך כמבואי עיר מבקעה׃ בפרסות סוסיו ירמס
will he his the With is that a (men) as your
trample horses of hoofs .breached city enter ,gates

776 5797 4676 41:91 2719 5971 2351 3605
את־כל־חוצותיך עמך בחרב יהרג ומצבות עזך לארץ
the to your the and shall He the by Your your all
ground strength of pillars ,kill sword people .streets

2346 2040 7404 962 24:28 7997 3381
12 תרד׃ ושללו חילך ובזזו רכלתך והרסו חומותיך
,walls your they And your and your they And go shall
raze shall .merchandise plunder ,wealth spoil shall .down

4325 8432 6083 60 86 68 54:22 2532 1004
ובתי חמדתך יתצו ואבניך ועציך ועפרך בתוך מים
the the in your and your and your And .destroy your and
water of midst dust timbers stones desirable houses

[13]And I will make cease the
noise of your songs; and the
sound of your harps shall
not be heard any more.
[14]And I will make you like a
shining rock. You shall be a
spreading place for nets;
you shall not be built any
more; for I, Jehovah, have
spoken, declares the Lord
Jehovah.
[15]So says the Lord
Jehovah to Tyre: Shall not
the coastlands shake at the
sound of your fall, when the
slain groan, in the slaying of
the slaughter in your midst?
[16]Then shall come down
from their thrones all the
rulers of the sea and lay
aside their robes, and strip
off their embroidered garments. They shall be
clothed *with* tremblings;
they shall sit on the ground,
and shall tremble at *every*
moment, and be appalled at
you. [17]And they shall take
up a lament for you, and say
to you, How you are
perished, who lived by the
seas, the city well-praised,
which was strong in the
sea, she and her inhabi-
tants, who put their terror
on all her inhabitants!
[18]Now the coasts shall
tremble *in* the day of your
fall. And the coasts that *are*
by the sea shall be troubled
at your going. [19]For so says
the Lord Jehovah: When I
shall make you a ruined city,
like the cities that do not
have inhabitants; when I
shall bring up the deep on
you, and shall cover you
with great waters; [20]and I
shall bring you down with
those who go into the Pit,
with the people of old time;
and I shall set you in the
earth's lowest parts, in
places ruined from days of
old, with ones who go to
the Pit, so that you have no
inhabitants; but I gave glory
in the land of the living—[21]I

8085 3808 3658 6963 7892 1995 7673 7760
13 ישימו׃ והשבתי המון שיריך וקול כנוריך לא ישמע
be shall not your the and your the will I And shall they
heard harps of sound ;songs of noise cease make .set

3808 1961 2764 4894 5553 6706 5414 5750
14 עוד׃ ונתתיך לצחיח סלע משטח חרמים תהיה לא
not you nets spreading A .rock a like will I And any
;be shall of place shining you make .more

3068 136 5002 1696 3068 5750 1129
תבנה עוד כי אני יהוה דברתי נאם אדני יהוה׃
.Jehovah the states have Jehovah I for any shall you
Lord ,spoken ;more built be

602 4658 6963 6865 3068 136 559 3541
15 כה אמר אדני יהוה לצור הלא מקול מפלתך באנק
when ,fall your the at Shall to Jehovah the says Thus
groan of sound not :Tyre Lord

3381 339 7493 8432 2026 2027 2491
16 חלל בהרג הרג בתוכך ירעשו האיים׃ וירדו מעל
from shall Then the shake your in the when the
down come ?coastlands ,midst slaughter slaying slain

4598 5493 3220 5387 3605 3678
כסאותם כל נשיאי הים והסירו את־מעיליהם ואת־בגדי
garments and ,robes their lay and the the all their
aside sea of rulers thrones

2729 3427 776 5921 3847 2731 6584 7553
רקמתם יפשטו חרדות ילבשו על־הארץ ישבו וחרדו
shall and they the on shall They (with) .off strip their
tremble ,sit shall ground ,clothed be tremblings embroidered

559 7015 5375 8074 7281
17 לרגעים ושממו עליך׃ ונשאו עליך קינה ואמרו לך איך
How to say and a for they And .you at be and (every) at
,you ,lament you up take shall appalled ,moment

2389 1961 834 1984 5892 3220 3427 6
אבדת נושבת מימים העיר ההללה אשר היתה חזקה
strong was which well- city the the by who are you
,praised ,seas lived ,perished

6258 3427 3605 2851 5414 834 3427 3220
18 בים היא וישביה אשר־נתנו חתיתם לכל־יושביה׃ עתה
Now her on their put who her and she the in
.dwellers all terror ,dwellers ,sea

3220 339 926 4658 3117 339 2729
יחרדו האין יום מפלתך ונבהלו האיים אשר־בים
the by that the shall And .fall your the (in) the shall
sea (are) coasts troubled be of day coasts tremble

5892 5414 3068 136 559 3541 3588 3318
19 מצאתך׃ כי כה אמר אדני יהוה בתתי אתך עיר
a you I When :Jehovah the says thus For your at
city make shall Lord .going

8415 5927 3427 5892 2717
נחרבת כערים אשר לא־נושבו בהעלות עליך את־תהום
,deep the on shall I when have not that the like ,ruined
you up bring ;dwellers cities

5971 953 3381 3381 7227 4325 3680
20 וכסוך המים הרבים׃ והורדתיך את־יורדי בור אל־עם
the with the who those with shall I and ;great waters shall and
of people ,pit into go down you bring you cover

5769 2723 8482 776 3427 5769
עולם והושבתיך בארץ תחתיות כחרבות מעולם את־
with days from places in lowest the in shall I and old
,old of ruined ,parts earth's you set ,time

2416 776 6643 5414 3427 3808 4616 953 3381
יורדי בור למען לא תשבי ונתתי צבי בארץ חיים׃
the the in glory I but have you not so the who ones
—living of land gave dwellers that ,pit to go

will give you terrors; and you will not be. Though you are sought, yet you shall not be found any more forever, declares the Lord Jehovah.

CHAPTER 27

[1]And the word of Jehovah was to me, saying, [2]And you, son of man, take up a lament for Tyre. [3]And say to Tyre, O you who dwell at the entrances of the sea, a merchant of the peoples for many coastlands, so says the Lord Jehovah: O Tyre, you have said, I *am* perfect of beauty. [4]In the heart of the seas are your borders; your builders have perfected your beauty. [5]They have made for you all your planks of fir-trees of Senir; they have taken a cedar from Lebanon to make a mast for you. [6]They have made your oars *of* the oaks of Bashan; they made your deck *with* ivory from the coasts of Chittim, daughter of Assyria. [7]Your sail was of fine linen, with embroidered work from Egypt, an ensign for you; violet and purple from the coasts of Elishah was your covering. [8]The residents of Sidon and Arvad were rowers to you. Your wise ones, O Tyre, were in you; they your sailors. [9]The elders of Gebal and her wise men were with you, reinforcing your seams. All the ships of the sea and their seamen were with you, to exchange your merchandise. [10]Persia and Lud and Lydia were in your army, men of war *to* you; they hung the shield and the helmet in you; they gave your splendor. [11]The sons of Arvad and your army *were* on your walls all around; and warriors were in your towers. They hung

5769 5750 4672 3808 1245 369 5414 1091
21 בַּלָּהוֹת אֶתְּנֵךְ וְאֵינֵךְ וּתְבֻקְשִׁי וְלֹא־תִמָּצְאִי עוֹד לְעוֹלָם
,forever any more shall you found be yet not you Though ,sought are you and .be not will I terrors you give

3068 136 5002
נְאֻם אֲדֹנָי יְהוִה׃
.Jehovah the Lord states

CAP. XXVII כז

CHAPTER 27

6865 5375 120 1121 559 3068 1697 1961
1
2 וַיְהִי דְבַר־יְהוָה אֵלַי לֵאמֹר׃ וְאַתָּה בֶן־אָדָם שָׂא עַל־צֹר
Tyre for take up ,man son of ,you And ,saying ,me to Jehovah the of word And was

7402 3220 3996 3427 6865 559 7015
3 קִינָה׃ וְאָמַרְתָּ לְצוֹר הַיֹּשַׁבְתִּי עַל־מְבוֹאֹת יָם רֹכֶלֶת
mer- of chant a ,sea the of entrances the at dwell who you O ,Tyre to say And a .lament

6865 3068 136 559 3541 7227 339 5971
הָעַמִּים אֶל־אִיִּים רַבִּים כֹּה אָמַר אֲדֹנָי יְהוִה צוֹר אַתְּ
you O Tyre :Jehovah the Lord says thus ,many coast- lands for the peoples

3634 1129 1366 3220 3820 3308 3632 589 559
4 אָמַרְתְּ אֲנִי כְּלִילַת יֹפִי׃ בְּלֵב יַמִּים גְּבוּלָיִךְ בֹּנַיִךְ כָּלְלוּ
have perfected your builders your are ;borders the seas the in of heart ;beauty perfect of I (am) have ,said

730 3871 3605 1129 8149 1265 3308
5 יָפְיֵךְ׃ בְּרוֹשִׁים מִשְּׂנִיר בָּנוּ לָךְ אֵת כָּל־לֻחֹתָיִם אֶרֶז
a cedar your ;planks all for you They made have Senir of of fir-trees your .beauty

6213 1316 437 8650 6213 3947 3844
6 מִלְּבָנוֹן לָקָחוּ לַעֲשׂוֹת תֹּרֶן עָלָיִךְ׃ אַלּוֹנִים מִבָּשָׁן עָשׂוּ
They made have Bashan of the (of) oaks for .you mast a make to have they taken from Lebanon

8336 3794 339 838 8127 7175 4880
7 מִשּׁוֹטָיִךְ קַרְשֵׁךְ עָשׂוּ־שֵׁן בַּת־אֲשֻׁרִים מֵאִיֵּי כִּתִּים׃ שֵׁשׁ
fine Of linen .Chittim the from of coasts of daughter Assyria (with) ,ivory they made your deck your ;oars

8504 5251 1961 4666 1961 4714 7553
בְּרִקְמָה מִמִּצְרַיִם הָיָה מִפְרָשֵׂךְ לִהְיוֹת לָךְ לְנֵס תְּכֵלֶת
purple ;ensign a for you be to you what out spread was from Egypt em- with work broidered

1961 719 6721 3427 4374 1961 473 339 713
8 וְאַרְגָּמָן מֵאִיֵּי אֱלִישָׁה הָיָה מְכַסֵּךְ׃ יֹשְׁבֵי צִידוֹן וְאַרְוַד הָיוּ
were and Arvad Sidon resi- of dents The your ,covering was Elishah the from of coasts and purple

1380 2205 2259 1961 6865 2450 7751
9 שָׁטִים לָךְ חֲכָמַיִךְ צוֹר הָיוּ בָךְ הֵמָּה חֹבְלָיִךְ׃ זִקְנֵי גְבַל
Gebal The of elders your .sailors they (were) in ,you were O ,Tyre wise Your ,ones to rowers ,you

4419 3220 591 3605 919 2388 1961 2450
וַחֲכָמֶיהָ הָיוּ בָךְ מַחֲזִיקֵי בִּדְקֵךְ כָּל־אֳנִיּוֹת הַיָּם וּמַלָּחֵיהֶם
their and seamen the sea the of ships All your .seams rein- forcing with were you her and men wise

2428 1961 6316 3865 6539 4627 6148 1961
10 הָיוּ בָךְ לַעֲרֹב מַעֲרָבֵךְ׃ פָּרַס וְלוּד וּפוּט הָיוּ בְחֵילֵךְ
your in ,army were and Lydia and Lud Persia your .merchandise to exchange with you were

1926 5414 8518 3553 4043 4421 582
אַנְשֵׁי מִלְחַמְתֵּךְ מָגֵן וְכוֹבַע תִּלּוּ־בָךְ הֵמָּה נָתְנוּ הֲדָרֵךְ׃
your .splendor gave they in ;you they hung the and helmet the shield war ;you (to) men of

4026 1575 5439 2346 5921 2428 719 1121
11 בְּנֵי אַרְוַד וְחֵילֵךְ עַל־חוֹמוֹתַיִךְ סָבִיב וְגַמָּדִים בְּמִגְדְּלוֹתַיִךְ
your in towers and warriors all ,around walls your on your and (were) army Arvad The of sons

their weapons on your walls
all around; they have
perfected your beauty.
12 Tarshish *was* your trader,
from the multitude of *your*
wealth; with silver, iron, tin,
and lead, they gave for your
wares. 13 Javan, Tubal, and
Meshech, they *were* your
merchants; they gave the
souls of men and vessels of
bronze for your goods.
14 From the house of
Togarmah they gave horses
and war-horses and mules
for your wares. 15 The sons
of Dedan *were* your mer-
chants; many coast-lands
were the traffic of your
hand. Tusks of ivory and
ebony they brought as your
gift. 16 Syria *was* your trader,
from the multitude of your
works, with emeralds,
purple, and embroidered
work, and fine linen, and
coral, and rubies they gave
for your wares. 17 Judah
and the land of Israel *were*
your merchants; with wheat
from Minnith and Pannag,
and honey and oil and balm
they gave for your goods.
18 Damascus *was* your
trader in the multitude of
your works, from the multitude of all *your* wealth; in
the wine of Helbon, and
white wool. 19 And Dan and
Javan going about gave for
your wares; smooth iron,
cassia, and cane were
among your goods.
20 Dedan *was* your merchant
in loose cloths for riding.
21 Arabia and all the princes
of Kedar, they *were* traders
of your hand, in lambs and
rams and goats; in them
was your trade.
22 The merchants of
Sheba and Raamah *were*
your merchants; with the
chief of all the spices, and
with every precious stone,
and gold, they gave for your
wares. 23 Haran, and Can-
neh, and Eden; the mer-
chants of Sheba, Asshur,
Chilmad *were* your mer-
chants; 24 they *were* your
merchants in perfect things,
in violet cloth, and

3308 3634 5439 2346 5921 8518 7982 1961
הָיוּ שִׁלְטֵיהֶם תִּלּוּ עַל־חוֹמוֹתַיִךְ סָבִיב הֵמָּה כָּלְלוּ יָפְיֵךְ׃
your have they all walls your on They their .were
.beauty perfected ;around hung weapons

5777 913 1270 3701 1952 3605 7230 5503 8659
12 תַּרְשִׁישׁ סֹחַרְתֵּךְ מֵרֹב כָּל־הוֹן בְּכֶסֶף בַּרְזֶל בְּדִיל וְעוֹפֶרֶת
,lead and ,tin ,iron with (your) the from your Tarshish
,silver ;wealth of plenty trader (was)

120 5315 7402 4902 8422 3120 5801 5414
13 נָתְנוּ עִזְבוֹנָיִךְ׃ יָוָן תֻּבַל וָמֶשֶׁךְ הֵמָּה רֹכְלָיִךְ בְּנֶפֶשׁ אָדָם
men the your they and Tubal ,Javan your they
of souls ;merchants (were) Meshech .wares for gave

5483 8425 1004 4627 5414 5178 3627
14 וּכְלֵי נְחֹשֶׁת נָתְנוּ מַעֲרָבֵךְ׃ מִבֵּית תּוֹגַרְמָה סוּסִים
horses Togarmah the From your for they bronze and
of house .goods gave of vessels

339 7402 1719 1121 5801 5414 6505 6571
15 וּפָרָשִׁים וּפְרָדִים נָתְנוּ עִזְבוֹנָיִךְ׃ בְּנֵי דְדָן רֹכְלַיִךְ אִיִּים
coast- your Dedan The your they mules and war- and
lands merchants (were) of sons .wares for gave horses

814 7725 1894 8127 7161 3027 5506 7227
רַבִּים סְחֹרַת יָדֵךְ קַרְנוֹת שֵׁן וְהוֹבְנִים הֵשִׁיבוּ אֶשְׁכָּרֵךְ׃
your as they ebony and ivory Tusks your the many
.gift brought of .hand of traffic (were)

948 7553 713 5306 4639 7230 5503 758
16 אֲרָם סֹחַרְתֵּךְ מֵרֹב מַעֲשָׂיִךְ בְּנֹפֶךְ אַרְגָּמָן וְרִקְמָה וּבוּץ
fine and em- and purple with your the from your Syria
,linen ,work broidered ,jewels .works of plenty trader (was)

3478 776 3063 5801 5414 3539 7215
17 וְרָאמֹת וְכַדְכֹּד נָתְנוּ בְּעִזְבוֹנָיִךְ׃ יְהוּדָה וְאֶרֶץ יִשְׂרָאֵל
Israel the and Judah your for They and ,coral and
of land .wares gave rubies

5414 6875 8081 1706 6436 4511 2406 7402
הֵמָּה רֹכְלָיִךְ בְּחִטֵּי מִנִּית וּפַנַּג וּדְבַשׁ וָשֶׁמֶן וָצֹרִי נָתְנוּ
they and oil and and and (from) With your they
gave balm honey ,Pannag Minnith wheat .merchants (were)

1952 3605 7230 4639 7230 5503 1834 4627
18 מַעֲרָבֵךְ׃ דַּמֶּשֶׂק סֹחַרְתֵּךְ בְּרֹב מַעֲשַׂיִךְ מֵרֹב כָּל־הוֹן
(your) all the from your the in your Damascus your for
,wealth of plenty ,works of plenty trader (was) .goods

5414 5801 235 3120 2051 6713 6785 2465 3196
19 בְּיֵין חֶלְבּוֹן וְצֶמֶר צָחַר׃ וְדָן וְיָוָן מְאוּזָּל בְּעִזְבוֹנַיִךְ נָתָנוּ
;gave your for going and And .white and Helbon the in
wares about Javan Dan wool of wine

7402 1719 1961 4627 7070 6916 6219 1270
20 בַּרְזֶל עָשׁוֹת קִדָּה וְקָנֶה בְּמַעֲרָבֵךְ הָיָה׃ דְּדָן רֹכַלְתֵּךְ
your Dedan .were your among and ,cassia ,smooth iron
merchant (was) goods cane

5503 6938 5387 3605 6152 7396 2667 899
21 בְּבִגְדֵי־חֹפֶשׁ לְרִכְבָּה׃ עֲרַב וְכָל־נְשִׂיאֵי קֵדָר הֵמָּה סֹחֲרֵי
traders they ,Kedar the and ,Arabia .riding for loose in
of (were) of princes all cloths

7614 7402 5503 6260 352 3733 3027
22 יָדֵךְ בְּכָרִים וְאֵילִים וְעַתּוּדִים בָּם סֹחֲרָיִךְ׃ רֹכְלֵי שְׁבָא
Sheba The your (was) in ,goats and rams and lambs in your
of merchants .trade them .hand

3368 68 3605 1314 3605 7218 7402 7484
וְרַעְמָה הֵמָּה רֹכְלָיִךְ בְּרֹאשׁ כָּל־בֹּשֶׂם וּבְכָל־אֶבֶן יְקָרָה
precious stone with and the all the with your they and
every spices of chief ;merchants (were) ,Raamah

804 7614 7402 5729 3656 2771 5801 5414 2091
23 וְזָהָב נָתְנוּ עִזְבוֹנָיִךְ׃ חָרָן וְכַנֵּה וָעֶדֶן רֹכְלֵי שְׁבָא אַשּׁוּר
Asshur ,Sheba the and and ,Haran your for they and
of merchants Eden Canneh .wares gave ,gold

8504 1545 4360 7402 3638
24 כִּלְמַד רֹכַלְתֵּךְ׃ הֵמָּה רֹכְלַיִךְ בְמַכְלֻלִים בִּגְלוֹמֵי תְּכֵלֶת
violet cloth in perfect in your they your Chilmad
of ,things merchants (were) ;merchants (were)

embroidered work, and in carpets of many colors, with tightly bound cords, and cedars among your merchandise. 25The ships of Tarshish *were* the travelers of your goods. And you were filled and made very glorious in the heart of the seas. 26Your rowers made you come into great waters; the east wind has broken you in the heart of the seas. 27Your wealth and your wares, your goods, your seamen, and your pilots reinforcing your seams, and the traders of your goods, and all men of war to you, who *are* in you, and all your assembly which *is* in your midst, shall fall into the heart of the seas, in the day of your ruin. 28At the sound of your sailor's cry the pasture lands will shake. 29And all handling the oar will come out from their ships, the seamen, all the sailors of the sea; on the land they will stand 30and will make heard their voice against you and will cry bitterly, and will make go up dust on their heads; they will wallow in the ashes.

31And they will be bald for you and gird with sackcloth. And they will weep for you with bitterness of soul, a bitter wailing. 32And they will lift up for you a lament *in* their mourning and lament over you: Who is like Tyre as her quiet in the sea's midst? 33When your wares went out from the seas, you satisfied many peoples. With the plenty of your riches and your goods, you enriched the kings of the earth. 34At *this time* you are broken by the seas, in the depths of the waters; your goods and all your assembly in your midst have fallen. 35All the residents of the coasts are appalled at you; and their kings are

729 2280 2256 1264 1595 75:53
וְרִקְמָה וּבִגְנְזֵי בְּרֹמִים בַּחֲבָלִים חֲבֻשִׁים וַאֲרֻזִים
cedars and | tightly ,bound | cords with | ,colors many | in and of carpets | embroi- and work dered

4390 4627 7788 8659 591 4819
25 בְּמַרְכֻלְתֵּךְ׃ אֳנִיּוֹת תַּרְשִׁישׁ שָׁרוֹתַיִךְ מַעֲרָבֵךְ וַתִּמָּלְאִי
you And filled were | .goods your | the (were) of travelers | Tarshish | The of ships | your among .merchandise

7751 935 7227 4325 3220 3820 3966 3513
26 וַתִּכְבְּדִי מְאֹד בְּלֵב יַמִּים׃ בְּמַיִם רַבִּים הֱבִאוּךְ הַשָּׁטִים
rowers | brought have you | great | into waters | the .seas | the in of heart | very | made and glorious

5801 1952 3220 3820 7665 6921 7307
27 אֹתָךְ רוּחַ הַקָּדִים שְׁבָרֵךְ בְּלֵב יַמִּים׃ הוֹנֵךְ וְעִזְבוֹנַיִךְ
your and wares | Your wealth | the .seas | the in of heart | has you broken | east | the wind | ;Your

4627 6148 919 2388 2259 4419 4627
מַעֲרָבֵךְ מַלָּחַיִךְ וְחֹבְלָיִךְ מַחֲזִיקֵי בִדְקֵךְ וְעֹרְבֵי מַעֲרָבֵךְ
your goods | the and of traders | your ,seams | rein- forcing | your and sailors | your ,seamen | your ,goods

8432 6951 3605 834 4421 582 3605
וְכָל־אַנְשֵׁי מִלְחַמְתֵּךְ אֲשֶׁר־בָּךְ וּבְכָל־קְהָלֵךְ אֲשֶׁר בְּתוֹכֵךְ
your in ,midst | which (is) | your assembly | and all | in ,you | who (are) | war you to | men of | and all

2259 2201 6963 4658 3117 3220 3820 5307
28 יִפְּלוּ בְּלֵב יַמִּים בְּיוֹם מַפַּלְתֵּךְ׃ לְקוֹל זַעֲקַת חֹבְלָיִךְ
your sailors | the of cry | the at of sound | your .ruin | the in of day | the seas | the into of heart | shall fall

4880 8610 3605 591 3381 4054 7493
29 יִרְעֲשׁוּ מִגְרֹשׁוֹת׃ וְיָרְדוּ מֵאֳנִיּוֹתֵיהֶם כֹּל תֹּפְשֵׂי מָשׁוֹט
,oar the | who handle | all | their from ships | shall And come down | pasture The .lands | will shake

8085 5975 776 3220 2259 4419
30 מַלָּחִים כֹּל חֹבְלֵי הַיָּם אֶל־הָאָרֶץ יַעֲמֹדוּ׃ וְהִשְׁמִיעוּ עָלַיִךְ
against you | will and make heard | shall they stand | the land | on | the ;sea | the of sailors | all | the seamen

665 7218 5921 6083 5927 4751 2199 6963
בְּקוֹלָם וְיִזְעֲקוּ מָרָה וְיַעֲלוּ עָפָר עַל־רָאשֵׁיהֶם בָּאֵפֶר
the in ashes | their ;heads | on | dust | shall and make go up | bitterly | shall and cry | their ,voice

1058 8242 2296 7142 7139 6428
31 יִתְפַּלָּשׁוּ׃ וְהִקְרִיחוּ אֵלַיִךְ קָרְחָה וְחָגְרוּ שַׂקִּים וּבָכוּ אֵלַיִךְ
for they and you weep shall | with ;sackcloth | and | bald | ,you for be the And smooth be shall | shall they .wallow

6969 7015 5704 5375 4751 4553 5315 4751
32 בְּמַר־נֶפֶשׁ מִסְפֵּד מָר׃ וְנָשְׂאוּ אֵלַיִךְ בְּנִיהֶם קִינָה וְקוֹנְנוּ
and lament | a lament | their (in) mourning | for you | they And up take shall | .bitter | a (with) wailing | soul | with of bitterness

3220 5801 3318 3220 8432 1822 6865 4310 5921
33 עָלַיִךְ מִי כְצוֹר כְּדֻמָה בְּתוֹךְ הַיָּם׃ בְּצֵאת עִזְבוֹנַיִךְ מִיַּמִּים
from ,seas the | your wares | went When out | the ?sea | the in of midst | her as quiet is who | like ,Tyre (is) | Who | over :you

4428 6238 4627 1952 7230 7227 5971 7646
הִשְׂבַּעַתְּ עַמִּים רַבִּים בְּרֹב הוֹנַיִךְ וּמַעֲרָבַיִךְ הֶעֱשַׁרְתְּ מַלְכֵי־
kings the of | you enriched | your and ;goods | your the riches | With of plenty | .many peoples | you satisfied

3605 4627 4325 4615 3220 7665 6256 776
34 אָרֶץ׃ עֵת נִשְׁבֶּרֶת מִיַּמִּים בְּמַעֲמַקֵּי־מָיִם מַעֲרָבֵךְ וְכָל־
all and | your goods | the ;waters | the by of depths | the from ,seas | are you broken | At (time this) | the .earth

8074 339 3427 3605 5307 8432 6951
35 קְהָלֵךְ בְּתוֹכֵךְ נָפָלוּ׃ כֹּל יֹשְׁבֵי הָאִיִּים שָׁמְמוּ עָלַיִךְ
,you at | are appalled | the coasts | resi- the of dents | All | have .fallen | your in midst | your assembly

horribly terrified; *their* faces tremble. [36]The traders among the peoples hiss over you; you have become terrors. And you shall not be forever.

CHAPTER 28

[1]And the word of Jehovah *came* to me, saying, [2]Son of man, say to the ruler of Tyre, So says the Lord Jehovah, Because your heart is lifted up, and you have said, I *am* a god; I sit in the seat of gods, in the heart of the seas—yet you *are* a man, and not God, though you give your heart as the heart of gods—[3]Behold, you *are* wiser than Daniel; every *one of the* secret *things* are not hidden *to* you. [4]With your wisdom and with your understanding you have made riches for yourself, and have worked gold and silver into your treasuries. [5]By your great wisdom, by your trade you have multiplied your riches, and your heart is lifted up because of your riches. [6]So the Lord Jehovah says this: Because you have given your heart as the heart of gods, [7]therefore, behold, I will cause to come on you awesome strangers *of* the nations. And they shall draw their swords against the beauty of your wisdom, and will profane your splendor. [8]They shall cause you to go down to the Pit, and you shall die the deaths of the slain in the heart of the seas. [9]Will you still say, I *am of the* gods, before him who strikes you? But you *are* a man, and not God, in the hands of him who pierces you. [10]You shall die the deaths of the uncircumcised, by the hand of strangers. For I have spoken, says the Lord Jehovah.

[11]And the word of Jehovah was to me, saying, [12]Son of man, lift up a lament over the king of Tyre, and say to him, So

---

8319 5971 5503 6440 7481 8175 8178 4428

36 וּמַלְכֵיהֶם שָׂעֲרוּ שַׂעַר רָעֲמוּ פָּנִים׃ סֹחֲרִים בָּעַמִּים שָׁרְקוּ

hiss the among peoples The traders (their) faces tremble ;horribly are terrified their and kings

5769 5704 369 1961 1091 5921

עָלַיִךְ בַּלָּהוֹת הָיִית וְאֵינֵךְ עַד־עוֹלָם׃

.forever you And be not shall have you .become terrors over ;you

CAP. XXVIII כח

CHAPTER 28

3541 6865 5057 559 120/1121 559 3068 1697 1961

1 וַיְהִי דְבַר־יְהוָה אֵלַי לֵאמֹר׃
2 בֶּן־אָדָם אֱמֹר לִנְגִיד צֹר כֹּה

Thus ,Tyre the to of ruler say ,man Son of ,saying ,me to Jehovah the of word And was

4186 410 559 3820 1361 3282 3068 136 559

אָמַר ׀ אֲדֹנָי יֱהוִה יַעַן גָּבַהּ לִבְּךָ וַתֹּאמֶר אֵל אָנִי מוֹשַׁב

the in of seat I ,(am) a god you and ,said have your heart is Because lifted up :Jehovah the Lord says

3820 5414 410 3808 120 3220 3820 430

אֱלֹהִים יָשַׁבְתִּי בְּלֵב יַמִּים וְאַתָּה אָדָם וְלֹא־אֵל וַתִּתֵּן לִבְּךָ

your heart though you give ,God and not a (are) man you yet the —seas the in of heart sit I gods

3808 5640 1840 2450 2009 430 3820

3 כְּלֵב אֱלֹהִים׃ הִנֵּה חָכָם אַתָּה מִדָּנִאֵל כָּל־סָתוּם לֹא

not secret (things) every (of one) than ;Daniel you (are) wiser ,Behold —gods the as of heart

2091 6213 2428 6213 8394 2451 6004

4 עֲמָמוּךָ׃ בְּחָכְמָתְךָ וּבִתְבוּנָתְךָ עָשִׂיתָ לְּךָ חַיִל וַתַּעַשׂ זָהָב

gold have and worked ,riches for yourself have you made your with and understanding your With wisdom hidden are .you (to)

2428 7235 7404 2451 7230 214 3701

5 וָכֶסֶף בְּאוֹצְרוֹתֶיךָ׃ בְּרֹב חָכְמָתְךָ בִּרְכֻלָּתְךָ הִרְבִּיתָ חֵילֶךָ

your ,riches have you multiplied your by trade your ,wisdom By great your .treasuries into and silver

3068 136 559 3541 3651 2428 3824 1361

6 וַיִּגְבַּהּ לְבָבְךָ בְּחֵילֶךָ׃ לָכֵן כֹּה אָמַר אֲדֹנָי יֱהוִה

:Jehovah the Lord says thus Therefore of because —riches your your heart is and up lifted

935 2005 3651 430 3820 3824 5414 3282

7 יַעַן תִּתְּךָ אֶת־לְבָבְךָ כְּלֵב אֱלֹהִים׃ לָכֵן הִנְנִי מֵבִיא עָלֶיךָ

on you will bring behold I ,therefore ,gods the as of heart your heart have you given Be- cause

2490 2451 3308 5921 2719 7324 1471 6184 2114

זָרִים עָרִיצֵי גּוֹיִם וְהֵרִיקוּ חַרְבוֹתָם עַל־יְפִי חָכְמָתֶךָ וְחִלְּלוּ

will and profane your ,wisdom the against of beauty their swords they And draw shall the .nations awe- some strangers

3220 3820 2491 4463 4191 3381 7845 3314

8 יִפְעָתֶךָ׃ לַשַּׁחַת יוֹרִדוּךָ וָמַתָּה מְמוֹתֵי חָלָל בְּלֵב יַמִּים׃

the .seas the in of heart the slain the of deaths you and die shall They shall ,you bring the to Pit your .splendor

3808 120 2026 6440 430 559 559

9 הֶאָמֹר תֹּאמַר אֱלֹהִים אָנִי לִפְנֵי הֹרְגֶךָ וְאַתָּה אָדָם וְלֹא־

and not man a (are) But you who him ?you kills before I ,(am) gods ,say you Will still

2114 4191 6189 4194 2490 3027 410

10 אֵל בְּיַד מְחַלְלֶךָ׃ מוֹתֵי עֲרֵלִים תָּמוּת בְּיַד־זָרִים כִּי אֲנִי

I For strangers' hand by shall You die uncir- cumcised the of deaths the who him .you kills the in of hand God

3068 1697 1961 3068 136 5002 1696

11 וַיְהִי דְבַר־יְהוָה אֵלַי׃ דִּבַּרְתִּי נְאֻם אֲדֹנָי יֱהוִה׃

to ,me Jehovah the of word And was .Jehovah the Lord says have ,spoken

3541 559 6865 4428 5921 7015 5375 120 1121 559

12 לֵאמֹר׃ בֶּן־אָדָם שָׂא קִינָה עַל־מֶלֶךְ צוֹר וְאָמַרְתָּ לּוֹ כֹּה

Thus to ,him say and Tyre the of king over a lament up lift ,man Son of ,saying says the Lord Jehovah: You seal the measure, full of wisdom and perfect in beauty. 13You have been in Eden the garden of God; every precious stone *was* your covering, the ruby, the topaz, and the diamond, the beryl, the onyx, and the jasper; the sapphire, the turquoise, and the emerald, and gold. The workmanship of your tabrets and of your pipes in you—in the day you were created, they were prepared. 14You *were* the anointed cherub that covers, and I had put you in the holy height of God, *where* you were. You walked up and down in the midst of the stones of fire. 15You were perfect in your ways from the day you were created, until iniquity was found in you. 16By the multitude of your trade they filled your midst *with* violence, and you sinned. So I cast you profaned from the height of God, and I destroyed you, O covering cherub, from among the stones of fire. 17Your heart was lifted up because of your beauty; you corrupted your wisdom because of your splendor. I have cast you to the ground. I will put you before kings, that they may see you. 18By the host of your iniquities, by the iniquity of your trade, you have profaned your holy places; thus I brought a fire from your midst; it shall devour you, and I will give you for ashes on the earth, in the sight of all who see you. 19All who know you among the peoples shall be appalled at you; you shall be terrors, and you will not be forever.

20And the word of Jehovah was to me, saying, 21Son of man, set your face against Sidon and prophesy against her. 22And say, So says the Lord Jehovah, Behold, I *am* against you, O Sidon, and I will be glorified in your midst. And they shall know that I *am* Jehovah, when I have done judgments in her, and shall be sanctified by her. 23And I will send a

3632 2451 4393 8508 2856 3068 136 559
אמר אדני יהוה אתה חותם תכנית מלא חכמה וכליל
and wisdom full the seal You :Jehovah the says
in perfect of ,measure Lord

124 45 40 3368 68 3605 1961 430 1508 5731 3308
13 יפי׃ בעדן גן־אלהים היית כל־אבן יקרה מסכתך אדם
the your precious stone every have You God the Eden in .beauty
,ruby ,covering (was) ;been of garden

1304 5306 5601 3471 7718 8658 3095 6357
פטדה ויהלם תרשיש שהם וישפה ספיר נפך וברקת
the and tur- the the the and the the the and the
emerald ,quoise ,sapphire ,jaspers onyx ,beryl ,diamond ,topaz

3559 1254 3117 53 45 8596 4399 2091
וזהב מלאכת תפיך ונקביך בך ביום הבראך כוננו׃
were they were you the in in of and your work- The and
.prepared created day —you pipes your tabrets of manship .gold

1961 430 6944/2022 5414 5526 4473 3742
14 את־כרוב ממשח הסוכך ונתתיך בהר קדש אלהים היית
(where) God holy the in I and that anointed the You
.were you of height you put had ,covers cherub (were)

3117 1870 8549 1980 784 68 8432
15 בתוך אבני־אש התהלכת׃ תמים אתה בדרכיך מיום
the from your in You were walked You fire the the in
day ways perfect .down and up of stones of midst

8432 4390 7404 7230 5766 4672 5704 1254
16 הבראך עד־נמצא עולתה בך׃ ברב רכלתך מלו תוכך
your they your the By in iniquity was until were you
midst filled trade of plenty .you found ,created

5526 3742 6 430 2022 2490 2398 2555
חמס ותחטא ואחללך מהר אלהים ואבדך כרוב הסוכך
,covering O I and ,God the from cast I So you and (with)
cherub ,you destroyed of height profaned you .sinned ,violence

5921 2451 7843 3308 38 20 1361 784 68 8432
17 מתוך אבני־אש׃ גבה לבך ביפיך שחת חכמתך על־
because your cor- you your for Your was .fire the from
of wisdom rupted ;beauty heart up lifted of stones among

7200 5414 4428 6440 79 93 776 3314
יפעתך על־ארץ השלכתיך לפני מלכים נתתיך לראוה
they that will I kings before have I the to your
see may ,you put .you cast ground .splendor

3318 4720 2490 74 04 57 66 57 71 7230
18 בך׃ מרב עוניך בעול רכלתך חללת מקדשיך ואוצא־
I thus holy your have you your the by your the By .you
brought ;places profaned ,trade of iniquity ,iniquities of host

5869 776 59 21 665 5414 398 8432 784
אש מתוכך היא אכלתך ואתנך לאפר על־הארץ לעיני
the in the on for will I and shall it your from a
of sight earth ashes you give ,you devour ;midst fire

1961 1091 8074 5971 3045 3605 7200 3605
19 כל־ראיך׃ כל־יודעיך בעמים שממו עליך בלהות היית
shall you terrors at be shall the among who All see who all
,be ;you appalled peoples you know .you

559 3068 1697 1961 5769/5704 369
20 ואינך עד־עולם׃ ויהי דבר־יהוה אלי לאמר׃
,saying ,me to Jehovah the And .forever you and
of word was be will not

3541 559 5012 6721 6440 7760 120 1121
21
22 בן־אדם שים פניך אל־צידון והנבא עליה׃ ואמרת כה
Thus ,say And against and Sidon against your set ,man Son
.her prophesy face of

3045 8432 3513 6721 2005 3068 136 559
אמר אדני יהוה הנני עליך צידון ונכבדתי בתוכך וידעו
they And your in will I and O against ,Behold :Jehovah the says
know shall .midst glorified be ,Sidon ,you (am) I Lord

7971 6942 8201 6213 3068
23 כי־אני יהוה בעשותי בה שפטים ונקדשתי בה׃ ושלחתי־
will I And by be shall and judgments in I when ,Jehovah I that
send .her sanctified her done have (am)

plague into her, and blood into her streets. And the slain will fall in her midst by the sword, on her from all around. And they shall know that I *am* Jehovah.

[24]And there will not be a pricking brier or a painful thorn to the house of Israel any more, from all who surround them, who hate them. And they shall know that I *am* the Lord Jehovah. [25]So says the Lord Jehovah: When I have gathered the house of Israel from the peoples of whom they are dispersed among them, and have been sanctified in them in the sight of the nations, then they shall dwell on their land which I have given to My servant Jacob. [26]And they shall dwell in it securely, and shall build houses and plant vineyards. Yes, they shall dwell securely, when I have done judgments on all those who hate them round about them. And they shall know that I *am* Jehovah their God.

2719 8432 2491 5307 2351 1818 1698
בה דבר ודם בחוצותיה ונפלל חלל בתוכה בחרב
the by sword | her in midst | the slain | will And fall | her into .streets | and blood | a ,plague | into her

24 1004 5750 1961/3808 3068 3045 5439
עליה מסביב וידעו כי־אני יהוה׃ ולא־יהיה עוד לבית
the to of house | any more | will And be not | .Jehovah | I that (am) | they And know shall | all from .around | on her

7590 54:39 3605 3510 6975 3992 5544 3478
ישראל סלון ממאיר וקוץ מכאב מכל סביבתם השאטים
hate who | surround who ,them | from all | painful | a or thorn | pricking | brier a | Israel

25 136 559 3068 136 3045
אותם וידעו כי אני אדני יהוה׃ כה־אמר אדני
the Lord | says | Thus | .Jehovah | the Lord | I (am) | that they And know shall | .them

63.27 834 5971 34.78 1004 6908 3068
יהוה בקבצי ׀ את־בית ישראל מן־העמים אשר נפצו
are they dispersed | of whom | the peoples | from | Israel | the of house | have I When gathered | Jeho- :vah

834 127 3427 1471 5869 6942
בם ונקדשתי בם לעיני הגוים וישבו על־אדמתם אשר
which | their land | on | they then dwell shall | the ,nations | the in of sight | in them | have and sanctified been | among ,them

26 1004 1129 982 3427 3290 5650 5414
נתתי לעבדי ליעקב׃ וישבו עליה לבטח ובנו בתים
houses | shall and build | securely | it in | they And dwell shall | .Jacob | My to servant | have I given

7590 36.05 82.01 62.13 982 3427 37.54 5193
ונטעו כרמים וישבו לבטח בעשותי שפטים בכל השאטים
who those hate | on all | judgments | I when have done | securely | they ,Yes dwell shall | .vineyards | and plant

430 3068 3045 5439
אתם מסביבתם וידעו כי אני יהוה אלהיהם׃
their .God | Jehovah | I (am) | that they And know shall | about round | them

CAP. XXIX כט

CHAPTER 29

CHAPTER 29

[1]In the tenth year, in the tenth *month*, in the twelfth of the month, the word of Jehovah was to me, saying, [2]Son of man, set your face against Pharaoh king of Egypt, and prophesy against him and against Egypt, all of it. [3]Speak and say, So says the Lord Jehovah: Behold, I *am* against you, Pharaoh king of Egypt, great monster who lies in the midst of his rivers, who has said, My river *is* mine, and I have made it. [4]But I will put hooks in your jaws, and I will cause to stick to your scales the fish of your rivers; and I will bring you up from amidst your rivers, and all the fish of your

1 1697 1961 2320 6240 6240 2320 6224 8141
בשנה העשירית בעשרי בשנים עשר לחדש היה דבר־
the of word | was | the of ,month | (day) | the in twelfth | the in ,(month) | ,tenth the tenth | year In

2 4428 6547 6440 7760 120 1121 559 3068
יהוה אלי לאמר׃ בן־אדם שים פניך על־פרעה מלך
king of | Pharaoh against | your face | set | ,man | Son of | ,saying | to ,me | Jehovah

3 559 1696 3605 4714 5012 4714
מצרים והנבא עליו ועל־מצרים כלה׃ דבר ואמרת
,say and | Speak | .it of all | ,Egypt | and against | him | and prophesy | ,Egypt

4714 44.28 6547 2005 30.68 136 559
כה־אמר ׀ אדני יהוה הנני עליך פרעה מלך־מצרים
,Egypt | king of | Pharaoh | against ,you | ,Behold (am) I | :Jehovah | the Lord | says | Thus

2975 559 834 2975 8432 7257 1419 8577
התנים הגדול הרבץ בתוך יאריו אשר אמר לי יארי
My river | mine (is) | has ,said | who | his ,rivers | the in of midst | who lies | great | monster

4 1710 1692 3895 2 397 5414 6213
ואני עשיתני׃ ונתתי חחים בלחייך והדבקתי דגת־
the of fish | will I and stick to cause | your in ,jaws | hooks | I But put will | made have .it | and I

3605 2975 8432 5927 7193 2975
יאריך בקשקשתיך והעליתיך מתוך יאריך ואת כל־
all | and | your ,rivers | from amidst | will I and up you bring | your to ,scales | your rivers

rivers shall stick to your scales. [5]And I will leave you to the wilderness, you and all the fish of your rivers; you shall fall on the open field; you shall not be removed or gathered. I have given you to the beasts of the field and to the birds of the heavens for food. [6]And all the inhabitants of Egypt shall know that I *am* Jehovah, because they have been a staff of reed to the house of Israel. [7]When they seized you by your hand, you broke and tore off all their shoulder. And when they leaned on you, you shattered and made all their loins stand.

[8]So the Lord Jehovah says this: Behold, I will bring on you a sword and cut off from you man and beast. [9]And the land of Egypt shall become for a desolation and a waste; and they shall know that I *am* Jehovah, because he has said, The River is mine, and I have made it. [10]So, behold, I *am* against you and against your rivers; and I will give the land of Egypt for an utter waste *and* a desolation, from Migdol *to* Syene, even to the border of Ethiopia. [11]The foot of man shall not pass through it; and the foot of beast shall not pass through it; and you shall not dwell forty years. [12]And I will make the land of Egypt a desolation in the midst of the lands that are desolate; and her cities shall be desolate among the wasted cities forty years. And I will disperse Egypt among the nations, and sow them among the lands.

[13]For so says the Lord Jehovah: At the end of forty years I will gather Egypt

4057 5203 1692 7193 2975 1710
5 דְּגַת יְאֹרֶיךָ בְּקַשְׂקְשֹׂתֶיךָ תִּדְבָּק׃ וּנְטַשְׁתִּיךָ הַמִּדְבָּרָה
the will I And .stick shall your to your the
,wilderness (to) you leave scales rivers of fish

3808 5307 7704 6440 2975 1710 3605
אוֹתְךָ וְאֵת כָּל־דְּגַת יְאֹרֶיךָ עַל־פְּנֵי הַשָּׂדֶה תִּפּוֹל לֹא
not shall you field the on your the all and you
.fall open ;rivers of fish

5414 8064 5775 776 2416 6908 3808 622
תֵאָסֵף וְלֹא תִקָּבֵץ לְחַיַּת הָאָרֶץ וּלְעוֹף הַשָּׁמַיִם נְתַתִּיךָ
have I the the to and the the to .gathered or shall You
you given heavens of birds field of beasts removed be

1961 3282 3068 4714 3427 3605 3045 402
6 לְאָכְלָה׃ וְיָדְעוּ כָּל־יֹשְׁבֵי מִצְרַיִם כִּי אֲנִי יְהוָה יַעַן הֱיוֹתָם
have they be- ,Jehovah I that Egypt the all shall And for
been cause (am) of dwellers know .food

7533 3709 8610 3478 1004 7070 4938
7 מִשְׁעֶנֶת קָנֶה לְבֵית יִשְׂרָאֵל׃ בְּתָפְשָׂם בְּךָ בַכַּפְּךָ תֵּרוֹץ
you your by you they When .Israel the to reed staff a
broke ,palm seized of house of

5975 7665 8172 3801 3605 1234
וּבָקַעְתָּ לָהֶם כָּל־כָּתֵף וּבְהִשָּׁעֲנָם עָלֶיךָ תִּשָּׁבֵר וְהַעֲמַדְתָּ
made and shat- you on they when And the all to tore and
stand tered ,you leaned .shoulder them off

2009 3068 136 559 4975 3605
8 לָהֶם כָּל־מָתְנָיִם׃ לָכֵן כֹּה אָמַר אֲדֹנָי יְהוִה הִנְנִי
,Behold :Jehovah the says thus Therefore .loins the all to
I Lord them

1961 929 120 3772 2719 935
9 מֵבִיא עָלַיִךְ חֶרֶב וְהִכְרַתִּי מִמֵּךְ אָדָם וּבְהֵמָה׃ וְהָיְתָה
shall And and man from cut and sword a on will
become .beast you off you bring

3282 3068 3045 2721 8077 4714 776
אֶרֶץ־מִצְרַיִם לִשְׁמָמָה וְחָרְבָּה וְיָדְעוּ כִּי־אֲנִי יְהוָה יַעַן
be- ,Jehovah I that they and a and a for Egypt the
cause (am) know shall ;waste desolation of land

2975 2005 6213 2975 559
10 אָמַר יְאֹר לִי וַאֲנִי עֲשִׂיתִי׃ לָכֵן הִנְנִי אֵלֶיךָ וְאֶל־יְאֹרֶיךָ
your and against ,Behold There- made have and mine The has he
,rivers against you (am) I ,fore .(it) I (is) River ,said

4024 8077 2723 2723 4714 776 5414
וְנָתַתִּי אֶת־אֶרֶץ מִצְרַיִם לְחָרְבוֹת חֹרֶב שְׁמָמָה מִמִּגְדֹּל
from a (and) utter an for Egypt the I and
Migdol ,desolation waste of land give will

7272 120 7272 5674 3808 3568 1366 5704 5482
11 סְוֵנֵה וְעַד־גְּבוּל כּוּשׁ׃ לֹא תַעֲבָר־בָּהּ רֶגֶל אָדָם וְרֶגֶל
the and ;man the it pass shall Not .Ethiopia the even (to)
of foot of foot through of border to ,Syene

5414 8141 705 3427 3808 5674 3808 929
12 בְּהֵמָה לֹא תַעֲבָר־בָּהּ וְלֹא תֵשֵׁב אַרְבָּעִים שָׁנָה׃ וְנָתַתִּי
I And .years forty shall you and ;it pass shall not beast
make will dwell not through

5892 8074 776 8432 8077 4714 776
אֶת־אֶרֶץ מִצְרַיִם שְׁמָמָה בְּתוֹךְ אֲרָצוֹת נְשַׁמּוֹת וְעָרֶיהָ
her and are that the the in a Egypt the
cities ;desolate lands of midst desolation of land

6327 8141 705 8077 1961 2717 5892 8432
בְּתוֹךְ עָרִים מָחֳרָבוֹת תִּהְיֶיןָ שְׁמָמָה אַרְבָּעִים שָׁנָה וַהֲפִצֹתִי
will I And .years forty desolate be shall wasted the among
disperse cities

559 776 2219 1471 4714
13 אֶת־מִצְרַיִם בַּגּוֹיִם וְזֵרִיתִים בָּאֲרָצוֹת׃ כִּי כֹה אָמַר
says so For the among sow and the among Egypt
.lads them nations

4714 6908 8141 705 7093 3068 136
אֲדֹנָי יְהוִה מִקֵּץ אַרְבָּעִים שָׁנָה אֲקַבֵּץ אֶת־מִצְרַיִם מִן
from Egypt will I years forty the At :Jehovah the
gather of end Lord

from the peoples where they are scattered there. [14]And I will return the captivity of Egypt and will make them return *to* the land of Pathros, to the land of their origin. And they shall be a lowly kingdom there. [15]It shall be the lowest of the kingdoms, and shall not lift itself any more above the nations. And I will diminish them so that they will not rule over the nations. [16]And it shall not be any more as confidence for the house of Israel, recalling the iniquity of their turning after them. And they shall know that I *am* the Lord Jehovah.

[17]And it came about, in the twenty-seventh year, in the first *month*, in the first of the month, the word of Jehovah was to me, saying, [18]Son of man, Nebuchadnezzar king of Babylon made his army to serve a great service against Tyre. Every head was made bald, and every shoulder was rubbed bare. Yet there was no hire to him or to his army from Tyre, for the service that he had served against it. [19]Therefore, so says the Lord Jehovah: Behold, I will give to Nebuchadnezzar king of Babylon the land of Egypt. And he shall carry her host and spoil her spoil, and seize her plunder. And it shall be hire for his army. [20]For his labor which he served against it, I have given him the land of Egypt, because they worked for Me, declares the Lord Jehovah.

[21]In that day I will make a horn bud to the house of Israel, and I will give to you the opening of the mouth in their midst. And they shall know that I *am* Jehovah.

4714 7621 7725 8033 6327 834 5971
14 הָעַמִּים אֲשֶׁר־נָפֹצוּ שָׁמָּה׃ וְשַׁבְתִּי אֶת־שְׁבוּת מִצְרַיִם
,Egypt the will I And .there were they where the
of captivity return scattered peoples

8033 1961 4351 776 6624 776 7725
וַהֲשִׁבֹתִי אֹתָם אֶרֶץ פַּתְרוֹס עַל־אֶרֶץ מְכוּרָתָם וְהָיוּ שָׁם
there they And their the to ,Pathros the (to) them will and
be shall .origin of land of land return make

3808 8217 1961 4467 8217 4467
15 מַמְלָכָה שְׁפָלָה׃ מִן־הַמַּמְלָכוֹת תִּהְיֶה שְׁפָלָה וְלֹא־
and the shall It the of .lowly a
not lowest be kingdoms kingdom

1471 7287 1115 4591 1471 5750 5375
תִתְנַשֵּׂא עוֹד עַל־הַגּוֹיִם וְהִמְעַטְתִּים לְבִלְתִּי רְדוֹת בַּגּוֹיִם׃
the over will they that so will I And the above any lift shall
.nations rule not them lessen nations more itself

6437 5771 2142 4009 3478 1004 5750 1961 3808
16 וְלֹא יִהְיֶה־עוֹד לְבֵית יִשְׂרָאֵל לְמִבְטָח מַזְכִּיר עָוֺן בִּפְנוֹתָם
turning their the recalling as Israel the for any shall it And
, of iniquity ,confidence of house more be not

6242 1961 3068 136 3045 310
17 אַחֲרֵיהֶם וְיָדְעוּ כִּי אֲנִי אֲדֹנָי יֱהוִה׃ וַיְהִי בְּעֶשְׂרִים
the in it And .Jehovah the I that they And after
twenty- ,was Lord (am) know shall .them

3068 1697 1961 2320 259 7223 8141 7651
וָשֶׁבַע שָׁנָה בָּרִאשׁוֹן בְּאֶחָד לַחֹדֶשׁ הָיָה דְבַר־יְהוָה אֵלַי
to Jehovah the was the of the in the in ,year seventh
,me of word ,month first ,(month) first

2428 5656 884 4428 5019 120 1121 559
18 לֵאמֹר׃ בֶּן־אָדָם נְבוּכַדְרֶאצַּר מֶלֶךְ־בָּבֶל הֶעֱבִיד אֶת־חֵילוֹ
his caused Babylon king Nebuchadnezzar ,man Son ,saying
army serve to of of

4803 3801 3605 7139 7218 3605 6865 1419 5656
עֲבֹדָה גְדוֹלָה אֶל־צֹר כָּל־רֹאשׁ מֻקְרָח וְכָל־כָּתֵף מְרוּטָה
rubbed was shoulder and was head Every .Tyre against great a
.bare every ,bald made service

5647 834 5647 6865 2428 1961 3808 7939
וְשָׂכָר לֹא־הָיָה לוֹ וּלְחֵילוֹ מִצֹּר עַל־הָעֲבֹדָה אֲשֶׁר־עָבַד
had he that the for from to or to there not Yet
served service ,Tyre army his him was wages

5019 5414 2005 3068 136 559
19 עָלֶיהָ׃ לָכֵן כֹּה אָמַר אֲדֹנָי יֱהוִה הִנְנִי נֹתֵן לִנְבוּכַדְרֶאצַּר
Nebuchadnezzar to will ,Behold Jeho- the says thus Therefore against
give I :vah Lord .it

7997 7997 1995 5375 4714 776 884 4428
מֶלֶךְ־בָּבֶל אֶת־אֶרֶץ מִצְרָיִם וְנָשָׂא הֲמֹנָהּ וְשָׁלַל שְׁלָלָהּ
her and her he And .Egypt the Babylon king
,spoil spoil host carry shall of land of

5414 5649 834 6468 2428 7939 1961 957 962
20 וּבָזַז בִּזָּהּ וְהָיְתָה שָׂכָר לְחֵילוֹ׃ פְּעֻלָּתוֹ אֲשֶׁר־עָבַד בָּהּ נָתַתִּי
have I against he which his For his for wages it And plun- her and
given ,it served labor .army be shall .der seize

3117 3068 136 5002 6213 834 4714 776
לוֹ אֶת־אֶרֶץ מִצְרָיִם אֲשֶׁר עָשׂוּ לִי נְאֻם אֲדֹנָי יֱהוִה׃ בַּיּוֹם
In .Jehovah the states for they because ,Egypt the him
day Lord ,Me worked of land

6310 6610 5414 3478 1004 7161 6779
21 הַהוּא אַצְמִיחַ קֶרֶן לְבֵית יִשְׂרָאֵל וּלְךָ אֶתֵּן פִּתְחוֹן־פֶּה
the the will I to and ,Israel the to horn a will I that
mouth of opening give you of house bud make

3068 3045 8432
בְּתוֹכָם וְיָדְעוּ כִּי־אֲנִי יְהוָה׃
.Jehovah I that they And their in
(am) know shall .midst

CAP. XXX ל

CHAPTER 30

CHAPTER 30

¹And the word of Jehovah was to me, saying, ²Son of man, prophesy and say, So says the Lord Jehovah: Howl, Alas for the day! ³For the day *is* near, even the day of Jehovah *is* near, a day of clouds; it shall be the time of the nations. ⁴And the sword shall come on Egypt, and anguish shall be in Ethiopia, when the slain shall fall in Egypt, and they shall take her host; and her foundations shall be razed. ⁵Ethiopia, and Lydia, and Lud, and all the mixed people; and Chub, and the sons of the land of the covenant with them, shall fall by the sword.

⁶So says Jehovah: Even those leaning on Egypt shall fall, and the pride of her power shall go down. From Migdol to Syene they shall fall with her by the sword, declares the Lord Jehovah. ⁷And they will be ruined amidst the wasted lands; and her cities shall be in the midst of the desolated cities. ⁸And they shall know that I *am* Jehovah, when I set a fire in Egypt, and all her helpers shall be crushed. ⁹In that day messengers shall go out from before Me in ships, to terrify the confident Ethiopia, and anguish shall be on them, as in the day of Egypt; for behold it is coming.

¹⁰So says the Lord Jehovah: I will make the multitude of Egypt cease by the hand of Nebuchadnezzar king of Babylon. ¹¹He and his people with him, awesome of the nations, shall be brought to corrupt the land. And they shall draw their swords against Egypt and fill the lands *with* the slain. ¹²And I will make the rivers dry, and sell the land into the

---

1
3541	559		5012	120	1121		559		3068	1697	1961
Thus	say and	prophesy	,man	Son of		,saying		to Jehovah	the	And
				me					of word	was

2

3
7138	3117	7138		3117	1929	32 13	3068	136	559
(is) even the	(is)	For	the	Alas	,Howl	:Jehovah	the	says
near	,day	near					Lord	

4
4714	2719	935	1961	1471	6256	6051	3117	3068	3117
,Egypt on	the	shall And	shall it	the	the	the ;clouds a	of	the
	sword	come		.be	nations	of time	of day	Jehovah	day

1995	3947	4714		2491	5307	3:56:8	12479	1961
her	they and	,Egypt in	the	when	in	anguish	shall and
;host	take shall		slain	fall shall	,Ethiopia		be

5
1121	3552	6153	3605	3865	3865	3568	3247	2040
the and	and mixed the	and	and	and ,Ethiopia	foun- her	shall and
of sons	,Chub	,people	all	,Lud	,Lydia		dations	razed be

6
3068	559		5307	2719	1285	776
:Jehovah	says	Thus	shall	the by	with	the	the
			.fall	sword	them covenant	of land

2719	54,82	4024	5997	1347	3381	47:14	5564	5307
the by	to	Migdol	From	her	the	go and	,Egypt	those shall Even
sword	Syene			.power	of pride	down		on leaning	fall

7
8074	776	8432		3068	136	5307
the	lands	amidst	they And	.Jehovah	the	states with	they
,wasted			ruined be will	Lord		,her fall shall

8
3068	3045	1961	2717	5892	8432	5892
,Jehovah	I that	they And	.be shall	the	cities	the in	her and
(am)	know shall			desolated		of midst	cities

9
3117	5826	36 05	7665	47:14	784	5414
that	day	In	her	all	shall and	-	,Egypt in	a	I when
			.helpers		crushed be			fire	set

983	3568	2729	67:16	644 10	4397	33:18
con-	the	terrify to	in	before from	messengers go shall
fident	Ethiopia		ships	Me	out

935	1961
935		4714	3117		24:79	1961
is it	,behold	for	;Egypt	in as	on	anguish	shall and
.coming				of day the	,them		be

10
3027	4714	1995	7673	3068	136	559
by	Egypt	multi- the	will I	:Jehovah	the	says	Thus
hand		of tude	cease make		Lord	

11
1471	6184	5971	884	4428	5019
the	awe-	with	his and	He	.Babylon king	Nebuchadnezzar's
,nations	of some	,him	people			of

4714	2719	7324	776	7843	935
Egypt	against	their	they And	the	corrupt to	be shall
	swords		draw shall	.land		brought

12
4376	2724	2975	6213	2491	776	43190
sell and	dry	the	I And	(with)	the	fill and
	,land	rivers	make will	.slain the	land	

hand of evil ones. And I will waste the land, and her fullness, by the hand of strangers. I Jehovah have spoken.

¹³So says the Lord Jehovah: I will also destroy the idols, and I will make vanities cease from Noph. And there shall not any longer be a prince of the land of Egypt. And I will put fear in the land of Egypt. ¹⁴And I will make Pathros desolate, and will set a fire in Zoan, and will do judgments in Thebes. ¹⁵And I will pour my fury on Sin, the strength of Egypt. And I will cut off the multitude of Thebes. ¹⁶And I will set a fire in Egypt; Sin shall greatly anguish; and Thebes shall be broken through; and Noph *shall have* daily woes; the young men of Aven and Pibeseth shall fall by the sword; and they shall go into captivity. ¹⁸At Tehaphnehes the day will be held back, when I shatter there the yokes of Egypt. And the pride of her strength shall cease in her; a cloud shall cover her; and her daughters shall go into captivity. ¹⁹And I will do judgments in Egypt. And they shall know that I *am* Jehovah.

²⁰And it was, in the eleventh year, in the first *month* in the seventh of the month, the word of Jehovah was to me, saying, ²¹Son of man, I have shattered the arm of Pharaoh king of Egypt. And behold, it shall not be bound up to give healing, to set a bandage to bind it, to make it strong to handle the sword. ²²So the Lord Jehovah says this: Behold, I *am* against Pharaoh king of Egypt, and I will shatter his arms, the strong one, and the shattered one. And I will cause the sword to fall out

---

	2114	3027	4393	776	8074	7451	3027	776
	וַהֲשִׁמֹּתִי	אֶרֶץ	וּמְלֹאָהּ	בְּיַד־				אֶת־הָאָרֶץ
	strangers	the by	her and	the	will I And	evil	the into	the
		hand	fullness	land	waste	ones	of hand	land

13 כֹּה־אָמַר אֲדֹנָי יְהוִֹה וְהַאֲבַדְתִּי
also will I :Jehovah the says Thus   (30.68 136   559)
destroy   Lord
have Jehovah I .spoken   (1696 3068)
אֲנִי יְהוָה דִּבַּרְתִּי

גִּלּוּלִים וְהִשְׁבַּתִּי אֱלִילִים מִנֹּף וְנָשִׂיא מֵאֶרֶץ־מִצְרַיִם לֹא
not Egypt the of a And from vanities will I and the
       of land prince   of .Noph   cease make idols

14 יִהְיֶה־עוֹד וְנָתַתִּי יִרְאָה בְּאֶרֶץ מִצְרָיִם: וַהֲשִׁמֹּתִי אֶת־
will I And .Egypt the in fear I And any be shall
desolate make   of land   put will .longer

15 פַּתְרוֹס וְנָתַתִּי אֵשׁ בְּצֹעַן וְעָשִׂיתִי שְׁפָטִים בְּנֹא: וְשָׁפַכְתִּי
will I And in judgments will and ,Zoan in a will and ,Pathros
pour   .Thebes   do   fire set

16 חֲמָתִי עַל־סִין מָעוֹז מִצְרָיִם וְהִכְרַתִּי אֶת־הֲמוֹן נֹא: וְנָתַתִּי
I And .Thebes the will I And .Egypt the ,Sin on My
set will of multitude   off cut of strength   fury

אֵשׁ בְּמִצְרַיִם חוּל תָּחוּל סִין וְנֹא תִּהְיֶה לְהִבָּקֵעַ וְנֹף צָרֵי
woes and broken be shall and Sin greatly :Egypt in a
Noph through Thebes anguish   fire

17 יוֹמָם: בַּחוּרֵי אָוֶן וּפִי־בֶסֶת בַּחֶרֶב יִפֹּלוּ וְהֵנָּה בַּשְּׁבִי תֵלַכְנָה:
.go shall into and shall the by and Aven young the .daily
captivity they ,fall sword Pibeseth of men

18 וּבִתְחַפְנְחֵס חָשַׂךְ הַיּוֹם בְּשִׁבְרִי־שָׁם אֶת־מֹטוֹת מִצְרַיִם
.Egypt the there I when the be will At
of yokes shatter ,day back held Tehaphnehes

וְנִשְׁבַּת־בָּהּ גְּאוֹן עֻזָּהּ הִיא עָנָן יְכַסֶּנָּה וּבְנוֹתֶיהָ בַּשְּׁבִי
into her and shall a her her the in shall And
captivity daughters ,cover cloud ;strength of pride her cease

19 תֵּלַכְנָה: וְעָשִׂיתִי שְׁפָטִים בְּמִצְרָיִם וְיָדְעוּ כִּי־אֲנִי יְהוָה:
Jehovah I that they And .Egypt in judgments I And .go shall
(am) know shall   do will

20 וַיְהִי בְּאַחַת עֶשְׂרֵה שָׁנָה בָּרִאשׁוֹן בְּשִׁבְעָה לַחֹדֶשׁ הָיָה
was the of the in the in year the in And
,month seventh (month) first   eleventh ,was it

21 דְבַר־יְהוָה אֵלַי לֵאמֹר: בֶּן־אָדָם אֶת־זְרוֹעַ פַּרְעֹה מֶלֶךְ־
king Pharaoh the ,man Son ,saying ,me to Jehovah the
of of arm of   of word

מִצְרַיִם שָׁבָרְתִּי וְהִנֵּה לֹא־חֻבְּשָׁה לָתֵת רְפֻאוֹת לָשׂוּם
set to ,healing give to shall it not And have I Egypt
bound be ,behold .shattered

22 חִתּוּל לְחָבְשָׁהּ לְחָזְקָהּ לִתְפֹּשׂ בֶּחָרֶב: לָכֵן כֹּה־אָמַר
says thus Therefore the to make to bind to
.sword handle strong it it bandage

אֲדֹנָי יְהוִֹה הִנְנִי אֶל־פַּרְעֹה מֶלֶךְ־מִצְרַיִם וְשָׁבַרְתִּי אֶת־
will I and ,Egypt king Pharaoh against Be- :Jehovah the
shatter   of (am) I ,hold   Lord

זְרֹעֹתָיו אֶת־הַחֲזָקָה וְאֶת־הַנִּשְׁבָּרֶת וְהִפַּלְתִּי אֶת־הַחֶרֶב
the will I And the and strong the
sword fall to cause .one shattered one ,arms his

out of his hand. [23]And I will scatter Egypt among the nations, and will sow them through the lands. [24]And I will strengthen the arms of the king of Babylon, and put My sword in his hand. But I will shatter the arms of Pharaoh, and he will groan with the groanings of the slain before him. [25]But I will make the arms of the king of Babylon stronger, and the arms of Pharaoh shall fall; and they shall know that I *am* Jehovah, when I put My sword into the king of Babylon's hand —and he will stretch it against the land of Egypt. [26]And I will scatter Egypt among the nations, and sow them among the lands. And they shall know that I *am* Jehovah.

776 2219 1471 4714 6327 3027
23 מִיָּדוֹ׃ וַהֲפִצוֹתִי אֶת־מִצְרַיִם בַּגּוֹיִם וְזֵרִיתִים בָּאֲרָצוֹת׃
the through | will and | the among | Egypt | will I And | of out
;lands | them sow | nations | scatter | .hand his

3027 2719 5414 884 4428 2220 2388
24 וְחִזַּקְתִּי אֶת־זְרֹעוֹת מֶלֶךְ בָּבֶל וְנָתַתִּי אֶת־חַרְבִּי בְּיָדוֹ
his in | My | put and ,Babylon | the | the | will I And
.hand | sword | of king | of arms | strengthen

6440 2491 5009 5008 6547 2220 7665
וְשָׁבַרְתִּי אֶת־זְרֹעוֹת פַּרְעֹה וְנָאַק נַאֲקוֹת חָלָל לְפָנָיו׃
before | the | the with | he and | Pharaoh | arms the | will I But
.him | slain | of groanings | groan will | of | shatter

5307 6547 2220 884 4428 2220 2388
25 וְהַחֲזַקְתִּי אֶת־זְרֹעוֹת מֶלֶךְ בָּבֶל וּזְרֹעוֹת פַּרְעֹה תִּפֹּלְנָה
;fall shall | Pharaoh | the and | ,Babylon | the | the | will I But
of arms | of king | of arms | strengthen

5186 884 4428 3027 2719 5414 3068 3045
וְיָדְעוּ כִּי־אֲנִי יְהוָה בְּתִתִּי חַרְבִּי בְּיַד מֶלֶךְ־בָּבֶל וְנָטָה
he and ,Babylon's the | into | My | I when ,Jehovah | I that they and
stretch will | of king hand | sword | put | (am) | know shall

14:71 4714 6327 4714 776
26 אוֹתָהּ אֶל־אֶרֶץ מִצְרָיִם׃ וַהֲפִצוֹתִי אֶת־מִצְרַיִם בַּגּוֹיִם
the among | Egypt | will I And | .Egypt | the against | it
,nations | scatter | of land

3068 3045 776 2219
וְזֵרִיתִי אוֹתָם בָּאֲרָצוֹת וְיָדְעוּ כִּי־אֲנִי יְהוָה׃
.Jehovah | I that they And | the among | them | and
(am) | know shall | .lands | sow

CAP. XXXI. לא

CHAPTER 31

1961 2321 259 7992 81:41 6240 259 1961
1 וַיְהִי בְּאַחַת עֶשְׂרֵה שָׁנָה בַּשְּׁלִישִׁי בְּאֶחָד לַחֹדֶשׁ הָיָה
was | the of | the on | the in | ,year | the in | it And
,month | first | ,(month) third | eleventh | was

4428 6547 559 120 1121 559 3068 1697
2 דְבַר־יְהוָה אֵלַי לֵאמֹר׃ בֶּן־אָדָם אֱמֹר אֶל־פַּרְעֹה מֶלֶךְ־
king | Pharaoh | to | speak ,man Son | ,saying | ,me to Jehovah | the
of | of | of word

804 2009 1433 1819 4310 1995 4714
3 מִצְרַיִם וְאֶל־הֲמוֹנוֹ אֶל־מִי דָּמִיתָ בְגָדְלֶךָ׃ הִנֵּה אַשּׁוּר
Assyria ,Behold | your in | you are whom To | his | and | Egypt
(was) | ?greatness | like | ;host | to

5668 996 6967 1362 6751 2793 6057 3303 38:44 730
אֶרֶז בַּלְּבָנוֹן יְפֵה עָנָף וְחֹרֶשׁ מֵצַל וּגְבַהּ קוֹמָה וּבֵין עֲבֹתִים
thick the and | ;height in | and | shade | and branches (with) | in | a
boughs among | exalted | forest | fair ,Lebanon | cedar

7311 8415 1430 4325 6788 1961
4 הָיְתָה צַמַּרְתּוֹ׃ מַיִם גִּדְּלוּהוּ תְּהוֹם רֹמְמָתְהוּ אֶת־
with | him made | deep the | him made | The | .top his | was
high | ;great | waters

7971 8585 4302 5439 1980 5104
נַהֲרֹתֶיהָ הֹלֵךְ סְבִיבוֹת מַטָּעָהּ וְאֶת־תְּעָלֹתֶיהָ שִׁלְחָה אֶל
to | sent she | her | and | her | all | was (it) | her
out | channels | ,planting | around | going | rivers

7704 6086 3605 6967 1361 7704 6086 3605
5 כָּל־עֲצֵי הַשָּׂדֶה׃ עַל־כֵּן גָּבְהָא קֹמָתוֹ מִכֹּל עֲצֵי הַשָּׂדֶה
the | the above | his | was | Therefore | the | the all
,field | of trees all | height | up lifted | .field | of trees

7227 4325 6288 748 5634 7235
וַתִּרְבֶּינָה סַרְעַפֹּתָיו וַתֶּאֱרַכְנָה פֹּארֹתָו מִמַּיִם רַבִּים
,many | of because | his | became and | his | were and
waters the | branches | long | ,boughs | multiplied

6288 8478 8064 5775 3605 7077 5589 7971
6 בְּשַׁלְּחוֹ׃ בִּסְעַפֹּתָיו קִנְנוּ כָּל־עוֹף הַשָּׁמַיִם וְתַחַת פֹּארֹתָיו
his | and | the | the | All nested | his in | his in
branches | under | ,heavens | of birds | boughs | .sending

CHAPTER 31

[1]And it came about, in the eleventh year, in the third *month*, on the first of the month, the word of Jehovah was to me,saying, [2]Son of man, speak toi Pharaoh king of Egypt and to his host: To whom are you like in your greatness? [3]Behold, Assyria *was* a cedar in Lebanon, *with* fair branches and forest shade, and exalted in height; and his top was among the thick boughs. [4]The waters made him great; the deep made him high with her rivers, going all around her planting; and she sent out her channels to all the trees of the field. [5]Therefore his height was lifted up above all the trees of the field, and his boughs were multiplied, and his branches became long, because of the many waters, in his sending. [6]All the birds of the heavens nested in his boughs, and under his branches all the

beasts of the field gave birth; and in his shadow dwelt all great nations. [7]And he was fair in his greatness, in the length of his branches. For his root was to many waters. [8]The cedars did not overshadow him in the garden of God; the fir-trees were not like his boughs; and the plane trees were not like his branches. Every tree in the garden of God was not like him in his beauty. [9]I have made him beautiful by his many branches, and all the trees of Eden that *were* in the garden of God envied him.

[10]So the Lord Jehovah says this: Because you were exalted in height, and he has set his top among the thick boughs, and his heart is lifted up in his height; [11]so I have given him into the mighty hand of the nations. He shall surely deal with him; I have expelled him for his evil. [12]And strangers have cut him off, the fearful of the nations, and have left him. His branches have fallen on the mountains and in all the valleys, and his boughs have been broken in all the ravines of the land. And all the people of the land have gone from his shadow, and have left him. [13]All the birds of the heavens shall dwell on his ruin, and on his branches shall be all the beasts of the field, [14]in order that all the trees *by* the waters may not be exalted in their height, and do not give their top among the thick boughs; and do not stand up in their mighty exaltation, all drinking waters. For all of them are given to death, to the earth's lowest parts, in the midst of the sons of men, with those going down *into* the Pit.

[15]So says the Lord Jehovah: In the day he went down to Sheol, I caused a

3033 7227 1471 3605 3427 6738 7704 2416 3605 3205
7 ילדו כל חית השדה ובצלו ישבו כל גוים רבים׃ וייף
he And .great nations all dwelt in and the the all gave
fair was shadow his ,field of beasts birth

7227 4325 8328 1961 1808 753 1433
בגדלו בארך דליותיו כי־היה שרשו אל־מים רבים׃
.many waters to root his was For his the in his in
.branches of length ,greatness

1819 3808 1265 430 1588 6004 3808 730
8 ארזים לא־עממהו בגן־אלהים ברושים לא דמו אל־
to were not fir the ;God the in over- not The
like trees of garden him shadow cedars

430 1588 6086 3605 6288 1961 3808 6196 5589
סעפתיו וערמנים לא־היו כפארתיו כל־עץ בגן־אלהים
God the in tree Every his like were not the and his
of garden .branches trees plane ,boughs

7065 1808 7230 6213 3303 3308 1819 3808
9 לא־דמה אליו ביפיו׃ יפה עשיתיו ברב דליותיו ויקנאהו
envied and his by have I beautiful his in to was not
him ,branches many him made .beauty him like

559 430 1588 834 5731 6086 3605
10 כל־עצי־עדן אשר בגן האלהים׃ לכן כה אמר
says thus Therefore .God the in that Eden the all
of garden (were) of trees

6788 5414 1363 1361 834 3282 3068 136
אדני יהוה יען אשר גבהת בקומה ויתן צמרתו אל־
to top his he and ,height in were you that Be- :Jehovah the
set has exalted cause Lord

1471 3027 5414 6967 3824 7311 5688 996
11 בין עבותים ורם לבבו בגבהו׃ ואתנהו ביד איל גוים
the the hand in have I so his in his is and thick the among
.nations of mighty him given ;height heart up lifted ,boughs

6184 2114 3772 1644 7562 6213 6213
12 עשו יעשה לו כרשעו גרשתהו׃ ויכרתהו זרים עריצי
fear- the ,strangers have And have I his for with shall He surely
of ful off him cut .him expelled evil ;him deal

1808 5307 1516 3605 2022 5203 1471
גוים ויטשהו אל־ההרים ובכל־גאיות נפלו דליותיו
his have the in and the On have and the
,branches fallen valleys all mountains .him left ,nations

3605 6738 3381 776 650 3605 6288 7665
ותשברנה פראתיו בכל־אפיקי הארץ וירדו מצלו כל־
all his from have And the the all in his have and
shadow gone .land of ravines boughs broken been

8064 5775 3605 7931 4658 5203 776 5971
13 עמי הארץ ויטשהו׃ על־מפלתו ישכנו כל־עוף השמים
the the all shall fall his On have and the the
,heavens of birds dwell .him left ,land of people

1361 3808 834 4616 7704 2416 3605 1961 6288
14 ואל־פראתיו היו כל חית השדה׃ למען אשר לא־יגבהו
be may not that order in the the all shall his and
exalted ,field of beasts be branches on

6788 5414 3808 4325 6086 3605 6967
בקומתם כל־עצי־מים ולא־יתנו את־צמרתם אל־בין
among top their give and the (by) the all their in
not ,waters trees height ,

3605 4325 8354 3605 1363 352 5975 3808 5688
עבתים ולא־יעמדו אליהם בגבהם כל־שתי מים כי כלם
of all For .waters drink- all their in their stand and thick the
them ing ,exaltation mighty up not ;boughs

3381 120 1121 8432 8432 776 4194 5414
נתנו למות אל־ארץ תחתית בתוך בני אדם אל־יורדי
those with ,men the the in ,parts lowest the to ,death to are
down going of sons of midst earth's given

56 7585 3381 3117 3068 136 559 953
15 בור׃ כה־אמר אדני יהוה ביום רדתו שאלה האבלתי
a caused I ,Sheol to went he the In :Jehovah the says Thus the (into)
.mourning down day Lord .Pit

mourning. I covered over him the deep, and I held back her rivers; and many waters were confined. And I darkened Lebanon on him, and all the trees of the field wilted away because of him. [16]I made the nations shake at the sound of his fall, when I cast him down to Sheol with those going down *in* the Pit. And all the trees of Eden shall be cheered in the earth's lowest parts, the choice and best of Lebanon, all that drink waters. [17]They also went down with him into Sheol, to the slain of the sword, even his arm, who dwelt in his shadow in the midst of the nations.

[18]To whom are you like in glory and greatness among Eden's trees? Yet you shall go down with the trees of Eden to the earth's lowest parts. You shall lie amidst the uncircumcised, with the slain of the sword. He is Pharaoh and all *his* host, declares the Lord Jehovah.

7227 4325 3607 5104 4513 8415 3680
כִּסֵּתִי עָלָיו אֶת־תְּהוֹם וָאֶמְנַע נַהֲרוֹתֶיהָ וַיִּכָּלְאוּ מַיִם רַבִּים
.many waters were and confined her ,rivers held I and back held the deep over him I covered

6963 5969 7704 6086 3605 3844 6937
16 וָאַקְדִּר עָלָיו לְבָנוֹן וְכָל־עֲצֵי הַשָּׂדֶה עָלָיו עֻלְפֶּה׃ מִקּוֹל
the at of sound wilted .away because him of the field the of trees and all ;Lebanon on him I And darkened

3381 7585 3381 1471 7493 4658
מַפַּלְתּוֹ הִרְעַשְׁתִּי גוֹיִם בְּהוֹרִדִי אֹתוֹ שְׁאוֹלָה אֶת־יוֹרְדֵי בוֹר
the (in) .Pit those with down going Sheol to him I when down cast the nations made I shake fall his

3844 2896 4005 5731 6086 3605 8432 776 5162
וַיִּנָּחֲמוּ בְּאֶרֶץ תַּחְתִּית כָּל־עֲצֵי־עֵדֶן מִבְחַר וְטוֹב־לְבָנוֹן
,Lebanon and of best the choice ,Eden the of trees all parts lowest the in earth's shall And be cheered

2719 2491 7585 3381 1571 4325 8354
17 כָּל־שֹׁתֵי מָיִם׃ גַּם־הֵם אִתּוֹ יָרְדוּ שְׁאוֹלָה אֶל־חַלְלֵי־חָרֶב
the ,sword the of slain to Sheol went into down with him They also .waters that drink all

3519 1819 4310 1471 8432 6738 3427 2220
18 וּזְרֹעוֹ יָשְׁבוּ בְצִלּוֹ בְּתוֹךְ גּוֹיִם׃ אֶל־מִי דָמִיתָ כָּכָה בְּכָבוֹד
glory in like you are whom To the .nations the in of midst his in shadow who dwelt his even ,arm

8482 776 5731 6086 3381 5731 6086 1433
וּבְגֹדֶל בַּעֲצֵי־עֵדֶן וְהוּרַדְתָּ אֶת־עֲצֵי־עֵדֶן אֶל־אֶרֶץ תַּחְתִּית
.parts lowest the earth's to Eden's trees with you Yet down go shall ?Eden's trees among great- and ness

3605 6547 2719 2491 7901 6189 8432
בְּתוֹךְ עֲרֵלִים תִּשְׁכַּב אֶת־חַלְלֵי־חֶרֶב הוּא פַרְעֹה וְכָל־
all and Pharaoh He (is) the .sword the of slain with shall you lie uncir- cumcised the Amidst

3068 136 5002 1995
הֲמוֹנֹה נְאֻם אֲדֹנָי יְהוִֹה׃
.Jehovah the Lord states (his) ,host

CAP. XXXII. לב

CHAPTER 32

CHAPTER 32

[1]And it happened in the twelfth year, in the twelfth month, on the first of the month, the word of Jehovah was to me, saying, [2]Son of man, take up a lament over Pharaoh, king of Egypt, and say to him, You were like a young lion of the nations, but you *are* like the monster in the seas. And you gushed in your rivers, and stirred up the waters with your feet, and fouled their rivers. [3]So says the Lord Jehovah: So I will spread out My net over you, with an assembly of many peoples; and they will lift you up in My net. [4]Then I will leave you on the land; I will hurl you on the face of the field, and will make all

2320 259 2320 6240 8147 8141 6240 8147 1961
1 וַיְהִי בִּשְׁתֵּי עֶשְׂרֵה שָׁנָה בִּשְׁנֵי־עָשָׂר חֹדֶשׁ בְּאֶחָד לַחֹדֶשׁ
the of ,month the on first ,month the in twelfth ,year the twelfth in it And ,was

7015 5375 120 1121 559 3068 1697 1961
2 הָיָה דְבַר־יְהוָה אֵלַי לֵאמֹר׃ בֶּן־אָדָם שָׂא קִינָה עַל־
over a lament take up ,man Son of ,saying to ,me Jehovah the of word was

1819 1471 3715 559 4714 4428 6547
פַּרְעֹה מֶלֶךְ־מִצְרַיִם וְאָמַרְתָּ אֵלָיו כְּפִיר גּוֹיִם נִדְמֵיתָ
were you ;like the nations young A of lion ,him to say and ,Egypt king of Pharaoh

4325 1804 5104 1518 3220 8577
וְאַתָּה כַּתַּנִּים בַּיַּמִּים וַתָּגַח בִּנְהָרוֹתֶיךָ וַתִּדְלַח־מַיִם
the waters stirred and up your in ,rivers you And gushed the in .seas the like monster but (are) you

3068 136 559 5104 7515 7272
3 בְּרַגְלֶיךָ וַתִּרְפֹּס נַהֲרוֹתָם׃ כֹּה אָמַר אֲדֹנָי יְהוִֹה
:Jehovah the Lord says Thus their ,rivers fouled and your with ,feet

5927 7227 5971 6951 7568 6566
וּפָרַשְׂתִּי עָלֶיךָ אֶת־רִשְׁתִּי בִּקְהַל עַמִּים רַבִּים וְהֶעֱלוּךָ
will they and up you lift ;many peoples an with of assembly ,net My over you will I Thus out spread

7931 2904 7704 6440 776 5203 2764
4 בְּחֶרְמִי׃ וּנְטַשְׁתִּיךָ בָאָרֶץ עַל־פְּנֵי הַשָּׂדֶה אֲטִילֶךָ וְהִשְׁכַּנְתִּי
will and dwell make will I ,you hurl the field the on of face the on ;land will I Then you leave My in .net

the birds of the heavens to dwell on you; and I will fill the beasts of all the earth from you. ⁵And I will put your flesh on the mountains, and fill the valleys *with* your height. ⁶And I will also make the land drink your discharge of your blood, to the mountains; and the ravines shall be full of you. ⁷And I will cover the heavens when *I* quench you, and will darken their stars. I will cover the sun with a cloud, and the moon shall not give its light. ⁸I will darken all the shining lights in the heavens over you, and will give darkness on your land, declares the Lord Jehovah. ⁹I will also vex the heart of many peoples when I bring your breaking among the nations, to the lands which you have not known. ¹⁰And I will make many people appalled at you, and their kings will be horribly afraid at you, when I make to fly My sword before their faces. And they shall quake at *every* moment, *each* man for his own life, in the day of your fall.

¹¹For so says the Lord Jehovah: The sword of the king of Babylon shall come on you. ¹²By the swords of the mighty I will make your host fall, *by* the fearful of the nations, all of them. And they shall spoil the pride of Egypt, and all its multitude shall be destroyed. ¹³I will also destroy all her beasts from on the great waters; and the foot of man shall not stir them any longer; and the hoofs of beasts shall not stir them up. ¹⁴Then I will make their waters settle and cause their rivers to run as oil says the Lord Jehovah. ¹⁵When I shall make the land of Egypt a waste, and the land shall be wasted of its fullness; when I shall strike all those who dwell in it;

---

776 ,3605 2416   7646   8064 :   5775 ,3605 .
עָלֶיךָ כָּל־עֹוף הַשָּׁמַיִם וְהִשְׂבַּעְתִּי מִמְּךָ חַיַּת כָּל־הָאָרֶץ:
the all the from will I and the the all on
.earth of beasts you fill ,heavens of birds you

5   7419   1516   4390   2022   1320   5414
וְנָתַתִּי אֶת־בְּשָׂרְךָ עַל־הֶהָרִים וּמִלֵּאתִי הַגֵּאָיֹות רָמוּתֶךָ:
your valleys the fill and the on your I And
.height (with) mountains flesh put will

6   4390   650   2022   1818   6823 776 8248
וְהִשְׁקֵיתִי אֶרֶץ צָפָתְךָ מִדָּמְךָ אֶל־הֶהָרִים וַאֲפִקִים יִמָּלְאוּן מִמֶּךָּ:
be shall the and the to your dis- your the also will I
full ravines ;mountains ,blood of charge land drink make
.you of

7   3556   6937   8064 :   3518   3680
וְכִסֵּיתִי בְכַבֹּותְךָ שָׁמַיִם וְהִקְדַּרְתִּי אֶת־כֹּוכְבֵיהֶם
;stars their darken and the (I) when I And
,heavens you quench cover will

8   216 3974   3605 216   215 3808   3394 3680   6051 8121
שֶׁמֶשׁ בֶּעָנָן אֲכַסֶּנּוּ וְיָרֵחַ לֹא־יָאִיר אֹורֹו: כָּל־מְאֹורֵי אֹור
lights the All .light its shall not the and will I a with the
of shining give moon ,cover cloud sun

136   5002   776   2822 5414   6937   8064
בַּשָּׁמַיִם אַקְדִּירֵם עָלֶיךָ וְנָתַתִּי חֹשֶׁךְ עַל־אַרְצְךָ נְאֻם אֲדֹנָי
the states your on darkness will and over will I the in
Lord ,land give you darken heavens

9   1471   7667   935   5971   5971 38 20 : 3707 3068
יְהוִה: וְהִכְעַסְתִּי לֵב עַמִּים רַבִּים בַּהֲבִיאִי שִׁבְרְךָ בַּגֹּויִם
the among your I when ,many peoples the also will I .Jehovah
,nations breaking bring of heart vex

10   5971   8074   3045 3808   834   776
עַל־אֲרָצֹות אֲשֶׁר לֹא־יְדַעְתָּם: וַהֲשִׁמֹּותִי עָלֶיךָ עַמִּים
peoples you at will I And have you not which the to
appalled make .known lands

2719   5774   8178   8175   4428   7227
רַבִּים וּמַלְכֵיהֶם יִשְׂעֲרוּ עָלֶיךָ שַׂעַר בְּעֹופְפִי חַרְבִּי עַל־
on My I when ,horribly you at be will their and ,many
sword fly make afraid kings

4658 3117 5315 : 376   7281   2729 6440
פְּנֵיהֶם וְחָרְדוּ לִרְגָעִים אִישׁ לְנַפְשֹׁו בְּיֹום מַפַּלְתֶּךָ:
.fall your the in his for (each) (every) at they And their
of day ,life own man ,moment quake shall .faces

11   2719   935   884   4428 2719 3068 136   559
12   כִּי כֹּה אָמַר אֲדֹנָי יְהוִה חֶרֶב מֶלֶךְ־בָּבֶל תְּבֹואֶךָ: בְּחַרְבֹות
the By come shall Babylon The :Jehovah the says thus For
of swords .you on of king sword Lord

1347   7703   3605 1471   6184 19:95   5307   1368
גִּבֹּורִים אַפִּיל הֲמֹונֶךָ עָרִיצֵי גֹויִם כֻּלָּם וְשָׁדְדוּ אֶת־גְּאֹון
pride the they And of all the fear- the your will I the
of spoil shall .them ,nations of ful fall make mighty

929   3605   6   1995   36 05 8045 4714 :
מִצְרַיִם וְנִשְׁמַד כָּל־הֲמֹונָהּ: וְהַאֲבַדְתִּי אֶת־כָּל־בְּהֶמְתָּהּ
beasts her all destroy .it of the all shall and ,Egypt
also will I the multitude destroyed be

6541   5750   120   7272   1804 38 08 7227 4325
מֵעַל מַיִם רַבִּים וְלֹא תִדְלָחֵם רֶגֶל־אָדָם עֹוד וּפַרְסֹות
the and any man the stir shall and the the from
of hoofs ;longer of foot up them not ;great waters on

8081   5104   4325   8257
בְּהֵמָה לֹא תִדְלָחֵם: אָז אַשְׁקִיעַ מֵימֵיהֶם וְנַהֲרֹותָם כַּשֶּׁמֶן
oil as their and their will I Then stir shall not beasts
rivers ,waters settle make .up them

15   8077   47 14   776   5414 3068 136   5002 32 12
אֹולִיךְ נְאֻם אֲדֹנָי יְהוִה: בְּתִתִּי אֶת־אֶרֶץ מִצְרַיִם שְׁמָמָה
,waste a Egypt the I When .Jehovah the says to cause
of land make shall Lord ,run

3045   3427   3605   5221   439:3   776   8077
וּנְשַׁמָּה אֶרֶץ מִמְּלֹאָהּ בְּהַכֹּותִי אֶת־כָּל־יֹושְׁבֵי בָהּ וְיָדְעוּ
they then in those all I when its of the shall and
know shall ;it dwell who strike shall ;fulness land wasted be

then they shall know that I *am* Jehovah.

[16]This is the lament, and they shall lament her; the daughters of the nations shall lament her. Over Egypt and over all her multitude, they shall lament her, declares the Lord Jehovah.

[17]And it happened, in the twelfth year, in the fifteenth of the month, the word of Jehovah was to me, saying, [18]Son of man, wail over the host of Egypt, and bring it down, her and the daughters of the majestic nations, to the earth's lowest parts, with those going down *to* the Pit. [19]Than whom are you more lovely? Go down and be laid with the uncircumcised. [20]They shall fall in the midst of the slain of the sword. She is given to the sword; they draw her and all her multitudes. [21]The strong of the mighty shall speak to him from the midst of Sheol; they went with his helpers; they, the uncircumcised, lie slain by the sword. [22]There *is* Assyria and all her assembly; all around him *are* his graves; all of them *are* slain, fallen by the sword; [23]of whom are given her graves in the recesses of the Pit; and her assembly is all around her grave; all of them slain, fallen by the sword, because they gave terror in the land of the living. [24]There *is* Elam and all her multitude around her grave; all of them slain, fallen by the sword, who went down uncircumcised into the earth's lowest parts; who gave their terror in the land of the living. Yet they bore their shame with those going down *to* the Pit. [25]In the midst of the slain, they have put a bed for her, with all her multitude; her graves *are* all around him, all of them uncircumcised, slain by the sword; though their terror was given in the land

6969 1471 1323 7015 6969 3068
16 כִּי־אֲנִי יְהוָה׃ קִינָה הִיא וְקוֹנְנוּהָ בְּנוֹת הַגּוֹיִם תְּקוֹנֵנָּה
shall the daughters they and This the .Jehovah I that
lament nations' ;her lament shall ,(is) lament (am)

5002 7015 1995 3605 4714
אוֹתָהּ עַל־מִצְרַיִם וְעַל־כָּל־הֲמוֹנָהּ תְּקוֹנֵנָּה אוֹתָהּ נְאֻם
states ,her shall they her all and Egypt Over .her
lament ,multitude over

6240 2568 8141 6240 8147 1961 3068 136
17 אֲדֹנָי יְהוִה׃ וַיְהִי בִּשְׁתֵּי עֶשְׂרֵה שָׁנָה בַּחֲמִשָּׁה עָשָׂר
the in ,year the in it And .Jehovah the
fifteenth twelfth ,was Lord

5091 120 1121 559 3068 1697 1961 2320
18 לַחֹדֶשׁ הָיָה דְבַר־יְהוָה אֵלַי לֵאמֹר׃ בֶּן־אָדָם נְהֵה עַל־
over wail ,man Son ,saying ,me to Jehovah the was the of
of of word ,month

776 117 1471 1323 3381 4714 1995
הֲמוֹן מִצְרַיִם וְהוֹרִדֵהוּ אוֹתָהּ וּבְנוֹת גּוֹיִם אַדִּרִם אֶל־אֶרֶץ
the to the nations the and her bring and Egypt the
earth's majestic of daughters ,down him of host

7901 3381 5276 953 3381 8482
19 תַּחְתִּיּוֹת אֶת־יוֹרְדֵי בוֹר׃ מִמִּי נָעָמְתָּ רְדָה וְהָשְׁכְּבָה
be and Go you are Than the (to) those with lowest
laid down ?lovely whom Pit down going ,parts

4900 5414 2719 5307 2719 2491 8432 6189
20 אֶת־עֲרֵלִים׃ בְּתוֹךְ חַלְלֵי־חֶרֶב יִפֹּלוּ חֶרֶב נִתָּנָה מָשְׁכוּ
they is She the to They the the In the with
draw ;given sword .fall shall ,sword of slain of midst .uncircumcised

7585 8432 1368 1696 1995 3605
21 אוֹתָהּ וְכָל־הֲמוֹנֶיהָ׃ יְדַבְּרוּ־לוֹ אֵלֵי גִבּוֹרִים מִתּוֹךְ שְׁאוֹל
;Sheol the from the The to shall her and her
of midst mighty of strong him speak .multitudes all

804 8033 2719 2491 6189 7901 3381 5826
22 אֶת־עֹזְרָיו יָרְדוּ שָׁכְבוּ הָעֲרֵלִים חַלְלֵי־חָרֶב׃ שָׁם אַשּׁוּר
Assyria There the slain uncircum- the they they his with
.sword by ,cised ,lie ;went helpers

5307 2491 3605 6913 5439 6951 3605
וְכָל־קְהָלָהּ סְבִיבוֹתָיו קִבְרֹתָיו כֻּלָּם חֲלָלִים הַנֹּפְלִים
fallen (are) of all his around all her and
,slain them ;graves (are) him ;assembly all

6951 1961 953 3411 6900 5414 834 2719
23 בֶּחָרֶב׃ אֲשֶׁר נִתְּנוּ קִבְרֹתֶיהָ בְּיַרְכְּתֵי־בוֹר וַיְהִי קְהָלָהּ
her and the the in graves her are of the by
assembly is ,Pit of recesses given whom ;sword

5414 834 2719 5307 2491 3605 6913 5439
סְבִיבוֹת קְבֻרָתָהּ כֻּלָּם חֲלָלִים נֹפְלִים בַּחֶרֶב אֲשֶׁר־נָתְנוּ
they because the by fallen (are) of all her all
gave ,sword ,slain them ;grave around

6900 5439 1995 3605 5867 2416 776 2851
24 חִתִּית בְּאֶרֶץ חַיִּים׃ שָׁם עֵילָם וְכָל־הֲמוֹנָהּ סְבִיבוֹת קְבֻרָתָהּ
her around her and Elam There the the in terror
;grave multitude all (is) .living of land

776 6189 3381 834 2719 5307 2491 3605
כֻּלָּם חֲלָלִים הַנֹּפְלִים בַּחֶרֶב אֲשֶׁר־יָרְדוּ עֲרֵלִים ׀ אֶל־אֶרֶץ
the into uncircum- went who the by fallen (are) of all
earth's cised .down ,sword ,slain them

3639 5375 2416 776 2851 5414 834 8482
תַּחְתִּיּוֹת אֲשֶׁר נָתְנוּ חִתִּיתָם בְּאֶרֶץ חַיִּים וַיִּשְׂאוּ כְלִמָּתָם
their they Yet the the in their gave who lowest
shame bore .living of land terror ;parts

1995 3605 4904 5414 2491 8432 953 3381
25 אֶת־יוֹרְדֵי בוֹר׃ בְּתוֹךְ חֲלָלִים נָתְנוּ מִשְׁכָּב לָהּ בְּכָל־הֲמוֹנָהּ
her with for bed a They the the In the (to) those with
.multitude all ,her put have slain of midst .Pit down going

2851 5414 2719 2491 6189 3605 6913 5439
סְבִיבוֹתָיו קִבְרֹתֶהָ כֻּלָּם עֲרֵלִים חַלְלֵי־חֶרֶב כִּי־נִתַּן חִתִּיתָם
their was though the slain uncircum- of all Her around all
terror given ;sword by ,cised them ,graves (are) him

of the living, yet they have become their shame with those going down *to* the Pit; he is put among the slain.
[26]There *is* Meshech, Tubal, and all her multitude; all around him *are* her graves; all of them uncircumcised, slain by the sword; though they gave their terror in the land of the living. [27]And they shall not lie with the mighty of the uncircumcised who are fallen, who have gone down *to* Sheol with their weapons of war. And they have put their swords under their heads, but their iniquities shall be on their bones; though the terror of the mighty *was* in the land of the living. [28]And you shall be broken in the midst of the uncircumcised, and shall lie with the slain by the sword.
[29]There *is* Edom, her kings and all her rulers, who are placed in their might with the slain of the sword; they shall lie with the uncircumcised, and with those going down *to* the Pit. [30]These *are* the princes of the north, all of them, and all the Sidonians, who have gone down with the slain in their terror. They are ashamed of their might. And they lie uncircumcised with those slain by the sword, and bear their shame with those going down *to* the Pit. [31]Pharaoh shall see them, and be cheered over all his multitude, those slain by the sword, Pharaoh and all the army, declares the Lord Jehovah. [32]For I had put his terror in the land of the living; but he will be laid among the uncircumcised, with those slain by sword, Pharaoh and all his multitude, declares the Lord Jehovah.

2491 8432 953 3381 3639 5375 2416 776
בְּאֶרֶץ חַיִּים וַיִּשְׂאוּ כְלִמָּתָם אֶת־יוֹרְדֵי בוֹר בְּתוֹךְ חֲלָלִים
the the in the (to) those with their they yet the the in
slain of midst ;Pit down going shame become have ,living of land

6913 5439 1995 3605 8422 4902 8033 5414
26 נִתָּן׃ שָׁם מֶשֶׁךְ תֻּבַל וְכָל־הֲמוֹנָהּ סְבִיבוֹתָיו קִבְרוֹתֶהָ
.graves her around all her and Tubal ,Meshech There is he
(are) him ;multitude all (is) .put

2416 776 2851 5414 2719 2491 6189 3605
כֻּלָּם עֲרֵלִים מְחֻלְלֵי חֶרֶב כִּי־נָתְנוּ חִתִּיתָם בְּאֶרֶץ חַיִּים׃
the the in their they though the slain uncircum- of All
;living of land terror gave ;sword by ,cised (are) them

7585 3381 834 6189 5307 1368 7901 3808
27 וְלֹא יִשְׁכְּבוּ אֶת־גִּבּוֹרִים נֹפְלִים מֵעֲרֵלִים אֲשֶׁר יָרְדוּ־שְׁאוֹל
Sheol gone have who the of are who the with shall they and
(to) down ,uncircumcised ,fallen mighty lie not

5414 7218 8478 2719 5414 4421 3627
בִּכְלֵי־מִלְחַמְתָּם וַיִּתְּנוּ אֶת־חַרְבוֹתָם תַּחַת רָאשֵׁיהֶם וַתְּהִי
but their under their they And their , with
be shall ,heads swords put have .war of weapons

2416 776 1368 2851 6106 5771
28 עֲוֺנֹתָם עַל־עַצְמוֹתָם כִּי־חִתִּית גִּבּוֹרִים בְּאֶרֶץ חַיִּים׃ וְאַתָּה
And the the in mighty the the though their on their
you .living of land (was) of terror ,bones iniquities

123 8033 2719 2491 7901 7665 6189 8432
29 בְּתוֹךְ עֲרֵלִים תִּשָּׁבַר וְתִשְׁכַּב אֶת־חַלְלֵי־חָרֶב׃ שָׁמָּה אֱדוֹם
,Edom There the the with shall and be shall uncir- the the in
(is) .sword by slain lie ,broken cumcised of midst

2719 2491 1369 5414 834 5387 3605 4428
מְלָכֶיהָ וְכָל־נְשִׂיאֶיהָ אֲשֶׁר־נִתְּנוּ בִגְבוּרָתָם אֶת־חַלְלֵי־חָרֶב
the the with their in put are who her and her
;sword of slain might ,rulers all kings

6828 5257 8033 953 3381 7901 6189
30 הֵמָּה אֶת־עֲרֵלִים יִשְׁכָּבוּ וְאֶת־יֹרְדֵי בוֹר׃ שָׁמָּה נְסִיכֵי צָפוֹן
the the These the (to) those with and ,lie shall uncir- the with they
,north of princes (are) .Pit down going cumcised

1369 2851 2491 3381 834 6722 3605 3605
כֻּלָּם וְכָל־צִדֹנִי אֲשֶׁר־יָרְדוּ אֶת־חֲלָלִים בְּחִתִּיתָם מִגְּבוּרָתָם
their from their in the with gone have who the and of all
might .terror slain down ,Sidonians all ,them

3639 5375 2719 2491 6189 7901 954
בּוֹשִׁים וַיִּשְׁכְּבוּ עֲרֵלִים אֶת־חַלְלֵי־חֶרֶב וַיִּשְׂאוּ כְלִמָּתָם
their bear and the those with uncircum- they And are They
shame ,sword by slain cised lie .ashamed

1995 3605 5162 6547 7200 953 3381
31 אֶת־יוֹרְדֵי בוֹר׃ אוֹתָם יִרְאֶה פַרְעֹה וְנִחַם עַל־כָּל־הֲמוֹנֹה
his all over be and Pharaoh shall them the (to) those with
;multitude cheered see .Pit down going

31
5414 3068 136 5002 2428 3605 6547 2719 2491
32 חַלְלֵי־חֶרֶב פַּרְעֹה וְכָל־חֵילוֹ נְאֻם אֲדֹנָי יְהוִה׃ כִּי־נָתַתִּי
had I For .Jehovah the states the and Pharaoh the slain
put Lord ,army all sword by

2491 6189 8432 7901 2416 776 2851
אֶת־חִתִּיתוֹ בְּאֶרֶץ חַיִּים וְהֻשְׁכַּב בְּתוֹךְ עֲרֵלִים אֶת־חַלְלֵי־
those with uncir- the amidst will he But the the in terror his
by slain cumcised laid be ,living of land

3068 136 5002 1995 3605 6547 2719
חֶרֶב פַּרְעֹה וְכָל־הֲמוֹנֹה נְאֻם אֲדֹנָי יְהוִה׃
.Jehovah the states his and Pharaoh the
Lord ,multitude all ,sword

CAP. XXXIII לג

CHAPTER 33

[1]And the word of Jehovah was to me, saying, [2]Son of man, speak to the sons of your people and

5971 1121 1696 120 1121 559 3068 1697 1961
1
2 וַיְהִי דְבַר־יְהוָה אֵלַי לֵאמֹר׃ בֶּן־אָדָם דַּבֵּר אֶל־בְּנֵי־עַמְּךָ
your the to speak ,man Son ,saying ,me to Jehovah the And
people of sons of of word was

say to them: When I bring the sword on it, on a land, and take one man from the people of the land, their borders, and set him for a watchman to them; [3]and *when* he sees the sword coming on the land, and he blows the ram's horn and warns the people, and the hearer hears the sound of the ram's horn, [4]and does not take warning; and the sword comes and takes him; his blood shall be on his own head. [5]He heard the sound of the ram's horn, and did not take warning; his blood shall be on himself. But he who took warning, he shall deliver his soul. [6]But if the watchman sees the sword coming, and does not blow the ram's horn, and the people are not warned; and the sword comes and takes a soul from them, he is taken in his iniquity. But I will require his blood from the watchman's hand.

[7]And you, son of man, I have set you *as* a watchman to the house of Israel. And you shall hear the word from My mouth, and warn them from Me. [8]When I say to the wicked, O wicked one, surely you shall die; and you do not speak to warn the wicked one from his way, that wicked one shall die in his iniquity, but I will require his blood from your hand. [9]But you, if you warn the wicked from his way, to turn from it; and he does not turn from his way; he shall die in his iniquity. But you have delivered your soul. [10]And you, son of man, say to the house of Israel, This you have spoken, saying, Surely our transgressions and our sins *are* on us, and we are rotting in them, even then shall we live? [11]Say to them, *As* I live, declares the Lord Jehovah, I do not have

5971 3947 2719 935 776 559
וְאָמַרְתָּ אֲלֵיהֶם אֶרֶץ כִּי־אָבִיא עָלֶיהָ חָרֶב וְלָקְחוּ עַם־
the of people | take and | the ,sword | it on | I bring | When | a (on) land | :them to | say and

6822 5414 7097 259 376 776
הָאָרֶץ אִישׁ אֶחָד מִקְצֵיהֶם וְנָתְנוּ אֹתוֹ לָהֶם לְצֹפֶה׃
a for ;watchman | them to | him | set and | their from ,borders | one | man | the land

3 2094 7782 8628 776 935 2719 7200
וְרָאָה אֶת־הַחֶרֶב בָּאָה עַל־הָאָרֶץ וְתָקַע בַּשּׁוֹפָר וְהִזְהִיר
warns and | ram's the horn | he and blows | the ,land | on | coming | the sword | (when) and sees he

4 2094 3808 7782 6963 8085 8085 5971
אֶת־הָעָם׃ וְשָׁמַע הַשֹּׁמֵעַ אֶת־קוֹל הַשּׁוֹפָר וְלֹא נִזְהָר
takes ,warning | and not | ram's the horn | of sound the | hearer the | hears and | the ;people

5 6963 1961 7218 1818 3947 2719 935
וַתָּבוֹא חֶרֶב וַתִּקָּחֵהוּ דָּמוֹ בְרֹאשׁוֹ יִהְיֶה׃ אֵת קוֹל
The of sound | .be shall | his on head own | his blood | takes and ;him | the sword | and comes

5315 2094 1961 1818 2094 3808 8085 7782
הַשּׁוֹפָר שָׁמַע וְלֹא נִזְהָר דָּמוֹ בּוֹ יִהְיֶה וְהוּא נִזְהָר נַפְשׁוֹ
his soul | took who ,warning | But he | shall .be | on himself | his blood | took ;warning | and not | he ,heard | ram's the horn

6 8628 3808 935 2719 7200 6822 4422
מִלֵּט׃ וְהַצֹּפֶה כִּי־יִרְאֶה אֶת־הַחֶרֶב בָּאָה וְלֹא־תָקַע
does blow | and not | coming | the sword | sees he if | the But ,watchman | shall he .deliver

5315 3947 2719 935 2094 3808 5971 7782
בַּשּׁוֹפָר וְהָעָם לֹא־נִזְהָר וַתָּבוֹא חֶרֶב וַתִּקַּח מֵהֶם נָפֶשׁ
,soul a | from them | and takes | the sword | and comes | are ;warned | not | the and people | ram's the ,horn

1875 6822 3027 1818 3947 5771
הוּא בַּעֲוֹנוֹ נִלְקָח וְדָמוֹ מִיַּד־הַצֹּפֶה אֶדְרֹשׁ׃ וְאַתָּה
,you And | will I .require | watch- man's | the from hand | his But blood | is .taken | his in iniquity | he

7 6310 8085 3478 1004 5414 6822 120 1121
בֶּן־אָדָם צֹפֶה נְתַתִּיךָ לְבֵית יִשְׂרָאֵל וְשָׁמַעְתָּ מִפִּי
from Me | you And hear shall | .Israel | the to of house | have I you set | a watchman | ,man | son of

8 4191 7563 7563 559 2094 1697
דָּבָר וְהִזְהַרְתָּ אֹתָם מִמֶּנִּי׃ בְּאָמְרִי לָרָשָׁע רָשָׁע מוֹת
surely | O ,wicked | the to ,wicked | I When say | My from .mouth | them | warn and | the ,word

5771 7563 1870 7563 2094 1696 3808 4191
תָּמוּת וְלֹא דִבַּרְתָּ לְהַזְהִיר רָשָׁע מִדַּרְכּוֹ הוּא רָשָׁע בַּעֲוֹנוֹ
his in iniquity | wicked one | that | his from ,way | the wicked | warn to | do you speak | and not | shall you ;die

9 1870 7563 2094 1245 3027 1818 4191
יָמוּת וְדָמוֹ מִיָּדְךָ אֲבַקֵּשׁ׃ וְאַתָּה כִּי־הִזְהַרְתָּ רָשָׁע מִדַּרְכּוֹ
his from ,way | the wicked | you warn | if | But ,you | will I .require | from your hand | his but blood | shall ;die

4191 5771 1870 7725 3808 7725
לָשׁוּב מִמֶּנָּה וְלֹא־שָׁב מִדַּרְכּוֹ הוּא בַּעֲוֹנוֹ יָמוּת וְאַתָּה
you But | shall .die | his in iniquity | he | his from ,way | he turns | and not | from ;it | turn to

10 3478 1004 559 120 1121 5337 5315
נַפְשְׁךָ הִצַּלְתָּ׃ וְאַתָּה בֶן־אָדָם אֱמֹר אֶל־בֵּית יִשְׂרָאֵל
,Israel | the of house | to | say | ,man son of | ,you And | have .delivered | your soul

2403 6588 559 559
כֵּן אֲמַרְתֶּם לֵאמֹר כִּי־פְשָׁעֵינוּ וְחַטֹּאתֵינוּ עָלֵינוּ וּבָם
in and them | on (are) ,us | our and sins | our transgressions | Surely | ,saying | have you ,spoken | Thus

11 5002 2416 559 2421 4743
אֲנַחְנוּ נְמַקִּים וְאֵיךְ נִחְיֶה׃ אֱמֹר אֲלֵיהֶם חַי־אָנִי נְאֻם
states | ,live I (As) | :them to | Say | we shall ?live | and then | are ;rotting | we

pleasure in the death of the wicked, except in the wicked turning from his way, and *so to* live. Turn! Turn from your evil ways! For why will you die, O house of Israel?

12And you, son of man, say to the sons of your people, The righteousness of the righteous shall not deliver him in the day of his trespass. And the evil of the evil; in the day he turns from his wickedness, he shall not fall by it. And the righteous shall not be able to live by it, in the day he sins. 13Though I say to the righteous, He shall surely live; yet he trusts in his own righteousness, and commits iniquity; all his righteousness shall not be remembered. But he shall die for his iniquity which he has done. 14And though I say to the wicked, You shall surely die; if he turns from his sin and does justice and righteousness; 15*if* the wicked returns the pledge; he repays the thing stolen; he walks in the statutes of life, not doing iniquity; he shall surely live; he shall not die. 16All his sins which he has sinned shall not be remembered to him; he has done justice and righteousness; he shall surely live. 17Yet the sons of your people say, The way of the Lord is not fair. But they, *even* their way is not fair. 18When the righteous turns from his righteousness, and does iniquity, he shall even die by them. 19But if the wicked turns from his wickedness, and does justice and righteousness, he shall live by them. 20Yet you say, The way of the Lord is not fair. I shall judge you, each man by his ways, O house of Israel.

21And it happened in the twelfth year, in the tenth *month*, on the fifth of the

7451 7725 7563 4194 2654 3068 136
אדני יהוה אם־אחפץ במות הרשע כי אם־בשוב רשע
the the in except the the in have I not ,Jehovah the
wicked of turning ,wicked of death pleasure Lord

4191 4100 7451 1870 7725 7725 2421 1870
מדרכו וחיה שובו שובו מדרכיכם הרעים ולמה תמותו
you will why for ;evil your from turn ,Turn and his from
die ways .live way

5971 1121 559 120 1121 3478 1004
12 בית ישראל׃ ואתה בן־אדם אמר אל־בני־עמך
your the to say ,man son ,you And ?Israel O
people of sons of of house

3808 7563 7564 6588 3117 5337 3808 6662 6666
צדקת הצדיק לא תצילנו ביום פשעו ורשעת הרשע לא־
not the the And his the in deliver shall not the righteous- The
,evil of evil .trespass of day him righteous of ness

2421 3201 3808 6662 7562 7725 3117 3782
יכשל בה ביום שובו מרשעו וצדיק לא יוכל לחיות בה
by live to shall not the And his from he the in ,it by shall he
it able be righteous .wickedness turns day fall

982 2421 2421 6662 559 2398 3117
13 ביום חטאתו׃ באמרי לצדיק חיה יחיה והוא־בטח
trusts and shall he surely the to I Though .sins he the in
he —live ,righteous say day

5771 2142 3808 6666 3605 5766 6213 6666
על־צדקתו ועשה עול כל־צדקתו לא תזכרנה ובעולו
his for but be shall not his all ,iniquity and own his in
iniquity —remembered righteousness commits righteousness

7725 4191 4191 7563 559 4191 6213 834
14 אשר־עשה בו ימות׃ ובאמרי לרשע מות תמות ושב
he if shall You surely the to though And shall he for has he that
turns —die ,wicked say I .die it ,done

1500 7563 7725 2258 6666 4941 6213 2403
15 מחטאתו ועשה משפט וצדקה׃ חבל ישיב רשע גזלה
thing the the returns the righ- and justice and his from
robbed ,wicked pledge ;teousness does sin

2421 2421 5766 6213 1115 1980 2416 2708 7999
ישלם בחקות החיים הלך לבלתי עשות עול חיו יחיה
shall he surely ;iniquity doing not ,walks he life the in he
;live of statutes ,repays

4941 2142 3808 2398 834 2403 3605 4191 3808
16 לא ימות׃ כל־חטאתו אשר חטא לא תזכרנה לו משפט
justice to be shall not has he which his All shall he not
;him remembered sinned sins .die

1870 8505 3808 5971 1121 559 2421 2421 6213 6666
17 וצדקה עשה חיו יחיה׃ ואמרו בני עמך לא יתכן דרך
The fair is not your the say Yet shall he surely has he righ- and
of way ,people of sons .live ;done teousness

6666 6662 7725 8505 3808 1870 136
18 אדני והמה דרכם לא־יתכן׃ בשוב־צדיק מצדקתו
his from the When .fair is not their (and) But the
righteousness righteous turns way they .Lord

6213 7564 7563 7725 4191 5766 6213
19 ועשה עול ומת בהם׃ ובשוב רשע מרשעתו ועשה
does and his from the if But .them by shall he ,iniquity and
wickedness wicked turns die even does

8505 3808 559 2421 6666 4941
20 משפט וצדקה עליהם הוא יחיה׃ ואמרתם לא יתכן
fair is not you Yet shall he them by and justice
,say .live ,righteousness

3478 1004 8199 1870 376 136 1870
דרך אדני איש כדרכיו אשפוט אתכם בית ישראל׃
.Israel O ,you will I his by Each the the
of house judge ,ways man .Lord of way

2320 2568 6224 8141 6240 8147 1961
21 ויהי בשתי עשרה שנה בעשרי בחמשה לחדש
the of the on tenth the in ,year the in And
month fifth ,(month) twelfth was it

month of our exile, one who escaped out of Jerusalem came to me, saying, The city has been stricken.
22 And the hand of Jehovah was on me in the evening, before the escaped one came. And He had opened my mouth until that one came in the morning. And my mouth was opened, and I was no longer dumb.
23 And the word of Jehovah was to me, saying,
24 Son of man, the inhabitants of ruins are speaking, these in the land of Israel, saying, Abraham was one, and he possessed the land; but we *are* many; the land is given to us for a possession.
25 So say to them, So says the Lord Jehovah: You eat on the blood, and you lift your eyes up to your idols, and you shed blood. And shall you possess the land?
26 You stand on your sword, and you each do abominations, defiling his neighbor's wife. And shall you possess the land?
27 Say this to them, So says the Lord Jehovah: *As* I live, surely those in the ruins shall fall by the sword; and I will give the one who *is* on the face of the field to the beasts to be eaten; and those in the forts, and in the caves, shall die by the plague.
28 For I shall make the land desolate, and a waste; and the pride of her strength shall cease. And the heights of Israel shall be a waste, that none will go through.
29 And they shall know that I *am* Jehovah, when I have made the land desolate and a waste, because of all their abominations which they have done.

30 And you, son of man, the sons of your people are talking about you beside the walls, and in the doors

5221 559 3389 6412 935 1546
לְגָלוּתֵנוּ בָּא־אֵלַי הַפָּלִיט מִירוּשָׁלַםִ לֵאמֹר הֻכְּתָה
been has ,saying of out who one to came our of
stricken ,Jerusalem escaped me ,exile

6412 935 6440 6153 1961 3068 3027 5892
22 הָעִיר׃ וְיַד־יְהוָה הָיְתָה אֵלַי בָּעֶרֶב לִפְנֵי בּוֹא הַפָּלִיט
escaped the came before the in me on was Jehovah And The
.one ,evening of hand the .city

481 3808 6310 6605 1242 935 5704 6310 6605
וַיִּפְתַּח אֶת־פִּי עַד־בּוֹא אֵלַי בַּבֹּקֶר וַיִּפָּתַח פִּי וְלֹא נֶאֱלַמְתִּי
was I and my was And the in me to he until my had He And
dumb not mouth opened .morning came mouth opened

3427 120 1121 559 3068 1697 1961 5750
23 עוֹד׃ וַיְהִי דְבַר־יְהוָה אֵלַי לֵאמֹר׃
24 בֶּן־אָדָם יֹשְׁבֵי
resi- the ,man Son ,saying ,me to Jehovah the And any
of dents of of word was .longer

259 559 559 3478 127 428 2723
הֶחֳרָבוֹת הָאֵלֶּה עַל־אַדְמַת יִשְׂרָאֵל אֹמְרִים לֵאמֹר אֶחָד
one ,saying are Israel the in these ,ruins
,speaking of land

5414 7227 776 3423 85 1961
הָיָה אַבְרָהָם וַיִּירַשׁ אֶת־הָאָרֶץ וַאֲנַחְנוּ רַבִּים לָנוּ נִתְּנָה
given is us to ;many we but the he and ,Abraham was
(are) ;land possessed

136 559 559 4181 776
25 הָאָרֶץ לְמוֹרָשָׁה׃ לָכֵן אֱמֹר אֲלֵיהֶם כֹּה־אָמַר ׀ אֲדֹנָי
the says Thus ,them to say Therefore a for the
Lord .possession land

1818 1544 5375 5869 398 1818 3068
יְהוִה עַל־הַדָּם ׀ תֹּאכֵלוּ וְעֵינֵכֶם תִּשְׂאוּ אֶל־גִּלּוּלֵיכֶם וְדָם
and your to lift you your and ,eat You the on :Jehovah
blood ,idols up eyes blood

6213 2719 5975 3423 776 8210
26 תִּשְׁפֹּכוּ וְהָאָרֶץ תִּירָשׁוּ׃ עֲמַדְתֶּם עַל־חַרְבְּכֶם עֲשִׂיתֶן
do you your on stand You shall you the and ;shed you
,sword ?possess land

3423 776 2930 7453 802 376 8441
תּוֹעֵבָה וְאִישׁ אֶת־אֵשֶׁת רֵעֵהוּ טִמֵּאתֶם וְהָאָרֶץ תִּירָשׁוּ׃
shall you the and ;defiles his wife and abomina-
?possess land neighbor's each tions

3808 2416 3068 136 559 3541 559
27 כֹּה־תֹאמַר אֲלֵהֶם כֹּה־אָמַר אֲדֹנָי יְהוִה חַי־אָנִי אִם־לֹא
surely (As) :Jehovah the says Thus ,them to say Thus
,I live Lord

2416 7704 6440 834 5307 2719 2723 834
אֲשֶׁר בֶּחֳרָבוֹת בַּחֶרֶב יִפֹּלוּ וַאֲשֶׁר עַל־פְּנֵי הַשָּׂדֶה לַחַיָּה
the to field the the in he and shall the by the in those
beasts of face (is) who ,fall sword ruins

4191 1698 4631 4679 834 398 5414
נְתַתִּיו לְאָכְלוֹ וַאֲשֶׁר בַּמְּצָדוֹת וּבַמְּעָרוֹת בַּדֶּבֶר יָמוּתוּ׃
shall the by in and the in and be to will I
.die plague caves the forts those ,eaten him give

8074 5797 1347 7673 4923 8077 776 5414
28 וְנָתַתִּי אֶת־הָאָרֶץ שְׁמָמָה וּמְשַׁמָּה וְנִשְׁבַּת גְּאוֹן עֻזָּהּ וְשָׁמְמוּ
be shall And her the has and a and desolate the I For
waste a .strength of pride ceased ,waste land made have

5414 3068 3045 5674 369 3478 2022
29 הָרֵי יִשְׂרָאֵל מֵאֵין עוֹבֵר׃ וְיָדְעוּ כִּי־אֲנִי יְהוָה בְּתִתִּי אֶת־
I when ,Jehovah I that they Then go will that ,Israel the
made have (am) know shall .through none of heights

6213 834 8441 3605 4923 8077 776
הָאָרֶץ שְׁמָמָה וּמְשַׁמָּה עַל כָּל־תּוֹעֲבֹתָם אֲשֶׁר עָשׂוּ׃
have they which their all because a and desolate the
.done abominations of waste land

7023 681 1696 5971 1121 120 1121
30 וְאַתָּה בֶן־אָדָם בְּנֵי עַמְּךָ הַנִּדְבָּרִים בְּךָ אֵצֶל הַקִּירוֹת
walls the beside about talking are your the ,man son And
you people of sons of ,you

559 251 376 2297 259 1696 1004 6607
וּבְפִתְחֵי הַבָּתִּים וְדִבֶּר־חַד אֶת־אַחַד אִישׁ אֶת־אָחִיו לֵאמֹר
,saying his ,brother with each man ,one to one speaks and the ,houses the in and of doors

31 935 3068 935 1697 4100 8085 935
בֹּאוּ־נָא וְשִׁמְעוּ מָה הַדָּבָר הַיּוֹצֵא מֵאֵת יְהוָה׃ וְיָבוֹאוּ
they come And .Jehovah from which comes the (is) word what and hear now Come

1697 8085 5971 6440 3427 5971 3996
אֵלֶיךָ כִּמְבוֹא־עָם וְיֵשְׁבוּ לְפָנֶיךָ עַמִּי וְשָׁמְעוּ אֶת־דְּבָרֶיךָ
your ;words they and hear My (as) ,people before you they and sit ,people as come you to

310 6213 6310 5690 6213
וְאוֹתָם לֹא יַעֲשׂוּ כִּי־עֲגָבִים בְּפִיהֶם הֵמָּה עֹשִׂים אַחֲרֵי
(but) after ,produce they their with mouth much love For they .do will not them but

32 6963 3303 5690 7892 2009 1980 3820 1215
בִּצְעָם לִבָּם הֹלֵךְ׃ וְהִנְּךָ לָהֶם כְּשִׁיר עֲגָבִים יְפֵה קוֹל
voice a beautiful love ,songs a as of singer to (are) them And you ,lo .goes their heart un- their gain just

33 935 369 6213 1697 8085 5071 2895
וּמֵטִב נַגֵּן וְשָׁמְעוּ אֶת־דְּבָרֶיךָ וְעֹשִׂים אֵינָם אוֹתָם׃ וּבְבֹאָהּ
when So ,comes it .they not them are but doing your ,words they hear for an (on) ,instrument play and well

8432 1961 5030 3045 935 2009
הִנֵּה בָאָה וְיָדְעוּ כִּי נָבִיא הָיָה בְתוֹכָם׃
their in .midst has been a prophet that they then know will is it —coming ,behold

of the houses. And one speaks to another, each man with his brother, saying, Come now and hear what the word *is* which comes from Jehovah. [31]And they come to you as people come; and they sit before you *as* My people. And they hear your words; but they do not do them. For they produce much love with their mouth, *but* their heart goes after their unjust gain. [32]And, behold, you *are* to them as a song of love: a beautiful voice, and playing well on an instrument. For they hear your words, but they are not doing them. [33]So when it comes — behold, it is coming — then they will know that a prophet has been in their midst.

CAP. XXXIV לד

CHAPTER 34

1 7462 5012 120 1121 559 3068 1697 1961
2
וַיְהִי דְבַר־יְהוָה אֵלַי לֵאמֹר׃ בֶּן־אָדָם הִנָּבֵא עַל־רוֹעֵי
the of shepherds against prophesy ,man Son of ,saying ,me to Jehovah the of word And was

136 559 3541 7462 559 5012 3478
יִשְׂרָאֵל הִנָּבֵא וְאָמַרְתָּ אֲלֵיהֶם לָרֹעִים כֹּה־אָמַר אֲדֹנָי
the Lord says Thus the to ,shepherds ,them to say and Prophesy .Israel

3808 7462 1961 834 3478 7462 1945 3068
יְהוִה הוֹי רֹעֵי־יִשְׂרָאֵל אֲשֶׁר הָיוּ רֹעִים אוֹתָם הֲלוֹא
Should not them- !selves feeding are who Israel's shepherds Woe to Jeho- :vah

3 6785 398 2459 7462 7462 6629
הַצֹּאן יִרְעוּ הָרֹעִים׃ אֶת־הַחֵלֶב תֹּאכֵלוּ וְאֶת־הַצֶּמֶר
the with wool and eat You fat the the ?shepherds feed the flock

4 2470 7462 3808 6629 2076 1277 3847
תִּלְבָּשׁוּ הַבְּרִיאָה תִּזְבָּחוּ הַצֹּאן לֹא תִרְעוּ׃ אֶת־הַנַּחְלוֹת
weak The .feed you not the flock you ;sacrifice fat the ones clothe ;yourselves

3808 7665 7495 3808 2470 2388 3808
לֹא חִזַּקְתֶּם וְאֶת־הַחוֹלָה לֹא־רִפֵּאתֶם וְלַנִּשְׁבֶּרֶת לֹא
not the and broken have you ;healed not the sick and have you ,strengthened not

3808 6 7725 3808 5080 2280
חֲבַשְׁתֶּם וְאֶת־הַנִּדַּחַת לֹא הֲשֵׁבֹתֶם וְאֶת־הָאֹבֶדֶת לֹא
not the lost and have ,back brought not the banished And have you .up bound

5 1077 6327 6531 7287 2394 1245
בִקַּשְׁתֶּם וּבְחָזְקָה רְדִיתֶם אֹתָם וּבְפָרֶךְ׃ וַתְּפוּצֶינָה מִבְּלִי
for of lack were they And scattered with and .harshness them you rule with but force have you ;sought

6327 7704 2416 3605 402 1961 7462
רֹעֶה וַתִּהְיֶינָה לְאָכְלָה לְכָל־חַיַּת הַשָּׂדֶה וַתְּפוּצֶינָה׃
were they when .scattered field the the of beasts to all food for they and became a ;shepherd

[1]And the word of Jehovah was to me, saying, [2]Son of man, prophesy against the shepherds of Israel. Prophesy and say to them, to the shepherds, So says the Lord Jehovah: Woe to the shepherds of Israel who are feeding themselves! Should not the shepherds feed the flock? [3]You eat the fat, and clothe yourselves with the wool; you sacrifice the fat ones; you do not feed the flock. [4]You have not made the weak strong, and you have not healed the sick; and you have not bound up the broken. And the banished have not been brought back, and you have not sought the lost; but you rule them with force and with harshness. [5]And they were scattered for lack of a shepherd. And they became food to all the beasts of the field, when they were

scattered. ⁶My sheep strayed through all the mountains and on every high hill. And My sheep were scattered on all the face of the earth, and none searched, and none sought *for them*. ⁷For this reason, shepherds, hear the word of Jehovah: ⁸*As* I live, declares the Lord Jehovah, surely because My sheep became a prey, and My sheep became food for all the beasts of the field, from not having *a* shepherd; and *because* My shepherds did not search *for* My sheep, but the shepherds fed themselves, and did not feed the flock; ⁹therefore, O shepherds, hear the word of Jehovah: ¹⁰So says the Lord Jehovah: Behold, I *am* against the shepherds, and I will require My sheep from their hand, and cause them to cease from pasturing the sheep. And the shepherds shall no longer feed themselves, for I will deliver My sheep from their mouth; and they will not be food to devour.

¹¹For so says the Lord Jehovah: Behold, I Myself will search for My sheep, and seek them out. ¹²As a shepherd seeks his flock in the day that he is among his scattered sheep, so I will seek out My sheep, and will deliver them from all the places where they were scattered, in a day of cloud and thick cloud. ¹³And I will bring them out from the peoples, and gather them from the lands, and will bring them to their land, and feed them on the mountains of Israel, by the ravines, and in all the dwelling-places of the land. ¹⁴I will feed them in a good pasture, and on the high mountains of Israel their fold shall be; they shall lie there in a good fold, and they shall feed *in a* fat

---

6

3605	7311	1389	3605	5921	2022	3605	6629	7686
all	And .high on	hill	every	and on	the mountains	through all	My sheep	strayed

7

36 ·51	1245	369	1875	369	6629	6327	776	6440
There-fore	sought (them for)	and none	searched	and none	My sheep	were scattered	the earth	the face of

8

30·68	136	5002	2416	3068	1697	8085	7462
,Jehovah Lord	the states (As)	,I live	:Jehovah the	of word	the hear	shep-herds

3605	402	6629	1961	957	6629	3282
all for	food for My sheep	and	a for became ,prey	My sheep	be-came	surely cause

7462	6629	7462	1875	38·08	7462	369	7704	2416
but fed	My (for) My shepherds	did search not	And .shepherd no having	the ,field	from of beasts

8085	746·2	7462	38·08	7462	7462
hear	O There- ,shepherds fore	did .feed	not	My flock selves	them- the shepherds

10

7462	2005	3068	136	559/3541	3068	1697
the shepherds	against ,Behold (am) I	,Jehovah the Lord	says Thus	:Jehovah the of word

380·8	6629	7462	7673	3027	6629	1875
And not .sheep	the pastoring	from cause to	them pasturing	and cease	their from hand	My sheep	will I and require

1961	8808	6310	6629	5337	7462	5750	7462
will they be	and their not ,mouth	from My sheep	will I for deliver	them- ,selves	the shepherds	any longer	shall feed

11

2005	3068	136	559	3541	402	3859
My-self	,Behold :Jehovah I Lord	the says	thus For	.devour to	food

12

3117	5739	74·62	1243	1239	6629	1875
the in day	his flock	a shepherd	seeks As	seek and .out them	sheep My	search will for

5337	6629	1239	6567	6629	8432	1961
will and deliver	My sheep	will I out seek	so .scattered	his sheep	among	he that is

6205	6051	3117	8033	6327	4725	3605
thick and cloud .cloud	a in of day	there were scattered	they where	the places	from all	them

13

935	776	5971	3318
will and them bring ,lands	from the peoples	gather and them	will I And out them bring

3605	650	3478	2022	7462	127
in and all	the ,ravines	by Israel	the of mountains	feed and them	their to land

14

4791	2022	7462	2896	4829	776	4186
high mountains	the on and ,them	will I feed	good a in	the pasture	dwell- the land of ings

8082	4827	2896	5116	7257	8033	5116	1961	3478
fat	(a in) and pasture	,good	a in fold	shall they lie	there	their ;fold	shall be	Israel of

pasture, all the mountains
of Israel. 15 I will feed My
sheep, and I will make them
lie down, declares the Lord
Jehovah. 16 I will seek the
lost, and I will return the
banished. And I will bind up
the broken, and I will make
the weak strong. But I will
destroy the fat and the
strong; I will feed them with
judgment. 17 And you, My
flock, so says the Lord
Jehovah: Behold, I judge
between lamb and lamb,
between rams and he-
goats. 18 Is it a small thing
to you to have fed on the
good pasture, but you must
trample the rest of your
pastures with your feet?
And have you drunk of the
clear waters, but the rest
you must foul with your
feet?
19 And My sheep, *what*
your feet have trampled,
they must feed on. And
what your feet fouled, they
must drink. 20 So the Lord
Jehovah says this to them:
Behold, I Myself will even
judge between the fat lamb
and the lean lamb. 21 Be-
cause you have thrust with
side and with shoulder, and
have pushed all the weak
with your horns, until you
have scattered them to the
outside; 22 I also will save
My sheep, and they shall no
longer be for a prey; and I
will judge between lamb
and lamb. 23 And I will raise
up over them one shepherd.
And He shall feed them; My
servant David, He shall feed
them; and He shall be to
them for a shepherd. 24 And
I, Jehovah, will be their
God; and My servant David
shall be a ruler among
them. I, Jehovah, have
spoken. 25 And I will cut a
covenant of peace with
them, and make evil beasts
cease out of the land. And
they shall live in the
wilderness securely, and

7257 369 6629 7462 3478 2022 7462
15 תִּרְעֶינָה אֶל־הָרֵי יִשְׂרָאֵל׃ אֲנִי אֶרְעֶה צֹאנִי וַאֲנִי אַרְבִּיצֵם
them make will and My feed will I .Israel the all shall they
,down lie I ,sheep of mountains feed

7725 5080 1245 6 3068 136 5002
16 נְאֻם אֲדֹנָי יְהוִה׃ אֶת־הָאֹבֶדֶת אֲבַקֵּשׁ וְאֶת־הַנִּדַּחַת אָשִׁיב
will I the and will I lost the .Jehovah the states
.return banished seek Lord

8082 2388 2470 2280 7665
וְלַנִּשְׁבֶּרֶת אֶחֱבֹשׁ וְאֶת־הַחוֹלָה אֲחַזֵּק וְאֶת־הַשְּׁמֵנָה וְאֶת־
and the But will I the and will I the And
fat .strengthen weak ,up bind broken

559 3541 6629 859 4941 7462 8045 2389
17 הַחֲזָקָה אַשְׁמִיד אֶרְעֶנָּה בְמִשְׁפָּט׃ וְאַתֵּנָה צֹאנִי כֹּה אָמַר
says thus My ,you And with will I will I strong the
,flock .judgment them feed .destroy

6260 352 7716 7716 8199 2005 3068 136
אֲדֹנָי יְהוִה הִנְנִי שֹׁפֵט בֵּין־שֶׂה לָשֶׂה לָאֵילִים וְלָעַתּוּדִים׃
.he-goats and (between) and lamb be- judge ,Behold :Jehovah the
rams ,lamb tween I Lord

7429 4829 3498 7462 2896 4829 4592
18 הַמְעַט מִכֶּם הַמִּרְעֶה הַטּוֹב תִּרְעוּ וְיֶתֶר מִרְעֵיכֶם תִּרְמְסוּ
must you your the but have to good the to a it Is
trample pastures of rest ,on fed pasture you thing small

7272 3499 8354 4325 4950 7272
בְּרַגְלֵיכֶם וּמִשְׁקַע־מַיִם תִּשְׁתּוּ וְאֵת הַנּוֹתָרִים בְּרַגְלֵיכֶם
your with rest the but have you waters of And your with
feet ,drunk clear the ?feet

7272 4833 7462 7272 4823 6629 7515
19 תִּרְפֹּשׂוּן׃ וְצֹאנִי מִרְמַס רַגְלֵיכֶם תִּרְעֶינָה וּמִרְפַּשׂ רַגְלֵיכֶם
your (with) what and must they your have (what) My And must you
feet fouled is ,on feed feet trampled ,sheep .foul

2005 3068 136 559 3541 8354
20 תִּשְׁתֶּינָה׃ לָכֵן כֹּה אָמַר אֲדֹנָי יְהוִה אֲלֵיהֶם הִנְנִי
,Behold :them to Jehovah the says thus Therefore (must) they
I Lord .drink

6654 3282 7330 7716 996 1274 7716 8199
21 אֲנִי וְשָׁפַטְתִּי בֵּין־שֶׂה בִרְיָה וּבֵין שֶׂה רָזָה׃ יַעַן בְּצַד
with Because the lamb and fat the lamb between even will My-
side .lean judge self

2470 3605 5055 7161 1920 3801
וּבְכָתֵף תֶּהְדֹּפוּ וּבְקַרְנֵיכֶם תְּנַגְּחוּ כָּל־הַנַּחְלוֹת עַד אֲשֶׁר
that until the all have with and have you with and
,weak pushed horns your ,thrust shoulder

3808 6629 3467 2351 6327
22 הֲפִיצוֹתֶם אוֹתָנָה אֶל־הַחוּצָה׃ וְהוֹשַׁעְתִּי לְצֹאנִי וְלֹא־
and My will I but the to them have you
not ,sheep save ;outside scattered

5921 6965 7716 7716 996 8199 957 5750 1961
23 תִהְיֶינָה עוֹד לָבַז וְשָׁפַטְתִּי בֵּין שֶׂה לָשֶׂה׃ וַהֲקִמֹתִי עֲלֵיהֶם
over will I And and lamb be- will I and a for any shall they
them up raise .lamb tween judge ;prey longer be

7462 1732 5650 7462 259 7462
רֹעֶה אֶחָד וְרָעָה אֶתְהֶן אֵת עַבְדִּי דָוִיד הוּא יִרְעֶה אֹתָם
,them shall He David My ,them He And .one shepherd
feed servant feed shall

430 1961 3068 7462 1961
24 וְהוּא יִהְיֶה לָהֶן לְרֹעֶה׃ וַאֲנִי יְהוָה אֶהְיֶה לָהֶם לֵאלֹהִים
,God to be will Jehovah And a for to shall He and
them I shepherd them be

3772 1696 3068 8432 5387 1732 5650
25 וְעַבְדִּי דָוִד נָשִׂיא בְתוֹכָם אֲנִי יְהוָה דִּבַּרְתִּי׃ וְכָרַתִּי לָהֶם
with I And have Jehovah I among ruler a David My and
them cut will .spoken them servant

4057 3427 776 7451 2416 7673 7965 1285
בְּרִית שָׁלוֹם וְהִשְׁבַּתִּי חַיָּה־רָעָה מִן־הָאָרֶץ וְיָשְׁבוּ בַמִּדְבָּר
the in they And the out evil beasts make and ,peace cove- a
wilderness live shall .land of cease of nant

sleep in the forests. [26]And I will make them and the places around My hill a blessing. And I will bring down the shower in its season; there shall be showers of blessing. [27]And the tree of the field shall yield its fruit, and the earth shall yield its increase. And they shall be securely on their land. And they shall know that I *am* Jehovah, when I have broken the staffs of their yoke, and have rescued them from the hand of those who enslaved them. [28]And they shall not any more be a prey to the nations; and the beast of the land shall not eat them; but they shall live securely, and no one shall terrify *them*. [29]And I will raise up for them a planting place of name; and they shall not any more *be of* those gathered *by* famine in the land. And *they* shall not any more bear the shame of the nations. [30]And they shall know that I, Jehovah their God *am* with them; and they *are* My people, the house of Israel, declares the Lord Jehovah. [31]And you, My sheep, the sheep of My pasture, you *are* men; I *am* your God, declares the Lord Jehovah.

1389 5439 3293 3462 982
26 לָבֶטַח וְיָשְׁנוּ בַּיְּעוֹרִים׃ וְנָתַתִּי אוֹתָם וּסְבִיבוֹת גִּבְעָתִי
hill My the and around places them I And make will the in .forests sleep and securely

1293 1653 1653 3381 1293
27 בְּרָכָה וְהוֹרַדְתִּי הַגֶּשֶׁם בְּעִתּוֹ גִּשְׁמֵי בְרָכָה יִהְיוּ׃ וְנָתַן
shall give And there .be shall blessing shower of its in ;season showers will I And down bring a .blessing

127 2981 776 6529 7704 6086
עֵץ הַשָּׂדֶה אֶת־פִּרְיוֹ וְהָאָרֶץ תִּתֵּן יְבוּלָהּ וְהָיוּ עַל־אַדְמָתָם
their land on they And be shall its .increase shall yield the and earth ,fruit its the field the of tree

5923 4133 7665 3068 982
לָבֶטַח וְיָדְעוּ כִּי־אֲנִי יְהוָה בְּשִׁבְרִי אֶת־מֹטוֹת עֻלָּם
their yoke the of staffs have I when broken ,Jehovah I (am) that they and know shall ;securely

959 5647 5337
28 וְהִצַּלְתִּים מִיַּד הָעֹבְדִים בָּהֶם׃ וְלֹא־יִהְיוּ עוֹד בַּז לַגּוֹיִם
the to ,nations a prey any more they And be shall not .their slavers' from hand have and them rescued

2729 982 398 776 2476
וְחַיַּת הָאָרֶץ לֹא תֹאכְלֵם וְיָשְׁבוּ לָבֶטַח וְאֵין מַחֲרִיד׃
shall .terrify and none ,securely they but live shall eat shall .them not the land the and of beast

7458 622 4302 6965
29 וַהֲקִמֹתִי לָהֶם מַטָּע לְשֵׁם וְלֹא־יִהְיוּ עוֹד אֲסֻפֵי רָעָב
famine those of gathered any more they shall and not ;name of planting a place for them will I And up raise

3068 3639 5375 776
30 בָּאָרֶץ וְלֹא־יִשְׂאוּ עוֹד כְּלִמַּת הַגּוֹיִם׃ וְיָדְעוּ כִּי־אֲנִי יְהוָה
Jehovah I that they And know shall the .nations the of shame any more shall bear and not the in ,land

3068 136 1004 430
אֱלֹהֵיהֶם אִתָּם וְהֵמָּה עַמִּי בֵּית יִשְׂרָאֵל נְאֻם אֲדֹנָי יְהוִה׃
.Jehovah the Lord states ,Israel the of house My (are) ,people and they with ;them (am) their God

430 120 4830 6629 6629 859
31 וְאַתֵּן צֹאנִי צֹאן מַרְעִיתִי אָדָם אַתֶּם אֲנִי אֱלֹהֵיכֶם נְאֻם
states ,God your (and) (am) I you ,(are) men My ,pasture the of sheep My ,sheep And ,you

3068 136
אֲדֹנָי יְהוִה׃
.Jehovah the Lord

CAP. XXXV לה

CHAPTER 35

CHAPTER 35

[1]And the word of Jehovah was to me, saying, [2]Son of man, set your face against Mount Seir, and prophesy against it. [3]And say to it, So says the Lord Jehovah: Behold, I *am* against you, Mount Seir; and I will stretch My hand against you; and I will make you a ruin and a waste. [4]I will lay your cities waste, and you shall be a ruin. And they shall know that I *am* Jehovah. [5]Because there was to you never-ending enmity, and you poured out

7760 120 1121 559 3068
1
2 וַיְהִי דְבַר־יְהוָה אֵלַי לֵאמֹר׃ בֶּן־אָדָם שִׂים פָּנֶיךָ עַל־הַר
Mount against your face set ,man Son of ,saying ,me to Jehovah the of word And was

3068 136 559 5012 8165
3 שֵׂעִיר וְהִנָּבֵא עָלָיו׃ וְאָמַרְתָּ לּוֹ כֹּה אָמַר אֲדֹנָי יְהוִה
:Jehovah the Lord says Thus ,it to say And against it and prophesy Seir

8077 5414 3027 5186 8165 2022 2009
הִנְנִי אֵלֶיךָ הַר־שֵׂעִיר וְנָטִיתִי יָדִי עָלֶיךָ וּנְתַתִּיךָ שְׁמָמָה
ruin a will I and you make against ,you My hand will I and stretch ,Seir Mount against ,you ,Behold (am) I

8077 7760 2723 4923
4 וּמְשַׁמָּה׃ עָרֶיךָ חָרְבָּה אָשִׂים וְאַתָּה שְׁמָמָה תִהְיֶה וְיָדַעְתָּ
you and know shall shall ;be ruin a you and will I ,lay waste your cities a and .waste

1121 5064 5769 342 3068
5 כִּי־אֲנִי יְהוָה׃ יַעַן הֱיוֹת לְךָ אֵיבַת עוֹלָם וַתַּגֵּר אֶת־בְּנֵי־
the of sons you and poured ever- ,lasting enmity to you there Because was .Jehovah I that (am)

the sons of Israel to the hands of the sword in the time of their calamity, in the time of *the* iniquity of the end. ⁶Therefore, *As* I live, declares the Lord Jehovah, surely for blood I appoint you, and blood shall pursue you. Since you have not hated blood, so blood shall pursue you. ⁷And I will make Mount Seir a ruin and a waste, and cut off from it the one passing through, and the one returning. ⁸And I will fill his mountains *with* his slain. In your hills and *in* your valleys, and *in* your every torrent, the slain by the sword shall fall in them. ⁹I will make you forever those ruins, and your cities shall not be inhabited. And you shall know that I *am* Jehovah. ¹⁰Because you have said, These two nations and these two lands will be mine, and we shall possess it—Jehovah was there — ¹¹therefore, *As* I live, declares the Lord Jehovah, I will act by your anger and by envy which you have done out of your hatred against them; and I will be known among them when I have judged you. ¹²And you shall know that I *am* Jehovah. I have heard all your revilings which you have spoken against the mountains of Israel, saying, Desolation! They are given to us for food! ¹³And you magnified with your mouth against Me, and have multiplied your words against Me; I have heard. ¹⁴So says the Lord Jehovah: As all the earth rejoices, I will make you a ruin. ¹⁵As you rejoiced at the inheritance of the house of Israel, because *they were a* ruin, so I will do to you. You shall be a ruin, O Mount Seir, and all Edom, all of it! And they shall know that I *am* Jehovah.

6
2416 3651 | 7093/5771 6256 | :343 6256 2719 3027 | 3478
לָכֵן חַי־ : קֵץ עֲוֺן בְּעֵת אֵידָם בְּעֵת חֶרֶב אֵידָם עַל־יְדֵי יִשְׂרָאֵל
(As) there-live ,fore | ;end's the iniquity the in | their the in calamity of time sword of time | to Israel the hands

38,08 518 7291 1818 6213 1818 3068 136 ~5002
אִם־לֹא יִרְדְּפֶךָ וְדָם כִּי־לְדָם אֶעֶשְׂךָ יְהֹוִה אֲדֹנָי נְאֻם אָנִי
not Since pur-shall and do I for surely ,you make blood ,Jehovah Lord the states I

7
8077 :8165 2022 5414 7291 1818 8130 1818
דָם שָׂנֵאתָ וְדָם יִרְדְּפֶךָ : וְנָתַתִּי אֶת־הַר שֵׂעִיר לְשִׁמְמָה
a for Seir Mount I And pur-shall ;you sue blood ,hated | so have you blood

8
2022 4390 7725 5674 3772 8077
וּשְׁמָמָה וְהִכְרַתִּי מִמֶּנּוּ עֹבֵר וָשָׁב : וּמִלֵּאתִי אֶת־הָרָיו
his will I And the and passer-the from cut and a and
mountains fill returnee through it off waste

15307 2719 2491 650 36,05 1516 1389 2491
חֲלָלָיו גִּבְעוֹתֶיךָ וְגֵאוֹתֶיךָ וְכָל־אֲפִיקֶיךָ חַלְלֵי־חֶרֶב יִפְּלוּ
shall the the your (in) and (in) and your (In) his (with)
fall sword the slain by ,torrent all ,valleys your hills .slain

9
3045 3427 38,08 5892 5414 15769 8077
בָהֶם : שִׁמְמוֹת עוֹלָם אֶתֶּנְךָ וְעָרֶיךָ לֹא תֵשַׁבְנָה וִידַעְתֶּם
you And be shall not your and will I forever Those .them in
know shall .inhabited cities ,you make ruins

10
8147 1471 81,47 559 3282 3068
כִּי־אֲנִי יְהֹוָה : יַעַן אֲמָרְךָ אֶת־שְׁנֵי הַגּוֹיִם וְאֶת־שְׁתֵּי
these and nations These have you Because .Jehovah I that
two two ,said (am)

11
2416 36,51 1961 8033 3068 3423 1961 776
הָאֲרָצוֹת לִי תִהְיֶינָה וִירֵשְׁנוּהָ וַיהוָה שָׁם הָיָה : לָכֵן חַי־אָנִי
I (As) there- —was there Jeho-Yet we and be will mine lands
live fore vah —it possess shall

6213 834 7068 639 6213 3068 136 ~5002
נְאֻם אֲדֹנָי יְהֹוִה וְעָשִׂיתִי כְּאַפְּךָ וּכְקִנְאָתְךָ אֲשֶׁר עָשִׂיתָה
have you which by and your by will I ,Jehovah the states
done envy anger act Lord

12
3045 8199 3045 8130
מִשִּׂנְאָתֶךָ בָּם וְנוֹדַעְתִּי בָם כַּאֲשֶׁר אֶשְׁפְּטֶךָ : וְיָדַעְתָּ כִּי
that you And have I when among will I and against of out
know shall .you judged them known be ;them hatred your

559 834 5007 36,05 8085 3068
אֲנִי יְהֹוָה שָׁמַעְתִּי אֶת־כָּל־נָאֲצוֹתֶיךָ אֲשֶׁר אָמַרְתָּ עַל־
against have you which your all have I .Jehovah I (am)
spoken revilings heard

13
1431 402 5414 8074 559 3478 2022
הָרֵי יִשְׂרָאֵל לֵאמֹר שָׁמֵמוּ לָנוּ נִתְּנוּ לְאָכְלָה : וַתַּגְדִּילוּ
you And .food for are they To !Desolation ,saying .Israel the
magnified given us of mountains

8085 1697 6280 63:10
עָלַי בְּפִיכֶם וְהַעְתַּרְתֶּם עָלַי דִּבְרֵיכֶם אֲנִי שָׁמָעְתִּי :
have I your against have and your with against
.heard ;words Me multiplied mouth Me

14
6213 8077 776 36,05 8056 3068 136 559 3541
כֹּה אָמַר אֲדֹנָי יְהֹוִה כִּשְׂמֹחַ כָּל־הָאָרֶץ שְׁמָמָה אֶעֱשֶׂה־
will I ruin a ;earth the all rejoices As : Jehovah the says Thus
make Lord

15
8077 3478 1004 5159 8057
לָּךְ : כְּשִׂמְחָתְךָ לְנַחֲלַת בֵּית־יִשְׂרָאֵל עַל אֲשֶׁר־שָׁמֵמָה
(a was) that because Israel the the at you As .you
,ruin of house of inheritance rejoiced

3605 123 3605 8165 2022 1961 8077 6213 3651
כֵּן אֶעֱשֶׂה־לָּךְ שְׁמָמָה תִהְיֶה הַר־שֵׂעִיר וְכָל־אֱדוֹם כֻּלָּהּ
of all ,Edom and Seir O shall you ruin A to will I so
.it all Mount ,be .you do

3068 3045
וְיָדְעוּ כִּי־אֲנִי יְהֹוָה :
.Jehovah I that they And
(am) know shall

CAP. XXXVI לו

CHAPTER 36

3478 2022 559 3478 2022 5012 120 1121
1 ואתה בן־אדם הנבא אל־הרי ישראל ואמרת הרי ישראל
,Israel O ,say and Israel the to prophesy ,man son And
of heights of mountains of ,you

341 559 3282 3068 136 559 3541 3068 1697 8085
2 שמעו דבר־יהוה׃ כה אמר אדני יהוה יען אמר האויב
the has Be- :Jehovah the says Thus .Jehovah the hear
enemy said cause Lord of word

1961 4181 5769 1116 1889
3 עליכם האח ובמות עולם למורשה היתה לנו׃ לכן
There- .us to have a For ever- heights !Aha against
fore become possession lasting ,you

7602 8074 3282 3282 3068 136 559 3541 559 5012
הנבא ואמרת כה אמר אדני יהוה יען ביען שמות ושאף
and the be- yea Be- :Jehovah the says Thus ,say and prophesy
crushing wasting cause ,cause Lord

5927 1471 7611 4181 1961 5439
אתכם מסביב להיותכם מורשה לשארית הגוים ותעלו
you and the the to a you that all from you of
lifted were ,nations of rest possession be might around

8085 3478 2022 3651 5971 1681 3956 8193
4 על־שפת לשון ודבת־עם׃ לכן הרי ישראל שמעו
hear ,Israel mountains There- the and the the on
of ,fore .people's talking tongue of lip

1389 2022 3068 136 559 3068 136 1697
דבר־אדני יהוה כה־אמר אדני יהוה להרים ולגבעות
to and the to Jehovah the says Thus :Jehovah the the
,hills the mountains Lord Lord of word

5800 5892 8074 2723 1516 650
לאפיקים ולגאיות ולחרבות השממות ולערים הנעזבות
,forsaken to and ,desolation the to to and the to
cities the of wastes ,valleys the ravines

3651 5439 1471 7611 3933 957 1961/834
5 אשר היו לבז וללעג לשארית הגוים אשר מסביב׃ לכן
there- all that the the to a and a be- which
,fore ;around (are) nations of rest mocking prey came

1696 7068 784 3068 136 559 3541
כה־אמר אדני יהוה אם־לא באש קנאתי דברתי על־
against have I My the in Surely :Jehovah the says thus
spoken jealousy of fire Lord

776 5414 834 3605 123 1471 7611
שארית הגוים ועל־אדום כלא אשר נתנו־את־ארצי ׀
My have who all ,Edom and the rest the
land given her of against ,nations of

4616 5315 7589 3824 8057 4181
להם למורשה בשמחת כל־לבב בשאט נפש למען
to soul scorn- with the all joy with a for them- to
of ing ,heart of possession selves

559 3478 127 5612 957 4054
6 מגרשה לבז׃ לכן הנבא על־אדמת ישראל ואמרת
say and Israel the concerning prophesy There- a for (it make)
of land fore prey land open

3068 136 559 3541 1516 650 1389 2022
להרים ולגבעות לאפיקים ולגאיות כה־אמר ׀ אדני יהוה
:Jehovah the says Thus to and the to to and the to
Lord ,valleys the ,ravines ,hills the mountains

5375 1471 3639 3282 1696 2534 7068
הנני בקנאתי ובחמתי דברתי יען כלמת גוים נשאתם׃
have you the the because have My in and My in ,Behold
.borne nations of shame spoken fury jealousy I

3027 5375 3068 136 559 3541
7 לכן כה אמר אדני יהוה אני נשאתי את־ידי אם־
sure- ;hand My have I :Jehovah the says thus Therefore
up lifted Lord

CHAPTER 36

[1]And you, son of man, prophesy to Israel's mountains and say, O heights of Israel, hear the word of Jehovah. [2]So says the Lord Jehovah: Because the enemy has spoken against you, *saying,* Aha! Everlasting heights have become a possession to us. [3]So prophesy and say, So says the Lord Jehovah: Because; yea, because of the wasting and crushing of you from all around, that you might be a possession to the rest of the nations, and you were lifted on the lip of the tongue, and the talking of the people; [4]so mountains of Israel, hear the word of the Lord Jehovah: So says the Lord Jehovah to the mountains and to the hills, to the ravines and to the valleys, to the wastes of desolation, and to the forsaken cities, which became a prey and a mocking to the rest of the nations that *are* all around. [5]So the Lord Jehovah says this: Surely I have spoken in the fire of My jealousy against the rest of the nations, and against Edom, all *those* of her who have given My land to themselves for a possession with all joy of heart, with scorning of soul, in order to *make it* open land for a prey. [6]So prophesy concerning the land of Israel, and say to the mountains and to the hills, to the ravines and to the valleys, So says the Lord Jehovah: Behold, I have spoken in My jealousy and in My fury, because you have borne the shame of the nations. [7]So the Lord Jehovah says this: I have lifted up My hand;

surely the nations that
surround you, they shall
bear their shame. [8]But you,
O mountains of Israel, you
shall put out your branches
and your fruit you shall bear
for My people Israel. For
they are drawing near to
come. [9]For behold, I *am*
for you, and I will turn to
you, and you shall be tilled
and sown. [10]And I will
multiply men on you, all the
house of Israel; all of it. And
the cities shall be inhabited,
and the wastes shall be
built. [11]And I will multiply
men on you, and beast, and
they will grow and be fruitful. And I will make you
dwell as you formerly *were;*
and I will do better than at
your beginnings. And you
shall know that I *am*
Jehovah. [12]I will cause
men to walk on you, My
people Israel; and they shall
possess you, and you will
be an inheritance to them,
and will not any more in-
crease their bereavement.
[13]So says the Lord
Jehovah: Because they said
to you, You *are* a devourer
of men; and you have
bereaved your nations;
[14]so you shall no longer
devour men; and you shall
not make your nations fall
any more, declares the Lord
Jehovah. [15]And I will not
let you hear the shame of
the nations any longer; and
you shall not bear the
disgrace of the peoples any
more; and you shall not
cause your nations to fall
any more, declares the Lord
Jehovah.
[16]And the word of
Jehovah was to me, say-
ing, [17]Son of man, *when*
the house of Israel dwelt on
their land, they even defiled
it by their ways and by their
doings—as the defilement
of woman's impurity, their
way was before Me. [18]So I
poured out My fury on
them, because of the blood
that they had poured out on
the land, and for their idols
by which they defiled it.

5375 3639 5439 1471
8 לֹא הַגּוֹיִם אֲשֶׁר־לָכֶם מִסָּבִיב הֵמָּה כְּלִמָּתָם יִשָּׂאוּ׃ וְאַתֶּם
But shall their they ,surround you that the ly
,you .bear shame nations

3478 5971 5375 6529 5414 6057 3478 2022
הָרֵי יִשְׂרָאֵל עַנְפְּכֶם תִּתֵּנוּ וּפֶרְיְכֶם תִּשְׂאוּ לְעַמִּי יִשְׂרָאֵל
.Israel My for shall you your and shall you your ,Israel moun- O
people bear fruit out put branches of tains

5647 6437 2005 935 7126
9 כִּי קֵרְבוּ לָבוֹא׃ כִּי הִנְנִי אֲלֵיכֶם וּפָנִיתִי אֲלֵיכֶם וְנֶעֱבַדְתֶּם
shall you and ,you to I and ,you for ,behold for ;come to they For
tilled be turn will (am) I near draw

3605 3478 1004 3605 120 7235 2232
10 וְנִזְרַעְתֶּם׃ וְהִרְבֵּיתִי עֲלֵיכֶם אָדָם כָּל־בֵּית יִשְׂרָאֵל כֻּלֹּה
of all ,Israel the all ,men you on will I And .sown and
it of house multiply

120 5921 7235 1129 2723 5892 3427
11 וְנֹשְׁבוּ הֶעָרִים וְהֶחֳרָבוֹת תִּבָּנֶינָה׃ וְהִרְבֵּיתִי עֲלֵיכֶם אָדָם
man you on will I And be shall the and the shall And
multiply .built wastes ,cities in dwelt be

2895 6927 3427 6509 7235 929
וּבְהֵמָה וְרָבוּ וּפָרוּ וְהוֹשַׁבְתִּי אֶתְכֶם כְּקַדְמוֹתֵיכֶם וְהֵטִבֹתִי
will I and ;(were) you as you will I and be and will and and
better do formerly dwell make ,fruitful grow ,beast

3212 3068 3045 7221
12 מֵרִאשֹׁתֵיכֶם וִידַעְתֶּם כִּי־אֲנִי יְהוָה׃ וְהוֹלַכְתִּי עֲלֵיכֶם
you on cause will I .Jehovah I that you And your at than
walk to (am) know shall .beginnings

3808 5159 1961 3423 3478 5971 120
אָדָם אֶת־עַמִּי יִשְׂרָאֵל וִירֵשׁוּךָ וְהָיִיתָ לָהֶם לְנַחֲלָה וְלֹא־
and an to you and they and ;Israel My ,men
not ,inheritance them be will ,you possess will people

559 3282 3068 136 559 3541 7921 5750 3254
13 תוֹסִף עוֹד לְשַׁכְּלָם׃ כֹּה אָמַר אֲדֹנָי יְהוִה יַעַן אֹמְרִים
they Be- :Jehovah the says Thus their to any add
said cause Lord .bereavement longer

120 1961 1471 7921 120 398
14 לָכֶם אֹכֶלֶת אָדָם אַתְּ וּמְשַׁכֶּלֶת גּוֹיַיִךְ הָיִית׃ לָכֵן אָדָם
men there- ;have you your bereaved and You men de- a ,you to
fore nations (are) of vourer

3068 136 5002 5750 3782 3808 1471 5750 398 3808
לֹא־תֹאכְלִי עוֹד וְגוֹיַיִךְ לֹא תְכַשְּׁלִי־עוֹד נְאֻם אֲדֹנָי יְהוִה׃
.Jehovah the states any shall you not your and any shall you not
Lord ;more fall make nations ,longer devour

3808 5971 2781 1471 3639 5750 8085 3808
15 וְלֹא־אַשְׁמִיעַ אֵלַיִךְ עוֹד כְּלִמַּת הַגּוֹיִם וְחֶרְפַּת עַמִּים לֹא
not the the and the the any you will I And
peoples of disgrace ;nations of shame longer hear let not

3068 136 5002 5750 3782 1471 5750 5375
תִשְׂאִי־עוֹד וְגוֹיַיִךְ לֹא־תַכְשִׁלִי עוֹד נְאֻם אֲדֹנָי יְהוִה׃
.Jehovah the states any shall you not your and any shall you
Lord more fall to cause nations ;longer bear

3478 1004 120 1121 559 3068 1697 1961
16
17 וַיְהִי דְבַר־יְהוָה אֵלַי לֵאמֹר׃ בֶּן־אָדָם בֵּית יִשְׂרָאֵל
Israel the (when) ,man Son ,saying ,me to Jehovah the And
of house of of word was

5949 1870 2930 127 3427
יֹשְׁבִים עַל־אַדְמָתָם וַיְטַמְּאוּ אוֹתָהּ בְּדַרְכָּם וּבַעֲלִילוֹתָם
their by and their by it even they their on dwelt
.doings ways defiled land

5921 2534 8210 6440 1870 1961 5079 2932
18 כְּטֻמְאַת הַנִּדָּה הָיְתָה דַרְכָּם לְפָנָי׃ וָאֶשְׁפֹּךְ חֲמָתִי עֲלֵיהֶם
them on My I Thus before their was woman's a de- the as
fury poured .Me way impurity of filement

2930 1544 776 5921 8210 1818
עַל־הַדָּם אֲשֶׁר־שָׁפְכוּ עַל־הָאָרֶץ וּבְגִלּוּלֵיהֶם טִמְּאוּהָ׃
they their for and the on they that the because
.it defiled (which by) idols ,land out poured had blood of

[19]And I scattered them among the nations, and they were sown among the lands; I judged them by their way and by their doings. [20]And *when* they entered into the nations, there where they went; they even profaned My holy name, by saying to them, These *are* the people of Jehovah, and they are gone out of His land. [21]But I had pity for My holy name which the house of Israel had profaned among the nations, there where they went.

[22]Therefore, say to the house of Israel, So says the Lord Jehovah: I do not do *this* for your sake, O house of Israel, but only for My holy name, which you profaned among the nations, there where you went. [23]And I will sanctify My great name which was profaned among the nations, which you profaned among them. And the nations shall know that I *am* Jehovah, declares the Lord Jehovah, when I am sanctified in you in their eyes. [24]For I will take you from the nations, and gather you out of all the lands, and bring you into your land. [25]Then I will sprinkle clean waters on you, and you shall be clean. I will cleanse you from all your defilement and from all your idols. [26]And I will also give you a new heart; and I will put a new spirit within you. And I will take away the stony heart out of your flesh, and I will give to you a heart of flesh. [27]And I will put My Spirit within you, and cause you *to* walk in My statutes; and you shall keep My judgments, and do them. [28]And you shall dwell in the land that I gave to your fathers. And you shall be a people to Me, and I will be God to

5949 1870 776 2219 1471 6327
19 וָאָפִיץ אֹתָם בַּגּוֹיִם וַיִּזָּרוּ בָּאֲרָצוֹת כְּדַרְכָּם וְכַעֲלִילוֹתָם
their by and their by the among they and among them I And
doings way ;lands sown were ,nations the scattered

2490 8033 935 1471 935 8199
20 שְׁפַטְתִּים׃ וַיָּבוֹא אֶל־הַגּוֹיִם אֲשֶׁר־בָּאוּ שָׁם וַיְחַלְּלוּ אֶת־
even they ,there they where the into (when) And judged I
profaned went nations entered they .them

3318 776 428 3068/5971 559 6944 8034
שֵׁם קָדְשִׁי בֶּאֱמֹר לָהֶם עַם־יְהוָה אֵלֶּה וּמֵאַרְצוֹ יָצָאוּ׃
are they of out and These Jehovah the ,them to saying by My name
.gone land His (are) of people ,holy

1471 3478 1004 2490 6944 8034 2550
21 וָאֶחְמֹל עַל־שֵׁם קָדְשִׁי אֲשֶׁר חִלְּלֻהוּ בֵּית יִשְׂרָאֵל בַּגּוֹיִם
the among Israel the had which My name for I But
nations of house profaned ,holy pity had

3541 3478 1004 559 8033 935
22 אֲשֶׁר־בָּאוּ שָׁמָּה׃ לָכֵן אֱמֹר לְבֵית־יִשְׂרָאֵל כֹּה
Thus ,Israel the to say Therefore .there they where
of house went

3478 1004 6213 4616 3808 3068 136 559
אָמַר אֲדֹנָי יְהוִה לֹא לְמַעַנְכֶם אֲנִי עֹשֶׂה בֵּית יִשְׂרָאֵל כִּי
but ,Israel O do I your for Not :Jehovah the says
of house ,(this) sake Lord

8033 935 1471 2490 834 6944
אִם־לְשֵׁם־קָדְשִׁי אֲשֶׁר חִלַּלְתֶּם בַּגּוֹיִם אֲשֶׁר־בָּאתֶם שָׁם׃
.there went you where the among you which My for only
nations profaned holy name

2490 834 1471 2490 1419 8034 6942
23 וְקִדַּשְׁתִּי אֶת־שְׁמִי הַגָּדוֹל הַמְחֻלָּל בַּגּוֹיִם אֲשֶׁר חִלַּלְתֶּם
you which the among was which great name My will I And
profaned ,nations profaned sanctify

6942 3068 136 5002 3068 1471 3045 8432
בְּתוֹכָם וְיָדְעוּ הַגּוֹיִם כִּי־אֲנִי יְהוָה נְאֻם אֲדֹנָי יְהוִה בְּהִקָּדְשִׁי
am I when ,Jehovah the states ,Jehovah I that the shall And amidst
sanctified Lord (am) nations know .them

6908 1471 4480 3947 5869
24 בָכֶם לְעֵינֵיהֶם׃ וְלָקַחְתִּי אֶתְכֶם מִן־הַגּוֹיִם וְקִבַּצְתִּי אֶתְכֶם
you gather and the from you I For their in you in
,nations take will .eyes

2236 127 935 776 3605
25 מִכָּל־הָאֲרָצוֹת וְהֵבֵאתִי אֶתְכֶם אֶל־אַדְמַתְכֶם׃ וְזָרַקְתִּי
will I Then your into you bring and the of out
sprinkle .land ,lands all

3605 2932 3605 2891 2889 4325
עֲלֵיכֶם מַיִם טְהוֹרִים וּטְהַרְתֶּם מִכֹּל טֻמְאוֹתֵיכֶם וּמִכָּל־
from and your From shall you and ,clean waters you on
all ;defilement all .clean be

7307 2319 3820 5414 2891 1544
26 גִּלּוּלֵיכֶם אֲטַהֵר אֶתְכֶם׃ וְנָתַתִּי לָכֶם לֵב חָדָשׁ וְרוּחַ
a and ;new heart a you will I .you will I idols your
spirit give also cleanse

1320 68 3820 5493 7130 5414 2319
חֲדָשָׁה אֶתֵּן בְּקִרְבְּכֶם וַהֲסִרֹתִי אֶת־לֵב הָאֶבֶן מִבְּשַׂרְכֶם
your of out stony heart the will I And within will I new
.flesh away turn you put

6213 7130 5414 7307 1320 3820 5414
27 וְנָתַתִּי לָכֶם לֵב בָּשָׂר׃ וְאֶת־רוּחִי אֶתֵּן בְּקִרְבְּכֶם וְעָשִׂיתִי
and within will I My And .flesh heart a you to I and
make you put Spirit of give will

3427 6213 8104 4941 1980 2706 834
28 אֵת אֲשֶׁר־בְּחֻקַּי תֵּלֵכוּ וּמִשְׁפָּטַי תִּשְׁמְרוּ וַעֲשִׂיתֶם׃ וִישַׁבְתֶּם
you And do and shall you My and you (for) My in that
dwell shall .them keep judgments ;walk (to) statutes (is) which

5971 1961 1 5414 776
בָּאָרֶץ אֲשֶׁר נָתַתִּי לַאֲבֹתֵיכֶם וִהְיִיתֶם לִי לְעָם וְאָנֹכִי
I and a to you And your to gave I that the in
,people Me be shall .fathers land

2932 3605 3467 430 1961
29 אֱהְיֶה לָכֶם לֵאלֹהִים׃ וְהוֹשַׁעְתִּי אֶתְכֶם מִכֹּל טֻמְאוֹתֵיכֶם
your from you will I .God you to be will
,defilements all save also

7458 5414 3808 7235 1715 7121
וְקָרָאתִי אֶל־הַדָּגָן וְהִרְבֵּיתִי אֹתוֹ וְלֹא־אֶתֵּן עֲלֵיכֶם רָעָב׃
a you on will I and ,it and grain for will I and
.famine put not increase call

3808 4616 7704 8570 6086 6529 7235
30 וְהִרְבֵּיתִי אֶת־פְּרִי הָעֵץ וּתְנוּבַת הַשָּׂדֶה לְמַעַן אֲשֶׁר לֹא־
not that order in the the and tree the the will I And
,field of produce of fruit multiply

1870 2142 1471 7458 2781 5750 3947
31 תִקְחוּ עוֹד חֶרְפַּת רָעָב בַּגּוֹיִם׃ וּזְכַרְתֶּם אֶת־דַּרְכֵיכֶם
ways your shall you Then among famine the any will you
remember .nations the of disgrace more receive

5869 6962 2896 4611 7451
הָרָעִים וּמַעַלְלֵיכֶם אֲשֶׁר לֹא־טוֹבִים וּנְקֹטֹתֶם בִּפְנֵיכֶם עַל
for own your in will you and were not that your and evil
eyes yourselves despise ,good doings

5002 6213 4616 8441 5771
32 עֲוֹנֹתֵיכֶם וְעַל תּוֹעֲבוֹתֵיכֶם׃ לֹא לְמַעַנְכֶם אֲנִי־עֹשֶׂה נְאֻם
states am I your for not your and your
(this) doing sake .abominations for iniquities

1004 1870 3637 954 3045 3068 136
אֲדֹנָי יְהוִה יִוָּדַע לָכֶם בּוֹשׁוּ וְהִכָּלְמוּ מִדַּרְכֵיכֶם בֵּית
house O your for con- and Be .you to it let ;Jehovah the
of ,ways founded ashamed known be Lord

3605 1891 3117 3068 136 559 3541 3478
33 יִשְׂרָאֵל׃ כֹּה אָמַר אֲדֹנָי יְהוִה בְּיוֹם טַהֲרִי אֶתְכֶם מִכֹּל
from you cleanse I the In :Jehovah the says Thus .Israel
all day Lord

776 2723 1129 5892 3427 5771
34 עֲוֹנוֹתֵיכֶם וְהוֹשַׁבְתִּי אֶת־הֶעָרִים וְנִבְנוּ הֶחֳרָבוֹת׃ וְהָאָרֶץ
the And the shall and the make will I your
land .wastes built be ,cities inhabited ,iniquities

5674 3605 5869 8077 1961 8478 5647 8074
הַנְּשַׁמָּה תֵּעָבֵד תַּחַת אֲשֶׁר הָיְתָה שְׁמָמָה לְעֵינֵי כָּל־עוֹבֵר׃
also all the in ruin a being rather be shall desolated
.by pass of sight than cultivated

2717 5892 5731 1588 1961 8074 1977 776 559
35 וְאָמְרוּ הָאָרֶץ הַלֵּזוּ הַנְּשַׁמָּה הָיְתָה כְּגַן־עֵדֶן וְהֶעָרִים הֶחֳרֵבוֹת
wasted the And .Eden like has was that This land they And
cities of garden the become desolated ,say shall

1471 3045 3427 1219 2040 8074
36 וְהַנְשַׁמּוֹת וְהַנֶּהֱרָסוֹת בְּצוּרוֹת יָשָׁבוּ׃ וְיָדְעוּ הַגּוֹיִם אֲשֶׁר
that the shall And (and) fortified are razed and and
nations know .inhabited desolated

2040 1129 3068 5439 7604
יִשָּׁאֲרוּ סְבִיבוֹתֵיכֶם כִּי אֲנִי יְהוָה בָּנִיתִי הַנֶּהֱרָסוֹת
razed the built Jehovah I that around all - are
.(places) you left

3541 6213 1696 3068 8074 5193
37 נָטַעְתִּי הַנְּשַׁמָּה אֲנִי יְהוָה דִּבַּרְתִּי וְעָשִׂיתִי׃ כֹּה
Thus will and have Jehovah I which that (and)
.(it) do spoken ;desolated was planted

6213 3478 1004 1875 2088 5750 3068 136 559
אָמַר אֲדֹנָי יְהוִה עוֹד זֹאת אִדָּרֵשׁ לְבֵית־יִשְׂרָאֵל לַעֲשׂוֹת
act to Israel the by will I this Yet :Jehovah Lord the says
of house sought be

6629 6944 6629 120 6629 7235
38 לָהֶם אַרְבֶּה אֹתָם כַּצֹּאן אָדָם׃ כְּצֹאן קָדָשִׁים כְּצֹאן
the as ,holy a As (with) a like them will I for
of flock flock .men flock increase .them

you. 29 I will also save you from all your defilements, and I will call for grain and increase it; and I will not put a famine on you. 30 And I will multiply the fruit of the tree, and the produce of the field, in order that you will not any more receive the disgrace of famine among the nations. 31 Then you shall remember your evil ways and your doings that were not good; and you will despise yourselves in your own eyes for your iniquities and for your abominations. 32 I am not doing *this* for your sake, declares the Lord Jehovah; let it be known to you. Be ashamed and confounded for your ways, O house of Israel.

33 So says the Lord Jehovah: In the day I cleanse you from all your iniquities, I will cause the cities *to be* inhabited, and the wastes shall be built. 34 And the desolated land shall be cultivated, rather than being a ruin in the sight of all who also pass by. 35 And they shall say, This land that was desolated has become like the Garden of Eden. And the wasted and desolated and razed cities are fortified *and* inhabited. 36 And the nations shall know, *those* left all around you, that I, Jehovah, built the razed *places*, and planted that which was desolated. I, Jehovah, have spoken, and will do *it*.

37 So says the Lord Jehovah: Yet *for* this I will be sought *unto* by the house of Israel, to act for them, *that* I will increase them like a flock *with* men. 38 As a holy flock, as the flock of Jerusalem in

her appointed *feasts*, so the wasted cities shall be filled *with* flocks of men. And they shall know that I *am* Jehovah.

CHAPTER 37

[1]The hand of Jehovah was on me, and brought me by the Spirit of Jehovah, and made me rest in the midst of a valley; and it was full of bones. [2]And He made me pass among them all around. And, behold, very many *were* on the face of the valley. And, behold! *They were* very dry. [3]And He said to me, Son of man,, can these bones live? And I said, O Lord Jehovah, You know. [4]And He said to Me, Prophesy to these bones and say to them, O dry bones, hear the word of Jehovah: [5]So says the Lord Jehovah to these bones: Behold, I will make breath enter into you, and you shall live. [6]And I will put sinews on you, and will bring flesh on you, and spread skin over you, and put breath in you, and you shall live. And you shall know that I *am* Jehovah. [7]So I prophesied as I was commanded. And as I prophesied, there was a noise. And, behold, a shaking! And the bones drew near, a bone to its bone. [8]And I watched. And, behold! The sinews and the flesh came up on them, and the skin spread over them from above. But there *was* no breath in them. [9]Then He said to me, Prophesy to the Spirit. Prophesy, son of man, and say to the Spirit, So says the

4393 2717 5892 1961 3651 4150 3389
יְרוּשָׁלַ͏ִם בְּמוֹעֲדֶיהָ כֵּן תִּהְיֶינָה הֶעָרִים הֶחֳרֵבוֹת מְלֵאוֹת
filled wasted the be shall so her in ,Jerusalem
cities ,(feasts) appointed

3068 3045 120 6629
צֹאן אָדָם וְיָדְעוּ כִּי־אֲנִי יְהוָה׃
.Jehovah I that they and ;men (with)
(am) know shall of flocks

CAP. XXXVII לז

CHAPTER 37

1 8432 5117 3068 7307 3318 3068 3027 5921 1961
הָיְתָה עָלַי יַד־יְהוָה וַיּוֹצִאֵנִי בְרוּחַ יְהוָה וַיְנִיחֵנִי בְּתוֹךְ
the in made and Jehovah the by brought and ,Jehovah The on was
of midst rest me of Spirit me of hand me

2 5439 5674 6106 4393 1237
הַבִּקְעָה וְהִיא מְלֵאָה עֲצָמוֹת׃ וְהֶעֱבִירַנִי עֲלֵיהֶם סָבִיב ׀
all among made He and ,bones was it and ;valley a
them pass me of full

3002 2009 1237 6440 3966 7227 2009 5439
סָבִיב וְהִנֵּה רַבּוֹת מְאֹד עַל־פְּנֵי הַבִּקְעָה וְהִנֵּה יְבֵשׁוֹת
(were They) ,And .valley the the on very many And .around
dry !behold of face (were) ,behold

3 428 6106 2421 120 1121 559 3966
מְאֹד׃ וַיֹּאמֶר אֵלַי בֶּן־אָדָם הֲתִחְיֶינָה הָעֲצָמוֹת הָאֵלֶּה
?these bones live can ,man Son ,me to He And .very
of said

4 5012 559 3045 3068 136 559
וָאֹמַר אֲדֹנָי יְהוִה אַתָּה יָדָעְתָּ׃ וַיֹּאמֶר אֵלַי הִנָּבֵא עַל־
to Prophesy ,me to He And .know You ,Jehovah O I And
said Lord ,said

8085 3002 6106 559 428 6106
הָעֲצָמוֹת הָאֵלֶּה וְאָמַרְתָּ אֲלֵיהֶם הָעֲצָמוֹת הַיְבֵשׁוֹת שִׁמְעוּ
hear ,dry bones O ,them to say and these bones

5 428 6106 3068 136 559 3541 3068 1697
דְּבַר־יְהוָה׃ כֹּה אָמַר אֲדֹנָי יְהוִה לָעֲצָמוֹת הָאֵלֶּה
:these bones to Jehovah the says Thus .Jehovah the
Lord of word

6 1517 5921 5414 2421 7307 3644 935 2009
הִנֵּה אֲנִי מֵבִיא בָכֶם רוּחַ וִחְיִיתֶם׃ וְנָתַתִּי עֲלֵיכֶם גִּדִים
,sinews you on will I And you and ,breath into make will I ,Behold
put .live shall you enter

5414 5785 7159 1320 5921 5927
וְהַעֲלֵתִי עֲלֵיכֶם בָּשָׂר וְקָרַמְתִּי עֲלֵיכֶם עוֹר וְנָתַתִּי בָכֶם
you in put and ,skin you spread and ,flesh you on will and
over up bring

7 6680 5012 3068 3045 2421 7307
רוּחַ וִחְיִיתֶם וִידַעְתֶּם כִּי־אֲנִי יְהוָה׃ וְנִבֵּאתִי כַּאֲשֶׁר צֻוֵּיתִי
was I as I So .Jehovah I that you And you and ,breath
.commanded prophesied (am) know shall .live shall

6106 6106 7126 7494 5012 6963 1961
וַיְהִי־קוֹל כְּהִנָּבְאִי וְהִנֵּה־רַעַשׁ וַתִּקְרְבוּ עֲצָמוֹת עֶצֶם אֶל־
to bone a ,bones the draw And a And I as a And
near !shaking ,behold .prophesied noise was

8 7159 5927 1320 1517 5921 2009 7200 6106
עַצְמוֹ׃ וְרָאִיתִי וְהִנֵּה־עֲלֵיהֶם גִּדִים וּבָשָׂר עָלָה וַיִּקְרַם
spread and came the and The them on and I And .bones its
over ,up flesh sinews !behold ,watched

9 5012 559 369 7307 4605 5785
עֲלֵיהֶם עוֹר מִלְמָעְלָה וְרוּחַ אֵין בָּהֶם׃ וַיֹּאמֶר אֵלַי הִנָּבֵא
Prophesy to He Then .them in not But .above from the them
,me said (was) breath skin

559 7307 559 120 1121 5012 7307
אֶל־הָרוּחַ הִנָּבֵא בֶן־אָדָם וְאָמַרְתָּ אֶל־הָרוּחַ כֹּה־אָמַר ׀
says Thus the to say and ,man son ,prophesy the to
,breath of :breath

Lord Jehovah: Come from the four winds, O Spirit, and breathe on these slain ones, that they may live. [10] So I prophesied as He commanded me, and the Spirit came into them. And they lived, and stood on their feet, a very, very great army.

[11] Then He said to me, Son of man, these bones *are* all the house of Israel. Behold, they say, Our bones are dried, and our hope is perished, we are cut off to ourselves. [12] So prophesy and say to them, So says the Lord Jehovah: Behold, I will open your graves, and cause you to come up out of your graves, O My people, and will bring you to the land of Israel. [13] And you shall know that I *am* Jehovah when I have opened your graves, and have brought you up out of your graves, O My people. [14] And I shall put My Spirit in you, and you shall live. And I will put you on your own land. And you shall know that I, Jehovah, have spoken, and have done *it*, says Jehovah.

[15] And the word of Jehovah was to me, saying, [16] And you, son of man, take one stick to yourself and write on it, For Judah, and for his companions, the sons of Israel. Then take another stick and write on it, For Joseph, the stick of Ephraim and all the house of Israel, his companions. [17] And draw them one to one for yourself, into one stick. And they shall become for oneness in your hand. [18] And when the sons of your people shall speak to you, saying, Will you not declare to us what *these* mean to you? [19] Say to

---

אֲדֹנָי יְהוָה מֵאַרְבַּע רוּחוֹת בֹּאִי הָרוּחַ וּפְחִי בַּהֲרוּגִים

the Lord :Jehovah the from winds four ,Come O Spirit, and breathe on slain ones

2026 5301 7307 935 7307 702 3068 136

10 הָאֵלֶּה וְיִחְיוּ׃ וְהִנַּבֵּאתִי כַּאֲשֶׁר צִוָּנִי וַתָּבוֹא בָהֶם הָרוּחַ

these ,that they live may So I prophesied as He com-manded me and came them into the breath

73,07 935 6680 5012 2421 428

11 וַיִּחְיוּ וַיַּעַמְדוּ עַל־רַגְלֵיהֶם חַיִל גָּדוֹל מְאֹד מְאֹד׃ וַיֹּאמֶר

and they lived and stood on their feet a army great very ,very Then He said

559 3966 3966 1419 12428 17272 5975 2421

אֵלַי בֶּן־אָדָם הָעֲצָמוֹת הָאֵלֶּה כָּל־בֵּית יִשְׂרָאֵל הֵמָּה הִנֵּה

me to Son man of ,bones these ,these all the house of Israel they ,Behold.

2009 3478 1004 3605 428 6106 120: 1121

אֹמְרִים יָבְשׁוּ עַצְמוֹתֵינוּ וְאָבְדָה תִקְוָתֵנוּ נִגְזַרְנוּ לָנוּ׃

say they are dried Our bones ,and is and our hope —perished is are we off cut to ourselves.

1504 8615 6 6106 3001 559

12 לָכֵן הִנָּבֵא וְאָמַרְתָּ אֲלֵיהֶם כֹּה־אָמַר אֲדֹנָי יְהוָה הִנֵּה

There-fore prophesy and say ,them to Thus says the Lord :Jehovah ,Behold

2009 3068 136 559 559 3541 559 5012 3651

אֲנִי פֹתֵחַ אֶת־קִבְרוֹתֵיכֶם וְהַעֲלֵיתִי אֶתְכֶם מִקִּבְרוֹתֵיכֶם

I will open your ,graves and to cause come up you out of your graves,

6913 6605 59,127 6913 6605

13 עַמִּי׃ וְהֵבֵאתִי אֶתְכֶם אֶל־אַדְמַת יִשְׂרָאֵל׃ וִידַעְתֶּם כִּי־אֲנִי

My O ,people will and bring you to the land of .Israel And you know shall that I (am)

5971 935 127 3478 3045 5971

יְהוָה בְּפִתְחִי אֶת־קִבְרוֹתֵיכֶם וּבְהַעֲלוֹתִי אֶתְכֶם

,Jehovah when I have opened your ,graves have and up brought you

3068 6605 6913 59,127 5927

14 מִקִּבְרוֹתֵיכֶם עַמִּי׃ וְנָתַתִּי רוּחִי בָכֶם וִחְיִיתֶם וְהִנַּחְתִּי

out of your ,graves My O .people And I My Spirit put shall ,you in you and shall live ,I will and put

6913 5971 5414 7307 24:21 3240

אֶתְכֶם עַל־אַדְמַתְכֶם וִידַעְתֶּם כִּי אֲנִי יְהוָה דִּבַּרְתִּי וְעָשִׂיתִי

you on your own .land And you shall know that I Jehovah have spoken have and done (it),

853 127 3068 1696 3045 6213

15 וַיְהִי דְבַר־יְהוָה אֵלַי לֵאמֹר׃ וְאַתָּה

16 And the word of was Jehovah me to ,saying And ,you

1961 1697 3068 559 559

נְאֻם־יְהוָה׃ .Jehovah says

5002 3068

בֶן־אָדָם קַח־לְךָ עֵץ אֶחָד וּכְתֹב עָלָיו לִיהוּדָה וְלִבְנֵי

son man, of to take yourself stick one and write on ,it For Judah for and of sons the

1121 120: 6086 259 3789 5921 3063 1121:

17 יִשְׂרָאֵל חֲבֵרוֹ וּלְקַח עֵץ אֶחָד וּכְתוֹב עָלָיו לְיוֹסֵף עֵץ

,Israel his .companions Then take stick one (another) and write on ,it Joseph, For stick the

3478 2272 3947 6086 259 3789 5921 3127: 6086

אֶפְרַיִם וְכָל־בֵּית יִשְׂרָאֵל חֲבֵרוֹ׃ וְקָרַב אֹתָם אֶחָד אֶל־

Ephraim, and the all house of ,Israel his .companions And draw them one to

669: 1004: 3478 2272 259: 7126 259

18 אֶחָד לְךָ לְעֵץ אֶחָד וְהָיוּ לַאֲחָדִים בְּיָדֶךָ׃ וְכַאֲשֶׁר יֹאמְרוּ

one for yourself stick one and shall become for one-ness your in .hand And when shall speak

259 6086: 259 1961 259 3027 559

אֵלֶיךָ בְּנֵי עַמְּךָ לֵאמֹר הֲלוֹא־תַגִּיד לָנוּ מָה־אֵלֶּה לָךְ׃

you to sons of your ,people ,saying Will not declare us to what (mean) these ?you

1121 5971 559 38108 5046 4100 428

them, So says the Lord Jehovah: Behold, I will take the stick of Joseph which *is* in the hand of Ephraim, and the tribes of Israel, his companions; and I will put them with him, with the stick of Judah, and will make them one stick; and they shall be one in My hand.

[20]And the sticks shall be in your hand, the ones *on* which you write before their eyes. [21]And say to them, So says the Lord Jehovah: Behold, I will take the sons of Israel from among the nations, there where they have gone, and will gather them from all around, and will bring them into their own land. [22]And I will make them one nation in the land, on the mountains of Israel; and one king shall be for a king to all of them. And they shall not be two nations still; and they will not be split into two kingdoms any more. [23]And they will not still be defiled with their idols, even with their filthy idols, not with all of their transgressions. But I will save them out of all their dwelling-places, in them where they have sinned; and I will cleanse them. And they shall be to Me for a people; and I will be to them for God. [24]And My Servant, David, *shall be* king over them. And there shall be one Shepherd to all of them. And they shall walk in My judgments and keep My statutes, and do them. [25]And they shall dwell on the land that I have given to My servant, to Jacob, *there* where your fathers dwelt in it. And they shall dwell on it, they and their sons, and the sons of their sons, forever. And My Servant, David *shall be* a ruler to them forever. [26]And I will cut a covenant

6086 3947 2009 3068 136 559 3541 1696

19 דבר אלהם כה־אמר אדני יהוה הנה אני לקח את־עץ

the of stick | will take | I ,Behold | :Jehovah | the Lord | says | Thus | ,them to | Say

5414 2272 3478 7636 669 3027 834 3127

יוסף אשר ביד־אפרים ושבטי ישראל חברו ונתתי אותם

them | I and put will | his ,companions | ,Israel | the and of tribes | ,Ephraim | the in of hand | which (is) | ,Joseph

3027 259 1961 259 6086 6213 3063 6086

עליו את־עץ יהודה ועשיתם לעץ אחד והיו אחד בידי׃

My in .hand | one | they and be shall | ,one | stick | will and them make | ,Judah | the with of stick | with ,him

1696 5869 3027 5921 3789 834 6086 1961

20 21 והיו העצים אשר תכתב עליהם בידך לעיניהם׃ ודבר

And say | their before .eyes | your in hand | them on | write you | which | the sticks | And be shall

1121 3947 2009 3068 136 559 3541

אלהם כה־אמר אדני יהוה הנה אני לקח את־בני

the of sons | will take | I | ,Behold | :Jehovah | the Lord | says | Thus | ,them to

6908 8033 1980 1471 996 3478

ישראל מבין הגוים אשר הלכו־שם וקבצתי אתם

them | will and gather | ,there | have they gone | where | the nations | from among | Israel

1471 6213 127 935 5439

22 מסביב והבאתי אותם אל־אדמתם׃ ועשיתי אתם לגוי

nation | them | will I And make | own their .land | into | them | will and bring | all from around

4428 3605 1961 259 4428 3478 2022 776 259

אחד בארץ בהרי ישראל ומלך אחד יהיה לכלם למלך

a for .king | them to all | shall be | one | king and | ,Israel | the on of mountains | the in ,land | one

4467 8147 5750 2673 3808 1471 8147 5750 1961 3808

ולא יהיה־עוד לשני גוים ולא יחצו עוד לשתי ממלכות

kingdoms | into two | still | will they split be | and not | ,nations | two | still | they be shall | And not

3605 8251 1544 5750 2930 3808 5750

23 עוד׃ ולא יטמאו עוד בגלוליהם ובשקוציהם ובכל

with nor of all | their with ;idols filthy | and | their with ;idols | still | will they defiled be | And not | any .more

2398 4186 3605 3467 6588

פשעיהם והושעתי אתם מכל מושבתיהם אשר חטאו

have they sinned | where | dwelling places | their | of out all | them | will I But save | trans- their .gressions

1961 5971 1961 2891

בהם וטהרתי אותם והיו־לי לעם ואני אהיה להם

to them | be will I | and | a for ,people | to Me | they So be shall | .them | will I and cleanse | in ,them

1961 259 7462 5921 4428 1732 5650 430

24 לאלהים׃ ועבדי דוד מלך עליהם ורועה אחד יהיה

there be shall | one | And shepherd | over .them | (be shall) king | David | My And servant | .God for

3427 6213 8104 2708 3212 4941 3605

25 לכלם ובמשפטי ילכו וחקותי ישמרו ועשו אותם׃ וישבו

they And dwell shall | .them | and do | ,keep | My and ,statutes | shall they ,walk | My in And judgments | all to .them of

3427 3290 5650 5414 776 5921

על־הארץ אשר נתתי לעבדי ליעקב אשר ישבו־בה

in it | dwelt | where | ,Jacob to | My to ,servant | have I given | that | the land | on

1121 1121 1121 3427

אבותיכם וישבו עליה המה ובניהם ובני בניהם עד־

for | their sons | the and of sons | their and ,sons | they | ,it on | they And dwell shall | your .fathers

1285 3772 5769 5387 5650 1732 5769

26 עולם ודוד עבדי נשיא להם לעולם׃ וכרתי להם ברית

cove- a of nant | with them | I And cut will | .forever | them to | ruler a | servant My (be shall) | And David | .ever

of peace with them; it shall
be an everlasting covenant
with them. And I will place
them and multiply them.
And I will give My
sanctuary in their midst
forever. [27]And My tabernacle shall be with them.
And I will be their God, and
they shall be for a people
to Me. [28]And the nations
shall know that I, Jehovah,
sanctify Israel, when My
sanctuary shall be in their
midst forever.

7235		1285	1961		5769	5414				7965
שׁלוֹם בְּרִית עוֹלָם יִהְיֶה אוֹתָם וְנָתַתִּי וְהִרְבֵּיתִי אוֹתָם										

them, and will I And with shall It ever- an .peace
multiply them place them be lasting covenant

5414		4720	8432		5769		1961		4908
וְנָתַתִּי אֶת־מִקְדָּשִׁי בְּתוֹכָם לְעוֹלָם: וְהָיָה מִשְׁכָּנִי עֲלֵיהֶם									27

with My shall And .forever their in My I and
them tabernacle be midst sanctuary put will

1961			430		1961		5971	3045	1471
וְהָיִיתִי לָהֶם לֵאלֹהִים וְהֵמָּה יִהְיוּ־לִי לְעָם: וְיָדְעוּ הַגּוֹיִם									28

the shall And a for to shall they and ,God for them to I And
nations know people Me be be will

3068	6942				3478	1961	4720		8432
כִּי אֲנִי יְהוָה מְקַדֵּשׁ אֶת־יִשְׂרָאֵל בִּהְיוֹת מִקְדָּשִׁי בְּתוֹכָם									

their in My when ,Israel sanctify Jehovah I that
midst sanctuary be shall

5769
לְעוֹלָם: °

.forever

CAP. XXXVIII לח
CHAPTER 38

CHAPTER 38

[1]And the word of
Jehovah was to me, say-
ing, [2]Son of man, set your
face against Gog, the land
of Magog, the prince of
Rosh, Meshech, and Tubal;
and prophesy against him.
[3]And say, So says the Lord
Jehovah: Behold, I *am*
against you, O Gog, the
prince of Rosh, Meshech,
and Tubal. [4]And I will turn
you back and put hooks into
your jaws. And I will bring
you and all your army out,
horses and horsemen, all of
them clothed most per-
fectly, a great assembly
with buckler and shield,
all of them swordsmen:
[5]Persia, Ethiopia, and Libya
with them; all of them *with*
shield and helmet; [6]Gomer
and all his bands; the house
of Togarmah *from* the
recesses of the north, and
all his bands; many peoples
with you. [7]Be prepared;
yea, prepared for yourself,
you and all your assembly
that are assembled to you;
and be a guard to them.
[8]After many days you shall
be visited. In the after years
you shall come into the land
turned back from the sword,
gathered out of many
peoples, on the mountains

1463		6440	7760	120/1121		559		3068	1697	1961
וַיְהִי דְבַר־יְהוָה אֵלַי לֵאמֹר: בֶּן־אָדָם שִׂים פָּנֶיךָ אֶל־גּוֹג										1 2

,Gog against your set ,man Son ,saying ,me to Jehovah the And
face of of word was

559		5012	8422	4902	7220	5387	40:31	776
אֶרֶץ הַמָּגוֹג נְשִׂיא רֹאשׁ מֶשֶׁךְ וְתֻבָל וְהִנָּבֵא עָלָיו: וְאָמַרְתָּ								3

,say And against and and Meshech Rosh the Magog the
him prophesy ,Tubal of prince of land

4902	7200	5387	1463	413	3068	136	559	3541
כֹּה אָמַר אֲדֹנָי יְהוִה הִנְנִי אֵלֶיךָ גּוֹג נְשִׂיא רֹאשׁ מֶשֶׁךְ								

Meshech ,Rosh the O against ,Behold :Jehovah the says Thus
of prince ,Gog ,you (am) I Lord

3318	3895	2377	5414	7725	8422
וְתֻבָל: וְשׁוֹבַבְתִּיךָ וְנָתַתִּי חַחִים בִּלְחָיֶיךָ וְהוֹצֵאתִי אוֹתְךָ					4

you will I And your into hooks put and will I And and
out bring ,jaws back you turn .Tubal

6951	36:05	4358	3847	6571	5483	2428/3605
וְאֶת־כָּל־חֵילֶךָ סוּסִים וּפָרָשִׁים לְבֻשֵׁי מִכְלוֹל כֻּלָּם קָהָל						

a of all most clothed and horses your all and
assembly ,them perfectly ,horsemen army

6316	3568	6539	3605	2719	8610	40:43	6793	7227
רַב צִנָּה וּמָגֵן תֹּפְשֵׂי חֲרָבוֹת כֻּלָּם: פָּרַס כּוּשׁ וּפוּט								5

and Ethiopia ;Persia of all ,sword handlers and (with) great
Libya :them of ,shield buckler

8425	1004	102	3605	1586	3553	4043/36:05
אִתָּם כֻּלָּם מָגֵן וְכוֹבָע: גֹּמֶר וְכָל־אֲגַפֶּיהָ בֵּית תּוֹגַרְמָה						6

Togarmah the her and Gomer and (with) of all with
of house ;bands all ;helmet shield them ,them

3559	7227	5971	102	3605	6828	3411
יַרְכְּתֵי צָפוֹן וְאֶת־כָּל־אֲגַפָּיו עַמִּים רַבִּים אִתָּךְ: הִכֹּן						7

Be with many peoples his all and the the (from)
,prepared .you ,bands ;north of recesses

1961	6950	6951	3605	3559
וְהָכֵן לְךָ אַתָּה וְכָל־קְהָלֶךָ הַנִּקְהָלִים עָלֶיךָ וְהָיִיתָ לָהֶם				

to be and ,you to are that your and you for pre- and
them assembled assembly all ,yourself pared

935	8141	319	6485	7227	3117	4929
לְמִשְׁמָר: מִיָּמִים רַבִּים תִּפָּקֵד בְּאַחֲרִית הַשָּׁנִים תָּבוֹא						8

shall you years the In shall you many After a for
come after .visited be days .guard

5921	7227	5971	6908	2719	7725	776
אֶל־אֶרֶץ מְשׁוֹבֶבֶת מֵחֶרֶב מְקֻבֶּצֶת מֵעַמִּים רַבִּים עַל						

on ,many of out gathered the from turned the into
peoples ,sword back land

of Israel which have been for a continual waste, but he has been brought out of the peoples; and they shall dwell securely, all of them. [9]And you shall go up; you shall come like a storm; you shall be like a cloud to cover the land, you and all your bands, and many peoples with you.

[10]So says the Lord Jehovah: And it shall be in that day, words shall come up into your heart, and you shall devise an evil plan. [11]And you shall say, I will go up to the land of open spaces; I will go *to* those at ease, who live securely, all of them living with no walls; and there are no bars and gates to them; [12]in order to spoil a spoil, and to steal a prize; to turn your hand on the inhabited waste places, and on the people gathered out of the nations, who have gotten livestock and goods; who dwell in the center of the earth. [13]Sheba and Dedan and the merchants of Tarshish, and all its young lions, shall say to you, Have you come to spoil a spoil? Have you gathered your assembly to steal a prize, to carry away silver and gold, to take away livestock and goods, to spoil a great spoil?

[14]So prophesy, son of man, and say to Gog, So says the Lord Jehovah: Shall you not know in that day when My people Israel dwells securely? [15]And you shall come from your place out of the recesses of the north, you and many peoples with you, all of them riding on horses; a great assembly; a mighty army. [16]And you shall come up on My people Israel like a cloud, to cover the land. It shall be in the after days; and I will bring you against My land, so that the nations

הרי ישראל אשר־היו לחרבה תמיד והיא מעמים
the of out he but con- a for have which Israel the
peoples ,tinual waste been of mountains

9 הוצאה וישבו לבטח כלם: ועלית כשאה תבוא כענן
a like shall you a like you And of all ,securely they and been has
cloud ;come storm ;up go shall .them dwell shall ;out brought

לכסות הארץ תהיה אתה וכל־אגפיך ועמים רבים אותך:
with many and your and you shall you the cover to
.you peoples ,bands all ,be land

10 כה אמר אדני יהוה והיה ביום ההוא יעלו
shall that day in it And :Jehovah the says Thus
up come be shall Lord

11 דברים על־לבבך וחשבת מחשבת רעה: ואמרת אעלה
will I you And .evil plan an you and your into words
up go say shall devise shall ,heart

על־ארץ פרזות אבוא השקטים ישבי לבטח כלם ישבים
living of all ,securely who those will I open the to
them live ,ease at (to) go ;spaces of land

12 באין חומה ובריח ודלתים אין להם: לשלל שלל ולבז
to and a spoil to ;them to there and bars and ;walls with
steal ,spoil not are gates no

בז להשיב ידך על־חרבות נושבות ואל־עם מאסף מגוים
of out gathered the and ;in dwelt waste the on your turn to a
.nations the people on places hand ;prize

13 עשה מקנה וקנין ישבי על־טבור הארץ: שבא ודדן
and Sheba .earth the the in who and livestock have who
,Dedan of center dwell ;goods gotten

וסחרי תרשיש וכל־כפיריה יאמרו לך הלשלל שלל
spoil a to Have ,you to shall young its and ,Tarshish the and
spoil say ,lions all of merchants

אתה בא הלבז בז הקהלת קהלך לשאת ׀ כסף וזהב
and silver carry to your you a Have ?come you
;gold away ;assembly gathered prize steal to

14 לקחת מקנה וקנין לשלל שלל גדול: לכן הנבא בן
son ,prophesy There- ?great spoil a spoil to and livestock take to
of ,fore ;goods away

אדם ואמרת לגוג כה אמר אדני יהוה הלוא ׀ ביום
day in Shall :Jehovah the says Thus ,Gog to say and ,man
not Lord

15 ההוא בשבת עמי ישראל לבטח תדע: ובאת ממקומך
your from you And you securely Israel My when that
place come shall ?know people dwells

מירכתי צפון אתה ועמים רבים אתך רכבי סוסים כלם
of all horses riding with many and you the the of out
,them on ,you peoples north of recesses

16 קהל גדול וחיל רב: ועלית על־עמי ישראל כענן לכסות
cover to a like Israel My on you And .mighty a and ,great as- a
,cloud people up come shall army sembly

הארץ באחרית הימים תהיה והבאותיך על־ארצי למען
so My against will I and shall It days the in the
that ,land you bring ,be after .land

may know Me, when I shall be sanctified in you before their eyes, O Gog. 17So says the Lord Jehovah: Are you he of whom I have spoken in former days, by the hand of My servants, the prophets of Israel, who prophesied in those days *and* years, to bring you against them? 18And it shall be on that day, when Gog comes against the land of Israel, declares the Lord Jehovah, My fury shall come up in My face. 19And in My jealousy, in the fire of My wrath, I have spoken. Surely, in that day there shall be a great quaking in the land of Israel. 20And the fish of the sea, and the birds of the heavens, and the beasts of the field, and all creeping things that creep on the earth, and all men who *are* on the face of the earth, shall quake at My face. And the mountains shall be thrown down, and the steep places shall fall, and every wall shall fall to the ground. 21And I shall call a sword against him on all My mountains, declares the Lord Jehovah. *Each* man's sword shall be against his brother. 22And I will judge him with a plague and with blood, and an overflowing shower, and hailstones. I will rain fire and brimstone on him, and on his bands, and on the many peoples who *are* with him. 23And I will magnify Myself and sanctify Myself. And I will be known in the eyes of the many nations; and they shall know that I *am* Jehovah.

דַּעַת הַגּוֹיִם אֹתִי בְּהִקָּדְשִׁי בְךָ לְעֵינֵיהֶם גּוֹג׃ כֹּה 17

Thus O their before in shall I when Me the may
Gog, eyes you sanctified be nations know

אָמַר אֲדֹנָי יְהוִה הַאַתָּה־הוּא אֲשֶׁר־דִּבַּרְתִּי בְּיָמִים קַדְמוֹנִים

former days in have I of he Are :Jehovah the says
spoken whom you Lord

בְּיַד עֲבָדַי נְבִיאֵי יִשְׂרָאֵל הַנִּבְּאִים בַּיָּמִים הָהֵם שָׁנִים לְהָבִיא

bring to (many) those days in who ,Israel the ser- My the by
years prophesied of prophets vants of hand

18 אֹתְךָ עֲלֵיהֶם׃ וְהָיָה בַּיּוֹם הַהוּא בְּיוֹם בּוֹא גוֹג עַל־

against Gog comes when ,that day on it And against you
be shall ?them

אַדְמַת יִשְׂרָאֵל נְאֻם אֲדֹנָי יְהוִה תַּעֲלֶה חֲמָתִי בְּאַפִּי׃

My in My come shall ,Jehovah the states ,Israel the
.face fury up Lord of land

19 וּבְקִנְאָתִי בְאֵשׁ־עֶבְרָתִי דִּבַּרְתִּי אִם־לֹא בַּיּוֹם הַהוּא יִהְיֶה

there that day in Surely have I My the in My in And
be shall .spoken ,wrath of fire ,jealousy

20 רַעַשׁ גָּדוֹל עַל אַדְמַת יִשְׂרָאֵל׃ וְרָעֲשׁוּ מִפָּנַי דְּגֵי הַיָּם וְעוֹף

the and the the My at shall And ,Israel the in great a
of birds ,sea of fish face shake of land shaking

הַשָּׁמַיִם וְחַיַּת הַשָּׂדֶה וְכָל־הָרֶמֶשׂ הָרֹמֵשׂ עַל־הָאֲדָמָה וְכָל

and the on that creeping and the the and the
all ,earth creep things all ,field of beasts ,heavens

הָאָדָם אֲשֶׁר עַל־פְּנֵי הָאֲדָמָה וְנֶהֶרְסוּ הֶהָרִים וְנָפְלוּ

shall and the be shall And the the on who men
fall ,mountains down cast .earth of face (are)

21 הַמַּדְרֵגוֹת וְכָל־חוֹמָה לָאָרֶץ תִּפּוֹל׃ וְקָרָאתִי עָלָיו לְכָל־

on against will I And shall the to wall and steep the
all him call .fall ground every ,places

הָרַי חֶרֶב נְאֻם אֲדֹנָי יְהוִה חֶרֶב אִישׁ בְּאָחִיו תִּהְיֶה׃

.be shall his against (Each) sword .Jehovah the states ,sword a My
brother man's Lord mountains

22 וְנִשְׁפַּטְתִּי אִתּוֹ בְּדֶבֶר וּבְדָם וְגֶשֶׁם שׁוֹטֵף וְאַבְנֵי אֶלְגָּבִישׁ

;hail and over- a and with and a with him will I And
of stones ,flowing shower .blood plague judge

אֵשׁ וְגָפְרִית אַמְטִיר עָלָיו וְעַל־אֲגַפָּיו וְעַל־עַמִּים רַבִּים אֲשֶׁר

who many the and his and on will I and fire
(are) peoples on ,bands on ,him rain brimstone

23 אִתּוֹ׃ וְהִתְגַּדִּלְתִּי וְהִתְקַדִּשְׁתִּי וְנוֹדַעְתִּי לְעֵינֵי גּוֹיִם רַבִּים

,many ,nations the in will I And sanctify and will I And with
of eyes known be .Myself Myself magnify .him

וְיָדְעוּ כִּי־אֲנִי יְהוָה׃

.Jehovah I that they and
(am) know shall

CAP. XXXIX לט

CHAPTER 39

1And you, son of man, prophesy against Gog and say, So says the Lord Jehovah: Behold, I *am*

1 וְאַתָּה בֶן־אָדָם הִנָּבֵא עַל־גּוֹג וְאָמַרְתָּ כֹּה אָמַר אֲדֹנָי יְהוִה

:Jehovah the says Thus ,say and ,Gog against proph- ,man son And
Lord esy of ,you

against you, O Gog, the prince of Rosh, Meshech, and Tubal. [2]And I will turn you back, and lead you on. And I will bring you up from the recesses of the north, and will bring you on the mountains of Israel. [3]And I will strike your bow out of your left hand; and *I* will cause your arrows to fall out of your right hand. [4]You shall fall on the mountains of Israel, you and all your bands, and the people who *are* with you. I will give you for food to the birds of prey, a bird of every wing; and *to* the beasts of the field. [5]You shall fall on the face of the field, for I have spoken, declares the Lord Jehovah. [6]And I will send a fire on Magog, and on the secure inhabitants of the coasts. And they shall know that I *am* Jehovah.

[7]And I will make My holy name known in the midst of My people Israel. And I will not let My holy name be profaned any more. And the nations shall know that I *am* Jehovah, the Holy One of Israel. [8]Behold! It is coming, and it shall be done, declares the Lord Jehovah. That *is* the day of which I have spoken. [9]And the inhabitants of the cities of Israel shall go out, and shall set afire and burn the weapons; even the shield and the buckler, the bow and the arrows, and the hand-staff, and the spears. And they shall burn them *with* fire seven years. [10]And they shall not take wood out of the field, and shall not cut down out of the forest. For they shall burn the weapons *with* fire. And they shall plunder those who plundered them, and rob those who robbed them, declares the Lord Jehovah.

[11]And it will be on that day, I will give to Gog a place there, a grave in Israel, the valley of those who pass by, east of the sea. And it shall stop those who pass by. And they shall

7725 8422 4902 7220 5387 1463 2005
2 הנני אליך גוג נשיא ראש משך ותבל׃ ושבבתיך
will I And and Meshech ,Rosh the O against ,Behold
back you turn .Tubal of prince ,Gog ,you (am) I

2022/5921 935 6828 3411 5927 8338
וששאתיך והעליתיך מירכתי צפון והבאותך על־הרי
the on bring will and the the from will I And lead and
of mountains you ,north of recesses up you bring .on you

3225 3027 2671 8040 3027 7198 5221 3478
3 ישראל׃ והכיתי קשתך מיד שמאולך וחציך מיד ימינך
your of out your and your of out your will I And .Israel
right hand arrows ,left hand bow strike

5971 102 3605 5307 3478 2022 5921 5307
4 אפיל׃ על־הרי ישראל תפול אתה וכל־אגפיך ועמים
the and your and ,you you Israel the On cause will
peoples ,bands all ,fall shall of mountains .fall to

5414 7704 2416 3611/3605 6833 5861 834
אשר אתך לעיט צפור כל־כנף וחית השדה נתתיך
will I the the and ,wing every bird a birds the to with who
you give field of beasts of ,prey of .you (are)

136 5002 1696 5307 7704 6440 402
5 לאכלה׃ על־פני השדה תפול כי אני דברתי נאם אדני
the states have I for shall you the the On .food for
Lord ,spoken ,fall field of face

3045 982 339 3427 4031 784/7971 3068
6 יהוה׃ ושלחתי־אש במגוג ובישבי האיים לבטח וידעו
they And .securely the the on and on a will I And .Jehovah
know shall coasts of dwellers ,Magog fire send

3478 5971 8432 3045 6944/8034 3068
7 כי־אני יהוה׃ ואת־שם קדשי אודיע בתוך עמי ישראל
.Israel My the in will I My name And .Jehovah I that
people of midst known make holy (am)

3068 1471 3045 5750 6944 8034 2490
ולא־אחל את־שם־קדשי עוד וידעו הגוים כי־אני יהוה
,Jehovah I that the shall And any My name let will I And
(am) nations know more holy profaned be not

3068 136 5002 1961 935 2009 3478 6918
8 קדוש בישראל׃ הנה באה ונהיתה נאם אדני יהוה
.Jehovah the states is it and has it ,Behold .Israel in Holy the
Lord ,done come One

1197 3478 5892 3427 3318 1696 834 3117
9 הוא היום אשר דברתי׃ ויצאו ישבי ערי ישראל ובערו
shall and ,Israel the resi- the shall And have I of the That
afire set of cities of dents out go .spoken which day (is)

3027 4731 2671 7198 6793 4043 5402 5400
והשיקו בנשק ומגן וצנה בקשת ובחצים ובמקל יד
the the and the and the the and the and the burn and
,hand of staff ,arrows bow ,buckler ,shield :weapons

6086 5375/3808 8141 7651 784 1197 7420
10 וברמח ובערו בהם אש שבע שנים׃ ולא־ישאו עצים מן
out wood they And .years seven (with) them they And the and
of take shall not fire burn shall .spears

784 1197 5402 3293 2404 3808 7704
השדה ולא יחטבו מן־היערים כי בנשק יבערו־אש
(with) shall they the for the out cut and the
.fire burn weapons ;forest of down not ,field

3068 136 5002 962 962 7998 7997
ושללו את־שלליהם ובזזו את־בזזיהם נאם אדני יהוה׃
.Jehovah the states who those and who those they And
Lord them robbed rob them spoiled spoil shall

3478 6913 8033 4725 1463 5414 3117 1961
11 והיה ביום ההוא אתן לגוג מקום־שם קבר בישראל
,Israel in grave a ,there place a to will I that day on it And
Gog give be will

6912 5674 2629 3220 6926 5674 1516
גי העברים קדמת הים וחסמת היא את־העברים וקברו
they And who those it shall And the east who those the
bury shall .by pass up stop .sea of by pass of valley

bury Gog and all his multitude there, and *they* shall call *it* The Valley of the Multitude of Gog. [12]And the house of Israel shall bury them, in order to cleanse the land, seven months. [13]And the people of the land shall bury. And it shall be for a name to them, the day when I *am* glorified, declares the Lord Jehovah. [14]And they shall separate men who continually pass through the land, burying those who passed through, who remain on the face of the earth, to cleanse it. At the end of seven months, they shall make a search. [15]And *as* they pass, those who pass through the land, and *any* man sees a bone, then he shall build a post beside it, until the buriers have buried it in The Valley of the Multitude of Gog. [16]And also the name of the city *is* The Multitude. And they shall cleanse the land.

[17]And you, son of man, So says the Lord Jehovah: Say to the bird of every wing, and to every beast of the field: Gather yourselves and come; collect yourselves from all around to My sacrifice which I sacrifice for you, a great sacrifice on the mountains of Israel, so that you may eat flesh and drink blood. [18]You shall eat the flesh of the mighty, and drink the blood of the princes of the earth; *of* rams, lambs, goats, *and* bulls, all of them fatlings of Bashan. [19]And you shall eat fat until satiated; and drink blood until drunkenness, of My sacrifice which I have sacrificed for you. [20]And you shall be satiated at My table, *with* horses and chariots, and mighty men, all the men of war, declares the Lord Jehovah. [21]And I will put My glory among the nations, and all the nations shall see My judgments which I have

6912 1463 1995 1516 7121 1995 3605 1463 8033
12 שָׁם אֶת־גּוֹג וְאֶת־כָּל־הֲמוֹנֹה וְקָרְאוּ גֵּיא הֲמוֹן גּוֹג׃ וּקְבָרוּם
shall And .Gog Mul- the The shall and his all and Gog there
them bury of titude of Valley ,(it) call ,multitude

2320 7617 776 2891 4616 3478 1004
בֵּית יִשְׂרָאֵל לְמַעַן טַהֵר אֶת־הָאָרֶץ שִׁבְעָה חֳדָשִׁים׃
.months seven the cleanse to in ,Israel the
,land order of house

5002 3513 3117 8034 1961 776 5971 6912
13 וְקָבְרוּ כָּל־עַם הָאָרֶץ וְהָיָה לָהֶם לְשֵׁם יוֹם הִכָּבְדִי נְאֻם
states I when the a for to it And the the shall And
,glorified am day name them be shall .land of people (them) bury

6912 776 5674 914 582 8548 3068 136
14 אֲדֹנָי יְהוִה׃ וְאַנְשֵׁי תָמִיד יַבְדִּילוּ עֹבְרִים בָּאָרֶץ מְקַבְּרִים
burying the pass who shall they contin- And .Jehovah the
,land through separate ually men Lord

7097 2891 776 6440 5921 3498 5674
אֶת־הָעֹבְרִים אֶת־הַנּוֹתָרִים עַל־פְּנֵי הָאָרֶץ לְטַהֲרָהּ מִקְצֵה
the at cleanse to the the on remain who who those
of end ;it ,earth of face ,through passed

7200 776 5674 5674 2713 2320 7651
15 שִׁבְעָה־חֳדָשִׁים יַחְקֹרוּ׃ וְעָבְרוּ הָעֹבְרִים בָּאָרֶץ וְרָאָה
(any) and the who those (as) And shall they months seven
sees ,land through pass ,pass they .search a make

6912 6912 5704 6725 681 1128 120 6106
עֶצֶם אָדָם וּבָנָה אֶצְלוֹ צִיּוּן עַד קָבְרוּ אֹתוֹ הַמְקַבְּרִים
buriers the it have until a beside he then ,man a
buried ,post it build shall bone

776 2891 1995 5892/8034 1571 1463 1995 1516
16 אֶל־גֵּיא הֲמוֹן גּוֹג׃ וְגַם שֶׁם־עִיר הֲמוֹנָה וְטִהֲרוּ הָאָרֶץ׃
the they And The (is) the the And .Gog Mul- the The in
.land cleanse shall .Multitude city of name also of titude of Valley

3605 6833 559 3068 136 559 3541 120 1121
17 וְאַתָּה בֶן־אָדָם כֹּה־אָמַר ׀ אֲדֹנָי יְהוִה אֱמֹר לְצִפּוֹר כָּל־
every the to Say :Jehovah the says Thus ,man son And
of bird Lord of ,you

5439 622 935 6908 7704 2416 3605 3671
כָּנָף וּלְכֹל ׀ חַיַּת הַשָּׂדֶה הִקָּבְצוּ וָבֹאוּ הֵאָסְפוּ מִסָּבִיב עַל־
to all from your- collect and Gather the beast to and wing
around selves ;come yourselves :field of every

3478 2022 14:19 2077 2076 834 2077
זִבְחִי אֲשֶׁר אֲנִי זֹבֵחַ לָכֶם זֶבַח גָּדוֹל עַל הָרֵי יִשְׂרָאֵל
,Israel the on great a for sacrifice I which My
of mountains sacrifice ,you sacrifice

1818 398 1368 1320 1818 8354 1320 398
18 וַאֲכַלְתֶּם בָּשָׂר וּשְׁתִיתֶם דָּם׃ בְּשַׂר גִּבּוֹרִים תֹּאכֵלוּ וְדַם־
the and shall You the the .blood drink and flesh you that so
of blood ,eat mighty of flesh eat may

4806 6499 6260 3733 352 8354 776 5387
נְשִׂיאֵי הָאָרֶץ תִּשְׁתּוּ אֵילִים כָּרִים וְעַתּוּדִים פָּרִים מְרִיאֵי
fatlings (of) (of) and (of) (of) ,drink the the
of ,bulls ,goats ,lambs ,rams earth of princes

7943 1818 8354 7654 2459 398 3605 1316
19 בָשָׁן כֻּלָּם׃ וַאֲכַלְתֶּם־חֵלֶב לְשָׂבְעָה וּשְׁתִיתֶם דָּם לְשִׁכָּרוֹן
until blood drink and until fat you And of all Bashan
,drunkenness ,satiated eat shall .them

5483 7979 7646 2076 834 2077
20 מִזִּבְחִי אֲשֶׁר־זָבַחְתִּי לָכֶם׃ וּשְׂבַעְתֶּם עַל־שֻׁלְחָנִי סוּס
(with) My at shall you So for have I which My of
horses table satiated be .you sacrificed sacrifice

5414 3068 136 5002 4421 376 3605 1368 7393
21 וָרֶכֶב גִּבּוֹר וְכָל־אִישׁ מִלְחָמָה נְאֻם אֲדֹנָי יְהוִה׃ וְנָתַתִּי
I And .Jehovah the states ,war the and mighty (with) and
put will Lord of men all men ,chariots

6213 834 4941 1471 3605 7200 1471 3519
אֶת־כְּבוֹדִי בַּגּוֹיִם וְרָאוּ כָל־הַגּוֹיִם אֶת־מִשְׁפָּטִי אֲשֶׁר עָשִׂיתִי
have I which My the all shall and among My
,done judgments nations see ,nations the glory

done, and My hand that I have laid on them. ²²So the house of Israel shall know that I *am* Jehovah their God, from that day and onward. ²³And the nations shall know that the house of Israel was exiled for their iniquity. Because they betrayed Me, so I hid My face from them and gave them into the hand of their enemies. And they fell by the sword, all of them. ²⁴According to their uncleanness and according to their sins, I have done to them, and have hidden My face from them. ²⁵So the Lord Jehovah says thus: Now I will return the captivity of Jacob, and will have mercy on all the house of Israel, and will be jealous for My holy name. ²⁶And also *after* they have borne their shame, and all their treachery which they have done against Me, when they dwell on their land securely, and no one terrifies; ²⁷when I have returned them from the peoples, and gathered them out of the hand of their enemies, and am sanctified in them in the sight of many nations; ²⁸then they shall know that I *am* Jehovah their God, who exiled them among the nations. But I have gathered them to their own land, and have not left any of them there. ²⁹And I will not any more hide My face from them; for I have poured out My Spirit on the house of Israel, declares the Lord Jehovah.

CHAPTER 40
¹In the twenty-fifth year of our exile, in the beginning of the year, in the tenth of the month, in the fourteenth year after the city was struck, on that same

---

22

  3027   7760   3027 3045 1004 3478

וְאֶת־יָדִי אֲשֶׁר־שַׂמְתִּי בָהֶם: וְיָדְעוּ בֵּית יִשְׂרָאֵל כִּי אֲנִי

I   that   Israel   the   shall   So   on   have I   that   My   and
(am)   of house   know   .them   laid   hand

23

1471   3045   1973   3117   430   3068

יְהוָה אֱלֹהֵיהֶם מִן־הַיּוֹם הַהוּא וָהָלְאָה: וְיָדְעוּ הַגּוֹיִם כִּי

that   the   shall   And   and   that   day   from   their   Jehovah
nations   know   .onward   God

6440 5641   4603   834   3282 3478 1004   1540 5071

בַּעֲוֹנָם גָּלוּ בֵית־יִשְׂרָאֵל עַל אֲשֶׁר מָעֲלוּ־בִי וָאַסְתִּר פָּנַי

My   I thus   ,Me   they   that   Be-   .Israel   the   was their for
face   hid   betrayed   cause   of house exiled iniquity

24

2932   3605   2719   5307   6862   3027 5414

מֵהֶם וָאֶתְּנֵם בְּיַד צָרֵיהֶם וַיִּפְּלוּ כֻלָּם: כְּטֻמְאָתָם

their to As   of all   the by   they And   their the into gave and from
uncleanness   .them ,sword   fell   .enemies of hand them   them

25

559   354.1   6440   5641   6213   6588

וּכְפִשְׁעֵיהֶם עָשִׂיתִי אֹתָם וָאַסְתִּר פָּנַי מֵהֶם: לָכֵן כֹּה אָמַר

says thus There-   from   My   have and   ,them   have I   to according and
fore   .them face   hidden   to done trespasses their

3605 7355   3290   7622   7725   6258 3068 136

אֲדֹנָי יְהוִה עַתָּה אָשִׁיב אֶת־שְׁבוּת יַעֲקֹב וְרִחַמְתִּי כָּל־

all   have will and   ,Jacob   of captivity   will I   Now   :Jehovah the
the   on mercy   return   Lord

26

36:39   5375   6944   8034   7065   3478 1004

בֵּית יִשְׂרָאֵל וְקִנֵּאתִי לְשֵׁם קָדְשִׁי: וְנָשׂוּ אֶת־כְּלִמָּתָם וְאֶת־

and   their   they (after)   My   name for   will and   ,Israel   house
shame   also borne have ;holy   jealous be   of

982   127   5921   3427   4604   834   4603 36:05

כָּל־מַעֲלָם אֲשֶׁר מָעֲלוּ־בִי בְּשִׁבְתָּם עַל־אַדְמָתָם לָבֶטַח

securely   their   on   they when against they   which   their   all
land   dwell   ,Me done have   treachery

27

6908   5971   7725   2729 369

וְאֵין מַחֲרִיד: בְּשׁוֹבְבִי אוֹתָם מִן־הָעַמִּים וְקִבַּצְתִּי אֹתָם

them   and   the   from   them have I   When   .terrifies   no and
gathered peoples   returned have   one

28

3045   7227 1471   5869   6942   341   776

מֵאַרְצוֹת אֹיְבֵיהֶם וְנִקְדַּשְׁתִּי בָם לְעֵינֵי הַגּוֹיִם רַבִּים: וְיָדְעוּ

they then ;many   nations   in   in   am from   of out
know shall   1471   of sight them sanctified ,enemies'   lands

3664   1546   430 3068

כִּי אֲנִי יְהוָה אֱלֹהֵיהֶם בְּהַגְלוֹתִי אֹתָם אֶל־הַגּוֹיִם וְכִנַּסְתִּים

have I   But   the   among   them   exiles who   their   Jehovah I   that
them gathered .nations   God   (am)

5750 5641   3808   8033   5750 3498   127

29

אֶל־אַדְמָתָם וְלֹא־אוֹתִיר עוֹד מֵהֶם שָׁם: וְלֹא־אַסְתִּיר עוֹד

any   will I   And   .there   of   any   have and   own their   to
more hide   not   them   left not   ,land

5002   3478 1004   7307   8210   6440

פָּנַי מֵהֶם אֲשֶׁר שָׁפַכְתִּי אֶת־רוּחִי עַל־בֵּית יִשְׂרָאֵל נְאֻם

states   ,Israel   the   on   My   have I   for   from   My
of house   Spirit   out poured   them face
3068 136

אֲדֹנָי יְהוִה:

.Jehovah the
Lord

CAP. XL מ

CHAPTER 40

1

6218   8141   7218   1546   8141   2568   6242

בְּעֶשְׂרִים וְחָמֵשׁ שָׁנָה לְגָלוּתֵנוּ בְּרֹאשׁ הַשָּׁנָה בֶּעָשׂוֹר

the in   the   the in   our of   year   fifth   the In
tenth   ,year   of beginning   exile   twenty-

5892   5221   310   8141   6240   702   2320

לַחֹדֶשׁ בְּאַרְבַּע עֶשְׂרֵה שָׁנָה אַחַר אֲשֶׁר הֻכְּתָה הָעִיר

the   was   after   year   the in   the of
,city   struck   fourteenth   ,month

day the hand of Jehovah
was on me, and brought me
there. ²In the visions of
God, He brought me into
the land of Israel, and made
me rest on a very high
mountain. And it went up,
as the structure of a city on
the south. ³And He brought
me there; and, behold, a
man whose appearance
was as the appearance of
bronze, and a line of flax
and a measuring reed in his
hand, and he stood in the
gate. ⁴And the man said
to me, Son of man, look
with your eyes, and hear
with your ears, and set your
heart on all that I shall show
you. For in order to show
you, you are brought here.
Declare to the house of
Israel all that you see.

⁵And, behold, a wall on the
outside of the house all
around. And a measuring
reed *was* in the man's hand,
six cubits, with a cubit and a
span. So he measured the
breadth of the building, one
reed; and the height, one
reed. ⁶And he came to the
gate which faced eastward,
and went up its steps and
measured the threshold of
the gate, one reed wide;
even the one threshold, one
reed wide. ⁷And a room,
one reed long and one reed
wide; and between the
rooms *were* five cubits. And
the threshold of the gate
from beside the porch of the
gate, from the house, *was*
one reed.

⁸And he measured the
porch of the gate from the
house, one reed. ⁹And he
measured the porch of the
gate, eight cubits; and its
pillars, two cubits; also the
porch of the gate from the

בְּעֶצֶם | הַיּוֹם הַזֶּה הָיְתָה עָלַי יַד־יְהֹוָה וַיָּבֵא אֹתִי שָׁמָּה:
6106 ... 3117 ... 2088 ... 1961 ... 3027 3068 ... 935 ... 8033

same on | day that was the on of hand Jehovah and me there.
day me and brought

בְּמַרְאוֹת אֱלֹהִים הֱבִיאַנִי אֶל־אֶרֶץ יִשְׂרָאֵל וַיְנִיחֵנִי אֶל־
4759 ... 430 ... 935 ... 776 ... 3478 ... 5117

2 the In of visions God brought He the into land of Israel made and me rest me on

הַר גָּבֹהַ מְאֹד וְעָלָיו כְּמִבְנֵה־עִיר מִנֶּגֶב: וַיָּבֵא אוֹתִי
2022 39 66 5927 ... 4011 5892 ... 5045 ... 935

3 mountain high very up went and as the of structure city a south. He And brought me on the

שָׁמָּה וְהִנֵּה־אִישׁ מַרְאֵהוּ כְּמַרְאֵה נְחֹשֶׁת וּפְתִיל־פִּשְׁתִּים
8033 ... 2009 376 ... 47 58 4758 ... 5178 6616 6593

there; behold, man a and whose appearance as the of appearance bronze, a and of line flax

בְּיָדוֹ וּקְנֵה הַמִּדָּה וְהוּא עֹמֵד בַּשָּׁעַר: וַיְדַבֵּר אֵלַי הָאִישׁ
3027 7070 4060 ... 5975 8179 ... 1696 376

4 his in hand, a and measur- reed ling the in He stood And the me to said .gate man,

בֶּן־אָדָם רְאֵה בְעֵינֶיךָ וּבְאָזְנֶיךָ שְׁמַע וְשִׂים לִבְּךָ לְכֹל
1121 120 7200 ... 5892 241 ... 8085 7760 ... 3820 3605

Son man, look your with eyes your with and ears, hear, and set your all on heart

אֲשֶׁר־אֲנִי מַרְאֶה אוֹתָךְ כִּי לְמַעַן הַרְאוֹתְכָה הֻבָאתָה
834 ... 7200 ... 4616 ... 7200 935

that I shall show .you For in order show you to you are brought

הֵן הַגֵּד אֶת־כָּל־אֲשֶׁר־אַתָּה רֹאֶה לְבֵית יִשְׂרָאֵל: וְהִנֵּה
2009 5046 834 ... 7200 1004 3478 ... 2009

5 .here Declare all that you see the to house of Israel .behold And,

חוֹמָה מִחוּץ לַבַּיִת סָבִיב סָבִיב וּבְיַד הָאִישׁ קְנֵה הַמִּדָּה
2346 2351 ... 1004 376 5439 5439 ... 3027 7070 4060

a wall on the outside the of house all ,around and in hand man's the the reed a measuring

שֵׁשׁ־אַמּוֹת בָּאַמָּה וָטֹפַח וַיָּמָד אֶת־רֹחַב הַבִּנְיָן קָנֶה אֶחָד
8337 520 520 8667 ... 2948 4058 ... 7341 1146 7070 259

six (of) a with cubit a and span he So measured the breadth the of building, reed ;one

וְקוֹמָה קָנֶה אֶחָד: וַיָּבֹא אֶל־שַׁעַר אֲשֶׁר פָּנָיו דֶּרֶךְ
6967 7070 259 ... 935 8179 ... 834 6440 1870

6 the and height reed .one Then he came to the gate which faced the way

הַקָּדִימָה וַיַּעַל בְּמַעֲלֹתָו וַיָּמָד אֶת־סַף הַשַּׁעַר קָנֶה אֶחָד
6921 5927 ... 4609 4058 ... 5592 8179 7070 259

east up went its steps and measured of threshold the gate, reed one

רֹחַב וְאֵת סַף אֶחָד קָנֶה אֶחָד רֹחַב: וְהַתָּא קָנֶה אֶחָד
7341 ... 5592 259 7070 259 7341 ... 8372 70 70 259

7 ;wide even the one threshold one reed ,one .wide And a room, reed one

אֹרֶךְ וְקָנֶה אֶחָד רֹחַב וּבֵין הַתָּאִים חָמֵשׁ אַמּוֹת וְסַף
753 7070 259 7341 ... 996 8372 2568 520 5592

long and reed one .wide And between rooms the five (were) .cubits And the of threshold

הַשַּׁעַר מֵאֵצֶל אֻלָם הַשַּׁעַר מֵהַבַּיִת קָנֶה אֶחָד: וַיָּמָד אֶת־
8179 681 ... 197 8179 ... 1004 7070 259 ... 4058

the gate from beside the porch the of gate the from house reed one. He also measured

8 אֻלָם הַשַּׁעַר מֵהַבַּיִת קָנֶה אֶחָד: וַיָּמָד אֶת־אֻלָם הַשַּׁעַר
197 8179 ... 1004 7070 259 ... 4058 197 8179

the of porch the gate the from house .one reed Then he measured of porch the gate

9 שְׁמֹנֶה אַמּוֹת וְאֵילָו שְׁתַּיִם אַמּוֹת וְאֻלָם הַשַּׁעַר מֵהַבַּיִת:
8083 520 ... 352 8147 520 ... 197 8179 1004

eight .cubits And its pillars two .cubits And the of porch the gate the from .house

house. ¹⁰And the gate-rooms eastward *were* three from here, and three from there; one measure to the three of them; and one measure *was* to the pillars, from here and from there. ¹¹And he measured the breadth of the gate-opening, ten cubits; the length of the gate *was* thirteen cubits. ¹²And the border in front of the rooms *was* one cubit; and the border from here, one cubit. And the room *was* six cubits from here, and six cubits from there. ¹³And he measured the gate of the room from roof to roof, twenty-five cubits wide, door to door. ¹⁴He also made the pillars, sixty cubits, even to the court-pillar, *from* the gate round *and* round. ¹⁵And on the face of the entrance gate, to the face of the porch of the inner gate, *was* fifty cubits; ¹⁶and latticed windows *were* to the rooms, and to their pillars inside the gate round *and* round; and so for the porches; and windows *were* round *and* round inside; and to a pillar *were* palm trees.

¹⁷And he brought me into the outer court. And, behold, chambers, and a pavement made for the court round *and* round. Thirty chambers *were* on the pavement. ¹⁸And the pavement by the side of the gates to equal the length of the gates *was* the lower pavement. ¹⁹And he measured the breadth from the face of the lower gate to the face of the inner court, on the outside, a hundred cubits eastward and northward. ²⁰And the gate which faces the way of the north of

---

10

the And	the	the on	east	three	from here	and three	from there	the gate	the rooms of
83172	8179	1870	6921	7969	6311	7969	63111		

one measure (was) | three the to | and measure | one | the to pillars | here | from and from there
6311 | 6311 | 352 | 259 | 4060 | 7969 | 259 | 4060

11 the gate | The length of | cubits ten | the opening of | the breadth | he And measured
8179 | 753 | 520 | 6235 | 8179 | 6607 | 7311 | 4058

12 one | (was) the | front in | the rooms of | border | cubits | thirteen (was)
259 | 520 | 8372 | 6440 | 13766 | 520 | 6240 | 7969 | 259

and | from | cubits six | the room And (was) | from | the | one | and cubit
6242 | 520 | 8337 | 83172 | 6311 | 1366 | 259 | 520

13 (was it) wide | to | the the from | the from gate | he And measured | there
7341 | 1406 | 8372 | 4058 | 6311 | 520

14 sixty | the pillars | the also He made | door | to door | cubits | five
8246 | 352 | 6213 | 6607 | 5048 | 6607 | 520 | 2568

15 the And of face on | round the (from) | the gate | court of pillar to | even ,cubits
6440 | 5439 | 5439 | 8179 | 269 | 3852 | 520

fifty (was) | inner | gate the | of porch | of face | to | the entrance | of gate
2572 | 6442 | 8179 | 197 | 6144 | 2978 | 8179

16 their pillars | to and | the rooms | to | latticed | and windows | —cubits
361 | 8372 | 331 | 2474 | 520

windows and | the for | and | round | the | inside
2472 | 361 | 3651 | 5439 | 8179 | 6441

17 into | he And brought | palm (were) | each and | inside | round
935 | 8561 | 352 | 6441 | 5439

round | the for court | made | a and pavement | chambers | And behold, | outer court
5439 | 2691 | 6213 | 7531 | 3957 | 2009 | 2435 | 2691

18 the by of side | the And pavement | the pavement | on (were) | chambers | Thirty (and) round
3801 | 7531 | 7531 | 3957 | 7970 | 5439

19 he Then measured | lower | the (was) pavement | the gates | of length | equal to gates the
4058 | 8481 | 7531 | 8179 | 753 | 5980 | 8179

the on outside, | inner | court | the to of face | lower | the gate | the from of face breadth
2351 | 6442 | 2691 | 6440 | 8481 | 8179 | 6440 | 7341

20 the faces of way | which | the And gate | and northward. | eastward | cubits | a hundred
1870 | 6440 | 834 | 8179 | 6828 | 6921 | 520 | 3967

the outer court, he measured its length and its breadth. 21And its rooms *were* three from here, and three from there. And its pillars and its porches were as the first measure—its length fifty cubits, and its breadth twenty-five cubits. 22And its windows, and its porches, and its palm trees *were* as the measure of the gate that faces eastward. And they went up to it by seven steps; and its porches *were* before them. 23And the gate of the inner court *was* across from the gate toward the north and toward the east. And he measured from gate to gate, a hundred cubits. 24And he led me southward. And, behold, a gate southward! And he measured its pillars and its porches according to these measures. 25And windows *were* in it, and its porches round *and* round like these windows. Fifty cubits *were* the length, and twenty-five cubits the breadth. 26And seven steps *were* going up to it, and its porches before them. And palm trees *were* to it, one from here and one from there, to its pillars. 27And a gate *was* to the inner court southward. And he measured from gate to gate, southward, a hundred cubits.

28And he brought me to the inner court by the south gate. And he measured the south gate by these measures. 29And its rooms, and its pillars, and its porches *were* as three measures. And windows *were* to it, and its porches round *and* round. *It was* fifty cubits long, and twenty-five cubits wide. 30And the porches round *and* round

8372 7341 753 4058 2435 2691 6828
21 הצפון לחצר החיצונה מדד ארכו ורחבו: ותאו
its And | its and | its | he | ,outer | the of | the
rooms | .breadth | length | measured | | court | north

4060 1961 361 352 6311 7991 6311 7969
שלושה מפו ושלשה מפו ואילו ואלמו היה כמדת
the as | were | its and | its And | from | and | from | (were)
of measure | | porches | pillars | .there | three | here | three

6242 2568 7341 753 520 2572 7223 8179
השער הראשון חמשים אמה ארכו ורחב חמש ועשרים
twenty-five | the and | Its | cubits | (was) | .first | the
| breadth ,length | | | fifty | | gate

6440 834 8179 4060 8561 361 2474 520
22 באמה: וחלונו ואלמו ותימרו כמדת השער אשר פניו
faces | that | gate the | as (were) | its and | its and | its And | .cubits
| | | of measure the | trees palm | ,porches | ,windows |

6440 361 5927 7651 4609 6921 1870
דרך הקדים ובמעלות שבע יעלו־בו ואילמו לפניהם:
(were) | its and | to | they | seven | by And | the | the
.them before | porches | ;it | up went | | steps | .east | of way

4058 6921 6828 8179 5048 6442 2691 8179
23 ושער לחצר הפנימי נגד השער לצפון ולקדים וימד
he And | toward and | the toward | the | across | inner | the | the And
measured | .east the | north | gate | from | (was) | court | of gate

2009 1864 1870 3212 520 3967 8179 8179
24 משער אל־שער מאה אמה: ויולכני דרך הדרום והנה־
and | the | the | he And | .cubits | a | gate | to | from
behold | ,south | of way | me led | | hundred | | | gate

428 4060 361 352 4058 1864 1870 8179
שער דרך הדרום ומדד אילו ואילמו כמדות האלה:
.these | according | its and | its | he And | the | the | gate a
| measures to | porches | pillars | measured | .south | of way |

428 2474 5439 5439 361 2474
25 וחלונים לו ולאילמו סביב ׀ סביב כהחלנות האלה
.these | windows like | (and) | round | its and | ,it in | win- And
| | round | | porches | | (were) dows

4609 520 6242 2568 7341 753 520 2572
26 חמשים אמה ארך ורחב חמש ועשרים אמה: ומעלות
steps And | .cubits | twenty-five | the and | The | cubits | (was)
| | | breadth | ,length | | fifty

6311 259 8561 6440 361 5930 7651
שבעה עלותו ואילמו לפניהם ותמרים לו אחד מפו
from | one | ,it to | palm And | before | its and | going | seven
here | | | (were) trees | .them | porches | ,it to up | (were)

1864 1870 6442 2691 8179 352 6311 259
27 ואחד מפו אל־אילו: ושער לחצר הפנימי דרך הדרום
the | the | inner | the to | a And | its | to | from | one and
.south | of way | | court (was) | gate | .pillars | | there |

935 520 3967 1864 1870 8179 8179 4058
28 וימד משער אל־השער דרך הדרום מאה אמות: ויביאני
he And | .cubits | a | the | the | gate | to | from | he And
me brought | | hundred | south | of way | | | gate | measured

1864 8179 4058 1864 8179 6442 2691
אל־חצר הפנימי בשער הדרום וימד את־השער הדרום
south | the | he And | the | gate by | inner | the | to
| gate | measured | .south | | | court |

428 4060 361 352 8372 428 4060
29 כמדות האלה: ותאו ואלו ואלמו כמדות האלה
.these | as (were) | its and | its and | its And | .these | by
| measures | porches | pillars | rooms | | measures

753 520 2572 5439 5439 361 2474
וחלונות לו ולאלמו סביב ׀ סביב חמשים אמה ארך
long | cubits | (was It) | (and) | round | its and | to | win- And
| | fifty | .round | | porches | ,it | (were) dows

753 5439 5439 361 520 2568 6242 7341
30 ורחב עשרים וחמש אמות: ואלמות סביב ׀ סביב ארך
long | (and) | round | the And | .cubits | five | twenty- | and
| round | | porches | | | | wide

were twenty-five cubits long, and five cubits wide. 31And its porches *were* toward the outer court; and palm trees on its pillars. And its stairway *had* eight steps.

32And he brought me into the inner court eastward. And he measured the gate by these measures. 33And its rooms, and its pillars, and its porches *were* as these measures. And windows *were* to it, and to its porches round *and* round. *It was* fifty cubits long and twenty-five cubits wide. 34And its porches *were* toward the outer court. And palm trees *were* on its pillars from here and from there. And its stairway *had* eight steps.

35And he brought me to the north gate, and measured by these measures, 36its rooms, its posts, and its porches. And windows *were* to it round *and* round. *It was* fifty cubits long and twenty-five cubits wide. 37And its pillars *were* toward the outer court. And palm trees *were* on its pillars, from here and from there; and its stairway *had* eight steps. 38And the chamber and its door *was* by the pillars of the gates; they washed the burnt offering there.

39And in the porch of the gate *were* two tables from here, and two tables from there, to slaughter on them the burnt offering, and the sin offering, and the guilt offering. 40And to the side outside, as one goes up to the door of the gate northward *were* two tables. And on the other side at the porch of the gate *were* two tables. 41Four tables *were* from here, and four tables from there, by the side of

361 520 2568 7341 520 6242 2568
31 חמש ועשרים אמה ורחב חמש אמות: ואלמו אל־
toward its And (were) porches .cubits five wide and cubits twenty- five

4608 8083 4609 352 8561 2436 2691
החצר החיצונה ותמרים אל־אילו ומעלות שמונה מעלו:
its .stairway eight (had) steps And its .pillars on palm And (were) trees .outer the court

8179 4058 6921 1870 6442 2691 935
32 ויביאני אל־החצר הפנימי דרך הקדים וימד את־השער
the gate he And measured the .east the of way inner court the into he And me brought

428 4060 361 352 8372 428 4060
33 כמדות האלה: ותאו ואלו ואלמו כמדות האלה
.these as measures its and (were) porches its and pillars its And rooms .these by measures

520 2572 753 5439 5439 361 2474
וחלונות לו ולאלמו סביב | סביב ארך חמשים אמה
cubits fifty (was It) long (and) .round round its to and porches ,it to win- And (were) dows

2435 2691 361 520 6242 2568 7341
34 ורחב חמש ועשרים אמה: ואלמו לחצר החיצונה
.outer the toward court its And (were) porches .cubits twenty- five and wide

4608 4609 8083 6311 6311 352 8561
ותמרים אל־אילו מפו ומפו ושמנה מעלות מעלו:
its .stairway steps (had) eight And from and there from here its pillars on palm And (were) trees

8372 428 4060 4058 6828 8179 935
35 ויביאני אל־שער הצפון ומדד כמדות האלה:
36 תאו
its ,rooms ;these by measures and measured north the gate to he And me brought

520 2572 753 5439 5439 2474 361 352
אלו ואלמו וחלונות לו סביב | סביב ארך חמשים אמה
cubits fifty (was It) long (and) .round round it to win- and (were) dows its and ;porches its posts

2435 2691 352 520 6242 2568 7341
37 ורחב חמש ועשרים אמה: ואילו לחצר החיצונה
.outer the toward court its And (were) pillars .cubits twenty- five and wide

4608 4609 8083 6311 6311 352 8561
ותמרים אל־אילו מפו ומפו ושמנה מעלות מעלו:
its .stairway steps (had) eight And from and there from here its ,pillars on palm And (were) trees

5930 1740 8033 8179 352 6607 3957
38 ולשכה ופתחה באילים השערים שם ידיחו את־העלה:
burnt the .offering they washed there ,gates the the by of pillars its and (was) door the And chamber

6311 7979 8147 6311 7979 8147 8179 197
39 ובאלם השער שנים שלחנות מפו ושנים שלחנות מפה
from ,there tables two and from here tables (were) two the gate the in And of porch

3801 816 2403 5930 7919
40 לשחוט אליהם העלה והחטאת והאשם: ואל־הכתף
the side And to guilt the and .offering sin the and offering burnt the offering them on to slaughter

7979 8147 6828 8179 6607 5927 2351
מחוצה לעולה לפתח השער הצפונה שנים שלחנות
.tables (were) two ,northward the gate the to of door one as up goes ,outside

7979 8147 8179 197 834 312 3801
ואל־הכתף האחרת אשר לאלם השער שנים שלחנות:
.tables (were) two the ,gate the at of porch which (was) ,other the side And on

3801 6311 7979 702 6311 7979 702
41 ארבעה שלחנות מפה וארבעה שלחנות מפה לכתף
the by of side from ,there tables (were) four and from ,here tables (were) Four

the gate, eight tables; they slaughter on them. **42**And the four tables for burnt offering *were* cut stone, one cubit and a half long, and one cubit and a half wide, and one cubit high. They also rested on them the instruments with which they slaughtered, by them the burnt offering and the sacrifice.

43And the double hooks, one span, were fastened in the house round *and* round; and the flesh of the offering on the tables. **44**And from the outside to the inner court *were* the chambers of the singers in the inner court, which *was* at the side of the north gate. And their face *was* southward; one at the side of the east gate looked the way of the north. **45**And he said to me, This chamber facing southward *is* for the priests, the keepers of the charge of the house. **46**And the chamber facing northward *is* for the priests, the keepers of the charge of the altar. They *are* the sons of Zadok who come near to Jehovah, of the sons of Levi, to minister to Him. **47**And he measured the court: a hundred cubits long and a hundred cubits wide, a square. And the altar *was* before the house.

48And he brought me to the porch of the house, and measured *each* pillar of the porch, five cubits from here, and five cubits from there. And the gate *was* three cubits wide from here, and three cubits from there. **49**The length of the porch *was* twenty cubits, and eleven cubits wide, even

---

42
8179	8083	7979		7979	702	7979
the	eight	tables;	them on	they	the And	tables
;gate			.slaughter	them on	four	

5930	68	1496.	753.	520	259	26.7	7431	520
burnt for	stone	(were)	cut	long	a	and	and	cubit
offering					cubit	one	a	wide
half								

259	2677	363	5201	259	3240	3627
one	a and	high	also they	them On	the	the
half			rested		instruments	

43
834	7919	5930	2077	8240	2948
with	they	the	the and	the And	span
which	slaughtered	burnt	.sacrifice	,hooks double	
		offering	them by		

259	3559	1004	5439	5439	7979	1320
,one	fastened	house	round.	round	tables	the (was) the
	were	the in	(and)	And	the	of flesh

44
7033	2351	8179	6442	3957	7891	2691
the	the from And	the to	(were)	inner	of chambers	the in
.offering	outside	gate	the	singers	court

6442	834	380.1	8179	6828	1865	1870	6440
,inner	which	(was)	gate	at	the	the	the
			of side	the	of way	south	:south

45
259	380.1	8179	6921	6440	1870	6828	1696
one	at	the	east	looked	of way	.north	he And
		gate of side		the			said

2090	39.57	834	64.40	1864	3548	8104
This	,chamber	whose	the	the	the for (is)	the
to		(is) face	south,		of keepers	
,me				.priests		

46
4931	1004	39.57	834	64.40	1870	6828	3548
the	the	And	whose	the	the	the	the for (is)
of charge	.house	chamber	(is) face	north	of way		,priests

2091	4931	4196	6659.	7131	1121
of sons	of	charge the the	.altar	Zadok	who come	They (are)
	keepers				near,

47
520	3967	753.	24.91	4058.	8334	3068
cubits	a	long	the	he So	serve to	,Jehovah	to ,Levi
	hundred		:court	measured	.Him	

48
7341	3967	520	7251	4196	6440	1004	935
and	a	,cubits	square a	the and	before	the	he And
wide	hundred		(was) altar		.house	me brought

197	1004	4058	352	3548	2568	520	6311	2568
of porch	pillar	measured	(each)	and	the	the	to
porch of				five	cubits	from	five
						here	

49
520	6311	7341	8179	7969	520	6311	7969	520
cubits	from	And	gate the	three	cubits	from	and	cubits
	here	(was) wide				.there	three

6311	753	197	6242	520	520	6249	6240	520
from	of length	The	the	(was)	,cubits	and	eleven	,cubits
.there	porch		twenty			wide

with the steps by which
they went up to it. And
columns *were* by the pillars,
one from here, and one
from there.

259	352		5982	5927	834	4609
אֶחָ֑ד	אֵלַ֣יִם אֶל־הָאֵלִ֔ים	וְעֹמְדִ֖ים	אֵלָ֑יו יַֽעֲל֣וּ	אֲשֶׁ֣ר	וּבְמַעֲל֗וֹת
one	the by ,pillars	(were) And columns	.it to they up went	which	the with even steps

6311	259	6311
מִפֹּֽה׃ וְאֶחָ֖ד		מִפֹּ֥ה
from .there	and one	from ,here

CAP. XLI מא

CHAPTER 41

[1] And he brought me to
the temple and measured
the pillars, six cubits wide
from here, and six cubits
wide from there—the width
of the tent. [2] And the door
was ten cubits wide. And
the sides of the door *were*
five cubits from here and
five cubits from there. And
he measured its length,
forty cubits; and twenty
cubits wide. [3] And he went
inside and measured the
pillars of the door, two
cubits. And the door *was*
six cubits; and the width of
the door, seven cubits.
[4] And he measured its
length, twenty cubits; and
the width, twenty cubits, to
the face of the temple. And
he said to me, This *is* the
Holy of Holies.

[5] And he measured the
wall of the house, six cubits;
and the width of *each* side
chamber, four cubits round
and round the house all
around. [6] And the side
chambers *were* a side
chamber over a side
chamber, three *stories*, and
thirty times. And *they*
entered the wall which *was*
of the house for the side
chambers round *and* round,
that they may be fastened;
but they were not fastened
in the wall of the house.
[7] And a widening and a
winding upwards *and*
upwards for the side
chambers —for the wind-
ing around of the house
went upward *and* upward,
round *and* round the house.
On account of this the
width of the house *went* up,

1

7341	520	8337	352	4058	1964	935
רֹ֔חַב	אַמּ֣וֹת שֵׁשׁ־	אֶת־הָאֵילִ֗ים וַיָּ֣מָד				וַיְבִיאֵ֖נִי אֶל־הַהֵיכָ֑ל
wide	cubits six ,pillars the and the measured temple					to he Then brought me

2

6607	7341	168	7341	6311 7341	520	8337	6311
הַפֶּ֔תַח וְרֹ֣חַב		הָאֹֽהֶל׃ רֹֽחַב־מִפּ֖וֹ			אַמּ֣וֹת וְשֵׁשׁ־		מִפֹּ֛ה
door the And (was) wide		.tent the the of width ,there		from broad	cubits and	six ,here	from

2568	6311	520	2568	6607	3801	520	6235
אַמּ֣וֹת	מִפּ֖וֹ	וְחָמֵ֥שׁ	אַמּ֣וֹת	חָמֵ֣שׁ הַפֶּ֔תַח	וְכִתְפ֤וֹת	אַמּ֑וֹת	עֶ֣שֶׂר
five and	here,	from	cubits	five door the (were)	the sides of	.cubits	ten

6242	7341	520	705	753	4058	6311	520
עֶשְׂרִֽים׃	וְרֹ֖חַב	אַמָּ֑ה	אַרְבָּעִ֣ים	אָרְכּ֖וֹ	וַיָּ֥מָד	מִפּ֖וֹ	אַמּ֥וֹת
twenty	wide and ,cubits		forty	its	he And measured .there	from	cubits

3

520	8147	6607	352	4058	6441	935	520
אַמּֽוֹת׃	שְׁתַּ֣יִם	הַפֶּ֖תַח אֵֽיל־ וַיָּ֥מָד			לִפְנִ֔ימָה	וּבָ֣א	אַמּֽוֹת׃
;cubits	two	the door of ,pillars the and measured			inside	he Then went	.cubits

4

4058	520	7651	6607	7341	520	8337	6607
וַיָּ֥מָד אֶת־	אַמּ֑וֹת	שֶׁ֣בַע	הַפֶּ֖תַח וְרֹ֥חַב		אַמּ֔וֹת שֵׁ֣שׁ		וְהַפֶּ֗תַח
he So measured	.cubits	seven	door the the and of width		cubits six		the and (was) door

1964	6440	520	6242	520	6242	753
הַהֵיכָ֑ל אֶל־פְּנֵ֖י		אַמָּ֔ה	וְרֹ֣חַב עֶשְׂרִ֣ים	אַמָּ֔ה	עֶשְׂרִ֣ים	אָרְכּ֞וֹ
the the to ,cubits temple of face			twenty the and ,cubits width		twenty	its ,length

5

8337	1004	7023	4058	6944	6944	2088	559
שֵׁ֣שׁ	הַבַּ֖יִת קִֽיר־ וַיָּ֥מָד			הַקֳּדָשִֽׁים׃	קֹ֖דֶשׁ זֶ֥ה		וַיֹּ֣אמֶר אֵלַ֔י
six	house of wall the he And measured			.holies the	holy (is) This		he to me said

520	5439	5439	520	702	6763	7341	520
אַמּ֑וֹת	סָבִ֣יב לַבַּ֖יִת	סָבִ֣יב	אַמּ֤וֹת	אַרְבַּ֨ע	הַצֵּלָ֜ע וְרֹ֨חַב		אַמּ֔וֹת
the (and) round ,cubits house round			(was) side (each) the and four chamber of width				;cubits

6

6741	7970	7969	6763	6763	6763	5439
סָבִֽיב׃	פְּעָמִ֔ים וּשְׁלֹשִׁ֣ים	שָׁל֤וֹשׁ	אֶל־צֵלָ֜ע צֵלָ֨ע		וְהַצְּלָע֡וֹת	
.times	thirty and	three	side a over side a side the And (stories) ,chamber chamber (were)		chambers ,around	all

1961	5439	5439	6763	1004	834	7023	935
לִֽהְי֣וֹת	סָבִ֣יב	לַצְּלָע֖וֹת		אֲשֶׁר־לַבַּ֛יִת		בַּקִּ֧יר וּבָא֞וֹת	
they that (and) be may ,round		side the for chambers		house (was) wall of which the		the (they) And wall entered	

7

5437	7337	1004	7023	270	1961	3808	270
וְנָסַ֣ב	וְרָחֲבָ֨ה	הַבָּ֑יִת בַּקִּ֣יר		אֲחוּזִ֖ים		אֲחוּזִ֔ים וְלֹֽא־	
a and winding	a And widening	.house the the in of wall		fastened	they but ,fastened	were not	

4605	1004	5437	6763	4605	4605
לְמַ֨עְלָה֩	הַבַּ֜יִת מֽוּסַב־ כִּ֣י		לַצְּלָע֗וֹת	לְמַ֣עְלָה	לְמַ֨עְלָה
(went) upward	the winding the For house of around		side the for .chambers	upwards	upwards (and)

4605	1004	7341	1004	5439	5439	4605
לְמָֽעְלָה׃		לַבַּ֜יִת רֹ֣חַב עַל־כֵּ֞ן	סָבִ֣יב		סָבִ֣יב	
(went) .upward		the of the Therefore house width	(and) round .house round			(and) ,upward

and so *from* the lowest it went up to the highest, by the middle *story*. [8]I also saw the height of the house round *and* round, the foundations of the side chambers *were* a full reed, six cubits by joining. [9]The width of the wall which *was* for the side chamber to the outside *was* five cubits, and that which *was* left between the side chambers that *were* of the house. [10]And between the chambers *was* the width of twenty cubits circling the house round *and* round. [11]And the door of the side chamber *was* toward the open space, one door northward, and one door southward. And the width of the place of the open space *was* five cubits round *and* round. [12]And the building that *was* before the separate area at the end of the way of the west *was* seventy cubits wide. And the wall of the building *was* five cubits wide round *and* round; and its length, ninety cubits.

[13]And he measured the house, a hundred cubits long. And the separate area, and the building and its wall *were* a hundred cubits long. [14]And the width of the face of the house, and the separate area toward the east, a hundred cubits. [15]And he measured the length of the building to the face of the separate area which *was* on its rear; and its gallery from here and from there *was* a hundred cubits; and the inner temple, and the porches of the court, [16]the thresholds, and the latticed windows, and the galleries all around, their three *stories* opposite the threshold, were paneled *with* wood round *and* round; and *from* the ground up to the windows, and the windows were covered; [17]to that above the door, even to the inner house, and outside, and to all the wall

1004 7200 8484 5945 5927 8481
8 וְכֵן הַתַּחְתּוֹנָה יַעֲלֶה עַל־הָעֶלְיוֹנָה לַתִּיכוֹנָה׃ וְרָאִיתִי לַבַּיִת
the of / house — also I saw — the by .(story) middle — the highest — to — went it up — the (from) lowest — and so
8337 7070 4393 6763 4328 5439 5439 1363
גֹּבַהּ סָבִיב ׀ סָבִיב מיסדות הַצְּלָעוֹת מְלוֹ הַקָּנֶה שֵׁשׁ
(of) six — reed — (were) full a — side the chambers — foun- the of dations — (and) ,round — round — the height
2568 2351 6763 834 7023 7341 679 520
9 אַמּוֹת אַצִּילָה׃ רֹחַב הַקִּיר אֲשֶׁר־לַצֵּלָע אֶל־הַחוּץ חָמֵשׁ
five — outside (was) — to — the side chamber (was) the for which — ,wall the — The of width — .joining — cubits by
3957 996 1004 834 6763 1004 3240 834 520
10 אַמּוֹת וַאֲשֶׁר מֻנָּח בֵּית צְלָעוֹת אֲשֶׁר לַבָּיִת׃ וּבֵין הַלְּשָׁכוֹת
the chambers — And between — the of .house — that (were) — side the chambers — be- tween — (was) what left — and, cubits
6607 5439 5439 1004 5439 520 6242 7341
11 רֹחַב עֶשְׂרִים אַמָּה סָבִיב לַבַּיִת סָבִיב ׀ סָבִיב׃ וּפֶתַח
the And of door — (and) .round — round — the house — circling — cubits — twenty — the (was) of width
1864 259 6607 6828 1870 259 6607 3240 6763
הַצֵּלָע לַמֻּנָּח פֶּתַח אֶחָד דֶּרֶךְ הַצָּפוֹן וּפֶתַח אֶחָד לַדָּרוֹם
the toward .south — one — door and — the ,north — the of way — one — door — the to ,space open — side the chamber
1146 5439 5439 520 2568 3240 4725 7341
12 וְרֹחַב מְקוֹם הַמֻּנָּח חָמֵשׁ אַמּוֹת סָבִיב ׀ סָבִיב׃ וְהַבִּנְיָן
the And building — (and) .round — round — cubits — (was) five — open the space — the of place — the And of width
520 7657 7341 3220 1870 6285 1508 6440 834
אֲשֶׁר אֶל־פְּנֵי הַגִּזְרָה פְּאַת דֶּרֶךְ־הַיָּם רֹחַב שִׁבְעִים אַמָּה
.cubits — (was) seventy — wide — the west — the of way — the at end — sep- the area arate — before — that (was)
8673 753 5439 5439 7341 520 2568 1146 7023
וְקִיר הַבִּנְיָן חָמֵשׁ־אַמּוֹת רֹחַב סָבִיב ׀ סָבִיב וְאָרְכּוֹ תִּשְׁעִים
(was) ninety — its and length — (and) ,round — round — wide — cubits — (was) five — the building — the And of wall
1140 1508 520 3967 753 1004 4058 520
13 אַמָּה׃ וּמָדַד אֶת־הַבַּיִת אֹרֶךְ מֵאָה אַמָּה וְהַגִּזְרָה וְהַבִּנְיָה
the and building — the And ,area separate — .cubits — a hundred — long — ,house the — he So measured — .cubits
1508 1004 6440 7341 520 3967 753 7023
14 וְקִירוֹתֶיהָ אֹרֶךְ מֵאָה אַמָּה׃ וְרֹחַב פְּנֵי הַבַּיִת וְהַגִּזְרָה
the and area separate — house the — the the And of face of width — .cubits — a hundred — long — its and (were) wall
1508 6440 1146 753 4058 520 3967 6921
15 לַקָּדִים מֵאָה אַמָּה׃ וּמָדַד אֹרֶךְ־הַבִּנְיָן אֶל־פְּנֵי הַגִּזְרָה
separate the area — the to of face — the building — the of length — he And measured — .cubits — a hundred — the toward east
1964 520 3967 6311 6311 862 310 834
אֲשֶׁר עַל־אַחֲרֶיהָ וְאַתּוּקֶיהָא מִפּוֹ וּמִפּוֹ מֵאָה אַמָּה וְהַהֵיכָל
the and temple — ,cubits — a hundred — from and from there here — its and gallery — its ;rear — on — which (was)
331 2472 5592 2691 197 6442
16 הַפְּנִימִי וְאֻלַמֵּי הֶחָצֵר׃ הַסִּפִּים וְהַחַלּוֹנִים הָאֲטֻמוֹת
,latticed — the and windows — the ,thresholds — ,court the — the and of porches — inner
5439 6086 7824 5592 5048 7969 5439 862
וְהָאַתִּיקִים ׀ סָבִיב לִשְׁלָשְׁתָּם נֶגֶד הַסַּף שְׂחִיף עֵץ סָבִיב ׀
round — (with) wood — were panelled — the ,threshold — opposite — three their ,(stories) — all around — the galleries — and
3680 2474 2474 776 5439
17 סָבִיב וְהָאָרֶץ עַד־הַחַלֹּנוֹת וְהַחַלֹּנוֹת מְכֻסּוֹת׃ עַל־מֵעַל
above — to that — were ;covered — the and windows — the to ,windows — up — (from) and ground the — (and) ;round
5437 7023 3605 2351 6442 1004 5704 6607
הַפֶּתַח וְעַד־הַבַּיִת הַפְּנִימִי וְלַחוּץ וְאֶל־כָּל־הַקִּיר סָבִיב ׀
round — the wall — all — and to — and ,outside — ,inner — the house — even to — the ,door

round *and* round inside and outside by measure. [18]And it was made *with* cherubs and palm trees; and a palm tree *was* between cherub and cherub. [19]And two faces *were* to a cherub, the face of a man toward the palm tree from here, and a young lion's face toward the palm tree from there. It was made to all the house round *and* round. [20]From the ground to above the door, cherubs and palm trees *were* made, and *on* the wall of the temple. [21]The temple doorposts *were* squared, and the face of the sanctuary, the appearance as *its* appearance. [22]The altar of wood *was* three cubits high, and its length two cubits. And its corners, and its length, and its walls *were* wood. And he said to me, This *is* the table that *is* before Jehovah. [23]And two doors *were* to the temple and the sanctuary. [24]And two doors *were* to *each* of the doors, two turning doors—two for the one door, and two for the other door. [25]And cherubs and palm trees were made on them, on the doors of the temple, like those made on the walls; and thick wood on the face of the porch outside. [26]And latticed windows, and palm trees, *were* from here and from there, on the sides of the porch, and the side chambers of the house, and wooden *canopies*.

8561 3742 6213 4060 2351 6442 5439
18 סָבִיב בַּפְּנִימִי וּבַחִיצוֹן מִדּוֹת׃ וְעָשׂוּי כְּרוּבִים וְתִמֹרִים
palm and (with) it And by and inside (and)
.trees cherubs made was .measure outside round

120 6440 3742 6440 8147 3742 3742 996 8561
19 וְתִמֹרָה בֵּין־כְּרוּב לִכְרוּב וּשְׁנַיִם פָּנִים לַכְּרוּב׃ וּפְנֵי אָדָם
man a the to (were) faces two And and cherub (was) a and
of face ,cherub a .cherub between tree palm

6213 6311 8561 3715 6311 6311 8561
אֶל־הַתִּמֹרָה מִפֹּו וּפְנֵי־כְפִיר אֶל־הַתִּמֹרָה מִפֹּו עָשׂוּי אֶל־
to was It from palm the toward young a and from palm the toward
made ;there tree lion's face ,here tree

6607 5704 776 5439 5439 1004 3605
20 כָּל־הַבַּיִת סָבִיב ׀ סָבִיב׃ מֵהָאָרֶץ עַד־מֵעַל הַפֶּתַח
the above to the From (and) round the all
door ground .round house

4201 1964 1964 7023 6213 8561 3742
21 הַכְּרוּבִים וְהַתִּמֹרִים עֲשׂוּיִם וְקִיר הַהֵיכָל׃ הַהֵיכָל מְזוּזַת
door- The the (on) and ,made palm and (were)
posts temple .temple of wall the trees cherubs

7969 6086 4196 4758 4758 6944 6440 7251
22 רְבֻעָה וּפְנֵי הַקֹּדֶשׁ הַמַּרְאֶה כַּמַּרְאֶה׃ הַמִּזְבֵּחַ עֵץ שָׁלוֹשׁ
(was) wood altar The (its) as ap- the the the and (were)
three of .appearance pearance ,sanctuary of face ,squared

753 4740 520 8147 753 1364 520
אַמּוֹת גָּבֹהַּ וְאָרְכּוֹ שְׁתַּיִם אַמּוֹת וּמִקְצֹעוֹתָיו לוֹ וְאָרְכּוֹ
its and to its And .cubits (was) its and ,high cubits
,length it (are) corners two length

3068 6440 834 7979 2088 1696 6086 7023
וְקִירֹתָיו עֵץ וַיְדַבֵּר אֵלַי זֶה הַשֻּׁלְחָן אֲשֶׁר לִפְנֵי יְהוָה׃
.Jehovah before that the This to he And .wood its and
(is) table (is) ,me said (were) walls

23
1817 1817 8147 6944 1964 1817 8147
24 וּשְׁתַּיִם דְּלָתוֹת לַהֵיכָל וְלַקֹּדֶשׁ׃ וּשְׁתַּיִם דְּלָתוֹת לַדְּלָתוֹת
(each) to (are) doors two And the and the to doors two And
doors the of .sanctuary temple (were)

1817 8147 259 1817 8147 1817 5437 8147
שְׁתַּיִם מוּסַבּוֹת דְּלָתוֹת שְׁתַּיִם לְדֶלֶת אֶחָת וּשְׁתֵּי דְלָתוֹת
the for and ,one the for two —doors turning two
door two door

3742 1964 1817 6213 312
25 לָאַחֶרֶת׃ וַעֲשׂוּיָה אֲלֵיהֶן אֶל־דַּלְתוֹת הַהֵיכָל כְּרוּבִים
cherubs the doors the on ,them on were And .other
temple of made

197 6440 6086 5646 7023 6213 8561
וְתִמֹרִים כַּאֲשֶׁר עֲשׂוּיִם לַקִּירוֹת וְעָב עֵץ אֶל־פְּנֵי הָאוּלָם
porch the the on wood and the on those like palm and
of face thick ;walls made trees

3801 6311 6311 8561 331 2474 2351
26 מֵהַחוּץ׃ וְחַלּוֹנִים אֲטֻמוֹת וְתִמֹרִים מִפֹּו וּמִפֹּו אֶל־כִּתְפוֹת
sides the on from and from palm and laticed windows And .outside
of ,there here trees

5646 1004 6763 197
הָאוּלָם וְצַלְעוֹת הַבַּיִת וְהָעֻבִּים׃
thick and the side the and the
.(planks) ,house of chambers porch

CAP. XLII מב

CHAPTER 42

CHAPTER 42

[1]And he brought me out into the outer court northward. And he brought me into the chamber that *was* across from the separate area, which *was* in front of the building to the north.

935 6828 1870 1870 2435 2691 3318
1 וַיּוֹצִאֵנִי אֶל־הֶחָצֵר הַחִיצוֹנָה הַדֶּרֶךְ דֶּרֶךְ הַצָּפוֹן וַיְבִאֵנִי
he And the toward way the ,outer the into he Then
me brought .north court out me brought

1146 5048 834 1508 5048 834 3957
אֶל־הַלִּשְׁכָּה אֲשֶׁר נֶגֶד הַגִּזְרָה וַאֲשֶׁר־נֶגֶד הַבִּנְיָן אֶל־
to the front in and separate the across that the into
building of (was) which area from (was) chamber

[2]To the face of *its* length *was* a hundred cubits, *toward* the north door, and fifty cubits wide. [3]Across from the twenty *cubits* which *were* to the inner court, and opposite the pavement which *was* to the the outer court, gallery on the face of gallery, in three *stories*. [4]And before the chambers *was* a walk ten cubits wide, to the inside, a way of one cubit. And their doors *were* toward the north. [5]And the upper chambers *were* shorter, for the galleries used up more *space* than the lower and middle ones in the building. [6]For they *were* in three *stories*, and there *were* no columns to them like the columns of the courts. So *the third* was made narrower than the lower and middle *stories* from the ground.

[7]And the wall that *was* outside near the chambers the way of the outer court, on the face of the chambers, its length *was* fifty cubits. [8]For the length of the chambers that *were* in the outer court *was* fifty cubits. And, behold, in the face of the temple *was* a hundred cubits. [9]And under these chambers *was* the entrance on the east side as one goes into them from the outer court. [10]In the width of the wall of the court eastward, to the face of the separate area, and to the face of the building *were* chambers. [11]And the way before them looked like the chambers which *were* northward; as their length, so their width. And all their exits *were* as their patterns, and as their doors. [12]And as the doors of the chambers that *were* southward there *was* a door in

7341 6828 6607 3967 520 753 6440 6828
2 הַצָּפוֹן׃ אֶל־פְּנֵי אֹרֶךְ אַמּוֹת הַמֵּאָה פֶּתַח הַצָּפוֹן וְהָרֹחַב
wide and ,north the a (was) (its) the To the
door ,hundred cubits length of face .north

5048 6442 2691 834 6242 5048 520 2572
3 חֲמִשִּׁים אַמּוֹת׃ נֶגֶד הָעֶשְׂרִים אֲשֶׁר לֶחָצֵר הַפְּנִימִי וְנֶגֶד
and the court for which the Across .cubits fifty
opposite ,inner (were) twenty from

862 6440 862 2435 2691 834 7531
רִצְפָה אֲשֶׁר לֶחָצֵר הַחִיצוֹנָה אַתִּיק אֶל־פְּנֵי־אַתִּיק
,gallery the on gallery the court to which the
of face outer (was) pavement

7341 520 6235 4109 3957 6440 7992
4 בַּשְּׁלִשִׁים׃ וְלִפְנֵי הַלְּשָׁכוֹת מַהֲלַךְ עֶשֶׂר אַמּוֹת רֹחַב אֶל־
to ,wide cubits ten a (was) the And three in
walk chambers before .(stories)

3957 6828 6607 259 520 1870 6442
5 הַפְּנִימִית דֶּרֶךְ אַמָּה אֶחָת וּפִתְחֵיהֶם לַצָּפוֹן׃ וְהַלְּשָׁכוֹת
the And the toward their And .one cubit a the
chambers .north (were) doors of way ,inside

8481 2007 862 3198 7114 5945
הָעֶלְיוֹנֹת קְצֻרוֹת כִּי־יוֹכְלוּ אַתִּיקִים מֵהֵנָּה מֵהַתַּחְתֹּנוֹת
the from than than the consumed for (were) upper
lower ,them galleries more ,shorter

5982 369 2009 8027 1146 8484
6 וּמֵהַתִּיכֹנוֹת בִּנְיָן׃ כִּי מְשֻׁלָּשׁוֹת הֵנָּה וְאֵין לָהֶן עַמּוּדִים
(were) to and they three in For the in middle and
columns them not ,(were) (stories) .building ones

8484 8481 680 2691 5982
כְּעַמּוּדֵי הַחֲצֵרוֹת עַל־כֵּן נֶאֱצַל מֵהַתַּחְתּוֹנוֹת וּמֵהַתִּיכֹנוֹת
middle the and the than made was So .courts the the like
(stories) lower narrower (third the) of columns

2691 1870 3957 5980 2351 834 1448 776
7 מֵהָאָרֶץ׃ וְגָדֵר אֲשֶׁר־לַחוּץ לְעֻמַּת הַלְּשָׁכוֹת דֶּרֶךְ הֶחָצֵר
the the the near outside that the And the from
court of way chambers (was) wall .ground

520 2572 753 3957 6440 2435
8 הַחִצוֹנָה אֶל־פְּנֵי הַלְּשָׁכוֹת אָרְכּוֹ חֲמִשִּׁים אַמָּה׃ כִּי־
For .cubits (was) length its ,chambers the the on outer
fifty of face

2009 520 2572 2435 2691 834 3957 753
אֹרֶךְ הַלְּשָׁכוֹת אֲשֶׁר לֶחָצֵר הַחִצוֹנָה חֲמִשִּׁים אַמָּה וְהִנֵּה
And .cubits (was) outer the in that the the
,behold fifty court (was) chambers of length

428 3957 8478 520 3967 1964 6440
9 עַל־פְּנֵי הַהֵיכָל מֵאָה אַמָּה׃ וּמִתַּחְתָּה לְשָׁכוֹת הָאֵלֶּה
these chambers under And .cubits a (was) the the in
(was) hundred temple of face

7341 2435 2691 2007 935 6921 3996
10 הַמָּבוֹא מֵהַקָּדִים בְּבֹאוֹ לָהֵנָּה מֵהֶחָצֵר הַחִצֹנָה׃ בְּרֹחַב
the in .outer the from into one as the on the
of width court them goes ,side east entrance

1146 6440 1508 6440 6921 1870 2691 1444
גֶּדֶר הֶחָצֵר דֶּרֶךְ הַקָּדִים אֶל־פְּנֵי הַגִּזְרָה וְאֶל־פְּנֵי הַבִּנְיָן
the the to and separate the the to the the the the
building of face ,area of face ,east of way court of wall

1870 834 3957 4758 6440 1870 3957
11 לְשָׁכוֹת׃ וְדֶרֶךְ לִפְנֵיהֶם כְּמַרְאֵה הַלְּשָׁכוֹת אֲשֶׁר דֶּרֶךְ
the which the looked before the And (were there)
of way (were) chambers like them way .chambers

4941 4161 3605 7341 753 6828
הַצָּפוֹן כְּאָרְכָּן כֵּן רָחְבָּן וְכֹל מוֹצָאֵיהֶן וּכְמִשְׁפְּטֵיהֶן
their as their And their so their as the
,patterns exits all .width (was) ,length ;north

6607 1864 1870 834 3957 6607 6607
12 וּכְפִתְחֵיהֶן׃ וּכְפִתְחֵי הַלְּשָׁכוֹת אֲשֶׁר דֶּרֶךְ הַדָּרוֹם פֶּתַח
(there) south the the that the the as And their as and
door a (was) of way (were) chambers of doors .doors

the head of the way, the way directly in the face of the wall, the way of the east, as one enters them.

[13]And he said to me, The north chambers, the south chambers which *are* to the face of the separate area, they *are* holy chambers, there where the priests shall eat, who approach to Jehovah, the holiest of the holy *things*. There they shall lay the holiest of the holy *things*, even the food offering, and the sin offering, and the guilt offering. For the place *is* holy. [14]When the priests enter, then they shall not go out of the sanctuary into the outer court, but they shall lay their clothes there by which they minister by them; for they *are* holy. They shall put on other clothes and shall approach to that *which is* for the people.

[15]And he finished measuring the inner house. And he brought me forth the way of the gate whose face *is* eastward, and measured round *and* round. [16]He measured the east side with the measuring reed, five hundred reeds with the measuring reed, all around. [17]He measured the north side, five hundred reeds with the measuring reed all around. [18]He measured the south side, five hundred reeds with the measuring reed. [19]He turned to the west side, measuring five hundred reeds with the measuring reed. [20]By the four sides he measured it. It had a wall round *and* round, five hundred *reeds* long, and five hundred *reeds* wide, to separate between the holy and the common.

6921 1870 1903 1448 6440 1870 1870 7218
בְּרֹאשׁ דֶּרֶךְ דֶּרֶךְ בִּפְנֵי הַגְּדֶרֶת הֲגִינָה דֶּרֶךְ הַקָּדִים
,east the | the of way | directly | wall the | the of face | the way | the ,way | the in of head

834 1864 3957 6828/3957 559 935
13 בְּבוֹאָן׃ וַיֹּאמֶר אֵלַי לִשְׁכוֹת הַצָּפוֹן לִשְׁכוֹת הַדָּרוֹם אֲשֶׁר
which (are) | south | the chambers | ,north | the chambers | to ,me | he Then said | one as .them enters

8033 398 834 6918 3957 1508 6440
אֶל־פְּנֵי הַגִּזְרָה הֵנָּה ׀ לִשְׁכוֹת הַקֹּדֶשׁ אֲשֶׁר יֹאכְלוּ־שָׁם
there | shall eat | where | ,holy | chambers | they (are) | sep- the arate ,area | the to of face

3240 8033 6944 6944 3068 7138 834 3548
הַכֹּהֲנִים אֲשֶׁר־קְרוֹבִים לַיהוָה קָדְשֵׁי הַקֳּדָשִׁים שָׁם יַנִּיחוּ ׀
shall they There lay | holy .(things) | the of holiest | to Jehovah | approach | who | the priests

4725 816 2403 4503 6944 6944
קָדְשֵׁי הַקֳּדָשִׁים וְהַמִּנְחָה וְהַחַטָּאת וְהָאָשָׁם כִּי הַמָּקוֹם
the (is) place | For | the and .offering guilt | sin the and ,offering | the even ,offering food | holy ,(things) | the of holiest

2691 6944 3318 3808 3548 935 6944
14 קָדֹשׁ׃ בְּבֹאָם הַכֹּהֲנִים וְלֹא־יֵצְאוּ מֵהַקֹּדֶשׁ אֶל־הֶחָצֵר
the court | into | the of sanctuary | shall they then out go | not | ,priests the | When enter | .holy

6944 8334 834 899 3240 8033 2691
הַחִיצוֹנָה וְשָׁם יַנִּיחוּ בִגְדֵיהֶם אֲשֶׁר־יְשָׁרְתוּ בָהֵן כִּי־קֹדֶשׁ
holy | for | by ;them | they minister | by which | their clothes | shall they but lay there | (the of) ,court

3615 5971 834 7126 312 899 3847
15 הֵנָּה יִלְבְּשׁוּ בְּגָדִים אֲחֵרִים וְקָרְבוּ אֶל־אֲשֶׁר לָעָם׃ וְכִלָּה
he And ended | the for .people | that (is which) | to | shall and approach | other | clothes | shall they on put | they ;(are)

834 8179 1870 3318 6442 1004 4060
אֶת־מִדּוֹת הַבַּיִת הַפְּנִימִי וְהוֹצִיאַנִי דֶּרֶךְ הַשַּׁעַר אֲשֶׁר
whose | the gate | the of way | brought he and forth me | inner | the house | measuring

6921 7307 4058 5439 5439 4058 6921 1870 6440
16 פָּנָיו דֶּרֶךְ הַקָּדִים וּמְדָדוֹ סָבִיב ׀ סָבִיב׃ מָדַד רוּחַ הַקָּדִים
east | the side | He measured | (and) . round | round | meas- and it ured | the ,east | the of way | face (is)

5439 4060 7070 7070 520 568 4060 7070
בִּקְנֵה הַמִּדָּה חֲמֵשׁ־אמוֹת קָנִים בִּקְנֵה הַמִּדָּה סָבִיב׃
all .around | the ,measuring | with reed | reeds | hundred five | ,measuring the with reed

5439 4060 7070 7070 3967 2568 6828 7307 4058
17 מָדַד רוּחַ הַצָּפוֹן חֲמֵשׁ־מֵאוֹת קָנִים בִּקְנֵה הַמִּדָּה סָבִיב׃
all .around | the ,measuring | with reed | reeds | hundred five | ,north | side the | He measured

4060 7070 7070 3967 3568 4058 1864 7307
18 אֵת רוּחַ הַדָּרוֹם מָדַד חֲמֵשׁ־מֵאוֹת קָנִים בִּקְנֵה הַמִּדָּה׃
the .measuring | with reed | reeds | hundred five | He ,measured | south | side the

4060 7070 7070 3967 3568 4058 3220 7307 5437
19 סָבַב אֶל־רוּחַ הַיָּם מָדַד חֲמֵשׁ־מֵאוֹת קָנִים בִּקְנֵה הַמִּדָּה׃
the .measuring | with reed | reeds | hundred | five | measuring | ,west | side the | to | He turned

2568 753 5439 5439 2346 4058 7307 702
20 לְאַרְבַּע רוּחוֹת מְדָדוֹ חוֹמָה לוֹ סָבִיב ׀ סָבִיב אֹרֶךְ חֲמֵשׁ
five | long | (and) round | round | It had | a wall | meas- He .it ured | sides | the by four

2455 6944 996 914 3967 2568 7341 3967
מֵאוֹת וְרֹחַב חֲמֵשׁ מֵאוֹת לְהַבְדִּיל בֵּין הַקֹּדֶשׁ לְחֹל׃
the and .common | the holy | between | to separate | ,hundred | five | and wide | hundred ,(reeds)

CAP. XLIII מג

CHAPTER 43

CHAPTER 43

[1]And he led me to the gate, the gate that faces eastward. [2]And, behold, the glory of the God of Israel came from the way of the east. And His voice *was* like the voice of many waters. And the earth shone from His glory. [3]And the appearance of the vision which I saw *was* as the appearance which I saw when I came to destroy the city; and as the appearance that I saw by the river Chebar. And I fell on my face. [4]And the glory of Jehovah come into the house, the way of the gate facing eastward. [5]And the Spirit took me up and brought me into the inner court. And, behold, the glory of Jehovah filled the house!

[6]And I heard *one* speaking to me from the house. And standing beside me was a Man. [7]And He said to me, Son of man, the place of My throne and the place of the soles of My feet, there where I will dwell among the sons of Israel forever, even the house of Israel shall not defile My holy name any more; they nor their kings, by their fornication, nor by the corpses of their kings in their high places. [8]In their setting of their threshold *by* My threshold, and their door post beside My door post, and the wall between Me and them; even they have defiled My holy name by their abominations that they have done. And I consumed them in My anger. [9]Now *let* them put away their fornication, and the corpses of their kings from Me, and I will dwell in their midst forever.

[10]You, son of man, declare to the house of

[interlinear column — read right to left]

1　וַיּוֹלִכֵנִי אֶל־הַשַּׁעַר שַׁעַר אֲשֶׁר פֹּנֶה דֶּרֶךְ הַקָּדִים׃
2009　6921　1870　6437　834　8179　8179　3212
And .east the the faces that the ,gate the to he And
behold	of way	gate	me led

2　כְּבוֹד אֱלֹהֵי יִשְׂרָאֵל בָּא מִדֶּרֶךְ הַקָּדִים וְקוֹלוֹ כְּקוֹל מַיִם
4325　6963　6963　6921　1870　935　3478　430　3519
waters the like His And the the from came Israel the glory the
of voice voice .east of way of God of

3　וְהָאָרֶץ הֵאִירָה מִכְּבֹדוֹ׃ וּכְמַרְאֵה הַמַּרְאֶה אֲשֶׁר
834　4759　3519　215　776　7227
which the the as And His from shone the And .many
vision of appearance .glory earth

רָאִיתִי כַּמַּרְאֶה אֲשֶׁר־רָאִיתִי בְּבֹאִי לְשַׁחֵת אֶת־הָעִיר
589:2　7843　935　7200　834　4758　7200
.city the to I when saw I which the as ,saw I
destroy came appearance

4　וּמַרְאוֹת כַּמַּרְאֶה אֲשֶׁר רָאִיתִי אֶל־נְהַר כְּבָר וָאֶפֹּל אֶל־
4758　15307　3529　5104　7200　834　4758
on I And .Chebar the by saw I that the as the And
fell river appearance appearances

פָּנָי׃ וּכְבוֹד יְהוָה בָּא אֶל־הַבַּיִת דֶּרֶךְ שַׁעַר אֲשֶׁר פָּנָיו
6440　834　8179　1870　1004　935　3068　3519　6440
its of the the the into came Jehovah the And my
face which gate of way ,house of glory .face

5　דֶּרֶךְ הַקָּדִים׃ וַתִּשָּׂאֵנִי רוּחַ וַתְּבִיאֵנִי אֶל־הֶחָצֵר הַפְּנִימִי
1870　6921　5375　7307　935　2691　6442
.inner the into brought and the took So .east the the (is)
court me Spirit up me of way

6　וְהִנֵּה מָלֵא כְבוֹד־יְהוָה הַבָּיִת׃ וָאֶשְׁמַע מִדַּבֵּר אֵלַי מֵהַבָּיִת
2009　4390　3519　3068　1004　8085　1696　1004
the from (one) I And the Jehovah the filled ,And
;house me speaking heard house of glory ,behold

7　וְאִישׁ הָיָה עֹמֵד אֶצְלִי׃ וַיֹּאמֶר אֵלַי בֶּן־אָדָם אֶת־מְקוֹם
376　1961　5975　681　559　1121　120　4725
the ,man Son to He And beside standing was a and
of place ,me said .me Man

כִּסְאִי וְאֶת־מְקוֹם כַּפּוֹת רַגְלַי אֲשֶׁר אֶשְׁכָּן־שָׁם בְּתוֹךְ בְּנֵי
36:78　4725　3709　72:72　834　7931　8033　8432　1121
the among there will I where My the the and My
of sons dwell ,feet of soles of place throne

יִשְׂרָאֵל לְעוֹלָם וְלֹא יְטַמְּאוּ עוֹד בֵּית־יִשְׂרָאֵל שֵׁם קָדְשִׁי
3478　5769　380:8　2930　5750　1004　3478　8034　6944
My name Israel the still shall even .forever Israel
,holy of house defile not

8　הֵמָּה וּמַלְכֵיהֶם בִּזְנוּתָם וּבְפִגְרֵי מַלְכֵיהֶם בָּמוֹתָם׃ בְּתִתָּם
4428　2184　4428　6297　4428　1116　54:14
their In their kings their by nor their nor they
of giving .places high of corpses the ,fornication ,kings

סִפָּם אֶת־סִפִּי וּמְזוּזָתָם אֵצֶל מְזוּזָתִי וְהַקִּיר בֵּינִי וּבֵינֵיהֶם
55:92　5592　4201　681　4201　7023　996
;them and between the and door My beside their and My (by) their
Me wall ,post post door ,threshold threshold

וְטִמְּאוּ אֶת־שֵׁם קָדְשִׁי בְּתוֹעֲבוֹתָם אֲשֶׁר עָשׂוּ וָאֲכַל אֹתָם
2930　8034　6944　8441　834　62:13　3615
them I Thus have they that their by My name they even
consumed .done abominations holy defiled have

9　בְּאַפִּי׃ עַתָּה יְרַחֲקוּ אֶת־זְנוּתָם וּפִגְרֵי מַלְכֵיהֶם מִמֶּנִּי
639　62:58　7368　2184　6297　4428
from their the and their them (let) Now My in
,Me ,kings of corpses ,fornication away put .anger

וְשָׁכַנְתִּי בְתוֹכָם לְעוֹלָם׃ **10**　אַתָּה בֶן־אָדָם הַגֵּד אֶת־
7931　8432　5769　1121　120　5046
declare ,man son ,You .forever their in will I and
of midst dwell

Israel the *temple* house, and they will blush from their iniquities. And let them seal up the measure its size. 11And if they are ashamed of all that they have done, the form of the house, and its arrangement, and its exits, and its entrances, and all its forms, and all its statutes, and all its forms, and all its laws, make known to them. And write them in their sight, so that they may observe all its form, and all its statutes, and do them. 12This *is* the law of the house: On the top of the mountain *is* all its border, round *and* round, *being* most holy. Behold, this *is* the law of the house.

13And these *are* the measures of the altar by the cubit—the cubit *is* a cubit and a span—even the base *shall be* a cubit, and the width a cubit, and its border on its lip all around *shall be* one span. And this *is* the upper part of the altar. 14And from the base *on* the ground to the lower ledge *shall be* two cubits, and the width one cubit. And from the smaller ledge to the greater ledge *shall be* four cubits, and the width a cubit. 15And the altar hearth *shall be* four cubits, and from the altar hearth and upward *shall be* four horns. 16And the altar hearth *shall be* twelve *cubits* long, and twelve wide, square in its four sides. 17And the ledge *shall be* fourteen long, fourteen wide, in its four sides. And the border around it *shall be* a half cubit, and the base for it a cubit all around. And its steps *shall* face the east.

18And He said to me, Son of man, so says the Lord

4058 5771 3637 1004 3478 1004
בֵּית־יִשְׂרָאֵל אֶת־הַבַּיִת וְיִכָּלְמוּ מֵעֲוֹנוֹתֵיהֶם וּמָדְדוּ אֶת־
them let And their from they and (temple) the Israel the (to)
measure .iniquities blush will house of house

8498 1004 6690 6213 834 3605 3637 518 8508
11 תָּכְנִית׃ וְאִם־נִכְלְמוּ מִכֹּל אֲשֶׁר־עָשׂוּ צוּרַת הַבַּיִת וּתְכוּנָתוֹ
its and the the have they that of are they And (its)
arrangement ,house of form ,done all ashamed if .size

6699 3605 2708 3605 6699 3605 4426 4161
וּמוֹצָאָיו וּמוֹבָאָיו וְכָל־צוּרֹתָו וְאֵת כָּל־חֻקֹּתָיו וְכָל־צוּרֹתָו
its and its all and its and its and its and
,forms all ,statutes ,forms all ,entrances exits

3605 8104 5869 3789 3045 8451 3605
וְכָל־תּוֹרֹתָו הוֹדַע אוֹתָם וּכְתֹב לְעֵינֵיהֶם וְיִשְׁמְרוּ אֶת־כָּל־
all they that so their in And to make its and
observe may ,sight (it) write them known ,laws all

1004 8451 2088 6213 2708 3605 6699
12 צוּרָתוֹ וְאֶת־כָּל־חֻקֹּתָיו וְעָשׂוּ אוֹתָם׃ זֹאת תּוֹרַת הַבָּיִת
the the This .them do and its all and its
:house of law (is) ,statutes ,form

2009 6944 6944 5439 5439 1366 3605 2022 7218
עַל־רֹאשׁ הָהָר כָּל־גְּבֻלוֹ סָבִיב ׀ סָבִיב קֹדֶשׁ קָדָשִׁים הִנֵּה־
,Behold .holy (being) (and) round its all (is) the the On
most ,round ,border mountain of top

520 520 4196 4060 428 1004 8451 2088
13 זֹאת תּוֹרַת הַבָּיִת׃ וְאֵלֶּה מִדּוֹת הַמִּזְבֵּחַ בָּאַמּוֹת אַמָּה
the the by the meas- the And the law the this
(is) cubit —cubit altar of ures (are) these !house of (is)

8193 1366 7341 520 520 2436 2947 520
אַמָּה וָטֹפַח וְחֵיק הָאַמָּה וְאַמָּה־רֹחַב וּגְבוּלָהּ אֶל־שְׂפָתָהּ
edge its on its and the a and (be shall) even a and a
border ,width cubit ,cubit a base the —span cubit

5704 776 2436 4196 1354 2088 259 2239 5439
14 סָבִיב זֶרֶת הָאֶחָד וְזֶה גַּב הַמִּזְבֵּחַ׃ וּמֵחֵיק הָאָרֶץ עַד־
to the (on) from And .altar's the height And .one (be shall) all
ground base the (is) this span around

259 520 7341 520 8147 8481 5835
הָעֲזָרָה הַתַּחְתּוֹנָה שְׁתַּיִם אַמּוֹת וְרֹחַב אַמָּה אֶחָת
.one cubit the and ,cubits (be shall) lower the
width two ledge

520 702 1419 5835 5704 6996 5835
וּמֵהָעֲזָרָה הַקְּטַנָּה עַד־הָעֲזָרָה הַגְּדוֹלָה אַרְבַּע אַמּוֹת
,cubits (be shall) greater ledge the to smaller the from And
four ledge

4605 741 520 702 741 2025 520 7341
15 וְרֹחַב הָאַמָּה׃ וְהַהַרְאֵל אַרְבַּע אַמּוֹת וּמֵהָאֲרִאֵיל וּלְמַעְלָה
and the from and ,cubits (be shall) the And (one) the and
upward hearth altar four hearth altar .cubit width

8147 753 6240 8147 741 2025 702 7161
16 הַקְּרָנוֹת אַרְבַּע׃ וְהָאֲרִאֵיל שְׁתֵּים עֶשְׂרֵה אֹרֶךְ בִּשְׁתֵּים
two ,long (cubits) (be shall) the And .four (be shall)
twelve hearth altar horns

702 5835 7253 702 7251 7341 6240
17 עֶשְׂרֵה רֹחַב רָבוּעַ אֶל אַרְבַּעַת רְבָעָיו׃ וְהָעֲזָרָה אַרְבַּע
(be shall) the And .sides its four the in square wide (and)
four- ledge of ten

7253 702 7341 6235 702 753 6240
עֶשְׂרֵה אֹרֶךְ בְּאַרְבַּע עֶשְׂרֵה רֹחַב אֶל־אַרְבַּעַת רְבָעֶיהָ
.sides its four the in wide (and) four ,long ten (and)
of ten (cubits)

5439 520 2436 520 2677 5439 1366
וְהַגְּבוּל סָבִיב אוֹתָהּ חֲצִי הָאַמָּה וְהַחֵיק־לָהּ אַמָּה סָבִיב
all (be shall) for the and ,cubit a half it around the And
.around cubit a it base (be shall) border

559 120 1121 559 6921 6437 4609
18 וּמַעֲלֹתֵהוּ פְּנוֹת קָדִים׃ וַיֹּאמֶר אֵלַי בֶּן־אָדָם כֹּה אָמַר
says thus .man Son ,me to He And .east the face its And
of said steps

Jehovah: These *are* the statutes of the altar in the day of its being made to offer on it burnt offerings, and to sprinkle on it blood.
19And you shall give to the priests of the Levites, they who *are* from the seed of Zadok, who approach to Me, declares the Lord Jehovah, to minister to Me, a bull, a son of the herd, for a sin offering. 20And you shall take of its blood and put *it* on its four horns, and on the four corners of the ledge, and on the border all around. And you shall cleanse it and atone for it. 21And you shall take the bull of the sin offering, and he shall burn *it* at the appointed *place* of the house outside the sanctuary.
22And on the second day you shall bring a buck of the goats, perfect, for a sin offering. And they shall cleanse the altar, as they cleansed *it* with the bull. 23When you have finished cleansing, you shall bring a perfect bull, a son of the herd, and a ram out of the flock, perfect. 24And you shall bring them before Jehovah, and the priests shall throw salt on them; and they shall offer them *for* a burnt offering to Jehovah. 25For seven days you shall daily prepare a he-goat *for* a sin offering. And they shall prepare a bull, a son of the herd, and a ram out of the flock, perfect *ones*. 26They shall atone seven days *for* the altar, and cleanse it, and consecrate *it*. 27And when the days are completed, it shall be on the eighth day and forward, the priests shall make your burnt offerings, and your peace offerings, on the altar. And I will accept you, declares the Lord Jehovah.

19

offer to	being its made	the in day of	altar the	the of statutes	These (are)	Jehovah the Lord	:Jehovah the
5927	6213	3117	4196:	2708	428	3068:	136

אֲדֹנָי יְהֹוִה אֵלֶּה חֻקּוֹת הַמִּזְבֵּחַ בְּיוֹם הֵעָשׂוֹתוֹ לְהַעֲלוֹת

the Levites	priests the of	to you And give shall	blood on	to and sprinkle it	burnt offerings,	it on
3881 3548		5414	1818	2236	5930	

עָלָיו עוֹלָה וְלִזְרֹק עָלָיו דָּם: וְנָתַתָּה אֶל־הַכֹּהֲנִים הַלְוִיִּם

Jehovah the Lord	states ,Me to	who approach	,Zadok the from they of seed (are) whom	
3068 136	5002	7138	6659 2233:	834

אֲשֶׁר הֵם מִזֶּרַע צָדוֹק הַקְּרֹבִים אֵלַי נְאֻם אֲדֹנָי יְהֹוִה

20

on put and (it)	its of blood take shall	you And	sin a for offering.	the son a herd of	,bull	serve to ,Me
54/14:	1818	3947	2403	1241 1121	6499	4334

לְשָׁרְתֵנִי פַּר בֶּן־בָּקָר לְחַטָּאת: וְלָקַחְתָּ מִדָּמוֹ וְנָתַתָּה עַל־

the border on of	and	,ledge the	corners the of four on	and	,horns its	four
1366	58 :35		6438	702	7161	702

אַרְבַּע קַרְנֹתָיו וְאֶל־אַרְבַּע פִּנּוֹת הָעֲזָרָה וְאֶל־הַגְּבוּל

21

sin the ,offering	the of bull	you And take shall	atone and .it for	it	you So cleanse shall	all .around
2403	6499	3947:	3722	2398		5439

סָבִיב וְחִטֵּאתָ אֹתוֹ וְכִפַּרְתָּהוּ: וְלָקַחְתָּ אֵת הַפָּר הַחַטָּאת

22

shall you bring	the second day	on And .sanctuary	the	outside the house of (place)	set at shall he and burn
7126	8145 3117	4720	2351 1004:	4662	8313

וּשְׂרָפוֹ בְּמִפְקַד הַבַּיִת מִחוּץ לַמִּקְדָּשׁ: וּבַיּוֹם הַשֵּׁנִי תַּקְרִיב

as	altar the	they And cleanse shall	sin a for .offering	perfect	the buck a goats of
	4196	2398 2403		8549 5795	8163

שְׂעִיר־עִזִּים תָּמִים לְחַטָּאת וְחִטְּאוּ אֶת־הַמִּזְבֵּחַ כַּאֲשֶׁר

23

,perfect	a herd of son	a ,bull bring	shall you (it)	a cleansing have you When	finished	.bull (it) cleansed the with they
8549	1241 1121	6499 7226	2398	3615		6499 2891

חִטֵּאו בַפָּר: בְּכַלּוֹתְךָ מֵחַטֵּא תַּקְרִיב פַּר בֶּן־בָּקָר תָּמִים

24

shall and cast	,Jehovah before	shall you them bring	.perfect	the out flock of	a and ram
7993	3068 6440	7126	8549	6629	352

וְאַיִל מִן־הַצֹּאן תְּמִימִם: וְהִקְרַבְתָּם לִפְנֵי יְהֹוָה וְהִשְׁלִיכוּ

(For) seven	to	burnt a offering (for)	them they and offer shall	,salt	them on	priests the
7651	3068	5930 5927	44 17:		3548	

הַכֹּהֲנִים עֲלֵיהֶם מֶלַח וְהֶעֱלוּ אוֹתָם עֹלָה לַיהֹוָה: שִׁבְעַת

out a and of ram	the a herd of son	a And ,bull	.daily	sin a (for) offering	he- a goat	shall you days prepare
352	1241 1121	6499 3117		2403	8163	6213 3117

יָמִים תַּעֲשֶׂה שְׂעִיר־חַטָּאת לַיּוֹם וּפַר בֶּן־בָּקָר וְאַיִל מִן־

26

the (for) ,altar	shall they atone	shall they days Seven	shall they prepare	perfect	the flock
4196	3722 3117	7651	6213	8549	6629

הַצֹּאן תְּמִימִם יַעֲשׂוּ: שִׁבְעַת יָמִים יְכַפְּרוּ אֶת־הַמִּזְבֵּחַ

27

the on shall it day (that) be	,days the	when And	his fill and	,it	and cleanse
3117	1961 3117	3615	3027	4390	2891

וְטִהֲרוּ אֹתוֹ וּמִלְאוּ יָדָו: וִיכַלּוּ אֶת־הַיָּמִים וְהָיָה בַיּוֹם

burnt ,offerings	your	altar the on	priests the shall make	and	eighth ,forward
5930		4196	3548 6213 1973:		8066

הַשְּׁמִינִי וָהָלְאָה יַעֲשׂוּ הַכֹּהֲנִים עַל־הַמִּזְבֵּחַ אֶת־עוֹלֹתֵיכֶם

.Jehovah the Lord	states ,you	will I And accept	peace your .offerings	and
3068 136	5002	75•21	8002	

וְאֶת־שַׁלְמֵיכֶם וְרָצִאתִי אֶתְכֶם נְאֻם אֲדֹנָי יְהֹוִה:

CAP. XLIV מד

CHAPTER 44

CHAPTER 44

[1]And he brought me back the way of the gate of the outer sanctuary, facing east. And it was shut. [2]And Jehovah said to me, This gate shall be shut; it will not be opened. And a man shall not enter by it, because Jehovah, the God of Israel, has entered by it; so it shall be shut. [3]*As for* the prince, *as* prince he shall sit in it to eat bread before Jehovah. He shall enter by the way of the porch of the gate, and by his way shall go out.

[4]And he brought me by the way of the north gate, to the face of the house. And I looked, and, behold, the glory of Jehovah filled the house of the Lord! And I fell on my face. [5]And Jehovah said to me, Son of man, set your heart and see with your eyes, and hear with your ears all that I say to you of all the statutes of the house of Jehovah, and of all its laws. And set your heart to the entrance of the house, with all the exits of the sanctuary. [6]And you shall say to the rebellious *ones*, to the house of Israel, So says the Lord Jehovah: Enough to you, of all your abominations, O house of Israel; [7]when you brought in the sons of aliens, uncircumcised of heart and uncircumcised of flesh, to be in My sanctuary, to profane it—*even* My house, when you bring near My bread, the fat and the blood. And they have broken My covenant by all your abominations. [8]And you have not kept the charge of My holy things, but you have set *them* as keepers of My charge in My sanctuary, for themselves. [9]So says

1 וַיָּשֶׁב אֹתִי דֶּרֶךְ שַׁעַר הַמִּקְדָּשׁ הַחִיצוֹן הַפֹּנֶה קָדִים וְהוּא
it And .east facing outer the sanctuary the of gate the of way me he Then back brought

2 סָגוּר׃ וַיֹּאמֶר אֵלַי יְהוָה הַשַּׁעַר הַזֶּה סָגוּר יִהְיֶה לֹא
not ;be shall shut This gate ,Jehovah me to said Then was shut

יִפָּתֵחַ וְאִישׁ לֹא־יָבֹא בוֹ כִּי יְהוָה אֱלֹהֵי־יִשְׂרָאֵל בָּא בוֹ
by .it has entered ,Israel the of God ,Jehovah Be- cause by .it shall not enter a and man be will it ;opened

3 וְהָיָה סָגוּר׃ אֶת־הַנָּשִׂיא נָשִׂיא־הוּא יֵשֶׁב־בּוֹ לֶאֱכָל־לֶחֶם
bread eat to in it shall sit he (as) prince ,prince the (As) (for) .shut it thus be shall

לִפְנֵי יְהוָה מִדֶּרֶךְ אוּלָם הַשַּׁעַר יָבוֹא וּמִדַּרְכּוֹ יֵצֵא׃
go shall .out by and way his shall He ,enter gate the the of porch the by of way .Jehovah before

4 וַיְבִיאֵנִי דֶּרֶךְ־שַׁעַר־הַצָּפוֹן אֶל־פְּנֵי הַבַּיִת וָאֵרֶא וְהִנֵּה מָלֵא
filled and !behold I And ,looked the .house the to of face north the gate the of way he Then me brought

5 כְבוֹד־יְהוָה אֶת־בֵּית יְהוָה וָאֶפֹּל אֶל־פָּנָי׃ וַיֹּאמֶר אֵלַי
me to said And my .face on I And fell !Jehovah the of house Jehovah The of glory

יְהוָה בֶּן־אָדָם שִׂים לִבְּךָ וּרְאֵה בְעֵינֶיךָ וּבְאָזְנֶיךָ שְׁמָע אֵת
hear with and ears your with your ,eyes and see your heart set ,man Son ,Jehovah of

כָּל־אֲשֶׁר אֲנִי מְדַבֵּר אֹתָךְ לְכָל־חֻקּוֹת בֵּית־יְהוָה וּלְכָל־
of and all ,Jehovah the of house the of statutes all of you to say I that all

תּוֹרֹתָו וְשַׂמְתָּ לִבְּךָ לִמְבוֹא הַבַּיִת בְּכָל מוֹצָאֵי הַמִּקְדָּשׁ׃
the .sanctuary exits the of with all the ,house the to of entrance your heart set And its .laws

6 וְאָמַרְתָּ אֶל־מֶרִי אֶל־בֵּית יִשְׂרָאֵל כֹּה אָמַר אֲדֹנָי יְהוִה
:Jehovah the Lord says Thus ,Israel the of house to the ,rebellious to you And say shall

7 רַב־לָכֶם מִכָּל־תּוֹעֲבוֹתֵיכֶם בֵּית יִשְׂרָאֵל׃ בַּהֲבִיאֲכֶם בְּנֵי־
the of sons you when in brought ,Israel O of house your ,abominations of all to Enough ,you

נֵכָר עַרְלֵי־לֵב וְעַרְלֵי בָשָׂר לִהְיוֹת בְּמִקְדָּשִׁי לְחַלְּלוֹ אֶת־
to —it profane My in ,sanctuary be to ,flesh uncir- of cumcised and heart uncir- of cumcised ,aliens

בֵּיתִי בְּהַקְרִיבְכֶם אֶת־לַחְמִי חֵלֶב וָדָם וַיָּפֵרוּ אֶת־בְּרִיתִי
My covenant they And broken have the and .blood the fat My ,bread you when near bring My (even) ,house

8 אֶל כָּל־תּוֹעֲבוֹתֵיכֶם׃ וְלֹא שְׁמַרְתֶּם מִשְׁמֶרֶת קָדָשָׁי
holy My ,things the of charge have you kept And not your .abominations all by

9 וַתְּשִׂימוּן לְשֹׁמְרֵי מִשְׁמַרְתִּי בְּמִקְדָּשִׁי לָכֶם׃ כֹּה־אָמַר
says Thus them- for .selves My in sanctuary charge My keepers as of have you but (them) set

the Lord Jehovah: Sons of an alien, uncircumcised of heart and uncircumcised of flesh, shall not enter into My sanctuary, or any son of an alien who *is* among the sons of Israel. ¹⁰But the Levites who have gone far from Me, when Israel went astray, who went astray from Me, *going* after their idols; even they shall bear their iniquity. ¹¹Yet they shall be ministers in My sanctuary, overseers at the gates of the house, and ministering *in* the house. They shall slaughter the burnt offering and the sacrifice for the people; and

they shall stand before them, to minister to them. ¹²Because they ministered to them before their idols, and became a stumbling-block of iniquity to the house of Israel, therefore I have lifted up My hand against them, declares the Lord Jehovah; and they shall bear their iniquity. ¹³And they shall not come near to Me to serve as priest to Me, nor come near to any of My holy things, to the holiest of the holy things; but they shall bear their shame and their abominations which they have done. ¹⁴But I will give them *to be* keepers of the charge of the house for all its service, and for all that shall be done in it.

¹⁵But the priests, the Levites, the sons of Zadok, who kept the charge of My sanctuary when the sons of Israel went astray from Me, they shall come near to Me to minister to Me. And they shall stand before Me to bring near to Me the fat and the blood, declares the Lord Jehovah. ¹⁶They shall enter into My sanctuary, and they shall come near to My table, to minister to Me. And they shall keep My charge. ¹⁷And it shall be, when they enter in the gates of the inner court,

---

	935	3808	1320		6189	3820	6189	5236	1121	3605	3068	136
אֲדֹנָי	יְהוִה	כָּל־בֶּן־נֵכָר	עֶרֶל	לֵב	וְעֶרֶל	בָּשָׂר	לֹא	יָבוֹא				
the	Lord	:Jehovah	an	heart uncir-	and heart uncir-	of cumcised	flesh uncir-	of cumcised	,flesh	not	shall enter

10 | כִּי | אֶל־מִקְדָּשִׁי | לְכָל־בֶּן־נֵכָר | אֲשֶׁר | בְּתוֹךְ | בְּנֵי יִשְׂרָאֵל׃ |

3478	1121	8432	834	5236	1121	3605	4720
.Israel	the of sons	among	who	an	son	or	,sanctuary
				alien	of	any	My into

¹⁰ וְהַלְוִיִּם אֲשֶׁר רָחֲקוּ מֵעָלַי בִּתְעוֹת יִשְׂרָאֵל אֲשֶׁר תָּעוּ

8582	834	3478	8582	7368	834	3881
went	who	,Israel	went when	from	gone have	the	But
astray			astray	Me	far	Levites

11 | מֵעָלַי אַחֲרֵי גִלּוּלֵיהֶם וְנָשְׂאוּ עֲוֺנָם׃ וְהָיוּ בְמִקְדָּשִׁי מְשָׁרְתִים |

8334	4720	5771	5375	1544	310
,ministers	My in they Yet	their and they	their	after	from
	sanctuary be shall	.iniquity bear shall	—idols		Me

פְּקֻדּוֹת אֶל־שַׁעֲרֵי הַבַּיִת וּמְשָׁרְתִים אֶת־הַבָּיִת הֵמָּה

1004	8334	100:4	8179	6486
They	the (in)	and	the	the	at	overseers
	.house	ministering	house	of gates

יִשְׁחֲטוּ אֶת־הָעֹלָה וְאֶת־הַזֶּבַח לָעָם וְהֵמָּה יַעַמְדוּ לִפְנֵיהֶם

6440	5975	5971	2077	5930	7819
before	shall	and	the for	the	and burnt the	shall
them	stand		,people	sacrifice	offering	slaughter

12 | לְשָׁרְתָם׃ יַעַן אֲשֶׁר יְשָׁרְתוּ אוֹתָם לִפְנֵי גִלּוּלֵיהֶם וְהָיוּ |

1961	1544	6440	8334	834	3282	8334
and	,idols their	before	them	they	that Because	minister to
became						.them to

לְבֵית־יִשְׂרָאֵל לְמִכְשׁוֹל עָוֺן עַל־כֵּן נָשָׂאתִי יָדִי עֲלֵיהֶם

3027	5375	5771	4383	3478	1004
against	My	have I	therefore	;iniquity	stumbling-a	Israel	the to
,them	hand	up lifted			of block	of house

13 | נְאֻם אֲדֹנָי יְהוִה וְנָשְׂאוּ עֲוֺנָם׃ וְלֹא־יִגְּשׁוּ אֵלַי לְכַהֵן לִי |

3547	3808	5066	5771	5375	3068	136	5002
to serve to	to	shall they And	their	they and	;Jehovah	the	states
,Me priest as	Me	near come not	.iniquity bear shall			Lord	

וְלָגֶשֶׁת עַל־כָּל־קָדָשַׁי אֶל־קָדְשֵׁי הַקֳּדָשִׁים וְנָשְׂאוּ כְּלִמָּתָם

3639	5375	6944	6944	6944	3605	5066
their	they but	holy the	to	holy My	any	to come to nor
shame	bear shall	,things	of holiest	,things	of	near

14 | וְתוֹעֲבוֹתָם אֲשֶׁר עָשׂוּ׃ וְנָתַתִּי אוֹתָם שֹׁמְרֵי מִשְׁמֶרֶת |

4931	8104	5414	6213	834	8441
the	keepers	them	I But	have they	which	their and
of charge	of	(be to)	give will	.done		abominations

15 | הַבַּיִת לְכֹל עֲבֹדָתוֹ וּלְכֹל אֲשֶׁר יֵעָשֶׂה בּוֹ׃ וְהַכֹּהֲנִים |

3548	6213	6213	3605	5656	3605	1004
the But	.it in	be shall	that	for and	its	for	the
,priests	done		all	,service	all	house

הַלְוִיִּם בְּנֵי צָדוֹק אֲשֶׁר שָׁמְרוּ אֶת־מִשְׁמֶרֶת מִקְדָּשִׁי בִּתְעוֹת

8582	4720	4931	8104	834	6659	1121	3881
went when	My	charge the	kept	who	,Zadok	the	the
astray	sanctuary	of			of sons	,Levites

בְּנֵי־יִשְׂרָאֵל מֵעָלַי הֵמָּה יִקְרְבוּ אֵלַי לְשָׁרְתֵנִי וְעָמְדוּ לְפָנַי

6440	5925	5647	7126	3478	1121
before And	serve to	Me	shall they	from	Israel
Me stand shall	.Me	approach	,Me		of sons

16 | לְהַקְרִיב לִי חֵלֶב וָדָם נְאֻם אֲדֹנָי יְהוִה׃ הֵמָּה יָבֹאוּ אֶל־ |

935	3068	136	5002	1818	2459	7126
into	shall	They	.Jehovah	the	states the and	the to	to	bring to
enter			Lord	,blood	fat	Me	near

מִקְדָּשִׁי וְהֵמָּה יִקְרְבוּ אֶל־שֻׁלְחָנִי לְשָׁרְתֵנִי וְשָׁמְרוּ אֶת־

8104	8334	7979	7126	4720
they and	serve to	My	to come shall	and	My
keep shall	,Me	table	near	they	,sanctuary

17 | מִשְׁמַרְתִּי׃ וְהָיָה בְּבוֹאָם אֶל־שַׁעֲרֵי הֶחָצֵר הַפְּנִימִית בִּגְדֵי |

899	6442	2691	8179	935	1961	4931
gar- with	,inner	the	the	in	they When	it And	.charge My
ments		court	of gates		enter	,be shall

they shall be clothed with linen garments. And wool shall not come up on them while they minister in the gates of the inner court, and in the house. [18]Turbans of linen shall be on their heads, and linen under-garments shall be on their loins. They shall not gird with sweat. [19]And when they go out into the outer court, to the outer court to the people, they shall put off their garments by which they ministered in them, and lay them in the holy chambers. And they shall put on other garments, and they shall not sanctify the people with their own garments. [20]And they shall not shave their heads; and they shall not send forth long hair; they shall surely trim their heads. [21]And every priest shall not drink wine when they enter into the inner court. [22]And they shall not take a widow, or a divorcee, for wives for themselves; but they shall only take virgins of the seed of the house of Israel, or a widow who is the widow of a priest.

[23]And they shall teach My people between the holy and the common, and between the unclean and the clean, to make them known. [24]And in a dispute, they shall stand to judge; they shall judge it by My judgments. And they shall observe My laws and My statutes in My appointed *feasts*; and they shall sanctify My sabbaths. [25]And he shall not come to a dead man, to defile *himself*; but for father, or for mother, or for a son, or for a daughter, for a brother, or for a sister who has not had a husband, they may defile themselves. [26]And after he is cleansed, they shall count seven days for him. [27]And in the day he goes into the sanctuary,

8179 8334 6785 5927 3808 3847 6593
פִּשְׁתִּים יִלְבָּשׁוּ וְלֹא־יַעֲלֶה עֲלֵיהֶם צֶמֶר בְּשָׁרְתָם בְּשַׁעֲרֵי
the in they while wool them on shall And be shall they linen
of gates minister up come not .clothed

7218 1961 8336 6287 1004 6442 2691
18 הֶחָצֵר הַפְּנִימִית וָבָיְתָה׃ פַּאֲרֵי פִשְׁתִּים יִהְיוּ עַל־רֹאשָׁם
their on shall bleached Turbans in and ,inner the
heads be (linen) of .house the court

3154 2296 3808 4975 1961 6593 4370
וּמִכְנְסֵי פִשְׁתִּים יִהְיוּ עַל־מָתְנֵיהֶם לֹא יַחְגְּרוּ בַּיָּזַע׃
with shall They not .loins their on shall linen under- and
.sweat gird be of garments

2435 2691 2435 2691 3318
19 וּבְצֵאתָם אֶל־הֶחָצֵר הַחִיצוֹנָה אֶל־הֶחָצֵר הַחִיצוֹנָה אֶל־
to outer the to ,outer the into when And
court court out go they

8334 834 899 6584 5971
הָעָם יִפְשְׁטוּ אֶת־בִּגְדֵיהֶם אֲשֶׁר־הֵמָּה מְשָׁרְתִם בָּם
in ministered they by their shall they the
,them which garments off put ,people

3808 312 899 3847 6944 3597 3240
וְהִנִּיחוּ אוֹתָם בְּלִשְׁכֹת הַקֹּדֶשׁ וְלָבְשׁוּ בְּגָדִים אֲחֵרִים וְלֹא־
and ,other garments they And .holy the in them lay and
not on put shall chambers

6545 1548 3808 7218 899 5971 6942
20 יְקַדְּשׁוּ אֶת־הָעָם בְּבִגְדֵיהֶם׃ וְרֹאשָׁם לֹא יְגַלֵּחוּ וּפֶרַע
long and they not their And own their with the shall they
hair ,shave shall .heads .garments people sanctify

8354 3808 3196 7218 3697 3697 7971 3808
21 לֹא יְשַׁלֵּחוּ כָּסוֹם יִכְסְמוּ אֶת־רָאשֵׁיהֶם׃ וְיַיִן לֹא־יִשְׁתּוּ
shall not And .heads their shall they trimming shall they not
drink wine trim ;forth send

1644 490 6442 2691 935 3548 3605
22 כָּל־כֹּהֵן בְּבוֹאָם אֶל־הֶחָצֵר הַפְּנִימִית׃ וְאַלְמָנָה וּגְרוּשָׁה
a or a And .inner the into they when priest every
divorcee widow court enter

3478 1004 2233 1330 802 3947/3808
לֹא־יִקְחוּ לָהֶם לְנָשִׁים כִּי אִם־בְּתוּלֹת מִזֶּרַע בֵּית יִשְׂרָאֵל
,Israel the the of virgins But for for shall they not
of house of seed only .wives themselves take

5971 3947 3548 490 1961 834 490
23 וְהָאַלְמָנָה אֲשֶׁר תִּהְיֶה אַלְמָנָה מִכֹּהֵן יִקָּחוּ׃ וְאֶת־עַמִּי
My And shall they priest a the is who a and
people .take of widow widow

7379 3045 2889 2931 2455 6944 3384
24 יוֹרוּ בֵּין קֹדֶשׁ לְחֹל וּבֵין־טָמֵא לְטָהוֹר יוֹדִעֻם׃ וְעַל־רִיב
a And make to the and un- the and the and the between they
dispute in .known them ,clean clean between ,common holy teach shall

8451 8199 4941 8199 5975
הֵמָּה יַעַמְדוּ לִשְׁפֹּט בְּמִשְׁפָּטַי וּשְׁפָטֻהוּ וְאֶת־תּוֹרֹתַי
My And shall they My by —judge to shall they
laws .it judge judgments stand

6942 7676 8104 4150 3605 2708
וְאֶת־חֻקֹּתַי בְּכָל־מוֹעֲדַי יִשְׁמֹרוּ וְאֶת־שַׁבְּתוֹתַי יְקַדֵּשׁוּ׃
shall they My and shall they appointed My in My and
.sanctify sabbaths ;observe (feasts) statutes

1121/517 1 2930 935 3808 120 4191
25 וְאֶל־מֵת אָדָם לֹא יָבוֹא לְטָמְאָה כִּי אִם־לְאָב וּלְאֵם וּלְבֵן
for or for or for but defile to shall he not man a And
,son a ,mother ,father ;(himself) ;come dead to

310 2930 376 1961 3808 834 269 251 1323
26 וּלְבַת לְאָח וּלְאָחוֹת אֲשֶׁר־לֹא־הָיְתָה לְאִישׁ יִטַּמָּאוּ׃ וְאַחֲרֵי
And de- may they a has not who a for or a for a for or
after .themselves file ,husband had sister ,brother ,daughter

6944 935 3117 5608 3117 7651 2893
27 טָהֳרָתוֹ שִׁבְעַת יָמִים יִסְפְּרוּ־לוֹ׃ וּבְיוֹם בֹּאוֹ אֶל־הַקֹּדֶשׁ
the into he in And for shall they days seven is he
,sanctuary goes day the .him count ,cleansed

to the inner court, to minister in the sanctuary, he shall bring his sin offering, declares the Lord Jehovah. ²⁸And it shall be to them for an inheritance —I am their inheritance; and you shall not give them possession in Israel—I *am* their possession. ²⁹They shall eat the food offering and the sin offering and the guilt offering. And every devoted thing in Israel shall be theirs. ³⁰And the first of all the firstfruits of all, and every *one of the* heave offerings of all, of all your heave offerings, shall be for the priests. And you shall give to the priest the first of your dough, to cause a blessing to rest on your house. ³¹The priests shall not eat *of* every corpse and torn thing, of birds, or of beasts.

5002	2403	7126	6944		8334	6442	2691
אֶל־הֶחָצֵר הַפְּנִימִית לְשָׁרֵת בַּקֹּדֶשׁ יַקְרִיב חַטָּאתוֹ נְאֻם							
states	sin his	shall he	the in	minister to	,inner	the	to
	,offering	bring	,sanctuary				court

28
.272	5159			5159		1961	3068	136
פֹס- and ;inheritance ;inheritance .Jehovah the							
אֲדֹנָי יְהוִֹה: וְהָיְתָה לָהֶם לְנַחֲלָה אֲנִי נַחֲלָתָם וַאֲחֻזָּה							
pos- and	their	(am) I	an for	them to	it And	.Jehovah	the
session	;inheritance		,inheritance		be shall		Lord

29
2403		4503	272		3478	5414 3808
לֹא־תִתְּנוּ לָהֶם בְּיִשְׂרָאֵל אֲנִי אֲחֻזָּתָם: הַמִּנְחָה וְהַחַטָּאת						
sin the and	food the	their	I	;Israel in	them shall you not	
offering	offering	.possession (am)			give	

1961		3478	2764	3605	398	.816
וְהָאָשָׁם הֵמָּה יֹאכְלוּם וְכָל־חֵרֶם בְּיִשְׂרָאֵל לָהֶם יִהְיֶה:						
shall	to	Israel in	devoted and	;eat shall	They	the and
.be	them		thing every			offering guilt

30
8641	3605	3605		8641	3605	3605	1061	36 105	7225
וְרֵאשִׁית כָּל־בִּכּוּרֵי כֹל וְכָל־תְּרוּמַת כֹּל מִכֹּל תְּרוּמוֹתֵיכֶם							
heave- your	of	,all	heave	and	,all	all the	the And
,offerings	all		of offerings	every	of firstfruits	of first	of first

5117	3548		5414	6182	7225	1961	3548
לַכֹּהֲנִים יִהְיֶה וְרֵאשִׁית עֲרִסוֹתֵיכֶם תִּתְּנוּ לַכֹּהֵן לְהָנִיחַ						
cause to	the to	shall you	dough	your	the And	shall	the for
rest to	priest	give		of first	.be	priests	

31
5775		2966	5038	3605	1004	1293
בְּרָכָה אֶל־בֵּיתֶךָ: כָּל־נְבֵלָה וּטְרֵפָה מִן־הָעוֹף וּמִן־						
of or	birds of	torn and	corpse	Every	your	a
		thing			.house	blessing

3548	398	38 :08	929
הַבְּהֵמָה לֹא יֹאכְלוּ הַכֹּהֲנִים:			
.priests the	shall	not	,beasts
eat			

CAP. XLV מה
CHAPTER 45

CHAPTER 45

¹And when you make fall by lot the land for an inheritance, you shall offer a heave offering to Jehovah, a holy *portion* of the land. The length shall be twenty-five thousand *cubits* long, and the width ten thousand. It *shall be* holy in all its borders all around. ²Of this there shall be for the sanctuary five hundred by five hundred *cubits*, square all around; and fifty cubits of open space *shall be* all around. ³And from this measure you shall measure the length, twenty-five thousand *cubits*, and the width, ten thousand. And in it shall be the sanctuary, the holiest of the holy. ⁴It is the holy *portion* of the land for the priests; it shall be for the ministers of the sanctuary, who come near to minister to Jehovah. And

1
3068	8641	7311	5159	776	5307
וּבְהַפִּילְכֶם אֶת־הָאָרֶץ בְּנַחֲלָה תָּרִימוּ תְרוּמָה לַיהוָה					
to	heave- a	shall you	an for	the	you And
,Jehovah	offering	offer	,inheritance	land	lot by fall make

7341	753	50 15	6242	25 68	753	776	6944
קֹדֶשׁ מִן־הָאָרֶץ אֹרֶךְ חֲמִשָּׁה וְעֶשְׂרִים אֶלֶף אֹרֶךְ וְרֹחַב						
the and	,long thousand	twenty-	(be shall)	The	the	of	holy a
width	(cubits)	five		length	.land		(portion)

2
2088	1961	5439	1366	3605	6944	505	6235
עֲשָׂרָה אֶלֶף קֹדֶשׁ־הוּא בְּכָל־גְּבוּלָהּ סָבִיב: מֹדּוּ					
this Of	there	all	around-	its	in	It	holy ,thousand	ten
	be shall		.around	borders	all	(be shall)	

5439	7251	3967	2568	3967	2568	6944
אֶל־הַקֹּדֶשׁ חֲמֵשׁ מֵאוֹת בְּחָמֵשׁ מֵאוֹת מְרֻבָּע סָבִיב						
all	square	hundred	five by	hundred	five	the for
,around	(cubits)					sanctuary

3
4058	2063	4060	5439	4054	520	2572
וַחֲמִשִּׁים אַמָּה מִגְרָשׁ לוֹ סָבִיב: וּמִן־הַמִּדָּה הַזֹּאת תָּמוֹד					
shall you	this	measure And	all	to	open of	cubits	And
measure		from	.around	it	space		fifty

1961	505	6235	7341	505	6242	2568	753
אֹרֶךְ חֲמִשָּׁה וְעֶשְׂרִים אֶלֶף וְרֹחַב עֲשֶׂרֶת אֲלָפִים וּבְתוֹכוֹ						
shall	And thousand	ten	the and thousand	twenty-	(cubits)	five	the
be	it in	(cubits)	width	,(cubits)			length

4
3548	776	6944	6944	6944	4720
יִהְיֶה הַמִּקְדָּשׁ קֹדֶשׁ קָדָשִׁים: קֹדֶשׁ מִן־הָאָרֶץ הוּא לַכֹּהֲנִים					
the for	it	the	of holy The	holy the	holiest the	the
,priests	(is)	land	.(places)	(portion)	of	,sanctuary

1961	3068	8334	7131	1961	4720	8334
מְשָׁרְתֵי הַמִּקְדָּשׁ יִהְיֶה הַקְּרֵבִים לְשָׁרֵת אֶת־יְהוָה וְהָיָה					
it And	.Jehovah	to	come who	shall it	the	the
be shall		to minister	near	,be	sanctuary	of ministers

it shall be for them a place for their houses, and a holy place for the sanctuary. [5]And twenty-five *cubits in* length, and ten thousand *in* width shall be for the Levites, the ministers of the house, for them, for a possession, twenty rooms.

[6]And you shall give the possession of the city, five thousand *cubits* wide and twenty-five thousand long, beside the heave offering of the holy *lot*—it shall be for the whole house of Israel. [7]And *a portion shall be* for the prince, from here, and from there, for the heave offering of the holy *place*, and of the possession of the city, to the face of the heave offering of the holy *place*, from the west side westward, and from the east side eastward. And the length *shall be* alongside one of the portions, from the west border to the east border. [8]It shall be for a land to him, for a possession in Israel; and My princes shall not oppress My people any more. And they shall give the land to the house of Israel according to their tribes.

[9]So says the Lord Jehovah: Enough for you, O princes of Israel! Turn away violence and oppression, and do justice and righteousness. Lift off your acts of violence from My people, declares the Lord Jehovah. [10]Let there be a just balance, and a just ephah, and a just bath to you. [11]The ephah and the bath shall be one measure that the bath may contain the tenth of the homer; and the tenth of the homer the ephah. Its measure shall be to the homer. [12]And the shekel *shall be* twenty gerahs: twenty shekels, *and* twenty-five shekels, fifteen shekels

---

5 לָהֶם מָלֽוֹם לְבָתִּ֔ים וּמִקְדָּ֖שׁ לַמִּקְדָּ֑שׁ׃ וַחֲמִשָּׁ֣ה וְעֶשְׂרִ֗ים
4725 · 1004 · 6944 · 6944 · 2568 · 6242
for · them · a for · a place · place holy · houses · their for · a and · the for · sanctuary. · five And · twenty-

אֶ֤לֶף אֹ֙רֶךְ֙ וַעֲשֶׂ֤רֶת אֲלָפִ֣ים רֹ֔חַב יִהְיֶ֥ה לַלְוִיִּ֖ם מְשָׁרְתֵ֣י
505 · 753 · 6235 · 505 · 7341 · 1961 · 3881 · 8334
(in) thousand · ,length (cubits) · ten and · (in) thousand (cubits) · ,width · be shall · ,Levites · the for · the ministers of

6 הַבַּ֑יִת לָהֶ֥ם לַאֲחֻזָּ֖ה עֶשְׂרִ֥ים לְשָׁכֹֽת׃ וַאֲחֻזַּ֣ת הָעִ֗יר תִּתְּנ֣וּ
1004 · 272 · 6242 · 3957 · 272 · 5892 · 5414
,house · —them —possession · a for · for the · twenty · .chambers · the city of · the And · give shall you

חֲמֵ֣שֶׁת אֲלָפִ֣ים רֹ֗חַב וְאֹ֙רֶךְ֙ חֲמִשָּׁ֤ה וְעֶשְׂרִ֣ים אֶ֔לֶף לְעֻמַּ֖ת
2568 · 505 · 7341 · 753 · 2568 · 6242 · 505 · 5980
five · thousand (cubits) · and wide · long · five · twenty- · thousand (cubits) · beside,

7 תְּרוּמַ֣ת הַקֹּ֑דֶשׁ לְכָל־בֵּ֥ית יִשְׂרָאֵ֖ל יִהְיֶֽה׃ וְלַנָּשִׂ֣יא מִזֶּ֣ה
8641 · 6944 · 3605 · 1004 · 3478 · 1961 · 5387 · 6311
heave- the · holy the · whole · house · Israel · be shall It · for And · from · offering · (lot) · of · .be · prince the · here

וּמִזֶּ֣ה לִתְרוּמַ֣ת הַקֹּ֗דֶשׁ וְלַאֲחֻזַּ֣ת הָעִ֔יר אֶל־פְּנֵ֥י תְרוּמַ֖ת
6311 · 8641 · 6944 · 272 · 5892 · 272 · 8641 · 6440
from and · heave- for · holy the · (lot's) · possession · ,city the · the of · heave- the · there · offering · of and · face · of · offering

הַקֹּ֑דֶשׁ וְאֶל־פְּנֵ֞י אֲחֻזַּ֤ת הָעִ֙יר֙ מִפְּאַ֣ת יָ֣ם יָ֔מָּה וּמִפְּאַ֥ת
6944 · 6440 · 272 · 5892 · 6285 · 3220 · 3220 · 6285
holy the · the to and · the · the of · the from · west · west- · from and · (lot's) · of face · possession · city, · side · ,ward side the

קֵ֖דְמָה קָדִ֑ימָה וְאֹ֗רֶךְ לְעֻמּ֤וֹת אַחַ֣ד הַחֲלָקִ֔ים מִגְּב֥וּל יָ֖ם
6924 · 6921 · 753 · 5980 · 259 · 2506 · 1366 · 3220
east · eastward. · length · alongside · (be shall) · portions, · border · west · of one · the · the from

8 אֶל־גְּב֥וּל קָדִֽימָה׃ לָאָ֗רֶץ יִֽהְיֶה־לּ֥וֹ לַאֲחֻזָּ֖ה בְּיִשְׂרָאֵ֑ל וְלֹֽא־
1366 · 6921 · 776 · 1961 · 272 · 3478 · 3808
border the · to · .east · land · a for · to shall It · him · a for · be · .possession · Israel in · ,and not

יוֹנ֤וּ עוֹד֙ נְשִׂיאַ֔י אֶת־עַמִּ֑י וְהָאָ֛רֶץ יִתְּנ֥וּ לְבֵ֥ית־יִשְׂרָאֵ֖ל
3238 · 5750 · 5387 · 5971 · 776 · 5414 · 1004 · 3478
shall · still · My · My · .people · the And · shall they · the to · Israel · oppress · princes · land · give · of house

9 לְשִׁבְטֵיהֶֽם׃ כֹּֽה־אָמַ֞ר אֲדֹנָ֣י יְהוִ֗ה רַב־לָכֶ֛ם נְשִׂיאֵ֥י
7626 · 559 · 136 · 3068 · 7227 · 5387
to according · Thus · says · the · ,Jehovah · Enough · for · O · .tribes their · Lord · ,you · of princes

יִשְׂרָאֵ֖ל חָמָ֣ס וָשֹׁ֣ד הָסִ֔ירוּ וּמִשְׁפָּ֥ט וּצְדָקָ֖ה עֲשׂ֑וּ הָרִ֡ימוּ
3478 · 2555 · 7701 · 5493 · 4941 · 6666 · 6213 · 7311
!Israel · Violence · op- and · turn · justice and · and · .do · Lift · pression · away, · righteousness · off

10 גְּרֻשֹֽׁתֵיכֶם֙ מֵעַ֣ל עַמִּ֔י נְאֻ֖ם אֲדֹנָ֣י יְהוִֽה׃ מֹֽאזְנֵי־צֶ֜דֶק וְאֵֽיפַת־
1646 · 5921 · 5971 · 5002 · 136 · 3068 · 3976 · 6664 · 374
your of acts · from · My · states · Just · balances · Jehovah. · the · ,people · and a · violence · Lord · .ephah

11 צֶ֧דֶק וּבַת־צֶ֛דֶק יְהִ֖י לָכֶֽם׃ הָאֵיפָ֣ה וְהַבַּ֗ת תֹּ֤כֶן אֶחָד֙ יִהְיֶ֔ה
6664 · 1324 · 6664 · 1961 · 374 · 1324 · 8506 · 259 · 1961
,just · a and · just · be there · .you to · let · The · the and · measure · one · shall · bath · ephah · .be

לָשֵׂ֣את מַעְשַׂ֣ר הַחֹ֔מֶר הַבָּ֑ת וַעֲשִׂירִ֥ת הַחֹ֖מֶר הָאֵיפָ֑ה אֶל־
5375 · 4643 · 2563 · 1324 · 6224 · 2563 · 374
may that · the · the · the and · the · the · to · contain · of tenth · homer · ,bath · of tenth · homer · .ephah

12 הַחֹ֖מֶר יִהְיֶ֥ה מִדָּתֽוֹ׃ וְהַשֶּׁ֖קֶל עֶשְׂרִ֣ים גֵּרָ֑ה עֶשְׂרִ֨ים
2563 · 1961 · 4971 · 8255 · 6213 · 1626 · 6242
the · be shall · Its · .measure · the And · (be shall) · .gerahs · Twenty · homer · shekel · twenty

שְׁקָלִ֜ים חֲמִשָּׁ֧ה וְעֶשְׂרִ֛ים שְׁקָלִ֖ים עֲשָׂרָ֥ה וַחֲמִשָּׁ֖ה שֶֽׁקֶל׃
8255 · 2568 · 6242 · 8255 · 6235 · 2568 · 8255
,shekels · five · twenty- · ,shekels · fifteen (and) · ,shekels

shall be a maneh to you.
13This *is* the heave offering
that you shall offer: the
sixth of an ephah of a homer
of wheat, and the sixth of an
ephah of a homer of barley.
14And the statute of oil, the
bath of oil, the tenth of the
bath out of the cor; *of* ten
baths, a homer; for ten
baths *are* a homer; 15and
one lamb out of the flock,
out of two hundred, out of
the watered *land* of Israel;
for a food offering, and for a
burnt offering, and for
peace offerings, to atone for
them, declares the Lord
Jehovah. 16All the people
of the land shall be at this
heave offering for the prince
in Israel. 17And burnt
offerings shall be on the
prince, and a food offering,
and drink offerings, in the
feasts and on the new
moons and on the sab-
baths, in all the appointed
feasts of the house of Israel.
He shall prepare the sin
offering, and the food
offering, and the burnt
offering, and the peace
offerings, to atone for the
house of Israel.
18So says the Lord
Jehovah: In the first *month*,
on the first of the month,
you shall take a perfect bull,
a son of the herd, and
cleanse the sanctuary.
19And the priest shall take of
the blood of the sin offering,
and put *it* on the door posts
of the house, and on the
four corners of the ledge of
the altar, and on the gate-
posts of the inner court.
20And so you shall do on the
seventh of the month for
each man who goes astray,
and for the simple. And you
shall atone for the house.
21In the first *month*, in the
fourteenth day of the
month, the Passover shall
be to you, a feast of seven

8341 7311 834 8641 2088 1961 4488
13 הַמָּנֶה יִהְיֶה לָכֶם׃ זֹאת הַתְּרוּמָה אֲשֶׁר תָּרִימוּ שִׁשִּׁית
the of sixth | shall you :offer | that | heave- the offering | This (is) | .you to | be shall | maneh a

8184 2563 374 8345 2406 2563 374
הָאֵיפָה מֵחֹמֶר הַחִטִּים וְשִׁשִּׁיתֶם הָאֵיפָה מֵחֹמֶר הַשְּׂעֹרִים׃
.barley | a of homer | an ephah | the and of sixth | wheat | a of homer | an ephah

6235 3734 1324 4643 8081 1324 8181 2706
14 וְחֹק הַשֶּׁמֶן הַבַּת הַשֶּׁמֶן מַעְשַׂר הַבַּת מִן־הַכֹּר עֲשֶׂרֶת
ten (of) | the —cor | out of | the bath | the of tenth | ,oil | the of bath | ,oil | the And of statute

259 7716 2563 1324 6235 2563 1324
15 הַבַּתִּים חֹמֶר כִּי־עֲשֶׂרֶת הַבַּתִּים חֹמֶר׃ וְשֶׂה־אַחַת מִן
of out | one lamb and | ;homer a | (are) baths | then | for | ,homer a | baths

5930 4503 3478 4945 3967 6629
הַצֹּאן מִן־הַמָּאתַיִם מִמַּשְׁקֵה יִשְׂרָאֵל לְמִנְחָה וּלְעוֹלָה
burnt a for and ,offering | a for ,offering food | ;Israel | the of out of (land) watered | two ,hundred | out of | the ,flock

5971 3605 3068 136 5002 3722 8002
16 וְלִשְׁלָמִים לְכַפֵּר עֲלֵיהֶם נְאֻם אֲדֹנָי יְהוִה׃ כֹּל הָעָם
the of people | All | .Jehovah | the Lord | states | for them | to atone | peace for and ,offerings

3478 5387 2088 8641 1961 776
17 הָאָרֶץ יִהְיוּ אֶל־הַתְּרוּמָה הַזֹּאת לַנָּשִׂיא בְּיִשְׂרָאֵל׃ וְעַל־
And on | .Israel in | the for prince | this | heave- offering | to | shall be | the land

2320 2282 5262 4503 5930 1961 5387
הַנָּשִׂיא יִהְיֶה הָעוֹלוֹת וְהַמִּנְחָה וְהַנֵּסֶךְ בַּחַגִּים וּבֶחֳדָשִׁים
the on and ,moons new | the in feasts | drink and ,offerings | food a and offering | burnt ,offerings | shall be | the prince

6213 3478 1004 4150 3605 7676
וּבַשַּׁבָּתוֹת בְּכָל־מוֹעֲדֵי בֵּית יִשְׂרָאֵל הוּא־יַעֲשֶׂה אֶת־
shall prepare | He | .Israel | the of house | appointed the all in of feasts | the on and ,sabbaths

3722 8002 5930 4503 2403
הַחַטָּאת וְאֶת־הַמִּנְחָה וְאֶת־הָעוֹלָה וְאֶת־הַשְּׁלָמִים לְכַפֵּר
to atone | peace the ,offerings | and | burnt the ,offering | and | food the ,offering | and | sin the .offering

7223 3068 136 559 3478 1004
18 בְּעַד בֵּית־יִשְׂרָאֵל׃ כֹּה־אָמַר אֲדֹנָי יְהוִה בָּרִאשׁוֹן
the In ,(month) first | :Jehovah | the Lord | says Thus | .Israel | the of house | for

2398 8549 1241 1121 6499 3947 2320 259
בְּאֶחָד לַחֹדֶשׁ תִּקַּח פַּר־בֶּן־בָּקָר תָּמִים וְחִטֵּאתָ אֶת־
and cleanse | ,perfect | the ,herd | son a of | a ,bull | shall you take | the of ,month | the on first

4201 5414 2403 1818 3548 3947 4720
19 הַמִּקְדָּשׁ׃ וְלָקַח הַכֹּהֵן מִדַּם הַחַטָּאת וְנָתַן אֶל־מְזוּזַת
door the of posts | on | put and (it) | sin the offering | the of of blood | the priest | shall And take | the .sanctuary

8179 4201 4196 5835 6438 702 1004
הַבַּיִת וְאֶל־אַרְבַּע פִּנּוֹת הָעֲזָרָה לַמִּזְבֵּחַ וְעַל־מְזוּזַת שַׁעַר
the of gate | the of posts | and on | the of ,altar | the ledge | corners of | the four | and on | the ,house

376 2320 7651 6213 3651 6442 2691
20 הֶחָצֵר הַפְּנִימִית׃ וְכֵן תַּעֲשֶׂה בְּשִׁבְעָה בַחֹדֶשׁ מֵאִישׁ
each for man | the of month | the on (day) seventh | shall you do | And so | .inner | the court

702 7223 1004 3722 6612 7686
21 שֹׁגֶה וּמִפֶּתִי וְכִפַּרְתֶּם אֶת־הַבָּיִת׃ בָּרִאשׁוֹן בְּאַרְבָּעָה
the in four- | first the In ,(month) | the .house | shall you And for atone | for and .simple the | goes who astray

3117 7620 2282 6453 1961 2320 3117 6240
עָשָׂר יוֹם לַחֹדֶשׁ יִהְיֶה לָכֶם הַפֶּסַח חַג שְׁבֻעוֹת יָמִים
;days | seven | a of feast | the ,Passover | you to | there be shall | the of ,month | day | (and) tenth

days; unleavened bread is
eaten. [22]And the prince
shall prepare on that day for
himself and for the people
of the land, a bull *for* a sin
offering. [23]And seven days
of the feast he shall prepare
a burnt offering to Jehovah,
seven bulls and seven rams,
perfect *ones*, daily *for* the
seven days, and *for* a sin
offering a kid of the goats
daily. [24]And a food offering of an ephah for a bull,
and an ephah for a ram, he
shall prepare; also of oil, a
hin for an ephah. [25]In the
seventh *month*, in the
fifteenth day of the month,
at the feast, he shall prepare
like these seven days, as
the sin offering, as the burnt
offering, as the food
offering, and as the oil.

4682 398 6213 5387 3117 3605
22 מַצּוֹת יֵאָכֵל׃ וְעָשָׂה הַנָּשִׂיא בַּיּוֹם הַהוּא בַּעֲדוֹ וּבְעַד כָּל־
all and for that on the shall And is unleavened
for himself day prince prepare .eaten bread

5971 776 6499 2403 7651 2282/3317 6213 5930
23 עַם הָאָרֶץ פַּר חַטָּאת׃ וְשִׁבְעַת יְמֵי־הֶחָג יַעֲשֶׂה עוֹלָה
burnt a shall he the days And sin a (for) a the the
offering prepare feast of seven .offering bull land of people

3068 7651 6499 7651 352 8549 3117 7651
לַיהוָה שִׁבְעַת פָּרִים וְשִׁבְעַת אֵילִים תְּמִימִם לַיּוֹם שִׁבְעַת
the daily perfect rams seven and bulls seven to
seven (for) ,Jehovah

3117 2403 8163 5795 3117 4503 374 6499
24 הַיָּמִים וְחַטָּאת שְׂעִיר עִזִּים לַיּוֹם׃ וּמִנְחָה אֵיפָה לַפָּר
a for an food a And .daily the a a (for) and ,days
,bull ephah of offering goats of kid offering sin

374 352 6213 8081 1969 374 7637 2568
25 וְאֵיפָה לָאַיִל יַעֲשֶׂה וְשֶׁמֶן הִין לָאֵיפָה׃ בַּשְּׁבִיעִי בַּחֲמִשָּׁה
the in the In an for a of and shall he a for an and
five ,month) seventh .ephah hin oil ,prepare ,ram ephah

6240 2320 2282 6213 428 7651 3117 2403
26 עָשָׂר יוֹם לַחֹדֶשׁ בֶּחָג יַעֲשֶׂה כָאֵלֶּה שִׁבְעַת הַיָּמִים כַּחַטָּאת
sin the as days seven like shall he the at the of day (and)
,offering these prepare ,feast ,month tenth

5930 4503 8081
כָּעֹלָה וְכַמִּנְחָה וְכַשָּׁמֶן׃
as and food the as the as
.oil the offering ,offering burnt

CAP. XLVI. מו

CHAPTER 46

CHAPTER 46

[1]So says the Lord
Jehovah: The gate of the
inner court that faces the
east shall be shut the six
working days. But on the
sabbath day it shall be
opened, and in the day of
the new moon it shall be
opened. [2]And the prince
shall enter by way of the
porch of the gate from
outside, and shall stand by
the gatepost. And the
priests shall prepare his
burnt offering, and his
peace offerings. And he
shall worship at the
threshold of the gate. Then
he shall go out, but the gate
shall not be shut until the
evening. [3]And the people
of the land shall worship *at*
the door of that gate on the
sabbaths, and on the new
moons, before Jehovah.
[4]And the burnt offering that
the prince shall bring to
Jehovah on the sabbath
day *shall be* six perfect
lambs, and a perfect ram.
[5]And the food offering *shall
be* an ephah for a ram, and a
food offering for the lambs,
a gift of his hand, and a hin
of oil to an ephah.

3541 559 136 3068 8179 2691 6442 6437 6921
1 כֹּה־אָמַר אֲדֹנָי יְהוִה שַׁעַר הֶחָצֵר הַפְּנִימִית הַפֹּנֶה קָדִים
east faces that inner court the The :Jehovah the says Thus
of gate Lord

1961 5462 8337 3117 4639 3117 7676 6605 3117
יִהְיֶה סָגוּר שֵׁשֶׁת יְמֵי הַמַּעֲשֶׂה וּבְיוֹם הַשַּׁבָּת יִפָּתֵחַ וּבְיוֹם
in and be shall it the on But .working days the shut shall
of day the ,opened Sabbath day six be

2320 6605 935 5387 1870 197 8179 5975/2351
2 הַחֹדֶשׁ יִפָּתֵחַ׃ וּבָא הַנָּשִׂיא דֶּרֶךְ אוּלָם הַשַּׁעַר מִחוּץ וְעָמַד
shall and from the the way by the shall And be shall it new the
stand ,outside gate of porch of prince enter .opened moon

4201 8179 6213 3548 5930 8002
עַל־מְזוּזַת הַשַּׁעַר וְעָשׂוּ הַכֹּהֲנִים אֶת־עוֹלָתוֹ וְאֶת־שְׁלָמָיו
peace his and burnt his the shall and the the by
,offerings offering priests prepare ,gate of post

7812 4670 8179 3318 8179 3808 5462 5704
וְהִשְׁתַּחֲוָה עַל־מִפְתַּן הַשַּׁעַר וְיָצָא וְהַשַּׁעַר לֹא־יִסָּגֵר עַד־
until be shall not the but he Then .gate the the at shall he and
shut gate ,out go shall of threshold worship

6153 7812 5971 776 6607 8179 7676
3 הָעָרֶב׃ וְהִשְׁתַּחֲווּ עַם־הָאָרֶץ פֶּתַח הַשַּׁעַר הַהוּא בַּשַּׁבָּתוֹת
the on ,that gate the (at) the the shall And the
Sabbaths of door land of people worship .evening

2320 6440 3068 5930 834 7126 5387 3068
4 וּבֶחֳדָשִׁים לִפְנֵי יְהוָה׃ וְהָעֹלָה אֲשֶׁר־יַקְרִב הַנָּשִׂיא לַיהוָה
to the shall that burnt the And Jeho- before the on and
Jehovah prince bring offering .vah moons new

3117 7676 8337 3532 8549 352 8549 4503
5 בְּיוֹם הַשַּׁבָּת שִׁשָּׁה כְבָשִׂים תְּמִימִם וְאַיִל תָּמִים׃ וּמִנְחָה
food the And .perfect a and ,perfect lambs (be shall) the on
offering ram six Sabbath day

374 352 3532 4503 4991 3027 8081 1969 374
אֵיפָה לָאַיִל וְלַכְּבָשִׂים מִנְחָה מַתַּת יָדוֹ וְשֶׁמֶן הִין לָאֵיפָה׃
an to a oil and his gift a food a for and a for (be shall)
.ephah hin of ,hand of ,offering lambs the ,ram ephah an

6And in the day of the
new moon: a perfect bull, a
son of the herd; and six
lambs, and a ram, they shall
be perfect; 7and an ephah
for a bull and an ephah for a
ram, he shall prepare *as* a
food offering; and for the
lambs as his hand can
reach; and a hin of oil to an
ephah. 8And when the
prince shall enter, he shall
enter by way of the porch of
the gate, and by its way he
shall leave. 9But when the
people of the land come
before Jehovah at the
appointed feasts, he who
enters by way of the north
gate to worship shall leave
by way of the south gate.
And he who enters by way
of the south gate shall leave
by way of the north gate. He
shall not return by way of
the gate by which he came
in, but shall leave opposite
it.

10And the prince shall go
in among them when they
go in, and he shall leave
when they leave. 11And in
the feasts, and in the
appointed feasts, the food
offering shall be an ephah
to a bull, and an ephah to a
ram, and to the lambs a gift
of his hand; and a hin of oil
to an ephah. 12And when
the prince prepares a free
offering, a burnt offering or
peace offerings *as a* free
offering to Jehovah, then
one shall open to him the
gate facing east. And he
shall prepare his burnt
offering and his peace
offerings as he does on the
sabbath day. And he shall
leave; and the gate is shut
after he leaves. 13And you
shall prepare a burnt offering daily to Jehovah, a
perfect lamb, a son of a
year; from dawn to dawn
you shall prepare it. 14And
you shall prepare a food
offering for it from dawn to
dawn, a sixth of an ephah,
and a third of a hin of oil to
wet the fine flour; a food
offering to Jehovah— per-
fect statutes forever. 15So
they shall prepare the lamb,
and the food offering, and

352 3522 8337 8549 1241 1121 6499 2320 3117
6 וּבְיוֹם הַחֹדֶשׁ פַּר בֶּן־בָּקָר תְּמִימִם וְשֵׁשֶׁת כְּבָשִׂם וָאָיִל
a and ram lambs six and perfect the son a herd of a bull new the moon in And of day

4503 6213 352 374 6499 374 1961 8549
7 תְּמִימִם יִהְיוּ׃ וְאֵיפָה לַפָּר וְאֵיפָה לָאַיִל יַעֲשֶׂה מִנְחָה
food a ,offering shall he prepare a for ,ram an and ephah a for ,bull an And ephah shall they .be perfect

935 374 1969 8081 3027 5381 3832
8 וְלַכְּבָשִׂים כַּאֲשֶׁר תַּשִּׂיג יָדוֹ וְשֶׁמֶן הִין לָאֵיפָה׃ וּבְבוֹא
when And enter shall an to .ephah a hin of and oil his ,hand can reach as (as much) the for and rams

5971 935 3318 1870 935 8179 197 1870 5387
9 הַנָּשִׂיא דֶּרֶךְ אוּלָם הַשַּׁעַר יָבוֹא וּבְדַרְכּוֹ יֵצֵא׃ וּבְבוֹא עַם־
the of people when But come shall he .out go by and way its shall he ,enter gate the the of porch way by of the ,prince

6828 8179 1870 935 4150 3068 6440 776
הָאָרֶץ לִפְנֵי יְהוָה בַּמּוֹעֲדִים הַבָּא דֶּרֶךְ שַׁעַר צָפוֹן
north the gate way by of who he enters appoint- ed the at ,feasts Jehovah before the land

3318 5045 8179 1870 935 5045 8179 1870 3318 7812
לְהִשְׁתַּחֲוֺת יֵצֵא דֶּרֶךְ־שַׁעַר נֶגֶב וְהַבָּא דֶּרֶךְ־שַׁעַר נֶגֶב יֵצֵא
shall leave south the gate way by of he And enters who .south the gate way by of shall worship leave to

935 834 8179 1870 7725 3808 6828 8179 1870
דֶּרֶךְ־שַׁעַר צָפוֹנָה לֹא יָשׁוּב דֶּרֶךְ הַשַּׁעַר אֲשֶׁר־בָּא בוֹ כִּי
but ,in he came which by the gate by of way shall he return not ;north the gate way by of

3318 3318 935 935 8432 5387 3318 5226
10 נִכְחוֹ יֵצֵאוּ׃ וְהַנָּשִׂיא בְּתוֹכָם בְּבוֹאָם יָבוֹא וּבְצֵאתָם יֵצֵאוּ׃
shall he .leave when and leave they go shall ,in they when in go their in midst the And prince shall out go opposite it

352 374 6499 374 4503 1961 4150 2282
11 וּבַחַגִּים וּבַמּוֹעֲדִים תִּהְיֶה הַמִּנְחָה אֵיפָה לַפָּר וְאֵיפָה לָאָיִל
a to ,ram an and ephah a to ,bull an ephah food the offering shall be the in and feasts appointed the in And feasts

5387 6213 374 1969 8081 3027 4991 3532
12 וְלַכְּבָשִׂים מַתַּת יָדוֹ וְשֶׁמֶן הִין לָאֵיפָה׃ וְכִי־יַעֲשֶׂה הַנָּשִׂיא
the prince prepares And when an to .ephah a hin of and oil his ,hand gift a of the to and rams

8179 6605 3068 5071 8002 5930 5071
נְדָבָה עוֹלָה אוֹ־שְׁלָמִים נְדָבָה לַיהוָה וּפָתַח לוֹ אֶת־הַשַּׁעַר
the gate to him one then open shall to ,Jehovah free (as) offering peace offerings or burnt a offering free a ,offering

6213 8002 5930 6213 6921 6437
הַפֹּנֶה קָדִים וְעָשָׂה אֶת־עֹלָתוֹ וְאֶת־שְׁלָמָיו כַּאֲשֶׁר יַעֲשֶׂה
does he as peace his offerings and burnt his offering he And prepare shall .east facing

3532 3318 310 8179 5462 3318 7676 3117
13 בְּיוֹם הַשַּׁבָּת וְיָצָא וְסָגַר אֶת־הַשַּׁעַר אַחֲרֵי צֵאתוֹ׃ וְכֶבֶשׂ
a And ram he .out go after gate the is and shut he And ;leave shall the .Sabbath on day

1242 1242 3068 3117 5930 6213 8549 8141 1121
בֶּן־שְׁנָתוֹ תָּמִים תַּעֲשֶׂה עוֹלָה לַיּוֹם לַיהוָה בַּבֹּקֶר בַּבֹּקֶר
dawn to from dawn to ;Jehovah daily burnt a offering shall you ,prepare ,perfect a year son a of

8345 1242 1242 6213 4503 6213
14 תַּעֲשֶׂה אֹתוֹ׃ וּמִנְחָה תַעֲשֶׂה עָלָיו בַּבֹּקֶר בַּבֹּקֶר שִׁשִּׁית
sixth a of dawn to from dawn for it shall you prepare a And offering food .it shall you prepare

3068 4503 5560 7450 1969 7992 8081 374
הָאֵיפָה וְשֶׁמֶן שְׁלִישִׁית הַהִין לָרֹס אֶת־הַסֹּלֶת מִנְחָה לַיהוָה
to ,Jehovah food a offering fine the ;flour to moisten ,hin a third a of oil and an ,ephah

4503 3532 6213 8548 5769 2708
15 חֻקּוֹת עוֹלָם תָּמִיד׃ וְעָשׂוּ אֶת־הַכֶּבֶשׂ וְאֶת־הַמִּנְחָה וְאֶת־
and food the .offering and ,ram the And prepare shall .perfect forever statutes

the oil, from dawn to dawn
as a burnt offering con-
tinually.

¹⁶So says the Lord
Jehovah: If the prince gives
a gift to sons *of* his
inheritance, it shall be to his
sons; it *is* their possession
by inheritance. ¹⁷But if he
gives it *as* a gift of his
inheritance to one of his
servants, then it shall be his
until the year of liberty; then
it shall return to the prince.
His inheritance *is* only his
sons'; it shall be theirs.
¹⁸And the prince shall not
take of the people's inheritance, oppressing them
from their possession. He
shall bequeath *to* his sons
from his possession, so that
My people shall not be
dispersed, each man from
his possession.

¹⁹And he brought me
through the entry which
was at the side of the gate,
into the holy chambers for
the priests, facing north.
And, behold, there *was* a
place on the two sides
westward. ²⁰And he said to
me, This *is* the place, there
where the priests shall boil
the guilt offering, and the
sin offering, where they
shall bake the food offering,
so as not to bring *them* out
to the outer court to sanctify
the people. ²¹And *he led*
me out to the outer court.
And he made me pass by
the four corners of the
court. And, behold, a court
in *each* corner of the court,
a court in *each* corner of the
court. ²²In the four corners
of the court *were* enclosed
courts; forty *cubits* long and
thirty wide; one measure to
the four of them, being
made in corners. ²³And a
row *was* around in them,
around the four of them;
and boiling places were

16

136	559	3541		8548	5930	1242		1242	8081
הָאֲדֹנָ֣י	אָמַ֣ר	כֹּֽה־	תָּמִ֑יד		עוֹלַ֖ת	בַּבֹּ֥קֶר		בַּבֹּ֣קֶר	הַשֶּׁ֗מֶן
the Lord	says	Thus	.continually	burnt a offering	to	from dawn		dawn	oil the

1121		5159	1121	376		4979	5387	54	14	30.68
לְבָנָ֔יו	הִ֣יא	נַחֲלָת֤וֹ	מִבָּנָ֣יו	לְאִ֨ישׁ	מַתָּנָ֗ה	הַנָּשִׂ֜יא	כִּֽי־יִתֵּ֨ן	יְהֹוִ֗ה		
his sons to	it	his (of) inheritance	man (any) to	gift a	the prince	gives	If	Jeho- vah:

17

259		5159	4979	5414		5159	272	1961
לְאַחַ֣ד	מִנַּחֲלָת֗וֹ	מַתָּנָ֣ה	וְכִֽי־יִתֵּ֤ן	בְּנַחֲלָ֑ה	הִ֖יא	אֲחֻזָּתָ֥ם	תִּֽהְיֶ֔ה	
one to	his (of) inheritance	gift a	he if But	.inheritance	(is) it	their possession	;be shall

389	5387	7725	1865		8141	5704		1961		5650
אַ֚ךְ	לַנָּשִׂ֣יא	וְשָׁבַ֣ת	הַדְּר֔וֹר	שְׁנַ֣ת	עַד־	ל֔וֹ	וְהָ֣יְתָה	מֵעֲבָדָ֔יו		
only	the prince to	return shall	;liberty the	of year	until	to him	it then	his of servants,

18

5971		5159	5387	3947	3808	1961		1121	5159
הָעָ֜ם	מִֽנַּחֲלַ֨ת	הַנָּשִׂ֡יא	וְלֹֽא־יִקַּ֣ח	תִּֽהְיֶֽה	לָהֶ֥ם	בָּנָ֛יו	נַֽחֲלָת֖וֹ		
the people's	of inheritance	prince the	shall And take not	shall it be	them to	sons'	his (is) in- heritance

3808	834		1121	5157	272		272	3238
לֹֽא־	אֲשֶׁ֣ר	לְמַ֙עַן֙	אֶת־בָּנָ֔יו	יַנְחִ֣ל	מֵאֲחֻזָּת֗וֹ	לְהֽוֹנֹתָ֖ם	מֵאֲחֻזָּתָ֑ם	
not	that	so	his sons (to)	shall he bequeath	his from possession	oppressing them	their from possession;

19

3801	834		3996	935		272	5971	6327
עַל־כָּתֵ֣ף	אֲשֶׁר֙	בַּמָּבוֹא֩	וַיְבִיאֵ֡נִי	מֵאֲחֻזָּתֽוֹ	אִ֖ישׁ	עַמִּ֛י	יָפֻ֧צוּ	
the of side	which (was)	entry the through	me brought he And	.possession his from	man	,people My	dis- persed be

6828	6437	3548		6944	3957		8179
צָפ֑וֹנָה	הַפֹּנ֣וֹת	אֶל־הַכֹּֽהֲנִ֗ים	הַקֹּ֜דֶשׁ	אֶל־הַלִּשְׁכ֨וֹת	הַשַּׁ֩עַר֩		
.north	facing	,priests the	holy	the into	gate the

20

4725		2088	559	3220		3411	47.25	8033	2009
הַמָּק֗וֹם	זֶ֣ה	אֵלַ֔י	וַיֹּ֣אמֶר	יָֽמָּה	בַּיַּרְכָתַ֖יִם	מָק֛וֹם	וְהִנֵּה־שָׁ֧ם		
place the (is)	This	,me to	he And said	west- .ward	two the sides on	place a (was)	there ,behold And

	2403		816	3548		8033	1310
אֲשֶׁ֨ר	יְבַשְּׁל֤וּ־שָׁם֙	הַכֹּֽהֲנִ֔ים	אֶת־הָֽאָשָׁ֖ם	וְאֶת־הַֽחַטָּ֑את			
where	priests the there shall boil	guilt the offering	sin the and ,offering	where

2435		2691	3318	1115		4503	644
הַחִ֣יצוֹנָ֔ה	אֶל־הֶֽחָצֵ֤ר	הוֹצִ֣יא	לְבִלְתִּ֥י	אֶת־הַמִּנְחָ֑ה		אֵפ֣וּ	
outer the court	to	bring to out (them)	not so that	food the ;offering	shall they bake

21

5674	2435		2691	331.8		5971	6942
וַיַּֽעֲבִירֵ֖נִי	הַחִ֣יצֹנָ֔ה	אֶל־הֶֽחָצֵ֤ר	וַיּֽוֹצִיאֵ֙נִי֙	אֶת־הָעָֽם׃		לְקַדֵּ֖שׁ	
pass me made he and	,outer	court the	to (led he) And me out	.people the	to sanctify

2691	2691	4740		269	2009	2691	4740	701
הֶֽחָצֵ֔ר	בְּמִקְצֹ֣עַ	חָצֵ֗ר	וְהִנֵּה־	הֶֽחָצֵ֑ר	מִקְצוֹעֵ֣י	אֶל־אַרְבַּ֖עַת		
court	of corner (each) in	court a	,And behold	.court of corner	the	four the	by

22

7000		2691	2691	4740		702		2691	4740
קְטֻר֑וֹת	חֲצֵר֣וֹת	הֶֽחָצֵ֖ר	בְּמִקְצֹעֹ֥ת	בְּאַרְבַּ֜עַת		בְּמִקְצֹ֥עַ הֶֽחָצֵ֖ר׃			
:enclosed	(were) courts	the	corners	the In four		the (each) in of corner court	

702		259	4060	7341		7970	753	705
לְאַרְבַּעְתָּֽם	אַחַ֖ת	מִדָּ֥ה	רֹ֔חַב	וּשְׁלֹשִׁ֣ים		אֹ֨רֶךְ֙	אַרְבָּעִ֤ים	
four the to them of	one (was)	measure	,wide	thirty and		long	forty (cubits)

23

	4018	702		4740
וּמְבַשְּׁל֣וֹת	לְאַרְבַּעְתָּ֑ם	סָבִ֖יב	בָּהֶ֔ם	סָבִ֣יב וְט֨וּר מְקֻצָּעֽוֹת׃
boiling and places	four the ,them of	around	,them in (was)	a And row made being .corners in

made under the rows
round about. 24And he
said to me, These *are* the
houses of those who boil,
where the ministers of
the house shall boil there
the sacrifice of the
people.

CHAPTER 47

1And he led me back to
the door of the house.
And, behold, water came
out from under the thres-
hold of the house east-
ward. For the face of the
house *is* east, and the
water came down from
under the right side of the
house, at the south from
the altar. 2And he led me
out by way of the north
gate, and led me around
the way outside to the
outer gate, by the way
facing east. And, behold,
water was trickling out of
the right side.
3When the man went
out eastward, and the
line in his hand, he
measured a thousand cu-
bits. And he passed me
through the water, water
to the ankles. 4And he
measured a thousand,
and passed me through
the water, water *to* the
knees. And he measured
a thousand, and passed
me through water *to* the
loins. 5And he measured
a thousand, *and there
was* a torrent which I was
not able to pass; for the
water had risen, water to
swim *in*; a torrent that
could not be passed.
6And he said to me, Have
you seen, son of man?
And he led me and made
me return to the lip of the
torrent. 7When I returned,
then, behold, on the lip of
the torrent *were* many
trees on this side and on
that side. 8And he said to
me, These waters go out
toward the eastern circuit,
and go down into the
Arabah, and enter the sea.
They are brought out into
the sea, and the waters
shall be healed. 9And it
shall be, every soul that
lives, which swarms in
every *place*, there where
the two torrents go, *that
soul* shall live. And there

1004 428 559 5439 2918 8478 6213
24 עָשׂוּי מִתַּחַת הַטִּירוֹת סָבִיב׃ וַיֹּאמֶר אֵלַי אֵלֶּה בֵּית
the of houses | These (are) | ,me to | he Then said | round .about | rows the | under | were made

5971 2077 1004 8334 8033 1310 834 1310
הַמְבַשְּׁלִים אֲשֶׁר יְבַשְּׁלוּ־שָׁם מְשָׁרְתֵי הַבַּיִת אֶת־זֶבַח הָעָם׃
the .people | sacri- the of fice | the house | the of ministers | there | shall boil | where | who those ,boil

CAP. XLVII מז

CHAPTER 47

4670 8478 3318 4325 2009 1004 6607 7725
1 וַיְשִׁבֵנִי אֶל־פֶּתַח הַבַּיִת וְהִנֵּה־מַיִם יֹצְאִים מִתַּחַת מִפְתַּן
thres- the of hold | from under | came out | water | ,And ,behold | .house the | the of door | to | led he And back me

8478 3381 4325 6921 1004 6440 6921 1004
הַבַּיִת קָדִימָה כִּי־פְנֵי הַבַּיִת קָדִים וְהַמַּיִם יֹרְדִים מִתַּחַת
from under | came down | the and water | ,east | the (is) house | the For of face | .eastward | the house

8179 1870 3318 4196 5045 3233 1004 3801
2 מִכֶּתֶף הַבַּיִת הַיְמָנִית מִנֶּגֶב לַמִּזְבֵּחַ׃ וַיֹּצִאֵנִי דֶּרֶךְ־שַׁעַר
the gate | way by of | led he Then out me | the from .altar | the at south | ,right | the house | the of side

6921 6437 1870 2351 8179 2351 1870 5437 6828
צָפוֹנָה וַיְסִבֵּנִי דֶּרֶךְ חוּץ אֶל־שַׁעַר הַחוּץ דֶּרֶךְ הַפּוֹנֶה קָדִים
.east | facing | the by way | ,outer gate the to | outside the way | me led and around | ,north

6921 376 3318 3233 3801 6379 4325 2009
3 וְהִנֵּה־מַיִם מְפַכִּים מִן־הַכָּתֵף הַיְמָנִית׃ בְּצֵאת־הָאִישׁ קָדִים
east- ward | the man | went When out | .right | the side | out of | was trickling | water | ,And ,behold

657 4325 4325 5674 520 505 4058 3027 6957
וְקָו בְּיָדוֹ וַיָּמָד אֶלֶף בָּאַמָּה וַיַּעֲבִרֵנִי בַמַּיִם מֵי אָפְסָיִם׃
the .ankles | water (to) | the through ,water | he and me passed | ,cubits | thou- a sand | he measured | his in the ,hand | and line

5674 505 4058 1290 4325 4325 5674 505 4058
4 וַיָּמָד אֶלֶף וַיַּעֲבִרֵנִי בַמַּיִם מַיִם בִּרְכָּיִם וַיָּמָד אֶלֶף וַיַּעֲבִרֵנִי
passed and through me | thou-a sand | he And measured | the .knees | water (to) | through ;water the | pass-and me ed | thou-a ,sand | he And measured

1342 5674 3201 3808 834 5158 505 4058 4975 4325
5 מֵי מָתְנָיִם׃ וַיָּמָד אֶלֶף נַחַל אֲשֶׁר לֹא־אוּכַל לַעֲבֹר כִּי־גָאוּ
had risen | for | ;pass to | was I able | not | which | a torrent | thou-a ,sand | he And measured | the .loins | water (to)

7200 559 5674 3808 834 5158 7813 4325 4325
6 הַמַּיִם מֵי שָׂחוּ נַחַל אֲשֶׁר לֹא־יֵעָבֵר׃ וַיֹּאמֶר אֵלַי הֲרָאִיתָ
you Have ,seen | ,me to | he And said | be could .passed | not | that | a torrent | ,(in) swim | to water | the ,water

2009 7725 5158 8193 7725 3212 120 1121
7 בֶן־אָדָם וַיֹּלִכֵנִי וַיְשִׁבֵנִי עַל־שְׂפַת הַנָּחַל׃ בְּשׁוּבֵנִי וְהִנֵּה
then ,behold | I When ,returned | the .torrent | of lip the | to | made and return me | he Then me led | ?man | son of

4325 559 2088 2088 3966 7227/6086 5158 8193
8 אֶל־שְׂפַת הַנַּחַל עֵץ רַב מְאֹד מִזֶּה וּמִזֶּה׃ וַיֹּאמֶר אֵלַי הַמַּיִם
waters | to ,me | he And said | on and side (that) | this on | very | many trees | the torrent | of lip the | on

6160 3381 6930 1552 3318 428
הָאֵלֶּה יוֹצְאִים אֶל־הַגְּלִילָה הַקַּדְמוֹנָה וְיָרְדוּ עַל־הָעֲרָבָה
Arabah the into | go and down | ,eastern | the circuit | toward | out go | These

3605 1961 4325 7495 3318 3220 3220 935
9 וּבָאוּ הַיָּמָּה אֶל־הַיָּמָּה הַמּוּצָאִים וְנִרְפְּאוּ הַמָּיִם׃ וְהָיָה כָל־
every | it And ,be will | the .waters | shall be healed | and | are they brought out | the sea | into | ;sea the | and enter

2421 5158/8033 935 834 3605 834 8317 834 2416 5315
נֶפֶשׁ חַיָּה אֲשֶׁר־יִשְׁרֹץ אֶל כָּל־אֲשֶׁר יָבוֹא שָׁם נַחֲלַיִם יִחְיֶה
shall .live | two the torrents | there | go | ,where | every (place) | in | swarms | which | that lives | soul

shall be very many fish,
because these waters shall
come there. And they shall
be healed. And all shall live
there where the torrent
goes. 10And it will be, the
fisherman shall stand on it;
from En-gedi even to En-
eglaim, a spreading place
for nets shall be there; their
fish shall be by its kind, like
the fish of the Great Sea,
very many. 11Its swamps
and its marshes shall not
even be healed; they shall
be given to salt. 12And all
trees *for* food shall go up by
the torrent, on its bank on
this *side* and on that; its leaf
shall not fade, and its fruit
shall not fail; it will bear by
its months, because its
waters come out from the
sanctuary. And its fruit shall
be for food, and its leaf for
healing.
13So says the Lord
Jehovah: This *shall be* the
border by which you shall
inherit the land, by the
twelve tribes of Israel.
Joseph *shall have two*
portions. 14And you shall
inherit it, each man like his
brother, that I lifted up My
hand to give it to your
fathers; even this land shall
fall to you for an inheritance. 15And this *is* the
border of the land to the
north side, from the Great
Sea, the way of Hethlon, to
the entrance of Zedad:
16Hamath, Berothah, Sib-
raim, which *is* between the
border of Damascus and the
border of Hamath; Hazer-
hatticon, which *is* by the
border of Hauran. 17And the
border shall be from the sea
to Hazar-enon, *at* the
border of Damascus; and
the north northward, even
the border of Hamath. And
this is the north side.
18And you shall measure
the east side from between
Hauran, and Damascus, and
Gilead, and the land of

והיה הדגה רבה מאד כי באו שמה המים האלה וירפאו
shall they And .these waters there shall be- ,very many fish there And
.healed be come cause be shall

10 וחי כל אשר־יבוא שמה הנחל׃ והיה יעמדו עליו דוגים
fish- the it on shall it And the there goes where all And
;erman stand be will .torrent live shall

מעין גדי ועד־עין עגלים משטוח לחרמים יהיו למינה תהיה
shall its by there for spreading a ,Eneglaim even from
be kind ;be shall nets place to Engedi

11 דגתם כדגת הים הגדול רבה מאד׃ בצאתו וגבאיו ולא
even its and its ,very many .Great the the like their
not marshes swamps Sea of fish ,fish

12 ירפאו למלח נתנו׃ ועל־הנחל יעלה על־שפתו מזה
this on lip its on go shall the And shall they for be shall
(side) up torrent by .given be salt ;healed

ומזה כל־עץ־מאכל לא־יבול עלהו ולא־יתם פריו לחדשיו
its by its shall and its shall not (for) trees all on and
months .fruit fail not ,leaf fade ,food (side) that

יבכר כי מימיו מן־המקדש המה יוצאים והיו פריו
its And .out come they the from its because will It
fruit be shall sanctuary ,waters ,bear

13 למאכל ועלהו לתרופה׃ כה אמר אדני יהוה גה
This :Jehovah the says Thus .healing for its and ,food for
(be shall) Lord leaf

גבול אשר תתנחלו את־הארץ לשני עשר שבטי ישראל
.Israel of tribes ten (and) two land the shall you by the
inherit which border

14 יוסף חבלים׃ ונחלתם אותה איש כאחיו אשר נשאתי
up lifted I which his like each ,it shall you And (two) Joseph
,brother man inherit .portions (have shall)

את־ידי לתתה לאבתיכם ונפלה הארץ הזאת לכם
you to this land shall and your to it give to hand My
fall ;fathers

15 בנחלה׃ וזה גבול הארץ לפאת צפונה מן־הים הגדול
,Great the from ,north the to the bor- the And in- an for
Sea side land of der this .heritance

16 הדרך חתלן לבוא צדדה׃ חמת ברותה סברים אשר
which ,Sibraim ,Berothah ,Hamath ,Zedad the to ,Hethlon way the
(is) of entrance of

בין־גבול דמשק ובין גבול חמת חצר התיכון אשר אל־
by which ,hatticon Hazer- ;Hamath the and Damascus the between
(is) of border of border

17 גבול חורן׃ והיה גבול מן־הים חצר עינון גבול דמשק
Damascus the (at) ,enon Hazar- the from the shall And .Hauran the
of border (to) sea border be of border

18 וצפון צפונה וגבול חמת ואת פאת צפון׃ ופאת קדים
east the And .north (is this) And .Hamath the even north- the and
side side the of border ,ward north

מבין חורן ומבין דמשק ומבין הגלעד ומבין ארץ ישראל
Israel the and ,Gilead and ,Damascus and Hauran from
of land between

Israel, *shall be* the Jordan, from the border to the Eastern Sea. And *this is* the east side. ¹⁹And the south side, southward from Tamar, to the waters of Meriboth-kadesh, the torrent to the Great Sea. And *this is* the south side to the Negeb. ²⁰And the west side *is* the Great Sea from the border until beside the entrance of Hamath. this *is* the west side.

²¹And you shall divide this land for yourselves by the tribes of Israel. ²²And it will be, you shall make it fall by lot for an inheritance to yourselves, and to the aliens who sojourn among you, who shall father sons among you. And they shall be to you as native-born among the sons of Israel. They shall be allotted an inheritance among the tribes of Israel. ²³And it shall be, in the tribe in it which the alien sojourns, there you shall give his inheritance, declares the Lord Jehovah.

CHAPTER 48

¹And these *are* the names of the tribes: From the north end, at the hand of the way of Hethlon *to* the entrance of Hamath, Hazarenon, the border of Damascus northward, at the hand of Hamath; and there shall be to it an east side *and a* west: *To* Dan, one *part*. ²And by the border of Dan, from the east side to the west side, Asher, one *part*. ³And by the border of Asher, from the east side to the west side, Naphtali, one *part*. ⁴And by the border of Naphtali, from the east side even to the west side, Manasseh, one *part*. ⁵And by the border of Manasseh, from the east side to the west side, Ephraim, one *part*. ⁶And by the border of

---

19

6921	6285		4058	6931	3220	1366		3383
.east	(is this)	And shall you	,Eastern	the	to the	from	(be shall)
	side the		.measure	Sea		border	Jordan the

5159	6:946	4808	4325		848:6	5045	6285
to	the	,kadesh Meriboth-	the to	from	south-	Negeb	the And
	torrent	of waters	,Tamar	ward		side

20

1419	3220	6285	5045	6285		1419	3220
Great	the	west the And	the to	south	(is this)	and	,Great	the
	Sea	(is)	side	,Negeb		side the		Sea

21

25 05		3220/6285	2574	935	5227	13:66
shall you And	.west	the	This	.Hamath	the	until	the from
divide		side	(is)	of entrance	beside	border

5307	19-61	3478	7626	2063	776
it make shall you	it And	.Israel	the by	for	this	land
			of tribes	yourselves

22

1121	3205	834	8432	1481	1616	5159
sons	shall	who	among	who	the to	and	your-	to	an	for
	father		,you		sojourn aliens	,selves		inheritance

5307	3478	1121	249	1961	8432
shall They	with	.Israel	the among	native- as	to	they And	among
fall	make	you		of sons	the	born	you	be shall	.you

23

1481	1616/83.4	7626	1961	3478	7626	8432	5159
stays	the	which	the in	it And	.Israel	the	among	in-an
	alien		tribe	,be shall		of tribes		heritance

3068	.136	5002	5159	5414	8033
.Jehovah	the	states	in- his	shall you	there	in
	Lord		,heritage	give		,it

CAP. XLVIII. מח

CHAPTER 48

1

2855	1870	3027	6828	7097	7626	8034	428
,Hethlon	the	the at	north	the From	the	the	the these And
	of way	of hand		end	:tribes	of names (are)

2574	3027	1834	1366	= 2704 =		935
-Hamath	the at	north-	Damascus	the	,enon	Hazar-	,Hamath the (to)
	of hand	ward		of border		of entrance

2

6285	18.35	1366	259	1835	3220	6921	1961
the from	,Dan	the	by And	one	.Dan	(and)	east	side a to there and
side		of border		(part)		,west		it be shall

3

6285	836	1366	259	836	3220	6285	6921
the from	,Asher	the	And	one	Asher	,west	the	to	east
side		of border	by	(part)		side

4

5321	1366	259	5321	3220	6285	6921
,Naphtali	the	And	one	Naphtali	,west	the	even	east
	of border	by	(part)		side		to

5

1366	259	4519	3220	6285	6921	6285
the	And	one	Manasseh	,west	the	to	east	the from
of border	by	(part)		side		side

6

259	669	3220	6285	6921	6285	4519
And	one	Ephraim	,west	the	to	east	the from	Manasseh
by	(part)		side		side

Ephraim, from the east side even to the west side, Reuben, one *part*. [7]And by the border of Reuben, from the east side even to the west side, Judah, one *part*. [8]And by the border of Judah, from the east side to the west side, shall be the heave offering which you shall offer—twenty-five thousand *cubits* wide and long, as one of the parts, from the east side to the west side. And the sanctuary shall be in its midst. [9]The heave offering that you shall offer to Jehovah *shall be* twenty-five thousand *cubits* long and ten thousand cubits wide. [10]And for these shall be the holy heave offering for the priests: northward, twenty-five thousand; and westward, ten thousand *cubits* wide; and eastward, ten thousand wide; and southward, twenty-five thousand *cubits* long. And the sanctuary of Jehovah shall be in its midst, [11]for the priests who are sanctified, of the sons of Zadok who have kept My charge, who did not go astray when the sons of Israel went astray, as the Levites went astray. [12]And the heave offering shall be theirs, from the heave offering of the land, the holiest of the holy places, by the border of the Levites.

[13]And the Levites *shall have* alongside the border of the priests twenty-five thousand *cubits* long and ten thousand wide. All the length *shall be* twenty-five thousand, and the width ten thousand. [14]And they shall not sell *any* of it, and shall not trade, and shall not cause to pass away the firstfruits of the land. For *it is* holy to Jehovah.

259 7205 3220 6285 6921 6285 669 1366
גבול אפרים מפאת קדים ועד־פאת־ימה ראובן אחד׃
one Reuben ,west the even east the from Ephraim the
.(part) side to side of border

7 259 3063 3220 6285 6921 6285 7205 1366
ועל גבול ראובן מפאת קדים עד־פאת־ימה יהודה אחד׃
one Judah ,west the to east the from Reuben the And
.(part) side side of border by

8 1961 3220 6285 6921 6285 3063 1366
ועל גבול יהודה מפאת קדים עד־פאת ימה תהיה
be shall ,west the to east the from ,Judah the And
side side of border by

753 7341 505 6242 2568 7311 834 8641
התרומה אשר־תרימו חמשה ועשרים אלף רחב וארך
and wide thousand twenty- five shall you which heave- the
,long (cubits) offer offering

1961 3220 6285 6921 6285 2506 259
כאחד החלקים מפאת קדימה עד־פאת־ימה והיה
shall And .west the to east the from ,parts the one as
be side side of

9 753 3068 7311 8641 8432 4720
המקדש בתוכו׃ התרומה אשר תרימו ליהוה ארך
long to shall you that heave- The its in the
Jehovah offer offering .midst sanctuary

10 428 505 6235 7341 505 6242 2568
חמשה ועשרים אלף ורחב עשרת אלפים׃ ולאלה
for And thousand ten wide and thousand twenty- (be shall)
these .(cubits) ,(cubits) five

6242 2568 6828 3548 6944 8641 1961
תהיה תרומת־הקדש לכהנים צפונה חמשה ועשרים
twenty- five northward the for holy heave- the shall
:priests offering be

6235 7341 6921 505 6235 6235 7341 505
אלף וימה רחב עשרת אלפים וקדימה רחב עשרת
ten wide and thousand ten wide and thou-
eastward ,(cubits) westward ,sand

4720 1961 505 6242 2568 753 5045 505
אלפים ונגבה ארך חמשה ועשרים אלף והיה מקדש־
the shall And thousand twenty- five long and thousand
of sanctuary be .(cubits) southward (cubits)

11 8104 834 6659 1121 6942 3548 8432 3068
יהוה בתוכו׃ לכהנים המקדש מבני צדוק אשר שמרו
have who ,Zadok the of are who the for its in Jehovah
kept of sons ,sanctified priests ;midst

8582 3478 1121 8582 8582 3808 4931
משמרתי אשר לא־תעו בתעות בני ישראל כאשר תעו
went as ,Israel the went when go did not who My
astray of sons astray astray ,charge

12 6944 776 8641 8642 1961 3881
הלוים׃ והיתה להם תרומיה מתרומת הארץ קדש
the land the heave- the from heave- the ,them to shall And the
of holiest of offering offering be .Levites

13 3548 1366 5980 3881 3881 1366 6944
קדשים אל־גבול הלוים׃ והלוים לעמת גבול הכהנים
the the along- the And the the by holy the
,priests of border side ,Levites .Levites of border places

753 3605 505 6235 7341 753 505 6242 2568
חמשה ועשרים אלף ארך ורחב עשרת אלפים כל־ארך
the All thousand ten wide and long thousand twenty- (have shall)
length .(cubits) (cubits) five

14 4376 3808 505 6235 7341 505 6242 2568
חמשה ועשרים אלף ורחב עשרת אלפים׃ ולא־ימכרו
shall they And thousand ten the and thousand twenty- (be shall)
sell not .(cubits) width ,(cubits) five

3068 6944 776 7225 5674 3808 4171 3808
ממנו ולא ימר ולא יעבור ראשית הארץ כי־קדש ליהוה׃
to (is it) For the first- the to cause and shall and of (any)
.Jehovah holy .land of fruits away pass not ,trade not ,it

[15]And the five thousand being left in the width in front of the twenty-five thousand, it *is* common for the city, for dwelling, and for open land. And the city shall be in its midst. [16]And these *shall be* its measures: the north side, four thousand and five hundred; and the south side, four thousand and five hundred *cubits*; and the east side, four thousand and five hundred; and the west side, four thousand and five hundred *cubits*. [17]And the open land shall be of the city northward, two hundred and fifty *cubits*; and southward, two hundred and fifty; and eastward, two hundred and fifty; and westward, two hundred and fifty *cubits*. [18]And the remainder in length alongside the heave offering of the holy *parts shall be* ten thousand eastward, and ten thousand westward. And it shall be alongside the heave offering of the holy *part*. And its produce shall be for bread to those who serve the city. [19]And he who serves the city shall serve it out of all the tribes of Israel. [20]All the heave offering *shall be* twenty-five thousand by twenty-five thousand *cubits*; foursquare. You shall offer the holy heave offering, to the possession of the city. [21]And the remainder *is* for the prince, on this *side* and on that, of the holy heave offering, and of the possession of the city, in the front of the twenty-five thousand of the heave offering to the east border, and westward in the front of the twenty-five thousand to the west border; alongside the parts of the prince. And it shall be a holy heave

6242 2568 644 0 7341 3498 505 2568
15 וְהַחֲמֵשֶׁת אֲלָפִים הַנּוֹתָר בָּרֹחַב עַל־פְּנֵי חֲמִשָּׁה וְעֶשְׂרִים
twenty- five the front in the in are that thousand the And
of width left five

8432 5892 1961 4054 4186 5892 2455 505
אֶלֶף חֹל־הוּא לָעִיר לְמוֹשָׁב וּלְמִגְרָשׁ וְהָיְתָה הָעִיר בְּתוֹכֹה׃
its in the shall And for and for the for it com- thousand
midst city be .land open ,dwelling ,city (is) mon

505 702 3967 2568 6828 6285 4060 428
16 וְאֵלֶּה מִדּוֹתֶיהָ פְּאַת צָפוֹן חֲמֵשׁ מֵאוֹת וְאַרְבַּעַת אֲלָפִים
thousand four and hundred five north the its these And
;(cubits) side :measures (be shall)

6285 505 702 3967 2568 2568 5045 6285
וּפְאַת־נֶגֶב חֲמֵשׁ חֲמֵשׁ מֵאוֹת וְאַרְבַּעַת אֲלָפִים וּמִפְּאַת
the and thousand four and hundred (even) ,five south the and
side ;(cubits) five side

2568 3220 6285 505 702 3967 2568 6921
קָדִים חֲמֵשׁ מֵאוֹת וְאַרְבַּעַת אֲלָפִים וּפְאַת־יָמָּה חֲמֵשׁ
five ,west the and thousand four and hundred five ,east
side ;(cubits)

6828 5892 4054 1961 505 702 3967
17 מֵאוֹת וְאַרְבַּעַת אֲלָפִים׃ וְהָיָה מִגְרָשׁ לָעִיר צָפוֹנָה
,northward the of open the And thousand four and hundred
city land be shall .(cubits)

2572 6921 3967 2572 5045 3967 2572
חֲמִשִּׁים וּמָאתַיִם וָנֶגְבָּה חֲמִשִּׁים וּמָאתַיִם וְקָדִימָה חֲמִשִּׁים
fifty east- and two and fifty south- and two and fifty
ward ;hundred ward ;hundred

5980 753 3498 3967 2572 3220 3967
18 וּמָאתַיִם וְיָמָּה חֲמִשִּׁים וּמָאתָיִם׃ וְהַנּוֹתָר בָּאֹרֶךְ לְעֻמַּת
alongside in the And . two and fifty west- and two and
length remainder .hundred ward ;hundred

505 6235 6921 505 6235 6944 8641
תְּרוּמַת הַקֹּדֶשׁ עֲשֶׂרֶת אֲלָפִים קָדִימָה וַעֲשֶׂרֶת אֲלָפִים
thousand ten and eastward thousand (be shall) holy the heave- the
(cubits) (cubits) ten (parts) of offering

3899 8393 1961 6944 8641 5980 1961 3220
יָמָּה וְהָיָה לְעֻמַּת תְּרוּמַת הַקֹּדֶשׁ וְהָיְתָה תְבוּאָתֹה לְלֶחֶם
for its shall And holy the heave- the alongside it And west-
bread produce be .(part) of offering be shall .ward

3478 7626 3605 5647 5892 5647 5892 5647
19 לְעֹבְדֵי הָעִיר׃ וְהָעֹבֵד הָעִיר יַעַבְדוּהוּ מִכֹּל שִׁבְטֵי יִשְׂרָאֵל׃
.Israel the of out serve shall the he And the those to
of tribes all it city serves who .city serve who

6242 2568 505 6242 2568 8641 3605
20 כָּל־הַתְּרוּמָה חֲמִשָּׁה וְעֶשְׂרִים אֶלֶף בַּחֲמִשָּׁה וְעֶשְׂרִים
twenty- five by thousand twenty- (be shall) heave- the All
five offering

5892 272 6944 8641 7311 7243 505
אֶלֶף רְבִיעִית תָּרִימוּ אֶת־תְּרוּמַת הַקֹּדֶשׁ אֶל־אֲחֻזַּת הָעִיר׃
.city the the to ,holy heave- the shall You four ;thousand
of possession offering offer square

272 6944 8641 2088 5387 3498
21 וְהַנּוֹתָר לַנָּשִׂיא מִזֶּה וּמִזֶּה לִתְרוּמַת־הַקֹּדֶשׁ וְלַאֲחֻזַּת
the of and ,holy heave- the of on and this on for (is) the And
of possession offering that (side) prince the remainder

1366 8641 505 6242 2568 6440 5892
הָעִיר אֶל־פְּנֵי חֲמִשָּׁה וְעֶשְׂרִים אֶלֶף תְּרוּמָה עַד־גְּבוּל
the to heave- the thousand twenty- five the front in the
border offering of of ,city

3220 1366 505 6242 2568 6440 3220 6921
קָדִימָה וְיָמָּה עַל־פְּנֵי חֲמִשָּׁה וְעֶשְׂרִים אֶלֶף עַל־גְּבוּל יָמָּה
;west the to thousand twenty- five the front in and ,east
border of westward

4720 6944 8641 1961 5387 2506 5980
לְעֻמַּת חֲלָקִים לַנָּשִׂיא וְהָיְתָה תְּרוּמַת הַקֹּדֶשׁ וּמִקְדַּשׁ
the and ;holy heave- a it And the of parts the alongside
of sanctuary offering be shall .prince

offering, and the sanctuary of the house in its midst. [22]And to the prince shall be from the possession of the Levites, and from the city's possession, amidst *that* which *is* for the prince; between the border of Judah and the border of Benjamin.

[23]And the rest of the tribes: From the east side to the west side, Benjamin, one *part*. [24]And by the border of Benjamin, from the east side to the west side, Simeon, one *part*. [25]And by the border of Simeon, from the east side to the west side, Issachar, one *part*. [26]And by the border of Issachar, from the east side to the west side, Zebulun, one *part*. [27]And by the border of Zebulun, from the east side to the west side, Gad, one *part*. [28]And by the border of Gad to the south side southward, from Tamar to the waters of Meriboth-kadesh, to the torrent to the Great Sea. [29]This *is* the land which you shall make fall by lot for an inheritance to the tribes of Israel, and these their parts, declares the Lord Jehovah.

[30]And these *are* the exits of the city on the north side, four thousand and five hundred measures. [31]And the gates of the city *shall be* by the names of the tribes of Israel: three gates northward—the gate of Reuben, one; the gate of Judah, one; the gate of Levi, one. [32]And at the east side four thousand five hundred, and three gates: even the gate of Joseph, one; the gate of Benjamin, one; the gate of Dan, one. [33]And the south side, four thousand and five hundred measures, and three gates: the gate of

834 8432 58:92 272 38,81 272 8432 1004
22 הַבַּיִת בְּתוֹכֹה׃ וּמֵאֲחֻזַּת הַלְוִיִּם וּמֵאֲחֻזַּת הָעִיר בְּתוֹךְ אֲשֶׁר
(that) which amidst the city's from and possession the Levites the from And of possession its in .midst the house

5387 1144 1366 3063 1366 996 1961 5387
לַנָּשִׂיא יִהְיֶה בֵּין ׀ גְּבוּל יְהוּדָה וּבֵין גְּבוּל בִּנְיָמִן לַנָּשִׂיא
the to prince —Benjamin the of border and Judah the of border between ↔is the for prince

1144 3220 6285 6921 6285 7626 3499 1961
23 יִהְיֶה׃ וְיֶתֶר הַשְּׁבָטִים מִפְּאַת קָדִימָה עַד־פְּאַת־יָמָּה בִּנְיָמִן
Benjamin ,west the side to east the from side the ,tribes the And of rest shall .be

3220 6285 6921 6285 1144 1366 259
24 אֶחָד׃ וְעַל ׀ גְּבוּל בִּנְיָמִן מִפְּאַת קָדִימָה עַד־פְּאַת־יָמָּה
,west the side to east the from side ,Benjamin the of border by And one .(part)

6285 6921 6285 8095 1366 259 8095
25 שִׁמְעוֹן אֶחָד׃ וְעַל ׀ גְּבוּל שִׁמְעוֹן מִפְּאַת קָדִימָה עַד־פְּאַת־
the side to east the from side ,Simeon the of border And by one .(part) Simeon

6921 6285 348.5 1366 259 3485 3220
26 יָמָּה יִשָּׂשכָר אֶחָד׃ וְעַל ׀ גְּבוּל יִשָּׂשכָר מִפְּאַת קָדִימָה
east the from side Issachar the of border by And .part one Issachar ,west

6921 6285 2074 1366 259 2074 3220 6285
27 עַד־פְּאַת־יָמָּה זְבוּלֻן אֶחָד׃ וְעַל ׀ גְּבוּל זְבוּלֻן מִפְּאַת קָדִימָה
east the from side ,Zebulun the of border And by one .(part) Zebulun ,west the side to

8486 5045 6285 1410 1366 259 1410 3220 6285
28 עַד־פְּאַת־יָמָּה גָּד אֶחָד׃ וְעַל גְּבוּל גָּד אֶל־פְּאַת נֶגֶב תֵּימָנָה
south- ward Negeb the side to Gad the of border by And one .(part) Gad ,west the side to

1419 3220 5159 6946 4808 4325 85:59 1366 19 61
וְהָיָה גְבוּל מִתָּמָר מֵי מְרִיבַת קָדֵשׁ נַחֲלָה עַל־הַיָּם הַגָּדוֹל׃
.Great the Sea to the to torrent ,Kadesh Meribath- of waters the from Tamar the border even be shall

428 3478 7626 5159 5307 834 776 2063
29 זֹאת הָאָרֶץ אֲשֶׁר־תַּפִּילוּ מִנַּחֲלָה לְשִׁבְטֵי יִשְׂרָאֵל וְאֵלֶּה
and these ,Israel the to of tribes an for inheritance shall you which lot by fall make the land This (is)

5892 8444 428 3068 136 5002 4256
30 מַחְלְקוֹתָם נְאֻם אֲדֹנָי יְהוִה׃ וְאֵלֶּה תּוֹצְאֹת הָעִיר
the city the of exits these And (are) .Jehovah the Lord states ,parts their

8179 4060 505 702 3967 2568 68:28 6285
31 מִפְּאַת צָפוֹן חֲמֵשׁ מֵאוֹת וְאַרְבַּעַת אֲלָפִים מִדָּה׃ וְשַׁעֲרֵי
the And of gates .measures thousand four and hundred five ,north the on side

6828 7969 8179 3478 7626 8034 5892
הָעִיר עַל־שְׁמוֹת שִׁבְטֵי יִשְׂרָאֵל שְׁעָרִים שְׁלוֹשָׁה צָפוֹנָה
north- ;ward three gates :Israel the of tribes the of names (be shall) by the city

259 38:78 8179 259 3063 8177 259 7205 8179
32 שַׁעַר רְאוּבֵן אֶחָד שַׁעַר יְהוּדָה אֶחָד שַׁעַר לֵוִי אֶחָד׃ וְאֶל־
at And .one ,Levi the of gate ;one Judah the of gate ;one Reuben the of gate

8179 505 702 3967 2568 6921 6285
פְּאַת קָדִימָה חֲמֵשׁ מֵאוֹת וְאַרְבַּעַת אֲלָפִים וּשְׁעָרִים
gates and thousand ;(cubits) four and hundred five ,east side the

259 1835 8179 259 1144 8179 259 3127 8179 7969
שְׁלֹשָׁה וְשַׁעַר יוֹסֵף אֶחָד שַׁעַר בִּנְיָמִן אֶחָד שַׁעַר דָּן אֶחָד׃
.one ,Dan the of gate ;one ,Benjamin the of gate ;one ,Joseph the of gate even :three

8179 40:60 505 702 3967 2568 5045 6285
33 וּפְאַת־נֶגְבָּה חֲמֵשׁ מֵאוֹת וְאַרְבַּעַת אֲלָפִים מִדָּה וּשְׁעָרִים
gates and ;measures thousand four and hundred five south the And side

Simeon, one; the gate of Issachar, one; the gate of Zebulun, one. [34]The west side, four thousand and five hundred, their gates three: the gate of Gad, one; the gate of Asher, one; the gate of Naphtali, one. [35]All around *it shall be* eighteen thousand *cubits*. And the name of the city from *that* day *shall be* JEHOVAH IS THERE.

2074 8179 259 3485 8179 259 8095 8179 259

שְׁלֹשָׁה׃ שַׁעַר שִׁמְעוֹן אֶחָד שַׁעַר יִשָּׂשכָר אֶחָד שַׁעַר זְבוּלֻן

,Zebulun the of gate ;one ,Issachar the of gate ;one ,Simeon the of gate :three

8179 505 702 3967 2568 3220 6285 259

34 אֶחָד׃ פְּאַת־יָמָּה חֲמֵשׁ מֵאוֹת וְאַרְבַּעַת אֲלָפִים שַׁעֲרֵיהֶם

their gates thousand ;(cubits) four and hundred five west The side .one

259 5321 8179 259 836 8179 259 1410 8179 7969

שְׁלֹשָׁה שַׁעַר גָּד אֶחָד שַׁעַר אָשֵׁר אֶחָד שַׁעַר נַפְתָּלִי אֶחָד׃

.one ,Naphtali the of gate ;one Asher the of gate ;one ,Gad the of gate :three

8033 3068 3117 5892 8034 505 6240 8083 5439

35 סָבִיב שְׁמֹנָה עָשָׂר אָלֶף וְשֵׁם־הָעִיר מִיּוֹם יְהוָה ׀ שָׁמָּה׃

(is) .there Jehovah (that) :day from the city the of name And .(cubits) thousand (be shall it) eighteen All around

דניאל

LIBER DANIELIS

(THE) BOOK OF DANIEL

CAPUT. I א

CHAPTER 1

A LITERAL TRANSLATION
OF THE BIBLE
THE BOOK OF DANIEL

CHAPTER 1

[1]In the third year of the reign of Jehoiakim, king of Judah, Nebuchadnezzar the king of Babylon came to Jerusalem and besieged it. [2]And the Lord gave Jehoiakim, king of Judah, into his hand, with part of the vessels of the house of God, which he carried into the land of Shinar to the house of his god. And he brought the vessels into the treasure house of his god.

[3]And the king spoke to Ashpenaz, the chief of his eunuchs, that he should bring *some* of the sons of Israel, and of the king's seed, and of the nobles; [4]young men *in* whom was no blemish, but who were of good appearance and skillful in all wisdom, having knowledge and understanding learning, even those *with* strength in them to stand in the king's palace, and to teach them the writing and the language of the Chaldeans. [5]And the king set them the portion of a day in its day, from the king's food, and the wine of his drinking; even to rear them three years so that at their end they may stand before the king. [6]And there were among them of the sons of Judah, Daniel, Hananiah, Mishael and Azariah, [7]to whom the chief of the eunuchs gave names. For he called Daniel, Belteshazzar; and Hananiah, Shadrach; and Mishael, Meshach; and Azariah, Abednego.

935 3068 4428 3079 4438 7969 8141
1 בִּשְׁנַת שָׁלוֹשׁ לְמַלְכוּת יְהוֹיָקִים מֶלֶךְ־יְהוּדָה בָּא
came ,Judah king Jehoiakim the of third the In
of of reign year

136 5414 6696 3389 894 4428 5019
2 נְבוּכַדְנֶאצַּר מֶלֶךְ־בָּבֶל יְרוּשָׁלַםִ וַיָּצַר עָלֶיהָ׃ וַיִּתֵּן אֲדֹנָי
the And .it and (to) Babylon king Nebuchadnezzar
Lord gave beseiged Jerusalem of

430 1004 3627 7417 3063 4428 3079 3027
בְּיָדוֹ אֶת־יְהוֹיָקִים מֶלֶךְ־יְהוּדָה וּמִקְצָת כְּלֵי בֵית־הָאֱלֹהִים
,God the the part with Judah king Jehoiakim his
of house of vessels of of hand

1004 935 3627 430 1004 8152 776 935
וַיְבִיאֵם אֶרֶץ־שִׁנְעָר בֵּית אֱלֹהָיו וְאֶת־הַכֵּלִים הֵבִיא בֵּית
the took he the And his the (to) Shinar the bore he and
house into vessels .god of house of land to them

935 5631 7227 828 4428 559 430 214
3 אוֹצַר אֱלֹהָיו׃ וַיֹּאמֶר הַמֶּלֶךְ לְאַשְׁפְּנַז רַב סָרִיסָיו לְהָבִיא
bring to his chief the to the said And his treasure
eunuchs of ,Ashpenaz king .god of

3206 6579 4410 2233 3478 1121
4 מִבְּנֵי יִשְׂרָאֵל וּמִזֶּרַע הַמְּלוּכָה וּמִן־הַפַּרְתְּמִים׃ יְלָדִים
young ,nobles the and ,royal of and ,Israel the of
men of seed the of sons

3605 7919 4758 2698 3971 3605 369 834
אֲשֶׁר אֵין־בָּהֶם כָּל־מאוּם וְטוֹבֵי מַרְאֶה וּמַשְׂכִּילִים בְּכָל־
all in having and look but ,blemish any in not (in)
understanding of good them was whom

5975 3581 4093 995 1847 3045 2451
חָכְמָה וְיֹדְעֵי דַעַת וּמְבִינֵי מַדָּע וַאֲשֶׁר כֹּחַ בָּהֶם לַעֲמֹד
to in (with) even ,learning and knowledge having ,wisdom
stand them strength those understanding

4487 3778 3956 5612 3925 4428 1964
5 בְּהֵיכַל הַמֶּלֶךְ וּלְלַמְּדָם סֵפֶר וּלְשׁוֹן כַּשְׂדִּים׃ וַיְמַן לָהֶם
to And the the and the teach to and the in
them set .Chaldeans of tongue writing them ,king's palace

4960 3196 4428 6598 3117 3117 1697 4428
הַמֶּלֶךְ דְּבַר־יוֹם בְּיוֹמוֹ מִפַּת־בַּג הַמֶּלֶךְ וּמִיֵּין מִשְׁתָּיו
his the and the food from its in a the king the
,drinking of wine king's day day of portion

1961 4428 6440 5975 7117 7969 8141 1430
6 וּלְגַדְּלָם שָׁנִים שָׁלוֹשׁ וּמִקְצָתָם יַעַמְדוּ לִפְנֵי הַמֶּלֶךְ׃ וַיְהִי
And .king the before they at that so three years to and
were stand may end their them rear

7760 5838 4332 2608 1840 3063 1121 854
7 בָהֶם מִבְּנֵי יְהוּדָה דָּנִיֵּאל חֲנַנְיָה מִישָׁאֵל וַעֲזַרְיָה׃ וַיָּשֶׂם
and and Mishael ,Hananiah ,Daniel :Judah the of among
assigned ,Azariah of sons them

1095 1840 7760 8034 5631 8269
לָהֶם שַׂר הַסָּרִיסִים שֵׁמוֹת וַיָּשֶׂם לְדָנִיֵּאל בֵּלְטְשַׁאצַּר
;Belteshazzar for he and ;names the the for
,Daniel assigned eunuchs of chief ,them

5664 5838 4335 4332 7714 2608
וְלַחֲנַנְיָה שַׁדְרַךְ וּלְמִישָׁאֵל מֵישַׁךְ וְלַעֲזַרְיָה עֲבֵד נְגוֹ׃
.Abednego tor and ;Meshach for and ;Shadrach for and
,Azariah ,Mishael ,Hananiah

8 And Daniel laid on his heart that he would not defile himself with the king's food, or with the wine of his drinking. So he asked of the chief of the eunuchs that he might not defile himself. 9 And God had given Daniel kindness and compassion before the chief of the eunuchs. 10 And the chief of the eunuchs said to Daniel, I fear my lord the king, who has chosen your food and your drink. For why should he see your faces worse looking than the boys who *are* in your term? Then you would forfeit my head to the king. 11 And Daniel said to Melzar, whom the chief of the eunuchs had set over Daniel, Hananiah, Mishael, and Azariah, 12 I beg you, test your servants ten days. And let vegetables be given to us, that we may eat, and water that we may drink. 13 Then let our faces be seen before you, our look and the look of the boys who eat of the king's food. And as you see, deal so with your servants. 14 And he listened to them in this matter, and tested them for ten days. 15 And at the end of ten days their faces looked better and fatter of flesh than all the boys who were eating the king's food. 16 So Melzar took away their food and the wine that they were to drink, and he gave them vegetables.

17 As for these four boys, God gave them knowledge and skill in all writing and wisdom. And Daniel had understanding in all visions

4428 6598 1351 3808 3820 5921 1840 7760
8 וישם דניאל על־לבו אשר לא־יתגאל בפתבג המלך
the king's | food with | would he not himself defile | that | his heart | upon | Daniel | But laid

1351 3808 5631 8269 1245 4960 3196
וביין משתיו ויבקש משר הסריסים אשר לא יתגאל׃
might he .himself defile | not | that | the eunuchs | the of chief | he So sought | his .drinking | the or of wine

8269 6440 7356 2617 1840 430 5414
9 ויתן האלהים את־דניאל לחסד ולרחמים לפני שר
the of chief | before | and compassion | kindness | Daniel | God | had Now given

3373 1840 5631 8269 559 5635
10 הסריסים׃ ויאמר שר הסריסים לדניאל ירא אני את־
I | fear | Daniel to | the eunuchs | the of chief | said And | the .eunuchs

4960 3978 4487 834 4428 113
אדני המלך אשר מנה את־מאכלכם ואת־משתיכם
;drink your | and | food your | has appointed | who | the ,king | my lord

834 3206 2196 6440 7200 4100 834
אשר למה יראה את־פניכם זעפים מן־הילדים אשר
who (are) | boys the | than | worse looking | faces your | he should see | why | for

1840 559 4428 7218 2325 1524
11 כגילכם וחיבתם את־ראשי למלך׃ ויאמר דניאל אל־
to | Daniel | Then said | the to .king | my head | would you Then forfeit | your in ?term

2608 1840 5921 5631 8269 4487 834 4453
המלצר אשר מנה שר הסריסים על־דניאל חנניה
,Hananiah | Daniel | over | the eunuchs | chief the of | had he appointed | whom | the ,overseer

5414 6235 3117 5650 5254 5838 4332
12 מישאל ועזריה׃ נס־נא את־עבדיך ימים עשרה ויתנו־
let and given be | ,ten | days | your servants | Please test | and ,Azariah | ,Mishael

6440 7200 8354 4325 398 2235
13 לנו מן־הזרעים ונאכלה ומים ונשתה׃ ויראו לפניך
before you | let Then seen be | we that .drink may | and water | we that ,eat may | the vegetables | (some) of | to us

4428 6598 398 3206 4758 7200
מראינו ומראה הילדים האכלים את פתבג המלך
the ;king's | food | eat who | boys the | the and of look | our look

2088 1697 8085 5650 6213 7200
14 וכאשר תראה עשה עם־עבדיך׃ וישמע להם לדבר הזה
,this | to matter | to them | he So listened | your .servants | with | deal | you ,see | as And

4758 7200 6235 3117 7117 6235 3117 5254
15 וינסם ימים עשרה׃ ומקצת ימים עשרה נראה מראיהם
their appearance | looked | ,ten | days | the at And of end | .ten | days | and them tested

6598 398 3206 3605 1320 1277 2896
טוב ובריאי בשר מן־כל־הילדים האכלים את פתבג
food | were who eating | the boys | all than | flesh | and of fatter | better

4960 3196 6598 5375 4453 1961 4428
16 המלך׃ ויהי המלצר נשא את־פתבגם ויין משתיהם
their ,drinks | the and of wine | their food | took away | the overseer | So | the .king's

5414 702 428 3206 2235 5414
17 ונתן להם זרענים׃ והילדים האלה ארבעתם נתן להם
to them | gave | ,four | these | for as And boys | .vegetables | to them | he and gave

995 1840 2451 5612 3605 7919 4093 430
האלהים מדע והשכל בכל־ספר וחכמה ודניאל הבין
had skill | but Daniel | and ;wisdom | writing | in all | and insight | knowledge | God

and dreams.
18 Now at the end of the days that the king had said to bring them in, the chief of the eunuchs brought them in before Nebuchadnezzar.
19 And the king talked with them. And among them all was found none like Daniel, Hananiah, Mishael, and Azariah. So they stood before the king.
20 And *in* any matter of wisdom *and* understanding that the king asked from them, he found them ten times better than all the horoscopists *and* the conjurers who *were* in all his kingdom.
21 And Daniel continued to the first year of king Cyrus.

18 בְּכָל־חָזוֹן וַחֲלֹמוֹת׃ וּלְמִקְצָת הַיָּמִים אֲשֶׁר־אָמַר הַמֶּלֶךְ

the king / had said / when / the days, / the at end of / Now / and dreams. / visions / in all

19 לַהֲבִיאָם וַיְבִיאֵם שַׂר הַסָּרִיסִים לִפְנֵי נְבֻכַדְנֶצַּר׃ וַיְדַבֵּר

And spoke / .Nebuchadnezzar / before / the eunuchs / chief the of / them brought then / bring to in them

אִתָּם הַמֶּלֶךְ וְלֹא נִמְצָא מִכֻּלָּם כְּדָנִיֵּאל חֲנַנְיָה מִישָׁאֵל

Mishael / ,Hananiah / like Daniel / all among them / was found / but none / the ,king / with them

20 וַעֲזַרְיָה וַיַּעַמְדוּ לִפְנֵי הַמֶּלֶךְ׃ וְכֹל דְּבַר חָכְמַת בִּינָה אֲשֶׁר

that / under-standing / wisdom (or) / matter of / And any / the .king / before / they so stood / and ,Azariah

בִּקֵּשׁ מֵהֶם הַמֶּלֶךְ וַיִּמְצָאֵם עֶשֶׂר יָדוֹת עַל־כָּל־הַחַרְטֻמִּים

horoscopists the all better than / hands ten / found he them / the ,king / from them / sought

21 הָאַשָּׁפִים אֲשֶׁר בְּכָל־מַלְכוּתוֹ׃ וַיְהִי דָּנִיֵּאל עַד־שְׁנַת אַחַת

first / the year / until / Daniel / And continued / his .kingdom / in all / who (were) / the (and) conjurers

לְכוֹרֶשׁ הַמֶּלֶךְ׃

the .king / Cyrus of

CAP. II ב

CHAPTER 2

CHAPTER 2

1 And in the second year of the reign of Nebuchadnezzar, Nebuchadnezzar was dreaming dreams, and his spirit was troubled, and his sleep was finished on him.
2 And the king said to call to the horoscopists, and to the conjurers, and to the sorcerers, and to the Chaldeans, to tell to the king his dreams. And they came and stood before the king.
3 And the king said to them, I have dreamed a dream, and my spirit was troubled to know the dream.
4 And the Chaldeans spoke to the king *in* Aramaic, O king, live forever! Tell your servants the dream, and we will reveal the meaning.
5 The king answered and said to the Chaldeans, The word *is* certainly gone from me. If you will not make known the dream and its meaning to me, you will be made into *mere* members, and your houses shall be made an outhouse.
6 But if you show the dream and its meaning,

1 וּבִשְׁנַת שְׁתַּיִם לְמַלְכוּת נְבֻכַדְנֶצַּר חָלַם נְבֻכַדְנֶצַּר חֲלֹמוֹת

,dreams / Nebuchad-nezzar / dreamed / Nebuchad-,nezzar / the of reign / second / in And year the

2 וַתִּתְפָּעֶם רוּחוֹ וּשְׁנָתוֹ נִהְיְתָה עָלָיו׃ וַיֹּאמֶר הַמֶּלֶךְ לִקְרֹא

call to / king the / said Then / .him on / was finished / his and sleep / his ,spirit / was and troubled

לַחַרְטֻמִּים וְלָאַשָּׁפִים וְלַמְכַשְּׁפִים וְלַכַּשְׂדִּים לְהַגִּיד לַמֶּלֶךְ

the to king / tell to / the to and ,Chaldeans / the to and ,sorcerers / the to and ,conjurers / the to ,horoscopists

3 חֲלֹמֹתָיו וַיָּבֹאוּ וַיַּעַמְדוּ לִפְנֵי הַמֶּלֶךְ׃ וַיֹּאמֶר לָהֶם הַמֶּלֶךְ

,king the / to them / said And / .king the / before / and stood / they So came / his .dreams

4 חֲלוֹם חָלַמְתִּי וַתִּפָּעֶם רוּחִי לָדַעַת אֶת־הַחֲלוֹם׃ וַיְדַבְּרוּ

Then spoke / .dream the / know to / my spirit / was and troubled / have I ,dreamed / a dream

הַכַּשְׂדִּים לַמֶּלֶךְ אֲרָמִית מַלְכָּא לְעָלְמִין חֱיִי אֱמַר חֶלְמָא

the dream / Tell / live / forever / ,king O / —Aramaic / the to —king / the Chaldeans

5 לְעַבְדָיךְ וּפִשְׁרָא נְחַוֵּא׃ עָנֵה מַלְכָּא וְאָמַר לְכַשְׂדָּיֵא מִלְּתָה

The word / the to ,Chaldeans / said and / The king / answered / will we .reveal / the and meaning / your to ,servants

מִנִּי אַזְדָּא הֵן לָא תְהוֹדְעוּנַּנִי חֶלְמָא וּפִשְׁרֵהּ הַדָּמִין

(mere) members / its and meaning / the dream / make will you me to known / not / If / (is) .assured / from me

6 תִּתְעַבְדוּן וּבָתֵּיכוֹן נְוָלִי יִתְּשָׂמוּן׃ וְהֵן חֶלְמָא וּפִשְׁרֵהּ

its and meaning / the dream / But if / be shall .made / out- an house / your and houses / be will you into made you shall receive gifts and a present and great honor from before me. Therefore, reveal the dream and its meaning to me. 7They again answered and said, Let the king tell his servants the dream, and we will reveal its meaning. 8The king answered and said, For I know that you buy time, that on account of all, you see the thing *is* certainly gone from me. 9But if you will not make the dream known to me, *there is* one law for you. For you have agreed upon lying and deceiving words to speak before me, until the time has changed. Therefore, tell me the dream; then I shall know that you can reveal the meaning to me.

10The Chaldeans replied before the king and said, There is not a man on the earth who can reveal the king's matter, because not any king, lord, or ruler has asked such a thing from any horoscopists, or conjurer, or Chaldean. 11And the thing that the king asks *is* rare. And there is no other who may reveal it before the king, except the gods, whose dwelling is not with flesh. 12Then the king was enraged and angered. And he commanded all the wise men of Babylon to be destroyed. 13And the law went out that the wise men should be killed. And they looked for Daniel and his companions, to be killed.

14Then Daniel replied *with* counsel and insight to Arioch the chief of the king's executioners, who had gone out to kill the wise men of Babylon. 15He

תהחון מתנן ונבזבה ויקר שגיא תקבלון מן־קדמי להן

There- fore before me from shall you receive great honor and a present and ,gifts make you known

7 חלמא ופשרה החוני׃ ענו תנינות ואמרין מלכא חלמא

the dream king the ,said and again They replied reveal me to its and meaning the dream

8 יאמר לעבדוהי ופשרה נהחוה׃ ענה מלכא ואמר מן־

For ,said and The king answered will we reveal. the and meaning his to servants Let tell

יציב ידע אנה די עדנא אנתון זבנין כל־קבל די חזיתון

see you that account of on all ,buy you time that I know certain

9 די אזדא מני מלתא׃ די הן־חלמא לא תהודענני חדה־

one law reveal will you me to not the dream if But the word. from me (is) assured that

היא דתכון ומלה כדבה ושחיתה הזדמנתון למאמר

speak to have you agreed upon corrupt and lying words for your ,law (is)

קדמי עד די עדנא ישתנא להן חלמא אמרו לי ואנדע

I and know shall to me tell the dream There- fore is changed. the time until before ,me

10 די פשרה תהחונני׃ ענו כשדיא קדם־מלכא ואמרין

,said and king the before the Chaldeans answered can you me to reveal. its meaning that

לא־איתי אנש על־יבשתא די מלת מלכא יוכל להחויה

make to ,known able is the king's matter who the earth on a man There is not

כל־קבל די כל־מלך רב ושליט מלה כדנה לא שאל

has asked not like this thing a or lord ,chief ,king any because

11 לכל־חרטם ואשף וכשדי׃ ומלתא די־מלכה שאל יקירה

(is) rare. asks the king that the And thing or Chaldean. or ,conjurer horoscopist any

ואחרן לא איתי די יחוננה קדם מלכא להן אלהין די

(the) ,gods except ,king the before may it reveal who there is no And other

12 מדרהון עם־בשרא לא איתוהי׃ כל־קבל דנה מלכא

king the ,Thereupon was .is not flesh with whose dwelling

בנס וקצף שגיא ואמר להובדה לכל חכימי בבל׃

.Babylon wise the of men all destroy to he And commanded .very and angered very enraged

13 ודתא נפקת וחכימיא מתקטלין ובעו דניאל וחברוהי

his and companions Daniel they And sought be should .killed the that men wise went out the And law

14 להתקטלה׃ באדין דניאל התיב עטא וטעם

and insight (with) counsel answered Daniel Then .killed be to

לאריוך רב־טבחיא די מלכא די נפק לקטלה לחכימי

wise the of men kill to had out gone who the king's execu- tioners the of chief the to Arioch answered and said to Arioch, the chief of the king's body-guard, Why *is* the decree so hasty from before the king? And Arioch made the thing known to Daniel. [16]And Daniel went in and asked of the king that he would give him time, and he would show the king the meaning. [17]Then Daniel went to his house and declared the thing to Hananiah, Mishael and Azariah, his companions, [18]that they might pray for the mercies of God in Heaven about this secret, that Daniel and his companions should not perish with the rest of the wise men of Babylon.

[19]Then the secret was revealed to Daniel in a night vision, and Daniel blessed the God of Heaven. [20]Daniel answered and said, Blessed be the name of God forever and ever, for wisdom and might *are* His. [21]And He changes the times and the seasons; He causes to pass away kings, and sets up kings; He gives wisdom to the wise, and knowledge to those who know understanding. [22]He reveals the deep and secret things; He knows what *is* in the darkness, and the light dwells in Him. [23]I thank You and praise You, O God of my fathers, who has given me wisdom and might, and has made me know what we ask of You. For You have revealed to us the king's matter.

[24]Then Daniel went in to Arioch, whom the king had chosen to destroy the wise men of Babylon. He went

4101 4430 7990 746 560 6032 895
15 בָּבֶל׃ עָנֵה וְאָמַר לְאַרְיוֹךְ שַׁלִּיטָא דִּי־מַלְכָּא עַל־מָה
Why (is) ,king's the captain Arioch to said and He answered .Babylon

740 3046 4406 116 44 30 6925 4480 2685 1882
דָתָא מְהַחְצְפָה מִן־קֳדָם מַלְכָּא אֱדַיִן מִלְּתָא הוֹדַע אַרְיוֹךְ
Arioch made known the matter Then ?king the before from urgent so the decree

5415 2166 1768 44 30 1480 1156 5954 1841 1841
16 לְדָנִיֵּאל׃ וְדָנִיֵּאל עַל וּבְעָא מִן־מַלְכָּא דִּי זְמָן יִנְתֵּן־לֵהּ
him he give would time that the king from and asked went in Then Daniel .Daniel to

1005 1847 116 4430 2324 6591
17 וּפִשְׁרָא לְהַחֲוָיָה לְמַלְכָּא׃ אֱדַיִן דָּנִיֵּאל לְבַיְתֵהּ
his to house Daniel Then the to .king would he known make the that meaning

304 6 4406 2269 5839 4333 2608 2 36
אֲזַל וְלַחֲנַנְיָה מִישָׁאֵל וַעֲזַרְיָה חַבְרוֹהִי מִלְּתָא הוֹדַע׃
made ;known the matter his ,companions and ,Azariah ,Mishael to and Hananiah ,went

1768 1836 7328 8064 426 6925/4480 1156 7359
18 וְרַחֲמִין לְמִבְעֵא מִן־קֳדָם אֱלָהּ שְׁמַיָּא עַל־רָזָה דְּנָה דִּי
that ,this about secret Heaven the of God before from they that ask might for mercies

895 2445 7606 5974 2269 1841 7 38 09
לָא יְהֹבְדוּן דָּנִיֵּאל וְחַבְרוֹהִי עִם־שְׁאָר חַכִּימֵי בָבֶל׃
.Babylon wise the of men the with of rest his and companions Daniel perish should not

689 1841 116 1541/7328 39 16 2376 1841 116
19 אֱדַיִן לְדָנִיֵּאל בְּחֶזְוָא דִּי־לֵילְיָא רָזָא גֲלִי אֱדַיִן דָּנִיֵּאל בָּרִךְ
blessed Daniel Then was revealed the secret the of night a in vision Daniel to Then

426 8036 19 31 560 1841 6032 8065 426
20 לֶאֱלָהּ שְׁמַיָּא׃ עָנֵה דָנִיֵּאל וְאָמַר לֶהֱוֵא שְׁמֵהּ דִּי־אֱלָהָא
God of the name Be ,said and Daniel answered .Heaven the of God

1370 2452 5957 5704 5957 4480 1289
מְבָרַךְ מִן־עָלְמָא וְעַד־עָלְמָא דִּי חָכְמְתָא וּגְבוּרְתָא דִּי־
(are) the and power the wisdom for ,ever and forever blessed

4430 5709 2166 5732 8133 1932
21 לֵהּ־הִיא׃ וְהוּא מְהַשְׁנֵא עִדָּנַיָּא וְזִמְנַיָּא מְהַעְדֵּה מַלְכִין
kings makes He away pass the and ;seasons the times changes He And to .Him

3046 4486 2445 2552 3052 4430 6966
וּמְהָקֵים מַלְכִין יָהֵב חָכְמְתָא לְחַכִּימִין וּמַנְדְּעָא לְיָדְעֵי
those to know who and knowledge the to ,men wise the wisdom He gives .kings sets and up

28:16 4101 3046 5642 5994 15 41 999
22 בִינָה׃ הוּא גָּלֵא עַמִּיקָתָא וּמְסַתְּרָתָא יָדַע מָה בַחֲשׁוֹכָא
the in ,darkness what (is) He knows secret and .things deep the deep reveals He under- .standing

7624 3029 2 426 8271 5974 50 94
23 וּנְהוֹרָא עִמֵּהּ שְׁרֵא׃ לָךְ ׀ אֱלָהּ אֲבָהָתִי מְהוֹדֵא וּמְשַׁבַּח
praise and thank my ,fathers O of God To ,You .dwells with Him the and light

30 46 3705 3052 1370 2452 576
אֲנָה דִּי חָכְמְתָא וּגְבוּרְתָא יְהַבְתְּ לִי וּכְעַן הוֹדַעְתַּנִי דִּי־
what made has know me and now to ;me has given the and power the wisdom who ,I

1836 6903 3606 3046 4430 4406 44:80 1156
24 בְעֵינָא מִנָּךְ דִּי־מִלַּת מַלְכָּא הוֹדַעְתֶּנָא׃ כָּל־קֳבֵל דְּנָה
that account of on all made have You .us to known the king's matter For from .You we asked

895 2445 7 4430 4483 746 5922 5954 1841
דָּנִיֵּאל עַל עַל־אַרְיוֹךְ דִּי מַנִּי מַלְכָּא לְהוֹבָדָה לְחַכִּימֵי בָבֶל
;Babylon wise the of men destroy to the king had appointed whom ,Arioch to went in Daniel

and said this to him, Do not destroy the wise men of Babylon. Bring me in before the king, and I will show the meaning to the king. [25]Then Arioch quickly brought Daniel in before the king, and spoke this to him, I have found a man of the captives of Judah who will make the meaning known to the king. [26]The king answered and said to Daniel, whose name *was* Belteshazzar, Are you able to reveal to me the dream which I have seen, and its meaning? [27]Daniel replied before the king and said, The secret which the king has demanded cannot be shown to the king by the wise men, the conjurers, the horoscopists, *or* the fortune-tellers. [28]But there is a God in Heaven who reveals secrets, and makes known to king Nebuchadnezzar what shall be in the latter days. Your dream, and the visions of your head on your bed, *was* this:

[29]As for you, O king, your thoughts came on your bed, what should happen after this. And He who reveals secrets makes known to you what shall occur. [30]But as for me, this secret is not revealed to me for *any* wisdom that I have more than any living man, but so that the meaning might be made known to the king, and that you might know the thoughts of your heart.

[31]You, O king, were seeing. And, behold, a certain great image! That great image stood before you with a brilliant brightness; and its form *was* dreadful. [32]The head of this

5954 7 409 895 2445 560 3652 236
אֱזַל ׀ וְכֵן אֲמַר־לֵהּ לְחַכִּימֵי בָבֶל אַל־תְּהוֹבֵד הַעֵלְנִי
me Bring in | Do destroy | not | Babylon | wise the of men | to ,him | he said | and thus | he went

746 116 2324 4430 6591 4430 6925
25 קֳדָם מַלְכָּא וּפִשְׁרָא לְמַלְכָּא אֲחַוֵּא׃ אֱדַיִן אַרְיוֹךְ
Arioch | Then | will I .declare | the to king | the and meaning | the ,king | before

560 3652 4430 6925 1841 5954 927
בְּהִתְבְּהָלָה הַנְעֵל לְדָנִיֵּאל קֳדָם מַלְכָּא וְכֵן אֲמַר־לֵהּ דִּי־
to ,him | he spoke | and thus | the ,king | before | Daniel | brought in | hurriedly

4430 6591 3061 1547 1123 1400 4672
הַשְׁכַּחַת גְּבַר מִן־בְּנֵי גָלוּתָא דִּי יְהוּד דִּי פִשְׁרָא לְמַלְכָּא
the to king | the meaning | who Judah | of | exiles | the of | man a | have I found

1046 8036 1841 560 4430 6032 3046
26 יְהוֹדַע׃ עָנֵה מַלְכָּא וְאָמַר לְדָנִיֵּאל דִּי שְׁמֵהּ בֵּלְטְשַׁאצַּר
,Belteshazzar | name whose (was) | ,Daniel to | said and | The king | answered | make will .known

6032 6591 2370 2493 3046 3546 383
27 הַאִיתָךְ כָּהֵל לְהוֹדָעֻתַנִי חֶלְמָא דִּי־חֲזֵית וּפִשְׁרֵהּ׃ עָנֵה
answered | its and ?meaning | have I which seen | the dream | make to me to known | able | you Are

3809 1793 4430 7328 560 4430 6925 1841
דָּנִיֵּאל קֳדָם מַלְכָּא וְאָמַר רָזָה דִּי־מַלְכָּא שָׁאֵל לָא
not | has ,asked | the which king | The secret | ,said and | the king | before | Daniel

4430 2324 3202 1505 2749 826 2445
חַכִּימִין אָשְׁפִין חַרְטֻמִּין גָּזְרִין יָכְלִין לְהַחֲוָיָה לְמַלְכָּא׃
the to .king | declare to | are able | astrologers | horo- ,scopists | ,conjurers | wise the ,men

4430 3046 7328 1541 8065 426 383 1297
28 בְּרַם אִיתַי אֱלָהּ בִּשְׁמַיָּא גָּלֵא רָזִין וְהוֹדַע לְמַלְכָּא
King to | makes and known | secrets | who reveals | Heaven in | God a | there is | But

2376 2493 3118 320 1934 4101 5020
נְבוּכַדְנֶצַּר מָה דִּי לֶהֱוֵא בְּאַחֲרִית יוֹמַיָּא חֶלְמָךְ וְחֶזְוֵי
the and of visions | Your dream | .days | the in latter | be shall | what | Nebuchad- nezzar

4430 607 1836 4903 5922 7217
29 רֵאשָׁךְ עַל־מִשְׁכְּבָךְ דְּנָה הוּא׃ אַנְתְּה מַלְכָּא
,king O | for As you | ;(was) | this | bed your | on | your head

1541 1836 314 1934 4101 1934 4903 5922 7476
רַעְיוֹנָךְ עַל־מִשְׁכְּבָךְ סְלִקוּ מָה דִּי לֶהֱוֵא אַחֲרֵי דְנָה וְגָלֵא
the And of Revealer | .this | after | should happen | what | came up | your bed | on | your thoughts

383 2452 3809 576 1934 3046 7328
30 רָזַיָּא הוֹדְעָךְ מָה־דִי לֶהֱוֵא׃ וַאֲנָה לָא בְחָכְמָה דִּי־אִיתַי
there that is | of because wisdom | not | as And ,me for | come shall .pass to | what | make secrets you to known

1701 5922 3861 1541 1836 7328 2417 3606
בִּי מִן־כָּל־חַיַּיָּא רָזָא דְנָה גֱּלִי לִי לָהֵן עַל־דִּבְרַת דִּי
that order in | but | to ,me | is revealed | this | secret | living any man | more than | with me

3046 3825 7476 3046 4430 6591
פִשְׁרָא לְמַלְכָּא יְהוֹדְעוּן וְרַעְיוֹנֵי לִבְבָךְ תִּנְדַּע׃
might you .know | your heart | the that of thoughts | making ,known | the to king | the meaning

1797 6755 7690 2298 6755 431 1934 2370 4430 607
31 אַנְתְּה מַלְכָּא חָזֵה הֲוַיְתָ וַאֲלוּ צְלֵם חַד שַׂגִּיא צַלְמָא דִּכֵּן
That | image | !great certain image | and behold | ,were seeing | ,king O | ,You

6755 1763 7299 6903 6966 3493 2122 7229
32 רַב וְזִיוֵהּ יַתִּיר קָאֵם לְקָבְלָךְ וְרֵוֵהּ דְּחִיל׃ הוּא צַלְמָא
image's | That | (was) .terrifying | its and appearance | ,you before | stood | extra- ordinary | an with brightness | great

image *was* of fine gold; its breasts and its arms *were* of silver; its belly and its thighs *were* of bronze; [33]its legs *were* of iron; its feet *were* partly of iron and partly of clay. [34]You continued until a stone was cut out without hands, which struck the image on its feet of iron and clay, and broke them to pieces. [35]Then the iron, the clay, the bronze, the silver, and the gold were together broken to pieces; and *they* became like the chaff of the summer threshing floors. And the wind carried them away, so that no trace was found for them. And the stone that struck the image became a great mountain and filled the whole earth.

[36]This *is* the dream; and we will tell the meaning of it before the king. [37]You, O king, *are* the king of kings. For the God of Heaven has given you the kingdom, the power, and the strength, and the honor. [38]And wherever the sons of men, the animals of the field, and the birds of the sky dwell, He has given *them* into your hand, and has made you ruler over them all. You *are* the head of gold. [39]And in your place shall arise another kingdom lower than yours, and another third kingdom of bronze, which shall rule in all the earth. [40]And the fourth kingdom shall be *as* strong as iron. Inasmuch as iron crushes and smashes all things, and as the iron that shatters all these, it will crush and shatter. [41]And as to that you saw, the feet and the toes, shall be partly of potters' clay and partly of

רֵאשֵׁהּ דִּי־דְהַב טָב חֲדוֹהִי וּדְרָעוֹהִי דִּי כְסַף מְעוֹהִי
its belly ;silver (were) of its and arms its breast ,fine gold of head (was)

33 וְיַרְכָתֵהּ דִּי נְחָשׁ׃ שָׁקוֹהִי דִּי פַרְזֶל רַגְלוֹהִי מִנְּהוֹן דִּי
of partly feet its (were) ;iron of legs its (were) ;bronze of its and thighs

34 פַרְזֶל וּמִנְּהוֹן דִּי חֲסַף׃ חָזֵה הֲוַיְתָ עַד דִּי הִתְגְּזֶרֶת אֶבֶן
a stone cut was out until You continued seeing .clay of and partly iron

דִּי־לָא בִידַיִן וּמְחָת לְצַלְמָא עַל־רַגְלוֹהִי דִּי פַרְזְלָא וְחַסְפָּא
clay and iron of feet its on the image which struck ,hands without

35 וְהַדֵּקֶת הִמּוֹן׃ בֵּאדַיִן דָּקוּ כַחֲדָה פַּרְזְלָא חַסְפָּא נְחָשָׁא
the bronze the clay the ,iron together were crushed Then .them and crushed

כַּסְפָּא וְדַהֲבָא וַהֲווֹ כְּעוּר מִן־אִדְּרֵי־קַיִט וּנְשָׂא הִמּוֹן רוּחָא
the wind them And away took .summer the of floors threshing the chaff like and became the gold and ;silver the

וְכָל־אֲתַר לָא־הִשְׁתְּכַח לְהוֹן וְאַבְנָא ׀ דִּי־מְחָת לְצַלְמָא
the image struck that the But stone for .them found was not trace any so that

36 הֲוָת לְטוּר רַב וּמְלָת כָּל־אַרְעָא׃ דְּנָה חֶלְמָא וּפִשְׁרֵהּ
its and meaning the ;dream This (is) the .earth whole filled and great a mountain became

37 נֵאמַר קֳדָם־מַלְכָּא׃ אַנְתָּה מַלְכָּא מֶלֶךְ מַלְכַיָּא דִּי אֱלָהּ
the of God for ,kings the of king the ,king O (are) ,You .king the before will we tell

38 שְׁמַיָּא מַלְכוּתָא חִסְנָא וְתָקְפָּא וִיקָרָא יְהַב־לָךְ׃ וּבְכָל־
where- And .you to has given the and honor the and strength the ,power the ,kingdom Heaven

דִּי דָאְרִין בְּנֵי־אֲנָשָׁא חֵיוַת בָּרָא וְעוֹף־שְׁמַיָּא יְהַב בִּידָךְ
your into ,hand He given has the or ,sky of birds the ,field of animals the ,men of sons the dwells ever

39 וְהַשְׁלְטָךְ בְּכָלְּהוֹן אַנְתָּה הוּא רֵאשָׁה דִּי דַהֲבָא׃ וּבָתְרָךְ
in And place your .gold of head that You (are) of all .them over has and rule you made

תְּקוּם מַלְכוּ אָחֳרִי אֲרַעא מִנָּךְ וּמַלְכוּ תְלִיתָיָא אָחֳרִי דִּי
of another third and kingdom than ,yours lower another kingdom shall arise

40 נְחָשָׁא דִּי תִשְׁלַט בְּכָל־אַרְעָא׃ וּמַלְכוּ רְבִיעָיָא תֶּהֱוֵא
be shall the fourth And kingdom the .earth in all rule shall which ,bronze

תַקִּיפָה כְּפַרְזְלָא כָּל־קֳבֵל דִּי פַרְזְלָא מְהַדֵּק וְחָשֵׁל כֹּלָּא
all ;things and smashes crushes iron much as (as) in ,iron as strong (as)

41 וּכְפַרְזְלָא דִּי־מְרָעַע כָּל־אִלֵּין תַּדִּק וְתֵרֹעַ׃ וְדִי־חֲזַיְתָה
you ,saw as And that and .shatter will it crush ,these all shatters that like and iron the

רַגְלַיָּא וְאֶצְבְּעָתָא מִנְּהֵן חֲסַף דִּי־פֶחָר וּמִנְּהֵן פַּרְזֶל
,iron and of partly (the) potter of clay partly of the and toes the feet

iron, *the* kingdom shall be divided. But there shall be in it the strength of iron, because you saw the iron mixed with clay of the potter. [42]And *as* the toes of the feet *were* partly of iron and partly of clay, *so* the kingdom shall be partly strong and partly fragile. [43]And as you saw the iron mixed with the clay of the clay, they shall be mixed with the seed of men. But they shall not adhere to one another, even as iron does not mix with clay.

[44]And in the days of these kings, the God of Heaven shall set up a kingdom which shall never be destroyed. And the kingdom shall not be left to other people. It shall break in pieces and destroy all these kingdoms, and it shall stand forever. [45]Because you saw that the stone was cut out of the mountain without hands, and that it broke the iron, the bronze, the clay, the silver, and the gold in pieces; the great God has made known to the king what shall occur after this. And the dream *is* certain, and the meaning of it is trustworthy.

[46]Then king Nebuchadnezzar fell on his face and worshiped Daniel. And he commanded an offering, even to offer incense to him. [47]The king answered Daniel and said, Your God truly *is* a God of gods and a Lord of kings, and a Revealer of secrets, since you could reveal this secret. [48]Then the king made Daniel great, and gave many great gifts to him. And

1934 6523 5326 1934 6386 4437
מַלְכוּ פְלִיגָה תֶּהֱוֵה וּמִן־נִצְבְּתָא דִּי־פַרְזְלָא לֶהֱוֵא־בַהּ
in shall there the of the But .be shall divided (the)
,it be iron strength of kingdom

677 2635 2635 6151 6523 2370 6903 3606
42 כָּל־קֳבֵל דִּי חֲזַיְתָה פַּרְזְלָא מְעָרַב בַּחֲסַף טִינָא׃ וְאֶצְבְּעָת
the (as) And the with mixed iron the saw you because
of toes .clay of clay

1934 4437 7118 2635 4480 6523 4480 7271
רַגְלַיָּא מִנְּהֵין פַּרְזֶל וּמִנְּהֵין חֲסַף מִן־קְצָת מַלְכוּתָא תֶּהֱוֵה
be shall the partly (so) ,clay and iron partly feet the
kingdom of partly of (were)

6151 6523 2370/1768 8406 1934 4480 8624
43 תַקִּיפָא וּמִנַּהּ תֶּהֱוֵא תְבִירָה׃ דִּי חֲזַית פַּרְזְלָא מְעָרַב
mixed iron the saw you And .fragile shall it and strong
as ,be partly

1690 3809 606 2234 1934 6151 2635 2635
בַּחֲסַף טִינָא מִתְעָרְבִין לֶהֱוֺן בִּזְרַע אֲנָשָׁא וְלָא־לֶהֱוֺן דָּבְקִין
shall they But .men the with be shall they the with
adhere not of seed mixed clay of clay

2635 6151 3809 6523 1888 1836 5979 1836
דְּנָה עִם־דְּנָה הָא־כְדִי פַרְזְלָא לָא מִתְעָרַב עִם־חַסְפָּא׃
the with mix does not iron the as even ,another to one
.clay

4437 8064 426 6966 581 4430 3118
44 וּבְיוֹמֵיהוֹן דִּי מַלְכַיָּא אִנּוּן יְקִים אֱלָהּ שְׁמַיָּא מַלְכוּ דִּי
which a Heaven the shall ,these kings of the in And
kingdom of God up set days

7662 3809 321 5922 4437 2255 3809 5957
לְעָלְמִין לָא תִתְחַבַּל וּמַלְכוּתָה לְעַם אָחֳרָן לָא תִשְׁתְּבִק
be shall not another to the And be shall not forever
.left peoples kingdom .destroyed

5957 6966 1932 4437 459 3606 5487 1855
תַּדִּק וְתָסֵיף כָּל־אִלֵּין מַלְכְוָתָא וְהִיא תְּקוּם לְעָלְמַיָּא׃
forever shall and ,kingdoms these all make and will It
stand it of end an crush

3028 3809 69 1505 2906 2370 6903 3606
45 כָּל־קֳבֵל דִּי־חֲזַיְתָ דִּי מִטּוּרָא אִתְגְּזֶרֶת אֶבֶן דִּי־לָא בִידַיִן
,hands without (the) cut was the of out that you Because
stone mountain saw

7229 426 1722 3701 2635 5174 6523 1855
וְהַדֶּקֶת פַּרְזְלָא נְחָשָׁא חַסְפָּא כַּסְפָּא וְדַהֲבָא אֱלָהּ רַב
great (the) the and the the the the it that and
God —gold ,silver clay ,bronze ,iron crushed

2493 3330 1836 1934 4101 4430 3046
הוֹדַע לְמַלְכָּא מָה דִּי לֶהֱוֵא אַחֲרֵי דְנָה וְיַצִּיב חֶלְמָא
the cer- And .this after shall what the to made has
dream (is) tain happen king known

5308 5020 4430 116 6591 540
46 וּמְהֵימַן פִּשְׁרֵהּ׃ בֵּאדַיִן מַלְכָּא נְבוּכַדְנֶצַּר נְפַל
fell Nebuchadnezzar King Then its trust- and
.meaning worthy

5260 560 5208 4541 5457 1841 600 5922
עַל־אַנְפּוֹהִי וּלְדָנִיֵּאל סְגִד וּמִנְחָה וְנִיחֹחִין אֲמַר לְנַסָּכָה
offer to he and an and ,worshiped Daniel and his on
commanded incense ,offering ,face

426 1768 7287 500 1841 4630 6032
47 לֵהּ׃ עָנֵה מַלְכָּא לְדָנִיֵּאל וְאָמַר מִן־קְשֹׁט דִּי אֱלָהֲכוֹן
,God your truth Of ,said and Daniel The answered to
king .him

1541 3202 7328 1541 4430 4756 416 426
הוּא אֱלָהּ אֱלָהִין וּמָרֵא מַלְכִין וְגָלֵה רָזִין דִּי יְכֵלְתָּ לְמִגְלֵא
to you since ,secrets a and ,kings Lord and gods a He
reveal able were of Revealer of of God (is)

7260 4979 7236 1841 4430 116 1836 7328
48 רָזָא דְנָה׃ אֱדַיִן מַלְכָּא לְדָנִיֵּאל רַבִּי וּמַתְּנָן רַבְרְבָן
great gifts and made Daniel king the Then .this secret
,great

he made him ruler over all the province of Babylon, and chief of the prefects over all the wise men of Babylon.

[49]And Daniel asked of the king, and he set Shadrach, Meshach, and Abednego over the affairs of the province of Babylon. But Daniel *sat* in the gate of the king.

CHAPTER 3

[1]Nebuchadnezzar the king made an image of gold, whose height *was* sixty cubits; its breadth, six cubits. He set it up in the plain of Dura, in the province of Babylon. [2]Then Nebuchadnezzar the king sent to gather the satraps, the prefects, the governors, the counselors, the treasurers, the judges, the justices; and all the officials of the provinces *were ordered* to come to the dedication of the image that Nebuchadnezzar the king had set up. [3]Then were gathered the satraps, the prefects, the governors, the counselors, the treasurers, the judges, the justices, and all the officials of the provinces, to the dedication of the image that Nebuchadnezzar the king had set up. And they stood before the image that Nebuchadnezzar had set up. [4]Then the herald cried with strength, To you it is commanded, O peoples, nations, and languages; [5]at the time you hear the sound of the horn, the pipe, zither, the lyre, harp, bagpipe, and all kinds of music, you shall fall down and worship the golden image that Nebuchadnezzar the king has set up.

5460 895 4083 3606 5922 7981 3052 7690
שַׂגִּיאָן יְהַב־לֵהּ וְהַשְׁלְטֵהּ עַל כָּל־מְדִינַת בָּבֶל וְרַב־סִגְנִין
and Babylon the all over made he And to gave many
Chief-Prefect of province ruler him .him

5922 4483 4430 1156 1841 895 2445 3606 5922
49 עַל כָּל־חַכִּימֵי בָבֶל׃ וְדָנִיֵּאל בְּעָא מִן־מַלְכָּא וּמַנִּי עַל
over he and the of asked Then .Babylon wise the all over
appointed king Daniel of men

1841 5663 4336 7715 895 4083 5673
עֲבִידְתָּא דִּי מְדִינַת בָּבֶל לְשַׁדְרַךְ מֵישַׁךְ וַעֲבֵד נְגוֹ וְדָנִיֵּאל
Daniel But and Meshach ,Shadrach ,Babylon the of the
(sat) .Abednego of province business

4430 8651
בִּתְרַע מַלְכָּא׃
the the in
.king of gate

CAP. III ג

CHAPTER 3

8361 520 7314 1722 6755 5648 4430 5020
1 נְבוּכַדְנֶצַּר מַלְכָּא עֲבַד צְלֵם דִּי־דְהַב רוּמֵהּ אַמִּין שִׁתִּין
,sixty (was) its ,gold of an made king the Nebuchadnezzar
cubits height image

895 4083 1757 1236 6966 8353 520 6613
פְּתָיֵהּ אַמִּין שִׁת אֲקִימֵהּ בְּבִקְעַת דּוּרָא בִּמְדִינַת בָּבֶל׃
.Babylon the in ,Dura the in set He .six cubits its
of province of plain up it breadth

5460 324 3673 7972 4430 5020
2 וּנְבוּכַדְנֶצַּר מַלְכָּא שְׁלַח לְמִכְנַשׁ לַאֲחַשְׁדַּרְפְּנַיָּא סִגְנַיָּא
the the gather to sent the Nebuchadnezzar
,prefects ,satraps together king

7984 3606 8614 1884 1411 148 6347
וּפַחֲוָתָא אֲדַרְגָּזְרַיָּא גְדָבְרַיָּא דְּתָבְרַיָּא תִּפְתָּיֵא וְכֹל שִׁלְטֹנֵי
officials the and the the the the the and
of all ,magistrates ,judges ,treasurers ,counselors ;governors

5020 6966 6755 2597 858 4083
מְדִינָתָא לְמֵתֵא לַחֲנֻכַּת צַלְמָא דִּי הֲקֵים נְבוּכַדְנֶצַּר
Nebuchadnezzar set had that the the to come to the
up image of dedication ,provinces

6347 5460 324 3673 116 4430
3 מַלְכָּא׃ בֵּאדַיִן מִתְכַּנְּשִׁין אֲחַשְׁדַּרְפְּנַיָּא סִגְנַיָּא וּפַחֲוָתָא
the the the were Then .king the
governors ,prefects ,satraps gathered

4083 7984 8614 1884 1411 148
אֲדַרְגָּזְרַיָּא גְדָבְרַיָּא דְתָבְרַיָּא תִּפְתָּיֵא וְכֹל שִׁלְטֹנֵי מְדִינָתָא
the the and the the the the
provinces of officials all ,magistrates ,judges ,treasurers ,counselors

6903 6966 4430 5020 6966 6755 2597
לַחֲנֻכַּת צַלְמָא דִּי הֲקֵים נְבוּכַדְנֶצַּר מַלְכָּא וְקָאֲמִין לָקֳבֵל
before they and ;king the Nebuchadnezzar had that the dedi- to
stood up set image's cation

2429 7123 3744 5020 6966 6755
4 צַלְמָא דִּי הֲקֵים נְבוּכַדְנֶצַּר׃ וְכָרוֹזָא קָרֵא בְחָיִל לְכוֹן
To with shouted the Then .Nebuchadnezzar had that the
you strength herald up set image

7032 8088 5732 3966 524 5972 560
5 אָמְרִין עַמְמַיָּא אֻמַּיָּא וְלִשָּׁנַיָּא׃ בְּעִדָּנָא דִּי־תִשְׁמְעוּן קָל
the hear you that the at and nations O com- is it
of sound time ;languages ,peoples manded

5481 6460 5443 7030 4953 7162
קַרְנָא מַשְׁרוֹקִיתָא קִיתָרֹס שַׂבְּכָא פְּסַנְתֵּרִין סוּמְפֹּנְיָה
,bagpipe ,harp the ,zither ,pipe the the
lyre ,horn

6966 1722 6755 5457 5308 2170 2178 3606
וְכֹל זְנֵי זְמָרָא תִּפְּלוּן וְתִסְגְּדוּן לְצֶלֶם דַּהֲבָא דִּי הֲקֵים
set has that golden the worship and shall you ,music kinds and
up image down fall of all

[6]And whoever does not fall down and worship, at that moment they will be thrown into the middle of a burning, fiery furnace. [7]Then at that time, when all the people heard the sound of the horn, the pipe, zither, the lyre, harp, and all kinds of music, all the peoples, the nations, and the languages fell down, worshiping the golden image that Nebuchadnezzar the king had set up.

[8]Then at that time men, Chaldeans, came near and slandered the Jews. [9]They answered and said to king Nebuchadnezzar, O king, live forever! [10]You, O king, have made a decree that every man who shall hear the sound of the horn, the pipe, zither, the lyre, harp, and the bagpipe, and all kinds of music, shall fall down and worship the golden image. [11]And whoever does not fall down and worship, he should be thrown into the middle of a burning, fiery furnace. [12]There are men, Jews, whom you have set over the business of the province of Babylon: Shadrach, Meshach, and Abednego. These men, O king, do not pay attention to you. They do not serve your gods, or worship the golden image which you have set up.

[13]Then Nebuchadnezzar in anger and wrath commanded to bring Shadrach, Meshach, and Abednego. Then they brought these men before the king. [14]Nebuchadnezzar spoke

8160 5457 5358 3809/4479 4430 5020
6 נבוכדנצר מלכא: ומן־די־לא יפל ויסגד בה־שעתא
moment At and does not who- And .king the Nebuchadnezzar
that ,worship down fall ever

1836 6903 3606 3345 5135 861 7412
7 יתרמא לגוא־אתון נורא יקדתא: כל־קבל דנה בה
at ,Thereupon .burning fire a amidst will be
that of furnace cast

4953 7162 7032 5972 3606 8088 1768 2166
זמנא כדי שמעין כל־עממיא קל קרנא משרוקיתא
pipe the the the the all heard when ,time
horn of sound peoples

5972 3606 5308 2170 2178 3606 64:60 5443 7030
קיתרס שבכא פסנתרין וכל זני זמרא נפלין כל־עממיא
the all fell ,music kinds and ,harp the ,zither
,peoples down of all ,lyre

5020 6966 17:22 67:55 5457 39:61 524
אמיא ולשניא סגדין לצלם דהבא די הקים נבוכדנצר
Nebuchad- had that golden the worshiping the and the
nezzar up set image languages ,nations

3778 1400 7127 21:66 1836 6903 3606 4430
8 מלכא: כל־קבל דנה בה־זמנא קרבו גברין כשדאין
,Chaldeans ,men came time at ,Thereupon the
near that .king

5020 560 6032 3062 7170 399
9 ואכלו קרציהון די יהודיא: ענו ואמרין לנבוכדנצר
Nebuchad- to said and They .Jews the of bits the and
nezzar answered chewed

2942 7761 4430 607 2418 5957 4430 4430
10 מלכא מלכא לעלמין חיי: אנתה מלכא שמת טעם
a have ,king O ,You !live forever ,king O the
decree set ,King

7030 4953 7162 7032 8088 606 3606
די־כל־אנש די ישמע קל קרנא משרקיתא קיתרס
zither ,pipe the the the shall who man every that
horn of sound hear

6755 5457 5308 2170 2178 3606 54:81 6460 5443
שבכא פסנתרין וסיפניא וכל זני זמרא יפל ויסגד לצלם
the and fall shall ,music kinds and the and ,harp ,lyre the
image worship down of all ,bagpipe

5135 861 7412 5457 5308 3809 4479 1722
11 דהבא: ומן־די־לא יפל ויסגד יתרמא לגוא־אתון נורא
fire a amidst be shall he and fall does not who- And .golden
of furnace thrown ,worship down ever

5673 5922 4483 3487 1400 383 3345
12 יקדתא: איתי גברין יהודאין די־מנית יתהון על־עבידת
the over them you whom ,Jewish ,men There .burning
of business set have are

3809 479 1400 5665 4336 7715 89:5 4083
מדינת בבל שדרך מישך ועבד נגו גבריא אלך לא
not Those men and Meshach ,Shadrach :Babylon pro- the
.Abednego of vince

67:55 6399 38:09 426 2942 44:30 7760
שמו עליך מלכא טעם לאלהיך לא פלחין ולצלם
the and do they not your ;attention ,king O ,you to do
image ,serve gods attend

5020 116 5457 38:09 6966 1722
13 דהבא די הקימת לא סגדין: באדין נבוכדנצר
,Nebuchadnezzar Then do they not have you which golden
.worship up set

116 5665 4336 7715 858 560 2528 7266
ברגז וחמא אמר להיתיה לשדרך מישך ועבד נגו באדין
Then .Abednego ,Meshach ,Shadrach bring to com- and in
manded wrath anger

560 5020 6032 4430 6925 858 479 1400
14 גבריא אלך היתיו קדם מלכא: ענה נבוכדנצר ואמר
and Nebuchadnezzar an- .king the before they those men
said swered brought

and said to them, *Is it* true, O Shadrach, Meshach, and Abednego? Do you not serve my gods, nor worship the golden image which I have set up? [15]Now if you are ready, at the time you hear the sound of the horn, the pipe, zither, the lyre, harp, and bagpipe, and all kinds of music, fall down and worship the image which I have made. But if you do not worship, in that moment you shall be thrown into the middle of a burning, fiery furnace. And who *is* that god who shall deliver you out of my hand? [16]Shadrach, Meshach, and Abednego answered and said to the king, O Nebuchadnezzar, we have no need to return a word to you on this matter. [17]If it is *so that* our God whom we serve is able to deliver us from the burning, fiery furnace, then He will deliver out of your hand, O king. [18]And if not, let it be known to you, O king, that we will not serve your gods, or worship the golden image which you have set up.

[19]Then Nebuchadnezzar was filled with wrath, and the form of his face was changed against Shadrach, Meshach, and Abednego. He spoke and commanded to heat the furnace seven times more than it was usual to heat it. [20]And he commanded mighty men of valor, who *were* in his army, to tie up Shadrach, Meshach, and Abednego, to throw *them* into the burning, fiery furnace. [21]Then these men were tied up in

383 3809 426 =5665= 4336 7715 6656
להון הצדא שדרך מישך ועבד נגו לאלהי לא איתיכון
are you not gods my and ,Meshach O it Is to
Abednego ,Shadrach true ,them

2006 3705 3457 38,09 6966 1722 67,55 6399
15 פלחין ולצלם דהבא די הקימת לא סגדין׃ כען הן
if Now are you not have I which golden the and ,serving
?worshiping up set image

7162 7032 8088 5732 6263 383
איתיכון עתידין די בעדנא די־תשמעון קל קרנא
,horn the the hear you that the at ,ready are you
of sound time

2178 3606 54 81 6460 5443 7030 4953
משרוקיתא קיתרס שבכא פסנתרין וסומפניה וכל ׀ זני
kinds and and ,harp ,lyre the ,zither pipe the
of all bagpipe

54 57 2006 5648 6755 5457 5308 2170
זמרא תפלון ותסגדון לצלמא די־עבדת והן לא תסגדון
do you not But have I which the and fall ,music
,worship if .made image worship down

4479 3345 5135 861 7411 8160
בה־שעתא תתרמון לגוא־אתון נורא יקדתא ומן־הוא
(is) And .burning fire a amidst shall you moment in
that who of furnace cast be that

=5665= 4336 7715 6032 3028 7804 426
16 אלה די־ישיזבנכון מן־ידי׃ ענו שדרך מישך ועבד נגו
and Meshach ,Shadrach an- my out deliver shall who god
Abednego swered ?hand of you

1836 5922 586 2818 5020 4430 560
ואמרין למלכא נבוכדנצר לא־חשחין אנחנה על־דנה
this on we (have) not Nebuchad- O the to said and
,matter need ,nezzar ,king

6399 586 426 2006 8421 6600
17 פתגם להתבותך׃ הן איתי אלהנא די־אנחנא פלחין
serve we whom God our is it If return to word a
(that) .you to

4430 3028 3345 5135 861 7804 3202
יכל לשיזבותנא מן־אתון נורא יקדתא ומן־ידך מלכא
,king O from then burning fire the from us deliver to is
,hand your of furnace able

3809 426 44,30 3046 3809 2006 7804
18 ישיזב׃ והן לא ידיע להוא־לך מלכא די לאלהיך לא־
not gods your that ,king O to be it let ,not But will He
,you known if .(us) deliver

5457 38,09 6966 1722 67,55 6399 383
איתנא פלחין ולצלם דהבא די הקימת לא נסגד׃
will we not have you which golden the and ,serve will we
.worship up set image

600 67,55 2528 4391 5020 116
19 באדין נבוכדנצר התמלי חמא וצלם אנפוהי
face his the and ,wrath was Nebuchadnezzar Then
of expression with filled

228 560 6032 =5665= 4336 7715 59,22 8133
אשתנו על־שדרך מישך ועבד נגו ענה ואמר למזא
heat to and He and Meshach ,Shadrach against was
directed answered Abednego changed

1401 1400 228 2370 1768 5922 7655 2298
20 לאתונא חד־שבעה על די חזה למזיה׃ ולגברין גברי־
mighty men And heat to was it than more seven times the
of .it usual furnace

=5665= 4336 7715 37,29 560 2429 242,9
חיל די בחילה אמר לכפתה לשדרך מישך ועבד נגו
nego and Meshach ,Shadrach bind to he his in who valor
Abed- ordered ,army (were)

37,29 479 1400 116 3345 5735 861 7411
21 למרמא לאתון נורא יקדתא׃ באדין גבריא אלך כפתו
were those men Then .burning fire the into throw to
bound of furnace (them)

their slippers, their tunics, and their mantles, and their *other* clothes, and were thrown into the middle of the burning, fiery furnace. [22]Then, because the king's command was urgent, and the furnace exceedingly hot, the flame of the fire killed those men who took up Shadrach, Meshach, and Abednego. [23]And these three men, Shadrach, Meshach, and Abednego, fell down bound into the middle of the burning, fiery furnace. [24]Then Nebuchadnezzar the king was amazed. And he rose up in haste; he spoke and said to his royal officials, Did we not throw three men bound into the middle of the fire? They replied and said to the king, True, O king. [25]He answered and said, Lo, I see four men loose, walking in the middle of the fire, and there is no harm among them. And the form of the fourth is like a son of *the* gods.

[26]Then Nebuchadnezzar came near to the door of the burning, fiery furnace. He answered and said, Shadrach, Meshach, and Abednego, servants of the most high God, come forth and come *here*. Then Shadrach, Meshach, and Abednego came out of the middle of the fire. [27]And the satraps, the prefects, the governors, and the king's officials assembled, *and* saw these men *on whose* bodies the fire had no power, and the hair of their head was not scorched, nor were their slippers changed, nor had the smell of fire clung on

7411 3837 3737 6361 5622
בסרבליהון פטישיהון וכרבלתהון ולבושיהון ורמיו
were and thrown | their and clothes (other) | their and turbans | their tunics | slippers their in

22 4406 4480 1836 6903 3605 3345 5135 861 1459
לגוא־אתון נורא יקדתא׃ כל־קבל דנה מן־די מלת
word | because | ,Thereupon | .burning | fire | the of furnace | amidst

1768 479 1400 3493 228 861 2685 4430
מלכא מחצפה ואתונא אזה יתירה גבריא אלך די
who | those | men | ,exceedingly | was heated | the and furnace | ,urgent was | the king's

1768 7631 1994 6992 5665 4336 7715 5267
הסקו לשדרך מישך ועבד נגו קטל המון שביבא די
of | flame the | them | killed | and Abednego | Meshach | ,Shadrach | up took

23 5665 4336 7715 8532 479 1400 5135
נורא׃ וגבריא אלך תלתהון שדרך מישך ועבד נגו
and Abednego | Meshach | ,Shadrach | three the ,them of | ,those | men But | .fire the

24 116 3729 3345 5135 861 1459 5308
נפלו לגוא־אתון־נורא יקדתא מכפתין׃ אדין
Then | .bound | burning | fire | the of furnace | amidst | fell down

560 6032 927 6965 8429 4430 5020
נבוכדנצר מלכא תוה וקם בהתבהלה ענה ואמר
said and | he answered | ;haste in | he and up rose | was ;amazed | king the | Nebuchad-nezzar

3729 5135 1459 7412 8532 1400 3809 1907
להדברוהי הלא גברין תלתה רמינא לגוא־נורא מכפתין
?bound | the fire | the into of midst | we did throw | three | men | Not | royal his to officials

25 576 1888 560 6032 4430 3330 4430 560 6032
ענין ואמרין למלכא יציבא מלכא׃ ענה ואמר הא־אנה
I | ,Behold | ,said and | He answered | .king O | ,Certainly | the to ,king | said and | They answered

3809 2257 1459 1981 8271 702 1400 2370
חזה גברין ארבעה שרין מהלכין בגוא־נורא וחבל לא־
not | and injury | the ,fire | the in of midst | walking | loose | four | men | see

426 1247 1821 7244 1768 7299 383
איתי בהון ורוה די רביעיא דמה לבר־אלהין׃
.gods (the) | a of son | like is | the fourth | of | the and look | among ;them | there is

26 6032 3345 5135 861 8651 5020 7127 116
באדין קרב נבוכדנצר לתרע אתון נורא יקדתא ענה
an-swered | he ;burning | fire | fur-nace | the of | the to of door | Nebuchadnezzar | drew near | Then

5943 426 1768 5649 5665 4336 7715 560
ואמר שדרך מישך ועבד־נגו עבדוהי די־אלהא עליא
most ,high | God the | of | servants | and ,Abednego | ,Meshach | ,Shadrach | and ,said

1459 5665 4336 7715 5312 858 5312
פקו ואתו באדין נפקין שדרך מישך ועבד נגו מן־גוא
from amidst | and Abednego | Meshach | ,Shadrach | came out | Then | and .come | come out

27 1907 6347 5460 324 3673 5135
נורא׃ ומתכנשין אחשדרפניא סגניא ופחותא והדברי
royal and officials | the ,governors | the ,prefects | the ,satraps | Then gathered | the .fire

1655 5135 7981 3809 1768 479 1400 2370 4430
מלכא חזין לגבריא אלך די לא־שלט נורא בגשמהון
their over ,body | the fire | had power | not | those | men | saw | the ,king's

7382 8133 3809 5622 2761 3809 7217 8177
ושער ראשהון לא התחרך וסרבליהון לא שנו וריח
the and of smell | were ,changed | not | slippers their | and was ,scorched | not | their head | the and of hair

them. [28]Nebuchadnezzar spoke and said, Blessed *be* the God of Shadrach, Meshach, and Abednego, who has sent His Angel and has delivered His servants who trusted in Him, and have changed the king's words, and have given their bodies that they might not serve nor worship any god except their own God. [29]And a decree is given by me, that every people, nation, and language who speak anything amiss about the God of Shadrach, Meshach, and Abednego, he will be made into *mere* members and his house shall be made an outhouse. Because there is no other God who is able to deliver like this. [30]Then the king made Shadrach, Meshach, and Abednego prosper in the province of Babylon.

CHAPTER 4

[1]The king, Nebuchadnezzar, to all the peoples, the nations and the tongues that dwell in all the earth: Your peace be multiplied. [2]It seemed good before me to declare the signs and the wonders that the most high God has done with me. [3]How great *are* His signs! And how mighty *are* His wonders! His kingdom *is* an everlasting kingdom, and His dominion *is* from generation to generation.

426 1289 560 5020 60 32 5709 3809 5135
28 נור לא עדת בהון: ענה נבוכדנצר ואמר בריך אלההון
God the Blessed ,said and Nebuchad- answered on did not fire
be nezzar ,them cling

7804 4398 797 2 1768 5665 4336 7715 1768
די־שדרך מישך ועבד נגו די־שלח מלאכה ושיזב
has and His has who and Meshach ,Shadrach of
delivered angel sent ,Abednego

3052 81:33 4430 4406 5922 7365 5649
לעבדוהי די התרחצו עלוהי ומלת מלכא שניו ויהבו
have and have the and ,Him in trusted who His
given changed king's word servants

3861 426 36 06 5457 3809 6399 3809 1768 1655
גשמיהון די לא־יפלחון ולא־יסגדון לכל־אלה להן
except god any might they and they not that their
worship not serve might bodies

1768 3961 524 597 4 3606 1768 2942 7760 4480 426
29 לאלההון: ומני שים טעם די כל־עם אמה ולשן די־
who and nation peo- every that a is by And own their
language ,ple ,decree given me .God

5665 4336 7715 1768 426 5922 7955 560
יאמר שלה על־אלההון די־שדרך מישך ועבד נגוא
and Meshach ,Shadrach of the about anything speaks
,Abednego God amiss

383 38 09 6903 3606 7739 5122 1005 5648 1917 .told I
הדמין יתעבד וביתה נולי ישתוה כל־קבל די לא איתי
there not since be will out- an his and will he (from)
is ,made house house ,taken be limbs

4430 116 1836 5338 3202 1768 321 426
30 אלה אחרן די־יכל להצלה כדנה: באדין מלכא
king the Then .this like deliver to able is who another God

895 4083 5665 4336 7715 6744
הצלח לשדרך מישך ועבד נגו במדינת בבל:
.Babylon the in and Meshach ,Shadrach made
of province Abednego prosper

1753 3961 524 59 72 360 6 4430 5020
31 נבוכדנצר מלכא לכל־עממיא אמיא ולשניא די־דארין
dwell that the and the the all to ,king the Nebuchad-
languages nations ,peoples nezzar

5974 5647 1768 8540 852 7680 8000 772 3606
32 בכל־ארעא שלמכון ישגא: אתיא ותמהיא די עבד עמי
with has that the and The be Your the in
me done wonders signs .increased peace :earth all

72 :60 4101 852 2324 6925 8232 5943/2126
33 אלהא עליא שפר קדמי להחויה: אתוהי כמה רברבין
great How His .declare to before seemed it most the
!(are) signs me good high God

7985 5957 4437 4437 8624 8540
ותמהוהי כמה תקיפין מלכותה מלכות עלם ושלטנה
His and ever- an king- His mighty how His And
(is) dominion ,lasting kingdom (is) dom !(are) wonders

1859 1859 5974
עם־דר ודר:
to gen- from
.generation eration

CAP. IV ד

CHAPTER 4

[4]I, Nebuchadnezzar, was at ease in my house, and flourishing in my palace. [5]I saw a dream and it terrified me, and *the* thoughts on my bed and the visions of my head troubled

2493 1965 7487 1005 1961 7954 5020 576
1
2 אנה נבוכדנצר שלה הוית בביתי ורענן בהיכלי: חלם
a .palace my in flourish- my in was ease at Nebuchadnezzar ,I
dream ing ,house

927 7217 2376 4903 2031 1763 2372
חזית וידחלנני והרהרין על־משכבי וחזוי ראשי יבהלנני:
troubled my the and bed my on (the) and it and saw I
.me head of visions conceptions ,me terrified

me. [6]So I made a decree to bring in all the wise men of Babylon before me, that they might make known to me the meaning of the dream. [7]Then the horoscopists, the conjurers, the Chaldeans, and the fortune-tellers came in. And I told the dream before them, but they did not make its meaning known to me.

[8]But at last Daniel came in before me, whose name *was* Belteshazzar, according to the name of my god, and in whom *is* the spirit of the holy gods. And I told the dream before him, *saying,* [9]O Belteshazzar, master of the horoscopists, because I know that the spirit of the holy gods *is* in you, and no secret troubles you, tell me the visions of my dream that I have seen, and its meaning. [10]As to the visions of my head on my bed; I was looking, and, behold, a tree *was* in the middle of the earth. And its height *was* great. [11]The tree became great and strong, and its height reached to the sky; and its appearance to the end of the earth. [12]Its leaves *were* beautiful, and its fruit plentiful, and food for all *was* in it. The animals of the field sought shade under it, and the birds of the sky dwelt in its branches; and all flesh was fed from it. [13]I was looking in the visions of my head on my bed. And, behold, a watcher, even a holy one, came down from Heaven. [14]He cried with might and said this: Cut down the tree, and cut off its branches. Shake off its leaves, and scatter its fruit. Let the animals flee from under it, and the birds *leave* its branches. [15]But leave the stump of its roots in the earth, even with a fetter of iron and bronze, in the grass of the field. And let it be wet with the dew of the

6591 895 2445 3606 6925 5954 2942 7760 4480
3 ומני שים טעם להנעלה קדמי לכל חכימי בבל די־פשר
mean- that Babylon wise the all before bring to a was by So
ing of men me in decree set me

3779 826 2749 5954 116 3046 2493
4 חלמא יהודענני׃ באדין עללין חרטמיא אשפיא כשדיא
the the horo- the came Then make they the
,Chaldeans ,conjurers ,scopists in .know me dream's

3046 3809 6591 6925 576 560 2493 1505
וגזריא וחלמא אמר אנה קדמיהון ופשרה לא־מהודעין
did they not its but before I told the and the and
known make meaning :them dream ,gazers

1096 8036 1841 6925 5922 318
5 לי׃ ועד אחרין על קדמי דניאל די־שמה בלטשאצר
,Belteshazzar name whose ,Daniel before came last But to
(was) me in at .me

6925 2493 430 7308 426 8036
כשם אלהי ודי רוח־אלהין קדישין בה וחלמא קדמוהי
him before the and in holy the the and and my by
dream ;him (is) gods of spirit ,god's name

7308 3046 576 2749 7229 1096 560
6 אמרת׃ בלטשאצר רב חרטמיא די ׀ אנה ידעת די רוח
the that knew I because horo- the chief ,Belteshazzar O :said I
of spirit ,scopists of

2493 2376 598 3809 7328 3606 6922 426
אלהין קדישין בך וכל־רז לא־אנס לך חזוי חלמי די־
that my the .you does not secret any in holy the
dream of visions baffle ,you (is) gods

1934 2370 4903 5922 7217 2376 560 6591 2370
7 חזית ופשרה אמר׃ וחזוי ראשי על־משכבי חזה הוית
,was I looking ,bed my on my the to As tell its and have I
head of visions .(me) meaning seen

8631 363 7236 7690 7314 772 1459 363 431
8 ואלו אילן בגוא ארעא ורומה שגיא׃ רבה אילנא ותקף
and The became (was) its and the the in a and
,strong tree great .great height ,earth of middle tree ,behold

6074 772 3606 5491 2379 8065 4291 7314
9 ורומה ימטא לשמיא וחזותה לסוף כל־ארעא׃ עפיה
Its the all the to its and the to reached its and
foliage .earth of end appearance ,sky height

2927 8460 3606 4203 7690 4 8209
שפיר ואנבה שגיא ומזון לכלא־בה תחתוהי תטלל ׀
sought it under in all For and ,abundant its and (was)
shade .it (was) .food fruit ,lovely

3606 2110 4480 8064 6853 1753 6056 1251 2423
חיות ברא ובענפוהי ידרון צפרי שמיא ומנה יתזין כל־
all was from and the birds the dwelt its in and the ani- The
fed it ,sky of branches ,field of mals

5894 431 4903 5922 7217 2376 1934 2370 1321
10 בשרא׃ חזה הוית בחזוי ראשי על־משכבי ואלו עיר
a ,lo and ,bed my on my the in was I looking .flesh
,watcher head of visions

363 1414/560 3652 2429 7123 5182 8064 4480 6922
11 וקדיש מן־שמיא נחת׃ קרא בחיל וכן אמר גדו אילנא
the Cut he and with He came Heaven from a even
tree down ,said thus ,might cried .down one holy

2423 5111 4 921 6074 5426 6056 7113
וקצצו ענפוהי אתרו עפיה ובדרו אנבה תנד חיותא מן־
from the Let its and its shake its cut and
animals flee .fruit scatter foliage off branches off

772 8330 6136 1297 6056 4480 6853 8479
12 תחתוהי וצפריא מן־ענפוהי׃ ברם עקר שרשוהי בארעא
the in its the But its from the and ,it under
earth roots of stump .branches birds

2920 1251 1883 5174 6523 613 7662
שבקו ובאסור די־פרזל ונחש בדתאא די ברא ובטל
with and the of the in and iron of with even ,leave
of dew the ,field grass ,bronze fetter a

heavens, and his portion *be* with the animals in the grass of the earth. [16]Let his heart be changed from man's, and let the heart of an animal be given to him. And let seven times pass over him. [17]This matter *is* by the decree of the watchers, and the command by the word of the holy ones; so that the living may know that the most High rules in the kingdom of men, and gives it to whomever He will; and *He* sets up over it the lowest of men. [18]I, Nebuchadnezzar, have seen this dream. Now you, O Belteshazzar, declare its meaning, since all the wise men of my kingdom are not able to reveal the meaning to me. But you *are* able, for the spirit of the holy gods *is* in you.

[19]Then Daniel, whose name *was* Belteshazzar, was stunned for one hour, and his thoughts troubled him. The king spoke and said, Belteshazzar, do not let the dream, or its meaning trouble you. Belteshazzar answered and said, My lord, the dream *is* to those who hate you, and its meaning *is* to your foes. [20]The tree that you saw, which became great and strong, whose height reached to the heavens, and its sight to all the earth; [21]and its leaves *being* beautiful, and its fruit plentiful; and food for all *being* in it; under which the animals of the field lived, and in its branches the birds of the sky had their home: [22]It *was* you, O king, for you have become great and strong. For your greatness has grown, and reaches to the heavens; and your rule *is* to the end of the earth.

13 שְׁמַיָּא יִצְטַבַּע וְעִם־חֵיוְתָא חֲלָקֵהּ בַּעֲשַׂב אַרְעָא׃ לִבְבֵהּ
3825 772 6215 2538 2423 5974 6647 8065
his heart | the ,earth | the in of grass | (be let) lot his | the animals | and with | him let ,wet be | the heaven

מִן־אֲנָשָׁא יְשַׁנּוֹן וּלְבַב חֵיוָא יִתְיְהִב לֵהּ וְשִׁבְעָה עִדָּנִין
5732 7655 3052 2423 3825 8133 606 4480
times | seven And | to .him | be let given | the beast | the and of heart | be Let ,changed | man's the (heart) | from

14 יַחְלְפוּן עֲלוֹהִי׃ בִּגְזֵרַת עִירִין פִּתְגָמָא וּמֵאמַר קַדִּישִׁין
6922 3983 6600 5894 1510 5922 2499
holy the (is) ones | (the) and of command | the ,word | the (is) watchers | the By of decree | .him over | pass let

שְׁאֶלְתָא עַד־דִּבְרַת דִּי יִנְדְּעוּן חַיַּיָּא דִּי־שַׁלִּיט עִלָּיָא
5943 7990 2417 3046 1701 7595
Most the High | (is) Master | that | the living | may know | that so | ,affair the

בְּמַלְכוּת אֲנָשָׁא וּלְמַן־דִּי יִצְבֵּא יִתְּנִנַּהּ וּשְׁפַל אֲנָשִׁים יְקִים
6966 606 8215 5415 6634 4479 606 4437
sets He up | men | the and of lowliest | gives He ,it | He ,wishes | to and whomever | ;men | king- the in of dom

15 עֲלַהּ׃ דְּנָה חֶלְמָא חֲזֵית אֲנָה מַלְכָּא נְבוּכַדְנֶצַּר וְאַנְתְּה
607 5020 4430 576 2370 2493 1836 5922
Now you | .Nebuchadnezzar | King | ,I | have seen | the dream | This (is) | .it over

בֵּלְטְשַׁאצַּר פִּשְׁרֵא אֱמַר כָּל־קֳבֵל דִּי כָּל־חַכִּימֵי
2445 3606 1760 6903 3606 560 6591 1096
wise the of men | all | much as in as | ,tell | its meaning | ,Belteshazzar O

מַלְכוּתִי לָא־יָכְלִין פִּשְׁרָא לְהוֹדָעֻתַנִי וְאַנְתְּה כָּהֵל דִּי
3546 607 3202 6591 3046 3202 3809 4437
for | are ,able | you But | known make to .me | the meaning | are able | not | my kingdom

16 רוּחַ־אֱלָהִין קַדִּישִׁין בָּךְ׃ אֱדַיִן דָּנִיֵּאל דִּי־שְׁמֵהּ בֵּלְטְשַׁאצַּר
1096 8036 1840 116 6922 426 7308
,Belteshazzar | name whose (was) | ,Daniel | Then | in .you | holy (is) | the gods | the of spirit

אֶשְׁתּוֹמַם כְּשָׁעָה חֲדָה וְרַעְיֹנֹהִי יְבַהֲלֻנֵּהּ עָנֵה מַלְכָּא וְאָמַר
560 4430 6032 2298 927 7476 2298 8160 8075
and ,said | The king | answered | troubled .him | his and thoughts | ,a | for moment | was stunned

בֵּלְטְשַׁאצַּר חֶלְמָא וּפִשְׁרֵא אַל־יְבַהֲלָךְ עָנֵה בֵלְטְשַׁאצַּר
1096 6032 927 409 6591 2493 1096
Belteshazzar | answered | let do .you trouble | not | its and ;meaning | the dream | ,Belteshazzar

17 וְאָמַר מָרִאי חֶלְמָא לְשָׂנְאָךְ וּפִשְׁרֵהּ לְעָרָךְ׃ אִילָנָא
363 6146 6591 8131 2493 4756 560
tree The | your to .adversaries | its and meaning | your to haters | the (be) dream | My ,lord | ,said and

דִּי חֲזַיְתָ דִּי רְבָה וּתְקִף וְרוּמֵהּ יִמְטֵא לִשְׁמַיָּא וַחֲזוֹתֵהּ
2379 8065 4291 7314 8631 7236 2370
its and appearance | the to sky | reached | whose height | and ,strong | became great | which you ,saw | that

18 לְכָל־אַרְעָא׃ וְעָפְיֵהּ שַׁפִּיר וְאִנְבֵּהּ שַׂגִּיא וּמָזוֹן לְכֹלָּא־
3606 4203 7690 4 8209 6074 772 3606
(was) all for | and food | (was) ,abundant | its and fruit | (was) ,lovely | its and foliage | the ;earth | all to

בֵהּ תְּחֹתוֹהִי תְּדוּר חֵיוַת בָּרָא וּבְעַנְפוֹהִי יִשְׁכְּנָן צִפְּרֵי
6853 7932 6056 1251 2423 1753 8460
the of birds | dwelt | its in and branches | the ,field | the of animals | dwelled | under which | ;it in

19 שְׁמַיָּא׃ אַנְתְּה־הוּא מַלְכָּא דִּי רְבַית וּתְקֵפְתְּ וּרְבוּתָךְ
7238 8631 7236 4430 607 8065
your for greatness | and ,strong | have you great became | for | ,king O | it (is) | You | .sky the

20 רְבָת וּמְטָת לִשְׁמַיָּא וְשָׁלְטָנָךְ לְסוֹף אַרְעָא׃ וְדִי חֲזָא
2370 772 5491 7985 8065 4291 7236
saw as | And as | .earth the | the to of end | your and dominion | ,sky the to | and reached | has grown

[23]And as the king saw a watcher and a holy one coming down from Heaven, and saying, Cut the tree down, and destroy it. Yet leave the stump of its roots in the earth, even with a fetter of iron and bronze in the grass of the field. And let him be wet with the dew of the heavens, and his portion *be* with the animals of the field, until seven times pass over him. [24]This *is* the meaning, O king, and this the decree of the Most High, which has come on my lord the king: [25]And you shall be driven from men, and your dwelling shall be with the animals of the field; and you shall be fed with the grass like oxen. And you shall be wet *with* the dew of the heavens, and seven times shall pass over you, until you know that the Most High *is* Ruler in the kingdom of men; and He gives it to whomever He desires. [26]And they that commanded to leave the stump of the tree roots: your kingdom *shall be* enduring to you, after you have realized that Heaven rules. [27]So, O king, let my advice be pleasing to you; even break off your sins by righteousness, and your iniquities by pitying the poor; whether there will be duration to your prosperity.

[28]All this came on the king, Nebuchadnezzar. [29]At the end of twelve months he walked in the palace of the kingdom of Babylon. [30]The king spoke and said, *Is* this not great Babylon that I have built for the house of the kingdom, by the might of my power, and for the honor of my majesty? [31]The word *was* still in the king's voice *when* a voice came down from Heaven,

363 1414 560 8065 4480 5182 6922 5894 4430
מַלְכָּא עִיר וְקַדִּישׁ נָחִת ׀ מִן־שְׁמַיָּא וְאָמַר גֹּדּוּ אִילָנָא
tree the Cut and ,Heaven from coming a and a king the
down ,saying down ,one holy ,watcher

613 7662 772 8330 6136 1297 2255
וְחַבְּלוּהִי בְּרַם עִקַּר שָׁרְשׁוֹהִי בְּאַרְעָא שְׁבֻקוּ וּבֶאֱסוּר
a with even leave the in roots its the But destroy and
band earth of stump .it

6647 8065 2920 1251 1768 1883 5174 6523
דִּי־פַרְזֶל וּנְחָשׁ בְּדִתְאָא דִּי בָרָא וּבְטַל שְׁמַיָּא יִצְטַבַּע
him let the the with and the of the in and iron of
;wet be heavens of dew field grass tender ,bronze

2499 5732 7655 5704 2508 1251 2423 5974
וְעִם־חֵיוַת בָּרָא חֲלָקֵהּ עַד דִּי־שִׁבְעָה עִדָּנִין יַחְלְפוּן עֲלוֹהִי׃
over by pass times seven until (be let) the ani- the and
:him lot his field of mals with

4756 4291 1768 1932 5943 1510 4430 6591 1836
21 דְּנָה פִשְׁרָא מַלְכָּא וּגְזֵרַת עִלָּאָה הִיא דִּי מְטָת עַל־מַרְאִי
my on has which this Most the the and ;king O the this
lord come (is) High of decree ,meaning (is)

1934 1251 2423 5974 606 2957 4430
22 מַלְכָּא׃ וְלָךְ טָרְדִין מִן־אֲנָשָׁא וְעִם־חֵיוַת בָּרָא לֶהֱוֵה
shall the ani- the and ,men from be shall And :king the
be field of mals with driven you

8065 2920 2939 8450 6215 4070
מְדֹרָךְ וְעִשְׂבָּא כְתוֹרִין ׀ לָךְ יְטַעֲמוּן וּמִטַּל שְׁמַיָּא לָךְ
you the the of And be shall you like with and your
,heavens of dew .fed oxen grass the ;abode

3046 1768 5704 2499 5732 7655 6647
מְצַבְּעִין וְשִׁבְעָה עִדָּנִין יַחְלְפוּן עֲלָךְ עַד ׀ דִּי־תִנְדַּע דִּי־
that you until over shall times seven and be shall
know ,you by pass ,wet

5415 6634 1768 4474 606 4437 5943 7990
שַׁלִּיט עִלָּאָה בְּמַלְכוּת אֲנָשָׁא וּלְמַן־דִּי יִצְבֵּא יִתְּנִנַּהּ׃
gives He He to and ;men the for Most the (is)
.it ,wishes whomever of kingdom High Ruler

4437 363 1768 8330 6136 7662 560
23 וְדִי אֲמַרוּ לְמִשְׁבַּק עִקַּר שָׁרְשׁוֹהִי דִּי אִילָנָא מַלְכוּתָךְ
your the of roots the the leave to they in And
kingdom :tree of stump commanded that

4430 3861 8065 7990 1768 3046 7011
24 לָךְ קַיָּמָא מִן־דִּי תִנְדַּע דִּי שַׁלִּטִן שְׁמַיָּא׃ לָהֵן מַלְכָּא
,king O ,Therefore .Heaven rules that have you after (be shall) for
realized enduring you

2604 5758 6562 6665 2408 8232 4431
מִלְכִּי יִשְׁפַּר עֲלָךְ וַחֲטָיָךְ בְּצִדְקָה פְרֻק וַעֲוָיָתָךְ בְּמִחַן
by your and break righ- by your and ,you to be let my
pitying iniquities ,off teousness sins pleasing counsel

5020 4291 3606 7963 754 1934 2006 6033
25 עֲנָיִן הֵן תֶּהֱוֵא אַרְכָה לִשְׁלֵוְתָךְ׃ כֹּלָּא מְטָא עַל־נְבוּכַדְנֶצַּר
Nebuchad- on came All your to duration there if the
nezzar (this) .prosperity be will ;poor

4437 1965 6236 8648 3393 7118 4430
26 מַלְכָּא׃ לִקְצָת יַרְחִין תְּרֵי־עֲשַׂר עַל־הֵיכַל מַלְכוּתָא
the the in ,twelve months the at ,king the
kingdom of palace of end

1932 1668 3809 560 4430 6032 1934 1981 895
27 דִּי בָבֶל מְהַלֵּךְ הֲוָה׃ עָנֵה מַלְכָּא וְאָמַר הֲלָא דָא־הִיא
this (Is) and The answered he walking Babylon of
not ,said king .was

2627 8632 4437 1005 1129 576 1768 7229 895
בָּבֶל רַבְּתָא דִּי־אֲנָה בֱנַיְתַהּ לְבֵית מַלְכוּ בִּתְקַף חִסְנִי
my the by ,royal the for have I that the Babylon
power of might palace it built ,great

8065 7032 4430 6433 4406 5751 1923 3367
28 וְלִיקָר הַדְרִי׃ עוֹד מִלְּתָא בְּפֻם מַלְכָּא קָל מִן־שְׁמַיָּא
Heaven from a ,king's the in The still my the for and
voice mouth (was) word ?majesty of honor

saying, O king Nebuchadnezzar, to you it is declared: The kingdom has been taken from you! 32And you shall be driven from men; and your dwelling *shall be* with the animals of the field. You shall be fed with the grass like oxen, and times shall pass over you until you know that the Most High *is* Ruler in the kingdom of men, and that He gives it to whomever He desires.

33The same hour the thing was fulfilled on Nebuchadnezzar. And he was driven from men, and he ate the grass like oxen; and his body was wet with the dew of the heavens, until his hair had grown like eagles *feathers*, and his nails like birds' *claws*. 34And at the end of the days, I, Nebuchadnezzar, lifted up my eyes to Heaven, and my understanding returned to me, and I blessed the Most High. And I praised and honored Him who lives forever, whose kingdom *is* an everlasting kingdom, and His rule from generation to generation. 35And all the inhabitants of the earth are counted as nothing. And He does according to His will among the army of Heaven, and *among* the inhabitants of the earth. And no one is able to strike His hand, or say to Him, What are You doing? 36At that time my reason returned to me, and the glory of my kingdom, my majesty, and my brightness returned to me. And my advisers and my nobles sought to me. And I was reestablished in my kingdom, and excellent greatness was added to me. 37Now I, Nebuchadnezzar, praise and exalt and honor the King of Heaven, for all His works *are* truth, and His ways *are* justice. And He is able to humble those who walk in pride.

נפל לך אמרין נבוכדנצר מלכא מלכותא עדת מנך:
from been has the ,king O Nebuchadnezzar is it To :fell
!you taken kingdom ,declared you

29 ומן־אנשא לך טרדין ועם־חיות ברא מדרך עשבא
the ;abode your the ani- the and be shall you men And
grass field of mals with ,driven from

כתורין לך יטעמון ושבעה עדנין יחלפון עליך עד | די־
until over pass shall times seven and be shall you oxen like
you by ,fed

תנדע די־שליט עליא במלכות אנשא ולמן די־יצבא
He that and ,men the in Most the (is) that you
,wishes whomever to of kingdom High Ruler know

30 יתננה: בה־שעתא מלתא ספת על־נבוכדנצר ומן־אנשא
men and Nebuchad- on was the ,moment In gives He
from :nezzar fulfilled thing its .it

טריד ועשבא כתורין יאכל ומטל שמיא גשמה יצטבע
wet was his the from and ,ate he oxen like the and was he
body ,heavens of dew the grass ,driven

31 עד די שערה כנשרין רבה וטפרוהי כצפרין: ולקצת
the at And birds' like his and had eagles' like his until
of end .(claws) nails ,grown (feathers) hair

יומיא אנה נבוכדנצר עיני | לשמיא נטלת ומנדעי עלי
to my and lifted Heaven to my ,Nebuchadnezzar ,I the
me reason eyes .days

יתוב ולעליא ברכת ולחי עלמא שבחת והדרת די שלטנה
whose ;honored and I who Him and ,blessed I the and re-
(is) dominion praised forever lives High Most ,turned

32 שלטן עלם ומלכותה עם־דר ודר: וכל־דארי ארעא כלה
as the the all And gen- to gen- from His and ever- an
nothing earth of dwellers .eration eration kingdom ,lasting dominion

חשיבין וכמצביה עבד בחיל שמיא ודארי ארעא ולא
And the the (in) and Heaven the in He according And are
none .earth of dwellers of army does will His to .counted

33 איתי די־ימחא בידה ויאמר לה מה עבדת: בה־זמנא
time At You are What to say or his with can who there
that ?doing ,Him ,hand strike is

מנדעי | יתוב עלי וליקר מלכותי הדרי וזוי יתוב עלי
to returned my and my my the and to returned my
.me luster majesty ,kingdom of glory ,me reason

ולי הדברי ורברבני יבעון ועל־מלכותי התקנת ורבו
and re- was I my and ,sought my and my And
greatness ,settled kingdom over nobles advisers me to

34 יתירה הוספת לי: כען אנה נבוכדנצר משבח ומרומם
exalt and praise ,Nebuchadnezzar ,I Now .me to was exceed-
added ing

ומהדר למלך שמיא די כל־מעבדוהי קשט וארחתה
His and truth His all for ,Heaven the and
ways (are) works of King glorify

דין ודי מהלכין בגוה יכל להשפלה:
.humble to is He in walking And jus-
able pride those .tice

CAP. V ה

CHAPTER 5

[1]Belshazzar the king made a great feast to a thousand of his nobles. And he drank wine before the thousand. [2]When tasting the wine, Belshazzar commanded the golden and silver vessels brought, those his father Nebuchadnezzar had taken out of the temple which *was* in Jerusalem; that the king might drink with them, and his nobles, his wives, and his concubines. [3]Then they brought the golden vessels that were taken out of the temple of the house of God in Jerusalem. And the king, his nobles, his wives, and his concubines drank with them; [4]they drank wine and praised the gods of gold, and of silver, and of bronze, of iron, wood, and stone.

[5]At that moment fingers of a man's hand came out and wrote on the plaster of the wall of the king's palace across from the lampstand. And the king saw the part of the hand that wrote. [6]Then the king's color was changed, and his thoughts troubled him, so that the joints of his loins shook, and his knees knocked one against *the other*. [7]The king cried aloud to bring in the conjurers, the Chaldeans, and the fortunetellers. The king spoke and said to the wise men of Babylon, Any man who can read this writing and reveal its meaning shall be clothed with purple, and *have* a chain of gold around his neck. And he shall rule third in the kingdom.

CHAPTER 5

6903 506 7261 7229 3900 5648 4430 1113
1 בֵּלְשַׁאצַּר מַלְכָּא עֲבַד לְחֶם רַב לְרַבְרְבָנוֹהִי אֲלַף וְלָקֳבֵל
the in and a his for great a made king the Belshazzar
of presence ,thousand ,nobles feast

2562 2942 560 1113 8355 2562 506
2 אַלְפָּא חַמְרָא שָׁתֵה׃ בֵּלְשַׁאצַּר אֲמַר ׀ בִּטְעֵם חַמְרָא
,wine the when com- Belshazzar he wine the
tasting manded .drank thousand

5020 5312 1768 3701 1722 3984 858
לְהַיְתָיָה לְמָאנֵי דַּהֲבָא וְכַסְפָּא דִּי הַנְפֵּק נְבוּכַדְנֶצַּר
Nebuchadnezzar had those and gold the bring to
taken ,silver of vessels

1430 8355 3390 1768 1965 2
אֲבוּהִי מִן־הֵיכְלָא דִּי בִירוּשְׁלֶם וְיִשְׁתּוֹן בְּהוֹן מַלְכָּא
,king the with might that in which the out his
them drink Jerusalem (was) temple of father

1722 3984 858 116 3904 7695 7261
3 וְרַבְרְבָנוֹהִי שֵׁגְלָתֵהּ וּלְחֵנָתֵהּ׃ בֵּאדַיִן הַיְתִיו מָאנֵי דַהֲבָא
gold the they Then his and wives his his and
of vessels brought .concubines ,nobles

8355 3390 1768 426 1005 1768 1965 5312
דִּי הַנְפִּקוּ מִן־הֵיכְלָא דִּי־בֵית אֱלָהָא דִּי בִירוּשְׁלֶם וְאִשְׁתִּיו
And in which God the of the out been had that
drank .Jerusalem (was) of house temple of taken

2562 8355 3904 7695 7261 44 30
4 בְּהוֹן מַלְכָּא וְרַבְרְבָנוֹהִי שֵׁגְלָתֵהּ וּלְחֵנָתֵהּ׃ אִשְׁתִּיו חַמְרָא
wine they his and ,wives his his and the with
drank ;concubines ,nobles king them

636 6523 5174 3701 1722 426 7624
וְשַׁבַּחוּ לֵאלָהֵי דַּהֲבָא וְכַסְפָּא נְחָשָׁא פַרְזְלָא אָעָא
,wood ,iron ,bronze ,silver and ,gold gods the and
of praised

6903 3790 606 3028 677 5312 8160 69
5 וְאַבְנָא׃ בַּהּ־שַׁעֲתָה נְפַקוּ אֶצְבְּעָן דִּי יַד־אֱנָשׁ וְכָתְבָן לָקֳבֵל
opposite and a hand of fingers came moment At and
wrote ,man's out that .stone

4430 4430 1768 1965 3597 1768 1528 5043
נֶבְרַשְׁתָּא עַל־גִּירָא דִּי־כְתַל הֵיכְלָא דִּי מַלְכָּא וּמַלְכָּא
the And the of the wall the of the on lamp- the
king king palace of plaster stand

8133 2122 4430 116 3790 3028 6447 2370
6 חָזֵה פַּס יְדָה דִּי כָתְבָה׃ אֱדַיִן מַלְכָּא זִיוֹהִי שְׁנוֹהִי
was his king the Then .wrote that the the saw
,changed color hand of palm

1668 755 8271 2783 7001 927 7476
וְרַעְיֹנֹהִי יְבַהֲלוּנֵּהּ וְקִטְרֵי חַרְצֵהּ מִשְׁתָּרַיִן וְאַרְכֻבָּתֵהּ דָּא
one his and ,shook his the and troubled his and
knees loins of joints ,him thoughts

3779 826 5954 2429 4430 7123 5368 1668
7 לְדָא נָקְשָׁן׃ קָרֵא מַלְכָּא בְּחַיִל לְהֶעָלָה לְאָשְׁפַיָּא כַּשְׂדָּיֵא
the the bring to with The cried .knocked against
,Chaldeans ,conjurers in might king this

606 3606 896 2445 560 4430 6032 1505
וְגָזְרַיָּא עָנֵה מַלְכָּא וְאָמַר ׀ לְחַכִּימֵי בָבֶל דִּי כָל־אֱנָשׁ
man Any ,Babylon wise the to said and The answered the and
of men king .gazers

3548 711 2324 6591 1836 3792 7123
דִּי־יִקְרֵה כְּתָבָה דְנָה וּפִשְׁרֵהּ יְחַוִּנַּנִי אַרְגְּוָנָא יִלְבַּשׁ
be shall purple declare its and this writing can who
with clothed me to meaning read

7981 4437 8523 6676 1722 2002
וְהַמְנוּכָא דִּי־דַהֲבָא עַל־צַוְּארֵהּ וְתַלְתִּי בְמַלְכוּתָא יִשְׁלַט׃
shall he the in And his around gold of the and
.rule kingdom third .neck (be shall) necklace

[8]Then all the king's wise men came in. But they could not read the writing, or make the meaning known to the king. [9]Then king Belshazzar was greatly troubled, and his face was changing on him, and his nobles were perplexed.

[10]The queen came in to the banquet house because of the words of the king and his nobles. The queen spoke and said, O king, live forever. Do not let your thoughts trouble you, and do not let your face be changed. [11]There is a man in your kingdom in whom *is* the spirit of the holy gods. And in the days of your father light and understanding and wisdom was found in him, like the wisdom of the gods. Your father, king Nebuchadnezzar, your father the king appointed him master of the horoscopists, conjurers, Chaldeans *and* fortune-tellers, [12]because an excellent spirit, and knowledge, and understanding, explaining of dreams, and revealing of hard sentences, and the unraveling of knots, were found in this Daniel, whom the king named Belteshazzar. Now let Daniel be called, and he will reveal the meaning.

[13]Then Daniel was thrust in before the king. The king spoke and said to Daniel, Are you that Daniel who *is* of the sons of the exiled of Judah, whom my father the king brought out of Judah? [14]I have even heard of you, that the spirit of the gods *is* in you, and light, and excellent wisdom, and understanding are found in you. [15]And now the wise men and the conjurers have been thrust in before me, so

7123 3793 3546 3809 4430 2445 3606 5954 116
8 אֱדַיִן עָלְלִין כֹּל חַכִּימֵי מַלְכָּא וְלָא־כָהֲלִין כְּתָבָא לְמִקְרֵא
read to | the writing | were they able | But not | the .king's | wise men | all | came in | Then

1113 4430 116 4430 3046 6591
9 וּפִשְׁרָא לְהוֹדָעָה לְמַלְכָּא׃ אֱדַיִן מַלְכָּא בֵלְשַׁאצַּר
Belshazzar | King | Then | the to .king | make to known | the or meaning

7672 7261 5922 8133 2122 927 7690
שַׂגִּיא מִתְבָּהַל וְזִיוֺהִי שָׁנַיִן עֲלוֹהִי וְרַבְרְבָנוֹהִי מִשְׁתַּבְּשִׁין׃
were .perplexed | his and nobles | on ,him | was changing | his and face | was ,terrified | greatly

4961 1005 7261 4430 4406 6903 4433
10 מַלְכְּתָא לָקֳבֵל מִלֵּי מַלְכָּא וְרַבְרְבָנוֹהִי לְבֵית מִשְׁתְּיָא
the banquet- | to house | his and ,nobles | the king | words the of | because of | ,queen The

409 24:18 5957 4430 560 443 6032 5954
עַלַּלַת עֲנָת מַלְכְּתָא וַאֲמֶרֶת מַלְכָּא לְעָלְמִין חֱיִי אַל־
not | !live | forever | ,king O | ,said and | queen the answered | ;came

4437 1400 383 8133 409 2122 7476 927
11 יְבַהֲלוּךְ רַעְיוֹנָךְ וְזִיוָיךְ אַל־יִשְׁתַּנּוֹ׃ אִיתַי גְּבַר בְּמַלְכוּתָךְ
your in kingdom | a man | There is | be let .changed | not | your and face | your ,thoughts | let Do alarm

7924 5094 2 3118 6922 426 7308/1768
דִּי רוּחַ אֱלָהִין קַדִּישִׁין בֵּהּ וּבְיוֹמֵי אֲבוּךְ נַהִירוּ וְשָׂכְלְתָנוּ
and ,insight | ,light | your father | the in And of days | in .(is) whom | holy | gods the | the of spirit

5020 4430 7912 426 2452 2452
וְחָכְמָה כְּחָכְמַת־אֱלָהִין הִשְׁתְּכַחַת בֵּהּ וּמַלְכָּא נְבוּכַדְנֶצַּר
Nebuchad-nezzar | King And | in .him | found was | ,gods (the) | the like of wisdom | and wisdom

2 6966 1505 3779 826 2749 7229 2
אֲבוּךְ רַב חַרְטֻמִּין אָשְׁפִין כַּשְׂדָּאִין גָּזְרִין הֲקִימֵהּ אֲבוּךְ
your father | appointed ;him | star-gazers | ,Chaldeans (and) | ,conjurers | horo-scopists | the chief of | your ,father

7924 4486 3493 7308 1768 6903 3606 4430
12 מַלְכָּא׃ כָּל־קֳבֵל דִּי רוּחַ ׀ יַתִּירָא וּמַנְדַּע וְשָׂכְלְתָנוּ
and (in) insight | and ,knowledge | ,extraordinary | an spirit | (was this) because | ;king the

7912 7001 8271 280 263 2493 6590
מְפַשַּׁר חֶלְמִין וְאַחֲוָיַת אֲחִידָן וּמְשָׁרֵא קִטְרִין הִשְׁתְּכַחַת
found were | ,problems | and solving | ,riddles | and of showing | ,dreams | inter-preting

1841 3705 1096 8036 7761 4430 1841
בֵּהּ בְּדָנִיֵּאל דִּי־מַלְכָּא שָׂם־שְׁמֵהּ בֵּלְטְשַׁאצַּר כְּעַן דָּנִיֵּאל
Daniel | Now | .Belteshazzar | his name | gave | the king | whom | ,Daniel | in this

6925 5954 1841 116 2324 6591 7123
13 יִתְקְרֵי וּפִשְׁרָה יְהַחֲוֵה׃ בֵּאדַיִן דָּנִיֵּאל הֻעַל קֳדָם
before | was in brought | Daniel | Then | will he .declare | the and meaning | be let ,called

1841 607 1841 560 4430 6032 4430
מַלְכָּא עָנֵה מַלְכָּא וְאָמַר לְדָנִיֵּאל אַנְתְּה־הוּא דָנִיֵּאל דִּי־
who (is) | Daniel | (Are) that | you | ,Daniel to | said and | The king | answered | the .king

3061 2 4430 858 1768 3061 1547 1123
מִן־בְּנֵי גָלוּתָא דִּי יְהוּד דִּי הַיְתִי מַלְכָּא אַבִי מִן־יְהוּד׃
?Judah | out of | my father | the king | brought whom | ,Judah of | the removed | the of sons

2452 7924 5094 426 7308 8088
14 שִׁמְעֵת עֲלָךְ דִּי רוּחַ אֱלָהִין בָּךְ וְנַהִירוּ וְשָׂכְלְתָנוּ וְחָכְמָה
and wisdom | and ,insight | and ,light | in ,you | (the) (is) gods | the that of spirit | ,you of | I Even heard have

826 2445 6925 5954 3705 7912 3493
15 יַתִּירָה הִשְׁתְּכַחַת בָּךְ׃ וּכְעַן הֻעַלּוּ קָדָמַי חַכִּימַיָּא אָשְׁפַיָּא
the ,conjurers | wise the ,men | before me | been have in brought | And now | in .you | found are | extra-ordinary

that they might read this writing, and make the meaning known to me. But they could not show the meaning of the thing. [16]And I have heard of you, that you can interpret meanings, and unravel knots. Now if you can read the writing, and reveal its meaning to me, you shall be clothed with purple and *have* a golden chain around your neck; and you will rule third in the kingdom.

[17]Then Daniel answered and said before the king, Let your gifts be to yourself, and give your rewards to another. Yet I will read the writing to the king, and make the meaning known to him. [18]O king, the most high God gave your father Nebuchadnezzar a kingdom, and majesty, and glory, and honor. [19]And for the majesty that He gave him, all peoples, nations, and languages trembled and feared before him. He killed whom He desired, and whom he desired, he kept alive. And whom He would, he set up; and whom he desired, he put down. [20]But when his heart was lifted up, and his mind hardened in pride, he was put down from the throne of his kingdom, and they took his glory from him. [21]And he was driven from the sons of men. And his heart was made like the animals, and his home *was* with the wild asses. They fed him with grass like oxen, and his body was wet with the dew of the heavens, until he knew that the most high God *is* Ruler in the kingdom of men; and that He appoints over it whomever He desires.

3546 3809 2324 6591 7123 1836 3792
דִּי־כְתָבָה דְנָה יִקְרוֹן וּפִשְׁרֵהּ לְהוֹדָעֻתַנִי וְלָא־כָהֲלִין
were they But known make its and might they this writing so
able not .me to meaning ,read that

3202 1768 8088 576 2324 4406 6591
16 פִּשַׁר־מִלְּתָא לְהַחֲוָיָה׃ וַאֲנָה שִׁמְעֵת עֲלָךְ דִּי־תִוּכֻל
are you that ,you of have I And .declare to meaning the
able heard thing the of

3792 3202 2006 3705 8271 7001 6590 6591
פִּשְׁרִין לְמִפְשַׁר וְקִטְרִין לְמִשְׁרֵא כְּעַן הֵן תִּוּכֻל כְּתָבָא
the are you if Now .solve to and to meanings
writing able problems ,interpret

1768 2002 3848 711 3046 6591 7123
לְמִקְרֵא וּפִשְׁרֵהּ לְהוֹדָעוּתַנִי אַרְגְּוָנָא תִלְבַּשׁ וְהַמְנוּכָא דִּי
of the and will you purple known make to its and ,read to
necklace ,with clothed be ,me to meaning

7981 4437 8531 6676 1722
דַהֲבָא עַל־צַוְּארָךְ וְתַלְתָּא בְמַלְכוּתָא תִּשְׁלַט׃
will you the in third and your around gold
.rule kingdom ,neck (be shall)

1934 4979 4430 6925 560 1841 6032 116
17 בֵּאדַיִן עָנֵה דָנִיֵּאל וְאָמַר קֳדָם מַלְכָּא מַתְּנָתָךְ לָךְ לֶהֶוְיָן
,be let to Your the before said and Daniel answered Then
yourself gifts ,king

6591 4430 7123 3792 1297 3052 321 5023
וּנְבִזְבְּיָתָךְ לְאָחֳרָן הַב בְּרַם כְּתָבָא אֶקְרֵא לְמַלְכָּא וּפִשְׁרָא
the and the to will I the Yet .give to your and
meaning ,king read writing another presents

7238 4437 5943 426 4430 607 3046
18 אֲהוֹדְעִנֵּהּ׃ אַנְתְּה מַלְכָּא אֱלָהָא עִלָּאָה מַלְכוּתָא וּרְבוּתָא
and the Most the ,king O (for As) make will I
greatness ,kingdom High God ,you .him to known

1768 7238 2 5020 3052 1923 3367
19 וִיקָרָא וְהַדְרָה יְהַב לִנְבֻכַדְנֶצַּר אֲבוּךְ׃ וּמִן־רְבוּתָא דִּי
that the And your Nebuchadnezzar gave and and
greatness from .father splendor ,majesty

1763 2112 1934 3961 524 5972 3606 3052
יְהַב־לֵהּ כֹּל עַמְמַיָּא אֻמַּיָּא וְלִשָּׁנַיָּא הֲווֹ זָאעִין וְדָחֲלִין מִן
from and shaking were the and the the all to He
fearing languages ,nations ,peoples ,him gave

2418 6634 1934 1768 6992 6634 1934 1768 6925
קֳדָמוֹהִי דִּי־הֲוָא צָבֵא הֲוָה קָטֵל וְדִי־הֲוָה צָבֵא הֲוָה מַחֵא
kept he ,wished he and ;killed he ,wished he Whom before
alive whom .him

8214 7934 6634 1934 1768 7313 1934 6634 1934 1768
וְדִי־הֲוָה צָבֵא הֲוָה מָרִים וְדִי־הֲוָא צָבֵא הֲוָא מַשְׁפִּל׃
.humbled he wished he and ;exalted he ,wished he And
whom whom

3764 5182 2103 8631 7308 3825 7313
20 וּכְדִי רִם לִבְבֵהּ וְרוּחֵהּ תִּקְפַת לַהֲזָדָה הָנְחַת מִן־כָּרְסֵא
the from was he act to grew his and his was But
of throne deposed ,insolently hard spirit ,heart lifted when

2957 606 1123 5709 3367 4437
21 מַלְכוּתֵהּ וִיקָרָה הֶעְדִּיו מִנֵּהּ׃ וּמִן־בְּנֵי אֲנָשָׁא טְרִיד
was he men the And from taken was (his) and his
,driven of sons from .him away majesty ,kingdom

8450 6215 4070 6167 5974 7739 2421 5974 3825
וְלִבְבֵהּ עִם־חֵיוְתָא שַׁוִּי וְעִם־עֲרָדַיָּא מְדוֹרֵהּ עִשְׂבָּא כְתוֹרִין
oxen like grass his (was) wild the and was the like his and
;dwelling asses with ;made animals heart

1768 3046 5704 6647 1655 8065 2920 2939
יְטַעֲמוּנֵּהּ וּמִטַּל שְׁמַיָּא גִּשְׁמֵהּ יִצְטַבַּע עַד דִּי־יְדַע דִּי
that he until ;wet was body his the (with) and fed they
knew heavens of dew the ,him

6966 6634 1768 4479 606 4437 5943 426 7990
שַׁלִּיט אֱלָהָא עִלָּאָה בְּמַלְכוּת אֲנָשָׁא וּלְמַן־דִּי יִצְבֵּא יְהָקֵים
He He that and ;men the in Most the (is)
appoints ,wishes whomever of kingdom High God Ruler

[22]And you, his son, O Belshazzar, have not bowed your heart, though you knew all this. [23]But you have lifted yourself up against the Lord of Heaven. And they have brought the vessels of His house before you. And you, and your nobles, your wives, and your concubines have drunk wine from them. And you have praised the gods of silver, and gold, bronze, iron, wood, and stone, which do not see, nor hear, and do not know. And you have not glorified the God in whose hand your breath *is*, and to whom belong all your ways. [24]Then the part of the hand was sent from Him. And this writing was written.

[25]And this is the writing that was written: A MINA, A MINA, A SHEKEL, AND HALF-MINAS. [26]This *is* the meaning of the thing: A MINA, God has numbered your kingdom, and finished it. [27]A SHEKEL, You are weighed in the balances, and found lacking. [28]HALF-MINAS, your kingdom is divided, and given to *the* Medes and Persians.

[29]Then Belshazzar commanded, and they clothed Daniel with purple, and a necklace of gold around his neck. And they made a proclamation concerning him, that he should be the third ruler in the kingdom.

[30]In that night Belshazzar, the king of the Chaldeans, was killed.

22 עליה׃ ואנתה ברה בלשאצר לא השפלת לבבך כל־

even your heart have humbled not ,Belshazzar O ,son his you And .it over

23 קבל די כל־דנה ידעת׃ ועל־מרא שמיא ׀ התרוממת

have you yourself exalted Heaven the of Lord against But you knew this all though

ולמאניא די־ביתה היתיו קדמך ואנתה ורברבניך

your and nobles ,you and before ;you have they brought His house of the and vessels

שגלתך ולחנתך חמרא שתין בהון ולאלהי כספא ודהבא

,gold and silver the And of gods with .them have drunk wine your and ,concubines your wives

נחשא פרזלא אעא ואבנא די לא־חזין ולא־שמעין ולא

and not do ,hear and not do ,see not which and ,stone wood ,iron (of) ,bronze

ידעין שבחת ולאלהא די־נשמתך בידה וכל־ארחתך

,ways your and all whose in hand your life-breath (is) the God But have you .praised do ,know

24 לה לא הדרת׃ באדין מן־קדמוהי שליח פסא די־ידא

the of .hand the palm was sent before Him from Then have you .glorified not Him

25 וכתבא דנה רשים׃ ודנה כתבא די רשים מנא מנא

A ,MINA A ,MINA was written that the writing this And (is) was .written this And writing

26 תקל ופרסין׃ דנה פשר מלתא מנא מנה־אלהא

God has numbered A ,MINA the :thing's meaning This (is) and HALF-MINAS A SHEKEL

27 מלכותך והשלמה׃ תקל תקילתה במאזניא והשתכחת

found and the on ,scales are You weighed A SHEKEL finished and .it your kingdom

28 חסיר׃ פרס פריסת מלכותך ויהיבת למדי ופרס׃

and .Persians (the) to Medes given and Your kingdom divided is HALF-MINAS .lacking

29 באדין ׀ אמר בלשאצר והלבשו לדניאל ארגונא

(with) ;purple Daniel they and clothed ,Belshazzar commanded Then

והמונכא די־דהבא על־צוארה והכרזו עלוהי די־להוא

he was that about ,him they And proclaimed .neck his around gold of the and necklace

30 שליט תלתא במלכותא׃ בה בליליא קטיל בלאשצר

Belshazzar was killed night In that the .kingdom in third the ruler

מלכא כשדיא׃

the .Chaldeans king the of

CAP. VI ו

CHAPTER 6

[31]And Darius the Mede took the kingdom, *being* a son of sixty-two years.

1 ודריוש מדיא קבל מלכותא כבר שנין שתין ותרתין׃

.two and sixty years a when of son the kingdom took over the Mede And Darius

CHAPTER 6

[1]It pleased Darius to set over the kingdom a hundred and twenty satraps, that they might be over the kingdom. [2]And over them *were* three presidents—Daniel *was* one of them—so that these satraps might give account to them, and the king should have no loss. [3]Then this Daniel was preferred above the presidents and satraps, because an excellent spirit *was* in him. And the king was planning to set him over all the kingdom.

[4]Then the presidents and satraps sought to find occasion against Daniel concerning the kingdom. But they could find no occasion or fault, because he *was* trustworthy. And no error or fault *was* found in him. [5]Then these men said, We shall not find any occasion against this Daniel unless we find *it* against him concerning the law of his God. [6]Then these presidents and satraps gathered together to the king and said this to him, King Darius, live forever. [7]All the presidents of the kingdom, the prefects, and the satraps, the officials and the governors, have planned together to establish a royal law, and to make a strong ban, that whoever shall ask a petition of any god or man for thirty days, except from you, O king, he shall be thrown into the den of lions. [8]Now, O king, establish the ban

324 4437 6966 1868 6925 8232
2 שְׁפַר קֳדָם דָּרְיָוֶשׁ וַהֲקִים עַל־מַלְכוּתָא לַאֲחַשְׁדַּרְפְּנַיָּא
satraps the kingdom over set to Darius before It seemed good

5922 4437 3606 1934 1768 6243 3969
3 מְאָה וְעֶשְׂרִין דִּי לֶהֱוֺן בְּכָל־מַלְכוּתָא׃ וְעֵלָּא מִנְּהוֺן
them over and ,kingdom the whole over they be might that and ,twenty a hundred

324 1934 1768 4480 2298 1841 8532 5632
סָרְכִין תְּלָתָה דִּי דָנִיֵּאל חַד מִנְּהוֺן דִּי־לֶהֱוֺן אֲחַשְׁדַּרְפְּנַיָּא
satraps might so that of them one Daniel (was) —three presidents

116 5142 1934 3809 4430 2941 3052 459
4 אִלֵּין יָהֲבִין לְהוֺן טַעְמָא וּמַלְכָּא לָא־לֶהֱוֵא נָזִק׃ אֱדַיִן
Then suffer .loss would not the and king ,account to give them these

3606 324 5632 5330 1934 1836 1841
דָּנִיֵּאל דְּנָה הֲוָא מִתְנַצַּח עַל־סָרְכַיָּא וַאֲחַשְׁדַּרְפְּנַיָּא כָּל־
satraps the and the presidents above distinguishing himself was this Daniel

6966 6246 4430 3493 7308 6903
קֳבֵל דִּי־רוּחַ יַתִּירָא בֵּהּ וּמַלְכָּא עֲשִׁית לַהֲקָמוּתֵהּ עַל־
over appoint to him was planning the And king in .him superb (was) a spirit because

5931 1156 1934 324 5632 116 4437 3606
5 כָּל־מַלְכוּתָא׃ אֱדַיִן סָרְכַיָּא וַאֲחַשְׁדַּרְפְּנַיָּא הֲווֺ בָעַיִן עִלָּה
pretext seeking were the and satraps the presidents Then the .kingdom all

7844 5931/3606 4437 6655 1841 7912
לְהַשְׁכָּחָה לְדָנִיֵּאל מִצַּד מַלְכוּתָא וְכָל־עִלָּה וּשְׁחִיתָה
fault or pretext But any .kingdom the concerning against Daniel find to

7960 3606 540 6903 3606 7912 3202 3809
לָא־יָכְלִין לְהַשְׁכָּחָה כָּל־קֳבֵל דִּי־מְהֵימַן הוּא וְכָל־שָׁלוּ
error And any he .(was) trustworthy because ,find to they able were not

560 479 1400 116 7912 3809 7844
6 וּשְׁחִיתָה לָא הִשְׁתְּכַחַת עֲלוֺהִי׃ אֱדַיִן גֻּבְרַיָּא אִלֵּךְ אָמְרִין
,said these men Then .him in found was not fault or

7912 3861 5931 3606 1836 1841 7912 3809
דִּי לָא נְהַשְׁכַּח לְדָנִיֵּאל דְּנָה כָּל־עִלָּא לָהֵן הַשְׁכַּחְנָא
(it) find we unless pretext any this against Daniel shall we find Not

459 324 5632 116 426 1882
7 עֲלוֺהִי בְּדָת אֱלָהֵהּ׃ אֱדַיִן סָרְכַיָּא וַאֲחַשְׁדַּרְפְּנַיָּא אִלֵּן
these the and satraps the presidents Then .God his the in law of against him

5957 4430 1868 560 3652 4430 7284
הַרְגִּשׁוּ עַל־מַלְכָּא וְכֵן אָמְרִין לֵהּ דָּרְיָוֶשׁ מַלְכָּא לְעָלְמִין
forever ,King Darius O to ,him they said and thus ,king the to gathered together

324 5460 4437 5632 3606 3272 2418
8 חֱיִי׃ אִתְיָעַטוּ כֹּל סָרְכֵי מַלְכוּתָא סִגְנַיָּא וַאֲחַשְׁדַּרְפְּנַיָּא
satraps the and the prefects the kingdom of presi-dents the All counsel took together !live

1768 633 7010 4430 6966 6966 6347 1907
הַדָּבְרַיָּא וּפַחֲוָתָא לְקַיָּמָה קְיָם מַלְכָּא וּלְתַקָּפָה אֱסָר דִּי
that ,ban make to and strong ,royal a statute to establish the and governors royal the ,officials

3861 8533 3118 5704/606 426 3606 1159 1156 1768 3606
כָל־דִּי־יִבְעֵא בָעוּ מִן־כָּל־אֱלָהּ וֶאֱנָשׁ עַד־יוֺמִין תְּלָתִין לָהֵן
except ,thirty days for man or god any of a petition shall ask whoever

6966 4430 3705 744 1358 7412 4430
9 מִנָּךְ מַלְכָּא יִתְרְמֵא לְגֹב אַרְיָוָתָא׃ כְּעַן מַלְכָּא תְּקִים
establish ,king O ,Now .lions the into of pit shall he thrown be ,king O from you

and sign the document, so that it may not be changed, according to the law of the Medes and Persians, which does not pass away. [9]All on account of this, king Darius signed the document and the ban.

[10]And when he had learned that the document was signed, Daniel went to his house. And his windows *were* open in his roof-room toward Jerusalem. He knelt on his knees three times in the day, and prayed and praised before his God, as he did before. [11]Then these men met together and found Daniel praying and seeking mercy before his God. [12]Then they came near and spoke before the king concerning the king's ban, *saying*, Have you not signed a ban that every man who shall ask of any god or man within thirty days, except of you, O king, *that he* shall be thrown into the lions' den? The king answered and said, The thing *is* certain, according to the law of the Medes and Persians, which does not pass away.

[13]Then they answered and said before the king, Daniel, who *is* of the sons of the captivity of Judah, has not respected you, O king, or the ban that you have signed, but he makes his prayer three times in the day. [14]Then the king, when he heard the word, was very displeased with himself. And he set *his* heart on Daniel, to deliver him. And he labored until sundown to deliver him. [15]Then these men met before the king and said to the king, O king,

6540 4075 1882 8133 38,09 3792 7560 633
אֱסָרָא וְתִרְשֻׁם כְּתָבָא דִּי לָא לְהַשְׁנָיָה כְּדָת־מָדַי וּפָרַס
and ,Persians the Medes the as of law be may changed it not so that the document sign and ban the

3792 7560 1868 44,30 1836 6903 3606 5709 38,09/1768
10 דִּי־לָא תֶעְדֵּא׃ כָּל־קֳבֵל דְּנָה מַלְכָּא דָּרְיָוֶשׁ רְשַׁם כְּתָבָא
the document signed Darius King ,this account of on All pass does not which .away

10:05 3792 7560 1768 3046 1841 5633
11 וֶאֱסָרָא׃ וְדָנִיֵּאל כְּדִי יְדַע דִּי־רְשִׁים כְּתָבָא עַל לְבַיְתֵהּ
his to .house he went the ,document was signed that he knew when And ,Daniel the and .ban

8532 2166 3390 5049 5952 6606 3557
וְכַוִּין פְּתִיחָן לֵהּ בְּעִלִּיתֵהּ נֶגֶד יְרוּשְׁלֶם וְזִמְנִין תְּלָתָה
three And times .Jerusalem toward his in roof-chamber to him open (were) And windows

6925 3029 6739 1291 1289 3118
בְּיוֹמָא הוּא ׀ בָּרֵךְ עַל־בִּרְכוֹהִי וּמְצַלֵּא וּמוֹדֵא קֳדָם
before and praised prayed and his knees on knelt he the in ,day

116 1836 6928 5648 1934 6903 3606 426
12 אֱלָהֵהּ כָּל־קֳבֵל דִּי־הֲוָא עָבֵד מִן־קַדְמַת דְּנָה׃ אֱדַיִן
Then .this before from doing he was which all ,God his

6925 2604 1156 1841 7912 7284 479 1400
גֻּבְרַיָּא אִלֵּךְ הַרְגִּשׁוּ וְהַשְׁכַּחוּ לְדָנִיֵּאל בָּעֵא וּמִתְחַנַּן קֳדָם
before seeking mercy and praying Daniel found and assembled those men

633 4430 6925 560 7127 116 426
13 אֱלָהֵהּ׃ בֵּאדַיִן קְרִבוּ וְאָמְרִין קֳדָם־מַלְכָּא עַל־אֱסָר
ban con- cerning king the before spoke and they came near Then .God his

3606 1156 1768 606 3606 7560 633 38,09 44,30
מַלְכָּא הֲלָא אֱסָר רְשַׁמְתָּ דִּי כָל־אֱנָשׁ דִּי־יִבְעֵא מִן־כָּל־
any of shall ask who man any that you Have signed a ban not the ;king's

1358 74,12 44,30 8533 3118 5704 606 426
אֱלָהּ וֶאֱנָשׁ עַד־יוֹמִין תְּלָתִין לָהֵן מִנָּךְ מַלְכָּא יִתְרְמֵא לְגוֹב
the into of pit be shall thrown ,king O from ,you except ,thirty days for man or god

6540 4075 1882 4406 3330 560 4430 6032 744
אַרְיָוָתָא עָנֵה מַלְכָּא וְאָמַר יַצִּיבָא מִלְּתָא כְּדָת־מָדַי וּפָרַס
and ,Persians the Medes the of law by thing The (is) certain ,said and The king answered ?lions

1841 4430 6925 560 6032 116 5709 3809 1768
14 דִּי־לָא תֶעְדֵּא׃ בֵּאדַיִן עֲנוֹ וְאָמְרִין קֳדָם מַלְכָּא דִּי דָנִיֵּאל
,Daniel ,king the before said and they answered Then pass does not which .away

2942 4430 7761/3809 3061 1547 1123 1768
דִּי מִן־בְּנֵי גָלוּתָא דִּי יְהוּד לָא־שָׂם עֲלָךְ מַלְכָּא טְעֵם
attention ,king O ,you to set has not ,Judah of the exile the of sons who (is)

1159 1156 3118 8532 2166 7560 633
וְעַל־אֱסָרָא דִּי רְשַׁמְתָּ וְזִמְנִין תְּלָתָה בְּיוֹמָא בָּעֵא בָּעוּתֵהּ׃
his .petition asks he the in day three but times have you signed that the to ban or

888 7690 8088 4406 1768 4430 116
15 אֱדַיִן מַלְכָּא כְּדִי מִלְּתָא שְׁמַע שַׂגִּיא בְּאֵשׁ עֲלוֹהִי וְעַל
And on with .himself was he displeased very he ,heard the word when the ,king Then

7712 1934 8122 4606 5704 7804 1097/7760 1841
דָּנִיֵּאל שָׂם בָּל לְשֵׁיזָבוּתֵהּ וְעַד מֶעָלֵי שִׁמְשָׁא הֲוָא מִשְׁתַּדַּר
striving was he the sun the of going And until deliver to .him (his) heart he set Daniel

560 4430 7284 428 1400 116 5538
16 לְהַצָּלוּתֵהּ׃ בֵּאדַיִן גֻּבְרַיָּא אִלֵּךְ הַרְגִּשׁוּ עַל־מַלְכָּא וְאָמְרִין
said and the king before assembled those men Then deliver to .him

know that the law of the Medes and Pesians *is* that every ban or law which the king enacts may not be changed. [16]And the king commanded. And they caused to arrive Daniel, and *they* threw *him* into the lions' den. The king spoke and said to Daniel, Your God, whom you constantly serve, will deliver you. [17]And a stone was brought and laid on the mouth of the den. And the king sealed it with his own signet, and with the signet of his nobles, that the affair may not change concerning Daniel.

[18]Then the king went to his palace and spent the night fasting. And diversions were not brought before him; and his sleep fled from him. [19]Then the king rose up in the dawn, in the daylight, and hurried to the lions' den. [20]And when he came to the den, he cried with a grieved voice to Daniel; the king spoke and said to Daniel, O Daniel, servant of the living God, your God whom you always serve, is He able to deliver you from the lions? [21]Then Daniel said to the king, O king, live forever. [22]My God has sent His Angel, and He has shut the mouths of the lions. And they have not hurt me, because in His sight purity was found in me. And also before you, O king, I have done no harm. [23]Then the king was exceedingly happy for him. And *he* commanded to bring up Daniel from the den. And Daniel was brought out of the den, and no harm was found on him,

7010 633 3606 65 40 4075 1882 44 30 3046 4330
למלכא דע מלכא די־דת למדי ופרס די־כל־אסר וקים
and ban every (is) and (the) of the that ,king O ,Know the to
statute that Persians Medes law ,king

560 4430 116 8133 3809 6966 4430 1768
17 די־מלכא יהקים לא להשניה׃ באדין מלכא אמר
,ordered the Then be may not establishes the which
king .changed king

4430 6032 744 1358 7412 1841 858
והיתיו לדניאל ורמו לגבא די אריותא ענה מלכא
The answered .lions the of the into threw and Daniel they And
king pit (him) brought

8411 63 99 607 426 1841 560
ואמר לדניאל אלהך די אנתה פלח־לה בתדירא הוא
He ,constantly serve you whom Your ,Daniel to and
,God said

2857 1358 6433 7760 2298 69 858 7804
18 ישיזבנך׃ והיתית אבן חדה ושמת על־פם גבא וחתמה
sealed And the the on laid and a stone was And deliver will
it .pit of mouth brought .you

6640 8133 3809 7261 5824 4430
מלכא בעזקתה ובעזקת רברבנוהי די לא־תשנא צבו
the might not that his the with and his with king the
affair change ,nobles of signet ,signet

3809 1761 29:08 956 1965 4430 2 36 116 1841
19 בדניאל׃ אדין אזל מלכא להיכלה ובת טות ודחון לא־
not and ;fasting and his to king the went Then concerning
diversions night the spent palace .Daniel

4430 116 5075 8139 6925 5954
20 הנעל קדמוהי ושנתה נדת עלוהי׃ באדין מלכא
king the Then from fled his and before were
.him sleep ;him brought

744 1768 1358 927 5053 6966 8238
בשפרפרא יקום בנגהא ובהתבהלה לגבא די־אריותא
the of the to haste and the in arose the in
lions pit in ,daylight dawn

6032 2200 6088 7032 1841 1358 7127 236
21 אזל׃ וכמקרבה לגבא לדניאל בקל עציב זעק ענה
an- he sorrowful a with Daniel to the to when And .went
swered ;cried voice ,pit near drew he

1768 426 2417 426 5649 1841 1841 560 4430
מלכא ואמר לדניאל דניאל עבד אלהא חיא אלהך די
whom your ,living the servant O ,Daniel to said and king the
God God of ,Daniel

744 7804 3202 8411 6399 607
אנתה פלח־לה בתדירא היכל לשיזבותך מן־אריותא׃
?lions the from deliver to He is ,constantly serve you
you able

426 2418 5957 4430 4449 44 30 5974 1841 116
22
23 אדין דניאל עם־מלכא מלל מלכא לעלמין חיי׃ אלהי
God My .live forever ,king O ,spoke king the with Daniel Then

6903 3606 2255 3809 744 6433 5463 4398 79 72
שלח מלאכה וסגר פם אריותא ולא חבלוני כל־קבל
because have they And the mouths He and His has
me harmed not .lions' shut has ,angel sent

2257 4430 6925 638 7912 2136 6925
די קדמוהי זכו השתכחת לי ואף קדמיך מלכא חבולה
harm ,king O before And in found was inno- before
,you also .me cence Him

1841 2868 7690 4430 116 5648 3809
24 לא עבדת׃ באדין מלכא שגיא טאב עלוהי ולדניאל
Daniel And for glad greatly king the Then have I not
.him was .done

2257 3606 1358 1841 5267 1360 5267 560
אמר להנסקה מן־גבא והסק דניאל מן־גבא וכל־חבל
harm and ,pit the out Daniel was and the from bring to he
any of brought ;pit up said

Left column (English commentary):

because he trusted in his God.

24And the king commanded, and they brought those men who had accused Daniel. And they threw *them* into the lions' den; them, their sons, and their wives. And the lions overpowered them, and crushed all their bones before they reached to the bottom of the den.

25Then king Darius wrote to all the peoples, the nations, and the languages who were living in all the earth: Peace be multiplied to you. 26I make a decree that in all the domain of my kingdom men shall tremble and fear before the God of Daniel. For He *is* the living God and endures forever, and His kingdom *is* the one which shall not be destroyed. And His rule *shall be* to the end. 27He delivers and rescues, and He works signs and wonders in the heavens and in the earth, He who has delivered Daniel from the power of the lions.

28And this Daniel was made to prosper in the reign of Darius, and in the reign of Cyrus the Persian.

Interlinear (Daniel 6:25–29):

25 לָא־הִשְׁתְּכַ֣ח בֵּ֔הּ דִּ֥י הֵימִ֖ן בֵּאלָהֵֽהּ׃ וַאֲמַ֣ר מַלְכָּ֔א וְהַיְתִ֗יו

they and ,king the And   his in   he because   on   found was   not
brought   ordered   .God   trusted   ,him

גֻּבְרַיָּ֤א אִלֵּךְ֙ דִּֽי־אֲכַ֣לוּ קַרְצ֣וֹהִי דִּ֣י דָֽנִיֵּ֔אל וּלְגֹ֥ב אַרְיָוָתָ֖א

lions the into And   .Daniel   of   bits the   had who   those   men
of pit the   chewed

רְמ֑וֹ אִנּ֤וּן בְּנֵיהוֹן֙ וּנְשֵׁיהֹ֔ן וְלָא־מְט֞וֹ לְאַרְעִ֣ית גֻּבָּ֗א עַ֤ד דִּֽי־

before the   the to   did they And   their and   their ,them   they
pit   of bottom   reach   not   .wives   sons   cast

26 שְׁלִ֣טֽוּ בְהוֹן֙ אַרְיָ֣וָתָ֔א וְכָל־גַּרְמֵיה֖וֹן הַדִּֽקוּ׃ בֵּאדַ֣יִן דָּרְיָ֣וֶשׁ

Darius   Then   they   their   and ;lions the   them   over-
.crushed   bones   all   powered

מַלְכָּ֗א כְּתַ֞ב לְֽכָל־עַֽמְמַיָּ֡א אֻמַיָּ֣א וְלִשָּֽׁנַיָּא֩ דִּֽי־דָאֲרִ֨ין בְּכָל־

all in   were who   the and   the   the   to   wrote   King
living   languages   ,nations   ,peoples   all

27 אַרְעָ֖א שְׁלָמְכ֥וֹן יִשְׂגֵּֽא׃ מִן־קָֽדָמַי֮ שִׂ֣ים טְעֵם֒ דִּ֣י ׀ בְּכָל־

all in   that   a   was   before from   be   Your   the
,decree   given   me   ;increased   peace   :earth

שָׁלְטָ֣ן מַלְכוּתִ֗י לֶהֱוֹ֤ן זָאֲעִין֙ וְדָ֣חֲלִ֔ין מִן־קֳדָ֖ם אֱלָהֵ֣הּ דִּֽי־

of   God the   before   fear and   tremble (men)   my   domain
shall   ,kingdom's

דָֽנִיֵּ֑אל דִּי־ה֣וּא ׀ אֱלָהָ֤א חַיָּא֙ וְקַיָּ֣ם לְעָֽלְמִ֔ין וּמַלְכוּתֵהּ֙

His and   ,forever   and   living   God the   He For   .Daniel
kingdom   (is)

28 דִּֽי־לָ֣א תִתְחַבַּ֔ל וְשָׁלְטָנֵ֖הּ עַד־סוֹפָֽא׃ מְשֵׁיזִ֣ב וּמַצִּ֗ל וְעָבֵד֙

He and   and   He   the (be shall)   His and   be shall not the (is)
works   ,rescues   delivers   .end   to   dominion   ,destroyed which one

אָתִ֣ין וְתִמְהִ֔ין בִּשְׁמַיָּ֖א וּבְאַרְעָ֑א דִּ֚י שֵׁיזִ֣ב לְדָֽנִיֵּ֔אל מִן־יַ֖ד

the from   Daniel   has who   the in and   the in   and   signs
of hand   delivered   ;earth   heavens   wonders

29 אַרְיָוָתָֽא׃ וְדָנִיֵּ֣אל דְּנָ֔ה הַצְלַ֖ח בְּמַלְכ֣וּת דָּרְיָ֑וֶשׁ וּבְמַלְכ֖וּת

the in and   ,Darius   the in   made was   this   Daniel   So   .lions the
of reign   of reign   prosper to

כּ֥וֹרֶשׁ פָּרְסָאָֽה׃

.Persian the   Cyrus

CAP. VII ז

Left column (Chapter 7 commentary):

CHAPTER 7
1In the first year of Belshazzar, king of Babylon, Daniel saw a dream and visions of his head on his bed. Then he related the dream, giving the sum of the matters. 2Daniel spoke and said, In my vision by night I was looking. And, behold, the four winds of the heavens were stirring up the Great Sea. 3And four great beasts came up from

---

Interlinear (Daniel 7:1–3):

1 בִּשְׁנַ֣ת חֲדָ֗ה לְבֵלְאשַׁצַּר֙ מֶ֣לֶךְ בָּבֶ֔ל דָּנִיֵּאל֙ חֵ֣לֶם חֲזָ֔ה וְחֶזְוֵ֥י

and   saw   a   Daniel ,Babylon king   of   first   the In
of visions   dream   of   Belshazzar   year

רֵאשֵׁ֖הּ עַֽל־מִשְׁכְּבֵ֑הּ בֵּאדַ֨יִן֙ חֶלְמָ֣א כְתַ֔ב רֵ֥אשׁ מִלִּ֖ין אֲמַֽר׃

he   the   sum the   he   the   Then   .bed his   on   his
.related   matters   of   ;wrote   dream   head

2 עָנֵ֤ה דָֽנִיֵּאל֙ וְאָמַ֔ר חָזֵ֥ה הֲוֵ֛ית בְּחֶזְוִ֖י עִם־לֵֽילְיָ֑א וַאֲר֗וּ

And   .night by   my in   was I   looking ,said and   Daniel   an-
!behold   vision   swered

3 אַרְבַּע֙ רוּחֵ֣י שְׁמַיָּ֔א מְגִיחָ֖ן לְיַמָּ֥א רַבָּֽא׃ וְאַרְבַּ֣ע חֵיוָ֣ן

beasts   four And   .great   sea the   were   the   The   four
stirring   heavens   of winds

the sea, different from one another. [4]The first *was* like a lion and had eagle's wings. I watched until its wings were torn off. And it was lifted up from the earth, and made to stand on two feet like a man; and a man's heart was given to it. [5]And, behold, another beast, a second, like a bear. And it was raised up on one side, and three ribs *were* in its mouth between its teeth. And they said this to it, Rise up, eat up much flesh. [6]After theis I watched, and, behold, another like a leopard, which had four wings of a bird on its back. For also the beast *had* four heads. And rulership was given to it. [7]And after this I looked in the night visions. And, behold, the fourth beast, fearful and terrifying, and very strong! And it *had* great iron teeth. It devoured and crushed, and stamped what was left with its feet. And it *was* different from all the beasts that *were* before it; and it had ten horns. [8]I was thinking about the horns; and, behold, another little horn came up among them, before whom three of the first horns were pulled up by the roots. And, behold, in this horn *were* eyes like the eyes of the man, and a mouth speaking great things.

[9]I was looking until the thrones were set up, and the Ancient of Days sat, whose robe *was* white as snow, and the hair of His head like pure wool. His throne *was like* flames of fire; its wheels *like* burning fire. [10]A stream of fire

4 רַבְרְבָן סָלְקָן מִן־יַמָּא שָׁנְיָן דָּא מִן־דָּא׃ קַדְמָיְתָא כְאַרְיֵה
a like lion, The (was) first from this. different this the from sea came up great
וְגַפִּין דִּי־נְשַׁר לַהּ חָזֵה הֲוֵית עַד דִּי־מְּרִיטוּ גַפַּיהּ וּנְטִילַת
was it And lifted up the wings. torn were off until was I looking .it to an (were) eagle of and wings
מִן־אַרְעָא וְעַל־רַגְלַיִן כֶּאֱנָשׁ הֳקִימַת וּלְבַב אֱנָשׁ יְהִיב לַהּ׃
.it to was given man's a and heart to made ;stand a like man two feet and on the from earth,
5 וַאֲרוּ חֵיוָה אָחֳרִי תִנְיָנָה דָּמְיָה לְדֹב וְלִשְׂטַר־חַד הֳקִמַת
was it raised up one on And side .bear a like ,second a ,another beast And ,behold
וּתְלָת עִלְעִין בְּפֻמַּהּ בֵּין שִׁנַּהּ וְכֵן אָמְרִין לַהּ קוּמִי אֲכֻלִי
devour ,Arise :it to said they And thus its between .teeth its in mouth ribs (were) and three
6 בְּשַׂר שַׂגִּיא׃ בָּאתַר דְּנָה חָזֵה הֲוֵית וַאֲרוּ אָחֳרִי כִּנְמַר
a like ,leopard another ,and ,behold was I looking this After .much flesh
וְלַהּ גַּפִּין אַרְבַּע דִּי־עוֹף עַל־גַּבַּיהּ וְאַרְבְּעָה רֵאשִׁין לְחֵיוְתָא
the to ;beast heads (were) four also its ;side on a bird of four wings and it to
7 וְשָׁלְטָן יְהִיב לַהּ׃ בָּאתַר דְּנָה חָזֵה הֲוֵית בְּחֶזְוֵי לֵילְיָא
the ;night of in visions was I looking this After .it to was given and dominion
וַאֲרוּ חֵיוָה רְבִיעָיָה דְּחִילָה וְאֵימְתָנִי וְתַקִּיפָא יַתִּירָה וְשִׁנַּיִן
And teeth .exceedingly strong and and ,terrifying frightful the ,fourth beast ,and ,behold
דִּי־פַרְזֶל לַהּ רַבְרְבָן אָכְלָה וּמַדְּקָה וּשְׁאָרָא בְּרַגְלַהּ
feet its with what and left was and ,crushed It devoured .great it to iron of (were)
רָפְסָה וְהִיא מְשַׁנְּיָה מִן־כָּל־חֵיוָתָא דִּי קָדָמַהּ וְקַרְנַיִן
horns and before ;it that (were) the beasts all from was different it And it .trampled
8 עֲשַׂר לַהּ׃ מִשְׂתַּכַּל הֲוֵית בְּקַרְנַיָּא וַאֲלוּ קֶרֶן אָחֳרִי זְעֵירָה
little another horn and ,behold the ,horns was I considering .it to ten (were)
סִלְקָת בֵּינֵיהֵן וּתְלָת מִן־קַרְנַיָּא קַדְמָיָתָא אֶתְעֲקַרוּ מִן
from were uprooted first the horns of and three among ;them came up
קֳדָמַהּ וַאֲלוּ עַיְנִין כְּעַיְנֵי אֲנָשָׁא בְּקַרְנָא־דָא וּפֻם מְמַלִּל
speaking a and mouth ,this (were) horn on the man the like of eyes eyes And ,behold before .it
9 רַבְרְבָן׃ חָזֵה הֲוֵית עַד דִּי כָרְסָוָן רְמִיו וְעַתִּיק יוֹמִין יְתִב
,sat Days the and of Ancient were ,up set thrones until was I looking great .things
לְבוּשֵׁהּ כִּתְלַג חִוָּר וּשְׂעַר רֵאשֵׁהּ כַּעֲמַר נְקֵא כָּרְסְיֵהּ
His throne .pure like wool His head the and of hair ,white snow as whose (was) robe
10 שְׁבִיבִין דִּי־נוּר גַּלְגִּלּוֹהִי נוּר דָּלִק׃ נְהַר דִּי־נוּר נָגֵד וְנָפֵק
and issued ,ran fire of A river .burning (were) fire its wheels ;fire of (like was) flames

went out and came out from before Him. A thousand thousands served Him, and a myriad myriads stood before Him. The court was set, and the books were opened. [11]Then I was looking because of the voice of the great words which the horn spoke. I was looking until the beast was killed, and his body was destroyed, and given to the burning flame. [12]And the rest of the beasts, their dominion was taken away. Yet length of life was given them for a season and a time. [13]I was looking in the night visions. And, behold, *one* like the Son of man came with the clouds of the heavens. And He came to the Ancient of Days. And they brought Him near before Him. [14]And dominion was given to Him, and glory, and a kingdom, that all peoples, nations, and languages should serve Him. His dominion *is* an everlasting dominion which shall not pass away, and His kingdom that which shall not be destroyed.

[15]I, Daniel, was distressed in my spirit in its sheath, and the visions of my head troubled me. [16]And I came near one of those who stood by and asked him the truth of all this. And he told me and made me know the meaning of the things. [17]These great beasts *are* four; *they are* four kings; they shall rise up out of the earth. [18]But the saints of the Most High shall receive the kingdom and possess the kingdom forever, even forever and ever. [19]Then I wanted to know the truth of the fourth beast, which was different from all of them, very frightening, whose teeth *were* of iron and its

6925 7240 7240 8120 506 506 6925
מִן־קֳדָמוֹהִי אֶלֶף אַלְפִים יְשַׁמְּשׁוּנֵּהּ וְרִבּוֹ רִבְוָן קָדָמוֹהִי
before Him myriads a myriad and served ,Him thousands a thousand before ;Him from

116 1934 2370 6606 5609 3488 1780 6966
11 יְקוּמוּן דִּינָא יְתִב וְסִפְרִין פְּתִיחוּ׃ חָזֵה הֲוֵית בֵּאדַיִן
then ,was I looking were .opened books and ,sat The court .stood

5707 1934 2370 4449 7162 1768 7260 4406 7032
מִן־קָל מִלַּיָּא רַבְרְבָתָא דִּי קַרְנָא מְמַלֱּלָה חָזֵה הֲוֵית עַד
until was I looking ,spoke the horn which great the words the for of sound

785 3346 3052 1655 7 2423 6992
דִּי קְטִילַת חֵיוְתָא וְהוּבַד גִּשְׁמַהּ וִיהִיבַת לִיקֵדַת אֶשָּׁא׃
.fire the of burning the to given and his body was and destroyed the beast was killed

3052 2417 754 7985 5709 2423 7606
12 וּשְׁאָר חֵיוָתָא הֶעְדִּיו שָׁלְטָנְהוֹן וְאַרְכָה בְחַיִּין יְהִיבַת לְהוֹן
to them was given life of Yet length their .dominion taken was away the ;beasts the And of rest

6050/5974 718 3916 2376 1934 2370 5732 2166 5705
13 עַד־זְמַן וְעִדָּן׃ חָזֵה הֲוֵית בְּחֶזְוֵי לֵילְיָא וַאֲרוּ עִם־עֲנָנֵי
the of clouds with and ,behold ,night the in of visions was I looking a and .season a for time

4291 3118 6268 5705 1934 858 606 1247 8065
שְׁמַיָּא כְּבַר אֱנָשׁ אָתֵה הֲוָא וְעַד־עַתִּיק יוֹמַיָּא מְטָה
He .came Days the of Ancient to and ,was coming man like (one) of Son the the heavens

3606 4437 3367 7985 3052 7127 6925
14 וּקְדָמוֹהִי הַקְרְבוּהִי׃ וְלֵהּ יְהִב שָׁלְטָן וִיקָר וּמַלְכוּ וְכֹל
that all a and ,kingdom and ,glory ,dominion was given to And Him brought they .near Him before And Him

5957 7985 [illegible] 6399 3961 524 5972
עַמְמַיָּא אֻמַיָּא וְלִשָּׁנַיָּא לֵהּ יִפְלְחוּן שָׁלְטָנֵהּ שָׁלְטָן עָלַם
ever- lasting an dominion His (is) dominion shall .serve Him the and languages the ,nations the ,peoples

3735 2255 3809 1768 4437 5709 3809
15 דִּי־לָא יֶעְדֵּה וּמַלְכוּתֵהּ דִּי־לָא תִתְחַבַּל׃ אֶתְכְּרִיַּת
was distressed be shall .destroyed not which His and kingdom pass shall ,away not which

7127 927 7217 2376 5085 1459 1841 576 7308
16 רוּחִי אֲנָה דָנִיֵּאל בְּגוֹא נִדְנֶה וְחֶזְוֵי רֵאשִׁי יְבַהֲלֻנַּנִי׃ קִרְבֵת
came I near alarmed .me my head the and of visions its ,sheath amidst ,Daniel ,I My spirit

1836 3606 1156 3330 6966 2298
עַל־חַד מִן־קָאֲמַיָּא וְיַצִּיבָא אֶבְעֵא־מִנֵּהּ עַל־כָּל־דְּנָה
.this all of from him asked the and truth who those of ,by stood one to

7260 2423 459 3046 4406 6591 560
17 וַאֲמַר־לִי וּפְשַׁר מִלַּיָּא יְהוֹדְעִנַּנִי׃ אִלֵּין חֵיוָתָא רַבְרְבָתָא
,great beasts These known made .me to the things of the and meaning ,me he And told

6902 772 6966 4430 702 702 581
18 דִּי אִנּוּן אַרְבַּע אַרְבְּעָה מַלְכִין יְקוּמוּן מִן־אַרְעָא׃ וִיקַבְּלוּן
shall But receive the .earth out of shall they arise ;kings four (are) ,four which (are)

5705 5957/5705 4437 2631 5946 6922 4437
מַלְכוּתָא קַדִּישֵׁי עֶלְיוֹנִין וְיַחְסְנוּן מַלְכוּתָא עַד־עָלְמָא וְעַד
even ,forever the kingdom and possess Most the High holy the of ones the kingdom

7244 2423 3321 6634 116 5957 5957
19 עָלַם עָלְמַיָּא׃ אֱדַיִן צְבִית לְיַצָּבָא עַל־חֵיוְתָא רְבִיעָיְתָא
,fourth the beast of know to truth the I desired Then (and) .ever forever

6523 1768 8128 3493 1763 3606 8133 1934
דִּי־הֲוָת שָׁנְיָה מִן־כָּלְּהֵון דְּחִילָה יַתִּירָה שִׁנַּהּ דִּי־פַרְזֶל
,iron (were) of its teeth ,very frightening of all ,them from different was which

nails bronze; *who* devoured *and* crushed, and trampled what was left with its feet. [20]And of the ten horns that *were* on its head, and the other which came up, and before whom three fell; even that horn that *had* eyes, and a mouth speaking great things, and its look *was* greater than his fellows; [21]I watched, and that horn made war with the saints and overcame them, [22]until the Ancient of Days came. And judgment was given to the saints of the Most High; and the time came that the saints possessed the kingdom. [23]And He said, The fourth beast shall be the fourth kingdom on earth, which shall be different from all kingdoms, and shall devour all the earth, and shall trample it down and crush it. [24]And the ten horns out of this kingdom *are* ten kings; they shall rise; and another shall rise after them. And he shall be different from the first, and he shall humble three kings. [25]And he shall speak words against the Most High, and shall wear out the saints of the Most High. And he intends to change times and law. And they shall be given into his hand until a time and times and one-half time. [26]But the judgment shall sit, and they shall take away his rulership, to cut off and to destroy until the end. [27]And the kingdom and rulership, and the greatness of the kingdom under all the heavens, shall be given to the people of the saints of the Most High, whose kingdom *is* an everlasting kingdom. And all kingdoms shall serve and obey Him. [28]Here *is* the end of the matter. As for me, Daniel,

וטפריה די־נחש אכלה מדקה ושארא ברגליה רפסה׃
,trampled feet its with what and (and) ate (who) ,bronze of its and
left was ,crushed ,up nails

20 ועל־קרניא עשר די בראשה ואחרי די סלקת ונפלו
fell and came which the and its on that ten the and
up other ,head (were) horns of

מן־קדמיה תלת וקרנא דכן ועינין לה ופם ממלל
speaking a and ,it to eyes and that even ,three before from
mouth (were) horn him

21 רברבן וחזוה רב מן־חברתה׃ חזה הוית וקרנא דכן
that and ,was I looking its than (was) its and great
horn .fellows greater look ;things

22 עבדא קרב עם־קדישין ויכלה להון׃ עד די־אתה עתיק
the came until ;them pre- and holy (His) with war made
of Ancient over vailed ,ones

יומיא ודינא יהב לקדישי עליונין וזמנא מטה ומלכותא
the that came the And Most the the for was the and ,Days
kingdom time .High of saints given judgment

23 החסנו קדישין׃ כן אמר חיותא רביעיתא מלכו רביעיא
the kingdom fourth The ,said he So holy (His) pos-
fourth beast .ones sessed

תהוא בארעא די תשנא מן־כל־מלכותא ותאכל כל־
all shall and king- the all from be shall which the on shall
devour doms different ;earth be

24 ארעא ותדושנה ותדקנה׃ וקרניא עשר מנה מלכותה
kingdom of out ten the And crush and trample and the
(are) this horns .it ,it ;earth

עשרה מלכין יקמון ואחרן יקום אחריהון והוא ישנא
be shall And after shall and shall they ;kings ten
different he .them rise another ;rise

25 מן־קדמיא ותלתה מלכין יהשפל׃ ומלין לצד עליא
the against And shall he kings three and the from
High Most words .humble ones previous

ימלל ולקדישי עליונין יבלא ויסבר להשניה זמנין ודת
and times change to he and wear shall Most the the and shall he
.law intends ,out High of ones holy ,speak

26 ויתיהבון בידה עד־עדן ועדנין ופלג עדן׃ ודינא יתב
will the But .time one and and a until his into they And
sit court half ,times time hand given be shall

27 ושלטנה יהעדון להשמדה ולהובדה עד־סופא׃ ומלכותא
the And the until to and to shall they his and
kingdom .end destroy exterminate ,away take dominion

ושלטנא ורבותא די מלכות תחות כל־שמיא יהיבת
be shall the all under the of the and the and
given ,heavens kingdoms greatness ,dominion

לעם קדישי עליונין מלכותה מלכות עלם וכל שלטניא
the And ever- an whose Most the holy the the to
dominion all .lasting kingdom (is) kingdom ,High of ones of people

28 לה יפלחון וישתמעון׃ עד־כה סופא די־מלתא אנה
As the of end the Here .obey and shall Him
,me for .matter (is) serve

my thoughts troubled me much, and my face changed on me. But I kept the matter in my heart.

CHAPTER 8

[1]In the third year of the reign of king Belshazzar, a vision appeared to me, Daniel, after that which appeared to me at the first. [2]And I looked in a vision. And it happened when I looked, I *was* at Shushan the citadel which *is* in the province of Elam. And in a vision I looked, and I was by the Canal of Ulai. [3]Then I lifted up my eyes and looked. And, behold, a ram was standing before the canal, having two horns. And the two horns *were* high, but one *was* higher than the other, and the higher one came up last. [4]I saw the ram pushing westward and northward and southward, so that no beasts could stand before him, nor *any* who could deliver out of his hand. But he did according to his will, and became great. [5]And I was considering, and, behold, a he-goat came from the west, over the face of all the earth, and did not touch the ground. And the goat *had* an outstanding horn between his eyes. [6]And he came to the ram with two horns, which I had seen standing before the canal. And he ran to it in the fury of his power. [7]And I saw him touched beside the ram. And he was moved with anger against him, and struck the ram and shattered his two horns. And there was no power in the ram to stand before him. But he threw him down to

4406 8133 2122 927 7476 7690 1841
דָּנִיֵּאל שַׂגִּיא ׀ רַעְיוֹנַי יְבַהֲלֻנַּנִי וְזִיוַי יִשְׁתַּנּוֹן עֲלַי וּמִלְּתָא
the But .me on changed my and alarmed my greatly ,Daniel
matter color ,me thoughts

5202 3821
בְּלִבִּי נִטְרֵת׃
.kept I my in
heart

CAP. VIII ח

CHAPTER 8

7200 2377 4430 1112 4438 7969 8141
1 בִּשְׁנַת שָׁלוֹשׁ לְמַלְכוּת בֵּלְאשַׁצַּר הַמֶּלֶךְ חָזוֹן נִרְאָה אֵלַי
to appeared a ,king the Belshazzar the of third the In
;me vision of reign year

2377 7200 8462 7200 310 1840
2 אֲנִי דָנִיֵּאל אַחֲרֵי הַנִּרְאָה אֵלַי בַּתְּחִלָּה׃ וָאֶרְאֶה בֶּחָזוֹן
the in I And the at me to which that after ,Daniel (to)
,vision looked .beginning appeared .me

4082 5867 834 1002 7800 7200 1961
וַיְהִי בִּרְאֹתִי וַאֲנִי בְּשׁוּשַׁן הַבִּירָה אֲשֶׁר בְּעֵילָם הַמְּדִינָה
the Elam in which the at I I when it and
.province (is) citadel Shushan (was) ,looked ,was

5869 5375 195 180 1961 2377 7200
3 וָאֶרְאֶה בֶּחָזוֹן וַאֲנִי הָיִיתִי עַל־אוּבַל אוּלָי׃ וָאֶשָּׂא עֵינַי
my I Then .Ulai the by was I and the in I And
eyes up lifted of Canal vision looked

7161 180 6440 5975 259 352 2009 7200
וָאֶרְאֶה וְהִנֵּה ׀ אַיִל אֶחָד עֹמֵד לִפְנֵי הָאֻבָל וְלוֹ קְרָנָיִם
two to and the before was a ram and and
.horns it ,canal standing ,behold ,looked

1364 8145 1364 259 1364 7161
וְהַקְּרָנַיִם גְּבֹהוֹת וְהָאַחַת גְּבֹהָה מִן־הַשֵּׁנִית וְהַגְּבֹהָה
the and the than higher one but (were) two the And
one higher ,other (was) ,high horns

6828 3220 5055 352 7200 314 5927
4 עֹלָה בָּאַחֲרֹנָה׃ רָאִיתִי אֶת־הָאַיִל מְנַגֵּחַ יָמָּה וְצָפוֹנָה
north- and west- butting ram the saw I .last came
ward ward up

6213 3027 5337 369 6440 5975 3808 2416 3605 5045
וָנֶגְבָּה וְכָל־חַיּוֹת לֹא־יַעַמְדוּ לְפָנָיו וְאֵין מַצִּיל מִיָּדוֹ וְעָשָׂה
he And from could and before might not beasts that so and
did .hand his deliver none ,him stand all ,southward

935 5795 6842 2009 995 1961 1430 7522
5 כִרְצֹנוֹ וְהִגְדִּיל׃ וַאֲנִי ׀ הָיִיתִי מֵבִין וְהִנֵּה צְפִיר־הָעִזִּים בָּא
came the a and ,considering was I And became and his by
goats of male ,behold .great ,will

6842 776 5060 369 776 3605 6440 4628
מִן־הַמַּעֲרָב עַל־פְּנֵי כָל־הָאָרֶץ וְאֵין נוֹגֵעַ בָּאָרֶץ וְהַצָּפִיר
he- the And the touch did and the all the over ,west the from
(had) goat .ground not ,earth of face

935
834 7161 1167 352 5869 996 2380 7161
6 קֶרֶן חָזוּת בֵּין עֵינָיו׃ וַיָּבֹא עַד־הָאַיִל בַּעַל הַקְּרָנַיִם אֲשֶׁר
which two the with the to he And his between con- an
horns ram came eyes spicuous horn

7200 3581 2534 7323 180 6440 5975 7200
7 רָאִיתִי עֹמֵד לִפְנֵי הָאֻבָל וַיָּרָץ אֵלָיו בַּחֲמַת כֹּחוֹ׃ וּרְאִיתִיו
saw I And his the in it to he and the before standing had I
him .power of fury ran ,canal seen

7665 352 5221 4843 352 681 5060
מַגִּיעַ ׀ אֵצֶל הָאַיִל וַיִּתְמַרְמַר אֵלָיו וַיַּךְ אֶת־הָאַיִל וַיְשַׁבֵּר
and the and against became he And the beside touched
shattered ram struck ,him furious .ram

7993 6440 5975 352 3581 1961 3808 1161 8147
אֶת־שְׁתֵּי קְרָנָיו וְלֹא־הָיָה כֹחַ בָּאַיִל לַעֲמֹד לְפָנָיו וַיַּשְׁלִיכֵהוּ
threw he But before to the in power there And its two
down him .him stand ram was not .horns

the ground, and trampled him. And no one could deliver the ram from his hand. 8Then the he-goat became very great. And when he was mighty, the great horn was broken. And in its place came up four outstanding *ones* toward the four winds of the heavens. 9And out of one of them came a little horn, which became very great, toward the south, and toward the east, and toward the bountiful *land*. 10And it became great, *even* to the host of the heavens. And it made fall *some* of the host, and of the stars, to the ground, and trampled them. 11Yea, he magnified himself even to the leader of the host. And the daily *sacrifice* was taken away by him, and the place of his sanctuary was cast down. 12And a host was given with the daily *sacrifice* because of transgression. And it threw the truth down to the ground; and it worked and prospered.

13Then I heard a certain holy one speaking, and another holy one said to that one who spoke, Until when *is* the vision, the regular *sacrifice*, and the desolating transgression, to give both the sanctuary and the host to be trampled? 14And he said to me, For two thousand, three hundred evenings *and* mornings; then the sanctuary will be vindicated.

15And it happened when I, Daniel, had seen the vision, then I sought meaning. And, behold, the form of a man stood before me. 16And I heard a man's voice between the *banks* of Ulai, and he called and said, Gabriel, make this one understand the vision. 17And he came beside my place. And when he came, I feared and fell on my face. But he said to me, O son of man, understand; for the vision *is* for the time of the end. 18And while he was speaking with me, I was

6842 3027 352 5337 1961 3808 7429 776
8 אַרְצָה וַיִּרְמְסֵהוּ וְלֹא־הָיָה מַצִּיל לָאַיִל מִיָּדוֹ׃ וּצְפִיר
the Then his from the deliver could and trampled and the to
of male .hand ram none ,him ground

5795 1419 5704 3966 6105 7665 7161 1419
הָעִזִּים הִגְדִּיל עַד־מְאֹד וּכְעָצְמוֹ נִשְׁבְּרָה הַקֶּרֶן הַגְּדוֹלָה
.great horn the was when And .very became the
broken ,mighty was he great goats

8064 7307 702 8478 702 2380 5927
וַתַּעֲלֶנָה חָזוּת אַרְבַּע תַּחְתֶּיהָ לְאַרְבַּע רוּחוֹת הַשָּׁמָיִם׃
the winds the toward ,place its in four con- came And
.heavens of four spicuous up

3499 1430 4704 259 7161 3318 259
9 וּמִן־הָאַחַת מֵהֶם יָצָא קֶרֶן־אַחַת מִצְּעִירָה וַתִּגְדַּל־יֶתֶר
,very be- and ,little a horn came of one And
great came them of out

6635 5704 1430 6643 4217 5045
10 אֶל־הַנֶּגֶב וְאֶל־הַמִּזְרָח וְאֶל־הַצֶּבִי׃ וַתִּגְדַּל עַד־צְבָא
the to (even) it And boun- the and ,east the and the toward
of host ,great became .(land) tiful toward toward south

7429 3556 6635 776 5307 8064
הַשָּׁמָיִם וַתַּפֵּל אַרְצָה מִן־הַצָּבָא וּמִן־הַכּוֹכָבִים וַתִּרְמְסֵם׃
trampled and ,stars the and host the of the to it And the
.them of ground fall made .heavens

7999 8548 7311 1430 6635 8269 5704
11 וְעַד שַׂר־הַצָּבָא הִגְדִּיל וּמִמֶּנּוּ הֻרַם הַתָּמִיד וְהֻשְׁלַךְ
was and regular the was by and magnified he the ruler to Even
down cast ,(sacrifice) removed him ,himself host of the

7993 6580 8548 5414 6635 4720 4349
12 מְכוֹן מִקְדָּשׁוֹ׃ וְצָבָא תִּנָּתֵן עַל־הַתָּמִיד בְּפָשַׁע וְתַשְׁלֵךְ
it and through regular the with was a And His place the
down cast ;trespass (sacrifice) given host .sanctuary of

6944 259 8085 6743 6213 776 571
13 אֱמֶת אַרְצָה וְעָשְׂתָה וְהִצְלִיחָה׃ וָאֶשְׁמְעָה אֶחָד־קָדוֹשׁ
holy a I Then and it and the to truth
one certain heard .prospered worked ;ground

5704 1696 6422 6918 259 559 1696
מְדַבֵּר וַיֹּאמֶר אֶחָד קָדוֹשׁ לַפַּלְמוֹנִי הַמְדַבֵּר עַד־מָתַי
when Until ,spoke who that to holy another said and ,speaking
(is) one one

4823 6635 6944 5414 8074 6588 8548 2377
הֶחָזוֹן הַתָּמִיד וְהַפֶּשַׁע שֹׁמֵם תֵּת וְקֹדֶשׁ וְצָבָא מִרְמָס׃
be to the and the both to ,desolating the and regular the the
?trampled host sanctuary give trespass (sacrifice) ,vision

6663 3967 7969 505 1242 6153 5704 559
14 וַיֹּאמֶר אֵלַי עַד עֶרֶב בֹּקֶר אַלְפַּיִם וּשְׁלֹשׁ מֵאוֹת וְנִצְדַּק
be will then hun- and two mornings evenings For ,me to he And
vindicated ;dred three thousand (and) said

998 1245 2377 1840 7200 1961 6944
15 קֹדֶשׁ׃ וַיְהִי בִּרְאֹתִי אֲנִי דָנִיֵּאל אֶת־הֶחָזוֹן וָאֲבַקְשָׁה בִינָה
;meaning I then the Daniel I when it And (the)
sought ,vision seen had ,was .sanctuary

996 120 6963 8085 1397 4758 5048 5975 2009
16 וְהִנֵּה עֹמֵד לְנֶגְדִּי כְּמַרְאֵה־גָבֶר׃ וָאֶשְׁמַע קוֹל־אָדָם בֵּין
be- man's a voice I And .man a the like before there then
tween heard of appearance me stood ,behold

4758 1975 995 1403 559 7121 195
אוּלָי וַיִּקְרָא וַיֹּאמַר גַּבְרִיאֵל הָבֵן לְהַלָּז אֶת־הַמַּרְאֶה׃
the this make ,Gabriel ,said and he and ,Ulai
.vision (man) discern called

559 6440 5307 1204 935 5977 681 935
17 וַיָּבֹא אֵצֶל עָמְדִי וּבְבֹאוֹ נִבְעַתִּי וָאֶפְּלָה עַל־פָּנָי וַיֹּאמֶר
he But .face my on fell and was I when And my beside he So
said afraid ,came he .place came

1696 2377 7093 6256 120 1121 995
18 אֵלַי הָבֵן בֶּן־אָדָם כִּי לְעֶת־קֵץ הֶחָזוֹן׃ וּבְדַבְּרוֹ עִמִּי
with he as And the the the for for ,man O ,Discern ,me to
,me speaking was .vision end of time (is) of son

5977 5975 :5060 776 6440 7290
נִרְדַּמְתִּי עַל־פָּנַי אָרְצָה וַיִּגַּע־בִּי וַיַּעֲמִידֵנִי עַל־עָמְדִי׃
.place my on | me made and stand | he But me touched | the to .ground | my on face | lay I stunned

2195 319 1961 834 :3045 2005 559
19 וַיֹּאמֶר הִנְנִי מוֹדִיעֲךָ אֵת אֲשֶׁר־יִהְיֶה בְּאַחֲרִית הַזָּעַם כִּי
For (is it) | in- .dignation | the last of end | the in | shall happen | what | make will know you | ,Behold I | he And said

4074 4428 7161 1167 7200 834 352 7093 4150
20 לְמוֹעֵד קֵץ׃ הָאַיִל אֲשֶׁר־רָאִיתָ בַּעַל הַקְּרָנָיִם מַלְכֵי מָדָי
Media | the of kings | :horns two | with | you saw | which | The ram | (the) .end | the for of time set

834 1419 7161 3120 4428 8163 6842 6539
21 וּפָרָס׃ וְהַצָּפִיר הַשָּׂעִיר מֶלֶךְ יָוָן וְהַקֶּרֶן הַגְּדוֹלָה אֲשֶׁר
that (is) | great | the And horn | .Greece | the of king | ,shaggy | the And he-goat | and .Persia

5925 7665 7223 4428 5869 996
22 בֵּין־עֵינָיו הוּא הַמֶּלֶךְ הָרִאשׁוֹן׃ וְהַנִּשְׁבֶּרֶת וַתַּעֲמֹדְנָה
stood and up | that for as And ,broken was which | .first | king the | (is) | its between eyes

3581 3808 5975 1471 4438 702 8478 702
אַרְבַּע תַּחְתֶּיהָ אַרְבַּע מַלְכֻיוֹת מִגּוֹי יַעֲמֹדְנָה וְלֹא בְכֹחוֹ׃
its with .power | but not | stand shall up | of out nation the | kingdoms | four | its in ,place | four

6440/5794 4428 5975 6586. 8552 443 :8 319
23 וּבְאַחֲרִית מַלְכוּתָם כְּהָתֵם הַפֹּשְׁעִים יַעֲמֹד מֶלֶךְ עַז־פָּנִים
,face strong of | king a | shall up stand | trans- gressors | the | have when finished | their kingdom | the in And of time latter

7843 6381 3581 38 08 3581 6105 2420 995
24 וּמֵבִין חִידוֹת׃ וְעָצַם כֹּחוֹ וְלֹא בְכֹחוֹ וְנִפְלָאוֹת יַשְׁחִית
shall he ,destroy | And marvelously | his by .power own | but not | his mighty and ,power | ;intrigues | and at skilled

6918 6099 7843 6213 6743
25 וְהִצְלִיחַ וְעָשָׂה וְהִשְׁחִית עֲצוּמִים וְעַם־קְדֹשִׁים׃ וְעַל־
And through | .holy the | and people | mighty the | destroy and | and ,accomplish | shall he and ,prosper

7843 7962 1430 3824 :3027 4820 6743 7922
שִׂכְלוֹ וְהִצְלִיחַ מִרְמָה בְּיָדוֹ וּבִלְבָבוֹ יַגְדִּיל וּבְשַׁלְוָה יַשְׁחִית
shall he destroy | be and ;ease at | will he himself lift | his in And heart own | his in .hand | deceit | make will he succeed | his skill

4758 7665 3027 657 5975 8269 8269 7227
26 רַבִּים וְעַל שַׂר־שָׂרִים יַעֲמֹד וּבְאֶפֶס יָד יִשָּׁבֵר׃ וּמַרְאֵה
the And of vision | be shall he .broken | a hand | with- out | but shall he ,up stand | rulers | the of Ruler | Also against | .many

2377 5640 571 559 834 1242 6153
הָעֶרֶב וְהַבֹּקֶר אֲשֶׁר נֶאֱמַר אֱמֶת הוּא וְאַתָּה סְתֹם הֶחָזוֹן
the ,vision | Shut up | But !you | .(is) it | true | ,told was | that | the and morning | the evening

3117 2470 1961/2470 1840 7227 3117
27 כִּי לְיָמִים רַבִּים׃ וַאֲנִי דָנִיֵּאל נִהְיֵיתִי וְנֶחֱלֵיתִי יָמִים
.days | was I And (for) sick | .sick was | Daniel | ,I And | .many | for days | for (is it)

4758 8074 4428 4399 6213 6965
וָאָקוּם וָאֶעֱשֶׂה אֶת־מְלֶאכֶת הַמֶּלֶךְ וָאֶשְׁתּוֹמֵם עַל־הַמַּרְאֶה
,vision the | at | was I And amazed | the .king's | business | did and | I Then arose

995 369
וְאֵין מֵבִין׃
under- .standing | not but was

CAP. IX ט

CHAPTER 9

834 4074 2233 325 1121 1867 259 8141
1 בִּשְׁנַת אַחַת לְדָרְיָוֶשׁ בֶּן־אֲחַשְׁוֵרוֹשׁ מִזֶּרַע מָדָי אֲשֶׁר
who | the ,Medes | the of of seed | ,Ahasuerus | the of son | Darius of | first | the In year

---

stunned, on my face toward the ground. But he touched me and made me stand.
19And he said, Behold, I will make you know what shall happen in the last end of the indignation. For *it is* for the time appointed *for* the end.
20The ram which you saw with two horns *is* the kings of Media and Persia.
21And the shaggy goat *is* the king of Greece. And the great horn that *is* between his eyes is the first king.
22And as for that which was broken, and four stood up in its place, four kingdoms shall stand up out of the nation, but not in its power.
23And in the latter time of their kingdom, when the transgressors have come to the full, a king strong of face, and skilled at intrigues, shall stand up.
24And his power shall be mighty, but not by his own power. And he shall destroy marvelously; and he shall prosper, and work, and destroy the mighty, and the holy people.
25And also through his skill he will make deceit succeed in his hand. And he will lift himself up in his heart, and be at ease; he shall destroy many. He shall also stand up against the Ruler of rulers, but he shall be broken without a hand.
26And the morning and evening vision that was told *is* true. But you shall shut up the vision; for it *shall be* for many days.
27And I, Daniel, was faint. And I was sick *for* days. Afterwards I got up and did the king's business. And I was amazed at the vision. But there was no understanding.

CHAPTER 9

1In the first year of Darius, the son of Ahasuerus, of the seed of the Medes, who was made king over the realm of the Chaldeans, [2]in the first year of his reign, I, Daniel, understood the number of the years by books, which came as the word of Jehovah to Jeremiah the prophet, that He would accomplish seventy years in the desolations of Jerusalem.

[3]And I set my face toward the Lord God, to seek by prayer and holy desires, with fasting, and sackcloth, and ashes. [4]And I prayed to Jehovah my God, and made my confession, saying, O Lord, the great and awesome God, keeping the covenant and mercy to those who love Him, and to those who keep His commandments; [5]we have sinned and have committed iniquity, and have done evilly, and have rebelled, even by departing from Your commandments and from Your judgments. [6]And we have not listened to Your servants the prophets, who spoke in Your name to our kings, our rulers, and our fathers, and to all the people of the land. [7]O Lord, righteousness *belongs* to You, but to us the shame of our faces, as *it is* this day; to the men of Judah, and to the dwellers of Jerusalem, and to all Israel, both near and at a distance, through all the lands where You have scattered them, because of their sin which they have sinned against You. [8]O Lord, shame of face *belongs* to us, to our kings, to our rulers, and to our fathers, because we have sinned against You. [9]To the Lord our God *belong* mercies, and pardons, for we have rebelled against Him. [10]We have not obeyed the voice of the Lord our God, to walk in His laws which he set before us by His servants the prophets. [11]Yea, all Israel has transgressed

4427 259 8141 3778 4438 4427
2 הָמְלַךְ עַל מַלְכוּת כַּשְׂדִּים׃ בִּשְׁנַת אַחַת לְמָלְכוֹ אֲנִי
,I his of first the In the king- the over made was
,reign year ,Chaldeans of dom king

1697 1961 834 8141 4557 5612 995 1840
דָּנִיֵּאל בִּינֹתִי בַּסְּפָרִים מִסְפַּר הַשָּׁנִים אֲשֶׁר הָיָה דְבַר־
word the came which years the the the by understood ,Daniel
of (as) of number ,books

7657 3389 2723 4390 5030 3414 3068
יְהוָה אֶל־יִרְמִיָה הַנָּבִיא לְמַלֹּאות לְחָרְבוֹת יְרוּשָׁלַםִ שִׁבְעִים
seventy —Jerusalem the for would He that the Jeremiah to Jehovah
of desolations accomplish ,prophet

8605 1245 430 136 6440 5414 8141
3 שָׁנָה׃ וָאֶתְּנָה אֶת־פָּנַי אֶל־אֲדֹנָי הָאֱלֹהִים לְבַקֵּשׁ תְּפִלָּה
by seek to ,God the toward face my set I And .years
prayer Lord

430 3068 6419 665 8242 6685 8469
4 וְתַחֲנוּנִים בְּצוֹם וְשַׂק וָאֵפֶר׃ וָאֶתְפַּלְלָה לַיהוָה אֱלֹהַי
,God my to prayed I And .dust and and with sup- and
Jehovah sackcloth fasting ,plications

8104 3372 1419 410 136 577 559 3034
וָאֶתְוַדֶּה וָאֹמְרָה אָנָּא אֲדֹנָי הָאֵל הַגָּדוֹל וְהַנּוֹרָא שֹׁמֵר
who and great God the O ,pray I ,said and and
keeps ,awesome ,Lord confessed

5753 2398 4687 8104 157 2617 1285
5 הַבְּרִית וְהַחֶסֶד לְאֹהֲבָיו וּלְשֹׁמְרֵי מִצְוֹתָיו׃ חָטָאנוּ וְעָוִינוּ
did and have we com- His those to and who those to and cove- the
,iniquity sinned ;mands keep who ,Him love lovingkindness nant

3808 4941 4687 5493 4775 7561
6 וְהִרְשַׁעְנוּ וּמָרָדְנוּ וְסוֹר מִמִּצְוֹתֶךָ וּמִמִּשְׁפָּטֶיךָ׃ וְלֹא
And Your from and Your from and have and have and
not ,judgments commands turned ,rebelled ,evilly done

8034 1696 834 5030 5650 8085
שָׁמַעְנוּ אֶל־עֲבָדֶיךָ הַנְּבִיאִים אֲשֶׁר דִּבְּרוּ בְּשִׁמְךָ אֶל־
to Your in spoke who the Your to have we
name ,prophets servants listened

136 776 5971 3605 1 8269 4428
7 מְלָכֵינוּ שָׂרֵינוּ וַאֲבֹתֵינוּ וְאֶל כָּל־עַם הָאָרֶץ׃ לְךָ אֲדֹנָי
O (belongs) the the all and our and our our
,Lord ,You to .land of people to ,fathers ,leaders ,kings

3427 3063 376 2088 3117 6440 1322 6666
הַצְּדָקָה וְלָנוּ בֹּשֶׁת הַפָּנִים כַּיּוֹם הַזֶּה לְאִישׁ יְהוּדָה וּלְיוֹשְׁבֵי
res- to and Judah the to ;this (at) as (our) the to but righ-
of idents of men day ,faces of shame us teousness

776 3605 7350 7138 3478 3605 3389
יְרוּשָׁלַםִ וּלְכָל־יִשְׂרָאֵל הַקְּרֹבִים וְהָרְחֹקִים בְּכָל־הָאֲרָצוֹת
lands the through who and are who ,Israel to and ,Jerusalem
all ,afar are near all

136 4604 834 4603 8033 5080 834
8 אֲשֶׁר הִדַּחְתָּם שָׁם בְּמַעֲלָם אֲשֶׁר מָעֲלוּ־בָךְ׃ אֲדֹנָי לָנוּ
us to O against have they which their for ,there have You where
(is) ,Lord .You done unfaithfulness them sown

2398 834 8269 4428 6440 1322
בֹּשֶׁת הַפָּנִים לִמְלָכֵינוּ לְשָׂרֵינוּ וְלַאֲבֹתֵינוּ אֲשֶׁר חָטָאנוּ
have we because our to and our to our to ,faces shame
sinned ,fathers ,rulers ,kings of

4775 5547 7356 430 136
9 לָךְ׃ לַאדֹנָי אֱלֹהֵינוּ הָרַחֲמִים וְהַסְּלִחוֹת כִּי מָרַדְנוּ בּוֹ׃
against have we for ,pardons and mercies our Lord the To against
.Him rebelled God (belong) .You

834 8451 3212 430 3068 6963 8085 3808
10 וְלֹא שָׁמַעְנוּ בְּקוֹל יְהוָה אֱלֹהֵינוּ לָלֶכֶת בְּתוֹרֹתָיו אֲשֶׁר־
which His in walk to ,God our Jehovah the have we And
laws of voice obeyed not

5674 3478 3605 5030 5650 3027 6440 5414
11 נָתַן לְפָנֵינוּ בְּיַד עֲבָדָיו הַנְּבִיאִים׃ וְכָל־יִשְׂרָאֵל עָבְרוּ אֶת־
has Israel And .prophets the His by before He
transgressed all servants us set

Your law, and turned aside, that they might not obey Your voice. For this reason the curse has poured out on us, and the oath that is written in the law of Moses the servant of God, because we have sinned against Him.

[12]And He has confirmed His words which He spoke against us, and against our judges who judge us, by bringing on us a great evil. For under the whole heavens *it* has not been done as *it* has been done to Jerusalem. [13]As it is written in the law of Moses, all this evil has come on us. Yet we did not make our prayer before Jehovah our God, that we might turn from our perversities and understand Your truth. [14]And Jehovah has looked on the evil, and has made it come on us. For Jehovah our God *is* righteous in all His works which He does. For we did not obey His voice. [15]And now, O Lord our God, *You* who have brought Your people out of the land of Egypt with a mighty hand, and who has made for Himself a name, as *it is* this day, we have sinned; we have done wrong.

[16]O Lord, I pray to You, according to all Your righteousness, let Your anger and Your fury be turned away from Your city Jerusalem, Your holy mountain. For because of our sins and of our fathers' iniquities, Jerusalem and Your people *have become* a reproach to all those around us. [17]And now, hear, O our God, the prayer of Your servant, and his holy desires, and cause Your face to shine on Your sanctuary that *is* desolate, for the sake of the Lord. [18]O my God, bow down Your ear and hear; open Your eyes and see our ruins; and the city which is called

422 54,13 6963 8085 11,15 5493 84:51
תּוֹרָתֶךָ וְסוֹר לְבִלְתִּי שְׁמוֹעַ בְּקֹלֶךָ וַתִּתַּךְ עָלֵינוּ הָאָלָה
the curse | us on | has And out poured | Your voice. | obeying | not | and veered | Your law,

3588 430 5650 4872 8451 3789 834 76,21
וְהַשְּׁבֻעָה אֲשֶׁר כְּתוּבָה בְּתוֹרַת מֹשֶׁה עֶבֶד־הָאֱלֹהִים כִּי
be- cause | God, | the of servant | Moses | the in of law | written is | that | oath the and

1696 834 1697 6965 2398
12 חָטָאנוּ לוֹ׃ וַיָּקֶם אֶת־דְּבָרָיו אֲשֶׁר־דִּבֶּר עָלֵינוּ וְעַל־
and against | against us | He spoke | which | words His | has He And confirmed | Him. | have we sinned

834 1419 7451 935 8199 834 8199
שֹׁפְטֵינוּ אֲשֶׁר שְׁפָטוּנוּ לְהָבִיא עָלֵינוּ רָעָה גְדֹלָה אֲשֶׁר
which | great, | evil a | us on | by bringing | us judged, | who | our judges

3389 6213 8064 36,05 8478 6213 3808
לֹא־נֶעֶשְׂתָה תַּחַת כָּל־הַשָּׁמַיִם כַּאֲשֶׁר נֶעֶשְׂתָה בִּירוּשָׁלִָם׃
Jerusalem to. | has it done been | as | the heavens | whole | under | been has done | not

935 2088 7451 3605 48:72 8451 3789
13 כַּאֲשֶׁר כָּתוּב בְּתוֹרַת מֹשֶׁה אֵת כָּל־הָרָעָה הַזֹּאת בָּאָה
has come | this | evil | all | Moses, | the in of law | is it written | As

5771 7725 430 3068 6440 2470 3808
עָלֵינוּ וְלֹא־חִלִּינוּ אֶת־פְּנֵי ׀ יְהוָה אֱלֹהֵינוּ לָשׁוּב מֵעֲוֺנֵנוּ
our from perversities | we that turn might | God our, | Jehovah | the before of face | made we prayer our | Yet not | us on.

935 7451 3068 8245 571 7919
14 וּלְהַשְׂכִּיל בַּאֲמִתֶּךָ׃ וַיִּשְׁקֹד יְהוָה עַל־הָרָעָה וַיְבִיאֶהָ
has and it brought | evil the, | over | Jehovah | has And watched | truth Your. | under- and stand

62:13 834 4639 3605 430 3068 6662
עָלֵינוּ כִּי־צַדִּיק יְהוָה אֱלֹהֵינוּ עַל־כָּל־מַעֲשָׂיו אֲשֶׁר עָשָׂה
does He. | which | His works | all | in | God our | Jehovah | righteous (is) | For | us on.

3318 834 430 136 6258 6963 8085 3808
15 וְלֹא שָׁמַעְנוּ בְּקֹלוֹ׃ וְעַתָּה ׀ אֲדֹנָי אֱלֹהֵינוּ אֲשֶׁר הוֹצֵאתָ
brought has | who | God our, | Lord O | now And, | His voice. | did we obey | And not

3117 8034 6213 23:88 3027 4714 776 5971
אֶת־עַמְּךָ מֵאֶרֶץ מִצְרַיִם בְּיָד חֲזָקָה וַתַּעַשׂ־לְךָ שֵׁם כַּיּוֹם
(it is) as day | a name | for has and Yourself made | mighty, | a with hand | Egypt | the of out of land | Your people

639 4994 7725 6666 3605 136 7561 2398 2088
16 הַזֶּה חָטָאנוּ רָשָׁעְנוּ׃ אֲדֹנָי כְּכָל־צִדְקֹתֶךָ יָשָׁב־נָא אַפְּךָ
Your anger | please let back turn | righ- Your teousness, | according all to | O Lord, | have we evilly done. | have we sinned, | this;

5771 2399 6944 2022 33:89 5891 2534
וַחֲמָתְךָ מֵעִירְךָ יְרוּשָׁלִַם הַר־קָדְשֶׁךָ כִּי בַחֲטָאֵינוּ וּבַעֲוֺנוֹת
and of iniquities | of because sins our | For | Your mountain holy. | Jerusalem, | Your from city | Your and fury

6258 5439 3605 2781 5971 33 89
17 אֲבֹתֵינוּ יְרוּשָׁלִַם וְעַמְּךָ לְחֶרְפָּה לְכָל־סְבִיבֹתֵינוּ׃ וְעַתָּה ׀
And now | those us around. | all to | (become have) reproach a | Your people | and Jerusalem | our fathers,

6440 215 8469 5650 8605 430 8085
שְׁמַע אֱלֹהֵינוּ אֶל־תְּפִלַּת עַבְדְּךָ וְאֶל־תַּחֲנוּנָיו וְהָאֵר פָּנֶיךָ
Your face | make and shine | his supplications, | and to | Your servant | prayer the of | to | our O God, | listen,

241 430 51 86 136 4616 8076 4720
18 עַל־מִקְדָּשְׁךָ הַשָּׁמֵם לְמַעַן אֲדֹנָי׃ הַטֵּה אֱלֹהַי ׀ אָזְנְךָ
Your ear | my O God, | Incline, | the Lord's. | for sake | (is) that desolate, | Your sanctuary | on

7121 834 58:92 8074 7200 5869 6491 8085
וּשְׁמָע פְּקַח עֵינֶיךָ וּרְאֵה שֹׁמְמֹתֵינוּ וְהָעִיר אֲשֶׁר־נִקְרָא
called is | which | the and city | our desolations, | see and | Your eyes | Open | and hear.

by Your name. For we do not present our prayers before You on account of our righteousnesses, but because of Your great mercies. [19]O Lord, hear! O Lord, forgive! O Lord, listen and act! Do not delay, for Your own sake, O my God; for Your name is called on Your city and on Your people.

[20]And while I was speaking and praying and confessing my sin, and the sin of my people Israel, and making my cry fall before Jehovah my God for the holy mountain of my God; [21]and while I was setting my prayer in order, then the man, Gabriel, whom I had seen in the vision at the beginning, touched me in *my* severe exhaustion, about the time of the evening sacrifice. [22]And he enlightened me, and talked with me, and said, O Daniel, I have now come out to give you skill in understanding. [23]At the beginning of your prayers, the word came forth, and I have come to reveal. For you *are* greatly beloved. Then understand the matter and pay attention to the vision:

[24]Seventy weeks are decreed as to your people, and as to your holy city, to finish the transgression, and to make an end of sins, and to make atonement for iniquity, and to bring in everlasting righteousness, and to seal up the vision and prophecy, and to anoint the Most Holy. [25]Know, then, and understand *that* from the going out of a word to restore and to rebuild Jerusalem, to Messiah *the* Prince, *shall be* seven weeks and sixty-two weeks. The street shall be built again, and the wall, even in times of affliction. [26]And after sixty-two weeks, Messiah shall be cut off, but

שִׁמְךָ עָלֶיהָ כִּי ׀ לֹא עַל־צִדְקֹתֵינוּ אֲנַחְנוּ מַפִּילִים תַּחֲנוּנֵינוּ
our supplication do present we our righteousnesses on account of not For it on Your name

19 לְפָנֶיךָ כִּי עַל־רַחֲמֶיךָ הָרַבִּים׃ אֲדֹנָי ׀ שְׁמָעָה אֲדֹנָי ׀ סְלָחָה
!forgive ,Lord O !hear ,Lord O .great Your mercies because of but before You

אֲדֹנָי הַקֲשִׁיבָה וַעֲשֵׂה אַל־תְּאַחַר לְמַעַנְךָ אֱלֹהַי כִּי־שִׁמְךָ
Your name for my God ,O Your sake own for ,delay Do not !act and listen ,Lord O

20 נִקְרָא עַל־עִירְךָ וְעַל־עַמֶּךָ׃ וְעוֹד אֲנִי מְדַבֵּר וּמִתְפַּלֵּל
praying and was speaking I And while Your .people and on Your city on called is

וּמִתְוַדֶּה חַטָּאתִי וְחַטַּאת עַמִּי יִשְׂרָאֵל וּמַפִּיל תְּחִנָּתִי
sup- plication my causing fall to and ,Israel my people the of sin and ,sin my con- fessing and

21 לִפְנֵי יְהוָה אֱלֹהַי עַל הַר־קֹדֶשׁ אֱלֹהָי׃ וְעוֹד אֲנִי מְדַבֵּר
was speaking I and while ;God my holy the of mountain for God my Jehovah before

בַּתְּפִלָּה וְהָאִישׁ גַּבְרִיאֵל אֲשֶׁר רָאִיתִי בֶחָזוֹן בַּתְּחִלָּה
the at ,beginning the in vision had I seen whom ,Gabriel the then man ,prayer in

22 מֻעָף בִּיעָף נֹגֵעַ אֵלַי כְּעֵת מִנְחַת־עָרֶב׃ וַיָּבֶן וַיְדַבֵּר עִמִּי
with ,me talked and he And distinguished evening the .sacrifice about of time the ,me touched (my) in weary weariness

23 וַיֹּאמַר דָּנִיֵּאל עַתָּה יָצָאתִי לְהַשְׂכִּילְךָ בִינָה׃ בִּתְחִלַּת
be- the of ginning At under- .standing you give to in skill have I come now O ,Daniel ,said and

תַּחֲנוּנֶיךָ יָצָא דָבָר וַאֲנִי בָּאתִי לְהַגִּיד כִּי חֲמוּדוֹת אָתָּה
;you greatly beloved are for to ,declare have come and I the ,word came forth your supplications

24 וּבִין בַּדָּבָר וְהָבֵן בַּמַּרְאֶה׃ שָׁבֻעִים שִׁבְעִים נֶחְתַּךְ עַל־
to as are decreed Seventy weeks the .vision and understand matter the so heed

עַמְּךָ ׀ וְעַל־עִיר קָדְשֶׁךָ לְכַלֵּא הַפֶּשַׁע וּלְחָתֵם חַטָּאוֹת
,sins make to and of end an trans- the gression finish to ,holy your city as and to your ,people

וּלְכַפֵּר עָוֺן וּלְהָבִיא צֶדֶק עֹלָמִים וְלַחְתֹּם חָזוֹן וְנָבִיא
and prophecy vision seal to and up ,everlasting righteous- ness to and bring in ,iniquity to and for atone

25 וְלִמְשֹׁחַ קֹדֶשׁ קָדָשִׁים׃ וְתֵדַע וְתַשְׂכֵּל מִן־מֹצָא דָבָר
the word the of issuing from under- and stand Then ,know .Most Holy the to and anoint

לְהָשִׁיב וְלִבְנוֹת יְרוּשָׁלַםִ עַד־מָשִׁיחַ נָגִיד שָׁבֻעִים שִׁבְעָה
seven (be shall) weeks (the) Prince Messiah to ,Jerusalem to and rebuild to restore

וְשָׁבֻעִים שִׁשִּׁים וּשְׁנַיִם תָּשׁוּב וְנִבְנְתָה רְחוֹב וְחָרוּץ
ditch and (with) plaza be shall it built Again .two and sixty weeks and

26 וּבְצוֹק הָעִתִּים׃ וְאַחֲרֵי הַשָּׁבֻעִים שִׁשִּׁים וּשְׁנַיִם יִכָּרֵת
be shall off cut ,two and sixty weeks the And after .times the in even of affliction

not *for* Himself. And the people of a coming prince shall destroy the city and the sanctuary. And its end *shall be* with the flood, and ruins are determined, until the end *shall be* war.

27 And he shall confirm a covenant with the many *for* one week. And in the middle of the week he shall cause the sacrifice and the offering to cease; and on a corner *of the altar,* desolating abominations, even until *the* end. And that which was decreed shall pour out on the desolator.

935 5057 5971 7843 6944 5892 369 4899
מָשִׁיחַ וְאֵין לוֹ וְהָעִיר וְהַקֹּדֶשׁ יַשְׁחִית עַם נָגִיד הַבָּא
.coming a the destroy shall the and the And to and ,Messiah
prince of people sanctuary city .Him is not
1396 8074 2782 4421 7093 5704 7858 7093
27 וְקִצּוֹ בַשֶּׁטֶף וְעַד קֵץ מִלְחָמָה נֶחֱרֶצֶת שֹׁמֵמוֹת׃ וְהִגְבִּיר
he And .desolations are (be shall) (the) and (be shall) its And
confirm shall determined ;war end until ,flood the with end
2077 7673 7620 2677 259 7620 7227 1285
בְּרִית לָרַבִּים שָׁבוּעַ אֶחָד וַחֲצִי הַשָּׁבוּעַ יַשְׁבִּית ׀ זֶבַח
sacrifice shall he week the in And .one (for) the with a
cease make of half the week many covenant
5413 2782 3617 5704 8074 8251 3671 5921 4503
וּמִנְחָה וְעַל כְּנַף שִׁקּוּצִים מְשֹׁמֵם וְעַד־כָּלָה וְנֶחֱרָצָה תִּתַּךְ
shall which that And (the) even a abominations wing a and and
out pour decreed was .end until ,desolator as upon ,offering
8074
עַל־שֹׁמֵם׃
the on
.desolator

CAP. X י

CHAPTER 10

1 In the third year of Cyrus king of Persia, a thing was revealed to Daniel, whose name was called Belteshazzar. And the thing *was* true, and a great conflict. And he understood the thing, and *had* understanding of the vision. 2 In those days I, Daniel, was mourning three weeks of days. 3 I ate no food for delight, and no flesh or wine came into my mouth. I did not anoint myself at all until three weeks of days were fulfilled. 4 And in the twenty-fourth day of the first month, as I was by the hand of the great river, which *is* Tigris, 5 then I lifted up my eyes and looked: And, behold, a certain man was clothed in linen, whose loins were wrapped in fine gold from Uphaz. 6 His body *was* also like the beryl, and his face looked like lightning. And his eyes *were* like torches of fire; and his arms and his feet in color like polished bronze; and the sound of his words *were* as the noise of a multitude. 7 And I, Daniel, alone saw the

1840 1540 1697 6539 4428 3566 7969 8141
1 בִּשְׁנַת שָׁלוֹשׁ לְכוֹרֶשׁ מֶלֶךְ פָּרַס דָּבָר נִגְלָה לְדָנִיֵּאל
,Daniel to was a ,Persia king Cyrus third the In
revealed thing of year
1419 6635 1697 571 1095 8034 7121 834
אֲשֶׁר־נִקְרָא שְׁמוֹ בֵּלְטְשַׁאצַּר וֶאֱמֶת הַדָּבָר וְצָבָא גָדוֹל
.great a and ,thing the And .Belteshazzar whose was
conflict (was) true name called
3117 4758 998 1697 995
2 וּבִין אֶת־הַדָּבָר וּבִינָה לוֹ בַּמַּרְאֶה׃ בַּיָּמִים הָהֵם אֲנִי
,I those days In the in to under- and the he And
.vision him (was) standing word understood
2532 3899 3117 7620 7969 56 1961 1840
3 דָּנִיֵּאל הָיִיתִי מִתְאַבֵּל שְׁלֹשָׁה שָׁבֻעִים יָמִים׃ לֶחֶם חֲמֻדוֹת
desirable food .days weeks three mourning was ,Daniel
of
5704 5480 3808 5480 6310 935 3808 3196 1320 398 3808
לֹא אָכַלְתִּי וּבָשָׂר וָיַיִן לֹא־בָא אֶל־פִּי וְסוֹךְ לֹא־סָכְתִּי עַד
until did I not at and my to did not and and ,ate I not
myself anoint all ,mouth come wine flesh
702 6242 3117 3117 7620 7969 4390
4 מְלֹאת שְׁלֹשֶׁת שָׁבֻעִים יָמִים׃ וּבְיוֹם עֶשְׂרִים וְאַרְבָּעָה
fourth and twenty the in And .days of weeks three were
day fulfilled
1419 5104 3027 1961 7223 2320
לַחֹדֶשׁ הָרִאשׁוֹן וַאֲנִי הָיִיתִי עַל יַד הַנָּהָר הַגָּדוֹל הוּא
which ,great the the by was I as ,first the of
(is) river of side month
3847 259 376 2009 7200 5869 5375 2313
5 חִדָּקֶל׃ וָאֶשָּׂא אֶת־עֵינַי וָאֵרֶא וְהִנֵּה אִישׁ־אֶחָד לָבוּשׁ
was certain a and and my I then ,Tigris
in clothed man ,behold :looked eyes up lifted
6440 8658 1472 210 3800 2296 4975 906
6 בַּדִּים וּמָתְנָיו חֲגֻרִים בְּכֶתֶם אוּפָז׃ וּגְוִיָּתוֹ כְתַרְשִׁישׁ וּפָנָיו
his and the like his also Uphaz fine in were his and ,linen
face ,beryl (was) body from gold girded loins
5869 4772 2220 784 3940 5869 1300 4758
כְּמַרְאֵה בָרָק וְעֵינָיו כְּלַפִּידֵי אֵשׁ וּזְרֹעֹתָיו וּמַרְגְּלֹתָיו כְּעֵין
the as his and his and ,fire torches like his and ;lightning the like
of eyes feet arms of eyes of appearance
1840 7200 1995 6963 1697 6963 7044 5178
7 נְחֹשֶׁת קָלָל וְקוֹל דְּבָרָיו כְּקוֹל הָמוֹן׃ וְרָאִיתִי אֲנִי דָנִיֵּאל
,Daniel ,I saw And mul- a the as his the and ,polished bronze
.titude of noise words of sound

vision. For the men who were with me did not see the vision. But a great trembling fell on them, so that they fled to hide themselves. [8]Then I was left alone, and saw this great vision; and there remained no strength in me. For my glory was turned within me to corruption, and I kept no strength. [9]Yet I heard the sound of his words. And when I heard the sound of his words, then I was on my face, stunned; and my face *was* toward the ground.

[10]And, behold, a hand touched me and set me shaking on my knees and the palms of my hands. [11]And he said to me, O Daniel, a man greatly beloved, understand the words that I speak to you, and stand up. For I am now sent to you. And when he had spoken this word to me, I stood, trembling. [12]And he said to me, Do not fear, Daniel. For from the first day that you set your heart to understand, and to humble yourself before your God, your words were heard. And I have come because of your words. [13]But the king of the kingdom of Persia withstood me twenty-one days. But, lo, Michael, one of the first rulers, came to help me. And I stayed there with the kings of Persia. [14]Now I have come to make you understand what shall happen to your people in the latter days. For the vision *is* yet for *many* days. [15]And when he had spoken such words to me, I set my face to the ground, and I became speechless.

[16]And, behold, *one* in form as the sons of men

7200 3808 1961 834 582 4758 905
לבדי את־המראה והאנשים אשר־היו עמי לא־ראו את־
did not with were who the while ,vision the alone
see me men

2244 1272 5307 1419 2731 61 4758
המראה אבל חרדה גדלה נפלה עליהם ויברחו בהחבא׃
hide to they and ,them on fell great a But .vision the
.themselves fled trembling

2063 1419 4758 7200 7604
8 ואני נשארתי לבדי ואראה את־המראה הגדלה הזאת
,this great vision saw and alone left was I Then

6113 3808 4889 2015 1935 3581 7604 3808
ולא־נשאר־בי כח והודי נהפך עלי למשחית ולא עצרתי
kept I and ,corruption to within was my For .strength in there and
not me turned glory me remained not

1697 6963 8085 1697 6963 8085 3581
9 כח׃ ואשמע את־קול דבריו וכשמעי את־קול דבריו
his the I when And his the heard I Yet .strength
,words of sound heard .words of sound

5060 3027 2009 776 6440 6440 7290 1961
10 ואני הייתי נרדם על־פני ופני ארצה׃ והנה־יד נגעה
touched a And the toward my and my on lying was I then
hand ,behold .ground (was) face ,face stunned

376 1840 559 3027 3709 1290 5128
11 בי ותניעני על־ברכי וכפות ידי׃ ויאמר אלי דניאל איש־
man a O ,me to he And my the and my on me set and ,me
,Daniel said .hands of palms knees shaking

5975 1696 834 1697 995 2532
חמדות הבן בדברים אשר אנכי דבר אליך ועמד על־
in and you to speak I that words the under- greatly
stand stand ,beloved

1697 1696 7971 6258 5977
עמדך כי עתה שלחתי אליך ובדברו עמי את־הדבר
word with he when And .you to sent I am now For your
me spoken had .place

1840 3372 408 559 7460 5977 2088
12 הזה עמדתי מרעיד׃ ויאמר אלי אל־תירא דניאל כי ׀
for ,Daniel Do not ,me to he Then .trembling stood I ,this
,fear said

6031 995 3820 5414 834 7223 3117
מן־היום הראשון אשר נתת את־לבך להבין ולהתענות
humbling and to your set you that first the from
yourself understand heart day

8269 1697 935 1697 8085 430 6440
13 לפני אלהיך נשמעו דבריך ואני־באתי בדבריך׃ ושר ׀
the But your for have I And your were your before
of leader .words come .words heard ,God

4317 2009 3117 259 6242 5975 6539 4438
מלכות פרס עמד לנגדי עשרים ואחד יום והנה מיכאל
,Michael But .days and twenty against stood Persia king- the
,lo one me of dom

8033 5414 5826 935 7223 8269 259
אחד השרים הראשנים בא לעזרני ואני נותרתי שם
there stayed I And help to came ,first rulers the of one
me

7136 834 995 935 6539 4428 681
14 אצל מלכי פרס׃ ובאתי להבינך את אשר־יקרה
shall what make to I Now .Persia kings the with
happen understand you come have of

1696 3117 2377 5750 3117 319 5971
15 לעמך באחרית הימים כי־עוד חזון לימים׃ ובדברו עמי
with he when And .days for the yet For .days latter the in your to
me spoken had vision (is) people

1823 2009 481 776 6440 5414 428 1697
16 כדברים האלה נתתי פני ארצה ונאלמתי׃ והנה כדמות
in (one) And became I and the to my set I ,these according
as form ,behold .speechless ground face words to

touched my lips. And I opened my mouth and spoke, and said to him who stood before me, O lord, my pangs have come over me, because of the vision, and I have no strength left. ¹⁷For how can the servant of my lord speak this with this my lord? For as for me, there is no power left in me; yea, there is no breath left in me. ¹⁸And again *one* in form as a man touched me, and made me strong. ¹⁹And he said, O man greatly beloved, do not fear. Peace to you. Be strong. Yea, be strong! And when he had spoken to me, I was made strong. And *I* said, Speak, my lord, for you have made me strong. ²⁰And he said, Do you know why I have come to you? And now I will return to fight with the ruler of Persia. And when I have gone out, then, lo, the ruler of Greece shall come. ²¹But I will tell you what is written in the Scripture of Truth. And no one makes himself strong with Me in these things, except Michael your ruler.

559	1696	63,10 6605	8193	5060 120	1121
וְאֹמְרָה	וַאֲדַבְּרָה	וָאֶפְתַּח־פִּי	עַל־שְׂפָתָי	נֹגֵעַ אָדָם	בְּנֵי
said and	spoke and	my mouth opened and	my lips my on touched	men	the of sons

3808	6735 2015	47,58	113	50,48 5975	
וְלֹא	עָלַי צִירַי	נֶהֶפְכוּ	בַּמַּרְאָה אֲדֹנִי	לְנֶגְדִּי וָאֹמְרָה	
not and	me pangs	turned	visions the ,lord O before	him to	

stood, have over me

113	1696 2088 11,13	5650 32,01 1963	3581	6113
כֹּחַ	עִם־אֲדֹנִי זֶה לְדַבֵּר עֶבֶד יוּכַל וְהֵיךְ			עָצַרְתִּי
my lord	with speak this my lord of servant can how For			.strength have I left

7604	3808 5397 3581	5975 3808 6258	2088
נִשְׁאֲרָה־בִּי	לֹא וּנְשָׁמָה כֹחַ לִי־יַעֲמָד־בִּי	מֵעַתָּה וַאֲנִי	זֶה
.me in is there not ,yea ;power in is not hence-forth ,me for as For ?this			

3372 408 559	2388	120 4758	5060 3254
אַל־תִּירָא	וַיֹּאמֶר וַיְחַזְּקֵנִי	אָדָם כְּמַרְאֵה	בִּי וַיֹּסֶף וַיִּגַּע
fear do not he And make and ,man a in (one) me touched Then said. strong me as form again			

2388	2388 2388	7965 2532 376	
אִישׁ־חֲמֻדוֹת	שָׁלוֹם לָךְ חֲזַק וַחֲזָק וּבְדַבְּרוֹ עִמִּי הִתְחַזָּקְתִּי		
made was I to he when And be ,yea be to Peace greatly O stronger me spoken had .strong ;strong ,you .loved man			

4100 3045 559	2388	11,3 1696 559	
וָאֹמְרָה	יְדַבֵּר אֲדֹנִי כִּי חִזַּקְתָּנִי וַיֹּאמֶר הֲיָדַעְתָּ לָמָּה		
why you Do he And made you for my Let I And know .said .strong me .lord speak .said			

| 6539 8269 3898 7725 6258 935 |
| בָּאתִי אֵלֶיךָ וְעַתָּה אָשׁוּב לְהִלָּחֵם עִם־שַׂר פָּרַס וַאֲנִי |
| And .Persia the with fight to will I now And ?you to have I I when of ruler return come |

| 3791 7559 3046 61 935 3120 8269 2009 3318 |
| יֹצֵא וְהִנֵּה שַׂר־יָוָן בָּא׃ אֲבָל אַגִּיד לְךָ אֶת־הָרָשׁוּם בִּכְתָב |
| the in is what you will I But shall Greece the then have of writing inscribed tell .come of ruler ,lo ,out gone |

| 4317 428 2381 259 369 571 |
| אֱמֶת וְאֵין אֶחָד מִתְחַזֵּק עִמִּי עַל־אֵלֶּה כִּי אִם־מִיכָאֵל |
| Michael except these in with himself makes one And .truth things me strong not |

| 8269 |
| שַׂרְכֶם׃ |
| your .ruler |

CHAPTER 11

CHAPTER 11

¹And I, in the first year of Darius the Mede, I was standing for a supporter and for a fortress for him. ²And now I will declare to you the truth: Behold, three kings will yet stand up in Persia. And the fourth *shall be rich in* all greater riches. And when he is strong by his rulers he will stir up all the kingdom of Greece. ³And a mighty king will stand up and will rule with great authority and do according to his will. ⁴And when he stands up his kingdom will be broken, and *it* will be divided to the

4581	2388	5977	4075	1867	259	8141	
וּלְמָעוֹז	לְמַחֲזִיק	עָמְדִי	לְדָרְיָוֶשׁ	הַמָּדִי	אַחַת	בִּשְׁנַת	וַאֲנִי
a for and	a for	my	,Mede the	Darius of	first	the in	And
fortress	supporter	standing				year	,I

4428	7969	5750 2009	5046	571	62,58		
מְלָכִים	שְׁלֹשָׁה	עוֹד הִנֵּה־לָךְ	אַגִּיד	אֱמֶת	וְעַתָּה	לוֹ	
kings	three	yet ,Behold	.you to will I	truth	the now And	for tell	.him

2393	3605	1419 6239	6238	7243	6539	5975
עֹמְדִים	לְפָרַס וְהָרְבִיעִי יַעֲשִׁיר עֹשֶׁר־גָּדוֹל מִכֹּל וּכְחֶזְקָתוֹ					
he when And .all greater riches (be shall) the and ;Persia in shall strong is (in) rich fourth up stand						

1368	4428 5975	3120 4438	36,05 5782 6239
בְעָשְׁרוֹ	יָעִיר אֵת כָּל־מַלְכוּת יָוָן׃ וְעָמַד מֶלֶךְ גִּבּוֹר		
,mighty king a shall And .Greece the all shall he his by up stand of kingdom up stir ,rulers			

4438	7665 5975	7522 6213 7227 4910 4910	
וּמָשַׁל	מִמְשָׁל רַב וְעָשָׂה כִּרְצוֹנוֹ׃ וּכְעָמְדוֹ תִּשָּׁבֵר מַלְכוּתוֹ		
his be shall when And to according do and great with shall and kingdom broken ,up stands he .will his authority rule

four winds of the heavens, and not to his posterity, nor according to his authority with which he ruled. For his kingdom will be pulled up and *given* to others besides these.

5And the king of the south shall be strong. And *one* of his rulers, even he shall overcome him, and he will rule; his rule *shall be* a great rule. 6And at the end of the years, they shall unite, and the daughter of the king of the south shall come to the king of the north to make a treaty. But she shall not keep the power of the arm. And he will not stand, nor his arm. But she will be given up, and those who brought her, and her begetter, and her supporter in *the* times. 7But the shoots of her roots will rise *in* his place, and he shall come to the army, and will enter into the fortress of the king of the north. And he will act against them, and will show power. 8And he will also bring their gods with their molten images, with vessels of their possessions, silver and gold, into exile *to* Egypt. And *for* years he shall stand *away* from the king of the north. 9And the king of the south will come into *his* kingdom, and will return to his own land. 10But his sons shall be stirred up, and will gather a host of great forces. And *one* will certainly come and overflow, and pass through. And he will return to his fortress, and be stirred up. 11And the king of the south will be furious, and will go out and fight with him, with the king of the north. And he will raise a great host. But the host will be given into his hand. 12And capturing the host, his heart will be lifted up. And he will make fall myriads, but he will not have power. 13For the king of the north will return and will raise a host greater than the former; and at the end of the times, years, he will certainly come with a great army and with much equipment. 14And in those times many

4475 3808 319 3808 8064 7307 702 2673
ותחץ לארבע רוחות השמים ולא לאחריתו ולא כמשלו
to according nor his to and ,heavens the winds the to be shall and
authority his ,posterity not of four divided

4910 3588 5428 4438 312 3808 4428
אשר משל כי תנתש מלכותו ולאחרים מלבד־אלה׃
.these besides (given) and his be shall For he with
others to ,kingdom up pulled .ruled which

5 2388 4428 5045 8269 2388 5921 4910 4474
ויחזק מלך־הנגב ומן־שריו ויחזק עליו ומשל ממשל
rule A he and on will he and his And .south the the shall And
.rule will ,him strong be ,rulers of (one) of king strong be

6 7227 4475 7093 8141 2266 1323 4428 5045
רב ממשלתו׃ ולקץ שנים יתחברו ובת מלך־הנגב
the of king the and join shall they ,years the at And (be shall) great
south's daughter ,together of end .rule his

935 413 4428 6828 6213 4339 3808 6113 3581
תבוא אל־מלך הצפון לעשות מישרים ולא־תעצר כוח
the shall she But an make to the king the to shall
of power keep not .agreement north of come

2220 3808 5975 2220 5414 1931 935 3205
הזרוע ולא יעמד וזרעו ותנתן היא ומביאיה והילדה
her and who those and she be shall But his nor shall he And the
,begetter ,her brought up given .arm ,stand not .arm

7 2388 6256 5975 5342 8328 3653 935 413
ומחזקה בעתים׃ ועמד מנצר שרשיה כנו ויבא אל־
to he and (in) ,roots her the of will But (those) in her and
come shall ,place his of shoots stand .times supporter

2428 935 4581 4428 6828 6213 2388
החיל ויבא במעוז מלך הצפון ועשה בהם והחזיק׃
shall and against he And the king the the into shall and the
.power show them act shall .north of of fortress enter army

8 1571 430 5257 3627 2532 3701 2091
וגם אלהיהם עם־נסכיהם עם־כלי חמדתם כסף וזהב
and silver their vessels with their with gods their And
gold possessions of images molten also

7628 935 4714 1931 8141 5975 4428 6828
בשבי יבא מצרים והוא שנים יעמד ממלך הצפון׃
.north the the from shall years he And .Egypt (to) will he into
of king stand bring exile

9 935 4428 5045 7725 127 1121 1624
10 ובא במלכות מלך הנגב ושב אל־אדמתו׃ ובנו יתגרו
be shall his But .land own his to will and the king the (his) into and
up stirred sons return ,south of kingdom come will

622 1995 2428 7227 935 935 7857 5674 7725
ואספו המון חילים רבים ובא בוא ושטף ועבר וישב
he And pass and over-and cer- (one) And .great forces mul-a shall and
return shall .through flow tainly come shall of titude gather

11 1624 5704 4581 4843 4428 5045 3318 3898
ויתגרו עד־מעזה׃ ויתמרמר מלך הנגב ויצא ונלחם עמו
with and will and the king the shall And his to be and
,him fight out go south of furious become .fortress ,up stirred

4428 6828 5975 1995 7227 5414 1995 3027
עם־מלך הצפון והעמיד המון רב ונתן ההמון בידו׃
his into the shall But .great host a he And .north the the with
.hand host given be raise shall of king

12 5375 1995 5375 3824 5307 7239 3808 5810
13 ונשא ההמון ירום לבבו והפיל רבאות ולא יעוז׃ ושב
shall For shall he but ,myriads will he And his be shall the cap-And
return .strong be not , fall make ,heart up lifted ,host turing

4428 6828 5975 1995 7227 7223 7093 6256
מלך הצפון והעמיד המון רב מן־הראשון ולקץ העתים
,times the at and .former the than greater host a shall and ,north the the
of end the raise of king

14 8141 935 935 2428 1419 7399 7227 6256
שנים בוא יבוא בחיל גדול וברכוש רב׃ ובעתים ההם
those times in And .much with and great a with cer- shall he ,years
equipment army tainly come

shall stand up against the king of the south. And the sons of the violent ones of your people shall lift up to make stand *the* vision; but they shall stumble. ¹⁵And the king of the north shall come and pour out a siegemound, and seize a fortified city. But the south's arms shall not stand, nor his chosen people; for there will be no strength to stand. ¹⁶But he coming against him will do as he wills, and none shall stand before him. And he shall stand in the glorious land, and destruction in his hand. ¹⁷And he will set his face to go in with the strength of all his kingdom, and upright ones with him; so he shall do. And he shall give the daughter of women to him, to destroy it. But she will not stand, nor be for him. ¹⁸And he shall turn his face to the coasts, and shall capture many. But a ruler shall make cease his reproach for him, but his reproach will return to him. ¹⁹And he shall turn his face to the fortresses of his land, but he will stumble and fall, and will not be found. ²⁰And one who sends an exactor shall stand in his place, *for* the glory of *the* kingdom. But within a few days he will be broken, but not in anger, and not in battle. ²¹And a despised one shall stand up in his place, and they shall not give to him the honor of the king; but he will enter while at ease and seize *the* kingdom by intrigues. ²²And the forces of the overflow will be swept from before him, and they will be broken, and also the ruler of a covenant. ²³And after they join him, he will practice deceit. For he will come and be strong with a few people. ²⁴He will enter safely, even into the rich places of *the* province. And he shall do what his fathers nor his father's father have not done. He shall plunder and spoil, and scatter goods among them.

רבים יעמדו על־מלך הנגב ׀ ובני ׀ פריצי עמך ינשאו
5375 5971 6530 1121 5045 44 28 5975 7227
lift shall / your / violent / the / the / And / the / / the / against / stand shall / many
up / people / of ones / of sons / .south / of king / / / up

15 להעמיד חזון ונכשלו׃ ויבא מלך הצפון וישפך סוללה
5550 8210 6828 44 28 935 3782 2377 5975
siege a / pour and / the / the / shall So / shall they but / (the) / establish to
mound / out / north / of king / come / .stumble / ;vision

ולכד עיר מבצרות וזרעות הנגב לא יעמדו ועם מבחריו
4005 5971 5975 38 08 50 45 2220 4013 5892 3920
his of / nor / shall / not / the / the And / .fortified / city a and
choice / people / ,stand / south of / arms / / / seize

16 ואין כח לעמד׃ ויעש הבא אליו כרצונו ואין עומד
5975 369 7522 1935 6213 5975 3581 369
shall / and / he as / against / who he / will But / .stand to / strength / for
stand / none / wills / him / comes / do / / be will not

17 לפניו ויעמד בארצ־הצבי וכלה בידו׃ וישם ׀ פניו לבוא
935 6440 7760 3027 3617 6643 776 5975 6440
go to / his / He Also / his in / and / ,glorious the / in / he And / before
in / face / set shall / .hand / destruction / / land / stand shall / .him

בתקף כל־מלכותו וישרים עמו ועשה ובת הנשים יתן
5414 802 1323 6213 3477 4438 36 05 8633
shall he / women / the And / he so / with / upright and / his / whole / the with
give / of daughter / .do shall / him / ones / ,kingdom / of strength

18 לו להשחיתה ולא תעמד ולא־לו תהיה׃ וישב ׀ פניו
6440 7725 1961 38 08 5975 38 08 7843
his / he And / .be / for nor / shall she / But / destroy to / to
face / turn shall / / him / ,stand / not / .it / him

לאים ולכד רבים והשבית קצין חרפתו לו בלתי חרפתו
2781 21115 2781 7101 76 73 7227 3920 339
his / but / for / his / ruler a / shall But / .many shall and / the to
reproach / reproach / / ,him reproach / cease make / / capture / coasts

19 ישב לו׃ וישב ׀ פניו למעוזי ארצו ונכשל ונפל ולא
38 08 5307 37 82 776 4581 64 40 7725 7725
and fall and / will he but / own his / the toward / his / he Then / to / shall
not / stumble / ,land / of fortresses / face turn shall / .him / return

20 ימצא׃ ועמד על־כנו מעביר נוגש הדר מלכות ובימים
3117 4438 1925 5065 5674 3653 5975 4672
within But / (the) / the (for) / an / who one / his / shall Then / be shall
days / .kingdom / of glory / exactor / sends / place / stand / .found

21 אחדים ישבר ולא באפים ולא במלחמה׃ ועמד על־
5975 4421 38 08 639 38 08 766 5 259
in / shall And / .battle / in / and / anger in / but / will he / few a
up stand / / not / ,broken be / 3653

כנו נבזה ולא־נתנו עליו הוד מלכות ובא בשלוה והחזיק
2388 79 62 935 4438 1935 5414 959
seize and / while / he But / king- the / honor / to / they and de- / his
ease at enter will / dom / him / give shall not / ,spised place

22 מלכות בחלקלקות׃ וזרעות השטף ישטפו מלפניו
6440 7858 7857 2220 2579 4438
before from / shall / the / the And / .intrigues by / (the)
him / swept be / overflow / of forces / / kingdom

23 וישברו וגם נגיד ברית׃ ומן־התחברות אליו יעשה
6213 2266 1285 5057 1571 7665
shall he / to / join they / And / a / ruler the and will they and
practice / him / themselves / after / ,covenant of / also ,broken be

24 מרמה ועלה ועצם במעט־גוי׃ בשלוה ובמשמני מדינה
4082 4924 1796 2 4592 6105 5927 4820
(the) / the into / even / ,Safely / .people / a with shall and / he For / .deceit
province of / places rich / / few strong / be come shall

יבא ועשה אשר לא־עשו אבתיו ואבות אבתיו בזה
961 62 13 935
Plunder / his / nor / his / have not / what / he And / will he
.fathers' / fathers / fathers / .done / do shall / .enter

ושלל ורכוש להם יבזור ועל מבצרים יחשב מחשבתיו
428 4 2835 4013 967 7339 7998
plots his / shall he / the / And shall he / among / and / and
devise / ,strongholds against / .scatter them / goods / ,spoil

And he shall devise his plots against the strongholds, even for a time. [25]And he will stir up his power and his heart against the king of the south with a great army. And the king of the south will be stirred to battle with a great and very mighty army. But he shall not stand, for they shall devise plots against him. [26]Yea, those who eat his food shall break him, and his army shall overflow. And many will fall down slain. [27]And both of these kings, their hearts *seek* to do evil, and they will speak false at one table. But it shall not prosper, for *the* end *comes* at the appointed time. [28]And he will return to his land with great wealth. And his heart *shall be* against *the* holy covenant. And he will act, and he will return to his land. [29]At the appointed time he will return and come against the south, but it will not be as the former or as the latter.

[30]For the ships of Chittim will come against him. And he shall be grieved, and turn back, and be furious against *the* holy covenant. And he shall act, and will return, and will heed those forsaking *the* holy covenant. [31]And forces will stand from him, and they will profane the sanctuary, the fortress. And *they* shall remove the regular *sacrifice*; and they will place the desolating abomination. [32]And he will ruin by flatteries those who do evil against *the* covenant. But the people who know their God will be strong, and will work. [33]And those who understand among the people will teach many; yet they will stumble by the sword, and by flame; by exile and spoil, *for* days. [34]And when they stumble, they shall be helped with a little help. But many will join them, with hypocrisy. [35]And *many* of those who understand shall stumble, to refine and to purge them, and *to* make white, to the time of *the* end. For *it is* yet for the appointed time. [36]And the

1419 2428 5045 4428 3824 3581 5782 6256
25 וְעַד־עֵת׃ וְיָעֵר כֹּחוֹ וּלְבָבוֹ עַל־מֶלֶךְ הַנֶּגֶב בְּחַיִל גָּדוֹל
.great a with the the against his and his he And a even
army south of king heart power stir will .time for

3966 6099 1419 2428 4421 1624 5045 4428
וּמֶלֶךְ הַנֶּגֶב יִתְגָּרֶה לַמִּלְחָמָה בְּחַיִל־גָּדוֹל וְעָצוּם עַד־מְאֹד
.very and great a with battle to be shall the the And
mighty army up stirred south of king

6598 398 4284 2803 5975
26 וְלֹא יַעֲמֹד כִּי־יַחְשְׁבוּ עָלָיו מַחֲשָׁבוֹת׃ וְאֹכְלֵי פַת־בָּגוֹ
food his those Even .plots against shall they for shall he But
eat who him devise ,stand not

8147 7227 2491 5307 7857 2428 7665
27 יְשַׁבְּרוּהוּ וְחֵילוֹ יִשְׁטוֹף וְנָפְלוּ חֲלָלִים רַבִּים׃ וּשְׁנֵיהֶם
both And .many slain shall And over- shall his and break shall
,them of down fall .flow army ,him

3808 1696 3577 259 7979 7451 3824 4428
הַמְּלָכִים לְבָבָם לְמֵרָע וְעַל־שֻׁלְחָן אֶחָד כָּזָב יְדַבֵּרוּ וְלֹא
But shall they lie(s) one table and do to hearts their ,kings the
not .speak at ,evil (be shall)

1419 7339 776 7725 4150 7093 5750 6743
28 תִצְלָח כִּי־עוֹד קֵץ לַמּוֹעֵד׃ וְיָשֹׁב אַרְצוֹ בִּרְכוּשׁ גָּדוֹל
.great wealth with his he And set the at (the) still for shall it
land to return will .time end ,prosper

7725 4150 776 7725 6213 6944 1285 3824
29 וּלְבָבוֹ עַל־בְּרִית קֹדֶשׁ וְעָשָׂה וְשָׁב לְאַרְצוֹ׃ לַמּוֹעֵד יָשׁוּב
will he the At .land his he and he and ;holy (the) against his And
return time set to return shall ,do shall covenant heart

935 314 7223 1961 3808 5045 935
30 וּבָא בַנֶּגֶב וְלֹא־תִהְיֶה כָרִאשֹׁנָה וְכָאַחֲרֹנָה׃ וּבָאוּ בוֹ
against will For the as or former the as shall it But against and
him come .latter be not .south the come

6213 6944 1285 2194 7725 3512 3794 6716
צִיִּים כִּתִּים וְנִכְאָה וְשָׁב וְזָעַם עַל־בְּרִית־קוֹדֶשׁ וְעָשָׂה
he And .holy (the) against be and turn and shall he Then .Kittim ships
,work shall covenant furious back grieved be of

5975 2220 6944 1285 5800 995 7725
31 וְשָׁב וְיָבֵן עַל־עֹזְבֵי בְּרִית קֹדֶשׁ׃ וּזְרֹעִים מִמֶּנּוּ יַעֲמֹדוּ
shall from And .holy (the) for- the and he and
,stand him arms covenant of sakers heed return will

8251 5414 8548 5493 4581 4720 2490
וְחִלְּלוּ הַמִּקְדָּשׁ הַמָּעוֹז וְהֵסִירוּ הַתָּמִיד וְנָתְנוּ הַשִּׁקּוּץ
the they and regular the shall and the ,sanctuary the they and
abomination put shall ,(sacrifice) remove ;fortress profane will

430 3045 5971 2514 2610 1285 7561 8074
32 מְשׁוֹמֵם׃ וּמַרְשִׁיעֵי בְרִית יַחֲנִיף בַּחֲלַקּוֹת וְעַם יֹדְעֵי אֱלֹהָיו
their who the But by shall he (the) evildoers And that
God know people .flatteries defile ,covenant against .desolates

2719 3782 7227 995 5971 995 7919 6213 2388
33 יַחֲזִקוּ וְעָשׂוּ׃ וּמַשְׂכִּילֵי עָם יָבִינוּ לָרַבִּים וְנִכְשְׁלוּ בְּחֶרֶב
the by will they Yet .many will (the) who those And will and be will
sword stumble instruct people among understand .work ,strong

4592 5828 5826 3782 3117 961 7628 3852
34 וּבְלֶהָבָה בִּשְׁבִי וּבְבִזָּה יָמִים׃ וּבְהִכָּשְׁלָם יֵעָזְרוּ עֵזֶר מְעָט
a help shall they they when And (for) by and by by and
.little with helped be ,stumble shall .days ,spoil exile flame

3782 7919 2519 7227 3867
35 וְנִלְווּ עֲלֵיהֶם רַבִּים בַּחֲלַקְלַקּוֹת׃ וּמִן־הַמַּשְׂכִּילִים יִכָּשְׁלוּ
shall who those And .hypocrisy with many them to shall But
,stumble understand of join

4150 5750 7093 6256 3835 1305 6884
לִצְרוֹף בָּהֶם וּלְבָרֵר וְלַלְבֵּן עַד־עֵת קֵץ כִּי־עוֹד לַמּוֹעֵד׃
the for (is it) For (the) the to make and to and them to
.time set still .end of time ,white ,purge refine

410 3605 1431 7311 4428 7522 6213
36 וְעָשָׂה כִרְצוֹנוֹ הַמֶּלֶךְ וְיִתְרוֹמֵם וְיִתְגַּדֵּל עַל־כָּל־אֵל וְעַל
even ;god every above and shall he And .king the according will And
against magnify himself exalt will his to do

king shall do according to
his will. And he shall exalt
and magnify himself above
every god; *he* shall even
speak marvelous things
against the God of gods,
and shall prosper until the
fury is fulfilled. For that
which is decreed shall be
done. 37He shall not regard
the God of his fathers, nor
the desire of women, nor
love any god. For he shall
magnify himself above all.
38But in his place he shall
honor the god of forces; and
he shall honor a god whom
his fathers did not know,
with gold and silver, and
with precious stones, and
desirable things. 39And he
shall act in the strongholds
of *the* fortresses with a
foreign god, whom he shall
acknowledge. He shall multiply in glory; and he shall
cause them to rule over
many, and shall divide the
land for a price.
40And at the end-time,
the king of the south shall
push at him. And the king of
the north shall come
against him like a tempest,
with chariots and with
horsemen, and with many
ships. And he shall go into
the lands, and shall overflow and pass over. 41He
shall also enter into the
glorious land, and many
shall be stumbled. But
these shall escape out of
his hand: Edom and Moab,
and the chief of the sons of
Ammon. 42He shall also
stretch out his hand on the
lands; and the land of Egypt
shall not escape. 43But he
shall have power over the
treasures of gold and silver,
and over the precious
things of Egypt. And the
Libyans and the Ethiopians
shall be at his steps. 44But
news from the east and
from the north shall trouble
him. Then he will go out
with great fury to destroy
and to devote many to de-
struction. 45And he shall
plant his palace tents
between *the* seas in the
glorious holy mountain. Yet
he shall come to his end,
and no helper is *there to*
help him.

2782 2195 3615 6743 6381 1696 410 410
אֵל אֵלִים יְדַבֵּר נִפְלָאוֹת וְהִצְלִיחַ עַד־כָּלָה זַעַם כִּי נֶחֱרָצָה
which that For the is until shall and marvelous shall gods the
decreed is .fury fulfilled succeed ,things speak of God

802 2532 995 38:08 430 6213
37 נֶעֱשָׂתָה׃ וְעַל־אֱלֹהֵי אֲבֹתָיו לֹא יָבִין וְעַל־חֶמְדַּת נָשִׁים
,women desire the and will he not his of God the And be shall
of not to go fathers .done

4501 433 1430 3605 5921 995 38:08 433 3605
38 וְעַל־כָּל־אֱלוֹהַּ לֹא יָבִין כִּי עַל־כֹּל יִתְגַּדָּל׃ וְלֶאֱלֹהַּ מָעֻזִּים
fortresses the But shall he all above For will he not god any and
of god .himself magnify .regard

3513 3045 38:08 834 433 3513 3653
עַל־כַּנּוֹ יְכַבֵּד וְלֶאֱלוֹהַּ אֲשֶׁר לֹא־יְדָעֻהוּ אֲבֹתָיו יְכַבֵּד
shall he his did not which the and shall he his in
honor ,fathers know god ;honor place

4013 6213 2532 3368 68 3701 2091
39 בְּזָהָב וּבְכֶסֶף וּבְאֶבֶן יְקָרָה וּבַחֲמֻדוֹת׃ וְעָשָׂה לְמִבְצְרֵי
fort- the in he And with and ,precious with and with and with
of tresses do shall .things desirable stones silver gold

4910 3519 7227 5234 834 52:36 433 4581
מָעֻזִּים עִם־אֱלוֹהַּ נֵכָר אֲשֶׁר הִכִּיר יַרְבֶּה כָבוֹד וְהִמְשִׁילָם
will he and ;glory shall He shall he whom ,alien god an with (the)
rule them make increase .acknowledge fortresses

5055 709.3 6256 4242 2505 127 7235
40 בָּרַבִּים וַאֲדָמָה יְחַלֵּק בִּמְחִיר׃ וּבְעֵת קֵץ יִתְנַגַּח עִמּוֹ
with engage shall (the) the at And a for divide shall the and ,many over
him butting in end of time .price land

6571 7393 6828 44:28 44:28 8175 5045 44:28
מֶלֶךְ הַנֶּגֶב וְיִשְׂתָּעֵר עָלָיו מֶלֶךְ הַצָּפוֹן בְּרֶכֶב וּבְפָרָשִׁים
horse- with and with ,north the the against come will And the king the
,men ,chariots of king him tempest a as .south of

776 935 5674 7857 776 935 7227 591
41 וּבָאֳנִיּוֹת רַבּוֹת וּבָא בָאֲרָצוֹת וְשָׁטַף וְעָבָר׃ וּבָא בְּאֶרֶץ
the into shall He pass and shall and the into he And .many with and
land enter also .over overflow lands come shall ships

4124 123 3027 44:22 378.2 7221 6643
הַצְּבִי וְרַבּוֹת יִכָּשֵׁלוּ וְאֵלֶּה יִמָּלְטוּ מִיָּדוֹ אֱדוֹם וּמוֹאָב
and ,Edom of out escape shall these But be will many and ,glorious
Moab :hand his .stumbled

471:4 776 776 3027 79:71 5983 1121 7225
42 וְרֵאשִׁית בְּנֵי עַמּוֹן׃ וְיִשְׁלַח יָדוֹ בַּאֲרָצוֹת וְאֶרֶץ מִצְרַיִם
Egypt the and the against his will also and ;Ammon the the and
of land ;lands hand out stretch of sons of chief

3605 3701 2091 4362 4910 6413 1961 3808
43 לֹא תִהְיֶה לִפְלֵיטָה׃ וּמָשַׁל בְּמִכְמַנֵּי הַזָּהָב וְהַכֶּסֶף וּבְכֹל
over and and gold the over he But .escape shall not
all ,silver of treasures rule will

926 8052 4703 3569 3864 4714 2532
44 חֲמֻדוֹת מִצְרָיִם וְלֻבִים וְכֻשִׁים בְּמִצְעָדָיו׃ וּשְׁמֻעוֹת יְבַהֲלֻהוּ
trouble shall news But His in the and the And .Egypt's desirable
him .steps Ethiopians Libyans things

2763 8045 1419 2534 3318 6828 4217
מִמִּזְרָח וּמִצָּפוֹן וְיָצָא בְּחֵמָא גְדֹלָה לְהַשְׁמִיד וּלְהַחֲרִים
devote to and destroy to great fury with he Then from and the from
destruction to out go will .north the east

3318 6944 6643 2022 3220 996 643 168 5193 7227
45 רַבִּים׃ וְיִטַּע אָהֳלֵי אַפַּדְנוֹ בֵּין יַמִּים לְהַר־צְבִי־קֹדֶשׁ וּבָא
he Yet .holy glorious the in (the) between tents he And .many
come shall mountain ,seas palace plant shall

5826 369 7093
עַד־קִצּוֹ וְאֵין עוֹזֵר לוֹ׃
for a not and his to
.him helper is ,end

CAP. XII יב

CHAPTER 12

CHAPTER 12

[1]And at that time Michael shall stand up, the great ruler who stands for the sons of your people. And there shall be a time of distress, such as has not been from the existence of a nation until that time. And at that time your people shall be delivered, everyone that shall be found written in the Book. [2]And many of those sleeping in the earth's dust shall awake, some to everlasting life, and some to reproaches *and* to everlasting loathing. [3]And those who are wise shall shine as the brightness of the firmament; and those who turn many to righteousness as the stars forever and ever. [4]But you, O Daniel, shut up the words, and seal the book, to the end-time. Many shall run to and fro, and knowledge shall be increased.

[5]Then I, Daniel, looked. And, behold, another two stood there, the one on this *side*, and one on that *side* of the river's edge. [6]And *one* said to the man clothed in linen, who *was* on the waters of the river, How long until the end of these wonders? [7]And I heard the man clothed in linen, who *was* on the waters of the river, when he held up his right and his left *hand* to Heaven, and swore by Him who lives forever, that it *shall be* for a time, times, and a half. And when they have made an end of scattering the power of the holy people, all these *things* shall be finished. [8]And I heard, but I did not understand. Then I said, O my lord, what *shall be* the end of these *things*? [9]And He said, Go, Daniel! For the words *are* closed up and

1121 5975 1419 8269 4317 5975 6256
1 וּבָעֵת הַהִיא יַעֲמֹד מִיכָאֵל הַשַּׂר הַגָּדוֹל הָעֹמֵד עַל־בְּנֵי
the for who great the ,Michael shall that at And
of sons stands ruler up stand time

5750 1471 1961 1961 6864 6256 1961 5971
עַמֶּךָ וְהָיְתָה עֵת צָרָה אֲשֶׁר לֹא־נִהְיְתָה מִהְיוֹת גּוֹי עַד
until a the from has not such ,distress a there And your
nation of existence been as of time be shall .people

3789 4672 3605 5971 4422 6256 6256
הָעֵת הַהִיא וּבָעֵת הַהִיא יִמָּלֵט עַמְּךָ כָּל־הַנִּמְצָא כָּתוּב
written shall that every- your be shall ,that at And- .that time
found be one ,people delivered time

2416 428 6974 6083 127 3463 7227 5612
2 בַּסֵּפֶר׃ וְרַבִּים מִיְּשֵׁנֵי אַדְמַת־עָפָר יָקִיצוּ אֵלֶּה לְחַיֵּי
life to some shall dust ground the those of many And the in
,awake of in sleep who .Book

2094 7919 5769 1860 2781 428 5769
3 עוֹלָם וְאֵלֶּה לַחֲרָפוֹת לְדִרְאוֹן עוֹלָם׃ וְהַמַּשְׂכִּלִים יַזְהִרוּ
shall are who those And ever- to (and) to and ever-
shine wise .lasting abhorrence reproaches some lasting

5703 5769 3556 7227 6663 7549 2096
כְּזֹהַר הָרָקִיעַ וּמַצְדִּיקֵי הָרַבִּים כַּכּוֹכָבִים לְעוֹלָם וָעֶד׃
and forever stars the as many turn- those and firm- the the as
.ever righteousness to ing ament of shine

7093 6256 5612 2856 1697 5640 1840
4 וְאַתָּה דָנִיֵּאל סְתֹם הַדְּבָרִים וַחֲתֹם הַסֵּפֶר עַד־עֵת קֵץ
(the) the to book the seal and words the shut O ,you But
.end of time up Daniel

2009 1840 7200 1847 7235 7227 7751
5 יְשֹׁטְטוּ רַבִּים וְתִרְבֶּה הַדָּעַת׃ וְרָאִיתִי אֲנִי דָנִיֵּאל וְהִנֵּה
and ,Daniel ,I looked Then .knowledge shall and ,Many roam shall
,behold increased be around

2008 259 2975 8193 2008 259 5975 312 8147
שְׁנַיִם אֲחֵרִים עֹמְדִים אֶחָד הֵנָּה לִשְׂפַת הַיְאֹר וְאֶחָד הֵנָּה
that on and the the of this on one were other two
(side) one ,river of lip (side) ,standing

4605 834 906 3847 376 559 2975 8193
6 לִשְׂפַת הַיְאֹר׃ וַיֹּאמֶר לָאִישׁ לְבוּשׁ הַבַּדִּים אֲשֶׁר מִמַּעַל
on who ,linen clothed the to (one) And the the of
(was) in man said .river of lip

376 8085 6382 7093 5704 2975 4325
7 לְמֵימֵי הַיְאֹר עַד־מָתַי קֵץ הַפְּלָאוֹת׃ וָאֶשְׁמַע אֶת־הָאִישׁ ׀
man the I And the the when Until the waters the
heard ?wonders of end (is) ,river of

3225 7311 2975 4325 4605 834 906 3847
לְבוּשׁ הַבַּדִּים אֲשֶׁר מִמַּעַל לְמֵימֵי הַיְאֹר וַיָּרֶם יְמִינוֹ
his he when the the on who ,linen clothed
right up held ,river of waters (was) in

6256 5769 2416 7650 8064 8040
וּשְׂמֹאלוֹ אֶל־הַשָּׁמַיִם וַיִּשָּׁבַע בְּחֵי הָעוֹלָם כִּי לְמוֹעֵד
a for that ,forever Him by swore and the to left his and
time (is it). lives who heavens (hand)

3605 3615 6944 5310 3615 2677 4150
מוֹעֲדִים וָחֵצִי וּכְכַלּוֹת נַפֵּץ יַד־עַם־קֹדֶשׁ תִּכְלֶינָה כָל־
all be shall ,holy people's the break- when And a and times
finished power ing finish they .half

319 4100 113 559 995 3808 8085 428
8 אֵלֶּה׃ וַאֲנִי שָׁמַעְתִּי וְלֹא אָבִין וָאֹמְרָה אֲדֹנִי מָה אַחֲרִית
end the what my O I And did I but ,heard And these
of (be shall) ,lord ,said .understand not I .(things)

1697 1856 5640 1840 3212 559 428
9 אֵלֶּה׃ וַיֹּאמֶר לֵךְ דָּנִיֵּאל כִּי־סְתֻמִים וַחֲתֻמִים הַדְּבָרִים
words the sealed and closed (are) For !Daniel ,Go he And these
up ,said ?(things)

sealed until the end-time.
10 Many shall be purified and made white and tested. But the wicked shall do wrong. And not one of the wicked shall understand; but the wise shall understand.
11 And from the time the regular *sacrifice* shall be taken away, and the abomination that makes desolate set up, a thousand, two hundred and ninety days *shall occur*.

12 Blessed is he who waits and comes to *the* thousand, three hundred and thirty-five days.
13 But you go on to the end; for you shall rest and stand in your lot at the end of the days.

7561 7227 6884 3835 1305 7093 6256

10 עַד־עֵת קֵץ׃ יִתְבָּרְרוּ וְיִתְלַבְּנוּ וְיִצָּרְפוּ רַבִּים וְהִרְשִׁיעוּ

do shall But .Many and made and be shall (the) the until
wickedly refined white purified .end of time

6256 995 7919 7563 995 3808 7563

11 רְשָׁעִים וְלֹא יָבִינוּ כָּל־רְשָׁעִים וְהַמַּשְׂכִּלִים יָבִינוּ׃ וּמֵעֵת

from And will wise the but the all will and the
time .discern ;wicked of discern not ;wicked

3967 505 3117 8074 8251 5414 8548 5493

הוּסַר הַתָּמִיד וְלָתֵת שִׁקּוּץ שֹׁמֵם יָמִים אֶלֶף מָאתַיִם

two a (be shall) that abomi- the set and regular the be shall
hundred thousand days desolates nation up (sacrifice) taken

3967 7969 505 3117 5060 2442 835 8673

12 וְתִשְׁעִים׃ אַשְׁרֵי הַמְחַכֶּה וְיַגִּיעַ לְיָמִים אֶלֶף שְׁלֹשׁ מֵאוֹת

hundred three (the) days to and who he Blessed .ninety and
thousand comes waits (is)

1486 5975 5117 7093 3212 2568 7970

13 שְׁלֹשִׁים וַחֲמִשָּׁה׃ וְאַתָּה לֵךְ לַקֵּץ וְתָנוּחַ וְתַעֲמֹד לְגֹרָלְךָ

your for and you and the to go But .five and thirty
lot stand rest shall ;end on you

3117 7093

לְקֵץ הַיָּמִין׃

the the at
.days of end

הושע

A LITERAL TRANSLATION
OF THE BIBLE
THE BOOK OF HOSEA

CHAPTER 1

[1]The word of Jehovah that was to Hosea, the son of Beeri, in the days of Uzziah, Jotham, Ahaz *and* Hezekiah, kings of Judah; and in the days of Jeroboam, the son of Joash, king of Israel. [2]The beginning of the speaking of Jehovah by Hosea. And Jehovah said to Hosea, Go, take to yourself a wife of harlotry, and children of harlotry. For the land has utterly gone lusting away from Jehovah. [3]And he went and took Gomer, the daughter of Diblaim, who conceived and bore him a son. [4]And Jehovah said to him, Call his name God Will Sow; for yet *in* a little *while* I will visit the blood of Jezreel on the house of Jehu, and will cause the kingdom of the house of Israel to cease. [5]And it shall be in that day, I will break the bow of Israel in the valley of Jezreel.

[6]And she conceived again, and bore a daughter. And He said to him, Call her name No-Mercy, for I will not again still have mercy *on* the house of Israel; but I will completely take them away. [7]And I will have mercy on the house of Judah, and will save them by Jehovah their God. And I will not save them by bow or by sword, or by battle, by horses, or by horsemen.

[8]And she having weaned No-Mercy, she conceived

LIBER HOSEAE

(THE) BOOK OF HOSEA

CAPUT. I א

CHAPTER 1

5818 3117 882 1121 1954 19 61 3068 1697
1 דבר-יהוה אשר היה אל-הושע בן-בארי בימי עזיה
,Uzziah the in ,Beeri the Hosea to was that Jehovah The
of days of son of word

3101 1121 3379 3117 3063 44 28 3169 271 3147
יותם אחז יחזקיה מלכי יהודה ובימי ירבעם בן-יואש
,Joash the Jeroboam in and ;Judah kings ,Hezekiah ,Ahaz ,Jotham
of son of days the of

3068 559 1954 3068 1696 84 62 3478 44 28
2 מלך ישראל: תחלת דבר-יהוה בהושע ויאמר יהוה אל-
to Jehovah And by Jehovah the be- The .Israel king
said :Hosea of speaking of ginning of

2181 2181 21 83 32 06 2183 802 3947 32 12 1954
הושע לך קח-לך אשת זנונים וילדי זנונים כי-זנה תזנה
goes surely For .harlotry and harlotry wife a to take ,Go ,Hosea
whoring of children of yourself

1691 1323 15 86 39 47 3212 3068 310 776
3 הארץ מאחרי יהוה: וילך ויקח את-גמר בת-דבלים
,Diblaim the Gomer took and he So .Jehovah away land the
of daughter went from

3157 8034 7121 3068 559 1121 32 05 2029
4 ותהר ותלד-לו בן: ויאמר יהוה אליו קרא שמו יזרעאל
.Jezreel his Call to Jehovah said And a to bore and she and
name ,him .son him conceived

3058 1004 5921 3157 1818 6485 45 92 5750
כי-עוד מעט ופקדתי את-דמי יזרעאל על-בית יהוא
,Jehu the on Jezreel the will I and little a yet For
of house of blood visit ,(while)

7665 3117 1961 3157 1004 4468 7673
5 והשבתי ממלכות בית ישראל: והיה ביום ההוא ושברתי
will I that ,that day in it And .Jezreel the kingdom the will and
break be shall of house of cease make

132 3 3205 5750 2029 3157 6010 34 78 7198
6 את-קשת ישראל בעמק יזרעאל: ותהר עוד ותלד בת
a bore and again she And .Jezreel the in Israel the
.daughter conceived of valley of bow

7355 5750 3254 3808 7355 38 08 8034 7121 559
ויאמר לו קרא שמה לא רחמה כי לא אוסיף עוד ארחם
have will more I not for ,Mercy No her Call to He And
on mercy again name ,him said

3063 1004 5375 5375 34 78 1004
7 את-בית ישראל כי-נשא אשא להם: ואת-בית יהודה
Judah the But .them take will I com- but ;Israel the
of house away pletely of house

7198 34 62 3808 430 3068 3467 73 55
ארחם והושעתים ביהוה אלהיהם ולא אושיעם בקשת
bow by save will I But .God their Jeho- by save will and have will I
them not vah them .on mercy

3808 1580 6571 5483 44 21 2719
8 ובחרב ובמלחמה בסוסים ובפרשים: ותגמל את-לא
No she And .horsemen by and, horses by, battle by and by and
weaned had ,sword

and bore a son. ⁹Then He said, Call his name Not-My-People; for you *are* not My people, and I will not be for you.

9

7355	2029		3205	1121	559		7121	8034	3808	5971	
,Mercy	and she	a son	,bore	and	conceived	He Then	said,	Call	his	name	Not	My

38.08	59.71		38.08	1961			
My Not	l-and	not	will	be	for	you

People; for you *(are)* not My People,

CAP. II ב

CHAPTER 2

1

1961	4557	1121	3478		3220	834	3808	4058	3808
be shall	the number	of sons of	Israel	the	as	the sea	of sand,	is not	which	the	and not ,measured

5608	1961		4725		559		3808	
.bered	be shall	,and num-	it And	of place	,the in	which	is it	said	to them,	Not My	people	;(are)	you

2

559		1121	410	2416		6908	1121	3063	1121	3478
shall it	to	them, of	God	.living the	Sons	gathered	the be shall	And	Judah	the and	Israel

31.62	7760		72.18	259	59.27	776	1419	3117
to-gether	shall and	set	themselves	head	one	for	;land the out	they And	.up go shall	the great	for	of day (be shall)

3

3157	559	251	5971		259	269		7355	7378
.Jezreel	,brothers	;people	your	A	and to	your	.sisters	,Mercy	;Strive

4

517		7378		38.08	802		38.08	376	5493
your	with	mother	;strive	she for	not	My	(is)	wife	am)	I and	not	her	.band	hus-	let And	turn her

5

21.83	6440		5005	996		7699		6584
harlotry	,face	her from	her	and	adultery	,breasts	her	from	between	,breasts her	lest	I strip	her

6

776	67:23	4191	6772		1121	38.08	7355
of land	,drought	a like	kill and	,her	.thirst with	her	And	not	will I	for

| | | | | | | 3205 | 3117 | 3322 | | 6174 |
| naked, | her | set and | out | of day | the | as | ,born | her | being | set and | .wilderness | her | as | the | place and | her | .6174 |

7

1121		2183		2181	517	3001		2029
of sons	the	harlotry	they	For	.(are)	a is	For	harlot	;mother	shamefully	ceived	con-	who	she acted	has	.them	,pity

559		310		7157	5414		3899	4325		6785
,said she	Let	me go	after	,lovers my	the	givers of	bread	my and	my	water,	my and	my	wool

8

6593		8081	8250		36.51	7753		1870	5518
my and	flax.	my and	oil	my	.drink	fore,	I hold	There-	be-	hedge	way your	,thorns with

9

1443		1448		5410	38.08		4672	7291
I and	up wall	her	,wall	paths her	not	shall she	find,	shall she And	pursue

157		5381/38.08	1245		38.08	4672		559
,lovers her	but	shall she	overtake	search	for	,them	but	shall she	not	.find	them,	shall she Then	,say shall

¹⁰Yet the number of the sons of Israel shall be as the sand of the sea, which is not measured nor numbered. And it shall be, in the place where it is said to them, You *are* not My people, it shall be said to them, Sons of the Living God. ¹¹And the sons of Judah and the sons of Israel shall be gathered together, and shall set over themselves one head. And they shall go up out of the land; for great *shall be* the day of Jezreel.

CHAPTER 2

¹Say to your brothers, A people; and to your sisters, Mercy. ²Strive! Strive with your mother, for she *is* not My wife; and I *am* not her husband. Therefore, let her put away her harlotry from her face, and her adulteries from between her breasts; ³that I not strip her naked, and set her out as in the day that she was born; and make her as the wilderness; and place her like a dry land; and kill her with thirst. ⁴And I will not have pity for her sons, for they *are* the sons of harlotry. ⁵For their mother is a harlot; she who conceived them has acted shamefully. For she said, I will go after my lovers who give my bread and my water, my wool and my flax, my oil and my drink.

⁶Therefore, behold, I will hedge your way with thorns, and I will wall up her wall, that she shall not find her paths; ⁷and she shall follow after her lovers, but she shall not overtake them. And she shall look for them, but she shall not find *them*. Then she shall say,

I will go and return to my first husband, for then *it was* better with me than now. [8]For she did not know that I gave her grain and wine and oil, and I multiplied her silver and the gold they prepared for Baal. [9]So I will return and take My grain in its time, and My wine in its season. And I will take back My wool and My flax *she uses* to cover her nakedness. [10]And now I will uncover her shamefulness to the eyes of her lovers; and a man shall not deliver her out of My hand. [11]I will also cause all her joy to cease, her feast days, her new moons, and her sabbaths, and all her solemn feasts. [12]And I will destroy her vines and her fig-trees, of which she has said, They *are* my rewards that my lovers have given me. And I will set them for a forest, and the beasts of the field shall eat them. [13]And I will visit on her the days of the Baals, *in* which she burned *incense* to them. Yea, she adorned herself with her noserings, and her jewels, and she went after her lovers and forgot Me, says Jehovah.

[14]Therefore, behold, I will lure her and bring her *to* the wilderness, and speak to her heart. [15]And from there I will give her vineyards to her, and the valley of Achor for a door of hope. And she shall answer there, as in the days of her youth, and as in the day when she came up out of the land of Egypt. [16]And at that day, says Jehovah, you shall call Me, My husband; and you shall no more call me, My Baal. [17]For I will take away the names of the Baals out of her mouth; and they shall no more be remembered by their name. [18]And in that day I will cut a covenant for

6258 227 2896 7223 376 7725 3212
אֵלְכָה וְאָשׁוּבָה אֶל־אִישִׁי הָרִאשׁוֹן כִּי טוֹב לִי אָז מֵעָתָּה׃
than then for (was it) for ,first my to might I that me Let
.now Me better husband return go

8492 1715 5414 3045 3808
10 וְהִיא לֹא יָדְעָה כִּי אָנֹכִי נָתַתִּי לָהּ הַדָּגָן וְהַתִּירוֹשׁ
new and grain her to gave I that did not she For
wine know

7725 3651 1168 6213 2091 7235 3701 3323
11 וְהַיִּצְהָר וְכֶסֶף הִרְבֵּיתִי לָהּ וְזָהָב עָשׂוּ לַבָּעַל׃ לָכֵן אָשׁוּב
will I There- the for they and to multi- I silver and olive and
return fore .Baal made gold her plied oil

6785 5337 4150 8492 6256 1715 3947
וְלָקַחְתִּי דְגָנִי בְּעִתּוֹ וְתִירוֹשִׁי בְּמוֹעֲדוֹ וְהִצַּלְתִּי צַמְרִי
wool My will I And its in My and its in My take and
recover .season wine new ,time grain

5040 1540 6258 6172 3680 6593
12 וּפִשְׁתִּי לְכַסּוֹת אֶת־עֶרְוָתָהּ׃ וְעַתָּה אֲגַלֶּה אֶת־נַבְלֻתָהּ
folly her will I now And her cover to My and
uncover .nakedness flax

3605 7673 3027 5337 376 157 5869
13 לְעֵינֵי מְאַהֲבֶיהָ וְאִישׁ לֹא־יַצִּילֶנָּה מִיָּדִי׃ וְהִשְׁבַּתִּי כָּל־
all will I And My from shall not a and ,lovers her the to
cease make .hand her deliver man of eyes

8074 4150 3605 7676 2320 2282 4885
14 מְשׂוֹשָׂהּ חַגָּהּ חָדְשָׁהּ וְשַׁבַּתָּהּ וְכֹל מוֹעֲדָהּ׃ וַהֲשִׁמֹּתִי
will I And solemn her and her and new her her ,joy her
destroy .feasts all ,sabbaths ,moons ,feasts

5414 866 559 834 8384 1612
גַּפְנָהּ וּתְאֵנָתָהּ אֲשֶׁר אָמְרָה אֶתְנָה הֵמָּה לִי אֲשֶׁר נָתְנוּ
have that ,me to they Rewards has she of her and her
given (are) ,said which ,tree fig vines

6485 7704 2416 398 3293 7760 157
15 לִי מְאַהֲבָי וְשַׂמְתִּים לְיַעַר וַאֲכָלָתַם חַיַּת הַשָּׂדֶה׃ וּפָקַדְתִּי
will I And .field the the eat shall and a for will I And .lovers My to
visit of beasts them forest them set me

5141 5710 6999 1168 3117
עָלֶיהָ אֶת־יְמֵי הַבְּעָלִים אֲשֶׁר תַּקְטִיר לָהֶם וַתַּעַד נִזְמָהּ
nose her decks and to she whom ,Baals the the her on
rings (in) herself ,them burned of days

3068 5002 7911 157 310 1980 2484
וְחֶלְיָתָהּ וַתֵּלֶךְ אַחֲרֵי מְאַהֲבֶיהָ וְאֹתִי שָׁכְחָה נְאֻם־יְהוָה׃
.Jehovah says ,forgets Me but ,lovers her after goes and her and
jewels

1696 4057 1980 6601 2009
16 לָכֵן הִנֵּה אָנֹכִי מְפַתֶּיהָ וְהֹלַכְתִּיהָ הַמִּדְבָּר וְדִבַּרְתִּי עַל־
to speak and the (to) her bring and her lure I ,behold There-
wilderness fore

6607 5911 6010 8033 3754 5414 3820
17 לִבָּהּ׃ וְנָתַתִּי לָהּ אֶת־כְּרָמֶיהָ מִשָּׁם וְאֶת־עֵמֶק עָכוֹר לְפֶתַח
an for Achor the and from her her to I And her
of entrance of valley ,there vineyards give will .heart

776 5927 3117 5271 3117 8033 6030 8615
תִּקְוָה וְעָנְתָה שָּׁמָּה כִּימֵי נְעוּרֶיהָ וּכְיוֹם עֲלוֹתָהּ מֵאֶרֶץ־
the from went she as and ,youth her the as ,there she And .hope
of land up when day the of days answer shall

376 7121 3068 5002 3117 1961 4714
18 מִצְרָיִם׃ וְהָיָה בַיּוֹם־הַהוּא נְאֻם־יְהוָה תִּקְרְאִי אִישִׁי
hus- My shall you ,Jehovah says ,that day in it And .Egypt
,band ,call be shall

1168 8034 5493 1167 5750 7121 3808
19 וְלֹא־תִקְרְאִי־לִי עוֹד בַּעְלִי׃ וַהֲסִרֹתִי אֶת־שְׁמוֹת הַבְּעָלִים
Baals the names the will I For .Baal My ,more Me call shall and
of away take not

3117 1285 3772 8034 5750 2142 3808 6310
20 מִפִּיהָ וְלֹא־יִזָּכְרוּ עוֹד בִּשְׁמָם׃ וְכָרַתִּי לָהֶם בְּרִית בַּיּוֹם
day in a for will I And their by more shall they And her from
covenant them cut .name remembered be not .mouth

them with the beasts of the field, and with the birds of the sky, and the creeping things of the ground. And I will break the bow and the sword, and the battle out of the earth, and I will make them to lie down safely. [19]And I will betroth you to Me forever. Yes, I will betroth you to Me in righteousness, and in judgment, and in mercy, and in compassions. [20]I will even betroth you to Me in faithfulness. And you shall know Jehovah. [21]And it shall be in that day, I will answer, says Jehovah. I will answer the heavens, and they shall answer the earth. [22]And the earth shall hear the grain, and the wine, and the oil; and they shall hear Jezreel. [23]And I will sow her to Me in the earth. And I will have mercy on No-Mercy. And I will say to Not-My-People, You *are* My people! And he shall say, My God!

21

127	7431	8064 :	5775	7704	2416
הַהוּא | עִם־חַיַּת | הַשָּׂדֶה | וְעִם־עוֹף | הַשָּׁמַיִם | וְרֶמֶשׂ | הָאֲדָמָה |

.ground the | the and | sky the | the and | field the | the with | that
| | of things creeping | | of birds with | | | of beasts

7901	776	7665	4421	2719	71·98
וְקֶשֶׁת | וְחֶרֶב | וּמִלְחָמָה | אֶשְׁבּוֹר | מִן־הָאָרֶץ | וְהִשְׁכַּבְתִּים |

make will I and | .earth the out of | will I break | battle and | and | bow And
| | | | | down lie them | | sword

6664	781	5769	781	982
לָבֶטַח: | וְאֵרַשְׂתִּיךְ | לִי | לְעוֹלָם | וְאֵרַשְׂתִּיךְ | לִי | בְּצֶדֶק |

righ- in | Me to | will I ,Yes | .forever | Me to | will I And | .securely
teousness | | you betroth | | | you betroth

22

3045	530	2617	49:41
וּבְמִשְׁפָּט | וּבְחֶסֶד | וּבְרַחֲמִים: | וְאֵרַשְׂתִּיךְ | לִי | בֶּאֱמוּנָה | וְיָדַעַתְּ |

you And | faith- in to | will I And | in and | in and | in and
know shall | .fulness | Me you betroth | .compassions | ,mercy | ,judgment

6030	3068/5002	6030	3117	1961	3068
אֶת־יְהוָה:: | תִּהְיֶה | בַּיּוֹם | הַהוּא | אֶעֱנֶה | נְאֻם־יְהוָה | אֶעֱנֶה |

will I | .Jehovah says | will I | that | day in it And | .Jehovah
answer | | answer | | ,answer | | be shall

23

24

6030	776	776	6030	8064
אֶת־הַשָּׁמַיִם | וְהֵם | יַעֲנוּ | אֶת־הָאָרֶץ: | וְהָאָרֶץ | תַּעֲנֶה | אֶת־ |

shall | the and | the | shall | and ,heavens the
answer | | answer earth | | ;earth | answer | | they

3157	6030	3323	8492	1715
הַדָּגָן | וְאֶת־הַתִּירוֹשׁ | וְאֶת־הַיִּצְהָר | וְהֵם | יַעֲנוּ | אֶת־יִזְרְעֶאל: |

,Jezreel | shall and | olive the and | and | new the | and the
| answer they | ;oil | | wine | | grain

25

3808	559	7355	38.08	7355	776	2232
וּזְרַעְתִּיהָ | לִי | בָּאָרֶץ | וְרִחַמְתִּי | אֶת־לֹא | רֻחָמָה | וְאָמַרְתִּי | לְלֹא |

Not to | will I And | .Mercy | No | will I And | the in to | will I And
say | | | | on mercy have | .earth | Me | her sow

430.	559	5971	5971
עַמִּי | עַמִּי־אַתָּה | וְהוּא | יֹאמַר | אֱלֹהָי: |

!God My | shall | And | you | My | My
| ,say | he | !(are) people | ,People | People

CAP. III ג

CHAPTER 3

1

5003	7453	157	802:	157	3212	30.68	559
וַיֹּאמֶר | יְהוָה | אֵלַי | עוֹד | לֵךְ | אֱהַב־אִשָּׁה | אֲהֻבַת | רֵעַ | וּמְנָאָפֶת |

an yet | a loved | a | love | ,Go | ,again to | Jehovah said Then
,adulteress | ,friend | by | woman | | .me

430	6437	3478	1121	3068	160
כְּאַהֲבַת | יְהוָה | אֶת־בְּנֵי | יִשְׂרָאֵל | וְהֵם | פֹּנִים | אֶל־אֱלֹהִים |

gods | to | turn | they and | ,Israel | the (toward) | Jeho- to according
| | | | of sons | | vah | of love the

6240	2568	3739	6025	809.	157	312
אֲחֵרִים | וְאֹהֲבֵי | אֲשִׁישֵׁי | עֲנָבִים: | וָאֶכְּרֶהָ | לִי | בַּחֲמִשָּׁה | עָשָׂר |

fifteen | with | for bar- | I So | .grapes | raisin | love and | other
| | ,me | her gained | | of cakes

2

3

3117	559	8184	3963	8184	3701
כֶּסֶף | וְחֹמֶר | שְׂעֹרִים | וְלֵתֶךְ | שְׂעֹרִים: | וָאֹמַר | אֵלֶיהָ | יָמִים |

days | ,her to | I And | .barley | a and | ,barley | a and | (of pieces)
| | said | | of half | | ot homer | silver

1571	376.	1961	38.08	2181	38.08	3427	7227
רַבִּים | תֵּשְׁבִי | לִי | לֹא | תִזְנִי | וְלֹא | תִהְיִי | לְאִישׁ | וְגַם־אֲנִי | אֵלָיִךְ: |

.you to | I so | a to | be | nor shall | You not | with shall | you Many
| | ,me | | | | | | | stay

4

8269	369	4428	369	3478	1121	3342.7	7227.	3117
כִּי | יָמִים | רַבִּים | יֵשְׁבוּ | בְּנֵי | יִשְׂרָאֵל | אֵין | מֶלֶךְ | וְאֵין | שָׂר |

,prince and | king no | ,Israel | the | shall | many | days For
no | | | | of sons | stay | | | | (with)

5

7725	310	8655	646	369	4676	369	2077	369
וְאֵין | זֶבַח | וְאֵין | מַצֵּבָה | וְאֵין | אֵפוֹד | וּתְרָפִים: | אַחַר | יָשֻׁבוּ |

shall Afterward | .teraphim | or ephod | no and | ,pillar | and | sacri- | and
return | | | | | no | | ,fice | | no

CHAPTER 3

[1]And Jehovah said to me, Go again. Love a woman loved by a friend, yet an adulteress, according to the love of Jehovah toward the sons of Israel, who turn to other gods, and love raisin-cakes of grapes. [2]So I bought her for myself with fifteen *pieces of* silver, and *for* a homer of barley, and a half of barley. [3]And I said to her, You shall stay with me many days. You shall not be a harlot, nor be to a man; and I also *will be* for you. [4]For the sons of Israel shall stay many days *with* no king, and no ruler, and *with* no sacrifice, and no pillars, and no ephod or teraphim. [5]Afterward the

sons of Israel shall return and seek Jehovah their God, and David their king. And they shall fear Jehovah and His goodness in the ends of the days.

CHAPTER 4

1 Sons of Israel, hear the word of Jehovah, for Jehovah *has* a quarrel with the inhabitants of the land; for there is no truth, and no mercy, and no knowledge of God in the land. 2 Lying, and swearing, and killing, and stealing, and the committing of adultery increase, and blood touches against blood. 3 On account of this the land shall mourn, and every one living in it shall droop, with the beasts of the field, and the birds of the heavens; yes, also the fish of the sea shall be removed. 4 Yet let not a man strive with nor reprove a man. For your people *are* as a priest striven with. 5 And you shall stumble *in* the day; and the prophet also shall stumble with you *at* night, and I will cut off your mother.

6 My people are cut off for lack of knowledge. Because you rejected the knowledge, I also rejected you from being priest to Me. Since you have forgotten the law of your God, I will forget your sons; even I. 7 As they were increased, so they sinned against Me. I will change their glory into shame. 8 They eat up the sin of My people, and they lift their vitality to their iniquity. 9 And it will be, Like people, like priest. And I will visit their ways on them, and repay them for their deeds. 10 For they shall eat and not have enough. They shall fornicate and not increase, because they have ceased heeding Jehovah. 11 Fornication and wine, and new wine, take away the heart.

12 My people seek advice by their wooden *idols*, and their rod declares to them. For the spirit of harlotry has led *them* astray. And they

---

4428 1732 430 3068 1245 3478 1121

בְּנֵי יִשְׂרָאֵל וּבִקְשׁוּ אֶת־יְהוָה אֱלֹהֵיהֶם וְאֵת דָּוִד מַלְכָּם

.king their David and God their Jehovah shall and seek Israel the of sons

3117 319 2898 3068 6342

וּפָחֲדוּ אֶל־יְהוָה וְאֶל־טוּבוֹ בְּאַחֲרִית הַיָּמִים׃

.days the the in of ends good- His and ness Jehovah they And fear shall

CAP. IV. ד

CHAPTER 4

3427 3068 7379 3478 1121 3068 1697 8085

1 שִׁמְעוּ דְבַר־יְהוָה בְּנֵי יִשְׂרָאֵל כִּי רִיב לַיהוָה עִם־יוֹשְׁבֵי

in- the of habitants with Jehovah to (is) quarrel a For .Israel sons of ,Jehovah the of word Hear

776 430 1847 369 2617 571 776

הָאָרֶץ כִּי אֵין־אֱמֶת וְאֵין־חֶסֶד וְאֵין־דַּעַת אֱלֹהִים בָּאָרֶץ׃

the in ;land God knowl- of edge and no ,mercy and no ,truth no for is the ,land

5060 1818 1818 6555 5003 1589 7523 3584 422

2 אָלֹה וְכַחֵשׁ וְרָצֹחַ וְגָנֹב וְנָאֹף פָּרָצוּ וְדָמִים בְּדָמִים נָגָעוּ׃

.touches against blood blood and ;increase doing ,adultery and and stealing and killing and ,lying ;swearing

7704 2416 3427 3605 535 776 56 3651

3 עַל־כֵּן תֶּאֱבַל הָאָרֶץ וְאֻמְלַל כָּל־יוֹשֵׁב בָּהּ בְּחַיַּת הַשָּׂדֶה

field the the with of beasts ,it in lives who every- one shall and droop the ,land shall mourn There- fore

7378 376 622 3220 1709 1571 8064 5775

4 וּבְעוֹף הַשָּׁמַיִם וְגַם־דְּגֵי הַיָּם יֵאָסֵפוּ׃ אַךְ אִישׁ אַל־יָרֵב

let with strive not man a Yet be shall .removed the sea the of fish ,Yes also .heavens the with and of birds the

3782 3117 3782 3548 7378 5971 376 3198 408

5 וְאַל־יוֹכַח אִישׁ וְעַמְּךָ כִּמְרִיבֵי כֹהֵן׃ וְכָשַׁלְתָּ הַיּוֹם וְכָשַׁל

shall and stumble the (in) ,day you So stumble shall a .priest as (are) with striven your For people a .man reprove and not

1097 5971 1820 517 1820 3915 5030

6 גַּם־נָבִיא עִמְּךָ לַיְלָה וְדָמִיתִי אִמֶּךָ׃ נִדְמוּ עַמִּי מִבְּלִי

lack for of My people de- stroyed are your .mother will I and off cut (at) ,night with you the also prophet

3547 3985 3988 1847 3588 1847

הַדָּעַת כִּי־אַתָּה הַדַּעַת מָאַסְתָּ וְאֶמְאָסְאךָ מִכַּהֵן לִי

to .Me being from priest rejected I also you ,rejected the knowledge you Because knowl- .edge

3651 7230 1121 7911 430 8451 7911

7 וַתִּשְׁכַּח תּוֹרַת אֱלֹהֶיךָ אֶשְׁכַּח בָּנֶיךָ גַּם־אָנִי׃ כְּרֻבָּם כֵּן

so were they As ,increased .I even your ;sons will I forget ,God your law the of you Since forgotten have

398 5971 2403 4171 7036 3519 2398

8 חָטְאוּ־לִי כְּבוֹדָם בְּקָלוֹן אָמִיר׃ חַטַּאת עַמִּי יֹאכֵלוּ וְאֶל־

to and they ,up eat My people sin The of will I .change shame into Their glory against .Me they sinned

1870 5921 6485 3548 5971 1961 5315 5375 5771

9 עֲוֺנָם יִשְׂאוּ נַפְשׁוֹ׃ וְהָיָה כָעָם כַּכֹּהֵן וּפָקַדְתִּי עָלָיו דְּרָכָיו

their ;ways on them will I And visit like, priest like ,people it And ;be will .soul their they lift their iniquity

6555 3808 2181 7646 3808 398 7725 4611

10 וּמַעֲלָלָיו אָשִׁיב לוֹ׃ וְאָכְלוּ וְלֹא יִשְׂבָּעוּ הִזְנוּ וְלֹא יִפְרֹצוּ

;increase and not shall They ,fornicate have .enough and not they For eat shall to .them will I return their and doings

3820 3947 8492 3196 2184 8104 5800 3068 3588

11 כִּי־אֶת־יְהוָה עָזְבוּ לִשְׁמֹר׃ זְנוּת וְיַיִן וְתִירוֹשׁ יִקַּח־לֵב׃

the .heart take new and wine and wine Fornica- tion .heed to have they ceased Jehovah because

8582 2183 7307 5046 4731 7592 6086 5971

12 עַמִּי בְּעֵצוֹ יִשְׁאָל וּמַקְלוֹ יַגִּיד לוֹ כִּי רוּחַ זְנוּנִים הִתְעָה

led has .astray harlotry the of spirit For to .them declares their and rod seek ,advice their by wood My people fornicated from under their God. 13 They sacrifice on the tops of the mountains, and burn incense on the hills, under oak and poplar and terebinth, because its shade is good. Therefore, your daughters shall be harlots, and your brides shall commit adultery. 14 I will not punish your daughters when they fornicate, nor your brides when they commit adultery. For the *men* themselves go aside with harlots; and they sacrifice with temple prostitutes. The people *who* do not understand are thrust down.

15 Israel, though you do harlotry, do not let Judah become guilty. And do not come *to* Gilgal, nor go up to Beth-aven, nor swear, *As* Jehovah lives. 16 For Israel is stubborn, like a stubborn heifer. Now Jehovah will feed them as a lamb in a roomy place. 17 Ephraim *is* joined to idols. Let him alone. 18 Their drink is sour. They are continually fornicating; her shields dearly love shame. 19 The wind binds her up in her wings; and they shall be ashamed because of their sacrifices.

5921 2076 2022 7218 5921 430 8478 2181
13 וַיִּזְנוּ מִתַּחַת אֱלֹהֵיהֶם׃ עַל־רָאשֵׁי הֶהָרִים יְזַבֵּחוּ וְעַל־
on and sac- they the tops the On their from they And
,rifice mountains of .God under fornicated

6738 2896 424 3839 437 8478 6999 1389
הַגְּבָעוֹת יְקַטֵּרוּ תַּחַת אַלּוֹן וְלִבְנֶה וְאֵלָה כִּי־טוֹב צִלָּהּ
(is) good for and and oak under in- burn hills the
.shade its ,terebinth poplar ,cense

6485 3808 5003 3618 1323 2181
14 עַל־כֵּן תִּזְנֶינָה בְּנוֹתֵיכֶם וְכַלּוֹתֵיכֶם תְּנָאַפְנָה׃ לֹא־אֶפְקוֹד
will I not commit shall your and your be shall Therefore
punish .adultery brides ,daughters harlots

5003 3618 2181 1323 5921
עַל־בְּנוֹתֵיכֶם כִּי תִזְנֶינָה וְעַל־כַּלּוֹתֵיכֶם כִּי תְנָאַפְנָה כִּי־הֵם
they For com- they when your not they when your on
.adultery mit brides ,fornicate ,daughters

995 3808 5971 2076 6948 6504 2181
עִם־הַזֹּנוֹת יְפָרֵדוּ וְעִם־הַקְּדֵשׁוֹת יְזַבֵּחוּ וְעָם לֹא־יָבִין
under- do not the and they temple and go harlots with
stand (who) people ;sacrifice prostitutes with ;apart

408 3063 816 408 3478 2181 3832
15 יִלָּבֵט׃ אִם־זֹנֶה אַתָּה יִשְׂרָאֵל אַל־יֶאְשַׁם יְהוּדָה וְאַל־
not And .Judah be let not ,Israel you do Though thrust are
guilty harlotry .down

3068 2416 7650 408 205 1007 5927 428 1537 935
תָּבֹאוּ הַגִּלְגָּל וְאַל־תַּעֲלוּ בֵּית אָוֶן וְאַל־תִּשָּׁבְעוּ חַי־יְהוָה׃
.Jehovah (As) ,swear nor ,aven to go nor (to) do
lives Beth- to up ,Gilgal come

3532 3068 7462 6258 3478 5637 5637 6510
16 כִּי כְּפָרָה סֹרֵרָה סָרַר יִשְׂרָאֵל עַתָּה יִרְעֵם יְהוָה כְּכֶבֶשׂ
a like Jehovah feed will Now .Israel is ,stubborn a as For
lamb them stubborn heifer

5435 5493 3240 669 6091 2266 4800
17
18 בַּמֶּרְחָב׃ חֲבוּר עֲצַבִּים אֶפְרָיִם הַנַּח־לוֹ׃ סָר סָבְאָם
their turned Has .him Let (is) idols Joined a in
.drink aside alone .Ephraim to .place roomy

7307 6887 4043 7036 3053 157 2181 2181
19 הַזְנֵה הִזְנוּ אָהֲבוּ הֵבוּ קָלוֹן מָגִנֶּיהָ׃ צָרַר רוּחַ אוֹתָהּ
her The binds her shame dearly love they. Contin-
wind up .shields ;fornicate ually

2077 954 3671
בִּכְנָפֶיהָ וְיֵבֹשׁוּ מִזִּבְחוֹתָם׃
their of because they and her in
.sacrifices ashamed be shall ;wings

CAP. V. ה

CHAPTER 5

1 Hear this, O priests, and listen, house of Israel. And give ear, house of the king. For the judgment *is* toward you, because you have been a snare to Mizpah, and a net spread on Tabor. 2 And revolters have gone deep *in* slaughtering; and I chasten all of them. 3 I know Ephraim, and Israel has not hidden from me. For now, O Ephraim, you have fornicated; Israel is defiled. 4 Their doings will not allow

4428 1004 3478 1004 7181 3548 2063 8085
1 שִׁמְעוּ־זֹאת הַכֹּהֲנִים וְהַקְשִׁיבוּ בֵּית יִשְׂרָאֵל וּבֵית הַמֶּלֶךְ
,king the And !Israel house ,listen and ;priests O ,this Hear
of house of

7561 4709 1961 6341 4941 238
הַאֲזִינוּ כִּי לָכֶם הַמִּשְׁפָּט כִּי־פַח הֱיִיתֶם לְמִצְפָּה וְרֶשֶׁת
net a and ,Mizpah to have you a for the (is) toward For !ear give
been snare judgment you

4148 6009 7846 7819 8396 5921 6566
2 פְּרוּשָׂה עַל־תָּבוֹר׃ וְשַׁחֲטָה שֵׂטִים הֶעְמִיקוּ וַאֲנִי מוּסָר
chasten I and gone have revolters (in) And .Tabor on spread
,deep slaughtering

3582 3808 3478 669 3045 3605
3 לְכֻלָּם׃ אֲנִי יָדַעְתִּי אֶפְרַיִם וְיִשְׂרָאֵל לֹא־נִכְחַד מִמֶּנִּי כִּי
For from has not Israel and ,Ephraim know I .all them
.Me hidden

4611 5414 3808 3478 2930 669 2181 6258
4 עַתָּה הִזְנֵיתָ אֶפְרַיִם נִטְמָא יִשְׂרָאֵל׃ לֹא יִתְּנוּ מַעַלְלֵיהֶם
deeds Their will not .Israel defiled is O have you ,now
(them) allow ;Ephraim ,fornicated

them to turn to their God. For the spirit of fornication is in their midst, and they do not know Jehovah. 5And the pride of Israel answers to his face. So Israel and Ephraim shall stumble in their iniquity. Judah shall also stumble with them. 6They shall go with their flocks and with their herds to seek Jehovah, but they shall not find; He has withdrawn Himself from them. 7They have acted treacherously against Jehovah, for they have brought forth strange sons. Now a new moon shall devour them with their portions.

8Blow a horn in Gibeah, a trumpet in Ramah. Cry aloud, Beth-aven; after you, O Benjamin. 9Ephraim shall be desolate in the day of correction. Among the tribes of Israel, I have made known that which is confirmed. 10The rulers of Judah were as removers of a border; I will pour out My wrath on them like water. 11Ephraim is oppressed, crushed in judgment; because he was pleased, he walked after the command. 12Therefore, I *am* as a moth to Ephraim, and to the house of Judah as rottenness. 13When Ephraim saw his sickness, and Judah his wound, then Ephraim went to Assyria, and sent to king Jareb. Yet he could not heal you, nor did he cure you of your wound. 14For I *am* to Ephraim as the lion, and as the young lion to the house of Judah; I, *even* I tear and go; I take away, and no one rescues.

15I will go; I will return to My place until they confess their guilt and seek My face. In their affliction they will seek Me diligently.

3808 3068 7130 2184 7307 430 7725
לָשׁוּב אֶל־אֱלֹהֵיהֶם כִּי רוּחַ זְנוּנִים בְּקִרְבָּם וְאֶת־יְהוָה לֹא
not Jehovah and their in (is) forni- the For their to to
,midst cation of spirit .God return

5
3782 669 3478 6440 3478 1347 6030 3045
יָדָעוּ׃ וְעָנָה גְאוֹן־יִשְׂרָאֵל בְּפָנָיו וְיִשְׂרָאֵל וְאֶפְרַיִם יִכָּשְׁלוּ
shall and Israel So his to Israel the shall So they
stumble Ephraim .face of pride answer .know

6
3212 1241 6629 3063 1571 3782 5771
בַּעֲוֺנָם כָּשַׁל גַּם־יְהוּדָה עִמָּם׃ בְּצֹאנָם וּבִבְקָרָם יֵלְכוּ
They with and their with with Judah also stumbles their in
go shall herds their flocks .them .iniquity

7
898 3068 2502 4672 3808 3068 1245
לְבַקֵּשׁ אֶת־יְהוָה וְלֹא יִמְצָאוּ חָלַץ מֵהֶם׃ בַּיהוָה בָּגָדוּ
did They against from has He shall they but ,Jehovah seek to
,deceit Jehovah .them withdrawn ;find not

2506 2320 398 6258 3205 2114 1121
כִּי־בָנִים זָרִים יָלָדוּ עַתָּה יֹאכְלֵם חֹדֶשׁ אֶת־חֶלְקֵיהֶם׃
.portions their with new a de- shall Now have they strange sons for
moon them vour .borne

8
1008 7321 7414 2689 1390 7782 8628
תִּקְעוּ שׁוֹפָר בַּגִּבְעָה חֲצֹצְרָה בָּרָמָה הָרִיעוּ בֵּית
Beth- Cry ;Ramah in a in a Blow
,aloud trumpet ,Gibeah horn

9
8433 3117 1961 8047 669 1144 310 205
אָוֶן אַחֲרֶיךָ בִּנְיָמִין׃ אֶפְרַיִם לְשַׁמָּה תִהְיֶה בְּיוֹם תּוֹכֵחָה
.correction the in shall waste a Ephraim O after ;aven
of day become .Benjamin ,you

10
3063 8269 1961 539 3045 3478 7626
בְּשִׁבְטֵי יִשְׂרָאֵל הוֹדַעְתִּי נֶאֱמָנָה׃ הָיוּ שָׂרֵי יְהוּדָה
Judah The were is what made have I ,Israel the Among
of chiefs .confirmed known of tribes

11
6231 5678 4325 8210 1366 5253
כְּמַסִּיגֵי גְּבוּל עֲלֵיהֶם אֶשְׁפּוֹךְ כַּמַּיִם עֶבְרָתִי׃ עָשׁוּק
oppressed My the like will I them on a removers as
.wrath water out pour ;border of

12
6673 310 1980 2974 4941 6231 669
אֶפְרַיִם רְצוּץ מִשְׁפָּט כִּי הוֹאִיל הָלַךְ אַחֲרֵי־צָו׃ וַאֲנִי
I And the after he was he for ,judgment crushed (is)
(am) .command walked ,pleased in ,Ephraim

13
669 7200 3063 1004 7538 669 6211
כָעָשׁ לְאֶפְרָיִם וְכָרָקָב לְבֵית יְהוּדָה׃ וַיַּרְא אֶפְרַיִם אֶת־
Ephraim When .Judah the to as and Ephraim to a as
saw of house rottenness moth

7971 804 669 3212 4205 3063 2483
חָלְיוֹ וִיהוּדָה אֶת־מְזֹרוֹ וַיֵּלֶךְ אֶפְרַיִם אֶל־אַשּׁוּר וַיִּשְׁלַח
sent and Assyria to Ephraim then his Judah and his
went ,wound sickness

1455 3808 7495 3201 3808 7378 4428
אֶל־מֶלֶךְ יָרֵב וְהוּא לֹא יוּכַל לִרְפֹּא לָכֶם וְלֹא־יִגְהֶה מִכֶּם
you he and you heal to was not he Yet .Jareb King to
cured not able

14
3063 1004 3715 669 7826 4205
מָזוֹר׃ כִּי אָנֹכִי כַשַּׁחַל לְאֶפְרַיִם וְכַכְּפִיר לְבֵית יְהוּדָה
;Judah the to the as and ,Ephraim to the as I For (the of)
of house lion young lion (am) .wound

15
7725 3212 5337 369 5375 3212 2963
אֲנִי אֲנִי אֶטְרֹף וְאֵלֵךְ אֶשָּׂא וְאֵין מַצִּיל׃ אֵלֵךְ אָשׁוּבָה
Me let will I .rescues no and take I ;go and tear (even) ,I
return ;go one ,away

6862 6440 1245 816 5704 4725
אֶל־מְקוֹמִי עַד אֲשֶׁר־יֶאְשְׁמוּ וּבִקְשׁוּ פָנָי בַּצַּר לָהֶם
to the In My and confess they until place My to
,them distress .face seek guilt their

7836
יְשַׁחֲרֻנְנִי׃
seek will they
.diligently Me

CHAPTER 6

[1]Come and let us return
to Jehovah. For He has torn,
and He will heal us. He has
stricken, and He will bind us
up. [2]After two days He
will bring us to life. In the
third day He will raise us up,
and we shall live before
Him. [3]Then we shall know,
we who follow on to know
Jehovah. His going forth is
established as the dawn.
And He shall come to us as
the rain, as the latter *and*
former rain to the earth.
[4]O Ephraim, what shall I
do to you? O Judah, what
shall I do to you? For your
goodness is like a morning
cloud, and it goes away like
the early dew. [5]So I have
hewn *them* by the
prophets; I have slain them
by the words of My mouth;
and your judgments *have
been as* the light that goes
forth. [6]For I desired mercy,
and not sacrifice; and the
knowledge of God more
than burnt offerings. [7]But,
like Adam, they have
broken the covenant; they
have acted like traitors
against Me there. [8]Gilead
is a city of those who work
iniquity, slippery with
bloodmarks. [9]And as troops
of robbers wait for a man,
the company of priests
murder *in* the way to
Shechem; for they have
done wickedness. [10]I have
seen a horrible thing in the
house of Israel: the fornication of Ephraim *is* there;
Israel is defiled. [11]Also, O
Judah, a harvest is
appointed to you, when I
return the captivity of My
people.

CHAPTER 7

[1]When I would have
healed Israel, then the
iniquity of Ephraim was
uncovered, and the wick-
edness of Samaria. For they
have worked falsehood.
And a thief comes; a troop
of robbers plunders out-
side. [2]And they do not say

CAP. VI ו

CHAPTER 6

5221 7495 2963 3068 7725 3212
1 לְכוּ וְנָשׁוּבָה אֶל־יְהוָה כִּי הוּא טָרָף וְיִרְפָּאֵנוּ יַךְ
He will He but has He For .Jehovah to let and Come
,struck .us heal ,torn return us

2421 6965 7992 3117 3117 2421 2280
2 וְיַחְבְּשֵׁנוּ׃ יְחַיֵּנוּ מִיֹּמָיִם בַּיּוֹם הַשְּׁלִישִׁי יְקִמֵנוּ וְנִחְיֶה
shall we and will He third the In two after will He will He but
live up us lift day .days us revive .up us bind

3559 7837 3068 3045 7291 3045 6440
3 לְפָנָיו׃ וְנֵדְעָה נִרְדְּפָה לָדַעַת אֶת־יְהוָה כְּשַׁחַר נָכוֹן
is the As .Jehovah know to us let let Then before
sure ,dawn pursue ,know us .Him

6213 4100 776 3384 4456 1653 935 4161
4 מוֹצָאוֹ וְיָבוֹא כַגֶּשֶׁם לָנוּ כְּמַלְקוֹשׁ יוֹרֶה אָרֶץ׃ מָה אֶעֱשֶׂה
do I shall What the (to) former the as ,us to the as He and going His
.earth rain rain latter rain come shall ;forth

1242 6051 2617 3063 6213 4100 669
לְּךָ אֶפְרַיִם מָה אֶעֱשֶׂה־לְּךָ יְהוּדָה וְחַסְדְּכֶם כַּעֲנַן־בֹּקֶר
,morning a like your For ?Judah O to I shall What ?Ephraim O to
of cloud (is) faithfulness ,you do ,you

2026 5030 2672 1980 7925 2919
5 וְכַטַּל מַשְׁכִּים הֹלֵךְ׃ עַל־כֵּן חָצַבְתִּי בַּנְּבִיאִים הֲרַגְתִּים
slain have I the by have I So (and) rising like and
them ;prophets hewn .going ,early ;dew the

3808 2654 2617 3318 216 4941 6310 561
6 בְּאִמְרֵי־פִי וּמִשְׁפָּטֶיךָ אוֹר יֵצֵא׃ כִּי חֶסֶד חָפַצְתִּי וְלֹא־
and ,desired I faith- For (that) the (as) your and My the by
not fulness .forth goes light ,judgments ,mouth of words

1285 5674 120 5930 430 1847 2077
7 זָבַח וְדַעַת אֱלֹהִים מֵעֹלוֹת׃ וְהֵמָּה כְּאָדָם עָבְרוּ בְרִית
;covenant have like ,they But than more God the and sacri-
transgressed ,Adam .offerings burnt of knowledge ;fice

1818 6121 205 6466 7151 1568 898 8033
8 שָׁם בָּגְדוּ בִי׃ גִּלְעָד קִרְיַת פֹּעֲלֵי אָוֶן עֲקֻבָּה מִדָּם׃
from slippery ,trouble those city a Gilead against did they there
.blood work who of (is) .Me deceit

7926 7523 1870 3548 2267 1416 376 2442
9 וּכְחַכֵּי אִישׁ גְּדוּדִים חֶבֶר כֹּהֲנִים דֶּרֶךְ יְרַצְּחוּ־שֶׁכְמָה כִּי
for to murder the (in) priests com- the of troops a as And
;Shechem way of pany ,robbers man for wait

2184 8033 8186 7200 3478 1004 6213 2154
10 זִמָּה עָשׂוּ׃ בְּבֵית יִשְׂרָאֵל רָאִיתִי שַׁעֲרִירִיָּה שָׁם זְנוּת
har- the there horrible a have I Israel the In have they wicked-
of lotry :thing seen of house .done ness

7725 7102 7896 3063/1571 3478 2930 669
11 לְאֶפְרַיִם נִטְמָא יִשְׂרָאֵל׃ גַּם־יְהוּדָה שָׁת קָצִיר לָךְ בְּשׁוּבִי
I when for a set is O ,Also .Israel is Ephraim
return ,you harvest ,Judah defiled ;(is)

5971 7622
שְׁבוּת עַמִּי׃
My cap- the
.people of tivity

CAP. VII ז

CHAPTER 7

8111 5771 669 5771 1540 3478 7495
1 כְּרָפְאִי לְיִשְׂרָאֵל וְנִגְלָה עֲוֹן אֶפְרַיִם וְרָעוֹת שֹׁמְרוֹן כִּי
For .Samaria the and ,Ephraim the was then ,Israel would I When
of wickedness of iniquity uncovered healed have

559 1077 2351 1416 6584 935 1590 8267 6466
2 פָעֲלוּ שָׁקֶר וְגַנָּב יָבוֹא פָּשַׁט גְּדוּד בַּחוּץ׃ וּבַל־יֹאמְרוּ
do they And .outside troop a plunders ;comes a And false- have they
say not robbers of thief .hood worked

within their hearts that I remember all their evil. Now their own doings have hemmed them in. They are before My face. 3They make the king glad with their evil, and the rulers with their lies. 4They *are* all adulterers, like an oven heated by the baker; he ceases from stirring, from kneading the dough while it is leavened. 5*In* the day of our king, the rulers have sickened themselves *with* the heat of wine. He stretches out his hand with scorners. 6For they have brought their heart near, like an oven, while they lie in wait. Their baker sleeps all night; in the morning, it burns like a flaming fire. 7They are all hot as an oven, and devour their judges. All their kings have fallen; not one among them calls to Me. 8Ephraim mixed himself among the peoples. Ephraim is a cake not turned. 9Strangers have eaten up his strength, yet he does not know. Yea, gray hairs are sprinkled on him, yet he does not know. 10And the pride of Israel testifies to his face. And they do not return to Jehovah their God, nor seek Him in all this.

11Ephraim also is like a silly dove without heart; they call *to* Egypt; they go to Assyria. 12When they go, I will spread My net over them; I will bring them down like the birds of the heavens; I will chastise them, as a report to their congregation. 13Wo to them! For they have fled from Me. Ruin to them! For they have transgressed against Me. Though I would redeem them, yet they have spoken lies against Me. 14And they have not cried to Me with their heart, when they howled on their beds. They gather themselves for grain and wine; they turn against Me. 15Though I

5048 4611 5437 6258 2142 7451 3605 3824
ללבבם כל־רעתם זכרתי עתה סבבום מעלליהם נגד
Before own their .doings hemmed have in them Now re- I .member their all evil their in (that) hearts

3 8269 3585 4428 8056 7451 1961 6440
פני היו׃ ברעתם ישמחו־מלך ובכחשיהם שרים׃
.rulers the their with and lies the .king made they glad their With evil they .are My face

4 5782 7673 644 1197 8574 3644 5003 3605
כלם מנאפים כמו תנור בערה מאפה ישבות מעיר
from ,stirring he ceases the by :baker heated an oven like ,adulterers They all (are)

5 2534 8269 2470 4428 3117 2556 5704 1217 3888
מלוש בצק עד־חמצתו׃ יום מלכנו החלו שרים חמת
the (with) of heat the rulers sickened themselves our king the (In) of day is it .leavened while the ,dough from kneading

6 693 3820 8574 7126 3945 3027 4900 3196
מיין משך ידו את־לצצים׃ כי־קרבו כתנור לבם בארבם
lie they .wait in while their ,heart the like oven they For near brought .scorners with his hand put He out .wine

3852 784 1197 1242 644 3463 3915 3605
כל־הלילה ישן אפהם בקר הוא בער כאש להבה׃
.flame a as of fire burns it the In ,morning their ,baker sleeps the night All

7 5307 4428 3605 8199 398 8574 2552 3605
כלם יחמו כתנור ואכלו את־שפטיהם כל־מלכיהם נפלו
have .fallen kings their All .judges their and devour the as oven are hot They all

8 669 1101 5971 669 7121 369
אין־קרא בהם אלי׃ אפרים בעמים הוא יתבולל אפרים
Ephraim mixes .himself he the among peoples Ephraim (is) to .Me among them calls Not one

9 3045/3808 1961 3381 2114 398 2015 1077 5692 1961
היה עגה בלי הפוכה׃ אכלו זרים כחו והוא לא ידע
does (it) know not he yet his ,strength Strangers have eaten .turned not a cake is

10 3478 1347 6030 3045 3808 2236 7872 1571
גם־שיבה זרקה בו והוא לא ידע׃ וענה גאון־ישראל
Israel the of pride And testifies know does not .(it) he yet on sprinkled ,him gray hairs ,Yea

3605 1245 3808 430 3068 7725 /3808 6440
בפניו ולא־שבו אל־יהוה אלהיהם ולא בקשהו בכל־
all in Him seek nor ,God their Jehovah to do they return not But his to ,face

11 7121 4714 3820 369 6601 3138 669 1961 2063
זאת׃ ויהי אפרים כיונה פותה אין לב מצרים קראו
they .call Egypt (To) .heart with- out silly a as dove Ephraim Also is .this

12 5775 7568 6566 3212 1980 804
אשור הלכו׃ כאשר ילכו אפרוש עליהם רשתי כעוף
like of birds ;net My them on will I spread they ,go when .go they (To) Assyria

13 188 5712 8088 3256 3381 8064
השמים אורידם איסרם כשמע לעדתם׃ אוי להם כי־
For !them to Woe their to .congregation a as report chastise will I .them bring will I .down them the heavens

6299 6586 7701 5074
נדדו ממני שד להם כי־פשעו בי ואנכי אפדם והמה
they yet ,them re- deem would I Though against .Me have they trespassed For to !them Ruin from .Me have they fled

14 3213 3820 2199 3808 3577 1696
דברו עלי כזבים׃ ולא־זעקו אלי בלבם כי ייליליו על־
on they howled when their with ,heart to Me And they have not cried .lies against Me have spoken

15 5493 1481 8492 1715 4904
משכבותם על־דגן ותירוש יתגוררו יסורו בי׃ ואני
Though I against .Me they turn gather They :themselves new and wine grain for .beds their

bound, I made their arms strong; yet they think evil against Me. 16 They return, *but* not to the *Most* High. They are like a treacherous bow. Their rulers shall fall by the sword, from the rage of the tongue. This *shall be* their scorn in the land of Egypt.

5920 3808 7725 7451 2803 2220 2388 3256
16 יסרתי חזקתי זרועתם ואלי יחשבו־רע׃ ישובו לא על
the to not re- They .evil they yet ;arms their strengthen I ,bound
High (but) ,turn think Me against

2097 3956 2195 8269 2719 5307 74:23 7198 1961
היו כקשת רמיה יפלו בחרב שריהם מזעם לשונם זו
This their the from Their the by shall .treachery a as They
(is) .tongue of rage ,rulers sword fall of bow are

4714 776 3933
לעגם בארץ מצרים׃
.Egypt the in their
of land scorn

CAP. VIII ח

CHAPTER 8

1 *Put* a horn to your mouth. *He comes* like an eagle against the house of Jehovah, because they have broken My covenant and have sinned against My law. 2 Israel shall cry to Me, My God, we know You. 3 Israel has thrown off good; the enemy shall pursue him. 4 They have set up kings, but not by Me. They have made rulers, but I did not know. They made idols for themselves *with* their silver and their gold, so that they may be cut off.

5 O Samaria, your calf has cast *you* off. My anger is kindled against them. Until when will they not attain purity? 6 For it also *came* from Israel: The craftsman made it, but *it is* not God. For the calf of Samaria shall be splinters. 7 For they sow the wind, and they reap the whirlwind. He has no stalk; the bud shall make no flour. If it does make *it*, strangers will swallow it up. 8 Israel is swallowed up. They are now among the nations as a vessel in which is no pleasure. 9 For they have gone up to Assyria, a wild ass alone by himself. Ephraim has hired lovers. 10 Yes, though they have hired among the nations, now I will gather them. And they began to be few, from the burden of the king of rulers. 11 Because Ephraim has made many altars to sin; they are altars to him to sin. 12 I will write the great things of My law for him; they were counted as a

:1285 5674 3282 3068 1004 5404 7782 2441
1 אל־חכך שפר כנשר על־בית יהוה יען עברו בריתי
My have they for ,Jehovah the against (comes He) a your (Put)
,covenant overpassed of house eagle an as :horn mouth to

2186 3478 3045 430 2199 6586 8451
2 ועל־תורתי פשעו׃ לי יזעקו אלהי ידענוך ישראל׃
3 זנח
has .Israel know we My shall To have law My and
off cast ,You ,God ,cry Me .trespassed against

7786 38:08 4427 5704 7291 341 2896 3478
4 ישראל טוב אויב ירדפו׃ הם המליכו ולא ממני השירו
made They by but set have They shall the ;good Israel
,princes Me not ,kings up .him pursue enemy

3772 4676 6091 6213 2091 3701 3045 38:08
ולא ידעתי כספם וזהבם עשו להם עצבים למען יכרת׃
may they that so ,idols for They their and their (with) I but
.off cut be them made gold silver .(it) knew not

5356 3201 38:08 5704 639 2734 81:11 5695 2186
5 זנח עגלך שמרון חרה אפי בם עד־מתי לא יוכלו נקין׃
?purity they will not when Until against My is .Samaria Your cast has
attain .them anger kindled calf off (you)

430 38:08 6213 2796 3478
6 כי מישראל והוא חרש עשהו ולא אלהים הוא כי־
For .(is) God and ,it made The it also Israel from For
not artisan .(came)

7114 5492 22:32 7307 8111 5695 :1961 7616
7 שבבים יהיה עגל שמרון׃ כי רוח יזרעו וסופתה יקצרו
shall they the and they the For .Samaria the shall splinters
.reap tempest sow wind of calf be

2114 62:13 194 7058 6213 1097 6780 369 7054
קמה אין־לו צמח בלי יעשה־קמח אולי יעשה זרים
strangers does it If .flour shall not bud the to is A
make make ;him not stalk

2656 369 3627 1471 1961 6258 3478 1104 1104
8 יבלעהו׃ נבלע ישראל עתה היו בגוים ככלי אין־חפץ
pleasure is a as the among they Now .Israel swallowed is swallow shall
no vessel nations are up .up it

8566 669 909 6501 804 5927
9 בו׃ כי־המה עלו אשור פרא בודד לו אפרים התנו
has Ephraim by alone wild a to have they For in
hired ,himself ass Assyria up gone which

4592 2490 6908 6258 1471 8566 1571 158
10 אהבים׃ גם כי־יתנו בגוים עתה אקבצם ויחלו מעט
,few they And will I now the among they though ,Yes .lovers
(be to) began .them gather ,nations hired have

2398 4196 669 7235 8269 44:27 4853
11 ממשא מלך שרים׃ כי־הרבה אפרים מזבחות לחטא
—sin to altars Ephraim made has For .rulers king the the from
many of of burden

2114 8451 7230 3789 2398 4196 1961
12 היו־לו מזבחות לחטא׃ אכתוב־לו רבי תורתי כמו־זר
a as My great the for will I —sin to altars to they
stranger ;law of things him write him are

stranger. [13]They sacrifice flesh *for* the sacrifices of My offerings, and they eat. Jehovah *was* not pleased with them. Now he will remember their iniquity and punish their sins. They shall return *to* Egypt. [14]For Israel has forgotten his Maker and builds temples. And Judah has multiplied fortified cities; but I will send a fire on his cities, and it shall burn up her citadels.

CHAPTER 9

[1]O Israel, do not rejoice for joy, like the peoples. For you have gone lusting away from your God. You have loved a reward on all threshing-floors of grain. [2]The floor and the winepress shall not feed them, and the new wine shall fail in her. [3]They shall not live in the land of Jehovah. But Ephraim shall return to Egypt; and they shall eat unclean things in Assyria. [4]They shall not offer wine to Jehovah. They shall not be pleasing to Him. Their sacrifices *shall be* like the bread of trouble to them; all who eat it shall be defiled; for their bread *is* for their person; it shall not come into the house of Jehovah.

[5]What will you do in the day of meeting, and in the day of the feast of Jehovah? [6]For, lo, they have gone from destruction. Egypt shall gather them; Memphis shall bury them. Nettles shall possess the desirable things of their silver; thorns *shall be* in their tents. [7]The days of her visitation have come; the days of retribution have come. Israel shall know. The prophet *is* a fool; the spiritual man *is* insane, because of the greatness of your iniquity and your great hatred. [8]Ephraim *is* a watchman with my God. The prophet *is* a snare of a fowler on all his ways; hatred *is* in the house of his God. [9]They have deeply corrupted, as *in* days of

7521 38:08 3068 398 1320 2076 1890 2077 2803
13 נֶחְשָׁבוּ׃ זִבְחֵי הַבְהָבַי יִזְבְּחוּ בָשָׂר וַיֹּאכֵלוּ יְהוָה לֹא רָצָם
ac- did not Jehovah they and flesh they My the For were they
.them cept .eat sacrifice gifts of sacrifices .counted
7725 4714 2403 6485 5771 2142
עַתָּה יִזְכֹּר עֲוֺנָם וְיִפְקֹד חַטֹּאתָם הֵמָּה מִצְרַיִם יָשׁוּבוּ׃
shall Egypt (to) They .sins their and their will He Now
.return visit iniquity remember
7235 30:63 1964 1129 6213 3478 7911
14 וַיִּשְׁכַּח יִשְׂרָאֵל אֶת־עֹשֵׂהוּ וַיִּבֶן הֵיכָלוֹת וִיהוּדָה הִרְבָּה
has Judah And .temples and his Israel has For
multiplied builds ,Maker forgotten
759 398 5892 784 7971 1219 5892
עָרִים בְּצֻרוֹת וְשִׁלַּחְתִּי־אֵשׁ בְּעָרָיו וְאָכְלָה אַרְמְנֹתֶיהָ׃
her shall it and his on a will I but inacces- cities
.citadels consume ,cities fire send :sible

CAP. IX ט

CHAPTER 9

430 2181 5971 1524 3478 8055 408
1 אַל־תִּשְׂמַח יִשְׂרָאֵל׀אֶל־גִּיל כָּעַמִּים כִּי זָנִיתָ מֵעַל אֱלֹהֶיךָ
your away have you For the as ,joy for ,Israel O do not
.God from fornicated .peoples rejoice
7462 38:08 3342 1637 1715 1637 3605 868 157
2 אָהַבְתָּ אֶתְנָן עַל כָּל־גָּרְנוֹת דָּגָן׃ גֹּרֶן וָיֶקֶב לֹא יִרְעֵם
feed shall not the and The .grain grain all on harlot's a have You
,them winepress floor of floors hire loved
669 7725 3068 776 3427 38:08 3584 8492
3 וְתִירוֹשׁ יְכַחֶשׁ בָּהּ׃ לֹא יֵשְׁבוּ בְּאֶרֶץ יְהוָה וְשָׁב אֶפְרַיִם
Ephraim But .Jehovah the in They not .her in shall new and
return shall of land live shall fail wine
38:08 3196 3068 5258 38:08 398 2931 804 4714
4 מִצְרַיִם וּבְאַשּׁוּר טָמֵא יֹאכֵלוּ׃ לֹא־יִסְּכוּ לַיהוָה יַיִן וְלֹא
And .wine to They not shall they unclean in and ;Egypt to
not Jehovah pour shall .eat things Assyria
2930 398 3605 205 3899 2077 6148
יֶעֶרְבוּ־לוֹ זִבְחֵיהֶם כְּלֶחֶם אוֹנִים לָהֶם כָּל־אֹכְלָיו יִטַּמָּאוּ
be shall eat who all to trouble the as (are) Their to shall they
;defiled it ;them of bread sacrifices .Him pleasing be
3117 6213 4100 3068 1004 935 38:08 5315 3899
5 כִּי־לַחְמָם לְנַפְשָׁם לֹא יָבוֹא בֵּית יְהוָה׃ מַה־תַּעֲשׂוּ לְיוֹם
the in you will What .Jehovah the into shall it not their for their for
of day do of house come ;person (is) bread
4714 77:01 1980 2009 3068 2282 3117 4150
6 מוֹעֵד וּלְיוֹם חַג־יְהוָה׃ כִּי־הִנֵּה הָלְכוּ מִשֹּׁד מִצְרַיִם
Egypt from have they ,behold ,For ?Jehovah the in and meet-
.destruction gone of feast of day the ,ing
2336 34:23 7058 37:01 4261 6912 4644 6908
תְּקַבְּצֵם מֹף תְּקַבְּרֵם מַחְמַד לְכַסְפָּם קִמּוֹשׁ יִירָשֵׁם חוֹחַ
thorns shall nettles their of Desirable bury shall Memphis shall
;possess ,silver things .them ;them gather
3045 7966 3117 935 6486 3117 935 168
7 בְּאָהֳלֵיהֶם׃ בָּאוּ ׀ יְמֵי הַפְּקֻדָּה בָּאוּ יְמֵי הַשִּׁלֻּם יֵדְעוּ
shall .retribution the have her The have (be shall)
know of days come ,visitation of days come .tents their in
7227 5771 7230 7307 376 7696 50:30 191 3478
יִשְׂרָאֵל אֱוִיל הַנָּבִיא מְשֻׁגָּע אִישׁ הָרוּחַ עַל רֹב עֲוֺנְךָ וְרַבָּה
and your great for the The (is) the a (is) ,Israel
much iniquity ,spirit man of insane .prophet fool
3352 6341 5030 430 669 6822 4895
8 מַשְׂטֵמָה׃ צֹפֶה אֶפְרַיִם עִם־אֱלֹהָי נָבִיא פַּח יָקוֹשׁ עַל־
on a snare The my with Ephraim a (your)
fowler's (is) prophet .God (is) watchman .hatred
3117 7843 6009 430 1004 4895 1870 3605
9 כָּל־דְּרָכָיו מַשְׂטֵמָה בְּבֵית אֱלֹהָיו׃ הֶעְמִיקוּ שִׁחֵתוּ כִּימֵי
(in) as cor- have They .God his the in hatred ;ways his all
of days the rupted deeply of house (is)

Gibeah. He will remember
their iniquity; He will punish
their sins.
[10]I found Israel like
grapes in the wilderness. I
saw your fathers as the
firstfruit in the fig-tree at her
first time. They came *to*
Baal-peor and set them-
selves apart to a shameful
thing. And they became
hateful like that which they
loved. [11]Ephraim is like a
bird; their glory shall fly
away from birth, and from
the womb, and from con-
ception. [12]Though they
nourish their sons, yet I will
make them childless, without a man. Yea, woe also to
them when I turn away from
them! [13]As when I looked
toward Tyre, Ephraim was
planted in a pleasant place.
But Ephraim shall bring
forth his sons to the slayer.
[14]O Jehovah, give them.
What will you give them?
Give them a miscarrying
womb and dry breasts. [15]All
their wickedness *is* in
Gilgal, for there I hated
them. I will drive them out
of My house for the
wickedness of their doings;
I will love them again;
all their rulers *are* revolters.
[16]Ephraim *is* stricken; their
root is dried up; they shall
bear no fruit. Yea, though
they bear, yet I will yet put to
death the beloved ones of
their womb. [17]My God shall
reject them because they
did not listen to Him. And
they shall be wanderers
among the nations.

הַגִּבְעָה יִזְכּוֹר עֲוֺנָם יִפְקוֹד חַטֹּאותָם׃ 10 כַּעֲנָבִים בַּמִּדְבָּר
the in wilderness grapes Like .sins their will He visit their ;iniquity recall Gibeah

מָצָאתִי יִשְׂרָאֵל כְּבִכּוּרָה בִתְאֵנָה בְּרֵאשִׁיתָהּ רָאִיתִי
saw I its beginning at the in tree fig the As firstfruit .Israel found I

אֲבוֹתֵיכֶם הֵמָּה בָּאוּ בַעַל־פְּעוֹר וַיִּנָּזְרוּ לַבֹּשֶׁת וַיִּהְיוּ
they And became to .shame and separated peor Baal- (to) came They .fathers your

11 שִׁקּוּצִים כְּאָהֳבָם׃ אֶפְרַיִם כָּעוֹף יִתְעוֹפֵף כְּבוֹדָם מִלֵּדָה
from ,birth ,glory their fly shall away a like bird for As ,Ephraim which that like .loved they hateful ,things

12 וּמִבֶּטֶן וּמֵהֵרָיוֹן׃ כִּי אִם־יְגַדְּלוּ אֶת־בְּנֵיהֶם וְשִׁכַּלְתִּים
make will I yet ,childless them their ,sons they nourish Though from and .conception from and ,womb the

13 מֵאָדָם כִּי־גַם־אוֹי לָהֶם בְּשׂוּרִי מֵהֶם׃ אֶפְרַיִם כַּאֲשֶׁר־
when as ,Ephraim from !them I when turn to them woe also ,Yes without .man a

רָאִיתִי לְצוֹר שְׁתוּלָה בְנָוֶה וְאֶפְרַיִם לְהוֹצִיא אֶל־הֹרֵג
the to slayer bring (shall) forth But Ephraim a in .meadow planted was toward ,Tyre looked I

14 בָּנָיו׃ תֵּן־לָהֶם יְהוָה מַה־תִּתֵּן תֵּן־לָהֶם רֶחֶם מַשְׁכִּיל
miscarrying a womb to Give them will what ?give You ;Jehovah to Give ,them his .sons

15 וְשָׁדַיִם צֹמְקִים׃ כָּל־רָעָתָם בַּגִּלְגָּל כִּי־שָׁם שְׂנֵאתִים עַל
for hated I ;them there for ,Gilgal in (is) their evil All .dry and breasts

רֹעַ מַעַלְלֵיהֶם מִבֵּיתִי אֲגָרְשֵׁם לֹא אוֹסֵף אַהֲבָתָם כָּל־
all ;them love will I again not will I ;them drive of out house My doings their the of evil

16 שָׂרֵיהֶם סֹרְרִים׃ הֻכָּה אֶפְרַיִם שָׁרְשָׁם יָבֵשׁ פְּרִי בְלִי־
not fruit is ;up dried their root ;Ephraim is stricken .revolters rulers their (are)

17 יַעֲשׂוּן גַּם כִּי יֵלֵדוּן וְהֵמַתִּי מַחֲמַדֵּי בִטְנָם׃ יִמְאָסֵם אֱלֹהַי
My ,God reject shall them their .womb beloved the of ones I yet kill will they though ,bear ,Yes they .make shall

כִּי לֹא שָׁמְעוּ לוֹ וְיִהְיוּ נֹדְדִים בַּגּוֹיִם׃
among .nations the wanderers they and be shall to ;Him did they listen not be- cause

CHAPTER 10

[1]Israel *is* a luxuriant
vine; he bears fruit for
himself. According to the
plenty of his fruit he has
increased the altars. They
have made beautiful
images according to the
goodness of his land;
their heart is divided.
[2]Now they shall be guilty;
He shall break down
their altars; He shall
spoil their pillars. [3]For

CAP. X י

CHAPTER 10

1 גֶּפֶן בּוֹקֵק יִשְׂרָאֵל פְּרִי יְשַׁוֶּה־לּוֹ כְּרֹב לְפִרְיוֹ הִרְבָּה
has he increased his of ,fruit the As plenty for .himself He bears fruit Israel .(is) luxuriant A vine

2 לַמִּזְבְּחוֹת כְּטוֹב לְאַרְצוֹ הֵיטִיבוּ מַצֵּבוֹת׃ חָלַק לִבָּם עַתָּה
Now their .heart is divided .pillars have they goodly his of land the As goodness .altars the

3 יֶאְשָׁמוּ הוּא יַעֲרֹף מִזְבְּחוֹתָם יְשֹׁדֵד מַצֵּבוֹתָם׃ כִּי עַתָּה
now For .pillars their shall He despoil their ;altars shall down break He shall they ;guilty be

now they shall say, We have no king, because we did not fear Jehovah. What then should a king do for us? [4]They have spoken words, swearing falsely to cut a covenant. So judgment springs up like hemlock in the furrows of the field. [5]The people of Samaria shall dread because of the calves of Beth-aven. For its people shall mourn over it; also its priests *who* rejoiced on it for its glory; because it has departed from it. [6]It shall also be carried to Assyria, a present to king Jareb. Ephraim shall receive shame, and Israel shall be ashamed of his own counsel. [7]Samaria is cut off; her king is as a bough on the face of the water. [8]Also, the sin of Israel, the high places of Aven shall be destroyed. The thorn and the thistle shall come up on their altars. And they shall say to the mountains, Cover us; and to the hills, Fall on us.

[9]O Israel, you have sinned from the days of Gibeah. There they stood; the battle against the sons of iniquity did not overtake them in Gibeah. [10]When I desire, I shall bind them; and the peoples shall be gathered against them, when they bind themselves to their perversities. [11]And Ephraim *is* a trained heifer, loving to tread out. But I passed over on the goodness of her neck; I will make Ephraim to ride; Judah shall plow; Jacob shall break clods for him. [12]Sow to yourselves in righteousness, reap as mercy. Break up your plowed ground. For *it is* time to seek Jehovah, until He comes and rains righteousness on you. [13]You have plowed wickedness; you have reaped iniquity. You have eaten the fruit of lies because you trusted in your way, in the multitude of your mighty men. [14]And an uproar shall rise up among your peoples. And all your

4100 4428 3068 3372 3808 4428 369 559
יֹאמְרוּ אֵין מֶלֶךְ לָנוּ כִּי לֹא יָרֵאנוּ אֶת־יְהוָה וְהַמֶּלֶךְ מַה־
What the then .Jehovah did we not be- ,us to king No shall they
king fear cause (is) ,say

6524 1285 3772 7723 422 1697 1696 6213
4 יַּעֲשֶׂה־לָּנוּ׃ דִּבְּרוּ דְבָרִים אָלוֹת שָׁוְא כָּרֹת בְּרִית וּפָרַח
So cove- a cut to empti- swearing ,words have They for should
up springs .nant ness spoken ?us do

1481 1007 5697 7704 8525 4941 7219
5 כָּרֹאשׁ מִשְׁפָּט עַל תַּלְמֵי שָׂדָי׃ לְעֶגְלוֹת בֵּית אָוֶן יָגוּרוּ
shall aven Beth- of Because the fur- the on judgment as
dread of calves the .field of rows hemlock

5923 3649 5971 56 8111 7934
שְׁכַן שֹׁמְרוֹן כִּי־אָבַל עָלָיו עַמּוֹ וּכְמָרָיו עָלָיו יָגִילוּ עַל־
for re- (who) it on its and its over shall For .Samaria's people
joiced ,priests ;people it mourn

4428 4503 2986 804 1571 1540 3519
6 כְּבוֹדוֹ כִּי־גָלָה מִמֶּנּוּ׃ גַּם־אוֹתוֹ לְאַשּׁוּר יוּבָל מִנְחָה לְמֶלֶךְ
king to a be shall Assyria to it Also .it from has it be- its
present ,carried departed cause ,glory

1820 6098 3478 954 3947 669 1322 7378
7 יָרֵב בָּשְׁנָה אֶפְרַיִם יִקָּח וְיֵבוֹשׁ יִשְׂרָאֵל מֵעֲצָתוֹ׃ נִדְמֶה
cut is own his from Israel shall and shall Ephraim shame .Jareb
off .counsel ashamed be ,receive

205 1116 8045 4325 6440 7110 4428 8111
8 שֹׁמְרוֹן מַלְכָּהּ כְּקֶצֶף עַל־פְּנֵי־מָיִם׃ וְנִשְׁמְדוּ בָּמוֹת אָוֶן
,Aven high the be shall Also the the on a as ,king her ,Samaria
of places destroyed .waters of face bough

559 4196 5927 1863 6975 3478 2403
חַטַּאת יִשְׂרָאֵל קוֹץ וְדַרְדַּר יַעֲלֶה עַל־מִזְבְּחוֹתָם וְאָמְרוּ
they And .altars their on come shall the and The .Israel sin the
say shall up thistle thorn of

1390 3117 5308 1389 3680 2022
9 לֶהָרִים כַּסּוּנוּ וְלַגְּבָעוֹת נִפְלוּ עָלֵינוּ׃ מִימֵי הַגִּבְעָה
Gibeah the From .us on Fall the to and Cover the to
of days ,hills ;us ,mountains

4421 1390 5381 3808 5975 8033 3478 2398
חָטָאתָ יִשְׂרָאֵל שָׁם עָמָדוּ לֹא־תַשִּׂיגֵם בַגִּבְעָה מִלְחָמָה
battle the Gibeah in over- not they There .Israel O have you
them takes ;stood ,sinned

631 5971 622 631 185 5932 1121
10 עַל־בְּנֵי עַלְוָה׃ בְּאַוָּתִי וְאֶסֳּרֵם וְאֻסְּפוּ עֲלֵיהֶם עַמִּים בְּאָסְרָם
they when ,peoples against shall And will I then I When .injustice the against
themselves bind them gathered be them bind desire of sons

1758 157 3925 5697 669 5771 8147
11 לִשְׁתֵּי עֹינֹתָם׃ וְאֶפְרַיִם עֶגְלָה מְלֻמָּדָה אֹהַבְתִּי לָדוּשׁ וַאֲנִי
I But tread to love I ;trained heifer a (is) And their to
.out Ephraim .perversities two

3063 2790 66 7392 6677 2898 5674
עָבַרְתִּי עַל־טוּב צַוָּארָהּ אַרְכִּיב אֶפְרַיִם יַחֲרוֹשׁ יְהוּדָה
;Judah shall ;Ephraim make will I ;neck her the on passed
plow ride to of goodness over

5214 2617 6440 7114 6666 2232 3290 7702
12 יְשַׂדֶּד־לוֹ יַעֲקֹב׃ זִרְעוּ לָכֶם לִצְדָקָה קִצְרוּ לְפִי־חֶסֶד נִירוּ
Break .mercy as reap righ- in your- to Sow .Jacob for shall
up ,teousness selves him harrow

6664 3384 935 5704 3068 1875 6256 5215
לָכֶם נִיר וְעֵת לִדְרוֹשׁ אֶת־יְהוָה עַד־יָבוֹא וְיֹרֶה צֶדֶק לָכֶם׃
to righ- rains and He until ,Jehovah seek to For plowed to
.you teousness comes time .ground you

3585 6259 398 7114 5766 7562 2790
13 חֲרַשְׁתֶּם־רֶשַׁע עַוְלָתָה קְצַרְתֶּם אֲכַלְתֶּם פְּרִי־כָחַשׁ כִּי־
because ,lies the have You have you iniquity wicked- have You
of fruit eaten .reaped ;ness plowed

3605 5971 7588 6965 1368 7230 1870 982
14 בָטַחְתָּ בְדַרְכְּךָ בְּרֹב גִּבּוֹרֶיךָ׃ וְקָאם שָׁאוֹן בְּעַמֶּךָ וְכָל־
And your among an shall And your in your in you
all .peoples uproar arise .warriors many ,way trusted

strongholds shall be spoiled, as the ruin *of* Beth-arbel in the day of battle. The mother was dashed in pieces on *her* sons. [15]So He does to you, Bethel, because of your great evil. In the dawn the king of Israel shall be completely cut off.

CHAPTER 11

[1]When Israel *was* a child, then I loved him, and I called My son out of Egypt. [2]*As* they called to them, so they went from their face. They sacrifice to the Baals, and burn incense to graven images. [3]I also taught Ephraim to go; he took them on their arms. But they did not know that I healed them. [4]I drew them with cords of a man, with bands of love. And I was to them as those who lift off the yoke on their jaws; and I gently give food to him.

[5]He shall not return to the land of Egypt, but he, Assyria, *shall be* his king, because they refused to return. [6]And the sword shall whirl in his cities and shall end his bars, and shall consume, because of their own counsels. [7]And My people are bent on backsliding from Me. And they call him to the Most High; no one at all would exalt *Him*.

[8]How shall I give you up, Ephraim? Shall I deliver you, Israel? How shall I make you like Admah? Shall I set you as Zeboim? My heart has turned within Me; My compassions are kindled together. [9]I will not carry out the heat of My anger; I will not return to destroy Ephraim. For I *am* God, and not a man, the Holy One in your midst. And I will not enter into the city. [10]They shall walk after Jehovah; He shall roar as a lion. When He roars, then sons shall tremble from the west. [11]They trembled as a bird

4421 3117 1009 8020 7701 7703 4013
מִבְצָרֶיךָ יוּשַּׁד כְּשֹׁד שַׁלְמַן בֵּית אַרְבֵאל בְּיוֹם מִלְחָמָה
.battle | the in of day | arbel | (of) Beth- | by Shalman | the as ruin | be shall ,despoiled | strong- holds your

7451 6440 1008 6213 3602 7376 1121 517
15 אֵם עַל־בָּנִים רֻטָּשָׁה׃ כָּכָה עָשָׂה לָכֶם בֵּית־אֵל מִפְּנֵי רָעַת
great because of | ,el Beth- | to ,you | He does | So | dashed was .pieces in | (her) sons | on | The mother

3478 4428 1820 1820 7837 7451
רָעַתְכֶם בַּשַּׁחַר נִדְמֹה נִדְמָה מֶלֶךְ יִשְׂרָאֵל׃
.Israel | king the of | be shall off cut | completely | the In dawn | your evil

CAP. XI יא

CHAPTER 11

7121 1121 7121 4714 157 3478 5288
1
2 כִּי נַעַר יִשְׂרָאֵל וָאֹהֲבֵהוּ וּמִמִּצְרַיִם קָרָאתִי לִבְנִי׃ קָרְאוּ
they (As) called | .son My | called I | of out and Egypt | loved I then ,him | Israel ,(was) | a child | When

6999 6456 2076 1168 6440 1980
לָהֶם כֵּן הָלְכוּ מִפְּנֵיהֶם לַבְּעָלִים יְזַבֵּחוּ וְלַפְּסִלִים יְקַטֵּרוּן׃
burn .incense | to and images carved | they sacrifice | the to Baals | their from ;face | they went | so | to ,them

3045 3808 2220 3947 669 7270
3 וְאָנֹכִי תִרְגַּלְתִּי לְאֶפְרַיִם קָחָם עַל־זְרוֹעֹתָיו וְלֹא יָדְעוּ כִּי
that | did they know | But not | His .arms | on | took He them | ;Ephraim | to taught walk | I Also

1961 160 5688 4900 120 2256 7495
4 רְפָאתִים׃ בְּחַבְלֵי אָדָם אֶמְשְׁכֵם בַּעֲבֹתוֹת אַהֲבָה וָאֶהְיֶה
I And was | .love | bands with of | drew I ;them | a man | With of cords | healed I .them

7725 3808 398 5186 3895 5923 7311
5 לָהֶם כִּמְרִימֵי עֹל עַל לְחֵיהֶם וְאַט אֵלָיו אוֹכִיל׃ לֹא יָשׁוּב
shall He return | not | give I .food | to him | And gently | their .jaws | on | the yoke | those as off lifting | to them

2342 7725 3985 4428 804 4714 776
6 אֶל־אֶרֶץ מִצְרַיִם וְאַשּׁוּר הוּא מַלְכּוֹ כִּי מֵאֲנוּ לָשׁוּב׃ וְחָלָה
shall And whirl | to .return | re- fused | they | for | his ,king | he (be shall) | but ,Assyria | ,Egypt | the of land | to

5971 4156 398 905 3615 5892 2719
7 חֶרֶב בְּעָרָיו וְכִלְּתָה בַדָּיו וְאָכָלָה מִמֹּעֲצוֹתֵיהֶם׃ וְעַמִּי
My And people | their of because .counsels own | shall and consume | his bars | bring shall and end an to | his in cities | the sword

3498 7311 3808 3162 7121 5920 4878 8511
8 תְלוּאִים לִמְשׁוּבָתִי וְאֶל־עַל יִקְרָאֻהוּ יַחַד לֹא יְרוֹמֵם׃ אֵיךְ
How | exalt would .(Him) | not | at all | call they him | to | And High Most the | backsliding to .Me from | bent are

7760 126 5414 349 3478 4042 669 5414
אֶתֶּנְךָ אֶפְרַיִם אֲמַגֶּנְךָ יִשְׂרָאֵל אֵיךְ אֶתֶּנְךָ כְאַדְמָה אֲשִׂימְךָ
I Shall you set | ?Admah like | I shall you make | How | ?Israel | shall (How) you deliver I | ?Ephraim | I shall ,up you give

6213 3808 5150 3648 3162 3820 5921 2015 6636
9 כִּצְבֹאיִם נֶהְפַּךְ עָלַי לִבִּי יַחַד נִכְמְרוּ נִחוּמָי׃ לֹא אֶעֱשֶׂה
will I out carry | not | com- passions | My | are kindled | together | My ;heart | within Me | has turned | ?Zeboim as

3808 410 669 7843 7725 3808 639 2740
חֲרוֹן אַפִּי לֹא אָשׁוּב לְשַׁחֵת אֶפְרָיִם כִּי אֵל אָנֹכִי וְלֹא־
and not | I (am) | God | For | .Ephraim | destroy to | will I return | not | My ;anger | the of heat

3212 3068 310 5892 935 3808 6918 7130 376
10 אִישׁ בְּקִרְבְּךָ קָדוֹשׁ וְלֹא אָבוֹא בְּעִיר׃ אַחֲרֵי יְהוָה יֵלְכוּ
they .walk shall | Jehovah | After | the into .city | will I enter | And not | Holy the .One | your in midst | a ,man

2729 3117 1121 2729 7580 7580 738
11 כְּאַרְיֵה יִשְׁאָג כִּי־הוּא יִשְׁאַג וְיֶחֶרְדוּ בָנִים מִיָּם׃ יֶחֶרְדוּ
did They tremble | the from .west | sons | shall then tremble | ,roars | He When | shall He .roar | a As lion

from Egypt, and like a dove from the land of Assyria. And I will make them live in their houses, says Jehovah. 12 Ephraim circles around Me with lies; and the house of Israel *circles* with deceit; but Judah still rules with God, and is faithful with the saints.

CHAPTER 12

1 Ephraim feeds on wind, and follows after the east wind; all the day he multiplies lies and ruin. And they cut a covenant with Assyria; and oil is carried into Egypt. 2 Jehovah also has a quarrel with Judah, and will punish Jacob according to his ways; He will repay him according to his deeds.

3 He took his brother by the heel in the womb, and by his strength he contended with God. 4 Yes, he wept and pleaded to Him, and he contended with the Angel, and overcame. He found us *at* Bethel, and He spoke with us there, 5 even Jehovah, the God of hosts. Jehovah *is* his memorial. 6 Now, then, return to your God; keep mercy and judgment, and wait on your God continually.

7 He *is* a merchant; the scales of deceit *are* in his hand; he loves to oppress. 8 And Ephraim said, I am rich; I have found much wealth for myself. *In* all my labors they shall find in me no iniquity that *is* sin. 9 And I *am* Jehovah, your God from the land of Egypt; yet I will make you live in tents, as in the days of congregating. 10 Also I have spoken by the prophets, and I have multiplied visions; and the prophets use parables. 11 *Is* Gilead evil? Surely they have been vanity. They sacrificed bulls in Gilgal; yea, their altars

3427 804 776 3128 4714 6833
כְצִפּוֹר מִמִּצְרַיִם וּכְיוֹנָה מֵאֶרֶץ אַשּׁוּר וְהוֹשַׁבְתִּים עַל־
in | will I And | .Assyria | the from | as and | from | a as
live them make | of land | dove a | ,Egypt | bird

3068 5002 1004
בָּתֵּיהֶם נְאֻם־יְהוָה׃
.Jehovah says | their
,houses

CAP. XII יב

CHAPTER 12

5704 3290 3478 1004 4820 669 3585 5437
1 סְבָבֻנִי בְכַחַשׁ אֶפְרַיִם וּבְמִרְמָה בֵּית יִשְׂרָאֵל וִיהוּדָה עֹד
still | but | ;Israel | the | with and | ;Ephraim | with | surrounds
Judah | of house | deceit | lying | Me

7291 7307 7462 669 539 6918 410 7300
2 רָד עִם־אֵל וְעִם־קְדוֹשִׁים נֶאֱמָן׃ אֶפְרַיִם רֹעֶה רוּחַ וְרֹדֵף
and | wind | feeds | Ephraim | is | holy the | and | ,God with | rules
pursues | on | .faithful | ones | with

3772 804 1285 7235 7701 3577 3117 3605 6921
קָדִים כָּל־הַיּוֹם כָּזָב וָשֹׁד יַרְבֶּה וּבְרִית עִם־אַשּׁוּר יִכְרֹתוּ
,cut they | Assyria with | a And | mul- he | and | lies | the | All | east the
covenant | .tiplies | ruin | day | .wind

6485 3063 3068 7379 2986 4714 8081
3 וְשֶׁמֶן לְמִצְרַיִם יוּבָל׃ וְרִיב לַיהוָה עִם־יְהוּדָה וְלִפְקֹד עַל־
to even | ,Judah with | to (is) | a And | is | Egypt into | and
visit | Jehovah | quarrel | .carried | oil

251 6117 990 7725 4611 1870 3290
4 יַעֲקֹב כִּדְרָכָיו כְּמַעֲלָלָיו יָשִׁיב לוֹ׃ בַּבֶּטֶן עָקַב אֶת־אָחִיו
his | took he | the In | to | will He | to according | to according | Jacob
,brother | heel the | by womb | .him | repay | acts his | ;ways his

1058 3201 4397 7786 430 8280 202
5 וּבְאוֹנוֹ שָׂרָה אֶת־אֱלֹהִים׃ וַיָּשַׂר אֶל־מַלְאָךְ וַיֻּכָל בָּכָה
wept he | and | Angel the with | he ,Yes | .God | with | con- he | by and
;overcame | contended | tended | strength his

3068 1696 8033 4672 1008 2589
6 וַיִּתְחַנֶּן־לוֹ בֵּית־אֵל יִמְצָאֶנּוּ וְשָׁם יְדַבֵּר עִמָּנוּ׃ וַיהוָה
even | ,us with | He | and | finds He | el | (At) | to | and
Jehovah | speaks | there | ,us | Beth- | Him pleaded

2617 7725 430 2143 3068 6635 430
7 אֱלֹהֵי הַצְּבָאוֹת יְהוָה זִכְרוֹ׃ וְאַתָּה בֵּאלֹהֶיךָ תָשׁוּב חֶסֶד
mercy | ;return | your to | Therefore | his | Jehovah | .hosts | the
God | you | .memorial | (is) | of God

3976 3027 3667 8548 430 7121 8104 4941
8 וּמִשְׁפָּט שְׁמֹר וְקַוֵּה אֶל־אֱלֹהֶיךָ תָּמִיד׃ כְּנַעַן בְּיָדוֹ מֹאזְנֵי
scales | his in | a (is He) | .always | God your | on | and | ,keep | and
of | (are) hand | ;merchant | wait | judgment

4672 6238 389 669 559 157 6231 4820
9 מִרְמָה לַעֲשֹׁק אָהֵב׃ וַיֹּאמֶר אֶפְרַיִם אַךְ עָשַׁרְתִּי מָצָאתִי
have I | am I | yet | ,Ephraim | said And | he | to | ;deceit
found | ;rich | .loves | oppress

2399 834 5771 4672 3808 3018 3605 202
10 אוֹן לִי כָּל־יְגִיעַי לֹא יִמְצְאוּ־לִי עָוֺן אֲשֶׁר־חֵטְא׃ וְאָנֹכִי
I And | .sin | that | iniquity | in | shall they | not | my | (in) | for wealth
(am) | (is) | me | find | labors | all | ;me

3117 168 3427 5704 4714 776 430 3068
יְהוָה אֱלֹהֶיךָ מֵאֶרֶץ מִצְרָיִם עֹד אוֹשִׁיבְךָ בָאֳהָלִים כִּימֵי
the as | ,tents in | make will I | yet | ,Egypt | the from | your | Jehovah
of days | live you | of land | ,God

3027 7235 2377 5030 1696 4150
11 מוֹעֵד׃ וְדִבַּרְתִּי עַל־הַנְּבִיאִים וְאָנֹכִי חָזוֹן הִרְבֵּיתִי וּבְיַד
the by and | have | visions | I and | ,prophets the | by | have I | Also | .meeting
of hand | multiplied | spoken

1537 1961 7723 389 205 1568 1819 5030
12 הַנְּבִיאִים אֲדַמֶּה׃ אִם־גִּלְעָד אָוֶן אַךְ־שָׁוְא הָיוּ בַּגִּלְגָּל
Gilgal In | they | vanity | Surely | ?evil | Gilead | (Is) | use | prophets the
.been have | .likenesses

are as heaps in the furrows of the field. [12]And Jacob fled into the field of Syria, and Israel served for a wife; yea, he shepherded for a wife. [13]And by a prophet Jehovah brought up Israel out of Egypt, and by a prophet he was kept safe. [14]Ephraim has provoked *Me* to anger most bitterly. And he shall leave his blood to him, and his Lord shall turn his reproach to him.

1272 7704 8525 1530 4196 1571 2076 7794
13 שְׁוָרִים זִבֵּחוּ גַּם מִזְבְּחוֹתָם כְּגַלִּים עַל תַּלְמֵי שָׂדָי׃ וַיִּבְרַח
fled And the fur- the on as altars their ,Yes they bullocks
field of rows heaps (are) .sacrificed
8104 802 802 3478 5647 758 7704 3290
יַעֲקֹב שְׂדֵה אֲרָם וַיַּעֲבֹד יִשְׂרָאֵל בְּאִשָּׁה וּבְאִשָּׁה שָׁמָר׃
kept he a for and a for Israel and ,Syria the into Jacob
.watch wife ;wife served of field
8104 5030 4714 3478 3068 5927 5030
14 וּבְנָבִיא הֶעֱלָה יְהוָה אֶת־יִשְׂרָאֵל מִמִּצְרָיִם וּבְנָבִיא נִשְׁמָר׃
was he a by and ,Egypt from Israel Jehovah brought a by And
.guarded prophet up prophet
7725 2781 5203 5921 1818 8563 669 3707
15 הִכְעִיס אֶפְרַיִם תַּמְרוּרִים וְדָמָיו עָלָיו יִטּוֹשׁ וְחֶרְפָּתוֹ יָשִׁיב
shall his and shall he on Therefore most Ephraim made has
turn reproach ,leave him blood his .bitterly angry (Me)
136
לוֹ אֲדֹנָיו׃
.Lord his to
him

CHAPTER 13

[1]When Ephraim spoke trembling, he was lifted up in Israel. But he offended in Baal, and he died. [2]And now they sin more and more, and have made themselves a molten image of their silver; idols according to their own understanding, all of it the work of the craftsmen. They say to them, Let men, those who sacrifice, kiss calves. [3]Therefore, they shall be as the morning cloud, and as the early dew that passes away; as chaff storm-driven from the threshing floor, and as the smoke out of the window. [4]Yet I *am* Jehovah, your God from the land of Egypt; and you shall know no other gods than Me. For there is no Savior besides Me.

[5]I have known you in the wilderness, in the land of great dryness. [6]According to their pasture, so they were filled. They were filled, and their heart was lifted up. On account of this they have forgotten Me. [7]Now I am as a lion to them; I will watch by the way like a leopard. [8]I will meet them like a bear whose cubs are taken away; and *I* will tear the lining of their heart. And as a lion, I will devour them there; the beast of the field shall tear them.

[9]O Israel, you are destroyed, but your help *is* in Me. [10]Where *is* your

CAP. XIII יג

CHAPTER 13

1168 816 3478 5375 7578 669 1696
1 כְּדַבֵּר אֶפְרַיִם רְתֵת נָשָׂא הוּא בְּיִשְׂרָאֵל וַיֶּאְשַׁם בַּבַּעַל
,Baal in he but ;Israel in he up lifted ,trembling Ephraim When
offended (himself) spoke
3701 4541 6213 2398 3254 6258 4191
2 וַיָּמֹת׃ וְעַתָּה יוֹסִפוּ לַחֲטֹא וַיַּעֲשׂוּ לָהֶם מַסֵּכָה מִכַּסְפָּם
their of casted a them- have and ,sin more they now And he and
,silver image selves made more and .died
559 3605 2796 4639 6091 8394
כִּתְבוּנָם עֲצַבִּים מַעֲשֵׂה חָרָשִׁים כֻּלֹּה לָהֶם הֵם אֹמְרִים
,say they Of of all craftsmen work ,idols their by
them .it of skill
2919 1242 6051 1961 3651 5401 5695 120 2076
3 זֹבְחֵי אָדָם עֲגָלִים יִשָּׁקוּן׃ לָכֵן יִהְיוּ כַּעֲנַן־בֹּקֶר וְכַטַּל
as and morning a as they Therefore let calves ,men who They
dew the of cloud be shall .kiss them ,sacrifice
699 6227 1637 5590 4671 1980 7925
4 מַשְׁכִּים הֹלֵךְ כְּמֹץ יְסֹעֵר מִגֹּרֶן וּכְעָשָׁן מֵאֲרֻבָּה׃ וְאָנֹכִי
I Yet the of out as and the from storm as ,go to rising
,(am) .window smoke ;floor driven chaff early
3045 3808 2108 430 4714 776 430 3068
יְהוָה אֱלֹהֶיךָ מֵאֶרֶץ מִצְרָיִם וֵאלֹהִים זוּלָתִי לֹא תֵדָע
shall you not other gods and ,Egypt the from God your Jehovah
.know Me than of land
8514 776 4057 3045 1115 369 3467
5 וּמוֹשִׁיעַ אַיִן בִּלְתִּי׃ אֲנִי יְדַעְתִּיךָ בַּמִּדְבָּר בְּאֶרֶץ תַּלְאֻבוֹת׃
.drought the in the in known have I besides not a For
of land ,wilderness you .Me is Savior
7911 3820 7311 7646 7646 4830
6 כְּמַרְעִיתָם וַיִּשְׂבָּעוּ שָׂבְעוּ וַיָּרָם לִבָּם עַל־כֵּן שְׁכֵחוּנִי׃
for- have they therefore their he and were They were so to According
.Me gotten ;heart up lifted filled .filled they ,pasture their
6298 7789 1870 5246 7826
7
8 וָאֱהִי לָהֶם כְּמוֹ־שָׁחַל כְּנָמֵר עַל־דֶּרֶךְ אָשׁוּר׃ אֶפְגְּשֵׁם
meet will I will I the by a as ;lion a as to Now
them .watch way leopard them am I
2416 3833 8033 398 3820 5458 7167 7909 1677
כְּדֹב שַׁכּוּל וְאֶקְרַע סְגוֹר לִבָּם וְאֹכְלֵם שָׁם כְּלָבִיא חַיַּת
the a as there will I And their the will and ,bereaved a as
of beast ;lion them devour .heart of lining tear bear
165 5828 3478 7843 1234 7704
9
10 הַשָּׂדֶה תְּבַקְּעֵם׃ שִׁחֶתְךָ יִשְׂרָאֵל כִּי־בִי בְעֶזְרֶךָ׃ אֱהִי
Where .help your in but ,Israel O are You tear shall the
(is) (is) Me ,destroyed .them field

king? Where is any other who may save you in all your cities? And *where are* your judges of whom you said, Give to me a king and rulers? ¹¹I give to you a king in My anger, and take *him* away in My fury. ¹²The iniquity of Ephraim *is* bound up; his sin *is* hidden. ¹³The pains of a woman in travail shall come to him; he *is* not a wise son; for he cannot stand still in the time of the breaking forth of sons. ¹⁴I will ransom them from the hand of Sheol; I will redeem them from death. O death, where *are* your plagues? O Sheol, where *is* your ruin? Repentance is hidden from My eyes.

¹⁵Though he is fruitful among brothers, an east wind shall come. The wind of Jehovah shall come up from the wilderness, and his spring shall be ashamed, and his fountain shall be dried up. He shall plunder the treasure of all desirable vessels. ¹⁶Samaria shall be desolate, for she has rebelled against her God. They shall fall by the sword. Their infants shall be dashed in pieces, and their pregnant women shall be ripped up.

CHAPTER 14

¹O Israel, return to Jehovah your God, for you have fallen by your sin. ²Take words with you and return to Jehovah. Say to Him, Take away all iniquity, and receive *us* well; that we may repay with the calves of our lips. ³Assyria shall not save us; we will not ride on horses. We shall not say any more to the work of our hands, Our gods! For in You the fatherless finds mercy.

⁴I will heal their backslidings; I will love them freely; for My anger has turned away from him. ⁵I will be as the dew to Israel; he shall blossom as the lily, and cast out his roots like Lebanon. ⁶His branches shall go and his beauty shall

	559	834	8199	5892	3605	3462	645	44.28
	,said you	of whom	your and judges	your cities;	in all	may he that you save	,now	king your

11

	5678	3947	639	4428	5414	8269	44.28	5414
	My in fury.	take and away	My in anger	a to king	to I you give	?rulers	a king	to Give me

12 13

	935	3205	2256	2403	6845	669.	5771	6887
	shall woman a come	travail in of pains	.sin his (is)	hidden	;Ephraim of iniquity	The (is)	the bound is .up	

	1121	4866	5975	3808	6256	24:50	38:08	1121
	.sons of out breaking	of time the in	does he not stand	(in) for time the	,wise not	a	son (is) ;him	he to

14

	162	419.4	16.98	1350	4194	62:99	7585	3027
	where O (is)	your ;death,	Where plagues	re-will I (are) them deem	From .them ransom	will I death.	Sheol's them	from hand

15

	6500	251	996	5869	5640	5164	758:5	6987
	is ,fruitful	brothers among	he Though	My from .eyes	is hid	Repent- ance	O ?Sheol	your ,ruin

	2717	4726	954	5927	4057	3068	7307	6921	935
	shall and up dried be	his ,spring	shall and dry become	the from ,up wilderness	comes the from Jehovah	The of wind	east an .wind	shall come	

	2532	3627	3605	214	815:4		4599
	.desire	vessels of	all of	trea-sure	the shall plunder	He	his ,fountain

CAP. XIV יד

CHAPTER 14

1

	5768	53:07	2719	430	4784	8111	816
	infants Their .fall shall	they the By sword	her against .God	has she rebelled	for ,Samaria	be shall desolate	

2

	3068	5704	3478	7725	1234	2030	7321
	Jehovah to	,Israel O	,Return	ripped .up	preg-nant women	their and be shall ,dashed	

3

	7725	1697	3947	5771	3782	430
	to return and	words	you with Take	your by .iniquity	have you fallen	,God your

	6499	7999	2896	3947	5771	5375	3605	559	3068
	the of calves (with)	will we and repay	receive and well (us)	ini-quity	Take away	all	,Him to Say	Jehovah	

4

	3808	73:92	38:08	5483	3462	38:08	804	8193
	And not	will we not .ride	not on horse	save shall .us	not	Assyria	.lips our	

	3490	7355	834	3027	4639	430	5750	559
	the .orphan	finds mercy	in You	For our .hands	the to of work	!gods Our	any more	shall we say

5 6

	1961	639	7725	5071	157	4878	7495
	will I be	from away .him	My has anger turned	for ;freely	will I them love	back-sliding;their	will I heal

7

	32:12	3844	8328	5221	7799	6524	6524	3478	2919
	shall go	in .Lebanon	his and roots out cast	the ,lily	as shall he blossom	;Israel to	the as dew

be like the olive-tree; and his scent like *is* as Lebanon to Him. [7]They who live under his shadow shall return; they shall live *like* the grain, and blossom like the vine; their memorial *shall be* as the wine of Lebanon. [8]Ephraim *shall say,* What *is* to me any more with idols? I eyed *him*; and I surveyed him; I *am* as a green cypress tree; your fruit is found from Me. [9]Who *is* wise and discerns these things? *Who is* discerning and knows them? For the ways of Jehovah are right, and the righteous shall walk in them. But transgressors shall stumble in them.

3427 7725 3844 7381 1935 2132 1961 3127
8 יֹֽנְקוֹתָיו וִיהִי כַזַּיִת הוֹדוֹ וְרֵיחַ לוֹ כַּלְּבָנוֹן׃ יָשֻׁבוּ יֹשְׁבֵי
who live They shall return as (is) .Lebanon to him and smell his beauty in the olive tree as he shall be and ,branches His

669 3844 3196 2143 1612 6524 1715 2421 6738
9 בְצִלּוֹ יְחַיּוּ דָגָן וְיִפְרְחוּ כַגָּפֶן זִכְרוֹ כְּיֵין לְבָנוֹן׃ אֶפְרַיִם
Ephraim ,(say shall) .Lebanon the as of wine their memory the as ,vine and blossom the shall they ,grain (as) live his in ;shadow

7488 1265 7789 6030 6091 5750 4100
מַה־לִּי עוֹד לָעֲצַבִּים אֲנִי עָנִיתִי וַאֲשׁוּרֶנּוּ אֲנִי כִּבְרוֹשׁ רַעֲנָן
.green a as cypress I sur-veyed him I and (am) ; (him) eyed I I ?idols with any more to me What (is)

3045 995 428 996 2450 4310 4672 6529
10 מִמֶּנִּי פֶּרְיְךָ נִמְצָא׃ מִי חָכָם וְיָבֵן אֵלֶּה נָבוֹן וְיֵדָעֵם כִּי־
For knows ?them and Dis-cerning, these ?things and discerns wise Who (is) .found is Your fruit From Me

3782 6586 3212 6662 3068 1870 3477
יְשָׁרִים דַּרְכֵי יְהוָה וְצַדִּקִים יֵלְכוּ בָם וּפֹשְׁעִים יִכָּשְׁלוּ בָם׃
in .them shall stumble trans-gressors But in .them shall walk the righteous and ,Jehovah the of ways (are) right

יואל

LIBER JOELIS

(THE) BOOK OF JOEL

CAPUT. I. א

CHAPTER 1

A LITERAL TRANSLATION
OF THE BIBLE
THE BOOK OF JOEL

CHAPTER 1

[1]The word of Jehovah that was to Joel, the son of Pethuel. [2]Hear this, you old men; and give ear, all you people of the land. Has this been in your days, or even in the days of your fathers? [3]Tell your sons about it, and your sons to their sons, and their sons to another generation:

[4]What was left by the cutter, the swarming locust ate; and that left by the swarming locust, the locust larvae ate; and that left by the locust larvae, the stripping locust ate. [5]Awake, drunkards, and weep. And wail, all wine-drinkers, over the grape must; for it is cut off from your mouth. [6]For a nation has come up on my land, strong and without number; its teeth *are* the teeth of a lion; and it has the jaw teeth of a lioness. [7]He has laid my vine waste, and has splintered my fig-tree. He has stripped it, and *he* threw *it* away; its branches grow white.

[8]Wail like a virgin girded with sackcloth, over the husband of her youth. [9]The food offering and the drink offering have been cut off from the house of Jehovah; the priests, Jehovah's ministers, mourn. [10]The field is wasted; the land mourns, for the grain is wasted. The new wine is dried up; the oil-tree droops. [11]Be ashamed, farmers; howl, vine-dressers; for the wheat and for the barley, because the harvest of the field has perished. [12]The vine is dried up, and the fig-tree

1 2
8085 6602 1121 3100 1961 834 3068 1697
דְּבַר־יְהוָה אֲשֶׁר הָיָה אֶל־יוֹאֵל בֶּן־פְּתוּאֵל׃ שִׁמְעוּ
Hear of son the Joel to was that of word The
.Pethuel Jehovah

2063 1961 776 3427 3605 238 2205 2063
זֹאת הַזְּקֵנִים וְהַאֲזִינוּ כֹּל יוֹשְׁבֵי הָאָרֶץ הֲהָיְתָה זֹּאת
this Has the dwellers all give and old you ,this
been land of ,ear ;men

3
1121 5608 1121 1 3117 518 3117
בִּימֵיכֶם וְאִם בִּימֵי אֲבֹתֵיכֶם׃ עָלֶיהָ לִבְנֵיכֶם סַפֵּרוּ וּבְנֵיכֶם
your and ,Recount your to about your the in or your in
sons sons it ?fathers of day even ,days

4
697 398 1501 3499 312 1755 1121 1121
לִבְנֵיהֶם וּבְנֵיהֶם לְדוֹר אַחֵר׃ יֶתֶר הַגָּזָם אָכַל הָאַרְבֶּה
swarming the ate the was What .another gen- to their and their to
;locust ,cutter by left eration sons sons

2625 398 3218 3499 3218 398 697 3499
וְיֶתֶר הָאַרְבֶּה אָכַל הַיָּלֶק וְיֶתֶר הַיֶּלֶק אָכַל הֶחָסִיל׃
strip- the ate locust the and locust the ate swarming the and
.locust ping ,larvae of left ;larvae locust of left

5
6071 3196 8354 3605 3213 1058 7910 6974
הָקִיצוּ שִׁכּוֹרִים וּבְכוּ וְהֵילִלוּ כָּל־שֹׁתֵי יָיִן עַל־עָסִיס כִּי
for the over wine all wail and and ,drunkards ,Awake
,must grape of drinkers ;weep

6
4557 369 6099 776 5927 1471 6310 3772
נִכְרַת מִפִּיכֶם׃ כִּי־גוֹי עָלָה עַל־אַרְצִי עָצוּם וְאֵין מִסְפָּר
(with) and strong my on has a For your from is it
;number not ,land up come nation .mouth off cut

7
8047 1612 8033 3833 4973 738 8127 8127
שִׁנָּיו שִׁנֵּי אַרְיֵה וּמְתַלְּעוֹת לָבִיא לוֹ׃ שָׂם גַּפְנִי לְשַׁמָּה
,waste my has It .has it a of the and a teeth its
vine laid lioness teeth jaw ,lion's teeth

8299 3835 7993 2834 2834 7111 8384
וּתְאֵנָתִי לִקְצָפָה חָשֹׂף חֲשָׂפָהּ וְהִשְׁלִיךְ הִלְבִּינוּ שָׂרִיגֶיהָ׃
its grow threw and stripped it com- ,fragmented my and
branches white ;away (it) it pletely tree fig

8 9
4503 3772 5271 1167 8242 2296 1330 421
אֱלִי כִּבְתוּלָה חֲגֻרַת־שַׂק עַל־בַּעַל נְעוּרֶיהָ׃ הָכְרַת מִנְחָה
food The been have her the over with girded a like Wail
offering off cut .youth of husband ,sackcloth virgin

10
7703 3068 8334 3548 56 3068 1004 5262
וָנֶסֶךְ מִבֵּית יְהוָה אָבְלוּ הַכֹּהֲנִים מְשָׁרְתֵי יְהוָה׃ שֻׁדַּד
are .Jehovah ministers the mourn :Jehovah the from the and
wasted of priests of house libation

1535 8492 3001 1715 7703 127 56 7704
שָׂדֶה אָבְלָה אֲדָמָה כִּי שֻׁדַּד דָּגָן הוֹבִישׁ תִּירוֹשׁ אֻמְלַל
droops new the is the is for the mourns The
;wine up dried ,grain wasted ,land ,fields

11
2406 3755 3213 406 3001 3323
יִצְהָר׃ הֹבִישׁוּ אִכָּרִים הֵילִילוּ כֹּרְמִים עַל־חִטָּה וְעַל־
and the over vine- ,howl ;farmers Be oil the
over wheat ,dressers ashamed .tree

12
8384 3001 1612 7704 7105 6 8184
שְׂעֹרָה כִּי אָבַד קְצִיר שָׂדֶה׃ הַגֶּפֶן הוֹבִישָׁה וְהַתְּאֵנָה
the and dried is The the har- the has for the
,tree fig ;up vine .field of vest perished ;barley

droops; *the* pomegranate,
and the palm tree, and the
apple tree; all the trees of
the field are dried up,
because joy has dried up
from the sons of men.
[13]Gird up and lament,
priests. Howl, ministers of
the altar. Come, spend the
night in sackcloth, ministers of my God. For the food
offering and the drink
offering are held back from
the house of your God.
[14]Set apart a fast; call a
solemn assembly; gather
the elders, all the inhabitants of the land, *into* the
house of Jehovah your
God, and cry out to
Jehovah.. [15]Alas for the
day! For the day of Jehovah
is at hand. Yea, it will come
as a destruction from the
Almighty. [16]Is not the food
cut off before your eyes, joy
and gladness from the
house of our God? [17]The
seed shrivels under their
clods; the storage bins are
laid waste; the granaries are
broken down, for the grain
has dried up. [18]How the
beasts groan! The herds of
livestock are vexed, for
there is no pasture for them.
Even the flocks of sheep are
perishing. [19]O Jehovah, to
You I will cry, for the fire has
burned up the pastures of
the wilderness, and the
flame has burned all the
trees of the field. [20]The
beasts of the field also cry
to You, for the rivers of
water are dried up, and the
fire has burned up the
pastures of the wilderness.

3001 7704 6086 3605/8598 8558 1571 7416 535
אֻמְלָלָה רִמּוֹן גַּם־תָּמָר וְתַפּוּחַ כָּל־עֲצֵי הַשָּׂדֶה יָבֵשׁוּ כִּי־
for are the the all the and the and pome- ;droops
.dried field of trees ,apple palm granate

3548 5594 2296 120 1121 8342 3001
13 הֹבִישׁ שָׂשׂוֹן מִן־בְּנֵי אָדָם׃ חִגְרוּ וְסִפְדוּ הַכֹּהֲנִים
;priests and Gird .men the from joy has
lament of sons up dried

430 8334 824:2 935 41:96 8334 32:13
הֵילִילוּ מְשָׁרְתֵי מִזְבֵּחַ בֹּאוּ לִינוּ בַשַּׂקִּים מְשָׁרְתֵי אֱלֹהָי
my ministers in lodge ,come the ministers howl
.God of ,sackcloth ;altar of

6685 6942 5262 4503 430 1004 4573
14 כִּי נִמְנַע מִבֵּית אֱלֹהֵיכֶם מִנְחָה וָנָסֶךְ׃ קַדְּשׁוּ־צוֹם
;fast a Set the and food the God your the from with- is For
apart .libation offering of house held

3068 1004 776 3427 3605 2205 622 6116 7121
קִרְאוּ עֲצָרָה אִסְפוּ זְקֵנִים כֹּל יֹשְׁבֵי הָאָרֶץ בֵּית יְהוָה
Jehovah the (in) the inhabi- the all the gather solemn a call
of house land of tants ,elders ;assembly

3117 7138 3117 162 3068 2199 430
15 אֱלֹהֵיכֶם וְזַעֲקוּ אֶל־יְהוָה׃ אֲהָהּ לַיּוֹם כִּי קָרוֹב יוֹם
day the at For the for Alas .Jehovah to cry and ;God your
of (is) hand !day out

3772 400 5869 5048 935 7706 7701 3068
16 יְהוָה וּכְשֹׁד מִשַּׁדַּי יָבוֹא׃ הֲלוֹא נֶגֶד עֵינֵינוּ אֹכֶל נִכְרָת
cut the our before (Is) will it the from as ,yea Jeho-
off food eyes not .come Almighty ruin a ;vah

8478 6507 5685 1524 8057 430 1004
17 מִבֵּית אֱלֹהֵינוּ שִׂמְחָה וָגִיל׃ עָבְשׁוּ פְרֻדוֹת תַּחַת
under The shrivels and joy ,God our the from
seed ?gladness of house

1715 3001 4460 2040 214 8074 4053
מֶגְרְפֹתֵיהֶם נָשַׁמּוּ אֹצָרוֹת נֶהֶרְסוּ מַמְּגֻרוֹת כִּי הֹבִישׁ דָּגָן׃
the has for the torn are store- the laid are ;clods their
.grain up dried ;granaries down ;houses waste

4829 369 1241 5739 943 929 584
18 מַה־נֶּאֶנְחָה בְהֵמָה נָבֹכוּ עֶדְרֵי בָקָר כִּי אֵין מִרְעֶה לָהֶם
for pasture not for live- The are the groan How
.them (is) ,stock of herds vexed !beasts

398 784 7121 3068 816 6629 5739 1571
19 גַּם־עֶדְרֵי הַצֹּאן נֶאְשָׁמוּ׃ אֵלֶיךָ יְהוָה אֶקְרָא כִּי־אֵשׁ אָכְלָה
has the for will I O To are sheep the Even
burned fire ;call ,Jehovah ,you .perishing of flocks

929 1571 7704 6086 3605 3857 385:2 40:57 4999
20 נְאוֹת מִדְבָּר וְלֶהָבָה לִהֲטָה כָּל־עֲצֵי הַשָּׂדֶה׃ גַּם־בַּהֲמוֹת
the Also the the all has the and the pas- the
of beasts .field of trees burned flame ;plains of tures

398 784 4325 650 3001 6165 7704
שָׂדֶה תַּעֲרוֹג אֵלֶיךָ כִּי יָבְשׁוּ אֲפִיקֵי מַיִם וְאֵשׁ אָכְלָה
has the and ,water rivers the have for long the
up eaten fire of up dried ;You field

4057 4999
נְאוֹת הַמִּדְבָּר׃
the of pas- the
.wilderness of tures

CAP. II. ב

CHAPTER 2

CHAPTER 2

[1]Blow a ram's horn in
Zion, and shout an alarm in
My holy mountain. Let all
the inhabitants of the land
tremble. For the day of
Jehovan approaches; *it is*
near; [2]a day of darkness
and gloominess; a day of

3427 3605 7264 6944 2022 7321 6726 7782 8628
1 תִּקְעוּ שׁוֹפָר בְּצִיּוֹן וְהָרִיעוּ בְּהַר קָדְשִׁי יִרְגְּזוּ כֹּל יֹשְׁבֵי
inhab- all Let .holy My in shout and in ram's a Blow
itants tremble mount alarm an ,Zion horn

3117 653 2822 3117 7138 3068 3117 935 776
2 הָאָרֶץ כִּי־בָא יוֹם־יְהוָה כִּי קָרוֹב׃ יוֹם חֹשֶׁךְ וַאֲפֵלָה יוֹם
a gloom- and dark- day a (is it) for ,Jehovah the for the
of day ;iness ness ;near of day comes ;land's

clouds and thick darkness;
as the dawn spread out on
the mountains —a great
and a strong people; there
has never been the like, nor
shall there ever be again to
the years of many genera-
tions; [3]a fire devours before it, and a flame burns
behind it; the land *is* as the
garden of Eden before
them, and behind them *is* a
desolate wilderness; yea,
also there is no escape to
them. [4]Their appearance is
like horses; and as war
horses, so they run. [5]They
shall leap like the noise of
chariots on the tops of the
mountains, like the noise of
flames of fire that devour
the chaff; as a strong people
set in order for battle.
[6]Before their face, the
people shall be pained; all
faces collect heat. [7]They
shall run as a mighty one;
they shall go up the wall as
men of war. And they each
go on his way; and they do
not change their paths.
[8]And each does not press
his brother; they *each* go in
his paths. And *if* they fall
behind their weapons, they
shall not be cut off. [9]They
shall rush on the city; they
shall run on the wall; they
shall climb up on the
houses; they shall enter in
by the windows, like a thief.
[10]The earth shall quake
before them; the heavens
shall shake. The sun and
moon shall grow dark, and
the stars shall gather in
their light. [11]And Jehovah
shall give His voice before
His army. For His camp *is*
very great. For he who does
His word *is* strong. For the
day of Jehovah *is* very great
and terrifying. And who can
endure it?

[12]Yet even now turn to
Me with all your heart, and
with fasting, and with
weeping, and with mourn-
ing, declares Jehovah.
[13]Yea, tear your heart, and
not your robes; and turn to
Jehovah your God. For He

3644 6099 7227 5971 2022 6566 7837 6205 6051
ענן וערפל כשחר פרש על־ההרים עם רב ועצום כמהו
it like and great a the on spread the as and clouds
;strong people ;mountains out dawn gloom

1755 1755 8141 5704 3254 3808 310 5769 1961 3808
לא נהיה מן־העולם ואחריו לא יוסף עד־שני דור ודור׃
gen- and gen- the to (be will) and ,it after the from has not
eration eration of years again not past been

3 776 5731 1588 3857 3857 310 784 398 6440
לפניו אכלה אש ואחריו תלהט להבה כגן־עדן הארץ
the garden the as a burns and ,fire devours Before
land Eden of ;flame it behind it

1961 3808 6413 1571 8077 4057 310 6440
לפניו ואחריו מדבר שממה וגם־פליטה לא־היתה לו׃
to is not escape ,yes ;desolation wilder- a and before
.them and of ness it behind

4
5 6963 7323 6571 4758 5483 4758
כמראה סוסים מראהו וכפרשים כן ירוצון׃ כקול
the As they so as and ap- its horses ap- the As
of noise .run ;horses war pearance (is) of pearance

398 784 3851 6963 7540 2022 7218 4818
מרכבות על־ראשי ההרים ירקדון כקול להב אש אכלה
that fire the the as they the the on chariots
devours of flames of noise ;leap mountains of heads

6 3605 5971 2342 6440 4421 6186 6099 5971 7179
קש כעם עצום ערוך מלחמה׃ מפניו יחילו עמים כל־
all the are Before .battle in set strong a as the
;peoples pained them for order people ,chaff

7 4421 582 7323 1368 6289 6908 6440
פנים קבצו פארור׃ כגבורים ירצון כאנשי מלחמה
battle men as shall they a As .heat collect faces
of ;run one mighty

734 5670 3808 3212 1870 376 2346 5927
יעלו חומה ואיש בדרכיו ילכון ולא יעבטון ארחותם׃
their they and they his on and the they
.paths change not ,go way each ;wall up go

8 7973 1157 3212 4546 1397 1766 3808 251 376
ואיש אחיו לא ידחקון גבר במסלתו ילכון ובעד השלח
the And they his in (each) ;presses not his And
weapon behind .go paths man brother each

9 5927 1004 7323 2346 8264 5892 1214 3808 5307
יפלו לא יבצעו׃ בעיר ישקו בחומה ירצון בבתים יעלו
they the on they the on they the On are they not they
;up go houses ;run wall ;rush city .off cut ,fall

10 8064 7493 776 7264 6440 1590 935 2474 1157
בעד החלונים יבאו כגנב׃ לפניו רגזה ארץ רעשו שמים
the shake the quakes Before a like they the by
,heavens ,earth them .thief enter windows

11 6963 5414 3068 5051 622 3556 6937 3394 8121
שמש וירח קדרו וכוכבים אספו נגהם׃ ויהוה נתן קולו
His gives And their gather the and grow and the
voice Jehovah .light in stars ,dark moon sun

1697 6213 6099 4264 3966 7227 2428 6440
לפני חילו כי רב מאד מחנהו כי עצום עשה דברו כי
For His who he strong for His very great for His before
.word does (is) ,camp (is) army

12 5002 6258 1571 3557 4310 3966 3372 3068 3117 1419
גדול יום־יהוה ונורא מאד ומי יכילנו׃ וגם־עתה נאם־
states even Yet can and ;very and Jehovah the great
,now ?it endure who fearful of day

4553 1065 6685 3824 3605 5704 8147 3068
יהוה שבו עדי בכל־לבבכם ובצום ובבכי ובמספד׃
with and with and with and your with to turn ,Jehovah
.wailing ,weeping ,fasting heart all Me

13 430 3068 7725 899 408 3824 7167
וקרעו לבבכם ואל־בגדיכם ושובו אל־יהוה אלהיכם
.God your Jehovah to and your and your And
return ,clothes not heart tear

is gracious and merciful; slow to anger, and of great kindness; and He pities concerning the evil. [14]Who knows *if* He will return and have pity and leave a blessing behind Him, a food offering and a drink offering for Jehovah your God?

[15]Blow a trumpet in Zion; sanctify a fast; call a solemn assembly. [16]Gather the people, sanctify the congregation, gather the elders, gather the children, and those who suck the breasts. Let the bridegroom go out of his room, and the bride out of her bridal room. [17]Let the priests, ministers of Jehovah, weep between the porch and the altar; and let them say, Have pity on Your people, O Jehovah, and do not give Your inheritance to shame, for a proverb among those of the nations. Why should they say among the peoples, Where *is* their God?

[18]Then Jehovah will be jealous for His land, and have pity on His people. [19]Yea, Jehovah will answer and say to His people, Behold, I will send you grain, and wine, and oil, and you shall be satisfied with it. And I will no more make you a curse among the nations. [20]But I will remove the northern *army* far from you, and will drive him into a dry and desolated land; with his face toward the eastern sea, and his rear toward the western sea. And his stench shall come up, and his ill odor shall come up, because he *was* doing great things.

[21]Fear not, O land; be glad and rejoice; for Jehovah *is* doing great things. [22]Fear not, beasts of the field, for the pastures of the wilderness grow green; for the tree bears its fruit; the fig-tree and the vine give their strength. [23]Then be glad, sons of Zion, and rejoice in Jehovah your God. For He

כִּי־חַנּוּן וְרַחוּם הוּא אֶרֶךְ אַפַּיִם וְרַב־חֶסֶד וְנִחָם עַל־
about He and great and anger slow He and For
repents ,kindness of (to) (is) merciful gracious

הָרָעָה׃ מִי יוֹדֵעַ יָשׁוּב וְנִחָם וְהִשְׁאִיר אַחֲרָיו בְּרָכָה 14
a behind and and will He knows Who .evil
,blessing Him leave repent return (if)

מִנְחָה וָנֶסֶךְ לַיהוָה אֱלֹהֵיכֶם׃ תִּקְעוּ שׁוֹפָר בְּצִיּוֹן 15
,Zion in a Blow ?God your for a and food a
trumpet Jehovah libation offering

קַדְּשׁוּ־צוֹם קִרְאוּ עֲצָרָה׃ אִסְפוּ־עָם קַדְּשׁוּ קָהָל קִבְצוּ 16
gather the sanctify Gather solemn a call sanctify
;assembly people the .assembly fast a

זְקֵנִים אִסְפוּ עוֹלָלִים וְיֹנְקֵי שָׁדָיִם יֵצֵא חָתָן מֵחֶדְרוֹ וְכַלָּה
the and his from the go let the suck- and the gather the
bride room groom out ;breast of lings children elders

מֵחֻפָּתָהּ׃ בֵּין הָאוּלָם וְלַמִּזְבֵּחַ יִבְכּוּ הַכֹּהֲנִים מְשָׁרְתֵי 17
ministers the let the and the Between her from
of ,priests weep ,altar porch .room bridal

יְהוָה וְיֹאמְרוּ חוּסָה יְהוָה עַל־עַמֶּךָ וְאַל־תִּתֵּן נַחֲלָתְךָ
in- Your do and Your on O Have let and Jehovah
heritance give not ,people ,Jehovah ,pity ,say them

לְחֶרְפָּה לִמְשָׁל־בָּם גּוֹיִם לָמָּה יֹאמְרוּ בָעַמִּים אַיֵּה
Where the among should Why the among a for shame to
(is) ,peoples say they nations of those proverb

אֱלֹהֵיהֶם׃ וַיְקַנֵּא יְהוָה לְאַרְצוֹ וַיַּחְמֹל עַל־עַמּוֹ׃ וַיַּעַן יְהוָה 18 19
Jehovah And His on have and His for Jehovah will Then ?God their
answer let .people pity land jealous be

וַיֹּאמֶר לְעַמּוֹ הִנְנִי שֹׁלֵחַ לָכֶם אֶת־הַדָּגָן וְהַתִּירוֹשׁ וְהַיִּצְהָר
,oil and ,wine and ,grain to (am) ,Behold His to say and
you sending I ,people

וּשְׂבַעְתֶּם אֹתוֹ וְלֹא־אֶתֵּן אֶתְכֶם עוֹד חֶרְפָּה בַּגּוֹיִם׃ וְאֶת־ 20
But the among a any you will I And with will you and
.nations shame more make not .it satisfied be

הַצְּפוֹנִי אַרְחִיק מֵעֲלֵיכֶם וְהִדַּחְתִּיו אֶל־אֶרֶץ צִיָּה וּשְׁמָמָה
and dryness a into will and ,you from re- will I the
;desolation of land him drive far move northener

אֶת־פָּנָיו אֶל־הַיָּם הַקַּדְמֹנִי וְסֹפוֹ אֶל־הַיָּם הָאַחֲרוֹן וְעָלָה
shall And .western the toward his and eastern the toward his with
up come sea rear sea face

בָאְשׁוֹ וְתַעַל צַחֲנָתוֹ כִּי הִגְדִּיל לַעֲשׂוֹת׃ אַל־תִּירְאִי אֲדָמָה 21
,land Fear not (was) great he for his shall and his
.doing things stench up come ,stink

גִּילִי וּשְׂמָחִי כִּי־הִגְדִּיל יְהוָה לַעֲשׂוֹת׃ אַל־תִּירְאוּ בַּהֲמוֹת 22
beasts be Do not (is) Jehovah great for be and rejoice
of afraid .doing things glad

שָׂדַי כִּי דָשְׁאוּ נְאוֹת מִדְבָּר כִּי־עֵץ נָשָׂא פִרְיוֹ תְּאֵנָה וָגֶפֶן
the and fig the its bears the For wil- the pas- the grow for the
vine tree fruit tree .derness of tures green ;field

נָתְנוּ חֵילָם׃ וּבְנֵי צִיּוֹן גִּילוּ וְשִׂמְחוּ בַּיהוָה אֱלֹהֵיכֶם כִּי־ 23
For .God your in be and rejoice ,Zion' And their give
Jehovah glad sons .strength

has given to you the early rain according to righteousness, and He will cause the rain to come down for you, the early rain and the latter rain in the first *month*. [24]And the floors shall be full with grain, and the winevats shall overflow with wine, and oil. [25]And I will restore to you the years which the swarming locust has eaten, the locust larvae, and the stripping locust, and the cutting locust, My great army which I sent among you. [26]And you shall eat fully and be satisfied; and you shall praise the name of Jehovah your God, who has dealt wondrously with you. And My people shall not be ashamed forever. [27]And you shall know that I *am* in the midst of Israel, and that I *am* Jehovah your God, and *there is* no other. And My people shall not be ashamed forever.

4175 1653 3381 6666 4175 5414
נָתַן לָכֶם אֶת־הַמּוֹרֶה לִצְדָקָה וַיּוֹרֶד לָכֶם גֶּשֶׁם מוֹרֶה
early the / the / to / made and to according / early the / to / has He
rain / ,rain / you / down come ,righteousness / rain / you / given

3342 7783 1250 1637 4390 7223 4456
24 וּמַלְקוֹשׁ בָּרִאשׁוֹן׃ וּמָלְאוּ הַגֳּרָנוֹת בָּר וְהֵשִׁיקוּ הַיְקָבִים
wine the / will and / (with) grain the / will And / the at / the and
vats / overflow / grain / floors / full be / .first / rain latter

398 834 8141 7999 3323 8492
25 תִּירוֹשׁ וְיִצְהָר׃ וְשִׁלַּמְתִּי לָכֶם אֶת־הַשָּׁנִים אֲשֶׁר אָכַל
has / which / years the / to / will I And / and / new (with)
eaten / you / restore / .oil / wine

7971 834 1419 2428 1501 2625 3218 697
הָאַרְבֶּה הַיֶּלֶק וְהֶחָסִיל וְהַגָּזָם חֵילִי הַגָּדוֹל אֲשֶׁר שִׁלַּחְתִּי
sent I / which / great / My / cut- the and / strip- the and / the / swarm- the
army ,locust ting / ,locust ping / ,larvae / ,locust ing

3068 8034 1984 7646 398 398
26 בָּכֶם׃ וַאֲכַלְתֶּם אָכוֹל וְשָׂבוֹעַ וְהִלַּלְתֶּם אֶת־שֵׁם יְהוָה
Jehovah / the / will you and / be and / fully / you And / among
of name / praise / ;satisfied / eat shall / .you

5971 954 3808 6381 6213 834 430
אֱלֹהֵיכֶם אֲשֶׁר־עָשָׂה עִמָּכֶם לְהַפְלִיא וְלֹא־יֵבֹשׁוּ עַמִּי
My / be will And / .wondrously / with / has / who / ,God your
people ashamed not / you / done

3068 3478 7130 3045 5769
27 לְעוֹלָם׃ וִידַעְתֶּם כִּי בְקֶרֶב יִשְׂרָאֵל אָנִי וַאֲנִי יְהוָה
Jehovah / I and / I / Israel / the in / that / you And / .forever
(am) ,(am) / of midst / know shall

5769 5971 954 3808 5750 369 430
אֱלֹהֵיכֶם וְאֵין עוֹד וְלֹא־יֵבֹשׁוּ עַמִּי לְעוֹלָם׃
.forever / My / be will and / any / and / ,God your
people / ashamed not / ,other (is) / not

CAP. III ג

CHAPTER 3

[28]And it shall be afterward, I will pour out My Spirit on all flesh. And your sons and your daughters shall prophesy; your old men shall dream dreams; your young men shall see visions. [29]And also I will pour out My Spirit on the slaves and on the slave-girls in those days. [30]And I will give signs in the heavens, and in the earth: blood, and fire, and columns of smoke. [31]The sun shall be turned to darkness, and the moon to blood, before the coming of the great and awesome day of Jehovah. [32]For it shall be, all who shall call on the name of Jehovah shall be saved. For salvation shall be in Mount Zion, and in Jerusalem, as Jehovah has

5012 1320 3605 7307 8210 310 1961
1 וְהָיָה אַחֲרֵי־כֵן אֶשְׁפּוֹךְ אֶת־רוּחִי עַל־כָּל־בָּשָׂר וְנִבְּאוּ
will And / .flesh / all / on / Spirit My / will I / ,afterward / it And
prophesy / out pour / be will

970 2472 2472 2205 1323 1121
בְּנֵיכֶם וּבְנוֹתֵיכֶם זִקְנֵיכֶם חֲלֹמוֹת יַחֲלֹמוּן בַּחוּרֵיכֶם
young your / will / dreams / old your / your and / your
men / dream / men / ;daughters / sons

3117 8198 5650 1571 7200 2377
2 חֶזְיֹנוֹת יִרְאוּ׃ וְגַם עַל־הָעֲבָדִים וְעַל־הַשְּׁפָחוֹת בַּיָּמִים
days in / the / and / slaves the / on / and / ;see will / visions
slave-girls / on / also

8064 4159 5414 7307 8210
3 הָהֵמָּה אֶשְׁפּוֹךְ אֶת־רוּחִי׃ וְנָתַתִּי מוֹפְתִים בַּשָּׁמַיִם
the in / signs / I And / .Spirit My / will I / those
heavens / give will / out pour

2822 2015 8121 6227 8490 784 1818 776
4 וּבָאָרֶץ דָּם וָאֵשׁ וְתִימְרוֹת עָשָׁן׃ הַשֶּׁמֶשׁ יֵהָפֵךְ לְחֹשֶׁךְ
dark- to / be will / sun the / ;smoke / columns and / and / blood / on and
ness / turned / of / fire / ;earth the

1961 3372 1419 3068 3117 935 6440 1818 3394
5 וְהַיָּרֵחַ לְדָם לִפְנֵי בּוֹא יוֹם יְהוָה הַגָּדוֹל וְהַנּוֹרָא׃ וְהָיָה
it For / and / great / Jehovah / the / the / before / to / the and
be will / .awesome / of day / of coming / blood / moon

3068 6726 2022 4422 3068 8034 7121 834 3605
כֹּל אֲשֶׁר־יִקְרָא בְּשֵׁם יְהוָה יִמָּלֵט כִּי בְּהַר־צִיּוֹן וּבִירוּשָׁלַםִ
Jerusalem and / Mount in / for / be will / ,Jehovah / the on / shall / who / (that)
in / Zion / ,saved / of name / call / all

said, and among the saved whom Jehovah shall call.

תִּהְיֶה פְּלֵיטָה כַּאֲשֶׁר אָמַר יְהוָה וּבַשְּׂרִידִים אֲשֶׁר
whom the saved and among ,Jehovah has said as ,salvation shall be

יְהוָה קֹרֵא׃
shall .call Jehovah

CAP. IV ד

CHAPTER 4

1 כִּי הִנֵּה בַּיָּמִים הָהֵמָּה וּבָעֵת הַהִיא אֲשֶׁר אָשׁוּב אֶת־
will I return (in) which ,that in and time those days in ,behold For

2 שְׁבוּת יְהוּדָה וִירוּשָׁלִָם׃ וְקִבַּצְתִּי אֶת־כָּל־הַגּוֹיִם וְהוֹרַדְתִּים
bring will and down them the ,nations all will I and gather and ;Jerusalem Judah the of exiles

אֶל־עֵמֶק יְהוֹשָׁפָט וְנִשְׁפַּטְתִּי עִמָּם שָׁם עַל־עַמִּי וְנַחֲלָתִי
in- my and heritance My for people there with them will I And judgment enter Jehosh- .aphat the of valley to

3 יִשְׂרָאֵל אֲשֶׁר פִּזְּרוּ בַגּוֹיִם וְאֶת־אַרְצִי חִלֵּקוּ׃ וְאֶל־עַמִּי
My for And people they .out shared My land and the in ,nations they scattered whom ,Israel

יַדּוּ גוֹרָל וַיִּתְּנוּ הַיֶּלֶד בַּזּוֹנָה וְהַיַּלְדָּה מָכְרוּ בַיַּיִן וַיִּשְׁתּוּ׃
they and .drank for ,wine was sold a and girl a for ,harlot boy a they and gave ;lots they cast

4 וְגַם מָה־אַתֶּם לִי צֹר וְצִידוֹן וְכֹל גְּלִילוֹת פְּלֶשֶׁת הַגְּמוּל
Repay- ment ?Philistia the of regions and all and ,Sidon Tyre to ,Me you what (are) And also

אַתֶּם מְשַׁלְּמִים עָלָי וְאִם־גֹּמְלִים אַתֶּם עָלַי קַל מְהֵרָה
speedily swiftly (and) (to) ,Me you (are) repaying And if (to) ?Me (are) restoring you

5 אָשִׁיב גְּמֻלְכֶם בְּרֹאשְׁכֶם׃ אֲשֶׁר־כַּסְפִּי וּזְהָבִי לְקַחְתֶּם
have you taken My and gold My silver (in) that your on ;head own re- your payment will I return

6 וּמַחֲמַדַּי הַטֹּבִים הֲבֵאתֶם לְהֵיכְלֵיכֶם׃ וּבְנֵי יְהוּדָה וּבְנֵי
the and of sons Judah the And of sons your to .temples have you brought good My and treasures

יְרוּשָׁלִַם מְכַרְתֶּם לִבְנֵי הַיְּוָנִים לְמַעַן הַרְחִיקָם מֵעַל
from re- might you them move that the ,Javanites the to of sons have you sold Jerusalem

7 גְּבוּלָם׃ הִנְנִי מְעִירָם מִן־הַמָּקוֹם אֲשֶׁר־מְכַרְתֶּם אוֹתָם
them have you sold the from place arousing them ,Behold (am) I their .border

8 שָׁמָּה וַהֲשִׁבֹתִי גְמֻלְכֶם בְּרֹאשְׁכֶם׃ וּמָכַרְתִּי אֶת־בְּנֵיכֶם
sons your I And sell will your on .head own re- your payment will I and return to ,there

וְאֶת־בְּנוֹתֵיכֶם בְּיַד בְּנֵי יְהוּדָה וּמְכָרוּם לִשְׁבָאיִם אֶל־גּוֹי
a to nation the to ,Sabeans will they and them sell ,Judah the of sons the into of hand your and daughters

9 רָחוֹק כִּי יְהוָה דִּבֵּר׃ קִרְאוּ־זֹאת בַּגּוֹיִם קַדְּשׁוּ
Sanctify among :nations the this Call has spoken Jehovah for ;off far

CHAPTER 3

[1]For, behold, in those days and in that time, *when* I bring again the exiles of Judah and Jerusalem, [2]I will also gather all nations, and will bring them down into the valley of Jehoshaphat. And I will enter into judgment with them there, for My people and My inheritance Israel, whom they have scattered among the nations, and they shared out My land. [3]And they have cast lots for My people. And *they* have given a boy for a harlot, and sold a girl for wine; and they drank. [4]And also, what *are* you to Me, Tyre and Sidon, and all the regions of Philistia? *Are* you restoring repayment *to* Me? And if you *are* repaying Me, I will turn your reward on your own head, swiftly, speedily; [5]*in* that you have taken My silver and My gold, and have carried My good treasures to your temples. [6]You have also sold the sons of Judah and the sons of Jerusalem to the sons of the Greeks, that you might remove them far from their border. [7]Behold, I *am* arousing them from the place where you have sold them, and will return your reward on your own head. [8]And I will sell your sons and your daughters into the hand of the sons of Judah; and they shall sell them to the Sabeans, to a nation far off. For Jehovah has spoken it.

[9]Proclaim this among the nations: Sanctify a war;

awaken the mighty men; let
all the men of war draw
near; let them come up.
[10]Beat your plowshares into
swords, and your pruning
hooks into spears. Let the
weak say, I *am* strong.
[11]Gather yourselves and
come, all you nations; and
gather yourselves together
all around. O Jehovah,
bring down Your mighty
ones. [12]Let the nations be
awakened and come up to
the valley of Jehoshaphat.
For there I will sit to judge
all the nations all around.
[13]Put in the sickle, for the
harvest is ripe. Come, go
down, for the press is full;
the vats overflow; for their
wickedness is great.
[14]Multitudes, multitudes in
the valley of decision! For
the day of Jehovah *is* near
in the valley of decision.
[15]The sun and the moon
shall be darkened, and the
stars shall gather in their
light; [16]and Jehovah roars
from Zion, and gives His
voice from Jerusalem. And
the heavens and the earth
quake. But Jehovah *is* a
refuge for His people, and a
fortress to the sons of
Israel. [17]And you shall
know that I *am* Jehovah
your God dwelling in Zion,
My holy mountain. And
Jerusalem shall be a holy
thing, and aliens shall no
more pass through her.

[18]And it shall be in that
day, the mountains shall
drop down new wine; and
the hills shall flow *with*
milk; and all the streams of
Judah shall flow *with*
waters. And a fountain shall
come forth from the house
of Jehovah, and *it* shall
water the valley of Shittim.
[19]Egypt shall be a ruin, and
Edom shall be a desolate
wilderness, from violence
done to the sons of Judah,
whose innocent blood they
poured out in their land.
[20]But Judah will dwell

4421 582 3605 5927 5066 1368 5782 4421
מִלְחָמָה הָעִירוּ הַגִּבּוֹרִים יִגְּשׁוּ יַעֲלוּ כֹּל אַנְשֵׁי הַמִּלְחָמָה׃
.war the all let draw let mighty the awaken ;war a
of men up come ,near ;men

559 2523 7420 4211 2719 855 3807
10 כֹּתּוּ אִתֵּיכֶם לַחֲרָבוֹת וּמַזְמְרֹתֵיכֶם לִרְמָחִים הַחַלָּשׁ יֹאמַר
let weak the ;spears to your and swords to your Beat
,say hooks pruning, plowshares

8033 6908 5439 1471 3605 935 5789 1368
11 גִּבּוֹר אָנִי׃ עוּשׁוּ וָבֹאוּ כָל־הַגּוֹיִם מִסָּבִיב וְנִקְבָּצוּ שָׁמָּה
to gather and all nations all and Hasten !(am) I mighty
.there yourselves around (you) come

6010 1471 5927 5782 1368 3068 3181
12 הַנְחַת יְהוָה גִּבּוֹרֶיךָ׃ יֵעוֹרוּ וְיַעֲלוּ הַגּוֹיִם אֶל־עֵמֶק
the to the come and be Let Your O Bring
of valley nations up aroused .ones mighty Jehovah down

5439 1477 3605 8199 3427 8033 3092
יְהוֹשָׁפָט כִּי שָׁם אֵשֵׁב לִשְׁפֹּט אֶת־כָּל־הַגּוֹיִם מִסָּבִיב׃
all the all judge to will I there For Jehosh-
.around nations sit .aphat

7783 1660 1390 3381 935 7102 1310 4038 7971
13 שִׁלְחוּ מַגָּל כִּי בָשַׁל קָצִיר בֹּאוּ רְדוּ כִּי־מָלְאָה גַּת הֵשִׁיקוּ
overflow the full is for go ;Come the ripe is for the Send
;press ,down .harvest ,sickle

2742 6010 1995 1995 7451 7227 3342
14 הַיְקָבִים כִּי רַבָּה רָעָתָם׃ הֲמוֹנִים הֲמוֹנִים בְּעֵמֶק הֶחָרוּץ
!decision the in multitudes ,Multitudes .evil their (is) for wine the
of valley great ,vats

6937 3391 8121 2742 6010 3068 3117 7138
15 כִּי קָרוֹב יוֹם יְהוָה בְּעֵמֶק הֶחָרוּץ׃ שֶׁמֶשׁ וְיָרֵחַ קָדָרוּ
grow the and The .decision the in Jehovah the (is) For
,dark moon sun of valley of day near

5414 3389 7580 6726 3068 5051 622 3556
16 וְכוֹכָבִים אָסְפוּ נָגְהָם׃ וַיהוָה מִצִּיּוֹן יִשְׁאָג וּמִירוּשָׁלַם יִתֵּן
give from and ,roars from and their gather the and
Jerusalem Zion Jehovah ,light in stars

1121 4581 5971 4218 3068 776 8064 7493 6963
קוֹלוֹ וְרָעֲשׁוּ שָׁמַיִם וָאָרֶץ וַיהוָה מַחֲסֶה לְעַמּוֹ וּמָעוֹז לִבְנֵי
the to a and His for a (is) But the and the and His
of sons fort people refuge Jehovah .earth heavens quake ,voice

2022 6726 7931 430 3068 3045 3478
17 יִשְׂרָאֵל׃ וִידַעְתֶּם כִּי אֲנִי יְהוָה אֱלֹהֵיכֶם שֹׁכֵן בְּצִיּוֹן הַר־
moun- in dwelling God your Jehovah I that you And .Israel
tain Zion (am) know shall

5750 5674 3808 2114 6944 3389 7961 6944
קָדְשִׁי וְהָיְתָה יְרוּשָׁלַם קֹדֶשׁ וְזָרִים לֹא־יַעַבְרוּ־בָהּ עוֹד׃
any through will not and holy a Jerusalem shall And My
.more her pass aliens ,thing be .holy

1384 6071 2022 5197 3117 1961
18 וְהָיָה בַיּוֹם הַהוּא יִטְּפוּ הֶהָרִים עָסִיס וְהַגְּבָעוֹת
the and new the will ,that day in it And
hills ,wine mountains drop be will

1004 4599 4325 3212 3063 650 3605 2461 3212
תֵּלַכְנָה חָלָב וְכָל־אֲפִיקֵי יְהוּדָה יֵלְכוּ מָיִם וּמַעְיָן מִבֵּית
the from a And (with) will of the and (with) will
of house spring .waters flow Judah streams all ,milk flow

8077 4714 7851 5158 8248 3318 3068
19 יְהוָה יֵצֵא וְהִשְׁקָה אֶת־נַחַל הַשִּׁטִּים׃ מִצְרַיִם לִשְׁמָמָה
a .Egypt .Shittim torrent the will and will Jehovah
desolation of valley water out go

3063 1121 2555 1961 8077 4057 123 1961
תִהְיֶה וֶאֱדוֹם לְמִדְבַּר שְׁמָמָה תִּהְיֶה מֵחֲמַס בְּנֵי יְהוּדָה
,Judah the vio- from will desolate wilder- a and will
of sons to lence become ness Edom become

3427 5769 3063 776 5355 1818 8210
20 אֲשֶׁר־שָׁפְכוּ דָם־נָקִיא בְּאַרְצָם׃ וִיהוּדָה לְעוֹלָם תֵּשֵׁב
will forever But their in innocent they whose
,dwell Judah .land blood out poured

forever, and Jerusalem to generation and generation.
21 And I will cleanse their blood *which* I did not cleanse; and Jehovah *is* dwelling in Zion.

3068	5352	1818	5352	1755	1755	3389	
21 וַיהוָה	לֹא־נִקֵּיתִי	דָּמָם	וְנִקֵּיתִי	וָדוֹר׃	לְדוֹר	וִירוּשָׁלַם	
and Jehovah	I (which) ,cleansed not	their blood	will I And cleanse	gen- and .eration	gen- to eration	and Jerusalem	

6726	7931
בְּצִיּוֹן׃	שֹׁכֵן
.Zion in	(is) dwelling

A LITERAL TRANSLATION
OF THE BIBLE
THE BOOK OF AMOS

CHAPTER 1

[1]The words of Amos, who was among the herdsmen of Tekoa, which he saw concerning Israel in the days of Uzziah, king of Judah, and in the days of Jeroboam, the son of Joash, king of Israel, two years before the earthquake. [2]And he said, Jehovah will roar from Zion, and utter His voice from Jerusalem. And the pastures of the shepherds shall mourn, and the top of Carmel shall dry up. [3]So says Jehovah: For three transgressions of Damascus, and for four, I will not turn back *from* it; for they have threshed Gilead with threshing sledges of iron. [4]But I will send a fire against the house of Hazael, and it shall devour the palaces of Ben-hadad. [5]I will also break the bar of Damascus, and cut off the inhabitant of the Valley of Aven, and him who holds the scepter from Beth-eden. And the people of Syria shall go captive to Kir, says Jehovah.

[6]So says Jehovah: For three transgressions of Gaza, and for four, I will not turn back *from* it; for they deported *as* exiles to deliver up a complete *population* to Edom. [7]But I will send a fire against the wall of Gaza, and it shall devour its palaces. [8]And I will cut off Ashdod's dwellers and him who holds the scepter from Ashkelon; and I will turn My hand against Ekron; and the remnant of the Philistines shall perish, says the Lord Jehovah.

ע מ ו ס

LIBER AMOS

(THE) BOOK OF AMOS

CAPUT. I א

CHAPTER 1

2372 834 8620 5349 1961 834 5986 1697
1 דִּבְרֵי עָמוֹס אֲשֶׁר־הָיָה בַנֹּקְדִים מִתְּקוֹעַ אֲשֶׁר חָזָה עַל־
con- he which from the among was who —Amos The
cerning saw .Tekoa shepherds of words

3101/1121 3379 3117 30 63 44 28 5818 3117 3478
יִשְׂרָאֵל בִּימֵי ׀ עֻזִּיָּה מֶלֶךְ־יְהוּדָה וּבִימֵי יָרָבְעָם בֶּן־יוֹאָשׁ
Joash the Jeroboam the in and ,Judah king Uzziah the in Israel
of son of days of of days

6726 3068 559 7794 6440 8147 34 78 44 28
2 מֶלֶךְ יִשְׂרָאֵל שְׁנָתַיִם לִפְנֵי הָרָעַשׁ׃ וַיֹּאמַר ׀ יְהוָה מִצִּיּוֹן
from Jehovah he And the before years two ,Israel king
Zion ,said .earthquake of

3001 7462 4999 56 6963 5414 3389 75 80
יִשְׁאָג וּמִירוּשָׁלִַם יִתֵּן קוֹלוֹ וְאָבְלוּ נְאוֹת הָרֹעִים וְיָבֵשׁ
shall and the pas- the shall And His will from and will
dry be ,shepherds of tures mourn .voice give Jerusalem roar

6588 79 169 3068 559 3541 3759 72 18
3 רֹאשׁ הַכַּרְמֶל׃ כֹּה אָמַר יְהוָה עַל־שְׁלֹשָׁה פִּשְׁעֵי
trans- three For :Jehovah says Thus .Carmel the
of gressions of top

2742 1758 7725 38 08 702 1834
דַמֶּשֶׂק וְעַל־אַרְבָּעָה לֹא אֲשִׁיבֶנּוּ עַל־דּוּשָׁם בַּחֲרֻצוֹת
threshing with they for will I not ,four and ,Damascus
of sledges threshed ;it withdraw for

398 2370 1004 784 7971 1568 1270
4 הַבַּרְזֶל אֶת־הַגִּלְעָד׃ וְשִׁלַּחְתִּי אֵשׁ בְּבֵית חֲזָאֵל וְאָכְלָה
it and ,Hazael the against a will I But .Gilead iron
devour shall of house fire send

3427 3772 18 34 1280 7665 1130 759
5 אַרְמְנוֹת בֶּן־הֲדָד׃ וְשָׁבַרְתִּי בְּרִיחַ דַּמֶּשֶׂק וְהִכְרַתִּי יוֹשֵׁב
the cut and ,Damascus the will I And .Hadad Ben- the
inhabitant off of bar down break of palaces

7024 758 5971 1540/1040/ 1004 7626 8551 205 1237
מִבִּקְעַת־אָוֶן וְתוֹמֵךְ שֵׁבֶט מִבֵּית עֶדֶן וְגָלוּ עַם־אֲרָם קִירָה
,Kir to Aram the shall And .Eden from the him and Aven the from
of people captive go Beth- scepter holds who of Valley

5804 6588 7969 30 68 559 3541 3068 559
6 אָמַר יְהוָה׃ כֹּה אָמַר יְהוָה עַל־שְׁלֹשָׁה פִּשְׁעֵי עַזָּה
Gaza trans- three For :Jehovah says Thus .Jehovah says
of gressions

8003 15 46 1540 7725 38 08 702
וְעַל־אַרְבָּעָה לֹא אֲשִׁיבֶנּוּ עַל־הַגְלוֹתָם גָּלוּת שְׁלֵמָה
complete a (as) they for will I not ,four and
(population) exiles deported ;it withdraw for

398 5804 2346 784 7971 123 5662
7 לְהַסְגִּיר לֶאֱדוֹם׃ וְשִׁלַּחְתִּי אֵשׁ בְּחוֹמַת עַזָּה וְאָכְלָה
it and ,Gaza the against fire a will I But .Edom to deliver to
devour shall of wall send up

831 7626 8551 795 3427 3772 759
8 אַרְמְנֹתֶיהָ׃ וְהִכְרַתִּי יוֹשֵׁב מֵאַשְׁדּוֹד וְתוֹמֵךְ שֵׁבֶט מֵאַשְׁקְלוֹן
;Ashkelon from the him and Ashdod from the also will I .palaces its
scepter holds who inhabitant off cut

559 6430 7611 6 6138 30 27 7725
וַהֲשִׁיבוֹתִי יָדִי עַל־עֶקְרוֹן וְאָבְדוּ שְׁאֵרִית פְּלִשְׁתִּים אָמַר
says ,Philistines the the shall and ;Ekron against My will I and
of remnant perish hand turn

9 So says Jehovah: For three transgressions of Tyre, and for four, I will not turn back *from* it; for they delivered up *as* exiles a complete *population* to Edom, and did not remember the covenant of brothers. 10 But I will send a fire against the wall of Tyre, and it shall devour its palaces.

11 So says Jehovah: For three transgressions of Edom, and for four, I will not turn back *from* it; for he pursued his brother with the sword, and corrupted his compassions, and his anger tore continually; and he kept it, his wrath, forever. 12 But I will send a fire against Teman, and it shall devour the palaces of Bozrah.

13 So says Jehovah: For three transgressions of the sons of Ammon, and for four, I will not turn back *from* it; for they ripped open the pregnant women of Gilead, to make their border larger. 14 But I will kindle a fire against the wall of Rabbah, and it shall devour its palaces; with a war-cry in the day of battle; with a tempest in the day of the windstorm. 15 And their king shall go into captivity, he and his rulers together, says Jehovah.

CHAPTER 2

1 So says Jehovah: For three transgressions of Moab, and for four, I will not turn back *from* it; for he burned the bones of the king of Edom into lime. 2 But I will send a fire against Moab, and it shall devour the palaces of Kerioth. And Moab shall die with uproar, with a war-cry, with the sound of the ram's horn. 3 And I will cut off the judge in its midst, and will kill all

אדני יהוה׃ 9 כה אמר יהוה על־שלשה פשעי־צר

,Tyre trans- three For :Jehovah says Thus .Jehovah the
of gressions Lord

ועל־ארבעה לא אשיבנו על־הסגירם גלות שלמה

complete a (as) they for will I not ,four and
(population) exiles up delivered ;it withdraw for

10 לאדום ולא זכרו ברית אחים׃ ושלחתי אש בחומת צר

,Tyre the against a will I But .brothers cove- the re- did and ,Edom to
of wall fire send of nant member not

11 ואכלה ארמנתיה׃ כה אמר יהוה על־שלשה

three For :Jehovah says Thus .palaces its shall it and
devour

פשעי אדום ועל־ארבעה לא אשיבנו על־רדפו בחרב

the with he for will I not ,four and ,Edom trans-
sword pursued ;it withdraw for of gressions

אחיו ושחת רחמיו ויטרף לעד אפו ועברתו שמרה נצח׃

.forever kept he his and his con- and his cor- and his
it wrath ,anger tinually tore compassions rupted ,brother

12 ושלחתי אש בתימן ואכלה ארמנות בצרה׃

.Bozrah palaces the shall it and against fire a will I So
of devour ,Teman send

13 כה אמר יהוה על־שלשה פשעי בני־עמון ועל־ארבעה

,four and ,Ammon the trans- three For :Jehovah says Thus
for of sons of gressions

לא אשיבנו על־בקעם הרות הגלעד למען הרחיב את־

enlarge order in ,Gilead preg- the ripped they for will I not
to of women nant open ;it withdraw

14 גבולם׃ והצתי אש בחומת רבה ואכלה ארמנותיה

,palaces its shall it and ,Rabbah the against a will I So their
devour of wall fire kindle .border

15 בתרועה ביום מלחמה בסער ביום סופה׃ והלך מלכם

their shall And the the in a with ,battle the in a with
king go .windstorm of day tempest of day war-cry

בגולה הוא ושריו יחדו אמר יהוה׃

.Jehovah says ,together his and he into
rulers ,exile

CAP. II ב

CHAPTER 2

1 כה אמר יהוה על־שלשה פשעי מואב ועל־ארבעה לא

not ,four and ,Moab trans- three For :Jehovah says Thus
for of gressions

2 אשיבנו על־שרפו עצמות מלך־אדום לשיד׃ ושלחתי־

will I But into Edom the bones the he for will I
send .lime of king of burned ;it withdraw

אש במואב ואכלה ארמנות הקריות ומת בשאון מואב

Moab with And .Kerioth palaces the shall it and against a
uproar die shall of devour ,Moab fire

3 בתרועה בקול שופר׃ והכרתי שופט מקרבה וכל־שריה

its and its from who he will I And ram's the with (and) a with
rulers all ,midst judges off cut .horn of sound the ,war-cry

his rulers with him, says Jehovah.
[4]So says Jehovah: For three transgressions of Judah, and for four, I will not turn back *from* it; for they despised the law of Jehovah, and they have not kept His statutes. Their lies after which their fathers walked led them astray.
[5]And I shall send a fire against Judah, and it shall devour the palaces of Jerusalem.
[6]So says Jehovah: For three transgressions of Israel, and for four, I will not turn back *from* it; for they sold the righteous for silver, and the poor for a pair of sandals,
[7]panting for the dust of the earth on the head of the helpless, and turning aside the way of the humble. And a man and his father will go *in* to the *same* girl, in order to profane the name of My holiness.
[8]And they will stretch out beside every altar, and on garments taken in pledge. And they will drink wine of those being fined *in* the house of God.
[9]Yet I destroyed the Amorite from before them, *whose* height *was* like the height of the cedars; and he *was* strong as the great trees. And I destroyed his fruit from above, and his roots from below.
[10]Also I brought you up from the land of Egypt, and led you in the wilderness forty years, to possess the land of the Amorite.
[11]And I raised up from your sons for prophets, and for Nazarites from your young men. *Is this* not even so, O sons of Israel, declares Jehovah?
[12]But you gave the Nazarites wine to drink, and you commanded the prophets, saying, Do not prophesy.
[13]Behold, I am pressed

7969 3068 559 3541 3068 559 2026
אֶהֱרוֹג עִמּוֹ אָמַר יְהוָה׃ 4 כֹּה אָמַר יְהוָה עַל־שְׁלֹשָׁה
three For :Jehovah says Thus .Jehovah says with him will I slay

3985 7725 3808 702 3063 6588
פִּשְׁעֵי יְהוּדָה וְעַל־אַרְבָּעָה לֹא אֲשִׁיבֶנּוּ עַל־מָאֳסָם אֶת־
they rejected for ;it withdraw will I not ,four and for ,Judah transgressions of

834 3577 8582 8104 3808 2706 3068 8451
תּוֹרַת יְהוָה וְחֻקָּיו לֹא שָׁמָרוּ וַיַּתְעוּם כִּזְבֵיהֶם אֲשֶׁר־
which their lies led And astray them have they .kept not His and statutes ,Jehovah law the of

398 3063 784 7971 310 1 1980
הָלְכוּ אֲבוֹתָם אַחֲרֵיהֶם׃ 5 וְשִׁלַּחְתִּי אֵשׁ בִּיהוּדָה וְאָכְלָה
shall it and devour against ,Judah fire a shall I But send after .them their fathers walked

7969 3068 559 3541 3389 759
אַרְמְנוֹת יְרוּשָׁלִָם׃ 6 כֹּה אָמַר יְהוָה עַל־שְׁלֹשָׁה
three For :Jehovah says Thus .Jerusalem palaces the of

3701 4376 7725 3808 702 3478 6588
פִּשְׁעֵי יִשְׂרָאֵל וְעַל־אַרְבָּעָה לֹא אֲשִׁיבֶנּוּ עַל־מִכְרָם בַּכֶּסֶף
for silver they sold for ;it withdraw will I not ,four and for ,Israel transgressions of

776 6083 7602 5275 34 6662
צַדִּיק וְאֶבְיוֹן בַּעֲבוּר נַעֲלָיִם׃ 7 הַשֹּׁאֲפִים עַל־עֲפַר־אֶרֶץ
the earth the of dust upon who Those trample pair a ,sandals of for the and poor the ,righteous

413 3212 1 376 5186 6035 1870 1800 7218
בְּרֹאשׁ דַּלִּים וְדֶרֶךְ עֲנָוִים יַטּוּ וְאִישׁ וְאָבִיו יֵלְכוּ אֶל־
to will go his and father a And man they ,divert the humble the and of way the ,helpless the on of head

2254 899 5921 6944 8034 2490 4616 5291
הַנַּעֲרָה לְמַעַן חַלֵּל אֶת־שֵׁם קָדְשִׁי׃ 8 וְעַל־בְּגָדִים חֲבֻלִים
in taken pledge garments And on My .holiness the of name profane order in to (same) the ,girl

430 1004 8354 6064 3196 4196 681 5186
יַטּוּ אֵצֶל כָּל־מִזְבֵּחַ וְיֵין עֲנוּשִׁים יִשְׁתּוּ בֵּית אֱלֹהֵיהֶם׃
their .God the (in) of house will they drink being those fined and of wine the ,altar every beside they out stretch

730 1363 834 6440 567 8045
9 וְאָנֹכִי הִשְׁמַדְתִּי אֶת־הָאֱמֹרִי מִפְּנֵיהֶם אֲשֶׁר כְּגֹבַהּ אֲרָזִים
the cedars the like of height who before from ,them Amorite the destroyed I Yet

8328 4605 6529 8045 437 2634 1363
גָּבְהוֹ וְחָסֹן הוּא כָּאַלּוֹנִים וָאַשְׁמִיד פִּרְיוֹ מִמַּעַל וְשָׁרָשָׁיו
his and roots from above his fruit I And destroyed the like .trees great he (was) strong and his (was) ;height

3212 4714 776 5927 8478
מִתָּחַת׃ 10 וְאָנֹכִי הֶעֱלֵיתִי אֶתְכֶם מֵאֶרֶץ מִצְרַיִם וָאוֹלֵךְ
led and Egypt the from of land you up brought I Also from .below

567 776 3423 8141 705 4057
אֶתְכֶם בַּמִּדְבָּר אַרְבָּעִים שָׁנָה לָרֶשֶׁת אֶת־אֶרֶץ הָאֱמֹרִי׃
the .Amorite land the of to possess ,years forty the in wilderness you

369 637 5139 970 5030 1121 6965
11 וָאָקִים מִבְּנֵיכֶם לִנְבִיאִים וּמִבַּחוּרֵיכֶם לִנְזִרִים הַאַף אֵין־
not even (it Is) for (some) .Nazarites your from and men young for (some) prophets your from sons I And up raised

3196 5139 8248 8248 3068 5002 3478 1121 2063
זֹאת בְּנֵי יִשְׂרָאֵל נְאֻם־יְהוָה׃ 12 וַתַּשְׁקוּ אֶת־הַנְּזִרִים יָיִן
,wine the Nazarites give you But drink to ?Jehovah declares ,Israel sons O of ,this

5781 2009 5012 3808 559 6680 5030
וְעַל־הַנְּבִיאִים צִוִּיתֶם לֵאמֹר לֹא תִּנָּבְאוּ׃ 13 הִנֵּה אָנֹכִי מֵעִיק
(am) pressed I ,Behold Do .prophesy not ,saying you ,commanded prophets the and to

under you, as a cart full *with* produce *is* pressed. [14]And refuge shall perish from the swift, and the strong shall not strengthen his power, nor shall the mighty deliver his life; [15]and he who handles the bow shall not stand; and he swift-footed shall not save; and he who rides the horse shall not save his life. [16]And the stout-hearted among the mighty shall run away naked in that day, declares Jehovah.

14 תחתיכם כאשר תעיק העגלה המלאה לה עמיר׃ ואבד
shall And cut (of) of full the cart the (is) as under
perish ,grain it produce (with) pressed ,you
מנוס מקל וחזק לא־יאמץ כחו וגבור לא־ימלט נפשו׃
his will not the and his shall not the and the from refuge
.life save mighty ,power strengthen strong ,swift
15 ותפש הקשת לא יעמד וקל ברגליו לא ימלט ורכב
he and save will not his with the And shall not bow the he And
rides who ,(himself) feet swift .stand handles who
16 הסוס לא ימלט נפשו׃ ואמיץ לבו בגבורים ערום ינוס
shall naked the among his the And his shall not the
flee mighty heart in one stout .life save horse
ביום־ההוא נאם־יהוה׃
.Jehovah declares ,that day in

CAP. III ג

CHAPTER 3

CHAPTER 3

[1]Hear this word that Jehovah has spoken against you, sons of Israel; against all the family which I brought up from the land of Egypt, saying, [2]You only have I known of all the families of the earth. On account of this I will punish you *for* all your iniquities. [3]Will two walk together unless they are agreed? [4]Will a lion roar in the forest when there is no prey for him? Will a young lion cry out of his den unless he has caught *something*? [5]Will a bird fall into a trap *on* the ground, and there is no bait for it? Will a trap spring up from the ground, and nothing at all be caught? [6]If a ram's horn is blowing in a city, will the people not also tremble? If there is a calamity in a city, has Jehovah not even done *it*? [7]For the Lord Jehovah will do nothing unless He reveals His secret to His servants the prophets? [8]A lion has roared; who will not fear? The Lord Jehovah has spoken; who will not prophesy?

[9]Make *it* heard at the

1 שמעו את־הדבר הזה אשר דבר יהוה עליכם בני ישראל
,Israel sons against Jehovah has which this word Hear
of ,you spoken
על כל־המשפחה אשר העליתי מארץ מצרים לאמר׃
,saying ,Egypt the from brought I which family the all against
of land up
2 רק אתכם ידעתי מכל משפחות האדמה על־כן אפקד
will I Therefore .earth the families the all of have I you Only
visit of known
3 עליכם את כל־עונתיכם׃ הילכו שנים יחדו בלתי אם־
unless ,together two walk Will your all you upon
.iniquities
4 נועדו׃ הישאג אריה ביער וטרף אין לו היתן כפיר
young a Will for is there when the in lion a roar Will are they
lion give ?him no prey forest ?agreed
5 קולו ממענתו בלתי אם־לכד׃ התפל צפור על־פח
trap a into bird a fall Will has he unless his from his
?caught den voice
הארץ ומוקש אין לה היעלה־פח מן־האדמה ולכוד לא
nothing at and the from trap a Will for there bait and the (on)
all ,ground up spring ?it not is ground
6 ילכוד׃ אם־יתקע שופר בעיר ועם לא יחרדו אם־תהיה
there If will not the ,city a in ram's a blown is If it
is ?tremble also people horn ?captures
7 רעה בעיר ויהוה לא עשה׃ כי לא יעשה אדני יהוה
Jehovah the do will not For has not even a in calamity
Lord ?(it) done Jehovah ,city
8 דבר כי אם־גלה סודו אל־עבדיו הנביאים׃ אריה שאג
has lion A the His to secret His He unless thing a
!roared .prophets servants counsel reveals
9 מי לא יירא אדני יהוה דבר מי לא ינבא׃ השמיעו
Make will not Who has Jehovah The will not Who
heard (it) ?prophesy !spoken Lord ?fear

עַל־אַרְמְנוֹת בְּאַשְׁדּוֹד וְעַל־אַרְמְנוֹת בְּאֶרֶץ מִצְרָיִם וְאִמְרוּ
,say and ,Egypt of land the in palaces the and at Ashdod in palaces the at

הֵאָסְפוּ עַל־הָרֵי שֹׁמְרוֹן וּרְאוּ מְהוּמֹת רַבּוֹת בְּתוֹכָהּ
its in midst many panics see and ,Samaria the of mountains on Gather yourselves

10 וַעֲשׁוּקִים בְּקִרְבָּהּ׃ וְלֹא־יָדְעוּ עֲשׂוֹת־נְכֹחָה נְאֻם־יְהוָה
,Jehovah declares ,right to (how) do do they know not For its in .midst and oppressions

11 הָאוֹצְרִים חָמָס וָשֹׁד בְּאַרְמְנוֹתֵיהֶם׃ לָכֵן כֹּה אָמַר
says thus Therefore .palaces their in and violence destruction those up storing

אֲדֹנָי יְהוִה צַר וּסְבִיב הָאָרֶץ וְהוֹרִד מִמֵּךְ עֻזֵּךְ וְנָבֹזּוּ
be will robbed and your fortress :from you lower will he And the !land all even around An :Jehovah enemy the Lord

12 אַרְמְנוֹתָיִךְ׃ כֹּה אָמַר יְהוָה כַּאֲשֶׁר יַצִּיל הָרֹעֶה מִפִּי
the from of mouth the shepherd snatches As :Jehovah says Thus .palaces your

הָאֲרִי שְׁתֵּי כְרָעַיִם אוֹ בְדַל־אֹזֶן כֵּן יִנָּצְלוּ בְּנֵי יִשְׂרָאֵל
,Israel the of sons be shall snatched so an ,ear a of piece or ,legs two the lion

13 הַיֹּשְׁבִים בְּשֹׁמְרוֹן בִּפְאַת מִטָּה וּבִדְמֶשֶׁק עָרֶשׂ׃ שִׁמְעוּ
Hear a (on) couch in and Damascus ,bed a a in of corner Samaria in those dwelling

14 וְהָעִידוּ בְּבֵית יַעֲקֹב נְאֻם־אֲדֹנָי יְהוִה אֱלֹהֵי הַצְּבָאוֹת׃ כִּי
For .hosts of God the ,Jehovah the Lord declares ,Jacob of house the in and testify

בְּיוֹם פָּקְדִי פִשְׁעֵי־יִשְׂרָאֵל עָלָיו וּפָקַדְתִּי עַל־מִזְבְּחוֹת בֵּית־
Beth- of altars the upon will I visit also upon ,him Israel of trans- gressions the I visit the in day

15 אֵל וְנִגְדְּעוּ קַרְנוֹת הַמִּזְבֵּחַ וְנָפְלוּ לָאָרֶץ׃ וְהִכֵּיתִי בֵית־
house will I And strike the to .ground and fall will the ,altar horns the of be will And chopped .el

הַחֹרֶף עַל־בֵּית הַקָּיִץ וְאָבְדוּ בָּתֵּי הַשֵּׁן וְסָפוּ בָּתִּים רַבִּים
,great the houses and swept away ;ivory the of houses shall and perish the ,summer house with the the winter

נְאֻם־יְהוָה׃
.Jehovah declares

palaces in Ashdod, and at the palaces in the land of Egypt; and say, Gather yourselves on the mountains of Samaria, and see many panics in its midst, and oppressions in its midst. [10]For they do not know to do right, declares Jehovah; those who store up violence and robbery in their palaces. [11]So the Lord Jehovah says this: An enemy! And *he shall be* all around the land; and he shall bring you down from your fortress; and your palaces shall be plundered. [12]So says Jehovah: As the shepherd takes two legs out of the mouth of the lion, or a piece of an ear, so shall the sons of Israel be taken out, those who dwell in Samaria in a corner of a bed, and in Damascus *on* a couch. [13]Hear and testify in the house of Jacob, declares the Lord Jehovah, the God of hosts. [14]For in the day I visit the transgressions of Israel on him, I will also visit on the altars of Bethel. And the horns of the altar will be chopped and will fall to the ground. [15]And I will strike the winter house with the summer house, and the houses of ivory shall perish. And the great houses shall be swept away, declares Jehovah.

CAP. IV ד

CHAPTER 4

1 שִׁמְעוּ הַדָּבָר הַזֶּה פָּרוֹת הַבָּשָׁן אֲשֶׁר בְּהַר שֹׁמְרוֹן הָעֹשְׁקוֹת
those oppressing ,Samaria of mountain the in who (are) ,Bashan of cows ,this word Hear

דַּלִּים הָרֹצְצוֹת אֶבְיוֹנִים הָאֹמְרֹת לַאֲדֹנֵיהֶם הָבִיאָה
Bring their to ,husbands those saying ,poor the those crushing the ,helpless

2 וְנִשְׁתֶּה׃ נִשְׁבַּע אֲדֹנָי יְהוִה בְּקָדְשׁוֹ כִּי הִנֵּה יָמִים בָּאִים
are coming the days ,behold that His by holiness Jehovah the Lord Has sworn we that .drink may

CHAPTER 4

[1]Hear this word, cows of Bashan who *are* in the mountain of Samaria, who press down the helpless, who crush the poor; who say to their husbands, Bring in, that we may drink. [2]The Lord Jehovah has sworn by His holiness that the days are coming that He will lift

you up with meathooks, and the last of you with fishhooks. [3]And you shall go out *at* the breaches, each woman before her. And you shall throw down the high place, declares Jehovah.

[4]Come into Bethel and transgress; multiply transgressing *at* Gilgal. And bring your sacrifices for the morning, your tithes for three days; [5]and offer a sacrifice of thanksgiving from that which is leavened; and cry out, call out the voluntary offerings! For so you love *to do*, sons of Israel, declares the Lord Jehovah.

[6]And I also have given you cleanness of teeth in all your cities, and lack of bread in all your places; and you have not returned to Me, declares Jehovah. [7]And I have also withheld the rain from you, when *it was* yet three months to the harvest. And I caused rain to fall on one city, and caused it not to rain on another city. One piece was rained on, and the piece where it did not rain was dried up. [8]So two or three cities staggered to one city in order to drink water, but they were not satisfied; yet you have not returned to Me, declares Jehovah. [9]I have struck you with blasting and mildew. The multitude of your gardens and your vineyards, and your figs, and your olives, *are* devoured by the creeping locust; yet you have not returned to Me, declares Jehovah. [10]I have sent a plague among you in the way of Egypt; I have killed your young men with the sword and your horses with captivity; and I have made the stench of your camps to come up even into your nostrils; yet you have not returned to Me, declares Jehovah. [11]I have overthrown among you, as God

1729 5518 319 6793 5375 5921
עֲלֵיכֶם וְנָשָׂא אֶתְכֶם בְּצִנּוֹת וְאַחֲרִיתְכֶן בְּסִירוֹת דּוּגָה׃
.fishing with the and with you He and upon
for hooks you of last ,hooks meat up lift will ,you

5002 2038 7993 5048 802 3318 6556
3 וּפְרָצִים תֵּצֶאנָה אִשָּׁה נֶגְדָּהּ וְהִשְׁלַכְתֶּנָה הַהַרְמוֹנָה נְאֻם־
declares high the shall you And before each shall you the (at) And
,place down throw .her woman ,out go breaches

935 6586 7235 1537 6586 1008 935 3068
4 יְהוָה׃ בֹּאוּ בֵית־אֵל וּפִשְׁעוּ הַגִּלְגָּל הַרְבּוּ לִפְשֹׁעַ וְהָבִיאוּ
And trans- increase (At) and ,el Beth- Enter .Jehovah
bring .gressing Gilgal !rebel

6999 4643 3117 7969 2077 1242
5 לַבֹּקֶר זִבְחֵיכֶם לִשְׁלֹשֶׁת יָמִים מַעְשְׂרֹתֵיכֶם׃ וְקַטֵּר
and ;tithes your days for your the for
burn three ,sacrifices morning

1121 157 3651 8085 5071 7121 8426 2557
מֵחָמֵץ תּוֹדָה וְקִרְאוּ נְדָבוֹת הַשְׁמִיעוּ כִּי כֵן אֲהַבְתֶּם בְּנֵי
sons love you so For announce voluntary and thank a that from
of ,(do to) .(them) ,offerings proclaim ,offering leavened

5356 5414 1571 3068 136 5002 3478
6 יִשְׂרָאֵל נְאֻם אֲדֹנָי יְהוִה׃ וְגַם־אֲנִי נָתַתִּי לָכֶם נִקְיוֹן
cleanness to have I And .Jehovah the declares ,Israel
of you given also Lord

3808 4725 3605 3899 2640 5892 3605 8127
שִׁנַּיִם בְּכָל־עָרֵיכֶם וְחֹסֶר לֶחֶם בְּכֹל מְקוֹמֹתֵיכֶם וְלֹא־
and ;places your all in bread and your in teeth
not of lack ,cities all

1653 4513 1571 3068 5002 7725
7 שַׁבְתֶּם עָדַי נְאֻם־יְהוָה׃ וְגַם אָנֹכִי מָנַעְתִּי מִכֶּם אֶת־הַגֶּשֶׁם
the from have I And .Jehovah declares to have you
,rain you withheld also ,Me returned

259 5892 4305 7105 2320 7969 5750
בְּעוֹד שְׁלֹשָׁה חֳדָשִׁים לַקָּצִיר וְהִמְטַרְתִּי עַל־עִיר אֶחָת
one city on made I And the to months three yet when
fall rain .harvest (was it)

2513 4305 259 2513 4305 3808 259 5892 5921
וְעַל־עִיר אַחַת לֹא אַמְטִיר חֶלְקָה אַחַת תִּמָּטֵר וְחֶלְקָה
a but rained was one portion made I not another city and
portion ,upon ;fall rain on

5892 7969 8147 5128 3001 5921 4305 3808
8 אֲשֶׁר־לֹא־תַמְטִיר עָלֶיהָ תִּיבָשׁ׃ וְנָעוּ שְׁתַּיִם שָׁלֹשׁ עָרִים
cities (or) two And .up dried it on did it not where
three staggered rain

7725 3808 7646 3808 4325 8354 259 5892
אֶל־עִיר אַחַת לִשְׁתּוֹת מַיִם וְלֹא יִשְׂבָּעוּ וְלֹא־שַׁבְתֶּם עָדַי
to have you and were they but ,water drink to one city to
,Me returned not ;satisfied not

1593 7235 3420 7711 5221 3068 5002
9 נְאֻם־יְהוָה׃ הִכֵּיתִי אֶתְכֶם בַּשִּׁדָּפוֹן וּבַיֵּרָקוֹן הַרְבּוֹת גַּנּוֹתֵיכֶם
your mul- the with and with you have I .Jehovah de-
gardens of titude ,mildew scorching struck clares

7725 3808 1501 398 2132 8384 3754
וְכַרְמֵיכֶם וּתְאֵנֵיכֶם וְזֵיתֵיכֶם יֹאכַל הַגָּזָם וְלֹא־שַׁבְתֶּם עָדַי
to have you and the was your and your and your and
,Me returned not ;locust devouring ,olives figs vinegards

2026 4714 1870 1698 7971 3068 5002
10 נְאֻם־יְהוָה׃ שִׁלַּחְתִּי בָכֶם דֶּבֶר בְּדֶרֶךְ מִצְרַיִם הָרַגְתִּי
have I .Egypt the in plague a among have I .Jehovah declares
killed of way you sent

4264 889 5927 5483 7628 970 2719
בַחֶרֶב בַּחוּרֵיכֶם עִם שְׁבִי סוּסֵיכֶם וָאַעֲלֶה בְּאֹשׁ מַחֲנֵיכֶם
your stench the made I and your the with young your the with
camps of up come to ;horses of captivity ,men sword

2015 3068 5002 7725 3808 639
11 וּבְאַפְּכֶם וְלֹא־שַׁבְתֶּם עָדַי נְאֻם־יְהוָה׃ הָפַכְתִּי בָכֶם
among have I .Jehovah declares to have you and into even
you overthrown ,Me returned not ;noses your

overthrew Sodom and Gomorrah, and you were like a firebrand plucked out of the burning; yet you have not returned to Me, declares Jehovah. [12]So I will do this to you, O Israel: Because of this I will do to you; prepare to meet your God, O Israel. [13]For, behold, He who forms mountains and creates the wind, and declares to man what His thought *is*; He who makes the dawn darkness, and treads on the high places of the earth; Jehovah, the God of Hosts, *is* His name.

5337 181 1961 6017 5467 430 4114
כְּמַהְפֵּכַת אֱלֹהִים אֶת־סְדֹם וְאֶת־עֲמֹרָה וַתִּהְיוּ כְּאוּד מֻצָּל
snatched a like you and ,Gomorrah and Sodom (of) God's like
firebrand were overthrow

6213 3068 5002 7725 3808 8316
12 מִשְּׂרֵפָה וְלֹא־שַׁבְתֶּם עָדַי נְאֻם־יְהוָה׃ לָכֵן כֹּה אֶעֱשֶׂה־
will I thus Therefore .Jehovah declares unto have you and the from
do ,Me returned not ,burning

430 7125 3559 6213 6118 3478
לְּךָ יִשְׂרָאֵל עֵקֶב כִּי־זֹאת אֶעֱשֶׂה־לָּךְ הִכּוֹן לִקְרַאת־אֱלֹהֶיךָ
,God your meet to prepare to will I this because :Israel O to
you do of you

4100 120 5041 7307 1254 2022 3335 2009 3478
13 יִשְׂרָאֵל׃ כִּי הִנֵּה יוֹצֵר הָרִים וּבֹרֵא רוּחַ וּמַגִּיד לְאָדָם מַה־
what to and the and mountains He ,behold For .Israel O
(is) man declares wind creates forms who

430 3068 776 1116 5921 1869 5890 7837 6213 7808
שֵּׂחוֹ עֹשֵׂה שַׁחַר עֵיפָה וְדֹרֵךְ עַל־בָּמֳתֵי אָרֶץ יְהוָה אֱלֹהֵי־
God the ,Jehovah the high the upon and ,darkness (into) who He His
of ,earth of places treads dawn makes ;thought

8034 6635
צְבָאוֹת שְׁמוֹ׃
His hosts
.name (is)

CAP. V ה

CHAPTER 5

CHAPTER 5

[1]Hear this word which I am lifting up against you, a dirge, O house of Israel. [2]The virgin of Israel has fallen, and not will rise again; she lies forsaken on her land; there is no one raising her up. [3]For so says the Lord Jehovah: The city that goes out *by* a thousand shall have a hundred left. And that which goes out *by* a hundred shall have ten left in the house of Israel.

[4]For so says Jehovah to the house of Israel: Seek Me, and live. [5]But do not seek Bethel, and do not enter Gilgal, and do not cross over to Beer-sheba; for Gilgal shall surely go into exile, and Bethel shall be for nothing. [6]Seek Jehovah, and live; that He not break out like a fire *on* the house of Joseph, and consume; and no one is putting it out for Bethel. [7]He abandoned those who turn justice and righteousness into wormwood *on* the earth. [8]He who created the Pleiades and Orion, and turns the deep darkness

1004 7015 5375 834 2088 1697 8085
1 שִׁמְעוּ אֶת־הַדָּבָר הַזֶּה אֲשֶׁר אָנֹכִי נֹשֵׂא עֲלֵיכֶם קִינָה בֵּית
O ,dirge a against am I which this word Hear
of house ,you lifting

5203 3478 1330 6965 3254 5307 3478
2 יִשְׂרָאֵל׃ נָפְלָה לֹא־תוֹסִיף קוּם בְּתוּלַת יִשְׂרָאֵל נִטְּשָׁה
lies she ;Israel virgin the arise will and has She .Israel
unattended of again not ,fallen

3068 136 559 3541 6965 369 127 5921
3 עַל־אַדְמָתָהּ אֵין מְקִימָהּ׃ כִּי כֹה אָמַר אֲדֹנָי יְהוִה
:Jehovah the says thus For raising is there her on
Lord .up her none ;land

7604 3967 3318 3967 7604 505 3318 5892
הָעִיר הַיֹּצֵאת אֶלֶף תַּשְׁאִיר מֵאָה וְהַיּוֹצֵאת מֵאָה תַּשְׁאִיר
have will hundred a that and ,hundred a have will thou- a goes that The
left (strong) forth goes which left (strong) sand forth city

1004 3068 559 3541 3478 1004 6235
4 עֲשָׂרָה לְבֵית יִשְׂרָאֵל׃ כִּי כֹה אָמַר יְהוָה לְבֵית
the to Jehovah says thus For .Israel the to ten
of house of house

3808 1537 1008 1875 2421 1875 3478
5 יִשְׂרָאֵל דִּרְשׁוּנִי וִחְיוּ׃ וְאַל־תִּדְרְשׁוּ בֵּית־אֵל וְהַגִּלְגָּל לֹא
not and ,el Beth- seek do But .live and ,Me Seek :Israel
Gilgal not

1008 1540 1540 1537 5674 3808 884 935
תָבֹאוּ וּבְאֵר שֶׁבַע לֹא תַעֲבֹרוּ כִּי הַגִּלְגָּל גָּלֹה יִגְלֶה וּבֵית
and go will surely Gilgal for cross do not sheba and do
Beth- ,exile into ;to over Beer- ;enter

784 6743 2421 3068 1875 1175 205 1961 1008
6 אֵל יִהְיֶה לְאָוֶן׃ דִּרְשׁוּ אֶת־יְהוָה וִחְיוּ פֶּן־יִצְלַח כָּאֵשׁ
a like He lest and ,Jehovah Seek for shall el
fire rush ;live .nothing be

3939 2015 1008 3518 369 398 31:27 1004
7 בֵּית יוֹסֵף וְאָכְלָה וְאֵין־מְכַבֶּה לְבֵית־אֵל׃ הַהֹפְכִים לְלַעֲנָה
into who Those .el for quench- there and and Joseph the (on)
wormwood turn Beth- (it) ing none is ,devour of house

2015 3684 3598 6213 3246 776 6666 4941
8 מִשְׁפָּט וּצְדָקָה לָאָרֶץ הִנִּיחוּ׃ עֹשֵׂה כִימָה וּכְסִיל וְהֹפֵךְ
and and the who He he the in righ- and ,justice
turns ,Orion Pleiades made ;abandoned earth teousness

into the morning, and He darkened the day *into* night; who calls for the waters of the sea, and pours them out on the face of the earth; Jehovah *is* His name; ⁹who causes destruction to flash out against the strong, and destruction comes against the fortress. ¹⁰They hate him who rebukes in the gate; and they despise him who speaks uprightly. ¹¹So, because of your trampling on the poor, and you take tribute of grain from him; you have built houses of hewn stones, but you shall not dwell in them; you have planted desirable vineyards, but you shall not drink wine from them. ¹²For I know your many transgressions, and your many sins: afflicting the just; taking of a bribe; and turning aside the poor in the gate. ¹³So the understanding ones shall keep silent in that time; for it *is* an evil time.

¹⁴Seek good, and not evil, that you may live; and so Jehovah the God of hosts *shall be* with you, as you have spoken. ¹⁵Hate evil, and love good, and establish justice in the gate. It may be that Jehovah the God of hosts will be gracious *to* the remnant of Joseph. ¹⁶So Jehovah, the God of Hosts, the Lord says this: Wailing *shall be* in all streets; and they shall say in all the highways, Alas! Alas! And they shall call the farmer to the mourning, and those knowing wailing to lamentation. ¹⁷And wailing *shall be* in all vineyards, for I will pass among you, says Jehovah. ¹⁸Woe to those desiring the day of Jehovah! What *is* this for you? The day of Jehovah *is* darkness, and not light; ¹⁹as if a man fled before a lion, and the bear met him; or he goes into the

---

3220	4325	7121	2821	3915	3117	6757	1242
לַבֹּקֶר צַלְמָוֶת וְיוֹם לַיְלָה הֶחְשִׁיךְ הַקּוֹרֵא לְמֵי־הַיָּם

the sea | of waters | who calls | He darkened; | (into) the night | and day | deep the darkness | the into morning

9
| 5794 | 7701 | 1082 | 8034 | 3068 | 776 | 6440 | 8210 |

וַיִּשְׁפְּכֵם עַל־פְּנֵי הָאָרֶץ יְהוָה שְׁמוֹ הַמַּבְלִיג שֹׁד עַל־עָז

the strong | on | destruction | flashes He with forth | His name | Jehovah (is) | the earth; | the face of | on | pours and out them

10
| 8549 | 1696 | 3198 | 8179 | 8130 | 935 | 4013 | 3282 | 8581 |

שָׂנְאוּ בַשַּׁעַר מוֹכִיחַ וְדֹבֵר תָּמִים יָבֹא

up-rightly speaks who | reproves | gate the in | They hate | .comes | the fortress | on | and destruction

11
| 3947 | 1280 | 4864 | 1800 | 1322 | 3282 | 8581 |

יַעַן בּוֹשַׁסְכֶם עַל־דָּל וּמַשְׂאַת־בַּר תִּקְחוּ מִמֶּנּוּ

from you | grain | the | on your | because There-fore | ,abhor | ;him take | of tribute | ,poor | trampling | of

| 3808 | 5193 | 2531 | 3754 | 3427 | 1129 | 1496 | 1004 |

בָּתֵּי גָזִית בְּנִיתֶם וְלֹא־תֵשְׁבוּ בָם כַּרְמֵי־חֶמֶד נְטַעְתֶּם וְלֹא

but | have you | desire | Vine- | in | shall you | but | have you hewn houses | not ,planted | of yards | .them dwell | not | ,built stones of

12
| 6099 | 6588 | 7227 | 3045 | 3196 | 8354 |

תִשְׁתּוּ אֶת־יֵינָם: כִּי יָדַעְתִּי רַבִּים פִּשְׁעֵיכֶם וַעֲצֻמִים

and | your (are) | many | know I | For | their | shall you | numerous | ,transgressions | .wine | drink

| 5186 | 8179 | 34 | 3724 | 3947 | 6662/6887 | 2403 |

חַטֹּאתֵיכֶם צֹרְרֵי צַדִּיק לֹקְחֵי כֹפֶר וְאֶבְיוֹנִים בַּשַּׁעַר הִטּוּ:

they | the in | the and | ,bribe a | taking | the oppressing | your (are) | .aside turn | gate | poor | of | ,righteous of | :sins

13
| 7451 | 6256 | 1826 | 6256 | 7919 |

לָכֵן הַמַּשְׂכִּיל בָּעֵת הַהִיא יִדֹּם כִּי עֵת רָעָה הִיא:

.(is) it | evil | an | for | keep will | that | in | who he | Therefore | time | ;silent | time | prudent is

14
| 430 | 3068 | 1961 | 2421 | 4616 | 7451 1408 | 2896 1875 |

דִּרְשׁוּ־טוֹב וְאַל־רָע לְמַעַן תִּחְיוּ וִיהִי־כֵן יְהוָה אֱלֹהֵי

God | ,Jehovah | so may and | may you so | ,evil and | good | Seek | of | be it | ;live | that | not

15
| 2896 | 157 | 7451 | 8130 | 559 | 6635 |

צְבָאוֹת אִתְּכֶם כַּאֲשֶׁר אֲמַרְתֶּם: שִׂנְאוּ־רָע וְאֶהֱבוּ טוֹב

,good | love and | evil | Hate | have you | as | with | hosts | ,spoken | you | (is)

| 6635 | 430 | 3068 | 2603 | 194 | 4941 | 8179 | 3322 |

וְהַצִּיגוּ בַשַּׁעַר מִשְׁפָּט אוּלַי יֶחֱנַן יְהוָה אֱלֹהֵי־צְבָאוֹת

hosts | God the | Jehovah | be will Perhaps | .justice | the in | and | of | gracious | gate | establish

16
| 6635 | 430 | 3068 | 559 | 3651 |

לָכֵן כֹּה־אָמַר יְהוָה אֱלֹהֵי צְבָאוֹת

hosts | God the | ,Jehovah | says thus | ,Therefore | .Joseph the (to) | of remnant

| 7611 | 3127 |

שְׁאֵרִית יוֹסֵף:

| 1930 | 559 | 2351 | 3605 | 45:53 | 7339 | 136 |

אֲדֹנָי בְּכָל־רְחֹבוֹת מִסְפֵּד וּבְכָל־חוּצוֹת יֹאמְרוּ הוֹ־הוֹ

!Alas | shall they | the | in and | ;wailing | squares | open In | the | !Alas | ,say | streets | all | (be will) | all | :Lord

17
| 3754 | 3605 | 5092 | 3045 | 4553 | 60 | 1406 | 7121 |

וְקָרְאוּ אִכָּר אֶל־אֵבֶל וּמִסְפֵּד אֶל־יוֹדְעֵי נֶהִי: וּבְכָל־כְּרָמִים

vineyards | in And | lamen- | those to | and | the | to | the | they And | all | .tation | knowing | wailing | ,mourning | farmer | call shall

18
| 183 | 1945 | 3068 | 559 | 7130 | 5674 | 4553 |

מִסְפֵּד כִּי־אֶעֱבֹר בְּקִרְבְּךָ אָמַר יְהוָה: הוֹי הַמִּתְאַוִּים

those | Woe | .Jehovah | says | your in | will I | for | (be will) | desiring | to | ,midst | pass | ,wailing

| 3808 | 2822 | 3068 | 3117 | 2088 | 4100 | 3068 | 3117 |

אֶת־יוֹם יְהוָה לָמָּה־זֶּה לָכֶם יוֹם יְהוָה הוּא־חֹשֶׁךְ וְלֹא־

and | darkness | it Jehovah | The | for | this | What | !Jehovah | day the | not | (is) | of day | ?you | (is) | of

19
| 935 | 1677 | 6293 | 738 | 6440 | 376 | 5127 | 216 |

אוֹר: כַּאֲשֶׁר יָנוּס אִישׁ מִפְּנֵי הָאֲרִי וּפְגָעוֹ הַדֹּב וּבָא

he or | the | met and | the | from | a | fled | (if) as | .light | enters | ;bear | him | ,lion | before | man

house and leans his hand
against the wall, and a
snake bites him. [20]*Shall*
not the day of Jehovah *be*
darkness, and not light;
even very dark, and not any
brightness in it?
[21]I hate, I despise your
feast days; and I will not
delight in your solemn
assemblies. [22]Though you
offer Me burnt offerings,
and your food offerings, I
will not be pleased; nor will
I regard the peace offerings
of your fat animals. [23]Take
the noise of your songs
away from Me; and I will not
hear the melody of your
stringed instruments. [24]But
let justice roll down like
waters, and righteousness
like an ever-flowing stream.
[25]Have you brought near
sacrifices and food offerings to Me forty years in the
wilderness, O house of
Israel? [26]Yea, you have
carried the booth of your
king and Kiyyun, your
images, the star of your
gods which you made for
yourselves! [27]Therefore, I
will cause you to go into
exile beyond Damascus,
says Jehovah, the God of
hosts *is* His name.

2822 3808 5175 5391 7023 3027 5564 1004
20 הֲבַיִת וְסָמַךְ יָדוֹ עַל־הַקִּיר וּנְשָׁכוֹ הַנָּחָשׁ׃ הֲלֹא־חֹשֶׁךְ
darkness (Is) the bites and the against his and the
not .snake him ,wall hand leans house

3985 8130 5051 650 216 3808 3068 3117
21 יוֹם יְהוָה וְלֹא־אוֹר וְאָפֵל וְלֹא־נֹגַהּ לוֹ׃ שָׂנֵאתִי מָאַסְתִּי
reject I ,hate I ?it in bright- and even ,light and ,Jehovah the
ness no gloomy not of day

5930 5927 6116 7306 3808 2282
22 חַגֵּיכֶם וְלֹא אָרִיחַ בְּעַצְּרֹתֵיכֶם׃ כִּי אִם־תַּעֲלוּ־לִי עֹלוֹת
burnt to offer you if For festive your in will I and feast your
,offerings Me up .assemblies delight not ,days

5493 5027 3808 4806 8002 7521 3808 4503
23 וּמִנְחֹתֵיכֶם לֹא אֶרְצֶה וְשֶׁלֶם מְרִיאֵיכֶם לֹא אַבִּיט׃ הָסֵר
Take will I not fattened your peace and will I not food your and
away .upon look animals of offerings ;pleased be ,offerings

4325 1556 8085 3808 5035 2172 7892 1995
24 מֵעָלַי הֲמוֹן שִׁרֶיךָ וְזִמְרַת נְבָלֶיךָ לֹא אֶשְׁמָע׃ וְיִגַּל כַּמַּיִם
like let But will I not your the and your the from
waters down roll .hear harps of melody ;songs of sound Me

5066 4503 2077 386 5158 6666 4941
25 מִשְׁפָּט וּצְדָקָה כְּנַחַל אֵיתָן׃ הַזְּבָחִים וּמִנְחָה הִגַּשְׁתֶּם־
you Did good and the ever- a like righ- and ,justice
near bring offerings sacrifices .flowing torrent teousness

5375 3478 1004 8141 705 4057
26 לִי בַמִּדְבָּר אַרְבָּעִים שָׁנָה בֵּית יִשְׂרָאֵל׃ וּנְשָׂאתֶם אֵת
you, Yea ?Israel house O ,years forty the in to
bore of wilderness Me

834 430 3556 6754 3594 4428 5522
סִכּוּת מַלְכְּכֶם וְאֵת כִּיּוּן צַלְמֵיכֶם כּוֹכַב אֱלֹהֵיכֶם אֲשֶׁר
which your star the your ,Kiyyun and your the
gods of ,images king of booth

559 1834 1973 1540 6213
27 עֲשִׂיתֶם לָכֶם׃ וְהִגְלֵיתִי אֶתְכֶם מֵהָלְאָה לְדַמָּשֶׂק אָמַר
says ,Damascus beyond you I ,Therefore your- for you
exile into take will ?selves made

8034 6635 430 3068
יְהוָה אֱלֹהֵי־צְבָאוֹת שְׁמוֹ׃
His hosts the ,Jehovah
.name (is) of God

CAP. VI ו

CHAPTER 6

CHAPTER 6

[1]Woe *to* those at ease in
Zion, and those trusting in
the mountain of Samaria,
those noted *as* the leader of
the nations! And the house
of Israel came to them.
[2]Cross to Calneh, and see;
and from there go to the
great Hamath; then go
down to Gath of the Philistines. *Are they* better than
these kingdoms, or their
border than your border?
[3]You who put the evil day
far away, and cause the seat
of violence to come near;
[4]who lie on beds of ivory,
and stretch themselves on
their couches; and those
eating the lambs from the
flock, and bull calves from
the midst of the stall;

7225 5344 8111 2022 982 6726 7600 1945
1 הוֹי הַשַּׁאֲנַנִּים בְּצִיּוֹן וְהַבֹּטְחִים בְּהַר שֹׁמְרוֹן נְקֻבֵי רֵאשִׁית
the those ,Samaria the in those and ,Zion in at those Woe
of chief (as) noted of mountain trusting ease (to)

3651 7200 3641 5674 3478 1004 935 1471
2 הַגּוֹיִם וּבָאוּ לָהֶם בֵּית יִשְׂרָאֵל׃ עִבְרוּ כַלְנֵה וּרְאוּ וּלְכוּ
and and to Cross !Israel house the to and the
go ;see Calneh over of them came ,nations

4467 2896 6430 1661 3381 7227 2574
3 מִשָּׁם חֲמַת רַבָּה וּרְדוּ גַת־פְּלִשְׁתִּים הֲטוֹבִים מִן־הַמַּמְלָכוֹת
kingdoms than (they Are) .Philistines the (to) go And the (to) from
better of Gath down .great Hamath there

5066 7451 3117 5077 1366 1366 7227 428
הָאֵלֶּה אִם־רַב גְּבוּלָם מִגְּבֻלְכֶם׃ הַמְנַדִּים לְיוֹם רָע וַתַּגִּישׁוּן
they but ,evil the who Those your than their greater or ,these
near bring day off thrust ?territory territory

640 5921 5628 8127 4296 7901 2555 7675
4 שֶׁבֶת חָמָס׃ הַשֹּׁכְבִים עַל־מִטּוֹת שֵׁן וּסְרֻחִים עַל־עַרְשׂוֹתָם
their on those and ,ivory beds on who those ;violence the
,couches sprawled of lie of seat

6527 4770 8432 5695 6629 3733 398
5 וְאֹכְלִים כָּרִים מִצֹּאן וַעֲגָלִים מִתּוֹךְ מַרְבֵּק׃ הַפֹּרְטִים עַ
to those the the from bull and the from lambs those and
improvising ;stall of midst calves flock eating

5those chanting with the mouth of the harp; they invent instruments of song for themselves like David; 6who drink bowls of wine, and they anoint with the best of oils; but they are not grieved for the breaking of Joseph!

7So now they shall go into exile with the first of the exiles, and the feast of those who stretch themselves shall cease. 8The Lord Jehovah has sworn by Himself, declares Jehovah, the God of hosts: I abhor the pride of Jacob, and hate his palaces; and I will shut up the city and its fullness. 9And it shall be, if ten men remain in one house, then they shall die. 10And his uncle shall lift him up, and he who burns him, to bring out the bones from the house; and he shall say to that one left in the recesses of the house, Are any still with you? And he shall say, No. Then he shall say, Hush! For not one shall mention the name of Jehovah. 11For, behold, Jehovah commands, and He will strike the great house into pieces, and the little house into cracks.

12Shall horses run on the rock? Or will one plow there with oxen? For you have turned justice into poison, and the fruit of righteousness into wormwood; 13those rejoicing for nothing; those saying, Have we not taken horns to ourselves by our own strength? 14For, behold, I will raise a nation up against you, O house of Israel, declares Jehovah, the God of hosts. And they shall oppress you from the entrance of Hamath to the torrent of the Arabah.

CHAPTER 7

1The Lord Jehovah made me see this: And, behold, He is forming locusts at the beginning of the coming up

Interlinear column:

6310	5035		17 32	2803		36 27	7892		8354		4219
the the	harp	;like	they	for	song instru-ments of	they	from those drinking	bowls	6		

פִּי־הַנֵּבֶל כְּדָוִיד חָשְׁבוּ לָהֶם כְּלֵי־שִׁיר: הַשֹּׁתִים בְּמִזְרְקֵי

the the of mouth ; harp like David invent they themselves for ments of song instru- they like for , song from those bowls drinking

3196	7225		8081	4886		2470 38 08		6666	3127

יַיִן וְרֵאשִׁית שְׁמָנִים יִמְשָׁחוּ וְלֹא נֶחְלוּ עַל־שֵׁבֶר יוֹסֵף:

, wine the with oils the best of they anoint but not (themselves) grieve do for the of breaking Joseph !

6258	5628		7 218 15 40	5493	4997	5628

לָכֵן עַתָּה יִגְלוּ בְּרֹאשׁ גֹּלִים וְסָר מִרְזַח סְרוּחִים:

There- now they into go exile first of exiles the will and the will cease feast of the sprawlers

7650 9 136	30 68	5002	3068	430	6635	8374

נִשְׁבַּע אֲדֹנָי יְהוִה בְּנַפְשׁוֹ נְאֻם־יְהוָה אֱלֹהֵי צְבָאוֹת מְתָאֵב

has sworn The Lord Jehovah by Himself Jehovah de-clares God the , hosts : abhor

4393 19 61	349 8	6235	582	1004	251	4191

אָנֹכִי אֶת־גְּאוֹן יַעֲקֹב וְאַרְמְנֹתָיו שָׂנֵאתִי וְהִסְגַּרְתִּי עִיר

the of pride Jacob , and his palaces hate I ; and I will shut up city the

375 7 1730	3318	6106	1004	559	5635

וּמְלֹאָהּ: וְהָיָה אִם־יִוָּתְרוּ עֲשָׂרָה אֲנָשִׁים בְּבַיִת אֶחָד וָמֵתוּ:

its and fullness. And it be will , if are left ten men in house one , then they die will.

3411	1004	5750	559	657	559	2013 38 08

וּנְשָׂאוֹ דּוֹדוֹ וּמְסָרְפוֹ לְהוֹצִיא עֲצָמִים מִן־הַבַּיִת וְאָמַר לַאֲשֶׁר

And will lift him up his uncle and his burner , to bring out the bones from the house , shall say that to (left one)

2142	8034	3068		2009	4687	3068	6680

בְּיַרְכְּתֵי הַבַּיִת הַעוֹד עִמָּךְ וְאָמַר אָפֶס וְאָמַר הָס כִּי לֹא

the in recesses of the house Are (any) still with you ? And he say will None. Then he say will Hush ! For not

2142	8034	3068		2009	4687	3068	5221 66 80

לְהַזְכִּיר בְּשֵׁם יְהוָה: כִּי־הִנֵּה יְהוָה מְצַוֶּה וְהִכָּה

must one mention of name the Jehovah. For , behold , Jehovah is com-manding , He and strike will

1004	7447		6996	1004	1223	7323	53 55

הַבַּיִת הַגָּדוֹל רְסִיסִים וְהַבַּיִת הַקָּטֹן בְּקִעִים: הַיְרֻצוּן בַּסֶּלַע

the house great (into) pieces and the house little (into) breaches. Do run the on rock

5483	2790	1241		2015	7219	49 41

סוּסִים אִם־יַחֲרוֹשׁ בַּבְּקָרִים כִּי־הֲפַכְתֶּם לְרֹאשׁ מִשְׁפָּט

?horses Or will one plow with (there) oxen ? For have you turned into poison justice

6529	6664	3937		8056	38 08 1697	559

וּפְרִי צְדָקָה לְלַעֲנָה: הַשְּׂמֵחִים לְלֹא דָבָר הָאֹמְרִים הֲלֹא

of fruit righteous-ness into wormwood ; those rejoicing no thing for those , saying not

2392	3947		7161	2005	69 65	1004

בְחָזְקֵנוּ לָקַחְנוּ לָנוּ קַרְנָיִם: כִּי הִנְנִי מֵקִים עֲלֵיכֶם בֵּית

by own our strength taken to our-selves horns? For behold I am rising up against you , O house

34 78	5002	3068	430	6635	1471/6635	3905	935

יִשְׂרָאֵל נְאֻם־יְהוָה אֱלֹהֵי הַצְּבָאוֹת גּוֹי וּלְחָצוּ אֶתְכֶם מִלְּבוֹא

Israel ; declares Jehovah God the of hosts a nation And they will oppress you the from of entrance

חֲמָת עַד־נַחַל הָעֲרָבָה:

Hamath to the of torrent the Arabah.

CHAPTER 7

3541	7200		136	3068	2009	3335	1462	8462	5927

כֹּה הִרְאַנִי אֲדֹנָי יְהוִה וְהִנֵּה יוֹצֵר גֹּבַי בִּתְחִלַּת עֲלוֹת

Thus showed me the Lord Jehovah and ; behold is He forming locusts the at of beginning the coming up of

of the late grass; even
behold, the late grass after
the mowings of the king.
²And it happened when it
had made an end of eating
the vegetation of the land,
then I said, Lord Jehovah, I
beg You, forgive. How can
Jacob stand? For he *is*
small. ³Jehovah repented
concerning this: It shall not
be, says Jehovah.
⁴The Lord Jehovah made
me to see this: And, behold,
the Lord Jehovah was
calling to contend by fire.
And it consumed the great
deep, and *it was* devouring
part of it. ⁵Then I said,
Lord Jehovah, I beg You,
stop. How can Jacob stand?
For he *is* small. ⁶Jehovah
repented concerning this: It
shall not be, says the Lord
Jehovah.
⁷He made me see this:
And, behold, the Lord was
standing by the plumbline-
wall, and a plumb-line in
His hand. ⁸And Jehovah
said to me, Amos, what do
you see? And I said, A
plumb-line. And the Lord
said, Behold, I will set a
plumb-line in the midst of
My people Israel. I will not
again pass over him any
more. ⁹And the high places
of Isaac shall be desolated;
and the holy places of Israel
shall be laid waste; and I
will rise against the house
of Jeroboam with the
sword.
¹⁰Then Amaziah the
priest of Bethel sent to
Jeroboam, the king of
Israel, saying, Amos has
plotted against you in the
midst of the house of Israel.
The land is not able to
endure all his words.
¹¹For so Amos says: Jero-
boam shall die by the
sword, and Israel shall
surely go into exile out of
his land. ¹²And Amaziah
said to Amos, Seer, go, flee
for yourself into the land of
Judah, and eat bread there,
and prophesy there. ¹³But

136,15 1961 44,28 1488 310 3954 3954
2 הַלֶּקֶשׁ וְהִנֵּה־לֶקֶשׁ אַחַר גִּזֵּי הַמֶּלֶךְ׃ וְהָיָה אִם־כִּלָּה
it when it And the the after tender the and late the
finished ,was .king of mowings plant behold ,grass

5545 3068 .136 559 776: 6212 398
לֶאֱכוֹל אֶת־עֵשֶׂב הָאָרֶץ וָאֹמַר אֲדֹנָי יְהוִה סְלַח־נָא מִי
How .Please for- ,Jehovah Lord I then the tender the eating
give said ,land plant

1961 38,08 20,63 3068 5162 6996 3290 6965
3 יָקוּם יַעֲקֹב כִּי קָטֹן הוּא׃ נִחַם יְהוָה עַל־זֹאת לֹא תִהְיֶה
shall it not ;this con- Jehovah re- ?(is) he small for ,Jacob can
be cerning pented stand

7378 7121 2009 30,68 136 7200 3541 3068 559
4 אָמַר יְהוָה׃ כֹּה הִרְאַנִי אֲדֹנָי יְהוִה וְהִנֵּה קֹרֵא לָרִב
to was And :Jehovah the showed Thus .Jehovah says
contend calling ,behold Lord me

398 72,27 8415 398 3068 136 784
בָּאֵשׁ אֲדֹנָי יְהוִה וַתֹּאכַל אֶת־תְּהוֹם רַבָּה וְאָכְלָה אֶת־
and ,great the was it And .Jehovah the by
devouring deep consuming Lord fire

6996 3290 6965 499,4 2308 3068 136 559 2506
5 הַחֵלֶק׃ וָאֹמַר אֲדֹנָי יְהוִה חֲדַל־נָא מִי יָקוּם יַעֲקֹב כִּי קָטֹן
small for ,Jacob can How !Please stop ,Jehovah Lord I Then the
stand said .portion

136 559 1961 38,08 1571 2088 3068 5162
6 הוּא׃ נִחַם יְהוָה עַל־זֹאת גַּם־הִיא לֹא תִהְיֶה אָמַר אֲדֹנָי
the says ,be shall not it Also :this con- Jehovah repented he
Lord cerning ?(is)

594 2346 5324 136 1961 7200 3541 3068
7 יְהוִה׃ כֹּה הִרְאַנִי וְהִנֵּה אֲדֹנָי נִצָּב עַל־חוֹמַת אֲנָךְ
plumb- a the by was the And showed He Thus .Jehovah
line of wall standing Lord ,behold ,me

559 5986 7200 4100 3068 559 594 3027
8 וּבְיָדוֹ אֲנָךְ׃ וַיֹּאמֶר יְהוָה אֵלַי מָה־אַתָּה רֹאֶה עָמוֹס וָאֹמַר
I And ?Amos are you What ,me to Jehovah said And a in and
,said seeing .plumbline hand His

38,08 3478 5971 7130 594 7760 2005 136 559 594
אֲנָךְ וַיֹּאמֶר אֲדֹנָי הִנְנִי שָׂם אֲנָךְ בְּקֶרֶב עַמִּי יִשְׂרָאֵל לֹא־
Not .Israel my the in plumb- a am Behold the said And a
people of midst line setting I ,Lord .plumbline

3478 4720 34,46 1116 8074 5674 5730 3254
9 אוֹסִיף עוֹד עֲבוֹר לוֹ׃ וְנָשַׁמּוּ בָּמוֹת יִשְׂחָק וּמִקְדְּשֵׁי יִשְׂרָאֵל
Israel the and ,Isaac high the be will And .him pass any will I
of places holy of places desolated over more again

558 7971 2719 3379 1004 6965 2717
10 יֶחֱרָבוּ וְקַמְתִּי עַל־בֵּית יָרָבְעָם בֶּחָרֶב׃ וַיִּשְׁלַח אֲמַצְיָה
Amaziah sent Then the with Jeroboam the against will I Then be will
.sword of house up rise .waste laid

7194 559 3478 44,28 3379 1008 3548
כֹּהֵן בֵּית־אֵל אֶל־יָרָבְעָם מֶלֶךְ־יִשְׂרָאֵל לֵאמֹר קָשַׁר עָלֶיךָ
against has ,saying ,Israel king the Jeroboam to el Beth- the
you conspired of of priest

3557 776 3201/3808 3478 1004 7130 5986
עָמוֹס בְּקֶרֶב בֵּית יִשְׂרָאֵל לֹא־תוּכַל הָאָרֶץ לְהָכִיל אֶת־
to the is Not .Israel the the in Amos
endure land able of house of midst

34,78 3379 4191 2719 59,86 559 1697 36,05
11 כָּל־דְּבָרָיו׃ כִּי־כֹה אָמַר עָמוֹס בַּחֶרֶב יָמוּת יָרָבְעָם וְיִשְׂרָאֵל
and ,Jeroboam shall the By ,Amos says thus For his all
Israel die sword .words

5986 558 559 127 1540 15,40
12 גָּלֹה יִגְלֶה מֵעַל אַדְמָתוֹ׃ וַיֹּאמֶר אֲמַצְיָה אֶל־עָמוֹס
,Amos to Amaziah said And .land his from go will surely
exile into

8033 3899 398 3063 776 1272 3212 2374
חֹזֶה לֵךְ בְּרַח־לְךָ אֶל־אֶרֶץ יְהוּדָה וֶאֱכָל־שָׁם לֶחֶם וְשָׁם
and bread there and ,Judah the to for flee ,go ,Seer O
there eat of land yourself

do not again prophesy at Bethel any more; for it *is* the king s holy place, and it *is* the royal house.
[14]Then Amos answered and said to Amaziah: I *was* not a prophet, nor *was* I a prophet's son. But I *was* a herdsman and a gatherer *from* sycamore trees.
[15]And Jehovah took me from behind the flock, and Jehovah said to me, Go, prophesy to My people Israel. [16]Now, then, hear the word of Jehovah: You say, Do not prophesy against Israel, and do not drop *words* against the house of Isaac. [17]So Jehovah says this: Your wife shall be a harlot in the city, and your sons and your daughters shall fall by the sword; and your land shall be divided by a line. And you shall die in a defiled land. And Israel shall surely go into exile from his land.

13 תִנָּבֵא׃ וּבֵית אֵל לֹא־תוֹסִיף עוֹד לְהִנָּבֵא כִּי מִקְדַּשׁ־מֶלֶךְ
the holy the king of place for ;prophesy any more do again not el (at) Beth- But .prophesy
14 הוּא וּבֵית מַמְלָכָה הוּא׃ וַיַּעַן עָמוֹס וַיֹּאמֶר אֶל־אֲמַצְיָה
:Amaziah to said and Amos Then answered .(is) it royal the and house ,(is) it
לֹא־נָבִיא אָנֹכִי וְלֹא בֶן־נָבִיא אָנֹכִי כִּי־בוֹקֵר אָנֹכִי וּבוֹלֵס
a and gatherer ,I (was) a herdsman For (was) I a prophet of son and not ,I (was) a prophet not
15 שִׁקְמִים׃ וַיִּקָּחֵנִי יְהוָה מֵאַחֲרֵי הַצֹּאן וַיֹּאמֶר אֵלַי יְהוָה לֵךְ
,Go ,Jehovah to me said and the flock behind from Jehovah took me And syc-amore trees (from)
16 הִנָּבֵא אֶל־עַמִּי יִשְׂרָאֵל׃ וְעַתָּה שְׁמַע דְּבַר־יְהוָה אַתָּה אֹמֵר
are saying You :Jehovah of word the hear ,now And .Israel my people to prophesy
17 לֹא תִנָּבֵא עַל־יִשְׂרָאֵל וְלֹא תַטִּיף עַל־בֵּית יִשְׂחָק׃ לָכֵן כֹּה־
thus There-fore .Isaac of house the against Do drip not ,and .Israel against Do prophesy not
אָמַר יְהוָה אִשְׁתְּךָ בָּעִיר תִּזְנֶה וּבָנֶיךָ וּבְנֹתֶיךָ בַּחֶרֶב יִפֹּלוּ
will fall ,the by sword your and daughters your and sons ,harlot a will be-come city the in Your wife :Jehovah says
וְאַדְמָתְךָ בַּחֶבֶל תְּחֻלָּק וְאַתָּה עַל־אֲדָמָה טְמֵאָה תָּמוּת
will you .die defiled land a upon ,you And be shall .divided line a by your and land
וְיִשְׂרָאֵל גָּלֹה יִגְלֶה מֵעַל אַדְמָתוֹ׃
.land his from go will surely exile into And Israel

CAP. VIII ח

CHAPTER 8

CHAPTER 8

[1]The Lord Jehovah made me see this: And, behold, a basket of summer fruit! [2]And He said, Amos, what do you see? And I said, A basket of summer fruit. And Jehovah said to me, The end has come on My people Israel; I will not again pass over him any more. [3]And they will howl the songs of the temple in that day, declares the Lord Jehovah. The dead bodies *shall be* many; in every place one shall throw *them* out, *saying*, Hush!
[4]Hear this, you who swallow up the poor, even to make the humble of the land to cease, [5]saying, when will the new moon have passed, so that we may buy grain? Or the sabbath, so that we may open the wheat, making smaller the ephah, and to enlarge the shekel, and to

1 2 כֹּה הִרְאַנִי אֲדֹנָי יְהוִה וְהִנֵּה כְּלוּב קָיִץ׃ וַיֹּאמֶר מָה־אַתָּה
you What said He And .summer fruit basket a of and ,behold ;Jehovah the Lord showed me Thus
רֹאֶה עָמוֹס וָאֹמַר כְּלוּב קָיִץ וַיֹּאמֶר יְהוָה אֵלַי בָּא הַקֵּץ
the end Has come to ,me Jehovah said And summer .fruit basket A of I And ,said ?Amos are ,seeing
3 אֶל־עַמִּי יִשְׂרָאֵל לֹא־אוֹסִיף עוֹד עֲבוֹר לוֹ׃ וְהֵילִילוּ שִׁירוֹת
songs the of they And howl will .him pass over any more will I again not ;Israel My people to
הֵיכָל בַּיּוֹם הַהוּא נְאֻם אֲדֹנָי יְהוִה רַב הַפֶּגֶר בְּכָל־מָקוֹם
place every in the ;corpses Many (be will) .Jehovah the Lord declares ,that day in the temple
4 הִשְׁלִיךְ הָס׃ שִׁמְעוּ־זֹאת הַשֹּׁאֲפִים אֶבְיוֹן וְלַשְׁבִּית
to and cease make the poor who you trample ,this Hear (saying) throws one !Hush ,out (them)
5 עֲנִוֵּי־אָרֶץ׃ לֵאמֹר מָתַי יַעֲבֹר הַחֹדֶשׁ וְנַשְׁבִּירָה שֶּׁבֶר
?grain we that so buy may new the ,moon have will When passed ,saying the earth of humble the
וְהַשַּׁבָּת וְנִפְתְּחָה־בָּר לְהַקְטִין אֵיפָה וּלְהַגְדִּיל שֶׁקֶל וּלְעַוֵּת
to and falsify the ,shekel to and enlarge the ephah to diminish the ,wheat open we that so may the Or ,sabbath

falsify the deceitful balances; [6]in order to buy the helpless with silver, and the poor for a pair of sandals; and sell the chaff of the wheat? [7]Jehovah has sworn by the pride of Jacob, Surely I will not ever forget all their works. [8]Shall not the land tremble for this, and all who dwell in it mourn? And all of it shall rise up like the light. And it shall overflow and sink like the Nile of Egypt.

[9]And it shall be in that day, declares the Lord Jehovah, that I will cause the sun to go down at noon, and I will darken the earth in the day of light. [10]And I will turn your feasts to mourning, and all your songs into a dirge. And I will bring up sackcloth on all loins, and baldness on every head. And I will make it like the mourning for an only one; and the end of it *shall be* like a bitter day.

[11]Behold, the days are coming, declares the Lord Jehovah, that I will send a famine into the land; not a famine for bread, nor a thirst for water, but rather *a famine* for hearing the words of Jehovah. [12]And they shall wander from sea to sea, and from the north even to east; they shall roam about to seek the word of Jehovah, and they shall not find *it*. [13]In that day the beautiful virgins and the young men shall faint with thirst. [14]They who swear by the guilt of Samaria, and say, *As* your God lives, O Dan! And, *As* the way of Beer-sheba lives! Even they shall fall, and not rise again.

5275 34 1800 3701 7069 4820 3976
6 מֹאזְנֵי מִרְמָה׃ לִקְנוֹת בַּכֶּסֶף דַּלִּים וְאֶבְיוֹן בַּעֲבוּר נַעֲלָיִם
of pair a for the and the with buy to ;deceit the
sandals poor helpless silver of balances

7911 3290 1347 3068 7650 7666 1250 3651
7 וּמַפַּל בַּר נַשְׁבִּיר׃ נִשְׁבַּע יְהוָה בִּגְאוֹן יַעֲקֹב אִם־אֶשְׁכַּח
will I Not ,Jacob the by Jehovah Has may we the the that
forget of pride sworn .sell wheat of chaff

56 776 7264 2063 4639 3605 5331
8 לָנֶצַח כָּל־מַעֲשֵׂיהֶם׃ הַעַל זֹאת לֹא־תִרְגַּז הָאָרֶץ וְאָבַל
and the will not this Because their all for
mourn ,land quake of ,works ever

2971 8258 1644 3605 216 5927 3427 3605
כָּל־יוֹשֵׁב בָּהּ וְעָלְתָה כָאֹר כֻּלָּהּ וְנִגְרְשָׁה וְנִשְׁקְעָה כִּיאוֹר
the like sinks and it and of all the like will And ?it in who all
of Nile down overflows ;it ,light up rise dwell

935 3068 136 5002 3117 1961 4714
9 מִצְרָיִם׃ וְהָיָה בַּיּוֹם הַהוּא נְאֻם אֲדֹנָי יְהוִה וְהֵבֵאתִי
will I And ,Jehovah the declares ,that day in it And .Egypt
down bring Lord be shall

2015 216 3117 776 2821 6672 8121
10 הַשֶּׁמֶשׁ בַּצָּהֳרָיִם וְהַחֲשַׁכְתִּי לָאָרֶץ בְּיוֹם אוֹר׃ וְהָפַכְתִּי
will I And .light the in the will I and ,noon at sun the
turn of day earth dark make

4975 3605 5921 5927 7015 7892 3605 60 2282
חַגֵּיכֶם לְאֵבֶל וְכָל־שִׁירֵיכֶם לְקִינָה וְהַעֲלֵיתִי עַל־כָּל־מָתְנַיִם
loins all on will I and a into your and to your
up bring ;dirge songs all ,mourning feasts

319 3173 60 7760 7142 7218 3605 5921 8242
שָׂק וְעַל־כָּל־רֹאשׁ קָרְחָה וְשַׂמְתִּיהָ כְּאֵבֶל יָחִיד וְאַחֲרִיתָהּ
it after and only an the like will I And .baldness head every and sack-
;son for mourning it make on cloth

7971 3068 136 5002 935 3117 2009 4751 3117
11 כְּיוֹם מָר׃ הִנֵּה יָמִים בָּאִים נְאֻם אֲדֹנָי יְהוִה וְהִשְׁלַחְתִּי
will I that ,Jehovah the declares are the ,Behold bitter- a like
send Lord ,coming days .ness of day

4325 6772 3808 3899 7458 776 7458
רָעָב בָּאָרֶץ לֹא־רָעָב לַלֶּחֶם וְלֹא־צָמָא לַמַּיִם כִּי אִם־
but for a and for a not the into a
rather ,water thirst not ,bread famine —land famine

5704 6828 3220 5128 3068 1697 8085
12 לִשְׁמֹעַ אֵת דִּבְרֵי יְהוָה׃ וְנָעוּ מִיָּם עַד־יָם וּמִצָּפוֹן וְעַד־
even from and ,sea to from they And .Jehovah the hear to
to north sea stagger will of words

3117 4672 3808 3068 1697 1245 7751 4217
13 מִזְרָח יְשׁוֹטְטוּ לְבַקֵּשׁ אֶת־דְּבַר־יְהוָה וְלֹא יִמְצָאוּ׃ בַּיּוֹם
day In will they and ,Jehovah the seek to will they the
.(it) find not of word about roam ;east

6772 970 3303 1330 5968
הַהוּא תִּתְעַלַּפְנָה הַבְּתוּלֹת הַיָּפוֹת וְהַבַּחוּרִים בַּצָּמָא׃
with the and beautiful virgins the faint will that
.thirst men young

1870 2416/1835 430 2416 559 8111 819 7650
14 הַנִּשְׁבָּעִים בְּאַשְׁמַת שֹׁמְרוֹן וְאָמְרוּ חֵי אֱלֹהֶיךָ דָּן וְחֵי דֶּרֶךְ
the (as) And O your (As) ,say and Samaria the by swearing Those
of way lives !Dan ,God lives of guilt

5750 6965 3808 5307 =884=
בְּאֵר־שָׁבַע וְנָפְלוּ וְלֹא־יָקוּמוּ עוֹד׃
.again rise and they so ,sheba Beer-
up not fall will

CAP. IX ט

CHAPTER 9

CHAPTER 9

[1]I saw the Lord standing by the altar. And He said, Strike the capital of the

3730 5221 559 4196 5324 136 7200
1 רָאִיתִי אֶת־אֲדֹנָי נִצָּב עַל־הַמִּזְבֵּחַ וַיֹּאמֶר הַךְ הַכַּפְתּוֹר
the Strike He And .altar the by standing the saw I
capital ,said Lord

door, and the thresholds will shake; and break them on the head of all of them. And I will kill the last of them with the sword. Not one of them who flees will flee, and not a fugitive of them will escape. ²And if they dig through into Sheol, from there My hand will take them. And if they go up to the heavens, from there I will bring them down. ³And if they hide themselves in the top of Carmel, I will search and take them out from there. And if they hide from My eyes in the bottom of the sea, from there I will command the serpent, and he will bite them. ⁴And if they go into exile before their enemies, from there I will command the sword, and it will kill them. And I will set My eyes on them for evil, and not for good.

⁵And the Lord Jehovah of hosts *is* He who touches the earth so that it melts; and all dwelling in it shall mourn. And all of it will rise up like the Nile, and sink down like the Nile of Egypt. ⁶*It is* He who builds His staircase in the heavens, and He has founded His firmament on the earth; He who calls for the sea-waters, and pours them out on the face of the earth— Jehovah *is* His name.

⁷Are you not like the sons of the Ethiopians to Me, O sons of Israel, declares Jehovah? Have I not brought Israel up out of the land of Egypt, and the Philistines from Caphtor, and the Syrians from Kir? ⁸Behold, the eyes of the Lord Jehovah *are* on the sinful kingdom, and I will destroy it from the face of the earth; only that I will not completely destroy the house of Jacob, declares Jehovah. ⁹For, behold, I will command, and I will shake the house of Israel among all the nations, as one shakes with a sieve; yet

---

Interlinear (read left to right):

7493	55 92	1214	7218	36 05	319	2719
וְיִרְעֲשׁוּ	הַסִּפִּים	וּבְצַעַם	בְּרֹאשׁ	כֻלָּם	וְאַחֲרִיתָם	בְּחֶרֶב
will and shake	the thresholds	break and them	the on head of	of all them.	the last And them of	the with sword

2 — 518 אָם — "If"

2864		5127	44 22	38 08/5127	44 22	518
אֶהֱרֹג		נָס	וְלֹא־יִמָּלֵט	לָהֶם	נָס	פָּלִיט
will I kill.	Not will flee	one of fleeing them	will and escape not	them	a of fugitive.

v2 — 2864 | 75 85 | 8033 | 8064 | 5927 | 518 | 3947 | 3027 | 8033 | 3381
| יַחְתְּרוּ | בִשְׁאוֹל | מִשָּׁם | יָדִי | תִקָּחֵם | וְאִם־יַעֲלוּ | הַשָּׁמַיִם | מִשָּׁם | אוֹרִידֵם |
| dig they though | into Sheol | there | from My hand | take them. | go they And shall | to up if | the heavens, | from there | bring will I down them. |

3 — 2664 | 8033 | 72 18 | 2244 | 518 | 3759 | 7218 | 8033
| וְאִם־יֵחָבְאוּ | בְּרֹאשׁ | הַכַּרְמֶל | מִשָּׁם | אֲחַפֵּשׂ |
| bring will I down them. | hide they And | themselves | the in top of | Carmel, | from there | search will I | them. |

| 3947 | 56 40 | 5048 | 5869 | 7172 | 3220 | 8033 | 6680
| וּלְקַחְתִּים | וְאִם־יִסָּתְרוּ | מִנֶּגֶד | עֵינַי | בְּקַרְקַע | הַיָּם | מִשָּׁם | אֲצַוֶּה |
| take will I and them | they hide if | from before | My eye | the in bottom of | sea, the | from there will I command |

4 — 5175 | 5391 | 32 12 | 762 8 | 6440 | 8033 | 341 | 8033
| אֶת־הַנָּחָשׁ | וּנְשָׁכָם | וְאִם־יֵלְכוּ | בַשְּׁבִי | לִפְנֵי | אֹיְבֵיהֶם | מִשָּׁם |
| the serpent, | and it bite them. | they And go if | into captivity | before | their enemies, | from there |

| 6680 | 2719 | 2026 | 7760 | 5869 | 7451
| אֲצַוֶּה | אֶת־הַחֶרֶב | וַהֲרָגָתַם | וְשַׂמְתִּי | עֵינַי | עֲלֵיהֶם | לְרָעָה |
| will I command | the sword, | and it kill them; | will I and set | My eye | them on | evil for, |

5 — 1 08/38 | 2896 | 136 | 68 30 | 6 35 | 5060 | 776 | 41 27
| וְלֹא | לְטוֹבָה | וַאדֹנָי | יְהוִה | הַצְּבָאוֹת | הַנּוֹגֵעַ | בָּאָרֶץ | וַתָּמוֹג |
| not | good .for | And the Lord | Jehovah | hosts of | who He touches | the earth | that so it melts, |

| 2975 | 59 27 | 3427 | 36 05 | 56 | 2975 | 59 27 | 3427
| וְאָבְלוּ | כָּל־יוֹשְׁבֵי | בָהּ | וְעָלְתָה | כַיְאֹר | כֻלָּהּ | וְשָׁקְעָה | כִּיאֹר |
| mourn and shall | who dwell all | in it, | And will rise up | the like Nile | of all it | and sink down | the like Nile |

6 — 4714 | 1129 | 8064 | 46 09 | 80 64 | 92 | 776 | 3245
| מִצְרָיִם | הַבּוֹנֶה | בַשָּׁמַיִם | מַעֲלוֹתָו | וַאֲגֻדָּתוֹ | עַל־אֶרֶץ | יְסָדָהּ |
| of Egypt. | who He builds | the in heavens | His staircase, | and His firmament | over the earth | it founded He; |

| 7121 | 43 25/32 20 | 8210 | 59 21 | 6440 | 776 | 3068 | 8034
| הַקֹּרֵא | לְמֵי־הַיָּם | וַיִּשְׁפְּכֵם | עַל־פְּנֵי | הָאָרֶץ | יְהוָה | שְׁמוֹ |
| who He calls | the for waters of sea | pours and them out | the on face of | earth— | Jehovah | His name. |

7 — 8808 | 1121 | 35 69 | 11 21 | 3478 | 1121 | 3478 | 5002 | 3068
| הֲלוֹא | כִבְנֵי | כֻשִׁיִּים | אַתֶּם | לִי | בְּנֵי | יִשְׂרָאֵל | נְאֻם־יְהוָה |
| Are not | the like sons | Ethiopians of | you | to me, | sons O | Israel, | Jehovah declares? |

| 38 08 | 3478 | 59 27 | 4714 | 776 | 6430 | 4467
| הֲלוֹא | אֶת־יִשְׂרָאֵל | הֶעֱלֵיתִי | מֵאֶרֶץ | מִצְרַיִם | וּפְלִשְׁתִּיִּים |
| not | Israel | up brought I Have | from of land | Egypt, | Philistines the and |

8 — 3731 | 758 | 7024 | 20 09 | 5869 | 136 | 3068 | 14467
| מִכַּפְתּוֹר | וַאֲרָם | מִקִּיר | הִנֵּה | עֵינֵי | אֲדֹנָי | יְהוִה | בַּמַּמְלָכָה |
| from Caphtor, | and Aram | Kir? from | Behold, the | eyes of | the Lord | Jehovah (are) | the on kingdom |

| 24 03/8045 | 127 | 6440 | 5921 | 8045 | 657 | 3588 | 657
| הַחַטָּאָה | וְהִשְׁמַדְתִּי | אֹתָהּ | מֵעַל | פְּנֵי | הָאֲדָמָה | אֶפֶס | כִּי | לֹא |
| sinful, | destroy will I and | it | from the | face of | earth; | that only | not |

9 — 8045 | 1004 | 3290 | 5002 | 3068 | 2009 | 595
| הַשְׁמֵיד | אַשְׁמִיד | אֶת־בֵּית | יַעֲקֹב | נְאֻם־יְהוָה | כִּי־הִנֵּה | אָנֹכִי |
| fully | destroy will I | the house of | Jacob. | Jehovah declares. | For behold, | I |

| 5128 | 1004 | 1471 | 3478 | 51 28
| מְצַוֶּה | וַהֲנִעוֹתִי | בְכָל־הַגּוֹיִם | אֶת־בֵּית | יִשְׂרָאֵל | כַּאֲשֶׁר | יִנּוֹעַ |
| com-manding, | shake will I and | among all nations the | the house of | Israel, | as | one shakes |

בִּכְבָרָה וְלֹא־יִפּוֹל צְרוֹר אָרֶץ׃ בַּחֶרֶב יָמוּתוּ כֹּל חַטָּאֵי 10
the of sinners all die shall the By sword the (to) ground a pebble shall fall yet not a with sieve

עַמִּי הָאֹמְרִים לֹא־תַגִּישׁ וְתַקְדִּים בַּעֲדֵינוּ הָרָעָה׃ בַּיּוֹם 11
day In the calamity us about come or front in will not near draw saying those My people

הַהוּא אָקִים אֶת־סֻכַּת דָּוִיד הַנֹּפֶלֶת וְגָדַרְתִּי אֶת־פִּרְצֵיהֶן
breaches its wall and up has that fallen David booth the of will I up raise that

וַהֲרִסֹתָיו אָקִים וּבְנִיתִיהָ כִּימֵי עוֹלָם׃ לְמַעַן יִירְשׁוּ אֶת־ 12
may they possess so that ;old the as of days will I and it rebuild will I ,up raise its And ruins

שְׁאֵרִית אֱדוֹם וְכָל־הַגּוֹיִם אֲשֶׁר־נִקְרָא שְׁמִי עֲלֵיהֶם נְאֻם־
declares upon them My name called is whom the nations and all Edom rem- nant the of

יְהוָה עֹשֶׂה זֹּאת׃ הִנֵּה יָמִים בָּאִים נְאֻם־יְהוָה וְנִגַּשׁ 13
shall and near draw ,Jehovah de- clares are coming the days ,Behold .this is who doing Jeho- vah

חוֹרֵשׁ בַּקֹּצֵר וְדֹרֵךְ עֲנָבִים בְּמֹשֵׁךְ הַזָּרַע וְהִטִּיפוּ הֶהָרִים
the mountains will And drip the .seed the of sower grapes he and treads who the ,reaper the plowman

עָסִיס וְכָל־הַגְּבָעוֹת תִּתְמוֹגַגְנָה׃ וְשַׁבְתִּי אֶת־שְׁבוּת עַמִּי 14
My people cap- of tivity the I And turn will be will .dissolved hills the and all ,must

יִשְׂרָאֵל וּבָנוּ עָרִים נְשַׁמּוֹת וְיָשָׁבוּ וְנָטְעוּ כְרָמִים וְשָׁתוּ אֶת־
and drink ,vineyards they and plant shall they and ,dwell shall are which ,desolate the cities they and build shall ,Israel

יֵינָם וְעָשׂוּ גַנּוֹת וְאָכְלוּ אֶת־פְּרִיהֶם׃ וּנְטַעְתִּים עַל־אַדְמָתָם 15
their ,land on will I And them plant their .fruit and eat gardens they And make shall their .wine

וְלֹא יִנָּתְשׁוּ עוֹד מֵעַל אַדְמָתָם אֲשֶׁר־נָתַתִּי לָהֶם אָמַר
says to ,them have I given which their land from again will they uprooted be and not

יְהוָה אֱלֹהֶיךָ׃
your .God Jehovah

not a grain shall fall *to* the ground. 10All the sinners of My people shall die by the sword, *those* who say, The evil shall not draw near, or come in front about us.

11In that day I will raise up the booth of David that has fallen, and will wall up its breaks. And I will raise up its ruins, and I will build it as the days of old; 12so that they may possess the remnant of Edom, and all the nations *on* whom My name is called, declares Jehovah who is doing this.

13Behold, the days are coming: The plowman and the reaper shall draw near, the treader of grapes, and he who draws along the seed. And the mountains will drip must, and all the hills will be dissolved. 14And I will turn back the captivity of My people Israel, and they shall build the cities which are desolate. And they shall dwell and they shall plant vineyards and drink their wine. 15And I will plant them on their land, and they will not be uprooted again from their land which I have given to them, says Jehovah your God.

ע ב ד י ה

LIBER OBADIAE

(THE) BOOK OF OBADIAH

CAPUT. I א

A LITERAL TRANSLATION OF THE BIBLE

THE BOOK OF OBADIAH

1 The vision of Obadiah: So says the Lord Jehovah concerning Edom: We have heard a message from Jehovah, and a messenger is sent among the nations; rise up, and let us rise up against her for battle. 2 Behold, I have given you *to be* small among the nations; you are greatly despised.

3 The pride of your heart has deceived you, dwelling in the clefts of the rock; his dwelling *is* lofty, saying in his heart, Who shall bring me down *to* the ground? 4 Though you rise high as the eagle, and though *you* set your nest between the stars, I will bring you down from there, declares Jehovah. 5 If thieves came to you, if destroyers by night —how you have been cut off!— Would they not have stolen until they had enough? If the grape-gatherers came to you, would they not leave gleanings? 6 How Esau is searched out! His hidden things are sought out! 7 All the men of your covenant have dismissed you to the border. The men who were at peace with you have deceived you *and* have prevailed over you. They are setting your bread *as* a snare under you; there *is* no understanding in him. 8 Shall I not in that day even destroy the wise out of Edom, and understanding out of the mount of Esau, declares Jehovah? 9 And your mighty ones, Teman, shall be afraid, so that each man from the mount of Esau may be cut off by slaughter.

10 Shame shall cover you from the violence against your brother Jacob, and you shall be cut off forever. 11 On the day of your standing on the other *side*, on the

8085 80 52 123 3068 136 559 5662 2377
1 חֲזוֹן עֹבַדְיָה כֹּה־אָמַר אֲדֹנָי יְהוִה לֶאֱדוֹם שְׁמוּעָה שָׁמַעְנוּ
have we heard · message a · concerning Edom · Jehovah · the Lord · says Thus · :Obadiah · The vision of

6965 6965 1471 6735 3068
מֵאֵת יְהוָה וְצִיר בַּגּוֹיִם שֻׁלָּח קוּמוּ וְנָקוּמָה עָלֶיהָ
against her · us let and up rise · Rise ,up · ;sent is · the among nations · a and messenger · ,Jehovah · from

3966 959 1471 5414 6996 2009 4421
2 לַמִּלְחָמָה׃ הִנֵּה קָטֹן נְתַתִּיךָ בַּגּוֹיִם בָּזוּי אַתָּה מְאֹד׃
.greatly · you (are) · being despised · the among ;nations · have I you given · small · ,Behold · .battle for

559 7931 4791 5553 2288 3427 5378 3820 2087
3 זְדוֹן לִבְּךָ הִשִּׁיאֶךָ שֹׁכְנִי בְחַגְוֵי־סֶּלַע מְרוֹם שִׁבְתּוֹ אֹמֵר
saying · his ;dwelling · lofty (is) · the ,rock · the in of clefts · dwelling · deceived has ,you · your heart · The of pride

3556 996 5404 1361 776 3381 4310 3820
4 בְּלִבּוֹ מִי יוֹרִדֵנִי אָרֶץ׃ אִם־תַּגְבִּיהַּ כַּנֶּשֶׁר וְאִם־בֵּין כּוֹכָבִים
the stars · between and though · the as ,eagle · rise you high · Though · the (to) ?ground · bring shall down me · Who · his in ,heart

935 1590 3068 5002 3381 7064 7760
5 שִׂים קִנֶּךָ מִשָּׁם אוֹרִידְךָ נְאֻם־יְהוָה׃ אִם־גַּנָּבִים בָּאוּ־לְךָ
to ,you · came · thieves · If · .Jehovah · declares · will I ,down you bring · from there · your ,nest · set to

518 1767 1589 1820 3915 7703 518
אִם־שׁוֹדְדֵי לַיְלָה אֵיךְ נִדְמֵיתָה הֲלוֹא יִגְנְבוּ דַּיָּם אִם־
If · their ?sufficiency · have they stolen · Would not · been have you !(them) like · how · by —night · those destroying · if

6215 2664 5956 7604 3808 935 1219
6 בֹּצְרִים בָּאוּ לָךְ הֲלוֹא יַשְׁאִירוּ עֹלֵלוֹת׃ אֵיךְ נֶחְפְּשׂוּ עֵשָׂו
!Esau · searched is out · How · ?gleanings · they leave · would not · to you · came · pick-ing grapes · those

1285 582 3605 7971 1366 5704 4710 1158
7 נִבְעוּ מַצְפֻּנָיו׃ עַד־הַגְּבוּל שִׁלְּחוּךָ כֹּל אַנְשֵׁי בְרִיתֶךָ
your ;covenant · men the of · all · have they ,you dismissed · the border · To · hidden his !things · are sought

8478 4204 7760 3899 7965 582 3201 5377
הִשִּׁיאוּךָ יָכְלוּ לְךָ אַנְשֵׁי שְׁלֹמֶךָ לַחְמְךָ יָשִׂימוּ מָזוֹר תַּחְתֶּיךָ
under ;you · a (as) snare · are they setting · Your bread · your .peace · men the of · over have (and) you prevailed · de-luded · they you

6 3068 5002 3117 8394 369
8 אֵין תְּבוּנָה בּוֹ׃ הֲלוֹא בַּיּוֹם הַהוּא נְאֻם־יְהוָה וְהַאֲבַדְתִּי
I even destroy · ,Jehovah declares · ,that · the in day · Shall not · in .him · under standing · there no is

8487 1368 2865 6215 2022 8394 123 2450
9 חֲכָמִים מֵאֱדוֹם וּתְבוּנָה מֵהַר עֵשָׂו׃ וְחַתּוּ גִבּוֹרֶיךָ תֵּימָן
Teman · your ,ones mighty · shall And afraid be · ?Esau · the from of mountain · under-standing · and Edom from · wise the ones

3290 251 2555 6993 6215 2022 376 3772 4616
10 לְמַעַן יִכָּרֶת־אִישׁ מֵהַר עֵשָׂו מִקָּטֶל׃ מֵחֲמַס אָחִיךָ יַעֲקֹב
Jacob · your brother · the from against violence · slaugh- ;ter · by · Esau · the from of mountain · each man · be may off cut · so that

3117 5048 5975 3117 5769 3772 955 3680
11 תְּכַסְּךָ בוּשָׁה וְנִכְרַתָּ לְעוֹלָם׃ בְּיוֹם עֲמָדְךָ מִנֶּגֶד בְּיוֹם
the on of day · ,opposite · your standing · the On of day · .forever · shall you off cut be · and ,shame · shall you cover

day that the strangers take
his force captive, and foreigners enter his gates, and
cast lots for Jerusalem,
even you *were* like one of
them.
12 But you should not
have looked on the day of
your brother, on the day of
his alienation; nor should
you have rejoiced over the
sons of Judah in the day of
their destruction; nor
should you have enlarged
your mouth in the day of
distress.
13 You should not
have entered into My
people's gate on the day of
his calamity, nor should you
have looked on his evil on
the day of his calamity; nor
should you have sent out
against his force in the day
of his calamity.
14 Nor
should you have stood on
the crossways to cut off
those of him who escaped.
Nor should you have shut
up his survivors in the day of
distress.
15 For the day of
Jehovah *is* near on all the
nations: As you have done,
it shall be done to you; your
reward shall return on your
head!
16 For as you have
drunk on My holy mount, *so*
all the nations shall
continually drink. Yea, they
shall drink and shall
swallow; and they will be as
if they had not been.
17 But the ones who
escaped shall be on Mount
Zion, and it shall be holy.
And the house of Jacob
shall possess their own
possessions.
18 And the
house of Jacob shall be a
fire, and the house of
Joseph a flame, and the
house of Esau for straw.
And they shall burn among
them, and consume them.
And no survivor shall be to
the house of Esau, for
Jehovah has spoken.
19 And *those of* Negeb shall
possess the mountain of
Esau, and the low country of
the Philistines; and they
shall possess Ephraim's
fields, and Samaria's fields;
and Benjamin *shall possess*
Gilead.
20 And the exiles of
this force to the sons of
Israel who shall possess
the land of the Canaanites
to Zarephath; even the
exiles of Jerusalem who *are*

3032 3389 8179 935 5235 2428 2114 7617
שבות זרים חילו ונכרים באו שערו ועל-ירושלם ידו
cast Jerusalem and his entered and his the taking
for gates foreigners ,force strangers captive

3117 251 3117 7200 408 259 1571 1486
12 גורל גם-אתה כאחד מהם: ואל-תרא ביום-אחיך ביום
the on your the on should you But of like you even ,lots
of day brother of day looked have not .them one (were)

1230 408 6 3117 3063 1121 8056 408 5235
נכרו ואל-תשמח לבני-יהודה ביום אבדם ואל-תגדל
should you and their the in Judah the over should you and es- his
enlarged have not ;destruction of day of sons rejoiced have not ;trangement

408 343 3117 5971 8179 935 408 6864 3117 6310
13 פיך ביום צרה: אל-תבוא בשער-עמי ביום אידם אל-
not their the on My the into should You not .distress the in your
;calamity of day people of gate entered have of day mouth

2428 7971 408 343 3117 7451 1571 7200
תרא גם-אתה ברעתו ביום אידו ואל-תשלחנה בחילו
his against should you and his the on his on you even should
force out sent have not ,calamity of day evil looked have

6412 3772 6563 5921 5975 408 343 3117
14 ביום אידו: ואל-תעמד על-הפרק להכרית את-פליטיו
his off cut to the upon should you And his the in
;escapees ,crossways stood have not .calamity of day

5921 3068 3117 7138 6864 3117 8300 5762 408
15 ואל-תסגר שרידיו ביום צרה: כי-קרוב יום-יהוה על-
upon Jehovah the near For .distress the in sur- his should you and
of day (is) of day vivors up shut have not

7218 7725 1576 6213 6213 1471 3605
כל-הגוים כאשר עשית יעשה לך גמלך ישוב בראשך:
your on shall your to shall it have you as the all
.head return reward ;you done be ,done ;nations

8548 1471 3605 8354 6944 2022 5921 8354
16 כי כאשר שתיתם על-הר קדשי ישתו כל-הגוים תמיד
con- the all shall holi- My the upon have you as For
.tinually nations drink ,ness of mountain drunk

6413 1961 6726 2022 1961 3808 1961 3886 8354
17 ושתו ולעו והיו כלוא היו: ובהר ציון תהיה פליטה
who those shall Zion the on But had they not as and swal- and they And
,escaped have be of mountain .been be will lowed ,drank

1004 1961 4180 3290 1004 3423 6944 1961
18 והיה קדש וירשו בית יעקב את מורשיהם: והיה בית-
the shall And own their Jacob the shall and ;holy it and
of house be .possessions of house possess be shall

1814 7179 6215 1004 3852 3130 1004 784 3290
יעקב אש ובית יוסף להבה ובית עשו לקש ודלקו בהם
among they And for Esau the and a Joseph the and a Jacob
them burn shall .straw of house ,flame of house ,fire

1696 3068 6215 1004 8300 1961 3808 398
ואכלום ולא-יהיה שריד לבית עשו כי יהוה דבר:
has Jehovah for ,Esau the to sur- a shall there And con- and
.spoken of house vivor be not .them sume

3423 6430 8219 6215 2022 5045 3423
19 וירשו הנגב את-הר עשו והשפלה את-פלשתים וירשו
they and ;Philistines the low the and ,Esau the (of those) shall And
possess shall of country of mountain Negev possess

1568 1144 8111 7704 669 7704
את-שדה אפרים ואת שדה שמרון ובנימן את-הגלעד:
.Gilead (with) and ;Samaria the and Ephraim fields the
Benjamin of fields of

6886 3669 834 3478 1121 2088 2828 1546
20 וגלת החל-הזה לבני ישראל אשר-כנענים עד-צרפת
;Zarephath (is) the who Israel the to this the And
to Canaanites (are) of sons force of exiles

5927 5045 5892 3423 5614 834 3389 1546
21 וגלת ירושלם אשר בספרד ירשו את ערי הנגב: ועלו
shall And the the shall they ;Sepharad in who Jerusalem the and
up go .Negev of cities possess (are) of exile

in Sepharad shall possess the cities of the Negeb.
21 And deliverers shall go up into the mountain of Zion to judge the mountain of Esau; and the kingdom shall be to Jehovah.

3068 1961 6215 2022 8199 6726 2022 3462

מוֹשִׁעִים בְּהַר צִיּוֹן לִשְׁפֹּט אֶת־הַר עֵשָׂו וְהָיְתָה לַיהוָה

to Jehovah | shall be and | ;Esau | the mountain of | to judge | Zion | into the mountain of | those delivering

4410

הַמְּלוּכָה׃

.Kingdom the

יונה

LIBER JONAE

(THE) BOOK OF JONAH

CAPUT. I א

CHAPTER 1

A LITERAL TRANSLATION OF THE BIBLE

THE BOOK OF JONAH

CHAPTER 1

[1]And the word of Jehovah was to Jonah, the son of Amittai, saying, [2]Rise up, go to Nineveh, the great city, and cry out against it; for their evil has come up before Me. [3]But Jonah rose up to flee to Tarshish from the presence of Jehovah. And *he* went down to Joppa, and he found a ship going to Tarshish. And he gave its fare, and went down into it, in order to go with them to Tarshish, from before the face of Jehovah.

[4]But Jehovah hurled a great wind into the sea, and there was a great storm in the sea, and the ship *was* thought to be broken. [5]And the sailors were afraid, and each man cried to his god. And they threw out the utensils in the ship, into the sea, to lighten *it* off of them. But Jonah had gone down into the hold of the ship; and he lay down, and was sound asleep. [6]And the chief of the seamen came near to him and said to him, What *is it* to you, O sound sleeper? Rise up and cry out to your God! It may be our god will notice us, and we will not perish. [7]And they said, each man to his companion, Come and let us cast lots, that we may know on whose account this evil *occurred* to us. And they cast lots, and the lot fell on Jonah. [8]And they said to him, Please tell us on account of whom *has* this evil *occurred* to us? What *is* your work? And

3212 6963 559 573 1121 3124 3068/1697 1961

1 וַיְהִי דְּבַר־יְהוָה אֶל־יו�ֹנָה בֶן־אֲמִתַּי לֵאמֹר׃ קוּם לֵךְ

2 go ,Arise ,saying ,Amittai the of son Jonah to Jehovah the of word And was

7451 5927 7121 1419 5892 5210

אֶל־נִינְוֵה הָעִיר הַגְּדוֹלָה וּקְרָא עָלֶיהָ כִּי־עָלְתָה רָעָתָם

their evil come up has for against it; cry out and ,great the city ,Nineveh to

3381 3068 64 40 8659 1272 3124 6965 6440

3 לְפָנָי׃ וַיָּקָם יוֹנָה לִבְרֹחַ תַּרְשִׁישָׁה מִלִּפְנֵי יְהוָה וַיֵּרֶד

went and to down Jeho- ;vah from before Tarshish to flee to Jonah rose But up before .Me

3381 7939 5414 8659 935 591 4572 3305

יָפוֹ וַיִּמְצָא אָנִיָּה ׀ בָּאָה תַרְשִׁישׁ וַיִּתֵּן שְׂכָרָהּ וַיֵּרֶד בָּהּ

into it went down and its ,fare he and gave ;Tarshish to going ship a he And found .Joppa

7307 2904 3068 3068 6440 8659 935

4 לָבוֹא עִמָּהֶם תַּרְשִׁישָׁה מִלִּפְנֵי יְהוָה׃ וַיהוָה הֵטִיל רוּחַ־

a wind hurled But Jehovah .Jehovah from before ,Tarshish to with them go to

2803 591 3220 1419 5591 1961 3220 1419

גְּדוֹלָה אֶל־הַיָּם וַיְהִי סַעַר־גָּדוֹל בַּיָּם וְהָאֳנִיָּה חִשְּׁבָה

(was) thought the and ship the in ,sea great a storm there and was the sea into great

2904 430 376 2199 4419 3372 7665

5 לְהִשָּׁבֵר׃ וַיִּירְאוּ הַמַּלָּחִים וַיִּזְעֲקוּ אִישׁ אֶל־אֱלֹהָיו וַיָּטִלוּ

they and hurled his ,gods to each man and cried the ,sailors were And afraid be to .broken

3124 5921 7043 3220 591 834 3627

אֶת־הַכֵּלִים אֲשֶׁר בָּאֳנִיָּה אֶל־הַיָּם לְהָקֵל מֵעֲלֵיהֶם וְיוֹנָה

And Jonah upon from .them lighten to (it) the sea into the in ship which (were) utensils the

7227 7126 7290 7901 5600 3411 3381

6 יָרַד אֶל־יַרְכְּתֵי הַסְּפִינָה וַיִּשְׁכַּב וַיֵּרָדַם׃ וַיִּקְרַב אֵלָיו רַב

the of chief him to came And near was and .asleep sound he and ,down laid ,ship the re- of cesses the into had down gone

430 7121 6963 7290 4100 559 2259

הַחֹבֵל וַיֹּאמֶר לוֹ מַה־לְּךָ נִרְדָּם קוּם קְרָא אֶל־אֱלֹהֶיךָ

your !God to cry out ,Arise sound O ?sleeper to What ,you (it is) to ,him said and the ,seamen

376 559 6 3808 430 6245 194

7 אוּלַי יִתְעַשֵּׁת הָאֱלֹהִים לָנוּ וְלֹא נֹאבֵד׃ וַיֹּאמְרוּ אִישׁ אֶל־

to each man they And said will we .perish and not ,us of the god take will notice Per- haps

2063 7451 7945 3045 1486 5307 3212 7453

רֵעֵהוּ לְכוּ וְנַפִּילָה גוֹרָלוֹת וְנֵדְעָה בְּשֶׁלְּמִי הָרָעָה הַזֹּאת

this (happened) evil whose on account may we that know ,lots us let and cast ,Go com- his ,panion

559 3124 1486 5307 1486 5307

8 לָנוּ וַיַּפִּלוּ גּוֹרָלוֹת וַיִּפֹּל הַגּוֹרָל עַל־יוֹנָה׃ וַיֹּאמְרוּ אֵלָיו

,him to they And said .Jonah on lot the fell and ,lots they And cast to .us

4399 4100 2063 7451 4310 4994 5046

הַגִּידָה־נָּא לָנוּ בַּאֲשֶׁר לְמִי־הָרָעָה הַזֹּאת לָנוּ מַה־מְּלַאכְתְּךָ

?work your What (is) to ?us this (is) evil whom account of on to us Please tell from where do you come? What *is* your country, and of what people *are* you? ⁹And he said to them, I *am* a Hebrew. And I fear Jehovah, the God of Heaven, who has made the sea and the dry land. ¹⁰And the men were terrified *with* fear; and said to him, What is this you have done? For the men knew that he was fleeing from before the face of Jehovah, because he had told them.

¹¹And they said to him, What shall we do to you, that the sea may be calm from on us? For the sea was going on and being stormy. ¹²And he said to them, Take me up and throw me out into the sea. And the sea will be calm from on you. For I know that this great storm *is* on you on account of me. ¹³But the men rowed to return to the dry land; but they were not able, for the sea was going on and being stormy against them. ¹⁴And they cried out to Jehovah, and said, We beseech You, O Jehovah; we beseech You, do not let us perish for this man's life; and do not lay innocent blood on us. For You, O Jehovah, have done as You desired. ¹⁵And they lifted Jonah up and threw him into the sea; and the sea ceased from its raging. ¹⁶Then the men feared Jehovah *with* a great fear, and offered a sacrifice to Jehovah, and vowed vows.

9
   370   935   4100   776   4100   5971   559
וַיֹּאמֶר אֲלֵהֶם עִבְרִי אָנֹכִי וְאֶת־יְהוָה אֱלֹהֵי הַשָּׁמַיִם אֲנִי יָרֵא

he And | (are) people | from And | your | What | you do | from And
said ?you | what | ?country (is) | ?come | where

3373 | 80 64 | 430 | 3068/5002 | 5680
אֲלֵהֶם עִבְרִי אָנֹכִי וְאֶת־יְהוָה אֱלֹהֵי הַשָּׁמַיִם אֲנִי יָרֵא
,fear I | heavens the | God the | Jehovah And | I | a
of | .(am) Hebrew | ,them to

10
  834 6213 3220 3006 3372 582 3373
אֲשֶׁר־עָשָׂה אֶת־הַיָּם וְאֶת־הַיַּבָּשָׁה וַיִּירְאוּ הָאֲנָשִׁים יִרְאָה

(with) | men the | were And | dry the | and the | has | who
fear | afraid | land | sea | made

582 | 3045 | 6213 | 4100 | 559 | 1419
גְדוֹלָה וַיֹּאמְרוּ אֵלָיו מַה־זֹּאת עָשִׂיתָ כִּי־יָדְעוּ הָאֲנָשִׁים כִּי

that the | knew For | have you | this What | to | they And | .great
men | ?done (is) | ,him | said

11
  6440 3068 1272 5046 559
מִלִּפְנֵי יְהוָה הוּא בֹרֵחַ כִּי הִגִּיד לָהֶם וַיֹּאמְרוּ אֵלָיו

to | they And | to | had he | for | was | he | Jehovah | from
him | said | .them | (it) told | ,fleeing | before

5490 | 3212 | 3220 | 59 | 3220 | 8367 | 6213
מַה־נַּעֲשֶׂה לָּךְ וְיִשְׁתֹּק הַיָּם מֵעָלֵינוּ כִּי הַיָּם הוֹלֵךְ וְסֹעֵר

being and was | the | For | upon from | the | may that | we shall What
.stormy on going | sea | ?us | sea calm become | you do

12
  559 75 53 04 29 20:32 8 367 3220
וַיֹּאמֶר אֲלֵיהֶם שָׂאוּנִי וַהֲטִילֻנִי אֶל־הַיָּם וְיִשְׁתֹּק הַיָּם

the | will Then | the | into | hurl and | me Lift | ,them to | he And
sea | calmed be | .sea | me | up | said

5921 | 2088 | 1419 | 5591 | 45 79 | 3045 | 5921
מֵעֲלֵיכֶם כִּי יוֹדֵעַ אָנִי כִּי בְשֶׁלִּי הַסַּעַר הַגָּדוֹל הַזֶּה עֲלֵיכֶם

upon | this | great | storm | account on | that I | know For | upon from
you (is) | me of | .you

13
  2864 582 7725 3006 3808 3201 3220
וַיַּחְתְּרוּ הָאֲנָשִׁים לְהָשִׁיב אֶל־הַיַּבָּשָׁה וְלֹא יָכֹלוּ כִּי הַיָּם

the | for | were they | but | the | to | bring to | the | But
sea | ,able | not | ,land dry | back | men | rowed

14
  3212 5490 7121 30 68 559 577 3068
הוֹלֵךְ וְסֹעֵר עֲלֵיהֶם וַיִּקְרְאוּ אֶל־יְהוָה וַיֹּאמְרוּ אָנָּה יְהוָה

O | ,Please ,said and | Jehovah to | they And | against | being and | was
,Jehovah | out cried | .them | stormy | on going

408 | 4994 | 6 | 5315 | 376 | 88:20 | 5414 | 408 | 59:21 | 1818
אַל־נָא נֹאבְדָה בְּנֶפֶשׁ הָאִישׁ הַזֶּה וְאַל־תִּתֵּן עָלֵינוּ דָּם

blood | upon | lay do | and | ,this | man's | because | us let | please not
us | not | life of | perish

15
  5355 3068 68:30 2654 6215 5375
נָקִיא כִּי־אַתָּה יְהוָה כַּאֲשֶׁר חָפַצְתָּ עָשִׂיתָ וַיִּשְׂאוּ

they And | You (so) | You | as | O | ,You | For | inno-
up lifted | .done have | .desired | ,Jehovah | cent

16
  5087 3372 2197 3220 5975 3220 2904 24:31
אֶת־יוֹנָה וַיְטִלֻהוּ וַיַּעֲמֹד הַיָּם מִזַּעְפּוֹ וַיִּירְאוּ

And | its from | the | stood and | the | into | hurled and | Jonah
feared | .raging | sea | (still) | ;sea | him

582 | 3373 | 1419 | 3068 | 2076 | 2077 | 68:3
הָאֲנָשִׁים יִרְאָה גְדוֹלָה אֶת־יְהוָה וַיִּזְבְּחוּ־זֶבַח לַיהוָה

to | sac- a | they and | ,Jehovah | great | a (with) | the
,Jehovah | rifice | offered | fear | men

5087 | 5088
וַיִּדְּרוּ נְדָרִים

.vows | and
vowed

CAP. II ב

CHAPTER 2

¹⁷And Jehovah had appointed a great fish to swallow Jonah. And Jonah was in the belly of the fish

1
  4487 3068 1710 11 04 3124 1961 3124 4578
וַיְמַן יְהוָה דָּג גָּדוֹל לִבְלֹעַ אֶת־יוֹנָה וַיְהִי יוֹנָה בִּמְעֵי

the in | Jonah | And | Jonah | to | great | a | Jeho- had Now
of belly | was | swallow | fish | vah appointed

three days and three nights.

CHAPTER 2

[1]And Jonah prayed to Jehovah his God out of the belly of the fish. [2]And *he* said, I cried out to Jehovah from my distress. And He answered me. Out of the belly of Sheol I cried for help, *and* You heard my voice. [3]For You cast me *into the* deep, into the heart of the seas; and the current surrounded me; all Your breakers and Your waves passed over me. [4]And I said, I am cast off from Your eyes; yet I will again look to Your holy temple. [5]Waters encompassed me, *even* to *my* soul; the depth surrounded me; seaweed *was* bound to my head. [6]I went down to the bases of the mountains; the earth with her bars *was* about me forever. But You brought up my life from the pit, O Jehovah my God. [7]When my soul fainted within me, I remembered Jehovah; and my prayer came to You, to Your holy temple. [8]Those who observe vanities of idolatry forsake their kindness; [9]but I will sacrifice to You with the voice of thanksgiving; I will fulfill that which I have vowed. Salvation *belongs* to Jehovah!

[10]And Jehovah spoke to the fish, and it vomited Jonah out onto the dry land.

CHAPTER 3

[1]And the word of Jehovah was to Jonah the second time, saying, [2]Rise up, go to Nineveh, the great city, and cry out to it the proclamation that I am declaring to you. [3]And Jonah rose up and went to Nineveh, according to the word of Jehovah. And

3124 6419 3915 7969 3117 7969 1709

2 הַדָּג שְׁלֹשָׁה יָמִים וּשְׁלֹשָׁה לֵילוֹת׃ וַיִּתְפַּלֵּל יוֹנָה אֶל־

to Jonah Then prayed .nights three and days three the fish

6864 7768 559 1710 1578 430 3068

3 יְהוָה אֱלֹהָיו מִמְּעֵי הַדָּגָה׃ וַיֹּאמֶר קָרָאתִי מִצָּרָה לִי

to me the from distress cried I out ,said and ,fish the the from of stomach his God Jehovah

696 8085 7768 7585 990 6030 3068

אֶל־יְהוָה וַיַּעֲנֵנִי מִבֶּטֶן שְׁאוֹל שִׁוַּעְתִּי שָׁמַעְתָּ קוֹלִי׃

my .voice You (and) heard cried I help for Sheol the From of belly He and .me answered Jehovah to

4867 3605 5437 5104 3220 3824 4688 7993

4 וַתַּשְׁלִיכֵנִי מְצוּלָה בִּלְבַב יַמִּים וְנָהָר יְסֹבְבֵנִי כָּל־מִשְׁבָּרֶיךָ

Your breakers All surrounded .me the and current waters the into of heart (the into) ,depths You For me threw

389 5869 6440 1644 559 5674 5924 1530

5 וְגַלֶּיךָ עָלַי עָבָרוּ׃ וַאֲנִי אָמַרְתִּי נִגְרַשְׁתִּי מִנֶּגֶד עֵינֶיךָ אַךְ

Only Your eyes from before am I off cast ,said I And .passed over me Your and waves

5315 5704 4325 661 6944 1964 5027 3254

6 אוֹסִיף לְהַבִּיט אֶל־הֵיכַל קָדְשֶׁךָ׃ אֲפָפוּנִי מַיִם עַד־נֶפֶשׁ

the .soul to Waters encompassed me Your .holy temple to look will I again

3381 2022 7095 7218 2282 5488 5437 8415

7 תְּהוֹם יְסֹבְבֵנִי סוּף חָבוּשׁ לְרֹאשִׁי׃ לְקִצְבֵי הָרִים יָרַדְתִּי

went I ;down the mountains the to of bases my to .head was bound seaweed surrounded ;me The deep

3068 2416 7845 5927 5769 1157 1280 776

הָאָרֶץ בְּרִחֶיהָ בַעֲדִי לְעוֹלָם וַתַּעַל מִשַּׁחַת חַיַּי יְהוָה

O Jehovah my ,life the from pit You But up brought .forever (was) me about her with bars the earth

935 2142 3068 5315 5848 430

8 אֱלֹהָי׃ בְּהִתְעַטֵּף עָלַי נַפְשִׁי אֶת־יְהוָה זָכָרְתִּי וַתָּבוֹא

came and I ;remembered Jehovah my ,soul within me fainted When my .God

7723 1892 8104 6944 1964 8605

9 אֵלֶיךָ תְּפִלָּתִי אֶל־הֵיכַל קָדְשֶׁךָ׃ מְשַׁמְּרִים הַבְלֵי־שָׁוְא

idolatry vanities of who Those to heed pay Your .holy temple to my ,prayer to You

5087 834 2076 8426 6963 5800 2617

10 חַסְדָּם יַעֲזֹבוּ׃ וַאֲנִי בְּקוֹל תּוֹדָה אֶזְבְּחָה־לָּךְ אֲשֶׁר נָדַרְתִּי

have I vowed that which to ;You will sacrifice thanks-giving the with of voice but I ;forsake their kindness

6958 1709 3068 589 3068 3444 7999

11 אֲשַׁלֵּמָה יְשׁוּעָתָה לַיהוָה׃ וַיֹּאמֶר יְהוָה לַדָּג וַיָּקֵא אֶת־

it and vomited the to ,fish Jehovah And spoke .Jehovah to salvation (belongs) will I fulfill

3006 3124

יוֹנָה אֶל־הַיַּבָּשָׁה׃

dry the .land on to Jonah

CAP. III ג

CHAPTER 3

5210 3212 6965 559 8145 3124 3068 1697 1961

1 וַיְהִי דְבַר־יְהוָה אֶל־יוֹנָה שֵׁנִית לֵאמֹר׃ קוּם לֵךְ אֶל־נִינְוֵה
2

,Nineveh to go ,Arise ,saying second the ,time Jonah to Jehovah the of word And came

7151 7121 1419 5892

הָעִיר הַגְּדוֹלָה וּקְרָא אֵלֶיהָ אֶת־הַקְּרִיאָה אֲשֶׁר אָנֹכִי

I that proclamation the it to cry and out great the city

3068 1697 5210 3212 3124 6965 1696

3 דֹּבֵר אֵלֶיךָ׃ וַיָּקָם יוֹנָה וַיֵּלֶךְ אֶל־נִינְוֵה כִּדְבַר יְהוָה

.Jehovah's according word to ,Nineveh to and went ,Jonah rose And up to .you de- am claring

Nineveh was a great city to God, of three days' journey. [4]And Jonah began to enter a day's journey into the city. And he cried out and said, Yet forty days and Nineveh shall be overthrown!

[5]And the men of Nineveh believed in God; and they called a fast, and put on sackclothes, from the greatest of them even to the least of them. [6]And the word touched even to the king of Nineveh, and he arose from his throne; and he took his robe from him, and covered himself *with* sackcloth; and sat on the ashes. [7]And he cried and said in Nineveh by the decree of the king and of his great ones, saying, Do not let man or beast, herd or flock, taste anything; do not let them feed nor let them drink water. [8]But let man and beast be covered *with* sackcloth. And let them call with strength to God. And let them each one turn from his evil way, and from the violence that *is* in their palms. [9]Who knows? He may turn, and God may repent and turn away from the glow of His anger, that we do not perish.

[10]And God saw their works, that they turned from their evil way. And God *was* compassionate over the evil that He had declared to do to them, and He did not do *it*.

ונינוה היתה עיר־גדולה לאלהים מהלך שלשת ימים׃
.days three a journey ,God to great city a was Now Nineveh

4 ויחל יונה לבוא בעיר מהלך יום אחד ויקרא ויאמר
,said and he And cried out .one day journey a of the into city to enter Jonah And began

5 עוד ארבעים יום ונינוה נהפכת׃ ויאמינו אנשי נינוה
Nineveh men the of And believed be shall !overthrown Nineveh and days forty Yet

באלהים ויקראו־צום וילבשו שקים מגדולם ועד־קטנם׃
their .least even to their from greatest sack- ;clothes put and on a fast they and proclaimed ;God in

6 ויגע הדבר אל־מלך נינוה ויקם מכסאו ויעבר אדרתו
robe his he and off took his from ,throne he and arose ,Nineveh the of king even to the word And touched

7 מעליו ויכס שק וישב על־האפר׃ ויזעק ויאמר בנינוה
in Nineveh said and he And cried the .ashes on sat and (with) sackcloth covered and him from

מטעם המלך וגדליו לאמר האדם והבהמה הבקר
the herd ,beast the and The man ,saying his and ,ones great the king's the by decree

והצאן אל־יטעמו מאומה אל־ירעו ומים אל־ישתו׃
them let .drink not and water them let not ,feed ;anything taste let not the and ,flock

8 ויתכסו שקים האדם והבהמה ויקראו אל־אלהים
God to let And call them .beast and man (with) sackcloth let But covered be

בחזקה וישבו איש מדרכו הרעה ומן־החמס אשר
that (is) the violence and from ,evil his from way each man let And turn with .strength

9 בכפיהם׃ מי־יודע ישוב ונחם האלהים ושב מחרון אפו
His ,anger the from of glow and turn God may and repent may He ;turn ,knows Who their in .palms

10 ולא נאבד׃ וירא האלהים את־מעשיהם כי־שבו מדרכם
their from way they that turned their ,deeds God saw And will we .perish that not

הרעה וינחם האלהים על־הרעה אשר־דבר לעשות־
do to had He declared that the evil over God And repented .evil

להם ולא עשה׃
did He .(it) do and not to ,them

CAP. IV ד

CHAPTER 4

[1]But it *was* a great calamity to Jonah's eye, and it kindled *anger in* him. [2]And he prayed to Jehovah, and said, Please, O Jehovah, *was* this not my word while I was on my own land? For this reason I

1
2 וירע אל־יונה רעה גדולה ויחר לו׃ ויתפלל אל־יהוה
Jehovah to he And prayed for .him was it and kindled ,great cal- lamity a Jonah's to eye it But

ויאמר אנה יהוה הלוא־זה דברי עד־היותי על־אדמתי
own my ?land on I was while my word this (Was) not O ,Jehovah ,Please ,said and

fled to Tarshish before, for I knew that You *are* a gracious God, and merciful, slow to anger, and of great kindness, and One who repents over calamity.
3And now, O Jehovah, please take my life from me. For better *is* my death than my life.
4And Jehovah said, Is anger rightly kindled in you?
5And Jonah went out from the city, and sat on the east of the city. And he made there a booth for himself, and sat under it in the shade until he should see what would happen in the city.
6And Jehovah God appointed a plant, and it came up over Jonah, to be shade over his head, in order to deliver him from his misery. And Jonah rejoiced over the plant *with* great joy.
7But God appointed a worm at the rising of the dawn of the next day; and it struck the plant; and it dried up.
8And it happened when the sun shone, God had ordained a scorching east wind; and the sun struck Jonah's head, so that he fainted; and he asked for his life to die. And he said, Better *is* my death than my life.
9And God said to Jonah, Is your anger rightly kindled over the plant? And he said, My anger is rightly kindled, *even* to death.
10And Jehovah said, You have had pity on the plant, for which you had not labored, nor made it grow — which was the son of a night, and perished the son of a night —
11and should I not have pity on Nineveh, the great city in which are

410 3045 8659 1272 6923 3651 5921
עַל־כֵּן קִדַּמְתִּי לִבְרֹחַ תַּרְשִׁישָׁה כִּי יָדַעְתִּי כִּי אַתָּה אֵל־
a God | You (are) | that know I | for | to Tarshish | flee | did I first at | Therefore

6258 7451 5921 5162 2617 7227 639 750 7349 2587
3 חַנּוּן וְרַחוּם אֶרֶךְ אַפַּיִם וְרַב־חֶסֶד וְנִחָם עַל־הָרָעָה׃ וְעַתָּה
And now | .calamity | over | One and repents who | ,grace | and of great | ,anger | slow | to ,compassionate | and ,gracious

559 2416 4194 2896 5315 3947 3068
4 יְהוָה קַח־נָא אֶת־נַפְשִׁי מִמֶּנִּי כִּי טוֹב מוֹתִי מֵחַיָּי׃ וַיֹּאמֶר
said And | my than .life | my death | better (is) | For | from .me | life my | please take | O ,Jehovah

3427 5892 3124 3318 2734 3190 3068
5 יְהוָה הַהֵיטֵב חָרָה לָךְ׃ וַיֵּצֵא יוֹנָה מִן־הָעִיר וַיֵּשֶׁב
sat and | the city | from | Jonah | Then out went | to ?you | anger Is kindled | rightly | ,Jehovah

5704 6738 8478 3427 5521 8033 6213 5892 6924
מִקֶּדֶם לָעִיר וַיַּעַשׂ לוֹ שָׁם סֻכָּה וַיֵּשֶׁב תַּחְתֶּיהָ בַּצֵּל עַד
until | the in shade | it under | sat and | a booth | there | for himself | he And made | the of .city | the on east

7021 430 3068 4487 5892 1961 4100 7200
6 אֲשֶׁר יִרְאֶה מַה־יִּהְיֶה בָּעִיר׃ וַיְמַן יְהוָה־אֱלֹהִים קִיקָיוֹן
,plant a | God | Jehovah | And appointed | the in .city | would happen | what | should he see

7451 5337 7218 5921 6738 1961 3124 5921 5927
וַיַּעַל ׀ מֵעַל לְיוֹנָה לִהְיוֹת צֵל עַל־רֹאשׁוֹ לְהַצִּיל לוֹ מֵרָעָתוֹ
his from .misery | him | to deliver | his ,head | over | shade | be to | Jonah | over | it and up came

430 4487 1419 8057 7021 5921 3124 8055
7 וַיִּשְׂמַח יוֹנָה עַל־הַקִּיקָיוֹן שִׂמְחָה גְדוֹלָה׃ וַיְמַן הָאֱלֹהִים
God | But appointed | .great | joy (with) | plant the | over | Jonah | And rejoiced

3001 7021 5221 4283 7837 5927 8438
תּוֹלַעַת בַּעֲלוֹת הַשַּׁחַר לַמָּחֳרָת וַתַּךְ אֶת־הַקִּיקָיוֹן וַיִּיבָשׁ׃
it and .up dried | ,plant the | it and struck | the of ;morrow | the dawn | the in of rising | worm a

2759 6921 7307 430 4487 8121 2224 1961
8 וַיְהִי ׀ כִּזְרֹחַ הַשֶּׁמֶשׁ וַיְמַן אֱלֹהִים רוּחַ קָדִים חֲרִישִׁית
scorching | east | an wind | God | had that appointed | the ,sun | when shone | it And ,was

5315 7592 5968 3124 7218 5921 8121 5221
וַתַּךְ הַשֶּׁמֶשׁ עַל־רֹאשׁ יוֹנָה וַיִּתְעַלָּף וַיִּשְׁאַל אֶת־נַפְשׁוֹ
life his | he And for asked | he that so .fainted | ,Jonah | the of head | on | sun the | And struck

3124 430 559 2416 4194 2896 559 4191
9 לָמוּת וַיֹּאמֶר טוֹב מוֹתִי מֵחַיָּי׃ וַיֹּאמֶר אֱלֹהִים אֶל־יוֹנָה
,Jonah | to | God | said And | my than .life | my death | Better (is) | he And ,said | .die to

5704 2734 3190 559 7021 5921 2734 3190
הַהֵיטֵב חָרָה־לְךָ עַל־הַקִּיקָיוֹן וַיֹּאמֶר הֵיטֵב חָרָה־לִי עַד־
(even) to | me Anger | rightly kindled is | he And ,said | ?plant the | over | to you | anger Is kindled | rightly

3808 834 7021 5921 2347 859 3068 559 4194
10 מָוֶת׃ וַיֹּאמֶר יְהוָה אַתָּה חַסְתָּ עַל־הַקִּיקָיוֹן אֲשֶׁר לֹא־
not | which | plant the | on | had compassion | You | ,Jehovah | said And | .death

6 3915 1121 1961 3915 1121 1431 3808 5998
עָמַלְתָּ בּוֹ וְלֹא גִדַּלְתּוֹ שֶׁבִּן־לַיְלָה הָיָה וּבִן־לַיְלָה אָבָד׃
it .perished | night a | the and of son | was | a night | the which of son | made you ,grow it | and not | with ,it | did you labor

3426 834 1419 5892 5210 5921 2347 3808 589
11 וַאֲנִי לֹא אָחוּס עַל־נִינְוֵה הָעִיר הַגְּדוֹלָה אֲשֶׁר יֶשׁ־בָּהּ
it in | there is | which | great | city the | Nineveh | on | have should compassion | not | And I

more than a hundred and twenty thousand men who do not know between *the* right *and the* left *hand*, and many cattle?

3225 996 3045 3808 834 120 7239 6240 7235

הַרְבֵּה מִשְׁתֵּים־עֶשְׂרֵה רִבּוֹ אָדָם אֲשֶׁר לֹא־יָדַע בֵּין־יְמִינוֹ

his right | between | do know | not | who | men | ten thousand | twelve | than | more

7227 929 8040

לִשְׂמֹאלוֹ וּבְהֵמָה רַבָּה׃

?many | cattle and | his to ,left

מ י כ ה

LIBER MICHAE

(THE) BOOK OF MICAH

CAPUT. I א

CHAPTER 1

A LITERAL TRANSLATION
OF THE BIBLE
THE BOOK OF MICAH

CHAPTER 1

[1]The word of Jehovah that was to Micah of Moresheth in the days of Jotham, Ahaz, *and* Hezekiah, kings of Judah, which he saw on Samaria and Jerusalem.

[2]Let the peoples hear, all of them. Pay attention, O earth, and its fullness. And let the Lord Jehovah be a witness against you, the Lord from His holy temple. [3]For, behold, Jehovah *is* coming out of His place, and will come down and walk on the high places of the earth. [4]And the mountains shall melt under Him, and the valleys shall cleave themselves, as wax before the fire, as waters poured out on a steep place. [5]All this *is* against the transgression of Jacob, and against the sins of the house of Israel. What *is* the transgression of Jacob? Is it not Samaria? And what *are* the high places of Judah? Are they not Jerusalem? [6]And I will make Samaria into ruins of the field, planting places for a vineyard. And I will pour down her stones into the valley; and I will uncover her foundations. [7]And all her carved images shall be beaten to pieces; and all her gifts *for harlotry* shall be burned with fire. And I will make all her idols a desolation. For she gathered *it* from the reward of a harlot, and they shall return to the reward of a harlot. [8]Because of this I will wail and howl; I will go stripped and naked; I will make a wailing like the jackals; yea, mourn like the daughters of an ostrich. [9]For her wounds *are* incurable; for it has come to

---

3147 3117 4183 4318 1961 3068 1697

1 דְּבַר־יְהוָה ׀ אֲשֶׁר הָיָה אֶל־מִיכָה הַמֹּרַשְׁתִּי בִּימֵי יוֹתָם

,Jotham the in of days the Morashthite Micah to was that Jehovah The of word

3389 8111 5921 2372 834 3063 4428 3169 271

אָחָז יְחִזְקִיָּה מַלְכֵי יְהוּדָה אֲשֶׁר־חָזָה עַל־שֹׁמְרוֹן וִירוּשָׁלִָם׃

and .Jerusalem Samaria upon he saw which ,Judah kings of ,Hezekiah Ahaz (and)

3068 136 1961 4393 776 7181 3605 5971 8085

2 שִׁמְעוּ עַמִּים כֻּלָּם הַקְשִׁיבִי אֶרֶץ וּמְלֹאָהּ וִיהִי אֲדֹנָי יְהוִה

Jehovah the Lord let and be its and ,fulness O earth Pay ,attention of all .them the ,peoples hear Let

3318 3068 2009 6944 1964 136 5707

3 בָּכֶם לְעֵד אֲדֹנָי מֵהֵיכַל קָדְשׁוֹ׃ כִּי־הִנֵּה יְהוָה יֹצֵא

com- out (is) ing Jehovah ,behold ,For His .holiness the from of temple the Lord a for ,witness against you

2022 4549 776 1116 5921 1869 3381 4725

4 מִמְּקוֹמוֹ וְיָרַד וְדָרַךְ עַל־בָּמֳתֵי־אָרֶץ׃ וְנָמַסּוּ הֶהָרִים

the mountains shall And melt the .earth high the of places upon and tread will and come down His from ,place

5064 4325 784 6440 1749 1234 6010 8478

תַּחְתָּיו וְהָעֲמָקִים יִתְבַּקָּעוּ כַּדּוֹנַג מִפְּנֵי הָאֵשׁ כְּמַיִם מֻגָּרִים

poured out as waters the ,fire before as wax cleave shall ,themselves the and valleys under ,Him

3478 1004 2403 3605 3290 6588 4174

5 בְּמוֹרָד׃ בְּפֶשַׁע יַעֲקֹב כָּל־זֹאת וּבְחַטֹּאות בֵּית יִשְׂרָאֵל

.Israel the of house the against and of sins ,this all Jacob the Against (is) of transgression a on .slope

3063 1116 4310 3117 3290 6588

מִי־פֶשַׁע יַעֲקֹב הֲלוֹא שֹׁמְרוֹן וּמִי בָּמוֹת יְהוּדָה הֲלוֹא

(they Are) not ?Judah high the of places And (are) what ?Samaria (it Is) not ?Jacob the What of transgression (is)

3754 4302 7704 5856 8111 7760 3389

6 יְרוּשָׁלִָם׃ וְשַׂמְתִּי שֹׁמְרוֹן לְעִי הַשָּׂדֶה לְמַטָּעֵי כָרֶם

vine- .yard a plantings ,field the into of ruins Samaria will I And make ?Jerusalem

3807 6456 3605 1540 3247 68 1516 5064

7 וְהִגַּרְתִּי לַגַּי אֲבָנֶיהָ וִיסֹדֶיהָ אֲגַלֶּה׃ וְכָל־פְּסִילֶיהָ יֻכַּתּוּ

be shall ,smashed graven her images And all will I bare lay her and foundations her ,stones the into valley will I And down pour

8077 7760 6091 3605 784 8313 868 3605

וְכָל־אֶתְנַנֶּיהָ יִשָּׂרְפוּ בָאֵשׁ וְכָל־עֲצַבֶּיהָ אָשִׂים שְׁמָמָה כִּי

For a .desolation will I make her idols and all with ,fire be shall burned her hires and all

7725 2181 868 6908 2181 868

8 מֵאֶתְנַן זוֹנָה קִבָּצָה וְעַד־אֶתְנַן זוֹנָה יָשׁוּבוּ׃ עַל־זֹאת

this Because of shall they .return a harlot the of hire to and ,(them) gath- ered she a harlot the from of hire

4553 6213 6174 7758 3212 3213 5594

אֶסְפְּדָה וְאֵילִילָה אֵילְכָה שֵׁילָל וְעָרוֹם אֶעֱשֶׂה מִסְפֵּד

wailing a will I make and ;naked stripped will I go ;howl and will I wail

935 4347 605 3284 1323 60 8577

9 כַּתַּנִּים וְאֵבֶל כִּבְנוֹת יַעֲנָה׃ כִּי אֲנוּשָׁה מַכּוֹתֶיהָ כִּי־בָאָה

has it come for her wounds incurable (are) For the ostrich the of daughters like and mourn the like ,jackals

Judah; it has reached to the gate of my people, to Jerusalem.

10 Do not declare *it* in Gath; do not sorely weep; in the house of Leaphrah wallow *in* dust. 11 Pass over to them, O dweller of Shaphir, in nakedness of shame. The dweller of Zaanan has not gone out; the mourning of Beth-ezel shall take from you its place of standing. 12 For be grieved for good, the inhabitant of Maroth, for evil came down from Jehovah to the gate of Jerusalem. 13 Inhabitant of Lachish, tie the chariot to the stallion; she *is* the beginning of sin to the daughter of Zion, for the transgressions of Israel were found in you. 14 So you shall give parting gifts to Moresheth-gath. The houses of Achzib *are* for a lying thing to the kings of Israel. 15 I will bring an heir to you again, O dweller of Mareshah. The glory of Israel shall come to Adullam. 16 Make yourself bald, and cut off *your hair* for the sons of your delight. Make your baldness increase like the eagle; for they go into exile from you.

3808 1661 3389 5971 8179 5060 30,63 5704
10 עַד־יְהוּדָה נָגַע עַד־שַׁעַר עַמִּי עַד־יְרוּשָׁלִָם׃ בְּגַת אַל־
not In Gath .Jerusalem to my people the of gate to has it reached ;Judah to

64•28 6083 1036 1004 1058 408 1058 5046
תַּגִּידוּ בָּכוֹ אַל־תִּבְכּוּ בְּבֵית לְעַפְרָה עָפָר הִתְפַּלָּשְׁתִּי׃
.wallow dust (in) Leaphrah the in of house ;weep do not weeping do ;(it) declare

3427 3318 38,08 132,2 6181 8208 3427 5674
11 עִבְרִי לָכֶם יוֹשֶׁבֶת שָׁפִיר עֶרְיָה־בֹשֶׁת לֹא יָצְאָה יוֹשֶׁבֶת
in- the of habitant gone has out Not .shame in of nakedness ,Shaphir inhab- O of itant to ,them Cross over

2342 5979 3947 1009 1004 4553 66:30
12 צַאֲנָן מִסְפַּד בֵּית הָאֵצֶל יִקַּח מִכֶּם עֶמְדָּתוֹ׃ כִּי־חָלָה
For grieved (is) standing its .place from you shall take Haezel Beth- the of wailing ;Zaanon

8179 3068 7451 3381 4796 3427 2896
לְטוֹב יוֹשֶׁבֶת מָרוֹת כִּי־יָרַד רָע מֵאֵת יְהוָה לְשַׁעַר
the to of gate Jehovah from evil came down for ;Maroth inhabi- the of tant for good

7225 3923 3427 7409 4818 7573 3389
13 יְרוּשָׁלִָם׃ רְתֹם הַמֶּרְכָּבָה לָרֶכֶשׁ יוֹשֶׁבֶת לָכִישׁ רֵאשִׁית
be- the of ginning ;Lachish inhabitant of the to stallion chariot the Tie .Jerusalem

3651 3478 6588 4672 67:26 1323 2403
14 חַטָּאת הִיא לְבַת־צִיּוֹן כִּי־בָךְ נִמְצְאוּ פִּשְׁעֵי יִשְׂרָאֵל׃ לָכֵן
There- fore .Israel trans- the of gressions were found in you for ,Zion the to of daughter she (is) sin

44 28 391 342 1004 4182 7964 5414
תִּתְּנִי שִׁלּוּחִים עַל מוֹרֶשֶׁת גַּת בָּתֵּי אַכְזִיב לְאַכְזָב לְמַלְכֵי
the to of kings a for deception (are) Achzib The of houses .Gath Moresheth to parting gifts shall you give

5725 5704 4762 3427 935 3423 57,50 3478
15 יִשְׂרָאֵל׃ עֹד הַיֹּרֵשׁ אָבִי לָךְ יוֹשֶׁבֶת מָרֵשָׁה עַד־עֲדֻלָּם
Adullam To .Mareshah inhabitant of to ,you will I bring the inheritor Again .Israel

7337 8588 1121 1494 7139 3478 3519 935
16 יָבוֹא כְּבוֹד יִשְׂרָאֵל׃ קָרְחִי וָגֹזִּי עַל־בְּנֵי תַּעֲנוּגָיִךְ הַרְחִבִי
Increase your .delight the for of sons and your- shear Make bald self .Israel glory the of shall come

1540 5404 7144
קָרְחָתֵךְ כַּנֶּשֶׁר כִּי־גָלוּ מִמֵּךְ׃
from .you go they into exile for the like ;eagle your baldness

CAP. II ב

CHAPTER 2

1 Woe to those plotting wickedness and preparing evil on their beds! In the light of the morning they practice it, because it is in the power of their hand. 2 And they covet fields, and seize *them*; and houses, and carry *them* away. And they oppress a man and his household, even a man and his inheritance. 3 So Jehovah says this: Behold, I *am* plotting an evil against this family, from which you shall not remove your necks; nor shall you go exalted, for it *is* an evil time.

1242 216 4904 59,21 7451 6466 205 2803 1945
1 הוֹי חֹשְׁבֵי־אָוֶן וּפֹעֲלֵי רָע עַל־מִשְׁכְּבוֹתָם בְּאוֹר הַבֹּקֶר
the morning the In of light !beds their on evil pre- and paring wick- edness those plotting Woe (to)

1004 14,97 7704 2530 3027 410 3426 6213
2 יַעֲשׂוּהָ כִּי יֶשׁ־לְאֵל יָדָם׃ וְחָמְדוּ שָׂדוֹת וְגָזָלוּ וּבָתִּים
and houses seize and ,(them) fields they And covet their .hand the in of power it is for do they it

3541 5159 376 1004 1397 6231 5375
3 וְנָשְׂאוּ וְעָשְׁקוּ גֶּבֶר וּבֵיתוֹ וְאִישׁ וְנַחֲלָתוֹ׃ לָכֵן כֹּה
thus Therefore his .inheritance and a even man his and ,household man a they And oppress carry and .off (them)

834 7451 2063 4940 2803 2005 3068 559
אָמַר יְהוָה הִנְנִי חֹשֵׁב עַל־הַמִּשְׁפָּחָה הַזֹּאת רָעָה אֲשֶׁר
which ,evil an this family against (am) plotting ,Behold I :Jehovah says

6256 73:17 1980 3808 66,77 4185 3808
לֹא־תָמִישׁוּ מִשָּׁם צַוְּארֹתֵיכֶם וְלֹא תֵלְכוּ רוֹמָה כִּי עֵת
time for ,exalted you shall go and not ;necks your from there shall you remove not

4In that day one shall lift up a parable against you, and lament a lament of lamenting; he says, We shall be completely laid waste; He has exchanged the share of my people. How He has removed *it* for me! To the apostate He has divided the fields. **5**So there shall not be for you one casting a line by lot in the congregation of Jehovah. **6**Do not drop *words as* they drop! They shall not drop *words* about these; they shall not draw back reproaches.

7House of Jacob, *it is* said, The Spirit of Jehovah is limited, if these *are* His doings. Do not My words do good with the one who walks upright? **8**Even yesterday My people has risen up *like* an enemy. You strip off an inner robe from before an outer garment, from those who pass by trustingly, those returning *from* war. **9**You have thrown the wives of My people out from the house of her delight; you have taken away My majesty forever from her children. **10**Rise up, and go! For because of destroying uncleanness, even a grievous destruction, this *is* not *your* rest. **11**If a man walks *with* wind, and he lies *in* deceit, saying, I will drop *words to* you for wine and for fermented drink, he shall even be a dropper of *words* for this people.

12I will surely gather all of you, Jacob; I will surely gather the remnant of Israel. I will set him together like the sheep of Bozrah, like a flock in the midst of its fold. They shall be in commotion because of men. **13**He breaking up has come before them; they have broken up and have passed through the gate, and have gone out of it. And their king shall pass before them, and Jehovah at the head of them.

4

5091	50`91	4912		5375	3117		7451
a lament and of lament	a ,parable		against you	shall one up lift	that	day In	it evil an .(is)

4.185	4171	5971	2506	77.03	7703	559	`5092
for has He !me (it)	How has He removed	my portion The of .exchanged	be shall we people of	.destroyed	Destroy- ing	he ,says	lament- ;ing

5

2256	79`93	1961	38`08	25`05	7704	7725
mea- a line suring	one casting you	for shall there not be	.divided fore	has He .divided	fields	one the To back turning

6

428	5197	5197	5197	408	3068	6951	1486
about ;these	shall they (words) drop	Not they	they (as) do	Not .Jehovah	the in	by of assembly lot

7

3068	7307	7114	32.90	1004	559	3639	5253/380`8
,Jehovah the of Spirit	Is limited	,Jacob of	house (is It)	,said	.reproaches back draw	shall not	

1980	3477	3190	1697	4.16`11	428
?walking up- one right	the with good	doing	My words	(Are) not	His ?doings	these if (are)

8

6584	143	8008	4136	69:65	341	5971	865.•
strip you ,off	a cloak	garment before	From .up	risen have	an as	My people ,yesterday	Even

9

1004	16:44	5971/802	4421	7725	983	5674
the from of house	My The driven	people of wives	.war (from)	returning dently	those confi- by passing	those from

10

32.112	6965	57`69	1926	3947	5768	8588
For and !go	Arise	.forever My	majesty	have you taken	her from children	her ;delight

11

3863	4834	2256	2254	2930	4496	2063.38.08
If !painful	a even (which)	destruction ,destroys	unclean- ness	because of	;rest	this not (is)

1961	7941	3196	5197	35.76	8267	7307	19180	376
he even fer- and be shall drink	mented wine	for for will I ;lies deceit	(in) and	he (with) walks wind	man a

12

6908	6908	36`105	3290	622	622	2088	5971	5197
will I gather	surely ,you of	of all ,Jacob	will I gather	Surely .this	people (word) a for dropper

8432	573`9	1203	66`29	7760	3162	3478	7611
the in of midst	a like flock	;Bozrah of sheep	the like will I him set	together ;Israel	rem- of nant

13

6555	64:40	6555	59`27	120	1949	1699
have they breached	;them before breaking through	one the up	the come Has men of	because	be will they commotion in	its pasture

3068	6440	44`28	5674
and Jehovah	,them before king	their through pass	shall And .it out gone	by have and the gate through passed

7218
their at .head

CAP. III ג

CHAPTER 3

1 וָאֹמַר שִׁמְעוּ־נָא רָאשֵׁי יַעֲקֹב וּקְצִינֵי בֵּית יִשְׂרָאֵל הֲלוֹא

And I said, Hear, please, heads of Jacob, and magistrates of the house of Israel. (Is it) not

2 לָכֶם לָדַעַת אֶת־הַמִּשְׁפָּט׃ שֹׂנְאֵי טוֹב וְאֹהֲבֵי רָעָה גֹּזְלֵי

for you to know justice? Those hating good and loving evil; those stripping

3 עוֹרָם מֵעֲלֵיהֶם וּשְׁאֵרָם מֵעַל עַצְמוֹתָם׃ וַאֲשֶׁר אָכְלוּ

their skin from upon them, and their flesh from upon their bones; and who eat

שְׁאֵר עַמִּי וְעוֹרָם מֵעֲלֵיהֶם הִפְשִׁיטוּ וְאֶת־עַצְמֹתֵיהֶם

the flesh of My people, and their skin from upon them to cause come off; and their bones

פִּצֵּחוּ וּפָרְשׂוּ כַּאֲשֶׁר בַּסִּיר וּכְבָשָׂר בְּתוֹךְ קַלָּחַת׃ אָז יִזְעֲקוּ

they break and shatter as that in the pot, and as flesh in the midst of a kettle. Then they shall cry out

4 אֶל־יְהוָה וְלֹא יַעֲנֶה אוֹתָם וְיַסְתֵּר פָּנָיו מֵהֶם בָּעֵת הַהִיא

to Jehovah, but not He will answer them. And He will hide His face from them in time that,

5 כַּאֲשֶׁר הֵרֵעוּ מַעַלְלֵיהֶם׃ כֹּה אָמַר יְהוָה עַל־

just as they have done evil (in) their doings. Thus says Jehovah concerning

הַנְּבִיאִים הַמַּתְעִים אֶת־עַמִּי הַנֹּשְׁכִים בְּשִׁנֵּיהֶם וְקָרְאוּ

the prophets those causing to err My people, those biting with their teeth, and they call out,

שָׁלוֹם וַאֲשֶׁר לֹא־יִתֵּן עַל־פִּיהֶם וְקִדְּשׁוּ עָלָיו מִלְחָמָה׃

Peace! And who(ever) does not give for their mouth, they even sanctify against him a war.

6 לָכֵן לַיְלָה לָכֶם מֵחָזוֹן וְחָשְׁכָה לָכֶם מִקְּסֹם וּבָאָה הַשֶּׁמֶשׁ

Therefore a night (be shall) for you from (apart) vision, and darkness for you from (apart) divining. And shall set the sun

7 עַל־הַנְּבִיאִים וְקָדַר עֲלֵיהֶם הַיּוֹם׃ וּבֹשׁוּ הַחֹזִים וְחָפְרוּ

on the prophets, and shall be black upon them the day. And shall be ashamed the seers, and shall blush

הַקֹּסְמִים וְעָטוּ עַל־שָׂפָם כֻּלָּם כִּי אֵין מַעֲנֵה אֱלֹהִים׃

those divining; and they shall cover over their mustache all of them, for there is no answer (from) God.

8 וְאוּלָם אָנֹכִי מָלֵאתִי כֹחַ אֶת־רוּחַ יְהוָה וּמִשְׁפָּט וּגְבוּרָה

But I am full of power, the Spirit of Jehovah, and justice and might,

9 לְהַגִּיד לְיַעֲקֹב פִּשְׁעוֹ וּלְיִשְׂרָאֵל חַטָּאתוֹ׃ שִׁמְעוּ־נָא

to declare to Jacob his transgression, and to Israel his sin. Hear, please,

זֹאת רָאשֵׁי בֵּית יַעֲקֹב וּקְצִינֵי בֵּית יִשְׂרָאֵל הַמְתַעֲבִים

this, heads of the house of Jacob, and magistrates of the house of Israel, those abhorring

10 מִשְׁפָּט וְאֵת כָּל־הַיְשָׁרָה יְעַקֵּשׁוּ׃ בֹּנֶה צִיּוֹן בְּדָמִים

justice, and all uprightness (who) pervert; those building Zion with bloodshed,

CHAPTER 3

1 And I said, Heads of Jacob, and magistrates of the house of Israel, please hear. *Is it* not for you to know justice? 2 Those hating good and loving evil, who pull their skin off them, and their flesh from their bones; 3 who also eat the flesh of My people, and cause their skin to come off from them; yea, they break their bones and shatter as that in the pot, and as flesh in the midst of the kettle. 4 Then they shall cry out to Jehovah, but He will not answer them. He will even hide His face from them in that time, as they have done evil in their doings.

5 So says Jehovah concerning the prophets who make My people err, who bite with their teeth and call out, Peace! And whoever does not give for their mouth, they even sanctify a war against him. 6 So a night shall be for you *without* vision; and darkness *without* divining. And the sun shall go down on the prophets, and the day shall be dark over them. 7 And the seers shall be ashamed, and the diviners shall blush, all of them; yea, they shall cover over their mustache, for there is no answer *from* God.

8 But I am full of power *by* the Spirit of Jehovah, and justice and might, to declare to Jacob his transgression, and his sin to Israel. 9 Heads of the house of Jacob, and magistrates of the house of Israel, *you* who abhor justice and pervert all equity, please hear this; 10 those building up Zion with blood, and

Jerusalem with iniquity.
11 Her leaders judge for a
bribe; and her priests teach
for pay; and her prophets
divine for silver; yet they
will lean on Jehovah, saying, *Is* not Jehovah among
us? No evil shall come on
us! 12 Therefore, on account
of you, Zion shall be plowed
as a field, and Jerusalem
shall become heaps, and
the mountain of the house
into high places of the
forest.

3354,8 8199 7810 7218 5766 3389
11 וִירוּשָׁלַם בְּעַוְלָה׃ רָאשֶׁיהָ ׀ בְּשֹׁחַד יִשְׁפֹּטוּ וְכֹהֲנֶיהָ
her and priests | ,judge | a for bribe | heads Her | with .iniquity | and Jerusalem

8172 3068 5921 7080 3701 5030 3384 4242
בִּמְחִיר יוֹרוּ וּנְבִיאֶיהָ בְּכֶסֶף יִקְסֹמוּ וְעַל־יְהוָה יִשָּׁעֵנוּ
will they ,lean | Jehovah | yet upon | ;divine | for silver | her and prophets | ,instruct | a for price

7451 935 3808 7130 3068 559
12 לֵאמֹר הֲלוֹא יְהוָה בְּקִרְבֵּנוּ לֹא־תָבוֹא עָלֵינוּ רָעָה׃ לָכֵן
There- ,fore | !evil | upon us | shall come | Not | our in ?midst | Jehovah | not (Is) | ,saying

2022 1961 5856 3389 2790 7704 6726 1558
בִּגְלַלְכֶם צִיּוֹן שָׂדֶה תֵחָרֵשׁ וִירוּשָׁלַם עִיִּין תִּהְיֶה וְהַר
the and of mount | shall ,be | ruins | Jerusalem and | be shall ,plowed | a (as) field | Zion | of because ,you

3293 1116 1004
הַבַּיִת לְבָמוֹת יָעַר׃
the .forest | the into of places high | the house

CAP. IV. ד

CHAPTER 4

1 But it shall be in the end
of the days, the mountain of
the house of Jehovah shall
be established on the top of
the mountains; and it shall
be lifted up from the hills;
and peoples shall flow on
it. 2 And many nations shall
come and say, Come, and
let us go up to the mountain
of Jehovah, and to the
house of the God of Jacob.
And He will teach us from
His ways, and we will walk
in His paths. For the law
shall go forth out of Zion,
and the word of Jehovah
from Jerusalem.
3 And He shall judge be-
tween many peoples, and
will decide for strong
nations afar off. And they
shall beat their swords into
plowshares, and their
spears into pruning hooks.
Nation shall not lift up a
sword against nation, nor
shall they learn war *any*
more. 4 But they shall each
one sit under his vine, and
under his fig-tree; and there
shall be no trembling. For
the mouth of Jehovah of
hosts has spoken. 5 For all
the peoples walk, *each* one
in the name of his god; but
we will walk in the name of
Jehovah our God forever
and ever. 6 In that day I will
gather the lame, declares

7218 3559 3068 1004 2022 1961 3117 319 1961
1 וְהָיָה ׀ בְּאַחֲרִית הַיָּמִים יִהְיֶה הַר בֵּית־יְהוָה נָכוֹן בְּרֹאשׁ
the on of head | founded | Jeho- vah | house the of | the of mountain | be shall | the ,days | end the of | in | it And be shall

1980 5971 5921 5102 1389 5375 2022
2 הֶהָרִים וְנִשָּׂא הוּא מִגְּבָעוֹת וְנָהֲרוּ עָלָיו עַמִּים׃ וְהָלְכוּ
shall And come | .peoples | upon it | shall and flow | the from ;hills | it | be shall and lifted | the ,mountains

1004 3068 2022 5927 3212 559 7227 1471
גּוֹיִם רַבִּים וְאָמְרוּ לְכוּ ׀ וְנַעֲלֶה אֶל־הַר־יְהוָה וְאֶל־בֵּית
house the of | and to | Jehovah | the of mountain | to | let and up go us | ,Come | ,say and | many nations

6726 734 3212 1870 3384 3290 430
אֱלֹהֵי יַעֲקֹב וְיוֹרֵנוּ מִדְּרָכָיו וְנֵלְכָה בְּאֹרְחֹתָיו כִּי מִצִּיּוֹן
from Zion | For | His in .paths | will we and walk | His from ,ways | will He And us instruct | .Jacob | the of God

5971 996 8199 3389 3068 1697 8451 3318
3 תֵּצֵא תוֹרָה וּדְבַר־יְהוָה מִירוּשָׁלָםִ׃ וְשָׁפַט בֵּין עַמִּים
peoples between | He And judge shall | from .Jerusalem | Jehovah | the and of word | the law | go shall forth

2719 3807 7350 6099 1471 3198 7227
רַבִּים וְהוֹכִיחַ לְגוֹיִם עֲצֻמִים עַד־רָחוֹק וְכִתְּתוּ חַרְבֹתֵיהֶם
their swords | they And hammer shall | far .distant | strong | for nations | will and decide | many

2719 1471 1471 5375 4211 2595 855
לְאִתִּים וַחֲנִיתֹתֵיהֶם לְמַזְמֵרוֹת לֹא־יִשְׂאוּ גּוֹי אֶל־גּוֹי חֶרֶב
a ,sword | a against nation | a nation | shall up lift | Not | pruning into .knives | their and spears | into ,plowshares

8478 1612 8478 376 3427 4421 5750 3925 3808
4 וְלֹא־יִלְמְדוּן עוֹד מִלְחָמָה׃ וְיָשְׁבוּ אִישׁ תַּחַת גַּפְנוֹ וְתַחַת
and under | his vine | under | (each) man | they But sit shall | .war | (any) more | shall they learn | and not

3605 1696 6635 3068 6310 2729 369 8384
5 תְּאֵנָתוֹ וְאֵין מַחֲרִיד כִּי־פִי יְהוָה צְבָאוֹת דִּבֵּר׃ כִּי כָּל־
all | For | has .spoken | hosts | Jehovah of | the For of mouth | .trembling | not and be will | his ;tree fig

3068 8034 3212 430 8034 376 3212/5971
הָעַמִּים יֵלְכוּ אִישׁ בְּשֵׁם אֱלֹהָיו וַאֲנַחְנוּ נֵלֵךְ בְּשֵׁם־יְהוָה
Jehovah | the in of name | will walk | we but | his ,god | the in of name | (each) man | ,walk | the peoples

622 3068/5002 3117 5703 5769 430
6 אֱלֹהֵינוּ לְעוֹלָם וָעֶד׃ בַּיּוֹם הַהוּא נְאֻם־יְהוָה אֹסְפָה
will I gather | ,Jehovah states | ,that | day In | and .ever | forever | God our

Jehovah, and I will gather
the banished, and the one I
have afflicted. 7And I will
make the lame into a
remnant, and her who was
cast off into a strong nation.
And Jehovah shall reign
over them in Mount Zion
from now on, and to forever.
8And you, tower of the
flock, the hill of the
daughter of Zion, it shall
happen to you; and the
rulers, the chief ones, shall
come, the kingdom of the
daughter of Jerusalem.
9Now why do you cry aloud,
an outcry? Is there not a
king among you? Has your
adviser perished? For pangs
have seized you like one
giving birth. 10Be in pain
and deliver, daughter of
Zion, like one giving birth.
For now you shall go out
from the city, and you shall
live in the field. And you
shall come to Babylon.
There you shall be snatched
back. There Jehovah shall
redeem you from the palm
of your enemies
11Now also many nations
are gathered against you,
saying, Let her be defiled,
and let our eyes look on
Zion. 12But they do not
know the plans of Jehovah,
nor do they understand His
counsel. For He has
gathered them like the
sheaf to the threshing floor.
13Rise up and thresh, O
daughter of Zion; for I will
make your horn iron, and I
will make your hoofs
bronze. And you shall crush
many peoples. And I will
devote their gain to
Jehovah, and their wealth
to the Lord of all the earth.

CHAPTER 5

1Now gather yourself
together, daughter of a
troop; one sets a siege
against us. They shall strike
the judge of Israel with a
rod on the cheek. 2And
you, Bethlehem Ephratah,
being least among the
thousands of Judah, out of

7 הַצֹּלֵעָה וְהַנִּדָּחָה אֲקַבֵּצָה וַאֲשֶׁר הֲרֵעֹתִי׃ וְשַׂמְתִּי אֶת־
will I And make | have I (to) evil done | and who(ever) | will I gather | the and banished | the lame
הַצֹּלֵעָה לִשְׁאֵרִית וְהַנַּהֲלָאָה לְגוֹי עָצוּם וּמָלַךְ יְהוָה עֲלֵיהֶם
over them | Jehovah shall and reign | ;strong a into nation | having she and removed been | a into ,remnant | the lame
8 בְּהַר צִיּוֹן מֵעַתָּה וְעַד־עוֹלָם׃ וְאַתָּה מִגְדַּל־עֵדֶר
the flock | tower of | ,you And | .forever to and | from now | Zion | the in of mountain
עֹפֶל בַּת־צִיּוֹן עָדֶיךָ תֵּאתֶה וּבָאָה הַמֶּמְשָׁלָה הָרִאשֹׁנָה
chief the :(ones) | ,rulers the | shall and come | shall it happen | you to | ,Zion the of daughter | of hill
9 מַמְלֶכֶת לְבַת־יְרוּשָׁלִָם׃ עַתָּה לָמָּה תָרִיעִי רֵעַ הֲמֶלֶךְ
king A | an ?outcry | cry you do aloud | why | Now | .Jerusalem | the of daughter | kingdom the of
10 אֵין בָּךְ אִם־יוֹעֲצֵךְ אָבָד כִּי־הֶחֱזִיקֵךְ חִיל כַּיּוֹלֵדָה׃ חוּלִי
in Be pain | one like .birth giving | pain | seized has For you | has ?perished | your adviser | Or | among ?you | is not
וָגֹחִי בַּת־צִיּוֹן כַּיּוֹלֵדָה כִּי־עַתָּה תֵצְאִי מִקִּרְיָה וְשָׁכַנְתְּ בַּשָּׂדֶה
the in ,field | you and abide | the from ,city | shall you out go | now For | one like .birth giving | ,Zion daugh- of ter | and ,deliver
וּבָאת עַד־בָּבֶל שָׁם תִּנָּצֵלִי שָׁם יִגְאָלֵךְ יְהוָה מִכַּף אֹיְבָיִךְ׃
your .enemies | the from of palm | Jehovah | shall you redeem | there | shall you ;delivered be | There | .Babylon | to | you and come shall
11 וְעַתָּה נֶאֶסְפוּ עָלַיִךְ גּוֹיִם רַבִּים הָאֹמְרִים תֶּחֱנָף וְתַחַז בְּצִיּוֹן
against Zion | let and look | her Let ,defiled be | ,saying | ,many nations | against you | are gathered | And now
12 עֵינֵינוּ׃ וְהֵמָּה לֹא יָדְעוּ מַחְשְׁבוֹת יְהוָה וְלֹא הֵבִינוּ עֲצָתוֹ
His .counsel | they do understand | and not | ,Jehovah | of plans the | do know | not | they But | our .eyes
13 כִּי קִבְּצָם כֶּעָמִיר גֹּרְנָה׃ קוּמִי וָדוֹשִׁי בַּת־צִיּוֹן כִּי־קַרְנֵךְ
your horn | for | ,Zion daugh- of ter | and thresh | Arise | the to .floor threshing | the like sheaf | has He them gathered | For
אָשִׂים בַּרְזֶל וּפַרְסֹתַיִךְ אָשִׂים נְחוּשָׁה וַהֲדִקּוֹת עַמִּים רַבִּים
.many | peoples | you and crush shall | ;bronze | will I make | your and hoofs | ,iron | will I make
14 וְהַחֲרַמְתִּי לַיהוָה בִּצְעָם וְחֵילָם לַאֲדוֹן כָּל־הָאָרֶץ׃ עַתָּה
Now | the .earth | all | the to of Lord | their and wealth | their ,gain unjust | to Jehovah | will I And consecrate
תִּתְגֹּדְדִי בַת־גְּדוּד מָצוֹר שָׂם עָלֵינוּ בַּשֵּׁבֶט יַכּוּ עַל־הַלְּחִי
the cheek | upon | shall they strike | a With rod | against .us | one sets | a siege | ;troop a | daugh of ter | band together
אֵת שֹׁפֵט יִשְׂרָאֵל׃
.Israel | one the judging

CAP. V ה

CHAPTER 5

1 וְאַתָּה בֵּית־לֶחֶם אֶפְרָתָה צָעִיר לִהְיוֹת בְּאַלְפֵי יְהוּדָה
,Judah | the among of thousands | being | least | ,Ephratha | Bethlehem | ,you And

you He shall come forth to Me, to become Ruler in Israel; and His goings forth *have been* from of old, from the days of eternity. [3]So He will give them over until the time the one giving birth has given birth; then the rest of His brothers shall return to the sons of Israel.

[4]And He shall stand and feed in the strength of Jehovah, in the majesty of the name of Jehovah His God. And they shall sit, for now He is great to the ends of the earth. [5]And this *One* shall be peace. When Assyria shall come into our land; and when he shall walk in our palaces, then we shall raise against him seven shepherds and eight anointed ones of man. [6]And they shall mar the land of Assyria with the sword, and the land of Nimrod at her entrances. And He shall deliver *us* from Assyria, when he comes into our land, and when he treads within our border. [7]And the remnant of Jacob shall be in the midst of many peoples as dew from Jehovah, as showers on a blade of grass, which does not wait for man, nor delay for the sons of men.

[8]And the remnant of Jacob shall be among the nations, in the midst of many peoples, like a lion among the beasts of the forest, like a young lion among the flocks of sheep — who both tramples and tears in pieces if he passes through—and there is no one to snatch back. [9]Your hands shall be high above your foes, and all your enemies shall be cut off. [10]And it shall be in that day, I will cut off your horses out of your midst, and I will destroy your chariots, declares Jehovah. [11]And I will cut off the cities of your land, and pull down all your fortresses. [12]And I will cut off sorceries out of your hand, and there shall not be fortune-tellers for you. [13]I will also cut off your carved images, and your pillars

6924 4162 3478 4910 1961 3318
מִמְּךָ לִי יֵצֵא לִהְיוֹת מוֹשֵׁל בְּיִשְׂרָאֵל וּמוֹצָאֹתָיו מִקֶּדֶם
(been have) His and ,Israel in one be- to shall He to of out
old of from forth comings ruling come forth come Me you

251 3499 3205 3205 6256/5704 54:14 3651 5769 3117
2 מִימֵי עוֹלָם׃ לָכֵן יִתְּנֵם עַד־עֵת יוֹלֵדָה יָלָדָה וְיֶתֶר אֶחָיו
His the then given has one the the until will He There- .eternity the from
brothers of rest ;birth birth giving time (over) them give fore of days

1347 3068 5797 7462 5975 3478 1121 7725
3 יְשׁוּבוּן עַל־בְּנֵי יִשְׂרָאֵל׃ וְעָמַד וְרָעָה בְּעֹז יְהוָה בִּגְאוֹן
the in ,Jehovah the in pas- and He And .Israel the to shall
of majesty of strength (us) ture stand shall of sons return

776 657 5704 1430 6258 3427 430 3068 8034
שֵׁם יְהוָה אֱלֹהָיו וְיָשָׁבוּ כִּי־עַתָּה יִגְדַּל עַד־אַפְסֵי־אָרֶץ׃
the the to is He now for they and His Jehovah the
.earth of ends great ,sit shall ;God of name

1869 776 935 804 7965 2088 1961
4 וְהָיָה זֶה שָׁלוֹם אַשּׁוּר כִּי־יָבוֹא בְאַרְצֵנוּ וְכִי יִדְרֹךְ
shall he and our into shall he when Assyria ,peace this shall And
tread when ;land come (One) be

5257 8083 7462 7651 6965 759
בְּאַרְמְנֹתֵינוּ וַהֲקֵמֹנוּ עָלָיו שִׁבְעָה רֹעִים וּשְׁמֹנָה נְסִיכֵי
anointed and shepherds seven against shall we then ,palaces our in
of ones eight him up raise

5248 776 2719 804 776 7462 120
5 אָדָם׃ וְרָעוּ אֶת־אֶרֶץ אַשּׁוּר בַּחֶרֶב וְאֶת־אֶרֶץ נִמְרֹד
Nimrod the and the with Assyria the shall they And .man
of land ,sword of land depasture

1869 776 935 804 5337 6607
בִּפְתָחֶיהָ וְהִצִּיל מֵאַשּׁוּר כִּי־יָבוֹא בְאַרְצֵנוּ וְכִי יִדְרֹךְ
shall he and our into shall he when from shall He And her at
tread when land come ,Assyria (us) deliver .entrances

7227 5971 7130 3290 7611 1961 1366
6 בִּגְבוּלֵנוּ׃ וְהָיָה שְׁאֵרִית יַעֲקֹב בְּקֶרֶב עַמִּים רַבִּים
many peoples the in Jacob remnant the shall And our within
of midst of be .border

376 6960 3808 834 6212 5921 7241 3068 2919
כְּטַל מֵאֵת יְהוָה כִּרְבִיבִים עֲלֵי־עֵשֶׂב אֲשֶׁר לֹא־יְקַוֶּה לְאִישׁ
for does not which ,grass blade a as ,Jehovah from dew as
man wait of (on) showers

7130 1471 3290 7611 1961 120 1121 3176 3808
7 וְלֹא יְיַחֵל לִבְנֵי אָדָם׃ וְהָיָה שְׁאֵרִית יַעֲקֹב בַּגּוֹיִם בְּקֶרֶב
the in the among Jacob remnant the And .man the for does and
of midst ,nations of be shall of sons delay not

6629/5739 3715 3293 929 738 7227 5971
עַמִּים רַבִּים כְּאַרְיֵה בְּבַהֲמוֹת יַעַר כִּכְפִיר בְּעֶדְרֵי־צֹאן
;sheep the among a like the the among a like ,many peoples
of flocks lion young ,forest of beasts lion

5921 3027 7311 5337 369 2963 7427 5674 834
8 אֲשֶׁר אִם־עָבַר וְרָמַס וְטָרַף וְאֵין מַצִּיל׃ תָּרֹם יָדְךָ עַל־
above Your be shall .delivering there and and both passes he if ,which
hand high none is —tears tramples through

5002 3117 1961 3772 341 3605 6862
9 צָרֶיךָ וְכָל־אֹיְבֶיךָ יִכָּרֵתוּ׃ וְהָיָה בַיּוֹם־הַהוּא נְאֻם
states ,that day in it And be shall your and your
be shall .off cut enemies all ,foes

3772 4818 6 7130 5483 3772 3068
10 יְהוָה וְהִכְרַתִּי סוּסֶיךָ מִקִּרְבֶּךָ וְהַאֲבַדְתִּי מַרְכְּבֹתֶיךָ׃ וְהִכְרַתִּי
will I And your will I and your from your will I that Jeho-
off cut .chariots destroy ,midst horses off cut ,vah

3027 3785 3772 4013 3605 2040 776 5892
11 עָרֵי אַרְצֶךָ וְהָרַסְתִּי כָּל־מִבְצָרֶיךָ׃ וְהִכְרַתִּי כְשָׁפִים מִיָּדֶךָ
your from sorceries will I And your all pull and your the
hand off cut .fortresses down ,land of cities

7130 4676 6456 3772 1961 3808 6049
12 וּמְעוֹנְנִים לֹא יִהְיוּ־לָךְ׃ וְהִכְרַתִּי פְסִילֶיךָ וּמַצֵּבוֹתֶיךָ מִקִּרְבֶּךָ
your from your and graven your will I And for there not and
;midst pillars ,images off cut .you be shall sorcerers

pillars from your midst. And you shall not any more worship the work of your hands. [14]And I will pluck your shrines from your midst, and I will destroy your cities. [15]And I will execute vengeance in anger and in fury *on* the nations, such as they have not heard.

7130 842 5422 3027 4639 5750 7812 3808
13 וְלֹא־תִשְׁתַּחֲוֶה עוֹד לְמַעֲשֵׂה יָדֶיךָ׃ וְנָתַשְׁתִּי אֲשֵׁירֶיךָ מִקִּרְבֶּךָ
your from your will I And your the to (any) shall you and
midst shrines up pluck .hands of work more down bow not

1471 5358 3534 639 6213 5892 8045
14 וְהִשְׁמַדְתִּי עָרֶיךָ׃ וְעָשִׂיתִי בְּאַף וּבְחֵמָה נָקָם אֶת־הַגּוֹיִם
the (on) vengeance in and in will I And your will I and
,nations fury anger perform .cities destroy

8085 38.08
אֲשֶׁר לֹא שָׁמֵעוּ׃
have they not such
.heard as

CAP. VI ו

CHAPTER 6

CHAPTER 6

[1]Hear now what Jehovah says: Rise up, contend with the mountains, and let the hills hear your voice. [2]Mountains, hear the contention of Jehovah; and *you* enduring foundations of the earth, for Jehovah has a quarrel with His people, and He will dispute with Israel. [3]My people, what have I done to you? And how have I made you weary? Answer against Me. [4]For I brought you up out of the land of Egypt, and redeemed you out of the house of slaves; and I sent Moses, Aaron and Miriam before you. [5]My people, remember now what Balak, king of Moab, planned, and what Balaam, the son of Beor, answered him from Shittim to Gilgal, so that you may know the righteousnesses of Jehovah.

[6]With what shall I come before Jehovah, *to* bow myself before the loftinesses of God? Shall I come before Him with burnt offerings, with calves, sons of a year? [7]Will Jehovah be pleased with thousands of rams, with ten thousands of torrents of oil? Shall I give my firstborn *for* my transgression, the fruit of my body *for* the sin of my soul? [8]He has declared to you, man, what *is* good; and what *does* Jehovah require of you, but to do justice, and to love mercy, and to walk humbly with your God? [9]The voice of Jehovah

2022 7378 6965 559 3068 4994 8085
1 שִׁמְעוּ־נָא אֵת אֲשֶׁר־יְהוָה אֹמֵר קוּם רִיב אֶת־הֶהָרִים
,mountains the contend ,Arise (is) Jehovah what please Hear
with :saying

3068 7379 2022 8085 6963 1389 8085
2 וְתִשְׁמַעְנָה הַגְּבָעוֹת קוֹלֶךָ׃ שִׁמְעוּ הָרִים אֶת־רִיב יְהוָה
,Jehovah the ,mountains ,Hear your hills the hear let and
of contention .voice

3478 5971 3068 7379 776 4146 386
וְהָאֵתָנִים מֹסְדֵי אָרֶץ כִּי רִיב לַיהוָה עִם־עַמּוֹ וְעִם־יִשְׂרָאֵל
Israel with and His with has con- a for the foundations the and
people Jehovah tention ;earth of constant

6030 3811 6213 4100 5971 3198
3 יִתְוַכָּח׃ עַמִּי מֶה־עָשִׂיתִי לְךָ וּמָה הֶלְאֵתִיךָ עֲנֵה בִי׃
against Answer I have And to I have what My will He
!Me ?you wearied how ?you done ,people .dispute

7971 6299 5650 1004 4714 776 5927
4 כִּי הֶעֱלִתִיךָ מֵאֶרֶץ מִצְרַיִם וּמִבֵּית עֲבָדִים פְּדִיתִיךָ וָאֶשְׁלַח
I and redeemed I servants from and ,Egypt the from brought I For
sent ;you of house the of land up you

3289 2142 5971 4813 175 4872 6440
5 לְפָנֶיךָ אֶת־מֹשֶׁה אַהֲרֹן וּמִרְיָם׃ עַמִּי זְכָר־נָא מַה־יָּעַץ
planned what please re- My and ,Aaron ,Moses before
member ,people .Miriam

7851 1160/1121 1109 6030 4100 4124 4428 1111
בָּלָק מֶלֶךְ מוֹאָב וּמֶה־עָנָה אֹתוֹ בִּלְעָם בֶּן־בְּעוֹר מִן־הַשִּׁטִּים
Shittim from ,Beor the Balaam him an- and ,Moab king Balak
of son swered what of

3068 6923 4100 3068 6666 3045 4616 1537/5704
6 עַד־הַגִּלְגָּל לְמַעַן דַּעַת צִדְקוֹת יְהוָה׃ בַּמָּה אֲקַדֵּם יְהוָה
,Jehovah I shall With .Jehovah righ- the may you so ,Gilgal to
before come what of teousness know that

8141 1121 5695 5930 6923 4791 430 3721
אִכַּף לֵאלֹהֵי מָרוֹם הַאֲקַדְּמֶנּוּ בְעוֹלוֹת בַּעֲגָלִים בְּנֵי שָׁנָה׃
?year a of sons with burnt with come I Shall lofti- the to bow
of ,calves ,offerings Him before ?nesses of God down

5414 8081 5158 7233 352 505 3068 7521
7 הֲיִרְצֶה יְהוָה בְּאַלְפֵי אֵילִים בְּרִבְבוֹת נַחֲלֵי־שָׁמֶן הַאֶתֵּן
I Shall ?oil torrents myriads with ,rams with Jehovah be Will
give of of thousands pleased

120 5046 5315 2403 990 6529 6588 1060
8 בְּכוֹרִי פִּשְׁעִי פְּרִי בִטְנִי חַטַּאת נַפְשִׁי׃ הִגִּיד לְךָ אָדָם
,man to has He ?soul my the (for) my fruit the my (for) my
,you declared of sin womb of transgression firstborn

4941 6213 1875 3068 4100 2896
מַה־טּוֹב וּמָה־יְהוָה דּוֹרֵשׁ מִמְּךָ כִּי אִם־עֲשׂוֹת מִשְׁפָּט
,justice do to except from (is) Jehovah and ;good what
you seeking what (is)

3068 6963 430 3212 6800 2617 160
9 וְאַהֲבַת חֶסֶד וְהַצְנֵעַ לֶכֶת עִם־אֱלֹהֶיךָ׃ קוֹל יְהוָה
Jehovah The your with walk to to and ,grace to and
of voice ?God humble be love

calls out to the city; and one *of* sound wisdom will see Your name; hear the rod, and *Him* who appointed it.
[10]Are there yet in the house of the wicked the treasures of wickedness, and a cursed ephah of leanness? [11]Shall I *declare* wicked balances *to be* pure, or a bag of deceitful weights? [12]*For* her rich ones are full of violence, and her inhabitants speak a lie; and their tongue *is* deceit in their mouth. [13]And I also have made *you* sick, to strike you, making you desolate because of your sins. [14]You shall eat, but not be satisfied; and your hunger *shall be* in your midst. And you shall draw back, but shall not save; and that which you save, I will give up to the sword. [15]You shall sow, but you shall not reap, You shall tread the olive, but you shall not anoint with oil; and new wine, but shall not drink wine.
[16]And *one* has kept himself *as to* the statutes of Omri, and all the works of the house of Ahab; and you walk in their counsels, so that I may give you for a horror, and her inhabitants for a hissing. And you shall bear the shame of My people.

3259 4310 4294 8085 8034 7200 8454 7121 5892
לעיר יקרא ותושיה יראה שמך שמעו מטה ומי יעדה׃
appointed and the ,Hear Your will one sound and calls the to
?it who rod ;name see wisdom ;out city

2194 7332 374 7562 214 7563 1004 784 5750
10 עוד האש בית רשע אצרות רשע ואיפת רזון זעומה׃
?cursed leanness an and wicked- the the the in is Yet
of ephah ,ness of treasures wicked of house there

834 4820 68 3599 7562 3976 2135
11 האזכה במאזני רשע ובכיס אבני מרמה׃
12 אשר
Which ?fraud weights a and wickedness of scales I Shall
of of bag pure (declare)

7423 3956 8267 1696 3427 2555 4390 6223
עשיריה מלאו חמס וישביה דברו־שקר ולשונם רמיה
(is) their and ,lie a speak her and ,violence are rich her
deceit tongue inhabitants of full ,ones

2403 8074 5221 2470 1571 6310
13 בפיהם׃ וגם־אני החליתי הכותך השמם על־חטאתיך
your because desolate to strike to made have I So their in
.sins of (you) ,you sick (you) also .mouth

3808 5253 7130 3545 7646 3808 398
14 אתה תאכל ולא תשבע וישחך בקרבך ותסג ולא
but will you And in be will your and be but shall You
not ,back draw .midst your hunger ;satisfied not eat

7114 3808 2232 5414 2719 6403 6403
15 תפליט ואשר תפלט לחרב אתן׃ אתה תזרע ולא תקצור
shall you but shall You will I the to you what and keep shall
.reap not ,sow .give sword ,save ;safe

3196 8354 3808 8492 8081 5480 3808 2132 1869
אתה תדרך־זית ולא־תסוך שמן ותירוש ולא תשתה־יין׃
.wine shall you but new and (with) shall you but the shall You
drink not wine ;oil anoint not ,olive tread

1980 256 1004 4639 3605 6018 2708 8104
16 וישתמר חקות עמרי וכל מעשה בית־אחאב ותלכו
you and ,Ahab the work the and ,Omri the (to as) has (one) And
walk of house of all of statutes himself kept

8322 3427 8047 5414 4616 4156
במעצותם למען תתי אתך לשמה וישביה לשרקה
a for her and a for you may I that so their in
;hissing inhabitants ,horror give ,counsels

5375 5971 2781
וחרפת עמי תשאו׃
shall you My the And
.bear people of disgrace

CAP. VII ז

CHAPTER 7

[1]Woe to me! For I am like the gatherings of summer fruit, like the gleanings of the vintage. There is no cluster to eat; my soul desires the early fig. [2]The pious has perished from the earth, and the upright is not among mankind. All of them lie in wait for blood; each one hunts his brother *with* a net. [3]Both palms *are* on evil, to do *it* well. The ruler *is* asking for a bribe; also the judge. And the great one speaks the lust of his soul; he *does*, and they weave it together. [4]The best of them *is* like a thorn;

811 369 1208 5955 7019 625 480
1 אללי לי כי הייתי כאספי־קיץ כעללת בציר אין־אשכול
cluster a There the the like ripe the like I For to Woe
(grapes of) not is .vintage of gleanings ,fruit of gatherings am !me

3477 776 2623 6 5315 183 1083 398
2 לאכול בכורה אותה נפשי׃ אבד חסיד מן־הארץ וישר
the and the from the Has my craves early the ;eat to
upright ,earth pious perished .soul fig

6679 251 376 693 1818 3605 369 120
באדם אין כלם לדמים יארבו איש את־אחיהו יצודו
hunts his (each) in lie for of All not among
brother, man ;wait bloodshed them .is man

8199 7592 8269 3190 3709 7451 2764
3 חרם׃ על־הרע כפים להיטיב השר שאל והשפט
the also (is) The do to both evil Upon a (with)
,judge ,asking ruler .well (it) ,palms (are) .net

2896 5686 5315 1942 1696 1419 7966
4 בשלום והגדול דבר הות נפשו הוא ויעבתוה׃ טובם
Their they and he his the speaks the and a for
best .it interweave ,(does) ;soul of lust (man) great ,bribe

the upright more than a hedge of thorns. The day of your watchers, your visitation is coming; now their shame shall be.

[5] Put no faith in a companion; put no trust in a friend; keep the door of your mouth from her who lies *in* your bosom; [6]for son despises father; a daughter rises up against her mother, the daughter-in-law against her mother-in-law; a man's enemies *are* the men of his house. [7]But I will look to Jehovah; I will wait for the God of my salvation; my God will hear me.

[8]Rejoice not against me, my enemy; for *if* I fall I shall arise. For *if* I sit in darkness, Jehovah is a light to me. [9]I will bear the fury of Jehovah because I have sinned against Him; until He pleads my cause and brings forth justice for me. He will bring me out to the light; I shall see His righteousness. [10]And my enemy shall see; and shame shall cover her, the one saying to me, Where *is* He, Jehovah your God? My eyes shall look on her; now she shall be for a trampling, as the mud of the streets. [11]A day of building your walls, that day the limit shall be far removed; [12]that day he shall come even to you from Assyria and the besieged cities, and from the siege even to the River, and from sea to sea, and mountain *to* mountain. [13]But the land shall become a waste because of those dwelling in it, from the fruit of their doings.

[14]Feed Your people with Your rod, the flock of Your possession, dwelling alone *in* the thicket, amidst Carmel. Let them pasture *in* Bashan and Gilead, as *in* days of old. [15]As the days of your coming out from the land of Egypt, I will cause him to see extraordinary things.

[16]The nations shall see and be ashamed from all their might; they shall set the hand on *their*

Interlinear (Hebrew, right-to-left)

Micah 7:4–16

```
6258   935    6486    6822    3117   4534         3477   2312
now  is  your   your  The a than more the  like (is)
coming  visitation ,watchers of day .thorn-hedge upright ;thorn at

441    982    408    74:53   539   3808       3998        1961
5  a  in  put do  not  a in  put do  Not  their  be shall
;friend  trust  ;companion  faith  .confusion

1323  1   5034  1121   6310  6607  8104  2436         7901
6  a ;father  is  son For  your  the  guard  your (in) her from
daughter  despising  .mouth of opening  bosom  reclining

1004  582  376   341   2545   3618    517   6965
7  I But own his the (are)  a  ene- the her against the her against rises
.house of men  man  of mies ;law-in-mother bride ,mother  up

4301   8085    3468    4301   3176   6822   3068
8  Not my hear will  me ;salvation of God  wait will I  look will  to
!God  for the  ;salvation of God  Jehovah

3068  2822  3427   6965  5307    341   8056
Jehovah in sit I  for  shall I fall I  for over my ,rejoice do
;darkness (if)  ;arise (if) ;me  ,enemy

5704  2398  3588  53:75  2197        216
9  (when)until against have I because will I Jehovah The  for a (is)
Him  sinned  bear  of rage .me  light

6666  7200   216   3318   4941   6213  1379  7378
His  shall I  the to  will He  my  and  my  He
.righteousness see  light out me bring .justice makes case contends

3068  575  559   955    3680   341   200
10 Jehovah Where ,me to one the ,shame  shall and  my  shall And
He (is)  saying  her cover ;enemy  see

2916  4823  1961  6258  7200   5869  430
the like  a for  shall she  now ;her on  look will  My  your
of mud trampling  become  eyes  ?God

3117  27,06  7368    3117  1447   1129  3117  2351
11  (in) the be shall  that (in) your  building day A  the
12  day ;limit remote  day ;walls (stone) of  .streets

4692   4692  5892  804    935:  5704
the from and ,siege the and Assyria from shall he to even that
siege  of cities  come  you

8077  776  776  1961         2022  2022  3220 3220/ 510:4/5704
13 a the shall And the (to) and from and the  even
desolation  land  become .mountain mountain ,sea sea ,River to

7626  5971  7462            4611   6529  3427
14 Your with Your Pasture  Your rod  .doings their the from those because
rod  people  of fruit ,it in dwelling of

1316  7462  3760  8432  3293  910  7931            5759 6629
(in) them Let .Carmel the in the (in) alone dwelling Your flock the
Bashan  pasture  of midst ;thicket  ,possession of

7200  4714  776   3318  3117         5769 3117  1568
15 cause will I ,Egypt the from your  the As  .old (in) as  and
see to him  of land out coming of days  of days the Gilead

5921 3027 7760 1369  3605  954   1471 7200  6381
16 over the shall they their  from be and the Shall extraordinary
hand set  forces  all ashamed nations see .things
```

mouth; their ears shall be deaf. 17 They shall lick the dust like a snake; they shall tremble out of their holes like crawlers of the earth; they shall dread Jehovah our God; they shall fear from You. 18 Who *is* a God like You, forgiving iniquity and passing by the transgression of the remnant of His possession? He does not make strong His anger forever, for He delights *in* grace. 19 He will return *to* show us compassion; He will trample our iniquities; and You will cast all their sins into the depths of the sea. 20 You will give faithfulness to Jacob *and* kindness to Abraham, which You have sworn to our fathers from the days of old.

776 2119 517 5 6083 3847 2790 241 6310

17 פֶּה אָזְנֵיהֶם תֶּחֱרַשְׁנָה׃ יְלַחֲכוּ עָפָר כַּנָּחָשׁ כְּזֹחֲלֵי אֶרֶץ

the earth; like crawlers of the like snake, the dust shall They lick be deaf. shall their ears the mouth;

3372 63 42 430 3068 4526 7264

יִרְגְּזוּ מִמִּסְגְּרֹתֵיהֶם אֶל־יְהוָה אֱלֹהֵינוּ יִפְחָדוּ וְיִרְאוּ מִמֶּךָּ׃

(from) You. shall they fear shall they dread; our God Jehovah to their fastnesses; of out shall they tremble

5159 7611 6588 5674 5771 5375 410

18 מִי־אֵל כָּמוֹךָ נֹשֵׂא עָוֹן וְעֹבֵר עַל־פֶּשַׁע לִשְׁאֵרִית נַחֲלָתוֹ

His possession? remnant of the of transgression the over and passing iniquity, lifting off like You a God (is) Who

7355 7725 2617 2654 639 5703 2388 3808

19 לֹא־הֶחֱזִיק לָעַד אַפּוֹ כִּי־חָפֵץ חֶסֶד הוּא׃ יָשׁוּב יְרַחֲמֵנוּ

show (to) mercy us; will He turn, He. grace desires for His anger, for ever He does strong make not

2403 3605 3220 4688 7971 5771 3533

יִכְבֹּשׁ עֲוֹנֹתֵינוּ וְתַשְׁלִיךְ בִּמְצֻלוֹת יָם כָּל־חַטֹּאותָם׃

sins their. all the sea the into of depths will You and cast our iniquities; will He trample

1 7650 834 85 2617 3290 571 5414

20 תִּתֵּן אֱמֶת לְיַעֲקֹב חֶסֶד לְאַבְרָהָם אֲשֶׁר־נִשְׁבַּעְתָּ לַאֲבֹתֵינוּ

our to fathers have You sworn which Abraham, to kindness Jacob, to faithfulness will You give

6924 3117

מִימֵי קֶדֶם׃

old. the from of days

A LITERAL TRANSLATION
OF THE BIBLE
THE BOOK OF NAHUM

CHAPTER 1

[1]The burden of Nineveh: The book of the vision of Nahum the Elkoshite.
[2]God *is* jealous, and Jehovah is avenging; Jehovah is avenging, and is a possessor of wrath. Jehovah takes vengeance against His foes, and He keeps *wrath* against His enemies. [3]Jehovah *takes* long *to* anger, and *is* great of power, and He does not by any means acquit *the guilty*. Jehovah *has* His way in the tempest and in the storm, and the clouds *are* the dust of His feet. [4]He rebukes the sea and makes it dry, and dries up the rivers. Bashan and Carmel wither; and the flower of Lebanon withers. [5]The mountains quake from Him, and the hills melt; and the earth is lifted up from before Him, even the world and all who dwell in it. [6]Who can stand before His fury? And who can rise against the heat of His anger? His wrath is poured out like fire, and the rocks are broken down because of Him. [7]Jehovah *is* good *for a* stronghold in the day of distress; and He knows those who trust in Him. [8]But with a flood passing through, He will make a complete end of its place, and darkness shall pursue His enemies.
[9]What are you plotting against Jehovah? He will make an utter end; distress shall not rise up a second time. [10]For as thorns are woven together, and as their drunkards are drunken, they shall be devoured like fully dried straw. [11]One who devises evil against Jehovah has come forth from you, one counseling worthlessness. [12]So says Jehovah, Though secure, and so many, yet they will

נחום

LIBER NAHUM

(THE) BOOK OF NAHUM

CAPUT. I א

CHAPTER 1

5358 7072 410 512 5151 2377 5612 5210 4853
1 2 מַשָּׂא נִינְוֵה סֵפֶר חֲזוֹן נַחוּם הָאֶלְקֹשִׁי׃ אֵל קַנּוֹא וְנֹקֵם
is and ,jealous God .Elkoshite the Nahum the book the :Nineveh The
avenging (is) of vision of of burden
5201 68:62 3068 5358 2534 1167 3068 5358 3068
יְהוָה נֹקֵם יְהוָה וּבַעַל חֵמָה נֹקֵם יְהוָה לְצָרָיו וְנוֹטֵר הוּא
He keeps and against Jehovah takes .wrath a and Jehovah is ;Jehovah
(wrath) ,foes His vengeance of possessor avenging
5352 38:08 5352 35:81 1419 639 750 3068 341
3 לְאֹיְבָיו׃ יְהוָה אֶרֶךְ אַפַּיִם וּגְדָול־כֹּחַ וְנַקֵּה לֹא יְנַקֶּה
does He not by and power and ,anger long Jehovah His against
,acquit means any of great (before) (is) .enemies
1605 72:72 80 6051 1870 8183 5492 3068
4 יְהוָה בְּסוּפָה וּבִשְׂעָרָה דַּרְכּוֹ וְעָנָן אֲבַק רַגְלָיו׃ גּוֹעֵר
He His the (are) the and His the in and the in Jehovah
rebukes .feet of dust clouds ,way storm tempest (is)
376:0 13.16 535 3001 5104 3605 2717 3220
בַּיָּם וַיַּבְּשֵׁהוּ וְכָל־הַנְּהָרוֹת הֶחֱרִיב אֻמְלַל בָּשָׁן וְכַרְמֶל
and Bashan withers dries He rivers the and makes and the
;Carmel .up all ,dry it ,sea
4127 1389 7493 2022 535 3844 6525
5 וּפֶרַח לְבָנוֹן אֻמְלָל׃ הָרִים רָעֲשׁוּ מִמֶּנּוּ וְהַגְּבָעוֹת הִתְמֹגָגוּ
melt hills the and because quake The .withers Lebanon the and
,Him of mountains of flower
2195 6440 3427 3605 8398 776 5375
6 וַתִּשָּׂא הָאָרֶץ מִפָּנָיו וְתֵבֵל וְכָל־יֹשְׁבֵי בָהּ׃ לִפְנֵי זַעְמוֹ
His Before .it in the and the even be- from the is and
fury inhabitants all world Him fore earth up lifted
6697 784 5413 2534 639 2740 6965 4310 59:75 4310
מִי יַעֲמוֹד וּמִי יָקוּם בַּחֲרוֹן אַפּוֹ חֲמָתוֹ נִתְּכָה כָאֵשׁ וְהַצֻּרִים
the and like poured is His His the against can And can who
rocks ,fire out wrath ?anger of heat rise who ?stand
26.20 3045 6864 3117 4581 30:68 2896 5422
7 נִתְּצוּ מִמֶּנּוּ׃ טוֹב יְהוָה לְמָעוֹז בְּיוֹם צָרָה וְיֹדֵעַ חֹסֵי בוֹ׃
in who those He and dis- the in (a for) Jehovah good because broken are
.Him trust knows tress of day stronghold .Him of down
2822 7291 341 4725 6213 36:17 56:7 4 7858
8 וּבְשֶׁטֶף עֹבֵר כָּלָה יַעֲשֶׂה מְקוֹמָהּ וְאֹיְבָיו יְרַדֶּף־חֹשֶׁךְ׃
.darkness will His and its of will He complete a passing with But
pursue enemies ,place make destruction through flood a
6965 38:08 6.21.3 36:17 30:68 2803 4100
9 מַה־תְּחַשְּׁבוּן אֶל־יְהוָה כָּלָה הוּא עֹשֶׂה לֹא־תָקוּם
shall not will He complete a ?Jehovah against you are What
up rise .make destruction plotting
5433 5435 54:40 5518 5704 6864 6471
10 פַּעֲמַיִם צָרָה׃ כִּי עַד־סִירִים סְבֻכִים וּכְסָבְאָם סְבוּאִים
are who their like and are thorns as For .Distress second a
,drunken drunkards ;interwoven as long time
7451 3068 28.03 33:18 43:93 3002 7179 398
11 אֻכְּלוּ כְּקַשׁ יָבֵשׁ מָלֵא׃ מִמֵּךְ יָצָא חֹשֵׁב עַל־יְהוָה רָעָה
,evil Jehovah against one come has Out .fully dried like shall they
plotting forth you of straw devoured be
3651 8003 30:68 559 35:41 1100 3289
12 יֹעֵץ בְּלִיָּעַל׃ כֹּה אָמַר יְהוָה אִם־שְׁלֵמִים וְכֵן
and ,complete Though ,Jehovah says Thus .worthlessness one
so counseling

be cut off, and will vanish. And though I have afflicted you, I will not afflict you any more. 13And now I will break his yoke from on you, and will tear away your bonds. 14And Jehovah has commanded about you, not *one* of your name shall be sown any more; I will cut off the carved image and the molten image out of the house of your gods; I will appoint your grave, for you are despised.

15Behold! The feet of Him bearing good news *is* on the mountains, making heard, Peace! O Judah, celebrate your feasts; fulfill your vows; for the worthless will not continue to pass through among you; he is completely cut off.

CHAPTER 2

1The one scattering is coming up against your face. Guard the rampart; watch the way; make the loins strong; exceedingly firm up *your* power. 2For Jehovah has turned the glory of Jacob, as the glory of Israel. For the plunderers have plundered them, and have destroyed their vine branches. 3The shield of his mighty ones has become red; the mighty men *are* clothed in scarlet; the chariots will flame like iron *torches* in the day of preparation; and the cypresses are made to quiver. 4The chariots run madly in the streets; they shall rush to and fro in the plazas. Their appearance *is* like torches; they dart about like the lightnings. 5He shall remember its nobles; they shall stumble in their walking; they shall hurry to its wall, and the covering shall be set up. 6The gates of the rivers shall be opened, and the palace shall be melted. 7And she who stood firm is uncovered and caused to go away; and her slavegirls are moaning like the sound of doves, beating on their breast.

8And Nineveh *is* like a pool of water from her days;

13 רַבִּים וְכֵן נָגֹזּוּ וְעָבָר וְעִנִּתִךְ לֹא אֲעַנֵּךְ עוֹד׃ וְעַתָּה

now And any will I not I Though and be will they yet ,many
.more you afflict ,you afflicted .vanish off cut therefore

14 אֶשְׁבֹּר מֹטֵהוּ מֵעָלָיִךְ וּמוֹסְרֹתַיִךְ אֲנַתֵּק׃ וְצִוָּה עָלֶיךָ יְהוָה

,Jehovah about has And will I your and upon from his will I
you commanded .away tear bonds ,you yoke break

לֹא־יִזָּרַע מִשִּׁמְךָ עוֹד מִבֵּית אֱלֹהֶיךָ אַכְרִית פֶּסֶל וּמַסֵּכָה

the and graven the will I your of Out any your from be shall not
;image cast image off cut gods of house the .more name sown (one)

אָשִׂים קִבְרֶךָ כִּי קַלּוֹתָ׃

are you for your will I
.despised ,grave appoint

CAP. II ב

CHAPTER 2

1 הִנֵּה עַל־הֶהָרִים רַגְלֵי מְבַשֵּׂר מַשְׁמִיעַ שָׁלוֹם חָגִּי יְהוּדָה

O Celebrate !Peace are bearing Him feet the the Upon ,Behold
,Judah heard making news good of mountains

חַגַּיִךְ שַׁלְּמִי נְדָרָיִךְ כִּי לֹא יוֹסִיף עוֹד לַעֲבוֹר־בָּךְ בְּלִיַּעַל

the among pass to any will not for your fulfill your
;worthless you through more continue ;vows ;feasts

2 כֻּלֹּה נִכְרָת׃ עָלָה מֵפִיץ עַל־פָּנַיִךְ נָצוֹר מְצֻרָה צַפֵּה־

watch the Guard your against one the com- Is is he com-
,rampart .face scattering up ing .off cut pletely

3 דֶרֶךְ חַזֵּק מָתְנַיִם אַמֵּץ כֹּחַ מְאֹד׃ כִּי שָׁב יְהוָה אֶת־גְּאוֹן

the Jehovah has For exceed- the firm the strengthen the
of glory turned .ingly power up ,loins ,way

יַעֲקֹב כִּגְאוֹן יִשְׂרָאֵל כִּי בְקָקוּם בֹּקְקִים וּזְמֹרֵיהֶם שִׁחֵתוּ׃

have they their and those emptied have For .Israel the like ,Jacob
.destroyed branches vine ,emptying them of glory

4 מָגֵן גִּבֹּרֵיהוּ מְאָדָּם אַנְשֵׁי־חַיִל מְתֻלָּעִים בְּאֵשׁ־פְּלָדוֹת

iron the with in clothed valor the become has mighty his The
(be shall) of fire ;scarlet (are) of men ;red ones of shield

5 הָרֶכֶב בְּיוֹם הֲכִינוֹ וְהַבְּרֹשִׁים הָרְעָלוּ׃ בַּחוּצוֹת יִתְהוֹלְלוּ

as run the In made are the and pre- his the in the
mad if streets .quiver to cypresses ;paration of day chariotry

הָרֶכֶב יִשְׁתַּקְשְׁקוּן בָּרְחֹבוֹת מַרְאֵיהֶן כַּלַּפִּידִם כַּבְּרָקִים

the Like .torches like ap- Their open the in rush shall They the
lightnings (is) pearance .squares fro and to .chariots

6 יְרוֹצֵצוּ׃ יִזְכֹּר אַדִּירָיו יִכָּשְׁלוּ בַּהֲלִיכוֹתָם יְמַהֲרוּ חוֹמָתָהּ

,wall its shall They their in shall They its shall He dart they
to hurry .walking stumble .nobles remember .about

7 וְהֻכַן הַסֹּכֵךְ׃ שַׁעֲרֵי הַנְּהָרוֹת נִפְתָּחוּ וְהַהֵיכָל נָמוֹג׃

be shall the and be shall rivers the gates The the shall and
.melted palace ,opened of .covering up set

8 וְהֻצַּב גֻּלְּתָה הֹעֲלָתָה וְאַמְהֹתֶיהָ מְנַהֲגוֹת כְּקוֹל יוֹנִים

,doves the like are her and to made and un- is who she And
of sound moaning handmaids ,away go covered firm stood

9 מְתֹפְפֹת עַל־לִבְבֵהֶן׃ וְנִינְוֵה כִבְרֵכַת־מַיִם מִימֵי הִיא

;her the from water a like (is) But their on beating
of days of pool Nineveh .breast

yet they are fleeing. Stand! Stand! *they cry;* but no one turns himself. [9]Seize the silver, seize the gold, for there is no end to the treasures; riches from all precious objects. [10]*She is* empty, even waste, even devastated. And the heart is melted, and the knees knocking; and trembling *is* in all the loins; and all of their faces collect heat. [11]Where *is* the den of the lions, and the feeding place of the young lions, where the lion *and* the lioness walked, *and* the lion's cub, and none shall terrify *them*. [12]The lion tears in pieces, enough for his cubs, and strangles for his lionesses, and has filled his holes *with* prey, even his lairs *with* torn prey. [13]Behold, I *am* against you, declares Jehovah of hosts; and I will burn her chariots in the smoke, and the sword shall devour your young lions. And I will cut off your prey from the earth, and the voice of your messengers shall not be heard any more.

וְהֵמָּה נָסִים עִמְדוּ עֲמֹדוּ וְאֵין מַפְנֶה׃ בֹּזּוּ כֶסֶף בֹּזּוּ 10
Plunder the Plunder turns who there but !Stand !Stand are Now
!silver .himself none is ,(cry they) .fleeing they

זָהָב וְאֵין קֵצֶה לַתְּכוּנָה כָּבֹד מִכֹּל כְּלִי חֶמְדָּה׃ בּוּקָה 11
(is She) .precious objects from riches the to end there For the
empty all treasure no is !gold

וּמְבוּקָה וּמְבֻלָּקָה וְלֵב נָמֵס וּפַק בִּרְכַּיִם וְחַלְחָלָה בְּכָל־
all in trembling and ,knees the and is the And and even
(is) of knocking ,melted heart .devastated waste

מָתְנַיִם וּפְנֵי כֻלָּם קִבְּצוּ פָארוּר׃ אַיֵּה מְעוֹן אֲרָיוֹת 12
,lions the den the Where .heat collect of all the and ,loins the
of (is) them of faces

וּמִרְעֶה הוּא לַכְּפִרִים אֲשֶׁר הָלַךְ אַרְיֵה לָבִיא שָׁם גּוּר
the ,there the lion walked where the for the and
of cub lioness (and) ,lions young place feeding

אַרְיֵה וְאֵין מַחֲרִיד׃ אַרְיֵה טֹרֵף בְּדֵי גֹרוֹתָיו וּמְחַנֵּק 13
and ,cubs his enough in tears lion The terrify shall and ;lion a
strangles for pieces .(them) none

לְלִבְאֹתָיו וַיְמַלֵּא־טֶרֶף חֹרָיו וּמְעֹנֹתָיו טְרֵפָה׃ הִנְנִי אֵלַיִךְ 14
against Behold torn (with) his even his (with) has and his for
,you (am) I .prey lairs ,holes prey filled ,lionesses

נְאֻם יְהוָה צְבָאוֹת וְהִבְעַרְתִּי בֶעָשָׁן רִכְבָּהּ וּכְפִירַיִךְ
your and her the in will I and ,hosts Jehovah declares
lions young ,chariots smoke burn of

תֹּאכַל חָרֶב וְהִכְרַתִּי מֵאֶרֶץ טַרְפֵּךְ וְלֹא־יִשָּׁמַע עוֹד
any be shall and your the from will I And the shall
more heard not ,prey earth off cut .sword devour

קוֹל מַלְאָכֵכֵה׃
your the
.messengers of voice

CAP. III. ג

CHAPTER 3

[1]Woe to the bloody city! All of it *is* a lie, full of plunder; the prey is not withdrawn. [2]The sound of a whip, and the sound of rattling of a wheel, and a galloping horse, and of a bounding chariot. [3]The horseman lifts up both the gleam of the sword and the lightning of the spear; and many *are* slain; and *there are* a mass of dead bodies, and no end of corpses; they stumble on their dead bodies, [4]because of the many harlotries of the well-favored harlot, the mistress of sorceries who sells nations by her harlotries, and families by her sorceries. [5]Behold, I *am* against you, declares Jehovah of hosts, and I will uncover your skirts over

CHAPTER 3

הוֹי עִיר דָּמִים כֻּלָּהּ כַּחַשׁ פֶּרֶק מְלֵאָה לֹא יָמִישׁ טָרֶף׃ 1
the is not ;of full plunder ,lie a of All !blood the Woe
.prey withdrawn (is) it of city (to)

קוֹל שׁוֹט וְקוֹל רַעַשׁ אוֹפָן וְסוּס דֹּהֵר וּמֶרְכָּבָה מְרַקֵּדָה׃ 2
.bounding a and ,galloping a and a the the and ,whip a The
chariot horse ,wheel of clatter of sound of sound

פָּרָשׁ מַעֲלֶה וְלַהַב חֶרֶב וּבְרַק חֲנִית וְרֹב חָלָל וְכֹבֶד פָּגֶר 3
corpses a and (are) and the the and the the and mount- is The
of mass ,slain many ;spear of lightning ,sword of gleam ,ing horseman

וְאֵין קֵצֶה לַגְּוִיָּה יִכְשְׁלוּ בִּגְוִיָּתָם׃ מֵרֹב זְנוּנֵי זוֹנָה טוֹבַת 4
well the harlotries Because their on they the to an not and
harlot of many of .corpses stumble ;bodies end is

חֵן בַּעֲלַת כְּשָׁפִים הַמֹּכֶרֶת גּוֹיִם בִּזְנוּנֶיהָ וּמִשְׁפָּחוֹת
families and her by nations sells who sorceries the ,favored
,harlotries of mistress

בִּכְשָׁפֶיהָ׃ הִנְנִי אֵלַיִךְ נְאֻם יְהוָה צְבָאוֹת וְגִלֵּיתִי שׁוּלַיִךְ 5
your will I and ,hosts Jehovah declares against ,Behold her by
skirts uncover of ,you (am) I .sorceries

your face; and I will cause the nations to see your nakedness, and the kingdoms your shame. ⁶And I will cast filth on you, and will disgrace you. And I will set you as a spectacle. ⁷And it shall be that all those who look on you shall flee from you, and shall say, Nineveh is laid waste; who shall weep for her? From where shall I seek comforters for you?

⁸Are you better than No Amon that dwelt among the Nile branches, waters surrounding her, whose rampart *was* the sea, the waters her wall? ⁹Ethiopia and Egypt *were* her strength; yea, without end; Put and Lubim were among your helpers; ¹⁰yet she *went* into exile; she went into captivity; also her young ones were dashed to pieces at the head of all the streets; and they cast lots for her honored ones; and all her great ones were bound in chains. ¹¹You also shall be drunken; you shall be hidden; you also shall seek a fortress from the enemy. ¹²All your fortresses are fig-trees with the firstfruits; if they are shaken, then they shall fall on the mouth of the eater. ¹³Behold, your people *are* women in your midst; the gates of your land shall surely be opened to your enemies; the fire shall devour your bars.

¹⁴Draw water of the siege for you! Strengthen your fortifications; go into the clay and tread in the mortar; make the mold strong. ¹⁵There fire will devour you, the sword shall cut you off; it will eat you up like the locust larvae. Make yourself as many as the larvae, multiply yourself like the locusts. ¹⁶You have increased your merchants above the stars of the heavens; the locust larvae shall strip off and fly away. ¹⁷Your princes *are* like the locusts, and your officials *are* a swarm of locusts that camp in the hedges in the cold day; the sun rises, and they flee, and the place where they *are* is not

---

6 עַל־פָּנָיִךְ וְהַרְאֵיתִי גוֹיִם מַעְרֵךְ וּמַמְלָכוֹת קְלוֹנֵךְ׃ וְהִשְׁלַכְתִּי
7993   7036   4467   46:26   1471   7200   6440   59:21
will I And   your   the and   your   the cause will I and your over
   cast   .shame   kingdoms nakedness nations see to   ,face

7 עָלַיִךְ שִׁקֻּצִים וְנִבַּלְתִּיךְ וְשַׂמְתִּיךְ כְּרֹאִי׃ וְהָיָה כָל־רֹאַיִךְ
7200   3605   1961   72:10   7760   5034   8051   59:21
seeing all   it And   a as   will I And   will and   filth   you on
you   .be shall .spectacle you set   you disdain

יִדּוֹד מִמֵּךְ וְאָמַר שָׁדְּדָה נִינְוֵה מִי יָנוּד לָהּ מֵאַיִן אֲבַקֵּשׁ
1245   370   5110 4310   5210 7703   559   5074
I shall From   for   will who ;Nineveh laid is   shall and   from   shall
seek   where   ?her lament   waste   ,say   you away flee

8 מְנַחֲמִים לָךְ׃ הֲתֵיטְבִי מִנֹּא אָמוֹן הַיֹּשְׁבָה בַּיְאֹרִים מַיִם
4325 2975   3427   527:   4996   3190   5162
waters the among   that   ,Amon than   you Are   for   comforters
     ,branches Nile dwell   -No better   ?you

9 סָבִיב לָהּ אֲשֶׁר־חֵיל יָם מִמַּיִם חוֹמָתָהּ׃ כּוּשׁ עָצְמָה וּמִצְרַיִם
4714   6109   3568   2346   3220/3220 : 2426   5439
;Egypt and   (her) Ethiopia   her   the   the   whose   ,her   sur-
   might (was)   ?wall   waters ,sea (was) rampart   rounding

10 וְאֵין קֵצֶה פּוּט וְלוּבִים הָיוּ בְּעֶזְרָתֵךְ׃ גַּם־הִיא לַגֹּלָה
14:73   1571   5833   1961 3864   6316   7097   369
into   she Yet   your among were Lubim and   Put   ;end   even
exile   (went)   helpers   without

הָלְכָה בַשֶּׁבִי גַּם עֹלָלֶיהָ יְרֻטְּשׁוּ בְּרֹאשׁ כָּל־חוּצוֹת וְעַל־
2351   7218   7376   5768   1571 7628:   1980
and ;streets the all   the at   dashed were   her also   into   she
for   of head   pieces to   young ;captivity went

11 נִכְבַּדֶּיהָ יַדּוּ גוֹרָל וְכָל־גְּדוֹלֶיהָ רֻתְּקוּ בַזִּקִּים׃ גַּם־אַתְּ
1571   2131   7576   1419 3605   14:86   3032   3513
you Also   .chains in   were   her   and   ,lots they   her
      bound ones great   all   cast ones honored

12 תִּשְׁכְּרִי תְּהִי נַעֲלָמָה גַּם־אַתְּ תְּבַקְשִׁי מָעוֹז מֵאוֹיֵב׃ כָּל־
36:105   341   4581   1245   1571   59:36   1961   7937
All   the from   a   seek shall   you also ;hidden shall you be shall
   .enemy fortress   be   ;drunken

מִבְצָרַיִךְ תְּאֵנִים עִם־בִּכּוּרִים אִם־יִנּוֹעוּ וְנָפְלוּ עַל־פִּי
6310   5307   5128   1061   8384   40:13
the upon they then   are they if   first- the   with   fig (are)   your
of mouth fall shall   ,shaken   ;fruits   trees   fortresses

13 אוֹכֵל׃ הִנֵּה עַמֵּךְ נָשִׁים בְּקִרְבֵּךְ לְאֹיְבַיִךְ פָּתוֹחַ נִפְתְּחוּ
6605   6605   341   7130   802   5971   2009   398
be shall   surely   your to   your in   (are)   your Behold   the
opened   enemies   ;midst   women people   .eater

14 שַׁעֲרֵי אַרְצֵךְ אָכְלָה אֵשׁ בְּרִיחָיִךְ׃ מֵי מָצוֹר שַׁאֲבִי־לָךְ
7579   4692   4325   1280   784:   1398   776   8179
for   draw   the   Water   gate your   the   shall   your gates the
!yourself   siege   of   .bars   fire devour   ;land   of

חַזְּקִי מִבְצָרָיִךְ בֹּאִי בַטִּיט וְרִמְסִי בַחֹמֶר הַחֲזִיקִי מַלְבֵּן׃
4404   2388   2563   7429   2916   935   4013   2388
the   make   the in   and   the   into go   your Strengthen
.mold   strong ;mortar   tread   clay   ;fortifications

15 שָׁם תֹּאכְלֵךְ אֵשׁ תַּכְרִיתֵךְ חֶרֶב תֹּאכְלֵךְ כַּיָּלֶק הִתְכַּבֵּד
3513   3218   1398   2719:   3772   784:   1398   8003
Multiply   the as   shall it   the   cut shall   ,fire devour will Com-
yourself   .larvae you devour ;sword   off you   you   pletely

כַּיֶּלֶק הִתְכַּבְּדִי כָּאַרְבֶּה׃ הִרְבֵּית רֹכְלַיִךְ מִכּוֹכְבֵי הַשָּׁמָיִם
8064   3556   7402   7235   697   3513   3218:
the   the than more   your   have You   the like   multiply   the as
;heavens   of stars merchants increased   .locusts   ;yourself   .larvae

16 יֶלֶק פָּשַׁט וַיָּעֹף׃ מִנְּזָרַיִךְ כָּאַרְבֶּה וְטַפְסְרַיִךְ כְּגוֹב גֹּבָי
1462   1462   2951   697   4502   57:74 6884   32:18
locusts a (are)   your and   the like   nobles Your fly and   shall   the
   of swarm officials ,locusts   (are)   .away off strip larvae

17 הַחוֹנִים בַּגְּדֵרוֹת בְּיוֹם קָרָה שֶׁמֶשׁ זָרְחָה וְנוֹדַד וְלֹא־נוֹדַע
3045   38:08 5074   2224   8121   7135   3117   1448   2583
is   and they and   ,rises sun the   ;cold the in   the in   that
known not   ,flee   of day   hedges   camp

known. 18Your shepherds
slumber, O king of Assyria;
your nobles are lying down.
Your people are scattered
on the mountains, and no
one is gathering. 19There is
no healing for your fracture;
your wound is severe. All
who hear of your report
shall clap the palm over
you; for on whom has your
wickedness not continually
passed?

6335 117 7931 804 4428 7462 5123 335 4725

18 מְקוֹמָם אַיָּם׃ נָמוּ רֹעֶיךָ מֶלֶךְ אַשּׁוּר יִשְׁכְּנוּ אַדִּירֶיךָ נָפֹשׁוּ

are scattered | your .nobles | lying down | Are | .Assyria | king of | O | Your ,shepherds | slumber | where .(are) they | their place

2470 7667 3545 369 6908 369 2022 5921 5971

19 עַמְּךָ עַל־הֶהָרִים וְאֵין מְקַבֵּץ׃ אֵין־כֵּהָה לְשִׁבְרֶךָ נַחְלָה

(is) severe | your fracture | for | healing | Not is | .collecting | any | and is not | the mountains | on | Your people

3808 4310 5921 5921 3709 8628 8085 8085 3605 4347

מַכָּתֶךָ כֹּל ׀ שֹׁמְעֵי שִׁמְעֲךָ תָּקְעוּ כַף עָלֶיךָ כִּי עַל־מִי לֹא־

not | whom | on | for | over ;you | the palm | shall clap | your report | those of hearing | All | your .wound

8548 7451 5674

עָבְרָה רָעָתְךָ תָּמִיד׃

?continually | your evil | has passed

A LITERAL TRANSLATION OF THE BIBLE

THE BOOK OF HABAKKUK

CHAPTER 1

1 The burden which Habakkuk the prophet saw: 2 O Jehovah, until when shall I cry for help, and You will not save? I cry out to You, Violence! But You do not save. 3 Why do You show me evil, and You look upon toil? For destruction and violence *are* before me; and there is strife, and contention rises up. 4 On account of this the law has become helpless, and justice does not continually go forth. For the wicked hems in the righteous, so justice goes forth, being perverted. 5 Look among the nations and see, and be amazed, be amazed. For a work is working in your days *which* you will not believe, though it be told to you. 6 For, behold, I raise up the Chaldeans, the bitter and impetuous nation which is going into the broad spaces of the land, to possess dwellings not his own. 7 He *is* terrible and fearful; his judgment and his glory comes from himself. 8 His horses also are swifter than leopards, and are fiercer than the evening wolves. And their horsemen spread themselves, and their horsemen come from afar; they shall fly as the eagle hurrying to eat. 9 All of him shall come for violence; the gathering of their faces *is* forward; and they gather captives like the sand. 10 And he shall scoff against the kings, and officials *shall be* a scorn to him. He shall scorn every fortress, and he shall heap up dirt, and capture it. 11 Then he sweeps on *like* a wind; and he transgresses, and is guilty; *crediting* this

חבקוק

LIBER HABAKKUK

(THE) BOOK OF HABAKKUK

CAPUT. I א

CHAPTER 1

7768 3068 5704 5030 2265 2372 834 4853
1 2 הַמַּשָּׂא אֲשֶׁר חָזָה חֲבַקּוּק הַנָּבִיא: עַד־אָנָה יְהוָה שִׁוַּעְתִּי
I shall Jehovah ,when Until the Habakkuk saw which The
.aid for call .prophet burden

7200 4100 3467 3808 2555 2199 8085 3808
3 וְלֹא תִשְׁמָע אֶזְעַק אֵלֶיךָ חָמָס וְלֹא תוֹשִׁיעַ: לָמָּה תַרְאֵנִי
You do Why You But !Violence to cry I will You and
me show !save not ,You out ?hear not

5375 4066 7379 1961 5048 2555 7701 5027 5999 205
אָוֶן וְעָמָל תַּבִּיט וְשֹׁד וְחָמָס לְנֶגְדִּי וַיְהִי רִיב וּמָדוֹן יִשָּׂא:
rises and ,strife and (are) and And You toil and ,evil
.up contention is ;me before violence ruin ?behold

7563 4941 5331 3318 3808 8451 6313
4 עַל־כֵּן תָּפוּג תּוֹרָה וְלֹא־יֵצֵא לָנֶצַח מִשְׁפָּט כִּי רָשָׁע
the For .justice continually goes and the become has Therefore
wicked forth not ,law helpless

7200 6127 4941 3318 3651 5921 6662 3803
5 מַכְתִּיר אֶת־הַצַּדִּיק עַל־כֵּן יֵצֵא מִשְׁפָּט מְעֻקָּל: רְאוּ
See being justice goes therefore the entraps
.perverted forth ;righteous

3808 3117 6467 6466 8539 8539 5027 1471
בַגּוֹיִם וְהַבִּיטוּ וְהִתַּמְּהוּ תְּמָהוּ כִּי־פֹעַל פֹּעֵל בִּימֵיכֶם לֹא
(which) your in is a For be be and and the among
not ,days working work !amazed ,amazed ,behold nations

1471 3778 6965 2005 5608 539
6 תַאֲמִינוּ כִּי יְסֻפָּר: כִּי־הִנְנִי מֵקִים אֶת־הַכַּשְׂדִּים הַגּוֹי
the ,Chaldeans the am ,behold ,For be it though will you
nation up raising I .you told ,believe

4908 3423 776 4800 3212 4116 4751
הַמַּר וְהַנִּמְהָר הַהוֹלֵךְ לְמֶרְחֲבֵי־אֶרֶץ לָרֶשֶׁת מִשְׁכָּנוֹת
dwellings to the broad the into is that and bitter
possess land of spaces going ,impetuous

3318 7613 4941 3372 366 3808
7 לֹּא־לוֹ: אָיֹם וְנוֹרָא הוּא מִמֶּנּוּ מִשְׁפָּטוֹ וּשְׂאֵתוֹ יֵצֵא:
came his and his from ;(is) he and Terrible to not
.forth majesty judgment himself fearful .him

6571 6335 6153 2061 2300 5483 5246 7043
8 וְקַלּוּ מִנְּמֵרִים סוּסָיו וְחַדּוּ מִזְּאֵבֵי עֶרֶב וּפָשׁוּ פָּרָשָׁיו
Their out spread the the than are and his than are And
,horsemen .evening of wolves fiercer ,horses leopards swifter

3605 398 2363 5404 5774 935 7350 6571
9 וּפָרָשָׁיו מֵרָחוֹק יָבֹאוּ יָעֻפוּ כְּנֶשֶׁר חָשׁ לֶאֱכוֹל: כֻּלֹּה
of All .eat to hurrying the as shall they shall from their and
him eagle fly ;come afar horsemen

7628 2349 622 6921 6440 4041 935 2555
לְחָמָס יָבוֹא מְגַמַּת פְּנֵיהֶם קָדִימָה וַיֶּאֱסֹף כַּחוֹל שֶׁבִי:
.captives the like they and (are) their gath- the shall for
sand gather ,forward faces of ering ;come violence

4013 3605 4890 7336 7046 4428
10 וְהוּא בַּמְּלָכִים יִתְקַלָּס וְרֹזְנִים מִשְׂחָק לוֹ הוּא לְכָל־מִבְצָר
fortress to he to (be shall) and shall the against And
every ,him scorn a officials ,scoff kings he

816 5674 7307 2498 227 3920 6083 6651 7831
11 יִשְׂחָק וַיִּצְבֹּר עָפָר וַיִּלְכְּדָהּ: אָז חָלַף רוּחַ וַיַּעֲבֹר וְאָשֵׁם
is and he and a (as) he Then capture and dirt shall he and shall
,guilty transgresses ,wind on sweeps .it up heap ,scorn

power of his to his god.
¹²Are You not from of old,
Jehovah our God, my Holy
One? We shall not die,
Jehovah, for You have
appointed him for judg-
ment. And, *my* Rock, You
have established him for
correction. ¹³*You are* of
purer eyes than to behold
evil, and You are not able to
look upon vexation. Why do
you look on those who deal
deceitfully? Will You be
silent when the wicked
swallows *one* more
righteous than he? ¹⁴For
You make man like the fish
of the sea, like creeping
things with no ruler over
him. ¹⁵He takes up all of
him with the hook; he drags
him with his net and
gathers him with his seine;
on account of this he
rejoices and exults. ¹⁶So he
sacrifices to his net, and
burns incense to his seine;
because by them his
portion *is* fat, and his food is
rich. ¹⁷Shall he therefore
empty his net, and shall he
not spare to continually slay
nations?

CHAPTER 2

¹I will stand on my guard,
and set myself on the
tower, and watch to see
what He will say against
me, and what I shall return
on my rebuke. ²And
Jehovah answered me and
said, Write the vision, and
engrave *it* on the tablets,
that he who reads it may
run. ³For the vision *is* still
for the appointed time, but
it does not lie. Though it
delays, wait for it; because
it will surely come; it will
not tarry. ⁴Behold, the soul
of him is puffed up *and* is
not upright; but the just
shall live by his faith.

⁵And also wine indeed
betrays a proud man, and
he is not content; who
widens his soul like Sheol,
and he *is* like death, and is

12

6918	430	3068	6924			430	3581/2098
קָדְשִׁי	אֱלֹהַי	יְהוָה	מִקֶּדֶם	אַתָּה	הֲלוֹא	לֵאלֹהוֹ	זוּ כֹחוֹ

my Holy | my God, | Jehovah | from old of, | You | Are | his god. | his to | his this power

3245	2198	6697	7760	4941	3068	4191	38:08

יְסַדְתּוֹ לְהוֹכִיחַ וְצוּר שַׂמְתּוֹ לְמִשְׁפָּט יְהוָה נְמוּת לֹא

estab- you to .him lished correct ,Rock .him set judgment ;Jehovah shall we Not die

13

4100	3201	38:08	5999	5027	7451:	7200	5869	2889

לָמָּה תּוּכַל לֹא אֶל־עָמָל וְהַבִּיט רָע מֵרְאוֹת עֵינַיִם טְהוֹר

why are You not vexa- upon to and ,evil to than eyes Purer
;able tion look view (are You) of

14

6213		6662	7563	1104	2790:	898:	5027

וַתַּעֲשֶׂה מִמֶּנּוּ צַדִּיק רָשָׁע בְּבַלַּע תַּחֲרִישׁ בּוֹגְדִים תַּבִּיט

You For than more (one) the when You Will dealing those You do
make ?he righteous wicked swallows silent be ?deceitfully watch

15

5927	2443	3605	4910	7431	3220	1709	120

הֶעֱלָה בְּחַכָּה כֻּלֹּה לֹא־מָשַׁל בּוֹ כְּרֶמֶשׂ הַיָּם כִּדְגֵי אָדָם

takes he a with Everyone over one not creep- like the the like man
;up hook him of .him ruling (is) ,things ing ,sea of fish

1524	8056		4365	622	2764	1641

וְיָגִיל יִשְׂמַח עַל־כֵּן בְּמִכְמַרְתּוֹ וְיַאַסְפֵהוּ בְחֶרְמוֹ יְגֹרֵהוּ

and he therefore his with gathers and his with drags he
.exults rejoices ;fishnet him ,net him

16

8082	1992	4365	6999	2764	2076

שָׁמֵן בְּחֶלְקָה כִּי לְמִכְמַרְתּוֹ וִיקַטֵּר לְחֶרְמוֹ יְזַבֵּחַ עַל־כֵּן

grows them by be- cause ;fishnet burns and his to he Therefore
fat fat incense net sacrifices

17

202:6	8548	2764	7324	3651	1277	3978	2506

לַהֲרֹג וְתָמִיד חֶרְמוֹ יָרִיק כֵּן הַעַל בְּרִאָה וּמַאֲכָלוֹ חֶלְקוֹ

slay to and ,net his he ,Therefore .rich is his and his
continually empty shall food portion

		2550	38:08	1471

גּוֹיִם לֹא יַחְמוֹל:

he shall not nations
?spare

CAP. II ב

CHAPTER 2

1

7200	68:22	4692	3321	5975	4931	59:21

עַל־מִשְׁמַרְתִּי אֶעֱמֹדָה וְאֶתְיַצְּבָה עַל־מָצוֹר וַאֲצַפֶּה לִרְאוֹת

see to will I guard my On
watch bulwark the on set and myself ,stand

2

3068	6030	8433	59:21	7725	4100	1696 4100

יְהוָה וַיַּעֲנֵנִי עַל־תּוֹכַחְתִּי אָשִׁיב וּמָה מַה־יְדַבֶּר־בִּי

Jehovah an- And my upon shall I and against will He what
me swered .rebuke return what ,me say

7121	7323	4616	3871	59:21	874	23:77	3789	559

בוֹ קוֹרֵא יָרוּץ לְמַעַן עַל־הַלֻּחוֹת וּבָאֵר חָזוֹן כְּתֹב וַיֹּאמֶר

.it is who may he so the on en- and the Write ,said and
reading run that tablets (it) grave ,vision

3

4102	3576	38:08	7093	6315	41:50	2377	5750

לַמּוֹעֵד חָזוֹן עוֹד כִּי וְלֹא יְכַזֵּב לַקֵּץ וְיָפֵחַ אִם־יִתְמַהְמָהּ

,delays it Though does and the to it but the for the still Fór
.lie not ,end pants ,time set (is) vision

4

3474	3808	6075	2009	309	38:08	935	935	2442

לוֹ חַכֵּה־לוֹ כִּי יָבֹא בֹא כִּי־אַחֵר לֹא יָבֹא עֻפְּלָה הִנֵּה לֹא־יָשְׁרָה

,upright is not puffed is ,Behold will it not will it surely for for wait
;come .tarry ;it

5

1397	898	3196	637	2421	530	6662	5315

גָּבֶר בּוֹגֵד כִּי־הַיַּיִן וְאַף יִחְיֶה בֶּאֱמוּנָתוֹ וְצַדִּיק נַפְשׁוֹ

a betrays the ,indeed And shall his by the but in his
man wine also .live faith just him soul

4194	5315	75:85	7337:	834	5115	38:08	3093

כַמָּוֶת וְהוּא נַפְשׁוֹ כִשְׁאוֹל הִרְחִיב אֲשֶׁר יִנְוֶה וְלֹא יָהִיר

like he and his Sheol like widens who is he and ,proud
,death (is) ,soul ;content not

not satisfied, but gathers all the nations to himself, and collects all the peoples to himself. [6]Shall not all of these lift up a parable against him, and a mocking riddle to him, and say, Woe to him who increases *what is* not his! How long, then, shall he load the pledges on himself? [7]Shall not those who strike you rise up suddenly, and *those* who shake you awake, and you become a prize to him? [8]Because you have plundered many nations, all the rest of the people shall plunder you, because of the blood of men, and the violence of the land, and the city, and all those dwelling in it.

[9]Woe *to* him who robs evil booty for his house, to set his nest on high, to be delivered from the hand of evil! [10]You have advised shame for your house, to make an end of many peoples, and are sinning *in* your soul. [11]For the stone shall cry out from the wall, and the beam shall answer it from the wood.

[12]Woe *to* him who builds a town with blood, and establishes a city by iniquity! [13]Behold, is it not for Jehovah of hosts that the people labor only for fire; yea, nations weary themselves only for vanity? [14]For the earth shall be filled with the knowledge of the glory of Jehovah, as the waters cover the sea.

[15]Woe *to* him who causes his friend to drink, pouring out your wineskin, and also making *him* drunk, so as to look upon their nakedness! [16]You are filled with shame instead of glory; you drink also, and *will* be seen as uncircumcised. The cup of the right hand of Jehovah shall turn on you, and disgrace *shall be* your glory. [17]For the violence of Lebanon shall cover you, and the ruin of beasts shall terrify them because of the blood of men, and the violence of the land, the city, and all those dwelling in it.

[18]What does an image

5971 3605 6908 1471 3605 622 7646 3808
וְלֹא יִשְׂבָּע וַיֶּאֱסֹף אֵלָיו כָּל־הַגּוֹיִם וַיִּקְבֹּץ אֵלָיו כָּל־הָעַמִּים׃
the all to and the all to but sat- is and
;peoples himself collects ,nations himself gathers ,isfied not

2420 4426 5375 4912 3605 428
6 הֲלוֹא־אֵלֶּה כֻלָּם עָלָיו מָשָׁל יִשָּׂאוּ וּמְלִיצָה חִידוֹת לוֹ
to riddle a and ,up lift a against of all ,these shall
,him mocking parable him ,them not

5671 5921 3513 5704 3808 7235 1945 559
וְיֹאמַר הוֹי הַמַּרְבֶּה לֹּא־לוֹ עַד־מָתַי וּמַכְבִּיד עָלָיו עַבְטִיט׃
the upon he even when Until to (is what) one the Woe and
?pledges himself loading (is) !him not increasing (to) ,say

4933 1961 2111 3364 5391 6965 6621
7 הֲלוֹא פֶתַע יָקוּמוּ נֹשְׁכֶיךָ וְיִקְצוּ מְזַעְזְעֶיךָ וְהָיִיתָ לִמְשִׁסּוֹת
prize a you and who those be and who those rise suddenly Shall
become you shake aroused you strike up not

5971 3499 3605 7997 7227 1471 7997 3588
8 לָמוֹ׃ כִּי־אַתָּה שַׁלּוֹתָ גּוֹיִם רַבִּים יְשָׁלּוּךָ כָּל־יֶתֶר עַמִּים
the the all shall ,many nations have you Because to
,peoples of rest you plunder plundered ?him

1945 3427 3605 7151 776 2555 120 1818
9 מִדְּמֵי אָדָם וַחֲמַס־אֶרֶץ קִרְיָה וְכָל־יֹשְׁבֵי בָהּ׃ הוֹי
Woe .it in those and the and the the and ,man from
(to) dwelling all city land of violence of blood the

7451 3709 5337 7064 4791 7760 1004 7451 1215 1214
בֹּצֵעַ בֶּצַע רָע לְבֵיתוֹ לָשׂוּם בַּמָּרוֹם קִנּוֹ לְהִנָּצֵל מִכַּף־רָע׃
!evil the from be to his the in set to his for evil gain the him
of palm delivered ,nest height ,house of gaining

5315 2398 7227 5971 7096 1004 3289 1322
10 יָעַצְתָּ בֹּשֶׁת לְבֵיתֶךָ קְצוֹת־עַמִּים רַבִּים וְחוֹטֵא נַפְשֶׁךָ׃
your (in) are and ,many peoples make to your for shame have You
,soul sinning of end an house counselled

1129 1945 6030 6086 3714 2199 7023 68
11
12 כִּי־אֶבֶן מִקִּיר תִּזְעָק וְכָפִיס מֵעֵץ יַעֲנֶנָּה׃ הוֹי בֹּנֶה
him (to) Woe shall the from the and cry shall from the For
building .it answer wood beam ,out wall the stone

3068 2009 5766 7151 3559 1818 5892
13 עִיר בְּדָמִים וְכוֹנֵן קִרְיָה בְּעַוְלָה׃ הֲלוֹא הִנֵּה מֵאֵת יְהוָה
Jehovah from ,behold it Is by city a and with a
of ,not !iniquity establishing ,blood town

3286 7385 1767 3816 784 1767 5971 3021 6635
צְבָאוֹת וְיִיגְעוּ עַמִּים בְּדֵי־אֵשׁ וּלְאֻמִּים בְּדֵי־רִיק יִעָפוּ׃
grow emptiness only and ;fire only peoples that ,hosts
.weary for nations for toil

3680 4325 3068 3519 3045 776 4390
14 כִּי תִּמָּלֵא הָאָרֶץ לָדַעַת אֶת־כְּבוֹד יְהוָה כַּמַּיִם יְכַסּוּ
cover the as ,Jehovah glory the the with the be shall For
waters of of knowledge earth filled

7937 2573 5595 7453 8248 1945 3220
15 עַל־יָם׃ הוֹי מַשְׁקֵה רֵעֵהוּ מְסַפֵּחַ חֲמָתְךָ וְאַף שַׁכֵּר
making and your pouring his causing him Woe the over
drunk also ,wineskin out ,friend drink to (to) .sea

8354 3519 7036 7646 4589 5027
16 לְמַעַן הַבִּיט עַל־מְעוֹרֵיהֶם׃ שָׂבַעְתָּ קָלוֹן מִכָּבוֹד שְׁתֵה
drink from (with) are You their upon look order in
;glory shame satiated !nakedness to

5921 7022 3068 3225 3563 5921 5437 6188 1571
גַם־אַתָּה וְהֵעָרֵל תִּסּוֹב עָלֶיךָ כּוֹס יְמִין יְהוָה וְקִיקָלוֹן עַל־
on disgrace ,Jehovah right the the upon Shall seen be and you also
of hand of cup you turn !uncircumcised

1818 2865 929 7701 3680 3844 2555 3519
17 כְּבוֹדֶךָ׃ כִּי־חֲמַס לְבָנוֹן יְכַסֶּךָּ וְשֹׁד בְּהֵמוֹת יְחִיתַן מִדְּמֵי
the from shall beasts the and shall Lebanon the For your
of blood them terrify of ruin ,you cover of violence .glory

6459 3276 4100 3427 3605 7151 776 2555 120
18 אָדָם וַחֲמַס־אֶרֶץ קִרְיָה וְכָל־יֹשְׁבֵי בָהּ׃ מָה־הוֹעִיל פֶּסֶל
an does What .it in those and the the the and ,man
,image profit dwelling all ,city ,land of violence

profit, for its maker has carved it; a molten image, and a teacher of falsehood. For does the maker trust in his work on it, to make mute idols? [19]Woe *to* him who says to the wood, Awake! To a mute stone, Rise up, it shall teach! Behold, it *is* overlaid *with* gold and silver, but no breath is in its midst. [20]But Jehovah *is* in His holy temple; let all the earth be silent before Him.

3335 3335 982 8267 3384 4541 33:36 6458
כִּי פְסָלוֹ יֹצְרוֹ מַסֵּכָה וּמוֹרֶה שָׁקֶר כִּי־בָטַח יֹצֵר יִצְרוֹ
his work | the maker | trusts For | false-?hood | an and of instructor | casted a image | its ;maker | carved has | for it

6974 6086 559 1945 483 457 6213 59:21
19 עָלָיו לַעֲשׂוֹת אֱלִילִים אִלְּמִים׃ הוֹי אֹמֵר לָעֵץ הָקִיצָה
!Awake | the to wood | one the saying | Woe (to) | ?mute | idols | make to | upon it

3701 2095 8610 2009 3384 1748 68 5782
עוּרִי לְאֶבֶן דּוּמָם הוּא יוֹרֶה הִנֵּה־הוּא תָּפוּשׂ זָהָב וָכֶסֶף
and ,silver | (with) gold | is overlaid | it ,Behold | shall !instruct | it | ;silent | a to stone | !Arise

6440 2013 69.44 1964 3068 7130 369 7307 3605
20 וְכָל־רוּחַ אֵין בְּקִרְבּוֹ׃ וַיהוָה בְּהֵיכַל קָדְשׁוֹ הַס מִפָּנָיו
before ,Him | be silent | His ;holiness | the in (is) of temple | But Jehovah | its in .midst | not is | breath | and any

776 3605
כָּל־הָאָרֶץ׃
.earth the | all

CAP. III ג

CHAPTER 3

CHAPTER 3

[1]A prayer of Habakkuk the prophet concerning erring ones:

[2]*O* Jehovah, I have heard Your report; I am afraid, Jehovah. Give new life *to* Your work in the midst of years; in the midst of years make known; in anger remember compassion. [3]God comes from Teman, and the Holy One from Mount Paran. Selah. His majesty covers the heavens, and His praise fills the earth. [4]And *His* brightness is as the light; rays from His hand *are* His, and there *was* a covering of His strength. [5]A plague goes before Him, and lightning went forth at His feet. [6]He stood and measured the earth; He looked and shook nations; and the ancient mountains were shattered; the eternal hills bowed down; the goings of eternity *are* His.

[7]I saw the tents of Cushan under calamity; the curtains of the land of Midian trembled. [8]Did Jehovah burn against rivers? Or *was* Your anger against the rivers? Or Your fury against the sea? *For* You ride on horses; Your chariots of salvation [9]Naked You bare Your bow; *according to* the oaths of the rods of *Your* word.

8088 8085 3068 7691 5921 5030 2265 8605
1 תְּפִלָּה לַחֲבַקּוּק הַנָּבִיא עַל שִׁגְיֹנוֹת׃
2 יְהוָה שָׁמַעְתִּי שִׁמְעֲךָ
Your report | have I heard | ,Jehovah | erring .ones | con- cerning | the ,prophet | Habakkuk of | A prayer

8141 7130 2421 8141 7130 6467 3068 3372
יָרֵאתִי יְהוָה פָּעָלְךָ בְּקֶרֶב שָׁנִים חַיֵּיהוּ בְּקֶרֶב שָׁנִים
years | the in of midst | it give ;life | ,years | the in of midst | Your (to) work | Jeho- ,vah | am I ;afraid

6918 935 8487 433 2142 7355 7267 3045
3 תּוֹדִיעַ בְּרֹגֶז רַחֵם תִּזְכּוֹר׃ אֱלוֹהַּ מִתֵּימָן יָבוֹא וְקָדוֹשׁ
the and One Holy | ,comes | from Teman | God | .remember | com- passion | anger in | make ;known

4390 8416 1935 8064 3680 5542 6290 2022
מֵהַר־פָּארָן סֶלָה כִּסָּה שָׁמַיִם הוֹדוֹ וּתְהִלָּתוֹ מָלְאָה
fills | His and praise | His ,majesty | the heavens | covers | .Selah | .Paran | the from of mountain

2253 8033 3027 7161 1961 216 5051 776
4 הָאָרֶץ׃ וְנֹגַהּ כָּאוֹר תִּהְיֶה קַרְנַיִם מִיָּדוֹ לוֹ וְשָׁם חֶבְיוֹן
a (was) of covering | and there | to (are) ,His | from hand His | rays | ;is | the as light | (His) And brightness | the .earth

4058 5975 7272 7565 3318 1698 3212 6440 5797
5 עֻזֹּה׃ לְפָנָיו יֵלֶךְ דָּבֶר וְיֵצֵא רֶשֶׁף לְרַגְלָיו׃
6 עָמַד וַיְמֹדֶד
and measured | He stood | His at .feet | lightning | and forth went | ,plague a | goes | Before Him | His .strength

1389 7817 57:03/2042 6327 14:71 5425 7200 776
אֶרֶץ רָאָה וַיַּתֵּר גּוֹיִם וַיִּתְפֹּצְצוּ הַרְרֵי־עַד שַׁחוּ גִּבְעוֹת
the of hills | bowed down | ;ancient | the mountains | were and shattered | ;nations | and shook | He looked | the ;earth

3572 168 7200 205 8478 5769 1979 5769
7 עוֹלָם הֲלִיכוֹת עוֹלָם לוֹ׃ תַּחַת אָוֶן רָאִיתִי אָהֳלֵי כוּשָׁן
;Cushan | tents the of | saw I | calamity | Under | to .Him | (are) | eternity | goings the of | ;eternity

3068 2734 5104 4080 776 3407 7264
8 יִרְגְּזוּן יְרִיעוֹת אֶרֶץ מִדְיָן׃ הֲבִנְהָרִים חָרָה יְהוָה אִם
Or (was) | ?Jehovah | burn | against | Did rivers | Midian | the of land | the of curtains | trembled

5483 5921 7392 5678 3220 639 5104
בַּנְּהָרִים אַפֶּךָ אִם־בַּיָּם עֶבְרָתֶךָ כִּי תִרְכַּב עַל־סוּסֶיךָ
Your ,horses | on | You ride | (For) | Your ?fury | against sea the | Or | Your ?anger | the against rivers

4294 7621 7198 6181 5783 3444 4818
9 מַרְכְּבֹתֶיךָ יְשׁוּעָה׃ עֶרְיָה תֵעוֹר קַשְׁתֶּךָ שְׁבֻעוֹת מַטּוֹת
rods the of | (to according) oaths the of | Your ;bow | You bare | Naked | .salvation | Your of chariots

Selah. You have cut
through the earth *with*
rivers. 10They saw You;
mountains trembled. The
storm of water passed over;
the deep gave its voice *and*
lifted up its hands on high.
11The sun *and* moon stood
still in their dwelling. At the
light of Your arrows they go,
at the shining of Your
gleaming spear. 12You
march into the land in fury.
You thresh nations in
anger. 13You went forth for
the salvation of Your
people, for the salvation of
Your anointed. You struck
the head from the house of
the wicked, to bare the
foundation to the neck.
Selah.

14You pierced the head of
his warriors with his shafts;
they rush to scatter me;
their rejoicing *is* to devour
the meek in a secret place.
15You trod in the sea with
Your horses, the foaming of
many waters. 16I heard,
and my belly trembled; my
lips quivered at the sound.
Rottenness entered into my
bones, and I trembled
within myself that I might
rest for the day of distress;
to come up against the
people, he cuts him off.

17Though the fig-tree
shall not blossom; and fruit
is not on the vines; the work
of the olive fails; and the
fields make no food; the
flock is cut off from the fold;
and no herd *is* in the
stalls; 18yet I will exult in
Jehovah; I will rejoice in the
God of my salvation.
19Jehovah the Lord *is* my
might, and He sets my feet
like hinds' *feet*, and He will
make me to walk on my
high places.

To the chief singer, on
my stringed instruments.

2230 2022 2342 7200 776 1234 5104 5542 561
10 אמר סלה נהרות תבקע־ארץ: ראוך יחילו הרים זרם
mountains (and) Saw the have You (with) .Selah (Your)
gushing whirled You .earth split rivers .word

3394 8121 5375 3027 7315 6963 8415 5414 5674 4325
11 מים עבר נתן תהום קולו רום ידיהו נשא: שמש ירח
the (and) The lifted it its high its the gave passed water
moon sun .up hands ;voice deep ;over

2195 2595 1300 5051 1980 2671 216 2073 5975
12 עמד זבלה לאור חציך יהלכו לנגה ברק חניתך: בזעם
fury In Your light- the the at they Your the At (their) in stood
.spear of ning of splendor ,march arrows of light .dwelling

3468 5971 3468 3318 1471 1758 639 776 6805
13 תצעד־ארץ באף תדוש גוים: יצאת לישע עמך לישע
the for Your the for went You .nations You In the march You
of saving people of salvation forth thresh anger .land into

5750 3247 6168 7563 1004 7218 4272 4899
את־משיחך מחצת ראש מבית רשע ערות יסוד עד
to foun- the bare to the the from the You Your
dation ,wicked of house head struck .anointed

6327 5590 6518 7218 4294 5344 5542 6677
14 צואר סלה: נקבת במטיו ראש פרזו יסערו להפיצני
scatter to rush they his head the his with You .Selah the
;me ;warriors of shafts pierced .neck

2563 5483 3220 1869 4565 6041 398 5951
15 עליצתם כמו־לאכל עני במסתר: דרכת בים סוסיך חמר
foam- the Your the (in) You the to the to (is) their
of ing ,horses sea trod .place secret meek devour as rejoicing

935 8193 6750 6963 990 7264 8085 7227 4325
16 מים רבים: שמעתי ותרגז בטני לקול צללו שפתי יבוא
Enters my quivered the at my and heard I .many waters
.lips sound ;belly trembled

5927 6869 3117 5117 834 7264 8478 6106 7538
רקב בעצמי ותחתי ארגז אשר אנוח ליום צרה לעלות
come to ;distress the for might I that I within and my into rotten-
up of day rest ,trembled myself ,bones ness

3584 1612 2981 369 6524 3808 8384 1464 5971
17 לעם יגודנו: כי־תאנה לא־תפרח ואין יבול בגפנים כחש
(and) the on produce and does not fig the Though cuts he against
fails .vines is not ,bud tree .him off people

369 6629 4356 1504 400 6213 3808 7709 2132 4639
מעשה־זית ושדמות לא־עשה אכל גזר ממכלה צאן ואין
and the the from (is) and ,food make not the and the the
is not ,flock fold off cut fields ,olive of work

3468 430 1523 5937 3068 7517 1241
18 בקר ברפתים: ואני ביהוה אעלוזה אגילה באלהי ישעי:
sal- my the in will I ,exult will in I yet the in herd
.vation of God rejoice Jehovah ,stalls

3381 1116 5921 355 7272 7760 2428 136 3068
19 יהוה אדני חילי וישם רגלי כאילות ועל־במותי ידרכני
will He high my and the like my He and my (is) the Jehovah
.walk me make places on ,hinds' feet set ,might Lord

5068 5329
למנצח בנגינותי:
stringed my on chief the To
.instruments ,musician

צפניה

LIBER ZEPHANIAE

(THE) BOOK OF ZEPHANIAH

CAPUT. I א

CHAPTER 1

A LITERAL TRANSLATION OF THE BIBLE

THE BOOK OF ZEPHANIAH

CHAPTER 1

[1]The word of Jehovah which was to Zephaniah the son of Cushi, the son of Gedaliah, the son of Amariah, the son of Hezekiah, in the days of Josiah the son of Amon, king of Judah:

[2]I will completely snatch away all from on the face of the ground, declares Jehovah. [3]I will snatch away man and beast: I will snatch away the birds of the heavens and the fish of the sea, and the stumbling-blocks, *even* the wicked. And I will cut off man from the face of the ground, declares Jehovah. [4]I will also stretch out My hand on Judah, and on all the inhabitants of Jerusalem. And I will cut off the remnant of Baal from this place, the name of the idol-worshipers, with the priests; [5]and those bowing to the host of the heavens on the housetops; and those bowing, swearing to Jehovah and swearing by Malcham *too*; [6]and those drawing back from after Jehovah, and who have not sought Jehovah, nor asked of Him. [7]Be silent before the face of the Lord Jehovah, for the day of Jehovah *is* near. For Jehovah has appointed a sacrifice; He has consecrated His called ones. [8]And it shall be in the day of the sacrifice of Jehovah, I will punish the rulers and the king's sons, and all those clothed *in* foreign clothing. [9]And I will punish

1436/1121 3569/1121 6846 19,61 834 3068 1697
1 דְּבַר־יְהוָה ׀ אֲשֶׁר הָיָה אֶל־צְפַנְיָה בֶן־כּוּשִׁי בֶן־גְּדַלְיָה
,Gedaliah the ,Cushi the Zephaniah to was which Jehovah The
of son of son of word

3063 44,28 526 1121 2977 3117 2396 1121 568 1121
בֶּן־אֲמַרְיָה בֶּן־חִזְקִיָּה בִּימֵי יֹאשִׁיָּהוּ בֶן־אָמוֹן מֶלֶךְ יְהוּדָה׃
.Judah king ,Amon the ,Josiah the in ,Hezekiah the ,Amariah the
of of son of days of son of son

622 3068 5002 127 6440 5921 36,05 622 622
2 אָסֹף אָסֵף כֹּל מֵעַל פְּנֵי הָאֲדָמָה נְאֻם־יְהוָה׃
3 אָסֵף
will I .Jehovah statement the the from all will I com-
gather of ground of face on away snatch pletely

4384 32:20 1709 8064 5775 622 929 120
אָדָם וּבְהֵמָה אָסֵף עוֹף־הַשָּׁמַיִם וּדְגֵי הַיָּם וְהַמַּכְשֵׁלוֹת
stumbling the and the the and the the will I and man
,blocks ,sea of fish heavens of birds snatch ,beast

127 6440 5921 120 3772 7563
אֶת־הָרְשָׁעִים וְהִכְרַתִּי אֶת־הָאָדָם מֵעַל פְּנֵי הָאֲדָמָה
the the from man will I And .wicked the (even)
,ground of face on off cut

3389 3427 36,05 30:63 3027 5186 3068 5002
4 נְאֻם־יְהוָה׃ וְנָטִיתִי יָדִי עַל־יְהוּדָה וְעַל כָּל־יוֹשְׁבֵי יְרוּשָׁלָ͏ִם
.Jerusalem those all and Judah against My will I And Jehovah state-
in dwelling against hand out stretch of ment

8034 1168 7604 2088 4725 3772
וְהִכְרַתִּי מִן־הַמָּקוֹם הַזֶּה אֶת־שְׁאָר הַבַּעַל אֶת־שֵׁם
the ,Baal remnant the this place from will I And
of name of off cut

1406 7812 3548 3649
5 הַכְּמָרִים עִם־הַכֹּהֲנִים׃ וְאֶת־הַמִּשְׁתַּחֲוִים עַל־הַגַּגּוֹת
the on those and ;priests the with the
roofs bowing idolators

30:68 7650 7812 8064 6635
לִצְבָא הַשָּׁמָיִם וְאֶת־הַמִּשְׁתַּחֲוִים הַנִּשְׁבָּעִים לַיהוָה
to swearing those and the the to
,Jehovah ,bowing ;heavens of host

834 3068 310 5472 4445 7650
6 וְהַנִּשְׁבָּעִים בְּמַלְכָּם׃ וְאֶת־הַנְּסוֹגִים מֵאַחֲרֵי יְהוָה וַאֲשֶׁר
and ,Jehovah from drawing those and by swearing yet
who after back ;Malcham

3068 136 6440 20:13 1875 38:08 3068 1245
7 לֹא־בִקְשׁוּ אֶת־יְהוָה וְלֹא דְרָשֻׁהוּ׃ הַס מִפְּנֵי אֲדֹנָי יְהוִה
,Jehovah the before Be asked have and ,Jehovah have not
Lord silent .Him of not sought

7121 6942 2077 3068 3559 30:68 3117 7138
כִּי קָרוֹב יוֹם יְהוָה כִּי־הֵכִין יְהוָה זֶבַח הִקְדִּישׁ קְרֻאָיו׃
called His has He a Jehovah has For !Jehovah the (is) for
.ones consecrated ;sacrifice appointed of day near

5921 8269 59:21 6485 30,68 2077 3117 1961
8 וְהָיָה בְּיוֹם זֶבַח יְהוָה וּפָקַדְתִּי עַל־הַשָּׂרִים וְעַל־
and the upon will I that ,Jehovah the the in it And
upon rulers visit of sacrifice of day ,be shall

6485 5237 44,03 3847 36,05 44,28 1121
9 בְּנֵי הַמֶּלֶךְ וְעַל כָּל־הַלֹּבְשִׁים מַלְבּוּשׁ נָכְרִי׃ וּפָקַדְתִּי
will I And .foreign (in) those all and the the
visit clothing clothed upon ,king of sons

all those who leap on the threshold in that day, who fill their master's houses *with* violence and deceit. [10]And it shall be in that day, declares Jehovah, the sound of a cry from the Fish Gate, and a howling from the Second, and a great breaking from the hills. [11]Howl, dwellers of Maktesh, for all the people of Canaan have perished; all those carrying silver are cut off. [12]And it shall be in that time, I will search Jerusalem with lamps, and punish the men being settled on their lees; who say in their heart, Jehovah will not do good, nor will He do evil. [13]And their goods shall become a prize, and their houses a waste. They shall also build houses, but not live *there*; and they shall plant vineyards, but not drink their wine.

[14]The great day of Jehovah *is* near; *it is* near and rushing greatly, the sound of the day of Jehovah. The mighty man shall cry out bitterly there. [15]That day *is* a day of wrath, a day of adversity and distress, a day of waste and ruin, a day of darkness and gloom, a day of clouds and thick darkness; [16]a day of the ram's horn and alarm against the fortified cities, and against the high towers. [17]And I will bring distress to men, and they shall walk like the blind, because they have sinned against Jehovah. And their blood shall be poured out as dust, and their flesh like dung. [18]Their silver and their gold shall not be able to deliver them in the day of the wrath of Jehovah. But

1004 4390 3117 4670 5921 1801 3605 5921
עַל כָּל־הַדּוֹלֵג עַל־הַמִּפְתָּן בַּיּוֹם הַהוּא הַמְמַלְאִים בֵּית
house the those ,that day in the on those all upon
of filling threshold leaping

5002 3117 1961 4820 2555 113
10 אֲדֹנֵיהֶם חָמָס וּמִרְמָה׃ וְהָיָה בַיּוֹם הַהוּא נְאֻם־
statement ,that day in it And and (with) their
of be shall .deceit violence masters

7667 4932 3215 1709 8179 6818 6963 3068
יְהוָה קוֹל צְעָקָה מִשַּׁעַר הַדָּגִים וִילָלָה מִן־הַמִּשְׁנֶה וְשֶׁבֶר
a and the from a and the from cry a the ,Jehovah
breaking ,Second howling ,Fish Gate of sound

3605 1820 4389 3427 3213 1389 1419
11 גָּדוֹל מֵהַגְּבָעוֹת׃ הֵילִילוּ יֹשְׁבֵי הַמַּכְתֵּשׁ כִּי נִדְמָה כָּל־
all have for ,Maktesh dwellers ,Howl the from great
perished of .hills

6256 1961 3701 5187 3605 3772 3667 5971
12 עַם כְּנַעַן נִכְרְתוּ כָּל־נְטִילֵי כָסֶף׃ וְהָיָה בָּעֵת
time in it And .silver those all cut are ;Canaan the
be shall carrying off of people

582 5921 6485 5216 3389 2664
הַהִיא אֲחַפֵּשׂ אֶת־יְרוּשָׁלִַם בַּנֵּרוֹת וּפָקַדְתִּי עַל־הָאֲנָשִׁים
men the upon visit and ,lamps with Jerusalem will I ,that
out search

3068 3190 3824 559 8105 5921 7087
הַקֹּפְאִים עַל־שִׁמְרֵיהֶם הָאֹמְרִים בִּלְבָבָם לֹא־יֵיטִיב יְהוָה
,Jehovah do will Not their in those their on being
good ,heart saying ;lees settled

1129 8077 1004 4933 2428 1961 7489
13 וְלֹא יָרֵעַ׃ וְהָיָה חֵילָם לִמְשִׁסָּה וּבָתֵּיהֶם לִשְׁמָמָה וּבָנוּ
they And a their and ,prize a their shall And will He and
build shall .desolation houses wealth become .evil do not

7138 3196 8354 3754 5193 3427 3808 1004
14 בָתִּים וְלֹא יֵשֵׁבוּ וְנָטְעוּ כְרָמִים וְלֹא יִשְׁתּוּ אֶת־יֵינָם׃ קָרוֹב
near (Is) .wine their drink but ,vineyards they and dwell but ,houses
not plant shall ,(there) not

4751 3068 3117 6963 3966 4118 7138 1419 3068 3117
יוֹם־יְהוָה הַגָּדוֹל קָרוֹב וּמַהֵר מְאֹד קוֹל יוֹם יְהוָה מַר
Bit- .Jehovah the the ,greatly and (is It) the Jehovah day
terly of day of sound hurrying near .great of

6864 3117 3117 5678 3117 1368 8033 6873
15 צֹרֵחַ שָׁם גִּבּוֹר׃ יוֹם עֶבְרָה הַיּוֹם הַהוּא יוֹם צָרָה
adversity day ,that (is) wrath day A the there shall
of day of .man mighty out cry

6051 3117 653 2822 3117 4875 7722 3117 4691
וּמְצוּקָה יוֹם שֹׁאָה וּמְשׁוֹאָה יוֹם חֹשֶׁךְ וַאֲפֵלָה יוֹם עָנָן
clouds a and darkness a ,ruin and waste a and
of day ,gloom of day of day ,distress

1219 5892 8643 7782 3117 6205
16 וַעֲרָפֶל׃ יוֹם שׁוֹפָר וּתְרוּעָה עַל הֶעָרִים הַבְּצֻרוֹת וְעַל
and ,fortified the against and ram's the a thick and
against cities alarm horn of day ,darkness

3588 5787 1980 120 6887 1364 6438
17 הַפִּנּוֹת הַגְּבֹהוֹת׃ וַהֲצֵרֹתִי לָאָדָם וְהָלְכוּ כַּעִוְרִים כִּי
be- blind like they and ,man to will I And .high the
cause ,men walk shall distress bring towers

1571 1561 3894 6083 1818 8210 2398 3068
18 לַיהוָה חָטָאוּ וְשֻׁפַּךְ דָּמָם כֶּעָפָר וּלְחֻמָם כַּגְּלָלִים׃ גַּם־
Also .dung like their and like their be shall And they against
flesh ,dust blood out poured .sinned Jehovah

3068 5678 3117 5337 3201 3808 2091 3701
כַּסְפָּם גַּם־זְהָבָם לֹא־יוּכַל לְהַצִּילָם בְּיוֹם עֶבְרַת יְהוָה
.Jehovah the the in deliver to be shall not their and their
of wrath of day them able gold silver

all the earth shall be consumed by the fire of His jealousy. For He shall make a full, yea, a speedy end of all the dwellers in the land.

CHAPTER 2

[1]Gather yourselves, even gather, O nation not being longed for; [2]before the birth of the decree, the day shall pass like the chaff, yet not before the hot anger of Jehovah comes on you; yet not before the day of the anger of Jehovah comes on you. [3]Seek Jehovah, all the meek of the earth who have done His justice; seek righteousness; seek meekness. It may be you shall be hidden in the day of the anger of Jehovah.

[4]For Gaza shall be forsaken, and Ashkelon a ruin. They shall drive Ashdod out at the noonday, and Ekron shall be rooted up. [5]Woe *to* the inhabitants of the seacoast, the nation of the Cherethites! The word of Jehovah *is* against you, Canaan, the land of the Philistines; I will destroy you so *there* not *shall be* an inhabitant. [6]And the seacoast shall be pastures, meadows of shepherds, and folds for the flock. [7]And the coast shall be for the remnant of the house of Judah; they shall feed on them. In the houses of Ashkelon, they shall lie down in the evening; for Jehovah their God shall visit them and return their captivity.

[8]I have heard the reproach of Moab, and the curses of the sons of Ammon, *with* which they have cursed My people and have magnified *themselves* on their border. [9]So *as* I live, declares Jehovah of hosts, the God of Israel, surely Moab shall be as Sodom, and the sons of Ammon like Gomorrah, a possession of nettles, and a

6213 3617 389 3615 776 3605 398 7068 784
וּבְאֵשׁ קִנְאָתוֹ תֵּאָכֵל כָּל־הָאָרֶץ כִּי־כָלָה אַךְ־נִבְהָלָה יַעֲשֶׂה
shall He speedy a ,yea ,full a For the all be shall His the by But
make end .earth consumed jealousy of fire
776 3427 3605
אֵת כָּל־יֹשְׁבֵי הָאָרֶץ׃
the in- the all (of)
.earth of habitants

CAP. II ב

CHAPTER 2

4671 2706 3205 2962 3700 3808 1471 7197 7197
1 הִתְקוֹשְׁשׁוּ וָקוֹשּׁוּ הַגּוֹי לֹא נִכְסָף׃ בְּטֶרֶם לֶדֶת חֹק כְּמֹץ
2
the like the birth the before being not O even Gather
chaff ,decree of ;for longed nation ,gather ;yourselves
2962 3068 639 2740 935 2962 3117 5674
עָבַר יוֹם בְּטֶרֶם ׀ לֹא־יָבוֹא עֲלֵיכֶם חֲרוֹן אַף־יְהוָה בְּטֶרֶם
before ,Jehovah the heat the on . comes not yet the shall
yet of anger of you before ,day pass
6035 3068 1245 3068 639 3117 5921 935 3808
3 לֹא־יָבוֹא עֲלֵיכֶם יוֹם אַף־יְהוָה׃ בַּקְּשׁוּ אֶת־יְהוָה כָּל־עַנְוֵי
the all ,Jehovah Seek .Jehovah the the you on comes not
of meek of anger of day
194 6038 1245 6664 1245 6466 4941 834 776
הָאָרֶץ אֲשֶׁר מִשְׁפָּטוֹ פָּעָלוּ בַּקְּשׁוּ־צֶדֶק בַּקְּשׁוּ עֲנָוָה אוּלַי
Perhaps meek- seek righteous- seek have His who the
.ness ,ness ;done justice ,earth
831 1961 5800 5804 3068 639 3117 5640
4 תִּסָּתְרוּ בְּיוֹם אַף־יְהוָה׃ כִּי עַזָּה עֲזוּבָה תִהְיֶה וְאַשְׁקְלוֹן
Ashkelon and shall abandoned Gaza For .Jehovah the the in shall you
,be of anger of day hidden be
6131 6138 1644 6672 795 8077
לִשְׁמָמָה אַשְׁדּוֹד בַּצָּהֳרַיִם יְגָרְשׁוּהָ וְעֶקְרוֹן תֵּעָקֵר׃
be shall Ekron and shall they the in —Ashdod deso- a
.uprooted ,out her drive noonday ;lation
3667 3068 1697 3774 1471 3220 2256 3427 1945
5 הוֹי יֹשְׁבֵי חֶבֶל הַיָּם גּוֹי כְּרֵתִים דְּבַר־יְהוָה עֲלֵיכֶם כְּנַעַן
,Canaan against Jehovah The Chere- the the ,sea the coast the those Woe
,you (is) of word !thites of nation of on dwelling (to)
3220 2256 1961 3427 369 6 6430 776
6 אֶרֶץ פְּלִשְׁתִּים וְהַאֲבַדְתִּיךְ מֵאֵין יוֹשֵׁב׃ וְהָיְתָה חֶבֶל הַיָּם
the the shall And in- an be so cause will I and the the
sea of coast be .habitant not perish to you Philistines of land
1004 7611 2256 1961 6629 1448 7462 3741 5116
7 נְוֹת כְּרֹת רֹעִים וְגִדְרוֹת צֹאן׃ וְהָיָה חֶבֶל לִשְׁאֵרִית בֵּית
the rem- the for the shall And the folds and ,shepherds mea- pas-
of house of nant coast be .flock for (for) dows ,tures
7257 6153 831 1004 7462 5921 3063
יְהוּדָה עֲלֵיהֶם יִרְעוּן בְּבָתֵּי אַשְׁקְלוֹן בָּעֶרֶב יִרְבָּצוּן כִּי
for shall they the in ,Ashkelon the in shall they upon ;Judah
,down lie evening of houses :pasture them
2781 8085 7622 7725 430 3068 6485
8 יִפְקְדֵם יְהוָה אֱלֹהֵיהֶם וְשָׁב שְׁבוּתָם׃ שָׁמַעְתִּי חֶרְפַּת
con- the have I their and their Jehovah visit shall
of tempt heard .captivity return God them
5921 1430 5971 2778 834 5983 1121 1421 4124
מוֹאָב וְגִדּוּפֵי בְּנֵי עַמּוֹן אֲשֶׁר חֵרְפוּ אֶת־עַמִּי וַיַּגְדִּילוּ עַל־
upon have and My have they (with) ,Ammon the the and Moab
great become people cursed which of sons of reproaches
3478 430 6635 3068 5002 2416/3651 1366
9 גְּבוּלָם׃ לָכֵן חַי־אָנִי נְאֻם יְהוָה צְבָאוֹת אֱלֹהֵי יִשְׂרָאֵל כִּי
surely ,Israel God the ,hosts Jehovah ,declares ,I (as) There- their
of of live ,fore .border
2738 4476 6017 5983 1121 1961 5467 4124
מוֹאָב כִּסְדֹם תִּהְיֶה וּבְנֵי עַמּוֹן כַּעֲמֹרָה מִמְשַׁק חָרוּל
nettles pos- a :Gomorrah like Ammon and ,be shall like Moab
of session of sons the Sodom

pit of salt, and a ruin forever. The remnant of My people shall plunder them, and the rest of the nation shall possess them. [10]They shall have this for their pride, because they have cursed and magnified *themselves* against the people of Jehovah of hosts. [11]Jehovah *will be* frightening to them; for He will *make* all the gods of the earth lean, and *each* man from his place, and all the coasts of the nations, will bow to Him.

[12]You also, O Ethiopians, *shall be* pierced by My sword. [13]And He will stretch out His hand against the north, and destroy Assyria, and will make Nineveh a desolation, dry like the desert. [14]And flocks shall lie down in her midst; all the beasts of a nation; both the pelican and the bittern shall lodge in the capitals of its pillars. A voice shall sing at the window; ruin *shall be* at the doorsill; for the cedar-work He will bare. [15]This *is* the joyful city, dwelling confidently, who says in her heart, I *am*, and there is yet no *other*. How she has become a ruin, a resting-place for animals! Everyone who passes near her shall hiss; he shall shake his hand!

3499 962 5971 7611 5769 8077 4417 953
ומכרה־מלח ושממה עד־עולם שארית עמי יבזום ויתר
the and shall My remnant The .forever to a and ,salt a and
of rest ,them spoil people of desolation of pit

1430 2978 1347 8478 5157 1471
10 גוי ינחלום׃ זאת להם תחת גאונם כי חרפו ויגדלו על־
against have and have they for their instead to This inherit shall the
great become cursed ,pride of them (be shall) .them nations

3605 73:29 3068 3372 6635 3068 5971
11 עם יהוה צבאות׃ נורא יהוה עליהם כי רזה את כל־
all will He for to Jehovah (be Will) .hosts Jehovah
lean (make) ;them frightening of people

1471 339 3605 4725 376 7812 776 430
אלהי הארץ וישתחוו־לו איש ממקומו כל איי הגוים׃
the the all his from (each) to will and the gods the
nations of islands ,place man ,Him bow ,earth of

6828 3027 5186 1992 2719 2491 3569 1571
12 גם־אתם כושים חללי חרבי המה׃
13 ויט ידו על־צפון
the against His He And they My pierced O ,you Also
north hand extends (are) sword by ,Ethiopians

4057 6723 8077 5210 77:60 804 6
ויאבד את־אשור וישם את־נינוה לשממה ציה כמדבר׃
the like dry a Nineveh will and ,Assyria makes and
.desert ,desolation make perish

70:90 6893 2416 3605 5739 8432 7257
14 ורבצו בתוכה עדרים כל־חיתו־גוי גם־קאת גם־קפד
the and the both a ani- his all ,flocks her in shall And
bittern pelican ;nation of mals midst down lie

731 55:92 2721 2474 7891 6963 3885 3730
בכפתריה ילינו קול ישורר בחלון חרב בסף כי ארזה
cedar- the for the on ruin the at shall A shall pillar its in
work ,doorsill (be will) ;window sing voice .lodge capitals

559 983 3427 5947 5892 6168
15 ערה׃ זאת העיר העליזה היושבת לבטח האמרה
one the ,confidently dwelling joyful the city This will He
saying (is) .bare lay

24:16 4769 80:47 1961 5750 657 38:24
בלבבה אני ואפסי עוד איך היתה לשמה מרבץ לחיה
for resting a a has she How (other) and I her in
!animals place ,desolation become .still is none (am) ,heart

30 27 5128 8319 5674 3605
כל עובר עליה ישרק יניע ידו׃
his shall he shall near passing Every-
!hand shake ;hiss her one

CAP. III ג

CHAPTER 3

[1]Woe *to* her rebelling and being defiled, *to* the oppressing city! [2]She did not listen to the voice; she did not take correction; she did not trust in Jehovah; she did not draw near to her God. [3]Her rulers within her *are* roaring lions; her judges *are* evening wolves; they do not gnaw bones for the morning. [4]Her prophets *are* proud, men of deceit; her priests have profaned the sanctuary; they have done violence *to* the Law. [5]The righteous Jehovah *is* in her midst; He will not act perversely.

3808 6963 8085 3808 3238 5892 1351 4754 1945
1 הוי מראה ונגאלה העיר היונה׃
2 לא שמעה בקול לא
not the to did she Not !oppressing the being and her Woe
;voice listen city defiled rebelling (to)

7126 38:08 430 982 3068 4148 3947
לקחה מוסר ביהוה לא בטחה אל־אלהיה לא קרבה׃
did she not her to did she not Jehovah in correc- did she
.near draw God ;trust tion take

38:08 6153 2061 8199 7580 738 71:30 8269
3 שריה בקרבה אריות שאגים שפטיה זאבי ערב לא
not the (are) her ;roaring (are) her in Her
(even) ;evening of wolves judges lions midst rulers

24:90 35:48 900 582 63:48 50:30 1242 1633
4 גרמו לבקר׃ נביאיה פחזים אנשי בגדות כהניה חללו־
have her ;deceit of men (are) Her the for they do
profaned priests ,proud prophets ,morning bones gnaw

59:66 6213 38:08 7130 6662 3068 8451 2554 69:44
5 קדש חמסו תורה׃ יהוה צדיק בקרבה לא יעשה עולה
;iniquity will He not her in the Jehovah the they holy the
do ;midst (is) righteous .law violated ;place

Every morning He gives His justice to the light; He fails not, but the perverse knows no shame. [6]I have cut off nations; their towers are ruined. I made their streets waste, so that none passes by. Their cities are laid waste, without a man, there being no inhabitant. [7]I said, Surely you will fear Me; you will receive instruction; then her dwelling shall not be cut off, all that I appointed for her. But they rose up early; they corrupted all their doings.

[8]Therefore, wait for Me, declares Jehovah, for the day I rise up to the prey. For My judgment *is* to gather the nations, for Me to gather the kingdoms, to pour My fury out on them, all My hot anger. For all the earth shall be burned up with the fire of My jealousy. [9]For then I will *give* a clear lip to the peoples, to call all of them by the name of Jehovah, to serve Him *with* one shoulder. [10]From beyond the rivers of Ethiopia, My worshipers, the daughter of My scattered ones, shall bring My food offering. [11]In that day you shall not be ashamed from all your doings *in* which you have transgressed against Me. For then I will take away those who rejoice in your pride out of your midst, and you shall not again be proud any more in My holy mountain. [12]I will also leave a poor and weak people in your midst, and they shall trust in the name of Jehovah. [13]The remnant of Israel shall not do iniquity, nor speak lies. And a deceitful tongue shall not be found in their mouth. For they shall feed and lie down; and no one shall frighten *them*.

[14]Shout for joy, daughter of Zion; shout, Israel! Be glad and rejoice with all the heart, daughter of Jerusalem. [15]Jehovah has turned off your judgments; He has turned away your

5767 38,08 57:37 38,08 216 5414 4941 1242 1242
בַּבֹּקֶר בַּבֹּקֶר מִשְׁפָּטוֹ יִתֵּן לָאוֹר לֹא נֶעְדָּר וְלֹא־יוֹדֵעַ עַוָּל
the perverse knows but not He does not fail the to light He gives His justice by morning morning

2351 2717 6438 8074 1471 3772 1322
6 בֹּשֶׁת׃ הִכְרַתִּי גוֹיִם נָשַׁמּוּ פִּנּוֹתָם הֶחֱרַבְתִּי חוּצוֹתָם
their streets have I waste laid their towers are desolated ;nations have I off cut ,shame

559 8034 376 1097 5892 6650 5674 1097
7 מִבְּלִי עוֹבֵר נִצְדּוּ עָרֵיהֶם מִבְּלִי־אִישׁ מֵאֵין יוֹשֵׁב׃ אָמַרְתִּי
,said I inhab-itant an there being not from a man that is not their cities laid waste Are passing by. that so (is) none

45:83 3772 41:48 3947 3372
אַךְ־תִּירְאִי אוֹתִי תִּקְחִי מוּסָר וְלֹא־יִכָּרֵת מְעוֹנָהּ כֹּל אֲשֶׁר־
that all her dwelling be shall off cut and not correc-tion will you receive ;Me will you fear Surely

36:51 5949 7843 7925 403 6485
8 פָּקַדְתִּי עָלֶיהָ אָכֵן הִשְׁכִּימוּ הִשְׁחִיתוּ כֹּל עֲלִילוֹתָם׃ לָכֵן
There-fore their doings. all they corrupted rose they ;early But for her. I appointed

622 4941 5706 6965 3117 30:68 5002 2442
חַכּוּ־לִי נְאֻם־יְהוָה לְיוֹם קוּמִי לְעַד כִּי מִשְׁפָּטִי לֶאֱסֹף
to gather justice My (is) For the to prey. rise I up the for day ;Jehovah declares for Me, wait

639 2740 3605 2195 8210 4467 6908 1471
גּוֹיִם לְקָבְצִי מַמְלָכוֹת לִשְׁפֹּךְ עֲלֵיהֶם זַעְמִי כֹּל חֲרוֹן אַפִּי
My anger. heat the of all My ,fury on them pour to out the ,kingdoms Me for collect to the ,nations

5971 2015 776 3605 398 7068 784
9 כִּי בְּאֵשׁ קִנְאָתִי תֵּאָכֵל כָּל־הָאָרֶץ׃ כִּי־אָז אֶהְפֹּךְ אֶל־עַמִּים
the peoples to change will I then For the earth. all be shall consumed My jealousy the with of fire For

259 7926 5647 30:68 8034 71:21 1305 8193
שָׂפָה בְרוּרָה לִקְרֹא כֻלָּם בְּשֵׁם יְהוָה לְעָבְדוֹ שְׁכֶם אֶחָד׃
.one (with) shoulder serve to Him ,Jehovah the by of name all them of call to ,clear lip a

3117 4503 2986 6327 6282 3568 5104 5676
10 מֵעֵבֶר לְנַהֲרֵי־כוּשׁ עֲתָרַי בַּת־פּוּצַי יוֹבִלוּן מִנְחָתִי׃ בַּיּוֹם
11
day In food My .offering shall bring of daughter the ones scattered My wor-shipers ,My Ethiopia the of rivers From across

227 6586 834 5949 3605 954 38:08
הַהוּא לֹא תֵבוֹשִׁי מִכֹּל עֲלִילֹתַיִךְ אֲשֶׁר פָּשַׁעַתְּ בִּי כִּי־אָז
then For against .Me have you transgressed (in) which your doings from all shall you ashamed be not that

2022 5750 1361 3254 38:08 1346 5947 71:30 5493
אָסִיר מִקִּרְבֵּךְ עַלִּיזֵי גַּאֲוָתֵךְ וְלֹא־תוֹסִפִי לְגָבְהָה עוֹד בְּהַר
the in of hill still be high shall you again and not your (in) ,majesty those rejoicing your from midst will I withdraw

3068 8034 2620 1800/6041/5971 7130 7604 4944
12 קָדְשִׁי׃ וְהִשְׁאַרְתִּי בְקִרְבֵּךְ עַם עָנִי וָדָל וְחָסוּ בְּשֵׁם יְהוָה׃
.Jehovah the of name in they trust shall and ;weak and poor a people your in midst will I And leave My .holiness

390:8 3577 1696 38:08 5766 6213 38:08 34:78 6041
13 שְׁאֵרִית יִשְׂרָאֵל לֹא־יַעֲשׂוּ עַוְלָה וְלֹא־יְדַבְּרוּ כָזָב וְלֹא־
and not ;lies speak and not ,iniquity shall do not Israel The rem-nant of

369 7257 7462 8649 3956 6310 4672
יִמָּצֵא בְּפִיהֶם לְשׁוֹן תַּרְמִית כִּי־הֵמָּה יִרְעוּ וְרָבְצוּ וְאֵין
and is none lie and ,down shall pasture they For .deceit a of tongue their in mouth be shall found

5937 8056 34:78 7321 67:26/1323 7442 2729
14 מַחֲרִיד׃ רָנִּי בַּת־צִיּוֹן הָרִיעוּ יִשְׂרָאֵל שִׂמְחִי וְעָלְזִי
and rejoice glad be ;Israel ,shout ;Zion daugh-ter of Shout joy for frightening .(them)

341 6437 4941 3068 5493 3389 1323 3820
15 בְּכָל־לֵב בַּת יְרוּשָׁלִָם׃ הֵסִיר יְהוָה מִשְׁפָּטַיִךְ פִּנָּה אֹיְבֵךְ
your .enemy has He turned your ,judgments Jehovah turned Has away .Jerusalem daughter the of with ,heart all

enemy. Jehovah, the King of Israel, is in your midst; you shall not fear evil any more. 16In that day it shall be said to Jerusalem, Fear not! Zion, do not let your hands droop. 17Jehovah your God *is* mighty in your midst; He will save. He will rejoice over you with joy; He is silent in His love. He rejoices over you with a joyful shout. 18I will gather the afflicted ones from the appointed place; they were from you, a lifting up *of* reproach over her. 19Behold, at that time I will deal with all those who afflict you. And I will save her who is lame, and gather her who was thrust out. And I will give them for a praise and for a name in all the land of their shame. 20In that time I will bring you, even in the time I gather you. For I will give you for a name and for a praise among all the peoples of the earth, when I turn back your captivity before your eyes, says Jehovah.

16 מֶלֶךְ יִשְׂרָאֵל ׀ יְהוָה בְּקִרְבֵּךְ לֹא־תִירְאִי רָע עוֹד׃ בַּיּוֹם
3117 5750 7451 3372 3808 7130 3068 3478 4428
day In (any) more evil shall you fear not your in midst; (is) Jehovah ,Israel The of King

הַהוּא יֵאָמֵר לִירוּשָׁלַםִ אַל־תִּירָאִי צִיּוֹן אַל־יִרְפּוּ יָדָיִךְ׃
3027 7503 6726 3372 408 3389 559
your !hands let do droop Not !Zion ,fear do Not ,Jerusalem to shall it said be that

17 יְהוָה אֱלֹהַיִךְ בְּקִרְבֵּךְ גִּבּוֹר יוֹשִׁיעַ יָשִׂישׂ עָלַיִךְ בְּשִׂמְחָה
8057 7797 3467 1368 7130 430 3068
.joy with over you will He rejoice will He .save (is) ;mighty your in midst your God Jehovah

18 יַחֲרִישׁ בְּאַהֲבָתוֹ יָגִיל עָלַיִךְ בְּרִנָּה׃ נוּגֵי מִמּוֹעֵד אָסַפְתִּי
622 4150 3013 7440 1524 160 2790
will I ;gather the from place appointed Those afflicted shout a with .joy of over you He rejoices His in ;love is He silent

19 מִמֵּךְ הָיוּ מַשְׂאֵת עָלֶיהָ חֶרְפָּה׃ הִנְנִי עֹשֶׂה אֶת־כָּל־
3605 6213 2005 2781 5921 2186 1961
all will with deal I ,Behold (of) .reproach over her lifting a up they ,were from you

מְעַנַּיִךְ בָּעֵת הַהִיא וְהוֹשַׁעְתִּי אֶת־הַצֹּלֵעָה וְהַנִּדָּחָה אֲקַבֵּץ
6908 5080 6760 3467 6256 6031
will I .gather being her out thrust and being her ,lame will I And save .that at time afflicting you

20 וְשַׂמְתִּים לִתְהִלָּה וּלְשֵׁם בְּכָל־הָאָרֶץ בָּשְׁתָּם׃ בָּעֵת הַהִיא
6256 1322 776 3605 8034 8416 5414
that In time their .shame the of land in all for and name a a for praise will I And them give

אָבִיא אֶתְכֶם וּבָעֵת קַבְּצִי אֶתְכֶם כִּי־אֶתֵּן אֶתְכֶם לְשֵׁם
8034 5414 6908 6256 935
a for name you will I For give .you My gathering even in of time the ,you will I bring

וְלִתְהִלָּה בְּכֹל עַמֵּי הָאָרֶץ בְּשׁוּבִי אֶת־שְׁבוּתֵיכֶם לְעֵינֵיכֶם
5869 7622 7725 776 5971 854 8416
your before ,eyes your captivity I when return the ,earth the of peoples among all for and praise a

אָמַר יְהוָה׃
3068 559
.Jehovah says

A LITERAL TRANSLATION OF THE BIBLE

THE BOOK OF HAGGAI

CHAPTER 1

1 In the second year of Darius the king, in the sixth month, in the first day of the month, the word of Jehovah came by Haggai the prophet to Zerubbabel, the son of Shealtiel, governor of Judah; and to Joshua, the son of Jehozadak, the high priest, saying:
2 So speaks Jehovah of hosts, saying, This people says, The time has not come, the time for the house of Jehovah to be built. 3 And the word of Jehovah was by Haggai the prophet, saying, 4 Is it time for you yourselves to live in your roofed houses, and this house to lie waste? 5 And now, so says Jehovah of hosts: Set your heart on your ways; 6 you have sown much, and bring in little; *you* eat, but are not satisfied; *you* drink, but not to be filled; *you* dress, but there is no warmth to one; and he who hires himself hires himself for a bag of holes.

7 So says Jehovah of hosts: Set your heart on your ways. 8 Go up the mountain and bring wood, and build this house. And I will be pleased with it, and I will be glorified, says Jehovah. 9 *You* looked for much, and, behold, little! And when you brought *it* home, then I blew on it. Why, declares Jehovah of hosts? Because of My house that *is* ruined, and

LIBER HAGGAI

(THE) BOOK OF HAGGAI

CAPUT. I א

CHAPTER 1

259 3117 8345 2320 44:28 1867 8147 8141
1 בשנת שתים לדריוש המלך בחדש הששי ביום אחד
the day in the in ,king the Darius of the year In first ,sixth month second
1121 2216 5030 2292 3068 1697 1961 2320
לחדש היה דבר־יהוה ביד־חגי הנביא אל־זרבבל בן
son ,Zerubbabel to the Haggai by Jehovah the came the of of prophet of word ,month
35 48 3087 1121 3091 30:63 6346 7597
שאלתיאל פחת יהודה ואל־יהושע בן־יהוצדק הכהן
priest ,Jehozadak son ,Joshua and ,Judah governor ,Shealtiel of to of
2088 5971 559 6635 3068 559 3541 559 1419
2 הגדול לאמר: כה אמר יהוה צבאות לאמר העם הזה
This people ,saying ,hosts Jehovah says Thus ,saying ,high the of
1697 1961 1129 3068 1004 6256 935 6256 38 08 559
3 אמרו לא עת־בא עת־בית יהוה להבנות: ויהי דבר
the Then .built be to Jehovah's for the is The not ,says of word came house time ,come time
3427 6256 559 5030 2292 3068
4 יהוה ביד־חגי הנביא לאמר: העת לכם אתם לשבת
live to your- for is It ,saying the Haggai by Jehovah selves you time prophet
3068 559 62:58 2717 2088 1004 5603 1004
5 בבתיכם ספונים והבית הזה חרב: ועתה כה אמר יהוה
Jehovah says thus And lie to this and ,roofed your in of now ?waste house houses
935 72 35 2232 1870 59 21 3824 7760 6635
6 צבאות שימו לבבכם על־דרכיכם: זרעתם הרבה והבא
and much have you ;ways your on your Set :hosts in bring sown heart
369 3847 79:37 369 8354 7654 369 398 4592
מעט אכול ואין־לשבעה שתו ואין־לשכרה לבוש ואין־
but (you) be to but (you) be to but (you) ;little is not ,dress ;filled not ,drink ;satisfied not eat
35 41 5344 6872 7936 7936 2527
7 לחם לו והמשתכר משתכר אל־צרור נקוב: כה
Thus .holes a for sells who he and to warmth of bag himself himself sells ;one
5927 1870 59 21 3824 7760 6635 3068 559
8 אמר יהוה צבאות שימו לבבכם על־דרכיכם: עלו
Go your on your Set :hosts Jehovah says up ,ways heart of
559 3513 7521 1004 1129 6086 935 2022
ההר והבאתם עץ ובנו הבית וארצה־בו ואכבד אמר
says will I and with will I And the and wood bring and the ,glorified be ,it pleased be .house build mountain
5301 1004 935 4592 2009 72 35 6437 3068
9 יהוה: פנה אל־הרבה והנה למעט והבאתם הבית ונפחתי
I then ,home when And !little and much for (You) Jeho- blew (it) brought you behold looked .vah
27:17 1004 328.2 66:35 3068 5002/4100 3282
בו יען מה נאם יהוה צבאות יען ביתי אשר־הוא חרב
,ruined is that My Because ?hosts Jehovah says ,Why .it on house of of

you, *each* man, run to his own house. [10]On account of this the heavens above you have held back the dew, and the earth is held back *from* her produce. [11]And I called for a drought in the land, and on the mountains, and on the grain, and on the new wine, and on the oil, and on that which the ground produces, and on man, and on livestock, and on all the labor of your hands.

[12]Then Zerubbabel, the son of Shealtiel, and Joshua, the son of Jehozadak, the high priest, and all the remnant of the people, obeyed the voice of Jehovah their God, and the words of Haggai the prophet, as Jehovah their God had sent him. And the people feared before Jehovah. [13]And Haggai the messenger of Jehovah spoke the message of Jehovah to the people, saying, I *am* with you, says Jehovah. [14]And Jehovah stirred up the spirit of Zerubbabel, the son of Shealtiel, governor of Judah, and the spirit of Joshua, the son of Jehozadak, the high priest, and the spirit of all the remnant of the people. And they came and worked on the house of Jehovah of hosts, their God, [15]in the twenty-fourth day of the sixth month, in the second year of Darius the king.

8064 3607 5921 3651 5921 1004 376 7323
10 וְאַתֶּם רָצִים אִישׁ לְבֵיתוֹ׃ עַל־כֵּן עֲלֵיכֶם כָּלְאוּ שָׁמַיִם
the held have above Therefore his to (each) run and
heavens back you .house man you

5921 776 2721 7121 2981 3607 776 2919
11 מִטָּל וְהָאָרֶץ כָּלְאָה יְבוּלָהּ׃ וָאֶקְרָא חֹרֶב עַל־הָאָרֶץ וְעַל־
and the on a I And her (from) held is the and from
on ,land drought for called .produce back earth ,dew

834 5921 33:23 5921 8492 5921 1715 2022
הֶהָרִים וְעַל־הַדָּגָן וְעַל־הַתִּירוֹשׁ וְעַל־הַיִּצְהָר וְעַל אֲשֶׁר
that and the and new the and the and the
which on ,oil on ,wine on ,grain on ,mountains

3013 3605 5921 929 120 127 3318
תּוֹצִיא הָאֲדָמָה וְעַל־הָאָדָם וְעַל־הַבְּהֵמָה וְעַל כָּל־יְגִיעַ
the all and ,cattle and ,man and the brings
of labor on on on ,ground forth

1121 3091 7597 1121 2216 8085 3709
12 כַּפָּיִם׃ וַיִּשְׁמַע זְרֻבָּבֶל ׀ בֶּן־שַׁלְתִּיאֵל וִיהוֹשֻׁעַ בֶּן־
the and ,Shealtiel the Zerubbabel Then your
of son Joshua of son obeyed .palms

3068 6963 59.71 7611 3605 14 19 3548 3687
יְהוֹצָדָק הַכֹּהֵן הַגָּדוֹל וְכֹל ׀ שְׁאֵרִית הָעָם בְּקוֹל יְהוָה
Jehovah the the the and the priest ,Jehosadak
of voice ,people of remnant all ,high

3068 7971 5030 2292 1697 430
אֱלֹהֵיהֶם וְעַל־דִּבְרֵי חַגַּי הַנָּבִיא כַּאֲשֶׁר שְׁלָחוֹ יְהוָה
Jehovah sent had as the Haggai the and their
him ,prophet of words ,God

4397 2292 559 3068 6440 5971 3372 430
13 אֱלֹהֵיהֶם וַיִּירְאוּ הָעָם מִפְּנֵי יְהוָה׃ וַיֹּאמֶר חַגַּי מַלְאַךְ
the Haggai Then .Jehovah before the And their
of messenger spoke people feared .God

3008 5002 559 5971 3068 4400 3068
יְהוָה בְּמַלְאֲכוּת יְהוָה לָעָם לֵאמֹר אֲנִי אִתְּכֶם נְאֻם־יְהוָה׃
.Jehovah says with I ,saying the to Jehovah's message .Jehovah
,you (am) ,people

3063 6396 7597 1121 2216 7307 30 68 5782
14 וַיָּעַר יְהוָה אֶת־רוּחַ זְרֻבָּבֶל בֶּן־שַׁלְתִּיאֵל פַּחַת יְהוּדָה וְאֶת־
and ,Judah governor ,Shealtiel the Zerubbabel the Jehovah And
of of son of spirit stirred

7611 3605 73 07 14 19 35 48 3087 1121 3091 73 07
רוּחַ יְהוֹשֻׁעַ בֶּן־יְהוֹצָדָק הַכֹּהֵן הַגָּדוֹל וְאֶת־רוּחַ כֹּל שְׁאֵרִית
rem- the all the and the priest , Jehosadak son Joshua the
of nant of spirit ,high of of spirit

430 6635 3068 1004 43 99 6213 935 5971
הָעָם וַיָּבֹאוּ וַיַּעֲשׂוּ מְלָאכָה בְּבֵית־יְהוָה צְבָאוֹת אֱלֹהֵיהֶם׃
,God their hosts Jehovah the on work and they And the
of of house did came .people

8147 8141 8345 2320 702 6242 3117
15 בְּיוֹם עֶשְׂרִים וְאַרְבָּעָה לַחֹדֶשׁ בַּשִּׁשִּׁי בִּשְׁנַת שְׁתַּיִם
the year in the month of fourth twenty- the in
second ,sixth day

44 28 1867
לְדָרְיָוֶשׁ הַמֶּלֶךְ׃
.king the Darius of

CAP. II ב

CHAPTER 2

[1]In the seventh *month*, on the twenty-first of the month, the word of Jehovah was by Haggai the prophet, saying, [2]Now speak to Zerubbabel, the son of Shealtiel, governor

2292 30:68 1697 1961 2320 259 6242 7637
1 בַּשְּׁבִיעִי בְּעֶשְׂרִים וְאֶחָד לַחֹדֶשׁ הָיָה דְּבַר־יְהוָה בְּיַד־חַגַּי
Haggai by Jehovah the came the of first the on the In
of word ,month twenty- ,(month) seventh

6346 7597 1121 2216 49.94/559 559 5030
2 הַנָּבִיא לֵאמֹר׃ אֱמָר־נָא אֶל־זְרֻבָּבֶל בֶּן־שַׁלְתִּיאֵל פַּחַת
governor ,Shealtiel son Zerubbabel to Now speak ,saying the
of of ,prophet

of Judah, and to Joshua, the son of Jehozadak, the high priest, and to the remnant of the people, saying, [3]Who is left among you who saw this house in her former glory? And how do you see it now? When compared to it, *is it* not as nothing in your eyes? [4]Yet now be strong, O Zerubbabel, says Jehovah. And be strong, O Joshua, son of Jehozadak, the high priest. And be strong and work, all people of the land, says Jehovah. For I *am* with you, declares Jehovah of hosts. [5]The word that I covenanted with you when you came out of Egypt, so My Spirit remains among you; do not fear. [6]For so says Jehovah of hosts: Yet once, it *is* a little while, and I will shake the heavens and the earth and the sea and the dry land. [7]And I will shake all the nations; and the desire of all nations shall come. And I will fill this house *with* glory, says Jehovah of hosts. [8]The silver *is* Mine, and the gold *is* Mine, says Jehovah of hosts. [9]The glory of this latter house shall be greater than that of the former, says Jehovah of hosts. And in this place I will give peace, says Jehovah of hosts.

[10]In the twenty-fourth of the ninth *month*, in the second year of Darius, the word of Jehovah came to Haggai the prophet, saying, [11]So says Jehovah of hosts: Now ask the priests the law

7611 1419 3548 3087 1121 3091 3063
יהודה ואל־יהושע בן־יהוצדק הכהן הגדול ואל־שארית
rem- the and ,high the priest Jehosadak son ,Joshua and ,Judah
of nant to of to

1004 7200 834 76:04 4310 559 5971
3 העם לאמר׃ מי בכם הנשאר אשר ראה את־הבית
house saw who left is among Who ,saying the
you ,people

6248 7200 7223 3519
הזה בכבודו הראשון ומה אתם ראים אתו עתה הלוא
(it Is) ?now it see you do And ?former its in this
,not how glory

3068/5002 2216 2388 6258 5869 369 3644
4 כמהו כאין בעיניכם׃ ועתה חזק זרבבל נאם־יהוה
.Jehovah says O be now Yet your in as like
,Zerubbabel ,strong ?eyes nothing it

5971 3605 2388 1419 3548 3097 1121 3091 2388
וחזק יהושע בן־יהוצדק הכהן הגדול וחזק כל־עם
people all be And the priest Jehosadak son O be And
of ,strong .high of ,Joshua ,strong

6635 3068 5002 6213 3068 5002 776
הארץ נאם־יהוה ועשו כי־אני אתכם נאם יהוה צבאות׃
.hosts Jehovah says with I For and ,Jehovah says the
of ,you (am) .work land

7307 4714 3318 3772 834 1697
5 את־הדבר אשר־כרתי אתכם בצאתכם ממצרים ורוחי
My so of out you when with cut I which The
Spirit Egypt came you word

3068 559 3372 408 8432 5975
6 עמדת בתוככם אל־תיראו׃ כי כה אמר יהוה
Jehovah says thus For .fear do not among abides
of ;you

8064 7493 4592 259 5750 66:35
צבאות עוד אחת מעט היא ואני מרעיש את־השמים
the shake will I and it little a ,once Yet :hosts
heavens ,(is) while

3605 7493 2724 3220 776
7 ואת־הארץ ואת־הים ואת־החרבה׃ והרעשתי את־כל־
all will I And dry the and the and the and
shake .ground sea earth

2088 1004 43 90 1471 36 05 2532 935 14:71
הגוים ובאו חמדת כל־הגוים ומלאתי את־הבית הזה
this house will I And the all the shall and the
fill .nations of desire come ,nations

5002 2091 7301 6635 3068 559 3519
8 כבוד אמר יהוה צבאות׃ לי הכסף ולי הזהב נאם
says the and The (is) .hosts Jehovah says (with)
,gold Me to ,silver Me to of ,glory

374 2088 1004 3519 19 61 1419 6635 3068
9 יהוה צבאות׃ גדול יהיה כבוד הבית הזה האחרון
latter this house The be will greater .hosts Jehovah
of glory of

79:65 5414 2088 4725 6635 3068 559 722:3
מן־הראשון אמר יהוה צבאות ובמקום הזה אתן שלום
,peace will I this in And .hosts Jehovah says the than
give place of ,former

8671 702 6242 6635 3068 559
10 נאם יהוה צבאות׃ בעשרים וארבעה לתשיעי
the of fourth the In .hosts Jehovah says
,(month) ninth twenty- of

5030 2292 30 :68 1697 1961 1867 8147 8141
בשנת שתים לדריוש היה דבר־יהוה ביד־חגי הנביא
the Haggai by Jehovah the came ,Darius of the year in
,prophet of word second

3548 4994 7592 6635 3068 559 35 41 559
11 לאמר׃ כה אמר יהוה צבאות שאל־נא את־הכהנים
the Now ask :hosts Jehovah says Thus ,saying
priests of

saying, [12]Behold, one
bears holy flesh in the *skirt*
of his garment, and touches
his *skirt* to the bread, or
boiled food, or wine, or oil,
or any food, will it become
holy? And the priests
answered and said, No.
[13]And Haggai said, If the
unclean of body touches
these, is it unclean? And the
priests answered and said,
It is unclean. [14]And Haggai
answered and said, So *is*
this people, and so *is* this
nation before Me, declares
Jehovah. And so *is* every
work of their hands, and
that which they offer there
is unclean. [15]And now, I
ask you, set your heart on it;
from this day and onward,
before the placing of a
stone on a stone in the
temple of Jehovah; [16]from
then onward, *one* came to a
heap of twenty *measures*,
and there were *but* ten; *one*
came to the wine vat to
draw out fifty from the wine
trough, and there were *but*
twenty. [17]I struck you with
blight, and with mildew,
and with hail, in all the
labors of your hands; yet
you did not *turn* to Me, says
Jehovah. [18]Now set your
heart from this day and
forward, from the twenty-
fourth day of the ninth
month, from the day that
Jehovah's temple was es-
tablished. Set your heart:
[19]*Is* the seed still in the
barn? Yes, as yet the vine,
and the fig-tree, and the
pomegranate, and the olive-
tree have not brought forth.
From this day I will bless
them.

[20]And a second time the
word of Jehovah came to
Haggai, in the twenty-
fourth of the month, saying,
[21]Speak to Zerubbabel the

5060 899 3671 6942 1320 376 5375 2009 559 8451
12 תורה לאמר׃ הן ישא־איש בשר־קדש בכנף בגדו ונגע
and touches | his garment | the in of wing | holy | flesh | man a carried | Be- ,hold | ,saying | ,law the

8081 176 3196 176 5138 3899 3671
בכנפו אל־הלחם ואל־הנזיד ואל־היין ואל־שמן ואל־
or | ,oil | or | ,wine | or | boiled food | or | the ,bread | to | his wing

559 3808 559 3548 6030 6944 3978 3605
13 כל־מאכל היקדש ויענו הכהנים ויאמרו לא׃ ויאמר
said And | .No | ,said and | priests the | And answered | ?holy become it will | ,food | any

3548 6030 2930 428 3605 2931 5060 2292
חגי אם־יגע טמא־נפש בכל־אלה היטמא ויענו הכהנים
priests the | And answered | ?unclean it is | ,these | any of | body the of unclean | touches If | Hag- ,gai

1471 3651 2088 5971 3651 559 2292 6030 2931 559
14 ויאמרו יטמא׃ ויען חגי ויאמר כן העם־הזה וכן־הגוי
nation and (is) so | ,this | people | So (is) | ,said and | Haggai | And answered | be shall It .unclean | ,said and

834 3027 4639 3605 3651 3068 5002 6440 2088
הזה לפני נאם־יהוה וכן כל־מעשה ידיהם ואשר
that and which | their ,hands | work (of) | every | And (is) so | .Jehovah states | before ,Me | this

3117 3824 4994 7760 6258 2891 8033 7126
15 יקריבו שם טמא הוא׃ ועתה שימו־נא לבבכם מן־היום
day from | your heart | now | set | ,now And | .is | unclean | there | they offer

3068 1964 68 68 7760 2962 4605
הזה ומעלה מטרם שום־אבן אל־אבן בהיכל יהוה׃
;Jehovah | the in of temple | a stone | on | stone a | the of placing | Before | and :onward | this

935 6235 1961 6242 6194 935
16 מהיותם בא אל־ערמת עשרים והיתה עשרה בא אל־
to | (one) came | (but) ;ten | there and were | twenty ,(measures) | heap a of | to | (one) came | then from ,on

5221 6242 1961 6333 2572 2834 3342
17 היקב לחשף חמשים פורה והיתה עשרים׃ הכיתי
struck I | (but) .twenty | there and were | the from ,trough wine | fifty | draw to of out | wine the vat

3027 4639 3605 1259 3420 7711
אתכם בשדפון ובירקון ובברד את כל־מעשה ידיכם
your ;hands | the (of) work | (in) all | with and ,hail | with and ,mildew | with ,blight | you

3117 3824 4994/7760 3068 5002 369
18 ואין־אתכם אלי נאם־יהוה׃ שימו־נא לבבכם מן־היום
day from | your heart | Now | set | .Jehovah says | to ,Me | did you (turn) | yet not

3117 8671 702 6242 3117 4605 2088
הזה ומעלה מיום עשרים וארבעה לתשיעי למן־היום
the day | from | the of ,(month) ninth | fourth | the twenty- | from day | and ,onward | this

2233 5750 3824 7760 3068 1964 3245
19 אשר־יסד היכל־יהוה שימו לבבכם׃ העוד הזרע
seed the still (Is) ;heart your set ;Jehovah's temple was established that

5375 3808 2132 6086 7416 8384 1612 5704 4035
במגורה ועד־הגפן והתאנה והרמון ועץ הזית לא נשא
have ;borne | not | the olive | the tree | and ,pomegranate | the ,tree-fig | and vine the | Even | ?barn the in

8145 3068 1697 1961 1288 2088 3117
20 מן־היום הזה אברך׃ ויהי דבר־יהוה שנית אל־
to | second a time | Jehovah | the of word | And came | will I .bless | this | day from

2216 559 559 2320 702 6242 2292
21 חגי בעשרים וארבעה לחדש לאמר׃ אמר אל־זרבבל
Zerubbabel to | Speak | ,saying | the of ,month | fourth | the in twenty- | Haggai

governor of Judah, saying, I will shake the heavens and the earth. [22]And I will overthrow the throne of the kingdoms; and I will destroy the strength of the kingdoms of the nations. And I will overthrow the chariots and their riders; and the horses and their riders will come down, each one by the sword of his brother. [23]In that day, says Jehovah of hosts, I will take you, O Zerubbabel, My servant, the son of Shealtiel, says Jehovah, and will make you like a signet; for I have chosen you, declares Jehovah of hosts.

776 8064 7493 559 3063 6346
פַּחַת־יְהוּדָה לֵאמֹר אֲנִי מַרְעִישׁ אֶת־הַשָּׁמַיִם וְאֶת־הָאָרֶץ׃
the earth | and | the heavens | shake will | I | ,saying | ,Judah | gov- ernor | the of

1471 4467 2392 8045 4467 3678 2015
22 וְהָפַכְתִּי כִּסֵּא מַמְלָכוֹת וְהִשְׁמַדְתִּי חֹזֶק מַמְלְכוֹת הַגּוֹיִם
the nations. | kingdoms of | the of strength | the destroy | will I and | the ,kingdoms' | the throne | will I And overthrow

376 7392 5483 3381 7392 4818 2015
וְהָפַכְתִּי מֶרְכָּבָה וְרֹכְבֶיהָ וְיָרְדוּ סוּסִים וְרֹכְבֵיהֶם אִישׁ
(each) man | their ,riders | and horses | the | will and down come | their ;riders | and | the chariots | will I And overthrow

3947 6635 3068 5002 3117 251 2719
23 בְּחֶרֶב אָחִיו׃ בַּיּוֹם הַהוּא נְאֻם־יְהֹוָה צְבָאוֹת אֶקָּחֲךָ
will I ,you take | ,hosts of | Jehovah | states | ,that | day In | his .brother | the by of sword

2368 7760 3068 5002 5650 7597 1121 2216
זְרֻבָּבֶל בֶּן־שְׁאַלְתִּיאֵל עַבְדִּי נְאֻם־יְהֹוָה וְשַׂמְתִּיךָ כַּחוֹתָם
a like ;(ring) signet | will and you make | ,Jehovah | states | My ,servant | Shealtiel | son of | Zerub- O babel

6635 3068 5002 977
כִּי־בְךָ בָחַרְתִּי נְאֻם יְהֹוָה צְבָאוֹת׃
.hosts of | Jehovah | states | have I ,chosen | you for

זכריה

LIBER ZACHARIAE

(THE) BOOK OF ZECHARIAH

CAPUT. I א

A LITERAL TRANSLATION OF THE BIBLE

THE BOOK OF ZECHARIAH

CHAPTER 1

[1]In the eighth month, in the second year of Darius, the word of Jehovah came to Zechariah, the son of Berechiah, the son of Iddo the prophet, saying, [2]Jehovah has been very angry with your fathers. [3]And you say to them, So says Jehovah of hosts: Turn to Me, says Jehovah of hosts, and I will turn to you, says Jehovah of hosts. [4]Do not be as your fathers, to whom the former prophets have proclaimed to them, saying, So says Jehovah of hosts: Turn now from your evil ways and your evil doings; but they did not hear or give heed to Me, says Jehovah. [5]Your fathers, where *are* they? And the prophets, do they live forever? [6]But My words and My statutes which I commanded My servants the prophets, did they not overtake your fathers? And they returned and said, As Jehovah of hosts purposes to do to us, according to our ways and according to our deeds, so He has done with us.

[7]On the twenty-fourth day of the eleventh month, it *is* the month Shebat, in the second year of Darius, the word of Jehovah was to Zechariah, the son of Berechiah, the son of Iddo the prophet, saying, [8]I saw at night. And, behold!

CHAPTER 1

3068 1697 1961 1869 8147 8141 8066 2320
1 בַּחֹדֶשׁ הַשְּׁמִינִי בִּשְׁנַת שְׁתַּיִם לְדָרְיָוֶשׁ הָיָה דְבַר־יְהוָה
Jehovah the was ,Darius of the year in the In
of word second ,eighth month

3068 7107 559 5030 5714/1121 1296 1121 2148
2 אֶל־זְכַרְיָה בֶּן־בֶּרֶכְיָה בֶּן־עִדּוֹ הַנָּבִיא לֵאמֹר׃ קָצַף יְהוָה
Jehovah was ,saying the Iddo son ,Berechiah son Zechariah to
angry ,prophet of of

3068 559 3541 559 7110 1
3 עַל־אֲבוֹתֵיכֶם קָצֶף׃ וְאָמַרְתָּ אֲלֵהֶם כֹּה אָמַר יְהוָה
Jehovah says Thus ,them to Therefore .anger your with
of say you fathers

7725 6635 3068 559 7725 6635
צְבָאוֹת שׁוּבוּ אֵלַי נְאֻם יְהוָה צְבָאוֹת וְאָשׁוּב אֲלֵיכֶם
,you to I and ,hosts Jehovah says to Turn :hosts
turn will of ,Me

7121 834 1 1961 408 6635 3068 559
4 אָמַר יְהוָה צְבָאוֹת׃ אַל־תִּהְיוּ כַאֲבֹתֵיכֶם אֲשֶׁר קָרְאוּ־
pro- have to your as be Do not .hosts Jehovah says
claimed whom ,fathers of

6635 3068 559 3541 559 7223 5030
אֲלֵיהֶם הַנְּבִאִים הָרִאשֹׁנִים לֵאמֹר כֹּה אָמַר יְהוָה צְבָאוֹת
:hosts Jehovah says Thus ,saying ,former the prophets them to
of

7181 3808 7451 4611 7451 1870 4994 7725
שׁוּבוּ נָא מִדַּרְכֵיכֶם הָרָעִים וּמַעֲלְלֵיכֶם הָרָעִים וְלֹא שָׁמְעוּ
did they but ;evil from and evil your from now Turn
listen not doings your ways

5030 3068 5002 8085 3808
5 וְלֹא־הִקְשִׁיבוּ אֵלַי נְאֻם־יְהוָה׃ אֲבוֹתֵיכֶם אַיֵּה־הֵם וְהַנְּבִאִים
the And ?they where Your .Jehovah says to give did and
,prophets (are) ,fathers ,Me heed not

5650 6680 834 2706 1697 2421 5769
6 הַלְעוֹלָם יִחְיוּ׃ אַךְ ׀ דְּבָרַי וְחֻקַּי אֲשֶׁר צִוִּיתִי אֶת־עֲבָדַי
My com- I which My and My But they do forever
servants manded statutes words ?live

2161 559 7725 1 5381 5030
הַנְּבִיאִים הֲלוֹא הִשִּׂיגוּ אֲבֹתֵיכֶם וַיָּשׁוּבוּ וַיֹּאמְרוּ כַּאֲשֶׁר זָמַם
pur- As ,said and they And your they did not the
poses returned ?fathers overtake ,prophets

6213 3651 4611 1870 6213 6635 3068
יְהוָה צְבָאוֹת לַעֲשׂוֹת לָנוּ כִּדְרָכֵינוּ וּכְמַעֲלָלֵינוּ כֵּן עָשָׂה
has He so according and to according ,us to do to hosts Jehovah
done ,deeds our to ways our of

2320 6240 6249 702 6242 3117
7 אִתָּנוּ׃ בְּיוֹם עֶשְׂרִים וְאַרְבָּעָה לְעַשְׁתֵּי־עָשָׂר חֹדֶשׁ הוּא־
(is) it, ,month the of and the day On with
eleventh fourth twenty- .us

3068 1697 1961 1867 8147 8141 7627 2320
חֹדֶשׁ שְׁבָט בִּשְׁנַת שְׁתַּיִם לְדָרְיָוֶשׁ הָיָה דְבַר־יְהוָה אֶל־
to Jehovah the came ,Darius of the year in ,Shebat the
of word second month

3915 7200 559 5030 5714 1121 1296 1121 2148
8 זְכַרְיָה בֶּן־בֶּרֶכְיָהוּ בֶּן־עִדּוֹא הַנָּבִיא לֵאמֹר׃ רָאִיתִי הַלַּיְלָה
,night saw I ,saying the Iddo son ,Berechiah son Zecha-
at ,prophet of of ,riah

A Man riding on a red horse. And He stood among the myrtle trees that *were* in the ravine. And behind Him *were* red, sorrel, and white horses. [9]Then I said, My lord, what *are* these? And the angel who was speaking with me said to me, I will show you what these *are*. [10]And the Man who stood among the myrtle trees answered and said, These *are* those whom Jehovah has sent to walk to and fro through the earth. [11]And they answered the Angel of Jehovah who stood among the myrtle trees, and said, We have walked to and fro through the earth; and, behold, all the earth sits still and is at peace.

[12]And the Angel of Jehovah answered and said, O Jehovah of hosts, until when will You not have pity on Jerusalem, and on the cities of Judah, against which You have cursed these seventy years? [13]And Jehovah answered the angel who was talking with me *with* good words *and* comforting words. [14]So the angel who was talking with me said to me, Cry out, saying, So says Jehovah of hosts: I am jealous for Jerusalem and for Zion, with a great jealousy. [15]And with great anger I am angry at the nations at ease; *in* that I was but a little angry, and they gave help for evil. [16]Therefore, so says Jehovah: I have returned to Jerusalem with compassions; My house shall be built in it, says Jehovah of hosts; and a line shall be stretched over Jerusalem. [17]Cry out again, saying, So

1918 996 5921 122 5483 5921 7392 376 2009
וְהִנֵּה־אִישׁ רֹכֵב עַל־סוּס אָדֹם וְהוּא עֹמֵד בֵּין הַהֲדַסִּים
myrtle the among stood He And red a on riding a and
trees .horse man ,behold

3836 8320 122 5483 310 4699
אֲשֶׁר בַּמְּצֻלָה וְאַחֲרָיו סוּסִים אֲדֻמִּים שְׂרֻקִּים וּלְבָנִים׃
and ,sorrel ,red horses behind And the in that
.white (were) Him .ravine (were)

9 1696 4397 559 113/428 4100 559
וָאֹמַר מָה־אֵלֶּה אֲדֹנִי וַיֹּאמֶר אֵלַי הַמַּלְאָךְ הַדֹּבֵר בִּי אֲנִי
I with was who the me to said And My ,these What I Then
,me speaking angel ?Lord (are) said

10 1918 996 5975 376 6030 428 4100 7200
אַרְאֶךָּ מָה־הֵמָּה אֵלֶּה׃ וַיַּעַן הָאִישׁ הָעֹמֵד בֵּין־הַהֲדַסִּים
the among who man the And .these (are) what you make
trees myrtle stood answered see

11 6030 776 1980 3068 7971 834 428 559
וַיֹּאמַר אֵלֶּה אֲשֶׁר שָׁלַח יְהוָה לְהִתְהַלֵּךְ בָּאָרֶץ׃ וַיַּעֲנוּ
they And the in walk to Jehovah has those These ,said and
answered .earth about sent whom (are)

1980 559 1918 996 5975 3068 4397
אֶת־מַלְאַךְ יְהוָה הָעֹמֵד בֵּין הַהֲדַסִּים וַיֹּאמְרוּ הִתְהַלַּכְנוּ
have We ,said and myrtle the among who Jehovah the
about walked trees stood of Angel

12 3068 4397 6030 8252 3427 776 3605 2009 776
בָאָרֶץ וְהִנֵּה כָל־הָאָרֶץ יֹשֶׁבֶת וְשֹׁקָטֶת׃ וַיַּעַן מַלְאַךְ יְהוָה
Jeho- Angel the Then at is and sits the all and the in
vah of answered .peace earth ,behold ,earth

7355 3808 5704 6635 3068 559
וַיֹּאמַר יְהוָה צְבָאוֹת עַד־מָתַי אַתָּה לֹא־תְרַחֵם אֶת־
have will not You when Until ,hosts O ,said and
on compassion of Jehovah

8141 7657 2194 834 3063 5892 3389
יְרוּשָׁלִַם וְאֵת עָרֵי יְהוּדָה אֲשֶׁר זָעַמְתָּה זֶה שִׁבְעִים שָׁנָה׃
?years seventy these have You which ,Judah the and Jerusalem
cursed of cities

13 1697 2896 1697 1696 4397 3068 6030
וַיַּעַן יְהוָה אֶת־הַמַּלְאָךְ הַדֹּבֵר בִּי דְּבָרִים טוֹבִים דְּבָרִים
(and) (with) words with was who the Jehovah And
words ,good me speaking Angel answered

14 3541 559 7121 1696 4397 559 5150
נִחֻמִים׃ וַיֹּאמֶר אֵלַי הַמַּלְאָךְ הַדֹּבֵר בִּי קְרָא לֵאמֹר כֹּה
Thus ,saying Cry with was who the me to said So .comforting
out ,me speaking Angel

1419 7068 6726 3389 7065 6635 3068 559
אָמַר יְהוָה צְבָאוֹת קִנֵּאתִי לִירוּשָׁלִַם וּלְצִיּוֹן קִנְאָה גְדוֹלָה׃
great a (with) for and for am I :hosts Jehovah says
jealousy Zion Jerusalem jealous of

15 7107 7600 1471 7107 1419 7110
וְקֶצֶף גָּדוֹל אֲנִי קֹצֵף עַל־הַגּוֹיִם הַשַּׁאֲנַנִּים אֲשֶׁר אֲנִי קָצַפְתִּי
was I (in) ;ease at the at am I great with And
angry that nations angry anger

16 7725 3068 559 3541 3651 7451 5826 4592
מְעָט וְהֵמָּה עָזְרוּ לְרָעָה׃ לָכֵן כֹּה־אָמַר יְהוָה שַׁבְתִּי
have I :Jehovah says thus Therefore .evil for helped then a
returned they little

6635 3068 5002 1129 1004 7356 3389
לִירוּשָׁלִַם בְּרַחֲמִים בֵּיתִי יִבָּנֶה בָּהּ נְאֻם יְהוָה צְבָאוֹת
;hosts Jehovah says ,it in be shall My with to
of built house ;compassions Jerusalem

17 559 3541 559 7121 5750 3389 5921 5186 6957
וְקָוֶה יִנָּטֶה עַל־יְרוּשָׁלִָם׃ עוֹד קְרָא לֵאמֹר כֹּה אָמַר
says Thus ,saying ,out Cry again .Jerusalem over be will a and
stretched line

says Jehovah of hosts: My cities shall again overflow with goodness, and Jehovah shall yet comfort Zion, and shall yet choose Jerusalem.

[18]Then I lifted up my eyes and looked. And, behold, four horns! [19]And I said to the angel who was talking with me, What *are* these? And he answered me, These *are* the horns that have scattered Judah, Israel, and Jerusalem. [20]And Jehovah showed me four craftsmen. [21]And I said, What *are* these coming to do? And He spoke, saying, These *are* the horns which have scattered Judah, so that no man lifts up his head. But these have come to terrify them, to throw down the horns of the nations who lifted up *their* horn over the land of Judah, to scatter it.

CHAPTER 2

[1]I lifted up my eyes again and looked. And, behold, A man, and a measuring line in his hand! [2]And I said, Where are you going? And he said to me, To measure Jerusalem, to see what *is* its breadth and what its length. [3]And, behold, the angel who was talking with me went out, and another angel went out to meet him, [4]and said to him, Run, speak to this young man, saying, Jerusalem shall be inhabited, *as* towns without walls, for the multitude of men and livestock in her midst. [5]And I will be to her a wall of fire all around, and I will be for glory in her midst, declares Jehovah.

[6]Ho! Ho! Flee then from

5750 3068 51 62 2896 5892 6327 5750 6635 3068
יְהוָה צְבָאוֹת עוֹד תְּפוּצֶנָה עָרַי מִטּוֹב וְנִחַם יְהוָה עוֹד
again Jehovah shall and from My shall again :hosts Jehovah
comfort goodness cities overflow of

3389 5750 977 67:26
אֶת־צִיּוֹן וּבָחַר עוֹד בִּירוּשָׁלִָם׃
.Jerusalem again shall and Zion
choose

CAP. II ב

CHAPTER 2

559 7161 702 2009 7200 5869 5375
1 וָאֶשָּׂא אֶת־עֵינַי וָאֵרֶא וְהִנֵּה אַרְבַּע קְרָנוֹת׃
2 וָאֹמַר אֶל־
to I And .horns four and and eyes my I Then
said ,behold ;looked up lifted

7161 428 559 428/4100 1696 4397
הַמַּלְאָךְ הַדֹּבֵר בִּי מָה־אֵלֶּה וַיֹּאמֶר אֵלַי אֵלֶּה הַקְּרָנוֹת
horns the These ,me to he And ?these What with was who the
(are) said (are) ,me speaking angel

7200 3389 3478 3063 2219
3 אֲשֶׁר זֵרוּ אֶת־יְהוּדָה אֶת־יִשְׂרָאֵל וִירוּשָׁלִָם׃ וַיַּרְאֵנִי
And and ,Israel ,Judah have that
me showed .Jerusalem scattered

6213 935 428 4100 559 2796 702 3068
4 יְהוָה אַרְבָּעָה חָרָשִׁים׃ וָאֹמַר מָה אֵלֶּה בָאִים לַעֲשׂוֹת
?do to coming these What I Then .craftsmen four Jehovah
(are) ,said

6310 3063 2219 834 7161 428 559 559
וַיֹּאמֶר לֵאמֹר אֵלֶּה הַקְּרָנוֹת אֲשֶׁר־זֵרוּ אֶת־יְהוּדָה כְּפִי־
so ,Judah have which horns the These ,saying He And
that scattered (are) ,spoke

2334 2729 428 935 7218 5375 376
אִישׁ לֹא־נָשָׂא רֹאשׁוֹ וַיָּבֹאוּ אֵלֶּה לְהַחֲרִיד אֹתָם לְיַדּוֹת
throw to ,them terrify to these have But his lifts not man a
down come .head up

2219 3063 776 7161 5375 1471 7161
אֶת־קַרְנוֹת הַגּוֹיִם הַנֹּשְׂאִים קֶרֶן אֶל־אֶרֶץ יְהוּדָה לְזָרוֹתָהּ׃
scatter to ,Judah the against (their) lifted who the the
.it of land horn up nations of horns

4060 2256 3027 376 2009 7200 5869 5375
5 וָאֶשָּׂא עֵינַי וָאֵרֶא וְהִנֵּה־אִישׁ וּבְיָדוֹ חֶבֶל מִדָּה׃
a line in and man A And and my I And
!measuring hand his !behold .saw eyes lifted

3389 40:58 559 1980 559
6 וָאֹמַר אָנָה אַתָּה הֹלֵךְ וַיֹּאמֶר אֵלַי לָמֹד אֶת־יְרוּשָׁלִַם
,Jerusalem To ,me to he And are you Where ! Then
measure said ?going ,said

1696 43:97 2009 753 7341 4100 7200
7 לִרְאוֹת כַּמָּה־רָחְבָּהּ וְכַמָּה אָרְכָּהּ׃ וְהִנֵּה הַמַּלְאָךְ הַדֹּבֵר
was who the And its what and its what see to
speaking angel ,behold .length (is) breadth (is)

7323 559 7125 3318 312 4397 3318
8 בִּי יֹצֵא וּמַלְאָךְ אַחֵר יֹצֵא לִקְרָאתוֹ׃ וַיֹּאמֶר אֵלָו רֻץ
,Run to said and meet to went another and went with
,him ,him forth angel ,forth me

7230 3389 3427 6519 559 1975 5288 1696
דַּבֵּר אֶל־הַנַּעַר הַלָּז לֵאמֹר פְּרָזוֹת תֵּשֵׁב יְרוּשָׁלִַם מֵרֹב
the for ,Jerusalem will open (like) ,saying ,this young to speak
of multitude dwell country man

2346 30:68 5002 1961 8432 929 120
9 אָדָם וּבְהֵמָה בְּתוֹכָהּ׃ וַאֲנִי אֶהְיֶה־לָּהּ נְאֻם־יְהוָה חוֹמַת
wall a ,Jehovah says to be will For her in and men
of ,her I .midst cattle

5227 1945 1945 8432 1961 3519 5439 784
10 אֵשׁ סָבִיב וּלְכָבוֹד אֶהְיֶה בְתוֹכָהּ׃ הוֹי הוֹי וְנֻסוּ
Flee !Ho !Ho her in will I for and all fire
then .midst be glory ,around

the land of the north, says Jehovah. For I have scattered you as the four winds of the heavens, declares Jehovah. [7]Ho, O Zion! Escape, you who live with the daughter of Babylon. [8]For so says Jehovah of hosts: He has sent Me after glory, to the nations who plundered you; for he who touches you touches the pupil of His eye. [9]For, behold, I will shake My hand over them, and they shall be a prize for their servants. And you shall know that Jehovah has sent Me.

[10]Sing and rejoice, O daughter of Zion. For, lo, I come; and I will dwell among you, says Jehovah. [11]And many nations shall be joined to Jehovah in that day, and they shall be My people; and I will dwell among you; and you shall know that Jehovah of hosts has sent Me to you. [12]And Jehovah shall possess Judah, His portion in the holy land, and *He* shall again choose Jerusalem. [13]All flesh, be silent before Jehovah. For He is raised up out of His holy habitation.

8064 7307 702 3068/5002 6828 776
מֵאֶרֶץ צָפוֹן נְאֻם־יְהוָה כִּי כְּאַרְבַּע רוּחוֹת הַשָּׁמַיִם
the winds the as for ;Jehovah says the the from / heavens of four ,north of land

3427 4422 3050 1945 3068 5002 6566
11 פֵּרַשְׂתִּי אֶתְכֶם נְאֻם־יְהוָה׃ הוֹי צִיּוֹן הִמָּלְטִי יוֹשֶׁבֶת
who you Escape !Zion O ,Ho .Jehovah says ,you have I / with live scattered

3519 310 6635 3068 559 3541 894/1323
12 בַּת־בָּבֶל׃ כִּי כֹה אָמַר יְהוָה צְבָאוֹת אַחַר כָּבוֹד
glory After :hosts Jehovah says thus For .Babylon the / of of daughter

5060 5060 7997 1471 7971
שְׁלָחַנִי אֶל־הַגּוֹיִם הַשֹּׁלְלִים אֶתְכֶם כִּי הַנֹּגֵעַ בָּכֶם נֹגֵעַ
touches you who he for ;you who the to has He / touches plundered nations ,Me sent

7998 1961 5921 3027 5130 2005 5869 892
13 בְּבָבַת עֵינוֹ׃ כִּי הִנְנִי מֵנִיף אֶת־יָדִי עֲלֵיהֶם וְהָיוּ שָׁלָל
prize a they and over My will ,behold ,For His the / be shall ,them hand wave I .eye of pupil

7442 7971 6635 3068 3045 5650
14 לְעַבְדֵיהֶם וִידַעְתֶּם כִּי־יְהוָה צְבָאוֹת שְׁלָחָנִי׃ רָנִּי
Sing sent has hosts Jehovah that you And their for / .Me of know shall ,servants

3068 5002 8432 7931 935 2005 6726 1323 8056
וְשִׂמְחִי בַּת־צִיּוֹן כִּי הִנְנִי־בָא וְשָׁכַנְתִּי בְתוֹכֵךְ נְאֻם־יְהוָה׃
.Jehovah says your in I and ,come ,lo For ,Zion O and / midst dwell will I of daughter ,rejoice

5971 1961 3117 3068 7227 1471 3867
15 וְנִלְווּ גוֹיִם רַבִּים אֶל־יְהוָה בַּיּוֹם הַהוּא וְהָיוּ לִי לְעָם
a for to they and ,that day in Jehovah to many nations will and / ;people Me be will joined be

7971 6635 3068 3045 8432 7931
וְשָׁכַנְתִּי בְתוֹכֵךְ וְיָדַעַתְּ כִּי־יְהוָה צְבָאוֹת שְׁלָחַנִי אֵלָיִךְ׃
.you to sent has hosts Jehovah that you and your in I and / Me of know shall ,midst dwell will

977 6944 127 2508 3063 3068 5157
16 וְנָחַל יְהוָה אֶת־יְהוּדָה חֶלְקוֹ עַל אַדְמַת הַקֹּדֶשׁ וּבָחַר
will and ,holy the land in His ,Judah Jehovah will And / choose portion inherit

5782 3068 6440 1320 3605 2013 3389 5750
17 עוֹד בִּירוּשָׁלָםִ׃ הַס כָּל־בָּשָׂר מִפְּנֵי יְהוָה כִּי נֵעוֹר
is He for ;Jehovah before ,flesh all Be .Jerusalem again / aroused ,silent

6944 4583
מִמְּעוֹן קָדְשׁוֹ׃
His from / .holy habitation

CAP. III ג

CHAPTER 3

CHAPTER 3

[1]And he made me see Joshua the high priest standing before the Angel of Jehovah, and Satan standing at his right hand to accuse him. [2]And Jehovah said to Satan, Jehovah rebuke you, Satan! And, Jehovah who has chosen Jerusalem rebuke you! Is this not a brand plucked out of the fire? [3]And Joshua was clothed with filthy

3068 4397 6440 5975 1419 3548 3091 7200
1 וַיַּרְאֵנִי אֶת־יְהוֹשֻׁעַ הַכֹּהֵן הַגָּדוֹל עֹמֵד לִפְנֵי מַלְאַךְ יְהוָה
,Jehovah the before standing high the Joshua He And / of Angel priest see me made

7854 3068 559 7853 3225 5975 7854
2 וְהַשָּׂטָן עֹמֵד עַל־יְמִינוֹ לְשִׂטְנוֹ׃ וַיֹּאמֶר יְהוָה אֶל־הַשָּׂטָן
,Satan to Jehovah said And accuse to his at standing and / .him hand right Satan

3389 977 3068 1605 7854 3068 1605
יִגְעַר יְהוָה בְּךָ הַשָּׂטָן וְיִגְעַר יְהוָה בְּךָ הַבֹּחֵר בִּירוּשָׁלָםִ
!Jerusalem has who you Jehovah And !Satan ,you Jehovah rebuke / chosen rebuke

899 3847 1961 3091 784 5337 181 2088
3 הֲלוֹא זֶה אוּד מֻצָּל מֵאֵשׁ׃ וִיהוֹשֻׁעַ הָיָה לָבֻשׁ בְּגָדִים
with clothed was Now the from Is a this not / garments Joshua ?fire snatched brand

garments, and he stood before the Angel. [4]And He answered and spoke to those who stood before Him, saying, Take away the filthy garments from him. And He said to him, Behold, I have caused your iniquity to pass from you, and I will clothe you with ceremonial robes. [5]And I said, Let them set a clean turban on his head. And they set a clean turban on his head, and clothed him with clothing. And the Angel of Jehovah stood by. [6]And the Angel of Jehovah charged Joshua, saying, [7]So says Jehovah of hosts: If you will walk in My ways, and if you will keep My charge, then you shall also judge My house, and shall also keep My courts; and I will give you room to walk among these who stand by.

[8]Hear now, O Joshua the high priest, you and your friends who are sitting before you, for they *are* men of symbol. For, behold, I will bring forth My Servant, the Branch. [9]For behold, the stone which I have set before Joshua: on one stone *are* seven eyes; behold, I will engrave its engraving, says Jehovah of hosts, and I will remove the iniquity of that land in one day. [10]In that day, says Jehovah of hosts, you shall call *each* man to his neighbor to *sit* under the vine and under the fig-tree.

5975 559 6030 4397 6440 5975 6674
4 צוֹאִים וְעֹמֵד לִפְנֵי הַמַּלְאָךְ׃ וַיַּעַן וַיֹּאמֶר אֶל־הָעֹמְדִים
who those standing were | to | and spoke | He And answered | the .Angel | before | he and stood | ,filthy

559 6674 899 5493 559 6440
לְפָנָיו לֵאמֹר הָסִירוּ הַבְּגָדִים הַצֹּאִים מֵעָלָיו וַיֹּאמֶר אֵלָיו
to him | He And said | from .him | filthy | the garments | Remove | ,saying | before Him

559 42,54 3847 577.1 5674 7200
5 רְאֵה הֶעֱבַרְתִּי מֵעָלֶיךָ עֲוֺנֶךָ וְהַלְבֵּשׁ אֹתְךָ מַחֲלָצוֹת׃ וָאֹמַר
I And ,said | festal .garments | with you | will I and clothe | your ,iniquity | from you | have I pass to caused | ,See

5921 2889 6797 7760 7218 5921 2889 6797 7760
יָשִׂימוּ צָנִיף טָהוֹר עַל־רֹאשׁוֹ וַיָּשִׂימוּ הַצָּנִיף הַטָּהוֹר עַל־
on | clean | turban a | they So sat | his ,head | on | clean | a turban | them Let set

4397 5649 5975 3068 4397 899 3847 7218
6 רֹאשׁוֹ וַיַּלְבִּשֻׁהוּ בְּגָדִים וּמַלְאַךְ יְהוָה עֹמֵד׃ וַיָּעַד מַלְאַךְ
the of Angel | And charged | .stood | Jehovah | the and of Angel | with ,clothes | clothed and him | his head

1870 6635 3068 559 559 3091 3068
7 יְהוָה בִּיהוֹשֻׁעַ לֵאמֹר׃ כֹּה־אָמַר יְהוָה צְבָאוֹת אִם־בִּדְרָכַי
My in ways | If | :hosts of | Jehovah | says Thus | ,saying | ,Joshua | Jehovah

1004 1777 1571 8104 4931 518 1980
תֵּלֵךְ וְאִם אֶת־מִשְׁמַרְתִּי תִשְׁמֹר וְגַם־אַתָּה תָּדִין אֶת־בֵּיתִי
My house | shall judge | you | then also | will you ,keep | My service | if and | you ,walk will

5975 996 1980 5414 2691 8104 1571
וְגַם תִּשְׁמֹר אֶת־חֲצֵרָי וְנָתַתִּי לְךָ מַהְלְכִים בֵּין הָעֹמְדִים
are who by standing | among | goings | to you | I and give will | My ,courts | shall keep | and also

7453 1419 3548 3091 4994/8085 428
8 הָאֵלֶּה׃ שְׁמַע־נָא יְהוֹשֻׁעַ ׀ הַכֹּהֵן הַגָּדוֹל אַתָּה וְרֵעֶיךָ
your and friends | you | ,high | the priest | O Joshua | ,now Hear | .these

935 2005 4159 582 64 :40 3427
הַיֹּשְׁבִים לְפָנֶיךָ כִּי־אַנְשֵׁי מוֹפֵת הֵמָּה כִּי־הִנְנִי מֵבִיא אֶת־
will forth bring | ,behold I | ,For | they .(are) | symbol | men of | for | before ;you | are who sitting

3091 6440 5414 834 68 2009 6780 5650
9 עַבְדִּי צֶמַח׃ כִּי ׀ הִנֵּה הָאֶבֶן אֲשֶׁר נָתַתִּי לִפְנֵי יְהוֹשֻׁעַ
;Joshua | before | have I given | which | the stone | behold | For | the .Branch | My Servant

3078 5002 6603 6605 2005 5869 7651 259 68 5921
עַל־אֶבֶן אַחַת שִׁבְעָה עֵינָיִם הִנְנִי מְפַתֵּחַ פִּתֻּחָהּ נְאֻם יְהוָה
Jehovah of | says | its engraving | will engrave | ,behold I | ;eyes | seven | one (are) | stone | on

3117 259 3117 776 5771 4185 6635
10 צְבָאוֹת וּמַשְׁתִּי אֶת־עֲוֺן הָאָרֶץ־הַהִיא בְּיוֹם אֶחָד׃ בַּיּוֹם
day In | .one | day in | that | land iniquity the of | I and remove will | ,hosts

8478 7453 376 7121 6635 3068 5002
הַהוּא נְאֻם יְהוָה צְבָאוֹת תִּקְרְאוּ אִישׁ לְרֵעֵהוּ אֶל־תַּחַת
under | to (sit) | his to neighbor | (each) man | shall you invite | ,hosts of | Jehovah | says | ,that

8384 8472 1612
גֶּפֶן וְאֶל־תַּחַת תְּאֵנָה׃
the .tree fig | under | and | the vine

CAP. IV ד

CHAPTER 4

CHAPTER 4

[1]And the angel who was speaking with me came again and awakened me, as a man that is awakened out

8142 5782 834 376 5782 1696 4397 7725
1 וַיָּשָׁב הַמַּלְאָךְ הַדֹּבֵר בִּי וַיְעִירֵנִי כְּאִישׁ אֲשֶׁר־יֵעוֹר מִשְּׁנָתוֹ׃
his from ,sleep | is awakened | who | a as man | awoke and ,me | with me | was who speaking | the angel | And returned

of his sleep. [2]And *he* said to me, What do you see? And I said, I see, and behold, a lampstdand, all of it gold; and a bowl *is* on its top. And its seven lamps *are* on it, and seven spouts each to the seven lamps on its top; [3]and two olive trees *are* beside it, one on the right of the bowl, and one on its left. [4]And I answered and spoke to the angel who was talking with me, saying, What *are* these, my lord? [5]And the angel who was speaking with me answered and said to me, Do you not know what these *are*? And I said, No, my lord. [6]Then he answered and spoke to me, saying, This *is* the word of Jehovah to Zerubbabel, saying, Not by might, nor by power, but by My Spirit, says Jehovah of hosts. [7]Who *are* you, O great mountain? Before Zerubbabel *you shall become* a plain. And he shall bring forth the top-stone with shouts: Grace! Grace to it!

[8]And the word of Jehovah was to me, saying, [9]The hands of Zerubbabel have laid the foundation of this house; his hands shall also finish *it*. And you shall know that Jehovah of hosts has sent me to you. [10]For who has despised the day of small things? For they shall rejoice and shall see the plummet stone in the hand of Zerubbabel. These seven are the eyes of Jehovah; they run to and fro through all the earth.

[11]And I answered and said to him, What *are* these two olive trees on the right of the lampstand, and on its left? [12]And I answered a second time and said to him, What *are* the two clusters of olives which *are* beside the two golden

4501 2009 7200 559 7200 4100 559
2 וַיֹּאמֶר אֵלַי מָה אַתָּה רֹאֶה וָאֹמַר רָאִיתִי וְהִנֵּה מְנוֹרַת
lamp- a and see I I And do you What ,me to and
of stand ,behold ,said ?see said

7651 5921 521 6 7651 7218 59 21 15 31 36 05 2091
זָהָב כֻּלָּהּ וְגֻלָּהּ עַל־רֹאשָׁהּ וְשִׁבְעָה נֵרֹתֶיהָ עָלֶיהָ שִׁבְעָה
seven on (are) its And .top its on a and of all ,gold
it lamps seven bowl ,it

2132 8147 7218 5921 834 5216 4166 7651
3 וְשִׁבְעָה מוּצָקוֹת לַנֵּרוֹת אֲשֶׁר עַל־רֹאשָׁהּ׃ וּשְׁנַיִם זֵיתִים
olive two and ;top its on which the to spouts and
trees (are) lamps seven

559 6030 8040 59 21 259 1543 3225 259
4 עָלֶיהָ אֶחָד מִימִין הַגֻּלָּה וְאֶחָד עַל־שְׂמֹאלָהּ׃ וָאַעַן וָאֹמַר
and I So left. its on one and the the on one beside
said answered ,bowl of right ,it

4397 6030 113 428 4100 559 1696 4397
5 אֶל־הַמַּלְאָךְ הַדֹּבֵר בִּי לֵאמֹר מָה־אֵלֶּה אֲדֹנִי׃ וַיַּעַן הַמַּלְאָךְ
the Then my these What ,saying with was who the to
angel answered ?lord (are) ,me speaking angel

559 428 4100 3045 559 1697
הַדֹּבֵר בִּי וַיֹּאמֶר אֵלַי הֲלוֹא יָדַעְתָּ מָה־הֵמָּה אֵלֶּה וָאֹמַר
I And ?these (are) what you Do not ,me to said and with was who
,said know me speaking

3068 1697 2088 559 559 6030 113 3808
6 לֹא אֲדֹנִי׃ וַיַּעַן וַיֹּאמֶר אֵלַי לֵאמֹר זֶה דְּבַר־יְהוָה אֶל־
to Jehovah the This ,saying ,me to said and he Then my ,No
of word (is) answered .lord

559 7307 3581 38 08 24 28 559 2216
זְרֻבָּבֶל לֵאמֹר לֹא בְחַיִל וְלֹא בְכֹחַ כִּי אִם־בְּרוּחִי אָמַר
says My by but by nor by Not ,saying Zerub-
Spirit ,power ,might ,babel

4334 2216 6440 1419 2022 4310 6635 3068
7 יְהוָה צְבָאוֹת׃ מִי־אַתָּה הַר־הַגָּדוֹל לִפְנֵי זְרֻבָּבֶל לְמִישֹׁר
!plain a Zerubbabel Before ?great O ,you Who .hosts Jehovah
(become) mountain (are) of

2580 2580 86 63 72 22 68 3318
וְהוֹצִיא אֶת־הָאֶבֶן הָרֹאשָׁה תְּשֻׁאוֹת חֵן ׀ חֵן לָהּ׃
to Grace !Grace (with) top stone the he And
!it ,shouts out bring shall

2088 1004 3448 2216 3027 559 3068 1697 1961
8
9 וַיְהִי דְבַר־יְהוָה אֵלַי לֵאמֹר׃ יְדֵי זְרֻבָּבֶל יִסְּדוּ הַבַּיִת הַזֶּה
;this house have Zerubbabel The ,saying ,me to Jehovah the And
founded of hands of word was

7971 6635 3068 3045 1214 3027
וְיָדָיו תְּבַצַּעְנָה וְיָדַעְתָּ כִּי־יְהוָה צְבָאוֹת שְׁלָחַנִי אֲלֵיכֶם׃
.you to sent has hosts Jehovah that you and shall his and
Me of know shall ;(it) finish hands

3027 913 68 7200 8056 6996 3117 96 4310
10 כִּי מִי בַז לְיוֹם קְטַנּוֹת וְשָׂמְחוּ וְרָאוּ אֶת־הָאֶבֶן הַבְּדִיל בְּיַד
in plummet stone the shall and they For small the has who For
hand see rejoice shall ?things of day despised

3605 7751 3068 5869 428 7651 2216
זְרֻבָּבֶל שִׁבְעָה־אֵלֶּה עֵינֵי יְהוָה הֵמָּה מְשׁוֹטְטִים בְּכָל־
all in roam they ,Jehovah the these seven Zerub-
around of eyes (are) —babel's

5921 428 2132 8147 4100 559 6030 776
11 הָאָרֶץ׃ וָאַעַן וָאֹמַר אֵלָיו מַה־שְּׁנֵי הַזֵּיתִים הָאֵלֶּה עַל־
on these olive two What to said and I Then the
trees (are) ,him answered .earth

559 8145 6030 8040 5921 4501 3225
12 יְמִין הַמְּנוֹרָה וְעַל־שְׂמֹאולָהּ׃ וָאַעַן שֵׁנִית וָאֹמַר אֵלָיו
to said and second a I And ?left its and lamp- the the
,him time answered on stand of right

2091 6804 8147 834 2132 7641 8147 4100
מַה־שְּׁתֵּי שִׁבֲּלֵי הַזֵּיתִים אֲשֶׁר בְּיַד שְׁנֵי צַנְתְּרוֹת הַזָּהָב
,gold of pipes the beside which olives clusters the What
two (are) of two (are)

pipes, emptying the golden *oil* from themselves? [13]And he spoke to me, saying, Do you not know what these *are*? And I said, No, my lord. [14]And he said, These *are* the two sons of fresh oil who stand by the Lord of the whole earth.

CHAPTER 5

[1]And I again lifted up my eyes and looked. And, behold, a flying scroll! [2]And he said to me, What do you see? And I answered, I see a flying scroll; its length *is* twenty cubits, and its width ten cubits. [3]And he said to me, This *is* the curse that goes forth over the face of the whole earth. For from now on everyone who steals shall be cut off according to it; and everyone who swears from now on shall be cut off according to it. [4]And I will bring it forth, says Jehovah of hosts. And it shall go into the house of the thief, and into the house of the one who swears falsely by My name. And it shall remain in the midst of his house, and shall bring it to an end, and its timber and its stones.

[5]Then the angel who was speaking with me went out and said to me, Now lift up your eyes and see what this that goes forth *is*. [6]And I said, What *is* it? And he said, This is the ephah that goes forth. And he said, This is their form in all the earth. [7]And, behold, a lead cover was lifted up, and a woman *was* sitting in the middle of the ephah. [8]And he said, This *is* wickedness. And he threw her into the midst of the ephah; and he threw the lead stone over its opening. [9]And I lifted up my eyes and looked. And, behold, two women came

ZECHARIAH 4:13–14 (interlinear)

13	559:	559	2091	7324
	הַמְרִיקִים מֵעֲלֵיהֶם הַזָּהָב : וַיֹּאמֶר אֵלַי לֵאמֹר הֲלוֹא
	not	,saying ,me to	he And golden the	from are which
			spoke	themselves emptying
			?(oil)	

14	1121 8147	?428	559	?.113/38 08 559	?428 4100 3045
	יָדַעְתָּ מָה־אֵלֶּה וָאֹמַר לֹא אֲדֹנִי : וַיֹּאמֶר אֵלֶּה שְׁנֵי בְנֵי
	sons the	These	he Then	my No I And	these what you Do
	of two	(are)	,said	,lord ,said	?(are) know

	776 ,3605 113	5975	3323
	הַיִּצְהָר הָעֹמְדִים עַל־אֲדוֹן כָּל־הָאָרֶץ :
	the	all the by	are who	fresh
	.earth	of Lord	standing	oil

CAP. V ה
CHAPTER 5

1 2	559	5774	4039 2009	7200	5869 5375	7725
	וַיֹּאמֶר : עָפָה וְהִנֵּה מְגִלָּה וָאֶרְאֶה עֵינַי וָאֶשָּׂא וָאָשׁוּב
	he And	.flying	scroll a and and	;looked	my lifted I	And
	said		,behold		eyes up	turning

	753	57:74 40,39	72.00	559;	7200	4100
	אֵלַי מָה אַתָּה רֹאֶה וָאֹמַר אֲנִי רֹאֶה מְגִלָּה עָפָה אָרְכָּה
	lengths its ;flying scroll a	see I	I And	?see do you	What	to .me
	(is)		,said			

3	2063	559	520	6235	7341 520:	6242
	עֶשְׂרִים בָּאַמָּה וְרָחְבָּהּ עֶשֶׂר בָּאַמָּה : וַיֹּאמֶר אֵלַי זֹאת
	This	,me to	he And	.cubits	ten	its and	cubits twenty
	(is)					width

	1589, 3605	776 36,05	6440 ,5921	3318	2422:
	הָאָלָה הַיּוֹצֵאת עַל־פְּנֵי כָל־הָאָרֶץ כִּי כָל־הַגֹּנֵב מִזֶּה
	hence- who	all For	the whole	the over	goes that	the
	forth steal		.earth	of face	forth	curse

4	5002	3318	5352	76:50	,3605 53,52
	כָּמוֹהָ נִקָּה וְכָל־הַנִּשְׁבָּע מִזֶּה כָּמוֹהָ נִקָּה : הוֹצֵאתִיהָ נְאֻם
	says	will I	be will	according hence- who	and be will accord-
	,out it bring	off cut	it to	forth swear	all ;off cut it to ing

	8034	7650	1004	15,90 1004	,6635 3068
	יְהוָה צְבָאוֹת וּבָאָה אֶל־בֵּית הַגַּנָּב וְאֶל־בֵּית הַנִּשְׁבָּע בִּשְׁמִי
	My by	who him the the	the into it And	.hosts Jehovah
	name	swears of house into	thief of house	go shall of
				,935	

	68	6086	36,15 10 04	8432	3885	8267
	לַשֶּׁקֶר וְלָנֶה בְּתוֹךְ בֵּיתוֹ וְכִלַּתּוּ וְאֶת־עֵצָיו וְאֶת־אֲבָנָיו :
	its	and its and	shall and his	within	it And	.falsely
	.stones	timber	it end	,house	remain shall

5	72,00	,58,69 4994 5375	559	1696	,4397 3318:
	וַיֵּצֵא הַמַּלְאָךְ הַדֹּבֵר בִּי וַיֹּאמֶר אֵלַי שָׂא נָא עֵינֶיךָ וּרְאֵה
	see and	your now Lift	,me to	said and	with was who	the went Then
		eyes up			me speaking angel	forth

6	374	2063, 559	4100	559	,2063, 3318	4100
	מָה הַיּוֹצֵאת הַזֹּאת : וָאֹמַר מַה־הִיא וַיֹּאמֶר זֹאת הָאֵיפָה
	the	This	?it What	I And	.(is) this	goes that what
	ephah	(is)	(is)	,said	,said	forth

7	5777	3603 2009	,3605	5869 2063, 559	33:18
	הַיּוֹצֵאת וַיֹּאמֶר זֹאת עֵינָם בְּכָל־הָאָרֶץ : וְהִנֵּה כִּכַּר עֹפֶרֶת
	lead a	cover And the	all in their This	he And	goes that
			appearance (is)	,said	.forth

8	559,	374	8432	3427	259;	802,	5375
	נִשֵּׂאת וְזֹאת אִשָּׁה אַחַת יוֹשֶׁבֶת בְּתוֹךְ הָאֵיפָה : וַיֹּאמֶר
	he And	the	the in	sitting	a	woman	and lifted was
	,said	.ephah	of midst				(is) this ;up

	,7993	374	8432	79,93	75,64	2063
	זֹאת הָרִשְׁעָה וַיַּשְׁלֵךְ אֹתָהּ אֶל־תּוֹךְ הָאֵיפָה וַיַּשְׁלֵךְ אֶת־
	he and	the	the into	her	he And	.wickedness This
	cast		the into		cast	(is)
		;ephah of midst				

9	8147	,2009	7200 58,69	,5325	6310	5777	68
	אֶבֶן הָעֹפֶרֶת אֶל־פִּיהָ : וָאֶשָּׂא עֵינַי וָאֵרֶא וְהִנֵּה שְׁתַּיִם
	two	and	and	my	I Then	its	on	lead	the
		,behold	,looked	eyes	up lifted	.opening			stone

out. And the wind *was* in their wings; for they had wings like the wings of the stork. And they lifted up the ephah between the earth and the heavens. ¹⁰And I said to the angel who was speaking with me, Where are they going with the ephah? ¹¹And he said to me, To build a house for it in the land of Shinar; and it shall be fixed and established there on its own place.

2624	3671	3671	2007	:3671	7307	3318	802
נָשִׁים יוֹצְאוֹת וְרוּחַ בְּכַנְפֵיהֶם וְלָהֵנָּה כְנָפַיִם כְּכַנְפֵי הַחֲסִידָה
the stork	the like	wings	they for	their in	the And	came	women
	of wings		(had)	;wings	(was) wind	.out	

	639		8064		776		374	5375
10	וַתִּשֶּׂנָה אֶת־הָאֵיפָה בֵּין הָאָרֶץ וּבֵין הַשָּׁמָיִם: וָאֹמַר אֶל־
	to	I Then	said	.heavens	the	and	the between	the	ephah	they And	up lifted

374		3212				1696
	4397
הַמַּלְאָךְ הַדֹּבֵר בִּי אָנָה הֵמָּה מוֹלִכוֹת אֶת־הָאֵיפָה:
the	with	going	they	Where	with	was who	the
?ephah				me		speaking	angel

3240	3559	8152	776	1004	1129		559
11	וַיֹּאמֶר אֵלַי לִבְנוֹת־לָהּ בַיִת בְּאֶרֶץ שִׁנְעָר וְהוּכַן וְהֻנִּיחָה
set and	will it and	;Shinar	the in	a	for	To	,me to	he And
	fixed be		of land	house	it	build		said

				4369/5921	8033
שָׁם עַל־מְכֻנָתָהּ:
own its	on there
	.place

CAP. VI ו

CHAPTER 6

¹And again my eyes lifted up and looked. And, behold, four chariots were coming from between two mountains; and the mountains were mountains of bronze. ²Red horses *were* in the first chariot; and black horses in the second chariot; ³and white horses in the third chariot; and horses *with* dappled, strong *colors were* in the fourth chariot. ⁴And I answered and said to the angel who was talking with me, What *are* these, my lord? ⁵And the angel answered and said to me, These *are* the four spirits of Heaven who go forth from standing before the Lord of all the earth. ⁶The black horses in it go into the north country; and the white go after them; and the dappled ones go toward the south country. ⁷And the strong-*colored ones* went forth and sought to go, to walk to and fro in the earth. And he said, Go! Walk to and fro in the earth. So they walked to and fro in the earth. ⁸And he cried out to me, and

3318		4818	702	2009	72:00	5869	5375	7725
1	וָאָשֻׁב וָאֶשָּׂא עֵינַי וָאֶרְאֶה וְהִנֵּה אַרְבַּע מַרְכָּבוֹת יֹצְאוֹת
were		chariots	four	and	and	my	lifted	And
coming				,behold	;looked	eyes	up	again

7723		4818		5178	2022	2022	2022	8147	996
2	מִבֵּין שְׁנֵי הֶהָרִים וְהֶהָרִים הָרֵי נְחֹשֶׁת: בַּמֶּרְכָּבָה הָרִאשֹׁנָה
first		the With		.bronze	moun-	the And	moun-	two	from
		chariot			of tains	mountains	tains	between	

7838		5783	8145	4818	122		5483
סוּסִים אֲדֻמִּים וּבַמֶּרְכָּבָה הַשֵּׁנִית סוּסִים שְׁחֹרִים:
;black	horses	second	with and	;red	(were)
			chariot the		horses

72:43		4818	3836	5483	7992		4818
3	וּבַמֶּרְכָּבָה הַשְּׁלִשִׁית סוּסִים לְבָנִים וּבַמֶּרְכָּבָה הָרְבִעִית
fourth		the with and	;white	horses	third	the with and
		chariot				chariot

1696		4397	559	60 30	554	1261	5483
4	סוּסִים בְּרֻדִּים אֲמֻצִּים: וָאַעַן וָאֹמַר אֶל־הַמַּלְאָךְ הַדֹּבֵר
was who	the	to	said and	I Then	strong (and)	dappled	horses
speaking	angel					.(colored)	answered

	702	428	559		4397	6030	113	428/ 4100
5	בִּי מָה־אֵלֶּה אֲדֹנִי: וַיַּעַן הַמַּלְאָךְ וַיֹּאמֶר אֵלַי אֵלֶּה אַרְבַּע
four the	These	to	said and	angel the	Then	my	,these	What with
(are)		me				?lord	answered	(are) ,me

	776	3605	113	3320	3318	8064	7307
רוּחוֹת הַשָּׁמָיִם יוֹצְאוֹת מֵהִתְיַצֵּב עַל־אֲדוֹן כָּל־הָאָרֶץ:
the	all	the	before standing from	go who	forth	spirits
;earth		of Lord			,heavens	of

68:28	776		3318	78:38	5483		834
6	אֲשֶׁר־בָּהּ הַסּוּסִים הַשְּׁחֹרִים יֹצְאִים אֶל־אֶרֶץ צָפוֹן
the	country	into	forth go	black	horses the	with which
;north						it (are)

776		3318	32:12	1245		3318	3836
וְהַלְּבָנִים יָצְאוּ אֶל־אַחֲרֵיהֶם וְהַבְּרֻדִּים יָצְאוּ אֶל־אֶרֶץ
a	to	go	the and	after	into	go	the and
country	forth		ones dappled	;them	(north the)	forth	white

776		1980	3212	1245		3318	554	8486
7	הַתֵּימָן: וְהָאֲמֻצִּים יָצְאוּ וַיְבַקְשׁוּ לָלֶכֶת לְהִתְהַלֵּךְ בָּאָרֶץ
the in	walk to	go to	sought and	went	strong the	And	the
.earth	fro and to			forth	(ones colored)		.south

2199	776	1980		776	1980	32 12/559
8	וַיֹּאמֶר לְכוּ הִתְהַלְּכוּ בָאָרֶץ וַתִּתְהַלַּכְנָה בָּאָרֶץ: וַיַּזְעֵק
he Then	the in	walked they So	the in	to walk	,Go	he And
out cried	.earth	fro and to	.earth	fro and		,said

spoke to me, saying, Behold, these who go toward the north country have caused My Spirit to rest in the north country.
9 [9]And the word of Jehovah was to me, saying. [10]Take from Heldai, from Tobijah, and from Jedaiah, from the exiles who have come from Babylon; and in that day you go and enter into the house of Josiah, the son of Zephaniah. [11]And take silver and gold, and make crowns, and set on the head of Joshua, the son of Jehozadak, the high priest. [12]And speak to him, saying, So says Jehovah of hosts, saying, Behold! The Man whose name is THE BRANCH! And He shall spring up out of His place, and He shall build the temple of Jehovah. [13]Even He shall build the temple of Jehovah; and He shall bear the majesty, and shall sit and rule on His throne. And He shall be a priest on His throne; and the counsel of peace shall be between the two of them. [14]And the crowns shall be for a memorial in the temple of Jehovah, to Helem, and to Tobijah, and to Jedaiah, and to Hen, the son of Zephaniah. [15]And the distant ones shall come and build in the temple of Jehovah. And you shall know that Jehovah of hosts has sent me to you. And *this* shall be, if you will diligently obey the voice of Jehovah your God.

5117 68:28 776 3318 72.00 559 1696 854
אתי וידבר אלי לאמר ראה היוצאים אל־ארץ צפון הניחו
set have the country to who those ,See ,saying ,me to and to
rest at north forth go spoke me

559 3068 1697 1961 6828 776 7307
9 את־רוחי בארץ צפון׃ ויהי דבר־יהוה אלי לאמר׃
,saying to Jehovah the And the in My
,me of word was .north country Spirit

3048 2900 2469 1473 3947
10 לקוח מאת הגולה מחלדי מאת טוביה ומאת ידעיה
,Jedaiah and ,Tobijah from from the from Take
from ,Heldai ,exiles

6846 1121 2977 1004 935 3117 935
ובאת אתה ביום ההוא ובאת בית יאשיה בן־צפניה
Zepha- the Josiah the and that day in you go and
,niah of son of house enter

5850 6213 2091 3701 3947 894 935
11 אשר־באו מבבל׃ ולקחת כסף־וזהב ועשית עטרות
;crowns and and silver take and from have who
make gold ;Babylon come

559 1419 3548 3087 1121 3091 7218 7760
12 ושמת בראש יהושע בן־יהוצדק הכהן הגדול׃ ואמרת
speak And .high the Jehosadak the Joshua the on set and
priest of son of head (it)

6780 376 559 6635 3068 559 3541 559
אליו לאמר כה אמר יהוה צבאות לאמר הנה־איש צמח
BRANCH A !Behold ,saying ,hosts Jehovah says Thus ,saying ,him to
(is) ,man of

1129 3068 1964 1129 67 79 8478 8034
13 שמו ומתחתיו יצמח ובנה את־היכל יהוה׃ והוא יבנה
shall Even .Jehovah the He and will He from And His
build He of temple build will ,sprout place His .name

1961 3678 5921 4910 3427 1935 5375 3068 1964
את־היכל יהוה והוא־ישא הוד וישב ומשל על־כסאו והיה
He and His on rule and shall and the shall and ,Jehovah the
be shall ;throne sit majesty bear He of temple

5850 8147 996 1961 7965 6098 3678 5921 3548
14 כהן על־כסאו ועצת שלום תהיה בין שניהם׃ והעטרת
the And two the between shall peace the and His on a
crowns .them of be of counsel ;throne priest

2146 6846 1121 2581 3048 2900 2494 1961
תהיה לחלם ולטוביה ולידעיה ולחן בן־צפניה לזכרון
a for Zephaniah the to and to and to and to shall
reminder of son Hen ,Jedaiah ,Tobijah ,Helem be

3045 3068 1964 1129 935 7350 3068 1964
15 בהיכל יהוה׃ ורחוקים יבאו ובנו בהיכל יהוה וידעתם
you and ,Jehovah the in and shall the And .Jehovah the in
know shall of temple build come ones distant of temple

8085 8085 518 1961 7971 6635 3068
כי־יהוה צבאות שלחני אליכם והיה אם־שמוע תשמעון
listen you diligently if it And .you to sent has hosts Jeho- that
to ,be will me of vah

430 3068 6963
בקול יהוה אלהיכם׃
.God your Jehovah the
of voice

CAP. VII ז

CHAPTER 7

CHAPTER 7

1 [1]And in the fourth year of king Darius, the word of Jehovah was to Zechariah, in the fourth of the ninth month, in Chislev. [2]And Sharezer and Regemmelech, and his men, had

30 68 1697 1961 4428 1867 702 8141 1961
1 ויהי בשנת ארבע לדריוש המלך היה דבר־יהוה אל־
to Jehovah the came ,king the Darius of fourth the in it And
of word year was

1004 7971 3691 8671 2320 702 2148
2 זכריה בארבעה לחדש התשעי בכסלו׃ וישלח בית־
Beth- had Now .Chislev in ,ninth the month of the in Zechariah
sent fourth

sent *to* Bethel to seek the favor of the face of Jehovah, [3]to speak to the priests who *belong* to the house of Jehovah of hosts, and to the prophets, saying, Should I weep in the fifth month, consecrating myself as I have done these many years?

[4]The the word of Jehovah of hosts was to me, saying, [5]Speak to all the people of the land, and to the priests, saying, When you fasted and mourned in the fifth and seventh *months*, even those seventy years, did you truly fast to Me, *even* to Me? [6]And when you ate, and when you drank, was it not for those eating, and for those drinking? [7]Are not *these* the words which Jehovah proclaimed by the former prophets, when Jerusalem was inhabited, and prosperous, with her cities all around her; and the Negeb and the Shephelah were inhabited?

[8]And the word of Jehovah was to Zechariah, saying, [9]So says Jehovah of hosts, saying, Judge true judgment, and practice kindness and pity, *each* man with his brother. [10]And do not oppress the widow, or the fatherless, the alien, or the poor. And do not devise evil in your heart, of a man *against* his brother. [11]But they refused to listen, and gave a stubborn shoulder, and they made their ears heavy from hearing. [12]And they made their heart adamant from hearing the law and the words which Jehovah of hosts has sent through His Spirit, by the former prophets. And great wrath was from Jehovah of hosts.

3068 6440 2470 582 7278 8272 410
אֶל שַׂרְאֶצֶר וְרֶגֶם מֶלֶךְ וַאֲנָשָׁיו לְחַלּוֹת אֶת־פְּנֵי יְהוָה׃
.Jehovah the the seek to his and melech and Sherezer el
of face of favor men Regem-

5030 6635 3068 1004 3548 559
3 לֵאמֹר אֶל־הַכֹּהֲנִים אֲשֶׁר לְבֵית־יְהוָה צְבָאוֹת וְאֶל־הַנְּבִיאִים
the and ,hosts Jehovah the to who the to to
,prophets to of of house (belong) priests speak

6213 5144 2549 2320 1058 559
לֵאמֹר הַאֶבְכֶּה בַּחֹדֶשׁ הַחֲמִשִׁי הִנָּזֵר כַּאֲשֶׁר עָשִׂיתִי זֶה
these have I as consecrating ,fifth the in I Should ,saying
done myself month weep

559 6635 3068 1697 1961 8141
4 כַּמֶּה שָׁנִים׃ וַיְהִי דְבַר־יְהוָה צְבָאוֹת אֵלַי לֵאמֹר׃
,saying ,me to hosts Jehovah the And ?years many
of of word came

6684 559 3548 776 5971 3605 559
5 אֱמֹר אֶל־כָּל־עַם הָאָרֶץ וְאֶל־הַכֹּהֲנִים לֵאמֹר כִּי־צַמְתֶּם
you When ,saying the and the the all to Speak
fasted ,priests to ,land of people

6684 6684 8141 7657 7637 2549 5594
וְסָפוֹד בַּחֲמִישִׁי וּבַשְּׁבִיעִי וְזֶה שִׁבְעִים שָׁנָה הֲצוֹם צַמְתֻּנִי
you did truly ,years seventy even seventh and the in and
,Me for fast those ,(months) fifth mourned

398 3808 8354 398
6 אָנִי׃ וְכִי תֹאכְלוּ וְכִי תִשְׁתּוּ הֲלוֹא אַתֶּם הָאֹכְלִים וְאַתֶּם
for and those (for) (it was) you and ate you And (just)
,you ;eating ,you not ,drank when when ?Me

3068 7121 834 1697 8354
7 הַשֹּׁתִים׃ הֲלוֹא אֶת־הַדְּבָרִים אֲשֶׁר קָרָא יְהוָה בְּיַד
by Jehovah pro- which the (these) (Are) those
claimed words not ?drinking

5892 7961 3427 3389 1961 7223 5030
הַנְּבִיאִים הָרִאשֹׁנִים בִּהְיוֹת יְרוּשָׁלַםִ יֹשֶׁבֶת וּשְׁלֵוָה וְעָרֶיהָ
her with and inhabited Jerusalem was when ,former the
cities prosperous prophets

3068 1697 1961 3427 8219 5045 5439
8 סְבִיבֹתֶיהָ וְהַנֶּגֶב וְהַשְּׁפֵלָה יֹשֵׁב׃ וַיְהִי דְּבַר־יְהוָה
Jehovah the And in- were the and the and around all
of word was ?habited Lowland Negeb ,her

4941 559 6635 3068 559 3541 559 2148
9 אֶל־זְכַרְיָה לֵאמֹר׃ כֹּה אָמַר יְהוָה צְבָאוֹת לֵאמֹר מִשְׁפַּט
judgment ,saying ,hosts Jehovah says Thus ,saying ,Zechariah to
of

490 251 376 6213 7356 2617 8199 571
10 אֱמֶת שְׁפֹטוּ וְחֶסֶד וְרַחֲמִים עֲשׂוּ אִישׁ אֶת־אָחִיו׃ וְאַלְמָנָה
the And his with (each) practice and and Judge true
widow .brother man compassion kindness

2803 408 251 376 7451 6231 408 6041 1616 3490
וְיָתוֹם גֵּר וְעָנִי אַל־תַּעֲשֹׁקוּ וְרָעַת אִישׁ אָחִיו אַל־תַּחְשְׁבוּ
do not his man a the And do not the or the the or
devise brother (against) of evil .oppress ,poor ,alien ,orphan

241 5637 3802 5414 7181 3985 3824
11 בִּלְבַבְכֶם׃ וַיְמָאֲנוּ לְהַקְשִׁיב וַיִּתְּנוּ כָתֵף סֹרָרֶת וְאָזְנֵיהֶם
their and stubborn a gave and to they But your in
ears shoulder listen refused .heart

8451 8085 8068 7760 3820 8085 3513
12 הִכְבִּידוּ מִשְּׁמוֹעַ׃ וְלִבָּם שָׂמוּ שָׁמִיר מִשְּׁמוֹעַ אֶת־הַתּוֹרָה
law the from adamant they their And from made they
hearing made heart .hearing heavy

7307 6635 3068 7971 834 1697
וְאֶת־הַדְּבָרִים אֲשֶׁר שָׁלַח יְהוָה צְבָאוֹת בְּרוּחוֹ בְּיַד
by through hosts Jehovah has which the and
Spirit His of sent words

6635 3068 1419 7110 1961 7223 5030
הַנְּבִיאִים הָרִאשֹׁנִים וַיְהִי קֶצֶף גָּדוֹל מֵאֵת יְהוָה צְבָאוֹת׃
.hosts Jehovah from great wrath Thus .former the
of came prophets

¹³And it will be, just as He called, and they did not listen; so they called, and I did not listen, says Jehovah of hosts. ¹⁴But I stormed them away on all the nations whom they did not know. And the land is desolated behind them, from passing and from returning—for they made the land of desire a waste.

13

559	8085	3808	7121	3651	8085	3808	7121	1961

וַיְהִי כַאֲשֶׁר־קָרָא וְלֹא שָׁמֵעוּ כֵּן יִקְרְאוּ וְלֹא אֶשְׁמָע אָמַר

| says | did I | and | they | so | they | and | He | just | it And |
| | listen, | not | called | called | listened | not | called | as | be will |

14

3045	834	1471	5921	5590	6635	3068

יְהוָה צְבָאוֹת: וָאֵסָעֲרֵם עַל כָּל־הַגּוֹיִם אֲשֶׁר לֹא־יְדָעוּם

| did they | not | whom | the | all | on | I And | .hosts | Jehovah |
| .them know | | | nations | | away them stormed | | | of |

776	7760	7725	5674	310	8047	776

וְהָאָרֶץ נָשַׁמָּה אַחֲרֵיהֶם מֵעֹבֵר וּמִשָּׁב וַיָּשִׂימוּ אֶרֶץ

| the | they for | from and | from | behind | is | the So |
| of land | made | ,returning | passing | them | desolated | land |

8074	2532

חֶמְדָּה לְשַׁמָּה:

| .waste a | desire |

CAP. VIII ח

CHAPTER 8

CHAPTER 8

¹And the word of Jehovah was, saying, ²So says Jehovah of hosts: I was jealous for Zion *with* great jealousy, and I was jealous for her *with* great wrath. ³So says Jehovah: I have returned to Zion, and will dwell in the midst of Jerusalem. And Jerusalem shall be called a city of truth, and the mountain of Jehovah of hosts, the holy mountain. ⁴So says Jehovah of hosts: There shall yet be old men and old women sitting in the streets of Jerusalem; and *each* man *with* his staff in his hand because of *their* many days. ⁵And the streets of the city shall be full of boys and girls playing in its streets. ⁶So says Jehovah of hosts: If it is marvelous in the eyes of the remnant of this people in those days, will it also be marvelous in My eyes, says Jehovah of hosts? ⁷So says Jehovah of hosts: Behold, I will save My people from the east country, and from the land of the setting sun. ⁸And I will bring them, and they shall live in the midst of Jerusalem. And they shall be for a people to Me, and I will be their God, in

1
2

6635	3068	559	559	6635	3068	1697	1961

וַיְהִי דְּבַר־יְהוָה צְבָאוֹת לֵאמֹר: כֹּה אָמַר יְהוָה צְבָאוֹת

| :hosts | Jehovah | says | Thus | ,saying | ,hosts | Jehovah | the | And |
| of | | | | | | of of word | came |

7065	1419	2534	1419	7068	6726	7065

קִנֵּאתִי לְצִיּוֹן קִנְאָה גְדוֹלָה וְחֵמָה גְדוֹלָה קִנֵּאתִי לָהּ:

| for | was I | great | (with) and | great | (with) | for | was I |
| .her | jealous | | wrath | | jealousy | Zion | jealous |

3

3389	8432	7931	6726	7725	3068	559	354.1

כֹּה אָמַר יְהוָה שַׁבְתִּי אֶל־צִיּוֹן וְשָׁכַנְתִּי בְּתוֹךְ יְרוּשָׁלִַם

| .Jerusalem | the in | will and | Zion to | have I | Jehovah | says | Thus |
| | of midst | dwell | | returned | | | |

2022	6635	3068	2022	571	5892	3389	7121

וְנִקְרְאָה יְרוּשָׁלִַם עִיר־הָאֱמֶת וְהַר־יְהוָה צְבָאוֹת הַר

| moun- | ,hosts | Jehovah | the and | ,truth | city a | Jerusalem | shall And |
| tain | | of mountain | mountain | | | | called be |

2205	7931	5750	6635	3068	559	3541	69.44

הַקֹּדֶשׁ: כֹּה אָמַר יְהוָה צְבָאוֹת עֹד יֵשְׁבוּ זְקֵנִים

| Old | will | again | :hosts | Jehovah | says | Thus | .holy the |
| men | sit | | of | | | | |

4

3117	7230	3027	4938	376	3389	7339	2205

וּזְקֵנוֹת בִּרְחֹבוֹת יְרוּשָׁלִָם וְאִישׁ מִשְׁעַנְתּוֹ בְּיָדוֹ מֵרֹב יָמִים:

| .days | from | his in | his (with) | a and | ,Jerusalem | the in | old and |
| | many the | ,hand | staff | man | | of plazas | women |

5

7339	7832	3207	3206	4390	5892	7339

וּרְחֹבוֹת הָעִיר יִמָּלְאוּ יְלָדִים וִילָדוֹת מְשַׂחֲקִים בִּרְחֹבֹתֶיהָ:

| .plazas its in | playing | girls and | boys | be shall | the | And |
| | | | | | of full | city | of plazas |

6

7611	5869	6381	6635	3068	559	354.1

כֹּה אָמַר יְהוָה צְבָאוֹת כִּי יִפָּלֵא בְּעֵינֵי שְׁאֵרִית

| the | the in | is it | If | :hosts | Jehovah | says | Thus |
| of remnant | of eyes | difficult | | | | | |

6635	3068	5002	6381	5869	1571	1996	3117	2088	5971

הָעָם הַזֶּה בַּיָּמִים הָהֵם גַּם־בְּעֵינַי יִפָּלֵא נְאֻם יְהוָה צְבָאוֹת:

| ?hosts | Jehovah | says | it will | My in | also | ,those | days in | this | people |
| | | | | :difficult be | eyes | | | | |

7

776	5971	3467	2009	6635	3068	559	3541

כֹּה אָמַר יְהוָה צְבָאוֹת הִנְנִי מוֹשִׁיעַ אֶת־עַמִּי מֵאֶרֶץ

| the from | My | save will | ,Behold | :hosts | Jehovah | says | Thus |
| of land | people | | | | | | of |

8432	7931	935	8121	3996	776	4217

מִזְרָח וּמֵאֶרֶץ מְבוֹא הַשָּׁמֶשׁ: וְהֵבֵאתִי אֹתָם וְשָׁכְנוּ בְּתוֹךְ

| the in | they and | ,them | will I | .sun | the | from and | the |
| of midst | live shall | | bring will | | setting | of land | rising |

8

571	430	1961	5971	1961	3389

יְרוּשָׁלִָם וְהָיוּ־לִי לְעָם וַאֲנִי אֶהְיֶה לָהֶם לֵאלֹהִים בֶּאֱמֶת

| truth in | ,God for | to | be will | and | a for | will they And | .Jerusalem |
| | them | | | | ,people | Me to be | |

truth and in righteousness.
[9]So says Jehovah of hosts: Let your hands be strong, you who hear in these days these words by the mouth of the prophets, that in the day the house of Jehovah of hosts is laid, the temple *is* to be built. [10]For before those days there was no wage for man, nor was there wage for animal; and there was no peace to him from the adversary who went out or came in. For I sent every man, a man against his neighbor. [11]But now I *will* not *be* to the remnant of this people as in former days, says Jehovah of hosts. [12]For there *shall be* peace *for* the seed; the vine shall give its fruit and the ground shall give its produce; and the heavens shall give their dew; and I will cause the remnant of this people to inherit all these. [13]And it shall be, as you were a curse among the nations, O house of Judah and house of Israel, so I will save you, and you shall be a blessing. Do not fear; let your hands be strong. [14]For so says Jehovah of hosts: As I purposed to punish you when your fathers provoked Me to wrath, says Jehovah of hosts; and I did not repent; [15]so again I have purposed in these days to do good to Jerusalem, and the house of Judah. Do not fear.

[16]These *are* the things that you shall do. *Let each* man speak the truth with his neighbor. Judge *with* truth and justice *for* peace in your gates. [17]And let each devise no evil in your heart *against* his neighbor;

3027 2388 6635 3068 559/3541 6666
9 ובצדקה׃ כה־אמר יהוה צבאות תחזקנה ידיכם
your hands, be Let strong :hosts Jehovah of says Thus in and .righteousness

5030 6310 428 1697 428 3117 8085
השמעים בימים האלה את הדברים האלה מפי הנביאים
the prophets, the of mouth from these words these days in who (you) hear

1129 1964 6635 3068 1004 3245 3117 834
10 אשר ביום יסד בית־יהוה צבאות ההיכל להבנות׃ כי
For .rebuild to the temple ,hosts' Jehovah of house is founded the in day that

929 7939 19:61 38:08 120 7939 19:96 3117 6440
לפני הימים ההם שכר האדם לא נהיה ושכר הבהמה
animal for wages or there was not man for wages those days before

3605 7971 6862 7965 935 5927
איננה וליוצא ולבא אין־שלום מן־הצר ואשלח את־כל־
every I sent for ;adversary the from ,peace not for coming him or for going him and was ,not

7223 3117 38:08 6258 7453 376 120
11 האדם איש ברעהו׃ ועתה לא כימים הראשנים אני
I (be will) former days the as not But now his against .neighbor a man ,man

7965 2233 6635 3068 5002 2088 5971 7611
12 לשארית העם הזה נאם יהוה צבאות׃ כי־זרע השלום
(have will) ,peace the seed For .hosts Jehovah of says ,this people the to of remnant

5414 8064 2981 5414 776 6529 5414 1612
הגפן תתן פריה והארץ תתן את־יבולה והשמים יתנו
will give the and heavens ?produce its will give the and land its fruit will give the vine

428 3605 2088 5971 7611 5157 29:19
טלם והנחלתי את־שארית העם הזה את־כל־אלה׃
.(things) these all this people remnant the will I and inherit to cause their ;dew

1004 3063 1004 1471 7045 19:61
13 והיה כאשר הייתם קללה בגוים בית יהודה ובית
and of house Judah O of house the among ,nations curse a were you as it And be shall

3372 1293 1961 3467 3478
ישראל כן אושיע אתכם והייתם ברכה אל־תיראו
;fear Do not .blessing a you and be shall ,you will I save so ,Israel

6635 3068 559 3541 3027 2388
14 תחזקנה ידיכם׃ כי כה אמר יהוה צבאות כאשר
As :hosts Jehovah of says thus For your .hands be let strong

3068 559 1 7107 7489 2161
זממתי להרע לכם בהקציף אבתיכם אתי אמר יהוה
Jehovah of says ,Me fathers your provoking to wrath in you harm to pur- I posed

428 3117 2161 7725 3661 5162 38:08 6635
15 צבאות ולא נחמתי׃ כן שבתי זממתי בימים האלה
these days in have I purposed again so ,repent did I not and ,hosts

428 3372 3063 1004 3389 3190
16 להיטיב את־ירושלם ואת־בית יהודה אל־תיראו׃ אלה
These (are) .fear do not ;Judah the and of house Jerusalem do to good to

571 7453 376 571 1696 6213 1697
הדברים אשר תעשו דברו אמת איש את־רעהו אמת
(with) truth his with ;neighbor (each) man truth Let speak shall you .do that things the

7453 7451 376 8179 8199 7965 4941
17 ומשפט שלום שפטו בשעריכם׃ ואיש את־רעת רעהו
his neighbor the of harm And each .gates your in judge (for) peace and justice

and do not love a false oath. For all these I hate, says Jehovah.
[18]And the word of Jehovah of hosts was to me, saying, [19]So says Jehovah of hosts: The fast of the fourth *month*, and the fast of the fifth, and the fast of the seventh, and the fast of the tenth, shall become for joy and gladness and cheerful feasts to the house of Judah, even love truth and peace. [20]So says Jehovah of hosts: There shall yet come people, and inhabitants of many cities; [21]and the inhabitants of one shall go to another, saying, Let us go at once to seek the favor of the face of Jehovah, and to seek Jehovah of hosts; I will go also. [22]And many peoples and strong nations shall come to seek Jehovah of hosts in Jerusalem, and to seek the favor of the face of Jehovah. [23]So says Jehovah of hosts: In those days ten men out of all languages of the nations shall take hold, and will seize the skirt of a man, a Jew, saying, Let us go with you, for we have heard that God *is* with you.

157 408 8267 7621 3824 2803 408
אַל־תַּחְשְׁבוּ בִּלְבַבְכֶם וּשְׁבֻעַת שֶׁקֶר אַל־תֶּאֱהָבוּ כִּי אֶת־
For .love do not false a oath and your in let not
;heart devise

3068 1697 1961 3068 5002 8130 428 3605
18 כָּל־אֵלֶּה אֲשֶׁר שָׂנֵאתִי נְאֻם־יְהוָה׃ וַיְהִי דְּבַר־יְהוָה
Jehovah the And .Jehovah says ,hate I these all
of word was

7243 6685 6635 3068 559 3451 559 6635
19 צְבָאוֹת אֵלַי לֵאמֹר׃ כֹּה־אָמַר יְהוָה צְבָאוֹת צוֹם הָרְבִיעִי
fourth the The :hosts Jehovah says Thus ,saying ,me to hosts
,(month) of fast of

1004 1961 6224 6685 7637 6685 2549 6685
וְצוֹם הַחֲמִישִׁי וְצוֹם הַשְּׁבִיעִי וְצוֹם הָעֲשִׂירִי יִהְיֶה לְבֵית־
the to shall the the and the the and the the and
of house be tenth of fast ,seventh of fast ,fifth of fast

7965 571 2896 4150 80:57 8342 3063
יְהוּדָה לְשָׂשׂוֹן וּלְשִׂמְחָה וּלְמֹעֲדִים טוֹבִים וְהָאֱמֶת וְהַשָּׁלוֹם
peace and even ,cheerful for and for and joy for Judah
truth feasts gladness

5971 935 5750 6635 3068 559 34 51 157
20 אֱהָבוּ׃ כֹּה אָמַר יְהוָה צְבָאוֹת עֹד אֲשֶׁר יָבֹאוּ עַמִּים
peoples There again :hosts Jehovah says Thus .love
come shall of

559 259 259 342 7 1980 7227 5892 3427
21 וְיֹשְׁבֵי עָרִים רַבּוֹת׃ וְהָלְכוּ יֹשְׁבֵי אַחַת אֶל־אַחַת לֵאמֹר
,saying ,another to one resi- the will and ;many cities resi- and
(city) of dents go of dents

6635 3068 1245 3068 6440 2470 1980 1980
נֵלְכָה הָלוֹךְ לְחַלּוֹת אֶת־פְּנֵי יְהוָה וּלְבַקֵּשׁ אֶת־יְהוָה צְבָאוֹת
;hosts Jehovah to and ;Jehovah the the seek to at us Let
of seek of face of favor once go

1245 6099 1471 7227 5971 935 1980
22 אֵלְכָה גַּם־אָנִי׃ וּבָאוּ עַמִּים רַבִּים וְגוֹיִם עֲצוּמִים לְבַקֵּשׁ
seek to mighty and many peoples shall And .I also go will
nations come

3068 6440 2470 3389 6635 3068
אֶת־יְהוָה צְבָאוֹת בִּירוּשָׁלִַם וּלְחַלּוֹת אֶת־פְּנֵי יְהוָה׃
.Jehovah the seek to and in hosts Jehovah
of face of favor the ,Jerusalem of

6235 2388 3117 6635 3068 559 3451
23 כֹּה־אָמַר יְהוָה צְבָאוֹת בַּיָּמִים הָהֵמָּה אֲשֶׁר יַחֲזִיקוּ עֲשָׂרָה
ten take shall those days In :hosts Jehovah says Thus
hold of

3064 376 3671 2388 1471 3956 3605 582
אֲנָשִׁים מִכֹּל לְשֹׁנוֹת הַגּוֹיִם וְהֶחֱזִיקוּ בִּכְנַף אִישׁ יְהוּדִי
,Jew a ,man a the they and the languages of out ,men
of skirt seize will ,nations of all

430 8085 1980 559
לֵאמֹר נֵלְכָה עִמָּכֶם כִּי שָׁמַעְנוּ אֱלֹהִים עִמָּכֶם׃
.you with (is) God have we for with Let ,saying
that heard ,you go us

CAP. IX ט

CHAPTER 9

[1]The burden of the word of Jehovah against the land of Hadrach; and its resting place, Damascus—when the eye of man, and all the tribes of Israel *shall be* toward Jehovah —[2]and Hamath also borders on it; Tyre and Sidon, though *they are* very wise; [3]and Tyre shall build a fortress for herself, and shall pile up silver like the dust, and gold

3068 4496 1834 2317 776 3068 1697 4853
1 מַשָּׂא דְבַר־יְהוָה בְּאֶרֶץ חַדְרָךְ וְדַמֶּשֶׂק מְנֻחָתוֹ כִּי לַיהוָה
toward when rest- its and ;Hadrach against Jehovah the bur- The
Jehovah —place ing Damascus of land the of word of den

6865 1379 2574 1571 3478 7626 3605/120 5869
2 עֵין אָדָם וְכֹל שִׁבְטֵי יִשְׂרָאֵל׃ וְגַם־חֲמָת תִּגְבָּל־בָּהּ צֹר
Tyre ;it on borders Hamath and —Israel the all and man eye the
also of tribes (be shall) of

3701 6651 4693 6865 1129 39 66 2449 6721
3 וְצִידוֹן כִּי חָכְמָה מְאֹד׃ וַתִּבֶן צֹר מָצוֹר לָהּ וַתִּצְבָּר־כֶּסֶף
silver shall and for for- a Tyre And .very (are they) though and
up pile herself .tress build shall wise ,Sidon

like the mud of the streets;
4 behold, the Lord will expel
her, and He will strike her
wealth in the sea, and she
shall be consumed with
fire. 5 Ashkelon shall see
and fear; Gaza also shall
writhe in great pain; and
Ekron shall be ashamed for
her hope. And the king shall
perish from Gaza, and Ashkelon shall not be inhabited.
6 And a bastard shall dwell in
Ashdod, and I will cut off
the pride of the Philistines.
7 And I will take away his
bloods out of his mouth,
and his idolatries from between his teeth. But the
remnant, even he *shall be*
for our God. And he shall be
as a governor in Judah, and
Ekron, like a Jebusite.
8 And I will camp around My
house because of an army,
because of him who passed
by, and because of him who
returns. And no tyrant shall
pass through them any
more. For now I have seen
with My eyes.
9 Rejoice greatly, O
daughter of Zion! Shout, O
daughter of Jerusalem!
Behold, your King comes to
you! He *is* righteous and
victorious; lowly and riding
on an ass, even on a colt,
the son of an ass. 10 And I
will cut off the chariot from
Ephraim, and the horse
from Jerusalem. And the
battle bow shall be cut off,
and He shall speak peace to
the nations. And His
dominion *shall be* from sea
to sea, and from the River to
the ends of the earth.
11 Also you, by the blood of
your covenant I have freed
your prisoners from the pit;
no water is in it. 12 Turn to
the stronghold, O prisoners
of hope! Even today I de-
clare I will return double to
you. 13 When I have bent
Judah for Me *as* a bow; I
filled *it* with Ephraim; and I
will stir up your sons, O
Zion, against your sons, O
Greece, and make you as
the sword of a mighty man.
14 Then Jehovah will be
seen over them, and His
arrow shall go out as
lightning; and the Lord

5221 3423 136 2009 2351 2966 2742 6083
4 כֶּעָפָר וְחָרוּץ כְּטִיט חוּצוֹת׃ הִנֵּה אֲדֹנָי יוֹרִשֶׁנָּה וְהִכָּה
He and expel will the ,behold the the like and like
strike will her Lord ;streets of mud gold ,dust

5804 3372 831 7200 398 784 2428 3220
5 בַיָּם חֵילָהּ וְהִיא בָּאֵשׁ תֵּאָכֵל׃ תֵּרֶא אַשְׁקְלוֹן וְתִירָא וְעַזָּה
Gaza and Ashkelon see will be will with and her the in
also ;fear .devoured fire she ,wealth sea

5804 4428 6 4007 3001 6138 3966 2342
וְתָחִיל מְאֹד וְעֶקְרוֹן כִּי־הֹבִישׁ מֶבָּטָהּ וְאָבַד מֶלֶךְ מֵעַזָּה
from the will and her be will for and ,great writhe shall
,Gaza king perish ;hope ashamed Ekron pain in

1347 3772 795 4464 3427 3427 3808 831
6 וְאַשְׁקְלוֹן לֹא תֵשֵׁב׃ וְיָשַׁב מַמְזֵר בְּאַשְׁדּוֹד וְהִכְרַתִּי גְּאוֹן
pride will I and ,Ashdod in a will And be will not and
off cut bastard dwell .inhabited Ashkelon

7604 8127 996 8251 6310 1818 5493 6430
7 פְלִשְׁתִּים׃ וַהֲסִרֹתִי דָמָיו מִפִּיו וְשִׁקֻּצָיו מִבֵּין שִׁנָּיו וְנִשְׁאַר
the And his from his and his from his will I And the
,remnant .teeth between abominations mouth bloods away take .Philistines

2983 6138 3063 441 1961 430 1571
גַּם־הוּא לֵאלֹהֵינוּ וְהָיָה כְּאַלֻּף בִּיהוּדָה וְעֶקְרוֹן כִּיבוּסִי׃
a like and ,Judah in a as he And our for he even
.Jebusite Ekron chief be shall .God (be will)

5750 5674/3808 5674 7725 4675 1004 2583
8 וְחָנִיתִי לְבֵיתִי מִצָּבָה מֵעֹבֵר וּמִשָּׁב וְלֹא־יַעֲבֹר עֲלֵיהֶם עוֹד
again them shall not and from and the from an from My will I And
pass ,returner the passer ,army house about camp

6726/1323/3966 1523 5869 7200 6258 5065
9 נֹגֵשׂ כִּי־עַתָּה רָאִיתִי בְעֵינָי׃ גִּילִי מְאֹד בַּת־צִיּוֹן
!Zion O ,greatly Rejoice My with have I now For an
of daughter eyes seen oppressor

3467 6662 935 4428 2009 3389/1323 7321
הָרִיעִי בַּת־יְרוּשָׁלַםִ הִנֵּה מַלְכֵּךְ יָבוֹא לָךְ צַדִּיק וְנוֹשָׁע
and righteous to is Your !Behold !Jerusalem O ,Shout
victorious !you coming King of daughter

3772 860 1121 5895 5921 2543 5921 7392 6041
10 הוּא עָנִי וְרֹכֵב עַל־חֲמוֹר וְעַל־עַיִר בֶּן־אֲתֹנוֹת׃ וְהִכְרַתִּי
will I And she- a the a even ,ass an on and humble He
off cut .ass of son ,colt on riding ;(is)

4421 7198 3772 3389 5483 669 7393
רֶכֶב מֵאֶפְרַיִם וְסוּס מִירוּשָׁלַםִ וְנִכְרְתָה קֶשֶׁת מִלְחָמָה
war bow the shall And from the and from the
of off cut be .Jerusalem horse ,Ephraim chariot

657 5704 5104 3220 4915 1471 7965 1696
וְדִבֶּר שָׁלוֹם לַגּוֹיִם וּמָשְׁלוֹ מִיָּם עַד־יָם וּמִנָּהָר עַד־אַפְסֵי
the to from and ,sea to (be will) His And the to peace He and
of ends River the sea from dominion .nations speak shall

953 615 7971 1285 1818 1571 776
11 אָרֶץ׃ גַּם־אַתְּ בְּדַם־בְּרִיתֵךְ שִׁלַּחְתִּי אֲסִירַיִךְ מִבּוֹר אֵין
not the from your have I your the by ,you Also the
is ;pit prisoners freed covenant of blood .earth

5046 3117 1571 8615 615 1225 7725 4325
12 מַיִם בּוֹ׃ שׁוּבוּ לְבִצָּרוֹן אֲסִירֵי הַתִּקְוָה גַּם־הַיּוֹם מַגִּיד
I today Even !hope the pris- O the to Turn .it in water
declare of oners ,stronghold

4390 7198 3063 1869 7725 4932
13 מִשְׁנֶה אָשִׁיב לָךְ׃ כִּי־דָרַכְתִּי לִי יְהוּדָה קֶשֶׁת מִלֵּאתִי
filled I a (as) Judah for have I For to will I double
with (it) ,bow Me bent you restore

2719 7760 3120 1121 6726 1121 5782 669
אֶפְרַיִם וְעוֹרַרְתִּי בָנַיִךְ צִיּוֹן עַל־בָּנַיִךְ יָוָן וְשַׂמְתִּיךְ כְּחֶרֶב
the as make and O your against O your will I and ,Ephraim
of sword you ,Greece ,sons ,Zion ,sons up stir

3068 136 2671 1300 3318 7200 5921 3068 1368
14 גִּבּוֹר׃ וַיהוָה עֲלֵיהֶם יֵרָאֶה וְיָצָא כַבָּרָק חִצּוֹ וַאדֹנָי יְהוִה
Jehovah the and His light- as shall and will over then mighty a
Lord ;arrow ning out go ,appear them Jehovah ;man

Jehovah shall blow the ram's horn, and shall go forth with the windstorms of the south. [15]Jehovah of hosts shall defend them. And they shall devour and trample on the sling-stones. And they shall drink and be boisterous, as with wine. And they shall be full like a bowl, like the corners of the altar. [16]And Jehovah their God shall save them in that day as the flock of His people; for *they are as* stones of a crown, lifted up as a banner over His land. [17]For how great *is* its goodness, and how great its beauty! Grain shall make the young men flourish, and new wine the virgins.

15

1598	6635	3068	8486	5592	19,80	86,28	7782
בְּשׁוֹפָר	צְבָאוֹת	יְהוָה	תֵּימָן׃	בְּסַעֲרוֹת	וְהָלַךְ	יִתְקַע	יָגֵן
will	hosts	Jehovah	the	the with	shall and	shall	ram's the
protect	of		south	of windstorms	forth go	blow	horn

3196	1993	8354	70:50	68	3533	398	
עֲלֵיהֶם	וְאָכְלוּ	וְכָבְשׁוּ	אַבְנֵי־קֶלַע	וְשָׁתוּ	וְהָמוּ	כְּמוֹ־יָיִן	
.wine as	be and	they And	the	and	they And	.them	
with boisterous drink shall	.sling of stones	trample	devour shall				

16

430	3068	34:67	4196	2106	4219	4390
אֱלֹהֵיהֶם	יְהוָה	וְהוֹשִׁיעָם	מִזְבֵּחַ	כְּזָוִיּוֹת		וּמָלְאוּ
their	Jehovah	will And	the	the like	a as	they And
God		them save	.altar	of corners	,bowl	full be will

5921	5264	5145:	68	5971	6629	3117
עַל־	מִתְנוֹסְסוֹת	אַבְנֵי־נֵזֶר	כִּי	עַמּוֹ	כְּצֹאן	בַּיּוֹם הַהוּא
over	as up lifted	(as are they)	for	His	the as	that day in
	banner a	crown a of stones		;people	of flock	

17

8492	970:	1715	3308	2998		127
וְתִירוֹשׁ	בַּחוּרִים	דָּגָן	וּמַה־יָּפְיוֹ		כִּי	אַרְצוֹ׃
new and	young the	Grain	its and	its	how For	.land His
wine	men		!beauty	goodness (great)		

1330	5107
בְּתֻלוֹת׃	יְנוֹבֵב
the	make shall
.virgins	flourish

CAP. X י

CHAPTER 10

CHAPTER 10

[1]Ask rain from Jehovah in the time of the latter rain. Jehovah shall make storm clouds, and He gives them showers of rain, grass to everyone in the field. [2]For the family idols speak iniquity, and the diviners have seen a lie, and have told false dreams. They comfort in vain. Therefore, they wandered like a flock. They were troubled because there was no shepherd. [3]My anger is kindled against the shepherds; and I will punish the he-goats. For Jehovah of hosts has visited His flock, the house of Judah, and made them as His splendid horse in battle. [4]From Him *came* the cornerstone; from Him the nail; from Him the battle bow; from Him every oppressor together. [5]And they shall be like mighty ones who trample the mud of the streets in the battle. And they shall fight because Jehovah *is* with them, and they shall make the riders of horses ashamed. [6]And I will make stronger the house of Judah; and I will save the

1

2385	6213	3068	4456	6256	4306	3068	7592
חֲזִיזִים	עֹשֶׂה	יְהוָה	מַלְקוֹשׁ	בְּעֵת	מָטָר	מֵיְהוָה	שַׁאֲלוּ
thunder	shall	Jehovah	latter the the	in	rain	from	Ask
bolts	make		rain	of time		Jehovah	

2

8655	77.04	6212	376	5414	1653	4306
כִּי הַתְּרָפִים	בַּשָּׂדֶה׃	עֵשֶׂב	לְאִישׁ	לָהֶם	יִתֵּן	וּמְטַר־גֶּשֶׁם
family the For	the in	grass (each) to	to	,them	He	showers and
idols	.field		man		gives	rain of

1696	7723	2472.	8267	2372	7080	205	1696
דִּבֵּרוּ־אָוֶן	וְהַקּוֹסְמִים	חָזוּ	שֶׁקֶר	וַחֲלֹמוֹת	הַשָּׁוְא	יְדַבֵּרוּ	
have	false	and	.lie a	have	the and	,iniquity speak
.told	dreams			seen	diviners	

7462	369	6031	6629	5265	5162	1892
הֶבֶל יְנַחֵמוּן	עַל־כֵּן	נָסְעוּ	כְמוֹ־צֹאן	יַעֲנוּ	כִּי־אֵין	רֹעֶה׃
.shepherd	not for	they	;flock a like	they	Therefore	they
	is ,afflicted are		up pulled		.comfort	vain

3

3068	6485	6485	6260	6:39	2734	7462
עַל־הָרֹעִים	חָרָה	אַפִּי	וְעַל־הָעַתּוּדִים	אֶפְקוֹד	כִּי־פָקַד	יְהוָה
Jehovah	has For	will I	the	and	My	is	the against
of	visited	.punish	he-goats		-anger kindled	shepherds

1935	5483	77.60	30:63	1004	5739	6635
צְבָאוֹת אֶת־עֶדְרוֹ	וְשָׂם אוֹתָם	כְּסוּס הוֹדוֹ			אֶת־בֵּית יְהוּדָה	
His	as	them and	,Judah	the	His	hosts
splendid horse	made		of house		flock	

4

4421	7198	34:89	6438	4421
בַּמִּלְחָמָה׃	מִמֶּנּוּ פִנָּה	מִמֶּנּוּ יָתֵד		
,battle	the	from	the	from cor- The	From	.battle	in
	of bow	Him	,nail	Him ;nerstone	Him

2916	947.	1368	1961	3162	5065	3605	3318
מִמֶּנּוּ יָצָא	כָל־נוֹגֵשׂ יַחְדָּו׃	בּוֹסִים בְּטִיט	וְהָיוּ כְגִבֹּרִים				
mud the	who	mighty like	they And	.together	every	came	from
of	trample	ones	be shall		oppressor	out	Him

7392	3001	3068	44:21	3898	2351
חוּצוֹת בַּמִּלְחָמָה	וְנִלְחֲמוּ	כִּי יְהוָה	עִמָּם	וְהֹבִישׁוּ רֹכְבֵי	
riders	shall they and	with	Jehovah because	they And	the in	the
of	ashamed make	,them (is)	fight shall	.battle	streets

6

3467	3127	1004	3063	1004	1396	5483
סוּסִים׃	וְגִבַּרְתִּי	אֶת־בֵּית יְהוּדָה	וְאֶת־בֵּית יוֹסֵף	אוֹשִׁיעַ		
will I	Joseph	the	and	,Judah	the	will I And	horses
,save		of house		of house		strenghten	

house of Joseph; and I
will return to save them;
for I have pity on them.
And they shall be as
though I had not rejected
them; for I *am* Jehovah
their God, and I will
answer them. 7And
Ephraim shall be like a
mighty one, and their
heart shall be glad as *by*
wine. And their sons shall
see and be glad; their
heart shall rejoice in
Jehovah. 8I will whistle
for them and gather them;
for I have redeemed them.
And they will be many as
they were many. 9And I
will sow them among the
peoples, and they shall
remember Me in the dis-
tances and they shall live
with their sons and return.
10And I will return to save
them out of the land of
Egypt, and I will gather
them out of Assyria. And I
will bring them into the
land of Gilead and Leb-
anon; for *room* shall not
be found for them. 11And
he shall pass through the
sea of distress, and strike
the waves in the sea; and
all the depths of the Nile
shall dry up. And the pride
of Assyria shall be
humbled, and the scepter
of Egypt shall go away.
12And I will make them
strong in Jehovah; and
they will walk in His
name, says Jehovah.

CHAPTER 11

1Open your doors, O
Lebanon, so that the fire
may devour your cedars.
2Howl, juniper, for the
cedar has fallen; because
the majestic *trees* have
been devastated. Howl, O
oaks of Bashan, for the
inaccessible forest has
come down.
3A voice of the shep-
herds' wail; for their splendor is devastated; a voice
of the roaring of young
lions; for the Jordan's
pride is devastated. 4For
so says Jehovah my God:
Feed the flock of the
slaughter; 5those buying
them kill them, and *they*
hold themselves inno-
cent. And those selling
them say, Blessed be
Jehovah, for I am rich;

2186 3808 1961 7355 3467 7725
וְהוֹשְׁבוֹתִים כִּי רִחַמְתִּים וְהָיוּ כַּאֲשֶׁר לֹא־זְנַחְתִּים כִּי
for had I not though as they And pity have I for to will I and
them rejected be shall .them on save them return

8056 669 1368 1961 6030 430 3068
7 אֲנִי יְהוָה אֱלֹהֵיהֶם וְאֶעֱנֵם׃ וְהָיוּ כְגִבּוֹר אֶפְרַיִם וְשָׂמַח
shall and ,Ephraim a like shall And will I and their Jehovah I
glad be man mighty be .them answer ,God (am)

3068 3820 1523 8056 7200 1121 3196 3820
לִבָּם כְּמוֹ־יָיִן וּבְנֵיהֶם יִרְאוּ וְשָׂמֵחוּ יָגֵל לִבָּם בַּיהוָה׃
.Jehovah in their shall be and shall their And .wine as their
heart rejoice ;glad see sons (in) heart

7235 7235 6299 6908 8319
8 אֶשְׁרְקָה לָהֶם וַאֲקַבְּצֵם כִּי פְדִיתִים וְרָבוּ כְּמוֹ רָבוּ׃
were they as they And re- have I for gather and for shall I
.many many be will .them deemed ;them them whistle

1121 2421 2142 4801 5971 2232
9 וְאֶזְרָעֵם בָּעַמִּים וּבַמֶּרְחַקִּים יִזְכְּרוּנִי וְחָיוּ אֶת־בְּנֵיהֶם
their with they and shall they the in and the among will I And
sons live shall ;Me remember distances ,peoples them sow

6908 804 4714 776 3467 7725 7725
10 וָשָׁבוּ׃ וַהֲשִׁבוֹתִים מֵאֶרֶץ מִצְרַיִם וּמֵאַשּׁוּר אֲקַבְּצֵם וְאֶל־
And will I from and ,Egypt the from return will I And and
to .them gather Assyria of land them save to .return

3220 5674 4672 3808 935 3844 1568 776
11 אֶרֶץ גִּלְעָד וּלְבָנוֹן אֲבִיאֵם וְלֹא יִמָּצֵא לָהֶם׃ וְעָבַר בַּיָּם
the by He And for (room) be shall and will I and Gilead the
of sea pass will .them found not ;them bring Lebanon of land

3381 2975 4688 3605 3001 1530 3220 5221 6864
צָרָה וְהִכָּה בַיָּם גַּלִּים וְהוֹבִישׁוּ כֹּל מְצוּלוֹת יְאֹר וְהוּרַד
be will And the the all shall and the the in shall and dis-
humbled .Nile of depths up dry ;waves sea strike ,tress

8034 3068 1396 5493 4714 7626 804 1347
12 גְּאוֹן אַשּׁוּר וְשֵׁבֶט מִצְרַיִם יָסוּר׃ וְגִבַּרְתִּים בַּיהוָה וּבִשְׁמוֹ
His in and in will I And turn shall Egypt the and ,Assyria the
name ;Jehovah them strengthen .away of scepter of pride

3068 5002 1980
יִתְהַלָּכוּ נְאֻם יְהוָה׃
.Jehovah says will they
,walk

CAP. XI יא

CHAPTER 11

1265 3213 730 784 398 1817 3844 6605
1
2 פְּתַח לְבָנוֹן דְּלָתֶיךָ וְתֹאכַל אֵשׁ בַּאֲרָזֶיךָ׃ הֵילֵל בְּרוֹשׁ
O ,Howl your the that so your O ,Open
,juniper .cedars fire devour may ,doors ,Lebanon

1316 437 3213 7703 117 834 730 5307
כִּי־נָפַל אֶרֶז אֲשֶׁר אַדִּרִים שֻׁדָּדוּ הֵילִילוּ אַלּוֹנֵי בָשָׁן כִּי
for ;Bashan O ,Howl been have majestic the because the has for
of oaks .destroyed (trees) ;cedar fallen

155 7703 7462 3215 6963 1208 3293 3381
3 יָרַד יַעַר הַבָּצוּר׃ קוֹל יִלְלַת הָרֹעִים כִּי שֻׁדְּדָה אַדַּרְתָּם
their is for the the voice A .inaccessible the come has
;splendor destroyed ;shepherds of wail of forest down

559 3541 3383 1347 7703 3715 7581 6963
4 קוֹל שַׁאֲגַת כְּפִירִים כִּי שֻׁדַּד גְּאוֹן הַיַּרְדֵּן׃ כֹּה אָמַר
says Thus .Jordan the is for ;lions young the voice a
of pride destroyed of roaring of

2026 7069 2028 6629 7462 430 3068
5 יְהוָה אֱלֹהָי רְעֵה אֶת־צֹאן הַהֲרֵגָה׃ אֲשֶׁר קֹנֵיהֶן יַהַרְגֻן
kill buy who Those the the Feed my Jehovah
them them .slaughter of flock :God

7462 6238 3068 1288 559 4376 816 3808
וְלֹא יֶאְשָׁמוּ וּמֹכְרֵיהֶן יֹאמַר בָּרוּךְ יְהוָה וַאעְשִׁר וְרֹעֵיהֶם
their and I for ,Jehovah Blessed ,say who those And held are and
shepherds ;rich am be them sell .guilty not

and their shepherds do not pity them. [6]For I will not again pity the dwellers of the land, says Jehovah. But, lo, I will make the men come out, each one into his neighbor's hand, and into his king's hand. And they shall bruise the land, and I will not deliver out of their hand. [7]And I fed the flock of slaughter, even the poor of the flock. And I took two staffs for Myself: the one I called Kindness; and the other I called Union. And I fed the flock. [8]I also cut off three shepherds in one month. And My soul was impatient with them, and their soul also detested Me. [9]Then I said, I will not feed you; that which dies, let it die; and that which is to be cut off, let it be cut off. And those left, let them eat, each woman her neighbor's flesh.

[10]And I took My staff Kindness and broke it apart, to break My covenant which I had cut with all the peoples. [11]And it was broken in that day; and so the poor of the flock who were watching Me knew that it *was* the word of Jehovah. [12]And I said to them, If *it is* good in your eyes, give My price; and if not, let it go. And they weighed My price, thirty *pieces* of silver. [13]And Jehovah said to Me, Throw it to the potter, the splendid price at which I was valued by them. And I took the thirty *pieces of* silver and threw it to the potter in the house of Jehovah. [14]Then I broke My second staff Union apart, that I might break the brotherhood between Judah and Israel.

776 3427 5750 2550 38,08 5921 2550 3808
6 לֹא יַחְמוֹל עֲלֵיהֶן׃ כִּי לֹא אֶחְמוֹל עוֹד עַל־יֹשְׁבֵי הָאָרֶץ
the the upon again will I not For upon have do not
.land of inhabitants pity have ,them pity

7453 3027 376 120 4672 3068
נְאֻם־יְהוָה וְהִנֵּה אָנֹכִי מַמְצִיא אֶת־הָאָדָם אִישׁ בְּיַד־רֵעֵהוּ
his into each the make will I But .Jehovah says
neighbor's hand man ,men fall ,lo

7462 3027 5337 38,08 776 3807 4428 3027
7 וּבְיַד מַלְכּוֹ וְכִתְּתוּ אֶת־הָאָרֶץ וְלֹא אַצִּיל מִיָּדָם׃ וָאֶרְעֶה
I So of out will I and the they and his into and
fed .hand their deliver not ,land bruise will ;king's hand

4731 8147 3947 6629 6041 3651 20,28 6629
אֶת־צֹאן הַהֲרֵגָה לָכֵן עֲנִיֵּי הַצֹּאן וָאֶקַּח־לִי שְׁנֵי מַקְלוֹת
:staffs two for I And the the even the the
Myself took .flock of poor ,slaughter of flock

7462 22,54 7121 259 5278 7121 259
לְאַחַד קָרָאתִי נֹעַם וּלְאַחַד קָרָאתִי חֹבְלִים וָאֶרְעֶה אֶת־
I And .Union called I the and Kind- called I one the
fed other ,ness

7114 259 3391 7462 7969 3582 6629
8 הַצֹּאן׃ וָאַכְחִד אֶת־שְׁלֹשֶׁת הָרֹעִים בְּיֶרַח אֶחָד וַתִּקְצַר
was And .one in shepherds three I And the
impatient month destroyed .flock

7462 38,08 559 973 5315 1571 5315
9 נַפְשִׁי בָּהֶם וְגַם־נַפְשָׁם בָּחֲלָה בִי׃ וָאֹמַר לֹא אֶרְעֶה
will I not I Then '.Me detested their and with My
feed ,said soul also ,them soul

398 7604 35,82 3582 4191 4191
אֶתְכֶם הַמֵּתָה תָמוּת וְהַנִּכְחֶדֶת תִּכָּחֵד וְהַנִּשְׁאָרוֹת תֹּאכַלְנָה
them let who those and be it let to is what and it let is What .you
eat left are .destroyed destroyed be ;die ,die to

1438 5278 4731 3947 7468 802
10 אִשָּׁה אֶת־בְּשַׂר רְעוּתָהּ׃ וָאֶקַּח אֶת־מַקְלִי אֶת־נֹעַם וָאֶגְדַּע
broke and ,Kindness My I And its the each
pieces in staff took .neighbor of flesh woman

5971 36,05 3772 834 1285 6565
אֹתוֹ לְהָפֵיר אֶת־בְּרִיתִי אֲשֶׁר כָּרַתִּי אֶת־כָּל־הָעַמִּים׃
the all with had I which My break to ,it
.peoples cut covenant

8104 6629 6041 3651 3045 1931 3117 6565
11 וַתֻּפַר בַּיּוֹם הַהוּא וַיֵּדְעוּ כֵן עֲנִיֵּי הַצֹּאן הַשֹּׁמְרִים אֹתִי כִּי
that Me were who the the so and ;that day in it And
watching flock of poor knew broken was

3053 5869 2896 559 3068 1697
12 דְבַר־יְהוָה הוּא׃ וָאֹמַר אֲלֵיהֶם אִם־טוֹב בְּעֵינֵיכֶם הָבוּ
give your in good If ,them to I And it Jehovah the
eyes (is it) said .(was) of word

3701 7970 7939 8254 2308 38,08 518 7939
שְׂכָרִי וְאִם־לֹא חֲדָלוּ וַיִּשְׁקְלוּ אֶת־שְׂכָרִי שְׁלֹשִׁים כָּסֶף׃
.silver thirty My they And it let ,not but My
(of pieces) price weighed .go if price

834 33,66 145 3335 79,93 30,68 559
13 וַיֹּאמֶר יְהוָה אֵלַי הַשְׁלִיכֵהוּ אֶל־הַיּוֹצֵר אֶדֶר הַיְקָר אֲשֶׁר
at price the the to it Throw to Jehovah And
which splendid ,potter ,Me said

79,93 3701 7970 3947 3365
יָקַרְתִּי מֵעֲלֵיהֶם וָאֶקְחָה שְׁלֹשִׁים הַכֶּסֶף וָאַשְׁלִיךְ אֹתוֹ
it threw and silver thirty the I And .Them by was I
(of pieces) took valued

8145 4731 1438 3335 3068 1004
14 בֵּית יְהוָה אֶל־הַיּוֹצֵר׃ וָאֶגְדַּע אֶת־מַקְלִי הַשֵּׁנִי אֵת
,second staff My broke I And the to Jehovah the in
pieces in .potter of house

3478 3063 996 264 6565 22,54
הַחֹבְלִים לְהָפֵר אֶת־הָאַחֲוָה בֵּין יְהוּדָה וּבֵין יִשְׂרָאֵל׃
.Israel and Judah between the break to ,Union
between brotherhood

[15]And Jehovah said to me, Take to yourself yet the instruments of a foolish shepherd. [16]For, lo, I will raise up a shepherd in the land; he shall not visit those who are cut off, nor will he seek the young; nor will heal that which is broken; nor will he sustain that which stands. But he shall eat the flesh of the fat, and tear their hooks in pieces. [17]Woe *to* the worthless shepherd who abandons the flock! The sword *shall be* on his arm, and on his right eye. His arm shall be completely withered, and his right eye shall be totally darkened.

15 2009 196 7462 3627 3947 5750 3068 559
16 וַיֹּאמֶר יְהוָה אֵלַי עוֹד קַח־לְךָ כְּלִי רֹעֶה אֱוִלִי׃ כִּי הִנֵּה
,lo ,For .foolish shep- a tools to Take again ,me to Jehovah And
herd's yourself said

3808 5288 6485 3808 3582 776 7462 6965
אָנֹכִי מֵקִים רֹעֶה בָּאָרֶץ הַנִּכְחָדוֹת לֹא־יִפְקֹד הַנַּעַר לֹא־
not the will he not going those the in a will I
young ,for care ruin to ;land shepherd up raise

1320 3557 3808 5324 7495 3808 7665 1245
יְבַקֵּשׁ וְהַנִּשְׁבֶּרֶת לֹא יְרַפֵּא הַנִּצָּבָה לֹא יְכַלְכֵּל וּבְשַׂר
the but will he not which that will he not which that and will he
of flesh ,sustain stands ,heal broken is seek

17 5800 451 7473 1945 6561 6541 398 1277
הַבְּרִיאָה יֹאכַל וּפַרְסֵיהֶן יְפָרֵק׃ הוֹי רֹעִי הָאֱלִיל עֹזְבִי
who worthless the Woe shall he their and shall he fat the
abandons shepherd to .off tear hoofs ,eat

5869 3001/3001 2220 3225 5869 2220 2719 6629
הַצֹּאן חֶרֶב עַל־זְרוֹעוֹ וְעַל־עֵין יְמִינוֹ זְרֹעוֹ יָבוֹשׁ תִּיבָשׁ וְעֵין
and be shall totally his his eye and his (be shall) The the
eye ,withered arm ;right against arm against sword !flock

3543 3543 3225
יְמִינוֹ כָּהֹה תִכְהֶה׃
be shall totally his
.darkened right

CAP. XII יב

CHAPTER 12

[1]The burden of the word of Jehovah for Israel, says Jehovah, who stretches forth the heavens, and lays the foundation of the earth, and forms the spirit of man within him. [2]Behold, I will make Jerusalem a cup of trembling to all the peoples all around, and it shall also be against Judah in the siege against Jerusalem.

[3]And in that day I will make Jerusalem a heavy stone for all the peoples; all who lift it shall be slashed, and all the nations of the earth will be gathered against it. [4]In that day I will strike every horse with terror, and his rider with madness, says Jehovah. And I will open My eyes on the house of Judah, and I will strike every horse of the peoples with blindness. [5]And the leaders of Judah shall say in their heart, The inhabitants of Jerusalem *shall be* my strength in Jehovah of hosts their God.

[6]In that day I will make the leaders of Judah like a hearth of fire among the wood, and like a torch of fire

1 3245 8064 5186 3068 5002 3478 3068 1697 4853
מַשָּׂא דְבַר־יְהוָה עַל־יִשְׂרָאֵל נְאֻם־יְהוָה נֹטֶה שָׁמַיִם וְיֹסֵד
and hea- the who ,Jehovah says ,Israel for Jehovah the bur- The
founds ,vens spreads of word of den

2 3389 7760 595 2009 7130 120 7307 3335 776
אֶרֶץ וְיֹצֵר רוּחַ־אָדָם בְּקִרְבּוֹ׃ הִנֵּה אָנֹכִי שָׂם אֶת־יְרוּשָׁלַםִ
Jerusalem will I ,Behold his in man the and the
make .midst of spirit forms ,earth

4692 1961 3063 1571 5439 5971 3605 7478 5592
סַף־רַעַל לְכָל־הָעַמִּים סָבִיב וְגַם עַל־יְהוּדָה יִהְיֶה בַמָּצוֹר
the in shall it Judah against and all the to reeling a
siege be also ,around peoples all of cup

3 68 3389 7760 3117 1961 3389
עַל־יְרוּשָׁלָםִ׃ וְהָיָה בַיּוֹם־הַהוּא אָשִׂים אֶת־יְרוּשָׁלַםִ אֶבֶן
a Jerusalem will I that day in it And .Jerusalem against
stone make ,be will

622 8295 8295 6006 3605 5971 3605 4614
מַעֲמָסָה לְכָל־הָעַמִּים כָּל־עֹמְסֶיהָ שָׂרוֹט יִשָּׂרֵטוּ וְנֶאֶסְפוּ
be will and be will severely lift who all the all for heavy
gathered ,lacerated it ;peoples

4 3605 5221 3068 5002 3117 776 1471 3605
עָלֶיהָ כֹּל גּוֹיֵי הָאָרֶץ׃ בַּיּוֹם הַהוּא נְאֻם־יְהוָה אַכֶּה כָל־
every will I ,Jehovah says ,that day In the the all against
strike .earth of nations it

6491 3063 1004 5921 7697 7392 8541 5483
סוּס בַּתִּמָּהוֹן וְרֹכְבוֹ בַּשִּׁגָּעוֹן וְעַל־בֵּית יְהוּדָה אֶפְקַח אֶת־
will I Judah the And with its and with horse
open of house on .madness rider ,panic

5 3063 441 559 5788 5221 5971 5483 3605/5869
עֵינַי וְכֹל סוּס הָעַמִּים אַכֶּה בַּעִוָּרוֹן׃ וְאָמְרוּ אַלֻּפֵי יְהוּדָה
Judah the shall And with will I the horse and My
of leaders say .blindness strike peoples of every ,eyes

430 6635 3068 3389 3427 556 3820
בְּלִבָּם אַמְצָה לִי יֹשְׁבֵי יְרוּשָׁלַםִ בַּיהוָה צְבָאוֹת אֱלֹהֵיהֶם׃
their hosts through Jerusalem The me to (be shall) their in
.God of Jehovah of dwellers strength ,heart

6 6086 784 3595 3063 441 7760 3117
בַּיּוֹם הַהוּא אָשִׂים אֶת־אַלֻּפֵי יְהוּדָה כְּכִיּוֹר אֵשׁ בָּעֵצִים
the among fire a like Judah the will I that day In
,wood of hearth of leaders make

among cut grain. And they shall devour all the peoples all around, on the right hand and on the left hand. And Jerusalem shall be inhabited again in her place, in Jerusalem. [7]Jehovah also shall save the tents of Judah first, so that the glory of the house of David and the glory of the inhabitants of Jerusalem may not be magnified above Judah. [8]In that day Jehovah shall defend around the inhabitants of Jerusalem. And it will be, he who is feeble among them in that day *shall be* like David; and the house of David *shall be* like God, like the Angel of Jehovah before them.

[9]And it shall be in that day, I will seek to destroy all the nations that come against Jerusalem. [10]And I will pour on the house of David, and on the inhabitants of Jerusalem, the Spirit of grace and of prayers. And they shall look on Me whom they have pierced; and they shall mourn for Him, as one mourns for an only *son*, and shall be bitter over Him, like the bitterness over the firstborn. [11]In that day the mourning in Jerusalem shall be great, like the mourning of Hadad-rimmon in the valley of Megiddo. [12]And the land shall mourn, each family apart: the family of the house of David apart, and their wives apart; the family of the house of Nathan apart, and their wives apart; [13]the family of the house of Levi apart, and their wives apart; the family of Shimei apart, and their wives apart; [14]all the families who remain, each family apart, and their wives apart.

8040 5921 3225 5921 398 5995 784 3940
וכלפיד אש בעמיר ואכלו על־ימין ועל־שמאול את־
left the and the on they And among fire like and
hand on hand right devour shall .grain cut of torch a

3389 8478 5750 3389 3427 5439 5971 3605
כל־העמים סביב וישבה ירושלם עוד תחתיה בירושלם׃
in her in again Jerusalem And all the all
.Jerusalem ,place dwells .around peoples

1430 3808 7223 3063 168 3068 3467
7 והושיע יהוה את־אהלי יהודה בראשנה למען לא־תגדל
be may not that so ,first Judah the Jehovah And
magnified of tents save shall

3063 5921 3389 3427 8597 1732 1004 8597
תפארת בית־דויד ותפארת ישב ירושלם על־יהודה׃
.Judah above Jerusalem in- the the and David the glory the
of habitants of glory of house of

3782 1961 3389 3427 3068 1598 3117
8 ביום ההוא יגן יהוה בעד יושב ירושלם והיה הנכשל
who he it And .Jerusalem the around Jehovah shall that In
feeble is ,be will of inhabitants protect day

4397 430 1732 1004 1732 3117 854
בהם ביום ההוא כדויד ובית דויד כאלהים כמלאך
the like (be shall) David the and (be shall) that day in among
of Angel ,God like of house ;David like them

8045 1245 3117 1961 6440 3068
9 יהוה לפניהם׃ והיה ביום ההוא אבקש להשמיד את־
destroy to will I that day in it And before Jehovah
seek ,be shall ,them

1004 5921 8210 3389 935 1471 3605
10 כל־הגוים הבאים על־ירושלם׃ ושפכתי על־בית
the on will I And .Jerusalem against that the all
of house out pour come nations

5027 8469 2580 7307 3389 3427 5921 1732
דויד ועל ׀ יושב ירושלם רוח חן ותחנונים והביטו אלי
on they And and grace the ,Jerusalem in- the and ,David
Me look shall .prayers of Spirit of habitants on

4843 3173 5594 4553 1856 834
את אשר־דקרו וספדו עליו כמספד על־היחיד והמר
will and only an for one as for they and have they whom
bitter be ,son mourns ,Him mourn shall ,pierced

4553 1430 3117 1060 5921 4843 5921
11 עליו כהמר על־הבכור׃ ביום ההוא יגדל המספד
the be will that day In the over the like over
mourning great .firstborn bitterness Him

5594 4023 1237 1910 4553 3389
12 בירושלם כמספד הדדרמון בבקעת מגדון׃ וספדה
shall And .Megiddo the in Hadad-rimmon the like in
mourn of valley of mourning ,Jerusalem

1732 1004 4940 905 4940 4940 776
הארץ משפחות משפחות לבד משפחת בית־דויד
David the family the ;alone families families the
of house of (by) ,land

905 802 905 5416 1004 4940 905 802 905
לבד ונשיהם לבד משפחת בית־נתן לבד ונשיהם לבד׃
;alone their and ,alone Nathan the family the ;alone their and ,alone
wives of house of wives

8097 4940 905 802 905 3878/1004 4940
13 משפחת בית־לוי לבד ונשיהם לבד משפחת השמעי
Shimei family the ;alone their and ,alone Levi the family the
of wives of house of

4940 7604 4940 3605 905 802 905
14 לבד ונשיהם לבד׃ כל המשפחות הנשארות משפחת
family are who families the all ;alone their and ,alone
left wives

905 802 905 4940
משפחת לבד ונשיהם לבד׃
.alone their and ,alone family (by)
wives

CAP. XIII יג

CHAPTER 13

CHAPTER 13

1In that day a fountain shall be opened to the house of David, and to the inhabitants of Jerusalem, for sin and for impurity.

2And it shall be in that day, I will cut off the names of the idols out of the land, and they shall be remembered no more, says Jehovah of hosts. And I also will cause the prophets and the unclean spirit to pass out of the land. 3And it shall be, when any shall prophesy again, his father and his mother who gave birth to him shall say to him then, You shall not live; for you speak lies in the name of Jehovah. And his father and his mother who gave him birth shall thrust him through when he prophesies. 4And it shall be in that day, the prophets shall be ashamed, each one of his vision, when he prophesies; and they shall not wear a hairy garment to deceive. 5But he shall say, I am not a prophet; I *am* a man, I *am* a tiller of the ground; for a man caused me to buy from my youth. 6And *one* shall say to him, What *are* these wounds between your hands? Then he shall answer, *Those* with which I was struck *in* the house of those who love me.

7O sword, awake against My Shepherd, and against the Man *who is* My companion, says Jehovah of hosts. Strike the Shepherd, and the sheep will be scattered. And I will turn My hand on the little ones. 8And it shall be in all the land, says Jehovah, two parts in it shall be cut off *and* perish, but the third shall be left in it. 9And I will bring the third part through the fire, and will refine them as silver is refined. And / will try them as gold is tried. They shall

3389 3427 1732 1004 66:05 4726 1961 3117
1 בַּיּוֹם הַהוּא יִהְיֶה מָקוֹר נִפְתָּח לְבֵית דָּוִיד וּלְיֹשְׁבֵי יְרוּשָׁלִָם
Jerusalem the to and David the to opened a be shall that In
of inhabitants of house fountain day

6635 3068 5002 3117 1961 5079 2403
2 לְחַטַּאת וּלְנִדָּה׃ וְהָיָה בַיּוֹם הַהוּא נְאֻם ׀ יְהוָה צְבָאוֹת
,hosts Jehovah says ,that day in it And for and sin for
of ,be shall ,impurity

5750 2142 3808 776 6097 8034 3772
אַכְרִית אֶת־שְׁמוֹת הָעֲצַבִּים מִן־הָאָרֶץ וְלֹא יִזָּכְרוּ עוֹד
.again be will they and the from idols the the will I
recalled not ,land of names off cut

776 5674 2932 7307 5030 1571
וְגַם אֶת־הַנְּבִיאִים וְאֶת־רוּחַ הַטֻּמְאָה אַעֲבִיר מִן־הָאָרֶץ׃
the from will I unclean the and prophets the And
.land pass to cause spirit also

3205 517 1 559 5750 376 5012 1961
3 וְהָיָה כִּי־יִנָּבֵא אִישׁ עוֹד וְאָמְרוּ אֵלָיו אָבִיו וְאִמּוֹ יֹלְדָיו
gave who his and his to shall then ,again a shall when it And
,birth him mother father him say man prophesy ,be shall

1 1856 3068 8034 1696 8267 24:21 3808
לֹא תִחְיֶה כִּי שֶׁקֶר דִּבַּרְתָּ בְּשֵׁם יְהוָה וּדְקָרֻהוּ אָבִיהוּ
his shall And .Jehovah the in speak you lies for shall you not
father him pierce of name ;live

5030 954 3117 1961 5012 3205 517
4 וְאִמּוֹ יֹלְדָיו בְּהִנָּבְאוֹ׃ וְהָיָה ׀ בַּיּוֹם הַהוּא יֵבֹשׁוּ הַנְּבִיאִים
the be shall that day in it And he when gave who his and
,prophets ashamed ,be shall .prophesies birth him mother

4616 8181 155 3847 38:08 50:12 2384 376
אִישׁ מֵחֶזְיֹנוֹ בְּהִנָּבְאֹתוֹ וְלֹא יִלְבְּשׁוּ אַדֶּרֶת שֵׂעָר לְמַעַן
order in hairy a shall they and he when his of (each)
to garment wear not ;prophesies vision man

127 5647 376 5030 38:08 559 3582
5 כַּחֵשׁ׃ וְאָמַר לֹא נָבִיא אָנֹכִי אִישׁ־עֹבֵד אֲדָמָה אָנֹכִי
;(am) I the tiller a ,man a ;(am) I a not he But .deceive
ground of prophet ,say shall

428 4347 4100 559 5271 7069 120
6 כִּי־אָדָם הִקְנַנִי מִנְּעוּרָי׃ וְאָמַר אֵלָיו מָה הַמַּכּוֹת הָאֵלֶּה
these wounds What ,him to (one) And my from me caused a for
(are) say shall .youth buy to man

2719 157 1004 5221 834 559 3027 996
7 בֵּין יָדֶיךָ וְאָמַר אֲשֶׁר הֻכֵּיתִי בֵּית מְאַהֲבָי׃ חֶרֶב
O who those the (in) was I with (Those) he And your be-
sword .me love of house struck which ,say shall ?hands tween

5221 6635 3068 5002 5997 1397 7462 5782
עוּרִי עַל־רֹעִי וְעַל־גֶּבֶר עֲמִיתִי נְאֻם יְהוָה צְבָאוֹת הַךְ
strike ;hosts Jehovah says My the and My against awake
of ,Associate Man against ,Shepherd

6819 3027 7725 6629 6327 7462
אֶת־הָרֹעֶה וּתְפוּצֶיןָ הַצֹּאן וַהֲשִׁבֹתִי יָדִי עַל־הַצֹּעֲרִים׃
little the against My will I And the be will and the
.ones hand turn .sheep scattered Shepherd

1478 3772 8147 6310 3068/5002 776 3605 1961
8 וְהָיָה בְכָל־הָאָרֶץ נְאֻם־יְהוָה פִּי־שְׁנַיִם בָּהּ יִכָּרְתוּ יִגְוָעוּ
(and) be shall it in two parts ,Jehovah says the all in it And
,perish off cut ,land ,be shall

784 7992 935 3498 7992
9 וְהַשְּׁלִשִׁית יִוָּתֶר בָּהּ׃ וְהֵבֵאתִי אֶת־הַשְּׁלִשִׁית בָּאֵשׁ
through third the will I And .it in be shall the but
,fire the (part) bring left third

2091 974 974 3701 6884 6884
וּצְרַפְתִּים כִּצְרֹף אֶת־הַכֶּסֶף וּבְחַנְתִּים כִּבְחֹן אֶת־הַזָּהָב
.gold is as test and ,silver is as will and
tested them refined them refine

call on My name, and I will answer them. I will say, It *is* My people, and he shall them. I will say, It is My people, and they shall say, Jehovah *is* my God.

CHAPTER 14

[1]Behold, the day of Jehovah comes, and your spoil shall be divided among you. [2]For I will gather all the nations to battle against Jerusalem. And the city shall be captured, and the houses plundered, and the women ravished. And half the city shall go into captivity, and the rest of the people shall not be cut off from the city. [3]And Jehovah shall go out and fight against those nations, like the day He fought in the day of battle.

[4]And His feet shall stand in that day on the Mount of Olives, which *is* before Jerusalem on the east; and the Mount of Olives shall divide from its middle, from the east and to the west, a very great valley. And half of the mountain shall move toward the north, and half of it toward the south. [5]And you shall flee to the valley of My mountains, for the valley of the mountains shall reach to Azal. And you shall flee as you fled from before the earthquake in the days of Uzziah, king of Judah. And Jehovah my God shall come, *and* all the saints with You. [6]And it will be in that day, there shall not be light; the glorious ones will shrink. [7]And it will be one day which shall be known to Jehovah; not day and not night, but it will be, there will be light at evening time. [8]And it shall be in that day, living waters shall go out from Jerusalem; half of them *shall go* toward the eastern sea, and

5971 559 6030 8034 7121
הוּא יִקְרָא בִשְׁמִי וַאֲנִי אֶעֱנֶה אֹתוֹ אָמַרְתִּי עַמִּי הוּא וְהוּא
and it My will I ;them will I and My on will They
he ,(is) people ,say answer name call

430 3068 559
יֹאמַר יְהוָה אֱלֹהָי׃
.God my Jehovah shall
(is) ,say

CAP. XIV יד

CHAPTER 14

622 7130 7998 2505 3068 935 3117 2009
1 2 הִנֵּה יוֹם־בָּא לַיהוָה וְחֻלַּק שְׁלָלֵךְ בְּקִרְבֵּךְ׃ וְאָסַפְתִּי
will I And your in your shall and of is the ,Behold
gather .midst spoil divided be ,Jehovah coming day

5892 3920 4421 3389 1471 3605
אֶת־כָּל־הַגּוֹיִם ׀ אֶל־יְרוּשָׁלִַם לַמִּלְחָמָה וְנִלְכְּדָה הָעִיר
the be shall And .battle to Jerusalem against the all
city captured nations

1473 5892 2677 3318 7693 802 1004 8155
וְנָשַׁסּוּ הַבָּתִּים וְהַנָּשִׁים תִּשָּׁגַלְנָה וְיָצָא חֲצִי הָעִיר בַּגּוֹלָה
into the half shall And .ravished the and the and
,exile city go women ,houses plundered

1471 3898 3068 3318 5892 3772 5971 3499
3 וְיֶתֶר הָעָם לֹא יִכָּרֵת מִן־הָעִיר׃ וְיָצָא יְהוָה וְנִלְחַם בַּגּוֹיִם
against and Jehovah shall Then the from be shall not the the and
nations fight out go .city off cut people of rest

3117 7272 5975 7128 3117 3898 3117
4 הָהֵם כְּיוֹם הִלָּחֲמוֹ בְּיוֹם קְרָב׃ וְעָמְדוּ רַגְלָיו בַּיּוֹם־הַהוּא
that day in His shall And .battle the in He the like ,those
feet stand of day fought day

2022 1234 6924 3389 6440 834 2132 2022 5921
עַל־הַר הַזֵּיתִים אֲשֶׁר עַל־פְּנֵי יְרוּשָׁלִַם מִקֶּדֶם וְנִבְקַע הַר
the shall and the on Jerusalem front in which ,Olives the on
of Mount split ;east of (is) of Mount

2677 4185 3966 1419 1516 3220 4217 2677 2132
הַזֵּיתִים מֵחֶצְיוֹ מִזְרָחָה וָיָמָּה גֵּיא גְּדוֹלָה מְאֹד וּמָשׁ חֲצִי
half will And .very great a to even the from its from Olives
of move valley ,west the east middle

1516 5060 2022 1516 5127 5045 2677 6828 2022
5 הָהָר צָפוֹנָה וְחֶצְיוֹ נֶגְבָּה׃ וְנַסְתֶּם גֵּיא־הָרַי כִּי־יַגִּיעַ גֵּי־
the shall for of valley the you And south- half and ,northward the
of valley reach ;mountains my to flee shall .ward it of mountain

3117 7494 6440 5127 5127 682 2022
הָרִים אֶל־אָצַל וְנַסְתֶּם כַּאֲשֶׁר נַסְתֶּם מִפְּנֵי הָרַעַשׁ בִּימֵי
the in the from fled you as you And .Azal to the
of days earthquake before flee shall mountains

6918 3605 430 3068 935 3063 4428 5818
עֻזִּיָּה מֶלֶךְ־יְהוּדָה וּבָא יְהוָה אֱלֹהַי כָּל־קְדֹשִׁים עִמָּךְ׃
with holy the (and) my Jehovah shall And .Judah king Uzziah
.you ones all ,God come of

7087 6918 216 1961 3808 3117 1961
6 וְהָיָה בַּיּוֹם הַהוּא לֹא־יִהְיֶה אוֹר יְקָרוֹת יְקִפָּאוֹן׃
will glorious the ;light there not ,that day in it And
.shrink ones be shall be shall

1961 3915 3808/3117 3068 3045 259 3117 1961
7 וְהָיָה יוֹם־אֶחָד הוּא יִוָּדַע לַיהוָה לֹא־יוֹם וְלֹא־לָיְלָה וְהָיָה
it but ,night and day not to shall which one day it And
be will not ;Jehovah known be be will

4325 3318 3117 1961 216 1961 6153 6256
8 לְעֵת־עֶרֶב יִהְיֶה־אוֹר׃ וְהָיָה ׀ בַּיּוֹם הַהוּא יֵצְאוּ מַיִם־
waters shall that day in it And .light there ,evening the at
out go be will be will of time

3220 2677 6931 3220 2677 3389 2416
חַיִּים מִירוּשָׁלִַם חֶצְיָם אֶל־הַיָּם הַקַּדְמוֹנִי וְחֶצְיָם אֶל־הַיָּם
sea the to half and ,eastern sea the to half from living
them of them of ;Jerusalem

half of them toward the western sea; in summer and in winter it shall be. [9]And Jehovah shall be king over all th earth. In that day there shall be one Jehovah, and His name one. [10]All the land shall be turned as a plain from Geba to Rimmon south of Jerusalem. And it shall rise and dwell in its place, from Benjamin's gate to the place of the first gate, to the Corner Gate, and *from* the Tower of Hananeel to the king's winepresses. [11]And they shall live in it. And there shall not again be a shutting in, but Jerusalem shall dwell safely.

[12]And this shall be the plague with which Jehovah will strike all the peoples who have fought against Jerusalem. Their flesh shall rot while they stand on their feet; and their eyes shall rot in their sockets; and their tongues shall rot in their mouth. [13]And it shall be in that day, a great panic of Jehovah shall be among them; and they shall each one lay hold of his neighbor, and his hand shall rise up against the hand of his neighbor. [14]And Judah also shall fight at Jerusalem. And the wealth of the surrounding nations shall be gathered, gold, and silver, and clothing, very much. [15]And so shall be the plague of the horse, the mule, the camel, and the ass, and all the beasts which shall be in those camps, like this plague.

[16]And it shall be, everyone who is left from all the nations which came up against Jerusalem shall go up from year to year to worship the King, Jehovah of hosts, and to keep the Feast of Tabernacles. [17]And it shall be, whoever will not go up from the

5921 4428 3068 1961 1961 2779 7019 314
9 הָאַחֲרוֹן בַּקַּיִץ וּבָחֹרֶף יִהְיֶה׃ וְהָיָה יְהוָה לְמֶלֶךְ עַל־
over king Jehovah And shall be shall it .be in and winter in summer ;western

259 8034 259 3068 1961 3117 776 3605
כָּל־הָאָרֶץ בַּיּוֹם הַהוּא יִהְיֶה יְהוָה אֶחָד וּשְׁמוֹ אֶחָד׃
.one His and name ,one Jehovah there be shall that day in the earth; all

3389 5045 7417 1387 6160 776 3605 5437
10 יִסּוֹב כָּל־הָאָרֶץ כָּעֲרָבָה מִגֶּבַע לְרִמּוֹן נֶגֶב יְרוּשָׁלִָם
.Jerusalem south of to Rimmon from Geba a like plain the land All be will turned

8179 4725 1144 8179 8478 3427 7213
וְרָאֲמָה וְיָשְׁבָה תַחְתֶּיהָ לְמִשַּׁעַר בִּנְיָמִן עַד־מְקוֹם שַׁעַר
the gate the of place to Benjamin's from gate her in ,place and dwell it And rise will

4428 3342 5704 2606 4026 6438 8179 7223
הָרִאשׁוֹן עַד־שַׁעַר הַפִּנִּים וּמִגְדַּל חֲנַנְאֵל עַד יִקְבֵי הַמֶּלֶךְ׃
the .king's wine presses to Hananeel from and of tower the ,Corner Gate the to ,first

983 3389 3427 5750 1961 3808 2764 3427
11 וְיָשְׁבוּ בָהּ וְחֵרֶם לֹא יִהְיֶה־עוֹד וְיָשְׁבָה יְרוּשָׁלִַם לָבֶטַח׃
.safely Jerusalem shall but dwell ,again shall be not a And in shutting in they And ,it dwell shall

3605 3068 5062 834 4046 1961 2063
12 וְזֹאת ׀ תִּהְיֶה הַמַּגֵּפָה אֲשֶׁר יִגֹּף יְהוָה אֶת־כָּל־
all Jehovah will strike (with) which the plague be shall And this

5975 1320 4743 3389 6633 834 5971
הָעַמִּים אֲשֶׁר צָבְאוּ עַל־יְרוּשָׁלִָם הָמֵק ׀ בְּשָׂרוֹ וְהוּא עֹמֵד
is standing while he his flesh will He rot make .Jerusalem against have fought who the peoples

6310 4743 3956 2356 4743 5869 7272
עַל־רַגְלָיו וְעֵינָיו תִּמַּקְנָה בְחֹרֵיהֶן וּלְשׁוֹנוֹ תִּמַּק בְּפִיהֶם׃
their in .mouth will rot his and tongue their in ;sockets rot will his and eyes his feet on

2388 854 7227 3068 4103 1961 3117 1961
13 וְהָיָה בַּיּוֹם הַהוּא תִּהְיֶה מְהוּמַת־יְהוָה רַבָּה בָּהֶם וְהֶחֱזִיקוּ
they and seize shall among ;them great Jehovah a of panic be shall that day in it And ,be shall

3063 1571 7453 3027 5927 3027 7453 3027 376
14 אִישׁ יַד רֵעֵהוּ וְעָלְתָה יָדוֹ עַל־יַד רֵעֵהוּ׃ וְגַם־יְהוּדָה
Judah And also his .neighbor the against of hand his hand will and up rise his ,neighbor's hand (each) man

3701 2091 5439 1471 3605 2428 622 3389 3898
תִּלָּחֵם בִּירוּשָׁלִָם וְאֻסַּף חֵיל כָּל־הַגּוֹיִם סָבִיב זָהָב וָכֶסֶף
and silver gold surround- ,ing the nations all the of wealth shall And gathered be at .Jerusalem shall fight

6505 5483 4046 1961 3651 3966 7230 899
15 וּבְגָדִים לָרֹב מְאֹד׃ וְכֵן תִּהְיֶה מַגֵּפַת הַסּוּס הַפֶּרֶד
the ,mule the ,horse the of plague be shall And so .very much and clothing

1992 4264 1961 834 929 3605 2543 1581
הַגָּמָל וְהַחֲמוֹר וְכָל־הַבְּהֵמָה אֲשֶׁר יִהְיֶה בַּמַּחֲנוֹת הָהֵמָּה
,those camps in shall be which the cattle and all the and ,ass the ,camel

1471 3605 3498 3605 1961 2063 4046
16 כַּמַּגֵּפָה הַזֹּאת׃ וְהָיָה כָּל־הַנּוֹתָר מִכָּל־הַגּוֹיִם
the nations from all is who left every- one it And ,be shall .this like plague

7812 8141 8141 1767/5927 3389 935
הַבָּאִים עַל־יְרוּשָׁלִָם וְעָלוּ מִדֵּי שָׁנָה בְשָׁנָה לְהִשְׁתַּחֲוֹת
worship to year to year from shall up go Jerusalem against which up came

1961 5521 2282 2287 6635 3068 4428
17 לְמֶלֶךְ יְהוָה צְבָאוֹת וְלָחֹג אֶת־חַג הַסֻּכּוֹת׃ וְהָיָה אֲשֶׁר
who- ever it And ,be shall .booths the of feast to and keep ,hosts Jehovah of the ,King

families of the earth to Jerusalem to worship the King, Jehovah of hosts, there shall even be no rain on them. [18]And if the family of Egypt does not go up, nor come in, then *the rain* shall not be on them; *but* the plague with which Jehovah shall strike the nations who do not come up to keep the Feast of Tabernacles. [19]This shall be Egypt's offense, and the offense of all nations who do not come up to keep the Feast of Tabernacles.

[20]In that day there shall be on the bells of the horses, HOLY TO JEHOVAH. And the pots in the house of Jehovah shall be like the bowls before the altar. [21]And every pot in Jerusalem and in Judah shall be holy to Jehovah of hosts. And all those who sacrifice shall come and take of them, and boil in them. And in that day there shall not be a trader in the house of Jehovah of hosts any more.

7812 3389 776 4940 5927 3808
לֹא־יַעֲלֶה מֵאֵת מִשְׁפְּחוֹת הָאָרֶץ אֶל־יְרוּשָׁלִַם לְהִשְׁתַּחֲוֹת
worship to Jerusalem to earth the families the of from will up go not

518 1653 1961 5921 3808 6635 3068 4428
18 לְמֶלֶךְ יְהוָה צְבָאוֹת וְלֹא עֲלֵיהֶם יִהְיֶה הַגָּשֶׁם׃ וְאִם־
if And .rain the be shall them on even not ,hosts Jehovah of the King

1961 5921 3808 935 3808 5927 4714 4940
מִשְׁפַּחַת מִצְרַיִם לֹא־תַעֲלֶה וְלֹא בָאָה וְלֹא עֲלֵיהֶם תִּהְיֶה
be will ;(rain) them on then not does and ,enter not up go does not Egypt family the of

2287 5927 3808 1471 3068 5221 834 4046
הַמַּגֵּפָה אֲשֶׁר יִגֹּף יְהוָה אֶת־הַגּוֹיִם אֲשֶׁר לֹא יַעֲלוּ לָחֹג
to keep do up come not who nations the Jehovah will strike (with) which (same) the plague

3605 2403 4714 2403 1961 2063 5521 2282
19 אֶת־חַג הַסֻּכּוֹת׃ זֹאת תִּהְיֶה חַטַּאת מִצְרַיִם וְחַטַּאת כָּל־
all the of offense and Egypt's offense be shall this .booths the of feast

3117 5521 2282 2287 5927 3808 834 1471
20 הַגּוֹיִם אֲשֶׁר לֹא יַעֲלוּ לָחֹג אֶת־חַג הַסֻּכּוֹת׃ בַּיּוֹם הַהוּא
that day In .booths the of feast keep to do up come not who nations

5518 1961 3068 6944 5483 4698 5921 1961
יִהְיֶה עַל־מְצִלּוֹת הַסּוּס קֹדֶשׁ לַיהוָה וְהָיוּ הַסִּירוֹת
pots the And be shall TO JEHOVAH HOLY the ,horses of bells the on there be shall

5518 1961 4196 6440 4219 3068 1004
21 בְּבֵית יְהוָה כַּמִּזְרָקִים לִפְנֵי הַמִּזְבֵּחַ׃ וְהָיָה כָּל־סִיר
pot every And be shall .altar the before bowls the like Jehovah the in of house

3605 935 6635 3068 6944 3063 3389
בִּירוּשָׁלִַם וּבִיהוּדָה קֹדֶשׁ לַיהוָה צְבָאוֹת וּבָאוּ כָּל־
all shall And come .hosts to of Jehovah holy Judah in and Jerusalem in

5750 3669 1961 3808 1310 3947 2026
הַזֹּבְחִים וְלָקְחוּ מֵהֶם וּבִשְּׁלוּ בָהֶם וְלֹא־יִהְיֶה כְנַעֲנִי עוֹד
again trader a there be shall not And .them in boil and of them take and who those sacrifice

3117 6635 3068 1004
בְּבֵית־יְהוָה צְבָאוֹת בַּיּוֹם הַהוּא׃
.that day in hosts Jehovah of the in of house

מ ל א כ י

LIBER MALACHIAE

(THE) BOOK OF MALACHI

CAPUT. I. א

A LITERAL TRANSLATION
OF THE BIBLE
THE BOOK OF MALACHI

CHAPTER 1

1 [1]The burden of the word
2 of Jehovah to Israel by the
hand of Malachi:
[2]I have loved you, says
Jehovah. But you say, In
what *way* have You loved
us? *Was* not Esau the
brother to Jacob? Yet I
3 loved Jacob, declares
Jehovah; [3]and I have hated
Esau, and have made his
mountains a desolation,
4 and his inheritance for the
jackals of the wilderness.
[4]If Edom says, We are
beaten down, but we will
return and build the ruined
places; so says Jehovah of
hosts: They shall build, but I
will tear down. And they
shall call them the region of
wickedness, and the
people *with* whom Jehovah
is indignant until forever.
5 [5]And you shall see, and you
shall say, Jehovah will be
magnified beyond the
6 border of Israel.
[6]A son honors *his* father,
and a servant his master. If
then I *am* a father, where *is*
My honor? And if I *am* a
master, where *is* My fear?
says Jehovah of hosts to
you, O priests who despise
My name. But you say, In
what *way* have we despised
Your name? [7]*You* are
offering defiled food on My
7 altar, and you say, In what
way have we defiled You? In
your saying, The table of
Jehovah, it *is* to be
despised. [8]And if you offer
the blind for sacrifice, is it
not evil? And if you offer the
8 lame and the sick, is it not
evil? Bring it now to your
governor. Will he accept

157 4401 3027 3478 3068 1697 4853
משא דבר־יהוה אל־ישראל ביד מלאכי׃ אהבתי אתכם
,you have I :Malachi the by Israel to Jehovah the bur- The
loved of hand . of word of den

6215 251 157 559 3068 559
אמר יהוה ואמרתם במה אהבתנו הלוא־אח עשו
Esau brother (Was) You have what In you but ;Jehovah says
not ?us loved (way) ,say

8130 6215 3290 157 3608/5002 3290
ליעקב נאם־יהוה ואהב את־יעקב׃ ואת־עשו שנאתי
have I Esau and ,Jacob I Yet .Jehovah states to
,hated loved ?Jacob

4057 8568 5159 8077 2022 7760
ואשים את־הריו שממה ואת־נחלתו לתנות מדבר׃ כי
If wil- the the for his and deso- a his have and
.derness of jackals inheritance lation mountains made

3068 559 3541 2723 1129 7725 7567 123 559
תאמר אדום רששנו ונשוב ונבנה חרבות כה אמר יהוה
Jehovah says thus ruined the and we but are We ,Edom says
of ;places build return will ,down beaten

7564 1366 7121 2040 1129 6635
צבאות המה יבנו ואני אהרוס וקראו להם גבול רשעה
wicked- the them they And tear will but shall They :hosts
,ness of region call shall .down I build

7200 5869 5769/5704 3068 2194 834 5971
והעם אשר־זעם יהוה עד־עולם׃ ועיניכם תראינה ואתם
and ,see shall your And .forever till Jehovah is (with) the and
you eyes indignant whom people

1 3512 1121 3478 1366 5921 3068 1431 559
תאמרו יגדל יהוה מעל לגבול ישראל׃ בן יכבד אב
(his) honors A .Israel the to above Jehovah be May shall
father son of border magnified ,say

113 518 3519 1 518 113 5650
ועבד אדניו ואם־אב אני איה כבודי ואם־אדונים אני
I master a And My where I a now his a and
,(am) if ?honor (is) ,(am) father if ;master servant

8034 959 3548 6635 3068 559 4172
איה מוראי אמר ׀ יהוה צבאות לכם הכהנים בוזי שמי
My de- ,priests O ,you to hosts Jehovah says My where
?name of spisers of ?fear (is)

3899 4196 5066 8034 959 4100 559
ואמרתם במה בזינו את־שמך׃ מגישים על־מזבחי לחם
food My on (are You) Your we have what In you But
altar presenting ?name despised (way) ,say

3068 7979 559 1351 4100 559 1351
מגאל ואמרתם במה גאלנוך באמרכם שלחן יהוה
Jehovah The your In we have what In you and ,defiled
of table ,saying ?You defiled (way) ,say

5066 7451 369 2076 5787 5066 959
נבזה הוא׃ וכי־תגשון עור לזבח אין רע וכי תגישו
you And ?evil it is for the you And .(is) it despic-
present if not ,sacrifice blind present if able

176 7521 6346 7126 7451 369 2470 6455
פסח וחלה אין רע הקריבהו נא לפחתך הירצך או
or he Will your to now it Bring ?evil it is the and the
you accept .governor not sick lame

you or lift up your face, says Jehovah of hosts? [9]And now entreat the face of God, that He favor us. This has been by your hands; will He lift up your faces, says Jehovah of hosts? [10]Who *is* even among you that will shut the doors, and you not kindle *fire on* My altar in vain! There is no delight to Me in you, says Jehovah of hosts. I will not be pleased with a food offering from you. [11]For from the east to the west, My name *shall be* great among the nations, and everywhere incense shall be offered to My name; and a pure food offering. For My name *shall be* great among the nations, says Jehovah of hosts.

[12]But you are profaning it when you say, The table of the Lord, it *is* polluted; and its fruit, His food, is to be despised. [13]You also have said, Behold, what weariness! And you have puffed at it, says Jehovah of hosts. And you bring plunder, and the lame, and the sick; and you bring the meal offering. Should I accept it from your hand, says Jehovah? [14]But cursed *be* a deceiver, and there is a male in his flock, yet he vows *it*, but sacrifices a blemished *one* to the Lord. For I *am* a great king, says Jehovah of hosts; and My name *is* feared among the nations.

410/6440 4994 2470 6258 6635 3068 559 6440 5375
9 הֲיִשָּׂא פָנֶיךָ אָמַר יְהוָה צְבָאוֹת׃ וְעַתָּה חַלּוּ־נָא פְנֵי־אֵל
God the now Entreat And .hosts Jehovah says your he will
of face ,now of ?face up lift

3068 559 6440 5375 1961 3027 2603
וִיחָנֵנוּ מִיֶּדְכֶם הָיְתָה זֹּאת הֲיִשָּׂא מִכֶּם פָּנִים אָמַר יְהוָה
Jehovah says ?faces from He will ;this has your By He that
of you up lift been hands .us favor

4196 215 3808 1817 5462 1571 4310 6635
10 צְבָאוֹת׃ מִי גַם־בָּכֶם וְיִסְגֹּר דְּלָתַיִם וְלֹא־תָאִירוּ מִזְבְּחִי
My (on) you and ,doors the and among even Who .hosts
altar (fire) kindle not shut would you (is)

3808 4503 6635 3068 559 2656 369 2600
חִנָּם אֵין־לִי חֵפֶץ בָּכֶם אָמַר יְהוָה צְבָאוֹת וּמִנְחָה לֹא־
not food a And .hosts Jehovah says ,you in delight to Nor in
offering of Me is .vain

1419 3997 81.43 4217 3027 7521
11 אֶרְצֶה מִיֶּדְכֶם׃ כִּי מִמִּזְרַח־שֶׁמֶשׁ וְעַד־מְבוֹאוֹ גָּדוֹל
great going its and sun the the from For your from will I
in of rising .hand accept

4503 8034 5066 6999 4825 3605 1471 8034
שְׁמִי בַּגּוֹיִם וּבְכָל־מָקוֹם מֻקְטָר מֻגָּשׁ לִשְׁמִי וּמִנְחָה
food and My to be shall ,incense place in and among name My
offering ,name presented every ,nations the (be shall)

6635 3068 559 1471 8034 1419 2889
12 טְהוֹרָה כִּי־גָדוֹל שְׁמִי בַּגּוֹיִם אָמַר יְהוָה צְבָאוֹת׃ וְאַתֶּם
But .hosts Jehovah says the among My great for ;pure a
you of ,nations name (be shall)

5108 1351 113 7979 559 2490
מְחַלְּלִים אוֹתוֹ בֶּאֱמָרְכֶם שֻׁלְחַן אֲדֹנָי מְגֹאָל הוּא וְנִיבוֹ
its and ,(is) defiled the The you when ,it (are)
fruit Lord of table ,say profaning

5301 4972 2009 559 400 959
13 נִבְזֶה אָכְלוֹ׃ וַאֲמַרְתֶּם הִנֵּה מַתְּלָאָה וְהִפַּחְתֶּם אוֹתוֹ
it have you And what ,Behold you And His de- is
at sniffed !weariness ,said have .food spicable

6455 1419 935 6635 3068 559
אָמַר יְהוָה צְבָאוֹת וַהֲבֵאתֶם גָּזוּל וְאֶת־הַפִּסֵּחַ וְאֶת־
and the and the you And .hosts Jehovah says
lame stolen bring of

3027 7521 4503 935 2470
הַחוֹלֶה וַהֲבֵאתֶם אֶת־הַמִּנְחָה הַאֶרְצֶה אוֹתָהּ מִיֶּדְכֶם
your from it I Should meal the you and the
?hand accept .offering bring ,sick

2076 5087 2145 5739 3426 5280 779 3068 559
14 אָמַר יְהוָה׃ וְאָרוּר נוֹכֵל וְיֵשׁ בְּעֶדְרוֹ זָכָר וְנֹדֵר וְזֹבֵחַ
sac- but he and a his in and a (be) But .Jehovah says
rifices ,(it) vows ,male flock is there ,deceiver cursed

6635 3068 559 1419 4428 136 7843
מָשְׁחָת לַאדֹנָי כִּי מֶלֶךְ גָּדוֹל אָנִי אָמַר יְהוָה צְבָאוֹת
;hosts Jehovah says I great king a For the to blem- a
of ,(am) .Lord (one) ished

1471 3372 8034
וּשְׁמִי נוֹרָא בַגּוֹיִם׃
the among (is) My and
.nations feared name

CAP. II ב

CHAPTER 2

[1]And now, O priests, this command *is* to you. [2]If you will not hear, and if you will not set *it* on *your* heart to give glory to My name, says

8085 3808/518 3548 2063 4687 6258
1 וְעַתָּה אֲלֵיכֶם הַמִּצְוָה הַזֹּאת הַכֹּהֲנִים׃
2 אִם־לֹא תִשְׁמְעוּ
will you not If .priests O ,this command you to And
,hear (is) now

3068 559 8034 3519 5414 3820 7760 3808
וְאִם־לֹא תָשִׂימוּ עַל־לֵב לָתֵת כָּבוֹד לִשְׁמִי אָמַר יְהוָה
Jehovah says My to glory give to heart upon will you not and
of ,name set if

Jehovah of hosts, then I will send the curse on you, and I will curse your blessings. And indeed, I have cursed it, because you *are* not setting *it* on *your* heart. ³Behold, I *am* rebuking your seed, and I will spread dung on your faces, the dung of your solemn feasts; and one will lift you up to it. ⁴And you shall know that I have sent this command to you; to be My covenant with Levi, says Jehovah of hosts. ⁵My covenant with him was life and peace, and I gave them to him *for fear;* and he feared Me, and he is put in awe before My name. ⁶The law of truth was in his mouth, and no iniquity was not found in his lips. In peace and in uprightness he walked with Me, and he turned many from iniquity. ⁷For the lips of the priest should guard knowledge; and they should seek the law from his mouth; for he *is* the messenger of Jehovah of hosts. ⁸But you have turned out of the way; you have caused many to stumble at the law. You have corrupted the covenant of Levi, says Jehovah of hosts. ⁹So I have also made you despised and low to all the people, just as you have not kept My ways, but *are* lifting up faces in the law. ¹⁰Is there not one father to us all? *Has* not one God created us? Why do we act deceitfully, *each* man with his brother, to profane the covenant of our fathers?

¹¹Judah has dealt treacherously, and has done an abomination in Israel and in Jerusalem; for Judah has profaned the holy *place* of Jehovah, which He loves; and married a daughter of a foreign god. ¹²Jehovah will cut off from the tents of

---

2182 — MALACHI 2:3 (Interlinear)

2:2 (cont.)

1293	779	779	3994		7971	66:35
צְבָאוֹת וְשִׁלַּחְתִּי בָכֶם אֶת־הַמְּאֵרָה וְאָרוֹתִי אֶת־בִּרְכוֹתֵיכֶם						
your blessings;	I and the curse will	, curse	you on	I then	, hosts	send will

3

	1605	2005	3820	7760	3588 779	1571
וְגַם אָרוֹתִיהָ כִּי אֵינְכֶם שָׂמִים עַל־לֵב: הִנְנִי גֹעֵר לָכֶם						
you to (am) Behold .heart on (are) you because have I and						
rebuking I not , it cursed indeed						

5375	2282	6569	6440	6569	2219	2233
אֶת־הַזֶּרַע וְזֵרִיתִי פֶרֶשׁ עַל־פְּנֵיכֶם פֶּרֶשׁ חַגֵּיכֶם וְנָשָׂא						
one and your the your on dung , seed the						
lift will , feasts of dung , faces spread will						

4

4687				3045		
אֶתְכֶם אֵלָיו: וִידַעְתֶּם כִּי שִׁלַּחְתִּי אֲלֵיכֶם אֵת הַמִּצְוָה						
command you to have I that you And .it to you						
sent know shall						

5

1285	6635	3068	559	3878	1285	1961	2063
הַזֹּאת לִהְיוֹת בְּרִיתִי אֶת־לֵוִי אָמַר יְהוָה צְבָאוֹת: בְּרִיתִי							
My covenant .hosts Jehovah says , Levi with My be to this							

3372	4172	5414	7965	2416		1961
הָיְתָה אִתּוֹ הַחַיִּים וְהַשָּׁלוֹם וָאֶתְּנֵם־לוֹ מוֹרָא וַיִּירָאֵנִי						
he and (for) to I and , peace and life with was						
, Me feared ; fear him them gave him						

6

5771	6310	1961	571	8451	2865	8034	6440
וּמִפְּנֵי שְׁמִי נִחַת הוּא: תּוֹרַת אֱמֶת הָיְתָה בְּפִיהוּ וְעַוְלָה							
and his in was truth The .he put is My from and							
iniquity , mouth of law awe in name before							

7227	19 80	4334	7965	8193	4672 3808	
לֹא־נִמְצָא בִשְׂפָתָיו בְּשָׁלוֹם וּבְמִישׁוֹר הָלַךְ אִתִּי וְרַבִּים						
many and with he in and peace In his on was not						
, Me walked uprightness .lips found						

7

1245	8451	1847	3104	3548	8193	5771	7725
הֵשִׁיב מֵעָוֹן: כִּי־שִׂפְתֵי כֹהֵן יִשְׁמְרוּ־דַעַת וְתוֹרָה יְבַקְשׁוּ							
should they the and know- should the lips the For from							
seek law ; ledge guard priest of .iniquity turned							

8

5493		4397	6635	3068		6310
מִפִּיהוּ כִּי מַלְאַךְ יְהוָה־צְבָאוֹת הוּא: וְאַתֶּם סַרְתֶּם מִן						
from have you But .(is) he hosts Jehovah the for his from						
turned of of messenger ; mouth						

559	3878	1285	7843	8451	7227	3782	1870
הַדֶּרֶךְ הִכְשַׁלְתֶּם רַבִּים בַּתּוֹרָה שִׁחַתֶּם בְּרִית הַלֵּוִי אָמַר							
says ! Levi cove- the have you the at many made have you the							
of nant corrupted ; law stumble ; way							

9

3605	8217	959	5414		1571	6635	3068
יְהוָה צְבָאוֹת: וְגַם־אֲנִי נָתַתִּי אֶתְכֶם נִבְזִים וּשְׁפָלִים לְכָל							
all to and despised you have I And .hosts Jehovah							
abased made also of							

6440	5375	1870	8104	369	6310	5971	
הָעָם כְּפִי אֲשֶׁר אֵינְכֶם שֹׁמְרִים אֶת־דְּרָכַי וְנֹשְׂאִים פָּנִים							
faces (are) but My (are) not you because the							
up lifting , ways keeping people							

10

1254	259	410		1961		259	8451
בַּתּוֹרָה: הֲלוֹא אָב אֶחָד לְכֻלָּנוּ הֲלוֹא אֵל אֶחָד בְּרָאָנוּ							
created one God (Has) us to one father not Is the in							
? us not ? all there .law							

11

898		1285	2490		251	376	898	4100
מַדּוּעַ נִבְגַּד אִישׁ בְּאָחִיו לְחַלֵּל בְּרִית אֲבֹתֵינוּ: בָּגְדָה								
acted has our cove- the to his with (each) act we do Why								
deceitfully ? fathers of nant profane , brother man deceitfully								

2490		3389	3478	6213		8441	3063
יְהוּדָה וְתוֹעֵבָה נֶעֶשְׂתָה בְיִשְׂרָאֵל וּבִירוּשָׁלִָם כִּי חִלֵּל							
has for in and Israel in been has an and , Judah							
profaned ; Jerusalem done abomination							

12

3772	5236	1166	157	834	3068	6944	3063
יְהוּדָה קֹדֶשׁ יְהוָה אֲשֶׁר אָהֵב וּבָעַל בַּת־אֵל נֵכָר: יַכְרֵת							
cut May foreign a a and He which Jehovah the Judah							
off . god of daughter married , loves of holy							

Jacob the man who does it, stirring, and answering, or offering a food offering to Jehovah of hosts. [13]And this *is* a second *thing* you have done; covering the altar of Jehovah *with* tears, *with* weeping and groaning; yet not facing toward the food offering, and taking *it with* delight from your hand.

[14]Yet you say, On what *cause*? Because Jehovah has been witness between you and the wife of your youth, against whom you have dealt treacherously; and she *is* your companion and your covenant wife. [15]And has He not made one? Yet the vestige of the Spirit *is in* him. And what *of* the one? He was seeking a seed of God. Then guard your spirit, and do not deal treacherously with the wife of your youth. [16]Jehovah, the God of Israel, says, He hates sending away, and to cover *with* violence on his garment, says Jehovah of hosts. Then guard your spirit, and do not act treacherously.

[17]You have wearied Jehovah with your words. Yet you say, In what have we wearied Him? When you say, Every evildoer *is* good in the eyes of Jehovah, and He delights in them; or, Where *is* the God of justice?

5066 3290 168 6030 5782 6213 834 376 3068
יְהוָה לָאִישׁ אֲשֶׁר יַעֲשֶׂנָּה עֵר וְעֹנֶה מֵאָהֳלֵי יַעֲקֹב וּמַגִּישׁ
pre- or Jacob the from an- and stirring —it does who the Jehovah
senting of tents —swering man

1832 3680 6213 8145 2063 6635 3068 4503
13 מִנְחָה לַיהוָה צְבָאוֹת׃ וְזֹאת שֵׁנִית תַּעֲשׂוּ כַּסּוֹת דִּמְעָה
(with) (you) :do you a this And .hosts to food a
tears cover second (is) of Jehovah offering

4503 6437 5750 369 603 1065 3068 4196
אֶת־מִזְבַּח יְהוָה בְּכִי וַאֲנָקָה מֵאֵין עוֹד פְּנוֹת אֶל־הַמִּנְחָה
food the toward (any) yet from and (with) ,Jehovah the
offering facing being not ;groaning weeping of altar

3068 4100 5921 559 3027 7521 3947
14 וְלָקַחַת רָצוֹן מִיֶּדְכֶם׃ וַאֲמַרְתֶּם עַל־מָה עַל כִּי־יְהוָה
Jehovah On what On you Yet your from (with) and
that ?(cause) ,say .hand delight taking

898 5271 802 996 996 5749
הֵעִיד בֵּינְךָ וּבֵין ׀ אֵשֶׁת נְעוּרֶיךָ אֲשֶׁר אַתָּה בָּגַדְתָּה בָּהּ
;against dealt have you whom youth your the the and between been has
deceitfully of wife you witness

7307 7604 6213 259 3808 1285 802 2278
15 וְהִיא חֲבֶרְתְּךָ וְאֵשֶׁת בְּרִיתֶךָ׃ וְלֹא־אֶחָד עָשָׂה וּשְׁאָר רוּחַ
the a And He did one But your the and com- your and
Spirit of vestige ?make not .covenant of wife panion (is) she

7307 8104 430 2233 1245 259 4100
לוֹ וּמָה הָאֶחָד מְבַקֵּשׁ זֶרַע אֱלֹהִים וְנִשְׁמַרְתֶּם בְּרוּחֲכֶם
,spirit your guard And .God seed a was He ?one the And to (is)
of seeking (of) what .him

3068 559 7971 8130 898 408 5271 802
16 וּבְאֵשֶׁת נְעוּרֶיךָ אַל־יִבְגֹּד׃ כִּי־שָׂנֵא שַׁלַּח אָמַר יְהוָה
,Jehovah says sending hates He deal not your with and
,away deceitfully youth of wife the

6635 3068 559 3830 5921 2555 3680 3478 430
אֱלֹהֵי יִשְׂרָאֵל וְכִסָּה חָמָס עַל־לְבוּשׁוֹ אָמַר יְהוָה צְבָאוֹת
.hosts Jehovah says his on (with) to and ,Israel the
of ,garment violence cover of God

3068 3021 898 3808 7307 8104
17 וְנִשְׁמַרְתֶּם בְּרוּחֲכֶם וְלֹא תִבְגֹּדוּ׃ הוֹגַעְתֶּם יְהוָה
Jehovah have You act do and your guard And
wearied .deceitfully not spirit

6213 559 3021 4100 559 1697
בְּדִבְרֵיכֶם וַאֲמַרְתֶּם בַּמָּה הוֹגַעְנוּ בֶּאֱמָרְכֶם כָּל־עֹשֵׂה
doer Every you When we have what In you Yet your with
of ,say ?Him wearied (way) ,say .words

430 176 2654 3068 5869 2896 7451
רָע טוֹב ׀ בְּעֵינֵי יְהוָה וּבָהֶם הוּא חָפֵץ אוֹ אַיֵּה אֱלֹהֵי
the Where ,or ;delights He in and ,Jehovah the in (is) evil
of God (is) them of eyes good

4941
הַמִּשְׁפָּט׃
?justice

CAP. III ג

CHAPTER 3

[1]Behold, I *am* sending My messenger, and he will clear the way before Me. And the Lord whom you *are* seeking shall suddenly come to His temple, even the Angel of the Covenant, in whom you delight. Behold, He comes, says Jehovah of hosts. [2]But who can endure the day of

935 6597 6440 1870 6437 4397 7971 2005
1 הִנְנִי שֹׁלֵחַ מַלְאָכִי וּפִנָּה־דֶרֶךְ לְפָנָי וּפִתְאֹם יָבוֹא אֶל־
to shall And before the he and mes- My (am) ,Behold
come suddenly .Me way clear will ,senger sending I

834 1285 4397 1245 834 113 1964
הֵיכָלוֹ הָאָדוֹן ׀ אֲשֶׁר־אַתֶּם מְבַקְשִׁים וּמַלְאַךְ הַבְּרִית אֲשֶׁר
(in) the the even (are) you whom the His
whom ,covenant of Angel ,seeking Lord ,temple

3557 4310 6635 3068 559 935 2655
2 אַתֶּם חֲפֵצִים הִנֵּה־בָא אָמַר יְהוָה צְבָאוֹת׃ וּמִי מְכַלְכֵּל
can But .hosts Jehovah says He ,Behold (are) you
endure who of ,comes delighting

His coming? And who will stand when He appears? For He *is* like a refiner's fire, and like fuller's soap. [3]And He shall sit as a refiner and purifier of silver; and He shall purify the sons of Levi, and purge them like gold and like silver, that they may be offerers of a food offering in righteousness to Jehovah. [4]Then the food offering of Judah and Jerusalem shall be pleasing to Jehovah, as *in* the days of old, and as *in* former years. [5]And I will come near to you for judgment; and I will be a swift witness against the sorcerers, and against the adulterers, and against those swearing to a lie; and against those who extort from the hired laborer's pay; and turning away the widow, and the fatherless, and the alien, and not fearing Me, says Jehovah of hosts. [6]For I *am* Jehovah, *I* change not. Because of this you sons of Jacob are not destroyed.

[7]From the days of your fathers, you have turned aside from My statutes, and have not kept *them*. Return to Me, and I will return to you, says Jehovah of hosts. But you say, In what *way* shall we return? [8]Will a man rob God? Yet you have robbed Me. But you say, In what have we robbed You? In the tithe and the offering! [9]You *are* cursed with a curse; for you *are* robbing Me, the nation, all of it. [10]Bring all the tithe into the storehouse, so that there may be food in My house. And test Me now with this, says Jehovah of hosts, whether I will not open the windows of the heavens for you, and pour out a blessing, until there is no sufficiency. [11]And I will rebuke your devourer, and he shall not decay the fruit of your ground against

אֶת־יוֹם בּוֹאוֹ וּמִי הָעֹמֵד בְּהֵרָאוֹתוֹ כִּי־הוּא כְּאֵשׁ מְצָרֵף
a refiner's | like fire | He (is) | For | His at ?appearing | (be will) standing | And who | His ?coming | the of day

3 וּכְבֹרִית מְכַבְּסִים׃ וְיָשַׁב מְצָרֵף וּמְטַהֵר כֶּסֶף וְטִהַר אֶת־
He and purify shall | ;silver | pur- and of ifier | a (as) refiner | He And sit shall | .fuller's | like and soap

בְּנֵי־לֵוִי וְזִקַּק אֹתָם כַּזָּהָב וְכַכָּסֶף וְהָיוּ לַיהוָה מַגִּישֵׁי מִנְחָה
offerings of | presenters | to Jehovah | they that be may | like and ,silver | like gold | them | and purge | ,Levi the of sons

4 בִּצְדָקָה׃ וְעָרְבָה לַיהוָה מִנְחַת יְהוּדָה וִירוּשָׁלִַם כִּימֵי
(in) as of days | and ,Jerusalem | Judah | food the of offering | to Jehovah | shall Then pleasing be | righ- in .teousness

5 עוֹלָם וּכְשָׁנִים קַדְמֹנִיּוֹת׃ וְקָרַבְתִּי אֲלֵיכֶם לַמִּשְׁפָּט וְהָיִיתִי ׀
I and be will | for ;judgment | you to | will I And near draw | .former | (in) as and years | old

עֵד מְמַהֵר בַּמְכַשְּׁפִים וּבַמְנָאֲפִים וּבַנִּשְׁבָּעִים לַשָּׁקֶר
a to ,lie | against and swearing those | against and adulterers the | the against sorcerers | swift | a witness

וּבְעֹשְׁקֵי שְׂכַר־שָׂכִיר אַלְמָנָה וְיָתוֹם וּמַטֵּי־גֵר וְלֹא יְרֵאוּנִי
fearing ,Me | and not | turning and ,alien the away | the and ,orphan | the widow | hired the ,laborer's | hire | against and of extorters

6 אָמַר יְהוָה צְבָאוֹת׃ כִּי אֲנִי יְהוָה לֹא שָׁנִיתִי וְאַתֶּם בְּנֵי־
sons of | and you | do ;change | not | Jehovah | I | For | .hosts | Jehovah of | says

7 יַעֲקֹב לֹא כְלִיתֶם׃ לְמִימֵי אֲבֹתֵיכֶם סַרְתֶּם מֵחֻקַּי וְלֹא
and not | My from statutes | have you turned | your ,fathers | the From of days | come have .end an to | not | Jacob

שְׁמַרְתֶּם שׁוּבוּ אֵלַי וְאָשׁוּבָה אֲלֵיכֶם אָמַר יְהוָה צְבָאוֹת
.hosts | Jehovah of | says | ,you to | I and return will | to Me | Return | kept have (them)

8 וַאֲמַרְתֶּם בַּמֶּה נָשׁוּב׃ הֲיִקְבַּע אָדָם אֱלֹהִים כִּי אַתֶּם
you | Yet | ?God | man a | rob Will | we shall ?return | what In (way) | you But ,say

קֹבְעִים אֹתִי וַאֲמַרְתֶּם בַּמֶּה קְבַעֲנוּךָ הַמַּעֲשֵׂר וְהַתְּרוּמָה׃
the and !offering | the (In) tithe | we have ?You robbed | what In (way) | you But ,say | .Me | (are) robbing

9
10 בַּמְּאֵרָה אַתֶּם נֵאָרִים וְאֹתִי אַתֶּם קֹבְעִים הַגּוֹי כֻּלּוֹ׃ הָבִיאוּ
Bring | of all .it | the nation | (are) robbing | you | for Me | being ;cursed | you (are) | a With curse

אֶת־כָּל־הַמַּעֲשֵׂר אֶל־בֵּית הָאוֹצָר וִיהִי טֶרֶף בְּבֵיתִי וּבְחָנוּנִי
And Me test | My in .house | food | that be may | stored goods | the of house | into | the tithe | all

נָא בָּזֹאת אָמַר יְהוָה צְבָאוֹת אִם־לֹא אֶפְתַּח לָכֶם אֵת
for you | will I open | not | if | ,hosts | Jehovah of | says | in ,this | now

11 אֲרֻבּוֹת הַשָּׁמַיִם וַהֲרִיקֹתִי לָכֶם בְּרָכָה עַד־בְּלִי־דָי׃ וְגָעַרְתִּי
will I And rebuke | suffi- .ciency | not until (is) | a blessing | for you | pour and out | the heavens | win- the of dows

לָכֶם בָּאֹכֵל וְלֹא־יַשְׁחִת לָכֶם אֶת־פְּרִי הָאֲדָמָה וְלֹא־
and not | the ,ground | the of fruit | to you | shall he decay to cause | and not | the devourer | for you

you; nor shall your vine miscarry against you in the field, says Jehovah of hosts. 12And all nations shall call you blessed; for you shall be a delightful land, says Jehovah of hosts

13Your words have been strong against Me, says Jehovah. Yet you say, What have we spoken together against you? 14You have said, It *is* vain to serve God. And, What profit *is it* that we have kept His charge, and that we have walked as mourners before Jehovah of hosts? 15And now we *are* calling the arrogant blessed. Not only are the doers of wickedness built up, they also test God, and escape.

16Then those fearing Jehovah spoke together, *each* man to his neighbor. And Jehovah gave attention and heard. And a book of remembrance was written before Him for those who feared Jehovah, and for those esteeming His name. 17And they shall be Mine, says Jehovah of hosts, for the day that I will make up *My* treasure. And I will pity them as a man has pity on his son who serves him. 18Then you shall again see the *difference* between the righteous and the wicked, between him who serves God and him who does not serve Him.

CHAPTER 4

1For, behold, the day is coming, burning like a fire-pot; and all the proud, and every doer of wickedness, shall be chaff. And the coming day will set them ablaze, says Jehovah of hosts, which will not leave root or branches to them.

2But to you who fear My name, the Sun of righteousness shall rise up, and healing *will be* on His wings. And you shall go out and frisk like calves of the stall. 3And you shall tread under the wicked, for they shall be ashes under the

833 6635 3068 559 770 4 1612 7921

12 תְשַׁכֵּל לָכֶם הַגֶּפֶן בַּשָּׂדֶה אָמַר יְהוָה צְבָאוֹת׃ וְאִשְּׁרוּ

shall And blessed call .hosts Jehovah of says the in ,field the vine against you will miscarry

3068 559 2656 776 1961 1471 3605

אֶתְכֶם כָּל־הַגּוֹיִם כִּי־תִהְיוּ אַתֶּם אֶרֶץ חֵפֶץ אָמַר יְהוָה

Jehovah of says ,delight a of land you be shall for the ;nations all you

559 3068 559 1697 2388 6635

13 צְבָאוֹת׃ חָזְקוּ עָלַי דִּבְרֵיכֶם אָמַר יְהוָה וַאֲמַרְתֶּם

you Yet ,say .Jehovah says your ,words against Me been Have strong .hosts

4100 430 5647 7723 559 1696

14 מַה־נִּדְבַּרְנוּ עָלֶיךָ׃ אֲמַרְתֶּם שָׁוְא עֲבֹד אֱלֹהִים וּמַה־

,and What ,God serve To (is) vanity have You ,said against ?You we have What together spoken

3068 6440 6941 1980 4931 8104 1215

בֶּצַע כִּי שָׁמַרְנוּ מִשְׁמַרְתּוֹ וְכִי הָלַכְנוּ קְדֹרַנִּית מִפְּנֵי יְהוָה

Jehovah of before as mourners have we walked and that His ,charge have we kept that unjust profit

6213 1129/1571 2086 833 6258 6635

15 צְבָאוֹת׃ וְעַתָּה אֲנַחְנוּ מְאַשְּׁרִים זֵדִים גַּם־נִבְנוּ עֹשֵׂי

doers of are Not up built only the arrogant calling (are) blessed we And now ?hosts

3068 3373 1696 227 4422 430 974 1571 7564

16 רִשְׁעָה גַּם בָּחֲנוּ אֱלֹהִים וַיִּמָּלֵטוּ׃ אָז נִדְבְּרוּ יִרְאֵי יְהוָה

Jehovah the of fearers spoke together Then and .escape God they also test wicked- ,ness

2146 5612 3489 7181 3068 7181 7453 376

אִישׁ אֶל־רֵעֵהוּ וַיַּקְשֵׁב יְהוָה וַיִּשְׁמָע וַיִּכָּתֵב סֵפֶר זִכָּרוֹן

remem- brance book a of was and written and ;heard Jehovah gave and attention his ,neighbor to (each) man

3068 559 1961 8034 2803 3068 3373 6440

17 לְפָנָיו לְיִרְאֵי יְהוָה וּלְחֹשְׁבֵי שְׁמוֹ׃ וְהָיוּ לִי אָמַר יְהוָה

Jehovah of says to they And ,Me be shall His .name those for and esteeming Jehovah the for of fearers before Him

5921 2550 5459 6213 3117 6635

צְבָאוֹת לַיּוֹם אֲשֶׁר אֲנִי עֹשֶׂה סְגֻלָּה וְחָמַלְתִּי עֲלֵיהֶם

them on will I and pity have (My) ;treasure make will I up that the for day ,hosts

7200 7725 2550 1121 5921 376 2550

18 כַּאֲשֶׁר יַחְמֹל אִישׁ עַל־בְּנוֹ הָעֹבֵד אֹתוֹ׃ וְשַׁבְתֶּם וּרְאִיתֶם

see and you And return shall .him serving his son on man a has pity as

5647 3808 430 5647 996 7561 6662 996

19 בֵּין צַדִּיק לְרָשָׁע בֵּין עֹבֵד אֱלֹהִים לַאֲשֶׁר לֹא עֲבָדוֹ׃ כִּי

For serving .Him not him and God him serving be- tween the and ,wicked the between righteous

6213 3605 2086 3605 1961 8574 1197 935 3117 2009

הִנֵּה הַיּוֹם בָּא בֹּעֵר כַּתַּנּוּר וְהָיוּ כָל־זֵדִים וְכָל־עֹשֵׂה

of doer every and the arrogant all will and be a like fire-pot burning is coming the day ,behold

6635 3068 559 935 3117 3857 7179 7564

רִשְׁעָה קַשׁ וְלִהַט אֹתָם הַיּוֹם הַבָּא אָמַר יְהוָה צְבָאוֹת

,hosts Jehovah of says ,coming the day them will And ablaze set .chaff wicked- ness

8034 3373 2224 6057 8328 6057 834

20 אֲשֶׁר לֹא־יַעֲזֹב לָהֶם שֹׁרֶשׁ וְעָנָף׃ וְזָרְחָה לָכֶם יִרְאֵי שְׁמִי

My name fearing you for shall And rise or .branches root to them will not leave which

5695 6335 3318 3671 4832 6666 8121

שֶׁמֶשׁ צְדָקָה וּמַרְפֵּא בִּכְנָפֶיהָ וִיצָאתֶם וּפִשְׁתֶּם כְּעֶגְלֵי

like of calves frisk and you And out go shall His on .wings and healing righteousness the of Sun

3701 8478 665 1961 7563 6072 4770

21 מַרְבֵּק׃ וְעַסּוֹתֶם רְשָׁעִים כִּי־יִהְיוּ אֵפֶר תַּחַת כַּפּוֹת

the of soles under ashes they be shall for the ,wicked you And trample shall .stall soles of your feet in the day which I *am* preparing, says Jehovah of hosts.

[4]Remember the law of My servant Moses, which I commanded him in Horeb for all Israel, the statutes and judgments.

[5]Behold, I *am* sending you Elijah the prophet before the coming of the great and dreadful day of Jehovah. [6]And he shall turn the heart of the fathers to the sons, and the heart of the sons to their fathers, that I not come and strike the earth *with* utter destruction.

2142 6635 3068 559 6213 834 3117 7272

22 רַגְלֵיכֶם בַּיּוֹם אֲשֶׁר־אֲנִי עֹשֶׂה אָמַר יְהוָה צְבָאוֹת׃ זִכְרוּ

Remember .hosts of Jehovah says ,preparing (am) I which the day in feet your

3478 3605 2722 6680 834 5650 4872 8451

23 תּוֹרַת מֹשֶׁה עַבְדִּי אֲשֶׁר צִוִּיתִי אוֹתוֹ בְחֹרֵב עַל־כָּל־יִשְׂרָאֵל

,Israel all for in Horeb him I commanded which My ,servant Moses the of Law

5030 452 79 71 2009 4941 2706

24 חֻקִּים וּמִשְׁפָּטִים׃ הִנֵּה אָנֹכִי שֹׁלֵחַ לָכֶם אֵת אֵלִיָּה הַנָּבִיא

the prophet Elijah to you (am) sending I ,Behold the and judgments the statutes

1 3820 7725 3372 1419 3068 3117 935 6440

לִפְנֵי בּוֹא יוֹם יְהוָה הַגָּדוֹל וְהַנּוֹרָא׃ וְהֵשִׁיב לֵב־אָבוֹת

of heart the fathers the he And turn shall the and .fearful the great Jehovah day the of before of coming

5221 935 1 1121 3820 1121

עַל־בָּנִים וְלֵב בָּנִים עַל־אֲבוֹתָם פֶּן־אָבוֹא וְהִכֵּיתִי אֶת־

strike and I come lest their ,fathers to the sons the and of heart the ,sons to

2764 776

הָאָרֶץ חֵרֶם׃

utter (with) .destruction the land